TEACHER'S EDITION

PRENTICE HALL

WORLD
HISTORY
THE MODERN ERA

Elisabeth Gaynor Ellis

Anthony Esler

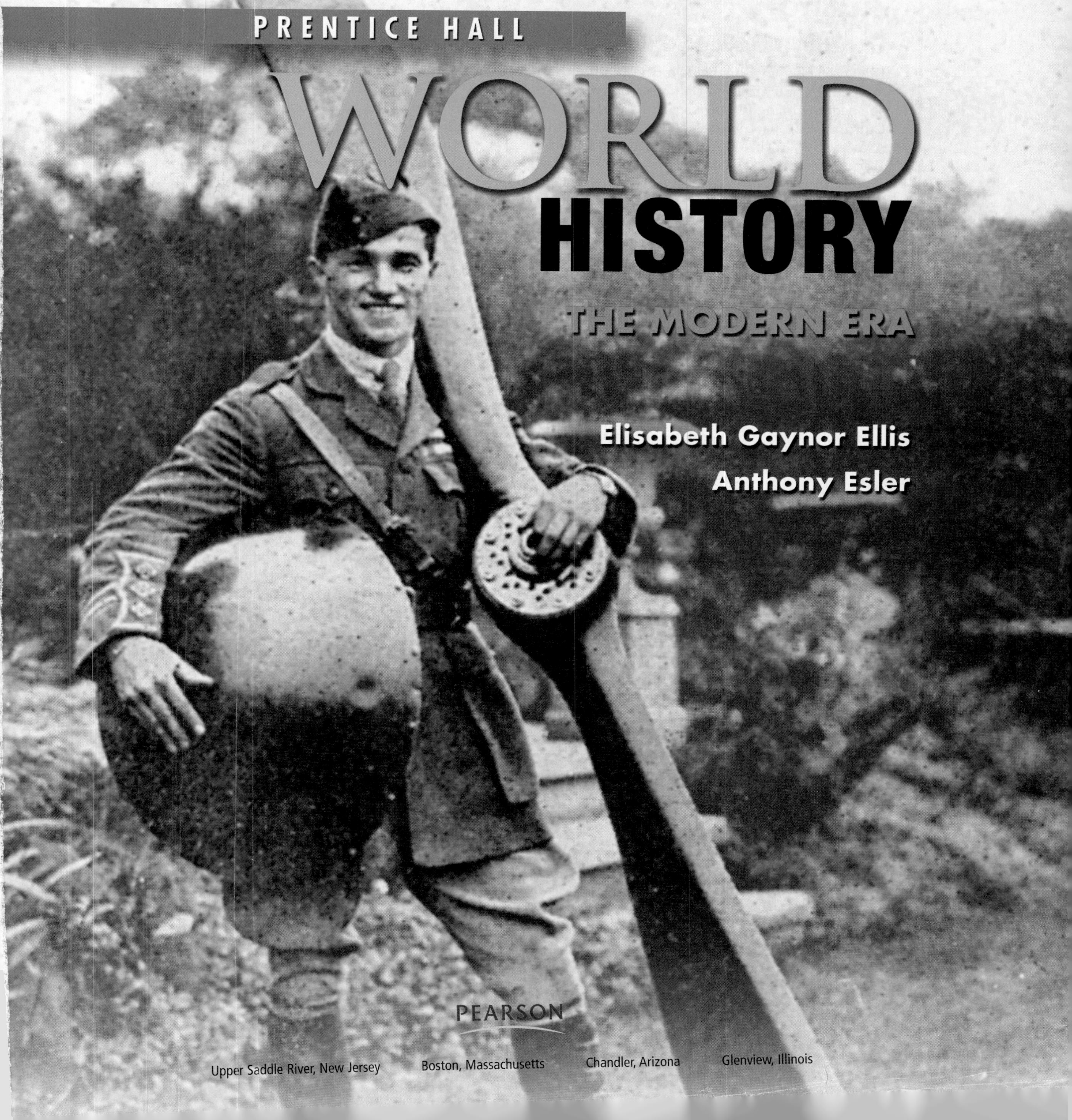

PEARSON

Upper Saddle River, New Jersey   Boston, Massachusetts   Chandler, Arizona   Glenview, Illinois

Authors

Elisabeth Gaynor Ellis

Elisabeth Gaynor Ellis holds a BS from Smith College and an MA and MS from Columbia University. Before she began writing textbooks, Ms. Ellis taught World Cultures, European History, and Russian Studies in Ardsley, New York. Ms. Ellis co-authored Prentice Hall's *World Cultures: A Global Mosaic*, and *World History: Connections to Today* with Dr. Anthony Esler. Ms. Ellis has also written other social studies materials, including *America's Holidays*, individual state histories, and a variety of Teacher's Edition materials. Ms. Ellis is currently working on a middle grades curriculum on Korea as well as a historical novel.

Anthony Esler

Anthony Esler is an emeritus professor of history at the College of William and Mary in Williamsburg, Virginia. His books include several studies of the conflict of generations in world history, half a dozen historical novels, and two other surveys of world and Western history besides this one. He is a member of the American Historical Association, the World History Association, and the Authors Guild. He has received Fulbright, Social Science Research Council, and other research grants, and is listed in the *Directory of American Scholars*, the *Directory of Poets and Fiction Writers*, and *Who's Who in America*. Books by Dr. Esler include *Bombs, Beards, and Barricades, Forbidden City*, and *The Human Venture*.

Senior Consultant
Burton F. Beers

Burton F. Beers is a retired professor of History from North Carolina State University. He has taught European history, Asian history, and American history. Dr. Beers has published numerous articles in historical journals and several books, including *The Far East: A History of Western Impacts and Eastern Responses*, with Paul H. Clyde, and *World History: Patterns of Civilization*.

Program Consultant

Grant Wiggins, Ed.D., is the President of Authentic Education in Hopewell, New Jersey. He earned his Ed.D. from Harvard University and his B.A. from St. John's College in Annapolis. Wiggins consults with schools, districts, and state education departments on a variety of reform matters; organizes conferences, workshops, and develops print materials and Web resources on curricular change. He is the co-author, with Jay McTighe, of *Understanding by Design* and the *Understanding by Design Handbook,* the award-winning and highly successful material on curriculum.

Cover and title page image: World War I British pilot and fighting ace, Captain Albert Ball, posing with propeller and nose cone, 1917.

Acknowledgments appear on page 869, which constitutes an extension of this copyright page.

ISBN-13: 978-0-13-372395-3

ISBN-10: 0-13-372395-X

2 3 4 5 6 7 8 9 10 V052 13 12 11

The Concept Connector Solution

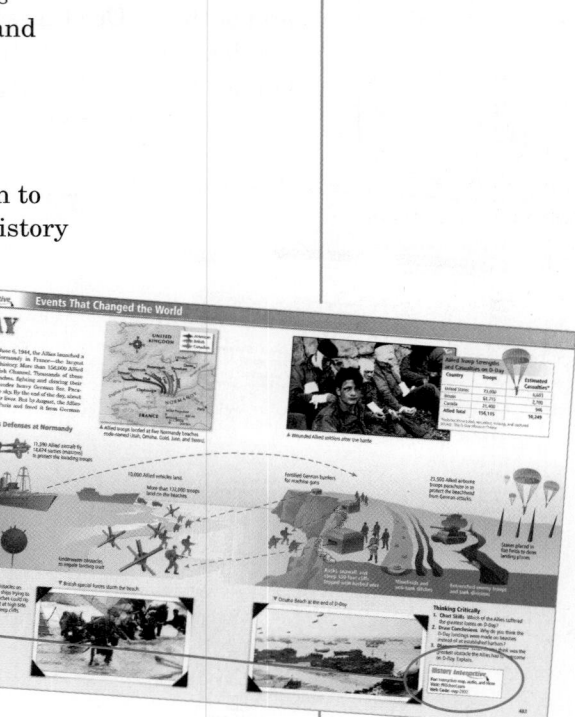

The Concept Connector Solution is an engaging way for you to connect with World History. As you study different civilizations, you will again and again encounter enduring Essential Questions and issues that people have wrestled with throughout history and that still challenge us today. The Concept Connector Solution will help you:

- **Connect to experience the past**
- **Connect to succeed today**
- **Connect to understand today and tomorrow**

Connect to Experience the Past

Experience the excitement of history for yourself. Video, audio, and digital interactivities make history come alive as you experience and interact with people and events of the past.

WITNESS HISTORY VIDEO

With a Discovery Channel video program for every chapter, the sights and sounds of each era come to life through historical reenactments and expert analysis.

WITNESS HISTORY 🔊 AUDIO

Audio symbols throughout your text let you know when you can listen to primary sources, music, and sounds from the past on your Witness History Audio CD or Interactive Textbook.

History *Interactive* **Geography** *Interactive*

Use the Web Codes to go online for interactive animations, maps, timelines, and more. Listen to the people who were there and see dramatic images of the past.

Go Online at PHSchool.com

History *Interactive*

For: Interactive map, audio, and more
Visit: PHSchool.com
Web Code: nap-2941

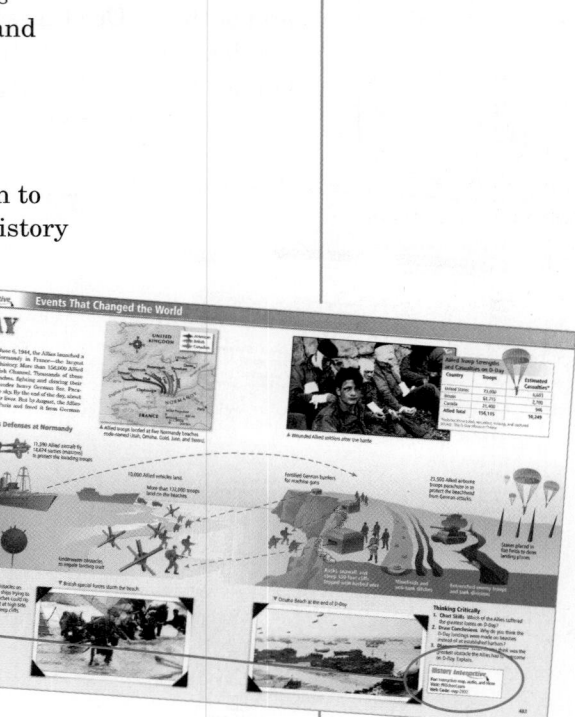

Connect to Succeed Today

Prentice Hall World History's Concept Connector Solution provides you with a variety of strategies and tools to help you truly understand the past, demonstrate your knowledge of world history, and succeed on quizzes, projects, and high-stakes tests.

21st Century Skills Handbook

The 21st Century Skills Handbook at the front of your textbook lets you brush up on important skills that you will use throughout your World History course and throughout your life. With 21st century knowledge and skills, you will succeed in school and succeed in life. Skills instruction to help you read, learn, and demonstrate your knowledge of world history includes:

- Reading Informational Texts
- Writing Handbook
- Geography Skills Handbook
- Critical Thinking About Texts, Visuals, and Media Sources
- Speaking and Listening

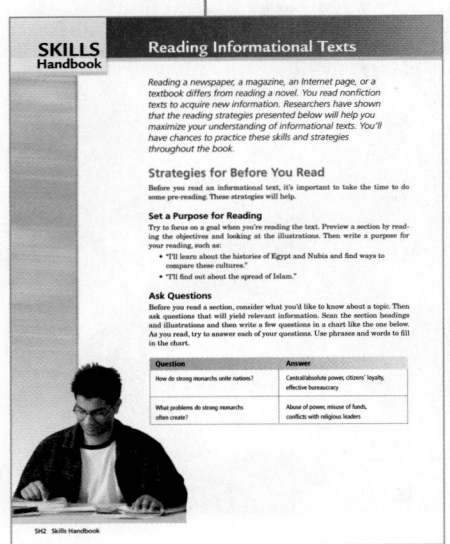

Note Taking

At the start of every section, you'll find suggestions on how to take notes using graphic organizers, timelines, and outlines. Use these to take notes in your own notebook, in your Reading and Note Taking Study Guide, or on the Note Taking Worksheets which you can download.

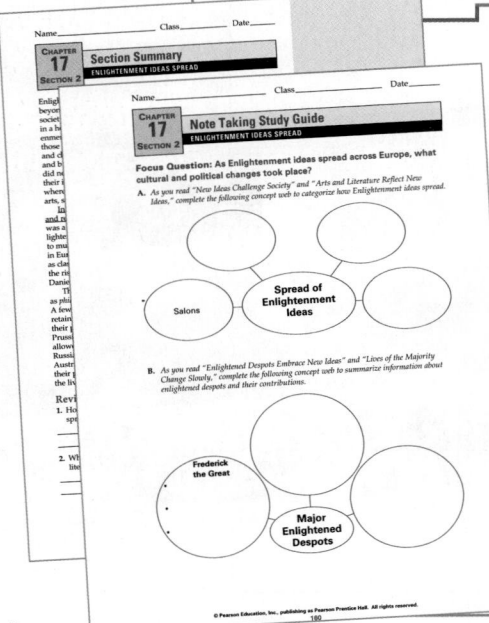

Reading and Note Taking Study Guide

Use your print or online study guide to develop vocabulary, practice reading and note taking skills, and record main ideas in different graphic formats. Use the easy-to-read summaries to help you learn the main ideas.

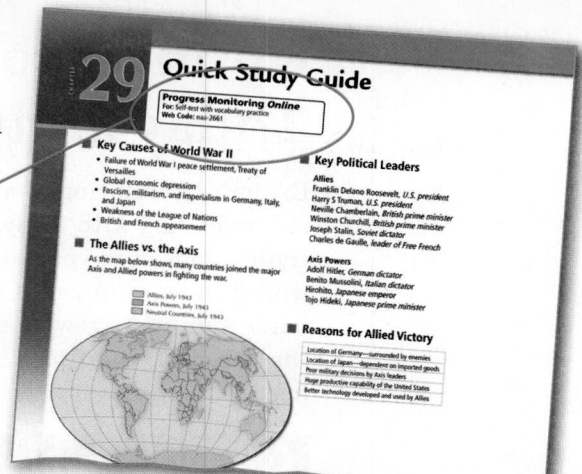

Progress Monitoring Online

Web codes at the end of every section take you to online quizzes with multiple choice questions on section content and vocabulary. At the end of each chapter, you'll find an online self-test on chapter content and a crossword puzzle to test your vocabulary mastery.

Go Online at PHSchool.com

Progress Monitoring *Online*
For: Self-test with vocabulary practice
Web Code: naa-2961

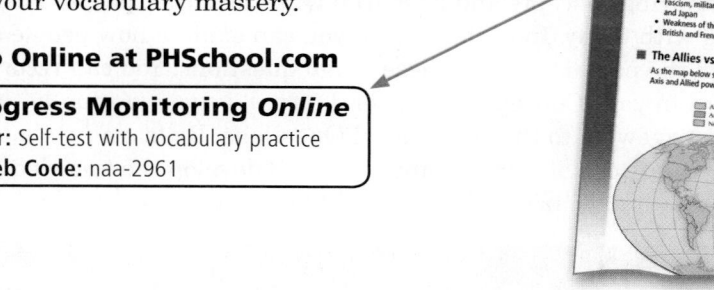

Quick Study Guides

At the end of each chapter, use the Quick Study Guide to make sure you have mastered the chapter contents and are ready for tests. Each Quick Study Guide organizes and reviews main ideas in a variety of formats, including:

- charts, graphs, and tables
- maps and illustrations
- graphic organizers and concept webs
- outlines and summaries
- timelines (Interactive timelines available online at PHSchool.com)

Document-Based Assessment

At the end of each chapter, the Document-Based Assessment contains several documents followed by multiple-choice questions that help you analyze documents and practice your map, graph, visual learning, and critical reading skills. A writing task helps you compare, contrast, and draw conclusions about the various documents.

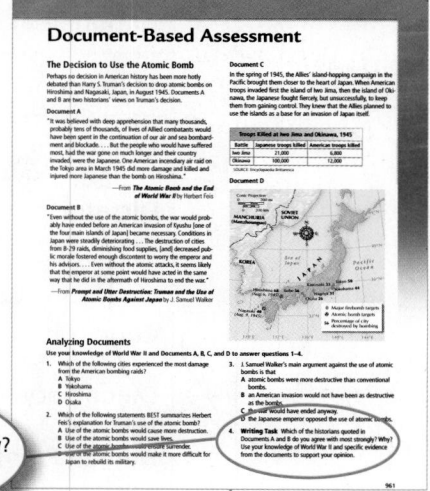

the Japanese emperor opposed the use of ato...

4. **Writing Task** Which of the historians quoted in Documents A and B do you agree with most strongly? Why? Use your knowledge of World War II and specific evidence from the documents to support your opinion.

Connect to Understand Today and Tomorrow

Explore 18 enduring concepts and Essential Questions that people are still wrestling with today. In each chapter, you can explore how people and civilizations of the past dealt with these tough questions. You can record what you learn in your Concept Connector Journal, as you gradually build your own answers to these Essential Questions. By learning about the Essential Questions of world history, you will develop the knowledge needed to understand your world today and tomorrow.

Concept	Essential Question
Belief Systems	How do religions and belief systems affect society?
Geography's Impact	How do geography and people affect one another?
Conflict	When, if ever, should people go to war?
Cultural Diffusion	Why does cultural diffusion occur?
Trade	What are the intended and unintended effects of trade?
Science and Technology	What are the benefits and costs of science and technology?
Political Systems	How do political systems rise, develop and decline?
Impact of the Individual	How can an individual change the world?
Economic Systems	How should resources and wealth be distributed?
Revolution	Why do political revolutions occur?
Nationalism	How can nationalism be a unifying and a divisive force?
Migration	Under what circumstances do people migrate?
Empire	How does a state gain or lose power over others?
Dictatorship	Why do people sometimes support dictators?
Genocide	Why do people sometimes commit the crime of genocide?
Cooperation	With whom should we cooperate and why?
Democracy	Under what conditions is democracy most likely to succeed?
Human Rights	How are human rights won or lost?

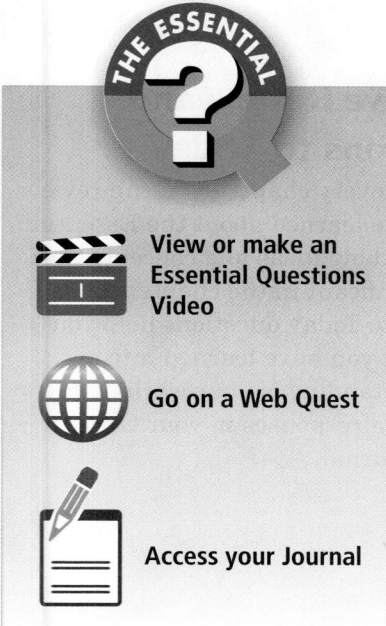

View or make an Essential Questions Video

Go on a Web Quest

Access your Journal

View Concept Connector Online

It's all here! As you start or finish a chapter, you can go online to find out which Essential Questions are most pertinent to the chapter. For each Essential Question, you can explore a full-page feature, engage in various interactivities, pursue a Web Quest, or make and submit your own video or digital presentation. You will record what you learn in your Concept Connector Journal. Finally, you will transfer your knowledge of the past into a better understanding of your world today and tomorrow.

Go Online at PHSchool.com
Web Code: nah-3008

Concept Connector Feature Pages

Each of the 18 Essential Questions is highlighted in a full-page feature. Suppose the question is "When, if ever, should people go to war?" The full-page feature in the chapter you are studying will show you how people of that time dealt with conflict. A timeline will give you ideas on why people of other times and places went to war or avoided war. Most importantly, you will transfer your knowledge and explore how people today are still dealing with conflict and war.

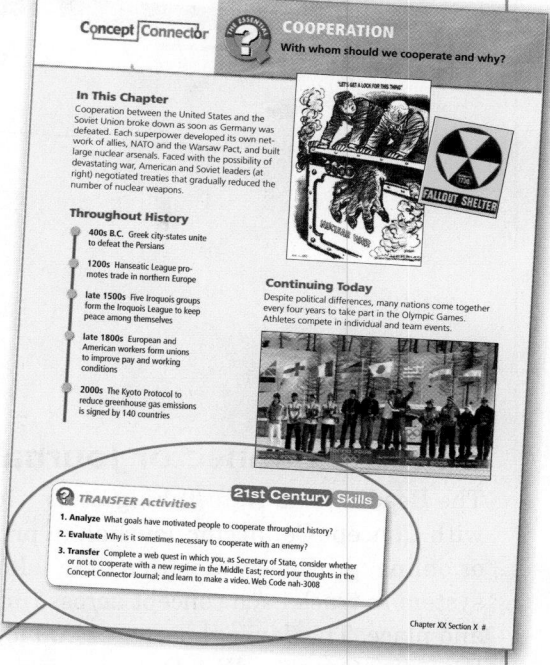

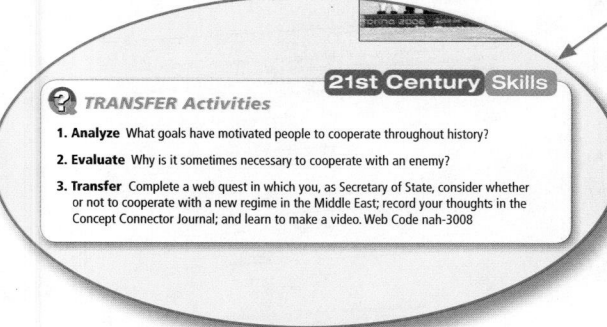

TRANSFER Activities
21st Century Skills

1. **Analyze** What goals have motivated people to cooperate throughout history?

2. **Evaluate** Why is it sometimes necessary to cooperate with an enemy?

3. **Transfer** Complete a web quest in which you, as Secretary of State, consider whether or not to cooperate with a new regime in the Middle East; record your thoughts in the Concept Connector Journal; and learn to make a video. Web Code nah-3008

Transfer Activities and Student-Made Projects Online

After working with the full-page feature, you can go online to transfer what you have learned about the past into a clearer understanding of what's happening in your world today. You might go on a Web Quest, play a role-playing game, interact with digital primary resources, or make and submit your own video or digital presentation.

Cumulative Review and Connections to Today

At the end of every chapter, you can review what you have learned about the Essential Questions and big ideas and concepts that are most significant in the chapter. The Connections to Today questions help you transfer what you have learned into a better understanding of your world today. You can record responses in your Concept Connector Journal.

Concept Connector Journal

The Reading and Note Taking Study Guide with Concept Connector Journal, in print or online, provides you with a note taking system to track each concept across time and place. The Journal prepares you for Essential Question Web Quests, activities, and essays. The essays are just like thematic essays on high-stakes tests. In your essays, you will respond to enduring Essential Questions on big ideas and concepts by drawing on your knowledge of different historical eras and civilizations.

A message for you from Grant Wiggins

The Concept Connector Solution will help you gain understanding of big ideas—not just for "the test," but for life. Essential Questions are the foundation of the system. Each Essential Question is designed to guide your inquiry into important ideas of World History. How is an essential question different from any other question?

There are three basic kinds of questions that you face as a student.

1. The factual question: *When did World War II begin?* The answer is in the textbook.

2. The opinion question: *Should the United States have dropped the atomic bomb on Japan?* The answer is your personal response, based on your values and the facts that you know.

3. The Essential Question: *When, if ever, should people go to war?* This is clearly an important and timeless question that is not linked to only one chapter or era. You will build an answer to this question as you study history, do research, and complete a Web Quest. But, in some ways, you will never be finished answering the question because it is a question that every generation must face, from your great grandparents who lived through major wars in the twentieth century to you who will face the conflicts of the twenty-first century.

Essential Questions are challenging, but need not be overwhelming. Take a step-by-step approach.

Step 1. Don't become buried by a blizzard of facts. Look for the key ideas, themes, and trends implied by the question, around which facts are presented. What is the key issue or dispute? What matters to us in the present about this past event? Use the Concept Connector Journal to take notes not only on the facts, but also on ideas about the question that are sparked by those facts in the text. Think about the question throughout the course and note details related to it regularly in your journal.

Step 2. You often need to question the question itself. Consider the question above: *When, if ever, should people go to war?* Does *when* refer to events outside the country? For example, someone might say that we should go to war when our allies are invaded. Or does *when* refer to the politics inside our own country in terms of the decision-making process? Then, the answer to *when* might be that we should only go to war when all citizens strongly support the cause. The question refers to both meanings, and both should be carefully considered.

Step 3. Consider the alternatives, weigh the evidence and arguments, and reach a thoughtful conclusion—like a jury member. All important historical and political questions can be looked at from different points of view. The best historians carefully explore alternative narratives, theories, and arguments. They know all sides of an argument, and they can offer good reasons why their argument is a better explanation than the alternatives. By exploring Essential Questions in this way, you will build understandings that will have lasting value beyond the classroom—and be more thoughtful about issues that you will face in the future.

"I want you to really see the value of history! That's our aim here: to help you achieve useful and interesting insight. We want you to understand . . . the goal is understanding, not superficial knowledge." —Grant Wiggins, World History Program Consultant

▲ Mali sculpture, c. 1300

▼ Goddess Athena supervising a vote

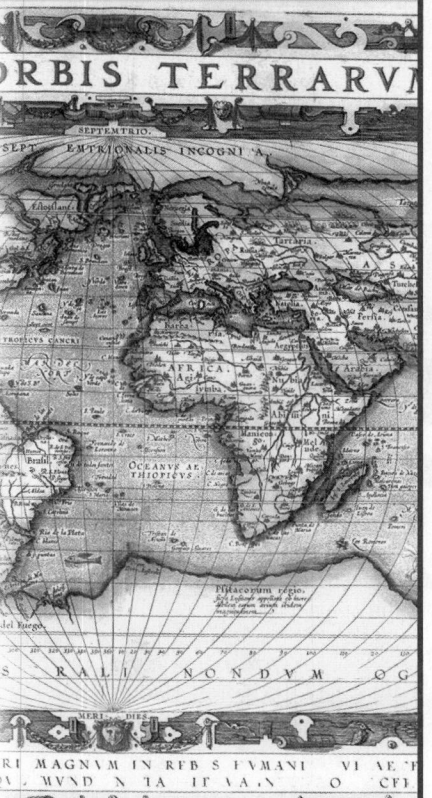

▲ Map of the world, 1560

UNIT 2 ENLIGHTENMENT AND REVOLUTION (1700–1850)

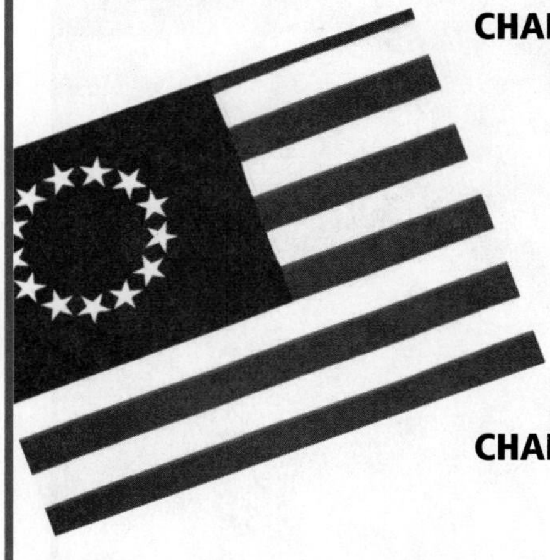

▲ Thirteen-star flag of the original colonies

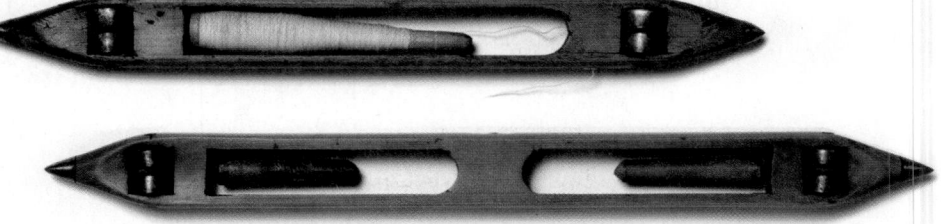

▶ Shuttles used to speed up the weaving process

▲ Chinese Imperial
embroidered robe

▼ Mexico's coat of arms (below); sheet music of a patriotic song of World War I (right)

▼ German children greet Berlin airlift plane.

▼ The world's first iron bridge, Shropshire, England

▲ Agricultural development assistance in Zambia, Africa

SPECIAL FEATURES AND MULTIMEDIA

Witness History: Janina's War Story

"It was 10:30 in the morning and I was helping my mother and a servant girl with bags and baskets as they set out for the market. . . . Suddenly the high-pitch scream of diving planes caused everyone to freeze. . . . Countless explosions shook our house followed by the *rat-tat-tat* of strafing machine guns. We could only stare at each other in horror. Later reports would confirm that several German Stukas had screamed out of a blue sky and . . . dropped several bombs along the main street—and then returned to strafe the market. The carnage was terrible." ◀))) AUDIO

—Janina Sulkowska,
Krzemieniec, Poland, September 12, 1939

WITNESS HISTORY ◀))) AUDIO

Primary source audio accounts throughout the text bring the voices and sounds of history to life.*

***Available on Witness History Audio CD and online at PHSchool.com.**

WITNESS HISTORY VIDEO

**Witness History Discovery School™ videos for each chapter bring
the events you read about in the text to life.**

History *Interactive* — Events That Changed the World

**Audio, video, and animation-filled features help you explore
major turning points in history.**

Concept Connector

**Explore World History's essential questions and go beyond the facts to
connect with the issues that people are still wrestling with today.**

Primary Sources

Full-page excerpts allow you to relive history through eyewitness accounts and documents.

In-text Primary Sources

Gain insights as you read by reading the words of people who were there.

Traveler's Tales

View historic places through the eyes of those who traveled there.

COMPARING VIEWPOINTS

Explore issues by analyzing two opposing viewpoints.

HUMANITIES

Experience great literature and arts from around the world.

BIOGRAPHIES

Meet fascinating history makers.

▼ Marie Curie

INFOGRAPHICS

Photographs, maps, charts, illustrations, audio, and text help you understand the significance of important historical events and developments.

Julius Caesar ▶

Document Based Assessment

Practice the art and science of a historian by analyzing an event through examining multiple historical documents, data, and images.

Cause and Effect

**Diagrams help you see the short- and long-term causes and effects
of history's most important events.**

Charts and Graphs

Diagrams and data help you understand history through visuals.

Charts and Graphs

Maps Geography *Interactive*

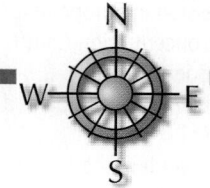

Interactive maps and Audio Guided Tours for each map with a Web code help you understand where history happened.

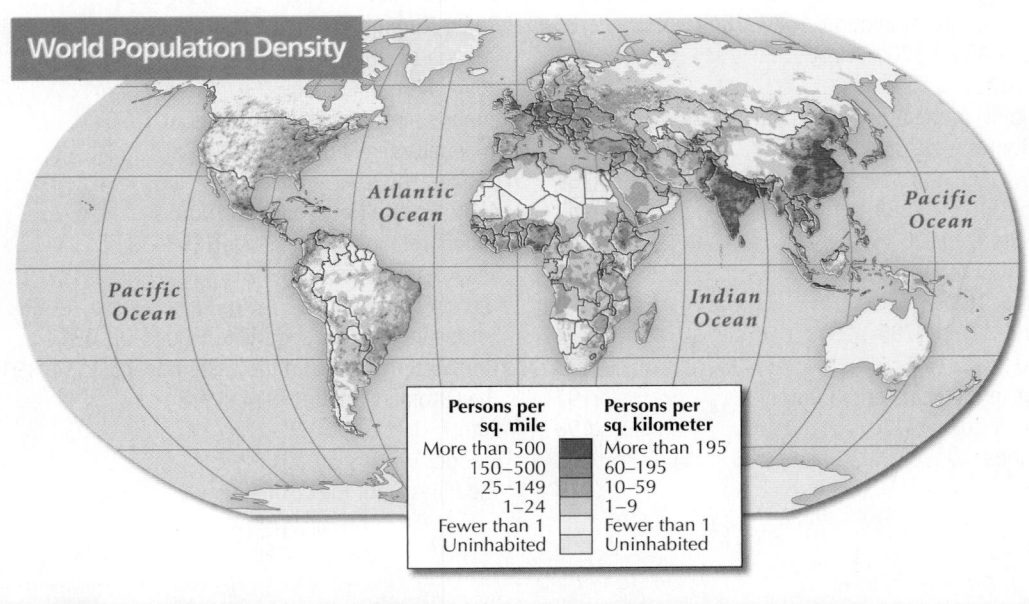

World Population Density

Persons per sq. mile	Persons per sq. kilometer
More than 500	More than 195
150–500	60–195
25–149	10–59
1–24	1–9
Fewer than 1	Fewer than 1
Uninhabited	Uninhabited

Raising the achievement level of all students is the number one challenge facing teachers today. To assist in meeting this challenge, we've enlisted a team of respected authors and consultants who specialize in world history education, reading in the content areas, and differentiated instruction. In the following pages, you'll find the key elements woven throughout this program that assure teaching and learning success.

Pacing GUIDE

Choose your course from the chart below. Then use the **Daily Pacing Guide** on this and the following pages to help plan the number of days that can be allotted to chapters or sections to meet your curriculum needs.

Chapter/Section	World History		Ancient History		Modern History	
	Periods	**Blocks**	**Periods**	**Blocks**	**Periods**	**Blocks**
Connecting With Past Learnings Part 1: Early Civilizations*						
1 Toward Civilizations (Prehistory–3000 B.C.)					.5	.25
2 First Civilizations: Africa and Asia (3200 B.C.–500 B.C.)					1	.5
3 Early Civilizations in India and China (2600 B.C.–256 B.C.)					.5	.25
Connecting With Past Learnings Part 2: Empires of the Ancient World*						
1 Empires of India and China (600 B.C.–A.D. 550)					.5	.25
2 Ancient Greece (1750 B.C.–133 B.C.)					1.5	.75
3 Ancient Rome and the Rise of Christianity (509 B.C.–A.D. 476)					1.5	.75
4 Civilizations of the Americas (1400 B.C.–A.D. 1570)					.5	.25
Connecting With Past Learnings Part 3: Regional Civilizations*						
1 The Rise of Europe (500– 1300)					.5	.25
2 The High and Late Middle Ages (1050–1450)					1	.5
3 The Byzantine Empire and Russia (330–1613)					.5	.25
4 Muslim Civilizations (622–1629)					1	.5
5 Kingdoms and Trading States of Africa (730 B.C. –A.D. 1591)					.5	.25
6 Spread of Civilizations in East Asia (500–1650)					.5	.25
TOTAL					10	5

*****Modern Era edition only**

1 Period = 50 minutes   **1 Block = 100 minutes**

Chapter/Section	World History		Ancient History		Modern History	
	Periods	**Blocks**	**Periods**	**Blocks**	**Periods**	**Blocks**
Foundations of Civilization (Prehistory–300 B.C.)						
1 Understanding Our Past	1	.5	3	1.5		
2 Turning Point: The Neolithic Revolution	1	.5	3	1.5		
3 Beginnings of Civilization	1	.5	3	1.5		
TOTAL	3	1.5	9	4.5		
Ancient Middle East and Egypt (3200 B.C.–500 B.C.)						
1 City-States of Ancient Sumer	1	.5	3	1.5		
2 Invaders, Traders, and Empire Builders	1	.5	3	1.5		
3 Kingdom on the Nile	.5	.25	2.5	1.25		
4 Egyptian Civilization	1.5	.75	3	1.5		
5 Roots of Judaism	1	.5	2.5	1.25		
TOTAL	5	2.5	14	7		
Ancient India and China (2600 B.C.–A.D. 550)						
1 Early Civilizations of India and Pakistan	1.5	.75	3.5	1.75		
2 Hinduism and Buddhism	1.5	.75	3.5	1.75		
3 Powerful Empires of India	1	.5	2	1		
4 Rise of Civilization in China	1.5	.75	3.5	1.75		
5 Strong Rulers Unite China	1.5	.75	3.5	1.75		
TOTAL	7	3.5	16	8		
Ancient Greece (1750 B.C.–133 B.C.)						
1 Early People of the Aegean	.5	.25	2.5	1.25		
2 The Rise of Greek City-States	1.5	.75	4	2		
3 Conflict in the Greek World	1	.5	2.5	1.25		
4 The Glory That Was Greece	2	1	4	2		
5 Alexander and the Hellenistic Age	2	1	4	2		
TOTAL	7	3.5	17	8.5		
Ancient Rome and the Rise of Christianity (509 B.C.–A.D. 476)						
1 The Roman World Takes Shape	1	.5	2	1		
2 From Republic to Empire	1.5	.75	4	2		
3 The Roman Achievement	1	.5	3	1.5		
4 The Rise of Christianity	2	1	4	2		
5 The Long Decline	2.5	1.25	5	2.5		
TOTAL	8	4	18	9		

Pacing GUIDE

Chapter/Section	World History		Ancient History		Modern History	
	Periods	**Blocks**	**Periods**	**Blocks**	**Periods**	**Blocks**
Civilizations of the Americas (Prehistory–A.D. 1570)						
1 Civilizations of Mesoamerica	2	1	4	2		
2 Andean Cultures of South America	1	.5	3	1.5		
3 Peoples of North America	1	.5	3	1.5		
TOTAL	**4**	**2**	**10**	**5**		
The Rise of Europe (500–1300)						
1 The Early Middle Ages	1	.5	2.5	1.25		
2 Feudalism and the Manor Economy	1	.5	2.5	1.25		
3 The Medieval Church	1	.5	3	1.5		
4 Economic Recovery Sparks Change	2	1	4	2		
TOTAL	**5**	**2.5**	**12**	**6**		
The High and Late Middle Ages (1050–1450)						
1 Royal Power Grows	1	.5	4	2		
2 The Holy Roman Empire and the Church	1.5	.75	3	1.5		
3 The Crusades and the Wider World	1.5	.75	3	1.5		
4 Learning and Culture Flourish	1	.5	3	1.5		
5 A Time of Crisis	1	.5	3	1.5		
TOTAL	**6**	**3**	**16**	**8**		
The Byzantine Empire, Russia, and Eastern Europe (330–1613)						
1 The Byzantine Empire	2	1	4	2		
2 The Rise of Russia	1	.5	3	1.5		
3 Shaping Eastern Europe	1	.5	3	1.5		
TOTAL	**4**	**2**	**10**	**5**		
Muslim Civilizations (622–1629)						
1 The Rise of Islam	1.5	.75	3	1.5		
2 Building a Muslim Empire	1.5	.75	3	1.5		
3 Muslim Civilization's Golden Age	1	.5	3	1.5		
4 India's Muslim Empires	1	.5	3	1.5		
5 The Ottoman and Safavid Empires	2	1	3	1.5		
TOTAL	**7**	**3.5**	**15**	**7.5**		

Chapter/Section	World History		Ancient History		Modern History	
	Periods	**Blocks**	**Periods**	**Blocks**	**Periods**	**Blocks**
Kingdoms and Trading States of Africa (730 B.C.–A.D. 1591)						
1 Early Civilizations of Africa	1	.5	3	1.5		
2 Kingdoms of West Africa	1	.5	4	2		
3 Kingdoms and Trading States of East Africa	1	.5	3	1.5		
4 Societies in Medieval Africa	1	.5	2	1		
TOTAL	**4**	**2**	**12**	**6**		
The Spread of Civilization in East and Southeast Asia (500–1650)						
1 Two Golden Ages of China	2	1	4	2		
2 The Mongol and Ming Empires	2	1	3.5	1.75		
3 Korea and Its Traditions	1	.5	2	1		
4 The Emergence of Japan and the Feudal Age	1	.5	3.5	1.75		
5 Diverse Cultures of Southeast Asia	1	.5	2	1		
TOTAL	**7**	**3.5**	**15**	**7.5**		
The Renaissance and Reformation (1300–1650)						
1 The Renaissance in Italy	1.5	.75	4	2	4	2
2 The Renaissance in the North	1	.75	3	1.5	1.5	.75
3 The Protestant Reformation	.5	.25	3	1.5	3	1.5
4 Reformation Ideas Spread	1.5	.75			1.5	.75
5 The Scientific Revolution	1.5	.75			2	1
TOTAL	**6**	**3**	**10**	**5**	**12**	**6**
The Beginnings of Our Global Age: Europe, Africa, and Asia (1415–1796)						
1 The Search for Spices	1.5	.75	4	2	1	.5
2 Turbulent Centuries in Africa	1.5	.75			2	1
3 European Footholds in South and Southeast Asia	1	.5			1	.5
4 Encounters in East Asia	1	.5			1	.5
TOTAL	**5**	**2.5**	**4**	**2**	**5**	**2.5**
The Beginnings of Our Global Age: Europe and the Americas (1492–1750)						
1 Conquest in the Americas	1	.5			2	1
2 Spanish and Portuguese Colonies in the Americas	1	.5	2	1	1.5	.75
3 Struggle for North America	1	.5			1	.5
4 The Atlantic Slave Trade	1	.5			2	1
5 Effects of Global Contact	2	1			1.5	.75
TOTAL	**6**	**3**	**2**	**1**	**8**	**4**

Pacing GUIDE

Chapter/Section	World History		Ancient History		Modern History	
	Periods	**Blocks**	**Periods**	**Blocks**	**Periods**	**Blocks**
The Age of Absolutism (1550–1800)						
1 Spanish Power Grows	1	.5			1	.5
2 France Under Louis XIV	1	.5			2	1
3 Parliament Triumphs in England	2	1			2.5	1.25
4 Rise of Austria and Prussia	1	.5			1	.5
5 Absolute Monarchy in Russia	1	.5			1.5	.75
TOTAL	6	3			8	4
The Enlightenment and the American Revolution (1700–1800)						
1 Philosophy in the Age of Reason	1.5	.75			2	1
2 Enlightenment Ideas Spread	1	.5			2	1
3 Birth of the American Republic	1.5	.75			1	.5
TOTAL	4	2			5	2.5
The French Revolution and Napoleon (1789–1815)						
1 On the Eve of Revolution	1.5	.75			2.5	1.25
2 The French Revolution Unfolds	1.5	.75			2	1
3 Radical Days of the Revolution	1	.5			1.5	.75
4 The Age of Napoleon	2	1			3	1.5
TOTAL	6	3			9	4.5
The Industrial Revolution Begins (1750–1850)						
1 Dawn of the Industrial Age	.5	.25			2	1
2 Britain Leads the Way	1.5	.75			1	.5
3 Social Impact of the Industrial Revolution	1	.5			2	1
4 New Ways of Thinking	1	.5			2	1
TOTAL	4	2			7	3.5
Revolutions in Europe and Latin America (1790–1848)						
1 An Age of Ideologies	1	.5			2	1
2 Revolutions of 1830 and 1848	.5	.25			1	.5
3 Revolts in Latin America	1.5	.75			2	1
TOTAL	3	1.5			5	2.5
Life in the Industrial Age (1800–1914)						
1 The Industrial Revolution Spreads	1.5	.75			2	1
2 The Rise of the Cities	1	.5			2	1
3 Changing Attitudes and Values	1	.5			2	1
4 Arts in the Industrial Age	.5	.25			1	.5
TOTAL	4	2			7	3.5

Chapter/Section	World History		Ancient History		Modern History	
	Periods	**Blocks**	**Periods**	**Blocks**	**Periods**	**Blocks**
Nationalism Triumphs in Europe (1800–1914)						
1 Building a German Nation	1	.5			2	1
2 Germany Strengthens	1	.5			1.5	.75
3 Unifying Italy	1	.5			1.5	.75
4 Nationalism Threatens Old Empires	.5	.25			0.5	.25
5 Russia: Reform and Reaction	1.5	.75			2.5	1.25
TOTAL	**5**	**2.5**			**8**	**4**
Growth of Western Democracies (1815–1914)						
1 Democratic Reform in Britain	1	.5			1	.5
2 Social and Economic Reform in Britain	1	.5			1.5	.75
3 Division and Democracy in France	1	.5			1	.5
4 Expansion of the United States	1	.5			1.5	.75
TOTAL	**4**	**2**			**5**	**2.5**
The New Imperialism (1800–1914)						
1 Building Overseas Empires	1.5	.75			1.5	.75
2 The Partition of Africa	1.5	.75			2	1
3 European Claims in Muslim Regions	1	.5			1.5	.75
4 The British Take Over India	1	.5			1.5	.75
5 China and the New Imperialism	1	.5			1.5	.75
TOTAL	**6**	**3**			**8**	**4**
New Global Patterns (1800–1914)						
1 Japan Modernizes	1.5	.75			2.5	1.25
2 Imperialism in Southeast Asia and the Pacific	1	.5			2	1
3 Self-Rule for Canada, Australia, and New Zealand	1	.5			1	.5
4 Economic Imperialism in Latin America	1.5	.75			1.5	.75
TOTAL	**5**	**2.5**			**7**	**3.5**
World War I and the Russian Revolution (1914–1924)						
1 The Great War Begins	1.5	.75			2	1
2 A New Kind of War	1	.5			2	1
3 Winning the War	1	.5			1.5	.75
4 Making the Peace	1	.5			1.5	.75
5 Revolution and Civil War in Russia	1.5	.75			3	1.5
TOTAL	**6**	**3**			**10**	**5**

Pacing GUIDE

Chapter/Section	World History		Ancient History		Modern History	
	Periods	**Blocks**	**Periods**	**Blocks**	**Periods**	**Blocks**
Nationalism and Revolution Around the World (1910–1939)						
1 Struggle in Latin America	1	.5			1.5	.75
2 Nationalism in Africa and the Middle East	1.5	.75			2	1
3 India Seeks Self-Rule	.5	.25			1	.5
4 Upheavals in China	1	.5			2	1
5 Conflicting Forces in Japan	1				1.5	.75
TOTAL	**5**	**2.5**			**8**	**4**
The Rise of Totalitarianism (1919–1939)						
1 Postwar Social Changes					2	1
2 The Western Democracies Stumble	.5	.25			1	.5
3 Fascism in Italy	1	.5			2	1
4 The Soviet Union Under Stalin	1.5	.75			2.5	1.25
5 Hitler and the Rise of Nazi Germany	1.5	.75			2.5	1.25
TOTAL	**5**	**2.5**			**10**	**5**
World War II and Its Aftermath (1931–1955)						
1 From Appeasement to War	1	.5			2	1
2 The Axis Advances	1	.5			2	1
3 The Allies Turn the Tide	1.5	.75			2	1
4 Victory in Europe and the Pacific	1	.5			1	.5
5 The End of World War II	1.5	.75			2	1
TOTAL	**6**	**3**			**9**	**4.5**
The Cold War (1945–1991)						
1 The Cold War Unfolds	2	1			3	1.5
2 The Industrialized Democracies	1	.5			2	1
3 Communism Spreads in East Asia	1.5	.75			2	1
4 War in Southeast Asia	1.5	.75			2	1
5 The End of the Cold War	3	1.5			3	1.5
TOTAL	**9**	**4.5**			**12**	**6**
New Nations Emerge (1945–Present)						
1 Independent Nations of South Asia	1	.5			1.5	.75
2 New Nations of Southeast Asia	1	.5			1.5	.75
3 African Nations Gain Independence	1	.5			1.5	.75
4 The Modern Middle East	2	1			2.5	1.25
TOTAL	**5**	**2.5**			**7**	**3.5**

Planning

1 Period = 50 minutes　　　　**1 Block = 100 minutes**

Chapter/Section	World History		Ancient History		Modern History	
	Periods	**Blocks**	**Periods**	**Blocks**	**Periods**	**Blocks**
Regional Conflicts (1945–Present)						
1 Conflicts Divide Nations	.5	.25			1	.5
2 Struggles in Africa	1	.5			2	1
3 Conflicts in the Middle East	1.5	.75			2	1
TOTAL	**3**	**1.5**			**5**	**2.5**
The Developing World (1945–Present)						
1 The Challenges of Development	1.5	.75			2	1
2 Africa Seeks a Better Future	1	.5			2	1
3 China and India: Two Giants of Asia	1	.5			2	1
4 Latin America Builds Democracy	1.5	.75			2	1
TOTAL	**5**	**2.5**			**8**	**4**
The World Today						
1 Industrialized Nations After the Cold War	1	.5			1	.5
2 Globalization	1	.5			2	1
3 Social and Environmental Challenges	1	.5			1	.5
4 Security in a Dangerous World	1	.5			2	1
5 Advances in Science and Technology	1	.5			1	.5
TOTAL	**5**	**2.5**			**7**	**3.5**

Research on Differentiated Instruction

Why do we need differentiated instruction?

The wide range of academic diversity in schools today presents both a challenge and an opportunity to all teachers. Because the challenge of accommodating all students is so urgent, we need to plan and teach to include all learners in a new way.

The importance of differentiated instruction Why is it so important to modify our planning and instruction in light of the increased diversity in our classes? First, each of our students is expected to master the key content that is tied to district or state outcome examinations. In other words, if students are in our classes, we are expected to teach to enable them to be successful on these high-stakes exams.

Second, when adolescents encounter failure in meeting rigorous curriculum demands, they often lose hope in their ability to be successful—they may mentally disengage from school, seek out "success" by acting out inappropriately, or even drop out of school. Thus, when we work with struggling learners, the costs for not successfully meeting their needs can be significant.

Meeting the needs of highly capable students is equally challenging. They must be "stretched" to learn new materials and engage in higher order thinking about the curriculum.

In short, the most successful teachers understand the complexity of the academic diversity in their classes and design their lessons and learning experiences accordingly.

What the research tells us The literature on differentiated instruction tells us that active instruction is that which increases the achievement levels of four major subgroups of students—special needs, low-, average-, and high-achieving—equally. If one sub-group benefits significantly more than others from a teacher's attempt to differentiate instruction for the entire class, eventually the attempt will be dropped because a significant portion of the class is not making gains.

To reach the needs of low-achieving students in any class, steps must be taken to ensure that instruction is systematic and explicit. That is, to the degree that the sequence of learning is not clear and new information to be mastered is not clearly taught, the students who struggle most in learning will continue to struggle and will fall further behind their classmates.

Finally, the long-term effects of any instructional practice will be enhanced if a majority of teachers use and reinforce that practice. For example, if Teacher A teaches her class to use a particular learning strategy to master new vocabulary, students will better learn and apply that strategy if it is used and reinforced by all teachers. Effective differentiated instruction is in part dependent on teachers having an opportunity to coordinate the use of similar materials and reinforce critical learning strategies.

How do we provide inclusive instruction?

One of the most important roles that teachers play in effectively providing differentiated instruction is to see themselves as a "mediator" in the learning process. That is, the chances of students learning complex content is greatly enhanced if teachers understand **(a)** the specific difficulties of learners in their class, **(b)** why the curriculum content they are teaching is difficult (Is it abstract, dense, etc.?), and **(c)** the unique features of the curriculum materials and the particular challenges they present in learning. In light of these three factors, the most effective teachers are those who help "mediate" (or manipulate or transform) the content in such a way as to make it understandable and memorable to all their students.

What is the result of differentiated instruction?

While improving student outcomes is a major goal of differentiated instruction, it is important to remember that when teachers are successful in reaching a large majority of students in their classes, an environment of cooperation, learning, and respect emerges. Teachers intent on successfully differentiating their instruction communicate a message that the "work" of this community is learning for *everyone*. Everyday practices and routines are based on cooperation in accomplishing this work, and the interests and learning needs of everyone in the community are taken seriously.

Don Deshler
Don Deshler, Ph.D., is the Chair of Prentice Hall's Differentiated Instruction Board. He assembled a distinguished panel of national experts to serve on the board, who offer extensive experience in educating special needs students, English language learners, less proficient readers, and gifted and talented students. This team informs Prentice Hall's approach to differentiated instruction and offers guidance on the development of new materials based on this approach. Deshler is the Director of the Center for Research on Learning at the University of Kansas.

Effective Classroom Implementation

The mission of *Prentice Hall World History* is to provide standards-based instruction in ways that allow all learners to participate and to achieve. Because not all students learn in the same manner nor have the same abilities, our program provides options so that all learners work toward the same essential understandings and skills, but use different content, processes, and products to get there. Our effective support helps you close the achievement gap.

Teaching Support Helps You Modify Instruction

The *Teacher's Edition* provides continuous professional development throughout the program, starting with strategies for specific populations at the beginning of this textbook. Differentiated Instruction boxes throughout each chapter offer specific suggestions for modifying instruction to accommodate all learners. Direct instruction creates opportunities to build a community of learners who can learn from and about one another. Together, these tools help you provide all learners with meaningful access to the curriculum.

> **Differentiated Instruction** Solutions for All Learners
>
> **L1 Special Needs** **L2 Less Proficient Readers** **L2 English Language Learners**
>
> Divide students into pairs. Have each pair construct a concept map of the strategies used to fight a total war. Students should determine the main ideas surrounding this concept and determine supporting ideas for each main idea. Then have pairs use their concept maps to discuss why each strategy was important to winning the war.
>
> Use the following study guide resources to help students acquiring basic skills:
>
> **Adapted Reading and Note Taking Study Guide**
> - Adapted Reading Strategies
> - Adapted Concept Connector
> - Adapted Section Summary

Varied Resources Address Different Populations

Prentice Hall World History resources are designed to help students of all abilities master core content. The *Reading and Note Taking Study Guide* is one such aid that encourages literacy and provides a framework for vocabulary development and learning. With three versions (On-level, Adapted, and Spanish), this note taking system provides the required support for all levels. The program also delivers content through a wide variety of formats—including text, transparencies, audio, video, and interactive text—that appeal to all of your students.

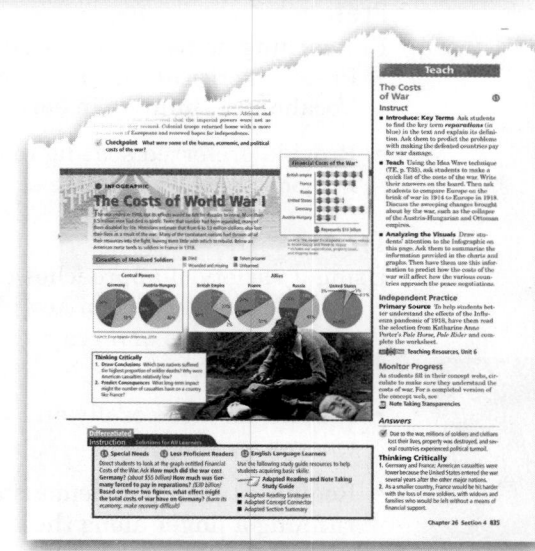

Leveled Review and Assessments Give You More Options

The On-level, Adapted, and Spanish Study Guides review content in different formats. The *ExamView*® Test Bank CD-ROM offers leveled tests and makes it easy to adapt tests based on individual needs.

Differentiated Instruction

Strategies for Differentiated Instruction

Differentiated instruction can be fostered through modifying instruction to address individual needs. Lesson plans in this *Teacher's Edition* provide differentiated instruction strategies and suggest ancillary support such as the three levels of the *Reading and Note Taking Study Guide.* The following pages provide general guidelines for modifying instruction for special needs students, English language learners, less proficient readers, gifted and talented students, and advanced readers.

SPECIAL NEEDS

Students with special education needs require unique cognitive, behavioral, social, and physical strategies. To help create a classroom that supports the participation and achievement of all students, set clear expectations and provide reasonable choices. Plan lessons with individual adaptations and modifications. Offer instructional activities that foster the development of relationships among students and between students and teachers.

Preteach
Preteaching helps prepare students for learning.
- Preteach critical social studies terms, people, and places and high-use academic words using the Vocabulary Builders in each section.

- Provide preferred seating in the front of the class for students who read lips or for interpreters. Provide space for a guide dog as necessary.

Teach
Using a variety of approaches enhances lessons.
- Provide an overview of key ideas and concepts presented in the text using outlines, maps, or the text summaries and graphic organizers provided in the *Adapted Reading and Note Taking Study Guide.*

- Present all ideas orally and visually, and when possible, incorporate tactile and kinesthetic experiences as well.

- Require students to demonstrate that they are listening and following along (e.g., taking notes, running a finger along the text).

- Incorporate active reading strategies (e.g., choral reading, paired reading).

- Provide adaptive materials as appropriate (e.g., enlarged print, Braille edition, captions for the video program).

- Incorporate the same comprehension and learning strategies over time to allow for mastery.

Assess
Students need to know what is expected.
- Assess students' understanding by asking them to write questions about what they have learned, identify what they find unclear or confusing, or complete short quick writes of key points.

- When students work in groups or pairs, set up procedures that maintain each student's accountability (e.g., writing, drawing, or response).

- Make sure that you have adequately scaffolded tasks for special needs students and equipped them with writing instruction and practice that builds spoken prerequisite skills.

- When appropriate, have students manage and chart their academic performance, homework and assignment completion, and behavior.

- Provide outlines of what is to be done, with suggested dates and timelines for project completion.

ENGLISH LANGUAGE LEARNERS

Students who are learning English are the fastest-growing segment of the school-age population. These students require frontloading, or preteaching, in order to grasp challenging literacy tasks, such as those encountered in a social studies textbook. Since English language learners may be approaching an assignment with limited background knowledge and weak English vocabulary, concentrate on activities that build strong conceptual and linguistic foundations, guide them through the text's organization, and model appropriate comprehension strategies.

Preteach

English language learners require extra preparation.

- Use Word Knowledge Rating Forms (provided in the ***Skills Handbook***) to determine understanding of essential words. Introduce these words in meaningful contexts, through simple sentences drawing on familiar issues, scenarios, and vocabulary. Ask students to write the definitions in their own words and then define the words when they occur within the reading.

- Utilize realia and visuals (e.g., photographs, objects from everyday life, color transparencies) to make concepts less abstract.

- Lead a quick "text tour," focusing students' attention on illustrations, titles and subtopics, and boldfaced words.

Teach

Many of these techniques will benefit all learners.

- Get students physically involved with the page, using sticky notes to focus and guide their reading.

- Encourage students to read while listening to a recording of the same passage as it is read aloud, such as on the ***Student Edition Audio.*** Spanish-language speakers can also listen to section summaries on the ***Spanish Guided Reading Audio.***

- Use the text summaries and graphic organizers provided in the ***Spanish Reading and Note Taking Study Guide.***

- Have students read the same brief passage several times to build word recognition, fluency, and reading rate.

- Praise students' efforts to experiment with new language in class, both in writing and in speaking.

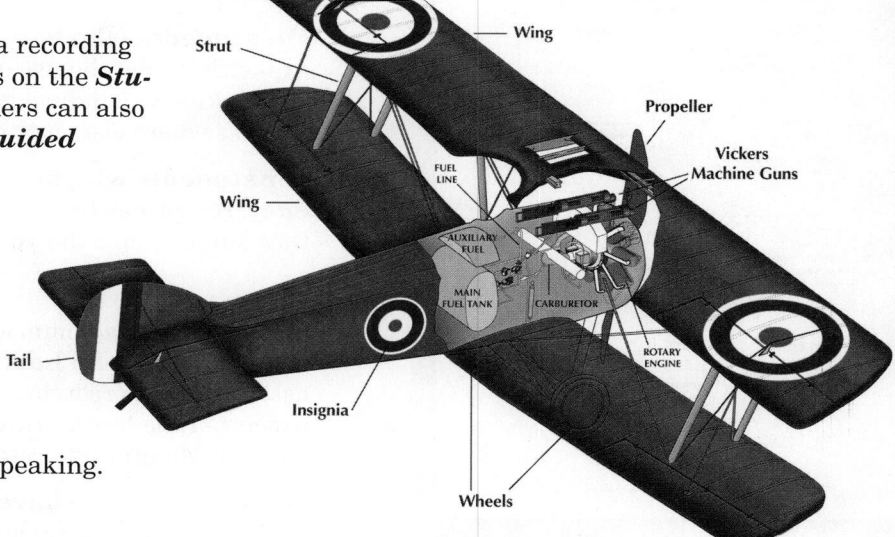

Assess

Students will demonstrate learning in different ways.

- Ask students to demonstrate their understanding by drawing upon different language skills: formal and informal writing assignments, posters, small group tasks, and oral presentations.

- Make sure students understand assessment criteria in advance. Distribute rubrics provided in the ***Assessment Rubrics.*** Whenever possible, provide models of work for students to emulate, along with a non-model that fails to meet the specified assessment criteria.

Differentiated Instruction

LESS PROFICIENT READERS

Less proficient readers are students who begin the year one or more years below grade level yet do not qualify for special education services. They may or may not be English language learners. They may be under-prepared for academic challenges due to difficulties with attention and memory, learning strategies, or vocabulary and reading fluency. It is especially important to engage these students in challenging lessons while incorporating support or instructional scaffolding to increase their likelihood of success.

Preteach

Preteaching helps build students' confidence.
- **For students who have difficulties with attention and memory,** gain attention by requesting a simple physical response (e.g. "Everyone, eyes on me please"). Then keep the lesson pace brisk—a "perky not pokey" pace is helpful.

- **For students who have difficulties with learning strategies,** clarify the rationale for learning a new strategy. Directly teach any pre-requisite skills needed to perform the strategy. Make strategies concrete by having students fill out the K-W-L chart provided in the ***Skills Handbook.***

- **For students who have difficulties with vocabulary and fluency,** directly teach meanings of critical vocabulary required for full understanding of the lesson.

Teach

Lessons have to address specific, different needs.
- **For students who have difficulties with attention and memory,** emphasize connections between new and known information. Engage students in a collaborative "read/reflect/discuss/note" cycle, filling out a graphic organizer from the ***Adapted Reading and Note Taking Study Guide.***

- **For students who have difficulties with learning strategies,** explicitly model the use of the strategy, including a significant focus on thinking aloud during the execution of each step in the strategy. Discuss where else in or out of school students could use the strategy.

- **For students who have difficulties with vocabulary and fluency,** revisit newly acquired vocabulary during discussion. Suggest that students use the Vocabulary Practice Online.

Assess

Assessment must accommodate unique needs.
- **For students who have difficulties with attention and memory,** ask students to reorganize, prioritize, and otherwise reflect on the key aspects of the lesson. Have them explain their graphic organizers to a partner. Monitor and reteach as necessary.

- **For students who have difficulties with learning strategies,** explicitly include strategies as part of quizzes, reports, projects, and other formal assessments.

- **For students who have difficulties with vocabulary and fluency,** randomly call on students to provide examples of the vocabulary word under examination.

GIFTED AND TALENTED STUDENTS AND ADVANCED READERS

Gifted and talented students and advanced readers need modified instruction to achieve their highest potential. They tend to understand complex concepts quickly, learn more rapidly and in greater depth, and may have interests that are different from their peers. Teachers can modify pacing and offer enrichment to allow for exploring topics in-depth, manipulating ideas in novel ways, and making connections to other disciplines.

Preteach

These students may have extensive background.
- Before beginning a new unit, have students write, verbalize, or draw on what they know about the topic and present this information to peers.

- Ask students to brainstorm what they'd like to learn, and then work with them to create a plan for advanced study based on their interests.

Teach

Activate students' ability to think creatively and see connections.
- Help students adjust the pace of their learning, by speeding through concepts they master quickly or by slowing down to study content in depth. The *Teacher's Edition* provides ideas for ways to extend content in the Extend part of the lesson plan.

- Challenge students to tackle more complex topics and offer frequent opportunities to focus on abstract ideas.

- Provide opportunities for in-depth research on student-directed topics. Have students explore topics on the Internet and under your direction.

- Encourage students to make connections between content they are learning and other disciplines such as language arts, science, and math. For example, students might want to read fiction about the historical period they are studying.

Assess

Assessment can take many forms.
- Have students be responsible for part of the assessment of their learning. Allow them to plan, design, and monitor the project or assignment.

- Encourage students to apply standards-based understandings to new situations. Challenge them to take information and use it in novel ways.

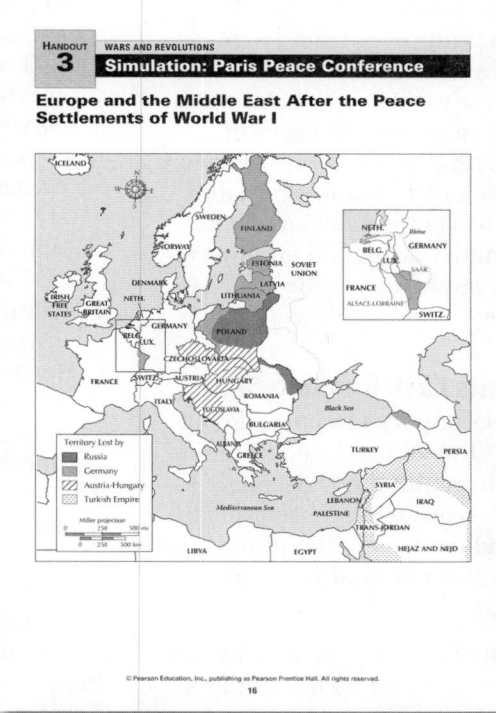

Research on Reading

Why do many students have difficulty reading textbooks? How can we help students read to learn social studies? In the pages that follow, we examine the research on the challenge of reading textbooks, show how Prentice Hall has responded to this research, and offer direct, systematic, and explicit strategies to help your students.

What Is Skilled Reading?

Recent research (Snow et al., 2002) suggests that skillful and strategic reading is a long-term developmental process in which "readers learn how to simultaneously extract and construct meaning through interaction with written language." In other words, successful readers know how to decode all types of words, read with fluency and expression, have well-developed vocabularies, and possess various comprehension strategies such as note taking and summarizing to employ as the academic reading task demands.

Many Students Lack Reading Skills

Sadly, many secondary students do not have solid reading skills. Even students quite skilled in reading novels, short stories, and adolescent magazines typically come to secondary school ill-equipped for the rigors of informational texts, or reading to learn.

Many students tend to dive right into a social studies chapter as if reading a recreational story. They don't first preview the material to create a mental outline and establish a purpose in reading. They have not yet learned other basic strategies, such as reading a section more than once, taking notes as they read, and reading to answer specific questions.

The Unique Demands of Textbooks

The differences between textbooks and the stories or adolescent magazines students are used to reading are dramatic. The most distinctive challenges include:

1. **Conceptual content** Content-area textbooks are laden with new and largely unfamiliar concepts (such as *human-environment interaction* and *nationalism*).
2. **Vocabulary load** The unique vocabulary used in academic texts is often referred to as *academic language.* Academic language consists of high-use academic words, such as *currency* and *restore,* and discipline-specific vocabulary (or "Key Terms"), such as *agrarian* and *legislature.*
3. **Paragraph and organizational patterns** Academic texts are constructed using unfamiliar organizational patterns such as cause-effect, problem-solution, categorization, chain of events, or comparison and contrast.
4. **Sentence structures** Because the purpose of textbooks is to communicate complex information as efficiently as possible, readers will come across sophisticated sentence structures.

Academic texts present such a significant challenge to most students that linguists and language researchers liken them to learning a foreign language (Schleppegrell, 2002). In other words, most secondary students are second-language learners: they are learning the academic language of informational texts.

The Need for Vocabulary Instruction

There is a clear consensus among literacy researchers that accelerating vocabulary growth is a vital and often neglected component of a comprehensive reading program (Baumann and Kameenui, 2004). Numerous studies have documented the strong and reciprocal relationship between vocabulary knowledge and reading comprehension. Research focused on school age second-language learners similarly concludes that vocabulary knowledge is the single best predictor of their academic achievement across subject matter domains.

Educators therefore need to make robust intentional vocabulary instruction a high priority. Intensive instruction should be focused on words related to central lesson concepts (or "Key Terms") and high-use academic words. Academic word lists developed by researchers can help educators determine appropriate high-use academic words (Coxhead, 2000; Xue and Nation, 1984).

Kate Kinsella
Kate Kinsella, Ed.D is a faculty member in the Department of Secondary Education at San Francisco State University and specializes in second-language acquisition and adolescent literacy.

Kevin Feldman
Kevin Feldman, Ed.D is Director of Reading and Early Intervention with the Sonoma County Office of Education and an independent educational consultant.

Effective Classroom Implementation

Research illustrates that virtually all students benefit from direct, systematic, and explicit instruction in reading informational texts (Baker and Gersten, 2000). *Prentice Hall World History* accomplishes this task in three steps: **(1)** Before reading—instructional frontloading **(2)** During reading—guided instruction **(3)** After reading—reflection and study.

Before Reading

If you emphasize preteaching, or "frontloading" your instruction, you will help structure learning to ensure student success.

Build Vocabulary To prepare students to read, introduce the key terms, people, and places at the beginning of each section. Vocabulary Builder terms are located in the margins next to where they appear in the student text and at the beginning of each section in the *Teacher's Edition*.

Set a Purpose Setting a purpose asks students to predict and anticipate what they will read. The Set a Purpose section at the beginning of each chapter in the *Teacher's Edition* includes a number of strategies for accomplishing this goal. These strategies are supported in the *Skills Handbook* and in the *Note Taking Transparencies*.

Additional Reading Strategies At the beginning of each section, the Note Taking activity asks students to focus on one reading skill, such as identifying the main idea, or recognizing sequence. It then provides a graphic organizer to help students apply the skill to the content. Detailed graphic organizers are located in the *Reading and Note Taking Study Guides*.

During Reading

As you read each section, use the direct instruction provided in the *Teacher's Edition* to help guide students through the text. Further practice in reading skills is located in the *Skills Handbook* and in the *Note Taking Transparencies*.

Active Reading To encourage active reading, the student text builds in questions for students to self-test their comprehension at the end of every section of text.

Guided Instruction In the *Teacher's Edition,* the lesson plan introduces a variety of strategies to teach the lesson, including Quick Activities to help keep students interested and engaged.

Note Taking To promote active reading, ask students to fill in the graphic organizers located at the beginning of each section and throughout the chapters as they read. This not only gives students practice in taking notes, but also reinforces content and reading skills introduced at the beginning of the section.

After Reading

During the reflection and study phases, formally check for student understanding. If necessary provide remediation. Provide activities that challenge students to apply content in a new way.

Provide Review Direct students to the Quick Study Guide at the end of every chapter. Encourage students to use the Note Taking graphic organizers and Concept Connector worksheets for additional review.

Assess Learning Use the Assess and Reteach portion of the lesson plan to check for student understanding. At the end of each section, the assessment returns to the Focus Question. Students should use their completed graphic organizers to answer it. Encourage students to take the self-quizzes and tests with vocabulary practice online.

Prepare to Read

Build Background Knowledge L3
Remind students that there had not been a large-scale European war since Napoleon's time. Have them predict how war might have changed since 1815.

Set a Purpose L3
- **WITNESS HISTORY** Read the selection aloud or play the audio.
  AUDIO **Witness History Audio CD,** track 26.3
  Ask **Why did the soldier find the singing of the birds so touching?** *(The peaceful, ordinary singing of the birds was such a contrast to the death and destruction surrounding him.)*
- **Focus** Point out the Section Focus Question and write it on the board. Tell students to refer to this question as they read. *(Answer appears with Section 2 Assessment answers.)*
- **Preview** Have students preview the Section Objectives and the list of Terms, People, and Places.
- **Note Taking** As they read, have students fill in the chart identifying details about the battlefronts.
  Reading and Note Taking Study Guide

Answer

✓ Russia mobilized quickly in the east, causing Germany to divert troops there. The British and French stopped the weakened German advance at the Marne.

...supplies to Britain. To defend against the submarines, the Allies organized convoys, or groups of merchant ships protected by warships.

✓ **Checkpoint** What made World War I much more deadly than previous wars?

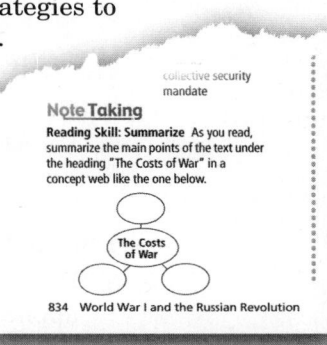

collective security
mandate

Note Taking

Reading Skill: Summarize As you read, summarize the main points of the text under the heading "The Costs of War" in a concept web like the one below.

The Costs
of War

834 World War I and the Russian Revolution

Reading and Discussion Strategies for Improving Comprehension

In response to today's environment of NCLB legislation and testing reform, Prentice Hall asked Dr. Kate Kinsella and Dr. Kevin Feldman to provide specific instructional strategies you can use to improve student comprehension. Their guidance informed the development of the *World History Teacher's Edition.* In addition to the materials and strategies outlined on the previous page, the lesson plans in this Teacher's Edition incorporate the following instructional strategies to enhance students' comprehension.

Reading Comprehension Strategies

There is no single magical strategy that will solve all of the difficulties that students encounter in reading challenging content area texts. Students in mixed-ability classrooms depend on teachers to use a consistent set of research-informed and classroom-tested strategies in a patient and recursive manner—not the occasional or random use of different strategies. Some strategies, such as Pre-Reading, are designed to eventually become the responsibility of the student to use independently. These are coded as student self-directed (SSD). Other strategies meant always to be used with the guidance of the teacher, such as the discussion strategies, are coded as teacher directed (TD).

How to Teach a Reading Strategy

A strategy is a plan of action or a series of steps to accomplish a task. Strategy instruction essentially consists of a teacher showing less-skilled younger readers how to successfully tackle a reading "strategically." The essence of how to teach a strategy can be summed up in three phases (Archer, 2001) as "I do it, We do it, You do it."

I do it

1. Explain the rationale: What is the purpose? How can this help you?
2. Demonstrate how to perform the strategy.

We do it

3. Guide the students in the steps of the strategy.
4. Direct students in practicing the strategy with a partner.
5. Re-model, providing feedback as necessary.

You do it

6. Direct students to perform the strategy while clarifying a clear "evidence check" of strategy application (e.g., turn in your Pre-Reading Outline) for accountability.

The amount of teacher support at the "I do it" and "We do it" phases of strategy instruction will vary widely depending upon the difficulty of the content and literacy levels of your students. It is important to realize that it will take several teacher-directed experiences with a new reading strategy before students will be able to successfully apply it on their own.

BEFORE READING

This program provides three key strategies to prepare students for the demands of reading and comprehending each chapter: Preread the Chapter: Why and How, Word Knowledge Rating, and K-W-L.

Preread the Chapter: Why and How (SSD)

Purpose: To build background knowledge, provide an overview of the topics, acquaint students with the structure and organization of the text, and establish the necessity of reading to learn from demanding text in more than one way.

1. Distribute the Preread the Chapter: Why and How worksheet from the **Skills Handbook** to help focus students' attention on each step in the prereading process. Later, this guide can serve as a written record that students have preread when assigned to do so independently.

2. Model how to use the Why and How checklist to preview chapter and section materials. You may also wish to read each heading and subheading aloud, clarify section structure (e.g. cause-effect relationships), frame the topics as questions to read to answer, and help students identify unfamiliar words and model ways to find clues to their meanings.

Word Knowledge Rating (TD)

Purpose: To teach students essential content terms and high use academic words they will need to understand and be able to use in reading, discussion, and writing tasks.

1. Have students pronounce each word, clarify the part of speech, and then rate how well they think they know the word on the Word Knowledge Rating Form. For difficult or polysyllabic words, break them into syllables and pronounce them with the students.

2. Explain what the word means in common "student friendly" language using synonyms and antonyms when possible.

3. Provide concrete examples to clarify the meaning and rephrase the example, having students pronounce the target word as they fill in their form.

K-W-L (TD)

Purpose: To engage students in thinking about a topic before, during, and after reading. The K-W-L worksheet guides students to reflect on what they **K**now, clarify what they **W**ant to learn (or expect to learn), and identify what they **L**earn as they read.

1. Distribute the K-W-L worksheet from the **Skills Handbook.** Structure a brief brainstorming session with the group to identify what they already know (or think they know) about a topic. List the student's name and idea on the board and encourage students to generate questions at points of ambiguity. (Note: If the students have very limited background knowledge about a topic,

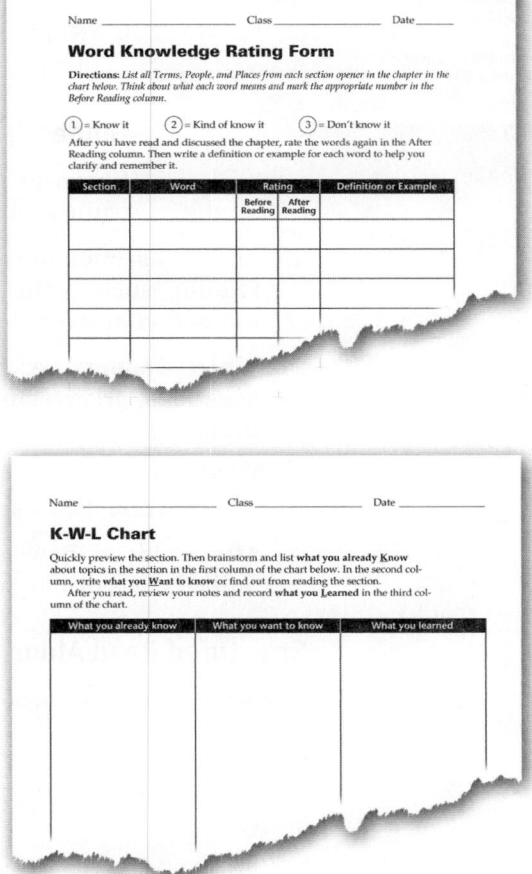

focus on building background knowledge or providing key information directly rather than attempting to activate what is not present.)

2. Guide students to record key ideas from the brainstorming session under the What You Already Know section of the chart.

3. Teach students how to ask questions based on the topic they predict the chapter will address, even when they know very little about it (e.g. who, what, when, where, why, how, effects of, etc.). Have them record these questions in the second column of the chart.

4. After reading and/or at key junctures in the text, facilitate a discussion answering key questions and clarifying any lingering confusion about key concepts. Have students fill in the final column of the chart.

DURING READING

This program supports student comprehension during reading by providing three key strategies: Paragraph Shrinking, Guided Questioning/Silent Reading, and Structured Reading Aloud.

Paragraph Shrinking (SSD)

Purpose: To teach students a basic strategy for summarizing essential information in each paragraph as they read.

1. Read the paragraph to yourself (you may choose to do this aloud if many students can't decode all of the words).

2. Identify the topic—what the paragraph is mainly about.

3. Clarify the two or three most essential details related to the topic.

4. Shrink the paragraph—state the topic and one or two key details in 15 words or less.

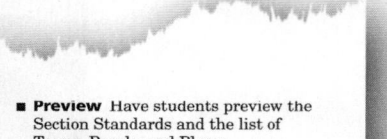

■ **Preview** Have students preview the Section Standards and the list of Terms, People, and Places.

■ **Note Taking** Have students read this section using the Paragraph Shrinking strategy (TE, p. T20). As they read, have students fill in the timeline summarizing events in Russia.

Reading and Note Taking Study Guide, p. 99

Guided Questioning/Silent Reading (TD)

Purpose: To ensure students' accountably, focus their attention on critical issues while reading silently.

1. Assign a section to read silently. Pose a question for the whole class to answer from their silent reading, such as the question at the end of each subsection. Model how one thinks while reading to find answers to a question.

2. When students get used to reading to answer the subsection questions, pose more in-depth questions, progressing from factual recall to questions that stimulate interpretative or applied thinking.

3. Teach students to ask and answer their own questions as they read. Model this process by reading a section aloud and answering your own questions as you read.

4. After students have read the section, direct them to share answers with a partner before a brief unified class discussion to clarify issues, key vocabulary, and related concepts.

Structured Read Aloud (TD)

Purpose: To provide basic access to the text, build fluency, and ensure active reading by all students.

1. Choose a passage and direct students to "read aloud silently using their inner voices." Be sure students understand that reading is an active process, and their job is to follow along—eyes riveted to each word, saying the words to themselves as you read aloud.

2. Tell students to be on their "reading toes," for you will be leaving out an occasional word and their task is to chorally supply the word.

3. Provide a simple focus question for students to think about while they are reading along silently and chiming in on words you leave out.

4. After reading a section aloud and filling in the words you've left out, briefly partner students to clarify their answers to the section focus question at the beginning of the section. Follow up with a whole class discussion as the topic warrants.

AFTER READING:

After reading strategies help students synthesize and consolidate key information and study for quizzes and tests. This program supports reading comprehension after reading by providing two key strategies: Vocabulary Study (below) and Responding to Chapter Questions (p. 606d).

Vocabulary Study (SSD)

Purpose: To teach students processes for reviewing and studying critical vocabulary terms.

1. **Read-Cover-Recite-Check (RCRC): Verbal Rehearsal**

   - **Read** Read the new vocabulary word and definition, thinking about examples of the word from your own experience.

   - **Cover** Cover the vocabulary word/definitions with your hand.

   - **Recite** Tell yourself the word–definition–examples–visualizations associated with the definition.

   - **Check** Lift your hand and check your study list. Tell yourself any corrections or changes.

2. **Vocabulary Study Cards (SSD)**

Guide students in selecting a few essential terms, including key concepts, to create vocabulary study cards.
   - On the unlined side of a 5 × 7 card:
     a. write the part of speech next to the word;
     b. write a phonetic pronunciation that you understand;
     c. in the lower left-hand corner, write any related word forms introduced during vocabulary instruction. If you know the word in another language, note the translation.

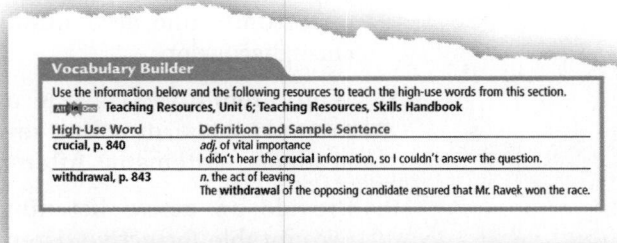

   - On the lined side of the card:
     a. on the top line fill in any "reminder words" (e.g. synonyms);
     b. copy the sentence from the reading/lesson that contains the new word;
     c. copy the relevant dictionary/glossary definition;
     d. write an example sentence from your own experience if possible.

   - Use RCRC to independently study the cards.

   - Partner students for additional study, asking them to take turns asking and answering.

READING

STRATEGIES FOR STRUCTURING ACADEMIC DISCUSSION

Every secondary teacher recognizes that active engagement in classroom activities is an essential prerequisite to academic success. Yet time and again research verifies the fact that many students, especially those less academically prepared, sit passively in classrooms watching the teacher and their higher-performing peers apply reading strategies and react to lesson content. The discussion strategies outlined below are designed to increase the odds that every student is actively and academically responding during every lesson phase.

Strategy 1: Idea Wave

Purpose: To support all students in actively listening and responding academically to a single, critical prereading (e.g., brainstorming) or postreading (e.g., review, application) question within a more elaborate unified-class discussion.

1. Pose an open-ended question or task (*e.g., Identify three possible reasons for the Industrial Revolution.*)

2. Provide a model response on the board (*e.g., The Scientific Revolution had started people thinking about new ideas and inventions.*)

3. Give students time to consider what they know about the topic and record a number of responses.

4. Provide two or three sentence starters and ask students to write one or two of their ideas using a sentence starter. These starters should include key academic vocabulary and sentence structures that students wouldn't ordinarily use in casual conversation. (*e.g., One possible reason for the Industrial Revolution was that Enlightenment thinkers had created a ripe environment for change.*)

5. As students are jotting down ideas, "nominate" a few volunteers to jumpstart the subsequent class discussion. Get a few answers from students who wouldn't ordinarily respond voluntarily and bolster their confidence by affirming their idea prior to the actual discussion.

6. Read aloud your model response and have students read along with you a second time to build reading fluency.

7. Have students "rehearse" their responses and build reading fluency and confidence by sharing it first with a partner. This partnering stage also ensures that every student has an opportunity and accountability to respond even if not included in the subsequent unified-class discussion.

8. Whip around the class in a relatively fast-paced and structured manner (e.g., down rows, around tables), directing several students to share an idea (i.e., reading aloud their complete academic statement). After this structured debriefing, call on a few volunteers.

9. Provide an active listening and notetaking task during the discussion. Hold students accountable for active listening by asking them to jot down two ideas, such as two perspectives with which you agree, two additional examples, etc.

10. After several contributions, if there tends to be repetition, ask students to point out similarities in responses rather than simply stating that their idea has already been mentioned. Require that students use language for acknowledging other ideas: e.g., *My idea builds upon ___'s idea. I also believe that. . . .*

Strategy 2: Think-Write-Pair-Share

Purpose: To engage students in responding to instruction.

1. **Think** Students listen while the teacher poses a question or task related to the reading or classroom discussion. The level of questions should vary from lower level literal to higher order inferential or analytical.

2. **Write** Provide quiet thinking or writing time for students to deal with the question and go back to the text or review notes. Have students record their ideas in their notebooks. If you are only posing one or two more demanding and essential questions instead of several, consider providing academic sentence starters for students to complete as a means of encouraging more thoughtful and formal responses: *e.g., How did the accomplishments of the Industrial Revolution affect peoples' everyday lives? It ___ enabled people to ___.*

3. **Pair/Share** Cue students to find a partner and share their written response, noting similarities and differences. Teach students to encourage one another to clarify and justify their responses. To add more accountability for active listening, ask students to share their partner's idea during the structured debriefing and require that they begin their response with a citation expression: *e.g., My partner ___ pointed out / emphasized / indicated / predicted that ___ enabled people to ___ during the Industrial Revolution.*

4. Randomly call on students to share during a unified class discussion after they have all rehearsed answers with their partners.

5. Invite any volunteers to contribute additional ideas and points of view to the discussion after calling on a reasonable number of students randomly.

6. Direct students to go back to notes and add any important information garnered during the partner and class discussions.

Strategy 3: Numbered Heads

Purpose: To support and engage all students in responding to a series of questions to assess reading comprehension and/or review lesson content.

1. Seat students in groups of four and number off one through four.

2. After posing a particular question or task, specify the amount of time students have to discuss their response (allow only 30 seconds to $1\frac{1}{2}$ minutes or students wander off task) and monitor students' interactions to identify comprehension issues, probe thinking, etc.

3. Remind students to pay close attention to the comments of each group member because you will be randomly selecting one student to represent the best thinking of the entire group.

4. Call a number (one through four) and ask all students with that number to raise their hands, ready to respond to the topic at hand in a teacher-directed, whole-class discussion.

5. Add comments, extend key ideas, ask follow-up questions, and make connections between individual student's comments to create a lively whole-class discussion.

6. Provide any summary comments required to ensure that all students understand critical points.

Research on Writing

Teachers often assume that if they teach content effectively, their students will be able to communicate what they have learned in writing on state assessments. The performance of many students on the writing tasks found in state tests tells us that this isn't true. Many students falter when asked to write because they don't know how to construct a response that shows what they have learned. Teachers can help students improve their performance by embedding expository writing tasks in class activities, homework assignments, and tests throughout the year.

Bringing Writing Into the Social Studies Classroom

A good way to begin a writing program is with short-answer writing prompts. Because these questions can be answered in a sentence or two, they are less intimidating to students. Even so, short-answer does not mean easy. Good responses to such questions are clear, detailed, and complete.

From short-answer questions move on to more complex constructed response prompts. Ideally these tasks should reflect what your students are likely to encounter on state assessments. This may be thematic essays, position papers, or document-based questions.

As you introduce each kind of prompt, take time with students to work through the process of analyzing the task and framing their response. To be successful, students will need to learn how to analyze the prompt, budget their time and answer space, plan and write their response, and then edit their first drafts.

Embedding Writing in Assessment

As students become familiar with a type of writing prompt, embed similar tasks in your class assessments. A good prompt will:

- test what students have been taught, whether defined by state standards or your own course outline;
- communicate what is expected of students in terms of format, length, and level of detail, such the number of examples or reasons; and
- be doable in the time and space allocated for the task.

> *Teachers can help students improve their performance by embedding expository writing tasks in class activities, homework assignments, and tests throughout the year.*

A good prompt provides multiple access points to help students with different learning styles, backgrounds, and abilities engage with the task. This may be done by breaking the task into parts that build from lower- to higher-order thinking skills. This sequencing provides a point of entry for weaker students who may not be capable of completing the entire task and enables them to respond in a limited way.

Bringing Students Into the Scoring Process

The goal of a writing program should be to empower students to assess and improve their own work. For this to happen, students need to have a clear vision of what good writing looks like and how to bring their own work up to that standard.

An effective way to communicate your expectations is through the consistent use of generic rubrics and/or scoring guides. Generic rubrics describe levels of performance on various traits of a written task, such as writing mechanics or development of a clear thesis statement. Scoring guides, in contrast, describe levels of performance for each specific task.

Teachers can use both of these tools to communicate efficiently with students about their written work. More important, once students are trained in the use of rubrics and scoring guides, they can use these tools to evaluate their own and other students' work. As students take on this responsibility, they begin to internalize performance standards.

Planning and implementing a writing program takes time and effort. But the potential payoffs are significant. Not only will your students become more competent and confident writers, but their test scores will also reflect those gains.

Diane Hart
Diane Hart is a writer and consultant in history and social studies. She is a former teacher at the elementary, secondary, and college levels and is an active member of both the National and California Councils for the Social Studies.

Effective Classroom Implementation

Prentice Hall World History provides a systematic approach to writing. It embeds detailed, step-by-step writing instructions so students can build their writing skills, and it provides opportunities for continuous practice throughout the course.

Teach the Steps

The **Skills Handbook** introduces the core steps of writing at the beginning of the Student Edition. It supplies students with the basic building blocks for writing different types of assignments—narrative, expository, research, persuasive, biographical, and assessment essays. Detailed worksheets and transparencies support the **Skills Handbook.**

Practice the Steps

Quick Writes at the end of every section provide simple prompts that allow students to practice short-answer responses and practice each step of the writing process, such as writing a thesis, gathering details, and crafting a conclusion.

Put the Steps Together

Writing About History assignments in every chapter put the steps for writing an essay together to form a more complex writing assignment with scaffolded instruction. Each type of writing assignment appears multiple times to encourage mastery.

Prepare for Challenging Essays

Essential Question Review and Connections to Today as well as full page Concept Connector features and the Concept Connector Handbooks help students prepare for the thematic essays that are common on both social studies exams and high-stakes assessments. Students may keep track of key concepts on the **Note Taking and Concept Connector Journal,** which is available online. Practice in writing for Document-Based Assessments appears at the end of every chapter.

Provide Clear Expectations

Assessment Rubrics allow teachers to provide clear expectations and consistent grading. They will allow students to learn how to assess their own writing, edit their work, and internalize standards. Rubrics for evaluating essays on the SAT and ACT appear in the **Skills Handbook.**

● **Writing About History**

Quick Write: Write a Thesis Statement
Suppose that you are writing an essay on the effects of Ottoman Turkey's decision to join the Central Powers during World War I. Answer the questions below. Use your answers to create a thesis statement for the essay.
• Why were the Dardanelles important to the Allies?
• Who won the Battle of Gallipoli?
• What impact do you think Gallipoli had on the Russian war effort?

● **Writing About History**

Writing a Cause and Effect Essay World War I was a definitive event of the 1900s. Write an essay in which you analyze the causes and effects of an event that took place during the World War I era. Consider using one of the following topics: Archduke Francis Ferdinand's assassination or Russia's March Revolution.

Prewriting
• Choose the topic listed above that interests you most, or choose another topic that appeals to you.
• Consider multiple causes and immediate and long-term effects of the event you've chosen. Create a cause-and-effect chart to identify your essay's most important points.

Drafting
• Develop a thesis and find information to support it.
• Choose an organizational structure for your essay.
• Write an introduction, several body paragraphs, and a conclusion. State the cause-and-effect relationship you are focusing on clearly in your introduction, and follow up your points in the conclusion.

Revising
• As you review your essay, make sure that each body paragraph supports or develops the cause-and-effect relationship you laid out in your thesis statement.
• Use the guidelines for revising your essay on page SH12 of the Writing Handbook.

848

Concept Connector

? Essential Question Review

To connect prior knowledge with what you have learned in this chapter, answer the questions below in your Concept Connector journal. Use the journal in the Reading and Note Taking Study Guide to record your answers (or go to www.phschool.com Web Code: nad-2607).

1. **Conflict** By 1914, the Balkans were known as the "powder keg of Europe." That same year, a Serbian terrorist assassinated Austrian Archduke Francis Ferdinand and his wife. Write a paragraph explaining why, in addition to avenging the assassination, Austria-Hungary and Germany went to war against Serbia. Think about the following:
   • nationalism
   • international rivalries
   • militarism

2. **Revolution** Compare the Russian Revolution and the French Revolution. How were they similar and different? Create a chart comparing the two revolutions in the following categories:
   • causes
   • duration/phases
   • leaders
   • world reaction
   • results

3. **Cooperation** In his farewell address, President George Washington warned against "entangling alliances." Prewar treaties between European powers were intended to promote peace by creating alliances that no country would dare attack. Identify other reasons for the formation of these prewar European alliances. Do you think the true cause of World War I was entangling alliances? Why or why not?

■ Connections To Today

1. **Conflict: The Balkan Powder Keg** The formation of Yugoslavia after World War I fulfilled the dream of a South Slav state in the Balkans. Yet unrest continued, erupting as recently as 2008. Conduct research and create a timeline of major events in the Balkans from 1918 to the present.

2. **Genocide: Memory and the Armenian Genocide** The Republic of Turkey still maintains that the deportation of the Turkish Armenian population during World War I was a result of civil unrest, not a genocide. Armenian advocacy groups disagree and wage an ongoing campaign for recognition of the Armenians' experience as a planned genocide. Find out where the campaign stands now. Summarize your findings in an essay.

Armenian Genocide in the Ottoman Empire

Research on Media Literacy

Defining Media Literacy

Research shows that social studies educators do not agree on a universal definition of the term *media literacy* (Hamot, Gregory, et al, *Media Literacy in Social Studies Teacher Education: Relating Meaning to Practice,* 1997). Some understand it to mean teaching students how to *use technology*. Others see it as meaning teaching them how to *evaluate the media*. In fact, we need to teach students *both* the technical and the critical thinking aspects of media literacy in order to equip them with the skills they need to navigate today's electronic and media-rich era.

As every teacher and parent knows, not only are teenagers spending more time than ever before with more types of technologies, but they are "managing to pack increasing amounts of media content into the same amount of time each day" (Kaiser Family Foundation, 2005). In fact, a Senate report of the Committee on Commerce, Science, and Transportation found that "children spend, on average, 28 hours per week watching television [per year], which is more time than they spend in school [per year]" (S. Report. No. 171, 1995).

How do we as teachers channel this familiarity and time spent with technology toward technology that teaches and informs as well as entertains? How do we ensure that we and our students are taking full advantage of the opportunities for learning that technology in the classroom can provide? And how do we make sure that our students are critical consumers of the media with which they are surrounded on a daily basis?

Teaching With and About Technology

Studies indicate that students in "technology-rich environments" experience increased achievement in all major subject areas (Sivin-Kachela, 1998). By integrating technology into the classroom, teachers not only help students learn the critical tools they need to thrive in a digital age, they also enhance social studies content.

Technology provides easily accessible ways to present core content and engage students. Audio and video bring dynamic moments to life. Primary sources provide the personal experience. The Internet unlocks a myriad array of materials. Together, these materials make history come alive in the classroom.

Teaching Critical Thinking About Media

Media can be a powerful tool not just to teach using technology, but also to teach critical thinking skills. Studies show that media literacy training increases students' ability to access, analyze, and evaluate media messages (Yates, 2001). Students need to learn to analyze what they see and hear as well as what they read. In a social studies course, primary sources and documents include quotations as well as political cartoons, fine art, and artifacts of all sorts. These are ideal instruments for fostering critical thinking skills, including

- comparing viewpoints;
- identifying bias and prejudice;
- evaluating evidence;
- interpreting past events and issues within the context in which the event unfolded;
- understanding the meaning, implication, and impact of historical events.

By embedding these media skills into the course, you not only enhance key concepts, but also teach students key analysis skills, many of which are tested on high-stakes exams and in document-based assessments. In addition, media-literate students will become more effective consumers, decision-makers, and citizens, able to succeed in the classroom and beyond.

> *Studies indicate that students in "technology-rich environments" experience increased achievement in all major subject areas (Sivin-Kachela, 1998).*

Judith Mahnke

Judith Mahnke has been teaching in public schools in San Francisco for over 20 years. She teaches Modern World Civilization, Advanced Placement United States History, Psychology, and Sociology. She is a teacher consultant for the California Geographic Alliance and has served on the board of the California Council for Social Studies for many years.

Effective Classroom Implementation

Media literacy is essential for students in today's classroom as well as in the world at large. *Prentice Hall World History* supports media literacy in an exciting variety of ways, helping students at all levels become more active and engaged learners.

Before Reading

- **Witness History** audio uniquely engages students' interest with primary source quotes, music, and sounds of the era. Look for the audio symbol 🔊 at the beginning of every chapter and section. The *Teacher's Edition* helps you use the *Witness History* audio to introduce every lesson.

During Reading

- **Geography Interactive** provides an audio guided tour to improve geographic literacy. Each chapter also contains an Interactive map, timeline, or diagram to enhance learning.

- **History Interactive** timelines extend students' knowledge of events as they occurred chronologically and help students understand the world events that occurred simultaneously.

- **Witness History Discovery School**™ video program contains high-interest videos and DVDs to enhance learning and bring history alive.

- **Political Cartoons** throughout the text challenge students with in-depth analysis questions.

- **Fine art, unique photos, posters, and artifacts** pique student interest and challenge their critical thinking skills.

- **Document-Based Assessment** provides a full page of primary sources, political cartoons, fine art, and charts and graphs followed by questions in a high-stakes exam format.

- **Note Taking Study Guide Online** contains leveled Note Taking Graphic Organizers and Concept Connector Journal pages that students fill in as they read the text.

- **Extend Online** activities with step-by-step instruction appear in the *Teacher's Edition* in every chapter.

After Reading

- **Progress Monitoring Online** with vocabulary practice online allows students to interactively monitor their own learning.

- *ExamView*® **Test Bank CD-ROM** allows teachers to easily create customized tests from banks of thousands of questions. Questions can be sorted by difficulty level to provide leveled quizzes and tests for differentiated instruction.

Research on Assessment

Frequent and numerous local, state, and federal mandates insist on systematic, ongoing assessment to assure that learning is targeted to outcomes and that students are indeed learning. We cannot expect this demand to be lifted or for it to be significantly altered.

A genuine strength of the texts we have assembled for your use is that learning outcomes (or objectives) that are specific to plan and guide instruction include companion assessments to monitor your instruction effort. Research demonstrates that reliance on assessment, especially formative assessment, is associated with greater learning. We have engaged in one of the time-honored procedures for sound, effective, and comprehensive instruction: teach-test-reteach and review and retest. This model works!

Assessment as a Process

Assessment needs to be seen and used as a *process*, not merely an activity that independently evaluates instruction or student learning, as mandates are often viewed. As a process, the goal of assessment is to assemble information from a variety of sources (unit tests, document assessments, AYP tests, locally crafted tests, specific instructor checklists, etc.), including professional judgment, to focus, guide, and support instruction and subsequently student learning.

With the range of resources the series provides (both instructional supports and multiple diverse assessments), testing and assessment become a sequential and progressive process that provides the opportunity for regular assessments that inform both instructors and students. As information accumulates and you use this information to tailor your instruction, research shows that student learning advances and accelerates—and achievement itself serves as a motivation for increased learning.

What is Formative Assessment?

As you set out to use assessments, become familiar with the major yet differing roles of assessments. First, plan for formative assessments across the school term. Formative assessment refers to all those activities undertaken by teachers, and by their students, in assessing themselves. These activities provide information to be used as feedback to modify teaching and learning activities. As an integrated approach to assessment and instruction, formative assessments emphasize mastery of specific course material, as opposed to evaluation of performance or assignment of grades (summative assessments).

Formative assessments are conducted throughout the instructional process to monitor students' progress and provide feedback on strengths and weaknesses. The key to formative assessment is the role of feedback. Feedback allows students to correct conceptual errors and encourages instructors to modify instructional activities in light of their effectiveness. Since formative assessments are designed to guide learning and are not used as an outcome measure, they are generally considered a low stakes assessment. Formative tests may be graded or non-graded based on instructor purpose and preference. Such assessments become "formative" when the evidence gathered is actually used by instructors to guide and adapt teaching to meet the needs of students in mastering the outcomes targeted.

What is Summative Assessment?

Instructors are also advised to incorporate summative assessments into their instructional plan. Summative assessments are used when instruction comes to the point where a judgment regarding progress or standing is called for. A summative test is a test that "counts," a test that tends to be comprehensive, a test for which students are expected to prepare and to take seriously, and a test that clearly impacts one's "grade." Nevertheless from the instructor's perspective, we need to use results from summative testing somewhat like that of formative: to inform instruction that could lead to the need for review and rehearsal of material already covered before moving on to new and different topics.

Assessment Today

We are in an age of assessment-driven reform. Teachers today are expected to be data-driven decision makers. The roles and use of formative and summative assessments is perhaps among the soundest approaches to achieve such capacity. Create a plan, then use assessments to inform yourself about the successes and achievements of your students and to alert yourself to shortcomings or outcomes that do not meet your expectations. Gather diverse but complementary information, study it filtered by your, parent, and school standards, and then go forward with lessons and units knowing what you students need and have accomplished.

John Poggio

John Poggio, Ph.D. is co-Director of the Center for Educational Testing and Evaluation and a Professor of Educational Psychology and Research at the University of Kansas. He has authored over 200 papers, articles, technical reports, book chapters, tests, and a text on topics relating to testing, assessment, evaluation, and statistical analysis in education.

Effective Classroom Implementation

In the past, it was common practice to teach a lesson, administer a test, grade it, and move on. Today we know that continuous assessment of student progress with immediate intervention contributes to high performance (Just for Kids, 2001). *Prentice Hall World History* helps you use data-driven assessment to inform teaching and point your students toward excellence.

Diagnose Readiness

AYP Monitoring Assessments—including diagnostic tests and a full year of benchmark tests with remediation suggestions—help you assess initial student readiness and monitor content mastery.

Track Understanding

- *Progress Monitoring Transparencies* allow you to check student understanding of each section on a daily basis.

- **Progress Monitoring *Online*** lets students assess their understanding of content and get instant vocabulary practice.

Assess Progress, Report Results, and Prescribe Remediation

- *ExamView*® **Test Bank CD-ROM** allows teachers to create customized tests from banks of thousands of questions. Questions can be sorted by difficulty levels to provide leveled quizzes and tests for differentiated instruction.

- The *EZData*™ *Scoring System* grades tests in seconds and allows you to analyze data and decide on remediation.

- *Assessment Rubrics* includes reproducible rubrics for students and instruction for rubric use for teachers.

Prepare for Standardized Assessment

Concept Connector and Document-Based Assessments get students ready for high-stakes world history assessments. Quick Study Guides enable students to check their understanding and prepare for test-taking success.

EZData™
Scoring System

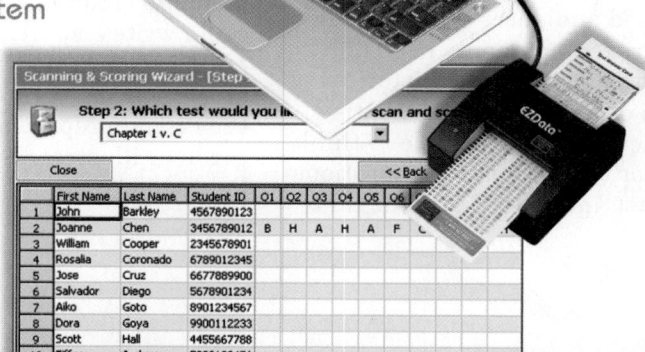

Research on Document-Based Assessment

The Value of Document-Based Assessment

For years, teachers have understood the value of having our students read and analyze documents to acquire knowledge and develop critical thinking skills. Document analysis has become an important assessment tool as well. Both the College Board Advanced Placement examinations and many state-mandated assessments use document-based questions, including a writing task in which students think critically about a variety of sources and then present their analysis in an essay.

Primary sources are historical records produced at the time of the event or period that they describe, or soon thereafter. These sources may include written accounts, such as diaries, speeches, government records, law codes, religious texts, and period cartoons, photographs, and artifacts. They are distinct from secondary sources, which are produced well after the events that they describe and interpret.

Teach With Primary Sources

Teaching students to examine historical documents involves asking the right questions. The first questions to ask are those for which students can find concrete answers. The answers to these questions will give students the information that forms a basis for critical thinking. Then students can consider the following questions: What kind of document is it? Who wrote this document? What was the writer's background? Who is the intended audience? Why was this document written? Students need to understand the purpose of a historical document in order to analyze it. Ultimately, students need to be able to think historically, or to ask their own questions about the past and to evaluate the infor-

mation in the documents. However, students must not evaluate the past in terms of the present. They must examine primary sources in the context of the times when they were produced.

Differentiate Instruction

As we attempt to differentiate instruction for students' differing abilities and learning styles, we can use document analysis for small group or whole class discussion, individual written reports, in-class presentations, role playing, or other instructional strategies. Students need direct instruction in using primary sources and conflicting interpretations of historical events, as well as repeated opportunities to practice these skills in class and in independent practice. Regardless of the strategy, teachers must generate one or two well-crafted questions about the document. This may be more difficult than it appears at first glance. The purpose of the questions is to help students find the kernel of information that the document offers. These questions can be used to spark a class discussion or as a focus for independent practice.

Extend Learning

Some teachers use documents to help students apply the concepts they are learning and to extend that learning beyond the textbook. For example, based on analysis of several primary sources, students could prepare an oral presentation taking a stand on an issue in history. They could use primary-source documents to create a museum display. They could write a speech or a news article, taking the position of someone who lived at the time the source was created. Or, they could prepare a poster, magazine cover, or illustrated timeline that highlights information from primary sources.

Prepare Students for Testing

Working with primary sources will not only increase students' appreciation for history and their critical thinking skills. It will also help to prepare them for document-based questions on state and College Board examinations. The skills they will need for these examinations include the following:

- applying information students have learned in their study of world history
- evaluating the reliability of historical sources
- identifying the point of view of these sources and determining bias
- identifying problems and considering alternative solutions
- categorizing information as political, social, or economic
- considering issues from multiple perspectives
- building support for a position by choosing accurate, relevant evidence

Steven Goldberg

Steven Goldberg is the District Chairperson of Social Studies for the City School District of New Rochelle, New York. He is past president of both the New York State Council for the Social Studies and the New York Social Studies Supervisory Association.

Effective Classroom Implementation

The primary source documents in *Prentice Hall World History* encourage students to appreciate the drama of history as it happened and to apply the critical thinking skills of a practicing historian. In addition, today's standardized tests are increasingly likely to include Document-Based Assessment. *Document-Based Assessment* at the end of every chapter in the student text helps students master key content and practice the increasingly essential skills—including writing essays—they need for success. The *Teacher's Edition* and the *Document-Based Assessment* workbook provide effective support and further practice.

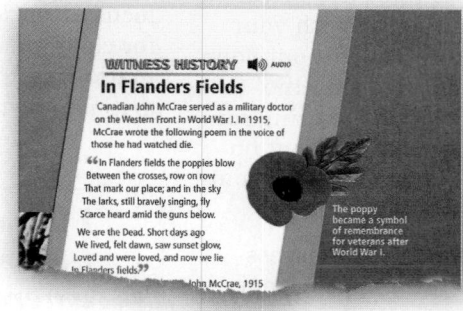

Develop and Assess Critical Thinking Skills

- In primary sources throughout the text, students gain insights by reading the words of the people who were there. Artifacts, fine art, unique photos, posters, and period cartoons pique students' interest and challenge critical thinking skills.

- Full-page primary source excerpts allow students to relive history through eyewitness accounts and documents.

- Primary source audio accounts bring the voices of history alive.

Prepare Students for Standardized Tests

- *Document-Based Assessment* in the student text provides a full page of primary sources, political cartoons, fine art, and charts and graphs followed by questions in a high-stakes test format. Scaffolded assessment includes questions in standardized test format that require students to analyze each document. A Writing Task follows each set of documents and requires analysis of all of the documents on the page plus relevant information from the chapter.

- The *Document-Based Assessment* workbook supplements the student text. The booklet is divided into eight activities, each of which explores a broad topic of world history within a historical context. Each topic contains six to eight primary and secondary source documents.

Every document-based activity is divided into two parts. In Part A, students study and analyze each document and answer a question about it. In Part B, students write an essay that answers a document-based question about the topic. In writing this essay, students must use the documents to support their points as well as other information they have gained from the text.

Build Test-Taking Skills

- Students master understanding of document-based questions they will face on standardized tests. *Document-Based Assessment* gives them practice in finding the kernel of information in each document quickly and accurately as well as in writing the short essays required on many state and College Board tests.

- Each chapter in the *Teacher's Edition* includes a Tip that helps students achieve results on all of their high stakes exams.

CONCLUSION

Connect Students to the Drama of History

I do my research by shadowing teenagers through their day in high school to pinpoint the moments when they are genuinely engaged by what is transpiring in the classroom. My ultimate goal is to identify specific classroom episodes where young people find genuine meaning, worth, and value in their academic experiences, and to understand what teachers can do to cultivate engagement.

The students I shadow typically experienced their class time as listless and tedious. As one student put it, "Sitting in class is like being in the car with your parents on a long road trip without your CD player." They identified the chief culprits for their boredom: unwavering routine, relentless lecture, detachment on the teacher's part, and content that mattered little to their world.

Despite this generally grim assessment, I have witnessed numerous episodes where students experienced the classroom as provocative, enchanting, memorable, and enjoyable. Animated by the experience of learning, they would say things like, "I can't believe how fast class went" or "That was intense!" or the ubiquitous, "today was cool." After watching hundreds of class sessions and analyzing the episodes with students and teachers who experienced them, I noted several commonalities.

Where students were engaged and motivated, the teachers viewed the students as unabashed and savvy consumers and they saw themselves as marketers locked in a fierce competition to secure their students' attention. These teachers didn't show up to class expecting compliance and focus. Instead, they devoted themselves to devising approaches that would generate buzz and energy. Here is a sampling of approaches:

Manipulate the pace and rhythm of classroom experiences

One teacher veered between an almost frenetic pace of questioning-and-answer discussion followed by long spans of quiet journaling time. She told me that her model for pace was music television. "I try and jar them into paying attention with lots of transitions, quick back and forth followed by some slow times. I see myself as a DJ at a party."

Teachers also manipulated routines to focus attention, taking students outside for class, introducing a subject with dramatic video footage, using music and gripping primary source materials.

I have witnessed numerous episodes where students experienced the classroom as provocative, enchanting, memorable, and enjoyable.

Frame the curriculum in ways that provide relevance

I almost never shadowed students who found intrinsic fascination with the subject matter at hand. In fact, the default response on the part of most students was "Why should *I* care about the industrial revolution? Why—other than the fact you will test me on this—should I delve into a study of how World War I occurred?" Students responded enthusiastically to teachers who helped students make meaningful connections to the subject matter.

To make this happen, some teachers connected the past to the present. Others had students take on the role of historical figures. For example, students studying the industrial revolution examined a series of photographs depicting children at work in the factories and composed journal entries describing their daily life as a child laborer. Other teachers utilized the principles of problem-based learning to create simulations where students had to resolve real historical dilemmas. These varied approaches require intense preparation and pedagogical skill on the part of the teacher, but done well they provide stimulating ways for students to showcase their content knowledge and practice their emerging skills.

Infuse your classroom with your personal presence

The students told me again and again: "Energy and passion matter." Teachers who connected with students told poignant personal stories, conveyed their own passion for the subject matter, expressed emotion, and conveyed their delight in what makes history puzzling and interesting. Their enthusiasm for the questions at the heart of the content modeled for students what it means to be a student of history. The episodes of inspired learning that I witnessed were always catalyzed by a teacher devoted to creating a space for students to express their emerging understandings.

Sam M. Intrator
Sam M. Intrator is an associate professor of Education and Child Study at Smith College in Northampton, MA. His book *Tuned in and Fired Up: How Teaching Can Inspire Genuine Learning* (Yale University Press) explores how students experience their academic learning.

SKILLS Handbook

Contents

A series of handbooks provide skills instruction to help you read, learn, and demonstrate your knowledge of world history.

21st Century Skills

SKILLS HANDBOOK

SKILLS HANDBOOK

Objectives

- Learn how to read nonfiction critically by using pre-reading, reading, and after-reading strategies.
- Use a systematic approach to write narrative, persuasive, expository, research, biographical, and assessment essays.
- Learn, review, and practice essential geography skills.
- Use a systematic approach to critically analyze and evaluate texts, visuals, and media sources.
- Learn strategies for active participation in group discussions and debates, for developing and presenting oral or multimedia presentations, and for active listening.

Objective

As you teach this section, keep students focused on the following objective to help them master core content.

- Learn how to read informational materials critically by using pre-reading, during reading, and after reading strategies.

Prepare to Read

Build Background Knowledge L3

Ask students what types of reading they have done recently. For each, ask **What kind of text is this? What information can you learn from it? What strategies can help you understand it?** Explain that to understand these types of information, readers must apply a variety of strategies before, during, and after reading.

Teach

Strategies for Before You Read L3

Instruct

- **Introduce** Ask students to read the headings under *Strategies for Before You Read* and describe any strategies with which they are already familiar.

  Preread the Chapter worksheets
  Teaching Resources, Skills Handbook, pp. 1–2

- **Teach** Point out that to set a purpose for reading, it is useful to read headings and look at illustrations.

  Transparency 1: Set a Purpose for Reading

   Note Taking Transparencies, 1

  Set a Purpose for Reading worksheet
  Teaching Resources, Skills Handbook, p. 5

- Point out that asking questions is another key prereading step. Ask a volunteer to point to a passage anywhere in the student text, then lead the class in asking and answering questions.

  Transparency 2: Ask Questions

  Note Taking Transparencies, 2

  Ask Questions worksheet
  Teaching Resources, Skills Handbook, p. 6

Reading Informational Texts

Reading a newspaper, a magazine, an Internet page, or a textbook differs from reading a novel. You read nonfiction texts to acquire new information. Researchers have shown that the reading strategies presented below will help you maximize your understanding of informational texts. You'll have chances to practice these skills and strategies throughout the book.

Strategies for Before You Read

Before you read an informational text, it's important to take the time to do some pre-reading. These strategies will help.

Set a Purpose for Reading

Try to focus on a goal when you're reading the text. Preview a section by reading the objectives and looking at the illustrations. Then write a purpose for your reading, such as:

- "I'll learn about the histories of Egypt and Nubia and find ways to compare these cultures."
- "I'll find out about the spread of Islam."

Ask Questions

Before you read a section, consider what you'd like to know about a topic. Then ask questions that will yield relevant information. Scan the section headings and illustrations and then write a few questions in a chart like the one below. As you read, try to answer each of your questions. Use phrases and words to fill in the chart.

Question	Answer
How do strong monarchs unite nations?	Central/absolute power, citizens' loyalty, effective bureaucracy
What problems do strong monarchs often create?	Abuse of power, misuse of funds, conflicts with religious leaders

Predict

Engage in the reading process by making predictions about what you are preparing to learn. Scan the section headings and the visuals. Then write a prediction, such as:

- "I will find out what caused feudalism in Europe to develop and later to disappear."

Keep your predictions in mind as you read—do they turn out to be accurate or do you need to revise them?

Use Prior Knowledge

Research shows that if you connect the new information in your reading to your prior knowledge, you'll be more likely to remember the new information. You'll also see the value of studying history if you see how it connects to the present. After previewing a section, create a chart like this one. Complete the chart as you read the section.

What I Know	What I Want to Know	What I Learned
Many people today are Calvinists or Lutherans.	How and when did these religions begin?	John Calvin and Martin Luther led people to start new Protestant churches during the sixteenth-century Reformation.

Strategies for During Reading

It's important to be an active reader. Use these strategies as you read an informational text.

Reread or Read Ahead

If you don't understand a certain passage, reread it to look for connections among the words and sentences. For example, look for cause-and-effect words that link ideas, or sequence words that show when events took place. Or, try reading ahead to see if the ideas are clarified later on. Once you find new clarifying information, return to the confusing text and read it again with the new information in mind.

Paraphrase

To paraphrase is to restate information in your own words, as in the example below. Paraphrasing is a good way to check your understanding of the reading. Think of it this way—if you can explain it to someone else, you understand it.

Original Paragraph	Paraphrase
When Ireland won independence in 1922, Britain retained control of six northern counties where there was a Protestant majority. Faced with widespread discrimination, Catholics demanded civil rights and the reunification of Ireland. Protestants wanted to remain part of Britain.	After Irish independence in 1922, Britain controlled six Protestant-dominated counties in the north. People in these counties divided along religious lines: Catholics called for both civil rights and reunification of the Irish nation; Protestants supported British control.

L1 Special Needs   L2 Less Proficient Readers   L2 English Language Learners

If students need extra practice paraphrasing and summarizing, have them choose a paragraph at random from their books. Ask them to paraphrase that paragraph, using the steps on in their text as a guide. If students have omitted key information, point this out. Then ask students to summarize the same text. Discuss how the paraphrases and summaries differ and the uses for each.

- Encourage students to use their experiences and reading to predict what might happen in a given situation. For example, what do they predict might happen in the next presidential election? How might unfolding events affect this prediction?

Transparency 3: Predict

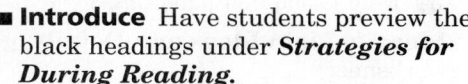 Note Taking Transparencies, 3

Predict worksheet
Teaching Resources, Skills Handbook, p. 7

- Model how to use the K-W-L chart. Point out that the first column lists what a reader knows before reading, the second lists the reader's questions, and third is completed after reading.

Transparency 4: Use Prior Knowledge

Note Taking Transparencies, 4

Use Prior Knowledge worksheet
Teaching Resources, Skills Handbook, p. 8

Independent Practice

Ask students to choose a section of text from anywhere in their student book and practice the pre-reading steps they have studied.

Monitor Progress

Circulate to make sure that students are filling in their worksheets accurately.

Strategies for During Reading   L3

Instruct

- **Introduce** Have students preview the black headings under *Strategies for During Reading.*

- **Teach** Explain that rereading or reading ahead can help students clarify a passage that is at first difficult to understand.

Transparency 5: Reread or Read Ahead

Note Taking Transparencies, 5

Reread or Read Ahead worksheet
Teaching Resources, Skills Handbook, p. 9

- Have a student read aloud the original paragraph and paraphrase about Irish independence, then discuss how the two versions differ.

Transparency 6: Paraphrase

📖 Note Taking Transparencies, 6

Paraphrase worksheet
Teaching Resources, Skills Handbook, p. 10

- Ask students to read the Original Paragraph and the Summary on the student page and explain how they differ. Then ask **How are paraphrasing and summarizing different? How does each help you read critically?** *(Paraphrasing involves restating the text in your own words. Summarizing involves stating the main ideas of a text in your own words.)*

Transparency 7: Summarize

📖 Note Taking Transparencies, 7

Summarize worksheet
Teaching Resources, Skills Handbook, p. 11

- Ask students to look at the main ideas and details highlighted in the sample text and outline. Ask **How is the main idea shown in the outline? How are the details shown?** *(The main idea is shown as an outline section heading. The details are shown beneath that heading as subordinate entries.)* **How do the details listed here support the main idea?** *(Each gives an example of a European seeking or finding routes in the Americas.)*

Transparency 8: Main Ideas and Details

📖 Note Taking Transparencies, 8

Identify Main Ideas and Details worksheet
Teaching Resources, Skills Handbook, p. 12

Summarize

Summarizing—a version of paraphrasing—can also help you confirm your understanding of the text. Summarizing focuses on restating the main ideas of a passage, as you can see in the example below. Include a few important details, such as the time period, to orient yourself or other readers to the text.

Original Paragraph	Summary
Ottoman expansion threatened the crumbling Byzantine empire. After several failed attempts to capture Constantinople, Muhammad II finally succeeded in 1453. Over the next 200 years, the Ottoman empire continued to expand.	The Byzantine empire gave way to the Ottoman empire around 1453, resulting in 200 years of Ottoman rule.

Identify Main Ideas and Details

A main idea is the most important point in a paragraph or section of text. Some main ideas are stated directly, but others are implied. You must determine these yourself by reading carefully. Pause occasionally to make sure you can identify the main idea.

Main idea →

> Europeans continued to seek new routes around or through the Americas. In 1513, the Spanish adventurer Vasco Núñez de Balboa, with the help of Native Americans, hacked a passage through the tropical forests of Panama to reach what he called the South Sea. In November 1529, Spanish nobleman Ferdinand Magellan sailed through a passage at the tip of South America. After a difficult journey filled with brutal storms, rushing tides, and unpredictable winds, Magellan's ships emerged into Balboa's South Sea, which Magellan renamed the Pacific—that is, peaceful—Ocean.

Main ideas are supported by details. Record main ideas and details in an outline format like the one shown here.

Main idea →
Details →

> European Exploration in the Americas
> I. Continued as Europeans sought new routes around or through the Americas
>   A. Balboa and Native Americans found a passage across Panama.
>   B. Balboa named the South Sea.
>   C. Magellan found passage around tip of South America.
>   D. Magellan reached the South Sea and renamed it the Pacific Ocean.

Vocabulary

Here are several strategies to help you understand the meaning of a word you do not recognize.

Use Context Clues You can often define an unfamiliar word with clues from the surrounding text. For example, in the sentence "Crusaders fought on and off for more than 200 years, and many died for their cause," the words *fought* and *died* are clues indicating that a Crusader was someone who fought wars. Context clues can be in the same sentence as the unfamiliar word or in nearby sentences or paragraphs.

Analyze Word Parts Use your knowledge of word parts to help you define unfamiliar words. Break the word into its parts—root, prefix, suffix. What do you know about these parts? For example, the suffixes *–ify* and *–ation* mean "make into" and "action or process." The word *desertify* means "turn into a desert." *Desertification* means "the process of turning into a desert."

Recognize Word Origins Another way to figure out the meaning of an unfamiliar word is to understand the word's origins. Use your knowledge of Greek or Latin roots, for example, to build meaning. The words *formation* and *reformation* contain the Latin root *form,* which means "shape." *Formation* is the shape in which something is arranged. *Reformation* is a change in the shape of an idea or institution.

Analyze the Text's Structure

Just as you organize a story about your weekend to highlight the most important parts, authors will organize their writing to stress their key ideas. Analyzing text structure can help you tap into this organization. In a social studies text, the author frequently uses one of the structures listed in the chart at right to organize information. Learn to identify structures in texts and you'll remember text information more effectively.

Analyze the Author's Purpose

Different reading materials are written with different goals, or purposes. For example, this book is written to teach you about world history. The technical manual that accompanies computer software is written to teach readers how to use the product. In a newspaper, some articles will be written to inform readers about news events, while editorials will be written to persuade readers to accept a particular view about those events.

An author's purpose influences not only how the material is presented but also how you read it. Thus you must identify the purpose, whether it is stated directly or merely suggested. If it is not directly stated, use clues in the text—such as opinion words in an editorial—to identify the author's purpose.

Structures for Organizing Information

Compare and Contrast Here, an author highlights similarities and differences between two or more ideas, cultures, processes, people, etc. Look for clue words such as *on the other hand* or *similarly.*

Sequence Here, an author recounts the order in which events occurred or steps were taken. History is often told in chronological sequence but can also involve flashbacks from later times to earlier times. Look for sequence words such as *initially, later,* and *ultimately.*

Cause and Effect Here, an author highlights the impact of one event on another or the effects of key events. Cause and effect is critical to understanding history because events in one time often strongly influence those in later times. Look for clue words such as *because, so,* or *as a result.*

21st Century Skills

SKILLS HANDBOOK

- Review each vocabulary strategy with students. Model the strategies with the examples provided, then help students find other examples in their texts or in other written materials.

Transparency 9: Use Context Clues

🖳 Note Taking Transparencies, 9

Vocabulary: Use Context Clues worksheet

Teaching Resources, Skills Handbook, p. 13

Transparency 10: Analyze Word Parts

🖳 Note Taking Transparencies, 10

Vocabulary: Analyze Word Parts worksheet

Teaching Resources, Skills Handbook, p. 14

Transparency 11: Recognize Word Origins

🖳 Note Taking Transparencies, 11

Vocabulary: Recognize Word Origins worksheet

Teaching Resources, Skills Handbook, p. 15

- Explain that identifying the structure of a text helps the reader understand and remember. Then direct students to the three common structures for organizing information in the boxed text. Ask them to describe each type of structure in their own words, and then to brainstorm topics that lend themselves to each.

Transparency 12: Analyze the Text's Structure

🖳 Note Taking Transparencies, 12

Analyze the Text's Structure worksheet

Teaching Resources, Skills Handbook, p. 16

- Explain that understanding the author's purpose, or goal, helps readers know how to read a text. Discuss different approaches to reading different kinds of texts, such as a computer manual, an editorial, and a textbook.

Transparency 13: Analyze the Author's Purpose

🖳 Note Taking Transparencies, 13

Analyze the Author's Purpose worksheet

Teaching Resources, Skills Handbook, p. 17

Differentiated Instruction Solutions for All Learners

L1 Special Needs   **L2 Less Proficient Readers**   **L2 English Language Learners**

Have students who need extra vocabulary practice choose a passage of text from anywhere in the Student Edition. Ask them to identify unfamiliar words, then use context clues, word parts, and word origins to define the words. Then have them check definitions in a reference source and write sentences containing the words. Ask students to share their sentences with the class. Can other students understand the unfamiliar words, based on the paragraph content and glossary?

- Explain that another important step in evaluating informational text is distinguishing between facts and opinions and recognizing bias. Ask each student to write one fact and one opinion, on any subject, in their notebooks and explain their choices.

Transparency 14: Distinguish Between Facts and Opinions/ Recognize Bias

📖 Note Taking Transparencies, 14

Distinguish Between Facts and Opinions/Recognize Bias worksheet
Teaching Resources, Skills Handbook, p. 18

- Tell students that identifying evidence is another way to read critically. Ask them to look again at the language highlighted in the sample editorial. Ask **Does the evidence presented in this passage convince you that Carlosa was a brilliant leader?** *(No, the writer does not back up his or her assertion with evidence.)*

Transparency 15: Identify Evidence

📖 Note Taking Transparencies, 15

Identify Evidence worksheet
Teaching Resources, Skills Handbook, p. 19

- Explain that *credible* means believable and reliable. Explain that credibility is especially important in evaluating sources on the Web. Direct students to the checklist for evaluating Web sites. Ask them to think about Web sites they have visited. **Do those Web sites pass the checklist's test? Why or why not?**

Transparency 16: Evaluate Credibility

📖 Note Taking Transparencies, 16

Evaluate Credibility worksheet
Teaching Resources, Skills Handbook, p. 20

Independent Practice

Ask students to bring in an editorial from the local newspaper or distribute copies of an appropriate editorial. Have students work in groups to apply the *Strategies for During Reading* they have learned.

Monitor Progress

Circulate to make sure that students are applying reading strategies correctly.

Distinguish Between Facts and Opinions/Recognize Bias

It's important to read actively, especially when reading informational texts. Decide whether information is factual—which means it can be proven—or if it includes opinions or bias—that is, people's views or evaluations.

Anytime you read material that conveys opinions, such as an editorial, keep an eye out for author bias. This bias might be revealed in the use of emotionally charged words or faulty logic. For example, the newspaper editorial below includes factual statements (in blue) and opinion statements (in red). Underlined words are emotionally charged words—they'll get a rise out of people. Faulty logic (in green) may include circular reasoning that returns to its beginning and either/or arguments that ignore other possibilities.

> **Editorial**
> In 1993, the people of Brazil voted to keep their government a republic rather than revert to a monarchy. Voters chose between the two options in a special election. Clearly, anyone who favored monarchy was a reactionary dinosaur who maliciously wanted to undermine Brazil's progress. The republican format allows Brazilians to vote for their leaders directly. As a result, our brilliant leader Fernando Henrique Carlosa spearheaded life-saving reforms to Brazil's dying and antiquated economic system. In a monarchy, this would be impossible.

Identify Evidence

Read critically. Don't accept an author's conclusion automatically. Identify and evaluate the author's evidence. Does it justify the conclusion in quantity and content? An author may present facts to support a claim, but there may be more to the story than facts. For example, what evidence does the writer of the editorial above present to support the claim that a monarch could not help Brazil's economy? Perhaps a monarch would use his or her more centralized authority to achieve more sweeping and rapid reforms.

Evaluate Credibility

After you evaluate evidence, check an author's credentials. Consider his or her level of experience and expertise about the topic. Is he or she likely to be knowledgeable *and* objective about the topic? Evaluating credibility is especially important with sites you may visit on the Internet. Ask the following questions to determine if a site and its author are reliable.

- Who sponsors the Web site? Is it a respected organization, a discussion group of individuals, or a single person?

- What is the source of the Web site's information? Does the site list sources for facts and statements?

- Does the Web site creator include his or her name and credentials?

- Is the information on the Web site balanced and objective or biased to reflect only one point of view?

- Can you verify the Web site's information using two other sources, such as an encyclopedia or news agency?

- Is the information current? Is there a date on the Web site to show when it was created or last updated?

Strategies for After Reading

Evaluate Understanding

Evaluate how well you understand what you've read.

- Go back to the questions you asked yourself before reading. Try to answer each of them.
- Check the predictions you made and revise them if appropriate.
- Draw a conclusion about the author's evidence and credibility.
- Check meanings of unfamiliar words in the dictionary to confirm your definitions.

Recall Information

Before moving on to new material, you should be able to answer the following questions fully:

- What is the text about?
- What is the purpose of the text?
- How is the text structured?

You should also be able to place the new information in the context of your prior knowledge of the topic.

Strategies for After Reading

Instruct

- **Introduce** Explain that *Strategies for After Reading* allow readers to confirm understanding and successfully file information for future use.

- **Teach** Ask volunteers to read each bulleted strategy under *Evaluate Understanding* aloud. Discuss why each of the strategies is useful. Which do students think are the most important?

  Transparency 17: Evaluate Understanding

  Note Taking Transparencies, 17

  Evaluate Understanding worksheet
  Teaching Resources, Skills Handbook, p. 21

- Ask volunteers to read each bulleted strategy under *Recall Information.* Explain that students should use this checklist to make sure that they understand new material before moving on.

  Transparency 18: Recall Information

  Note Taking Transparencies, 18

  Recall Information worksheet
  Teaching Resources, Skills Handbook, p. 22

Independent Practice

Have students choose one of the sample texts they read or discussed in *Reading Informational Texts.* Ask them to write answers to the final three bulleted questions on this page.

Monitor Progress

If students cannot answer the *Strategies for After Reading* questions, urge them to reread their chosen text and apply *Strategies for During Reading* again.

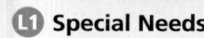 **Special Needs**    **Less Proficient Readers**   **English Language Learners**

If students are struggling, tell them to approach the task of reading an informational text by asking themselves the following questions as they read: **What** is this text mainly about? **What** are its main ideas? **Which** words are unfamiliar and **how** can I figure out their meanings? **Why** did the author write this? **How**

has the author made his or her points, using facts, opinions, or biased text? **What** evidence has the author used to support the main idea? **Who** is the author, and what sources has he or she used? Have them practice asking and answering these questions on an editorial or newspaper article of your choice.

Objective

As you teach this section, keep students focused on the following objective to help them master core content.

■ Use a systematic approach to write narrative, persuasive, expository, research, biographical, and assessment essays.

Prepare to Read

Build Background Knowledge ⑬

Ask students to identify writing assignments they have completed for school and outside writing they have done, such as letters, lists, or stories. Explain that all these types of writing share a few main writing purposes: to tell a story, to explain or share information about a topic or person, to persuade, or to demonstrate one's mastery of a topic.

Teach

Narrative Essay ⑬

Instruct

■ **Introduce** Tell students that they will be asked to write narrative essays for school as a way of linking personal experience to a topic they are studying. They may also need to write a narrative essay for job or college applications that ask about how an applicant's experiences prepare him or her for the task ahead.

■ **Teach** Discuss the *Prewriting* suggestions listed in the text and ask volunteers to name specific instances where they might apply each ("I read in the paper about opportunities for new immigrants in my neighborhood. I would like to write about the struggles that my family has had as immigrants.") Then choose a topic such as "A New Immigrant's Experiences" and work through different scenarios for audience and purpose. Ask **Is the intended audience people who have shared the experience or people who know nothing about it? How will the answer to that question affect the way the essay is written?**

SKILLS Handbook

Writing Handbook

Writing is one of the most powerful communication tools you will use for the rest of your life. Research shows that writing about what you read actually helps you learn new information and ideas. A systematic approach to writing— including prewriting, drafting, revising, and proofing—can help you write better, whether you're writing an essay or a research paper.

Narrative Essay

Narrative writing tells a story, often about a personal experience. In social studies, this story might be a narrative essay that recounts how a recent or historical event affected you or your family.

① Prewriting

Choose a topic. The focus of your essay should be an experience of significance to you. Use these ideas as a guide.

- **Look at photos** that show you and/or your family. Perhaps you attended a political rally or visited an important historical monument.
- **Scan the news** in print or through electronic media. Consider how current events relate to you and your family.
- **Brainstorm** with family or friends about recent events. How did you respond to these events? Jot down ideas like the ones below.

Connections to History This Year
— trip to art museum: Renaissance painters
— historical books: World War II Africa
— mock debate: Vietnam War

Consider audience and purpose.

- Keep your **audience's** knowledge and experience level in mind. Make sure you provide any necessary background information.
- Choose a **purpose** as well. If you want to entertain, include humorous details. To convey how the experience changed you, you might share more serious insights.

Gather details. Collect the facts and details you need to tell your story.

- **Research** any background about the historical event that readers might need to know about.
- **List details** about your own experience as it relates to the event.

② Drafting

Identify the climax, or most interesting part of your story. Then logically organize your story into a beginning, middle, and end. Narratives are usually told in chronological order.

Open strongly with an engaging sentence, such as the one below, that will catch your reader's attention.

Use sensory details, such as sights, sounds, or smells, to make the story vivid for readers. Describe people's actions and gestures. Pinpoint and describe locations.

Write a conclusion that sums up the significance of the event or situation you have experienced.

> I never expected to find myself arguing to support America's role in Vietnam. Our recent mock debate on the Vietnam War gave me new insight about this complex time in my nation's history. Research took me inside the perspective of those who supported the War and its goals. On the day of the debate, my hands were covered in sweat and my heart pounded as I stood to explain this currently unpopular position.

Strong opening engages the reader.

Insight or significance tells the reader what this event means to you.

Sensory details help the reader envision the experience.

③ Revising

Add dialogue or description. Dialogue, or conveying a person's thoughts or feelings in his or her own words, can make a narrative more effective. Look for places where the emotions are especially intense. In the model, this might be when the writer's opponents respond to the debate position.

First Draft	Revised Original
At the debate, my hands were wet and my heart beat fast.	On the day of the debate, my hands were covered in sweat and my heart pounded.

Revise word choice. Replace general words with more specific, colorful ones. Choose vivid action verbs, precise adjectives, and specific nouns to convey your meaning. Look at the example above. Notice how much more effective the revised version is at conveying the experience.

Read your draft aloud. Listen for grammatical errors and statements that are unclear. Revise your sentences as necessary.

④ Publishing and Presenting

Share by reading aloud. Highlight text you want to emphasize and then read your essay aloud to the class. Invite and respond to questions.

- Refer students to the Writing Rubrics (p. SH23) so they know what is expected.

- Students may find it helpful to write out the main events of their narratives in chronological order. They can then expand this list of events into an outline as they add details that will flesh out the story. They can also explore re-arranging the events to allow for a flashback or other narrative break. Students might then list sensory details in a web graphic organizer to make their narratives more vivid.

- Reassure students that dialogue will not suit every narrative. If their narrative has only one character, students may wish to use inner dialogue to show the character's thoughts or may prefer to describe those thoughts through the narrator's voice.

- Review the example under *First Draft* and *Revised Original*. Then ask students to write simple sentences with general words on the board and work together to replace them with more specific, colorful options.

- Display **Transparency 19: Narrative Essay.**

   Note Taking Transparencies, 19

- Have students fill in the **Narrative Essay** worksheet.
  Teaching Resources, Skills Handbook, p. 23

Independent Practice

Tell students to write a narrative essay about a recent experience that surprised them or changed them or their perspective in some way. Invite students to use one of the prewriting topic finders or to brainstorm topics with a peer.

Monitor Progress

Pair students to review each other's essays. Invite peer reviewers to identify at least two successful aspects of their partner's work before focusing on areas needing further work. Refer partners to the Writing Rubrics on p. SH23 for additional evaluation criteria. Circulate to answer questions as needed.

Expository Writing

Instruct

- **Introduce** Tell students that expository writing may be the type of writing they will use most often in school. Assignments often ask students to explain a process, compare and contrast, examine cause and effect, or describe a problem and solution.

- **Teach** Direct students to the *Ask Questions* strategy for choosing a topic. Brainstorm a list of questions and answers that answer the question "how." Choose one topic and guide students to create steps in a process essay on that topic.

- Display **Transparency 20: Explain a Process.**

  📖 Note Taking Transparencies, 20

- Have students fill in the **Expository Essay: Explain a Process** worksheet.
  Teaching Resources, Skills Handbook, p. 24

- Lead students through the compare/contrast grab bag strategy for choosing a topic to compare and contrast. Then, using the Venn diagram at the bottom of the text as a model, help them create a similar graphic organizer to compare and contrast their topics.

- Display **Transparency 21: Expository Essay: Compare and Contrast.**

  📖 Note Taking Transparencies, 21

- Have students fill in the **Expository Essay: Compare and Contrast** worksheet.
  Teaching Resources, Skills Handbook, p. 25

- Direct students to "take a mental walk" with a world or regional map. Lead them through choosing a problem based on their "mental walk" and suggest solutions to it.

- Display **Transparency 23: Expository Essay: Problem and Solution.**

  📖 Note Taking Transparencies, 23

- Have students fill in the **Expository Essay: Problem and Solution** worksheet.
  Teaching Resources, Skills Handbook, p. 27

- Refer students to the Writing Rubrics on p. SH23 for clarification of writing expectations.

Expository Writing

Expository writing explains ideas or information in detail. The strategies on these pages examine each of several expository writing styles.

① Prewriting

Choose a topic. In social studies, the focus of your writing might be explaining a historical process, comparing and contrasting cultural trends, explaining causes and effects of current events, or exploring problems societies have faced and the solutions they have sought. These ideas are a guide.

- **Ask questions.** For process writing, consider the question *how*. Think about *how* people in history have accomplished their goals, such as building a giant monument. Identify the steps and procedures involved.

> **Question: How did great thinkers of the 1600s change people's view of the world?**
>
> Answer: They developed the scientific method.

- **Create a compare/contrast grab bag.** With a small group, write on separate slips of paper examples from each category: ideas, cultures, or time periods. Mix the slips in a bag and choose two. Compare and contrast the two ideas, cultures, or time periods.

- **Interview** someone who made a major change in lifestyle, such as moving from one culture to another. Find out how and why the person did this. Understanding *why* is the basis of any cause and effect essay.

- **Take a mental walk.** Study a map and envision taking a tour of the region. Think about problems each area you visit might face, such as armed conflict, natural disaster, or governmental change. Choose a problem and suggest solutions for it.

Consider audience and purpose. Consider how much your readers know about the problem, comparison, event, or process you will address. Suit your writing to your audience's knowledge or plan to give explanations of unfamiliar terms and concepts.

Gather details. Collect the facts and details you need to write your essay.

Research the topic. Use books, the Internet, or interviews of local experts. List facts, details, and other evidence related to your topic. Also consider your personal experience. For example, you might know about a process from personal experience or have witnessed the effects of a historic legal decision.

Create a graphic organizer. For cause-and-effect or problem-solution essays, use a two-column chart. Process writing can be listed as a bulleted list of steps. A Venn diagram can help you compare and contrast.

World War I
- new weapons used: machine guns, poison gas, submarines
- 8.5 million military deaths

- fought by two powerful alliances
- began in Europe, then spread

World War II
- new weapon used: atomic bomb
- 20 million military deaths

Identify causes and effects. List possible explanations for events. Remember that many events result from multiple causes. Identify effects both large and small. Note that some events may have effects that in turn cause other events. Look for causes and effects in all your expository essays. For example, in a process explanation, one step often causes the next.

Fine-tune your ideas. For a problem-solution essay, decide what you will suggest as a solution. Keep your solution narrow to be achievable in cost, effort, and timing. Make sure no one has tried it before, or if it has been tried and it failed, address the failure.

❷ Drafting

Match structure to purpose. Typically, process writing and cause-and-effect writing are written in sequence order. Problem-solution essays benefit from block organization, which presents the entire problem and proposes a solution. For compare/contrast essays, you can organize by subject or by point.

| By subject: Discuss the events and outcomes of World War I, and then compare and contrast these with those of World War II. |
| By point: Introduce a category, such as use of new weapons. Relate both wars to this category, comparing or contrasting them along the way. |

Give background. To discuss events from history, first orient the reader to time and place. Choose the important facts but don't overwhelm the reader with detail. If you need to, return to prewriting to narrow your topic further.

Elaborate for interest and emphasis. Give details about each point in your essay. For example, add facts that make the link between events so that a cause-and-effect relationship is clear. Also, readers will support proposed solutions more if your details clearly show how these solutions will solve the stated problem. Use facts and human experiences to make your essay vivid.

Connect to today. Even when you write about historical events, you may find links to today. Explore these links in your essay.

> Mexico's population underwent great change during the mid–twentieth century. **Population shifted from rural areas to urban areas. The nation's society went from largely agricultural to largely industrial and urban. Urban populations exploded, with Mexico City alone growing from 1.5 million people in 1940 to nearly 20 million later in the century. These changes resulted from several causes.**
>
> First, land reform begun in the 1930s failed. The millions of acres redistributed by then–President Lázaro Cárdenas proved arid and unproductive. Second, the rural population was growing rapidly. This placed increased demands on the land. The land became even more depleted and unproductive. **Finally, several Mexican governments in turn shifted their attention from the small rural peasant farmer toward larger scale farming operations.**
>
> Mexico's shifting population and changing economic patterns yielded new problems for its leaders by late in the twentieth century.

Identify the topic to orient readers.

Chronological order walks readers through the cause-effect sequence.

Elaboration supports the relationship you are highlighting.

Connection to today tells readers why this matters to them.

- Make a three-column list on the board. Label the first "Event," the second "Causes," and the third "Effects." Have students brainstorm a list of current events and fill in causes and effects for each.

- Have students fill in the **Expository Essay: Cause and Effect** worksheet. **Teaching Resources, Skills Handbook,** p. 26

- Display **Transparency 22: Expository Essay: Cause and Effect.**
  📖 **Note Taking Transparencies,** 22

- Read the ***Drafting*** steps with students. Then make two columns on the board, one listing types of essays mentioned in the text (process writing, cause and effect, etc.) and the other listing types of organization (sequence, block organization, etc.) Have students come to the board to match the type of essay with its typical organization.

- Encourage students to experiment with different organizational patterns for compare/contrast essays. Ask students to suppose that they are writing an essay comparing soccer and basketball. Ask **Which type of organization would you choose? Why?** *(Sample: There are advantages and disadvantages to both, but I prefer by subject as it's easier to be sure that I've included all the information. / I prefer by point because it's easier to see connections.)*

- Model the steps in drafting an expository essay by working through the sample essay on Mexico.

Differentiated Instruction
Solutions for All Learners

L1 Special Needs **L2 Less Proficient Readers** **L2 English Language Learners**

If students are struggling with writing essays, urge them to return to the prewriting phase and check their assumptions. Is the topic narrow enough? Do they have enough information? Then encourage them to draft a brief outline of the main paragraphs or ideas they wish to cover before they begin to write. You may also encourage them to write for five or ten minutes on any subject as a "warm-up" to writing a more formal essay.

- Read the *Revising* steps with students. Challenge students to use each transition word in the text in a sentence as well as add their own examples of transition words. Ask **Why is the Revised sample more effective than the First Draft?** *(It shows the order of events.)*

- Explain that even professional writers ask their peers to review their work. Peers often use each other as "talking partners" to help clarify ideas that need further explanation.

- Read the *Publishing and Presenting* steps with students. Have students choose a publishing option from those listed, or suggest one of their own. Ask them to explain why they feel their essay is best suited to this presentation format.

Independent Practice

Tell students to write an expository essay about a current issue related to popular culture (music, films, books, video games, fashion, etc.). Have them use one of the prewriting steps listed, then choose the type of essay that best suits the topic.

Monitor Progress

Circulate to make sure that students are filling in their worksheets correctly and to provide guidance with planning and writing their essays.

3 Revising

Add transition words. Make cause-and-effect relationships clear with words such as *because, as a result,* and *so.* To compare or contrast ideas, use linking words, such as *similarly, both, equally* or *in contrast, instead, yet.* Use words such as *first, second, next,* and *finally* to help readers follow steps in a process. Look at the following examples. In the revised version, a reader knows the correct order in which to perform the steps.

First Draft	Revised
Scientists form an educated guess called a hypothesis. They test that hypothesis with an experiment.	Next, scientists form an educated guess called a hypothesis. Then, they test that hypothesis with an experiment.

Remember purpose. Shape your draft so that it answers the question or thesis you began with. For a problem-solution essay—in which your purpose is to sell your solution—that means anticipating opposing arguments and responding to them. For cause-and-effect, you want to stress the way one event leads to the next. Always tell readers *why* they should care about your topic.

Review organization. Confirm that your ideas flow in a logical order. Write main points on index cards. Reorganize these until you are satisfied that the order best strengthens your essay.

Add details. Make sure you haven't left out any steps in your essay, and don't assume readers will make the connections. For example, you might forget to state explicitly that a process must be repeated in order to produce accurate results. Add more background if necessary for clarity.

Revise sentences and words. Look at your sentence length. Vary it to include both short and long sentences. Then scan for vague words, such as *good.* Replace them with specific and vibrant words, such as *effective.* Use technical terms only when necessary, and then define them.

Peer review. Ask a peer to read your draft. Is it clear? Can he or she follow your ideas? Revise areas of confusion.

4 Publishing and Presenting

Collect in a class manual. Contribute your process explanation to a class manual of *History How-To's.*

Submit to a library. Find a specialized library, such as a presidential library. Mail your essay to the library's publications or public relations department.

Seek publication. If your historical events or issues are local, seek publication in a local historical magazine or contact a historical society. You might speak to their members.

Mail to an advocacy group. Find a local, national, or international organization that is concerned with your topic. Send them your essay and ask for comments on its ideas. Make sure to include a self-addressed stamped envelope and a note explaining your essay and offering thanks for its review.

Research Writing

❶ Prewriting

Choose a topic. Often, a teacher will assign your research topic. You may have flexibility in choosing your focus or you may have the opportunity to completely define your topic. These ideas are a guide.

- **Catalog scan.** Using a card or electronic catalog, search for topics that interest you. When a title looks promising, find the book on the shelves. Libraries usually use the Dewey Decimal Classification system to group research materials by subject, so you should find other books on similar subjects nearby. You can use them all to decide on your final topic.

- **Notes review.** Review your social studies notes from the last month or so. Jot down topics that you found interesting. Then repeat the process with your other classes. For example, you might find a starting point for research into the Scientific Revolution from a math theorem.

- **Social studies categories game.** With a group, brainstorm categories in social studies. For example, you might list key world leaders or important wars. Within each category, take turns adding subtopics. The chart below looks at different transportation topics.

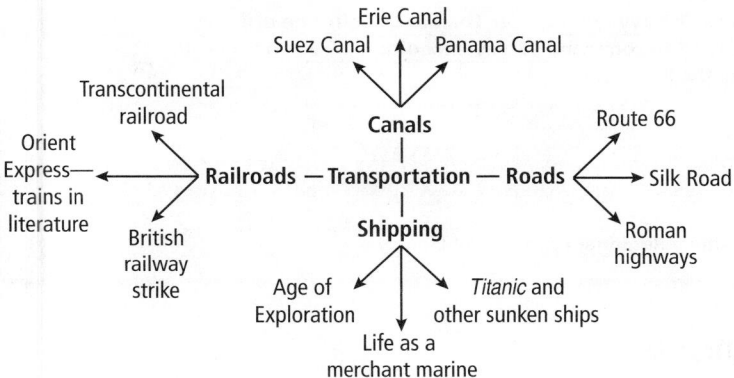

You can use sources such as newspapers to get ideas.

Daily News
November 17, 1869
Volume 1
The Suez Canal Opens!

Research Writing

Instruct

- **Introduce** Clarify that research writing results in an essay based heavily on information from outside sources beyond the writer's own knowledge. In addition to school, research writing is often required in job settings, such as when an employer needs to learn about a new technology.

- **Teach** Read the steps for prewriting research essays with students. Invite students to share any questions they may have.

- Point out the several techniques for finding or refining a research topic. Urge students to choose topics that they think would interest general readers, but that also interest them as writers. Research writing is time-consuming, and an interest in the topic will help students stay focused.

- Model dividing subjects into categories by working through the transportation topics web in the text. Then divide students into groups to choose a topic and create a web like the one shown.

 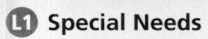

- Review the sample notecards on the text page. Ask students to identify and define each piece of information on the cards. Ask **How does the researcher identify his or her sources?** *(by numbering the cards)* Strongly encourage students to document facts as they write. It can be very time-consuming to return to a stack of index cards to find one piece of information.

- Refer students to the Writing Rubrics on p. SH23 for clarification of writing expectations.

- Read the ***Drafting*** steps with students. To help students fine-tune a thesis, tell them to ask themselves questions such as the following: **Based on your research, what are the main ideas you wish to get across? Do you support or oppose the ideas and actions you have researched?** Urge students to discuss these questions with a peer if they are still struggling with a thesis statement.

- Display **Transparency 24: Research Writing.**

  📖 Note Taking Transparencies, 24

- Have students fill in the **Research Writing** worksheet.
  Teaching Resources, Skills Handbook, p. 28

Analyze the audience. Your research and your paper should be strongly influenced by the audience. How much will readers know about this topic and how much will you have to teach them?

Gather details. Collect the facts and details you need to write your paper. Use resources beyond the typical history books. Look at nonfiction books such as memoirs or collections of letters. Also look at magazine and newspaper articles. Consider news magazines, as well as those focused on topics such as history or travel. You may find interviews with experts on your topic or travel articles about a region that interests you. Search the Internet, starting with online encyclopedias, news organizations, and history Web sites.

Organize evidence and ideas. Use note cards to record information and to help you organize your thoughts. Start with a general thesis statement in mind. Then begin reading and taking notes. Write a heading at the top of each note card to group it under a subtopic. Note a number or title to identify the information source. In the examples below, the number 3 is used. Use the same number for an additional source card containing the bibliographic information you will need.

Heading

Information source I.D. number

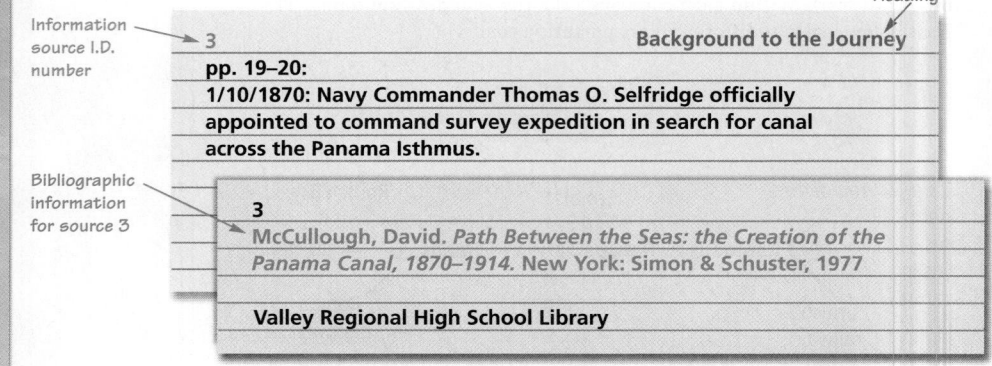

3   Background to the Journey

pp. 19–20:
1/10/1870: Navy Commander Thomas O. Selfridge officially appointed to command survey expedition in search for canal across the Panama Isthmus.

Bibliographic information for source 3

3
McCullough, David. *Path Between the Seas: the Creation of the Panama Canal, 1870–1914.* New York: Simon & Schuster, 1977

Valley Regional High School Library

❷ Drafting

Fine-tune your thesis. Review your notes to find relationships between ideas. Shape a thesis that is supported by the majority of your information, then check that it is narrow enough to address thoroughly in the allotted time and space. Remember, you can fine-tune your thesis further as you draft or even when you revise.

Organize to fit your purpose. Do you want to persuade readers of a particular position about your topic, compare and contrast aspects of the topic, or show a cause-and-effect relationship? Organize appropriately—for example, by looking at parts of a whole to examine events leading to building and completing the Panama Canal.

Make an outline. Create an outline in which you identify each topic and subtopic in a single phrase. You can then turn these phrases into sentences and later into the topic sentences of your draft paragraphs. Study the example at the top of the next page to see how to do this well.

Write by paragraph. Write an introduction, at least three body paragraphs, and a conclusion. Address a subtopic of your main topic in each body paragraph. Support all your statements with the facts and details you gathered.

Building the Panama Canal

Outline
I. Introduction
II. Why the Canal Was Built
III. How the Canal Was Built
   A. Physical Challenges
   B. Medical Challenges
IV. Conclusion

Introduction
Ever since Christopher Columbus first explored the Isthmus of Panama, the Spanish had been looking for a water route through it. They wanted to be able to sail west from Spain to Asia without sailing around South America. However, it was not until 1914 that the dream became a reality.

Conclusion
It took eight years and more than 70,000 workers to build the Panama Canal. It remains one of the greatest engineering feats of modern times.

An outline helps you structure your information.

Each body paragraph looks at a part of the whole topic.

The introduction puts the topic in a context of time and place. The entire paragraph conveys the thesis: Building the Panama Canal was a dream that took centuries to achieve.

The conclusion recaps key points and leaves readers with a final statement to remember.

❸ Revising

Add detail. Mark points where more details would strengthen your statements. Look at the following examples. Notice the added details in the revised version. When adding facts, make certain that they are accurate.

First Draft	Revised
The Navy excursion was a huge undertaking. Supplies were gathered to support the team for many months.	The Navy excursion was a huge undertaking. Supplies were gathered to support the team for many months, including more than 600 pairs of shoes, 100 miles of telegraph wire, 2,500 pounds of coffee, and 10,000 pounds of bread! (McCullough 20).

Make the connection for readers. Help readers find their way through your ideas. First, check that your body paragraphs and the information within them flow in a logical sequence. If they do not, revise to correct this. Then add transition words to link ideas and paragraphs.

Give credit. Check that you have used your own words or given proper credit for borrowed words. You can give credit easily with parenthetical notes. These include the author's last name and the relevant page number from the source. For example, you could cite the note card here as (McCullough 19–20).

❹ Publishing and Presenting

Plan a conference. Gather a group of classmates and present your research projects. You may each wish to create visual materials to accompany your presentations. After you share your papers, hold a question and answer session.

■ Review the sample outline on this page. Discuss each step in the outline, pointing out how the information is organized in a clear, logical fashion. Explain that each paragraph of the paper would link to an outline entry. Point out that the Introduction puts the topic in context and conveys the thesis statement, while the Conclusion recaps key points and ends with a memorable statement.

■ Read the ***Revising*** steps with students. Review the sample first draft and discuss how the added details in the revision make the Navy excursion easier to understand.

■ An important step in revising a research paper is rereading to confirm that each fact is documented. Stress the importance of documenting each fact. If a fact cannot be documented, it should be cut.

■ Read the ***Publishing and Presenting*** suggestion with students. Point out that students should anticipate likely questions classmates might ask and prepare general answers. If possible, provide access to computers so that students can create accompanying visuals such as multimedia presentations.

Independent Practice
Have students consider and choose topics for a research paper. Once they have selected a topic, have them work in groups to list possible sources for information.

Monitor Progress
Circulate to make sure that students are filling in their worksheets correctly and provide guidance with selecting topics and brainstorming sources of information.

Differentiated Instruction
Solutions for All Learners

L1 Special Needs **L2 Less Proficient Readers**   **L2 English Language Learners**

If students are struggling with research essays, urge them to return to the prewriting phase and check their assumptions. Is the topic narrow enough? Do they have enough information? If not, where can they look

for more information? Encourage them to draft a brief outline of the main paragraphs or ideas they wish to cover, and then fill in supporting details.

Persuasive Essay

Instruct

- **Introduce** Show students an editorial from a current newspaper or magazine. Explain that this is a real-world example of persuasive writing. Invite students to suggest additional applications for persuasive writing, such as film reviews or advertisements.

- **Teach** Read the steps for prewriting persuasive essays with students. Tell them that the purpose of writing a persuasive essay is to convince other people to share your point of view. However, persuasive essays must use solid, reliable evidence and arguments to make the writer's points.

- Review the suggestions for choosing a topic (Round-table discussion, Textbook flip, Make connections). Using their study of world history, the text, and current events, lead students through an example of each strategy. Point out that writers should search for topics they can make a personal connection with. Writing persuasively is more effective with a strong point of view.

- Direct students to scan the graphic organizer about education in developing nations. Ask **Why are there more items listed under Pro than under Con?** *(The organizer supports a position in favor of public education.)*

- Refer students to the Writing Rubrics on p. SH23 for clarification of writing expectations.

- Have students fill in the **Persuasive Essay** worksheet.
  Teaching Resources, Skills Handbook, p. 29

- Display **Transparency 25: Persuasive Essay.**
  🎞 Note Taking Transparencies, 25

- Read the ***Drafting*** steps with students. Have a volunteer read aloud the sample thesis statement. Point out that its strength is that it clearly states a position in the first sentence, then gives an overarching reason to support that position. Readers then know exactly what to expect from the essay to follow.

Persuasive Essay

Persuasive writing supports an opinion or position. In social studies, persuasive essays often argue for or against positions on historical or current issues.

❶ Prewriting

Choose a topic. Choose a topic that provokes an argument and has at least two sides. Use these ideas as a guide.

- **Round-table discussion.** Talk with classmates about issues you have studied recently. Outline pro and con positions about these issues.
- **Textbook flip.** Scan the table of contents or flip through the pages of your textbook. Focus on historical issues that engage your feelings.
- **Make connections.** Relate current events to history. Develop a position for or against a situation of importance today using historical evidence.

Narrow your topic.

- **Cover part of the topic** if you find too many pros and cons for a straightforward argument.
- **Use looping.** Write for five minutes on the general topic. Circle the most important idea. Then write for five minutes on that idea. Continue looping until the topic is manageable.

Consider your audience. Choose arguments that will appeal to the audience for your writing and that are likely to persuade them to agree with your views.

Gather evidence. Collect the evidence to support your position convincingly.

- **Identify pros and cons.** Use a graphic organizer like the one below to list points on both sides of the issue.

Position: Education is key to improving life in developing nations.	
Pro ⟵	⟶ **Con**
• Education allows people to get higher-paying jobs. • With more money, people can help boost the economy. • With education, people can better handle disease and disaster.	• Building new schools may cost more than the government has available for education. • Some countries have other large problems to handle, such as serious diseases.

- **Interview** adults who have lived or worked in developing nations. What do they think? Ask them for reasons to support their views.
- **Research** to get your facts straight. Read articles or books about life in developing nations.

❷ Drafting

State your thesis. Clearly state your position, as in this example:

> Education is the key to revitalizing developing nations. Once many people are educated, many other problems can be solved.

Use your introduction to provide a context for the issue. Tell your readers when and why the issue arose, and identify the important people involved.

Sequence your arguments. Open or close with your strongest argument. If you close with the strongest argument, open with the second-best argument.

Acknowledge opposition. State, and then refute, opposing arguments.

Use facts and details. Include quotations, statistics, or comparisons to build your case. Include personal experiences or reactions to the topic, such as those a family member might have shared when interviewed.

Write a conclusion that restates your thesis and closes with a strong, compelling argument.

> Many people living in developing nations want to improve life in their countries. They want the people to have everything they need, such as food and clean water, electricity, medicines, and even fun items like televisions and bicycles. Education is the key to revitalizing developing nations. Once many people are educated, many other problems can be solved.
>
> Education allows people to get higher-paying jobs. With more money, people can help boost the economy. As well, education is an added tool people can use to deal with other problems. It's true that building new schools costs a lot. And in some places, people face many other major problems such as serious diseases. But education will only help them handle these issues....

Background orients readers.

Thesis identifies your main argument.

Supporting argument clarifies your thesis.

Opposing argument, noted and refuted, adds to your position.

3 Revising

Add information. Extra details can generate interest in your topic. For example, add a quotation from a news article that assesses the role of education in a developing nation or a poor area.

Review arguments. Make sure your arguments are logically sound and clearly developed. Avoid faulty logic such as circular reasoning (arguing a point by merely restating it differently). Evidence is the best way to support your points. Look at the following examples. Notice how much more effectively the revised version supports the argument.

First Draft	Revised
Education allows people to make more money, which is helpful.	Education allows people to get higher-paying jobs. With more money, people can help boost the economy.

Use transition words to guide readers through your ideas.

- To show contrast: *however, although, despite*
- To point out a reason: *since, because, if*
- To signal conclusion: *therefore, consequently, so, then*

4 Publishing and Presenting

Persuasive Speech. Many persuasive essays are delivered orally. Prepare your essay as a speech, highlighting words for emphasis and adding changes in tone, volume, or speed.

- Remind students to research as necessary to provide specific supporting information. Ask **Why is an argument that is supported with facts and examples more effective than one that is unsupported?** *(It appeals to the reader's intelligence rather than just stating an emotional position.)*

- Review the sample draft in the text. Ask **Where does the main argument appear?** *(at the end of the first paragraph)* **Where else could it appear for equal effectiveness?** *(at the beginning of the first paragraph)*

- Walk students through the features of the sample draft, identifying the highlighted elements and confirming students' understanding.

- Read the ***Revising*** steps with students. Point out that to revise a persuasive essay, students should check for areas where information should be added, faulty logic, or places transition words could help guide readers through the argument.

- Discuss the sample first draft and revision. Ask **Why is the revision an improvement over the first draft?** *(It is more specific and contains more details.)*

- Read the ***Publishing and Presenting*** suggestion with students. Model how you use emphasis, gesture, tone, volume, or speed in your own presentations. Stress that persuasive speech should be delivered with feeling, but never involve shouting or emotional extremes. These distract listeners from the speaker's ideas.

Independent Practice

Tell students to write a persuasive essay about a topic that matters to them, such as restrictions to popular media, length or timing of the high school day, military draft for young men and women, or the value of competitive sports in high school. Pair students to discuss their positions. One partner will state his or her topic and position. The other partner will refute it. Students will then switch roles and repeat with the second student's topic.

Monitor Progress

Circulate to make sure that students are filling in their worksheets correctly and staying focused on their topics for a persuasive essay.

Differentiated Instruction   Solutions for All Learners

L1 Special Needs   L2 Less Proficient Readers   L2 English Language Learners

If students are having trouble organizing their ideas, divide them into groups and assign each group a topic from the ***Independent Practice*** activity. Urge each member of the group to write one important idea on a slip of paper or index card. Then have students within the group categorize the ideas that fit together. Point out that each category belongs in its own paragraph with its own topic sentence.

Biographical Writing

⑬

Instruct

- **Introduce** List several key people that the class has recently studied or has studied in a previous course. Tell students that biographical writing will allow them to explore and understand the lives of such people. In addition, biographical writing is used to tell about authors in book reviews, to describe political candidates, and to introduce new employees.

- **Teach** Read the steps for prewriting biographical essays with students. Invite and answer any questions students may have.

- Have students scan the table of contents of their text to identify at least one possible biography subject. Ask students to explain why this person interests them.

- Invite volunteers to read aloud the entries for the Name Game. Point out that each entry includes a brief idea of the person's views. Tell students that they may add their responses to these views. As with a persuasive essay, any views included must be supported with evidence.

- Review the example for how to follow an episode. Trace the path of ideas from Martin Luther to the event (the Diet of Worms) to the background about that event. Stress the importance of understanding and explaining background and historical context when discussing a person's actions.

- Refer students to the Writing Rubrics on p. SH23 for clarification of writing expectations.

- Display **Transparency 26: Biographical Writing.**

  📖 Note Taking Transparencies, 26

- Have students fill in the **Biographical Writing** worksheet.
Teaching Resources, Skills Handbook, p. 30

Biographical Writing

❶ Prewriting

Choose a topic. Biographical writing tells the story of a real person's life. For social studies, you should focus on the life of an important historical or current figure. The following ideas are a guide.

- **Find a hero.** Think about a person from history whom you admire—for example, a world leader, a great thinker, or an inventor. Remember to choose someone about whom information is easily available.

- **Name game.** On an index card, write the name of a person in the news today. Write a sentence or phrase explaining what makes this person interesting to you, as on the examples below. With a group, shuffle all the cards and then take turns drawing topics. If you like, trade your topic with a friend.

Martin Luther
He thought the Bible—not the pope—should guide a person's actions.

Wangari Maathai
She thinks preserving the environment can improve people's lives.

- **Table of Contents scan.** Your history book lists the short biographies that are included in the text. Scan this listing in the book's Table of Contents for three possible subjects. Read the biography of each subject before you make a final choice.

Focus your approach. Decide how you want to approach your subject. For example, you could emphasize the person's influence on historical events, or you could show how personal experiences affected his or her achievements.

Gather details. Collect the facts and details you need to write your paper. Use the research methods for gathering information explained on page SH14. In particular, check biographical source materials in the reference section of the library.

Isolate episodes. As you learn about your subject, focus on the particular episodes that seem to be most important. Then learn more about the events surrounding these episodes and take notes on them, as in the example below.

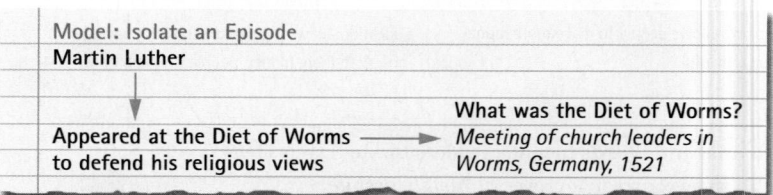

Model: Isolate an Episode	
Martin Luther	
↓	
	What was the Diet of Worms?
Appeared at the Diet of Worms ⟶ to defend his religious views	*Meeting of church leaders in Worms, Germany, 1521*

Focus your fact-gathering. Your goal is to bring this person's life to readers—to share facts and opinions relating to that life and respond to them with your own conclusions. As you determine the main points you wish to make about this person, find facts to support your assertions. Make sure to give enough factual background for readers to appreciate your points.

② Drafting

Focus your essay. In a single paper, you will probably need to focus on an aspect of your subject's life or on a quick overview of major events in that life.

Organize important events. Choose the events you will discuss, and then order them in a logical way. Biographies are usually organized chronologically.

Reveal your subject. Include direct description of your subject, which allows you to convey information quickly. Balance this with quotations or examples of the person's actions, which lend color and authenticity to your essay.

Open strongly. Get readers' attention immediately with an engaging quotation, an interesting fact about your subject, or an anecdote that sets the tone.

"Here I stand, I cannot do otherwise." Martin Luther spoke these words at the Diet of Worms in 1521. The Diet, a conference of religious leaders, had summoned Luther to explain his controversial religious views.

Martin Luther was born in 1483 into a German family. Raised a Catholic, Luther entered a monastery after experiencing a religious calling. He became both devout and committed to strict observance. Over time, this approach brought him into conflict with the Church. For example, Luther felt that the Catholic Church should not sell indulgences, or guarantees of good grace after death.

Luther developed new ideas about the Church and its leadership. At the core were his beliefs that people should have a direct relationship to the Bible and that the Church and the pope stood in the way of this. In his 95 Theses, Luther called for widespread reforms in the Catholic Church and later in the German government. Because his views were contrary to accepted beliefs, Luther was called in front of the Diet of Worms. He refused to back down, so the Church expelled him in 1521.

A quote gets the readers attention and quickly establishes the subject's personality.

The biography will focus on this aspect of Luther's life.

Chronological organization helps readers see the development of Luther's ideas.

The conclusion brings the biography back to its initial anecdote.

---

③ Revising

Examine word choice. Bring your subject to life with vivid adjectives, specific verbs, and precise nouns. Then link your chronological organization with words that show sequence. The draft above uses dates as well as phrases such as *over time* to show the sequence of Luther's life and religious growth.

Make connections for readers. For example, the sentence below connects Luther's life to current times by linking it to the modern Lutheran Church.

Although Luther himself never called for a new church, today the Protestant branch named for him claims more than 5 million members in America alone.

Give credit. Cite sources for any facts, statistics, or quotations you include. If several pieces of information in a paragraph come from a single source, you may cite the source once at the end of the paragraph. Always check with your teacher for specific bibliographic requirements.

④ Publishing and Presenting

Create a biographical character. Use what you've learned about this person's life to appear as that person. If you wish, wear a costume. Explain who you are and what is most important to you. Ask and answer questions.

■ Read the *Drafting* steps with students. Discuss the issues of chronology and sequence. Explain that while biographies are usually written in chronological order, writers may want to jump backward in time to include information from earlier times. Childhood background, for example, might explain the subject's actions or attitudes.

■ Ask students to read the model draft in the text. Ask **How does the opening anecdote work to get readers' attention?** *(It begins dramatically by introducing Martin Luther in a tight situation, which makes readers wonder how he'll respond.)*

■ Read the *Revising* steps with students. Ask them to write two or three sentences about a person with whom they are familiar. Supply them with colored pens or pencils. Have them examine their word choice by circling adjectives, verbs, and nouns each in a different color, then deciding if any of these words need replacing with more effective words.

■ Read the *Publishing and Presenting* steps with students. Review ways that students can convey information about a biographical character. For example, they might use tone of voice, show a characteristic gesture or physical trait, or repeat a well-known quotation.

Independent Practice

Tell students to write a biographical essay about a current or historical person that interests them. Urge them to consider people they know personally, as well as those from the public arena. Pair them with a partner to brainstorm for likely sources of information.

Monitor Progress

Circulate to make sure that students are filling in their worksheets correctly. Offer suggestions about students' choice of subjects, research, and drafting of their biographical essays.

Differentiated Instruction
Solutions for All Learners

L4 Advanced Readers L4 Gifted and Talented Students

Help more advanced students refine their writing skills by practicing strong openings for biographical and other essays. Ask each student to choose an historic or other figure to research. Then have them write at least two different strong openings for a biographical essay on that person. One opening should be a quotation and the other should be an interesting fact or event that captures important information about the person. Ask students to read their openings aloud and have classmates guess who the biography will be about.

Writing for Assessment Ⓛ3

Instruct

- **Introduce** Ask students to name the in-class and high-stakes tests they have completed recently. Discuss how many of these included writing components. Note with the class how often students are asked to write for assessment. Developing strategies for successful assessment writing greatly enhances students' chances for school success.

- **Teach** Read the steps for prewriting assessment responses with students. Invite and answer any questions students may have.

- Highlight the issue of question choice. Ask **Why might choosing a particular question be important?** *(It allows you to focus on areas of greater knowledge or on structures you find easier to work with.)*

- Review the list of key words in the text. Provide students with a few questions from a recent assessment. Ask them to identify key words in each question, underlining them as shown in the sample question.

- Remind students that prewriting for assessment includes quickly plotting your answer to make sure you have chosen the best question, measuring your time, and gathering facts and details.

Writing for Assessment

Assessment writing differs from all other writing that you do. You have fewer choices as a writer, and you almost always face a time limit. In social studies, you'll need to write both short answers and extended responses for tests. While these contrast in some ways, they share many requirements.

❶ Prewriting

Choose a topic. Short-answer questions seldom offer a topic choice. For extended response, however, you may have a choice of more than one question. Use the following strategies to help you navigate that choice.

- **Examine the question.** To choose a question you can answer effectively, analyze what each question is asking. Use key words such as those listed below to help you choose topics and respond to short-answer questions in which the topic is given.

Key Words	What You Need in an Answer
Explain	Give a clear, complete account of how something works or why something happened.
Compare/Contrast	Show how two or more things are alike and different.
Define	Give examples to explain meaning.
Argue, Convince, Support, Persuade	Take a position on an issue and present strong reasons to support your side of the issue.
Summarize	Provide the most important elements of a subject.
Evaluate/Judge	Assign a value or explain an opinion.
Interpret	Support a thesis with examples from the text.

Notice in the examples below that the key words are underlined:

Short answer: <u>Describe</u> one way that Chief Joseph showed his <u>military expertise</u>.

Extended response: According to the author of this article, Chief Joseph was both a <u>peace chief</u> and a <u>military genius</u>. Use information from the article to <u>support this conclusion</u>.

- **Plot your answer.** After choosing a question, quickly plot the answer in your mind. Do you have the information to answer this question? If the answer is *no*, try another question.

Measure your time. Your goal is to show the instructor that you've mastered the material. To stay focused on this goal, divide your time: one-quarter on prewriting; half on drafting; one-quarter on revising. For short-answer questions, determine how much of the overall test time you can spend on each question. Don't spend more than that.

Gather details. Organize the facts and details you need to write your answer. For short-answer questions, this usually involves identifying exactly what information is required.

Use a graphic organizer. For extended response, divide your topic into subtopics that fit the type of question. Jot down facts and details for each. For the question on Chief Joseph, the following organizer would be effective:

Chief Joseph of the Nez Percé
Peace Chief
• traded peacefully with white settlers (1)
• reluctantly went to war (2)
• famous speech, "I will fight no more forever." (3)
Military Genius
• won battles with fewer warriors than opposing troops had (a)
• avoided capture for many months (b)
• led his people more than 1,000 miles (c)
• knew when to surrender for the good of his people (c)

② Drafting

Choose an organization that fits the question. With a short-answer question, write one to three complete sentences. With extended response, you'll need more elaborate organization. For the question on Chief Joseph, organize your points by importance within each subtopic. For a summary or explanation, use chronological order. For compare/contrast, present similarities first, then differences.

Open and close strongly. Start your answer by restating the question or using its language to state your position. This helps you focus and shows the instructor that you understand the question. Finish with a strong conclusion that restates your position. For short answer, include some language from the question in your response.

One way that Chief Joseph showed his military expertise was by defeating U.S. Army troops despite having fewer warriors than they had.

Support your ideas. Each paragraph should directly or indirectly support your main idea. Choose facts that build a cohesive argument. The numbered sentences in the draft below show how this writer organized support.

Chief Joseph was both a peace chief and a military genius. He was a peace chief because he traded peacefully with white settlers for many years. (1) He went to war reluctantly after the government ordered his people to move to a reservation. (2) When he finally surrendered, he said in a famous speech, "I will fight no more forever." (3)   Chief Joseph was also a military genius. He fought off U.S. Army forces with fewer warriors than they had, (a) and he avoided capture for many months. (b) He led his people more than 1,000 miles (c) before he made the decision to surrender. Chief Joseph will long be remembered for his dual roles as peace chief and military genius.

The opening restates the question and presents the main idea.

The writer uses information from the graphic organizer, in order of importance.

The writer supports the second subtopic.

The conclusion recaps the main idea and again uses the question's language.

- Have students compare the Extended Response question on Chief Joseph with the graphic organizer outlining an answer. Ask **How is the question reflected in the headings of the graphic organizer? How will this help the writer plan a response?** *(Each underlined key element has a main heading in the organizer. This allows the writer to plan supporting details for each required point in the question.)*

- Refer students to the Writing Rubrics on p. SH23 for clarification of writing expectations.

- Have students fill in the **Writing for Assessment** worksheet. **Teaching Resources, Skills Handbook**, p. 31

- Display **Transparency 27: Writing for Assessment.**
    🏛 Note Taking Transparencies, 27

- Read the ***Drafting*** steps with students. Review the discussion about choosing an organization to fit purpose. Then ask students to suggest appropriate possible organizations for each of the question types shown under Key Words.

- Stress the value of restating the question at the beginning of the answer. This is immensely useful in focusing the writer's response. Have students link the opening sentence of the sample response to the question about Chief Joseph. Ask them to circle words that appear in both texts. *(Chief Joseph, both, peace chief, military genius)*

L1 Special Needs   **L2 Less Proficient Readers**   **L2 English Language Learners**

Emphasize the importance of reading directions and looking for key words in writing an assessment essay. For students who need extra practice, have them copy the chart on the student page onto a piece of notebook paper. They should list "key words" on the left side of the paper and "What you need in an answer" on the left, then fold the paper in half. For each key word, have them describe what they need in an answer. If they get stuck, they can unfold their paper to remind themselves, then try again.

- Read the ***Revising*** steps with students. Have them read the First Draft and Revised examples in the text. Ask students to list words added to the Revised version, and then explain how each addition or change makes the text about Chief Joseph more effective.

- Emphasize the importance of good time management. Tell students that revising can be a critical step in assessment writing, and to resist the impulse to skip it. Have students complete the organizational check by circling the main idea in each paragraph of an essay.

- Show students some samples of assessment essays you have scored highly. Ask them to identify the strengths in each essay.

- Read the ***Publishing and Presenting*** step with students. Remind students to make all corrections neatly in the space between lines. They can use standard editing marks to indicate insertions and deletions.

Independent Practice

Give students a sample assessment question on a topic they are familiar with. Allow them an appropriate amount of time to respond to the question.

Monitor Progress

Circulate to make sure that students are filling in their worksheets accurately. Make sure that they are staying on task and monitoring their time appropriately as they complete the ***Independent Practice*** activity. If students are spending too much time on planning, give them a discreet reminder to move on to the next step. If students appear stuck, refer them back to the prewriting steps and urge them repeat their examination of the question.

❸ Revising

Examine word choice. Replace general words with specific words. Add transitions where these improve clarity. Read the following examples. The revised version shows the relative importance of the writer's supporting evidence.

First Draft	Revised
Chief Joseph was both a peace chief and a military genius. He was a peace chief because he traded peacefully with white settlers for many years. He went to war reluctantly...	Chief Joseph was both a peace chief and a military genius. He was a peace chief for several reasons. First, he traded peacefully with white settlers for many years. Second, he went to war reluctantly...

Check organization. Make sure your introduction includes a main idea and defines subtopics. Review each paragraph for a single main idea. Check that your conclusion summarizes the information you've presented.

❹ Publishing and Presenting

Edit and proof. Check spelling, grammar, and mechanics. Make sure that tenses match, that subjects agree with verbs, and that sentences are not too long. Finally, confirm that you have responded to all the questions you were asked to answer.

Writing Rubric

Use this chart, or rubric, to evaluate your writing.

SAT	
SCORE OF 6 An essay in this category is **outstanding**, demonstrating **clear and consistent mastery**, although it may have a few minor errors. A typical essay • effectively and insightfully develops a point of view on the issue and demonstrates outstanding critical thinking, using clearly appropriate examples, reasons, and other evidence to support its position • is well organized and clearly focused, demonstrating clear coherence and smooth progression of ideas • exhibits skillful use of language, using a varied, accurate, and apt vocabulary • demonstrates meaningful variety in sentence structure • is free of most errors in grammar, usage, and mechanics	**SCORE OF 3** An essay in this category is **inadequate**, but demonstrates **developing mastery**, and is marked by **one or more** of the following weaknesses: • develops a point of view on the issue, demonstrating some critical thinking, but may do so inconsistently or use inadequate examples, reasons, or other evidence to support its position • is limited in its organization or focus, but may demonstrate some lapses in coherence or progression of ideas • displays developing facility in the use of language, but sometimes uses weak vocabulary or inappropriate word choice • lacks variety or demonstrates problems in sentence structure • contains an accumulation of errors in grammar, usage, and mechanics
SCORE OF 5 An essay in this category is **effective**, demonstrating **reasonably consistent mastery**, although it will have occasional errors or lapses in quality. A typical essay • effectively develops a point of view on the issue and demonstrates strong critical thinking, generally using appropriate examples, reasons, and other evidence to support its position • is well organized and focused, demonstrating coherence and progression of ideas • exhibits facility in the use of language, using appropriate vocabulary • demonstrates variety in sentence structure • is generally free of most errors in grammar, usage, and mechanics	**SCORE OF 2** An essay in this category is **seriously limited**, demonstrating **little mastery**, and is flawed by **one or more** of the following weaknesses: • develops a point of view on the issue that is vague or seriously limited, demonstrating weak critical thinking, providing inappropriate or insufficient examples, reasons, or other evidence to support its position • is poorly organized and/or focused, or demonstrates serious problems with coherence or progression of ideas • displays very little facility in the use of language, using very limited vocabulary or incorrect word choice • demonstrates frequent problems in sentence structure • contains errors in grammar, usage, and mechanics so serious that meaning is somewhat obscured
SCORE OF 4 An essay in this category is **competent**, demonstrating **adequate mastery**, although it will have lapses in quality. A typical essay • develops a point of view on the issue and demonstrates competent critical thinking, using adequate examples, reasons, and other evidence to support its position • is generally organized and focused, demonstrating some coherence and progression of ideas • exhibits adequate but inconsistent facility in the use of language, using generally appropriate vocabulary • demonstrates some variety in sentence structure • has some errors in grammar, usage, and mechanics	**SCORE OF 1** An essay in this category is **fundamentally lacking**, demonstrating **very little** or **no mastery**, and is severely flawed by one or more of the following weaknesses: • develops no viable point of view on the issue, or provides little or no evidence to support its position • is disorganized or unfocused, resulting in a disjointed or incoherent essay • displays fundamental errors in vocabulary • demonstrates severe flaws in sentence structure • contains pervasive errors in grammar, usage, or mechanics that persistently interfere with meaning
	SCORE OF 0 Essays not written on the essay assignment will receive a score of zero.

Writing Rubrics L3

Instruct

- **Introduce** Poll students on how many plan to take the SAT exam. Explain that an important part of these exams now involves essay writing.

- **Teach** Explain that the *Writing Rubric* on this page shows students how their essays on the SAT exam will be scored. Ask volunteers to name the four criteria that are used to rate essays for the SAT. Then ask students to explain in their own words the qualities that distinguish a strong essay from a weak essay.

- Have students fill in the **Writing Rubrics** worksheet.
  Teaching Resources, Skills Handbook, p. 32

- Display **Transparency 28: Writing Rubrics.**
  📖 Note Taking Transparencies, 28

Independent Practice

Ask students to choose the best essay they have written so far and evaluate it using the rubrics on this page.

Monitor Progress

Collect students' essays and self-evaluations. Meet with students to go over good points and areas for improvement.

Objective

As you teach this section, keep students focused on the following objective to help them master core content.

■ Learn, review, and practice essential geography skills.

Prepare to Read

Build Background Knowledge L3

Point out that geography is part of students' everyday lives as they follow a route to school or plan a trip away from home. Discuss why knowledge of geography is essential to the study of history.

Teach

Analyze the Five Themes of Geography

Instruct

■ **Introduce** Ask students what it means to identify location, such as the location of their school. Ask **What other questions might you ask when studying geography?** Coach students to elicit as many of the five themes as possible.

■ **Teach** Have students read the bullet points under *Analyze the Five Themes of Geography* and give examples of each theme from their reading and knowledge of history and geography so far. Use

Transparency 29: Analyze the Five Themes of Geography

📖 Note Taking Transparencies, 29

Analyze the Five Themes of Geography worksheet
Teaching Resources, Skills Handbook, p. 33

Independent Practice

Have students complete the Practice and Apply questions.

Monitor Progress

As students answer the questions, circulate to confirm their understanding.

Geography Skills Handbook

Analyze the Five Themes of Geography

The five themes of geography are tools you can use to analyze geographic information given in photographs, charts, maps, and text.

- **Location** answers the question "Where is it?" The answer might be an absolute location, such as 167 River Lane, or a relative location, such as six miles west of Mill City.
- **Regions** are areas that share at least one common feature. Climate, culture, and government are features that can be used to define a region.
- **Place** identifies natural and human features that make a place different from other places. Landforms, climate, plants, animals, people, culture, and languages are features that can be used to identify a specific place.
- **Movement** answers the question "How do people, goods, and ideas move from place to place?"
- **Human-Environment Interaction** focuses on the relationship between people and the environment. Humans often make changes to the environment, and the environment often affects how humans live.

Use the photograph and steps that follow to analyze the five themes of geography.

The Nile River in Egypt

Read supporting information such as a caption or key. Use this information and your own knowledge of the world to determine location and region.

Analyze the content. Consider the elements of the visual or text to develop ideas about region, place, movement, and human-environment interaction.

Practice and Apply the Skill

Use the photograph above to answer the following questions:

1. How might you describe the relative location of the fields of crops?
2. What is the climate region shown here? How do you know?
3. What elements in the scene identify this specific place?
4. How do you think people, goods, and ideas move to and from this place?
5. How have the people of this area changed their environment?

Answers

1. in the desert along the Nile in Egypt
2. dry and hot; desert, camels, palm trees
3. desert, river, camel, irrigated farmland
4. by boat along the river, by camel through the desert
5. through irrigation

Understand Latitude and Longitude

Geographers divide the globe along imaginary horizontal lines called parallels of latitude. They measure these parallels in degrees (°) north or south of the Equator, which itself is a line of latitude. Geographers also divide the globe along imaginary vertical lines called meridians of longitude. They measure these meridians in degrees east or west of the Prime Meridian, a line of longitude running through Greenwich, England. All meridians intersect at the North Pole and the South Pole. Together, the lines of latitude and longitude form a grid that gives an absolute location for every place on Earth. Use the globes and the steps that follow to understand latitude and longitude.

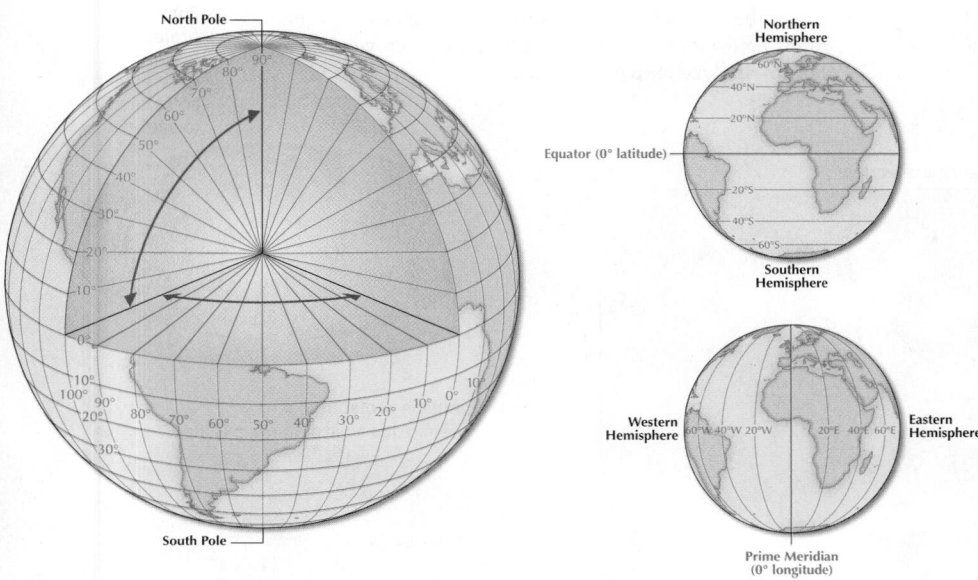

Study purpose. Study the two main globes to understand why geographers divide the globe into parallels and meridians. Study the two smaller globes to understand the role of the Equator and the Prime Meridian as starting points for measuring parallels and meridians.

Read labels and captions. Read the labels and captions to understand how to determine the latitude and longitude of a given location, as well as to identify which hemispheres it sits in.

Identify absolute location. You can use lines of latitude and longitude together to identify the absolute location of any spot on Earth.

Practice and Apply the Skill

Use the text and globes above to answer the following questions:

1. Which part of the location 67° N, 55° E represents the longitude?
2. What line of latitude lies halfway from the Equator to the North Pole?
3. Do lines of latitude ever intersect one another? Explain.
4. If you followed the 70° W line of longitude north to the North Pole and then continued on the same line south, what line of longitude would you be on? (Hint: The globe, like a circle, has a total of 360 degrees.)

Understand Latitude and Longitude

Instruct

- **Introduce** Draw a sphere on the board labeled "Earth." Draw a horizontal line through the center labeled "Equator" and sketch in lines of latitude (parallels). Do the same for the Prime Meridian and lines of longitude (meridians). Ask volunteers to label the hemispheres.

- **Teach** Have students read the steps under *Understand Latitude and Longitude* and share any questions they have. Referring them to a world map, ask **Which continents are in the Northern and Southern Hemispheres? Which are in the Western and Eastern?** *(Northern: North America, Europe, Asia, most of Africa; Southern: South America, Australia. Western: North and South America, Eastern: Asia, Australia, and most of Europe and Africa.)* Use

  Transparency 30: Understand Latitude and Longitude

  📖 Note Taking Transparencies, 30

  Understand Latitude and Longitude worksheet
  Teaching Resources, Skills Handbook, p. 34

Independent Practice

Have students complete the Practice and Apply questions.

Monitor Progress

Circulate to make sure that students are answering the Practice and Apply questions correctly.

Answers

1. 55° E
2. 45° N
3. No; they run parallel to each other, which means they do not intersect.
4. 110° E

Analyze Map Projections 🔢

Instruct

- **Introduce** Ask **Can you flatten an orange peel without stretching or tearing it?** Point out that cartographers face much the same problem of distortion and loss of accuracy when they try to show Earth on a flat surface. The different types of maps—or projections—shown on the text page are different solutions to this problem.

- **Teach** Have students read the steps under **Analyze Map Projections** and share any questions they have. Then have them skim their textbooks to find and analyze additional examples of map projections. Use

  Transparency 32: Analyze Map Projections

  📖 Note Taking Transparencies, 32

  Analyze Map Projections worksheet **Teaching Resources, Skills Handbook,** p. 36

Independent Practice

Have students complete the Practice and Apply questions. Discuss their responses as a class.

Monitor Progress

As students complete the questions, circulate to provide guidance. If necessary, ask additional questions to help facilitate understanding.

Answers

1. The Mercator projection; it accurately shows directions. The equal-area projection and Robinson projection do not show direction clearly.
2. the equal-area map; the sizes of the landmasses are equal relative to one another.
3. The Mercator parallels stretch landmasses out vertically, while its meridians stretch the surface horizontally because they do not curve like meridians on a globe.
4. By compromising between the Mercator and equal-area projections, the Robinson gives a more useful general picture of the world.

Analyze Map Projections

Because maps are flat, they cannot show the correct size and shape of every feature on Earth's curved surface. Mapmakers must shrink some places and stretch others. Different types of map projections distort Earth's surface in different ways. Mapmakers choose the projection that has the least distortion for the information they are presenting.

Same-shape map projections such as the Mercator projection accurately show the shapes of landmasses. However, they distort sizes and distances. Equal-area map projections show the correct size of landmasses but distort shapes, especially at the edges of a map. The Robinson projection keeps the size and shape relationships of most continents and oceans but distorts the size of the polar regions. Use the maps below and the steps that follow to help you learn how to analyze map projections.

Mercator projection

The greatest distortion is at the far northern and southern latitudes.

Equal-area projection The sizes of landmasses are accurate relative to one another.

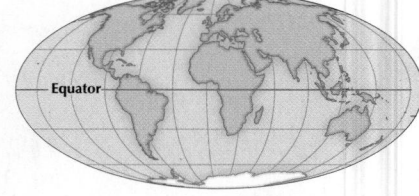

Robinson projection The entire top edge of the map is the North Pole.

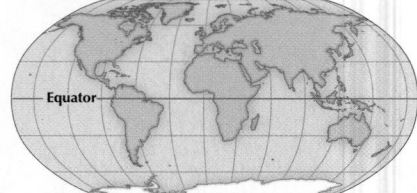

The entire bottom edge of the map is the South Pole.

Identify each projection. Study the appearance of each type of projection.

Read labels and captions. Read the labels and captions to understand the important details of each projection.

Compare the maps. Compare the shape of the maps and then the shapes of landmasses on them. Last, compare the amount of curvature of the lines of latitude and longitude on the maps.

Practice and Apply the Skill

Use the maps above to answer the following questions:

1. If you wanted to plot a course to sail from one port to another on the most direct route, which map projection would work best? Why?

2. Which map shows the most accurate relative size of Antarctica, the white region on each map? Why?

3. How do the grid lines on the Mercator projection vary from a globe's?

4. Why do you think many maps in this book use the Robinson projection?

Read Maps

Maps can show many different kinds of information. A physical map represents what a region looks like by showing its major physical features, such as mountains and plains. A political map focuses on elements related to government, such as nations, borders, and cities. Special-purpose maps provide information on a specific subject—for example, land use, population distribution, or trade routes. Road maps and weather maps are two kinds of special purpose maps.

Mapmakers provide clues to help you read maps and gather the information they offer. Use the map below and the steps that follow to practice reading a map.

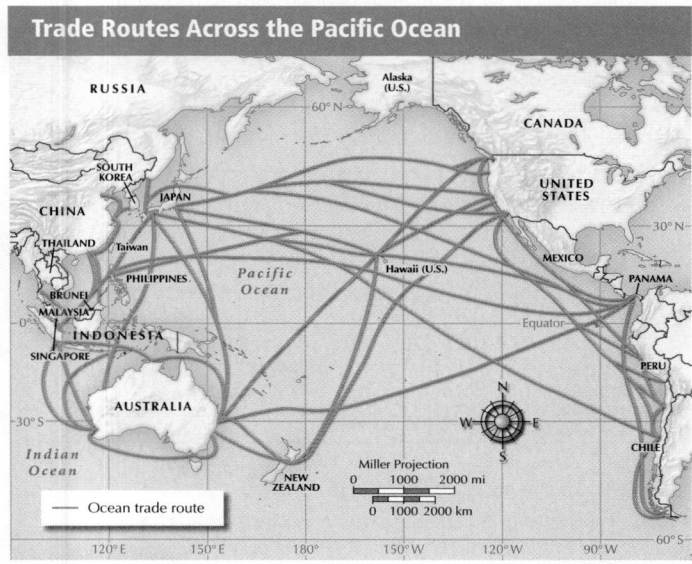

Trade Routes Across the Pacific Ocean

— Ocean trade route

Read the title. The title tells you the subject of the map.

Read the key. The key explains the symbols, lines, and colors and the map.

Use the scale bar and compass rose. Use the scale bar to determine distances between places on the map. Use the compass rose to determine the relative directions of places on the map.

Practice and Apply the Skill

Use the map above to answer the following questions.

1. What is the purpose of this map? What part of the world does it show?

2. What do the blue lines represent?

3. How many trade routes go through New Zealand?

4. When goods travel from the United States to Australia, in what direction do they travel?

5. What generalization could you make about trade across the Pacific Ocean based on this map?

Read Maps

Instruct

- **Introduce** Explain that maps can show different types of information. **What does the map on this page show?** (trade routes across the Pacific) Brainstorm a list of different ways that the focus on this same geographic area could be different (physical features, political entities, weather, natural resources, economic activity, etc.).

- **Teach** Have students read the steps under *Read Maps* and share any questions they have. Emphasize the importance of using the key when analyzing maps. Use

  Transparency 33: Read Maps

  📖 Note Taking Transparencies, 33

  Read Maps worksheet
  Teaching Resources, Skills Handbook, p. 37

Independent Practice

Have students complete the Practice and Apply questions. Discuss their responses as a class.

Monitor Progress

Circulate to make sure students are answering the Practice and Apply questions accurately and to answer any additional questions they may have.

Answers

1. to show trade routes across the Pacific; the Pacific Rim
2. ocean trade routes
3. 4; 2
4. southwest
5. There is a significant amount of trade crossing the Pacific Ocean.

Step-by-Step Instruction

Objective

As you teach this section, keep students focused on the following objective to help them master core content.

■ Use a systematic approach to critically analyze and evaluate texts, visuals, and media sources.

Prepare to Read

Build Background Knowledge ⒀

Give students five minutes to list as many visual and media sources they can think of, such as political cartoons, advertisements, graphs, and timelines. Explain that responding critically to these materials will help them be more active readers.

Teach

Analyze Graphic Data ⒀

Instruct

■ **Introduce** Tell students that they will encounter graphs frequently, in textbooks, tests, or newspapers.

■ **Teach** Have students read the steps under *Analyze Graphic Data*. Invite a student to read the graph titles and describe the main topic of each.

Transparency 35: Analyze Graphic Data

▢ Note Taking Transparencies, 35

Analyze Graphic Data worksheet
Teaching Resources, Skills Handbook, p. 39

Independent Practice

Have students complete the Practice and Apply questions.

Monitor Progress

Make sure students can identify each feature of the graphs.

Answers

1. *Travel Times to London;* how long it took to travel to London from three different cities during three different time periods
2. Birmingham and Manchester in 1750; it became faster.
3. blue; Protestant ownership increased, Catholic ownership decreased; Protestants gained political power.
4. Yes, one could use colored bars instead of wedges.

SH28

Critical Thinking
About Texts, Visuals, and Media Sources

Analyze Graphic Data

The study of history requires that you think critically about the text you're reading as well as any visuals or media sources. This section of the Skills Handbook will allow you to practice and apply some important skills for critical thinking.

Graphs show numerical facts in picture form. Bar graphs and line graphs compare things at different times or places, such as changes in school enrollment. Circle graphs show how a whole is divided into parts. To interpret a graph, look closely at its features. Use the graphs below and the steps that follow to practice analyzing graphic data.

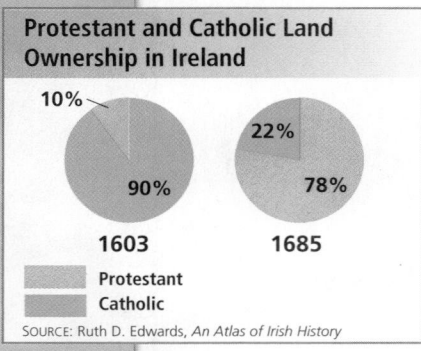

Protestant and Catholic Land Ownership in Ireland

10%

90%

1603

22%

78%

1685

▢ Protestant
▢ Catholic

SOURCE: Ruth D. Edwards, *An Atlas of Irish History*

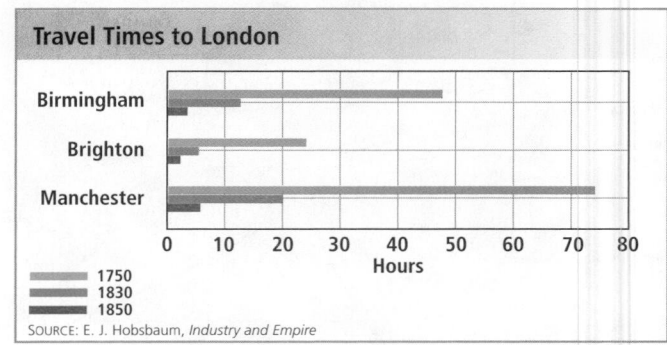

Travel Times to London

Birmingham

Brighton

Manchester

0 10 20 30 40 50 60 70 80
Hours

▢ 1750
▢ 1830
▢ 1850

SOURCE: E. J. Hobsbaum, *Industry and Empire*

Read the title to learn the main topic of the graph.

Use labels and the key to read the data given in the graph. The bar graph is labeled in hours, with intervals of 10 hours. The keys on all three graphs assign different colors to different groups or dates.

Interpret the graph. Look for interesting patterns in the data. Look at changes over time or compare information for different groups.

Practice and Apply the Skill

Use the graphs above to answer the following questions:

1. What is the title of the bar graph? What is its topic?
2. Which cities show the longest travel times to London, and in which years? What does this tell you about changes in transportation?
3. What color on the circle graphs shows Catholic land ownership? How did Irish land ownership change over time? What might explain this change?
4. Could the information in the circle graph be shown as a bar graph? Explain.

Analyze Images

Television, film, the Internet, and print media all carry images that seek to convey information or influence attitudes. To respond, you must develop the ability to understand and interpret visuals. Use the photograph below and the steps that follow to practice analyzing images.

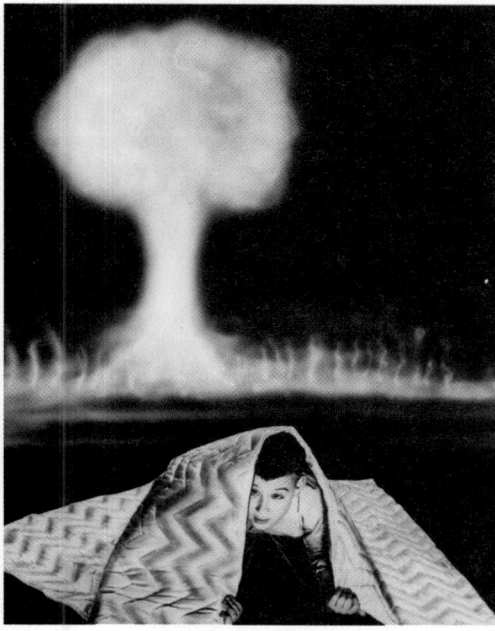

In the 1950s, people everywhere worried about nuclear attack. This 1954 image advertised a bogus "radiation-resistant" blanket.

Identify the content. Look at all parts of the image and determine which are most important.

Note emotions. Study facial expressions and body positions. Consider the emotions they may suggest.

Read captions/credits. Gather information about the image, such as when it was produced.

Study purpose. Consider who might have created this image. Decide if the purpose was to entertain, inform, or persuade.

Consider context. Determine the context in which the image was created—in this case, the Cold War between the United States and the Soviet Union.

Respond. Decide if a visual's impact achieves its purpose—to inform, to entertain, or to persuade.

Practice and Apply the Skill

Use the photograph above to answer the following questions:

1. What are the three main images in this photograph?

2. What feelings are conveyed by the boy's facial expression?

3. What do you think the photograph's purpose is?

4. When was this image produced? How did historical context influence its production?

Analyze Images

Instruct

- **Introduce** Write the saying "A picture is worth a thousand words" on the board. Ask students what they think it means. Point out how important it is to recognize and critically evaluate the message in every visual image, especially if that message is meant to persuade viewers.

- **Teach** Have students read the steps under *Analyze Images* and share any questions they have. Then ask students in turn to complete one step in analyzing the image on the text page and share their findings with the class. Invite other students to add information or comment on the findings. Reach consensus on the content, emotions, background, purpose, and context of the "radiation-resistant" blanket advertisement pictured.

Transparency 36: Analyze Images

📖 Note Taking Transparencies, 36

Analyze Images worksheet
Teaching Resources, Skills Handbook, p. 40

Independent Practice

Have students complete the Practice and Apply questions. Discuss their responses as a class.

Monitor Progress

As students complete the practice questions, allow them to ask questions if they are confused. Remind them to look for key words in the questions that will help them identify what information is being sought.

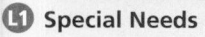 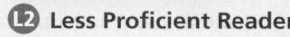
Answers

1. the mushroom cloud, the child's face, and the blanket
2. anxiety and fear
3. to sell blankets
4. 1954; Cold War anxiety meant there was a market for a blanket such as this.

Analyze Timelines

Instruct

- **Introduce** Point out that timelines are essential to the study of history because they allow readers to quickly and easily see a progression of events. In addition, timelines help readers place events in an overall context.

- **Teach** Have students read the steps under *Analyze Timelines* and share any questions they have. Then ask a volunteer to read the title of the timeline aloud. Ask **How do the entries on the top of the timeline differ from those on the bottom?** (*Events on the top are from a particular chapter on the Industrial Revolution; those on the bottom are global events happening during the same time period.*) Have volunteers read the timeline entries out loud. Ask students to identify events that fall into similar categories.

Transparency 37: Analyze Timelines

📖 Note Taking Transparencies, 37

Analyze Timelines worksheet
Teaching Resources, Skills Handbook, p. 41

Independent Practice

Have students complete the Practice and Apply questions. Discuss their responses as a class.

Monitor Progress

As students complete the questions, circulate to check on students with difficulties. Remind them to read the timeline from left to right, and to use the progression of dates from earliest to latest as a guide.

Answers

1. emancipation of the serfs, 1861
2. 1807
3. 32
4. Darwin published *On the Origin of Species.*

SH30

Analyze Timelines

Timelines show the order in which events occur as well as the amount of time that passes between events. To understand a timeline, study its labels and captions carefully. Use the timeline below and the steps that follow to practice analyzing timelines

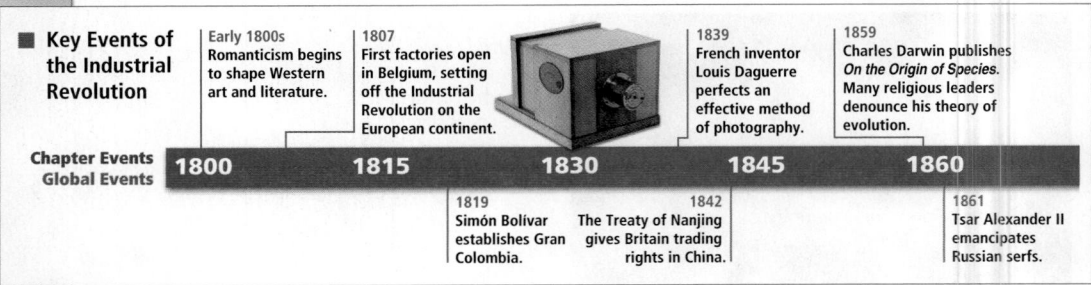

■ Key Events of the Industrial Revolution

Early 1800s Romanticism begins to shape Western art and literature.

1807 First factories open in Belgium, setting off the Industrial Revolution on the European continent.

1839 French inventor Louis Daguerre perfects an effective method of photography.

1859 Charles Darwin publishes *On the Origin of Species.* Many religious leaders denounce his theory of evolution.

Chapter Events / Global Events

1800   1815   1830   1845   1860

1819 Simón Bolívar establishes Gran Colombia.

1842 The Treaty of Nanjing gives Britain trading rights in China.

1861 Tsar Alexander II emancipates Russian serfs.

Identify time units. Find the main time units of the timeline. Determine how much time is represented by the entire timeline.

Read each entry. Read each of the entries on the timeline. Connect each entry to the events before and after it.

Look for patterns among the events shown. Determine if any of the entries fall into a common category. Think about whether the events might be causes and/or effects.

Practice and Apply the Skill

Use the timeline above to answer the following questions.

1. What is the most recent event on the timeline? When did it take place?
2. When did the first factories open in Belgium?
3. How many years after the first factories opened did Louis Daguerre perfect his method of photography?
4. What happened in 1859?

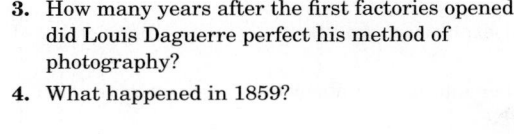

Simón Bolívar

Differentiated Instruction Solutions for All Learners

L1 Special Needs   L2 Less Proficient Readers   L2 English Language Learners

To help students who need further practice analyzing timelines, ask them to create a simple timeline of their own lives so far, or of the life of a friend or public fig-

ure. Then have them create a double timeline by adding a timeline underneath the first that records important events outside of, but concurrent with, the person's life.

Analyze Primary Sources

Primary sources include official documents and firsthand accounts of events or visual evidence such as photographs, paintings, and political cartoons. Such sources provide valuable information about the past. Use the excerpt below and the steps that follow to learn to analyze primary sources.

The following excerpt is a translation from *The Satires*, a series of poems written in Latin by Juvenal about life in Rome in the first century A.D. In this excerpt, Juvenal recounts a friend's reasons for moving away from Rome.

Read the headnote, caption, or attribution line. Determine the source's historical context—who wrote it, when, and why.

Read the primary source. Identify and define unfamiliar words. Then look for the writer's main point.

Identify facts and opinions. Facts can be proven. Opinions reflect a person's views or feelings. Use opinion clues to help: exaggeration, phrases such as "I think," or descriptive words such as "gorgeous."

Identify bias and evaluate credibility. Consider whether the author's opinions suggest bias. Evaluate other factors that might lead to author bias, such as his or her previous experiences. Decide if the author knows enough to be credible and was objective enough to be reliable. Determine whether the source might be propaganda, that is, material published to promote a policy, idea, or cause.

Practice and Apply the Skill

Political cartoons reflect an artist's observations about events of the time. They often use symbols to represent things or exaggeration to make a point. Use the cartoon at right to answer the following questions.

1. Who is the author of this primary source?
2. What does the bulldozer represent?
3. What is exaggerated in this cartoon?
4. What opinion is the cartoonist expressing?
5. Do you think the cartoonist's opinion is valid? Why or why not?

This cartoon by Arcadio Esquivel of Costa Rica comments on environmental destruction.

Analyze Primary Sources 🔵L3

Instruct

- **Introduce** Ask students to locate examples of primary sources in their texts, including photographs, political cartoons, and quotations. Explain that primary sources convey or support main ideas in the writing. Readers must identify the key ideas in the primary source material and link them to surrounding text.

- **Teach** Have students read the steps under *Analyze Primary Sources* and share any questions they have. Then have a student read the introduction to the primary source quotation on the text page and the quotation itself aloud. Work as a group to paraphrase it, then help students work through the steps in the text to analyze the quotation.

Transparency 38: Analyze Primary Sources

📖 Note Taking Transparencies, 38

Analyze Primary Sources worksheet Teaching Resources, **Skills Handbook,** p. 42

Independent Practice

Have students complete the Practice and Apply questions. Discuss their responses as a class.

Monitor Progress

As students complete the questions, circulate to provide guidance. If necessary, ask additional questions to help facilitate understanding. (What is the size of Earth at the beginning of the cartoon? What is its size at the end? What does this change in size suggest?)

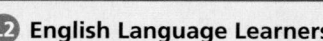
Answers

1. Arcadio Esquivel
2. progress
3. the size of the bulldozer relative to the size of the world
4. that progress is destroying the environment
5. Sample: The cartoon may be making a valid point but is vastly exaggerated.

Compare Viewpoints

Instruct

- **Introduce** Recall a recent school, local, or national election. Identify a key issue in the candidates' debate and the differing viewpoints they expressed about it. Stress that voters had to understand, compare, and choose among the different viewpoints expressed.

- **Teach** Have students read the steps under *Compare Viewpoints.* Then organize students into pairs. Have each partner read one of the primary sources on the text page and its introduction, explain its main idea, and list one supporting reason that the writer gave. Ask partners to share ideas about which viewpoint makes most sense to them.

  Transparency 39: Compare Viewpoints

  Note Taking Transparencies, 39

  Compare Viewpoints worksheet

  Teaching Resources, Skills Handbook, p. 43

Independent Practice

Have students complete the Practice and Apply questions. Discuss their responses as a class.

Monitor Progress

As students complete the questions, circulate to provide assistance as needed. If students are struggling, read through the Compare Viewpoints steps with them. Confirm their understanding of the key concepts, then urge them to try again to answer the questions.

Answers

1. King Henri Christophe—Haiti, early 1800s; Leo Tolstoy—Russia, around 1900
2. Henri Christophe argues that educated citizens can resist tyranny. Tolstoy uses an analogy of training a puppy to argue that rote learning alone will not help children live a moral life.
3. Sample: The king's frame of reference is a largely uneducated population, so he is concerned with basic education. Tolstoy's frame of reference is people who already have a basic education.
4. He says *has to be* rather than *is*.
5. Yes, it makes sense that educated citizens would be better able to resist tyranny and that citizens educated in mind and character will contribute more to society.

Critical Thinking

Compare Viewpoints

A person's viewpoint is shaped by subjective influences such as feelings, prejudices, and past experiences. Two politicians will recommend different policies to address the same problem. Comparing such viewpoints will help you understand issues and form your own views. The excerpts below offer two different views on the purpose of education. Use the excerpts and the steps that follow to learn about comparing viewpoints.

King Henri Christophe of Haiti set up schools for outstanding students. He believed these schools would secure Haiti's new and hard-won freedom. In 1817, he wrote:

Primary Source

  ❝To form good citizens we must educate our children. From our national institutions will proceed a race of men capable of defending by their knowledge and talents those rights so long denied by tyrants. It is from these sources that light will be diffused among the whole mass of the population.❞

—Henri Christophe, 1817

Leo Tolstoy, a Russian aristocrat of the late 1800s, became a famous novelist as a young man. As he grew older, he increasingly focused on social issues in his writing. In 1902, he wrote:

Primary Source

  ❝You can take a puppy and feed him, and teach him to carry something, and enjoy the sight of him; but it is not enough to rear and bring up a man, and teach him Greek: he has to be taught to live, that is, to take less from others, and give more.❞

—Leo Tolstoy, 1902

Identify the authors. Determine when and where the authors lived.

Examine the viewpoints. Identify the author's main idea and evaluate his or her supporting arguments. Determine whether the arguments are logical and the evidence is sufficient to support the main idea. Confirm that the evidence is valid by doing research if necessary.

Determine the author's frame of reference. Consider how the author's attitudes, beliefs, and past experiences might affect his or her viewpoint.

Recognize facts and opinions. Identify which statements are opinions and which are facts. Opinions represent the author's viewpoint.

Evaluate each viewpoint's validity. Decide whether the viewpoints are based on facts and/or reasonable arguments. Consider whether or not you agree with the viewpoints.

Practice and Apply the Skill

Use the excerpts above to answer the following questions.

1. Who are the authors of these two documents? Where and when did each one live?
2. What is each man's main argument about education? What evidence or supporting arguments does each provide?
3. How might each man's frame of reference affect his viewpoint?
4. How does Tolstoy's phrase "he has to be taught to live" signal an opinion?
5. Are these two viewpoints based on reasonable arguments? Explain.

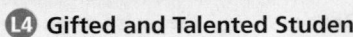

Differentiated Instruction   Solutions for All Learners

L4 Advanced Readers   **L4 Gifted and Talented Students**

Ask students who need more of a challenge to find two viewpoints on a single topic having to do with current events. Viewpoints may be from the editorial page of a newspaper, from news magazines written from different perspectives, or from the Internet.

Review students' choices and help them make copies for the class. Then have students lead the class through a discussion that works through the steps for comparing viewpoints in the text.

Synthesize Information

Just as you might ask several friends about a movie before deciding to see it, you can combine information from different sources to develop a fuller understanding of any topic. This process, called synthesizing, will help you become better informed. Study the documents below about developments in the 1400s and 1500s. Then use the steps that follow to learn to synthesize information.

Critical Thinking

Document A

This caravel helped Europeans sail across and into the wind.

Document B

Improved Technology

Several improvements in technology helped Europeans navigate the vast oceans of the world. Cartographers, or mapmakers, created more accurate maps and sea charts. European sailors learned to use the astrolabe, an instrument developed by the ancient Greeks and perfected by the Arabs, to determine their latitude at sea.

Europeans also designed larger and better ships. The Portuguese developed the caravel, which combined the square sails of European ships with Arab lateen, or triangular, sails. Caravels also adapted the sternpost rudder and numerous masts used on Chinese ships. The new rigging made it easier to sail across or even into the wind.

Document C

Hardships on the Uncharted Sea

In his journal, Italian sailor Antonio Pigafetta detailed the desperate conditions Magellan's sailors experienced as they crossed the Pacific Ocean:

Primary Source

66We remained three months and twenty days without taking in provisions or other refreshments, and we only ate old biscuit reduced to powder, and full of grubs, and stinking from the dirt which the rats had made on it. . . . we drank water that was yellow and stinking. We also ate the ox hides which were under the main-yard [and] were very hard on account of the sun, rain, and wind. . . .99

—Journal of Antonio Pigafetta

Identify thesis statements. Before you can synthesize, you must understand the thesis, or main idea, of each source.

Compare and contrast. Analyze how the information and ideas in the sources are the same or different. When several sources agree, the information is more reliable and thus more significant.

Draw conclusions and generalize. Look at all the information. Use it to draw conclusions that form a single picture of the topic. Make a generalization, or statement that applies to all the sources.

Practice and Apply the Skill

Use the documents above to answer the following questions.

1. What is the main idea of each source?

2. Which sources support the idea that European sailors became better equipped to sail the seas?

3. What view does Antonio Pigafetta contribute to the topic?

4. Draw a conclusion about European ocean exploration in the early 1500s.

21st Century Skills   SKILLS HANDBOOK

Synthesize Information

Instruct

- **Introduce** Direct students to a poster in the classroom or halls, or to another piece of media containing both visual and textual information. Ask them to identify information from each part of the poster. Tell them that this process is synthesizing information.

- **Teach** Have students read the steps under *Synthesize Information* and share any questions they have. Invite volunteers to identify and describe each document in the text. Ask **What kind of source is this?** *(Document A is a drawing. Document B is explanatory text. Document C is a primary source journal entry.)* Then discuss the kind of information each source can provide (visual, firsthand account, background). As a whole, how do they contribute to a fuller understanding of the topic than one document alone?

Transparency 40: Synthesize Information

Note Taking Transparencies, 40

Synthesize Information worksheet
Teaching Resources, Skills Handbook, p. 44

Independent Practice

Have students complete the Practice and Apply questions. Discuss their responses as a class.

Monitor Progress

If students are struggling to answer the questions, model how to create a 3-column main idea chart. Make a column for each source and list its main idea. Urge students to refer to this information as they answer the questions.

Answers

1. Document A: The caravel helped Europeans sail more easily; Document B: Improvements in technology helped Europeans explore the oceans; Document C: Crossing the ocean was a wretched experience.
2. Documents A and B
3. that ocean travel was miserable
4. Ocean travel was difficult for Europeans in the early 1500s, but advancing technology began to ease the task.

Analyze Cause and Effect ⓑ

Instruct

- **Introduce** Identify a recent school success, such as an athletic victory or well-received artistic production. Ask students what factors contributed to the success. List these on the board. Then ask students how the success has affected the school community. List effects on the board. Explain that like this event, events in history result from actions and attitudes, and in turn cause new actions and attitudes.

- **Teach** Have students read the steps under *Analyze Cause and Effect* and share any questions they have. Have students read the bulleted items in the boxed text on the student page. Poll the class to identify the central event. Then work through the bulleted items one at a time. Ask students if they think each is a cause or an effect and to explain their reasoning.

  Transparency 41: Analyze Cause and Effect

  📖 Note Taking Transparencies, 41

  Analyze Cause and Effect worksheet
  Teaching Resources, Skills Handbook, p. 45

Independent Practice

Have students complete the Practice and Apply questions. Discuss their responses as a class.

Monitor Progress

If students are struggling to answer the questions, review the definitions of long-term and short-term causes with them. Review their charts and ask questions to redirect if necessary. **Sample: Why do you think this event is a (cause/effect)?**

Analyze Cause and Effect

One of a historian's main tasks is to understand the causes and effects of the event he or she is studying. Study the facts below, which are listed in random order. Then use the steps that follow to learn how to analyze cause and effect.

In the 1980s and 1990s, the Soviet Union underwent a major change in its economy and government. As a result, the Soviet Union ceased to exist. This list shows key elements in that change.

- Low output of crops and consumer goods
- Soviets want to ensure influence in neighboring Afghanistan, so they invade that nation in 1979
- Soviet Union breaks up into 15 republics after its central government collapses
- Changeover to market economy in Russia
- Ethnic and nationalist movements to achieve independence from Soviet Union
- Cold War with United States leads to high military spending
- Food and fuel shortages
- Rise to power of Mikhail Gorbachev in 1985
- Russian republic approves a new constitution
- Baltic states of Estonia, Latvia, and Lithuania demonstrate for independence
- Cold War ends

Identify the central event. Determine to what event or issue all the facts listed relate.

Locate clue words. Use words such as *because, so,* and *due to* to spot causes and effects.

Identify causes and effects. Causes precede the central event and contribute to its occurrence. Effects come after the central event. They occur or emerge as a result of it.

Consider timeframe. Decide if causes have existed for a long period of time or emerged just prior to the central event. Short-term causes are usually single or narrowly defined events. Long-term causes usually arise from ongoing conditions.

Make recommendations. Use what you've learned to suggest actions or make predictions.

Practice and Apply the Skill

Use the list above to answer the following questions:

1. Which item on the list describes the central event whose causes and effects can be determined?
2. Name three facts that are long-term causes.
3. Name three facts that are probably short-term causes.
4. Name three facts that were most likely effects of the central event.

Answers

1. the collapse of the Soviet Union
2. low output of crops and consumer goods; high military spending for Cold War; ethnic and nationalist movements for independence
3. food and fuel shortages, 1979 war with Afghanistan, rise to power of Mikhail Gorbachev, Baltic states demonstrate for independence
4. changeover to market economy, Russian republics approve a new constitution, Cold War ends

L1 Special Needs   L2 Less Proficient Readers

To help students who need further practice analyzing cause and effect, ask students to use the boxed list in the text to create a cause and effect graphic organizer. Ask them to draw three large boxes on a sheet of paper, with arrows leading from the first box to the second, and from the second to the third. Have them

L2 English Language Learners

write the central event from the list in their text in the center box, with causes in the left-hand box and effects in the right-hand box. Explain that they can use this type of graphic organizer to help them understand causes and effects in history and current events.

Problem Solving and Decision Making

You will face many problems in your life, from disputes with friends to how to vote on issues facing your nation. You will be most likely to find solutions if you make decisions in a logical way. Study the situation outlined below. Then use the steps that follow to learn the skills of problem solving and decision making.

A Problem for Japan and China

In the 1800s, Japan and China faced a problem. Industrialized nations had developed machinery and weapons that were superior to those that the Japanese and Chinese had. Some industrialized nations used their new power to demand special trading privileges in Asia.

Options for Japan and China

Option	Advantages	Disadvantages
1. Give in to demands of the industrialized powers.	• Avoid conflict. •	• Native merchants lose profits to foreigners.
2. Give in to demands, but also build modern machines and weapons.	• •	• •
3. Refuse the demands and reject much of the new technology.	• •	• •

The Decisions

- The Japanese government decided to follow option 2.
- The Chinese government decided to follow option 3.

Effects of the Decisions

- Japan quickly became a modern industrial and military power. Although it demilitarized after suffering defeat in World War II, it remains one of the world's leading industrial powers.
- China was weakened by a century of conflict with Great Britain and other major powers, and was invaded and occupied by Japan. Foreign nations gained special privileges in China. Today, China is still struggling to become a leading industrial power.

Identify the problem. You cannot solve a problem until you examine it and understand it.

Gather information and identify options. Most problems have many solutions. Identify as many solution options as possible.

Consider advantages and disadvantages. Analyze each option by predicting benefits and drawbacks.

Decide on and implement the solution. Pick the option with the most desirable benefits and least important drawbacks.

Evaluate the decision. After time, reexamine your solution. If necessary, make a new decision.

Practice and Apply the Skill

Use information from the box above to answer the following questions:

1. What problem did China and Japan face? What caused this problem?
2. Describe an option that Japan or China could have chosen other than those in the list.
3. Identify two advantages and two disadvantages for options 2 and 3.
4. Why do you think China and Japan chose the options they did?

Problem Solving and Decision Making

Instruct

- **Introduce** Invite volunteers to share a problem from their lives, such as too much homework or an annoying younger sibling. Ask students to contribute ideas for solving these problems.

- **Teach** Have students read the steps under *Problem Solving and Decision Making* and share any questions they have. Read the boxed text as a class. Ask **What is the main idea?** *(China and Japan responded differently to the challenge of keeping up with industrialized nations.)* Ask students to identify the possible solutions listed on the chart, and identify additional advantages and disadvantages of each. Poll students on whether they think each nation made a wise decision. Invite volunteers to explain their votes.

Transparency 42: Problem Solving and Decision Making

📖 Note Taking Transparencies, 42

Problem Solving and Decision Making worksheet
Teaching Resources, Skills Handbook, p. 46

Independent Practice

Have students complete the Practice and Apply questions. Discuss their responses as a class.

Monitor Progress

If students are struggling to answer question #4, direct them to reread the text under Options for Japan and China. Confirm that students understand the choices each nation made.

Answers

1. Some industrialized nations were demanding trading rights. They had superior machinery and weapons.
2. refuse the demands but still accept and pursue new technology
3. Option 2: avoid conflict and gain power over time, but native merchants lose profits, and money is needed to fund modernization; Option 3: keep profits for native merchants and minimize foreign influences but failure to modernize and possible military conflict
4. China probably valued limiting foreign influence and maintaining traditions most highly. Japan probably wished to avoid conflict, but also wanted to modernize.

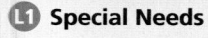 **Special Needs**  **Less Proficient Readers** L2 **English Language Learners**

To help students who need further practice in problem solving and decision making, ask them to name a problem they have solved or decision they have made in their own lives. Examples may include whether to find an after school job, play a sport, or make an important purchase. Using the chart in the text as a model, ask students to create their own problem solving and decision making chart based on their own decisions. Charts should include a description of the problem, options, decision(s), and effects of the decision(s).

Draw Inferences and Conclusions

Instruct

- **Introduce** Ask students what kind of day it is outside and what they would expect to feel outside. Discuss the clues students used to answer, such as previous experiences with days that look like this. Point out that we draw inferences and conclusions every day.

- **Teach** Have students read the steps under *Draw Inferences and Conclusions.* Then help them use the boxed text and illustrations on the student page to practice the skill. Ask **What do you know from the illustrations?** *(that Watt lived a long time ago and was associated with the steam engine.)* Given this information, what inferences and conclusions can they draw about Watt?

Transparency 43: Drawing Inferences and Conclusions

Note Taking Transparencies, 43

Drawing Inferences and Conclusions worksheet
Teaching Resources, Skills Handbook, p. 47

Independent Practice

Have students complete the Practice and Apply questions. Discuss their responses as a class.

Monitor Progress

If students are struggling to answer the last question, ask them to compare the steam engine to another invention, such as television, the telephone, or the camera. How have these inventions been improved over the years?

Draw Inferences and Conclusions

Text and artwork may not contain all the facts and ideas you need to understand a topic. You may need to add information from your own experience or knowledge, or use information that is implied but not directly stated in the text or artwork. Study the biography below. Then use the steps that follow to learn how to draw inferences and conclusions.

BIOGRAPHY

James Watt

How did a clever Scottish engineer become the "Father of the Industrial Revolution"? After repairing a Newcomen steam engine, James Watt (1736–1819) had become fascinated with the idea of improving the device. Within a few months, he knew he had a product that would sell. Still, Watt lacked the money needed to produce and market it.

Fortunately, he was able to form a partnership with the shrewd manufacturer Matthew Boulton. They then founded Soho Engineering Works in Birmingham, England, to manufacture steam engines. Watt's version of the steam engine shown here had a separate condensing chamber and was patented in 1769. Eventually, a measure of mechanical and electrical power, the watt, would be named for James Watt. **How might the Industrial Revolution have been different if Watt had not found a business partner?**

Study the facts. Determine what facts and information the text states.

Summarize information. Confirm your understanding of the text by briefly summarizing it.

Ask questions. Use *who, what, when, where, why,* and *how* questions to analyze the text and learn more. For example, you might compare and contrast, or look for causes or effects.

Add your own knowledge. Consider what you know about the topic. Use this knowledge to evaluate the information.

Draw inferences and conclusions. Use what you learned from the text and your own knowledge to draw inferences and conclusions about the topic.

Practice and Apply the Skill

Use the biography above to answer these questions.

1. Who is discussed in the biography? When did he live?
2. Briefly summarize the text.
3. How do Watt's accomplishments still have an impact on our lives today?
4. Why do you think Watt wanted to improve a technology that already existed?

Answers

1. James Watt, 1736–1819
2. Sample: Watt became the Father of the Industrial Revolution by improving and selling the steam engine.
3. We still measure electrical power in watts.
4. Sample: He had ideas to make it more useful and efficient.

Use the Internet for Research

The Internet is a valuable research tool that provides links to millions of sources of information created by businesses, governments, schools, organizations, and individuals all over the world. Follow the steps to learn how you could use the Internet to research the European Renaissance.

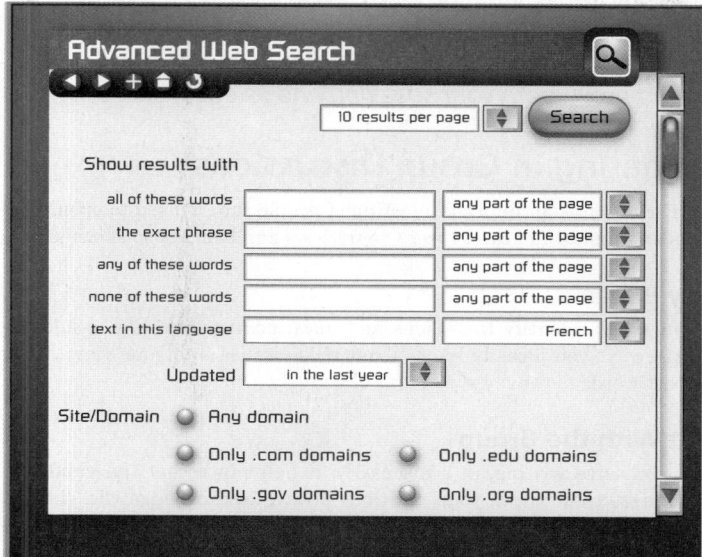

Sample search engine

Begin a search. Use search engines on the Internet to help you find useful Web sites. Type in key words that briefly summarize your topic. Use *and* between words to find documents containing all your keywords. Use *or* between words to find documents containing any one of several keywords.

Find reliable information. Universities, museums, libraries, and government agencies are usually the most reliable and useful for social studies research. The URLs for education sites end in *.edu*, government sites in *.gov*, and not-for-profit organization sites in *.org*. Read each site summary and choose those most likely to be reliable. Click on links to access individual sites.

Evaluate Web sites. Explore each Web site. Note its sponsor and when it was last updated.

Use advanced searches. Try advanced search options. Limit by date or type of site, such as educational institutions. Try new or different key words if you still don't get what you need.

Practice and Apply the Skill

Use a computer connected to the Internet to answer the following questions:

1. What key words might you use to learn about the European Renaissance? Type them into a search engine Web site and see what results you get.

2. Which of the first ten sites that came up in your search is most likely to be reliable? Why?

3. Who is the sponsor of the site you chose? What does this suggest about its quality or its possible bias?

Use the Internet for Research ⓛ₃

Instruct

- **Introduce** Invite volunteers to tell how and why they have most recently used the Internet. Then, discuss the many ways that people use the Internet, listing students' ideas on the board. If necessary, point out that research is a major asset of the Internet.

- **Teach** Have students read the steps under *Use the Internet for Research* and share any questions they have. Then invite students to name a topic of interest to them. As a group, discuss key words that would be good research starting points. Identify the more and less effective ideas, and give reasons for each decision. For example, it may be better to search by words likely to appear in a Web site than by the topic of the Web site.

- Display **Transparency 44: Use the Internet for Research.**

  📖 Note Taking Transparencies, 44

- Have students fill in the **Use the Internet for Research** worksheet.
  Teaching Resources, Skills Handbook, p. 48

Independent Practice

Have students complete the Practice and Apply questions. Discuss their responses as a class.

Monitor Progress

Circulate to make sure that students are finding appropriate and useful information on the Internet about the European Renaissance.

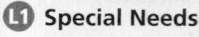 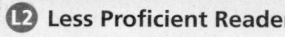
Answers

1. European and Renaissance
2. Students should choose sites that are sponsored by reliable sources such as universities and museums.
3. Answers will vary according to individual searches.

Objective

As you teach this section, keep students focused on the following objective to help them master core content.

- Learn strategies for active participation in group discussions and debates, for developing and presenting oral or multimedia presentations, and for active listening.

Prepare to Read

Build Background Knowledge L3

Review recent oral presentations or class discussions. Ask students to share areas where they felt prepared and where they would have liked more skill training.

Teach

Participating in Group Discussions/Debating L3

Instruct

- **Introduce** Emphasize that discussions and debates are opportunities for students to share and discuss their views.

- **Teach** Have students read the steps under *Participating in Group Discussion* and *Debating.* Suggest that they keep a notepad and pencil at hand during discussions and debates to jot down reminders of their thoughts.

- Display **Transparency 45: Participating in Group Discussions.**
  📖 Note Taking Transparencies, 45

- Have students fill in the **Participating in Group Discussions** worksheet.
  Teaching Resources, Skills Handbook, p. 49

- Discuss why debates are useful ways to present controversy and air points of view.

- Display **Transparency 46: Debating.**
  📖 Note Taking Transparencies, 46

- Have students fill in the **Debating** worksheet.
  Teaching Resources, Skills Handbook, p. 50

Independent Practice

Have students choose an issue from their current studies and explore it in discussion. Then help them organize a formal debate.

Monitor Progress

Encourage students to fully participate in their groups and debates and to display good listening/speaking techniques.

Speaking and Listening

Speaking and listening are forms of communication you use every day. In certain situations, however, specific skills and strategies can increase the effectiveness of your communication. The strategies offered in this section will help you improve both your speaking and listening skills.

Participating in Group Discussions

A group discussion is an informal meeting of people that is used to openly discuss ideas and topics. You can express your views and hear those of others.

Identify Issues

Before you speak, identify the issues and main points you want to address. Incorporate what you already know about these issues into your views. Then find the best words to convey your ideas effectively.

Interact With the Group

As with persuasive writing, in a discussion it helps to accept the validity of opposing views, then argue your position. Always acknowledge the views of others respectfully, but ask questions that challenge the accuracy, logic, or relevance of those views.

Debating

A debate is a formal argument about a specific issue. Explicit rules govern the procedure of a debate, with each debater or team given an allotted time to make arguments and respond to opposing positions. You may also find yourself arguing a position you don't personally hold.

Prepare Your Arguments

If you support a position, use your existing knowledge of it to direct your research. If you personally oppose an assigned position, use that knowledge to identify likely opposing arguments. Generate an outline and then number note cards to highlight key information for each of your main points.

Avoid Common Pitfalls

Stay focused on your arguments. Be aware of words that may reveal bias, such as *unpatriotic.* Speak assertively, but avoid getting overly emotional. Vary the pitch and tone of your voice to keep listeners engaged. Try to speak actively, rather than just reading aloud, and use eye contact and gestures to emphasize your message.

Giving an Oral or Multimedia Presentation

An oral or multimedia presentation provides an audience with information through a variety of media.

Choose Media

If you are limited to speaking only, focus your time on developing a presentation that engages listeners. If you can include other media, consider what kind of information each form of media conveys most effectively.

Maps	Graphs/charts	Pictures	Diagrams	Audio/video
Clarify historical or geographical information	Show complicated information in an accessible format	Illustrate objects, scenes, or other details	Show link between parts and a whole or a process	Brings the subject to life and engages audience

Generate Text

Gather information using library and online sources. Develop your most important ideas in the body of your presentation. Back up assertions with solid facts and use multimedia examples to illustrate key points.

Present With Authority

Practice your presentation to gain comfort with the text and the presentation sequence. Experiment with the timing of how to include multimedia elements. Make sure you have the necessary equipment and know how to use it.

Active Listening

Active listening is a key component of the communication process. Like all communication, it requires your engaged participation.

Focus Your Attention on Ideas

Look at and listen to the speaker. Think about what you hear and see. Which ideas are emphasized or repeated? What gestures or expressions suggest strong feelings? Can you connect the speaker's ideas to your own experiences?

Listen to Fit the Situation

Active listening involves matching your listening to the situation. Listen critically to a speech given by a candidate for office. Listen empathetically to the feelings of a friend. Listen appreciatively to a musical performance.

Ask Questions

Try to think of questions while you're listening. Look at these examples:

Open-ended	Closed	Fact
Why do you think it is so important for young people to vote?	Do you support the current voting age of 18?	How many people aged 18–25 voted in the most recent election?

Differentiated Instruction
Solutions for All Learners

L1 Special Needs L2 Less Proficient Readers L2 English Language Learners

To help students who need further practice, review the steps for participating in group discussions, debating, giving presentations, and active listening. Then have students evaluate their own performance in each of these areas, suggesting strengths and areas for improvement. Meet with individual students to review areas needing improvement that they noted or that you observed. Review listening and speaking skills as needed.

Giving an Oral or Multimedia Presentation/ Active Listening L3

Instruct

- **Introduce** Tell students that you give an oral presentation every day in the classroom. It requires you to convey ideas orally, but also to listen so that you can respond to students' ideas and needs. Remind students that they too must use these presenting and speaking skills often in the classroom.

- **Teach** Have students read the steps under *Giving an Oral or Multimedia Presentation* and review the types of media presented in the text. Stress the importance of thorough preparation and sufficient practice, including a run-through with visuals and equipment.

- Display **Transparency 47: Giving an Oral or Multimedia Presentation.**

  Note Taking Transparencies, 47

- Have students fill in the **Giving an Oral or Multimedia Presentation** worksheet.
  Teaching Resources, Skills Handbook, p. 51

- **Teach** Ask students what it means to be an active listener. *(being an engaged participant by focusing your attention and listening to fit the situation)*

- Display **Transparency 48: Active Listening.**

  Note Taking Transparencies, 48

- Have students fill in the **Active Listening** worksheet.
  Teaching Resources, Skills Handbook, p. 52

Independent Practice

Ask students to brainstorm a list of current topics of interest. Assign them brief oral or multimedia presentations on these topics. Invite them to present their work as the remaining students listen actively.

Monitor Progress

Redirect attention if any students are not focusing on the presentations. Develop and share with students a collection of nonverbal cues to indicate that time is running out, or that they need to speak more slowly or more loudly, etc.

Connecting With Past Learnings

Section	Core Instruction L3	Differentiated Instruction L1 L2 L4	

Part 1
A Global View: Early Civilizations

 2 periods, 1 block

SECTIONS
- Toward Civilization (Prehistory–3000 B.C.)
- First Civilizations: Africa and Asia (3200 B.C.–500 B.C.)
- Early Civilizations in India and China (2600 B.C.–256 B.C.)

Core Instruction L3

All in One Teaching Resources, Modern Review Unit
Vocabulary Builder: Dictionary Skills, p. 2
Reading Strategy: Compare and Contrast, p. 3

Reading and Note Taking Study Guide
Note Taking Study Guide, pp. 8, 10, 12
Section Summaries, pp. 9, 11, 13
Concept Connector, p. 233

Note Taking Transparencies, 101–103

Color Transparencies, 6

Witness History Discovery School™
video program, *Secrets of the Iceman; The Nile: Where Egypt Began; Discovering Ancient Shang China*

Teaching Resources, Skills Handbook
Prereading the Chapter, pp. 1–2
Word Knowledge Rating Form, p. 3
K-W-L Chart, p. 4

Differentiated Instruction L1 L2 L4

L1 Adapted Reading and Note Taking Study Guide
Note Taking Study Guide, pp. 8, 10, 12 SN
Section Summaries, pp. 9, 11, 13 SN
Concept Connector, p. 233 SN

L2 Adapted Reading and Note Taking Study Guide
Note Taking Study Guide, pp. 8, 10, 12 LPR
Section Summaries, pp. 9, 11, 13 LPR
Concept Connector, p. 233 LPR

Spanish Reading and Note Taking Study Guide
Note Taking Study Guide, pp. 8, 10, 12 ELL
Section Summaries, pp. 9, 11, 13 ELL
Concept Connector, p. 233 ELL

L4 All in One Teaching Resources, Modern Review Unit
Link to Literature: From *The Source* by James Michener, p. 4 AR, GT
Viewpoints: The Origin of Law, p. 5 AR, GT
Biography: Imhotep, p. 6 AR, GT
Link to Literature: From *The Tale of Sinuhe*, p. 7 AR, GT

*Student Edition Audio SN
Differentiated Instruction Activity, Teacher's Edition, pp. 5, 9 SN

*Guided Reading Audio, Spanish ELL
*Student Edition Audio LPR
Differentiated Instruction Activity, Teacher's Edition, pp. 5, 9 LPR, ELL

Link to Literature: The Man Who Forgot, p. 8 AR, GT
Differentiated Instruction Activity, Teacher's Edition, p. 7 AR, GT
Extend Activity, Teacher's Edition, p. 10 AR, GT

Focus Question *How did the first civilizations evolve?*

Part 2
A Global View: Empires of the Ancient World

 4 periods, 2 blocks

SECTIONS
- Empires of India and China (600 B.C.–A.D. 550)
- Ancient Greece (1750 B.C.–133 B.C.)
- Ancient Rome and the Rise of Christianity (509 B.C.– A.D. 476)
- Civilizations of the Americas (1400 B.C.–A.D. 1570)

All in One Teaching Resources, Modern Review Unit
Vocabulary Builder: Make Connections, p. 15
Reading Strategy: Identify Supporting Details, p. 16

Reading and Note Taking Study Guide
Note Taking Study Guide, pp. 14, 16, 18, 20
Section Summaries, pp. 15, 17, 19, 21
Concept Connector, p. 270

Note Taking Transparencies, 104–107

Color Transparencies, 15, 24, 36

Witness History Discovery School™
video program, *Asoka's Elephant Warriors; Alexander the Great; Rome: The Rise of Empire; The Mummies of Peru*

L1 Adapted Reading and Note Taking Study Guide
Note Taking Study Guide, pp. 14, 16, 18, 20 SN
Section Summaries, pp. 15, 17, 19, 21 SN

L2 Adapted Reading and Note Taking Study Guide
Note Taking Study Guide, pp. 14, 16, 18, 20 LPR
Section Summaries, pp. 15, 17, 19, 21 LPR
Concept Connector, p. 270 LPR

L4 All in One Teaching Resources, Modern Review Unit
Link to Literature: Sita and Rama's First Meeting, p. 17 AR, GT
Traveler's Tales: The Silk Road, p. 18 AR, GT
Viewpoints: The Values of Sparta and Athens, p. 19 AR, GT
Link to Literature: From *The History of the Decline and Fall of the Roman Empire* by Edward Gibbon, p. 20 AR, GT
Biography: Nezahualcoyotl, p. 21 AR, GT

Concept Connector, p. 270 SN
Differentiated Instruction Activity, Teacher's Edition, pp. 17, 19, 21 SN

Spanish Reading and Note Taking Study Guide
Note Taking Study Guide, pp. 14, 16, 18, 20 ELL
Section Summaries, pp. 15, 17, 19, 21 ELL
Concept Connector, p. 270 ELL
Differentiated Instruction Activity, Teacher's Edition, pp. 17, 19, 21 LPR, ELL

All in One Teaching Resources, Modern Review Unit
Simulation: A Medieval Manor, pp. 41–44
Extend Activity, Teacher's Edition, p. 22 AR, GT

Focus Question *What characteristics were shared by ancient empires around the world?*

***Audio Support is available for all sections.**

Section	Core Instruction (L3)	Differentiated Instruction (L1) (L2) (L4)

Part 3
A Global View: Regional Civilizations

 4 periods, 2 blocks

SECTIONS
- The Rise of Europe (500–1300)
- The High and Late Middle Ages (1050–1450)
- The Byzantine Empire and Russia (330–1613)
- Muslim Civilizations (622–1629)
- Kingdoms and Trading States of Africa (730 B.C.–A.D. 1591)
- The Spread of Civilizations in East Asia (500–1650)

Focus Question *How did regional civilizations expand the scope of world history?*

All in One Teaching Resources, Modern Review Unit
Vocabulary Builder: Word Maps, p. 28
Reading Strategy: Categorize, p. 29

Reading and Note Taking Study Guide
Note Taking Study Guide, pp. 22, 24, 26, 28, 30, 32
Section Summaries, pp. 23, 25, 27, 29, 31, 33
Concept Connector, pp. 237, 247, 300

Note Taking Transparencies, 108–113

Color Transparencies, 42, 63

Witness History Discovery School™ video program, *The Rise of Feudalism, The Black Death; Byzantine Empire; Suleiman the Magnificent; Zimbabwe: Lost City of Africa; The Samurai of Japan*

(L1) Adapted Reading and Note Taking Study Guide
Note Taking Study Guide, pp. 22, 24, 26, 28, 30, 32 **SN**
Section Summaries, pp. 23, 25, 27, 29, 31, 33 **SN**
Concept Connector, pp. 237, 247, 300 **SN**

(L2) Adapted Reading and Note Taking Study Guide
Note Taking Study Guide, pp. 22, 24, 26, 28, 30, 32 **LPR**
Section Summaries, pp. 23, 25, 27, 29, 31, 33 **LPR**
Concept Connector, pp. 247, 300 **LPR**

(L4) All in One Teaching Resources, Modern Review Unit
Primary Source: A Vassal Pledges His Loyalty, p. 30 **AR, GT**
Primary Source: The Magna Carta, p. 31
Biography: Ivan III, p. 32
Link to Literature: From the Quran, p. 33
Traveler's Tales: Ibn Battuta, p. 34

Differentiated Instruction Activity, Teacher's Edition, pp. 27, 29, 33, 35, 37 **SN**

Spanish Reading and Note Taking Study Guide
Note Taking Study Guide, pp. 22, 24, 26, 28, 30, 32 **ELL**
Section Summaries, pp. 23, 25, 27, 29, 31, 33 **ELL**
Concept Connector, pp. 247, 300 **ELL**

Differentiated Instruction Activity, Teacher's Edition, pp. 27, 29, 33, 35, 37 **LPR**

Differentiated Instruction Activity, Teacher's Edition, p. 31 **AR, GT**

Extend Activity, Teacher's Edition, p. 38 **AR, GT**

Assessment Resources
- *ExamView*® **Test Bank CD-ROM,** Modern Review Unit
- **All in One Teaching Resources, Modern Review Unit,** Tests A and B, pp. 9–14, 22–27, 35–40
- **Assessment Rubrics**

Differentiated Instruction Key

L1 Special Needs	**LPR** Less Proficient Readers
L2 Basic to Average	**AR** Advanced Readers
L3 All Students	**SN** Special Needs Students
L4 Average to Advanced	**GT** Gifted and Talented
	ELL English Language Learner

The Discovery of Agriculture

Agriculture most likely began with the simple practice of harvesting edible grains found growing wild, part of the normal food-gathering procedures of Old Stone Age people. Alert gatherers might sometimes encourage the ripening of the crop by extra care—for instance, by watering plants at the end of a dry summer. But the great breakthrough came when bands of *Homo sapiens sapiens* learned to plant some of the grain in order to guarantee a harvest the following year. Wherever this occurred—with wheat and barley in the Near East, millet in North China, corn in Central America—the wandering days of the hunting band were numbered and a new way of life was set in train. . . .

Life thus grew in complexity as the Neolithic centuries rolled on. The settled agricultural peoples of the Near East, like their fellows in many parts of the globe, learned to cultivate their crops with care, to weed and irrigate, to use the manure produced by their stock to fertilize their croplands. They discovered how to breed stock for meat and for strength, how to use milk, milk products, and other animal and vegetable products seldom utilized by their hunting-and-gathering predecessors. First in the rain-watered hills, then in the river valleys that provided the most fertile land, these prehistoric farmers reaped a greater bounty than nature had normally provided for their Paleolithic ancestors.

Above all, they grew in numbers. Farming was hard work, probably more demanding than hunting and gathering had been. But agriculture had the great advantage of feeding many more people from the same tract of land than could be fed by hunting and gathering. One estimate suggests that whereas the foraging economy could support one person per square kilometer, even primitive farming could feed fifty persons from a single square kilometer. From this population growth came the Neolithic agricultural village and—in time—the city, the political state, and all their history.

—Anthony Esler, *The Human Venture: From Prehistory to the Present,* (Upper Saddle River, New Jersey: Pearson Education, 2004), pp. 21–23

Extend Online

Recent Digs

Have students examine recent archaeological discoveries and excavations. Have each student choose a recent field site and write an essay about the artifacts unearthed and the information uncovered. Use the steps below.

Prepare for the Activity Tell students that archaeology is the study of past peoples and cultures through their material remains. These remains include buildings and artifacts such as tools, weapons, and stone sculptures (such as the dog created by an artist in Mesopotamia around 2000 B.C., shown at left). Archaeologists find and analyze artifacts to learn about life during prehistory as well as during historical times. This helps them draw conclusions about the beliefs, values, and activities of our ancestors. Since archaeologists make new discoveries frequently, at times they must revise their theories in light of the new evidence.

Conduct the Activity For help in starting the activity, send students to **Web Code nbe-0101.** Students will view images and maps of recent archaeological digs and read the field notes and personal journals of the archaeologists. Ask students choose one dig site to explore and then write an essay describing it. Ensure they describe what is being excavated, examples of artifacts that were found, and information revealed by these discoveries.

Follow-Up Conduct a class discussion based on the following questions: How do scholars study the past? What techniques do archaeologists use? What types of obstacles do historians have to overcome to give a straightforward account of events? In what ways do archaeologists work with new technologies and other scholars?

Differentiated Instruction   Solutions for All Learners

Give One, Get One L2

Use the following steps to help foster independent reflection and peer interaction before a class discussion.

1. Pose a thought-provoking question to the class.

2. Allow students to consider what they may already know about the topic and jot down a number of potential responses.

3. Ask students to place a check mark next to the two or three ideas that they perceive as their strongest and then draw a line after their final idea to separate their ideas from those that they will gather from classmates.

4. Give students a set amount of time (about eight to ten minutes) to get up from their seats and share ideas with a classmate. After finding a partner, the two students should exchange papers and quietly read each other's idea. Then they should discuss the ideas briefly, select one idea from their partner's list, and add it to their own, making sure to accurately copy the idea and their partner's name. Then have students exchange partners.

5. At the end of the exchange period, facilitate a unified class discussion. Call on a volunteer to share one new idea acquired from a conversation partner. The student whose idea has just been reported will then share the next idea, pulled from a different conversation partner.

Modeling Reading and Writing Skills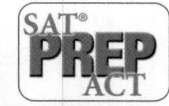

Set a Purpose for Reading Tell students that setting a purpose for reading will provide them with a reading focus or goal. It helps them know what information to look for in the text. Explain that first, they should preview the section headings and visuals. Next, they should use the information they gleaned to set a purpose. Then they should read the text looking for that information.

Model this skill by looking through Part 1, noting both the red and black headings and the visuals. In Part 1 Section 1, point out the image of the funeral mask of King Tutankhamen and the map of New Kingdom Egypt, 1450 B.C., which shows the empires of the Egyptians and the Hittites. Note that the headings refer to the study of ancient civilizations in Africa and Asia. Explain that now that you know what this part is about, you can set a purpose to fit what you've previewed: to learn about the development of ancient civilizations. Ask students to list other purposes for reading this section. *(Sample: to find out the religious beliefs of the ancient civilizations, to learn the technologies used in ancient China)*

Ask Questions Explain that asking questions about the headings, subheadings, and visuals will help students understand and remember the text. Then students should read to answer their own questions. This is but another strategy to help students interact with the text and better comprehend it.

Model the process. Look at the second red heading in Part III, Section 2 (page 26): Feudalism and the Manor Economy. Turn this into questions: What was feudalism? How did the manor economy work? Then read aloud to find the answers, and note them on the board. Ask students to turn the next black heading into a question. Write their responses on the board. Then, as a class, read to find the answers to their questions.

Review Unit

Connecting With Past Learnings

Unit Overview

Part 1 focuses on the beginnings of civilization to the rise of ancient Egypt, the ancient Middle East, and the growth of civilizations in India and China.
Key Concept: Belief Systems

Part 2 deals with empires of India and China, ancient Greece and Rome, the rise of Christianity, and the emergence of civilizations in the Americas.
Key Concept: Geography's Impact

Part 3 focuses on the development of regional civilizations and cultural patterns that linked people of many different lands.
Key Concepts: Conflict, Cultural Diffusion, Trade

Connecting With Past Learnings:
From Prehistory to Early Modern Times

Queen Nefertiti

T o understand modern world history requires familiarity with the history of ancient and medieval times. Events, concepts, and relationships that began thousands of years ago continue to have an impact on contemporary life.

This unit serves as a review of key developments from prehistory to early modern times. It focuses on major trends and revolutionary ideas of earlier eras—trends and ideas that transformed people and their cultures in new ways. Highlights include the emergence of river valley civilizations, the cultures of Greece and Rome, and the growth of empires and regional civilizations.

Neolithic pottery, *c.* 6000 B.C.

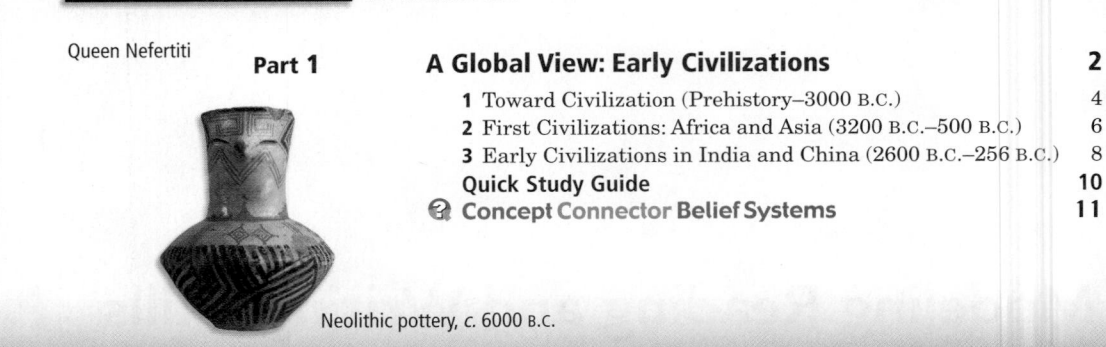

Namib desert, Namibia

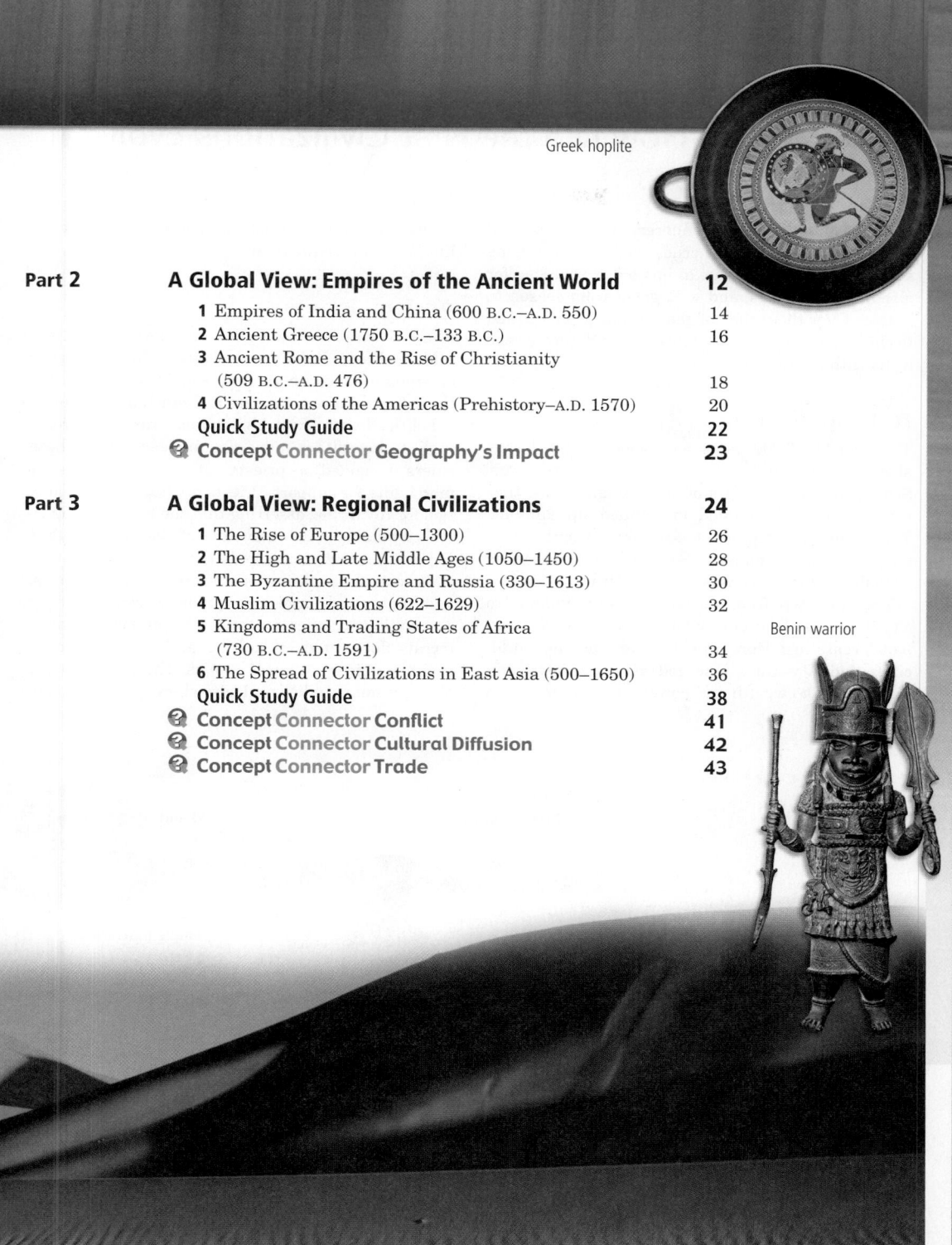

Greek hoplite

Benin warrior

Understanding the Big Picture

The Modern Review Unit, Connecting With Past Learnings, covers prehistory to early modern times and is divided into three main parts: Early Civilizations, Empires of the Ancient World, and Regional Civilizations. Each part is introduced by a summary essay, A Global View, and a global timeline. Each timeline provides a chronology of major events and developments in Africa, the Americas, Asia and Oceania, and Europe. By studying the timelines, students may compare developments in various regions and note examples of global interaction. Ask students to preview the unit, noting the ideas covered in the timelines and main headings.

Introduce the Unit

To introduce this unit, use these questions to start a discussion with your students.

Science and Technology
How do you think farming changed people's lives?

Geography's Impact
How do you think seas and rivers benefited the rise of civilization?

Trade
How do you think trade affected the development of regional civilizations?

Cultural Diffusion
As contact between different regions of the world increased, how do you think art and literature changed?

Home Improvement
The *Letter Home* includes a summary of the Modern Review Unit content that students will be studying.

All in One Teaching Resources, Modern
      Review Unit, p. 1

All in One Review Unit Directory

- **Letter Home,** p. 1
- **Vocabulary Builder,** pp. 2, 15, 28
- **Reading Strategy,** pp. 3, 16, 29
- **Enrichment**
   Biography, pp. 6, 21, 32
   Link to Literature, pp. 4, 7, 8, 17, 33

   Primary Source, pp. 20, 30, 31
   Traveler's Tales, pp. 18, 34
   Viewpoints, pp. 5, 19
- **Test Forms A and B,** pp. 9–14, 22–27, 35–40
- **Unit Simulation,** pp. 41–44

PART 1

A Global View: Early Civilizations

How Did the First Civilizations Evolve?

Technology Resources

- Student**EXPRESS** CD-ROM, Modern Review Unit, Part 1
- Teacher**EXPRESS** CD-ROM, Modern Review Unit, Part 1
- Presentation**EXPRESS**™ **Premium DVD** Modern Review Unit, Part 1
- *ExamView*® **Test Bank CD-ROM,** English and Spanish, Modern Review Unit, Part 1
- **Guided Reading Audio,** Spanish, Modern Review Unit, Part 1
- **Student Edition on Audio,** Modern Review Unit, Part 1
- **Witness History Discovery School**™ video program, *Secrets of the Iceman, The Nile: Where Egypt Began, Discovering Ancient Shang China*
- **Experience It! Multimedia Pack**

The first humans were wanderers. Wearing animal skins and equipped with crude spears and digging sticks, they followed game animals and searched for ripening fruit, roots, and wild grain from season to season. Over thousands of generations, they learned to chip stone tools, to make fire, and to decorate cave walls with pictures of animals.

Farming Villages

Then, about 10,000 years ago, some human beings abandoned the wandering life of hunter-gatherers. Settling into tiny villages of stone or mud huts, they raised crops and herded or penned up animals. Thanks to these dependable food sources, agricultural villages grew in number. Some of them began to specialize in arts and crafts, trade, and war.

The next step, from scattered farming villages to city-based civilizations, came a little more than 5,000 years ago. Here and there around the world, cities and city-states emerged. Kings, priests, and traders rose to wealth and power. And the invention of writing symbolized the emergence of a new way of life. We call it civilization.

Ancient Societies

Early civilizations took shape in North Africa, the Middle East, India, and China. Although they emerged in isolation across a widely scattered area, these first civilized societies had much in common.

Politically, the first civilizations turned increasingly to hereditary monarchs for leadership. These rulers depended on priests, officials, aristocrats, or merchants for support. Priests provided divine sanction for royal rule, asserting that the kings of Sumerian city-states were "stewards of the gods" or that Egypt's pharaohs were gods themselves. Royal officials carried out the ruler's decrees, collected taxes, and supervised large-scale public works, including city walls and irrigation projects. Landowning aristocrats dominated agriculture and often served as military officers in royal armies. The merchants of Mesopotamia, India, and elsewhere grew wealthy

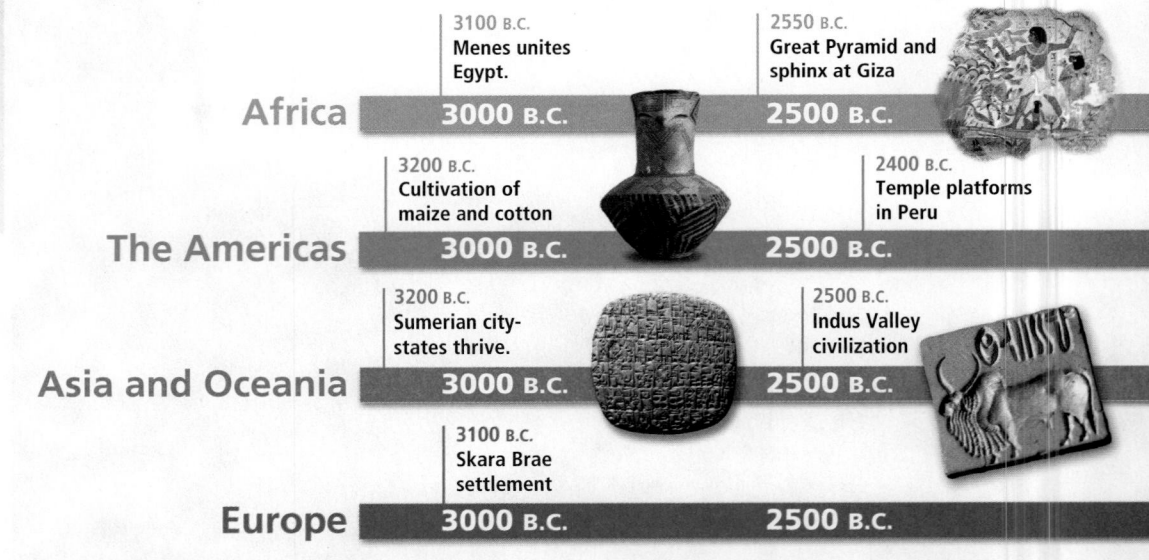

Africa
3000 B.C.   2500 B.C.
3100 B.C. **Menes unites Egypt.**
2550 B.C. **Great Pyramid and sphinx at Giza**

The Americas
3000 B.C.   2500 B.C.
3200 B.C. **Cultivation of maize and cotton**
2400 B.C. **Temple platforms in Peru**

Asia and Oceania
3000 B.C.   2500 B.C.
3200 B.C. **Sumerian city-states thrive.**
2500 B.C. **Indus Valley civilization**

Europe
3000 B.C.   2500 B.C.
3100 B.C. **Skara Brae settlement**

Bibliography

For the Teacher

Green, Kevin. *Archaeology: An Introduction.* 3rd ed. Philadelphia: University of Pennsylvania Press, 1995.

Ikram, Salima. *Death and Burial in Ancient Egypt.* Harlow: Longman, 2003.

Possehl, Gregory. *The Indus Civilization: A Contemporary Perspective.* Walnut Creek: AltaMira Press, 2002.

For the Student

L1 Lauber, Patricia. *Painters of the Cave.* Washington, D.C.: National Geographic Society, 1998.

L2 Smith, Stuart Tyson and Nancy Stone Bernard. *Valley of the Kings.* Series: Digging for the Past. New York: Oxford University Press, 2003.

L3 Mann, Kenny. *The Ancient Hebrews.* Series: Cultures of the Past. New York: Benchmark Books, 1999.

from trade, paid taxes, and strengthened the state economically.

Cities like Mohenjo-Daro or Babylon became the centers of political power and economic development. Most people, however, continued to live in small villages and cultivate the soil. These peasant majorities provided a foundation for the more elaborate lifestyles of their social superiors.

Ancient Cultures

These early civilizations built on the cultural achievements of the simpler societies from which they grew. Architects constructed elaborate royal palaces, temples such as the ziggurats of Mesopotamia, and royal tombs such as the pyramids of Egypt. Sculptors carved beautiful statues of gods, goddesses, and rulers. Painters depicted scenes of everyday life or military victories. The development of writing preserved some of the world's oldest literature, from the Egyptian *Tale of Sinuhe* and Sumerian *Epic of Gilgamesh* to India's *Mahabharata* and ancient China's *Book of Songs*.

Major advances in science and technology may also be traced to ancient times. From metalworking and textiles to mathematics and astronomy, early civilizations contributed greatly to humanity's store of skills. Religions also grew more complex, producing early scriptures, including the Vedas of India. While most ancient societies were polytheistic, the Hebrew people of the Middle East introduced monotheism, the worship of one single, all-powerful God.

Looking Ahead

A thousand years before the time of Jesus, civilization was still a rare phenomenon. Most people on all continents still lived in food-gathering bands, in farming villages, or as nomadic herders. But the future belonged to the islands of civilizations that were emerging here and there around the world.

Assessment

Choose two events and two pictures from the timeline below. For each, write a sentence explaining how it relates to the themes expressed in the Global View essay.

2050 B.C.	1472 B.C.	1279–1213 B.C.	730–670 B.C.
Middle Kingdom of Egypt begins.	**Reign of Natshepsut begins.**	**Reign of Ramses II**	**Nubian rule over Egypt**

2000 B.C. **1500** B.C. **1000** B.C. **500** B.C.

2000 B.C.	1500 B.C.	900 B.C.	500 B.C.
Permanent towns in Valley of Mexico	**Rise of Olmec civilization**	**Chavin culture in Peru**	**Adena mounds in Ohio**

2000 B.C. **1500** B.C. **1000** B.C. **500** B.C.

2000 B.C.	1766 B.C.	1100 B.C.	539 B.C.
Development of Chinese writing	**Shang dynasty in China emerges.**	**Assyrians expand power.**	**Persian empire created.**

2000 B.C. **1500** B.C. **1000** B.C. **500** B.C.

2000 B.C.	1600 B.C.	750 B.C.
Bronze Age in Europe	**Height of Minoan civilization**	**Greeks colonize the Mediterranean.**

2000 B.C. **1500** B.C. **1000** B.C. **500** B.C.

Part 1 Resources

- All in One Vocabulary Builder; Reading Strategy; Enrichments; Chapter Tests
- AYP Monitoring Assessments
- *ExamView* Test Bank CD-ROM
- Guided Reading Audio (Spanish)
- Student Edition Audio

Previewing Part 1

- **Introduce** Write the question that introduces Part 1 on the board: *How did the first civilizations evolve?* Ask students to predict answers to this question based on the red headings and the timeline. Have them revise their predictions as they read the essay. Tell students to keep this question in mind and to continue to revise their predictions as they read Part 1.

- **Teach** Have students work together in small groups to paraphrase ideas in the Global View essay. Invite students to share and compare their paraphrased sentences with those of other groups. For help in paraphrasing, refer students to the **Skills Handbook,** p. SH3.

- **Analyzing the Visuals** Discuss the timeline with students. Ask **Which society arose first?** *(Sumerian city-states)* **What events happened around 1500 B.C.?** *(reign of Hatshepsut begins, rise of Olmecs, Shang dynasty emerges in China, height of Minoan civilization)* Then have students answer the Assessment question.

Have students access **Web Code nbd-0101** for the **Note Taking Study Guide** *Online,* as an alternative to the *Reading and Note Taking Study Guide* booklet.

Answer

Students' sentences should reflect an ability to analyze and classify information in a concise format. For detailed guidelines on assessing student activities, see **Assessment Rubrics.**

Prepare to Read

Build Background Knowledge ⑬

Ask students to suppose that they lived 5,000 years ago during the Bronze Age. Ask **How would you use the resources of your environment to create a civilization?** As students list ideas, write them on the board under these categories: agriculture, building projects, tools and works of art.

Set a Purpose ⑬

- **Preview** Have volunteers read aloud the main ideas that begin each section of Part 1. Ask them to summarize these ideas in 3 to 5 sentences.

- **Reading Skill** Have students use the *Reading Strategy: Compare and Contrast* worksheet. Then have students read this section using the Structured Read Aloud strategy (TE, p. T21).

  All in One Teaching Resources,
  Modern Review Unit, p. 3

- **Vocabulary Builder** To help students develop vocabulary skills, have them use the *Vocabulary Builder: Dictionary Skills* worksheet.

  All in One Teaching Resources,
  Modern Review Unit, p. 2

1 Toward Civilization

(Prehistory–3000 B.C.)

Ancient Mesopotamian carving of a carpenter at work

Main Ideas

- About 10,000 years ago, during the Neolithic period, or New Stone Age, people learned to farm.
- By about 5,000 years ago, the advances made by early farming communities led to the rise of civilizations.
- Historians define seven basic features common to most early civilizations: well-organized central governments, complex religions, job specialization, social classes, arts and architecture, public works, and writing.

Historians call the earliest period of human history the Old Stone Age, or the Paleolithic Period. This long period dates from the time of the first stone toolmakers to about 10,000 B.C. Paleolithic people were **nomads,** moving from place to place to follow game animals and search for edible plants. They lived in small hunting and food-gathering bands of about 20 to 30 people.

Stone Age people learned to adapt to their environment for survival. Men and women made simple tools and weapons such as digging sticks, spears, and axes. They developed spoken language, which let them cooperate as they worked. During the ice ages, people invented clothing made of animal skins and learned to build fires.

The Growth of Farming

About 10,000 years ago, nomadic bands made a dramatic breakthrough. They learned to farm. By producing their own food, they could remain in one place. This change from nomadic to settled farming life ushered in the New Stone Age, or Neolithic Period. Neolithic farmers established permanent villages and developed new skills and tools.

People also learned to tame some of the animals they once hunted. Rather than wait for migrating animals to return each year, the new village dwellers rounded them up and herded the animals or penned them in enclosures. This practice enabled people to have meat, and eventually animal labor, without leaving villages and farms.

Because people could now settle in one place, agriculture led to a growth in population. This growth in population led, in turn, to increased interaction among human communities.

Village life also reshaped the roles of women and men. Heads of families formed a council of elders to make important decisions. Often, a village chief emerged. During times of want, warfare increased. Success in battle enabled some men to gain status as warriors. These warriors had power over both women and other men. The status of women declined, though they did not lose all their influence or rights.

About 5,000 years ago, the advances made by early farming communities led people to a new stage of development—the emergence of civilizations.

Beginnings of Civilization

Historians define eight basic features common to most early civilizations. These features are: (1) cities, (2) well-organized central governments, (3) complex religions, (4) job specialization, (5) social classes, (6) arts and architecture, (7) public works, and (8) writing.

In Africa and Asia, the first cities emerged after farmers began raising crops in fertile lands along river valleys. The nutrient-rich soils and a reliable source of water allowed farmers to produce surplus, or extra, crops. These surpluses provided more food and helped populations to expand. As populations increased, some villages grew into cities.

In these cities, some of the people were able to work at jobs other than farming. This was a radical departure from the traditional economies of the Stone Age. In fact, many aspects of life were dramatically different than they had been before.

Connect to Our World

Connections to Today From its origins in the Neolithic Age, agriculture remains a predominant human activity today. Nearly 50 percent of the world's people still engage in some form of agriculture. While less than 3 percent of people in industrialized countries work in agriculture, in developing countries the figure is around 60 percent. In industrialized nations, modern science and technology have revolutionized the growing, cultivating, and harvesting of plants, as well as food processing and distribution. In less-developed regions, practices still resemble those of ancient times, including the use of human and animal labor and slash-and-burn techniques.

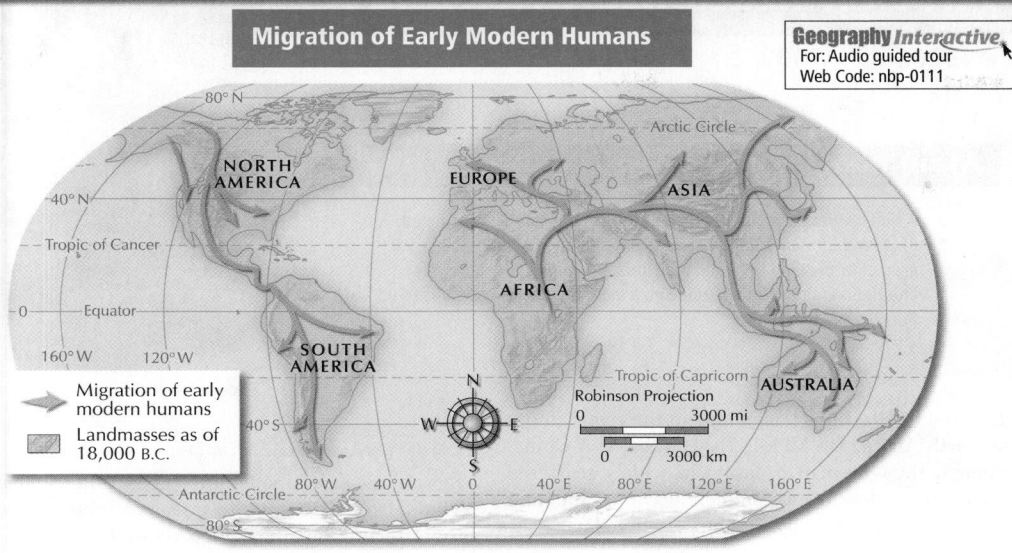

Migration of Early Modern Humans

Geography *Interactive*
For: Audio guided tour
Web Code: nbp-0111

Geography and History
Once *Homo sapiens* had emerged, they migrated along the various routes shown above. Many of these routes followed the paths of large herd animals.

Organized Governments The challenge of farming in a river valley contributed to the development of city governments. To control flooding and channel waters to fields, early farmers worked together. Through cooperation, they built dikes, dug canals, and carved out irrigation ditches. Such projects required leadership and well-organized governments. Some city governments grew powerful and complex. Over time, government bureaucracies grew. A **bureaucracy** is a system of managing government through specialized departments run by appointed officials.

Social Classes Social organization also became more complex. People were ranked in social classes according to their jobs. Priests and nobles were usually at the top. Next came wealthy merchants, followed by **artisans**, or skilled craftworkers. Below them stood the vast majority of people, who were peasant farmers. Slaves were at the lowest social level.

A critical new skill emerged—writing. Priests probably developed writing in order to record the amount of grain collected or other information. Early writing was made up of **pictographs**, or simple drawings that represented ideas. As writing grew more complex, specially trained people called scribes learned to read and write.

The First Empires As ancient rulers gained more and more power, they conquered territories beyond the boundaries of their cities. Some were able to conquer many cities and villages, creating empires. An **empire** is a group of states, territories, and peoples ruled by one person. While empire building brought painful defeat for conquered peoples, it also helped limit war and establish connections between neighboring communities.

Assessment

1. **Identify (a)** Old Stone Age **(b)** New Stone Age
2. **Define (a)** nomad **(b)** bureaucracy **(c)** artisan **(d)** pictograph **(e)** empire
3. What dramatic breakthrough allowed nomadic bands to settle in villages for the first time?

L1 Special Needs **L2 Less Proficient Readers** **L2 English Language Learners**

To help students better read this section on the rise of civilization, have them use sticky notes or a clear transparency sheet as they read this section. Ask them to number each step in the rise of the first civilizations, starting with (1) people farmed the land in rich river valleys. Ensure they understand how this led to

(2) farmers produced surpluses, (3) they stored food for the future, (4) the extra food could support expanding populations, (5) villages grew into cities, and (6) people were able to do other work than farming. Then have them transfer this information into a cause-and-effect chart.

Toward Civilization   **L3**

Instruct

- **Introduce** Display **Color Transparency 6: Prehistory to Civilization.** Outline the basic features that define civilization. For each feature, ask students to list an example from modern society.

  📖 **Color Transparencies, 6**

- **Teach** Trace the development of civilization. Ask **How did people live in the Old Stone Age?** *(moved from place to place in search of food)* **How did the Neolithic Age change the way people lived?** *(Once they learned to farm, they produced their own food, rather than hunting and gathering; they began to live in permanent settlements, rather than leading a nomadic life.)* Then discuss the advantages and disadvantages of the first empires.

- **Quick Activity** Show students *Secrets of the Iceman* from the **Witness History Discovery School**™ video program. Discuss how archaeologists have studied the Iceman to learn more about life during the Neolithic Age.

Independent Practice

- **Note Taking** Have students fill in the outline with the rise of civilization.

  🗒 **Reading and Note Taking Study Guide, p. 10**

- **Link to Literature** Have students read the excerpt from James Michener's *The Source* and complete the worksheet. Discuss the process historians use to study ancient civilizations.

  All in One **Teaching Resources, Modern Review Unit, p. 4**

Monitor Progress

As students fill in their outlines, circulate to make sure they understand the conditions under which the first civilizations arose. For a completed version of the outline, see

📖 **Note Taking Transparencies, 101**

Answers

1–2. Answers should reflect an understanding of the terms listed.

3. learning to farm

Instruct

- **Introduce: Key Terms** Ask students to find and define the key terms *monotheistic* and *ethics* (in blue). Ask students to describe their own moral standards of behavior or those that they have learned about at home, in school, in religious settings, or through reading.

- **Teach** Discuss the various early civilizations that evolved in ancient Africa and Asia. Ask **What accomplishments arose from each of the ancient Egyptian Kingdoms?** *(The Old Kingdom produced a strong central government. The Middle Kingdom produced cultural diffusion through trade and warfare. The New Kingdom produced a large empire.)* **What key geographic challenge did early Sumerians face?** *(They had to learn to control the flooding waters of the Tigris and Euphrates rivers.)* **How have laws and traditions helped Jews maintain close-knit communities while living outside of Israel?** *(They have given the Jews a set of central ideas around which to build similar communities everywhere they go.)*

- **Quick Activity** Show students *The Nile: Where Egypt Began* from the **Witness History Discovery School**™ video program. Discuss the ways in which geography helped shape ancient Egypt.

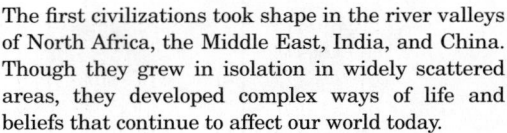

2 First Civilizations: Africa and Asia

(3200 B.C.–500 B.C.)

Main Ideas

- A rich civilization emerged in the valley of the Nile River in Egypt.
- Independent Sumerian city-states developed in Mesopotamia, an area of fertile land between the Tigris and Euphrates rivers.
- The Hebrews developed Judaism, a monotheistic religion based on the worship of one God.

Funeral mask of King Tutankhamen

The first civilizations took shape in the river valleys of North Africa, the Middle East, India, and China. Though they grew in isolation in widely scattered areas, they developed complex ways of life and beliefs that continue to affect our world today.

Ancient Kingdoms of the Nile

More than 5,000 years ago, a rich farming civilization grew in the valley of the Nile River in Egypt. To control the Nile's annual floods, village people learned to cooperate. They built dikes, reservoirs, and irrigation ditches to channel the river and store water for the dry season. Eventually, these villages joined together into two kingdoms. About 3100 B.C., King Menes united these kingdoms, creating the world's first unified state along the Nile.

After Menes' reign, the history of ancient Egypt can be divided into three main periods: the Old Kingdom (about 2575 B.C.–2130 B.C.), the Middle Kingdom (about 1938 B.C.–1630 B.C.), and the New Kingdom (about 1539 B.C.–1075 B.C.).

During the Old Kingdom, pharaohs (FEHR ohz), or the Egyptian rulers, organized a strong central state. They built majestic pyramids to serve as tombs. During the Middle and New Kingdoms, trade and warfare brought Egypt into contact with other civilizations. New ideas, customs, and technologies spread from one people to another in a process called cultural diffusion. Powerful New Kingdom pharaohs such as Queen Hatshepsut and Ramses II established a large empire that eventually reached the Euphrates River. After Ramses II, Egyptian power slowly declined.

Egyptian Civilization

Egyptians worshiped many gods and goddesses. They also built tombs to preserve their bodies for the afterlife and they filled them with items that they would need in their new lives.

Egyptian society was organized into classes. The pharaoh, who was considered both a god and a king, ruled at the top. Next came the nobles, who fought the pharaoh's wars. A tiny class of merchants and artisans developed. Farmers and slaves were at the bottom of society.

City-States of Ancient Sumer

To the northeast of the Nile lies the Fertile Crescent, an arc of soil-rich land. More than 5,000 years ago, the independent city-states of Sumer grew along the Tigris and Euphrates rivers in a part of the Fertile Crescent called Mesopotamia. A city-state is a political unit made up of a city and the surrounding lands.

Floods and Irrigation Control of the Tigris and Euphrates rivers was the key to the development of a civilization in the Sumerian city-states. Villagers built dikes and irrigation ditches. Using clay bricks, Sumerians built ziggurats, or soaring pyramid-temples.

The city-states of Sumer often fought for control of land and water. War leaders gained importance and eventually became hereditary rulers. A social hierarchy (HY ur ahr kee), or system of ranks, emerged. The highest rank included the ruling family, leading officials, and high priests.

History Background

Sumerians Invent Writing By 3100 B.C., Sumerians had invented the earliest known writing. It was later called cuneiform, from the Latin word *cuneus* for "wedge," because scribes wrote by making wedge-shaped marks on clay tablets. Cuneiform grew out of a system of pictographs used to record goods brought to temple storehouses. Later, the Sumerians developed symbols to represent more complicated thoughts. As their writing evolved, the Sumerians used it to record not only economic exchanges, but also myths, prayers, laws, and business contracts. Sumerian scribes had to go through years of difficult schooling to acquire their skills. Discipline was strict. Untidy copying or talking in class could be punished by caning. Students who did well often learned about religion, mathematics, and literature, as well.

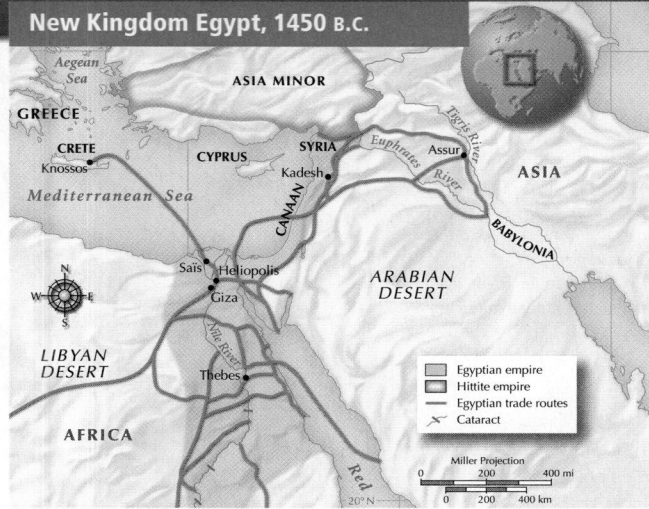

New Kingdom Egypt, 1450 B.C.

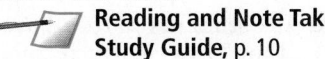

Geography *Interactive*
For: Audio guided tour
Web Code: nbp-0231

Geography and History
During the years of the New Kingdom, powerful and ambitious pharaohs created a large empire. At its height, around 1450 B.C., the Egyptian empire reached as far north as Syria and the Euphrates River.

Advances in Learning

By 3100 B.C., Sumerians had invented the earliest form of writing, called **cuneiform** (kyoo NEE uh fawrm). **Scribes,** or the specially trained people who knew how to read and write, maintained records for the kingdom.

Invaders, Traders, and Empires

Mesopotamia's location at a geographical crossroads made it tempting to invaders, some of whom built great empires. Sargon, the ruler of Akkad, conquered the city-states of Sumer about 2300 B.C. He built the first empire known to history.

About 1790 B.C., Hammurabi (hah muh RAH bee), king of Babylon, brought much of Mesopotamia under his control. He published a remarkable set of laws, known as the Code of Hammurabi. This code was the first major collection of laws in history. In 539 B.C., Persian armies overthrew Babylon.

Warfare and trade in Mesopotamia spread ideas and technology around the Mediterranean world. Knowledge of ironworking became common throughout the region. An Assyrian king founded one of the first libraries. The Phoenicians created an alphabet and the Persians improved trade by encouraging the use of coins among merchants.

The Roots of Judaism

Among the many peoples who occupied the Fertile Crescent were the Hebrews. According to the Torah, the Hebrews' most sacred text, they once lived in Mesopotamia. About 2000 B.C., they migrated into a region known as Canaan.

The early Hebrews developed Judaism, which is a **monotheistic** religion (based on the belief in one true God). They recorded events and laws, such as the Ten Commandments, in the Torah. **Prophets,** or spiritual leaders, urged the Hebrews to obey God's law. These prophets preached a strong code of **ethics,** or moral standards of behavior. They urged both personal morality and social justice, calling on the rich and powerful to protect the poor and weak.

By 1000 B.C., the Hebrews established the kingdom of Israel. A famous ruler, King Solomon, built a splendid temple dedicated to God, at Jerusalem. Eventually the kingdom split into two parts. A series of invading armies captured the Hebrew kingdoms.

During their captivity, the Hebrews became known as Jews. They lived mainly under foreign rulers until about 2,000 years ago, when many were forced to leave their homeland. This **diaspora** (dy AS pur uh), or scattering of people, sent Jews to different parts of the world. Wherever they settled, they built close-knit communities and kept their traditions. Today, Judaism is considered one of the world's major religions for its unique contribution to religious thought.

Assessment

1. **Identify (a)** Nile River **(b)** Fertile Crescent **(c)** Mesopotamia **(d)** Hebrews
2. **Define (a)** pharaoh **(b)** cultural diffusion **(c)** city-state **(d)** ziggurat **(e)** hierarchy **(f)** cuneiform **(g)** scribe **(h)** monotheistic **(i)** prophet **(j)** ethics **(k)** diaspora
3. Name two geographic locations where early civilizations developed.

Independent Practice

■ **Note Taking** Have students fill in the outline of the first civilizations in Africa and Asia.

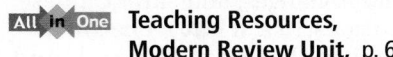 **Reading and Note Taking Study Guide,** p. 10

■ Have students access **Web Code nbp-0231** to take the **Geography Interactive Audio Guided Tour.**

■ **Biography** To help students better understand aspects of ancient Egyptian culture, have them read the biography *Imhotep* and complete the worksheet.

All in One Teaching Resources, Modern Review Unit, p. 6

Monitor Progress

As students fill in their outlines, circulate to make sure they understand the distinct characteristics of the early civilizations of the Middle East and Egypt. For a completed version of the outline, see

📖 **Note Taking Transparencies,** 102

Answers

1. **(a)** river in Egypt **(b)** a region of rich soil shaped like an arc that includes the eastern Mediterranean coast and Mesopotamia **(c)** the land between the Tigris and Euphrates rivers **(d)** a monotheistic people who occupied the region of Canaan in the eastern Mediterranean
2. **(a)** an Egyptian ruler **(b)** the spread of ideas, customs, and technologies from one people to another **(c)** a political unit made up of a city and the surrounding lands **(d)** a pyramid-temple **(e)** system of ranks **(f)** a form of writing invented by the Sumerians **(g)** a specially trained person who knew how to read and write and who kept records **(h)** based on the worship of one God **(i)** spiritual leader **(j)** moral standards of behavior **(k)** scattering of people
3. Sample: the Nile River, the Fertile Crescent, Mesopotamia

Early Civilizations in India and China ⑬

Instruct

- **Introduce** Ask students to recall the civilizations they have reviewed thus far. Based on their previous reading, have them predict the characteristics of the Indus, Ganges, and early Chinese civilizations. Have students read ahead to see if their predictions were accurate.

- **Teach** Discuss the characteristics of the Indus, Ganges, and early Chinese civilizations. Ask **What were some similarities between Harrapa and Mohenjo-Daro?** (*Both were carefully planned in a grid pattern and featured complex plumbing.*) **How did the Aryan civilization differ from the Indus Valley civilization that came before it?** (*Responses should address differences in where and how these people lived, the structure of their societies, and their religious beliefs.*) **In what ways did geographic isolation affect how the Chinese viewed the world and their place in it?** (*Because great barriers separated China from the rest of the world, they had limited contact and believed that China was the center of the earth and the sole source of civilization.*)

- **Quick Activity** Show students *Discovering Ancient Shang China* from the **Witness History Discovery School**™ video program. Discuss how the Shang set up and ruled the first dynasty in China.

---

3 Early Civilizations in India and China

(2600 B.C.–256 B.C.)

Main Ideas

- India's first civilization grew in the Indus River valley.
- The Aryans later built a new civilization along the Ganges River.
- During the Shang and Zhou dynasties, the ancient Chinese made significant achievements in many areas.

The Hindu god Shiva

As civilizations took shape in the Nile Valley and Fertile Crescent, people in India and China carved out their own civilizations. These grew along the fertile river valleys of Asia.

Cities of the Indus Valley

India's first civilization emerged in the Indus River valley about 2600 B.C. The people of the Indus flourished there for 700 years, building a civilization that covered the largest area of any in ancient times. Its two main cities, Mohenjo-Daro and Harappa, were both carefully planned. Each city was laid out in a grid pattern, with blocks larger than modern city blocks. Houses had complex plumbing systems, with baths, drains, and water chutes that led to underground sewers.

Most Indus people were farmers. Powerful leaders, perhaps priest-kings, made sure the cities had a reliable supply of grain. Merchants and traders sailed with cargoes of cotton cloth, grain, copper, and pearls all the way to the cities of Sumer.

By 1750 B.C., the quality of life in the Indus Valley cities was declining. Around this time, there is evidence of severe floods that ravaged cities and farms along the Indus River. By 1700 B.C., many of the cities along the Indus had been abandoned.

Kingdoms of the Ganges

As the Indus Valley civilization declined, peoples herding horses and cattle migrated from Central Asia into northwestern India. They spoke an Indo-European language related to English and other European languages. Over several centuries, these peoples spread into northern India and intermarried with the existing residents. Their descendants called themselves Aryans.

In time, Aryans spread eastward to the forests of the Ganges River basin. They made tools of iron and built walled cities. By 500 B.C., a new Indian civilization had emerged. It consisted of many rival kingdoms that shared a common culture.

Most of what we know about the Aryans comes from the Vedas, a collection of prayers, hymns, and other religious teachings. Aryan priests memorized and recited the Vedas for a thousand years before they were written down.

Society The Aryans divided people into social classes by occupation. The highest-ranking group was the priests; followed by the warriors; a third group of herders, farmers, artisans, and merchants; and a fourth group made up farmworkers, servants, and other laborers. The fifth and lowest group were the dalits, who had to do jobs that no one else wanted. Over time, these divisions gave way to a more complex system of castes. **Castes** are social groups into which people are born and which they cannot leave.

Religious Beliefs Aryans were **polytheistic**. That is, they believed in many gods. As society developed and changed, people moved toward the notion of a single spiritual power beyond the many gods of the Vedas. They called this power **brahman** and believed it lived in all things. Some Aryans became **mystics**, or individuals who devote their lives to seeking spiritual truth.

Link to Literature

The *Mahabharata* The Aryans maintained a strong oral tradition, memorizing and reciting ancient hymns and epic poems. One epic poem, the *Mahabharata* has served as a major source of social and religious doctrine for India for many hundreds of years. Through its 100,000 verses, we hear echoes of the battles that rival Aryan tribes fought to gain control of the Ganges region. One episode, a lengthy poem known as the *Bhagavad-Gita* (BUG uh vud GEE tuh), reflects important religious beliefs about the immortality of the soul and the value of the performing one's duty. In its verses, the god Krishna instructs Prince Arjuna on the importance of duty over personal desires and ambitions.

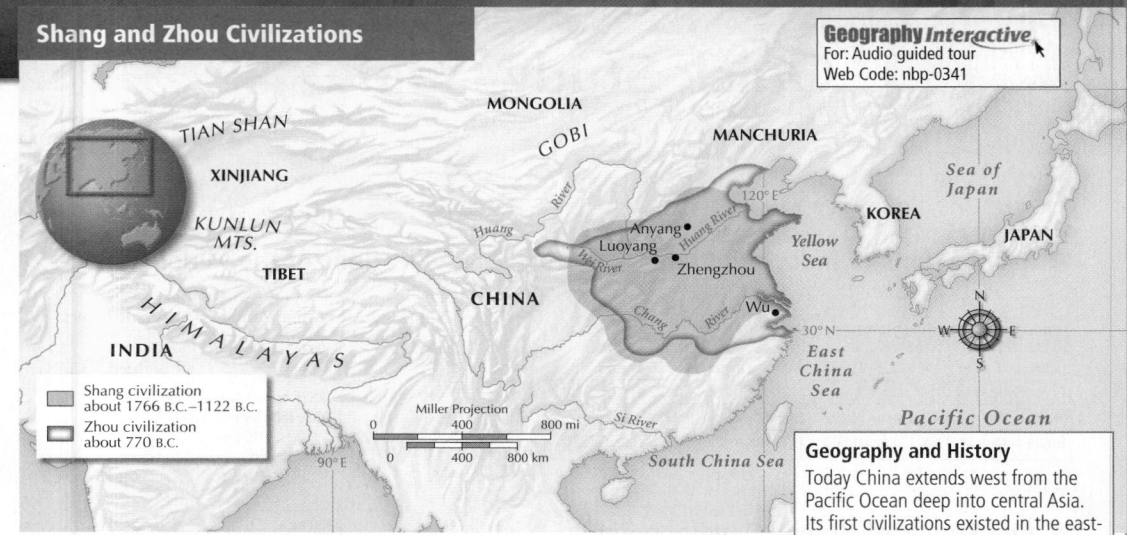

Shang and Zhou Civilizations

MONGOLIA
GOBI
MANCHURIA
TIAN SHAN
XINJIANG
Sea of Japan
KUNLUN MTS.
Anyang
Luoyang
Huang River
Yellow Sea
KOREA
JAPAN
TIBET
Huang River
Zhengzhou
CHINA
120° E
HIMALAYAS
Chang River
Wu
30° N
East China Sea
INDIA
Wei River
Si River
Pacific Ocean
South China Sea
90° E

Shang civilization about 1766 B.C.–1122 B.C.
Zhou civilization about 770 B.C.

Miller Projection
0   400   800 mi
0   400   800 km

Geography *Interactive*
For: Audio guided tour
Web Code: nbp-0341

Geography and History
Today China extends west from the Pacific Ocean deep into central Asia. Its first civilizations existed in the eastern part of the modern-day country.

Early Civilizations in China

Long distances and physical barriers separated China from Egypt, the Middle East, and India. This isolation contributed to the Chinese belief that China was at the center of the Earth and the sole source of civilization. This led the ancient Chinese to call their land the Middle Kingdom.

Geography Great barriers blocked the easy movement of the Chinese to the outside world. High mountains, brutal deserts, thick jungles, and the vast Pacific Ocean lay between China and the rest of the world. Still, the people of China found ways to trade with neighboring peoples. In time, Chinese products reached the Middle East and beyond.

Chinese history began in the Huang He valley, where Neolithic people learned to farm. As in other places, the need to control a major river through large water projects probably led to the rise of a strong central government.

The Shang and Zhou Dynasties About 1650 B.C., a Chinese people called the Shang came to power in northern China. In 1027 B.C., the Zhou (joh) people overthrew the Shang. The Zhou dynasty lasted until 256 B.C. A **dynasty** is a ruling family. To justify their rebellion against the Shang, the Zhou dynasty promoted the idea of the Mandate of Heaven, or the divine right to rule. Later, this idea expanded to explain the **dynastic cycle**, or the rise and fall of dynasties. If rulers became corrupt, the Chinese believed that Heaven withdrew its support, or mandate, and the dynasty fell.

Religion By Shang times, the Chinese had developed complex religious beliefs. They prayed to many gods and nature spirits. Over time, Chinese religious practices came to center on respect for ancestors. The Chinese called on the spirits of their ancestors to bring good fortune to the family. The Chinese also believed that the universe reflected a balance between two forces, yin and yang. Yin was linked to the Earth and female forces, while yang stood for Heaven and male forces.

Science and Technology During the Shang and Zhou periods, the Chinese studied the movement of the planets, recorded eclipses, and created an accurate calendar. They developed the technology of bronzemaking and silkmaking. Under the Zhou dynasty, the Chinese made the first books. They bound strips of wood or bamboo together and drew characters on the flat surfaces. By 256 B.C., China was a large, wealthy, and highly developed center of civilization.

Assessment

1. **Identify (a)** Mohenjo-Daro **(b)** Aryans **(c)** Vedas **(d)** Zhou dynasty
2. **Define (a)** caste **(b)** polytheistic **(c)** brahman **(d)** mystic **(e)** dynasty **(f)** dynastic cycle
3. Name the five basic groups, or castes, into which the Aryans divided people.
4. What were some of the religious beliefs of the Chinese during the Shang dynasty?

Independent Practice

■ **Note Taking** Have students fill in the outline detailing the early civilizations in India and China.
  Reading and Note Taking Study Guide, p. 12

■ Have students access **Web Code nbp-0341** to take the **Geography Interactive Audio Guided Tour.**

■ **Link to Literature** To help students better understand ancient Chinese ideas, have them read the selection *The "Man Who Forgot"* and complete the worksheet.
  All in One **Teaching Resources, Modern Review Unit,** p. 8

Monitor Progress

As students fill in their outlines, circulate to make sure they understand the developments in the civilizations of India and China. For a completed version of the outline, see
  Note Taking Transparencies, 103

Answers

1. **(a)** a city of the Indus River Valley civilization **(b)** nomadic people who overran the cities of the Indus region **(c)** a collection of Aryan prayers, hymns, and other religious teachings **(d)** a Chinese dynasty that lasted from 1027 B.C. to 256 B.C.
2. **(a)** an unchangeable social group into which a person is born **(b)** believing in many gods **(c)** a single spiritual power believed to exist in all things **(d)** an individual who devotes his or her life to seeking spiritual truth **(e)** ruling family **(f)** the rise and fall of dynasties
3. priests; warriors; herders, farmers, artisans, and merchants; and conquered non-Aryans
4. The Chinese of the Shang Dynasty believed in many gods and nature spirits. Over time, their religious practices centered on veneration of ancestors. They also believed in two universal, balanced forces, yin and yang.

Differentiated Instruction   Solutions for All Learners

L1 Special Needs   L2 Less Proficient Readers

For this activity, ask students to divide a lined piece of paper in half lengthwise to create a "double journal." On one side of the divided line, instruct students to list in bullet points factual information about Indus Valley, Aryan, or ancient Chinese society as they read pages

L2 English Language Learners

8–9 in their text. On the opposite side of the page, ask students to write a journal entry from the perspective of any citizen living in one of these early cultures.

Assess and Reteach

- Have students use the charts and graphs on this page to review the material in Part 1.

- For additional review, remind students to refer to the **L3**

   Reading and Note Taking Study Guide
  Note Taking Study Guide, pp. 8, 10, 12
  Section Summaries, pp. 9, 11, 13

- When students have completed their study of this section, distribute Tests A and B.

  All in One Teaching Resources, Modern Review Unit, pp. 9–14

Extend **L4**

To extend students' understanding of how scholars piece together the past, see this section's Professional Development pages for the Extend Online activity on recent archaeological digs.

Quick Study Guide

■ Civilizations of India and China

India		China	
Indus civilization	2600 B.C. to 1900 B.C.	Shang dynasty	1766 B.C. to 1122 B.C.
Aryan civilization	1500 B.C. to ?	Zhou dynasty	1122 B.C. to 256 B.C.
Maurya empire	321 B.C. to 185 B.C.	Qin dynasty	221 B.C. to 206 B.C.
Gupta empire	A.D. 320 to A.D. 550	Han dynasty	202 B.C. to A.D. 220

■ Key Stages of Human Development

Old Stone Age
- creation of stone, bone, and wood tools and weapons
- use of fire
- spoken language
- ability to travel across water in boats
- belief in a spiritual world
- creation of cave paintings
- burial of the dead

New Stone Age
- farming and domestication of plants and animals
- settling of permanent villages
- dominance of family, economic, and political life by men
- gaining of prestige by warriors
- appearance of differences in wealth
- creation of first calendars
- more elaborate tools and new technologies

Rise of Civilizations
- production of surpluses of food
- expansion of population
- development of cities, civilizations, and governments
- government oversight of large-scale projects
- belief in polytheistic religions
- job specialization
- development of social classes
- development of arts and architecture
- invention of writing systems
- expansion of some cities into city-states and empires
- cultural diffusion

■ Civilizations of the Middle East

Civilization	Time Period	Notable Rulers
Sumer	3200 B.C.–1900 B.C.	
Egypt	Old Kingdom 2575 B.C.–2130 B.C. Middle Kingdom 1938 B.C.–1630 B.C. New Kingdom 1539 B.C.–1075 B.C.	Hatshepsut Thutmose III Ramses II
Akkad	2300 B.C.–2150 B.C.	Sargon
Babylon	Old 1790 B.C.–1595 B.C. New 626 B.C.–539 B.C.	Hammurabi Nebuchadnezzar
Hittite	1650 B.C.–1200 B.C.	
Assyria	1350 B.C.–609 B.C.	Assurbanipal
Israel	1000 B.C.–586 B.C.	David Solomon
Persia	539 B.C.–323 B.C.	Cyrus the Great Darius I

■ Key Innovations

Sumer: social hierarchy; cuneiform writing; advances in astronomy and mathematics
Egypt: bureaucracy; pyramids; mummification; social hierarchy; hieroglyphic-based writing; papyrus; advances in science and mathematics; 365-day calendar
Babylon: legal code; advances in astronomy and mathematics
Hittites: iron working
Assyrians: legal regulations of royal household; libraries
Israel: monotheistic religion, Judaism
Persians: use of coins and money economy
Phoenicians: alphabet
India: plumbing system; sewers; caste system
China: water projects; strong central government; advances in astronomy, mathematics, technology, and writing with characters

---

Differentiated
Instruction   Solutions for All Learners

L1 Special Needs **L2 Less Proficient Readers**
Use the following study guide resources to help students acquiring basic skills:

 **Adapted Reading and Note Taking Study Guide**
- Adapted Note Taking Study Guide, pp. 8, 10, 12
- Adapted Section Summaries, pp. 9, 11, 13

L2 English Language Learners
Use the following study guide resources to help Spanish-speaking students:

 **Spanish Reading and Note Taking Study Guide**
- Spanish Note Taking Study Guide, pp. 8, 10, 12
- Spanish Section Summaries, pp. 9, 11, 13

BELIEF SYSTEMS

How do religions and belief systems affect society?

Belief Systems

Objectives
- Describe ways that belief systems shape societies.
- Understand that many governments reflect belief systems.
- Complete a Web Quest on belief systems.

In This Chapter
Belief systems can influence not only rules of conduct and social structure but also art and architecture. Hinduism, Buddhism, Confucianism, and Daoism are all belief systems that originated in India or China in ancient times. The painting of the Buddha (right) is in the Jokhang Temple in Tibet. For centuries, the temple has attracted millions of monks and pilgrims, who carry prayer wheels and chant sacred mantras.

Throughout History

First century B.C. Jewish teachings stress religious duties and ethical conduct.

500–1500 A.D. The Christian church gains political power in Europe.

600s Arabs are united under Islam.

1600s Puritans stress education so people can read the Bible.

1700s–1800s Religious groups in the United States and Britain fight to end slavery.

2000s Religious differences affect the politics of nations and the world.

Continuing Today
Today, billions of people identify themselves as belonging to a specific religion or belief system. The extent of religious influence in a given country varies, however. In a theocracy, such as Iran, religious leaders make sure that laws conform to Islamic teachings.

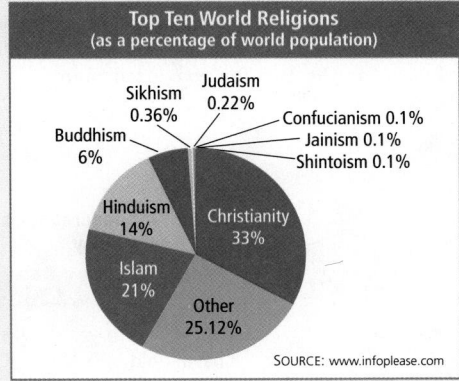

Top Ten World Religions
(as a percentage of world population)

- Sikhism 0.36%
- Judaism 0.22%
- Confucianism 0.1%
- Jainism 0.1%
- Shintoism 0.1%
- Buddhism 6%
- Hinduism 14%
- Islam 21%
- Christianity 33%
- Other 25.12%

SOURCE: www.infoplease.com

Build Background Knowledge 🔳
Help students develop a definition of religion. Ask: How does a religion differ from a belief system, such as Confucianism?

Instruct 🔳
- Direct students' attention to the Essential Question: **How do religions and belief systems affect society?** Have students read the text beneath "Asoka Rules by Moral Example" in Section 3. Ask: **How did Asoka's beliefs shape his empire?**
- Ask students to look at Continuing Today and the corresponding graph. Ask volunteers to give examples of how conflicting belief systems affect society today.
- Assign the Web Quest activity.

Independent Practice
Concept | Connector Have students fill in the Web Quest reflection question on belief systems in their Concept Connector Journal.

Reading and Note Taking Study Guide, p. 235

Monitor Progress
Circulate to make sure that students are filling in their Concept Connector Journal. Ensure they understand why belief systems occur.

21st Century Skills

❓ TRANSFER Activities

1. Analyze Throughout history, how has religion affected society?

2. Draw Conclusions Why does what people believe affect what they do?

3. Transfer Complete a Web quest in which you analyze the influence of religion on a specific country; record your thoughts in the Concept Connector Journal; and learn to make a video. Web Code nbh-0308

History Background

Forms of Worship The ways that people worship varies from belief system to belief system. In some religions, such as Christianity and Judaism, worshipers commonly gather in a central location—a church or synagogue—where a religious leader addresses the group. For Hindus, daily worship may take place at a shrine, at a temple, or in the home. In each setting, Hindus worship different gods, such as one associated with a particular caste at a temple and their own family deity at their shrine at home. Muslims often take time out wherever they may be to pray toward Mecca at specific times each day. Buddhists may meditate at home, at a temple, in nature, or anywhere, at anytime they choose.

Transfer Activities
1. Religion has been a force behind social changes and has united and divided people and nations throughout history.
2. Core beliefs guide human behavior. People will generally not behave in ways that violate those beliefs or will use their beliefs to justify their behavior.
3. Students' work should be evaluated against the rubric at Web Code nbh-0308.

A Global View: Empires of the Ancient World

What Characteristics Were Shared by Ancient Empires Around the World?

Empires combining many cities and small countries emerged in various parts of the world in ancient times. Some of the largest of these empires took shape in India, China, Europe, and, later, in the Americas.

These larger political structures had many things in common. Most empires were built by military conquest and ruled by hereditary emperors through appointed governors or lesser kings. Empires everywhere developed powerful centralized bureaucracies like those of China or imposed universal legal codes like Roman law. Emperors protected far-flung trade routes and built large cities, canals, highways, and other public works. They also sponsored the spread of major religions, such as Buddhism in India and Christianity throughout the Roman empire.

Eastern Empires

In India, the Maurya dynasty united the states along the Ganges in about 300 B.C. The Hindu faith continued to flourish, but after 500 B.C., followers of a reformer known as the Buddha converted many Indians to Buddhism.

Shi Huangdi unified the states of eastern China around 200 B.C. After that, for most of China's history, the Han and later dynasties ruled a vast united nation. Philosophers like Confucius, as well as Buddhist missionaries, laid the groundwork for many basic Chinese beliefs.

Classical Civilizations of Europe

The earliest European civilizations emerged among the peoples of two neighboring Mediterranean peninsulas. These people were the Greeks and the Romans. The Greeks built a brilliant civilization centered in independent city-states, while the Romans later constructed a huge empire that spanned three continents.

Two earlier societies—those of the sea-trading Minoans and the warlike Mycenaeans—gave way to the Greek city-states before 500 B.C. Led by Athens and Sparta, the bustling little Greek cities traded with many peoples, Athens also developed an early form of democratic government. Though they often

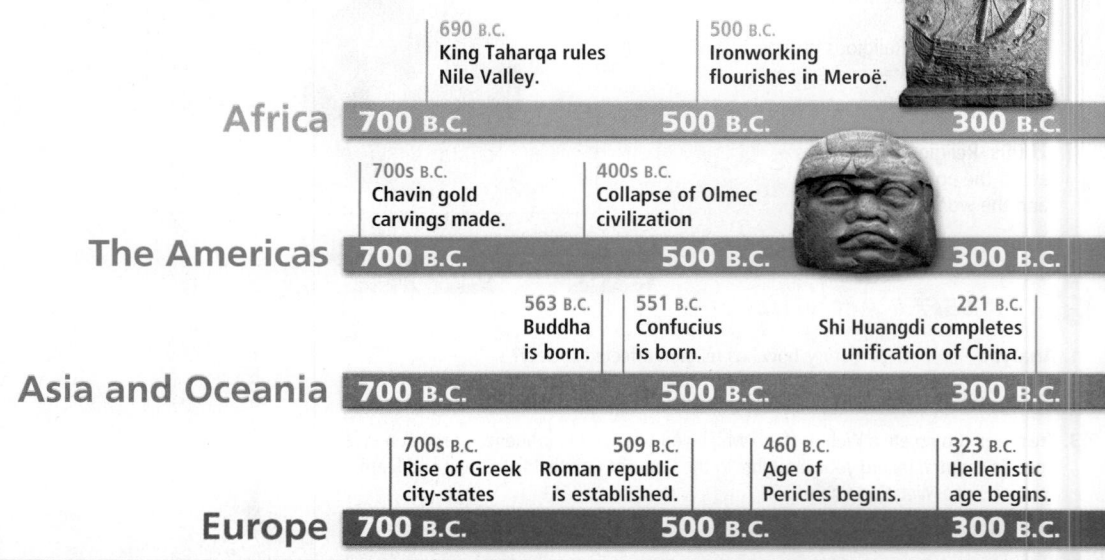

Africa

690 B.C. King Taharqa rules Nile Valley.

500 B.C. Ironworking flourishes in Meroë.

700 B.C.   500 B.C.   300 B.C.

The Americas

700s B.C. Chavin gold carvings made.

400s B.C. Collapse of Olmec civilization

700 B.C.   500 B.C.   300 B.C.

Asia and Oceania

563 B.C. Buddha is born.

551 B.C. Confucius is born.

221 B.C. Shi Huangdi completes unification of China.

700 B.C.   500 B.C.   300 B.C.

Europe

700s B.C. Rise of Greek city-states

509 B.C. Roman republic is established.

460 B.C. Age of Pericles begins.

323 B.C. Hellenistic age begins.

700 B.C.   500 B.C.   300 B.C.

Bibliography

For the Teacher

Adkins, Lesley and Roy A. Adkins. *Handbook to Life in Ancient Rome.* New York: Facts on File, 2004.

Adovasio, J.M. and Jake Page. *The First Americans: In Pursuit of Archaeology's Greatest Mystery.* New York: Random House, 2002

Burger, Richard L. and Lucy C. Salazar, eds. *Machu Picchu: Unveiling the Mystery of the Incas.* New Haven: Yale University Press, 2004.

For the Student

L2 Watkins, Richard. *Gladiator.* Boston: Houghton Mifflin, 1997.

L3 Hall, Eleanor J. *Ancient Chinese Dynasties.* Series: World History. San Diego: Lucent, 2000.

L4 Nardo, Don. *The Rise of Christianity.* Series: Turning Points in World History. San Diego: Greenhaven Press, 1999.

fought with one another, the Greeks created a common body of art, science, and philosophy that laid the foundations of Western civilization.

The Romans learned much from the Greeks. Their expanding empire swept around the Mediterranean and then spread northward across Western Europe. Dominated first by its aristocratic Senate, Rome came to be ruled by powerful emperors after the reign of Augustus Caesar.

During the reign of Augustus, Jesus was born in the region of Judea. Christianity spread widely in Roman times. The new religion survived the fall of Rome to become the core of European culture in later centuries.

American Civilizations

Across the Atlantic Ocean, civilizations also emerged in the Americas. Hunters and food-gatherers gradually settled into agricultural villages. In some regions, religious ceremonial centers emerged, then city-states and empires.

In Mexico, the Maya city-states built magnificent temples and mastered complex mathematics. Peru saw a number of regional empires flourish. In the A.D. 1300s and 1400s, the Aztecs established a pow-erful empire in Mexico, while the Inca built an even larger one in the high Andes of Peru.

Looking Ahead

Some of these mighty empires of Europe, Asia, and the Americas would serve as models for other generations in later centuries. From the Great Wall of China to the Incan royal road through the Andes, these empires left behind impressive monuments. The civilizations of China and India, Greece and Rome, together forged cultural legacies that still influence the world today.

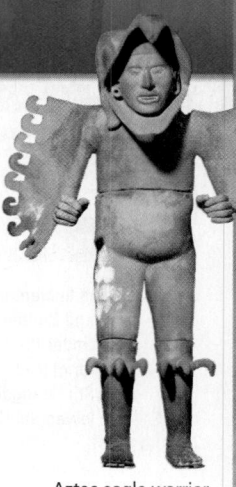

Aztec eagle warrior

Assessment

Choose two events and two pictures from the timeline below. For each, write a sentence explaining how it relates to the themes expressed in the Global View essay.

| 146 B.C. **Destruction of Carthage** | 23 B.C. **Roman attack on Nubia fails.** | | A.D. 350 **Axum converts to Christianity.** |

100 B.C. | **A.D. 100** | **A.D. 300** | **A.D. 500**

| | A.D. 100s **Mochica civilization rises.** | A.D. 200s **Hopewell culture flourishes.** | A.D. 500s **Height of Maya civilization** |

100 B.C. | **A.D. 100** | **A.D. 300** | **A.D. 500**

 | A.D. 100 **Paper is invented in Han China.** | A.D. 370 **Gupta golden age begins.** |

100 B.C. | **A.D. 100** | **A.D. 300** | **A.D. 500**

| 27 B.C. **Pax Romana begins.** | A.D. 135 **Jewish diaspora begins.** | | A.D. 476 **Western Roman empire falls.** |

100 B.C. | **A.D. 100** | **A.D. 300** | **A.D. 500**

Part 2 Resources

- **All in One** Vocabulary Builder; Reading Strategy; Enrichments; Chapter Tests
- AYP Monitoring Assessments
- *ExamView* Test Bank CD-ROM
- Guided Reading Audio (Spanish)
- Student Edition Audio

Previewing Part 2

- **Introduce** Write the question that introduces Part 2 on the board: *What characteristics were shared by ancient empires around the world?* Ask students to predict answers to this question based on the red headings and the timeline. Have them revise their predictions as they read the essay. Tell students to keep this question in mind and to continue to revise their predictions as they read Part 2.

- **Teach** Have students work together in small groups to summarize ideas in the Global View essay. Invite students to share and compare their summaries with those of other groups. For help in summarizing, refer students to the **Skills Handbook,** p. SH4.

- **Analyzing the Visuals** Discuss the timeline with students. Ask **What events happened in Europe around the same time that ironworking flourished in Africa?** *(The Roman republic was established.)* **When did the Gupta golden age begin in Asia?** *(A.D. 370)* Then have students answer the Assessment question.

Have students access **Web Code nbd-0102** for the **Note Taking Study Guide** *Online,* as an alternative to the *Reading and Note Taking Study Guide* booklet.

Answer

Students' sentences should reflect an ability to analyze and classify information in a concise format. For detailed guidelines on assessing student activities, see **Assessment Rubrics.**

Prepare to Read

Build Background Knowledge L3
Ask students to study the titles and illustrations in Part 2. Have them make predictions about what they will learn.

Set a Purpose L3

- **Preview** Have students read aloud the main ideas that begin each section of Part 2. Ask them to summarize these ideas in 3 to 5 sentences.

- **Reading Skill** Have students use the *Reading Strategy: Identify Supporting Details* worksheet. Then have students read this section using the Paragraph Shrinking strategy (TE, p. T20).

  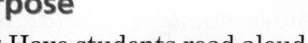 **Teaching Resources, Modern Review Unit**, p. 16

- **Vocabulary Builder** To help students develop vocabulary skills, have them use the *Vocabulary Builder: Make Connections* worksheet.

  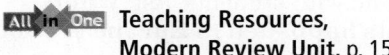 **Teaching Resources, Modern Review Unit**, p. 15

1 Empires of India and China

(600 B.C.–A.D. 550)

Colossal rock sculpture of Buddha

Main Ideas

- In ancient India, two major religions developed—Hinduism and Buddhism.
- Under the Maurya and Gupta empires, India grew into a center of trade.
- Shi Huangdi united all of China. Under the Han rulers who followed Shi Huangdi, Chinese civilization made huge advances.

Between 600 B.C. and A.D. 550, strong, unified empires emerged in India and China. These civilizations established patterns in government, religion, and philosophy that influenced later cultures.

Hinduism and Buddhism

Two major religions, Hinduism and Buddhism, grew in ancient India. Hinduism has no single founder and no single sacred text. It grew from the beliefs of the different groups who settled in India. Even so, all Hindus share certain basic beliefs.

Hindus believe that everything is part of the unchanging, all-powerful spiritual force called brahman. The most important Hindu gods are Brahma, Vishnu, and Shiva. Each can take many forms, human or animal, to represent the various aspects of brahman with which he is associated. The goal of life for Hindus is to achieve union with brahman. **Reincarnation** is the rebirth of the soul in another bodily form. Reincarnation allows people to work toward union with brahman through several lifetimes.

Another major religion, Buddhism, emerged after 500 B.C. While it shared many Hindu traditions, Buddhism differed from Hinduism. It urged people to seek enlightenment through meditation, rather than through the priests, formal rituals, and many gods of Hinduism.

Buddhism's founder was Siddhartha Gautama. He was known as the Buddha, which means the "Enlightened One." The Buddha taught that desire causes suffering. To overcome suffering, people should rid themselves of desire by following the Eightfold Path. The Buddha describes the Eight-fold Path as "right views, right aspirations, right speech, right conduct, right livelihood, right effort, right mindfulness, and right contemplation." Buddhists seek **nirvana**, or union with the universe and release from the cycle of rebirth.

Buddhism spread from India to Sri Lanka and across East Asia and mainland Southeast Asia. After about A.D. 500, however, it gave way in India to Hinduism, which also spread to Sri Lanka.

Powerful Empires of India

For centuries, northern India was a battleground. Then, in 321 B.C., Chandragupta Maurya (chun druh GUP tuh MOWR yuh) forged the first great Indian empire. The Maurya dynasty eventually conquered much of India.

Chandragupta's grandson, Asoka, turned his back on violent conquest and converted to Buddhism. He ruled by moral example. His policies brought peace and wealth. Asoka also paved the way for the spread of Buddhism throughout Asia.

After Asoka's death, rivals battled for power. Despite unrest, India traded with civilizations in Africa, the Middle East, and Central and Southeast Asia. Then, about 500 years after the Mauryas, the Gupta dynasty again united much of India. Under the Guptas, who ruled from A.D. 320 to about A.D. 540, India enjoyed a golden age of peace and achievement.

History Background

Asoka During his rule of Maurya India, Asoka converted to Buddhism, rejected violence, and resolved to rule by moral example. Asoka's conversion to Buddhism was so complete that he extended the Buddhist prohibition of violence to violence against animals. He gave up hunting and banned the slaughter of animals in royal kitchens. Asoka made his personal convictions the law of the land, which he stated in edicts written on stone pillars. On one pillar he proclaimed a list of protected species. It included several kinds of birds and fish and "all four-footed creatures that are neither useful nor edible." It also declared that "one animal is not to be fed to another." On certain Buddhist holidays, horses could not be branded and the sale of fish was prohibited.

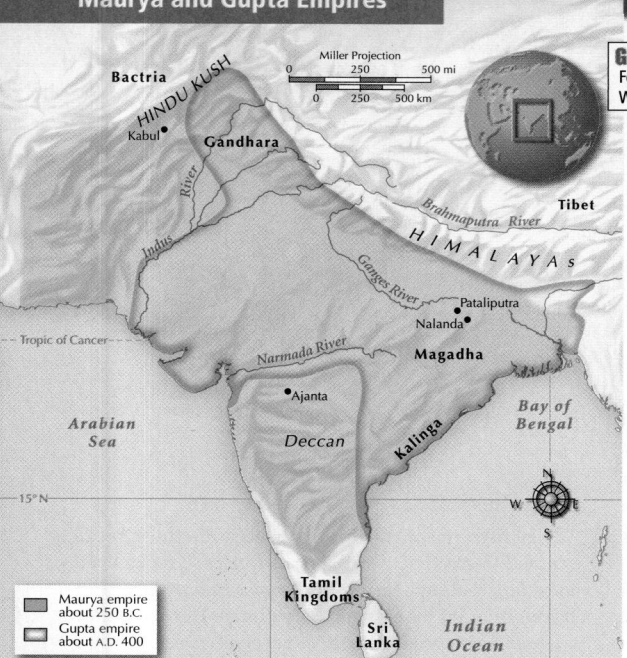

Geography *Interactive,*
For: Audio guided tour
Web Code: nbp-0331

Maurya empire about 250 B.C.

Gupta empire about A.D. 400

Geography and History
India's diverse people were seldom united. Yet the Maurya and, later, the Guptas were able to unite much of the subcontinent.

Pillars of Indian Life Most Indians of that period were village peasants. Then, as today, the village and the family maintained order in daily life. The caste system also greatly influenced Indian society. Caste rules governed every part of life—including where people lived and how they earned a living. Despite its inequalities, caste created a stable social order.

Philosophy and Religion in China

China's most influential philosopher, Confucius, was born in 551 B.C. A brilliant scholar, Confucius took little interest in religious matters. He was concerned with social order and good government. He taught that harmony resulted when people accepted their place in society. He put **filial piety,** or respect for parents, above all other duties. Confucius' ideas came to influence every area of

Chinese life and eventually spread to neighboring countries.

Another Chinese philosopher, Hanfeizi, introduced ideas that differed sharply from the ideas of Confucius. He insisted that the only way to achieve order in society was to pass strict laws and to impose harsh punishments. Hanfeizi's teachings came to be known as Legalism. Many feudal rulers, including the Qin emperor who united China in 221 B.C., believed Legalism was the most effective way to maintain order.

A third philosophy, Daoism, arose around the same time. Daoists sought to live in harmony with nature, rather than to bring order to human affairs. They viewed government as unnatural and therefore the cause of many problems.

Strong Rulers Unite China

When the Zhou dynasty weakened, a powerful new ruler, Shi Huangdi, rose to unify all of China. He spent 20 years conquering the warring states. He built a strong government and set the stage for China's classical age. His most remarkable and costly achievement was the building of the Great Wall.

After Shi Huangdi died, a new dynasty, the Han, was founded. It lasted from 206 B.C. to A.D. 220. Under Han rulers, the Chinese made huge advances in trade, government, technology, and the arts. The Silk Road, which eventually stretched 4,000 miles, linked China to the Fertile Crescent. The Han empire brought 400 years of unity to China.

Assessment

1. **Identify (a)** Siddhartha Gautama **(b)** Confucius **(c)** Shi Huangdi **(d)** the Han dynasty
2. **Define (a)** reincarnation **(b)** nirvana **(c)** filial piety
3. What are two basic teachings of Hinduism?

L4 Advanced Readers   L4 Gifted and Talented

Explain to students that this activity is called "Dear Confucius." After students have learned about Confucius by reading the text, ask them to do additional research on the ideas of Confucius. Then ask them to apply these ideas to modern-day situations. Students should write an advice column with questions for Confucius to respond to. Ask them to apply the ideas of Confucius by crafting a plausible response that Confucius himself might have provided.

Teach

Empires of India and China

- **Instruct** Display **Color Transparency 15: The Spread of Hinduism.** Trace the spread of Hinduism and Buddhism, two important religions. Tell students that both began in India but that Buddhism spread to China as well. Ask students to name modern nations where these religions are prominent.
  Color Transparencies, 15

- **Teach** Have students discuss features of Hinduism and Buddhism, as well as ways that religion and philosophy influenced early empires of ancient India and China. Ask **Why do you think the philosophies of Confucianism and Daoism were able to be absorbed into Buddhism in China?** *(because Buddhism emphasized some of the same ideas as Confucianism and Daoism, such as treating others well and respecting the natural world)*

- **Quick Activity** Show students *Asoka's Elephant Warriors* from the **Witness History Discovery School™** video program. Discuss how Asoka's conversion to Buddhism influenced his rule.

Independent Practice

- **Note Taking** Have students fill in the outline of empires of India and China.
  Reading and Note Taking Study Guide, p. 14

- **Traveler's Tales** Have students complete the worksheet *Zhang Qian and the Origin of the Silk Road.*
   **Teaching Resources, Modern Review Unit,** p. 18

Monitor Progress

Circulate to make sure students understand how the empires of India and China established patterns in government, religion, and philosophy. For a completed version of the outline, see
  Note Taking Transparencies, 104

Answers

1–2. Answers should reflect an understanding of the terms listed.
3. Sample: that everything is part of a spiritual force called brahman; that the goal of life is to achieve union with brahman; and that reincarnation allows people to work toward nirvana through several lifetimes.

- **Introduce: Key Terms** Ask students to find and define the key terms *polis* and *acropolis* (in blue). Point out that the polis was the basic political unit of ancient Greece, as the nation is the basic political unit of our world today.

- **Teach** Ask **How did ideas spread through the Mediterranean region?** *(through trade)* Then trace the development of direct democracy in Athens. Then ask **How did the city-states of Athens and Sparta differ?** *(Athens: limited democracy, only males participated; Sparta: military society, women gained status as men were often at war)* **What factors led to the Hellenistic civilization?** *(Alexander and his armies founded new cities. The conquering Greeks adopted local customs and local people assimilated Greek customs. This blending created Hellenistic culture.)*

- **Quick Activity** Show students *Alexander the Great* from the **Witness History Discovery School™** video program. Then display **Color Transparency 24: Empire of Alexander.** Discuss how Alexander was able to conquer such a large extent of the known world.
  - **Color Transparencies, 24**

2 Ancient Greece

(1750 B.C.–133 B.C.)

Interior vase detail of a Greek hoplite warrior

Main Ideas

- Through trading contacts, Minoan and Mycenaean cultures borrowed many ideas from older civilizations.
- After the Persian Wars, democracy flourished in Athens.
- Guided by a belief in reason, Greek philosophers, writers, and artists used their genius to seek order in the universe.

Unlike many other civilizations, Greek civilization did not rise in a fertile river valley. Instead, it grew in a rugged corner of southeastern Europe. Over time, independent Greek city-states created a civilization that set a standard of excellence for later civilizations. Greek ideas about the universe, the individual, and government still live on in the world today.

Early People of the Aegean

The island of Crete in the Aegean Sea was home to the Minoan people, the earliest civilization in the region. The Minoans were traders who set up outposts throughout the Aegean world and on the Greek mainland. Through contact with Egypt and Mesopotamia, this early people gained ideas and technology that they adapted to their own culture. Minoan civilization reached its height between about 1600 B.C. and 1500 B.C. By about 1400 B.C., Minoan civilization had vanished. A natural disaster may have helped destroy these island people.

The Mycenaeans, another civilization of sea traders, soon dominated the Greek mainland and Crete. They flourished between about 1400 B.C. and 1200 B.C. The Mycenaeans, too, absorbed both Egyptian and Mesopotamian ideas, which they passed on to later Greeks. They are best remembered for the Trojan War. The poet Homer described the conflict in his two epic poems, the *Iliad* and the *Odyssey*. These poems reveal much about the values and religion of the ancient Greeks. The heroes display honor and courage. Such ideals greatly influenced Greek culture. Three thousand years later, the epics of Homer and the ideals of the ancient Greeks continue to inspire us.

The Rise of Greek City-States

When Mycenaean civilization declined, the Greeks seemed to step backward. For centuries, Greeks lived in small, isolated farming villages. Eventually, they began to build many small city-states. However, they frequently warred among themselves. Despite their differences, Greeks shared a common culture, including their language, religion, and festivals. They became skilled sailors and traders. Eventually, Greek colonies took root all around the Mediterranean. Greek ideas and culture spread.

As their world expanded after 750 B.C., the Greeks evolved a unique version of the city-state, called the **polis**. Typically, Greeks built cities on two levels. On a hilltop stood the **acropolis** (uh KRAH puh lis), or high city. There, the Greeks dedicated temples to the gods and goddesses. On flatter ground below lay the walled main city with its marketplace, theater, public buildings, and homes.

Governing the City-States At first, the ruler of the polis was a king. A government in which a king or queen exercises central power is a **monarchy**. Slowly, power shifted to a class of noble landowners. The result was an **aristocracy**, or rule by a landholding elite. As trade expanded, a new middle class of wealthy merchants, farmers, and artisans formed in some cities. They challenged the land-owning nobles for power and came to rule some city-states. The result was a form of government called an oligarchy. An **oligarchy** is government by a small, powerful elite, usually from the business class.

History Background

Training for Boys At age seven, Spartan boys were taken from their mothers and placed in "packs" under the control of a "Warden" of the city-state. They learned to read and write and even to sing and memorize poetry, but the focus of their education was to harden and discipline them for battle by instilling the values of fitness, obedience, and courage. Boys built their own beds from brush using their bare hands rather than knives. They rarely bathed. After age twelve, they received but one cloak to wear each year. Packs of boys were trained to fight each other. Tests of courage were severe, forcing boys to run a gauntlet of whips or to survive alone for a time. Disobedience was severely punished by beatings. The result was that young Spartans learned to obey and respect their laws—which forbade them to flee in battle but to always stand firm: to conquer or die.

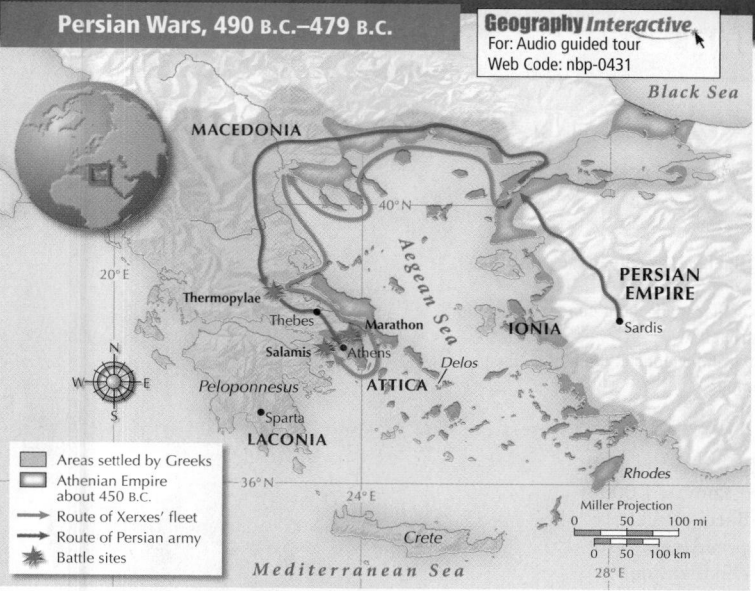

Persian Wars, 490 B.C.–479 B.C.

Geography *Interactive*
For: Audio guided tour
Web Code: nbp-0431

MACEDONIA

Black Sea

40° N

20° E

Thermopylae

Thebes

Marathon

Salamis

Athens

Aegean Sea

IONIA

Delos

Sardis

PERSIAN
EMPIRE

Peloponnesus

ATTICA

Sparta

LACONIA

Rhodes

36° N

24° E

Crete

Miller Projection

0   50   100 mi

0   50   100 km

Mediterranean Sea

28° E

- Areas settled by Greeks
- Athenian Empire about 450 B.C.
- Route of Xerxes' fleet
- Route of Persian army
- ✴ Battle sites

Geography and History
When the Persian empire turned its mighty army against Greece, the Greek city-states briefly joined forces to defend their independence.

Sparta and Athens In the Greek city-state of Sparta, a warrior society took root. Spartan boys trained for military service. Because men were occupied with war, some women gained responsibilities such as running their family's estate. The city-state of Athens evolved into a **democracy**, or government by the people. By modern standards, Athenian democracy was quite limited. Only male citizens participated.

Victory and Defeat in the Greek World When the Persians threatened the Greeks, the city-states briefly joined together to defend themselves. After the Persian Wars, Athens thrived. Under the leadership of Pericles, a Greek statesman who ruled from 460 B.C. to 429 B.C., democracy and culture flourished. Athens developed a **direct democracy**. Under this system, a large number of male citizens took part in the day-to-day affairs of government. Athenian power and influence increased.

The Glory That Was Greece

Greeks had great confidence in the power of the human mind. Many Greek artists, writers, and philosophers denied that events were caused by the gods. Instead, they used observation and reason to find causes for what happened. Philosophers and teachers like Socrates, Plato, and Aristotle developed new ideas about truth, reason, justice, and government. People developed new styles of art and architecture, that reflected those ideas. Philosophers, poets, and dramatists set the standard for what later Europeans called the classic style.

Alexander and the Hellenistic Age

While the Greek city-states warred among themselves, King Philip of neighboring Macedonia built a superb army. Eventually, Philip controlled all of Greece. When he died, his 20-year-old son Alexander took the throne. Over the next 12 years, this confident young man earned the title Alexander the Great. His conquests spread Greek civilization throughout the Mediterranean world and across the Middle East to the outskirts of India.

Alexander's conquests linked a vast area. Greek culture blended with Persian, Egyptian, and Indian cultures to create the Hellenistic civilization. Art, science, mathematics, and philosophy flourished. Even as Greek political power waned, Greek ideas came to dominate the Mediterranean world. This legacy later influenced the civilizations of Rome and Western Europe.

Assessment

1. **Identify (a)** Homer **(b)** Pericles **(c)** Alexander
2. **Define (a)** polis **(b)** acropolis **(c)** monarchy **(d)** aristocracy **(e)** oligarchy **(f)** democracy **(g)** direct democracy
3. What cultural ties united the Greek world?
4. How were Greek city-states governed?
5. Why did many Greek philosophers and writers reject the belief that events were caused by the whims of the gods?

L1 Special Needs   **L2 Less Proficient Readers**

Guide students in using word parts to learn vocabulary. Write the words *aristocracy* and *democracy* on the board. Point out that both words share the suffix *-ocracy,* which means a form of government. Both words then must relate to forms of government. Next, tell students that the Greek word *aristos* means *the best.* Therefore, this word must mean government by the best, or rule by a

L2 English Language Learners

privileged elite. Model this again using the word *democracy.* Ask students to predict what the Greek word *demos* means *(the people).* Ask them to then use the root words to come up with a definition. *(Sample: government by the people, majority rule)* Finally, ask students to use these skills to come up with definitions for the words *oligarchy* and *monarchy.*

Independent Practice

- **Note Taking** Have students fill in the outline describing ancient Greece.

  📄 **Reading and Note Taking Study Guide**, p. 18

- Have students access **Web Code nbp-0431** to take the **Geography Interactive Audio Guided Tour.**

- **Viewpoints** To help students better understand the contrasts between Sparta and Athens, have them read the selection *The Values of Sparta and Athens* and complete the worksheet.

  All in One **Teaching Resources, Modern Review Unit,** p. 19

Monitor Progress

As students fill in their outlines, circulate to make sure they understand the lasting legacies of the Greeks. For a completed version of the outline, see

🏛 **Note Taking Transparencies,** 105

Answers

1. **(a)** Greek poet known for two epic poems, the *Iliad* and the *Odyssey* **(b)** Greek statesman in Athens **(c)** Macedonian king whose vast conquests spread Greek civilization

2. **(a)** Greek city-state **(b)** hilltop city **(c)** government in which a single ruler exercises power **(d)** rule by a landholding elite **(e)** government by a small, powerful elite, usually from the business class **(f)** government by the people **(g)** government in which a large number of people take part in day-to-day affairs of government

3. The Greeks shared the same language, values, festivals, and religion.

4. Each Greek city-state governed itself independently. Some were monarchies; others were oligarchies, aristocracies, democracies, and direct democracies.

5. Many Greek thinkers placed great confidence in the power of the human mind. Using observation and reason, they sought rational explanations for events and developed new ideas about truth.

■ **Introduce** Have students read this section looking for evidence of how Rome's culture resembled or differed from that of ancient Greece. Make a list on the board.

■ **Teach** Point out that the republic was a new form of government in the ancient world. Have students explain how it differed from the Greek system of direct democracy. Then ask **What factors led to civil wars in the Roman republic?** *(New wealth led to corruption.)* **What events marked the end of the Roman republic and the beginning of the Roman empire?** *(Octavian took control and became Emperor Augustus.)* **How did the Romans show their admiration for Greek literature, philosophy, and the arts?** *(They copied and improved upon Greek style in sculpture, architecture, and engineering.)* **What new belief attracted many followers to Jesus?** *(the belief that Jesus was the true messiah who would bring spiritual salvation and eternal life to those who believed in him)*

■ **Quick Activity** Show students *Rome: The Rise of Empire* from the **Witness History Discovery School™** video program. Discuss how powerful emperors helped Rome grow and prosper.

3 Ancient Rome and the Rise of Christianity

(509 B.C.–A.D. 476)

Soldiers and Roman officers of the Praetorian Guard

Main Ideas

● Conquest and diplomacy helped the Romans spread their rule from Spain to Egypt.
● During the Pax Romana, Roman emperors brought peace, order, and prosperity to the lands they controlled.
● Christianity, which began in Roman-held lands in the Middle East, spread throughout the Roman empire.

Rome expanded across the Mediterranean and grew into a huge, diverse empire. Rome's 1,000-year history had many lasting effects. Probably none was more important than the spread westward into Europe of key elements of the civilizations of Greece, Egypt, and the Fertile Crescent.

The Roman World Takes Shape

Rome began as a small city-state in Italy. The Romans were an Indo-European people who settled along the Tiber River in small villages. Their neighbors, the Etruscans, ruled much of central Italy, including Rome. After the Romans threw over the hated Etruscan king in 509 B.C., they resolved never to be ruled by a monarch again. Instead, they set up a **republic,** a government in which officials are chosen by the people. At first, the most powerful people in government were **patricians,** or members of the landholding upper class. Eventually, commoners, or **plebeians,** also gained the right to be elected to the Roman senate.

As Rome's political system changed, its armies expanded Roman power across Italy. By about 270 B.C., Rome occupied all of Italy. Rome's success was due partly to skillful diplomacy and partly to its efficient, well-disciplined army. Furthermore, Rome generally treated its defeated enemies with mercy. By 133 B.C., Roman power reached from Spain to Egypt.

From Republic to Empire

Military victories put the Romans in control of busy trade routes. Incredible riches flooded into Rome from conquered lands. This new wealth, however, had disturbing consequences. Increased corruption and self-interest replaced virtues such as simplicity, hard work, and devotion to duty. Attempts to reform the system led to a backlash. For 100 years, Rome faced a series of civil wars.

Eventually, a powerful Roman general named Octavian restored order. Although he was not called a king, he exercised absolute power. Taking the name Augustus, he ruled from 31 B.C. to A.D. 14, and brought the 500-year-old republic to an end. A new age dawned—the age of the Roman empire.

As Rome's first emperor, Augustus helped the empire recover from the long period of unrest. He laid the foundation for a stable government and undertook economic reforms. The 200-year span that began with Augustus and ended with emperor Marcus Aurelius is known as the Pax Romana, or "Roman Peace." During this time, Roman emperors brought peace, order, unity, and prosperity to the lands under their control. People were able to move easily within the Roman empire, spreading ideas and knowledge.

History Background

The Distraction of Entertainment Throughout the Roman empire, rich and poor alike loved spectacular forms of entertainment. At the Circus Maximus, Rome's largest racecourse, chariots thundered around an oval course, making dangerously tight turns at either end. Fans bet feverishly on their favorite team and successful charioteers were hailed as heroes. Gladiator contests were even more popular.

During the Pax Romana, the general prosperity hid underlying social and economic problems. To the emperors who paid for the amusements with the taxes they collected from the empire, these amusements were a way to pacify the city's restless mobs. In much the same spirit, the government provided free grain to feed the poor. Critics warned against this policy of "bread and circuses," but few listened.

A fish and the cross, symbols of Christianity

The Roman Achievement

Through war and conquest, Rome spread its civilization to distant lands. Yet, the civilization that developed was not simply Roman. Rather, Rome acted as a bridge between the east and the west by borrowing and transforming Greek and Hellenistic achievements. This blend of cultures became known as Greco-Roman civilization.

The Romans greatly admired Greek culture. They took Greek ideas and adapted them to their own ways. Roman sculptors, for instance, used the Greek idea of realism to reveal an individual's character in each stone portrait. Roman architects improved on design elements such as the arch and the dome. Above all, Romans excelled as engineers. They built roads, bridges, aqueducts, and harbors throughout the empire. Many of these remained standing long after Rome fell.

Probably the greatest legacy of Rome was its commitment to the rule of law and to justice. These ideas still shape Western civilization today. The rule of law fostered unity and stability. Roman law would become the basis for legal systems in Europe and Latin America.

The Rise of Christianity

Early in the Pax Romana, a new religion, Christianity, sprang up in Roman-held lands in the Middle East. Its leading figure was a Jew named Jesus. Jesus was born around 4 B.C. in Bethlehem. He was prophesied to be the **messiah,** or savior sent by God to lead the Jews to freedom. The teachings of Jesus were firmly rooted in the Jewish religion. He believed in one God and accepted the Ten Commandments, a collection of laws that Jews believe God gave them.

At the same time, Jesus preached new beliefs. He called himself the Son of God and taught that his mission was to bring salvation and eternal life to all of God's children—anyone who would believe in him. He extended the Jewish ideas of mercy and sympathy for the poor and helpless to include forgiveness and love for enemies.

To some Jews and Romans, Jesus was a dangerous troublemaker. Eventually, he was executed. But his disciples, or followers, believed that Jesus had risen from the dead, talked with them, and then ascended into heaven. Slowly, a few Jews accepted the teaching that Jesus was the messiah, or the Christ, from the Greek for "the anointed one." These people became the first Christians.

For a while, these first Christians remained a **sect,** or small group, within Judaism. But then Paul, a Jew from Asia Minor, set to work to spread the new faith to non-Jews. At first, Rome persecuted Christians. Nevertheless, Christians organized into a church and grew in strength. Eventually, Christianity reshaped Roman beliefs.

The Long Decline

After the death of the emperor Marcus Aurelius in A.D. 180, turmoil rocked the Roman empire. Eventually, the empire split into two parts, east and west, each with its own ruler. In the west, a corrupt government, poverty and unemployment, and declining moral values contributed to the decline. Germanic peoples along the northern borders began to claim territory from the weakened empire. Then foreign invaders marched into Italy and, in 476, took over Rome itself.

But the Roman empire did not disappear from the map. The eastern Roman empire continued to prosper under the emperor Constantine and other emperors. In time, the eastern Roman empire would become known as the Byzantine empire. It would endure for another 1,000 years.

Assessment

1. **Identify (a)** Augustus **(b)** Pax Romana **(c)** Jesus
2. **Define (a)** republic **(b)** patrician **(c)** plebeian **(d)** messiah **(e)** sect
3. Why did Rome change from a republic to an empire ruled by an emperor?
4. Give an example of a Roman achievement that continues to influence Western civilization today.
5. Describe the relationship between Christianity and Judaism.

Independent Practice

■ <u>Note Taking</u> Have students fill in the outline showing the rise and fall of the Roman Empire.

Reading and Note Taking Study Guide, p. 18

■ **Link to Literature** To help students better understand the end of the Roman Empire, have them read the excerpt from Edward Gibbon's *The History of the Decline and Fall of the Roman Empire* and complete the worksheet.

All in One Teaching Resources, Modern Review Unit, p. 20

Monitor Progress

As students fill in their outlines, circulate to make sure they understand how Rome grew from a single city to a huge, diverse empire. For a completed version of the outline, see

Note Taking Transparencies, 106

Answers

1. **(a)** Rome's first emperor **(b)** 200-year span of prosperity and order—the Roman Peace **(c)** the Jewish teacher whose life and teachings gave rise to Christianity
2. **(a)** government in which officials are chosen by the people **(b)** member of the landholding upper class **(c)** commoner **(d)** savior sent by God **(e)** small religious group
3. Wealth corrupted the values of the Romans and a series of civil wars brought turmoil. Eventually an emperor rose to restore order.
4. Some students may mention Roman commitment to the rule of law, or styles of sculpture and architecture.
5. Christianity was founded on the teachings of Jesus, who was a Jew. Christianity grew out of Judaism, extending some of its ideas and adding new ones.

Instruct

- **Introduce** Display **Color Transparency 36: Pueblo Bonito.** Tell students that the Anasazi, but one of the civilizations of the Americas, built these elaborate cliff dwellings. Based on what they already know about early civilizations, have students predict what they will learn about civilizations in the Americas. Then have them read to confirm their predictions.

  🏛 **Color Transparencies,** 36

- **Teach** Create a chart on the board with the headings *Maya, Aztec, Inca, Anasazi,* and *Mound Builders.* Have students volunteer information about each group, focusing on location, time period, religious beliefs, social structure, advances, and achievements. Then ask **What is each civilization best known for?** *(Maya: writing and calendar; Aztecs: complex social structure, rebellious conquered subjects; Inca: quipus, Quechua language, road system; Anasazi: pueblos, cliff dwellings; Mound Builders: giant earthen mounds)*

- **Quick Activity** Show students *The Mummies of Peru* from the **Witness History Discovery School**™ video program. Discuss the insight that mummies and artifacts offer into the lives of the Chiribaya and other early peoples.

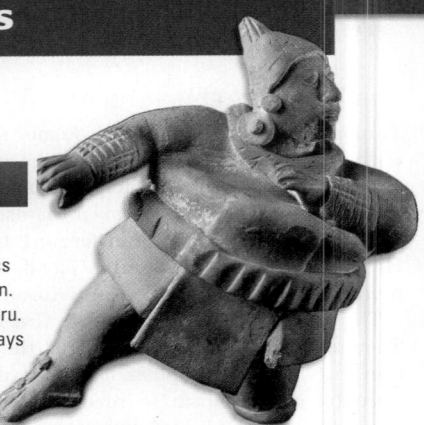

Main Ideas

- Between A.D. 300 and A.D. 900, Maya civilization flourished from southern Mexico through Central America. In the 1400s, the Aztecs conquered most of Mexico and built a highly developed civilization.
- By the 1500s, the Inca established a centralized government in Peru.
- Eight culture groups developed in North America. Their diverse ways of life were strongly influenced by geography.

Mesoamerican ball player

The first American civilization, the Olmecs, began in the tropical forest along the Mexican Gulf Coast. Olmec society lasted from about 1500 B.C. to 500 B.C. Later, other advanced civilizations developed in Mesoamerica and South America, including those of the Maya, Aztecs, and Inca. Diverse groups of people lived in North America.

Civilizations of Middle America

The first settlers in the Americas were nomadic hunters who probably migrated across a land bridge between Siberia and Alaska. Gradually, they populated two vast continents. These early people adapted to a variety of climates and resources. Between 8500 B.C. and 2000 B.C., Neolithic people in Mexico, or perhaps farther south, began to raise a variety of crops, including corn, beans, and squash, and tamed animals.

The Maya Although the Olmec civilization was the first in the Americas, more is known about the Maya city-states of Central America. Maya farmers cleared the rain forests to produce maize, or corn, to feed their cities. Maya society was divided into social classes. Each city-state had its own ruling chief. Priests held great power. Pyramid temples and palaces served as altars and burial places. The Maya developed a hieroglyphic writing system and an accurate calendar. Today, millions of people in Central America speak Maya languages.

The Aztecs Several hundred years after the decline of Maya civilization, the Aztecs conquered most of Mexico. By 1500, the Aztec empire numbered about 30 million people. War brought immense wealth as well as power to the Aztecs. **Tribute,** or payment from conquered peoples, helped the Aztecs turn their capital into a magnificent city.

The Aztecs developed a complex social structure with a single ruler or emperor at the top. A large class of priests performed the various rituals and sacrifices needed to please the many Aztec gods. Conquered peoples often supplied both tribute and human sacrifices for Aztec religious rituals. As a result, the conquered peoples were unhappy and they often rebelled. When armies from Spain later arrived, they found allies among the peoples who were ruled by the Aztecs.

The World of the Inca

In South America, for more than 2,000 years, civilizations rose and fell. Then in the 1400s, the Inca came down from the Andes mountains of Peru. Led by Pachacuti, a skilled warrior and leader, they rapidly conquered an empire that stretched 2,500 miles down the Andes and along the Pacific coast. By the 1500s, the Inca had established a centralized government in Peru, ruled by a god-king and a powerful class of priests.

Inca Government The emperor had absolute power over the Inca empire. He claimed to be divine and lived in splendor. From the capital at Cuzco, he ran an efficient government. His chain of command reached to every village. Specially trained officials kept records on quipus, collections

History Background

The Aztec Capital In A.D. 1325, the Aztecs founded their capital city, Tenochtitlán. According to Aztec legend, the gods had told the Aztecs to search for an eagle holding a snake in its beak and perching atop a cactus. When they saw this sign, they would know where to build their capital. Indeed, they finally saw the sign on a swampy island in Lake Texcoco, and there they built their city. Today, Mexico City sits atop this same site.

As their population grew, the Aztecs found ingenious ways to create more farmland in their lake environment. They built chinampas, artificial islands made of mud piled atop reed mats that were anchored to the shallow lake-bed with willow trees. On these floating gardens, the Aztecs raised maize, squash, and beans.

Ancestral Puebloan cliff dwelling at Mesa Verde, Colorado

of knotted colored strings, which probably noted dates and events as well as statistics.

Inca Achievements The Inca worked to unite their conquered peoples. They imposed their own language, Quechua (KECH wuh), and religion on the people. They also created one of the great road systems in history. It was even more extensive than the roads that united the Roman empire. The Inca roads wound more than 14,000 miles through mountains and deserts. In the 1500s, civil war broke out in the Inca empire. The fighting weakened the empire at the moment that Spanish invaders were about to arrive.

Peoples of North America

Before 1500, many groups of Native Americans with diverse ways of life lived in North America. Regional culture groups in the Arctic, Subarctic, Northwest Coast, California, Great Basin, Plateau, Southwest, Plains, Southeast, and Northeast were strongly influenced by geography.

The Ancestral Puebloans The best-known society of the desert southwest is that of the Ancestral Puebloans. These resourceful people built large villages, later called pueblos by the Spanish, of stone and adobe brick. At the center of their village life was the kiva. A **kiva** is a large underground chamber used for religious rituals. In the mid-1100s, the Ancestral Puebloans began to build housing complexes in the shadow of canyon walls. Cliffs offered protection from raiders. By the late 1200s, drought forced the Ancestral Puebloans to abandon their cliff dwellings. However, their traditions survive today among the Hopi and other Pueblo Indians.

The Mound Builders Far to the east of the Ancestral Puebloans, in the Mississippi and Ohio river valleys, other farming cultures emerged as early as 1000 B.C. The Hopewell people left behind giant earthen mounds in many different shapes. Objects found in Hopewell mounds suggest that trade networks stretched from the Gulf of Mexico to the Great Lakes. By about A.D. 800, this culture was replaced by the Mississippians, who grew corn and other crops. They built large towns and ceremonial centers. Their greatest center, Cahokia in present-day Illinois, housed as many as 20,000 people by about 1100.

Variations in climate and resources encouraged the development of different cultures. In the far north, the Inuits adapted to frozen terrain. Along the Northwest Coast, rich food sources encouraged the growth of wealthy societies. In the Northeast, warring farming villages eventually settled their differences and formed the Iroquois League. This was an alliance of five Iroquois groups who were known as the Five Nations. Member nations governed their own villages but met jointly in a council when they needed to address larger issues.

Assessment

1. **Identify (a)** Olmecs **(b)** Maya **(c)** Aztecs **(d)** Inca **(e)** Ancestral Puebloans **(f)** Mississippians
2. **Define (a)** tribute **(b)** kiva
3. Who ruled the Maya city-states?
4. Describe two steps the Incas took to unite their empire.

Independent Practice

■ **Note Taking** Have students fill in the outline describing the civilizations of the Americas.

    Reading and Note Taking Study Guide, p. 20

■ **Biography** To help students learn more about the political structure of the Aztecs, have them read the biography *Nezahualcoyotl*, about the Aztec poet-king, and complete the worksheet.

    All in One Teaching Resources, Modern Review Unit, p. 21

Monitor Progress

As students fill in their outlines, circulate to make sure they understand how the characteristics of the civilizations of the Americas were similar and different. For a completed version of the outline, see

    Note Taking Transparencies, 107

Differentiated Instruction   Solutions for All Learners

L1 Special Needs   L2 Less Proficient Readers

Have students create flashcards for each civilization in the text. Provide each student with a topic such as architecture, agriculture, art, government, warfare, cities, social life, families, religion, medicine, science, or technology. Give each student five notecards. After reviewing their topic in the text, have them create an

L2 English Language Learners

illustration on one side of the card and two to three bullet-pointed facts on the other. Students should complete five cards, one each for the Maya, Aztecs, Inca, Anasazi, and Mound Builders, and should display and explain their cards to classmates. Explain that students will not find information about every topic for every culture.

Answers

1. **(a)** the first American civilization **(b)** a civilization of independent city-states in Central America **(c)** a highly developed civilization in Mexico **(d)** a civilization that emerged from the Andes Mountain of South America **(e)** early Native Americans of the desert southwest **(f)** early North American farming culture that built Cahokia
2. **(a)** payment that conquered people **(b)** large underground chamber used by the Anasazi for religious rituals
3. a chief
4. They imposed their language and religion on conquered people; they created a complex system of roads.

Assess and Reteach

- Have students use the charts and graphs on this page to review the material.

- For additional review, remind students to refer to the **L3**

  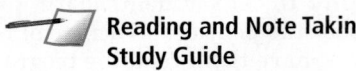 **Reading and Note Taking Study Guide**

  Note Taking Study Guide, pp. 14, 16, 18, 20
  Section Summaries, pp. 15, 17, 19, 21

- When students have completed their study of this section, distribute Tests A and B.

  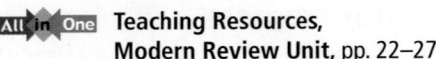 **Teaching Resources, Modern Review Unit, pp. 22–27**

Extend **L4**

Tell students that in different civilizations, road systems and trade routes have played various roles in connecting peoples. Ask student groups to discuss what forms of cooperation have been enabled by the use of roads and trade routes. Ensure they consider the Chinese, the Romans, and the Inca.

Quick Study Guide

■ Philosophies Founded in China

Confucianism	Daoism
• Founded by Confucius	• Possibly founded by Laozi
• Focuses on worldly goals of ensuring social order and good government	• Focuses on living in harmony with nature
• Stresses accepting one's place in society and behaving correctly	• Stresses simple ways of nature and the virtue of yielding
• Views government as responsible for setting a good example for people and for being run by well-educated people	• Views government as unnatural and as a body that should govern the people as little as possible

■ Religions Founded in India

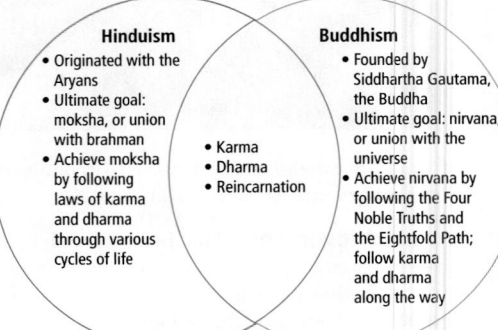

Hinduism
- Originated with the Aryans
- Ultimate goal: moksha, or union with brahman
- Achieve moksha by following laws of karma and dharma through various cycles of life

- Karma
- Dharma
- Reincarnation

Buddhism
- Founded by Siddhartha Gautama, the Buddha
- Ultimate goal: nirvana, or union with the universe
- Achieve nirvana by following the Four Noble Truths and the Eightfold Path; follow karma and dharma along the way

■ Key Greek Political Leaders

Leader	Accomplishments
Solon	Athenian archon who introduced reforms making the government more democratic and the economy more profitable
Pisistratus	Athenian tyrant who gave poor citizens a voice in government and weakened the aristocracy
Cleisthenes	Athenian leader who created the Council of 500 and made the assembly a legislature
Themistocles	Athenian leader who was victorious at the Battle of Marathon
Pericles	Athenian statesman who instituted direct democracy in Athens, increased participation in government, provided salaries for government employees, and encouraged the cultural development of Athens
Philip II	Macedonian king who conquered Greece
Alexander the Great	Macedonian leader who conquered an empire stretching from Greece to India and encouraged the spread of Greek culture throughout his empire

■ Key Roman Rulers

Ruler	Dates	Key Accomplishments
Julius Caesar	100 B.C.(?)–44 B.C.	• Attempted to make reforms to help save the ailing republic • Made himself absolute ruler
Octavian/ Augustus	63 B.C.–A.D. 14	• Declared Exalted One and first citizen by the Senate • First ruler of the Pax Romana
Marcus Aurelius	A.D. 121–A.D. 180	• Last great emperor of the Pax Romana
Diocletian	A.D. 245–A.D. 316	• Divided the empire into two parts, eastern and western
Constantine	A.D. 280 (?)–A.D. 337	• Moved Roman power eastward by building a new capital at Constantinople • Granted toleration to Christians through the Edict of Milan

■ Cultures of North America

Culture Area	Culture Groups
Arctic	Aleut, Inuit
Subarctic	Beaver, Chipewyan, Cree, Ingalik, Kutchin, Montagnais, Naskapi, Ojibwa, Tanaina
Northwest Coast	Apache, Bella Coola, Chinook, Haida, Kwakiutl, Navajo, Nootka, Tlingit
California	Chumash, Maidu, Miwok, Mojave, Pomo, Paiute, Shastan, Shoshone
Great Basin	Paiute, Shoshone, Ute
Plateau	Nez Percé, Spokan, Sushwap
Southwest	Anasazi, Apache, Hohokam, Navajo, Papago, Pima, Pueblos
Plains	Arapaho, Blackfoot, Cheyenne, Comanche, Cree, Crow, Hidatsa, Kiowa, Mandan, Omaha, Pawnee, Sioux, Wichita
Southeast	Calusa, Catawba, Chickasaw, Choctaw, Creek, Delaware, Iroquois, Mississippians, Natchez, Seminole
Northeast	Adena, Algonquins, Hopewell, Iroquois, Micmac, Winnebago

Differentiated Instruction   Solutions for All Learners

L1 Special Needs   L2 Less Proficient Readers

Use the following study guide resources to help students acquiring basic skills:

 **Adapted Reading and Note Taking Study Guide**

- Adapted Note Taking Study Guide, pp. 14, 16, 18, 20
- Adapted Section Summaries, pp. 15, 17, 19, 21

L2 English Language Learners

Use the following study guide resources to help Spanish-speaking students:

 **Spanish Reading and Note Taking Study Guide**

- Spanish Note Taking Study Guide, pp. 14, 16, 18, 20
- Spanish Section Summaries, pp. 15, 17, 19, 21

Concept Connector

GEOGRAPHY'S IMPACT

How do geography and people affect one another?

In This Chapter

Because they lived in vastly different geographic areas, early Americans interacted with their environment in a variety of ways. Mayan farmers burned rain forests to clear the land. High in the Andes, Incas carved out roads to tie their empire together (right) and built terraces to farm. Desert dwellers, like the Hohokam, built irrigation systems.

Throughout History

- **3200 B.C.** Early civilizations begin to develop in river valleys.

- **1300 B.C.** Divided by mountains and water, Greeks live in separate city-states.

- **1800s A.D.** European nations compete to control Africa and its rich resources.

- **1800s** The United States expands westward across the continent.

- **2000s** Oil reserves in the Middle East make the region strategically important.

Continuing Today

Despite modern technology, geography still plays an important role in human activities. This woman is laying down hay barriers to hold back advancing desert sands.

21st Century Skills

❓ *TRANSFER Activities*

1. **Analyze** How has geography influenced history?

2. **Predict** What geographic issues might affect how people live in the future?

3. **Transfer** Complete a Web quest analyzing the impact of geography; record your thoughts in the Concept Connector Journal; and learn to make a video. Web Code nbh-0608

Concept Connector ❓

Geography's Impact

Objectives

- Understand how people shape the land in which they live.
- Describe how geography affects human activity.
- Complete a Web Quest on geography's impact.

Build Background Knowledge

Check students' understanding of the term *geography's impact*. Review students' response to the Warm-Up in the Concept Connector Journal as a starting point for a discussion of the impact of geography on their lives..

Instruct

- Direct students' attention to the essential question: **How go geography and people affect one another?** Tell them to look at the section entitled **In This Chapter.** How did the early Americans change their environment?

- Have students look at the section entitled **Continuing Today** and the corresponding image. Ask them to describe how the picture shows geography and people affecting one another.

- Assign the Web Quest on geography's impact.

Independent Practice

Concept Connector Have students fill in the Web Quest reflection question on geography's impact in their Concept Connector Journal.

 Reading and Note Taking Study Guide, p. 273

Monitor Progress

Circulate to make sure that students are filling in their Concept Connector Journal. Ensure they understand why geography had an impact.

Transfer Activities

1. Geographic features have influenced how and where civilizations have developed, have turned the tide in wars, and have helped shape how people live.

2. Depletion of natural resources, global warming, pollution, erosion, and deforestation are some of the issues that may affect how people live.

3. Students' work should be evaluated against the rubric at Web Code nbh-0608.

23

Technology Resources

- Student**EXPRESS** CD-ROM,
  Modern Review Unit, Part 3

- Teacher**EXPRESS** CD-ROM,
  Modern Review Unit, Part 3

- Presentation**EXPRESS**™
  Premium DVD Modern Review
  Unit, Part 3

- *ExamView*® **Test Bank CD-ROM,**
  English and Spanish, Modern Review
  Unit, Part 3

- **Guided Reading Audio,** Spanish,
  Modern Review Unit, Part 3

- **Student Edition on Audio,**
  Modern Review Unit, Part 3

- **Witness History Discovery School**™
  video program, *The Rise of Feudalism;
  The Black Death; Byzantine Empire;
  Suleiman the Magnificent; Zimbabwe:
  Lost City of Africa; The Samurai of
  Japan*

- **Experience It! Multimedia Pack**

PART 3 A Global View: Regional Civilizations

How Did Regional Civilizations Expand the Scope of World History?

During the period of roughly a thousand years from 500 to 1500, sprawling regional civilizations came to dominate much of the world. Extending beyond the borders of any single empire, regional civilizations linked diverse nations within a shared culture.

Shared Cultures

Sometimes regional civilizations were based on a common religion that spread to a number of neighboring countries. Sometimes a powerful empire would influence its neighbors until they all shared a common regional culture. Sometimes geographic features, such as grassy plains or mountains, influenced all the people who lived there, producing a single regional style of civilization.

Important regional civilizations between 500 and 1500 included Christian Europe, the Muslim zone of Eurasia and North Africa, the trading states of Africa south of the Sahara, and the Chinese sphere of influence in East Asia.

Christendom and Islam

Two of the major regional civilizations that took shape during this period were based on a common religion. These were the civilizations of the Christian and Muslim zones.

Within each of these regions, diverse peoples shared powerful religious beliefs. Both Christians and Muslims felt a duty to spread their religions, and the civilizations that went with them, to neighboring peoples. Both of these crusading faiths, therefore, brought cultural unity to many peoples and nations.

Christianity had already spread around the Mediterranean and westward across Europe in Roman times. During the Middle Ages, the Christian religion and related institutions spread across Eastern Europe as well. These influential medieval institutions included feudalism, the manor system, and the medieval Christian churches, which were the Roman Catholic in the West and the Greek Orthodox in the East.

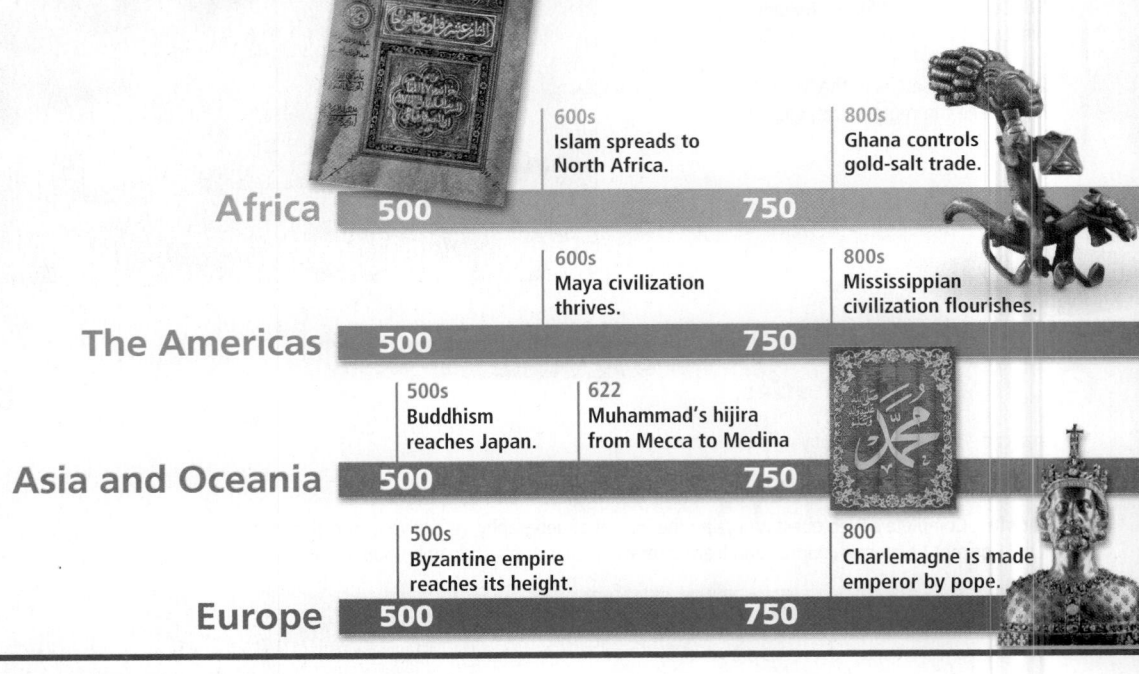

Africa 500 750
- **600s** Islam spreads to North Africa.
- **800s** Ghana controls gold-salt trade.

The Americas 500 750
- **600s** Maya civilization thrives.
- **800s** Mississippian civilization flourishes.

Asia and Oceania 500 750
- **500s** Buddhism reaches Japan.
- **622** Muhammad's hijira from Mecca to Medina

Europe 500 750
- **500s** Byzantine empire reaches its height.
- **800** Charlemagne is made emperor by pope.

Bibliography

For the Teacher

Kelly, John. *The Great Mortality: An Intimate History of the Black Death, the Most Devastating Plague of All Time.* New York: HarperCollins, 2005

Stierlin, Henri. *Islamic Art and Architecture: From Isfahan to the Taj Mahal.* New York: Thames & Hudson, 2002.

For the Student

- L1 Ingram, Scott. *The Song Dynasty.* San Diego: Gale, Blackbirch Press, 2003.

- L2 Macaulay, David. *Mosque.* Boston: Houghton Mifflin, 2003.

- L4 Wood, Frances. *The Silk Road: Two Thousand Years in the Heart of Asia.* Berkeley: University of California Press, 2003.

The Prophet Muhammad proclaimed the Muslim faith in the 600s. Believers spread Islam far across North Africa, western Asia, and parts of southern Europe. With the religion came literacy, cities, long-distance trade, and development in philosophy and art. Islam thus shaped the culture of many peoples, from Muhammad's own Arabian neighbors to the Eurasian steppes, from western Africa to India and Southeast Asia.

Africa and Asia

Other regions of Africa and Asia saw the rise of other kinds of regional civilizations during this period. Across Africa, geography and trade linked many peoples, while in East Asia the influence of China imposed a common culture on a wide region.

In West Africa, peoples of the grasslands built a series of similar kingdoms and empires. All profited greatly from their commercial ties to Muslim traders from the north and the gold mines of the Guinea coast to the south. On the other side of the continent, African rulers and Muslim merchants from the north constructed a string of commercial city-states down the East African coast. These coastal trading cities linked India and China to inner Africa and the Mediterranean.

In East Asia, China's looming power continued to influence surrounding states, especially Korea and Japan. From the Chinese empire, the Japanese and Korean people adapted Confucian philosophy, belief in divine emperors, and the Chinese version of Buddhism, among other things. A common civilization, often described as Confucian, thus united this vast region.

Looking Ahead

Regional civilizations were a step beyond kingdoms and empires. They brought common economic and cultural characteristics to regions that were still too large for political unification. Next, regional civilizations headed toward global interdependence. This step would be taken only after European expansion began in 1492.

Assessment

Choose two events and two pictures from the timeline below. For each, write a sentence explaining how it relates to the themes expressed in the Global View essay.

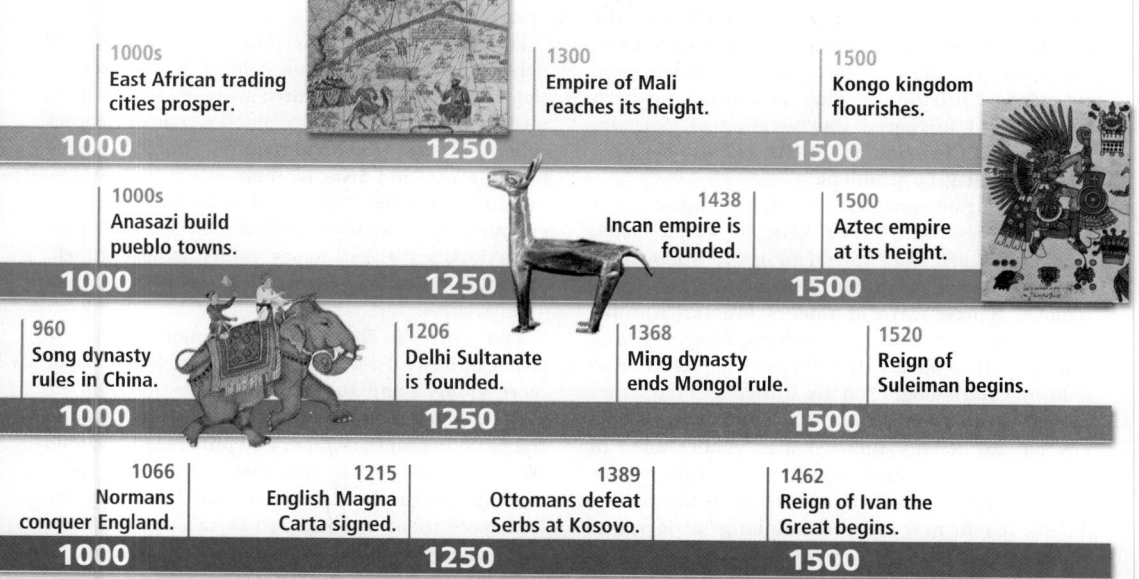

1000s
East African trading cities prosper.

1300
Empire of Mali reaches its height.

1500
Kongo kingdom flourishes.

1000 **1250** **1500**

1000s
Anasazi build pueblo towns.

1438
Incan empire is founded.

1500
Aztec empire at its height.

1000 **1250** **1500**

960
Song dynasty rules in China.

1206
Delhi Sultanate is founded.

1368
Ming dynasty ends Mongol rule.

1520
Reign of Suleiman begins.

1000 **1250** **1500**

1066
Normans conquer England.

1215
English Magna Carta signed.

1389
Ottomans defeat Serbs at Kosovo.

1462
Reign of Ivan the Great begins.

1000 **1250** **1500**

Part 3 Resources

- ■ All in One Vocabulary Builder; Reading Strategy; Enrichments; Chapter Tests
- ■ AYP Monitoring Assessments
- ■ *ExamView* Test Bank CD-ROM
- ■ Guided Reading Audio (Spanish)
- ■ Student Edition Audio

Previewing Part 3

- ■ **Introduce** Write the question that introduces Part 3 on the board: *How did regional civilizations expand the scope of world history?* Ask students to predict answers to this question based on the red headings and the timeline. Have them revise their predictions as they read the essay. Tell students to keep this question in mind and continue to revise their predictions as they read Part 3.

- ■ **Teach** Have students work together in small groups to identify main ideas and details in the Global View essay. Invite students to share and compare their findings with those of other groups of students. For help in identifying main ideas and details, refer students to the **Skills Handbook,** p. SH4.

- ■ **Analyzing the Visuals** Discuss the timeline with students. Ask **Which came first, the Empire of Mali or the Song dynasty?** *(the Song dynasty)* **What happened in Europe around 800?** *(Charlemagne was made emperor by the pope.)* Then have students answer the Assessment question.

Have students access **Web Code nbd-0103** for the **Note Taking Study Guide** *Online,* as an alternative to the *Reading and Note Taking Study Guide* booklet.

Answer

Students' sentences should reflect an ability to analyze and classify information in a concise format. For detailed guidelines on assessing student activities, see **Assessment Rubrics.**

Prepare to Read

Build Background Knowledge ⓛ₃

Ask students to study the titles and illustrations in Part 3. Have them make predictions about what they will learn.

Set a Purpose ⓛ₃

- **Preview** Have volunteers read aloud the main ideas that begin each section of Part 3. Ask them to summarize these ideas in 3 to 5 sentences.

- **Reading Skills** Have students use the *Reading Strategy: Categorize* worksheet. Teach Part 3 using the Guided Questioning strategy (TE, p. T20).

   **Teaching Resources, Modern Review Unit**, p. 29

- **Vocabulary Builder** To help students develop vocabulary skills, have them use the *Vocabulary Builder: Word Maps* worksheet.

   **Teaching Resources, Modern Review Unit**, p. 28

1 The Rise of Europe

(500–1300)

A town charter from King John, 1215

Main Ideas

- In the 800s, a ruler named Charlemagne temporarily reunited much of Europe. He revived learning and furthered the blending of German, Roman, and Christian traditions.
- Feudalism, the manor economy, and the Roman Catholic Church were dominant forces during the Middle Ages.

When Germanic peoples ended Roman rule in the West, they began to create a new civilization. Their culture differed greatly from that of the Romans. They had no cities and no written laws. Instead, they lived in small communities, ruled by elected kings whose chief role was to lead them in war. Europe became a fragmented, largely isolated region.

The Early Middle Ages

Between 400 and 700, Germanic invaders carved Europe into small kingdoms. Then around 800, Western Europe had a moment of unity when Charlemagne (SHAHR luh mayn), or Charles the Great, built an empire reaching across France, Germany, and part of Italy. He revived learning, extended Christian civilization into northern Europe, and furthered the blending of German, Roman, and Christian traditions. He also set up a strong, efficient government.

After Charlemagne died in 814, his empire crumbled. The resultant power struggle, which lasted almost 30 years, came to an end in 843 when Charlemagne's grandsons divided his empire into three regions. A new wave of raiders overran Europe, plundering and looting. Muslims, Magyars, and Vikings all attacked the fragmented territories held by Charlemagne's heirs. Kings and emperors proved too weak to maintain law and order. People needed to defend their homes and lands. In response to that basic need for protection, a new system, called feudalism, evolved. The rise of feudalism led to new networks linking all levels of European society.

Feudalism and the Manor Economy

Under the system of **feudalism**, powerful local lords divided their large landholdings among the lesser lords. In exchange for land and protection, these lesser lords, or **vassals**, pledged service and loyalty to the greater lord. A lord granted his vassal a **fief** (feef), or estate. It included the peasants who worked the land. Feudalism gave a strict order to medieval society.

Feudal lords battled constantly for power. Many nobles trained from boyhood for a future occupation as a **knight**, or mounted warrior. In the later medieval period, knights adopted a code of conduct called **chivalry**. Chivalry required knights to be brave, loyal, and true to their word. In warfare, knights had to fight fairly and be generous to their enemies. Since warfare often meant seizing lands, lords fortified their homes to withstand attack. Medieval strongholds gradually became sprawling stone castles.

The heart of the medieval economy was the **manor**, or lord's estate. Most manors included one or more villages and surrounding lands. Most of the peasants on a manor were **serfs**, who were bound to the land. Peasants could not be purchased and sold like enslaved people, but they spent their lives working for the lord of the manor. In return, the lord gave them the right to farm some land for themselves, as well as protection from invaders.

History Background

The Manor Court The self-sufficiency of the manor extended beyond economic matters to the legal realm. The manor court was usually held in the lord's hall, although the parish church might be used. In some cases, the oldest tree in the village was designated as the official court site. The court had jurisdiction over minor criminal, manorial, and civil matters—serious matters were referred to the king or a higher lord. Criminal matters included stealing wood from the lord's forest, selling underweight bread, poor plowing, or assault. Civil and manorial matters included the choosing of village officials and the recording of changes in land holding, inheritances, and dowries. The manor court was composed mostly of serfs and so afforded some protection against the arbitrary caprice of the lord; those peasants who spoke up often saw justice served.

Ivory carving showing monks at work

The Medieval Church After the fall of Rome, the Christian Church split into an eastern and a western church. The western church, headed by the pope, became known as the Roman Catholic Church. As the Church grew stronger and wealthier, it became the most powerful secular, or worldly, force in medieval Europe. Some Church leaders, including the pope, ruled over their own territories, like feudal lords. Additionally, Church officials were often appointed to high government positions by the ruling nobility because they were the only educated people. Eventually, the pope claimed to have authority over all secular rulers.

By the end of the Middle Ages, Christianity was practiced throughout Europe and by minorities in neighboring parts of Asia.

The Church had considerable power throughout Europe. Christians believed that all people sinned and risked eternal suffering. The only way to avoid eternal suffering was to believe in Christ and participate in church worship. Christians also believed that nobles and kings required the Church's blessing. The Church could control the powerful by threatening to condemn them.

The very success of the church brought problems. As its wealth and power grew, discipline weakened. Throughout the Middle Ages, there were calls for reform in the church.

Economic Expansion and Change By the 1000s, advances in agriculture and commerce spurred economic revival throughout Europe. People used new iron plows to improve farming, and windmills to grind grain into flour. The adoption of the three-field system enabled peasants to expand crop production. New trade routes and goods also increased wealth. Traders and their customers first did business at local trade fairs. Later, merchants settled in local towns and attracted artisans who made goods for them to sell. Soon, towns became trade and manufacturing centers. Merchant guilds, or associations, came to dominate life in medieval towns. In the growing towns, the old social order of nobles, clergy, and peasant gradually changed. By 1000, merchants, traders, and artisans formed a new social class—the middle class. By 1300, Western Europe's economic revival was making momentous changes in medieval life.

A monarch knighting a young man on the battlefield

Assessment

1. **Identify (a)** Germanic tribes **(b)** Charlemagne **(c)** Roman Catholic Church
2. **Define (a)** feudalism **(b)** vassal **(c)** fief **(d)** knight **(e)** chivalry **(f)** manor **(g)** serf **(h)** secular **(i)** guild
3. What effect did Charlemagne's rule have on Europe?
4. How was medieval society organized under feudalism?

- **Introduce** Remind students that lords and the Church often had more power than monarchs under feudalism. Ask students to predict what kinds of power struggles might result.

- **Teach** Trace the rise of conflict between Church, nobles, and monarchs. Ask **How did English kings after William the Conqueror increase royal power?** *(They built a tax-collecting system, strengthened finances and the law, broadened the royal justice system, and developed the basis of common law.)* **Why was the Magna Carta so important?** *(It limited the king's power and, later, the government's power, and it established that ordinary people had some rights.)* **Why did Europeans participate in the Crusades?** *(conquest of the Holy Land)* **How did the Black Death affect the authority of the Church?** *(It weakened Church authority since the Church could not protect people.)*

- **Quick Activity** Show students *The Black Death* from the **Witness History Discovery School™** video program. Discuss the conditions that helped to spread the plague and the effects that the disease had on life in Europe.

2 The High and Late Middle Ages

(1050–1450)

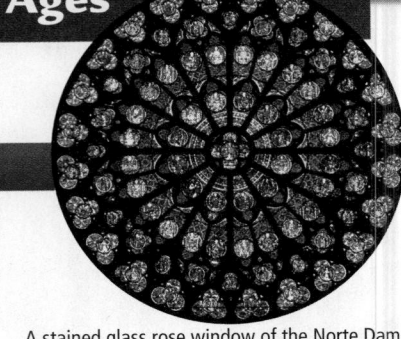

A stained glass rose window of the Norte Dame Cathedral, Paris (above), and a German imperial crown (left)

Main Ideas

- During the High Middle Ages, feudal monarchs began to build a framework for the modern nation-state.
- European contacts with the Middle East during the Crusades revived interest in trade and exploration.
- Beginning in the 1300s, famine, plague, and war marked the decline of medieval Europe.

During the early Middle Ages, hundreds of feudal nobles ruled over territories of varying size. Most were loyal to a king or other overlord, but royal rulers had little power. During the High Middle Ages, feudal monarchs started to increase their power. Slowly, over the next several centuries, these monarchs built the framework for what would become the European nations of today.

Growth of Royal Power in England

When William the Conqueror took the throne of England in 1066, he helped unify England and strengthen the monarchy. William's successors built a system of tax collecting. They also strengthened finances and law. Other English kings broadened the system of royal justice and developed the basis for English **common law,** or law that is based on custom and court rulings. A jury system also developed. A **jury,** or group of men sworn to speak the truth, determined which cases should be brought to trial.

Evolving Traditions As the English kings strengthened the throne, they conflicted with nobles and the Church. Out of those struggles came traditions of government that would influence the modern world. In the early 1200s, a group of nobles checked the growing power of the English kings. They forced King John to sign the Magna Carta, or great charter.

The Magna Carta The Magna Carta contained two basic ideas that in the long run would shape government traditions in England. First, it said that the nobles had certain rights. Over time, the rights that originally had been granted to nobles applied to all English citizens. Second, the Magna Carta made clear that the monarch, like his or her subjects, must obey the law. This included respecting the legal rights of the people. The king also agreed not to raise new taxes without first consulting his Great Council of lords and clergy. Eventually, the Great Council became the Parliament.

The Holy Roman Empire and the Church

The Holy Roman Empire arose from the patchwork of many Germanic states that formed after the death of Charlemagne. When a single ruler united the separate kingdoms, the pope crowned him "emperor." His successors took the title Holy Roman emperor.

During the early Middle Ages, the Church had spread its influence across Europe. By the High Middle Ages, both popes and monarchs were extending their authority. Explosive conflicts erupted. Popes clashed with the Holy Roman emperors who ruled lands from Germany to Italy. Some conflicts arose over who would control appointments to high Church offices. Eventually, some popes claimed the right to remove kings and emperors from the throne. Refusal to obey the Church could possibly result in excommunication. **Excommunication** was a harsh penalty. It meant that

History Background

Effects of the Black Death The significance of the Black Death is not in the outbreak of disease, but in the profound political, social, and economic consequences of high rates of mortality throughout Europe. Short-term consequences included an end to wars, a decline in trade, and a reduction in the amount of land under cultivation. However, the economic depression of the late fourteenth century was a pre-cursor to the creation of a more dynamic European society. The Black Death was a catalyst for the end of the feudal and manorial system. Labor shortages gave serfs and peasants new options as their labor was in high demand. Lords were often forced to offer better terms of service. Both agricultural and urban workers experienced wage increases.

someone could not receive the **sacraments**, or sacred rituals of the Church.

In the 1200s, the Church reached its peak of power. However, during the following century, the papacy entered a period of decline.

Europeans Look Outward

In 1050, Western Europe was barely emerging from isolation. However, several civilizations in the Middle East and Asia had long been thriving political and economic powers. Muslims, as believers in the Islamic faith are called, had built a great empire and created a major civilization. It reached from Spain across North Africa and the Middle East to India.

The Crusades Begin In the eastern Mediterranean, Byzantine civilization was a rival to Islam. The Byzantines were Christians. In the 1050s, Muslim Turks invaded the Byzantine empire. They also attacked Christian pilgrims to the Holy Land, or Palestine, in the Middle East. The Byzantine emperor asked the pope in Rome for help. Soon, thousands of Christians from Europe left for the Holy Land to fight the Muslims. They fought a series of **crusades**, or holy wars.

Effects of the Crusades For 200 years, crusaders marched and fought. For a time, they held parts of Palestine. The Crusades failed in their chief goal—the conquest of the Holy Land. Instead, they left a bitter legacy of religious hatred behind them. However, the Crusades increased European trade, heightened papal power, and increased the power of feudal monarchs. Contacts with the Muslim world also introduced Christians to little-known regions. Europeans also gained access to the scientific and technical knowledge of the Muslim world and other Asian civilizations.

Learning, Literature, and the Arts

As economic and political conditions improved in the High Middle Ages, a revival of learning took place. Schools sprang up around the great cathedrals, eventually becoming the first universities. Ideas and texts that had originated in ancient Greece reached the universities through the works of Muslim scholars. New writings began to be

Pope Innocent III (in red) approving the rules of the friars of Saint Francis (kneeling)

produced in the **vernacular**, or everyday languages of ordinary people. Spain's great epic, *Poem of the Cid,* told of conflict with Islam. Famed Italian poet Dante Alighieri (DAHN tay ah leeg YEH ree) wrote the *Divine Comedy,* an imaginary journey into hell and purgatory.

A Time of Crisis

In the late Middle Ages, a series of disasters struck. Bubonic plague raged throughout the world and eventually throughout Europe. Unsanitary conditions aided the spread of the disease, which was called the Black Death. Approximately one in three people died, more than in any war in history.

The plague brought social upheaval and plunged the European economy to a low ebb. Unable to provide sufficient comfort to people, the Church faced opposition and reform efforts. Famine and war added to the turmoil of the period. Western Europe would not fully recover from the effects of the Black Death for 100 years.

Assessment

1. **Identify (a)** Magna Carta **(b)** Holy Roman Empire **(c)** Black Death
2. **Define (a)** common law **(b)** jury **(c)** excommunication **(d)** sacrament **(e)** crusade **(f)** vernacular
3. What principles were established in the Magna Carta?
4. What were the results of the Crusades?

Answers

1. **(a)** the great charter; it contained key ideas that shaped English government **(b)** German states united by a single ruler who was crowned emperor by the pope **(c)** bubonic plague
2. **(a)** law that is the same for everyone **(b)** group of citizens sworn to speak the truth **(c)** most serious penalty for disobedience to the Roman Catholic Church **(d)** sacred ritual of the Roman Catholic Church **(e)** holy war **(f)** everyday language of ordinary people
3. All nobles (and, later, all English citizens) had certain rights; the monarch must obey the law.
4. increased trade, increased power for the pope and monarchs, increased knowledge of the world outside of Europe.

Instruct

- **Introduce** Ask volunteers to read the Main Ideas on the student page aloud. Then ask students to predict which aspects of Greco-Roman culture might have been the most influential in the Byzantine empire. Have them revise their list as they read.

- **Teach** Discuss the expansion and contraction of the Byzantine Empire. Ask **What was one of Justinian's most important contributions?** *(created Justinian's Code to organize laws of ancient Rome.)* **What was the lasting impact of the Russian rulers, Ivan the Great and Ivan the Terrible?** *(They established authoritarian rule in Russia.)* **What people migrated into Eastern Europe during its early development?** *(Slavs from Russia, large groups from Asia, Germans, and Jewish settlers)*

- **Quick Activity** Show students *Byzantine Empire* from the **Witness History Discovery School™** video program. Ask them to describe how the Byzantine Empire preserved Greek and Roman culture.

3 The Byzantine Empire and Russia

(330 –1613)

Empress Theodora

Main Ideas

- After the fall of Rome, Greco-Roman heritage survived in the Byzantine empire.
- Traders and missionaries brought Byzantine culture and Eastern Orthodox Christianity to Russia and Eastern Europe.
- Invasions and migrations created a mix of ethnic and religious groups in Eastern Europe.

The fall of Rome left Europe divided. To the west, medieval civilization began to grow. To the east, the Roman empire survived as the Byzantine empire. Byzantine civilization later influenced Eastern Europe and Russia, bringing Greek culture and Eastern Orthodox Christianity to the region.

The Byzantine Empire

As German invaders pounded the Roman empire in the west, emperors moved their base to the eastern Mediterranean. By 330, the emperor Constantine had rebuilt the Greek city of Byzantium. He renamed it Constantinople. In time, the eastern Roman empire became known as the Byzantine empire. During the Middle Ages, Constantinople thrived, controlling key trade routes that linked Europe and Asia.

Justinian's Code The most famous Byzantine emperor was Justinian, who ruled from 527 to 565. He was aided by his wife, Theodora. Justinian set up a commission to collect and organize the laws of ancient Rome. The result was known as Justinian's Code. By the 1100s, Justinian's Code had reached Western Europe, influencing the laws and principles of the Roman Catholic Church as well as medieval monarchs. The code thus preserved and spread the heritage of Roman law.

Byzantine Christianity As in Western Europe, Christianity was important in the Byzantine empire. But a division grew between Byzantine Christians and Roman Catholics. In the Byzantine empire, the emperor controlled Church affairs, rejecting the pope's claim to authority over all Christians. Further, Byzantine clergy retained the right to marry. By 1054, a number of such controversies caused a schism, or permanent split, between the Eastern (Greek) Orthodox and Roman Catholic churches.

By the time of the schism, the Byzantine empire was declining. In 1453, Constantinople fell to the Ottoman empire. The ancient Christian city, renamed Istanbul, eventually became a great center of Muslim culture.

Byzantine Heritage For 1,000 years, Byzantine civilization had thrived, blending Christian beliefs with Greek science, philosophy, arts, and literature. The Byzantines also expanded upon Roman achievements in engineering and law. When the empire fell in the 1400s, Greek scholars left Constantinople to teach at Italian universities. They took valuable Greek manuscripts to the West. They also brought their knowledge of Greek and Byzantine culture. The work of these scholars contributed to the European cultural flowering known as the Renaissance.

The Rise of Russia

The early history of Russia began in the fertile area of present-day Ukraine. During Roman times, a people called the Slavs lived in this area. Then, in the 700s and 800s, the Vikings began to travel on Russian rivers, trading and collecting tribute from the Slavs. The Vikings also traded with Constantinople. Eventually, the city of Kiev in Ukraine became the center of the first Russian state. Kiev served as a vital trade center.

Connect to Our World

Connections to Today Today, Moscow is the capital of Russia and covers 386 square miles. At the center of the city stands the Kremlin, a fortified red-brick enclosure crowned by 20 towers. The Kremlin was built by Italians at the invitation of Ivan the Great in the fifteenth century. Russians across the country set their clocks and watches to the radio broadcast of the chiming of the clock in the belfry of the Savior Tower. The leading industries in Moscow today are engineering and metalworking, and the city boasts several notable vehicle production plants. Moscow is also home to the famous Gum department store, which traces its roots back to medieval trade fairs.

Growth of Russia, 1300–1584

Geography *Interactive*
For: Audio guided tour
Web Code: nbp-0921

Moscow, about 1300
Land added, 1300–1462
Land added, 1462–1533
Land added, 1533–1584
Empire of the Golden Horde, 1300
Battle site

Geography and History
Between 1300 and 1584, the lands ruled by Russian princes and tsars grew from a small area around Moscow to a large area in Asia and Eastern Europe.

Trade brought Kiev into the Byzantine sphere of influence. Constantinople eventually sent missionaries to convert the Slavs to Christianity. About 863, two Greek monks adapted the Greek alphabet so they could translate the Bible into Slavic languages. This alphabet became the written script still used in Russia and Ukraine. A class of educated Russian priests grew. Russians adapted Byzantine art, music, and architecture.

The Mongol Conquest In the early 1200s, the Mongols of central Asia overran land from China to Eastern Europe. Though they were fierce conquerors, the Mongols were generally tolerant rulers. But the absolute power of the Mongols served as a model for later Russian rulers. Mongol rule also cut Russia off from Western Europe at a time when Europeans were making rapid advances in the arts and sciences.

Rise of Moscow Eventually, the princes of Moscow gained power and defeated the Mongols. Between 1462 and 1505, Ivan III, known as Ivan the Great, brought much of northern Russia under his rule. He and his successors took the title tsar,

the Russian word for Caesar. Ivan III built the framework for absolute rule. His grandson, Ivan IV, further centralized royal power and introduced Russia to a tradition of extreme absolute power that earned him the title "Ivan the Terrible."

Shaping Eastern Europe

In Eastern Europe, no single ethnic group dominated the region. An **ethnic group** is a large group of people who share the same language and cultural heritage. Over time, many groups settled in Eastern Europe. In the early Middle Ages, the Slavs spread across Eastern Europe. Waves of Asian peoples moved into the area, among them the Huns, Avars, Bulgars, Khazars, and Magyars. Germanic people added to the mix.

Later, Byzantine missionaries carried Eastern Orthodox Christianity, as well as Byzantine culture, throughout the Balkans. At the same time, German knights and missionaries spread Roman Catholic Christianity to the area. In the late Middle Ages, Eastern Europe was a refuge for many Jewish settlers when Western European Christians persecuted them.

Many kingdoms and small states arose in Eastern Europe. Poland often had to battle Germans, Russians, and Mongols to survive. The Magyars of Hungary controlled parts of present-day Slovakia and Romania. By the late 1100s, the Serbs built a kingdom in the Balkan peninsula. By the 1500s, however, the Ottoman Turks ruled over much of southeastern Europe.

Assessment

1. **Identify (a)** Constantinople **(b)** Justinian **(c)** Kiev **(d)** Ivan III
2. **Define (a)** schism **(b)** tsar **(c)** ethnic group
3. Describe the legacy of Byzantine civilization.
4. What element of Mongol rule continued to influence the tsars, even after they ousted the Mongols from Russia?

Independent Practice

- **Note Taking** Have students fill in the outline describing important events of the Byzantine empire and the rise of Russia.

  Reading and Note Taking Study Guide, p. 26

- Have students access **Web Code nbp-0921** to take the **Geography Interactive Audio Guided Tour.**

- **Biography** To help students better understand the power of Russian monarchs, have them read the biography *Ivan the Great* and complete the worksheet.

  All in One Teaching Resources, Modern Review Unit, p. 32

Monitor Progress

As students fill in their outlines, circulate to make sure they understand important events of the Byzantine empire and the rise of Russia For a completed version of the outline, see

Note Taking Transparencies, 110

Answers

1. **(a)** the Greek city of Byzantium, which the Roman Emperor renamed after himself and made the eastern capital of the empire **(b)** Byzantine emperor who set up a code of laws **(c)** important early city and trade center in the Ukraine **(d)** the first Russian tsar, also called Ivan the Great
2. **(a)** a permanent division in a church **(b)** title of the ruler of the Russian empire **(c)** large group of people who share the same language and cultural heritage
3. Byzantine civilization blended Christian beliefs with Greek science, philosophy, arts, and literature, influencing the cultures of Russia and Eastern Europe. It also preserved Roman law and the classic works of ancient Greece.
4. The Mongol rulers had exercised absolute power. Russian tsars followed this model and set the framework for their own absolute rule.

Muslim Civilizations ⓛ

Instruct

- Display **Color Transparency 63: Spread of Islam.** Explain that Islam spread from the Arabian peninsula to the Indus Valley after the death of Muhammad in 632.

  📖 **Color Transparencies,** 63

- **Teach** Discuss the key features of Islam. Ask **What are the Five Pillars of Islam?** *(belief in one God, daily prayer, charity to the poor, fasting, and the hajj)* **What are some key accomplishments of Muslim civilization's golden age?** *(algebra; contributions to astronomy, philosophy, medicine, and art; architecture such as domed mosques)* **Who were the Muslims who invaded India?** *(Turkish and Afghan warriors)* **What city did the Ottomans seize and what did they call it?** *Constantinople; Istanbul)*

- **Quick Activity** Show students *Suleiman the Magnificent* from the **Witness History Discovery School™** video program. Discuss how under Suleiman, the Ottoman Empire reached the height of its power and prestige.

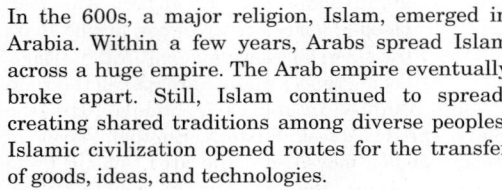

4 Muslim Civilizations

(622–1629)

Main Ideas

- The religion of Islam emerged on the Arabian peninsula in the 600s.
- Muslim civilization eventually created cultural ties among diverse peoples across three continents.
- By the 1500s, the Mughals, Ottomans, and Safavids dominated the Muslim world.

Muslim scholars studying with the Greek philosopher Aristotle

In the 600s, a major religion, Islam, emerged in Arabia. Within a few years, Arabs spread Islam across a huge empire. The Arab empire eventually broke apart. Still, Islam continued to spread, creating shared traditions among diverse peoples. Islamic civilization opened routes for the transfer of goods, ideas, and technologies.

Rise of Islam

Muhammad, the prophet of Islam, was born in Mecca in western Arabia about 570. According to Muslim belief, Muhammad was called in a vision to become the messenger of God. He spent the rest of his life spreading Islam. Eventually, thousands of Arabs embraced the new religion.

Like Judaism and Christianity, Islam is monotheistic. Muslims believe in one all-powerful, compassionate God. All Muslims accept five basic duties, known as the Five Pillars of Islam. They include belief in one God, daily prayer, charity to the poor, fasting, and the **hajj**, or pilgrimage to Mecca. Muslims also hold that the Quran contains the sacred word of God and is the final authority on all matters. Over time, Muslim scholars have applied the teachings of the Quran to every aspect of daily life. In this way, Islam is both a religion and a way of life.

Islam Spreads

When Muhammad died in 632, Abu Bakr was elected to be the first **caliph**, or successor to Muhammad. He launched a breathtaking military campaign to conquer territory across the Byzantine and Persian empires. A key reason for the Arabs'

swift and wide-ranging conquests was their belief in the holiness of their faith and certainty of paradise for those who fell in battle.

A series of rulers led the conquests that carried Islam from the Atlantic to the Indus Valley. Eventually, the Abbasid dynasty moved the capital of Islam to Baghdad and ruled until 1258. Under the Abbasids, Baghdad exceeded Constantinople in size and wealth. But as the 1200s drew to a close, the Arab empire had fragmented and fallen. Independent Muslim caliphates and states were scattered across North Africa and the Iberian peninsula in Europe, while Mongol converts to Islam ruled the Muslim Middle East.

Golden Age of Muslim Civilization

The advancing Muslim empire united people from diverse cultures, blending the cultures of Arabs, Persians, Africans, and Europeans. Muslim society was more open than that of medieval Europe. People could advance in society, especially through religious, scholarly, or military achievements. Muslim leaders imposed a tax on non-Muslims but allowed Christians, Jews, and others to practice their own faiths. Many non-Muslims converted to Islam. In later centuries, Turkish and Mongol converts helped spread Islam far across Asia.

Between 750 and 1350, Muslim merchants established a vast trading network. Islamic ideas, products, and technology spread across the Muslim world and beyond. Muslims pioneered the study of algebra and made contributions in the fields of astronomy, philosophy, and literature, as well as advances in medicine. Islamic art reached new heights. Artisans developed elaborate mosaics of

History Background

Quran *Quran* means "recitation," and Muhammad orally recited the words as they were revealed to him. They were later written down by his followers. The Quran contains rhymed or semi-rhymed verses whose grace and poetry are difficulty to translate. Devout Muslims try to memorize the entire book. Before touching the Quran, Muslims ritually cleanse and prepare in mind, body, and spirit. Veneration of the Quran is also expressed in the ornate calligraphy and decoration of each page. The Quran includes the teachings of earlier Jewish and Christian prophets such as Noah, Moses, Abraham, Solomon, Jesus, and John the Baptist. Many Qurans have a wide margin so readers may turn the pages without touching the words. The leather cover also protects the holy book from damage.

The Arabian Peninsula

Miller Projection
0   200   400 mi
0   200 400 km

- Muslim lands by 632
- Boundary of Byzantine empire
- → Route of Hijra

BYZANTINE EMPIRE
Syria
Jerusalem
PERSIAN EMPIRE
Tigris R.
Euphrates R.
Arabian Desert
Red Sea
Persian Gulf
Medina
Mount Hira
Mecca
ARABIAN PENINSULA
Rub Al Khali (Empty Quarter)
Yemen
Arabian Sea
Gulf of Aden
Nile R.
20° N
40° E
50° E
10° N

Geography *Interactive*
For: Audio guided tour
Web Code: nbp-0141

Geography and History
Fleeing persecution in Mecca in 622, Muhammad and his followers journeyed to Medina. By the time of his death in 632, thousands had adopted Islam.

abstract and geometric patterns. In the field of architecture, domed **mosques,** or houses of worship, came to dominate Muslim cities. Baghdad became a great Muslim center of learning.

Muslims in India

About 1000, Turkish converts to Islam began making raids into India. A Muslim **sultan,** or ruler, defeated Hindu armies in the late 1100s. He set up a capital in Delhi. His successors founded the Delhi sultanate, which lasted from 1206 to 1526.

Muslims and Hindus Muslim rule brought changes to India. Widespread destruction of Buddhist monasteries contributed to the decline of Buddhism as a major religion in India. Many Hindus were killed. Eventually, Muslim rulers grew more tolerant and Indian Muslims absorbed elements of Hindu culture.

Mughal India In 1526, Turkish and Mongol invaders again poured into India. At their head rode Babur. He swept away the remnants of the Delhi sultanate and set up the Mughal dynasty, which ruled from 1526 to 1857. In the late 1600s, economic hardship sparked rebellions against the Mughal dynasty. Eventually, European traders began to work against the once-powerful Mughal empire.

The Ottoman and Safavid Empires

While the Mughals ruled India, two other dynasties, the Ottomans and the Safavids, dominated the Middle East and parts of Eastern Europe. All three empires owed much of their success to new weapons, including cannons and muskets.

The Ottoman Empire The Ottomans were Turkish-speaking nomadic people who had migrated from Central Asia. In the 1300s, they moved across Asia Minor and into the Balkans. In 1453, they captured Constantinople and renamed it Istanbul. The Ottoman empire was a powerful force for 500 years. Under the sultan Suleiman (soo lay MAHN), who ruled from 1520 to 1566, the Ottoman empire enjoyed its golden age. Ottoman poets adapted Persian and Arab models to produce works in the Turkish language. Painters produced detailed miniatures and illuminated manuscripts. Architects designed hundreds of mosques and palaces. At its height, the empire stretched from Hungary to Arabia and Mesopotamia and across North Africa.

The Safavid Empire By the 1500s, the Safavids (sah FAH vidz), a Turkish-speaking Muslim dynasty, had united a strong empire in present-day Iran. The outstanding Safavid ruler, Shah Abbas the Great, ruled from 1588 to 1629. Abbas revived the glory of ancient Persia. His capital became a center for the international silk trade. In the late 1700s, a new dynasty, the Qajars (kuh JAHRZ) won control of Iran. They ruled until 1925.

Assessment

1. **Identify (a)** Muhammad **(b)** Baghdad **(c)** Mughal dynasty **(d)** Ottoman empire
2. **Define (a)** hajj **(b)** caliph **(c)** mosque **(d)** sultan
3. What are some of the teachings of Islam?
4. How did Islam spread far beyond Arabia so quickly?

Independent Practice

- **Note Taking** Have students fill in the outline describing Muslim civilizations.
  Reading and Note Taking Study Guide, p. 28
- Have students access **Web Code nbp-0141** to take the **Geography Interactive Audio Guided Tour.**
- **Link to Literature** To help students learn more about the Quran, have them read the excepts from it and answer the questions on the worksheet.
  All in One Teaching Resources, Modern Review Unit, p. 33

Monitor Progress

As students fill in their outlines, circulate to make sure they understand the key ideas of Islam and the accomplishments and the spread of Muslim civilization. For a completed version of the outline, see

Note Taking Transparencies, 111

Answers

1. **(a)** founder of Islam **(b)** early capital of Islam **(c)** Islamic dynasty that conquered and ruled India from 1526 to 1857 **(d)** an Islamic empire that captured Constantinople and was powerful for 500 years.
2. **(a)** pilgrimage to Mecca **(b)** successor to Muhammad **(c)** Muslim house of worship **(d)** Muslim ruler
3. There is one God; Muslims should pray daily, fast, give to the poor, and make a pilgrimage to Mecca; and the Quran is the word of God as revealed to Muhammad.
4. Muslim armies conquered regions from the Atlantic Ocean to the Indus River and many people converted to Islam. Also, Muslim traders spread Islam peacefully.

- **Introduce** Ask students what they would do if they had too much of one item and not enough of another. Guide students to see that this situation often leads to trade. Ask students to predict how trade might influence the cultures of Africa.

- **Teach** Discuss the impact of trade on kingdoms in Africa. Ask **How did trade affect Nubia and North Africa?** *(Trade brought contact with other regions, peoples, and ideas.)* **What were the most important goods traded in West Africa and why?** *(gold and salt; gold could be traded to Europeans, salt was needed for health in the hot climate.)* **How was Axum's trade network similar to those in West Africa?** *(Both linked Africa to the Mediterranean world; both connected the interior to coastal regions.)* **What is the difference between a nuclear family and an extended family?** *A nuclear family consists of the parents and their children; an extended family includes grandparents, aunts, uncles, etc.)*

- **Quick Activity** Show students *Zimbabwe: Lost City of Africa* from the **Witness History Discovery School**™ video program. Discuss how archaeologists have determined that Great Zimbabwe was the center of a thriving African culture.

5 Kingdoms and Trading States of Africa

(730 B.C.–A.D. 1591)

Bronze plaque of Benin warriors in their battle dress

Main Ideas

- Between 800 and 1600, a series of powerful West African kingdoms controlled the rich Sahara trade route.
- Indian Ocean trade routes led to the growth of wealthy city-states along the East African coast.

Vast migrations of people have contributed to the rich diversity of African cultures. One such series of migrations, called the Bantu migrations, probably occurred because of changes in the environment. Over a period of a thousand years, Bantu-speakers from West Africa moved south and east to populate most of southern Africa. Today, as many as one third of Africans speak a language in the Bantu family.

Early Civilizations of Africa

Long before the Bantu migrations, important civilizations rose and flourished in Africa. While ancient Egyptian civilization developed in Northern Africa, another Nile civilization—called Nubia, or Kush—took shape to the south.

The Kingdom of Nubia For thousands of years, powerful kings and queens reigned over Nubia. From time to time, the Egyptians to the north conquered the land, but Nubians always regained their independence. As a result of conquest and trade, Nubian rulers adopted many Egyptian traditions. By 500 B.C., Nubian rulers moved their capital to Meroë (MEHR oh ay), a thriving trade center. Meroë produced iron for tools and weapons. Finally, about A.D. 350, invading armies from the neighboring African kingdom of Axum overran the kindom of Nubia.

North Africa Unlike Nubia, North Africa and Egypt were ruled, for a time, by the Greeks and then the Romans. Under Roman rule, Christianity spread to the cities of North Africa. Islam eventually replaced Christianity as the main religion of the region. North Africa benefited from the blossoming of Muslim civilization. Linked into a global trade network, North African ports did a busy trade in grain, wine, ivory, and gold.

Kingdoms of West Africa

By A.D. 100, settled farming villages on the western savannas were expanding. Soon trade networks linked the savanna to forest lands in the south and then sent goods across the Sahara.

By A.D. 200, camels, brought to North Africa from Asia, had revolutionized trade across the Sahara. Camel caravans created new, profitable trade networks. Gold and salt were the major products. North Africans sought gold to trade in exchange for European goods. West Africans traded gold to North Africans in exchange for an equally valuable item, salt. People need salt in their diet to stay healthy, especially in hot, tropical areas.

The Kingdom of Ghana By A.D. 800, the rulers of the Soninke people had united many farming villages to form the kingdom of Ghana. The king controlled gold-salt trade routes across West Africa. So great was the flow of gold that Arab writers called Ghana "land of gold." Over time, Muslim merchants established Islam in Ghana.

History Background

Timbuktu An African proverb said that "Salt comes from the north, gold from the south, and silver from the country of white men, but the word of God and the treasures of wisdom are to be found only in Timbuktu." Timbuktu was an important learning center for Muslims of Africa and beyond. The city's scholars, many of whom had studied in Mecca or Egypt, attracted students from diverse areas. But as a result of the Moroccan conquest of Songhai, Timbuktu suffered a rapid decline. The new Moroccan rulers doubted the loyalty of the city's scholars and ordered that they be arrested. Some were killed and many others were exiled. For years thereafter, Timbutktu continued to experience invasions and instability, and its importance as an educational center declined.

African Kingdoms and Trading States

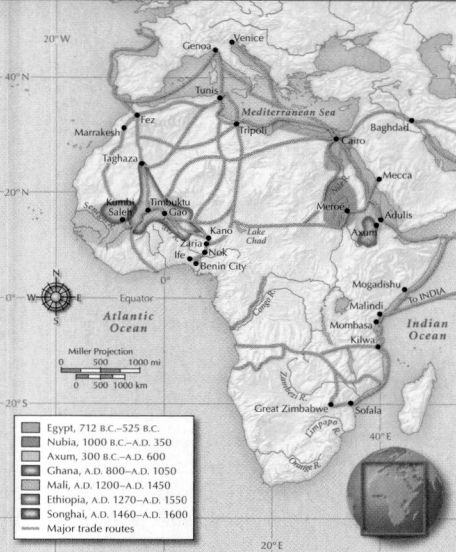

Geography *Interactive*
For: Audio guided tour
Web Code: nbp-1121

Geography and History
From 1000 B.C. in Nubia to the 1500s in Songhai, Africans built strong kingdoms in East and West Africa. Many of which developed because of profitable trade with other lands.

Muslim art, technology, and philosophy were influential as well. When the empire of Ghana declined in the late 1100s, it was swallowed up by a new rising power, the kingdom of Mali.

The Kingdom of Mali Mali emerged by 1250. It controlled both the gold-mining regions to the south and the salt supplies of the Sahara. The greatest emperor of Mali was Mansa Musa (MAHN sah MOO sah), who came to the throne in 1312. Musa expanded Mali's borders. A convert to Islam, Musa journeyed to Mecca in 1324 to fulfill the hajj. Musa's pilgrimage forged new ties with Muslim states and brought scholars and artists to Mali.

The Kingdom of Songhai As Mali weakened in the 1400s, a new West African kingdom, Songhai (SAWNG hy), arose. Songhai forged the largest state that had ever existed in West Africa. The kingdom controlled trade routes and wealthy cities like Timbuktu, a leading center of learning. Songhai prospered until about 1586. At that time, civil war and invasion weakened and splintered the empire.

Trade Routes of East Africa

By the time the kingdom of Axum conquered Nubia about A.D. 350, Axum had long been an important trading center. Located southeast of Nubia, Axum linked trade routes between Africa, India, and the Mediterranean world. A powerful Axum king converted to Christianity in the 300s. At first, Christianity strengthened Axum's ties to the Mediterranean world. However, in the 600s, Islam came to dominate North Africa, leaving Axum an isolated island of Christianity. Over time the kingdom of Axum slowly declined.

As Axum declined, a string of trading cities gradually rose along the East African coast. Since ancient times, traders had visited this coast. In the 600s, Arab and Persian merchants set up Muslim communities under the protection of local African rulers. By 1000, port cities were thriving from trade across the Indian Ocean.

Societies in Medieval Africa

Factors such as Africa's varied geography, diverse climates, and later migration and trade played major roles in how early societies developed throughout the continent. In some medieval African societies, the **nuclear family** was typical, with parents and children living and working together, while in other communities the family included several generations. Political patterns varied depending in part on the size and culture of the community.

Across Africa, religious beliefs were varied and complex. Some Africans followed traditional beliefs and were polytheistic. By 1000, both Christianity and Islam had spread to many regions of Africa. African societies preserved their values and history through both oral and written literature. In West Africa, **griots** (GREE ohz), or professional storytellers, recited ancient stories as they still do today.

Assessment

1. **Identify (a)** Bantu migrations **(b)** Nubia **(c)** Ghana **(d)** Mansa Musa **(e)** Axum
2. **Define (a)** nuclear family **(b)** griot
3. How did Nubian civilization prosper?
4. How did the gold-salt trade develop between West Africa and North Africa?

L1 Special Needs   L2 Less Proficient Readers
Explain to students that they can build their reading skills by posing questions and then looking for answers in the text. Model the skill using the first subheading, Early Civilizations of Africa, and asking: **How did Egypt influence Nubia?** Then, work with students to find the answer. Have students continue the exercise by writing two questions and their answers for each subsection.

Use the following study guide resources to help students acquiring basic skills:

Adapted Reading and Note Taking Study Guide
■ Adapted Note Taking Study Guide, p. 30
■ Adapted Section Summary, p. 31

Independent Practice

■ **Note Taking** Have students fill in the outline detailing the kingdoms and trading states of Africa.

Reading and Note Taking Study Guide, p. 30

■ Have students access **Web Code nbp-1121** to take the **Geography Interactive Audio Guided Tour.**

■ **Traveler's Tales** Have students read the selection *Ibn Battuta* and answer the questions on the worksheet.

All in One Teaching Resources, Modern Review Unit, p. 34

Monitor Progress

As students fill in their outlines, make sure they understand details about the kingdoms and trading states of Africa. For a completed version of the outlines, see

Note Taking Transparencies, 112

Answers

1. **(a)** series of migrations in which the Bantu people from West Africa moved south and east to populate most of southern Africa **(b)** a powerful North African civilization that thrived along the Nile **(c)** a wealthy West African trading kingdom **(d)** the greatest emperor of Mali **(e)** an important trading center located southeast of Nubia
2. **(a)** family unit consisting of parents and children **(b)** professional African poet
3. from trade and iron-making
4. North Africans wanted gold for trade with Europeans, while West Africans needed salt to stay healthy and to preserve food. Each possessed an item of trade that was desirable to the other.

- **Introduce** Ask students what a "golden age" is. Have volunteers identify other periods they consider to be a golden age, and explain why.

- **Teach** Trace the spread of civilization through the cultures of East Asia. Ask **How did the Tang and Song dynasties structure society?** *(well-ordered, with emperor and aristocrats at the top, then two classes of gentry, followed by the peasantry)* **What are some key accomplishments of the Ming Dynasty?** *(civil service exams, revival of Confucian learning, thriving economy and cities, global sea exploration)* **How did Chinese influence first begin to reach Korea?** *(during the Han dynasty, when the Korean peninsula was within the Chinese zone of influence)* **How did Chinese culture come to Japan?** *(initially through Korea, but in the early 600s, the Japanese began traveling to China to learn about its culture)* **How did the Tokugawa shogunate affect Japanese society?** *(Peace and stability increased, trade and culture flourished, and society became conservative.)*

- **Quick Activity** Show students *The Samurai of Japan* from the **Witness History Discovery School™** video program. Ask **How did the samurai use military technology to maintain and increase their power?** *(The samurai sword was hard enough to hold a sharp edge and flexible enough to absorb blows. Samurai made their armor from flexible materials that helped cushion a sword's blow. The samurai adopted guns from Europeans.)*

6 The Spread of Civilizations in East Asia

(500–1650)

Main Ideas

- China expanded and grew rich under the powerful Tang and Song dynasties.
- During the 1200s and 1300s, the Mongols ruled much of Asia. After the fall of the Mongols, the Ming restored Chinese culture and later imposed a policy of isolation.
- During the 1100s, Japan created a feudal society ruled by powerful military lords.

The Western Market of the Tang dynasty specialized in foreign goods.

After the Han dynasty collapsed in A.D. 220, China remained a divided land for nearly 400 years. Various Chinese dynasties rose and fell. Then in the 500s, China reemerged as a united empire. For a short period, the Sui dynasty ruled. Then a Sui general and his son, Tang Taizong, led a successful revolt and established their own dynasty, the Tang.

Two Golden Ages of China

Under the rule of the Tang dynasty (618–907), China was restored to its earlier glory. Tang armies marched deep into Central Asia and surrounding regions. They forced neighboring lands to become **tributary states**. That is, while these states remained independent, their rulers had to acknowledge Chinese supremacy and send regular tribute to the Tang emperor. Tang emperors restored the bureaucracy. They redistributed land to the peasants. They also completed a system of canals to encourage internal trade and transportation. The Tang dynasty finally collapsed in 907. The Song dynasty soon rose to take its place.

In 960, the Song reunited much of China to rule for 319 years. The Song period was a golden age. Chinese wealth and culture dominated East Asia even when its armies did not. Farming and foreign trade expanded. Paper money came into use. China's cities, which had been mainly centers of government, now prospered as centers of trade. Several cities even had populations over one million.

The first empress of China, Wu Zhao

Government and Society Under the Tang and Song, China was a well-ordered society. Besides the emperor and the aristocratic families, the two main classes were the gentry and the peasantry. The gentry were wealthy landowners who valued scholarship more than physical labor. Most scholar-officials at court came from this class. The peasants farmed on the land. However, even peasants could move up in society through education and government service.

Cultural Achievements A rich economy supported the thriving culture of Tang and Song China. Prose and poetry flourished. Scholars produced works on philosophy, religion, and history. Painting and calligraphy became essential skills for the scholar-gentry.

The Mongol and Ming Empires

In the early 1200s, the Mongols dominated Asia. They invaded China and finally toppled the Song dynasty in 1279. The Mongols established peace and order within their domains. Political stability set the stage for economic growth. Under the protection of the Mongols, trade flourished along the Silk Road and across Eurasia.

Ming Dynasty In 1368, a rebel Chinese army pushed the Mongols back beyond the Great Wall. A new dynasty, the Ming—meaning brilliant—sought to reassert Chinese greatness after years of foreign rule. The Ming restored the civil service exams. Confucian learning again became the road to success. Chinese cities were home to many industries, and the economy thrived.

History Background

Zheng He In 1405, Zheng He launched the first of seven sea expeditions. He departed at the head of a fleet of 62 huge ships and over 200 smaller ones, carrying a crew of about 28,000 sailors. Between 1405 and 1433, Zheng He explored the coasts of Southwest Asia and India and the entrances to the Red Sea and the Persian Gulf. He also visited a number of ports in East Africa. In the wake of these expeditions, Chinese merchants settled in Southeast Asia and India and became a permanent presence in their trading centers. One result of these voyages was the importation of exotic animals, such as giraffes, into China. The voyages showed local rulers the power and strength of the Chinese empire.

Exploration Early Ming rulers proudly sent Chinese fleets into distant waters. The Chinese admiral Zheng He (jeng heh) commanded hundreds of vessels carrying 25,000 sailors during a series of expeditions. His goal was to promote trade and collect tribute. Zheng He's fleet explored as far as the coasts of East Africa.

Korea and Its Traditions

As early as Han times, China extended its influence to peoples beyond the Middle Kingdom. To the northeast, the Korean peninsula lay within the Chinese zone of influence. While Korea absorbed many Chinese traditions over the centuries, it also maintained its own identity. Additionally, Koreans improved on a number of Chinese inventions. They advanced Chinese woodblock printing techniques by creating movable metal type to print books. They also created an alphabet for the sounds of their language that was easier to use than Chinese characters. Its use led to an extremely high literacy rate in Korea.

The Emergence of Japan

Like Korea, Japan felt the powerful influence of Chinese civilization early in its history. Even so, the Japanese continued to maintain their own distinct culture. The surrounding seas both protected and isolated Japan. While Japan was close enough to the mainland to learn from China, it was too far away for China to conquer.

By about A.D. 500, Japan's first and only dynasty—the Yamato—dominated Honshu, the largest Japanese island. In the early 600s, the Yamato dynasty sent young Japanese nobles to study in China. They returned to Japan spreading Chinese thought, technology, and arts. For a time, the Japanese modeled much of their society on Chinese culture and government. Eventually, however, the Japanese chose to adopt some Chinese ways while discarding or changing others.

Japan's Feudal Age

In theory, the emperor headed Japanese society. In fact, he was a powerless, though revered, figurehead. Real power lay in the hands of the **shogun**, or supreme military commander. He distributed lands to vassal lords who agreed to support him with their armies in time of need. These great warrior lords were called **daimyo** (DY myoh). They, in turn, granted land to lesser warriors called **samurai**, meaning "those who serve." Samurai were the fighting aristocracy in the constant struggle for power. Japan had evolved into a feudal society.

In 1603, Tokugawa Ieyasu (toh koo gah wah ee AY ah soo) founded the Tokugawa shogunate, which ruled Japan until 1868. The Tokugawas brought peace and stability to Japan. They imposed central government control on all of Japan and created a unified, orderly society. Trade flourished, merchants prospered, and prosperity contributed to a flowering of culture. Still, the shoguns were extremely conservative. They tried to preserve samurai virtues and ancient beliefs. This commitment would bring them into sharp conflict with the foreigners who arrived in the 1500s.

Assessment

1. **Identify (a)** Tang **(b)** Song **(c)** Mongols **(d)** Ming **(e)** Tokugawa
2. **Define (a)** tributary state **(b)** shogun **(c)** daimyo **(d)** samurai
3. How did the Tang and Song dynasties benefit China?
4. Who held the most power in feudal Japan?

Differentiated Instruction   Solutions for All Learners

L1 Special Needs   L2 Less Proficient Readers
Pair students who have difficulty reading with those who are more proficient. Have the proficient students guide the others to find the key details about the Tang, Song, and Ming dynasties and the Tokugawa shogunate by finding the answers to the key questions of journalism: *Who, What, Where, When, Why,* and *How.*

L2 English Language Learners
Use the following study guide resources to help students acquiring basic skills:

 Adapted Reading and Note Taking Study Guide
- Reading and Note Taking Study Guide, p. 32
- Adapted Section Summary, p. 33

Independent Practice

Have students fill in the outline showing the spread of civilizations in East Asia.

 Reading and Note Taking Study Guide, p. 32

Monitor Progress

As students fill in their outlines, circulate to make sure they understand the how civilization in East Asia spread. For a completed version of the outlines see

 Note Taking Transparencies, 113

Answers

1. **(a)** dynasty that reunited and ruled China from 618 to 907 **(b)** dynasty that presided over a golden age in China from 960–1079 **(c)** Asians who invaded and ruled China **(d)** dynasty that pushed out the Mongols and restored Chinese greatness **(e)** shogunate that ruled Japan from 1603 to 1868
2. **(a)** state that remains independent but sends tribute to an overlord **(b)** Japanese supreme military commander **(c)** Japanese warrior lord **(d)** lesser warrior who served a daimyo
3. Under these two dynasties, China enjoyed political stability, efficient government, thriving agriculture, and expanding trade. The arts and sciences flourished.
4. the shogun, or supreme military commander

Assess and Reteach

- Have students use the charts and graphs on this page and the following pages to review the material in Part 3.
- For additional review, remind students to refer to the **L3**

 **Reading and Note Taking Study Guide**

Note Taking Study Guide, pp. 22, 24, 26, 28, 30, 32

Section Summaries, pp. 23, 25, 27, 29, 31, 33

- When students have completed their study of this section, distribute Tests A and B.

All in One **Teaching Resources, Modern Review Unit,** pp. 35–40

Extend **L4**

Have student pairs write letter from a citizen in one of the cultures in Part 3 to a citizen in another of the cultures. Have students ask and answer questions about their respective cultures.

Quick Study Guide

PART 3

■ The Church

Daily Life	Economic Power	Political Power
• Mass • Sacraments • Religious calendar • Aid to needy • Moral guidance	• Owned large tracts of land • People willed riches to Church • Agricultural and commercial activity in monasteries.	• Papal supremacy • Threat of excommunication, interdict • Raised own armies • Clergy served in governments • Moral authority

■ Evolution of English Government

1066	**Norman Conquest** William, Duke of Normandy, defeats King Harold of the Anglo-Saxons at Hastings.
1086	***Domesday Book*** King William uses this census, or survey of people and property, as a basis for taxation.
1160–1180s	**Common Law** Henry II uses accepted customs to lay the foundation for the English legal system.
1215	**Magna Carta** King John approves this document limiting royal power and extending rights to nobles and freemen.
1295	**Model Parliament** King Edward I expands Parliament to include representatives of common people as well as lords and clergy.

■ Economic Recovery

Agricultural Revolution →	Revival of Trade →	Towns and the Middle Class
• Production increases. • Population grows.	• Warfare decreases. • Travel becomes safer. • Desire for foreign goods increases. • Trade fairs develop. • Towns and cities grow.	• As towns grow, merchants gain power. • Guilds form and become powerful. • Modern business practices develop. • The middle class gains power. • Trade and commerce gain importance.

■ Power Shifts in the High Middle Ages

England	France	Holy Roman Empire
William the Conqueror consolidates royal power, limiting power of lords.	Hugh Capet is elected king by French nobles who feel he is weak.	Otto is crowned Holy Roman emperor, but nobles and Church officials wield power.
Henry II strengthens royal courts, and tries to make clergy accountable to them.	Capetian kings make throne hereditary, take lands from nobles, build a bureaucracy.	Henry IV is excommunicated by Pope Gregory VII, and then forgiven.
King John approves Magna Carta, limiting monarch's power.	Louis IX improves royal government, ends serfdom, creates strong national feeling.	Henry IV forces Pope Gregory VII into exile.
Parliament develops under Edward I.	After Philip IV clashes with Pope Boniface, French monarchs gain more control over popes.	Frederick Barbarossa and Frederick II try to conquer Italy but fail.
During Hundred Years' War, monarchs ask Parliament for funds, increasing Parliament's power.	During Hundred Years' War, English are expelled from most of France, increasing French national feeling.	Holy Roman Empire remains fragmented.

Key Muslim Empires

Empire	Muhammad and First Successors (632–661)	Umayyad (661–750) (756–1031 in Spain)	Abbasid (750–1258)	Mughal (1526–1857)	Ottomans (late 1200s–1924)	Safavids (early 1500s–1722)
Key Leader(s)	• Muhammad • Abu Bakr • Umar • Ali	• Mu'awiyah	• Abu al-Abbas • al-Mansur • Harun al-Rashid	• Babur • Akbar • Jahangir • Shah Jahan • Aurangzeb	• Mehmet II • Suleiman • Selim II	• Shah Abbas
Capital	Mecca	Damascus (Cordóba in Spain)	Baghdad	Delhi, Agra	Istanbul	Isfahan

The Byzantine Empire, Eastern Europe and Russia in 1300

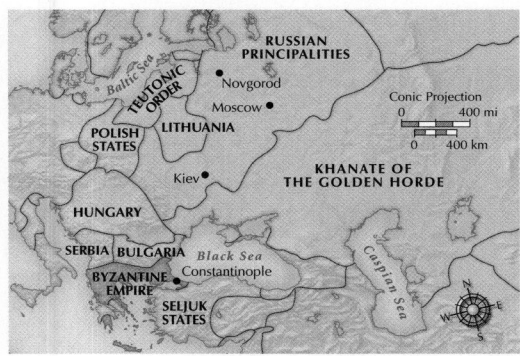

Key Political Leaders

Byzantine empire
• Constantine established Constantinople (named for himself) as the capital of the eastern Roman empire; converted to Christianity
• Justinian, emperor during the Byzantine empire's golden age

Russia
• Rurik, Rus prince who ruled Novgorod
• Princess Olga of Kiev, converted to Christianity
• Yaroslav the Wise, presided over golden age in Kiev
• Ivan the Great, expanded Russia and centralized power
• Ivan the Terrible, tsar who established absolute power

Eastern Europe
• Queen Jadwiga, queen of Poland, joint ruler of Poland-Lithuania
• Duke Wladislaw Jagiello, Lithuanian duke, joint ruler of Poland-Lithuania
• Stefan Dusan, ruler of Serbia

Spread of the Arab Empire

Cause and Effect	
Long-Term Causes	**Immediate Causes**
• Weakness of Byzantine and Persian empires • Economic and social changes in Arabia	• Tribes of Arabia unified by Islam around a central message • Wide acceptance of religious message of Islam • Easy acceptance of social ideas of Islam, such as equality among believers

Spread of Islam	
Immediate Effects	**Long-Term Effects**
• Islam spreads from the Atlantic coast to the Indus River valley • Centers of learning flourish in Cairo, Córdoba, and elsewhere	• Muslim civilization emerges • Linking of Europe, Asia, and Africa through Muslim trade network • Arabic becomes shared language of Muslims • Split between Sunni and Shiites

History Background

An International Trade Network Muslim merchants spread products, technologies, knowledge, and culture. From India they brought back the Indian number system—the familiar "Arabic numerals" and zero now used everywhere—and introduced it to the Western world. Traders also brought sugar from India and papermaking from China back. At the same time, they brought Islam to many new regions. As more people converted and learned Arabic, a common language and religion helped the global exchange grow and thrive. Extensive trade and a money economy led Muslims to pioneer new business practices. They created partnerships, bought and sold on credit, formed banks to change currency, and invented the predecessors of todays bank checks. The English word *check* comes from the Arabic word *sakh*.

Quick Study Guide

■ Major African Kingdoms and Trading States

Kingdom or State	Date	Location	Religion	Economic Base
Egypt	2575 B.C.–1075 B.C.	North Africa	Local religion	Trade
Nubia	1100 B.C.–A.D. 350	Northeast Africa	Local religion	Trade and iron ore
Ghana	800–1050	West Africa	Islam	Gold
Mali	1235–1400s	West Africa	Local religion and Islam	Gold and salt
Songhai	1460–1591	West Africa	Local religion and Islam	Trade
Benin	1300s–1500s	West Africa	Local religion	Pepper, ivory, and slaves
Axum	350–600s	East Africa	Christianity	Trade
Great Zimbabwe	1300s–1500s	East Africa	Unknown	Trade

■ Important Ancient and Medieval African Rulers

Ruler	Kingdom	Accomplishment
Piankhi	Nubia	Conquered Egypt and brought it under Nubian control
Sundiata	Mali	Defeated Sumanguru and founded the empire of Mali
Mansa Musa	Mali	Expanded Mali's borders and based justice system on the Quran
Askia Muhammad	Songhai	Expanded Songhai's territory and improved the government by setting up bureaucracies
Amina	Hausa city-states	Gained control of many Saharan trade routes
King Ezana	Axum	Conquered Nubia and made Christianity the official religion
King Lalibela	Ethiopia	Sponsored the building of the Lalibela churches

■ China's Influence on Its Neighbors

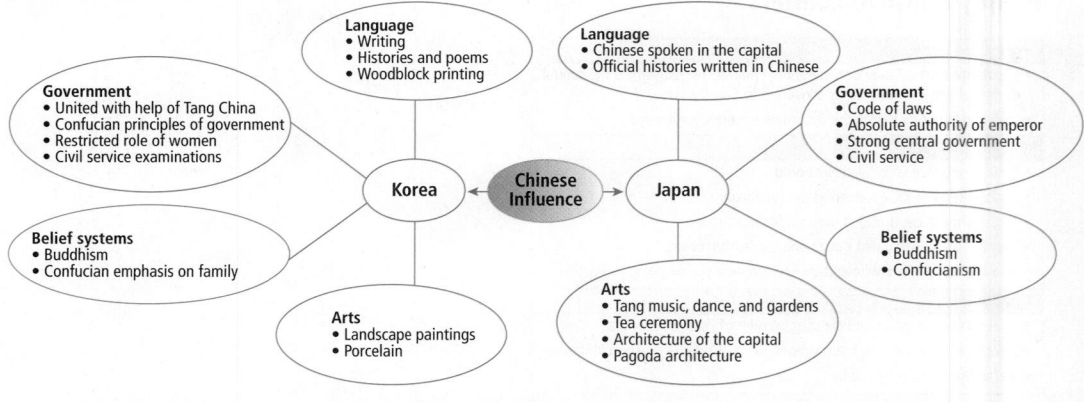

History Background

China's Civil Service System Han emperors adopted the idea that civil servants should win their positions by merit, rather than through family ties as had occurred in the past. Much later, in the 580s, the Sui dynasty set up a formal system of civil service exams, which were given at the local, provincial, and national levels. In theory, any man could take the exams. In practice, only those who could afford years of study, such as the sons of wealthy landowners or officials, could hope to succeed. The civil service system remained in use until 1912. It put men trained in Confucian thought at every level of government and created an enduring system of values. Dynasties rose and fell, but Confucian influence survived.

Conflict

Objectives
- Understand the reasons that people go to war.
- Complete a Web Quest on conflict.

In This Chapter
During the Middle Ages, people repeatedly chose to deal with their differences by waging war. Conflicts over power, territory, and beliefs sparked both the Crusades and the Reconquista (right). Like many other wars, they sowed the seeds of future discord.

Throughout History

264 B.C.–146 B.C. Romans fight Carthage for control of the western Mediterranean.

711 A.D. Muslim forces spread Arab rule into Spain.

1756–1763 In the Seven Years' War, Britain and France struggle for global power

1861 Conflict over slavery leads to the American Civil War.

1914 A series of alliances pull European nations into World War I.

1961 Eritrea begins a 30-year struggle for independence from Ethiopia.

Continuing Today
The origin of many conflicts today can be traced to the past. Long-standing rivalries make it hard to gain or maintain lasting peace in many parts of the globe.

Conflicts in the World Today

21st Century Skills

 TRANSFER Activities

1. **Analyze** Why have nations gone to war in the past?

2. **Evaluate** List in order of importance what you consider to be just causes for war. Explain the reason for your choices.

3. **Transfer** Complete a Web quest analyzing the reasons why states do or don't go to war; record your thoughts in the Concept Connector Journal; and learn to make a video. Web Code nbh-0808

Build Background Knowledge
Check students' understanding of the term *conflict*. Ask students to describe from their own experience why conflicts occur. Why do some simmer down while others heat up?

Instruct
- Direct students' attention to the essential question: **When, if ever, should people go to war?** Have them look at the section entitled **In This Chapter** and the corresponding image. Ask students to describe why people went to war during the Crusades and the Reconquista.

- Tell the students to read the section entitled **Continuing Today** and to look at the corresponding map. Have students compare the Map of the Crusades in this chapter with the map on this page. Is there still conflict in the same region? What are the issues in Middle Eastern conflicts today?

- Assign the Web Quest on conflict.

Independent Practice
Concept Connector Have students fill in the Web Quest reflection question on conflict in their Concept Connector Journal.

 Reading and Note Taking Study Guide, p. 238

Monitor Progress
Circulate to make sure that students are filling in their Concept Connector Journal. Facilitate discussion about when or if war is justified.

Transfer Activities
1. Nations have gone to war to gain territory, because of religious and ethnic differences, to defend themselves, and for many other reasons.
2. Answers will vary. Students might indicate that self-defense, coming to the aid of another nation, or to topple a tyrannical government are just reasons to go to war.
3. Students' work should be evaluated against the rubric at Web Code nbh-0808.

Link to Literature

Shakespeare's Source The Wars of the Roses have spawned many works of fiction and nonfiction alike. Some of the best-known works are plays by William Shakespeare based on the lives of kings Henry VI and Richard III. Shakespeare's depiction of Richard as a hunchbacked murderer of his two young nephews became part of historical memory. There is little evidence that he was a hunchback, although he may have been responsible for the disappearance of his young nephews, the heirs to the throne. However, Shakespeare's depiction of an evil tyrant became popularly accepted and set up Richard's adversary, Henry Tudor, as a hero. Henry was the grandfather of Queen Elizabeth, monarch at the time Shakespeare's play was published.

Cultural Diffusion

Objectives

- Define cultural diffusion.
- Describe how migration and trade spread ideas from one culture to another.
- Complete a web quest on cultural diffusion.

Build Background Knowledge L3

- Ask students to name their favorite foods and write their responses on the board. Have students identify the country of origin for each food. Point out that food is just one element that shows how different cultures influence each other.

Instruct L3

- Directs students' attention to the Essential Question. **How does cultural diffusion occur?** Have a student read In This Chapter aloud. Ask: **How did various cultures spread?** Remind students that cultural diffusion is not usually a replacement of one culture by another, but rather a gradual blending of two cultures.

- Have students use the map to compare the African language groups with the Bantu migration routes. Ask: **How do the routes of migration explain the language patterns?**

- Assign the Web Quest on cultural diffusion.

Independent Practice

Concept Connector Have students fill in the Web Quest reflection question on cultural diffusion in their Concept Connector Journal.

 Reading and Note Taking Study Guide, p. 248

Monitor Progress

Circulate to make sure that students are filling in their Concept Connector Journal. Ensure they understand how cultural diffusion occurs.

Transfer Activities

1. Both spread their own cultural traits and absorb traditions of other people.
2. Students may mention the loss or modification of customs and traditions and the spread of new ideas, technology, and trade.
3. Students' work should be evaluated against the rubric at Web Code nbh-1108.

CULTURAL DIFFUSION
How does cultural diffusion occur?

In This Chapter

During their migration, Bantu-speaking peoples from West Africa slowly diffused, or spread, their language over much of the African continent. Language, religion, and cultural traits have moved along the way of migrations, trade routes, and invading armies. Travelers changed and were changed by the cultures with whom they came in contact.

Throughout History

- **1200 A.D.** Migration of Hittite ironsmiths spreads technology of weapon making.

- **586 B.C.** Exiled Jews take their laws and traditions to other lands.

- **600s–700s A.D.** Arab armies carry Muslim culture to conquered lands.

- **1455** The printing press speeds the exchange of ideas.

- **1800s** Imperialism spreads Western influence in Africa and Asia.

Language and the Bantu Migrations

Miller Projection
0   500   1000 mi
0   500 1000 km

Language Groups, c. A.D. 1500
- Afro-Asiatic
- Nilo-Saharan
- Niger-Congo other than Bantu
- Bantu
- Khoisan
- Austronesian
- Igbo Language
- Bantu homeland, c. 2000 B.C.
- Bantu migrations, to A.D. 500

Continuing Today

American culture has had a major impact around the world. The popularity of baseball has spread from the United States around the world, leading to a World Baseball Classic.

21st Century Skills

? TRANSFER Activities

1. **Analyze** How are methods of cultural diffusion similar?

2. **Evaluate** What are some costs and benefits of cultural diffusion?

3. **Transfer** Complete a Web quest in which you analyze how cultures diffuse today; record your thoughts in the Concept Connector Journal; and learn to make a video. Web Code nbh-1108

Careers

Chef The migration of groups of people was the impetus behind the arrival of such foods as pizza, bagels, and sushi into the United States. These foods spread throughout the U.S. in part through the work of chefs because some the foods reflected their own heritage or because they were interested in the cuisines of other cultures. Some chefs cook in a style called *fusion* that reflects a blend of ingredients and cooking methods from different cuisines. Many cooks learn in high school or vocational school, but top chefs must undergo years of training in specialized culinary institutes. These jobs are plentiful, but competition is fierce. Chefs need creativity, imagination, good technical knowledge, nutritional knowledge, great manual skills—and good taste.

TRADE

What are the intended and unintended effects of trade?

In This Chapter

As routes became safer, trade along the ancient Silk Road increased. Merchants traveled in both directions between China and the Mediterranean Sea. Along with porcelain, silk, and spices came religion, art, architecture, and ideas. For more than a thousand years, the network of trade routes helped shape the tastes and cultures of people in much of Asia and Europe.

Throughout History

600s B.C. Greek traders bring goods and the Phoenician alphabet back to Greece.

1400s A.D. The search for a new trade route to Asia brings Europeans to the Americas.

1500s–1800s Slave trade enriches merchants but destroys African societies.

1700s New crops from the Americas boost farm output in China.

1850s–1860s Western demands for trade lead to modernization of Japan.

Continuing Today

Trade involves the movement of goods. Sometimes, unexpected cargo goes along for the ride. One invasive species, the zebra mussel, arrived in the United States in the bilge tank of an East European cargo ship. Zebra mussels clog water intake pipes and upset the ecosystem of the Great Lakes region.

21st Century Skills

? TRANSFER Activities

1. Analyze How has trade had more than just economic impact?

2. Evaluate What limits, if any, should there be on trade?

3. Transfer Complete a Web quest in which you investigate the pros and cons of free trade; record your thoughts in the Concept Connector Journal; and learn to make a video. Web Code nbh-1208

Careers

International Marketing The rise of global trade networks and of multinational corporations—companies with operations in many different countries—has increased the need for workers who specialize in international marketing. This is the field of business that focuses on the best ways to introduce, promote, and sell products in more than one country. A bachelor's or master's degree in business with courses in international marketing and related subjects is helpful to obtain these jobs. Knowledge of one or more foreign languages and deep understanding of other cultures is also helpful.

Concept Connector

Trade

Objectives

- Understand the reasons that people trade.
- Describe the consequences of trade, both intentional and unintentional.
- Complete a Web Quest on trade.

Build Background Knowledge

Ask students to explain why they think trade is important. Review students' Concept Connector Journal entries for this theme.

Instruct

- Direct students' attention to the essential question: **What are the intended and unintended consequences of trade?** Have them look at the section entitled **In This Chapter.** Discuss how trade brings new types of foods, people, products, and culture into a land.

- Ask students to look at the section entitled **Continuing Today** and the corresponding image. Ask: **Why do you think nations limit the agricultural and animal products they allow to be brought into their country?**

- Assign a Web Quest on trade.

Independent Practice

Concept Connector Have students fill in the Web Quest reflection question on trade in their Concept Connector Journal.

 Reading and Note Taking Study Guide, p. 303

Monitor Progress

Circulate to make sure that students are filling in their Concept Connector Journal. Ensure that students are aware of the intended and unintended consequences of trade.

Transfer Activities

1. Trade can bring positive aspects of one land to another, but it can also lead to unintended consequences, such as war.
2. Answers will vary. Students might indicate that limits should be placed on dangerous products. They might mention taxes and regulations for businesses and goods.
3. Students' work should be evaluated against the rubric at Web Code nbh-1208.

Early Modern Times
1300–1800

Unit Overview

Unit 1 studies the major developments that led to the emergence of modern Europe and an age of global conquest, interdependence, and exchange.

Chapter 1 examines the Renaissance, Reformation, and Scientific Revolution.
Concepts: Cultural Diffusion, Science

Chapter 2 describes the growth of the European trading empires in Asia.
Concepts: Conflict, Cultural Diffusion, Empire, Technology, Trade

Chapter 3 studies the impact of Europe's age of exploration on the Americas, Africa, and Europe itself.
Concepts: Economic Systems, Empire, Genocide, Trade

Chapter 4 focuses on the role of absolute monarchs in Europe from the 1500s through the 1700s.
Concepts: Democracy, Political Systems, Revolution

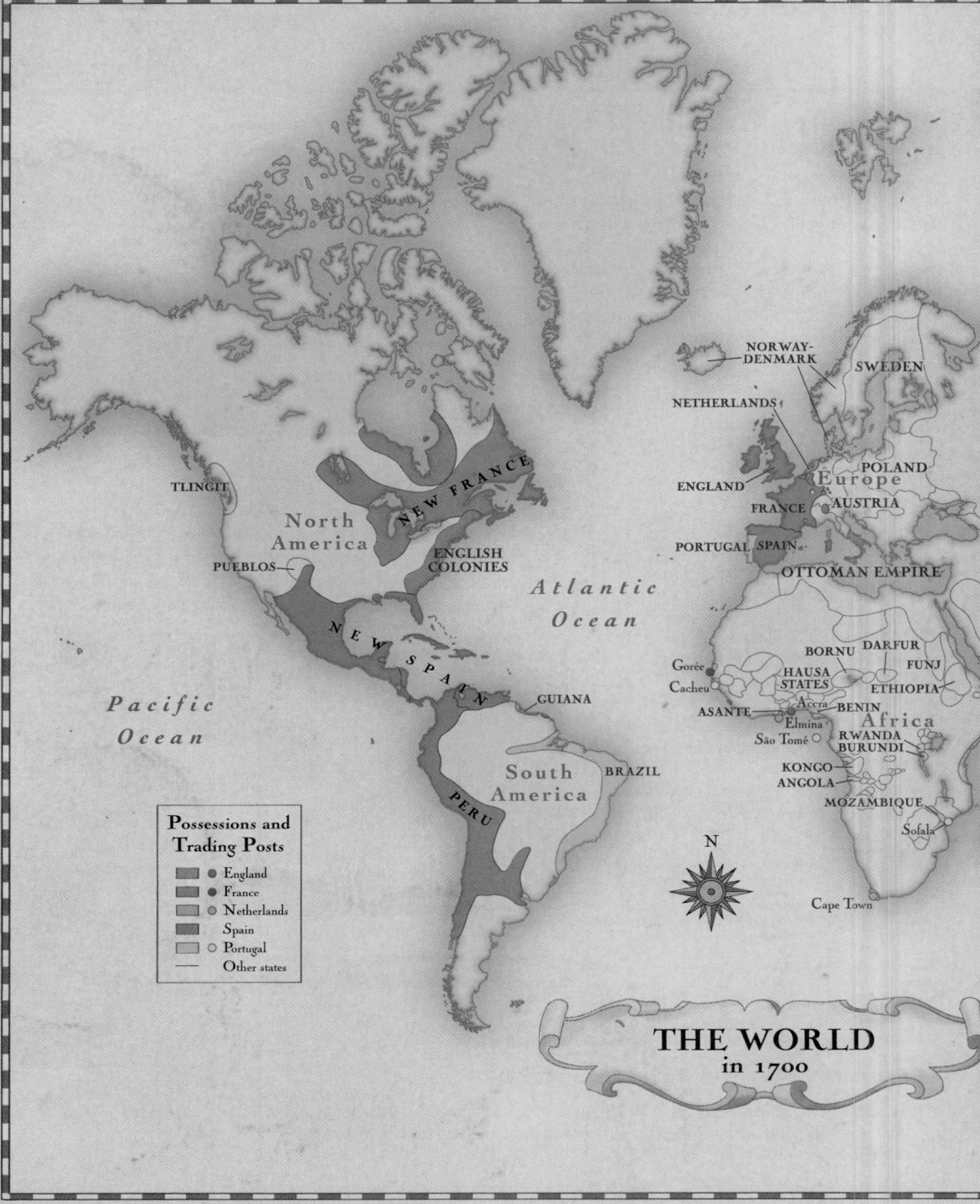

Possessions and Trading Posts

- England
- France
- Netherlands
- Spain
- Portugal
- Other states

THE WORLD
in 1700

About the Map

Beginning in the 1400s, Europeans explored the coasts of Africa and the Americas in search of a sea route to Asia so that they could gain control of the rich trade in Asian spices and luxury goods. By 1700, Europeans had established trading posts along the coasts of Africa and Asia. However, Europeans were confined to trading posts, small islands, and narrow coastal strips on those continents. Europeans were not yet a match for the powerful states that maintained their independence in the interiors of Africa and Asia. Chinese and Mughal emperors, for example, ruled much larger populations in 1700 than any European king. In the Americas, however, European countries had conquered vast territories by 1700 with the aid of metal weapons, firearms, horses, and contagious disease. France, England, Spain, and Portugal all controlled large American colonies.

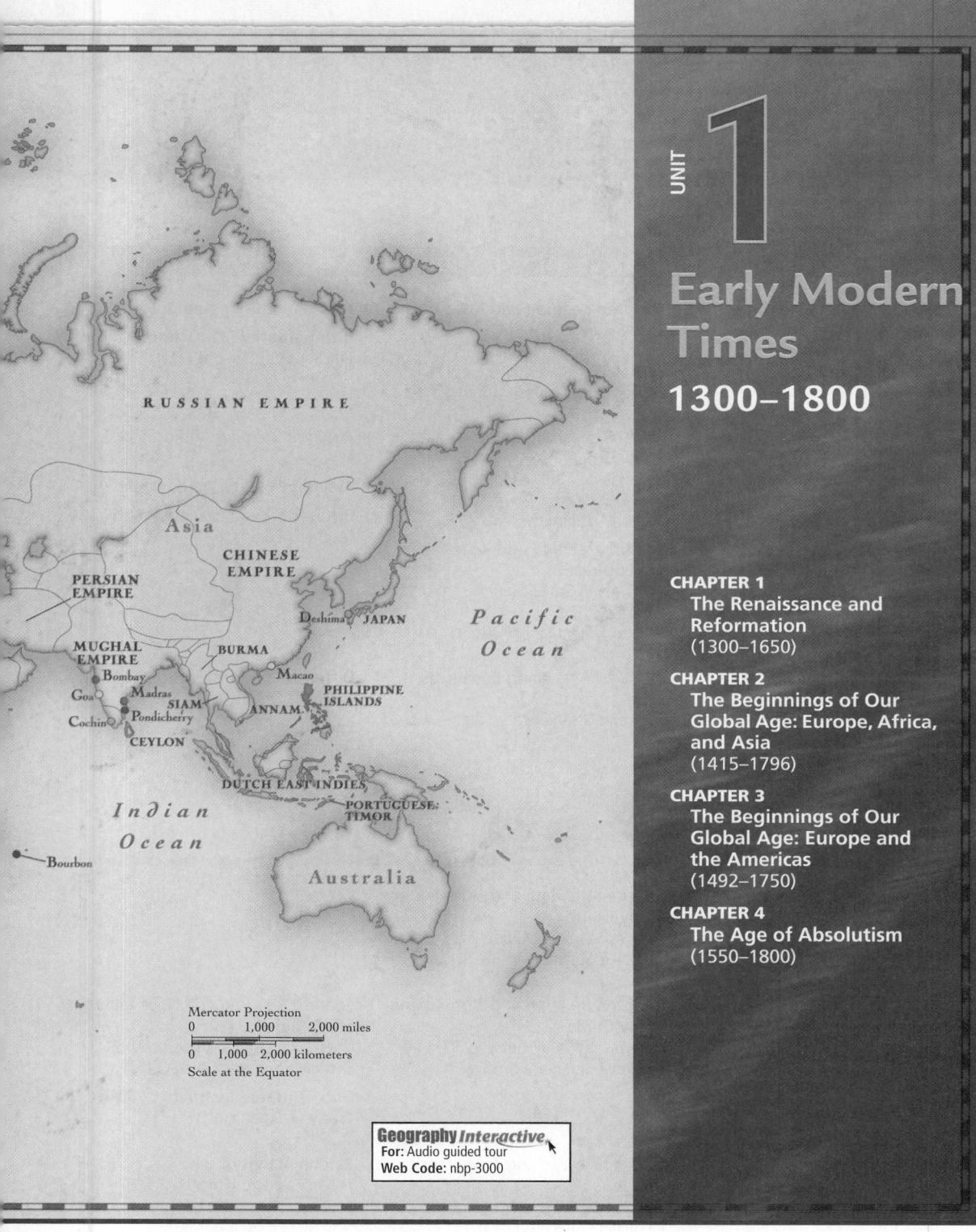

1

Early Modern Times

1300–1800

CHAPTER 1
The Renaissance and Reformation
(1300–1650)

CHAPTER 2
The Beginnings of Our Global Age: Europe, Africa, and Asia
(1415–1796)

CHAPTER 3
The Beginnings of Our Global Age: Europe and the Americas
(1492–1750)

CHAPTER 4
The Age of Absolutism
(1550–1800)

RUSSIAN EMPIRE

Asia

CHINESE EMPIRE

PERSIAN EMPIRE

Deshima JAPAN

MUGHAL EMPIRE

BURMA

Bombay

Goa

Madras

SIAM

Macao

PHILIPPINE ISLANDS

Cochin

Pondicherry

ANNAM

CEYLON

Pacific Ocean

DUTCH EAST INDIES

Indian Ocean

PORTUGUESE TIMOR

Bourbon

Australia

Mercator Projection
0   1,000   2,000 miles
0   1,000   2,000 kilometers
Scale at the Equator

Geography *Interactive*
For: Audio guided tour
Web Code: nbp-3000

Geographic Literacy

Point out that the map on these pages shows that early modern Europeans were extending their reach around the world. Ask **On which continents did European powers have possessions or trading posts?** (*Asia, Africa, and the Americas*) **On which continents were the largest European possessions located in 1700?** (*North and South America*) **List four large empires that were not controlled by European colonial powers in 1700.** (*Ottoman, Russian, Chinese, Persian, Mughal*) **List four African states that were not controlled by European colonial powers in 1700.** (*Asante, Benin, Hausa States, Darfur, Funj, Ethiopia, Rwanda, Burundi, Kongo*)

Looking Ahead

Ask students to read the chapter titles to the right of the map. Ask **Based on these titles and your study of the map, what do you predict you will learn about in this unit?** (*how Europeans set out on voyages of exploration and established trading empires in Asia, Africa, and the Americas*) Explain that students will also learn about the blossoming of art and culture during the Renaissance, the religious reformation that established Protestant churches, and the absolute monarchs who arose during the Age of Absolutism.

A note on the projection:
Although the Mercator projection distorts the sizes of continents, it was widely used for maps after its invention in 1569.

Home Involvement
The *Letter Home* includes a summary of the Early Modern Times content that students will be studying.
All in One Teaching Resources, Unit 1, p. 1

The Renaissance and Reformation

CHAPTER PLANNER

Section	Core Instruction (L3)	Differentiated Instruction (L1) (L2) (L4)	
Section 1 *The Renaissance in Italy* **4 periods, 2 blocks** **OBJECTIVES** ■ Describe the characteristics of the Renaissance and understand why it began in Italy. ■ Identify Renaissance artists and explain how new ideas affected the arts of the period. ■ Understand how writers of the time addressed Renaissance themes. **Focus Question** *What were the ideals of the Renaissance, and how did Italian artists and writers reflect these ideals?*	**All in One Teaching Resources, Unit 1** Reading Strategy: Main Ideas, p. 8 Vocabulary Builder: Word Parts, p. 7 Outline Map: Europe About 1600, p. 14 Geography Quiz, p. 15 Section 1 Quiz, p. 2 **Reading and Note Taking Study Guide** Note Taking Study Guide, pp. 34–35 Section 1 Summary, p. 36 **Note Taking Transparencies,** 114 **WITNESS HISTORY Audio CD** An Artist Becomes a Biographer, Giorgio Vasari **Progress Monitoring Transparencies,** 53 **Color Transparencies,** 77, 79, 81 **Witness History Discovery School™** video program, *Machiavelli's* The Prince **Teaching Resources, Skills Handbook** Prereading the Chapter, pp. 1–2 Word Knowledge Rating Form, p. 3 K-W-L Chart, p. 4	**(L1) Adapted Reading and Note Taking Study Guide** Note Taking Study Guide, pp. 34–35 **SN** Section 1 Summary, p. 36 **SN** **(L2) Adapted Reading and Note Taking Study Guide** Note Taking Study Guide, pp. 34–35 **LPR** Section 1 Summary, p. 36 **LPR** **Spanish Reading and Note Taking Study Guide** Note Taking Study Guide, pp. 34–35 **ELL** Section 1 Summary, p. 36 **ELL** **(L4) All in One Teaching Resources, Unit 1** Biography: Isabella d'Este, p. 9 **AR, GT**	***Student Edition Audio** **SN** **Differentiated Instruction Activity,** Teacher's Edition, p. 49 **SN** ***Guided Reading Audio,** Spanish **ELL** ***Student Edition Audio** **LPR** **Differentiated Instruction Activity,** Teacher's Edition, p. 49 **LPR, ELL** **Differentiated Instruction Activity,** Teacher's Edition, p. 53 **AR, GT** **Extend Activity,** Teacher's Edition, p. 54 **AR, GT**
Section 2 *The Renaissance in the North* **1.5 periods, .75 block** **OBJECTIVES** ■ Explain how the printing revolution shaped European society. ■ Describe the themes that northern European artists, humanists, and writers explored. **Focus Question** *How did the Renaissance develop in northern Europe?*	**All in One Teaching Resources, Unit 1** Section 2 Quiz, p. 3 **Reading and Note Taking Study Guide** Note Taking Study Guide, p. 37 Section 2 Summary, p. 38 **Note Taking Transparencies,** 115 **WITNESS HISTORY Audio CD** An Expanding World **Progress Monitoring Transparencies,** 54 **Color Transparencies,** 80	**(L1) Adapted Reading and Note Taking Study Guide** Note Taking Study Guide, p. 37 **SN** Section 2 Summary, p. 38 **SN** **(L2) Adapted Reading and Note Taking Study Guide** Note Taking Study Guide, p. 37 **LPR** Section 2 Summary, p. 38 **LPR** **(L4) All in One Teaching Resources, Unit 1** Link to Literature: From *Macbeth* by William Shakespeare p. 11 **AR, GT** Biography: Desiderius Erasmus, p. 12 **AR, GT**	**Spanish Reading and Note Taking Study Guide** Note Taking Study Guide, p. 37 **ELL** Section 2 Summary, p. 38 **ELL** **Differentiated Instruction Activity,** Teacher's Edition, p. 57 **LPR** **Extend Activity,** Teacher's Edition, p. 59 **AR, GT**

*Audio support is available for all sections.

Assessment Resources
- **Progress Monitoring Transparencies,** 53–57
- **SuccessTracker™,** Chapter 1
- **Document-Based Assessment,** pp. 41–53
- ***ExamView®* Test Bank CD-ROM,** Chapter 1
- **All in One Teaching Resources, Unit 1,** Chapter Tests A and B, pp. 16–21
- **Progress Monitoring *Online* Quizzes,** Chapter 1
- **Assessment Rubrics**

Differentiated Instruction Key
(L1) Special Needs	**LPR**	Less Proficient Readers
(L2) Basic to Average	**AR**	Advanced Readers
(L3) All Students	**SN**	Special Needs Students
(L4) Average to Advanced	**GT**	Gifted and Talented
	ELL	English Language Learner

Section	Core Instruction **L3**	Differentiated Instruction **L1 L2 L4**	
Section 3 *The Protestant Reformation* ⏱ **3 periods, 1.5 blocks** **OBJECTIVES** ■ Summarize the factors that encouraged the Protestant Reformation. ■ Analyze Martin Luther's role in shaping the Protestant Reformation. ■ Explain the teachings and impact of John Calvin. **Focus Question** *How did revolts against the Roman Catholic Church affect northern European society?*	**All in One Teaching Resources, Unit 1** Section 3 Quiz, p. 4 **Reading and Note Taking Study Guide** Note Taking Study Guide, p. 39 Section 3 Summary, p. 40 **Note Taking Transparencies**, 116 **WITNESS HISTORY Audio CD** A Monk Rebels **Progress Monitoring Transparencies**, 55	**L1 Adapted Reading and Note Taking Study Guide** Note Taking Study Guide, p. 39 SN Section 3 Summary, p. 40 SN **L2 Adapted Reading and Note Taking Study Guide** Note Taking Study Guide, p. 39 LPR Section 3 Summary, p. 40 LPR **L4 All in One Teaching Resources, Unit 1** Biography: Desiderius Erasmus, p. 12 AR, GT Primary Source: From the Ninety-Five Theses of Martin Luther, 1517, p. 13 AR, GT	**Differentiated Instruction Activity,** Teacher's Edition, pp. 62, 64 SN **Spanish Reading and Note Taking Study Guide** Note Taking Study Guide, p. 39 ELL Section 3 Summary, p. 40 ELL **Differentiated Instruction Activity,** Teacher's Edition, pp. 62, 64 LPR, ELL **Extend Activity,** Teacher's Edition, p. 65 AR, GT
Section 4 *Reformation Ideas Spread* ⏱ **1.5 periods, .75 block** **OBJECTIVES** ■ Describe the new ideas that Protestant sects embraced. ■ Understand why England formed a new church. ■ Analyze how the Catholic Church reformed itself. ■ Explain why many groups faced persecution during the Reformation. **Focus Question** *How did the Reformation bring about two different religious paths in Europe?*	**All in One Teaching Resources, Unit 1** Section 4 Quiz, p. 5 **Reading and Note Taking Study Guide** Note Taking Study Guide, p. 41 Section 4 Summary, p. 42 **Note Taking Transparencies**, 117 **WITNESS HISTORY Audio CD** A King Speaks Out **Progress Monitoring Transparencies**, 56 **Color Transparencies**, 78	**L1 Adapted Reading and Note Taking Study Guide** Note Taking Study Guide, p. 41 SN Section 4 Summary, p. 42 SN **L2 Adapted Reading and Note Taking Study Guide** Note Taking Study Guide, p. 41 LPR Section 4 Summary, p. 42 LPR **L4 Differentiated Instruction Activity,** Teacher's Edition, p. 69 AR, GT **Extend Activity,** Teacher's Edition, p. 71 AR, GT	**Differentiated Instruction Activity,** Teacher's Edition, p. 67 SN **Spanish Reading and Note Taking Study Guide** Note Taking Study Guide, p. 41 ELL Section 4 Summary, p. 42 ELL **Differentiated Instruction Activity,** Teacher's Edition, p. 67 LPR, ELL
Section 5 *The Scientific Revolution* ⏱ **2 periods, 1 block** **OBJECTIVES** ■ Explain how new discoveries in astronomy changed the way people viewed the universe. ■ Understand the new scientific method and how it developed. ■ Analyze the contributions that Newton and other scientists made to the Scientific Revolution. **Focus Question** *How did discoveries in science lead to a new way of thinking for Europeans?*	**All in One Teaching Resources, Unit 1** Section 5 Quiz, p. 6 **Reading and Note Taking Study Guide** Note Taking Study Guide, p. 43 Section 5 Summary, p. 44 Concept Connector, pp. 247, 295 **Note Taking Transparencies**, 118 **WITNESS HISTORY Audio CD** Mountains on the Moon **Progress Monitoring Transparencies**, 57 **Color Transparencies**, 76	**L1 Adapted Reading and Note Taking Study Guide** Note Taking Study Guide, p. 43 SN Section 5 Summary, p. 44 SN Concept Connector, pp. 247, 295 SN **L2 Adapted Reading and Note Taking Study Guide** Note Taking Study Guide, p. 43 LPR Section 5 Summary, p. 44 LPR Concept Connector, pp. 247, 295 LPR **L4 All in One Teaching Resources, Unit 1** Viewpoints: Does the Earth Move?, p. 10 AR, GT	**Differentiated Instruction Activity,** Teacher's Edition, p. 73 SN **Spanish Reading and Note Taking Study Guide** Note Taking Study Guide, p. 43 ELL Section 5 Summary, p. 44 ELL Concept Connector, pp. 247, 295 ELL **Differentiated Instruction Activity,** Teacher's Edition, p. 73 LPR, ELL **Extend Activity,** Teacher's Edition, pp. 46c, 76 AR, GT

Author's Notes

The Renaissance of Western Art

The word *renaissance* means "rebirth," and the age was so called by its own leading intellectual lights, the classical scholars of Renaissance Italy. They thought of their era as one of cultural rebirth, a revival of the wisdom and art of what was for them Europe's greatest age—the ancient world of Periclean Greece and Augustan Rome. The legacy of ancient Rome especially enthralled them. They did a splendid job of imbuing Renaissance culture with Latin literature and Roman history and mythology. Indeed, it is almost impossible to read Renaissance literature or look at much Renaissance art without some knowledge of ancient Rome.

The study of classical culture, in contrast with the study of things divine, was known in the Renaissance as *humanism*. The men who began to read the Latin classics seriously again after a thousand years were called humanists. They were a varied lot of classical scholars—teachers and writers, poets and philosophers, pious Christians and libertines. The first of them, the fourteenth-century Italian poet Petrarch, wrote Renaissance love poems and medieval meditations on death with equal enthusiasm. The most famous sixteenth-century humanist, Erasmus, was equally admired for his editions of the New Testament and for his worldly satires on every aspect of Renaissance life, including the sins of organized religion.

The humanists as a group performed one great service for the modern West. They recovered much of our Western heritage of ancient Greek and Latin literature, lost and moldering in forgotten corners of obscure monastic libraries, unhonored and unread. They also attempted, with more modest success, to "civilize" the sword-swinging medieval nobility by a strong infusion of ancient culture. They did not produce the race of Platonic philosopher-kings they hoped for. But they did produce the first really literate aristocracy Europe had had for ten centuries—a first step at least toward matching the more cultivated courtier classes of the Muslim East or China's Confucian scholar bureaucrats.

—Anthony Esler, *The Human Venture From Prehistory to the Present*, (Upper Saddle River, New Jersey: Pearson Education, 2004), p. 372

Extend Online

Galileo and the Scientific Method

Have students research several of Galileo's experiments. Divide the class into groups and assign each group one of the experiments to discuss and demonstrate to the class. Use the steps below to help students complete the activity.

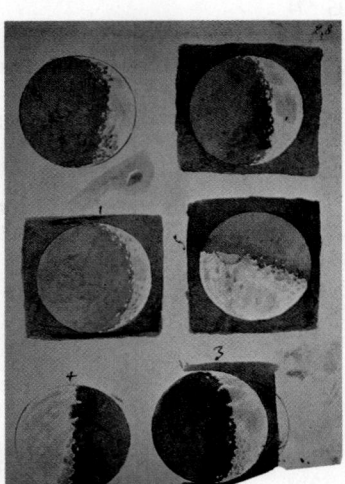

Prepare for the Activity Remind students that Galileo was a revolutionary thinker. When he invented an astronomical telescope, he not only viewed the moon (see his sketches shown at left), he also refuted Aristotle's and Ptolemy's theories about the universe.

Galileo applied new techniques to scientific research, using mathematics as a way to measure and gather data.

Conduct the Activity For help in starting the activity, send students to **Web Code nbe-1301.** Students will view several models of Galileo's experiments. Then each group will create a model of their assigned experiment and present it to the class. Be sure that students illustrate the experiment's possible hypotheses, scientific steps, and conclusions clearly.

Follow-Up Conduct a class discussion based on the following questions: Based on these experiments, what was Galileo most interested in studying? How do you think this contributed to his study of the universe and planetary location? How do you think his experiments influenced other thinkers, both from the Renaissance and modern times? Which of these techniques do you use in your experiments in science class?

Differentiated Instruction   Solutions for All Learners

Creating a Word Bank L2

Research suggests that students will best learn new vocabulary words through frequent encounters. For this reason, the text continues to use high-use words after they are introduced.

You can also encourage frequent encounters by asking students to create a word bank. This can help them process, reflect, and integrate new terms into their vocabulary. To begin, have students make a list of key terms and high-use words from this chapter. Then have students take the list home and see how many examples of these words they can find in current periodicals. Have students bring in their examples and ensure they are accurate. Then have students tape or paste the examples on their list next to the word and place these sheets in their notebooks. They may use this as a study guide later.

Peer Editing L2

Writing is a key component of any social studies class. Peer editing of essays can be a valuable tool that significantly improves the quality of student work. It allows students to see samples of writing, so they may internalize what is appropriate and acceptable in an essay. It also helps students develop confidence in their writing. As they read each other's essays, ask students to consider the following:

■ Is a thesis statement evident in the first paragraph?
■ Is appropriate and accurate historical information used to support the thesis statement?
■ Does the essay end with a well-thought out conclusion that revisits the main argument?

Provide students with a rubric to use when critiquing their classmates' work. Encourage students to be both constructive and specific in their feedback. Remind them to also edit for grammar and spelling.

Modeling Reading and Writing Skills

Vocabulary: Analyze Word Parts Tell students that when they come across an unfamiliar word, they can often break it into word parts—roots, suffixes, and prefixes—to help them recognize it and pronounce it. Remind them that the root is the base of a word with its own meaning, and that prefixes and suffixes are added to a word to change its meaning.

Model this skill by reading aloud the words *disorder and disunity* under the heading *A New Worldview Evolves* in Section 1. Point out the prefix *dis-* means the "opposite of." Since *order* means "organization" or "arrangement", the opposite must be disruption and confusion. Have students repeat this process with the word *disunity.*

Acknowledge Opposition Explain that in this chapter students will be writing a persuasive essay. (See Writing About History, p. 80.) Point out that in a persuasive essay, students need to acknowledge opposing arguments and make counter arguments to refute these. List the following arguments on the board and ask students to provide opposing arguments. Remind them that arguments should be constructed logically.

A Junk food should be banned from schools because American teenagers have poor nutritional habits.
B. Teenagers should be able to get into R-rated films if their parents give permission.
C. Video games lead to violent behavior by inciting aggressive feelings in those who play them.

As each opposing argument is presented, invite another student to counter it or do so yourself. Provide the following example as a guide:

A. Opposing argument: Teenagers should be given information to make informed decisions about food because developing decision-making habits is important. **Counter argument:** Students can develop decision-making as they choose between equally healthy options.

CHAPTER 1

Teach With Technology

PresentationEXPRESS™
Premium DVD

- Teach this chapter's core content using **PresentationExpress™ Premium,** which includes dynamic lecture notes, interactive game shows, songs, videos, and the ***ExamView®*** *QuickTake* assessment tool.
- To introduce this chapter using **PresentationExpress™ Premium,** start by asking students **Which of the following statements do you most agree with? (A) All people should remain faithful to the religion of their ancestors. (B) All people should follow the religion of their political leaders. (C) People should be free to choose their own religion. (D) People should be free not to follow a religion.** Take a class poll or record students' answers using the QuickTake feature and discuss their responses. Point out that in this chapter, they will read how Europeans used military and political means to spread their religious beliefs during the Renaissance and Reformation. Continue introducing the chapter using the chapter opener slideshow and Witness History audio.

Technology Resources

- Student**EXPRESS** CD-ROM, Chapter 1
- Teacher**EXPRESS** CD-ROM, Chapter 1
- Presentation**EXPRESS™** **Premium DVD,** Chapter 1
- **WITNESS HISTORY Audio CD,** Chapter 1
- ***ExamView*** **Test Bank CD-ROM,** English and Spanish, Chapter 1
- **Guided Reading Audio,** Spanish, Chapter 1
- **Student Edition Audio,** Chapter 1
- **Witness History Discovery School™** video program, *Machiavelli's "The Prince"*
- **Experience It! Multimedia Pack**

CHAPTER 1

The Renaissance and Reformation

1300–1650

Bibliography

For the Teacher

Collinson, Patrick. *The Reformation: A History.* New York: Modern Library, 2004.

Jardine, Lisa. *Ingenious Pursuits: Building the Scientific Revolution.* New York: Nan A. Talese, 1999.

Picard, Liza. *Elizabeth's London: Everyday Life in Elizabethan London.* St. Martin's Press, 2004.

For the Student

L3 Stanley, Diane. *Leonardo da Vinci.* New York: William Morrow, 1996.

L2 Nettleton, Pamela Hill. *William Shakespeare: Playwright and Poet.* Minneapolis: Compass Point Books, 2005.

L1 Langley, Andrew. *Leonardo and His Times.* London: Dorling Kindersley, 1999.

WITNESS HISTORY 🔊 AUDIO

Painting a Renaissance Marvel

For four years, painter and sculptor Michelangelo stood on top of a high scaffold, painting the enormous ceiling of the Sistine Chapel in Rome. He hadn't wanted to take the job, but the pope had insisted. Michelangelo wrote a poem about the work:

❝My belly is shoved up under my chin . . .
My beard faces skyward and the back of my neck is wedged into my spine . . .
My face is richly carpeted with a thick layer of paint from my brush . . .
I don't want to be here and I'm no painter.❞

Listen to the Witness History audio to hear more about Michelangelo's work and how it came to symbolize the great period of cultural rebirth that transformed Europe.

◄ An art restorer uses computer technology to restore a portion of the frescoes in the Sistine Chapel.

Bust of Michelangelo sculpted in the mid-1500s

Chapter Preview

Chapter Focus Question How did the Renaissance shape European art, thought, and religion?

Section 1
The Renaissance in Italy

Section 2
The Renaissance in the North

Section 3
The Protestant Reformation

Section 4
Reformation Ideas Spread

Section 5
The Scientific Revolution

Use the ☑ **Quick Study Timeline** at the end of this chapter to preview chapter events.

A Gutenberg bible

A gold coin from 1545 celebrating Henry VIII as head of the Church of England

Concept Connector ONLINE

To explore Essential Questions related to this chapter, go to PHSchool.com
Web Code: nbd-1307

Previewing the Chapter

■ **WITNESS HISTORY** Read the Witness History selection aloud or play the accompanying audio. Point out the themes the selection touches on, including the close relationship between Renaissance art and the Church, and the importance of the work of talented artists like Michelangelo. Explain to students that works like the Sistine Chapel have come to symbolize both the Roman Catholic Church and the Renaissance.

🔊 AUDIO **Witness History Audio CD,** Painting a Renaissance Marvel

■ **Analyzing the Visuals** Have students study the detail of the mural shown in the photo. Remind them that this is only a small detail of an enormous work that took years to paint. **What questions do the photo and the Witness History selection bring to mind about the Renaissance or Michelangelo in particular?** (*Example: What might compel an artist to undertake such a huge painting project?*) Have students write these questions down in their notebooks. Remind them to return to them as they read the chapter.

■ **Focus** Write the Chapter Focus Question on the board. Tell students to keep this question in mind as they read the chapter. (*Answer appears with Chapter Assessment answers.*) Have students preview the section titles for this chapter.

Step-by-Step Instruction

Objectives

As you teach this section, keep students focused on the following objectives to help them answer the Section Focus Question and master core content.

- Describe the characteristics of the Renaissance and understand why it began in Italy.
- Identify Renaissance artists and explain how new ideas affected the arts of the period.
- Understand how writers of the time addressed Renaissance themes.

Prepare to Read

Build Background Knowledge L3

Based on their previous reading about the Middle Ages, have students predict how Europe would change during the Renaissance.

Set a Purpose L3

- **WITNESS HISTORY** Read the selection aloud or play the audio.

  ◀)) AUDIO **Witness History Audio CD,** An Artist Becomes a Biographer

  Ask **Why was Vasari's book so important?** (*It gave firsthand information about Renaissance artists from a knowledgeable source.*)

- **Focus** Point out the Section Focus Question and write it on the board. Tell students to refer to this question as they read. (*Answer appears with Section 1 Assessment answers.*)

- **Preview** Have students preview the Section Objectives and the list of Terms, People, and Places.

- **Reading Skill** Have students use the *Reading Strategy: Main Ideas* worksheet.

  All in One Teaching Resources, Unit 1, p. 8

- **Note Taking** Have students read this section using the Structured Read Aloud strategy (TE, p. T20). Have them fill in the outline with the main themes of the Italian Renaissance.

  Reading and Note Taking Study Guide, pp. 34–35

A detail from the Uffizi

WITNESS HISTORY ◀)) AUDIO

An Artist Becomes a Biographer

In 1546, a young artist named Giorgio Vasari dined at the Cardinal's residence in Rome. The conversation turned to the amazing artistic achievement of Renaissance Italy. Vasari decided to record a tribute to all the important Italian artists who had contributed to this remarkably creative time period. Four years later, Vasari published his book *Lives of the Most Eminent Painters, Sculptors, and Architects.* A true "Renaissance man"— he was an able painter and architect as well as a writer—Vasari also became a biographer and historian of his era.

Focus Question What were the ideals of the Renaissance, and how did Italian artists and writers reflect these ideals?

Vasari designed the Uffizi Gallery in Florence, which houses his self-portrait.

The Renaissance in Italy

Objectives

- Describe the characteristics of the Renaissance and understand why it began in Italy.
- Identify Renaissance artists and explain how new ideas affected the arts of the period.
- Understand how writers of the time addressed Renaissance themes.

Terms, People, and Places

humanism	Leonardo
humanities	Michelangelo
Petrarch	Raphael
Florence	Baldassare Castiglione
patron	Niccolò Machiavelli
perspective	

Note Taking

Reading Skill: Identify Main Ideas As you read, create an outline like the one below to record main ideas about the Italian Renaissance.

> I. What was the Renaissance?
>   A. A changing worldview
>   1.
>   2.
>   B. A spirit of adventure

A new age had dawned in Western Europe, given expression by remarkable artists and thinkers. Europeans called this age the Renaissance, meaning "rebirth." It began in the 1300s and reached its peak around 1500. The Renaissance marked the transition from medieval times to the early modern world.

What Was the Renaissance?

The Renaissance was a time of creativity and great change in many areas—political, social, economic, and cultural. It marked a slow shift from an agricultural to an urban society, in which trade assumed greater importance than in the past. It was also a time when creative thinking and new technology let people comprehend and describe their world more accurately.

A New Worldview Evolves During the Renaissance, creative minds set out to transform their own age. Their era, they felt, was a time of rebirth after what they saw as the disorder and disunity of the medieval world.

Renaissance thinkers had a reawakened interest in the classical learning of Greece and Rome, which medieval scholars had preserved. They continued to use Latin as the language of the Church as well as for scholarship. Yet they produced new attitudes toward culture and learning. Medieval scholars had focused more on religious beliefs and spirituality. In contrast, Renaissance thinkers explored the richness and variety of human experience in

Vocabulary Builder

Use the information below and the following resources to teach the high-use words from this section. **All in One Teaching Resources, Unit 1,** p. 7; **Teaching Resources, Skills Handbook,** p. 3

High-Use Words	Definitions and Sample Sentences
comprehend, p. 48	*v.* to understand; take in They could not **comprehend** the speaker's words at first because he spoke so softly.
emerge, p. 48	*v.* to develop; rise from; become known A bustling new town began to **emerge** from the ruins of the old city.

the here and now. At the same time, society placed a new emphasis on individual achievement. Indeed, the Renaissance ideal was a person with talents in many fields.

A Spirit of Adventure The Renaissance supported a spirit of adventure and a wide-ranging curiosity that led people to explore new worlds or to reexamine old ones. Navigators who sailed across the ocean, scientists who looked at the universe in new ways, and writers and artists who experimented with new forms and techniques all shared that spirit. In part, that spirit of adventure came from a new view of man himself. As Italian thinker Pico della Mirandola asserted in 1486: "To [man] it is granted to have whatever he chooses, to be whatever he wills."

Expressing Humanism At the heart of the Italian Renaissance was an intellectual movement known as **humanism.** Humanists studied the classical culture of Greece and Rome, but used that study to increase their understanding of their own times. Though most humanists were pious Christians, they focused on worldly subjects rather than on the religious issues that had occupied medieval thinkers. Humanists believed that education should stimulate the individual's creative powers. They emphasized the **humanities**—subjects such as grammar, rhetoric (the study of using language effectively), poetry, and history—that had been taught in ancient Greek and Roman schools.

Francesco **Petrarch** (PEE trahrk), a Florentine who lived in the 1300s, was an early Renaissance humanist, poet, and scholar. He assembled a library of Greek and Roman manuscripts in monasteries and churches. In later years his efforts and those of others encouraged by his example enabled the works of Cicero, Homer, and Virgil to again become known to Western Europeans.

✔ **Checkpoint** What were the main characteristics of the Renaissance?

Italy: Cradle of the Renaissance

The Renaissance began in Italy. Over the next hundred years it spread to the rest of Europe, eventually transforming the entire Western world. Italy was the place where the Renaissance emerged for several reasons.

Italy's History and Geography Renaissance thinkers had a new interest in ancient Rome. Italy had been the center of the Roman empire, and people could study its art and architecture. The Roman Catholic Church, based in Rome, supported many artists and scholars.

Italy's location on the Mediterranean Sea also encouraged trade with the Muslim world just across the sea. Ships carrying a variety of goods docked at Italy's many ports. Banking, manufacturing, and merchant networks developed to support trade. Italian merchants led the growth of trade across Europe during the late Middle Ages. Trade provided the wealth that fueled Italy's Renaissance.

Trade routes also carried new ideas that were important in shaping the Renaissance. Muslim scholars had preserved and developed the scientific and technical knowledge of ancient Greece and Rome, which had been forgotten in medieval Europe. Contact through trade gave Italy access to the Muslim world's wealth of knowledge.

Michelangelo's *David*
Michelangelo sculpted his masterpiece *David* out of a block of marble left over from another sculpture. Completed in 1504, the statue was commissioned to express the power and strength of Florence.

Vocabulary Builder

comprehend—(kahm pree HEND) *v.* understand; take in

emerge—(ee MURJ) *v.* develop; rise from; become known

L1 Special Needs **L2 Less Proficient Readers**

To help students understand the changes during the Renaissance, ask them to create a two-column chart. In the first column, have them list how people viewed the world in the Middle Ages. Then have students read this section and list the new ideas of the Renaissance in the second column. They can use this chart to summarize the changes during the Renaissance.

L2 English Language Learners

Use the following resources to help students acquire basic skills:

Reading and Note Taking Study Guide
- Adapted Note Taking Study Guide, pp. 34–35
- Adapted Section Summary, p. 36

What Was the Renaissance?

Instruct

- **Introduce: Vocabulary Builder**
  Have students read the Vocabulary Builder term and definition. Ask them to predict what new ideas people might have begun to **comprehend** during the Renaissance.

- **Teach** As you discuss the meaning of the Renaissance, ask **What does the Witness History selection mean by the term** *Renaissance man*? *(someone of broad achievement with talent in many areas)* Then ask **What other qualities could you add to a description of a Renaissance man?** *(curiosity, interest in classical learning, adventurous spirit, belief in importance of education)* **Why did these characteristics emerge so strongly during the Renaissance rather than the Middle Ages?** *(During the Middle Ages, people were more focused on religion and spirituality. The Renaissance brought a new interest in the material and human worlds and an appreciation for individual achievement.)*

- **Quick Activity** Display **Color Transparency 77:** *Pietà,* **by Michelangelo.** Use the lesson suggested in the transparency book to guide a discussion on how Renaissance artists modeled their works on the art of classical Greece and Rome and revived interest in those cultures. Discuss how this piece reflects classical elements, such as form and style.

  📖 Color Transparencies, 77

Independent Practice

Have students fill in the Outline Map *Europe About 1600* and label the main states and kingdoms.

 Teaching Resources, Unit 1, p. 14

Monitor Progress

Circulate to make sure students are filling in their Outline Maps accurately. Administer the Geography Quiz.

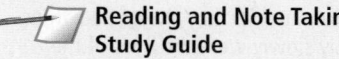 Teaching Resources, Unit 1, p. 15

Answer

✔ a new worldview based on human experience, an emphasis on education and humanism, and a spirit of adventure and curiosity

Italy: Cradle of the Renaissance

Instruct

- **Introduce: Vocabulary Builder**
  Have students read the Vocabulary Builder term, *emerge,* and its definition. Remind them of the meaning of the word *Renaissance.* Ask students to make a connection between the two words.

- **Teach** Emphasize how Italy's city-states differed from political structures in the rest of Europe. Ask **How did the city-state structure encourage the Renaissance?** *(City-states were competitive, encouraging innovative ideas; wealthy rulers of city-states were patrons to artists; cities had greater concentrations of artists, artisans, and scholars; trade was well established in the city-states.)*

- **Quick Activity** Direct students to the map on the next page. Point out Italy's location on the Mediterranean Sea. Have students trace Italy's trade routes on the map. Ask them why they think the cities of Genoa and Venice became such important centers of trade.

Independent Practice

- Display **Color Transparency 81: Venice as a Center of Trade.** Ask students to choose a geographic area that could be considered a crossroads of trade today. Have them write a paragraph explaining what factors—geographic, cultural, or other—make it a crossroads.

  Color Transparencies, 81

- Have students access **Web Code nbp-1311** to take the **Geography Interactive Audio Guided Tour** and then have them answer the map skills questions in the text.

Monitor Progress

Reread the title of this section, Italy: Cradle of the Renaissance. Ask students to explain why the term *cradle* is used here to describe the growth of the Renaissance in Italy. Ensure that students understand the reasons why Italy was the birthplace of the Renaissance.

Answers

Caption elegant clothing and furniture, servants, bags of money

✓ It was a crossroads of trade and had been the center of the classical world.

Italian Bankers
An illuminated manuscript from the late 1400s depicts a typical scene in an Italian banking house. *How is the wealth of the banker shown in this image?*

Italy's Vibrant City-States Unlike the kingdoms of most of the rest of Europe, Italy was divided into many small city-states. Each Italian city-state was controlled by a powerful family and dominated by a wealthy and powerful merchant class. These merchant families exerted both political and economic leadership, and their interest in art and emphasis on personal achievement helped to shape the Italian Renaissance.

The Medici (MED uh chee) family of **Florence,** for example, ranked among the richest merchants and bankers in Europe. Cosimo de' Medici gained control of the Florentine government in 1434, and the family continued as uncrowned rulers of the city for many years. Cosimo's grandson Lorenzo, known as "the Magnificent," represented the Renaissance ideal. A clever politician, he held Florence together during difficult times in the late 1400s. He was also a generous **patron,** or financial supporter, of the arts. At Lorenzo's invitation, poets and philosophers frequently visited the Medici palace. Artists learned their craft by sketching ancient Roman statues displayed in the Medici gardens.

The Medicis' great wealth and influence transformed Florence. Perhaps more than any other city, it came to symbolize the energy and brilliance of the Italian Renaissance. Like the ancient city of Athens, it produced a dazzling number of gifted poets, artists, architects, scholars, and scientists in a relatively short span of time.

✓ **Checkpoint** Why was Italy a favorable setting for the Renaissance?

Renaissance Art Flowers

The Renaissance attained its most glorious expression in its paintings, sculpture, and architecture. Wealthy patrons, popes, and princes played a major role in this artistic flowering. Ordinary people—who were beginning to appreciate human experiences not related to the Church—also played a role.

Reflecting Humanist Thought Renaissance art reflected the ideas of humanism. Like artists of the Middle Ages, Renaissance artists portrayed religious themes. However, they often set religious figures such as Jesus and Mary against classical Greek or Roman backgrounds. Painters also produced portraits of well-known figures of the day, reflecting the humanist interest in individual achievement. Renaissance artists studied ancient Greek and Roman works and revived many classical forms. The sculptor Donatello, for example, created a life-size statue of a soldier on horseback. It was the first such figure done since ancient times.

Using New Artistic Techniques Roman art had been very realistic, but in medieval times art became much more stylized. Renaissance painters returned to the realism of classical times by developing new techniques for representing both humans and landscapes. In particular, the rules of **perspective** allowed Renaissance artists to create realistic art. By making distant objects smaller than those close to the viewer, artists could paint scenes that appeared three-dimensional.

History Background

Italian Renaissance Society Not all people experienced the Renaissance in the same way. While the upper class enjoyed lives made easier by wealth and enriched by art and ideas, most Italians of the time lived and worked much as they always had: from hand to mouth. Only slowly were the lives of the working classes affected by the Renaissance.

In addition, the Renaissance occurred against a background of extreme violence. Families within city-states feuded and fought, as Shakespeare immortalized in his late-1500s play *Romeo and Juliet.* Italian city-states were constantly at war with one another. Yet none of this social conflict dampened the spirit of the Renaissance. Indeed, people looked to new, innovative Renaissance ideas to help them solve the problems of their time.

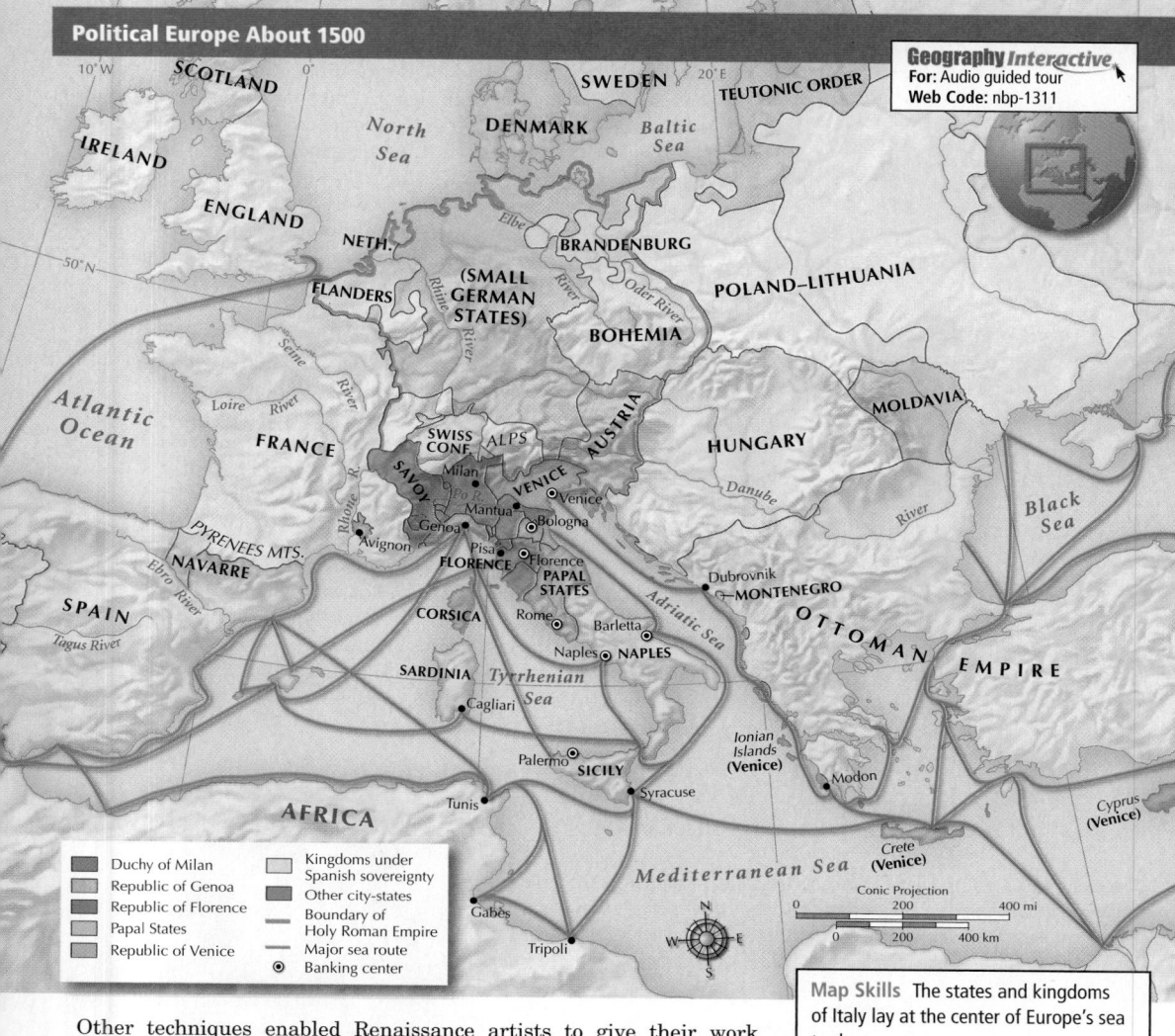

Geography *Interactive*
For: Audio guided tour
Web Code: nbp-1311

Map legend:
- Duchy of Milan
- Republic of Genoa
- Republic of Florence
- Papal States
- Republic of Venice
- Kingdoms under Spanish sovereignty
- Other city-states
- Boundary of Holy Roman Empire
- Major sea route
- ⊙ Banking center

Map Skills The states and kingdoms of Italy lay at the center of Europe's sea trade.

1. **Locate** (a) Florence (b) Palermo (c) Crete
2. **Identify** Which republic controlled Crete? Which kingdom controlled Sicily?
3. **Apply Information** Why were so many banking centers located in Italy?

Other techniques enabled Renaissance artists to give their work energy and realism. Renaissance painters used shading to make objects look round and real, and new oil paints to reflect light. Painters and sculptors also studied human anatomy and drew from observing live models. As a result, they were able to portray the human body much more accurately than medieval artists had done.

Architecture: A "Social Art" Architecture was transformed in Renaissance Italy. Architect Leon Alberti described architecture as a "social art," meant to blend beauty with utility and improvement of society. Architects rejected the Gothic style of the late Middle Ages as disorderly. Instead, they adopted the columns, arches, and domes that had been favored by the Greeks and Romans. For the cathedral in Florence, Filippo Brunelleschi (broo nay LAYS kee) created a majestic dome, which he modeled on the dome of the Pantheon in Rome. Like other Renaissance artists, Brunelleschi was multitalented. He studied art and sculpture with Donatello and was an accomplished engineer, inventing many of the machines used to construct his dome.

Renaissance Art Flowers 🔢

Instruct

- **Introduce: Key Terms** Ask students to find the key term *humanism* (in blue) in the text and explain its meaning. Ask **How do Leonardo's notebooks reflect humanist themes?** (*He had a special interest in the human body and in drawing figures realistically; his notebook-keeping indicates his active curiosity about the world around him.*) **How did an interest in humanism lead to the development of new art techniques?** (*Artists looked for new techniques that would let them draw, paint, and sculpt more realistically.*)

- **Teach** Review the lives and achievements of Leonardo, Michelangelo, and Raphael. Remind students that each of these artists created great religious works, which were often commissioned by popes. Ask **How did Renaissance artists differ from medieval artists in their treatment of religious themes?** (*Religious figures were shown realistically, in more natural settings; religious paintings included classical themes.*)

- **Quick Activity** Display **Color Transparency 79:** *School of Athens.* Together with students, identify all of the Renaissance elements that are blended in the painting: the classical statues of ancient philosophers; the emphasis on learning (several of the figures are perusing books or diagrams); the use of perspective. Also explain to students that several of the figures in the painting are actually of famous Renaissance artists, including Leonardo and Raphael himself.

  🏛 **Color Transparencies,** 79

Careers

Conservators Archivists, curators, and conservators work to preserve cultural objects. For instance, art conservators, or restorers, first analyze materials to identify any damage and its cause. Next they determine how best to repair the material and prevent future damage. Then they restore it to maintain its original characteristics. Art restorers work on a variety of objects, from paintings and paper to ceramics and furniture. While most work takes place in laboratories, art restorers also spend time in museums, art galleries, and private homes, advising on collections. They help determine how artwork is stored, monitor environmental conditions, and help set up exhibits. This work combines scientific, historical, and visual art skills.

Answers

Map Skills
1. Review locations with students.
2. Venice; Spain
3. Its central location made it ideal for supplying loans to traders.

Independent Practice

Biography To help students better understand women's role in Renaissance art and society, have them read the biography *Isabella d'Este* and answer the questions on the worksheet.

All in One Teaching Resources, Unit 1, p. 9

Monitor Progress

After students have read the biography, read them the History Background note at the bottom of this page. Then ask them to write a paragraph explaining whether they think d'Este was a typical Renaissance woman or an unusual one. Use the Think-Write-Pair-Share strategy (TE, p. T23) to have students share their findings with each other.

Leonardo da Vinci Artist **Leonardo** da Vinci (duh VIN chee) (1452–1519) had an endless curiosity that fed a genius for invention. He made sketches of nature and of models in his studio, and dissected corpses to learn how bones and muscles work. As a result, Leonardo's paintings grip people with their realism. The *Mona Lisa* is a portrait of a woman whose mysterious smile has baffled viewers for centuries. *The Last Supper*, showing Jesus and his apostles on the night before the crucifixion, is both a moving religious painting and a masterpiece of perspective. Because Leonardo experimented with a new type of paint, much of *The Last Supper* decayed over the years. However, it has recently been restored.

Leonardo thought of himself as an artist. Yet his talents and accomplishments ranged over many areas, including botany, anatomy, optics, music, architecture, and engineering. He made sketches for flying machines and undersea boats centuries before the first airplane or submarine was actually built. Though most of his paintings are lost today, his many notebooks survive as a testament to his genius and creativity.

Michelangelo Artist **Michelangelo** Buonarroti (1475–1564), like Leonardo, had many talents—he was a sculptor, engineer, painter, architect, and poet. Michelangelo has been called a "melancholy genius" because his work reflects his many life-long spiritual and artistic struggles. In his twenties, he created marble masterpieces such as *David* and the

● INFOGRAPHIC

The Discovery of Perspective

Before the 1400s, artists did not know how to create perspective, or the technique of showing distant objects on flat surfaces the way the eye actually sees them. The discovery of perspective revolutionized art. Using simple geometry, Renaissance artists could for the first time reproduce what their eyes actually saw.

Brunelleschi is credited with inventing perspective. His many studies (left) helped him design Florence's Duomo, completed in 1436. At 185 feet (56 m) high, it was the largest domed structure built since A.D. 125. ▶

Artist Leon Alberti refined Brunelleschi's ideas. ▶ He wrote books explaining the rules of perspective, and developed the "perspective net" (right). To show perspective, the artist looks over an eyepiece and through the net at a model (far right). Then he reproduces the outlines of the model on paper with grids corresponding to those on the net.

Link to Art

Renaissance Women Most upper-class Renaissance women led domestic lives, running their households, attending court, or serving in religious orders. While these women often received a classical humanist education, they were expected to use their skills privately. A very few women overcame the Renaissance limits on education and training to become professional artists. Sometimes these women kept their activity secret, allowing their work to be passed off by their husbands as their own. Much more rarely, a woman artist gained professional acceptance on her own terms. In the 1500s, Sofonisba Anguissola (soh foh NEEZ bah ahn GWEE soh lah), an Italian noblewoman, became court painter to King Philip II of Spain.

Pietà. The *Pietà* captures the sorrow of the Biblical Mary as she cradles her dead son Jesus on her knees. Michelangelo's heroic statue of *David*, the Biblical shepherd who killed the giant Goliath, recalls the harmony and grace of ancient Greek tradition.

One of Michelangelo's greatest projects was painting a series of huge murals to decorate the ceiling of the Sistine Chapel in Rome. The enormous task, which took four years to complete and left the artist partially crippled, depicted the biblical history of the world from the Creation to the Flood. Michelangelo was also a talented architect. His most famous design was for the dome of St. Peter's Cathedral in Rome. It served as a model for many later structures, including the United States Capitol building in Washington, D.C.

Raphael A few years younger than Michelangelo, **Raphael** (rah fah EL) (1483–1520) was widely admired both for his artistic talent and "his sweet and gracious nature." Raphael studied the works of the great masters but developed his own style of painting that blended Christian and classical styles. He is probably best known for his tender portrayals of the Madonna, the mother of Jesus. In *The School of Athens,* Raphael pictured an imaginary gathering of great thinkers and scientists, including Plato, Aristotle, Socrates, and the Arab philosopher Averroës. With typical Renaissance self-confidence, Raphael included the faces of Michelangelo, Leonardo—and himself.

✔ **Checkpoint** How were Renaissance ideals reflected in the arts?

History *Interactive*
For: Interactive The Last Supper
Visit: www.PHSchool.com
Web Code: nbp-1312

Leonardo eagerly explored perspective in his mural *The Last Supper.* He uses converging lines, like those shown below, to create a vanishing point. This vanishing point draws the viewer's eye to the space above Jesus, and gives the painting the illusion of space and depth. ▶

Thinking Critically
1. **Apply Information** Why was the invention of perspective necessary for artists to achieve realism in painting?
2. **Analyze Visuals** What other techniques bring the eye to the central figure of Jesus in *The Last Supper?*

Writing for a New Society ⑬

Instruct

- **Introduce** Ask students if they recognize the key term ***Machiavellian.*** Elicit meanings, then explain that the word came from Machiavelli and his book *The Prince.* Have students read the subsection titled Machiavelli's Successful Prince and then engage in a brief debate between those who agree with Machiavelli and those who side with his critics.

- **Teach** Review the two writers discussed in the section and their motivations for writing. Ask **What Renaissance ideals did each of these men espouse?** *(Castiglione: the multi-talented man; Machiavelli: political realism)* **Why might these ideas have particularly appealed to people during the Renaissance?** *(Emerging from the stagnation of the medieval world, they would have embraced a vision of their society as better than the past.)*

- **Quick Activity** Show students *Machiavelli's "The Prince"* from the **Witness History Discovery School**™ video program. Ask them to list the factors that may have inspired Machiavelli to write *The Prince. (his experience as a diplomat, his understanding of government, power, and conflict in his native Italy, and the rise of interest in the humanities)*

Independent Practice

Ask students if "how-to" books are still written today. Have pairs of students create lists of subjects a "how-to" writer might address today to help people succeed in society.

Monitor Progress

As students fill in their outlines, circulate to make sure they understand the main themes of the Italian Renaissance. For a completed version of the outline, see
📖 **Note Taking Transparencies,** 114

Answers

✔ Artists emphasized classical subjects and the human form, and they employed new techniques for showing subjects more realistically.

Thinking Critically
1. Without it, artists could not show objects as the eye sees them.
2. Jesus appears in the center and in front of the windows, and most apostles are looking in his direction.

Assess and Reteach

Assess Progress **L3**

- Have students complete the Section Assessment.
- Administer the Section Quiz.
- **All in One** Teaching Resources, **Unit 1,** p. 2
- To further assess student understanding, use

   Progress Monitoring Transparencies, 53

Reteach

If students need more instruction, have them read the section summary.

 Reading and Note Taking **L3**
Study Guide, p. 36

 Adapted Reading and **L1** **L2**
Note Taking Study Guide, p. 36

 Spanish Reading and **L2**
Note Taking Study Guide, p. 36

Extend **L4**

Point out the Infographic about perspective. Divide students into small groups. Have each group discuss why the discovery of perspective was such an important milestone in the development of Renaissance art. Then have each group present its conclusions to the class.

Answers

PRIMARY SOURCE His wide-ranging talents and avid curiosity reflect Renaissance ideals.

✓ Writers focused on the human experience in the world around them.

In the mid-1500s, Giorgio Vasari wrote a biography of Leonardo da Vinci, whose self-portrait is shown here. Why is Leonardo da Vinci described today as an ideal "Renaissance man"?

Primary Source

❝Sometimes, in supernatural fashion, beauty, grace, and talent are united beyond measure in one single person. . . . This was seen by all mankind in Leonardo da Vinci . . . so great was his genius, and such its growth, that to whatever difficulties he turned his mind, he solved them with ease. In him was great bodily strength . . . with a spirit and courage ever royal and magnanimous; and the fame of his name so increased, that not only in his lifetime was he held in esteem, but his reputation became even greater among posterity after his death.❞ 🔊 AUDIO

Writing for a New Society

Italian writers reflected the trademark Renaissance curiosity and interest in the humanities. Humanists and historians wrote works of philosophy and scholarship. Other writers developed a literature of guidebooks to help ambitious men and women who wanted to achieve success in the Renaissance world.

Castiglione's Ideal Courtier The most widely read of these handbooks was *The Book of the Courtier*. Its author, **Baldassare Castiglione** (kahs teel YOH nay), describes the manners, skills, learning, and virtues that a member of the court should have. Castiglione's ideal courtier was a well-educated, well-mannered aristocrat who mastered many fields, from poetry to music to sports.

Castiglione's ideal differed for men and women. The ideal man, he wrote, is athletic but not overactive. He is good at games, but not a gambler. He plays a musical instrument and knows literature and history but is not arrogant. The ideal woman offers a balance to men. She is graceful and kind, lively but reserved. She is beautiful, "for outer beauty," wrote Castiglione, "is the true sign of inner goodness."

Machiavelli's Successful Prince Niccolò Machiavelli (mahk ee uh VEL ee) wrote a guide for rulers on how to gain and maintain power. Unlike ancient writers such as Plato, Machiavelli did not discuss leadership in terms of high ideals. Instead, his book *The Prince* looked at real rulers in an age of ruthless power politics. Machiavelli stressed that the end justifies the means. He urged rulers to use whatever methods were necessary to achieve their goals.

Machiavelli saw himself as an enemy of oppression and corruption, but critics attacked his cynical advice. (In fact, the term "Machiavellian" came to refer to the use of deceit in politics.) Later students of government, however, argued that Machiavelli provided a realistic look at politics. His work continues to spark debate because it raises important ethical questions about the nature of government and the use of power.

✓ **Checkpoint** How did Renaissance writings express realism?

 SECTION 1 Assessment

> **Progress Monitoring Online**
> **For:** Self-quiz with vocabulary practice
> **Web Code:** nba-1311

Terms, People, and Places
1. For each term, person, or place listed at the beginning of the section, write a sentence explaining its significance.

Note Taking
2. **Reading Skill: Identify Main Ideas** Use your completed outline to answer the Focus Question: What were the ideals of the Renaissance, and how did Italian artists and writers reflect these ideals?

Comprehension and Critical Thinking
3. **Make Generalizations** How was the Renaissance worldview different from that of the Middle Ages?
4. **Summarize** In what ways did Italian city-states encourage the Renaissance?
5. **Synthesize Information** How did humanism influence Renaissance painting and sculpture?
6. **Recognize Ideologies** Why were nature and human nature important to Renaissance artists and writers?

● **Writing About History**
Quick Write: Generate Arguments Consider the following thesis statement for a persuasive essay: Renaissance Italy produced some of the greatest writers and thinkers that the world has ever known. Next, generate a number of arguments that support that thesis. Rank your arguments in order of importance.

Section 1 Assessment

1. Sentences should reflect an understanding of each term, person, and place listed at the beginning of the section.
2. Artists, architects, and writers used realistic techniques. Their work reflected the Renaissance ideals of humanism, an appreciation of the classics, and curiosity.
3. The medieval worldview was shaped by religion; it accepted tradition and the idea

that only God was perfect. In contrast, the Renaissance worldview was shaped by inquiry, exploration, and the idea that humans could perfect themselves.
4. Their connections to trade brought wealth that spurred the Renaissance and spread new ideas. The competition among city-states encouraged new ways of thinking.
5. Artists focused on human beings, their achievements, and their relationship to God.
6. They thought that art should reflect the reality of human experience.

● **Writing About History**
Responses should show an understanding that each argument should support the thesis statement, and arguments should be ranked.

For additional assessment, have students access **Progress Monitoring Online** at **Web Code nba-1311.**

The Prince by Niccolò Machiavelli

Florentine Niccolò Machiavelli (1469–1527) served in the government as a diplomat for fourteen years before becoming a full-time writer and scholar. In 1513, he used his experience in politics and his studies of ancient Roman history to write a book called *The Prince*. In this book, Machiavelli combined his personal experience of politics with his knowledge of the past to offer a guide to rulers on how to gain and maintain power.

A portrait of Niccolò Machiavelli painted in the late 1500s

Here the question arises: is it better to be loved than feared, or vice versa? I don't doubt that every prince would like to be both; but since it is hard to accommodate these qualities, if you have to make a choice, to be feared is much safer than to be loved. For it is a good general rule about men, that they are ungrateful, fickle[1], liars and deceivers, fearful of danger and greedy for gain. While you serve their welfare, they are all yours, offering their blood, their belongings, their lives, and their children's lives, as we noted above—so long as the danger is remote. But when the danger is close at hand, they turn against you. Then, any prince who has relied on their words and has made no other preparations will come to grief; because friendships that are bought at a price, and not with greatness and nobility of soul, may be paid for but they are not acquired, and they cannot be used in time of need. People are less concerned with offending a man who makes himself loved than one who makes himself feared: the reason is that love is a link of obligation which men, because they are rotten, will break any time they think doing so serves their advantage; but fear involves dread of punishment, from which they can never escape.

Still, a prince should make himself feared in such a way that, even if he gets no love, he gets no hate either; because it is perfectly possible to be feared and not hated, and this will be the result if only the prince will keep his hands off the property of his subjects or citizens, and off their women. When he does have to shed blood, he should be sure to have a strong justification and manifest[2] cause; but above all, he should not confiscate[3] people's property, because men are quicker to forget the death of a father than the loss of a patrimony[4]. Besides, pretexts[5] for confiscation are always plentiful; it never fails that a prince who starts living by plunder can find reasons to rob someone else. . . .Returning to the question of being feared or loved, I conclude that since men love at their own inclination but can be made to fear at the inclination of the prince, a shrewd prince will lay his foundations on what is under his own control, not on what is controlled by others.

---

1. **fickle** (FIK ul) *adj.* changeable
2. **manifest** (MAN uh fest) *adj.* clear; plain to see
3. **confiscate** (KAHN fis kayt) *v.* to seize or take

4. **patrimony** (PA truh moh nee) *n.* property or inheritance
5. **pretexts** (PREE teksts) *n.* excuses; false reasons

WITNESS HISTORY VIDEO

Watch *Machiavelli's The Prince* to explore the world of an important "Renaissance man" on the **Witness History Discovery School**™ video program.

DISCOVERY SCHOOL

Thinking Critically

1. **Summarize Information** Why does Machiavelli believe that it is better for a prince to be feared than to be loved?
2. **Make Comparisons** Reread the section of the text titled Castiglione's Ideal Courtier. Is Machiavelli's description of an ideal prince consistent with that of Castiglione's courtier? Why or why not?

Niccolò Machiavelli: *The Prince*

Objectives

- Explain why Machiavelli believes that it is better for a prince to be feared than loved.
- Identify the qualities Machiavelli believes successful prince needs to have.

Build Background Knowledge L3

Ask students what qualities they think an ideal leader should have. As they identify qualities, write them on the board.

Instruct

- Remind students of the meaning of the term *Machiavellian*. After students have read the selection, ask them if they think the common usage of the term accurately describes Machiavelli's prince. *(Students should note that Machiavelli points out that even a feared leader must act justly so as not to incite hatred.)* Have students identify specific words or phrases from the excerpt to support their views.

- Point out that although the subject of *The Prince* is political leaders, Machiavelli spends a good deal of time talking about people in general. Ask **What is Machiavelli's general view of people?** *(He has a critical view; he describes them as "greedy," "fickle," and "liars.")* **How might his experience as a diplomat have shaped that view?** *(He may have observed diplomats who used any means necessary to get what they wanted.)*

Monitor Progress

Have students return to the qualities they identified in the background exercise. Ask them to write a paragraph explaining whether Machiavelli would agree that a leader should have these qualities.

Thinking Critically

1. He says that people's love is fickle and untrustworthy, while people's fear can be counted on at all times.
2. Answers should suggest that they are not consistent, because Castiglione's courtier is well-mannered, not arrogant, and always attuned to those around him, while Machiavelli's prince is concerned with his own power.

Objectives

As you teach this section, keep students focused on the following objectives to help them answer the Section Focus Question and master core content.

■ Explain how the printing revolution shaped European society.

■ Describe the themes that northern European artists, humanists, and writers explored.

Prepare to Read

Build Background Knowledge L3

Have students predict the effect of Italy's Renaissance on northern Europe.

Set a Purpose L3

■ **WITNESS HISTORY** Read the selection aloud or play the audio.

🔊)) AUDIO **Witness History Audio CD,** An Expanding World

Ask **Why does Rabelais compare his time to that of Plato and Cicero?** *(Renaissance humanists measured their own time against the classical period.)*

■ **Focus** Point out the Section Focus Question and write it on the board. Tell students to refer to this question as they read. *(Answer appears with Section 2 Assessment answers.)*

■ **Preview** Have students preview the Section Objectives and the list of Terms, People, and Places.

■ **Note Taking** Have students read this section using the Paragraph Shrinking strategy (TE, p. T20), and have them fill in the chart with the main features of the Renaissance in the North.

✐ **Reading and Note Taking Study Guide,** p. 37

Answer

✔ It enabled books to be produced more cheaply, raised literacy rates, and spread new ideas quickly.

WITNESS HISTORY 🔊)) AUDIO
An Expanding World

❝ All the world is full of knowing men, of most learned schoolmasters, and vast libraries; and it appears to me as a truth, that neither in Plato's time, nor Cicero's . . . there was ever such conveniency for studying, as we see at this day there is. ❞
—François Rabelais, 1532

Scholars and artists throughout northern Europe in the 1500s lived in an exciting time. The newly invented printing press made the world seem smaller. All over Europe, the world of knowledge was expanding in ways that would have been unthinkable in medieval times.

Focus Question How did the Renaissance develop in northern Europe?

A modern artist depicts Gutenberg and his printing press; at top right is a Bible Gutenberg printed *circa* 1455.

The Renaissance in the North

Objectives
• Explain how the printing revolution shaped European society.
• Describe the themes that northern European artists, humanists, and writers explored.

Terms, People, and Places

Johann Gutenberg	Erasmus
Flanders	Thomas More
Albrecht Dürer	utopian
engraving	Shakespeare
vernacular	

Note Taking

Reading Strategy: Identify Main Ideas Keep track of the main ideas of the section by creating a chart like the one below. Add boxes to complete the chart.

```
          Renaissance in the North
   ┌───────────┬──────────┬──────────┐
   Printing    Artists and  Humanists
   Revolution  Writers
   ┌───────┐   ┌───────┐   ┌───────┐
   └───────┘   └───────┘   └───────┘
```

As the Renaissance began to flower in Italy, northern Europe was still recovering from the ravages of the Black Death. But by the 1400s, the cities of the north began to enjoy the economic growth—and the wealth—needed to develop their own Renaissance.

The Printing Revolution

An astounding invention aided the spread of the Renaissance. In about 1455, **Johann Gutenberg** (GOOT un burg) of Mainz, Germany, printed the first complete edition of the Bible using a printing press with movable type. A printing revolution had begun that would transform Europe. Before the printing press, there were only a few thousand books in all of Europe. These books had been slowly copied out by hand. By 1500, according to some estimates, 15 to 20 million volumes had been produced on printing presses.

The printing revolution brought immense changes. Printed books were cheaper and easier to produce than hand-copied works. With books more readily available, more people learned to read. Readers gained access to a broad range of knowledge, from medicine and law to mining. As printing presses were established in Italy and other parts of Europe, printed books exposed educated Europeans to new ideas and new places.

✔ **Checkpoint** What was the impact of the printing press?

Vocabulary Builder

Use the information below and the following resources to teach the high-use word from this section.
All in One Teaching Resources, Unit 1, p. 7; **Teaching Resources, Skills Handbook,** p. 3

High-Use Word	Definition and Sample Sentence
prosperous, p. 57	*adj.* successful; wealthy The **prosperous** lawyer lived in a large, expensive home.

Northern Renaissance Artists

The northern Renaissance began in the prosperous cities of **Flanders,** a region that included parts of present-day northern France, Belgium, and the Netherlands. Flanders was a thriving center of trade for northern Europe. From Flanders, the Renaissance spread to Spain, France, Germany, and England.

Flemish Painters In the 1400s, Jan van Eyck was one of the most important Flemish painters. Van Eyck's portrayals of townspeople as well as religious scenes abound in rich, realistic details. In the 1500s, Flemish painter Pieter Bruegel (BROY gul) used vibrant colors to portray lively scenes of peasant life, earning him the nickname "Peasant Bruegel." Bruegel also addressed religious and classical themes, but he set them against a background of common people.

In the 1600s, Peter Paul Rubens blended the realistic tradition of Flemish painters like Bruegel with the classical themes and artistic freedom of the Italian Renaissance. As a scholar and humanist, Rubens had a wide knowledge of mythology, the Bible, and classical history. Many of his enormous paintings portray these themes.

Dürer: "Leonardo of the North" German painter **Albrecht Dürer** (DYOOR ur) was one of the first northern artists to be profoundly affected by Renaissance Italy. In 1494, he traveled to Italy to study the Italian masters. He soon became a pioneer in spreading Renaissance ideas to northern Europe. At the same time, his own methods influenced artists in Italy. Because of his wide-ranging interests, which extended far beyond art, he is sometimes called the "Leonardo of the North."

Dürer's important innovation was to apply the painting techniques he had learned in Italy to **engraving.** In engraving, an artist etches a design on a metal plate with acid. The artist then uses the plate to make prints. Dürer had studied engraving in his goldsmith father's workshop and perfected the technique. Many of Dürer's engravings and paintings portray religious upheaval, one of the northern Renaissance's most powerful themes.

✓ **Checkpoint** What themes did northern Renaissance artists explore?

Northern Humanists and Writers

Northern European humanists and writers also helped spread Renaissance ideas. Humanist scholars stressed education and classical learning, hoping to bring about religious and moral reform. Though humanist scholars wrote mainly in Latin, other writers began writing in the **vernacular,** or everyday language of ordinary people. This appealed to a new, middle class audience who lived in northern towns and cities.

Erasmus: Making Humanism Popular The Dutch priest and humanist Desiderius **Erasmus** (ih RAZ mus), born in 1466, was one of the most important scholars of the age. He wrote texts on a number of subjects and used his knowledge of classical languages to produce a new Greek edition of the Bible.

Vocabulary Builder

prosperous—(PRAHS pur us) *adj.*
successful; wealthy

Dürer, Artist and Gentleman
In Germany artists were viewed merely as skilled craftsmen, prompting Dürer to comment that "[In Italy] I am a gentleman, at home I am a parasite." He worked hard to change that view, learning languages and court manners to promote himself. Dürer painted this self-portrait in 1498 when he was 26 years old. *Judging from the painting, how did Dürer view his own importance?*

Northern Humanists and Writers

Instruct

- **Introduce: Key Terms** Tell students that while both northern and Italian humanists emphasized education and learning, northern humanists put a greater focus on religious themes. Then point out the key term *vernacular* (in blue) in the text and review its meaning. Ask **Why did humanists like Erasmus call for translating the Bible into the vernacular?** (*He believed that all people should have access to religious and classical learning.*) **How did More's visions of a utopian society fit in with the ideas of Erasmus?** (*More believed in a society in which all people were educated.*)

- **Teach** Describe the growth of interest in fiction and plays in Renaissance Europe. Ask **What contributed to the popularity of this kind of entertainment?** (*A growing middle class had more money and time for such entertainments; because of the printing press, literacy had risen, and books and plays were more widely available.*) **How did popular writers spread humanistic ideas?** (*They helped raise literacy by writing in the vernacular; they focused on individuals and religious themes.*)

Independent Practice

Link to Literature To help students better understand the popular literature of the Renaissance, have them read the excerpt from *Macbeth* by William Shakespeare and complete the worksheet.

All in One Teaching Resources, Unit 1, p. 11

Monitor Progress

As students fill in their charts, circulate to make sure they understand how the Renaissance developed in the north. For a completed version of the chart, see
Note Taking Transparencies, p. 115

● INFOGRAPHIC Realism in Northern European Art

Northern European artists eagerly pursued realism in their art. The new technique of oil painting allowed them to produce strong colors and a hard surface that could survive the centuries. They also used oils to achieve depth and to create realistic details. Artists placed a new emphasis on nature, recording in their art what they actually saw. Landscapes became a major theme, not just the backdrop to human activities.

▲ Pieter Bruegel the Elder is best known for his scenes of daily life. In *Winter Landscape With Skaters and a Bird Trap*, every detail—from the bare trees to the people walking on ice—conveys the white and frozen reality of northern Europe in winter.

Erasmus helped spread Renaissance humanism to a wider public. He called for a translation of the Bible into the vernacular. He scorned those who ". . . don't want the holy scriptures to be read in translation by the unlearned . . . as if the chief strength of the Christian religion lay in people's ignorance of it. . . ." To Erasmus, an individual's chief duties were to be open-minded and to show good will toward others. As a priest, he was disturbed by corruption in the Church and called for reform.

Sir Thomas More's Ideal Society Erasmus's friend, the English humanist Sir **Thomas More,** also pressed for social reform. In *Utopia,* More describes an ideal society in which men and women live in peace and harmony. No one is idle, all are educated, and justice is used to end crime rather than to eliminate the criminal. Today, the word **utopian** has come to describe any ideal society often with the implication that such a society is ultimately impractical.

Rabelais's Comic Masterpiece The French humanist François Rabelais (rab uh LAY) had a varied career as a monk, physician, Greek scholar, and author. In *Gargantua and Pantagruel,* he chronicles the adventures of two gentle giants. On the surface, the novel is a comic tale of travel and war. But Rabelais uses his characters to offer opinions on religion, education, and other serious subjects. Like More and Erasmus, Rabelais was deeply religious, but had doubts about the organized church.

Shakespeare Writes for All Time The towering figure of Renaissance literature was the English poet and playwright William **Shakespeare.** Between 1590 and 1613, he wrote 37 plays that are still performed around the world. Fellow playwright and poet Ben Jonson correctly predicted at the time that Shakespeare ". . . was not of an age, but for all time."

History Background

Rise of the Middle Class The plague, with its decimation of the European population, had far-reaching consequences for Western Europe's society and economy. With fewer farmworkers available, agricultural production dropped. Those who survived demanded higher wages or moved to the cities to take up jobs vacated by artisans who had died. At the time when the landowning class was weakening, artisans and merchants in the cities found themselves in positions of growing power. With less competition, they could charge higher prices for their goods. This new middle class continued to gain strength as the Renaissance took hold.

Oils made from linseed, walnuts, or poppies were mixed with colored pigments to make oil paint. Oil paints have two qualities that allow them to achieve realism— they can blend together, thus creating more realistic colors, and they reflect light, adding depth and glow.

Jan van Eyck refined and spread the technique of oil painting. In *Portrait of Giovanni Arnolfini and His Wife*, van Eyck layered oil paints to create the shimmering fabrics the couple wore.

Albrecht Dürer kept extensive notebooks on nature. He used his avid curiosity and his keen powers of observation to paint amazingly realistic pictures of plants and animals.

Thinking Critically
1. **Analyze Images** What realistic details appear in van Eyck's painting?
2. **Compare and Contrast** Compare these paintings with the Cranach woodcut in Section 3. How do the artists' intentions differ?

Shakespeare's genius was in expressing universal themes in everyday, realistic settings. His work explores Renaissance ideals such as the complexity of the individual and the importance of the classics. At the same time, his characters speak in language that common people can understand and appreciate. Shakespeare's love of words also vastly enriched the English language. More than 1,700 words appeared for the first time in his works.

✓ **Checkpoint** What Renaissance ideas did Shakespeare's work address?

SECTION 2 Assessment

Progress Monitoring *Online*
For: Self-quiz with vocabulary practice
Web Code: nba-1321

Terms, People, and Places
1. What do the key people listed at the beginning of the section have in common? Explain.

Note Taking
2. **Reading Skill: Identify Main Ideas** Use your completed chart to answer the Focus Question: How did the Renaissance develop in northern Europe?

Comprehension and Critical Thinking
3. **Predict Consequences** What impact would the printing press have on religious reform movements of the 1500s?
4. **Analyze Information** How did northern Renaissance artists blend Italian Renaissance ideas with their own?
5. **Identify Point of View** How did Erasmus's training as a priest sharpen his critique of the Church?
6. **Synthesize Information** What factors encouraged the use of the vernacular in literature in Renaissance society?

● **Writing About History**
Quick Write: Generate Arguments List a number of arguments that could be used to oppose your thesis in a persuasive essay. For example, reread the thesis statement in the Section 1 Quick Write. Then use the information from Section 2 to generate arguments opposing your thesis. Be sure to cite important northern European artists and technological developments. Organizing your arguments into a pro-and-con chart can be helpful.

Assess Progress [L3]
- Have students complete the Section Assessment.
- Administer the Section Quiz.
   Teaching Resources, Unit 1, p. 3
- To further assess student understanding, use
  🏛 **Progress Monitoring Transparencies,** 54

Reteach
If students need more instruction, have them read the section summary.
 Reading and Note Taking Study Guide, p. 38 [L3]

Adapted Reading and Note Taking Study Guide, p. 38 [L1] [L2]

Spanish Reading and Note Taking Study Guide, p. 38 [L2]

Extend [L4]
Biography To help students better understand humanism during the Renaissance, have them read the biography *Desiderius Erasmus* and complete the worksheet.
 Teaching Resources, Unit 1, p. 12

Answers

Thinking Critically
1. a natural setting; everyday objects; realistic colors and lighting; accurate human forms
2. Cranach's woodcut instructively illustrates a particular point. Van Eyck's painting is meant to observe a realistic setting.

✓ an emphasis on the individual; realism; and the importance of the classics

---

Section 2 Assessment
1. Sentences should reflect an understanding of each term, person, or place listed at the beginning of the section.
2. Trade encouraged the spread of ideas, as did the printing press. Artists and writers developed and spread new ideas and techniques to increasingly larger audiences.
3. Religious reformers could use the printing press to spread their ideas to large numbers of people quickly.

4. Dürer used Italian painting techniques to refine the German art of engraving; Flemish artists used oil painting to express humanist themes.
5. He had firsthand knowledge of church abuses, and his religious training gave him specific ideas for reform.
6. Answers should include the growth of the middle class, the humanist emphasis on education, and the printing press.

● **Writing About History**
Responses should be specific, compelling arguments to support the student's thesis and should include details from the text. Responses should also indicate student understanding of what makes a strong argument.

For additional assessment, have students access **Progress Monitoring** *Online* at **Web Code nba-1321.**

Shakespeare's Globe Theatre

Objectives

- Describe the design of the Globe Theater.
- Understand how Shakespeare's plays were suited for performance in this type of theater.

Build Background Knowledge

Have students recall plays they have seen or participated in. Ask them what the theater looked like and how the stage was constructed. Ask them how an outdoor performance might differ from a performance staged indoors.

Instruct

- Ask students to study the visuals on this page and read the captions. Have them compare the diagram of the theater to the photo.
- Ask **Why was the theater so popular in Shakespeare's time?** (*People were eager to explore human experience.*) **Are Shakespeare's plays as relevant today as they once were?** (*Some students may suggest that because they address universal themes the plays will always be relevant; others may suggest that because Shakespeare's language is not readily understandable to all people today, his plays are not as relevant.*)

Monitor Progress

Ask students why it was important for Shakespeare to have a specific theater at which to perform his plays. (*Sample A playwright needed to have his plays produced—and the productions attended by paying customers —in order to make a living from his craft. There was no better way for Shakespeare to ensure that his plays would be staged than to have his own theater.*)

Thinking Critically

1. Open-air theaters allow the production to use natural light, which can make scenes seem more realistic. But the absence of a roof allows outside noise, as well as weather, to filter in.
2. Shakespeare wrote about themes and situations that were relevant to people of all classes. Also, the theater was constructed in such a way that all people could find seats appropriate to what they could pay.

Shakespeare's Globe Theatre

In his play *As You Like It,* William Shakespeare wrote that "all the world's a stage." When it came to showcasing his own work, however, the playwright chose the Globe Theatre. In 1599, when the English people were increasingly eager for plays and other sorts of entertainment, Shakespeare and his company of actors built the Globe on the south bank of London's Thames River. The three-story, open-air theater could seat 3,000 people and had a stage more than 40 feet wide. Shakespeare wrote many of his plays—including *Hamlet, Macbeth,* and *Othello*—specifically to be performed at the Globe Theatre. Twenty of Shakespeare's plays were performed there during his lifetime. During a performance of his play *Henry VII* in 1613, onstage cannon fire ignited the theater's thatched roof and destroyed the building.

▲ William Shakespeare

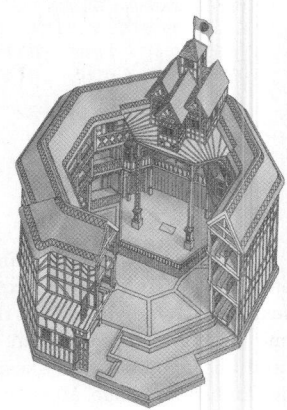

The 1997 reconstruction of the Globe Theatre (below) is faithful to the original. Wealthy theatergoers in the seventeenth century sat in galleries along the theater's walls. Poorer people bought cheap seats on the ground in front of the stage.

The center of the theater was open to the sky. Because the theater had no interior lights, plays were performed in the afternoon to let in as much light as possible.

The theater's round shape meant that the audience surrounded the stage on three sides. The stage was not curtained off, further drawing the audience into the action. ▶

Thinking Critically

1. **Draw Inferences** What are the advantages and disadvantages of staging productions in an open-air theater like the Globe?
2. **Synthesize Information** What about Shakespeare's plays drew people from all social classes to the theater?

History Background

Building the Globe Theatre The construction of the original Globe was accompanied by controversy. Richard Burbage and his acting company, The Lord Chamberlain's Men, had been performing at a stage called "The Theatre" on the outskirts of London. After their lease expired, the landlord threatened to tear the building down. Instead, Burbage and his associates dismantled The Theatre, carried the materials to a new site, and used them to build the Globe. When their absentee landlord returned to London, he promptly sued, but The Lord Chamberlain's Men won the case.

Luther is shown tacking his 95 Theses to a church door in Wittenberg. At top right is a print block from a printing press.

WITNESS HISTORY ◀ AUDIO

A Monk Rebels

❝ I have cast the die. . . . I will not reconcile myself to them [the Roman Catholic Church] for all eternity. . . . Let them condemn and burn all that belongs to me; in return I will do as much for them. . . . Now I no longer fear, and I am publishing a book in the German tongue about Christian reform, directed against the pope, in language as violent as if I were addressing the Antichrist. ❞
—Martin Luther, 1520

Focus Question How did revolts against the Roman Catholic Church affect northern European society?

The Protestant Reformation

Objectives
- Summarize the factors that encouraged the Protestant Reformation.
- Analyze Martin Luther's role in shaping the Protestant Reformation.
- Explain the teachings and impact of John Calvin.

Terms, People, and Places

indulgences	John Calvin
Martin Luther	predestination
Wittenberg	Geneva
Charles V	theocracy
diet	

Note Taking

Reading Skill: Identify Main Ideas Use a concept web like the one below to record main ideas about the Reformation. Add circles as necessary.

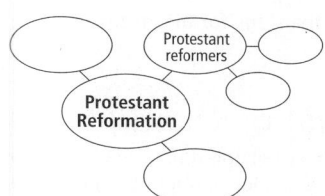

In the 1500s, the Renaissance in northern Europe sparked a religious upheaval that affected Christians at all levels of society. Northern European calls for church reform eventually unleashed forces that would shatter Christian unity. This movement is known as the Protestant Reformation.

Background to the Reformation

Many northern Europeans faced a great deal of uncertainty in their lives. As in Renaissance Italy, most people were poor and life could be violent. Fixed medieval economies were giving way to more uncertain urban, market-based economies, and wealth was distributed unequally. Renaissance humanist ideas found fertile ground in this uncertain society. Spread by the printing press, humanist ideas such as a return to classical education and an emphasis on social reform quickly took root. Many people looked for ways to shape a society that made more sense to them. Increasingly, they used humanist ideas to question a central force in their lives—the Church.

Church Abuses Beginning in the late Middle Ages, the Church had become increasingly caught up in worldly affairs. Popes competed with Italian princes for political power. They fought long wars to protect the Papal States against invasions by secular rulers. They plotted against powerful monarchs who tried to seize control of the Church within their lands. The Church also fought to expand its own interests.

Vocabulary Builder

Use the information below and the following resources to teach the high-use words from this section.
All in One Teaching Resources, Unit 1, p. 7; **Teaching Resources, Skills Handbook,** p. 3

High-Use Words	Definitions and Sample Sentences
radical, p. 63	*adj.* extreme; calling for change They decided that **radical** changes were necessary to solve the organization's many problems.
doctrine, p. 63	*n.* practice; teaching She always followed the **doctrine** of "listen and learn."

SECTION 3

Step-by-Step Instruction

Objectives

As you teach this section, keep students focused on the following objectives to help them answer the Section Focus Question and master core content.

- Summarize the factors that encouraged the Protestant Reformation.
- Analyze Martin Luther's role in shaping the Protestant Reformation.
- Explain the teachings and impact of John Calvin.

Prepare to Read

Build Background Knowledge L3

Ask students to predict how the changing religious worldview expressed in Renaissance art would affect the practice of religion in Europe.

Set a Purpose L3

- **WITNESS HISTORY** Read the selection aloud or play the audio.
  - AUDIO **Witness History Audio CD,** A Monk Rebels

  Ask **What kind of language does Luther use to make his points?** *(He uses dramatic language, talking of "casting the die for all eternity.")* **What was Luther's purpose in using such language?** *(He is making it clear that reconciliation with the Catholic Church is impossible.)*

- **Focus** Point out the Section Focus Question and write it on the board. Tell students to refer to this question as they read. *(Answer appears with Section 3 Assessment answers.)*

- **Preview** Have students preview the Section Objectives and the list of Terms, People, and Places.

- **Note Taking** Have students read this section using the Guided Questioning strategy (TE, p. T20). As they read, have students fill in the concept web showing the main ideas about the Reformation.

   Reading and Note Taking Study Guide, p. 39

Teach

Background to the Reformation ⬢L3

Instruct

- **Introduce** Read aloud the paragraph under the red heading Background to the Reformation. Discuss with students why people leading such a life would crave stability and order. Then ask students to write short phrases that a person a hundred years from now might use to describe students' lives today.

- **Teach** Ask students to find the word *worldly* in the text under the black heading Church Abuses. Help them explore the meaning of the term by using the context of the related sentences. Then explore why people were so opposed to the Church's involvement in worldly affairs. Ask **Why did people begin to question the Church at this time?** *(Renaissance thought encouraged people to question and examine the world around them.)*

- **Analyzing the Visuals** Have students examine the woodcut on this page. In groups, have them discuss what the woodcut says about indulgences and other Church abuses.

Independent Practice

Biography Have students look back to the biography of Erasmus. Have them use what they have learned about him to write a short summary of his critique of the Catholic Church.

⬛ All in One **Teaching Resources, Unit 1,** p. 12

Monitor Progress

As students fill in their concept webs, circulate to make sure students understand the major causes of the Protestant Reformation. For a completed version of the concept web see

📖 **Note Taking Transparencies,** 116

Answers

Analyzing Art
1. Protestantism
2. Possible details: The Protestant scene is orderly, with peaceful baptisms and communion taking place; the Catholic scene is disorderly, showing an angry God and greedy churchmen.

✔ anger about Church practices such as selling indulgences; societal upheaval as a result of a changing economy; the ability of the printing press to spread ideas quickly

Analyzing Art

Protestant Art German artist Lucas Cranach the Elder expressed his views of Protestantism (left panel) and Catholicism (right panel) in this woodcut made in 1545. He wrote that the work was meant to show the difference between the "true religion" and the "false idolatrous teaching."

A Angels float peacefully in the sky above Luther.

B A preaching Martin Luther is shown as having a direct connection to God above.

C A Catholic clergyman sells indulgences.

D The pope counts bags of money.

1. According to Cranach, which of the religions shown is the "true religion"?
2. Find another detail in the painting that expresses the artist's opinion.

Like other Renaissance rulers, popes led lavish lives, supported the arts, and hired artists to beautify churches. To finance such projects, the Church increased fees for services such as marriages and baptisms. Some clergy also sold **indulgences.** According to Church teaching, an indulgence was a lessening of the time a soul would have to spend in purgatory, a place where souls too impure to enter heaven atoned for sins committed during their lifetimes. In the Middle Ages, the Church had granted indulgences only for good deeds. By the late 1400s, however, indulgences could be bought with money.

Many Christians protested such practices, especially in northern Europe. Christian humanists such as Erasmus urged a return to the simple ways of the early Christian church. They stressed Bible study and rejected what they saw as the worldliness of the Church.

Early Revolts Against the Church Long before the Protestant Reformation, a few thinkers protested against the Church more strongly. In England in the 1300s, John Wycliffe launched a systematic attack against the Church, using sermons and writings to call for change. After his death, his followers met secretly to keep alive the movement he started. Jan Hus, born about 40 years after Wycliffe in what is now the Czech Republic, led a reform movement for which he was executed.

✔ **Checkpoint** What factors set the stage for the Protestant Reformation?

Martin Luther: Catalyst of Change

In 1517, protests against Church abuses erupted into a full-scale revolt. The man who triggered the revolt was a German monk and professor of theology named **Martin Luther.**

Differentiated Instruction Solutions for All Learners

L1 Special Needs **L2 Less Proficient Readers**

Help students understand why someone who had dedicated his life to the Church would then decide to protest against it. First, ask students to think about groups that they belong to. Then ask them to think of a time when they disagreed with the group's decision. How did they feel about the group? Did they speak out? If so, what was their motivation? *(Sample: to bring about change)* How is it different when someone outside the group criticizes it? Reinforce that Luther's goal was not to bring down the Church but rather to change it, as he did not agree with some of its practices.

As a young man, Luther prayed and fasted and tried to lead a holy life. He once remarked that "... if ever a monk got into heaven by monkery, so should I also have gotten there." Still, he found himself growing disillusioned with what he saw as Church corruption and worldliness. At last, an incident in the town of Wittenberg prompted him to take action.

Writing the 95 Theses In 1517, a priest named Johann Tetzel set up a pulpit on the outskirts of **Wittenberg,** in Germany. He offered indulgences to any Christian who contributed money for the rebuilding of the Cathedral of St. Peter in Rome. Tetzel claimed that purchase of these indulgences would assure entry into heaven not only for the purchasers but for their dead relatives as well.

To Luther, Tetzel's actions were the final outrage, because they meant that poor peasants could not get into heaven. He drew up 95 Theses, or arguments, against indulgences. Among other things, he argued that indulgences had no basis in the Bible, that the pope had no authority to release souls from purgatory, and that Christians could be saved only through faith. In accordance with the custom of the time, he may have posted his list on the door of Wittenberg's All Saints Church.

Igniting a Firestorm Almost overnight, copies of Luther's 95 Theses were printed and distributed across Europe, where they stirred furious debate. The Church called on Luther to recant, or give up his views. Luther refused. Instead, he developed even more <u>radical</u> new <u>doctrines</u>. Before long, he was urging Christians to reject the authority of Rome. He wrote that the Church could only be reformed by secular, or non-Church, authorities.

In 1521, Pope Leo X excommunicated Luther. Later that year, the new Holy Roman emperor, **Charles V,** summoned Luther to the **diet** at the city of Worms. The word diet, or assembly of German princes, comes from a Middle English word meaning "a day for a meeting." Luther went, expecting to defend his writings. Instead, the emperor simply ordered him to give them up. Luther again refused to recant.

Charles declared Luther an outlaw, making it a crime for anyone in the empire to give him food or shelter. Still, Luther had many powerful supporters and thousands hailed him as a hero. They accepted his teachings and, following his lead, renounced the authority of the pope.

Vocabulary Builder

radical—(RAD ih kul) *adj.* extreme; calling for change
doctrine—(DAHK trin) *n.* practice; teaching

BIOGRAPHY

Martin Luther
"I am rough, boisterous, stormy, and altogether warlike," concluded Martin Luther (1483–1546). Luther's strong personality allowed him to take on the powerful Catholic Church. As a monk, Luther closely studied the Bible and came to believe that only its words—and not the pope or the Catholic Church—should dictate a person's actions.

When he appeared at the Diet of Worms, Luther (right) was 37 years old. Though depressed and fearful about the confrontation, he is said to have affirmed, "Here I stand, I cannot do otherwise." When he refused to retract his statements, an order was given to destroy his books. Yet his influence grew, leading to a deep division within Christianity and the founding of a new church that took his name. **Why did Luther refuse to retract his statements?**

History Background

Luther's German Bible Luther's translation of the Bible into German has been called his noblest achievement. Luther spent many years on this translation. In order to get just the right German words for describing animal sacrifices in the Old Testament, he visited butcher shops and asked what the various parts of a goat or sheep were called. Luther also wrestled with the names of birds and animals. He wrote a friend, "I can handle the stag, roebuck, and chamois [kinds of deer], but what in the Devil am I to do with the tragelaphus, pygargus, oryx, and camelopard?"

In describing Biblical events, Luther often made them seem as if they had taken place in the forests and castles of Germany. His work made the Bible come alive to people for whom it had previously been distant and strange.

Instruct

- **Introduce: Vocabulary Builder** Have students read the Vocabulary Builder terms and definitions. Who do they think will be called *radical?* What *doctrines* in the text will most likely be described as radical?

- **Teach** Discuss the reasons that compelled Luther to draw up his 95 Theses. Ask **What were Luther's main objections to the Catholic Church?** *(the sale of indulgences; the unquestioned authority of the pope; the secondary role of the Bible)* **Why did Luther gain an immediate following?** *(Some people genuinely wanted to end Church corruption; others wanted to take power from the Church to make themselves more powerful.)*

- **Quick Activity** Ask students to read the biography of Martin Luther in their text. In groups, have them discuss the Church's response. Ask **What did the Church do when he refused to take back his statements?** *(burned his books)* Remind students of the importance of the printing press in spreading Reformation ideas. Ask each group to predict what Luther's impact might have been if the printing press had not yet been invented. Use the Numbered Heads strategy (TE, p. T23) to have groups of students share their findings with the class.

Independent Practice

Primary Source To help students better understand Luther's main objections to the Catholic Church, have them read the selection *From the 95 Theses of Martin Luther, 1517* and answer the questions on the worksheet.

All in One Teaching Resources, Unit 1, p. 13

Monitor Progress

Ask students to select one of Luther's 95 Theses and explain how it directly challenges a Catholic doctrine.

Answer

BIOGRAPHY He believed that the salvation of Christians was at stake.

Switzerland's Reformation

Instruct

- **Introduce: Key Terms** Explain to students that once the idea of challenging the Catholic Church took hold, people like John Calvin looked beyond Luther to develop their own Protestant ideas and doctrines. Point out the key term **predestination** (in blue) in the text. Explain that this belief was one of the core beliefs of Calvinism.

- **Teach** Ask **Why did Calvinists believe that they were the "chosen people"?** *(They believed that God had chosen them specifically to build a true Christian society.)* **What aspects of Calvinism might have appealed to people in a time of uncertainty?** *(the idea that if they lived good lives, that meant that God had already chosen them to gain salvation)*

- **Analyzing the Visuals** Have students look at the image of the Calvinist Temple in Lyon. Have groups brainstorm a list of clues in the photo that demonstrate the break between Calvin and the Catholic Church. Then have groups share their lists with the class.

Independent Practice

Have students review the chart on this page comparing the tenets of Catholicism, Lutheranism, and Calvinism. Have them turn the material in the chart into a narrative form—an essay, an article, or another format of their choice.

Monitor Progress

Check Reading and Note Taking Study Guide entries for student understanding of how the Reformation spread.

Comparing Catholicism, Lutheranism, and Calvinism

	Catholicism	Lutheranism	Calvinism
Salvation	Salvation is achieved through faith and good works.	Salvation is achieved through faith.	God alone predetermines who will be saved.
Sacraments	Priests perform seven sacraments, or rituals—baptism, confirmation, marriage, ordination, communion, anointing the sick, and repentance.	Accepts some of the sacraments, but rejects others because rituals cannot erase sin—only God can.	Accepts some of the sacraments, but rejects others because rituals cannot erase sin—only God can.
Head of Church	Pope	Elected councils	Council of elders
Importance of the Bible	Bible is one source of truth; Church tradition is another.	Bible alone is source of truth.	Bible alone is source of truth.
How Belief Is Revealed	Priests interpret the Bible and Church teachings for the people.	People read and interpret the Bible for themselves.	People read and interpret the Bible for themselves.

Chart Skills *Who was the head of the Lutheran church? Why was this an important difference from the organization of the Catholic Church?*

Luther's Teachings At the heart of Luther's teachings were several beliefs, shown in the chart at left. All Christians, he said, have equal access to God through faith and the Bible. Like Erasmus and other humanist scholars, Luther wanted ordinary people to be able to read and study the Bible, so he translated parts of it into German. He also wanted every town to have a school so that all children could learn to read the Bible. Luther wanted to change other church practices. He banned indulgences, confession, pilgrimages, and prayers to saints. He simplified the elaborate ritual of the mass and instead emphasized the sermon. And he permitted the clergy to marry.

Luther's Ideas Spread The new printing presses spread Luther's writings throughout Germany and Scandinavia, prompting him to declare that "Printing was God's highest act of grace." Fiery preachers denounced Church abuses. By 1530, the Lutherans were using a new name, Protestant, for those who "protested" papal authority.

Many clergy saw Luther's reforms as the answer to Church corruption. A number of German princes, however, embraced Lutheran beliefs for more selfish reasons. Some saw Lutheranism as a way to throw off the rule of both the Church and the Holy Roman emperor. Others welcomed a chance to seize Church property in their territories, and use it for their own purposes. Still other Germans supported Luther because of feelings of national loyalty. They were tired of German money going to support churches and clergy in Italy.

The Peasants' Revolt Many peasants also took up Luther's banner. They hoped to gain his support for social and economic change. In 1524, a Peasants' Revolt erupted across Germany. The rebels called for an end to serfdom and demanded other changes in their harsh lives. However, Luther strongly favored social order and respect for political authority. As the Peasants' Revolt grew more violent, Luther denounced it. With his support, nobles suppressed the rebellion, killing tens of thousands of people and leaving thousands more homeless.

The Peace of Augsburg During the 1530s and 1540s, Charles V tried to force Lutheran princes back into the Catholic Church, but with little success. Finally, after a number of brief wars, Charles and the princes reached a settlement. The Peace of Augsburg, signed in 1555, allowed each prince to decide which religion—Catholic or Lutheran—would be followed in his lands. Most northern German states chose Lutheranism. The southern German states remained largely Catholic.

 Checkpoint How did Luther's teachings affect people and society in northern Europe?

Answers

Chart Skills elected councils; because it means that members of the church derived their own authority from God and the Bible rather than from the pope

✓ Luther's teachings lead to the establishment of a new church and sparked a period of social upheaval and violence as people fought over religious beliefs.

Switzerland's Reformation

Swiss reformers also challenged the Catholic Church. Ulrich Zwingli, a priest and an admirer of Erasmus, lived in the Swiss city of Zurich. Like Luther, he stressed the importance of the Bible and rejected elaborate church rituals. Many of his ideas were adopted by Zurich's city council. The other reformer was **John Calvin,** who would profoundly affect the direction of the Reformation.

Calvin was born in France and trained as a priest and lawyer. In 1536, he published a widely-read book that set forth his religious beliefs and explained how to organize and run a Protestant church. Calvin shared many of Luther's beliefs. But he put forth a number of ideas of his own. He preached **predestination,** the idea that God had long ago determined who would gain salvation. To Calvinists, the world was divided into two kinds of people—saints and sinners. Calvinists tried to live like saints, believing that only those who were saved could live truly Christian lives.

In 1541, Protestants in the Swiss city-state of **Geneva** asked Calvin to lead their community. Calvin set up a **theocracy,** or government run by church leaders. Calvin's followers in Geneva came to see themselves as a new "chosen people" entrusted by God to build a truly Christian society. Calvinists stressed hard work, discipline, thrift, honesty, and morality. Citizens faced fines or other harsher punishments for offenses such as fighting, swearing, laughing in church, or dancing. To many Protestants, Calvinist Geneva seemed like a model community.

Reformers from all over Europe visited Geneva and then returned home to spread Calvin's ideas. By the late 1500s, Calvinism had taken root in Germany, France, the Netherlands, England, and Scotland. This new challenge to the Roman Catholic Church set off bloody wars of religion across Europe. In Germany, Catholics and Lutherans opposed Calvinists. In France, wars raged between French Calvinists and Catholics. Calvinists in the Netherlands avoided persecution by preaching in the remote countryside. In England, some Calvinists sailed to the Americas in the early 1600s to escape persecution at home. In Scotland, a Calvinist preacher named John Knox led a religious rebellion, overthrowing the Catholic queen.

✓ **Checkpoint** How were Calvin's ideas put into practice?

A Calvinist Church, 1564
The Calvinist belief in simplicity is reflected in the design of this church. No images other than scriptures and coats of arms decorate the church, and the preacher's pulpit is the center of focus.

SECTION 3 Assessment

Progress Monitoring *Online*
For: Self-quiz with vocabulary practice
Web Code: nba-1331

Terms, People, and Places
1. For each term, person, or place listed at the beginning of the section, write a sentence explaining its significance.

Note Taking
2. **Reading Skill: Identify Main Ideas** Use your completed concept web to answer the Focus Question: How did revolts against the Roman Catholic Church affect northern European society?

Comprehension and Critical Thinking
3. **Synthesize Information** Why did the sale of indulgences become a critical issue during the Renaissance but not during the Middle Ages?
4. **Compare Points of View** How did Luther's ideas differ from those expressed by the Catholic Church?
5. **Draw Inferences** How might Luther have felt about the Calvinist theocracy in Geneva?

● **Writing About History**
Quick Write: Choose Strongest Argument Consider this thesis statement: The Reformation was the most important event in European history. List possible arguments for a persuasive essay that supports this thesis. Review each one and choose the strongest. Make sure that factual points in the text support your argument.

---

4 Step-by-Step Instruction

Objectives

As you teach this section, keep students focused on the following objectives to help them answer the Section Focus Question and master core content.

- Describe the new ideas that Protestant sects embraced.
- Understand why England formed a new church.
- Analyze how the Catholic Church reformed itself.
- Explain why many groups faced persecution during the Reformation.

Prepare to Read

Build Background Knowledge L3

Considering the importance of religion to Europeans before the Reformation, have students predict how the split between Protestants and Catholics would have affected life in Europe.

Set a Purpose L3

- **WITNESS HISTORY** Read the selection aloud or play the audio.

  🔊)) AUDIO **Witness History Audio CD,**
  A King Speaks Out

  What does Henry's description of himself tell you about the importance of Catholicism to Catholic rulers? *(It indicates that these rulers believed that Catholicism was an integral part of their rule.)*

- **Focus** Point out the Section Focus Question and write it on the board. Tell students to refer to this question as they read. *(Answer appears with Section 4 Assessment answers.)*

- **Preview** Have students preview the Section Objectives and the list of Terms, People, and Places.

Answer

✔ Protestants who rejected infant baptism; some also sought radical change.

Painter Hans Holbein shows Henry VIII as a commanding and regal king. A gold medal (top right) celebrates King Henry as the head of the Church of England.

WITNESS HISTORY 🔊)) AUDIO

A King Speaks Out

Henry VIII, the Catholic king of England, was deeply disturbed by Luther's teachings. In 1521 he wrote to the pope to express his displeasure.

❝ . . . we believe that no duty is more incumbent on a Catholic sovereign than to preserve and increase the Catholic faith . . . so when we learned that the pest of Martin Luther's heresy had appeared in Germany and was raging everywhere . . . we bent all our thoughts and energies on uprooting [those heresies] in every possible way. . . . ❞

Just a few years later, Henry would break with the Catholic Church and set England on the path to becoming a Protestant country.

Focus Question How did the Reformation bring about two different religious paths in Europe?

Reformation Ideas Spread

Objectives
- Describe the new ideas that Protestant sects embraced.
- Understand why England formed a new church.
- Analyze how the Catholic Church reformed itself.
- Explain why many groups faced persecution during the Reformation.

Terms, People, and Places

sect	compromise
Henry VIII	Council of Trent
Mary Tudor	Ignatius of Loyola
Thomas Cranmer	Teresa of Avila
Elizabeth	ghetto
canonize	

Note Taking

Reading Skill: Identify Main Ideas As you read about the spread of the Protestant Reformation, record the main ideas in a flowchart like this one below. Add more boxes as necessary.

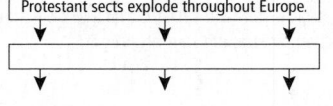

Protestant sects explode throughout Europe.

Throughout Europe, Catholic monarchs and the Catholic Church fought back against the Protestant challenge by taking steps to reform the Church and to restore its spiritual leadership of the Christian world. Still, Protestant ideas continued to spread.

An Explosion of Protestant Sects

As the Reformation continued, hundreds of new Protestant **sects,** or religious groups that had broken away from an established church, sprang up. Many of these followed variations on the teachings of Luther, Calvin, and Zwingli. Some sects, however, had ideas that were even more radical—such as rejecting infant baptism. Infants, they argued, are too young to understand what it means to accept the Christian faith. They became known as Anabaptists.

A few Anabaptist sects sought radical social change as well. Some wanted to abolish private property. Others sought to speed up the coming of God's day of judgment by violent means. When radical Anabaptists took over the city of Munster in Germany, even Luther advised his supporters to join Catholics in suppressing the threat to the traditional order. Most Anabaptists, however, were peaceful. They called for religious toleration and separation of church and state. Despite harsh persecution, these groups influenced Protestant thinking in many countries. Today, the Baptists, Mennonites, and Amish all trace their religious ancestry to the Anabaptists.

✔ **Checkpoint** Who were the Anabaptists?

Vocabulary Builder

Use the information below and the following resources to teach the high-use word from this section.
🔲 **Teaching Resources, Unit 1,** p. 7; **Teaching Resources, Skills Handbook,** p. 3

High-Use Word	Definition and Sample Sentence
rigorous, p. 70	*adj.* strict; thorough He began a **rigorous** exercise program to get into shape.

The English Reformation

In England, religious leaders like John Wycliffe had called for Church reform as early as the 1300s. By the 1520s, some English clergy were exploring Protestant ideas. The break with the Catholic Church, however, was the work not of religious leaders but of King **Henry VIII.**

Henry VIII Seeks an Annulment At first, Henry VIII stood firmly against the Protestant revolt. The pope even awarded him the title "Defender of the Faith" for a pamphlet that he wrote denouncing Luther.

In 1527, however, an issue arose that set Henry at odds with the Church. After 18 years of marriage, Henry and his Spanish wife, Catherine of Aragon, had only one surviving child, **Mary Tudor.** Henry felt that England's stability depended on his having a male heir. He had already fallen in love with a young noblewoman named Anne Boleyn, who served the Queen. He hoped that if he married her she would bear him a son. Because Catholic law does not permit divorce, he asked the pope to annul, or cancel, his marriage. Popes had annulled royal marriages before. But this pope refused. He did not want to offend the Holy Roman emperor Charles V, Catherine's nephew.

Breaking With the Church Henry was furious. Spurred on by his advisors, many of whom leaned toward Protestantism, he decided to take over the English church. Guided by his chancellor Thomas Cromwell, he had Parliament pass a series of laws. They took the English church from the pope's control and placed it under Henry's rule. At the same time, Henry appointed **Thomas Cranmer** archbishop of the new church. Cranmer annulled the king's marriage, and in 1533 Henry married Anne Boleyn. Soon, Anne gave birth to a daughter, **Elizabeth.**

In 1534, Parliament passed the Act of Supremacy, making Henry "the only supreme head on Earth of the Church of England." Many loyal Catholics refused to accept the Act of Supremacy and were executed for treason. Among them was the great English humanist Sir Thomas More, who served in Henry's government but tried to resign in protest. More was later **canonized,** or recognized as a saint, by the Catholic Church.

Strengthening the Church of England Between 1536 and 1540, royal officials investigated Catholic convents and monasteries. Claiming that they were centers of immorality, Henry ordered them closed. He then confiscated, or seized, their lands and wealth. Henry shrewdly granted some of these lands to nobles and other high-ranking citizens. He thus secured their support for the Anglican Church, as the new Church of England was called. Despite these actions, Henry was not a religious radical. He rejected most Protestant doctrines. Aside from breaking away from Rome and allowing use of the English Bible, he kept most Catholic forms of worship.

Religious Turmoil When Henry died in 1547, he had only one surviving son—despite having married six times. Nine-year-old Edward VI inherited the throne. The young king and his advisors were devout Protestants and took steps to make England a truly Protestant country. Under Edward, Parliament passed new laws bringing Protestant reforms to England. Thomas Cranmer drew up the Protestant *Book of Common Prayer,* which became required reading in all of the country's church services. Though it outlined a moderate form of Protestant service, it sparked uprisings. These uprisings were harshly suppressed.

 BIOGRAPHY

Elizabeth I
The life of Elizabeth I (1533–1603) did not start favorably. When she was only two years old her mother, Anne Boleyn, was beheaded so that her father, Henry VIII, could remarry. The young princess grew up in isolation. Still, Henry VIII was affectionate to his daughter and saw to it that she received a rigorous education. Even as a teenager she was well-respected for her sharp mind, fluency in languages, and understanding of philosophy and theology.

Under the reign of her half-sister Mary Tudor, Elizabeth became both a rallying symbol for Protestants and a target for Catholics. Though arrested and imprisoned, she survived her sister to become queen of England at age 25. The well-loved Elizabeth used her talents to unify England, expand its international power, and encourage a period of great artistic flowering. **Why do you think the period under Elizabeth's reign is now called the Elizabethan Age?**

■ **Note Taking** Have students read this section using the Guided Questioning strategy (TE, p. T20). As they read, have students fill in the flowchart with the main ideas about the spread of the Reformation.

✐ **Reading and Note Taking Study Guide,** p. 41

Teach

An Explosion of Protestant Sects ⓛ₃

Instruct

■ **Introduce** Display **Color Transparency 78: The Spread of Protestantism.** Emphasize to students how quickly Protestantism spread during this period. Have students identify Protestant sects in this country and speculate on where they originated.

🏛 **Color Transparencies,** 78

■ **Teach** Ask **Why did the Catholic Church remain unchallenged for so long?** *(Before the Renaissance, people did not think of denying the Church's authority.)* Ask **Why did Protestants develop many different sects, rather just embracing Lutheranism?** *(People had different criticisms of Catholicism and different ideas about what the ideal Christian faith should be.)*

■ **Quick Activity** Ask students to find news articles about religious conflict in the world today. Have student groups discuss each article and compare it to the religious turmoil of the Reformation.

Independent Practice

Have students use the results of their Quick Activity discussions to write a paragraph comparing the spread of the Protestant Reformation to religious events today.

Monitor Progress

Ask students why some Protestants joined with Catholics to oppose other Protestants. Check that students understand that different Protestant sects held very different beliefs and that many of them were competing for power.

Answer

BIOGRAPHY Elizabeth reigned for more than 40 years and was such a strong, influential leader that her rule shaped the age she lived in.

Differentiated Instruction Solutions for All Learners

ⓛ₁ Special Needs   ⓛ₂ Less Proficient Readers   ⓛ₂ English Language Learners

To help students explain why England formed its own church, have students read this section looking for evidence of the reasons for the break with the Church. Ask them to create a bulleted list of their findings. Then have them use their lists to write a one-sentence summary of this subsection. Have students repeat this strategy for each subsection, using the section objectives as a guide.

Use the following resources to help students acquire basic skills:

✐ **Adapted Reading and Note Taking Study Guide**

■ Adapted Note Taking Study Guide, p. 41
■ Adapted Section Summary, p. 42

The English Reformation ⓭

Instruct

- **Introduce** After students have read about Henry VIII's break with the Catholic Church, have them reread the Witness History quotation. Explore with students how Henry's actions could be so different from his earlier words. Ask students if they think Henry would have still broken with the Church if Luther's teachings had not become popular.

- **Teach** Ask **How did Henry gain support for his Anglican Church?** *(He kept some forms of Catholic worship and gave Church lands to important people.)* **What actions did Queen Elizabeth take to turn England toward Protestantism?** *(She firmly established Protestant practices but retained Catholic rituals and ceremonies, thus bringing about Protestantism gradually and without great opposition.)* Discuss with students why Elizabeth was able to unite the country while Edward and Mary had failed to do so. Ask **How might Mary's burning of "heretics" have strengthened the Protestant cause in England?** *(Protestants may have banded together in opposition to such cruel punishment.)*

- **Analyzing the Visuals** Ask students to review the timeline on this page and the next. Have them use content from the text to add important events to the timeline.

Independent Practice

Have students review the map two pages ahead. Ask them to summarize the geographical impact of the Protestant Reformation.

Monitor Progress

- Have students read aloud the headings of this section, and summarize the content under each.

- As students fill in their flowcharts, circulate to make sure they understand how the Protestant Reformation spread. For a completed version of the flowchart see

  📖 **Note Taking Transparencies,** 117

Answer

☑ Henry VIII declared the Church of England independent of Rome when the pope refused to grant him a divorce from Catherine of Aragon.

When Edward died in his teens, his half-sister Mary Tudor became queen. She was determined to return England to the Catholic faith. Under Queen Mary hundreds of English Protestants, including Archbishop Cranmer, were burned at the stake for heresy.

The Elizabethan Settlement On Mary's death in 1558, the throne passed to 25-year-old Elizabeth, the daughter of Henry VIII and Anne Boleyn. For years, Elizabeth had survived court intrigues, including the religious swings under Edward and Mary. As queen, Elizabeth had to determine the future of the Church of England. Moving cautiously at first, she slowly enforced a series of reforms that over time came to be called the Elizabethan settlement.

The queen's policies were a **compromise,** or acceptable middle ground, between Protestant and Catholic practices. The Church of England preserved much Catholic ritual, and it kept the hierarchy of bishops and archbishops. Unlike Henry, the queen did not call herself "supreme head" of the church, but she reaffirmed that the monarch was the "supreme governor" over spiritual matters in England. At the same time, Elizabeth restored a version of the *Book of Common Prayer,* accepted moderate Protestant doctrine, and allowed English to replace Latin in church services. Her sensible compromises, which satisfied most Catholics and Protestants, largely ended decades of religious turmoil.

During a long reign, Elizabeth used all her skills to restore unity to England. Even while keeping many Catholic traditions, she made England a firmly Protestant nation. After her death, England faced new religious storms. But it escaped the endless religious wars that tore apart France and many other European states during the 1500s.

☑ **Checkpoint** Why was the Church of England established?

Major Events of the English Reformation

1521 Henry VIII writes to the pope to condemn Luther's teachings.

1529 Parliament begins passing laws to make Henry VIII head of the church in England.

1533 Henry VIII divorces Catherine of Aragon and marries Anne Boleyn.

1534 Parliament passes the Act of Supremacy.

King Henry the eyght.

Connect to Our World

Connections to Today The Reformation would have a significant impact on the spread of Christianity throughout the world. European explorers brought Christianity to Africa, Asia, and the Americas. North America became a refuge for Protestants. Today, Christianity has more adherents worldwide than any other religion, with 554 million Christians in Europe, 395 million in Africa, 325 million in Asia, and 270 million in North America, and 25 million in Oceania. Latin America has the highest concentration of Christians, with 93 percent of the population, or 501 million people.

The Catholic Reformation

As the Protestant Reformation swept across northern Europe, a vigorous reform movement took hold within the Catholic Church. Led by Pope Paul III, it is known as the Catholic Reformation, or the Counter-Reformation. During the 1530s and 1540s, the pope set out to revive the moral authority of the Church and roll back the Protestant tide. He also appointed reformers to end corruption within the papacy itself. They and their successors led the Catholic Reformation for the rest of the century.

Council of Trent To establish the direction that reform should take, the pope called the Council of Trent in 1545. Led by Italian cardinal Carlo Borromeo, the council met off and on for almost 20 years. The council reaffirmed the traditional Catholic views that Protestants had challenged. It declared that salvation comes through faith and good works. According to the council, the Bible, while a major source of religious truth, is not the only source. The council also took steps to end abuses in the Church. It provided stiff penalties for worldliness and corruption among the clergy. It also established schools to create a better-educated clergy who could challenge Protestant teachings.

Empowering the Inquisition Pope Paul strengthened the Inquisition to fight Protestantism. As you have read, the Inquisition was a Church court set up during the Middle Ages. The Inquisition used secret testimony, torture, and execution to root out heresy. It also prepared the *Index of Forbidden Books*, a list of works considered too immoral or irreligious for Catholics to read. The list included books by Luther and Calvin, as well as earlier works by Petrarch and other humanists.

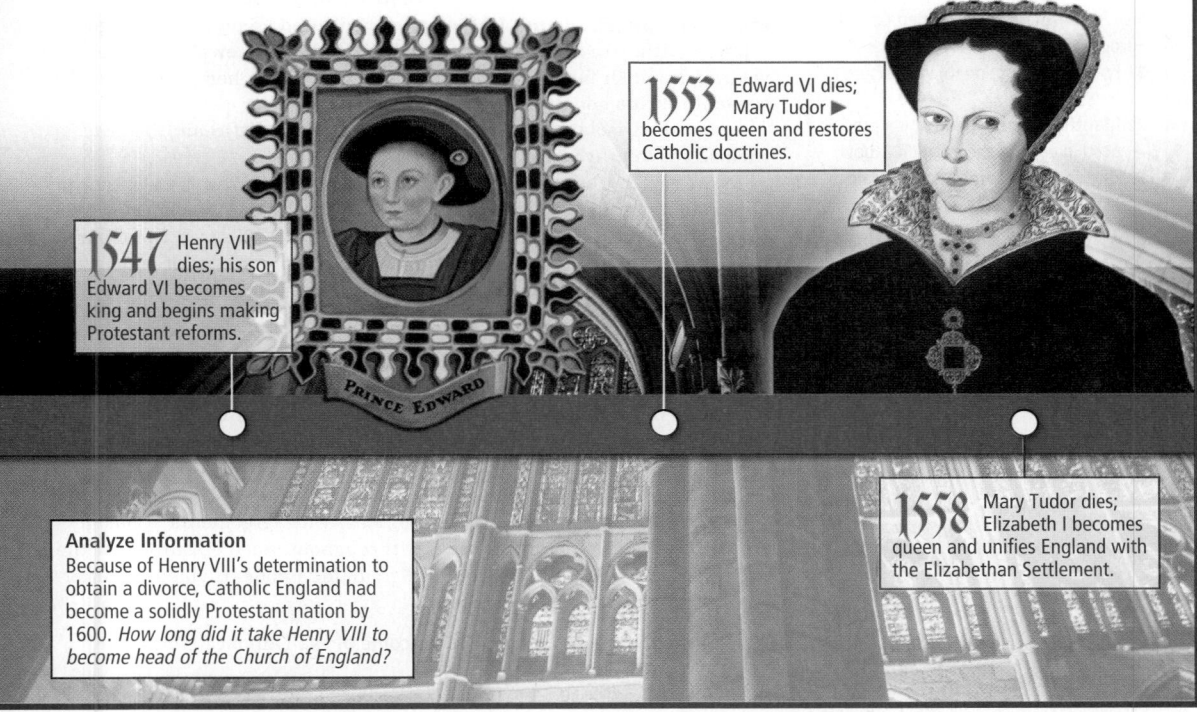

1547 Henry VIII dies; his son Edward VI becomes king and begins making Protestant reforms.

PRINCE EDWARD

1553 Edward VI dies; Mary Tudor ▶ becomes queen and restores Catholic doctrines.

1558 Mary Tudor dies; Elizabeth I becomes queen and unifies England with the Elizabethan Settlement.

Analyze Information
Because of Henry VIII's determination to obtain a divorce, Catholic England had become a solidly Protestant nation by 1600. *How long did it take Henry VIII to become head of the Church of England?*

L4 Advanced Readers   L4 Gifted and Talented

Challenge students to compare how the Catholic Reformation and the Protestant Reformation responded to the growing problems within the church. Ask them to make a three-column chart, listing the problems in the church, the Catholic reaction, and the Protestant reform. Then ask students to write a short answer to the following question: In what ways can the Catholic Reformation be considered a Counter-Reformation?

Instruct

- **Introduce: Vocabulary Builder**
  Have students read the Vocabulary Builder term and definition. Ask **Why might the Catholic Church have wanted to establish a *rigorous* religious order at the time of the Reformation?** *(The Church wanted to strengthen itself and train its priests strictly to spread Catholicism.)*

- **Teach** Remind students that the Catholic Reformation is also known as the Counter-Reformation. Ask **What does the term Counter-Reformation imply about the causes of this movement?** *(that it was a specific response to the Protestant Reformation)* **What were the basic components of the Catholic Reformation?** *(reform of Church practices; strengthening the Inquisition; founding new religious orders meant to bolster Catholicism)*

- **Quick Activity** Have groups of students discuss the ways in which the Jesuits were Renaissance men. Have them use specific examples from the text to support their arguments.

Independent Practice

Have students make a timeline of events titled The Catholic Reformation. Direct them to use the timeline shown at left as a model.

Monitor Progress

Ask students to summarize the causes and effects of the Catholic Reformation.

Answer

Analyze Information five years

Widespread Persecution ⓛ

Instruct

- **Introduce: Key Terms** Point out the key term *ghetto* in the text. Ask students first for definitions of the word. Then ask them where they have heard the term used, and how it was used. Finally, have them read the word in its historical context in the text.

- **Teach** Ask **Why was religious persecution widespread during the Reformation?** *(People were struggling to establish their own faiths as the one true religion.)* **Why was persecution of Jews and "witches" especially harsh?** *(In a time of insecurity, people looked for others to blame, especially those most unlike themselves.)*

- **Quick Activity** Ask students to read the text under the heading Conducting Witch Hunts. Ask them if they have heard the term "modern-day witch hunt." Help explain the term. Then use the Think-Write-Pair-Share Strategy (TE, p. T22) and ask students to discuss ways in which people are persecuted today.

Independent Practice

Have students use the results from their Quick Activity discussion to write a paragraph that compares persecution during the Renaissance and Reformation with persecution today.

Monitor Progress

Check Reading and Note Taking Study Guide entries for student understanding.

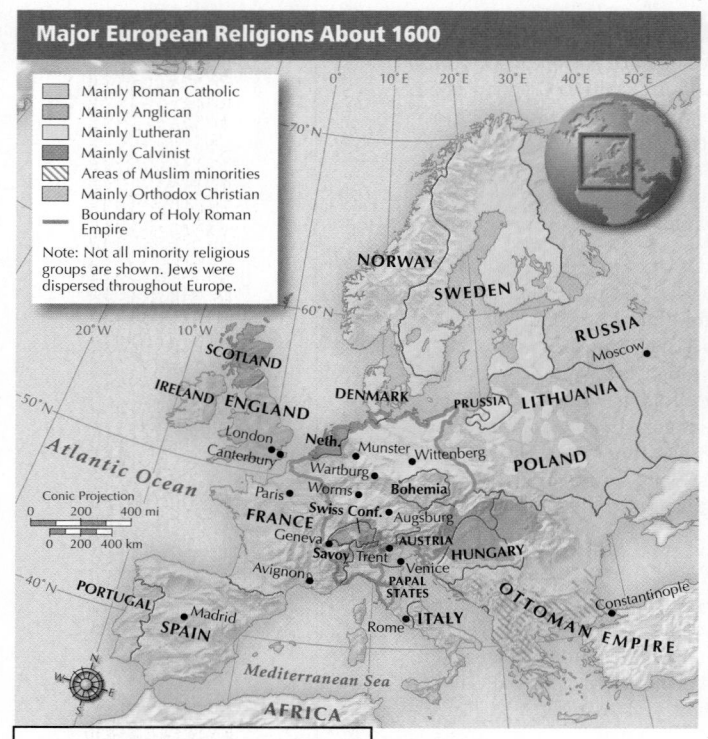

Major European Religions About 1600

- Mainly Roman Catholic
- Mainly Anglican
- Mainly Lutheran
- Mainly Calvinist
- Areas of Muslim minorities
- Mainly Orthodox Christian
- Boundary of Holy Roman Empire

Note: Not all minority religious groups are shown. Jews were dispersed throughout Europe.

Map Skills By 1600, the spread of Protestantism had transformed Catholic Europe.

1. **Locate** (a) London (b) Wittenberg (c) Rome
2. **Identify** Identify the religion practiced in each of the locations above.
3. **Understand Main Ideas** Explain why most people in each region were practicing that religion by 1600.

Geography *Interactive*
For: Audio guided tour
Web Code: nbp-1341

Vocabulary Builder
rigorous—(RIG ur us) *adj.* strict; thorough

Founding the Jesuits In 1540, the pope recognized a new religious order, the Society of Jesus, or Jesuits. The order was founded by **Ignatius of Loyola,** a Spanish knight raised in the crusading tradition. After his leg was shattered in battle, he found comfort reading about saints who had overcome mental and physical torture. Vowing to become a "soldier of God," Ignatius drew up a strict program for the Jesuits. It included spiritual and moral discipline, rigorous religious training, and absolute obedience to the Church. Led by Ignatius, the Jesuits embarked on a crusade to defend and spread the Catholic faith worldwide.

To further the Catholic cause, Jesuits became advisors to Catholic rulers, helping them combat heresy in their lands. They set up schools that taught humanist and Catholic beliefs and enforced discipline and obedience. Daring Jesuits slipped into Protestant lands in disguise to minister to Catholics. Jesuit missionaries spread their Catholic faith to distant lands, including Asia, Africa, and the Americas.

Teresa of Avila As the Catholic Reformation spread, many Catholics experienced renewed feelings of intense faith. **Teresa of Avila** symbolized this renewal. Born into a wealthy Spanish family, Teresa entered a convent in her youth. Finding convent routine not strict enough, she established her own order of nuns. They lived in isolation, eating and sleeping very little and dedicating themselves to prayer and meditation.

Impressed by her spiritual life, her superiors in the Church asked Teresa to reorganize and reform Spanish convents and monasteries. Teresa was widely honored for her work, and after her death the Church canonized her. Her spiritual writings rank among the most important Christian texts of her time, and are still widely read today.

Legacy of the Catholic Reformation By 1600, the majority of Europeans remained Catholic. Tireless Catholic reformers, like Francis de Sales in France, had succeeded in bringing back Protestant converts. Moreover, renewed piety found expression in literature and art. Across Catholic Europe, charity flourished and church abuses were reduced.

Still, Protestantism had gained a major foothold on the continent. The Reformation and the Catholic Reformation stirred up intense feeling and debate. Religious conflict played into heated disagreements about government, which would erupt into war throughout much of Europe. At the end, Europe would remain—and still remains today—divided by differing interpretations of Christianity.

✔ **Checkpoint** What was the outcome of the Catholic Reformation?

Answers

Map Skills
1. Review locations with students.
2. London: Anglican; Wittenberg: Lutheran; Rome: Roman Catholic
3. Political leaders in each region had adopted that religion and persecuted members of other religions.

✔ Europe remained mainly Catholic; the Church initiated reforms; a new piety was expressed in the arts.

History Background

Evidence of Witchcraft As the witchcraft mania spread in Europe, popular superstitions came to be treated as legal truths. Until the late 1600s, most magistrates accepted that there were physical tests for witchcraft. If the body of the accused exhibited unusual marks, the person was considered to be a witch. If the accused had body parts that were insensitive to the prick of a needle, the person was judged to be a witch. Storms and diseases were also taken as signs of sorcery. Witch hunts also took place across the Atlantic in the English colonies. In 1692, a witch hunt broke out in the town of Salem, Massachusetts. Accusations spread like wildfire throughout the town. Before the witch hunt ended the following year, at least 200 people had been named as witches. Twenty of them had been executed.

Widespread Persecution

During this period of heightened religious passion, persecution was widespread. Both Catholics and Protestants fostered intolerance and persecuted radical sects like the Anabaptists, people they thought were witches, and Jews.

Conducting Witch Hunts Between 1450 and 1750, tens of thousands of women and men died as victims of witch hunts. Those accused of being witches, or agents of the devil, were usually women. Most victims of the witch hunts died in the German states, Switzerland, and France, all centers of religious conflict. When the wars of religion came to an end, the persecution of witches also declined.

Scholars have offered various reasons for this persecution, but most agree that it had to do with people's twin beliefs in Christianity and magic. Most people believed that among them were witches who practiced magical deeds, often with the aid of the devil. Thus witches were seen as anti-Christian. Because witches often behaved in non-traditional ways, many people accused of witchcraft were often social outcasts, such as beggars. Midwives and herbalists were also targeted.

Persecuting Jews For many Jews in Italy, the early Renaissance had been a time of relative prosperity. While Spain had expelled its Jews in 1492, Italy allowed them to remain. Still, pressure remained strong on Jews to convert. In 1516, Venice ordered Jews to live in a separate quarter of the city called the **ghetto.** Other Italian cities soon followed.

During the Reformation, restrictions on Jews increased. At first, Luther hoped that Jews would be converted to his teachings. When they did not convert, he called for them to be expelled from Christian lands and for their synagogues to be burned. In time, some German princes did expel Jews. In the 1550s, Pope Paul IV placed added restrictions on Jews. Even Emperor Charles V, who supported toleration of Jews in the Holy Roman Empire, banned them from Spanish territories and new American colonies. From the early 1500s on, many Jews migrated to the Mediterranean parts of the Ottoman Empire and to the Netherlands.

✔ **Checkpoint** Why were Jews and other people persecuted?

Teresa of Avila wrote a book in 1610 describing her work with reforming Catholic convents and monasteries.

Primary Source

❝ At about this time there came to my notice the harm and havoc that were being wrought in France by these Lutherans and the way in which their unhappy sect was increasing. . . . I wept before the Lord and entreated Him to remedy this great evil. I felt that I would have laid down a thousand lives to save a single one of all the souls that were being lost there. And, seeing that I was a woman, and a sinner . . . I determined to do the little that was in me. . . . ❞

Progress Monitoring *Online*
For: Self-quiz with vocabulary practice
Web Code: nba-1341

SECTION 4 Assessment

Terms, People, and Places
1. Place each of the key terms at the beginning of this section into one of the following categories: politics, culture, economy, or geography. Write a sentence for each term explaining your choice.

Note Taking
2. **Reading Skill: Identify Main Ideas** Use your completed flowchart to answer the Focus Question: How did the Reformation bring about two different religious paths in Europe?

Comprehension and Critical Thinking
3. **Identify Point of View** Why were the Anabaptists considered to be radical?
4. **Understand Sequence** How did reforms cause England to become a Protestant country?
5. **Recognize Ideologies** Why might the Catholic Church have found the ideas of Ignatius to be particularly relevant to the Catholic Reformation?
6. **Make Comparisons** Why did witch hunting decline with the end of the religious wars, while persecution of Jews did not?

● **Writing About History**
Quick Write: Decide on an Organizational Strategy Write a thesis statement for a persuasive essay about the spread of the Reformation. List your supporting arguments, from strongest to weakest. Then make an outline that shows where your arguments will appear and how they relate to your thesis statement. You may want to save your strongest argument for the last paragraph of body text before your conclusion.

Objectives

As you teach this section, keep students focused on the following objectives to help them answer the Section Focus Question and master core content.

■ Explain how new discoveries in astronomy changed the way people viewed the universe.

■ Understand the new scientific method and how it developed.

■ Analyze the contributions that Newton and other scientists made to the Scientific Revolution.

Prepare to Read

Build Background Knowledge ⑬

Emphasize that changes in science happened at the same time as social, political, and artistic changes of the Renaissance. Remind students that many artists were interested in science and nature, and their art reflected those interests.

Set a Purpose ⑬

■ **WITNESS HISTORY** Read the selection aloud or play the audio.

🔊 AUDIO **Witness History Audio CD,** Mountains on the Moon

Ask **What Renaissance characteristics does Galileo display in this story?** *(He shows great curiosity and inventiveness; he shows a worldview expanded by re-examining the universe.)*

■ **Focus** Point out the Section Focus Question and write it on the board. Tell students to refer to this question as they read. *(Answer appears with Section 5 Assessment answers.)*

■ **Preview** Have students preview the Section Objectives and the list of Terms, People, and Places.

■ **Note Taking** Have students read this section using the Paragraph Shrinking strategy (TE, p. T20). As they read, have students fill in the table showing the important people of the Scientific Revolution.

✏️ **Reading and Note Taking Study Guide,** p. 43

An 1800s artist imagines Galileo at work, peering into the sky. Galileo's telescope is shown at top right.

Mountains on the Moon

In 1609, Italian astronomer Galileo Galilei heard of a new Dutch invention, the telescope. It was designed to help people see distant enemy ships. Galileo was interested for another reason—he wondered what would happen if he trained a telescope on the night sky. So he built his own telescope for this purpose. When he pointed it at the sky, he was amazed. The new telescope allowed him to see mountains on the moon, fiery spots on the sun, and four moons circling the planet Jupiter. "I did discover many particulars in Heaven that had been unseen and unheard of until this our age," he later wrote.

Focus Question How did discoveries in science lead to a new way of thinking for Europeans?

The Scientific Revolution

Objectives

• Explain how new discoveries in astronomy changed the way people viewed the universe.

• Understand the new scientific method and how it developed.

• Analyze the contributions that Newton and other scientists made to the Scientific Revolution.

Terms, People, and Places

Nicolaus Copernicus	scientific method
heliocentric	hypothesis
Tycho Brahe	Robert Boyle
Johannes Kepler	Isaac Newton
Galileo	gravity
Francis Bacon	calculus
René Descartes	

Note Taking

Reading Skills: Identify Main Ideas Use a table like the one below to record information about important people of the Scientific Revolution.

Thinkers of the Scientific Revolution	
Nicolaus Copernicus	Developed sun-centered universe theory

The Renaissance and the Reformation facilitated the breakdown of the medieval worldview. In the mid-1500s, a profound shift in scientific thinking brought about the final break with Europe's medieval past. Called the Scientific Revolution, this movement pointed toward a future shaped by a new way of thinking about the physical universe. At the heart of the Scientific Revolution was the assumption that mathematical laws governed nature and the universe. The physical world, therefore, could be known, managed, and shaped by people.

Changing Views of the Universe

Until the mid-1500s, Europeans' view of the universe was shaped by the theories of the ancient writers Ptolemy and Aristotle. More than 1,000 years before the Renaissance, they had taught that Earth was the center of the universe. Not only did this view seem to agree with common sense, it was accepted by the Church. In the 1500s and 1600s, however, people began to question this view.

Copernicus Challenges Ancient Astronomy In 1543, Polish scholar **Nicolaus Copernicus** (koh PUR nih kus) published *On the Revolutions of the Heavenly Spheres*. In it, he proposed a **heliocentric,** or sun-centered, model of the universe. The sun, he said, stands at the center of the universe. Earth is just one of several planets that revolve around the sun.

Vocabulary Builder

Use the information below and the following resources to teach the high-use words from this section.
All in One **Teaching Resources, Unit 1,** p. 7; **Teaching Resources, Skills Handbook,** p. 3

High-Use Words	Definitions and Sample Sentences
contradict, p. 73	*v.* to go against The evidence **contradicted** the scientist's original theory.
philosopher, p. 73	*n.* a person who is an expert in the study of knowledge The **philosopher** Aristotle developed a system of logic.

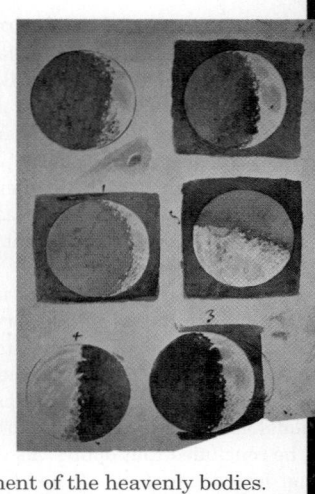
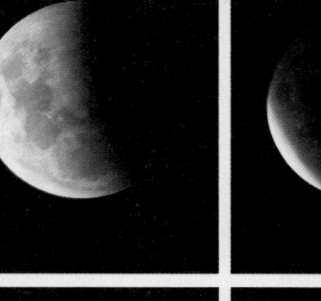

Most experts rejected this revolutionary theory. In Europe at the time, all scientific knowledge and many religious teachings were based on the arguments developed by classical thinkers. If Ptolemy's reasoning about the planets was wrong, people believed, then the whole system of human knowledge might be called into question. But in the late 1500s, the Danish astronomer **Tycho Brahe** (TEE koh BRAH uh) provided evidence that supported Copernicus's theory. Brahe set up an astronomical observatory. Every night for years, he carefully observed the sky, accumulating data about the movement of the heavenly bodies.

After Brahe's death, his assistant, the brilliant German astronomer and mathematician **Johannes Kepler,** used Brahe's data to calculate the orbits of the planets revolving around the sun. His calculations supported Copernicus's heliocentric view. At the same time, however, they showed that each planet does not move in a perfect circle, as both Ptolemy and Copernicus believed, but in an oval-shaped orbit called an ellipse.

Galileo's "Heresies" Scientists from many different lands built on the foundations laid by Copernicus and Kepler. In Italy, **Galileo** Galilei assembled an astronomical telescope. As you have read, he observed that the four moons of Jupiter move slowly around that planet—exactly, he realized, the way Copernicus said that Earth moves around the sun.

Galileo's discoveries caused an uproar. Other scholars attacked him because his observations <u>contradicted</u> ancient views about the world. The Church condemned him because his ideas challenged the Christian teaching that the heavens were fixed in position to Earth, and perfect.

In 1633, Galileo was tried before the Inquisition, and for the rest of his life he was kept under house arrest. Threatened with death unless he withdrew his "heresies," Galileo agreed to state publicly in court that Earth stands motionless at the center of the universe. Legend has it that as he left the court he muttered, "And yet it moves."

✓ Checkpoint Why was Copernicus's theory seen as radical?

A New Scientific Method

Despite the opposition of the Church, by the early 1600s a new approach to science had emerged, based upon observation and experimentation. During the Renaissance, the works of the ancient Greek <u>philosopher</u> Plato were rediscovered. Plato taught that man should look beyond simple appearances to learn nature's truths. He believed that mathematics, one of the greatest human achievements, was the key to learning these truths. His teachings were rediscovered by Renaissance scientists and helped shape people's view of the physical world.

Views of the Moon
Galileo sketched the views of the moon he saw through his telescope in 1609 (left). Pictures of the moon taken through a modern telescope (right) look remarkably similar.

Vocabulary Builder
contradict—(kahn truh DIKT) v. to go against

Vocabulary Builder
philosopher—(fih LAHS uh fur) n. a person who is an expert in the study of knowledge

Teach

Changing Views of the Universe

Instruct

■ **Introduce: Vocabulary Builder** Have students read the Vocabulary Builder terms and definitions. Ask them to predict how the word *contradict* might apply to Galileo's discoveries and the teachings of the Catholic Church.

■ **Teach** Ask **Why was Galileo threatened with death because of his theories?** *(The Church feared that if its teachings on this matter were called into question, then all of its teachings could be questioned.)* **How might the experience of the Reformation have shaped the Church's response?** *(The Church had already seen itself as under attack by the Protestant Reformation. It was more aware than ever that it was in danger of losing authority.)*

■ **Quick Activity** Point out the key term *heliocentric* (in blue) in the text. Explain to students how radical this theory was at the time. Have students formulate reasons why the Church was particularly opposed to this theory.

Independent Practice

Viewpoints To help students better understand the changing worldview of the time, have them read the selection *Does the Earth Move?*, which is from the correspondence between Galileo and Kepler, and complete the worksheet.

All in One **Teaching Resources, Unit 1,** p. 10

Monitor Progress

As students fill in their tables, circulate to make sure they understand the significance of the key scientists of the Scientific Revolution. For a completed version of the table, see

 Note Taking Transparencies, 118

Answer

✓ It contradicted both Church teachings and common sense.

A New Scientific Method

L3

Instruction

- **Introduce: Vocabulary Builder**
  Have students read the Vocabulary Builder term and definition. Ask them to speculate on why the work of a ***philosopher*** could be important to a scientist. Use the Think-Write-Pair-Share strategy (TE, p. T23) to structure group discussion.

- **Teach** Ask **What were the contributions of the philosophers Bacon and Descartes?** *(Their belief that truth can only be known after a process of investigation helped bring about the scientific method.)* **Why might a rigorous scientific method have particularly appealed to non-scientists?** *(Non-scientists could be assured that scientific conclusions were based on an established method of inquiry rather than on the idiosyncrasies of a particular scientist.)*

- **Quick Activity** Have student groups develop a quiz based on information in this section. Groups should first organize main ideas and key facts. Then they should decide on a format for their quiz—for example, multiple choice, matching, or a combination of questions. Finally, students should write their quizzes and present them to other groups to complete.

Independent Practice

To make sure that students understand that the Renaissance, Reformation, and Scientific Revolution were linked, have students construct a timeline that shows major events from all three.

Monitor Progress

Circulate to see that Quick Activity quizzes accurately reflect the material on the scientific method and that groups have correctly answered the questions.

Answers

✓ Bacon emphasized experimentation and observation, while Descartes emphasized human reasoning.

Diagram Skills because it allows other scientists to uncover possible errors or to use the results as a starting point for further investigation

Bacon and Descartes: Revolutionary Thinkers The new scientific method was really a revolution in thought. Two giants of this revolution were the Englishman **Francis Bacon** and the Frenchman **René Descartes** (day KAHRT). Each devoted himself to understanding how truth is determined. Both Bacon and Descartes, writing in the early 1600s, rejected Aristotle's scientific assumptions. They also challenged the scholarly traditions of the medieval universities that sought to make the physical world fit in with the teachings of the Church. Both argued that truth is not known at the beginning of inquiry but at the end, after a long process of investigation.

Bacon and Descartes differed in their methods, however. Bacon stressed experimentation and observation. He wanted science to make life better for people by leading to practical technologies. Descartes emphasized human reasoning as the best road to understanding. In his *Discourse on Method* (1637), he explains how he decided to discard all traditional authorities and search for provable knowledge. Left only with doubt, he concluded that doubt was the only thing he could not question, and that in order to doubt he had to exist as a rational, thinking being. Therefore he made his famous statement, "I think, therefore I am."

A Step-by-Step Process Over time, a step-by-step process of discovery evolved that became known as the **scientific method.** The scientific method required scientists to collect and accurately measure data. To explain the data, scientists used reasoning to propose a logical **hypothesis,** or possible explanation. They then tested the hypothesis with further observation or experimentation. Mathematical calculations were used to convert the observations and experiments into scientific laws. After reaching a conclusion, scientists repeated their work at least once—and usually many times—to confirm and refine their hypotheses or formulate better ones.

✓ **Checkpoint** How did Bacon and Descartes each approach the new scientific method?

Diagram Skills The scientific method, still used today, is based on careful observation and measurement of data. *Why is Step 7 an important part of the process?*

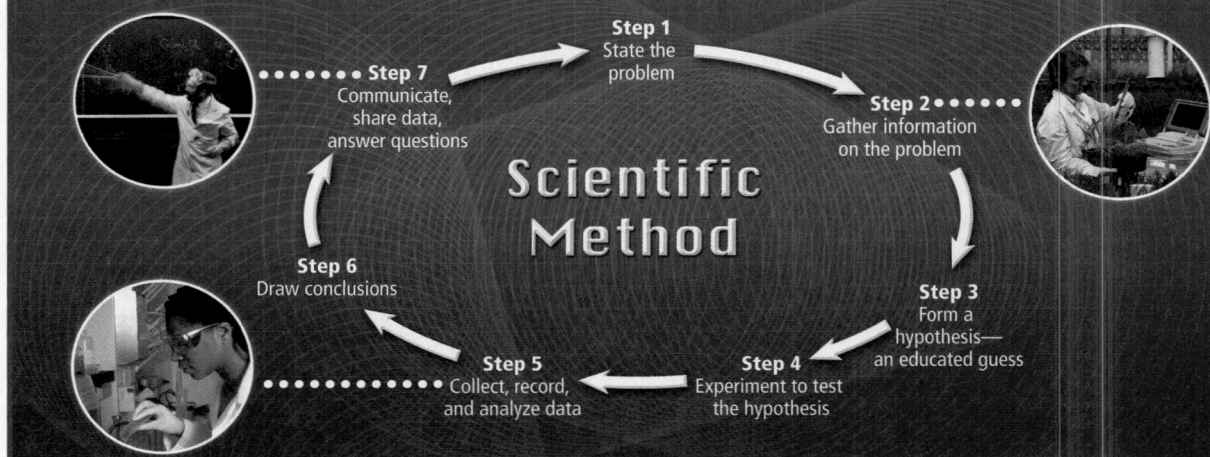

Scientific Method

Step 1 State the problem

Step 2 Gather information on the problem

Step 3 Form a hypothesis— an educated guess

Step 4 Experiment to test the hypothesis

Step 5 Collect, record, and analyze data

Step 6 Draw conclusions

Step 7 Communicate, share data, answer questions

History Background

Kepler's Laws Johannes Kepler wanted to know why Mars didn't appear where it was supposed to, based on mathematical calculations. Thanks to exact measurements by his mentor, Tycho Brahe, Kepler had excellent records of how Mars' position in the sky seemed to change. But the positions seemed wrong. They didn't fit any known theory of planetary move-ment. Racking his brain to work out a better theory, he finally came up with three principles of planetary motion, now known as Kepler's laws. Kepler was so exhilarated that he wrote, "Has not God himself waited 6,000 years for someone to contemplate his work with understanding?"

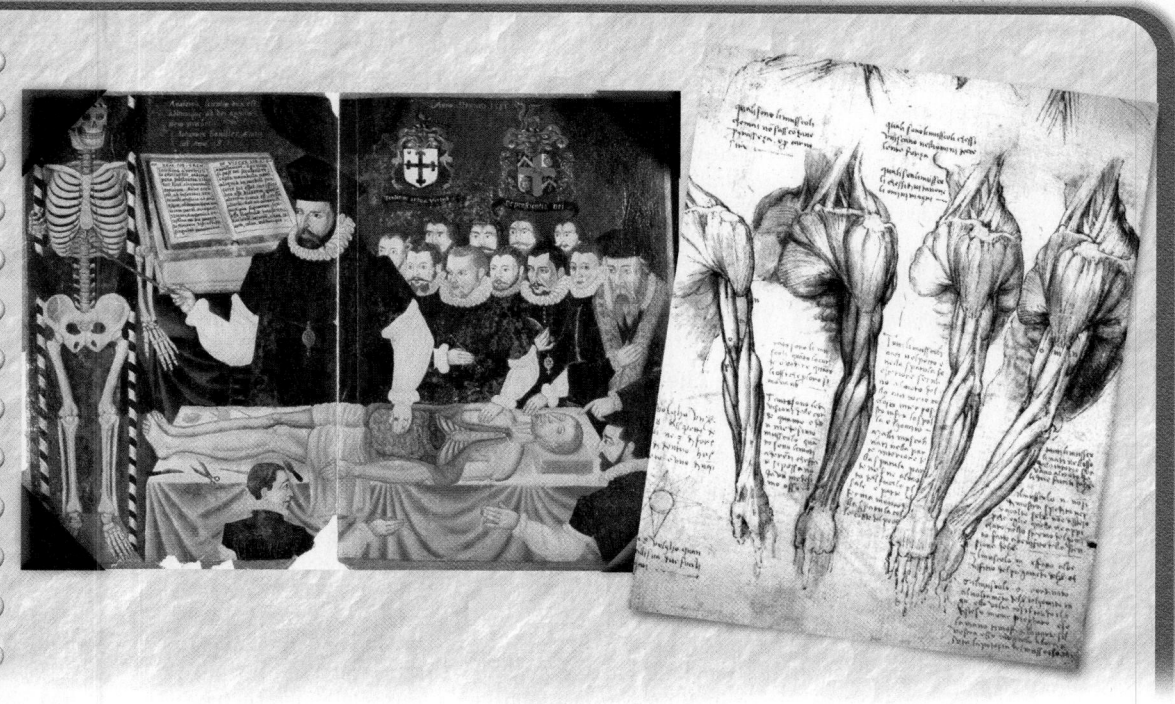

Breakthroughs in Medicine and Chemistry

The 1500s and 1600s saw dramatic changes in many branches of science, especially medicine and chemistry. The rapid changes in science and technology that began in this period still continue to this day.

Exploring the Human Body Medieval physicians relied on the works of the ancient physician Galen. Galen, however, had made many errors, in part because he had limited knowledge of human anatomy. During the Renaissance, physicians made new efforts to study the human body. In 1543, Andreas Vesalius (vuh SAY lee us) published *On the Structure of the Human Body,* the first accurate and detailed study of human anatomy. Vesalius used whatever means he could to increase his knowledge of anatomy. He used friendships with people of influence to get invitations to autopsies. He also autopsied bodies that he himself obtained—counting on friends in the local government to look the other way.

In the early 1540s, French physician Ambroise Paré (pa RAY) developed a new and more effective ointment for preventing infection. He also developed new surgical techniques, introduced the use of artificial limbs, and invented several scientific instruments. Then in the early 1600s, William Harvey, an English scholar, described the circulation of the blood for the first time. He showed how the heart serves as a pump to force blood through veins and arteries. Later in the century, the Dutch inventor Anton van Leeuwenhoek (LAY wun hohk) perfected the microscope and became the first human to see cells and microorganisms. These pioneering scientists opened the way for further discoveries.

Human Anatomy
Renaissance artists and scientists, determined to learn how things really worked, studied nature with great curiosity. In the 1400s, Leonardo drew the muscles of the human arm with amazing accuracy (right). Renaissance doctors learned much about human anatomy from dissections (left). *How does this painting from the 1500s reflect the advances in scientific thinking?*

Breakthroughs in Medicine and Chemistry/Isaac Newton Links the Sciences **L3**

Instruct

- **Introduce** Discuss the contributions and importance of Isaac Newton. Mention that his contributions to science are sometimes referred to as the "Newtonian Revolution." Ask students to discuss why Newton's work was revolutionary.

- **Teach** Review the rapid changes that occurred in medicine and chemistry at this time. Emphasize the expanding worldview, characterized by Leonardo's anatomical drawings, that led to greater knowledge of the human body. Discuss the visual titled Human Anatomy, Past and Present on this page. Ask **How is knowledge of the human body still expanding today?** *(Scientists are constantly developing and refining new technologies such as MRIs, computers, and lasers to give us more accurate views of the body.)*

- **Quick Activity** Display **Color Transparency 76: Hans Holbein's *The Ambassadors*** to investigate the links between Renaissance art and science. Use the lesson suggested in the transparency book to guide a discussion.
  ▥ **Color Transparencies,** 76

Independent Practice

Have students write a paragraph about a recent scientific discovery or debate. Paragraphs should include details describing the discovery or debate and an explanation of its significance.

Monitor Progress

Check Reading and Note Taking Study Guide entries for student understanding of the major figures of the Scientific Revolution and their accomplishments.

Answers

Caption It shows medical students engaged in learning about human anatomy by direct observation—an essential part of the scientific method.

✔ Boyle established that all matter is composed of tiny particles that behave in certain knowable ways.

Assess Progress

- Have students complete the Section Assessment.
- Administer the Section Quiz.

 Teaching Resources, Unit 1, p. 6

- To further assess student understanding, use

  Progress Monitoring Transparencies, 57

Reteach

If students need more instruction, have them read the section summary.

 Reading and Note Taking Study Guide, p. 44

 Adapted Reading and Note Taking Study Guide, p. 44

 Spanish Reading and Note Taking Study Guide, p. 44

Extend

See this chapter's Professional Development pages for the Extend Online activity on Galileo's experiments.

Answers

✔ He posited that objects he observed falling to Earth must have been pulled by the same forces that moved the planets.

PRIMARY SOURCE It suggests that Newton was highly respected and seen as a symbol of his time.

An English poet wrote the following as an epitaph for Newton's gravestone. What does it suggest about how people of the time viewed Newton's importance?

Primary Source

❝Nature and Nature's Laws lay hid in night,
  God said, Let Newton be! and all was light.❞
—Alexander Pope, *Epitaphs*

Transforming Chemistry The branch of science now called chemistry was in medieval times called alchemy. Alchemists believed that any substance could be transformed into any other substance, and many of them tried unsuccessfully to turn ordinary metals into gold. With the advances of the Scientific Revolution, the experiments of alchemists were abandoned. However, some of their practices—especially the manipulation of metals and acids—set the stage for modern chemistry.

In the 1600s, English chemist **Robert Boyle** refined the alchemists' view of chemicals as basic building blocks. He explained all matter as being composed of tiny particles that behave in knowable ways. Boyle distinguished between individual elements and chemical compounds, and explained the effect of temperature and pressure on gases. Boyle's work opened the way to modern chemical analysis of the composition of matter.

✔ **Checkpoint** How did Boyle transform the science of chemistry?

Isaac Newton Links the Sciences

As a student in England, **Isaac Newton** devoured the works of the leading scientists of his day. By age 24, he had formed a brilliant theory to explain why the planets moved as they did. According to one story, Newton saw an apple fall from a tree. He wondered whether the force that pulled that apple to Earth might not also control the movements of the planets. In the next 20 years, Newton perfected his theory. Using mathematics, he showed that a single force keeps the planets in their orbits around the sun. He called this force **gravity.**

In 1687, Newton published a book explaining the law of gravity and other workings of the universe. Nature, argued Newton, follows uniform laws. All motion in the universe can be measured and described mathematically. To many, Newton's work seemed to link the sciences just as gravity itself bound the universe together.

For more than 200 years, Newton's laws held fast. In the early 1900s, startling new theories of the universe called some of his ideas into question. Yet his laws of motion and mechanics continue to have many practical uses. For example, **calculus**—a branch of mathematics partially developed by Newton and used to explain his laws—is still applied today.

✔ **Checkpoint** How did Newton use observations of nature to explain the movements of the planets?

SECTION 5 Assessment

Progress Monitoring *Online*
For: Self-quiz with vocabulary practice
Web Code: nba-1351

Terms, People, and Places

1. What do all of the key people listed at the beginning of this section have in common? Explain.

Note Taking

2. **Reading Skill: Identify Main Ideas** Use your completed table to answer the Focus Question: How did discoveries in science lead to a new way of thinking for Europeans?

Comprehension and Critical Thinking

3. **Recognize Ideologies** Why did the theories of Copernicus and Galileo threaten the views of the Church?
4. **Make Generalizations** In what ways did the scientific method differ from earlier approaches to learning?
5. **Recognize Cause and Effect** What impact did Renaissance ideas have on medicine?
6. **Synthesize Information** How did Newton use the ideas of Plato?

● **Writing About History**

Quick Write: Write a Conclusion Write a conclusion to a persuasive essay about the Scientific Revolution. Your conclusion should restate a thesis statement, supported by one or two strong arguments. You may want to end your essay with a quotation. For example, you could use the Pope quotation to support a thesis that Newton's ideas were the most important of the Scientific Revolution.

---

4. Before, people learned accepted truths, dictated by tradition or religion. The scientific method was based on the idea that truth could come only through investigation.
5. The Renaissance worldview led people to explore the human body in new ways to see how it really worked, sparking new discoveries in anatomy and medicine.
6. He used Plato's emphasis on mathematics and reality to discover nature's laws.

● **Writing About History**

Conclusions should strongly restate the thesis, but should not be merely repetitive.

For additional assessment, have students access **Progress Monitoring *Online*** at **Web Code nba-1351.**

Concept Connector

SCIENCE AND TECHNOLOGY
What are the benefits and costs of science and technology?

In This Chapter

Science and religion clashed during the Scientific Revolution as new theories and discoveries conflicted with traditional views. Galileo was tried and imprisoned by the Inquisition (right) for claiming that Earth revolved around the sun.

Throughout History

1400 B.C. Hittites use iron for tools and weapons.

850 A.D. Chinese develop explosives used in fireworks and guns.

1700s New farming methods raise output but displace workers.

1800s Industrialization increases standards of living and pollution.

2000s The Internet leads to increased communication and computer-based fraud.

Continuing Today

Nuclear energy generates electrical power without the carbon emissions of fossil fuels. However, environmentalists (below) are among those who warn of the dangers of nuclear waste and the possibility of the accidental release of radioactive ions into the atmosphere.

21st Century Skills

? TRANSFER Activities

1. **Analyze** Why do science and technology have both costs and benefits?

2. **Evaluate** Does science have a greater potential for helping society, or for hurting society? Why?

3. **Transfer** Complete a Web quest in which you identify a successful innovator; record your thoughts in the Concept Connector Journal; and learn to make a video. Web Code nbh-1308

 Concept Connector

Science

Objectives
- Identify both positive and negative effects of science and technology.
- Understand that conflicts arise over costs versus benefits.
- Complete a Web Quest on science and technology.

Build Background Knowledge
Have students share their answers to the WARM-UP on Science and Technology in their Concept Connector Journal. Discuss whether or not the convenience of the automobile is worth the 114 lives a day lost in auto accidents.

Instruct
- Direct students' attention to the Essential Question: **What are the benefits and costs of science and technology?** Have students review what led to Galileo's trial by the Inquisition. Why might new ideas lead to conflict in society?
- Ask students to look at the Continuing Today image and read the caption. Ask: **What are these protestors implying about the cost of using nuclear power?**
- Assign a Web Quest on science and technology.

Independent Practice
Concept Connector Have students fill in the reflection question on the Web Quest on science and technology in their Concept Connector Journal.

 Reading and Note Taking Study Guide, p. 297

Monitor Progress
Circulate to make sure that students are filling in their Concept Connector journal. Ensure they understand the results of scientific and technological advances.

Transfer Activities
1. People can use the same item for good or evil purposes.
2. Answers will vary but should be supported with logical reasoning.
3. Students' work should be evaluated against the rubric at Web Code nbh-1308.

- Have students use the Quick Study Guide to prepare for this chapter's tests. Students may wish to refer to the following pages as they review:

Major Themes of the Renaissance
Section 1, pp. 48–50; Section 2, p. 57

Important Figures of the Scientific Revolution
Section 5, pp. 72–76

Causes and Effects of the Protestant Reformation
Section 2, pp. 57–58; Section 3, pp. 61–65; Section 4, pp. 66–71

Key Events of the Renaissance and Reformation
Section 1, pp. 48–50, 52–53; Section 2, p. 56; Section 3, p. 63; Section 4, p. 67; Section 5, pp. 72–73

- For additional review, remind students to refer to the **L3**

🖊 **Reading and Note Taking Study Guide**
Note Taking Study Guide, pp. 34–35, 37, 39, 41, 43
Section Summaries, pp. 36, 38, 40, 42, 44

- Have students access **Web Code nbp-1361** for this chapter's **History** *Interactive* timeline, which includes expanded entries and additional events.

- If students need more instruction on analyzing timelines, have them read the **Skills Handbook,** p. SH30.

- When students have completed their study of the chapter, distribute Chapter Tests A and B.

All in One Teaching Resources, Unit 1, pp. 16–21

For **Progress Monitoring Online,** refer students to the Self-test with vocabulary practice at **Web Code nba-1361.**

Quick Study Guide

Progress Monitoring *Online*
For: Self-test with vocabulary practice
Web Code: nba-1361

■ Major Themes of the Renaissance

- Importance of classical learning
- Emphasis on the individual
- Adventurous spirit and willingness to experiment
- Focus on realism in art and literature
- Questioning of traditional religious ideas

■ Important Figures of the Scientific Revolution

Person	Achievement	Date
Nicolaus Copernicus	Developed the sun-centered model of the universe	1543
Tycho Brahe and Johannes Kepler	Built astronomical observatory to calculate the planetary orbits; supported Copernicus's views	Late 1500s
Galileo Galilei	Developed telescope to view the planets and confirmed Copernicus's theory	1600
Francis Bacon	Called for new scientific method	Early 1600s
René Descartes	Developed new philosophy of human reasoning	Early 1600s
Isaac Newton	Developed laws of gravity and motion; invented calculus	Late 1600s
Robert Boyle	Identified basic building blocks of matter, opening the way for modern chemistry	Late 1600s

■ Causes and Effects of the Protestant Reformation

Cause and Effect	
Long-Term Causes	**Immediate Causes**
• Roman Catholic Church becomes more worldly.	• Johann Tetzel sells indulgences in Wittenberg.
• Humanists urge a return to simple religion.	• Martin Luther posts 95 Theses.
• Shift to more uncertain, urban-based economies causes people to look for society that makes more sense to them.	• Luther translates the Bible into German.
	• The printing press spreads reform ideas.
• Monarchs and other leaders question the pope's authority and wealth.	• Calvin and other reformers preach against Roman Catholic traditions.

The Protestant Reformation	
Immediate Effects	**Long-Term Effects**
• Peasants' Revolt	• Religious wars in Europe
• Catholic Reformation	• Founding of Lutheran, Calvinist, Anglican, Presbyterian, and other Protestant churches
• Strengthening of the Inquisition	• Weakening of Holy Roman Empire
• Luther's calls for Jewish expulsion result in Jewish migration to Eastern Europe	• Increased anti-Semitism

■ Key Events of the Renaissance and the Reformation

1300s
The Renaissance begins in the city-states of Italy.

1434
The Medici family gains control of Florence's government.

Chapter Events
World Events

1300   **1350**   **1400**

1324
Mansa Musa makes hajj.

1368
The Ming dynasty is founded in China.

1450
The kingdom of Songhai emerges in West Africa.

Differentiated Instruction   **Solutions for All Learners**

L1 Special Needs   **L2 Less Proficient Readers**
For students acquiring basic skills:

🖊 **Adapted Reading and Note Taking Study Guide**
Adapted Note Taking Study Guide, pp. 34–35, 37, 39, 41, 43
Adapted Section Summaries, pp. 36, 38, 40, 42, 44

L2 English Language Learners
For Spanish-speaking students:

🖊 **Spanish Reading and Note Taking Study Guide**
Spanish Note Taking Study Guide, pp. 34–35, 37, 39, 41, 43
Spanish Section Summaries, pp. 36, 38, 40, 42, 44

Concept Connector

Essential Question Review

To connect prior knowledge with what you have learned in this chapter, answer the questions below in your Concept Connector journal. Use the journal in the Reading and Note Taking Study Guide to record your answers (or go to www.phschool.com **Web Code: nbd-1307**).

1. **Cultural Diffusion** The Renaissance that emerged in Italy and northern Europe from about 1300 to 1500 and the flowering of Muslim civilization under the Abbasid dynasty from about 750 to 850 are both described as golden ages. Why were these periods in history considered golden ages? How and why did the ideas of Islam and the Renaissance spread?

2. **Science** During the Scientific Revolution, there were many advances in science, mathematics, philosophy and medicine. These developments challenged existing ideas and changed how people looked at the world. How were the ideas of the Scientific Revolution a break from the past? How do these changes affect our understanding of the world today?

■ Connections to Today

1. **Technology: The Communications Revolution** During the Renaissance, new technology like the printing press revolutionized life. Consider the various impacts that the printing press had during the Renaissance, in areas ranging from literacy to religion. Then choose a modern technology that has had a comparable effect. Write two paragraphs explaining why the technology you chose is as important in terms of its impact today as the printing press was in Renaissance times.

2. **Science: Its Global Impact** The Scientific Revolution transformed technology, government, economy, and society in Europe. Use of the scientific method allowed Europeans to improve farming techniques and ways of manufacturing goods. It helped them to improve mapmaking and navigation techniques and to sail across oceans. European governments found that these changes increased their income and their power, and so many of them supported scientific research. As you will read in the next two chapters, Europe's improved sea power, military technology, and economic might allowed it to conquer parts of Africa and Asia and most of the Americas. Considering these developments, explain how the world today is different from the world before the Scientific Revolution.

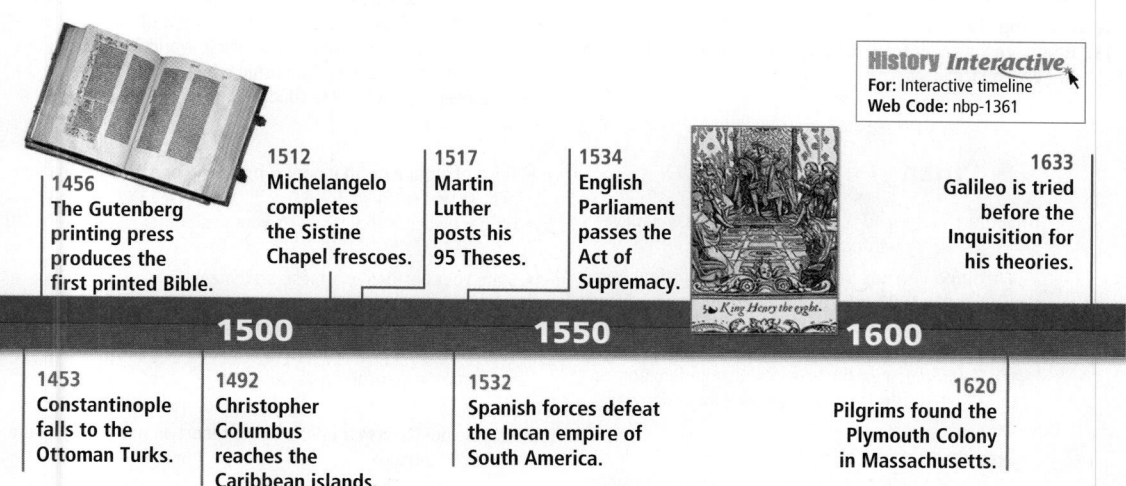

History Interactive
For: Interactive timeline
Web Code: nbp-1361

| 1456 The Gutenberg printing press produces the first printed Bible. | 1512 Michelangelo completes the Sistine Chapel frescoes. | 1517 Martin Luther posts his 95 Theses. | 1534 English Parliament passes the Act of Supremacy. | | 1633 Galileo is tried before the Inquisition for his theories. |

1500 **1550** **1600**

| 1453 Constantinople falls to the Ottoman Turks. | 1492 Christopher Columbus reaches the Caribbean islands. | 1532 Spanish forces defeat the Incan empire of South America. | 1620 Pilgrims found the Plymouth Colony in Massachusetts. |

Concept Connector

Tell students that the main concepts for this chapter are Cultural Diffusion and Science and then ask them to answer the Essential Question Review questions on this page. Discuss the Connections to Today topics and ask students to answer the questions that follow.

Essential Question Review

1. Students should be able to describe the achievements of these cultures. Responses should show how the two were similar because of the importance of trade and the rise of wealthy trade centers. Renaissance merchants, like Muslim traders, spread both wealth and ideas.

2. Answers will vary. Students should draw upon the chapter to describe how the developments of the Scientific Revolution changed how people thought about the world. Students should draw on one or more of these developments to discuss how they have affected us today.

Connections to Today

1. Answers will vary. The invention chosen by the student should have a clear and wide-ranging impact similar to that of the printing press.

2. Answers will vary. Students should draw on chapter content and background knowledge to explain how the Scientific Revolution changed the world.

For additional review of this chapter's core concepts, remind students to refer to the **ⓛ3**

Reading and Note Taking Study Guide
Concept Connector, pp. 247, 295

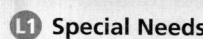
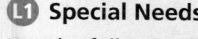

Differentiated
Instruction **Solutions for All Learners**

ⓛ1 Special Needs **ⓛ2 Less Proficient Readers**

Use the following study guide resources to help students acquiring basic skills:

Adapted Reading and Note Taking Study Guide
Adapted Concept Connector, pp. 247, 295

ⓛ2 English Language Learners

Use the following study guide resources to help Spanish-speaking students:

Spanish Reading and Note Taking Study Guide
Spanish Concept Connector, pp. 247, 295

Chapter Assessment

Terms, People, and Places

1. patron
2. vernacular
3. predestination
4. compromise
5. heliocentric

Main Ideas

6. Artists and writers adopted both a new realism and an emphasis on humanity.

7. It quickly spread the works of humanists and other Renaissance writers to a large audience.

8. Artists developed new techniques to paint more realistically; writers addressed the themes of humanism and wrote in the vernacular.

9. Renaissance thinkers began to question the Church as the sole source of truth, opening the way for people to question the Church on more specific issues as well.

10. It needed to prevent large numbers of people from embracing Protestantism and thereby weakening the authority of the Church.

11. Scientists began to question accepted teaching, relying instead on their own observations and reasoning to get to the truth.

Chapter Focus Question

12. Renaissance thought was profoundly affected by a new worldview that embraced curiosity, exploration, and the importance of humanity. Renaissance people remained religious, but they no longer accepted religious authority unquestioningly. Instead, they used their expanding knowledge in other fields to shape their own religious thinking.

Critical Thinking

13. Italy's Mediterranean location, between Europe and the East, encouraged trade. Trade, and with it a flow of new ideas and wealth, encouraged the development and spread of the Renaissance.

14. It broke with medieval times by questioning religious authority and by emphasizing the importance of the human world. It continued medieval ways by highly valuing religion and a sharply defined social structure.

Chapter Assessment

Terms, People, and Places

Complete each sentence by choosing the correct answer from the list of terms below. You will not use all of the terms.

patron	indulgence	ghetto
humanism	predestination	heliocentric
vernacular	compromise	hypothesis
utopian		

1. Lorenzo de' Medici was a _____ of the Florentine arts.
2. Rabelais and Shakespeare wrote in the _____ to appeal to the common people.
3. Calvin's belief in _____ set him apart from Catholics.
4. Elizabeth's sensible _____ helped keep England unified in the face of religious conflict.
5. Copernicus's _____ theory of the universe challenged the accepted teachings of the Church.

Main Ideas

Section 1 (pp. 48–54)
6. How did the new Renaissance worldview shape the work of Italian Renaissance artists and writers?

Section 2 (pp. 56–59)
7. What was the role of the printing press in spreading Renaissance ideas?
8. How did northern European artists and writers apply Renaissance ideas in their work?

Section 3 (pp. 61–65)
9. How did the Renaissance open the door to the Protestant Reformation?

Section 4 (pp. 66–71)
10. Why did the Church respond with its Catholic Reformation?

Section 5 (pp. 72–76)
11. How were the scientists of the Scientific Revolution influenced by Renaissance ideas?

Chapter Focus Question

12. How did the Renaissance shape European art, thought, and religion?

Critical Thinking

13. **Geography and History** How did Italy's geography encourage the spread of the Renaissance?
14. **Analyze Information** In what ways was the Renaissance a break with medieval times? In what ways was it a continuation of medieval times?
15. **Predict Consequences** Under what circumstances are religious beliefs likely to inspire anger or violence?
16. **Analyze Visuals** What Renaissance theme does the bas-relief below express?

17. **Test Conclusions** The Renaissance and Scientific Revolution are often described as eras of human progress. Evaluate whether this is an accurate description.
18. **Recognize Cause and Effect** Why did England escape the kinds of religious wars that tore apart other European nations?
19. **Synthesize Information** An English author wrote, "The preaching of sermons is speaking to a few of mankind, but printing books is talking to the whole world." How does this statement suggest a relationship between two of the key events discussed in this chapter?

● Writing About History

In this chapter's five Section Assessments, you developed skills for writing a persuasive essay.

Writing a Persuasive Essay European history from 1300 to the 1600s was a time of great change, discovery, and religious upheaval. Write a persuasive essay that presents your position on either the Renaissance, the Reformation, or the Scientific Revolution. Consult page SH16 of the Writing Handbook for additional help.

Prewriting
● Choose a topic and decide what your main position will be.

● Think of arguments that both support and oppose your position, and answer them.
● Gather evidence that supports your position.

Drafting
● State your position in a thesis statement.
● Organize your arguments into a draft outline.
● Write the introduction, body text, and closing arguments. Be sure to support your arguments with a variety of points, including facts, comparisons, and statistics.

Revising
● Use the guidelines for revising your report on page SH17 of the Writing Handbook.

---

15. Sample: When there is great uncertainty—whether financial, social, or religious—people are more likely to feel threatened by those with different religious beliefs or ways of life.

16. the importance of education

17. Answers may agree with this description because great discoveries were made, advancing science and enriching art. Other answers may suggest that most people did not benefit greatly from the period's advances and still lived in poverty.

18. Queen Elizabeth's efforts to make compromises satisfied both Protestants and Catholics and averted religious warfare.

19. The Protestant Reformation could not have spread so quickly nor had such a great impact without the invention of the printing press.

Document-Based Assessment

The Impact of the Printing Press

In a time when new ideas and discoveries were commonplace, the invention of the printing press was no less than astonishing in its impact. Documents A, B, and D describe the spread of printing during the Renaissance. Document C, written by a historian in the 1500s, describes its impact at the time.

Document A

"In 1455 all Europe's printed books could have been carried in a single wagon. Fifty years later, the titles ran to tens of thousands, the individual volumes to millions. Today, books pour off presses at the rate of 10,000 million *a year*. That's some 50 million tons of paper. Add in 8,000 to 9,000 daily newspapers, and the Sundays, and the magazines, and the figure rises to 130 million tons . . . It would make a pile 700 meters [2,297 feet] high—four times the height of the Great Pyramid."

—From *Gutenberg: How One Man Remade the World with Words* by John Man

Document B

"Printing spread from Mainz to Strasbourg (1458), Cologne (1465), Augsburg (1468), Nuremberg (1470), Leipzig (1481), and Vienna (1482). German printers, or their pupils, introduced the 'divine' art to Italy in 1467, Switzerland and Bohemia in 1468, France and the Netherlands in 1470, Spain, England, Hungary, and Poland between 1474 and 1476, Denmark and Sweden in 1482–1483. By 1500 the presses had issued about six million books in approximately forty thousand editions, more books, probably, than had been produced in western Europe since the fall of Rome . . . Now individuals could afford to own books, where before they had normally been owned almost exclusively by institutions—monasteries, cathedral chapters, and colleges."

—From *The Foundation of Early Modern Europe, 1460–1559* by Eugene F. Rice, Jr.

Document C

"As if to offer proof that God has chosen us to accomplish a special mission, there was invented in our land a marvelous new and subtle art, the art of printing. This opened German eyes even as it is now bringing enlightenment to other countries. Each man became eager for knowledge, not without feeling a sense of amazement at his former blindness."

—From *Address to the Estates of the Empire* by Johann Sleidan

Document D

The Spread of Printing in Renaissance Europe

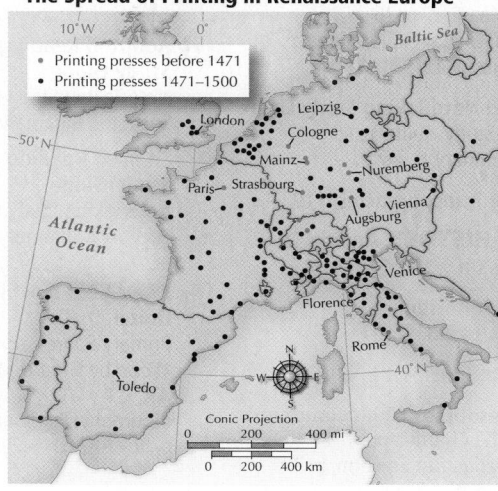

- Printing presses before 1471
- Printing presses 1471–1500

Analyzing Documents

Use your knowledge of the Renaissance and Documents A, B, C, and D to answer questions 1–4.

1. According to Document B, the increased supply and lower cost of books had what effect?
   A More people became teachers.
   B More people became printers.
   C More people bought books.
   D More people bought printing presses.

2. What information about printing can be found only on Document D?
   A specific dates when printing presses were introduced
   B areas where the concentration of printing presses was densest
   C numbers of printing presses introduced into selected cities
   D countries where printing presses were introduced

3. What does German historian Sleidan, in Document C, imply is the *most important* role of the printing press?
   A spreading the Protestant religion
   B teaching German history to other countries
   C making books cheaper
   D giving Germans more knowledge

4. **Writing Task** How did the invention of the printing press affect the spread of the Reformation? Use specific evidence from the documents above, along with information from this chapter, to support your answer.

Writing About History

As students begin the assignment, refer them to page SH16 of the **Writing Handbook** for help in writing a persuasive essay. Remind them of the steps they should take to complete their assignment, including prewriting, drafting, and revising. For help in revising, remind them to use the guidelines on page SH17 of the **Writing Handbook.**

Students' essays should make a clear argument, supported with specific details and facts. Essays should have a clear structure, with an introduction, a body, and a conclusion. They should show evidence that the student has considered opposing points of view. For scoring rubrics for writing assignments, see **Assessment Rubrics,** p. 8.

Answers

1. C
2. B
3. A
4. Responses should show a clear understanding that the printing press had a dramatic impact on the spread of the Reformation, and should be supported with specific examples from the chapter and the documents.

The Beginnings of Our Global Age: Europe, Africa, and Asia

Section	Core Instruction L3	Differentiated Instruction L1 L2 L4	
Section 1 *The Search for Spices* **1 period, .5 block** **OBJECTIVES** ■ Understand European motivation for exploring the seas. ■ Analyze early Portuguese and Spanish explorations. ■ Describe European searches for a direct route to Asia. **Focus Question** *How did the search for spices lead to global exploration?*	**All in One Teaching Resources, Unit 1** Reading Strategy: Identify Causes and Effects, p. 27 Vocabulary Builder: Use Context Clues to Determine Meaning, p. 26 Outline Map: Global Explorations, p. 34 Section 1 Quiz, p. 22 **Reading and Note Taking Study Guide** Note Taking Study Guide, p. 45 Section 1 Summary, p. 46 **Note Taking Transparencies,** 119 **WITNESS HISTORY Audio CD** The Search is On **Progress Monitoring Transparencies,** 58 **Color Transparencies,** 82 **Teaching Resources, Skills Handbook** Prereading the Chapter, pp. 1–2 Word Knowledge Rating Form, p. 3 K-W-L Chart, p. 4	**L1 Adapted Reading and Note Taking Study Guide** Note Taking Study Guide, p. 45 **SN** Section 1 Summary, p. 46 **SN** **L2 Adapted Reading and Note Taking Study Guide** Note Taking Study Guide, p. 45 **LPR** Section 1 Summary, p. 46 **LPR** **Spanish Reading and Note Taking Study Guide** Note Taking Study Guide, p. 45 **ELL** Section 1 Summary, p. 46 **ELL** **L4 All in One Teaching Resources, Unit 1** Primary Source: *1569 Map of the World* by Gerard Mercator, p. 28 **AR, GT** Biography: Ferdinand Magellan, p. 30 **AR, GT**	*Student Edition Audio **SN** **Differentiated Instruction Activity,** Teacher's Edition, p. 85 **SN** *Guided Reading Audio, Spanish **ELL** *Student Edition Audio **LPR** **Differentiated Instruction Activity,** Teacher's Edition, p. 85 **LPR, ELL** **Differentiated Instruction Activity,** Teacher's Edition, p. 88 **AR, GT** **Extend Activity,** Teacher's Edition, p. 89 **AR, GT**
Section 2 *Turbulent Centuries in Africa* **2 periods, 1 block** **OBJECTIVES** ■ Describe how the Portuguese established footholds on Africa's coasts. ■ Analyze how European actions affected the slave trade and the rise of African states. ■ Explain how the European presence in Africa expanded. **Focus Question** *What effects did European exploration have on the people of Africa?*	**All in One Teaching Resources, Unit 1** Section 2 Quiz, p. 23 **Reading and Note Taking Study Guide** Note Taking Study Guide, p. 47 Section 2 Summary, p. 48 **Note Taking Transparencies,** 120 **WITNESS HISTORY Audio CD** Great Seabirds Arrive, Chronicle of the Discovery and Conquest of Guinea **Progress Monitoring Transparencies,** 59 **Color Transparencies,** 85	**L1 Adapted Reading and Note Taking Study Guide** Note Taking Study Guide, p. 47 **SN** Section 2 Summary, p. 48 **SN** **L2 Adapted Reading and Note Taking Study Guide** Note Taking Study Guide, p. 47 **LPR** Section 2 Summary, p. 48 **LPR** **L4 Extend Activity,** Teacher's Edition, p. 93 **AR, GT**	**Differentiated Instruction Activity,** Teacher's Edition, p. 91 **SN** **Spanish Reading and Note Taking Study Guide** Note Taking Study Guide, p. 47 **ELL** Section 2 Summary, p. 48 **ELL** **Differentiated Instruction Activity,** Teacher's Edition, p. 91 **LPR, ELL**

*Audio support is available for all sections.

Section	Core Instruction L3	Differentiated Instruction L1 L2 L4	
Section 3 *European Footholds in South and Southeast Asia* **1 period, .5 block** **OBJECTIVES** ■ Summarize how Portugal built a trading empire in South and Southeast Asia. ■ Analyze the rise of Dutch and Spanish dominance in the region. ■ Understand how the decline of Mughal India affected European traders in the region. **Focus Question** *How did European nations build empires in South and Southeast Asia?*	**All in One Teaching Resources, Unit 1** Section 3 Quiz, p. 24 **Reading and Note Taking Study Guide** Note Taking Study Guide, p. 49 Section 3 Summary, p. 50 **Note Taking Transparencies,** 121 **WITNESS HISTORY Audio CD** Gunfire Over Malacca **Progress Monitoring Transparencies,** 60 **Color Transparencies,** 86, 87	**L1 Adapted Reading and Note Taking Study Guide** Note Taking Study Guide, p. 49 SN Section 3 Summary, p. 50 SN **L2 Adapted Reading and Note Taking Study Guide** Note Taking Study Guide, p. 49 LPR Section 3 Summary, p. 50 LPR **L4 All in One Teaching Resources, Unit 1** Primary Source: The Portuguese Reach India, p. 29 AR, GT Primary Source: An Unusual Dinner Party, p. 31 AR, GT	**Differentiated Instruction Activity,** Teacher's Edition, p. 97 SN **Spanish Reading and Note Taking Study Guide** Note Taking Study Guide, p. 49 ELL Section 3 Summary, p. 50 ELL **Differentiated Instruction Activity,** Teacher's Edition, p. 97 LPR, ELL **Extend Activity,** Teacher's Edition, p. 98 AR, GT
Section 4 *Encounters in East Asia* **1 period, .5 block** **OBJECTIVES** ■ Describe European contacts with Ming China. ■ Understand the Manchu conquest and its impact on European trade. ■ Analyze the factors that led Korea to isolate itself from other nations. ■ Summarize Japan's attitudes toward foreign trade and how they changed over time. **Focus Question** *How were European encounters in East Asia shaped by the worldviews of both Europeans and Asians?*	**All in One Teaching Resources, Unit 1** Outline Map: World During the Age of Discovery, p. 33 Geography Quiz, p. 35 Section 4 Quiz, p. 62 **Reading and Note Taking Study Guide** Note Taking Study Guide, p. 51 Section 4 Summary, p. 52 Concept Connector, pp. 237, 262, 295, 300 **Note Taking Transparencies,** 122 **WITNESS HISTORY Audio CD** A Jesuit in China **Progress Monitoring Transparencies,** 61 **Color Transparencies,** 83, 84, 88 **Witness History Discovery School™** video program, *Manchu China and the West*	**L1 Adapted Reading and Note Taking Study Guide** Note Taking Study Guide, p. 51 SN Section 4 Summary, p. 52 SN Concept Connector, pp. 237, 262, 295, 300 SN **L2 Adapted Reading and Note Taking Study Guide** Note Taking Study Guide, p. 51 LPR Section 4 Summary, p. 52 LPR Concept Connector, pp. 237, 262, 295, 300 LPR **L4 All in One Teaching Resources, Unit 1** Viewpoints: Japan's Shoguns Reject the West, p. 32 AR, GT Simulation: Closing Japan to Foreigners, pp. 84–87 AR, GT	**Differentiated Instruction Activity,** Teacher's Edition, p. 100 SN **Spanish Reading and Note Taking Study Guide** Note Taking Study Guide, p. 51 ELL Section 4 Summary, p. 52 ELL Concept Connector, pp. 237, 262, 295, 300 ELL **Differentiated Instruction Activity,** Teacher's Edition, p. 100 LPR, ELL **Extend Activity,** Teacher's Edition, p. 103 AR, GT

Assessment Resources

- **Progress Monitoring Transparencies,** 58–61
- **SuccessTracker™,** Chapter 2
- **Document-Based Assessment,** pp. 41–53
- *ExamView®* **Test Bank CD-ROM,** Chapter 2
- **All in One Teaching Resources, Unit 1,** Chapter Tests A and B, pp. 36–41
- **Progress Monitoring** *Online* **Quizzes,** Chapter 2
- **Assessment Rubrics**

Differentiated Instruction Key

L1 Special Needs	**LPR** Less Proficient Readers
L2 Basic to Average	**AR** Advanced Readers
L3 All Students	**SN** Special Needs Students
L4 Average to Advanced	**GT** Gifted and Talented
	ELL English Language Learner

CHAPTER PLANNER

Author's Notes

Conquest and Commerce

There were missionaries eager for converts and young men mad for glory among these Western imperialists. But there were probably more who went out to the far places of the earth, as a chronicler who marched with Cortés put it, "to grow rich as all men desire to do." And like empire builders from one end of history to the other, Europeans brought home many things from conquered lands. . . .

Asia was the first objective. The original goal of the Western voyagers had been to find a sea route to the spices and luxury goods of the Far East that would be cheaper and surer than the overland routes controlled by other peoples. First the Portuguese, then the Dutch, French, and English broke into the trade of the Indian Ocean and Southeast Asia, and soon they were its masters.

In the holds of caravels and lumbering East Indiamen (large merchant ships), Europeans brought home silk, tea, porcelain, and spices such as pepper, cloves, and cinnamon from China; cottons and precious stones from India; coffee from Arabia and the Middle East; drugs, saltpeter for gunpowder, indigo dye—the list is almost endless. Europe's consumption of pepper doubled in the first half of the sixteenth century. In the seventeenth, coffee and tea became national drinks in Europe. Indian cotton would spawn a whole new industry in Britain and trigger the Industrial Revolution. The long-range consequences of Asian imports were even more incalculable than their immediate impact.

On the way to Asia, European vessels had to sail around the second-largest continent—Africa. They found profitable commodities here too: pepper and cloves, gold and ivory—and, above all, slaves. Laboring men and women became Africa's primary contribution to the burgeoning wealth of the West. Europeans did not invent the African slave trade. Slavers from the Muslim lands of North and East Africa had raided and traded for slaves in that continent for centuries. It had always been a profitable business for the intruders and a deeply destructive experience for African society. But the European onslaught was to have a much larger impact on the history of the world as a whole.

—Anthony Esler, *The Human Venture From Prehistory to the Present*, (Upper Saddle River, New Jersey: Pearson Education, 2004), pp. 464–466

Extend Online

The Spice Trade

Have students research various travel routes of the spice trade. Ask them to analyze the possible problems a sea captain might encounter and identify solutions. Use the steps below to help students complete the activity.

Prepare for the Activity Explain that the spice trade, which sparked the beginnings of a global age, could be a tricky venture. Christopher Columbus set out for the East Indies in order to find a route to the spices and riches found there. When he landed in the Caribbean, he wrote that he believed he had found such spices as nutmeg, rhubarb, and cinnamon. As proof, he brought back a sample of the cinnamon, which turned out to be bark from an unidentified tree. Besides finding the unexpected, explorers encountered rough seas, pirates, and other dangers.

Conduct the Activity For help in starting the activity, send students to **Web Code nbe-1401.** Students will take the role of a sea captain about to embark on a trading voyage. In pairs, have students make decisions about cargo, crew, trade route, and piracy. Have them draw a map of their voyage and make a list of their expenses, goods, crew, problems encountered and their proposed solutions. Then have them present their journey to the class.

Follow-Up Conduct a class discussion based on the following questions: What choices did you find the most difficult to make regarding your voyages? What other obstacles might explorers have encountered? How did trade add to the European understanding of the world?

Differentiated Instruction   Solutions for All Learners

Mapping Word Definitions ⓛ²

To help students learn unfamiliar words, introduce them to the strategy of mapping word definitions. Research shows that this technique helps students develop the ability to investigate word meanings independently and provide elaborated definitions (as opposed to simple one- or two-word definitions). Research also indicates that effective vocabulary strategies require students to go beyond simply looking up dictionary definitions or examining the context. Vocabulary learning must be based on the learner's dynamic engagement in constructing meaning.

- Model mapping word definitions by using the following steps for the high-use word *unify*.
- Define the word in your own words—*to make whole, to bring together into one*
- Provide a synonym or example—*unite, combine*
- Use the word in a sentence—*By combining the north and south high schools into one school, the school board unified the town.*
- Provide a non-example—*collaborate*

Revising the Text ⓛ⁴

Advanced readers typically understand that in a conflict, each group's perspective on the event can differ tremendously. To reinforce this, ask students to rewrite a section of text explaining a conflict from one side's perspective. Follow the steps below:

1. Assign members of the class a selection of reading from their text that discusses an event or conflict that involves more than one group.

2. Ask students to choose one of the groups involved and research their role in the event.

3. Have students rewrite the text to reflect the perspective of their chosen group.

Revisions should include changes in word choice that may make the reader more sympathetic to the selected group, mention events that were omitted from this text, and include explanations for why the selected group acted in a certain way.

Modeling Reading and Writing Skills

Signal Words: Cause and Effect Tell students that recognizing causes and effects helps them to clarify the relationships among events or situations. Point out that noting signal words can help them identify these relationships. Clue words such as *reason, because, produced,* and *purpose* indicate possible causes. Words such as *brought about, led to, outcome, produced, reaction, result, so, then, therefore,* and *this* indicate possible effects.

Model how to identify cause-and-effect relationships by reading aloud the last sentence on page 85. Draw students' attention to the word *because* and point out that this word signals an effect. The effect is that the tip became known as the Cape of Good Hope. The cause of the name is that this tip, at the southern end of Africa, opened a sea route to Asia.

Gather Details Explain that in this chapter students will be writing a biographical essay. (See Writing About History, p. 106.) Tell students that for such an essay, they will need to research the life and historical importance of

their subject. Point out that there are many sources for biographical information. Ask students to share their ideas for sources. Then post the following sources on the board and discuss techniques for using each one.

1. Internet: key word search by name; biographical reference Web sites; topic reference Web sites such as European Explorers or Renaissance Artists

2. Biographical dictionaries or encyclopedias

3. Periodicals: search in Readers' Guide to Periodicals or similar reference

4. Topic specific books: visit a library or bookstore; use online booksellers for partial access to texts

5. Expert Interview: speak with history teacher at local high school, college, or university

6. Quotations: books; online databases

Remind students of the importance of using current and reliable sources, and stress the need to accurately quote and cite source materials to avoid plagiarism.

The Beginnings of Our Global Age: Europe, Africa, and Asia

1415–1796

Teach With Technology

PresentationEXPRESS™
Premium DVD

- Teach this chapter's core content using **PresentationExpress™ Premium,** which includes dynamic lecture notes, interactive game shows, songs, videos, and the *ExamView® QuickTake* assessment tool.

- To introduce the chapter using **PresentationExpress™ Premium,** start by asking students **Which of the following statements do you most agree with? A) Spreading religion is a valid reason for conquering other people. B) Obtaining wealth is a valid reason for conquering other people. C) Spreading democracy is a valid reason for conquering other people. D) There are no valid reasons for conquering other people.** Take a class poll or record students' answers using the QuickTake feature and discuss their responses. Point out that in this chapter, they will read about the motives for European exploration and its effects on people around the world. Continue introducing the chapter using the chapter opener slide show and Witness History audio.

Technology Resources

- Student**EXPRESS** CD-ROM, Chapter 2
- Teacher**EXPRESS** CD-ROM, Chapter 2
- Presentation**EXPRESS**™ **Premium DVD,** Chapter 2
- **WITNESS HISTORY** Audio CD, Chapter 2
- *ExamView* **Test Bank CD-ROM,** English and Spanish, Chapter 2
- **Guided Reading Audio,** Spanish, Chapter 2
- **Student Edition Audio,** Chapter 2
- **Witness History Discovery School**™ video program, *Manchu China and the West*
- **Experience It! Multimedia Pack**

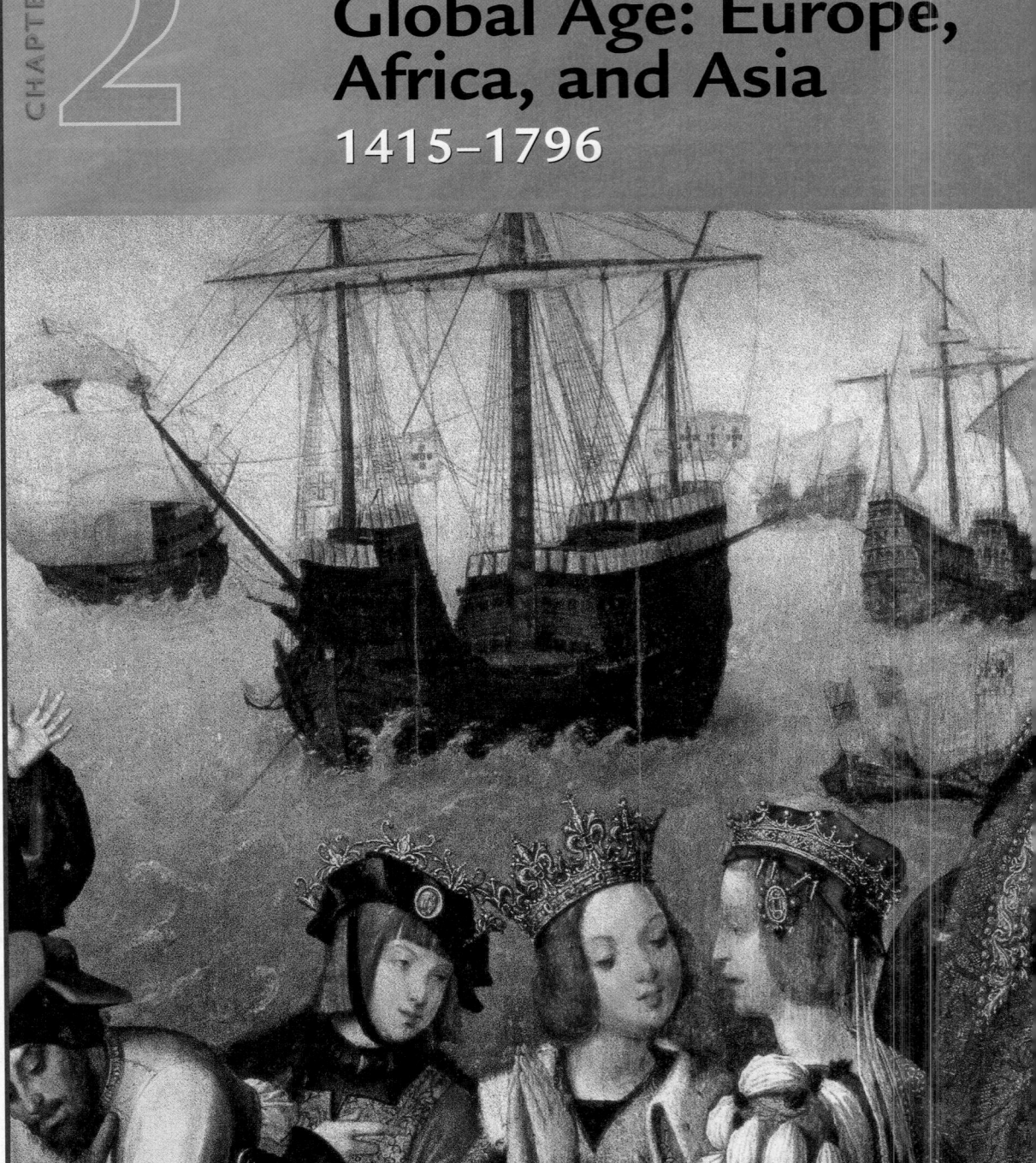

Bibliography

For the Teacher
Birmingham, David. *Trade and Empire in the Atlantic, 1400–1600.* London: Routledge, 2000.

Fritze, Ronald H. *New Worlds: The Great Voyages of Discovery, 1400–1600.* Westport, Conn.: Praegar Publishers, 2002.

Turner, Jack. *Spice: The History of a Temptation.* New York: Alfred A. Knopf, 2004.

For the Student
L2 Martell, Hazel M. *Exploring Africa.* Series: Voyages of Discovery. New York: P. Bedrick Books, 1997.

L3 Wiesner, Merry E. *The Age of Voyages, 1350–1600.* New York: Oxford University Press, 2005.

L4 Milton, Giles. *Samurai Williams: The Englishman Who Opened the East.* New York: Farrar, Straus and Giroux, 2003.

WITNESS HISTORY 🔊 AUDIO

Around the World and Into History

In 1519, a fleet of five Spanish ships with more than 250 crew sailed from Spain. Ferdinand Magellan, the captain, had been commissioned to sail around the Americas to the Spice Islands. Three years later, a single battered ship limped back into a Spanish harbor. On board were just 18 malnourished, skeletal sailors, so weak they could barely walk. Magellan and all but one of the ship's officers had perished. The survivors told an amazing tale. One recorded in his journal:

A pottery dish in the Muslim Spanish style shows a *nao*, a light sailing ship developed in the 1400s.

❝From the time we left that bay . . . until the present day, we had sailed 14,460 leagues [nearly 60,000 miles], and furthermore had completed the circumnavigation of the world from east to west.❞

Listen to the Witness History audio to hear more about this historic voyage.

◄ A Portuguese painting from 1522 tells the story of the martyrdom of Ursula, a medieval Catholic saint. The religious story and the sailing ships in the background express the themes of the age of exploration.

African statue of a Portuguese soldier

Chapter Preview

Chapter Focus Question How did European voyages of exploration lead to European empires in the Eastern Hemisphere?

Section 1
The Search for Spices

Section 2
Turbulent Centuries in Africa

Section 3
European Footholds in South and Southeast Asia

Section 4
Encounters in East Asia

Use the ☑ **Quick Study Timeline** at the end of this chapter to preview chapter events.

Chinese silk robe from the Qing dynasty

❓ **Concept Connector ONLINE**
To explore Essential Questions related to this chapter, go to PHSchool.com
Web Code: nbd-1407

Chapter-Level Resources

All in One Vocabulary Builder; Reading Strategy; Enrichments; Outline Maps; Geography Quiz; Chapter Tests
■ Document-Based Assessments
■ AYP Monitoring Assessments
■ *ExamView* Test Bank CD-ROM
■ Guided Reading Audio (Spanish)
■ Student Edition Audio

Previewing the Chapter

■ **WITNESS HISTORY** To help students understand the perilous nature of Magellan's historic voyage, ask them to brainstorm obstacles that Magellan and his crew might have faced, such as storms, lack of food and water, and so on. Elicit from students less obvious obstacles, such as lack of accurate maps or lack of means to communicate with anyone on land. Then read the Witness History selection aloud or play the accompanying audio. Make sure that students understand the great danger of the voyage, and the impact the voyage would have on politics, economics, people, and technology.

🔊 AUDIO **Witness History Audio CD,** Around the World and Into History

■ **Analyzing the Visuals** Have students describe the scene in the painting, and then read its caption. Ask **What role do you think religion will play in the Age of Exploration?** *(Sample: Desire to convert others could be a motive for exploration and also a cause of hostility.)*

■ **Focus** Write the Chapter Focus Question on the board. Tell students to keep this question in mind as they read the chapter. *(Answer appears with Chapter Assessment answers.)* Have students preview the section titles for this chapter.

Differentiated Instruction Solutions for All Learners

The following Teacher's Edition strategies are suitable for students of varying abilities.

L1 Special Needs Students, pp. 85, 91, 96, 100, 105 **SN**

L2 English Language Learners, pp. 85, 91, 96, 100, 105 **ELL**

L2 Less Proficient Readers, pp. 85, 91, 96, 100, 105 **LPR**

L4 Gifted and Talented Students, pp. 88, 101 **GT**

L4 Advanced Readers, pp. 88, 101 **AR**

Note Taking Study Guide With Concept Connector Journal
For online access: Web code: nbd-1407
For print alternative: Reading and Note Taking Study Guide booklet

Objectives

As you teach this section, keep students focused on the following objectives to help them answer the Section Focus Question and master core content.

- Understand European motivation for exploring the seas.
- Analyze early Portuguese and Spanish explorations.
- Describe European searches for a direct route to Asia.

Build Background Knowledge ⓛ

Point out that the age of exploration began during the Renaissance. Ask students to recall key ideas and developments of the Renaissance. Then have them predict how these ideas would affect overseas exploration by Europeans.

Set a Purpose ⓛ

- **WITNESS HISTORY** Read the selection aloud or play the audio.

  ◀)) AUDIO **Witness History Audio CD,** The Search Is On

  Ask **What did the Indonesian ruler mean by his statement?** *(Because of differences in climate, spices could not be grown in Europe.)* **Why was this significant?** *(The only way for Europeans to get spices was to trade with Asia.)*

- **Focus** Point out the Section Focus Question and write it on the board. Tell students to refer to this question as they read. *(Answer appears with Section 1 Assessment answers.)*

- **Preview** Have students preview the Section Objectives and the list of Terms, People, and Places.

- **Reading Skill** Have students use the *Reading Strategy: Identify Causes and Effects* worksheet.

  All in One **Teaching Resources, Unit 1,** p. 27

Answer

✓ the desire for spices; Renaissance and religious ideals

A French traveler in the 1400s illustrated workers harvesting pepper in southern India; a clove plant is shown at left.

The Search for Spices

Objectives
- Understand European motivations for exploring the seas.
- Analyze early Portuguese and Spanish explorations.
- Describe European searches for a direct route to Asia.

Terms, People, and Places

Moluccas	Line of Demarcation
Prince Henry	Treaty of Tordesillas
cartographer	Ferdinand Magellan
Vasco da Gama	circumnavigate
Christopher Columbus	

Note Taking

Reading Skill: Identify Causes and Effects Examine the text for clues that signal cause and effect. Then use a flowchart like this one to record major causes and effects of European exploration.

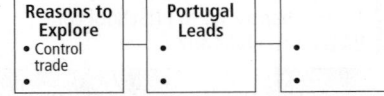

Reasons to Explore	Portugal Leads	
• Control trade	•	•
	•	•

Throughout history, groups of people—from the ancient Greeks to Muslim Arabs and the Vikings of Scandinavia—had explored the seas, trading and migrating over long distances. The European sailors of the 1400s began a dramatic new period of exploration.

Motivations for Exploring the Seas

Europeans traded with Asians long before the Renaissance. The Crusades introduced Europeans to many luxury goods from Asia, carried on complex overland routes through the Mongol empire of the 1200s and 1300s. The Black Death and the breakup of the Mongol empire disrupted that trade. By the 1400s, though, Europe's population was growing, along with its demand for trade goods. The most valued items were spices, used to preserve food, add flavor to meat, and make medicines and perfumes. The chief source of spices was the **Moluccas,** an island chain in present-day Indonesia, which Europeans then called the Spice Islands.

In the 1400s, Arab and Italian merchants controlled most trade between Asia and Europe. Muslim traders brought prized goods to eastern Mediterranean ports, and Italian traders carried them to European markets. Europeans outside Italy knew that it would be more profitable to gain direct access to Asia. They were also driven by Renaissance curiosity to seek new lands.

✓ **Checkpoint** What factors encouraged European exploration?

Vocabulary Builder

Use the information below and the following resources to teach the high-use word from this section.

All in One **Teaching Resources, Unit 1,** p. 26; **Teaching Resources, Skills Handbook,** p. 3

High-Use Word	Definition and Sample Sentence
authority, p. 87	*n.* the power to give commands and enforce obedience When the president of the company is absent, the vice president has the **authority** to make decisions.

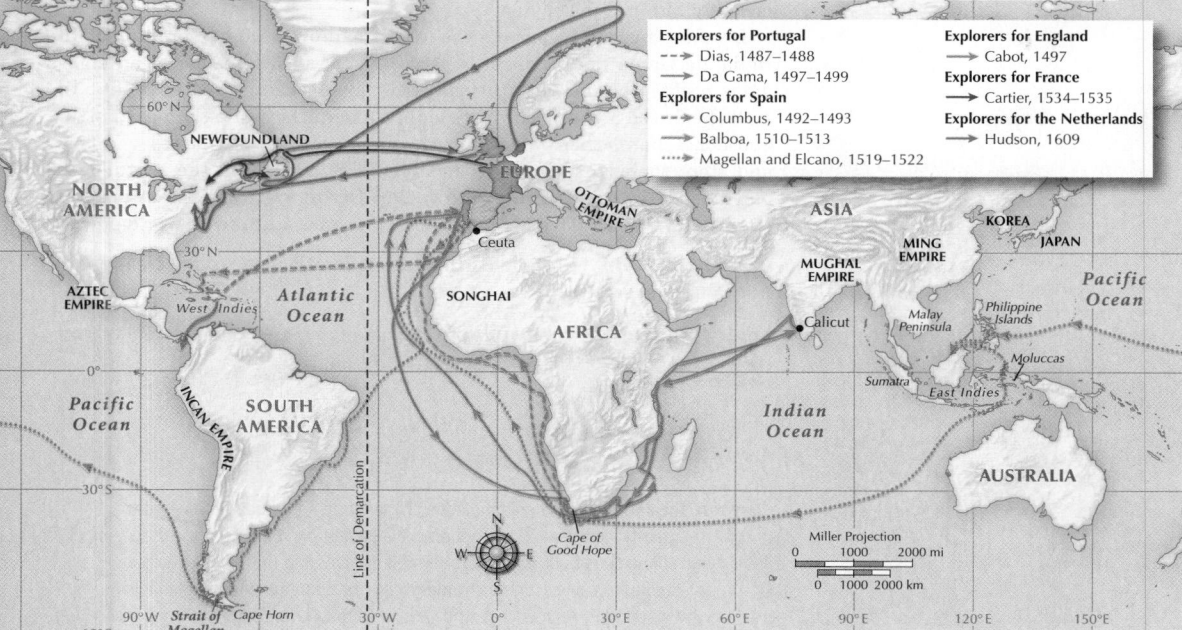

Geography *Interactive*

For: Audio guided tour
Web Code: nbp-1411

Early Voyages of European Exploration, 1487–1609

Map Skills Spain, England, France, and the Netherlands quickly followed Portugal's lead in exploring the world by ship.

1. **Locate** (a) West Indies (b) East Indies (c) Line of Demarcation (d) Strait of Magellan

2. **Describe** Describe the route of Columbus.

3. **Draw Inferences** Why do you think explorers from different countries followed similar routes?

Explorers for Portugal
- - → Dias, 1487–1488
──→ Da Gama, 1497–1499

Explorers for Spain
- - → Columbus, 1492–1493
──→ Balboa, 1510–1513
········ Magellan and Elcano, 1519–1522

Explorers for England
──→ Cabot, 1497

Explorers for France
──→ Cartier, 1534–1535

Explorers for the Netherlands
──→ Hudson, 1609

Portugal Sails East

Prince Henry led the way in sponsoring exploration for Portugal, a small nation next to Spain. First, Prince Henry's navigators discovered and claimed the Madeira and Azores islands to the west and southwest of Portugal. By 1415, Portugal had expanded into Muslim North Africa, seizing the port of Ceuta (SYOO tah) on the North African coast.

Mapping the African Coast Prince Henry saw great promise in Africa. The Portuguese could convert Africans—most of whom practiced either Islam or tribal religions—to Christianity. He also believed that in Africa he would find the sources of riches the Muslim traders controlled.

Finally, Prince Henry hoped to find an easier way to reach Asia, which meant going around Africa. The Portuguese felt that with their expert knowledge and technology, they could accomplish this feat. At Sagres, in southern Portugal, Henry gathered scientists, **cartographers,** or mapmakers, and other experts. They redesigned ships, prepared maps, and trained captains and crews for long voyages. Henry's ships then slowly worked their way south to explore the western coast of Africa.

Henry died in 1460, but the Portuguese continued their quest. In 1488, Bartholomeu Dias rounded the southern tip of Africa. Despite the turbulent seas around it, the tip became known as the Cape of Good Hope because it opened the way for a sea route to Asia.

Differentiated

Instruction   **Solutions for All Learners**

L1 Special Needs   **L2 Less Proficient Readers**

Ask students to create a chart with two columns. Label the columns "reasons to stay" and "reasons to explore." Ask students to complete the chart with the reasons why people move or why they prefer to stay in one place. Then discuss how these same reasons would have applied in the Age of Exploration. Discuss the risks that overseas explorers were taking.

L2 English Language Learners

Use the following resources to help students acquire basic skills.

Adapted Reading and Note Taking Study Guide

■ Adapted Note Taking Study Guide, p. 45
■ Adapted Section Summary, p. 46

■ **Note Taking** Have students read this section using the Paragraph Shrinking strategy (TE, p. T20). As they read, have students fill in the flowchart showing the major causes and effects of early European exploration.

> **Reading and Note Taking Study Guide,** p. 45

Teach

Motivations for Exploring **L3**

Instruct

■ **Introduce: Key Terms** Have students find the key term *Moluccas* (in blue) in the text, and identify its European name. Then have students locate the islands on the map on this page and trace the European sea routes to it.

■ **Teach** Discuss why Europeans searched for new trade routes. Ask **Why did Europeans find potentially dangerous sea routes preferable to overland routes?** *(They were quicker; they eliminated Arab middlemen; they allowed Europeans to get goods more cheaply by going straight to the source.)*

■ **Quick Activity** Have small groups of students identify an item that is of great value today, such as oil. Ask them to identify who controls that item, and discuss what prevents people from obtaining it. Using the Numbered Heads strategy (TE, p. T23), have each group report its findings.

Independent Practice

Have students access **Web Code nbp-1411** to take the **Geography Interactive Audio Guided Tour** and then answer the map skills questions.

Monitor Progress

As students fill in their flowcharts, circulate to make sure they have identified the main causes and effects of early European exploration. For a completed version of the flowchart, see

📖 **Note Taking Transparencies,** 119

Answers

Map Skills
1. Review locations with students.
2. Columbus sailed west to the West Indies across the Atlantic, then sailed east back to Spain.
3. Sample: Because of geography and the technology of the time, there were few viable routes.

Chapter 2 Section 1 85

Portugal Sails East 🔵 L3

Instruct

■ **Introduce** As students read about Prince Henry, point out that Prince Henry himself never sailed on a voyage of exploration. Ask **What motivated Prince Henry to make overseas exploration one of his life goals?** *(He wanted to make Portugal a world power; he hoped to gain converts to Christianity.)* **Did Prince Henry fulfill his goals?** *(He made Portugal a world power, but he did not succeed in spreading Christianity. He also encouraged advances in navigation and mapmaking.)*

■ **Teach** Ask **What was Vasco da Gama's major accomplishment?** *(He found a sea route to India.)* **How did da Gama establish a foothold for a Portuguese empire?** *(He left Portuguese merchants in India and forced a treaty upon an Indian ruler.)*

■ **Analyzing the Visuals** Display **Color Transparency 82: European Explorations for Spices, About 1500.** Use the lesson suggested in the transparency book to guide a discussion.

  🏛 **Color Transparencies, 82**

Independent Practice

Primary Source To help students better understand the role of cartography in the age of exploration, have them read the selection *Mercator Projection* and answer the questions on the worksheet.

  All in One Teaching Resources, Unit 1, p. 28

Monitor Progress

Ask students to write a paragraph explaining how and why Portugal took the lead in overseas exploration. Check that students have emphasized the key role of Prince Henry.

Answer

✔ The Portuguese established forts or took over cities that were centers of trade; over time, they connected them into a large empire.

Seeking India In 1497, Portuguese navigator Vasco da Gama followed in Dias's footsteps, leading four ships around the Cape of Good Hope. Da Gama, however, had plans to go farther. After a ten-month voyage, da Gama reached the great spice port of Calicut on the west coast of India. On the long voyage home, the Portuguese lost half their ships, and many sailors died of hunger, thirst, and scurvy, a disease caused by a lack of vitamin C in the diet.

Despite the hard journey, the venture proved highly profitable. In India, da Gama had acquired a cargo of spices that he sold at an enormous profit. He quickly outfitted a new fleet, seeking greater profits. In 1502, he forced a treaty on the ruler of Calicut. Da Gama then left Portuguese merchants there whose job was to buy spices when prices were low and store them until the next fleet could return. Soon, the Portuguese had seized key ports around the Indian Ocean, creating a vast trading empire. Da Gama's voyages confirmed Portugal's status as a world power.

✔ **Checkpoint** How did Portuguese exploration lead to the creation of a trading empire?

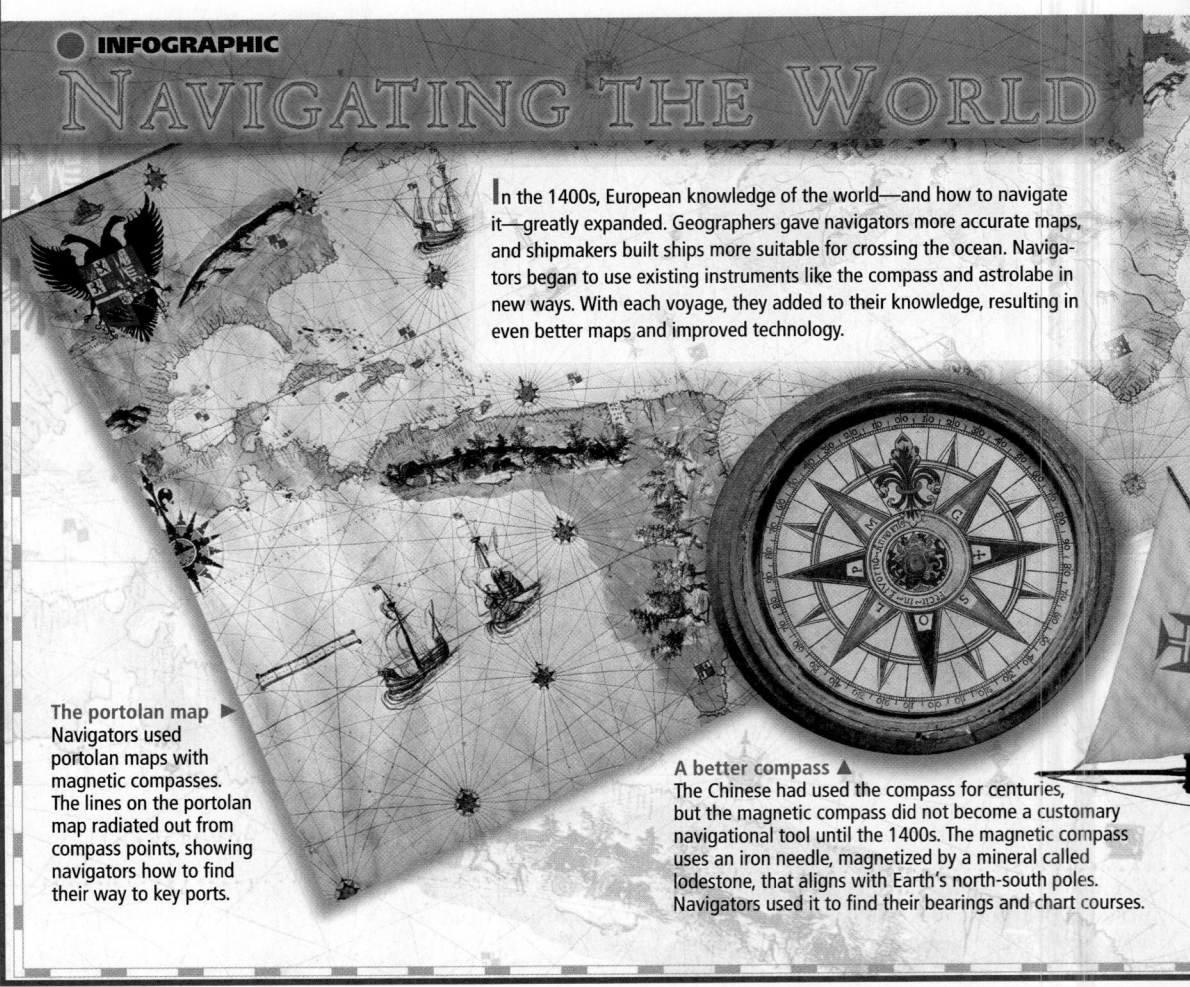

● **INFOGRAPHIC**

NAVIGATING THE WORLD

In the 1400s, European knowledge of the world—and how to navigate it—greatly expanded. Geographers gave navigators more accurate maps, and shipmakers built ships more suitable for crossing the ocean. Navigators began to use existing instruments like the compass and astrolabe in new ways. With each voyage, they added to their knowledge, resulting in even better maps and improved technology.

The portolan map ▶
Navigators used portolan maps with magnetic compasses. The lines on the portolan map radiated out from compass points, showing navigators how to find their way to key ports.

A better compass ▲
The Chinese had used the compass for centuries, but the magnetic compass did not become a customary navigational tool until the 1400s. The magnetic compass uses an iron needle, magnetized by a mineral called lodestone, that aligns with Earth's north-south poles. Navigators used it to find their bearings and chart courses.

History Background

Navigation—Past and Present The astrolabe made long sea voyages possible—but the navigation tool wasn't easy to use. To use the astrolabe, the sailor needed to hold it steady so that he could take a reading on a star or the sun. The ship's deck often heaved and rolled, making it nearly impossible to hold the astrolabe still. As a result, errors of hundreds of miles were often made. Keeping accurate time was another problem. Early explorers used an hourglass to mark the passage of each half hour. Forgetting to turn over the glass was disastrous; each minute lost could put a ship 15 miles off course.

Today, sailors navigate using GPS, or the Global Positioning System. Based on a network of satellites in orbit around Earth, GPS can pinpoint a location to within 50 feet, no matter where the user is.

Columbus Sails West

News of Portugal's successes spurred other people to look for a sea route to Asia. An Italian navigator from Genoa, named **Christopher Columbus,** wanted to reach the East Indies—a group of islands in Southeast Asia, today part of Indonesia—by sailing west across the Atlantic. Like most educated Europeans, Columbus knew that Earth was a sphere. A few weeks sailing west, he reasoned, would bring a ship to eastern Asia. His plan made sense, but Columbus greatly underestimated Earth's size. And he had no idea that two continents lay in his path.

Reaching Faraway Lands Portugal refused to sponsor him, but Columbus persuaded Ferdinand and Isabella of Spain to finance his voyage. To increase their <u>authority</u>, the Spanish rulers had taken radical measures, including expelling Jews from Spain. They hoped their actions would strengthen Catholicism. However, the loss of some of Spain's most affluent and cultured people weakened the nation. The rulers hoped Columbus's voyage would bring wealth and prestige.

Vocabulary Builder

authority—(uh THAWR uh tee) *n.* the power to give commands and enforce obedience

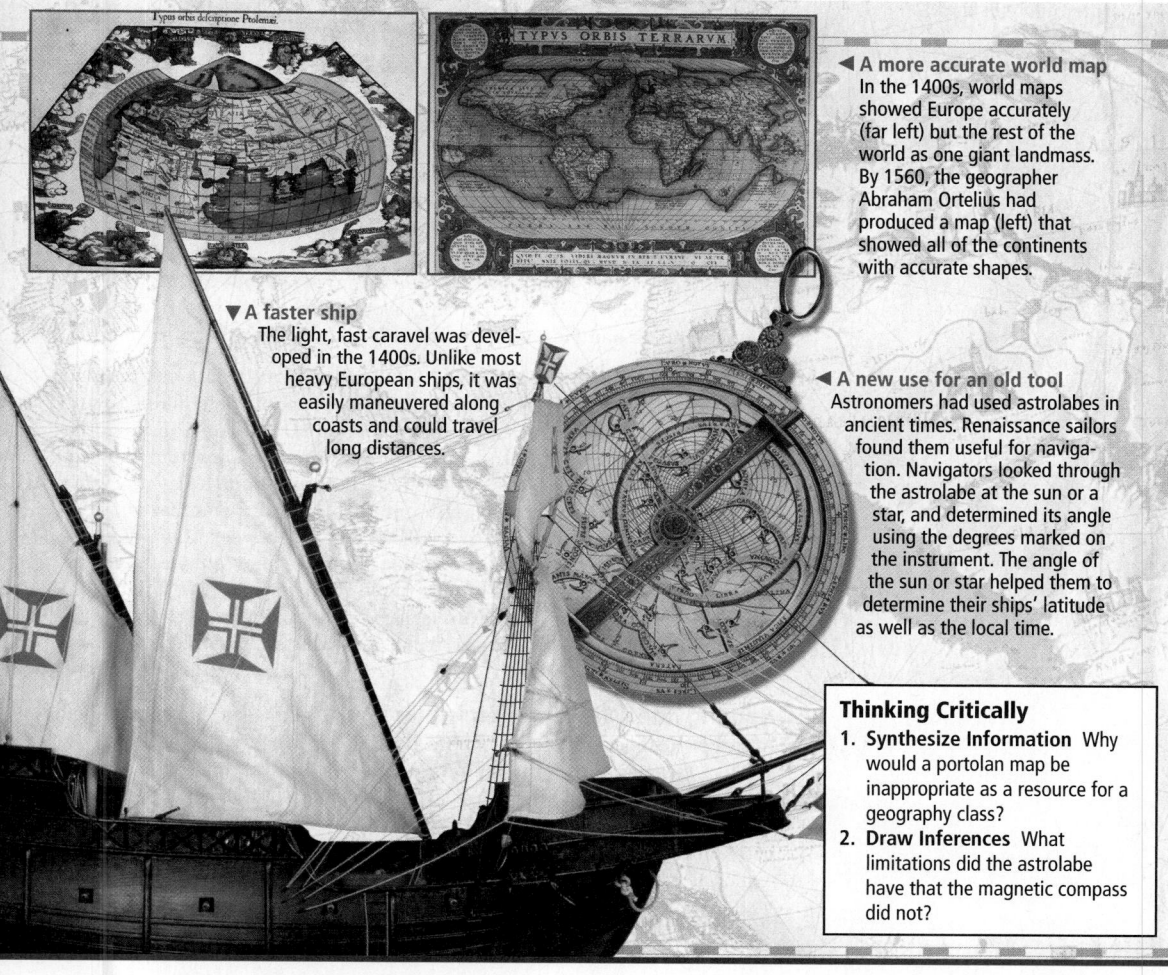

◄ **A more accurate world map**
In the 1400s, world maps showed Europe accurately (far left) but the rest of the world as one giant landmass. By 1560, the geographer Abraham Ortelius had produced a map (left) that showed all of the continents with accurate shapes.

▼ **A faster ship**
The light, fast caravel was developed in the 1400s. Unlike most heavy European ships, it was easily maneuvered along coasts and could travel long distances.

◄ **A new use for an old tool**
Astronomers had used astrolabes in ancient times. Renaissance sailors found them useful for navigation. Navigators looked through the astrolabe at the sun or a star, and determined its angle using the degrees marked on the instrument. The angle of the sun or star helped them to determine their ships' latitude as well as the local time.

Thinking Critically
1. **Synthesize Information** Why would a portolan map be inappropriate as a resource for a geography class?
2. **Draw Inferences** What limitations did the astrolabe have that the magnetic compass did not?

Link to Science

Scurvy This vitamin C deficiency disease was a frequent problem for sailors, who often did not eat enough fresh fruits and vegetables while at sea. One sufferer described the horror of scurvy in graphic terms: "It rotted all my gums, which gave out a black and putrid blood. My thighs and lower legs were black and gangrenous, and I was forced to use my knife each day to cut into the flesh in order to release this black and foul blood. I also used my knife on my gums, which were livid and growing over my teeth. . . . Many of our people died of it every day."

Native Americans from what is now Canada were familiar with the disease and offered afflicted Europeans a cure made from brewed hemlock branches. It wasn't until 1753 that Scottish naval surgeon James Lind prescribed the consumption of orange, lemon, or lime juice, all loaded with vitamin C, as a preventive and curative measure.

Columbus Sails West

Instruct

■ **Introduce: Vocabulary Builder** Have students read the Vocabulary Builder term and definition. Ask them to predict who might ***authorize*** a European voyage of exploration.

■ **Teach** Emphasize the importance of the voyages of Columbus in shaping European knowledge of the world. Ask **What were the main accomplishments of Columbus?** *(Columbus was the first European to reach the Americas, and he motivated other explorers.)* **How did the Treaty of Tordesillas affect competition among European nations? Why?** *(It intensified competition, because European nations felt they needed to claim land quickly before there was nothing left to discover.)*

■ **Analyzing the Visuals** Have students review the Infographic on these pages. Ask students to compare the two world maps on this page, and then explain how new technology helped produce the more accurate world map.

Independent Practice

Have students fill in the Outline Map *Global Explorations*, labeling the major routes with the correct explorer.

All in One **Teaching Resources, Unit 1,** p. 34

Monitor Progress

Circulate to make sure students are filling in their Outline Maps accurately by labeling the routes with the correct explorer.

Answers

Thinking Critically
1. It doesn't show geographical locations or features accurately; its only use is as a navigation tool.
2. Unlike the magnetic compass, the astrolabe could not be used when bad weather limited the sky's visibility.

The Search for a Direct Route Continues ⓵

Instruct

- **Introduce: Key Terms** Have students find the key term *circumnavigate* (in blue) in the text. Elicit from students the difficulties that Magellan would have had to overcome to carry out this feat. Point out the quotation by Pigafetta at the end of this section. Have students discuss what compelled him to make that statement.

- **Teach** As you describe Magellan's voyage, trace it on a world map. Ask **Why did European monarchs fund such risky voyages by navigators?** *(They were willing to take risks in exchange for the possibility of claiming new lands, finding a northwest passage, or discovering sources of wealth.)* **What was Magellan's basic mistake when planning and carrying out his voyage?** *(He greatly underestimated the size of the Pacific Ocean.)*

- **Quick Activity** Have students take on the roles of sailors aboard Magellan's ship. Explain that they have just passed through the Strait of Magellan. Ask them to debate whether they should return to Spain the way they came or keep going across the Pacific. Students should use maps and information from the section to support their positions.

Independent Practice

Biography To help students better understand the age of exploration, have them read the biography *Ferdinand Magellan* and answer the questions on the worksheet.

All in One Teaching Resources, Unit 1, p. 30

Monitor Progress

Check Reading and Note Taking Study Guide entries for student understanding.

Answers

BIOGRAPHY Henry appears to be a solemn, thoughtful, and impressive figure.

✔ His discoveries prompted Spain to obtain the treaty, ensuring that the lands Columbus discovered, along with future discoveries, would belong to Spain.

BIOGRAPHY

Henry the Navigator
All of the European explorers owed a debt to Prince Henry (1394–1460), whose Christian faith, curiosity, and national pride ushered in the great age of European exploration. The English nicknamed Henry "the Navigator." Yet Henry himself, who sponsored and encouraged navigators, geographers, and merchants, never traveled the seas. Henry's work required financial risks, and his enthusiasm motivated his navigators to take great personal risks. Henry also inspired generations of later explorers. **What characteristics does the artist ascribe to Henry (center figure in black)?**

On August 3, 1492, Columbus sailed west with three small ships, the *Niña*, the *Pinta*, and the *Santa María*. Although the expedition encountered good weather and a favorable wind, no land came into sight for many weeks. Provisions ran low, and the crew became anxious. Finally, on October 12, land was spotted.

Columbus spent several months cruising the islands of the Caribbean. Because he thought he had reached the Indies, he called the people of the region "Indians." In 1493, he returned to Spain to a hero's welcome. In three later voyages, Columbus remained convinced that he had reached the coast of East Asia. Before long, though, other Europeans realized that Columbus had found a route to previously unknown continents.

Dividing the Globe in Half In 1493 Ferdinand and Isabella appealed to the Spanish-born Pope Alexander VI to support their claim to the lands of the new world. The pope set a **Line of Demarcation,** dividing the non-European world into two zones. Spain had trading and exploration rights in any lands west of the line. Portugal had the same rights east of the line. The specific terms of the Line of Demarcation were agreed to in the **Treaty of Tordesillas,** signed between the two countries in 1494. The actual line was unclear, because geography at the time was imprecise. However, the treaty made it obvious to both Spain and Portugal—and to other European nations, eager to defy what they saw as Spain and Portugal's arrogance—that they needed to build their own empires quickly.

Naming the Western Hemisphere An Italian sea captain named Amerigo Vespucci wrote a journal describing his voyage to Brazil. In 1507, a German cartographer named Martin Waldseemüller used Vespucci's descriptions of his voyage to publish a map of the region, which he labeled "America." Over time, the term "Americas" came to be used for both continents of the Western Hemisphere. The islands Columbus had explored in the Caribbean became known as the West Indies.

✔ **Checkpoint** How did Columbus influence the Treaty of Tordesillas?

The Search for a Direct Route Continues

Though Europeans had claimed vast new territories, they had not yet found a direct route to Asia. The English, Dutch, and French explored the coast of North America unsuccessfully for a "northwest passage," or a route from the Atlantic Ocean to the Pacific through the Arctic islands. Meanwhile, in 1513 the Spanish adventurer Vasco Núñez de Balboa, helped by local Indians, hacked a passage westward through the tropical forests of Panama. From a ridge on the west coast, he gazed at a huge body of water. The body of water that he named the South Sea was in fact the Pacific Ocean.

On September 20, 1519, a minor Portuguese nobleman named **Ferdinand Magellan** set out from Spain with five ships to find a way to reach the Pacific. Magellan's ships sailed south and west, through storms and calms and tropical heat. At last, his fleet reached the coast of South America. Carefully, they explored each bay, hoping to find one that would lead to the Pacific. In November 1520, Magellan's ships entered a bay at the southern tip of South America. Amid brutal storms, rushing tides, and unpredictable winds, Magellan found a passage that later became known as the Strait of Magellan. The ships emerged into Balboa's South Sea. Magellan renamed the sea the Pacific, from the Latin word meaning *peaceful*.

Their mission accomplished, most of the crew wanted to return to Spain the way they had come. Magellan, however, insisted that they push on across the Pacific to the East Indies. Magellan underestimated the size of the Pacific. Three more weeks, he thought, would bring them to the Spice Islands. Magellan was wrong. For nearly four months, the ships plowed across the uncharted ocean. Finally, in March 1521, the fleet reached the Philippines, where Magellan was killed. On September 8, 1522, nearly three years after setting out, the survivors—one ship and 18 sailors—reached Spain. The survivors had been the first people to **circumnavigate,** or sail around, the world. Antonio Pigafetta, one of the few survivors of the expedition, observed: "I believe of a certainty that no one will ever again make such a voyage."

✔ **Checkpoint**   What was the significance of Balboa's discovery?

SECTION 1 Assessment

Progress Monitoring *Online*
For: Self-quiz with vocabulary practice
Web Code: nba-1411

Terms, People, and Places
1. For each term, person, or place listed at the beginning of the section, write a sentence explaining its significance.

Note Taking
2. **Reading Skill: Identify Causes and Effects** Use your completed flowchart to answer the Focus Question: How did the search for spices lead to global exploration?

Comprehension and Critical Thinking
3. **Recognize Cause and Effect** How did the Renaissance motivate European explorers?
4. **Recognize Ideologies** How did Prince Henry's Christian faith shape his role as a sponsor of exploration?
5. **Identify Alternatives** If Columbus had understood the real geography of the world, would he still have made his voyage? Why or why not?
6. **Predict Consequences** What effect might Magellan's circumnavigation of the world have on English, Dutch, and French explorers?

● Writing About History
Quick Write: Gather Information Choose one of the following people from this section for a biographical essay: Prince Henry, Christopher Columbus, or Ferdinand Magellan. Gather information about the person you chose. Note events that were both directly and indirectly influenced by this person.

Objectives

As you teach this section, keep students focused on the following objectives to help them answer the Section Focus Question and master core content.

■ Describe how the Portuguese established footholds on Africa's coasts.

■ Analyze how European actions affected the slave trade and the rise of African states.

■ Understand how the European presence in Africa expanded.

A Benin ivory carving (right) depicts a Portuguese sailor in a ship. Iron weights (top) were used in western Africa to weigh gold.

WITNESS HISTORY 🔊 AUDIO

Great Seabirds Arrive

A Portuguese captain named Alvise Cadamosto reached West Africa in the mid-1400s. He described the reaction of the West Africans to the sight of his ship:

❝ It is said that the first time they saw sails . . . they believed they were great seabirds with white wings, which were flying and had come from some strange place. . . . Some thought the ships were fishes, others that they were ghosts that went by night, at which they were terrified. **❞**
—Alvise Cadamosto, 1455

Focus Question What effects did European exploration have on the people of Africa?

Turbulent Centuries in Africa

Objectives
• Describe how the Portuguese established footholds on Africa's coasts.
• Analyze how European actions affected the slave trade and the rise of African states.
• Explain how the European presence in Africa expanded.

Terms, People, and Places

Mombasa	Osei Tutu
Malindi	monopoly
plantation	Oyo empire
Affonso I	Cape Town
missionary	Boers
Asante kingdom	

Note Taking

Reading Skill: Identify Effects As you read, record effects of European exploration in Africa in a chart like the one below.

```
        Effects of European Exploration
   ┌──────────┬──────────┬──────────┐
 European      Slave      New African
 Footholds     Trade       States
```

European encounters with Africa had occurred for hundreds of years. Yet the European explorers who arrived in the 1400s brought great and unforeseen changes to Africa's peoples and cultures.

Portugal Gains Footholds

As you have read, the Portuguese who explored Africa's coasts in the 1400s were looking for a sea route to Asia that bypassed the Mediterranean. They also wanted to buy goods directly from their source, rather than trading through Arab middlemen.

The Portuguese began carrying out their strategy in West Africa, building small forts to collect food and water and to repair their ships. They also established trading posts to trade muskets, tools, and cloth for gold, ivory, hides, and slaves. These were not colonies peopled by settlers. Instead, the Portuguese left just enough men and firepower to defend their forts.

From West Africa, the Portuguese sailed around the continent. They continued to establish forts and trading posts, but they also attacked existing East African coastal cities such as **Mombasa** and **Malindi,** which were hubs of international trade. With cannons blazing, they expelled the Arabs who controlled the East African trade network and took over this thriving commerce for themselves. Each conquest added to their growing trade empire.

Over the next two centuries, some Portuguese explorers managed to reach parts of present-day Congo, Zambia, and Zimbabwe, establishing limited trade. In general, however, the Portuguese did not venture far from the coasts. They knew little about Africa's interior, and they lacked accurate maps or other resources to help them explore there. Furthermore, Africans in the interior, who wanted to control the gold trade, resisted such exploration. As a result of all these factors, when the Portuguese empire declined in the 1600s, the Portuguese did not leave a strong legacy in Africa.

✅ **Checkpoint** Why did the Portuguese establish a presence mainly along the African coast?

The African Slave Trade Explodes

In the 1500s and 1600s, Europeans began to view slaves as the most important item of African trade. Slavery had existed in Africa, as elsewhere around the world, since ancient times. Egyptians, Greeks, Romans, Persians, Indians, and Aztecs often enslaved defeated foes. The English word *slave* comes from the large number of Slavs taken from southern Russia to work as unpaid laborers in Roman times.

The Arab empire also used slave labor, often captives from East Africa. In the Middle East, enslaved Africans often worked on farming estates. Others became artisans, soldiers, or merchants. Some rose to prominence in the Muslim world even though they were slaves.

Europeans Enter the Slave Trade Portuguese traders quickly joined the profitable slave trade, followed by other European traders. Europeans bought large numbers of slaves to perform labor on their plantations—large estates run by an owner or an owner's overseer—in the Americas and elsewhere. Rich Europeans also bought slaves as exotic household servants. By the 1500s, European participation had encouraged a much broader Atlantic slave trade.

Europeans seldom went into Africa's interior to take part in slave raids. Instead, they relied on African rulers and traders to seize captives in the interior and bring them to coastal trading posts and forts. There, the captives were exchanged for textiles, metalwork, rum, tobacco, weapons, and gunpowder. Over the next 300 years, the slave trade grew into a huge and profitable business to fill the need for cheap labor. Each year, traders shipped tens of thousands of enslaved Africans across the Atlantic to work on sugar, rice, tobacco, and other plantations in the Americas. These slaves were considered to be property, and they had no hope of bettering their situations.

African Leaders Resist Some African leaders tried to slow down or stop the transatlantic slave trade. But in the end, the system that supported the trade was simply too strong for them. An early voice raised against the slave trade was that of **Affonso I,** ruler of Kongo in west-central Africa. As a young man, Affonso had been tutored by Portuguese **missionaries,** who hoped to convert Africans to Christianity.

A Valuable Commodity
Since ancient times, gold was a valuable trade good in western Africa. Beginning in the 1500s, it became an important part of the slave trade. Europeans melted down African gold jewelry like the pieces above to make gold coins.

A Portuguese observer described the first ship of African slaves arriving in Portugal in 1444 from West Africa. Judging from the writer's words, what was his opinion of what he saw?

Primary Source

❝Some kept their heads low and their faces bathed in tears, looking at each other . . . others struck themselves in the face and threw themselves to the ground; and others sang sad songs—although we did not understand their words, the sound told of their great sorrow. . . . The mothers threw themselves flat on the ground. They were beaten but they refused to give up their children.❞
—From *Chronicle of the Discovery and Conquest of Guinea*

🔊 AUDIO

New African States/The European Presence Expands

 L3

Instruct

- **Introduce: Vocabulary Builder**
  Have students read the Vocabulary Builder terms and definitions. Ask students to suggest ways that the two terms are related.

- **Teach** Ask **How did kingdoms like the Asante and Oyo respond to the growing slave trade?** *(They gained power by conquering other Africans and by increasing their involvement with European traders.)* **Why did many Africans at this time turn against other Africans?** *(Many Africans felt that if they did not gain power for themselves, they might be obliterated.)* Using the Numbered Heads strategy (TE, p. T23), ask students to predict how the expansion of European power in Africa would affect the slave trade.

- **Quick Activity** Point out the sentence in the text: "The Boers held to a Calvinist belief that they were the elect, or chosen, of God." Have small groups discuss why this belief may have caused the Boers to view Africans as inferiors. Students may want to review the section in an earlier chapter on the Protestant Reformation.

Independent Practice

Have students access **Web Code nbp-1421** to take the **Geography Interactive Audio Guided Tour** and then answer the map skills questions.

Monitor Progress

- Check answers to map skills questions.
- Check Reading and Note Taking Study Guide entries for student understanding. Ask students to summarize how European countries affected the African states.

Answers

Map Skills

1. Review locations with students.
2. Asante, Oyo, Dahomey, Benin, Bornu, Darfur, and Kongo.
3. Most were located in coastal areas because that is where the Europeans were based.

✔ Europeans became involved in the slave trade, seeking larger numbers of slaves for their plantations; African states expanded the slave trade to meet European needs and gain wealth.

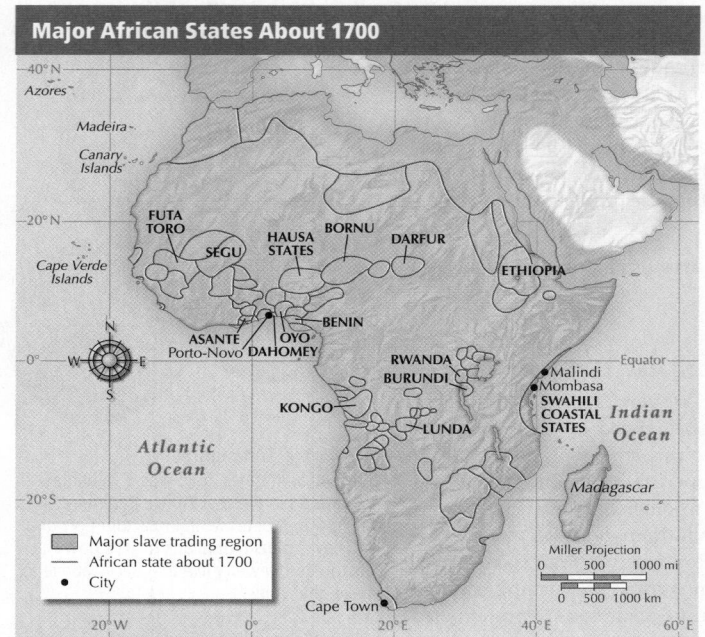

Major African States About 1700

Map Skills By about 1700, many of Africa's states and kingdoms were involved in the slave trade.
1. **Locate** (a) Malindi (b) Kongo (c) Asante (d) Bornu
2. **Describe** Which states were part of a major slave trading region?
3. **Synthesize Information** In general, where were most slave trading regions located? Explain.

Geography *Interactive*
For: Audio guided tour
Web Code: nbp-1421

Vocabulary Builder
dominate—(DAHM uh nayt) *v.* to rule or control by superior power

Vocabulary Builder
unified—(YOO nuh fyd) *v.* combined into one

After becoming king in 1505, he called on the Portuguese to help him develop Kongo as a modern Christian state. But he became alarmed as more and more Portuguese came to Kongo each year to buy slaves. Affonso wanted to maintain contact with Europe but end the slave trade. His appeal failed, and the slave trade continued.

In the late 1700s, another African ruler tried to halt the slave trade in his lands. He was the almany (from the Arabic words meaning "religious leader") of Futa Toro, in present-day Senegal. Since the 1500s, French sea captains had bought slaves from African traders in Futa Toro. In 1788, the almany forbade anyone to transport slaves through Futa Toro for sale abroad. However, the inland slave traders simply worked out a new route to the coast. Sailing to this new market, the French captains easily purchased the slaves that the almany had prevented them from buying in Futa Toro.

✔ **Checkpoint** How did the African slave trade expand?

New African States Arise

The slave trade had major effects on African states in the 1600s and 1700s. In West Africa, for example, the loss of countless numbers of young women and men resulted in some small states disappearing forever. At the same time, there arose new states whose way of life depended on the slave trade. The rulers of these powerful new states waged war against other Africans to dominate the slave trade.

The Asante Kingdom The **Asante kingdom** (uh SAHN teh) emerged in the area occupied by present-day Ghana. In the late 1600s, an able military leader, **Osei Tutu,** won control of the trading city of Kumasi. From there, he conquered neighboring peoples and unified the Asante kingdom. The Asante faced a great challenge in the Denkyera, a powerful neighboring enemy kingdom. Osei Tutu realized that in order to withstand the Denkyera, the people of his kingdom needed to be firmly united. To do this, he claimed that his right to rule came from heaven, and that people in the kingdom were linked by spiritual bonds. This strategy paid off when the Asante defeated the Denkyera in the late 1600s.

Under Osei Tutu, government officials, chosen by merit rather than by birth, supervised an efficient bureaucracy. They managed the royal monopolies on gold mining and the slave trade. A **monopoly** is the exclusive control of a business or industry. The Asante traded with Europeans on the coast, exchanging gold and slaves for firearms. They also played rival Europeans against one another to protect themselves. In this way, they built a wealthy, powerful state.

The Oyo Empire The **Oyo empire** arose from successive waves of settlement by the Yoruba people of present-day Nigeria. It began as a relatively small forest kingdom. Beginning in the late 1600s, however, its leaders used wealth from the slave trade to build up an impressive army. The Oyo empire used the army to conquer the neighboring kingdom of Dahomey. At the same time, it continued to gain wealth by trading with European merchants at the port city of Porto-Novo.

✓ **Checkpoint** What caused some African states to grow?

The European Presence Expands

Following the Portuguese example, by the 1600s several European powers had established forts along the western coast of Africa. As Portuguese power declined in the region, British, Dutch, and French traders took over their forts. Unlike the Portuguese, they established permanent footholds throughout the continent.

In 1652, Dutch immigrants arrived at the southern tip of the continent. They built **Cape Town,** the first permanent European settlement, to supply ships sailing to or from the East Indies. Dutch farmers, called **Boers,** settled around Cape Town. Over time, they ousted, enslaved, or killed the people who lived there. The Boers held a Calvinist belief that they were the elect, or chosen, of God. They looked on Africans as inferiors and did not respect their claims to their own land. In the 1700s, Boer herders and ivory hunters began to push north from the Cape Colony. Their migrations would eventually lead to battle with several African groups.

By the mid-1600s, the British and French had both reached present-day Senegal. The French established a fort in the region around 1700. In the late 1700s, stories about British explorers' search for the source of the Nile River sparked an interest in Africa among Europeans, especially the French and British. In 1788, the British established the African Association, an organization that sponsored explorers to Africa. Over the next century, European exploration of Africa would explode.

✓ **Checkpoint** How did the European presence in Africa expand?

Elmina Castle
European traders called the places where they held and traded slaves "castles." Built by the Portuguese in 1482, Elmina Castle in present-day Ghana was used as a base for trading slaves, gold, and imported European products.

Progress Monitoring *Online*
For: Self-quiz with vocabulary practice
Web Code: nba-1421

SECTION 2 Assessment

Terms, People, and Places
1. What do many of the key terms and people listed at the beginning of the section have in common? Explain.

Note Taking
2. **Reading Skill: Identify Effects** Use your completed chart to answer the Focus Question: What effects did European exploration have on the people of Africa?

Comprehension and Critical Thinking
3. **Determine Relevance** How did the Portuguese strategy of building forts instead of permanent colonies affect Portugal's history in Africa?
4. **Recognize Cause and Effect** How did Europeans change the nature of African slavery?
5. **Analyze Information** Why did the Asante and Oyo need to trade with Europeans to maintain power?
6. **Predict Consequences** Would the Europeans have taken the same course in Africa if the people there had been Christian like themselves?

● **Writing About History**
Quick Write: Write a Thesis Statement Write a thesis statement that will support a biographical essay about either Osei Tutu or Affonso I. Remember that the facts and events you cite in your essay should support your thesis statement. For example, the following thesis statement is not supported by the facts in the text: Affonso I was instrumental in slowing the slave trade in Africa.

Answers

✓ The slave trade gave some states the resources to expand and conquer their neighbors.

✓ Various Europeans took over the forts of the declining Portuguese, and worked to establish more permanent footholds.

Section 2 Assessment

1. Most of the terms relate to European exploration or to African leaders and places with which Europeans had contact.
2. Some Africans grew wealthy from trade with Europeans. However, European exploration had mainly negative effects on Africans, including the takeover of African cities and the loss of people to the slave trade.

3. Portugal was unable to establish a long-term presence in the region.
4. The slave trade grew and slaves became commodities with little hope of receiving better treatment.
5. Without wealth from the European trade, they could not have defeated their neighbors.
6. Answers will vary. Some students may suggest that Europeans would have treated Africans better if they were Christians. Others may suggest that even people of

the same religion can come into conflict if their interests are not the same.

● **Writing About History**
Thesis statements should express a clear and distinctive perspective about either Osei Tutu or Affonso I.

King Affonso I: *Letter to King John III of Portugal*

Objectives

■ Understand Affonso's reasons for asking Portugal to help end the slave trade in Africa.

■ Analyze the language Affonso uses in hopes of convincing King John.

Build Background Knowledge ⓛ

Have students recall what they have learned about Portuguese efforts to win converts to Christianity in Africa. As students read the selection, have them consider whether Affonso's conversion to Christianity made any difference in his relations with King John of Portugal.

Instruct ⓛ

■ As students read the selection, have them list each of the negative effects that Affonso says Portugal's involvement in the slave trade has produced. When students have finished, have them write a master list on the board. *(Lists should include: weakening of Affonso's power over vassals; lessening of Kongo's security and peace; corruption; depopulation)*

■ Point out that Affonso uses religious language that he hopes will appeal to the Portuguese king. Ask **What are some examples of this language?** *(He refers to God, priests, and the holy sacrament.)* **What does he hope to accomplish by using such language?** *(He wants to appeal to King John's responsibility as a Christian king.)*

Monitor Progress

Have students return to the Build Background Knowledge exercise. Ask them to use specific quotations from the selection to write a paragraph that answers the question they were to consider: *Does Affonso's status as a Christian make any difference in his relations with King John of Portugal?*

Thinking Critically

1. Affonso believes they no longer respect him as a ruler, because they can get the things they want directly from the Europeans.

2. priests and teachers, and wine and flour for religious sacraments

King Affonso I: *Letter to King John III of Portugal*

In 1490, the Portuguese converted the son of a Kongo king to Christianity and then helped him take his father's throne. The new king, born Nzinga Mbemba, was renamed Affonso. King Affonso soon realized that his relationship with Portugal had extremely negative consequences, as can be seen from his letter to King John III of Portugal in 1526. In this letter, the king of Kongo appeals to the king of Portugal to end the slave trade.

Sir, Your Highness of Portugal should know how our Kingdom is being lost in so many ways. This is caused by the excessive freedom given by your officials to the men and merchants who are allowed to come to this Kingdom to set up shops with goods and many things which have been prohibited by us. Many of our vassals, whom we had in obedience, do not comply[1] because they have the things in greater abundance than we ourselves. It was with these things that we had them content and subjected under our jurisdiction[2], so it is doing a great harm not only to the service of God, but to the security and peace of our Kingdoms and State as well.

And we cannot reckon how great the damage is, since the mentioned merchants are taking every day our natives, sons of the land and the sons of our noblemen and vassals and our relatives. The thieves and men of bad conscience grab them wishing to have the things and wares of this Kingdom which they are ambitious of; they grab them and get them to be sold. And so great, Sir, is the corruption and licentiousness[3] that our country is being completely depopulated, and your Highness should not agree with this nor accept it as in your service. And to avoid it we need from those your Kingdoms no more than some priests and a few people to teach in schools, and no other goods except wine and flour for the holy sacrament.

That is why we beg of Your Highness to help and assist us in this matter, commanding your factors[4] that they should not send here either merchants or wares, because it is our will that in these kingdoms there should not be any trade of slaves nor outlet for them. Concerning what is referred to above, again we beg of Your Highness to agree with it otherwise we cannot remedy such an obvious damage.

1. **comply** (kum PLY) *v.* agree to a request
2. **jurisdiction** (joor is DIK shun) *n.* area of authority or power
3. **licentiousness** (ly SEN shus nis) *n.* lack of morality
4. **factors** (FAK turs) *n.* agents

▲ A Congolese brass and wood crucifix dating from the 1500s blends Christian and traditional African symbols.

▲ King John III of Portugal

Thinking Critically

1. **Identify Causes** What does King Affonso believe has caused his vassals to become disobedient?

2. **Analyze Information** What specifically does King Affonso say he still needs from the Portuguese?

Commander Afonso de Albuquerque (right); a Portuguese rifle (top)

WITNESS HISTORY 🔊 AUDIO

Gunfire Over Malacca

In 1511, a Portuguese fleet commanded by Afonso de Albuquerque (AL buh kur kee) dropped anchor off Malacca, a rich Islamic trading port that controlled the sea route linking India, Southeast Asia, and China. The fleet remained at anchor for several weeks before opening fire. According to a Malaysian account:

66 The cannon balls came like rain. And the noise of the cannon was as the noise of thunder in the heavens and the flashes of fire of their guns were like flashes of lightning in the sky: and the noise of their matchlocks [guns] was like that of groundnuts [peanuts] popping in the frying pan. 99
—From the *Malay Annals*

Focus Question How did European nations build empires in South and Southeast Asia?

European Footholds in South and Southeast Asia

Objectives
- Summarize how Portugal built a trading empire in South and Southeast Asia.
- Analyze the rise of Dutch and Spanish dominance in the region.
- Understand how the decline of Mughal India affected European traders in the region.

Terms, People, and Places

Afonso de Albuquerque	Dutch East India Company
Mughal empire	sovereign
Goa	Philippines
Malacca	sepoys
outpost	

Note Taking

Reading Skill: Identify Causes and Effects As you read this section, fill in a chart like the one below with the causes and effects of European exploration in South and Southeast Asia.

Portugal	Netherlands	Spain	Britain
•	•	•	•
•	•	•	•

Portugal was the first European power to gain a foothold in Asia. The Portuguese ships were small in size and number, but the firepower of their shipboard cannons was unmatched. In time, this superior firepower helped them win control of the rich Indian Ocean spice trade and build a trading empire in Asia.

Portugal Builds an Eastern Empire

After Vasco da Gama's voyage, the Portuguese, under **Afonso de Albuquerque's** command, burst into the Indian Ocean. By that time, Muslim rulers, originally from central Asia, had established the **Mughal empire** throughout much of India. The southern regions of India, however, were still controlled by a patchwork of local princes. The Portuguese won these princes to their side with promises of aid against other Europeans. With these southern footholds, Albuquerque and the Portuguese hoped to end Muslim power and turn the Indian Ocean into a "Portuguese lake."

A Rim of Trading Outposts In 1510, the Portuguese seized the island of **Goa** off the coast of India, making it their major military and commercial base. Albuquerque burned coastal towns and crushed Arab fleets at sea. The Portuguese took the East Indies port of **Malacca** in 1511, massacring the city's Muslims.

Vocabulary Builder

Use the information below and the following resources to teach the high-use word from this section.
All in One **Teaching Resources, Unit 1,** p. 26; **Teaching Resources, Skills Handbook,** p. 3

High-Use Word	Definition and Sample Sentence
strategic, p. 96	*adj.* important to carrying out a plan of action In the chess match, the man's **strategic** placement of his bishop led him to win the game.

Objectives

As you teach this section, keep students focused on the following objectives to help them answer the Section Focus Question and master core content.

- Summarize how Portugal built a trading empire in South and Southeast Asia.
- Analyze the rise of Dutch and Spanish dominance in the region.
- Understand how the decline of Mughal India affected European traders in the region.

Prepare to Read

Build Background Knowledge L3

Ask students to recall how and why the Portuguese began exploration in Africa, and what kind of presence they established. Then have them predict what impact the Portuguese might have in South and Southeast Asia.

Set a Purpose L3

- **WITNESS HISTORY** Read the selection aloud or play the audio.

   AUDIO **Witness History Audio CD,** Gunfire Over Malacca

  Ask **What do these descriptions suggest about Malaysians' experience with gunfire up to that time?** *(They suggest that Malaysians had not experienced gunfire before, and thus described it with words from their natural surroundings.)*

- **Focus** Point out the Section Focus Question and write it on the board. Tell students to refer to this question as they read. *(Answer appears with Section 3 Assessment answers.)*

- **Preview** Have students preview the Section Objectives and the list of Terms, People, and Places.

- **Note Taking** Have students read this section using the Guided Questioning strategy (TE, p. T20). As they read, have students fill in the chart showing the effects of European exploration.

  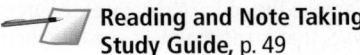 **Reading and Note Taking Study Guide,** p. 49

Portugal Builds an Eastern Empire/Rise of the Dutch ⑬

Instruct

- **Introduce: Vocabulary Builder**
  Have students read the Vocabulary Builder term and definition. Then point out the heading Rise of the Dutch. Ask students to predict how a ***strategic*** settlement could have helped the Dutch rise in the region.

- **Teach** Return to the predictions students made in the Build Background Knowledge activity. Ask **Why was Portugal unable to establish a long-term presence in the region?** *(It did not have the resources to conquer territory or establish inland trade; its missionaries' harsh methods incited a backlash among local people.)* **Why were the strategies of the Dutch more successful?** *(The Dutch established permanent colonies with close ties to local people; they concentrated more on trade than on missionary work.)*

- **Quick Activity** Display **Color Transparency 87: The Wreck of the *Flor de la Mar*.** Use the lesson suggestion in the transparency book to guide a discussion about the importance of Malacca to Europeans.

  📺 **Color Transparencies,** 87

Independent Practice

Primary Source To help students better understand the goals of both European explorers and Muslim merchants, have them read the selection *The Portuguese Reach India* and then answer the questions that follow.

All·in·One **Teaching Resources, Unit 1,** p. 29

Monitor Progress

As students fill in their charts, circulate to make sure they understand the causes and effects of European exploration in South and Southeast Asia.

📺 **Note Taking Transparencies,** 121

Answers

✔ They used force and diplomacy to establish coastal trading posts, which they turned into a trading empire.

Caption Sample: They depicted early encounters in the ways that made the most sense to them.

In less than 50 years, the Portuguese had built a trading empire with military and merchant **outposts,** or distant areas under their control, rimming the southern seas. They used the cities they had seized on the east coast of Africa to resupply and repair their ships. For most of the 1500s, Portugal controlled the spice trade between Europe and Asia.

A Limited Impact Despite their sea power, the Portuguese lacked resources and faced too much resistance to make great inroads into the region. They made harsher efforts to convert local people to Christianity than they had in Africa, attacking Muslims and destroying Hindu temples. Still, by 1600 the Portuguese had converted fewer than a million people to Christianity. The conversion rate was especially low among Asian Muslims.

✔ **Checkpoint** How did the Portuguese control the spice trade?

Rise of the Dutch

The Dutch were the first Europeans to challenge Portuguese domination of Asian trade. The land we know today as the Netherlands included a group of provinces and prosperous trading cities on the North Sea. In the early 1500s it was part of the Holy Roman Empire, but later the Protestant northern provinces won independence. The independent Netherlands entered vigorously into competition for overseas influence.

Building a Mighty Sea Power In 1599, a Dutch fleet returned to Amsterdam from Asia after more than a year's absence. It carried a cargo of pepper, cloves, and other spices. The success of this voyage led to a frenzy of overseas activity. Soon Dutch warships and trading vessels had made the Netherlands a leader of European commerce. Dutch power set up colonies and trading posts around the world. With their strategic settlement at Cape Town, the Netherlands had a secure foothold in the region.

A Powerful Dutch Company In 1602, a group of wealthy Dutch merchants formed the **Dutch East India Company.** From the beginning, this company had an unusual amount of power. Unlike Portuguese and Spanish traders, whose expeditions were tightly controlled by government, the Dutch East India Company had full **sovereign** powers. With its power to build armies, wage war, negotiate peace treaties, and govern overseas territory, it came to dominate the region.

Vocabulary Builder

strategic—(struh TEE jik) *adj.* important to carrying out a plan of action

Different Perspectives
A European artist (right) shows the king of Sri Lanka and a Dutch explorer meeting as equals. In the Indian painting to the left, Europeans are shown as vassals bringing gifts to India's ruler. *How did European and Asian artists bring their own perspectives to early encounters?*

History Background

Still Life in Holland In the 1600s, Holland enjoyed a golden age of art. After years of war in the Low Countries, there was finally peace at home and the wealth provided by the overseas trade created a consumer class with enough disposable income to support the arts. Affluent burghers bought paintings and portraits to hang in their homes.

Amsterdam became not only a major commercial port, but also a rich cultural center that attracted artists such as Johannes Vermeer, Rembrandt von Rijn, and Willem Kalf. Rembrandt and his students developed the genre of the still life, depicting inanimate objects such as fruit or flowers. While other artists focused on religious or courtly themes, the Dutch turned toward nature. So prominent were these new kinds of paintings during the 1600s that the Dutch words *stilleven* and *landschap* were adapted into English as "still life" and "landscape."

Asserting Dutch Dominance In 1641, the Dutch captured Malacca from the Portuguese and opened trade with China. Soon they were able to enforce a monopoly in the Spice Islands, controlling shipments to Europe as well as much of the trade within Southeast Asia. Like the Portuguese, the Dutch used military force to further their trading goals. Yet they forged closer ties with local rulers than the Portuguese had. Many Dutch merchants married Asian women.

In the 1700s, the growing power of England and France contributed to the decline of the Dutch trading empire in the East. Still, the Dutch maintained an empire in Indonesia until the 1900s.

✔ **Checkpoint** How did the Dutch build up a strong presence in Southeast Asia?

Symbols of the Dutch Empire
The Dutch painting *Jacob Mathieusen and His Wife* (c. 1650) shows a senior official in the Dutch East India Company overlooking the Dutch fleet in Batavia, Indonesia. A slave holds a parasol, an Asian symbol of power. *How can you tell that the artist was European?*

Spain Seizes the Philippines

While the Portuguese and Dutch set up bases on the fringes of Asia, Spain took over the **Philippines.** Magellan had claimed the archipelago for Spain in 1521. Within about 50 years, Spain had conquered and colonized the islands, renaming them for the Spanish king Philip II. Unlike most other peoples of Southeast Asia, the Filipinos were not united. As a result, they could be conquered more easily.

In the spirit of the Catholic Reformation, Spanish priests set out to convert the Filipino people to Christianity. Later, missionaries from the Philippines tried to spread Catholic teachings in China and Japan.

The Philippines became a key link in Spain's overseas trading empire. The Spanish shipped silver mined in Mexico and Peru across the Pacific to the Philippines. From there, they used the silver to buy goods in China. In this way, large quantities of American silver flowed into the economies of East Asian nations.

✔ **Checkpoint** Why was Spain able to conquer the Philippines easily?

Spain Seizes the Philippines/ Mughal India L3

Instruct

- **Introduce** Display **Color Transparency 86:** *Jacob Mathieusen and His Wife.* Explain that the man shown in the painting is a senior merchant of the Dutch East India Company in the mid-1600s. Have students look for details that give clues to the rise of European merchants in South and Southeast Asia.

  🏛 **Color Transparencies,** 86

- **Teach** Emphasize that as Europeans established a growing presence in South and Southeast Asia, their goal broadened from dominating trade to building empires. Ask **What was the strategic importance of the Philippines?** *(It was located between Europe and the Americas.)* **How did an interest in trade goods lead to British domination of India?** *(The British East India Company gradually used its trade wealth to dominate the country.)*

- **Quick Activity** Have student groups construct annotated timelines, charting European policies and actions in South and Southeast Asia between the 1500s and 1700s. Have each group focus on Portugal, the Netherlands, Spain, Britain, or France.

Independent Practice

Primary Source To help students better understand how European traders influenced Indian culture, have them read the selection *An Unusual Dinner Party* and answer the questions.

All in One **Teaching Resources, Unit 1,** p. 31

Monitor Progress

Check Reading and Note Taking Study Guide entries for student understanding.

Differentiated
Instruction   Solutions for All Learners

L1 Special Needs **L2 Less Proficient Readers**

Have students suppose that they are going to open a franchise in their local town. Ask them to list the preparations that would need to be made before opening. Explain that European explorers faced similar challenges as they set up trading posts. List the preparations that they would need to make in order to develop a successful trading post.

L2 English Language Learners

Use the following resources to help students acquire basic skills.

📐 **Adapted Reading and Note Taking Study Guide**
■ Adapted Note Taking Study Guide, p. 49
■ Adapted Section Summary, p. 50

Answers

✔ by using their sea power to set up colonies, setting up the Dutch East India Company, and establishing permanent ties with locals

✔ The Filipinos were not united as a people.

Caption the style of painting; the depiction of the Dutch official as powerful

Assess and Reteach

Assess Progress

- Have students complete the Section Assessment.

- Administer the Section Quiz.

All in One Teaching Resources, Unit 1, p. 24

- To further assess student understanding, use

  Progress Monitoring Transparencies, 60

Reteach

If students need more instruction, have them read the section summary.

Reading and Note Taking Study Guide, p. 50

Adapted Reading and Note Taking Study Guide, p. 50

Spanish Reading and Note Taking Study Guide, p. 50

Extend

Remind students that while South and Southeast Asia's geography makes the region a center of trade, it has also brought great challenges. Have student groups research one type of major storm (hurricanes, typhoons, or tsunamis) that has struck the region in the past 500 years. Ask groups to make a map of the region, include details of specific storms on the appropriate spots on the map, and summarize the impact of such storms on the region.

Answer

✓ It made alliances with local leaders and organized armies of sepoys to drive out the French; it used its wealth to weaken the Mughal empire.

An Indian Sepoy
An Indian officer in the British army poses with his wife in this Indian painting dating from the 1700s.

Mughal India and European Traders

For two centuries, the Mughal empire had enjoyed a period of peace, strength, and prosperity. European merchants were dazzled by India's splendid Mughal court and its many luxury goods.

A Center of Valuable Trade Mughal India was the center of the valuable spice trade. It was also the world leader in textile manufacturing, exporting large quantities of silk and cotton cloth. The Mughal empire was larger, richer, and more powerful than any kingdom in Europe. When Europeans sought trading rights, Mughal emperors saw no threat in granting them. The Portuguese—and later the Dutch, English, and French—thus were permitted to build forts and warehouses in Indian coastal towns.

A Great Empire Shatters Over time, the Mughal empire weakened. Conflicts between Hindu and Muslim princes rekindled. Years of civil war drained Mughal resources. Rulers then increased taxes, sparking rebellions. Corruption became widespread, and the central government collapsed. As Mughal power faltered, French and English traders fought for power. Like the Dutch, both the British and the French had established East India companies. These companies made alliances with local officials and independent rajahs, or local chiefs. Each company organized its own army of sepoys, or Indian troops.

By the mid-1700s, the British and the French had become locked in a bitter struggle for global power. The fighting involved both nations' lands in Asia and the Americas. In India, the British East India Company used an army of British troops and sepoys to drive out the French. The company then forced the Mughal emperor to recognize its right to collect taxes in the northeast. By the late 1700s, it had used its great wealth to dominate most of India.

✓ **Checkpoint** How did Britain gain control of India?

SECTION 3 Assessment

Progress Monitoring *Online*
For: Self-quiz with vocabulary practice
Web Code: nba-1431

Terms, People, and Places

1. For each term, person, or place listed at the beginning of the section, write a sentence explaining its significance.

Note Taking

2. **Reading Skill: Identify Causes and Effects** Use your completed flowchart to answer the Focus Question: How did European nations build empires in South and Southeast Asia?

Comprehension and Critical Thinking

3. **Draw Inferences** You read that the Portuguese did not attempt to conquer inland territory. What does that tell you about their assessment of the inland empires?

4. **Analyze Information** Why did the leaders of the Netherlands give so much power to the Dutch East India Company?

5. **Identify Central Issues** What about the location of the Philippines made it a valuable asset for Spain?

6. **Identify Assumptions** The Mughal empire gave trading rights to several European countries. What assumptions about the power of those countries does this show?

● **Writing About History**
Quick Write: Present Evidence to Support a Thesis Write a biographical essay about Afonso de Albuquerque. First, think of a thesis statement that describes the main points you want to make. Then write the main body text, referring frequently to your thesis statement. The details in a biographical essay should directly support your main point. For example, if your thesis is that Albuquerque was a violent man, you would include details about his takeover of Malacca.

Section 3 Assessment

1. Sentences should reflect an understanding of each term, person, or place listed at the beginning of the section.
2. They built strategic outposts to control the spice trade; established colonies; and with their wealth and power began to influence or even take over the local governments, thus establishing empires.

3. They perceived these empires as being stronger than their own forces.
4. Sample: Actions could occur much more quickly if the company's leaders could make their own decisions.
5. It was ideally situated across the Pacific from Spain's American colonies.
6. Sample: This shows that their power, even with concessions, was not great enough to be a threat to Mughal rulers.

● **Writing About History**
Responses should develop the body of the essay, using biographical details about Afonso de Albuquerque that clearly support the thesis statement.

For additional assessment, have students access **Progress Monitoring *Online*** at **Web Code nba-1431.**

A Chinese watercolor portrays Matteo Ricci with European objects, including a model of the universe. A geography book that Ricci translated into Chinese is shown at the top.

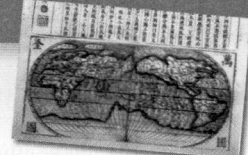

WITNESS HISTORY 🔊 AUDIO

A Jesuit in China

In 1583, a young Jesuit priest arrived in China. He had studied Chinese and immediately impressed Chinese rulers with his fluency as well as his knowledge of European science. Matteo Ricci recognized that the Chinese would not accept a European religion "unless it be seasoned with an intellectual flavoring." In his nearly 30 years in China, Ricci translated five European books into Chinese. Ricci adopted Chinese dress and established friendships with Confucian scholars. When he died in 1610 at age 58, he was buried near the emperor. Much of Europe's knowledge about China came from Ricci's writings.

Focus Question How were European encounters in East Asia shaped by the worldviews of both Europeans and Asians?

Encounters in East Asia

Objectives

• Describe European contacts with Ming China.
• Understand the Manchu conquest and its impact on European trade.
• Analyze the factors that led Korea to isolate itself from other nations.
• Summarize Japan's attitudes toward foreign trade and how they changed over time.

Terms, People, and Places

Macao	Qing
Guangzhou	Qianlong
Matteo Ricci	Lord Macartney
Manchus	Nagasaki

Note Taking

Reading Skill: Understand Effects Fill in a chart like the one below with effects of European contacts in East Asia.

```
        European Contacts in East Asia

    China          Korea          Japan
    •              •              •
    •              •              •
```

Portuguese ships first reached China from their base in Malacca in 1514. To the Chinese, the Portuguese, like other foreigners, were barbarians. Europeans, by contrast, wrote enthusiastically about China. In 1590, a visitor described Chinese artisans "cleverly making devices out of gold, silver and other metals," and wrote with approval: "They daily publish huge multitudes of books."

European Contact With Ming China

European interest in China and other parts of East Asia continued to grow. The Ming, however, had no interest in Europe—since, as a Ming document proclaimed, "our empire owns the world."

The Ming Limit Trade The Portuguese wanted Chinese silks and porcelains, but had little to offer in exchange. European textiles and metalwork were inferior to Chinese products. The Chinese therefore demanded payment in gold or silver. The Ming eventually allowed the Portuguese a trading post at **Macao** near Canton, present-day **Guangzhou** (GWAHNG joh). Later, they let Dutch, English, and other Europeans trade with Chinese merchants. Foreigners could trade only at Canton under the supervision of <u>imperial</u> officials. When each year's trading season ended, they had to sail away.

Vocabulary Builder

Use the information below and the following resources to teach the high-use words from this section.
All in One **Teaching Resources, Unit 1,** p. 26; **Teaching Resources, Skills Handbook,** p. 3

High-Use Words	Definitions and Sample Sentences
imperial, p. 100	*adj.* relating to an emperor or empire We knew the document was approved by the emperor because it had an **imperial** stamp.
allegiance, p. 103	*n.* loyalty or devotion to a cause or person The knights swore **allegiance** to the new king and promised to protect him.

Teach

European Contact With Ming China ⓛ3

Instruct

- **Introduce: Vocabulary Builder**
Have students read the Vocabulary Builder term and definition. Ask them to consider if an *imperial* officer could help facilitate trade or hinder it.

- **Teach** Explain that Ming China was a powerful, unified empire. Ask **How did the Ming view Europeans?** *(as backward and uncivilized, with only inferior objects to trade)* **Did the arrival of the Jesuits change this view?** *(Yes, in that the Chinese respected many of the Jesuits as intellectuals, though they still saw their own culture as far superior to that of Europe.)*

- **Quick Activity** Have students examine the Infographic on this page. Assign small groups of students a trade item shown in the Infographic. Have them use the information there, as well as additional information in the text, to trace the item from its origin to a European market.

Independent Practice

Have students fill in the Outline Map *World During the Age of Discovery*, noting the areas of European influence.

All in One Teaching Resources, Unit 1, p. 33

Monitor Progress

- Circulate to make sure students are accurately filling in their Outline Map, by correctly labeling the names of countries and regions and noting areas of European influence. Administer the Geography Quiz.

All in One Teaching Resources, Unit 1, p. 35

- As students fill in their charts, circulate to make sure they have identified the main effects of European contacts in East Asia.

📺 Note Taking Transparencies, 122

Answer

✔ They were not interested in any European trade items.

Vocabulary Builder

imperial—(im PIHR ee ul) *adj.* relating to an emperor or empire

---

Seeking Converts Portuguese missionaries arrived in China along with the traders. In later years the Jesuits—from Spain, Italy, and Portugal—arrived. Most Jesuits had a broad knowledge of many subjects, and the Chinese welcomed the chance to learn about Renaissance Europe from these scholars. The brilliant Jesuit priest **Matteo Ricci** (mah TAY oh REE chee) made a particularly strong impression on the Chinese. Still, Ricci and other priests had little success spreading their religious beliefs in China. They did, however, become important sources of information for Europeans who knew little about China.

✔ **Checkpoint** Why did Ming China demand that Europeans pay for goods with gold or silver?

The Manchu Conquest

By the early 1600s, the aging Ming dynasty was decaying. Revolts erupted, and Manchu invaders from the north pushed through the Great Wall. The **Manchus** ruled a region in the northeast, Manchuria, that had long been influenced by Chinese civilization. In 1644, victorious Manchu armies seized Beijing and made it their capital.

● **INFOGRAPHIC**

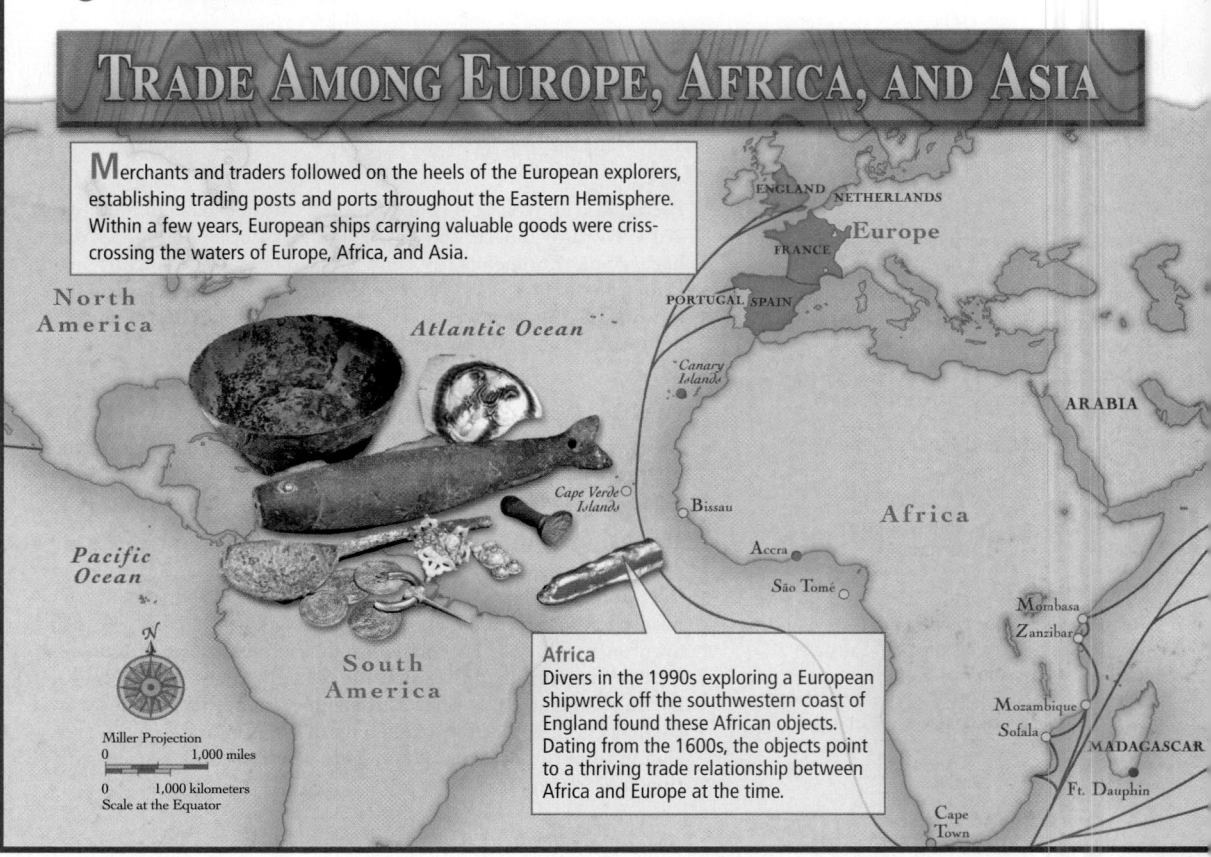

TRADE AMONG EUROPE, AFRICA, AND ASIA

Merchants and traders followed on the heels of the European explorers, establishing trading posts and ports throughout the Eastern Hemisphere. Within a few years, European ships carrying valuable goods were criss-crossing the waters of Europe, Africa, and Asia.

Africa
Divers in the 1990s exploring a European shipwreck off the southwestern coast of England found these African objects. Dating from the 1600s, the objects point to a thriving trade relationship between Africa and Europe at the time.

Miller Projection
0   1,000 miles
0   1,000 kilometers
Scale at the Equator

Differentiated Instruction   Solutions for All Learners

ⓛ1 Special Needs   ⓛ2 Less Proficient Readers

Discuss ways to respond when confronted by a bully. Ask students to list the pros and cons of the following options: fighting back, negotiating, and giving in. Explain to students that Asian countries faced a similar set of choices when confronted with European expansion. Each country had to decide how to respond based on the possible outcome of each response.

ⓛ2 English Language Learners

Use the following resources to help students acquire basic skills.

📝 **Adapted Reading and Note Taking Study Guide**

- Adapted Note Taking Study Guide, p. 51
- Adapted Section Summary, p. 52

Founding the Qing Dynasty The Manchus set up a new dynasty called the **Qing** (ching). The Manchus won the support of Chinese scholar-officials because they adopted the Confucian system of government. For each top government position, the Qing chose two people, one Manchu and one Chinese. Local government remained in the hands of the Chinese, but Manchu troops stationed across the empire ensured loyalty.

Two rulers oversaw the most brilliant age of the Qing. Kangxi (kahng shee), who ruled from 1661 to 1722, was an able administrator and military leader. He extended Chinese power into Central Asia and promoted Chinese culture. Kangxi's grandson **Qianlong** (chyahn lung) had an equally successful reign from 1736 to 1796. He expanded China's borders to rule the largest area in the nation's history. Qianlong retired after 60 years because he did not want to rule longer than his grandfather had.

Spreading Peace and Prosperity The Chinese economy expanded under both emperors. New crops from the Americas, such as potatoes and corn, had been introduced into China. These crops boosted farm output, which in turn contributed to a population boom. China's population rose from 140 million in 1740 to over 300 million by 1800. The silk, cotton, and porcelain industries expanded. Internal trade grew, as did the demand for Chinese goods from all over the world.

WITNESS HISTORY VIDEO

Watch *Manchu China and the West* on the **Witness History Discovery School**™ video program to learn more about the interactions between two very different cultures.

DISCOVERY SCHOOL

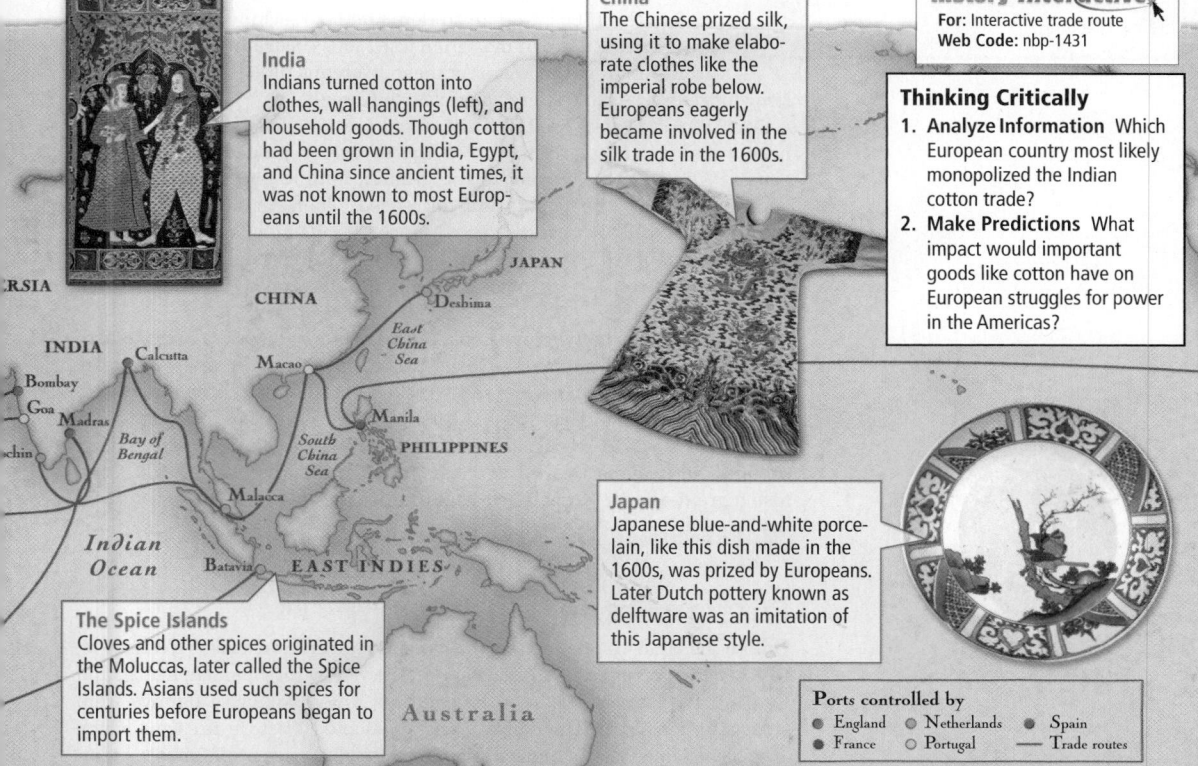

India
Indians turned cotton into clothes, wall hangings (left), and household goods. Though cotton had been grown in India, Egypt, and China since ancient times, it was not known to most Europeans until the 1600s.

China
The Chinese prized silk, using it to make elaborate clothes like the imperial robe below. Europeans eagerly became involved in the silk trade in the 1600s.

Japan
Japanese blue-and-white porcelain, like this dish made in the 1600s, was prized by Europeans. Later Dutch pottery known as delftware was an imitation of this Japanese style.

The Spice Islands
Cloves and other spices originated in the Moluccas, later called the Spice Islands. Asians used such spices for centuries before Europeans began to import them.

History Interactive
For: Interactive trade route
Web Code: nbp-1431

Thinking Critically
1. **Analyze Information** Which European country most likely monopolized the Indian cotton trade?
2. **Make Predictions** What impact would important goods like cotton have on European struggles for power in the Americas?

Ports controlled by
- England
- Netherlands
- Spain
- France
- Portugal
— Trade routes

The Manchu Conquest

Instruct

- **Introduce** Display **Color Transparency 83: Goldfish from China.** Explain that as a result of contact with the Chinese, the goldfish (in art and as a pet) spread to Europe. Have students think of other Asian goods that may have been introduced to Europe at this time.
  - Color Transparencies, 83

- **Teach** Explain that with the Manchu conquest, China became more powerful and successful. Ask **What factors contributed to peace and prosperity in Qing China?** *(A population boom raised output and strengthened the economy; Qing government practices strengthened the empire.)* **What effect did this prosperity have on trade with Europeans?** *(The Chinese continued to restrict trade with Europeans, because they saw their success as a justification of their limited trade policies.)*

- **Quick Activity** Show students *Manchu China and the West* from the **Witness History Discovery School**™ video program. Ask them what factors led to the failure of Macartney's mission. Then discuss whether cultural impasses, such as Lord Macartney's inability to communicate with Emperor Qianlong, occur today.

Independent Practice

- Display **Color Transparency 84: Europe Spreads Its Influence.** Ask students to review the transparency, and then write a paragraph explaining whether China was wise to limit trade.
  - Color Transparencies, 84

- Have students access **Web Code nbp-1441** to take the **Geography Interactive Audio Guided Tour** and then answer the map skills questions.

Monitor Progress

- As students write their paragraphs, circulate to ensure they are supporting their points with valid examples.

L4 Advanced Readers   L4 Gifted and Talented

Share with students that the Chinese civil service system was established so that civil service positions would be assigned based on merit, instead of on special or inherited privilege. Men were therefore recruited based on how they performed on a civil service examination. Over time, this exam became more complex and difficult. Have students research to find out more about China's civil service exam, specifically on the varying levels that were given and what subjects were covered. With a partner, ask students to write a mini exam based on the information they find.

Answers

Thinking Critically
1. England
2. Sample: Competition over cotton-producing lands in the Americas would intensify struggles for power.

Korea Chooses Isolation/ Foreign Traders in Japan L3

Instruct

■ **Introduce: Vocabulary Builder** Have students read the Vocabulary term and definition. Have them predict how **allegiance** to a certain faith could provoke hostility.

■ **Teach** Explain that while Korea and Japan were both isolated geographically, they had contact with the peoples of East Asia for many years before their encounters with Europeans. Still, both countries chose a path of isolation. Ask **What was Korea's main reason for choosing isolation?** *(a desire to avoid being controlled by its more powerful neighbors—China and Japan)* **How was Japan's path to isolation different?** *(Japan also feared European power, but its leaders also felt that only in isolation could they keep the necessary control over their own people.)*

■ **Analyzing the Visuals** Have students view the Japanese screen on the next page. Ask them to identify how the art reflects Japanese attitudes toward Europeans.

Independent Practice

Viewpoints To help students better understand the way different historians view Japan's decision to pursue isolationism, have them read the selection *Japan's Shoguns Reject the West,* and answer the questions on the worksheet. Then, in small groups, have them discuss how the two viewpoints differed.

All in One Teaching Resources, Unit 1, p. 32

Monitor Progress

Check Reading and Note Taking Study Guide entries for student understanding.

Emperor Qianlong wrote a letter to King George III denying Britain's request for more trading rights and permanent ambassadors. How does Emperor Qianlong's language express his view that China is superior to Britain?

Primary Source

 As to your entreaty to send one of your nationals . . . to my Celestial Court, this request is contrary to all usage of my dynasty and cannot possibly be entertained. . . .

I have but one aim in view, namely, to maintain a perfect governance and to fulfill the duties of the State: strange and costly objects do not interest me. . . . Our dynasty's majestic virtue has penetrated unto every country under Heaven, and Kings of all nations have offered their costly tribute by land and sea. As your Ambassador can see for himself, we possess all things. I set no value on objects strange or ingenious, and have no use for your country's manufactures. **99**

Rejecting Contact With Europeans The Qing maintained the Ming policy of restricting foreign traders. Still, Europeans kept pressing to expand trade to cities other than Guangzhou. In 1793, **Lord Macartney** arrived in China at the head of a British diplomatic mission. He brought samples of British-made goods to show the Chinese the advantages of trade with Westerners. The Chinese, who looked on the goods as rather crude products, thought they were gifts offered as tribute to the emperor.

Further misunderstandings followed. Macartney insisted on an audience with the emperor. The Chinese told Macartney he would have to perform the traditional kowtow, touching his head to the ground to show respect to the emperor. Macartney refused. He also offended the Chinese by speaking of the natural superiority of the English. The negotiations faltered.

At the time, Qianlong's attitude seemed justified by China's successes. After all, he already ruled the world's greatest empire. Why should he negotiate with a nation as distant as Britain? In the long run, however, his policy proved disastrous. In the 1800s, China would learn that its policy of ignoring Westerners and their technology would have undesired consequences.

✔ **Checkpoint** How did the Qing respond to Britain's diplomatic mission?

Korea Chooses Isolation

Before the 1500s, Korean traders had far-reaching contacts across East Asia. A Korean map from the 1300s accurately outlines lands from Japan to the Mediterranean. Koreans probably acquired this knowledge from Arab traders who came to Korea.

In 1592, and again in 1597, the Japanese invaded Korea. The Japanese were driven out in 1598, but the invasions proved disastrous for Korea. Villages were burned to the ground, famine and disease became widespread, and the population decreased. Then, in 1636, before the country was fully recovered, the Manchus invaded Korea. When the Manchus set up the Qing dynasty in China, Korea became a tributary state. It was run by its own government but forced to acknowledge China's supremacy.

Devastated by the two invasions, Korean rulers adopted a policy of isolation, excluding foreigners except the Chinese and a few Japanese. When European sailors were shipwrecked on Korean shores, they were imprisoned and held as spies. Although Korea had few contacts with much of the world for almost 250 years, Koreans on tribute missions brought back maps as well as books on scientific discoveries. This was also a great age for Korean arts and literature.

✔ **Checkpoint** Why did Korea become isolated?

Foreign Traders in Japan

Unlike the Chinese or Koreans, the Japanese at first welcomed Westerners. In 1543, the Portuguese reached Japan, followed by the Spanish, Dutch, and English. They arrived at a turbulent time, when Japanese daimyo were struggling for power. The daimyo quickly adopted Western firearms which may have helped the Tokugawa shoguns centralize power and impose order.

Answers

History Background

The Japanese Invasion of Korea Japan's invasion of Korea in the 1590s had long-lasting consequences for all three nations involved. For Ming China, which aided Korea early in the war, the large cost weakened the dynasty, which was already in decline. When the Manchus later challenged the Ming dynasty, the Ming did not have the resources to successfully fight back. In Korea, towns and temples were destroyed. Cultural objects were ransacked or stolen, and the conflict hardened Korean feelings against foreigners. Japan is the only nation to have benefited from the fighting. The stolen books and artwork aided scholastic development, as did the movable type printing machine, which they stole and imitated. They also took Korean prisoners, including potters and weavers who helped build Japan's growing ceramic and textile industry.

Jesuits, such as the Spanish priest Francis Xavier, found the Japanese curious about Christianity. A growing number of Japanese adopted the new faith. The Japanese also welcomed the printing press the Jesuits brought. The Tokugawa shoguns, however, grew increasingly hostile toward foreigners. After learning that Spain had seized the Philippines, they may have seen the newcomers as threats. They also worried that Japanese Christians—who may have numbered as many as 300,000— owed their <u>allegiance</u> to the pope, rather than to Japanese leaders. In response, the Tokugawas expelled foreign missionaries. They brutally persecuted Japanese Christians, killing many thousands of people.

By 1638, the Tokugawas had turned against European traders as well. Japan barred all European merchants and forbade Japanese to travel abroad. To further their isolation, they outlawed the building of large ships, thereby ending foreign trade. In order to keep informed about world events, they permitted just one or two Dutch ships each year to trade at a small island in **Nagasaki** harbor.

Japan remained isolated for more than 200 years. Art and literature flourished, and internal trade boomed. Cities grew in size and importance, and some merchant families gained wealth and status. By the early 1700s, Edo (present-day Tokyo) had a million inhabitants, more than either London or Paris.

✔ **Checkpoint** Why did the Tokugawas turn against Europeans?

Bringing Trade and Christianity
This 1600s decorative screen shows Japanese people meeting a Portuguese ship carrying European goods and missionaries. *Did the presence of missionaries help or hurt European-Japanese trade relations?*

Vocabulary Builder
<u>allegiance</u>—(uh LEE juns) *n.* loyalty or devotion to a cause or person

---

SECTION **4** Assessment

Progress Monitoring *Online*
For: Self-quiz with vocabulary practice
Web Code: nba-1441

Terms, People, and Places
1. Place each of the key terms, people, or places listed at the beginning of the section into one of the following categories: politics, culture, government, or geography. Write a sentence for each term explaining your choice.

Note Taking
2. **Reading Skill: Understand Effects** Use your completed chart to answer the Focus Question: How were European encounters in East Asia shaped by the worldviews of both Europeans and Asians?

Comprehension and Critical Thinking
3. **Analyze Credibility** Reread the quotation from the Ming document on page 461. Do you think its characterization of China is credible? Explain.
4. **Draw Inferences** What do Qing China's trade policies with Europeans in the 1700s tell you about the state of the Qing economy?
5. **Make Comparisons** Why did both Japan and Korea respond to increased foreign contact by going into isolation?
6. **Synthesize Information** Why did Japan allow limited contact with the Dutch, but not with the Spanish or Portuguese?

● **Writing About History**
Quick Write: Write a Conclusion Write a sentence to conclude a biographical essay about Matteo Ricci. Read the information about Ricci in this section. Then construct a broad summary sentence that covers the main point you want to make about his life. For example, if your thesis is that Ricci believed Chinese culture to be superior to European culture, you would include that point in your summary sentence.

Assess and Reteach

Assess Progress L3

■ Have students complete the Section Assessment.
■ Administer the Section Quiz.
All in One Teaching Resources, Unit 1, p. 25
■ To further assess student understanding, use
▦ **Progress Monitoring Transparencies,** 61

Reteach
If students need more instruction, have them read the section summary.

 Reading and Note Taking Study Guide, p. 52 L3

 Adapted Reading and Note Taking Study Guide, p. 52 L1 L2

 Spanish Reading and Note Taking Study Guide, p. 52 L2

Extend L4
Display **Color Transparency 88: European Knowledge of the World.** Use the lesson suggested in the transparency book to guide a discussion about how Europeans' knowledge of the world expanded as their contact with people and places outside of Europe increased.
▦ **Color Transparencies,** 88

Answer

✔ They came to see Europeans as a threat to their power, and they feared that Japanese Christians would shift their allegiance from Japan to the pope.

Section 4 Assessment

1. Sentences should reflect an understanding of each term, person, or place listed at the beginning of the section as well as the proper categorization.
2. Europeans considered the world theirs to discover. Most Asian peoples saw themselves at the center of culture and Europeans on the fringes. Some Asians had a practical world view that allowed them to avoid destructive conflict.
3. Sample: It is not credible because China did not control the whole world; it is somewhat credible because at that time in its history, China dominated most of Asia.
4. They suggest that China had a very strong, self-sustained economy.
5. Both were small nations that thought they could survive more easily by remaining isolated.
6. Because the Dutch did not send large numbers of missionaries, the Japanese may have felt less threatened by them.

● **Writing About History**
Summary statements should be broad enough to cover the person's life and should also support a specific thesis statement.

For additional assessment, have students access **Progress Monitoring *Online*** at Web Code nba-1441.

- Have students use the Quick Study Guide to prepare for this chapter's test. Students may wish to refer to the following pages as they review:

Causes of European Exploration
Section 1, pp. 84–85, 87–89

European Footholds in the Eastern Hemisphere
Section 1, pp. 85–86; Section 2, p. 90; Section 3, pp. 95–98

Important European Explorers
Section 1, pp. 86–89

Major Asian Dynasties and Empires
Section 3, p. 98; Section 4, pp. 99–103

Europe, Africa, and Asia 1415–1796
Section 1, pp. 84–89; Section 2, pp. 90–93; Section 3, pp. 95–98; Section 4, pp. 99–103

- For additional review, remind students to refer to the **L3**

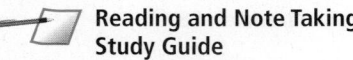
    Reading and Note Taking Study Guide
Note Taking Study Guide, pp. 45, 47, 49, 51
Section Summaries, pp. 46, 48, 50, 52

- Have students access **Web Code nbp-1451** for this chapter's **History Interactive** timeline, which includes expanded entries and additional events.

- If students need more instruction on analyzing timelines, have them read the **Skills Handbook,** p. SH30.

- When students have completed their study of the chapter, distribute Chapter Tests A and B.

All in One **Teaching Resources, Unit 1,**
    pp. 36–41

For **Progress Monitoring Online,** refer students to the Self-test with vocabulary practice at **Web Code nba-1451.**

Quick Study Guide

Progress Monitoring *Online*
For: Self-test with vocabulary practice
Web Code: nba-1451

■ Causes of European Exploration

- Desire for Asian luxury goods such as spices, gold, and silks
- Motivation to spread Christianity
- Strategic need to gain more direct access to trade
- Desire to gain glory for country
- Renaissance curiosity to explore new lands
- Competition with other European countries

■ European Footholds in the Eastern Hemisphere

Country	Date	Foothold	Reason for Interest
Portugal	1502	Calicut, India	Spices
Portugal	1510	Goa, India	Military and commercial base
Portugal	1511	Malacca, Southeast Asia	Center of sea trade
Spain	1521	The Philippines	Center of sea trade
Portugal	1589	Mombasa, East Africa	Hub of international trade
Netherlands	1652	Cape Town, southern Africa	Strategic port for repairing and resupplying ships
Great Britain	1757	Northeastern India	Spices, trade goods

■ Important European Explorers

Explorer	Accomplishment
Vasco da Gama (Portugal)	Sailed around Cape of Good Hope; established ports on Indian Ocean
Christopher Columbus (Spain)	Sailed west across Atlantic Ocean to Caribbean
Vasco Núñez de Balboa (Spain)	Crossed Panama, reaching Pacific Ocean
Ferdinand Magellan (Spain)	Circumnavigated the globe

■ Major Asian Dynasties and Empires

Ruler	Location	Description	European Contact
Mughal empire	India	Major trading empire	After two centuries of peace and prosperity, civil war between Muslim and Hindu princes weakened empire; European powers took control in 1700s
Ming dynasty	China	Prosperous dynasty that had sponsored overseas exploration	Allowed some trade with Europeans and sought out European learning; revolts in the 1600s led to overthrow by the Manchus
Qing dynasty	China	Powerful dynasty that expanded China's borders and promoted Chinese culture	Increasingly restricted European trading rights
Choson dynasty	Korea	Chinese-influenced Confucian state	Had few contacts with the outside world except for China and Japan
Tokugawa shogunate	Japan	Powerful warrior kingdom	Welcomed Europeans at first but then expelled missionaries and most traders

■ Europe, Africa, and Asia 1415–1796

1492
Christopher Columbus reaches the Caribbean.

1498
Portuguese explorer Vasco da Gama rounds Africa and reaches India.

1522
Magellan's expedition circumnavigates the globe.

Chapter Events
Global Events

1450	1500	1550

1453
The Ottoman Turks take Constantinople, ending the Byzantine empire.

1500
The kingdom of Kongo thrives in Africa.

1556
Akbar begins the Mughal reign in India.

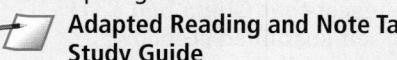

Differentiated
Instruction **Solutions for All Learners**

L1 Special Needs **L2 Less Proficient Readers** **L2 English Language Learners**

Use the following study guide resources to help students acquiring basic skills:

Adapted Reading and Note Taking Study Guide
Adapted Note Taking Study Guide, pp. 45, 47, 49, 51
Adapted Section Summaries, pp. 46, 48, 50, 52

Use the following study guide resources to help Spanish-speaking students:

Spanish Reading and Note Taking Study Guide
Spanish Note Taking Study Guide, pp. 45, 47, 49, 51
Spanish Section Summaries, pp. 46, 48, 50, 52

Concept Connector

 Essential Question Review

To connect prior knowledge with what you have learned in this chapter, answer the questions below in your Concept Connector journal. Use the journal in the Reading and Note Taking Study Guide to record your answers (or go to www.phschool.com **Web Code:** nbd-1407). In addition, record information about the following concepts:
- Technology: the compass
- Trade: Dutch trading empire; Indian trade in Southeast Asia

1. **Empire** With the founding of the Qing Empire, the Manchus established one of China's most successful dynasties. Identify policies the Qing Dynasty used to gain the support of the Chinese people and explain how these policies helped the Qing to expand their empire.

2. **Conflict** As the French and British began to establish global empires in the 1600s and 1700s, they frequently came into conflict. Review the Causes of European Exploration on the opposite page. Then create a list of factors that would cause conflict between two European countries pursuing global empires during this period. Consider military, economic, and political goals.

3. **Trade** As trade brought different nations into greater contact with one another from the 1400s to the 1700s, there were both winners and losers. What were some of the costs and benefits of international trade in this era? How did some states demonstrate their resistance to this expanded contact? Consider the impact on the following:
   - economics
   - politics
   - society

■ **Connections to Today**

1. **Trade: The Dutch Trading Empire** In the 1500s, the Dutch began establishing an overseas trade empire in Southeast Asia, using the tools of sea power and monopolistic trade policies. Today, the Dutch are not known for their sea power or overseas domination, yet the strong economy of the Netherlands still depends heavily on trade. Research Dutch trade, including its global rank in exports, the number and types of companies owned by the Dutch in the United States, and the role of multinational companies in the economy of the Netherlands. Write two paragraphs summarizing the importance of trade to the Netherlands today.

2. **Technology: The Compass** European exploration would not have been possible without the compass. The compass allowed navigators to find direction accurately, rather than relying on the sun, stars, and moon. Consider the events and discoveries that the compass made possible. Then think of recent technological inventions that have had profound impacts on the world today. Which technology do you consider to be equivalent in its impact to the compass? Why?

Timeline:

1602	1641	1736
The Dutch establish the Dutch East India Company.	The Dutch take Malacca from the Portuguese.	China's emperor Qianlong begins his reign.

History *Interactive*
For: Interactive timeline
Web Code: nbp-1451

1600	1650	1700	1750

1603	1642	1756
The Tokugawas come to power in Japan.	The English Civil War begins.	The Seven Years' War breaks out between Britain and France.

Differentiated
Instruction — Solutions for All Learners

L1 Special Needs   L2 Less Proficient Readers

Use the following study guide resources to help students acquiring basic skills:

 Adapted Reading and Note Taking Study Guide
Adapted Concept Connector, pp. 237, 247, 262, 295, 300

L2 English Language Learners

Use the following study guide resources to help Spanish-speaking students:

Spanish Reading and Note Taking Study Guide
Spanish Concept Connector, pp. 237, 262, 295, 300

Concept Connector

Tell students that the main concepts for this chapter are: Technology, Trade, Cultural Diffusion, Empire, and Conflict. Then ask them to answer the Essential Question Review questions on this page. Discuss the Connections to Today topics and ask students to answer the questions that follow.

Essential Question Review

1. The Manchus won the support of the Chinese people by adopting a Confucian system of government. By working with the Chinese and showing respect for their culture, the rulers were able to increase the power of the empire and expand its borders.

2. Factors that would cause conflict include: disputes over trading rights or trade routes, conflicts over exploration rights and land claims, competition to build their own empires quickly, and desire to monopolize trade.

3. Students should be able to identify how European powers benefited from the trade by gaining natural resources, slaves, and access to ports. They should be able to show which societies did not welcome the trade, identifying their resistance to slavery, conversion to Christianity, and the mixing of cultures.

Connections to Today

1. Students might say that in today's world of multinational companies, it is not always clear where major trade centers are located.

2. Answers should be supported with evidence and show a clear impact.

For additional review of this chapter's **L3** core concepts, remind students to refer to the

 **Reading and Note Taking Study Guide**
Concept Connector, pp. 237, 262, 295, 300

Chapter Assessment

Terms, People, and Places

1. A cartographer is a mapmaker. Henry the Navigator sponsored cartographers at Sagres.

2. Circumnavigating the globe took many months, during which time sailors often got scurvy from a lack of fresh fruits and vegetables.

3. Europeans used large numbers of slaves to raise labor-intensive cash crops on their plantations.

4. An outpost is a distant area under a country's control. Europeans used outposts as bases for trade, merging them into an empire.

5. They needed the support of local Indian troops to succeed.

6. By maintaining power over key industries, it was able to play European rivals off against each other.

Main Ideas

7. Europeans' desire to eliminate middlemen encouraged them to sail to the Spice Islands themselves; in doing so, they made discoveries.

8. As Europeans followed new sea routes, they established outposts that they later used to expand their presence.

9. African towns and cities were taken over; European exploration and its role in trade increased the slave trade.

10. By leading Europe in exploration, Portugal was able to establish footholds earlier than other European nations.

11. They turned it into a permanent colony with large numbers of settlers, making it a geographical and economic base for an overseas empire.

12. It had little impact at first, but over time it weakened the empire.

13. Europeans established missions in China with little success, and in Japan with greater success. Europeans gained very limited trade concessions in China and in Japan, until they were restricted.

14. They did not feel that Europeans had much to offer them.

Chapter Focus Question

15. They brought great advances in geography, navigation, and technology, and made Europeans aware of the world's resources. Europeans used the knowl-

Chapter Assessment

Terms, People, and Places

1. Define **cartographer**. How did Prince Henry encourage the work of cartographers?
2. Write a sentence or two that shows why scurvy was a problem for sailors who **circumnavigated** the globe.
3. What was the role of European **plantations** in the growth of slavery?
4. Define **outpost**. Why were European outposts important in the development of overseas empires?
5. Why did European trading companies organize armies of **sepoys** in India?
6. How did the Asante kingdom use **monopolies** to keep its power?

Main Ideas

Section 1 (pp. 84–89)
7. How did the European interest in the spice trade lead to the discovery of new routes and lands?

Section 2 (pp. 90–93)
8. How did new sea routes lead to an expanded European presence in Africa?
9. What impact did Portuguese exploration have on the people of Africa?

Section 3 (pp. 95–98)
10. How did Portugal gain dominance of the spice trade?
11. How did the Dutch use their foothold in Cape Town to develop an overseas trade empire?
12. What effect did European trade have on the Mughal empire?

Section 4 (pp. 99–103)
13. Summarize European attempts to establish trade and missions in East Asia.
14. Why were the Dutch able to maintain a presence in Japan even when other Europeans were kicked out?

Chapter Focus Question
15. How did European voyages of exploration lead to European empires in the Eastern Hemisphere?

Critical Thinking
16. **Predict Consequences** What might have happened if Asian explorers, rather than Europeans, had first reached the Americas?
17. **Geography and History** How did Japan's geography allow the Tokugawas to maintain a long period of isolation?
18. **Draw Conclusions** Did missionaries hurt or help European attempts to establish trade in Asia? Explain your answer.
19. **Analyze Visuals** The woodcut below was made in 1555 by a Swedish geographer. What does it tell you about European knowledge of the world before the age of exploration?

20. **Recognize Cause and Effect** How did competition among European countries affect overseas exploration and conquest?

● **Writing About History**

In this chapter's four Section Assessments, you developed skills for writing a biographical essay.

Writing a Biographical Essay Many great Europeans, Africans, and Asians shaped the history of our global age. Write about one of the following important people in a biographical essay: Ferdinand Magellan, Affonso I, Afonso de Albuquerque, Emperor Qianlong, or Matteo Ricci. Consult page SH18 of the Writing Handbook for additional help.

Prewriting
• Choose the person who interests you the most. Take notes about this person and his role in shaping the age of global exploration.

• Draw conclusions about the person you have chosen. Think about how you can turn these conclusions into main points for your essay.

Drafting
• Write an introduction and a thesis statement. Your thesis statement should summarize the main point you want to make about the person you chose.
• Write the body text, introducing details and evidence that support your thesis statement. Then write a conclusion.

Revising
• Use the guidelines for revising your essay on page SH19 of the Writing Handbook.

edge and skills they gained to establish outposts, take over profitable trade routes, and create empires.

Critical Thinking

16. Students might suggest that Asians could not have had the same impact because they lacked firepower and unity. Europeans at least had similar languages, a common religion (Christianity), and a well-established history of diplomacy.

17. It was an island nation and the easternmost Asian country, the farthest from Europe.

18. They often roused hostility that hurt trade efforts, especially in East Asia.

19. that it was limited, relying mainly on myth

20. It stimulated exploration as nations competed to control trade. It also encouraged conquest as nations competed to gain land and territory.

Document-Based Assessment

Why Did Europeans Explore the Seas?

In the 1400s, Europeans began to embark on long and dangerous voyages to unknown destinations. Why did this age of exploration begin? In Documents A and B, a contemporary observer and a modern-day historian describe the impetus behind these early expeditions.

Document A

"The discovery of the new Western World followed, as an incidental consequence, from the long struggle of the nations of Europe for commercial supremacy and control of the traffic with the East. In all these dreams of the politicians and merchants, sailors and geographers, who pushed back the limits of the unknown world, there is the same glitter of gold and precious stones, the same odour of far-fetched spices."

—Sir Walter Raleigh, 1509

Document B

"The starting point for the European expansion out of the Mediterranean and the Atlantic continental shelf had nothing to do with, say, religion or the rise of capitalism—but it had a great deal to do with pepper. . . . . [Pepper] comprised more than half of all the spice imports into Italy over a period of more than a century. No other single spice came within one-tenth of the value of pepper. . . . However, since about 1470 the Turks had been impeding the overland trade routes east from the Mediterranean. As a result the great Portuguese, Italian, and Spanish explorers all sailed west or south in order to reach the Orient. The Americas were discovered as a by-product in the search for pepper."

—From *Seeds of Change* by Henry Hobhouse

This page from a sixteenth-century book about navigation depicts England's Queen Elizabeth in the ship at the right. ▶

Document C

◀ This fifteenth-century painting depicts Henry the Navigator, standing at right in round black hat. A Portuguese prince, Henry did much to advance maritime exploration and the fields of navigation and cartography.

Document D

Analyzing Documents

Use your knowledge of European exploration and Documents A, B, C, and D to answer questions 1–4.

1. Documents A and B both make the point that the discovery of new lands was motivated by
   A religious fanaticism.
   B adventurous dreams.
   C wanting to make money.
   D Renaissance ideals.

2. What motivation for exploration is implied in Document C?
   A the search for spices
   B the desire to please king or country
   C the desire to spread Christianity
   D both B and C

3. What does Document D suggest about how European monarchs viewed exploration?
   A They saw it as vitally important to their nations.
   B They viewed exploration as interesting but unnecessary.
   C They saw it as important but not worth spending money on.
   D They had no opinion about exploration.

4. **Writing Task** Using information from the chapter, assess the various motivations for exploration. Are there any that are not shown in these documents? Choose the motivation you think was the most compelling for Europeans. Use specific evidence from the chapter and documents to support your argument.

● Writing About History

As students begin the assignment, refer them to page SH18 of the **Writing Handbook** for help in writing a biographical essay. Remind them of the steps they should take to complete their assignment, including prewriting, drafting, and revising. For help in revising, remind them to use the guidelines on page SH19 of the **Writing Handbook.**

Students' biographical essays should have a clear thesis statement, supported with specific facts. Essays should end with a broad summary statement that relates directly to the thesis. For scoring rubrics for writing assignments, see **Assessment Rubrics,** p. 8.

Document-Based Assessment

■ To help students understand the documents on this page, give them the following **TIP: As you read, think about causes and effects. Ask yourself, What happened (effect)? Why did it happen (cause)?**

■ To provide students with further practice in answering Document-Based Assessment Questions, go to 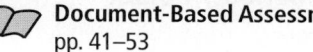 **Document-Based Assessment,** pp. 41–53

■ If students need more instruction on drawing inferences and conclusions, have them read the **Skills Handbook,** p. SH36.

Answers

1. C
2. D
3. A
4. Responses should emphasize Europeans' motivations for wealth and control of trade, and should be supported with specific evidence from the documents and the chapter. Motivations not included here could be competition among European nations, Renaissance curiosity, or scientific inquiry.

CHAPTER 3

The Beginnings of Our Global Age: Europe and the Americas

CHAPTER PLANNER

Section	Core Instruction **L3**	Differentiated Instruction **L1 L2 L4**	
Section 1 *Conquest in the Americas* ⏱ **2 periods, 1 block** **OBJECTIVES** ■ Analyze the results of the first encounters between the Spanish and Native Americans. ■ Explain how Cortés and Pizarro gained control of the Aztec and Incan empires. ■ Understand the short-term and long-term effects of the Spanish on the peoples of the Americas. **Focus Question** *How did a small number of Spanish conquistadors conquer huge Native American empires?*	**All in One** Teaching Resources, Unit 1 Reading Strategy: Recognize Sequence, p. 48 Vocabulary Builder: Make Connections, p. 47 Section 1 Quiz, p. 42 **Reading and Note Taking Study Guide** Note Taking Study Guide, p. 53 Section 1 Summary, p. 54 **Note Taking Transparencies,** 123 **WITNESS HISTORY** Audio CD Moctezuma Hears Strange News, Mayan Life **Progress Monitoring Transparencies,** 62 **Color Transparencies,** 89, 90, 93 **Teaching Resources, Skills Handbook** Prereading the Chapter, pp. 1–2 Word Knowledge Rating Form, p. 3 K-W-L Chart, p. 4	**L1** Adapted Reading and Note Taking Study Guide Note Taking Study Guide, p. 53 **SN** Section 1 Summary, p. 54 **SN** **L2** Adapted Reading and Note Taking Study Guide Note Taking Study Guide, p. 53 **LPR** Section 1 Summary, p. 54 **LPR** **Spanish Reading and Note Taking Study Guide** Note Taking Study Guide, p. 53 **ELL** Section 1 Summary, p. 54 **ELL** **L4** **All in One** Teaching Resources, Unit 1 Primary Source: The Broken Spears, p. 49 **AR, GT** Primary Source: The Massacre in the Temple of Tenochtitlán, p. 51 **AR, GT** Traveler's Tales: Bernal Diaz and the Conquest of New Spain, p. 52 **AR, GT**	*Student Edition Audio **SN** Differentiated Instruction Activity, Teacher's Edition, p. 111 **SN** *Guided Reading Audio, Spanish **ELL** *Student Edition Audio **LPR** Differentiated Instruction Activity, Teacher's Edition, p. 111 **LPR, ELL** Differentiated Instruction Activity, Teacher's Edition, p. 112 **AR, GT** Extend Activity, Teacher's Edition, pp. 108c, 114 **AR, GT**
Section 2 *Spanish and Portuguese Colonies in the Americas* ⏱ **2 periods, 1 block** **OBJECTIVES** ■ Explain how Spain ruled its empire in the Americas. ■ Analyze the major features of Spanish colonial society and culture. ■ Describe how Portugal and other European nations challenged Spanish power. **Focus Question** *How did Spain and Portugal build colonies in the Americas?*	**All in One** Teaching Resources, Unit 1 Section 2 Quiz, p. 43 **Reading and Note Taking Study Guide** Note Taking Study Guide, p. 55 Section 2 Summary, p. 56 **Note Taking Transparencies,** 124A, 124B **WITNESS HISTORY** Audio CD A Missionary Protests **Progress Monitoring Transparencies,** 63	**L1** Adapted Reading and Note Taking Study Guide Note Taking Study Guide, p. 55 **SN** Section 2 Summary, p. 56 **SN** **L2** Adapted Reading and Note Taking Study Guide Note Taking Study Guide, p. 55 **LPR** Section 2 Summary, p. 56 **LPR** **L4** **All in One** Teaching Resources, Unit 1 Viewpoints: Two Views of the Treatment of Indians, p. 50 **AR, GT**	Differentiated Instruction Activity, Teacher's Edition, p. 116 **SN** Spanish Reading and Note Taking Study Guide Note Taking Study Guide, p. 55 **ELL** Section 2 Summary, p. 56 **ELL** Differentiated Instruction Activity, Teacher's Edition, p. 116 **LPR, ELL** Extend Activity, Teacher's Edition, p. 119 **AR, GT**

*Audio support is available for all sections.

Assessment Resources

- **Progress Monitoring Transparencies,** 62–66
- **SuccessTracker™,** Chapter 3
- **Document-Based Assessment,** pp. 41–53
- *ExamView®* **Test Bank CD-ROM,** Chapter 3
- **All in One** Teaching Resources, Unit 1, Chapter Tests A and B, pp. 57–62
- **Progress Monitoring** *Online* Quizzes, Chapter 3
- **Assessment Rubrics**

Differentiated Instruction Key

L1 Special Needs		**LPR**	Less Proficient Readers
L2 Basic to Average		**AR**	Advanced Readers
L3 All Students		**SN**	Special Needs Students
L4 Average to Advanced		**GT**	Gifted and Talented
		ELL	English Language Learner

Section	Core Instruction L3	Differentiated Instruction L1 L2 L4	
Section 3 *Struggle for North America* ⏱ **1 period, .5 block** **OBJECTIVES** ■ Explain why the colony of New France grew slowly. ■ Analyze the establishment and growth of the 13 English colonies. ■ Understand why Europeans competed for power in North America and how their struggle affected Native Americans. **Focus Question** *How did European struggles for power shape the North American continent?*	**All in One Teaching Resources, Unit 1** Outline Map: Claims in the Americas in the 1700s, p. 54 Outline Map: North America in 1763, p. 55 Geography Quiz, p. 56 Section 3 Quiz, p. 44 **Reading and Note Taking Study Guide** Note Taking Study Guide, p. 57 Section 3 Summary, p. 58 **Note Taking Transparencies**, 125 **WITNESS HISTORY Audio CD** A Piece of the Past **Progress Monitoring Transparencies**, 64 **Color Transparencies**, 91	**L1 Adapted Reading and Note Taking Study Guide** Note Taking Study Guide, p. 57 SN Section 3 Summary, p. 58 SN **L2 Adapted Reading and Note Taking Study Guide** Note Taking Study Guide, p. 57 LPR Section 3 Summary, p. 58 LPR **L4 Differentiated Instruction Activity,** Teacher's Edition, p. 121 AR, GT	**Differentiated Instruction Activity,** Teacher's Edition, p. 123 SN **Spanish Reading and Note Taking Study Guide** Note Taking Study Guide, p. 57 ELL Section 3 Summary, p. 58 ELL **Differentiated Instruction Activity,** Teacher's Edition, p. 123 LPR, ELL **Extend Activity,** Teacher's Edition, p. 124 AR, GT
Section 4 *The Atlantic Slave Trade* ⏱ **2 periods, 1 block** **OBJECTIVES** ■ Explain how triangular trade worked. ■ Understand the nature of the Middle Passage and describe its effects. ■ Analyze the impact of the Atlantic slave trade. **Focus Question** *How did the Atlantic slave trade shape the lives and economies of Africans and Europeans?*	**All in One Teaching Resources, Unit 1** Section 4 Quiz, p. 45 **Reading and Note Taking Study Guide** Note Taking Study Guide, p. 59 Section 4 Summary, p. 60 **Note Taking Transparencies**, 126 **WITNESS HISTORY Audio CD** Forced Into Slavery **Progress Monitoring Transparencies**, 65 **Witness History Discovery School™** video program, *The Atlantic Slave Trade*	**L1 Adapted Reading and Note Taking Study Guide** Note Taking Study Guide, p. 59 SN Section 4 Summary, p. 60 SN **L2 Adapted Reading and Note Taking Study Guide** Note Taking Study Guide, p. 59 LPR Section 4 Summary, p. 60 LPR **L4 All in One Teaching Resources, Unit 1** Biography: Joseph Cinque, p. 53 AR, GT	**Differentiated Instruction Activity,** Teacher's Edition, p. 127 SN **Spanish Reading and Note Taking Study Guide** Note Taking Study Guide, p. 59 ELL Section 4 Summary, p. 60 ELL **Differentiated Instruction Activity,** Teacher's Edition, p. 127 LPR, ELL **Extend Activity,** Teacher's Edition, p. 128 AR, GT
Section 5 *Effects of Global Contact* ⏱ **1.5 periods, .75 block** **OBJECTIVES** ■ Explain how European exploration led to the Columbian Exchange. ■ Analyze the commercial revolution. ■ Understand the impact that mercantilism had on European and colonial economies. **Focus Question** *How did the voyages of European explorers lead to new economic systems of Europe and its colonies?*	**All in One Teaching Resources, Unit 1** Section 5 Quiz, p. 46 **Reading and Note Taking Study Guide** Note Taking Study Guide, p. 61 Section 5 Summary, p. 62 Concept Connector, pp. 242, 259, 262, 267, 300 **Note Taking Transparencies**, 127A, 127B **WITNESS HISTORY Audio CD** Uniting the World **Progress Monitoring Transparencies**, 66 **Color Transparencies**, 92, 94	**L1 Adapted Reading and Note Taking Study Guide** Note Taking Study Guide, p. 61 SN Section 5 Summary, p. 62 SN Concept Connector, pp. 242, 259, 262, 267, 300 SN **L2 Adapted Reading and Note Taking Study Guide** Note Taking Study Guide, p. 61 LPR Section 5 Summary, p. 62 LPR Concept Connector, pp. 242, 259, 262, 267, 300 LPR **L4 Extend Activity,** Teacher's Edition, p. 133 AR, GT	**Differentiated Instruction Activity,** Teacher's Edition, pp. 131, 134 SN **Spanish Reading and Note Taking Study Guide** Note Taking Study Guide, p. 61 ELL Section 5 Summary, p. 62 ELL Concept Connector, pp. 242, 259, 262, 267, 300 ELL **Differentiated Instruction Activity,** Teacher's Edition, pp. 131, 134 LPR, ELL

Author's Notes

The Western Predominance

The degree of global sovereignty exercised by Western people at this point in history remains debatable. . . . Many historians detect a systematic European global dominance emerging over these early centuries. Other scholars, however, emphasize the much greater degree of western power achieved during the second great wave of imperial conquest in the 1800s and early 1900s.

Between 1500 and 1800, these specialists assert, most non-Western peoples were still little affected by the long reach of Western ships and guns, soldiers, traders, and missionaries. The millions of Native Americans and Africans who became subjects or slaves of Europeans after 1500 would certainly have disagreed

with this view. But European intercontinental empires would in fact impact many more peoples during the New Imperialism of the nineteenth and twentieth centuries, when Western predominance turned almost all of Africa and most of Asia into Western colonies, protectorates, or spheres of influence. . . .

The global power balance, however, did shift dramatically between 1500 and 1800. In 1500 the most powerful nation in the world was certainly China. The most dynamic expanding culture was probably that of the Muslim center of Eurasia. In Africa and the Americas, independent centers of empire were developing in the Western Sudan, Mexico, and Peru. Pluralism prevailed, and Europe was by no means the greatest of world civilizations.

As 1800 approached, all this had clearly changed. European power had destroyed the American empires, and the African kingdoms had declined in a welter of wars and slave trading. The Western nations, meanwhile, had repulsed and outflanked the Islamic lands, pushed into an Indian Ocean formerly dominated by Muslim traders, and replaced Muslim power in Southeast Asia with European power. The rulers of India were being slowly sucked into the maw of European dependency. Everywhere except East Asia, the weight of Western political predominance was being felt as the eighteenth century drew to a close.

—Anthony Esler, *The Human Venture From Prehistory to the Present*, (Upper Saddle River, New Jersey: Pearson Education, 2004), pp. 468–469

Extend Online

Pizarro and the Incas

Have students research Francisco Pizarro's conquest of the Inca empire in Peru. Ask them to write an eyewitness account from the perspective of the Inca. Use the steps below to complete the activity.

Prepare for the Activity Tell students that when Pizarro set out to explore the land that is now Peru, he experienced years of disappointment and disaster. When his second expedition ran into trouble, the governor sent ships to retrieve his men. However, Pizarro was determined to continue his exploration. He drew a line in the sand and asked his group to stay with him. Thirteen men joined him. Later, when they fought the Inca empire, they were aided by such factors as cultural misunderstandings and disease.

Conduct the Activity For help in starting the activity, send students to **Web Code nbe-1501,** where students will read the dramatic story of Pizarro and Peru. They will read primary sources and a chronological account of Pizarro's conquest. Ask students to list the reasons Pizarro defeated the Inca. Then have students write a narrative of the conquest from the viewpoint of the Inca, focusing on one section of the chronology. Be sure students highlight at least one of the factors from their lists. Then have students share their eyewitness accounts with the class.

Follow-Up Conduct a class discussion based on the following questions: What events might have changed if the outcome had been different? What were the primary motivations for the Spanish conquistadors? Which factor was most significant in influencing the outcome? What other events might have changed if the outcome had been different?

WITNESS HISTORY 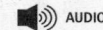 AUDIO

A Heavenly City

By the 1400s, the Aztec city of Tenochtitlán was one of the largest and most well-planned cities in the world. Aztec wealth had provided clean streets, beautiful gardens, and overflowing storehouses. An Aztec poem written in the early 1500s expressed the writer's pride in the great city:

66Proudly stands the city of Mexico— Tenochtitlán.
Here no one fears to die in war . . .
Keep this in mind, oh princes . . .
Who could attack Tenochtitlán?
Who could shake the foundation of heaven?99

Just a few years after this poem was written, Tenochtitlán would fall to an unknown invader from far away. Listen to the Witness History audio to hear more about the end of the Aztec empire.

◀ Contemporary Mexican artist Diego Rivera depicts the Totonacs, Indians who were conquered by the Aztecs and later joined the Spanish.

Aztec feather shield made during the time of Moctezuma

Chapter Preview

Chapter Focus Question How did European colonization of the Americas shape global economies and societies?

Section 1
Conquest in the Americas

Section 2
Spanish and Portuguese Colonies in the Americas

Section 3
Struggle for North America

Section 4
The Atlantic Slave Trade

Section 5
Effects of Global Contact

Use the ☑ **Quick Study Timeline** at the end of this chapter to preview chapter events.

Portuguese colonial carving made from brazilwood

Canadian powder horn showing fur trading routes

② Concept Connector ONLINE

To explore Essential Questions related to this chapter, go to PHSchool.com
Web Code: nbd-1507

Chapter-Level Resources

All in One Vocabulary Builder; Reading Strategy; Enrichments; Outline Maps; Geography Quiz; Chapter Test
■ Document-Based Assessments
■ AYP Monitoring Assessments
■ *ExamView* Test Bank CD-ROM
■ Guided Reading Audio (Spanish)
■ Student Edition Audio

Previewing the Chapter

■ **WITNESS HISTORY** Point out that when Europeans first arrived in North America, the continent was already occupied by diverse groups of Native Americans with different cultures, languages, and societies. Read the Witness History selection aloud or play the accompanying audio. Ask **What do the selection and the poem tell you about Tenochtitlán and the people who founded it?** *(The Aztecs must have been a powerful, wealthy people. The poem suggests that they were well aware of their success, almost to the point of arrogance.)* Have students predict the impact of European voyages on the culture, economy, government, technology, and geography of the peoples of the Americas.

🔊 AUDIO **Witness History Audio CD,** A Heavenly City

■ **Analyzing the Visuals** Ask students to describe the scene shown in the painting. Ask **What clues does the painting offer about Totonac society?** *(Sample: They were wealthy, judging from the elaborate costumes and architecture; religion and rituals were important to them, judging from the temples and the people dancing.)*

■ **Focus** Write the Chapter Focus Question on the board. Tell students to keep this question in mind as they read the chapter. *(Answer appears with Chapter Assessment answers.)* Have students preview the section titles for this chapter.

Note Taking Study Guide With Concept Connector Journal
For online access: Web code: nbd-1507
For print alternative: Reading and Note Taking Study Guide booklet

Objectives

As you teach this section, keep students focused on the following objectives to help them answer the Section Focus Question and master core content.

- Analyze the results of the first encounters between the Spanish and Native Americans.

- Explain how Cortés and Pizarro gained control of the Aztec and Incan empires.

- Understand the short-term and long-term effects of the Spanish on the peoples of the Americas.

Prepare to Read

Build Background Knowledge ⓛ

Ask students to recall interactions between Europeans, Africans, and Asians. Have them predict what the pattern of interaction would be between Europeans and peoples of the Americas.

Set a Purpose ⓛ

- **WITNESS HISTORY** Read the selection aloud or play the audio. Ask **What is the main idea of this passage?** *(The messengers' report of unusual newcomers fills Moctezuma with fear.)*

  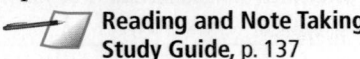 AUDIO **Witness History Audio CD,** Moctezuma Hears Strange News

- **Focus** Point out the Section Focus Question and write it on the board. Tell students to refer to this question as they read. *(Answer appears with Section 1 Assessment answers.)*

- **Preview** Have students preview the Section Objectives and the list of Terms, People, and Places.

- **Reading Skill** Have students use the *Reading Strategy: Recognize Sequence* worksheet.

  All in One Teaching Resources, Unit 1, p. 48

- **Note Taking** Have students read this section using the Structured Read Aloud strategy (TE, p. T20). As they read, have students fill in the chart sequencing Spain's actions in the Americas.

  Reading and Note Taking Study Guide, p. 137

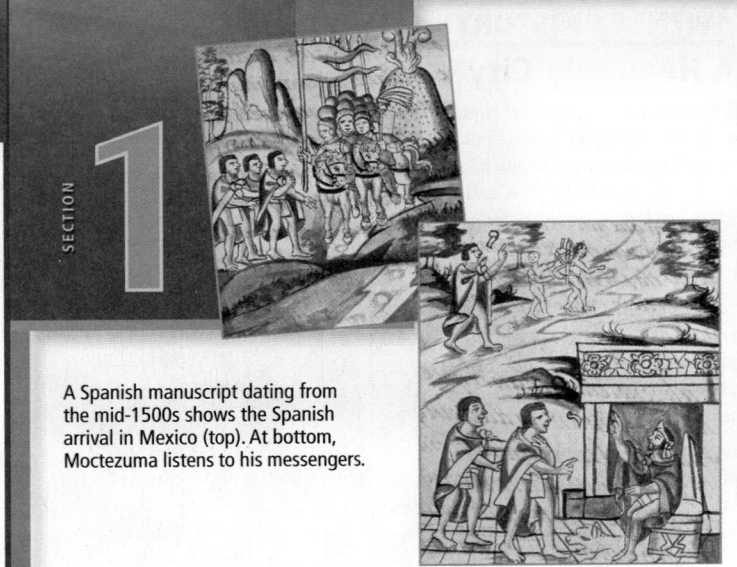

A Spanish manuscript dating from the mid-1500s shows the Spanish arrival in Mexico (top). At bottom, Moctezuma listens to his messengers.

SECTION 1

WITNESS HISTORY ⏴⏵ AUDIO

Moctezuma Hears Strange News

In 1519, the Aztec ruler Moctezuma heard an astounding report from his messengers. They described unusual people who had just arrived in the region—people with white skin and yellow hair, clad completely in iron, who rode "deer" as tall as a house and had dogs with burning yellow eyes. According to a Spanish translation of native accounts, "When Moctezuma heard this, he was filled with terror. It was as if his heart grew faint, as it shrank; he was overcome by despair."

Focus Question How did a small number of Spanish conquistadors conquer huge Native American empires?

Conquest in the Americas

Objectives

- Analyze the results of the first encounters between the Spanish and Native Americans.
- Explain how Cortés and Pizarro gained control of the Aztec and Incan empires.
- Understand the short-term and long-term effects of the Spanish on the peoples of the Americas.

Terms, People, and Places

conquistador	alliance
immunity	Moctezuma
Hernán Cortés	Francisco Pizarro
Tenochtitlán	civil war
Malinche	

Note Taking

Reading Skill: Recognize Sequence Keep track of the sequence of events that led to European empires in the Americas by completing a chart like the one below.

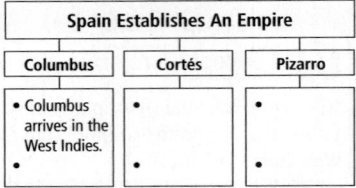

Spain Establishes An Empire		
Columbus	**Cortés**	**Pizarro**
• Columbus arrives in the West Indies. •	• •	• •

In 1492, explorer Christopher Columbus landed in the Caribbean islands that are now called the West Indies. The wave of exploration he spurred in the Americas would have drastic, far-reaching consequences for the people who already lived there.

First Encounters in the Americas

Columbus's first meeting with Native Americans began a cycle of encounter, conquest, and death that would be repeated throughout the Western Hemisphere.

Meeting the Taínos When Columbus first arrived in the West Indies, he encountered the Taíno (TY noh) people. The Taínos lived in villages and grew corn, yams, and cotton, which they wove into cloth. They were friendly and open toward the Spanish. Columbus noted that they were "generous with what they have, to such a degree as no one would believe but he who had seen it."

Despite this friendly reception, the Spanish treated the Taíno harshly. Columbus's men assaulted Taíno men and women, claimed their land for Spain, and seized some to take back to the Spanish king. The Spanish killed any Taínos who dared to resist. Columbus later required each Taíno to give him a set amount of gold. Any Taíno who failed to deliver was tortured or killed.

Columbus's encounter was repeated by a wave of Spanish **conquistadors** (kahn KEES tuh dawrz), or conquerors, who soon arrived in the Americas. They first settled on the islands of Hispaniola (now the Dominican Republic and Haiti), Cuba, and Puerto Rico.

Vocabulary Builder

Use the information below and the following resources to teach the high-use word from this section.
All in One Teaching Resources, Unit 1 p. 47; **Teaching Resources, Skills Handbook,** p. 3

High-Use Word	Definition and Sample Sentence
compel, p. 110	*v.* to force The bailiff **compelled** the witness to leave the courtroom.

Throughout the region, the conquistadors seized the Native Americans' gold ornaments and then made them pan for more gold. At the same time, the Spanish forced the Native Americans to convert to Christianity.

Guns, Horses, and Disease Although Spanish conquistadors only numbered in the hundreds as compared to millions of Native Americans, they had many advantages. Their guns and cannons were superior to the Native Americans' arrows and spears, and European metal armor provided them with better protection. They also had horses, which not only were useful in battle and in carrying supplies, but also frightened the Native Americans, who had never seen a horse.

Most importantly, an invisible invader—disease—helped the conquistadors take control of the Taínos and other Native Americans. Europeans unknowingly carried diseases such as smallpox, measles, and influenza to which Native Americans had no **immunity**, or resistance. These diseases spread rapidly and wiped out village after village. As a result, the Native American population of the Caribbean islands declined by as much as 90 percent in the 1500s. Millions of Native Americans died from disease as Europeans made their way inland.

✓ **Checkpoint** How did Spanish conquistadors treat the Taínos?

Cortés Conquers Mexico

From the Caribbean, Spanish explorers probed the coasts of the Americas. They spread stories of empires rich in gold, but they also told of fierce fighting people. Attracted by the promise of riches as well as by religious zeal, a flood of adventurers soon followed.

Cortés Advances on the Aztecs Among the earliest conquistadors was Hernán Cortés. Cortés, a landowner in Cuba, heard of Spanish expeditions that had been repelled by Indians. He believed that he could succeed where none had before. In 1519, he landed on the coast of Mexico with about 600 men, 16 horses, and a few cannons. He began an inland trek toward Tenochtitlán (teh nawch tee TLAHN), the capital of the Aztec empire. A young Indian woman named Malinche (mah LEEN chay), called Doña Marina by the Spanish, served as his translator and advisor. Malinche knew both the Maya and Aztec languages, and she learned Spanish quickly.

Malinche told Cortés that the Aztecs had gained power by conquering other groups of people. The Aztecs sacrificed thousands of their captives to the Aztec gods each year. Many conquered peoples hated their Aztec overlords, so Malinche helped Cortés arrange **alliances** with them. They agreed to help Cortés fight the Aztecs.

Moctezuma Faces a Dilemma Meanwhile, messengers brought word about the Spanish to the Aztec emperor Moctezuma (mahk tih ZOO muh). Terrified, he wondered if the leader of the pale-skinned, bearded strangers might be Quetzalcoatl (ket sahl koh AHT el), an Aztec god-king who had long ago vowed to return from the east. Because Moctezuma did not know for sure if Cortés was a god, he did not know how to respond to the news. He sent gifts of turquoise, feathers, and other goods with religious importance, but urged the strangers not to continue to Tenochtitlán.

Cortés, however, had no intention of turning back. He was not interested in the Aztec religious objects, but was extremely interested in the gold and silver ornaments that Moctezuma began sending him.

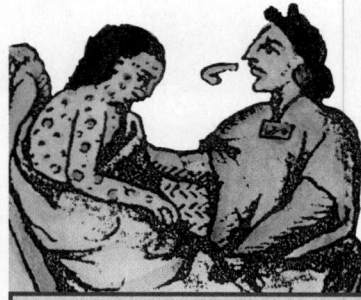

This passage from a Maya book written in the 1500s describes life before the arrival of the Spanish. What does the writer say was the main effect of Europeans on the Maya?

Primary Source AUDIO

❝ There was then no sickness;
They had then no aching bones;
They had then no high fever;
They had then no smallpox;
They had then no burning chest. . .
At that time the course of humanity was orderly.
The foreigners made it otherwise when they arrived here.❞

Malinche Shapes History
Malinche's parents sold her as a slave when she was a child, believing that she was born under an unlucky star. Despite her unfortunate beginning, she left a major mark on the history of the Americas.

Teach

First Encounters in the Americas L3

Instruct

■ **Introduce: Key Terms** Have students find the key term *conquistadors* (in blue) in the text and explain its meaning. Explain that these explorers and treasure-hunters conquered vast areas of land in the Americas for Spain, enslaving and killing Native Americans and plundering their wealth.

■ **Teach** Discuss the first encounters between conquistadors and Native Americans. Ask **What advantages did the Spanish have over Native Americans?** (*Though there were more Native Americans, the Spanish had guns and cannons that were superior to Native American arrows and spears; they used horses in battle and for labor; and they were immune to the diseases they brought.*) **What might the Taínos and other Native Americans have done differently to defend themselves against the conquistadors?** (*Students might suggest Native Americans could have been less trusting of newcomers, could have sought help from other Native Americans, and so on.*)

Independent Practice

Primary Source To help students better understand the Spanish conquest of the Aztecs, have them read the selection *Massacre in the Temple of Tenochtitlán* and complete the worksheet.

All in One Teaching Resources, Unit 1, p. 51

Monitor Progress

As students fill in their charts, circulate to make sure they understand how Europeans built American empires. For a completed version of the chart, see

📖 **Note Taking Transparencies**, 123

Differentiated
Instruction Solutions for All Learners

L1 Special Needs **L2 Less Proficient Readers**

Have students suppose that they came upon a lost Incan tribe in the rainforests of South America. Have students draw or write a story of their interaction with the tribe. Could they successfully communicate with the tribe? How so? How would the tribe respond to them? What would the likely condition of the tribe be in one year? In 50 years? In another 500 years?

L2 English Language Learners

Use the following resources to help students acquire basic skills:

 Adapted Reading and Note Taking Study Guide

■ Adapted Note Taking Study Guide, p. 137
■ Adapted Section Summary, p. 138

Answers

PRIMARY SOURCE They brought disease to the Maya.

✓ as inferiors

Cortés Conquers Mexico ⑬

Instruct

■ **Introduce: Vocabulary Builder**
Have students read the Vocabulary term and definition. Point out that Cortés used Moctezuma's fear that he might be a god, as well as the support of other Native American peoples who hated the Aztecs, to ***compel*** Moctezuma to give Aztec land and treasure to the Spanish. Use the Idea Wave strategy (TE, p. T22) and ask students to list other tactics that people use to ***compel*** others to do something.

■ **Teach** Explain how and why Cortés conquered the Aztecs. Ask **What motivated non-Aztec Native Americans to help Cortés fight the Aztecs?** *(The Aztecs conquered neighboring peoples and sacrificed thousands from those groups to their gods.)* **What conditions prevented Cortés from defeating the Aztecs in 1519, but enabled him to prevail in 1521?** *(In 1519, competing conquistadors arrived and in the fighting that followed, half the Spanish died. By 1521, European diseases had killed many Aztecs, allowing Cortés's brutal assault to succeed.)*

■ **Analyzing the Visuals** Direct students to the visuals in the Traveler's Tales feature on this page. Have students describe the city of Tenochtitlán, including its location, grid-like layout, great plaza with temple, and so on. Then display **Color Transparency 93: Templo Mayor,** which shows the religious and political center of the Aztec Empire. Ask students how the Spanish might have felt upon seeing it.
🏛 **Color Transparencies,** 93

Independent Practice

Traveler's Tales To extend students' understanding of the conquest of Mexico, have them read the selection *Bernal Díaz and the Conquest of New Spain* and complete the worksheet.

All in One **Teaching Resources, Unit 1,** p. 52

Monitor Progress

Check that students' responses on the worksheet reflect a solid understanding of the Traveler's Tales enrichment selection.

Answer

✓ They believed that Cortés might be one of their gods, and therefore were more welcoming than they might have been otherwise.

Traveler's Tales
EYEWITNESS ACCOUNT

Díaz Sets the Record Straight

Bernal Díaz del Castillo was a Spanish soldier who came to Cuba in 1514. In 1519, he accompanied Hernán Cortés on his conquest of the Aztecs. More than 40 years later, Díaz wrote his *True History* because he felt other accounts of the conquest—written by historians who had not been there—were inaccurate. He insisted that as an eyewitness of events he was a better historical source. For example, Díaz was there when Moctezuma took Cortés to the top of the great temple to look at Tenochtitlán, his magnificent capital city on the lake.

Vocabulary Builder
compel—(kum PEL) *v.* to force

Cortés became more determined than ever to reach Tenochtitlán. Fighting and negotiating by turns, Cortés led his forces inland toward the capital. At last, the Spanish arrived in Tenochtitlán, where they were dazzled by the grandeur of the city.

Tenochtitlán Falls to the Spanish Moctezuma welcomed Cortés to his capital. However, relations between the Aztecs and Spaniards soon grew strained. The Spanish scorned the Aztecs' religion and sought to convert them to Christianity. At the same time, as they remained in the city, they saw more of the Aztec treasure. They decided to imprison Moctezuma so they could gain control of the Aztecs and their riches.

Cortés compelled Moctezuma to sign over his land and treasure to the Spanish. In the meantime, a new force of Spanish conquistadors had arrived on the coast to challenge Cortés. In the confusion that followed—with various groups of Spanish, Aztecs, and Native Americans all fighting for control—the Aztecs drove the Spanish from the city. More than half of the Spanish were killed in the fighting, as was Moctezuma.

Cortés retreated to plan an assault. In 1521, in a brutal struggle, Cortés and his Indian allies captured and demolished Tenochtitlán. The Spanish later built Mexico City on the ruins of Tenochtitlán. As in the Caribbean, disease had aided their cause. Smallpox had spread among the Aztecs from the 1519 encounter, decimating the population.

✓ **Checkpoint** What impact did the Aztecs' religious beliefs have on Cortés's approach to Tenochtitlán?

Differentiated Instruction   Solutions for All Learners

L4 Advanced Readers   **L4 Gifted and Talented**

To challenge students, ask them to identify the knowledge that Moctezuma and his successors would have needed in order to better defend the Aztec empire against Cortés *(e.g. Cortés was not a god; he would kill for riches; his troops were carriers of deadly disease, and so on).* Have them also consider how

Moctezuma might have obtained this knowledge. Then have students write a short scenario in which Moctezuma is able to thwart the advances of the Spanish. Ask volunteers to read their scenarios to the class.

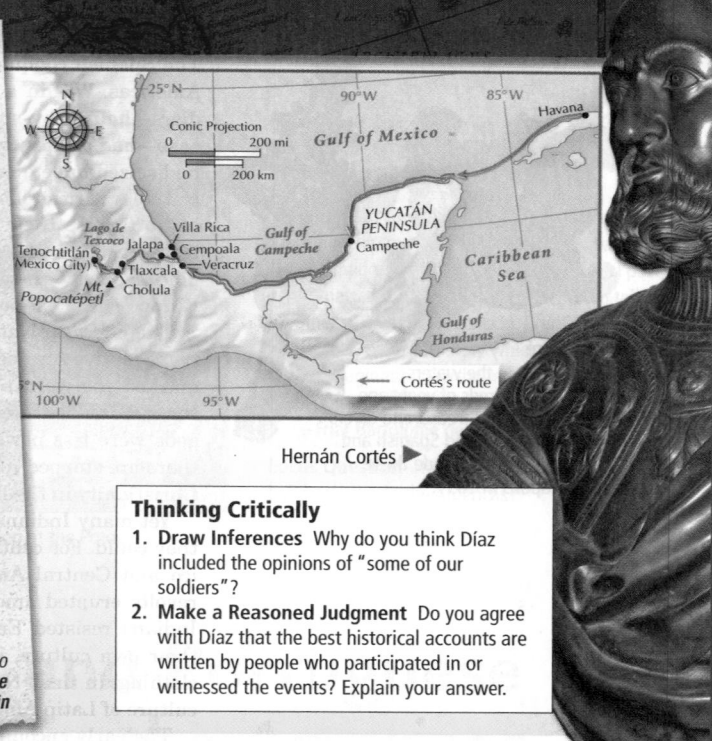

> "When we saw so all those cities and villages built in the water, and other great towns on dry land, and that straight and level causeway leading toward [Tenochtitlán], we were astounded. These great towns and [pyramids] and buildings rising from the water, all made of stone, seemed like an enchanted vision... Indeed, some of our soldiers asked whether it was not all a dream.... It was all so wonderful that I do not know how to describe this first glimpse of things never heard of, seen or dreamed of before."

> "We turned back to the great market and the swarm of people buying and selling. The mere murmur of their voices was loud enough to be heard more than three miles away. Some of our soldiers who had been in many parts of the world, in Constantinople, in Rome, and all over Italy, said that they had never seen a market so well laid out, so large, so orderly, and so filled with people."

— *Bernal Díaz del Castillo*
from *The True History of the Conquest of New Spain*

Hernán Cortés ▶

Thinking Critically

1. **Draw Inferences** Why do you think Díaz included the opinions of "some of our soldiers"?
2. **Make a Reasoned Judgment** Do you agree with Díaz that the best historical accounts are written by people who participated in or witnessed the events? Explain your answer.

Pizarro Takes Peru

Cortés's success inspired other adventurers, among them Spaniard **Francisco Pizarro** (pee SAHR oh). Pizarro was interested in Peru's Inca empire, which was reputed to have even more riches than the Aztecs. Pizarro arrived in Peru in 1532, just after the Incan ruler Atahualpa (ah tah WAHL puh) had won the throne from his brother in a bloody **civil war.** A civil war is fought between groups of people in the same nation.

Pizarro's secretary described Atahualpa as

Primary Source

> "a man of thirty years, good-looking and poised, somewhat stout, with a wide, handsome, and ferocious face, and the eyes flaming with blood . . ."
> —Francisco de Xerez

Atahualpa refused to become a Spanish vassal or convert to Christianity. In response, Pizarro, aided by Indian allies, captured him and slaughtered thousands of Inca. The Spanish demanded a huge ransom for the ruler. The Inca paid it, but the Spanish killed Atahualpa anyway.

Despite continuing resistance, Pizarro and his followers overran the Incan heartland. He had superior weapons, and the Inca were weakened by European diseases. From Peru, Spanish forces surged across Ecuador and Chile. Before long, Spain had added much of South America to its growing empire. Pizarro himself was killed by a rival Spanish faction a few years after he established the city of Lima.

✔ **Checkpoint** What factors encouraged Spanish success in Peru?

History Background

La Malinche Also known as Doña Marina, La Malinche was the daughter of Aztec nobles. Her mother sold her into slavery as a young girl; eventually, she and 19 other slaves were given to Cortés when he arrived in the Yucatan.

Cortés had been relying on a Spanish priest who spoke Mayan to interpret for him, but the priest could not speak the Aztec language. Malinche could. She spoke various Mayan dialects along with her native Aztec language and quickly learned Spanish. Her work as Cortés interpreter helped save thousands of lives since it allowed him to negotiate rather than fight. He acknowledged the tremendous contribution she made when he wrote: "After God, we owe this conquest of New Spain to Doña Marina."

Pizarro Takes Peru/ Effects of the Spanish Conquistadors   **L3**

Instruct

■ **Introduce** Display **Color Transparency 90: Inca Shirt.** Use the lesson suggested in the transparency book to guide a discussion about Incan culture.
  📖 **Color Transparencies,** 90

■ **Teach** Discuss Pizarro's conquest of the Inca and the broader effects of the Spanish conquest of the Americas. Ask students to **Compare and contrast Pizarro's conquest of the Inca to Cortés's conquest of the Aztec.** *(Like Cortés, Indian allies, superior weapons, and European disease aided Pizarro's success. Unlike Cortés, Pizarro's efforts followed a bloody civil war that probably weakened the Incas.)* **In what way did the Spanish conquest affect Native Americans who survived?** *(They were demoralized and hopeless. Their cultures and ways of life were often destroyed.)*

■ **Quick Activity** Display **Color Transparency 89: The Americas.** Use the lesson suggested in the transparency book to guide a discussion.
  📖 **Color Transparencies,** 89

Independent Practice

Primary Source To extend students' understanding of the impact of the Spanish conquest of the Americas on Native Americans, have them read the selection *The Broken Spears* and complete the worksheet.

All in One Teaching Resources, Unit 1, p. 49

Monitor Progress

Check Reading and Note Taking Study Guide entries for student understanding.

Answers

✔ the Inca civil war, Indian allies, superior weapons, and disease

Thinking Critically

1. Díaz's account gained credibility by stating that a number of his soldiers who had traveled to the great capitals of the world felt that Tenochtitlán was truly remarkable.
2. Sample: Firsthand accounts of events provide authenticity, but histories by people who read and synthesize a variety of firsthand accounts can provide a broader view.

Quick Study Guide

- Have students use the Quick Study Guide to prepare for this chapter's tests. Students may wish to refer to the following pages as they review:

Key Elements of Europe's Commercial Revolution
Section 5, pp. 130–133

Triangular Trade Routes
Section 4, pp. 125–127

Major European Settlements/Colonies in the Americas
Section 1, pp. 111–113; Section 2, p. 119; Section 3, pp. 120–122

The Native American Population Declines
Section 1, pp. 111–112, 114; Section 2, pp. 116, 119

Europe and the Americas, 1492–1750
Section 1, pp. 110–114; Section 2, pp. 115–119; Section 3, pp. 120–124; Section 4, pp. 125–128; Section 5, pp. 129–133

- For additional review, remind students to refer to the **L3**

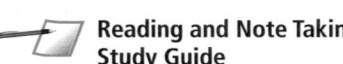 **Reading and Note Taking Study Guide**
Note Taking Study Guide, pp. 137, 139, 141, 143, 145
Section Summaries, pp. 138, 140, 142, 144, 146

- Have students access **Web Code nbp-1561** for this chapter's **History Interactive** timeline, which includes expanded entries and additional events.

- If students need more instruction on analyzing timelines, have them read the **Skills Handbook,** p. SH30.

- When students have completed their study of the chapter, distribute Chapter Tests A and B.

All in One Teaching Resources, Unit 1, pp. 42–47

> For **Progress Monitoring Online,** refer students to the Self-test with vocabulary practice at **Web Code nba-1561.**

Quick Study Guide

Progress Monitoring Online
For: Self-test with vocabulary practice
Web Code: nba-1561

■ Key Elements of Europe's Commercial Revolution

- **Columbian Exchange** Foods, ideas, technologies, and diseases are exchanged between the hemispheres, resulting in population growth.
- **Inflation** Rising prices occur along with an increase in the money supply.
- **Price Revolution** Rising prices are coupled with inflation.
- **Capitalism** People invest money to make a profit.
- **Mercantilism** European countries adopt mercantilist policies—such as establishing colonies, increasing exports, and limiting imports—to compete for trade and empire.

■ Triangular Trade Routes

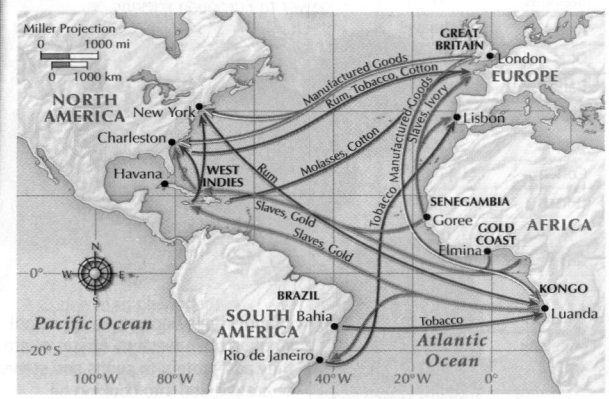

■ Major European Settlements/Colonies in the Americas

Date	Region Settled	Country	Purpose
1520s	Mexico	Spain	Find gold
1530s	Peru	Spain	Find gold
1530s	Brazil	Portugal	Establish settlements and plantations
Early 1500s	New France (eastern Canada)	France	Take part in fur trade and fishing
Early 1600s	13 colonies (present-day eastern United States)	England	Various reasons including establishing settlements and escaping religious persecution

■ The Native American Population Declines

Native American Population of Central Mexico

SOURCE: Nicolás Sánchez-Albornoz, *The Population of Latin America*

■ Europe and the Americas, 1492–1750

	1492 Columbus lands in the Americas.	1521 Cortés completes conquest of the Aztecs.	1530s Cartier explores the St. Lawrence River, claiming eastern Canada for France.	1607 British colonists found Jamestown, Virginia.

Chapter Events / Global Events

1500 — **1550** — **1600**

1498 Portuguese explorer da Gama rounds Africa and reaches India.

1526 The Mughal dynasty is founded in India.

Differentiated Instruction Solutions for All Learners

L1 Special Needs **L2 Less Proficient Readers**
For students acquiring basic skills:

Adapted Reading and Note Taking Study Guide
Adapted Note Taking Study Guide, pp. 137, 139, 141, 143, 145
Adapted Section Summaries, pp. 138, 140, 142, 144, 146

L2 English Language Learners
For Spanish-speaking students:

Spanish Reading and Note Taking Study Guide
Spanish Note Taking Study Guide, pp. 137, 139, 141, 143, 145
Adapted Section Summaries, pp. 138, 140, 142, 144, 146

Concept Connector

 Essential Question Review

To connect prior knowledge with what you have learned in this chapter, answer the questions below in your Concept Connector journal. Use the journal in the Reading and Note Taking Study Guide to record your answers (or go to www.phschool.com Web Code: nbd-1507). In addition, record information about the following concepts:

- Cooperation: Moctezuma welcomes Cortes and his men; Malinche helps the Spaniards
- Genocide: Native Americans

1. **Empire** Compare the establishment of the Spanish empire in the Americas with the establishment of the English empire in the Americas. Note similarities and differences in the following.
   - political systems
   - economic systems
   - religion
   - effects on the Native American population.

2. **Trade** The transatlantic slave trade expanded greatly between 1500 and 1800. Although some people reaped enormous profits from the slave trade, it resulted in disasters that went beyond the horrors of the Middle Passage. Who benefited most from slavery and why? What were some of the unintended consequences of the slave trade for African states and societies? How have the consequences of the slave trade influenced world history?

3. **Economic Systems** In the Middle Ages, wealth was based on the manorial system in which peasants worked on land owned by nobles. Following the Commercial Revolution, European nations adopted a policy of mercantilism to build their wealth and power.
   - How did mercantilism change the source and distribution of wealth in European society?

■ **Connections to Today**

1. **Cultural Diffusion** During the Columbian Exchange, people were exposed to goods, ideas, and diseases that changed their lives forever. Many of these exchanges were positive, such as the introduction of the horse to the Americas. Some were negative, such as the introduction of European diseases to the Americas. Think about similar exchanges that have happened in recent times. Research and write about a positive exchange and a negative exchange. To direct your research, consider topics such as disease, new technology, the introduction of fish or animals into non-native regions, and the availability of new foods.

2. **Trade** Throughout history, people and governments have worked to establish profitable trade methods. Some very successful trade methods have had terrible consequences for other people. Consider how Europe's commercial revolution was achieved in large part because of the Atlantic slave trade. Then think about trade practices today that, though profitable, might hurt some people. Write two to three paragraphs describing the pros and cons of modern trade practices. Consider the following:
   - trade pacts like NAFTA
   - voluntary labeling of products such as Fair Trade
   - practices such as child labor

1619
First cargo of African slaves arrives in Virginia.

1750s
Olaudah Equiano writes a book about his experiences during the Atlantic slave trade.

1763
The Treaty of Paris is signed, ending the French and Indian War.

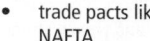

1650 **1700** **1750**

History Interactive
For: Interactive timeline
Web Code: nbp-1561

1630s
Japan bars foreign merchants from the country.

1687
Englishman Isaac Newton publishes his book explaining the laws of gravity.

1735
The reign of Chinese emperor Qianlong begins.

Concept Connector

Tell students that the main concepts for this chapter are Empire, Trade, Genocide, and Economic Systems, and then ask them to answer the Essential Question Review questions on this page. Discuss the Connections to Today topics and ask students to answer the questions that follow.

Essential Question Review

1. Students should go back to the chapters to locate information on the political and economic systems, religion, and the effects on the Native Americans in each conquest. With this information, they should be able to make comparisons between the two empires.

2. The slave trade made the merchants and traders extremely wealthy, and provided labor that helped colonial economies to expand. The lives of individual Africans were destroyed or cut short, and entire African societies were ruined.

3. Mercantilism took power and wealth away from the nobles who lost out when investment shifted from land to overseas ventures. Merchants who invested abroad acquired resources and became more powerful. The middle class developed and expanded, while poverty increased among laborers.

Connections to Today

1. Student research should be supported with specific examples and details.

2. Samples: Trade pacts can facilitate trade and lower prices but can also cause the loss of jobs; product labeling can affect consumers' buying habits; practices such as child labor can allow businesses to cut costs, but damage people's lives.

For additional review of this **L3** chapter's core concepts, remind students to refer to the

 Reading and Note Taking Study Guide
Concept Connector, pp. 242, 259, 262, 267, 300

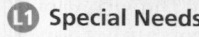

Chapter Assessment

Terms, People, and Places
1. encomienda   4. privateer
2. revenue   5. immunity
3. inflation   6. mutiny

Main Ideas

7. They conquered societies of great wealth, plundered them, and set the stage for colonization and more profits based on the labor of those they conquered or enslaved.

8. It decimated the Native American population through deadly diseases, killing, and brutalization of Indian workers.

9. Spain divided up its empire into provinces and set up the Council of the Indies to oversee its viceroys in the provinces. They in turn oversaw local officials and audiencias.

10. Peninsulares, people from Spain, were at the top of the social structure, followed by creoles, or people of Spanish descent born in the Americas. Mulattoes were people of mixed African and European descent, while mestizos were of mixed Indian and European descent; these groups were in the middle. At the bottom were peons, forced to labor to pay debt, and slaves.

11. They had landed outside the jurisdiction of any government and so created a compact to govern themselves.

12. Britain gained dominance in North America, including much of present-day Canada and the United States, while France retained land in the Caribbean.

13. It devastated African society, causing the enslavement and exportation of millions of men, women, and children.

14. Merchants made large profits buying and selling slaves and the other commodities of the triangular trade. European plantation owners profited from free slave labor.

15. They stimulated European economies, creating a price revolution, inflation, and eventually new economic policies such as mercantilism.

16. It increased global trade as nations strove to produce and export more than they imported and to collect treasuries full of gold and silver.

Chapter Assessment

Terms, People, and Places

Match the following terms with the definitions listed below.

immunity	inflation
revenue	encomienda
privateer	mutiny

1. the right to demand labor from Native Americans
2. income from taxes
3. rise in prices linked to an increase in the money supply
4. pirate operating under government approval
5. resistance
6. revolt

Main Ideas

Section 1 (pp. 110–114)
7. How did the explorations of conquistadors such as Hernán Cortés and Francisco Pizarro contribute to the Spanish empire in the Americas?
8. What effect did European exploration have on Native American populations?

Section 2 (pp. 115–119)
9. How did Spain structure its American empire?
10. Write a sentence or two explaining the role of each of the following in Spanish colonial society: peon, peninsular, creole, mulatto, and mestizo.

Section 3 (pp. 120–124)
11. Why did the Pilgrims make a compact when they arrived in North America?
12. What was the result of the British and French struggle in North America?

Section 4 (pp. 125–128)
13. How did triangular trade affect Africans?
14. How did the slave trade benefit Europeans?

Section 5 (pp. 129–133)
15. What impact did American gold and silver have on European economies?
16. How did the policy of mercantilism affect global economies?

Chapter Focus Question
17. How did European colonization of the Americas shape global economies and societies?

Critical Thinking

18. **Compare Points of View** You read that many Native Americans saw the Spanish takeover as a sign that their gods were less powerful than those of the Spanish. How did the Spanish likely interpret their victory?
19. **Predict Consequences** How would society in the United States today be affected if mysterious diseases wiped out 90 percent or more of the population?
20. **Analyzing Visuals** The painting below, titled *First Landing of Columbus*, was painted in 1803. Consider what you have learned in this chapter. Do you think this painting accurately shows that event? Explain your answer.

● Writing About History

In this chapter's four Section Assessments, you developed skills for writing a compare-contrast essay.

Writing a Compare and Contrast Essay The European nations that settled the Americas all wanted wealth and empire—but went about getting them in different ways. Write a compare and contrast essay that discusses two of the European powers involved in settling the Americas. Consult page SH9 of the Writing Handbook for additional help.

Prewriting
• Choose a topic that lends itself to comparison and contrast. Possibilities include important leaders, economic goals, interactions with Native Americans, or religious goals.
• Create graphic organizers, such as tables or Venn diagrams, to help you see similarities and differences.

Drafting
• Write an introduction and a thesis statement. Your thesis statement should summarize the main points you want to make about the things you are comparing.
• Write the body text, introducing details and evidence that support your thesis statement. Organize your text by subject or by point. Then write a conclusion.

Revising
• Use the guidelines for revising your essay on page SH12 of the Writing Handbook.

17. It fostered trade and led to a global economy, and it plundered the enormous wealth and resources of the Americas and transferred them to Europe. It changed societies by making valuable foods and technologies available and by imposing European religion and culture around the globe.

Critical Thinking

18. The Spanish probably believed they were victorious because God was on their side.

19. Sample: Knowledge would be lost, disease would probably run rampant, governmental and societal institutions would break down, and the horror of the situation might breed violence; certainly there would be widespread disorder.

20. Student answers should show careful examination of the details of the painting. Answers should show an understanding that the painting shows bias in depicting the Europeans as civilized victors and the Native Americans as backward and groveling.

Document-Based Assessment

The Impact of Piracy

In 1580, Admiral Francis Drake returned to England after circumnavigating the globe. A delighted Queen Elizabeth I knighted the commander when she visited his ship, the *Golden Hind*, in 1581. The British queen had good reason to be grateful. Drake's voyage brought huge revenues to the royal treasury and dealt a blow to her enemy, King Philip II of Spain. The documents below give different views of Drake's activities.

Document A

"Passing the Straits of Magellan, untraversed as yet by any Englishman, [Drake] swept the unguarded coast of [Chile] and Peru, loaded his bark with the gold-dust and silver-ingots of Potosí, and with the pearls, emeralds, and diamonds which formed the cargo of the great galleon that sailed once a year from Lima to Cadiz. With spoils of above half-a-million in value the daring adventurer steered undauntedly for the Moluccas, rounded the Cape of Good Hope, and after completing the circuit of the globe dropped anchor again in Plymouth harbour. . . . The welcome he received from Elizabeth on his return was accepted by Philip as an outrage which could only be expiated by war. . . . She met a request for Drake's surrender by knighting the free-booter, and by wearing in her crown the jewels he had offered her as a present."

—From *A Short History of the English People* by J.R. Green

Document B

"[The Ambassador urged his king] . . . that no foreign ship be spared, in . . . the . . . Indies, but that every one should be sent to the bottom, and not a soul on board of them allowed to live. This will be the only way to prevent the English and French from going to these parts to plunder, for at present there is hardly an Englishman who is not talking of undertaking the voyage, so encouraged are they by Drake's return."

—Don Bernardino de Mendoza,
Philip II's ambassador to London, around 1580

Document C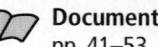

"To Lima we came the 13th of February; and, being entered the haven, we found there about twelve sail of ships lying fast moored at an anchor, having all their sails carried on shore; for the masters and merchants were here most secure, having never been assaulted by enemies, and at this time feared the approach of none such as we were. Our general rifled these ships, and found in one of them a chest full of reals of plate, and good store of silks and linen cloth. . . . In which ship he had news of another ship called the *Cacafuego*, which was gone toward Payta, and that the same ship was laden with treasure. Whereupon we stayed no longer here, but cutting all the cables of the ships in the haven, we let them drive whither they would, either to sea or to the shore; and with all speed we followed the *Cacafuego* which was gone toward Payta. . . ."

—From *Sir Francis Drake's Famous Voyage
Round the World, 1580* by Francis Pretty

Document D ▼

Analyzing Documents

Use your knowledge of American colonial history and Documents A, B, C, and D to answer questions 1–4.

1. According to Document A, Drake's exploits in Chile and Peru
   A were not commercially successful.
   B were done impulsively, without Queen Elizabeth's consent or approval.
   C gave King Philip II the excuse he'd been wanting to start a war against England.
   D met with outrage and anger from Queen Elizabeth and the English-speaking world.

2. According to Document B, what was Don Bernardino de Mendoza's main concern regarding Drake?
   A that Drake would return to the West Indies soon
   B that other seamen would copy Drake's exploits
   C that Spanish seamen would join future Drake expeditions
   D that other nations would join with England against Spain

3. Document D shows Queen Elizabeth I with Francis Drake. Which of the other documents does this one support?
   A Document A
   B Document B
   C Document C
   D Documents A, B, and C

4. **Writing Task** Write a news article about Drake's exploits that might have appeared in a Spanish newspaper around 1580. Use the documents along with information from the chapter to support your article.

The Age of Absolutism

Section	Core Instruction L3	Differentiated Instruction L1 L2 L4

Section 1
Spanish Power Grows

⏱ **1 period, .5 block**

OBJECTIVES
■ Describe the empire that Charles V inherited.
■ Analyze how Spanish power increased under Philip II.
■ Explain how the arts flourished during Spain's golden age.

Focus Question *How did Philip II extend Spain's power and help establish a golden age?*

Core Instruction (Section 1):

All in One Teaching Resources, Unit 1
Reading Strategy:
Compare and Contrast, p. 69
Vocabulary Builder:
Dictionary Skills, p. 68
Section 1 Quiz, p. 63

Reading and Note Taking Study Guide
Note Taking Study Guide, pp. 63–64
Section 1 Summary, p. 65

Note Taking Transparencies, 128

WITNESS HISTORY Audio CD
A Working Monarch

Progress Monitoring Transparencies, 67

Color Transparencies, 97

Teaching Resources, Skills Handbook
Prereading the Chapter, pp. 1–2
Word Knowledge Rating Form, p. 3
K-W-L Chart, p. 4

Differentiated Instruction (Section 1):

L1 Adapted Reading and Note Taking Study Guide
Note Taking Study Guide, pp. 63–64 SN
Section 1 Summary, p. 65 SN

*Student Edition Audio SN
Differentiated Instruction Activity, Teacher's Edition, p. 143 SN

L2 Adapted Reading and Note Taking Study Guide
Note Taking Study Guide, pp. 63–64 LPR
Section 1 Summary, p. 65 LPR

Spanish Reading and Note Taking Study Guide
Note Taking Study Guide, pp. 63–64 ELL
Section 1 Summary, p. 65 ELL

*Guided Reading Audio, Spanish ELL
*Student Edition Audio LPR
Differentiated Instruction Activity, Teacher's Edition, p. 143 LPR, ELL

L4 Differentiated Instruction Activity, Teacher's Edition, p. 145 AR, GT

Extend Activity, Teacher's Edition, p. 146 AR, GT

Section 2
France Under Louis XIV

⏱ **2 periods, 1 block**

OBJECTIVES
■ Understand how Henry IV rebuilt France after the wars of religion.
■ Explain how Louis XIV became an absolute monarch.
■ Describe how Versailles was a symbol of royal power.
■ Identify Louis XIV's successes and failures.

Focus Question *How did France become the leading power of Europe under the absolute rule of Louis XIV?*

Core Instruction (Section 2):

All in One Teaching Resources, Unit 1
Section 2 Quiz, p. 64

Reading and Note Taking Study Guide
Note Taking Study Guide, p. 66
Section 2 Summary, p. 67

Note Taking Transparencies, 129

WITNESS HISTORY Audio CD
Life at Versailles

Progress Monitoring Transparencies, 68

Color Transparencies, 95, 96

Differentiated Instruction (Section 2):

L1 Adapted Reading and Note Taking Study Guide
Note Taking Study Guide, p. 66 SN
Section 2 Summary, p. 67 SN

Differentiated Instruction Activity, Teacher's Edition, p. 149 SN

L2 Adapted Reading and Note Taking Study Guide
Note Taking Study Guide, p. 66 LPR
Section 2 Summary, p. 67 LPR

Spanish Reading and Note Taking Study Guide
Note Taking Study Guide, p. 66 ELL
Section 2 Summary, p. 67 ELL

Differentiated Instruction Activity, Teacher's Edition, p. 149 LPR

L4 All in One Teaching Resources, Unit 1
Link to Literature: The Would-Be Gentleman by Moliere, p. 70 AR, GT
Primary Source: A Busy Day at the Sun King's Court, p. 71 AR, GT

Extend Activity, Teacher's Edition, p. 152 AR, GT

*Audio support is available for all sections.

Assessment Resources
- **Progress Monitoring Transparencies,** 67–71
- **Test Prep,** Unit Study Sheets, pp. 94–96; Unit Test, pp. 15–19
- **SuccessTracker™,** Chapter 4
- **Document-Based Assessment,** pp. 41–53
- *ExamView® Test Bank CD-ROM,* Chapter 4
- **All in One Teaching Resources, Unit 1,** Chapter Tests A and B, pp. 78–83
- **Progress Monitoring *Online* Quizzes,** Chapter 4
- **Assessment Rubrics**

Differentiated Instruction Key
- **L1** Special Needs
- **L2** Basic to Average
- **L3** All Students
- **L4** Average to Advanced
- **LPR** Less Proficient Readers
- **AR** Advanced Readers
- **SN** Special Needs Students
- **GT** Gifted and Talented
- **ELL** English Language Learner

Section	Core Instruction L3	Differentiated Instruction L1 L2 L4

Section 3
Parliament Triumphs in England

🕐 **2.5 periods, 1.25 blocks**

OBJECTIVES
- Describe the Tudor monarchs' relations with Parliament.
- Analyze how clashes between the Stuarts and Parliament ushered in a century of revolution.
- Understand how the English Civil War and the development of the Common-wealth led to the Glorious Revolution.
- Explain the development of English constitutional government.

Focus Question *How did the British Parliament assert its rights against royal claims to absolute power in the 1600s?*

Core Instruction

All in One Teaching Resources, Unit 1
Section 3 Quiz, p. 65

Reading and Note Taking Study Guide
Note Taking Study Guide, p. 68
Section 3 Summary, p. 69

Note Taking Transparencies, 130

WITNESS HISTORY Audio CD
Charting a Collision Course, Thomas Hobbes

Progress Monitoring Transparencies, 69

Differentiated Instruction

L1 **Adapted Reading and Note Taking Study Guide**
Note Taking Study Guide, p. 68 **SN**
Section 3 Summary, p. 69 **SN**

Differentiated Instruction Activity, Teacher's Edition, p. 157 **SN**

L2 **Adapted Reading and Note Taking Study Guide**
Note Taking Study Guide, p. 68 **LPR**
Section 3 Summary, p. 69 **LPR**

Spanish Reading and Note Taking Study Guide
Note Taking Study Guide, p. 68 **ELL**
Section 3 Summary, p. 69 **ELL**

Differentiated Instruction Activity, Teacher's Edition, p. 157 **LPR, ELL**

L4 **All in One Teaching Resources, Unit 1**
Biography: George Fox, p. 72 **AR, GT**
Primary Source: From a letter of Oliver Cromwell to Colonel Robert Hammond, November 25, 1648, p. 73 **AR, GT**

Extend Activity, Teacher's Edition, p. 161 **AR, GT**

Section 4
Rise of Austria and Prussia

🕐 **1 period, .5 block**

OBJECTIVES
- Outline causes and results of the Thirty Years' War.
- Understand how Austria and Prussia emerged as great powers.
- Describe how European nations tried to maintain a balance of power.

Focus Question *How did the two great empires of Austria and Prussia emerge from the Thirty Years' War and subsequent events?*

All in One Teaching Resources, Unit 1
Outline Map: Europe After the Peace of Westphalia, p. 75
Geography Quiz, p. 77
Section 4 Quiz, p. 66

Reading and Note Taking Study Guide
Note Taking Study Guide, p. 70
Section 4 Summary, p. 71

Note Taking Transparencies, 131

WITNESS HISTORY Audio CD
War Rages in Germany

Progress Monitoring Transparencies, 70

Color Transparencies, 98

L1 **Adapted Reading and Note Taking Study Guide**
Note Taking Study Guide, p. 70 **SN**
Section 4 Summary, p. 71 **SN**

Differentiated Instruction Activity, Teacher's Edition, p. 164 **SN**

L2 **Adapted Reading and Note Taking Study Guide**
Note Taking Study Guide, p. 70 **LPR**
Section 4 Summary, p. 71 **LPR**

Spanish Reading and Note Taking Study Guide
Note Taking Study Guide, p. 70 **ELL**
Section 4 Summary, p. 71 **ELL**

Differentiated Instruction Activity, Teacher's Edition, p. 164 **LPR, ELL**

L4 **All in One Teaching Resources, Unit 1**
Viewpoints: Empress Maria Theresa, p. 74 **AR, GT**

Differentiated Instruction Activity, Teacher's Edition, p. 166 **AR, GT**

Extend Activity, Teacher's Edition, p. 167 **AR, GT**

Section 5
Absolute Monarchy in Russia

🕐 **1.5 periods, .75 block**

OBJECTIVES
- Explain how Peter the Great tried to make Russia into a modern state.
- Identify the steps Peter took to expand Russia's borders.
- Describe how Catherine the Great strengthened Russia.

Focus Question *How did Peter the Great and Catherine the Great strengthen Russia and expand its territory?*

All in One Teaching Resources, Unit 1
Outline Map: Eastern Europe in 1796, p. 76
Section 5 Quiz, p. 67

Reading and Note Taking Study Guide
Note Taking Study Guide, p. 72
Section 5 Summary, p. 73
Concept Connector, pp. 250, 287, 291

Note Taking Transparencies, 132

WITNESS HISTORY Audio CD
A Foreign Princess Takes the Throne, Alexander Pushkin

Progress Monitoring Transparencies, 71

Color Transparencies, 99, 100

Witness History Discovery School™ video program, *Peter the Great*

L1 **Adapted Reading and Note Taking Study Guide**
Note Taking Study Guide, p. 72 **SN**
Section 5 Summary, p. 73 **SN**
Concept Connector, pp. 250, 287, 291 **SN**

Differentiated Instruction Activity, Teacher's Edition, p. 169 **SN**

L2 **Adapted Reading and Note Taking Study Guide**
Note Taking Study Guide, p. 72 **LPR**
Section 5 Summary, p. 73 **LPR**
Concept Connector, pp. 250, 287, 291 **LPR**

Spanish Reading and Note Taking Study Guide
Note Taking Study Guide, p. 72 **ELL**
Section 5 Summary, p. 73 **ELL**
Concept Connector, pp. 250, 287, 291 **ELL**

Differentiated Instruction Activity, Teacher's Edition, p. 169 **LPR, ELL**

L4 **Differentiated Instruction Activity,** Teacher's Edition, p. 172 **AR, GT**

Extend Activity, Teacher's Edition, p. 173 **AR, GT**

PROFESSIONAL DEVELOPMENT

Author's Notes

"I am the State"

No ruler of the age embodied the spirit of royal absolutism as did Louis XIV (1643–1715), for whom the age is named. Who but the Sun King, the Grand Monarch, could have interrupted a diplomat's pompous references to "the French state" with an impatient but quite accurate *"l' état, c'est moi"*—"I am the state"—and have historians nodding sagely ever since?

Building royal power meant undermining local and regional power centers, and this Louis did with a will. The old independent-minded French aristocrats were turned into tame courtiers at Louis's court. Town officials became royal appointees. Royal regulations were imposed upon medieval guilds. Provincial courts called *parlements* were compelled to rubber-stamp royal decrees. The Estates General, France's embryonic Parliament, became a dead letter by virtue of never being summoned to meet during Louis's long reign.

In place of medieval regional autonomy, centralized royal institutions grew up. Central councils presided over by the king formulated government policies. Powerful royal masters such as the Marquis de Louvois, minister of war, and above all Jean Baptiste Colbert (1619–1683), chief minister for finances and many other matters, elaborated and then implemented them in the provinces, collecting taxes and army conscripts, regulating the economy, and providing at least some government protection in the countryside.

Perhaps the most impressive achievement of absolutism under Louis XIV, however, was the elaborate system of mercantilist regulation of the national economy developed by Colbert. The traditional goals of mercantilism were to increase national production, secure a favorable balance of trade in the goods produced, and thus guarantee a flow of payments in gold and silver bullion in the country. . . .

Under Colbert, then, an intricate structure of monopolies, chartered companies, protective tariffs, controls on wages, prices, and product quality, and colonial regulations was established to achieve these ends. All major powers practiced mercantilistic regulation of their economies. But few did so as efficiently and wholeheartedly as Louis and his first minister, Colbert.

—Anthony Esler, *The Human Venture From Prehistory to the Present,* (Upper Saddle River, New Jersey: Pearson Education, 2004), pp. 475–476

Extend Online

Rulers During the Age of Absolutism

Have students research the biography of one of the rulers during the Age of Absolutism. Have them create a résumé of that person's qualifications and accomplishments. Use the steps below to complete the activity.

Prepare for the Activity Tell students that during the reign of Elizabeth I (shown at left), she helped transform England from a relatively impoverished country into a major force in politics and trade. As she demonstrated, a ruler can greatly affect the course of one's country.

Conduct the Activity For help in starting the activity, send students to **Web Code nbe-1601.** Students will choose a ruler from this period and research his or her biography. Ask students to put together a résumé highlighting the skills and qualifications that ruler may have needed to assume that authority. Have them also list their accomplishments once in office. Then have them present their rulers' résumés to the class and take a poll as to which one the students would hire to be their ruler.

Follow-Up Conduct a class discussion based on the following questions: What were the characteristics of most leaders during the Age of Absolutism? How did each ruler affect the country where he or she ruled? How do they compare to leaders today? What characteristics would you want to see in a leader?

Differentiated Instruction   Solutions for All Learners

Sorting ⓛ2

A sorting activity can engage kinesthetic and tactile learners when you ask them to physically become part of the sort. First create placards with key terms and phrases. Then distribute one placard to each student and ask them to find other students with phrases associated with theirs. Tell them to form groups of a set number, such as five and the first group to correctly find all their matches wins.

To help students distinguish between different rulers during the Age of Absolutism, the placards could read as follows:

- Group 1: Spain; Philip II; Armada; Siglo de Oro; absolute ruler waged war to increase power.
- Group 2: France; Louis XIV; Versailles; the Fronde challenged absolutism; absolute ruler kept nobles busy with social functions so they wouldn't challenge his power.
- Group 3: England; John Locke; Parliament; Civil War challenged absolutism; political leaders developed the cabinet system.

- Group 4: Prussia; Hohenzollern; Frederick William I; ruler sparked war of Austrian succession; rulers united their holdings to create Prussia.
- Group 5: Russia; Peter the Great; St. Petersburg; absolute ruler sought a warm-water port; absolute ruler sought to modernize his country.

This activity forces students to recall and categorize the material. The competition and movement can help energize students. Initially, a student with the placard Spain might join with someone holding the placard France. However, once students see the key name Philip II, they should realize that the sort is not grouped by names of country but rather by things associated with each country.

You may increase or decrease the difficulty simply by changing the words on the placards. For instance, you could include a phrase that applies to more than one group, such as ruled by divine right, which applies to both Spain and France. By forcing students to form groups of five, they would need to decide which key term could also apply to another group.

Modeling Reading and Writing Skills

Vocabulary: Recognize Word Origins Tell students that by recognizing word parts, they can identify and understand many unfamiliar words. Remind them that many words come from Greek or Latin roots. For example, the suffix *-cracy* means a form of government. This suffix is part of the noun *democracy*, which is government ruled by the people, and *autocracy*, which is a government ruled by someone with unlimited power such as a monarch.

Write on the board the key term *elector*—based on the Latin root *electus* meaning "to choose." Point out that this root can be seen in the words *election* and *elect*. Then explain that the suffix *-or* means "someone who does something." Therefore, the word *elector* must mean someone who chooses.

Consider Your Audience Explain that in this chapter students will be writing a persuasive essay. (See Writing About History, p. 176.) Remind students that views about controversial issues are often products of a historical time. For example, historical audiences would be open

to arguments in favor of the Atlantic slave trade that modern audiences would find highly offensive. As they develop arguments, students should choose a contemporary or an historical audience and identify aspects of the arguments that will be most persuasive.

Model this skill by listing the following arguments on the board and ask students whether each is more appropriate for a historical or a modern audience:

1. Spanish missionaries helped Native Americans by converting many to Christianity. *(historical)*

2. The Spanish encomienda system was equivalent to slavery, and led to horrible exploitation. *(modern)*

Students should set up the context of their essay to fit their chosen audience. For example, for a historical context they might write a persuasive letter from an explorer to a monarch. For a modern context, they might write a standard formal essay but should provide the historical context and acknowledge historical views in their discussion.

Teach With Technology

PresentationEXPRESS™
Premium DVD

- Teach this chapter's core content using **PresentationExpress™ Premium,** which includes dynamic lecture notes, interactive game shows, songs, videos, and the *ExamView® QuickTake* assessment tool.

- To introduce this chapter using **PresentationExpress™ Premium,** start by asking students **Which of the following statements do you most agree with? (A) A government leader should never have absolute authority. (B) A government leader can exercise absolute authority if it will help advance a country's economy. (C) A government leader can exercise absolute authority when a country is under attack. (D) A government leader can exercise absolute authority whenever it will advance a country's interests.** Take a class poll or record students' answers using the QuickTake feature and discuss their responses. Point out that in this chapter, they will read about European monarchs who believed they had the right to rule with absolute powers. Continue introducing the chapter using the chapter opener slide show and Witness History audio.

Technology Resources

- Student**EXPRESS** CD-ROM, Chapter 4
- Teacher**EXPRESS** CD-ROM, Chapter 4
- Presentation**EXPRESS**™ **Premium DVD,** Chapter 4
- **WITNESS HISTORY** Audio CD, Chapter 4
- *ExamView* Test Bank CD-ROM, English and Spanish, Chapter 4
- **Guided Reading Audio,** Spanish, Chapter 4
- **Student Edition Audio,** Chapter 4
- **Witness History Discovery School**™ video program, *Peter the Great*
- **Experience It! Multimedia Pack**

The Age of Absolutism
1550–1800

Bibliography

For the Teacher
Cameron, Euan, ed. *Early Modern Europe: An Oxford History.* New York: Oxford University Press, 1999.

Levi, Anthony. *Cardinal Richelieu and the Making of France.* New York: Carroll & Graf, 2000.

Mortimer, Geoff. *Eyewitness Accounts of the Thirty Years War.* New York: Palgrave, 2002.

For the Student
L2 Greenblatt, Miriam. *Peter the Great and Tsarist Russia.* Tarrytown, N.Y.: Benchmark Books, 1999.

L3 Marrin, Albert. *The Sea King: Sir Francis Drake and His Times.* New York: Atheneum, 1995.

L4 Stalcup, Brenda, ed. *The Inquisition.* Series: Turning Points in World History. San Diego: Greenhaven, 2000.

WITNESS HISTORY AUDIO

A Child Becomes King

In 1643, the five-year-old heir to the French crown, Louis XIV, made his first public appearance. The tiny monarch climbed the throne and sat for hours as officials conducted the ceremony announcing the new reign. Louis XIV had been orphaned as a baby, and was a sickly, shy child. As a child, he would often bring a cat to government councils, stroking the fur as he sat in silence. Despite this quiet beginning, Louis XIV proved to be a strong, able ruler who came to symbolize the period of absolute monarchy we now call the "Age of Absolutism." Listen to the Witness History audio to hear more about this powerful king.

◄ Louis XIV receives foreign ambassadors at his Versailles court in 1678.

Chapter Preview

Chapter Focus Question What events led to the rise of absolute monarchies and the development of centralized nation-states in Europe?

Section 1
Spanish Power Grows

Section 2
France Under Louis XIV

Section 3
Parliament Triumphs in England

Section 4
Rise of Austria and Prussia

Section 5
Absolute Monarchy in Russia

Use the ☑ **Quick Study Timeline** at the end of this chapter to preview chapter events.

A French bishop's official seal

Oliver Cromwell's battle helmet

Carpentry tool owned by Peter the Great

Concept Connector ONLINE

To explore Essential Questions related to this chapter, go to PHSchool.com
Web Code: nbd-1607

Chapter-Level Resources

All in One Vocabulary Builder; Reading Strategy; Enrichments; Outline Maps; Geography Quiz; Chapter Tests
- Document-Based Assessments
- AYP Monitoring Assessments
- *ExamView* Test Bank CD-ROM
- Guided Reading Audio (Spanish)
- Student Edition Audio

Previewing the Chapter

- **WITNESS HISTORY** Begin by analyzing the chapter title, The Age of Absolutism. Explain why historians use this term today. Then read the Witness History selection aloud and listen to the accompanying audio. Ask students to consider how life would have been for young children expected to become absolute monarchs. How would it have differed from the lives of ordinary children? Make sure students understand the differences between absolute rule and rule of democratic leaders such as the president of the United States.

  AUDIO **Witness History Audio CD,** A Child Becomes King

- **Analyzing the Visuals** Have students identify Louis XIV in the painting. Ask them to point out details that give clues to Louis's status as absolute ruler of a powerful nation.

- **Focus** Write the Chapter Focus Question on the board. Tell students to keep this question in mind as they read the chapter. *(Answer appears with Chapter Assessment answers.)* Have students preview the section titles for this chapter.

Note Taking Study Guide With Concept Connector Journal
For online access: Web code: nbd-1607
For print alternative: Reading and Note Taking Study Guide booklet

Step-by-Step Instruction

Objectives

As you teach this section, keep students focused on the following objectives to help them answer the Section Focus Question and master core content.

- Describe the empire that Charles V inherited.
- Analyze how Spanish power increased under Philip II.
- Explain how the arts flourished during Spain's golden age. ·

Prepare to Read

Build Background Knowledge ⓛ

Ask students to predict how the trading empires built by European nations in Asia, Africa, and the Americas affected Europe's monarchs. Ask them to predict what European monarchs might do with their increased wealth.

Set a Purpose ⓛ

- **WITNESS HISTORY** Read the selection aloud or play the audio.

  ◄))) AUDIO **Witness History Audio CD,** A Working Monarch

  Ask **What were the advantages and drawbacks of Philip "keeping an eye on everything"?** (Sample: He could make sure government was running the way he wanted it to, but this created a situation where the nation depended too much on one person.)

- **Focus** Point out the Section Focus Question and write it on the board. Tell students to refer to this question as they read. (Answer appears with Section 1 Assessment answers.)

- **Preview** Have students preview the Section Objectives and the list of Terms, People, and Places.

- **Reading Skill** Have students use the Reading Strategy: Compare and Contrast worksheet.

  All in One Teaching Resources, Unit 1, p. 69

Philip II wears royal dress. In the background, his Armada heads to England.

A late 1500s Spanish coin commemorates Philip's rule.

WITNESS HISTORY ◄))) AUDIO

A Working Monarch

"It is best to keep an eye on everything," Philip II of Spain often said—and he meant it. As king of the most powerful nation in Europe, he gave little time to pleasure. Instead, he plowed through a mountain of paperwork each day, making notes on even the most trivial matters. But Philip's determination to "keep an eye on everything" extended far beyond trivia. It helped him build Spain into a strong centralized state. By the late 1500s, he had concentrated all power in his own hands. Over the next 200 years, other European monarchs would pursue similar goals.

Focus Question How did Philip II extend Spain's power and help establish a golden age?

Spanish Power Grows

Objectives

- Describe the empire that Charles V inherited.
- Analyze how Spanish power increased under Philip II.
- Explain how the arts flourished during Spain's golden age.

Terms, People, and Places

Hapsburg empire	divine right
Charles V	armada
Philip II	El Greco
absolute monarch	Miguel de Cervantes

Note Taking

Reading Skill: Identify Main Ideas and Supporting Details As you read about how Philip II extended Spanish power, create an outline to record details that support the main ideas in this section. This example will help you get started.

> I. Charles V Inherits Two Crowns
>   A. Ruling the Hapsburg Empire
>   1. Spain
>   2. Holy Roman Empire and Netherlands
>   B. Charles V abdicates

By the 1500s, Spain had shaken off its feudal past and emerged as the first modern European power. Queen Isabella and King Ferdinand had unified the country, enforced religious unity, and commanded the Spanish conquest of the Americas.

Charles V Inherits Two Crowns

In 1516, Ferdinand and Isabella's grandson, Charles I, became king of Spain, and thereby ruler of the Spanish colonies in the Americas as well.

Ruling the Hapsburg Empire When his other grandfather died in 1519, Charles I also became heir to the sprawling **Hapsburg empire,** which included the Holy Roman Empire and the Netherlands. As ruler of this empire, Charles took the name **Charles V.** Historians now usually refer to him by this title.

Ruling two empires involved Charles in constant warfare. As a devout Catholic, he fought to suppress Protestantism in the German states. After years of religious conflict, however, Charles was forced to allow the German princes to choose their own religion.

Charles also faced the Muslim Ottoman empire, which was based in Turkey but stretched across the Balkans. Under Suleiman, Ottoman forces advanced across central Europe to the walls surrounding Vienna, Austria. Although Austria held firm during the siege, the Ottomans occupied much of Hungary following their crushing victory at the Battle of Mohács. Ottoman naval forces also continued to challenge Spanish power in the Mediterranean.

Vocabulary Builder

Use the information below and the following resources to teach the high-use word from this section.
All in One Teaching Resources, Unit 1, p. 68; **Teaching Resources, Skills Handbook,** p. 3

High-Use Word	Definition and Sample Sentence
cumbersome, p. 143	adj. hard to handle because of size, weight, or many parts. The refrigerator was extremely **cumbersome** to move upstairs into a second-floor apartment.

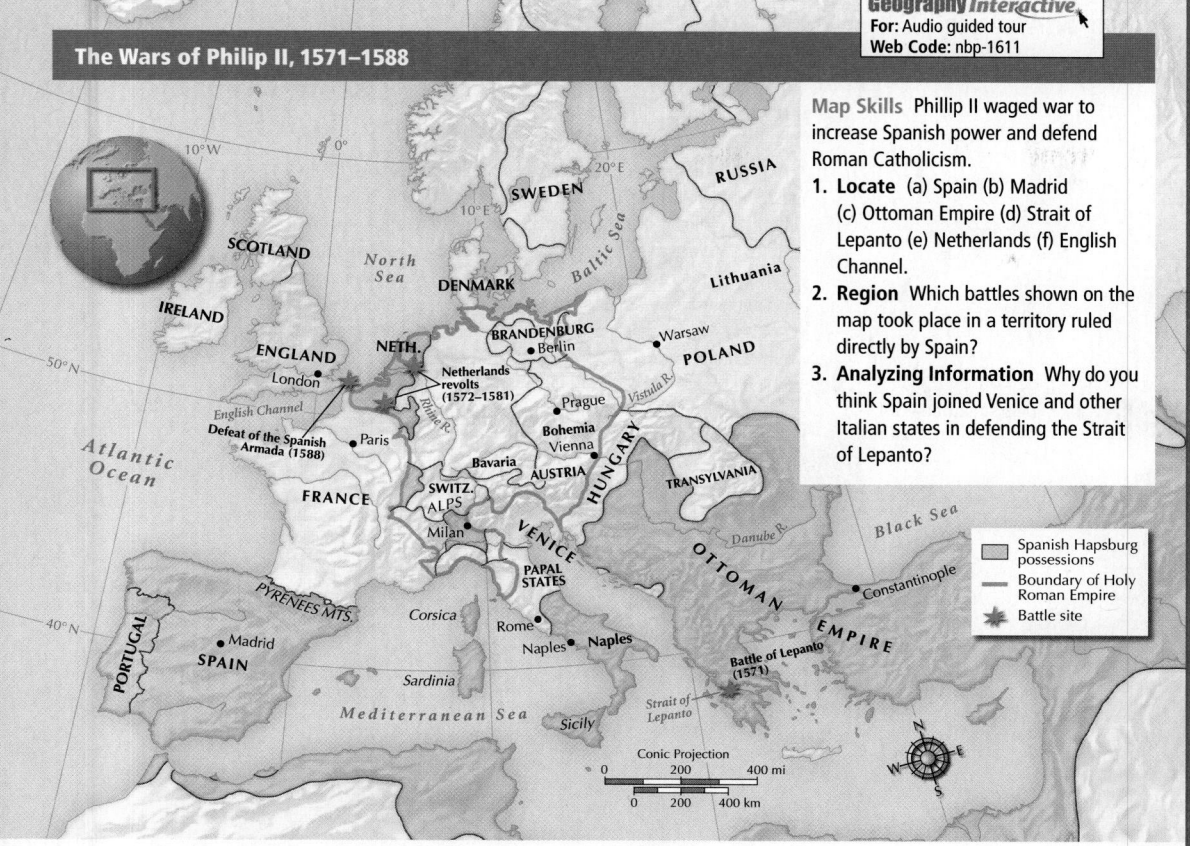

Geography *Interactive*
For: Audio guided tour
Web Code: nbp-1611

Map Skills Phillip II waged war to increase Spanish power and defend Roman Catholicism.

1. **Locate** (a) Spain (b) Madrid (c) Ottoman Empire (d) Strait of Lepanto (e) Netherlands (f) English Channel.
2. **Region** Which battles shown on the map took place in a territory ruled directly by Spain?
3. **Analyzing Information** Why do you think Spain joined Venice and other Italian states in defending the Strait of Lepanto?

Charles V Abdicates

The Hapsburg empire proved to be too scattered and <u>cumbersome</u> for any one person to rule effectively. Exhausted and disillusioned, Charles V gave up his titles and entered a monastery in 1556. He divided his empire, leaving the Hapsburg lands in central Europe to his brother Ferdinand, who became Holy Roman emperor. He gave Spain, the Netherlands, some southern Italian states, and Spain's overseas empire to his 29-year-old son Philip, who became Philip II.

✔ **Checkpoint** Why did Charles V divide the Hapsburg Empire?

Philip II Solidifies Power

During his 42-year reign, **Philip II** expanded Spanish influence, strengthened the Catholic Church, and made his own power absolute. Thanks in part to silver from Spanish colonies in the Americas, he made Spain the foremost power in Europe.

Centralizing Power Like his father, Philip II was hard working, devout, and ambitious. Unlike many other monarchs, Philip devoted most of his time to government work. He seldom hunted, never jousted, and lived as simply as a monk. The King's isolated, somber palace outside Madrid, known as the Escorial (es kohr YAHL), reflected his character. It served as a church, a residence, and a tomb for the royal family.

Vocabulary Builder

<u>cumbersome</u>—(KUM bur sum) *adj.* hard to handle because of size, weight, or many parts

L1 Special Needs **L2 English Language Learners** **L2 Less Proficient Readers**

Assign students to work in pairs. Have one student scan the text and read out the names of places. Have the other student locate each place named on the map. When they reach the Infographic, have students trade places. Then ask students to explain, using the map, why Philip's plan to invade England was likely to encounter difficulties.

Use the following resources to help students acquire basic skills:

 Adapted Reading and Note Taking Study Guide

■ Adapted Note Taking Study Guide, pp. 63–64
■ Adapted Section Summary, p. 65

■ **Note Taking** Have students read this section using the Paragraph Shrinking strategy (TE, p. T20). As they read, have students create an outline with information about Spain under Philip II.

 Reading and Note Taking Study Guide, pp. 63–64

Charles V Inherits Two Crowns   L3

Instruct

■ **Introduce: Vocabulary Builder** Have students read the Vocabulary Builder term and definition. Then direct their attention to the map. Ask them why it would be ***cumbersome*** for one person to rule the Holy Roman Empire and the Spanish Hapsburg possessions.

■ **Teach** Ask **With whom did Charles V go to war?** *(German states and the Ottoman Empire)* **What were the main reasons for these wars?** *(religion and competition for territory)*

■ **Analyzing the Visuals** Direct students' attention to the map. Have students compare this map to the map of religions on page 70. Then ask students which of the battles shown on the map on this page occurred on the boundaries between two religions. *(all of them)*

Independent Practice

Have students access **Web Code nbp-1611** to take the **Geography Interactive Audio Guided Tour** and then answer the map skills questions in the text.

Monitor Progress

Ask students what specific difficulties Charles faced in ruling two empires. *(lengthy communication delays, problems defending so many borders, differences in language and religion)*

Answers

✔ It was too difficult for one person to rule effectively.

Map Skills
1. Review locations with students.
2. the Netherlands revolts
3. Spain did not want the Ottomans to control the Mediterranean.

Philip II Solidifies Power L3

Instruct

- **Introduce: Key Terms** Ask students to find the key terms *absolute monarch* and *divine right* (in blue) in the text and explain their meanings. Ask **What groups might resist an absolute monarch?** (*Sample: feudal lords, religious officials, a parliament or legislative body, ministers*) Discuss how belief in divine right might affect how a monarch governed.

- **Teach** Trace the rise and decline of Spain's power. Ask **What was Philip's main military victory?** (*defeat of the Ottoman fleet*) **What were his two major defeats?** (*loss of the northern provinces of the Netherlands and the defeat of the Spanish Armada*) Discuss whether he was more successful overall than his father had been. Ask **How did Spain's colonies in the Americas lead to its economic decline?** (*Riches from the colonies led to neglect of farming and commerce and soaring inflation. Also, the government taxed and weakened the middle class.*)

- **Analyzing the Visuals** Have groups of students examine and discuss the Infographic on this page. Ask groups to list the strengths and weaknesses of each strategy Philip II used to solidify power. Then use the Numbered Heads strategy (TE, p. T23) to have groups share their responses with the class.

Independent Practice

Ask students to write a paragraph explaining why the defeat of the Spanish Armada was such an important event of the period.

Monitor Progress

As students create their outlines, circulate to make sure they identify the main events of Philip's rule. For a completed version of the outline, see

📖 **Note Taking Transparencies,** 128

Answers

Thinking Critically

1. They could cement alliances, prevent war, and bring wealth, land, or power.
2. They provided great wealth that helped to finance Spain's wars in Europe, but this wealth also caused inflation and undermined Spain's economic strength.

● **INFOGRAPHIC**

PHILIP II AND THE RISE OF SPAIN

Philip II's Marriages

Maria	Mary Tudor	Elizabeth Valois	Anna
Alliance: Portugal	Alliance: England	Allliance: France	Alliance: Austria

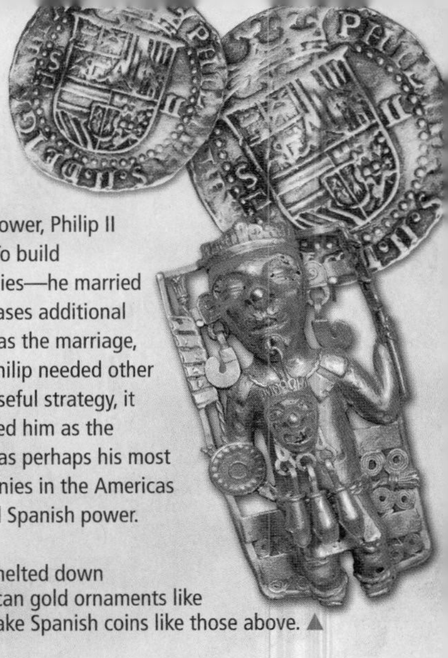

In his pursuit of building and extending Spanish power, Philip II had many tools in his arsenal. Marriage was one. To build important alliances—and to pacify potential enemies—he married a total of four times, gaining power and in some cases additional territory. Yet because alliances lasted only as long as the marriage, and Renaissance women often did not live long, Philip needed other ways to expand Spain's power. War was another useful strategy, it gained him the kingdom of Portugal and established him as the defender of the Roman Catholic Church. Wealth was perhaps his most important tool. Silver and gold from his colonies in the Americas fueled the Spanish economy and ensured Spanish power.

Philip's marriage to Mary Tudor in 1554 created an alliance with England until Mary's death four years later. ▼

The Spanish melted down Native American gold ornaments like this one to make Spanish coins like those above. ▲

Philip's victory against the Turks in the Battle of Lepanto assured his role as defender of the Catholic Church. ▼

Thinking Critically
1. **Apply Information** What various purposes could royal marriages serve during the age of absolutism?
2. **Understand Cause and Effect** How did Philip's colonies in the Americas affect his goals for Spain?

Philip surpassed Ferdinand and Isabella in making every part of the government responsible to him. He reigned as an **absolute monarch,** a ruler with complete authority over the government and the lives of the people. Like other European rulers, Philip asserted that he ruled by **divine right.** That is, he believed that his authority to rule came directly from God. Philip therefore saw himself as the guardian of the Roman Catholic Church. The great undertaking of his life was to defend

---

History Background

The Divine Right of Europe's Monarchs

Since the Middle Ages, Europe's monarchs had struggled to assert power over feudal lords. Some early monarchs were elected, but over time Europe's royal families retained power by making monarchy hereditary—passed down within families. They also developed an ideology to support their claims to absolute power. It reached its height in the 1600s when Jacques-Bénigne

Bossuet, a French bishop who admired Louis XIV, formulated the concept of the divine right of kings. Bossuet argued that monarchs were chosen by God and therefore should be obeyed absolutely. This idea allowed European kings and queens to bring all aspects of government, trade, and religion under their rule.

the Catholic Reformation and turn back the rising Protestant tide in Europe. Within his empire, Philip enforced religious unity, turning the Inquisition against Protestants and other people thought to be heretics.

Battles in the Mediterranean and the Netherlands Philip fought many wars as he attempted to advance Spanish Catholic power. In the Mediterranean, the Ottoman empire continued to pose a threat to European control of the region. At the Battle of Lepanto in 1571, Spain and its Italian allies soundly defeated an Ottoman fleet off the coast of Greece. Although the Ottoman Empire would remain a major power in the Mediterranean region for three more centuries, Christians still hailed the battle as a great victory and a demonstration of Spain's power.

During the last half of his reign, Philip battled rebels in the Netherlands. At the time, the region included 17 provinces that are today Belgium, the Netherlands, and Luxembourg. It was the richest part of Philip's empire. Protestants in the region resisted Philip's efforts to crush their faith. Protestants and Catholics alike opposed high taxes and autocratic Spanish rule, which threatened local traditions of self-government.

In the 1560s, riots against the Inquisition sparked a general uprising in the Netherlands. Savage fighting raged for decades. In 1581, the northern, largely Protestant provinces declared their independence from Spain and became known as the Dutch Netherlands. They did not gain official recognition, however, until 1648. The southern, mostly Catholic provinces of the Netherlands remained part of the Spanish Empire.

The Armada Sails Against England By the 1580s, Philip saw England's Queen Elizabeth I as his chief Protestant enemy. First secretly, then openly, Elizabeth had supported the Dutch against Spain. She encouraged English captains such as Francis Drake, known as sea dogs, to plunder Spanish treasure ships and loot Spanish cities in the Americas. To Philip's dismay, Elizabeth made the pirate Drake a knight.

To end English attacks and subdue the Dutch, Philip prepared a huge **armada,** or fleet, to carry a Spanish invasion force to England. In 1588, the Spanish Armada sailed with more than 130 ships, 20,000 men, and 2,400 pieces of artillery. The Spanish were confident of victory. "When we meet the English," predicted one Spanish commander, "God will surely arrange matters so that we can grapple and board them, either by sending some strange freak of weather or, more likely, just by depriving the English of their wits."

This prediction did not come to pass. In the English Channel, lumbering Spanish ships were outmaneuvered by the lighter, faster English ships. Strong winds favored the English, scattering the Armada. After further disasters at sea, the tattered remnants limped home in defeat.

An Empire Declines The defeat of the Armada marked the beginning of the end of Spanish power. Throughout the 1600s, Spain's strength and prosperity decreased. One reason for this decline was that Philip II's successors ruled far less ably than he had.

Spain Loses Territory
The Treaty of Munster, signed in 1648, recognized the independence of the Netherlands' Protestant provinces.

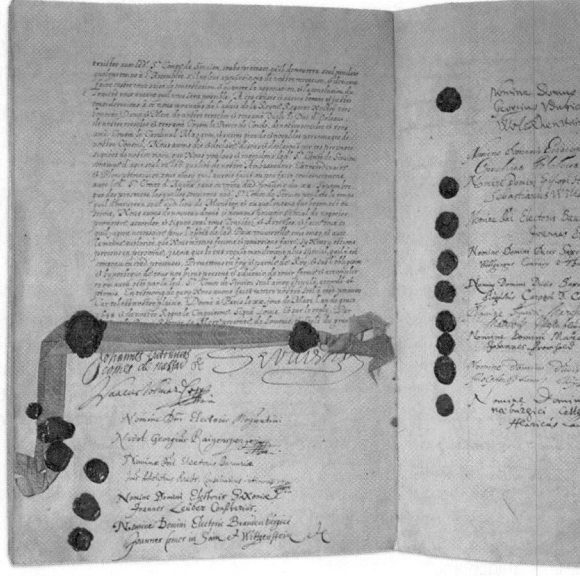

Instruct

- **Introduce** Display **Color Transparency 97: Spanish Tapestry.** Ask students what sort of scene is shown and what it says about the *Siglo de oro.* Ask who might have commissioned the tapestry, given the enormous labor and cost.
  📖 Color Transparencies, 97

- **Teach** Ask **What were the key themes of *Siglo de oro* painters and writers?** *(religion, nobles, royalty)* **How did the writer Cervantes chronicle the end of feudalism?** *(He satirized chivalry and those who pursued it.)*

- **Analyzing the Visuals** Direct students to the El Greco painting on the next page. Ask **How do El Greco's themes, atmosphere, and artistry reflect the age of Philip II?** *(They are both intensely religious, somber, exquisitely precise.)*

Independent Practice

Have students research a *Siglo de oro* painter or writer and write a letter to a Spanish king praising that person's work and recommending that the king provide the artist with royal support. Have students read their letters to the class.

Monitor Progress

Check Reading and Note Taking Study Guide entries for student understanding.

L4 Gifted and Talented   **L4 Advanced Readers**

Scholars have studied the defeat of the Spanish Armada extensively. According to one scholar, a newly found letter reveals that the Ottomans, at England's request, kept much of Spain's fleet busy in the Mediterranean. Another scholar, analyzing evidence found on Spanish ships, argues that the Spanish carried shot that did not fit their cannons. Others say Spanish ships were built for traditional naval battles, involving grappling and boarding. New, lighter, faster English ships evaded boarding while shooting with longer-range guns. Have students research and write an essay taking a position on the reasons for the defeat of the Armada and illustrate their essay with maps and diagrams. Then conduct a debate on the subject.

Assess and Reteach

Assess Progress L3

- Have students complete the Section Assessment.
- Administer the Section Quiz.

All in One Teaching Resources, Unit 1, p. 63

- To further assess student understanding, use

 Progress Monitoring Transparencies, 67

Reteach L1 L2

If students need more instruction, have them read the section summary.

 Reading and Note Taking Study Guide, p. 65 L3

 Adapted Reading and Note Taking Study Guide, p. 65 L1 L2

 Spanish Reading and Note Taking Study Guide, p. 65 L2

Extend L4

Have students choose two non-European countries that have a history of rule by monarchs. Have them research their countries' histories and write an essay addressing whether the monarch in each country claimed a divine right to rule or the backing of a god or gods.

Answers

✓ advancing Catholicism and increasing Spain's power

Caption Sample: A church tower points to the sky; a heavenly light bathes the city.

✓ It was a golden century of Spanish arts and literature, from 1550 to 1650.

View of Toledo
El Greco's painting shows the Spanish city of Toledo, where he lived for 40 years. This is El Greco's only landscape painting. *How does El Greco express religious themes in this painting?*

Economic problems were also to blame. Costly overseas wars drained wealth out of Spain almost as fast as it came in. Treasure from the Americas led Spain to neglect farming and commerce. The government heavily taxed the small middle class, weakening a group that in other European nations supported royal power. The expulsion of Muslims and Jews from Spain deprived the economy of many skilled artisans and merchants. Finally, the influx of American gold and silver led to soaring inflation.

As Spain's power dwindled in the 1600s and 1700s, Dutch, English, and French fleets challenged—and eventually surpassed—Spanish power both in Europe and around the world.

✓ **Checkpoint** What were Philip II's motivations for waging war?

Spain's Golden Age

The century from 1550 to 1650 is often referred to as Spain's *Siglo de Oro* (SEEG loh day OHR oh), or "golden century," for the brilliance of its arts and literature. Philip II was an enthusiastic patron of the arts and also founded academies of science and mathematics.

Among the famous painters of this period was a man called El Greco, meaning "the Greek." Though not Spanish by birth, El Greco is considered to be a master of Spanish painting. Born on the Greek island of Crete, El Greco had studied in Italy before settling in Spain. He produced haunting religious pictures and striking portraits of Spanish nobles. El Greco's use of vibrant colors influenced the work of Diego Velázquez (vuh LAHS kes), court painter to King Philip IV. Velázquez is perhaps best known for his vivid portraits of Spanish royalty.

Spain's golden century produced several outstanding writers. Lope de Vega (LOH pay duh VAY guh), a peasant by birth, wrote more than 1,500 plays, including witty comedies and action-packed romances. Miguel de Cervantes (sur VAN teez) was the most important writer of Spain's golden age. His *Don Quixote*, which pokes fun at medieval tales of chivalry, is considered to be Europe's first modern novel. Although *Don Quixote* mocks the traditions of Spain's feudal past, Cervantes depicts with affection both the foolish but heroic idealism of Don Quixote and the unromantic, earthy realism of his sidekick, Sancho Panza.

✓ **Checkpoint** What was the *Siglo de Oro*?

SECTION 1 Assessment

Progress Monitoring *Online*
For: Self-quiz with vocabulary practice
Web Code: nba-1611

Terms, People, and Places

1. For each term, person, or place listed at the beginning of the section, write a sentence explaining its significance.

Note Taking

2. **Reading Skill: Identify Main Ideas and Supporting Details** Use your completed outline to answer the Focus Question: How did Philip II extend Spain's power and help establish a golden age?

Comprehension and Critical Thinking

3. **Compare and Contrast** How were Charles V and Philip II alike and different in their goals of ensuring absolute power and strengthening Catholicism?

4. **Synthesize Information** Why did Spanish power and prosperity decline?

5. **Summarize** Why is the period from 1550 to 1650 considered Spain's golden age?

● Writing About History

Quick Write: Generate Arguments Choose a topic from this section that could be the subject of a persuasive essay—for example, whether England was really a threat to Spain. Then write two thesis statements, one arguing each side of your topic. Make sure that the arguments clearly explain opposite or differing opinions on the topic.

Section 1 Assessment

1. Sentences should reflect an understanding of each term, person, or place listed at the beginning of the section.
2. Philip II asserted absolute power, waged war, and supported the arts, all to extend Spain's power and prestige.
3. Both sought to ensure absolute power and strengthen Catholicism, but Philip was more determined and successful.

4. Costly wars, inflation, bad economic choices, and faulty leadership caused Spain's decline.
5. It was a period of unusual brilliance in the arts and literature.

● Writing About History

Each thesis statement should address a valid topic and be suitable for development in a persuasive essay. Students should take positions on two opposing sides of the topic and explain those positions clearly in their thesis statements.

For additional assessment, have students access **Progress Monitoring *Online*** at **Web Code nba-1611.**

Don Quixote by Miguel de Cervantes

Although the age of chivalry had long passed, stories about knights-errant were still popular in the early 1600s. The heroes of these stories were brave knights who traveled far and wide performing noble deeds. Miguel de Cervantes's novel *Don Quixote* satirizes such romances. His hero, the elderly Don Quixote, has read too many tales of chivalry. Imagining himself a knight-errant, he sets out across the Spanish countryside with his practical servant, Sancho Panza. In this famous excerpt, Don Quixote's noble motives give dignity to his foolish battle with the windmills.

J ust then they came in sight of thirty or forty windmills that rise from that plain, and no sooner did Don Quixote see them than he said to his squire: "Fortune is guiding our affairs better than we ourselves could have wished. Do you see over yonder, friend Sancho, thirty or forty hulking giants? I intend to do battle with them and slay them. With the spoils we shall begin to be rich, for this is a righteous war. . . ."

"What giants?" asked Sancho Panza.

"Those you see over there," replied his master, "with the long arms; some of them have them well-nigh[1] two leagues in length."

"Take care, sir," cried Sancho. "Those over there are not giants but windmills, and those things that seem to be armed are their sails, which when they are whirled around by the wind turn the millstone."

"It is clear," replied Don Quixote, "that you are not experienced in adventures. Those are giants, and if you are afraid, turn aside and pray whilst I enter into fierce and unequal battle with them."

Uttering these words, he clapped spurs to Rozinante, his steed, without heeding the cries of his squire, Sancho, who warned him that he was not going to attack giants, but windmills. But so convinced was he that they were giants that he neither heard his squire's shouts nor did he notice what they were, though he was very near them. Instead, he rushed on, shouting in a loud voice: "Fly not, cowards and vile caitliffs[2]; one knight alone attacks you!" At that moment a slight breeze arose and the great sails began to move. . . .

He ran his lance into the sail, but the wind twisted it with such violence that it shivered the lance in pieces and dragged both rider and horse after it, rolling them over and over on the ground, sorely damaged.

1. **well-nigh** (wel ny) *adv.* nearly
2. **caitliff** (KAYT lif) *n.* cowardly person

▲ Miguel de Cervantes

▼ An illustration from *Don Quixote* shows Sancho Panza shouting after his master, who is battling windmills.

Thinking Critically
1. **Synthesize Information** What values of chivalry motivate Don Quixote's attack on the windmills?
2. **Analyze Literature** How does Cervantes show both sides of Don Quixote—the noble and the foolish—in this excerpt?

History Background

Miguel de Cervantes As a young man, Cervantes fought in the battle at Lepanto; he was shot three times, his left hand permanently crippled. Returning from war, he was enslaved by Algerian pirates for five years. Although he returned a war hero, he was quickly forgotten. He wrote perhaps thirty unsuccessful plays. Desperate, he took a job provisioning the Spanish Armada but was charged with embezzling funds and jailed. Past fifty and wretchedly poor, Cervantes created his masterpiece, *Don Quixote,* a popular satire. With its lively and highly original characters and narrative, it is viewed today as the first modern European novel. Cervantes is often ranked with Shakespeare, his contemporary, as one of literature's most important writers.

Don Quixote by Miguel de Cervantes

Objectives
- Understand a key piece of literature from Spain's golden age.
- Describe the characters and themes of *Don Quixote* and its portrayal of medieval chivalry.

Build Background Knowledge 🔵
Ask students to recall what they know about the period of medieval chivalry. Then ask them to recall what they know about Spain during the time of Philip II. Have them list the features that stayed the same in European society and those that changed between the two time periods. Then have students predict how these factors might have affected Cervantes's writing.

Instruct
- Ask **What values do stories about knights and chivalry embrace?** *(individual heroism, Christian faith, and a spirit of adventure and travel)* **Where else were these values expressed during the time of Philip II?** *(in Spain's colonial expansion and in its religious wars)*
- Ask **In Don Quixote's mind, what are his motives for attacking the "giants"?** *(to prove his bravery, to gain riches, and to engage in a "righteous war")* **What qualities in Don Quixote does Cervantes seem to admire?** *(his courage, his desire to battle evil)* **What qualities in Don Quixote does Cervantes seem to mock?** *(his inability to see the obvious and to live in the present)*

Monitor Progress
Share with students the History Background note about Cervantes' life. Ask students to write a paragraph exploring how Cervantes' own background shaped his writing of *Don Quixote.* Have students include specific quotations from the selection in their paragraph.

Thinking Critically
1. the desire to prove his courage and prowess in battle, the desire to combat evil
2. He shows both sides by having Don Quixote voice his noble intentions while Sancho Panza points out the foolishness of Don Quixote's actions.

Objectives

As you teach this section, keep students focused on the following objectives to help them answer the Section Focus Question and master core content.

- Understand how Henry IV rebuilt France after the wars of religion.
- Explain how Louis XIV became an absolute monarch.
- Describe how Versailles was a symbol of royal power.
- Identify Louis XIV's successes and failures.

Prepare to Read

Build Background Knowledge ⑬

Ask students to recall what they know about the theory of the divine right of kings. Then ask them to predict how this theory might allow Louis XIV to strengthen royal power.

Set a Purpose ⑬

- **WITNESS HISTORY** Read the selection aloud or play the audio.

  🔊 AUDIO **Witness History Audio CD,** Life at Versailles

  Ask **Why did Louis XIV structure life at Versailles around rituals and extravagant events?** *(Doing so enabled him to keep the nobles under his control at court and thereby dependent on him.)*

- **Focus** Point out the Section Focus Question and write it on the board. Tell students to refer to this question as they read. *(Answer appears with Section 2 Assessment answers.)*

- **Preview** Have students preview the Section Objectives and the list of Terms, People, and Places.

- **Note Taking** Have students read this section using the Guided Questioning strategy (TE, p. T20). As they read, have students fill in the concept web with details about Louis XIV's rule.

  📝 **Reading and Note Taking Study Guide,** p. 66

A delicate, beaded shoe from Louis's era

WITNESS HISTORY 🔊 AUDIO

Life at Versailles

At Versailles, the palace court of Louis XIV, life revolved around the king. Nobles waited days or weeks for the honor of attending the king while he dressed or bathed. Every evening the king was at the center of a lavish entertainment, followed by a supper of dozens of rich dishes. The elaborate and extravagant rituals that governed life at court masked a very serious purpose—they were a way for Louis XIV to control every aspect of court life and ensure his absolute authority.

Focus Question How did France become the leading power of Europe under the absolute rule of Louis XIV?

Louis XIV rides a powerful horse, displaying his strength and abilities.

France Under Louis XIV

Objectives

- Understand how Henry IV rebuilt France after the wars of religion.
- Explain how Louis XIV became an absolute monarch.
- Describe how Versailles was a symbol of royal power.
- Identify Louis XIV's successes and failures.

Terms, People, and Places

Huguenots	intendant
Henry IV	Jean-Baptiste Colbert
Edict of Nantes	Versailles
Cardinal Richelieu	*levée*
Louis XIV	balance of power

Note Taking

Reading Skill: Identify Supporting Details As you read about the rule of Louis XIV and how he strengthened the monarchy, use a concept web like the one below to record details that support the main ideas in this section. Add as many circles as you need.

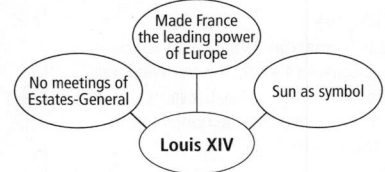

Made France the leading power of Europe

No meetings of Estates-General

Sun as symbol

Louis XIV

In the last half of the fifteenth century, France enjoyed a period of peace. After driving out the English, the French kings were able to solidify their power within their own realm. But in the 1500s, rivalry with Charles V of Spain and then religious conflict plunged the kingdom into turmoil.

Henry IV Restores Order

In the late 1500s France was torn apart by turbulent wars of religion. A century later, France was a strong, unified nation-state ruled by the most powerful monarch in Europe.

Religious Strife From the 1560s to the 1590s, religious wars between the Catholic majority and French Protestants, called **Huguenots** (HYOO guh nahts), tore France apart. Leaders on both sides used the strife to further their own ambitions.

The worst incident began on St. Bartholomew's Day (a Catholic holiday), August 24, 1572. While Huguenot and Catholic nobles were gathered for a royal wedding, a plot by Catholic royals led to the massacre of 3,000 Huguenots. In the next few days, thousands more were slaughtered. For many, the St. Bartholomew's Day Massacre symbolized the complete breakdown of order in France.

Bringing Peace to a Shattered Land In 1589, a Huguenot prince inherited the French throne as **Henry IV.** For four years Henry fought against fierce Catholic opposition to gain control of France. Finally, to end the conflict, he converted to Catholicism. "Paris is well worth a Mass," he is supposed to have said. To protect Protestants, however, in 1598 he issued the **Edict of Nantes** granting the Huguenots religious toleration and other freedoms.

Vocabulary Builder

Use the information below and the following resources to teach the high-use word from this section.

All in One **Teaching Resources, Unit 1,** p. 68; **Teaching Resources, Skills Handbook,** p. 3

High-Use Word	Definition and Sample Sentence
erode, p. 152	*v.* to wear away or disintegrate
	Many years of disappointment had **eroded** Robin's trust in people and the promises they made.

Henry IV then set out to repair France. His goal, he said, was not the victory of one sect over another, but "a chicken in every pot"—a good Sunday dinner for every peasant. Under Henry, the government reached into every area of French life. Royal officials administered justice, improved roads, built bridges, and revived agriculture. By building the royal bureaucracy and reducing the influence of nobles, Henry IV laid the foundations on which future French monarchs would build absolute power.

Cardinal Richelieu Strengthens Royal Authority When Henry IV was killed by an assassin in 1610, his nine-year-old son, Louis XIII, inherited the throne. For a time, nobles reasserted their power. Then, in 1624, Louis appointed **Cardinal Richelieu** (ree shul YOO) as his chief minister. This cunning, capable leader devoted the next 18 years to strengthening the central government.

Richelieu sought to destroy the power of the Huguenots and nobles—two groups that did not bow to royal authority. Although he allowed the Huguenots to practice their religion, he smashed their walled cities and outlawed their armies. Likewise, he defeated the private armies of the nobles and destroyed their fortified castles. While reducing their independence, Richelieu tied the nobles to the king by giving them high posts at court or in the royal army.

Richelieu also handpicked his able successor, Cardinal Mazarin (ma za RAN). When five-year-old **Louis XIV** inherited the throne in 1643, the year after Richelieu's death, Mazarin was in place to serve as chief minister. Like Richelieu, Mazarin worked tirelessly to extend royal power.

✓ **Checkpoint** What rights did the Edict of Nantes extend to Huguenots?

An Absolute Monarch Rises

Soon after Louis XIV became king, disorder again swept France. In an uprising called the *Fronde*, nobles, merchants, peasants, and the urban poor each rebelled in order to protest royal power or preserve their own. On one occasion, rioters drove the boy king from his palace. It was an experience Louis would never forget. When Mazarin died in 1661, the 23-year-old Louis resolved to take complete control over the government himself. "I have been pleased to entrust the government of my affairs to the late Cardinal," he declared. "It is now time that I govern them myself."

"I Am the State" Like his great-grandfather Philip II of Spain, Louis XIV firmly believed in his divine right to rule. He took the sun as the symbol of his absolute power. Just as the sun stands at the center of the solar system, he argued, so the Sun King stands at the center of the nation. Louis is often quoted as saying, *"L'état, c'est moi"* (lay TAH seh MWAH), which in English translates as "I am the state."

During his reign, Louis did not once call a meeting of the Estates General, the medieval council made up of representatives of all French social classes. In fact, the Estates General did not meet between 1614 and 1789. Thus, the Estates General played no role in checking royal power.

BIOGRAPHY

Cardinal Richelieu

Armand Richelieu's (1585–1642) parents expected great things from him. They even invited the king of France to attend Armand's christening, promising that someday he would be a leader of France.

The young boy also aspired to greatness as he was growing up. At first, he received training to become a disciplined and authoritative military officer. Then, at his family's request, he switched direction. At age 17, he began training to become a bishop in the Catholic Church. The path was different but the purpose was the same: to become a leader and to serve the monarch.

Over the next 40 years, Armand Richelieu rose to the highest levels of authority in both religious and political circles. He became the true power behind the throne of King Louis XIII. **What characteristics of Richelieu does the artist portray in this painting?**

Teach

Henry IV Restores Order

Instruct

■ **Introduce** Explain the religious wars between the Catholic majority and the Huguenots. Then display **Color Transparency 95: St. Bartholomew's Day Massacre.** Ask **What sort of place is shown?** *(royal castles, rich homes)* **What kinds of people are involved?** *(wealthy nobles).* Point out Notre Dame Cathedral and then ask **Why is it in the center of the scene?** *(as the center of Catholic faith)* Tell students that so many people were slaughtered in the ensuing months that bodies filled the rivers and people stopped eating fish.
🏛 **Color Transparencies,** 95

■ **Teach** Inform students that the St. Bartholomew's Day Massacre occurred on the future King Henry IV's wedding day. Ask **How did Henry IV reunite France?** *(by becoming Catholic, granting rights to Huguenots, and strengthening royal power)* **Which groups did Cardinals Richelieu and Mazarin weaken to increase royal power?** *(Huguenots and nobles)*

■ **Quick Activity** Henry IV and Richelieu made many improvements to France but also extended royal power. Hold a debate on whether their changes were ultimately good or bad for France.

Independent Practice

Tell students that Henry IV's goal—"A chicken in every pot"—became an enduring slogan. Have students create other slogans appropriate to the reign of either Henry IV or Louis XIII.

Monitor Progress

To check students' understanding, ask students to compare the reigns of Henry IV and Louis XIII to that of Philip II of Spain.

Answers

✓ religious toleration and other rights
BIOGRAPHY his seriousness and the power of his religious office

An Absolute Monarch Rises

Instruct

- **Introduce: Key Terms** Ask students to find the key term *intendant* (in blue) in the text and explain its meaning. Then have them reread the Witness History selection. Ask them to predict how intendants would help a king gain the absolute power Louis describes.

- **Teach** Ask **What was the *Fronde*?** *(an uprising soon after Louis XIV became king that protested the growing power of the royals)* **How did it affect Louis' reign?** *(He later took the government of France strongly in hand himself.)* Then discuss ways that Louis XIV kept the power of other groups in check. Then ask **How did Colbert boost the economy?** *(cleared land for farming, encouraged mining and industry, built luxury trades, put tariffs on imports, encouraged colonies, regulated trade)*

- **Quick Activity** Divide students into four groups, representing nobles, merchants, peasants, and the urban poor. Have each group list advantages and disadvantages brought by Louis XIV's reign. Then have all groups debate whether they should organize an uprising like the *Fronde*.

Independent Practice

Read aloud the Primary Source selection on this page. Then ask students to write a paragraph explaining ways in which Louis's and Colbert's policies reinforced the relationship between king and people, which is described by Bossuet. Use the Think-Write-Pair-Share strategy (TE, p. T23) to have students share their work with each other.

Monitor Progress

As students complete their concept webs, circulate to make sure they understand how Louis XIV strengthened royal power. For a completed version of the concept web, see

 Note Taking Transparencies, 129

Answers

✔ It symbolized his role as the all-powerful center of the nation.

PRIMARY SOURCE to rule with complete authority over his subjects

---

Louis XIV Strengthens Royal Power Louis spent many hours each day attending to government affairs. To strengthen the state, he followed the policies of Richelieu. He expanded the bureaucracy and appointed **intendants,** royal officials who collected taxes, recruited soldiers, and carried out his policies in the provinces. These and other government jobs often went to wealthy middle-class men. In this way Louis cemented his ties with the middle class, thus checking the power of the nobles and the Church. The king also built the French army into the strongest in Europe. The state paid, fed, trained, and supplied up to 300,000 soldiers. Louis used this highly disciplined army to enforce his policies at home and abroad.

Colbert Builds France's Finances Louis's brilliant finance minister, **Jean-Baptiste Colbert** (kohl behr), imposed mercantilist policies to bolster the economy. He had new lands cleared for farming, encouraged mining and other basic industries, and built up luxury trades such as lacemaking. To protect French manufacturers, Colbert put high tariffs on imported goods. He also fostered overseas colonies, such as New France in North America and several colonies in India, and regulated trade with the colonies to enrich the royal treasury. Colbert's policies helped make France the wealthiest state in Europe. Yet not even the financial genius of Colbert could produce enough income to support the huge costs of Louis's court and his many foreign wars.

✔ **Checkpoint**   Why did Louis XIV choose the sun as his symbol?

Versailles: Symbol of Royal Power

In the countryside near Paris, Louis XIV turned a royal hunting lodge into the immense palace of **Versailles** (ver SY). He spared no expense to make it the most magnificent building in Europe. Its halls and salons displayed the finest paintings and statues, and they glittered with chandeliers and mirrors. In the royal gardens, millions of flowers, trees, and fountains were set out in precise geometric patterns. Versailles became the perfect symbol of the Sun King's wealth and power. As both the king's home and the seat of government, it housed nobles, officials, and servants.

Conducting Court Ceremonies Louis XIV perfected elaborate ceremonies that emphasized his own importance. Each day began in the king's bedroom with a major ritual known as the *levée* (luh VAY), or rising. High-ranking nobles competed for the honor of holding the royal washbasin or handing the king his diamond-buckled shoes. At night, the ceremony was repeated in reverse. Wives of nobles vied to attend upon women of the royal family.

Rituals such as the *levée* served a serious purpose. French nobles were descendants of the feudal lords who held power in medieval times. At liberty on their estates, these nobles were a threat to the power of the monarchy. By luring nobles to Versailles, Louis turned them into courtiers angling for privileges rather than rival warriors battling for power. His tactic worked because he carefully protected their prestige and left them exempt from paying taxes.

The Sun King developed his philosophy of absolutism with the help of a brilliant bishop named Jacques Bénigne Bossuet (1627–1704). In his writings, Bossuet argued that the Bible shows that a monarch rules by the will of God. Therefore, opposition to the monarch is a sin. Bossuet also believed that, although the monarch should rule absolutely, it was God's will that he or she act only in the best interest of the nation. **According to Bossuet, what is the role of a king?**

Primary Source

❝ The royal power is absolute. . . . The prince need render account of his acts to no one. . . . Without this absolute authority [he] could neither do good nor repress evil. It is necessary that his power be such that no one can hope to escape him. . . . The prince . . . is not regarded as a private person: he is a public personage, all the state is in him; the will of all the people is included in his. As all perfection and all strength are united in God, so all the power of individuals is united in the person of the prince. ❞
—Bishop Jacques Bénigne Bossuet, "Politics Drawn from the Very Words of Scripture," 1679

History Background

Court Etiquette The strictness of etiquette at Versailles made it almost impossible to relax. A noble would never consider walking out of his court appointed place in a royal procession. Knocking on a door was forbidden. Instead, one was to scratch on the door with the fingernail of the little finger. Any digression from court etiquette subjected one to open derision and ridicule for days and might even result in banishment from court. One duchess who sat down at a gaming table when she was not playing was never invited to the Palace of Versailles again.

● INFOGRAPHIC

Separate Classes
LIFE IN FRANCE IN THE 1600S

It is no surprise that the life of Louis XIV is central to French history. Historians and social observers wrote volumes about this larger-than-life king, and buildings like Versailles survive as testaments to his legacy. Yet the vast majority of French people were not nobles, and never set foot in Versailles. They performed various jobs, from artisan, to soldier, to merchant. Rather than fancy balls, they enjoyed street plays and cockfights. Many were peasants, living hard and simple lives in the countryside. All of these people paid heavy taxes that supported the nobles' lavish lifestyles.

▲ A noblewoman is dressed in the romantic style of the time. French monarchs used Versailles' Hall of Mirrors, in the background above, for political and social ceremonies. In the foreground is a richly embroidered bag that a noble may have owned.

Women in the lower classes, like the woman below, might have been field workers, street vendors, or maids for noble families. In the background, French villagers tend livestock and wash clothes. ▼

"In France, nine-tenths of the people die of hunger, one-tenth of indigestion."
—Italian ambassador to Louis's court

Thinking Critically
1. **Draw Inferences** Read the quotation. Judging from the quotation, what is the speaker's view of the differences between nobles and commoners?
2. **Draw Conclusions** Why are the lives of nobles and royalty better documented than those of commoners?

Link to Dance

Ballet Brought to France from Italy by Caterina de' Medici (mother of Henry IV), ballet was originally a spectacle with elaborate costumes, songs, poetry, and dance. In the court of Louis XIV, the king and his courtiers performed the ballets themselves. At age fourteen, Louis danced the role of Apollo, god of the sun, and later became known as the Sun King. His courtiers had to learn and practice many complex dances and perform them at the king's whim. Courtiers stood and bowed in what became ballet's five foot positions. When he grew older, Louis stopped dancing, and so did his courtiers. Louis then started the first professional ballet school. Only later did ballet develop lighter costumes, slippers without heels, and dancing *en pointe.*

Assess Progress

- Have students complete the Section Assessment.

- Administer the Section Quiz.

 **Teaching Resources, Unit 1,** p. 64

- To further assess student understanding, use

   Progress Monitoring Transparencies, 68

Reteach

If students need more instruction, have them read the section summary.

 Reading and Note Taking Study Guide, p. 67

 Adapted Reading and Note Taking Study Guide, p. 67

 Spanish Reading and Note Taking Study Guide, p. 67

Extend

Hold a class debate on whether a U.S. president would ever say "I am the state." Ask students whether citizens might feel differently about such a statement at a time of crisis, such as an invasion.

Answers

✓ He kept them tied to the court; he exempted them from paying taxes.

✓ Waging war drained his treasury; expelling Huguenots removed some of his most productive subjects.

Patronizing the Arts The king and his court supported a "splendid century" of the arts. The age of Louis XIV came to be known as the classical age of French drama. In painting, music, architecture, and decorative arts, French styles became the model for all Europe. A new form of dance drama, ballet, gained its first great popularity at the French court. As a leading patron of culture, Louis sponsored the French Academies, which set high standards for both the arts and the sciences.

✓ **Checkpoint** How did Louis XIV secure support from the nobility?

A Strong State Declines

Louis XIV ruled France for 72 years—far longer than any other monarch. At the end of Louis's reign, France was the strongest state in Europe. However, some of Louis's decisions eventually caused France's prosperity to erode.

Waging Costly Wars Louis XIV poured vast resources into wars meant to expand French borders. However, rival rulers joined forces to check these ambitions. Led by the Dutch or the English, these alliances fought to maintain the **balance of power**. The goal was to maintain a distribution of military and economic power among European nations to prevent any one country from dominating the region.

In 1700, Louis's grandson Philip V inherited the throne of Spain. To maintain the balance of power, neighboring nations led by England fought to prevent the union of France and Spain. The War of the Spanish Succession dragged on until 1713, when an exhausted France signed the Treaty of Utrecht (YOO trekt). Philip remained on the Spanish throne, but France agreed never to unite the two crowns.

Persecuting Huguenots Louis saw France's Protestant minority as a threat to religious and political unity. In 1685, he revoked the Edict of Nantes. More than 100,000 Huguenots fled France, settling mainly in England, the Netherlands, Germany, Poland, and the Americas. The Huguenots had been among the hardest working and most prosperous of Louis's subjects. Their loss was a serious blow to the French economy, just as the expulsion of Spanish Muslims and Jews had hurt Spain.

✓ **Checkpoint** How did Louis's actions weaken France's economy?

Vocabulary Builder

erode—(ee ROHD) v. wear away or disintegrate

SECTION 2 Assessment

Progress Monitoring Online
For: Self-quiz with vocabulary practice
Web Code: nba-1621

Terms, People, and Places

1. What do each of the key terms, people, and places listed at the beginning of the section have in common? Explain.

Note Taking

2. **Reading Skill: Identify Supporting Details** Use your completed concept web to answer the Focus Question: How did France become the leading power of Europe under the absolute rule of Louis XIV?

Comprehension and Critical Thinking

3. **Draw Inferences** How did Henry IV's conversion to Catholicism help France unite?

4. **Identify Central Issues** What was the purpose of Louis XIV's extravagant palace and daily rituals?

5. **Recognize Ideologies** Why did other European nations form alliances to oppose France's plans to expand?

● **Writing About History**

Quick Write: Support Opinions With Evidence Choose a topic from the section, such as whether or not you think Louis XIV's reign was good for France. Make a list of evidence from the text that supports your opinion.

Section 2 Assessment

1. They all have to do with French government and power from the late 1500s to the early 1700s.

2. Louis XIV strengthened royal power, the army, the economy, and the arts to make France the leading power of Europe.

3. Because he was a Huguenot, Henry IV's conversion united France by healing the division between Huguenots and Catholics.

4. They kept the nobles busy in the king's court instead of battling for power.

5. They wanted to keep the balance of power so they would not be dominated by France or any other European nation.

● **Writing About History**

Responses should include a substantial list of evidence that clearly supports an opinion.

For additional assessment, have students access **Progress Monitoring Online** at **Web Code nba-1621.**

Concept Connector

THE ESSENTIAL ?

POLITICAL SYSTEMS

How do political systems rise, develop, and decline?

In This Chapter

Every society has developed some political system by which either the one, the few, or the many rule over others. Some rulers, like King Louis XIV of France (right), have claimed to hold absolute power. Louis XIV's abuse of his power sowed the seeds for the later overthrow of the French monarchy.

Throughout History

3300 B.C. The practice of rule by war leaders evolves into hereditary rule in ancient Sumer.

1766 B.C.–1911 A.D. In China, the idea of the Mandate of Heaven is used to explain why dynasties rise and fall.

321 B.C. Chandragupta Maurya forges an empire in India and maintains order with a well-organized bureaucracy.

900 A.D. Feudalism develops in Europe because individual monarchs are too weak to maintain law and order.

1556 Philip II of Spain asserts divine right, saying that his authority to rule comes directly from God.

1789 The United States Constitution creates the framework for the American federal system of government.

Continuing Today

With resistance to apartheid growing both in South Africa and in the international community, South Africa changed its constitution in 1996. Once a nation ruled by the minority population, South Africa became a nation with a democratic political system. Each election is another milestone in this transformation.

TRANSFER Activities

1. **Analyze** Throughout history, how have political systems developed?

2. **Evaluate** Why do you think political systems change over time?

3. **Transfer** Complete a Web Quest in which you research a particular political system; record your thoughts in the Concept Connector Journal; and learn to make a video. Web Code: nbh-1608

History Background

Democratization The late twentieth century saw many countries change from autocratic rule to democracy, a process scholars call *democratization*. One scholar, Samuel P. Huntington, sees three waves of democratization in history: in the early 1800s, just after World War II, and in the late 1900s. In some countries, democratization was followed by reversion to autocracy. Some scholars believe that trust, cooperation, and tolerance of differences are essential for democracy to survive. Sometimes, deep conflicts can lead to violence and a reassertion of control by one or a few. But in South Africa, Nelson Mandela, who became the president of the new democracy after being jailed for 27 years, kept the head of the old, racist regime as his vice president. This spirit of cooperation helped lead to a peaceful transition.

Concept Connector ?

Political Systems

Objectives
- Understand how a political system develops.
- Explain why political systems gain or lose support.
- Complete a web quest on political systems.

Build Background Knowledge
Have students think about the history of the government. Who ruled during the colonial period? Have them explain why and how the system changed. Check students' understanding of the term *political system*. Address any misunderstanding.

Instruct L3
- Direct students' attention to the Essential Question. **How do political systems rise, develop, and decline?** Have students give examples from the chapter of the rise and fall of the French and Spanish monarchies from the mid-1500s to 1800.
- Using the timeline, have students note reasons for the cycle of power. Ask: **What reason did rulers give for their absolute power? What would cause the rulers to lose power?**
- Assign the Web Quest on political systems.

Independent Practice
Concept Connector Have students fill in the Web Quest reflection question on political systems in their Concept Connector Journal.

 Reading and Note Taking Study Guide, p. 289

Monitor Progress
Circulate to make sure that students are filling in their Concept Connector journal. Ensure they understand how political systems rise, develop and decline.

Transfer Activities
1. Political systems develop to avoid chaos. They create governments to maintain order protect people from attack.
2. Possible answer: People find the system is not providing for their needs. The ruler may be abusing power, too many people may be suffering, or nation may be losing economic or international power.
3. Students' work should be evaluated against the rubric at Web Code nbh-1608.

Objectives

As you teach this section, keep students focused on the following objectives to help them answer the Section Focus Question and master core content.

- Describe the Tudor monarchs' relations with Parliament.
- Analyze how clashes between the Stuarts and Parliament ushered in a century of revolution.
- Understand how the English Civil War and the development of the Commonwealth led to the Glorious Revolution.
- Explain the development of English constitutional government.

Prepare to Read

Build Background Knowledge L3

Ask students to recall the significance of the Magna Carta and the power of the English Parliament. Ask them to predict how the English might respond to an absolute monarch.

Set a Purpose L3

- **WITNESS HISTORY** Read the selection aloud or play the audio.

  🔊 AUDIO **Witness History Audio CD,** Charting a Collision Course

  Ask students to compare this selection to the Witness History selection on page 148 and the primary source on page 150. Ask **How does the quotation from James I differ?** (*It says that kings not only are appointed by God but can themselves be called gods.*) Ask why James I's point of view might provoke anger.

- **Focus** Point out the Section Focus Question and write it on the board. Tell students to refer to this question as they read. (*Answer appears with Section 3 Assessment answers.*)

- **Preview** Have students preview the Section Objectives and the list of Terms, People, and Places.

Answer

✔ He needed Parliament's approval to levy new taxes and to obtain a divorce.

A portrait of King James of England painted around 1619 gives no hint of the monarch's frequent clashes with Parliament.

Charting a Collision Course

In 1603 James I, a monarch with strong ideas about his role, took the English throne. In 1610 the king made a speech to Parliament that would have quite the opposite effect of what he intended:

❝ The state of Monarchy is the supremest thing upon earth; for kings are not only God's lieutenants upon earth and sit upon God's throne, but even by God himself they are called gods. . . . Kings are justly called gods for that they exercise a manner or resemblance of Divine power upon earth. . . . And to the King is due both the affection of the soul and the service of the body of his subjects. . . .❞
—James I

Focus Question How did the British Parliament assert its rights against royal claims to absolute power in the 1600s?

Parliament Triumphs in England

Objectives

- Describe the Tudor monarchs' relations with Parliament.
- Analyze how clashes between the Stuarts and Parliament ushered in a century of revolution.
- Understand how the English Civil War and the development of the Commonwealth led to the Glorious Revolution.
- Explain the development of English constitutional government.

Terms, People, and Places

James I	limited monarchy
dissenter	constitutional
Puritans	government
Charles I	cabinet
Oliver Cromwell	oligarchy
English Bill of Rights	

Note Taking

Reading Skill: Identify Supporting Details As you read the section, use a flowchart to record details about the evolution of the English Parliament. One has been started for you.

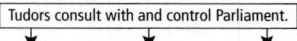

Tudors consult with and control Parliament.

In the 1600s, while Louis XIV perfected royal absolutism in France, political power in England took a different path. Despite attempts by English monarchs to increase royal authority, Parliament steadily expanded its own influence.

The Tudors Work With Parliament

From 1485 to 1603, England was ruled by Tudor monarchs. Although the Tudors believed in divine right, they shrewdly recognized the value of good relations with Parliament. As you have read, when Henry VIII broke with the Roman Catholic Church, he turned to Parliament to legalize his actions. Parliament approved the Act of Supremacy, making the monarch head of the Church of England.

A constant need for money also led Henry to consult Parliament frequently. Although he had inherited a bulging treasury, he quickly used up his funds fighting overseas wars. To levy new taxes, the king had to seek the approval of Parliament. Members of Parliament tended to vote as Henry's agents instructed. Still, they became accustomed to being consulted on important matters.

When Elizabeth I gained the throne, she too both consulted and controlled Parliament. Her advisors conveyed the queen's wishes to Parliament and forbade discussion of certain subjects, such as foreign policy or the queen's marriage. Her skill in handling Parliament helped make "Good Queen Bess" a popular and successful ruler.

✔ **Checkpoint** Why did Henry VIII work with Parliament?

Vocabulary Builder

Use the information below and the following resources to teach the high-use words from this section.
All in One **Teaching Resources, Unit 1,** p. 68; **Teaching Resources, Skills Handbook,** p. 3

High-Use Words	Definitions and Sample Sentences
suppress, p. 155	*v.* to keep from being revealed; to put down by force The government **suppressed** the news about the president's illness.
tolerate, p. 158	*v.* to respect others' beliefs without sharing them Although she was a Republican and he was a Democrat, they **tolerated** each other's political views for the sake of their friendship.

A Century of Revolution Begins

Elizabeth died childless in 1603. Her heir was her relative James Stuart, the ruling king of Scotland. The Stuarts were neither as popular as the Tudors nor as skillful in dealing with Parliament. They also inherited problems that Henry and Elizabeth had long <u>suppressed</u>. The result was a "century of revolution" that pitted the Stuart monarchs against Parliament.

The Stuarts Issue a Challenge The first Stuart monarch, James I, had agreed to rule according to English laws and customs. Soon, however, he was lecturing Parliament about divine right. "I will not be content that my power be disputed upon," he declared. Leaders in the House of Commons fiercely resisted the king's claim to absolute power.

James repeatedly clashed with Parliament over money and foreign policy. He needed funds to finance his lavish court and wage wars. When members wanted to discuss foreign policy before voting funds, James dissolved Parliament and collected taxes on his own.

James also clashed with dissenters, Protestants who differed with the Church of England. One group, called Puritans, sought to "purify" the church of Catholic practices. Puritans called for simpler services and a more democratic church without bishops. James rejected their demands, vowing to "harry them out of this land or else do worse."

Parliament Responds In 1625, Charles I inherited the throne. Like his father, Charles behaved like an absolute monarch. He imprisoned his foes without trial and squeezed the nation for money. By 1628, however, his need to raise taxes forced Charles to summon Parliament. Before voting any funds, Parliament insisted that Charles sign the Petition of Right. This document prohibited the king from raising taxes without Parliament's consent or from jailing anyone without legal justification.

Charles did sign the Petition, but he then dissolved Parliament in 1629. For 11 years, he ignored the Petition and ruled the nation without Parliament. During that time, he created bitter enemies, especially among Puritans. His Archbishop of Canterbury, William Laud, tried to force all clergy to follow strict Anglican rules, dismissing or imprisoning dissenters. Many people felt that the archbishop was trying to revive Catholic practices.

In 1637, Charles and Laud tried to impose the Anglican prayer book on Scotland. The Calvinist Scots revolted. To get funds to suppress the Scottish rebellion, Charles once again had to summon Parliament in 1640. When it met, however, Parliament launched its own revolt.

The Long Parliament Begins The 1640 Parliament became known as the Long Parliament because it lasted on and off until 1653. Its actions triggered the greatest political revolution in English history. In a mounting struggle with Charles I, Parliament tried and executed his chief ministers, including Archbishop Laud. It called for the abolition of bishops and declared that the Parliament could not be dissolved without its own consent.

Vocabulary Builder

suppressed—(suh PRESD) *v.* kept from being revealed; put down by force

A Voice for Absolutism

In 1651, two years after the English Civil War ended, English political philosopher Thomas Hobbes published *Leviathan*. In this book, he explained why he favored an absolute monarchy. How might people who supported Parliament over the monarch have argued against Hobbes's view?

Primary Source

❝During the time men live without a common power to keep them all in awe, they are in that condition which is called war. . . . In such condition, there is no place for industry. . . . no arts; no letters; no society; and, which is worst of all, continual fear and danger of violent death. And the life of man [is] solitary, poor, nasty, brutish, and short.❞
—Thomas Hobbes, *Leviathan*

History Background

Good Queen Bess When Elizabeth took the throne, England had suffered decades of religious and political turmoil. An observer noted: "The Queen poor. The realm exhausted. The nobility poor and decayed. Want of good captains and soldiers. The people out of order. Justice not executed." Due to Elizabeth's skillful management and striking speeches, England was a great power at the time of her death. In 1588, as English forces mustered to combat the Spanish Armada, she gave a stirring speech: "I am come amongst you . . . resolved in the midst and heat of battle, to live and die amongst you all. . . . I know I have the body but of a weak and feeble woman, but I have the heart and stomach of a king and of a King of England too."

■ **Note Taking** Have students read this section using the Structured Read Aloud strategy (TE, p. T20). As they read, have students create a flowchart with details about events that led to an increase in Parliament's power.

Reading and Note Taking Study Guide, p. 68

Teach

The Tudors Work With Parliament

Instruct

■ **Introduce** Discuss with students how the tradition of the English Parliament set England apart from other European nations. Explain that each English monarch had developed his or her own method for dealing with Parliament.

■ **Teach** Point out that the Tudor monarchs developed a good relationship with Parliament. Ask **How did Henry and Elizabeth handle Parliament?** *(They regularly consulted Parliament but controlled it through their agents.)*

■ **Quick Activity** Read aloud this speech that Elizabeth gave to Parliament and discuss its meaning: "Though God hath raised me high, yet this I count the glory of my crown, that I have reigned with your loves. . . . It is my desire to live nor reign no longer . . . than my life and reign shall be for your good. And though you have had, and may have, many princes more mighty and wise sitting in this seat, yet you never had, nor shall have, any that will be more careful and loving."

Independent Practice

Have students write an essay comparing Elizabeth's reign and her style of governing to either Philip II of Spain or Louis XIV of France.

Monitor Progress

To check student understanding, ask them how and why Parliament was involved in making the monarch the head of the Church of England.

Answer

PRIMARY SOURCE Sample: They might say that a body such as Parliament can provide the "common power" necessary for society to function productively.

A Century of Revolution Begins

Instruct

- **Introduce: Vocabulary Builder**
  Have students read the Vocabulary Builder term and its definition. Then have students reread the Witness History quotation. Ask them to speculate what practices an absolute monarch might *suppress*.

- **Teach** Explain that unlike the Tudors, the Stuart monarchs immediately clashed with various groups. Ask **Why do you think James and Charles suppressed dissenters?** *(perhaps because they feared religious dissent would lead to political dissent or even rebellion)* **How did Parliament respond?** *(by attacking the king's government and challenging his power)*

- **Quick Activity** Read aloud the Primary Source selection from the previous page or play the accompanying audio. Ask students to paraphrase this statement. Then divide students into two groups. Have them take the roles of people living in the 1600s. Stage a debate in which one group argues for Hobbes's view on absolute monarchy and another group argues against it.

  ◀))) AUDIO **Witness History Audio CD,**
  Thomas Hobbes, *Leviathan*

Independent Practice

Create a cause-and-effect chart on the board. Have students reproduce the chart individually and fill it in with each major action of James I and Charles I and each reaction from Parliament.

Monitor Progress

As students fill in their flowchart, circulate to make sure they summarize the most important events. For a completed version of the flowchart, see

🏛 **Note Taking Transparencies,** 130

Answer

✔ a legal document that prohibited the king from raising taxes without Parliament's consent or imprisoning people who had not violated laws

---

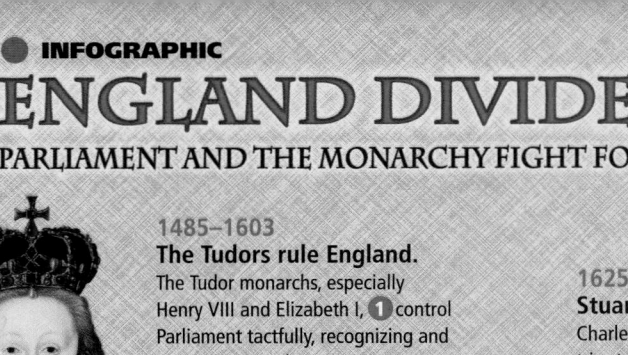

ENGLAND DIVIDED:
PARLIAMENT AND THE MONARCHY FIGHT FOR POWER

1485–1603
The Tudors rule England.
The Tudor monarchs, especially Henry VIII and Elizabeth I, ❶ control Parliament tactfully, recognizing and respecting its role in government.

1603–1625
Stuart king James I rules.
James I becomes king and immediately clashes with Parliament. In 1621, James scolds Parliament for usurping royal power, and Parliament responds with a declaration of its own rights. In the last Parliament of his reign, the aging James gives in to Parliament.

1625–1649
Stuart king Charles I rules.
Charles dissolves Parliament when it tries to expand powers to deal with an economic crisis. The Parliament of 1628 produces the Petition of Right, and later Parliaments ❷ clash with Charles over what they charge are violations of the document. Charles dissolves Parliament again.

1640–1653
The Long Parliament meets.
Faced with economic problems and invasions by Scotland, Charles is forced to call Parliament. The Long Parliament, as it became known, works to steadily expand its powers. Eventually Charles strikes back, adopting the motto "Give Caesar his Due."

Charles lashed back. In 1642, he led troops into the House of Commons to arrest its most radical leaders. They escaped through a back door and soon raised their own army. The clash now moved to the battlefield.

✔ **Checkpoint** What was the Petition of Right?

Fighting a Civil War

The civil war that followed lasted from 1642 to 1651. Like the *Fronde* that occurred about the same time in France, the English Civil War posed a major challenge to absolutism. But while the forces of royal power won in France, in England the forces of revolution triumphed.

Cavaliers and Roundheads At first, the odds seemed to favor the supporters of Charles I, called Cavaliers. Many Cavaliers were wealthy nobles, proud of their plumed hats and fashionably long hair. Well trained in dueling and warfare, the Cavaliers expected a quick victory. But their foes proved to be tough fighters with the courage of their convictions. The forces of Parliament were composed of country gentry, town-dwelling manufacturers, and Puritan clergy. They were called Roundheads because their hair was cut close around their heads.

The Roundheads found a leader of genius in **Oliver Cromwell**. A Puritan member of the lesser gentry, Cromwell proved himself to be a skilled general. He organized a "New Model Army" for Parliament, made up of officers selected for skill rather than social class, into a disciplined fighting force.

Link to Literature

The King James Bible A positive result of the king's dispute with the Puritans was his support of the Puritans' call for a new translation of the Bible. This version, known as the King James, appeared in 1611 and has had a lasting influence on English language and literature. The King James Version of the Bible represents one of the great literary achievements in English. The translators' mission was to create a text that both Anglicans and Puritans could use, expressed in the language of the day. Today scholars argue about the version's accuracy, but its poetic style and imagery still resonate in familiar excerpts, such as "Yea, though I walk through the valley of the shadow of death, I will fear no evil . . . " (Psalm 23).

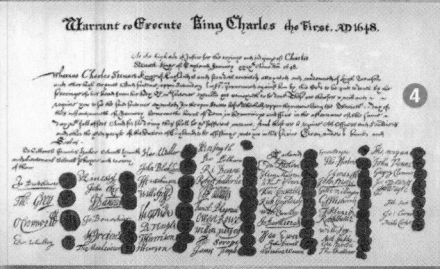

1642–1649
The English Civil War rages.
War breaks out **3** between Parliament's Roundheads (right) and Charles I's Cavaliers (left). The parliamentary forces, led by Oliver Cromwell, eventually win. In 1649, Charles is executed. **4**

1649–1660
The English Commonwealth begins and ends.
Abolishing the monarchy and House of Lords, Parliament rules as a commonwealth with Cromwell as leader. **5** Problems plague the nation, and the Commonwealth falls apart upon Cromwell's death in 1658. Groups in favor of monarchy begin to gain power.

1660–1685
The monarchy is restored.
Charles II works with Parliament to repair the shattered nation, but clashes with Parliament when he works to restore Catholicism. In 1678, Charles dissolves Parliament and builds the monarchy's power. His successor, James II, continues to push for Catholic power, and incites a backlash. James II flees England in 1688.

1688
The Glorious Revolution assures Parliament's power.
William and Mary become England's monarchs **6** with Parliament's blessing—provided that they agree to very limited powers under Parliament's domination.

XXVIII. WILLIAM the THIRD and MARY the SECOND, from 1688 to 1702.

WILLIAM the hero, with MARIA mild,
(He James's nephew, she his eldest child)
Fix'd freedom and the church, reform'd the coin,
Oppos'd the French, and settled Brunswick's line.

Thinking Critically
1. **Recognize Point of View** What does Charles I's usage of the phrase "Give Caesar his Due" tell you about his view of royal power?
2. **Recognize Ideologies** How did the religious beliefs of key people on this timeline shape political outcomes?

Cromwell's army defeated the Cavaliers in a series of decisive battles. By 1647, the king was in the hands of parliamentary forces.

A King Is Executed Eventually, Parliament set up a court to put the king on trial. It condemned him to death as "a tyrant, traitor, murderer, and public enemy." On a cold January day in 1649, Charles I stood on a scaffold surrounded by his foes. "I am a martyr of the people," he declared. Showing no fear, the king told the executioner that he himself would give the sign for him to strike. After a brief prayer, Charles knelt and placed his neck on the block. On the agreed signal, the executioner severed the king's neck with a single stroke.

The execution sent shock waves throughout Europe. In the past, a king had occasionally been assassinated or killed in battle. But for the first time, a ruling monarch had been tried and executed by his own people. The parliamentary forces had sent a clear message that, in England, no ruler could claim absolute power and ignore the rule of law.

✔ **Checkpoint** What was the result of the English Civil War?

Cromwell and the Commonwealth

After the execution of Charles I, the House of Commons abolished the monarchy, the House of Lords, and the established Church of England. It declared England a republic, known as the Commonwealth, under the leadership of Oliver Cromwell.

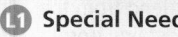

Fighting a Civil War

Instruct

■ **Introduce** Have a volunteer read aloud the description of Charles's execution, under the black heading A King Is Executed. Ask how different people in the crowd might have responded to the scene and Charles's words. Point out that he was head of the church and chose the Christian word "martyr." Ask how his words might affect future events in England and across Europe.

■ **Teach** Review the causes of the English Civil War and the events leading up to Charles I's execution. Ask **Who were the Cavaliers?** *(wealthy supporters of the king)* **Why did they expect a quick victory?** *(They were trained as soldiers.)* **What strengths did the Roundheads have?** *(religious conviction, discipline, and a skilled general, Cromwell)* Point out that after the Roundheads defeated the Cavaliers, Parliament put the king on trial. Then ask **What was the significance of King Charles's execution?** *(It showed that no ruler was above the law.)*

Independent Practice
Primary Source To make sure students understand the importance of Oliver Cromwell in shaping English history, have them read the excerpt from Oliver Cromwell's letter to Colonel Robert Hammond, November 25, 1648, and answer the questions that follow.

All in One Teaching Resources, Unit 1, p. 73

Monitor Progress

To check students' understanding, ask them to explain whom they would have supported in England's Civil War—Cromwell or Charles I—and why.

Answers

✔ Parliament won and had Charles I executed.

Thinking Critically
1. Likening himself to the emperor Caesar, Charles suggests that he is entitled to financial support without needing Parliament's approval.
2. Sample: Religious beliefs shaped the actions of the Stuart monarchs (suppressing Puritans) and Cromwell (setting up a Puritan-influenced commonwealth).

Cromwell and the Commonwealth

Instruct

- **Introduce: Vocabulary Builder**
  Have students read the Vocabulary Builder term and definition. Create two columns on the board. With students' help, list which beliefs were *tolerated* and which were not under Henry VIII, Elizabeth I, James I, Charles I, and Cromwell.

- **Teach** Explain that despite Cromwell's intention to set up a democratic republic, the Commonwealth became increasingly undemocratic. Ask **What did the Levellers want?** *(rights for poor men and for women)* **How did Cromwell seize power?** *(He used the army, first to suppress dissent, then to monopolize power.)* **What was the Restoration?** *(the return of the monarchy)*

- **Quick Activity** Direct students' attention to the feature title Our Puritan Heritage on the next page. Use the Think-Write-Pair-Share strategy (TE, p. T23) to initiate a class discussion about why universal education was important to the Puritans, why it was a revolutionary idea, and how education is related to democracy.

Independent Practice

Ask students to create a bulleted list of Cromwell's successes and failures. Then ask them to decide whether Cromwell should have been executed after he became a dictator. Students should explain their reasoning.

Monitor Progress

To check students' understanding, ask them to explain how the actions of Charles I influenced the rise of Cromwell.

Cromwell's Armor
Oliver Cromwell wore this helmet and sword when he led the English forces into Ireland.

Vocabulary Builder
tolerate—(TAHL er ayt) *v.* to respect other's beliefs without sharing them

Challenging the Commonwealth The new government faced many threats. Supporters of Charles II, the uncrowned heir to the throne, attacked England by way of Ireland and Scotland. Cromwell led forces into Ireland and brutally crushed the uprising. He then took harsh measures against the Irish Catholic majority that are still vividly remembered in that nation today. In 1652, Parliament passed a law exiling most Catholics to barren land in the west of Ireland. Any Catholic found disobeying this order could be killed on sight.

Squabbles also splintered forces within the Commonwealth. One group, called Levellers, thought that poor men should have as much say in government as the gentry, lawyers, and other leading citizens. "The poorest he that is in England hath a life to live as the greatest he," wrote one Leveller. In addition, female Levellers asserted their right to petition Parliament. These ideas horrified the gentry, who dominated Parliament. Cromwell suppressed the Levellers, as well as more radical groups who threatened ownership of private property. In 1653, as the challenges to order grew, Cromwell took the title Lord Protector. From then on, he ruled as a virtual dictator through the army.

Puritans: A Sobering Influence Under the Commonwealth, Puritans—with their goal of rooting out godlessness—gained a new voice in society. The English Civil War thus ushered in a social revolution as well as a political one.

Parliament enacted a series of laws designed to make sure that Sunday was set aside for religious observance. Anyone over the age of 14 who was caught "profaning the Lord's Day" could be fined. To the Puritans, theaters were frivolous. So, like John Calvin in Geneva, Cromwell closed all theaters. Puritans also frowned on taverns, gambling, and dancing.

Puritans felt that every Christian, rich and poor, must be able to read the Bible. To spread religious knowledge, they encouraged education for all people. By mid-century, families from all classes were sending their children to school, girls as well as boys. Puritans also pushed for changes in marriage to ensure greater fidelity. In addition to marriages based on business interests, they encouraged marriages based on love. Still, as in the past, women were seen mainly as caretakers of the family, subordinate to men.

Although Cromwell did not tolerate open worship by Roman Catholics, he believed in religious freedom for other Protestant groups. He even welcomed Jews back to England after more than 350 years of exile.

The Commonwealth Ends Oliver Cromwell died in 1658. Soon after, the Puritans lost their grip on England. Many people were tired of military rule and strict Puritan ways. In 1660, a newly elected Parliament invited Charles II to return to England from exile.

England's "kingless decade" ended with the Restoration, or return of the monarchy. Yet Puritan ideas about morality, equality, government, and education endured. In the following century, these ideas would play an important role in shaping the future of Britain's colonies in the Americas.

✔️ **Checkpoint** What was the Commonwealth?

From Restoration to Glorious Revolution

In late May 1660, cheering crowds welcomed Charles II back to London. John Evelyn, a supporter and diarist whose writings are an important source of information about English political and social history, wrote:

History Background

British Redcoats Cromwell was a fiery member of Parliament who proved a brilliant military strategist despite his lack of military training. He chose soldiers not for their social standing (as the king did) but for their proficiency. He instituted discipline and high moral standards in his New Model Army. He paid soldiers regularly, provided good weapons, and gave them brilliant red uniforms. In the heat of battle, the bright red coats helped soldiers tell friend from foe. The red color also camouflaged bloodstains from wounds, helping to keep morale high. He trained soldiers to regroup quickly in battle for a new charge. It was Britain's first professional army. After Cromwell's demise, Charles II kept the professional army, the discipline, and the red coats, which would become a symbol of British power around the world.

Answer

 The Commonwealth was the republic of England under Cromwell.

❝This day came in his Majesties Charles the Second to London after a sad, and long Exile . . . with a Triumph of above 20,000 horse and [soldiers], brandishing their swords, and shouting with unexpressible joy; the [ways strewn] with flowers, the bells ringing, the streetes hung with [tapestry].❞
—John Evelyn, *Diary*

Charles II With his charm and flashing wit, young Charles II was a popular ruler. He reopened theaters and taverns and presided over a lively court in the manner of Louis XIV. Charles reestablished the Church of England but encouraged toleration of other Protestants such as Presbyterians, Quakers, and Baptists.

Although Charles accepted the Petition of Right, he shared his father's belief in absolute monarchy and secretly had Catholic sympathies. Still, he shrewdly avoided his father's mistakes in dealing with Parliament.

James II is Forced to Flee Charles's brother, James II, inherited the throne in 1685. Unlike Charles, James practiced his Catholic faith openly. He angered his subjects by suspending laws on a whim and appointing Catholics to high office. Many English Protestants feared that James would restore the Roman Catholic Church.

In 1688, alarmed parliamentary leaders invited James's Protestant daughter, Mary, and her Dutch Protestant husband, William III of Orange, to become rulers of England. When William and Mary landed with their army late in 1688, James II fled to France. This bloodless overthrow of the king became known as the Glorious Revolution.

The English Bill of Rights Before they could be crowned, William and Mary had to accept several acts passed by Parliament in 1689 that became known as the English Bill of Rights. The Bill of Rights ensured the superiority of Parliament over the monarchy. It required the monarch to summon Parliament regularly and gave the House of Commons the "power of the purse," or control over spending. A king or queen could no longer interfere in parliamentary debates or suspend laws. The Bill of Rights also barred any Roman Catholic from sitting on the throne.

The Bill of Rights also restated the traditional rights of English citizens, such as trial by jury. It abolished excessive fines and cruel or unjust punishment. It affirmed the principle of *habeas corpus*. That is, no person could be held in prison without first being charged with a specific crime.

In addition, a separate Toleration Act, also of 1689, granted limited religious freedom to Puritans, Quakers, and other dissenters. Still, only members of the Church of England could hold public office. And Catholics were allowed no religious freedom.

Puritan girls spent hours working on embroidered samplers like this one. Such work was considered part of their education. ▼

Our Puritan Heritage

Decades before the Puritans gained power in England, Puritans living in the Massachusetts Bay colony worked to put into action their own ideas about religion and government. The Puritans knew that to assure survival of their beliefs and culture, they would have to educate their children to read and write. As soon as they were able, the Puritans began to set up schools, starting with the Boston Latin School in 1635 and then Harvard College (below) in 1636.

Eventually, the colonies became the United States. Over time, the rest of the country adopted the Puritan tradition of establishing public schools to help train children to become good citizens of their community. A literate, well-informed citizenry has continued to be a major aim of American schools to this day. **What other institutions help to train American children to be good citizens?**

Instruct

- **Introduce** Have a student read aloud the Primary Source selection, John Evelyn's description of crowds welcoming Charles II back to London. Ask them to speculate why people who were particularly tired of Puritan ways might have thrilled to the pageantry of the Restoration.

- **Teach** Explain that as in the past, religious faith became a contentious issue. Ask **How did James II anger his subjects?** *(by suspending laws and appointing Catholics to office)* **How was William and Mary's monarchy different from earlier monarchies?** *(They were invited by Parliament and had to acknowledge its supremacy.)* **What group was not included in the Toleration Act?** *(Catholics)*

- **Quick Activity** Have students volunteer provisions of the English Bill of Rights, and list them on the board. Then, with students' input, check off those that we inherited in our own Constitution and Bill of Rights.

Independent Practice

Biography To help students better understand the Quakers, have them read the biography *George Fox* and complete the worksheet.

All in One **Teaching Resources, Unit 1,** p. 72

Monitor Progress

To review this section, ask students how a limited monarchy differed from an absolute monarchy and the divine right of kings.

Connect to Our World

Civic Responsibility Habeas corpus, which means "you may have the body," requires that a prisoner must be brought before a judge and charged with a crime or be released. It is enshrined in Article I, Section 9 of the U.S. Constitution. However, it is not a right but a "privilege" that may be suspended "when in Cases of Rebellion or Invasion the public Safety may require it." President Abraham Lincoln suspended habeas corpus during the Civil War. Today, the United States, like other nations, imprisons people whom it suspects of planning terrorist acts, but who have not yet committed a crime.

Answer

Caption Sample: youth groups, volunteer organizations, religious institutions

Constitutional Government Evolves/A Society Still Ruled by the Few

Instruct

- **Introduce: Key Terms** Write the word *cabinet* on the board. Have students find the key term (in blue) in the text, learn its history, and explain its meaning. Tell students that members of the cabinet evolved into ministers with different areas of expertise, and one member became the prime (first) minister. Ask students what they know about the American cabinet and help them draw connections.

- **Teach** Explain that as constitutional government evolved, it still did not include all members of British society. Ask **What is a constitutional government?** *(a government whose power is defined and limited by law)* **Who made up Britain's first political parties?** *(Tories, who were mainly rural, conservative aristocrats, and Whigs, who were mainly urban businesspeople)* **How was Britain's government an oligarchy?** *(Power was held by a limited group of privileged people.)*

- **Quick Activity** On the board, write "monarch" at the very top and "landless poor" at the bottom. Call on students, and have each volunteer fill in one of the other groups to create a ranking of British society. Then circle the ones who held ruling power.

Independent Practice

Have students review the chart titled Influence of the Glorious Revolution on this page. Have them use details from the section and their own background knowledge to add other influences on the United States.

Monitor Progress

Check Reading and Note Taking Study Guide entries for student understanding.

Answers

 the bloodless overthrow of James II and the installation of William and Mary as monarchs

Chart Skills the English Bill of Rights

A Limited Monarchy The Glorious Revolution created not a democracy, but a type of government called **limited monarchy**, in which a constitution or legislative body limits the monarch's powers. English rulers still had much power, but they had to obey the law and govern in partnership with Parliament. In the age of absolute monarchy elsewhere in Europe, the limited monarchy in England was quite radical.

The Glorious Revolution also greatly influenced important political thinkers of the time, such as John Locke. Locke's ideas were later used by leaders of the American Revolution as the basis for their struggle, and are found in documents such as the Declaration of Independence.

✓ **Checkpoint** What was the Glorious Revolution?

Constitutional Government Evolves

In the century following the Glorious Revolution, three new political institutions arose in Britain: political parties, the cabinet, and the office of prime minister. The appearance of these institutions was part of the evolution of Britain's **constitutional government**—that is, a government whose power is defined and limited by law.

Political Parties Emerge In the late 1600s, political parties emerged in England as a powerful force in politics. At first, there were just two political parties—Tories and Whigs. Tories were generally aristocrats who sought to preserve older traditions. They supported broad royal powers and a dominant Anglican Church. Whigs backed the policies of the Glorious Revolution. They were more likely to reflect urban business interests, support religious toleration, and favor Parliament over the crown.

The Cabinet System The cabinet, another new feature of government, evolved in the 1700s after the British throne passed to a German prince. George I spoke no English and relied on the leaders in Parliament to help him rule. Under George I and his German-born son George II, a handful of parliamentary advisors set policy. They came to be referred to as the **cabinet** because of the small room, or "cabinet," where they met. In time, the cabinet gained official status.

The Prime Minister Leads the Cabinet Over time, the head of the cabinet came to be known as the prime minister. This person was always the leader of the majority party in the House of Commons. Eventually, the prime minister became the chief official of the British government. From 1721 to 1742, the able Whig leader Robert Walpole molded the cabinet into a unified body by requiring all members to agree on major issues.

Influence of the Glorious Revolution

Outcome in England

English Bill of Rights	Writings of John Locke	Constitutional Government
• People elect representatives to Parliament, which is supreme over monarch. • All citizens have natural rights.	• People have natural rights such as life, liberty, and property. • There is a social contract between people and government.	• Government is limited and defined by law. • Political parties, the cabinet, and the office of prime minister arise.

Impact on the United States

Colonists believed that they too had rights, including the right to elect people to represent them.	Locke's ideas shaped the American Revolution and the writing of the Declaration of Independence and the Constitution.	The new American nation formed a constitutional government with two parties and a cabinet; the American system included even more provisions for the separation of powers.

Chart Skills A common protest during the American Revolution was "no taxation without representation." *Which English outcome of the Glorious Revolution influenced that idea?*

History Background

Parliamentary Democracy The first model for a parliament was Rome's senate, a council of the elite. During feudal times, lords met to decide whether to support the king, leading in the 1300s to England's Magna Carta and its first parliament. A parliamentary democracy has a constitution, a parliament, and both a head of state (a monarch or, today, a president), which is a ceremonial position with limited powers, and a head of government (a prime minister), who is chosen by the parliament's ruling party from among its members. The prime minister, therefore, is not directly elected by the people and can be removed by the parliament. Because the executive and legislative branches are led by the same party, it is easier to pass reforms than in a republic. Most parliaments today include ordinary people as well as the elite and represent all the nation's people.

Although the title was not yet in use, Walpole is often called Britain's first prime minister. In time, the power of the prime minister would exceed that of the monarch. Other countries later adopted and adapted the cabinet system, including the United States.

✓ **Checkpoint** What three political institutions contributed to the evolution of Britain's constitutional government?

A Society Still Ruled by the Few

The decades that Walpole headed the cabinet were a time of peace and prosperity. But even as Parliament and the cabinet assumed new powers, British government was far from democratic. Rather, it was an **oligarchy**—a government in which the ruling power belongs to a few people.

In Britain, landowning aristocrats were believed to be the "natural" ruling class. The highest nobles held seats in the House of Lords. Other wealthy landowners and rich business leaders in the cities controlled elections to the House of Commons. The right to vote was limited to a relatively few male property owners.

Most Britons had neither the wealth nor the privileges of the upper class and lived very differently, making a meager living from the land. In the 1700s, even that poor existence was threatened. Wealthy landowners, attempting to increase agricultural production, bought up farms and took over common lands, evicting tenant farmers and small landowners. Because they controlled Parliament, they easily passed laws ensuring that their actions were legal. As a result many landless families drifted into towns, where they faced a harsh existence.

However, a relatively strong middle class—including merchants, craftspeople, and manufacturers—was growing. These prosperous and often wealthy people controlled affairs in the towns and cities. Some improved their social standing by marrying into the landed gentry. The middle class also produced talented inventors and entrepreneurs who would soon help usher in the Industrial Revolution.

✓ **Checkpoint** How did British society remain divided?

SECTION 3 Assessment

Progress Monitoring Online
For: Self-quiz with vocabulary practice
Web Code: nba-1631

Terms, People, and Places
1. Place each of the key terms at the beginning of the section into one of the following categories: politics, culture, or government. Write a sentence for each explaining your choice.

Note Taking
2. **Reading Skill: Identify Supporting Details** Use your completed flowchart to answer the Focus Question: How did the British Parliament assert its rights against royal claims to absolute power in the 1600s?

Comprehension and Critical Thinking
3. **Contrast** How did the Stuarts differ from the Tudors in their approach to Parliament?
4. **Identify Central Issues** In less than 100 years, England changed from a monarchy to a commonwealth and back to a monarchy. What central issue caused this political upheaval?
5. **Draw Conclusions** What were two results of the Glorious Revolution?
6. **Summarize** How did constitutional government evolve in England in the 1700s?

● **Writing About History**
Quick Write: Answer Opposing Arguments To write a strong persuasive essay you need to address arguments that could be raised to refute your own position. Choose a topic from this section—for example, whether Parliament had the right to replace James II—and list the arguments for and against your position.

The English Bill of Rights

Objectives

■ Describe the purpose and contents of the English Bill of Rights.

■ Understand how the English Bill of Rights influenced the evolution of constitutional government.

Build Background Knowledge ⑬

Ask students to recall what they know about the Glorious Revolution and the English Bill of Rights. Ask them to predict some of the rights this document guarantees.

Instruct

■ Point out that, like our Declaration of Independence, the English Bill of Rights begins with a list of grievances. Ask **According to the document, what did James II do wrong?** (*He threatened Protestantism and English law.*)

■ Ask **Who controls the monarch's budget?** (*Parliament*) **What must have happened in the past when subjects petitioned the king?** (*They were jailed.*) **Why was item 13 included?** (*Charles I had bypassed Parliament by not calling it for 11 years.*) **Where is freedom of speech guaranteed?** (*in Parliament*) **Why does item 10 sound familiar?** (*It is quoted exactly in the Eighth Amendment to the U.S. Constitution.*)

Monitor Progress

Ask students to compare the rights guaranteed in the English Bill of Rights overall to those guaranteed in the U.S. Bill of Rights. Ask how many years passed between the writing of these two documents. (*one hundred years, from 1689 to 1789*)

Thinking Critically

1. Item 6 means that a monarch could not keep an army to be used against citizens. It was included because Charles I sent troops into Parliament.

2. They included item 9 so that monarchs could not jail or punish members of Parliament for speaking out against them.

The English Bill of Rights

When the Catholic James II was forced from the English throne in 1688, Parliament offered the crown to his Protestant daughter Mary and her husband, William of Orange. But Parliament insisted that William and Mary submit to a Bill of Rights. This document, reflecting the long-standing struggle between monarch and Parliament, sums up the powers that Parliament had been seeking since the Petition of Right in 1628. This document ensured the superiority of Parliament over the monarchy and spelled out basic rights.

An engraving made in 1689 shows the new English rulers, William and Mary.

The original English Bill of Rights, now more than 300 years old, is carefully preserved in a museum in London, England.

Whereas, the late King James II ... did endeavor to subvert[1] and extirpate[2] the Protestant religion and the laws and liberties of this kingdom ... and whereas the said late King James II having abdicated the government, and the throne being vacant ... the said lords [Parliament] ... being now assembled in a full and free representative [body] of this nation ... do in the first place ... declare:

1. That the pretended power of suspending of laws or the execution of laws by regal authority without consent of Parliament is illegal. ...

4. That levying money for or to the use of the crown by pretense of prerogative[3] without grant of Parliament ... is illegal;

5. That it is the right of the subjects to petition the king, and all commitments and prosecutions for such petitioning are illegal.

6. That ... raising or keeping a standing army within the kingdom in time of peace, unless it be with consent of Parliament, is against law. ...

8. That election of members of Parliament ought to be free. ...

9. That the freedom of speech and debates or proceedings in Parliament ought not to be challenged or questioned in any court or place out of Parliament. ...

10. That excessive bail ought not to be required, nor excessive fines imposed, nor cruel and unusual punishments inflicted. ...

13. And that, for redress of all grievances and for the amending, strengthening, and preserving of the laws, Parliaments ought to be held frequently. ...

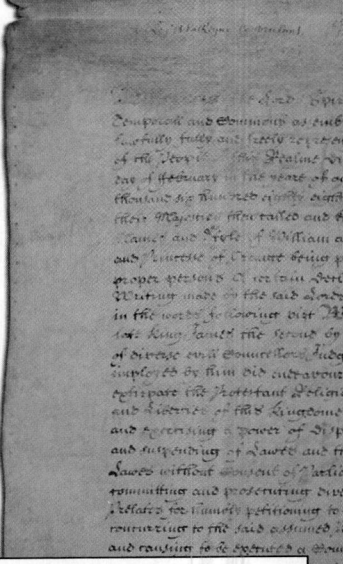

1. **subvert** (sub VURT) *v.* to destroy, overthrow, or undermine
2. **extirpate** (EKS tur payt) *v.* to eliminate
3. **prerogative** (pree RAHG uh tiv) *n.* a right

Thinking Critically

1. **Synthesize Information** What is the meaning of item 6, and why do you think it was included in the Bill of Rights?

2. **Draw Inferences** Why do you think the members of Parliament included item 9? Why do you think this item might have been important?

History Background

English Bill of Rights The Bill of Rights was read to William and Mary at their coronation in 1689, and William replied, "We thankfully accept what you have offered us." Although an important document in the history of democracy, the English Bill of Rights is not primarily a declaration of the rights of all citizens, as is the U.S. Bill of Rights. Instead, it outlines mainly the rights of Parliament and the limits on the power of the British crown to interfere with Parliament. The bill makes clear, however, that its writers believed they were doing "as their ancestors in like cases have usually done" in creating a document for the purpose of "vindicating and asserting their ancient rights and liberties." The provision giving Parliament the sole right to tax is the source of American colonists' claim of a right to "no taxation without representation."

Flemish artist Pieter Snayers painted several battles during the Thirty Years' War, including this one fought near Prague in 1620.

This silver flask held musket powder in the Thirty Years' War.

WITNESS HISTORY AUDIO

War Rages in Germany

The conflict known as the Thirty Years' War ravaged the German states of central Europe for much of the first half of the seventeenth century. A German family Bible contained this entry describing the war's end:

66 They say that the terrible war is now over. But there is still no sign of a peace. Everywhere there is envy, hatred, and greed: that's what the war has taught us. . . . We live like animals, eating bark and grass. No one could have imagined that anything like this would happen to us. Many people say that there is no God.99

Focus Question How did the two great empires of Austria and Prussia emerge from the Thirty Years' War and subsequent events?

Rise of Austria and Prussia

Objectives

- Outline causes and results of the Thirty Years' War.
- Understand how Austria and Prussia emerged as great powers.
- Describe how European nations tried to maintain a balance of power.

Terms, People, and Places

elector	War of the Austrian
Ferdinand	Succession
mercenary	Prussia
depopulation	Frederick William I
Peace of Westphalia	Frederick II
Maria Theresa	

Note Taking

Reading Skill: Identify Supporting Details As you read this section, use a table like the one below to record details about the emergence of Austria and Prussia as European powers.

Rise of Austria	Rise of Prussia
• Austrian ruler keeps title of Holy Roman Emperor.	• Hohenzollern rulers take over German states.
•	•

The Thirty Years' War took a terrible toll on the people of the German states. Finally, two great German-speaking powers, Austria and Prussia, rose out of the ashes. Like Louis XIV in France, their rulers perfected skills as absolute monarchs.

The Thirty Years' War Ravages Europe

By early modern times, as the French philosopher Voltaire later observed, the Holy Roman Empire was neither holy, nor Roman, nor an empire. Instead, by the seventeenth century it had become a patchwork of several hundred small, separate states. In theory, these states were ruled by the Holy Roman emperor, who was chosen by seven leading German princes called **electors.** In practice, the emperor had little power over the many rival princes. This power vacuum contributed to the outbreak of the Thirty Years' War. Religion further divided the German states. The north had become largely Protestant, while the south remained Catholic.

A Brutal War Begins The Thirty Years' War was actually a series of wars. It began in Bohemia, the present-day Czech Republic. **Ferdinand,** the Catholic Hapsburg king of Bohemia, sought to suppress Protestants and to assert royal power over nobles. In May 1618, a few rebellious Protestant noblemen tossed two royal officials out of a castle window in Prague. This act, known as the Defenestration of Prague, sparked a general revolt, which Ferdinand moved to suppress. As both sides sought allies, what began as a local conflict widened into a general European war.

Teach

The Thirty Years' War Ravages Europe L3

Instruct

- **Introduce: Vocabulary Builder**
  Have students read the Vocabulary Builder term and definition. Ask what Catholic rulers **aspired** to do in Europe. *(to eradicate Protestantism)*

- **Teach** Display **Color Transparency 98: The Holy Roman Empire, About 1618.** Ask students why the empire was difficult to rule and vulnerable to war. Point out that it really looked like a patchwork quilt. Then ask **What happened in the Defenestration of Prague?** *(Protestant nobles tossed royal officials out the window.)* **Why did the war spread through Europe?** *(The continent was divided by religion and shifting political alliances.)* **What were the results of the war in German states?** *(One third of the population died; German lands were divided into 360 mostly small, independent states.)*

  📖 **Color Transparencies,** 98

- **Quick Activity** Have students access **Web Code nbp-1641** to take the **Geography Interactive Audio Guided Tour** and then answer the map skills questions in the text.

Independent Practice

Have students fill in the Outline Map *Europe After the Peace of Westphalia.*

All in One Teaching Resources, Unit 1, p. 75

Monitor Progress

Circulate to make sure students are filling in their Outline Maps accurately. Administer the Geography Quiz.

All in One Teaching Resources, Unit 1, p. 77

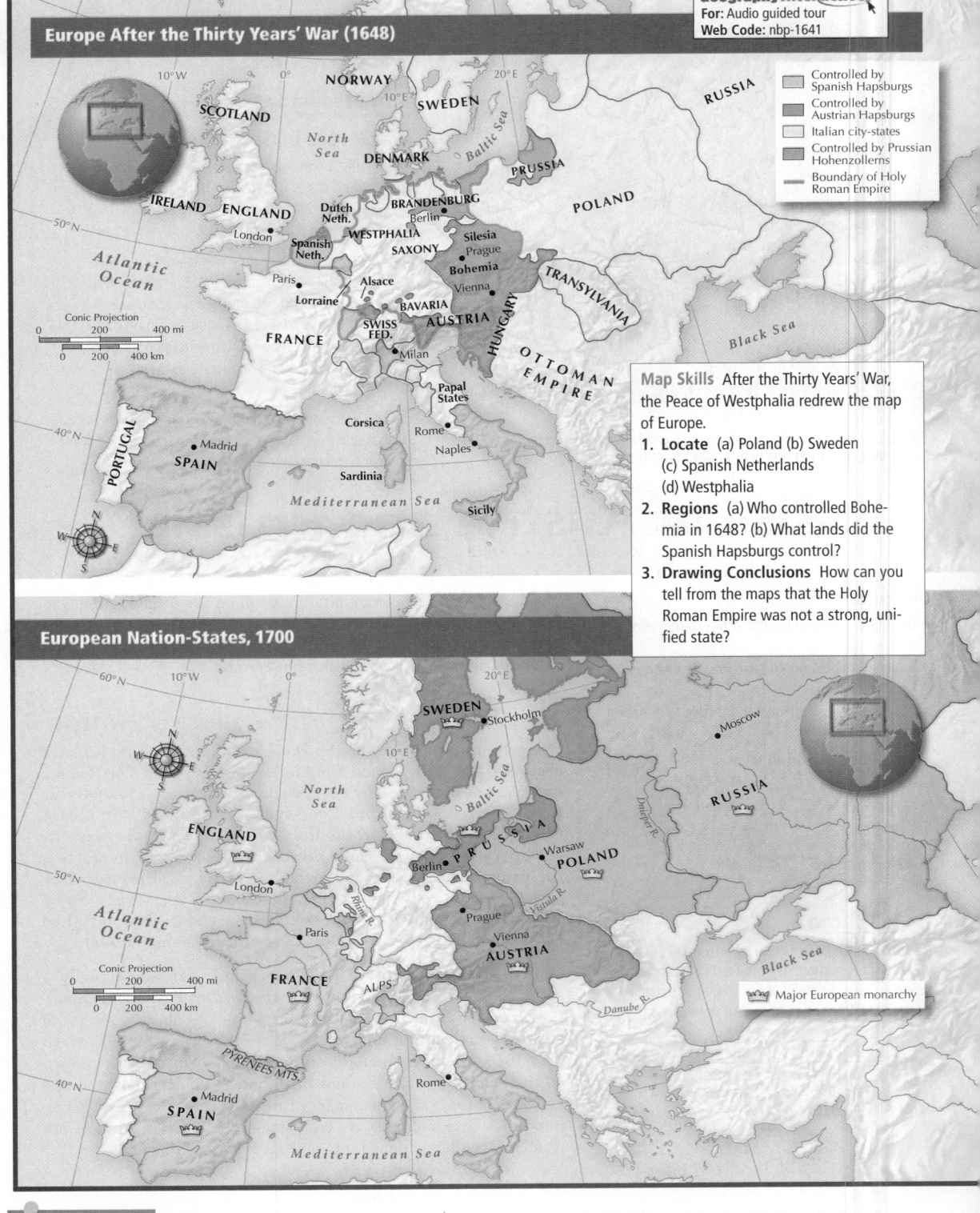

Geography *Interactive*
For: Audio guided tour
Web Code: nbp-1641

Europe After the Thirty Years' War (1648)

Controlled by Spanish Hapsburgs
Controlled by Austrian Hapsburgs
Italian city-states
Controlled by Prussian Hohenzollerns
Boundary of Holy Roman Empire

Map Skills After the Thirty Years' War, the Peace of Westphalia redrew the map of Europe.

1. **Locate** (a) Poland (b) Sweden (c) Spanish Netherlands (d) Westphalia
2. **Regions** (a) Who controlled Bohemia in 1648? (b) What lands did the Spanish Hapsburgs control?
3. **Drawing Conclusions** How can you tell from the maps that the Holy Roman Empire was not a strong, unified state?

European Nation-States, 1700

Major European monarchy

Answers

Map Skills

1. Review locations with students.
2. (a) Austrian Hapsburgs (b) Spain, Milan, Sardinia, Sicily, southern Italy, Spanish Netherlands, and other territories in the Holy Roman Empire
3. The map shows that areas within the Holy Roman Empire were ruled by several different powers, including Prussia and Spain.

Differentiated Instruction   Solutions for All Learners

L1 Special Needs   L2 Less Proficient Readers

Help students use word roots and associations to learn definitions. *Elector,* like *elect,* comes from the Latin word *electus,* "chosen." *Defenestration* comes from the Latin *fenestra,* or "window." *Depopulation* comes from the Latin *populus,* "people," as does the word *popular.* Have students write a definition of each word using a root or related word.

L2 English Language Learners

Use the following resources to help students acquire basic skills:

✏️ **Adapted Reading and Note Taking Study Guide**

- Adapted Note Taking Study Guide, p. 70
- Adapted Section Summary, p. 71

The following year, Ferdinand was elected Holy Roman Emperor. With the support of Spain, Poland, and other Catholic states, he tried to roll back the Reformation by force. In the early stages of the war, he defeated the Bohemians (who had rebelled when he became emperor) and their Protestant allies. Alarmed, Protestant powers like the Netherlands and Sweden sent troops into Germany. Before long, political motives outweighed religious issues. Catholic and Protestant rulers shifted alliances to suit their own interests. At one point, Catholic France joined Lutheran Sweden against the Catholic Hapsburgs.

A Terrible Loss of Life The fighting took a terrible toll. Roving armies of **mercenaries,** or soldiers for hire, burned villages, destroyed crops, and killed without mercy. Murder and torture were followed by famine and disease. Wolves, not seen in settled areas since the Middle Ages, stalked the deserted streets of once-bustling villages. The war led to a severe **depopulation,** or reduction in population. Exact statistics do not exist, but historians estimate that as many as one third of the people in the German states may have died as a result of the war.

Peace at Last Finally, in 1648, the exhausted combatants accepted a series of treaties, known as the **Peace of Westphalia.** Because so many powers had been involved in the conflict, the treaties <u>aspired</u> both to bring about a general European peace and to settle other international problems. Among the combatants France emerged a clear winner, gaining territory on both its Spanish and German frontiers. The Hapsburgs were not so fortunate. They had to accept the almost total independence of all the princes of the Holy Roman Empire. In addition, the Netherlands and the Swiss Federation (present-day Switzerland) won recognition as independent states.

The Thirty Years' War left German lands divided into more than 360 separate states—"one for every day of the year." These states still acknowledged the rule of the Holy Roman emperor. Yet each state had its own government, currency, church, armed forces, and foreign policy. The German states, potentially the most powerful nation in Europe if they could be unified, thus remained fragmented for another 223 years.

✔ **Checkpoint** What were some effects of the Peace of Westphalia?

Hapsburg Austria Changes its Focus

Though weakened by war, the Hapsburgs still wanted to create a strong united state. They kept the title "Holy Roman emperor," but focused their attention on expanding their own lands. To Austria, they would soon add Bohemia, Hungary, and, later, parts of Poland and some Italian states.

Challenges to Unity Uniting these lands proved difficult. Not only were they divided by geography, they included a number of diverse peoples and cultures as well. By the 1700s, the Hapsburg Empire included Germans, Magyars, Slavs, and others. In many parts of the empire, people had their own languages, laws, political assemblies, and customs.

The Hapsburgs did exert some control over these diverse peoples. They sent German-speaking officials to Bohemia and Hungary and settled Austrians on lands they had seized in these provinces. They also put down revolts in Bohemia and Hungary. Still, the Hapsburgs never developed a centralized governmental system like that of France.

Vocabulary Builder
<u>aspired</u>—(uh SPY urd) *v.* aimed; sought

Hapsburg Austria Changes its Focus

Instruct

- **Introduce** Have students locate the territory controlled by Hapsburg Austria on the map on the previous page. Have them compare it with the map of Europe in the back of the book and name modern countries that were once part of Hapsburg Austria.

- **Teach** Use the Numbered Heads strategy (TE, p. T23) and ask **What challenges did the Hapsburgs have in governing?** *(diverse peoples, languages, and cultures)* **Why was there doubt about the Austrian Succession?** *(The only heir was a young woman.)* **How did Maria Theresa rally support?** *(with a powerful speech to the Hungarian assembly)* **What were Maria Theresa's successes?** *(strengthening and centralizing power, easing the burden of peasants)*

- **Quick Activity** Have students study and analyze the portrait of Maria Theresa on the next page. Then have them write and read aloud a brief speech from Maria Theresa to the Hungarian assembly, asking them to defend her empire. Take a vote on the best speech.

Independent Practice

Viewpoints To help students better understand the reign of Maria Theresa, have them read the selection *Empress Maria Theresa* and complete the worksheet.

All in One Teaching Resources, Unit 1, p. 74

Monitor Progress

As students fill in their tables, circulate to make sure they understand how Austria emerged as a major power. For a completed version of the table, see

📖 **Note Taking Transparencies,** 131

Differentiated Instruction Solutions for All Learners

 Gifted and Talented   **Advanced Readers**

Rivals Maria Theresa of Austria and Frederick II of Prussia both emerged from unpromising beginnings to become great and powerful rulers. Both loved the arts. Both came to power in 1740; she was 24, and he was 28. One of his first acts was to invade the Hapsburg province of Silesia, which Maria Theresa called "the rape of Silesia." Frederick defended his action by saying "the passions of rulers have no other curb but the limits of their power." To his surprise, Maria Theresa vigorously defended her domain, although she never regained Silesia. In grudging respect, Frederick began to refer to her as "that man in Vienna." Have students research these two rivals and write a report comparing their lives and their reigns.

Answer

✔ France gained land, the Hapsburgs lost land, the Netherlands and Swiss Federation gained independence, and the German lands were even more divided.

Hohenzollern Prussia/ The Rivalry of Great Powers ⓛ₃

Instruct

- **Introduce** Read aloud the words of Frederick William that "nothing else in the world can confer upon a prince such fame and honor as the sword." Discuss with students whether this was true during this period and whether other absolute rulers would agree.

- **Teach** Explain that as Prussia emerged as a strong power, the concept of a balance of power among European nations took on greater urgency. Ask **How did the Hohenzollern consolidate power?** *(by seizing lands between their scattered holdings and setting up a central bureaucracy)* **What were the five main European powers?** *(Austria, Prussia, France, Britain, Russia)* Then have students look at the map titled European Nation-States, 1700, two pages back. Ask them to predict where war would break out next in Europe and explain their reasoning.

- **Analyzing the Visuals** Have students analyze the picture of young Frederick on the next page. Ask students to contrast this image of Frederick with the description in the text of Frederick's military prowess.

Independent Practice

Read aloud the quote that "Prussia is not a state which possesses an army, but an army which possesses a state." Tell students that Frederick William once savagely beat a soldier for having a button missing. Then have them write a short essay comparing Prussia and Sparta.

Monitor Progress

Check Reading and Note Taking Study Guide entries for student understanding.

Answers

✓ Maria Theresa's succession to the throne and Frederick II's invasion of Silesia.

PRIMARY SOURCE Sample: determination, leadership, ability to judge character and to delegate, and good communication skills

---

BIOGRAPHY

Maria Theresa
When Maria Theresa (1717–1780) became Hapsburg empress at the age of 23, her chances of remaining in power seemed very slim. She later said, "I found myself all at once without money, without troops, and without advice." A decade after her crowning she wrote, "I do not think anyone would deny that history hardly knows of a crowned head who started his rule under circumstances more grievous than those attending my accession."

But the determined empress survived. She appointed superb advisors and was able to maintain control of her empire. During her 40-year reign, Vienna became a center for music and the arts.

Maria Theresa had one thing in common with most women of her day—being a mother. She gave birth to a total of 16 children—11 girls and 5 boys. Among them were future emperors Joseph II and Leopold II and Queen Marie Antoinette of France. **What traits did Maria Theresa need to stay in power?**

A Woman Emperor Takes the Throne In the early 1700s, a new challenge threatened Hapsburg Austria. Emperor Charles VI had no male heir. His daughter, Maria Theresa, was intelligent and capable, but no woman had yet ruled Hapsburg lands in her own name. Charles persuaded other European rulers to recognize his daughter's right to succeed him. When he died, however, many ignored their pledge.

The War of the Austrian Succession Shortly after Charles's death in 1740, Frederick II of Prussia seized the rich Hapsburg province of Silesia. This action sparked the eight-year War of the Austrian Succession. Maria Theresa set off for Hungary to appeal for military help from her Hungarian subjects. The Hungarians were ordinarily unfriendly to the Hapsburgs. But she made a dramatic plea before an assembly of Hungarian nobles. According to one account, the nobles rose to their feet and shouted, "Our lives and blood for your Majesty!" She eventually got further help from Britain and Russia, who did not want Prussia to upset the balance of power by gaining new lands.

Maria Theresa never succeeded in forcing Frederick out of Silesia. Still, she did preserve her empire and win the support of most of her people. Equally important, she strengthened Hapsburg power by reorganizing the bureaucracy and improving tax collection. She even forced nobles and clergy to pay taxes and tried to ease the burden of taxes and labor services on peasants. As you will read, her son and successor, Joseph II, later extended many of her reforms.

✓ **Checkpoint** What caused the War of the Austrian Succession?

Hohenzollern Prussia

While Austria was molding a strong Catholic state, a region called Prussia emerged as a new Protestant power. In the 1600s, the Hohenzollern (HOH un tsahl urn) family ruled scattered lands across north Germany. In the century following the Peace of Westphalia, ambitious Hohenzollern rulers united their holdings, creating Prussia.

Creating a Bureaucracy Hohenzollerns rulers set up an efficient central bureaucracy. Frederick William I was a Prussian ruler who came to power upon the death of his father in 1713. He cleverly gained the loyalty of the Prussian nobles, called *Junkers* (YOON kerz), by giving them positions in the army and government. His tactic reduced the nobles' independence and increased his own control. Frederick also placed great emphasis on military values and forged one of the best-trained armies in Europe. One Prussian military leader boasted, "Prussia is not a state which possesses an army, but an army which possesses a state." By 1740, Prussia was strong enough to challenge its rival Austria.

A Crown Prince Learns the Art of War Frederick William made sure that, from an early age, his son Frederick was trained in the art of war. He wrote,

> **Primary Source**
>
> 66 His tutor must take the greatest pains to imbue my son with a sincere love for the soldier's profession and to impress upon him that nothing else in the world can confer upon a prince such fame and honor as the sword. 99

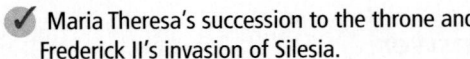

History Background

Frederick William King Frederick William of Prussia led a militaristic lifestyle that was impassioned, and at times, bizarre. In public, he always wore his military uniform. Like a good soldier, he regularly began his work day at five or six in the morning. At 10, he usually reported to the parade ground to drill or inspect the troops. Any lapse in military discipline might trigger his violent temper. Frederick William had an unusual admiration for tall soldiers, whom he regarded as possesing superior strength and stamina. Like a fanatical basketball coach seeking the championship, he sent scouts throughout much of Europe. Their mission was to entice, buy, and even kidnap the tallest soldiers for service in the Prussian army.

In fact, young Frederick II preferred playing the flute and writing poetry. His father despised these pursuits and treated the young prince so badly that he tried to flee the country. Discovering these plans, Frederick William put his son in solitary confinement. Then he forced the 18-year-old prince to watch as the friend who had helped him was beheaded.

Frederick's harsh military training had an effect. After becoming king in 1740, Frederick II lost no time in using his army. As you have read, he boldly seized Silesia from Austria, sparking the War of the Austrian Succession. In several later wars, Frederick continued to brilliantly use his disciplined army, forcing all to recognize Prussia as a great power. His exploits earned him the name Frederick the Great.

✓ **Checkpoint** How did Frederick William increase his power?

The Rivalry of Great Powers

By 1750, the great European powers included Austria, Prussia, France, Britain, and Russia. These nations formed various alliances to maintain the balance of power. Though nations sometimes switched partners, two basic rivalries persisted. Prussia battled Austria for control of the German states, while Britain and France competed to develop their overseas empires.

On occasion, these rivalries resulted in worldwide conflict. The Seven Years' War, which lasted from 1756 until 1763, was fought on four continents. Prussia, Austria, Russia, France, and Britain battled in Europe. Britain and France also fought in India and Africa. In North America, where the conflict is known as the French and Indian War, Native American groups took sides with the French or the British. The Treaty of Paris ending these wars gave Britain a huge empire, thus changing Europe's balance of power for the next hundred years.

✓ **Checkpoint** What were the two main rivalries after 1750?

Petitioning a King
Frederick the Great, strolling in his gardens, receives a petition from a common person. *What characteristics of Frederick does the artist hint at in the painting?*

Assess and Reteach

Assess Progress L3

- Have students complete the Section Assessment.
- Administer the Section Quiz.

 Teaching Resources, Unit 1, p. 66

- To further assess student understanding, use

 Progress Monitoring Transparencies, 70

Reteach L1 L2

If students need more instruction, have them read the section summary.

 Reading and Note Taking Study Guide, p. 155 L3

 Adapted Reading and Note Taking Study Guide, p. 155 L1 L2

 Spanish Reading and Note Taking Study Guide, p. 155 L2

Extend L4

The European Union (EU) today is a loose confederation of many independent states. Have students research the EU and write an essay comparing it with the Holy Roman Empire and predicting whether or not the EU is likely to be more successful and why.

Answers

✓ He controlled the Junkers, created an efficient bureaucracy, and established a strong army.

✓ England and France; Austria and Prussia

Caption Sample: compassion, fair-mindedness, cultural literacy

SECTION 4 Assessment

Progress Monitoring Online
For: Self-quiz with vocabulary practice
Web Code: nba-1641

Terms, People, and Places
1. For each term, person, or place listed at the beginning of the section, write a sentence explaining its significance.

Note Taking
2. **Reading Skill: Identify Supporting Details** Use your completed table to answer the Focus Question: How did the two great empires of Austria and Prussia emerge from the Thirty Years' War and subsequent events?

Comprehension and Critical Thinking
3. **Recognize Cause and Effect** What impact did the Thirty Years' War have on the German states?
4. **Compare** What two major powers emerged in Europe at the end of the Thirty Years' War? How were the goals of these two nations similar?
5. **Make Generalizations** How did European nations maintain a balance of power?

● **Writing About History**
Quick Write: Write a Thesis Statement Select a topic from the section that you might use as the subject of a persuasive essay—for example, whether Austria or Prussia was more successful at developing a strong nation-state. Then write a thesis statement that summarizes your opinion on this topic.

Section 4 Assessment

1. Sentences should reflect an understanding of each term, person, or place listed at the beginning of the section.
2. After war decimated the Holy Roman Empire, strong rulers Maria Theresa, Frederick William, and Frederick II consolidated power and territory to build their empires.
3. The war depopulated the German states and weakened their unity, resulting in the emergence of many small independent states.
4. Austria and Prussia; both sought to consolidate power, build a strong state, and extend their territory.
5. European nations maintained a balance of power through wars and shifting alliances.

● **Writing About History**
Thesis statements should be appropriate for development in a persuasive essay and express a clear opinion.

For additional assessment, have students access **Progress Monitoring Online** at **Web Code nba-1641.**

Step-by-Step Instruction

Objectives

As you teach this section, keep students focused on the following objectives to help them answer the Section Focus Question and master core content.

- Explain how Peter the Great tried to make Russia into a modern state.
- Identify the steps Peter took to expand Russia's borders.
- Describe how Catherine the Great strengthened Russia.

Prepare to Read

Build Background Knowledge L3

Ask students to recall what they know about the tsars, boyars, and serfs of Russia. Ask them to predict whether Russia's rulers during this time would act similarly to or differently from absolute monarchs elsewhere in Europe.

Set a Purpose L3

- **WITNESS HISTORY** Read the selection aloud or play the audio.

  🔊 AUDIO **Witness History Audio CD,** A Foreign Princess Takes the Throne

  Have students study the photos, captions, and Witness History text on this page. Ask them to predict the role of both Western European and Russian traditions on Catherine's rule.

- **Focus** Point out the Section Focus Question and write it on the board. Tell students to refer to this question as they read. *(Answer appears with Section 5 Assessment answers.)*

- **Preview** Have students preview the Section Objectives and the list of Terms, People, and Places.

- **Note Taking** Have students read this section using the Guided Questioning strategy (TE, p. T20). As they read, have students fill in the Venn diagram with details about the reigns of Peter the Great and Catherine the Great.

  ✏️ **Reading and Note Taking Study Guide,** p. 72

The palace (left) of Catherine the Great (far left) reflects both European and traditional Russian architectural styles.

WITNESS HISTORY 🔊 AUDIO

A Foreign Princess Takes the Throne

For twenty years, the German princess Catherine lived at the Russian court, enduring an unhappy marriage to the Russian heir apparent, who was widely considered to be insane. She filled her time reading, studying French philosophy, building alliances behind the scenes, and biding her time. When her husband became emperor in 1762, she called on her allies to act. Within a few months he had been deposed and Catherine proclaimed empress of Russia. Like Peter the Great before her, Catherine would rule with intelligence, a firm hand, and a mind set on modernization.

Focus Question How did Peter the Great and Catherine the Great strengthen Russia and expand its territory?

Absolute Monarchy in Russia

Objectives
- Explain how Peter the Great tried to make Russia into a modern state.
- Identify the steps Peter took to expand Russia's borders.
- Describe how Catherine the Great strengthened Russia.

Terms, People, and Places

Peter the Great	warm-water port
westernization	St. Petersburg
autocratic	Catherine the Great
boyar	partition

Note Taking

Reading Skill: Identify Main Ideas As you read this section, make a Venn diagram like the one below to compare events in the reigns of Peter the Great and Catherine the Great.

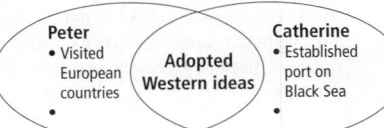

Peter
- Visited European countries

Adopted Western ideas

Catherine
- Established port on Black Sea

In the early 1600s, Russia was still a medieval state, untouched by the Renaissance or Reformation and largely isolated from Western Europe. As you have read, the "Time of Troubles" had plunged the country into a period of disorder and foreign invasions. The reign of the first Romanov tsar in 1613 restored a measure of order. Not until the end of the century, however, did a tsar emerge who was strong enough to regain the absolute power of earlier tsars. **Peter the Great,** as he came to be called, used his power to put Russia on the road to becoming a great modern power.

Peter the Great Modernizes Russia

Peter, just 10 years old when he took the throne in 1682, did not take control of the government until 1689. Although he was not well educated, the young tsar was immensely curious. He spent hours in the "German quarter," the Moscow neighborhood where many Dutch, Scottish, English, and other foreign artisans and soldiers lived. There, he heard of the new technology that was helping Western European monarchs forge powerful empires.

Journey to the West In 1697, Peter set out to learn about Western ways for himself. He spent hours walking the streets of European cities, noting the manners and homes of the people. He visited factories and art galleries, learned anatomy from a doctor, and even had a dentist teach him how to pull teeth. In England, Peter was impressed by Parliament. "It is good," he said, "to hear subjects speaking truthfully and openly to their king."

Vocabulary Builder

Use the information below and the following resources to teach the high-use word from this section.
All in One Teaching Resources, Unit 1, p. 68; **Teaching Resources, Skills Handbook** p. 3

High-Use Word	Definition and Sample Sentence
stipulate, p. 169	*v.* to make a specific demand The contract **stipulated** that the buyer had to pay in cash.

Peter brought to Russia a group of technical experts, teachers, and soldiers he had recruited in Europe. He then embarked on a policy of **westernization,** that is, the adoption of Western ideas, technology, and culture. But persuading fellow Russians to change their way of life proved difficult. To impose his will, Peter became the most **autocratic** of Europe's absolute monarchs, meaning that he ruled with unlimited authority.

Controlling the Church and the Nobles Peter pursued several related goals. He wanted to strengthen the military, expand Russian borders, and centralize royal power. To achieve his ends, he brought all Russian institutions under his control, including the Russian Orthodox Church. He also forced the haughty **boyars,** or landowning nobles, to serve the state in civilian or military positions.

Some changes had a symbolic meaning. For example, after returning from the West, Peter stipulated that boyars shave their beards. He also forced them to replace their old-fashioned robes with Western-style clothes. To end the practice of secluding upper-class women in separate quarters, he held grand parties at which women and men were expected to dance together. Russian nobles opposed this radical mixing of the sexes in public, but they had to comply.

Peter knew that nobles would serve the state only if their own interests were protected. Therefore, he passed laws ensuring that nobles retained control over their lands, including the serfs on those lands. In doing so, Peter strengthened serfdom. Under his rule serfdom spread in Russia, long after it had died out in Western Europe. Further, he forced some serfs to become soldiers or to work as laborers on roads, canals, and other government projects.

Modernizing With Force Using autocratic methods, Peter pushed through social and economic reforms. He imported Western technology, improved education, simplified the Russian alphabet, and set up academies for the study of mathematics, science, and engineering. To pay for his sweeping reforms, Peter adopted mercantilist policies, such as encouraging exports. He improved waterways and canals, developed mining and textile manufacturing, and backed new trading companies.

Peter had no mercy for any who resisted the new order. When elite palace guards revolted, he had more than 1,000 of the rebels tortured and executed. Then, as an example of his power, he left their rotting corpses outside the palace walls for months.

✓ **Checkpoint** What rewards and punishments did Peter use to solidify his control over the nobles?

Peter Expands Russia's Borders

From his earliest days as tsar, Peter worked to build Russia's military power. He created the largest standing army in Europe, built a world-class navy from scratch, and set out to extend Russian borders to the west and south.

Seeking a Warm-Water Port Russian seaports, located along the Arctic Ocean, were frozen over during the winter. To increase Russia's ability to trade with the West, Peter desperately wanted a **warm-water port**—one that would be free of ice all year round.

Vocabulary Builder

stipulated—(STIP yuh layt ed) *v.* made a specific demand

A Russian cartoon shows Peter the Great personally cutting off the beard of a boyar.

Teach

Peter the Great Modernizes Russia

Instruct

- **Introduce: Vocabulary Builder** Have students read the Vocabulary Builder term and definition. Ask what monarchs usually *stipulated* that lords should do, and what Peter *stipulated* that the boyars should do.

- **Teach** Describe Peter's goals for modernization. Ask **What aspects of the West did Peter choose to emulate?** *(technology, clothes, shaving of beards, women's social roles, education, mercantilism, manufacturing, trading, better armies)* **In what aspects did he differ from the West?** *(keeping and strengthening serfdom)* **How did he handle people who opposed him in Russia?** *(with severe repression)*

Independent Practice

Ask students to choose one of the following: boyar, upper-class woman, serf, church leader, merchant, palace guard, or person who knew Peter in Europe. Have students write a dialogue between that person and Peter about some aspect of culture or technology.

Monitor Progress

As students fill in their Venn diagram, circulate to make sure they are accurately comparing the reigns of Peter and Catherine. For a completed version of the Venn diagram, see

📖 **Note Taking Transparencies,** 132

Differentiated Instruction Solutions for All Learners

L1 Special Needs **L2 English Language Learners** **L2 Less Proficient Readers**

Help students use the map on the next page to better understand Russian expansion. Point out how much of Russia is in Asia (east of the Ural Mountains). Have pairs of students answer the following: How did Russia differ from other European nations? Why was the land added to the East so important? What was the significance of St. Petersburg's location? Why was Bering's exploration important for Russia?

Use the following resources to help students acquire basic skills:

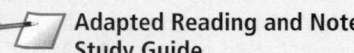 **Adapted Reading and Note Taking Study Guide**

- Adapted Note Taking Study Guide, p. 72
- Adapted Section Summary, p. 73

Answer

✓ Rewards: laws that favored the nobles, for example those strengthening serfdom. Punishments: stipulating that they change their customs; requiring them to serve the state.

Peter Expands Russia's Borders ⑬

Instruct

- **Introduce: Key Terms** Ask students to find the key term ***warm-water port*** (in blue) in the text and define it. Then display **Color Transparency 99: Russia Needs a Warm-Water Port.** Ask students to explain why ports are important to a nation, particularly to one of Russia's size. *(for trade)*

  🏛 **Color Transparencies,** 99

- **Teach** As you describe Russia's expansion, refer to the map two pages ahead. Ask **What happened in Peter's war with Sweden?** *(At first he was defeated, but after rebuilding the army he won land along the Baltic.)* **How was St. Petersburg different from Moscow?** *(It was a seaport, closer to Europe, European in design.)* Then refer students to the Infographic on this page. Discuss how the navy helped turn Russia into a world power.

- **Quick Activity** Show students *Peter the Great* from the **Witness History Discovery School™** video program. Then have students discuss whether they think Peter was a great monarch or a monstrous tyrant. As they name achievements and misdeeds, list them in two columns on the board. Ask students to weigh the evidence on the board. Then take a class vote on the matter.

Independent Practice

Web Code nbp-1651 will take students to an interactive map. Have students complete the interactivity and then answer the map skills questions in the text.

Monitor Progress

Read aloud the Primary Source selection on the next page or play the accompanying audio. Then ask students to explain what Pushkin is referring to.

🔊 AUDIO **Witness History Audio CD,** Alexander Pushkin

Answers

Map Skills
1. Review locations with students.
2. Those on the Baltic were frozen for part of the year.
3. Russia's territory would be smaller, and it would not have expanded as much in coastal areas.

The nearest warm-water coast was located along the Black Sea. To gain control of this territory, Peter had to push through the powerful Ottoman Empire. In the end, Peter was unable to defeat the Ottomans and gain his warm-water port, but the later Russian monarch Catherine the Great would achieve that goal before the century ended.

The Great Northern War In 1700, Peter began a long war against the kingdom of Sweden, which at the time, dominated the Baltic region. Early on, Russia suffered humiliating defeats. A Swedish force of only 8,000 men

● **INFOGRAPHIC**

Peter the Great and His Navy

As a sixteen-year-old boy, Peter found the hull of an old European sailing vessel in a storehouse. He restored the boat and taught himself to sail it on the lakes and rivers near Moscow. The find sparked a lifelong love for all things having to do with sailing. As tsar, Peter traveled to Europe to learn everything he could about shipbuilding. Armed with this knowledge, he created a European-style navy, thus turning Russia into a leading world power. In later years, Peter named the boat he had restored "the grandfather of the Russian navy." On his fifty-first birthday he sailed it into St. Petersburg harbor to meet its "grandchildren," Peter's navy.

A woodcut dating from the 1800s shows Peter, disguised as a ship's carpenter, learning from Dutch shipbuilders in the late 1600s. Peter's own carpentry tool and drawing are shown at bottom.

◀ A modern painter shows Peter as a common shipbuilder in the Netherlands.

A Russian artist who was a contemporary of Peter's shows St. Petersburg's harbor, filled with the ships that Peter had built. ▼

Russia's Navy Grows

Number of vessels / Year — 1705, 1714, 1725 (values: 0, 400, 800, 1200)

Thinking Critically
1. **Draw Inferences** Peter's motto was "I am a student and I seek teachers." How do you think this motto relates to his practice of passing himself off as a common man while studying in Europe?
2. **Make Comparisons** How did the absolute monarchies of Peter the Great and Louis XIV differ in terms of each monarch's dealings with common people?

Link to Geography

Siberia Russia's absolute monarchs needed a place to exile both criminals and political opponents for long periods of time. What place was better than the arctic region of Siberia? Siberia was far away from everything Russian and had an extremely inhospitable climate; temperatures could average −59°F (−51°C) in winter. There was little chance of escape, as it was almost impossible to survive alone in the vast, frozen, sparsely populated region. In fact, 10 to 15 percent of the exiles never made it to Siberia; they died along the way. The number of exiles grew from a trickle in the early 1600s to 2,000 a year by the early 1800s. After a revolt in 1825, the tsar sent 150,000 people off to their freezing fate. Today, the expression "sent to Siberia" still implies that a person is being punished or has become an outcast.

defeated a Russian army five times its size. Undaunted, Peter rebuilt his army, modeling it after European armies. Finally, in 1709, he defeated the Swedes and won territory along the Baltic Sea.

Building St. Petersburg On this land won from Sweden, Peter built a magnificent new capital city, **St. Petersburg.** Seeking to open a "window on the West," he located the city on the Baltic coast along the swampy shores of the Neva River. He forced tens of thousands of serfs to drain the swamps. Many thousands died, but Peter's plan for the city succeeded. He then invited Italian architects and artisans to design great palaces in Western style. Peter even planned the city's parks and boulevards himself. Just as Versailles became a monument to French absolutism, St. Petersburg became a great symbol of Peter's effort to forge a modern Russia.

Blazing Trails to the Pacific Russian traders and raiders also crossed the plains and rivers of Siberia, expanding the Russian empire to the east. Under Peter, Russia signed a treaty with China that recognized Russia's claim to lands north of China and defined the empires' common border.

In the early 1700s, Peter hired the Danish navigator Vitus Bering to explore what became known as the Bering Strait between Siberia and Alaska (see map on the next page). After Peter's death, Russian traders built outposts in Alaska and northern California. Few Russians moved east of the Ural Mountains at this time, but the expansion made Russia the largest country in the world. It still is today, nearly 300 years later.

Peter the Great's Legacy When Peter died in 1725, he left a mixed legacy. He had expanded Russian territory, gained ports on the Baltic Sea, and created a mighty army. He had also ended Russia's long period of isolation. From the 1700s on, Russia would be increasingly involved in the affairs of Western Europe. Yet many of Peter's ambitious reforms died with him. Nobles, for example, soon ignored his policy of service to the state.

Like earlier tsars, Peter the Great had used terror to enforce his absolute power. His policies contributed to the growth of serfdom, which served only to widen the gap between Russia and the West that Peter had sought to narrow.

✔ **Checkpoint** What impact did Peter's defeat of Sweden have on Russia's expansion?

Catherine the Great Follows Peter's Lead

Peter died without an heir and without naming a successor. This set off a power struggle within the Romanov family, from whom all the tsars had come since the early 1600s. Under a series of ineffective rulers, Russian nobles reasserted their independence. Then, a new monarch took the reins of power firmly in hand. She became known to history as **Catherine the Great.**

WITNESS HISTORY VIDEO

Watch *Peter the Great* on the **Witness History Discovery School**™ video program to learn more about this larger-than-life tsar.

Discovery SCHOOL

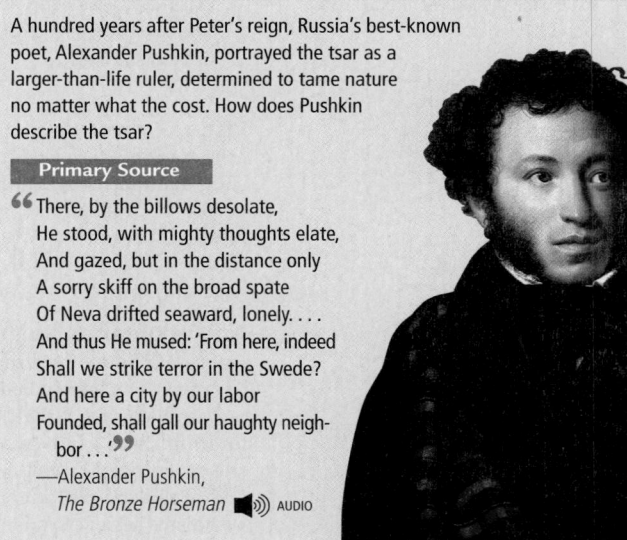

A hundred years after Peter's reign, Russia's best-known poet, Alexander Pushkin, portrayed the tsar as a larger-than-life ruler, determined to tame nature no matter what the cost. How does Pushkin describe the tsar?

Primary Source

66 There, by the billows desolate,
He stood, with mighty thoughts elate,
And gazed, but in the distance only
A sorry skiff on the broad spate
Of Neva drifted seaward, lonely. . . .
And thus He mused: 'From here, indeed
Shall we strike terror in the Swede?
And here a city by our labor
Founded, shall gall our haughty neighbor . . .' 99

—Alexander Pushkin,
The Bronze Horseman AUDIO

Catherine the Great Follows Peter's Lead   L3

Instruct

- **Introduce** Read aloud the following quote from Catherine: "The Extent of the Dominion [of Russia] requires an absolute Power to be vested in that Person who rules over it. . . ." Use the Think-Write-Pair-Share strategy (TE, p. T23) and ask students to explain her reasoning and whether there is any basis for it in history.

- **Teach** Point out that Catherine followed largely in Peter's footsteps, though many argue that she was even more powerful and ruthless. Ask **What changes did Catherine bring to Russia?** (*She reorganized government, created public education, encouraged Western culture, intensified serfdom, and expanded Russia's borders.*) **Why did both Peter and Catherine increase burdens on serfs?** (*to keep the loyalty of the boyars*) **How did Catherine differ from Peter in treatment of the boyars?** (*She granted them some rights.*)

- **Quick Activity** Display **Color Transparency 100: Partitions of Poland, 1701–1795.** Use the lesson suggested in the transparency book to guide a discussion about the carving up of Poland.

  📖 **Color Transparencies,** 100

History Background

Bering's Explorations Young Vitus Bering, a Danish navigator, joined the newly created Russian navy in 1703. In 1725 he was sent by Peter the Great to explore Asia's northeast coast. It took two years to move men and supplies across Siberia. Finally, he sailed through what is now the Bering Strait, proving that Russia was not connected to North America. On his return across Siberia, he became ill, and five of his children died. In 1741 he set off again, this time to explore the northwest coast of North America. He discovered the Aleutian Islands, but fell ill. Bering and 28 of his men died there on a barren island. Following his expedition, Spain rushed to establish settlements on North America's west coast. Russia, however, was more interested in the fur trade than in expanding onto a third continent.

Answers

✔ It gained Russia territory along the Baltic Sea, including the land for his new capital, St. Petersburg.

PRIMARY SOURCE Sample: He portrayed him as both imaginative and powerful.

Independent Practice

Have students fill in the Outline Map *Eastern Europe in 1796*.

All in One Teaching Resources, Unit 1, p. 76

Monitor Progress

- Check Reading and Note Taking Study Guide entries for student understanding.
- Circulate to make sure students are filling in their Outline Maps accurately.

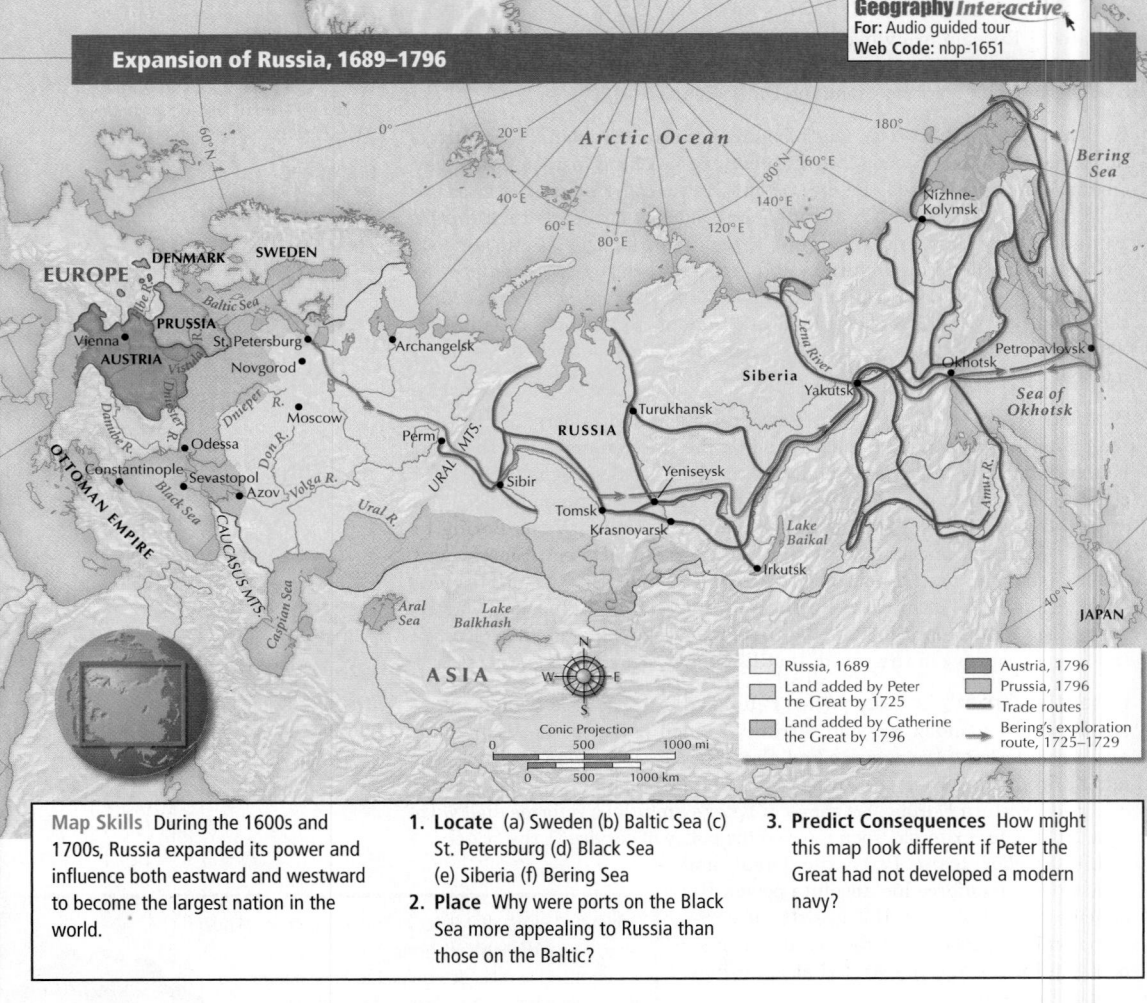

Geography *Interactive*
For: Audio guided tour
Web Code: nbp-1651

Expansion of Russia, 1689–1796

Map Skills During the 1600s and 1700s, Russia expanded its power and influence both eastward and westward to become the largest nation in the world.

1. **Locate** (a) Sweden (b) Baltic Sea (c) St. Petersburg (d) Black Sea (e) Siberia (f) Bering Sea
2. **Place** Why were ports on the Black Sea more appealing to Russia than those on the Baltic?
3. **Predict Consequences** How might this map look different if Peter the Great had not developed a modern navy?

Rise to Power A German princess by birth, Catherine came to Russia at the age of 15 to wed the heir to the Russian throne. She learned Russian, embraced the Russian Orthodox faith, and won the loyalty of the people. In 1762, a group of Russian army officers loyal to her deposed and murdered her mentally unstable husband, Tsar Peter III. Whether or not Catherine was involved in the assassination is uncertain. In any case, with the support of the military, she ascended the Russian throne.

An Enlightened Ruler Catherine proved to be an efficient, energetic empress. She reorganized the provincial government, codified laws, and began state-sponsored education for both boys and girls.

Like Peter the Great, Catherine embraced Western ideas and worked to bring Russia fully into European cultural and political life. At court, she encouraged French language and customs, wrote histories and plays, and organized performances. As you will read in the next chapter, she was also a serious student of the French thinkers who led the intellectual movement known as the Enlightenment.

Answers

Thinking Critically

1. He knew he would learn more if people thought he was a commoner, not a ruler.
2. Peter, driven by curiosity, had more dealings with common people than did Louis, who surrounded himself with nobles in Versailles. However, Peter treated some common people—serfs—more harshly than other European rulers.

Differentiated Instruction Solutions for All Learners

L4 Gifted and Talented **L4 Advanced Readers**

In 1787, Catherine the Great made a grand tour of her newly conquered lands in Ukraine and Crimea. Her deputy and former lover, Grigory Potemkin, had helped to conquer these lands from the Ottoman Empire, and Catherine put him in charge of their development. Potemkin colonized southern Russia with Bulgarians, Germans, Greeks, Jews, and Roma- nians, as well as Russians, and he developed the new port of Sevastopol. There he built Russia's first Black Sea naval fleet. Some believe he was the power behind the throne who helped Catherine achieve many of her dreams. Have students research this controversial figure and outline the plot and some scenes for a movie about his life.

A Ruthless Absolute Monarch Catherine was also an absolute monarch, like other European rulers of the time, and often she was among the most ruthless. She granted a charter to the boyars outlining important rights, such as exemption from taxes. She also allowed them to increase their stranglehold on the peasants. When peasants rebelled against the harsh burdens of serfdom, Catherine took firm action to repress them. As a result, conditions grew worse for Russian peasants. Under Catherine, even more peasants were forced into serfdom.

Like Peter the Great, Catherine was determined to expand Russia's borders. Waging the Russo-Turkish war against the Ottoman Empire gained her a warm-water port on the Black Sea in 1774. She also took steps to seize territory from neighboring Poland.

The Partitions of Poland In the 1770s, Catherine, King Frederick II of Prussia, and Emperor Joseph II of Austria hungrily eyed Poland. As you have read, the Polish-Lithuanian Commonwealth had once been a great European power. However, its rulers were unable to centralize their power or diminish the influence of the Polish nobility. The divided Polish government was ill-prepared to stand up to the increasing might of its neighbors, Russia, Prussia, and Austria.

To avoid fighting one another, the three monarchs agreed in 1772 to **partition,** or divide up, Poland. Catherine took part of eastern Poland, where many Russians and Ukrainians lived. Frederick and Joseph took control of Polish territory in the west. Poland was further partitioned in 1793. Then in 1795, Austria, Prussia, and Russia each took their final slices and the independent country of Poland vanished from the map. Not until 1919 would a free Polish state reappear.

 Checkpoint How were Catherine's goals similar to those of Peter?

Looking Ahead

By the mid-1700s, absolute monarchs ruled four of the five leading countries in Europe. Britain, with its strong Parliament, was the only exception. As these five nations competed with one another, they often ended up fighting to maintain a balance of power. At the same time, new ideas were in the air. Radical changes would soon shatter the French monarchy, upset the balance of power, and revolutionize European societies.

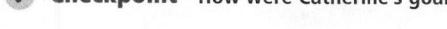

SECTION 5 Assessment

Progress Monitoring Online
For: Self-quiz with vocabulary practice
Web Code: nba-1651

Terms, People, and Places
1. For each term, person, or place listed in the beginning of the section, write a sentence explaining its significance.

Note Taking
2. **Reading Skill: Identify Main Ideas** Use your completed Venn diagram to answer the Focus Question: How did Peter the Great and Catherine the Great strengthen Russia and expand its territory?

Comprehension and Critical Thinking
3. **Identify Central Issues** What were three goals of Peter the Great and what was one step that he undertook to achieve each goal?
4. **Analyze Information** Why was obtaining a warm-water port a major priority for Peter?
5. **Compare Points of View** How did Peter and Catherine envision Russia's future?

● **Writing About History**
Quick Write: Write the Text Body Choose a topic from the section on which you might write a persuasive essay—for example: Was Peter the Great really "great"? Write the body of your text, using a list of points you have made to guide you. Remember to open and close the body of the text with particularly strong arguments.

Section 5 Assessment

1. Sentences should reflect an understanding of each term, person, or place listed at the beginning of the section.
2. Using autocratic methods, they westernized and modernized Russia, centralized royal power, improved the army, and expanded its territory through war, treaties, and exploration.
3. Goals (any 3): to westernize, strengthen the military, expand Russian borders, and centralize royal power. Reforms (any 3): bring the church under his control, force boyars to serve the state, force changes in social customs, strengthen serfdom, import technology, improve education, build military power.
4. A warm-water port would allow Russia to increase trade and become a major power.
5. Both envisioned that Russia would continue to grow and become more powerful by mastering Western technologies and practices.

● **Writing About History**
Responses should include a list of arguments that clearly support one side. An accompanying paragraph or group of paragraphs should restate these arguments in the form of sentences.

For additional assessment, have students access **Progress Monitoring Online** at Web Code nba-1651.

CHAPTER **4**

Quick Study Guide

■ Have students use the Quick Study Guide to prepare for this chapter's test. Students may wish to refer to the following pages as they review:

Key Rulers
Section 1, pp. 142–146; Section 2, pp. 148–152; Section 3, pp. 154–159; Section 4, pp. 163, 165–167; Section 5, pp. 168–173

Key Events
Section 1, pp. 507; Section 2, p. 510–511, 514; Section 3, pp. 518–519, 521–522; Section 4, pp. 525–529; Section 5, pp. 532–533; 535

Partition of Poland
Section 5, p. 173

Key Events in the Age of Absolutism
Section 1, p. 143; Section 2, p. 152; Section 3, p. 156; Section 4, p. 163; Section 5, pp. 168, 172–173

■ For additional review, remind students to refer to the **L3**

 Reading and Note Taking Study Guide
Note Taking Study Guide, pp. 63–64, 66, 68, 70, 72
Section Summaries, pp. 65, 67, 69, 71, 73

■ Have students access **Web Code nbp-1652** for this chapter's 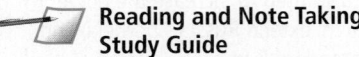 timeline, which includes expanded entries and additional events.

■ If students need more instruction on analyzing timelines, have them read the **Skills Handbook,** p. SH30.

■ When students have completed their study of the chapter, distribute Chapter Tests A and B.

All in One Teaching Resources, Unit 1, pp. 78–83

For **Progress Monitoring Online,** refer students to the Self-test with vocabulary practice at **Web Code nba-1652.**

CHAPTER **4**

Quick Study Guide

Progress Monitoring Online
For: Self-test with vocabulary practice
Web Code: nba-1652

■ Key Rulers

Spain: Charles V (Charles I of Spain); Philip II
France: Henry IV; Louis XIV
Britain: Henry VIII; Elizabeth I; James I; Charles I; Oliver Cromwell; Charles II; James II; William and Mary
Austria: Ferdinand; Charles VI; Maria Theresa
Prussia: Frederick William; Frederick the Great
Russia: Peter the Great; Catherine the Great

■ Key Events

- **Battle of Lepanto, 1571**—Spain and allies against Ottoman Empire
- **Netherlands rebellions, 1560s–1580s**—political and religious revolts against Spain
- **Spanish Armada attacks England, 1588**
- **St. Bartholomew's Day Massacre, 1572**—slaughter of French Huguenots
- **Thirty Years' War, 1618–1648**
- **English Civil War, 1642–1648**
- **The *Fronde,* 1648–1653**—uprising of various groups in France
- **Glorious Revolution, 1688**—bloodless change of monarchs in England
- **War of the Spanish Succession, 1700–1713**
- **Great Northern War, 1700–1721**—Russia and allies against Sweden
- **War of the Austrian Succession, 1740–1748**
- **Seven Years' War, 1756–1763**
- **Russo-Turkish War, 1768–1774**—Russia against the Ottoman Empire
- **Partitions of Poland, 1772, 1793, 1795**

■ Partitions of Poland, 1701–1795

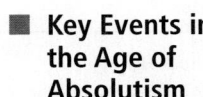

Conic Projection
0   200   400 mi
0   200   400 km

■ Key Events in the Age of Absolutism

Chapter Events
Global Events

| 1550 | 1600 | 1650 |

1556
Philip II becomes king of Spain.

1618
The Thirty Years' War begins.

1642
The English Civil War begins.

1556
Akbar the Great becomes emperor of Mughal India.

1607
British colonists found Jamestown.

Differentiated
Instruction   **Solutions for All Learners**

L1 Special Needs   **L2 Less Proficient Readers**

For students acquiring basic skills:

 Adapted Reading and Note Taking Study Guide
Adapted Note Taking Study Guide, pp. 63–64, 66, 68, 70, 72
Adapted Section Summaries, pp. 65, 67, 69, 71, 73

L2 English Language Learners

For Spanish-speaking students:

Spanish Reading and Note Taking Study Guide
Spanish Note Taking Study Guide, pp. 63–64, 66, 68, 70, 72
Spanish Section Summaries, pp. 65, 67, 69, 71, 73

Concept Connector

 Essential Question Review

To connect prior knowledge with what you have learned in this chapter, answer the questions below in your Concept Connector journal. Use the journal in the Reading and Note Taking Study Guide to record your answers (or go to www.phschool.com. **Web Code:** nbd-1607).

1. **Revolution** A revolution is a significant and widespread change in the social structure of a society or societies. Using this definition as a guide, discuss what makes the Glorious Revolution a revolution.

2. **Political Systems** Absolute monarchies were the dominant political system during the Age of Absolutism. Yet policies instituted by some monarchs weakened their empires and contributed to the decline of absolute monarchies as a political system. How did the use of absolute power by the following rulers weaken their empires?
   - Philip II
   - Louis XIV
   - Charles I
   - Peter the Great

3. **Democracy** The English Bill of Rights of 1688 granted basic rights to citizens, limited the power of the monarch, and gave Parliament the "power of the purse." These were critical steps in reducing the power of the monarchy and expanding the rights of the people. Write one or two paragraphs that summarize how these developments led to increased democracy in England.

■ Connections to Today

1. **Conflict** The Age of Absolutism was also an "age of religious conflicts." Many of these conflicts, primarily between Catholics and Protestants, were long lasting and extremely violent. Several caused major wars. Find and read a newspaper or Internet article about a country or region where religious conflict is still a concern today—for example, Bosnia, India, Iraq, Israel, or Northern Ireland. Write a two- or three-paragraph summary of what you learn.

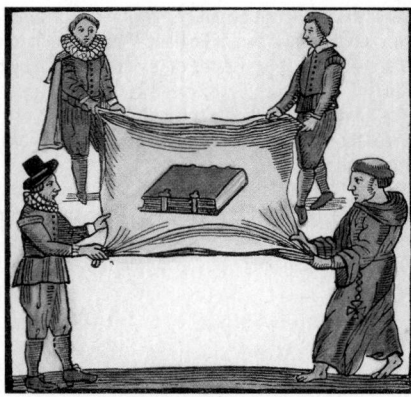

2. **Democracy** The English Bill of Rights is one of the source documents for ideas included in the American Declaration of Independence and the United States Constitution. Review the excerpt from the English Bill of Rights on page 162. Write a three-paragraph essay that summarizes how aspects of the English Bill of Rights are still present in American ideas of democracy today.

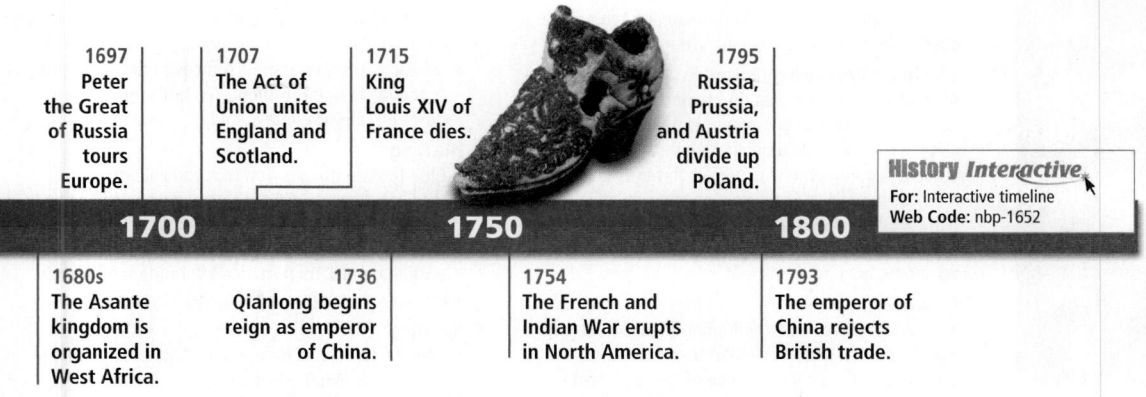

| 1697 Peter the Great of Russia tours Europe. | 1707 The Act of Union unites England and Scotland. | 1715 King Louis XIV of France dies. | 1795 Russia, Prussia, and Austria divide up Poland. |

1700 **1750** **1800**

| 1680s The Asante kingdom is organized in West Africa. | 1736 Qianlong begins reign as emperor of China. | 1754 The French and Indian War erupts in North America. | 1793 The emperor of China rejects British trade. |

History *Interactive*
For: Interactive timeline
Web Code: nbp-1652

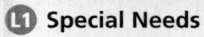 **Differentiated**
Instruction **Solutions for All Learners**

 Special Needs **Less Proficient Readers**
Use the following study guide resources to help students acquiring basic skills:

Adapted Reading and Note Taking Study Guide
Adapted Concept Connector, pp. 250, 287, 291

English Language Learners
Use the following study guide resources to help Spanish-speaking students:

Spanish Reading and Note Taking Study Guide
Spanish Concept Connector, pp. 250, 287, 291

Concept Connector

Tell students that the main concepts for this chapter are Revolution, Political Systems, and Democracy, and then ask them to answer the Essential Question Review questions on this page. Discuss the Connections to Today topics and ask students to answer the questions that follow.

Essential Question Review

1. Students should go back to the chapter to describe how the Glorious Revolution revolutionized the way the British government worked. They should be able to discuss why this was revolutionary, according to the definition. They should demonstrate an understanding of how this impacted the development of British society.

2. Students should go back to the chapter to examine the policies of each of the listed rulers. Using this information, they should be able to discuss how the decisions of those leaders weakened their empires.

3. Students should go back to the chapter and look up information on the English Bill of Rights and the transformation of the Parliament. This should allow them to summarize the effect that the Bill of Rights had on the development of democracy in England.

Connections to Today

1. Responses should describe the groups in conflict, give a brief history of the conflict, discuss the role of religion, and summarize the current situation.

2. Essays should mention at least a few of the following: the concept of a Bill of Rights; the idea that no one is above the law; the rights of due process, free elections, and free speech; and the ban on of cruel or unusual punishment.

For additional review of this chapter's core concepts, remind students to refer to the

Reading and Note Taking Study Guide
Concept Connector, pp. 250, 287, 291

Chapter Assessment

Terms, People, and Places

1. constitutional monarchy
2. divine right
3. habeas corpus
4. westernization
5. partition
6. absolute monarch

Main Ideas

7. Treasure from the Americas led to the neglect of farming and commerce and to soaring inflation.

8. A fleet sent by Spain in 1588 to invade England; it was defeated.

9. Sample: the sun and Versailles, both of which signified power and brilliance.

10. (a) Parliament executed the king's chief ministers and refused to be dissolved; Charles led troops into the House of Commons to arrest its radical leaders. (b) Charles I was executed, the monarchy was abolished, and Cromwell took power.

11. Parliament forced William and Mary to accept the English Bill of Rights, which ensured Parliament's supremacy over the monarchy.

12. King Ferdinand's suppression of Protestantism; the Defenestration of Prague; the rush to make alliances.

13. imposed requirements on nobles (or boyars), imported technology, improved education, simplified the alphabet, set up academies, improved waterways and canals, developed mining and textiles, and backed new trading companies

14. To get a warm-water port; it was finally achieved by Catherine's successful war against the Ottomans.

Chapter Focus Question

15. Strong rulers centralized power, reduced the influence of nobles and the church, fought wars to increase territory, and used the doctrine of divine right to justify absolute power.

Critical Thinking

16. Sample: European powers succeeded in balancing power, but to do so they had to fight many costly wars.

17. Louis meant that he held absolute power over every aspect of government.

18. Sample: yes, because it was a bloodless turnover of power and a victory for democracy.

Chapter Assessment

Terms, People, and Places

Complete each sentence by choosing the correct answer from the list of terms below. You will not use all the terms.

absolute monarch	constitutional monarchy
divine right	limited monarchy
balance of power	oligarchy
westernization	partition
habeas corpus	

1. After the Glorious Revolution, several new institutions marked the transition of England's government to a _____.
2. The theory of _____ states that monarchs rule by the will of God.
3. The English Bill of Rights sets out the principle of _____.
4. Peter the Great pursued a policy of _____ to make Russia more modern.
5. The _____ of Poland occurred in the 1700s when the rulers of Austria, Russia, and Prussia agreed to split that country among themselves.
6. In this period, nearly every major European nation was ruled by a(n) _____.

Main Ideas

Section 1 (pp. 142–146)
7. How did resources from the Spanish colonies in the Americas contribute to the decline of Spain?
8. What was the Spanish Armada?

Section 2 (pp. 148–152)
9. What were two symbols of the reign of Louis XIV and what was their significance?

Section 3 (pp. 154–161)
10. (a) What were the immediate causes of the English Civil War? (b) What were some important results?
11. How did the Glorious Revolution limit royal power in England?

Section 4 (pp. 163–167)
12. What events led to the start of the Thirty Years' War?

Section 5 (pp. 168–173)
13. What reforms did Peter the Great carry out?
14. What was one long-term goal of the Russian monarchs and how was it finally achieved?

Chapter Focus Question
15. What events led to the rise of absolute monarchies and the development of centralized nation-states in Europe?

Critical Thinking

16. **Draw Conclusions** Based on the material in the chapter, how effective do you think the policy of maintaining a balance of power was among European nations?
17. **Analyze Information** Explain what Louis XIV meant when he said, "I am the state."
18. **Test Conclusions** Based on what you have learned about the Glorious Revolution, do you think the name for that event is accurate? Why or why not?
19. **Compare** Compare the goals and policies of Peter the Great with those of one of the following monarchs: (a) Louis XIV (b) Frederick II (c) Maria Theresa.
20. **Synthesize Information** What was the historical significance of the execution of Charles I of England?
21. **Understand Effects** What was the general impact of the Thirty Years' War on Europe?

● **Writing About History**

In this chapter's five Section Assessments, you developed skills for writing a persuasive essay.

Writing a Persuasive Essay During the Age of Absolutism, strong monarchs created centralized nation-states whose governments they ruled with complete authority. Write a persuasive essay in which you argue a position on one aspect of this age. Consider topics such as: Was absolute monarchy an effective system? Was the divine right of kings a valid basis for rule? Consult page SH16 of the Writing Handbook for additional help.

Prewriting
• Choose a listed topic or another one that interests you, one that provokes an argument and has at least two sides. Then choose a side of the argument.

• Collect evidence, using a graphic organizer to list points on both sides of the issue.
• Research Internet or print sources to find materials that analyze your position from both sides. Take notes on relevant details, events, and people.

Drafting
• Clearly state the position that you will argue in a thesis statement. Use the rest of your introduction to provide readers necessary context about the issue.
• Make an outline to organize your argument and supporting details. Then choose information from your research that supports each part of your outline.

Revising
• Use the guidelines for revising your essay on page SH17 of the Writing Handbook.

---

19. Answers will vary, but all of these monarchs were absolute rulers who sought to expand their power and territory.

20. It was the first time a monarch had been deposed and executed by his own people.

21. It destabilized the region and ultimately led to new power alliances.

Document-Based Assessment

The Rise of Parliament

The struggle between English monarchs and Parliament raged through the seventeenth century, and was fought on battlefields and legal fronts. The documents below illustrate the points of view of a monarch, Parliament, and a well-known philosopher.

Document A

"THE KINGS THEREAFTER in Scotland were before any estates or ranks of men within the same, before any Parliaments were holden or laws made; and by them was the land distributed (which at first was wholly theirs), states erected and decerned, and forms of government devised and established. And it follows of necessity that the Kings were the authors and makers of the laws and not the laws of the Kings."

—From ***True Law of Free Monarchies***, 1598

Document B

"The Petition exhibited to his Majesty by the lords Spiritual and Temporal, and Commons, in this present Parliament assembled, concerning divers Rights and Liberties of the Subjects, with the King's Majesty's royal answer thereunto in full Parliament.
. . . Your subjects have inherited this freedom, that they should not be compelled to contribute to any tax, tallage, aid, or other like charge not set by common consent, in parliament.
. . . No man, of what estate or condition that he be, should be put out of his land or tenements, nor taken, nor imprisoned, nor disinherited nor put to death without being brought to answer by due process of law."

—From ***The Petition of Right***, 1628

Document C

"Men, being, as has been said, by nature all free, equal, and independent, no one can be . . . subjected to the political power of another without his own consent. The only way whereby anyone divests himself of his natural liberty, and puts on the bonds of civil society is by agreeing with other men to join and unite into a community. . . .
    It is evident, that *absolute monarchy*, which by some men is counted the only government in the world, is indeed *inconsistent with civil society*."

—From ***Two Treatises on Government*** by John Locke, 1690.

Document D

A mid-1600s engraving depicts Charles I as a political and religious martyr.

Analyzing Documents

Use your knowledge of the age of absolutism and Documents A, B, C, and D to answer questions 1–4.

1. What is the main point of Document A?
   A Kings are subject only to laws of parliament.
   B Kings make laws but are not subject to them.
   C Kings no longer have the power of life and death over subjects.
   D Parliament now has the power of life and death over subjects.

2. Document B is a declaration of whose rights?
   A the king's rights
   B Parliament's rights
   C subjects' rights
   D the landed aristocracy's rights

3. Document C
   A supports Document A.
   B supports Document B.
   C supports both Document A and Document B.
   D supports Document A and Document D.

4. **Writing Task** Would you describe the rise of Parliament in England as an evolution or a revolution? Use documents from this page along with information from the chapter in your response.

● Writing About History

As students begin the assignment, refer them to page SH16 of the **Writing Handbook** for help in writing a persuasive essay. Remind them of the steps they should take to complete their assignment, including prewriting, drafting, and revising. For help in revising, remind them to use the guidelines on page SH17 of the **Writing Handbook**.

Students' essays should have a clear and appropriate thesis that takes a position and is supported by facts, examples, and comparisons. Essays should contain an introduction, a body, and a conclusion. They should show evidence of reflection and be free of grammatical and spelling errors. For scoring rubrics for writing assignments, see **Assessment Rubrics**, p. 8.

Enlightenment and Revolution
1700–1850

Unit Overview

Unit 2 discusses an era of revolutions, beginning with the Enlightenment period and its connection with the American Revolution and continuing with the French Revolution, the Industrial Revolution, and other revolutions in Europe and Latin America.

Chapter 5 examines how Enlightenment ideas about freedom and government helped inspire the American Revolution and how that revolution led to the formation of the United States of America.
Concepts: Cooperation, Conflict, Impact of the Individual, Political Systems

Chapter 6 describes the causes and diverse phases of the French Revolution as well as the Age of Napoleon that followed it.
Concepts: Democracy, Nationalism, Revolution

Chapter 7 explores the origins and far-reaching impact of the radical shift to machine production known as the Industrial Revolution.
Concepts: Economic Systems, Technology

Chapter 8 studies the string of democratic revolutions that occurred in Europe during the mid-1800s and examines the wars of independence in Latin America.
Concepts: Conflict, Democracy, Empire, Nationalism, Revolution

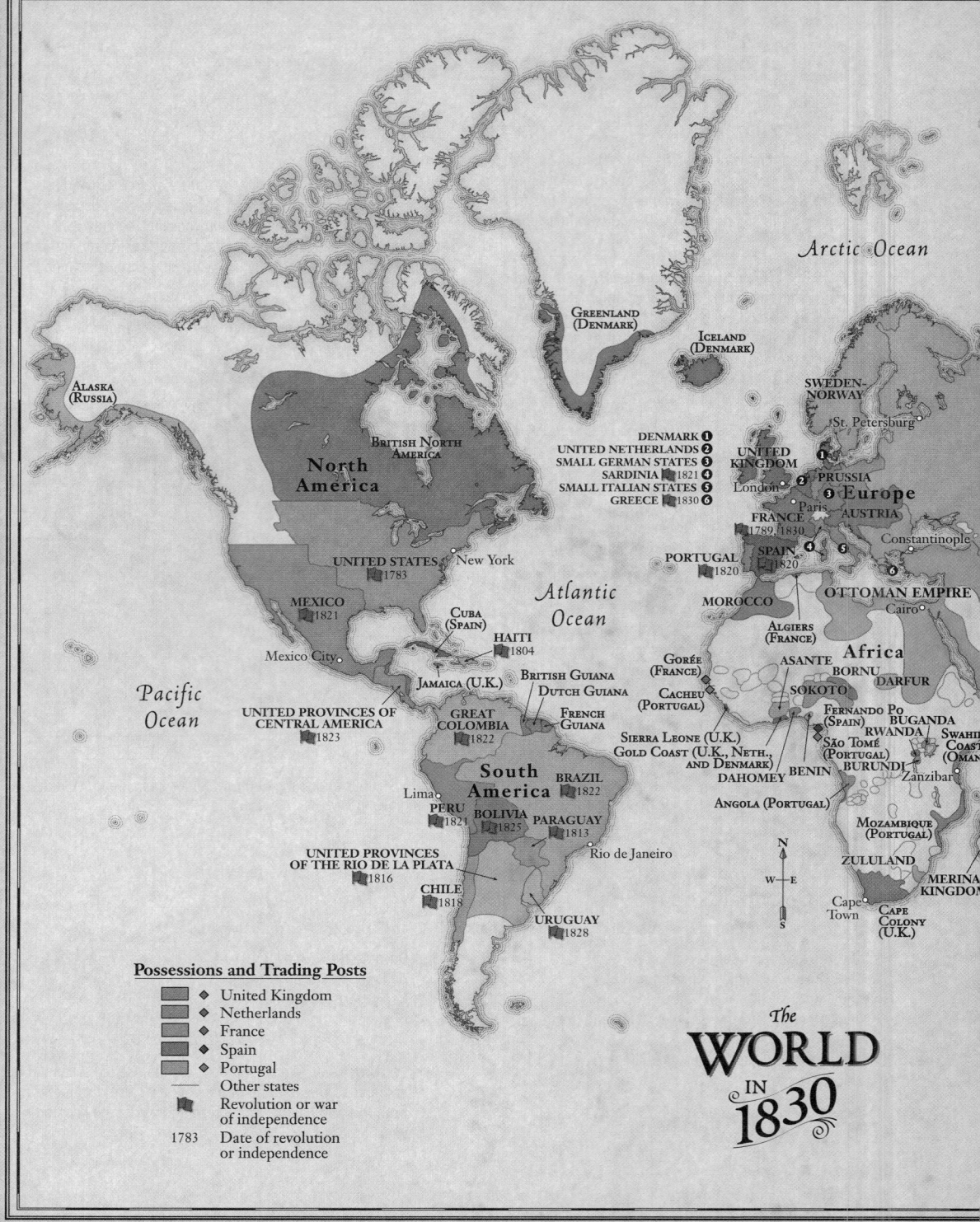

The WORLD IN 1830

Possessions and Trading Posts
- ◆ United Kingdom
- ◆ Netherlands
- ◆ France
- ◆ Spain
- ◆ Portugal
- Other states
- Revolution or war of independence
- 1783 Date of revolution or independence

About the Map

In the 1800s, European powers continued to rely on colonial possessions for access to raw materials. Those raw materials, in the hands of capitalists, helped fuel the Industrial Revolution. By 1830, the Industrial Revolution had spread from England to other European countries and the United States. Other revolutions, in the Americas and Europe, found their fuel in ideas. Enlightenment thinkers during the 1700s had stressed concepts such as liberty and equality. Revolutionaries in some of Britain's

American colonies were the first to take action against tyranny. They declared independence as the United States. France's revolution followed. The revolutionary spirit spread to Latin America, where former European colonies fought for independence in the early 1800s. By 1830, the huge Spanish empire had shrunk with the loss of its American colonies. Meanwhile, a wave of revolutions swept Western Europe between 1820 and 1830.

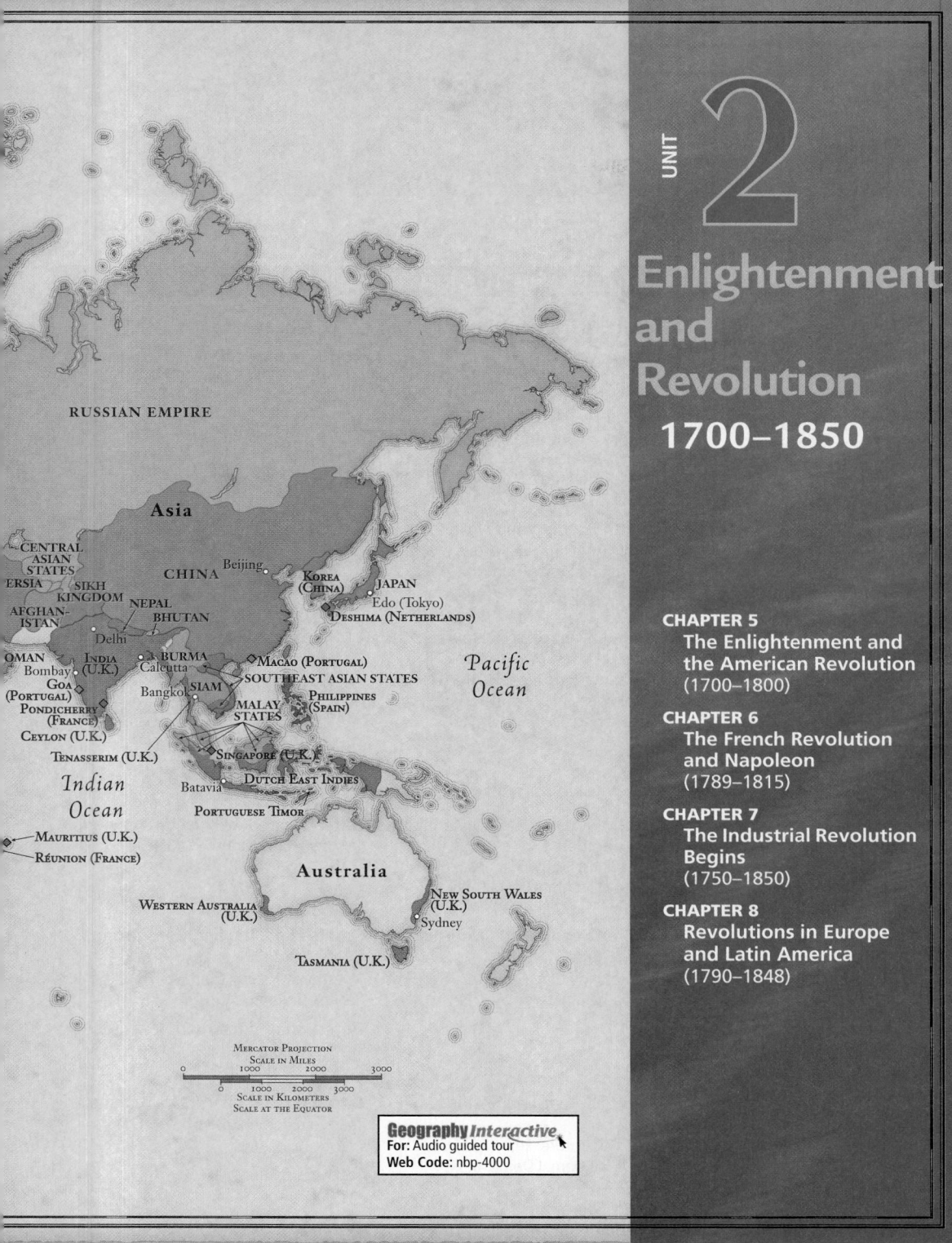

UNIT 2

Enlightenment and Revolution
1700–1850

RUSSIAN EMPIRE

Asia

CENTRAL ASIAN STATES
ERSIA
SIKH KINGDOM
AFGHAN-ISTAN
NEPAL
BHUTAN
CHINA   Beijing
KOREA (CHINA)
JAPAN
Edo (Tokyo)
DESHIMA (NETHERLANDS)

OMAN
Bombay
GOA (PORTUGAL)
PONDICHERRY (FRANCE)
CEYLON (U.K.)
INDIA (U.K.)
Delhi
Calcutta
BURMA
MACAO (PORTUGAL)
SOUTHEAST ASIAN STATES
SIAM
Bangkok
MALAY STATES
PHILIPPINES (SPAIN)
TENASSERIM (U.K.)
SINGAPORE (U.K.)

Pacific Ocean

Indian Ocean
Batavia
DUTCH EAST INDIES
PORTUGUESE TIMOR

MAURITIUS (U.K.)
RÉUNION (FRANCE)

Australia

WESTERN AUSTRALIA (U.K.)
NEW SOUTH WALES (U.K.)
Sydney

TASMANIA (U.K.)

MERCATOR PROJECTION
SCALE IN MILES
0   1000   2000   3000
0   1000   2000   3000
SCALE IN KILOMETERS
SCALE AT THE EQUATOR

Geography *Interactive*
For: Audio guided tour
Web Code: nbp-4000

CHAPTER 5
The Enlightenment and the American Revolution
(1700–1800)

CHAPTER 6
The French Revolution and Napoleon
(1789–1815)

CHAPTER 7
The Industrial Revolution Begins
(1750–1850)

CHAPTER 8
Revolutions in Europe and Latin America
(1790–1848)

Geographic Literacy

Remind students that overseas colonies played a key role in several nations' economies. Ask **In which region of the world were the major colonial powers located in 1830?** *(Europe)* Have students locate at least one possession or trading post for each of the European colonizers. Then ask **What country had the largest overseas empire in 1830?** *(the United Kingdom)* **Which country was the first to have a revolution or war for independence?** *(the United States)* **In which region of the world did wars or revolutions turn many former colonies into independent states?** *(the Americas)* Have students compare the size of selected colonial powers with the size of their possessions. Then ask how a small state can control a huge amount of territory. *(Sample: technologically advanced weapons; effective organization and administration; strategies to control local leaders)*

Looking Ahead

Ask students to read the chapter titles to the right of the map. Ask **Based on these titles and your study of the map, what do you predict you will learn about in this unit?** *(how various revolutions affected Europe and the Americas in the 1700s and 1800s)* Explain that students will also analyze the concept of nationalism as a force behind independence movements, and they will learn about the explosion of technology that accompanied the Industrial Revolution.

A note on the projection:
Although the Mercator projection distorts the sizes of continents, it was widely used for maps after its invention in 1569.

Home Involvement
The *Letter Home* includes a summary of the Enlightenment and Revolution content that students will be studying.
All in One **Teaching Resources, Unit 2,** p. 1

The Enlightenment and the American Revolution

CHAPTER PLANNER

Section	Core Instruction L3	Differentiated Instruction L1 L2 L4	

Section 1
Philosophy in the Age of Reason

 2 periods, 1 block

OBJECTIVES
- Explain how science led to the Enlightenment.
- Compare the ideas of Hobbes and Locke.
- Identify the beliefs and contributions of the *philosophes*.
- Summarize how economic thinking changed during this time.

Focus Question *What effects did Enlightenment philosophers have on government and society?*

Core Instruction L3

All in One Teaching Resources, Unit 2
Reading Strategy: Summarize, p. 6
Vocabulary Builder: Word Maps, p. 5
Section 1 Quiz, p. 2

Reading and Note Taking Study Guide
Note Taking Study Guide, p. 74
Section 1 Summary, p. 75

Note Taking Transparencies, 120

WITNESS HISTORY Audio CD
Rousseau Stirs Things Up

Progress Monitoring Transparencies, 72

Color Transparencies, 101, 102

Teaching Resources, Skills Handbook
Prereading the Chapter, pp. 1–2
Word Knowledge Rating Form, p. 3
K-W-L Chart, p. 4

L1 Adapted Reading and Note Taking Study Guide
Note Taking Study Guide, p. 74 **SN**
Section 1 Summary, p. 75 **SN**

L2 Adapted Reading and Note Taking Study Guide
Note Taking Study Guide, p. 74 **LPR**
Section 1 Summary, p. 75 **LPR**

Spanish Reading and Note Taking Study Guide
Note Taking Study Guide, p. 74 **ELL**
Section 1 Summary, p. 75 **ELL**

L4 **All in One Teaching Resources, Unit 2**
Biography: Voltaire, p. 7 **AR, GT**
Viewpoints: Enlightenment Views on Education, p. 10 **AR, GT**

*Student Edition Audio **SN**
Differentiated Instruction Activity, Teacher's Edition, p. 183 **SN**

*Guided Reading Audio (Spanish) **ELL**
*Student Edition Audio **LPR**
Differentiated Instruction Activity, Teacher's Edition, pp. 183, 187 **LPR, ELL**

Differentiated Instruction, Teacher's Edition, p. 185 **AR, GT**
Extend Activity, Teacher's Edition, p. 186 **AR, GT**

Section 2
Enlightenment Ideas Spread

 2 periods, 1 block

OBJECTIVES
- Identify the roles that censorship and salons played in the spread of new ideas.
- Describe how the Enlightenment affected the arts and literature.
- Understand how *philosophes* influenced enlightened despots.
- Explain why Enlightenment ideas were slow to reach most Europeans.

Focus Question *As Enlightenment ideas spread across Europe, what cultural and political changes took place?*

All in One Teaching Resources, Unit 2
Outline Map: Enlightenment Europe, p. 12
Section 2 Quiz, p. 3

Reading and Note Taking Study Guide
Note Taking Study Guide, p. 76
Section 2 Summary, p. 77

Note Taking Transparencies, 121A–121B

WITNESS HISTORY Audio CD
Mozart, the Musical Genius; Rococo Reaction; Opera

Progress Monitoring Transparencies, 73

L1 Adapted Reading and Note Taking Study Guide
Note Taking Study Guide, p. 76 **SN**
Section 2 Summary, p. 77 **SN**

L2 Adapted Reading and Note Taking Study Guide
Note Taking Study Guide, p. 76 **LPR**
Section 2 Summary, p. 77 **LPR**

L4 **All in One Teaching Resources, Unit 2**
Link to Literature: From *Robinson Crusoe*, by Daniel Defoe, p. 9 **AR, GT**
Primary Source: From Essay on the Reforms of Government, by Frederick II, p. 8 **AR, GT**

Differentiated Instruction Activity, Teacher's Edition, p. 191 **SN**

Spanish Reading and Note Taking Study Guide
Note Taking Study Guide, p. 76 **ELL**
Section 2 Summary, p. 77 **ELL**
Differentiated Instruction Activity, Teacher's Edition, p. 191 **LPR, ELL**

Differentiated Instruction Activity, Teacher's Edition, p. 192 **AR, GT**
Extend Activity, Teacher's Edition, p. 193 **AR, GT**

*Audio support is available for all sections.

Assessment Resources
- **Progress Monitoring Transparencies,** 72–74
- **SuccessTracker™,** Chapter 5
- **Document-Based Assessment,** pp. 54–66
- *ExamView®* **Test Bank CD-ROM,** Chapter 5
- **All in One Teaching Resources, Unit 2,** Chapter Tests A and B, pp. 15–20
- **Progress Monitoring *Online* Quizzes,** Chapter 5
- **Assessment Rubrics**

Differentiated Instruction Key
L1 Special Needs	**LPR** Less Proficient Readers
L2 Basic to Average	**AR** Advanced Readers
L3 All Students	**SN** Special Needs Students
L4 Average to Advanced	**GT** Gifted and Talented
	ELL English Language Learner

Section

Section 3
Birth of the American Republic

 1.5 periods, .75 block

OBJECTIVES
- Describe characteristics of Britain and the 13 English colonies in the mid-1700s.
- Outline the events that led to the American Revolution.
- Summarize the events and significance of the American Revolution.
- Analyze how the new Constitution reflected the ideas of the Enlightenment.

Focus Question *How did ideas of the Enlightenment lead to the independence and founding of the United States of America?*

Core Instruction ⓛ3

 Teaching Resources, Unit 2
Outline Map: The Thirteen Colonies, p. 5
Geography Quiz, p. 14
Section 3 Quiz, p. 4

Reading and Note Taking Study Guide
Note Taking Study Guide, p. 78
Section 3 Summary, p. 79
Concept Connector, pp. 237, 242, 247, 250, 278, 287

Note Taking Transparencies, 122

WITNESS HISTORY Audio CD
Paine's *Common Sense;* The Declaration of Independence

Progress Monitoring Transparencies, 74

Color Transparencies, 103, 104, 105, 106

Witness History Discovery School™
video program, *The Enlightenment and the American Revolution*

Differentiated Instruction ⓛ1 ⓛ2 ⓛ4

L1 Adapted Reading and Note Taking Study Guide
Note Taking Study Guide, p. 78 **SN**
Section 3 Summary, p. 79 **SN**
Concept Connector, pp. 237, 242, 247, 250, 278, 287 **SN**

L2 Adapted Reading and Note Taking Study Guide
Note Taking Study Guide, p. 78 **LPR**
Section 3 Summary, p. 79 **LPR**
Concept Connector, pp. 237, 242, 247, 250, 278, 287 **LPR**

Spanish Reading and Note Taking Study Guide
Note Taking Study Guide, p. 78 **ELL**
Section 3 Summary, p. 79 **ELL**
Concept Connector, pp. 237, 242, 247, 250, 278, 287 **ELL**

L4 Teaching Resources, Unit 2
Viewpoints: Two Views of the Battle of Cowpens, p. 11 **AR, GT**

Differentiated Instruction Activity,
Teacher's Edition, p. 200 **AR, GT**

Differentiated Instruction Activity,
Teacher's Edition, pp. 196, 198, 202 **SN**

Differentiated Instruction Activity,
Teacher's Edition, pp. 196, 198, 202 **LPR, ELL**

Extend Activity, Teacher's Edition, pp. 180c, 201 **AR, GT**

Author's Notes

The Enlightenment

The French *Encyclopedia,* edited by Denis Diderot and Jean d'Alembert, used this seemingly neutral form as a cloak for more subtle attacks on the "old regime," as the society of this age was later called. The influence of such works, particularly in the hands of the educated French bourgeoisie, was inexorably subversive, undermining faith in the major social institutions of the time.

Enlightenment philosophes were thus social critics, the most vigorous Europe had known for centuries. Voltaire and his colleagues attacked the churches of their day—Catholic and Protestant—as nests of superstition, fanaticism, and useless logic-chopping. They condemned the European aristo-cracy as mere decorations rather than pillars of society, daring to suggest that merit might be more important in determining a person's true value than inherited social position. And if kings and queens were less vigorously assaulted, it was primarily because the philosophes hoped to work through duly enlightened absolutists to build a more rational and more just world.

On the positive side, these same often satirical social critics found hope in the Scientific Revolution that a better society was possible once human reason was set to solving social problems. Another century or two of determined *social*-scientific inquiry, they believed, would uncover "natural laws" as valid in society as the laws of planetary motion or the law of gravity were in the material world. . . .

It was a period of revolutionary social thought that seemed to shed a dazzling new light on the way human society works. The subversive attacks of the philosophes fueled the fires on the impending American and French revolutions. Their social theories would provide support for the social engineering and big government, as well as the more revolutionary creeds, of our own time.

—Anthony Esler, *The Human Venture: From Prehistory to the Present,* (Upper Saddle River, New Jersey: Pearson Education, 2004), pp. 482–483

Extend Online

The Declaration of Independence

Have students learn more about how the Declaration of Independence was written. Ask them to create a guided tour for an exhibit of this important document.

Prepare for the Activity Tell students that Thomas Jefferson wrote and revised the Declaration of Independence multiple times. After he presented it to the Committee of Five, the committee (three of its members—Benjamin Franklin, John Adams, and Jefferson—are pictured at left) made further changes, as did the Continental Congress. They were careful to attack King George III and not the British Parliament, which represented the people. In targeting the king, they hoped that the revolt would appear to be against tyranny and that the king's enemies would come to their aid.

Conduct the Activity For help in starting the activity, send students to Web Code nbe-1701, where they will visit the exhibition of the original Declaration, now kept in the National Archives in Washington, D.C. Students should prepare a guided tour of the exhibit. Ask them to include information about how the document was created and its meaning today.

Follow-Up Conduct a class discussion based on the following questions: What does the Declaration of Independence stand for? How has the Declaration of Independence inspired those outside the United States? What does the document mean today?

Differentiated Instruction   Solutions for All Learners

Shared Reading L1 L2

Depending on their skill level, some readers may be unable to successfully complete a reading assignment at home or independently. They may only be able to understand the content sufficiently if the selection of text is read aloud in class and the meaning is clarified by the teacher. You may choose to do this in several ways:

■ **As a Class** Call on each student to read a paragraph out loud to the class, using stronger readers for longer selections and weaker readers for shorter selection. After each paragraph, ask the class a question to check for understanding of key concepts, and wait for volunteers.

■ **In Small Groups** Break the class into small groups, assigning each group a small selection of text. Each group is responsible for bullet pointing key information from that selection to present to the class. All members of the class should take notes as selections of text are presented.

Creating a Dialogue L2

In addition to learning social studies content, English Language Learners face the more daunting challenge of developing proficiency in English. To encourage students to use both written and spoken English and apply core content, have them create a dialogue. Follow these steps:

1. Divide students into groups and assign each group a scenario.

2. List key terms and high-use words on the board that must be included in the dialogue.

3. Require that every student in the group have a speaking role.

4. Have students submit a written copy of the script as part of the assessment on this activity.

Ask each group to perform their dialogues for the class to enhance the English language listening skills of students in the audience.

Modeling Reading and Writing Skills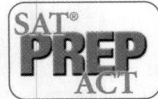

Examine the Question   Explain that in this chapter students will be writing for assessment. (See Writing About History, p. 206.) Remind them that a complete response to an assessment question will address every aspect of that question. As students read an essay question, they should look for key words that explain exactly what they should do to write a thorough answer. Key words include *examine the causes, analyze, compare and contrast, defend, distinguish between, examine, explore, evaluate, identify,* and *show.*

Model how to identify key words by writing on the board the following sample essay question: "Write an essay describing life in the colonies during the American Revolution." Point out the key word *describing.* The assignment is asking students to tell more about daily life in this time period. Then put on the board: "The American colonists declared independence in 1776. Write an essay justifying the colonists' rebellion against Britain." Underline the key word *justifying.* Tell students the assignment is asking them to show that the position is right or reasonable using facts, reasoning, and examples.

Summarize The ability to summarize effectively can help improve students' abilities to understand and remember the text. Tell students that good summarizers take notes on the text and then reread as they write. Poor summarizers read the text once and begin writing.

Model how to create a useful summary of Section 1 using the following steps:

1. Review structural aids, such as headings, key terms, reading checks, visual information, and captions.

2. Predict what you think you will learn about the text.

3. Read the selection, sorting through the main ideas and details. Reread the section and take notes on key words from topic sentences that express the main idea of each paragraph.

4. Organize the ideas in your notes. Cluster ideas that go together.

5. Write your summary. As you write, be sure to cross out any information that does not seem important.

The Enlightenment and the American Revolution
1700–1800

Teach With Technology
PresentationEXPRESS™
Premium DVD

- Teach this chapter's core content using **PresentationExpress™ Premium,** which includes dynamic lecture notes, interactive game shows, songs, videos, and the **ExamView®** *QuickTake* assessment tool.

- To introduce this chapter using **PresentationExpress™ Premium,** start by asking students **Which of the following statements do you most agree with? (A) Freedom of speech should always be protected. (B) Freedom of speech should be restricted during times of war. (C) Freedom of speech should be restricted if it harms someone. (D) Freedom of speech should be restricted if it endangers someone's life.** Take a class poll or record students' answers using the QuickTake feature and discuss their responses. Point out that in this chapter, they will read about various philosophers' ideas on freedom of speech, just government, checks and balances, and separation of powers. Continue introducing the chapter using the chapter opener slide show and Witness History audio.

Technology Resources

- Student**EXPRESS** CD-ROM, Chapter 5
- Teacher**EXPRESS** CD-ROM, Chapter 5
- Presentation**EXPRESS™ Premium DVD,** Chapter 5
- **WITNESS HISTORY** Audio CD, Chapter 5
- *ExamView* **Test Bank CD-ROM,** English and Spanish, Chapter 5
- **Guided Reading Audio,** Spanish, Chapter 5
- **Student Edition Audio,** Chapter 5
- **Witness History Discovery School**™ video program, *The Enlightenment and the American Revolution*
- **Experience It! Multimedia Pack**

Bibliography

For the Teacher
Fairweather, Maria. *Madame de Staël.* New York: Carroll & Graf, 2005.

Gaines, James R. *Evening in the Palace of Reason: Bach Meets Frederick the Great in the Age of Enlightenment.* New York: Fourth Estate, 2005.

Himmelfarb, Gertrude. *The Roads to Modernity: The British, French, and American Enlightenments.* New York: Knopf, 2004.

For the Student
L1 Vernon, Roland. *Introducing Mozart.* Parsipanny, NJ: Silver Burdett, 1996.

L2 Whitelaw, Nancy. *Catherine the Great and the Enlightenment in Russia.* Greensboro, NC: Morgan Reynolds Publishing, 2005.

L3 Brody, Miriam. *Mary Wollstonecraft.* New York: Oxford University Press, 2000.

Pens to Inspire Revolution

Enlightenment thinker Denis Diderot compiled a 28-volume work called the *Encyclopedia*, published between 1751 and 1772. This work was a forum for Enlightenment thinkers believed that with the power of reason, they could fix the problems of society. The *Encyclopedia* was banned in many places and censored in others. Yet it would prove to be a major influence in the years to come. It contains the passage below on freedom. Listen to the Witness History audio to hear more about this work.

66No man has received from nature the right to give orders to others. Freedom is a gift from heaven, and every individual of the same species has the right to enjoy it as soon as he is in enjoyment of his reason.99
—Denis Diderot

◄ Madame Geoffrin (far right in blue), in her famous salon where Enlightenment thinkers gathered to share ideas.

Denis Diderot bust

Rococo fan

Chapter Preview

Chapter Focus Question How did Enlightenment thinkers inspire revolutionaries to push for radical changes in government and society?

Section 1
Philosophy in the Age of Reason

Section 2
Enlightenment Ideas Spread

Section 3
Birth of the American Republic

Use the ☑ **Quick Study Timeline** at the end of this chapter to preview chapter events.

British tax stamp used in the American colonies

? Concept Connector ONLINE
To explore Essential Questions related to this chapter, go to PHSchool.com
Web Code: nbd-1707

Chapter-Level Resources

All in One Vocabulary Builder; Reading Strategy; Enrichments; Outline Maps; Geography Quiz; Chapter Tests
■ Document-Based Assessments
■ AYP Monitoring Assessments
■ *ExamView* Test Bank CD-ROM
■ Guided Reading Audio (Spanish)
■ Student Edition Audio

Previewing the Chapter

■ **WITNESS HISTORY** Ask students **What does it mean to be "enlightened"?** *(free from ignorance, prejudice, or superstition)* Explain that during the Enlightenment, philosophers emphasized political goals like individual freedom and limited government. Read the Witness History selection aloud or play the accompanying audio. Ask students how Diderot's words are reflected in the ideals of American government and in the United States today.

◄)) AUDIO **Witness History Audio CD,**
Pens to Inspire Revolution

■ **Analyzing the Visuals** Explain that Enlightenment writers, artists, and philosophers met in informal social gatherings called salons to discuss arts, science, and political ideas. This painting shows Madame Geoffrin's Paris salon. Point out the bust of Voltaire, who was in exile at the time, as well as Madame Geoffrin (bottom row, third from the right). Tell students that Diderot and other leading figures of the Enlightenment are also present. Ask **Do we have anything comparable to salons today?** *(Sample: weblogs, editorial pages, radio call-in shows, and professional conferences and societies)*

■ **Focus** Write the Chapter Focus Question on the board. Tell students to keep this question in mind as they read the chapter. *(Answer appears with Chapter Assessment answers.)* Have students preview the section titles for this chapter.

Differentiated Instruction Solutions for All Learners

The following Teacher's Edition strategies are suitable for students of varying abilities

L1 Special Needs Students, pp. 183, 191, 196, 198, 202 **SN**

L2 English Language Learners, pp. 183, 187, 191, 196, 198 **ELL**

L2 Less Proficient Readers, pp. 183, 187, 191, 196, 198, 202 **LPR**

L4 Gifted and Talented Students, pp. 185, 192, 200 **GT**

L4 Advanced Readers, pp. 185, 192, 200 **AR**

Note Taking Study Guide With Concept Connector Journal
For online access: Web code nbd-1707
For print alternative: Reading and Note Taking Study Guide booklet

Objectives

As you teach this section, keep students focused on the following objectives to help them answer the Section Focus Question and master core content.

- Explain how science led to the Enlightenment.
- Compare the ideas of Hobbes and Locke.
- Identify the beliefs and contributions of the *philosophes*.
- Summarize how economic thinking changed during this time.

Prepare to Read

Build Background Knowledge L3

Remind students that during the Scientific Revolution, scientists used reason to explain why things happened in the physical universe. Then ask them to predict what other aspects of life people could study using the new scientific method.

Set a Purpose L3

- **WITNESS HISTORY** Read the selection aloud or play the audio.

   AUDIO **Witness History Audio CD,** Rousseau Stirs Things Up

  Ask students to explain in their own words what Rousseau meant by "chains." What might have been some examples of such "chains" in his time? What are some examples today?

- **Focus** Point out the Section Focus Question and write it on the board. Tell students to refer to this question as they read. *(Answer appears with Section 1 Assessment answers.)*

- **Preview** Have students preview the Section Objectives and the list of Terms, People, and Places.

- **Reading Skill** Have students use the *Reading Strategy: Summarize* worksheet.

  All in One Teaching Resources, Unit 2, p. 6

Jean-Jacques Rousseau and quill pen

WITNESS HISTORY ◀)) AUDIO

Rousseau Stirs Things Up

In Jean-Jacques Rousseau's most important work, *The Social Contract,* he argued that in order to be free, people should do what is best for their community. Rousseau had many supporters who were inspired by his passionate writings. European monarchs, on the other hand, were angry that Rousseau was questioning authority. As a result, Rousseau worried about persecution for much of his life. The "chains" below represent the social institutions that confined society.

❝ Man is born free, and everywhere he is in chains. ❞
—Rousseau, *The Social Contract*

Focus Question What effects did Enlightenment philosophers have on government and society?

Philosophy in the Age of Reason

Objectives

- Explain how science led to the Enlightenment.
- Compare the ideas of Hobbes and Locke.
- Identify the beliefs and contributions of the *philosophes.*
- Summarize how economic thinking changed during this time.

Terms, People, and Places

natural law	Montesquieu
Thomas Hobbes	Voltaire
John Locke	Diderot
social contract	Rousseau
natural right	laissez faire
philosophe	Adam Smith

Note Taking

Reading Skill: Summarize Draw a table like the one shown here. As you read the section, summarize each thinker's works and ideas.

Thinkers' Works and Ideas	
Hobbes	*Leviathan,* social contract
Locke	
Montesquieu	

By the early 1700s, European thinkers felt that nothing was beyond the reach of the human mind. Through the use of reason, insisted these thinkers, people and governments could solve every social, political, and economic problem. In essence, these writers, scholars, and philosophers felt they could change the world.

Scientific Revolution Sparks the Enlightenment

The Scientific Revolution of the 1500s and 1600s had transformed the way people in Europe looked at the world. In the 1700s, other scientists expanded European knowledge. For example, Edward Jenner developed a vaccine against smallpox, a disease whose path of death spanned the centuries.

Scientific successes convinced educated Europeans of the power of human reason. **Natural law,** or rules discoverable by reason, govern scientific forces such as gravity and magnetism. Why not, then, use natural law to better understand social, economic, and political problems? Using the methods of the new science, reformers thus set out to study human behavior and solve the problems of society. In this way, the Scientific Revolution led to another revolution in thinking, known as the Enlightenment. Immanuel Kant, a German philosopher best known for his work *The Critique of Pure Reason,* was one of the first to describe this era with the

---

Vocabulary Builder

Use the information below and the following resources to teach the high-use word from this section.
All in One Teaching Resources, Unit 2 p. 5; Teaching Resources, Skills Handbook, p. 3

High-Use Word	Definition and Sample Sentence
philosophy, p. 185	*n.* the love of, or the search for, wisdom or knowledge Jonathan's **philosophy** of nature comes from his many hikes in the wilderness, where he observes wildlife.

---

word "Enlightenment." Despite Kant's skepticism about the power of reason, he was enthusiastic about the Enlightenment and believed, like many European philosophers, that natural law could help explain aspects of humanity.

✓ **Checkpoint** What convinced educated Europeans to accept the power of reason?

Hobbes and Locke Have Conflicting Views

Thomas Hobbes and **John Locke,** two seventeenth-century English thinkers, set forth ideas that were to become key to the Enlightenment. Both men lived through the upheavals of the English Civil War. Yet they came to very different conclusions about human nature and the role of government.

Hobbes Believes in Powerful Government Thomas Hobbes outlined his ideas in a work titled *Leviathan.* In it, he argued that people were naturally cruel, greedy, and selfish. If not strictly controlled, they would fight, rob, and oppress one another. Life in the "state of nature"— without laws or other control—would be "solitary, poor, nasty, brutish, and short."

To escape that "brutish" life, said Hobbes, people entered into a social contract, an agreement by which they gave up their freedom for an organized society. Hobbes believed that only a powerful government could ensure an orderly society. For him, such a government was an absolute monarchy, which could impose order and compel obedience.

Locke Advocates Natural Rights John Locke had a more optimistic view of human nature. He thought people were basically reasonable and moral. Further, they had certain **natural rights,** or rights that belonged to all humans from birth. These included the right to life, liberty, and property.

In *Two Treatises of Government,* Locke argued that people formed governments to protect their natural rights. The best kind of government, he said, had limited power and was accepted by all citizens. Thus, unlike Hobbes, Locke rejected absolute monarchy. England during this time experienced a shift in political power known as the Glorious Revolution. James II, an unpopular absolute monarch, left the throne and fled England in 1688. Locke later wrote that he thought James II deserved to be dethroned for violating the rights of the English.

Locke proposed a radical idea about this time. A government, he said, has an obligation to the people it governs. If a government fails its obligations or violates people's natural rights, the people have the right to overthrow that government. Locke's idea would one day influence leaders of the American Revolution, such as Benjamin Franklin, Thomas Jefferson, and James Madison. Locke's idea of the right of revolution would also echo across Europe and Latin America in the centuries that followed.

✓ **Checkpoint** How did Hobbes and Locke differ in their views on the role of government?

Hobbes Writes the *Leviathan*
The title page from *Leviathan* (1651) by Hobbes demonstrates his belief in a powerful ruler. The monarch here represents the Leviathan who rises above all of society.

■ **Note Taking** Have students read this section using the Paragraph Shrinking strategy (TE, p. T20). As they read, have students fill in the table describing each thinker's works and ideas.
Reading and Note Taking Study Guide, p. 74

Teach

Scientific Revolution/ Hobbes and Locke

Instruct

■ **Introduce: Key Terms** Ask students to find the key term *natural law* (in blue) in the text. Point out that during the 1500s and 1600s, scientists used natural law and the scientific method to challenge long-held beliefs.

■ **Teach** Compare Hobbes's and Locke's views on government. Then ask **In the 1700s, what type of government existed in most European states?** *(divine-right monarchy)* **How did Locke's ideas challenge Europe's traditional order?** *(His theory of natural rights contradicted the theory of divine rights.)* **What was the long-term effect of these ideas?** *(They influenced revolutions across the globe.)*

■ **Quick Activity** Ask students if they recognize Locke's ideas about natural rights in our government. Have them read the excerpt from John Locke's *Two Treatises of Government* at the end of this section. Then discuss if and when people have the right to overthrow their government.

Independent Practice

Pair students and have them write a dialogue between Locke and Hobbes on the dethroning of James II in England.

Monitor Progress

As students compose the dialogues, check to ensure they understand that Hobbes and Locke would have had different views on the dethroning.

Answers

✓ scientific successes

✓ Hobbes believed that the government needed to impose order and compel obedience. Locke thought governments should have limited power and be sanctioned by all citizens.

The *Philosophes* ⑬

Instruct

- **Introduce: Vocabulary Builder**
  Have students read the Vocabulary Builder term and definition. Ask students to define **philosophy** in their own words. Then ask students to explain who the *philosophes* were.

- **Teach** Create a two-column chart on the board, labeling one column "Thinker" and the other "Main Ideas." Ask volunteers to fill in the chart with the thinkers discussed in the section and each thinker's ideas and accomplishments. Then have students use the chart to summarize the main ideas of the Enlightenment. Using the Think-Write-Pair-Share strategy (TE, p. T23), ask students to discuss what made these ideas revolutionary in the 1700s.

- **Quick Activity** Display **Color Transparency 101: Enlightenment Ideas About Government.** Use the lesson suggested in the transparency book to guide a discussion. Ask how the *philosophes* helped create new assumptions about the proper use of power and the attributes of a just government.
  🏛 **Color Transparencies,** 101

Independent Practice

- **Biography** To help students better understand the courage it took to criticize powerful institutions, have them read *Voltaire* and complete the worksheet.
  All in One Teaching Resources, Unit 2, p. 7

- **Viewpoints** To help students learn about different viewpoints on education at the time, have them read *Enlightenment Views on Education* and complete the worksheet.
  All in One Teaching Resources, Unit 2, p. 10

Monitor Progress

As students fill in their tables, circulate to make sure they understand each thinker's ideas. For a completed version of the table, see
🏛 **Note Taking Transparencies,** 133

Answers

BIOGRAPHY Voltaire: the French authorities and enemies of freedom; Montesquieu: separation of the powers of government

---

● BIOGRAPHY

Voltaire
François-Marie Arouet, known as Voltaire (1694–1778) was an impassioned poet, historian, essayist, and philosopher who wrote with cutting sarcasm and sharp wit. Voltaire was sent to the Bastille prison twice due to his criticism of French authorities and was eventually banned from Paris. When he was able to return to France, he wrote about political and religious freedom. Voltaire spent his life fighting enemies of freedom, such as ignorance, superstition, and intolerance. **What did Voltaire attack in his writings?**

Montesquieu
Born to wealth, Charles Louis de Secondat (1689–1755) inherited the title Baron de Montesquieu from his uncle. Like many other reformers, he did not let his privileged status keep him from becoming a voice for democracy. His first book titled *Persian Letters* ridiculed the French government and social classes. In his work published in 1748, *The Spirit of the Laws*, he advanced the idea of separation of powers—a foundation of modern democracy. **What did Montesquieu think was necessary to protect liberty?**

The *Philosophes*

In the 1700s, there was a flowering of Enlightenment thought. This was when a group of Enlightenment thinkers in France applied the methods of science to understand and improve society. They believed that the use of reason could lead to reforms of government, law, and society. These thinkers were called **philosophes** (fee loh ZOHFS), which means "philosophers." Their ideas soon spread beyond France and even beyond Europe.

Montesquieu Advances the Idea of Separation of Powers An early and influential thinker was Baron de **Montesquieu** (MAHN tus kyoo). Montesquieu studied the governments of Europe, from Italy to England. He read about ancient and medieval Europe, and learned about Chinese and Native American cultures. His sharp criticism of absolute monarchy would open doors for later debate.

In 1748, Montesquieu published *The Spirit of the Laws*, in which he discussed governments throughout history. Montesquieu felt that the best way to protect liberty was to divide the various functions and powers of government among three branches: the legislative, executive, and judicial. He also felt that each branch of government should be able to serve as a check on the other two, an idea that we call checks and balances. Montesquieu's beliefs would soon profoundly affect the Framers of the United States Constitution.

Voltaire Defends Freedom of Thought Probably the most famous of the *philosophes* was François-Marie Arouet, who took the name **Voltaire.** "My trade," said Voltaire, "is to say what I think," and he did so throughout his long, controversial life. Voltaire used biting wit as a weapon to expose the abuses of his day. He targeted corrupt officials and idle aristocrats. With his pen, he battled inequality, injustice, and superstition. He detested the slave trade and deplored religious prejudice.

Voltaire's outspoken attacks offended both the French government and the Catholic Church. He was imprisoned and forced into exile. Even as he saw his books outlawed and even burned, he continued to defend the principle of freedom of speech.

Diderot Edits the *Encyclopedia* Denis **Diderot** (DEE duh roh) worked for years to produce a 28-volume set of books called the *Encyclopedia*. As the editor, Diderot did more than just compile articles.

History Background

Science and Philosophy Sociology, the study of human behavior and the development of human societies, came out of the science practiced by the eighteenth-century *philosophes*, in particular Baron de Montesquieu. He can legitimately be called the father of sociology. In his great treatise, *The Spirit of the Laws*, Montesquieu wrote that religion shapes politics, that political climate controls behavior, and that the extent of freedom in a society is determined by its institutions. He examined laws, customs, and behaviors of various societies. His method of study was to compare the features of past and present societies. This is similar to the methods of comparative sociology today.

His purpose was "to change the general way of thinking" by explaining ideas on topics such as government, <u>philosophy</u>, and religion. Diderot's *Encyclopedia* included articles by leading thinkers of the day, including Montesquieu and Voltaire. In these articles, the *philosophes* denounced slavery, praised freedom of expression, and urged education for all. They attacked divine-right theory and traditional religions. Critics raised an outcry. The French government argued that the *Encyclopedia* was an attack on public morals, and the pope threatened to excommunicate Roman Catholics who bought or read the volumes.

Despite these and other efforts to ban the *Encyclopedia,* more than 4,000 copies were printed between 1751 and 1789. When translated into other languages, the *Encyclopedia* helped spread Enlightenment ideas throughout Europe and across the Atlantic Ocean to the Americas.

Rousseau Promotes *The Social Contract*
Jean-Jacques Rousseau (roo SOH), believed that people in their natural state were basically good. This natural innocence, he felt, was corrupted by the evils of society, especially the unequal distribution of property. Many reformers and revolutionaries later adopted this view. Among them were Thomas Paine and Marquis de Lafayette, who were leading figures of the American and French Revolutions.

In 1762, Rousseau set forth his ideas about government and society in *The Social Contract*. Rousseau felt that society placed too many limitations on people's behavior. He believed that some controls were necessary, but that they should be minimal. Additionally, only governments that had been freely elected should impose these controls.

Rousseau put his faith in the "general will," or the best conscience of the people. The good of the community as a whole, he said, should be placed above individual interests. Rousseau has influenced political and social thinkers for more than 200 years. Woven through his work is a hatred of all forms of political and economic oppression. His bold ideas would help fan the flames of revolt in years to come.

Women Challenge the *Philosophes*
The Enlightenment slogan "free and equal" did not apply to women. Though the *philosophes* said women had natural rights, their rights were limited to the areas of home and family.

By the mid- to late-1700s, a small but growing number of women protested this view. Germaine de Staël in France and Catharine Macaulay and Mary Wollstonecraft in Britain argued that women were being excluded from the social contract itself. Their arguments, however, were ridiculed and often sharply condemned.

Wollstonecraft was a well-known British social critic. She accepted that a woman's first duty was to be a good mother but felt that a woman should be able to decide what was in her own interest without depending on her husband. In 1792, Wollstonecraft published *A Vindication of the Rights of Woman*. In it, she called for equal education for girls and boys. Only education, she argued, could give women the tools they needed to participate equally with men in public life.

✓ **Checkpoint** What topics were addressed by the *philosophes* in their *Encyclopedia* articles?

Vocabulary Builder

<u>philosophy</u>—(fih LAHS uh fee) *n.* love of, or the search for, wisdom or knowledge

Heated Debate
Rousseau (left) and Voltaire (right) are pictured here in the midst of an argument. Even though the *philosophes* were reform-minded, they disagreed about some issues. *Compare the beliefs of Rousseau and Voltaire.*

New Economic Thinking
L3

Instruct

■ **Introduce** Ask students to read the introductory sentences under the red heading New Economic Thinking. Have students predict how natural law could apply to economics. Then have them read to find out whether their predictions were accurate.

■ **Teach** Discuss the new economic thinking. Ask **What are two differences between the physiocrats and the mercantilists?** *(mercantilists: favored government regulation, believed in building wealth through trade; physiocrats: opposed government regulation, believed in building wealth through land productivity)* **How did Adam Smith's ideas build upon those of the physiocrats?** *(He agreed that government should not interfere with the economy.)* **According to Smith, what should rule the economy?** *(market forces of supply and demand)*

■ **Quick Activity** Display **Color Transparency 102: Law of Supply and Demand.** Use the lesson suggested in the transparency book to guide a discussion on the ways Smith's ideas are included in modern economic theory.

 Color Transparencies, 102

Independent Practice

Laissez-faire economists argue that society would be better off if the government did not interfere with business and the marketplace. Discuss what students believe to be the proper role of government in a nation's economy.

Monitor Progress

Check Reading and Note Taking Study Guide entries for student understanding.

Answers

✓ Answers may include topics such as slavery, freedom of expression, and education.

Caption Rousseau believed that a freely elected government should exercise minimal control over the people; Voltaire believed in free speech, equality, justice, and reason.

Assess Progress

- Have students complete the Section Assessment.
- Administer the Section Quiz.

 Teaching Resources, Unit 2, p. 2

- To further assess student understanding, use
  Progress Monitoring Transparencies, 72

Reteach

If students need more instruction, have them read the section summary.

 Reading and Note Taking Study Guide, p. 75

 Adapted Reading and Note Taking Study Guide, p. 75

 Spanish Reading and Note Taking Study Guide, p. 75

Extend

Organize the class into small groups. Have each group think of areas in modern society that are based on or represent Enlightenment ideas. *(Sample: government, human rights, education, gender roles)* Have them choose one Enlightenment idea and discuss the similarities and differences between that idea and the present-day manifestation of the idea.

Answer

 Smith believed the market would be more productive without government regulation.

New Economic Thinking

French thinkers known as physiocrats focused on economic reforms. Like the *philosophes,* physiocrats based their thinking on natural laws. The physiocrats claimed that their rational economic system was based on the natural laws of economics.

Laissez Faire Replaces Mercantilism Physiocrats rejected mercantilism, which required government regulation of the economy to achieve a favorable balance of trade. Instead, they urged a policy of **laissez faire** (les ay FEHR), allowing business to operate with little or no government interference. Physiocrats also supported free trade and opposed tariffs.

Smith Argues for a Free Market Scottish economist **Adam Smith** greatly admired the physiocrats. In his influential work *The Wealth of Nations,* he argued that the free market should be allowed to regulate business activity. Smith tried to show how manufacturing, trade, wages, profits, and economic growth were all linked to the market forces of supply and demand. Wherever there was a demand for goods or services, he said, suppliers would seek to meet that demand in order to gain profits. Smith was a strong supporter of laissez faire. However, he felt that government had a duty to protect society, administer justice, and provide public works. Adam Smith's ideas would help to shape productive economies in the 1800s and 1900s.

✓ **Checkpoint** Why did Smith support laissez faire?

Investors in Paris, France, 1720

SECTION 1 **Assessment**

Progress Monitoring Online
For: Self-quiz with vocabulary practice
Web Code: nba-1711

Terms, People, and Places

1. For each term, person, or place listed at the beginning of the section, write a sentence explaining its significance.

Note Taking

2. **Reading Skill: Summarize** Use your completed tables to answer the Focus Question: What effects did Enlightenment philosophers have on government and society?

Comprehension and Critical Thinking

3. **Summarize** How did the achievements of the Scientific Revolution contribute to the Enlightenment?

4. **Recognize Cause and Effect** What did the *philosophes* do to better understand and improve society?

5. **Synthesize Information** Explain the connection between the policy of laissez faire and natural economic laws.

● **Writing About History**

Quick Write: Explore a Topic On some essay tests, you may have a choice of topic. You should choose one that you feel most knowledgeable about. Choose from the following, and draft a single sentence that identifies the main idea:
(a) social contracts (b) freedom of speech (c) women in the mid-1700s

---

1. Sentences should reflect an understanding of each term, person, or place listed at the beginning of the section.
2. They contributed new ideas such as separation of powers and freely elected government.
3. They led to greater faith in the power of reason. People began to apply reason to human nature and government as well as to the physical world.
4. They applied the methods of science to study and improve society.
5. Laissez faire means allowing the free market to operate "naturally," or with little or no government interference.

● **Writing About History**

Sentences should show an understanding of the main idea of one of the three writing topics given.

> For additional assessment, have students access **Progress Monitoring Online** at **Web Code nba-1711.**

John Locke:
Two Treatises of Government

English philosopher John Locke (1632–1704) published *Two Treatises of Government* in 1690. Locke believed that all people had the same natural rights of life, liberty, and property. In this essay, Locke states that the primary purpose of government is to protect these natural rights. He also states that governments hold their power only with the consent of the people. Locke's ideas greatly influenced revolutions in America and France.

John Locke and a book of his writings

But though men, when they enter into society give up the equality, liberty, and executive power they had in the state of Nature into the hands of society . . . the power of the society or legislative constituted by them can never be supposed to extend farther than the common good. . . . Whoever has the legislative or supreme power of any commonwealth, is bound to govern by established standing laws, promulgated[1] and known to the people, and not by extemporary[2] decrees, by indifferent and upright judges, who are to decide controversies by those laws; and to employ the force of the community at home only in the execution of such laws, or abroad to prevent or redress foreign injuries and secure the community from inroads[3] and invasion. And all this to be directed to no other end but the peace, safety, and public good of the people. . . .

The reason why men enter into society is the preservation of their property; and the end while they choose and authorize a legislative is that there may be laws made, and rules set, as guards and fences to the properties of all the society, . . .

Whensoever, therefore, the legislative [power] shall transgress[4] this fundamental rule of society, and either by ambition, fear, folly, or corruption, endeavor to grasp themselves, or put into the hands of any other, an absolute power over the lives, liberties, and estates of the people, by this breach of trust they forfeit the power the people had put into their hands for quite contrary ends, and it devolves[5] to the people; who have a right to resume their original liberty, and by the establishment of a new legislative (such as they shall think fit), provide for their own safety and security. . . .

1. **promulgated** (PRAHM ul gayt id) *vt.* published or made known.
2. **extemporary** (ek STEM puh rehr ee) *adj.* without any preparation.
3. **inroads** (IN rohdz) *n.* advances at the expense of someone.
4. **transgress** (trans GRES) *vt.* go beyond; break.
5. **devolves** (dih VAHLVZ) *vt.* passes.

Thinking Critically

1. **Draw Inferences** According to Locke, how should a land be governed? Why do you think this is the case?
2. **Identify Central Issues** What does Locke say can happen if a government fails to protect the rights of its people?

John Locke: *Two Treatises of Government*

Objectives

- Explain the ideas presented in John Locke's *Two Treatises of Government.*
- Understand the impact of this document on the French and American revolutions.

Build Background Knowledge L3

Ask students to recall what they know about John Locke and his ideas on government. Tell them that Locke explained some of his ideas in this essay.

Instruct L3

- Direct students to the introduction at the top of the page. Then ask **What does Locke believe is the primary purpose of government?** *(to protect people's natural rights of life, liberty, and property)* Ask students to recall where else they have heard this idea. Point out that Locke's ideas about natural rights and the obligations of government later influenced Thomas Jefferson's writing of the Declaration of Independence. This document states that all men are created equal and are given "certain unalienable Rights, that among these are Life, Liberty and the pursuit of Happiness."

- As students read the selection, have them list each of Locke's ideas on government. When students have finished, have them compare their lists, and then create a master list on the board. *(Lists should include: People have natural rights; people form governments to protect their natural rights; if a government fails this obligation, the people have a right to overthrow that government.)*

Monitor Progress

To confirm students' understanding, ask them to briefly summarize Locke's ideas. How does modern American government incorporate his ideas?

Thinking Critically

1. by a government chosen by the people; Sample: All people have the same natural rights and should be able to choose the body that protects them.
2. The people can overthrow the government.

Opera

Objectives

■ Understand how opera developed.
■ List the key features of an opera.

Build Background Knowledge ⓛ

Ask students if they have ever seen a musical or opera. If they have, ask them to share their recollections with the class. Tell them that in opera, the music showcases the vocal range of the singers.

Instruct ⓛ

■ Play the selection from the Witness History audio that accompanies this page, or play an opera selection of your own choosing. Have students discuss the piece by comparing and contrasting it to other music that is familiar to them.

🔊 AUDIO **Witness History Audio CD,**
Opera

■ Ask students to study the visuals on this page. Point out the image of the modern opera singers, The Three Tenors, and the picture of one of Europe's oldest opera houses, La Scala. Ask **What can you conclude about opera from looking at these pictures?** (*Opera is a formal and elegant art form that is still popular today; attending an opera is an exciting visual and musical experience.*)

Monitor Progress

Ask **Why do you think operas are still written and performed today?** (*Sample: Audiences still enjoy the music and theatricality of opera and appreciate the tremendous skill of the performers.*)

Thinking Critically

1. Sample: Composers of opera must work not just with the orchestra, but with a plot line and words, as well as showcasing the singers' voices. Most symphonies feature only the orchestra.
2. It was appealing because it was a new form that composers and musicians could use to combine theater and music.

HUMANITIES / MUSIC

View of La Scala in Milan, mid-1800s ▼

Opera

Operas originated in Florence, Italy, in the seventeenth century. First called *drama per musica*, or drama through music, these musical performances typically involve large casts and elaborate sets and costumes. When Italian operas were performed in France, they emphasized glory and love, and included ballet and lavish stage settings to please the French court. Handel, Mozart, Verdi, Wagner, and Puccini composed some of the world's most famous operas. 🔊 AUDIO

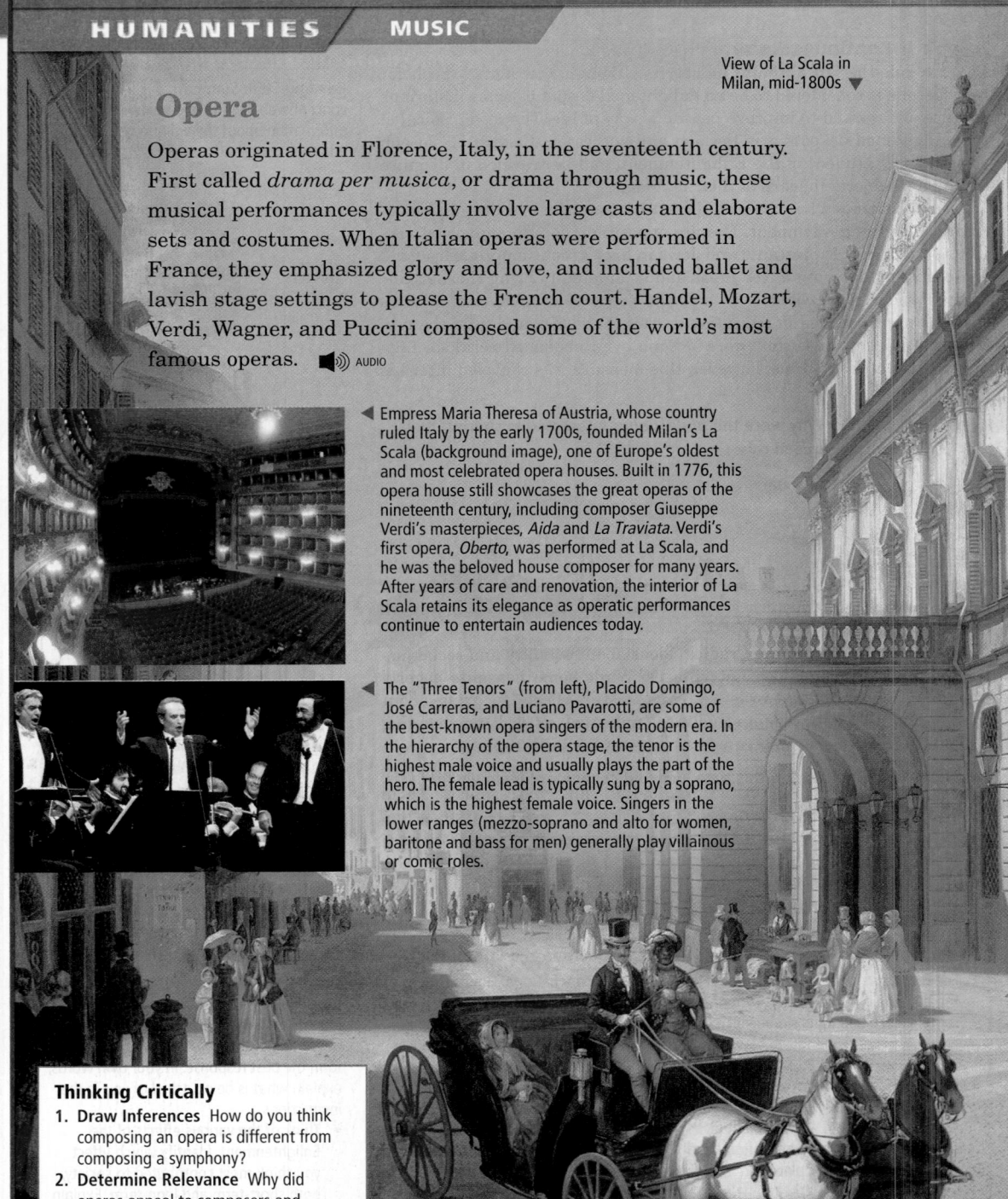

◄ Empress Maria Theresa of Austria, whose country ruled Italy by the early 1700s, founded Milan's La Scala (background image), one of Europe's oldest and most celebrated opera houses. Built in 1776, this opera house still showcases the great operas of the nineteenth century, including composer Giuseppe Verdi's masterpieces, *Aida* and *La Traviata*. Verdi's first opera, *Oberto*, was performed at La Scala, and he was the beloved house composer for many years. After years of care and renovation, the interior of La Scala retains its elegance as operatic performances continue to entertain audiences today.

◄ The "Three Tenors" (from left), Placido Domingo, José Carreras, and Luciano Pavarotti, are some of the best-known opera singers of the modern era. In the hierarchy of the opera stage, the tenor is the highest male voice and usually plays the part of the hero. The female lead is typically sung by a soprano, which is the highest female voice. Singers in the lower ranges (mezzo-soprano and alto for women, baritone and bass for men) generally play villainous or comic roles.

Thinking Critically

1. **Draw Inferences** How do you think composing an opera is different from composing a symphony?
2. **Determine Relevance** Why did operas appeal to composers and musicians during the Enlightenment?

History Background

Opera Opera is generally considered a European art form—traditionally, operas are performed in Italian, French, or German. It would take many years for well-known operas to come out of the United States. The best-known American opera, *Porgy and Bess*, was written in 1935 by George Gershwin and DuBose Howard. The opera, based on Howard's book *Porgy*, is the story of a black fishing town in South Carolina and the unlikely relationship between Bess, a woman with a sordid past, and Porgy, an old crippled man. At first, critics did not accept the work as an opera, and Gershwin himself chose to have it open on Broadway. Eventually, though, it was accepted as an opera and performed at major opera houses worldwide.

Thomas Paine

British tax stamp

WITNESS HISTORY 🔊 AUDIO

Paine's *Common Sense*

Early in 1776, English colonists in North America eagerly read the newly published *Common Sense*, by Thomas Paine. This pamphlet called on them to declare their independence from Britain and echoed the themes of the Enlightenment.

> 66 'Tis repugnant to reason, to the universal order of things, to all examples from former ages, to suppose that this Continent can long remain subject to any external power. 99
> —Thomas Paine, *Common Sense*

Focus Question How did ideas of the Enlightenment lead to the independence and founding of the United States of America?

Birth of the American Republic

Objectives

- Describe characteristics of Britain and its American colonies in the mid-1700s.
- Outline the events that led to the American Revolution.
- Summarize the events and significance of the American Revolution.
- Analyze how the new Constitution reflected the ideas of the Enlightenment.

Terms, People, and Places

George III	Yorktown, Virginia
Stamp Act	Treaty of Paris
George Washington	James Madison
Thomas Jefferson	Benjamin Franklin
popular sovereignty	federal republic

Note Taking

Reading Skill: Recognize Sequence As you read, complete a timeline like the one below with important dates that led up to the formation of the United States government.

French and Indian War ends.

1763

On the eve of the American Revolution, Britain was a formidable foe whose power stretched throughout the world. In addition, an ambitious new ruler sought to expand the powers of the monarchy.

Britain Becomes a Global Power

There are several key reasons for Britain's rise to global prominence:

- Location placed England in a position to control trade. In the 1500s and 1600s, English merchants sent ships across the world's oceans and planted outposts in the West Indies, North America, and India. From these tiny settlements, England would build a global empire.
- England offered a climate favorable to business and commerce and put fewer restrictions on trade than some of its neighbors.
- In the 1700s, Britain was generally on the winning side in European conflicts. With the Treaty of Utrecht, France gave Nova Scotia and Newfoundland to Britain. In 1763, the end of the French and Indian War and the Seven Years' War brought Britain all of French Canada. The British also monopolized the slave trade in Spanish America, which brought enormous wealth to British merchants.
- England's territory expanded closer to home as well. In 1707, England and Wales were united with Scotland to become the United Kingdom of Great Britain. Free trade with Scotland created a larger market for farmers and manufacturers. Ireland had come under English control during the 1600s. It was formally united with Great Britain in 1801.

Vocabulary Builder

Use the information below and the following resources to teach the high-use word from this section.
All in One Teaching Resources, Unit 2, p. 5; **Teaching Resources, Skills Handbook**, p. 3

High-Use Word	Definition and Sample Sentence
assert, p. 196	*vt.* to insist on being recognized He knew that if he didn't **assert** himself, his boss would give the promotion to someone else.

SECTION 3 **Step-by-Step Instruction**

Objectives

As you teach this section, keep students focused on the following objectives to help them answer the Section Focus Question and master core content.

- Describe characteristics of Britain and its American colonies in the mid-1700s.
- Outline the events that led to the American Revolution.
- Summarize the events and significance of the American Revolution.
- Analyze how the new Constitution reflected the ideas of the Enlightenment.

Prepare to Read

Build Background Knowledge

Ask students to recall what they already know about the American Revolution. Why did the colonists go to war? How was the new American Republic different from other governments at the time?

Set a Purpose

- **WITNESS HISTORY** Read the selection aloud or play the audio.

  🔊 AUDIO **Witness History Audio CD**, Paine's *Common Sense*

  Ask **How do Paine's words reflect Enlightenment ideals?** *(He points to reason and natural law—"the universal order of things"—as reasons why the colonies must be free from England.)*

- **Focus** Point out the Section Focus Question and write it on the board. Tell students to refer to this question as they read. *(Answer appears with Section 3 Assessment answers.)*

- **Preview** Have students preview the Section Objectives and the list of Terms, People, and Places.

- **Note Taking** Have students read this section using the Structured Read Aloud strategy (TE, p. T20). As they read, have students fill in the timeline showing important dates leading to the formation of the U.S. government.

   Reading and Note Taking Study Guide, p. 78

Britain Becomes a Global Power L3

Instruct

- **Introduce** Using the Think-Write-Pair-Share strategy, (TE, p. T23), ask students to list characteristics that would allow a nation to become a global power. *(wealth, trade, territory, victories in war, an ambitious ruler)* Write their responses on the board.

- **Teach** Ask **How did Britain exhibit the characteristics of a global power in the mid-1700s?** Match students' responses in the Introduce activity with their responses to this question.

- **Quick Activity** Display **Color Transparency 103:** *The Election II—Canvassing for Votes,* by **William Hogarth.** Use the lesson suggested in the transparency book to guide a discussion on the corruption of Britain's political system.

  📖 **Color Transparencies,** 103

Independent Practice

Link to Geography Have students work in groups to find the following maps using Internet and library resources: England before 1707, Great Britain after 1707 and before 1801, Great Britain after 1801, British colonies in the mid-1700s, British colonies in the mid-1800s. Ask them to explain the changes in Great Britain's territory. Have students share the maps they find with the class.

Monitor Progress

As students fill in their timelines, circulate to make sure they have correctly identified the sequence of events that led to the formation of the U.S. government. For a completed version of the timeline see

📖 **Note Taking Transparencies,** p. 135

Answers

Map Skills
1. Review locations with students.
2. Massachusetts
3. They are all located close to the coast, which would have been important for trade and travel.

✓ Each victory in war brought Britain more lands. In addition, Britain was in a position to control trade.

Geography *Interactive*
For: Audio guided tour
Web Code: nbp-1731

The Colonies That Became the United States

◄ The original flag of the United States

Map Skills Cities in the English colonies were busy centers of trade and important to Britain's economy.
1. **Locate** (a) Philadelphia (b) Massachusetts (c) Boston
2. **Region** Which colony had two separate pieces of land?
3. **Analyze Information** What do almost all the colonial cities have in common based on the map? Why was this important?

Vocabulary Builder
assert—(uh SURT) *vt.* to insist on being recognized

In 1760, George III began a 60-year reign. Unlike his father and grandfather, the new king was born in England. He spoke English and loved Britain. But George was eager to recover the powers the crown had lost. Following his mother's advice, "George, be a king!" he set out to reassert royal power. He wanted to end Whig domination, choose his own ministers, dissolve the cabinet system, and make Parliament follow his will. Gradually, George found seats in Parliament for "the king's friends." Then, with their help, he began to <u>assert</u> his leadership. Many of his policies, however, would prove disastrous.

✓ **Checkpoint** What led to Britain's rise to global prominence in the mid-1700s?

The Colonies in the Mid-1700s

By 1750, a string of prosperous colonies stretched along the eastern coast of North America. They were part of Britain's growing empire. Colonial cities such as Boston, New York, and Philadelphia were busy commercial centers that linked North America to the West Indies, Africa, and Europe. Colonial shipyards produced many vessels for this trade.

Britain applied mercantilist policies to its colonies in an attempt to strengthen its own economy by exporting more than it imported. To this end, in the 1600s, Parliament had passed the Navigation Acts to regulate colonial trade and manufacturing. For the most part, however, these acts were not rigorously enforced. Therefore, activities like smuggling were common and not considered crimes by the colonists.

Differentiated Instruction Solutions for All Learners

L1 Special Needs   **L2 Less Proficient Readers**   **L2 English Language Learners**

Have students scan the headings and visuals in the section. Then create two columns on the board, labeled *Britain* and *The American Colonies.* Have students volunteer information comparing and contrasting the two regions in the 1700s. Then ask students to use this chart to explain why the colonists would seek independence in 1776.

Use the following resources to help students acquire basic skills:

✏️ **Adapted Reading and Note Taking Study Guide**

- Adapted Note Taking Study Guide, p. 78
- Adapted Section Summary, p. 79

By the mid-1700s, the colonies were home to diverse religious and ethnic groups. Social distinctions were more blurred than in Europe, although wealthy landowners and merchants dominated government and society. In politics, as in much else, there was a good deal of free discussion. Colonists felt entitled to the rights of English citizens, and their colonial assemblies exercised much control over local affairs. Many also had an increasing sense of their own destiny separate from Britain.

✓ **Checkpoint** In what ways were the colonies already developing independence from Britain?

Colonists Express Discontent

The Seven Years' War and the French and Indian War in North America had drained the British treasury. King George III and his advisors thought that the colonists should help pay for these wars. To increase taxes paid by colonists, Parliament passed the Sugar Act in 1764, which imposed import taxes, and the **Stamp Act** in 1765, which imposed taxes on items such as newspapers and pamphlets. "No taxation without representation," the colonists protested. They believed that because they had no representatives in Parliament, they should not be taxed. Parliament repealed the Stamp Act in 1766, but then passed a Declaratory Act that said it had complete authority over the colonists.

Colonists Rebel Against Britain A series of violent clashes intensified the colonists' anger. In March 1770, British soldiers in Boston opened fire on a crowd that was pelting them with stones and snowballs. Colonists called the death of five protesters the Boston Massacre. Then in December 1773, a handful of colonists hurled a cargo of recently arrived British tea into the harbor to protest a tax on tea. The incident became known as the Boston Tea Party. When Parliament passed harsh laws to punish Massachusetts for the destruction of the tea, other colonies rallied to oppose the British response.

As tensions increased, fighting spread. Finally, representatives from each colony gathered in Philadelphia and met in a Continental Congress to decide what action to take. Among the participants were the radical yet fair-minded Massachusetts lawyer John Adams, who had defended the British soldiers involved in the Boston Massacre in their trial; Virginia planter and soldier **George Washington;** and political and social leaders from other colonies.

Colonists Declare Independence In April 1775, the ongoing tension between the colonists and the British exploded into war in Lexington and Concord, Massachusetts. This war is known as the Revolutionary War, or the American Revolution. The Congress met soon after and set up a Continental Army, with George Washington in command. Although many battles ended in British victories, the colonists were determined to fight at any cost. In 1776, the

Drafting the Declaration
Benjamin Franklin, John Adams, and Thomas Jefferson (from left to right)

The Declaration of Independence stands as one of the most important documents in all of history. It still serves as inspiration for people around the world. Where did some of the ideas of the Declaration originate?

> **Primary Source**

 We hold these truths to be self-evident, that all men are created equal, that they are endowed by their Creator with certain unalienable Rights, that among these are Life, Liberty and the pursuit of Happiness. That to secure these rights, Governments are instituted among Men, deriving their just powers from the consent of the governed; That whenever any Form of Government becomes destructive of these ends it is the Right of the People to alter or to abolish it, and to institute new Government, laying its foundation on such principles and organizing its powers in such form, as to them shall seem most likely to effect their Safety and Happiness. **"**
—*Declaration of Independence*, July 4, 1776   ◀))) AUDIO

The Colonies in the Mid-1700s

Instruct

- **Introduce** Using the map titled The Colonies That Became the United States on the previous page, remind students of the location and names of the colonies in the mid-1700s. Ask **Why were the colonies clustered together on the eastern seaboard?** *(They had been settled largely by immigrants from England; the population of the colonies had not yet grown to the point where people needed to move to the unsettled interior, especially since the Appalachian Mountains stood in the way.)*

- **Teach** Have students describe the English colonies in the mid-1700s. Ask **Which characteristics do you think would lead them on a collision course with Britain?** *(prosperity and growing self-confidence)*

- **Quick Activity** Ask students to discuss in small groups why colonists felt entitled to the rights of English citizens. Then have groups share their responses with the class.

Independent Practice

- Have students access **Web Code nbp-1731** to take the **Geography Interactive Audio Guided Tour** and then answer the maps skills questions in the text.

- Have students fill in the Outline Map *The Colonies That Became the United States.*

All in One Teaching Resources, Unit 2, p. 13

Monitor Progress

- Check answers to map skills questions.

- Check students' Outline Maps to make sure that they have accurately located the thirteen colonies. Administer the Geography Quiz.

All in One Teaching Resources, Unit 2, p. 14

Careers

Lawyers More than half of the signers of the Declaration of Independence were trained in the law. Lawyers work to advise and advocate in legal matters. They may represent parties in civil and criminal trials, research the intent of the law, and draft legal documents. Most specialize in an area of law, such as elder care, real estate, or the growing field of intellectual property. They spend much of their time in law libraries, offices, and courtrooms as they do research, meet with clients, and argue cases. Lawyers are analytical, persuasive, and articulate. To practice law, a person must have a bachelor's degree, a law degree, and a license to practice in a given state.

Answers

✓ Answers may include colonial prosperity, colonial assemblies having some control over local affairs, and the lack of enforcement of its laws by Britain.

PRIMARY SOURCE in France and England from Enlightenment thinkers such as Locke and Rousseau

Colonists Express Discontent

Instruct

- **Introduce** Read the Primary Source selection from the Declaration of Independence aloud or play the audio. Ask students to summarize the passage in their own words. Ask why the Declaration of Independence is one of the most important documents in all of history.

  🔊 AUDIO **Witness History Audio CD,** The Declaration of Independence

- **Teach** Ask **Why did the colonists object so strongly to the idea of no taxation without representation?** *(The British government was imposing its laws without any say from the colonists.)* **How did Enlightenment ideals influence the colonists' view of this issue?** *(The Enlightenment emphasized representative government.)*

- **Quick Activity** Display **Color Transparency 106:** *Tarring and Feathering Under The Liberty Tree,* showing colonists' discontent before the American Revolution with the famous English portrayal of tarring and feathering. Use the lesson suggested in the transparency book to guide a discussion.

  📖 **Color Transparencies,** 106

Independent Practice

Ask students to choose an event mentioned in the text, such as the passage of the Stamp Act or the Boston Massacre, and write two letters to the editor. One letter should be from the viewpoint of a colonist and one should be from the viewpoint of someone living in Britain.

Monitor Progress

As students compose their letters, circulate to make sure that they understand how the viewpoints of a colonist and of someone living in Britain would differ when viewing the same event.

Answers

BIOGRAPHY Washington: He was a patient, courageous, and determined leader. Madison: They were well-read intellectuals who supported Enlightenment ideals. Franklin: His scientific reputation preceded his visit to France, and he represented freedom, which was an Enlightenment ideal.

✔ individual freedom, government by the people, the right to "life, liberty, and property"

BIOGRAPHY

George Washington

When George Washington (1732–1799) was chosen to lead the American army, the British thought he would be a failure. Washington indeed faced many challenges, including an army that did not have weapons, uniforms, or bedding. He struggled to incorporate order and discipline and to instill pride and loyalty in his soldiers. Washington persevered to American victory. His success as a leader continued when he became the nation's first President. **How did Washington hold the army together through difficult times?**

James Madison

James Madison (1751–1836) arrived at the Constitutional Convention in Philadelphia in May 1787 with his thick notebooks on history and government. Madison chose a seat in front of the president's chair and kept detailed notes of the debates. Madison was greatly respected and quickly became the Convention's floor leader. His notebooks remained unpublished for more than 50 years, but they are now our main source of information about the birth of the Constitution. **What did the Framers of the Constitution have in common?**

Benjamin Franklin

Benjamin Franklin (1706–1790) was a philosopher, scientist, publisher, legislator, and diplomat. Sent by Congress to France in 1776 to seek financial and military support for the war, he soon became popular in France because of his intellect and wit. Those who admired America's goal of attaining freedom also admired Franklin. When Franklin returned to America after nine years, he served as a delegate to the Constitutional Convention as the eldest of the delegates. **Why was Franklin admired in France?**

Second Continental Congress took a momentous step, voting to declare independence from Britain. **Thomas Jefferson** of Virginia was the principal author of the Declaration of Independence, a document that reflects John Locke's ideas of the government's obligation to protect the people's natural rights to "life, liberty, and property."

The Declaration included another of Locke's ideas: people had the right "to alter or to abolish" unjust governments—a right to revolt. The principle of **popular sovereignty,** which states that all government power comes from the people, is also an important point in the Declaration. Jefferson carefully detailed the colonists' grievances against Britain. Because the king had trampled colonists' natural rights, he argued, the colonists had the right to rebel and set up a new government that would protect them. Aware of the risks involved, on July 4, 1776, American leaders adopted the Declaration, pledging "our lives, our fortunes, and our sacred honor" to creating and protecting the new United States of America.

✔ **Checkpoint** What Enlightenment ideas are reflected in the Declaration of Independence?

The American Revolution Continues

At first, the American cause looked bleak. The British had a large number of trained soldiers, a huge fleet, and greater resources. About one third of the American colonists were Loyalists, or those who supported Britain. Many others refused to fight for either side. The Americans lacked military resources, had little money to pay soldiers, and did not have a strategic plan.

Still, colonists had some advantages. One was the geography of the diverse continent. Since colonists were fighting on their own soil, they were familiar with its thick woods and inadequate roads. Other advantages were their strong leader, George Washington, and their fierce determination to fight for their ideals of liberty.

To counteract these advantages, the British worked to create alliances within the colonies. A number of Native American groups sided with the British, while others saw potential advantages in supporting the colonists' cause. Additionally, the British offered freedom to any enslaved people who were willing to fight the colonists.

France Provides Support The first turning point in the war came in 1777, when the Americans triumphed over the British at the Battle of Saratoga. This victory persuaded France to join the Americans against its old rival, Britain. The alliance brought the Americans desperately needed supplies, trained soldiers, and French warships. Spurred by the French example, the Netherlands and Spain added their support.

Hard times continued, however. In the brutal winter of 1777–1778, Continental troops at Valley Forge suffered from cold, hunger, and disease. Throughout this crisis and others, Washington was patient, courageous, and determined. He held the ragged army together.

WITNESS HISTORY VIDEO

Watch *The Enlightenment and the American Revolution* on the **Witness History Discovery School**™ video program to learn more about the American Revolution.

Discovery SCHOOL

Fearless Leader
George Washington directs his troops on the battlefield. *What traits did Washington possess that helped lead Americans to victory?*

The American Revolution Continues ⓛ³

Instruct

- **Introduce** Create a two-column chart on the board, labeling one column "disadvantages" and the other "advantages." Have students fill in the chart with the disadvantages and advantages of the colonists at the start of the Revolution. Ask **Would you have been able to predict colonial victory based on this list?** *(Answers will vary.)*

- **Teach** Ask **Why was the battle of Saratoga a turning point in the war?** *(The American victory persuaded the French to help the colonists.)* **Why was George Washington's leadership essential to the colonists' ultimate success?** *(He was able to hold the ragged colonial army together with his courage and determination.)*

- **Quick Activity** Show students *The Enlightenment and the American Revolution* from the **Witness History Discovery School**™ video program. Ask them to list three ways in which Enlightenment ideals influenced the American Revolution. *(Guided by the ideas of the Enlightenment, the founders of the United States promoted the ideals of equality, inalienable rights, and the people's right to abolish any government that denied these rights.)*

Independent Practice

- **Viewpoints** To help students better understand differing viewpoints during the war, have them read the selection *Two Views of the Battle of Cowpens* and complete the worksheet.

  All in One Teaching Resources, Unit 2, p. 11

Monitor Progress

- To check understanding, ask students to summarize the course of the war.

History Background

A Soldier's Philosophy The philosophical writings of the Enlightenment certainly influenced leading Americans such as Thomas Jefferson and Benjamin Franklin. However, more fundamental thoughts motivated many of the soldiers in the Continental Army.

When Captain Levi Preston was asked if he joined the fight for independence because of having read the writings of Locke and others on liberty, he replied, "Never heard of 'em. We read only the Bible, the Catechism, Watts's Psalms and Hymns, and the Almanack. Young man, what we meant in going for those red-coats was this: we always had governed ourselves, and we always meant to. They didn't mean we should."

Answer

Caption perseverance, strong leadership, and determination

A New Constitution L3

Instruct

- **Introduce** Point out that the United States Constitution has endured for over 200 years. Ask **What is the reason for its longevity?** *(It is based on enduring ideals such as government of, by, and for the people.)*

- **Teach** Ask students to list the main provisions of the Constitution, such as an elected president and the creation of a federal republic. Write their responses on the board. Then help them give present-day examples of each provision.

- **Analyzing the Visuals** Display **Color Transparency 104: Enlightenment Thinkers** on the Enlightenment ideas that inspired revolution and the principles of representative government. Then direct students to the Infographic on this page. Ask **What ideas of the Enlightenment were incorporated into the Constitution?** *(popular sovereignty, limited government, separation of powers, checks and balances)*

  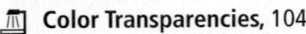 Color Transparencies, 104

Independent Practice

- Have students work in groups to research examples of checks and balances. Encourage students to use newspapers and magazines as well as Internet news services.

- **Web Code nbp-1732** will take students to an interactive diagram. Have students complete the interactivity and then answer the questions in the text.

Monitor Progress

Have students share their examples of checks and balances with the class. Then lead a discussion to further explore one or two of the most timely examples.

Answers

Thinking Critically
1. Sample: the right to freedom of speech, religion, and property ownership
2. For every branch of government, another branch has the power to veto or regulate. For example, the President has the power to veto legislation, the courts may declare congressional acts unconstitutional, and Congress has the ability to override presidential vetoes.

✓ familiarity with the terrain, strong leadership, and determination to achieve their ideals

---

INFOGRAPHIC

The Roots of American Democracy

The Framers of the United States Constitution were well educated and widely read. They were familiar with governments of ancient Greece and Rome and those of contemporary Great Britain and Europe. Political writings such as Montesquieu's *The Spirit of the Laws*, Rousseau's *Social Contract*, and Locke's *Two Treatises of Government* contained principles that greatly influenced the Framers in the development of the Constitution. Centuries later, these fundamental democratic principles of American government—popular sovereignty, limited government, separation of powers, and checks and balances—are still in place. The diagram here shows checks and balances, one of Montesquieu's ideas, which ensures that one branch does not accumulate too much power.

Checks and Balances

Congress may impeach judges; Senate may reject appointment of judges.

Courts may declare acts of Congress unconstitutional.

Judicial Branch

Legislative Branch

Courts may declare executive actions unconstitutional.

President appoints judges.

President may veto legislation.

Executive Branch

Congress may impeach the President and may override veto; Senate approves or rejects treaties and appointments.

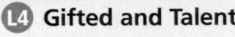 **History *Interactive***
For: Interactive diagram
Web Code: nbp-1732

Thinking Critically
1. **Draw Conclusions** What additional ideas might the Framers have learned from the political writings of the Enlightenment thinkers?
2. **Summarize** Explain how the basic principle of checks and balances works.

Treaty of Paris Ends the War In 1781, the French fleet blockaded the Chesapeake Bay, which enabled Washington to force the surrender of a British army at **Yorktown, Virginia.** With that defeat, the British war effort crumbled. Two years later, American, British, and French diplomats signed the **Treaty of Paris,** ending the war. In that treaty, Britain recognized the independence of the United States of America. The Americans' victory can be attributed to their resilient dedication to attaining independence.

✓ **Checkpoint** What advantages did the colonists have in battling Britain for their independence?

A New Constitution

The Articles of Confederation was the nation's first constitution. It proved to be too weak to rule the new United States effectively. To address this problem, the nation's leaders gathered once more in Philadelphia. Among them were George Washington, **James Madison,** and **Benjamin Franklin.**

During the hot summer of 1787, they met in secret to redraft the articles of the new constitution. The result was a document that established a government run by the people, for the people.

Enlightenment Ideas Have Great Impact The Framers of the Constitution had studied history and absorbed the ideas of Locke, Montesquieu, and Rousseau. They saw government in terms of a social contract into which "We the People of the United States" entered. They provided not only for an elective legislature but also for an elected president rather than a hereditary monarch. For the first President, voters would choose George Washington.

The Constitution created a **federal republic,** with power divided between the federal, or national, government and the states. A central feature of the new federal government was the separation of powers among the legislative, executive, and judicial branches, an idea borrowed directly from Montesquieu. Within that structure, each branch of government was provided with checks and balances on the other branches.

The Bill of Rights, the first ten amendments to the Constitution, was important to the passage of the Constitution. It recognized the idea that people had basic rights that the government must protect, such as freedom of religion, speech, and the press. The Bill of Rights, like the Constitution, put the *philosophes'* Enlightenment ideas into practice. In 1789, the Constitution became the supreme law of the land, which means it became the nation's fundamental law. This remarkable document has endured for more than 200 years.

Symbol of Freedom The Constitution of the United States created the most progressive government of its day. From the start, the new republic was a symbol of freedom to European countries and reformers in Latin America. Its constitution would be copied or adapted by many lands throughout the world. The Enlightenment ideals that had inspired American colonists brought changes in Europe too. In 1789, a revolution in France toppled the monarchy in the name of liberty and equality. Before long, other Europeans would take up the cry for freedom as well.

✓ **Checkpoint** Explain the influence of Enlightenment ideas on the United States Constitution and Bill of Rights.

The U.S. Bill of Rights

1st:	Guarantees freedom of religion, speech, press, assembly, and petition
2nd:	Right to bear arms
3rd:	Prohibits quartering of troops in private homes
4th:	Protects from unreasonable searches and seizures
5th:	No punishment without due process of law
6th:	Right to a speedy and public trial in the state where the offense was committed
7th:	Right to jury trial for civil cases if over $20
8th:	Prohibits excessive bail and cruel and unusual punishments
9th:	Civil rights are not restricted to those specified by these amendments.
10th:	Powers not granted to the national government belong to the states and to the people.

Chart Skills The first ten amendments to the United States Constitution are known as the Bill of Rights. *What is the significance of the 10th Amendment?*

SECTION 3 Assessment

Progress Monitoring Online
For: Self-quiz with vocabulary practice
Web Code: nba-1731

Terms, People, and Places

1. For each term, person, or place listed at the beginning of the section, write a sentence explaining its significance.

Note Taking

2. **Reading Skill: Recognize Sequence** Use your completed timeline to answer the Focus Question: How did ideas of the Enlightenment lead to the independence and founding of the United States of America?

Comprehension and Critical Thinking

3. **Make Generalizations** Describe society and politics in the 13 English colonies during the mid-1700s.
4. **Express Problems Clearly** Explain why conflict between the colonists and Britain increased after 1763.
5. **Identify Point of View** What reasons might a Loyalist have for opposing the American Revolution?
6. **Determine Relevance** Give two examples of why the Bill of Rights is important to you.

● **Writing About History**

Quick Write: Providing Elaboration To prove that you fully understand a subject, you need to include specific details. You should use facts, dates, names, examples, explanations, or quotes to support your answer. Write a paragraph to describe the events that led to the American Revolution. Then read through your response and add specific details where you can.

Section 3 Assessment

1. Sentences should reflect an understanding of each term, person, or place listed at the beginning of the section.
2. Ideas about freedom and representative government inspired leaders in the colonies to revolt and establish an independent republic.
3. The colonies were prosperous and home to diverse groups. There was a good deal of free discussion about politics and a sense of having a separate identity from Britain.
4. The colonists resented the new taxes that Britain imposed to help pay for the Seven Years' War. They opposed taxes without representation in Parliament.
5. The colonies belonged to Britain and therefore, the colonists owed allegiance to it. Britain also supported and protected the colonies.
6. Answers should show an understanding of the Bill of Rights.

● **Writing About History**
Responses should show a well-supported paragraph that uses specific details.

For additional assessment, have students access **Progress Monitoring Online** at **Web Code nba-1731.**

Assess and Reteach

Assess Progress L3

■ Have students complete the Section Assessment.
■ Administer the Section Quiz.
  All in One Teaching Resources, Unit 2, p. 5
■ To further assess student understanding, use
  📖 **Progress Monitoring Transparencies,** 74

Reteach

If students need more instruction, have them read the section summary.

 Reading and Note Taking Study Guide, p. 79 L3

 Adapted Reading and Note Taking Study Guide, p. 79 L1 L2

Spanish Reading and Note Taking Study Guide, p. 79 L2

Extend L4

See this chapter's Professional Development pages for the Extend Online activity on the Declaration of Independence.

Answers

Chart Skills It explicitly reserves all unenumerated powers to the people and the states, thereby limiting the power of the federal government.

✓ Students should cite separation of powers, checks and balances, individual freedom, and government by the people.

Spreading the Word of Revolution

Objectives

- Explain the ways newspapers spread the ideas behind the American Revolution.

- Analyze items that appeared in colonial newspapers.

- Understand the impact of the American Revolution on other parts of the world.

Build Background Knowledge **L3**

Ask students to brainstorm ways that the American colonists shared their growing anger toward the British. *(word of mouth, letters, newspapers, pamphlets)* Point out that newspapers became part of this propaganda machine, printing controversial political cartoons and essays.

Instruct **L3**

- Direct students to the newspaper engraving on the bottom of this page. Ask volunteers to describe how Paul Revere exaggerated the Boston Massacre to incite anger. Then have them look at the *Maryland Gazette* and its depiction of the Stamp Act. How would the skull and bones drawing incite anger? Then have students summarize the ways that newspapers spread the ideas of resistance and revolt.

- Direct students to the map at the top of the right hand page. Ask **What is the purpose of this map?** *(to show where revolutions took place around the globe)* **Which of the colonies revolted first?** *(the American colonies)* Display **Color Transparency 105: Revolutions Since 1776** and have students identify where subsequent revolutions took place. Then ask **Why was the American Revolution an important turning point in world history?** *(Its success and ideals inspired revolts around the globe.)*

  📽 **Color Transparencies, 105**

SPREADING THE WORD OF REVOLUTION

While Enlightenment thinkers had a profound impact on the leaders of the American Revolution, newspapers made a great impact on the colonists. Colonists depended on newspapers for information about the war and the economy. News about the war was the first great news event to report in America. Would the colonists be free? Or would English control continue? As demand increased, newspapers began publishing several times a week instead of weekly. The number of newspapers increased from 29 to 48 from 1770 to 1775. During this time, the American newspaper changed from a weak form of communication to a propaganda machine that included controversial political cartoons and essays.

Trouble for newspapers came in 1765 when the British government passed the Stamp Act. Newspapers were forced to pay the tax imposed by the Stamp Act or face heavy penalties. Colonists already felt they had no representation so they became even more discontented. Many newspapers strongly opposed the Stamp Act and showed their resentment in their pages with cartoons, editorial content, and typographical devices. The *Maryland Gazette*, for example, set a skull and crossbones on its front page where the tax stamp belonged (facing page). Others ceased publication. The strength of the press was evident when the British government was forced to repeal the Stamp Act. Newspapers had voiced protest effectively and would continue to be a powerful medium of communication for years to come.

◀ Engraving by Paul Revere of the 1770 Boston Massacre. Revere exaggerated the event to incite anger among the colonists against the British.

▼ Engraving of the Battle of Lexington, the first battle of the American Revolution. Demand for exciting news of the war led to the creation of more newspapers.

◀ The *Maryland Gazette*, October 10, 1765

1789 French Revolution begins.

1775 American Revolution begins.

1821 Mexico gains independence from Spain.

1791 Haitian revolt against France begins.

1821 Peru declares independence from Spain.

1819 Colombia achieves independence from Spain.

1825 Bolivia achieves independence from Spain.

1822 Brazil proclaims independence from Portugal.

1811 Paraguay proclaims independence from Spain.

1818 Chile declares independence from Spain.

EUROPE

NORTH AMERICA

AFRICA

SOUTH AMERICA

The first political cartoon (left) in an American newspaper was created by Benjamin Franklin and appeared in 1754. The Sons of Liberty, an organization that loudly opposed the Stamp Act, used newspapers (above) to increase colonial participation.

An Era of Revolutions

As word of revolution spread throughout the colonies, the news also spread throughout the world. The American Revolution had a great impact on other parts of the world because it established the first government with all powers based on the consent of its people. Americans' attainment of freedom inspired revolts in France, in Hispaniola (present-day Haiti), and throughout Latin America as shown on this map.

History *Interactive*
For: Interactive map, audio, and more
Visit: PHSchool.com
Web Code: nbp-1733

Thinking Critically
1. **Recognize Propaganda** Explain how the front page of the *Maryland Gazette* was used as a propaganda tool.
2. **Make Comparisons** How does the newspaper affect people's perceptions today?

Independent Practice

History *Interactive* To enrich and extend the lesson, have students access this unit's History Interactive map, audio, and slide show at **Web Code nbp-1733.**

Monitor Progress

Ask **How did the ideas of liberty spread throughout the American colonies and the world?** *(Sample: Newspapers helped to spread the ideas throughout the colonies, and then word of the American Revolution spread throughout the world.)*

History Background

Spreading the Word After the Declaration of Independence was adopted on July 4, 1776, the Continental Congress had to get the word out. They brought the approved version to John Dunlap, the official printer to Congress, who printed the first copies. These copies, in turn, were dispatched to the various assemblies and conventions, and to the officers of the Continental Army. George Washington ordered that it be read to his troops. Newspapers spread the message to the rest of the colonies. Within the first week, five broadsheets in Philadelphia alone had reprinted the Declaration.

Thinking Critically
1. It uses dramatic and inflammatory language such as "expiring" and "hopes of a resurrection to life again" and large lettering in the headline; it includes a skull and crossbones in the lower right corner.
2. Newspapers today influence public opinion with many of the same tools—images, cartoons, and articles.

Quick Study Guide

- Have students use the Quick Study Guide to prepare for this chapter's tests. Students may wish to refer to the following pages as they review:

Enlightenment Thinkers
Section 1, pp. 183–186

Enlightenment Ideas Influence Democracy
Section 1, pp. 183–185; Section 3, pp. 200–201

American Declaration of Independence: Main Ideas
Section 3, p. 198

The U.S. Bill of Rights
Section 3, p. 201

Key Events from 1700–1789
Section 1 pp. 184–186; Section 2, pp. 188–192; Section 3, pp. 197–198, 200

- For additional review, remind students to refer to the **L3**

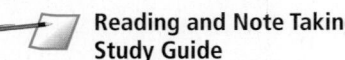 **Reading and Note Taking Study Guide**
Note Taking Study Guide, pp. 74, 76, 78
Section Summaries, pp. 75, 77, 79

- Have students access **Web Code nbp-1701** for this chapter's *History Interactive* timeline, which includes expanded entries and additional events.

- If students need more instruction on analyzing timelines, have them read the **Skills Handbook,** p. SH30.

- When students have completed their study of the chapter, distribute Chapter Tests A and B.

All in One Teaching Resources, Unit 2, pp. 15–20

For **Progress Monitoring Online,** refer students to the Self-test with vocabulary practice at **Web Code nba-1741.**

Quick Study Guide

Progress Monitoring Online
For: Self-test with vocabulary practice
Web Code: nba-1741

■ Enlightenment Thinkers

- **Thomas Hobbes:** social contract in which people give power to the government for an organized society
- **John Locke:** natural rights—life, liberty, and property
- **Baron de Montesquieu:** separation of powers; checks and balances
- **Voltaire:** battled corruption, injustice, and inequality; defended freedom of speech
- **Denis Diderot:** *Encyclopedia*
- **Jean-Jacques Rousseau:** social contract in which people follow the "general will" for true liberty
- **Adam Smith:** free market; laissez faire

■ Enlightenment Ideas Influence Democracy

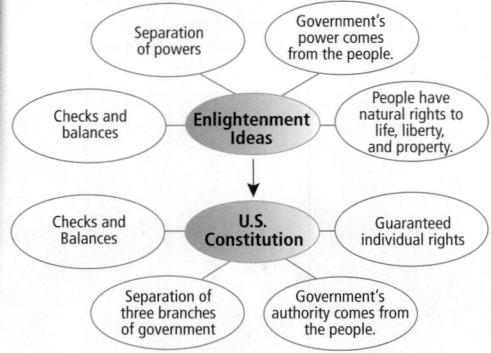

Separation of powers

Government's power comes from the people.

Checks and balances

Enlightenment Ideas

People have natural rights to life, liberty, and property.

Checks and Balances

U.S. Constitution

Guaranteed individual rights

Separation of three branches of government

Government's authority comes from the people.

■ American Declaration of Independence: Main Ideas

Declaration of Independence: Main Ideas
• All men are created equal and have natural rights to life, liberty, and the pursuit of happiness.
• It is the government's obligation to protect these rights.
• If a government fails to protect these rights, the people can revolt and set up a new government.

■ The U.S. Bill of Rights

The U.S. Bill of Rights
1st: Guarantees freedom of religion, speech, press, assembly, and petition
2nd: Right to bear arms
3rd: Prohibits quartering of troops in private homes
4th: Protects from unreasonable searches and seizures
5th: No punishment without due process of law
6th: Right to a speedy and public trial in the state where the offense was committed
7th: Right to jury trial for civil cases if over $20
8th: Prohibits excessive bail and cruel and unusual punishments
9th: Civil rights are not restricted to those specified by these amendments.
10th: Powers not granted to the national government belong to the states and to the people.

■ Key Events From 1700–1789

1700s France sees flowering of Enlightenment thought.

1721 Johann Sebastian Bach publishes his Brandenburg Concertos.

1740 Frederick II begins his reign in Prussia.

Chapter Events
Global Events

1720   1730   1740

1735 China's Emperor Qianlong begins his long reign.

Differentiated Instruction   Solutions for All Learners

L1 Special Needs   **L2 Less Proficient Readers**   **L2 English Language Learners**

For students acquiring basic skills:

Adapted Reading and Note Taking Study Guide
Adapted Note Taking Study Guides, pp. 74, 76, 78
Adapted Section Summaries, pp. 75, 77, 79

For Spanish-speaking students:

Spanish Reading and Note Taking Study Guide
Spanish Note Taking Study Guides, pp. 74, 76, 78
Spanish Section Summaries, pp. 75, 77, 79

Concept Connector

Essential Question Review

To connect prior knowledge with what you have learned in this chapter, answer the questions below in your Concept Connector journal. Use the journal in the Reading and Note Taking Study Guide to record your answers (or go to www.phschool.com Web Code: nbd-1707). In addition, record information about the following concepts:

- Cultural Diffusion: Roots of American Democracy
- Political Systems: federal government
- Democracy: The American Declaration of Independence
- Impact of the Individual: John Locke

1. **Cooperation** During the American Revolution economic and military aid from France helped the American colonists defeat the British. Suggest at least one reason why France would have helped the American colonists. What role did Benjamin Franklin play in the alliance forged between the two nations? What French military tactic made the colonists' defeat of the British army possible?

2. **Conflict** Inspired by the American Revolution, colonists in Central and South America rose up and fought for freedom from their colonial rulers. In addition, many revolutionary leaders in Central and South America were influenced by the ideas of the Enlightenment. Review the concept web "Enlightenment Ideas Influence Democracy" in the Quick Study Guide in this chapter. Which Enlightenment ideas would be most likely to cause conflict between colonists and their rulers? Why?

3. **Impact of the Individual** Many individuals contributed to the success of the American Revolution. Review Section 4 in this chapter and choose one individual who you believe made the most significant impact. Describe this individual's contribution and explain its importance to winning the American Revolution.

■ Connections to Today

1. **Democracy: Still Strong Today** As you have read, the Framers of the United States Constitution were inspired by Montesquieu, Rousseau, and Locke. Democratic revolutions around the world were inspired by the same Enlightenment ideas that had inspired American colonists. Even today, nations seeking a model for democratic government often turn to the Constitution of the United States. Research and write a newspaper article about one of these nations.

2. **Culture: Modern Salons** Salons provided a way for people to gather and share ideas, especially during the Enlightenment. Today, we know that many people do this without ever meeting in person—through the Internet. People are able to join chat rooms and newsgroups to share their thoughts. Many discussions on the Internet lack the serious-minded tone of a salon conversation and the benefit of face-to-face conversation. The Internet does, however, provide a sense of community, where people can gather to discuss ideas, even if it is a "virtual" living room. Compare salons of the Enlightenment and Internet chat rooms. Explain which you think is the better forum for sharing ideas, and why.

1751 Diderot publishes *Encyclopedia*.	1759 Voltaire publishes *Candide*.	1762 Rousseau publishes *The Social Contract*.	1776 American leaders sign the Declaration of Independence.

History *Interactive*
For: Interactive timeline
Web Code: nbp-1701

1750   1760   1770   1780

1754 French and Indian War begins.	1763 Treaty of Paris gives Britain control of Canada.	1789 The French Revolution begins.

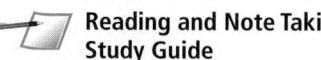

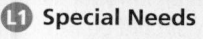
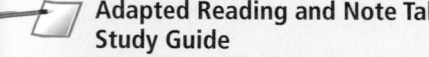
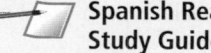
Concept Connector ❓

Chapter Assessment

Terms, People, and Places
1. federal republic
2. Montesquieu
3. rococo
4. Joseph II
5. Yorktown, Virginia
6. John Locke, natural rights

Main Ideas
7. A government has an obligation to its people, and the people have the right to overthrow that government if it fails its obligations.

8. Laissez faire is a policy that allows businesses to operate with little or no government interference.

9. Some monarchs accepted Enlightenment ideas and were thus called enlightened despots, or absolute rulers who used their power to bring about reform.

10. Britain sought to tax the colonies to pay for their defense, while colonists thought Britain had no right to tax them without representation.

11. The Bill of Rights recognized the natural rights stated by Locke and the duty the government had to protect them.

Chapter Focus Question
12. By introducing new ideas on liberty and government, Enlightenment thinkers inspired revolutionaries to question what existed and strive for a better, more just, society and system of government.

Critical Thinking
13. Responses should reflect *philosophes'* beliefs in the right of all people to life, liberty, and the pursuit of happiness.

14. Answers may include: Other areas in the world will most likely follow suit because people will desire freedom and equality when they see it is possible to attain them. Also, lower classes and colonies of large nations are oppressed around the world, so they are likely to seek freedom as well.

15. rococo: elegant and delicate

16. Answers should express the differences in power: the colonies were weak and unorganized, while Britain was strong and organized.

17. ideas connected with the Enlightenment, Magna Carta, English Bill of Rights, and the Glorious Revolution

Chapter Assessment

Terms, People, and Places

Complete each sentence by choosing the correct answer from the list of terms below. You will not use all of the terms.

natural rights	Montesquieu
John Locke	federal republic
laissez faire	Yorktown, Virginia
rococo	Frederick the Great
baroque	Treaty of Paris
Joseph II	Rousseau

1. In a _____, power is divided between the federal government and the states.
2. _____ advanced the idea of separation of powers.
3. The _____ style influenced by the Enlightenment was personal, elegant, and charming.
4. The enlightened despot who ended censorship was _____.
5. The American Revolution ended when George Washington forced the surrender of the British at _____.
6. _____ believed in _____, which are the rights to life, liberty, and property.

Main Ideas

Section 1 (pp. 182–186)
7. What idea did John Locke advocate for the role of a government?
8. Explain the economic policy of laissez faire.

Section 2 (pp. 188–193)
9. How did the Enlightenment affect some rulers in Europe, and what are these rulers known as?

Section 3 (pp. 195–201)
10. How did taxation create tensions between the American colonies and the British government?

● Writing About History

In this chapter's three Section Assessments, you developed skills for writing for assesssment.

Writing for Assessment Select either a philosopher from the Enlightenment or an important figure from the American Revolution. Explain how his or her actions, beliefs, and/or works contributed to improving society.

Prewriting
- Consider what you know about the people in this chapter and choose one who interests you.
- Develop a focus or main idea. Write a single sentence identifying the main idea you will develop.
- As you prepare to write your essay, make sure you understand the instructions. Circle verbs, nouns, or important phrases in the question.

Drafting
- Develop a thesis statement that identifies the focus of your essay.
- Make an outline for your essay and fill in facts and examples.
- Write an introduction to explain your thesis, a body to provide evidence for your thesis, and a conclusion.

Revising
- Even though time is limited on essay tests, you should still leave time to check your writing for accuracy and clarity.
- Use the guidelines for revising your essay on page SH22 of the Writing Handbook.

11. How does the Bill of Rights reflect a key Enlightenment idea?

Chapter Focus Question
12. How did Enlightenment thinkers inspire revolutionaries to push for radical changes in government and society?

Critical Thinking

13. **Synthesize Information** Choose one *philosophe* from this chapter and describe how he or she might respond to a human rights issue that has been in the news recently.
14. **Predict Consequences** Given the impact the Enlightenment thinkers had on the American Revolution, what can you predict will happen in other areas of the world? Explain why you predicted what you did.
15. **Analyzing Visuals** Identify the style of this painting and describe its characteristics.

16. **Make Comparisons** Compare Britain and its North American colonies in the mid-1700s.
17. **Analyze Information** What ideas about government do you think English settlers brought with them to the Americas?

● Writing About History

As students begin the assignment, refer them to p. SH20 of the **Writing Handbook** for help in writing for assessment. Remind them of the steps they should take to complete their assignment, including prewriting, drafting, and revising. For help in revising, remind them to use the guidelines on p. SH22 of the **Writing Handbook.**

Students' essays should have a clear thesis with supporting details and contain an introduction, a body, and a conclusion. They should be free of grammatical and spelling errors. For scoring rubrics, see **Assessment Rubrics**, p. 8.

Document-Based Assessment

Enlightenment Thought

Enlightenment thinkers believed in the possibility of social, political, and economic change. Often critical of society during this time, they were driven by the power of human reason and progress.

Document A

"Common sense is not so common."

—From ***Philosophical Dictionary*** by Voltaire

Document B

"A prince ought not to deem it beneath his dignity to state that he considers it his duty not to dictate anything to his subjects in religious matters, but to leave them complete freedom."

—From ***What Is Enlightenment?*** by Immanuel Kant

Document C

"A strange consequence that necessarily follows from the use of torture is that the innocent person is placed in a condition worse than that of the guilty, for if both are tortured, the circumstances are all against the former. Either he confesses the crime and is condemned, or he is declared innocent and has suffered a punishment he did not deserve."

—From ***On Crimes and Punishments*** by Marchese di Beccaria

Document D

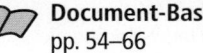

Diderot and Catherine the Great

Document E

Selected Enlightenment Thinkers			
Thinker	**Lifespan**	**Nationality**	**Key Work**
Jean DiAlembert	1717–1783	French	*Encyclopedia*
Jeremy Bentham	1748–1832	English	*The Principles of Morals and Legislation*
Cesare Beccaria	1738–1794	Italian	*Crimes and Punishment*
Denis Diderot	1713–1784	French	*Encyclopedia*
David Hume	1711–1776	Scottish	*Treatise of Human Nature*
Immanuel Kant	1724–1804	E. Prussian	*Critique of Pure Reason*
John Locke	1632–1704	English	*Essay Concerning Human Understanding*
Charles Montesquieu	1689–1755	French	*The Spirit of the Laws*
Jean-Jacques Rousseau	1712–1778	French	*The Social Contract*
Adam Smith	1723–1790	English	*The Wealth of Nations*
Voltaire	1694–1778	French	*Philosophical Dictionary*

Analyzing Documents

Use your knowledge of the Enlightenment and Documents A, B, C, D, and E to answer the questions below.

1. Kant believes in _____ based on Document B.
   - A freedom of religion
   - B freedom of speech
   - C the government making a religious choice for its people
   - D dignity

2. In Document C, the author condemned
   - A capital punishment.
   - B religion of any kind.
   - C torture.
   - D the Inquisition.

3. Catherine the Great and Diderot pictured in Document D are most likely
   - A sharing war stories.
   - B sharing Enlightenment ideas.
   - C planning the American Revolution.
   - D discussing population growth in France.

4. **Writing Task** Which of the above documents do you think best exemplifies the spirit of the Enlightenment? Why? Use your knowledge of the Enlightenment and specific information from the documents to support your opinion.

The French Revolution and Napoleon

Section	Core Instruction L3	Differentiated Instruction L1 L2 L4

Section 1
On the Eve of Revolution

⏱ **2.5 periods, 1.25 blocks**

OBJECTIVES
- Describe the social divisions of France's old order.
- List reasons for France's economic troubles in 1789.
- Explain why Louis XVI called the Estates-General and summarize what resulted.
- Understand why Parisians stormed the Bastille.

Focus Question *What led to the storming of the Bastille, and therefore, to the start of the French Revolution?*

All in One Teaching Resources, Unit 2
Reading Strategy: Recognize Sequence, p. 26
Vocabulary Builder: Use Context Clues to Determine Meaning, p. 25
Section 1 Quiz, p. 21

Reading and Note Taking Study Guide
Note Taking Study Guide, p. 80
Section 1 Summary, p. 81

Note Taking Transparencies, 136

WITNESS HISTORY Audio CD
Inciting Revolution

Progress Monitoring Transparencies, 75

Color Transparencies, 110

Teaching Resources, Skills Handbook
Prereading the Chapter, pp. 1–2
Word Knowledge Rating Form, p. 3
K-W-L Chart, p. 4

L1 Adapted Reading and Note Taking Study Guide
Note Taking Study Guide, p. 80 **SN**
Section 1 Summary, p. 81 **SN**

L2 Adapted Reading and Note Taking Study Guide
Note Taking Study Guide, p. 80 **LPR**
Section 1 Summary, p. 81 **LPR**

Spanish Reading and Note Taking Study Guide
Note Taking Study Guide, p. 80 **ELL**
Section 1 Summary, p. 81 **ELL**

L4 All in One Teaching Resources, Unit 2
Link to Literature: From *A Tale of Two Cities*, by Charles Dickens, p. 29 **AR, GT**

***Student Edition Audio** **SN**

Differentiated Instruction Activity,
Teacher's Edition, pp. 211, 214 **SN**

***Guided Reading Audio, Spanish** **ELL**
***Student Edition Audio** **LPR**

Differentiated Instruction Activity,
Teacher's Edition, pp. 211, 214 **LPR, ELL**

Extend Activity, Teacher's Edition, p. 215 **AR, GT**

Section 2
The French Revolution Unfolds

⏱ **2 periods, 1 block**

OBJECTIVES
- Explain how the political crisis of 1789 led to popular revolts.
- Summarize the moderate reforms enacted by the National Assembly in August 1789.
- Identify additional actions taken by the National Assembly as it pressed onward.
- Analyze why there was a mixed reaction around Europe to the events unfolding in France.

Focus Question *What political and social reforms did the National Assembly institute in the first stage of the French Revolution?*

All in One Teaching Resources, Unit 2
Section 2 Quiz, p. 22

Reading and Note Taking Study Guide
Note Taking Study Guide, pp. 82–83
Section 2 Summary, p. 84

Note Taking Transparencies, 137

WITNESS HISTORY Audio CD
Parisian Women Storm Versailles

Progress Monitoring Transparencies, 76

Color Transparencies, 107, 109

L1 Adapted Reading and Note Taking Study Guide
Note Taking Study Guide, pp. 82–83 **SN**
Section 2 Summary, p. 84 **SN**

L2 Adapted Reading and Note Taking Study Guide
Note Taking Study Guide, pp. 82–83 **LPR**
Section 2 Summary, p. 84 **LPR**

L4 All in One Teaching Resources, Unit 2
Biography: Olympe de Gouges, p. 30 **AR, GT**
Viewpoints: Two Views of the French Revolution, p. 31 **AR, GT**

Differentiated Instruction Activity,
Teacher's Edition, p. 217 **SN**

Spanish Reading and Note Taking Study Guide
Note Taking Study Guide, pp. 82–83 **ELL**
Section 2 Summary, p. 84 **ELL**

Differentiated Instruction Activity,
Teacher's Edition, p. 217 **LPR**

Differentiated Instruction Activity,
Teacher's Edition, p. 218 **AR, GT**

Extend Activity, Teacher's Edition, p. 221 **AR, GT**

*Audio support is available for all sections.

Section	Core Instruction ⓛ③	Differentiated Instruction ⓛ①ⓛ②ⓛ④	
Section 3 *Radical Days of the Revolution* **1.5 periods, .75 block** **OBJECTIVES** ■ Understand how and why radicals abolished the monarchy. ■ Explain why the Committee of Public Safety was created and why the Reign of Terror resulted. ■ Summarize how the excesses of the Convention led to the formation of the Directory. ■ Analyze how the French people were affected by the changes brought about by the revolution. **Focus Question** *What events occurred during the radical phase of the French Revolution?*	**All in One Teaching Resources, Unit 2** Section 3 Quiz, p. 23 **Reading and Note Taking Study Guide** Note Taking Study Guide, p. 85 Section 3 Summary, p. 86 **Note Taking Transparencies,** 138 **WITNESS HISTORY Audio CD** The Engine of Terror **Progress Monitoring Transparencies,** 77	**ⓛ① Adapted Reading and Note Taking Study Guide** Note Taking Study Guide, p. 85 SN Section 3 Summary, p. 86 SN **ⓛ② Adapted Reading and Note Taking Study Guide** Note Taking Study Guide, p. 85 LPR Section 3 Summary, p. 86 LPR **ⓛ④ All in One Teaching Resources, Unit 2** Primary Source: The Royal Family in Prison, p. 27 AR, GT Simulation: Trial in France, pp. 79–82 AR, GT	**Differentiated Instruction Activity,** Teacher's Edition, p. 224 SN **Spanish Reading and Note Taking Study Guide** Note Taking Study Guide, p. 85 ELL Section 3 Summary, p. 86 ELL **Differentiated Instruction Activity,** Teacher's Edition, pp. 224, 225 LPR, ELL **Extend Activity,** Teacher's Edition, pp. 208c, 228 AR, GT
Section 4 *The Age of Napoleon* **3 periods, 1.5 blocks** **OBJECTIVES** ■ Understand Napoleon's rise to power and why the French strongly supported him. ■ Explain how Napoleon built an empire and what challenges the empire faced. ■ Analyze the events that led to Napoleon's downfall. ■ Outline how the Congress of Vienna tried to create a lasting peace. **Focus Question** *Explain Napoleon's rise to power in Europe, his subsequent defeat, and how the outcome still affects Europe today.*	**All in One Teaching Resources, Unit 2** Outline Maps, pp. 32–33 Geography Quiz, p. 34 Section 4 Quiz, p. 24 **Reading and Note Taking Study Guide** Note Taking Study Guide, p. 87 Section 4 Summary, p. 88 Concept Connector, pp. 242, 250, 284, 291 **Note Taking Transparencies,** 139 **WITNESS HISTORY Audio CD** Enter Napoleon Bonaparte **Progress Monitoring Transparencies,** 78 **Color Transparencies,** 108, 111, 112 **Witness History Discovery School™** video program, *Napoleon's Lost Army*	**ⓛ① Adapted Reading and Note Taking Study Guide** Note Taking Study Guide, p. 87 SN Section 4 Summary, p. 88 SN Concept Connector, pp. 242, 250, 284, 291 SN **ⓛ② Adapted Reading and Note Taking Study Guide** Note Taking Study Guide, p. 87 LPR Section 4 Summary, p. 88 LPR Concept Connector, pp. 242, 250, 284, 291 LPR **ⓛ④ All in One Teaching Resources, Unit 2** Viewpoints: Two Views of Napoleon, p. 28 AR, GT	**Differentiated Instruction Activity,** Teacher's Edition, pp. 231, 233 SN **Spanish Reading and Note Taking Study Guide** Note Taking Study Guide, p. 87 ELL Section 4 Summary, p. 88 ELL Concept Connector, pp. 242, 250, 284, 291 ELL **Differentiated Instruction Activity,** Teacher's Edition, pp. 231, 233 LPR, ELL **Differentiated Instruction Activity,** Teacher's Edition, p. 237 AR, GT **Extend Activity,** Teacher's Edition, p. 238 AR, GT

Assessment Resources

- **Progress Monitoring Transparencies,** 75–78
- **SuccessTracker™,** Chapter 6
- **Document-Based Assessment,** pp. 54–66
- *ExamView*® **Test Bank CD-ROM,** Chapter 6
- **All in One Teaching Resources, Unit 2,** Chapter Tests A and B, pp. 35–40
- **Progress Monitoring *Online* Quizzes,** Chapter 6
- **Assessment Rubrics**

Differentiated Instruction Key

ⓛ①	Special Needs	LPR	Less Proficient Readers
ⓛ②	Basic to Average	AR	Advanced Readers
ⓛ③	All Students	SN	Special Needs Students
ⓛ④	Average to Advanced	GT	Gifted and Talented
		ELL	English Language Learner

Author's Notes

Napoleon Conquers Europe—and Meets His Waterloo

When General Napoleon returned from the Battle of the Pyramids, a cabal of Directory politicians tried to use him as a front for their own power.

But Napoleon Bonaparte (1769–1821) had a vision of his own destiny. A coup in 1799 made Napoleon "first consul" of France. His armies and a seemingly unending string of victories over the great powers of Europe did the rest. . . .

For a decade and a half, Napoleon Bonaparte ruled a larger European empire than anyone since ancient Rome. He crowned himself emperor of the French in 1804. By 1810 he, his family, and his generals ruled directly or indirectly over a collection of states that stretched from Spain to the frontiers of Russia, from the English Channel to the toe of Italy. Wherever his armies went, furthermore, Napoleon spread the ideals of the French Revolution. At home he was France's enlightened despot at last, streamlining institutions and modernizing laws with military efficiency.

It looked almost as if Europe might find the unity it had enjoyed in Roman times, under a child of the French Revolution.

But Europe's old regime fought back tenaciously against the "Corsican upstart." Britain, safe on its islands, would not make terms. Napoleon's invasion of Russia in 1812 was a fiasco—his first major setback. He had beaten three coalitions of great powers, but in 1813 a fourth defeated him at Leipzig, in the epochal Battle of the Nations. Temporarily exiled from Europe in 1814, Napoleon returned the following year for the miraculous Hundred Days that ended in 1815 with his final defeat at Waterloo.

It was the end of a great adventure—and the beginning of something even greater. For the revolution and its general had seeded Europe with radical ideas, images, and memories that would bear startling fruit for much of the coming century.

—Anthony Esler, *The Human Venture: From Prehistory to the Present*, (Upper Saddle River, New Jersey: Pearson Education, 2004), pp. 486–487

Extend Online

Songs of the Revolution

Have students listen to and analyze the music of the French Revolution. Use the steps below to help students complete the activity.

Prepare for the Activity Explain that when France declared war on Austria in 1792, a local politician remarked that the French soldiers lacked a good marching song. An army officer, Claude-Joseph Rouget de Lisle, heard this and quickly composed an anthem. "La Marseillaise," as it came to be known, grew increasingly popular throughout all of France and was sung at many public events. The Convention proclaimed it the French national anthem in 1795. When Napoleon came to power, he banned the song, due to its associations with the revolution. Later, it was reinstated as the country's national anthem.

Conduct the Activity For help in starting the activity, send students to **Web Code nba-1801.** Students will listen to music from the French Revolution, read the descriptions of the event for which the music was written, and read the accompanying lyrics, which have been translated from French to English. Have them note the tone of each piece, as well as its purpose.

Follow-Up Conduct a class discussion based on the following questions: What role did music play throughout the French Revolution? How did music reflect the changes that occurred in France during this time? Why do you think the French adopted "La Marseillaise" as their national anthem?

Differentiated Instruction   Solutions for All Learners

Deciphering Idioms ⓛ ⓛ

Some vocabulary and idiomatic expressions are potentially problematic for English Language Learners and Less Proficient Readers. The meanings of statements such as "reign of terror" and "power in the hands of the people" are not obvious to all students. To help students understand the meaning of these phrases, model these steps, using the phrase "Power in the hands of the people."

1. Use context clues and visuals to help decipher meaning. For example, the painting that opens this chapter shows the people taking power into their own hands.

2. Cite specific examples that illustrate the phrase, such as the French Revolution that students are about to study.

3. Discuss the appeal of the phrase. Would "power in the minds of the people" be just as vivid? Why or why not?

4. Ask students to find three examples of the phrase "power in the hands of the people" in the text.

Peer Editing ⓛ

Writing is a key component of any social studies class. While many English Language Learners should not have great difficulty in developing an argument or finding factual information to back it up, they often struggle with the mechanics of writing. Peer editing can be a valuable tool, as it allows students to see various samples of writing so they may internalize what is appropriate in an essay. As they read each other's essays, ask students to consider the following:

■ Is a thesis statement evident in the first paragraph?

■ Is appropriate and accurate historical information used to substantiate the thesis statement?

■ Does the essay end with a well-thought out conclusion that revisits the main argument?

Provide students with a rubric to use while critiquing their classmates' essays. Encourage students to be both constructive and specific in their feedback. Remind them to also edit for grammar and spelling.

Modeling Reading and Writing Skills

Gather Details   Tell students that in this chapter they will be writing a cause-and-effect essay (See Writing About History, p. 242.) Before they begin writing, they should make a list of the causes and effects of a selected event to help them organize the information. One way to gather details for each cause and each effect is to create either a concept web that shows the relationship between the facts or by showing a flowchart. Remind them to make sure that all the details support either a cause or an effect. To avoid including unnecessary details, cross out circles that do not back up the relationship.

Model this skill by writing *blizzard* on the board in the center of a web. From the cause, add these radiating circles as effects: bad driving conditions, power failure, school closures. Ask students to continue adding information to the web to gather more details. Then cross out details that are unnecessary to illustrate the cause-and-effect relationship.

Predict   Explain to students that making predictions can help them focus their reading and remember key content. Tell them that a prediction is an idea about what will come next. It can be based on information such as headings and visuals.

To demonstrate this skill, begin by reading aloud the headings and describing the visuals from Section 1. Point out that the images show conflict and the headings show mounting problems in France. Tell students that you predict the chapter will recount a looming crisis in France.

Teach With Technology

PresentationEXPRESS™
Premium DVD

- Teach this chapter's core content using **PresentationExpress™ Premium,** which includes dynamic lecture notes, interactive game shows, songs, videos, and the *ExamView® QuickTake* assessment tool.

- To introduce this chapter using **PresentationExpress™ Premium,** start by asking students **Which of the following statements do you most agree with? (A) People should never take part in political revolution. (B) People should take part in political revolution only if their family is in danger. (C) People should take part in political revolution only if their basic human rights are not met. (D) People should take part in political revolution whenever they disagree with their government.** Take a class poll or record students' answers using the QuickTake feature and discuss their responses. Point out that in this chapter, they will read about a historic revolution in France destined to inspire others around the world. Continue introducing the chapter using the chapter opener slide show and Witness History audio.

Technology Resources

- Student**EXPRESS** CD-ROM, Chapter 6
- Teacher**EXPRESS** CD-ROM, Chapter 6
- Presentation**EXPRESS™** Premium DVD, Chapter 6
- **WITNESS HISTORY** Audio CD, Chapter 6
- *ExamView* **Test Bank CD-ROM,** English and Spanish, Chapter 6
- **Guided Reading Audio,** Spanish, Chapter 6
- **Student Edition Audio,** Chapter 6
- **Witness History Discovery School™** video program, *Napoleon's Lost Army*
- **Experience It! Multimedia Pack**

The French Revolution and Napoleon
1789–1815

Bibliography

For the Teacher

Broers, Michael. *Europe Under Napoleon 1799–1815.* Arnold, 1996.

Doyle, William. *Origins of the French Revolution*, 3rd ed. Oxford University Press, 1999.

Godineau, Dominique. *The Women of Paris and Their French Revolution.* trans. K. Streip. University of California Press, 1998.

For the Student

- L2 Plain, Nancy. *Louis XVI, Marie-Antoinette and the French Revolution.* Marshall Cavendish, 2001.
- L3 Shuter, Jane, ed. *Helen Williams and the French Revolution.* Raintree Steck-Vaughn, 1996.
- L4 Walter, Jakob. *The Diary of a Napoleonic Foot Soldier,* ed. Marc Raeff. Penguin Group, 1993.

WITNESS HISTORY AUDIO

The Loss of Blood Begins

On July 14, 1789, after a daylong hunting expedition, King Louis XVI returned to his palace in Versailles. Hours earlier, armed Parisians had attacked the Bastille. They had cut the chains of the prison drawbridge, crushing a member of the crowd, and poured into the courtyard. Chaos ensued as shots rang out, blood was spattered, and heads were paraded down the streets on spikes. When Louis heard the news, he exclaimed, "Then it's a revolt?" "No, sire," replied the duke bearing the news, "it's a revolution!" The French Revolution had begun. Listen to the Witness History audio to hear more about the fall of the Bastille.

Plate declaring "Live Free or Die"

◀ *The Conquerors of the Bastille before the Hotel de Ville,* painted by Paul Delaroche.

Chapter Preview

Chapter Focus Question What were the causes and effects of the French Revolution, and how did the revolution lead to the Napoleonic era?

Drum from the French revolutionary period

Section 1
On the Eve of Revolution

Section 2
The French Revolution Unfolds

Section 3
Radical Days of the Revolution

Section 4
The Age of Napoleon

Bust of Napoleon Bonaparte

Use the ☑ **Quick Study Timeline** at the end of this chapter to preview chapter events.

Concept Connector ONLINE

To explore Essential Questions related to this chapter, go to PHSchool.com
Web Code: nbd-1807

Chapter-Level Resources

All in One Vocabulary Builder; Reading Strategy; Enrichments; Outline Maps; Geography Quiz; Chapter Tests
- Document-Based Assessments
- AYP Monitoring Assessments
- *ExamView* Test Bank CD-ROM
- Guided Reading Audio (Spanish)
- Student Edition Audio

Previewing the Chapter

- **WITNESS HISTORY** Read the Witness History selection aloud or play the accompanying audio. Ask **What is the difference between a "revolt" and a "revolution"?** *(revolt: uprising, rebellion; revolution: overthrow of government or social system)* Then ask students to think about the causes and effects of the American Revolution. Tell them they will learn about the causes and effects of the French Revolution in the chapter ahead.

  AUDIO **Witness History Audio CD,** The Loss of Blood Begins

- **Analyzing the Visuals** Tell students that the Bastille, a prison in Paris, was a symbol of royal power in the 1700s; it was used mainly for political prisoners. Anyone the king wished could be arrested on a secret warrant and kept there without trial. Ask students to study the painting. Point out that those who stormed the Bastille took what they found, including the keys to the prison, and paraded outside City Hall. Ask **What do you think provoked Parisians to storm the Bastille?** *(Sample: frustration with the way things were, unjust government, lack of representation)* **Why do you think they took practically everything they could carry?** *(Answers will vary.)*

- **Focus** Write the Chapter Focus Question on the board. Tell students to keep this question in mind as they read the chapter. *(Answer appears with Chapter Assessment answers.)* Have students preview the section titles for this chapter.

Note Taking Study Guide With Concept Connector Journal
For online access: Web code nbd-1807
For print alternative: Reading and Note Taking Study Guide booklet

---

Differentiated
Instruction **Solutions for All Learners**

The following Teacher's Edition strategies are suitable for students of varying abilities.

L1 Special Needs Students, pp. 211, 214, 217, 224, 231, 233 SN

L2 English Language Learners, pp. 214, 224, 225, 227, 231, 233 ELL

L2 Less Proficient Readers, pp. 211, 214, 217, 224, 231, 233 LPR

L4 Gifted and Talented Students, pp. 218, 237 GT

L4 Advanced Readers, pp. 218, 237 AR

Objectives

As you teach this section, keep students focused on the following objectives to help them answer the Section Focus Question and master core content.

- Describe the social divisions of France's old order.
- List reasons for France's economic troubles in 1789.
- Explain why Louis XVI called the Estates-General and summarize what resulted.
- Understand why Parisians stormed the Bastille.

Prepare to Read

Build Background Knowledge ⑬

Ask students to recall some of the ideas of the Enlightenment. Based on their previous reading, ask them to predict how these ideas might influence peasants and the middle class in countries with absolute monarchs, such as France.

Set a Purpose ⑬

- **WITNESS HISTORY** Read the selection aloud or play the audio.

  🔊 AUDIO **Witness History Audio CD,** Inciting Revolution

  Ask **According to Desmoulins, what elements do monarchies thrive on?** *(vices, concealments, and crimes)* **Why do you think the crowd would find this speech inspiring?** *(Sample: It appeals to a desire for an honest government.)*

- **Focus** Point out the Section Focus Question and write it on the board. Tell students to refer to this question as they read. *(Answer appears with Section 1 Assessment answers.)*

- **Preview** Have students preview the Section Objectives and the list of Terms, People, and Places.

- **Reading Skills** Have students use the *Reading Strategy: Recognize Sequence* worksheet.

  All in One Teaching Resources, Unit 2, p. 26

Camille Desmoulins and French Revolution banner

WITNESS HISTORY 🔊 AUDIO

Inciting Revolution

Camille Desmoulins was a French revolutionary leader and journalist who wrote pamphlets and journals to express his views on the revolution. He also spoke to Parisian crowds and his stirring speeches in 1789 were a cause of the storming of the Bastille prison on July 14, 1789. This excerpt is from one of his speeches, "Better to Die than not Live Free":

66 In a democracy, tho the people may be deceived, yet they at least love virtue. It is merit which they believe they put in power as substitutes for the rascals who are the very essence of monarchies. The vices, concealments, and crimes which are the diseases of republics are the very health and existence of monarchies. 99

Focus Question What led to the storming of the Bastille, and therefore, to the start of the French Revolution?

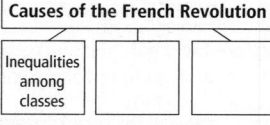

On the Eve of Revolution

Objectives

- Describe the social divisions of France's old order.
- List reasons for France's economic troubles in 1789.
- Explain why Louis XVI called the Estates-General and summarize what resulted.
- Understand why Parisians stormed the Bastille.

Terms, People, and Places

ancien régime	Jacques Necker
estate	Estates-General
bourgeoisie	cahier
deficit spending	Tennis Court Oath
Louis XVI	Bastille

Note Taking

Reading Skill: Recognize Multiple Causes Create a chart to identify causes of the French Revolution. Add as many boxes as you need.

```
          Causes of the French Revolution
           ┌──────────┬──────────┐
   Inequalities
   among
   classes
```

On April 28, 1789, unrest exploded at a Paris wallpaper factory. A rumor had spread that the factory owner was planning to cut wages even though bread prices were soaring. Enraged workers vandalized the owner's home.

Riots like these did not worry most nobles. They knew that France faced a severe economic crisis but thought financial reforms would ease the problem. The nobles were wrong. The crisis went deeper than government finances. Reform would not be enough. By July, the hungry, unemployed, and poorly paid people of Paris had taken up arms. Their actions would push events further and faster than anyone could have foreseen.

French Society Divided

In 1789, France, like the rest of Europe, still clung to an outdated social system that had emerged in the Middle Ages. Under this **ancien régime,** or old order, everyone in France was divided into one of three social classes, or **estates.** The First Estate was made up of the clergy; the Second Estate was made up of the nobility; and the Third Estate comprised the vast majority of the population.

The Clergy Enjoy Wealth During the Middle Ages, the Church had exerted great influence throughout Christian Europe. In 1789, the French clergy still enjoyed enormous wealth and privilege. The Church owned about 10 percent of the land, collected tithes, and paid no direct taxes to the state. High Church leaders such as bishops and abbots

Vocabulary Builder

Use the information below and the following resources to teach the high-use word from this section.

All in One Teaching Resources, Unit 2, p. 25; Teaching Resources, Skills Handbook, p. 3

High-Use Word	Definition and Sample Sentence
urban, p. 212	*adj.* of, relating to, or characteristic of a city Jack grew up in an **urban** environment where few people had a back yard.

were usually nobles who lived very well. Parish priests, however, often came from humble origins and might be as poor as their peasant congregations.

The First Estate did provide some social services. Nuns, monks, and priests ran schools, hospitals, and orphanages. But during the Enlightenment, *philosophes* targeted the Church for reform. They criticized the idleness of some clergy, the Church's interference in politics, and its intolerance of dissent. In response, many clergy condemned the Enlightenment for undermining religion and moral order.

Nobles Hold Top Government Jobs The Second Estate was the titled nobility of French society. In the Middle Ages, noble knights had defended the land. In the 1600s, Richelieu and Louis XIV crushed the nobles' military power but had given them other rights—under strict royal control. Those rights included top jobs in government, the army, the courts, and the Church.

At Versailles, ambitious nobles competed for royal appointments while idle courtiers enjoyed endless entertainments. Many nobles, however, lived far from the center of power. Though they owned land, they received little financial income. As a result, they felt the pinch of trying to maintain their status in a period of rising prices.

Many nobles hated absolutism and resented the royal bureaucracy that employed middle-class men in positions that once had been reserved for them. They feared losing their traditional privileges, especially their freedom from paying taxes.

Third Estate Is Vastly Diverse The Third Estate was the most diverse social class. At the top sat the **bourgeoisie** (boor zhwah ZEE), or middle class. The bourgeoisie included prosperous bankers, merchants, and manufacturers, as well as lawyers, doctors, journalists, and professors. The bulk of the Third Estate, however, consisted of rural peasants.

REVEIL DU TIERS ETAT.

Analyzing Political Cartoons

The Old Regime This cartoon represents the social order in France before the French Revolution. While a member of the Third Estate is beginning to express anger and rise up, a nobleman representing the Second Estate and a priest, representing the First Estate, recoil in surprise and fear.
1. How does the cartoonist portray the Third Estate? Explain why.
2. What were the differences among the social classes in pre-revolutionary France?

Seven Years' War and the American Revolution strained the treasury even further. Costs generally had risen in the 1700s, and the lavish court soaked up millions. To bridge the gap between income and expenses, the government borrowed more and more money. By 1789, half of the government's income from taxes went to paying the interest on this enormous debt. Also, in the late 1780s, bad harvests sent food prices soaring and brought hunger to poorer peasants and city dwellers.

To solve the financial crisis, the government would have to increase taxes, reduce expenses, or both. However, the nobles and clergy fiercely resisted any attempt to end their exemption from taxes.

Economic Reform Fails The heirs of Louis XIV were not the right men to solve the economic crisis that afflicted France. Louis XV, who ruled from 1715 to 1774, pursued pleasure before serious business and ran up more debts. **Louis XVI** was well-meaning but weak and indecisive. He did, however, wisely choose **Jacques Necker**, a financial expert, as an advisor. Necker urged the king to reduce extravagant court spending, reform government, and abolish burdensome tariffs on internal trade. When Necker proposed taxing the First and Second Estates, however, the nobles and high clergy forced him to dismiss him.

As the crisis deepened, the pressure for reform mounted. The wealthy and powerful classes demanded, however, that the king summon the **Estates-General**, the legislative body consisting of representatives of the three estates, before making any changes. A French king had not called the Estates-General for 175 years, fearing that nobles would use it to recover the feudal powers they had lost under absolute rule. To reform-minded nobles, the Estates-General seemed to offer a chance of carrying out changes like those that had come with the Glorious Revolution in England. They hoped that they could bring the absolute monarch under the control of the nobles and guarantee their own privileges.

✔ **Checkpoint** What economic troubles did France face in 1789, and how did they lead to further unrest?

France were faced with great hunger as bad harvests sent food prices soaring. People began to riot to demand bread. In the countryside, peasants began to attack the manor houses of the nobles. Arthur Young, an English visitor to France, witnessed these riots and disturbances. Why did the poor attack the nobles' homes?

Primary Source

❝ Everything conspires to render the present period in France critical: the [lack] of bread is terrible: accounts arrive every moment from the provinces of riots and disturbances, and calling in the military, to preserve the peace of the markets. ❞
—Arthur Young, *Travels in France During the Years 1787–1789*

Independent Practice

Have students work with a partner to write brief profiles for three of the following: nun, priest, nobleman, banker, manufacturer, lawyer, peasant, member of the royal family, journeyman, servant. In their profiles, students should identify the estate to which each person would have belonged in 1789, the privileges and complaints each might have had, and changes that each might have desired. After students have finished their profiles, invite volunteers to read them to the class.

Monitor Progress

- As students fill in their charts, circulate to make sure they understand that inequalities among classes was one of the causes of the French Revolution. For a completed version of the chart, see **Note Taking Transparencies, 136**
- If students need more instruction on identifying causes and effects, have them read the **Skills Handbook, p. SH36.**

Some were prosperous landowners who hired laborers to work for them. Others were tenant farmers or day laborers.

Among the poorest members of the Third Estate were <u>urban</u> workers. They included apprentices, journeymen, and others who worked in industries such as printing or cloth making. Many women and men earned a meager living as servants, construction workers, or street sellers of everything from food to pots and pans. A large number of the urban poor were unemployed. To survive, some turned to begging or crime.

From rich to poor, members of the Third Estate resented the privileges enjoyed by their social "betters." Wealthy bourgeois families in the Third Estate could buy political office and even titles, but the best jobs were still reserved for nobles. Urban workers earned miserable wages. Even the smallest rise in the price of bread, their main food, brought the threat of greater hunger or even starvation.

Because of traditional privileges, the First and Second Estates paid almost no taxes. Peasants were burdened by taxes on everything from land to soap to salt. Though they were technically free, many owed fees and services that dated back to medieval times, such as the corvée (kawr VAY), which was unpaid labor to repair roads and bridges. Peasants were

● INFOGRAPHIC

What Is the Third Estate?

"1. What is the Third Estate? *Everything.*
2. What has it been until now in the political order? *Nothing.*
3. What does it want to be? *Something.*"
—Abbé Emmanuel Sieyès

Sieyès, a clergyman before the revolution, captured the spirit of the Third Estate with these words in a pamphlet published in January 1789. The vast Third Estate—peasants, dentists, laborers, and more—comprising more than 95 percent of France, was ready to fight for equality.

▲ Ceramic bottle depicting dentist and patient

▲ *Woman of the French Revolution,* painting of a peasant woman by Jacques-Louis David

▼ Eighteenth-century French street traders

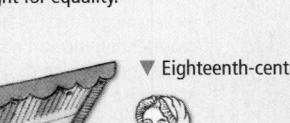   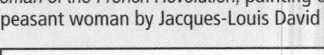

Thinking Critically
1. Identify Point of View. According to...

Louis XVI Calls the Estates-General/Parisians Storm the Bastille ⑬

Instruct

- **Introduce: Key Terms** Use the Idea Wave Strategy (TE, p. T22) and ask students to list ways they can express their opinions about something they do not like, such as an action taken by their state legislature. Then ask students to find the key term ***cahiers*** (in blue) in the text and explain that cahiers gave voice to the complaints of members of all three estates.

- **Teach** Remind students that economic problems forced Louis XVI to call the Estates-General, while social inequalities led the delegates of the Third Estate to take the Tennis Court Oath. Ask **Which do you think was a bigger factor in starting the French Revolution—economic troubles or social inequalities?** *(Sample: Answers will vary, but students should provide logical reasons for their choice.)*

- **Quick Activity** Display **Color Transparency 110: Bastille Prison.** Use the lesson suggested in the transparency book to guide a discussion on the storming of the Bastille.
   Color Transparencies, 110

Independent Practice

On the board, write the following idea from John Locke: "People have a natural right to life, liberty, and property. Rulers have a responsibility to protect these rights. People have the right to change a government that fails to do so." Have students write a paragraph explaining how this quote relates to the events of the meeting of the Estates-General.

Monitor Progress

- To check students understanding, ask **What three factors led to the start of the French Revolution?** *(social inequalities, economic troubles, inspiring Enlightenment ideas)*
- Check Reading and Note Taking Study Guide entries for student understanding.

The Oath Is Taken
Delegates of the Third Estate declare themselves to be the National Assembly, representing the people of France. They take the Tennis Court Oath (bottom), vowing to create a constitution. The National Assembly later issues the assignat (top) as currency to help pay the government's debts. *What was the significance of the Tennis Court Oath?*

Louis XVI Calls the Estates-General

As 1788 came to a close, France tottered on the verge of bankruptcy. Bread riots were spreading, and nobles, fearful of taxes, were denouncing royal tyranny. A baffled Louis XVI finally summoned the Estates-General to meet at Versailles the following year.

Estates Prepare Grievance Notebooks In preparation, Louis had all three estates prepare **cahiers** (kah YAYZ), or notebooks, listing their grievances. Many cahiers called for reforms such as fairer taxes, freedom of the press, or regular meetings of the Estates-General. In one town, shoemakers denounced regulations that made leather so expensive they could not afford to make shoes. Servant girls in the city of Toulouse demanded the right to leave service when they wanted and that "after a girl has served her master for many years, she receive some reward for her service."

The cahiers testified to boiling class resentments. One called tax collectors "bloodsuckers of the nation who drink the tears of the unfortunate from goblets of gold." Another one of the cahiers condemned the courts of nobles as "vampires pumping the last drop of blood" from the people. Another complained that "20 million must live on half the wealth of France while the clergy . . . devour the other half."

Delegates Take the Tennis Court Oath Delegates to the Estates-General from the Third Estate were elected, though only propertied men could vote. Thus, the delegates were mostly lawyers, middle-class officials, and writers. They were familiar with the writings of Voltaire, Rousseau, and other *philosophes*. They went to Versailles not only to solve the financial crisis but also to insist on reform.

The Estates-General convened in May 1789. From the start, the delegates were deadlocked over the issue of voting. Traditionally, each estate had met and voted separately. Each group had one vote. Under this system, the First and Second Estates always outvoted the Third Estate two to one. This time, the Third Estate wanted all three estates to meet in a single body, with votes counted "by head."

After weeks of stalemate, delegates of the Third Estate took a daring step. In June 1789, claiming to represent the people of France, they declared themselves to be the National Assembly. A few days later, the National Assembly found its meeting hall locked and guarded. Fearing that the king planned to dismiss them, the delegates moved to a nearby indoor tennis court. As curious spectators looked on, the delegates took their famous **Tennis Court Oath.** They swore "never to separate

Answer

Caption It showed the Third Estate's commitment to creating a constitution.

and to meet wherever the circumstances might require until we have established a sound and just constitution."

When reform-minded clergy and nobles joined the Assembly, Louis XVI grudgingly accepted it. But royal troops gathered around Paris, and rumors spread that the king planned to dissolve the Assembly.

✓ **Checkpoint** What actions did delegates of the Third Estate take when the Estates-General met in 1789?

Parisians Storm the Bastille

On July 14, 1789, the city of Paris seized the spotlight from the National Assembly meeting in Versailles. The streets buzzed with rumors that royal troops were going to occupy the capital. More than 800 Parisians assembled outside the Bastille, a grim medieval fortress used as a prison for political and other prisoners. The crowd demanded weapons and gunpowder believed to be stored there.

The commander of the Bastille refused to open the gates and opened fire on the crowd. In the battle that followed, many people were killed. Finally, the enraged mob broke through the defenses. They killed the commander and five guards and released the handful of prisoners who were being held there, but found no weapons.

The Bastille was a symbol to the people of France representing years of abuse by the monarchy. The storming of and subsequent fall of the Bastille was a wake-up call to Louis XVI. Unlike any other riot or short-lived protest, this event posed a challenge to the sheer existence of the regime. Since 1880, the French have celebrated Bastille Day annually as their national independence day.

✓ **Checkpoint** What was the significance of the storming of the Bastille?

Parisians storm the Bastille on July 14, 1789.

Progress Monitoring *Online*
For: Self-quiz with vocabulary practice
Web Code: nba-1811

SECTION 1 Assessment

Terms, People, and Places

1. What do many of the key terms, people, and places listed at the beginning of the section have in common? Explain.

Note Taking

2. **Reading Skill: Recognize Multiple Causes** Use your completed chart to answer the Focus Question: What led to the storming of the Bastille, and therefore, to the start of the French Revolution?

Comprehension and Critical Thinking

3. **Compare Point of View** How did the views of society differ between the nobles and peasants in 1789 France?

4. **Identify Point of View** Suppose that you are Jacques Necker. Write a paragraph that explains how your economic reform program will benefit France.

5. **Express Problems Clearly** What issues arose when Louis XVI called the Estates-General in 1789?

● **Writing About History**

Quick Write: Make a Cause-and-Effect Organizer Choose a specific event from this section and write it in the center of a piece of paper. List causes above it and effects below it. This will give you the details to include in your cause-and-effect essay. You may need to do additional research to gather more details.

Radicals Take Over

Instruct

- **Introduce: Key Terms** Ask students to find the key term *republic* (in blue) in the text and explain its meaning. Have them name countries in the world today that are republics. (*Sample: Brazil, Ethiopia, France, India, Nigeria, Philippines, United States*)

- **Teach** Ask **Why did European rulers and nobles denounce the French Revolution?** (*They feared that ideas of revolution would spread to their countries and bring an end to their power and privileges.*) **What factors led to the radical phase of the Revolution?** (*continuing economic problems and hostile factions competing for power*)

- **Analyze the Visuals** Display **Color Transparency 107:** *The French Plague.* Use the lesson suggested in the transparency book to further analyze the political cartoon on this page.

  🏛 **Color Transparencies,** 107

Independent Practice

Viewpoints To help students better understand the mixed reactions to the French Revolution, have them read the selection *Two Views of the French Revolution* and complete the worksheet.

⬛ **Teaching Resources, Unit 2,** p. 31

Monitor Progress

- Have students reread the passage on British statesman and writer Edmund Burke. Ask them to summarize his opinion of the French Revolution and describe how his predictions began to come true.

- Check Reading and Note Taking Study Guide entries for student understanding.

Answers

 It set up a limited monarchy, created a new Legislative Assembly, replaced the old provinces with 83 departments, abolished provincial courts, and reformed laws.

Analyzing Political Cartoons
1. They didn't want to lose their privileges and power and feared the influence of the Third Estate's actions.
2. as giant French rats whose tails form a guillotine

of war and peace. Lawmakers would be elected by tax-paying male citizens over age 25.

To make government more efficient, the constitution replaced the old provinces with 83 departments of roughly equal size. It abolished the old provincial courts, and it reformed laws.

To moderate reformers, the Constitution of 1791 seemed to complete the revolution. Reflecting Enlightenment goals, it ensured equality before the law for all male citizens and ended Church interference in government. At the same time, it put power in the hands of men with the means and leisure to serve in government.

Louis's Escape Fails Meanwhile, Marie Antoinette and others had been urging the king to escape their humiliating situation. Louis finally gave in. One night in June 1791, a coach rolled north from Paris toward the border. Inside sat the king disguised as a servant, the queen dressed as a governess, and the royal children.

The attempted escape failed. In a town along the way, Louis's disguise was uncovered by someone who held up a piece of currency with the king's face on it. A company of soldiers escorted the royal family back to Paris, as onlooking crowds hurled insults at the king. To many, Louis's dash to the border showed that he was a traitor to the revolution.

✓ **Checkpoint** What were the provisions of the Constitution of 1791?

Radicals Take Over

Events in France stirred debate all over Europe. Supporters of the Enlightenment applauded the reforms of the National Assembly. They saw the French experiment as the dawn of a new age for justice and equality. European rulers and nobles, however, denounced the French Revolution.

Rulers Fear Spread of Revolution European rulers increased border patrols to stop the spread of the "French plague." Fueling those fears were the horror stories that were told by émigrés (EM ih grayz)—nobles, clergy, and others who had fled France and its revolutionary forces. Émigrés reported attacks on their privileges, their property, their religion, and even their lives. Even "enlightened" rulers turned against France. Catherine the Great of Russia burned Voltaire's letters and locked up her critics.

Edmund Burke, a British writer and statesman who earlier had defended the American Revolution, bitterly condemned revolutionaries in Paris. He predicted all too accurately that the revolution would become more violent. "Plots and assassinations," he wrote, "will be anticipated by preventive murder and preventive confiscation." Burke warned: "When ancient opinions and rules of life are taken away . . . we have no compass to govern us."

Threats Come From Abroad The failed escape of Louis XVI brought further hostile rumblings from abroad. In August 1791, the king of Prussia and the

Analyzing Political Cartoons

The French Plague European rulers, nobles, and clergy (such as, from left, Catherine the Great of Russia, the Pope, Emperor Leopold II of Prussia, and George III of England) feared the revolution in France would spread to their countries. Many émigrés fueled the flames with their tales of attacks by the revolutionary government.
1. Why were European rulers against revolutionary ideas coming into their countries?
2. How does the cartoonist portray the "plague?"

Connect to Our World

Connections to Today Ask students to describe what the terms *left*, *right*, and *center* mean in politics today. Explain that the political use of these terms began with France's Legislative Assembly in 1791. Members with similar views always sat together in the meeting hall in Paris. On the right sat those who felt that reform had gone far enough and those who wanted to turn the clock back to 1788. In the center of the hall sat supporters of moderate reform. On the left were the Jacobins and other republicans who wanted to abolish the monarchy completely and bring about radical changes. Today, the terms *right, center,* and *left* continue to reflect those ideologies and seating arrangements.

emperor of Austria—who was Marie Antoinette's brother—issued the Declaration of Pilnitz. In this document, the two monarchs threatened to intervene to protect the French monarchy. The declaration may have been mostly a bluff, but revolutionaries in France took the threat seriously and prepared for war. The revolution was about to enter a new, more radical phase of change and conflict.

Radicals Fight for Power and Declare War In October 1791, the newly elected Legislative Assembly took office. Faced with crises at home and abroad, it survived for less than a year. Economic problems fed renewed turmoil. Assignats (AS ig nats), the revolutionary currency, dropped in value, causing prices to rise rapidly. Uncertainty about prices led to hoarding and caused additional food shortages.

In Paris and other cities, working-class men and women, called **sans-culottes** (sanz koo LAHTS), pushed the revolution into more radical action. They were called sans-culottes, which means "without breeches," because they wore long trousers instead of the fancy knee breeches that upper-class men wore. By 1791, many sans-culottes demanded a **republic,** or government ruled by elected representatives instead of a monarch.

Within the Legislative Assembly, several hostile factions competed for power. The sans-culottes found support among radicals in the Legislative Assembly, especially the Jacobins. A revolutionary political club, the **Jacobins** were mostly middle-class lawyers or intellectuals. They used pamphleteers and sympathetic newspaper editors to advance the republican cause. Opposing the radicals were moderate reformers and political officials who wanted no more reforms at all.

The National Assembly Declares War on Tyranny The radicals soon held the upper hand in the Legislative Assembly. In April 1792, the war of words between French revolutionaries and European monarchs moved onto the battlefield. Eager to spread the revolution and destroy tyranny abroad, the Legislative Assembly declared war first on Austria and then on Prussia, Britain, and other states. The great powers expected to win an easy victory against France, a land divided by revolution. In fact, however, the fighting that began in 1792 lasted on and off until 1815.

Sans-culotte, 1792

✓ **Checkpoint** How did the rest of Europe react to the French Revolution?

Progress Monitoring Online
For: Self-quiz with vocabulary practice
Web Code: nba-1821

SECTION 2 Assessment

Terms, People, and Places

1. For each term, person, or place listed at the beginning of the section, write a sentence explaining its significance.

Note Taking

2. **Reading Skill: Identify Supporting Details** Use your completed outline to answer the Focus Question: What political and social reforms did the National Assembly institute in the first stage of the French Revolution?

Comprehension and Critical Thinking

3. **Make Comparisons** How was the French Declaration of the Rights of Man and the Citizen similar to the American Declaration of Independence?

4. **Summarize** What did the Constitution of 1791 do, and how did it reflect Enlightenment ideas?

5. **Draw Inferences** Describe what happened to France's constitutional monarchy because of the French Revolution.

● **Writing About History**

Quick Write: Create a Flowchart As you prepare to write a cause-and-effect essay, you need to decide how to organize it. To do this, create a flowchart that shows the effects of the French Revolution on other countries. Do you want to write about the events in chronological order? By the importance of each event?

Objectives

■ Identify the basic principles of the French Declaration of the Rights of Man and the Citizen.

■ Understand how specific articles support the basic principles of the Declaration.

Build Background Knowledge L3

Ask students to recall what they know about the Declaration of the Rights of Man and the Citizen. Remind them that the document was modeled in part after the American Declaration of Independence, which was written 13 years earlier, in 1776, and based in part on the English Bill of Rights, written in 1689. Have students predict what kinds of statements the Declaration of the Rights of Man might contain.

Instruct L3

■ Go over each of the articles listed with students. Help students understand how each of the articles may have affected the lives of French citizens. Have students give one real-life example of each of the four natural rights listed under article 2.

■ Ask students how the Declaration of the Rights of Man and the Citizen reflects the slogan of the French Revolution, "Liberty, Equality, Fraternity."

Monitor Progress

Remind students that Enlightenment ideas influenced both the French Revolution and the Declaration of the Rights of Man and the Citizen. Present students with some Enlightenment ideas or have volunteers name the fundamental ones. *(Sample: right to life, liberty, and property)* Ask students to identify which articles reflect these ideas.

Thinking Critically

1. Article 6 states that all citizens are equal under the law and have the right to participate in government. This marked a significant change for most French citizens, who were not previously treated equally under the law.

2. Both stated that all men are created equal.

Declaration of the Rights of Man and the Citizen

Painting of the declaration

The National Assembly issued this document in 1789 after having overthrown the established government in the early stages of the French Revolution. The document was modeled in part on the English Bill of Rights and on the American Declaration of Independence. The basic principles of the French declaration were those that inspired the revolution, such as the freedom and equality of all male citizens before the law. The Articles below identify additional principles.

Therefore the National Assembly recognizes and proclaims, in the presence and under the auspices[1] of the Supreme Being, the following rights of man and of the citizen:

1. Men are born and remain free and equal in rights. Social distinctions may be founded only upon the general good.

2. The aim of all political association is the preservation of the natural and imprescriptible[2] rights of man. These rights are liberty, property, security, and resistance to oppression. . . .

4. Liberty consists in the freedom to do everything which injures no one else. . . .

5. Law can only prohibit such actions as are hurtful to society. . . .

6. Law is the expression of the general will. Every citizen has a right to participate personally, or through his representative, in its formation. It must be the same for all, whether it protects or punishes. All citizens, being equal in the eyes of the law, are equally eligible to all dignities and to all public positions and occupations, according to their abilities, and without distinction except that of their virtues and talents.

7. No person shall be accused, arrested, or imprisoned except in the cases and according to the forms prescribed by law. . . .

11. The free communication of ideas and opinions is one of the most precious of the rights of man. Every citizen may, accordingly, speak, write, and print with freedom. . . .

13. A common contribution is essential for the maintenance of the public [military] forces and for the cost of administration. This should be equitably distributed among all the citizens in proportion to their means.

1. **auspices** (AWS puh siz) *n.* approval and support
2. **imprescriptible** (im prih SKRIP tuh bul) *adj.* that which cannot be rightfully taken away

Thinking Critically

1. **Summarize** Summarize article 6. Why is this article especially significant?

2. **Identify Central Issues** What central idea does this declaration share with the American Declaration of Independence?

History Background

Origins of the Declaration of the Rights of Man and the Citizen In addition to being influenced by the American Declaration of Independence and the English Bill of Rights, the French Declaration of the Rights of Man and the Citizen drew its content from other sources as well. The constitutions of individual states such as New Hampshire and Virginia also influenced the Declaration.

The impact of Enlightenment philosophes is clearly seen in the document, too. Montesquieu's notion of separation of powers is represented, as are Locke's ideas on natural rights and Rousseau's theories on the general will and national sovereignty. The physiocrats' ideas about private property and Voltaire's notions of protecting individuals against arbitrary police action are also included.

SECTION 3

Marie Antoinette transported by cart to the guillotine

WITNESS HISTORY 🔊 AUDIO

The Engine of Terror

A new execution device called the guillotine was introduced during this phase of the revolution. With its large, diagonal blade that came crashing down from a great height, it cut off heads swiftly and accurately. Thousands of people were sent to the guillotine and executed without trial. In his novel *A Tale of Two Cities*, Charles Dickens describes daily life during the Reign of Terror:

❝ Along the Paris streets, the death-carts rumble, hollow and harsh. Six tumbrils [carts that carried condemned persons to the guillotine] carry the day's wine to La Guillotine. ❞

Focus Question What events occurred during the radical phase of the French Revolution?

Radical Days of the Revolution

Objectives
- Understand how and why radicals abolished the monarchy.
- Explain why the Committee of Public Safety was created and why the Reign of Terror resulted.
- Summarize how the excesses of the Convention led to the formation of the Directory.
- Analyze how the French people were affected by the changes brought about by the revolution.

Terms, People, and Places

suffrage	Napoleon
Robespierre	nationalism
Reign of Terror	Marseilles
guillotine	

Note Taking

Reading Skill: Recognize Sequence Make a timeline like the one shown here. Add dates and important events as you read this section.

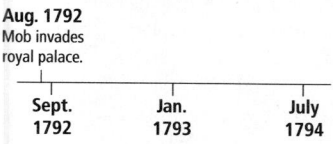

Aug. 1792
Mob invades
royal palace.

Sept. 1792	Jan. 1793	July 1794

In 1793, the revolution entered a radical phase. For a year, France experienced one of the bloodiest regimes in its long history as determined leaders sought to extend and preserve the revolution.

The Monarchy Is Abolished

As the revolution continued, dismal news about the war abroad heightened tensions. Well-trained Prussian forces were cutting down raw French recruits. In addition, royalist officers were deserting the French army, joining émigrés and others hoping to restore the king's power.

Tensions Lead to Violence Battle disasters quickly inflamed revolutionaries who thought the king was in league with the enemies. On August 10, 1792, a crowd of Parisians stormed the royal palace of the Tuileries and slaughtered the king's guards. The royal family fled to the Legislative Assembly, escaping before the mob arrived.

A month later, citizens attacked prisons that held nobles and priests accused of political offenses. About 1,200 prisoners were killed; among them were many ordinary criminals. Historians disagree about the people who carried out the "September massacres." Some call them bloodthirsty mobs. Others describe them as patriots defending France from its enemies. In fact, most were ordinary citizens fired to fury by real and imagined grievances.

Radicals Take Control and Execute the King Backed by Paris crowds, radicals then took control of the Assembly. Radicals

Vocabulary Builder

Use the information below and the following resources to teach the high-use word from this section.
All in One Teaching Resources, Unit 2, p. 25; **Teaching Resources, Skills Handbook,** p. 3

High-Use Word	Definition and Sample Sentence
radical, p. 224	*adj.* extreme; departure from the usual or traditional
	Christine always had long hair so it was a **radical** change when she cut it short.

SECTION 3 **Step-by-Step Instruction**

Objectives

As you teach this section, keep students focused on the following objectives to help them answer the Section Focus Question and master core content.

- Understand how and why radicals abolished the monarchy.
- Explain why the Committee of Public Safety was created and why the Reign of Terror resulted.
- Summarize how the excesses of the Convention led to the formation of the Directory.
- Analyze how the French people were affected by the changes brought about by the revolution.

Prepare to Read

Build Background Knowledge L3

Note that the French Revolution had a radical stage of excessive violence. Ask students to preview the pictures and brainstorm possible reasons for the atrocities that often take place in revolutions.

Set a Purpose L3

- **WITNESS HISTORY** Read the selection aloud or play the audio.

  🔊 AUDIO **Witness History Audio CD,** The Engine of Terror

  Point out that the picture shows Marie Antoinette in a tumbril. Ask **How does Dickens describe the tumbrils?** (*He calls them death-carts.*) **How do you think he feels about using the carts for those about to die?** (*Death is taken too lightly.*)

- **Focus** Point out the Section Focus Question and write it on the board. Tell students to refer to this question as they read. (*Answer appears with Section 3 Assessment answers.*)

- **Preview** Have students preview the Section Objectives and the list of Terms, People, and Places.

- **Note Taking** Have students read this section using the Guided Questioning strategy (TE, p. T20). As they read, have students fill in the timeline sequencing events from this section.

  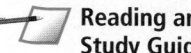 **Reading and Note Taking Study Guide,** p. 85

Teach

The Monarchy Is Abolished

Instruct

- **Introduce: Vocabulary Builder**
  Have students read the Vocabulary Builder term and explain its meaning. Have students talk about what has happened so far in the French Revolution and speculate on reasons why people might next take *radical* actions.

- **Teach** Discuss the violent events leading up to the king's execution. Ask **How did the war abroad affect the revolutionaries' behavior?** (*Battle losses inflamed their anger at the king and caused them to attack the royal palace and prisons.*) **How did the Jacobins try to wipe out the old order?** (*by seizing nobles' lands, abolishing titles of nobility, and executing the king*) **Why do you think the press celebrated Marie Antoinette's execution?** (*Sample: She had come to symbolize the excesses of the monarchy.*)

- **Quick Activity** Conduct the unit simulation, *Trial in France*, which reenacts the monarchy's trial for treason.

  All in One Teaching Resources, Unit 2, p. 79

Independent Practice

Primary Source To show students another perspective of the king, have them read the selection *The Royal Family in Prison* and complete the worksheet.

All in One Teaching Resources, Unit 2, p. 27

Monitor Progress

As students fill in their timelines, circulate to make sure they understand the sequence of events during the radical phase of the revolution. For a completed version of the timeline, see

🏛 **Note Taking Transparencies**, 138

Answers

✔ They called for a new legislative body, extended the right to vote to all male citizens, abolished the monarchy, established a republic, and executed the king and queen.

COMPARING VIEWPOINTS Students should support their opinions with specific examples.

Vocabulary Builder
radical—(RAD ih kul) *adj.* extreme; departure from the usual or traditional

called for the election of a new legislative body called the National Convention. **Suffrage,** the right to vote, was to be extended to all male citizens, not just to property owners.

The Convention that met in September 1792 was a more <u>radical</u> body than earlier assemblies. It voted to abolish the monarchy and establish a republic—the French Republic. Deputies then drew up a new constitution for France. The Jacobins, who controlled the Convention, set out to erase all traces of the old order. They seized lands of nobles and abolished titles of nobility.

During the early months of the Republic, the Convention also put Louis XVI on trial as a traitor to France. The king was convicted by a single vote and sentenced to death. On a foggy morning in January 1793, Louis mounted a scaffold in a public square in Paris. He started to speak, "Frenchmen, I die innocent. I pardon the authors of my death. I pray God that the blood about to be spilt will never fall upon the head of France. . . ." Then a roll of drums drowned out his words. Moments later, the king was beheaded. The executioner lifted the king's head by its hair and held it before the crowd.

In October, Marie Antoinette was also executed. The popular press celebrated her death. The queen, however, showed great dignity as she went to her death.

✔ **Checkpoint** What occurred after radicals took control of the Assembly?

■ COMPARING VIEWPOINTS

On the Execution of a King

On January 21, 1793, King Louis XVI of France was executed by order of the National Convention. Reaction to this event was both loud and varied throughout Europe. The excerpts below present two different views on this event. **Critical Thinking** *Which of the two viewpoints makes a better case for or against the execution of King Louis XVI? Cite examples from both statements to support your argument.*

For the Execution

The crimes of Louis XVI are unhappily all too real; they are consistent; they are notorious. Do we even have to ask the question of whether a nation has the right to judge, and execute, its highest ranking public official . . . when, to more securely plot against the nation, he concealed himself behind a mask of hypocrisy? Or when, instead of using the authority confided to him to protect his countrymen, he used it to oppress them? Or when he turned the laws into an instrument of violence to crush the supporters of the Revolution? Or when he robbed the citizens of their gold in order to subsidize their foes, and robbed them of their subsistence in order to feed the barbarian hordes who came to slaughter them? Or when he created monopolies in order to create famine by drying up the sources of abundance so that the people might die in misery and hunger? . . .

—Jean-Paul Marat

Against the Execution

The Republican tyrants of France have now carried their bloody purposes to the uttermost diabolical stretch of savage cruelty. They have murdered their King without even the shadow of justice, and of course they cannot expect friendship nor intercourse with any civilized part of the world. The vengeance of Europe will now rapidly fall on them; and, in process of time, make them the veriest wretches on the face of the earth. The name of Frenchman will be considered as the appellation of savage, and their presence shunned as a poison, deadly destructive to the peace and happiness of Mankind. It appears evident, that the majority of the National Convention, and the Executive Government of that truly despotic country, are comprised of the most execrable villains upon the face of the earth. . . .

—*London Times*, January 25, 1793

Differentiated Instruction — Solutions for All Learners

L2 Less Proficient Readers   L2 English Language Learners   L1 Special Needs

On the board, write the headings *Changes* and *Better/Worse.* Ask students to list the changes that occurred during the radical period of the French Revolution. For each item on the list, ask students whether the change made France a better or worse place for its citizens.

Use the following resources to help students acquire basic skills.

✏ **Adapted Reading and Note Taking Study Guide**

- Adapted Note Taking Study Guide, p. 85
- Adapted Section Summary, p. 86

Terror and Danger Grip France

By early 1793, danger threatened France on all sides. The country was at war with much of Europe, including Britain, the Netherlands, Spain, and Prussia. In the Vendée (vahn DAY) region of France, royalists and priests led peasants in rebellion against the government. In Paris, the sans-culottes demanded relief from food shortages and inflation. The Convention itself was bitterly divided between Jacobins and a rival group, the Girondins.

The Convention Creates a New Committee To deal with the threats to France, the Convention created the Committee of Public Safety. The 12-member committee had almost absolute power as it battled to save the revolution. The Committee prepared France for all-out war, issuing a *levée en masse,* or mass levy (tax) that required all citizens to contribute to the war effort. In addition, the 12 members of the Committee were in charge of trials and executions.

Spurred by revolutionary fervor, French recruits marched off to defend the republic. Young officers developed effective new tactics to win battles with masses of ill-trained but patriotic forces. Soon, French armies overran the Netherlands. They later invaded Italy. At home, they crushed peasant revolts. European monarchs shuddered as the revolutionaries carried "freedom fever" into conquered lands.

Robespierre "the Incorruptible" At home, the government battled counterrevolutionaries under the guiding hand of Maximilien **Robespierre** (ROHBZ pyehr). Robespierre, a shrewd lawyer and politician, quickly rose to the leadership of the Committee of Public Safety. Among Jacobins, his selfless dedication to the revolution earned him the nickname "the incorruptible." The enemies of Robespierre called him a tyrant.

Robespierre had embraced Rousseau's idea of the general will as the source of all legitimate law. He promoted religious toleration and wanted to abolish slavery. Though cold and humorless, he was popular with the sans-culottes, who hated the old regime as much as he did. He believed that France could achieve a "republic of virtue" only through the use of terror, which he coolly defined as nothing more than "prompt, severe, inflexible justice." "Liberty cannot be secured," Robespierre cried, "unless criminals lose their heads."

The Guillotine Defines the Reign of Terror Robespierre was one of the chief architects of the **Reign of Terror,** which lasted from September 1793 to July 1794. Revolutionary courts conducted hasty trials. Spectators greeted death sentences with cries of "Hail the Republic!" or "Death to the traitors!"

In a speech given on February 5, 1794, Robespierre explained why the terror was necessary to achieve the goals of the revolution:

Primary Source

66 It is necessary to stifle the domestic and foreign enemies of the Republic or perish with them. . . . The first maxim of our politics ought to be to lead the people by means of reason and the enemies of the people by terror. . . . If the basis of popular government in time of peace is virtue, the basis of popular government in time of revolution is both virtue and terror. 99
—Maximilien Robespierre, quoted in *Pageant of Europe* (Stearns)

BIOGRAPHY

Robespierre

Maximilien Robespierre (1758–1794) did not have an easy childhood. His mother died when he was only 6 years old. Two years later, his father abandoned him and his three siblings. The children's aunts and grandfather then raised them. Because of this, Robespierre assumed responsibilities at an early age. Eventually, he went to study law at the University of Paris. His performance was so noteworthy that he was chosen to deliver a speech to Louis XVI on the occasion of the king's coronation. But young Robespierre was snubbed. After listening to the address in a pouring rainstorm, the king and queen left without acknowledging Robespierre in any way. Years later, in 1789, Robespierre was elected to the Estates-General, where his career as a revolutionary began. **How do you think Robespierre's early life might have influenced his political ideas?**

Terror and Danger Grip France ⓵

Instruct

- **Introduce: Key Terms** Ask students to find the key term *Reign of Terror* (in blue) in the text and explain its meaning. Then ask them to predict what life in France might have been like during this period.

- **Teach** Ask **Why did the Convention create the Committee on Public Safety?** *(to deal with threats to France, both from internal rebellion and external war, and to save the Revolution)* **Did the actions taken by Robespierre and the Committee promote the original ideals of the Revolution or go against them? Explain.** *(Sample: They went against the ideals of equality and liberty by unfairly imprisoning people and performing executions after hasty trials.)*

- **Quick Activity** Direct students' attention to The Reign of Terror Infographic on the next page. Read the captions and discuss the visuals as a class. Note that many actions during the Reign of Terror were very undemocratic. Ask small groups of students to discuss whether a democratic government is ever justified in using nondemocratic means to protect itself and ensure its survival. Use the Numbered Heads strategy (TE, p. T23) and have groups share their conclusions with the class.

Independent Practice

Web Code nbp-1831 will take students to an interactive activity. Have students complete the interactivity and then answer the questions in the text.

Monitor Progress

To review this section, ask students to summarize the character of the revolution under the Committee of Public Safety. *(violent, radical)*

Differentiated Instruction   Solutions for All Learners

ⓛ English Language Learners

Direct students to read the key term *Reign of Terror.* Clarify that the word *reign* means a period of rule. Ask students to go through this section and find three sources of information that prove that this time of the French Revolution was the Reign of Terror. *(Sample: the brutality of the guillotine, the excessive use of the guillotine, the inflexible "justice" of Robespierre)*

Answer

BIOGRAPHY Sample: Growing up in poverty may have fueled his hatred of the old regime. This plus the snubbing by the king and queen probably influenced his decision to join the revolution.

The Revolution Enters Its Third Stage ⓛ

Instruct

- **Introduce: Key Terms** Ask students to find the name **_Napoleon_** (in blue) in the text. Ask students what they already know about Napoleon and list their responses on the board. Ask them to predict how Napoleon might change the course of the French Revolution.

- **Teach** Discuss the third stage of the French Revolution. Ask **What group took control of France after the Reign of Terror?** *(moderates)* **The slogan of the revolution was "Liberty, Equality, Fraternity." Why do you think citizens gave up all three of these ideals during the Reign of Terror?** *(Sample: They may have thought it was the only way to achieve those ideals for the future.)*

Independent Practice

Have pairs or groups of students create posters to support or oppose the reinstatement of a constitutional monarchy in France after the Reign of Terror.

Monitor Progress

To review this section, ask students to explain whether or not the Revolution moved in a more moderate direction after the Reign of Terror. *(Yes, it did.)*

Suspect were those who resisted the revolution. About 300,000 were arrested during the Reign of Terror. Seventeen thousand were executed. Many were victims of mistaken identity or were falsely accused by their neighbors. Many more were packed into hideous prisons, where deaths from disease were common.

The engine of the Terror was the **guillotine** (GIL uh teen). Its fast-falling blade extinguished life instantly. A member of the legislature, Dr. Joseph Guillotin (gee oh TAN), had introduced it as a more humane method of beheading than the uncertain ax. But the guillotine quickly became a symbol of horror.

Within a year, the Terror consumed those who initiated it. Weary of bloodshed and fearing for their own lives, members of the Convention turned on the Committee of Public Safety. On the night of July 27, 1794, Robespierre was arrested. The next day he was executed. After the heads of Robespierre and other radicals fell, executions slowed dramatically.

✔ **Checkpoint** Why did Robespierre think the Terror was necessary to achieve the goals of the revolution?

The Revolution Enters Its Third Stage

In reaction to the Terror, the revolution entered a third stage. Moving away from the excesses of the Convention, moderates produced another constitution, the third since 1789. The Constitution of 1795 set up a five-

● **INFOGRAPHIC**

THE REIGN OF TERROR

From autumn 1793 to midsummer 1794, the revolution in France was overshadowed by a time of terror as the Committee of Public Safety rounded up "suspected persons" all over France. Only about 15 percent of those sentenced to death by guillotine (model at left) were of the nobility and clergy. Most were artisans and peasants of the Third Estate. Prisons in Paris—which included places such as former mansions and palaces, religious premises, and colleges—became more and more crowded as the number of suspects increased. Once sentenced to death, the condemned might travel an hour to the guillotine by cart as onlookers threw mud at them.

Thieves stole ▲ items such as silver as émigrés fled the country due to the Terror.

◀ Interrogation of aristocratic prisoners at L'Abbaye prison

Link to Humanities

Revolutionary Language As part of the French Revolution, everyday language changed to reflect the abolition of social ranks and privileges. For example, people stopped using the formal *vous* for "you," which peasants had customarily used to address nobility or merchants, and instead used the informal *tu*, which in the past had been used only to address good friends. The titles *Monsieur* and *Madame* (literally, My Lord and My Lady) were tainted with class overtones. The proponents of social equality replaced these titles—by law—with "Citizen" and "Citizeness." In these ways, the leaders of the revolution attempted to erase the differences among social classes and create equality among all French citizens.

---

man Directory and a two-house legislature elected by male citizens of property. The middle class and professional people of the bourgeoisie were the dominant force during this stage of the French Revolution. The Directory held power from 1795 to 1799.

Weak but dictatorial, the Directory faced growing discontent. Peace was made with Prussia and Spain, but war with Austria and Great Britain continued. Corrupt leaders lined their own pockets but failed to solve pressing problems. When rising bread prices stirred hungry sans-culottes to riot, the Directory quickly suppressed them. Another threat to the Directory was the revival of royalist feeling. Many émigrés were returning to France, and devout Catholics, who resented measures that had been taken against the Church, were welcoming them. In the election of 1797, supporters of a constitutional monarchy won the majority of seats in the legislature.

As chaos threatened, politicians turned to **Napoleon** Bonaparte, a popular military hero who had won a series of brilliant victories against the Austrians in Italy. The politicians planned to use him to advance their own goals. To their dismay, however, before long Napoleon would outwit them all to become ruler of France.

✔ **Checkpoint** What changes occurred after the Reign of Terror came to an end?

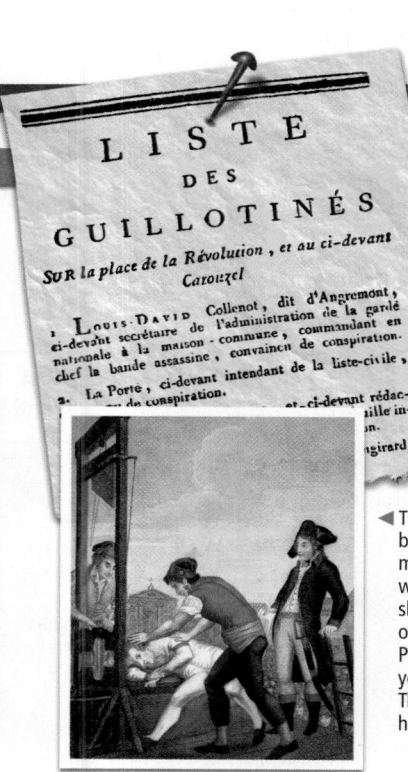

People never knew if friends or family might appear on a list of guillotine victims. There is some debate on the humane-ness of death by guillotine. Some authorities claim that even after the head has been severed, the victim could remain conscious for up to 30 seconds.

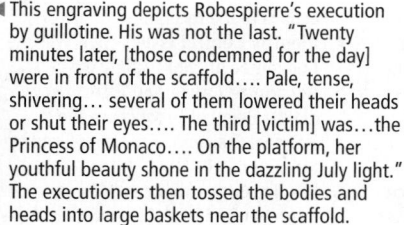
History *Interactive*
For: Interactive French Revolution
Web Code: nbp-1821

◄ This engraving depicts Robespierre's execution by guillotine. His was not the last. "Twenty minutes later, [those condemned for the day] were in front of the scaffold…. Pale, tense, shivering… several of them lowered their heads or shut their eyes…. The third [victim] was…the Princess of Monaco…. On the platform, her youthful beauty shone in the dazzling July light." The executioners then tossed the bodies and heads into large baskets near the scaffold.

Georges Danton, ▶ a Revolutionary leader, challenged the Terror and was guillotined.

Thinking Critically
1. **Identify Point of View** What were the goals of the Committee of Public Safety?
2. **Predict Consequences** How do you think life in France changed after the Terror came to an end?

Revolution Brings Change L3

Instruct

■ **Introduce: Key Terms** Ask students to find the key term ***nationalism*** (in blue) in the text and explain its meaning. Ask them to predict how national-ism in France might affect the future of the French Revolution.

■ **Teach** Have students name some of the major changes that occurred in France between 1789 and 1799. Ask **What did the red "liberty caps" and the tricolor symbolize?** *(The liberty and equality of all male citizens)* **What was the social impact of the revolution?** *(People developed a national identity, titles were eliminated, state schools were established, and slavery in French colonies was abolished.)*

■ **Quick Activity** Point out the images of French nationalism on the next page. Use the Idea Wave strategy (TE, p. T22) and ask students to brainstorm ways that people demonstrate nationalism today. *(Sample: displaying the flag, cele-brating national holidays, supporting their troops, cheering for their country at the Olympics)*

Independent Practice

Ask students to make a list of the ways France changed during the French Revo-lution and to rank what they think will be the most significant and lasting effect. Use the Think-Write-Pair-Share strategy (TE, p. T23) to have students share their rankings.

Monitor Progress

■ Tell students that some French parents gave their children names like Consti-tution, Republic, and August Tenth. To review this section, ask students the significance of each name.

■ Check Reading and Note Taking Study guide entries for student understanding.

Answers

✔ Moderates created the Constitution of 1795, which set up a five-man Directory and a two-house legislature.

Thinking Critically
1. to deal with the political threats from other countries in Europe and to deal with domestic enemies to the Revolution
2. Sample: People weren't as fearful of execution and began to look for more moderate solutions to political problems.

History Background

Women in the Revolution As the revolution progressed, women's right to express their views in public came under attack. In 1793, a committee of the National Convention declared that women lacked "the moral and physical strength necessary to prac-tice political rights." Women's revolutionary clubs were banned and violators were arrested. Women were imprisoned and sent to the guillotine.

However, women did gain some rights for a time. The government made divorce easier, a move that was aimed at weakening Church authority. Government officials also allowed women to inherit property, hop-ing to undermine the tradition of nobles leaving large estates to their oldest sons. However, these reforms and others did not last long after Napoleon gained power.

French Nationalism
"La Marseillaise" (top) and a revolutionary-period drum (bottom) helped rally the French people.

Revolution Brings Change

By 1799, the 10-year-old French Revolution had dramatically changed France. It had dislodged the old social order, overthrown the monarchy, and brought the Church under state control.

New symbols such as the red "liberty caps" and the tricolor confirmed the liberty and equality of all male citizens. The new title "citizen" applied to people of all social classes. All other titles were eliminated. Before he was executed, Louis XVI was called Citizen Capet, from the name of the dynasty that had ruled France in the Middle Ages. Elaborate fashions and powdered wigs gave way to the practical clothes and simple haircuts of the sans-culottes.

Nationalism Spreads Revolution and war gave the French people a strong sense of national identity. In earlier times, people had felt loyalty to local authorities. As monarchs centralized power, loyalty shifted to the king or queen. Now, the government rallied sons and daughters of the revolution to defend the nation itself. **Nationalism,** a strong feeling of pride in and devotion to one's country, spread throughout France. The French people attended civic festivals that celebrated the nation and the revolution. A variety of dances and songs on themes of the revolution became immensely popular.

By 1793, France was a nation in arms. From the port city of **Marseilles** (mahr say), troops marched to a rousing new song. It urged the "children of the fatherland" to march against the "bloody banner of tyranny." This song, "La Marseillaise" (mahr say ez), would later become the French national anthem.

Revolutionaries Push For Social Reform Revolutionaries pushed for social reform and religious toleration. They set up state schools to replace religious ones and organized systems to help the poor, old soldiers, and war widows. With a major slave revolt raging in the colony of St. Domingue (Haiti), the government also abolished slavery in France's Caribbean colonies.

✓ **Checkpoint** What changes occurred in France because of the French Revolution?

SECTION **3 Assessment**

Terms, People, and Places

1. Place each of the key terms at the beginning of the section into one of the following categories: politics, culture, geography, or technology. Write a sentence for each term explaining your choice.

Note Taking

2. **Reading Skill: Recognize Sequence** Use your completed timeline to answer the Focus Question: What events occurred during the radical phase of the French Revolution?

Comprehension and Critical Thinking

3. **Summarize** Summarize the goals and actions of the Jacobins.

4. **Identify Central Issues** Why was the Committee of Public Safety created?

5. **Recognize Cause and Effect** How did the Reign of Terror cause the National Convention to be replaced by the Directory?

6. **Predict Consequences** How do you think French nationalism affected the war between France and the powers of Europe?

● **Writing About History**

Quick Write: Provide Elaboration To illustrate each cause and effect of your essay, you should have supporting details, facts, and examples. Choose one of the events below and list as many specific details as possible. Then write a paragraph using the details you listed to explain what caused the event.

- Reign of Terror
- Execution of King Louis XVI
- Creation of the Committee of Public Safety

Art of Revolution

Revolutions have visual chronicles as well as written ones, and in the days before photography, these depictions were often rendered with paint. The French artist Jacques-Louis David (ZHAHK loo EE dah VEED) and the Spanish artist Francisco Goya both portrayed aspects of revolution on canvas, but they had differing viewpoints. David supported the early French Revolution and embraced the revolutionary spirit in his work. Goya, however, was a realist who showed human suffering and the horrors of war in his paintings.

▲ *Napoleon Crossing Mont Saint Bernard,* **Jacques-Louis David, 1801**
Imprisoned after moderates turned against the Reign of Terror, David barely escaped with his life. When Napoleon rose to power, David deftly switched his political allegiance to the new Emperor of France and became one of Bonaparte's chief portraitists. Notice the names carved into the rocks. David included these names of great past rulers to show Napoleon's level of greatness. David's depictions of Napoleon helped cement him as a strong and heroic leader.

▲ *The Third of May, 1808,* **Francisco José de Goya y Lucientes, 1814**
One of the consequences of the French Revolution and Napoleon's rise was that France soon found itself at war with the rest of Europe. Francisco Goya saw firsthand the impact of these wars. Born in northern Spain, he rose to become the official painter of the Spanish court. When Napoleon invaded Spain and deposed its king, Goya chronicled the horrors of the resulting guerrilla warfare.

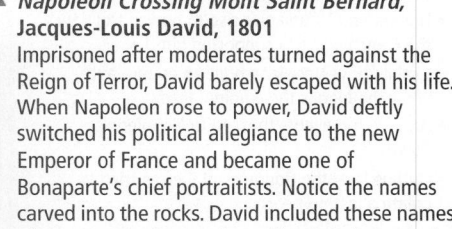

> **Thinking Critically**
> 1. **Compare Points of View** What elements in each painting express the viewpoint of the artist? How are the elements different?
> 2. **Recognize Ideologies** How do you think the ideology of the French Revolution led to the scene Goya portrays here?

History Background

Jacques-Louis David Before glorifying Napoleon and the imperial regime, Jacques-Louis David used his creative genius to promote the revolution. Of his drawing of the Tennis Court Oath, one critic wrote, "If you are not set on fire and consumed by patriotic flames . . . you are not worthy of liberty."

During the Reign of Terror, he continued to produce images that inspired a patriotic fervor. He did a number of martyr portraits and sketched people on the way to the guillotine, including Marie Antoinette. He also orchestrated state funerals and elaborate festivals. As the Terror ended, David was jailed; upon his release, he swore to remain out of politics—a vow he would keep for only a short while. Then he met Napoleon at a dinner in 1797, and offered to paint his portrait. Soon thereafter, Napoleon named him First Painter.

Art of Revolution

Objectives
■ Understand that historical events may be depicted in works of art.
■ Explain how viewpoints on the French Revolution were conveyed through art.

Build Background Knowledge L3
Ask students to recall an image or painting of a historical event they may have seen in a museum or history book. Ask students if they were able to tell what point of view the artist wanted to convey about the event from looking at the painting. Then have students look at the paintings on this page without reading the accompanying text and predict what they reflect about each artist's viewpoint.

Instruct L3
■ Have students study David's and Goya's paintings on this page, read the text, and confirm their predictions. Ask **How might you be able to tell which painting conveys approval of revolution and which does not?** *(Sample: The first painting shows Napoleon as strong and powerful, thereby embracing the revolutionary spirit. The second painting shows people being gunned down by Napoleon's soldiers, bleeding, and dying, thereby criticizing the revolution and its horrors.)*

■ Ask students to list ways that art can encourage nationalism. *(Sample: inspire pride, emotion)*

Monitor Progress
Have students write one paragraph summarizing how David's and Goya's backgrounds affected their art.

Thinking Critically
1. In the David painting, Napoleon, placed in the center of a canvas painted with vibrant colors, looks strong and powerful. In the Goya painting, the dark colors and blood evoke the fearsome brutality of French soldiers. Bright colors glorify Napoleon and the dark shadows show a sense of doom.
2. Initially, the ideology aimed to secure more rights and better opportunities for French citizens, but, as this scene shows, French defense of the revolution turned into a war against other nations that often disregarded other people's rights.

Objectives

As you teach this section, keep students focused on the following objectives to help them answer the Section Focus Question and master core content.

■ Understand Napoleon's rise to power and why the French strongly supported him.

■ Explain how Napoleon built an empire and what challenges the empire faced.

■ Analyze the events that led to Napoleon's downfall.

■ Outline how the Congress of Vienna tried to create a lasting peace.

Build Background Knowledge L3

Remind students that, in 1799, Napoleon was a popular military leader. Ask them to predict how his military background might influence France and Europe.

Set a Purpose L3

■ **WITNESS HISTORY** Read the selection aloud or play the audio.

🔊 AUDIO **Witness History Audio CD,** Enter Napoleon Bonaparte

Ask **How does Napoleon's statement after his victory at Lodi, Italy, reflect his ambition?** *(Napoleon felt he was only just beginning.)*

■ **Focus** Point out the Section Focus Question and write it on the board. Tell students to refer to this question as they read. *(Answer appears with Section 4 Assessment answers.)*

■ **Preview** Have students preview the Section Objectives and the list of Terms, People, and Places.

■ **Note Taking** Have students read this section using the Structured Read Aloud strategy (TE, p. T20). As they read, have students fill in the flowchart showing events that led to Napoleon's rise to power and to his defeat.

📖 **Reading and Note Taking Study Guide,** p. 87

Unfinished portrait of Napoleon by Jacques-Louis David and Napoleon's signature

Enter Napoleon Bonaparte

After the execution of King Louis XVI, France entered a state of confusion and chaos without a single leader. Meanwhile, Napoleon Bonaparte, a brilliant and ambitious captain in the French army, was rapidly rising in the military ranks. Soon enough, Napoleon would come to rule almost all of Europe. One of his earliest victories in Lodi, Italy, convinced him that he was only just beginning his successful rise to power:

❝ From that moment, I foresaw what I might be. Already I felt the earth flee from beneath me, as if I were being carried into the sky.**❞**
—Napoleon Bonaparte

Focus Question Explain Napoleon's rise to power in Europe, his subsequent defeat, and how the outcome still affects Europe today.

The Age of Napoleon

Objectives
• Understand Napoleon's rise to power and why the French strongly supported him.
• Explain how Napoleon built an empire and what challenges the empire faced.
• Analyze the events that led to Napoleon's downfall.
• Outline how the Congress of Vienna tried to create a lasting peace.

Terms, People, and Places

plebiscite	scorched-earth policy
Napoleonic Code	abdicate
annex	Congress of Vienna
Continental System	legitimacy
guerrilla warfare	Concert of Europe

Note Taking

Reading Skill: Identify Main Ideas As you read the section, use a flowchart to list the important events that led from Napoleon's rise to power to his defeat. Add boxes as you need them.

Napoleon quickly advances through military ranks.

↓   ↓   ↓

From 1799 to 1815, Napoleon Bonaparte would dominate France and Europe. A hero to some, an evil force to others, he gave his name to the final phase of the revolution—the Age of Napoleon.

Napoleon Rises to Power

Napoleon was born in Corsica, a French-ruled island in the Mediterranean. At age nine, he was sent to France to be trained for a military career. When the revolution broke out, he was an ambitious 20-year-old lieutenant, eager to make a name for himself.

Napoleon favored the Jacobins and republican rule. However, he found the conflicting ideas and personalities of the French Revolution confusing. He wrote to his brother in 1793: "Since one must take sides, one might as well choose the side that is victorious, the side which devastates, loots, and burns. Considering the alternative, it is better to eat than be eaten."

Victories Cloud Losses During the turmoil of the revolution, Napoleon rose quickly in the army. In December 1793, he drove British forces out of the French port of Toulon (too LOHN). He then went on to win several dazzling victories against the Austrians, capturing most of northern Italy and forcing the Hapsburg emperor to make peace. Hoping to disrupt British trade with India, he led an expedition to Egypt in 1798. The Egyptian campaign proved to be a disaster, but Napoleon managed to hide stories of the worst losses from his admirers in France. He did so by establishing a network of spies and censoring the press.

Vocabulary Builder

Use the information below and the following resources to teach the high-use word from this section.
All in One **Teaching Resources, Unit 2,** p. 25; **Teaching Resources, Skills Handbook,** p. 3

High-Use Word	Definition and Sample Sentence
anticipate, p. 232	*vt.* to foresee or expect Jon didn't **anticipate** rain, so he left his umbrella at home.

Success fueled Napoleon's ambition. By 1799, he moved from victorious general to political leader. That year, he helped overthrow the weak Directory and set up a three-man governing board known as the Consulate. Another constitution was drawn up, but Napoleon soon took the title First Consul. In 1800, he forced Spain to return Louisiana Territory to France. In 1802, Napoleon had himself named consul for life.

Napoleon Crowns Himself Emperor Two years later, Napoleon had acquired enough power to assume the title Emperor of the French. He invited the pope to preside over his coronation in Paris. During the ceremony, however, Napoleon took the crown from the pope's hands and placed it on his own head. By this action, Napoleon meant to show that he owed his throne to no one but himself.

At each step on his rise to power, Napoleon had held a plebiscite (PLEB uh syt), or popular vote by ballot. Each time, the French strongly supported him. As you will read, although the people theoretically had a say in government through their votes, Napoleon still held absolute power. This is sometimes called democratic despotism. To understand why people supported him, we must look at his policies.

✔ **Checkpoint** How did Napoleon rise to power so quickly in France?

Napoleon Reforms France

Napoleon consolidated his power by strengthening the central government. Order, security, and efficiency replaced liberty, equality, and fraternity as the slogans of the new regime.

To restore economic prosperity, Napoleon controlled prices, encouraged new industry, and built roads and canals. He set up a system of public schools under strict government control to ensure well-trained officials and military officers. At the same time, Napoleon backed off from some of the revolution's social reforms. He made peace with the Catholic Church in the Concordat of 1801. The Concordat kept the Church under state control but recognized religious freedom for Catholics. Revolutionaries who opposed the Church denounced the agreement, but Catholics welcomed it.

Napoleon won support across class lines. He encouraged émigrés to return, provided they take an oath of loyalty. Peasants were relieved when he recognized their right to lands they had bought from the Church and nobles during the revolution. The middle class, who had benefited most from the revolution, approved of Napoleon's economic reforms and the restoration of order after years of chaos. Napoleon also opened jobs to all, based on talent, a popular policy among those who remembered the old aristocratic monopoly of power.

Among Napoleon's most lasting reforms was a new code of laws, popularly called the **Napoleonic Code.** It embodied Enlightenment principles such as the equality of all citizens before the law, religious toleration, and the abolition of feudalism.

The Egyptian Campaign
The Battle of the Pyramids, July 21, 1798, painted by Louis-Francois Lejeune. *How did Napoleon hide the fact that the Egyptian campaign was a disaster?*

Napoleon Rises to Power/ Napoleon Reforms France L3

Instruct

■ **Introduce: Key Terms** Ask students to find the key term *Napoleonic Code* (in blue) in the text and explain its meaning. Point out that previous proclamations and laws in France, America, and England were not referred to by the name of any particular leader (the Declaration of the Rights of Man and the Citizen). Have students predict what having Napoleon's name attached to the Napoleonic Code might indicate about its laws.

■ **Teach** Discuss Napoleon's rise to power and the reforms he enacted. Ask **What do you think was the main reason Napoleon was able to gain absolute power in France?** *(Sample: He had the support of the French people.)* **Why do you think Napoleon was so popular?** *(Sample: He was popular with all classes; he took charge when people longed for order.)*

■ **Quick Activity** Display **Color Transparency 108:** *Bonaparte Crossing the Alps at the Grand-Saint-Bernard,* **by Jacques Louis David.** Point out the names carved in the rocks under the horse's back hoofs and discuss why the artist joined Napoleon's name to those of Hannibal and Charlemagne.
🏛 Color Transparencies, 108

Independent Practice

Viewpoints To help students understand others' views of Napoleon, have them read the selection *Two Views of Napoleon* and complete the worksheet.
All in One Teaching Resources, Unit 2, p. 28

Monitor Progress

As students fill in their flowcharts, circulate to make sure they understand the events that led to Napoleon's rise to power. For a completed version of the flowchart, see
🏛 Note Taking Transparencies, 78

Answers

✔ He was very ambitious, and his military successes helped him gain power.

Caption through censorship and a network of spies

Napoleon Builds an Empire

Instruct

- **Introduce: Vocabulary Builder**
  Have students read the Vocabulary Builder term and definition. Ask students what effect not being able to *anticipate* an enemy's actions might have during a time of war.

- **Teach** Trace Napoleon's various moves to acquire power. Ask **How did Napoleon use "forceful diplomacy" to gain power?** *(He put relatives and friends on some European thrones and forced other countries to sign treaties with France.)* **How did geography both help and hurt Britain during its war with France?** *(With the English Channel separating it from the rest of Europe, it was more difficult to attack. However, the Channel hurt Britain because a complete naval blockade could prevent any shipping to or from other countries.)*

- **Analyzing the Visuals** Have students look at the map on the next page, titled Napoleon's Power in Europe, 1812, and help them use the key to interpret it. Ask students to describe Napoleon's influence in different areas and to identify places where he did not hold power.

Vocabulary Builder

anticipate—(an TIS uh payt) *vt.* to foresee or expect

But the Napoleonic Code undid some reforms of the French Revolution. Women, for example, lost most of their newly gained rights and could not exercise the rights of citizenship. Male heads of households regained complete authority over their wives and children. Again, Napoleon valued order and authority over individual rights.

 Checkpoint What reforms did Napoleon introduce during his rise to power?

Napoleon Builds an Empire

From 1804 to 1812, Napoleon furthered his reputation on the battlefield. He successfully battled the combined forces of the greatest European powers. He took great risks and even suffered huge losses. "I grew up on the field of battle," he once said, "and a man such as I am cares little for the life of a million men." By 1812, his Grand Empire reached its greatest extent.

As a military leader, Napoleon valued rapid movements and made effective use of his large armies. He developed a new plan for each battle so opposing generals could never <u>anticipate</u> what he would do next. His enemies paid tribute to his leadership. Napoleon's presence on the battlefield, said one, was "worth 40,000 troops."

The Map of Europe Is Redrawn As Napoleon created a vast French empire, he redrew the map of Europe. He **annexed,** or incorporated into his empire, the Netherlands, Belgium, and parts of Italy and Germany. He also abolished the tottering Holy Roman Empire and created a 38-member Confederation of the Rhine under French protection. He cut Prussian territory in half, turning part of old Poland into the Grand Duchy of Warsaw.

Napoleon controlled much of Europe through forceful diplomacy. One tactic was placing friends and relatives on the thrones of Europe. For example, after unseating the king of Spain, he placed his own brother, Joseph Bonaparte, on the throne. He also forced alliances on European powers from Madrid to Moscow. At various times, the rulers of Austria, Prussia, and Russia reluctantly signed treaties with the "Corsican ogre," as the monarchs he overthrew called him.

In France, Napoleon's successes boosted the spirit of nationalism. Great victory parades filled the streets of Paris with cheering crowds. The people celebrated the glory and grandeur that Napoleon had gained for France.

Napoleon Strikes Britain Britain alone, of all the major European powers, remained outside Napoleon's European empire. With only a small army, Britain relied on its sea power to stop Napoleon's drive to rule the continent. In 1805, Napoleon prepared to invade England. But at the Battle of Trafalgar, fought off the southwest coast of Spain, British Admiral Horatio Nelson smashed the French fleet.

With an invasion ruled out, Napoleon struck at Britain's lifeblood, its commerce. He waged economic warfare through the **Continental System,** which closed European ports to British goods. Britain responded with its own blockade of European ports. A blockade involves shutting off ports to keep people or supplies from moving in or out. During their long struggle, both Britain and France seized neutral ships suspected of trading with the other side. British attacks on American ships sparked anger in the United States and eventually triggered the War of 1812.

History Background

A Double Victory At the Battle of Austerlitz, in 1805, Napoleon won not only on the field of battle. After his victory, Napoleon made a grand gesture that won him the loyalty and adoration of the masses. He announced in a public speech that he would adopt the children of all the French soldiers killed in the battle—a number that was in the thousands. To fulfill his promise, he ordered the state to pay for the children's support and education, to arrange marriages for the girls, and to find jobs for the boys. One final provision was perhaps the most cherished—he permitted "his children" to add the name Napoleon to theirs.

Answer

 He enacted reforms to improve the economy, established a public school system, and introduced the Napoleonic Code.

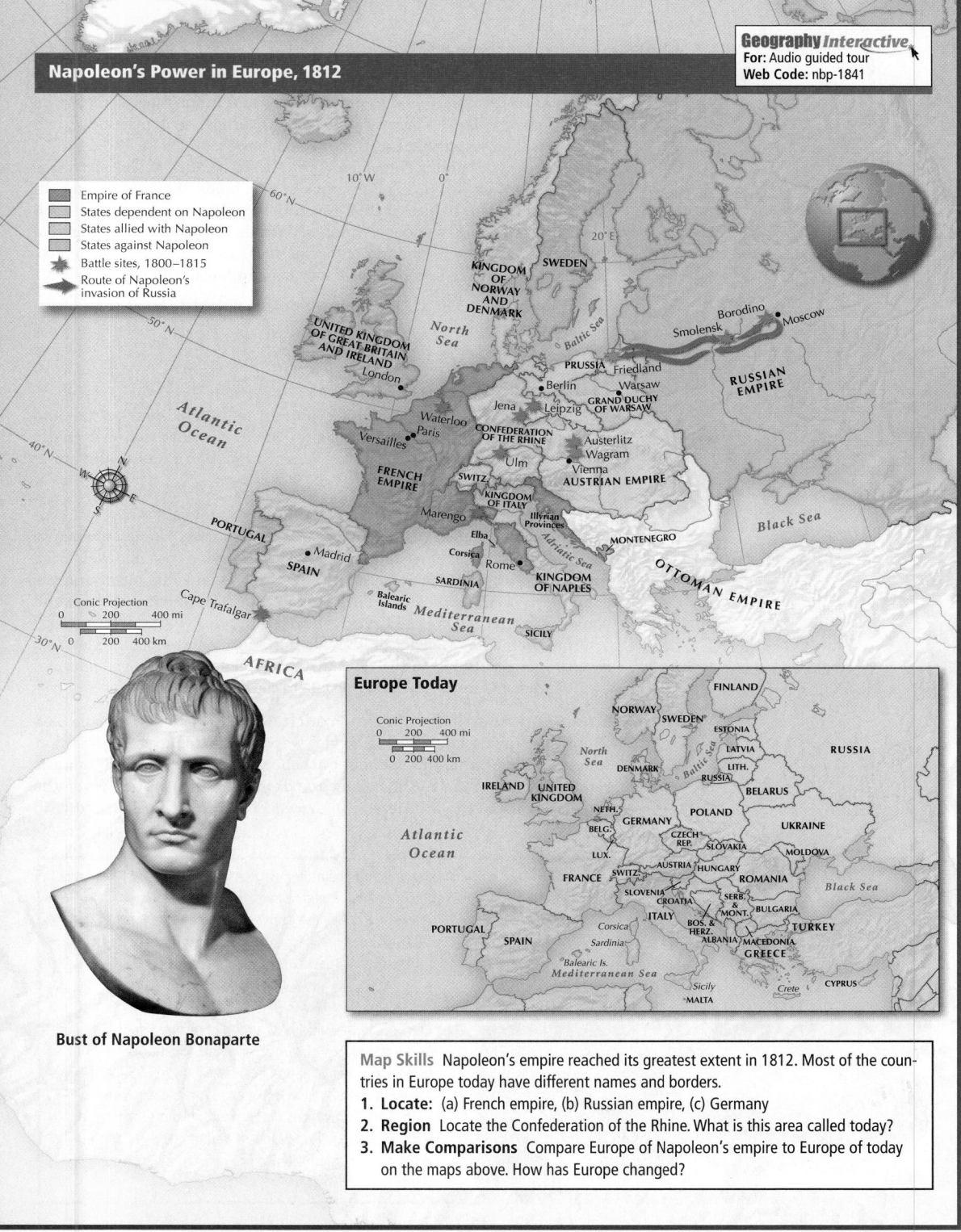

Napoleon's Power in Europe, 1812

Geography *Interactive*
For: Audio guided tour
Web Code: nbp-1841

Legend:
- Empire of France
- States dependent on Napoleon
- States allied with Napoleon
- States against Napoleon
- ★ Battle sites, 1800–1815
- ➤ Route of Napoleon's invasion of Russia

Conic Projection
0   200   400 mi
0   200   400 km

Bust of Napoleon Bonaparte

Europe Today

Conic Projection
0   200   400 mi
0   200   400 km

Map Skills Napoleon's empire reached its greatest extent in 1812. Most of the countries in Europe today have different names and borders.

1. **Locate:** (a) French empire, (b) Russian empire, (c) Germany
2. **Region** Locate the Confederation of the Rhine. What is this area called today?
3. **Make Comparisons** Compare Europe of Napoleon's empire to Europe of today on the maps above. How has Europe changed?

Independent Practice

Have students access **Web Code nbp-1841** to take the **Geography Interactive Audio Guided Tour** and then answer the map skills questions in the text.

Monitor Progress

- To check student understanding, have students define the key terms *annexed* and *Continental System* (in blue) and use each term in a sentence related to the Napoleonic Age.

- Check answers to Map Skills questions.

Differentiated Instruction   Solutions for All Learners

L2 Less Proficient Readers   **L2 English Language Learners**   **L1 Special Needs**

Direct students to look at the map, Napoleon's Power in Europe, 1812. Have students work in pairs to describe how Napoleon redrew the map of Europe. First, ask them to find the states that Napoleon had already added to his empire: the Netherlands, Belgium, and parts of Italy and Germany. Next, have them name the states allied with Napoleon and those

allied against him. Point out that Great Britain was the only major European power to remain outside the Napoleonic empire. Ask **What might be a geographic reason for this?** *(Sample: Sea power: enabled Britain's powerful navy to protect the country.)* Then ask students to discuss why Napoleon's military conquests would spread the ideas of revolution.

Answers

Map Skills

1. Review locations with students.
2. Germany
3. Smaller countries have replaced the Austrian and French Empires, the Confederation of the Rhine is now Germany, Italy has been united, and new countries have emerged in Eastern Europe.

Napoleon's Empire Faces Challenges

Instruct

- **Introduce: Key Terms** Have students find the key term ***guerrilla warfare*** (in blue) and explain its meaning. Ask them to name examples of other conflicts where guerrilla warfare has been used. Have them predict how guerrilla warfare might affect an advancing army.

- **Teach** Have students discuss the challenges Napoleon faced in Spain, Austria, and Russia. Ask **How did nationalism both help and harm Napoleon?** *(Nationalism helped Napoleon in France where it boosted morale and encouraged the army and the people to support him. In other countries, nationalism prompted people to oppose and fight against the rule of a foreign invader.)*

- **Quick Activity** Show students *Napoleon's Lost Army* from the **Witness History Discovery School**™ video program. Ask them how scientists are studying the remains of Napoleon's defeated army and what the researchers have found. *(By excavation in Lithuania, they discovered a mass grave of French soldiers, many of them between the ages of 20 and 25.)*

Independent Practice

Have students fill in the Outline Map *The Spread of Revolution* and label the places where Napoleon's army spread ideas of revolution.

All in One Teaching Resources, Unit 2, p. 33

Monitor Progress

Circulate to make sure students are filling in their Outline Maps accurately.

Answers

✔ He defeated European powers by moving large armies rapidly, taking risks, and being willing to suffer great losses. He annexed some lands and forced alliances on others. He put friends and family members on several European thrones.

PRIMARY SOURCE The French army was devastated. They were weak, gaunt, weaponless, and dressed in rags.

In the end, Napoleon's Continental System failed to bring Britain to its knees. Although British exports declined, Britain's powerful navy kept vital trade routes open to the Americas and India. Meanwhile, trade restrictions created a scarcity of goods in Europe, sent prices soaring, and intensified resentment against French power.

French armies under Napoleon spread ideas of the revolution across Europe. They backed liberal reforms in the lands they conquered. In some places, they helped install revolutionary governments that abolished titles of nobility, ended Church privileges, opened careers to men of talent, and ended serfdom and manorial dues. The Napoleonic Code, too, influenced countries in continental Europe and Latin America.

✔ **Checkpoint** How did Napoleon come to dominate most of Europe by 1812?

Napoleon's Empire Faces Challenges

In 1812, Napoleon continued his pursuit of world domination and invaded Russia. This campaign began a chain of events that eventually led to his downfall. Napoleon's final defeat brought an end to the era of the French Revolution.

Nationalism Works Against Napoleon Napoleon's successes contained seeds of defeat. Although nationalism spurred French armies to success, it worked against them too. Many Europeans who had welcomed the ideas of the French Revolution nevertheless saw Napoleon and his armies as foreign oppressors. They resented the Continental System and Napoleon's effort to impose French culture on them.

From Rome to Madrid to the Netherlands, nationalism unleashed revolts against France. In the German states, leaders encouraged national loyalty among German-speaking people to counter French influence.

Spain and Austria Battle the French Resistance to foreign rule bled French-occupying forces dry in Spain. Napoleon introduced reforms that sought to undermine the Spanish Catholic Church. But many Spaniards remained loyal to their former king and devoted to the Church. When the Spanish resisted the invaders, well-armed French forces responded with

As shown in this painting, the Russian winter took its toll on Napoleon's army. Philippe Paul de Ségur, an aide to Napoleon, describes the grim scene as the remnants of the Grand Army returned home. **What were the effects of this disaster in Russia?**

Primary Source

❝ In Napoleon's wake [was] a mob of tattered ghosts draped in . . . odd pieces of carpet, or greatcoats burned full of holes, their feet wrapped in all sorts of rags. . . . [We] stared in horror as those skeletons of soldiers went by, their gaunt, gray faces covered with disfiguring beards, without weapons . . . with lowered heads, eyes on the ground, in absolute silence. ❞
—*Memoirs of Philippe Paul de Ségur*

History Background

Napoleon's Retreat from Russia In June 1812, Napoleon eagerly took on the challenge of conquering Russia, calling it "my greatest and most difficult enterprise." A few months later, he would see things differently. After a disheartening battle outside Moscow, Napoleon hurried back to Paris to squelch rumors that he had been killed, leaving his shrinking army to retreat after him in the brutal Russian winter.

French troops experienced temperatures as low as −40°F. In their desperation to find shelter in the blinding snow, soldiers resorted to building huts using the frozen corpses of their fallen comrades, stacking them like logs to create walls. In June, Napoleon had crossed into Russia with more than 400,000 troops. By December, there were only 10,000 soldiers left.

brutal repression. Far from crushing resistance, however, the French response further inflamed Spanish nationalism. Efforts to drive out the French intensified.

Spanish patriots conducted a campaign of guerrilla warfare, or hit-and-run raids, against the French. (In Spanish, *guerrilla* means "little war.") Small bands of guerrillas ambushed French supply trains or troops before retreating into the countryside. These attacks kept large numbers of French soldiers tied down in Spain when Napoleon needed them elsewhere.

Spanish resistance encouraged Austria to resume hostilities against the French. In 1805, at the Battle of Austerlitz, Napoleon had won a crushing victory against an Austro-Russian army of superior numbers. Now, in 1809, the Austrians sought revenge. But once again, Napoleon triumphed—this time at the Battle of Wagram. By the peace agreement that followed, Austria surrendered lands populated by more than three million subjects.

The Russian Winter Stops the Grand Army Tsar Alexander I of Russia was once an ally of Napoleon. The tsar and Napoleon planned to divide Europe if Alexander helped Napoleon in his Continental System. Many countries objected to this system, and Russia became unhappy with the economic effects of the system as well. Yet another cause for concern was that Napoleon had enlarged the Grand Duchy of Warsaw that bordered Russia on the west. These and other issues led the tsar to withdraw his support from the Continental System. Napoleon responded to the tsar's action by assembling an army with soldiers from 20 nations, known as the Grand Army.

In 1812, with about 600,000 soldiers and 50,000 horses, Napoleon invaded Russia. To avoid battles with Napoleon, the Russians retreated eastward, burning crops and villages as they went. This scorched-earth policy left the French hungry and cold as winter came. Napoleon entered Moscow in September. He realized, though, that he would not be able to feed and supply his army through the long Russian winter. In October, he turned homeward.

The 1,000-mile retreat from Moscow turned into a desperate battle for survival. Russian attacks and the brutal Russian winter took a terrible toll. Fewer than 20,000 soldiers of the once-proud Grand Army survived. Many died. Others deserted. French general Michel Ney sadly concluded: "General Famine and General Winter, rather than Russian bullets, have conquered the Grand Army." Napoleon rushed to Paris to raise a new force to defend France. His reputation for success had been shattered.

 **Checkpoint** What challenges threatened Napoleon's empire and what led to the disaster in Russia?

Napoleon Falls From Power
A defeated Napoleon after his abdication on April 6, 1814, in a painting by Paul Delaroche

WITNESS HISTORY VIDEO

Watch *Napoleon's Lost Army* on the **Witness History Discovery School**™ video program to learn about Napoleon's invasion of Russia in 1812.

DISCOVERY SCHOOL'

Napoleon Falls From Power

Instruct

- **Introduce: Key Terms** Have students find the key term **abdicated** (in blue) and explain its meaning. Ask **Is a ruler who abdicates a position victorious or defeated?** *(defeated)*

- **Teach** Have students describe the events that led to Napoleon's ultimate fall from power. Ask **Do you think Napoleon was "the revolution on horseback" or a traitor to the revolution? Explain.** *(Students should give reasons for their opinions.)*

- **Quick Activity** Display **Color Transparency 111: The *Two Kings of Terror*.** Use the lesson suggested in the transparency book to guide a discussion on criticisms of Napoleon.
  🏛 **Color Transparencies,** 111

Independent Practice

Have students fill in the Outline Map *The French Revolution and Napoleon* and label key places related to the French Revolution and Napoleon.

All in One Teaching Resources, Unit 2, p. 32

Monitor Progress

- Circulate to make sure students are filling in their Outline Maps accurately.

- Administer the Geography Quiz.

All in One Teaching Resources, Unit 2, p. 34

Link to Humanities

1812 Overture Russian composer Pyotr Ilyich Tchaikovsky wrote his *1812 Overture* as a musical depiction of Napoleon's retreat from Moscow. It is a very dramatic piece that concludes with a round of cannon fire. Tchaikovsky used "La Marseillaise," the French national anthem, to symbolize the French. An orthodox chant, a folksong, and "God Save the Tsar" represent the Russians. If possible, obtain a recording of the *1812 Overture* to play for students. (Recordings of the overture are available in many libraries.) Have students discuss the different musical parts of the overture, and how each part might represent a different stage of the French army's Russian campaign. Ask them how they think Tchaikovsky's feelings about Napoleon's retreat may have been reflected in this musical composition.

Answer

✓ nationalism in individual European states, guerrilla warfare in Spain, Austria seeking revenge, and the devastating Russian winter

Leaders Meet at the Congress of Vienna

Instruct

- **Introduce: Key Terms** Ask students to find the key term *legitimacy* (in blue) and explain its meaning. Point out that the leaders at the Congress of Vienna wanted to restore their power and so brought back the previous rulers, the "legitimate" monarchs.

- **Teach** Have students name some accomplishments of the Congress of Vienna and list them on the board. Ask **Who was a part of the Quadruple Alliance, and what was its purpose?** *(Austria, Russia, Prussia, and Great Britain; its purpose was to protect the new order created by the Congress of Vienna by maintaining a balance of power and suppressing any uprisings)* **Do you think restoring the monarchy in France will help create a lasting peace in Europe? Why or why not?** *(Sample: No, because citizens who have experienced life without a social hierarchy during the French Revolution probably will not want to go back to having a king and royal family.)*

- **Quick Activity** Display **Color Transparency 112: Europe After the Congress of Vienna.** Use the lesson suggested in the transparency book to guide a discussion on the ways that the Congress of Vienna changed Europe.

  📖 **Color Transparencies,** 112

Answer

BIOGRAPHY Sample: He wanted whatever was in the best interests of Austria.

Napoleon Falls From Power

The disaster in Russia brought a new alliance of Russia, Britain, Austria, and Prussia against a weakened France. In 1813, they defeated Napoleon in the Battle of the Nations at Leipzig.

Napoleon Abdicates Briefly The next year, Napoleon **abdicated**, or stepped down from power. The victors exiled him to Elba, an island in the Mediterranean. They then recognized Louis XVIII, brother of Louis XVI, as king of France.

The restoration of Louis XVIII did not go smoothly. He agreed to accept the Napoleonic Code and honor the land settlements made during the revolution. However, many émigrés rushed back to France bent on revenge. An economic depression and the fear of a return to the old regime helped rekindle loyalty to Napoleon.

As the victorious allies gathered in Vienna for a general peace conference, Napoleon escaped his island exile and returned to France. Soldiers flocked to his banner. As citizens cheered Napoleon's advance, Louis XVIII fled. In March 1815, Napoleon entered Paris in triumph.

Crushed at the Battle of Waterloo Napoleon's triumph was short-lived. His star soared for only 100 days, while the allies reassembled their forces. On June 18, 1815, the opposing armies met near the town of Waterloo in Belgium. British forces under the Duke of Wellington and a Prussian army commanded by General Blücher crushed the French in an agonizing day-long battle. Once again, Napoleon was forced to abdicate and to go into exile on St. Helena, a lonely island in the South Atlantic. This time, he would not return.

Napoleon's Legacy Napoleon died in 1821, but his legend lived on in France and around the world. His contemporaries as well as historians today have long debated his legacy. Was he "the revolution on horseback," as he claimed? Or was he a traitor to the revolution?

No one, however, questions Napoleon's impact on France and on Europe. The Napoleonic Code consolidated many changes of the revolution. The France of Napoleon was a centralized state with a constitution. Elections were held with expanded, though limited, suffrage. Many more citizens had rights to property and access to education than under the old regime. Still, French citizens lost many rights promised so fervently by republicans during the Convention.

On the world stage, Napoleon's conquests spread the ideas of the revolution. He failed to make Europe into a French empire. Instead, he sparked nationalist feelings across Europe. The abolition of the Holy Roman Empire would eventually help in creating a new Germany. Napoleon's impact also reached across the

🔵 BIOGRAPHY

Prince Clemens von Metternich

As Austria's foreign minister, Metternich (1773–1859) used a variety of means to achieve his goals. In 1809, when Napoleon seemed vulnerable, Metternich favored war against France. In 1810, after France had crushed Austria, he supported alliance with France. When the French army was in desperate retreat from Russia, Metternich became the "prime minister of the coalition" that defeated Napoleon. At the Congress of Vienna, Metternich helped create a new European order and made sure that Austria had a key role in it. He would skillfully defend that new order for more than 30 years. **Why did Metternich's policies toward France change?**

Connect to Our World

Connections to Today During the French Revolution, the French National Assembly enacted the metric system as the measure of all things. They replaced the confusing array of measurements with a standardized system based on multiples of ten. Although Napoleon did away with some of the revolution's reforms, he did keep the metric system and his military conquests helped spread it across Europe. The scientists who developed it adopted the motto, "for all people, for all time." Today, most nations around the world use this measurement system for mathematics, science, and daily life. Nevertheless, the people of the United States are reluctant to abandon their traditional system of measure, called the U.S. Customary System, and "go metric."

Europe After the Congress of Vienna, 1815

Geography Interactive
For: Audio guided tour
Web Code: nbp-1842

Map Skills At the Congress of Vienna, European leaders redrew the map of Europe in order to contain France and keep a balance of power.

1. **Locate** (a) German Confederation, (b) Netherlands, (c) Vienna
2. **Region** Name three states that were in the German Confederation.
3. **Recognize Cause and Effect** Why did the Congress enlarge some of the countries around France?

Atlantic. In 1803, his decision to sell France's vast Louisiana Territory to the American government doubled the size of the United States and ushered in an age of American expansion.

 **Checkpoint** How did Napoleon impact Europe and the rest of the world?

Leaders Meet at the Congress of Vienna

After Waterloo, diplomats and heads of state again sat down at the **Congress of Vienna.** They faced the monumental task of restoring stability and order in Europe after years of war. The Congress met for 10 months, from September 1814 to June 1815. It was a brilliant gathering of European leaders. Diplomats and royalty dined and danced, attended concerts and ballets, and enjoyed parties arranged by their host, Emperor Francis I of Austria. The work fell to Prince Clemens von Metternich of Austria, Tsar Alexander I of Russia, and Lord Robert Castlereagh of Britain. Defeated France was represented by Prince Charles Maurice de Talleyrand.

Differentiated Instruction Solutions for All Learners

L4 Advanced Readers   L4 Gifted and Talented Students

Have the class analyze the different interests behind the Congress of Vienna. To begin, divide the class into five groups, and assign each group to represent one country at the Congress of Vienna: Austria, Russia, Prussia, Britain, and France. Ask them to research (1) Napoleon's impact on the delegate's country, (2) the goals and interests of the country for the Congress, and (3) how the country would like to reorganize Europe. Have them hold a roundtable discussion on how to create a lasting peace, with one student from each group assuming the role of the delegate and the others in the group acting as advisors. After the discussion, have each student write a brief paper outlining the attempt to create a lasting peace.

Independent Practice

- Have students access **Web Code nbp-1842** to take the **Geography Interactive Audio Guided Tour** and then answer the map skills questions in the text.

- Ask students to create a chart of the causes and lasting effects of the French Revolution. For a completed version, see the Quick Study page. If students need more instruction on analyzing cause and effect, have them read the **Skills Handbook,** p. SH36.

Monitor Progress

- To review this section, ask students to explain how the Congress of Vienna was a reaction to Napoleon's actions after the French Revolution.

- Check Reading and Note Taking Study Guide entries for student understanding.

- Check answers to Map Skills questions.

Answers

Map Skills
1. Review locations with students.
2. Bavaria, Hanover, and Saxony
3. to help prevent French expansion

✔ He spread the ideas of nationalism across Europe and facilitated American expansion with the Louisiana Territory and abolished the Holy Roman Empire, which would help create a new Germany.

Assess and Reteach

Assess Progress

- Have students complete the Section Assessment.
- Administer the Section Quiz.

All in One Teaching Resources, Unit 2, p. 24

- To further assess student understanding, use
  Progress Monitoring Transparencies, 78

Reteach

If students need more instruction, have them read the section summary.

 Reading and Note Taking Study Guide, p. 88

 Adapted Reading and Note Taking Study Guide, p. 88

Spanish Reading and Note Taking Study Guide, p. 88

Extend

Have students research and write a paper on one of two topics: how Napoleon and the ideals of the French Revolution are still reflected in France today, or how Napoleon and the French Revolution inspired change in another country.

Answer

 Goal: to create a lasting peace in Europe by establishing a balance of power and protecting the monarchy system; Outcome: a balance of power that lasted for the next 100 years but failed to anticipate new forces such as nationalism

Portrait of Louis XVIII

Congress Strives For Peace The chief goal of the Vienna decision makers was to create a lasting peace by establishing a balance of power and protecting the system of monarchy. Each of the leaders also pursued his own goals. Metternich, the dominant figure at the Congress, wanted to restore things the way they were in 1792. Alexander I urged a "holy alliance" of Christian monarchs to suppress future revolutions. Lord Castlereagh was determined to prevent a revival of French military power. The aged diplomat Talleyrand shrewdly played the other leaders against one another so France would be accepted as an equal partner.

The peacemakers also redrew the map of Europe. To contain French ambitions, they ringed France with strong countries. In the north, they added Belgium and Luxembourg to Holland to create the kingdom of the Netherlands. To prevent French expansion eastward, they gave Prussia lands along the Rhine River. They also allowed Austria to reassert control over northern Italy.

To turn back the clock to 1792, the architects of the peace promoted the principle of **legitimacy,** restoring hereditary monarchies that the French Revolution or Napoleon had unseated. Even before the Congress began, they had put Louis XVIII on the French throne. Later, they restored "legitimate" monarchs in Portugal, Spain, and the Italian states.

Congress Fails to See Traps Ahead To protect the new order, Austria, Russia, Prussia, and Great Britain extended their wartime alliance into the postwar era. In the Quadruple Alliance, the four nations pledged to act together to maintain the balance of power and to suppress revolutionary uprisings, especially in France. Another result of the Congress was a system known as the **Concert of Europe,** in which the powers met periodically to discuss any problems affecting the peace of Europe.

The Vienna statesmen achieved their immediate goals in creating a lasting peace. Their decisions influenced European politics for the next 100 years. Europe would not see war on a Napoleonic scale until 1914. They failed, however, to foresee how powerful new forces such as nationalism would shake the foundations of Europe and Latin America in the next decades.

 Checkpoint Explain the chief goal and outcome of the Congress of Vienna.

SECTION 4 Assessment

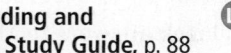

Progress Monitoring Online
For: Self-quiz with vocabulary practice
Web Code: nba-1841

Terms, People, and Places
1. For each term, person, or place listed at the beginning of the section, write a sentence explaining its significance.

Note Taking
2. **Reading Skill: Identify Main Ideas** Use your completed flowchart to answer the Focus Question: Explain Napoleon's rise to power in Europe, his subsequent defeat, and how the outcome still affects Europe today.

Comprehension and Critical Thinking
3. **Demonstrate Reasoned Judgment** If you were a French voter in 1803, how would you have voted on the plebiscite to make Napoleon emperor? Explain.
4. **Synthesize Information** Describe the resistance Napoleon encountered as countries grew to resent him.
5. **Make Comparisons** How does the peacekeeping solution adopted by the Congress of Vienna compare to today's peacekeeping missions?

● Writing About History
Quick Write: Clarify When you write a rough draft of a cause-and-effect essay, you should highlight the causes and effects. Use two highlighters, one to show causes, and the other to show effects. Eliminate causes or effects that do not support your main point, and add transitional phrases as needed. Write a paragraph about Napoleon's downfall. Highlight the causes and effects to evaluate the effectiveness of your paragraph.

Section 4 Assessment

1. Sentences should reflect an understanding of each term, person, or place listed at the beginning of the section.
2. Responses should show an understanding of the events from Napoleon's rise to his defeat as well as his legacy in Europe.
3. Responses should demonstrate an understanding of Napoleon's policies and France's instability.

4. The resistance was fueled by renewed nationalism in places such as Germany and the Netherlands. Countries fought the French army with tactics such as guerrilla warfare in Spain and the scorched-earth policy in Russia.
5. Answers may compare peacekeeping solutions from the Congress of Vienna to peacekeeping efforts of the UN or temporary alliances such as the coalition that defeated Iraq in the Persian Gulf War.

● Writing About History
Paragraphs should show an understanding of the causes and effects of Napoleon's downfall. The causes and effects should be highlighted.

For additional assessment, have students access **Progress Monitoring Online** at **Web Code nba-1841.**

IMPACT OF THE INDIVIDUAL

How can an individual change the world?

In This Chapter

Some people have such an effect on history that historians name entire eras after them. During the Napoleonic Era, Napoleon Bonaparte's conquests changed the map of Europe. At the same time, his decision to sell the Louisiana Territory to the United States forever altered the course of American history.

Throughout History

1700s B.C. Hammurabi sets up the first known code of laws.

500–400s B.C. The teachings of Confucius shape Chinese values.

1400s A.D. Brunelleschi revolutionizes art by finding a way to show perspective.

1517 Luther posts the 95 Theses and ignites the Protestant Reformation.

1558 Elizabeth I of England calms religious turmoil and expands international power.

1920s–1940s Gandhi urges nonviolent protest to win Indian independence from Britain.

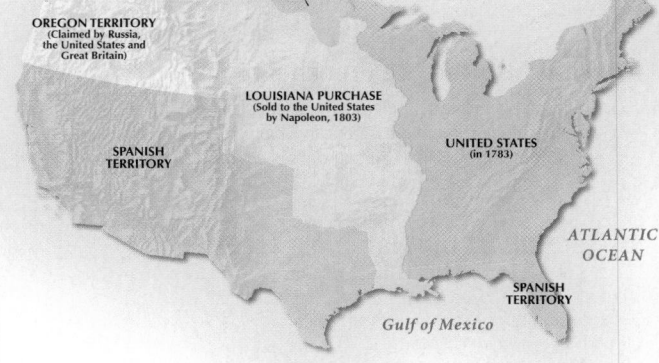

The Louisiana Purchase

Continuing Today

No one knows whose contributions will have the most impact in the years to come. Will it be a political leader? A person of great moral integrity? Or a brilliant scientist? Could it be you?

21st Century Skills

 TRANSFER Activities

1. **Analyze** How have individual people made lasting impacts on history?

2. **Evaluate** How could the small contributions of many individuals have as big an impact as the major contribution of one? Give an example.

3. **Transfer** Complete a Web quest in which you evaluate the impact of an individual; record your thoughts in the Concept Connector Journal; and learn to make a video. Web Code nbh-1808

History Background

Geography and the Battle of Waterloo To this day Waterloo symbolizes utter defeat. But on the morning of the battle, Napoleon felt certain of victory. "This whole affair will not be more serious than swallowing one's breakfast," he said.

But both weather and terrain conspired against him. First, he held off his attack until the rain-soaked ground could dry. (Cannonballs just stick in mud; they can do more damage bouncing along dry ground.) These lost hours gave the enemy time to move in more troops. Second, Napoleon ordered a frontal attack against an enemy positioned on an upward slope. The crest of its ridge helped shield the opposition from French artillery barrages. At Waterloo, more than 20,000 French soldiers died, and Napoleon suffered his final defeat.

Concept Connector

Impact of the Individual

Objectives

- Identify individuals who have made an impact on history.
- Understand that the contributions of one person can change the course of history.
- Complete a Web Quest on the impact of the individual.

Build Background Knowledge Ⓛ3

Have students volunteer the names of individuals whom they think have affected the flow of history and describe the nature of each person's influence.

Instruct Ⓛ3

- Direct students' attention to the Essential Question: **How can an individual change the world?** Have them read In This Chapter and look at the corresponding image. Ask volunteers to imagine how the world might be different if Napoleon had not sold the Louisiana Territory.

- Ask student to look at the time line and generalize about what qualities or opportunities a person needs in order to have a great impact. Ask: **Who today may have those qualities or that opportunity?**

- Assign the Web Quest on the impact of the individual.

Independent Practice

Concept Connector Have students fill in the reflection question on the Web Quest on the impact of the individual in their Concept Connector Journal.

 Reading and Note Taking Study Guide, p. 280

Monitor Progress

Circulate to make sure that students are filling in their Concept Connector journal. Have a class discussion about the effect an individual can have in your community.

Transfer Activities

1. Individuals have used political power or moral leadership to influence others.
2. When people gather together to support a cause, the weight of all their influence can change the world. Possible examples: voters, Peace Corps volunteers
3. Students' work should be evaluated against the rubric at Web Code nbh-1808.

Quick Study Guide

- Have students use the Quick Study Guide to prepare for this chapter's test. Students may wish to refer to the following pages as they review:

What Inspired the French Revolution?
Section 1, pp. 210–213

Causes and Effects of the French Revolution
Section 1, pp. 210–215; Section 2, pp. 217–222; Section 3, pp. 223–227; Section 4, pp. 230–238

Reforms of the National Assembly
Section 2, pp. 217–220

Key Events from 1789–1815
Section 1, pp. 215; Section 3, pp. 224–225; Section 4, pp. 231, 234–238

- For additional review, remind students to refer to the **L3**

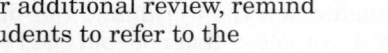
Reading and Note Taking Study Guide

Note Taking Study Guide, pp. 80, 82–83, 85, 87
Section Summaries, pp. 81, 84, 86, 88

- Have students access **Web Code nbp-1801** for this chapter's **History Interactive** timeline, which includes expanded entries and additional events.

- If students need more instruction on analyzing timelines, have them read the **Skills Handbook,** p. SH30.

- When students have completed their study of the chapter, distribute Chapter Tests A and B.

All in One Teaching Resources, Unit 2, pp. 35–40

For **Progress Monitoring Online,** refer students to the Self-test with vocabulary practice at **Web Code nba-1851.**

Quick Study Guide

Progress Monitoring Online
For: Self-test with vocabulary practice
Web Code: nba-1851

What Inspired the French Revolution?

- **Social:** Enlightenment ideas such as equality and justice
- **Political:** Ideas from the American Revolution
- **Economic:** Inequalities among classes; unrest due to extravagant monarchy

Reforms of the National Assembly

Political
• Proclaimed all male citizens equal before the law.
• Limited the power of the monarchy.
• Established the Legislative Assembly to make laws.
• Granted all tax-paying male citizens the right to elect members of the Legislative Assembly.

Social and Economic
• Abolished special privileges of the nobility.
• Announced an end to feudalism.
• Called for taxes to be levied according to ability to pay.
• Abolished guilds and forbade labor unions.
• Compensated nobles for lands seized by peasants.

Religious
• Declared freedom of religion.
• Took over and sold Church lands.
• Placed the French Catholic Church under control of the state.
• Provided that bishops and priests be elected and receive government salaries.

Causes and Effects of the French Revolution

Cause and Effect	
Long-Term Causes	**Immediate Causes**
• Corrupt and inconsistent leadership	• Huge government debt
• Prosperous members of Third Estate resent privileges of First and Second Estates.	• Poor harvests and rising price of bread
	• Failure of Louis XVI to accept financial reforms
• Spread of Enlightenment ideas	• Formation of National Assembly
	• Storming of Bastille

The French Revolution

Immediate Effects	Long-Term Effects
• Declaration of the Rights of Man and the Citizen adopted.	• Napoleon gains power.
	• Napoleonic Code established.
• France adopts its first written constitution.	• French public schools set up.
• Revolutionary France fights coalition of European powers.	• French conquests spread nationalism.
• Monarchy abolished; execution of king and queen.	• Congress of Vienna convenes to restore stability to Europe.
• Reign of Terror	• Revolutions occur elsewhere in Europe and in Latin America.

Connections to Today
• French law reflects Napoleonic Code.
• France eventually became a democratic republic.

Key Events From 1789–1815

Chapter Events
Global Events

1789 Parisians storm the Bastille on July 14, starting the French Revolution.	1793 Radicals execute the king and queen, which leads to the Reign of Terror.	1799 Napoleon overthrows the Directory.
1790	**1795**	**1800**
1789 The United States Constitution is ratified.	1793 China rejects British trade offer.	

L1 Special Needs   **L2 Less Proficient Readers**

For students acquiring basic skills:

Adapted Reading and Note Taking Study Guide
Adapted Note Taking Study Guide, pp. 80, 82–83, 85, 87
Adapted Section Summaries, pp. 81, 84, 86, 88

L2 English Language Learners

For Spanish-speaking students:

Spanish Reading and Note Taking Study Guide
Spanish Note Taking Study Guide, pp. 80, 82–83, 85, 87
Spanish Section Summaries, pp. 81, 84, 86, 88

Concept Connector

 Essential Question Review

To connect prior knowledge with what you have learned in this chapter, answer the questions below in your Concept Connector journal. Use the journal in the Reading and Note Taking Study Guide to record your answers (or go to www.phschool.com **Web Code:** nbd-1807). In addition, record information about the following concept:

• Cooperation: Coalitions against Napoleon

1. **Nationalism** During the French Revolution, the people were inspired to rally to the cause of freedom. How did the leaders of the revolution motivate the people? Consider the following.
   • songs
   • symbols
   • slogans

2. **Revolution** In 1524, German peasants rose up against the nobility in an effort to end serfdom. They hoped for but did not get the support of Martin Luther. The German nobility put down the rebellion and killed thousands of people. In the French Revolution, the Third Estate revolted against the Old Regime. Describe how the circumstances around the French Revolution were similar to and different from the Peasants' Revolt in Germany.

3. **Democracy** According to the text, "Napoleon's successes contained seeds of defeat." His conquests unleashed feelings of nationalism that led conquered countries to revolt against France. How did Napoleon strengthen democracy in France? How did he weaken democratic gains made during earlier phases of the Revolution? Focus on the following:
   • economic reforms
   • legal reforms
   • natural rights

■ Connections To Today

1. **Geography's Impact: Wars in the Middle East**
   Geography played an important role in Napoleon's defeat in Russia. Napoleon's Grand Army, once nearly 500,000 soldiers strong, shrank to about 20,000 due to the brutal Russian winter. Research newspaper and magazine articles to find how geography has impacted wars in the Middle East. Compile your research and write a script for your local newscast. Consider the following:
   • location
   • landforms
   • climate

   Burning oil pipeline, September 14, 2004, caused by sabotage in the Middle East

2. **Cooperation: United Nations** Diplomats and heads of states from the powers that defeated Napoleon—Austria, Russia, Prussia, and Great Britain—gathered at the Congress of Vienna in 1814. Their main goal was to restore peace after the French Revolution and Napoleonic era. Today, U.N. peacekeeping operations take place around the globe with the same goal of keeping or restoring peace. Research to find more information on the Congress of Vienna and U.N. peacekeeping operations. Draw a table to write facts about each in individual columns. Think about the following:
   • history and purpose of the organizations
   • definitions of "peacekeeping"

| 1804 Napoleon crowns himself emperor of France. | | 1812 Napoleon invades Russia. | 1814 Congress of Vienna meets. | 1815 Napoleon is defeated at Waterloo. |

1805 **1810** **1815**

| 1804 Haiti declares independence from France. | | 1812 The United States declares war on Britain. | |

History Interactive
For: Interactive timeline
Web Code: nbp-1801

Concept Connector

Tell students that the main concepts for this chapter are Democracy, Nationalism, Impact of the Individual, and Revolution, and then ask them to answer the Essential Question Review questions on this page. Discuss the Connections to Today topics and ask students to answer the questions that follow.

Essential Question Review

1. Students should go back to the chapter to find examples of songs, symbols, and slogans used in the French Revolution. These include the song *La Marseillaise*, the revolutionary drum, red "liberty caps," the title of "citizen," and "Citizen Capet."

2. In both revolutions, the poor revolted against the nobles over harsh conditions, violence, and tyranny. Unlike the Peasant Revolution, when the people received little support, the French Revolution had support from some aristocrats and clergy.

3. Napoleon strengthened French democracy through the Napoleonic Code and through numerous social and economic reforms. However, he undid some reforms of the French Revolution and strengthened the central government.

Connections to Today

1. Newscast scripts should depict how location and desert conditions impact war in the Middle East.

2. Tables should include accurate facts about the Congress of Vienna and UN peacekeeping operations.

For additional review of this chapter's core concepts, remind students to refer to the

Reading and Note Taking Study Guide
Concept Connector, pp. 242, 250, 284, 291

Chapter Assessment

Terms, People, and Places

1. Estates-General
2. deficit spending
3. nationalism
4. bourgeoisie
5. Olympe de Gouges
6. Maximilien Robespierre
7. plebiscite
8. sans-culotte
9. Napoleonic Code
10. abdicate

Main Ideas

11. Nobles got the best government positions; urban workers earned poor wages; peasants' taxes were high; nobles did not pay their fair share.

12. They declared themselves the National Assembly and took the Tennis Court Oath stating that they would meet until they established a constitution. They took this action because the other two estates rejected their idea to meet as a single body with votes to be counted by head, rather than by estate.

13. Sample: (a) declared that all men were equal and had natural rights (b) made bishops and priests elected and salaried officials (c) set up a limited monarchy and a new Legislative Assembly

14. a ruthless campaign against people suspected of being enemies of the revolution

15. controlled prices, encouraged new industry, promoted public schools and public works, instituted new law code

16. redrew national boundaries, surrounded France with strong countries, created Quadruple Alliance

Chapter Focus Question

17. Some causes of the French Revolution were social inequalities between the three estates, the spread of Enlightenment ideas, and economic problems such as huge government debt, rising bread prices, and the failure of Louis XVI to make financial reforms. The effects were the formation of the National Assembly, the storming of the Bastille, the adoption of the Declaration of Man and the Citizen, the abolition of the monarchy, and, eventually, the Reign of Terror. The chaos that ensued from the first ten years of the Revolution led the people

to support Napoleon, who stood for order, security, and efficiency.

Critical Thinking

18. They influenced people to believe that their natural rights and equality should be protected under the law; Enlightenment ideas were reflected in many of the laws created during the Revolution.

Chapter Assessment

Terms, People, and Places

Match the following terms with the definitions below.

sans-culotte	Olympe de Gouges
bourgeoisie	plebiscite
Napoleonic Code	deficit spending
abdicate	Maximilien Robespierre
Estates-General	nationalism

1. a meeting of the representatives of the three estates
2. situation in which a government spends more money than it takes in
3. strong feeling of devotion to one's country
4. the middle class
5. journalist who demanded equal rights for women
6. leader of the Committee of Public Safety
7. ballot in which voters have a direct say on an issue
8. working-class men and women in France; means "without breeches"
9. law code that embodied Enlightenment principles such as equality
10. step down from power

Main Ideas

Section 1 (pp. 210–215)

11. What caused discontent in the old French regime?
12. When the Estates-General convened in May 1789, what actions did members of the Third Estate take and why?

Section 2 (pp. 216–221)

13. Describe one reform that the National Assembly enacted through each of the following documents: **(a)** the Declaration of the Rights of Man and the Citizen, **(b)** the Civil Constitution of the Clergy, **(c)** the Constitution of 1791.

Section 3 (pp. 223–228)

14. What was the Reign of Terror?

Section 4 (pp. 230–238)

15. List the reforms that Napoleon made as leader of France.
16. How did the Congress of Vienna try to restore the balance of power in Europe?

Chapter Focus Question

17. What were the causes and effects of the French Revolution, and how did the revolution lead to the Napoleonic era?

Critical Thinking

18. **Draw Conclusions** What impact did Enlightenment ideas have on the French Revolution?
19. **Recognize Cause and Effect** Explain the events that led to the end of the monarchy.
20. **Geography and History** How did the geography of the Russian empire work against Napoleon's Grand Army?
21. **Analyzing Cartoons** In the cartoon shown here, the figure on the left represents the British, and the other figure represents Napoleon. What are the figures carving, and why?

● Writing About History

In this chapter's four Section Assessments, you developed skills for writing an expository essay.

Expository Essay: Cause and Effect There were many key events in the French Revolution and Napoleonic era that affected France and the rest of the world. Write an essay that explains the causes of one of the following events and discuss what resulted: Parisians storming the Bastille; Women marching on Versailles; Napoleon crowning himself emperor of the French. Consult page SH10 of the Writing Handbook for additional help.

Prewriting
• Consider what you know about these events and choose one that you think best shows cause and effect.

• Take time to research facts, descriptions, and examples, to clearly illustrate the causes and effects in your essay.

Drafting
• Choose one of the following to organize the causes and effects in your essay: show the chronological order of events, or order the events from the least important to the most important.
• As you draft your essay, illustrate each cause and effect with supporting facts and details.

Revising
• Review your entire draft to ensure you show a clear relationship between the causes and effects.
• Analyze each paragraph to check that you have provided a thorough set of facts and details.

---

19. War losses and radicals taking over the Assembly led to the end of the monarchy.

20. Sample: Distance and a cold climate took a huge toll on Napoleon's forces.

21. They are carving up the world because France and Britain want to divide the world between their empires.

Document-Based Assessment

Storming the Bastille

One of the most famous and dramatic moments of the French Revolution was the storming of the Bastille. This prison fortress with 90-foot-high walls symbolized the injustices of absolute monarchy. The following documents describe the event from different viewpoints.

Document A

"Shouts of 'Give us the Bastille' were heard, and nine hundred had pressed into the undefended outer courtyard, becoming angrier by the minute. . . . At about half past three in the afternoon the crowd was reinforced by companies of *gardes françaises* [French guards] and by defecting soldiers, including a number who were veterans of the American campaign. Two in particular, Second-Lieutenant Jacob Elie, the standard-bearer of the Infantry of the Queen, and Pierre-Augustin Hulin, the director of the Queen's laundry, were crucial in turning the incoherent assault into an organized siege."

—From *Citizens: A Chronicle of the French Revolution,* (1989) by Simon Schama

Document B

"How much the greatest event it is that ever happened in the world! and how much the best!"

—**Letter, July 30, 1789,** by Charles James Fox (1749–1806), British politician, on the fall of the Bastille

Document C

"The mob came closer and the governor declared his willingness to capitulate [give up]. . . The streets and houses, even the roofs were filled with people abusing and cursing me. Daggers, bayonets, pistols were constantly pointed at me. I did not know how I would be killed but was sure my last hour had come. Those who had no arms were throwing stones at me, the women wrenched their teeth and threatened me with their fists. Two soldiers behind me had already been killed by the furious mob and I am convinced I could not have reached City Hall had not one officer . . . escorted me."

—**"Reports of the Taking of the Bastille, July 14, 1789, by One of Its Defenders"** (1834) by Ludwig von der Fluhe (Swiss officer)

Document D

▼ *Demolition of the Bastille, 1789*

Analyzing Documents

Use your knowledge of the storming of the Bastille and Documents A, B, C, and D to answer questions 1–4.

1. In Document B, Charles James Fox was mostly likely enthusiastic about the fall of the Bastille because
   A he had a personal grudge against prison guards.
   B the people stood up to authority.
   C he supported King Louis XVI.
   D he was anxious to see what the people of France would do next.

2. Which document attempts to give an objective view of the storming of the Bastille?
   A Document B
   B Document A
   C Document C
   D Document D

3. In Document C, which words best indicate which side the author is on?
   A the governor declared his willingness to capitulate
   B daggers, bayonets, pistols
   C even the roofs were filled with people
   D furious mob

4. **Writing Task** Compare the four documents. Which lasting document best conveys the significance of the event? Use your knowledge of this event and specific evidence from the documents to support your opinion.

● Writing About History

As students begin the assignment, refer them to p. SH10 of the **Writing Handbook** for help in writing an expository essay. Remind them of the steps they should take to complete their assignment, including prewriting, drafting, and revising. For help in revising, remind them to use the guidelines on p. SH12 of the **Writing Handbook.**

Students' cause-and-effect essays should state the factors that caused the event of their choice and the effects that followed. They should be organized either chronologically or from least important effect to most important and should use supporting facts and details to illustrate causes and effects. The essays should be free of grammatical and spelling errors and should clearly show the relationship between causes and effects. For scoring rubrics for writing assignments, see **Assessment Rubrics,** p. 8.

Answers

1. B
2. B
3. D
4. Responses should show a clear understanding that the storming of the Bastille symbolized an attack on the monarchy itself and marked the beginning of the French Revolution. They should use specific evidence from the documents and the chapter to support their conclusions.

The Industrial Revolution Begins

Section	Core Instruction L3	Differentiated Instruction L1 L2 L4

Section 1
Dawn of the Industrial Age

 2 periods, 1 block

OBJECTIVES
- Analyze why life changed as industry spread.
- Summarize how an agricultural revolution led to the growth of industry.
- Outline the new technologies that helped trigger the Industrial Revolution.

Focus Question *What events helped bring about the Industrial Revolution?*

All in One Teaching Resources, Unit 2
Reading Strategy: Understand Effects, p. 46
Vocabulary Builder: Word Origins, p. 45
Section 1 Quiz, p. 41

Reading and Note Taking Study Guide
Note Taking Study Guide, p. 89
Section 1 Summary, p. 90

Note Taking Transparencies, 140

WITNESS HISTORY Audio CD
From Hand Power to Steam Power

Progress Monitoring Transparencies, 79

Color Transparencies, 116

Teaching Resources, Skills Handbook
Prereading the Chapter, pp. 1–2
Word Knowledge Rating Form, p. 3
K-W-L Chart, p. 4

L1 Adapted Reading and Note Taking Study Guide
Note Taking Study Guide, p. 89 SN
Section 1 Summary, p. 90 SN

L2 Adapted Reading and Note Taking Study Guide
Note Taking Study Guide, p. 89 LPR
Section 1 Summary, p. 90 LPR

Spanish Reading and Note Taking Study Guide
Note Taking Study Guide, p. 89 ELL
Section 1 Summary, p. 90 ELL

L4 Extend Activity,
Teacher's Edition, p. 249 AR, GT

*Student Edition Audio SN

Differentiated Instruction Activity, Teacher's Edition, p. 247 SN

*Guided Reading Audio, Spanish ELL

*Student Edition Audio LPR

Differentiated Instruction Activity, Teacher's Edition, p. 247 LPR

Section 2
Britain Leads the Way

 1 period, .5 block

OBJECTIVES
- Understand why Britain was the starting point for the Industrial Revolution.
- Describe the changes that transformed the textile industry.
- Explain the significance of the transportation revolution.

Focus Question *What key factors allowed Britain to lead the way in the Industrial Revolution?*

All in One Teaching Resources, Unit 2
Outline Map: Industrial Cities in Great Britain and Ireland, 1800–1850, p. 52
Geography Quiz, p. 53
Section 2 Quiz, p. 42

Reading and Note Taking Study Guide
Note Taking Study Guide, p. 91
Section 2 Summary, p. 92

Note Taking Transparencies, 141

WITNESS HISTORY Audio CD
Riding the Railway

Progress Monitoring Transparencies, 80

Color Transparencies, 113, 114, 115

L1 Adapted Reading and Note Taking Study Guide
Note Taking Study Guide, p. 91 SN
Section 2 Summary, p. 92 SN

L2 Adapted Reading and Note Taking Study Guide
Note Taking Study Guide, p. 91 LPR
Section 2 Summary, p. 92 LPR

L4 Extend Activity,
Teacher's Edition, p. 253 AR, GT

Differentiated Instruction Activity, Teacher's Edition, p. 251 SN

Spanish Reading and Note Taking Study Guide
Note Taking Study Guide, p. 91 ELL
Section 2 Summary, p. 92 ELL

Differentiated Instruction Activity, Teacher's Edition, p. 251 LPR, ELL

Section	Core Instruction L3	Differentiated Instruction L1 L2 L4	

Section 3
Social Impact of the Industrial Revolution

🕐 **2 periods, 1 block**

OBJECTIVES
- Explain what caused urbanization and what life was like in the new industrial cities.
- Compare and contrast the industrial working class and the new middle class.
- Understand how the factory system and mines changed the way people worked.
- Analyze the benefits and challenges of industrialization.

Focus Question *What were the social effects of the Industrial Revolution?*

All in One Teaching Resources, Unit 2
Section 3 Quiz, p. 43

Reading and Note Taking Study Guide
Note Taking Study Guide, p. 93
Section 3 Summary, p. 94

Note Taking Transparencies, 142

WITNESS HISTORY Audio CD
Stench and Sickness

Progress Monitoring Transparencies, 81

Color Transparencies, 117, 118

Witness History Discovery School™
video program, *In Old New York*

L1 Adapted Reading and Note Taking Study Guide
Note Taking Study Guide, p. 93 **SN**
Section 3 Summary, p. 94 **SN**

L2 Adapted Reading and Note Taking Study Guide
Note Taking Study Guide, p. 93 **LPR**
Section 3 Summary, p. 94 **LPR**

L4 All in One Teaching Resources, Unit 2
Link to Literature: From "The Excursion" by William Wordsworth, p. 51 **AR, GT**
Link to Literature: From *Mary Barton*, by Elizabeth Gaskell, p. 48 **AR, GT**
Viewpoints: Two Views on Child Labor in Factories, p. 47 **AR, GT**

Differentiated Instruction Activity,
Teacher's Edition, p. 255 **SN**

Spanish Reading and Note Taking Study Guide
Note Taking Study Guide, p. 93 **ELL**
Section 3 Summary, p. 94 **ELL**

Differentiated Instruction Activity,
Teacher's Edition, p. 255 **LPR, ELL**

Differentiated Instruction Activity,
Teacher's Edition, p. 257 **AR, GT**

Extend Activity,
Teacher's Edition, p. 258 **AR, GT**

Section 4
New Ways of Thinking

🕐 **2 periods, 1 block**

OBJECTIVES
- Understand laissez-faire economics and the beliefs of those who supported it.
- Describe the doctrine of utilitarianism.
- Summarize the theories of socialism.
- Explain Marx's views of the working class and the response to Marxism.

Focus Question *What new ideas about economics and society were fostered as a result of the Industrial Revolution?*

All in One Teaching Resources, Unit 2
Section 4 Quiz, p. 44

Reading and Note Taking Study Guide
Note Taking Study Guide, pp. 95–96
Section 4 Summary, p. 97
Concept Connector, pp. 259, 295

Note Taking Transparencies, 143

WITNESS HISTORY Audio CD
The Struggle of the Working Class

Progress Monitoring Transparencies, 82

L1 Adapted Reading and Note Taking Study Guide
Note Taking Study Guide, pp. 95–96 **SN**
Section 4 Summary, p. 97 **SN**
Concept Connector, pp. 259, 295 **SN**

L2 Adapted Reading and Note Taking Study Guide
Note Taking Study Guide, pp. 95–96 **LPR**
Section 4 Summary, p. 97 **LPR**
Concept Connector, pp. 259, 295 **LPR**

L4 All in One Teaching Resources, Unit 2
Biography: Jeremy Bentham, p. 49 **AR, GT**
Viewpoints: Responses to the Industrial Revolution, p. 50 **AR, GT**

Spanish Reading and Note Taking Study Guide
Note Taking Study Guide, pp. 95–96 **ELL**
Section 4 Summary, p. 97 **ELL**
Concept Connector, pp. 259, 295 **ELL**

Differentiated Instruction Activity,
Teacher's Edition, p. 262 **LPR, ELL**

Extend Activity,
Teacher's Edition, p. 264 **AR, GT**

Audio support is available for all sections.

Assessment Resources
- **Progress Monitoring Transparencies**, 79–82
- **SuccessTracker™**, Chapter 7
- **Document-Based Assessment**, pp. 54–66
- ***ExamView®* Test Bank CD-ROM**, Chapter 7
- **All in One Teaching Resources, Unit 2,** Chapter Tests A and B, pp. 54–59
- **Progress Monitoring *Online* Quizzes,** Chapter 7
- **Assessment Rubrics**

Differentiated Instruction Key
- **L1** Special Needs
- **L2** Basic to Average
- **L3** All Students
- **L4** Average to Advanced
- **LPR** Less Proficient Readers
- **AR** Advanced Readers
- **SN** Special Needs Students
- **GT** Gifted and Talented
- **ELL** English Language Learner

Author's Notes

Causes of the Industrial Revolution

Attempts to explain the Industrial Revolution that began in the eighteenth century, like explanations of the European overseas empires that emerged in the sixteenth, are many and controversial. Traditional accounts celebrated a handful of English inventors as the heroes of the great transformation. More theoretical economic explanations emphasized the concentration of large amounts of capital to pay for the costly process of industrialization. Some emphasized character traits seen as typically European, including rationality, individualism, or "industriousness," while others pointed to alleged weaknesses in other societies, from poor tropical soils or unproductive elites to "oriental despotism" in government. One widely discussed recent analysis, on the other hand, could find no major differences between the British and Chinese economies beyond coal and colonial supplies of cotton.

The issue, in short, is still being debated vigorously. Here, we will offer a number of causal factors, all centered in Britain, where the Industrial Revolution did in fact begin. While no one of these factors was unique to eighteenth-century Britain, all of them together may have combined to generate the first industrial "take-off" in history. This complex combination includes natural resources, labor, demand, capital, technology, and entrepreneurship.

Natural resources, especially coal and iron, were essential. So was a substantial labor force free from agricultural labor. An increased demand from a growing population is often cited, as is capital accumulation to pay the huge initial cost of tooling up for industrial production. Invention undoubtedly played a part, though in the more systematic form of an ongoing process of technological development. Perhaps most important, there was the role of the entrepreneur, the catalytic agent that brought all the other elements together, added a touch of factory management and marketing skills—and made the Industrial Revolution happen.

—Anthony Esler, *The Human Venture: From Prehistory to the Present*, (Upper Saddle River, New Jersey: Pearson Education, 2004), pp. 488–489

Extend Online

The Transportation Revolution

Have students analyze how improvements in technology and transportation fueled the Industrial Revolution. Have them write journal entries from the point of view of someone living during this time, chronicling how railways changed society. Use the steps below to help students complete the activity.

Prepare for the Activity Explain that the booming railroads transformed Britain, economically and socially.

Goods and people were able to travel across land more swiftly. Because of reduced shipping costs, both consumption and production grew. Middle-class families could now afford to travel, and so day trips became popular. Small resorts developed and professional sports also grew, as the rails allowed teams to travel and play each other.

Conduct the Activity For help in starting the activity, send students to **Web Code nbe-1901.** Students will view information about early railways during the Industrial Revolution and analyze primary sources and artifacts, like the train ticket shown here. Have them note the effects of the railroads on daily life. Have them write journal entries based on what they learn.

Follow-Up Conduct a class discussion based on the following questions: Why was the development of railways important to industrialization? How did it change people's daily lives? What were the economic and social benefits of railroads?

Differentiated Instruction Solutions for All Learners

Responding to Chapter Questions L1 L2

To teach students how to productively answer chapter questions, provide them with the following steps. These will also deepen their understanding of "study reading."

1. Read the chapter question silently and ask yourself—based on the question—what type of information will I be looking for?

> Why? = For what reasons? What are the reasons?
> How? = What was the process? What was the sequence?
> What? = Definition (What is _____ ?)
> What + signal word =
> > What are the <u>benefits</u> of _____?
> > What was the <u>reaction</u> to _____?

2. Skim the headings to find the section that addresses the question.

3. Re-read the section looking for the answer.

4. Record the answer in your own words, if possible turning the question into part of the answer. (e.g., *Why did the Industrial Age begin?* The Industrial Age began because...)

Independent Research L4

Challenge advanced readers by asking them to independently research material that goes beyond what is presented in the textbook. By honing their research skills, these advanced readers are learning to be independent thinkers and are developing skills that will aid them in future studies. The text provides an excellent base knowledge that students can use as a springboard for individual student research. You may assign students to research the personal backgrounds and biographies of historical individuals mentioned in a particular chapter. Students can be asked to conduct in-depth research on events that are only given passing mention by the text. Students should present their research to the class via a multimedia presentation or oral report.

Modeling Reading and Writing Skills

Narrow Your Topic Explain that in this chapter students will be writing an explanatory essay. (See Writing About History, p. 268.) Remind students that their topic should be suitable both for the resource materials available and for the space allotted for the essay. Tell them that they can use the table of contents and indexes of reference materials to further narrow their topic to one of an appropriate scope. They may also do a key word search in an electronic database or search engine to find similar topics.

To model this, take a broad topic from this program, such as the Industrial Revolution, and flip to the index of this book. Show students how it is further broken down into categories, such as arts during the, cause and effects of, child labor in the, cities in the, and communications during. Next, turn to the broad topic of economics. Show them that there are separate entries for economics of dependence and economic systems. Students can take these categories and subdivisions and use them as a starting place for research.

Use Prior Knowledge Remind students that they already know something about many topics, both from reading previous materials and from their own experiences. Explain that building on this prior knowledge gives readers a head start on learning new information.

To demonstrate this, have students look at the images throughout this chapter of developing technologies. Ask **What are some of today's developing technologies?** *(Sample: cell phones, the Internet, computers, video games, cars)* **What are some of the effects of technology?** *(Sample: It can change the way people perform tasks and the way society operates.)* Tell students that by using what they already know, they make connections between their own knowledge and the text, which will give them a greater understanding of the new content.

Teach With Technology

PresentationEXPRESS™
Premium DVD

- Teach this chapter's core content using **PresentationExpress™ Premium,** which includes dynamic lecture notes, interactive game shows, songs, videos, and the *ExamView® QuickTake* assessment tool.

- To introduce this chapter using **PresentationExpress™ Premium,** start by asking students **Which of the following statements do you most agree with? The greatest significance of the Industrial Revolution was— (A) the change in where people lived. (B) the change in working conditions. (C) the advances in transportation and communication. (D) development of new energy sources.** Take a class poll or record students' answers using the QuickTake feature and discuss their responses. Point out that in this chapter, they will read about the Industrial Revolution. Continue introducing the chapter using the chapter opener slide show and Witness History audio.

Technology Resources

- Student**EXPRESS** CD-ROM, Chapter 7

- Teacher**EXPRESS** CD-ROM, Chapter 7

- Presentation**EXPRESS™** **Premium DVD,** Chapter 7

- **WITNESS HISTORY** Audio CD, Chapter 7

- *ExamView* **Test Bank CD-ROM,** English and Spanish, Chapter 7

- **Guided Reading Audio,** Spanish, Chapter 7

- **Student Edition Audio,** Chapter 7

- **Witness History Discovery School™** video program, *In Old New York*

- **Experience It! Multimedia Pack**

The Industrial Revolution Begins
1750–1850

Bibliography

For the Teacher

Freese, Barbara. *Coal: A Human History.* Cambridge, Mass.: Perseus Books, 2003.

O'Brien, Patrick, and Roland Quinault, eds. *The Industrial Revolution and British Society.* Cambridge: Cambridge University Press, 1993.

Wrigley, E.A. *Continuity, Chance and Change: The Character of the Industrial Revolution in England.* Cambridge: Cambridge University Press, 1988.

For the Student

L2 Ross, Stewart. *The Industrial Revolution.* New York: Franklin Watts, 2000.

L3 Bland, Celia. *The Mechanical Age.* New York: Facts on File, 1995.

L4 Yancey, Diane. *Life in Charles Dickens' England.* San Diego: Lucent Books, 1999.

A Different Kind of Revolution

While the American Revolution and the French Revolution were being fought in the late 1700s, another kind of revolution took hold in Britain. Though not political, this revolution—known as the Industrial Revolution—brought about just as many changes to society. Paul Johnson, historian, describes this time period as "the age, above all in history, of matchless opportunities for penniless men with powerful brains and imaginations." Listen to the Witness History audio to hear more about the start of the Industrial Revolution.

◀ On September 27, 1825, the Stockton and Darlington Railway in England became the world's first steam railway to offer passenger and freight service.

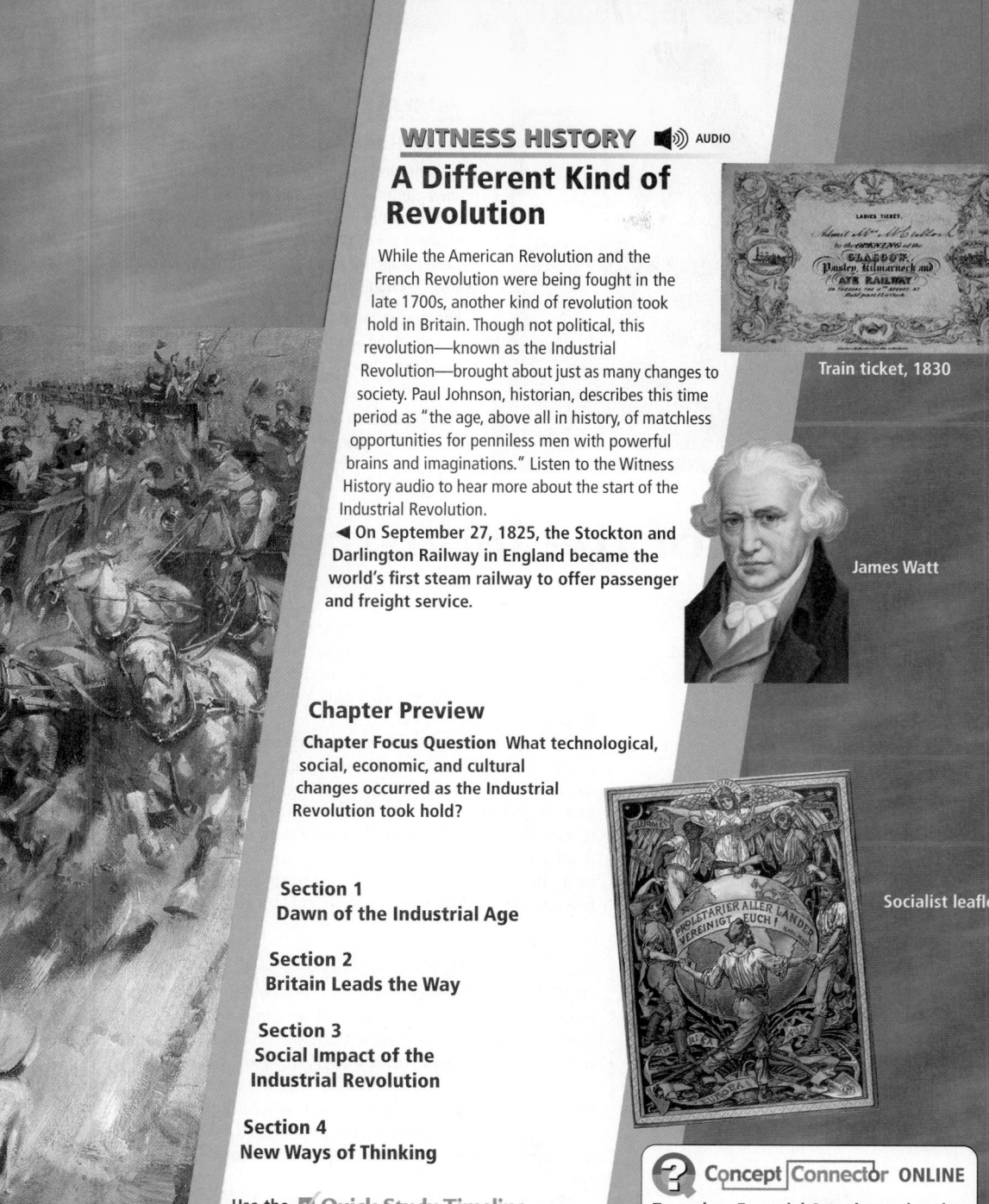

Train ticket, 1830

James Watt

Socialist leaflet

Chapter Preview

Chapter Focus Question What technological, social, economic, and cultural changes occurred as the Industrial Revolution took hold?

Section 1
Dawn of the Industrial Age

Section 2
Britain Leads the Way

Section 3
Social Impact of the Industrial Revolution

Section 4
New Ways of Thinking

Use the ✓ **Quick Study Timeline** at the end of this chapter to preview chapter events.

❓ Concept Connector ONLINE

To explore Essential Questions related to this chapter, go to PearsonSchool.com
Web Code: nbd-1907

Chapter-Level Resources

All in One Vocabulary Builder; Reading Strategy; Enrichments; Outline Maps; Geography Quiz; Chapter Tests
- Document-Based Assessments
- AYP Monitoring Assessments
- *ExamView* Test Bank CD-ROM
- Guided Reading Audio (Spanish)
- Student Edition Audio

Previewing the Chapter

- **WITNESS HISTORY** Read aloud the Witness History selection or play the accompanying audio. Discuss historian Paul Johnson's statement about "matchless opportunity." Then ask students to predict the ways that the Industrial Revolution would change society. *(Sample: faster transportation, growth of cities, increased pollution)* Tell them they will learn about these changes in the chapter ahead.

  🔊 AUDIO **Witness History Audio CD,** A Different Kind of Revolution

- **Analyzing the Visuals** Ask students to study the painting of the Stockton and Darlington Railway. Point out the young boy running alongside the train. Ask **What was the reaction to the development of the railroad?** *(Sample: excitement, optimism)*

- **Focus** Write the Chapter Focus Question on the board. Tell students to keep this question in mind as they read the chapter. *(Answer appears with Chapter Assessment answers.)* Have students preview the section titles for this chapter.

Note Taking Study Guide With Concept Connector Journal
For online access: Web code nbd-1907
For print alternative: Reading and Note Taking Study Guide booklet

Objectives

As you teach this section, keep students focused on the following objectives to help them answer the Section Focus Question and master core content.

- Analyze why life changed as industry spread.
- Summarize how an agricultural revolution led to the growth of industry.
- Outline the new technologies that helped trigger the Industrial Revolution.

Prepare to Read

Build Background Knowledge L3

Write the word *revolution* on the board. Ask students to list revolutions they have studied (including the Scientific Revolution) and the characteristics of revolutions. Tell them they will learn about the characteristics of the Industrial Revolution next.

Set a Purpose L3

- **WITNESS HISTORY** Read the selection aloud or play the audio.

  ◀)) AUDIO **Witness History Audio CD,** From Hand Power to Steam Power

  Ask **What effect did Boulton think steam power would have on the world?** *(It would benefit people by relieving them of hard manual labor.)* Ask students to predict whether steam power would "uplift civilization."

- **Focus** Point out the Section Focus Question and write it on the board. Tell students to refer to this question as they read. *(Answer appears with Section 1 Assessment answers.)*

- **Preview** Have students preview the Section Objectives and the list of Terms, People, and Places.

- **Reading Skill** Have students use the *Reading Strategy: Understand Effects* worksheet.

All in One Teaching Resources, Unit 2, p. 7

Matthew Boulton

WITNESS HISTORY ◀)) AUDIO

From Hand Power to Steam Power

For centuries, people used their own energy to provide the power for their work. While the idea of using steam power came about in the seventeenth century, it was not until engineer James Watt improved the steam engine that it could be applied to machinery. His financial partner Matthew Boulton, a successful manufacturer, proclaimed:

❝ I have at my disposal what the whole world demands, something which will uplift civilization more than ever by relieving man of all undignified drudgery. I have *steam power.* ❞

Focus Question What events helped bring about the Industrial Revolution?

Dawn of the Industrial Age

Objectives

- Analyze why life changed as industry spread.
- Summarize how an agricultural revolution led to the growth of industry.
- Outline the new technologies that helped trigger the Industrial Revolution.

Terms, People, and Places

anesthetic
enclosure
James Watt
smelt

Note Taking

Reading Skill: Recognize Multiple Causes Several key events led to the Industrial Revolution. As you read the section, create a flowchart of these causes. Add categories as needed.

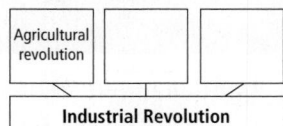

For thousands of years following the rise of civilization, most people lived and worked in small farming villages. However, a chain of events set in motion in the mid-1700s changed that way of life for all time. Today, we call this period of change the Industrial Revolution.

The Industrial Revolution started in Britain. The economic changes that Britain experienced affected people's lives as much as previous political changes and revolutions had. In contrast with most political revolutions, it was neither sudden nor swift. Instead, it was a long, slow, uneven process in which production shifted from simple hand tools to complex machines. From its beginnings in Britain, the Industrial Revolution has spread to the rest of Europe, North America, and around the globe.

Life Changes as Industry Spreads

In 1750, most people worked the land, using handmade tools. They lived in simple cottages lit by firelight and candles. They made their own clothing and grew their own food. In nearby towns, they might exchange goods at a weekly outdoor market.

Like their ancestors, these people knew little of the world that existed beyond their village. The few who left home traveled only as far as their feet or a horse-drawn cart could take them. Those bold adventurers who dared to cross the seas were at the mercy of the winds and tides.

With the onset of the Industrial Revolution, the rural way of life began to disappear. By the 1850s, many country villages had grown into industrial towns and cities. Those who lived there were able to buy clothing and food that someone else produced.

Vocabulary Builder

Use the information below and the following resources to teach the high-use word from this section.
All in One Teaching Resources, Unit 2, p. 45; Teaching Resources, Skills Handbook, p. 3

High-Use Word	Definition and Sample Sentence
statistics, p. 248	*pl.n.* data that is gathered and tabulated to present information The **statistics** from this season's basketball games showed that Jenny had scored more points than any other player.

Industrial-age travelers moved rapidly between countries and continents by train or steamship. Urgent messages flew along telegraph wires. New inventions and scientific "firsts" poured out each year. Between 1830 and 1855, for example, an American dentist first used an anesthetic, or drug that prevents pain during surgery; an American inventor patented the first sewing machine; a French physicist measured the speed of light; and a Hungarian doctor introduced antiseptic methods to reduce the risk of women dying in childbirth.

Still more stunning changes occurred in the next century, which created our familiar world of skyscraper cities and carefully tended suburbs. How and why did these great changes occur? Historians point to a series of interrelated causes that helped trigger the industrialization of the West. The "West" referred originally to the industrialized countries in Europe but today includes many more.

✔ **Checkpoint** Why was the Industrial Revolution a turning point in world history?

Agriculture Spurs Industry

Oddly enough, the Industrial Revolution was made possible in part by a change in the farming fields of Western Europe. From the first agricultural revolution some 11,000 years ago, when people learned to farm and domesticate animals, until about 300 years ago, farming had remained pretty much the same. Then, a second agricultural revolution took place that greatly improved the quality and quantity of farm products.

Farming Methods Improve The Dutch led the way in this new agricultural revolution. They built earthen walls known as dikes to reclaim land from the sea. They also combined smaller fields into larger ones to make better use of the land and used fertilizer from livestock to renew the soil.

In the 1700s, British farmers expanded on Dutch agricultural experiments. Educated farmers exchanged news of experiments through farm journals. Some farmers mixed different kinds of soils to get higher crop yields. Others tried out new methods of crop rotation. Lord Charles Townshend urged farmers to grow turnips, which restored exhausted soil. Jethro Tull invented a new mechanical device, the seed drill, to aid farmers. It deposited seeds in rows rather than scattering them wastefully over the land.

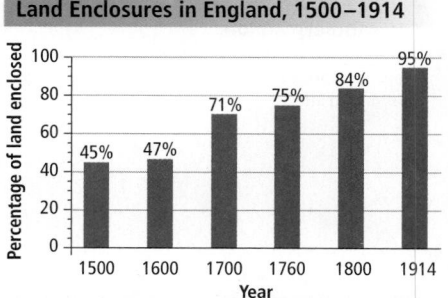

Land Enclosures in England, 1500–1914

Percentage of land enclosed: 45% (1500), 47% (1600), 71% (1700), 75% (1760), 84% (1800), 95% (1914)

Graph Skills According to the graph, between which years was the largest percentage of land enclosed? What was the result of these land enclosures?

SOURCE: *Oxford Atlas of World History*, 1999

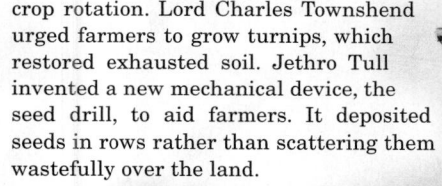

Jethro Tull's seed drill

■ **Note Taking** Have students read this section using the Guided Questioning strategy (TE, p. T20). As they read, have students fill in the flowchart showing the multiple causes of the Industrial Revolution.

Reading and Note Taking Study Guide, p. 89

Teach

Life Changes/Agriculture 🔵L3

Instruct

■ **Introduce: Vocabulary Builder** Have students read the Vocabulary Builder term and definition. Ask **What kinds of *statistics* might reflect the changes that occurred in the Industrial Revolution?** *(statistics on rural and urban population, factory production, product sales)*

■ **Teach** Trace the shift from simple hand tools to complex machines. Ask **How did farming methods improve during the second agricultural revolution?** *(Fertilizer and crop rotation led to higher crop yields; larger fields and new devices increased efficiency.)* **How did these changes help lead to the Industrial Revolution?** *(Greater efficiency reduced the need for labor. Farm laborers migrated to cities in search of work.)*

Independent Practice

Ask students to write a brief paragraph that explains how the practice of enclosures helped lead to the Industrial Revolution. They should use details from the text and from the bar graph on this page.

Monitor Progress

As students fill in their flowcharts, circulate to make sure they understand that an agricultural revolution and the population explosion helped lead to the Industrial Revolution. For a completed version of the flowchart, see

🏛 **Note Taking Transparencies**, 140

Answers

✔ The Industrial Revolution changed where and how people lived and how they worked and traveled.

Graph Skills between 1600 and 1700; farm output and profits rose, but small farmers were forced off the land and eventually migrated to cities to find work.

Differentiated Instruction Solutions for All Learners

🔵L1 **Special Needs** 🔵L2 **Less Proficient Readers**

Help students brainstorm ways that they use machines and machine-made items every moment of their lives, from the time their alarm clocks wake them in the morning until they turn the lights off at night. Then ask them to summarize what aspects of life were changed by the Industrial Revolution.

Use the following resources to help students acquire basic skills:

Adapted Reading and Note Taking Study Guide

■ Adapted Note Taking Study Guide, p. 89
■ Adapted Section Summary, p. 90

New Technology Becomes Key

Instruct

- **Introduce** Point out that the way we think of technology is a product of the Industrial Revolution. Use the Think-Write-Pair-Share Strategy (TE, p. T22) and Ask **Was technology a cause or a result of the Industrial Revolution? Why?** *(both; answers will vary.)*

- **Teach** Ask **Which two technologies contributed to the Industrial Revolution?** *(improvements to the steam engine and to iron production)* **How did these two technologies influence each other?** *(Better-quality iron was used to build steam engines; steam engines produced new uses for iron, such as locomotives.)*

- **Quick Activity** Display **Color Transparency 116: Steam-Powered Inventions.** Ask students to list what kinds of changes each invention led to. Then return to the Witness History quotation from Matthew Boulton, from the beginning of this section. Have students debate whether they agree or disagree with Boulton's statement that steam power will "uplift civilization," using the evidence in the chart.

  📖 **Color Transparencies,** 116

Independent Practice

Assign student groups to research one of the following inventors and his contribution to the Industrial Revolution: Henry Cort, Robert Fulton, John McAdam, Samuel F. B. Morse, George Stephenson, or John Wilkinson. Have the groups present their findings to the class.

Monitor Progress

- To review the section so far, have students explain the significance of Abraham Darby's experiments with coal. Point out the photo of the bridge completed by Abraham Darby III.

- Check Reading and Note Taking Study Guide entries for student understanding.

Answers

✔ Because of an agricultural revolution, people ate better and were healthier, which reduced death rates.

BIOGRAPHY Sample: Watt's improved steam engine might not have been marketed right away, which could have meant a delay in the spread of the Industrial Revolution.

Enclosure Increases Output but Causes Migration Meanwhile, rich landowners pushed ahead with **enclosure,** the process of taking over and consolidating land formerly shared by peasant farmers. In the 1500s, landowners had enclosed land to gain more pastures for sheep to increase wool output. By the 1700s, they wanted to create larger fields that could be cultivated more efficiently. The British Parliament facilitated enclosures through legislation.

As millions of acres were enclosed, farm output rose. Profits also rose because large fields needed fewer workers. But such progress had a large human cost. Many farm laborers were thrown out of work, and small farmers were forced off their land because they could not compete with large landholders. Villages shrank as cottagers left in search of work. In time, jobless farm workers migrated to towns and cities. There, they formed a growing labor force that would soon tend the machines of the Industrial Revolution.

Vocabulary Builder

statistics—(stuh TIS tiks) *pl.n.* data that are gathered and tabulated to present information

Population Multiplies The agricultural revolution contributed to a rapid growth of population. Precise population statistics for the 1700s are rare, but those that do exist are striking. Britain's population, for example, soared from about 5 million in 1700 to almost 9 million in 1800. The population of Europe as a whole shot up from roughly 120 million to about 180 million during the same period. Such growth had never before been seen.

Why did this population increase occur? First, the agricultural revolution reduced the risk of death from famine because it created a surplus of food. Since people ate better, they were healthier. Also, better hygiene and sanitation, along with improved medical care, further slowed deaths from disease.

✔ **Checkpoint** How did an agricultural revolution contribute to population growth?

BIOGRAPHY

James Watt

How did a clever Scottish engineer become the "Father of the Industrial Revolution"? After repairing a Newcomen steam engine, James Watt (1736–1819) became fascinated with the idea of improving the device. Within a few months, he knew he had a product that would sell. Still, Watt lacked the money needed to produce and market it.

Fortunately, he was able to form a partnership with the shrewd manufacturer Matthew Boulton. They then founded Soho Engineering Works in Birmingham, England, to manufacture steam engines. Watt's version of the steam engine shown here had a separate condensing chamber and was patented in 1769. Eventually, a measure of mechanical and electrical power, the watt, would be named for James Watt. **How might the Industrial Revolution have been different if Watt had not found a business partner?**

Link to Science

Watt, Horsepower, and Watts By preventing the loss of steam, Watt made steam engines more efficient and more powerful. He also attached a flywheel, converting the back-and-forth motion of the pistons into a circular motion to power not only pumps but all sorts of machinery. To market his engines, Watt needed to be able to describe their power. The best source of power at the time was horses. Watt found that a horse could lift 550 pounds of coal 10 feet (30 m) in 10 seconds, or 33,000 pounds per foot (0.3 m) per minute. He defined this value as one horsepower. Horsepower is still used for engines; trucks and SUVs today average more than 200 horsepower. Watt's name was later given to a measure of power: the watt. Common light bulbs measure 60 to 100 watts. One horsepower is equal to 745.56 watts.

New Technology Becomes Key

Another factor that helped trigger the Industrial Revolution was the development of new technology. Aided by new sources of energy and new materials, these new technologies enabled business owners to change the ways work was done.

An Energy Revolution During the 1700s, people began to harness new sources of energy. One vital power source was coal, used to develop the steam engine. In 1712, British inventor Thomas Newcomen had developed a steam engine powered by coal to pump water out of mines. Scottish engineer **James Watt** looked at Newcomen's invention in 1764 and set out to make improvements on the engine in order to make it more efficient. Watt's engine, after several years of work, would become a key power source of the Industrial Revolution. The steam engine opened the door not only to operating machinery but eventually to powering locomotives and steamships.

The Quality of Iron Improves Coal was also a vital source of fuel in the production of iron, a material needed for the construction of machines and steam engines. The Darby family of Coalbrookdale pioneered new methods of producing iron. In 1709, Abraham Darby used coal instead of charcoal to **smelt** iron, or separate iron from its ore.

Darby's experiments led him to produce less expensive and better-quality iron, which was used to produce parts for the steam engines. Both his son and grandson continued to improve on his methods. In fact, Abraham Darby III built the world's first iron bridge. In the decades that followed, high-quality iron was used more and more widely, especially after the world turned to building railroads.

✓ **Checkpoint** What new technologies helped trigger the Industrial Revolution?

Abraham Darby III completed the world's first iron bridge in 1779. The bridge still stands today.

SECTION 1 Assessment

Progress Monitoring Online
For: Self-quiz with vocabulary practice
Web Code: nba-1911

Terms, People, and Places
1. For each term, person, or place listed at the beginning of the section, write a sentence explaining its significance.

Note Taking
2. **Reading Skill: Recognize Multiple Causes** Use your completed flowchart to answer the Focus Question: What events helped bring about the Industrial Revolution?

Comprehension and Critical Thinking
3. **Recognize Cause and Effect** What were the immediate and long-term effects of the agricultural revolution that occurred in the 1700s?
4. **Predict Consequences** How do you think population growth contributed to the Industrial Revolution?
5. **Summarize** Explain how new sources of energy, specifically coal, contributed to the Industrial Revolution.

● Writing About History
Quick Write: Give Background To explain a historical process, you should first orient the reader to time and place. Ask yourself when and where the process occurred. Practice by explaining in one or two sentences how an agricultural revolution led to the Industrial Revolution.

Step-by-Step Instruction

Objectives

As you teach this section, keep students focused on the following objectives to help them answer the Section Focus Question and master core content.

- Understand why Britain was the starting point for the Industrial Revolution.
- Describe the changes that transformed the textile industry.
- Explain the significance of the transportation revolution.

Early train ticket

WITNESS HISTORY 🔊 AUDIO

Riding the Railway

One of the most important developments of the Industrial Revolution was the creation of a countrywide railway network. The world's first major rail line went from Liverpool to Manchester in England. Fanny Kemble, the most famous actress of the day, was one of the first passengers:

❝We were introduced to the little engine which was to drag us along the rails. . . This snorting little animal, . . . started at about ten miles an hour. . . . You can't imagine how strange it seemed to be journeying on thus, without any visible cause of progress other than the magical machine . . .❞

Train passengers in Britain

Focus Question What key factors allowed Britain to lead the way in the Industrial Revolution?

Britain Leads the Way

Objectives

- Understand why Britain was the starting point for the Industrial Revolution.
- Describe the changes that transformed the textile industry.
- Explain the significance of the transportation revolution.

Terms, People, and Places

capital	Eli Whitney
enterprise	turnpike
entrepreneur	Liverpool
putting-out system	Manchester

Note Taking

Reading Skill: Identify Causes and Effects Fill in the circles of a concept web like the one below with the key factors that helped Britain take an early lead in industrialization. In a separate concept web, fill in the effects of Britain's early lead.

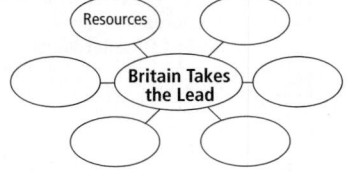

When agricultural practices changed in the eighteenth century, more food was able to be produced, which in turn fueled population growth in Britain. The agricultural changes also left many farmers homeless and jobless. These two factors led to a population boom in the cities as people migrated from rural England into towns and cities. This population increase, in turn, created a ready supply of labor to mine the coal, build the factories, and run the machines. The start of the Industrial Revolution in Britain can be attributed to many factors. Population growth was just one of them.

Why Britain?

What characteristics of eighteenth-century Britain made it ripe for industrialization? Historians cite several reasons for Britain's lead.

Natural Resources Abound Britain had the advantage of plentiful natural resources such as natural ports and navigable rivers. Rivers supplied water power and allowed for the construction of canals. These canals increased accessibility for trade and were instrumental in bringing goods to market. In addition, Britain was able to establish communications and transport relatively cheaply due to its easy accessibility to the sea from all points. Britain's plentiful supply of coal was fundamental to its industrialization and was used to power steam engines. Vast supplies of iron were available to be used to build the new machines.

Vocabulary Builder

Use the information below and the following resources to teach the high-use word from this section.
🔲 **Teaching Resources, Unit 2,** p. 45; **Teaching Resources, Skills Handbook,** p. 3

High-Use Word	Definition and Sample Sentence
decade, p. 253	*n.* ten-year periods In the **decade** from 1990 to 2000, the world witnessed a technological revolution led by the Internet.

The Effects of Demand and Capital In the 1700s, Britain had plenty of skilled mechanics who were eager to meet the growing demand for new, practical inventions. This ready workforce, along with the population explosion, boosted demand for goods. In order to increase the production of goods to meet the demand, however, another key ingredient was needed. Money was necessary to start businesses.

From the mid-1600s to 1700s, trade from a growing overseas empire helped the British economy prosper. Beginning with the slave trade, the business class accumulated **capital,** or money used to invest in enterprises. An **enterprise** is a business organization in an area such as shipping, mining, railroads, or factories. Many businessmen were ready to risk their capital in new ventures due to the healthy economy.

In addition to the advantages already cited, Britain had a stable government that supported economic growth. While other countries in Europe faced river tolls and other barriers, Britain did not. The government built a strong navy that protected its empire, shipping, and overseas trade. Although the upper class tended to look down on business people, it did not reject the wealth produced by the new entrepreneurs. These **entrepreneurs** were those who managed and assumed the financial risks of starting new businesses.

✓ **Checkpoint** What conditions in Britain paved the way for the Industrial Revolution?

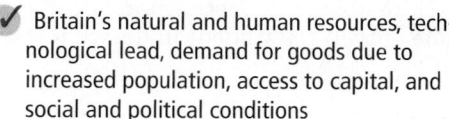
Shuttle used to speed up weaving process

Geography *Interactive*
For: Audio guided tour
Web Code: nbp-1921

Resources and Industries in England, 1750

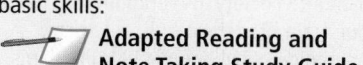

Map Skills Plentiful supplies of coal, advancements in the textile industry, iron smelting, and the manufacturing of iron goods contributed to Britain's position as the world's leading industrial nation in the late eighteenth century.
1. **Locate** (a) London (b) Manchester (c) Thames River
2. **Region** Identify the centers of woolen industry in England.
3. **Draw Inferences** What were the industrial advantages of the rivers during this time?

Legend:
- Coalfield
- Navigable river
- Copper mining and smelting
- Iron extraction and smelting
- Linen cloth
- Metalware and cutlery
- Shipbuilding
- Tin mining and smelting
- Woolen cloth

The Textile Industry/The Transportation Revolution ⑬

Instruct

- **Introduce: Vocabulary Builder**
  Have students read the Vocabulary Builder term and definition. Have students scan the text and identify the respective *decades* in which the spinning jenny and cotton gin were invented. *(1760s, 1790s)* Point out that the Industrial Revolution triggered a chain reaction in which key changes occurred in decades instead of centuries.

- **Teach** Display **Color Transparency 115: British Cotton Imports and Exports About 1840.** Ask **Which invention most affected imports?** *(cotton gin)* **Which inventions most affected exports?** *(flying shuttle, spinning jenny, water frame, factory)* **How did more British imports affect slavery in America?** *(To grow more cotton to export, planters bought more land and slaves, causing the economy to depend on slave labor.)*
  ⬛ **Color Transparencies,** 115

- **Quick Activity** Display **Color Transparency 113: Canals in Britain, 1800.** Ask students to trace various routes and ask **What was shipped on the canals?** *(coal, raw materials, finished textiles)* **What replaced the canals?** *(railroads)* Then display **Color Transparency 114: The Growth of Railways in Great Britain, 1840 and 1850.** Ask **Why was the route from Liverpool to Manchester so vital?** *(Liverpool was a key port; Manchester was a key industrial city.)* Have students compare the two maps. Which routes were important on both? Why?
  ⬛ **Color Transparencies,** 113 and 114

Independent Practice

Have students, working in pairs, develop a script for a tour of the early textile factories and workshops of the Industrial Revolution.

Monitor Progress

Check Reading and Note Taking Study Guide entries for student understanding.

Answers

Caption They made it more productive because things were being done much faster.

✔ inventions that increased production and the creation of factories

---

British Textile Inventions

These textile machines were constructed to increase cotton production. The flying shuttle sped up weaving, while the spinning jenny and the water frame increased the speed of spinning thread. How did these inventions change the textile industry?

John Kay's flying shuttle, 1733 ▶

◀ James Hargreaves' spinning jenny, 1764

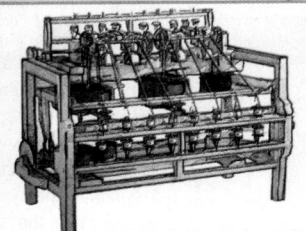
Richard Arkwright's water frame, 1769 ▶

The Textile Industry Advances

The Industrial Revolution first took hold in Britain's largest industry—textiles. In the 1600s, cotton cloth imported from India had become popular. British merchants tried to organize a cotton cloth industry at home. They developed the **putting-out system,** also known as cottage industry, in which raw cotton was distributed to peasant families who spun it into thread and then wove the thread into cloth in their own homes. Skilled artisans in the towns then finished and dyed the cloth.

Inventions Speed Production Under the putting-out system, production was slow. As the demand for cloth grew, inventors came up with a string of remarkable devices that revolutionized the British textile industry. For example, John Kay's flying shuttle enabled weavers to work so fast that they soon outpaced spinners. James Hargreaves solved that problem by producing the spinning jenny in 1764, which spun many threads at the same time. A few years later, in 1769, Richard Arkwright patented the water frame, which was a spinning machine that could be powered by water.

Meanwhile, in America, these faster spinning and weaving machines presented a challenge—how to produce enough cotton to keep up with England. Raw cotton grown in the South had to be cleaned of dirt and seeds by hand, a time-consuming task. To solve this, **Eli Whitney** invented a machine called the cotton gin that separated the seeds from the raw cotton at a fast rate. He finished the cotton gin in 1793, and cotton production increased exponentially.

Factories Are Born in Britain The new machines doomed the putting-out system. They were too large and expensive to be operated at home. Instead, manufacturers built long sheds to house the machines. At first, they located the sheds near rapidly moving streams, harnessing the water power to run the machines. Later, machines were powered by steam engines.

Spinners and weavers now came each day to work in these first factories, which brought together workers and machines to produce large quantities of goods. Early observers were awed at the size and output of these establishments. One onlooker noted: "The same [amount] of labor is now performed in one of these structures which formerly occupied the industry of an entire district."

✔ **Checkpoint** What led to the advancement of the British textile industry?

The Transportation Revolution

As production increased, entrepreneurs needed faster and cheaper methods of moving goods from place to place. Some capitalists invested in **turnpikes,** private roads built by entrepreneurs who charged travelers a toll, or fee, to use them. Goods traveled faster as a result, and turnpikes

---

Careers

Engineer The people who create cutting-edge inventions that improve our lives are often engineers. Engineers apply science to designing products or processes that are useful to society. The engineering field is divided into four main branches: civil, electrical, mechanical, and chemical. Civil engineers build dams, bridges, highways, large buildings, and power plants. Electrical engineers create everything from computers and electronics to missile guidance systems.

Mechanical engineers work on engines, machinery, air conditioning and heating, automobiles, airplanes, and spacecraft. Chemical engineers help protect the environment and create products such as medicines, plastics, synthetic fibers, metals, and food. There are many other specialties. Engineering requires good math skills, mechanical ability, and an interest in taking things apart and solving problems.

soon linked every part of Britain. Other entrepreneurs had canals dug to connect rivers together or to connect inland towns with coastal ports. Engineers also built stronger bridges and upgraded harbors to help the expanding overseas trade.

Canals Boom During the late 1700s and early 1800s, factories needed an efficient, inexpensive way to receive coal and raw materials and then to ship finished goods to market. In 1763, when the Bridgewater canal opened, it not only made a profit from tolls, but it cut in half the price of coal in Manchester. The success of this canal set off a canal-building frenzy. Entrepreneurs formed companies to construct canals for profit. Not all the canals that were built had enough traffic to support them, however, and bankruptcy often resulted. Then, beginning in the 1830s, canals lost their importance as steam locomotives made railroads the new preferred form of transportation.

Welcome the Steam Locomotive It was the invention of the steam locomotive that made the growth of railroads possible. In the early 1800s, pioneers like George Stephenson developed steam-powered locomotives to pull carriages along iron rails. The railroad did not have to follow the course of a river. This meant that tracks could go places where rivers did not, allowing factory owners and merchants to ship goods swiftly and cheaply over land. The world's first major rail line, from **Liverpool** to **Manchester,** opened in England in 1830. In the following <u>decades</u>, railroad travel became faster and railroad building boomed. By 1870, rail lines crisscrossed Britain, Europe, and North America.

One Thing Leads to Another As the Industrial Revolution got under way, it triggered a chain reaction. Once inventors developed machines that could produce large quantities of goods more efficiently, prices fell. Lower prices made goods more affordable and thus created more consumers who further fed the demand for goods. This new cycle caused a wave of economic and social changes that dramatically affected the way people lived.

 Checkpoint Why was the development of railroads important to industrialization?

Vocabulary Builder

<u>decades</u>—(DEK aydz) *n.* ten-year periods

Progress Monitoring *Online*
For: Self-quiz with vocabulary practice
Web Code: nba-1921

SECTION 2 Assessment

Terms, People, and Places
1. For each term, person, or place listed at the beginning of the section, write a sentence explaining its significance.

Note Taking
2. **Reading Skill: Identify Causes and Effects** Use your completed concept webs to answer the Focus Question: What key factors allowed Britain to lead the way in the Industrial Revolution?

Comprehension and Critical Thinking
3. **Analyze Information** Explain how each of the following helped contribute to demand for consumer goods in Britain: (a) population explosion, (b) general economic prosperity.
4. **Determine Relevance** What was the significance of new machines to the textile industry?
5. **Summarize** Explain how advances in transportation contributed to Britain's global trade.

● **Writing About History**
Quick Write: Create a Flowchart Flowcharts are useful tools to help you write an explanatory essay. Create a flowchart to show the changes that occurred in the textile industry. Be sure that the sequence of events is clear.

 Assess and Reteach

Assess Progress
■ Have students complete the Section Assessment.
■ Administer the Section Quiz.
All in One **Teaching Resources, Unit 2,** p. 42
■ To further assess student understanding, use
 Progress Monitoring Transparencies, 80

Reteach
If students need more instruction, have them read the section summary.
 Reading and Note Taking Study Guide, p. 92
 Adapted Reading and Note Taking Study Guide, p. 92
Spanish Reading and Note Taking Study Guide, p. 92

Extend
See this Chapter's Professional Development pages for the Extend Online activity on the transportation revolution.

Answer

 They allowed factory owners to ship raw materials and products quickly over land, not just by water.

Section 2 Assessment

1. Sentences should reflect an understanding of each term, person, or place listed at the beginning of the section.
2. natural and human resources, technological inventions, demand for goods due to increased population, access to capital, social and political conditions, creation of factories, and better transportation
3. (a) As population grew, demand increased because there were more people who needed more goods. (b) As people became more prosperous, they had more money to buy goods.
4. The new machines were faster and greatly increased production. Their size and expense led to the creation of factories, which increased production further.
5. Railroads allowed transportation over land, and steamships improved transportation over water, making it faster, cheaper, and easier to reach global markets.

● **Writing About History**
Responses should show a clear sequence of events and demonstrate how each change led to problems that led to the next change.

For additional assessment, have students access **Progress Monitoring *Online*** at **Web Code nba-1921.**

Objectives

As you teach this section, keep students focused on the following objectives to help them answer the Section Focus Question and master core content.

- Explain what caused urbanization and what life was like in the new industrial cities.
- Compare and contrast the industrial working class and the new middle class.
- Understand how the factory system and mines changed the way people worked.
- Analyze the benefits and challenges of industrialization.

Prepare to Read

Build Background Knowledge L3

Ask students to recall how life changed for rural farmers in the 1750s. Then ask them to predict what life would be like for those farmers who moved to cities.

Set a Purpose L3

- **WITNESS HISTORY** Read the selection aloud or play the audio.
  - 🔊 AUDIO **Witness History Audio CD,** Stench and Sickness

  Ask **How did conditions become so bad in industrial cities?** *(The move from the country to cities was rapid. Cities were not prepared to cope with the influx.)* **Why was little done to improve conditions initially?** *(Sample: Working people were poor and powerless to improve their lot.)*

- **Focus** Point out the Section Focus Question and write it on the board. Tell students to refer to this question as they read. *(Answer appears with Section 3 Assessment answers.)*

- **Preview** Have students preview the Section Objectives and the list of Terms, People, and Places.

- **Note Taking** Have students read this section using the Paragraph Shrinking strategy (TE, p. T20). As they read, have students fill in the table listing the benefits and challenges of industrialization.
  - ✏️ **Reading and Note Taking Study Guide,** p. 93

Monmouth Street, London

WITNESS HISTORY 🔊 AUDIO

Stench and Sickness

As more and more people moved to the cities to work, they had little choice about where to live. There was no public water supply, waste lined the unpaved streets, and disease spread rapidly in these unsanitary conditions. Dr. Southwood-Smith worked in two districts of London and wrote:

❝ Uncovered sewers, stagnant ditches and ponds, gutters always full of putrefying matter . . . It is not possible for any language to convey an adequate conception of the poisonous condition in which large portions of both these districts always remain, . . . from the masses of putrefying matter which are allowed to accumulate. ❞

Focus Question What were the social effects of the Industrial Revolution?

Social Impact of the Industrial Revolution

Objectives

- Explain what caused urbanization and what life was like in the new industrial cities.
- Compare and contrast the industrial working class and the new middle class.
- Understand how the factory system and mines changed the way people worked.
- Analyze the benefits and challenges of industrialization.

Terms, People, and Places

urbanization
tenement
labor union

Note Taking

Reading Skill: Understand Effects As you read the section, complete a table that lists benefits and challenges of industrialization.

Industrialization	
Benefits	**Challenges**
• Created jobs	• Crowded cities
•	•

The Industrial Revolution brought great riches to most of the entrepreneurs who helped set it in motion. For the millions of workers who crowded into the new factories, however, the industrial age brought poverty and harsh living conditions.

In time, reforms would curb many of the worst abuses of the early industrial age in Europe and the Americas. As standards of living increased, people at all levels of society would benefit from industrialization. Until then, working people would suffer with dangerous working conditions; unsafe, unsanitary, and overcrowded housing; and unrelenting poverty.

People Move to New Industrial Cities

The Industrial Revolution brought rapid **urbanization,** or the movement of people to cities. Changes in farming, soaring population growth, and an ever-increasing demand for workers led masses of people to migrate from farms to cities. Almost overnight, small towns around coal or iron mines mushroomed into cities. Other cities grew up around the factories that entrepreneurs built in once-quiet market towns.

The British market town of Manchester numbered 17,000 people in the 1750s. Within a few years, it exploded into a center of the textile industry. Its population soared to 40,000 by 1780 and 70,000 by 1801. Visitors described the "cloud of coal vapor" that polluted

---

Vocabulary Builder

Use the information below and the following resources to teach the high-use words from this section.
🔲 **Teaching Resources, Unit 2,** p. 45; **Teaching Resources, Skills Handbook,** p. 3

High-Use Words	Definitions and Sample Sentences
contaminated, p. 256	*adj.* unclean and impure; polluted You can no longer drink from the river because it is **contaminated** with chemicals from a nearby factory.
stress, p. 256	*vt.* to emphasize In her speech, the candidate **stressed** that she had the most experience.

the air, the pounding noise of steam engines, and the filthy stench of its river. This growth of industry and rapid population growth dramatically changed the location and distribution of two resources—labor and people.

✔ **Checkpoint** What led to the massive migration of people from farms to cities?

New Social Classes Emerge

The Industrial Revolution created a new middle class along with the working class. Those in the middle class owned and operated the new factories, mines, and railroads, among other industries. Their lifestyle was much more comfortable than that of the industrial working class.

When farm families moved to the new industrial cities, they became workers in mines or factories. Many felt lost and bewildered. They faced tough working conditions in uncomfortable environments. In time, though, factory and mine workers developed their own sense of community despite the terrible working conditions.

The Industrial Middle Class Those who benefited most from the Industrial Revolution were the entrepreneurs who set it in motion. The Industrial Revolution created this new middle class, or bourgeoisie (boor zhwah ZEE), whose members came from a variety of backgrounds. Some were merchants who invested their growing profits in factories. Others were inventors or skilled artisans who developed new technologies. Some rose from "rags to riches," a pattern that the age greatly admired.

Middle-class families lived in well-furnished, spacious homes on paved streets and had a ready supply of water. They wore fancy clothing and ate well. The new middle class took pride in their hard work and their determination to "get ahead." Only a few had sympathy for the poor. Women of the middle class did not leave the home to work but instead focused their energy on raising their children. This contrasted with the

Population Growth in London, c. 1750–1900

Population (in millions) vs **Year**

Graph Skills Population increased dramatically as factories sprung up in cities such as London (pictured here). How many more people were in London in 1900 than in 1750 according to the line graph?

SOURCE: *International Historical Statistics, Europe 1750–1993*, 1998

New Social Classes Emerge

Instruct

- **Introduce: Vocabulary Builder**
  Have students read the Vocabulary Builder terms and definitions. Ask students to predict what became **contaminated.** Then have them read to find out whether their predictions were accurate.

- **Teach** On the board, create two columns, labeled *Industrial Middle Class* and *Industrial Working Class.* Have students take turns listing the characteristics of each class, such as where they lived, where they worked, and what groups they joined.

- **Quick Activity** Display **Color Transparency 117:** *Tremendous Sacrifice.* Use the lesson suggested in the transparency book to guide a discussion on the results of industrialization.
  📖 **Color Transparencies,** 117

Independent Practice

Link to Literature To help students better understand how industrialization affected the working class, have them read the excerpt from Elizabeth Gaskell's *Mary Barton* and complete the worksheet.

All in One Teaching Resources, Unit 2, p. 48

Monitor Progress

To review this section, ask students to describe the lives and beliefs of a middle-class woman, a working-class child, a Luddite, and a Methodist.

Vocabulary Builder

<u>contaminated</u>—(kun TAM uh nayt id) *adj.* unclean and impure; polluted

Vocabulary Builder

<u>stressed</u>—(stresd) *vt.* emphasized

WITNESS HISTORY VIDEO

Watch *In Old New York* on the **Witness History Discovery School**™ video program to learn about life during the Industrial Age.

DISCOVERY SCHOOL

---

wealthy, who had maidservants to look after their children, and the working class, whose children were a part of the workforce.

The Industrial Working Class While the wealthy and the middle class lived in pleasant neighborhoods, vast numbers of poor struggled to survive in foul-smelling slums. They packed into tiny rooms in **tenements,** or multistory buildings divided into apartments. These tenements had no running water, only community pumps. There was no sewage or sanitation system, so wastes and garbage rotted in the streets. Sewage was also dumped into rivers, which created an overwhelming stench and <u>contaminated</u> drinking water. This led to the spread of diseases such as cholera.

Workers Stage Futile Protests Although **labor unions,** or workers' organizations, were illegal at this time, secret unions did exist among frustrated British workers. They wished to initiate worker reforms, such as increases in pay, but had no political power to effect change. Sometimes their frustration led to violence. The first instances of industrial riots occurred in England from 1811 to 1813. Groups of textile workers known as the Luddites (LUD yts) resisted the labor-saving machines that were costing them their jobs. Some of them smashed textile machines with sledgehammers and burned factories. They usually wore masks and operated at night. There was widespread support among the working class for these Luddite groups.

Workers Find Comfort in Religion Many working-class people found comfort in a religious movement called Methodism. This movement was influenced by the Industrial Revolution as people moved to cities and lost connections with their old churches. John Wesley had founded the Methodist movement in the mid-1700s. Wesley <u>stressed</u> the need for a personal sense of faith. He encouraged his followers to improve themselves by adopting sober, moral ways.

Methodist meetings featured hymns and sermons promising forgiveness of sin and a better life to come. Methodist preachers took this message of salvation into the slums. There, they tried to rekindle hope among the working poor. They set up Sunday schools where followers not only studied the Bible but also learned to read and write. Methodists helped channel workers' anger away from revolution and toward reform.

✔ **Checkpoint** How did members of the working class react to their new experiences in industrial cities?

Life in the Factories and Mines

The heart of the new industrial city was the factory. There, the technology of the machine age and the rapid pace of industrialization imposed a harsh new way of life on workers.

Factory Workers Face Harsh Conditions Working in a factory system differed greatly from working on a farm. In rural villages, people worked hard, but their work varied according to the season. Life was also hard for poor rural workers who were part of the putting-out system, but at least they worked at their own pace. In the grim factories of industrial towns, workers faced a rigid schedule set by the factory whistle.

History Background

The Peterloo Massacre On August 16, 1819, a crowd of more than 50,000 men, women and children in their Sunday best gathered in St. Peter's Field in Manchester. Speakers argued simply that workers had the right to vote and to be represented in Parliament. At the time, less than five percent of the men—mainly the rich gentry—could vote. Residents of Manchester and other new industrial cities had no representation at all. Local officials panicked at the size of the crowd. Troops on horseback waved their sabers and charged into the crowd, killing eleven and injuring hundreds. The speakers were arrested. Some were sent to prison for up to two years. Journalists who printed news of the event were also jailed, but one dubbed it the Peterloo Massacre, after the Battle of Waterloo, which had occurred four years earlier.

Answer

 Some staged futile protests; others turned to Methodism.

Working hours were long, with shifts lasting from 12 to 16 hours, six or seven days a week. Workers could only take breaks when the factory owners gave permission. Exhausted workers suffered accidents from machines that had no safety devices. They might lose a finger, a limb, or even their lives. In textile mills, workers constantly breathed air filled with lint, which damaged their lungs. Those workers who became sick or injured lost their jobs.

The majority of early factory workers were women rather than men. Employers often preferred to hire women workers because they thought women could adapt more easily to machines and were easier to manage. In addition, employers generally paid women half what they paid men.

Factory work created a double burden for women. Their new jobs took them out of their homes for 12 hours or more a day. They then returned to their tenements, which might consist of one damp room with a single bed. They had to feed and clothe their families, clean, and cope with such problems as sickness and injury.

Miners Face Worse Conditions The Industrial Revolution increased the demand for iron and coal, which in turn increased the need for miners. Although miners were paid more, working conditions in the mines were even worse than in the factories. They worked in darkness, and the coal dust destroyed their lungs. There were always the dangers of explosions, flooding, and collapsing tunnels. Women and children carted heavy loads of coal, sometimes on all fours in low passages. They also climbed ladders carrying heavy baskets of coal several times a day.

Children Have Dangerous Jobs Factories and mines also hired many boys and girls. These children often started working at age seven or eight, a few as young as five. Nimble-fingered and quick-moving, they changed spools in the hot and humid textile mills where sometimes they could not see because of all the dust. They also crawled under machinery to repair broken threads in the mills. Conditions were even worse for children who worked in the mines. Some sat all day in the dark, opening

Even children as young as five years old worked in the mines. James Kay-Shuttleworth worked as a physician among the different classes of the Industrial Revolution in Manchester. His profession allowed him to see the working conditions of poor in the cities. How was work in factories and mines different from work on the farm?

Primary Source

❝Whilst the engine runs, people must work—men, women, and children are yoked together with iron and steam. The animal machine is chained fast to the iron machine, which knows no suffering and weariness.❞
—James Kay-Shuttleworth, 1832

Life in the Factories and Mines/The Results of Industrialization

Instruct

■ **Introduce** Have students read the quotation from James Kay-Shuttleworth. Ask **According to Kay-Shuttleworth, how did factory owners view their workers?** (as machines) **Why was this view bad for the workers?** (Unlike machines, they needed rest and protection from injury.) Ask them to predict what would have to change for conditions to improve.

■ **Teach** On the board, create four columns, labeled *Factory Workers, Miners, Women Workers,* and *Child Laborers.* Using the Numbered Heads strategy (TE, p. T23), have students provide information to fill in the conditions faced by each group.

■ **Quick Activity** Show students *In Old New York* from the **Witness History Discovery School**™ video program. Ask students **What led to the creation of gangs?** (crime and poor social conditions) Ask them to give examples of things that gangs were involved with. (promotion of political candidates and creation of organized fire brigades)

Independent Practice

Viewpoints To help students appreciate different viewpoints about child labor, have them read the selection *Two Views on Child Labor in Factories* and complete the worksheet.

All in One Teaching Resources, Unit 2, p. 47

Monitor Progress

Check Reading and Note Taking Study Guide entries for student understanding.

Differentiated Instruction   Solutions for All Learners

L4 Advanced Readers   **L4 Gifted and Talented**

In the last thirty years, China has been experiencing rapid urbanization and industrialization. About 100 million people have moved from the countryside to the cities. Some observers worry that China is already experiencing some of the challenges of the Industrial Revolution, such as crowded cities, exploited workers,

and pollution. Have students research China's industrial revolution. Then have them write a report comparing the benefits and challenges of China's industrialization today to those of Britain's during the Industrial Revolution.

Answer

PRIMARY SOURCE Workers in the factories and mines had a rigid schedule and worked long hours. They could not take breaks when they wanted as they had on their farms.

and closing air vents. Others hauled coal carts in the extreme heat. Because children had helped with work on the farm, parents accepted the idea of child labor. The wages the children earned were needed to keep their families from starving.

Child labor reform laws called "factory acts" were passed in the early 1800s. These laws were passed to reduce a child's workday to twelve hours and also to remove children under the age of eight or nine from the cotton mills. Because the laws were generally not enforced, British lawmakers formed teams of inspectors to ensure that factories and mines obeyed the laws in the 1830s and 1840s. More laws were then passed to shorten the workday for women and require that child workers be educated.

✔ **Checkpoint** How did the Industrial Revolution affect the lives of men, women, and children?

Families could afford to take trips to such places as the zoo as wages increased.

The Results of Industrialization

Since the 1800s, people have debated whether the Industrial Revolution was a blessing or a curse. The early industrial age brought terrible hardships. In time, however, reformers pressed for laws to improve working conditions. Labor unions won the right to bargain with employers for better wages, hours, and working conditions. Eventually working-class men gained the right to vote, which gave them political power.

Despite the social problems created by the Industrial Revolution—low pay, dismal living conditions—the Industrial Age did have some positive effects. As demand for mass-produced goods grew, new factories opened, which in turn created more jobs. Wages rose so that workers had enough left after paying rent and buying food to buy a newspaper or visit a music hall. As the cost of railroad travel fell, people could visit family in other towns. Horizons widened and opportunities increased.

✔ **Checkpoint** Why was the Industrial Revolution seen as both a blessing and a curse?

SECTION 3 Assessment

Terms, People, and Places

1. What do each of the key terms listed at the beginning of the section have in common? Explain.

Note Taking

2. **Reading Skill: Understand Effects** Use your completed table to answer the Focus Question: What were the social effects of the Industrial Revolution?

Comprehension and Critical Thinking

3. **Analyze Information** How did the Industrial Revolution affect **(a)** cities and **(b)** population distribution?

4. **Synthesize Information** Explain how the Industrial Revolution changed the living conditions for both the middle class and the working class.

5. **Demonstrate Reasoned Judgment** Do you think increases in wages justify harsh working conditions? Why or why not?

● **Writing About History**

Quick Write: Gather Details When writing an explanatory essay, you should include facts, examples, and descriptions that help explain your topic. Make a list of details to help explain what life was like when people moved from rural areas to the new industrial cities.

Friedrich Engels: *The Condition of the Working Class in England in 1844*

In *The Condition of the Working Class in England in 1844*, Friedrich Engels recorded his observations of the wretched living conditions in poor areas of nineteenth-century England. In this excerpt, Engels describes working-class districts in Manchester. He depicts the misery and filth typical of the living areas of industrial workers.

Friedrich Engels, 1845

The houses are packed very closely together and since the bank of the river is very steep it is possible to see a part of every house. All of them have been blackened by soot, all of them are crumbling with age and all have broken window-panes and window-frames. In the background there are old factory buildings which look like barracks. On the opposite, low-lying bank of the river, one sees a long row of houses and factories. The second house is a roofless ruin, filled with refuse, and the third is built in such a low situation that the ground floor is uninhabitable and has neither doors nor windows. In the background one sees the paupers'[1] cemetery, and the stations of the railways to Liverpool and Leeds. . . .

The recently constructed extension of the Leeds railway which crosses the Irk at this point has swept away some of these courts and alleys, but it has thrown open to public gaze some of the others. So it comes about that there is to be found immediately under the railway bridge a court which is even filthier and more revolting than all the others. This is simply because it was formerly so hidden and secluded that it could only be reached with considerable difficulty [but is now exposed to the human eye]. I thought I knew this district well, but even I would never have found it had not the railway viaduct [elevated roadway] made a breach[2] in the slums at this point. One walks along a very rough path on the river bank, in between clothesposts and washing lines, to reach a chaotic group of little, one-storied, one-roomed cabins. Most of them have earth floors, and working, living and sleeping all take place in the one room. In such a hole, barely six feet long and five feet wide, I saw two beds—and what beds and bedding!—which filled the room, except for the fireplace and the doorstep. Several of these huts, as far as I could see, were completely empty, although the door was open and the inhabitants were leaning against the door posts. In front of the doors filth and garbage abounded. I could not see the pavement, but from time to time I felt it was there because my feet scraped it. . . .

1. **pauper** (PAW pur) *n.* poor person
2. **breach** (breech) *n.* break

Thinking Critically
1. **Draw Inferences** (a) How did the development of the railways affect the working-class districts? (b) How does Engels feel about the living conditions he observes?
2. **Make Generalizations** What seems to be Engels' general attitude toward the Industrial Revolution?

History Background

Friedrich Engels Engels was born in Germany in 1820. His father was the wealthy owner of a textile mill. When Engels moved to a town near Manchester, England, in 1842 he was already interested in radical politics. He took a position in a cotton plant that was partially owned by his father. Engels used his first-hand knowledge of the hardships of factory workers and his excellent writing skills to portray their lives.

Like *Uncle Tom's Cabin,* Engels' book outraged readers. Just four years later, Engels helped Karl Marx write *The Communist Manifesto,* one of the most influential books in history. They both believed that through revolution the new industrial working class would rise to power and transform society. In later years, Engels was a successful businessman (and capitalist) who used his income to support Marx and his writing.

Engels: *The Condition of the Working Class in England in 1844*

Objectives
- Understand living conditions in the new industrial city.
- Describe the hardships of the new industrial working class.

Build Background Knowledge
Ask students to recall what they know about the living conditions of the working class in the new industrial cities. Then ask them to speculate on why a writer might choose to describe those conditions.

Instruct
- Ask **What is the general condition of the buildings that Engels observes?** (*They are crumbling with age and some lack doors and windows. Many are one-room cabins with earth floors.*) **Why could Engels not see the pavement?** (*It was covered with filth and garbage.*)
- Discuss Engels' reasons for writing this passage. Ask **Why do you think Engels had never seen such sights before?** (*The working-class tenements were in a separate part of the city, away from the middle-class neighborhoods.*) **Who do you think was the target audience for this book?** (*probably upper- or middle-class people who could read and who would not know about the conditions described in Engels' book*)

Monitor Progress
Ask students to describe their reaction to the passage. Then ask **What was the author's purpose?** (*to educate readers and persuade them that reforms were needed*) Ask whether they think the work succeeded.

Thinking Critically
1. (a) The railway construction destroyed some areas but opened others to public view. (b) outraged
2. Engels is outraged at the poverty that the working class has suffered in the Industrial Revolution.

Objectives

As you teach this section, keep students focused on the following objectives to help them answer the Section Focus Question and master core content.

- Understand laissez-faire economics and the beliefs of those who supported it.
- Describe the doctrine of utilitarianism.
- Summarize the theories of socialism.
- Explain Marx's views of the working class and the response to Marxism.

Prepare to Read

Build Background Knowledge ⑬

Ask students to recall the conditions faced by the industrial working class and how people like Engels viewed their plight. Then have them predict what reformers might propose to improve conditions.

Set a Purpose ⑬

- **WITNESS HISTORY** Read the selection aloud or play the audio.

  🔊 AUDIO **Witness History Audio CD,** The Struggle of the Working Class

  Ask **According to *The Communist Manifesto*, how do owners view workers?** *(as part of the machinery)* **How does this affect workers?** *(They are given simple, boring tasks.)*

- **Focus** Point out the Section Focus Question and write it on the board. Tell students to refer to this question as they read. *(Answer appears with Section 4 Assessment answers.)*

- **Preview** Have students preview the Section Objectives and the list of Terms, People, and Places.

- **Note Taking** Have students read this section using the Structured Read Aloud (TE, p. T20) strategy. As they read, have students outline the new economic theories.

  📝 **Reading and Note Taking Study Guide,** pp. 95–96

SECTION 4

Workers on break, London

WITNESS HISTORY 🔊 AUDIO

The Struggle of the Working Class

Karl Marx and Friedrich Engels give their view on how the Industrial Revolution affected workers:

❝Owing to the extensive use of machinery and to division of labor, the work of the proletarians has lost all individual character, and, consequently, all charm for the workman. He becomes [a limb] of the machine, and it is only the most simple, most monotonous, and most easily acquired knack, that is required of him. . . .❞
—From *The Communist Manifesto*

Focus Question What new ideas about economics and society were fostered as a result of the Industrial Revolution?

New Ways of Thinking

Objectives
- Understand laissez-faire economics and the beliefs of those who supported it.
- Describe the doctrine of utilitarianism.
- Summarize the theories of socialism.
- Explain Marx's views of the working class and the response to Marxism.

Terms, People, and Places

Thomas Malthus	Robert Owen
Jeremy Bentham	Karl Marx
utilitarianism	communism
socialism	proletariat
means of production	social democracy

Note Taking

Reading Skill: Identify Main Ideas Write an outline like the one here to show the new economic and social theories.

```
I. Laissez-faire economics
   A. Adam Smith and free enterprise
      1.
      2.
II. Malthus on population
    A.
```

Everywhere in Britain, British economist **Thomas Malthus** saw the effects of the population explosion—crowded slums, hungry families, unemployment, and widespread misery. After careful study, in 1798 he published *An Essay on the Principle of Population*. He concluded that poverty was unavoidable because the population was increasing faster than the food supply. Malthus wrote: "The power of population is [far] greater than the power of the Earth to produce subsistence for man."

Malthus was one of many thinkers who tried to understand the staggering changes taking place in the early Industrial Age. As heirs to the Enlightenment, these thinkers looked for natural laws that governed the world of business and economics.

Laissez-Faire Economics

During the Enlightenment, physiocrats argued that natural laws should be allowed to operate without interference. As part of this philosophy, they believed that government should not interfere in the free operation of the economy. In the early 1800s, middle-class business leaders embraced this laissez-faire, or "hands-off," approach.

As you have learned, the main proponent of laissez-faire economics was Adam Smith, author of bestseller *The Wealth of Nations*. Smith asserted that a free market—the unregulated exchange of goods and services—would come to help everyone, not just the rich. The free market, Smith said, would produce more goods at lower prices, making them affordable to everyone. A growing economy would also encourage capitalists to reinvest

---

Vocabulary Builder

Use the information below and the following resources to teach the high-use word from this section.
All in One Teaching Resources, Unit 2, p. 45; **Teaching Resources, Skills Handbook,** p. 3

High-Use Word	Definition and Sample Sentence
formulate, p. 263	*vt.* to devise or develop, as in a theory or plan The coaches **formulated** a plan to stop the other team's high-scoring offense.

profits in new ventures. Supporters of this free-enterprise capitalism pointed to the successes of the Industrial Age, in which government had played no part.

Malthus Holds Bleak View Also a laissez-faire economist, Thomas Malthus predicted that population would outpace the food supply. The only checks on population growth, he said, were nature's "natural" methods of war, disease, and famine. As long as population kept increasing, he went on, the poor would suffer. He thus urged families to have fewer children and discouraged charitable handouts and vaccinations.

During the early 1800s, many people accepted Malthus's bleak view as the factory system changed people's lifestyles for the worse. His view was proved wrong, however. Although the population boom did continue, the food supply grew even faster. As the century progressed, living conditions for the Western world slowly improved—and then people began having fewer children. By the 1900s, population growth was no longer a problem in the West, but it did continue to afflict many nations elsewhere.

Ricardo Shares View Another influential British laissez-faire economist, David Ricardo, dedicated himself to economic studies after reading Smith's *The Wealth of Nations.* Like Malthus, Ricardo did not hold out hope for the working class to escape poverty. Because of such gloomy predictions, economics became known as the "dismal science." In his "Iron Law of Wages," Ricardo pointed out that wage increases were futile because increases would only cover the cost of necessities. This was because when wages were high, families often had more children instead of raising the family's current standard of living.

Both Malthus and Ricardo opposed any government help for the poor. In their view, the best cure for poverty was not government relief but the unrestricted "laws of the free market." They felt that individuals should be left to improve their lot through thrift, hard work, and limiting the size of their families.

✔ **Checkpoint** Explain the response to laissez-faire economics during the nineteenth century.

Population Theory
Thomas Malthus believed poor families should have fewer children to preserve the food supply. *What were the advantages of families with many children?*

Utilitarians For Limited Government

Other thinkers sought to modify laissez-faire doctrines to justify some government intervention. By 1800, British philosopher and economist **Jeremy Bentham** was advocating **utilitarianism,** or the idea that the goal of society should be "the greatest happiness for the greatest number" of its citizens. To Bentham, all laws or actions should be judged by their "utility." In other words, did they provide more pleasure or happiness than pain? Bentham strongly supported individual freedom, which he believed guaranteed happiness. Still, he saw the need for government to become involved under certain circumstances.

Laissez-Faire Economics/ Utilitarians for Limited Government ⓛ₃

Instruct

■ **Introduce** Direct students' attention to the image of the large family on this page. Ask **Did large families make life easier or harder for working people?** *(Large families meant more hands to work but also many mouths to feed.)* **What kinds of problems came with overpopulation?** *(lower wages, unemployment, poverty)*

■ **Teach** On the board, create three columns, labeled *Smith*; *Malthus and Ricardo*; and *Bentham and Mill.* Have students fill in each group of economists' ideas on business and the government's role.

■ **Quick Activity** Assign students to three groups to examine the beliefs of Smith, Malthus and Ricardo, or Bentham and Mill. Then organize a quick debate on the strengths and weaknesses of each system in terms of balancing individual freedom and public good.

Independent Practice

Biography To help students better understand utilitarianism, have them read the biography *Jeremy Bentham* and complete the worksheet.

All in One Teaching Resources, Unit 2, p. 49

Monitor Progress

As students fill in their outlines, circulate to make sure they understand the difference between laissez-faire economics and utiliarianism. For a completed version of the outline, see

▦ **Note Taking Transparencies,** 143

Answers

Caption Families with many children had more money coming in as the children went off to work at a young age.

✔ Government should not interfere in business because a free market eventually brings greater prosperity to everyone.

Socialist Thought Emerges ⓛ

Instruct

- **Introduce: Key Terms** Have students find the key term *socialism* (in blue) in the text and explain its meaning. Point out the word's root, *social,* and that it was supposed to lead to *social good,* a system that was good for all of *society.* Ask students to picture a society in which all work is shared and all property is owned in common. As a class, examine challenges that might arise.

- **Teach** Explain that Bentham and Mill wanted to reform laissez-faire economics, but socialists wanted to abolish capitalism entirely. Ask **What are the** ***means of production?*** *(farms, factories, railways, and other large businesses that produce and distribute goods)* **What is the name of the system in which individuals own the means of production?** *(capitalism)* **Why did socialists think that private ownership of the means of production was bad?** *(They believed it would always lead to wealth for the rich and injustice for poor workers.)*

- **Quick Activity** Direct students' attention to the Infographic on this page. Ask them to compare the actions Robert Owen took to those of other reformers of the time. Then have students complete the interactivity at **Web Code nbp-1941.**

Independent Practice

Have students write a paragraph comparing Thomas More's Utopia with Robert Owen's New Lanark. Paragraphs should analyze which aspects of New Lanark seem ideal and which do not.

Monitor Progress

To ensure understanding, have students look at their essays on More's Utopia and Owen's New Lanark. Ask students to explain whether New Lanark was socialist, capitalist, both, or neither.

Answers

✔ Mill believed government should intervene to prevent harm to its citizens, such as abuse of workers.

Thinking Critically
1. It appears that children at New Lanark attended classes instead of living in crowded, dirty conditions.
2. Students' answers should include specific reasons.

Bentham's ideas influenced the British philosopher and economist John Stuart Mill. Although he believed strongly in individual freedom, Mill wanted the government to step in to improve the hard lives of the working class. "The only purpose for which power can be rightfully exercised over any member of a civilized community, against his will," Mill wrote, "is to prevent harm to others." Therefore, while middle-class business and factory owners were entitled to increase their own happiness, the government should prevent them from doing so in a manner that would harm workers.

Mill further called for giving the vote to workers and women. These groups could then use their political power to win reforms. Most middle-class people rejected Mill's ideas. Only in the later 1800s were his views

● INFOGRAPHIC

> *"The population… is crowded into one dense mass of cottages. …This is an atmosphere loaded with the exhalation of a large manufacturing city."*
> —J.P. Kay

▲ The Industrial Age brought harsh living conditions and poverty as people crowded into cities.

Thinking Critically
1. **Make Generalizations** Based on the images, how did life for children at New Lanark differ from those who lived in industrial cities?
2. **Recognize Ideologies** Do you think Utopianism was an effective solution for the challenges of the Industrial Age? Why or why not?

Owen's Utopia

The poverty and filth of the Industrial Age did not sit well with Robert Owen, a British social reformer. Like other Utopians, he believed there was a way he could change society for the better. To prove his point, he set up his cotton mill in New Lanark, Scotland, as a model village. He insisted that the conditions in which people lived shaped their character. Owen reduced working hours, built homes for workers, started a school for children, and opened a company store where workers could buy food and clothes. He showed that an employer could offer decent living and working conditions and still run a profitable business. Between 1815 and 1825, about 20,000 people visited New Lanark to study Owen's reforms. The complex eventually fell into decline but visitors can still wander the village today.

> *"…[I have never seen] so much order, good government, tranquility, and rational happiness prevail."*
> —Visitor to New Lanark

History *Interactive*
For: Interactive Village
Web Code: nbp-1941

▲ Children attended geography classes and dance lessons at the school in New Lanark.

Differentiated Instruction — Solutions for All Learners

ⓛ Less Proficient Readers   ⓛ English Language Learners

Guide students in using word relationships to learn key terms. Tell them that the suffix *-ism* means practice of or belief in. For the key words *socialism, utilitarianism, capitalism,* and *communism,* have students write a sentence that explains the term using the root and suffix (e.g., "*Communism* is the belief in *communal* ownership of the means of production").

Use the following resources to help students acquire basic skills:

Adapted Reading and Note Taking Study Guide
- Adapted Note Taking Study Guide, pp. 95–96
- Adapted Section Summary, p. 97

slowly accepted. Today's democratic governments, however, have absorbed many ideas from Mill and the other utilitarians.

 Checkpoint What did John Stuart Mill see as the proper role of government?

Socialist Thought Emerges

While the champions of laissez-faire economics praised individual rights, other thinkers focused on the good of society in general. They condemned the evils of industrial capitalism, which they believed had created a gulf between rich and poor. To end poverty and injustice, they offered a radical solution—**socialism.** Under socialism, the people as a whole rather than private individuals would own and operate the means of production— the farms, factories, railways, and other large businesses that produced and distributed goods. Socialism grew out of the Enlightenment faith in progress and human nature and its concern for social justice.

Are Utopians Dreamers? A number of early socialists established communities in which all work was shared and all property was owned in common. When there was no difference between rich and poor, they said, fighting between people would disappear. These early socialists were called Utopians. The name implied that they were impractical dreamers. The Utopian **Robert Owen** set up a model community in New Lanark, Scotland, to put his own ideas into practice.

Owen Establishes a Utopia A poor Welsh boy, Owen became a successful mill owner. Unlike most industrialists at the time, he refused to use child labor. He campaigned vigorously for laws that limited child labor and encouraged the organization of labor unions.

 Checkpoint What did early socialists believe?

Karl Marx Calls for Worker Control

In the 1840s, **Karl Marx,** a German philosopher, condemned the ideas of the Utopians as unrealistic idealism. He formulated a new theory, "scientific socialism," which he claimed was based on a scientific study of history. He teamed up with another German socialist, Friedrich Engels, whose father owned a textile factory in England.

Marx and Engels wrote a pamphlet, *The Communist Manifesto*, which they published in 1848. "A spectre [ghost] is haunting Europe," it began, "the spectre of communism." Marx predicted a struggle between social classes that would lead to a classless society where all means of production would be owned by the community. In practice, however, **communism** later came to refer to a system in which governments led by a small elite controlled all economic and political life.

In *The Communist Manifesto*, Marx theorized that economics was the driving force in history. He argued that there was "the history of class struggles" between the "haves" and the "have-nots." The "haves" had always owned the means of production and thus controlled society and all its wealth. In industrialized Europe, Marx said, the "haves" were the bourgeoisie. The "have-nots" were the **proletariat,** or working class.

According to Marx, the modern class struggle pitted the bourgeoisie against the proletariat. In the end, he predicted, the proletariat would be

Vocabulary Builder

formulated—(FAWR myoo layt id) *vt.* devised or developed, as in a theory or plan

Karl Marx Calls for Worker Control/Marxism in the Future ⓛ

Instruct

- **Introduce: Vocabulary Builder** Have students read the Vocabulary Builder term and definition. Ask students to speculate about how the thinkers introduced in this section *formulated* their theories. Ask them what they think Marx meant when he said his theory was based on scientific study of history.

- **Teach** Explain Marx's ideas. Ask **According to Marx, what kind of struggle drove history?** *(the class struggle)* **Which two groups were in conflict?** *(the haves and have-nots)* **Who was the proletariat?** *(the working class)* **How would capitalism come to an end?** *(The workers would unite and overthrow it.)* **What would the ideal society look like?** *(classless, with wealth and means of production owned in common by all)* Review with students what happened when people tried to put Marxism into practice.

- **Quick Activity** Tell students that in the United States today, people continue to debate the degree to which government should intervene to alleviate social and economic problems. Use the Think-Write-Pair-Share strategy (TE, p. T23) to have students discuss this issue.

Independent Practice

Direct students' attention to the poster on page 264. Ask them which political ideas the poster expresses. Then have them create a poster for one of the political systems they have studied.

Monitor Progress

Check Reading and Note Taking Study Guide entries for student understanding.

History Background

Robert Owen Although Robert Owen had mixed success, he left many important legacies. He himself left school at the age of ten to work in the textile industry. When he became a wealthy factory co-owner, he fought for reforms in working hours, child labor, and education. Jeremy Bentham was one of the partners in Owen's New Lanark community, where education for workers' children included a nursery school, a new idea in Britain. In 1825, Owen left New Lanark and started a small cooperative agricultural community across the sea in New Harmony, Indiana. Although the community failed and depleted his resources, the cooperative movement later revived. There are many cooperatives today founded on Owen's ideas. Owen returned to Britain and helped establish the trade union movement, another important legacy.

Answer

 Early socialists believed that all property and all means of production should be owned by the people as a whole.

Assess Progress

- Have students complete the Section Assessment.

- Administer the Section Quiz.

 **Teaching Resources, Unit 2**, p. 44

- To further assess student understanding, use

   Progress Monitoring Transparencies, 82

Reteach

If students need more instruction, have them read the section summary.

 Reading and Note Taking Study Guide, p. 97

Adapted Reading and Note Taking Study Guide, p. 97

Spanish Reading and Note Taking Study Guide, p. 97

Extend

Viewpoints To help students appreciate different viewpoints about industrialization, have them read the selection *Responses to the Industrial Revolution* and complete the worksheet.

 Teaching Resources, Unit 2, p. 50

Answers

 The proletariat would overthrow capitalism through revolution, take control of the means of production, and create a classless society.

Marx was wrong about international revolution, and by the 1990s, few communist countries remained.

---

triumphant. Workers would then take control of the means of production and set up a classless, communist society. Such a society would mark the end of the struggles people had endured throughout history, because wealth and power would be equally shared. Marx despised capitalism. He believed it created prosperity for only a few and poverty for many. He called for an international struggle to bring about its downfall. "Workers of all countries," he urged, "unite!"

 Checkpoint What did Marx predict was the future of the proletariat?

Marxism in the Future

At first, Marxism gained popularity with many people around the world. Leaders of a number of reform movements adopted the idea that power should be held by workers rather than by business owners. Marx's ideas, however, would never be practiced exactly as he imagined.

Marxism Briefly Flourishes In the 1860s, German socialists adapted Marx's beliefs to form **social democracy,** a political ideology in which there is a gradual transition from capitalism to socialism instead of a sudden violent overthrow of the system. In the late 1800s, Russian socialists embraced Marxism, and the Russian Revolution of 1917 set up a communist-inspired government. For much of the 1900s, revolutionaries around the world would adapt Marxist ideas to their own situations and needs. Independence leaders in Asia, Latin America, and Africa would turn to Marxism.

Marxism Loses Appeal As time passed, however, the failures of Marxist governments would illustrate the flaws in Marx's arguments. He predicted that workers would unite across national borders to wage class warfare. Instead, nationalism won out over working-class loyalty. In general, people felt stronger ties to their own countries than to the international communist movement. By the end of the twentieth century, few nations remained with communist governments, while nearly every economy included elements of free-market capitalism.

 Checkpoint How accurate did Marx's predictions about social classes prove to be?

Workers of the World
An 1895 leaflet urges that "Workers of the World Unite," the slogan of the socialist movement of Marx (above) and Engels.

Section 4 Assessment

Progress Monitoring Online
For: Self-quiz with vocabulary practice
Web Code: nba-1941

Terms, People, and Places
1. For each term, person, or place listed at the beginning of the section, write a sentence explaining its significance.

Note Taking
2. **Reading Skill: Identify Main Ideas** Use your completed outline to answer the Focus Question: What new ideas about economics and society were fostered as a result of the Industrial Revolution?

Comprehension and Critical Thinking
3. **Identify Points of View** What were the views of laissez-faire economists (a) Adam Smith, (b) Thomas Malthus, and (c) David Ricardo?
4. **Compare Points of View** Contrast the approaches of utilitarians and socialists to solving economic problems.
5. **Synthesize Information** How might workplace reforms have altered Marxist predictions of world revolution?

● **Writing About History**
Quick Write: Write a Thesis Statement As in other types of essays, it is important to clearly state your thesis, or main idea, when writing an explanatory essay. Write a thesis statement followed by a short paragraph on one of the theories discussed in this section.

Section 4 Assessment

1. Sentences should reflect an understanding of each term, person, or place listed at the beginning of the section.
2. laissez-faire economics, utilitarianism, socialism, and communism (Marxism)
3. (a) Adam Smith believed in a free market. (b) Thomas Malthus believed population growth would lead to famine. (c) David

Ricardo formulated the "Iron Law of Wages," which stated that wage increases only encouraged larger families.
4. Utilitarians believed government should intervene to curb abuses; socialists wanted to abolish capitalism altogether and have the people own the means of production.
5. They might have lessened workers' suffering and made them less likely to stage revolutions.

● **Writing About History**

Responses should include a clear thesis statement about a political theory studied in this section. The rest of the paragraph should support or develop the thesis statement.

For additional assessment, have students access **Progress Monitoring Online** at **Web Code nba-1941.**

ECONOMIC SYSTEMS

How should resources and wealth be distributed?

"Please, sir, I want some more."

In This Chapter

In the United States and Europe, industry began to replace traditional agriculture by the mid-1800s. New ways of thinking emerged about how to answer these three key economic questions: (1) What will be produced? (2) How will it be produced? (3) Who will get the product? In the illustration from *Oliver Twist* (right), a young orphan asks for more food.

Throughout History

Prehistory Hunters and gatherers live off the land.

900s A.D. The self-sufficient manor is at the heart of the feudal economy.

1500s–1700s Under mercantalism, colonies exist to enrich European powers.

1800s In the free market system, individual businesses operate without government control.

1800s Industrial workers struggle to gain better wages and living conditions.

1900s Under communism, the Soviet government owns most businesses and property.

Continuing Today

The World Trade Organization (WTO) negotiates the rules of trade between nations. At an annual WTO meeting, protestors express their view that the rights of developing nations are insufficiently protected.

21st Century Skills

 **TRANSFER Activities**

1. **Analyze** Throughout history, how have answers to the key economic questions differed?

2. **Evaluate** Why does it matter who controls the economy?

3. **Transfer** Complete a Web quest in which you analyze how different economics systems allocate resources and wealth; record your thoughts in the Concept Connector Journal; and learn to make a video. Web Code nbh-1908

Economic Systems

Objectives

- Identify the three key economic questions.
- Understand that economic systems are based on the distribution of resources.
- Complete a web quest on economic systems.

Build Background Knowledge L3

Identify the three major economic systems and describe their main characteristics. *(market economy: buyers and sellers make key economic decisions; centrally planned economy: government makes the key economic decisions; mixed economy: free enterprise, with significant government role in economic decisions).*

Instruct L3

- Direct students' attention to the Essential Question: **How should resources and wealth be distributed?** Have students read In This Chapter and look at the corresponding cartoon. Ask: **How did the transition from an agricultural society to an industrial society change the economic pattern?**

- Assign the Web Quest activity.

Independent Practice

Concept Connector Have students fill in the Web Quest reflection question on economic systems in their Concept Connector Journal.

 Reading and Note Taking Study Guide, p. 260

Monitor Progress

Circulate to make sure that students are filling in their Concept Connector journal. Ensure they understand how resources and wealth are distributed.

Transfer Activities

1. Governments have chosen different economic systems to address the key economic questions.
2. Whoever controls the economy determines how resources are distributed.
3. Students' work should be evaluated against the rubric at Web Code nbh-1908.

History Background

Social Democracy Ferdinand Lassalle, son of a Jewish merchant, founded what became the first Social Democratic Party in Germany in the 1860s. He believed that revolution was unnecessary—that if workers could vote, they would force the state to reform. In the 1890s, in his book *Evolutionary Socialism,* Eduard Bernstein agreed, and he used scientific methods to refute Marxist theories of revolution. He used statistics to show that capitalism was not collapsing and workers' lives were not getting worse. Bernstein and others came to believe that democracy could be used to bring about socialist goals. Over the course of the twentieth century, social democratic parties in most countries came to believe in reforming capitalism rather than abolishing it. They prefer democracy to Marx's "dictatorship of the proletariat."

- Have students use the Quick Study Guide to prepare for this chapter's test. Students may wish to refer to the following pages as they review:

New Inventions and Ideas
Section 1, pp. 247–249; Section 2, pp. 252–253; Section 3, p. 256; Section 4, pp. 260–264

Effects of the Industrial Revolution
Section 1, pp. 246–248; Section 3, pp. 254–258; Section 4, pp. 260–264

Why Britain Industrialized First
Section 2, pp. 250–252

Responses to the Industrial Revolution
Section 4, pp. 260–264

Events From 1750–1850
Section 1, p. 248; Section 2, pp. 252–253; Section 4, pp. 263–264

- For additional review, remind **L3** students to refer to the

 Reading and Note Taking Study Guide
Note Taking Study Guide, pp. 89, 91, 93, 95–96
Section Summaries, pp. 90, 92, 93, 97

- Have students access **Web Code nbp-1901** for this chapter's **History** *Interactive* timeline, which includes expanded entries and additional events.

- If students need more instruction on analyzing a timeline, have them read the **Skills Handbook,** p. SH30.

- When students have completed their study of the chapter, distribute Chapter Tests A and B.

All in One Teaching Resources, Unit 2, pp. 54–59

For **Progress Monitoring Online,** refer students to the Self-test with Vocabulary Practice at **Web Code nba-1951.**

Quick Study Guide

Progress Monitoring *Online*
For: Self-test with vocabulary practice
Web Code: nba-1951

■ New Inventions and Ideas

Inventors and Thinkers	Inventions and Ideas
Jethro Tull	Seed drill
Thomas Newcomen	Steam engine
James Watt	Improved steam engine
John Kay	Flying shuttle
James Hargreaves	Spinning jenny
Richard Arkwright	Water frame
Eli Whitney	Cotton gin
George Stephenson	Steam-powered locomotive
John Wesley	Methodism
Adam Smith	Laissez-faire economics
Thomas Malthus	Population growth could outpace food supply.
Jeremy Bentham	Utilitarianism
Robert Owen	Utopian communities
Karl Marx	Communism, Marxism

■ Effects of the Industrial Revolution

Industrial Revolution

↓

- Population growth
- Rural to urban migration
- Growth of cities

↓

- Poor working conditions in factories
- Low wages
- Overcrowding in cities

↓

- Laissez-faire economics
- Utilitarianism
- Socialism
- Marxism

■ Why Britain Industrialized First

Industrial Revolution in Britain
Plentiful natural resources
Ready workforce
Prosperous economy
Availability of capital and demand
Stable government

■ Responses to the Industrial Revolution

- Bentham/Mill: utilitarianism
- Socialism
- Owen: utopianism
- Marx/Engels: communism

■ Events From 1750–1850

Early Industrial Revolution Events
Global Events

1760s Watt improves the steam engine.

1764 The spinning jenny is invented.

1750

1775

1762 Catherine the Great comes to power in Russia.

1770 Cook claims Australia for Britain.

1788 Futa Toro outlaws slave trade.

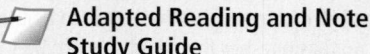

Differentiated Instruction Solutions for All Learners

L1 Special Needs **L2 Less Proficient Readers**

Use the following study guide resources to help students acquiring basic skills:

Adapted Reading and Note Taking Study Guide
Adapted Note Taking Study Guide, pp. 89, 91, 93, 95–96
Adapted Section Summaries, pp. 90, 92, 94, 97

L2 English Language Learners

Use the following study guide resources to help Spanish-speaking students:

Spanish Reading and Note Taking Study Guide
Spanish Note Taking Study Guide, pp. 89, 91, 93, 95–96
Spanish Section Summaries, pp. 90, 92, 94, 97

Concept Connector

Essential Question Review

To connect prior knowledge with what you have learned in this chapter, answer the questions below in your Concept Connector journal. Use the journal in the Reading and Note Taking Study Guide to record your answers (or go to www.phschool.com **Web Code:** nbd-1907). In addition, record information about the following concepts:

- Economic Systems: market economy
- Economic Systems: centrally planned economy
- Economic Systems: mixed economy

1. **Economic Systems** The Commercial Revolution in the 1500s gave rise to capitalism and mercantilism. The Industrial Revolution gave rise to new economic theories: laissez-faire economics, utilitarianism, and socialism. Compare capitalism and socialism. Think about how wealth is gained and distributed in each economic system.

2. **Technology** Once James Watt made improvements to Thomas Newcomen's steam engine, it became a key power source of the Industrial Revolution. In a similar way, hundreds of years earlier, the printing press had dramatically changed how people communicated and shared information. Compare the impact of the two developments. Consider the following:
   - who benefited from the use of the invention
   - how the work was done before the invention
   - why the invention was important

■ Connections to Today

1. **Migration: Twentieth Century Global Migrations** During the Industrial Revolution, rural workers migrated to urban areas to live and work. Today, people still migrate in various parts of the world. Do online and library research to find information on rural-to-urban migration in a country located in Asia or Africa. Write a brief newspaper article in which you compare the experiences of those who migrated then and now.

Strawberry pickers at work, South Africa

2. **People and the Environment: Population Growth** The population growth that occurred during the Industrial Revolution often created filth and unsanitary conditions as people crowded into tenements. The growth also caused an increase in the demand for products, which led to the opening of more factories. Do online and library research to find the history of population growth in the town or state in which you live. What are the patterns and results?

| 1800 Owen begins social reforms at New Lanark. | 1807 Fulton develops the first successful steamboat, the *Clermont*. | 1830 The Liverpool-Manchester Railroad opens. | | 1848 Marx and Engels publish *The Communist Manifesto.* |

History Interactive
For: Interactive timeline
Web Code: nbp-1901

1800 — 1825 — 1850

| 1804 Napoleon becomes the emperor of France. | 1814 Congress of Vienna meets to restore stability in Europe. | 1819 Bolívar captures Bogotá. | 1848 Revolutions sweep Europe. |

Concept Connector

Tell students that the main concepts for this chapter are Economic Systems, Technology, and then ask them to answer the Essential Question Review questions on this page. Discuss the Connections to Today topics and ask students to answer the questions that follow.

Essential Question Review

1. In capitalism, businesses naturally regulate themselves through competition and supply and demand. In socialism, the people own the means of production, sharing wealth with the other citizens of their society. Capitalists assume that people will prosper if left to make their own monetary decisions, and that the government does not need to regulate the economy. Socialists advocate government intervention to ensure that the needs of the people are met.

2. Student answers should demonstrate how both inventions changed the way people lived. The steam engine revolutionized transportation, greatly expanding how people traveled and traded. The printing press revolutionized how people learned, making it possible to disseminate information on a much wider scale. Prior to the steam engine, travel was dangerous and slow, making it harder to migrate and trade. Before the printing press, manuscripts had to be copied by hand, and most literate people did not own many books.

Connections to Today

1. Articles should highlight both geographical and historical differences. They may choose to focus on modern migration policies.

2. Students should trace the history of population growth or decline in their town or state. For periods of growth, they should mention environmental effects such as air and water pollution.

L3

For additional review of this chapter's core concepts, remind students to refer to the

 Reading and Note Taking Study Guide
Concept Connector, pp. 259, 295

Differentiated
Instruction   Solutions for All Learners

L1 Special Needs **L2 Less Proficient Readers**
Use the following study guide resources to help students acquiring basic skills:

 **Adapted Reading and Note Taking Study Guide**
Adapted Concept Connector, pp. 259, 295

L2 English Language Learners
Use the following study guide resources to help Spanish-speaking students:

 **Spanish Reading and Note Taking Study Guide**
Spanish Concept Connector, pp. 259, 295

Document-Based Assessment

New Economic and Social Theories

Various thinkers of the day attempted to understand and interpret the dramatic changes brought about by the Industrial Revolution. They responded with a wide range of explanations and solutions, as the documents below illustrate.

Document A

"As every individual, therefore, endeavours as much as he can both to employ his capital in the support of domestic industry, and so to direct that industry that its produce may be of the greatest value; every individual necessarily labours to render the annual revenue of the society as great as he can. . . . By preferring the support of domestic to that of foreign industry, he intends only his own security; and by directing that industry in such a manner as its produce may be of the greatest value, he intends only his own gain, and he is in this, as in many other cases, led by an invisible hand to promote an end which was no part of his intention. . . . every individual it is evident, can, in his local situation, judge much better than any statesman or lawgiver can do for him."

—From ***The Wealth of Nations*** by Adam Smith, 1776

Document B

"In those characters which now exhibit crime, the fault is obviously not in the individual, but the defects proceed from the system in which the individual was trained. Withdraw those circumstances which tend to create crime in the human character, and crime will not be created. Replace them with such as are calculated to form habits of order, regularity, temperance, industry; and these qualities will be formed. . . . Proceed systematically on principles of undeviating persevering kindness, yet retaining and using, with the least possible severity, the means of restraining crime from immediately injuring society, and by degrees even the crimes now existing in adults will also gradually disappear. . . ."

—From ***A New View of Society*** by Robert Owen, 1816

Document C

New Lanark Mills, Scotland

Document D

". . . the power of population is indefinitely greater than the power in the earth to produce subsistence for man. Population, when unchecked, increased in a geometrical ratio. Subsistence increases only in an arithmetical ratio. A slight acquaintance with numbers will show the immensity of the first power in comparison of the second. . . . No fancied equality, no agrarian regulations in their utmost extent, could remove the pressure of it even for a single century. And it appears, therefore, to be decisive against the possible existence of a society, all the members of which should live in ease, happiness, and comparative leisure; and feel no anxiety about providing the means of subsistence for themselves and families. Consequently, if the premises are just, the argument is conclusive against the perfectibility of the mass of mankind."

—From ***An Essay on the Principle of Population 1798***
by Thomas Malthus

Analyzing Documents

Use your knowledge of the new economic and social theories and Documents A, B, C, and D to answer the questions below.

1. According to Adam Smith in Document A, individuals promote the good of society because of
   A high ideals.
   B self-interest.
   C government pressure.
   D religion.

2. How did Robert Owen explain the fact that some people become criminals?
   A the invisible hand of fate
   B struggles between the ruling class and the oppressed
   C the influence of problems in society
   D the power of population over production

3. Thomas Malthus argued that a society where all individuals enjoy happiness, comfort, and pleasure is
   A only possible with increased agricultural output.
   B impossible because of the base nature of human greed.
   C impossible because of the pressures of population.
   D possible when people are treated decently and fairly.

4. **Writing Task** Suppose you were working in Britain in the year 1840. Which of the above economic philosophies would you support? Remember to identify your occupation and social class. Use your knowledge of the Industrial Revolution and the documents above to support your opinion.

● Writing About History

As students begin the assignment, refer them to page SH10 of the **Writing Handbook** for help in writing an explanatory essay. Remind them of the steps they should take to complete their assignment, including prewriting, drafting, and revising. For help in revising, remind them to use the guidelines on page SH12 of the **Writing Handbook.**

Students' explanatory essays should have a clear thesis supported by facts, examples, and comparisons with one or more other revolutions. They should contain an introduction, a body, and a conclusion. They should show evidence of reflection and be free of grammatical and spelling errors. For scoring rubrics for writing assignments, see **Assessment Rubrics,** p. 8.

Answers

1. B
2. C
3. C
4. Responses should show a clear understanding of the chosen economic philosophy and its effects on a person of the chosen occupation and social class. Students should use specific evidence from the documents and the chapter to support their conclusions.

Revolutions in Europe and Latin America

Section	Core Instruction **L3**	Differentiated Instruction **L1 L2 L4**

Section 1
An Age of Ideologies

🕐 **2 periods, 1 block**

OBJECTIVES
- Understand the goals of the conservatives.
- Explain how liberals and nationalists challenged the old order.
- Summarize the early challenges to the old order in Europe.

Focus Question *What events proved that Metternich was correct in his fears?*

Core Instruction (Section 1):

All in One Teaching Resources, Unit 2
Reading Strategy: Identify Main Ideas, p. 64
Vocabulary Builder: Visualizing Vocabulary, p. 63
Section 1 Quiz, p. 60

Reading and Note Taking Study Guide
Note Taking Study Guide, p. 98
Section 1 Summary, p. 99

Note Taking Transparencies, 144A–144B

WITNESS HISTORY Audio CD
A "Revolutionary Seed"

Progress Monitoring Transparencies, 83

Color Transparencies, 119

Teaching Resources, Skills Handbook
Prereading the Chapter, pp. 1–2
Word Knowledge Rating Form, p. 3
K-W-L Chart, p. 4

Differentiated Instruction (Section 1):

L1 Adapted Reading and Note Taking Study Guide
Note Taking Study Guide, p. 98 **SN**
Section 1 Summary, p. 99 **SN**

***Student Edition Audio** **SN**

Differentiated Instruction Activity,
Teacher's Edition, p. 273 **SN**

L2 Adapted Reading and Note Taking Study Guide
Note Taking Study Guide, p. 98 **LPR**
Section 1 Summary, p. 99 **LPR**

Spanish Reading and Note Taking Study Guide
Note Taking Study Guide, p. 98 **ELL**
Section 1 Summary, p. 99 **ELL**

***Guided Reading Audio**
(Spanish) **ELL**

***Student Edition Audio** **LPR**

Differentiated Instruction Activity,
Teacher's Edition, p. 273 **LPR, ELL**

L4 All in One Teaching Resources, Unit 2
Traveler's Tales: Writings of Lord Byron from Greece, p. 65 **AR, GT**

Extend Activity,
Teacher's Edition, p. 275 **AR, GT**

Section 2
Revolutions of 1830 and 1848

🕐 **1 period, .5 block**

OBJECTIVES
- Describe how French rebels won some reforms in 1830.
- Analyze how the spirit of reform spread in 1830.
- Explain the revolutions that surged through France and throughout the rest of Europe in 1848.

Focus Question *What were the causes and effects of the revolutions in Europe in 1830 and 1848?*

Core Instruction (Section 2):

All in One Teaching Resources, Unit 2
Outline Map: Revolutions in Europe, 1820s–1840s, p. 70
Geography Quiz, p. 72
Section 2 Quiz, p. 61

Reading and Note Taking Study Guide
Note Taking Study Guide, p. 100
Section 2 Summary, p. 101

Note Taking Transparencies, 132

WITNESS HISTORY Audio CD
More Revolution in the Wind

Progress Monitoring Transparencies, 84

Color Transparencies, 120, 121, 122

Witness History Discovery School™
video program, *Revolutionary France: Les Misérables*

Differentiated Instruction (Section 2):

L1 Adapted Reading and Note Taking Study Guide
Note Taking Study Guide, p. 100 **SN**
Section 2 Summary, p. 101 **SN**

Differentiated Instruction Activity,
Teacher's Edition, pp. 277, 280 **SN**

L2 Adapted Reading and Note Taking Study Guide
Note Taking Study Guide, p. 100 **LPR**
Section 2 Summary, p. 101 **LPR**

Spanish Reading and Note Taking Study Guide
Note Taking Study Guide, p. 100 **ELL**
Section 2 Summary, p. 101 **ELL**

Differentiated Instruction Activity,
Teacher's Edition, pp. 277, 280 **LPR, ELL**

L4 All in One Teaching Resources, Unit 2
Link to Literature: From *Les Misérables,* by Victor Hugo, p. 66 **AR, GT**
Primary Source: From *Reminiscences,* by Carl Shurz, p. 67 **AR, GT**

Extend Activity,
Teacher's Edition, p. 281 **AR, GT**

Section 3
Revolts in Latin America

 2 periods, 1 block

OBJECTIVES
- Explain the causes of discontent in Latin America.
- Describe Haiti's fight for freedom.
- Summarize the revolts in Mexico and Central America.
- Understand how revolutions ignited South America.

Focus Question *Who were the key revolutionaries that led the movements for independence in Latin America, and what were their accomplishments?*

All in One Teaching Resources, Unit 2
Outline Map: Latin American Independence, p. 71
Section 3 Quiz, p. 62

Reading and Note Taking Study Guide
Note Taking Study Guide, p. 102
Section 3 Summary, p. 103
Concept Connector, pp. 237, 250, 291

Note Taking Transparencies, 133

WITNESS HISTORY Audio CD
A Revolutionary Is Born

Progress Monitoring Transparencies, 85

Color Transparencies, 123, 124

L1 Adapted Reading and Note Taking Study Guide
Note Taking Study Guide, p. 102 **SN**
Section 3 Summary, p. 103 **SN**
Concept Connector, pp. 237, 250, 291 **SN**

L2 Adapted Reading and Note Taking Study Guide
Note Taking Study Guide, p. 102 **LPR**
Section 3 Summary, p. 103 **LPR**
Concept Connector, pp. 237, 250, 291 **LPR**

L4 All in One Teaching Resources, Unit 2
Biography: Toussaint L'Ouverture, p. 68 **AR, GT**
Primary Source: From the Decree of Hidalgo, p. 69 **AR, GT**

Differentiated Instruction Activity, Teacher's Edition, p. 284 **SN**

Spanish Reading and Note Taking Study Guide
Note Taking Study Guide, p. 102 **ELL**
Section 3 Summary, p. 103 **ELL**
Concept Connector, pp. 237, 250, 291 **ELL**

Differentiated Instruction Activity, Teacher's Edition, p. 284 **LPR, ELL**

Differentiated Instruction Activity, Teacher's Edition, p. 286 **AR, GT**

Extend Activity, Teacher's Edition, pp. 270c, 288 **AR, GT**

---

*Audio support is available for all sections.

Assessment Resources

- **Progress Monitoring Transparencies,** 83–85
- **Test Prep,** Unit Study Sheets, pp. 97–99; Unit Test, pp. 20–23
- **SuccessTracker™,** Chapter 8
- **Document-Based Assessment,** pp. 54–66
- *ExamView*® **Test Bank CD-ROM,** Chapter 8

- **All in One Teaching Resources, Unit 2,** Chapter Tests A and B, pp. 73–78
- **Progress Monitoring *Online* Quizzes,** Chapter 8
- **Assessment Rubrics**

Differentiated Instruction Key

L1	Special Needs	**LPR**	Less Proficient Readers
L2	Basic to Average	**AR**	Advanced Readers
L3	All Students	**SN**	Special Needs Students
L4	Average to Advanced	**GT**	Gifted and Talented
		ELL	English Language Learner

CHAPTER PLANNER

Author's Notes

The Spirit of Revolt

Social, economic, and political resentments had been building up for centuries among a variety of colonial groups. Conquered Indians resented the conquest and all the subsequent oppression. Black slaves were never reconciled to slavery. *Mestizos,* cut off by prejudice from other communities, envied the power of their fathers' European world and resented the oppression of their mothers' non-European people. *Criollos,* the chief builders of the colonial economy, saw no justice in the privileged social position and the political authority enjoyed by peninsular judges, bishops, military commanders, captains general, and viceroys. . . .

The most oppressed rebelled first—Indians in South America and black slaves in the Caribbean.

Tupac Amaru, who claimed descent from the Incas, was Jesuit-educated and wealthy. Nevertheless, he led a 1780 revolt of the brutally exploited Indians of the Peruvian Andes that briefly liberated Bolivia and parts of Peru and Argentina. Toussaint L'Ouverture, grandson of an African king, was a Haitian slave who had made his own fortune. Inspired by the French Revolution, he launched a ten-year rebellion against the French planters in Haiti (1791–1801). Tupac Amaru was captured and executed, many thousands of his followers slaughtered, his insurrection suppressed. Toussaint L'Ouverture freed Haiti but was betrayed to his enemies and died in a French prison. But the flame had been lit, in both South America and the Caribbean, and it would not go out.

Ironically, it was not the North American or French Revolutions that triggered Latin America's fifteen years of revolutionary upheaval, but the great empire builder Napoleon Bonaparte. Napoleon conquered both Spain and Portugal in the early 1800s and put puppet kings on their thrones. Even royalists in the Latin American colonies turned against these usurping monarchs in Madrid and Lisbon.

—Anthony Esler, *The Human Venture: From Prehistory to the Present,* (Upper Saddle River, New Jersey: Pearson Education 2004), pp. 520–521

Extend Online

Wars of Independence

Have students conduct research on the leaders of the independence movements in Latin America. Use the steps below to help students conduct the activity.

Prepare for the Activity Explain that as liberal ideas spread to Latin America from Europe, revolutionary movements arose to overthrow the European colonial powers. While reasons for discontent varied, Latin Americans all shared the goal of freedom. Strong leaders from a variety of backgrounds led the fight.

Conduct the Activity For help in starting the activity, send students to **Web Code nbe-2001.**

Tell students to suppose that they will write and direct a television miniseries about independence movements in Latin America. First, they need to create a list of characters to be portrayed in the drama. Have students, in small groups, research the biographies of the different leaders of the revolts in Latin America, including Simón Bolívar of Venezuela (pictured at left), Miguel Hidalgo of Mexico, José de San Martín of Argentina, and Toussaint L'Ouverture of Haiti. Ask each group to write up a detailed cast list, which includes the names, personalities, and motivations of those who will appear in this drama. Have them sketch out the major plot lines.

Follow-Up Conduct a class discussion based on the following questions: How are the leaders similar and different? What traits did independence leaders share? What goals did they share? What challenges did the different leaders face?

Differentiated Instruction   Solutions for All Learners

Providing Appropriate Resource Materials   L2

In order to maximize English language learner success in your social studies class, make sure that your classroom is provisioned with materials that can assist students struggling with English as a second language. These materials can help students better decipher text and assigned readings, write more coherently, and feel confident in their understanding of the content being taught. Materials that a teacher of English language learners should try to obtain include:

1. English dictionary for looking up unfamiliar terms

2. Two-way translation dictionaries for looking up words in their native language to obtain the equivalent word in English and for looking up unfamiliar words in English to find a definition in their native language.

3. Thesaurus to help students expand their English vocabulary. If a student essay repeatedly uses a basic vocabulary word such as "good," encourage students to use the thesaurus to incorporate a wider variety of words into their writing.

4. Grammar book to assist students in their writing.

5. A set of encyclopedias that provides brief and clear background information on a variety of topics. Often full-length books found in a school's library are daunting to English language learners beginning their historical research. Encyclopedias, particularly those aimed at K-12 students, allow students to research information without becoming overwhelmed by lengthy and difficult passages in English.

Modeling Reading and Writing Skills

Use Effective Language Explain that in this chapter students will be writing a persuasive essay. (See Writing About History, p. 292.) Point out that the words they choose can influence their reader's response to their arguments. When using a thesaurus to find synonyms or words with similar meanings, it is important to distinguish between a word's denotation and connotation. Explain that the denotation is a word's explicit meaning, which may be checked in a dictionary. A word's connotation is the implied meaning, or meaning given to it by a reader.

Write the words *clever* and *sly* on the board and ask students to describe a person who is characterized by each of these words. Point out that these words—*clever* and *sly*—have similar dictionary definitions, but opposite connotations. Including each of these words in a description will give a reader a different impression. Remind students that once they have drafted their essays, they should revise their word choice, replacing imprecise words with precise ones and paying attention to connotation as well as to words' explicit meanings.

Paraphrase Tell students that to paraphrase, they must restate what they have read in their own words. This will ensure that they comprehend the text. Explain that to paraphrase, they should replace some of the words in the passage and combine several words into one idea. They should also ensure that their paraphrased passage conveys the same ideas as the original passage and that it does not distort its meaning. Remind students that paraphrasing is especially useful when researching a paper, as it helps ensure that they don't plagiarize from their sources.

Model this skill by reading aloud the introductory paragraph to Section 1. Point out that one could combine the ideas of effects of the opposing ideologies and the aftermath of the Congress of Vienna. Then tell them that this paragraph says that two conflicting beliefs emerged after the Congress of Vienna, which caused chaos in the region. European leaders worked to preserve the old system, while others questioned it. Have students practice this skill with the next paragraph.

Teach With Technology

PresentationEXPRESS™
Premium DVD

■ Teach this chapter's core content using **PresentationExpress™ Premium,** which includes dynamic lecture notes, interactive game shows, songs, videos, and the *ExamView® QuickTake* assessment tool.

■ To introduce this chapter using **PresentationExpress™ Premium,** start by asking students **Which of the following statements do you most agree with? (A) People should wait for political change to occur on its own. (B) Violence is often the only way to bring political change. (C) Negotiation is the best way to bring political change. (D) Political change is pointless because it doesn't affect people's daily lives.** Take a class poll or record students' answers using the QuickTake feature and discuss their responses. Point out that in this chapter, they will read about revolutions in Europe and Latin America. Continue introducing the chapter using the chapter opener slide show and Witness History audio.

Technology Resources

■ Student**EXPRESS** CD-ROM, Chapter 8

■ Teacher**EXPRESS** CD-ROM, Chapter 8

■ Presentation**EXPRESS™** **Premium DVD,** Chapter 8

■ **WITNESS HISTORY** Audio CD, Chapter 8

■ *ExamView* **Test Bank CD-ROM,** English and Spanish, Chapter 8

■ **Guided Reading Audio,** Spanish, Chapter 8

■ **Student Edition Audio,** Chapter 8

■ **Witness History Discovery School™** video program, *Revolutionary France: Les Misérables*

■ **Experience It! Multimedia Pack**

Bibliography

For the Teacher

Dubois, Laurent. *Avengers of the New World: The Story of the Haitian Revolution.* Belknap Press, 2004.

Harvey, Robert. *Liberators: Latin America's Struggle for Independence.* Overlook Press, 2000.

Mansel, Philip. *Paris Between Empires: Monarchy and Revolution, 1814–1852.* St. Martin's Press, 2003.

For the Student

L1 Grant, R.G. *1848: Year of Revolution.* Thomson Learning, 1995.

L2 Stefoff, Rebecca. *Independence and Revolution in Mexico.* Facts on File, 1993.

L3 Goodnough, David. *Simon Bolivar: South American Liberator.* Enslow Publishers, 1998.

WITNESS HISTORY AUDIO

Freedom From Tyranny

Several revolutions erupted in Europe between 1815 and 1829, and the spread of revolutionary ideals would ignite new uprisings in 1830 and 1848. Also occurring during this time were the wars of independence in Latin America. These revolts began in the late 1700s and early 1800s and were inspired by the success of the American Revolution and the ideals of the French Revolution. Simón Bolívar was one of the great heroes in the fight for independence in Spanish South America. He helped win independence for Bolivia, Colombia, Ecuador, Peru, and Venezuela. Listen to the Witness History audio to learn more about revolutions in Europe and Latin America.

Simón Bolívar's crown

66A state too extensive in itself, or by virtue of its dependencies, ultimately falls into decay; its free government is transformed into a tyranny; it disregards the principles which it should preserve, and finally degenerates into despotism. The distinguishing characteristic of small republics is stability....99
—Simón Bolívar

◄ Bolívar fights Spanish troops in his endeavor to free South America.

French tricolor flag

Chapter Preview

Chapter Focus Question How did revolutionary ideals in Europe and Latin America ignite uprisings in the first half of the nineteenth century?

Section 1
An Age of Ideologies

Section 2
Revolutions of 1830 and 1848

Section 3
Revolts in Latin America

José de San Martín

Use the ☑ **Quick Study Timeline** at the end of this chapter to preview chapter events.

? Concept Connector ONLINE
To explore Essential Questions related to this chapter, go to PHSchool.com
Web Code: nbd-2007

Chapter-Level Resources

All in One Vocabulary Builder; Reading Strategy; Enrichments; Outline Maps; Geography Quiz; Chapter Tests
- Document-Based Assessments
- AYP Monitoring Assessments
- *ExamView* Test Bank CD-ROM
- Guided Reading Audio Spanish
- Student Edition Audio

Previewing the Chapter

- **WITNESS HISTORY** Point out that the late 1700s and first half of the 1800s were a period of change and revolution in Europe and Latin America. Ask students to explain the quotation in their own words. Then ask them to make a list of despotic governments with which they are familiar from their study of history. Does Bolívar's statement apply to any of these cases?

  ■))) AUDIO **Witness History Audio CD,** Freedom From Tyranny

- **Analyzing the Visuals** Ask students to study the mural of Bolívar in battle. Ask **What questions do the photos and the Witness History selection bring to mind?** *(What caused the fighting? What was the outcome of the battle? What is the significance of this scene?)* Write down students' questions. Tell students you are keeping a copy of these questions so that they can go back and answer them after they have read the chapter.

- **Focus** Write the Chapter Focus Question on the board. Tell students to keep this question in mind as they read the chapter. *(Answer appears with Chapter Assessment answers.)* Have students preview the section titles for this chapter.

Note Taking Study Guide With Concept Connector Journal
For online access: Web code nbd-2007
For print alternative: Reading and Note Taking Study Guide booklet

liberate, which means to free. Nationalism comes from *nation*. Have students write a definition of each ideology using a root or related word.

- Adapted Note Taking Study Guide, p. 98
- Adapted Section Summary, p. 99

1. determined men and women who supported freedom and progress
2. urged monarchs to crush revolts

Chapter Assessment

Terms, People, and Places

1. Thomas Malthus
2. proletariat, tenement
3. enterprise
4. utilitarianism
5. smelt
6. James Watt

Main Ideas

7. Farmers lost their farms or jobs and migrated to cities to find work.

8. An agricultural revolution reduced deaths from famine. Women who ate better had stronger babies who lived longer. Better hygiene, sanitation, and medical care also slowed deaths from disease.

9. Britain's natural and human resources, technological inventions, effects of demand and capital, and social and political conditions helped bring about the Industrial Revolution.

10. by speeding up production with new inventions and fostering the creation of factories

11. (a) long hours, low pay, and dangerous, unhealthy conditions (b) Women worked long hours, received only half of men's salaries, and also had to feed and care for their families.

12. He wanted the government to prevent abuse of workers and to give the vote to workers and women.

13. (a) He saw it as the history of class struggle, which would end in world revolution and power for the proletariat. (b) World revolution never happened, and by the 1990s, nearly all countries had incorporated elements of capitalism.

Chapter Focus Question

14. The Industrial Revolution caused massive technological changes in mechanization, the use of energy, and transportation. It resulted in rapid urbanization and the creation of both a prosperous new middle class and a working class that lived and worked in wretched conditions. It led to the development of laissez-faire capitalism, utilitarianism, socialism, and communism.

Critical Thinking

15. (a) Steam power led to greater mechanization and new forms of transporta-

---

Chapter Assessment

Terms, People, and Places

Complete each sentence by choosing the correct answer from the list of terms below. You will not use all of the terms.

smelt	James Watt
urbanization	Manchester
Thomas Malthus	tenement
proletariat	socialism
enterprise	utilitarianism

1. _____ predicted that population would outpace the food supply.
2. A member of the _____ most likely lived in a small, crowded building called a _____.
3. Investors in Britain were ready to risk their capital to invest in _____.
4. Those who advocated _____ believed that the goal of society was to bring about the greatest happiness for the greatest number.
5. To _____ involves separating iron from its ore.
6. _____ improved the efficiency and design of Newcomen's steam engine.

Main Ideas

Section 1 (pp. 244–247)
7. How did the enclosure movement affect farmers?
8. Identify three causes of the population explosion that occurred in the 1700s.

Section 2 (pp. 248–251)
9. Describe four factors that helped bring about the Industrial Revolution in England.

10. How did the Industrial Revolution transform the textile industry?

Section 3 (pp. 252–257)
11. (a) What were the main characteristics of factory work? (b) What challenges did factory work create for women?

Section 4 (pp. 258–263)
12. List the government reforms sought by John Stuart Mill.
13. (a) Describe Karl Marx's view of history. (b) How have events challenged that view?

Chapter Focus Question
14. What technological, social, economic, and cultural changes occurred as the Industrial Revolution took hold?

Critical Thinking

15. **Synthesize Information** What were the impacts of each of the following technologies: (a) steam power, (b) improved methods for smelting iron, (c) railroad?
16. **Geography and History** Explain the link between Britain's natural resources and its rise as an industrial nation.
17. **Analyze Information** Describe how the Industrial Revolution affected each of the following: (a) size of population, (b) cities, (c) working and living conditions, (d) women and children.
18. **Predict Consequences** If more people had supported utilitarianism, how do you think it would have influenced society?
19. **Recognize Ideologies** Explain the major differences between Adam Smith's free market ideas and Karl Marx's socialist ideas.

● Writing About History

In this chapter's Section Assessments, you developed skills for writing an expository essay.

Expository: Explanatory Essay During the late 1700s, the Industrial Revolution began to transform Britain. An agricultural revolution triggered a chain of events, and Britain sped ahead of the rest of the world to become the first industrial nation. But why is the Industrial Revolution considered to be a "revolution"? Write an explanatory essay to answer this question.

Prewriting
• Ask yourself what you need to know in order to write an effective explanation. Think about what you already know about revolutions.

• Do research to gather facts, descriptions, examples, and other details to clearly illustrate your point.

Drafting
• Create a Venn diagram to compare aspects of the Industrial Revolution to another revolution you have learned about, such as the American Revolution or the French Revolution.
• Write a thesis statement once you have a focus for your essay. Begin your introduction with an interesting lead-in to get your reader's attention.
• Be sure to include comparisons, analogies, and facts in your essay to support your explanation.

Revising
• Use the guidelines for revising your essay on page SH12 of the Writing Handbook.

---

tion. (b) Improved iron led to its use in the manufacture of bridges, machinery, and railroads. (c) The railroad allowed goods to be transported swiftly and cheaply.

16. Britain's coal and iron resources helped power and build machinery. Its ports and rivers provided transportation for goods.

17. (a) Population grew rapidly. (b) Cities became crowded, overwhelmed by waste, and polluted by industry. (c) Working and

living conditions improved for the middle class but were horrible for the working class. (d) Working-class women and children had dangerous and difficult jobs with long hours and low pay.

18. Answers should show an understanding of the characteristics of utilitarianism.

19. Smith: the free market would increase everyone's prosperity. Marx: free-market capitalism benefited the rich at the expense of the poor.

Europe Challenges the Old Order L3

Instruct

- **Introduce: Vocabulary Builder**
  Have students read the Vocabulary Builder term and definition. Ask students to list arguments that revolutionary *agitators* might have used during this period.

- **Teach** Have students point out the location of the Balkans on a map of Europe. Ask **Why were the Balkans a key area for revolt?** (*They were inhabited by people of different religions and ethnic groups.*) **How did European powers intervene in Greece?** (*They helped Greece win independence but imposed a German king.*) **Why might European powers support nationalism in some cases?** (*It might further their own interests.*)

- **Analyzing the Visuals** Ask them to describe the different views of battle and heroism that the two images convey and to explain the significance of the struggle between the Serbs and the Ottomans.

Independent Practice

Note Taking Have students fill in the chart showing details of revolts in Serbia, Greece, and other countries.

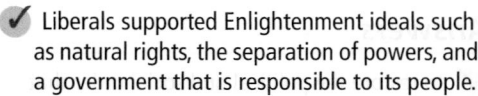
Reading and Note Taking Study Guide, p. 98

Monitor Progress

As students fill in their tables, circulate to make sure they include supporting details about revolts in Serbia, Greece, and other European nations in the 1820s. For a completed version of the table, see
📖 **Note Taking Transparencies,** 144B

In the 1800s, national groups who shared a common heritage set out to win their own states. Within the diverse Austrian empire, for example, various nationalist leaders tried to unite and win independence for each particular group. Nationalism gave people with a common heritage a sense of identity and the goal of creating their own homeland. At the same time, however, nationalism often bred intolerance and led to persecution of other ethnic or national groups.

✓ **Checkpoint** How did the liberalism of the early 1800s reflect Enlightenment ideals?

Central Europe Challenges the Old Order

Spurred by the ideas of liberalism and nationalism, revolutionaries fought against the old order. During the early 1800s, rebellions erupted in the Balkan Peninsula and elsewhere along the southern fringe of Europe. The Balkans, in southeastern Europe, were inhabited by people of various religions and ethnic groups. These peoples had lived under Ottoman rule for more than 300 years.

Serbia Seeks Independence The first Balkan people to revolt were the Serbs. From 1804 to 1813, the Serb leader Karageorge (ka rah JAWR juh) led a guerrilla war against the Ottomans. The intense struggle was unsuccessful, but it fostered a sense of Serbian identity. A revival of Serbian literature and culture added to the sense of nationhood.

In 1815, Milos Obrenovic (oh BRAY noh vich) led the Serbs in a second, more successful rebellion. One reason for the success was that Obrenovic turned to Russia for assistance. Like the Serbs, the Russian people were Slavic in language and Christian Orthodox in religion. By 1830, Russian support helped the Serbs win **autonomy,** or self-rule, within the

Serbs in Battle
Serb leader Karageorge (below left) leads the Serbs against the Ottomans at the Battle of Misar during the first Serbian rebellion. *(a) Why would this battle and others like it help lead to a sense of Serbian national identity? (b) Why was this sense of nationalism important for the Serbs?*

Connect to Our World

Connections to Today People in the United States today are also divided between conservatives and liberals. Today, however, both conservatives and liberals believe in democracy and capitalism. Unlike in the early 1800s, conservatives today tend to favor laissez-faire economics more than liberals do. Liberals tend to favor social democracy, or more government involvement in the economy.

Have students do research on the differences and similarities between liberals and conservatives in the United States today. Divide them into groups and have them present their findings in chart form.

Answers

✓ Liberals supported Enlightenment ideals such as natural rights, the separation of powers, and a government that is responsible to its people.

Caption (a) Those who died in the battles became martyrs, and survivors joined against an enemy who had killed Serbs. (b) This sense of nationalism united Serbs and fueled further struggles.

Ottoman empire. The Ottoman sultan later agreed to formal independence. In the future, Russia would continue to defend Serbian interests and affect events in the Balkans.

Greece Revolts to End Ottoman Rule In 1821, the Greeks revolted, seeking to end centuries of Ottoman rule. At first, the Greeks were badly divided. But years of suffering in long, bloody wars of independence helped shape a national identity. Leaders of the rebellion justified their struggle as "a national war, a holy war, a war the object of which is to reconquer the rights of individual liberty." The Greeks had the support of romantic writers such as English poet Lord Byron, who went to Greece to aid the fight for independence.

Admirers of Greece in Europe backed the Greek rebels. In the late 1820s, Britain, France, and Russia forced the Ottomans to grant independence to some Greek provinces. By 1830, Greece was independent. The European powers, however, pressured the Greeks to accept a German king, a move meant to show that they did not support the nationalism that brought about the revolution.

More Challenges Erupt Several other challenges to the Vienna peace settlement erupted in the 1820s. Revolts occurred along the southern fringe of Europe. In Spain, Portugal, and various states in the Italian peninsula, rebels struggled to gain constitutional governments.

Metternich urged conservative rulers to act decisively and crush the dangerous uprisings. In response, a French army marched over the Pyrenees to suppress a revolt in Spain. Austrian forces crossed the Alps to smash rebellious outbreaks in Italy.

Troops dampened the fires of liberalism and nationalism, but could not smother them. In the next decades, sparks would flare anew. Added to liberal and nationalist demands were the goals of the new industrial working class. By the mid-1800s, social reformers and <u>agitators</u> were urging workers to support socialism or other ways of reorganizing property ownership.

✓ **Checkpoint**   Why would a monarch order his army to suppress an uprising in another country?

Note Taking

Reading Skill: Identify Supporting Details As you read, fill in a table like the one below with supporting details about revolts in Serbia, Greece, and other countries during the early 1800s.

Serbia	Greece	Other Revolts
•	•	•
•	•	•

Vocabulary Builder

agitator—(AJ ih tayt ur) *n.* someone who attempts to arouse feeling for or against something, especially a political cause

---

Progress Monitoring Online
For: Self-quiz with vocabulary practice
Web Code: nba-2011

SECTION 1 Assessment

Terms, People, and Places

1. For each term, person, or place listed at the beginning of the section, write a sentence explaining its significance.

Note Taking

2. **Reading Skill: Identify Main Ideas** Use your completed charts to answer the Focus Question: What events proved that Metternich was correct in his fears?

Comprehension and Critical Thinking

3. **Identify Point of View** What were the goals of conservative leaders?
4. **Compare Points of View** (a) How did the political goals of liberals differ from those of conservatives? (b) How did nationalists threaten the borders set up by European monarchs?
5. **Recognize Cause and Effect** (a) Why did the Serbs and Greeks revolt? (b) Why were there uprisings in Spain, Portugal, and the Italian states?

● **Writing About History**

Quick Write: Choose a Topic To write an effective persuasive essay, you should begin with a clearly stated opinion or argument on an issue that has more than one side. Look back over Section 1, jotting down issues that have two or more sides. Then choose an issue and write a well-constructed sentence that states your opinion or argument against it.

Assess and Reteach

Assess Progress   L3

■ Have students complete the Section Assessment.

■ Administer the Section Quiz.

All in One Teaching Resources, Unit 2, p. 60

■ To further assess student understanding, use

📖 **Progress Monitoring Transparencies**, 83

Reteach

If students need more instruction, have them read the section summary.

✏️ **Reading and Note Taking Study Guide**, p. 99   L3

✏️ **Adapted Reading and Note Taking Study Guide**, p. 99   L1 L2

✏️ **Spanish Reading and Note Taking Study Guide**, p. 99   L2

Extend   L4

Traveler's Tales To help students better understand Greece during this period, have them read the selection *Writings of Lord Byron from Greece* and complete the worksheet.

All in One Teaching Resources, Unit 2, p. 65

Answer

✓ to prevent the uprisings and revolutionary ideas from spreading to their own countries

---

Section 1 Assessment

1. Sentences should reflect an understanding of each term, person, or place listed at the beginning of the section.
2. the Serb and Greek wars of independence and uprisings in Spain, in Portugal, and in various Italian states
3. restoring monarchies, traditional social hierarchies, and the established church; imposing peace by suppressing dissension
4. (a) Liberals wanted the protection of basic rights and governments based on written constitutions and separation of powers. Conservatives supported monarchies and established churches; they valued order and stability over change. (b) Nationalists wanted independence from foreign rule.
5. (a) Serbs and Greeks wanted freedom from Ottoman rule. (b) Rebels wanted to set up constitutional governments.

● **Writing About History**

Responses should state a clear opinion or position on an issue addressed in the section.

For additional assessment, have students access **Progress Monitoring Online** at Web Code nba-2011.

The Spirit of Reform Spreads

Instruct

- **Introduce** Direct students to the map on this page. Have them point out Brussels and its proximity to Paris (the source of revolution) and Britain. Then have students point out Cracow's location and proximity to Russia. Have students predict how these locations will affect the spread of revolution.

- **Teach** Create a Venn diagram on the board comparing the Belgian and Polish uprisings, and have students volunteer information to fill in. Then ask **What difference most affected the outcome of the two revolutions?** *(The Belgians had support from Britain and France, whereas the Poles had no support and were opposed by Russia.)*

- **Quick Activity** Show students *Revolutionary France: Les Misérables* from the **Witness History Discovery School™** video program. When they have finished watching, ask them to describe how the video depicts revolutionary France.

Independent Practice

Have students begin filling in the Outline Map *Revolutions in Europe, 1820s–1840s*, with names of countries, dates of uprisings, and outcomes. Make sure students leave room to add the 1848 revolutions later.

All in One Teaching Resources, Unit 2, p. 70

Monitor Progress

Circulate to make sure students are filling in their Outline Maps accurately and are including the July Revolution in France and the 1830 revolts.

Answer

✓ The Belgians gained independence from Holland, but the Polish rebellion was crushed by Russia.

---

capital. Britain and France believed thay they would benefit from the separation of Belgium and Holland and supported Belgian demands for independence. As a result, in 1831, Belgium became an independent state with a liberal constitution.

Rebels Fail in Poland Nationalists in Poland also staged an uprising in 1830. But, unlike the Belgians, the Poles failed to win independence for their country.

In the late 1700s, Russia, Austria, and Prussia had divided up Poland. Poles had hoped that the Congress of Vienna would restore their homeland in 1815. Instead, the great powers handed most of Poland to Russia.

In 1830, Polish students, army officers, and landowners rose in revolt. The rebels failed to gain widespread support, however, and were brutally crushed by Russian forces. Some survivors fled to Western Europe and the United States, where they kept alive the dream of freedom.

✓ **Checkpoint** How did the Belgian and Polish revolutions in 1830 end differently?

The French Revolt Again in 1848

In the 1840s, discontent began to grow in France once again. Radicals formed secret societies to work for a French republic. Utopian socialists called for an end to private ownership of property. Even liberals <u>denounced</u> Louis Philippe's government for corruption and called for expanded suffrage.

Near the end of the decade, discontent was heightened by a **recession**, or period of reduced economic activity. Factories shut down and people lost their jobs. Poor harvests caused bread prices to rise. Newspapers blamed government officials for some of the problems. With conditions much like those in 1789, Paris was again ripe for revolution.

Vocabulary Builder

<u>denounce</u>—(dee NOWNS) *vt.* to express harsh criticism of something or somebody, usually in public

---

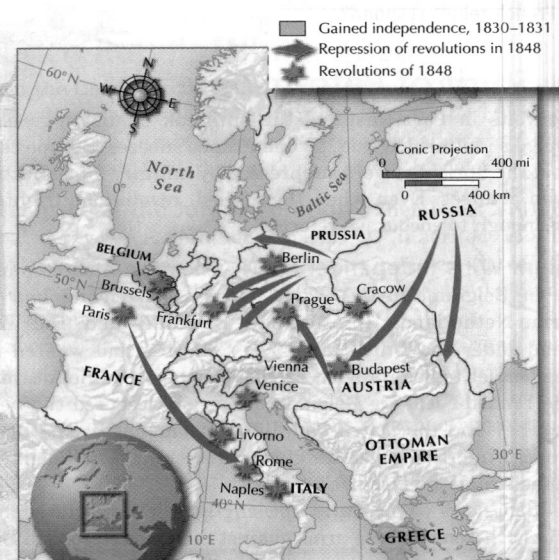

● **INFOGRAPHIC**

1848: The Year of Hope and Despair

Revolution in Europe spread like wildfire in the days and months of 1848. Although an outbreak in January occurred in Italy, France's successful February Revolution was the spark for other revolts throughout Europe. As shown on the map here, revolutions were not confined to one city or country. They engulfed the continent of Europe and numbered almost fifty in the first four months of the year alone. Despite the failures of the revolutions, Europe was transformed as governments and the rising middle class began to cooperate with one another.

Legend:
- Gained independence, 1830–1831
- Repression of revolutions in 1848
- Revolutions of 1848

Link to Music

Poland Has Not Yet Perished When Poland was partitioned by Prussia, Austria, and Russia in 1795, Poland ceased to exist as an independent state, but the Polish national spirit lived on. The country's national anthem, which begins with the words "Poland has not yet perished," was written in 1797. Parts of Poland became provinces of the Austrian Empire and of Prussia, which later became part of Germany. However, the largest portion of Poland lay within the Russian Empire, and the Russian province of Poland carried on the name of the divided nation. Russian Poland staged several armed revolts against Russian rule, including the 1830 uprising. Poles under German, Austrian, and Russian rule never abandoned their quest for reunification and independence. They finally achieved their goal in 1918, when Poland was reborn as an independent, united nation at the end of World War I.

Turmoil Spreads During "February Days" In February 1848, when the government took steps to silence critics and prevent public meetings, angry crowds took to the streets. During the "February Days," overturned carts, paving stones, and toppled trees again blocked the streets of Paris. Church bells rang alarms, while women and men on the barricades sang the revolutionary anthem "La Marseillaise." A number of demonstrators clashed with royal troops and were killed.

As the turmoil spread, Louis Philippe abdicated. A group of liberal, radical, and socialist leaders proclaimed the Second Republic. (The First Republic had lasted from 1792 until 1804, when Napoleon became emperor.)

From the start, deep differences divided the new government. Middle-class liberals wanted moderate political reforms. Socialists wanted far-reaching social and economic change and forced the government to set up national workshops to provide jobs for the unemployed.

The Working Class Loses Out During "June Days" By June, however, upper- and middle-class interests had won control of the government. They saw the national workshops as a waste of money and shut them down.

Furious, workers again took to the streets of Paris. This time, however, bourgeois liberals turned violently against the protesters. Peasants, who feared that socialists might take their land, also attacked the rioting workers. At least 1,500 people were killed before the government crushed the rebellion.

The fighting of the "June Days" left a bitter legacy. The middle class both feared and distrusted the socialists, while the working class harbored a deep hatred for the bourgeoisie.

A New Napoleon Comes to Power By the end of 1848, the National Assembly, now dominated by members who wanted to restore order,

FEBRUARY

Opposition grew as Louis Philippe refused to listen to the middle class, workers, or peasants. In February, crowds revolted in the streets. As the turmoil of the "February Days" spread, Louis Philippe abdicated and a group of liberal, radical, and socialist leaders proclaimed the Second Republic.

MARCH

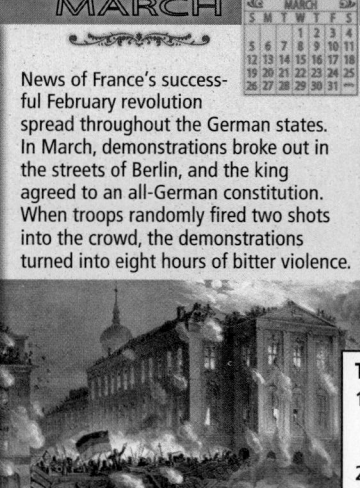

News of France's successful February revolution spread throughout the German states. In March, demonstrations broke out in the streets of Berlin, and the king agreed to an all-German constitution. When troops randomly fired two shots into the crowd, the demonstrations turned into eight hours of bitter violence.

JUNE

"June Days" in France again saw Paris streets crowded with angry protestors when the workshops for the unemployed were closed. Before this worker revolt ended, about 1,500 died in the first two days, while as many as 3,000 more were executed for their participation in the uprising.

Thinking Critically
1. **Make Comparisons** How were the "February Days" and the "June Days" similar and different?
2. **Recognize Ideologies** What ideals survived despite how quickly most rebellions throughout Europe were crushed?

Careers

Political Scientist In a democracy, it is not necessary to be a revolutionary to play an active role in creating social change. There are many careers in political science. For example, political activists work for organizations or candidates that promote policies they favor. Some work as lobbyists, trying to persuade government officials to create or enforce certain laws. Others serve as public relations specialists, informing the public about their causes. Still others work as pollsters, sampling public opinion. Many careers in political science involve working in local, state, national, or international government. Political science careers often require a college degree, but volunteer experience is also helpful. Perhaps the most important requirements are enthusiasm and an interest in improving society.

Revolution Surges Through Europe

Instruct

- **Introduce: Vocabulary Builder**
  Have students read the Vocabulary Builder term and definition on the facing page. Ask students to name some divisions that *emerged* during this period.

- **Teach** Create a chart on the board with two columns labeled Rebellion and Reaction. Using the Numbered Heads strategy (TE, p. T23), have students provide information about events in 1848 to fill in the chart.

- **Quick Activity** Direct students' attention to the serpent political cartoon on the next page. Then display **Color Transparency 122: *Europe: 1848 Uprisings.*** Ask students to compare how the rulers and the revolutionaries are portrayed in the two cartoons.

  🏛 **Color Transparencies,** 122

Independent Practice

- **Primary Source** To help students better understand the excitement of revolution in 1848, have them read the excerpt from Carl Schurz's *Reminiscences* and complete the worksheet.

  All in One Teaching Resources, Unit 2, p. 67

- Have students suppose they are conservative advisors to King Frederick William IV of Prussia. Have them write a paragraph advising the king whether to accept the crown offered by the Frankfurt assembly.

Monitor Progress

Check Reading and Note Taking Study Guide entries for student understanding.

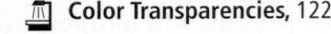

Cause and Effect

Long-Term Causes	Immediate Causes
• Spread of Enlightenment ideas	• Uprisings in Paris
• Growth of nationalism and liberalism	• Economic recession
• Poverty caused by the Industrial Revolution	• Poor harvests
	• Corrupt governments

The Revolutions of 1848

Immediate Effects	Long-Term Effects
• A new republic in France	• A new empire in France
• Fall of Metternich	• Successes for liberalism, nationalism, and socialism
• Promises of reform in Austria, Italy, and Prussia	• Germany and Italy united
	• Labor unions
	• Increased voting rights for men

Connections to Today

- Ongoing efforts to ensure basic rights for all citizens
- Ongoing efforts to ensure limited government and popular sovereignty worldwide

Analyze Cause and Effect The revolutions of 1848 were the result of new ways of thinking and hard times for workers. *Could one of these factors by itself have caused such widespread rebellion? Why or Why not?*

Italian revolutionary flag

---

issued a constitution for the Second Republic. It created a strong president and a one-house legislature. But it also gave the vote to all adult men, the widest suffrage in the world at the time. Nine million Frenchmen now could vote, compared with only 200,000 who had that right before.

When elections for president were held, the overwhelming winner was Louis Napoleon, nephew of Napoleon Bonaparte. The "new" Napoleon attracted the working classes by presenting himself as a man who cared about social issues such as poverty. At the same time, his famous name, linked with order and past French glory, helped him with conservatives.

Once in office, Louis Napoleon used his position as a stepping-stone to greater power. By 1852, he had proclaimed himself emperor, taking the title **Napoleon III.** Thus ended the short-lived Second Republic.

Like his celebrated uncle, Napoleon III used a plebiscite to win public approval for his seizure of power. A stunning 90 percent of voters supported his move to set up the Second Empire. Many thought that a monarchy was more stable than a republic or hoped that Napoleon III would restore the glory days of Napoleon Bonaparte.

Napoleon III, like Louis Philippe, ruled at a time of rapid economic growth. For the bourgeoisie, the early days of the Second Empire brought prosperity and contentment. In time, however, Napoleon III would embark on foreign adventures that would bring down his empire and end French leadership in Europe.

✔ **Checkpoint** How did the French revolutions of 1830 and 1848 differ?

Revolution Surges Through Europe

In 1848, revolts in Paris again unleashed a tidal wave of revolution across Europe. For opponents of the old order, it was a time of such hope that they called it the "springtime of the peoples." Although events in France touched off the revolts, grievances had been piling up for years. Middle-class liberals wanted a greater share of political power for themselves, as well as protections for the basic rights of all male citizens. Workers demanded relief from the miseries of the Industrial Revolution. And nationalists of all classes ached to throw off foreign rule.

Change in the Austrian Empire In the Austrian empire, revolts broke out in the major cities. Even though Metternich censored the press, books were smuggled to universities throughout the empire. Students demanded change. When workers joined the students on the streets of Vienna, Metternich resigned and fled in disguise.

Revolution continued to spread. In Budapest, Hungarian nationalists led by journalist **Louis Kossuth** demanded an independent government, an end to serfdom, and a written constitution to protect basic rights. In Prague, the Czechs made similar demands. Overwhelmed by events, the Austrian government agreed to the reforms. The gains were temporary, however.

Answers

Analyze Cause and Effect Sample: probably not, since major events usually have a variety of causes

✔ 1830 resulted in a constitutional monarchy; 1848 resulted in the Second Republic with a strong president and wider suffrage for men

Austrian troops soon regained control of Vienna and Prague and smashed the rebels in Budapest.

Revolts in Italy Uprisings also erupted in the Italian states. Nationalists wanted to end Hapsburg domination and set up a constitutional government. From Venice in the north to Naples in the south, Italians set up independent republics. Revolutionaries even expelled the pope from Rome and installed a nationalist government. Before long, the forces of reaction surged back here, too. Austrian troops ousted the new governments in northern Italy. A French army restored the pope to power in Rome. In Naples, local rulers canceled the reforms they had reluctantly accepted.

Rebellion in the German States In the German states, university students demanded national unity and liberal reforms. Economic hard times and a potato famine brought peasants and workers into the struggle. In Prussia, liberals forced King Frederick William IV to agree to a constitution written by an elected assembly. Within a year, though, he dissolved the assembly.

Throughout 1848, delegates from German states met in the Frankfurt Assembly. Divisions soon <u>emerged</u> over whether Germany should be a republic or a monarchy and whether to include Austria in a united German state. Finally, the assembly offered Prussia's Frederick William IV the crown of a united Germany. To their dismay, the conservative king rejected the offer because it came not from the German princes but from the people—"from the gutter," as he described it.

By 1850, rebellion faded, ending the age of liberal revolution that had begun in 1789. Why did the uprisings fail? The rulers' use of military force was just one reason. Another was that revolutionaries did not have mass support, and in many instances, constitutions that represented their principles were withdrawn or replaced. In the decades ahead, liberalism, nationalism, and socialism would win successes not through revolution, but through political activity.

✓ **Checkpoint** What was the outcome of most of the revolutions outside France in 1848?

Analyzing Political Cartoons

A Year of Revolution This English cartoonist comments on the revolutions of 1848 and the reaction of European rulers. Based on the cartoon,
1. What ideal led to the revolutions of 1848?
2. How did the revolutions affect Europe's monarchs?

Vocabulary Builder

emerge—(ee MURJ) *v.* to arise, appear, or come out of

SECTION 2 Assessment

Progress Monitoring Online
For: Self-quiz with vocabulary practice
Web Code: nba-2021

Terms, People, and Places
1. For each term, person, or place listed at the beginning of the section, write a sentence explaining its significance.

Note Taking
2. **Reading Skill: Identify Causes and Effects** Use your completed chart to answer the Focus Question: What were the causes and effects of revolutions in Europe in 1830 and 1848?

Comprehension and Critical Thinking
3. **Draw Conclusions** What were the conditions under which the people of France lived that led to revolution rather than peace?
4. **Analyze Information** **(a)** Where did revolution spread in 1830? **(b)** Were these revolutions successful? Explain.
5. **Make Generalizations** Why did most of the revolutions of 1848 fail to achieve their goals?

● **Writing About History**
Quick Write: Gather and Organize Evidence In order to write a well-organized persuasive essay, you need to gather evidence to support your position. Gather evidence from the section to support an essay on whether workers were justified in taking to the streets in 1830 and 1848. Then create a chart that lists both sides of the issue.

Assess and Reteach

Assess Progress

- Have students complete the Section Assessment.
- Administer the Section Quiz.

All in One Teaching Resources, Unit 2, p. 61

- To further assess student understanding, use
   Progress Monitoring Transparencies, 84

Reteach

If students need more instruction, have them read the section summary.

 Reading and Note Taking Study Guide, p. 101 ⓛ3

 Adapted Reading and Note Taking Study Guide, p. 101 ⓛ1 ⓛ2

 Spanish Reading and Note Taking Study Guide, p. 101 ⓛ2

Extend ⓛ4

Have students discuss whether European rulers could have prevented nationalist revolts by allowing reforms. Ensure that they explain their answers.

Answers

Analyzing Political Cartoons
1. liberty
2. They were threatened.

✓ Most of the revolutions succeeded at first but they were later crushed and their reforms canceled.

Section 2 Assessment

1. Sentences should reflect an understanding of each term, person, or place listed at the beginning of the section.
2. causes: liberals sought constitutions and basic rights, nationalists sought independence, and workers and peasants demanded better conditions; effects: in most countries other than Belgium, revolutions resulted in failure, the restoration of monarchy or empire, and the cancellation of any reforms.
3. absolute rule, government corruption, poverty
4. (a) Belgium and Poland (b) The Belgian revolution was successful in gaining independence, but the Polish revolution was not.
5. They were crushed by the armies and strength of the European powers.

● **Writing About History**
Charts should include several arguments on each side that are clearly related to the workers' revolting.

For additional assessment, have students access **Progress Monitoring Online** at **Web Code nba-2021**.

Revolution

Objectives

■ Identify reasons why people have revolted.

■ Understand that revolution has occurred throughout history.

■ Complete a Web Quest on revolution.

Build Background Knowledge L3

Ask students to discuss their understanding of the term *revolution*. Address any misconceptions. Have students discuss the circumstances that would have to exist for them to take part in a revolution.

Instruct L3

■ Direct students' attention to the Essential Question: **Why do political revolutions occur?** Have students read In This Chapter and look at the corresponding picture. Ask: **What conditions in Europe led to an outbreak of revolutions in 1830 and 1848? Why did they fail?**

■ Have students review the time line and Continuing Today. Discuss with them the various goals that have sparked revolutions throughout time.

■ Assign the Web Quest activity.

Independent Practice

Concept | Connector Have students fill in the Web Quest reflection question on revolution in their Concept Connector Journal.

 Reading and Note Taking Study Guide, p. 292

Monitor Progress

Circulate to make sure that students are filling in their Concept Connector journal. Ensure they understand why revolutions occur.

Transfer Activities

1. People have revolted to get rid of heavy taxes, gain economic freedom, address unequal distribution of wealth and overthrow oppressive leaders.
2. Every age has seen circumstances in which people have felt that their rulers were not meeting their needs and have been unwilling or unable to make peaceful changes.
3. Students' work should be evaluated against the rubric at Web Code nbh-2008.

Concept | Connector

REVOLUTION

Why do political revolutions occur?

In This Chapter

The wave of revolution that swept Europe in the early 1800s mainly involved a clash between liberal and conservative political ideas. Conservatives wanted to keep the power in the hands of established institutions; liberals wanted to distribute power more widely, especially to the middle class. In Germany (right), the military clashed with revolutionaries.

Throughout History

200s A.D. Han empire is overthrown when it burdens peasants with heavy taxes.

1524 German peasants revolt against nobles to end serfdom.

1688 The Glorious Revolution replaces the Catholic King of England James II with his Protestant daughter Mary.

1789 Unequal distribution of wealth and power sparks the French Revolution.

1867 Social and economic unrest lead to the overthrow of the Japanese shogun.

1917 Bolsheviks seize power in Russia and overthrow the tsar.

Continuing Today

An election in Ukraine, seen by many to be fraudulent, sparked a series of nonviolent protests. The government was forced to call for a revote, which led to a change of leadership.

21st Century Skills

 TRANSFER Activities

1. **Analyze** Throughout history, why have people revolted?

2. **Draw Conclusions** Why do you think every age in history has witnessed revolution?

3. **Transfer** Complete a Web quest in which you analyze the influence of religion on a specific country; record your thoughts in the Concept Connector Journal; and learn to make a video. Web Code nbh-2008

History Background

Comparative Theories of Revolution Political theorists have tried to come up with a comprehensive theory of revolutions. Theda Skocpol and other theorists have pointed to three main conditions. First, the state must be vulnerable. A vulnerable state is one that is facing external as well as internal pressures, such as war and economic problems. Second, there must be an elite group that is well positioned to be able to oppose the government (for example, nobles or middle-class liberals in a legislative body). Third, there must be a rural or peasant population that can be mobilized. Some theorists, such as Jack Goldstone, add that revolution occurs only when many people believe there is something wrong or unjust in the way the country is being governed.

Simón Bolívar

Crown awarded to Bolívar

WITNESS HISTORY ◀)) AUDIO

A Revolutionary Is Born

Like many wealthy Latin Americans, young Simón Bolívar was sent to Europe to complete his education. In Europe he became a strong admirer of the ideals of the Enlightenment and the French Revolution. One day while speaking with his Italian tutor about freedom and individual rights, he fell on his knees and swore an oath:

❝ I swear before God and by my honor never to allow my hands to be idle nor my soul to rest until I have broken the chains that bind us to Spain. ❞

Focus Question Who were the key revolutionaries that led the movements for independence in Latin America, and what were their accomplishments?

Revolts in Latin America

Objectives
- Explain the causes of discontent in Latin America.
- Describe Haiti's fight for freedom.
- Summarize the revolts in Mexico and Central America.
- Understand how revolutions ignited South America.

Terms, People, and Places

peninsular	Toussaint L'Ouverture
creole	Father Miguel Hidalgo
mestizo	Father José Morelos
mulatto	José de San Martín
Simón Bolívar	Dom Pedro

Note Taking

Reading Skill: Identify Main Ideas As you read the section, fill in a table like the one below with a country, a date, and a main idea about revolts in Latin America. Add rows as needed.

Revolts in Latin America		
Haiti	1791	Toussaint L'Ouverture

Liberal ideas were spreading to Latin America with explosive results. From Mexico to the tip of South America, revolutionary movements arose to overthrow the reigning European powers. By 1825, most of Latin America was freed from colonial rule.

Discontent Fans the Fires

By the late 1700s, the revolutionary fever that gripped Western Europe had spread to Latin America. There, discontent was rooted in the social, racial, and political system that had emerged during 300 years of Spanish rule.

Social and Ethnic Structures Cause Resentment Spanish-born **peninsulares,** members of the highest social class, dominated Latin American political and social life. Only they could hold top jobs in government and the Church. Many **creoles**—the European-descended Latin Americans who owned the haciendas, ranches, and mines—bitterly resented their second-class status. Merchants fretted under mercantilist policies that tied the colonies to Spain.

Meanwhile, a growing population of **mestizos,** people of Native American and European descent, and **mulattoes,** people of African and European descent, were angry at being denied the status, wealth, and power that were available to whites. Native Americans suffered economic misery under the Spanish, who had conquered the lands of their ancestors. In the Caribbean region and parts of South America, masses of enslaved Africans who worked on plantations longed for freedom.

Vocabulary Builder

Use the information below and the following resources to teach the high-use word from this section.
All in One Teaching Resources, Unit 2, p. 63; Teaching Resources, Skills Handbook, p. 3

High-Use Word	Definition and Sample Sentence
proclaim, p. 288	*vt.* to announce publicly or formally The mayor **proclaimed** that a statue would be erected to celebrate the town hero.

Teach

Discontent Fans the Fires ⓛ

Instruct

- **Introduce** Write the terms *peninsulares, creoles, mestizos,* and *mulattoes* on the board. Ask students to find the terms (in blue) in the text and explain their meanings. Discuss which of these groups would be most, and which least, content.

- **Teach** Display **Color Transparency 123: Composition of Mexico City Society, 1753.** Ask **Looking at the graph, what tensions would you expect to find?** (*resentment that power was concentrated in the hands of the few Europeans*) **How might this social structure affect Latin America?** (*Sample: It might cause discontent, which could lead to revolt.*)
  🏛 **Color Transparencies,** 123

- **Analyzing the Visuals** Have students analyze the portrait of Emperor Joseph on this page, including his stance, manner of dress, and surroundings. Ask students how Latin Americans may have viewed Emperor Joseph.

Independent Practice

Divide students into five groups representing creoles, mestizos, mulattoes, Native Americans, and African Americans. Have each group write a manifesto in favor of or opposed to rebellion. Ensure they include the injustices in their society and recommend a path to correct these injustices. Then have each group choose a student to deliver the manifesto to the class.

Monitor Progress

To check student understanding, ask them to explain how Napoleon affected events in Latin America.

Portrait of Joseph Bonaparte, King of Spain, 1808

The Enlightenment Inspires Latin Americans In the 1700s, educated creoles read the works of Enlightenment thinkers. They watched colonists in North America throw off British rule. Translations of the Declaration of Independence and the Constitution of the United States circulated among the creole elite.

During the French Revolution, young creoles like **Simón Bolívar** (boh LEE vahr) traveled in Europe and were inspired by the ideals of "liberty, equality, and fraternity." Yet despite their admiration for Enlightenment ideas and revolutions in other lands, most creoles were reluctant to act.

Napoleon Invades Spain The spark that finally ignited widespread rebellion in Latin America was Napoleon's invasion of Spain in 1808. Napoleon ousted the Spanish king and placed his brother Joseph on the Spanish throne. In Latin America, leaders saw Spain's weakness as an opportunity to reject foreign domination and demand independence from colonial rule.

✔️ **Checkpoint** Where did creoles get many of their revolutionary ideas?

Slaves Win Freedom for Haiti

Even before Spanish colonists hoisted the flag of freedom, revolution had erupted in a French-ruled colony on the island of Hispaniola. In Haiti, as the island is now called, French planters owned very profitable sugar plantations worked by nearly a half million enslaved Africans. Sugar plantations were labor-intensive. The slaves were overworked and underfed.

Toussaint L'Ouverture Leads a Slave Revolt Embittered by suffering and inspired by the talk of liberty and equality, the island's slaves rose up in revolt in 1791. The rebels were fortunate to find an intelligent and skillful leader in **Toussaint L'Ouverture** (too SAN loo vehr TOOR), a self-educated former slave. Although untrained, Toussaint was a brilliant general and inspiring commander.

Toussaint's army of former slaves faced many enemies. Some mulattoes joined French planters against the rebels. France, Spain, and Britain all sent armies against them. The fighting took more lives than any other revolution in the Americas. But by 1798, the rebels had achieved their goal: slavery was abolished, and Toussaint's forces controlled most of the island.

Haiti Wins Independence In 1802, Napoleon Bonaparte sent a large army to reconquer the former colony. Toussaint urged his countrymen to take up arms once again to resist the invaders. In April 1802 the French agreed to a truce, but then they captured Toussaint and carried him in chains to France. He died there in a cold mountain prison a year later.

The struggle for freedom continued, however, and late in 1803, with yellow fever destroying their army, the French surrendered. In January 1804, the island declared itself an independent country under the name Haiti. In the following years, rival Haitian leaders fought for power. Finally, in 1820, Haiti became a republic.

✔️ **Checkpoint** How were slaves instrumental in achieving Haiti's independence?

Answers

✔️ Creoles got their revolutionary ideas from reading Enlightenment thinkers and observing the American and French Revolutions.

✔️ The army of slaves who revolted in 1791 formed the army that then fought for Haiti's independence.

Mexico and Central America Revolt

The slave revolt in Haiti frightened creoles in Spanish America. Although they wanted power themselves, most had no desire for economic or social changes that might threaten their way of life. In 1810, however, a creole priest in Mexico, **Father Miguel Hidalgo** (hee DAL goh), raised his voice for freedom.

Father Hidalgo Cries Out for Freedom Father Hidalgo presided over the poor rural parish of Dolores. On September 15, 1810, he rang the church bells summoning the people to prayer. When they gathered, he startled them with an urgent appeal, "My children, will you be free?" Father Hidalgo's speech became known as "el Grito de Dolores"—the cry of Dolores. It called Mexicans to fight for independence.

A ragged army of poor mestizos and Native Americans rallied to Father Hidalgo and marched to the outskirts of Mexico City. At first, some creoles supported the revolt. However, they soon rejected Hidalgo's call for an end to slavery and his plea for reforms to improve conditions for Native Americans. They felt that these policies would cost them power.

After some early successes, the rebels faced growing opposition. Less than a year after he issued the "Grito," Hidalgo was captured and executed, and his followers scattered.

José Morelos Continues the Fight Another priest picked up the banner of revolution. **Father José Morelos** was a mestizo who called for wide-ranging social and political reform. He wanted to improve

Liberty!
Toussaint L'Ouverture and his army of former slaves battle for independence from France and an end to slavery. Although Toussaint achieved his goal of ending slavery, Haiti (see inset) did not become independent until after his death. *Why do you think Toussaint and his army were willing to risk death to achieve their goals?*

History Background

A Deadly, Microscopic Enemy French forces in Haiti were up against more than Toussaint L'Ouverture's brilliant leadership and valiant soldiers. They also had to fight an enemy they could not see or begin to understand: yellow fever. Although no one realized it then, yellow fever is a virus carried by mosquitoes and is extremely prevalent in tropical Haiti. Soldiers who caught the virus became dizzy and developed

high fevers and muscle aches. Their gums bled. Many became comatose and eventually died. Historians estimate that of the 60,000 French troops Napoleon sent to the Caribbean, more than 80 percent (48,000) contracted yellow fever and died, including General Leclerc, Napoleon's brother-in-law. Some 20,000 British troops also died of malaria and yellow fever before abandoning the island.

Instruct

- **Introduce** On the board, write the words Toussaint L'Ouverture told his troops on the eve of a critical battle: "We are fighting so that liberty—the most precious of all earthly possessions—may not perish." Ask **Why was liberty so important to Toussaint's army?** (They were former slaves.) **What can you tell about Toussaint from this quotation?** (He was very dedicated, zealous, and an inspired speaker.)

- **Teach** Explain that conditions for slaves in Haiti were extremely brutal, and the slaves retaliated with much violence when they revolted. Ask **Why do you think France, Spain, and Britain all sent troops to fight Toussaint's army?** (They probably feared the slave rebellion would spread, and they depended on the slave trade. They might also have wanted the lucrative colony of Haiti for themselves.) **Why might revolutionary France not have been very sympathetic with Toussaint's rebellion?** (It depended on money from Haiti's plantations.)

- **Analyzing the Visuals** Have students study the painting of Toussaint and his army in battle and the inset map. Ask them to describe Haiti's location and discuss what they may know about the country today. (It endures great poverty and political turmoil.) **What does the painting suggest about the difficulties Toussaint's army forced?** (They were fighting well-equipped and well-trained soldiers.)

Independent Practice

- **Biography** To help students better understand Haiti's revolution, have them read the biography *Toussaint L'Ouverture* and complete the worksheet.

All in One Teaching Resources, Unit 2, p. 68

Monitor Progress

To review the section so far, have students reread the black headings and summarize the content under each heading.

Answer

Caption They preferred death to a return to slavery.

Mexico and Central America Revolt

Instruct

- **Introduce** Inform students that Mexicans and Mexican Americans celebrate September 16 as independence day. Ask why the date is celebrated even though Father Hidalgo's rebellion failed. (*It was the day the struggle for independence began, like the Fourth of July in the United States.*)

- **Teach** Ask **Why do you think Mexico's first two independence leaders were priests?** (*Priests were among the best educated people. They also had close contact with poor mestizos and Native Americans and saw their living conditions.*) **What were Iturbide's motives for rebellion?** (*to seize power as emperor and avoid liberal reforms from Spain*) **Why do you think Iturbide was quickly overthrown?** (*Many of those who fought with him for independence wanted liberal reforms.*)

- **Quick Activity** Using the Think-Write-Pair-Share strategy (TE, p. T23), have students brainstorm slogans. Then ask each pair to create banners for the revolutionary forces of Fathers Hidalgo and Morelos.

Independent Practice

Primary Source To help students better understand Father Hidalgo's rebellion, have them read the selection *From the Decree of Hidalgo* and complete the worksheet.

All in One Teaching Resources, Unit 2, p. 69

Monitor Progress

As students fill in their charts, circulate to make sure they include the rebellions of Hidalgo, Morelos, and Iturbide. For a completed version of the chart, see

Note Taking Transparencies, 146

Answer

✓ When Spanish liberals forced the king to issue a constitution, Iturbide fought for independence to avoid liberal reforms.

---

conditions for the majority of Mexicans, abolish slavery, and give the vote to all men. For four years, Morelos led rebel forces before he, too, was captured and shot in 1815.

Spanish forces, backed by conservative creoles, hunted down the surviving guerrillas. They had almost succeeded in ending the rebel movement when events in Spain had unexpected effects.

Mexico Wins Independence In Spain in 1820, liberals forced the king to issue a constitution. This move alarmed Agustín de Iturbide (ee toor BEE day), a conservative creole in Mexico. He feared that the new Spanish government might impose liberal reforms on the colonies as well.

Iturbide had spent years fighting Mexican revolutionaries. Suddenly, in 1821, he reached out to them. Backed by creoles, mestizos, and Native Americans, he overthrew the Spanish viceroy. Mexico was independent at last. Iturbide took the title Emperor Agustín I. Soon, however, liberal Mexicans toppled the would-be monarch and set up the Republic of Mexico.

New Republics Emerge in Central America Spanish-ruled lands in Central America declared independence in the early 1820s. Iturbide tried to add these areas to his Mexican empire. After his overthrow, local leaders set up a republic called the United Provinces of Central America. The union soon fragmented into the separate republics of Guatemala, Nicaragua, Honduras, El Salvador, and Costa Rica.

✓ **Checkpoint** How did events in Spain affect the fight for Mexican independence?

Revolution Ignites South America

In South America, Native Americans had rebelled against Spanish rule as early as the 1700s, though with limited results. It was not until the 1800s that discontent among the creoles sparked a widespread drive for independence.

Bolívar Begins the Fight In the early 1800s, discontent spread across South America. Educated creoles like Simón Bolívar admired the French and American revolutions. They dreamed of winning their own independence from Spain.

In 1808, when Napoleon Bonaparte occupied Spain, Bolívar and his friends saw the occupation as a signal to act. In 1810, Bolívar led an uprising that established a republic in his native Venezuela. Bolívar's new republic was quickly toppled by conservative forces, however. For years, civil war raged in Venezuela. The revolutionaries suffered many setbacks. Twice Bolívar was forced into exile on the island of Haiti.

Then, Bolívar conceived a daring plan. He would march his army across the Andes and attack the Spanish at Bogotá, the capital of the viceroyalty of New Granada (present-day Colombia). First, he cemented an alliance with the hard-riding llaneros, or Venezuelan cowboys. Then, in a grueling campaign, he led an army through swampy lowlands and over the snowcapped Andes. Finally, in August 1819, he swooped down to take Bogotá from the surprised Spanish.

Other victories followed. By 1821, Bolívar had succeeded in freeing Caracas, Venezuela. "The Liberator," as he was now called, then moved south into Ecuador, Peru, and Bolivia. There, he joined forces with another great leader, **José de San Martín.**

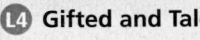
Differentiated Instruction   Solutions for All Learners

L4 Advanced Readers   L4 Gifted and Talented

Even before Toussaint L'Ouverture's slave revolt and the creole revolutions of the 1800s, a Native American named Tupac Amarú led a rebellion in Latin America. He claimed to be the great-grandson of the last Inca who had fought against the Spaniards in the 1500s, also named Tupac Amarú. Tupac Amarú II demanded an end to the brutal system of forced Indian labor.

Spanish officials rejected the demand. In 1780, Tupac Amarú organized a revolt. A large army crushed the rebellion and killed its leader, but his rebellion did call attention to the system of forced labor, which was eventually abolished. Have students research Tupac Amarú, write a brief biography, and create a design for a Web page about him.

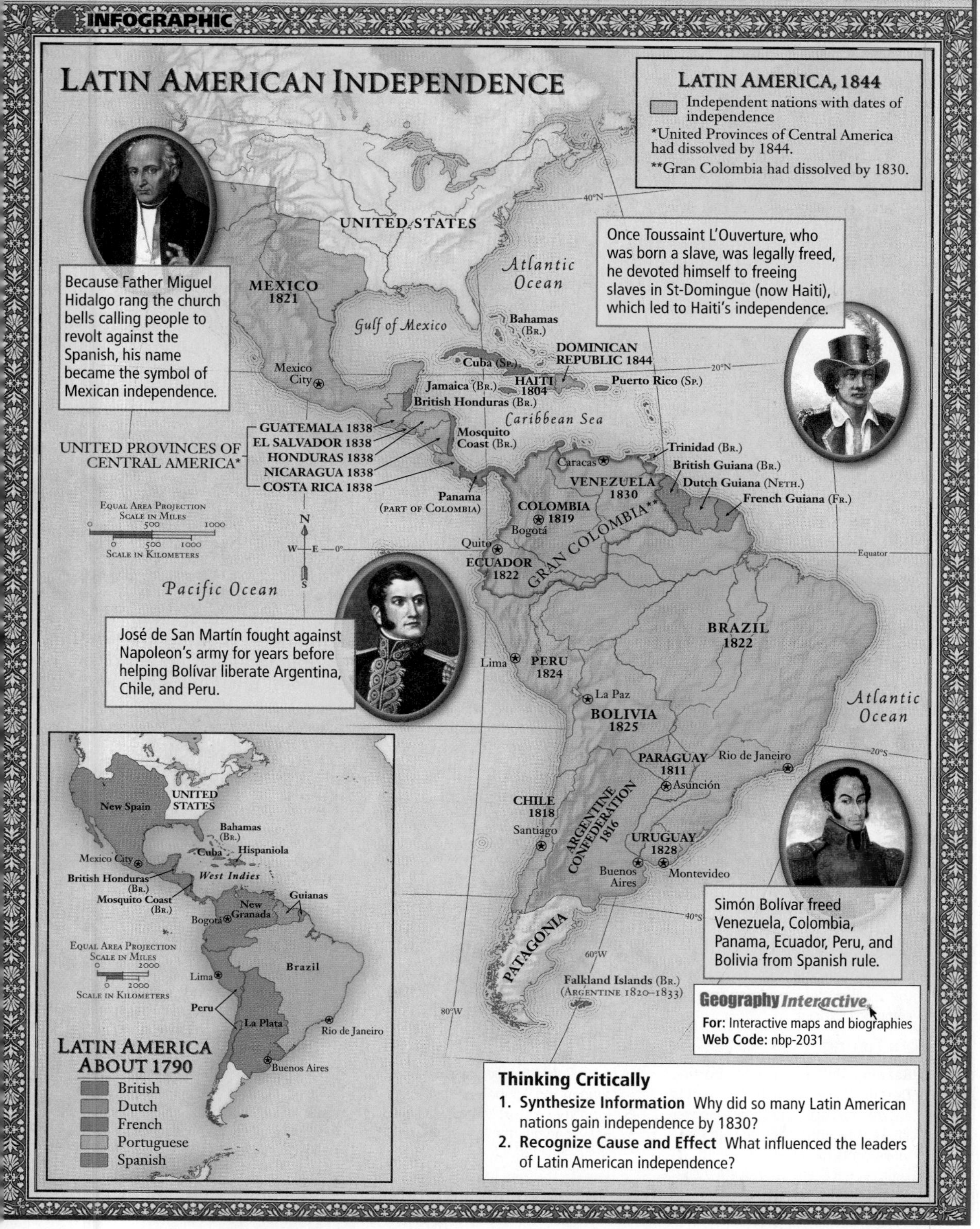

LATIN AMERICAN INDEPENDENCE

LATIN AMERICA, 1844

☐ Independent nations with dates of independence

*United Provinces of Central America had dissolved by 1844.

**Gran Colombia had dissolved by 1830.

Because Father Miguel Hidalgo rang the church bells calling people to revolt against the Spanish, his name became the symbol of Mexican independence.

Once Toussaint L'Ouverture, who was born a slave, was legally freed, he devoted himself to freeing slaves in St-Domingue (now Haiti), which led to Haiti's independence.

UNITED STATES

Atlantic Ocean

MEXICO 1821

Gulf of Mexico

Mexico City ⊛

Bahamas (BR.)

Cuba (SP.)

Jamaica (BR.)
British Honduras (BR.)

HAITI 1804

DOMINICAN REPUBLIC 1844

Puerto Rico (SP.)

Caribbean Sea

GUATEMALA 1838
EL SALVADOR 1838
HONDURAS 1838
NICARAGUA 1838
COSTA RICA 1838

Mosquito Coast (BR.)

Trinidad (BR.)

UNITED PROVINCES OF CENTRAL AMERICA*

Panama (PART OF COLOMBIA)

Caracas ⊛

VENEZUELA 1830

British Guiana (BR.)
Dutch Guiana (NETH.)
French Guiana (FR.)

EQUAL AREA PROJECTION
SCALE IN MILES
0   500   1000
0   500   1000
SCALE IN KILOMETERS

COLOMBIA ⊛ 1819
Bogotá

Quito
ECUADOR 1822

GRAN COLOMBIA**

Equator

Pacific Ocean

José de San Martín fought against Napoleon's army for years before helping Bolívar liberate Argentina, Chile, and Peru.

Lima ⊛ PERU 1824

BRAZIL 1822

La Paz

BOLIVIA 1825

Atlantic Ocean

PARAGUAY 1811
⊛ Asunción

Rio de Janeiro

CHILE 1818
Santiago

ARGENTINE CONFEDERATION 1816

URUGUAY 1828

Buenos Aires   Montevideo

Simón Bolívar freed Venezuela, Colombia, Panama, Ecuador, Peru, and Bolivia from Spanish rule.

PATAGONIA

Falkland Islands (BR.)
(ARGENTINE 1820–1833)

Geography *Interactive*
For: Interactive maps and biographies
Web Code: nbp-2031

LATIN AMERICA ABOUT 1790

New Spain

UNITED STATES

Bahamas (BR.)

Mexico City

Cuba · Hispaniola

British Honduras (BR.)

West Indies

Mosquito Coast (BR.)

Bogotá New Granada

Guianas

EQUAL AREA PROJECTION
SCALE IN MILES
0   2000
0   2000
SCALE IN KILOMETERS

Lima

Peru

La Plata

Brazil

Rio de Janeiro

Buenos Aires

☐ British
☐ Dutch
☐ French
☐ Portuguese
☐ Spanish

Thinking Critically

1. **Synthesize Information** Why did so many Latin American nations gain independence by 1830?
2. **Recognize Cause and Effect** What influenced the leaders of Latin American independence?

Revolution Ignites South America

Instruct

- **Introduce** Display **Color Transparency 124:** *Simón Bolívar Crossing the Andes.* Ask students to identify aspects of the painting that make Bolívar appear as a great hero. Explain that it was inspired by Jacques-Louis David's painting of Napoleon crossing the Alps.

  📖 **Color Transparencies, 124**

- **Teach** Ask **Why do you think it was so difficult for Bolívar and San Martín to win independence?** *(Power was concentrated in the hands of the peninsulares.)* Explain that South America had a much smaller and less powerful middle class than industrialized European countries did, which also made it difficult to pass liberal reforms. Ask **How did Dom Pedro keep power in Brazil?** *(by declaring independence and accepting a constitution)*

- **Quick Activity** Have students access **Web Code nbp-2031** to study the **Geography Interactive** maps and biographies. Discuss the transformation of Latin America from 1790 to 1844 and the significance of its leaders.

Independent Practice

Have students fill in the Outline Map *Latin American Independence* with names of countries, dates of revolutions, and outcomes.

All in One **Teaching Resources, Unit 2**, p. 71

Monitor Progress

- Check Reading and Note Taking Study Guide entries for student understanding.
- Circulate to make sure students are filling in their Outline Maps accurately.

Link to Geography

Crossing the Andes Two spectacular crossings of the Andes led to the liberation of South America. Revolutionary forces were no match for Spanish troops in direct combat. So José de San Martín came up with the fantastic idea of crossing the Andes from Argentina to launch a surprise attack on Chile. He crossed in great secrecy in January 1817 with 3,000 men, half of whom were former slaves. He lost many men, horses, and mules but succeeded in liberating Chile. He then invaded Peru by sea. Two years later, Simón Bolívar crossed the Andes in the north, surprising Spanish troops and liberating Colombia. In 1822 the two liberators met in Ecuador. San Martín told a friend, "There isn't enough room for Bolívar and me in Peru." San Martín withdrew, and Bolívar completed the liberation of Peru.

Answers

Thinking Critically

1. Strong leaders galvanized revolts.
2. Enlightenment ideals and the French and American revolutions

Dom Pedro, Emperor of Brazil

Vocabulary Builder

proclaim—(proh KLAYM) *vt.* to announce publicly or formally

San Martín Joins the Fight Like Bolívar, San Martín was a creole. He was born in Argentina but went to Europe for military training. In 1816, this gifted general helped Argentina win freedom from Spain. He then joined the independence struggle in other areas. He, too, led an army across the Andes, from Argentina into Chile. He defeated the Spanish in Chile before moving into Peru to strike further blows against colonial rule. San Martín turned his command over to Bolívar in 1822, allowing Bolívar's forces to win the final victories against Spain.

Freedom Leads to Power Struggles The wars of independence ended by 1824. Bolívar then worked tirelessly to unite the lands he had liberated into a single nation, called Gran Colombia. Bitter rivalries, however, made that dream impossible. Before long, Gran Colombia split into four independent countries: Colombia, Panama, Venezuela, and Ecuador.

Bolívar faced another disappointment as power struggles among rival leaders triggered destructive civil wars. Before his death in 1830, a discouraged Bolívar wrote, "We have achieved our independence at the expense of everything else." Contrary to his dreams, South America's common people had simply changed one set of masters for another.

Brazil Gains Independence When Napoleon's armies conquered Portugal, the Portuguese royal family fled to Brazil. When the king returned to Portugal, he left his son **Dom Pedro** to rule Brazil. "If Brazil demands independence," the king advised Pedro, "proclaim it yourself and put the crown on your own head."

In 1822, Pedro followed his father's advice. A revolution had brought new leaders to Portugal who planned to abolish reforms and demanded that Dom Pedro return. Dom Pedro refused to leave Brazil. Instead, he became emperor of an independent Brazil. He accepted a constitution that provided for freedom of the press, freedom of religion, and an elected legislature. Brazil remained a monarchy until 1889, when social and political turmoil led it to become a republic.

✓ **Checkpoint** How were the goals of the South American revolutions different from their results?

SECTION 3 Assessment

Terms, People, and Places

1. What do many of the key terms listed at the beginning of the section have in common? Explain.

Note Taking

2. **Reading Skill: Identify Supporting Details** Use your completed chart to answer the Focus Question: Who were the key revolutionaries that led the movements for independence in Latin America, and what were their accomplishments?

Comprehension and Critical Thinking

3. **Draw Conclusions** How did social structure contribute to discontent in Latin America?
4. **Analyze Information** (a) What was the first step on Haiti's road to independence? (b) Why did creoles refuse to support Hidalgo or Morelos?
5. **Identify Central Issues** Why did Bolívar admire the American and French revolutions?

● **Writing About History**

Quick Write: Use Effective Language Most effective persuasive essays contain memorable and convincing details and vivid, persuasive language. Suppose you were one of the revolutionary leaders mentioned in the section. Write notes for a speech in which you persuade others to join your cause. Include at least three compelling reasons why people should follow you.

Simón Bolívar: *Address to the Congress of Venezuela*

Encouraged by the revolutions in British North America and France, colonists in Spanish South America soon began to create a force for independence. Simón Bolívar was one of the leaders of this movement. The excerpt below is from Bolívar's Address to the Second National Congress of Venezuela, given in 1819. In this speech, Bolívar offers advice on what type of government to set up in Venezuela.

Statue of Bolívar as the Liberator, Mexico City

Subject to the threefold yoke of ignorance, tyranny, and vice, the American people have been unable to acquire knowledge, power, or [civic] virtue. The lessons we received and the models we studied, as pupils of such pernicious[1] teachers, were most destructive. . . .

If a people, perverted by their training, succeed in achieving their liberty, they will soon lose it, for it would be of no avail to endeavor to explain to them that happiness consists in the practice of virtue; that the rule of law is more powerful than the rule of tyrants, because, as the laws are more inflexible everyone should submit to their beneficent austerity; that proper morals, and not force, are the bases of law; and that to practice justice is to practice liberty.

Therefore, Legislators, your work is so much the more arduous[2], inasmuch as you have to reeducate men who have been corrupted by erroneous[3] illusions and false incentives[4]. Liberty, says Rousseau, is a succulent[5] morsel, but one difficult to digest. . . .

Legislators, meditate well before you choose. Forget not that you are to lay the political foundation for a newly born nation which can rise to the heights of greatness that Nature has marked out for it if you but proportion this foundation in keeping with the high plane that it aspires to attain. Unless your choice is based upon the peculiar . . . experience of Venezuelan people—a factor that should guide you in determining the nature and form of government you are about to adopt for the well-being of the people . . . the result of our reforms will again be slavery.

1. **pernicious** (pur NISH us) *adj.* harmful, injurious
2. **arduous** (AHR joo us) *adj.* difficult
3. **erroneous** (eh ROH nee us) *adj.* mistaken, wrong
4. **incentive** (in SEN tiv) *n.* reason for doing something
5. **succulent** (SUK yoo lunt) *adj.* juicy, tasty

Thinking Critically
1. **Analyze Literature** How did Bolívar feel the people of Latin America were prepared for new government?
2. **Draw Inferences** Do you think Bolívar was practical or idealistic? Use examples from the excerpt to defend your opinion.

History Background

Simón Bolívar Bolívar had visited the United States, but he judged its federal government to be "weak and complicated" and "difficult to adapt to Venezuela." During his times of refuge in Haiti, he observed its government and was persuaded to free the slaves, who later formed an important part of his forces. Bolívar's military campaign was still mired in difficulty when, in February 1819, he summoned a congress at Angostura. At the opening of the congress he gave this famous address. Later that year Bolívar crossed the Andes and marched triumphantly into Bogotá. In his address, Bolívar admitted the difficulties that Venezuelans faced. He envisioned a transitional period that would allow time for the people to be trained in the foundations of democracy.

Simón Bolívar: *Address to the Congress of Venezuela*

Objective
■ Describe Simón Bolívar's goals for South America and understand the difficulties Latin Americans faced creating democratic governments.

Build Background Knowledge ⬤
Ask students to recall what they know about Simón Bolívar's goals for the liberation of South America, especially those that met with disappointment. Ask them why they think it was so difficult to achieve liberal reforms such as freedom and individual rights.

Instruct ⬤
■ Discuss Bolívar's advice on government. Ask **Who does Bolívar believe were "pernicious teachers"?** *(Spanish colonial administrators)* **What attitude does Bolívar believe the people will have toward laws?** *(Because they have only seen corruption, they will not understand the importance of law in preserving liberty, and they will ignore the law.)* **What kind of government does Bolívar think they should choose for Venezuela?** *(one based on the specific experience of Venezuelans)*

■ Read aloud the last line of the third paragraph: "Liberty, says Rousseau, is a succulent morsel, but one difficult to digest. . . ." Ask students to discuss the meaning of this statement.

Monitor Progress
To review this feature, ask students to discuss whether Bolívar turned out to be right that a people "perverted by their training . . . will soon lose" their liberty once it is gained.

Thinking Critically
1. He thought they were very poorly prepared for new government by their experience with corrupt, tyrannical colonial government.
2. Responses may vary but should be supported with examples.

Quick Study Guide

- Have students use the Quick Study Guide to prepare for this chapter's test. Students may wish to refer to the following pages as they review:

Revolutions in Europe
Section 1, pp. 273–275; Section 2, pp. 280–281

Independence Movements in Latin America
Section 3, pp. 283–289

Events in France
Section 2, pp. 276–280

Age of Revolution
Section 2, pp. 276, 280–281; Section 3, pp. 284–286

- For additional review, remind students to refer to the **L3**

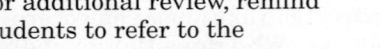 **Reading and Note Taking Study Guide**

Note Taking Study Guide, pp. 98, 100, 102
Summaries, pp. 99, 101, 103

- Have students access **Web Code nbp-2001** for this chapter's **History Interactive** timeline, which includes expanded entries and additional events.

- If students need more instruction on analyzing timelines, have them read the **Skills Handbook,** p. SH30.

- When students have completed their study of the chapter, distribute Chapter Test A and B.

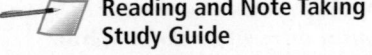 **Teaching Resources, Unit 2,** pp. 73–78

For **Progress Monitoring Online,** refer students to the Self-test with vocabulary practice at **Web Code nba-2041.**

Quick Study Guide

Progress Monitoring Online
For: Self-test with vocabulary practice
Web Code: naa-2041

■ Revolutions in Europe

Successful	Unsuccessful
Serbia (autonomy 1830)	Poland (1830)
Greece (1830)	Austria (1848)
Belgium (1830)	Italy (1848)
	Germany (1848)

■ Events in France

July 1830	1840	February 1848
• Rebels take control of Paris. • Constitutional monarchy proclaimed. • Louis Philippe becomes king.	• Recession heightens discontent.	• Rebels take to the streets. • Second Republic is proclaimed. • Louis Philippe abdicates.

June 1848	1850	1852
• Bourgeois liberals crush workers' rebellion.	• Louis Napoleon is voted president of the Second Republic.	• Louis Napoleon becomes emperor of the Second Empire.

■ Independence Movements in Latin America

Cause and Effect	
Long-Term Causes	**Immediate Causes**
• European domination • Spread of Enlightenment ideas • American and French Revolutions • Growth of nationalism	• Social injustices • Revolutionary leaders emerge. • Napoleon invades Spain.

Independence Movements	
Immediate Effects	**Long-Term Effects**
• Toussaint L'Ouverture leads slave revolt in Haiti. • Bolívar, San Martin, and others lead successful revolts. • Colonial rule ends in much of Latin America.	• Numerous independent nations in Latin America • Continuing efforts to achieve stable democratic governments and to gain economic independence

■ Age of Revolution

	1804	1810	1819	1821
	Haiti declares independence from France.	Father Miguel Hidalgo urges Mexicans to fight for independence from Spain.	Simón Bolívar seizes Bogotá from the Spanish.	Simón Bolívar liberates Caracas, Venezuela.

Chapter Events
Global Events — 1800 — 1810 — 1820

	1803	1814	1819	1823
	United States buys Louisiana from France.	Napoleon is banished to Elba.	The United States acquires Spanish Florida.	U.S. President James Monroe issues the Monroe Doctrine.

Differentiated Instruction Solutions for All Learners

L1 Special Needs **L2 Less Proficient Readers**

Use the following study guide resources to help students acquiring basic skills:

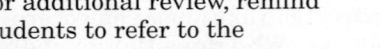 **Adapted Reading and Note Taking Study Guide**
Adapted Note Taking Study Guide, pp. 98, 100, 102
Adapted Section Summaries, pp. 99, 101, 103

L2 English Language Learners

Use the following study guide resources to help Spanish-speaking students:

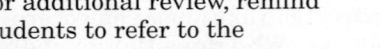 **Spanish Reading and Note Taking Study Guide**
Spanish Note Taking Study Guide, pp. 98, 100, 102
Spanish Section Summaries, pp. 99, 101, 103

Concept Connector

Essential Question Review

To connect prior knowledge with what you have learned in this chapter, answer the questions below in your Concept Connector journal. Use the journal in the Reading and Note Taking Study Guide to record your answers (or go to www.phschool.com **Web Code: nbd-2007**). In addition, record information about the following concepts:
- Conflict: European revolutionaries in 1830 and 1848
- Revolution: Latin American revolutions against European rulers

1. **Conflict** The early 1800s saw a clash of opposing ideologies. Conservatives favored monarchies as a political system. Liberals supported a republican form of government. How did conservatives benefit from the status quo, or existing state of affairs? Why did liberals and nationalists oppose the status quo? What steps did Prince Clemens von Metternich urge monarchs to take to maintain their power?

2. **Democracy** Before his death in 1830, Simón Bolívar wrote, "We have achieved our independence at the expense of everything else." What did he mean? How were the outcomes of Latin American revolutions similar to, and different from, the American Revolution? Think about the following:
   - social classes
   - constitutions
   - cooperation between the colonies

■ Connections to Today

1. **Independence: Mexican Independence Day** Today, the people of Mexico remember Father Hidalgo's speech as "el Grito de Dolores." Every September 15, the anniversary of the speech, the president of Mexico rings a bell—suggestive of the church bell in Dolores. The president then honors the Grito de Dolores by repeating the speech. The next day, September 16, marks the anniversary of the beginning of the fight against the Spanish. It is celebrated as Mexican Independence Day, a national holiday. Schools and businesses shut down, and people throw huge parties. Fireworks light the night sky. Why is the ringing of bells an important custom of Mexican Independence Day?

2. **Conflict: Chechnya and Russia** There are many struggles for independence in the world today. Certain Basques in Spain, Tibetans in China, and Chechens in Russia are all seeking their independence. In some cases, such as in Chechnya, revolutionaries resort to terrorism to fight for their goals. Conduct research and write a one-page report about Chechnya and why its revolutionaries seek independence from Russia.

1830		1848	
French revolutionaries battle the king's troops in the streets of Paris.		Revolutions break out across much of Europe.	**History** *Interactive* **For:** Interactive timeline **Web Code:** nbp-2001

1830   **1840**   **1850**

1839	1850
China and Britain clash in the Opium War.	Taiping Rebellion begins in China.

Concept Connector

Tell students that the main concepts for this chapter are Human Rights, Nationalism, Revolution, Democracy, and Conflict. Then ask students to answer the Essential Question Review questions on this page. Discuss the Connections to Today topics and ask students to answer the questions that follow.

Essential Question Review

1. Conservatives, mostly nobility and church leaders, stood to benefit from the status quo because they would be able to maintain their power if they could prevent revolutionary change. Liberals and nationalists sought greater freedom, equality, and individual rights. In order to prevent revolutionary change, Metternich urged monarchs to oppose freedom of the press, crush protest, and send troops to quell rebellions.

2. Bolívar was suggesting that the independence he helped achieve was a hollow victory because Gran Colombia could not maintain its unity, fracturing into four separate countries. In both the Latin American and American revolutions, there was a desire for independence and unity. But after the Latin American revolutions, power remained in the hands of the few people who owned land. After the American Revolution, a democracy was established in which many people owned land and shared power.

Connections to Today

1. The ringing of bells signifies liberty because it reminds Mexicans of Father Hidalgo ringing the bells at the church in Dolores.

2. Reports should give the history of Chechen nationalism and of Chechens' struggle for independence.

Chapter Assessment

Terms, People, and Places

1. ideology
2. autonomy
3. creole
4. recession
5. mestizo
6. Louis Philippe
7. José de San Martin
8. peninsular

Main Ideas

9. (a) restoring power to monarchies, hierarchies, and the church and suppressing dissension (b) written constitutions, separation of powers, and protection of basic rights (c) independence from foreign rule

10. Charles X suspended the legislature and restricted the press and the right to vote, which angered citizens and caused them to revolt.

11. The 1848 revolutions were eventually crushed, and reforms were canceled.

12. (a) Hidalgo and Morelos's revolts failed, but Iturbide led a successful revolt. (b) hardly at all

13. He liberated many countries in South America from Spanish rule.

Chapter Focus Question

14. Although uprisings were suppressed in the 1820s, liberal and nationalist ideals reignited revolutions in France in 1830 and 1848 that spread across Europe.

Critical Thinking

15. Liberalism and nationalism led to repeated uprisings, which were violently suppressed by determined conservatives.

16. Sample: They were accustomed to a society in which men with property held power; to include everyone would have been a radical step at the time.

17. (a) They admired Greek civilization and wanted to weaken the Ottomans. (b) No, and to discourage revolutions, they forced the Greeks to accept a German king.

18. (a) When there is an uprising in Paris, revolution spreads across Europe. (b) Yes: revolutions spread from France in 1830 and 1848.

19. Bolívar's Gran Colombia is divided into Venezuela, Colombia, and Ecuador.

Chapter Assessment

Terms, People, and Places

Match the following terms with the definitions below.

creole	peninsular
autonomy	ideology
Louis Philippe	mestizo
recession	José de San Martín

1. system of thought and belief
2. self-rule
3. person in Spain's colonies in the Americas who was an American-born descendant of Spanish settlers
4. period of reduced economic activity
5. person in Spain's colonies in the Americas who was of Native American and European descent
6. known as the "citizen king"
7. fought for freedom in South America
8. member of the highest class in Spain's colonies in the Americas

Main Ideas

Section 1 (pp. 634–637)
9. In the early 1800s, what were the main goals of (a) conservatives, (b) liberals, and (c) nationalists?

Section 2 (pp. 638–644)
10. What were the causes of the French revolution of 1830?
11. Describe the outcomes of the 1848 rebellions in Europe.

Section 3 (pp. 645–651)
12. (a) How did Mexico gain independence from Spain? (b) How did Mexico's independence change the lives of its people?
13. Why is Simón Bolívar known as "The Liberator"?

Chapter Focus Question
14. How did revolutionary ideals in Europe and Latin America ignite uprisings in the first half of the nineteenth century?

Critical Thinking

15. **Recognize Cause and Effect** How did the clash of conservatism, liberalism, and nationalism contribute to unrest in Europe in the 1800s?
16. **Draw Conclusions** Why do you think liberals of the early 1800s supported limited voting rights?
17. **Synthesize Information** In the 1820s, Britain, France, and Russia supported the Greek struggle for independence. (a) Why did these European powers support the Greeks? (b) Did the European powers usually respond to revolution in this way? Explain.
18. **Analyze Information** You have read Metternich's comment: "When France sneezes, Europe catches cold." (a) What did he mean by these words? (b) Was Metternich correct?
19. **Geography and History** Review the map in Section 3. How does the map show that Bolívar failed to achieve one of his dreams?
20. **Analyzing Visuals** The scene below is part of a famous mural by José Clemente Orozco. How do you think Orozco feels about Father Hidalgo?

21. **Geography and History** (a) How did climatic conditions help Haitians defeat the French? (b) Do you think the distance between Europe and Latin America affected the Latin American wars for independence? Explain.

● Writing About History

In this chapter's three Section Assessments, you developed skills for writing a persuasive essay.

Writing a Persuasive Essay The early 1800s were a time of revolution across Europe. Liberals and nationalists attempted to organize revolts that might overthrow Europe's colonial rule. Write a persuasive essay that a liberal or nationalist might have published in a local newspaper to persuade people to join a revolution.

Prewriting
- Take notes about the ideas that motivated revolutionaries in the early 1800s.
- Generate arguments that a liberal or nationalist might make.

Drafting
- Using a convincing thesis, or main argument, make an outline that organizes the essay.
- Write an attention-grabbing introduction, a body, and a conclusion.
- Open and close with your strongest argument.

Revising
- Make sure your arguments are logical and clearly explained. Provide additional evidence where needed.
- Use the guidelines for revising your report on page SH17 of the Writing Handbook.

---

20. Sample: that he was a larger-than-life figure who set Mexico's institutions on fire

21. (a) Haiti's tropical climate favored yellow fever, which killed thousands of French troops. (b) The distance helped colonists because it made it difficult for Europe to send troops and arms or to react quickly.

Document-Based Assessment

The Revolutions of 1848: The Aftermath

The revolutions of 1848 began spontaneously in February 1848 on the streets of Paris. Reformers won short-lived success with the abdication of Louis Philippe. Uprisings spread across Europe to Austria, Hungary, Germany, and Italy, among others. These rebellions were quelled in short order, as the documents below illustrate, but some reverberations were more lasting.

Document A

"[O]n June 23rd, 1848 . . . the proletarians of Paris were defeated, decimated [killed off so that a large part of the population was removed], crushed with such an effect that even now they have not yet recovered from the blow. And immediately, all over Europe, the new and old Conservatives and Counter-Revolutionists raised their heads with an effrontery [boldness] that showed how well they understood the importance of the event. The Press was everywhere attacked, the rights of meeting and association were interfered with, every little event in every small provincial town was taken profit of to disarm the people to declare a state of siege, to drill the troops in the new maneuvers and artifices [clever tricks] that Cavaignac [French general known for his harsh treatment of Parisian rebels] had taught them."

—From *The Paris Rising—Frankfort Assembly*
by Frederich Engels (February, 1852)

Document B

"[German] factory workers failed to win any lasting class advantages in 1848–1849 . . . Many artisans exerted themselves for the revolution; in October 1849 the magazine of the cigar workers estimated that three hundred in this industry alone had been forced to flee to Switzerland. . . . For German democrats— whether workers or from the middle class—the revolution left little immediate consolation. In a few states democrats retained large representation in the parliaments, but reactionary changes in the suffrage systems soon ended that. . . . But the long-range results of the revolution were not altogether negative. To be sure, those who worked for democracy after 1849 knew better than to try to create a republic. They also knew the futility of resorting to revolutionary violence. But their effort did not cease."

—From *The Democratic Movement in Germany, 1789–1914*
by John L. Snell

Document C

Metternich Flees Austria

Document D

"The rising of 1848 was a spontaneous expression of national feeling but completely uncoordinated and therefore defeated in detail. After it, once more patrolled by Austria, Italy sank back into inaction. . . . From the wreck of Italian political institutions in 1849 there was only one survival, the constitution granted by [King] Charles Albert in Piedmont [kingdom in northwestern Italy]. It provided for a Premier or President of the Council, who, like the Senate, was nominated by the King, and a Chamber of Deputies numbering two hundred and four, elected on a narrow franchise [vote]."

—From *The Evolution of Modern Italy* by Arthur James Whyte

Analyzing Documents

Use your knowledge of the revolutions of 1848 and Documents A, B, C, and D to answer questions 1–4.

1. Which words describe the attitude of the author of Document A toward the counter-revolutionaries?
   A admiration and pride
   B understanding and sympathy
   C hatred and disapproval
   D respect and sympathy

2. According to Document B, what strategies did the democrats of Germany follow after the revolution was put down?
   A revolutionary plots
   B voter-registration drives
   C underground efforts
   D parliamentary politics

3. In Document C, Prince Clemens von Metternich is
   A proud to resign.
   B continuing Austrian governance.
   C expressing nationalism.
   D unpopular and defeated.

4. **Writing Task** Describe the aftermath of the revolutions of 1848. If you had lived in 1849, would you have seen causes for optimism or pessimism? How would your answer be different from the viewpoint of the twenty-first century?

● Writing About History

As students begin the assignment, refer them to page SH13 of the **Writing Handbook** for help in writing a research paper. Remind them of the steps they should take to complete their assignment, including prewriting, drafting, and revising. For help in revising, remind them to use the guidelines on page SH15 of the **Writing Handbook.**

Students' essays should have a strong persuasive thesis supported by clearly stated liberal or nationalist arguments. They should contain an attention-grabbing introduction, a body, and a conclusion. They should show evidence of reflection and be free of grammatical and spelling errors. For scoring rubrics for writing assignments, see **Assessment Rubrics,** p. 8.

Industrialism and a New Global Age
1750–1914

Unit Overview

Unit 3 examines the century preceding the First World War, during which time industrialization took hold in many countries, and the strongest of them built or added to their overseas empires.

Chapter 9 studies the spread of the Industrial Revolution and how the mechanization of work and the urbanization brought about by this revolution affected society.
Concepts: Economic Systems, Science, Technology

Chapter 10 explores how European nationalism led to the unification of Germany and Italy, caused tensions to rise in Eastern Europe, and led to reform as well as repression in Russia.
Concepts: Empire, Nationalism, Revolution

Chapter 11 focuses on Britain, France, and the United States and the social and political changes that took place in these Western democracies during the 1800s.
Concepts: Cooperation, Democracy, Migration

Chapter 12 describes how European powers, spurred by the needs of industrialization, aggressively expanded their empires in the 1800s during the Age of Imperialism.
Concepts: Belief Systems, Empire, Genocide

Chapter 13 examines how imperialist domination in Africa, Asia, and Latin America affected subject peoples politically, economically, and culturally, while fueling tensions among the imperialists themselves.
Concepts: Cooperation, Geography's Impact, Migration

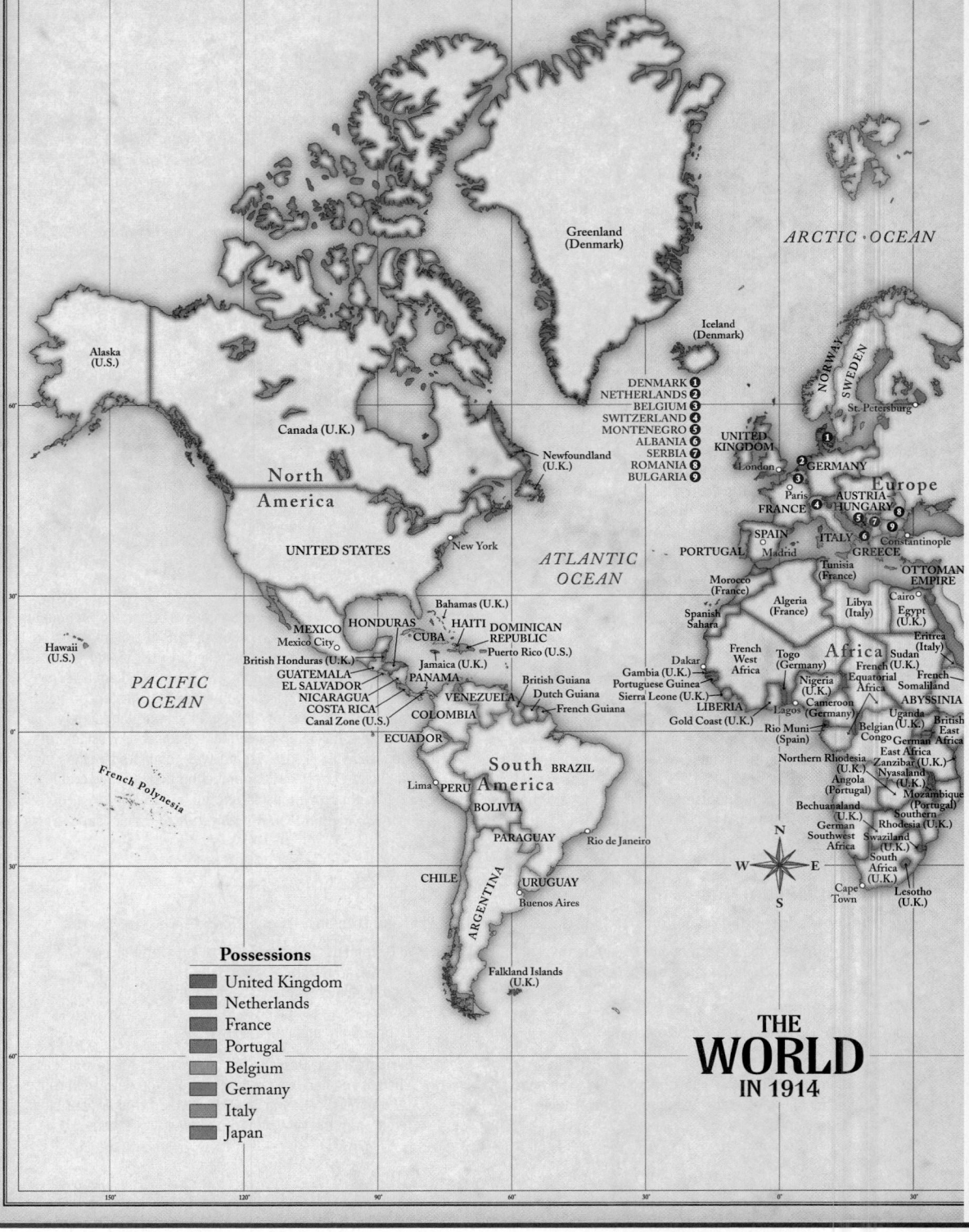

Possessions
- United Kingdom
- Netherlands
- France
- Portugal
- Belgium
- Germany
- Italy
- Japan

THE
WORLD
IN 1914

About the Map

The Industrial Revolution increased the wealth and power of the nations of Western Europe and the United States. During the 1800s, these Western powers competed for control of territory in Africa, southern Asia, and the Pacific. In India, Britain set up a system of colonial rule that introduced Western technology and culture and later provoked a strong independence movement. Starting in the 1870s, Europeans scrambled to colonize Africa. Only Ethiopia (or Abyssinia) and Liberia succeeded in maintaining their independence. In the early 1900s, Japan joined the competition for external possessions in East Asia. External possessions were a source of national prestige for Western powers and Japan, and they provided raw materials and consumer markets for growing industries. While powerful democracies controlled Western Europe, three large empires ruled over many distinct nationalities in Eastern Europe. During the early 1900s, nationalist tensions within Europe were growing.

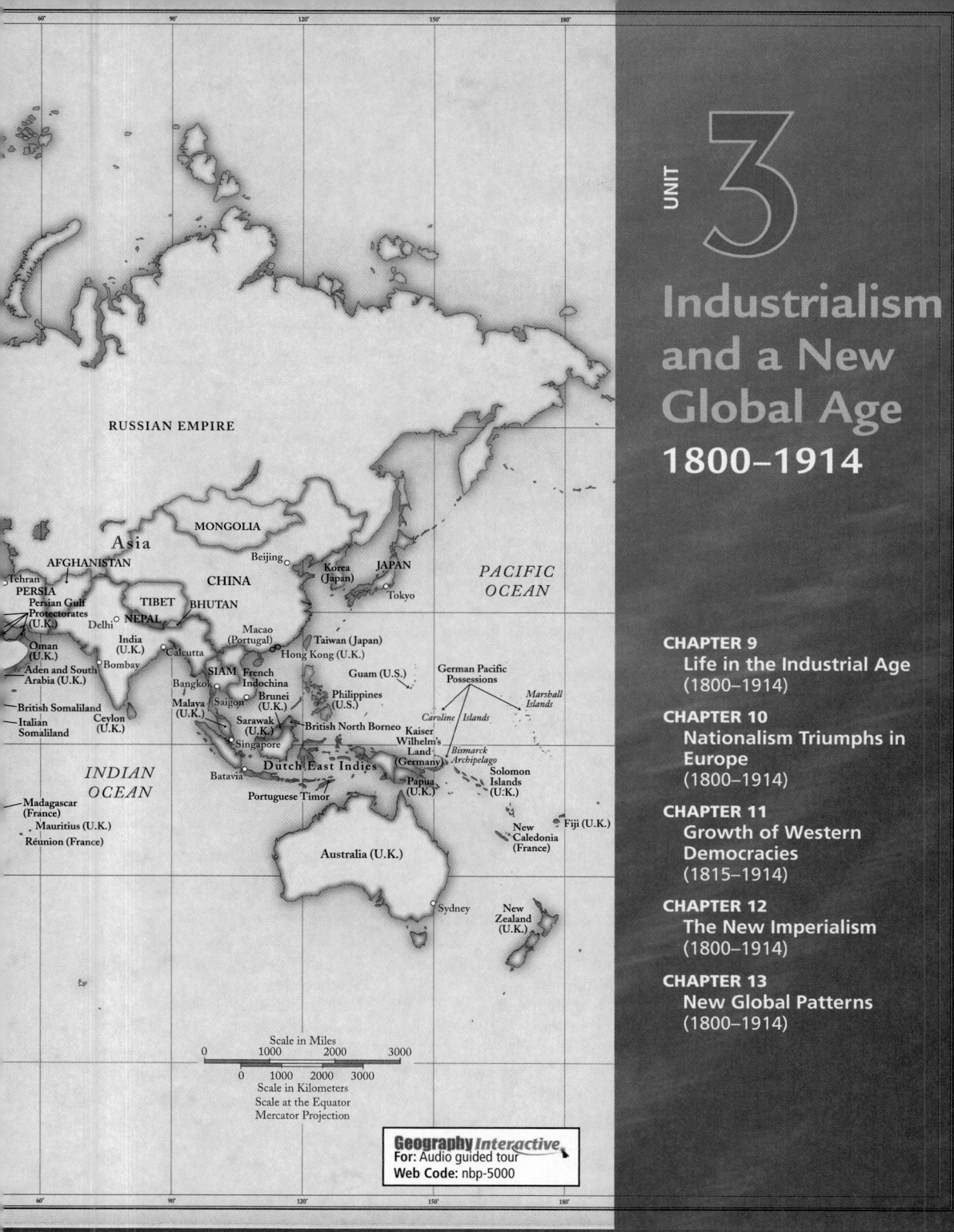

Geography *Interactive*
For: Audio guided tour
Web Code: nbp-5000

UNIT 3

Industrialism and a New Global Age

1800–1914

Geographic Literacy

Point out that the map on these pages shows that by 1914, Western powers and Japan had established extensive overseas empires. Ask **Which continents were most affected by European colonial expansion?** *(They managed to carve up Africa almost completely. Also, Britain gained control of Australia. Much of Asia was also under European control, especially if Russia is counted as a European power.)* **What nearby lands did Japan control in 1914?** *(Korea and the island of Taiwan)* **What new territories had the United States acquired?** *(Alaska, Hawaii, the Panama Canal Zone, Puerto Rico, Guam, and the Philippines)* **Why do you think these industrializing powers were so eager to take control of foreign lands?** *(Sample: They sought a steady supply of natural resources to keep their factories going, as well as markets for finished products. They also competed with one another for military advantage and political prestige throughout the world.)* **Three empires dominated Eastern Europe. Two of these were Germany and Austria-Hungary. What was the third?** *(the Russian Empire)*

Looking Ahead

Ask students to read the chapter titles to the right of the map. Ask **Based on these titles and your study of the map, what do you predict you will learn about in this unit?** *(social changes brought on by the Industrial Revolution, political changes in the West, and the imperialist expansion of Western powers and Japan)* Explain that students will also learn about a flood of immigration into the United States, nationalist movements in colonized regions, and three British colonies that gained independence.

A note on the projection:
Although the Mercator projection distorts the sizes of continents, it was widely used for maps after its invention in 1569.

> **Home Involvement**
> The *Letter Home* includes a summary of the Industrialism and A New Global Age content that students will be studying.
> All in One **Teaching Resources, Unit 3,** p. 1

Life in the Industrial Age

Section	Core Instruction L3	Differentiated Instruction L1 L2 L4	
Section 1 *The Industrial Revolution Spreads* 🕐 **2 periods, 1 block** **OBJECTIVES** ■ List the industrial powers that emerged in the 1800s. ■ Describe the impact of new technology on industry, transportation, and communication. ■ Understand how big business emerged in the late 1800s. **Focus Question** *How did science, technology, and big business promote industrial growth?*	**All in One Teaching Resources, Unit 3** Reading Strategy: Identify Supporting Details, p. 7 Vocabulary Builder: Word Origins, p. 6 Outline Map: Europe About 1870, p. 13 Geography Quiz, p. 14 Section 1 Quiz, p. 2 **Reading and Note Taking Study Guide** Note Taking Study Guide, p. 104 Section 1 Summary, p. 105 **Note Taking Transparencies,** 147 **WITNESS HISTORY Audio CD** The Steelmaking Process **Progress Monitoring Transparencies,** 86 **Color Transparencies,** 125, 126, 127 **Teaching Resources, Skills Handbook** Prereading the Chapter, pp. 1–2 Word Knowledge Rating Form, p. 3 K-W-L Chart, p. 4	**L1 Adapted Reading and Note Taking Study Guide** Note Taking Study Guide, p. 104 SN Section 1 Summary, p. 105 SN **L2 Adapted Reading and Note Taking Study Guide** Note Taking Study Guide, p. 104 LPR Section 1 Summary, p. 105 LPR **Spanish Reading and Note Taking Study Guide** Note Taking Study Guide, p. 104 ELL Section 1 Summary, p. 105 ELL **L4 All in One Teaching Resources, Unit 3** Link to Literature: From *Hard Times* by Charles Dickens, p. 10 AR, GT Simulation: Monopolies, pp. 104–107 AR, GT	*Student Edition Audio SN **Differentiated Instruction Activity,** Teacher's Edition, p. 301 SN *Guided Reading Audio, Spanish ELL *Student Edition Audio LPR **Differentiated Instruction Activity,** Teacher's Edition, p. 301 LPR, ELL **Differentiated Instruction Activity,** Teacher's Edition, p. 299 AR, GT **Extend Activity,** Teacher's Edition, p. 304 AR, GT
Section 2 *The Rise of the Cities* 🕐 **2 periods, 1 block** **OBJECTIVES** ■ Summarize the impact of medical advances in the late 1800s. ■ Describe how cities had changed by 1900. ■ Explain how working-class struggles led to improved conditions for workers. **Focus Question** *How did the Industrial Revolution change life in the cities?*	**All in One Teaching Resources, Unit 3** Section 2 Quiz, p. 3 **Reading and Note Taking Study Guide** Note Taking Study Guide, p. 106 Section 2 Summary, p. 107 **Note Taking Transparencies,** 148 **WITNESS HISTORY Audio CD** London Fog **Progress Monitoring Transparencies,** 87 **Color Transparencies,** 128 **Witness History Discovery School™** video program, *The Jungle: A View of Industrial America*	**L1 Adapted Reading and Note Taking Study Guide** Note Taking Study Guide, p. 106 SN Section 2 Summary, p. 107 SN **L2 Adapted Reading and Note Taking Study Guide** Note Taking Study Guide, p. 106 LPR Section 2 Summary, p. 107 LPR **L4 All in One Teaching Resources, Unit 3** Primary Source: The People of Paris Earn a Living, p. 8 AR, GT Viewpoints: Looking at London in the 1820s, p. 9 AR, GT	**Differentiated Instruction Activity,** Teacher's Edition, p. 306 SN **Spanish Reading and Note Taking Study Guide** Note Taking Study Guide, p. 106 ELL Section 2 Summary, p. 107 ELL **Differentiated Instruction Activity,** Teacher's Edition, p. 306 LPR, ELL **Differentiated Instruction Activity,** Teacher's Edition, p. 311 AR, GT **Extend Activity,** Teacher's Edition, p. 309 AR, GT

Section	Core Instruction L3	Differentiated Instruction L1 L2 L4	
Section 3 *Changing Attitudes and Values* ⏱ **2 periods, 1 block** **OBJECTIVES** ■ Explain what values shaped the new social order. ■ Understand how women and educators sought change. ■ learn how science challenged existing beliefs. **Focus Question** *How did the Industrial Revolution change the old social order and long-held traditions in the Western world?*	**All in One** Teaching Resources, Unit 3 Section 3 Quiz, p. 4 **Reading and Note Taking Study Guide** Note Taking Study Guide, p. 108 Section 3 Summary, p. 109 **Note Taking Transparencies**, 149 **WITNESS HISTORY** Audio CD Votes for Women **Progress Monitoring Transparencies**, 88 **Color Transparencies**, 129	**L1** **Adapted Reading and Note Taking Study Guide** Note Taking Study Guide, p. 108 SN Section 3 Summary, p. 109 SN	**Differentiated Instruction Activity,** Teacher's Edition, pp. 314, 316 SN
		L2 **Adapted Reading and Note Taking Study Guide** Note Taking Study Guide, p. 108 LPR Section 3 Summary, p. 109 LPR	**Spanish Reading and Note Taking Study Guide** Note Taking Study Guide, p. 108 ELL Section 3 Summary, p. 109 ELL **Differentiated Instruction Activity,** Teacher's Edition, pp. 314, 316 LPR, ELL
		L4 **All in One** Teaching Resources, Unit 3 Link to Literature: From *Pride and Prejudice*, by Jane Austen, p. 11 AR, GT	**Differentiated Instruction Activity,** Teacher's Edition, p. 317 AR, GT **Extend Activity,** Teacher's Edition, p. 318 AR, GT
Section 4 *Arts in the Industrial Age* ⏱ **1 period, .5 block** **OBJECTIVES** ■ Understand what themes shaped romantic art, literature, and music. ■ Explain how realists responded to the industrialized, urban world. ■ Describe how the visual arts changed. **Focus Question** *What artistic movements emerged in reaction to the Industrial Revolution?*	**All in One** Teaching Resources, Unit 3 Section 4 Quiz, p. 5 **Reading and Note Taking Study Guide** Note Taking Study Guide, p. 110 Section 4 Summary, p. 111 Concept Connector, pp. 259, 295 **Note Taking Transparencies**, 150 **WITNESS HISTORY** Audio CD Sunset; Ludwig van Beethoven **Progress Monitoring Transparencies**, 89 **Color Transparencies**, 130	**L1** **Adapted Reading and Note Taking Study Guide** Note Taking Study Guide, p. 110 SN Section 4 Summary, p. 111 SN Concept Connector, pp. 259, 295 SN	**Differentiated Instruction Activity,** Teacher's Edition, p. 320 SN
		L2 **Adapted Reading and Note Taking Study Guide** Note Taking Study Guide, p. 110 LPR Section 4 Summary, p. 111 LPR Concept Connector, pp. 259, 295 LPR	**Spanish Reading and Note Taking Study Guide** Note Taking Study Guide, p. 110 ELL Section 4 Summary, p. 111 ELL Concept Connector, pp. 259, 295 ELL **Differentiated Instruction Activity,** Teacher's Edition, p. 320 LPR, ELL
		L4 **All in One** Teaching Resources, Unit 3 Biography: Julia Margaret Cameron, p. 12 AR, GT	**Extend Activity,** Teacher's Edition, pp. 296c, 322 AR, GT

*Audio support is available for all sections.

Assessment Resources

- **Progress Monitoring Transparencies**, 86–89
- **SuccessTracker™**, Chapter 9
- **Document-Based Assessment**, pp. 66–78
- *ExamView*® **Test Bank CD-ROM**, Chapter 9
- **All in One** **Teaching Resources, Unit 3,** Chapter Tests A and B, pp. 15–20
- **Progress Monitoring** *Online* **Quizzes**, Chapter 9
- **Assessment Rubrics**

Differentiated Instruction Key

L1	Special Needs	**LPR**	Less Proficient Readers
L2	Basic to Average	**AR**	Advanced Readers
L3	All Students	**SN**	Special Needs Students
L4	Average to Advanced	**GT**	Gifted and Talented
		ELL	English Language Learner

Author's Notes

The Spread of the Industrial Revolution

By mid-century, competition between rival nations, between old and new industries, between countless small or middle-sized producers of the same good or service was widespread in Europe. Cloth making, coal mining, transportation all saw hundreds and even thousands of freely competing firms at work. "Competition," it was widely said, "is the life of trade and the law of progress."

In the last quarter of the century, however, there came a change. It was not a return to government regulation—that would not come on a large scale until the twentieth century. It was rather the rigorous curtailment of free competition by businessmen themselves. These limits on competition were the result of large-scale business combinations—the sort that American law would come to call "combination in restraint of trade."

The move toward monopoly combination that began in the 1870s was in part a defensive measure in the face of the sheer brutality of the fang-and-claw competition of the age. During the periodic depressions particularly, unregulated competition hurt all competitors and drove many into bankruptcy. Under such circumstances, many business leaders began to think that combination, not competition, might be the life of trade and even the law of survival. The result was the most amazing flower of nineteenth-century economic development: the rise of big business.

Some aggressive industrialists merged with or bought out either competitors or related industries to produce giant new *corporations*. Thus Albert Krupp, the German steelmaker, brought up coal and iron mines, ore boats, and even industries which used his steel. When complete, the Krupp family's industrial empire included machine-tool plants, railcar manufactures, a shipyard, and the arms industries for which his descendants would be most famous. . . .

This was the trend as the twentieth century got under way, and it has remained a main current of Western economic history since. Competition and entrepreneurship still play key innovative roles, but big business controls vast swathes of economic activity today.

—Anthony Esler, *The Human Venture: From Prehistory to the Present*, (Upper Saddle River, New Jersey: Pearson Education, 2004), p. 493

Extend Online

Impressionism and Post-Impressionism

Have students view paintings by impressionist and post-impressionist painters. Have them compare the use of light, style, and subject matter, and present their conclusions to the class. Use these steps to help students complete the activity.

Prepare for the Activity Explain that impressionist painters, such as Claude Monet, showed how light and atmosphere can affect perception. As Monet once wrote, "Everything changes, even stone."

Conduct the Activity For help in starting the activity, send students to **Web Code nbe-2101.** Students will view artwork by impressionist and post-impressionist painters and access resources such as video clips, biographies, and other background materials. Ask students to look through the images and compare how artists experimented with light and technique and how they began to portray modern city life. Then have students select one image to present to the class. Presentations should include a brief biography of the artist, a description of the image, and an explanation on the image's significance.

Follow-Up Conduct a class discussion based on the following questions: What aspects of these images were ground breaking? Why do the impressionist images continue to be popular today?

Differentiated Instruction   Solutions for All Learners

Experiential Learning L1 L2

For learners struggling to grasp core concepts and generalizations presented in the text, help students "experience" it. Design an activity that enables students to get their hands on the content. Follow the guidelines below.

1. Guide students through an experience. Divide the class into groups of five and designate half the groups as Batch 1 and the other half as Batch 2. Provide both batches with a stack of paper. Instruct the groups of Batch 1 to create paper airplanes using any design they like. Provide Batch 2 with specific instructions and a specific design to use to make their paper airplanes. Assign the groups of students in the second batch with specific steps. For example, one student might fold the paper in half and hand it to the next person on the assembly line for the next step. Have the groups work on their tasks for five to seven minutes.

2. Reflect on that experience. Ask the class the following questions: Which group made the most airplanes? Which group had the greatest variety of airplanes? Which group enjoyed the process of making airplanes (e.g., did anyone find their job repetitive or challenging)?

3. Act on that experience. Ask students to connect the airplane activity with the Industrial Revolution. Have them make three generalizations about its impact on the quality and price of goods and the quality of life. Though students cannot truly experience this type of work during the 1800s, use this learning strategy can to help them make general connections to the societal shift that took place at this time.

Modeling Reading and Writing Skills

Consider the Audience and Purpose Explain that in this chapter, students will be writing a problem-solution essay. (See Writing About History, p. 326.) Tell students that once they've defined the problem, they should identify whom it affects, what causes the problem, and then brainstorm and research solutions. Remind them that as they gather details, they should think about the target audience and identify the aspects of each solution that will have the strongest impact on this audience.

Write on the board the following:

- Problem: depletion of fossil fuels
- Solution: hybrid cars

Ask students to identify the appeal of this solution for each of the following audiences:

- Environmentalists
- Commuters

(Sample: environmentalists—the cars consume less fuel than those powered by gasoline, so they are less harmful to the environment; commuters—the cars use less gasoline, so commuters will save money.)

Identify Supporting Details Remind students that a text's main idea should be supported by details that provide further information about it. These details may explain the main idea or give examples or reasons. Use a concept web as a tool to identify supporting details and illustrate their connection to the main idea.

To model this, read aloud the first paragraph under *Medicine Contributes to the Population Explosion* in Section 2. Point out the main idea: that the decline in the death rate led to the growth of populations. Then note the details that support the main idea: improved nutrition, advances in medicine, and better public sanitation. All of these details are reasons why the death rate fell. As you list each item, have students add details to the main idea in the center of their concept web.

Teach With Technology

PresentationEXPRESS™
Premium DVD

- Teach this chapter's core content using **PresentationExpress™ Premium,** which includes dynamic lecture notes, interactive game shows, songs, videos, and the *ExamView® QuickTake* assessment tool.

- To introduce this chapter using **PresentationExpress™ Premium,** start by asking students **Which of the following statements do you most agree with? (A) Technology is always beneficial, as it makes life easier. (B) Technology can be beneficial, provided it doesn't control our life. (C) Technology can be destructive, as it breaks down traditions. (D) Technology is always destructive, as it makes life too hectic.** Take a class poll or record students' answers using the QuickTake feature and discuss their responses. Point out that in this chapter, they will read about how technology affected daily life. Continue introducing the chapter using the chapter opener slide show and Witness History audio.

Technology Resources

- Student**EXPRESS** CD-ROM, Chapter 9
- Teacher**EXPRESS** CD-ROM, Chapter 9
- Presentation**EXPRESS™** Premium DVD, Chapter 9
- **WITNESS HISTORY** Audio CD, Chapter 9
- *ExamView* **Test Bank CD-ROM,** English and Spanish, Chapter 9
- **Guided Reading Audio,** Spanish, Chapter 9
- **Student Edition Audio,** Chapter 9
- **Witness History Discovery School™** video program, *The Jungle: A View of Industrial America*
- **Experience It! Multimedia Pack**

Life in the Industrial Age
1800–1914

Bibliography

For the Teacher
Anderson, Bonnie S. *Joyous Greetings: The First International Women's Movement.* Oxford University Press, 2000.
Carmona, Michel. *Haussmann: His Life and Times, and the Making of Modern Paris.* Ivan R. Dee, 2002.
Flanders, Judith. *Inside the Victorian Home: A Portrait of Domestic Life in Victorian England.* W.W. Norton, 2003.

For the Student
L2 Freedman, Russell. *Kids at Work: Lewis Hine and the Crusade Against Child Labor.* Clarion Books, 1998.
L3 Ingpen, Robert, Philip Wilkinson, and Michael Pollard. *The Industrial Revolution.* Chelsea House, 1995.
L4 Dickens, Charles. *David Copperfield.* Penguin Books, 2004. First published in 1850.

Factory Life

In 1888, Nell Cusack, a reporter for the Chicago *Times,* worked undercover to write a series of newspaper articles about the conditions under which factory girls worked:

66 . . . The place was noisy with flying shuttles, clicking needles, and the whizzing wheels of the roaring machinery. . . . The clatter of the machines was deafening. . . . The room was low . . . and clouds of lint seemed floating about in space. Add to that poor light, bad ventilation, the exhalations of so many people, [and] the smell of dye from the cloth . . . and you have material for the make-up of [the] shop. All afternoon we sewed; sewed incessantly without uttering a syllable or resting a moment. **99**

Listen to the Witness History audio to learn more about factory life.

◀ **Spinner at a cotton mill in Whitnel, North Carolina, 1908**

German labor union poster

Banner from the National Union of Women's Suffrage Societies

Chapter Preview

Chapter Focus Question What were the technological, social, and economic effects of the Industrial Revolution?

Section 1
The Industrial Revolution Spreads

Section 2
The Rise of the Cities

Section 3
Changing Attitudes and Values

Section 4
Arts in the Industrial Age

The first commercially successful typewriter, 1875

Use the ☑ **Quick Study Timeline** at the end of this chapter to preview chapter events.

? Concept Connector ONLINE

To explore Essential Questions related to this chapter, go to PHSchool.com
Web Code: nbd-2107

Chapter-Level Resources

All in One Vocabulary Builder; Reading Strategy; Enrichments; Outline Maps; Geography Quiz; Chapter Tests
- Document-Based Assessments
- AYP Monitoring Assessments
- *ExamView* Test Bank CD-ROM
- Guided Reading Audio, Spanish
- Student Edition Audio

Previewing the Chapter

- **WITNESS HISTORY** Read the Witness History selection aloud or play the accompanying audio. Ask **What does the shop sound like?** *(loud, noisy with machines)* **What are the conditions that the factory girls worked in?** *(cramped, crowded)* **How do you think the Industrial Revolution affected everyday life?** *(Sample: It affected everything; as working conditions changed, so people's day-to-day lives probably changed.)*

  ◀)) AUDIO **Witness History Audio CD,** Factory Life

- **Analyzing the Visuals** Have students look carefully at the image shown here. Tell students that photography was one of the many technologies invented during the Industrial Revolution. Ask **What questions do the photograph and the Witness History bring to mind about the technology and inventions of the Industrial Revolution?** *(Examples: What was daily life like in the factories? How old were the youngest workers? How did working conditions change for children? What else was invented during the Industrial Revolution?)* Tell students that you will keep a copy of these questions and will refer back to them later.

- **Focus** Write the Chapter Focus Question on the board. Tell students to keep this question in mind as they read the chapter. *(Answer appears with Chapter Assessment Answers.)* Have students preview the section titles for this chapter.

Note Taking Study Guide With Concept Connector Journal
For online access: Web code: nbd-2107
For print alternative: Reading and Note Taking Study Guide booklet

---

Differentiated
Instruction Solutions for All Learners

The following Teacher's Edition strategies are suitable for students of varying abilities.

L1 Special Needs Students, pp. 301, 306, 314, 316, 320 SN

L2 English Language Learners, pp. 301, 306, 314, 316, 320 ELL

L2 Less Proficient Readers, pp. 301, 306, 314, 316, 320 LPR

L4 Gifted and Talented Students, pp. 299, 311, 317 GT

L4 Advanced Readers, pp. 299, 311, 317 AR

Objectives

As you teach this section, keep students focused on the following objectives to help them answer the Section Focus Question and master core content.

■ List the industrial powers that emerged in the 1800s.

■ Describe the impact of new technology on industry, transportation, and communication.

■ Understand how big business emerged in the late 1800s.

Prepare to Read

Build Background Knowledge L3

Ask students to recall the first phase of the Industrial Revolution during the mid-1700s. Based on their previous reading, ask them to predict what would happen in the second phase of the Industrial Revolution.

Set a Purpose L3

■ **WITNESS HISTORY** Read the selection aloud or play the audio.

🔊)) AUDIO **Witness History Audio CD,** The Steelmaking Process

Ask **What is the main idea of Bridge's quote?** *(The process of turning molten metal into steel is an amazing process to watch.)* **How does the painting reinforce this idea?** *(The steel mill is portrayed as huge and awe-inspiring.)*

■ **Focus** Point out the Section Focus Question and write it on the board. Tell students to refer to this question as they read. *(Answer appears with Section 1 Assessment answers).*

■ **Preview** Have students preview the Section Objectives and the list of Terms, People, and Places.

■ **Reading Skills** Have students use the *Reading Strategy: Identify Supporting Details* worksheet.

All in One Teaching Resources, Unit 3, p. 7

Painting of a nineteenth-century steel mill

The Industrial Revolution Spreads

Objectives

• List the industrial powers that emerged in the 1800s.

• Describe the impact of new technology on industry, transportation, and communication.

• Understand how big business emerged in the late 1800s.

Terms, People, and Places

Henry Bessemer	assembly line
Alfred Nobel	Orville and Wilbur Wright
Michael Faraday	Guglielmo Marconi
dynamo	stock
Thomas Edison	corporation
interchangeable parts	cartel

Note Taking

Reading Skill: Identify Main Ideas Fill in a chart like this one with the major developments of the Industrial Revolution.

```
        The Second Industrial Revolution

New Powers    Industry/Business    Transportation/
                                   Communication
  •                 •                    •
  •                 •                    •
```

The first phase of industrialization had largely been forged from iron, powered by steam engines, and driven by the British textile industry. By the mid-1800s, the Industrial Revolution entered a second phase. New industrial powers emerged. Factories powered by electricity used innovative processes to turn out new products. Changes in business organization contributed to the rise of giant companies. As the twentieth century dawned, this second Industrial Revolution transformed the economies of the Western world.

New Industrial Powers Emerge

During the early Industrial Revolution, Britain stood alone as the world's industrial giant. To protect its head start, Britain tried to enforce strict rules against exporting inventions.

For a while, the rules worked. Then, in 1807, British mechanic William Cockerill opened factories in Belgium to manufacture spinning and weaving machines. Belgium became the first European nation after Britain to industrialize. By the mid-1800s, other nations had joined the race, and several newcomers were challenging Britain's industrial supremacy.

Nations Race to Industrialize How were other nations able to catch up with Britain so quickly? First, nations such as Germany, France, and the United States had more abundant supplies of coal, iron, and other resources than did Britain. Also, they had the advantage of being able to follow Britain's lead. Like Belgium,

Vocabulary Builder

Use the information below and the following resources to teach the high-use word from this section.
All in One Teaching Resources, Unit 3, p. 6; Teaching Resources, Skills Handbook, p. 3

High-Use Word	Definition and Sample Sentence
dominate, p. 300	*v.* to rule or control by power or influence The leader of the group **dominated** the discussion and barely let anyone else speak.

Centers of Industry, 1871

Geography *Interactive*
For: Audio guided tour
Web Code: nbp-2111

CANADA

UNITED STATES

Pittsburgh • Boston

New York

Conic Projection
0   400 mi
0   400 km

MEXICO

Gulf of Mexico

Atlantic Ocean

NORWAY

SWEDEN

DENMARK

North Sea

Baltic Sea

Glasgow

Newcastle

UNITED KINGDOM

Liverpool • Manchester

Birmingham

London

Brussels • BELG.

NETH.

Hamburg

Berlin

Ruhr

GERMANY

Dresden

Frankfurt

LUX.
Saar

Munich

Vienna

AUSTRIA-HUNGARY

Paris

Limoges

FRANCE

Loire R.

Lyon

SWITZ.

Milan

Madrid

Barcelona

Marseille

ITALY

Adriatic Sea

PORTUGAL

SPAIN

Atlantic Ocean

Conic Projection
0   200   400 mi
0   200   400 km

Mediterranean Sea

Coal fields
Iron ore deposits
Major industrial cities

An increase in manufacturing created a demand for workers. Children began running machines and mining coal (right).

Primary Source

❝ Shut in from everything that is pleasant, with no chance to learn . . . grinding their little lives away in this dusty room, they are no more than the wire screens that separate the great lumps of coal from the small. They had no games; when their day's work is done, they are too tired for that. They know nothing but the difference between slate and coal. ❞

—"The Labor Standard," 1877

Map Skills Deposits of raw materials such as iron and coal were essential to a nation's industrial success.

1. **Locate** (a) Belgium (b) Germany (c) Saar (d) Ruhr
2. **Region** Which American city probably grew because of its location near coal fields?
3. **Draw Inferences** Why would you expect Lyon, France, to become a major industrial city?

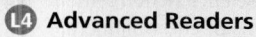

Differentiated Instruction   Solutions for All Learners

L4 Advanced Readers   L4 Gifted and Talented

To maintain its economic supremacy and combat industrial espionage, Britain enacted a law that forbade inventors and workers in key industries from emigrating. Have students debate the measures that a country should take today to protect such industries as computers, microelectronics, and defense technology. Some of the specific issues students might touch upon in their debate include patent rights, freedom of speech, freedom of movement, and national security.

- **Note Taking** Have students read this section using the Structured Read Aloud strategy (TE, p. T20). As they read, have students fill in the chart showing the major developments of the second Industrial Revolution.

    Reading and Note Taking Study Guide, p. 104

Teach

New Industrial Powers Emerge   L3

Instruct

- **Introduce: Vocabulary Builder** Have students read the Vocabulary Builder term and definition. Ask them to predict how the theme expressed by the word ***dominate*** would be key to understanding how the industrialized Western nations would influence the rest of the world.

- **Teach** Ask **How did Belgium, Germany, France, and the United States industrialize?** *(They had abundant supplies of natural resources, and they were able to borrow the ideas and technology of the British.)* **How did industrialization affect these nations?** *(The factory system allowed more people to buy cheaper goods than ever before; industrialization bolstered the economy by creating jobs; industrialized Western nations grew in power.)*

- **Quick Activity** Draw students' attention to the map on this page. Point out that the United Kingdom had the most major industrial cities. Ask students why they think the United Kingdom became an important center of industry. Have students access **Web Code nbp-2111** to take the **Geography Interactive Audio Guided Tour** and then answer the map skills questions in the text.

Answers

Map Skills
1. Review locations with students.
2. Pittsburgh
3. It was located near both coal fields and iron ore deposits.

Vocabulary Builder

<u>dominate</u>—(DAHM uh nayt) *v.* to rule or control by power or influence

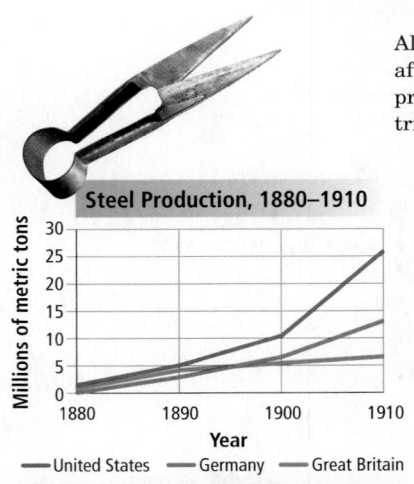

Steel Production, 1880–1910

Graph Skills By the late 1800s, steel was the major material used in manufacturing tools, such as the sheep shears (above). The graph shows the amount of steel produced by the United States, Germany, and Great Britain. *Between 1890 and 1910, which nation had the greatest increase in steel production? The smallest?*

SOURCES: *European Historical Statistics, 1750–1970; Historical Statistics of the United States*

latecomers often borrowed British experts or technology. The first American textile factory was built in Pawtucket, Rhode Island, with plans smuggled out of Britain. American inventor Robert Fulton powered his steamboat with one of James Watt's steam engines.

Two countries in particular—Germany and the United States—thrust their way to industrial leadership. Germany united into a powerful nation in 1871. Within a few decades, it became Europe's leading industrial power. Across the Atlantic, the United States advanced even more rapidly, especially after the Civil War. By 1900, the United States was manufacturing about 30 percent of the world's industrial goods, surpassing Britain as the leading industrial nation.

Uneven Development Other nations industrialized more slowly, particularly those in eastern and southern Europe. These nations often lacked natural resources or the capital to invest in industry. Although Russia did have resources, social and political conditions slowed its economic development. Only in the late 1800s, more than 100 years after Britain, did Russia lumber toward industrialization.

In East Asia, however, Japan offered a remarkable success story. Although Japan lacked many basic resources, it industrialized rapidly after 1868 because of a political revolution that made modernization a priority. Canada, Australia, and New Zealand also built thriving industries during this time.

Effects of Industrialization Like Britain, the new industrial nations underwent social changes, such as rapid urbanization. Men, women, and children worked long hours in difficult and dangerous conditions. As you will read, by 1900, these conditions had begun to improve in many industrialized nations.

The factory system produced huge quantities of new goods at lower prices than ever before. In time, ordinary workers were buying goods that in earlier days only the wealthy could afford. The demand for goods created jobs, as did the building of cities, railroads, and factories. Politics changed, too, as leaders had to meet the demands of an industrial society.

Globally, industrial nations competed fiercely, altering patterns of world trade. Because of their technological and economic advantage, the Western powers came to <u>dominate</u> the world more than ever before.

 Checkpoint What factors led to the industrialization of other nations after Britain?

Technology Sparks Industrial Growth

During the early Industrial Revolution, inventions such as the steam engine were generally the work of gifted tinkerers. They experimented with simple machines to make them better. By the 1880s, the pace of change quickened as companies hired professional chemists and engineers to create new products and machinery. The union of science, technology, and industry spurred economic growth.

Steel Production and the Bessemer Process American inventor William Kelly and British engineer **Henry Bessemer** independently developed a new process for making steel from iron. In 1856, Bessemer

Link to Literature

Science Fiction The dizzying rate of invention in the late 1800s inspired imaginative novelists like France's Jules Verne and England's H.G. Wells to pioneer a new literary form—science fiction. In his 1865 novel *From the Earth to the Moon,* Verne created one of the earliest pictures of space travel. He correctly predicted that space travelers would experience weightlessness.

Today, in print or on film, science fiction remains one of the most popular forms of entertainment. Inspired by modern advances in physics and computer technology, creators of television shows and movies, including *Star Trek, Star Wars,* and *Men in Black,* developed scripts that moved far beyond the visions of Verne's day.

Answers

Graph Skills United States; Great Britain

✔ Other nations had abundant supplies of natural resources and were able to use the ideas and technology that Britain had developed.

patented this process. Steel was lighter, harder, and more durable than iron, so it could be produced very cheaply. Steel quickly became the major material used in tools, bridges, and railroads.

As steel production soared, industrialized countries measured their success in steel output. In 1880, for example, the average German steel mill produced less than 5 million metric tons of steel a year. By 1910, that figure reached nearly 15 million metric tons.

Innovations in Chemistry Chemists created hundreds of new products, from medicines such as aspirin to perfumes and soaps. Newly developed chemical fertilizers played a key role in increasing food production.

In 1866, the Swedish chemist Alfred Nobel invented dynamite, an explosive much safer than others used at the time. It was widely used in construction and, to Nobel's dismay, in warfare. Dynamite earned Nobel a huge fortune, which he willed to fund the famous Nobel prizes that are still awarded today.

Electric Power Replaces Steam In the late 1800s, a new power source—electricity—replaced steam as the dominant source of industrial power. Scientists like Benjamin Franklin had tinkered with electricity a century earlier. The Italian scientist Alessandro Volta developed the first battery around 1800. Later, the English chemist Michael Faraday created the first simple electric motor and the first dynamo, a machine that generates electricity. Today, all electrical generators and transformers work on the principle of Faraday's dynamo.

In the 1870s, the American inventor Thomas Edison made the first electric light bulb. Soon, Edison's "incandescent lamps" illuminated whole cities. The pace of city life quickened, and factories could continue to operate after dark. By the 1890s, cables carried electrical power from dynamos to factories.

New Methods of Production The basic features of the factory system remained the same during the 1800s. Factories still used large numbers of workers and power-driven machines to mass-produce goods. To improve efficiency, however, manufacturers designed products with interchangeable parts, identical components that could be used in place of one another. Interchangeable parts simplified both the assembly and repair of products.

By the early 1900s, manufacturers had introduced another new method of production, the assembly line. Workers on an assembly line add parts to a product that moves along a belt from one work station to the next. A different person performs each task along the assembly line. This division of labor in an assembly line, like interchangeable parts, made production faster and cheaper, lowering the price of goods. Although dividing labor into separate tasks proved to be more efficient, it took much of the joy out of the work itself.

Electricity Lights Up Cities
This early dynamo (above) generated enough electricity to power lights in factories. Electricity changed life outdoors as well. *Judging from this print, how did electricity make life easier for people in the city?*

✓ **Checkpoint** What was the dynamo's impact on the Industrial Revolution?

Technology Sparks Industrial Growth

Instruct

■ **Introduce: Key Terms** Ask students to find the term *assembly line* (in blue) in the text and explain its meaning. Tell students that in assembly lines individual workers perform one specialized task repeatedly in making the final product. Ask **Why would specializing in specific tasks be more efficient than having a worker build an entire product from start to finish?** (*It is more efficient for workers to be in charge of one task than to require them to master every task that needs to be done, particularly in producing complex products such as automobiles.*)

■ **Teach** Ask **What power source replaced steam as the main source of industrial power?** (*electricity*) **Why was electricity important to industrialization?** (*Electricity transformed the pace of growth during the Industrial Revolution because cities could be lit up at night and factories could run after dark. It was the power source for the machines and assembly lines that mass-produced goods, making more products faster and more cheaply than ever before.*)

■ **Quick Activity** Display **Color Transparency 127: Technology: Blessing or Curse?** Use the lesson suggested in the transparency book to guide a discussion on modern technology.

▥ **Color Transparencies,** 127

Independent Practice

Link to Literature To help students understand the labor conditions in the factories, have them read the selection from Charles Dickens' *Hard Times* and complete the worksheet.

All in One Teaching Resources, Unit 3, p. 10

Monitor Progress

As students fill in their charts, circulate to make sure they understand the major developments in the second Industrial Revolution. For a completed version of the chart, see

▥ **Note Taking Transparencies,** 147

Answers

Caption They could travel at night.

✓ The dynamo generated electricity that powered the machines.

Transportation and Communication Advances

L3

Instruct

- **Introduce** Have students read how Marconi transmitted a transatlantic radio message in 1901. Use the Idea Wave strategy (TE, p. T22) and ask **How is radio used today? Why is it important?** *(entertainment, news, emergency broadcasts, weather warnings, communication)*

- **Teach** Ask **What did Nikolaus Otto invent?** *(a gasoline-powered internal combustion engine)* **What effect did his invention have on the Industrial Revolution?** *(Because it powers automobiles, threshers, reapers, and airplanes, it had a huge impact on transportation, farm production, and the economies of industrialized Western nations that produced these products.)*

- **Quick Activity** Display **Color Transparency 125: Inventors and Inventions.** Use the lesson suggested in the transparency book to guide a discussion on the new technologies of the industrial age.

  📖 **Color Transparencies,** 125

Independent Practice

Have students examine the Infographic, The Modern Office. Then ask them to write a paragraph on how advances in transportation and communication created massive change in business offices in the late 1800s.

Monitor Progress

Ask students to reread the introductory paragraph under the red heading Transportation and Communication Advances. Then ask them to explain the importance of the growth of railroads to industry.

Answers

Thinking Critically

1. As corporations expanded, they needed more office space.
2. Sample: Telephones would have had the greatest impact on offices because they would have enabled faster communication and therefore faster production.

● **INFOGRAPHIC**

The Modern Office

The Bessemer process prepared the way for the use of steel in building construction. Before steel, frameworks consisted of heavy iron. Steel provided a much lighter framework and enabled the construction of taller buildings. The first skyscrapers were between 10 and 20 stories high. They were built in the United States in the 1880s to house large corporations.

Elevators made it practical for buildings to have more than five or six stories.

Offices could be illuminated with **electric lights** both night and day.

Telephones allowed workers to send and receive messages faster than the telegraph.

Typewriters enabled workers to type information faster than they could write it by hand.

Thinking Critically
1. **Draw Inferences** Why did industrialization create a need for skyscrapers?
2. **Synthesize Information** What invention do you think had the most impact on offices? Explain.

Automobiles and subway systems permitted rapid transit to and from cities.

ILLUSTRATION NOT TO SCALE

Transportation and Communication Advances

During the Industrial Revolution, transportation and communications were transformed by technology. Steamships replaced sailing ships, and railroad building took off. In Europe and North America, rail lines connected inland cities and seaports, mining regions and industrial centers. In the United States, a transcontinental railroad provided rail service from the Atlantic to the Pacific. In the same way, Russians built the Trans-Siberian Railroad, linking Moscow in European Russia to Vladivostok on the Pacific. Railroad tunnels and bridges crossed the Alps in Europe and the Andes in South America. Passengers and goods rode on rails in India, China, Egypt, and South Africa.

The Automobile Age Begins The transportation revolution took a new turn when a German engineer, Nikolaus Otto, invented a gasoline-powered internal combustion engine. In 1886, Karl Benz received a patent for the first automobile, which had three wheels. A year later, Gottlieb Daimler (DYM lur) introduced the first four-wheeled automobile. People laughed at the "horseless carriages," but they quickly transformed transportation.

The French nosed out the Germans as early automakers. Then the American Henry Ford started making models that reached the breathtaking speed of 25 miles per hour. In the early 1900s, Ford began using the assembly line to mass-produce cars, making the United States a leader in the automobile industry.

Airplanes Take Flight The internal combustion engine powered more than cars. Motorized threshers and reapers boosted farm production. Even more dramatically, the internal combustion engine made possible sustained, pilot-controlled flight. In 1903, American bicycle makers **Orville and Wilbur Wright** designed and flew a flimsy airplane at Kitty Hawk, North Carolina. Although their flying machine stayed aloft for only a few seconds, it ushered in the air age.

Soon, daredevil pilots were flying airplanes across the English Channel and over the Alps. Commercial passenger travel, however, would not begin until the 1920s.

Rapid Communication A revolution in communications also made the world smaller. An American inventor, Samuel F. B. Morse, developed

---

Connect to Our World

Connections to Today Ever since the telegraph was invented in the mid-nineteenth century, people in business have been grumbling about the ever-increasing speed of business and communications. "The businessmen of the present day must be continually on the jump," said a New York merchant in 1868. "He *must* use the telegraph." New communication technologies, such as the telephone and then the fax machine, quickly became indispensable to business. With the advent of cell phones, personal handheld devices, and wireless Internet, people could conduct business from practically anywhere. Some relished the flexibility, while others resented that they could no longer leave work at the office.

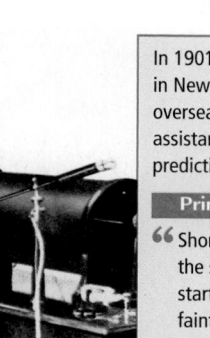

In 1901, Guglielmo Marconi (left) was in Newfoundland to receive the first overseas radio transmission from his assistant in England. Did Marconi's prediction come true? Explain.

Primary Source

66 Shortly before mid-day I placed the single earphone to my ear and started listening. . . . I heard, faintly but distinctly, *pip-pip-pip*. . . . I now felt for the first time absolutely certain that the day would come when mankind would be able to send messages without wires not only across the Atlantic, but between the farthermost ends of the earth.99

the telegraph, which could send coded messages over wires by means of electricity. His first telegraph line went into service between Washington, D.C. and Baltimore, in 1844. By the 1860s, an undersea cable was relaying messages between Europe and North America. This trans-Atlantic cable was an amazing engineering accomplishment for its day.

Communication soon became even faster. In 1876, the Scottish-born American inventor Alexander Graham Bell patented the telephone. By the 1890s, the Italian pioneer **Guglielmo Marconi** had invented the radio. In 1901, Marconi received a radio message, using Morse code, sent from Britain to Canada. Radio would become a cornerstone of today's global communications network.

✔ **Checkpoint** How did technological advances in transportation and communications affect the Industrial Revolution?

Business Takes a New Direction

By the late 1800s, what we call "big business" came to dominate industry. Big business refers to an establishment that is run by entrepreneurs who finance, manufacture, and distribute goods. As time passed, some big businesses came to control entire industries.

Rise of Big Business New technologies required the investment of large amounts of money, or capital. To get the needed capital, owners sold stock, or shares in their companies, to investors. Each stockholder became owner of a tiny part of a company. Large-scale companies, such as steel foundries, needed so much capital that they sold hundreds of thousands of shares. These businesses formed giant **corporations,** businesses that are owned by many investors who buy shares of stock. With large amounts of capital, corporations could expand into many areas.

Move Toward Monopolies Powerful business leaders created monopolies and trusts, huge corporate structures that controlled entire industries or areas of the economy. In Germany, Alfred Krupp inherited a steelmaking business from his father. He bought up coal and iron mines as well as ore deposits—supply lines or raw materials that fed the steel business. Later, he and his son acquired plants that made tools, railroad cars, and weapons. In the United States, John D. Rockefeller built Standard Oil Company into an empire. By gaining control of oil wells, oil refineries, and oil pipelines, he dominated the American petroleum industry.

Business Takes a New Direction

Instruct

■ **Introduce** Ask students to read the paragraph under the red heading Business Takes a New Direction. Ask **What is "big business"?** *(a large-scale business that is run by entrepreneurs who finance manufacture, and distribute goods)* Ask students to list what they know about big business today.

■ **Teach** Ask **How did company owners get the capital needed to run businesses?** *(They sold stock and formed giant corporations.)* **Why was there a move toward monopolies?** *(Business leaders who dominated entire industries could squeeze out competing companies and charge any price for a product or service.)* **What are the benefits of regulating monopolies?** *(Regulations would allow for competition, better pricing, and fair business practices.)*

■ **Quick Activity** Display **Color Transparency 126: Features of a Monopoly.** Use the lesson suggested in the transparency book to guide a discussion on the widespread concern about the harmful effects of monopolies in the late 1800s.

   Color Transparencies, 126

Independent Practice

Divide students into pairs. Ask them to explain the following terms to their partner: big business, monopoly, regulation.

Monitor Progress

Check Reading and Note Taking Study Guide entries for student understanding of the major developments of the second Industrial Revolution.

Answers

PRIMARY SOURCE Yes, advances in communications such as cellular phones and e-mail have made worldwide communication almost instantaneous.

✔ Advances in transportation and communication changed the way that people lived. People could travel faster and farther by steamship, railroad, car, and airplanes. They could also communicate nationally and internationally by telegraph, telephone, and radio.

Answers

Analyzing Political Cartoons favored; big business is a monster.

✓ Some believed that they created economic benefits, while others thought they exploited consumers and free enterprise.

Analyzing Political Cartoons

One View of Big Business To some critics, the growth of monopolies had a dangerous effect on society. This 1899 American cartoon shows a monopoly as an octopus-like monster. *Do you think this cartoonist favored or opposed government regulation of business? Explain.*

In their pursuit of profit, ruthless business leaders destroyed competing companies. With the competition gone, they were free to raise prices. Sometimes, a group of corporations would join forces and form a **cartel,** an association to fix prices, set production quotas, or control markets. In Germany, a single cartel fixed prices for 170 coal mines.

Move Toward Regulation The rise of big business and the creation of such great wealth sparked a stormy debate. Some people saw the Krupps and Rockefellers as "captains of industry" and praised their vision and skills. They pointed out that capitalists invested their wealth in worldwide ventures, such as railroad building, that employed thousands of workers and added to the general prosperity.

To others, the aggressive magnates were "robber barons." Destroying competition, critics argued, damaged the free-enterprise system, or the laissez-faire economy. Reformers called for laws to prevent monopolies and regulate large corporations. Despite questionable business practices, big business found support from many government leaders. By the early 1900s, some governments did move against monopolies. However, the political and economic power of business leaders often hindered efforts at regulation.

✓ **Checkpoint** Why were big business leaders "captains of industry" to some, but "robber barons" to others?

SECTION 1 Assessment

Terms, People, and Places

1. For each term, person, or place listed at the beginning of the section, write a sentence explaining its significance.

Note Taking

2. **Reading Skill: Identify Main Ideas** Use your completed chart to answer the Focus Question: How did science, technology, and big business promote industrial growth?

Comprehension and Critical Thinking

3. **Summarize** How did the Industrial Revolution spread in the 1800s?

4. **Draw Conclusions** How did technology help industry expand?

5. **Recognize Cause and Effect** How did the need for capital lead to new business organizations and methods?

6. **Predict** How might government change as a result of industrialization?

● **Writing About History**

Quick Write: Define a Problem Choose one topic from this section that you could use to write a problem-and-solution essay. For example, you could write about the impact of powerful monopolies. Make a list of details, facts, and examples that define the problems that monopolies pose to a free market.

---

304 Life in the Industrial Age

Charles Dickens with an illustration from one of his serialized novels

London Fog

Between 1850 and 1900, London's population more than doubled, rising from about 2.6 million people to more than 6.5 million people. With the rapid population growth came increased pollution and health problems:

❝ It was a foggy day in London, and the fog was heavy and dark. Animate [living] London, with smarting eyes and irritated lungs, was blinking, wheezing, and choking; inanimate [nonliving] London was a sooty spectre, divided in purpose between being visible and invisible, and so being wholly neither. ❞
—Charles Dickens, *Our Mutual Friend*

Focus Question How did the Industrial Revolution change life in the cities?

The Rise of the Cities

Objectives
• Summarize the impact of medical advances in the late 1800s.
• Describe how cities had changed by 1900.
• Explain how working-class struggles led to improved conditions for workers.

Terms, People, and Places

germ theory	Joseph Lister
Louis Pasteur	urban renewal
Robert Koch	mutual-aid society
Florence Nightingale	standard of living

Note Taking

Reading Skill: Identify Supporting Details As you read, look for the main ideas and supporting details and how they relate to each other. Use the format below to create an outline of the section.

```
I. Medicine and the population explosion
   A. The fight against disease
      1.
      2.
   B.
II.
```

The population explosion that had begun during the 1700s continued through the 1800s. Cities grew as rural people streamed into urban areas. By the end of the century, European and American cities had begun to take on many of the features of cities today.

Medicine Contributes to the Population Explosion

Between 1800 and 1900, the population of Europe more than doubled. This rapid growth was not due to larger families. In fact, families in most industrializing countries had fewer children. Instead, populations soared because the death rate fell. Nutrition improved, thanks in part to improved methods of farming, food storage, and distribution. Medical advances and improvements in public sanitation also slowed death rates.

The Fight Against Disease Since the 1600s, scientists had known of microscopic organisms, or microbes. Some scientists speculated that certain microbes might cause specific infectious diseases. Yet most doctors scoffed at this **germ theory**. Not until 1870 did French chemist **Louis Pasteur** (pas TUR) clearly show the link between microbes and disease. Pasteur went on to make other major contributions to medicine, including the development of vaccines against rabies and anthrax. He also discovered a process called pasteurization that killed disease-carrying microbes in milk.

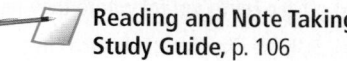

Medicine Contributes to the Population Explosion L3

Instruct

- **Introduce** Ask students to find the term *germ theory* (in blue). Ask **Why was it important to know that certain microbes cause disease?** *(Once the link was known, scientists and doctors could work on finding preventions and cures.)*

- **Teach** Ask **What happened to the population of Europe between 1800 and 1900? Why?** *(The population more than doubled due to a declining death rate.)* **Why was improved hospital care especially important to the poor?** *(While wealthier patients could be treated at home, the poor were admitted to hospitals that were often unsanitary. Improved care would increase their rate of recovery and survival.)*

- **Quick Activity** Read aloud Nightingale's statement under the heading Hospital Care Improves ("The very first . . . no harm.") Ask students to work in small groups and decide whether they agree or disagree with her statement. Use the Numbered Heads strategy (TE, p. T23) and have students share their responses with the class.

Independent Practice

Ask students to write a paragraph describing how the population growth in Europe was due, in part, to medical advances. Have students think about the impact of these advances both in the 1800s and today.

Monitor Progress

As students fill in their outlines, circulate to make sure they understand how main ideas and supporting details relate to each other. For a completed version of the outline, see

📖 **Note Taking Transparencies,** 148

Answers

BIOGRAPHY She improved sanitation by insisting that military and medical staff clean barracks, dig latrines, do laundry, and get the wounded off the bare ground where they lay.

✓ better diets, better hygiene, advances in medicine, and improved sanitation

◉ BIOGRAPHY

Florence Nightingale

When Florence Nightingale (1820–1910) arrived at a British military hospital in the Crimea in 1854, she was horrified by what she saw. The sick and wounded lay on bare ground. With no sanitation and a shortage of food, some 60 percent of all patients died. But Nightingale was a fighter. Bullying the military and medical staff, she soon had every available person cleaning barracks, digging latrines, doing laundry, and caring for the wounded. Six months later, the death rate had dropped to 2 percent.

Back in England, Nightingale was hailed as a saint. Ballads were even written about her. She took advantage of her popularity and connections to pressure the government for reforms. **How did Nightingale achieve reforms in British army hospitals?**

WITNESS HISTORY VIDEO

Watch *The Jungle: A View of Industrial America* on the **Witness History Discovery School™** video program to learn more about city life during the industrial age.

In the 1880s, the German doctor **Robert Koch** identified the bacterium that caused tuberculosis, a respiratory disease that claimed about 30 million human lives in the 1800s. The search for a tuberculosis cure, however, took half a century. By 1914, yellow fever and malaria had been traced to microbes carried by mosquitoes.

As people understood how germs caused disease, they bathed and changed their clothes more often. In European cities, better hygiene helped decrease the rate of disease.

Hospital Care Improves In the early 1840s, anesthesia was first used to relieve pain during surgery. The use of anesthetics allowed doctors to experiment with operations that had never before been possible.

Yet, throughout the century, hospitals could be dangerous places. Surgery was performed with dirty instruments in dank rooms. Often, a patient would survive an operation, only to die days later of infection. For the poor, being admitted to a hospital was often a death sentence. Wealthy or middle-class patients insisted on treatment in their own homes.

"The very first requirement in a hospital," said British nurse **Florence Nightingale,** "is that it should do the sick no harm." As an army nurse during the Crimean War, Nightingale insisted on better hygiene in field hospitals. After the war, she worked to introduce sanitary measures in British hospitals. She also founded the world's first school of nursing.

The English surgeon **Joseph Lister** discovered how antiseptics prevented infection. He insisted that surgeons sterilize their instruments and wash their hands before operating. Eventually, the use of antiseptics drastically reduced deaths from infection.

✓ **Checkpoint** Which factors caused population rates to soar between 1800 and 1900?

City Life Changes

As industrialization progressed, cities came to dominate the West. City life, as old as civilization itself, underwent dramatic changes in Europe and the United States.

City Landscapes Change Growing wealth and industrialization altered the basic layout of European cities. City planners created spacious new squares and boulevards. They lined these avenues with government buildings, offices, department stores, and theaters.

The most extensive **urban renewal,** or rebuilding of the poor areas of a city, took place in Paris in the 1850s. Georges Haussmann, chief planner for Napoleon III, destroyed many tangled medieval streets full of tenement housing. In their place, he built wide boulevards and splendid public buildings. The project put many people to work, decreasing the threat of social

Differentiated Instruction   Solutions for All Learners

L1 Special Needs   L2 Less Proficient Readers

Explain to students that the Industrial Revolution had both positive and negative effects on daily life. Have students create a chart entitled "Effects of the Industrial Revolution." The chart should have two columns: positive and negative. Ask students to read through this section of the chapter and record and categorize the effects in each column.

L2 English Language Learners

Use the following resources to help students acquire basic skills.

 **Adapted Reading and Note Taking Study Guide**

- Adapted Note Taking Study Guide, p. 106
- Adapted Section Summary, p. 107

unrest. The wide boulevards also made it harder for rebels to put up barricades and easier for troops to reach any part of the city.

Gradually, settlement patterns shifted. In most American cities, the rich lived in pleasant neighborhoods on the outskirts of the city. The poor crowded into slums near the city center, within reach of factories. Trolley lines made it possible to live in one part of the city and work in another.

Sidewalks, Sewers, and Skyscrapers Paved streets made urban areas much more livable. First gas lamps, and then electric street lights <u>illuminated</u> the night, increasing safety. Cities organized police forces and expanded fire protection.

Beneath the streets, sewage systems made cities much healthier places to live. City planners knew that clean water supplies and better sanitation methods were needed to combat epidemics of cholera and tuberculosis. In Paris, sewer lines expanded from 87 miles (139 kilometers) in 1852 to more than 750 miles (1200 kilometers) by 1911. The massive new sewer systems of London and Paris were costly, but they cut death rates dramatically.

By 1900, architects were using steel to construct soaring buildings. American architects like Louis Sullivan pioneered a new structure, the skyscraper. In large cities, single-family middle-class homes gave way to multistory apartment buildings.

Slum Conditions Despite efforts to improve cities, urban life remained harsh for the poor. Some working-class families could afford better clothing, newspapers, or tickets to a music hall. But they went home to small, cramped row houses or tenements in overcrowded neighborhoods.

In the worst tenements, whole families were often crammed into a single room. Unemployment or illness meant lost wages that could ruin a family. High rates of crime and alcoholism were a constant curse. Conditions had improved somewhat from the early Industrial Revolution, but slums remained a fact of city life.

Vocabulary Builder

illuminate—(ih LOO muh nayt) v. to light up; to give light to

Jacob Riis, a police reporter, photographer, and social activist in New York City published *How the Other Half Lives* in 1890 in an effort to expose the horrible living conditions of the city slums and tenements. Conditions among the urban working class in Britain (right) were similar to those in New York described by Riis:

Primary Source

66 Look into any of these houses, everywhere the same . . . . Here is a "flat" or "parlor" and two pitch-dark coops called bedrooms. . . . One, two, three beds are there, if the old boxes and heaps of foul straw can be called by that name; a broken stove with crazy pipe from which the smoke leaks at every joint, a table of rough boards propped up on boxes, piles of rubbish in the corner. The closeness and smell are appalling. How many people sleep here? The woman with the red bandanna shakes her head sullenly, but the bare-legged girl with the bright face counts on her fingers. . . "Six, sir!" 99

History Background

Wash Your Hands In 1848, physician Ignaz Philipp Semmelweis of Hungary noted that fewer patients died when doctors washed their hands frequently. He ordered students in his clinic to wash their hands using a solution of chlorinated lime, which disinfected their hands. Semmelweis believed that infection was caused by microscopic particles. Yet his theories were largely ignored, because health professionals believed that disease was caused by mysterious vapors and that cleanliness practices were irrelevant. When Louis Pasteur discovered microorganisms, the world was finally ready to believe that they might play a role in disease. Today, doctors and patients both know that sterilizing wounds and medical instruments is paramount in preventing disease.

Instruct

- **Introduce: Vocabulary Builder** Have students read the Vocabulary Builder term and definition. Ask them to predict how the word *illuminated* would be important to understanding life in the cities. Then display **Color Transparency 128: *Night Festival at the Universal Exposition of 1889*, by Antoine Roux II.** Use the lesson suggested in the transparency book to guide a discussion on how street lights changed city life.

  ⎗ Color Transparencies, 128

- **Teach** Discuss the effects of industrialization. Ask **Why did the poor live closer to city centers than the middle class did?** *(to be closer to the factories where they worked)* **How might the middle and upper classes have experienced city life differently than the working class did?** *(Working class families mainly flocked to the cities for jobs and housing and saw the harshness of the cities, while wealthier families were drawn to the cities for their cultural opportunities.)*

- **Quick Activity** Show students *The Jungle: A View of Industrial America* from the **Witness History Discovery School**™ video program. Ask them to explain the short-term and long-term reforms inspired by Upton Sinclair's *The Jungle*. *(short term: Congress passed laws mandating the inspection of meat and banning the use of filler in meat products; long term: better conditions for workers)* Have them also consider why Sinclair's book remains relevant today. *(Sample: It shows how a book can eventually lead to reform.)*

Independent Practice

Viewpoints To help students better understand that some people found cities exciting while others found them frightening, have them read the selection *Looking at London in the 1820s* and complete the worksheet.

All in One Teaching Resources, Unit 3, p. 9

Monitor Progress

Point out the photos of the working class and the moviegoers in this section. To help students review the section, ask them to explain how the images illustrate the positive and negative aspects of city life.

The Working Class Advances

Instruct

- **Introduce** Ask students to read the introductory sentences and two black headings under The Working Class Advances. Have students predict what they will learn under each heading. Then have them read to find out whether their predictions were accurate.

- **Teach** Ask **Why did workers form unions?** *(to improve working conditions, reduce long hours, and increase low pay)* Have students rank the reform laws that are discussed in their text in order of their importance. Using the Idea Wave strategy (TE, p. T22) ask students to explain why they ranked the reforms in this particular order.

- **Analyzing the Visuals** Refer students to the Cause-and-Effect chart on this page. Use the Think-Write-Pair-Share strategy (TE, p. T23) and ask students to list concrete ways that the Industrial Revolution continues to impact their daily lives.

Independent Practice

Primary Source To help students better understand the work that people did, have them read the selection *The People of Paris Earn a Living* and complete the worksheet.

All in One Teaching Resources, Unit 3, p. 8

Monitor Progress

Check Reading and Note Taking Study Guide entries for student understanding.

Cause and Effect

Causes

- Increased agricultural productivity
- Growing population
- New sources of energy, such as steam and coal
- Growing demand for mass-produced goods
- Improved technology
- Available natural resources, labor, and money
- Strong, stable governments

Industrial Revolution

Immediate Effects
- Rise of factories
- Changes in transportation and communication
- Urbanization
- New methods of production
- Rise of urban working class
- Growth of reform movements

Long-Term Effects
- Growth of labor unions
- Inexpensive new products
- Increased pollution
- Rise of big business
- Expansion of public education
- Expansion of middle class
- Competition for world trade
- Progress in medical care

Connections to Today

- Improvements in world health
- Growth in population
- Industrialization in developing nations
- New energy sources, such as oil and nuclear power
- Environmental pollution
- Efforts to regulate world trade

Analyze Cause and Effect The long-term effects of the Industrial Revolution touched nearly every aspect of life. *Identify two social and two economic effects of the Industrial Revolution.*

The Lure of the City Despite their drawbacks, cities attracted millions. New residents were drawn as much by the excitement as by the promise of work. For tourists, too, cities were centers of action.

Music halls, opera houses, and theaters provided entertainment for every taste. Museums and libraries offered educational opportunities. Sports, from tennis to bare-knuckle boxing, drew citizens of all classes. Few of these enjoyments were available in country villages.

✓ **Checkpoint** How did industrialization change the face of cities?

The Working Class Advances

Workers tried to improve the harsh conditions of industrial life. They protested low wages, long hours, unsafe conditions, and the constant threat of unemployment. At first, business owners and governments tried to silence protesters. By mid-century, however, workers began to make progress.

Labor Unions Begin to Grow Workers formed **mutual-aid societies,** self-help groups to aid sick or injured workers. Men and women joined socialist parties or organized unions. The revolutions of 1830 and 1848 left vivid images of worker discontent, which governments could not ignore.

By the late 1800s, most Western countries had granted all men the vote. Workers also won the right to organize unions to bargain on their behalf. Germany legalized labor unions in 1869. Britain, Austria, and France followed. By 1900, Britain had about three million union members, and Germany had about two million. In France, membership grew from 140,000 in 1890 to over a million in 1912.

The main tactic of unions was the strike, or work stoppage. Workers used strikes to demand better working conditions, wage increases, or other benefits from their employers. Violence was often a result of strikes, particularly if employers tried to continue operating their businesses without the striking workers. Employers often called in the police to stop strikes.

Pressured by unions, reformers, and working-class voters, governments passed laws to regulate working conditions. Early laws forbade employers to hire children under the age of ten. Later, laws were passed outlawing child labor entirely and banning the employment of women in mines. Other laws limited work hours and improved safety. By 1909, British coal miners had won an eight-hour day, setting a standard for workers in other countries. In Germany, and then elsewhere, Western governments established old-age pensions, as well as disability insurance for workers who were hurt or became ill. These programs protected workers from poverty once they were no longer able to work.

Answers

✓ With industrialization came more jobs, urban renewal, better sanitation, and entertainment, but it also created slum conditions and higher crime rates.

Analyze Cause and Effect Sample: Social effects include the expansion of the middle class and public education. Economic effects include the growth of labor unions and the rise of big business.

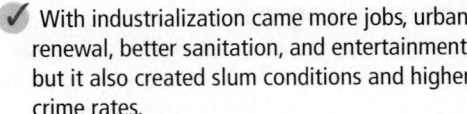

Careers

Urban Planner The people who determine the look and feel of our communities are often urban planners. Using data and computer modeling, they design an overall plan for a thriving community, be it a new town or an existing urban area. They must balance residential, commercial, industrial, and recreational needs. For example, they might not allow a school next to a factory, as it would not suit the purpose of either. They also consider such issues as traffic flow, environmental impact, and economic development. To create a sustainable plan, they work with civic and business leaders, local residents, and land developers, offering alternative approaches to land use. Most urban planners hold a master's degree in urban planning and work for the federal, state, or local government.

Family Life and Leisure
With standards of living rising, families could pursue activities such as going to the movies. This 1896 French poster (left) advertises the Cinématographe Lumière (loom YEHR), the most successful motion-picture camera and projector of its day. *What does the clothing of the people in the poster suggest about their social rank?*

Standards of Living Rise Wages varied throughout the industrialized world, with unskilled laborers earning less than skilled workers. Women received less than half the pay of men doing the same work. Farm laborers barely scraped by during the economic slump of the late 1800s. Periods of unemployment brought desperate hardships to industrial workers and helped boost union membership.

Overall, though, standards of living for workers did rise. The standard of living measures the quality and availability of necessities and comforts in a society. Families ate more varied diets, lived in better homes, and dressed in inexpensive, mass-produced clothing. Advances in medicine improved health. Some workers moved to the suburbs, traveling to work on subways and trolleys. Still, the gap between workers and the middle class widened.

✔ **Checkpoint** How did workers try to improve their living and working conditions?

Standards Monitoring *Online*
For: Self-quiz with vocabulary practice
Web Code: nba-2121

Terms, People, and Places
1. For each term, person, or place listed at the beginning of the section, write a sentence explaining its significance.

Note Taking
2. **Reading Skill: Identify Supporting Details** Use your completed outline to answer the Focus Question: How did the Industrial Revolution change life in the cities?

Comprehension and Critical Thinking
3. **Recognize Cause and Effect** Why did the rate of population growth increase in the late 1800s?
4. **Summarize** What are three ways that city life changed in the 1800s?
5. **Analyze Information** What laws helped workers in the late 1800s?
6. **Synthesize Information** How did the rise of the cities challenge the economic and social order of the time?

● **Writing About History**
Quick Write: Brainstorm Possible Solutions Choose one topic from this section, such as the hardships of city life, about which you could write a problem-solution essay. Use the text and your own knowledge to create a list of possible solutions to the problem that you've chosen to write about. Next, organize your list to rank the solutions from most effective to least effective.

Assess Progress L3
- Have students complete the Section Assessment.
- Administer the Section Quiz.

All in One **Teaching Resources, Unit 3,** p. 3
- To further assess student understanding, use
  Progress Monitoring Transparencies, 87

Reteach
If students need more instruction, have them read the section summary.

Reading and Note Taking Study Guide, p. 107 L3

Adapted Reading and Note Taking Study Guide, p. 107 L1 L2

Spanish Reading and Note Taking Study Guide, p. 107 L2

Extend L4
Have students scan newspaper headlines for present-day examples of the pros and cons of city life, the effect of technologies on daily life, or the role of labor unions.

Answers

Caption They were middle-class people who could afford nice clothes and leisure activities.

✔ through protest and pressure on the government

Section 2 Assessment
1. Sentences should reflect an understanding of each term, person, or place listed at the beginning of the section.
2. Sample: The poor crowded into slums and crime rates were high, but street lights made cities safer; sewers made cities healthier; trolley lines meant people could live farther from their jobs.
3. People were eating better and practicing better hygiene. Medical discoveries eliminated some diseases. Sanitation improved.
4. Sample: better transportation, street lights, new sewer systems
5. New laws allowed workers to unionize, expanded the right to vote, regulated working conditions, limited child labor, and set up pensions and disability insurance.
6. by bringing people from different classes into closer contact; by allowing people to work in one place and live in another

● **Writing About History**
Responses should show clearly organized solutions, ranked from the most effective to the least effective.

For additional assessment, have students access **Progress Monitoring *Online*** at **Web Code nba-2121.**

Electricity's Impact on Daily Life

Objectives
- Analyze the effect of electricity on daily life.
- Describe the importance of this invention.

Build Background Knowledge L3
Ask students to list the ways they used electricity on this day. Point out that electricity is considered to be one of the most important innovations made during the Industrial Age.

Instruct L3
- Direct students to the images on this page. Ask volunteers to read aloud the captions that describe each technology that relies on electricity. For each image, ask students to describe how the technology shown changed daily life.
- Refer students to the chart titled Electricity Customers in England and Wales. Ask **What is the purpose of this chart?** *(to measure the number of electricity customers in England and Wales, by decade)* **What decade saw the greatest increase in electricity customers?** *(1930s)* **What do you think accounts for the increase in the number of customers in the 1970s?** *(Sample: larger population and better infrastructure)* **What would you predict for the number of customers in 1990? Why?** *(Sample: 22 million; customers would increase at a slow, but steady rate as usage would be fairly widespread at this point in both rural and urban areas.)* **What do the numbers suggest about the impact of electricity in this time period?** *(Sample: While the growth of electricity customers has been dramatic during some decades and slower during others, it has had a deep impact on daily life for millions.)*

Electricity's Impact on Daily Life

Few technologies have transformed daily life as dramatically as electrification. Electric power lit up city streets, helped to improve workplace productivity, revolutionized life at home, and modernized rural farms and businesses. Although electrification began in urban areas of Europe and the United States in the 1880s, it took several decades to spread to rural areas. Electrification remains an ongoing process in developing nations today.

Installing insulators on an electric pole in 1940

Advertisement for household electrical appliances

An electric streetcar in England, around 1900

Electricity Customers in England and Wales	
Year	Customers in Millions
1920	0.9
1930	3.5
1940	9.6
1950	12.0
1960	15.5
1970	18.3
1980	20.3

SOURCE: Department of Trade and Industry, United Kingdom

History Background

The Slow Acceptance of Electricity Like the development of steam power and the railroad before it, the development of electricity caused fear and apprehension. People were concerned about health hazards from the new, untested technology. Poorly insulated wires were placed next to gas mains, causing frightening explosions that made the front page of the papers. Accidental electrocutions also made the front page. At first, electricity was unreliable and repairs were slow, as there were not enough technicians. People also did not understand the new technology; Mark Twain and L. Frank Baum both satirized the fear that electricity would fall into the wrong hands. Consequently, the use of electricity spread slowly. Advertisements of the 1920s were still trying to convince people that electricity was safe and beneficial.

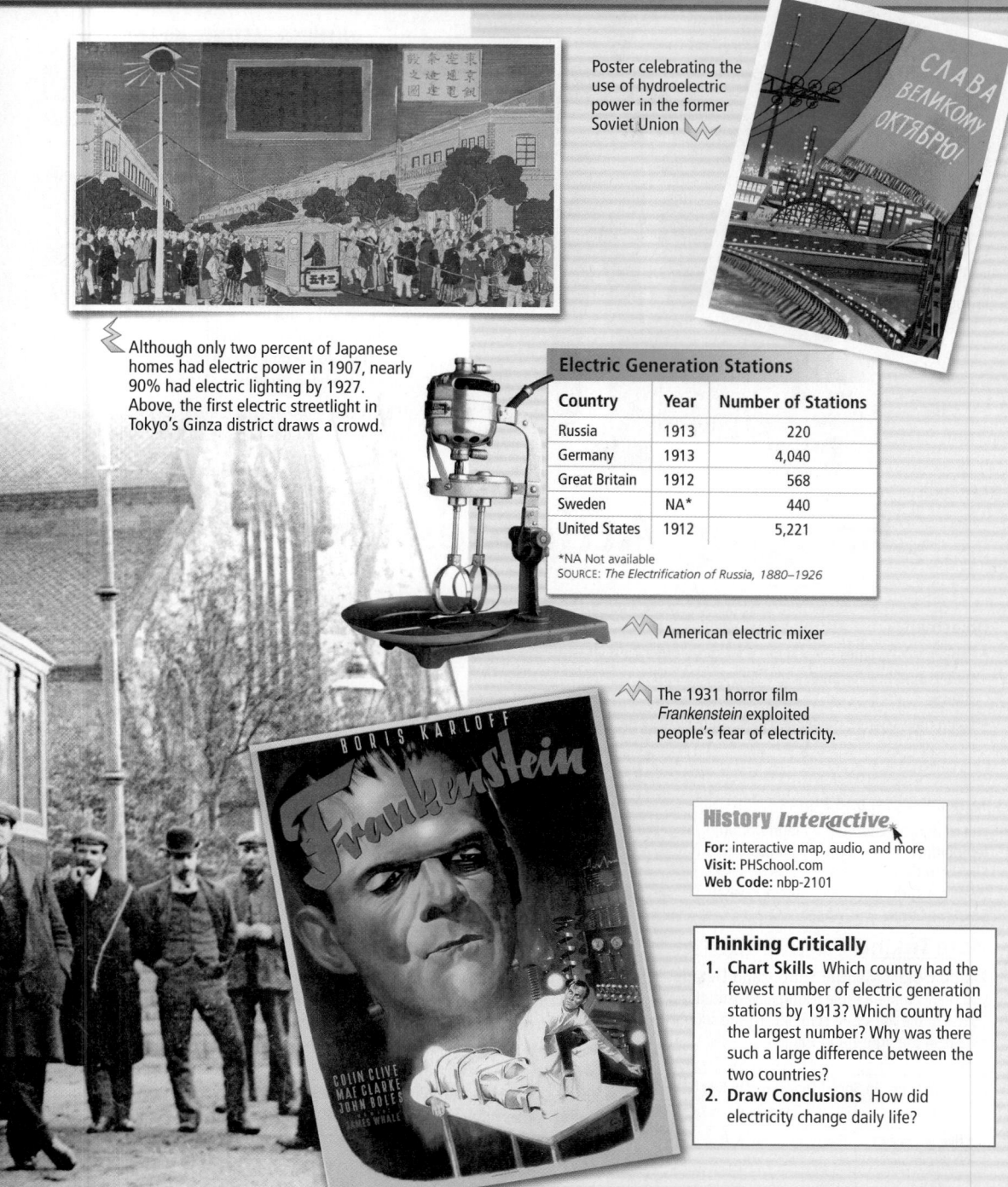

Poster celebrating the use of hydroelectric power in the former Soviet Union

Although only two percent of Japanese homes had electric power in 1907, nearly 90% had electric lighting by 1927. Above, the first electric streetlight in Tokyo's Ginza district draws a crowd.

American electric mixer

The 1931 horror film *Frankenstein* exploited people's fear of electricity.

Electric Generation Stations

Country	Year	Number of Stations
Russia	1913	220
Germany	1913	4,040
Great Britain	1912	568
Sweden	NA*	440
United States	1912	5,221

*NA Not available
SOURCE: *The Electrification of Russia, 1880–1926*

History *Interactive*
For: interactive map, audio, and more
Visit: PHSchool.com
Web Code: nbp-2101

Thinking Critically

1. **Chart Skills** Which country had the fewest number of electric generation stations by 1913? Which country had the largest number? Why was there such a large difference between the two countries?
2. **Draw Conclusions** How did electricity change daily life?

Thinking Critically

1. Russia; United States; Russia was further behind in industrializing, and the United States was steadily expanding.
2. Sample: Electricity changed the way people lighted and heated their homes. It changed modes of transportation and communication and increased productivity for businesses. Appliances made housework easier so many women began to work outside the home.

Objectives

As you teach this section, keep students focused on the following objectives to help them answer the Section Focus Question and master core content.

- Explain what values shaped the new social order.
- Understand how women and educators sought change.
- Learn how science challenged existing beliefs.

Suffragette arrested in London, 1914

Women's suffrage banner

Changing Attitudes and Values

Objectives

- Explain what values shaped the new social order.
- Understand how women and educators sought change.
- Learn how science challenged existing beliefs.

Terms, People, and Places

cult of domesticity	John Dalton
temperance movement	Charles Darwin
Elizabeth Cady Stanton	racism
women's suffrage	social gospel
Sojourner Truth	

Note Taking

Reading Skill: Identify Supporting Details As you read, create a table listing new attitudes and values in the left-hand column. List the supporting details in the right-hand column.

Changes in Social Order and Values	
Issue	**Change**
• New social order	•
• Rights for women	•
•	•

Demand for women's rights was one of many issues that challenged the traditional social order in the late 1800s. By then, in many countries, the middle class—aspiring to upper-class wealth and privilege—increasingly came to dominate society.

A New Social Order Arises

The Industrial Revolution slowly changed the social order in the Western world. For centuries, the two main classes were nobles and peasants. Their roles were defined by their relationship to the land. While middle-class merchants, artisans, and lawyers played important roles, they still had a secondary position in society. With the spread of industry, a more complex social structure emerged.

Three Social Classes Emerge By the late 1800s, Western Europe's new upper class included very rich business families. Wealthy entrepreneurs married into aristocratic families, gaining the status of noble titles. Nobles needed the money brought by the industrial rich to support their lands and lifestyle.

Below this tiny elite, a growing middle class was pushing its way up the social ladder. Its highest rungs were filled with mid-level business people and professionals such as doctors and scientists. With comfortable incomes, they enjoyed a wide range of material goods. Next came the lower middle class, which included teachers and office workers. They struggled to keep up with their "betters."

Workers and peasants were at the base of the social ladder. In highly industrialized Britain, workers made up more than 30 percent of the population in 1900. In Western Europe and the United States, the number of farmworkers dropped, but many families still worked the land. The rural population was higher in eastern and southern Europe, where industrialization was more limited.

Middle-Class Tastes and Values By mid-century, the modern middle class had developed its own way of life. A strict code of etiquette governed social behavior. Rules dictated how to dress for every occasion, how to give a dinner party, how to pay a social call, when to write letters, and how long to mourn for dead relatives.

Parents strictly supervised their children, who were expected to be "seen but not heard." A child who misbehaved was considered to reflect badly on the entire family. Servants, too, were seen as a reflection of their employers. Even a small middle-class household was expected to have at least a cook and a housemaid.

The Ideal Home Within the family, the division of labor between wife and husband changed. Earlier, middle-class women had helped run family businesses out of the home. By the later 1800s, most middle-class husbands went to work in an office or shop. A successful husband was one who earned enough to keep his wife at home. Women spent their time raising children, directing servants, and doing religious or charitable service.

Books, magazines, and popular songs supported a **cult of domesticity** that idealized women and the home. Sayings like "home, sweet home" were stitched into needlework and hung on parlor walls. The ideal woman was seen as a tender, self-sacrificing caregiver who provided a nest for her children and a peaceful refuge for her husband to escape from the hardships of the working world.

This ideal rarely applied to the lower classes. Working-class women labored for low pay in garment factories or worked as domestic servants. Young women might leave domestic service after they married, but often had to seek other employment. Despite long days working for wages, they were still expected to take full responsibility for child care and homemaking.

✔ **Checkpoint** How had the social order changed by the late 1800s?

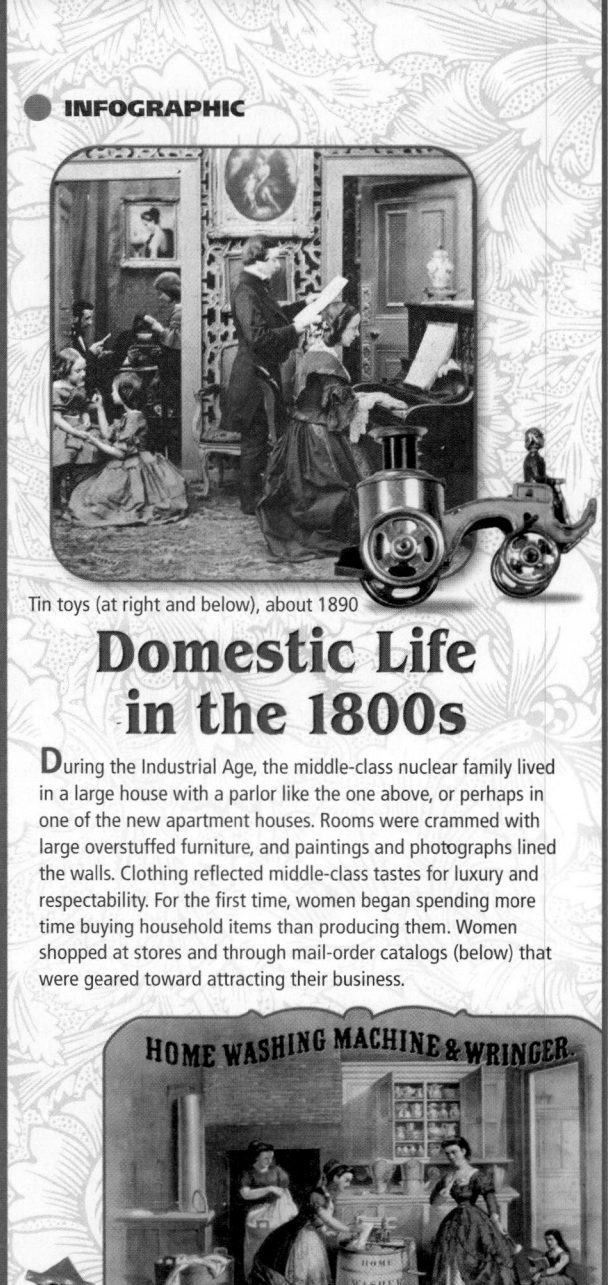

● **INFOGRAPHIC**

Tin toys (at right and below), about 1890

Domestic Life in the 1800s

During the Industrial Age, the middle-class nuclear family lived in a large house with a parlor like the one above, or perhaps in one of the new apartment houses. Rooms were crammed with large overstuffed furniture, and paintings and photographs lined the walls. Clothing reflected middle-class tastes for luxury and respectability. For the first time, women began spending more time buying household items than producing them. Women shopped at stores and through mail-order catalogs (below) that were geared toward attracting their business.

HOME WASHING MACHINE & WRINGER.

Thinking Critically
1. **Analyze Visuals** How do these images reflect a cult of domesticity?
2. **Make Comparisons** Compare and contrast the women in these two images. How are they similar? How are they different?

Teach

A New Social Order Arises **L3**

Instruct

■ **Introduce** Explain that the growth of industry brought the rise of a large middle class. Ask **Who made up the middle class?** *(business people and professionals, as well as teachers, office workers, shopkeepers, and clerks)*

■ **Teach** Ask **How did the division of labor in middle-class households change?** *(Most husbands went to work in an office or shop, while most wives stayed at home to raise their children.)* **Did the same division of labor happen in the working class?** *(No, working-class men and women both had to work in order to earn a living.)*

■ **Quick Activity** Direct students to the Infographic on this page. Ask them to discuss the similarities between the two images and what these similarities suggest.

Independent Practice

Link to Literature To help students better understand the social distinctions between the British middle and upper classes, have them read the excerpt from Jane Austen's *Pride and Prejudice* and complete the worksheet.

All in One Teaching Resources, Unit 3, p. 11

Monitor Progress

As students fill in their tables, circulate to make sure they understand how a new social order developed out of the Industrial Revolution. For a completed version of the table, see

▥ **Note Taking Transparencies,** 149

Answers

✔ Three distinct social classes emerged—upper, middle, and working class—and middle-class values and tastes were idealized.

Thinking Critically
1. These images show how the only suitable activities for women were confined to the home.
2. Similar: each image shows women performing domestic activities; different: they show two aspects of domestic expectations for women—learning how to entertain and supervising an everyday chore.

History Background

The Proper Victorians In England, the period from 1837 to 1901 is known as the Victorian Era because Queen Victoria's long reign spanned those years. Middle-class Victorians had a strict code of manners.

■ In respectable Victorian homes, fabric drapes concealed piano legs, which, like women's legs, were considered immodest if shown.

■ A widow was expected to dress in black from head to toe and never to remarry. In contrast, a widower

wore a black crepe band around his hat or sleeve and was expected to find a new wife quickly.

■ Wealthy businessmen wore knee-length frock coats and silk top hats to the office.

■ Women wore suffocating corsets pulled tightly enough to achieve the ideal waist measurement of 18 to 20 inches.

Women Work for Rights ⑬

Instruct

- **Introduce: Key Terms** Ask students to find the term ***temperance movement*** (in blue) in the text and define its meaning. Would students have supported the temperance movement if they had been alive then?

- **Teach** Ask **What rights had women won by the late 1800s?** *(the right to attend universities and to control their own property)* Ask **How did women's involvement in the abolition movement lead to some women campaigning for voting rights?** *(While campaigning for the rights of others, some women realized that they, too, were lacking political rights, such as the right to vote.)*

- **Quick Activity** Display **Transparency 129: Hugging a Delusion.** Use the lesson suggested in the transparency book to guide a discussion on the political cartoon on women's suffrage.
  🏛 **Color Transparencies,** 129

Independent Practice

Direct students to the quote by Sojourner Truth under the black heading The Suffrage Struggle. Ask students to write a paragraph about Truth's reaction to the statement that a woman's place was in the home. Ask them to explain her question, "Ain't I a woman?"

Monitor Progress

As students write their paragraphs on Sojourner Truth's quote, circulate to make sure they understand that as a former enslaved person, she had even fewer rights than a white woman. Be sure that students understand that she had been seen as property, but now worked for freedom and women's rights.

In an 1892 address, the American women's rights leader Elizabeth Cady Stanton argued that women should have an equal right to education. How does Stanton believe that an education would help women better control their own lives?

Primary Source

❝ . . . As an individual, she must rely on herself. . . . To throw obstacles in the way of a complete education is like putting out the eyes. . . . In talking of education, how shallow the argument that [men and women] must be educated for the special work [they propose] to do, and that all of the faculties not needed in this special work must lie dormant and utterly wither for lack of use, when, perhaps, these will be the very faculties needed in life's greatest emergencies! ❞ —"The Solitude of Self"

African American suffragist Sojourner Truth

Women Work for Rights

Some individual women and women's groups protested restrictions on women. They sought a broad range of rights. Across Europe and the United States, politically active women campaigned for fairness in marriage, divorce, and property laws. Women's groups also supported the temperance movement, a campaign to limit or ban the use of alcoholic beverages. Temperance leaders argued not only that drinking threatened family life, but that banning it was important for a productive and efficient workforce.

These reformers faced many obstacles. In Europe and the United States, women could not vote. They were barred from most schools and had little, if any, protection under the law. A woman's husband or father controlled all of her property.

Early Voices Before 1850, some women—mostly from the middle class—had campaigned for the abolition of slavery. In the process, they realized the severe restrictions on their own lives. In the United States, Lucretia Mott, **Elizabeth Cady Stanton,** and Susan B. Anthony crusaded against slavery before organizing a movement for women's rights.

Many women broke the barriers that kept them out of universities and professions. By the late 1800s, a few women trained as doctors or lawyers. Others became explorers, researchers, or inventors, often without recognition. For example, Julia Brainerd Hall worked with her brother to develop an aluminum-producing process. Their company became hugely successful, but Charles Hall received almost all of the credit.

The Suffrage Struggle By the late 1800s, married women in some countries had won the right to control their own property. The struggle for political rights proved far more difficult. In the United States, the Seneca Falls Convention of 1848 demanded that women be granted the right to vote. In Europe, groups dedicated to **women's suffrage,** or women's right to vote, emerged in the later 1800s.

Among men, some liberals and socialists supported women's suffrage. In general, though, suffragists faced intense opposition. Some critics claimed that women were too emotional to be allowed to vote. Others argued that women needed to be "protected" from grubby politics or that a woman's place was in the home, not in government. To such claims, **Sojourner Truth,** an African American suffragist, is believed to have replied, "Nobody ever helps me into carriages, or over mudpuddles, or gives me any best place! And ain't I a woman?"

On the edges of the Western world, women made faster strides. In New Zealand, Australia, and some western territories of the United States, women won the vote by the early 1900s. There, women who had "tamed the frontier" alongside men were not dismissed as weak and helpless. In the United States, Wyoming became the first state to grant women the right to vote. In Europe and most of the United States, however, the suffrage struggle succeeded only after World War I.

✓ **Checkpoint** What were the arguments against women's suffrage?

Answers

PRIMARY SOURCE She believes that a well-rounded education would better prepare women for the unexpected and teach women to be more independent.

✓ Women were too emotional to be allowed to vote; women needed to be protected from politics; a woman's place was traditionally at home and not out in society.

Growth of Public Education

By the late 1800s, reformers persuaded many governments to set up public schools and require basic education for all children. Teaching "the three Rs"—reading, writing, and 'rithmetic—was thought to produce better citizens. In addition, industrialized societies recognized the need for a literate workforce. Schools taught punctuality, obedience to authority, disciplined work habits, and patriotism. In European schools, children also received basic religious education.

Public Education Improves At first, elementary schools were primitive. Many teachers had little schooling themselves. In rural areas, students attended class only during the times when they were not needed on the farm or in their parents' shops.

By the late 1800s, more and more children were in school, and the quality of elementary education improved. Teachers received training at Normal Schools, where the latest "norms and standards" of educational practices were taught. Beginning in 1879, schools to train teachers were established in France. In England, schooling girls and boys between the ages of five and ten became compulsory after 1881. Also, governments began to expand secondary schools, known as high schools in the United States. In secondary schools, students learned the "classical languages," Latin and Greek, along with history and mathematics.

In general, only middle-class families could afford to have their sons attend these schools, which trained students for more serious study or for government jobs. Middle-class girls were sent to school primarily in the hope that they might marry well and become better wives and mothers. Education for girls did not include subjects such as science, mathematics, or physical education because they were not seen as necessary subjects for girls to learn.

Higher Education Expands Colleges and universities expanded in this period, too. Most university students were the sons of middle- or upper-class families. The university curriculum emphasized ancient history and languages, philosophy, religion, and law. By the late 1800s, universities added courses in the sciences, especially in chemistry and physics. At the same time, engineering schools trained students who would have the knowledge and skills to build the new industrial society.

Some women sought greater educational opportunities. By the 1840s, a few small colleges for women opened, including Bedford College in England and Mount Holyoke in the United States. In 1863, the British reformer Emily Davies campaigned for female students to be allowed to take the entrance examinations for Cambridge University. She succeeded, but as late as 1897, male Cambridge students rioted against granting degrees to women.

✔ **Checkpoint** Why did more children attend school in the late 1800s than before?

Public Education

Before 1870, the only formal education available for British children was in religious schools or "ragged schools," which taught poor children basic skills, such as reading. The Industrial Revolution changed that as it created a growing need for people to be better educated. *How does this 1908 photo of a science class in London illustrate the changes that had taken place in the British educational system?*

Growth of Public Education

Instruct

■ **Introduce** Ask students to read the introductory sentences and the two black headings under Growth of Public Education. Have students predict what they will learn under each heading. Then have them read to find out whether their predictions were accurate.

■ **Teach** Using the Numbered Heads strategy (TE, p. T23), ask **What basic education did schools teach by the late 1800s?** *(Teachers taught reading, writing, math, education, and the importance of being disciplined, punctual, obedient, and patriotic.)* **Why had colleges and universities changed their curriculums by the late 1800s?** *(The Industrial Revolution brought about a need for many people to be prepared to work in industries that required science and engineering knowledge and skills.)*

■ **Analyzing the Visuals** Point out the photograph of the schoolroom on this page. Ask students to identify similarities and differences between this school in the late 1800s and their schools today.

Independent Practice

Ask students to create an outline with Growth of Public Education as I. and the two black headings below it in their text as A. and B. Then ask students to write one paragraph explaining the purpose of schools today.

Monitor Progress

As students work on their paragraphs, circulate to ensure they understand that society needs a well-educated workforce and that, on a personal level, schooling opens up greater opportunities for an individual.

Connect to Our World

Connections to Today Schools encouraged physical fitness as well as learning. In the early 1800s, English schoolboys began playing a game that developed into soccer. School representatives drew up the first official rules in 1848. The game spread to the rest of Europe, then to Chile, Canada, and the United States. Today, soccer is probably the most widely played sport in the world.

In December 1891, American James Naismith, a physical education teacher, used a soccer ball to devise a game that could be played indoors during the long winter months. He hung up two peach basket goals, one at each end of the gym, and his YMCA athletes played the first game of basketball. The new game spread swiftly. As it grew more popular, it assumed its now familiar characteristics.

Answers

Caption It shows that education had changed because girls were being taught science in a large, bright classroom, and many supplies were available to them.

✔ Fewer children were needed to work on farms or in their parents' shops; the growing number of middle-class families could afford to send their children to school.

Science Takes New Directions L3

Instruct

- **Introduce: Vocabulary Builder** Have students read the Vocabulary Builder terms and definitions. Ask them to predict how the words *speculated* and *controversial* would be key to understanding how science challenged long-standing beliefs in the late 1800s.

- **Teach** Ask **What do John Dalton, Charles Lyell, and Charles Darwin have in common?** *(They all advanced startling scientific theories about the natural world.)* **Why was Darwin's idea controversial?** *(It contradicted the Bible.)* **How did Darwin's ideas become connected with racist ideas?** *(Some thinkers applied his theory of natural selection to human society in an unscientific way, with the belief that some races are superior to others.)*

- **Quick Activity Web Code nba-4174** will take students to an interactive map. Have students complete the interactivity on the Voyage of the HMS *Beagle* and then answer the questions in the text.

Independent Practice

Direct students to the Infographic on the Voyage of the HMS *Beagle* in their text. Ask them to find the Galápagos Islands, west of South America. Have them trace Darwin's voyage, and then explain to a partner its purpose and significance.

Monitor Progress

As students write their paragraphs, circulate to make sure they understand the purpose and significance of Darwin's voyage.

Vocabulary Builder

speculate—(SPEK yuh layt) *v.* to think about

Science Takes New Directions

Science in the service of industry brought great changes in the later 1800s. At the same time, researchers advanced startling theories about the natural world. Their new ideas challenged long-held beliefs.

Atomic Theory Develops A crucial breakthrough in chemistry came in the early 1800s when the English Quaker schoolteacher **John Dalton** developed modern atomic theory. The ancient Greeks had speculated that all matter was made of tiny particles called atoms. Dalton showed that each element has its own kind of atoms. Earlier theories put forth the idea that all atoms were basically alike. Dalton also showed how different kinds of atoms combine to make all chemical substances. In 1869, the Russian chemist Dmitri Mendeleyev (men duh LAY ef) drew up a table that grouped elements according to their atomic weights. His table became the basis for the periodic table of elements used today.

Debating the Earth's Age The new science of geology opened avenues of debate. In *Principles of Geology*, Charles Lyell offered evidence to

---

INFOGRAPHIC

Voyage of the HMS Beagle

In 1831, the HMS *Beagle* sailed from England on a five-year voyage around the world to survey and chart the oceans. Aboard was 22-year-old Charles Darwin, whose role was to observe, record, and collect samples of rocks, plants, animals, insects, and fossils. Some of the animals that he studied are pictured on the map. The specimens Darwin collected and studied helped him develop his theory of evolution. Controversy over Darwin's theory continues today.

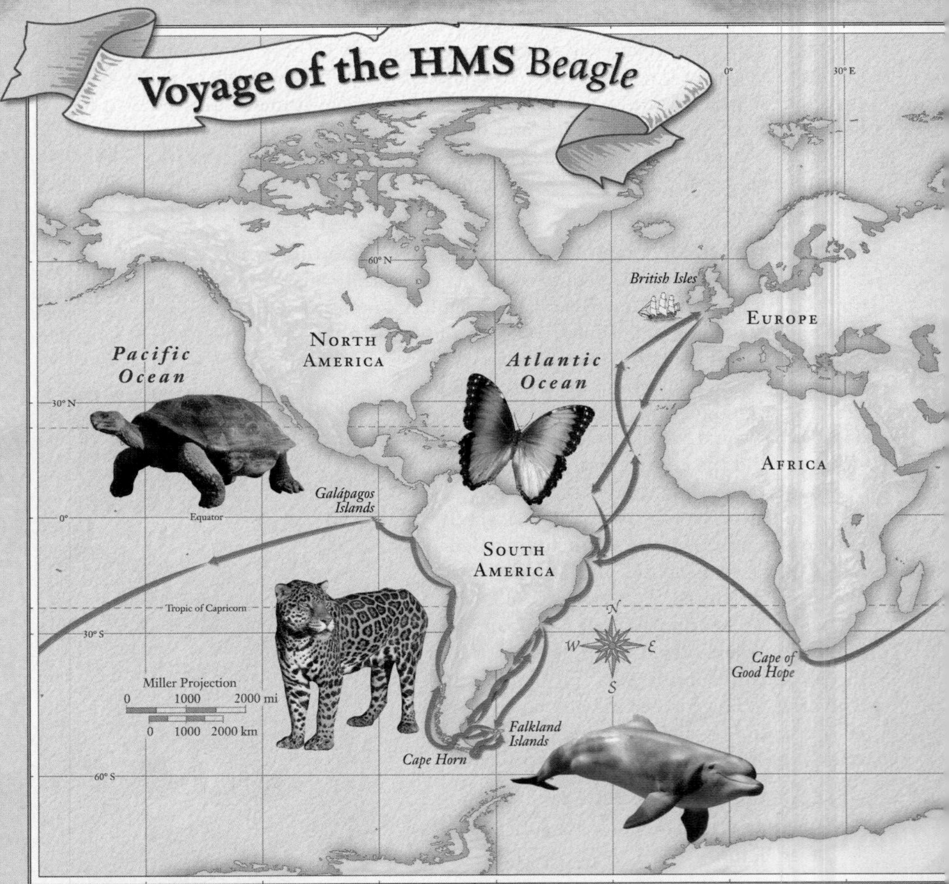

► Clockwise from upper right: blue common Morpho butterfly, bottlenose dolphin, jaguar, Galápagos tortoise

---

show that Earth had formed over millions of years. His successors concluded that Earth was at least two billion years old and that life had not appeared until long after Earth was formed. These ideas did not seem to agree with biblical accounts of creation.

Archaeology added other pieces to an emerging debate about the origins of life on Earth. In 1856, workers in Germany accidentally uncovered fossilized Neanderthal bones. Later scholars found fossils of other early modern humans. These archaeologists had limited evidence and often drew mistaken conclusions. But as more discoveries were made, scholars developed new ideas about early humans and their ancestors.

Darwin's Theory of Natural Selection The most <u>controversial</u> new idea came from the British naturalist **Charles Darwin**. In 1859, after years of research, he published *On the Origin of Species*. Darwin argued that all forms of life, including human beings, had evolved into their present state over millions of years. To explain the long, slow process of evolution, he put forward his theory of natural selection.

Darwin adopted Thomas Malthus's idea that all plants and animals produced more offspring than the food supply could support. As a result,

Vocabulary Builder

<u>controversial</u>—(kahn truh VUR shul) *adj.* that is or can be argued about or debated

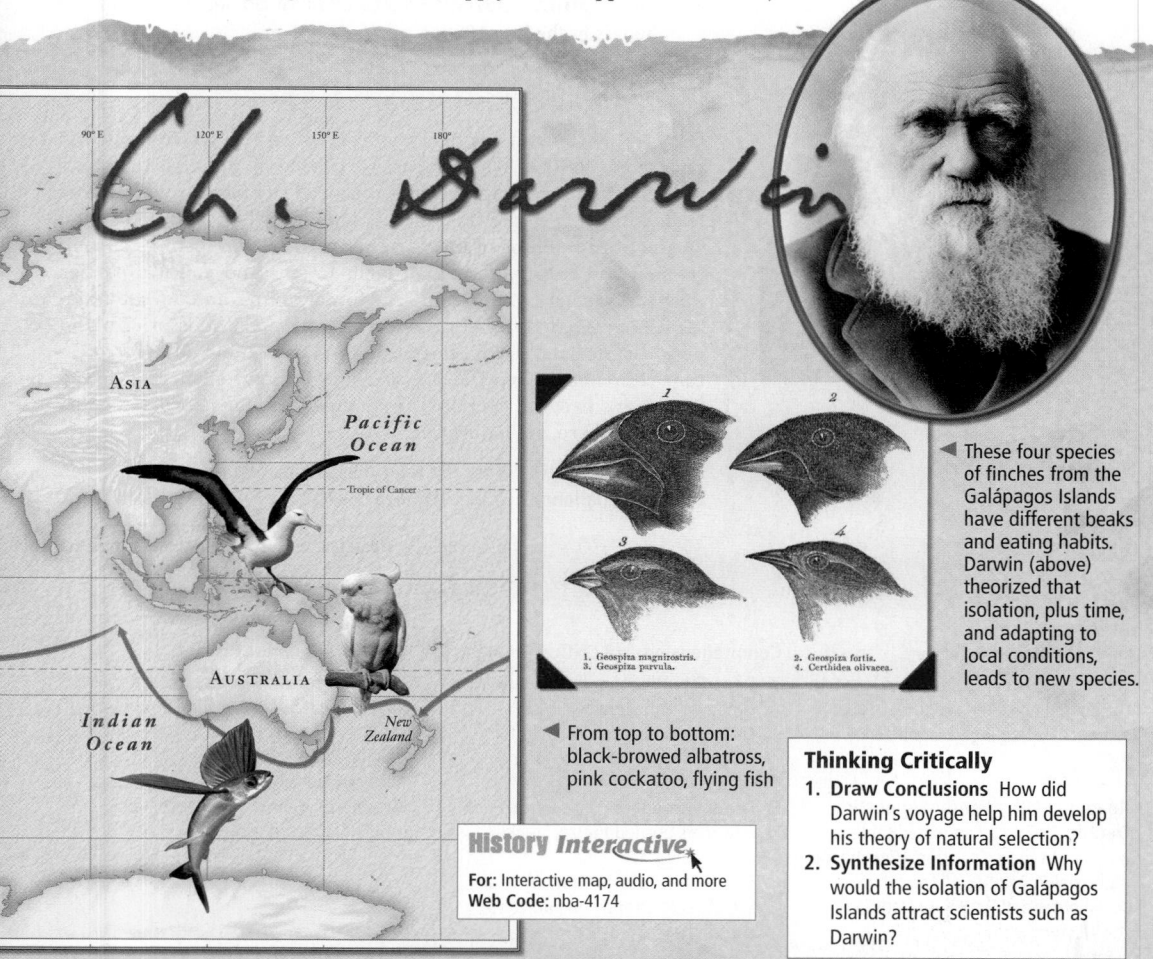

ASIA

Pacific Ocean

Tropic of Cancer

AUSTRALIA

New Zealand

Indian Ocean

◀ These four species of finches from the Galápagos Islands have different beaks and eating habits. Darwin (above) theorized that isolation, plus time, and adapting to local conditions, leads to new species.

1. *Geospiza magnirostris.* 2. *Geospiza fortis.*
3. *Geospiza parvula.* 4. *Certhidea olivacea.*

◀ From top to bottom: black-browed albatross, pink cockatoo, flying fish

History Interactive

For: Interactive map, audio, and more
Web Code: nba-4174

Thinking Critically

1. **Draw Conclusions** How did Darwin's voyage help him develop his theory of natural selection?
2. **Synthesize Information** Why would the isolation of Galápagos Islands attract scientists such as Darwin?

Religion in an Urban Age ⓲

Instruct

- **Introduce** Explain that despite new scientific thinking, religion had a major place in industrialized nations. Ask students to predict what this place might be, and then read to find out if their predictions were correct.

- **Teach** Ask **What was the purpose of the social gospel?** (*It encouraged Christians to do social service.*) **Why did living conditions in industrialized nations encourage compassionate and charitable feelings?** (*Industrialization created harsh living and working conditions for many people. People felt the need to push for reforms for the working poor, and religious organizations were one way to do that.*)

- **Analyzing the Visuals** Have students describe the photo of the Salvation Army on the next page and explain the significance of the image. Remind students that groups like the Salvation Army still exist today.

Independent Practice

Ask students to work in groups to generate a list of reasons why reforms and social services were needed and what religious groups could do to help fill this need. Have student groups share their lists with the class.

Monitor Progress

Check Reading and Note Taking Study Guide entries for student understanding.

Differentiated
Instruction   **Solutions for All Learners**

⓵ **Gifted and Talented Students**   ⓵ **Advanced Readers**

Ask students who need an extra challenge to do library and Internet research either on organizations in the late 1800s or early 1900s that provided help to the poor, or on such organizations today, such as the Salvation Army or Goodwill Industries. (Some organizations will span both periods.) Students should

provide a history of the organization, explain its purpose, and describe the social services it provided or provides. Ask students to report their findings to the rest of the class in the form of a news release from the organization.

Answers

Thinking Critically
1. By traveling, he was able to study different varieties of a given species and formulate theories about survival and evolution.
2. Because of their isolation, the few species that reached the islands had to adapt to their environments, making them an ideal place to study natural selection.

Assess Progress L3

- Have students complete the Section Assessment.
- Administer the Section Quiz.
- **Teaching Resources, Unit 3**, p. 4
- To further assess student under-standing, use
  - **Progress Monitoring Transparencies**, 88

Reteach

If students need more instruction, have them read the section summary.

- **Reading and Note Taking Study Guide**, p. 109 L3
- **Adapted Reading and Note Taking Study Guide**, p. 109 L1 L2
- **Spanish Reading and Note Taking Study Guide**, p. 109 L2

Extend L4

Have students scan newspaper headlines for examples of scientific advances. Then discuss the effect that these scientific advances could have on society.

Answers

Caption clothing and food to the urban poor, funds for hospitals and schools

✓ The research of Lyell and Darwin challenged traditional and biblical views.

✓ They worked for reform and social services.

The Salvation Army
By 1878, William and Catherine Booth had set up the Salvation Army in London to spread Christian teachings and provide social services. Their daughter, Evangeline (below), stands in front of one the kettles used to gather funds for the needy. *What services did religious organizations provide?*

---

he said, members of each species constantly competed to survive. Natural forces "selected" those with physical traits best adapted to their environment to survive and to pass the trait on to their offspring. This process of natural selection came to be known as "survival of the fittest."

Social Darwinism and Racism Although Darwin himself never promoted any social ideas, some thinkers used his theories to support their own beliefs about society. Applying the idea of survival of the fittest to war and economic competition came to be known as Social Darwinism. Industrial tycoons, argued Social Darwinists, were more "fit" than those they put out of business. War brought progress by weeding out weak nations. Victory was seen as proof of superiority.

Social Darwinism encouraged **racism,** the unscientific belief that one racial group is superior to another. By the late 1800s, many Europeans and Americans claimed that the success of Western civilization was due to the supremacy of the white race. As you will read, such powerful ideas would have a long-lasting impact on world history.

✓ **Checkpoint** How did science begin to challenge existing beliefs in the late 1800s?

Religion in an Urban Age

Despite the challenge of new scientific ideas, religion continued to be a major force in Western society. Christian churches and Jewish synagogues remained at the center of communities. Religious leaders influenced political, social, and educational developments.

The grim realities of industrial life stimulated feelings of compassion and charity. Christian labor unions and political parties pushed for reforms. Individuals, church groups, and Jewish organizations all tried to help the working poor. Catholic priests and nuns set up schools and hospitals in urban slums. Many Protestant churches backed the **social gospel,** a movement that urged Christians to social service. They campaigned for reforms in housing, healthcare, and education.

✓ **Checkpoint** How did religious groups respond to the challenges of industrialization?

SECTION 3 Assessment

Progress Monitoring Online
For: Self-quiz with vocabulary practice
Web Code: nba-2131

Terms, People, and Places

1. For each term, person, or place listed at the beginning of the section, write a sentence explaining its significance.

Note Taking

2. **Reading Skill: Identify Supporting Details** Use your completed table to answer the Focus Question: How did the Industrial Revolution change the old social order and long-held traditions in the Western world?

Comprehension and Critical Thinking

3. **Describe** What are three values associated with the middle class?
4. **Draw Conclusions** Why did the women's movement face strong opposition?
5. **Draw Inferences** Why do you think reformers pushed for free public education?
6. **Synthesize Information** Why did the ideas of Charles Darwin cause controversy?

● **Writing About History**

Quick Write: Write a Thesis Statement Imagine that you are writing a problem-solution essay on the unequal treatment of women in the 1800s. Based on what you have read in this section, write a thesis statement, or the main idea, for your problem-solution essay.

Section 3 Assessment

1. Sentences should reflect an understanding of each term, person, or place listed at the beginning of the section.
2. Three distinct social classes emerged (upper, middle, and working); middle-class tastes and values became a measuring stick for the working classes; women sought a political voice, the right to vote, and the chance to attend universities; scientists shook long-held religious beliefs.
3. luxury, respectability, and a strict etiquette
4. Men believed that women belonged in the home; they also thought that women were too emotional to vote.
5. Sample: It would improve opportunities for working-class children.
6. Darwin's ideas contradicted the widely accepted biblical account of creation.

● **Writing About History**

Responses should show include a clear and direct thesis statement that explains the main idea of the problem-solution essay.

For additional assessment, have students access **Progress Monitoring Online** at **Web Code nba-2131.**

Sunset

In the 1800s, many writers turned away from the harsh realities of industrial life to celebrate nature. The English poet William Wordsworth described the peace and beauty of sunset:

❝ It is a beauteous evening, calm and free,
The holy time is quiet as a Nun
Breathless with adoration; the broad sun
Is sinking down in its tranquillity. ❞
—William Wordsworth,
Complete Poetical Works

Focus Question What artistic movements emerged in reaction to the Industrial Revolution?

Albert Bierstadt, *Hetch Hetchy Canyon*, 1875

Arts in the Industrial Age

Objectives
• Understand what themes shaped romantic art, literature, and music.
• Explain how realists responded to the industrialized, urban world.
• Describe how the visual arts changed.

Terms, People, and Places

William Wordsworth	realism
William Blake	Charles Dickens
romanticism	Gustave Courbet
Lord Byron	Louis Daguerre
Victor Hugo	impressionism
Ludwig van Beethoven	Claude Monet
	Vincent van Gogh

Note Taking

Reading Skill: Identify Supporting Details Fill in a table like the one below with details about the artistic movements in the 1800s.

Major Artistic Movements of the 1800s		
Movement	**Goals/ Characteristics**	**Major Figures**
Romanticism	• Rebellion against reason	• Wordsworth
Realism	•	•
Impressionism	•	•

William Wordsworth, along with **William Blake,** Samuel Taylor Coleridge, and Percy Bysshe Shelley among others, was part of a cultural movement called romanticism. From about 1750 to 1850, romanticism shaped Western literature and arts.

The Romantic Revolt Against Reason

Romanticism does not refer to romance in the sense of an affectionate relationship, but rather to an artistic style emphasizing imagination, freedom, and emotion. Romanticism was a reaction to the neoclassical writers of the Enlightenment, who had turned to classical Greek and Roman literature and ideals that stressed order, harmony, reason, and emotional restraint. In contrast to Enlightenment literature, the works of romantic writers included simple, direct language, intense feelings, and a glorification of nature. Artists, composers, and architects were also followers of the movement.

The Romantic Hero Romantic writers created a new kind of hero—a mysterious, melancholy figure who felt out of step with society. "My joys, my grief, my passions, and my powers, / Made me a stranger," wrote Britain's George Gordon, **Lord Byron.** He himself was a larger-than-life figure equal to those he created. After a rebellious, wandering life, he joined Greek forces battling for freedom. When he died of a fever there, his legend bloomed. In fact, public interest in his poetry and adventures was so great that moody, isolated romantic heroes came to be described as "Byronic."

Vocabulary Builder

Use the information below and the following resources to teach the high-use words from this section.
All in One Teaching Resources, Unit 3, p. 6; **Teaching Resources, Skills Handbook,** p. 3

High-Use Words	Definitions and Sample Sentences
emphasis, p. 321	*n.* special attention given to something to make it stand out
The school placed more **emphasis** on scholarship than athletics.
intense, p. 322	*adj.* very strong or deep
Death Valley is known for its **intense** heat.

Objectives

As you teach this section, keep students focused on the following objectives to help them answer the Section Focus Question and master core content.

■ Understand what themes shaped romantic art, literature, and music.

■ Learn how realists responded to the industrialized, urban world.

■ Describe how the visual arts changed.

Prepare to Read

Build Background Knowledge ⓛ3

Ask students to recall how the Industrial Revolution affected all aspects of life. Ask them to predict how it would influence the way that people thought about, viewed, or listened to the arts.

Set a Purpose ⓛ3

■ **WITNESS HISTORY** Read the selection aloud or play the audio.
 AUDIO **Witness History Audio CD,** Sunset

Ask **What is the main idea of this stanza?** *(that the setting sun is calm, quiet, beautiful, and peaceful)* **How is Wordsworth's poem a reaction to industrial life?** *(By retreating to the beauty and power of nature, it turns away from industrialization and city life.)*

■ **Focus** Point out the Section Focus Question and write it on the board. Tell students to refer to this question as they read. *(Answer appears with Section 4 Assessment answers.)*

■ **Preview** Have students preview the Section Objectives and the list of Terms, People, and Places.

■ **Note Taking** Have students read this section using the Guided Questioning strategy (TE, p. T20). As they read, have them fill in the table describing the major artistic movements of the 1800s.

 **Reading and Note Taking Study Guide,** p. 110

The Romantic Revolt Against Reason

Instruct

- **Introduce** Read aloud the quotation by Lord Byron under the black heading The Romantic Hero ("My joys . . . / Made me a stranger") and discuss students' responses.

- **Teach** Explain that *romanticism* emphasizes imagination, emotion, and feeling as sources of knowledge. Ask **How was romanticism a reaction to Enlightenment ideas?** *(Romantics appealed to emotion rather than reason.)* Ask **What did romantic poetry, writing, music, and art have in common?** *(They all sought to excite strong emotions and intense feelings from the audience or viewer.)*

- **Quick Activity** Ask students to read the biography of Beethoven on this page. Then play the Witness History audio selection. Ask students to describe what classifies this piece as romantic. Then ask them to look at the painting on the previous page and describe the romantic qualities of that piece.

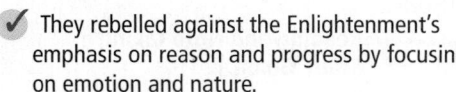 AUDIO **Witness History Audio CD,** Ludwig van Beethoven

Independent Practice

Have students work in groups to compare the romantic hero of the 1800s to the ideal of a romantic hero today. Ask **How are they similar or different?** *(Possible similarities: mysteriousness and melancholy; possible differences: audiences today prefer happy endings rather than the grim destiny met by heroes of the 1800s.)* Have each group create a Venn diagram with the characteristics discussed.

Monitor Progress

As students fill in their tables, circulate to make sure they understand the major features of artistic movements in the 1800s. For a completed version of the table, see

🏛 **Note Taking Transparencies,** 150

Answers

BIOGRAPHY His music aroused strong emotions.

✓ They rebelled against the Enlightenment's emphasis on reason and progress by focusing on emotion and nature.

BIOGRAPHY

Ludwig van Beethoven

An accomplished musician by age 12, composer Ludwig van Beethoven (1770–1827) agonized over every note of every composition. The result was stunning music that expresses intense emotion. The famous opening of his Fifth Symphony conveys the sense of fate knocking at the door. His Sixth Symphony captures a joyful day in the countryside, interrupted by a violent thunderstorm.

Beethoven's career was haunted by perhaps the greatest tragedy a musician can face. In 1798, he began to lose his hearing. Still, he continued to compose music he could hear only in his mind. **How did Beethoven's music reflect romanticism?**

 AUDIO

The romantic hero often hid a guilty secret and faced a grim destiny. German writer Johann Wolfgang von Goethe (GUR tuh) wrote the dramatic poem *Faust*. The aging scholar Faust makes a pact with the devil, exchanging his soul for youth. After much agony, Faust wins salvation by accepting his duty to help others. In *Jane Eyre,* British novelist Charlotte Brontë weaves a tale about a quiet governess and her brooding, Byronic employer, whose large mansion conceals a terrifying secret.

Inspired by the Past Romantic writers combined history, legend, and folklore. Sir Walter Scott's novels and ballads evoked the turbulent history of Scottish clans or medieval knights. Alexandre Dumas (doo MAH) and **Victor Hugo** re-created France's past in novels like *The Three Musketeers* and *The Hunchback of Notre Dame*.

Architects, too, were inspired by old styles and forms. Churches and other buildings, including the British Parliament, were modeled on medieval Gothic styles. To people living in the 1800s, medieval towers and lacy stonework conjured up images of a glorious past.

Music Stirs Emotions Romantic composers also tried to stir deep emotions. Audiences were moved to laughter or tears at Hungarian Franz Liszt's piano playing. The passionate music of German composer **Ludwig van Beethoven** combined classical forms with a stirring range of sound. He was the first composer to take full advantage of the broad range of instruments in the modern orchestra. In all, Beethoven produced nine symphonies, five piano concertos, a violin concerto, an opera, two masses, and dozens of shorter pieces. To many, he is considered the greatest composer of his day.

Other romantic composers wove traditional folk melodies into their works to glorify their nations' pasts. In his piano works, Frederic Chopin (shoh PAN) used Polish peasant dances to convey the sorrows and joys of people living under foreign occupation.

Romanticism in Art Painters, too, broke free from the discipline and strict rules of the Enlightenment. Landscape painters like J.M.W. Turner sought to capture the beauty and power of nature. Using bold brush strokes and colors, Turner often showed tiny human figures struggling against sea and storm.

Romantics painted many subjects, from simple peasant life to medieval knights to current events. Bright colors conveyed violent energy and emotion. The French painter Eugène Delacroix (deh luh KRWAH) filled his canvases with dramatic action. In *Liberty Leading the People*, the Goddess of Liberty carries the revolutionary tricolor as French citizens rally to the cause.

✓ **Checkpoint** How did romantic writers, musicians, and artists respond to the Enlightenment?

The Call to Realism

By the mid-1800s, a new artistic movement, **realism,** took hold in the West. Realism was an attempt to represent the world as it was, without the sentiment associated with romanticism. Realists often focused their work on the harsh side of life in cities or villages. Many writers and artists were committed to improving the lot of the unfortunates whose lives they depicted.

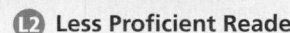 Differentiated
Instruction   Solutions for All Learners

L1 Special Needs   L2 Less Proficient Readers

Write the word *romantic* on the board. Ask students to suggest definitions for this word. Then explain that romanticism was a cultural movement that rejected reason as the only way to acquire knowledge and embraced emotion and imagination. Ask them to explain how romanticism is similar to and different from their definitions of *romantic*.

L2 English Language Learners

Use the following resources to help students acquire basic skills.

 **Adapted Reading and Note Taking Study Guide**

- Adapted Note Taking Study Guide, p. 110
- Adapted Section Summary, p. 111

Novels Depict Grim Reality The English novelist **Charles Dickens** vividly portrayed the lives of slum dwellers and factory workers, including children. In *Oliver Twist,* Dickens tells the story of a nine-year-old orphan raised in a grim poorhouse. In response to a request for more food, Oliver is smacked on the head and sent away to work. Later, he runs away to London. There he is taken in by Fagin, a villain who trains homeless children to become pickpockets. The book shocked many middle-class readers with its picture of poverty, mistreatment of children, and urban crime. Yet Dickens's humor and colorful characters made him one of the most popular novelists in the world.

French novelists also portrayed the ills of their time. Victor Hugo, who moved from romantic to realistic novels, revealed how hunger drove a good man to crime and how the law hounded him ever after in *Les Misérables* (lay miz ehr AHB). The novels of Émile Zola painted an even grimmer picture. In *Germinal*, Zola exposed class warfare in the French mining industry. To Zola's characters, neither the Enlightenment's faith in reason nor the romantic movement's feelings mattered at all.

Realism in Drama Norwegian dramatist Henrik Ibsen brought realism to the stage. His plays attacked the hypocrisy he observed around him. *A Doll's House* shows a woman caught in a straitjacket of social rules. In *An Enemy of the People,* a doctor discovers that the water in a local spa is polluted. Because the town's economy depends on its spa, the citizens denounce the doctor and suppress the truth. Ibsen's realistic dramas had a wide influence in Europe and the United States.

Arts Reject Romantic Ideas Painters also represented the realities of their time. Rejecting the romantic emphasis on imagination, they focused on ordinary subjects, especially working-class men and women. "I cannot paint an angel," said the French realist **Gustave Courbet** (koor BAY) "because I have never seen one." Instead, he painted works such as *The Stone Breakers,* which shows two rough laborers on a country road. Later in the century, *The Gross Clinic,* by American painter Thomas Eakins, shocked viewers with its realistic depiction of an autopsy conducted in a medical classroom.

✔ **Checkpoint** How did the realism movement differ from the romantic movement?

Realism in the Arts

Ⓐ Thomas Eakins's 1875 painting *The Gross Clinic* depicts the realism of medical school where students learn by performing autopsies. The artist included many realistic elements such as the surgical tools in the foreground and the reaction of the spectator at the far left.

Ⓑ Edvard Munch's 1898 painting shows an impression of Henrik Ibsen filled with psychological realism, similar to that found in Ibsen's plays.

Ⓒ This 1896 portrait of Ibsen shows photographic realism in the playwright's appearance and expression.

Ⓓ Victor Hugo's 1862 novel *Les Misérables* describes the reality of poverty, hunger, and corruption among the poor in Paris. This 1886 poster depicts the novel's main characters: the convict Jean Valjean at the center, and Cosette, the girl he adopts, at the right.

Vocabulary Builder

emphasis—(EM fuh sis) *n.* special attention given to something to make it stand out

---

Instruct

- **Introduce: Vocabulary Builder**
Have students read the Vocabulary Builder term and definition. Then have students read the introductory paragraph under this heading and each black heading. Use the Idea Wave strategy (TE, p. T22) and ask **If Charles Dickens were alive today, what kinds of people might he *emphasize* in his writing?** *(Sample: homeless people, the working poor, people suffering from disease, victims of war, political and economic refugees)*

- **Teach** Ask **What was the realist movement?** *(a rejection of the romantic emphasis on imagination and a focus on ordinary subjects, working-class men and women, and the harsh realities of industrial life)* **What is the aim of impressionist paintings?** *(to capture the eye's first impression of an object or scene)* **How does impressionist painting differ from photography?** *(Photography is much more realistic than impressionist painting.)*

- **Quick Activity** Point out that realism took many forms: paintings, plays, novels. Refer students to the Realism in the Arts feature on this page. As a class, have students discuss how each visual reflects features of realism. Then display **Color Transparency 130: *The Stone Breakers,* by Gustave Courbet.** Tell students that many critics denounced this work as vulgar and unspiritual. Ask students why they think his work caused such a reaction.

🎞 Color Transparencies, 130

Independent Practice

Biography To help students better understand the role of photography in the 1800s, have them read the biography *Julia Margaret Cameron* and complete the worksheet.

All in One Teaching Resources, Unit 3, p. 12

Monitor Progress

Check Reading and Note Taking Study Guide entries for student understanding.

Answer

✔ Realism represented the realities of industrialization and rejected the romantic emphasis on imagination and sentiment.

Link to Drama

"Immoral and Subversive" Henrik Ibsen originally planned to study medicine at the University of Norway. After failing his entrance examinations in Greek and arithmetic, he decided to work as a playwright and stage manager of the newly founded Norwegian Theater. He began writing historical and romantic plays for the small company before venturing into his "problem plays." These plays, one of which is *A Doll's House,* openly criticized social conventions of the 1800s, such as subjugation of women, political hypocrisy, bourgeois mediocrity, and corrupt journalism. These forthright attacks on social structures caused his critics to label him "immoral and subversive." Yet, Ibsen's willingness to probe the foundations of society eventually earned him the title of "father of modern drama."

Assess Progress 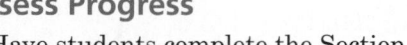 L3

- Have students complete the Section Assessment.
- Administer the Section Quiz.

All in One Teaching Resources, Unit 3, p. 5

- To further assess student understanding, use

 Progress Monitoring Transparencies, 89

Reteach

If students need more instruction, have them read the section summary.

 Reading and Note Taking Study Guide, p. 111 L3

 Adapted Reading and Note Taking Study Guide, p. 111 L1 L2

 Spanish Reading and Note Taking Study Guide, p. 111 L2

Extend L4

See this Chapter's Professional Development pages for the Extend Online activity on impressionism.

Answers

Caption intense colors, bold brush strokes, and the effects of light

 The realism of photography made some artists turn away from realistic painting.

Postimpressionism
This self-portrait of Dutch painter Vincent van Gogh shows his bandaged ear, which he cut off in a state of depression. *What postimpressionist features are demonstrated in Van Gogh's self-portrait?*

Vocabulary Builder
intense—(in TENS) *adj.* very strong or deep

The Visual Arts Take New Directions

By the 1840s, a new art form, photography, was emerging. **Louis Daguerre** (dah GEHR) in France and William Fox Talbot in England had improved on earlier technologies to produce successful photographs. At first, many photos were stiff, posed portraits of middle-class families or prominent people. Other photographs reflected the romantics' fascination with faraway places.

In time, photographers used the camera to present the grim realities of life. During the American Civil War, Mathew B. Brady preserved a vivid, realistic record of the corpse-strewn battlefields. Other photographers showed the harsh conditions in industrial factories or slums.

The Impressionists Photography posed a challenge to painters. Why try for realism, some artists asked, when a camera could do the same thing better? By the 1870s, a group of painters took art in a new direction, seeking to capture the first fleeting impression made by a scene or object on the viewer's eye. The new movement, known as **impressionism,** took root in Paris, capital of the Western art world.

Since the Renaissance, painters had carefully finished their paintings so that no brush strokes showed. But impressionists like **Claude Monet** (moh NAY) and Edgar Degas (day GAH) brushed strokes of color side by side without any blending. According to new scientific studies of optics, the human eye would mix these patches of color.

By concentrating on visual impressions rather than realism, artists achieved a fresh view of familiar subjects. Monet, for example, painted the cathedral at Rouen (roo AHN), France, dozens of times from the same angle, capturing how it looked in different lights at different times of day.

The Postimpressionists Later painters, called postimpressionists, developed a variety of styles. Georges Seurat (suh RAH) arranged small dots of color to define the shapes of objects. **Vincent van Gogh** experimented with sharp brush lines and bright colors. His unique brushwork lent a dreamlike quality to everyday subjects. Paul Gauguin (goh GAN) also developed a bold, personal style. In his paintings, people look flat, as in "primitive" folk art. But his brooding colors and black outlining of shapes convey intense feelings and images.

✓ **Checkpoint** How did photography influence the development of painting?

SECTION 4 **Assessment**

Progress Monitoring Online
For: Self-quiz with vocabulary practice
Web Code: nba-2141

Terms, People, and Places

1. For each term, person, or place listed at the beginning of the section, write a sentence explaining its significance.

Note Taking

2. **Reading Skill: Identify Supporting Details** Use your completed table to answer the Focus Question: What artistic movements emerged in reaction to the Industrial Revolution?

Comprehension and Critical Thinking

3. **Summarize** What are three subjects romantics favored?
4. **Draw Conclusions** What did Courbet mean when he said, "I cannot paint an angel because I have never seen one"? Do you agree with his attitude? Explain.
5. **Recognize Cause and Effect** In what ways were the new artistic styles of the 1800s a reaction to changes in society?

● **Writing About History**

Quick Write: Support a Solution Based on what you've read, list supporting information, such as details, data, and facts, for the following thesis statement of a problem-solution essay: Artists in the 1800s portrayed subjects realistically to make the public more aware of some of the grim problems of life in industrialized nations.

Impressionism

Impressionism was one of the most important art movements of the 1800s. It marked a departure from tradition, both in subject matter and painting technique. Artists sought to depict the human eye's first perception of a scene. Characterized by the use of unmixed primary colors and small, visible brush strokes, impressionism attempted to show the effects of direct or reflected light. Impressionist artists often painted outdoors for maximum effect.

▲ **Claude Monet,** *Impression: Sunrise,* **1872**
In the 1800s, "The Salon," an annual exhibition that accepted only traditional paintings, dominated the Parisian art scene. In 1874, a group of artists held their own exhibition at a local photographer's studio. Claude Monet's *Impression: Sunrise* was one of the works displayed. Monet's painting demonstrates several characteristics of impressionist work, including short, visible brush strokes and an idealized depiction of a landscape.

▲ **Edgar Degas,** *The Dancing Class,*
c. **1873–1875**
This painting by Edgar Degas shows the influence of the newly invented camera. Impressionists' paintings moved away from the traditional placement of subjects in favor of off-center compositions. Figures were also painted on the outermost parts of the canvas. Much like photographs, impressionist paintings were often snapshots of life rather than elaborate portraits.

▲ **Berthe Morisot,** *Eugène Manet and His Daughter at Bougival, c.* **1881**
French impressionist painter Berthe Morisot also participated in the first impressionist exhibit in 1874. Morisot's delicate, subtle paintings often portrayed her family and friends—as this one of her husband and daughter.

Thinking Critically
1. **Summarize** How did impressionism depart from tradition?
2. **Draw Conclusions** What are the advantages and disadvantages of painting outdoors?

History Background

The Value of Art Like other artists, impressionist painters still had to make a living, and the Salon's hostility toward their work made that task difficult. Many impressionists came to rely on Paul Durand-Ruel, a Paris art dealer who became one of the movement's earliest supporters. He tirelessly promoted impressionism, and eventually patronage began to build. Many of the initial collectors were middle-class businessmen drawn to the world depicted in the paintings. Americans, in particular, became reliable purchasers of impressionist art. The first museum exhibit devoted to impressionism was held at the Musée de Luxembourg in 1897. The impressionists received further exposure at the World's Fair in 1900. Today, the style pioneered by a few artistic renegades is one of the most popular styles in the world.

Impressionism

Objectives
■ Describe the emergence of the impressionist movement.
■ Explain how impressionist paintings tried to capture a moment in time.

Build Background Knowledge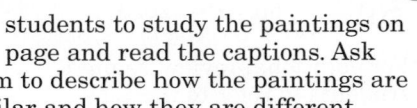
Have students use the ELBOW acronym to discuss the characteristics of impressionism: Everyday life, Light, Brush strokes, Outdoor settings, Weather and atmosphere. Divide the class into groups. Ask each group to select a painting by one of the impressionists. Have students discuss how ELBOW captures the essence of the particular work selected.

Instruct
Ask students to study the paintings on this page and read the captions. Ask them to describe how the paintings are similar and how they are different.

Monitor Progress
To review this section, ask students to list the technical innovations of impressionism, particularly the use of color. *(Sample: Impressionists used both short, visible strokes and primary colors such as red, blue, and yellow. These colors were often unmixed and applied in combinations that caused an even greater effect on the viewer's eye than more traditional methods.)*

Thinking Critically
1. It used unmixed primary colors; visible brush strokes; idealized depictions of objects. Subjects were sometimes off-center. Figures were sometimes on the periphery of the canvas.
2. Possible advantages: immediate connection between artist and subject; painters did not need to rely on sketches or memory in composing the final work; painters could capture one scene at different times and in different lights. Possible disadvantages: the artist was at the mercy of the weather and had to work more rapidly than in a studio.

- Have students use the Quick Study Guide to prepare for this chapter's test. Students may wish to refer to the following pages as they review:

Key People
Section 1, pp. 300–303; Section 2, pp. 305–306; Section 3, pp. 314, 316–318; Section 4, pp. 319–323

Life Expectancy in the Industrial Age
Section 2, pp. 305–306

Impact of the Industrial Revolution
Section 1, pp. 298–304; Section 2, pp. 305–309; Section 3, pp. 312–315

Key Events of the Industrial Revolution
Section 1, pp. 298–299, 302; Section 2, p. 308; Section 3, pp. 316–318; Section 4, pp. 319–320, 322

- For additional review, remind students to refer to the **L3**

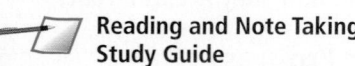 **Reading and Note Taking Study Guide**

Note Taking Study Guide, pp. 104, 106, 108, 110
Section Summaries, pp. 105, 107, 109, 111

- Have students access **Web Code nbp-2151** for this chapter's *History Interactive* timeline, which includes expanded entries and additional events.

- If students need more instruction on analyzing timelines, have them read the **Skills Handbook,** p. SH30.

- When students have completed their study of the chapter, distribute Chapter Tests A and B.

All in One Teaching Resources, Unit 3, pp. 15–20

For **Progress Monitoring** *Online,* refer students to the Self-test with vocabulary practice at **Web Code nba-2151.**

Progress Monitoring *Online*
For: Self-test with vocabulary practice
Web Code: nba-2151

■ Key People

Inventors/Developers
Henry Bessemer—steel processing
Michael Faraday—dynamo
Thomas Edison—electric light bulb
Gottlieb Daimler—automobile
Samuel F.B. Morse—telegraph
Alexander Graham Bell—telephone
Guglielmo Marconi—radio

Scientists
Louis Pasteur—vaccinations, pasteurization
Joseph Lister—antiseptics
John Dalton—modern atomic theory
Charles Darwin—theory of natural selection

Reformers
Florence Nightingale—sanitary measures in hospitals
Elizabeth Cady Stanton—women's rights
Susan B. Anthony—women's rights
William and Catherine Booth—Salvation Army

Artists, Writers, and Composers
William Wordsworth—romantic writer
Lord Byron—romantic writer
Ludwig van Beethoven—romantic composer
Charles Dickens—realist writer
Émile Zola—realist writer
Gustave Courbet—realist painter
Claude Monet—impressionist painter
Edgar Degas—impressionist painter
Vincent van Gogh—postimpressionist painter

■ Life Expectancy in the Industrial Age

Average Life Expectancy in Selected Industrial Areas, 1850–1910		
Year	Male	Female
1850	40.3 years	42.8 years
1870	42.3 years	44.7 years
1890	45.8 years	48.5 years
1910	52.7 years	56.0 years

SOURCE: E.A. Wrigley, *Population and History* (based on data for parts of Western Europe and the United States)

■ Impact of the Industrial Revolution

Key Effects of the Industrial Revolution		
Industrialization	**Urbanization**	**Social Structure**
• Germany, France, and the U.S. join Great Britain as industrial powers. • Rise of factories; new production methods • Advances in transportation and communication • Rise of big business • Growth of labor unions	• Advances in medicine and science • Population growth due to falling death rates • Higher standard of living	• Three social classes emerge • Middle class expands • Rise of urban working class • Reform movements grow • Public education expands

■ Key Events of the Industrial Revolution

Early 1800s
Romanticism begins to shape Western art and literature.

1807
First factories open in Belgium, setting off the Industrial Revolution on the European continent.

1839
French inventor Louis Daguerre perfects an effective method of photography.

Chapter Events
Global Events

| 1800 | 1815 | 1830 | 1845 |

1819
Simón Bolívar establishes Gran Colombia.

1842
The Treaty of Nanjing gives Britain trading rights in China.

Differentiated Instruction   Solutions for All Learners

L1 Special Needs   **L2 Less Proficient Readers**
For students acquiring basic skills:
Adapted Reading and Note Taking Study Guide
Adapted Note Taking, pp. 104, 106, 108, 110
Adapted Section Summaries, pp. 105, 107, 109, 111

L2 English Language Learners
For Spanish-speaking students:
Spanish Reading and Note Taking Study Guide
Spanish Note Taking, pp. 104, 106, 108, 110
Spanish Section Summaries, pp. 105, 107, 109, 111

Concept Connector

 Essential Question Review

To connect prior knowledge with what you have learned in this chapter, answer the questions below in your Concept Connector journal. Use the journal in the Reading and Note Taking Study Guide to record your answers (or go to www.phschool.com Web Code: nbd-2107).

1. **Science** Major shifts in how scientists thought about the world in the 1500s and 1600s led to a period called the Scientific Revolution. During this time, advances in mathematics, astronomy, medicine, chemistry, and other fields led to many new discoveries. In this chapter, you read about how scientific advances during the Industrial Revolution changed the way in which people lived and worked. Choose one scientific discovery or advance from the Scientific Revolution and one from the Industrial Revolution. In a few sentences, explain how these discoveries changed peoples' lives.

2. **Technology** During the High Middle Ages, an agricultural revolution brought about great change. Compare the technological changes that took place from about 1000 to 1300 to the changes that took place during the Industrial Revolution. Think about the following:
   * how a new invention or method may have solved a problem
   * how a new technology or methods sparked economic growth
   * how the invention or method changed peoples lives

3. **Economic Systems** The revival of trade during the High Middle Ages resulted in a commercial revolution. Hundreds of years later, the Industrial Revolution brought about changes in business. In what ways were the changes during the two periods similar? Think about the following:
   * new business practices
   * role of guilds and labor unions

■ Connections to Today

1. **Technology: Power Outage** In August 2003, people in Canada and the northeastern part of the United States found out just how much their lives depend on electricity. When an energy plant unexpectedly shut down, it led to the largest power outage in North America's history—more than 50 million people were left in the dark.

   Lights and elevators stopped working in skyscrapers, and workers had to carefully make their way down darkened stairways. Others were trapped on trains or stuck in traffic jams caused by inoperable traffic lights. Airports experienced extended delays. Business slowed because Internet servers were not functioning properly, phone systems crashed, computerized cash registers could not ring up sales, and ATMs went down. With today's linked power grids, the possibility of more massive blackouts that disrupt the lives of millions of people across county, state, and international lines is very real. What economic effects might a power outage have?

2. **Belief Systems: Social Darwinism** British philosopher and Social Darwinist Herbert Spencer coined the phrase "survival of the fittest," meaning that the strong grow in power and influence over the weaker members of society. Social Darwinists promoted the beliefs that the group was more important than the individual, and that privileged, powerful people had the right to make decisions about those whom they believed were inferior.

   These ideas had horrific consequences for people throughout the world. For example, they led to unethical medical experimentation on people of color, abuse of the mentally ill, and countless acts of violence toward people of "different" religions, races, and ethnicities. To what degree do you think Social Darwinism is still a part of our culture today?

1859
Charles Darwin publishes *On the Origin of Species*. Many religious leaders denounce his theory of evolution.

1869
Germany legalizes labor unions.

1903
Wilbur and Orville Wright conduct tests of their airplane at Kitty Hawk, North Carolina.

 **History** *Interactive*

For: Interactive timeline
Web Code: nbp-2151

 1860 **1875** **1890** **1905**

1861
Tsar Alexander II emancipates Russian serfs.

1884
European nations carve up Africa at the Berlin Conference.

1898
Spanish-American War is fought.

1914
The Panama Canal opens.

Concept Connector

Chapter Assessment

Terms, People, and Places

1. dynamo
2. stock
3. Racism
4. standard of living
5. mutual-aid society
6. Realism

Main Ideas

7. Sample: New technology, such as electricity, sparked industrial growth and made production faster and less expensive. New forms of transportation moved people and goods farther and faster. The telegraph and telephone connected people quickly over great distances.

8. New technologies required the investment of more money; big, powerful corporations allowed more people to invest in business.

9. Improved: safety increased, police and fire departments were better organized, disease declined, standard of living rose. Worsened: neighborhoods were overcrowded, the number of slums increased.

10. Before the Industrial Revolution, nobles and peasants made up the two main social classes, and their roles were defined by their relationship to the land. By the late 1800s, a large middle class had emerged.

11. that all atoms were alike, the age of Earth, and biblical accounts of creation

12. Romantics emphasized freedom, imagination, and emotion. Realists focused on ordinary subjects, the harsh side of city life, and the ills of the time.

Chapter Focus Question

13. New technology caused massive industrial growth and brought about the rise of the cities. Three distinct social classes emerged. As big business boomed, it employed thousands of workers, controlled the markets of entire industries, and enabled more people to invest in business.

Critical Thinking

14. Sample: New developments made it possible for people to move from one country to another and from rural to urban areas more easily.

Chapter Assessment

Terms, People, and Places

Choose the italicized term in parentheses that best completes each sentence.

1. A *(dynamo/cartel)* is a machine that generates electricity.
2. Business owners sell *(corporations/stock)*, or shares in their companies, to investors.
3. *(Racism/Germ theory)* is the belief that one racial group is superior to another.
4. The *(cult of domesticity/standard of living)* measures the quality and availability of necessities and comforts in a society.
5. A self-help group to aid sick or injured workers is called a *(social gospel/mutual-aid society)*.
6. *(Impressionism/Realism)* attempted to represent the world as it was.

Main Ideas

Section 1 (pp. 298–304)
7. Describe the impact of new technology on industry, transportation, and communication.
8. Why did big businesses emerge during the Industrial Revolution?

Section 2 (pp. 305–309)
9. How did the Industrial Revolution improve city life? How did it make city life worse?

Section 3 (pp. 312–318)
10. How did the Industrial Revolution influence the class structure of Western Europe?
11. What existing beliefs did new scientific theories challenge?

Section 4 (pp. 319–322)
12. How did artists, composers, writers, and others respond to industrialization?

Chapter Focus Question
13. What were the technological, social, and economic effects of the Industrial Revolution?

Critical Thinking

14. **Geography and History** How did technology affect the movement of people and goods in the 1800s and in the early 1900s?

15. **Identify Point of View** How might each of the following have viewed the Industrial Revolution: (a) an inventor, (b) an entrepreneur, (c) a worker?

16. **Draw Conclusions** Do you think women's lives improved as a result of the Industrial Revolution? Why or why not?

17. **Draw Inferences** Referring to *Oliver Twist*, Dickens wrote that "to show [criminals] as they really are, for ever skulking uneasily through the dirtiest paths of life . . . would be a service to society." How does his claim reflect the goals of realism?

18. **Summarize** How would you describe Victorian middle-class values?

19. **Demonstrate Reasoned Judgment** Some historians have suggested that we are now in a third phase of the Industrial Revolution, characterized by information technology and computers. Do you agree or disagree? Explain the reasons for your answer.

20. **Analyzing Visuals** Which artistic movement of the 1800s does *Cathedral of Rouen, Afternoon* (right) by Claude Monet reflect: romanticism, realism, or impressionism? Explain your reasoning.

● Writing About History

In this chapter's four Section Assessments, you developed skills for writing a problem-solution essay.

Writing a Problem-Solution Essay The second Industrial Revolution ushered in a period of great change to the modern world. Write a problem-solution essay about a topic relating to the content in this chapter.

Prewriting
- Choose the topic that interests you most. If you have a personal interest in a problem and its solution, your essay will be easier to develop.
- Narrow your topic.

- Make a list of details, facts, and examples that proves there is a problem. Then, identify the specific parts of your solution.

Drafting
- Develop a working thesis and choose information to support it.
- Organize the paragraphs in a logical order so that readers can understand the solution you propose.

Revising
- Use the guidelines for revising your essay on page SH12 of the Writing Handbook.

---

15. Sample: (a) as an opportunity to use creativity (b) as an opportunity for investment and profit (c) as an opportunity for an improved standard of living

16. Sample: Yes. Women in some countries won the right to vote and the right to get an education.

17. By portraying the criminal world, he may inspire society to solve the problem.

18. Values included a strict code of etiquette and respectability.

19. Students should support their opinion with relevant evidence.

20. Impressionism; answers include the use of individual brush strokes and natural light.

Document-Based Assessment

Birth of the Modern City

The birth of the modern city helped to define the Industrial Age. The documents below show that the modern city represented progress, but not without costs.

Document A

"The first shock of a great earthquake had, just at that period, rent the whole neighborhood to its center. Traces of its course were visible on every side. Houses were knocked down; streets broken through and stopped; deep pits and trenches dug in the ground; enormous heaps of earth and clay thrown up; buildings that were undermined and shaking, propped by great beams of wood. . . . In short, the yet unfinished and unopened Railroad was in progress; and, from the very core of all this dire disorder, trailed smoothly away, upon its mighty course of civilization and improvement."

—from ***Dombey and Son*** by Charles Dickens

Document B

Selected Inventions, 1824–1911	
Cement	1824
Locomotive	1830
Dynamite	1866
Telephone	1876
Cash register	1879
Electric trolley car	1884–1887
Steel alloy	1891
Self-starting auto	1911

SOURCE: *The World Almanac*, 2004

Document C

Population of Major Cities		
City	1850	1900
Berlin, Germany	419,000	1,889,000
London, England	2,685,000	6,586,000
Moscow, Russia	365,000	989,000
New York, United States	696,000	3,437,000
Paris, France	1,053,000	2,714,000

SOURCE: *International Historical Statistics*

Document D

Brooklyn Bridge, 1883

Analyzing Documents

Use your knowledge of the industrial age and Documents A, B, C, and D to answer questions 1–4.

1. The cause of the earthquake described in Document A was
   - A an underground fault in London.
   - B poorly constructed tall buildings.
   - C construction of a railroad.
   - D deep pits and trenches in the ground.

2. Which inventions from Document B had the most impact on New York City at the time Document D was created?
   - A trolley cars, steel alloy, cash registers
   - B dynamite, telephones, cash registers
   - C cement, locomotives, telephones
   - D cement, locomotives, dynamite

3. Which trend does Document C illustrate?
   - A the shift in population from Europe to the United States
   - B the shift in population from East Coast to West Coast
   - C the increase in population of cities
   - D the decrease in rural population

4. **Writing Task** What were the most significant features of the modern city? Why? Use the information from Documents A through D, as well as what you've learned in this chapter, to support your opinion.

● Writing About History

As students begin the assignment, refer them to page SH10 of the **Writing Handbook** for help in writing a problem-solution essay. Remind them of the steps they should take to complete their assignment, including prewriting, drafting, and revising. For help in revising, remind them to use the guidelines on page SH12 of the **Writing Handbook**.

Students' problem-solution essays should focus on a narrow topic that they can address effectively in their essay. They should develop a working thesis with specific details and examples to support it. Their essays should show evidence of thoughtful organization and be free of grammatical and spelling errors. For scoring rubrics for writing assignments, see **Assessment Rubrics,** p. 8.

 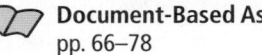

CHAPTER PLANNER

Section	Core Instruction L3	Differentiated Instruction L1 L2 L4	

Section 1
Building a German Nation

⏱ **2 periods, 1 block**

OBJECTIVES
- Identify several events that promoted German unity during the early 1800s.
- Explain how Bismarck unified Germany.
- Analyze the basic political organization of the new German empire.

Focus Question *How did Otto von Bismarck, the chancellor of Prussia, lead the drive for German unity?*

All in One Teaching Resources, Unit 3
Reading Strategy: Recognize Sequence, p. 27
Vocabulary Builder: Context Clues, p. 26
Outline Map: Unification of Germany, 1865–1871, p. 35
Section 1 Quiz, p. 21

Reading and Note Taking Study Guide
Note Taking Study Guide, p. 112
Section 1 Summary, p. 113

Note Taking Transparencies, 151

WITNESS HISTORY Audio CD
Blood and Iron

Progress Monitoring Transparencies, 90

Color Transparencies, 131

Teaching Resources, Skills Handbook
Prereading the Chapter, pp. 1–2
Word Knowledge Rating Form, p. 3
K-W-L Chart, p. 4

L1 **Adapted Reading and Note Taking Study Guide**
Note Taking Study Guide, p. 112 SN
Section 1 Summary, p. 113 SN

L2 **Adapted Reading and Note Taking Study Guide**
Note Taking Study Guide, p. 112 LPR
Section 1 Summary, p. 113 LPR

Spanish Reading and Note Taking Study Guide
Note Taking Study Guide, p. 112 ELL
Section 1 Summary, p. 113 ELL

L4 **Extend Activity,**
Teacher's Edition, p. 333 AR, GT

*Student Edition Audio SN

*Guided Reading Audio, Spanish ELL

*Student Edition Audio LPR

Differentiated Instruction Activity,
Teacher's Edition, p. 332 LPR

Section 2
Germany Strengthens

⏱ **1.5 periods, .75 block**

OBJECTIVES
- Describe how Germany became an industrial giant.
- Explain why Bismarck was called the Iron Chancellor.
- List the policies of Kaiser William II.

Focus Question *How did Germany increase its power after unifying in 1871?*

All in One Teaching Resources, Unit 3
Section 2 Quiz, p. 22

Reading and Note Taking Study Guide
Note Taking Study Guide, p. 114
Section 2 Summary, p. 115

Note Taking Transparencies, 152

WITNESS HISTORY Audio CD
The New German Empire

Color Transparencies, 132

Progress Monitoring Transparencies, 91

L1 **Adapted Reading and Note Taking Study Guide**
Note Taking Study Guide, p. 114 SN
Section 2 Summary, p. 115 SN

L2 **Adapted Reading and Note Taking Study Guide**
Note Taking Study Guide, p. 114 LPR
Section 2 Summary, p. 115 LPR

L4 **All in One Teaching Resources, Unit 3**
Viewpoints: Bismarck and His Strategies, p. 48 AR, GT

Spanish Reading and Note Taking Study Guide
Note Taking Study Guide, p. 114 ELL
Section 2 Summary, p. 115 ELL

Differentiated Instruction Activity,
Teacher's Edition, p. 336 AR, GT

Extend Activity,
Teacher's Edition, p. 337 AR, GT

*Audio support is available for all sections.

Assessment Resources
- **AYP Benchmark Assessments,** Benchmark Test 2, pp. 37–39; Midyear Outcome Test, pp. 40–42
- **Progress Monitoring Transparencies,** 90–94
- **SuccessTracker™,** Chapter 10
- **Document-Based Assessment,** pp. 66–78
- *ExamView*® **Test Bank CD-ROM,** Chapter 10
- **All in One Teaching Resources, Unit 3,** Chapter Tests A and B, pp. 37–42
- **Progress Monitoring** *Online* **Quizzes,** Chapter 10
- **Assessment Rubrics**

Differentiated Instruction Key
- L1 Special Needs
- L2 Basic to Average
- L3 All Students
- L4 Average to Advanced
- LPR Less Proficient Readers
- AR Advanced Readers
- SN Special Needs Students
- GT Gifted and Talented
- ELL English Language Learner

Section	Core Instruction L3	Differentiated Instruction L1 L2 L4	

Section 3
Unifying Italy

 1.5 periods, .75 block

OBJECTIVES
- List the key obstacles to Italian unity.
- Understand what roles Count Camillo Cavour and Giuseppe Garibaldi played in the struggle for Italy.
- Describe the challenges that faced the new nation of Italy.

Focus Question *How did influential leaders help to create a unified Italy?*

All in One Teaching Resources, Unit 3
Section 3 Quiz, p. 23

Reading and Note Taking Study Guide
Note Taking Study Guide, p. 116
Section 3 Summary, p. 117

Note Taking Transparencies, 153

WITNESS HISTORY Audio CD
Stirrings of Nationalism

Progress Monitoring Transparencies, 92

Color Transparencies, 133

L1 Adapted Reading and Note Taking Study Guide
Note Taking Study Guide, p. 116 SN
Section 3 Summary, p. 117 SN

L2 Adapted Reading and Note Taking Study Guide
Note Taking Study Guide, p. 116 LPR
Section 3 Summary, p. 117 LPR

L4 All in One Teaching Resources, Unit 3
Biography: Giuseppe Verdi, p. 29 AR, GT

Differentiated Instruction Activity,
Teacher's Edition, p. 339 SN

Spanish Reading and Note Taking Study Guide
Note Taking Study Guide, p. 116 ELL
Section 3 Summary, p. 117 ELL

Differentiated Instruction Activity,
Teacher's Edition, p. 339 LPR

Extend Activity,
Teacher's Edition, p. 342 AR, GT

Section 4
Nationalism Threatens Old Empires

 .5 period, .25 block

OBJECTIVES
- Describe how nationalism contributed to the decline of the Hapsburg empire.
- List the main characteristics of the Dual Monarchy.
- Understand how the growth of nationalism affected the Ottoman empire.

Focus Question *How did the desire for national independence among ethnic groups weaken and ultimately destroy the Austrian and Ottoman empires?*

All in One Teaching Resources, Unit 3
Outline Map: The Ottoman Empire, About 1815, p. 33
Outline Map: The Balkans, 1878, p. 34
Geography Quiz, p. 36
Section 4 Quiz, p. 24

Reading and Note Taking Study Guide
Note Taking Study Guide, p. 118
Section 4 Summary, p. 119

Note Taking Transparencies, 154

WITNESS HISTORY Audio CD
Balkan Nationalism

Progress Monitoring Transparencies, 93

Color Transparencies, 134, 135

L1 Adapted Reading and Note Taking Study Guide
Note Taking Study Guide, p. 118 SN
Section 4 Summary, p. 119 SN

L2 Adapted Reading and Note Taking Study Guide
Note Taking Study Guide, p. 118 LPR
Section 4 Summary, p. 119 LPR

L4 Extend Activity,
Teacher's Edition, p. 346 AR, GT

Differentiated Instruction Activity,
Teacher's Edition, p. 344 SN

Spanish Reading and Note Taking Study Guide
Note Taking Study Guide, p. 118 ELL
Section 4 Summary, p. 119 ELL

Differentiated Instruction Activity,
Teacher's Edition, p. 344 LPR, ELL

Section 5
Russia: Reform and Reaction

 2.5 periods, 1.25 blocks

OBJECTIVES
- Describe major obstacles to progress in Russia.
- Explain why tsars followed a cycle of absolutism, reform, and reaction.
- Explain why the problems of industrialization contributed to the outbreak of revolution.

Focus Question *Why did industrialization and reform come more slowly to Russia than to Western Europe?*

All in One Teaching Resources, Unit 3
Section 5 Quiz, p. 25

Reading and Note Taking Study Guide
Note Taking Study Guide, p. 120
Section 5 Summary, p. 121
Concept Connector, pp. 262, 284, 291

Note Taking Transparencies, 155

WITNESS HISTORY Audio CD
Plight of the Serfs

Progress Monitoring Transparencies, 94

Color Transparencies, 136

Witness History Discovery School™ video program, *Crisis and Revolution in Russia*

L1 Adapted Reading and Note Taking Study Guide
Note Taking Study Guide, p. 120 SN
Section 5 Summary, p. 121 SN
Concept Connector, pp. 262, 284, 291 SN

L2 Adapted Reading and Note Taking Study Guide
Note Taking Study Guide, p. 120 LPR
Section 5 Summary, p. 121 LPR
Concept Connector, pp. 262, 284, 291 LPR

L4 All in One Teaching Resources, Unit 3
Primary Source: *The Execution in Semyonovsky Square,* by Feodor Dostoyevsky, p. 31 AR, GT
Link to Literature: "How I Found America," by Anzia Yezierska, p. 30 AR, GT
Primary Source: *From Declaration of Alexander II Emancipating the Serfs,* p. 32 AR, GT

Differentiated Instruction Activity,
Teacher's Edition, p. 351 SN

Spanish Reading and Note Taking Study Guide
Note Taking Study Guide, p. 120 ELL
Section 5 Summary, p. 121 ELL
Concept Connector, pp. 262, 284, 291 ELL

Differentiated Instruction Activity,
Teacher's Edition, p. 351 LPR

Extend Activity,
Teacher's Edition, pp. 328c, 353 AR, GT

CHAPTER PLANNER

PROFESSIONAL DEVELOPMENT

Author's Notes

The Birth of the Modern Ideologies: Nationalism

In some ways *nationalism* blazed even more brightly than liberalism across the nineteenth-century sky. Nineteenth-century nationalists built on the teachings of the eighteenth-century German cultural nationalists who preached the importance of each people's national spirit. They also drew on the model of the French Revolution, which had unleashed powerful patriotic energies, both in France and in nations conquered by Napoleon. Nationalists in the nineteenth century dedicated their energies to unifying divided peoples such as the Italians and the Germans. Or they labored to win national self-determination for oppressed minorities such as the Eastern European, mostly Slavic peoples ruled by the Austrian, Russian, and Ottoman emperors. Later in the century, however, nationalism turned chauvinistic. It began to be used to justify the aggressive or expansionist policies of German or French or British governments.

Nationalists believed that common language and literature, history and custom welded a people into a larger whole—the nation. Some of them believed in a folk soul or folk spirit uniting a people spiritually. Many saw a national character that they shared with their fellow nationals: Frenchmen were naturally more civilized and artistic than other peoples, Germans more philosophical or scientific, Britons better at government and more practical, and so forth.

These apostles of nationality preached their patriotic creed in terms of native soil and blood—the black earth of Russia, for instance, or German or Anglo-Saxon blood. They expressed their loyalty with reverence for such concrete symbols as the national flag or the national anthem. They wept when the French Tricolor or the British Union Jack passed by, and they sang the "Marseillaise," "Britannia Rules the Waves," or "Germany Over All" with passion.

—Anthony Esler, *The Human Venture: From Prehistory to the Present*, (Upper Saddle River, New Jersey: Pearson Education, 2004), p. 492

Extend Online

The Winter Palace

Have students examine the Winter Palace in St. Petersburg, Russia. Ask them to discuss their observations on the Palace, compare it with what they have read about the lives of the peasants and serfs, and draw connections to the revolutions and reforms in Russia. Use these steps to help students complete the activity.

Prepare for the Activity Explain that beginning in the 1760s, the Winter Palace was the primary residence for the Russian tsars. It was the scene of many important events in Russian history, including Bloody Sunday, shown at left.

Conduct the Activity For help in starting the activity, send students to **Web Code nbe-2201,** where they can explore details of the Winter Palace. Ask students to view the photographs of the palace and write a paragraph summarizing their observations.

Follow-Up Conduct a class discussion based on the following questions: How would you describe the Winter Palace? Given their surroundings, how sympathetic do you think Russian tsars were toward the plight of Russian serfs and peasants? How do you think Russian peasants and serfs felt about the palace? Why do you think the palace became a key spot for demonstrations? Why do you think the Russians continue to preserve the palace, now a part of the State Hermitage Museum?

Differentiated Instruction Solutions for All Learners

Finding High-Interest Ideas L1 L2

Students will be more willing and interested in engaging in discussion if they are discussing a topic of high interest. As students read the chapter, ask them to write down one idea that could be used to conduct an interesting discussion. Ideas could relate to something they do not understand, something that seems interesting, or something that relates to something else they know, but should provoke interest and more ideas.

Model the process by giving students both rich and poor ideas for a discussion.

Rich idea: What factors led these serfs to revolt?

Poor idea: What kind of clothing did the serfs wear?

Revising the Text L4

Advanced readers typically understand that differing groups' perspectives on an event can vary tremendously. To reinforce this, ask students to rewrite a section of text explaining a conflict from one side's perspective. Follow the steps below:

1. Assign members of the class a selection of reading from their text that discusses an event or conflict that involves more than one nation or group.

2. Ask students to choose one of the nations or groups involved and research its role in the event.

3. Have students rewrite the text to reflect the perspective of the chosen nation or group.

Revisions should include changes in word choice that may make the reader more sympathetic to the perspective of the selected nation, events that were omitted from this text, and rationales for why the group acted in a certain way.

Modeling Reading and Writing Skills

Acknowledge Opposition Explain that in this chapter students will be writing a persuasive essay. (See Writing About History, p. 356.) Point out that in a persuasive essay, students need to acknowledge opposing arguments and make counter arguments to refute these. List the following arguments on the board and ask students to provide opposing arguments. Remind them that arguments should be constructed logically.

A Junk food should be banned from schools because American teenagers have poor nutritional habits.
B. Teenagers should be able to get into R-rated films if their parents give permission.
C. Video games lead to violent behavior by inciting aggressive feelings in those who play them.

As each opposing argument is presented, invite another student to counter it or do so yourself. Provide the following example as a guide:

A. Opposing argument: Teenagers should be given information to make informed decisions about junk food because developing decision-making habits is important.
Counterargument: Students can develop their decision-making habits as they choose among healthy options.

Identify Implied Main Ideas Explain to students that main ideas do not have to be directly stated. They may be implied. To determine an implied main idea, readers must look for the idea that links all the details in a section of text and then construct a sentence that states the main idea.

To model the skill, read aloud the text under the heading *Intrigue with France*, in Section 3. Point out the details: Cavour negotiated a secret deal with Napoleon, provoked war, and then annexed Lombardy. All three details are linked by Cavour's actions. The main idea, then, is that Cavour manipulated events to further Italian unification.

Teach With Technology

PresentationEXPRESS™
Premium DVD

- Teach this chapter's core content using **PresentationExpress™ Premium,** which includes dynamic lecture notes, interactive game shows, songs, videos, and the *ExamView® QuickTake* assessment tool.

- To introduce this chapter using **PresentationExpress™ Premium,** start by asking students **Which of the following statements do you most agree with? (A) Feeling pride in one's country is a citizen's responsibility. (B) Feeling little pride in one's country makes a person a troublemaker. (C) Feeling too much pride in one's country can be dangerous. (D) Expressing pride in one's country—in any fashion—is a citizen's right.** Take a class poll or record students' answers using the QuickTake feature and discuss their responses. Point out that in this chapter, they will read about various ways that nationalism—or pride in and devotion to one's country—shaped Europe in the 1800s. Continue introducing the chapter using the chapter opener slide show and Witness History audio.

Technology Resources

- Student**EXPRESS** CD-ROM, Chapter 10

- Teacher**EXPRESS** CD-ROM, Chapter 10

- Presentation**EXPRESS™** **Premium DVD,** Chapter 10

- **WITNESS HISTORY** Audio CD, Chapter 10

- *ExamView* Test Bank CD-ROM, English and Spanish, Chapter 10

- **Guided Reading Audio,** Spanish, Chapter 10

- **Student Edition Audio,** Chapter 10

- **Witness History Discovery School™** video program, *Crisis and Revolution in Russia*

- **Experience It! Multimedia Pack**

Nationalism Triumphs in Europe
1800–1914

Bibliography

For the Teacher
Blackbourn, David. *History of Germany, 1780–1918: The Long Nineteenth Century,* 2nd ed. Malden, MA: Blackwell Publishing, 2002.

Chapman, Tim. *Imperial Russia, 1801–1905.* New York: Routledge, 2001.

Glenny, Misha. *The Balkans: Nationalism, War and the Great Powers, 1804–1999.* Viking, 2000.

For the Student
L2 McGowen, Tom. *Frederick the Great, Bismarck, and the Building of the German Empire in World History.* Berkeley Heights, NJ: Enslow, 2002.

L3 Bachrach, Deborah. *The Crimean War.* San Diego, CA: Lucent, 1998.

L4 Garibaldi, Giuseppe. *My Life,* trans. by Stephen Parkin, London: Hesperus Press, 2004.

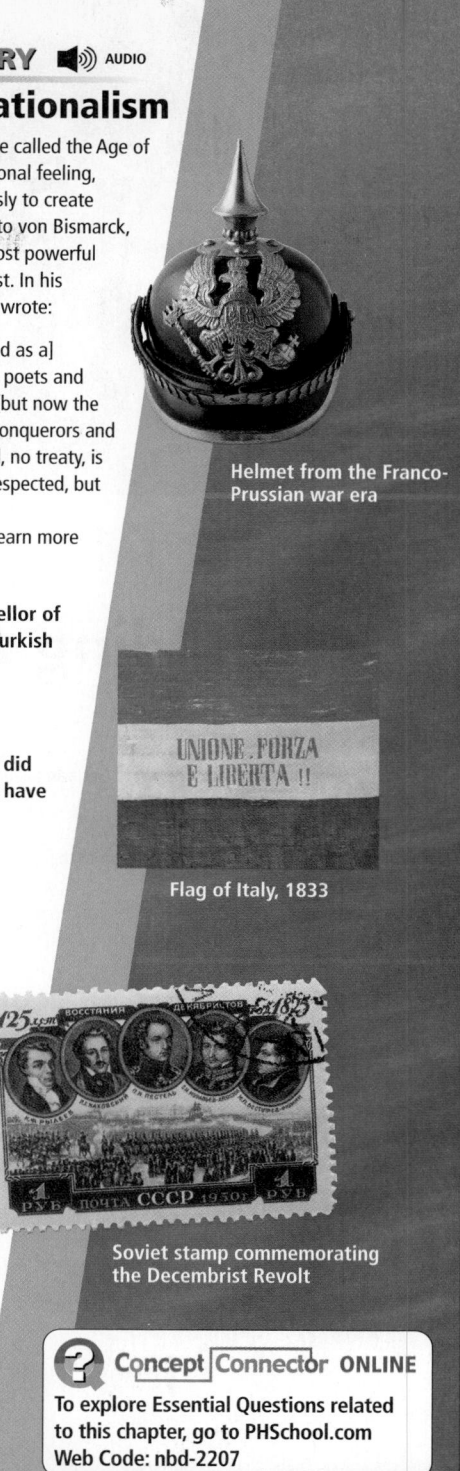

WITNESS HISTORY 🔊 AUDIO

The Price of Nationalism

The last half of the 1800s can be called the Age of Nationalism. By harnessing national feeling, European leaders fought ruthlessly to create strong, unified nations. Under Otto von Bismarck, Germany emerged as Europe's most powerful empire—but at a considerable cost. In his 1870 diary, Crown Prince Friedrich wrote:

❝[Germany had once been admired as a] nation of thinkers and philosophers, poets and artists, idealists and enthusiasts . . . [but now the world saw Germany as] a nation of conquerors and destroyers, to which no pledged word, no treaty, is sacred. . . . We are neither loved nor respected, but only feared.❞

Listen to the Witness History audio to learn more about nationalism.

Helmet from the Franco-Prussian war era

◀ Otto von Bismarck (center), chancellor of Germany, meets with European and Turkish leaders at the Congress of Berlin.

Chapter Preview

Chapter Focus Question What effects did nationalism and the demand for reform have in Europe?

Flag of Italy, 1833

Section 1
Building a German Nation

Section 2
Germany Strengthens

Section 3
Unifying Italy

Section 4
Nationalism Threatens Old Empires

Soviet stamp commemorating the Decembrist Revolt

Section 5
Russia: Reform and Reaction

Use the ☑ **Quick Study Timeline** at the end of this chapter to preview chapter events.

? Concept Connector ONLINE

To explore Essential Questions related to this chapter, go to PHSchool.com
Web Code: nbd-2207

Chapter-Level Resources

All in One Vocabulary Builder; Reading Strategy; Enrichments; Outline Maps; Geography Quiz; Chapter Tests
■ Document-Based Assessments
■ AYP Monitoring Assessments
■ *ExamView* Test Bank CD-ROM
■ Guided Reading Audio (Spanish)
■ Student Edition Audio

Previewing the Chapter

■ **WITNESS HISTORY** In the age of nationalism, Germany was formed out of smaller German states into one powerful nation. However, not everyone approved of the results. Explain that Crown Prince Friedrich was the son of William I of Prussia and later ruled, very briefly, as Emperor of Germany. Read aloud the Witness History selection or play the accompanying audio. Ask students to summarize Friedrich's complaint about the results of German nationalism and to explain why he might have felt that way, despite his position.

🔊 AUDIO **Witness History Audio CD,** The Price of Nationalism

■ **Analyzing the Visuals** Ask students to study the painting on this spread. Ask **What questions do the painting and the Witness History selection bring to mind?** (*Sample: Who is Bismarck? What did he do to make people fear Germany?*) Tell students to write down their questions to return to later.

■ **Focus** Write the Chapter Focus Question on the board. Tell students to keep this question in mind as they read the chapter. (*Answer appears with Chapter Assessment answers.*) Have students preview the section titles for this chapter.

Note Taking Study Guide With Concept Connector Journal
For online access: Web code: nbd-2207
For print alternative: Reading and Note Taking Study Guide booklet

Objectives

As you teach this section, keep students focused on the following objectives to help them answer the Section Focus Question and master core content.

- Identify several events that promoted German unity during the early 1800s.
- Explain how Bismarck unified Germany.
- Analyze the basic political organization of the new German empire.

Prepare to Read

Build Background Knowledge **L3**

Remind students that in this period, many peoples with a shared cultural and ethnic heritage were moved by nationalist feelings to establish their own political identities. Have students predict how nationalism might contribute to the creation of a German nation.

Set a Purpose **L3**

- **WITNESS HISTORY** Read the selection aloud or play the audio.

  ◀)) AUDIO **Witness History Audio CD,** Blood and Iron

  Ask **What's the main idea of Bismarck's speech?** (*Military force is more effective than slow political change or reform.*) **Based on the picture and speech, what kind of leader do you think Bismarck will be?** (*Sample: strong, forceful, and aggressive*)

- **Focus** Point out the Section Focus Question and write it on the board. Tell students to refer to this question as they read. (*Answer appears with Section 1 Assessment answers.*)

- **Preview** Have students preview the Section Objectives and the list of Terms, People, and Places.

- **Reading Skill** Have students use the *Reading Strategy: Recognize Sequence* worksheet.

All in One Teaching Resources, Unit 3, p. 27

Otto von Bismarck

Helmet from the Franco-Prussian war era

WITNESS HISTORY ◀)) AUDIO

Blood and Iron

Prussian legislators waited restlessly for Otto von Bismarck to speak. He wanted them to vote for more money to build up the army. Liberal members opposed the move. Bismarck rose and dismissed their concerns:

“ Germany does not look to Prussia's liberalism, but to her power. . . . The great questions of the day are not to be decided by speeches and majority resolutions—that was the mistake of 1848 and 1849—but by blood and iron! ”
—Otto von Bismarck, 1862

Focus Question How did Otto von Bismarck, the chancellor of Prussia, lead the drive for German unity?

Building a German Nation

Objectives

- Identify several events that promoted German unity during the early 1800s.
- Explain how Bismarck unified Germany.
- Analyze the basic political organization of the new German empire.

Terms, People, and Places

Otto von Bismarck	annex
chancellor	kaiser
Realpolitik	Reich

Note Taking

Reading Skill: Recognize Sequence Keep track of the sequence of events that led to German unification by completing a chart like the one below. Add more boxes as needed.

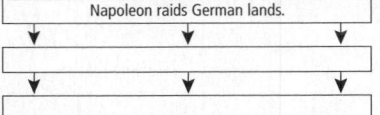

Napoleon raids German lands.

Otto von Bismarck delivered his "blood and iron" speech in 1862. It set the tone for his future policies. Bismarck was determined to build a strong, unified German state, with Prussia at its head.

Taking Initial Steps Toward Unity

In the early 1800s, German-speaking people lived in a number of small and medium-sized states as well as in Prussia and the Austrian Hapsburg empire. Napoleon's invasions unleashed new forces in these territories.

Napoleon Raids German Lands Between 1806 and 1812, Napoleon made important territorial changes in German-speaking lands. He annexed lands along the Rhine River for France. He dissolved the Holy Roman Empire by forcing the emperor of Austria to agree to the lesser title of king. He also organized a number of German states into the Rhine Confederation.

At first, some Germans welcomed the French emperor as a hero with enlightened, modern policies. He encouraged freeing the serfs, made trade easier, and abolished laws against Jews. However, not all Germans appreciated Napoleon and his changes. As people fought to free their lands from French rule, they began to demand a unified German state.

Napoleon's defeat did not resolve the issue. At the Congress of Vienna, Metternich pointed out that a united Germany would require dismantling the government of each German state. Instead, the peacemakers created the German Confederation, a weak alliance headed by Austria.

Vocabulary Builder

Use the information below and the following resources to teach the high-use word from this section.
All in One Teaching Resources, Unit 3, p. 26; **Teaching Resources, Skills Handbook,** p. 3

High-Use Word	Definition and Sample Sentence
edit, p. 333	*vt.* to make additions, deletions, or other changes to a piece of writing He **edited** his paper very carefully before handing it in to his professor.

Economic Changes Promote Unity In the 1830s, Prussia created an economic union called the *Zollverein* (TSAWL fur yn). It dismantled tariff barriers between many German states. Still, Germany remained politically fragmented.

In 1848, liberals meeting in the Frankfurt Assembly again demanded German political unity. They offered the throne of a united German state to Frederick William IV of Prussia. The Prussian ruler, however, rejected the notion of a throne offered by "the people."

✓ **Checkpoint** What was the German Confederation?

Bismarck Unites Germany

Otto von Bismarck succeeded where others had failed. Bismarck came from Prussia's Junker (YOONG kur) class, made up of conservative landowning nobles. Bismarck first served Prussia as a diplomat in Russia and France. In 1862, King William I made him prime minister. Within a decade, the new prime minister had become **chancellor**, or the highest official of a monarch, and had used his policy of "blood and iron" to unite the German states under Prussian rule.

Geography *Interactive*
For: Audio guided tour
Web Code: nbp-2211

Unification of Germany, 1865–1871

Royal house medal of the Hohenzollerns

Prussia, 1865
Added to Prussia, 1866
Added to form North German Confederation, 1867
Added to form German empire, 1871
Boundary of German empire, 1871
✳ Battle sites
Route of Prussian armies in Austro-Prussian War
Route of German armies in Franco-Prussian War

Map Skills In the early 1800s, people living in German-speaking states had local loyalties. By the mid-1800s, however, they were developing a national identity.

1. **Locate:** (a) Prussia (b) Silesia (c) Bavaria (d) Schleswig
2. **Region** What area did Prussia add to its territory in 1866?
3. **Analyzing Information** Why do you think Austrian influence was greater among the southern German states than among the northern ones?

History Background

Bismarck's Appointment The decision to make Bismarck prime minister came in the midst of a government crisis. Liberals in Prussia's parliament had blocked King William I's plans to reorganize and increase the army. After months of disagreement between king and parliament, the king was about to abdicate his throne in favor of his son. Then advisors suggested he turn to Bismarck. The two met and discussed the situation. Bismarck told the king that, in his view, parliamentary government "must be avoided at all costs, even if by a period of dictatorship." He went on: "I will rather perish with the King than forsake your Majesty in the contest with parliamentary government." Convinced that Bismarck would support his claims to royal power, William named him prime minister.

■ **Note Taking** Have students read this section using the Structured Read Aloud strategy (TE, p. T20). As they read, have students fill in the flowchart showing the sequence of events that led to German unification.

Reading and Note Taking Study Guide, p. 112

Teach

Steps Toward Unity L3

Instruct

■ **Introduce** Have students read the first paragraph under the red heading. Ask them to predict how a foreign invasion by Napoleon led to the rise of nationalist feelings among Germans.

■ **Teach** Ask **In what ways did Napoleon's rule bring about a desire for German unity?** *(The Rhine Confederation probably encouraged people to believe that German states could unite. Also, many Germans wanted to free themselves from French rule and unite into a strong German state.)* **What was the *Zollverein* and how did it encourage German unification?** *(It was a German economic union created by Prussia that did away with trade barriers; however, the states still remained politically divided.)*

Independent Practice

Have students write a letter from the perspective of someone who lived in a German state in the early 1800s to a cousin in another country, explaining what has changed since Napoleon invaded.

Monitor Progress

As students fill in their flowcharts, make sure that they understand that the German Confederation and the *Zollverein* were steps towards unification. For a completed version of the flowchart, see
📖 **Note Taking Transparencies,** 151

Answers

✓ a weak alliance headed by Austria that was created after the defeat of Napoleon

Map Skills
1. Review locations with students.
2. Schleswig, Holstein, Hanover, and parts of central Germany
3. Austria was geographically closer to many of the southern German states than was Prussia.

Bismarck Unites Germany/Birth of the German Empire

Instruct

- **Introduce: Key Terms** Ask students to find the key term *Realpolitik* (in blue) in the text and explain it. Ask students whether they think governments today follow the ideas of *Realpolitik*. Do students think leaders are justified in taking any kind of action—even those that are illegal or immoral—if it strengthens the nation?

- **Teach** Clarify for students that Bismarck's main goal was to increase Prussia's power, not to fulfill German nationalist aims. Then display **Color Transparency 131: Events Leading to German Unification** Discuss the steps Bismarck took to reach his goal of unification. Ask students to list examples when Bismarck employed *Realpolitik* as he worked to create a unified German state. Then ask **Who ruled Germany after it was united?** (*Prussia's King Wilhelm I became Germany's kaiser.*) **How did Prussia unite Germany?** (*By defeating Germany's traditional enemy, France, Prussia won the allegiance of Germans in other states.*)

  📺 **Color Transparencies,** 131

- **Quick Activity** Have students access **Web Code nbp-2211** to take the **Geography Interactive Audio Guided Tour** and then answer the map skills questions in the text.

Independent Practice

Have students fill in the Outline Map *Unification of Germany, 1865–1871* and label the territories and states that became part of Prussia in 1866 and those that formed the German empire in 1871.

All in One Teaching Resources, Unit 3, p. 35

Monitor Progress

- Check Reading and Note Taking Study Guide entries for student understanding.

- Check answers to map skills questions and the accuracy of Outline Maps.

Answer

PRIMARY SOURCE in von Moltke's view, to establish its power and assert its leadership of the German states

---

Master of Realpolitik Bismarck's success was due in part to his strong will. He was a master of **Realpolitik** (ray AHL poh lee teek), or realistic politics based on the needs of the state. In the case of Realpolitik, power was more important than principles.

Although Bismarck was the architect of German unity, he was not really a German nationalist. His primary loyalty was to the Hohenzollerns (hoh un TSAWL urnz), the ruling dynasty of Prussia, who represented a powerful, traditional monarchy. Through unification, he hoped to bring more power to the Hohenzollerns.

Strengthening the Army As Prussia's prime minister, Bismarck first moved to build up the Prussian army. Despite his "blood and iron" speech, the liberal legislature refused to vote for funds for the military. In response, Bismarck strengthened the army with money that had been collected for other purposes. With a powerful, well-equipped military, he was then ready to pursue an aggressive foreign policy. Over the next decade, Bismarck led Prussia into three wars. Each war increased Prussian prestige and power and paved the way for German unity.

Prussia Declares War With Denmark and Austria Bismarck's first maneuver was to form an alliance in 1864 with Austria. Prussia and Austria then seized the provinces of Schleswig and Holstein from Denmark. After a brief war, Prussia and Austria "liberated" the two provinces and divided up the spoils. Austria was to administer Holstein and Prussia was to administer Schleswig.

In 1866, Bismarck invented an excuse to attack Austria. The Austro-Prussian War lasted just seven weeks and ended in a decisive Prussian victory. Prussia then **annexed,** or took control of, several other north German states.

Bismarck dissolved the Austrian-led German Confederation and created a new confederation dominated by Prussia. Austria and four other southern German states remained independent. Bismarck's motives, as always, were strictly practical. Attempting to conquer Austria might have meant a long and risky war for Prussia.

War and Power

In 1866, Field Marshal Helmuth von Moltke analyzed the importance of Prussia's war against Austria. Why, according to von Moltke, did Prussia go to war against Austria?

Primary Source

❝ The war of 1866 was entered on not because the existence of Prussia was threatened, nor was it caused by public opinion and the voice of the people; it was a struggle, long foreseen and calmly prepared for, recognized as a necessity by the Cabinet, not for territorial expansion, for an extension of our domain, or for material advantage, but for an ideal end—the establishment of power. Not a foot of land was exacted from Austria. . . . Its center of gravity lay out of Germany; Prussia's lay within it. Prussia felt itself called upon and strong enough to assume the leadership of the German races. ❞

Austro-Prussian War painting (above) and a medal of victory (left)

Differentiated Instruction — Solutions for All Learners

L2 Less Proficient Readers

On the board, draw a timeline of German unification and include the following years: 1830s, 1848, 1862, 1864, 1866, 1870, and 1871. Ask students to use their completed graphic organizers to supply key events, and write their answers on the board. Then ask **What two main elements led to German unification?** (*militarism and diplomacy*)

Use the following resources to help students acquire basic skills.

Adapted Reading and Note Taking Study Guide

- Adapted Note Taking Study Guide, p. 112
- Adapted Section Summary, p. 113

France Declares War on Prussia In France, the Prussian victory over Austria angered Napoleon III. A growing rivalry between the two nations led to the Franco-Prussian War of 1870.

Germans recalled only too well the invasions of Napoleon I some 60 years earlier. Bismarck played up the image of the French menace to spur German nationalism. For his part, Napoleon III did little to avoid war, hoping to mask problems at home with military glory.

Bismarck furthered the crisis by rewriting and then releasing to the press a telegram that reported on a meeting between King William I and the French ambassador. Bismarck's underlining editing of the "Ems dispatch" made it seem that William I had insulted the Frenchman. Furious, Napoleon III declared war on Prussia, as Bismarck had hoped.

A superior Prussian force, supported by troops from other German states, smashed the badly organized and poorly supplied French soldiers. Napoleon III, old and ill, surrendered within a few weeks. France had to accept a humiliating peace.

✓ **Checkpoint** What techniques did Bismarck use to unify the German states?

Birth of the German Empire

Delighted by the victory over France, princes from the southern German states and the North German Confederation persuaded William I of Prussia to take the title **kaiser** (KY zur), or emperor. In January 1871, German nationalists celebrated the birth of the second **Reich,** or empire. They called it that because they considered it heir to the Holy Roman Empire.

A constitution drafted by Bismarck set up a two-house legislature. The Bundesrat (BOON dus raht), or upper house, was appointed by the rulers of the German states. The Reichstag (RYKS tahg), or lower house, was elected by universal male suffrage. Because the Bundesrat could veto any decisions of the Reichstag, real power remained in the hands of the emperor and his chancellor.

✓ **Checkpoint** How was the new German government, drafted by Bismarck, structured?

Vocabulary Builder

edit—(ED it) v. to make additions, deletions, or other changes to a piece of writing

---

SECTION 1 Assessment

Progress Monitoring Online
For: Self-quiz with vocabulary practice
Web Code: nba-2211

Terms, People, and Places
1. For each term, person, or place listed at the beginning of the section, write a sentence explaining its significance.

Note Taking
2. **Reading Skill: Recognize Sequence** Use your completed chart to answer the Focus Question: How did Otto von Bismarck, the chancellor of Prussia, lead the drive for German unity?

Comprehension and Critical Thinking
3. **Summarize** What territorial and economic changes promoted German unity?
4. **Analyze Information** Identify three examples of Bismarck's use of Realpolitik.
5. **Draw Conclusions** How did the emperor and his chancellor retain power in the new German government?

● **Writing About History**
Quick Write: Generate Arguments Choose one topic from this section that you could use to write a persuasive essay. For example, you could write about whether Germany's war against Austria was justifiable. Make sure that the topic you choose to write about has at least two sides that could provoke an argument.

Section 1 Assessment

1. Sentences should reflect an understanding of each term, person, or place listed at the beginning of the section.
2. Bismarck strengthened the army and directed the military in three successful wars. After the last victory, over France, leaders of most of the German states invited the Prussian king to become emperor of all Germany.
3. the annexation of the Rhine lands by Napoleon; the creation of the German Confederation, and the creation of the *Zollverein*
4. Sample: He used nonmilitary funds to build up the Prussian army, invented an excuse to attack Austria, and tricked Napoleon III into war with Prussia.
5. The upper house, which could veto decisions of the lower house, was appointed by the rulers of the German states.

● **Writing About History**
Topics should be drawn from the section and have at least two ideas that could provoke argument.

For additional assessment, have students access **Progress Monitoring Online** at **Web Code nba-2211.**

Objectives

As you teach this section, keep students focused on the following objectives to help them answer the Section Focus Question and master core content.

- Describe how Germany became an industrial giant.
- Explain why Bismarck was called the Iron Chancellor.
- List the policies of Kaiser William II.

Build Background Knowledge L3

Ask students to recall the methods Bismarck used to unify the German states. Based on their previous reading, have them predict what steps Bismarck might take to strengthen the newly created Germany.

Set a Purpose L3

- **WITNESS HISTORY** Read the selection aloud or play the audio.

   AUDIO **Witness History Audio CD,** The New German Empire

  Ask **What is the main idea of von Treitschke's article?** *(The territories of Alsace and Lorraine rightfully belong to Germany.)* **What does this suggest about the newly united Germany?** *(that it will try to grow in size and power)*

- **Focus** Point out the Section Focus Question and write it on the board. Tell students to refer to this question as they read. *(Answer appears with Section 2 Assessment answers.)*

- **Preview** Have students preview the Section Objectives and the list of Terms, People, and Places.

- **Note Taking** Have students read this section using the Paragraph Shrinking strategy (TE, p. T20). As they read, have students fill in the flowchart sequencing the causes and effects of a strong German nation.

  Reading and Note Taking Study Guide, p. 114

French bayonet

Prussian soldiers at Versailles

WITNESS HISTORY ◀)) AUDIO

The New German Empire

In 1870, German historian Heinrich von Treitschke (vawn TRYCH kuh) wrote a newspaper article demanding the annexation of Alsace and Lorraine from France. A year later, annexation became a condition of the peace settlement in the Franco-Prussian War:

❝ The sense of justice to Germany demands the lessening of France. . . . These territories are ours by the right of the sword, and . . . [by] virtue of a higher right—the right of the German nation, which will not permit its lost children to remain strangers to the German Empire. ❞

Focus Question How did Germany increase its power after unifying in 1871?

Germany Strengthens

Objectives

- Describe how Germany became an industrial giant.
- Explain why Bismarck was called the Iron Chancellor.
- List the policies of Kaiser William II.

Terms, People, and Places

Kulturkampf
William II
social welfare

Note Taking

Reading Skill: Recognize Sequence Keep track of the sequence of events described in this section by completing a chart like the one below. List the causes that led to a strong German nation.

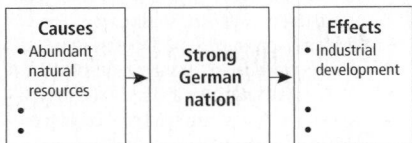

Causes	Strong German nation	Effects
• Abundant natural resources • •		• Industrial development • •

In January 1871, German princes gathered in the glittering Hall of Mirrors at the French palace of Versailles. They had just defeated Napoleon III in the Franco-Prussian War. Once home to French kings, the palace seemed the perfect place to proclaim the new German empire. To the winners as well as to the losers, the symbolism was clear: French domination of Europe had ended. Germany was now the dominant power in Europe.

Germany Becomes an Industrial Giant

In the aftermath of unification, the German empire emerged as the industrial giant of the European continent. By the late 1800s, German chemical and electrical industries were setting the standard worldwide. Among the European powers, German shipping was second only to Britain's.

Making Economic Progress Germany, like Great Britain, possessed several of the factors that made industrialization possible. Germany's spectacular growth was due in part to ample iron and coal resources, the basic ingredients for industrial development. A disciplined and educated workforce also helped the economy. The German middle class and educated professionals helped to create a productive and efficient society that prided itself on its sense of responsibility and deference to authority. Germany's rapidly growing population—from 41 million in 1871 to 67 million by 1914—also provided a huge home market along with a larger supply of industrial workers.

Vocabulary Builder

Use the information below and the following resources to teach the high-use words from this section.
All in One **Teaching Resources, Unit 3,** p. 26; **Teaching Resources, Skills Handbook,** p. 3

High-Use Words	Definitions and Sample Sentences
synthetic, p. 335	*adj.* prepared or made artificially Her jacket was made of **synthetic** fur because she did not like to wear real fur.
coordinate, p. 335	*vt.* to design or adjust so as to have harmonious action The florist **coordinated** different flowers to make a beautiful arrangement.

The new nation also benefited from earlier progress. During the 1850s and 1860s, Germans had founded large companies and built many railroads. The house of Krupp (kroop) boomed after 1871, becoming an enormous industrial complex that produced steel and weapons for a world market. Between 1871 and 1914, the business tycoon August Thyssen (TEES un) built a small steel factory of 70 workers into a giant empire with 50,000 employees. Optics was another important industry. German industrialist and inventor Carl Zeiss built a company that became known for its telescopes, microscopes, and other optical equipment.

Promoting Scientific and Economic Development German industrialists were the first to see the value of applied science in developing new products such as <u>synthetic</u> chemicals and dyes. Industrialists, as well as the government, supported research and development in the universities and hired trained scientists to solve technological problems in their factories.

The German government also promoted economic development. After 1871, it issued a single currency for Germany, reorganized the banking system, and <u>coordinated</u> railroads built by the various German states. When a worldwide depression hit in the late 1800s, Germany raised tariffs to protect home industries from foreign competition. The leaders of the new German empire were determined to maintain economic strength as well as military power.

✔ **Checkpoint** What factors did Germany possess that made industrialization possible there?

The Iron Chancellor

As chancellor of the new German empire, Bismarck pursued several foreign-policy goals. He wanted to keep France weak and isolated while building strong links with Austria and Russia. He respected British naval power but did not seek to compete in that arena. "Water rats," he said, "do not fight with land rats." Later, however, he would take a more aggressive stand against Britain as the two nations competed for overseas colonies.

BIOGRAPHY

Otto von Bismarck

Otto von Bismarck (1815–1898) spent his early years on his father's country estate. He worked briefly as a civil servant, but found the work boring. At 24, Bismarck resigned his post as a bureaucrat. "My ambition strives more to command than to obey," the independent-minded young man explained.

The resignation did not end his career in government. While he was a delegate to a United Diet that was called by Prussian King Frederick William IV, Bismarck's conservative views and passionate speeches in defense of government policies won him the support of the king. He then served as a diplomat to the German Federation. He became chancellor of the German empire in 1871, a position he held for 19 years. **What path did Bismarck take to win political power?**

Vocabulary Builder

<u>synthetic</u>—(sin THET ik) *adj.* prepared or made artificially

Vocabulary Builder

<u>coordinate</u>—(koh AWR dih nate) *v.* to design or adjust so as to have harmonious action

Link to Science

The Color Mauve The first synthetic dye was devised accidentally in 1856 by an 18-year-old chemistry student named William Henry Perkin. Searching for a synthetic form of quinine—the drug used to treat malaria—he instead produced a new chemical remarkable for its bright reddish purple color. Though Perkin named it "Tyrian Purple," the French name *mauveine* caught on. Soon, chemists were producing many new dyes, which quickly became part of clothing, wallpaper, and other decorative items. By the late 1800s German companies dominated the chemical and dye industries. Along with dyes, they turned out such new products as drugs like aspirin and, in the early 1900s, predecessors of modern plastics.

The Iron Chancellor/Kaiser William II ⓛ③

Instruct

- **Introduce** Display **Color Transparency 132:** *The Proclamation of Wilhelm as Kaiser of the New German Reich.* Point out that although the painting's subject is William I's coronation, Bismarck is prominent, in white, at the center of the work. Ask **What does this painting indicate about Bismarck's role in Germany's new position in Europe?** *(He will play a central role.)* **What generalization can be made about the predominance of military uniforms in this scene?** *(Military strength was important to the leaders of Germany.)*

  📖 **Color Transparencies,** 132

- **Teach** Ask **Why did Bismarck fear socialists?** *(They called for democratic and social reforms, and Bismarck thought that they would undermine the workers' support for the government.)* **How did Bismarck appeal to workers to woo them away from socialism?** *(He passed laws to protect workers. Germany became a pioneer in social reform.)* **How did Kaiser William II continue Bismarck's policies?** *(He continued to provide social welfare programs and build up the military.)*

- **Quick Activity** Ask student groups to make charts that compare Bismarck's and William II's personalities and ideas on government.

Independent Practice

Viewpoints To help students better understand competing views of Bismarck, have them read *Bismarck and His Strategies* and complete the worksheet.

All in One Teaching Resources, Unit 3, p. 28

Monitor Progress

Check Reading and Note Taking Study Guide entries for student understanding.

Answers

✔️ He felt that they were the two greatest threats to Germany because they drew people's allegiance away from the German state.

Analyzing Political Cartoons
1. by showing that it was a strategic and competitive partnership
2. Bismarck attempted to undermine the Catholic Church, but his moves ultimately increased people's loyalty to the church, which became more politically powerful.

Analyzing Political Cartoons

A Political Game of Chess This political cartoon shows Otto von Bismarck and Pope Pius IX trying to checkmate each other in a game of chess.

1. How does this cartoon reflect the relationship between Bismarck and the Catholic Church?
2. How did the conflict between church and state affect German politics in the 1870s?

On the domestic front, Bismarck applied the same ruthless methods he had used to achieve unification. The Iron Chancellor, as he was called, sought to erase local loyalties and crush all opposition to the imperial state. He targeted two groups—the Catholic Church and the Socialists. In his view, both posed a threat to the new German state.

Campaign Against the Church After unification, Catholics made up about a third of the German population. Bismarck, who was Lutheran, distrusted Catholics—especially the clergy—whose first loyalty, he believed, was to the pope instead of to Germany.

In response to what he saw as the Catholic threat, Bismarck launched the *Kulturkampf* (kool TOOR kahmpf), or "battle for civilization," which lasted from 1871 to 1878. His goal was to make Catholics put loyalty to the state above allegiance to the Church. The chancellor had laws passed that gave the state the right to supervise Catholic education and approve the appointment of priests. Other laws closed some religious orders, expelled the Jesuits from Prussia, and made it compulsory for couples to be married by civil authority.

Bismarck's moves against the Catholic Church backfired. The faithful rallied behind the Church, and the Catholic Center party gained strength in the Reichstag. A realist, Bismarck saw his mistake and worked to make peace with the Church.

Campaign Against the Socialists Bismarck also saw a threat to the new German empire in the growing power of socialism. By the late 1870s, German Marxists had organized the Social Democratic party, which called for parliamentary democracy and laws to improve conditions for the working class. Bismarck feared that socialists would undermine the loyalty of German workers and turn them toward revolution. Following a failed assassination plot against the kaiser, Bismarck had laws passed that dissolved socialist groups, shut down their newspapers, and banned their meetings. Once again, repression backfired. Workers were unified in support of the socialist cause.

Bismarck then changed course. He set out to woo workers away from socialism by sponsoring laws to protect them. By the 1890s, Germans had health and accident insurance as well as old-age insurance to provide retirement benefits. Thus, under Bismarck, Germany was a pioneer in social reform. Its system of economic safeguards became the model for other European nations.

Although workers benefited from Bismarck's plan, they did not abandon socialism. In fact, the Social Democratic party continued to grow in strength. By 1912, it held more seats in the Reichstag than any other party. Yet Bismarck's program showed that conditions for workers could be improved without the upheaval of a revolution. Later, Germany and other European nations would build on Bismarck's social policies, greatly increasing government's role in providing for the needs of its citizens.

✔️ **Checkpoint** Why did Bismarck try to crush the Catholic Church and the Socialists?

Kaiser William II

In 1888, **William II** succeeded his grandfather as kaiser. The new emperor was supremely confident in his abilities and wished to put his own stamp on Germany. In 1890, he shocked Europe by asking the dominating Bismarck to resign. "There is only one master in the Reich," he said, "and that is I."

William II seriously believed that his right to rule came from God. He expressed this view when he said:

❝My grandfather considered that the office of king was a task that God had assigned to him. . . . That which he thought I also think. . . . Those who wish to aid me in that task . . . I welcome with all my heart; those who oppose me in this work I shall crush.❞
—William II

Not surprisingly, William resisted efforts to introduce democratic reforms. At the same time, however, his government provided programs for **social welfare,** or programs to help certain groups of people. His government also provided services such as cheap transportation and electricity. An excellent system of public schools, which had flourished under Bismarck, taught students obedience to the emperor along with reading, writing, and mathematics.

Like his grandfather, William II lavished funds on the German military machine, already the most powerful in Europe. He also launched an ambitious campaign to expand the German navy and win an overseas empire to rival those of Britain and France. William's nationalism and aggressive military stance helped increase tensions on the eve of World War I.

Social Reform
Under Bismarck's leadership, Germany pioneered social reform. By 1884, Germans had health and accident insurance. By 1889, they had disability and old-age insurance. *Why did Bismarck introduce these social reforms?*

✓ **Checkpoint** Why did William II ask Bismarck to resign in 1890?

SECTION 2 Assessment

Progress Monitoring Online
For: Self-quiz with vocabulary practice
Web Code: nba-2222

Terms, People, and Places
1. For each term, person, or place listed at the beginning of the section, write a sentence explaining its significance.

Note Taking
2. **Reading Skill: Recognize Sequence** Use your completed chart to answer the Focus Question: How did Germany increase its power after unifying in 1871?

Comprehension and Critical Thinking
3. **Summarize** How did Germany become an industrial giant in the late 1800s?
4. **Demonstrate Reasoned Judgment** Do you think Bismarck's methods were justified by his social reforms? Explain.
5. **Draw Conclusions** Do you think the supporters of a democratic government in Germany in the late 1800s had hope of success? Explain.

● **Writing About History**
Quick Write: Answer Opposing Arguments To write a strong persuasive essay, you need to address arguments that can be used to contradict your position. Choose a topic from the section. For example, think about whether a government should guarantee that its citizens have adequate healthcare. List the arguments for and against your position on a piece of paper.

Section 2 Assessment

1. Sentences should reflect an understanding of each term, person, or place listed at the beginning of the section.
2. Germany emerged as an industrial giant, became economically stable, and made social reforms, all of which increased the new nation's power.
3. Germany had ample coal and iron resources, a disciplined and educated workforce, a growing population, and had made previous progress in building industries and railroads.
4. Sample: No, because an able politician should have been able to achieve these results without resorting to ruthlessness.
5. Sample: Because Bismarck and the emperor possessed most of the power, supporters of democratic government probably had little hope of success.

● **Writing About History**
Responses should describe a topic chosen from this section, and give at least three arguments in support of the position and three arguments against it.

For additional assessment, have students access **Progress Monitoring Online** at **Web Code nba-2222.**

Step-by-Step Instruction

Objectives

As you teach this section, keep students focused on the following objectives to help them answer the Section Focus Question and master core content.

- List the key obstacles to Italian unity.
- Understand what roles Count Camillo Cavour and Giuseppe Garibaldi played in the struggle for Italy.
- Describe the challenges that faced the new nation of Italy.

Prepare to Read

Build Background Knowledge L3

Ask students to recall the issues facing the German states during unification. Ask them to predict what kinds of issues nationalist leaders in Italy would face as they tried to unify their country.

Set a Purpose L3

- **WITNESS HISTORY** Read the selection aloud or play the audio.
  - 🔊 AUDIO **Witness History Audio CD,** Stirrings of Nationalism

  Ask **What event is Mazzini describing?** (*An Italian rebel was begging for money so that he could escape after a failed revolt against Austria.*) **Why was this significant to him?** (*He saw this as a turning point when he realized that the Italians should be free from foreign rule.*)

- **Focus** Point out the Section Focus Question and write it on the board. Tell students to refer to this question as they read. (*Answer appears with Section 3 Assessment answers.*)

- **Preview** Have students preview the Section Objectives and the list of Terms, People, and Places.

- **Note Taking** Have students read this section using the Guided Questioning strategy (TE, p. T20). As they read, have them fill in the timeline with events that led to Italy's unification.
  - 📝 **Reading and Note Taking Study Guide,** p. 116

Giuseppe Mazzini, around 1865

Flag of Italy, 1833

UNIONE FORZA E LIBERTA !!

WITNESS HISTORY 🔊 AUDIO

Stirrings of Nationalism

After a failed revolution against Austrian rule in northern Italy, many rebels, fearing retribution, begged for funds to pay for safe passage to Spain. Giuseppe Mazzini (mat SEE nee), still a boy, described his reaction to the situation:

❝ He (a rebel) held out a white handkerchief, merely saying, 'For the refugees of Italy.' My mother . . . dropped some money into the handkerchief. . . . That day was the first in which a confused idea presented itself to my mind . . . an idea that we Italians could and therefore ought to struggle for the liberty of our country. . . . ❞
—Giuseppe Mazzini, *Life and Writings*

Focus Question How did influential leaders help to create a unified Italy?

Unifying Italy

Objectives
- List the key obstacles to Italian unity.
- Understand what roles Count Camillo Cavour and Giuseppe Garibaldi played in the struggle for Italy.
- Describe the challenges that faced the new nation of Italy.

Terms, People, and Places

Camillo Cavour
Giuseppe Garibaldi
anarchist
emigration

Note Taking

Reading Skill: Recognize Sequence As you read, create a timeline showing the sequence of events from 1831 to 1871 that led to Italian unification.

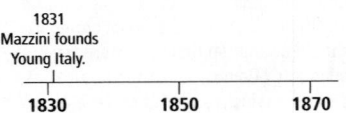

1831
Mazzini founds
Young Italy.

1830   1850   1870

Although the people of the Italian peninsula spoke the same language, they had not experienced political unity since Roman times. By the early 1800s, though, Italian patriots—including Mazzini, who would become a revolutionary—were determined to build a new, united Italy. As in Germany, unification was brought about by the efforts of a strong state and furthered by a shrewd, ruthless politician—Count **Camillo Cavour** (kah VOOR).

Obstacles to Italian Unity

For centuries, Italy had been a battleground for ambitious foreign and local princes. Frequent warfare and foreign rule had led people to identify with local regions. The people of Florence considered themselves Tuscans, those of Venice Venetians, those of Naples Neapolitans, and so on. But as in Germany, the invasions of Napoleon had sparked dreams of national unity.

The Congress of Vienna, however, ignored the nationalists who hoped to end centuries of foreign rule and achieve unity. To Prince Metternich of Austria, the idea of a unified Italy was laughable. At Vienna, Austria took control of much of northern Italy, while Hapsburg monarchs ruled various other Italian states. In the south, a French Bourbon ruler was put in charge of Naples and Sicily.

In response, nationalists organized secret patriotic societies and focused their efforts on expelling Austrian forces from northern Italy. Between 1820 and 1848, nationalist revolts exploded across the region. Each time, Austria sent in troops to crush the rebels.

Vocabulary Builder

Use the information below and the following resources to teach the high-use words from this section.
All in One Teaching Resources, Unit 3, p. 26; **Teaching Resources, Skills Handbook,** p. 3

High-Use Words	Definitions and Sample Sentences
constitute, p. 339	*vt.* to set up; establish You need eleven players to **constitute** a soccer team.
successor, p. 340	*n.* a person who succeeds another to an office or rank The senator decided not to run for reelection, and he campaigned for his assistant to become his **successor**.

Mazzini Establishes Young Italy In the 1830s, the nationalist leader Giuseppe Mazzini founded Young Italy. The goal of this secret society was "to <u>constitute</u> Italy, one, free, independent, republican nation." In 1849, Mazzini helped set up a revolutionary republic in Rome, but French forces soon toppled it. Like many other nationalists, Mazzini spent much of his life in exile, plotting and dreaming of a united Italy.

Nationalism Takes Root "Ideas grow quickly," Mazzini once said, "when watered by the blood of martyrs." Although revolution had failed, nationalist agitation had planted seeds for future harvests.

To nationalists like Mazzini, a united Italy made sense not only because of geography, but also because of a common language and history. Nationalists reminded Italians of the glories of ancient Rome and the medieval papacy. To others, unity made practical economic sense. It would end trade barriers among the Italian states and stimulate industry.

✓ **Checkpoint** What forces hindered Italian unity?

The Struggle for Italy

After 1848, leadership of the Risorgimento (ree sawr jee MEN toh), or Italian nationalist movement, passed to the kingdom of Sardinia, which included Piedmont, Nice, and Savoy as well as the island of Sardinia. Its constitutional monarch, Victor Emmanuel II, hoped to join other states to his own, thereby increasing his power.

Cavour Becomes Prime Minister In 1852, Victor Emmanuel made Count Camillo Cavour his prime minister. Cavour came from a noble family but favored liberal goals. He was a flexible, practical, crafty politician, willing to use almost any means to achieve his goals. Like Bismarck in Prussia, Cavour was a monarchist who believed in Realpolitik.

Once in office, Cavour moved first to reform Sardinia's economy. He improved agriculture, had railroads built, and encouraged commerce by supporting free trade. Cavour's long-term goal, however, was to end Austrian power in Italy and annex the provinces of Lombardy and Venetia.

Opposing Austrian Rule
In March 1848, nationalists in Venice took over the city's arsenal and declared the establishment of the Republic of Venice (left). Their success was short lived, however, as the republic was soon disbanded and Venice again fell under the rule of Austria in 1849. The image above is a draft of a speech written by Camillo Cavour in 1861.

Vocabulary Builder

constitute—(KAHN stuh toot) *v.* to set up; establish

The Struggle for Italy

Instruct

- **Introduce: Key Terms** Ask students to find the name *Camillo Cavour* (in blue) in the text and identify who he was. Ask students to think about how Cavour was different from and similar to Otto von Bismarck as they read.

- **Teach** Refer students to the Infographic on the next page. Ask students to trace the steps nationalists followed to unify Italy. Ask **How did Cavour further nationalist aims?** *(He reformed Sardinia's economy, then joined with Britain and France in the Crimean War, which gave Sardinia a part in the peace talks and gained the attention of Napoleon III. Cavour made an alliance with Napoleon in case of war with Austria, then he provoked that war. Sardinia won the war, and other northern states also revolted against Austria and then joined Sardinia.)*

- **Quick Activity** Display **Color Transparency 133: *Right Leg in the Boot at Last.*** Use the lesson suggested in the transparency book to guide a discussion on how the political cartoon illustrates the importance of Garibaldi's role in unification.

   🏛 **Color Transparency,** 133

Independent Practice

Web Code nbp-2232 will take students to an interactive timeline. Have students complete the interactivity and then answer the questions in the text.

Monitor Progress

Refer students to the visuals in the Infographic on the next page. To help students review the section so far, have them explain the significance of each of the nationalists pictured. *(Mazzini inspired more people to demand liberation; Garibaldi led troops in battle; Cavour organized the state.)*

Vocabulary Builder

<u>successor</u>—(suk SES ur) *n.* a person who succeeds another to an office or rank

---

Intrigue With France In 1855, Sardinia, led by Cavour, joined Britain and France against Russia in the Crimean War. Sardinia did not win territory, but it did have a voice at the peace conference. Sardinia also gained the attention of Napoleon III.

In 1858, Cavour negotiated a secret deal with Napoleon, who promised to aid Sardinia in case it faced a war with Austria. A year later, the shrewd Cavour provoked that war. With help from France, Sardinia defeated Austria and annexed Lombardy. Meanwhile, nationalist groups overthrew Austrian-backed rulers in several other northern Italian states. These states then joined with Sardinia.

Garibaldi's "Red Shirts" Next, attention shifted to the Kingdom of the Two Sicilies in southern Italy. There, Giuseppe Garibaldi (gah ree BAHL dee), a longtime nationalist and an ally of Mazzini, was ready for action. Like Mazzini, Garibaldi wanted to create an Italian republic. He did not hesitate, however, to accept aid from the monarchist Cavour. By 1860, Garibaldi had recruited a force of 1,000 red-shirted volunteers. Cavour provided weapons and allowed two ships to take Garibaldi and his "Red Shirts" south to Sicily. With surprising speed, Garibaldi's forces won control of Sicily, crossed to the mainland, and marched triumphantly north to Naples.

Unity at Last Garibaldi's success alarmed Cavour, who feared that the nationalist hero would set up his own republic in the south. To prevent this, Cavour urged Victor Emmanuel to send Sardinian troops to deal with Garibaldi. Instead, the Sardinians overran the Papal States and linked up with Garibaldi and his forces in Naples.

In a patriotic move, Garibaldi turned over Naples and Sicily to Victor Emmanuel. Shortly afterward, southern Italy voted to approve the move, and in 1861, Victor Emmanuel II was crowned king of Italy.

Two areas remained outside the new Italian nation: Rome and Venetia. Cavour died in 1861, but his <u>successors</u> completed his dream. Italy formed an alliance with Prussia in the Austro-Prussian War and won the province of Venetia. Then, during the Franco-Prussian War in 1870, France was forced to withdraw its troops from Rome. For the first time since the fall of the Roman empire, Italy was a united land.

 Checkpoint What steps did Camillo Cavour take to promote Italian unity?

Challenges Facing the New Nation

Italy faced a host of problems. Like the German empire that Bismarck cemented together out of many states, Italy had no tradition of unity. Few Italians felt ties to the new nation. Strong regional rivalries left Italy unable to solve critical national issues.

Divisions The greatest regional differences were between the north and the south. The north was richer and had more cities than the south. For centuries, northern Italian cities had flourished as centers of business and culture. The south, on the other hand, was rural and poor. Its population was booming, but illiterate peasants could extract only a meager existence from the exhausted farmland.

Hostility between Italy and the Roman Catholic Church further divided the nation. Popes bitterly resented the seizure of the Papal

---

History Background

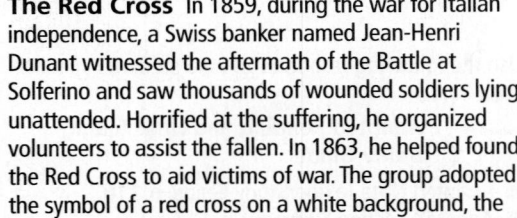

The Red Cross In 1859, during the war for Italian independence, a Swiss banker named Jean-Henri Dunant witnessed the aftermath of the Battle at Solferino and saw thousands of wounded soldiers lying unattended. Horrified at the suffering, he organized volunteers to assist the fallen. In 1863, he helped found the Red Cross to aid victims of war. The group adopted the symbol of a red cross on a white background, the reverse of the colors on the Swiss flag, in tribute to Dunant. At the group's suggestion, 16 nations met in Geneva, Switzerland the following year, where they adopted the first Geneva Convention. It established a set of rules to care for those hurt in war and was the beginning of international humanitarian law. Today, the Red Cross and its sister organization, the Red Crescent, operate in more than 180 countries.

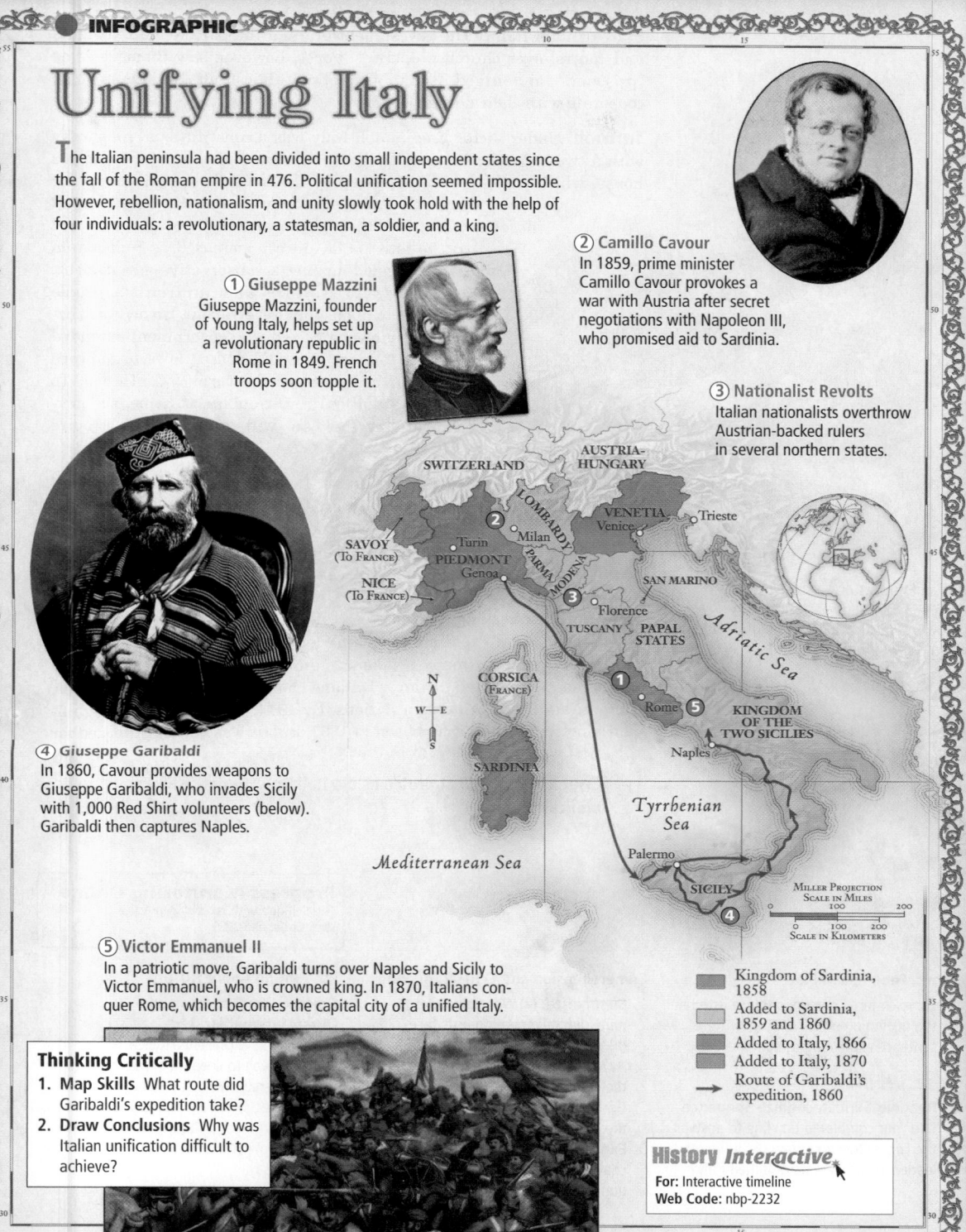

Unifying Italy

The Italian peninsula had been divided into small independent states since the fall of the Roman empire in 476. Political unification seemed impossible. However, rebellion, nationalism, and unity slowly took hold with the help of four individuals: a revolutionary, a statesman, a soldier, and a king.

① Giuseppe Mazzini
Giuseppe Mazzini, founder of Young Italy, helps set up a revolutionary republic in Rome in 1849. French troops soon topple it.

② Camillo Cavour
In 1859, prime minister Camillo Cavour provokes a war with Austria after secret negotiations with Napoleon III, who promised aid to Sardinia.

③ Nationalist Revolts
Italian nationalists overthrow Austrian-backed rulers in several northern states.

④ Giuseppe Garibaldi
In 1860, Cavour provides weapons to Giuseppe Garibaldi, who invades Sicily with 1,000 Red Shirt volunteers (below). Garibaldi then captures Naples.

⑤ Victor Emmanuel II
In a patriotic move, Garibaldi turns over Naples and Sicily to Victor Emmanuel, who is crowned king. In 1870, Italians conquer Rome, which becomes the capital city of a unified Italy.

Map labels: SWITZERLAND, AUSTRIA-HUNGARY, LOMBARDY, VENETIA, Venice, Trieste, SAVOY (To France), Turin, Milan, PIEDMONT, Genoa, PARMA, MODENA, NICE (To France), SAN MARINO, Florence, TUSCANY, PAPAL STATES, Adriatic Sea, CORSICA (France), Rome, KINGDOM OF THE TWO SICILIES, Naples, SARDINIA, Tyrrhenian Sea, Palermo, SICILY, Mediterranean Sea

MILLER PROJECTION
SCALE IN MILES
0 100 200
SCALE IN KILOMETERS
0 100 200

Legend:
- Kingdom of Sardinia, 1858
- Added to Sardinia, 1859 and 1860
- Added to Italy, 1866
- Added to Italy, 1870
- → Route of Garibaldi's expedition, 1860

Thinking Critically
1. **Map Skills** What route did Garibaldi's expedition take?
2. **Draw Conclusions** Why was Italian unification difficult to achieve?

History Interactive
For: Interactive timeline
Web Code: nbp-2232

Challenges Facing the New Nation

Instruct

- **Introduce: Key Terms** Ask students to find the key terms *anarchists* and *emigration* (in blue) in the text and explain their meanings. Ask students to predict how Italy's leaders would deal with these challenges.

- **Teach** Using the Numbered Heads strategy (TE, p. T23), have the class discuss and list the challenges that faced the newly unified Italy. Then ask **How did Italians deal with growing tensions?** *(They protested through a variety of means. Socialists organized strikes, anarchists used violence, and many people left Italy.)* **How did the government deal with Italy's problems?** *(It slowly extended suffrage and made some social reforms. It also distracted people by attempting to build an empire in Ethiopia.)* **Do you think the empire-building strategy was effective? Why or why not?** *(Sample: No, because Italians continued to emigrate.)*

- **Quick Activity** Have students study this section and develop a three-question quiz that can be answered by the information in the section. Then have students exchange their questions with a partner and answer them.

Independent Practice

Have students write an editorial about the problems faced by Italy either before or after unification.

Monitor Progress

Check Reading and Note Taking Study guide entries for understanding.

Connect to Our World

Connections to Today Currently, the nation of Italy covers all of the Italian peninsula except for two areas: Vatican City and San Marino. They are now two of the smallest independent states in Europe. When Italy was unified in 1870, the Pope lost control of the Papal States. However, in 1929, Italy recognized the independence of Vatican City, ruled by the Pope as the center of the Roman Catholic Church. This area, which includes St. Peter's Basilica, covers only about 108 acres and is surrounded by the city of Rome. The other independent state, San Marino, is near Italy's Adriatic coast. This republic was able to maintain its autonomy for nearly a thousand years because of its strong fortresses and its location in the mountains. It played a role in Italian unification, providing asylum to Garibaldi and other revolutionaries. Unified Italy signed a treaty with San Marino in 1862, recognizing its independence.

Answers

Thinking Critically
1. He went south from Genoa to Tuscany, then farther south to Sicily, then east and eventually north to Naples.
2. Sample: Each state had different goals, and many attempts at unification were thwarted by foreign interference.

Assess and Reteach

Assess Progress L3

- Have students complete the Section Assessment.
- Administer the Section Quiz.
- **All in One** Teaching Resources, Unit 3, p. 23
- To further assess student understanding, use
   Progress Monitoring Transparencies, 92

Reteach

If students need more instruction, have them read the section summary.

 Reading and Note Taking Study Guide, p. 117 L3

 Adapted Reading and Note Taking Study Guide, p. 117 L1 L2

 Spanish Reading and Note Taking Study Guide, p. 117 L2

Extend L4

Have students research one of the figures mentioned in this section *(Sample: Camillo Cavour, Giuseppe Garibaldi)* and write a short biography about their subject.

Answers

Caption to avoid the social unrest and get away from population increases

✓ The government faced opposition, regional divisions, and disputes with the Catholic Church, while the people experienced limited suffrage, social unrest, urbanization, and rapid population growth.

States and of Rome. The government granted the papacy limited rights and control over church properties. Popes, however, saw themselves as "prisoners" and urged Italian Catholics—almost all Italians—not to cooperate with their new government.

Turmoil Under Victor Emmanuel, Italy was a constitutional monarchy with a two-house legislature. The king appointed members to the upper house, which could veto bills passed by the lower house. Although the lower house consisted of elected representatives, only a small number of men had the right to vote.

In the late 1800s, unrest increased as radicals on the left struggled against a conservative government. Socialists organized strikes while **anarchists,** people who want to abolish all government, turned to sabotage and violence. Slowly, the government extended suffrage to more men and passed laws to improve social conditions. Still, the turmoil continued. To distract attention from troubles at home, the government set out to win an overseas empire in Ethiopia.

Economic Progress Despite its problems, Italy did develop economically, especially after 1900. Although the nation lacked important natural resources such as coal, industries did sprout up in northern regions. Industrialization, of course, brought urbanization as peasants flocked to the cities to find jobs in factories. As in other countries, reformers campaigned to improve education and working conditions.

The population explosion of this period created tensions. One important safety valve for many people was **emigration,** or movement away from their homeland. Many Italians left for the United States, Canada, and Latin American nations. By 1914, the country was significantly better off than it had been in 1861. But, it was hardly prepared for the great war that broke out in that year.

✓ **Checkpoint** What problems did Italians experience after unification?

Italian Emigration
Emigrants crowd the port of Naples (above). *Why did Italians immigrate to other countries in the early 1900s?*

SECTION 3 Assessment

Progress Monitoring Online
For: Self-quiz with vocabulary practice
Web Code: nba-2233

Terms, People, and Places

1. For each term, person, or place listed at the beginning of the section, write a sentence explaining its significance.

Note Taking

2. **Reading Skill: Recognize Sequence** Use your completed timeline to answer the Focus Question: How did influential leaders help to create a unified Italy?

Comprehension and Critical Thinking

3. **Summarize** (a) What obstacles to unity did Italian nationalists face? (b) What conditions favored unity?

4. **Analyze Information** (a) What was the source of conflict between Garibaldi and Cavour? (b) How was the conflict resolved?

5. **Express Problems Clearly** What challenges did Italians face after unification?

● **Writing About History**

Quick Write: Decide on an Organizational Strategy Using clear organization to present a logical argument is a good way to keep the reader's attention in a persuasive essay. Choose an issue from the section about which you could make an argument. Then write an outline showing how you would organize a persuasive essay.

Section 3 Assessment

1. Sentences should reflect an understanding of each term, person, or place listed at the beginning of the section.
2. Camillo Cavour applied *Realpolitik* to make alliances with other nations and increase Sardinia's power and territory. Mazzini inspired nationalists. Giuseppe Garibaldi recruited his Red Shirts to fight for unification.

3. **(a)** fragmentation into multiple states, regional loyalty, foreign interference **(b)** a common language, a common history, and nationalist opposition to Napoleon's invasions
4. **(a)** Cavour feared that Garibaldi would set up a rival nation in the south. **(b)** Garibaldi turned over his conquered territories to Victor Emmanuel II.
5. regional differences, disputes between the Church and the state, and opposition to a

conservative government; the nation also had to deal with social unrest, urbanization, and rapid population growth

● **Writing About History**
Responses should be in outline form and present a clear, organized argument about an issue covered in this section.

> For additional assessment, have students access **Progress Monitoring Online** at **Web Code nba-2233.**

Hungarian parliament passes legislation funding an army to fight against the Hapsburg empire, 1848

Austria-Hungarian empire flag

WITNESS HISTORY AUDIO

Balkan Nationalism

❝ How is it that they [European powers] cannot understand that less and less is it possible . . . to direct the destinies of the Balkans from the outside? We are growing up, gaining confidence, and becoming independent . . .❞
—Bulgarian statesman on the first Balkan War and the European powers

Focus Question How did the desire for national independence among ethnic groups weaken and ultimately destroy the Austrian and Ottoman empires?

Nationalism Threatens Old Empires

Objectives
- Describe how nationalism contributed to the decline of the Hapsburg empire.
- List the main characteristics of the Dual Monarchy.
- Understand how the growth of nationalism affected the Ottoman empire.

Terms, People, and Places
Francis Joseph
Ferenc Deák
Dual Monarchy

Note Taking

Reading Skill: Recognize Sequence Complete a table like the one below to keep track of the sequence of events that led Austria into the Dual Monarchy. Look for dates and other clues to sequence in the text.

Events in Austrian History	
1840	
1848	
1859	
1866	
1867	

Napoleon had dissolved the Holy Roman Empire, which the Hapsburgs had led for nearly 400 years. Austria's center of power had shifted to Central Europe. Additional wars resulted in continued loss of territory to Germany and Italy. Why did nationalism bring new strength to some countries and weaken others?

In Eastern and Central Europe, the Austrian Hapsburgs and the Ottoman Turks ruled lands that included diverse ethnic groups. Nationalist feelings among these subject peoples contributed to tensions building across Europe.

The Hapsburg Empire Declines

In 1800, the Hapsburgs were the oldest ruling house in Europe. In addition to their homeland of Austria, over the centuries they had acquired the territories of Bohemia and Hungary, as well as parts of Romania, Poland, Ukraine, and northern Italy.

Austria Faces Change Since the Congress of Vienna, the Austrian emperor Francis I and his foreign minister Metternich had upheld conservative goals against liberal forces. "Rule and change nothing," the emperor told his son. Under Francis and Metternich, newspapers could not even use the word *constitution,* much less discuss this key demand of liberals. The government also tried to limit industrial development, which would threaten traditional ways of life.

The Hapsburg Empire/ Dual Monarchy

Instruct **L3**

- **Introduce: Key Terms** Ask students to find the key term ***Dual Monarchy*** (in blue) in the text and explain what it was. Have them predict if this compromise would help restore or further erode Austrian power.

- **Teach** To show the luxurious life at the Vienna court of the Hapsburgs, display **Color Transparency 135: *Court Ball at the Hofburg.*** Discuss the events that led to the decline of the Austrian empire. Then ask **What made the Austrian empire vulnerable to nationalist efforts?** *(It was multinational and extremely fragmented, even within the various regions. Also, it was ethnically diverse, with Germans in the minority; fewer than a quarter of Austrian subjects even spoke German.)*

  📖 **Color Transparencies,** 135

- **Quick Activity** Have students access **Web Code nbp-2243** to take the **Geography Interactive Audio Guided Tour** and then answer the map skills questions in the text.

Independent Practice

Split students into two groups. Assign one group the role of Hungarians immediately after the creation of the Dual Monarchy. Assign the second group the role of Czechs from Bohemia. Have the groups discuss their stance on the Dual Monarchy among themselves, then have the two groups debate each other.

Monitor Progress

As students complete their tables, circulate to make sure they understand that the Dual Monarchy was a compromise to allow the Hungarians to have more control of their government and yet remain under Francis Joseph's rule. For a completed version of the table, see

📖 **Note Taking Transparencies** 154

Answers

✔ He made some limited reforms, such as granting a constitution that set up a legislature.

✔ Subject peoples other than Hungarians resented the Dual Monarchy, and unrest increased.

Austria, however, could not hold back the changes that were engulfing the rest of Europe. By the 1840s, factories were springing up. Soon, the Hapsburgs found themselves facing the problems of industrial life that had long been familiar in Britain—the growth of cities, worker discontent, and the stirrings of socialism.

A Multinational Empire Equally disturbing to the old order were the urgent demands of nationalists. The Hapsburgs presided over a multinational empire. Of its 50 million people at mid-century, fewer than a quarter were German-speaking Austrians. Almost half belonged to different Slavic groups, including Czechs, Slovaks, Poles, Ukrainians, Serbs, Croats, and Slovenes. Often, rival groups shared the same region. The empire also included large numbers of Hungarians and Italians. The Hapsburgs ignored nationalist demands as long as they could. When nationalist revolts broke out in 1848, the government crushed them.

Francis Joseph Grants Limited Reforms Amid the turmoil, 18-year-old **Francis Joseph** inherited the Hapsburg throne. He would rule until 1916, presiding over the empire during its fading days into World War I.

An early challenge came when Austria suffered its humiliating defeat at the hands of France and Sardinia in 1859. Francis Joseph realized he needed to strengthen the empire at home. Accordingly, he made some limited reforms. He granted a new constitution that set up a legislature. This body, however, was dominated by German-speaking Austrians. The reforms thus satisfied none of the other national groups that populated the empire. The Hungarians, especially, were determined to settle for nothing less than total self-government.

✔ **Checkpoint** What actions did Francis Joseph take to maintain power?

Formation of the Dual Monarchy

Austria's disastrous defeat in the 1866 war with Prussia brought renewed pressure for change from Hungarians within the empire. One year later, **Ferenc Deák** (DEH ahk), a moderate Hungarian leader, helped work out a compromise that created a new political power known as the **Dual Monarchy** of Austria-Hungary.

The Austria-Hungary Government Under the agreement, Austria and Hungary were separate states. Each had its own constitution and parliament. Francis Joseph ruled both, as emperor of Austria and king of Hungary. The two states also shared ministries of finance, defense, and foreign affairs, but were independent of each other in all other areas.

Nationalist Unrest Increases Although Hungarians welcomed the compromise, other subject peoples resented it. Restlessness increased among various Slavic groups, especially the Czechs in Bohemia. Some nationalist leaders called on Slavs to unite, insisting that "only through liberty, equality, and <u>fraternal</u> solidarity" could Slavic peoples fulfill their "great mission in the history of mankind." By the early 1900s, nationalist unrest often left the government paralyzed in the face of pressing political and social problems.

✔ **Checkpoint** How did Hungarians and Slavic groups respond to the Dual Monarchy?

Vocabulary Builder
<u>fraternal</u>—(fruh TUR nul) *adj.* brotherly

L1 Special Needs   **L2 Less Proficient Readers**   **L2 English Language Learners**

To help visual learners understand why nationalism challenged the Austrian and Ottoman empires, have them look at the map on the next page. Have them compare the ethnic borders in the main map with the political borders in the inset map. Ask **Why would these borders lead to tensions?** *(Many groups are split by borders and combined with other groups.)*

Use the following resources to help students acquire basic skills.

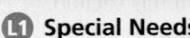 **Adapted Reading and Note Taking Study Guide**

- Adapted Note Taking Study Guide, p. 118
- Adapted Section Summary, p. 119

Major Nationalities in Eastern Europe, 1800–1914

Geography *Interactive*
For: Audio guided tour
Web Code: nbp-2243

GERMANY

POLES

WHITE RUSSIANS

GREAT RUSSIANS

CZECHS

POLES

UKRAINIANS

UKRAINIANS

FRANCE

SLOVAKS

SWITZ.

GERMANS

HUNGARIANS

ROMANIANS

ITALIANS

SLOVENES

ROMANIANS

GREAT RUSSIANS

ITALIANS

CROATS

ITALY

SERBIANS

ROMANIA

BOSNIAKS   SERBIA

ROMANIANS

Black Sea

Adriatic Sea

MONTENEGRINS

BULGARIANS

MONT.

ALBANIANS

30°E

40°N

Mediterranean Sea

MACEDONIANS

TURKS

10°E

GREEKS   *Aegean Sea*

Conic Projection
0   200   400 mi
0   200   400 km

GREECE

Colors reflect the major languages spoken
in Eastern Europe, 1800 to 1914.

The Balkans, 1878

RUSSIA

AUSTRIA-HUNGARY

Bosnia-
Herzegovina
(occupied by
Austria)

ROMANIA

SERBIA

Danube

Black Sea

ITALY

Bulgaria
(autonomous)

MONTENEGRO

Adriatic Sea

Eastern Rumelia
(semi-autonomous)

⊗ Constantinople

40°N

Conic Projection
0   300 mi
0   300 km

Aegean Sea

GREECE

Independent
Balkan states

Mediterranean Sea

Ottoman Empire

20°E   30°E   Crete

Map Skills In the late 1800s, the Balkans had become a center of conflict, as various peoples and empires competed for power.

1. **Locate** (a) Black Sea (b) Ottoman empire (c) Serbia (d) Greece (e) Austria-Hungary
2. **Place** Which four large seas border the Balkan Peninsula?
3. **Identify Central Issues** Why do you think competing interests in the Balkans led the region to be called a powder keg?

The Ottoman Empire Collapses

Instruct

- **Introduce** Explain to students that the Ottoman empire, like the Austrian empire, was enormous and contained many diverse states and ethnic groups. As they read, have students compare how nationalism affected the Ottoman empire with how nationalism affected the Austrian empire.

- **Teach** Ask **What made the Balkans, in particular, such an unstable area?** (*It consisted of many small states with nationalist movements, and it was the focus of competing interests and conflicts among the European powers.*) **What happened once the Ottoman empire began to fail?** (*European powers, such as Britain, Austria, and Russia, scrambled to divide up Ottoman lands.*)

- **Quick Activity** Display **Color Transparency 134: Europe, 1803 and 1914.** Use the lesson suggested in the transparency book to guide a discussion on the changes in Europe during this period.

  🏛 **Color Transparencies,** 134

Independent Practice

- To help students understand the different regions included in the Ottoman empire, have them fill in the Outline Map *The Ottoman Empire, About 1815.*

  All in One Teaching Resources, Unit 3, p. 33

- Have students fill in the Outline Map *The Balkans, 1878,* and label the Balkan states.

  All in One Teaching Resources, Unit 3, p. 34

Monitor Progress

- Check Reading and Note Taking Study Guide entries for student understanding.

- Circulate to make sure that students are filling in their Outline Maps accurately. Administer the Geography Quiz.

  All in One Teaching Resources, Unit 3, p. 36

Answers

Map Skills
1. Review locations with students.
2. Adriatic, Mediterranean, Aegean, and Black Sea
3. Sample: Different nationalist interests were causing unrest with no clear solution, and the region seemed ready to explode into war at any moment.

History Background

Religious Differences The peoples of the Balkans differ not only in their ethnicities, but also in their religions. Bosniaks and Albanians are Muslim. Although Romanians, Bulgarians, Greeks, Serbs, and Montenegrins all belong to Orthodox Christian Churches, each national church has its own hierarchy and an independent head. Croats are Roman Catholics. Hungarians, Czechs, and Slovaks are mainly Catholics, though some belong to Protestant churches.

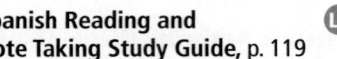

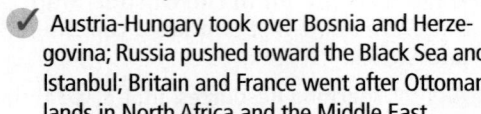

"The Sick Man of Europe"
Turkey's Abdul Hamid II (right) reacts to Bulgarian and Austrian rulers claiming parts of the Ottoman empire. *How does this cartoon show the Ottoman empire as "the sick man of Europe"?*

The Ottoman Empire Collapses

Like the Hapsburgs, the Ottomans ruled a multinational empire. It stretched from Eastern Europe and the Balkans to North Africa and the Middle East. There, as in Austria, nationalist demands tore at the fabric of the empire.

Balkan Nationalism Erupts In the Balkans, Serbia won autonomy in 1830, and southern Greece won independence during the 1830s. But many Serbs and Greeks still lived in the Balkans under Ottoman rule. The Ottoman empire was also home to other national groups, such as Bulgarians and Romanians. During the 1800s, various subject peoples staged revolts against the Ottomans, hoping to set up their own independent states.

European Powers Divide Up the Ottoman Empire Such nationalist stirrings became mixed up with the ambitions of the great European powers. In the mid-1800s, Europeans came to see the Ottoman empire as "the sick man of Europe." Eagerly, they scrambled to divide up Ottoman lands. Russia pushed south toward the Black Sea and Istanbul, which Russians still called Constantinople. Austria-Hungary took control of the provinces of Bosnia and Herzegovina. This action angered the Serbs, who also had hoped to expand into that area. Meanwhile, Britain and France set their sights on other Ottoman lands in the Middle East and North Africa.

War in the Balkans In the end, a complex web of competing interests contributed to a series of crises and wars in the Balkans. Russia fought several wars against the Ottomans. France and Britain sometimes joined the Russians and sometimes the Ottomans. Germany supported Austrian authority over the discontented national groups. But Germany also encouraged the Ottomans because of their strategic location in the eastern Mediterranean. In between, the subject peoples revolted and then fought among themselves. By the early 1900s, observers were referring to the region as the "Balkan powder keg." The explosion that came in 1914 helped set off World War I.

✔ **Checkpoint** How did the European powers divide up Ottoman lands?

SECTION 4 Assessment

Terms, People, and Places

1. For each term, person, or place listed at the beginning of the section, write a sentence explaining its significance.

Note Taking

2. **Reading Skill: Recognize Sequence** Use your completed table to answer the Focus Question: How did the desire for national independence among ethnic groups weaken and ultimately destroy the Austrian and Ottoman empires?

Comprehension and Critical Thinking

3. **Identify Alternatives** What alternatives did Francis Joseph have in responding to nationalist demands? How might Austrian history have been different if he had chosen a different course of action?

4. **Draw Conclusions** Why did the Dual Monarchy fail to end nationalist demands?

5. **Identify Central Issues** How did Balkan nationalism contribute to the decline of the Ottoman empire?

 Writing About History

Quick Write: Draft an Opening Paragraph In a persuasive essay, you want to grab the reader's attention by opening with a strong example, and then convincingly stating your views. Choose a topic from the section, such as whether the Hapsburgs or the Ottoman Turks could have built a modern, unified nation from their multinational empires. Then draft an opening paragraph.

NATIONALISM

How can nationalism be both a positive force and a negative force?

In This Chapter

Nationalism is a powerful force characterized by strong feelings of pride in and devotion to one's nation. In the 1800s, nationalism forged new nations and tore old empires apart. For example, nationalists who believed that all Italian-speaking people on the Italian peninsula should be united created the nation of Italy (right).

Throughout History

1776 Americans declare independence from Great Britain.

1800s Latin America colonies rise up in rebellion against Spain.

1800s The Ottoman Empire is weakened by nationalist movements.

1900s After World War II, African nations gain independence from colonial rulers.

1990s Nationalist feelings among diverse ethnic groups leads to war in Yugoslavia.

Continuing Today

People will fight to establish or preserve their national identity, defend their own land, or even aggressively grab the territory of others. In Canada, the English-speaking majority has sought to maintain national unity in the face of a movement by French Canadians to establish an independent Quebec.

21st Century Skills

 TRANSFER Activities

1. Analyze How has nationalism changed the course of history?

2. Evaluate Why do people respond to nationalism?

3. Transfer Complete a Web quest in which you decide if you would or would not support a nationalist movement; record your thoughts in the Concept Connector Journal; and learn to make a video. Web Code nbh-2208

History Background

The World Cup Every four years, a heated soccer competition called the World Cup arouses nationalistic feelings around the world. World Cup competitions have taken place every four years since 1930, except during World War II. In 2002, Brazil won its fifth World Cup title—a record. Ecstatic fans celebrated for three days, draped in green and gold, the colors of Brazil's flag.

While most of the nationalism inspired by the World Cup is light-hearted, the competition has led to tension and even violence. For example, in 1994, angry fans murdered Colombian player Andrés Escobar upon his return home from the World Cup because he had accidentally kicked the ball into his own team's net, crushing Colombia's hopes for the title.

Concept Connector

Nationalism

Objectives

- Define nationalism.
- Explain the impact a strong sense of nationalism can have on a country.
- Complete a web quest on nationalism.

Build Background Knowledge

Have students compare the terms *patriotism* and *nationalism*. Have students recall the sense of pride they felt as part of a team or school. Discuss in what ways this can inspire positive actions. Have them suggest any negative consequences to this pride.

Instruct

- Direct students' attention to the Essential Question: **How can nationalism be both a positive force and a negative force?** Have students recall how nationalism shaped events in German and Italian states in the 1800s. Discuss whether they would classify these events as positive or negative.
- Ask students to review the timeline. **How did a sense of nationalism affect the actions of people over the course of history?**
- Assign the Web Quest on nationalism.

Independent Practice

Concept Connector Have students fill in the Web Quest reflection question on nationalism in their Concept Connector Journal.

 Reading and Note Taking Study Guide, p. 285

Monitor Progress

Circulate to make sure that students are filling in their Concept Connector journal. Ensure they understand why nationalism occurs.

Transfer Activities

1. At times nationalism brought people together, and at other times, it caused competition and conflict.
2. Possible answer: It gives them a sense of identity. People like to feel connected to a powerful successful country.
3. Students' work should be evaluated against the rubric at Web Code nbh-2208.

Objectives

As you teach this section, keep students focused on the following objectives to help them answer the Section Focus Question and master core content.

- Describe major obstacles to progress in Russia.
- Explain why tsars followed a cycle of absolutism, reform, and reaction.
- Understand why the problems of industrialization contributed to the outbreak of revolution.

Prepare to Read

Build Background Knowledge ⬛️

Ask students to recall the development of the absolute monarchy in Russia. Based on their previous reading, ask them to predict how Russian rulers would react to forces for progress and reform that existed in the later 1800s.

Set a Purpose ⬛️

- **WITNESS HISTORY** Read the selection aloud or play the audio.
  - 🔊 AUDIO **Witness History Audio CD,** Plight of the Serfs

  Ask **How would you describe the life of a Russian serf?** *(They were virtually slaves and could be moved or sold against their wills.)* **To what group in American history could Russian serfs be compared?** *(slaves)*

- **Focus** Point out the Section Focus Question and write it on the board. Tell students to refer to this question as they read. *(Answer appears with Section 5 Assessment answers.)*

- **Preview** Have students preview the Section Objectives and the list of Terms, People, and Places.

- **Note Taking** Have students read this section using the Guided Questioning strategy (TE, p. T20). As they read, have students fill in the timeline sequencing events that led to Russia's 1905 revolution.

  ✏️ **Reading and Note Taking Study Guide,** p. 120

Russian peasant women clearing stones from a field

Plight of the Serfs

Although serfdom had almost disappeared in Western Europe by the 1700s, it survived in Russia. Masters exercised almost total power over their serfs. A noble turned revolutionary described the treatment of the serfs:

❝ I heard . . . stories of men and women torn from their families and their villages, and sold, or lost in gambling, or exchanged for a couple of hunting dogs, and then transported to some remote part of Russia to create a [master's] new estate; of children taken from their parents and sold to cruel . . . masters. ❞
—Peter Kropotkin, *Memoirs of a Revolutionist*

Focus Question Why did industrialization and reform come more slowly to Russia than to Western Europe?

Russia: Reform and Reaction

Objectives

- Describe major obstacles to progress in Russia.
- Explain why tsars followed a cycle of absolutism, reform, and reaction.
- Understand why the problems of industrialization contributed to the outbreak of revolution.

Terms, People, and Places

colossus	pogrom
Alexander II	refugees
Crimean War	Duma
emancipation	Peter Stolypin
zemstvo	

Note Taking

Reading Skill: Recognize Sequence Create a timeline of Russian events like the one below to keep track of the sequence of events that led to the revolution of 1905. Look for dates and other clues to sequence in the text.

```
1801
Alexander I
inherits throne.
|_____|_____|_____|_____|
1800     1850     1900     1950
```

Reformers hoped to free Russia from autocratic rule, economic backwardness, and social injustice. But efforts to modernize Russia had little success, as tsars imprisoned critics or sent them into exile.

Conditions in Russia

By 1815, Russia was not only the largest, most populous nation in Europe but also a great world power. Since the 1600s, explorers, soldiers, and traders seeking furs had expanded Russia's empire eastward across Siberia to the Pacific. Seeking ports, Peter the Great and Catherine the Great had added lands on the Baltic and Black seas. Seeking to contain the Ottoman and British empires, tsars in the 1800s expanded into the Caucasus and Central Asia. Russia thus acquired a huge multinational empire, part European and part Asian.

Other European nations looked on the Russian **colossus,** or giant, anxiously. Russia had immense natural resources. Its vast size gave it global influence. But many Europeans disliked its autocratic government and feared its expansion. At the same time, Russia remained economically undeveloped. By the 1800s, tsars saw the need to modernize but resisted reforms that would undermine their absolute rule.

Russia's Social Structure A great obstacle to progress was the rigid social structure. Landowning nobles dominated society and rejected any change that would threaten their power. The middle class was small and weak. Most Russians were serfs, or laborers bound to the land and to the landowners who controlled them.

Vocabulary Builder

Use the information below and the following resources to teach the high-use word from this section.

All in One Teaching Resources, Unit 3, p. 26; **Teaching Resources, Skills Handbook,** p. 3

High-Use Word	Definition and Sample Sentence
radical, p. 350	*n.* a person who favors great changes or reforms Martin Luther was a **radical** who wanted to change many things about the established church.

Most serfs were peasants. Others were servants, artisans, or soldiers forced into the tsar's army. As industry expanded, some masters sent serfs to work in factories but took much of their pay.

Many enlightened Russians knew that serfdom was inefficient. As long as most people had to serve the whim of their masters, Russia's economy would remain backward. However, landowning nobles had no reason to improve agriculture and took little interest in industry.

Ruling With Absolute Power For centuries, tsars had ruled with absolute power, imposing their will on their subjects. On occasion, the tsars made limited attempts at liberal reform, such as easing censorship or making legal and economic reforms to improve the lives of serfs. However, in each instance the tsars drew back from their reforms when they began to fear losing the support of nobles. In short, the liberal and nationalist changes brought about by the Enlightenment and the French Revolution had almost no effect on Russian autocracy.

✓ **Checkpoint** Describe the social structure that existed in Russia during the 1800s.

Emancipation and Stirrings of Revolution

Alexander II came to the throne in 1855 during the **Crimean War**. His reign represents the pattern of reform and repression used by his father and grandfather, Alexander I and Nicholas I. The Crimean War had broken out after Russia tried to seize Ottoman lands along the Danube River. Britain and France stepped in to help the Ottoman Turks, invading the Crimean peninsula that juts into the Black Sea. The war, which ended in a Russian defeat, revealed the country's backwardness. Russia had only a few miles of railroads, and the military bureaucracy was hopelessly inefficient. Many felt that dramatic changes were needed.

Freeing the Serfs A widespread popular reaction followed. Liberals demanded changes, and students demonstrated, seeking reform. Pressed from all sides, Alexander II finally agreed to reforms. In 1861, he issued a royal decree that required **emancipation,** or freeing of the serfs.

Freedom brought problems. Former serfs had to buy the land they had worked, but many were too poor to do so. Also, the lands allotted to peasants were often too small to farm efficiently or to support a family. Peasants remained poor, and discontent festered.

Still, emancipation was a turning point. Many peasants moved to the cities, taking jobs in factories and building Russian industries. Equally important, freeing the serfs boosted the drive for further reform.

Introducing Other Reforms Along with emancipation, Alexander II set up a system of local government. Elected assemblies, called **zemstvos,** were made responsible for matters such as road repair, schools, and agriculture. Through this system, Russians gained some experience of self-government at the local level.

The Decembrist Revolt
In 1825, army officers led an uprising known as the Decembrist Revolt (below). They had picked up liberal ideas while fighting in Western Europe and demanded reforms and a constitution. Tsar Nicholas I repressed the revolt. This stamp (inset) commemorates the 125th anniversary of the revolt. *How did the revolt symbolize Russia in the 1800s?*

History Background

Serfs The daily life of Russian serfs was scarcely better than that of workhorses or other animals. They lived in dirt-floored huts. Windows were covered with pigs' bladders, which allowed no light to enter. Pigs and calves slept in the huts along with the people. Fires that burned for warmth and cooking filled the homes with thick smoke. The labor requirements imposed on serfs had changed little over the centuries. They still had to work several days a week on their masters' estates, usually doing farm work. They also spent part of the year building roads, canals, and railways for the state. When Russia began to industrialize, serfs were compelled to live and work in factory towns under quasi-military discipline.

Conditions in Russia 🄻🄱

Instruct

- **Introduce: Key Terms** Ask students to find the key term *colossus* (in blue) in the text and define it. Point out that then, as now, Russia was an enormous country. Other European nations viewed it as mysterious, but also backward. As they read, ask students to consider what made this colossus different from other European countries.

- **Teach** Using the Think-Write-Pair-Share strategy (TE, p. T23), discuss how Russia's social structure, with an absolute ruler at the top, prevented reforms and progress. Ask **How did serfdom keep the Russian economy from advancing?** *(It encouraged the preservation of an agricultural base, rather than the development of industry, and so Russia did not develop a modern economy.)*

- **Quick Activity** Display **Color Transparency 136:** *Gambling with the Lives of Serfs.* Use the lesson suggested in the transparency book to analyze a political cartoon on the vast differences between serfs and nobles.
  📖 **Color Transparencies,** 136

Independent Practice

Primary Source To help students better understand how the tsars reacted to liberal ideas, have them read the selection from Feodor Dostoyevsky's *The Execution in Semyonovsky Square* and complete the worksheet.
All in One **Teaching Resources, Unit 3,** p. 31

Monitor Progress

As students complete their timelines, circulate to make sure they understand the events that led to the 1905 Revolution. For a completed version of the timeline, see
📖 **Note Taking Transparencies,** 155

Answers

✓ The majority were serfs at the bottom. There was a small middle class, a group of nobles above them, and the tsar at the top.

Caption It showed that even Russia's army, a group responsible for protecting the sovereign, didn't have faith in the tsar.

of each term, person, or place listed at the beginning of the section.
2. Russia was an autocracy that was still largely agricultural and based on serf labor. The tsars and nobles did not want to make changes or improvements that might undermine their authority and way of life.

5. Sample: Bloody Sunday revealed that the tsar feared the Russian people and was willing to use force to suppress them. Many Russians, realizing that peaceful reform was unlikely, were now willing to use violence against the tsar.

gave evidence that supports their view on a topic from this section.

For additional assessment, have students access **Progress Monitoring *Online*** at **Web Code nba-2255.**

Turning Point: Crisis and Revolution ③

Teach

■ **Introduce** Refer students to the two images on this page and ask them to describe the scene. Based on their previous reading, ask them to predict how discontented Russians will react to this

WITNESS HISTORY VIDEO

Watch *Crisis and Revolution in Russia* on the **Witness History Discovery School™** video program to examine the discontent in tsarist Russia.

DISCOVERY SCHOOL

focused on economic development. It encouraged the building of railroads to connect iron and coal mines with factories and to transport goods across Russia. It also secured foreign capital to invest in industry and transportation systems, such as the Trans-Siberian Railroad, which linked European Russia to the Pacific Ocean.

Political and social problems increased as a result of industrialization. Government officials and business leaders applauded economic growth. Nobles and peasants opposed it, fearing the changes it brought. Industrialization also created new social ills as peasants flocked to cities to work in factories. Instead of a better life, they found long hours and low pay in

---

CHAPTER 10

Quick Study Guide

■ Have students use the Quick Study Guide to prepare for this chapter's tests. Students may wish to refer to the following pages as they review:

Effects of Nationalism
Section 1, pp. 331–333; Section 2, pp. 334–336; Section 3, pp. 338–341; Section 4, pp. 343–346; Section 5, pp. 348–353

Unification in Europe
Section 1, p. 331; Section 3, p. 336; Section 4, p. 345

Key Leaders
Section 1, pp. 331–333; Section 2, p. 337; Section 3, pp. 338–342; Section 4, p. 344; Section 5, pp. 349–353

Key Events of Nationalism
Section 1, pp. 330–333; Section 3, pp. 339–340; Section 4, p. 346; Section 5, pp. 349, 352–353

■ For additional review, remind ③ students to refer to the

Reading and Note Taking Study Guide

Note Taking Study Guide, pp. 112, 114, 116, 118, 120
Section Summaries, pp. 113, 115, 117, 119, 121

■ Have students access **Web Code nbp-2264** for this chapter's **History** *Interactive* timeline, which includes expanded entries and additional events.

■ If students need more instruction on analyzing timelines, have them read the **Skills Handbook,** p. SH30.

■ When students have completed their study of the chapter, distribute Chapter Tests A and B.
Teaching Resources, Unit 3, pp. 37–72

> For **Progress Monitoring** *Online,* refer students to the Self-test with vocabulary practice at **Web Code nba-2266.**

354

CHAPTER 10

Quick Study Guide

> **Progress Monitoring** *Online*
> **For:** Self-test with vocabulary practice
> **Web Code:** nba-2266

■ Effects of Nationalism

Nationalism by Region				
Germany	**Italy**	**Austria**	**Balkans**	**Russia**
• German states unite under William I. • Empire takes leading role in Europe. • Bismarck becomes known as the Iron Chancellor.	• Mazzini founds Young Italy. • Garibaldi leads Red Shirts. • Victor Emmanuel II makes Cavour prime minister of Sardinia. • Italian states become unified by 1871.	• Francis I and Metternich uphold conservative goals. • Dual Monarchy with Hungary is set up. • Nationalist groups grow restless. • Empire becomes weakened.	• Serbians achieve autonomy in 1830. • Greeks achieve independence in the 1830s. • European nations divide up Ottoman lands. • "Balkan powder keg" helps set off World War I.	• Serfs are freed in 1861. • Alexander III encourages persecution and pogroms. • Russia enters the industrial age late. • Bloody Sunday leads to revolution in 1905. • Duma has limited power.

■ Unification in Europe, 1873

As the map below shows, nationalist movements led to the creation of several new nations across Europe.

■ Key Events of Nationalism

■ Key Leaders

Germany
Otto von Bismarck, *chancellor*
William I, *Prussian king, German kaiser*
William II, *kaiser*

Italy
Giuseppe Mazzini, *founder of Young Italy*
Victor Emmanuel II, *king*
Count Camillo Cavour, *prime minister*
Giuseppe Garibaldi, *leader of Red Shirts*

Austria-Hungary
Ferenc Deák, *Hungarian politician*
Francis Joseph, *Austrian emperor, Hungarian king*

Russia
Alexander II, *tsar of Russia*
Alexander III, *tsar of Russia*
Nicholas II, *tsar of Russia*

Key Events of Nationalism

Early 1800s	**1814**	**1830s**
Nationalism rises in Germany.	**The Congress of Vienna redraws the map of Europe after Napoleon's defeat.**	**Giuseppe Mazzini founds Young Italy to encourage Italian unification.**

Chapter Events
Global Events

1800	**1825**	**1850**

1804
Haiti declares independence from France.

1848
Revolutions take place throughout Europe.

Differentiated
Instruction Solutions for All Learners

① **Special Needs** **②** **Less Proficient Readers**	**②** **English Language Learners**
For students acquiring basic skills:	For Spanish-speaking students:
 **Adapted Reading and Note Taking Study Guide** Adapted Note Taking Study Guide, pp. 112, 114, 116, 118, 120 Adapted Section Summaries, pp. 113, 115, 117, 119, 121	**Spanish Reading and Note Taking Study Guide** Spanish Note Taking Study Guide, pp. 112, 114, 116, 118, 120 Spanish Section Summaries, pp. 113, 115, 117, 119, 121

Concept Connector

Essential Question Review

To connect prior knowledge with what you have learned in this chapter, answer the questions below in your Concept Connector journal. Use the journal in the Reading and Note Taking Study Guide to record your answers (or go to www.phschool.com **Web Code: nbd-2207**).

1. **Empire** In 1864, the Prussian prime minister, Otto von Bismarck, formed an alliance with Austria. Prussia and Austria then seized and "liberated" two provinces from Denmark. By 1871, German nationalists were celebrating the birth of the second Reich. Describe two actions that von Bismarck took between 1864 and 1871 that show why he was considered a master of Realpolitik. What was von Bismarck's ultimate goal? How did these events result in the formation of the second Reich?

2. **Nationalism** During the early 1800s, nationalist rebellions erupted in the Balkans. Many of the ethnic groups in the region hoped to overthrow Austrian and Ottoman rule and set up independent states of their own. Re-read Section 4 in this chapter. Take notes on the situation in the Balkans between 1800 and the early 1900s. Using your notes, create a timeline of the events in the Balkans leading up to 1914.

3. **Revolution** Many revolutions involve a conflict between tradition and progress. How did the conditions in Russia leading to the Revolution of 1905 demonstrate this conflict? Consider the actions of the tsar, the liberals, and the peasants. How did industrialization intensify the struggle between opposing factions?

■ Connections To Today

1. **Nationalism: The State of Nationalism Today** You've read how nationalism was a strong enough force in the 1800s to help unify nations, such as Italy and Germany, but threatened to destroy the Austrian and Ottoman empires. Do you think that nationalism is still a force in the world today? Conduct research to learn more about current nationalist issues. You may want to focus your research on Kurdistan, Northern Ireland, the former Yugoslavia, or Russia. Write two paragraphs on nationalism today, citing examples from current events to support your answer.

2. **Economic Systems: Social Welfare Programs** Under Otto von Bismarck, Germany was a pioneer in social reform, providing several social welfare programs to its citizens. By the 1890s, Germans had health and accident insurance as well as retirement benefits. Social welfare programs soon spread to other European nations. Conduct research to learn more about social welfare programs today. Compare social welfare programs in one country in Europe with those in the United States. How are they similar? How are they different?

1861	1870	1905
Tsar Alexander II frees the serfs.	**Bismarck provokes Franco-Prussian War to create a unified German empire.**	**Revolution breaks out in St. Petersburg after Bloody Sunday massacre.**

History *Interactive*
For: Interactive timeline
Web Code: nbp-2264

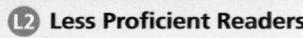
1875 **1900** **1925**

1861	1898	1914
The Civil War begins in the United States.	**The Philippines declares independence from Spain.**	**World War I begins.**

Concept Connector

Tell students that the main concepts for this chapter are Empire, Nationalism, and Revolution and ask them to answer the Essential Question Review questions on this page. Discuss the Connections to Today topics and ask students to answer the questions that follow.

Essential Question Review

1. In 1866, von Bismarck attacked his ally, Austria, and annexed territory. His 1870 editing of the Ems dispatch prompted France to declare war on Prussia. Bismarck wanted to unite the German states and bring more power to the Hohenzollerns. After France's defeat, the southern German states and the North German Confederation united.

2. Responses may include: 1800s: Subject peoples revolt against the Ottomans; 1830: Serbia wins autonomy from the Ottoman Empire; 1830s: Greece wins independence from the Ottomans; mid-1800s: European powers divide up the Ottoman empire; Early 1900s: The area is called the "Balkan powder keg," due to constant wars.

3. Russian tsars saw the need to modernize, but resisted reforms that would undermine absolute rule. Liberals demanded reforms. The tsar emancipated the serfs, though the nobles objected. As industrialization progressed, peasants flocked to the cities for work and found poor living and working conditions. Radicals and Socialists tried to win the support of these workers.

Connections to Today

1. Responses should be at least two paragraphs long and include examples and details from current world events to support their conclusions.

2. Responses should compare at least one type of social welfare program in the United States today, such as Medicare, with one in a European country, such as the National Health Service in Great Britain.

For additional review of this chapter's core concepts, remind students to refer to the

 Reading and Note Taking Study Guide
Concept Connector, pp. 262, 284, 291

Chapter Assessment

Terms, People, and Places

1. anarchist
2. Duma
3. kaiser
4. emancipation
5. chancellor
6. pogrom
7. emigration
8. *Realpolitik*
9. social welfare

Main Ideas

10. Bismarck's goal was to increase the power of the rulers of Prussia. He achieved that goal by using *Realpolitik* strategies: war, deceit, measured reforms, and propaganda.

11. It became an industrial giant, sought to keep France weak, and built alliances with Austria and Russia.

12. Camillo Cavour consolidated some states around Sardinia. Cavour then allied with France in case of a war with Austria and later provoked that war, which Sardinia and France won. Several northern states then broke away from Austria and joined Sardinia. In the south, Giuseppe Garibaldi took over the southern states, which he gave up so that they could unite with the northern states under the rule of Victor Emmanuel, Italy's first king.

13. Nationalist movements in both empires brought about unrest and demands for democratic reforms that weakened the ruling empire. The Ottoman empire's situation was complicated by the interference of European nations.

14. The Russian economy was based on agriculture and serf labor, and the nobles and the tsars resisted changes that might undermine their power.

Chapter Focus Question

15. Nationalism and the demand for reform led to the unification of Germany and its new position as a major power. They also led to the unification of Italy, the collapse of the Austrian and Ottoman empires, and revolution in Russia.

Critical Thinking

16. Bismarck was a practical practitioner of *Realpolitik*, not a romantic. To him nationalism was a tool to use to achieve his goals, not an ideal to strive for.

17. Both Bismarck and Cavour employed *Realpolitik*, and both wanted to increase the power of the rulers they

---

Chapter Assessment

Terms, People, and Places

Match the following definitions with the terms listed below.

chancellor	emigration
Realpolitik	emancipation
kaiser	pogrom
social welfare	Duma
anarchist	

1. someone who wants to abolish all government
2. elected national legislature in Russia
3. emperor of Germany
4. granting of freedom to serfs
5. the highest official of a monarch
6. violent attack on a Jewish community
7. movement away from one's homeland
8. realistic politics based on the needs of the state
9. programs to help people in need

Main Ideas

Section 1 (pp. 330–333)

10. What was Chancellor Otto von Bismarck's main goal? What policies did he follow to meet that goal?

Section 2 (pp. 334–337)

11. How did Germany increase its power in the late 1800s?

Section 3 (pp. 338–342)

12. Summarize the process by which Italy unified. Include information on the leaders who helped unify Italy.

Section 4 (pp. 343–346)

13. How did nationalism contribute to the decline of the Hapsburg and Ottoman empires?

Section 5 (pp. 348–353)

14. Why was Russia slow to industrialize?

Chapter Focus Question

15. What effects did nationalism and the demand for reform have in Europe?

Critical Thinking

16. **Make Comparisons** How did the nationalism represented by Bismarck differ from that embraced by liberals in the early 1800s?

17. **Make Comparisons** Compare and contrast the goals and methods of Cavour in Italy and Bismarck in Germany.

18. **Analyze Information** Tsar Alexander II declared that it is "better to abolish serfdom from above than to wait until it will be abolished by a movement from below." Explain his statement.

19. **Geography and History** How did regional differences contribute to continued divisions in Italy after unification?

20. **Analyzing Cartoons** How does this French cartoonist view Bismarck? Explain.

21. **Predict Consequences** Based on your reading of the chapter, predict the consequences of the following: (a) defeat of France in the Franco-Prussian War, (b) growth of German nationalism and militarism in the late 1800s, (c) failure to satisfy nationalist ambitions in Austria-Hungary, and (d) weakening of the Ottoman empire.

LE GRAND OGRE ALLEMAND.

● Writing About History

In this chapter's five Section Assessments, you developed skills to write a persuasive essay.

Writing a Persuasive Essay Some people define nationalism as excessive, narrow, or jingoist patriotism. A nationalist might be described as someone who boasts of his patriotism and favors aggressive or warlike policies. The rise of nationalism in Europe led to both division and unification. For example, it unified Germany, but it led Russian tsars to suppress the cultures of national minorities within the country. Nationalism remains a powerful force to this day for unifying countries and for sparking rivalries, conflicts, and bloodshed. Write a persuasive essay in which you support or oppose the idea that nationalism is an excessive form of patriotism.

Prewriting
- Collect the examples and evidence that you need to support your position convincingly.
- Use a graphic organizer to list points on both sides of the issue.

Drafting
- Focus on a thesis statement. Clearly state the position that you will prove. Use the rest of your introduction to provide readers with the necessary context about the issue.
- Acknowledge the opposition by stating, and then refuting, opposing arguments.

Revising
- Use the guidelines for revising your essay on page SH17 of the Writing Handbook.

---

served. However, Cavour believed in liberal ideals, while Bismarck was a monarchist and conservative.

18. Sample: He felt that if he did not end serfdom himself, revolutionaries would eventually do so. By freeing the serfs, he hoped to avoid revolution.

19. People still had local loyalties rather than loyalty to the nation. Southern Italy was poor and rural, while northern Italy was urban and more prosperous.

20. The cartoonist portrays Bismarck as a greedy ogre, gobbling everything in sight.

21. Sample: (a) instability in Europe, fear of Germany in Britain and other countries; (b) attempts to gain greater and greater territory, which could lead to war; (c) unrest and civil war; (d) the breakup of the Ottoman empire into small, unstable countries.

Document-Based Assessment

On the Crimean Front

In 1853, the British, the French, and their allies took on the vast Russian empire in the Crimean War. Called a "perfectly useless modern war," it was fought in the Black Sea region, although major campaigns took place well beyond that area. Like all wars, it was grim. More than 500,000 people died during the conflict.

Document A

"[The Crimean War] was one of the last times that the massed formations of cavalry and infantry were employed—the thin red line was to disappear forever. Henceforward, armies would rely on open, flexible formations and on trench warfare. For the British, it was the end of an era: never again would their soldiers fight in full-dress uniform. Never again would the colors be carried into the fray and the infantry would no longer march into battle to the stirring tunes of regimental bands. The Crimean War ushered in the age of the percussion cap rifle. The new Minie rifle was the decisive weapon, replacing the clumsy . . . musket. The weapon fired a cartridge, not a ball, with accuracy far superior to the old firelocks. . . ."

—From ***The Road to Balaklava,*** by Alexis S. Troubetzkoy

Document B

"I see men in hundreds rushing from the Mamelon [bastion] to the Malakoff [tower]. . . . with all its bristling guns. Under what a storm of fire they advance, supported by that impenetrable red line, which marks our own infantry! The fire from the Malakoff is tremendous—terrible. . . . Presently the twilight deepens, and the light of rocket, mortar, and shell falls over the town."

—From ***Journal kept during the Russian War: From the Departure of the Army from England in April 1854, to the Fall of Sebastopol,*** by Mrs. Henry Duberly, an army wife

Document C

"Men sent in there [French hospital] with fevers and other disorders were frequently attacked with the cholera in its worst form, and died with unusual rapidity, in spite of all that could be done to save them. I visited the hospital, and observed that a long train of . . . carts, filled with sick soldiers, were drawn up by the walls. . . . the quiet that prevailed was only broken now and then by the moans and cries of pain of the poor sufferers in the carts."

—From ***The British Expedition to the Crimea*** by W. H. Russell, ***Times*** correspondent

Document D

Treating Cholera

Analyzing Documents

Use your knowledge of the Crimean War and Documents A, B, C, and D to answer questions 1–4.

1. According to Document A, the Crimean War marked the end of
   A private soldiers in war.
   B most small wars in Europe.
   C old ways of fighting.
   D soldiers dying of diseases in military hospitals.

2. With what purpose did the author write Document B?
   A to help people understand the dangers of fighting with new weapons
   B to criticize inadequate technology
   C to describe the state of mind of the soldiers
   D to make the British public understand how quickly the war was progressing

3. With what purpose did the artist create Document D?
   A to help the British public understand the dangers of fighting with new weapons
   B to criticize the inadequate state of army hospitals
   C to describe the dangers of soldiering and soldiers' valor
   D to make the British public understand the toll that disease was taking on soldiers

4. **Writing Task** Suppose you are a surgeon working near the war front. Write a brief letter home describing your impressions. Use the four documents along with information from the chapter to write your letter.

● Writing About History

As students begin the assignment, refer them to page SH16 of the **Writing Handbook** for help in writing a persuasive essay. Remind them of the steps they should take to complete their assignment, including prewriting, drafting, and revising. For help in revising, remind them to use the guidelines on page SH17 of the **Writing Handbook.**

Students' persuasive essays should present a clear thesis with a specific point of view, include sequenced arguments supported by facts and details, and provide at least one oppositional argument. Essays should also be thoughtfully written, stay on the topic, and be free of grammatical and spelling errors. For scoring rubrics for writing assignments, see **Assessment Rubrics,** p. 8.

Document-Based Assessment

■ To help students understand the documents on this page, give them the following **TIP: Study each document to assess its context and purpose. Use your knowledge of the subject as well as the information given in the document and the attribution line to determine who created it, when, and why.**

■ To provide students with further practice in answering Document-Based Assessment Questions, go to 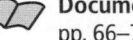 **Document-Based Assessment,** pp. 66–78

■ If students need more instruction on synthesizing information, have them read the **Skills Handbook,** p. SH33.

Answers

1. C
2. A
3. D
4. Letters should show a clear understanding of the medical issues during the Crimean War and should be written in the first person. They should also use specific evidence from the documents and the chapter to support their conclusions.

Growth of Western Democracies

Section	Core Instruction L3	Differentiated Instruction L1 L2 L4	
Section 1 *Democratic Reform in Britain* **1 period, .5 block** **OBJECTIVES** ■ Describe how reformers worked to change Parliament in the 1800s. ■ Understand the values that Queen Victoria represented. ■ Learn how the Liberal and Conservative parties helped bring a new era to British politics. **Focus Question** *How did political reform gradually expand suffrage and make the British Parliament more democratic during the 1800s?*	**All in One Teaching Resources, Unit 3** Vocabulary Builder: Word Maps, p. 47 Section 1 Quiz, p. 43 **Reading and Note Taking Study Guide** Note Taking Study Guide, p. 122 Section 1 Summary, p. 123 **Note Taking Transparencies, 143** **WITNESS HISTORY Audio CD** Two Nations **Progress Monitoring Transparencies, 95** **Color Transparencies, 137, 138** **Teaching Resources, Skills Handbook** Prereading the Chapter, pp. 1–2 Word Knowledge Rating Form, p. 3 K-W-L, p. 4	**L1 Adapted Reading and Note Taking Study Guide** Note Taking Study Guide, p. 122 SN Section 1 Summary, p. 123 SN **L2 Adapted Reading and Note Taking Study Guide** Note Taking Study Guide, p. 122 LPR Section 1 Summary, p. 123 LPR **Spanish Reading and Note Taking Study Guide** Note Taking Study Guide, p. 122 ELL Section 1 Summary, p. 123 ELL **L4 All in One Teaching Resources, Unit 3** Biography: Queen Victoria, p. 49 AR, GT	***Student Edition Audio** SN **Differentiated Instruction Activity,** Teacher's Edition, p. 362 SN ***Guided Reading Audio,** Spanish ELL ***Student Edition Audio** LPR **Differentiated Instruction Activity,** Teacher's Edition, p. 362 LPR **Extend Activity,** Teacher's Edition, p. 363 AR, GT
Section 2 *Social and Economic Reform in Britain* **1.5 periods, .75 block** **OBJECTIVES** ■ Identify the social and economic reforms benefiting British workers and others. ■ Describe how British women worked to win the right to vote. ■ Understand the causes of conflict between the British and the Irish nationalists. **Focus Question** *What social and economic reforms were passed by the British Parliament during the 1800s and early 1900s?*	**All in One Teaching Resources, Unit 3** Reading Strategy: Categorize, p. 48 Outline Map: Great Britain and Ireland, About 1870, p. 54 Section 2 Quiz, p. 44 **Reading and Note Taking Study Guide** Note Taking Study Guide, p. 124 Section 2 Summary, p. 125 **Note Taking Transparencies, 144** **WITNESS HISTORY Audio CD** No Surrender; The Irish Potato Famine **Progress Monitoring Transparencies, 96** **Witness History Discovery School™** video program, *The Great Hunger in Ireland*	**L1 Adapted Reading and Note Taking Study Guide** Note Taking Study Guide, p. 124 SN Section 2 Summary, p. 125 SN **L2 Adapted Reading and Note Taking Study Guide** Note Taking Study Guide, p. 124 LPR Section 2 Summary, p. 125 LPR **L4 All in One Teaching Resources, Unit 3** Primary Source: The London Street Markets, p. 50 AR, GT Primary Source: A Lecture on the Causes of the Irish Famine, p. 51 AR, GT	**Differentiated Instruction Activity,** Teacher's Edition, p. 365 SN **Spanish Reading and Note Taking Study Guide** Note Taking Study Guide, p. 124 ELL Section 2 Summary, p. 125 ELL **Differentiated Instruction Activity,** Teacher's Edition, p. 365 LPR **Differentiated Instruction Activity,** Teacher's Edition, p. 366 AR, GT **Extend Activity,** Teacher's Edition, pp. 358, 369 AR, GT

Section	Core Instruction (L3)	Differentiated Instruction (L1) (L2) (L4)	
Section 3 *Division and Democracy in France* 🕐 **1 period, .5 block** **OBJECTIVES** ■ List the domestic and foreign policies of Napoleon III. ■ Analyze the impact of the Dreyfus affair and other challenges of the Third Republic. ■ Describe the French government's steps toward reform in the early 1900s. **Focus Question** *What democratic reforms were made in France during the Third Republic?*	**All in One Teaching Resources, Unit 3** Section 3 Quiz, p. 45 **Reading and Note Taking Study Guide** Note Taking Study Guide, p. 126 Section 3 Summary, p. 127 **Note Taking Transparencies,** 158 **WITNESS HISTORY** Audio CD *Vive la France!* **Progress Monitoring Transparencies,** 97 **Color Transparencies,** 139, 140	(L1) **Adapted Reading and Note Taking Study Guide** Note Taking Study Guide, p. 126 SN Section 3 Summary, p. 127 SN (L2) **Adapted Reading and Note Taking Study Guide** Note Taking Study Guide, p. 126 LPR Section 3 Summary, p. 127 LPR (L4) **Differentiated Instruction Activity,** Teacher's Edition, pp. 372, 375 AR, GT	**Differentiated Instruction Activity,** Teacher's Edition, p. 374 SN **Spanish Reading and Note Taking Study Guide** Note Taking Study Guide, p. 126 ELL Section 3 Summary, p. 127 ELL **Differentiated Instruction Activity,** Teacher's Edition, p. 374 LPR **Extend Activity,** Teacher's Edition, p. 376 AR, GT
Section 4 *Expansion of the United States* 🕐 **1.5 periods, .75 block** **OBJECTIVES** ■ Describe how the territory of the United States changed during the 1800s. ■ Summarize how American democracy grew before and after the Civil War. ■ Analyze the impact of economic growth and social reform on the United States. **Focus Question** *How did the United States develop during the 1800s?*	**All in One Teaching Resources, Unit 3** Outline Map: Expansion of the United States, p. 55 Geography Quiz, p. 56 Section 4 Quiz, p. 46 **Reading and Note Taking Study Guide** Note Taking Study Guide, p. 128 Section 4 Summary, p. 129 Concept Connector, pp. 242, 250, 281 **Note Taking Transparencies,** 159 **WITNESS HISTORY** Audio CD *America!* **Progress Monitoring Transparencies,** 98 **Color Transparencies,** 141, 142	(L1) **Adapted Reading and Note Taking Study Guide** Note Taking Study Guide, p. 128 SN Section 4 Summary, p. 129 SN (L2) **Adapted Reading and Note Taking Study Guide** Note Taking Study Guide, p. 128 LPR Section 4 Summary, p. 129 LPR Concept Connector, pp. 242, 250, 281 LPR (L4) **All in One Teaching Resources, Unit 3** Traveler's Tales: From the Journals of Lewis and Clark, p. 53 AR, GT Viewpoints: Two Approaches to Abolition, p. 52 AR, GT	Concept Connector, pp. 242, 250, 281 SN **Spanish Reading and Note Taking Study Guide** Note Taking Study Guide, p. 128 ELL Section 4 Summary, p. 129 ELL Concept Connector, pp. 242, 250, 281 ELL **Differentiated Instruction Activity,** Teacher's Edition, p. 379 LPR, ELL **Extend Activity,** Teacher's Edition, p. 381 AR, GT

*Audio support is available for all sections.

Assessment Resources

- **Progress Monitoring Transparencies,** 95–98
- **SuccessTracker™,** Chapter 11
- **Document-Based Assessment,** pp. 67–79
- *ExamView®* **Test Bank CD-ROM,** Chapter 11
- **All in One Teaching Resources, Unit 3,** Chapter Tests A and B, pp. 57–62
- **Progress Monitoring** *Online* **Quizzes,** Chapter 11
- **Assessment Rubrics**

Differentiated Instruction Key

(L1) Special Needs		LPR	Less Proficient Readers
(L2) Basic to Average		AR	Advanced Readers
(L3) All Students		SN	Special Needs Students
(L4) Average to Advanced		GT	Gifted and Talented
		ELL	English Language Learner

Author's Notes

Britain's Age of Reform

The domestic history of Britain in the nineteenth century is . . . usually presented as a chronicle of social and political reform. Queen Victoria (ruled 1837-1901) presided over a parliamentary government that was able to change with the times, to meet the needs of a rapidly evolving industrial society. Politicians of various persuasions, from the Liberal William Gladstone to the Conservative Benjamin Disraeli, both guided and responded to the wishes of a growing electorate to produce the model of a functioning nineteenth-century Western democracy—social change through the ballot box.

Parliamentary reform bills extending the right to vote to one group after another provided the skeleton of Britain's age of reform. The great Reform Bill of 1832 gave new industrial cities such as Manchester and Birmingham—and the business middle classes everywhere—representation in Parliament. Disraeli's reform bill of 1867 granted the suffrage to factory workers, Gladstone's bill of 1884 awarded it to farm laborers, and the 1918 bill climaxed the women's suffrage movement by giving the vote to most women.

Other reform measures included laws designed to render the new industrial system more livable. Laws regulating women's working conditions and child labor were passed, as were factory-safety acts and legislation limiting the length of the working day. Public education began in Britain in the nineteenth century.

During the years before World War I, a Liberal government enacted such socialistic measures—as they then seemed—as the beginnings of public health service and old-age pensions.

There was tension, of course—the massive and sometimes violent demonstrations connected with the Reform Bill of 1832, the (failed) Chartist movement of the 1840s demanding universal manhood suffrage, and the women's campaign for the right to vote in the 1890s and early 1900s. But the system proved flexible and strong enough to contain and channel all such pressures. Change came comparatively peacefully through the democratic process.

—Anthony Esler, *The Human Venture: From Prehistory to the Present,* (Upper Saddle River, New Jersey: Pearson Education, 2004), p. 495

Extend Online

The Victorian Age

Have students research daily life in the Victorian Age. Use the following steps to help students complete the activity.

Prepare for the Activity Ask students to list the problems that industrialization caused in Britain. Then ask students to list the ways Britain attempted to solve them. *(Sample: labor unions, reform laws)* If necessary, remind students that during the Victorian Age, reformers worked for change in Britain. Reforms helped the working class, but women's suffrage remained controversial. Irish nationalists campaigned for home rule.

Conduct the Activity For help in starting the activity, send students to **Web Code nbe-2301.** Have students read the primary and secondary sources depicting life during the Victorian Age. Then have students focus on a specific aspect, such as education, factory life, or public health, and write a paragraph exploring the ways in which Britain changed during this period. Students should use specific information from the textbook and Web site. If necessary, have them conduct further research on the reforms. Then have students share their paragraphs with the class.

Follow-Up Conduct a class discussion based on the following questions: Would you have wanted to live during the Victorian Age? Why or why not? How did people adapt to the demands of an industrial society? How are these demands seen in the daily life of the family highlighted on the Web site? How did reformers respond to those demands? Whom did the reforms help? Who was left out by the reforms?

Differentiated Instruction   Solutions for All Learners

Cornell Note Taking L1 L2

Learning to efficiently take notes will help students read the text and review key information. The Cornell Note Taking strategy provides students with a structured way to read and record core content.

1. Students draw a vertical line two and a half inches from the left-hand side of notebook paper to create a Review Column.

2. Students take notes on the text material in the more spacious area to the right.

3. After taking notes on a section, students review their notes and write focused questions in the Review Column that elicit the specific content to the right. For example, if one section of the notes details the democratic reforms in Britain, the student would write the review question "What were the democratic reforms in Britain?" Formulating these review questions forces students to carefully review the section content and clarify the information in their minds.

4. To study their notes, students' cover up the right side of the page, read the review questions, and quiz themselves by checking their understandings and recall of critical content, rather than passively rereading information.

5. Students can be encouraged/required to write a brief summary of each section in their own words at the end of their notes to strengthen their review and increase the likelihood that they will retain the information.

Modeling Reading and Writing Skills

Gather Details Explain that in this chapter, students will be writing a compare and contrast essay. (See Writing About History, p. 384.) Ask students to think about articles or books they have read recently. Tell them that when writing a compare and contrast essay, they will often have to conduct further research into their subject. Ask students to list possible sources where they can find additional information. *(Sample: reliable Web sites, newspapers, magazines, reference books, encyclopedias)* Remind students that by using several different sources, they can ensure the information is current, accurate, and balanced.

Give them the following guidelines for improving accuracy.

1. Check to see when printed sources were published to make sure the information is up-to-date.

2. If you note discrepancies in the information given by two sources, check the facts in a third source. If three or more sources disagree, mention the disagreement in your paper.

3. Whenever possible, cross-check information from the Internet or from an interview by consulting other sources.

Vocabulary: Analyze Word Parts Explain that when students come across an unfamiliar word, they can break it into word parts—roots, suffixes, and prefixes—to help them recognize and pronounce it. Remind them that the root is the base of a word with its own meaning, and that prefixes and suffixes are added to a word to change its meaning.

Model this skill by reading aloud the word *requirement,* in the last line of the second paragraph under the heading *Reform Act of 1832,* in Section 1. Point out that the root *require* means to insist upon, demand, or to be in need of something. The suffix *-ment* means the result or process of an action. Therefore, the word *requirement* must mean that something is needed or demanded.

Growth of Western Democracies
1815–1914

Teach With Technology
PresentationEXPRESS™
Premium DVD

■ Teach this chapter's core content using **PresentationExpress™ Premium,** which includes dynamic lecture notes, interactive game shows, songs, videos, and the *ExamView® QuickTake* assessment tool.

■ To introduce this chapter using **PresentationExpress™ Premium,** start by asking students **Which of the following statements do you most agree with? (A) In a democracy, the government responds instantly to citizens' wishes. (B) In a democracy, citizens need only vote in elections to reform the government. (C) In a democracy, citizens must sometimes protest to win government reforms. (D) In a democracy, the only real way to change the government is through a revolution.** Take a class poll or record students' answers using the QuickTake feature and discuss their responses. Point out that in this chapter, they will read about the ways Britain, France, and the United States used democratic reforms in the 1800s and 1900s. Continue introducing the chapter using the chapter opener slide show and Witness History audio.

Technology Resources

■ Student**EXPRESS** CD-ROM, Chapter 11

■ Teacher**EXPRESS** CD-ROM, Chapter 11

■ Presentation**EXPRESS™** **Premium DVD,** Chapter 11

■ **WITNESS HISTORY** Audio CD, Chapter 11

■ *ExamView* Test Bank CD-ROM, English and Spanish, Chapter 11

■ **Guided Reading Audio,** Spanish, Chapter 11

■ **Student Edition Audio,** Chapter 11

■ **Witness History Discovery School™** video program, *The Great Hunger in Ireland*

■ **Experience It! Multimedia Pack**

Bibliography

For the Teacher
Anderson, Bonnie S. *Joyous Greetings: The First International Women's Movement.* Oxford University Press, 2000.

Arnstein, Walter L. *Queen Victoria.* Palgrave Macmillan, 2003.

Wawro, Geoffrey. *The Franco-Prussian War: The German Conquest of France in 1870–1871.* Cambridge University Press, 2003.

For the Student
L1 Wisler, G. Clifton. *When Johnny Went Marching: Young Americans Fight the Civil War.* HarperCollins, 2001.

L2 Bartoletti, Susan Campbell. *Black Potatoes: The Story of the Great Irish Famine, 1845–1850.* Houghton Mifflin, 2001.

L3 Swisher, Clarice. *Victorian England.* Lucent, 2000.

WITNESS HISTORY AUDIO

The People Demand Reform

A series of political reforms during the 1800s and early 1900s transformed Great Britain from a monarchy and aristocracy into a democracy. While some British politicians opposed the reforms, most sided in favor of reforming Parliament.

❝No doubt, at that very early period, the House of Commons did represent the people of England but. . . . the House of Commons, as it presently subsists, does not represent the people of England. . . . The people called loudly for reform, saying that whatever good existed in the constitution of this House—whatever confidence was placed in it by the people, was completely gone. ❞
—Lord John Russell, March 1, 1831

Listen to the Witness History audio to learn more about democratic developments in Britain.

◀ **Parliamentary Election of 1836**
Though most were unable to vote, many townspeople gathered in the marketplace to cheer or harass the candidates.

Chapter Preview

Chapter Focus Question How did Britain, France, and the United States slowly extend democratic rights during the 1800s and early 1900s?

Section 1
Democratic Reform in Britain

Section 2
Social and Economic Reform in Britain

Section 3
Division and Democracy in France

Section 4
Expansion of the United States

Use the ☑ Quick Study Timeline at the end of this chapter to preview chapter events.

Queen Victoria of Great Britain and Ireland

Badge commemorating a union strike in Britain, 1888

Advertisement for transportation to California during the Gold Rush

Concept Connector ONLINE
To explore Essential Questions related to this chapter, go to PHSchool.com
Web Code: nbd-2307

Chapter-Level Resources

All in One Vocabulary Builder; Reading Strategy; Enrichments; Outline Maps; Geography Quiz; Chapter Test
- Document-Based Assessments
- AYP Monitoring Assessments
- *ExamView* Test Bank CD-ROM
- Guided Reading Audio, Spanish
- Student Edition Audio

Previewing the Chapter

- **WITNESS HISTORY** Read the Witness History selection aloud or play the accompanying audio. Ask **According to Lord John Russell, whom did the House of Commons once represent?** *(the people)* **Whom does he think it represents now?** *(Sample: the elite)* **Why do you think Russell says that people's confidence in the House of Commons is now gone?** *(Sample: The government might not be acting in the interest of the people).* Tell students they will learn about democratic reforms in Britain in the chapter ahead.

   AUDIO **Witness History Audio CD,** The People Demand Reform

- **Analyzing the Visuals** Ask students to study the image of the Parliamentary Election of 1836 and have them read the caption. Ask **What does the townspeople's cheering and jeering of the candidates suggest about the political process?** *(Even those who could not vote were involved in the political process.)* Ask students to predict how the majority of people would gain a greater voice in the political process throughout the nineteenth century.

- **Focus** Write the Chapter Focus Question on the board. Tell students to keep this question in mind as they read the chapter. *(Answer appears with Chapter Assessment answers.)* Have students preview the section titles for this chapter.

Note Taking Study Guide With Concept Connector Journal
For online access: Web code: nbd-2307
For print alternative: Reading and Note Taking Study Guide booklet

---

SECTION 1

Step-by-Step Instruction

Objectives

As you teach this section, keep students focused on the following objectives to help them answer the Section Focus Question and master core content.

- Describe how reformers worked to change Parliament in the 1800s.
- Understand the values that Queen Victoria represented.
- Summarize how the Liberal and Conservative parties helped bring a new era to British politics.

Prepare to Read

Build Background Knowledge **L3**

Ask students to recall how the French tried to create a more democratic government. *(through revolution)* Have them suggest other ways that people can change how their government works.

Set a Purpose **L3**

- **WITNESS HISTORY** Read the selection aloud or play the audio.
   AUDIO **Witness History Audio CD,** Two Nations

  Ask **What is the stranger's main idea?** *(The rich and the poor occupy separate, unequal worlds.)* **How do the two images reveal the social divisions?** *(The two women represent the rich; the woman with the infant represents the poor.)* **What dangers are posed to British society by the deep divisions the stranger describes?** *(Sample: Those divisions might lead to revolution, as it did in France.)*

- **Focus** Point out the Section Focus Question and write it on the board. Tell students to refer to this question as they read. *(Answer appears with Section 1 Assessment answers).*

- **Preview** Have students preview the Section Objectives and the list of Terms, People, and Places.

SECTION 1

WITNESS HISTORY ◀)) AUDIO

Two Nations

One day a wealthy Englishman named Charles Egremont boasted to strangers that Victoria, the queen of England, "reigns over the greatest nation that ever existed."

"Which nation?" asks one of the strangers, "for she reigns over two. . . . Two nations; between whom there is no [communication] and no sympathy; who are as ignorant of each other's habits, thoughts, and feelings, as if they were . . . inhabitants of different planets."

What are these "two nations," Egremont asks. "THE RICH AND THE POOR," the stranger replies.
—Benjamin Disraeli, *Sybil*

Focus Question How did political reform gradually expand suffrage and make the British Parliament more democratic during the 1800s?

Fashions of the rich (above right), and poverty on the streets of London, circa 1877 (above)

Democratic Reform in Britain

Objectives
- Describe how reformers worked to change Parliament in the 1800s.
- Understand the values that Queen Victoria represented.
- Summarize how the Liberal and Conservative parties helped bring a new era to British politics.

Terms, People, and Places

rotten borough	Benjamin Disraeli
electorate	William Gladstone
secret ballot	parliamentary democracy
Queen Victoria	

Note Taking

Reading Skill: Identify Main Ideas As you read this section, complete an outline of the contents.

    I. Reforming Parliament
       A. Reformers press for change
          1.
          2.

In the 1800s, Benjamin Disraeli and other political leaders slowly worked to bridge Britain's "two nations" and extend democratic rights. Unlike some of its neighbors in Europe, Britain generally achieved change through reform rather than revolution.

Reforming Parliament

In 1815, Britain was a constitutional monarchy with a parliament and two political parties. Still, it was far from democratic. Although members of the House of Commons were elected, less than five percent of the people had the right to vote. Wealthy nobles and squires, or country landowners, dominated politics and heavily influenced voters. In addition, the House of Lords—made up of hereditary nobles and high-ranking clergy—could veto any bill passed by the House of Commons.

Reformers Press for Change Long-standing laws kept many people from voting. Catholics and non-Anglican Protestants, for example, could not vote or serve in Parliament. In the 1820s, reformers pushed to end religious restrictions. After fierce debate, Parliament finally granted Catholics and non-Anglican Protestants equal political rights.

An even greater battle soon erupted over making Parliament more representative. During the Industrial Revolution, centers of population shifted. Some rural towns lost so many people that they had few or no voters. Yet local landowners in these **rotten boroughs** still

---

Vocabulary Builder

Use the information below and the following resources to teach the high-use word from this section.
All in One **Teaching Resources, Unit 3**, p. 47; **Teaching Resources, Skills Handbook**, p. 3

High-Use Word	Definition and Sample Sentence
allocate, p. 361	*vt.* to distribute according to a plan The city council voted on how to **allocate** the city's funds to different projects.

sent members to Parliament. At the same time, populous new industrial cities like Manchester and Birmingham had no seats <u>allocated</u> in Parliament because they had not existed as population centers in earlier times.

Reform Act of 1832 By 1830, Whigs and Tories were battling over a bill to reform Parliament. The Whig Party largely represented middle-class and business interests. The Tory Party spoke for nobles, land-owners, and others whose interests and income were rooted in agriculture. In the streets, supporters of reform chanted, "The Bill, the whole Bill, and nothing but the Bill!" Their shouts seemed to echo the cries of revolutionaries on the continent.

Parliament finally passed the Great Reform Act in 1832. It redistributed seats in the House of Commons, giving representation to large towns and cities and eliminating rotten boroughs. It also enlarged the **electorate,** the body of people allowed to vote, by granting suffrage to more men. The Act did, however, keep a property requirement for voting.

The Reform Act of 1832 did not bring full democracy, but it did give a greater political voice to middle-class men. Landowning nobles, however, remained a powerful force in the government and in the economy.

The Chartist Movement The reform bill did not help rural or urban workers. Some of them demanded more radical change. In the 1830s, protesters known as Chartists drew up the People's Charter. This petition demanded universal male suffrage, annual parliamentary elections, and salaries for members of Parliament. Another key demand was for a **secret ballot,** which would allow people to cast their votes without announcing them publicly.

Twice the Chartists presented petitions with over a million signatures to Parliament. Both petitions were ignored. In 1848, as revolutions swept Europe, the Chartists prepared a third petition and organized a march on Parliament. Fearing violence, the government moved to suppress the march. Soon after, the unsuccessful Chartist movement declined. In time, however, Parliament would pass most of the major reforms proposed by the Chartists.

✓ **Checkpoint** How was the British Parliament reformed during the early 1800s?

The Victorian Age

From 1837 to 1901, the great symbol in British life was **Queen Victoria.** Her reign was the longest in British history. Although she exercised little real political power, she set the tone for what is now called the Victorian age.

Symbol of a Nation's Values As queen, Victoria came to embody the values of her age. These Victorian ideals included duty, thrift, honesty, hard work, and above all respectability. Victoria herself embraced a strict code of morals and manners. As a young woman, she married a German prince, Albert, and they raised a large family.

A Confident Age Under Victoria, the British middle class—and growing numbers of the working class—felt great confidence in the future. That confidence grew as Britain expanded its already huge empire.

Vocabulary Builder
allocate—(AL oh kayt) *vt.* to distribute according to a plan

Meeting of the Unions on Newhall Hill, Birmingham
The Birmingham Political Union's enormous rallies (above) and calls for reform are credited with the final passage of the Great Reform Bill of 1832. As one politician said of the BPU, "To this body, more than to any other, is confessedly due the triumph (such as it was) of the Reform Bill. Its well-ordered proceedings, extended organisation, and immense assemblages of people, at critical periods of its progress, rendered the measure irresistible."

■ **Note Taking** Have students read this section using the Structured Read Aloud strategy (TE, p. T20). As they read, have students outline the main ideas of Britain's reforms.

⟋◹ **Reading and Note Taking Study Guide,** p. 122

Teach

Reforming Parliament L3

Instruct

■ **Introduce: Vocabulary Builder**
Have students read the Vocabulary Builder term and definition. Explain that in this section they will learn how the British changed the way seats were **allocated** in Parliament.

■ **Teach** Share with students the History Background note at the bottom of this page. Then ask **What was the problem with rotten boroughs?** *(The population had shifted, but the seat distribution had not been changed.)* **How did the Reform Act of 1832 make Britain more democratic?** *(by enlarging the electorate and redistributing the seats in the House of Commons)* **Why were Chartists not satisfied with these reforms?** *(The bill did not help many rural or urban workers, who could not meet the property requirement.)*

■ **Quick Activity** Display **Color Transparency 137: Notices for Chartist Meetings, 1841.** Use the lesson suggested in the transparency book to guide a discussion on the Chartists.
▥ **Color Transparencies,** 137

Independent Practice

Have students draw a political cartoon for or against the Great Reform Act.

Monitor Progress

As students complete their outlines, circulate to make sure they understand the effects of Great Reform Act of 1832. For a completed version of the outline, see
▥ **Note Taking Transparencies,** 156

Answer

✓ Seats in Parliament were redistributed to reflect the movement of the population out of rotten boroughs and into cities; the electorate was expanded to include middle-class men.

History Background

Unfair Representation Before the passage of the Reform Act of 1832, more than one-fifth of the seats in Parliament were in rotten boroughs. Fifty of the representatives had fewer than fifty voters in their districts. Some members represented even fewer people. As Thomas Paine, an English political thinker, wrote, "The old town of Sarum, which contains not three houses, sends two members; and the town of Manchester, which contains upwards of sixty thousands souls, is not admitted to send any."

In addition to rotten boroughs, Britain also had "pocket boroughs," which were said to be in the pocket of the people or family who controlled them. They used coercion or bribes to influence the vote.

The Victorian Age/ A New Era in British Politics

L3

Instruct

- **Introduce: Key Terms** Direct students' attention to the key term **Queen Victoria** (in blue) and discuss the values she embodied. Ask them to predict how these values will influence reform.

- **Teach** Discuss the reform movements in Britain. Ask **Why did the House of Lords block further reforms advanced in the early 1900s?** *(They feared they were losing political power and influence.)* **How was this impasse resolved?** *(The government threatened to add so many new members that the reforms would pass anyway.)* Using the Think-Write-Pair-Share strategy (TE, p. T23), ask students to identify areas in which reforms were still needed at the close of the 1800s.

- **Quick Activity** Display **Color Transparency 138: *The Houses of Parliament* by Claude Monet.** Use the lesson suggested in the transparency book to guide a discussion on how British political parties changed in the 1800s.

  🏛 **Color Transparencies, 138**

Independent Practice

Biography To help students better understand Queen Victoria and her significance to Victorian society, have them read the biography *Queen Victoria* and complete the worksheet.

All in One **Teaching Resources, Unit 3,** p. 49

Monitor Progress

- To check student understanding, ask students to explain the extent of Britain's political reform. *(Almost all males had gained suffrage by 1918, while women had not.)*

- Check Reading and Note Taking Study Guide entries for student understanding.

Answers

Thinking Critically

1. the aristocrats, because they stood to lose the most power in Parliament
2. It gave the House of Commons more political power than the House of Lords.

✓ duty, thrift, honesty, hard work, and respectability; promoted reform because they were widely adopted by people at all levels of society

● **INFOGRAPHIC**

From Monarchy to Democracy in Britain

In the early 1800s, Britain's government was a monarchy and an aristocracy under the rule of Queen Victoria ① and the aristocrats and landowners in the House of Lords. ② A series of reforms during the 1800s and early 1900s transformed Britain's government into a democracy. The first of these reforms was the Great Reform Act of 1832, by which seats in the Parliament were redistributed to give more representation to growing industrial areas. The act also expanded the vote to include about one in five adult men. The Second Reform Act in 1867 was spearheaded by Benjamin Disraeli, ④ a Conservative leader who hoped to defeat his liberal rival William Gladstone ③ and

Victoria, the empress of India and ruler of some 300 million subjects around the world, became a revered symbol of British might.

During her reign, Victoria witnessed growing agitation for social reform. The queen herself commented that the lower classes "earn their bread and riches so deservedly that they cannot and ought not to be kept back." As the Victorian era went on, reformers continued the push toward greater social and economic justice.

✓ **Checkpoint** What values did Queen Victoria represent and how did these values relate to economic reform?

A New Era in British Politics

In the 1860s, a new era dawned in British politics. The old political parties regrouped under new leadership. Benjamin Disraeli forged the Tories into the modern Conservative Party. The Whigs, led by William Gladstone, evolved into the Liberal Party. Between 1868 and 1880, as the majority in Parliament swung between the two parties, Gladstone and Disraeli alternated as prime minister. Both fought for important reforms.

Expanding Suffrage Disraeli and the Conservative Party pushed through the Reform Bill of 1867. By giving the vote to many working-class men, the new law almost doubled the size of the electorate.

In the 1880s, it was the turn of Gladstone and the Liberal Party to extend suffrage. Their reforms gave the vote to farmworkers and most other men. By century's end, almost-universal male suffrage, the secret ballot, and other Chartist ambitions had been achieved. Britain had truly transformed itself from a constitutional monarchy to a parliamentary democracy, a form of government in which the executive leaders (usually

---

Differentiated Instruction Solutions for All Learners

L1 Special Needs **L2 Less Proficient Readers**

To help students trace the political changes in Britain, have them create a timeline of the democratic reforms. Have students mark the beginning of their timeline "Monarchy" and the end "Democracy." Ask students to place and briefly describe each change in Parliament. Ensure they include the Great Reform Act of 1832 and the Reform Bill of 1867 on their timelines.

Use the following study guide resources to help students acquiring basic skills.

📝 **Adapted Reading and Note Taking Study Guide**

- Adapted Note Taking Study Guide, p. 122
- Adapted Section Summary, p. 123

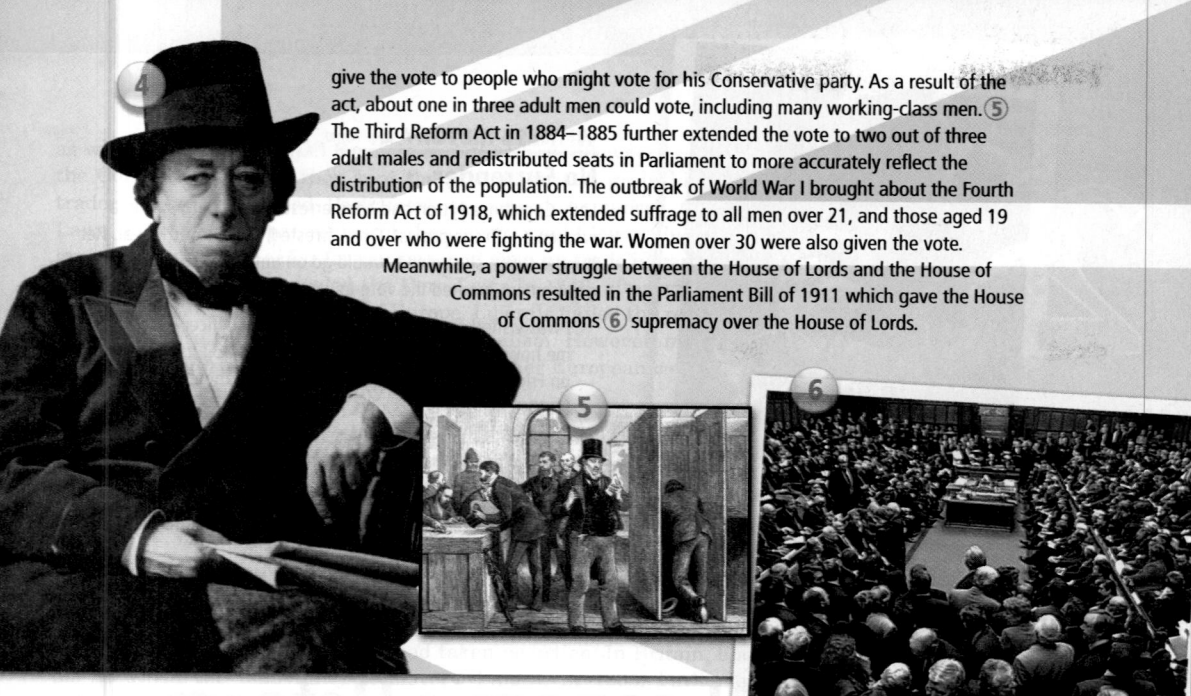

give the vote to people who might vote for his Conservative party. As a result of the act, about one in three adult men could vote, including many working-class men. The Third Reform Act in 1884–1885 further extended the vote to two out of three adult males and redistributed seats in Parliament to more accurately reflect the distribution of the population. The outbreak of World War I brought about the Fourth Reform Act of 1918, which extended suffrage to all men over 21, and those aged 19 and over who were fighting the war. Women over 30 were also given the vote.

Meanwhile, a power struggle between the House of Lords and the House of Commons resulted in the Parliament Bill of 1911 which gave the House of Commons ⑥ supremacy over the House of Lords.

a prime minister and cabinet) are chosen by and responsible to the legislature (parliament), and are also members of it.

Limiting the Lords In the early 1900s, many bills passed by the House of Commons met defeat in the House of Lords. In 1911, a Liberal government passed measures to restrict the power of the Lords, including their power to veto tax bills. The Lords resisted. Finally, the government threatened to create enough new lords to approve the law, and the Lords backed down. People hailed the change as a victory for democracy. In time, the House of Lords would become a largely ceremonial body with little power. The elected House of Commons would reign supreme.

✓ **Checkpoint** How was Parliament reformed during the late 1800s and early 1900s?

Thinking Critically
1. **Recognize Ideologies** Which group in the early 1800s do you think most feared the "democratization" of Britain? Why?
2. **Identify Central Issues** How did the Parliament Bill in 1911 reflect the same trends occurring as a result of the reform acts?

SECTION 1 Assessment

Progress Monitoring Online
For: Self-quiz with vocabulary practice
Web Code: nba-2312

Terms, People, and Places
1. What do each of the key terms listed at the beginning of the section have in common? Explain.

Note Taking
2. **Reading Skill: Identify Main Ideas** Use your completed outline to answer the Focus Question: How did political reform gradually expand suffrage and make the British Parliament more democratic during the 1800s?

Comprehension and Critical Thinking
3. **Summarize** How did the Reform Act of 1832 change Parliament?
4. **Categorize** What middle-class values are associated with the Victorian age?
5. **Identify Central Issues** What reforms did the Liberal and Conservative parties achieve?
6. **Draw Conclusions** Why do you think the Chartists demanded (a) a secret ballot, (b) salaries for members of Parliament?

● Writing About History
Quick Write: Gather Information If you were assigned to write a biographical essay on Queen Victoria, Benjamin Disraeli, or William Gladstone, what questions about these individuals would you want to answer in your essay? Choose one of these people and create a list of such questions about that person.

Section 1 Assessment

1. They all relate to Britain's government. The four terms highlight issues in British government of the 1800s; the three people are British political leaders.
2. Suffrage was extended to most men; representation was made fairer by getting rid of rotten boroughs.
3. It redistributed seats in the House of Commons, enlarged the electorate to include more men, and gave more of a political voice to middle-class men.
4. the values of duty, thrift, honesty, hard work, and respectability
5. They gave the right to vote to working-class men, farm workers and most other men, and restricted the power of the House of Lords, including their power to veto tax bills.
6. (a) so people could not use bribes or threats to influence votes (b) so people would not need wealth to serve in Parliament

● Writing About History
Questions should show an understanding of the feats and influence of the person chosen.

For additional assessment, have students access **Progress Monitoring Online** at **Web Code nba-2312.**

Quick Study Guide

- Have students use the Quick Study Guide to prepare for this chapter's test. Students may wish to refer to the following pages as they review:

  Democratic Reforms in Britain 1800s–Early 1900s
  Section 1, pp. 361–363

  Social and Economic Reforms in Britain 1800s–Early 1900s
  Section 2, pp. 364–367

  Key Events in France, 1800s–Early 1900s
  Section 3, pp. 371–376

  Key Events in the United States 1800s–Early 1900s
  Section 4, pp. 377–381

  Key Events in the Growth of Western Democracies
  Section 1, p. 361; Section 2, pp. 367–368; Section 3, pp. 373–375; Section 4, p. 379

- For additional review, remind students to refer to the

   Reading and Note Taking Study Guide **L3**

  Note Taking Study Guide, pp. 122, 124, 126, 128
  Section Summaries, pp. 123, 125, 127, 129

- Have students access **Web Code nbp-2308** for this chapter's **History Interactive** timeline, which includes expanded entries and additional events.

- If students need more instruction on analyzing timelines, have them read the **Skills Handbook,** p. SH30.

- When students have completed their study of the chapter, distribute Chapter Tests A and B.

  All in One Teaching Resources, Unit 3, pp. 57–62

> For **Progress Monitoring Online,** refer students to the Self-test with vocabulary practice at **Web Code nba-2307.**

Quick Study Guide

> **Progress Monitoring *Online***
> **For:** Self-test with vocabulary practice
> **Web Code:** nba-2307

■ Democratic Reforms in Britain 1800s–Early 1900s

- Redistribution of seats in the House of Commons from rural towns to growing cities (1832)
- Expansion of suffrage for men with property (1832)
- Expansion of suffrage for many working-class men (1867)
- Expansion of suffrage to farm workers and most men
- Introduction of secret ballot
- Power of the House of Lords restricted (1911)

■ Social and Economic Reforms in Britain 1800s–Early 1900s

- Slave trade prohibited (1807)
- Slavery in all British colonies abolished (1833)
- Repeal of high tariffs on grains (1846)
- Women and children under ten forbidden to work in mines (1842)
- Women and children limited to 10-hour workday (1847)
- Improvements in public health and housing
- Free elementary education
- Accident, health, and unemployment insurance
- Old-age pensions
- Suffrage extended to women over 30 (1918)

■ Key Events in France, 1800s–Early 1900s

1852	Napoleon III sets up Second Empire.
1856	France and Britain defeat Russia in Crimean War.
1863	Napoleon III sends troops and Archduke Maximilian to Mexico.
1860	France gains Nice and Savoy by helping Italian nationalists defeat Austria.
1870	Napoleon III captured in Franco-Prussian war; Four-month siege of Paris by Prussians; France defeated and Alsace Lorraine ceded to Germany; Republicans in Paris establish the Third Republic.
1871	Paris Commune uprising
1894	Dreyfus affair
1905	Separation of church and state established by law.

■ Key Events in the United States 1800s–Early 1900s

1803	Louisiana Purchase
1846–1848	Mexican War
1849	California Gold Rush
1861–1865	Civil War
1867	Purchase of Alaska
1869	Completion of Transcontinental Railroad
1882	Formation of Standard Oil Trust
1898	Spanish-American War; Hawaiian islands annexed
1908	Development of Henry Ford's Model T

■ Key Events in the Growth of Western Democracies

Europe and North America World Events

1832 Great Reform Act gives more British men suffrage and redistributes seats in House of Commons.	1845 Potato famine in Ireland begins.	1861–1865 American Civil War ends slavery in the United States.
1815	**1835**	**1855**
1821 Mexico wins independence from Spain.		1858 Britain begins rule of India.

Differentiated Instruction — Solutions for All Learners

L1 Special Needs L2 Less Proficient Readers

Use the following study guide resources to help students acquiring basic skills:

Adapted Reading and Note Taking Study Guide
Adapted Note Taking Study Guide, pp. 122, 124, 126, 128
Adapted Section Summaries, pp. 123, 125, 127, 129

L2 English Language Learners

Use the following study guide resources to help Spanish-speaking students:

Spanish Reading and Note Taking Study Guide
Spanish Note Taking Study Guide, pp. 122, 124, 126, 128
Spanish Section Summaries, pp. 123, 125, 127, 129

Concept Connector

Concept Connector

 Essential Question Review

To connect prior knowledge with what you have learned in this chapter, answer the questions below in your Concept Connector journal. Use the journal in the Reading and Note Taking Study Guide to record your answers (or go to www.phschool.com Web Code: nbd-2307). In addition, record information about the following concept:

• **Migration:** Westward Movement in the United States

1. **Cooperation** During France's Third Republic, political parties had to form coalitions—alliances of various parties—in order to form a government. In other countries, different groups often formed coalitions or alliances to achieve common goals. Identify and explain the goals of alliances that were formed in
   • Britain in the 1830s
   • France during the Dreyfus affair
   • the United States in the 1860s and 1890s

2. **Migration** By the mid-1800s, the United States had expanded its borders through wars and treaties. Americans believed that their nation was destined to spread across the entire continent. How did American migration to the West in the late 1800s differ from Irish migration to the United States during the same period? How did migration to the West affect the Native American population?

3. **Democracy** Democratic reforms swept through Britain, France, and the United States during the 1800s. Identify specific reforms that each country achieved during this period. Focus on the following:
   • suffrage
   • natural rights
   • government
   • workers' rights

■ Connections to Today

1. **Trade: Free Trade and Tariffs** The British Corn laws imposed high, protective tariffs on imported grains and kept the price of British grown grain high. Do library research to learn more about a current protective tariff that is opposed by those who favor free trade. Which country has imposed this tariff on imports? What goods are affected? Which groups oppose the tariff and why?

2. **Conflict: Northern Ireland** The southern counties of Ireland gained independence from Britain in 1922, but Northern Ireland remained under British rule. Conflict ensued between minority Catholics in Northern Ireland, who demanded the reunification of Ireland, and majority Protestants, who favored a continued union with Britain. In 1998, the main political parties signed a peace accord that would eventually bring self-rule to Northern Ireland. Do research to learn more about the status of peace in Northern Ireland.

3. **Conflict: Native Americans** The expansion of the United States proved to be devastating for most Native American groups in North America. By the 1890s, most surviving Native Americans had been driven onto reservations. Conduct library research to learn more about the status of Native Americans living in the United States today. Write a paragraph summarizing the information you find.

NATIONAL UNION OF WOMENS SUFFRAGE SOCIETIES

LAW-ABIDING   NO PARTY

History *Interactive*
For: Interactive timeline
Web Code: nbp-2308

1870 France defeated in the Franco-Prussian War; Third Republic established.	1897 Theodor Herzl organizes the First Zionist Congress for the purpose of founding a Jewish state.	1900s The women's suffrage movement grows in Britain and the United States.

1875   **1895**   **1915**

1869 The French-built Suez Canal opens in Egypt.	1889 Brazil becomes a republic.	1893 New Zealand is the first nation to give women the vote.	1910 The Union of South Africa is formed.

Concept Connector

Tell students that the main concepts for this chapter are Cooperation, Migration, and Democracy, and then ask them to answer the Essential Question Review questions on this page. Discuss the Connections to Today topics and ask students to answer the questions that follow.

Essential Question Review

1. In 1830s Britain, Chartists demanded universal male suffrage and a secret ballot. In France, the army, the government, and the Church pursued Dreyfus's trial and conviction. In the 1860s, abolitionists and women fought slavery. The Southern states formed the Confederate States of America. The 1890s saw farmers and city workers unite to form the Populist party.

2. American settlers headed west to acquire land or pan for gold. The impoverished Irish were escaping the "Great Hunger" caused by the potato blight. Some Native Americans resisted settlement on their lands, but they were outnumbered and forced to live on reservations.

3. In Britain, the Great Reform Act of 1832 gave representation to cities, extended suffrage, and transformed the government into a democracy. In France, unions were legalized and public education was extended to girls. In the United States, constitutional amendments banned slavery and gave African American men the vote.

Connections to Today

1. Answers should reflect current research on trade barriers and a specific example. They should also discuss goods affected, the country imposing the tariffs, and opposition to the tariff.

2. Answers should reflect thorough and accurate research about Northern Ireland and events since the Good Friday Agreement.

3. Students' paragraphs should include accurate information about some aspect of life for Native Americans today.

For additional review of this chapter's core concepts, remind students to refer to the

Reading and Note Taking Study Guide

Concept Connector, pp. 242, 250, 281

383

Chapter Assessment

Terms, People, and Places

1. It eliminated them by redistributing seats in the House of Commons.

2. women over 30 years old

3. so that landowners could not use money or power to influence voters

4. Merchants would have more opportunity for sales, and consumers would have lower prices.

5. There were so many political parties that no one could win a majority; several parties had to join together temporarily to govern.

6. Australia

7. legal separation of groups of people

8. a temporary government

Main Ideas

9. It redistributed seats in the House of Commons, granted the vote to more men; and, as a result, gave a greater political voice to middle-class men.

10. Parliament passed a law banning slavery in all British colonies.

11. There were only two parties in Britain but many in France. As a result, French parties needed to join in coalitions to form governments which made its government less stable than Britain's.

12. to build a Jewish state in Palestine

13. any two: obtain women's suffrage, eliminate child labor, limit working hours, regulate monopolies, give voters more power

Chapter Focus Question

14. In all three countries, the vote was eventually extended to all men, even if they did not own property. In the U.S., all women won suffrage in 1920; in Britain some women won that right in 1918, but all women did not receive it until 1928. In France, women did not have that right until after World War II. In the U.S., although African Americans technically had the right to vote, many were prevented from doing so.

Critical Thinking

15. that it was important for women to have a political voice outside of their husband's

16. Sample: France had deeper social and political divisions, which made it harder for groups to work together.

384

Chapter Assessment

Terms, People, and Places

1. How did the Great Reform Act of 1832 correct the problem of **rotten boroughs?**
2. What group of people was added to the British **electorate** in 1918?
3. Why did members of the Chartist movement demand the use of **secret ballots?**
4. Why did the opponents of the Corn Laws in Britain favor **free trade?**
5. Why did French politicians need to form **coalitions?**
6. Where did Britain establish **penal colonies?**
7. What is **segregation?**
8. What is a **provisional** government?

Main Ideas

Section 1 (pp. 360–363)
9. What were the effects of the Great Reform Act of 1832?

Section 2 (pp. 364–369)
10. How did British policy toward slavery change in 1833?

Section 3 (pp. 371–376)
11. How did the party system in France's Third Republic differ from the British party system?
12. What was the main goal of the Zionist movement?

Section 4 (pp. 377–381)
13. List two goals of the Progressives in the United States in the early 1900s.

Chapter Focus Question

14. How did Britain, France, and the United States slowly extend democratic rights during the 1800s and early 1900s?

Critical Thinking

15. **Analyzing Cartoons** What views of suffrage does this cartoon reflect?

16. **Draw Conclusions** Britain and France faced many similar political and social problems in the 1800s. Why do you think Britain was able to avoid the upheavals that plagued France?

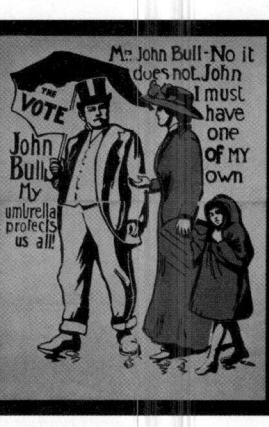

17. **Recognize Cause and Effect** (a) List two long-term causes and two immediate causes of the Great Hunger; (b) list two immediate effects. (c) Why do you think the famine sparked lasting feelings of bitterness against Britain?

18. **Synthesize Information** Describe how each of the following was related to nationalism: (a) the prestige of Queen Victoria, (b) the revolt of the Paris Commune, (c) the rise of Zionism.

19. **Geography and History** How did the geography of the United States encourage the American government to achieve its goal of Manifest Destiny?

● Writing About History

In this chapter's four Section Assessments, you developed skills for writing a compare and contrast essay.

Writing a Compare and Contrast Expository Essay
Conduct research and write a compare and contrast essay on the careers and accomplishments of Benjamin Disraeli and William Gladstone (left).

Prewriting
• Identify points of comparison and contrast for your essay. For example, you may want to compare and contrast the two men in terms of their background, political views, specific accomplishments, and impact on British politics. These categories will help you organize details in your essay.
• Create a Venn Diagram showing differences between the two men in the outside circles and similarities in the overlapping center.

• Collect the facts you need to write your essay.

Drafting
• Start with an engaging opening that defines the comparison/contrast and grabs readers' interest. This could be a quotation, surprising detail or statistic, or a question.
• Give details about each point of comparison to make it more accessible to readers. For example, you might give the years during which each man served as prime minister.
• Discuss the points about each man in the same order. You might even use similar sentence structure to emphasize this.

Revising
• Use the guidelines for revising your essay on page SH12 of the Writing Handbook.

---

17. (a) Long-term causes: The British controlled Irish farmland and used much of the land to produce food for export. The potato was the main source of food for the Irish. Immediate causes: A blight destroyed the potato crops for several years. The British continued to ship other food out of Ireland. (b) One million Irish people died of starvation or illness. Another million emigrated. (c) The Irish blamed the British for shipping food out

of Ireland when famine was devastating the country.

18. (a) Victoria's prestige helped the British feel proud of their country. (b) The Communards felt they were patriots who rejected the harsh peace with Germany. (c) Zionists believed that the Jewish people had a right to their own nation.

19. The U.S. was on the eastern part of a large continent; vast stretches of land lay to the west, seemingly there for the taking.

Document-Based Assessment

The Dreyfus Affair

On December 22, 1894, a French military court convicted an innocent Jewish man, Captain Alfred Dreyfus, of selling state secrets to Germany. Dreyfus was imprisoned on Devil's Island off of South America and his conviction was reversed only after nearly twelve years. The Dreyfus affair caused a great division between conservatives, who still disliked the outcome of the French Revolution and held strong anti-Semitic beliefs, and liberals, who viewed the case as a gross abuse of individual rights.

Document A

". . . if my voice ceased to be heard, it would mean that it had been extinguished forever, for if I have survived, it has been in order to insist on my honor—my property and the patrimony of our children—and in order to do my duty, as I have done it everywhere and always, and as it must always be done, when right and justice are on one's side, without ever fearing anything or anyone."

—From a letter to his wife Lucie, by Alfred Dreyfus, September 1898, published in *Cinq Années*

Document B

"I accuse the offices of War of having conducted in the press, particularly in L'Eclair and in L'Echo de Paris, an abominable campaign designed to mislead public opinion and to conceal their wrongdoing."

"Finally, I accuse the first Court Martial of having violated the law in convicting a defendant on the basis of a document kept secret, and I accuse the second Court Martial of having covered up . . . [and] knowingly acquitting a guilty man."

—From *"J'Accuse"* a letter to the President of the Republic by Émile Zola

Document C

"Un Diner En Famille"
    Translation: "It is agreed that there should be no talk of the affair! But they did talk about it . . ."

—From *Le Figaro* by Caran d'Ache, February, 1898

Analyzing Documents

Use your knowledge of the Dreyfus affair and Documents A, B, and C to answer questions 1–4.

1. In Document A, Dreyfus suggests that his wish to prove his innocence helped to—
   A keep him close to his family.
   B keep him alive.
   C make the Army take illegal actions.
   D make anti-Semitic groups angry.

2. Which statement best summarizes Zola's letter in Document B?
   A Although the French military convicted the wrong man, they attempted to carry out a fair trial.
   B The French military was fooled by handwriting experts, who tried to convict the wrong man.
   C The French military knowingly and illegally convicted an innocent man.
   D The French military showed that the army was anti-Semitic at the highest levels.

3. Document C illustrates—
   A why many French families believed Dreyfus was guilty.
   B why Dreyfus was convicted unfairly of treason.
   C how the Dreyfus case divided France.
   D how anti-Semitism was a factor in the Dreyfus case.

4. **Writing Task** On July 21, 1906, a French general knighted Alfred Dreyfus a member of the Legion of Honor. Well wishers attended the ceremony in the courtyard of the École Militaire. Some shouted "Long live Dreyfus." Suppose you were reporting on the event for an American newspaper. Write a news story, using the documents on this page along with information from the chapter.

Document-Based Assessment

■ To help students understand the documents on this page, give them the following **TIP: Study each document to assess its context and purpose. Use your knowledge of the subject as well as the information given in the document and the attribution line to determine who created it, when, and why.**

■ To provide students with further practice in answering Document-Based Assessment Questions, go to
    Document-Based Assessment, pp. 67–79

■ If students need more instruction on analyzing primary sources, have them read the **Skills Handbook,** p. SH31.

● Writing About History

As students begin the assignment, refer them to p. SH10 of the **Writing Handbook** for help in writing an expository essay. Remind them of the steps they should take to complete their assignment, including prewriting, drafting, and revising. For help in revising, remind them to use the guidelines on p. SH12 of the **Writing Handbook.**

Students' compare-and-contrast essays should highlight the similarities and differences between Disraeli and Gladstone. They should have a clear thesis with supporting details and contain an introduction, a body, and a conclusion. Their papers should show evidence of thoughtful and thorough research, be free of grammatical and spelling errors, and use correct bibliographical form. For scoring rubrics for writing assignments, see **Assessment Rubrics,** p. 8.

Answers

1. B
2. C
3. C
4. Responses should convey the complexities of the Dreyfus affair as well as the passionate feelings of people on both sides. They should be supported with specific evidence from the documents and the chapter.

The New Imperialism

Section	Core Instruction L3	Differentiated Instruction L1 L2 L4

Section 1
Building Overseas Empires

 1.5 periods, .75 block

OBJECTIVES
- Analyze the causes of the "new imperialism."
- Explain why Western imperialism spread so rapidly.
- Describe how imperial governments ruled their empires.

Focus Question *How did Western nations come to dominate much of the world in the late 1800s?*

All in One Teaching Resources, Unit 3
Reading Strategy: Identify Causes and Effects, p. 69
Vocabulary Builder: Context Clues, p. 68
Section 1 Quiz, p. 63

Reading and Note Taking Study Guide
Note Taking Study Guide, p. 130
Section 1 Summary, p. 131

Note Taking Transparencies, 160

WITNESS HISTORY Audio CD
The White Man's Burden

Progress Monitoring Transparencies, 99

Color Transparencies, 143, 144

Teaching Resources, Skills Handbook
Prereading the Chapter, pp. 1–2
Word Knowledge Rating Form, p. 3
K-W-L Chart, p. 4

L2 Adapted Reading and Note Taking Study Guide
Note Taking Study Guide, p. 130 SN
Section 1 Summary, p. 131 SN

L2 Adapted Reading and Note Taking Study Guide
Note Taking Study Guide, p. 130 LPR
Section 1 Summary, p. 131 LPR

Spanish Reading and Note Taking Study Guide
Note Taking Study Guide, p. 130 ELL
Section 1 Summary, p. 131 ELL

L4 Extend Activity, Teacher's Edition, p. 391 AR, GT

*Student Edition Audio SN

Differentiated Instruction Activity, Teacher's Edition, p. 389 SN

*Guided Reading Audio, Spanish ELL

*Student Edition Audio LPR

Differentiated Instruction Activity, Teacher's Edition, p. 389 LPR, ELL

Section 2
The Partition of Africa

 2 periods, 1 block

OBJECTIVES
- Analyze the forces that shaped Africa.
- Explain why European contact with Africa increased during the 1800s.
- Understand how Leopold II started a scramble for colonies.
- Describe how Africans resisted imperialism.

Focus Question *How did imperialist European powers claim control over most of Africa by the end of the 1800s?*

All in One Teaching Resources, Unit 3
Section 2 Quiz, p. 64

Reading and Note Taking Study Guide
Note Taking Study Guide, p. 132
Section 2 Summary, p. 133

Note Taking Transparencies, 161

WITNESS HISTORY Audio CD
Resisting Imperialism

Progress Monitoring Transparencies, 100

Color Transparencies, 145, 149

Witness History Discovery School™ video program, *The Scramble for African Colonies*

L1 Adapted Reading and Note Taking Study Guide
Note Taking Study Guide, p. 132 SN
Section 2 Summary, p. 133 SN

L2 Adapted Reading and Note Taking Study Guide
Note Taking Study Guide, p. 132 LPR
Section 2 Summary, p. 133 LPR

L4 All in One Teaching Resources, Unit 3
Viewpoints: Two Views of Imperialism in Africa, p. 70 AR, GT
Link to Literature: From "The Gentlemen of the Jungle," by Jomo Kenyatta, p. 71 AR, GT

Differentiated Instruction Activity, Teacher's Edition, p. 395 SN

Spanish Reading and Note Taking Study Guide
Note Taking Study Guide, p. 132 ELL
Section 2 Summary, p. 133 ELL

Differentiated Instruction Activity, Teacher's Edition, p. 395 LPR, ELL

Extend Activity, Teacher's Edition, pp. 386c, 398 AR, GT

*Audio support is available for all sections.

Assessment Resources
- **Progress Monitoring Transparencies**, 99–103
- **SuccessTracker™**, Chapter 12
- **Document-Based Assessment**, pp. 67–79
- *ExamView®* **Test Bank CD-ROM**, Chapter 12
- **All in One Teaching Resources, Unit 3,** Chapter Tests A and B, pp. 78–83
- **Progress Monitoring** *Online* **Quizzes,** Chapter 12
- **Assessment Rubrics**

Differentiated Instruction Key
L1 Special Needs	LPR Less Proficient Readers
L2 Basic to Average	AR Advanced Readers
L3 All Students	SN Special Needs Students
L4 Average to Advanced	GT Gifted and Talented
	ELL English Language Learner

Section	Core Instruction L3	Differentiated Instruction L1 L2 L4	

Section 3
European Claims in Muslim Regions

1.5 periods, .75 block

OBJECTIVES
- Analyze the sources of stress in Muslim regions.
- Explain the problems the Ottoman empire faced.
- Describe how Egypt sought to modernize.
- Understand European interest in Persia.

Focus Question *How did European nations extend their power into Muslim regions of the world?*

All in One Teaching Resources, Unit 3
Outline Map: The Ottoman Empire in the Late 1800s, p. 75
Section 3 Quiz, p. 65

Reading and Note Taking Study Guide
Note Taking Study Guide, p. 134
Section 3 Summary, p. 135

Note Taking Transparencies, 162

WITNESS HISTORY Audio CD
The Egyptian Campaign

Progress Monitoring Transparencies, 101

Color Transparencies, 63, 146

L1 Adapted Reading and Note Taking Study Guide
Note Taking Study Guide, p. 134 SN
Section 3 Summary, p. 135 SN

L2 Adapted Reading and Note Taking Study Guide
Note Taking Study Guide, p. 134 LPR
Section 3 Summary, p. 135 LPR

L4 All in One Teaching Resources, Unit 3
Viewpoints: Two Views on the Suez Canal, p. 72 AR, GT

Differentiated Instruction Activity, Teacher's Edition, p. 402 SN

Spanish Reading and Note Taking Study Guide
Note Taking Study Guide, p. 134 ELL
Section 3 Summary, p. 135 ELL

Differentiated Instruction Activity, Teacher's Edition, p. 402 LPR, ELL

Differentiated Instruction Activity, Teacher's Edition, p. 401 AR, GT

Extend Activity, Teacher's Edition, p. 404 AR, GT

Section 4
The British Take Over India

1.5 periods, .75 block

OBJECTIVES
- Understand the causes and effects of the Sepoy Rebellion.
- Explain how British rule affected India.
- Describe how Indians viewed Western culture.
- Identify the origins of Indian nationalism.

Focus Question *How did Britain gradually extend its control over most of India, despite opposition?*

All in One Teaching Resources, Unit 3
Outline Map: The British in India to 1858, p. 76
Geography Quiz, p. 77
Section 4 Quiz, p. 66

Reading and Note Taking Study Guide
Note Taking Study Guide, p. 136
Section 4 Summary, p. 137

Note Taking Transparencies, 163

WITNESS HISTORY Audio CD
Critical of British Rule

Progress Monitoring Transparencies, 102

Color Transparencies, 147

L1 Adapted Reading and Note Taking Study Guide
Note Taking Study Guide, p. 136 SN
Section 4 Summary, p. 137 SN

L2 Adapted Reading and Note Taking Study Guide
Note Taking Study Guide, p. 136 LPR
Section 4 Summary, p. 137 LPR

L4 All in One Teaching Resources, Unit 3
Biography: Rabindranath Tagore, p. 73 AR, GT

Differentiated Instruction Activity, Teacher's Edition, p. 407 SN

Spanish Reading and Note Taking Study Guide
Note Taking Study Guide, p. 136 ELL
Section 4 Summary, p. 137 ELL

Differentiated Instruction Activity, Teacher's Edition, p. 407 LPR, ELL

Differentiated Instruction Activity, Teacher's Edition, p. 408 AR, GT

Extend Activity, Teacher's Edition, p. 409 AR, GT

Section 5
China and the New Imperialism

1.5 periods, .75 block

OBJECTIVES
- Describe what trade rights Westerners sought in China.
- Explain the internal problems Chinese reformers tried to solve.
- Understand how the Qing dynasty fell.

Focus Question *How did Western powers use diplomacy and war to gain power in Qing China?*

All in One Teaching Resources, Unit 3
Section 5 Quiz, p. 67

Reading and Note Taking Study Guide
Note Taking Study Guide, p. 138
Section 5 Summary, p. 139
Concept Connector, pp. 233, 262, 267

Note Taking Transparencies, 164

WITNESS HISTORY Audio CD
Trading Opium for Tea

Progress Monitoring Transparencies, 103

Color Transparencies, 148

L1 Adapted Reading and Note Taking Study Guide
Note Taking Study Guide, p. 138 SN
Section 5 Summary, p. 139 SN
Concept Connector, pp. 233, 262, 267 SN

L2 Adapted Reading and Note Taking Study Guide
Note Taking Study Guide, p. 138 LPR
Section 5 Summary, p. 139 LPR
Concept Connector, pp. 233, 262, 267 LPR

L4 All in One Teaching Resources, Unit 3
Primary Source, p. 74 AR, GT

Differentiated Instruction Activity, Teacher's Edition, p. 414 SN

Spanish Reading and Note Taking Study Guide
Note Taking Study Guide, p. 138 ELL
Section 5 Summary, p. 139 ELL
Concept Connector, pp. 233, 262, 267 ELL

Differentiated Instruction Activity, Teacher's Edition, p. 414 LPR, ELL

Extend Activity, Teacher's Edition, p. 415 AR, GT

CHAPTER PLANNER

PROFESSIONAL DEVELOPMENT

Author's Notes

First the Treaties, Then the Troops

The scramble for Africa by competing European powers was carried out by politicians and diplomats in Europe and by explorers, missionaries, military commanders, economic developers, and others in Africa itself. By the end of the century, it had brought nine tenths of the world's second-largest continent under Western rule. . . .

On the African earth itself, it was first the treaties, then the troops. In the 1870s and 1880s, expeditions set out for the interior from the string of European settlements that had been scattered along the coasts since the heyday of the Old Imperialism. These handfuls of government officials or agents for trading companies negotiated treaties with Muslim monarchs and paramount chiefs, including the rulers of many of the newly evolving states. . . . In return for gifts, protection, and other benefits, African rulers thus accepted a European overlordship that many of them only partly understood.

The misunderstandings were thrashed out later, during the sometimes savage fighting of the 1890s and the early 1900s. The larger states of inner Africa resisted initial penetration. Other African peoples revolted later against the increasingly heavy hand of Western rule.

Recent scholarship suggests that we should not exaggerate the European mastery of the situation. Local rulers often knew the local situation much better than the intruders did and made quite advantageous terms, at least in the short run. In the early 1830s, after a dozen years of mounting British pressure on the Shanti of West Africa, the Ashanti princess Akyaawa Yikwan negotiated a key peace treaty that brought her people a vigorous revival of trade and postponed foreign rule for most of the rest of the century.

Rarely, however, was either resistance or diplomacy successful for long. The courage of the Africans was great, and their numbers often greater than those of the intruders. But a single Maxim machine gun could make numbers and courage suddenly irrelevant. From Egypt to the Cape, from the tree-studded grasslands of the western Sudan to the green hills of East Africa, European organization, discipline, ruthlessness, and firepower carried the day.

—Anthony Esler, *The Human Venture: From Prehistory to the Present*, (Upper Saddle River, New Jersey: Pearson Education, 2004), pp. 569–571

Extend Online

African Resistance to European Imperialism

Have students research types of resistance to the European presence in Africa. (The carving below is symbolic of the relationship at that time.) Ask them to choose one type of resistance—religious, royal, or political—and write a brief news article presenting their findings.

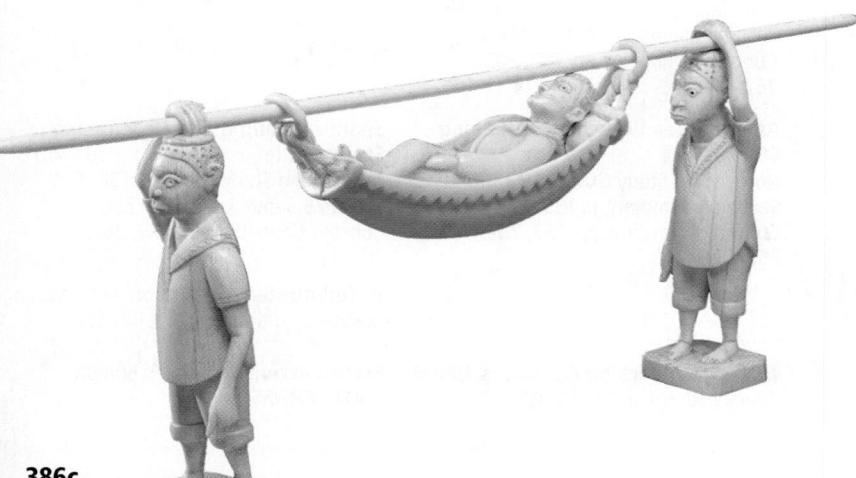

Prepare for the Activity Explain to students that there were several types of resistance to European imperialism, including armed rebellions like those inspired by Usman dan Fodio. Newspapers and other publications criticizing colonial rule had also begun to be widely circulated toward the end of the nineteenth century.

Conduct the Activity For help in starting the activity, send students to **Web Code nbe-2401.** Have students work in small groups and research one type of resistance. Have students note historical background, goals, outcome, groups involved, as well as any current information about their topic and present their findings in a short news article.

Follow-Up Have students read their articles to the class. Then discuss whether each type of resistance was ultimately successful. Ensure students explain their reasoning. Have them consider factors such as weapons, nationalism, education, and religion.

Differentiated Instruction Solutions for All Learners

Debate L4

Debates challenge students by asking them to use higher level thinking to consider, defend, and refute two opposing arguments. In order to do this effectively, they need to be well-versed in the topic being considered. Debates can be structured in a variety of ways. Here is one model that can be particularly effective:

1. Present an opinion-based question to students that can be logically answered several different ways.

2. Break students up into two groups, one representing each side.

3. Have students brainstorm justifications for their positions. Make sure that a "scribe" is appointed to write down group members' ideas.

4. Provide time for students to research their position.

5. Instruct students on each side to prepare a two minute opening statement that makes a compelling case for their position.

6. Begin the debate. A student from each side should read their opening statement, which is to be followed by questions from the opposing side. Any member of the group can respond to questions.

7. Conclude the debate by giving each team several minutes to create a brief closing statement to be read to the class.

Poster Assessments L2

Less Proficient Readers often have trouble discerning main points in the text. To help them find key information, suggest that they create bulletin boards or informative posters. These are both an excellent way to have them find key points in the text and present the information in an engaging manner. Additionally, the artistic or verbal component of the assignment often heightens student interest and confidence.

Provide students with a specific number of bullet points that they are required to put on their poster. Each bullet point should list an important main idea about their assigned topic. Students should add an illustration to accompany each bullet point. These poster assessments can be shared with classmates to review key information or displayed around the classroom for students to view.

Modeling Reading and Writing Skills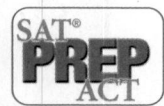

Revise Explain that in this chapter, students will be writing a persuasive essay. (See Writing About History, p. 418.) Tell students that after they have written a draft, they should go back and revise it. Remind them to consider their audience and purpose. Have them consider what sort of arguments would appeal to their target reader. For instance, they would write an advertisement targeted at eight-year-old elementary school students differently than one aimed at 19-year-old college students. Similarly, in a persuasive speech or position paper, they must consider how best to appeal to their audience. Have them return to their writing and consider both word choice and the strength of their arguments.

Vocabulary: Recognize Word Origins Tell students that by recognizing word parts, they can identify and understand many unfamiliar words. Remind them that many words come from Greek or Latin roots. For example, the prefix *uni-*, which means one, comes from the Latin word *unus*, which also means one. This prefix is part of the noun *unit* (the smallest whole number), the verb *unite* (to join into one, combine, make whole), and the adjective *universal* (covering the whole collectively).

To demonstrate this, begin by writing on the board: *vitality*—based on the Latin root *vit/viv* meaning "live." Model the process aloud. If I know that *vit* means "live," I can add a meaning for the suffix *-ity* to build a word. Since *-ity* means "state or quality of," vitality must mean "full of life."

Teach With Technology

PresentationEXPRESS™
Premium DVD

- Teach this chapter's core content using **PresentationExpress™ Premium,** which includes dynamic lecture notes, interactive game shows, songs, videos, and the *ExamView® QuickTake* assessment tool.

- To introduce this chapter using **PresentationExpress™ Premium,** start by asking students **Which of the following statements do you most agree with? (A) A stronger country has the right to take over a weaker country. (B) A strong country should never interfere with weaker countries. (C) A strong country should use its strength to help weaker countries. (D) A strong country should use its strength to gain the most economic advantages possible from weaker countries.** Take a class poll or record students' answers using the QuickTake feature and discuss their responses. Point out that in this chapter, they will read about how strong countries built empires by taking over weaker countries. Continue introducing the chapter using the chapter opener slide show and Witness History audio.

Technology Resources

- Student**EXPRESS** CD-ROM, Chapter 12

- Teacher**EXPRESS** CD-ROM, Chapter 12

- Presentation**EXPRESS™** **Premium DVD,** Chapter 12

- **WITNESS HISTORY** **Audio CD,** Chapter 12

- *ExamView* **Test Bank CD-ROM,** English and Spanish, Chapter 12

- **Guided Reading Audio,** Spanish, Chapter 12

- **Student Edition Audio,** Chapter 12

- **Witness History Discovery School™** video program, *The Scramble for African Colonies*

- **Experience It! Multimedia Pack**

Bibliography

For the Teacher

Marshall, P.J., ed. *The Cambridge Illustrated History of the British Empire.* New York: Cambridge University Press, 1996.

Spence, Jonathan D. *God's Chinese Son.* New York: Norton, 1996.

Vandervort, Bruce. *Wars of Imperial Conquest in Africa, 1830–1914.* Bloomington: Indiana University Press, 1998.

For the Student

L2 Worth, Richard. *Stanley and Livingstone and the Exploration of Africa in World History.* Berkeley Heights, N.J.: Enslow Publishers, 2000.

L3 Ngwane, Zolani. *Zulu.* New York: Rosen Publishing Group, 1997.

L4 Smith, Bonnie G. *Imperialism: A History in Documents.* Oxford University Press, 2000.

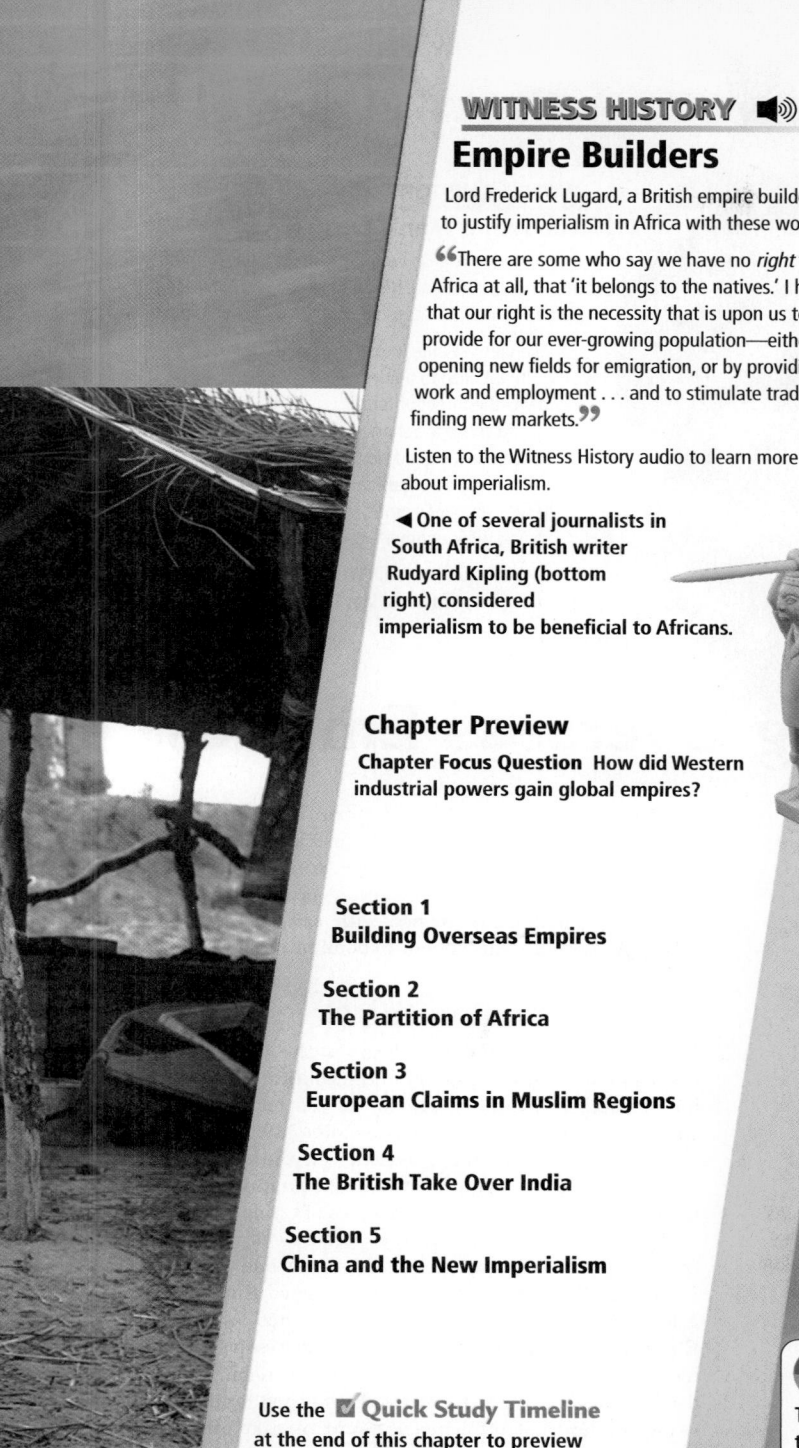

Empire Builders

Lord Frederick Lugard, a British empire builder, tried to justify imperialism in Africa with these words:

❝There are some who say we have no *right* to Africa at all, that 'it belongs to the natives.' I hold that our right is the necessity that is upon us to provide for our ever-growing population—either by opening new fields for emigration, or by providing work and employment . . . and to stimulate trade by finding new markets.**❞**

Listen to the Witness History audio to learn more about imperialism.

◄ **One of several journalists in South Africa, British writer Rudyard Kipling (bottom right) considered imperialism to be beneficial to Africans.**

Chapter Preview

Chapter Focus Question How did Western industrial powers gain global empires?

Section 1
Building Overseas Empires

Section 2
The Partition of Africa

Section 3
European Claims in Muslim Regions

Section 4
The British Take Over India

Section 5
China and the New Imperialism

Use the ☑ **Quick Study Timeline** at the end of this chapter to preview chapter events.

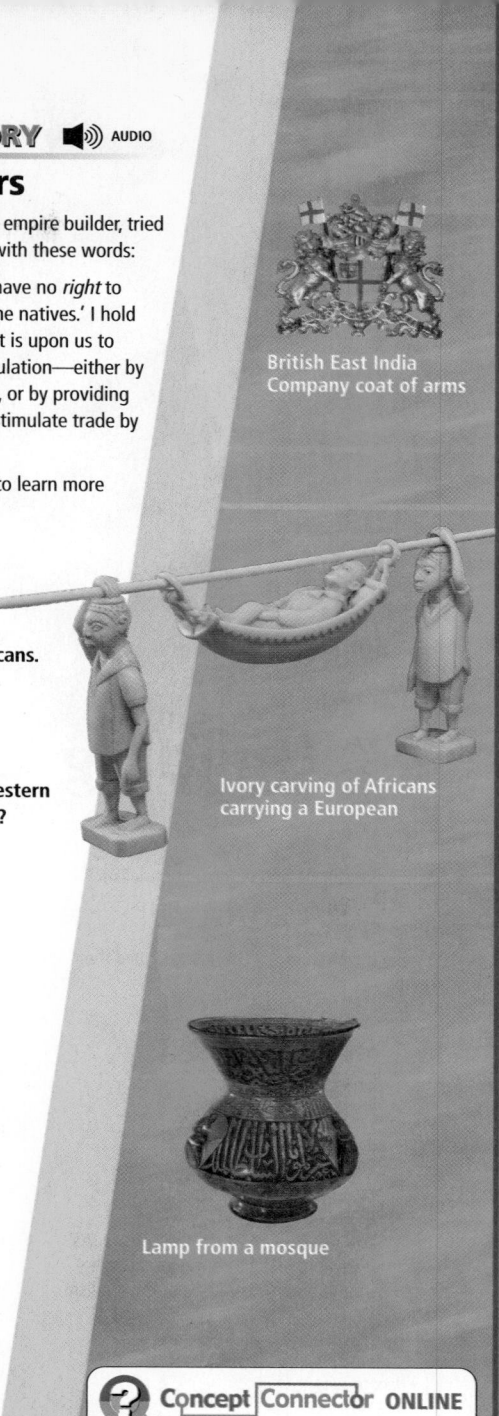

British East India Company coat of arms

Ivory carving of Africans carrying a European

Lamp from a mosque

? Concept Connector ONLINE
To explore Essential Questions related to this chapter, go to PHSchool.com
Web Code: nbd-2407

Chapter-Level Resources

All in One Vocabulary Builder; Reading Strategy; Enrichments; Outline Maps; Geography Quiz; Chapter Test,
- Document-Based Assessments
- AYP Monitoring Assessments
- *ExamView®* Test Bank CD-ROM
- Guided Reading Audio, Spanish
- Student Edition Audio

Previewing the Chapter

- **WITNESS HISTORY** Explain that from 1800 to 1914 Western industrial nations built empires in Africa and Asia. Read the Witness History selection aloud or play the audio. Ask **What are the opposing viewpoints in the selection?** *(that the British should stay out of Africa; that Britain has a right to extend its influence into Africa)* **Who are "the natives" and what is Lord Lugard's attitude toward them?** *(The "natives" are those who lived in Africa before the British arrived; Lugard views them with disdain.)*

  🔊 AUDIO **Witness History Audio CD,** Empire Builders

- **Analyzing the Visuals** Ask students to study the photo in the previous page. Ask **What questions do the photo and the Witness History selection bring to mind?** *(Sample: Will the European imperialists succeed? How will Africans react to them? What new markets will the imperialists find? How will all this affect Africa?)* Write questions on a flip chart to return to later.

- **Focus** Write the Chapter Focus Question on the board. Tell students to keep this question in mind as they read the chapter. *(Answer appears with Chapter Assessment answers.)* Have students preview the section titles for this chapter.

Note Taking Study Guide With Concept Connector Journal
For online access: Web code: nbd-2407
For print alternative: Reading and Note Taking Study Guide booklet

Objectives

As you teach this section, keep students focused on the following objectives to help them answer the Section Focus Question and master core content.

■ Analyze the causes of the "new imperialism."

■ Explain why Western imperialism spread so rapidly.

■ Describe how imperial governments ruled their empires.

Prepare to Read

Build Background Knowledge ⓛ

Write the words *empire* and *imperialism* on the board. Ask **How are these words related?** *(Empire means a group of states under one ruler; imperialism is the process of forming an empire by creating colonies.)* Ask students to recall earlier empires they have studied. Then have them predict the benefits and disadvantages of empire building in the 1800s.

Set a Purpose ⓛ

■ **WITNESS HISTORY** Read the selection aloud or play the audio.

  ◀)) AUDIO **Witness History Audio CD,** The White Man's Burden

Ask **Why would "the White Man" show pride?** *(He thinks he is superior.)* **Who does Kipling think profits from imperialism?** *(the subject peoples)* **Who do you think really profits from this relationship?** *(Answers will vary.)*

■ **Focus** Point out the Section Focus Question and write it on the board. Tell students to refer to this question as they read. *(Answer appears with Section 1 Assessment answers.)*

■ **Preview** Have students preview the Section Objectives and the list of Terms, People, and Places.

■ **Reading Skill** Have students use the worksheet *Reading Strategy: Identify Causes and Effects.*

All in One Teaching Resources, Unit 3, p. 69

English writer Rudyard Kipling

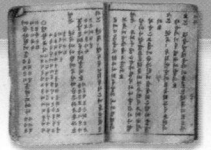

Missionary prayer book in Korean

WITNESS HISTORY ◀)) AUDIO

The White Man's Burden

Born in India, English writer Rudyard Kipling witnessed British imperialism firsthand. His 1899 poem "The White Man's Burden" summarizes his view of the duties of imperial nations:

❝ Take up the White Man's burden—
    In patience to abide,
To veil the threat of terror
    And check the show of pride;
By open speech and simple,
    An hundred times made plain,
To seek another's profit,
    And work another's gain.❞

Focus Question How did Western nations come to dominate much of the world in the late 1800s?

Building Overseas Empires

Objectives
• Analyze the causes of the "new imperialism."
• Explain why Western imperialism spread so rapidly.
• Describe how imperial governments ruled their empires.

Terms, People, and Places
imperialism
protectorate
sphere of influence

No̲te Taking

Reading Skill: Recognize Multiple Causes As you read the section, make a chart like the one below showing the multiple causes of imperialism in the 1800s.

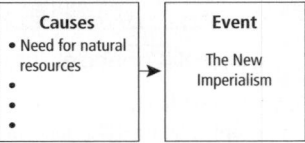

Causes		Event
• Need for natural resources • • •	→	The New Imperialism

Like Great Britain, other Western countries built overseas empires in the late 1800s. The Industrial Revolution had transformed the West. Advances in science and technology, industry, transportation, and communication provided Western nations with many advantages. Armed with new economic and political power, Western nations set out to dominate the world.

Motives Driving the New Imperialism

European imperialism did not begin in the 1800s. **Imperialism** is the domination by one country of the political, economic, or cultural life of another country or region. As you have learned, European states won empires in the Americas after 1492, established colonies in South Asia, and gained toeholds on the coasts of Africa and China. Despite these gains, between 1500 and 1800, Europe had little influence on the lives of the peoples of China, India, or Africa.

By the 1800s, however, Europe had gained considerable power. Strong, centrally governed nation-states had emerged, and the Industrial Revolution had greatly enriched European economies. Encouraged by their new economic and military strength, Europeans embarked on a path of aggressive expansion that today's historians call the "new imperialism." In just a few decades, beginning in the 1870s, Europeans brought much of the world under their influence and control. Like other key developments in world history, the new imperialism exploded out of a combination of causes.

Vocabulary Builder

Use the information below and the following resources to teach the high-use word from this section.

All in One **Teaching Resources, Unit 3,** p. 68; **Teaching Resources, Skills Handbook,** p. 3

High-Use Word	Definition and Sample Sentence
prestige, p. 389	*n.* the power to impress or influence because of success or wealth Even though Christine wasn't the most popular candidate for class president, her **prestige** still won her many votes.

Economic Interests Spur Expansion The Industrial Revolution created needs and desires that spurred overseas expansion. Manufacturers wanted access to natural resources such as rubber, petroleum, manganese for steel, and palm oil for machinery. They also hoped for new markets of consumers to whom they could sell their factory goods. Bankers sought ventures to invest their profits. In addition, colonies offered a valuable outlet for Europe's growing population.

Political and Military Motives Political and military issues were closely linked to economic motives. Steam-powered merchant ships and naval vessels needed bases around the world to take on coal and supplies. Industrial powers seized islands or harbors to satisfy these needs.

Nationalism played an important role, too. When France, for example, moved into West Africa, rival nations like Britain and Germany seized lands nearby to halt further French expansion. Western leaders claimed that colonies were needed for national security. They also felt that ruling a global empire increased a nation's <u>prestige</u> around the world.

Humanitarian and Religious Goals Many Westerners felt a genuine concern for their "little brothers" beyond the seas. Missionaries, doctors, and colonial officials believed they had a duty to spread what they saw as the blessings of Western civilization, including its medicine, law, and Christian religion.

Applying Social Darwinism Behind the idea of the West's civilizing mission was a growing sense of racial superiority. Many Westerners had embraced the ideas of Social Darwinism. They applied Darwin's ideas about natural selection and survival of the fittest to human societies. European races, they argued, were superior to all others, and imperial domination of weaker races was simply nature's way of improving the human species. As a result, millions of non-Westerners were robbed of their cultural heritage.

✔ **Checkpoint** What factors contributed to European imperialism in the 1800s?

Vocabulary Builder

<u>prestige</u>—(pres TEEZH) *n.* the power to impress or influence because of success or wealth

A Market for Goods

A driving force behind imperialism was the desire for access to new markets in which to sell goods. This British propaganda poster boasts that Africa would become a gold mine for British-made products. Britain's sense of national pride and aggressive foreign policy during this period came to be known as jingoism. *What does this poster show about the British attitude toward Africa?*

Teach

Motives Driving the New Imperialism

Instruct

■ **Introduce: Vocabulary Builder** Have students read the Vocabulary Builder term and definition. Tell students that **prestige** was very important to European powers. Ask **How might a nation increase its prestige?** *(by increasing its political, economic, or military power or by expanding the territory it controls)*

■ **Teach** Display **Color Transparency 143: Causes of the New Imperialism** and review the causes. Then ask students how the Industrial Revolution might have contributed to Western nations' sense of superiority.

▦ **Color Transparencies**, 143

■ **Quick Activity** Have students reread the Kipling quote. Ask **Who stood to "profit" or "gain" from each of the factors that led to the new imperialism?** *(mostly Western powers)*

Independent Practice

Organize students into four groups. Ask each group to examine one of the following motives for the new imperialism: economic, political/military, humanitarian/religious, Social Darwinist. Then have each group create a poster illustrating its motive.

Monitor Progress

As students fill in their charts, circulate to make sure they understand the political and social causes of imperialism. For a completed version of the chart, see
▦ **Note Taking Transparencies**, 160

Answers

✔ economic motives, political and military missions, humanitarian and religious beliefs, and Social Darwinist ideas

Caption It was seen as a new market to be explored and exploited.

The Rapid Spread of Western Imperialism/ Forms of Imperial Rule ⓛ

Instruct

- **Introduce: Key Terms** Write the key terms *colony, protectorate,* and *sphere of influence* on the board. Draw a circle around each term, overlapping part of all three circles. Use this three-way Venn diagram to lead a discussion comparing and contrasting these terms.

- **Teach** On the board, create four columns for Western Strengths and Weaknesses, Non-Western Strengths and Weaknesses. Have students volunteer information to fill in the chart. Make sure they include resistance groups under Non-Western Strengths and criticism at home under Western Weaknesses. Encourage students to identify strengths and weaknesses beyond those listed in the book, such as fighting on native versus foreign soil. Then use the Think-Write-Pair-Share strategy (TE, p. T23) to discuss whether Western and non-Western countries were matched in a fair fight.

- **Quick Activity** Display **Color Transparency 144: Responsibilities of Powerful Nations**. Have students identify the cartoonist's point of view. Then discuss whether or not powerful nations have responsibilities toward less powerful nations.

  🗔 **Color Transparencies, 144**

Independent Practice

Have students suppose that they are living in the 1800s and that the two views in Comparing Viewpoints are newspaper editorials. Have them write a letter to the editor arguing against one of the viewpoints.

Monitor Progress

- Circulate to ensure students understand both sides of the debate on imperialism.
- Check Reading and Note Taking Study Guide entries for student understanding.

Answers

COMPARING VIEWPOINTS that the English are a superior race; that the land belongs to its inhabitants, who have an established way of life

Caption They had superior weapons.

■ COMPARING VIEWPOINTS

European Conquest of Africa

The excerpts below present two different views on the partition of Africa by European nations in the 1800s. **Critical Thinking** *What is Cecil Rhodes's argument for imperialism? What is Chief Kabongo's argument against it?*

Favoring Imperialism	Opposing Imperialism
"I contend that we are the first race in the world and that the more of the world we inhabit the better it is for the human race. I contend that every acre added to our territory provides for the birth of more of the English race, who otherwise would not be brought into existence . . . . I believe it to be my duty to God, my Queen and my country to paint the whole map of Africa red, red from the Cape to Cairo. That is my creed, my dream and my mission." —*Cecil Rhodes*	"A Pink Cheek man came one day to our Council . . . and he told us of the King of the Pink Cheek who . . . lived in a land over the seas. 'This great king is now your king,' he said. This was strange news. For this land was ours. . . . We had no king, we elected our Councils and they made our laws. With patience, our leading Elders tried to tell this to the Pink Cheek. . . . But at the end he said, 'This we know, but in spite of this what I have told you is a fact. You have now a king . . . and his laws are your laws.'" —*Chief Kabongo of the Kikuyu in Kenya*

The Maxim Gun
Sir Hiram Maxim with his invention, the Maxim machine gun. *Why were European armies often able to defeat African or Asian forces?*

The Rapid Spread of Western Imperialism

From about 1870 to 1914, imperialist nations gained control over much of the world. Leading the way were soldiers, merchants, settlers, missionaries, and explorers. In Europe, imperial expansion found favor with all classes, from bankers and manufacturers to workers. Western imperialism expanded rapidly for a number of reasons.

Weakness of Non-Western States While European nations had grown stronger in the 1800s, several older civilizations were in decline, especially the Ottoman Middle East, Mughal (MOO gul) India, and Qing (ching) China. In West Africa, wars among African peoples and the damaging effect of the slave trade had undermined established empires, kingdoms, and city-states. Newer African states were not strong enough to resist the Western onslaught.

Western Advantages European powers had the advantages of strong economies, well-organized governments, and powerful armies and navies. Superior technology, including riverboats and the telegraph, as well as improved medical knowledge also played a role. Quinine and other new medicines helped Europeans survive deadly tropical diseases. And, of course, advances such as Maxim machine guns, repeating rifles, and steam-driven warships were very strong arguments in persuading Africans and Asians to accept Western control.

Resisting Imperialism Africans and Asians strongly resisted Western expansion into their lands. Some people fought the invaders, even though they had no weapons to equal the Maxim gun. Ruling groups in certain areas tried to strengthen their societies against outsiders by reforming their own Muslim, Hindu, or Confucian traditions. Finally, many

History Background

The Maxim Gun As English writer Hilaire Belloc wrote in this couplet, "Whatever happens, we have got/ the Maxim gun, and they have not." This weapon provided Western powers with a significant advantage in battle. Invented by Hiram Maxim in 1885, it was the first fully automatic machine gun. It could fire 500 rounds per minute, about as many as 100 rifles.

A later model was called the "Devil's Paintbrush" because of the way it mowed down charging soldiers. In 1893, fifty British soldiers with four Maxim guns fought off 5000 warriors in what is now Zimbabwe. The Austrian, German, Italian, and Russian armies also bought Maxim machine guns.

Western-educated Africans and Asians organized nationalist movements to expel the imperialists from their lands.

Facing Criticism at Home In the West itself, a small group of anti-imperialists emerged. Some argued that colonialism was a tool of the rich. Others said it was immoral. Westerners, they pointed out, were moving toward greater democracy at home but were imposing undemocratic rule on other peoples.

 Checkpoint How did Western imperialism spread through Africa and Asia so quickly?

Forms of Imperial Rule

The leading imperial powers developed several kinds of colonial rule. The French practiced direct rule, sending officials and soldiers from France to administer their colonies. Their goal was to impose French culture on their colonies and turn them into French provinces.

The British, by contrast, often used a system of indirect rule. To govern their colonies, they used sultans, chiefs, or other local rulers. They then encouraged the children of the local ruling class to get an education in Britain. In that way, they groomed a new "Westernized" generation of leaders to continue indirect imperial rule and to spread British civilization. Like France and other imperialist nations, however, Britain could still resort to military force if its control over a colony was threatened.

In a **protectorate,** local rulers were left in place but were expected to follow the advice of European advisors on issues such as trade or missionary activity. A protectorate cost less to run than a colony did, and usually did not require a large commitment of military forces.

A third form of Western control was the **sphere of influence,** an area in which an outside power claimed exclusive investment or trading privileges. Europeans carved out these spheres in China and elsewhere to prevent conflicts among themselves.

Indian princes and British army officers play polo in 1880.

 **Checkpoint** Compare and contrast how Britain and France ruled their colonies.

Progress Monitoring *Online*
For: Self-quiz with vocabulary practice
Web Code: nba-2411

Terms, People, and Places
1. What do each of the key terms listed at the beginning of the section have in common? Explain.

Note Taking
2. **Reading Skill: Recognize Multiple Causes** Use your completed chart to answer the Focus Question: How did Western nations come to dominate much of the world in the late 1800s?

Comprehension and Critical Thinking
3. **Explain** (a) What were three reasons for the rapid spread of Western imperialism? (b) How did people oppose it?
4. **Recognize Bias** Western colonial officials and missionaries thought that they had a duty to spread the "blessings of Western civilization" to their African and Asian "little brothers." How was this a biased viewpoint?

● **Writing About History**
Quick Write: Write a Thesis Statement Suppose that you are writing a persuasive essay using the point of view of an anti-imperialist from a Western nation trying to persuade the public that imperialism is wrong. Based on what you have read in this section, write a thesis statement for your essay.

Section 1 Assessment

1. All three terms relate to the domination of one country by another.
2. Western scientific, technological, and economic progress during the Industrial Revolution strengthened Western armed forces and allowed Western nations to dominate much of the world.
3. (a) Non-Western nations were in a weak state; Western powers had strong economies, governments, and armed forces; and they had superior technology. (b) through wars of resistance and nationalist movements and by adopting Western technologies and economic reforms
4. Western civilization was assumed to be superior and Westerners to be wiser and more advanced than their "little brothers."

Assess Progress
- Have students complete the Section Assessment.
- Administer the Section Quiz.

[All in One] **Teaching Resources, Unit 3,** p. 63
- To further assess student understanding, use
   Progress Monitoring Transparencies, 99

Reteach L1 L2
If students need more instruction, have them read the section summary.

 Reading and Note Taking Study Guide, p. 131 L3

 Adapted Reading and Note Taking Study Guide, p. 131 L1 L2

Spanish Reading and Note Taking Study Guide, p. 131 L2

Extend L4
Have students write an essay comparing the new European empires to one of the empires studied in a previous chapter. They should compare the forms of imperial rule and the factors that led to the spread of empire.

Answers

✓ Westerners had stronger economies, governments, and technology as well as the necessary manpower.

✓ France practiced direct rule whereas Britain often used indirect rule, through a local ruling class.

● **Writing About History**
The thesis statement should take a clear position and include reasons that can be supported by evidence in the section.

For additional assessment, have students access **Progress Monitoring *Online*** at **Web Code nba-2411.**

Objectives

As you teach this section, keep students focused on the following objectives to help them answer the Section Focus Question and master core content.

- Analyze the forces that shaped Africa.
- Explain why European contact with Africa increased during the 1800s.
- Understand how Leopold II started a scramble for colonies.
- Describe how Africans resisted imperialism.

Build Background Knowledge L3

Ask students to look at the map in this section and recall Africa's geography, peoples, religions, and trade. Have them predict which parts of Africa Europeans might seek to control first and why.

Set a Purpose L3

- **WITNESS HISTORY** Read the selection aloud or play the audio.

  🔊 AUDIO **Witness History Audio CD,** Resisting Imperialism

  Ask **How does the German officer probably perceive Chief Machemba?** *(as an inferior, his subject)* **How does Chief Machemba perceive himself?** *(as an equal)* **Based on this letter, how do you think Africans responded to imperialism?** *(They probably resisted it.)*

- **Focus** Point out the Section Focus Question and write it on the board. Tell students to refer to this question as they read. *(Answer appears with Section 2 Assessment answers.)*

- **Preview** Have students preview the Section Objectives and the list of Terms, People, and Places.

- **Note Taking** Have students read this section using the Paragraph Shrinking strategy (TE, p. T20). As they read, have them fill in the chart with causes and effects of Africa's partition.

  📝 **Reading and Note Taking Study Guide,** p. 132

African soldiers in German uniforms

WITNESS HISTORY 🔊 AUDIO

Resisting Imperialism

In 1890, Chief Machemba (mah CHEM bah) of the Yao (YAH oh) people in East Africa wrote in Swahili to a German officer:

❝ If it be friendship that you desire, then I am ready for it . . . but to be your subject, that I cannot be. . . . I do not fall at your feet, for you are God's creature just as I am.❞
—Chief Machemba, Letter to Herman von Wissman

Focus Question How did imperialist European powers claim control over most of Africa by the end of the 1800s?

The Partition of Africa

Objectives

- Analyze the forces that shaped Africa.
- Explain why European contact with Africa increased during the 1800s.
- Understand how Leopold II started a scramble for colonies.
- Describe how Africans resisted imperialism.

Terms, People, and Places

Usman dan Fodio	Boer War
Shaka	Samori Touré
paternalistic	Yaa Asantewaa
David Livingstone	Nehanda
Henry Stanley	Menelik II
King Leopold II	elite

Note Taking

Reading Skill: Identify Causes and Effects As you read the section, fill in the chart with information about the causes and effects of the partition of Africa by European nations.

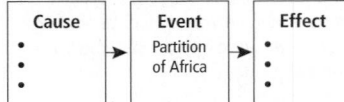

Cause	Event	Effect
•	Partition	•
•	of Africa	•
•		•

In the late 1800s, Britain, France, Germany, and other European powers began a scramble for African territories. Within about 20 years, the Europeans had carved up the continent and dominated millions of Africans. Although the Yao and others resisted, they could not prevent European conquest.

Africa in the Early 1800s

To understand the impact of European domination, we must look at Africa in the early 1800s, before the scramble for colonies began. Africa is a huge continent, nearly three times the size of Europe. Across its many regions, people spoke hundreds of languages and had developed varied governments. Some people lived in large centralized states, while others lived in village communities.

North Africa North Africa includes the enormous Sahara and the fertile land along the Mediterranean. Since long before 1800, the region was a part of the Muslim world. In the early 1800s, much of North Africa remained under the rule of the declining Ottoman empire.

Islamic Crusades in West Africa By the early 1800s, an Islamic revival spread across West Africa. It began among the Fulani people in northern Nigeria. The scholar and preacher **Usman dan Fodio** (oo SMAHN dahn foh DEE oh) denounced the corruption of the local Hausa rulers. He called for social and religious reforms based on the sharia, or Islamic law. Usman inspired Fulani herders and Hausa townspeople to rise up against their European rulers.

Vocabulary Builder

Use the information below and the following resources to teach the high-use word from this section.
All in One Teaching Resources, Unit 3, p. 68; **Teaching Resources, Skills Handbook,** p. 3

High-Use Word	Definition and Sample Sentence
domain, p. 397	*n.* territory over which rule or control is exercised The vegetable garden was my mother's **domain,** and she did not trust its care to anyone else.

Usman and his successors set up a powerful Islamic state in northern Nigeria. Under their rule, literacy increased, local wars quieted, and trade improved. Their success inspired other Muslim reform movements in West Africa. Between about 1780 and 1880, more than a dozen Islamic leaders rose to power, replacing old rulers or founding new states in the western Sudan.

In the forest regions, strong states like the Asante (uh SAHN teh) kingdom had arisen. The Asante traded with Europeans and Muslims and controlled several smaller states. However, these tributary states were ready to turn to Europeans or others who might help them defeat their Asante rulers.

East Africa Islam had long influenced the east coast of Africa, where port cities like Mombasa (mahm BAH suh) and Kilwa (KEEL wah) carried on profitable trade. The cargoes were often slaves. Captives were marched from the interior to the coast to be shipped as slaves to the Middle East. Ivory and copper from Central Africa were also exchanged for goods such as cloth and firearms from India.

Southern Africa In the early 1800s, the Zulus emerged as a major force in southern Africa under a ruthless and brilliant leader, **Shaka.** Between 1818 and 1828, Shaka waged relentless war and conquered many nearby peoples. He absorbed their young men and women into Zulu regiments. By encouraging rival groups to forget their differences, he cemented a growing pride in the Zulu kingdom.

His conquests, however, set off mass migrations and wars, creating chaos across much of the region. Groups driven from their homelands by the Zulus then migrated north, conquering still other peoples and creating their own powerful states. By the 1830s, the Zulus faced a new threat, the arrival of well-armed, mounted Boers, descendants of Dutch farmers who were migrating north from the Cape Colony. In 1814, the Cape Colony had passed from the Dutch to the British. Many Boers resented British laws that abolished slavery and otherwise interfered with their way of life. To escape British rule, they loaded their goods into covered wagons and started north. Several thousand Boer families joined this "Great Trek."

As the migrating Boers came into contact with Zulus, fighting quickly broke out. At first, Zulu regiments held their own. But in the end, Zulu spears could not defeat Boer guns. The struggle for control of the land would rage until the end of the century.

Impact of the Slave Trade In the early 1800s, European nations began to outlaw the transatlantic slave trade, though it took years to end. Meanwhile, the East African slave trade continued to Asia.

Some people helped freed slaves resettle in Africa. In 1787, the British organized Sierra Leone in West Africa as a colony for former slaves. Later, some free blacks from the United States settled in nearby Liberia. By 1847, Liberia had become an independent republic.

✔ **Checkpoint** What factors shaped each of the main regions of Africa during the early 1800s?

Zulu King Cetshwayo
A nephew of Shaka, Cetshwayo (kech WY oh) was the last of the great Zulu kings. He ruled a disciplined army of about 40,000 men until the British defeated him in 1879. *Why was Cetshwayo considered a threat to British colonial interests?*

Teach

Africa in the Early 1800s Ⓛ₃

Instruct

- **Introduce** Ask students what they recall about Africa's geography, key trading centers, and European trade routes. Have students look at the map on page 395. Point out the locations of the Fulani (northern Nigeria), the Asante (Gold Coast), Mombasa (British East Africa), Kilwa (German East Africa), and the Cape Colony (South Africa).

- **Teach** Ask **What effects did Islam have in Africa?** *(It often brought strong governments, higher literacy, peace, and trade.)* **What were two main forces of change in Africa before imperialism spread?** *(Any two: the slave trade, the Zulu conquests, spread of Islam, decline of Ottoman empire)*

- **Quick Activity** Display **Color Transparency 145: European Explorations of Africa.** Use the lesson suggested in the transparency book to guide a discussion on African exploration.
  📖 **Color Transparencies,** 145

Independent Practice

Divide students into four groups, one for each region of Africa. Have each group research their region in the early 1800s and create a poster showing a map of important towns and kingdoms and pictures of key people and activities. Groups should present their posters to the class.

Monitor Progress

Ensure that posters include thoughtful and accurate information about each region. For scoring rubrics for posters and maps, see **Assessment Rubrics,** pp. 6, 10.

Answer

Caption because of his powerful army

✔ In Muslim North Africa, the Ottoman empire was declining. In West Africa, new Muslim leaders and strong kingdoms like the Asante held power. In East Africa the slave trade continued to the East. In South Africa, Zulus and Boers battled for control.

History Background

Liberia Beginning in 1822, freed slaves fled the racism of the United States to settle in Liberia (Latin for "land of liberty"). In 1847, Liberia became independent and modeled its laws and constitution after those of the United States. From the beginning, local peoples resented the intrusion of the freed slaves as simply a different form of imperialism. The Westernized, Christian former slaves and their descendants made up only five to ten percent of the population, yet they imposed English as the official language, ran the government, and largely excluded African Liberians, who had their own languages and religions. In the 1980s and 1990s, these tensions finally erupted. The government was overthrown in 1980, and bitter and bloody civil wars continued through the 1990s.

European Contact Increases

Instruct

- **Introduce** Remind students that when Europeans first came to Africa in the 1400s and 1500s, they established coastal trading posts but did not venture inland. Explain that Europeans took an interest in Africa's interior in the 1800s.

- **Teach** Tell students that Europeans were fascinated by stories of the adventures of Stanley and Livingstone. Ask **Why were explorers and missionaries held in high regard by Europeans?** *(They had "noble" missions to pursue science and spread civilization to the "savages.")* **How might Africans have felt about these efforts?** *(They probably resented them.)*

- **Quick Activity** Organize a debate on whether or not imperialism was advantageous for Africans. Point out that Europeans brought medicine and education to Africa and ended slavery, but violated Africans' rights to self-determination, destroyed traditional societies, and exploited the people and their land and resources without fair compensation.

Independent Practice

Viewpoints To help students better understand the debate on imperialism, have them read *Two Views of Imperialism in Africa* and complete the worksheet.

All in One Teaching Resources, Unit 3, p. 70

Monitor Progress

As students fill in their charts, circulate to make sure they have included increased contact from missionaries and explorers as a cause that led to the partition of Africa. For a completed version of the graphic organizer, see

📖 **Note Taking Transparencies, 161**

Missionaries at Work
Missionaries conduct a baptism ceremony in the Lower Congo in 1907. Others performed communion with chalices and patens, or ceremonial plates, like those above. *Why did missionaries seek to convert people to Christianity?*

WITNESS HISTORY VIDEO

Watch *The Scramble for African Colonies* on the **Witness History Discovery School**™ video program to learn more about the partition of Africa.

DISCOVERY SCHOOL

European Contact Increases

From the 1500s through the 1700s, Europeans traded along the African coast. Africans wanted trade with Europeans but did not want to "house them." Resistance by Africans, difficult geography, and diseases all kept Europeans from moving into the interior regions of the continent. Medical advances and river steamships changed all that in the 1800s.

Explorers Advance Into Africa's Interior In the early 1800s, European explorers began pushing into the interior of Africa. Explorers like Mungo Park and Richard Burton set out to map the course and sources of the great African rivers such as the Niger, the Nile, and the Congo. They were fascinated by African geography, but they had little understanding of the peoples they met. All, however, endured great hardships while exploring Africa.

Missionaries Follow Explorers Catholic and Protestant missionaries followed the explorers. All across Africa, they sought to win people to Christianity. The missionaries were sincere in their desire to help Africans. They built schools and medical clinics alongside churches. They also focused attention on the evils of the slave trade. Still, missionaries, like most Westerners, took a **paternalistic** view of Africans, meaning they saw them as children in need of guidance. To them, African cultures and religions were "degraded." They urged Africans to reject their own traditions in favor of Western civilization.

Livingstone Blazes a Trail The best-known explorer and missionary was **Dr. David Livingstone.** For 30 years, he crisscrossed Africa. He wrote about the many peoples he met with more sympathy and less bias than did most Europeans. He relentlessly opposed the slave trade, which remained a profitable business for some African rulers and foreign traders. The only way to end this cruel traffic, he believed, was to open up the interior of Africa to Christianity and trade.

Livingstone blazed a trail that others soon followed. In 1869, the journalist **Henry Stanley** trekked into Central Africa to find Livingstone, who had not been heard from for years. He finally tracked him down in 1871 in what is today Tanzania, greeting him with the now-legendary phrase "Dr. Livingstone, I presume?"

✔ **Checkpoint** How did European contact with Africa increase in the late 1800s?

A Scramble for Colonies

Shortly afterward, **King Leopold II** of Belgium hired Stanley to explore the Congo River basin and arrange trade treaties with African leaders. Publicly, Leopold spoke of a civilizing mission to carry the light "that for millions of men still plunged in barbarism will be the dawn of a better era." Privately, he dreamed of conquest and profit. Leopold's activities in the Congo set off a scramble by other nations. Before long, Britain, France, and Germany were pressing rival claims to the region.

Berlin Conference To avoid bloodshed, European powers met at an international conference in 1884. It took place not in Africa but in Berlin, Germany. No Africans were invited to the conference.

Careers

Foreign Correspondent In the late 1800s, readers eagerly awaited Henry Stanley's dispatches from Africa to the *New York Herald*. Foreign correspondents include both journalists and photographers who capture images of the world in words or on film and send them back to local outlets. They work for newspapers, radio, or television; their careers often involve not only excitement and travel, but also long hours and danger, especially in times of war or natural disaster. Time differences may mean working in the middle of the night. Foreign correspondents often have a college degree in journalism or communications, but hands-on experience is also extremely valuable.

Answers

Caption They viewed African religions as inferior to Christianity.

✔ Medical advances and steamships allowed explorers and missionaries to push deep into Africa.

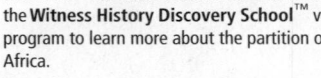

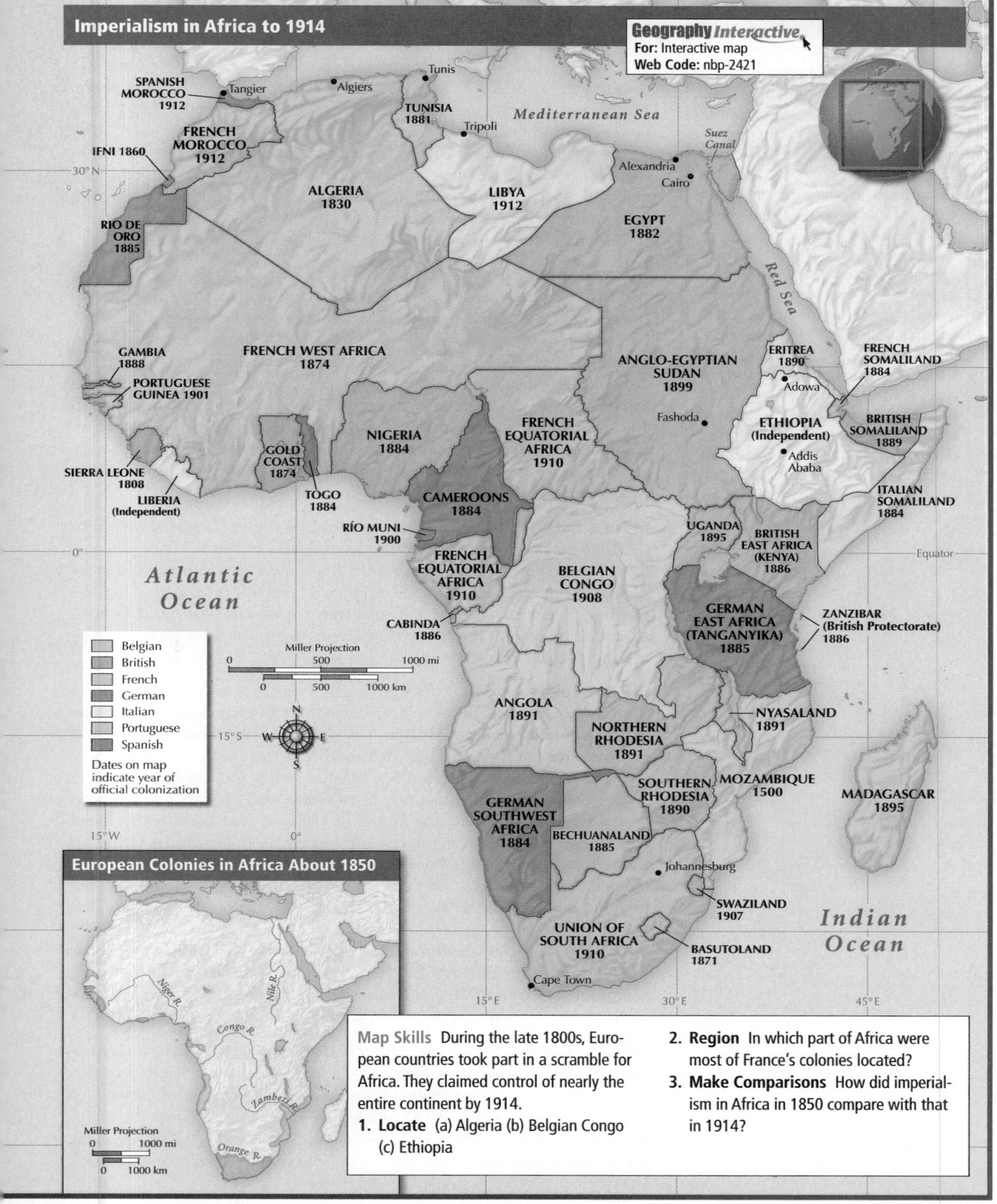

Imperialism in Africa to 1914

Geography *Interactive*.
For: Interactive map
Web Code: nbp-2421

Mediterranean Sea

SPANISH MOROCCO 1912 • Tangier
• Algiers
Tunis
TUNISIA 1881
• Tripoli

IFNI 1860
FRENCH MOROCCO 1912
30° N

ALGERIA 1830

LIBYA 1912

Suez Canal
• Alexandria
Cairo

RIO DE ORO 1885

EGYPT 1882

GAMBIA 1888
FRENCH WEST AFRICA 1874

ANGLO-EGYPTIAN SUDAN 1899

ERITREA 1890
• Adowa

FRENCH SOMALILAND 1884

PORTUGUESE GUINEA 1901

Fashoda •

ETHIOPIA (Independent)
• Addis Ababa

BRITISH SOMALILAND 1889

SIERRA LEONE 1808

NIGERIA 1884

FRENCH EQUATORIAL AFRICA 1910

GOLD COAST 1874

ITALIAN SOMALILAND 1884

LIBERIA (Independent)

TOGO 1884

CAMEROONS 1884

RÍO MUNI 1900

UGANDA 1895
BRITISH EAST AFRICA (KENYA) 1886

0°

FRENCH EQUATORIAL AFRICA 1910

BELGIAN CONGO 1908

Equator

Atlantic Ocean

CABINDA 1886

GERMAN EAST AFRICA (TANGANYIKA) 1885

ZANZIBAR (British Protectorate) 1886

Belgian
British
French
German
Italian
Portuguese
Spanish

Miller Projection
0   500   1000 mi
0   500   1000 km

ANGOLA 1891

NYASALAND 1891

Dates on map indicate year of official colonization

15° S

NORTHERN RHODESIA 1891

N
W   E
S

SOUTHERN RHODESIA 1890

MOZAMBIQUE 1500

MADAGASCAR 1895

15° W   0°

GERMAN SOUTHWEST AFRICA 1884

BECHUANALAND 1885

• Johannesburg

European Colonies in Africa About 1850

SWAZILAND 1907

Indian Ocean

Niger R.

Nile R.

UNION OF SOUTH AFRICA 1910

BASUTOLAND 1871

Congo R.

15° E   30° E   45° E

Miller Projection
0   1000 mi
0   1000 km

Zambezi R.

Orange R.

• Cape Town

Map Skills During the late 1800s, European countries took part in a scramble for Africa. They claimed control of nearly the entire continent by 1914.

1. **Locate** (a) Algeria (b) Belgian Congo (c) Ethiopia

2. **Region** In which part of Africa were most of France's colonies located?

3. **Make Comparisons** How did imperialism in Africa in 1850 compare with that in 1914?

A Scramble for Colonies L3

Instruct

- **Introduce** Have a volunteer read the sentence in the first paragraph with the quotation from King Leopold II. Ask students to recall the actual motives of European imperialism from Section 1. *(economic, political, military, humanitarian, religious, Social Darwinist)*

- **Teach** Display **Color Transparency 149: The Scramble for Africa (with overlays).** Have students compare the maps showing the spread of European colonies. Then ask **Why did countries want to control certain areas?** *(proximity to ports, trade routes)* **What did the European countries that seized the most territory in Africa have in common?** *(They were the most industrialized nations.)*

  📖 **Color Transparencies, 149**

- **Quick Activity** Show students *The Scramble for African Colonies* from the **Witness History Discovery School™** video program. Ask students to list abuses of Africans shown in the video. Then ask **Why did Europeans feel they had the "right" to treat Africans as they did?** You may want to replay or reread the chapter Witness History audio selection.

Differentiated Instruction Solutions for All Learners

L1 Special Needs L2 Less Proficient Readers

Have students look at the map on this page. Ask them to work in pairs and name the colonies seized by each country and the region(s) of Africa where they were located. **What two countries remained independent?** *(Ethiopia, Liberia)* Ask students to brainstorm possible reasons why these two nations successfully remained independent, when much of Africa did not.

L2 English Language Learners

Use the following resources to help students acquire basic skills:

Adapted Reading and Note Taking Study Guide

- Adapted Note Taking Study Guide, p. 132
- Adapted Section Summary, p. 133

Answers

Map Skills
1. Review locations with students.
2. North and West Africa
3. By 1914, European colonies had spread across most of the continent and very few regions remained independent.

- **Web Code nbp-2421** will take students to an interactive map. Have students complete the interactivity and then answer the questions in their text.

- Remind students that the Western powers did not invite any African nations to the Berlin Conference, where they established rules to govern how the continent could be divided up among the Western powers. Challenge students to write a paragraph explaining whether or not this was a wise decision.

Monitor Progress

- Have a student reread the last paragraph in this section. Ask **What did the German politician mean by "our place in the sun"?** *(the glory and prestige of having colonies)* Ask whether Europeans considered that they were putting Africans "in the shade."

- Check answers to map skills questions.

BIOGRAPHY

Cecil Rhodes

Cecil Rhodes (1853–1902) arrived in South Africa at age 17, determined to make his fortune. He got off to a slow start. His first venture, a cotton-farming project, failed. Then, Rhodes turned to diamond and gold mining. By the age of 40, he had become one of the richest men in the world.

However, money was not his real interest. "For its own sake I do not care for money," he once wrote. "I want the power." Rhodes strongly supported British imperialism in Africa. He helped Britain extend its African empire by 1,000,000 square miles and had an entire British colony named after himself—Rhodesia (now Zimbabwe). Rhodes also helped promote the policy of the separation of races in southern Africa. **How was Cecil Rhodes' desire for power illustrated by his actions?**

At the Berlin Conference, European powers recognized Leopold's private claims to the Congo Free State but called for free trade on the Congo and Niger rivers. They further agreed that a European power could not claim any part of Africa unless it had set up a government office there. This principle led Europeans to send officials who would exert their power over local rulers and peoples.

The rush to colonize Africa was on. In the 20 years after the Berlin Conference, the European powers partitioned almost the entire continent. As Europeans carved out their claims, they established new borders and frontiers. They redrew the map of Africa with little regard for traditional patterns of settlement or ethnic boundaries.

Horrors in the Congo Leopold and other wealthy Belgians exploited the riches of the Congo, including its copper, rubber, and ivory. Soon, there were horrifying reports of Belgian overseers brutalizing villagers. Forced to work for almost nothing, laborers were savagely beaten or mutilated. The overall population declined drastically.

Eventually, international outrage forced Leopold to turn over his personal colony to the Belgian government. It became the Belgian Congo in 1908. Under Belgian rule, the worst abuses were ended. Still, the Belgians regarded the Congo as a possession to be exploited. Africans were given little or no role in the government, and the wealth of their mines went out of the country to Europe.

France Extends Its Influence France took a giant share of Africa. In the 1830s, it had invaded and conquered Algeria in North Africa. The victory cost tens of thousands of French lives and killed many times more Algerians. In the late 1800s, France extended its influence along the Mediterranean into Tunisia. It also won colonies in West and Central Africa. At its height, the French empire in Africa was as large as the continental United States.

Britain Takes Its Share Britain's share of Africa was more scattered than that of France. However, it included more heavily populated regions with many rich resources. Britain took chunks of West and East Africa. It gained control of Egypt and pushed south into the Sudan.

In southern Africa, Britain clashed with the Boers, who were descendants of Dutch settlers. As you have read, Britain had acquired the Cape Colony from the Dutch in 1814. At that time, many Boers fled British rule, migrating north and setting up their own republics. In the late 1800s, however, the discovery of gold and diamonds in the Boer lands led to conflict with Britain. The **Boer War,** which lasted from 1899 to 1902, involved bitter guerrilla fighting. The British won in the end, but at great cost.

In 1910, the British united the Cape Colony and the former Boer republics into the Union of South Africa. The new constitution set up a government run by whites and laid the foundation for a system of complete racial segregation that would remain in force until 1993.

Others Join the Scramble Other European powers joined the scramble for colonies, in part to bolster their national image, while also furthering their economic growth and influence. The Portuguese carved out large colonies in Angola and Mozambique. Italy reached across the Mediterranean to occupy Libya and then pushed into the "horn" of Africa, at the southern end of the Red Sea. The newly united German empire took

Link to Literature

Things Fall Apart Nigerian writer Chinua Achebe was one of the first writers to show the period of imperialism from an African perspective. Unlike most European writers, he sympathetically portrayed traditional African culture and also showed the West's derision of it. In his 1958 masterpiece, *Things Fall* *Apart,* Achebe depicts the tragic effects of well-intentioned missionaries in a traditional Igbo village; he captures the benefits, losses, and confusion of a time when missionaries and colonialism gained a stranglehold on the region.

Answer

BIOGRAPHY He used his influence and money to help Britain further colonize Africa so he eventually had a colony named after him.

lands in eastern and southwestern Africa, including Cameroons and Togo. A German politician, trying to ease the worries of European rivals, explained, "We do not want to put anyone in the shade, but we also demand our place in the sun."

✓ **Checkpoint** How did King Leopold II set off a scramble for colonies in Africa?

Africans Resist Imperialism

Europeans met armed resistance across the continent. The Algerians battled the French for years. **Samori Touré** (sah MAWR ee too RAY) fought French forces in West Africa, where he was building his own empire. The British battled the Zulus in southern Africa and the Asante in West Africa. When their king was exiled, the Asante put themselves under the command of their queen, **Yaa Asantewaa** (YA uh ah sahn TAY wuh). She led the fight against the British in the last Asante war. Another woman who became a military leader was **Nehanda** (neh HAHN duh), of the Shona in Zimbabwe. Although a clever tactician, Nehanda was captured and executed. However, the memory of her achievements inspired later generations to fight for freedom.

In East Africa, the Germans fought wars against the Yao and Herero (huh REHR oh). Fighting was especially fierce in the Maji-Maji Rebellion of 1905. The Germans triumphed only after burning acres and acres of farmland, leaving thousands of local people to die of starvation.

Ethiopia Survives One ancient Christian kingdom in East Africa, Ethiopia, managed to resist European colonization and maintain its independence. Like feudal Europe, Ethiopia had been divided up among a number of rival princes who ruled their own <u>domains</u>. In the late 1800s, however, a reforming ruler, **Menelik II,** began to modernize his country. He hired European experts to plan modern roads and bridges and set up a Western school system. He imported the latest weapons and European officers to help train his army. Thus, when Italy invaded Ethiopia in 1896, Menelik was prepared. At the battle of Adowa (AH duh wuh), the Ethiopians smashed the Italian invaders. Ethiopia was the only African nation, aside from Liberia, to preserve its independence.

Vocabulary Builder

<u>domain</u>—(doh MAYN) *n.* territory over which rule or control is exercised

BIOGRAPHY

Menelik II

Before becoming emperor of Ethiopia, Menelik II (1844–1913) ruled the Shoa region in central Ethiopia. He ensured that he would succeed John IV as emperor by marrying his daughter to John's son. After John died in 1889, Menelik took the throne.

Menelik used profits from ivory sales to buy modern weapons. He then hired European advisors to teach his soldiers how to use the new guns. Menelik's army conquered neighboring lands and won a stunning victory over the Italians at Adowa. European nations rushed to establish diplomatic ties with Ethiopia. Around the world, people of African descent hailed Menelik's victory over European imperialism. **How did Menelik preserve Ethiopian independence?**

History Background

The Asante and the Golden Stool The Asante kingdom was a powerful, gold-rich nation in present-day Ghana. Among its most important symbols was a golden stool, believed to contain the soul and welfare of the nation. For decades the Asante resisted takeover by Europeans on all sides, but in 1896 King Prempeh I gave in to British demands to avoid the annihilation of his people. The British governor forced the king to lie in the dust before him—a humiliation—and sent him to prison. Then the governor ordered the golden stool brought for him to sit on—an even greater insult. Not even their king sat on the stool. The queen mother, Yaa Asantewa, soon led her people in a fierce rebellion against the British but they could not defeat the Maxim guns. The queen, still defiant, spat in the face of the British officer who took her prisoner.

Instruct

- **Introduce: Vocabulary Builder** Have students read the Vocabulary Builder term and definition. **What is an example of a *domain* in Africa?** *(African kingdoms, European colonies)* **How are most *domains* established?** *(through war, treaties or alliances)*

- **Teach** Ask **Who were the new African elite?** *(Westernized, middle- or upper-class Africans)* **How did the African elite view European society and their own traditions?** *(varied)* **Who do you predict will lead the African nationalist movements of the 1900s? Why?** *(probably the elite, who were familiar with Western democratic principles)*

- **Quick Activity** Divide students into groups. Ask each group to suppose that it leads an African nation. What methods will they use to resist imperialism? *(Sample: modernization, westernization, armed battle)*

Independent Practice

Link to Literature To help students better understand Africans' response to imperialism, have them read the excerpt from "The Gentlemen of the Jungle" by Jomo Kenyatta and complete the worksheet.

All in One Teaching Resources, Unit 3, p. 71

Monitor Progress

- To review this section, ask students to identify two ways Africans responded to imperialism. *(resistance, Westernization)*

- Check Reading and Note Taking Study Guide entries for student understanding.

Answers

✓ by sending explorers to the Congo and trying to establish treaties to dominate trade

BIOGRAPHY by obtaining and learning how to use Western weapons

Assess and Reteach

Assess Progress

- Have students complete the Section Assessment.
- Administer the Section Quiz.

 Teaching Resources, Unit 3, p. 64

- To further assess student understanding, use

   Progress Monitoring Transparencies, 100

Reteach

If students need more instruction, have them read the section summary.

Reading and Note Taking Study Guide, p. 133

Adapted Reading and Note Taking Study Guide, p. 133

Spanish Reading and Note Taking Study Guide, p. 133

Extend

See this Chapter's Professional Development pages for the Extend Online activity on African resistance to imperialism.

Answers

Caption that he may be an official or expert who visited or was educated in Europe

✓ Menelik II modernized and Westernized both his country and army and so Ethiopia was prepared to fight Western troops. They defeated Italy's invasion and remained independent.

An Asante King
A king of the Asante people in Ghana (center) sits surrounded by his people. *What do the clothes of the man to the left of the king suggest about his social rank?*

A New African Elite Emerges During the Age of Imperialism, a Western-educated African **elite**, or upper class, emerged. Some middle-class Africans admired Western ways and rejected their own culture. Others valued their African traditions and condemned Western societies that upheld liberty and equality for whites only. By the early 1900s, African leaders were forging nationalist movements to pursue self-determination and independence.

✓ **Checkpoint** How did Ethiopians resist imperialism?

SECTION 2 Assessment

Terms, People, and Places
1. For each term, person, or place listed at the beginning of the section, write a sentence explaining its significance.

Note Taking
2. **Reading Skill: Identify Causes and Effects** Use your completed chart to answer the Focus Question: How did imperialist European powers claim control over most of Africa by the end of the 1800s?

Comprehension and Critical Thinking
3. **Describe** Name one development in each region of Africa in the early 1800s.
4. **Analyze Information** What impact did explorers and missionaries have on Africa?
5. **Draw Inferences** (a) Why do you think the Europeans did not invite Africans to the Berlin Conference? (b) What might be the effect of this exclusion upon later African leaders?
6. **Summarize** How did Africans resist European imperialism?

● **Writing About History**
Quick Write: Generate Arguments One way to approach a persuasive essay is to create a list of arguments that you can include to persuade your audience. For practice, create a list of three arguments that could be used in a persuasive essay either in favor of or opposed to the European colonization of Africa.

Section 2 Assessment

1. Sentences should reflect an understanding of each term, person, or place listed at the beginning of the section.
2. Explorers and missionaries penetrated Africa. Then European countries divided and conquered Africa with superior arms.
3. In North Africa, the Ottoman empire was declining. In West Africa, new Muslim leaders held power. In East Africa, the slave trade continued. In South Africa, Zulus, Boers, and the British battled for control.
4. Explorers opened Africa's interior to other Europeans. Missionaries built schools and clinics but undermined African cultures.
5. (a) Sample: They believed they had the right to decide its fate. (b) Sample: They may have resented their exclusion.
6. Many Africans fought back in battle, and the African elite began organizing for independence.

● **Writing About History**
Responses should include three separate, well-reasoned arguments that clearly support either position.

For additional assessment, have students access **Progress Monitoring Online** at **Web Code nba-2421.**

On Trial for My Country
by Stanlake Samkange

European imperialists gained control over much of Africa by signing treaties with local rulers. In most cases, the chiefs did not understand what rights they were signing away. Cecil Rhodes used this tactic with King Lobengula, who thought that he was allowing the British only to dig on his land. Rhodes, however, took control of the kingdom, eventually naming it Rhodesia. The novel *On Trial for My Country* is a fictional account of a conversation between King Lobengula and his father.

"Why did you not stand up to Rhodes and prevent him from taking your country by strength? Why did you not fight?"

"I thought that if I appealed to the white men's sense of justice and fair play, reminding them how good I had been to them since I had never killed or ill-treated a white man, they might hear my word and return to their homes...."

"I . . . told them that I had not given them the road to Mashonaland."

"Yes, and they replied and told you that they had been given the road by their Queen and would only return on the orders of their Queen. What did you do then?"

"I mobilized[1] the army and told them to wait for my word."

"Did you give that word?"

"No."

"Were the soldiers keen to fight?"

"Yes, they were dying to fight."

"Why did you not let them fight?"

"I wanted to avoid bloodshed and war...."

"And you allowed them to flout[2] your word as king of the Amandebele? You let them have their way.... Is that right?....Why did you not . . . seek their protection and declare your country a British protectorate?"

". . . I knew that if I fought the white men I would be beaten. If I sought the white man's friendship and protection, there would be opposition to me or civil war. So I decided to pretend to the white men that if they came into the country I would fight, and hoped that they would be afraid and not come.... [T]hey called my bluff and came . . ."

"Was there no other way out of your dilemma?"

"I did consider marrying the Queen, but even though I hinted at this several times no one followed it up."

"I see!"

1. **mobilize** (MOH buh lyz) *v.* to assemble for war
2. **flout** (flowt) *v.* to mock

▲ King Lobengula of the Matabele nation in present-day Zimbabwe

Thinking Critically
1. **Synthesize Information** Why did King Lobengula want to avoid fighting the British?
2. **Analyze Literature** How does Samkange show that Lobengula's father disagreed with his son's decision?

History Background

Samkange's Story Stanlake Samkange, the author of *On Trial for My Country*, grew up in the British colony of Rhodesia (now Zimbabwe). Although fictional, *On Trial for My Country* explores the issues at the heart of the British colonization of Rhodesia. Rhodesia was colonized in the 1890s, largely through the will of one man, Cecil Rhodes, which it was then named after. *On Trial for My Country* sets up the literary device of both Lobengula, the leader of the Matabeles in Zimbabwe, and Rhodes having to defend their actions in the afterlife. Each is judged by a council of their own ancestors. Samkange does not reveal the heavenly decision, calling on readers to draw their own conclusions.

On Trial for My Country
by Stanlake Samkange

Objectives
- Understand the methods European imperialists used to gain control over Africa.
- Describe African rulers' response to imperialism.

Build Background Knowledge ⓛ
Ask students to recall the purposes of British imperialism. Have them predict how British imperialism affected the peoples of East and Southern Africa.

Instruct
- Ask **How did Cecil Rhodes gain control of what would become Rhodesia?** *(by signing a treaty with the local ruler, who did not understand the terms of the agreement)* **What options did Lobengula have to prevent the British from taking his country?** *(fight or declare the country a British protectorate)*
- Point out that King Lobengula wanted to appeal to Rhodes's sense of justice. Ask **Do you think this would be an effective strategy? Why or Why not?** *(Sample: No, because Rhodes had already tricked the ruler once and had proven that he did not play fair.)*

Monitor Progress
Ask students to summarize how King Lobengula's father questions his son about his actions, paying particular attention to the alternatives the father suggests.

Thinking Critically
1. He appealed to their sense of justice because he knew he could not win militarily.
2. His father shows his disagreement by continuing to question why his son did not allow his troops to fight when they were able and ready.

Objectives

As you teach this section, keep students focused on the following objectives to help them answer the Section Focus Question and master core content.

- Analyze the sources of stress in Muslim regions.
- Explain the problems the Ottoman empire faced.
- Describe how Egypt sought to modernize.
- Understand European interest in Persia.

Prepare to Read

Build Background Knowledge 🔼

Ask students to recall how nationalism weakened the Ottoman empire, which bordered Europe to the south and east. Then have students predict how European imperialism may affect the region.

Set a Purpose 🔼

- **WITNESS HISTORY** Read the selection aloud or play the audio.

  🔊 AUDIO **Witness History Audio CD,** The Egyptian Campaign

  Ask **Why do you think that Napoleon viewed the East as a place for glory?** *(Sample: the location of previous empires, the pyramids, spectacular art and architecture)*

- **Focus** Point out the Section Focus Question and write it on the board. Tell students to refer to this question as they read. *(Answer appears with Section 3 Assessment answers.)*

- **Preview** Have students preview the Section Objectives and the list of Terms, People, and Places.

- **Note Taking** Have students read this section using the Guided Questioning strategy (TE, p. T20). As they read, have students fill in the concept web showing effects of European imperialism in Muslim regions.

  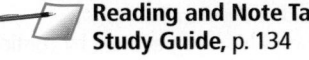 **Reading and Note Taking Study Guide,** p. 134

Poster of Napoleon in Egypt

NAPOLEON IN EGYPT

WITNESS HISTORY 🔊 AUDIO

The Egyptian Campaign

By 1797, Napoleon Bonaparte felt that Europe offered too few chances for glory. Setting his sights toward Africa in 1798, he invaded Egypt, a province of the Ottoman empire.

❝ Europe is a molehill. . . . We must go to the East. . . . All great glory has been acquired there. ❞

Focus Question How did European nations extend their power into Muslim regions of the world?

Lamp from a mosque

European Claims in Muslim Regions

Objectives
- Analyze the sources of stress in Muslim regions.
- Explain the problems the Ottoman empire faced.
- Describe how Egypt sought to modernize.
- Understand European interest in Persia.

Terms, People, and Places

Muhammad Ahmad	genocide
Mahdi	Muhammad Ali
pasha	concession
sultan	

Note Taking

Reading Skill: Understand Effects As you read, fill in a concept web like the one below with the effects of European imperialism in Muslim regions of the world.

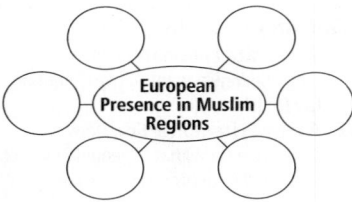

European Presence in Muslim Regions

Napoleon's Egyptian campaign highlighted Ottoman decline and opened a new era of European contact with Muslim regions of the world. European countries were just nibbling at the edges of Muslim countries. Before long, they would strike at their heartland.

Stresses in Muslim Regions

Muslim lands extended from western Africa to Southeast Asia. In the 1500s, three giant Muslim empires ruled much of this world—the Ottomans in the Middle East, the Safavids (sah FAH vidz) in Persia, and the Mughals in India.

Empires in Decline By the 1700s, all three Muslim empires were in decline. The decay had many causes. Central governments had lost control over powerful groups such as landowning nobles, military elites, and urban craft guilds. Corruption was widespread. In some places, Muslim scholars and religious leaders were allied with the state. In other areas, they helped to stir discontent against the government.

Rise of Muslim Reform Movements In the 1700s and 1800s, reform movements sprang up across various Muslim regions of Africa and Asia. Most stressed religious piety and strict rules of behavior. Usman dan Fodio led the struggle to reform Muslim practices in northern Africa. In the Sudan, **Muhammad Ahmad** (AHK mud) announced that he was the **Mahdi** (mahk DEE), the long-awaited savior of the faith. The Mahdi and his followers fiercely resisted British expansion into the region.

Vocabulary Builder

Use the information below and the following resources to teach the high-use word from this section.
All in One Teaching Resources, Unit 3, p. 68; **Teaching Resources, Skills Handbook,** p. 3

High-Use Word	Definition and Sample Sentence
bureaucracy, p. 401	*n.* government staffed by administrators and officials who follow rigid rules. To get the policy changed, Julio had to take his petition through the entire education **bureaucracy,** from his teacher to the principal to the school board to the state board of education.

Another Islamic reform movement, the Wahhabi (wah HAHB ee) movement in Arabia, rejected the schools of theology and law that had emerged in the Ottoman empire. In their place, they wanted to recapture the purity and simplicity of Muhammad's original teachings. Although the revolt was put down, the Wahhabi movement survived. Its teachings remain influential in the kingdom of Saudi Arabia today.

European Imperialism In addition to internal decay and stress, the three Muslim empires faced powerful threats from Western imperialists. Through diplomacy and military threats, European powers won treaties giving them favorable trading terms. They then demanded special rights for Europeans residing in Muslim lands. At times, European powers protected those rights by intervening in local affairs.

✔ **Checkpoint** How was Western imperialism a source of stress in Muslim regions of the world?

Problems for the Ottoman Empire

At its height, the Ottoman empire had extended across North Africa, Southeastern Europe, and the Middle East. By the early 1800s, however, it faced serious challenges. Ambitious **pashas,** or provincial rulers, had increased their power. Economic problems and corruption added to Ottoman decay.

Nationalist Revolts Break Out As ideas of nationalism spread from Western Europe, internal revolts weakened the multiethnic Ottoman empire. Subject peoples in North Africa, Eastern Europe, and the Middle East threatened to break away. In the Balkans, Greeks, Serbs, Bulgarians, and Romanians gained their independence. Revolts against Ottoman rule also erupted in Arabia, Lebanon, and Armenia. The Ottomans suppressed these uprisings, but Egypt slipped out of their control.

European Pressure Increases European states sought to benefit from the slow crumbling of the Ottoman empire. After seizing Algeria in the 1830s, France hoped to gain more Ottoman territory. Russia schemed to gain control of the Bosporus (BAHS puh rus) and the Dardanelles. Control of these straits would give the Russians access to the Mediterranean Sea. Britain tried to thwart Russia's ambitions, which it saw as a threat to its own power in the Mediterranean and beyond to India. And in 1898, the new German empire hoped to increase its influence in the region by building a Berlin-to-Baghdad railway.

Efforts to Westernize Since the late 1700s, several Ottoman rulers had seen the need for reform and looked to the West for ideas. They reorganized the bureaucracy and system of tax collection. They built railroads, improved education, and hired Europeans to train a modern military. Young men were sent to the West to study science and technology. Many returned with Western political ideas about democracy and equality.

The reforms also brought improved medical care and revitalized farming. These improvements,

Vocabulary Builder

bureaucracy (bur OK re see) *n.* government staffed by administrators and officials who follow rigid rules.

General Ismail Pasha (center) fought for the British army in the Crimean War.

(L4) **Advanced Readers** (L4) **Gifted and Talented**

Ask students to learn more about the Young Turks and their revolutionary movement, including its key leaders, the chronology of events leading up to the overthrow, and its main goals. Then challenge students to write a scene taken from an imaginary play that illuminates a crucial moment in the struggle of the Young Turks to gain power. The scene does not have to be strictly factual, but should be based on actual events. Suggestions include meetings between leaders to discuss strategies or goals, or the sultan Abdülhamid II's announcement that the constitution of 1876 will be restored. Refer students to language arts textbooks to review how scenes in plays are structured. Have students perform their scenes if appropriate.

Stresses in Muslim Regions/ Problems for the Ottoman Empire   (L3)

Instruct

- **Introduce** Display **Color Transparency 63: Historical Map Set** and review the spread of Islam. Point out that by the 1500s, three Muslim empires controlled land from western Africa to Southest Asia.

  🏛 **Color Transparencies,** 63

- **Teach** Ask students to identify the stresses that affected Muslim empires in the 1800s. *(government corruption, conflict over interpretations of Islam, European imperialism)* **How did these problems affect the Ottoman empire?** *(corruption allowed provincial rulers to grow powerful, the spread of Western ideas led sultans to reject reform, European imperialism threatened to compromise Ottoman territory)*

- **Quick Activity** Display **Color Transparency 146: The Berlin-to-Baghdad Railway 1913.** Have students identify nations through which the railway would pass. Ask **Why would the Ottomans agree to have the Germans build a railway?** *(Sample: They did not have the technology or capital to build it themselves.)* **Why did the Germans want to build it?** *(They would profit from it and make inroads into the area.)*

  🏛 **Color Transparencies,** 146

Independent Practice

Have students fill in the Outline Map *The Ottoman Empire in the Late 1800s*

All in One **Teaching Resources, Unit 3,** p. 75

Monitor Progress

- As students fill in their concept webs, circulate to make sure they understand the pressures that European imperialism placed on Muslim regions. For a completed version of the concept web, see

  🏛 **Note Taking Transparencies,** 162

- Circulate to make sure students are accurately labeling the regions of the Ottoman empire on their Outline Maps.

Answer

✔ Europeans gained better trading terms, demanded special treatment, and interfered in local affairs.

Egypt Seeks to Modernize ⑬

Instruct

- **Introduce** Reread or play the audio of Napoleon's Witness History selection at the beginning of this section. Explain that Napoleon was successful at first in Egypt, but then the British (concerned about trade with India) sent their navy to destroy the French fleet. The Ottomans sent Muhammad Ali to retake Egypt. Ask students to predict what effect Napoleon's escapade had on European powers. *(They, too, began to think about expanding into the Middle East.)*

- **Teach** Ask **How did Britain gain control of the Suez Canal?** *(Egypt was unable to pay its debts for the canal, so Britain bought Egypt's shares in it.)* Point out that European powers often gained control in this way. Explain that in 1882 Britain claimed it intervened to protect its investments in Egypt.

- **Analyzing the Visuals** Direct students to the Infographic on the next page. Ask **Why was the Suez Canal so important to European powers, particularly the British?** *(It provided access to their empires in India, East Asia, and Australia.)*

Independent Practice

- **Viewpoints** To help students understand the debate surrounding the construction of the Suez Canal, have them read the selection *Two Views on the Suez Canal* and complete the worksheet.

  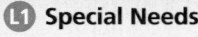 **Teaching Resources, Unit 3,** p. 72

- Divide the class into groups. Have each group research a different aspect of the Suez Canal, such as its political history, construction, and current use. Have each group design a web page (on paper). Put the pages together into a class web site.

Monitor Progress

To review this section, ask students to summarize how Britain gained control of Egypt.

Answer

✓ They led to population growth and conflict over foreign influence.

---

however, created a different set of problems. Better healthcare resulted in a population explosion that increased the already intense competition for the best land and led to unrest.

The adoption of Western ideas also increased tension. Many officials objected to changes that were inspired by a foreign culture. For their part, repressive **sultans,** rulers of the Ottoman Turkish empire, rejected reform and tried to rebuild the autocratic power enjoyed by earlier rulers.

Young Turks Demand Reform In the 1890s, a group of liberals formed a movement called the Young Turks. They insisted that reform was the only way to save the empire. In 1908, the Young Turks overthrew the sultan. Before they could achieve their planned reforms, however, the Ottoman empire was plunged into the world war that erupted in 1914.

Armenian Genocide Traditionally, the Ottomans had let minority nationalities live in their own communities and practice their own religions. By the 1890s, however, nationalism was igniting new tensions, especially between Turkish nationalists and minority peoples who sought their own states. These tensions triggered a brutal genocide of the Armenians, a Christian people concentrated in the eastern mountains of the empire. **Genocide** is a deliberate attempt to destroy a racial, political, or cultural group.

The Muslim Turks accused Christian Armenians of supporting Russian plans against the Ottoman empire. When Armenians protested repressive Ottoman policies, the sultan had tens of thousands of them slaughtered. Over the next 25 years, between 600,000 and 1.5 million Armenians were killed or died from disease and starvation.

✓ **Checkpoint** How were efforts to Westernize problematic for the Ottoman empire?

Egypt Seeks to Modernize

In the early 1800s, Egypt was a semi-independent province of the Ottoman empire, making great strides toward reform. Its success was due to **Muhammad Ali,** an ambitious soldier appointed governor of Egypt by the Ottomans. Ali used the opportunity created by Napoleon's invasion and the civil war that followed to seize power in 1805.

Muhammad Ali Introduces Reforms Muhammad Ali is sometimes called the "father of modern Egypt." He introduced a number of political and economic reforms, including improving tax collection, reorganizing the landholding system, and backing large irrigation projects to increase farm output. By expanding cotton production and encouraging the development of many local industries, Ali increased Egyptian participation in world trade.

Muhammad Ali also brought Western military experts to Egypt to help him build a well-trained, modern army. He conquered the neighboring lands of Arabia, Syria, and Sudan. Before he died in 1849, he had set Egypt on the road to becoming a major Middle Eastern power.

Building the Suez Canal Muhammad Ali's successors lacked his skills, and Egypt came increasingly under foreign control. In 1858, a French entrepreneur, Ferdinand de Lesseps (LAY seps), organized a company to build the Suez Canal. European nations gained power over the Ottomans by extending loans at high interest rates. In 1875, the ruler of

---

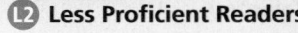 

Suez Canal

he Suez Canal is a waterway in Egypt that stretches for more than 100 miles (160 kilometers). It connects the Mediterranean and Red seas, shortening the travel distance from Western Europe to ports in East Africa and Asia. After it opened in 1869, European ships no longer had to sail around the southern tip of Africa. The canal reduced the trip from London, England, to Bombay, India, by 5,150 miles (8,280 kilometers). The canal averaged between one and two ships per day (below) in its first year of operation and travel time averaged about 40 hours. Today, oil tankers and cargo ships make up most of the canal's traffic with a travel time of about 14 hours.

Route Through the Suez Canal

Miller Projection

British rule or control
French rule or control
Italian rule or control
Ottoman empire, 1913
Russian empire
— Trade route
⚒ Known oilfields, 1914

▲ Construction of the Suez Canal began in 1859 and took workers 10 years to complete. Although digging was first done by hand, laborers later used dredgers and steam shovels to remove sediment.

Thinking Critically
1. **Draw Conclusions** Why was the Suez Canal an important waterway?
2. **Map Skills** Which countries benefited the most from the Suez Canal? Explain.

Geography Interactive
For: Audio guided tour
Web Code: nbp-2431

History Background

Iran and Imperialism Iran, as Persia was renamed in the 1930s, has continued to struggle with the effects of imperialism. In the 1920s, the British brought a Persian military officer, Reza Khan, to power. He soon declared himself shah, forced out Russian and British troops, and negotiated better terms with the British for oil. In 1941, the British, fearing Reza Shah would side with Germany in World War II, forced him out in favor of his son, Mohammad Reza. After the war, British and Russian troops withdrew. In the 1950s, Britain and the United States, fearing nationalization of the oil industry, carried out a coup and placed the shah in absolute power. He was overthrown by revolution in 1979. Iran was then taken over by an anti-Western, conservative Islamic regime, but some Iranians continue to seek democratic reforms.

Persia and the European Powers ⬤

Instruct

■ **Introduce: Key Terms** Ask students to find the key term *concession* (in blue) in the text and explain its meaning. Tell students that countries like Persia did not have the technology or capital to develop their own natural resources or build railways or mines. They granted European **concessions,** or special rights, so the Europeans could come in and develop Persia for them.

■ **Teach** Ask **How did the Qajar shahs try to resist European imperialism?** *(by reforming)* **What kinds of reforms did they make?** *(improved finances, built telegraph lines and railroads, created a new constitution)* **How did British and Russian troops end up in Persia?** *(These countries were granted oil concessions and sent troops to protect their investments.)* **What two groups objected?** *(Westernized nationalists and Muslim religious nationalists)* Point out that these two groups remain at odds in Iran to this day.

Independent Practice

Have students take the role of a British or Russian diplomat assigned to Persia. Have them write a letter back to their government outlining goals, obstacles, and progress in obtaining an oil concession.

Monitor Progress

Check Reading and Note Taking Study Guide entries for student understanding.

Answers

Thinking Critically
1. It connected Europe with eastern Africa, southern and eastern Asia, and Australia.
2. European countries that were able to increase trade

Oil flows out of one of the first oil wells to be drilled in Persia, around 1910.

Egypt was unable to repay loans he had contracted for the canal and other projects. To pay his debts, he sold his shares in the canal. The British bought the shares, gaining a controlling interest in the canal.

Becoming a British Protectorate When Egyptian nationalists revolted against foreign influence in 1882, Britain made Egypt a protectorate. In theory, the governor of Egypt was still an official of the Ottoman government. In fact, he followed policies dictated by Britain. Under British influence, Egypt continued to modernize. However, nationalist discontent simmered and flared into protests and riots.

✓ **Checkpoint** How did Egypt fall under British control?

Persia and the European Powers

Like the Ottoman empire, Persia faced major challenges in the 1800s. The Qajar (kah JAHR) shahs, who ruled Persia from 1794 to 1925, exercised absolute power. Still, they did take steps to introduce reforms. The government helped build telegraph lines and railroads and experimented with a liberal constitution. Reform, however, did not save Persia from Western imperialism. Russia wanted to protect its southern frontier and expand into Central Asia. Britain wanted to protect its interests in India.

For a time, each nation set up its own sphere of influence in Persia. The discovery of oil in the early 1900s heightened foreign interest in the region. Both Russia and Britain plotted for control of Persian oil fields. They persuaded the Persian government to grant them **concessions,** or special rights given to foreign powers. To protect their interests, they sent troops into Persia. Persian nationalists were outraged. The nationalists included two very different groups. Some Persians wanted to move swiftly to adopt Western ways. Others, led by Muslim religious leaders, condemned the Persian government and Western influences.

✓ **Checkpoint** How did Persia attract foreign interest in the early 1900s?

SECTION 3 Assessment

Terms, People, and Places
1. For each term, person, or place listed at the beginning of the section, write a sentence explaining its significance.

Note Taking
2. **Reading Skill: Understand Effects** Use your completed concept web to answer the Focus Question: How did European nations extend their power into Muslim regions of the world?

Comprehension and Critical Thinking
3. **Draw Conclusions** How did European nations take advantage of stresses in the Muslim world?
4. **Summarize** Describe two problems that contributed to Ottoman decline.
5. **Synthesize Information** How did Muhammad Ali modernize Egypt?
6. **Identify Central Issues** Why did Russia and Britain compete for power in Persia?

● Writing About History
Quick Write: Answer Opposing Arguments Suppose that you are writing a persuasive essay on whether the Suez Canal was a positive or negative development for Egypt. An effective way to make your arguments convincing is to address both sides of the topic. Create a chart noting facts and ideas that support your position on one side and arguments that might be used against your position on the other.

Queen Victoria writes letters as her Indian servant waits for his orders.

Critical of British Rule

In 1871, Indian nationalist Dadabhai Naoroji (DAH dah by now ROH jee) criticized British rule in India:

❝ [Indians] call the British system 'Sakar ki Churi' (SA kur kee CHOO ree), the knife of sugar. That is to say, there is no oppression, it is all smooth and sweet, but it is the knife notwithstanding. ❞

Focus Question How did Britain gradually extend its control over most of India, despite opposition?

British East India Company's coat of arms

The British Take Over India

Objectives
- Understand the causes and effects of the Sepoy Rebellion.
- Explain how British rule affected India.
- Describe how Indians viewed Western culture.
- Identify the origins of Indian nationalism.

Terms, People, and Places

sati	deforestation
sepoy	Ram Mohun Roy
viceroy	purdah

Note Taking

Reading Skill: Identify Causes and Effects As you read this section, make a flowchart to show the causes and effects of British rule in India.

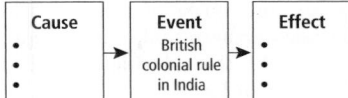

For more than 200 years, Mughal rulers governed a powerful empire in India. By the mid-1700s, however, the Mughal empire was collapsing from a lack of strong rulers. Britain then turned its commercial interests in the region into political ones.

East India Company and Rebellion

In the early 1600s, the British East India Company won trading rights on the fringe of the Mughal empire. As Mughal power declined, the company's influence grew. By the mid-1800s, it controlled three fifths of India.

Exploiting Indian Diversity The British were able to conquer India by exploiting its diversity. Even when Mughal power was at its height, India was home to many people and cultures. As Mughal power crumbled, India became fragmented. Indians with different traditions and dozens of different languages were not able to unite against the newcomers. The British took advantage of Indian divisions by encouraging competition and disunity among rival princes. Where diplomacy or intrigue did not work, the British used their superior weapons to overpower local rulers.

Implementing British Policies The East India Company's main goal in India was to make money, and leading officials often grew rich. At the same time, the company did work to improve roads, preserve peace, and reduce banditry.

East India Company and Rebellion ⓛ

Instruct

- **Introduce: Key Terms** Ask students to find the key term *sepoy* (in blue) in the text and explain its meaning. Explain that sepoys were Indian soldiers trained and led by British officers, who in turn answered to the British East India Company. Ask **What problems might this situation create?** *(conflicting loyalties, misuse of force for profit)* **Why did the British use this system?** *(cheap, easy to maintain)*

- **Teach** Ask **How did the British exploit Indian diversity?** *(They played different princes and peoples against each other.)* **What changes did the East India Company bring to India?** *(It improved roads, preserved peace, reduced banditry, introduced Western education and law, and pushed for social change.)* **How could the Sepoy Rebellion be interpreted as resulting from British feelings of superiority?** *(The rebellion flared because British rules did not take into consideration sepoys' religious practices, possibly because the British did not regard Indian religions as equal in importance to their own religion.)* **Why do you think the Sepoy Rebellion was so violent?** *(religious fervor and long-simmering resentment over British control)*

- **Quick Activity** Have students access **Web Code nbp-2441** to take the **Geography Interactive Audio Guided Tour** and then have them compare the area mainly affected by the Sepoy Rebellion with the total area under British control in 1858.

Independent Practice

Have students write a letter from an Indian sepoy to Queen Victoria protesting the treatment of Indians by the East India Company. Make sure they mention violations of their religious beliefs.

Monitor Progress

As students fill in their flowcharts, circulate to make sure they understand the causes of British rule in India. For a completed version of the flowchart, see

📖 **Note Taking Transparencies,** 163

⬤ **INFOGRAPHIC**

THE SEPOY REBELLION

In 1857, the British issued new rifles to the sepoys. Troops were told to bite off the tips of cartridges before loading them into the rifles (right). Sepoys believed the cartridges (below) were greased with animal fat—from cows, which Hindus considered sacred, and from pigs, which were forbidden to Muslims. When sepoys (right) refused to load the guns, they were imprisoned. Angry sepoys rebelled against British officers, sparking a massacre of British troops, as well as women and children.

◄ A Sepoy rebels against British forces.

By the early 1800s, British officials introduced Western education and legal procedures. Missionaries tried to convert Indians to Christianity, which they felt was superior to Indian religions. The British also pressed for social change. They worked to end slavery and the caste system and to improve the position of women within the family. One law banned sati (SUH tee), a Hindu custom practiced mainly by the upper classes. It called for a widow to join her husband in death by throwing herself on his funeral fire.

Growing Discontent In the 1850s, the East India Company made several unpopular moves. First, it required sepoys (SEE poyz), or Indian soldiers in its service, to serve anywhere, either in India or overseas. For high-caste Hindus, however, overseas travel was an offense against their religion. Second, the East India Company passed a law that allowed Hindu widows to remarry. Hindus viewed both moves as a Christian conspiracy to undermine their beliefs.

Then, in 1857, the British issued new rifles to the sepoys. Troops were told to bite off the tips of cartridges before loading them into the rifles. The cartridges, however, were greased with animal fat—either from cows, which Hindus considered sacred, or from pigs, which were forbidden to Muslims. When the troops refused the order to "load rifles," they were imprisoned.

Rebellion and Aftermath Angry sepoys rose up against their British officers. The Sepoy Rebellion swept across northern and central India. Several sepoy regiments marched off to Delhi, the old Mughal capital. There, they hailed the last Mughal ruler as their leader.

In some places, the sepoys brutally massacred British men, women, and children. But the British soon rallied and crushed the revolt. They then took terrible revenge for their earlier losses, torching villages and slaughtering thousands of unarmed Indians.

History Background

British East India Company Founded in the 1600s, the British East India Company was the predecessor of the transnational corporation. Until 1858 the company did largely as it pleased, enforcing its will with a private army. Its officers profited personally amid widespread corruption. Because of its monopoly, it could drive down prices, causing destitution among India's weavers, and sell high in Britain. It had many critics; even economist Adam Smith criticized its oppressive policies. Horace Walpole accused the company of having "murdered, deposed, plundered, usurped," and caused "famine in Bengal, in which millions perished" while the company hoarded rice for price gouging. Jawaharlal Nehru noted it was not accidental that a Hindustani word absorbed into the English language was *loot*. Edmund Burke pointed out that "every rupee of profit made by an Englishman is lost for ever to India."

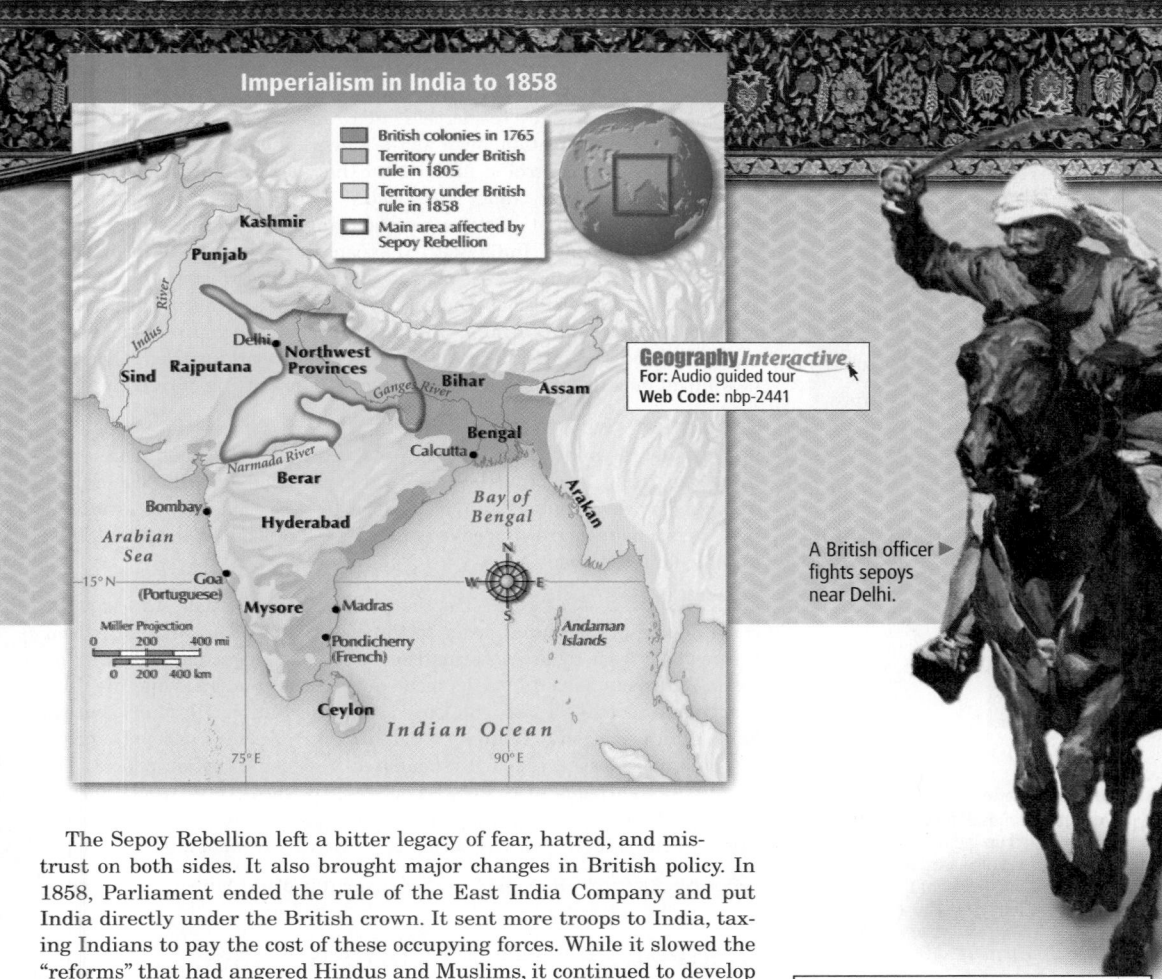

Imperialism in India to 1858

Legend:
- British colonies in 1765
- Territory under British rule in 1805
- Territory under British rule in 1858
- Main area affected by Sepoy Rebellion

Kashmir
Punjab
Sind
Rajputana
Delhi
Northwest Provinces
Bihar
Assam
Bengal
Calcutta
Berar
Bombay
Hyderabad
Arabian Sea
Goa (Portuguese)
Mysore
Madras
Pondicherry (French)
Bay of Bengal
Arakan
Andaman Islands
Ceylon
Indian Ocean

Miller Projection
0   200   400 mi
0   200   400 km

15°N
75°E   90°E

Geography *Interactive*
For: Audio guided tour
Web Code: nbp-2441

A British officer ▶ fights sepoys near Delhi.

The Sepoy Rebellion left a bitter legacy of fear, hatred, and mistrust on both sides. It also brought major changes in British policy. In 1858, Parliament ended the rule of the East India Company and put India directly under the British crown. It sent more troops to India, taxing Indians to pay the cost of these occupying forces. While it slowed the "reforms" that had angered Hindus and Muslims, it continued to develop India for Britain's own economic benefit.

✓ **Checkpoint** What were the causes of the Sepoy Rebellion in northern and central India?

Impact of British Colonial Rule

After 1858, Parliament set up a system of colonial rule in India called the British Raj. A British **viceroy** in India governed in the name of the queen, and British officials held the top positions in the civil service and army. Indians filled most other jobs. With their cooperation, the British made India the "brightest jewel" in the crown of their empire.

British policies were designed to incorporate India into the <u>overall</u> British economy. At the same time, British officials felt they were helping India to modernize. In their terms, modernizing meant adopting not only Western technology but also Western culture.

An Unequal Partnership Britain saw India both as a market and as a source of raw materials. To this end, the British built roads and an impressive railroad network. Improved transportation let the British sell

---

Thinking Critically
1. **Draw Conclusions** How was the Sepoy Rebellion a clash of cultures?
2. **Map Skills** Which regions were most affected by the Sepoy Rebellion?

Vocabulary Builder

<u>overall</u>—(OH vur awl) *adj.* total

Impact of British Colonial Rule 〔L3〕

Instruct

- **Introduce: Vocabulary Builder**
  Have students read the Vocabulary Builder term and definition. Ask students what the "*overall* British economy" included. (*Britain's own industries, its banks and trading companies, and its overseas trade*) Ask **What did it mean for India to be just a part of this overall economy?** (*India's interests were not a priority.*)

- **Teach** Ask students how trade benefited Britain, and how it benefited India. Then, on the board, write "British Raj," the name for British rule, and beneath it, create two columns to list the positive and negative effects of British rule on India. Using the Idea Wave strategy (TE, p. T22), have students volunteer information to go in each column. Then ask **How did British rule lead to famine?** (*Improvements in health and farming led to population growth that could not be sustained. In addition, farmers grew cash crops rather than food for themselves.*)

- **Quick Activity** Display **Color Transparency 147: Indian Tea Poster.** Use the lesson suggested in the transparency book to guide a discussion on trade in India.
  ▥ **Color Transparencies, 147**

Independent Practice

Have students fill in the Outline Map *The British in India to 1858* and shade the areas of India brought under British control.

〔All in One〕 **Teaching Resources, Unit 3, p. 76**

Monitor Progress

Circulate to make sure students are filling in their Outline Maps accurately. Administer the Geography Quiz.

〔All in One〕 **Teaching Resources, Unit 3, p. 77**

Differentiated
Instruction   Solutions for All Learners

〔L1〕 Special Needs   〔L2〕 Less Proficient Readers

Direct students to the Infographic on the Sepoy Rebellion. Have volunteers explain how each picture or artifact is related to the story of the rebellion. Have volunteers explain the sepoys' complaints and the British point of view. Then have students examine the photos in this section and identify advantages and disadvantages of British rule of India.

〔L2〕 English Language Learners

Use the following resources to help students acquire basic skills:

 **Adapted Reading and Note Taking Study Guide**
- Adapted Note Taking Study Guide, p. 136
- Adapted Section Summary, p. 137

Answers

✓ The Sepoy rebellion was caused by changes that violated Hindu beliefs: requiring sepoys to travel and to bite off greased cartridge tips and allowing widows to remarry.

Thinking Critically
1. The British forced Hindu and Muslim soldiers to do things that were against their religious beliefs.
2. northern and central India

Different Views on Culture/Indian Nationalism Grows

Instruct

- **Introduce** Have a volunteer read aloud the last sentence under the black heading Western Attitudes. Remind them that the word *arrogant,* used to describe Macaulay's statement, means "full of self-importance." Ask student to describe how this meaning suits Macaulay's quote.

- **Teach** Point out that leaders such as Ram Mohun Roy wanted to combine Western and Indian culture. Meanwhile, British leaders hoped that a Western-educated elite would strengthen British power. Ask **How did the British strategy backfire?** *(Western ideas led to nationalism and calls for self-rule.)*

- **Quick Activity** Have students take the role of Indian nationalists who are opening a new school. Have them decide whether they would establish the school in English, or in one of the major native Indian languages.

Independent Practice

Biography To help students better understand how educated Indians tried to blend Western with Indian culture, have them read the biography *Rabindranath Tagore* and complete the worksheet.

All in One **Teaching Resources, Unit 3,** p. 73

Monitor Progress

Check Reading and Note Taking Study Guide entries for student understanding.

Railroads and Trade
By building thousands of miles of railroads, the British opened up India's vast interior to trade. The British also encouraged Indians to grow tea (top photo) and jute (bottom photo). Today, tea is one of India's biggest crops. *What were some of the benefits of British rule?*

---

their factory-made goods across the subcontinent and carry Indian cotton, jute, and coal to coastal ports for transport to factories in England. New methods of communication, such as the telegraph, also gave Britain better control of India. After the Suez Canal opened in 1869, British trade with India soared. But it remained an unequal partnership, favoring the British. The British flooded India with inexpensive, machine-made textiles, ruining India's once-prosperous hand-weaving industry.

Britain also transformed Indian agriculture. It encouraged nomadic herders to settle into farming and pushed farmers to grow cash crops, such as cotton and jute, that could be sold on the world market. Clearing new farmlands led to massive **deforestation,** or cutting of trees.

Population Growth and Famine The British introduced medical improvements and new farming methods. Better healthcare and increased food production led to rapid population growth. The rising numbers, however, put a strain on the food supply, especially as farmland was turned over to growing cash crops instead of food. In the late 1800s, terrible famines swept India.

Benefits of British Rule On the positive side, British rule brought some degree of peace and order to the countryside. The British revised the legal system to promote justice for Indians regardless of class or caste. Railroads helped Indians move around the country, while the telegraph and postal system improved communication. Greater contact helped bridge regional differences and develop a sense of national unity.

The upper classes, especially, benefited from some British policies. They sent their sons to British schools, where they were trained for posts in the civil service and military. Indian landowners and princes, who still ruled their own territories, grew rich from exporting cash crops.

✓ **Checkpoint** How did British colonial rule affect Indian agriculture?

Different Views on Culture

Some educated Indians were impressed by British power and technology and urged India to follow a Western model of progress. These mostly upper-class Indians learned English and adopted Western ways. Other Indians felt that the answer to change lay with their own Hindu or Muslim cultures.

Indian Attitudes In the early 1800s, **Ram Mohun Roy** combined both views. A great scholar, he knew Sanskrit, Persian, and Arabic classics, as well as English, Greek, and Latin works. Roy felt that India could learn from the West. He was a founder of Hindu College in Calcutta, which provided an English-style education to Indians. Many of its graduates went on to establish English schools all over the region. While Roy saw the value of Western education, he also wanted to reform traditional Indian culture.

Roy condemned some traditions, such as rigid caste distinctions, child marriage, sati, and **purdah** (PUR duh), the isolation of women in separate quarters. But he also set up educational societies that helped revive pride in Indian culture. Because of his influence on later leaders, he is often hailed today as the founder of Indian nationalism.

Answers

✓ nomadic herders became farmers, farmers grew cash crops, clearing farmland led to deforestation, and the British introduced new farming methods.

Caption a degree of peace and order, improved communication and transportation, a fairer legal system, an increased sense of unity, and better educational opportunities for young men of the upper class

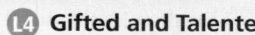

Western Attitudes The British disagreed among themselves about India. A few admired Indian theology and philosophy. As Western scholars translated Indian classics, they acquired respect for India's ancient heritage. Western writers and philosophers borrowed ideas from Hinduism and Buddhism.

However, most British people knew little about Indian achievements and dismissed Indian culture with contempt. In an essay on whether Indians should be taught in English or their own languages, British historian Thomas Macaulay arrogantly wrote that "a single shelf of a good European library is worth the whole native literature of India and Arabia."

 Checkpoint How did Indians and British view each other's culture in the 1800s?

Indian Nationalism Grows

During the years of British rule, a class of Western-educated Indians emerged. In the view of Macaulay and others, this elite class would bolster British power. As it turned out, exposure to European ideas had the opposite effect. By the late 1800s, Western-educated Indians were spearheading a nationalist movement. Schooled in Western ideals such as democracy and equality, they dreamed of ending imperial rule.

Indian National Congress In 1885, nationalist leaders organized the Indian National Congress, which became known as the Congress party. Its members believed in peaceful protest to gain their ends. They called for greater democracy, which they felt would bring more power to Indians like themselves. The Indian National Congress looked forward to eventual self-rule, but supported Western-style modernization.

Muslim League At first, Muslims and Hindus worked together for self-rule. In time, however, Muslims grew to resent Hindu domination of the Congress party. They also worried that a Hindu-run government would oppress Muslims. In 1906, Muslims formed the Muslim League to pursue their own goals. Soon, they were talking of a separate Muslim state.

 Checkpoint How are the origins of Indian nationalism linked to British rule?

SECTION 4 Assessment

Progress Monitoring Online
For: Self-quiz with vocabulary practice
Web Code: nba-2441

Terms, People, and Places
1. What do the key terms listed at the beginning of the section have in common?

Note Taking
2. **Reading Skill: Identify Causes and Effects** Use your completed flowchart to answer the Focus Question: How did Britain gradually extend its control over most of India, despite opposition?

Comprehension and Critical Thinking
3. **Recognize Cause and Effect** What were the causes and effects of the Sepoy Rebellion?
4. **Draw Conclusions** What were the positive and negative effects of British rule on Indians?
5. **Analyze Information** How did British rule lead to growing Indian nationalism?

● **Writing About History**
Quick Write: Draft an Opening Paragraph Write an opening paragraph for a persuasive essay on whether the British were right to pass laws that tried to reform the caste system. Remember that the first few sentences of your draft are your chance to build interest in your topic. Add details that will help grab the reader's attention.

Section 4 Assessment

1. Most of the terms are related to British imperialism in India *(sepoy, viceroy, deforestation)* or Hindu customs targeted by the British *(sati, purdah).*
2. The British East India Company exploited Indian diversity and used its monopoly to extend control over most of India; then the British government took over.
3. Cause: British rules that violated Hindu beliefs; Effects: distrust and hatred on both sides and more direct control of India by the British
4. Positive: improved transportation, communication, medical care, farming methods, order, justice, and education; Negative: exploitation, destruction of local industry, deforestation, and famine
5. Western-educated Indians learned ideas about democracy, which they applied to their situation.

Concept Connector

Empire

Objectives

- Identify ways empires have gained power.
- Understand that even once powerful empires can fall.
- Complete a Web Quest on empire.

Build Background Knowledge ℡

Review the characteristics of an empire with students. Ask: **Does the United States fulfill the criteria of an empire? Why or why not?**

Instruct

- Direct students' attention to the Essential Question: **What factors allow empires to rise and cause them to fall?**
- Have students review In This Chapter and the corresponding picture. Have volunteers identify the factors in its society that gave the British the ability to develop an empire.
- Direct students attention to the time line. Elicit from them why various factors strengthened or weakened empires. Ask volunteers for other factors that might influence the rise and fall of empires.
- Assign the Web Quest on empire.

Independent Practice

Concept Connector Have students fill in the reflection question on the Web Quest on empire in their Concept Connector Journal.

 Reading and Note Taking Study Guide, p. Modern 266

Monitor Progress

Circulate to make sure that students are filling in their Concept Connector Journal. Ensure they understand how empires occur.

Transfer Activities

1. Empires have developed because of strong bureaucracy, strong leaders, and good transportation networks. They have been weakened by waging costly wars.
2. Possible answer: Each empire eventually fails because of the cost of defending the empire and changes in leadership.
3. Students' work should be evaluated against the rubric at Web Code nbh-2408.

410

Concept Connector

 **EMPIRE**

What factors allow empires to rise and cause them to fall?

In This Chapter

Britain brought much of the globe under its control in the 1800s because of its industrial strength and powerful navy. The "jewel in the crown" of the British Empire was India (right). India supplied British factories with raw materials and served as a huge market for British manufactured goods. But in the twentieth century, independence movements in India and elsewhere broke the British Empire apart.

Throughout History

522 B.C.–486 B.C. Darius I unifies the Persian empire by setting up a strong bureaucracy and building hundreds of miles of roads

31 B.C.–A.D. 14 Emperor Augustus encourages loyalty by allowing Roman provinces a large measure of self-government.

1500s Spain used wealth from its empire in the Americas to wage wars in Europe, neglecting its own economic development.

1800s The French Empire rises and falls with the rise and fall of Napoleon I.

1990s Economic weakness and involvement in a long war in Afghanistan leads to the breakup of the Soviet Union.

Continuing Today

Although the Soviet Union has broken apart, Russia maintains its interest in the affairs of former Soviet states. Russia will flex its military muscle to keep them in line. Here Russian tanks roll into neighboring Georgia to support South Ossetia.

21st Century Skills

② TRANSFER Activities

1. **Analyze** Throughout history, how have different empires been strengthened or weakened?

2. **Evaluate** Why do you think no empire has even been able to maintain its influence forever?

3. **Transfer** Complete a Web quest, record your thoughts in the Concept Connector Journal, and learn to make a video. Web Code nbh-2408

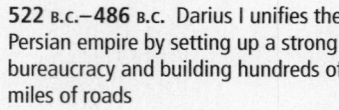

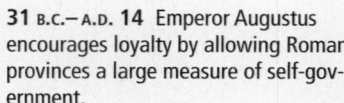

Lin Zexu,
Chinese official

WITNESS HISTORY 🔊 AUDIO

Trading Opium for Tea

By the 1830s, British merchant ships were arriving in China loaded with opium to trade with the Chinese for tea. In 1839, Chinese government official Lin Zexu (lin DZUH shoo) wrote a letter to Britain's Queen Victoria condemning the practice:

❝We have heard that in your own country opium is prohibited with the utmost strictness and severity—this is strong proof that you know full well how hurtful it is. . . . Since . . . you do not permit it to injure your own country, you ought not to have the injurious drug transferred to another country.❞

Britain's Union Jack

Focus Question How did Western powers use diplomacy and war to gain power in Qing China?

China and the New Imperialism

Objectives
- Describe what trade rights Westerners sought in China.
- Explain the internal problems Chinese reformers tried to solve.
- Understand how the Qing dynasty fell.

Terms, People, and Places

balance of trade	Taiping Rebellion
trade surplus	Sino-Japanese War
trade deficit	Open Door Policy
Opium War	Guang Xu
indemnity	Boxer Uprising
extraterritoriality	Sun Yixian

N̲o̲te Taking

Reading Skill: Recognize Multiple Causes As you read, create a flowchart like the one below in which you can record key events and developments that led to the decline of Qing China.

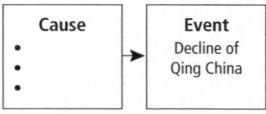

Cause	→	Event
•		Decline of
•		Qing China
•		

For centuries, Chinese regulations had ensured that China had a favorable **balance of trade** with other nations. A nation's balance of trade refers to the difference between how much a country imports and how much it exports. By the 1800s, however, Western nations were using their growing power to tilt the balance of trade with East Asia in their favor.

Trade Between Britain and China

Prior to the 1800s, Chinese rulers placed strict limits on foreign traders. European merchants were restricted to a small area in southern China. China sold them silk, porcelain, and tea in exchange for gold and silver. Under this arrangement, China enjoyed a **trade surplus,** or exported more than it imported. Westerners, on the other hand, had a **trade deficit** with China, buying more from the Chinese than they sold to them.

By the late 1700s, two developments were underway that would transform China's relations with the Western world. First, China entered a period of decline. Second, the Industrial Revolution created a need for expanded markets for European goods. At the same time, it gave the West superior military power.

The Opium War During the late 1700s, British merchants began making huge profits by trading opium grown in India for Chinese tea, which was popular in Britain. Soon, many Chinese had become addicted to the drug. Silver flowed out of China in payment for the drug, disrupting the economy.

Vocabulary Builder

Use the information below and the following resources to teach the high-use word from this section.
A̲l̲l̲ ̲i̲n̲ ̲O̲n̲e̲ **Teaching Resources, Unit 3,** p. 68; **Teaching Resources, Skills Handbook,** p. 3

High-Use Word	Definition and Sample Sentence
stipulate, p. 412	*v.* to specifically demand something in an agreement
	As part of their truce, Jess **stipulated** that her sister could no longer borrow her clothes without asking.

Trade Between Britain and China/The Taiping Rebellion Weakens China

Instruct

- **Introduce: Vocabulary Builder**
  Have students read the Vocabulary Builder term and definition. Ask them to predict how the Western powers obtained treaties with China that *stipulated* favorable conditions. *(threat of force)*

- **Teach** Write *trade surplus, trade deficit,* and *balance of trade* on the board and ask students to define them. Ask students **What did British traders hope to achieve by continuing to trade opium?** *(They hoped to end the trade deficit and create huge profits.)* **What were the results of the Opium War?** *(China signed the first of several unequal treaties with Europe powers.)* **How did European powers take advantage of the Taiping Rebellion?** *(They continued to push for more influence in China.)*

- **Quick Activity** On the board, create three columns, labeled Causes, Events, and Effects of the Taiping Rebellion. Then have students use the Infographic on the Taiping Rebellion and the text to supply information for each column.

Independent Practice

Have students access **Web Code nbp-2451** to take the **Geography Interactive Audio Guided Tour** and then answer the map skills questions in the text.

Monitor Progress

As students fill in their flowcharts, circulate to make sure they understand how the population explosion was a factor in the decline of the Qing dynasty. For a completed version of the flowchart, see
📖 **Note Taking Transparencies,** 164

Answer

✓ The British introduced opium; when the Chinese tried to stop the opium trade, the British responded with gunboats.

The Chinese government outlawed opium and executed Chinese drug dealers. They called on Britain to stop the trade. The British refused, insisting on the right of free trade.

In 1839, Chinese warships clashed with British merchants, triggering the **Opium War.** British gunboats, equipped with the latest in firepower, bombarded Chinese coastal and river ports. With outdated weapons and fighting methods, the Chinese were easily defeated.

Unequal Treaties In 1842, Britain made China accept the Treaty of Nanjing (NAHN jing). Britain received a huge **indemnity,** or payment for losses in the war. The British also gained the island of Hong Kong. China had to open five ports to foreign trade and grant British citizens in China **extraterritoriality,** the right to live under their own laws and be tried in their own courts.

The treaty was the first of a series of "unequal treaties" that forced China to make concessions to Western powers. A second war, lasting from 1856 to 1858, ended with France, Russia, and the United States pressuring China to sign treaties stipulating the opening of more ports to foreign trade and letting Christian missionaries preach in China.

✓ **Checkpoint** How did British trade with China trigger the Opium Wars?

The Taiping Rebellion Weakens China

By the 1800s, the Qing dynasty was in decline. Irrigation systems and canals were poorly maintained, leading to massive flooding of the Huang valley. The population explosion that had begun a century earlier created hardship

Vocabulary Builder

stipulate—(STIP yuh layt) *v.* to specifically demand something in an agreement

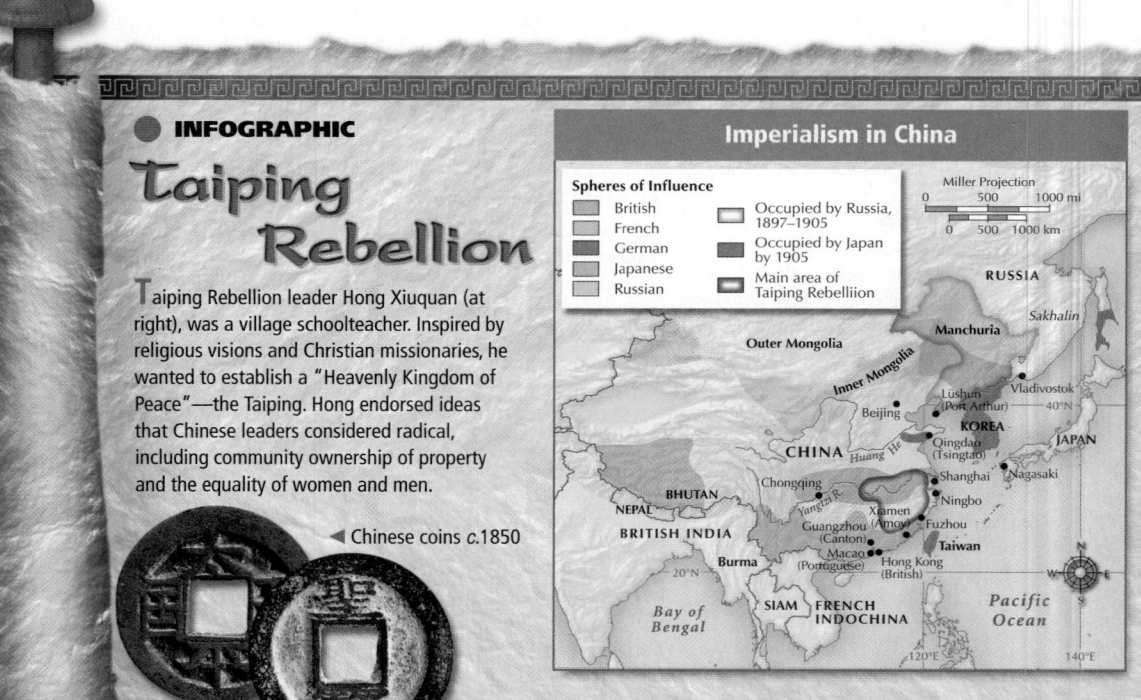

INFOGRAPHIC

Taiping Rebellion

Taiping Rebellion leader Hong Xiuquan (at right), was a village schoolteacher. Inspired by religious visions and Christian missionaries, he wanted to establish a "Heavenly Kingdom of Peace"—the Taiping. Hong endorsed ideas that Chinese leaders considered radical, including community ownership of property and the equality of women and men.

◄ Chinese coins c.1850

Imperialism in China

Spheres of Influence
- British
- French
- German
- Japanese
- Russian
- Occupied by Russia, 1897–1905
- Occupied by Japan by 1905
- Main area of Taiping Rebelliion

Miller Projection
0   500   1000 mi
0   500   1000 km

RUSSIA, Sakhalin, Outer Mongolia, Inner Mongolia, Manchuria, Vladivostok, Lüshun (Port Arthur), 40°N, Beijing, KOREA, JAPAN, CHINA, Huang He, Qingdao (Tsingtao), Nagasaki, Chongqing, Shanghai, BHUTAN, Yangzi R., Ningbo, NEPAL, Guangzhou (Canton), Xiamen (Amoy), Fuzhou, BRITISH INDIA, Macao (Portuguese), Taiwan, 20°N, Burma, Hong Kong (British), Bay of Bengal, SIAM, FRENCH INDOCHINA, Pacific Ocean, 120°E, 140°E

History Background

Lin Zexu and the Opium Tea Party Although China outlawed opium in 1729 and again in 1796, the British East India Company used its monopoly on opium growing in India to make enormous profits in China, where opium had ruinous effects. In 1838, Lin Zexu, a humane and just administrator, tried to stop the opium trade. Lin confined 350 foreign merchants in their trading houses until they signed an agreement not to import opium. They refused to sign but were released when they turned over twenty thousand chests of opium. Lin dumped some 3 million pounds of opium into the sea and wrote a letter to Queen Victoria. The British, outraged, sent gunships, which quickly overwhelmed China's antiquated defenses. Lin was blamed at first but later revered with monuments across China.

for China's peasants. An extravagant imperial court, tax evasion by the rich, and widespread official corruption added to the peasants' burden. As poverty and misery increased, peasants rebelled. The **Taiping Rebellion** (TY ping), which lasted from 1850 to 1864, was probably the most devastating peasant revolt in history. The leader, Hong Xiuquan (hong shyoo CHWAHN), called for an end to the hated Qing dynasty. The Taiping rebels won control of large parts of China and held out for 14 years. However, with the help of loyal regional governors and generals, the government crushed the rebellion.

The Taiping Rebellion almost toppled the Qing dynasty. It is estimated to have caused the deaths of between 20 million and 30 million Chinese. The Qing government survived, but it had to share power with regional commanders. During the rebellion, Europeans kept up pressure on China, and Russia seized lands in the north.

✔ **Checkpoint** How did the Taiping Rebellion and other internal problems weaken the Qing dynasty?

Launching Reform Efforts

By the mid-1800s, educated Chinese were divided over the need to adopt Western ways. Most saw no reason for new industries because China's wealth and taxes came from land. Although Chinese merchants were allowed to do business, they were not seen as a source of prosperity.

Scholar-officials also disapproved of the ideas of Western missionaries, whose emphasis on individual choice challenged the Confucian order. They saw Western technology as dangerous, too, because it threatened Confucian ways that had served China successfully for so long.

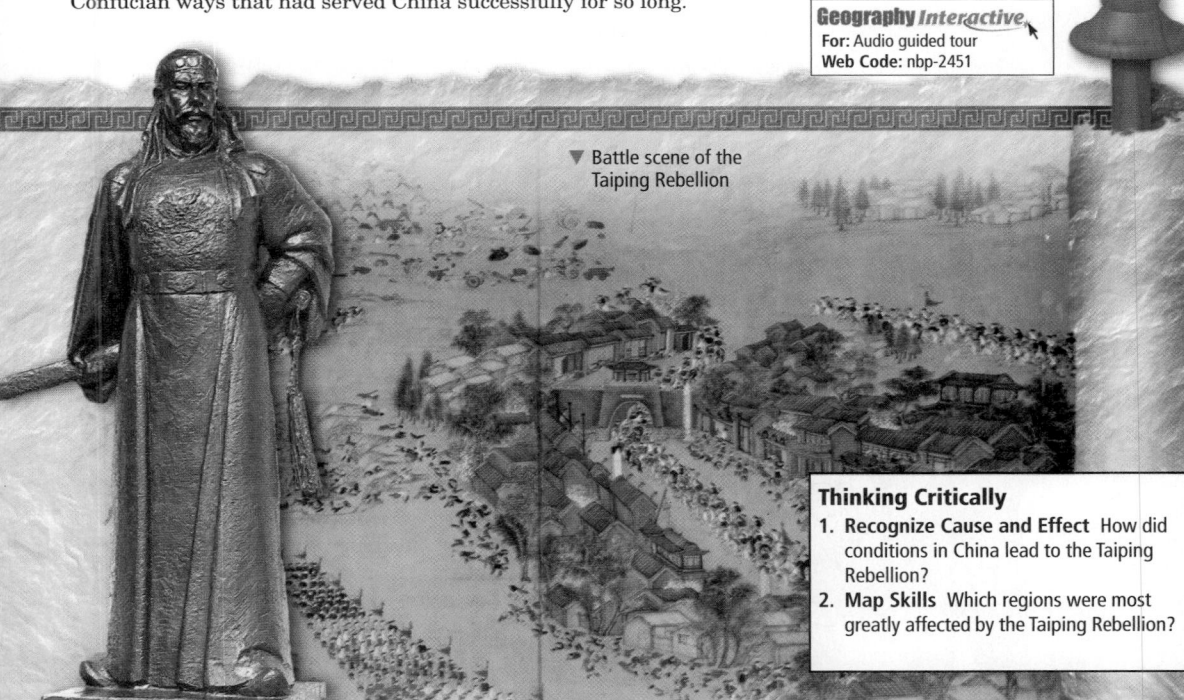

Geography *Interactive*
For: Audio guided tour
Web Code: nbp-2451

▼ Battle scene of the Taiping Rebellion

Thinking Critically
1. **Recognize Cause and Effect** How did conditions in China lead to the Taiping Rebellion?
2. **Map Skills** Which regions were most greatly affected by the Taiping Rebellion?

Launching Reform Efforts

 L3

Instruct

■ **Introduce** Point out that China's Confucian ideals had resulted in a successful government for more than 2,000 years. Ask **Why do you think China was so resistant to Western influence?** *(Sample: China's system had worked successfully for a very long time; they did not value new industry or merchants; and individualism and technology threatened Confucian ways.)* **What pushed China toward change?** *(losses in war)*

■ **Teach** Ask **Who won the First Sino-Japanese war, and why?** *(The Japanese won because of its modern army.)* Using the Think-Write-Pair-Share strategy (TE, p. T23), ask students to respond to this question: **How did efforts at reform both help and hurt China?** *(Reforms led to some improvements, but also to more internal conflict.)*

■ **Quick Activity** Display **Color Transparency 148: The Great Powers Divide China.** Ask students to identify the powers portrayed and explain what situation the cartoon is referring to. Then ask how the cartoonist views the great powers in China.
  📖 **Color Transparencies, 148**

Independent Practice

Primary Source To help students better understand Chinese views on reform, have them read the excerpt from "Exhortation to Study" by Chang Chi-tung and complete the worksheet.

All in One **Teaching Resources, Unit 3,** p. 74

Monitor Progress

To review this subsection, ask students to describe the viewpoints of conservatives such as Ci Xi and of reformers such as Guang Xu.

Answers

✔ Years of turmoil, as well as power given to regional leaders, weakened the Qing dynasty and made China vulnerable to European encroachment.

Thinking Critically
1. Living conditions for peasants worsened causing them to finally rise up under Hong Xiuquan's leadership.
2. areas of southeastern China

The Qing Dynasty Falls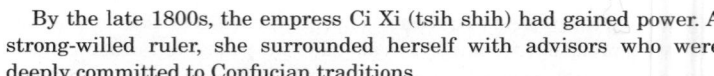

Instruct

- **Introduce: Key Terms** Ask students to find the key term *Boxer Uprising* (in blue) in the text and describe what it was. Ask **What grievances did the Chinese have against foreigners?** *(opium addiction, the undermining of Chinese culture by missionaries, foreign control, foreign troops, loss of wealth)*

- **Teach** Ask **How did the Boxer Uprising bring about change in China?** *(Its failure forced even conservatives to agree to institute social and economic reforms.)* **What were the Three Principles of the People?** *(Sun Yixian's principles for a new China: nationalism, democracy, and livelihood.)* **What challenges faced Sun Yixian's new republic?** *(Sample: creating conditions for democracy and capitalism after thousands of years of empire and loss of wealth to Western powers)*

- **Analyzing the Visuals** Tell students to compare the photo of the Boxer rebel on this page with the photo of Sun Yixian on the next page. Ask students how their dress reflects different responses to Western culture.

Independent Practice

Have students create a propaganda poster advocating change and representing the ideas of the Boxers, Chinese reformers, or Sun Yixian.

Monitor Progress

Check Reading and Note Taking Study Guide entries for student understanding.

The Boxer Rebellion
Suffering from the effects of floods and famine, poverty, and foreign aggression, Boxers (below) participated in an anti-foreign movement. In 1900, some 140,000 Boxers attempted to drive Westerners out of China. An international force eventually put down the uprising. *Why were Westerners and Western influences a source of discontent for the Boxers?*

By the late 1800s, the empress Ci Xi (tsih shih) had gained power. A strong-willed ruler, she surrounded herself with advisors who were deeply committed to Confucian traditions.

Self-Strengthening Movement In the 1860s, reformers launched the "self-strengthening movement." They imported Western technology, setting up factories to make modern weapons. They developed shipyards, railroads, mining, and light industry. The Chinese translated Western works on science, government, and the economy. However, the movement made limited progress because the government did not rally behind it.

War With Japan Meanwhile, the Western powers and nearby Japan moved rapidly ahead. Japan began to modernize after 1868. It then joined the Western imperialists in the competition for a global empire.

In 1894, Japanese pressure on China led to the Sino-Japanese War. It ended in disaster for China, with Japan gaining the island of Taiwan.

Carving Spheres of Influence The crushing defeat revealed China's weakness. Western powers moved swiftly to carve out spheres of influence along the Chinese coast. The British took the Chang River valley. The French acquired the territory near their colony of Indochina. Germany and Russia gained territory in northern China.

The United States, a longtime trader with the Chinese, did not take part in the carving up of China. It feared that European powers might shut out American merchants. A few years later, in 1899, it called for a policy to keep Chinese trade open to everyone on an equal basis. The imperial powers accepted the idea of an Open Door Policy, as it came to be called. No one, however, consulted the Chinese.

Hundred Days of Reform Defeated by Japan and humiliated by Westerners, Chinese reformers blamed conservative officials for not modernizing China. They urged conservative leaders to stop looking back at China's past and to modernize as Japan had.

In 1898, a young emperor, Guang Xu (gwahng shoo), launched the Hundred Days of Reform. New laws set out to modernize the civil service exams, streamline government, and encourage new industries. Reforms affected schools, the military, and the bureaucracy. Conservatives soon rallied against the reform effort. The emperor was imprisoned, and the aging empress Ci Xi reasserted control. Reformers fled for their lives.

✓ **Checkpoint** How did reformers try to solve China's internal problems?

The Qing Dynasty Falls

As the century ended, China was in turmoil. Anger grew against Christian missionaries who threatened traditional Chinese Confucianism. The presence of foreign troops was another source of discontent. Protected by extraterritoriality, foreigners ignored Chinese laws and lived in their own communities.

Boxer Uprising Anti-foreign feeling finally exploded in the Boxer Uprising. In 1899, a group of Chinese had formed a secret society, the Righteous Harmonious Fists. Westerners watching them

---

Differentiated
Instruction · **Solutions for All Learners**

L1 Special Needs **L2 Less Proficient Readers**

Form students into pairs and ask them to create a timeline of the events in China covered in this section, starting with the beginning of the Opium War in 1839. Tell them to approach the task by skimming each heading, identifying its main idea, and jotting down any dates that are mentioned. They should then assemble their timelines using their notes.

L2 English Language Learners

Use the following resources to help students acquire basic skills:

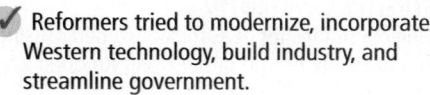 **Adapted Reading and Note Taking Study Guide**

- Adapted Note Taking Study Guide, p. 138
- Adapted Section Summary, p. 139

Answers

✓ Reformers tried to modernize, incorporate Western technology, build industry, and streamline government.

Caption because they ignored Chinese laws and customs

train in the martial arts dubbed them Boxers. Their goal was to drive out the "foreign devils" who were polluting the land with their un-Chinese ways, strange buildings, machines, and telegraph lines.

In 1900, the Boxers attacked foreigners across China. In response, the Western powers and Japan organized a multinational force. This force crushed the Boxers and rescued foreigners besieged in Beijing. The empress Ci Xi had at first supported the Boxers but reversed her policy as they retreated.

Aftermath of the Uprising China once again had to make concessions to foreigners. The defeat, however, forced even Chinese conservatives to support Westernization. In a rush of reforms, China admitted women to schools and stressed science and mathematics in place of Confucian thought. More students were sent abroad to study.

China also expanded economically. Mining, shipping, railroads, banking, and exports of cash crops grew. Small-scale Chinese industry developed with the help of foreign capital. A Chinese business class emerged, and a new urban working class began to press for rights.

Three Principles of the People Although the Boxer Uprising failed, the flames of Chinese nationalism spread. Reformers wanted to strengthen China's government. By the early 1900s, they had introduced a constitutional monarchy. Some reformers called for a republic.

A passionate spokesman for a Chinese republic was **Sun Yixian** (soon yee SHYAHN), also known as Sun Yat-sen. In the early 1900s, he organized the Revolutionary Alliance to rebuild China on "Three Principles of the People." The first principle was nationalism, or freeing China from foreign domination. The second was democracy, or representative government. The third was livelihood, or economic security for all Chinese.

Birth of a Republic When Ci Xi died in 1908 and a two-year-old boy inherited the throne, China slipped into chaos. In 1911, uprisings in the provinces swiftly spread. Peasants, students, local warlords, and even court politicians helped topple the Qing dynasty.

In December 1911, Sun Yixian was named president of the new Chinese republic. The republic faced overwhelming problems and was almost constantly at war with itself or foreign invaders.

✓ **Checkpoint** What caused the Qing dynasty to fall?

BIOGRAPHY

Sun Yixian

Sun Yixian (1866–1925) was not born to power. His parents were poor farmers. Sun's preparation for leadership came from his travels, education, and personal ambitions. In his teen years, he lived with his brother in Hawaii and attended British and American schools. Later on, he earned a medical degree.

Sun left his career in medicine to struggle against the Qing government. After a failed uprising in 1895, he went into exile. Sun visited many nations, seeking support against the Qing dynasty. When revolution erupted in China, Sun was in Denver, Colorado. He returned to China to begin his leading role in the new republic. **How did Sun's background prepare him to lead?**

SECTION 5 Assessment

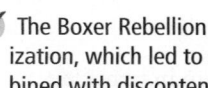

Progress Monitoring Online
For: Self-quiz with vocabulary practice
Web Code: nba-2451

Terms, People, and Places
1. For each term, person, or place listed at the beginning of the section, write a sentence explaining its significance.

Note Taking
2. **Reading Skill: Recognize Multiple Causes** Use your completed flowchart to answer the Focus Question: How did Western powers use diplomacy and war to gain power in Qing China?

Comprehension and Critical Thinking
3. **Draw Conclusions** How did Western powers gain greater trading rights in China?
4. **Summarize** (a) What internal problems threatened the Qing dynasty? (b) What were the goals of Chinese reformers?
5. **Synthesize Information** How was the Qing dynasty replaced by a republic?

● Writing About History
Quick Write: Write a Conclusion Before writing a persuasive essay, make a list of your arguments. In organizing the essay, it's often a good idea to save your strongest argument for last. For practice, write a concluding paragraph for a persuasive essay that either supports or opposes internal reform efforts to Westernize China in the 1800s.

Assess and Reteach

Assess Progress · L3
- Have students complete the Section Assessment.
- Administer the Section Quiz.
- **All in One** Teaching Resources, Unit 3, p. 67
- To further assess student understanding, use
  - Progress Monitoring Transparencies, 103

Reteach · L1 L2
If students need more instruction, have them read the section summary.

- Reading and Note Taking Study Guide, p. 139 · L1 L3
- Adapted Reading and Note Taking Study Guide, p. 139 · L1 L2
- Spanish Reading and Note Taking Study Guide, p. 139 · L1 L2

Extend · L4
Today, as China rapidly industrializes, it is flooding world markets with cheap industrial products. The United States has a record trade deficit with China. Have students research the issues and itemize how the trade deficit affects China's relationship with Western countries.

Answers

✓ The Boxer Rebellion led to greater Westernization, which led to nationalism, which combined with discontent and a weak emperor (a two-year-old) to topple the dynasty.

BIOGRAPHY It gave him access to ideas that he may not have otherwise discovered.

● Writing About History
Responses should include a strong, carefully considered argument that clearly supports or opposes Chinese reform efforts in the 1800s.

For additional assessment, have students access **Progress Monitoring Online** at **Web Code nba-2451.**

Quick Study Guide

- Have students use the Quick Study Guide to prepare for this chapter's test. Students may wish to refer to the following pages as they review:

Western Imperialism
Section 2, pp. 392–398; Section 3, pp. 400–404; Section 4, pp. 405–409; Section 5, pp. 411–415

Imports from Africa and Asia about 1870
Section 1, pp. 388–399

Key Events of the New Imperialism
Section 2, pp. 394–396; Section 3, p. 402; Section 4, pp. 406–407; Section 5, p. 415

- For additional review, remind students to refer to the **L3**

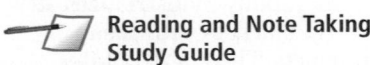 **Reading and Note Taking Study Guide**

Note Taking Study Guide, pp. 130, 132, 134, 136, 138
Section Summaries, pp. 131, 133, 135, 137, 139

- Have students access **Web Code nbp-2462** for this chapter's **History Interactive** timeline, which includes expanded entries and additional events.

- If students need more instruction on analyzing timelines, have them read the **Skills Handbook,** p. SH30.

- When students have completed their study of the chapter, distribute Chapter Tests A and B.

All in One Teaching Resources, Unit 3, pp. 78–83

For **Progress Monitoring Online,** refer students to the Self-test with vocabulary practice at **Web Code nba-2461.**

Quick Study Guide

Progress Monitoring Online
For: Self-test with vocabulary practice
Web Code: nba-2461

■ Western Imperialism

Africa	Muslim Regions	India	China
• Berlin Conference • Raw materials exploited • Boer War • Racial segregation in South Africa • Western-educated African elite • Nationalism grows	• Islamic reform movements • Internal revolts • Armenian genocide • Egypt modernizes	• British East India Company • Changes to legal and caste systems • Sepoy Rebellion • Indians forced to raise cash crops • Population growth and famine • Indian National Congress • Muslim League	• Opium War • Unequal trade treaties • Self-strengthening movement • Sino-Japanese War • Boxer Uprising

■ Imports from Africa and Asia about 1870

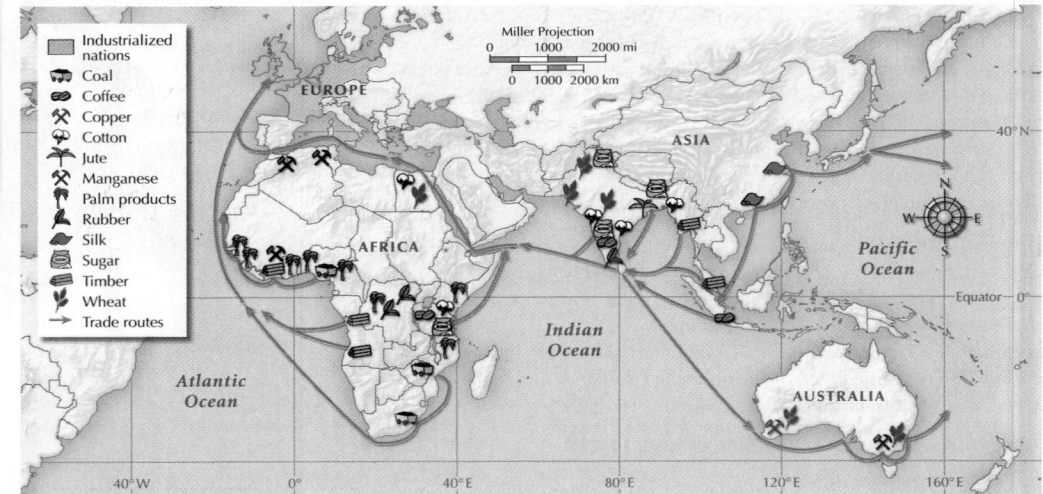

Industrialized nations
Coal
Coffee
Copper
Cotton
Jute
Manganese
Palm products
Rubber
Silk
Sugar
Timber
Wheat
→ Trade routes

Miller Projection

EUROPE
ASIA
AFRICA
Pacific Ocean
Indian Ocean
Atlantic Ocean
AUSTRALIA
Equator
40° N

■ Key Events of the New Imperialism

1805 Muhammad Ali is named governor of Egypt.

1830 France begins efforts to conquer Algeria in North Africa.

1857 The Sepoy Rebellion breaks out in India.

Chapter Events
Global Events

1800   **1825**   **1850**

1807 In the United States, Robert Fulton uses a steam engine to power a ship.

1848 Revolutions break out throughout much of Europe.

Differentiated Instruction   Solutions for All Learners

L1 Special Needs   **L2 Less Proficient Readers**

Use the following study guide resources to help students acquiring basic skills:

Adapted Reading and Note Taking Study Guide
Note Taking Study Guide, pp. 130, 132, 134, 136, 138
Section Summaries, pp. 131, 133, 135, 137, 139

L2 English Language Learners

Use the following study guide resources to help Spanish-speaking students:

Spanish Reading and Note Taking Study Guide
Note Taking Study Guide, pp. 130, 132, 134, 136, 138
Section Summaries, pp. 131, 133, 135, 137, 139

Concept Connector

 Essential Question Review

To connect prior knowledge with what you have learned in this chapter, answer the questions below in your Concept Connector journal. Use the journal in the Reading and Note Taking Study Guide to record your answers (or go to www.phschool.com Web Code: nbd-2407). In addition, record information about the following concepts:

1. **Belief Systems** Both foreign and Chinese belief systems influenced China during the 1800s. Some Chinese wanted to adopt Western ways, while others wanted to maintain Confucian ways. How did the choices China made influence its future relationship with Western nations? Do you think China's history would have been different if it had made the same choices as Japan? Why or why not?

2. **Genocide** In the 1890s, tensions between Muslim Turkish nationalists and Christian Armenians triggered a brutal genocide of the minority Armenians. It is estimated that more than one million Armenians were killed or died as a result. Review what you learned about Social Darwinism. How might a Social Darwinist explain the Armenian genocide?

3. **Empire** Powerful armies and navies, advanced weapons, and superior technologies were the tools of the "new imperialism." But the European powers also employed other strategies to gain and keep control over colonies. For example, in South Africa, the British set up a government run by whites and imposed a system of complete racial segregation. What were some of the other strategies Europeans used to control colonies or spheres of influence? Think about the following:
   - indirect rule
   - exploitation
   - trade
   - treaties

■ Connections to Today

1. **Economics: Trade and the Suez Canal** Reread the information in Section 3 on the Suez Canal. How did the opening of the Suez Canal in 1869 transform world trade? Then, find a recent newspaper or magazine article on the Suez Canal today. Do you think the canal is more or less important today than it was in 1869? Write two paragraphs on trade and the Suez Canal today, citing examples from current events to support your answer.

Suez Canal Traffic		
Year	Number of Ships	Net Tons
1975	5,579	50,441,000
1985	19,791	352,579,000
1995	15,051	360,372,000
2003	15,667	549,381,000

SOURCE: Leth Suez Transit Online, 2004

2. **People and the Environment: Famine** You have read how disaster struck Ireland in October 1845 when a deadly plant disease ruined the potato crop. In the late 1800s, famines also swept through India. What were the major causes of these famines? What was the effect of growing cash crops instead of food? Conduct research to learn more about the causes of hunger and malnutrition in the world today.

1884	Mid-1880s	1899	1911	1914
European officials meet at the Berlin Conference to settle rival land claims in Africa.	German engineers develop the first automobile.	Boer War erupts in South Africa.	Sun Yixian becomes president of Chinese republic.	World War I begins in Europe.

History Interactive,
For: Interactive timeline
Web Code: nbp-2462

1875   1900   1925

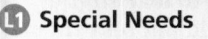

Concept Connector

Tell students that the main concepts for this chapter are Belief Systems, Empire, and Genocide, and then ask them to answer the Essential Question Review questions on this page. Discuss the Connections to Today topics and ask students to answer the questions that follow.

Essential Question Review

1. Students' answers may include information about China's "self-strengthening movement" and that China imported Western technology. If China had modernized as quickly as Japan, it may have resisted imperialist powers and avoided the internal strife that killed millions.

2. Responses may include the suggestion that because the Armenians were non-Muslim, they were considered an untrustworthy, problem population, or that the genocide was based on religious differences.

3. Responses should include indirect rule, using local rulers to govern; protectorates-local rulers advised by Europeans; and spheres of influence, where outside powers claimed exclusive trading privileges. Exploitation encouraged disunity among regional rivals, while unequal treaties forced countries to make concessions to foreigners.

Connections to Today

1. Responses should also include details on trade through the canal today (such as number of ships or total revenue) to support a clear thesis statement on whether the canal is more or less important today.

2. Responses should mention that population growth and growing cash crops instead of food helped lead to famine in the 1800s. Similar factors have led to hunger in the world today, but students may also mention drought, deforestation, and political issues.

For additional review of this chapter's core concepts, remind students to refer to the

↗ **Reading and Note Taking Study Guide**
Concept Connector, pp. 233, 262, 267

Chapter Assessment

Terms, People, and Places

1. imperialism
2. Sino-Japanese War
3. pasha
4. trade deficit
5. Muhammad Ali
6. Taiping Rebellion
7. genocide
8. indemnity

Main Ideas

9. economic, political, military, humanitarian, religious motives, and Social Darwinism

10. Many non-Western nations were weak whereas Western powers had strong economies, governments, and armed forces and superior technology.

11. Medical advances and steamships allowed explorers and missionaries to push deep into Africa.

12. King Leopold's activities in the Congo led to the Berlin Conference, which led to a scramble to carve out claims.

13. nationalist revolts, European pressure, efforts to Westernize, the Young Turks movement, and problems with Armenians

14. Muhammad Ali's modernization encouraged Western influence and eventually led to the construction of the Suez canal, but high-interest loans forced the Egyptian ruler to sell shares of the canal, giving the British a controlling interest.

15. British rule led to improved transportation, communication, medical care, farming methods, order, justice, and education but also led to exploitation, destruction of local industry, deforestation, and famine.

16. British rule led to schooling in Western ideals of democracy, which led to nationalism.

17. through military force

18. The defeat of the Boxer Rebellion led to greater Westernization, which led to nationalism, which combined with discontent and a weak emperor to topple the dynasty.

Chapter Focus Question

19. Western nations gained global empires by exploiting weaknesses in non-Western states and by using their economic and military power and superior technology to extend their influence.

Chapter Assessment

Terms, People, and Places

Match the following definitions with the terms listed below. You will not use all of the terms.

genocide
imperialism
indemnity
Sino-Japanese War
pasha
viceroy

trade surplus
trade deficit
Menelik II
Muhammad Ali
Taiping Rebellion
Boxer Uprising

1. the domination by one country of the political, economic, or cultural life of another country or region
2. war between China and Japan where Japan gained Taiwan
3. provincial ruler in the Ottoman empire
4. situation in which a country imports more than it exports
5. governor of Egypt, sometimes called the "father of modern Egypt"
6. peasant revolt in China from 1850–1864
7. a deliberate attempt to destroy an entire religious or ethnic group
8. payment for losses in war

Main Ideas

Section 1 (pp. 386–389)
9. Describe the four main motives of the new imperialists.
10. Why did Western imperialism spread so rapidly?

Section 2 (pp. 390–397)
11. How did European contact with Africa increase during the 1800s?
12. How did the scramble for African colonies begin?

Section 3 (pp. 398–402)
13. What problems faced the Ottoman empire in the 1800s?
14. How did the modernization of Egypt lead to British rule?

Section 4 (pp. 403–408)
15. Explain the impact of British colonial rule on India.
16. Describe the origins of Indian nationalism.

Section 5 (pp. 409–413)
17. How did westerners gain trading rights in China during the 1800s?
18. Why did the Qing dynasty come to an end?

Chapter Focus Question
19. How did Western industrial powers gain global empires?

Critical Thinking

20. **Geography and History** Why were the natural resources of Africa and Asia important to Europeans in the 1800s?

21. **Analyzing Cartoons** The political cartoon below shows a French soldier (left) and a British soldier (right) ripping apart a map. How do you think the situation depicted in the cartoon affected relations between Britain and France?

22. **Summarize** How did the Ottoman empire try to westernize?
23. **Predict Consequences** How do you think rivalries between religious groups affected anti-imperialism efforts in India? Explain your answer.
24. **Analyze Information** Why did Western industrial nations establish spheres of influence in China rather than colonies as they did in Africa and India?

● Writing About History

In this chapter's five Section Assessments, you developed skills for writing a persuasive essay.

Writing a Persuasive Essay During the 1800s, European powers embarked on a period of expansion known as the Age of Imperialism. Despite resistance, these powers brought much of the world under their control between 1870 and 1914. Write a persuasive essay from the point of view of a Chinese government official in which the official tries to persuade the British that the Treaty of Nanjing is too harsh and will lead to dangerous anti-foreign feelings. Consult page SH16 of the Writing Handbook for additional help.

Prewriting
- Make a list of what you believe to be the strongest arguments of the Chinese official.
- Organize the arguments from weakest to strongest.

Drafting
- Clearly state the position that you will prove in the thesis statement.
- Sequence your arguments so that you open or close with your strongest one.
- Write a conclusion that restates your thesis and closes with a strong argument.

Revising
- Review your arguments to make sure that you have explained them logically and clearly.

Critical Thinking

20. They needed them for industry, due to the Industrial Revolution.

21. Sample: It may have improved them because they divided territory without going to war.

22. It Westernized its government and military, built railroads, improved medical care and farming, and sent young men to receive a Western education.

23. Sample: They may have hindered anti-imperialist efforts by causing division and causing Muslims to fear that a Hindu-run India would oppress them.

24. Sample: to avoid conflict among themselves and possibly to avoid the expense of maintaining a colony in China

Document-Based Assessment

The Forgotten Genocide

The Armenian massacre has been called the "forgotten genocide." It refers to the destruction, between 1895 and 1923, of the Christian Armenians of Turkey under the Muslim Ottoman government. More than 2 million Armenians lived in Turkey before the genocide. Estimates of those killed vary from 600,000 to 1.5 million. The rest were driven from their ancestral home. Most perpetrators were freed, despite pledges by the Allies to punish them after World War I.

Document A

"As it got worse, all of us, and all the people, began gathering in our school. The word came around that the Turks were going on the streets and killing all the Armenians and leaving them on the streets. I, myself, was in school already, so I simply stayed there. Then orders came from the school that we, too, should run away. But where? All the buildings were on fire! The Turks were burning everything. There was a whole group of us running away from the school."

—Annalin, a survivor from Smyrna on events of 1922

Document B

"The massacre of Armenian subjects in the Ottoman Empire in 1896 . . . was amateur and ineffective compared with the largely successful attempt to exterminate [them] during the First World War in 1915. . . . [This] genocide was carried out under the cloak of legality by cold-blooded governmental action. These were not mass-murders committed spontaneously by mobs of private people. . . ."

—Arnold Toynbee, British historian, cited in *Experiences*

Document C

"The 1,000 Armenian houses are being emptied of furniture by the police one after the other. The furniture, bedding and everything of value is being stored in large buildings about the city. . . . The goods are piled in without any attempt at labeling or systematic storage. A crowd of Turkish women and children follow the police about like a lot of vultures and seize anything they can lay their hands on and when the more valuable things are carried out of the house by the police they rush in and take the balance. . . . I suppose it will take several weeks to empty all the houses and then the Armenian shops and stores will be cleared out."

—From a report to the American embassy by Oscar S. Heizer, American consul in Tebizond, July 1915

Document D

"The proportion of Armenians killed by the Turks in World War I out of the general number of Armenians in the Ottoman Empire was no less than that of the Jewish victims [during the Holocaust] out of the total Jewish population in Europe. Nor are the methods of killing unique. . . . The type of murder committed by the Germans in the USSR—mass machine-gunning—was the traditional method of mass murder in our century, and the death marches of Jews in the closing stages of the war had their precedent in the Armenian case as well. Nor is the fact that in the case of the Holocaust it was a state machine and a bureaucracy that was responsible for the murder unique, because there, too, the Young Turks had preceded the German Nazis in planning the execution of a population with such means as were modern at the time."

—From *Remembrance and Denial* by Richard G. Hovannisian

Analyzing Documents

Use your knowledge of the Armenian massacre and Documents A, B, C, and D to answer questions 1–4.

1. According to Document B, the 1915 massacre of Armenians
   A went unpunished.
   B was ineffective and unsuccessful.
   C was not as well documented as the 1896 massacre.
   D was committed with the knowledge of the Turkish government.

2. Document C shows that the Turkish police
   A tried to protect the property of Armenian citizens, despite their government's orders.
   B tried to help Armenian citizens as best they could.
   C took part in stealing the property of Armenian citizens.
   D protested to the American embassy to try to help their friends.

3. According to Document D, the Armenian Massacre and the Holocaust
   A were committed by the same people.
   B were carried out in a similar way.
   C had very few similarities, except for the large number of murders.
   D both took place in Germany.

4. **Writing Task** Ismayale Kemal Pasha, a governor in Marash, was described by one survivor as kind and justice-loving. He tried saving Armenian citizens, despite orders from his superiors to carry out the genocide without remorse. Suppose Ismayale Kemal Pasha explained his decision to help in a memoir. Write a brief explanation from his point of view. Use these documents along with information from the chapter in your writing.

● Writing About History

As students begin the assignment, refer them to page SH16 of the **Writing Handbook** for help in writing a persuasive essay. Remind them of the steps they should take to complete their assignment, including prewriting, drafting, and revising. For help in revising, remind them to use the guidelines on page SH17 of the **Writing Handbook**.

Students' essays should have a clear thesis statement supported by well-developed arguments that build from weakest to strongest. They should include a conclusion that ends with a strong argument. They should be polite toward their audience and free of grammatical and spelling errors. For scoring rubrics for writing assignments, see **Assessment Rubrics,** p. 8.

Answers

1. D
2. C
3. B
4. Responses should use specific evidence from the documents and the chapter to explain how the violence and destruction of the Armenian genocide caused Pasha to disobey his superiors.

CHAPTER PLANNER

Section	Core Instruction L3	Differentiated Instruction L1 L2 L4	
Section 1 *Japan Modernizes* **2.5 periods, 1.25 blocks** **OBJECTIVES** ■ Explain how problems in Japanese society and the opening of Japan to other countries led to the Meiji Restoration. ■ Describe the main reforms under the Meiji government. ■ Analyze the factors contributing to Japan's drive for empire. **Focus Question** *How did Japan become a modern industrial power, and what did it do with its new strength?*	**All in One Teaching Resources, Unit 3** Reading Strategy: Recognize Multiple Causes, p. 89 Vocabulary Builder: Dictionary Skills, p. 88 Section 1 Quiz, p. 84 **Reading and Note Taking Study Guide** Note Taking Study Guide, p. 140 Section 1 Summary, p. 141 **Note Taking Transparencies**, 165 **WITNESS HISTORY Audio CD** Changes for Japan **Progress Monitoring Transparencies**, 104 **Color Transparencies**, 150 **Teaching Resources, Skills Handbook** Prereading the Chapter, pp. 1–2 Word Knowledge Rating Form, p. 3 K-W-L Chart, p. 4	**L1 Adapted Reading and Note Taking Study Guide** Note Taking Study Guide, p. 140 **SN** Section 1 Summary, p. 141 **SN** **L2 Adapted Reading and Note Taking Study Guide** Note Taking Study Guide, p. 140 **LPR** Section 1 Summary, p. 141 **LPR** **Spanish Reading and Note Taking Study Guide** Note Taking Study Guide, p. 140 **ELL** Section 1 Summary, p. 141 **ELL** **L4 All in One Teaching Resources, Unit 3** Traveler's Tales: The First Japanese in America, p. 90 **AR, GT**	*Student Edition Audio **SN** Differentiated Instruction Activity, Teacher's Edition, p. 426 **SN** *Guided Reading Audio, Spanish **ELL** *Student Edition Audio **LPR** Differentiated Instruction Activity, Teacher's Edition, p. 426 **LPR, ELL** Differentiated Instruction Activity, Teacher's Edition, p. 423 **AR, GT** **Extend Activity,** Teacher's Edition, pp. 420c, 428 **AR, GT**
Section 2 *Imperialism in Southeast Asia and the Pacific* **2 periods, 1 block** **OBJECTIVES** ■ Outline how Europeans colonized Southeast Asia and how Siam avoided colonial rule. ■ Explain how the United States gained control over the Philippines. ■ Describe how imperialism spread to the Pacific islands. **Focus Question** *How did industrialized powers divide up Southeast Asia, and how did the colonized peoples react?*	**All in One Teaching Resources, Unit 3** Outline Map: Imperialism in Asia, p. 95 Section 2 Quiz, p. 85 **Reading and Note Taking Study Guide** Note Taking Study Guide, p. 142 Section 2 Summary, p. 143 **Note Taking Transparencies**, 166 **WITNESS HISTORY Audio CD** A Patriot's Dilemma **Progress Monitoring Transparencies**, 105 **Color Transparencies**, 151, 152	**L1 Adapted Reading and Note Taking Study Guide** Note Taking Study Guide, p. 142 **SN** Section 2 Summary, p. 143 **SN** **L2 Adapted Reading and Note Taking Study Guide** Note Taking Study Guide, p. 142 **LPR** Section 2 Summary, p. 143 **LPR** **L4 All in One Teaching Resources, Unit 3** Biography: King Mongkut of Siam, p. 92 **AR, GT** Biography: José Rizal, p. 91 **AR, GT**	**Spanish Reading and Note Taking Study Guide** Note Taking Study Guide, p. 142 **ELL** Section 2 Summary, p. 143 **ELL** Differentiated Instruction Activity, Teacher's Edition, p. 430 **LPR, ELL** **Extend Activity,** Teacher's Edition, p. 433 **AR, GT**

Audio support is available for all sections.

Assessment Resources

- **Progress Monitoring Transparencies**, 104–107
- **Test Prep** Unit Study Sheets, pp. 100–102; Unit Test, pp. 24–29
- **SuccessTracker™**, Chapter 13
- **Document-Based Assessment**, pp. 67–79

- *ExamView*® **Test Bank CD-ROM**, Chapter 13
- **All in One Teaching Resources, Unit 3,** Chapter Tests A and B, pp. 98–103
- **Progress Monitoring *Online* Quizzes,** Chapter 13
- **Assessment Rubrics**

Differentiated Instruction Key

L1 Special Needs		**LPR**	Less Proficient Readers
L2 Basic to Average		**AR**	Advanced Readers
L3 All Students		**SN**	Special Needs Students
L4 Average to Advanced		**GT**	Gifted and Talented
		ELL	English Language Learner

Section	Core Instruction **L3**	Differentiated Instruction **L1 L2 L4**	

Section 3
Self-Rule for Canada, Australia, and New Zealand

 1 period, .5 block

OBJECTIVES
- Describe how Canada achieved self-rule.
- Analyze how European settlement changed the course of Australian history.
- Summarize how New Zealand was settled and how it emerged as an independent nation.

Focus Question *How were the British colonies of Canada, Australia, and New Zealand settled, and how did they win self-rule?*

All in One Teaching Resources, Unit 3
Section 3 Quiz, p. 86

Reading and Note Taking Study Guide
Note Taking Study Guide, p. 144
Section 3 Summary, p. 145

Note Taking Transparencies, 167

WITNESS HISTORY Audio CD
O Canada!

Progress Monitoring Transparencies, 106

Color Transparencies, 153, 154

Witness History Discovery School™
video program, *Australia: The Story of a Penal Colony*

L1 Adapted Reading and Note Taking Study Guide
Note Taking Study Guide, p. 144 **SN**
Section 3 Summary, p. 145 **SN**

L2 Adapted Reading and Note Taking Study Guide
Note Taking Study Guide, p. 144 **LPR**
Section 3 Summary, p. 145 **LPR**

Spanish Reading and Note Taking Study Guide
Note Taking Study Guide, p. 144 **ELL**
Section 3 Summary, p. 145 **ELL**

L4 All in One Teaching Resources, Unit 3
Primary Source: From John Grant's Journals and Letters, p. 93 **AR, GT**

Differentiated Instruction Activity,
Teacher's Edition, p. 437 **SN**

Differentiated Instruction Activity,
Teacher's Edition, p. 437 **LPR, ELL**

Differentiated Instruction Activity,
Teacher's Edition, p. 435 **AR, GT**

Extend Activity,
Teacher's Edition, p. 438 **AR, GT**

Section 4
Economic Imperialism in Latin America

 1.5 periods, .75 block

OBJECTIVES
- Describe the political problems faced by Mexico and other new Latin American nations.
- List the ways industrialized nations affected Latin America.

Focus Question *How did Latin American nations struggle for stability, and how did industrialized nations affect them?*

All in One Teaching Resources, Unit 3
Outline Map: Imperialism in Latin America, p. 96
Geography Quiz, p. 97
Section 4 Quiz, p. 87

Reading and Note Taking Study Guide
Note Taking Study Guide, p. 146
Section 4 Summary, p. 147
Concept Connector, pp. 242, 270, 281

Note Taking Transparencies, 168A–168B

WITNESS HISTORY Audio CD
La Reforma

Progress Monitoring Transparencies, 107

Color Transparencies, 155

L1 Adapted Reading and Note Taking Study Guide
Note Taking Study Guide, p. 146 **SN**
Section 4 Summary, p. 147 **SN**
Concept Connector, pp. 242, 270, 281 **SN**

L2 Adapted Reading and Note Taking Study Guide
Note Taking Study Guide, p. 146 **LPR**
Section 4 Summary, p. 147 **LPR**
Concept Connector, pp. 242, 270, 281 **LPR**

L4 All in One Teaching Resources, Unit 3
Primary Source: From "Our America," by José Martí, p. 94 **AR, GT**

Differentiated Instruction Activity,
Teacher's Edition, p. 440 **SN**

Spanish Reading and Note Taking Study Guide
Note Taking Study Guide, p. 146 **ELL**
Section 4 Summary, p. 147 **ELL**
Concept Connector, pp. 242, 270, 281 **ELL**

Differentiated Instruction Activity,
Teacher's Edition, p. 440 **LPR, ELL**

Differentiated Instruction Activity,
Teacher's Edition, p. 442 **AR, GT**

Extend Activity,
Teacher's Edition, p. 445 **AR, GT**

CHAPTER PLANNER

Author's Notes

Material Impact of Imperialism

Materially, the New Imperialism thrust its way into other people's cultures as the Old Imperialism seldom had. The makers of the New Imperialism exploited and developed colonial regions with unmatched thoroughness and intensity. They reaped harvests, tapped trees, dug mines, drilled for oil from Brazil to Borneo. They unrolled barbed wire, strung up telegraph lines, laid rails, constructed harbor facilities. They built processing plants and even manufacturing plants in the colonies to turn raw materials into something closer to the use objects the Europeans, the Americans, and their other customers wanted.

The material impact was vast, cumulative, and accelerating. Irreplaceable natural resources—Congo copper, Arab oil—began to be drained from the land. Patterns of agriculture were drastically changed. Cash crops replaced subsistence farming until populations that formerly fed themselves came to depend on imported food for sheer survival.

Local industries were ruined by the competition of cheap Western machine-made alternatives. The Indian cotton industry was the world's leader in the seventeenth century. It was driven to the brink of extinction by the cotton mills of Manchester and Birmingham in the nineteenth.

Native peoples were often uprooted and forced into new patterns of life. The bright lights of cities built by Europeans lured African villagers away from their old lives and into new ones that were often rootless and demoralizing. European laws were forced on local people by fiat of colonial administrators. European customs spread with the temptation of jobs and contracts that went to those who accepted European ways.

Envious, resentful, filled with righteous wrath or a burning desire to live as these intruders did, the victims of this climactic phase of the Western conquest were drawn as by a great magnet in directions their ancestors could not have imagined.

—Anthony Esler, *The Human Venture: From Prehistory to the Present*, (Upper Saddle River, New Jersey: Pearson Education, 2004), pp. 586–587

Extend Online

Changes Reflected in Japanese Art

Have students examine Japanese woodblock prints for depictions of Japan's modernization in the late 1800s-early 1900s. Ask them to analyze one print and create a multimedia presentation with their conclusions. Use the steps below to help students complete the activity.

Prepare for the Activity

Explain that before the Meiji era, artists produced woodblock prints by hand in workshops. Their prints often depicted beautiful landscapes or the adventures of common people living in cities. As Japan modernized in the late 1800s, artists created prints in which they recorded the changes taking place around them.

Conduct the Activity For help in starting the activity, send students to Web Code nbe-2501. Students will view woodblock prints from the Meiji era. They should choose one print, describe it, and discuss how it reflects the changes in Japan during this period. They may need to conduct additional research about the Meiji era for this task. Have students create multimedia presentations displaying their research and chosen woodblock print.

Follow-Up Conduct a class discussion based on the following questions: What generalizations about Japan can you draw from the woodblock prints? How can art reflect changes in society? How do you think modernization affected Japan's culture? Were these effects positive or negative? How can you tell?

Differentiated Instruction   Solutions for All Learners

Shared Reading L1 L2

Depending on their skill level, some readers may be unable to successfully complete a reading assignment independently. They may only be able to understand the content sufficiently if the selection of text is read aloud in class and the meaning is clarified by the teacher. You may choose to do this in several ways:

■ **As a Class** Call on each student to read a paragraph out loud to the class. After each paragraph, ask the class a question to check for understanding of key concepts, and wait for volunteers.

■ **In Small Groups** Break the class into small groups, assigning each group a small selection of text. Each group is responsible for making a bulleted list of key information from that selection to present to the class. All members of the class should take notes as selections of text are presented.

Finding Patterns L4

Learning to find patterns in history helps students make connections among events and time periods and see relevance to their own times. Comparing the way several societies reacted to the demands of imperialism requires higher-level thinking and presents an excellent opportunity for this exercise.

Suggest that students keep a "Patterns Diary" in which they compare the actions of Japan in this chapter with those of China, discussed in the previous chapter. One column should be labeled China and the other Japan. Categories may include

■ Leaders
■ Treaties
■ Reactions to imperialism
■ Reforms
■ Changes to society

Students may also work together to develop their own list of categories. When they have completed their reading, have students draw three to five conclusions from their diaries.

Modeling Reading and Writing Skills

Choose an Organization Tell students that in this chapter they will practice writing for assessment. (See Writing about History, p. 448.) Explain that when writing with both time and space constraints, it can be helpful to follow a standard framework for writing paragraphs. This structure can ensure that students' writing makes the points asked for in the instructions and helps students fully answer the question. Tell students that they should begin with a topic sentence, then add three to five examples, using transition words to move from one example to the next example. Finally, they should end with a summary sentence.

Demonstrate this skill by showing students the first paragraph under *The Meiji Transformation* in Section 1. The first sentence expresses the main idea: reforming

Japan would be an enormous task. The next two sentences provide examples as to why this would be a difficult endeavor. The last line summarizes, or reiterates, the main point: change was difficult.

Vocabulary: Use Context Clues Explain that students can help determine the meaning of vocabulary words by looking for clues in the surrounding text. The sentence's context can provide clues to the words meaning.

Model this skill by pointing out the word *restore* in the last paragraph under the heading *External Pressure and Internal Revolt* in Section 1. The surrounding words explain that one leader was unseated, or taken out of power, and another was put in its place. Since the text explains that emperors once ruled Japan, restore must mean to reinstate.

New Global Patterns
1800–1914

Teach With Technology

PresentationEXPRESS™
Premium DVD

- Teach this chapter's core content using **PresentationExpress™ Premium,** which includes dynamic lecture notes, interactive game shows, songs, videos, and the *ExamView® QuickTake* assessment tool.

- To introduce this chapter using **PresentationExpress™ Premium,** start by asking students **Which of the following statements do you most agree with? (A) Countries must be economically strong to be free. (B) Countries must be militarily strong to be free. (C) Countries must be democratic to be free. (D) Countries must be technologically advanced to be free.** Take a class poll or record students' answers using the QuickTake feature and discuss their responses. Point out that in this chapter, they will learn how imperialism affected some countries while others broke free. Continue introducing the chapter using the chapter opener slide show and Witness History audio.

Technology Resources

- Student**EXPRESS** CD-ROM, Chapter 13
- Teacher**EXPRESS** CD-ROM, Chapter 13
- Presentation**EXPRESS™** **Premium DVD,** Chapter 13
- **WITNESS HISTORY** Audio CD, Chapter 13
- *ExamView* Test Bank CD-ROM, English and Spanish, Chapter 13
- **Guided Reading Audio,** Spanish, Chapter 13
- **Student Edition Audio,** Chapter 13
- **Witness History Discovery School™** video program, *Australia: The Story of a Penal Colony*
- **Experience It! Multimedia Pack**

Bibliography

For the Teacher
Buruma, Ian. *Inventing Japan, 1853–1964.* Modern Library, 2003.
Curtin, Philip D. *The World and the West.* Cambridge University Press, 2000.
Wasserman, Mark. *Everyday Life and Politics in Nineteenth Century Mexico: Men, Women, and War.* University of New Mexico Press, 2000.

For the Student
L3 Linnea, Sharon. *Princess Ka'iulani: Hope of a Nation, Heart of a People.* Eerdmans, 1999.
L2 Gaines, Ann Graham. *Commodore Perry Opens Japan to Trade in World History.* Enslow, 2000.
L1 Theunissen, Steve. *The Maori of New Zealand.* Lerner Publishing Group, 2002.

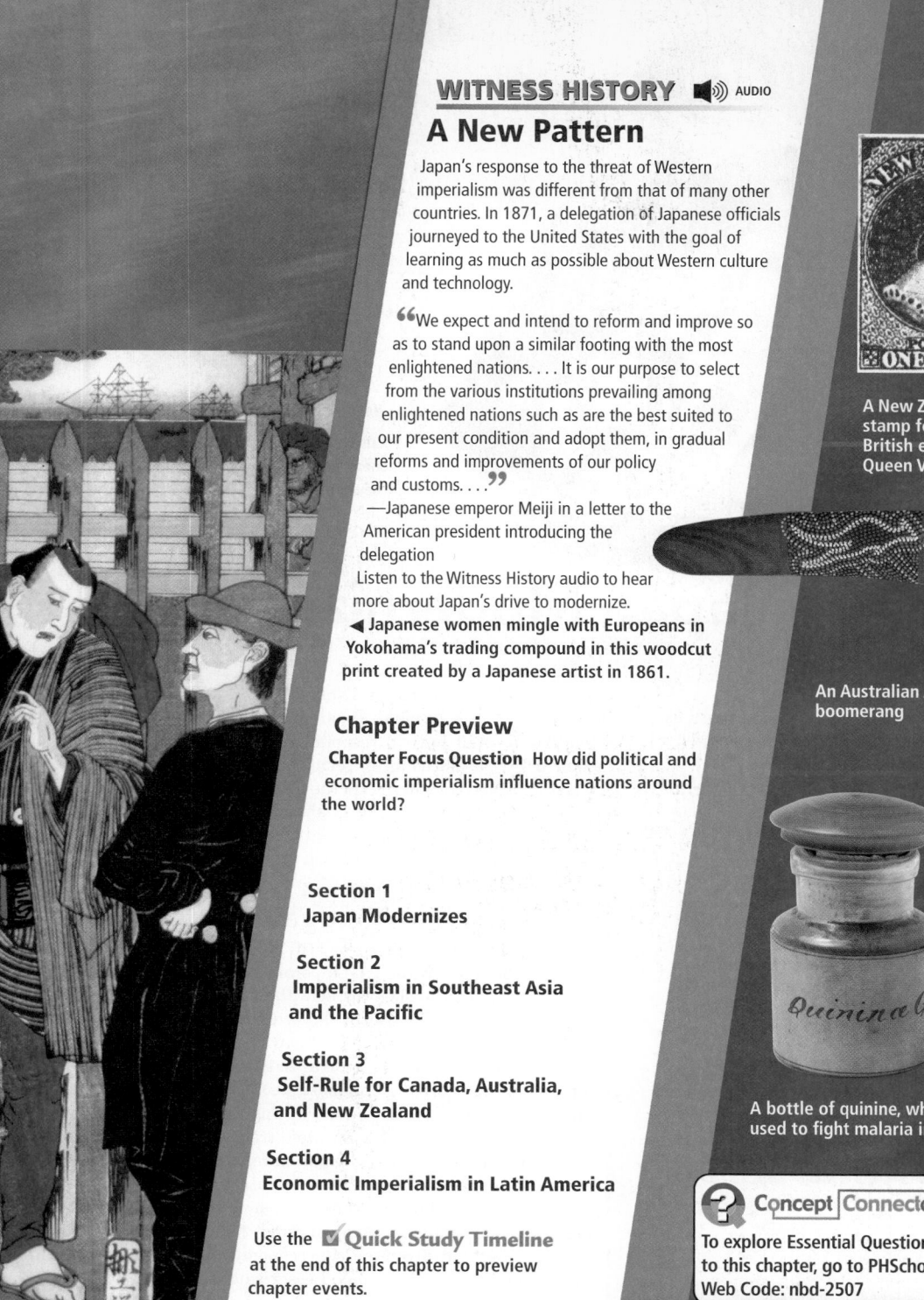

WITNESS HISTORY 🔊 AUDIO

A New Pattern

Japan's response to the threat of Western imperialism was different from that of many other countries. In 1871, a delegation of Japanese officials journeyed to the United States with the goal of learning as much as possible about Western culture and technology.

❝We expect and intend to reform and improve so as to stand upon a similar footing with the most enlightened nations. . . . It is our purpose to select from the various institutions prevailing among enlightened nations such as are the best suited to our present condition and adopt them, in gradual reforms and improvements of our policy and customs. . . .**❞**

—Japanese emperor Meiji in a letter to the American president introducing the delegation

Listen to the Witness History audio to hear more about Japan's drive to modernize.

◀ Japanese women mingle with Europeans in Yokohama's trading compound in this woodcut print created by a Japanese artist in 1861.

A New Zealand postage stamp featuring the British empire's Queen Victoria

An Australian Aborigine boomerang

A bottle of quinine, which was used to fight malaria in Panama

Chapter Preview

Chapter Focus Question How did political and economic imperialism influence nations around the world?

Section 1
Japan Modernizes

Section 2
Imperialism in Southeast Asia and the Pacific

Section 3
Self-Rule for Canada, Australia, and New Zealand

Section 4
Economic Imperialism in Latin America

Use the ☑ **Quick Study Timeline** at the end of this chapter to preview chapter events.

? Concept Connector ONLINE
To explore Essential Questions related to this chapter, go to PHSchool.com
Web Code: nbd-2507

Chapter-Level Resources

All in One Vocabulary Builder; Reading Strategy; Enrichments; Outline Maps; Geography Quiz; Chapter Tests
- Document-Based Assessments
- AYP Monitoring Assessments
- *ExamView* Test Bank CD-ROM
- Guided Reading Audio (Spanish)
- Student Edition Audio

Previewing the Chapter

- **WITNESS HISTORY** Read the Witness History selection aloud or play the accompanying audio. Ask students **What does Meiji tell the American president that he plans to do in Japan?** *(take what is good from "enlightened" nations and apply it to Japan)* **What is Meiji's purpose in borrowing from other nations?** *(to stand upon similar footing with them)* Have students discuss how Meiji's reaction to Western nations differs from those of leaders in the previous chapter.

  🔊 AUDIO **Witness History Audio CD,** A New Pattern

- **Analyzing the Visuals** Tell students that the central figure of the image on the previous page is a European woman dressed in the style of her day. Ask **What sort of interaction seems to be taking place between the European woman and the Japanese woman closest to her?** *(a friendly, perhaps curious, exchange of glances)* **Why might Japanese people have been curious about Europeans in 1861?** *(Japan had been following a policy of isolation for hundreds of years, so any foreigners would be unusual and possibly interesting to Japanese people.)*

- **Focus** Write the Chapter Focus Question on the board. Tell students to keep this question in mind as they read the chapter. *(Answer appears with Chapter Assessment answers.)* Have students preview the section titles for this chapter.

Note Taking Study Guide With Concept Connector Journal
For online access: Web code: nbd-2507
For print alternative: Reading and Note Taking Study Guide booklet

Objectives

As you teach this section, keep students focused on the following objectives to help them answer the Section Focus Question and master core content.

- Explain how problems in Japanese society and the opening of Japan to other countries led to the Meiji Restoration.
- Describe the main reforms under the Meiji government.
- Analyze the factors contributing to Japan's drive for empire.

Prepare to Read

Build Background Knowledge ⑬

Remind students that for more than two centuries Japan's leaders kept the island nation isolated. Discuss reasons why Japanese leaders might reverse this policy and open Japan to foreign influences.

Set a Purpose ⑬

- **WITNESS HISTORY** Read the selection aloud or play the audio.

  🔊 AUDIO **Witness History Audio CD,** Changes for Japan

  Discuss the implications of the emperor Meiji's poem about his hopes for change in Japan.

- **Focus** Point out the Section Focus Question and write it on the board. Tell students to refer to this question as they read. *(Answer appears with Section 1 Assessment answers.)*

- **Preview** Have students preview the Section Objectives and the list of Terms, People, and Places.

- **Reading Skill** Have students use the *Reading Strategy: Recognize Multiple Causes* worksheet.

  🔲 **Teaching Resources, Unit 3,** p. 89

- **Note Taking** Have students read this section using the Paragraph Shrinking strategy (TE, p. T20). As they read, have students fill in the cause and effect chart about the Meiji Restoration.

  📝 **Reading and Note Taking Study Guide,** p. 140

Emperor Meiji

A traditional Japanese fan

WITNESS HISTORY 🔊 AUDIO

Changes for Japan

The emperor Meiji wrote a poem to provide inspiration for Japan's efforts to become a modern country in the late 1800s:

❝ May our country,
   Taking what is good,
   and rejecting what is bad,
   Be not inferior
   To any other.❞

Focus Question How did Japan become a modern industrial power, and what did it do with its new strength?

Japan Modernizes

Objectives

- Explain how problems in Japanese society and the opening of Japan to other countries led to the Meiji Restoration.
- Describe the main reforms under the Meiji government.
- Analyze the factors contributing to Japan's drive for empire.

Terms, People, and Places

Matthew Perry	zaibatsu
Tokyo	homogeneous society
Meiji Restoration	First Sino-Japanese War
Diet	Russo-Japanese War

Note Taking

Reading Skill: Identify Causes and Effects As you read this section, identify the causes and effects of the Meiji Restoration in a chart like the one below.

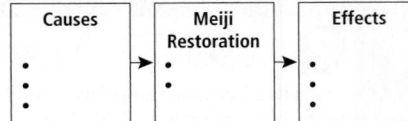

In 1853, the United States displayed its new military might, sending a naval force to make Japan open its ports to trade. Japanese leaders debated how to respond. While some resisted giving up their 215-year-old policy of seclusion, others felt that it would be wiser for Japan to learn from the foreigners.

In the end, Japan chose to abandon its centuries of isolation. The country swiftly transformed itself into a modern industrial power and then set out on its own imperialist path.

Discontent in Tokugawa Japan

In the early 1600s, Japan was still ruled by shoguns, or supreme military dictators. Although emperors still lived in the ceremonial capital of Kyoto, the shoguns held the real power in Edo. Daimyo, or landholding warrior lords, helped the shoguns control Japan. In 1603, a new family, the Tokugawas, seized power. The Tokugawa shoguns reimposed centralized feudalism, closed Japan to foreigners, and forbade Japanese people to travel overseas. The nation's only window on the world was through Nagasaki, where the Dutch were allowed very limited trade.

For more than 200 years, Japan developed in isolation. Internal commerce expanded, agricultural production grew, and bustling cities sprang up. However, these economic changes strained Japanese society. Many daimyo suffered financial hardship. They needed money in a commercial economy, but a daimyo's wealth was in land rather than cash. Lesser samurai were unhappy, too, because they lacked the money to live as well as urban merchants.

Vocabulary Builder

Use the information below and the following resources to teach the high-use words from this section.
🔲 **Teaching Resources, Unit 3,** p. 88; **Teaching Resources, Skills Handbook,** p. 3

High-Use Words	Definitions and Sample Sentences
emphasize, p. 423	*vt.* to stress The teacher underlined the word with a red marker to **emphasize** its importance.
thereby, p. 424	*adv.* by that means, because of that The player hit a home run, **thereby** breaking the tie and winning the game.

Merchants in turn resented their place at the bottom of the social ladder. No matter how rich they were, they had no political power. Peasants, meanwhile, suffered under heavy taxes.

The government responded by trying to revive old ways, <u>emphasizing</u> farming over commerce and praising traditional values. These efforts had scant success. By the 1800s, shoguns were no longer strong leaders, and corruption was common. Discontent simmered throughout Japan.

✔ **Checkpoint** By the mid-1800s, why did so many groups of people in Japan feel discontented?

Japan Opens Up

While the shoguns faced troubles at home, disturbing news of the British victory over China in the Opium War and the way in which imperialists had forced China to sign unequal treaties reached Japan. Surely, Japanese officials reasoned, it would not be long before Western powers turned towards Japan.

External Pressure and Internal Revolt The officials' fears were correct. In July 1853, a fleet of well-armed American ships commanded by Commodore **Matthew Perry** sailed into lower Tokyo Bay. Perry carried a letter from Millard Fillmore, the President of the United States. The letter demanded that Japan open its ports to diplomatic and commercial exchange.

The shogun's advisors debated what to do. Japan did not have the ability to defend itself against the powerful United States Navy. In the Treaty of Kanagawa in 1854, the shogun Iesada agreed to open two Japanese ports to American ships, though not for trade.

The United States soon won trading and other rights, including extraterritoriality and low taxes on American imports. European nations demanded and won similar rights. Like the Chinese, the Japanese felt humiliated by the terms of these unequal treaties. Some bitterly criticized the shogun for not taking a strong stand against the foreigners.

Vocabulary Builder

emphasizing—(EM fuh syz ing) *vt.* stressing

In the Japanese woodblock print below, Japanese boats go out to meet one of Commodore Matthew Perry's ships in Tokyo Bay. In response to Perry's expedition, the Japanese statesman Lord Ii considered Japan's strategy toward contact with foreign powers:

Primary Source

❝ There is a saying that when one is besieged in a castle, to raise the drawbridge is to imprison oneself. . . . Even though the Shogun's ancestors set up seclusion laws, they left the Dutch and Chinese to act as a bridge. . . . Might this bridge not now be of advantage to us in handling foreign affairs, providing us with the means whereby we may for a time avert the outbreak of hostilities and then, after some time has elapsed, gain a complete victory?❞

L4 Advanced Readers   **L4 Gifted and Talented**

When Commodore Matthew Perry arrived in Japan in July 1853, the Japanese shogun was unsure how to respond so he sought the recommendations of his advisors. Ask students to conduct further research on Commodore Perry's arrival in Japan. Suggest that they pay special attention to the shogun's decision and the factors he had to consider in making it. Then have students

recreate a meeting of the shogun and his advisors concerning Perry's arrival. Divide the class into three groups for the discussion: one group will argue for cooperation, one for resistance, and one will represent the shogun and remain undecided. Allow students time to prepare arguments for their side and questions for the other sides and then commence the meeting of the shogun's council.

Teach

Discontent in Tokugawa Japan/Japan Opens Up ⒀

Instruct

■ **Introduce: Vocabulary Builder**
Have students read the Vocabulary Builder terms and definitions. Ask them to list factors a ruler might consider when deciding what the government should *emphasize* under his or her reign.

■ **Teach** Using the Think-Write-Pair-Share strategy (TE, p. T23), have students work together to identify the internal and external pressures faced in Tokugawa Japan. (*internal: discontent of daimyo, lesser samurai, merchants, and peasants; failure of Tokugawa reform efforts; weakening of shogun's power; external: inability of Japan to defend itself against U.S. forces*) Ask **How did these pressures influence the signing of unequal treaties with foreign powers and the downfall of Tokugawa government?** (*Together, these factors weakened Japan so much that the shogun felt he had to sign the unequal treaties. This act brought on great criticism of the shogun and then revolt.*) **What was the Meiji reformers' main goal?** (*They wanted to adapt Western ways to Japanese needs so that Japan could withstand Western demands.*)

■ **Quick Activity** Read aloud the Primary Source selection. Ask students whether they agree with Lord Ii's opinion on contact with foreign powers. Then have students work in groups to discuss the decision by Japan's rulers to adapt to Western ways rather than continue to isolate Japan from foreign influence. Have groups list reasons in support of each position.

Answer

✔ The economy changed but the social structure remained the same, and the shoguns were no longer strong leaders.

Independent Practice

Traveler's Tales To help students learn more about Fukuzawa's impressions of the United States, have them read the selection *The First Japanese in America* and complete the worksheet.

All in One Teaching Resources, Unit 3, p. 90

Monitor Progress

As students fill in their cause-and-effect charts, circulate to make sure they understand that both internal and external pressures led to the opening of Japan. For a completed version of the chart, see

Note Taking Transparencies, 165

Traveler's Tales
EYEWITNESS ACCOUNT

Japanese Diplomat
Fukuzawa Yukichi Visits America

In 1860, writer and educator Fukuzawa Yukichi (1835–1901) joined the first Japanese diplomatic mission to the United States. When he returned home, he wrote articles and books explaining Western customs and practices to the Japanese. In this selection from his autobiography, Fukuzawa recalls his early impressions of San Francisco and discusses some of the differences between American and Japanese cultures and attitudes.

Foreign pressure deepened the social and economic unrest. In 1867, discontented daimyo and samurai led a revolt that unseated the shogun and "restored" the 15-year-old emperor Mutsuhito to power. When he was crowned emperor, Mutsuhito took the name Meiji (MAY jee), which means "enlightened rule." He moved from the old imperial capital in Kyoto to the shogun's palace in Edo, which was renamed **Tokyo,** or "eastern capital."

The Meiji Restoration The young emperor began a long reign known as the **Meiji Restoration.** This period, which lasted from 1868 to 1912, was a major turning point in Japanese history. The Meiji reformers, who ruled in the emperor's name, were determined to strengthen Japan. Their goal was summarized in their motto, "A rich country, a strong military." The emperor supported and embodied the reforms.

The new leaders set out to study Western ways, adapt them to Japanese needs, and thereby keep Japan from having to give in to Western demands. In 1871, members of the government traveled overseas to learn about Western governments, economies, technology, and customs. The government brought experts from Western countries to Japan and sent young samurai to study abroad, furthering Japan's knowledge of Western industrial techniques.

Vocabulary Builder
thereby—(THEHR by) *adv.* by that means, because of that

✓ **Checkpoint** How did Japan react when it was forced to accept unequal treaties?

History Background

An Eye-Opening Experience During the Tokugawa era, the Japanese had viewed other world cultures as inconsequential. The humiliating experience of being forced to accept Western demands made many Japanese people question this view. Over time, they reshaped their views of other societies. Fukuzawa argued that the technology, sciences, and humane laws of Western countries made them both "civilized and enlightened." Like Fukuzawa, whose observations students may read in the Traveler's Tales feature and worksheet, many Japanese officials went abroad to study Western ways. In 1871, about half the key Meiji leaders spent some time in the United States or Europe.

Answer

✓ Discontented samurai and daimyo restored the emperor to power and set about reforming Japan to allow it to compete more effectively with Western powers.

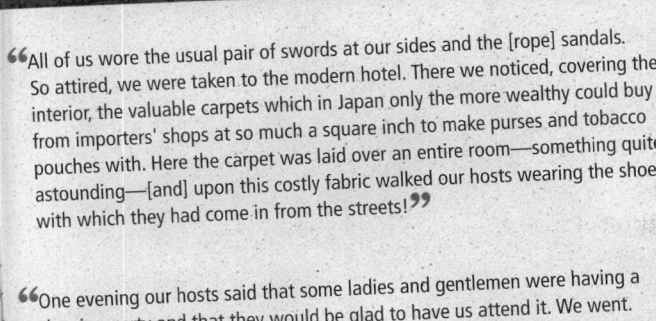

"All of us wore the usual pair of swords at our sides and the [rope] sandals. So attired, we were taken to the modern hotel. There we noticed, covering the interior, the valuable carpets which in Japan only the more wealthy could buy from importers' shops at so much a square inch to make purses and tobacco pouches with. Here the carpet was laid over an entire room—something quite astounding—[and] upon this costly fabric walked our hosts wearing the shoes with which they had come in from the streets!"

"One evening our hosts said that some ladies and gentlemen were having a dancing party and that they would be glad to have us attend it. We went. To our dismay we could not make out what they were doing. The ladies and gentlemen seemed to be hopping about the room together. As funny as it was, we knew it would be rude to laugh, and we controlled our expressions with difficulty as the dancing went on. These were but a few of the instances of our bewilderment at the strange customs of American society."

From *The Autobiography of Fukuzawa Yukichi*

◀ Fukuzawa Yukichi

◀ An American scene by a Japanese artist

▲ Calligraphy by Fukuzawa, which means "a spirit of independence and self-respect"

Thinking Critically
1. **Make Inferences** Why is Fukuzawa amazed that people in America walk on carpeting with their shoes on?
2. **Identify Point of View** What opinion do you think Fukuzawa has of American culture?

The Meiji Transformation

The Meiji reformers faced an enormous task. They were committed to replacing the rigid feudal order with a completely new political and social system and to building a modern industrial economy. Change did not come easily. In the end, however, Japan adapted foreign ideas with great speed and success.

A Modern Government The reformers wanted to create a strong central government, equal to those of Western powers. After studying various European governments, they adapted the German model. In 1889, the emperor issued the Meiji constitution. It set forth the principle that all citizens were equal before the law. Like the German system, however, it gave the emperor autocratic, or absolute, power. A legislature, or **Diet,** was formed, made up of one elected house and one house appointed by the emperor. Additionally, voting rights were sharply limited.

Japan then established a Western-style bureaucracy with separate departments to supervise finance, the army, the navy, and education. To strengthen the military, it turned to Western technology and ended the special privilege of samurai. In the past, samurai alone were warriors. In modern Japan, as in the West, all men were subject to military service.

Independent Practice

Break students into groups and assign them one of the following areas of change during the Meiji Restoration: government, industry, or society. Ask each group to create a poster or multimedia presentation describing the ways in which their assigned area changed. Have each group present to the class.

Monitor Progress

- Have students reread the last paragraph before the Checkpoint on the next page. Ask **By the 1890s, how had the more modernized Japan changed its relationship with the West?** *(Japan became more powerful, acquiring its own empire and revising the unequal treaties.)*

- If students need more instruction on identifying causes and effects, have them read the **Skills Handbook,** p. SH34.

Investment in Meiji Japan

Yen invested (in millions)

Type of economic activity	1883	1893
Trade	35.9	57.6
Manufacturing	14.7	68.3
Railways	12.1	57.9
Banking	75.4	111.6

Chart Skills Japanese women (above) work in a silk manufacturing factory in the 1890s. *How does the graph reflect the Meiji reformers' drive to industrialize Japan?*

SOURCE: S. Uyehara, *The Industry and Trade of Japan*

Industrialization Meiji leaders made the economy a major priority. They encouraged Japan's businesses to adopt Western methods. They set up a modern banking system, built railroads, improved ports, and organized a telegraph and postal system.

To get industries started, the government typically built factories and then sold them to wealthy business families who developed them further. With such support, business dynasties like the Kawasaki family soon ruled over industrial empires. These powerful banking and industrial families were known as **zaibatsu** (zy baht soo).

By the 1890s, industry was booming. With modern machines, silk manufacturing soared. Shipyards, copper and coal mining, and steel making also helped make Japan an industrial powerhouse. As in other industrial countries, the population grew rapidly, and many peasants flocked to the growing cities for work.

Changes in Society The constitution ended legal distinctions between classes, thus allowing more people to become involved in nation building. The government set up schools and a university. It hired Westerners to teach the new generation how to use modern technology.

Despite the reforms, class distinctions survived in Japan as they did in the West. Also, although literacy increased and some women gained an education, women in general were still assigned a secondary role in society. The reform of the Japanese family system, and women's position in it, became the topic of major debates in the 1870s. Although the government agreed to some increases in education for women, it dealt harshly with other attempts at change. After 1898, Japanese women were forbidden any political participation and legally were lumped together with minors.

An Amazing Success Japan modernized with amazing speed during the Meiji period. Its success was due to a number of causes. Japan had a strong sense of identity, partly because it had a **homogeneous society**— that is, its people shared a common culture and language. Economic growth during Tokugawa times had set Japan on the road to development. Japan also had experience in learning and adapting ideas from foreign nations, such as China.

Answer

Chart Skills The graph shows an increase in the amount of yen invested in various economic activities, showing that the Meiji reforms brought a strong increase in Japan's economic strength, particularly in industry.

The Japanese were determined to resist foreign rule. By the 1890s, Japan was strong enough to force Western powers to revise the unequal treaties. By then, it was already acquiring its own overseas empire.

✓ **Checkpoint** What changes did the reforms of the Meiji Restoration bring about in Japan?

Japan's Growing Military Strength

As in Western industrial nations, Japan's economic needs fed its imperialist desires. As a small island nation, Japan lacked many basic resources that were essential for industrial growth. It depended on other countries to obtain raw materials. Spurred by this dependency and a strong ambition to equal the West, Japan sought to build an empire. With its modern army and navy, it maneuvered for power in East Asia.

Korea in the Middle Imperialist rivalries put the spotlight on Korea. Located at a crossroads of East Asia, the Korean peninsula was a focus of competition among Russia, China, and Japan. Korea had been a tributary state to China for many years. A tributary state is a state that is independent but acknowledges the supremacy of a stronger state. Although influenced by China, Korea had its own traditions and government. Korea had also shut its doors to foreigners. It did, however, maintain relations with China and sometimes with Japan.

By the 1800s, Korea faced pressure from outsiders. As Chinese power declined, Russia expanded into East Asia. Then, as Japan industrialized, it too eyed Korea. In 1876, Japan used its superior power to force Korea to open its ports to Japanese trade.

Japan Gains Power As Japan extended its influence in Korea, it came into conflict with China. In 1894, competition between Japan and China in Korea led to the **First Sino-Japanese War.** ("Sino" means "Chinese.") Although China had greater resources, Japan had benefited from modernization. To the surprise of China and the West, Japan won easily. It used its victory to gain treaty ports in China and control over the island of Taiwan, thus joining the West in the race for empire.

Japan Rising
In this political cartoon, Japan is depicted marching over Korea on its way to Russia. *Why would Russia feel threatened by Japan's aggression in Korea?*

■ COMPARING VIEWPOINTS

Colonization in Korea

The excerpts below present two different views of the effect of Japan's control of Korea in the early 1900s. **Critical Thinking** *How do the two views on the results of colonization in Korea differ?*

Positive Effects	**Negative Effects**
Mining, fishery, and manufacturing have advanced. The bald mountains have been covered with young trees. Trade has increased by leaps and bounds. . . . Study what we are doing in Korea. . . . Japan is a steward on whom devolves [falls] the gigantic task of uplifting the Far East. —*Japanese academic Nitobe Inazo*	The result of annexation, brought about without any conference with the Korean people, is that the Japanese . . . by a false set of figures show a profit and loss account between us two peoples most untrue, digging a trench of everlasting resentment deeper and deeper. . . . —*From the Declaration of Korean Independence, 1919*

History Background

The Russo-Japanese War The Russo-Japanese War began and ended on the sea. On February 19, 1904, Japanese torpedo boats made a surprise attack on part of the Russian fleet, near Manchuria. Most of the Russian ships were wiped out. The rest of the Russian navy was based in the Baltic Sea, more than 10,000 miles away. Its ships began a slow 15-month journey around Africa. When they reached the waters of East Asia on May 27, 1905, the Japanese navy attacked again. Japan's faster ships and more accurate gunnery forced the Russians to surrender in a single day.

Japan's Growing Military Strength (13)

Instruct

- **Introduce** Have students read the introductory paragraph under Japan's Growing Military Strength and then have them predict how industrialization and economic needs might feed imperialist desires in Japan.

- **Teach** Discuss Japan's efforts to expand its influence in East Asia. Ask **Why did Japan seek greater influence in Korea?** *(Japan wanted to create an empire equal to those of Western powers and gain natural resources.)* **How did Japan assert its power in the region?** *(by armed warfare, defeating its rivals in the First Sino-Japanese War and the Russo-Japanese War)* **In what ways did Japan benefit from expansion into East Asia?** *(by gaining natural resources, territory, greater influence, and new ports)*

- **Analyze the Visuals** Direct students to study the political cartoon on this page and identify which countries the figures in the cartoon represent. Then have students discuss how a Korean nationalist and a Japanese nationalist might each react to the cartoon.

Independent Practice

Have students create a political cartoon or news article about imperialist rivalries in East Asia. They may represent pro-Japanese or anti-Japanese viewpoints, but should use details from the text to support their depictions.

Monitor Progress

Reread the red heading Japan's Growing Military Strength. Ask students to summarize the ways in which Japan expanded its empire in the late 1800s and early 1900s.

Answers

✓ The Meiji reforms brought about rapid industrialization, modernization, and changes in government and society in Japan.

Caption Russia may feel that it will be the next target of Japanese aggression.

COMPARING VIEWPOINTS The Japanese view is that colonization has improved Korea's economy, while the Korean view is that colonization has created nothing but resentment.

Assess Progress

■ Have students complete the Section Assessment.

■ Administer the Section Quiz.

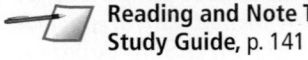 **Teaching Resources,** Unit 3, p. 84

■ To further assess student understanding, use

　 Progress Monitoring Transparencies, 104

Reteach

If students need more instruction, have them read the section summary.

 Reading and Note Taking Study Guide, p. 141 L3

 Adapted Reading and Note Taking Study Guide, p. 141 L1 L2

 Spanish Reading and Note Taking Study Guide, p. 141 L2

Extend L4

See this chapter's Professional Development pages for the Extend Online activity on the Meiji Restoration.

Answer

✔ Japan had few of the natural resources it needed to make industrial products. Expansion increased Japan's access to natural resources and enabled it to build an empire similar to those of the Western powers.

Ten years later, Japan successfully challenged Russia, its other rival for power in Korea and Manchuria. During the **Russo-Japanese War,** Japan's armies defeated Russian troops in Manchuria, and its navy destroyed almost an entire Russian fleet. For the first time in modern history, an Asian power humbled a European nation. In the 1905 Treaty of Portsmouth, Japan gained control of Korea as well as rights in parts of Manchuria.

The Japanese in Korea
In this illustration, Japanese soldiers march into Seoul, Korea's capital city. Japan controlled Korea from 1905 until 1945.

Japan Rules Korea Japan made Korea a protectorate. In 1910, it annexed Korea outright, absorbing the kingdom into the Japanese empire. Japan ruled Korea for 35 years. Like Western imperialists, the Japanese set out to modernize their newly acquired territory. They built factories, railroads, and communications systems. Development, however, generally benefited Japan. Under Japanese rule, Koreans produced more rice than ever before, but most of it went to Japan.

The Japanese were as unpopular in Korea as Western imperialists were elsewhere. They imposed harsh rule on their colony and deliberately set out to erase the Korean language and identity. Repression bred resentment. And resentment, in turn, nourished a Korean nationalist movement.

Nine years after annexation, a nonviolent protest against the Japanese began on March 1, 1919, and soon spread throughout Korea. The Japanese crushed the uprising and massacred many Koreans. The violence did not discourage people who worked to end Japanese rule. Instead, the March First Movement became a rallying symbol for Korean nationalists.

The Koreans would have to wait many years for freedom. Japan continued to expand in East Asia during the years that followed, seeking natural resources and territory. By the early 1900s, Japan was the strongest power in Asia.

✔ **Checkpoint** How did industrialization help start Japan on an imperialist course?

SECTION **1** **Assessment**

Progress Monitoring Online
For: Self-quiz with vocabulary practice
Web Code: nba-2511

Terms, People, and Places

1. Place each of the terms listed at the beginning of the section into one of the following categories: politics, culture, or economics. Write a sentence for each term explaining your choice.

Note Taking

2. **Reading Strategy: Identify Causes and Effects** Use your completed chart to answer the section Focus Question: How did Japan become a modern industrial power, and what did it do with its new strength?

Comprehension and Critical Thinking

3. **Identify Central Issues** What problems weakened shogun rule in Japan in the mid-1800s?

4. **Recognize Causes** What caused Japan to end over 200 years of seclusion?

5. **Draw Conclusions** List three ways in which Japan modernized. Explain how each of these actions helped strengthen Japan so it could resist Western pressure.

6. **Connect to Geography** Why was control of Korea desirable to both China and Japan?

● Writing About History

Quick Write: Choose a Topic When you write for assessment, you may occasionally be given a choice of topics. In that case, quickly jot down notes you could use to answer each prompt. Then, choose the prompt you know the most about. Practice this process using the two sample prompts below. Jot down notes about each prompt, choose one, and then write a sentence explaining why you chose that prompt.
- Explain how Japan modernized under the Meiji reformers.
- Summarize how and why Korea became a Japanese colony.

---

1. Sentences should reflect an understanding of each term, person, or place listed at the beginning of the section, as well as the proper categorization.

2. After domestic discontent and weakness in the face of foreign powers, the Japanese overthrew their shogun and restored the emperor to power. Reformers modernized and westernized the government, economy, and society. Japan used its power to protect itself and to start its own empire.

3. financial hardship, social resentment, heavy taxes, corruption

4. a display of power by the United States

5. Sample: Japan established a Western-style government, which strengthened the military; built modern factories, which boosted the economy; and ended legal distinctions among classes, which allowed more people to work toward nation-building.

6. Korea's location made it a major crossroads for all of East Asia.

● Writing About History

Sentences should clearly state a reason for each student's choice.

For additional assessment, have students access **Progress Monitoring Online** at **Web Code nba-2511.**

A European woman being transported in a rickshaw in French Indochina

Currency from a British colony in Malaya

WITNESS HISTORY ◀)) AUDIO

A Patriot's Dilemma

In 1867, Phan Thanh Gian, a Vietnamese official, faced a dilemma. The French were threatening to invade. As a patriot, Phan Thanh Gian wanted to resist. But as a devoted follower of Confucius, he was obliged "to live in obedience to reason." And based on the power of the French military, he concluded that the only reasonable course was to surrender:

❝ The French have immense warships, filled with soldiers and armed with huge cannons. No one can resist them. They go where they want, the strongest [walls] fall before them. ❞

Focus Question How did industrialized powers divide up Southeast Asia and the Pacific, and how did the colonized peoples react?

Imperialism in Southeast Asia and the Pacific

Objectives
- Outline how Europeans colonized Southeast Asia and how Siam avoided colonial rule.
- Explain how the United States gained control over the Philippines.
- Describe how imperialism spread to the Pacific islands.

Terms, People, and Places

French Indochina	Spanish-American War
Mongkut	Liliuokalani

Note Taking

Reading Skill: Identify Causes and Effects As you read, fill in a flowchart similar to the one below to record the causes, events, and effects of imperialism in Southeast Asia and the Pacific.

Causes		Events		Effects
• •	→	• • • •	→	• •

Leaders throughout Southeast Asia faced the same dilemma as Phan Thanh Gian did in 1867. As they had in Africa, Western industrial powers divided up the region in search of raw materials, new markets, and Christian converts.

Europeans Colonize Southeast Asia

Southeast Asia commands the sea lanes between India and China. The region had been influenced by both civilizations. From the 1500s through the 1700s, European merchants gained footholds in Southeast Asia, but most of the area remained independent. This changed in the 1800s. Westerners—notably the Dutch, British, and French—manipulated local rivalries and used modern armies and technology to colonize much of Southeast Asia.

The Dutch East Indies Established During the early 1600s, the Dutch East India Company established bases on the island of Java and in the Moluccas, or Spice Islands. From there, the Dutch slowly expanded to dominate the rest of the Dutch East Indies (now Indonesia). The Dutch expected their Southeast Asian colonies to produce profitable crops of coffee, indigo, and spices.

The British in Burma and Malaya In the early 1800s, rulers of Burma (present-day Myanmar) clashed with the British, who were expanding eastward from India. The Burmese suffered disastrous defeats in several wars. They continued to resist British rule, however, even after Britain annexed Burma in 1886.

Vocabulary Builder

Use the information below and the following resources to teach the high-use word from this section.
AllᵢₙOne Teaching Resources, Unit 3, p. 88; Teaching Resources, Skills Handbook, p. 3

High-Use Word	Definition and Sample Sentence
transition, p. 433	*n.* passage from one way to another Some scientists found the **transition** from working as a group in the field to working alone in the laboratory difficult.

Step-by-Step Instruction

SECTION 2

Objectives
As you teach this section, keep students focused on the following objectives to help them answer the Section Focus Question and master core content.

- Outline how Europeans colonized Southeast Asia and how Siam avoided colonial rule.
- Explain how the United States gained control over the Philippines.
- Describe how imperialism spread to the Pacific islands.

Prepare to Read

Build Background Knowledge ⓛ
In the last section, students learned how Japan's imperialist ambitions affected East Asia. This section examines the competition for colonies in Southeast Asia and the Pacific. Have students suggest reasons why industrialized nations might want colonies in Southeast Asia.

Set a Purpose ⓛ

- **WITNESS HISTORY** Read the selection aloud or play the audio.
   AUDIO **Witness History Audio CD,** A Patriot's Dilemma

  Ask **What reasons does Phan Thanh Gian give for favoring surrender?** *(Vietnam could not defeat the superior French forces, so fighting would be futile.)*

- **Focus** Point out the Section Focus Question and write it on the board. Tell students to refer to this question as they read. *(Answer appears with Section 2 Assessment answers.)*

- **Preview** Have students preview the Section Objectives and the list of Terms, People, and Places.

- **Note Taking** Have students read this section using the Structured Read Aloud strategy (TE, p. T20). As they read, have students fill in the flowchart recording the causes and effects of imperialism in Southeast Asia and the Pacific.

   Reading and Note Taking Study Guide, p. 142

Europeans Colonize Southeast Asia ⓛ

Instruct

- **Introduce** Ask students to read the introductory paragraph under the red heading Europeans Colonize Southeast Asia. Have them make predictions about how the colonizers and the colonized peoples viewed each other.

- **Teach** Use the Numbered Heads strategy (TE, p. T22) and ask students to list the ways in which European colonization affected Southeast Asia. Ask **What were the main reasons why the Dutch, British, and French established colonies in Southeast Asia?** *(All wanted raw materials for industrial development. France was also interested in Christian converts.)* **Who benefited most from the changes that the colonial powers made in Southeast Asia?** *(the colonial powers)*

- **Quick Activity** Have students access **Web Code nbp-2521** to take the **Geography Interactive Audio Guided Tour** and then answer the map skills questions in the text.

Independent Practice

- Have students fill in the Outline Map *Imperialism in Asia* and label key places in East Asia and Southeast Asia.

  All in One Teaching Resources, Unit 3, p. 95

- **Biography** To help students better understand the role of King Mongkut in modernizing Siam and preventing European colonization, have them read the selection *King Mongkut of Siam* and complete the worksheet.

  All in One Teaching Resources, Unit 3, p. 92

Monitor Progress

- As students fill in their flowcharts, circulate to make sure they understand the effects of imperialism on colonies and colonizers. For a completed version of the flowchart, see

  📖 **Note Taking Transparencies**, 166

- Check students' Outline Maps for accuracy.

Answer

✔ They fiercely resisted European rule.

At the same time, the British expanded their influence in Malaya. The busy port of Singapore grew up at the southern tip of the peninsula. Soon, natural resources and profits from Asian trade flowed through Singapore to enrich Britain.

French Indochina Seized The French, meanwhile, were building an empire on the Southeast Asian mainland. In the 1500s, Portuguese traders had set up a trading center in what today is Vietnam. Christian missionaries from France and other European countries moved into Vietnam and won some converts. Threatened by growing Western influence, Vietnamese officials tried to suppress Christianity by killing converts and missionary priests. Partly in response, France invaded Vietnam in 1858. The French also wanted more influence and markets in Southeast Asia.

The Vietnamese fought fiercely but could not withstand superior European firepower. By the early 1860s, France had seized a portion of southern Vietnam. Over the next decades, the French took over the rest of Vietnam and all of Laos and Cambodia. The French and other Westerners referred to these holdings as **French Indochina**. (Mainland Southeast Asia was known during this period as "Indochina.")

Siam Survives The kingdom of Siam (present-day Thailand) lay between British-ruled Burma and French Indochina. The king of Siam, **Mongkut** (mahng KOOT), who ruled from 1851 to 1868, did not underestimate Western power. He studied foreign languages and read widely on modern science and mathematics. He used this knowledge to negotiate with the Western powers and satisfy their goals in Siam by making agreements in unequal treaties. In this way, Siam escaped becoming a European colony.

Mongkut and his son, Chulalongkorn, (CHOO lah lawng kawrn) set Siam on the road to modernization. They reformed the government, modernized the army, and hired Western experts to teach Thais how to use the new technology. They abolished slavery and gave women some choice in marriage. As Siam modernized, Chulalongkorn bargained to remove the unequal treaties.

Colonial Southeast Asia During this period, many Chinese people migrated to Southeast Asia to take advantage of the economic opportunities there. They left China to escape hardship and turmoil. Despite local resentment, these communities formed vital networks in trade, banking, and other economic activities.

Two Paths in Southeast Asia
King Mongkut of Siam managed to keep his kingdom out of European control. In other parts of Southeast Asia, colonized peoples labored to produce export crops for their colonial rulers. Below, workers process sugar cane in the Philippines in the early 1900s.

By the 1890s, Europeans controlled most of Southeast Asia. They introduced modern technology and expanded commerce and industry. Europeans directed the mining of tin, the harvesting of rubber, and the building of harbors and railroads. But these changes benefited the European colonizers far more than they did the Southeast Asians.

✔ **Checkpoint** How did the Burmese and the Vietnamese respond to attempts to colonize them?

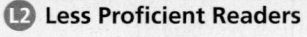 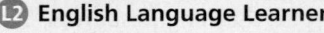

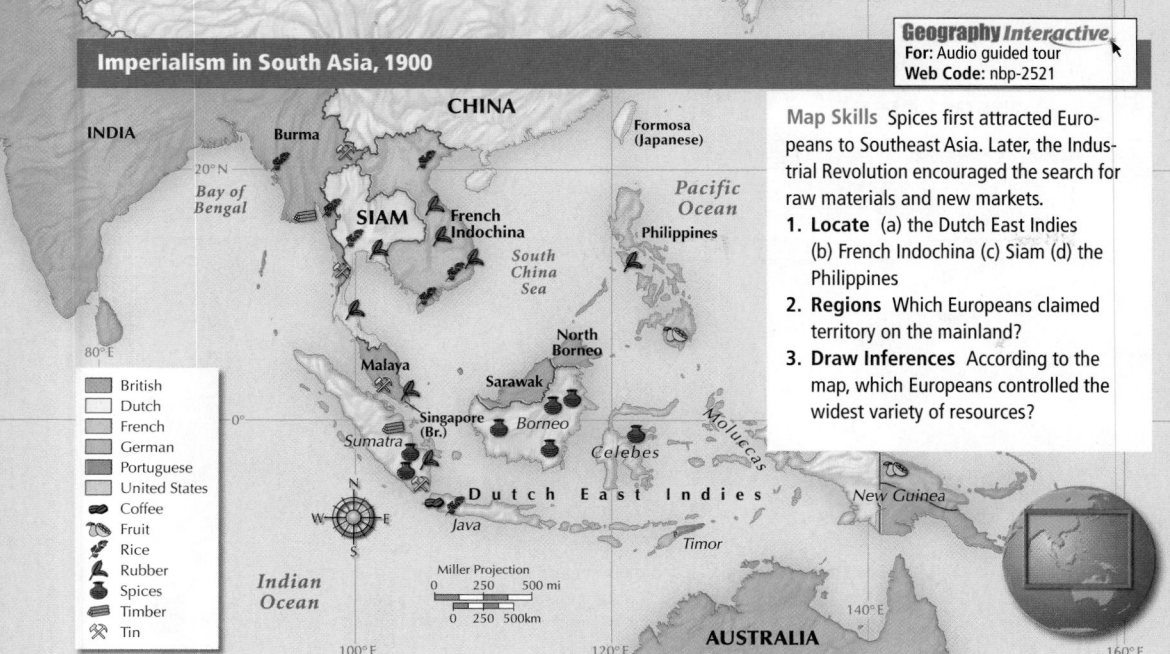

Imperialism in South Asia, 1900

Geography *Interactive*
For: Audio guided tour
Web Code: nbp-2521

INDIA

CHINA

Burma

20° N

Bay of Bengal

SIAM

French Indochina

Formosa (Japanese)

Pacific Ocean

Philippines

South China Sea

80° E

North Borneo

Malaya

Sarawak

Singapore (Br.)

Borneo

Sumatra

0°

Celebes

Moluccas

Java

Dutch East Indies

New Guinea

Timor

Indian Ocean

Miller Projection
0   250   500 mi
0   250   500km

AUSTRALIA

100° E   120° E   140° E   160° E

Legend:
- British
- Dutch
- French
- German
- Portuguese
- United States
- Coffee
- Fruit
- Rice
- Rubber
- Spices
- Timber
- Tin

Map Skills Spices first attracted Europeans to Southeast Asia. Later, the Industrial Revolution encouraged the search for raw materials and new markets.

1. **Locate** (a) the Dutch East Indies (b) French Indochina (c) Siam (d) the Philippines
2. **Regions** Which Europeans claimed territory on the mainland?
3. **Draw Inferences** According to the map, which Europeans controlled the widest variety of resources?

The United States and the Philippines

In the 1500s, Spain had seized the Philippines. Catholic missionaries spread Christianity among the Filipinos. As the Catholic Church gained enormous power and wealth, many Filipinos accused the Church of abusing its position. By the late 1800s, their anger fueled strong resistance to Spanish rule.

The opening of the Suez Canal in 1860 helped the economy of the Philippines by making trade with European countries easier. Some upper class Filipinos gained access to better education. Leaders such as José Rizal inspired Filipinos to work to gain better treatment from Spain.

The **Spanish-American War** broke out in 1898 between Spain and the United States over Cuba's attempts to win independence from Spain. During the war, American battleships destroyed the Spanish fleet, which was stationed in the Philippines. Encouraged by American naval officers, Filipino rebel leaders declared independence from Spain. Rebel soldiers threw their support into the fight against Spanish troops.

In return for their help, the Filipino rebels expected the Americans to recognize their independence. Instead, in the treaty that ended the war with Spain, the United States agreed to give Spain $20 million in return for control of the Philippines. Within the United States, debate raged over the treaty's ratification. American imperialists wanted to join the European competition for territory. Anti-imperialists wanted the United States to steer clear of foreign entanglements. The United States Senate ratified the treaty by only one vote over the required two-thirds majority.

Bitterly disappointed, Filipino nationalists renewed their struggle. From 1899 to 1901, Filipinos led by Emilio Aguinaldo (ah gee NAHL doh) battled American forces. Thousands of Americans and hundreds of thousands of Filipinos died. In the end, the Americans crushed the rebellion.

Link to Literature

The King of Siam Unlike many Southeast Asian leaders, King Mongkut pursued a policy of openness toward the West. His tolerance and willingness to negotiate with Western powers helped keep Siam independent. In 1944, a popular book by Margaret Landon brought King Mongkut to the attention of Western readers. Landon based her book, *Anna and the King of Siam*, on the memoirs of Anna Leonowens, a British teacher who served as a governess to King Mongkut's children at the royal court. Her depiction of the monarch as an inflexible and tyrannical ruler was inaccurate, but the book increased interest in Thailand (as it was later renamed). It also inspired the popular Broadway musical *The King and I*, two movies, and a television show.

The United States and the Philippines

 13

Instruct

- **Introduce: Vocabulary Builder** Have students read the Vocabulary Builder term and definition. Then have them locate the Philippines on the map on this page. Based on other Southeast Asian countries' responses to imperialism, have students predict how Filipinos would react to the *transition* from Spanish rule to American rule.

- **Teach** Ask **How did Filipino rebels become involved in the Spanish-American War?** *(They helped U.S. forces defeat the Spanish in the Philippines.)* **What led to armed conflict between the United States and the Filipino rebels?** *(The rebels expected the United States to recognize Filipino independence, but American officials bought the Philippines from Spain and claimed it as an American colony.)* **What was the outcome of the conflict?** *(The United States took control of the Philippines.)*

- **Quick Activity** Display **Color Transparency 151:** *What Will He Do With It?* Use the lesson suggested in the transparency book to discuss different views on the role of the United States in the Philippines. Discuss the political cartoon and whether the cartoonist supports or opposes U.S. imperialism.
  🏛 **Color Transparencies,** 151

Independent Practice

- **Web Code nbp-2522** will take students to an interactive Infographic. Have students complete the interactivity and then answer the questions in the text.

- **Biography** To learn more about the Filipino struggle for independence, have students read the biography *José Rizal* and complete the worksheet.
  All in One Teaching Resources, Unit 3, p. 91

Monitor Progress

Point out the Infographic on the next page. To check student understanding, have students summarize how imperialism affected Southeast Asia.

Answers

Map Skills
1. Review locations with students.
2. the British, the French
3. the Dutch

Western Powers Seize the Pacific Islands ⓵

Instruct

- **Introduce** Have students locate Samoa, the Hawaiian Islands, and other South Pacific island groups that were claimed by European nations or the United States on the map of Australia, New Zealand, and Oceania on page 782 of the Atlas. Ask students to predict the reasons that the United States and European countries would become interested in these islands.

- **Teach** Ask **Why did the industrialized powers want colonies on islands in the Pacific?** (*to serve as supply bases for British, French, and American whaling and sealing ships; for missionary work; to grow cash crops*) **How did the competition for colonies among Western powers influence the U.S. decision to annex Hawaii?** (*The competition for colonies provided American planters and supporters of annexation with a strong argument for their point of view.*)

- **Quick Activity** Have students debate Hawaii's annexation by the United States. Have them suggest arguments that imperialists and anti-imperialists might have made.

Independent Practice

Have students create a timeline showing the colonization of Southeast Asia and the Pacific. Have students decide which events were most significant.

Monitor Progress

- As students complete their timelines, circulate to confirm that the information is accurate and that events are in sequence. Ask each student to summarize the experience of one colony for the class.

- Check Reading and Note Taking Study Guide entries for student understanding.

Answers

Thinking Critically

1. Pre-colonial traditions were weakened when many community members migrated to find work to pay their taxes.
2. Sample: The rivals might fight each other when not restricted by colonial rule.

● INFOGRAPHIC

THE EFFECTS OF IMPERIALISM

Western imperialism had an enormous impact around the world. It affected different places in different ways. Some common effects are listed below.

Cultural
- Missionaries spread Christianity and European languages to colonized people as they established schools and hospitals. Above, a missionary works with children in Seoul, Korea.
- Some colonized peoples came to believe in Western superiority and lost confidence in their own culture.
- Pre-colonial traditions were weakened by economic and political disruption in some areas, especially where family members were forced to travel long distances to find work.

Political
- New colonial administrations changed traditional political units. In India, British rulers worked with local rulers to meet their goals. In the painting above, the British King Edward VII greets Indian leaders.
- Colonizers often defined the borders of their new colonies without an understanding of the local political or ethnic situations.
- Colonized people took on European ideas of nationalism and agitated for their own independence.

Economic
- To meet the export goals of their colonial rulers, colonized people often grew cash crops instead of food. This man (above) worked on a Malayan rubber plantation.
- As they became part of a money economy, some colonized people were forced to work for their colonial rulers so that they could pay their taxes.
- Imports of machine-made goods destroyed indigenous cottage industries.

A German collector's card (left) showing a Sumatran plantation. A carved stool from Gabon, Africa, (right) depicts a European missionary.

Thinking Critically
1. **Categorize** How is migrating to find work a cultural as well as an economic effect of imperialism?
2. **Predict Consequences** How might grouping several rival ethnic groups into one political unit cause friction when that region gains independence?

History *Interactive*
For: Interactive content
Web Code: nbp-2522

History Background

Annexing Hawaii The fight over Hawaii's annexation lasted for nearly a decade. In 1893, U.S. President Grover Cleveland delayed signing the annexation treaty drafted by sugar growers until events leading to the overthrow of Liliuokalani's government could be investigated. When the investigation showed that most Hawaiians opposed annexation, Cleveland refused to approve the treaty. In 1897, however, staunch imperialist William McKinley became president. McKinley negotiated a new treaty. Anti-imperialist lawmakers delayed its ratification for more than a year, but the Spanish-American War turned the tide. During the war, the use of the U.S. naval base at Pearl Harbor showed Americans Hawaii's strategic importance. In 1900, a resolution by Congress made Hawaii a U.S. territory.

The United States set out to modernize the Philippines through education, improved health care, and economic reforms. The United States also built dams, roads, railways, and ports. In addition, the United States promised Filipinos a gradual <u>transition</u> to self-rule some time in the future.

 Checkpoint How did the United States gain control of the Philippines?

Western Powers Seize the Pacific Islands

In the 1800s, the industrialized powers also began to take an interest in the islands of the Pacific. The thousands of islands splashed across the Pacific include the three regions of Melanesia, Micronesia, and Polynesia.

At first, American, French, and British whaling and sealing ships looked for bases to take on supplies in the Pacific. Missionaries, too, moved into the region and opened the way for political involvement.

In 1878, the United States secured an unequal treaty from Samoa, a group of islands in the South Pacific. The United States gained rights such as extraterritoriality and a naval station. Other nations gained similar agreements. As their rivalry increased, the United States, Germany, and Britain agreed to a triple protectorate over Samoa.

Beginning in the mid-1800s, American sugar growers pressed for power in the Hawaiian Islands. When the Hawaiian queen **Liliuokalani** (lih lee uh oh kuh LAH nee) tried to reduce foreign influence, American planters overthrew her in 1893. They then asked the United States to annex Hawaii, which it finally did in 1898. Supporters of annexation argued that if the United States did not take Hawaii, Britain or Japan might do so. By 1900, the United States, Britain, France, and Germany had claimed nearly every island in the Pacific.

 Checkpoint Why did some Americans think the United States should control Hawaii?

Vocabulary Builder

<u>transition</u>—(tran ZISH un) *n.* passage from one way to another

---

SECTION **2** Assessment

Progress Monitoring *Online*
For: Self-quiz with vocabulary practice
Web Code: nba-2521

Terms, People, and Places
1. For each term, person, or place listed at the beginning of the section, write a sentence explaining its significance.

Note Taking
2. **Reading Strategy: Identify Causes and Effects** Use your completed chart to answer the Focus Question: How did industrialized powers divide up Southeast Asia and the Pacific, and how did the colonized peoples react?

Comprehension and Critical Thinking
3. **Summarize** What steps did Siam take to preserve its independence?
4. **Draw Conclusions** Why were Filipino rebels disappointed when the United States took control of the Philippines?
5. **Synthesize Information** How did Hawaii become part of the United States?
6. **Make Comparisons** Compare the partition of Southeast Asia to the partition of Africa. How was it similar? How was it different?

● **Writing About History**
Quick Write: Examine the Question To answer a short answer or extended-response question effectively, first examine the question. Look for key words like *explain, compare,* or *persuade,* which will tell you what type of answer to provide. Then look for words that signal the topic. Identifying key words will help you focus and organize your response. Copy the prompt below and underline its key words.
• Compare Siam's relationship with imperial powers to that of Vietnam.

Assess and Reteach

Assess Progress
- Have students complete the Section Assessment.
- Administer the Section Quiz.
- **All in One** Teaching Resources, Unit 3, p. 85
- To further assess student understanding, use
  📖 **Progress Monitoring Transparencies,** 105

Reteach
If students need more instruction, have them read the section summary.

 Reading and Note Taking Study Guide, p. 143

 Adapted Reading and Note Taking Study Guide, p. 143

Spanish Reading and Note Taking Study Guide, p. 143

Extend
Display **Color Transparency 152: Inter-Cultural Influences** and point out the influence of African art on Picasso. Then ask students to research ways in which the culture of the colonies discussed in this section influenced the nations that ruled them.
📖 **Color Transparencies,** 152

Answers

 They bought the country from Spain for $20 million and then crushed a Filipino rebellion.

 If the United States did not take Hawaii, Britain or Japan might.

Section 2 Assessment

1. Sentences should reflect an understanding of each term, person, or place listed at the beginning of the section.
2. The Dutch took over the Dutch East Indies; the British took over Burma and Malaya; the French took over French Indochina; and the United States took over the Philippines and Hawaii. Colonized peoples often fought their colonizers but could not withstand them.
3. Siam avoided incidents that might provoke invasion. Its leaders reformed the government, modernized the army, and hired Western experts to teach them about new technology.
4. The rebels had thought the United States supported their cause.
5. The United States annexed Hawaii after American planters overthrew the queen.
6. As in Africa, the Western powers used military force and treaties to gain control of Southeast Asia. One difference is that the United States acquired the Philippines but had no colonies in Africa.

● **Writing About History**
Students should underline the word *compare.*

For additional assessment, have students access **Progress Monitoring *Online*** at **Web Code nba-2521.**

Objectives

As you teach this section, keep students focused on the following objectives to help them answer the Section Focus Question and master core content.

- Describe how Canada achieved self-rule.
- Analyze how European settlement changed the course of Australian history.
- Summarize how New Zealand was settled and how it emerged as an independent nation.

Prepare to Read

Build Background Knowledge [L3]

Remind students that unlike the colonized people of Southeast Asia and the Pacific, many of the North American colonists shared beliefs and spoke the same language with their colonial rulers. Have students predict how these similarities might affect their political relationship.

Set a Purpose [L3]

- **WITNESS HISTORY** Read the selection aloud or play the audio.
  - 🔊 AUDIO **Witness History Audio CD,** O Canada!

  Ask **How does George Brown view colonial rule by Britain?** *(He is very positive, expressing hope that all British colonies in North America will be united under British rule.)*

- **Focus** Point out the Section Focus Question and write it on the board. Tell students to refer to this question as they read. *(Answer appears with Section 3 Assessment answers.)*

- **Preview** Have students preview the Section Objectives and the list of Terms, People, and Places.

- **Note Taking** Have students read this section using the Paragraph Shrinking strategy (TE, p. T20). As students read, have them fill in the chart showing causes and effects of events in Canada, Australia, and New Zealand.

  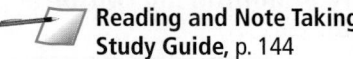 **Reading and Note Taking Study Guide,** p. 144

WITNESS HISTORY 🔊 AUDIO

O Canada!

In the early 1860s, the separate colonies of British North America considered whether they should join together to create one powerful confederation—Canada. George Brown, an influential politician who helped bring about the confederation, shared his dream for Canada:

❝ Sir, it may be that some among us will live to see the day when, as the result of [the confederation], a great and powerful people may have grown up in these lands—when the boundless forests all around us shall have given way to smiling fields and thriving towns—and when one united government, under the British flag, shall extend from shore to shore. ❞

Focus Question How were the British colonies of Canada, Australia, and New Zealand settled, and how did they win self-rule?

Settler's Log House (above) was painted in 1856 by a Dutch immigrant to Canada, Cornelius Krieghoff. The maple leaf (above right) is an emblem of Canada.

Self-Rule for Canada, Australia, and New Zealand

Objectives
- Describe how Canada achieved self-rule.
- Analyze how European settlement changed the course of Australian history.
- Summarize how New Zealand was settled and how it emerged as an independent nation.

Terms, People, and Places

confederation	indigenous
dominion	penal colony
métis	Maori

Note Taking

Reading Skill: Identify Cause and Effects As you read, record the causes and effects of the events you read about in a chart like this one.

Cause	Event	Effect
Loyalist Americans flee to Canada.	Up to 30,000 loyalists settle in Canada.	Ethnic tensions arise between English- and French-speaking Canadians.

Canada, Australia, and New Zealand won independence faster and easier than other British colonies in Africa or Asia. The language and cultural roots they shared with Britain helped. Racial attitudes also played a part. Imperialists in nations like Britain felt that whites, unlike non-whites, were capable of governing themselves.

Canada Achieves Self-Rule

When France lost Canada to Britain in 1763, thousands of French-speaking Catholic settlers remained. After the American Revolution, about 30,000 British loyalists fled to Canada. They were English-speaking Protestants. In addition, in the 1790s, several groups of Native American peoples still lived in eastern Canada. Others, in the west and the north, had not yet come into contact with European settlers.

Unrest in the Two Canadas To ease ethnic tensions, Britain passed the Constitutional Act of 1791. The act created two provinces: English-speaking Upper Canada (now Ontario) and French-speaking Lower Canada (now Quebec). French traditions and the Catholic Church were protected in Lower Canada. English traditions and laws guided Upper Canada.

Vocabulary Builder

Use the information below and the following resources to teach the high-use word from this section.
All in One Teaching Resources, Unit 3, p. 88; **Teaching Resources, Skills Handbook,** p. 3

High-Use Word	Definition and Sample Sentence
compile, p. 435	*vt.* to put together from several sources The family used local newspapers and magazines **to compile** a list of activities for the weekend.

During the early 1800s, unrest grew in both colonies. The people of Upper Canada resented the power held by a small group of elites who controlled the government. Lower Canada had similar problems. In 1837, discontent flared into rebellion in both places. Louis Joseph Papineau, the head of the French Canadian Reform party, led the rebellion in Lower Canada. William Lyon Mackenzie led the revolt in Upper Canada, crying, "Put down the villains who oppress and enslave our country!"

Britain Responds The British had learned from the American Revolution. While they hurried to put down the disorder, they sent an able politician, Lord Durham, to compile a report on the causes of the unrest. In 1840, Parliament acted on some of Durham's recommendations by passing the Act of Union. The act joined the two Canadas into one province. It also gave them an elected legislature that determined some domestic policies. Britain still controlled foreign policy and trade.

Canada Becomes a Dominion In the mid-1800s, thousands of English, Scottish, and Irish people immigrated to Canada. As the country grew, two Canadians, John Macdonald and George Étienne Cartier, urged **confederation,** or unification, of Britain's North American colonies. These colonies included Nova Scotia, New Brunswick, Prince Edward Island, and British Columbia, as well as the united Upper and Lower Canadas. The two leaders felt that confederation would strengthen the new nation against American ambitions and help its economic development.

Britain finally agreed, passing the British North America Act of 1867. The act created the Dominion of Canada. A **dominion** is a self-governing nation. As a dominion, Canada had its own parliament, modeled on that

Vocabulary Builder

compile—(kum PYL) *vt.* to put together from several sources

Geography *Interactive*
For: Audio guided tour
Web Code: nbp-2531

Canada, 1867–1914

Map Skills Canada grew throughout the latter half of the 1800s.

1. **Locate:** (a) Quebec (b) Ontario (c) British Columbia (d) Saskatchewan

2. **Movement** Why did British Columbia become a part of Canada before Alberta and Saskatchewan?

3. **Make Comparisons** Compare Nova Scotia's natural resources to those of Manitoba.

Legend:
- Gold
- Silver
- Copper
- Iron ore
- Coal
- Timber
- Fish
- Lobster
- Canadian Pacific Railway, 1885

Yukon River
Yukon Territory 1898
Northwest Territories 1870
Mackenzie R.
British Columbia 1871
Peace R.
Fraser R.
Alberta 1905
Saskatchewan 1905
Saskatchewan River
Manitoba 1870
Hudson Bay
Quebec 1867
Ontario 1867
New Brunswick 1867
Prince Edward Island 1873
Nova Scotia 1867
Atlantic Ocean
Pacific Ocean
UNITED STATES
140°W 130°W 70°N 60°N 50°N 60°W 50°W
Conic projection
0 200 400 mi
0 200 400 km

Teach

Canada Achieves Self-Rule L3

Instruct

- **Introduce: Key Terms** Ask students to locate the key terms **confederation** and **dominion** (in blue) in the text and explain their meanings. Have students describe possible advantages of a confederation for Canada. Then ask them to explain the difference between dominion and colonial status.

- **Teach** Ask **Why were the British alarmed by the unrest in Upper and Lower Canada?** *(They did not want a repeat of the American Revolution, in which they lost their other North American colonies.)* Then list these events on the board: Act of Union, British North America Act, and the opening of Canadian Pacific Railway. Using the Numbered Heads strategy (TE, p. T23), discuss how each event contributed to Canada's unification and peaceful transition to self-rule.

- **Quick Activity** Display **Color Transparency 153: Origins of Immigrants to Canada, 1860–1920.** Use the lesson suggested in the transparency book to guide a discussion on the reasons for Canada's growth during the mid-1800s.
  - **Color Transparencies,** 153

Independent Practice

Have students access **Web Code nbp-2531** to take the **Geography Interactive Audio Guided Tour** and then answer the map skills questions in the text.

Monitor Progress

As students fill in their charts, make sure they have correctly identified how these events affected Canada's relationship with Britain. For a completed version of the chart, see
  - **Note Taking Transparencies,** 167

Differentiated Instruction Solutions for All Learners

L4 Advanced Readers **L4 Gifted and Talented**

Tell students that Great Britain responded to colonial agitation very differently in Canada than in the United States. By the time that Canadian unrest began in the early 1800s, the British had learned from their experiences with their American colonies. Consequently, the result of colonial agitation in Canada was quite different from what it had been in the United States.

Ask students to create a chart that compares British action in the United States with British action in Canada. Students should create two columns, one for the U.S. and one for Canada and three rows: "British Action," "Short-term Effects," and "Long-term Effects." Students should fill in the chart with information from their reading. Then pair students to compare results.

Answers

Map Skills
1. Review locations with students.
2. Because it is on the coast, British Columbia could be reached more easily by ship than inland Alberta and Saskatchewan.
3. Nova Scotia: timber, fish, lobster, coal; Manitoba: timber, gold, silver, copper

Europeans in Australia ⬡

Instruct

- **Introduce: Key Terms** Have students find the key term *indigenous* (in blue) in the text and explain its meaning. Ask students to consider the effects of European settlers arriving in the Americas on the indigenous population there. Have them predict what might have occurred when Europeans arrived in Australia. Then have them read to find out whether their predictions were accurate.

- **Teach** Ask **Who were the first Europeans to settle in Australia?** *(British criminals being sent to the penal colony there)* **After free British citizens emigrated to Australia, why was Britain responsive to demands for self-rule in the early 1900s?** *(It feared the interference of other European powers and wanted to boost development.)* **How did Australia preserve its ties to Britain?** *(It recognized the British monarch as its head of state.)*

- **Quick Activity** Show students *Australia: The Story of a Penal Colony* from the **Witness History Discovery School**™ video program. Ask students to describe the daily life of British convicts in Australia. *(They did hard labor such as clearing the land to make the land comfortable for others; they were kept under constant watch and lived in small cells, waiting for their promised day of freedom.)*

Independent Practice

Primary Source To help students better understand life in the Australian penal colony, have them read the selection *From John Grant's Journals and Letters* and complete the worksheet.

All in One Teaching Resources, Unit 3, p. 93

Monitor Progress

To help students review the process by which Australia became an independent country, ask them to read aloud each black heading under Europeans in Australia and summarize its content.

Answers

Caption Aborigines were thrust aside or killed as more British settlers came to Australia.

✓ Britain allowed Canada to transition peacefully to self-rule.

Life in Australia
Australian Aborigines used boomerangs, like this one decorated with traditional motifs, to hunt and in battles. The first British settlers in Australia were convicted criminals. The convicts in the illustration below are being forced to carry heavy loads of shingles as part of their hard labor. *What happened to Aborigines as British settlement spread?*

---

of Britain. By 1900, Canada also had some control over its own foreign policy. Still, Canada maintained close ties with Britain.

Canada Grows Like the United States, Canada expanded westward in the 1800s. In 1885, the Canadian Pacific Railway opened, linking eastern and western Canada. Wherever the railroad went, settlers followed. It moved people and products, such as timber and manufactured goods across the country. In the late 1800s and early 1900s, more immigrants flooded into Canada from Germany, Italy, Poland, Russia, Ukraine, China, and Japan. They enriched Canada's economy and culture.

As in the United States, westward expansion destroyed the way of life of Native Americans in Canada. Most were forced to sign treaties giving up their lands. Some resisted. In central Canada, Louis Riel led a revolt of the **métis,** people of mixed Native American and French Canadian descent, in 1869 and again in 1885. Many métis were French-speaking Catholics who believed that the government was trying to take their land and destroy their language and religion. Government troops put down both uprisings. Riel was executed in 1885.

By 1914, Canada was a flourishing nation. Still, French-speaking Canadians were determined to preserve their separate heritage, making it hard for Canadians to create a single national identity. Also, the cultural and economic influence of the United States threatened to dominate Canada. Both issues continue to affect Canada today.

✓ **Checkpoint** How did the British respond to the Canadians' desire for self-rule?

Europeans in Australia

The Dutch in the 1600s were the first Europeans to reach Australia. In 1770, Captain James Cook claimed Australia for Britain. For a time, however, Australia remained too distant to attract European settlers.

The First Settlers Like most regions claimed by imperialist powers, Australia had long been inhabited by other people. The first settlers had reached Australia perhaps 40,000 years earlier, probably from Southeast Asia, and spread across the continent. These **indigenous,** or original, people were called Aborigines, a word used by Europeans to denote the earliest people to live in a place. Today, many Australian Aborigines call themselves Kooris. Isolated from the larger world, the Aborigines lived in small hunting and food-gathering bands, much as their Stone Age ancestors had. Aboriginal groups spoke as many as 250 distinct languages. When white settlers arrived in Australia, the indigenous population suffered disastrously.

A Penal Colony During the 1700s, Britain had sent convicts to its North American colonies, especially to Georgia. The American Revolution closed that outlet. Prisons in London and other cities were jammed.

To fill the need for prisons, Britain made Australia into a **penal colony,** or a place where convicted

---

Connect to Our World

Connections to Today The question of Québécois secession dominated Canadian politics in the late twentieth century. Many of the province's French-speaking majority felt that the economically stronger English-speaking minority discriminated against them. They also felt out of place in English-dominated Canada. In 1980, the province held its first vote on whether to declare itself a "sovereignty asso-ciation" in Canada. The referendum was defeated by 60 percent of voters, but the issue did not disappear. Separatists gained power in the Quebec government, and in 1995 another referendum was held, this time for full secession. Voters chose not to secede, by an extremely tight margin. The movement faded in the late 1990s, but separatists again began to push for independence in the early twenty-first century.

Geography *Interactive*
For: Audio guided tour
Web Code: nbp-2532

Map Skills British settlement in Australia started with penal settlements on both coasts and slowly spread into the interior of the continent.

1. **Locate** (a) Simpson Desert (b) Great Sandy Desert (c) Sydney (d) Perth
2. **Regions** What physical features probably slowed British settlement of Australia's interior?
3. **Draw Inferences** What types of economic activity do you think took place in the area of Australia that was settled by Europeans between 1831 and 1875?

---

criminals are sent to be punished. The first British ships, carrying about 700 convicts, arrived in Botany Bay, Australia, in 1788. The people who survived the grueling eight-month voyage faced more hardships on shore. Many were city dwellers with no farming skills. Under the brutal discipline of soldiers, work gangs cleared land for settlement.

The Colonies Grow In the early 1800s, Britain encouraged free citizens to emigrate to Australia by offering them land and tools. A prosperous wool industry grew up as settlers found that the land and climate suited sheepherding. In 1851, a gold rush in eastern Australia brought a population boom. Many gold hunters stayed on to become ranchers and farmers. They pushed into the rugged interior known as the Outback, carving out huge sheep ranches and wheat farms. As the newcomers settled in, they thrust aside or killed the Aborigines.

Achieving Self-Government Like Canada, Australia was made up of separate colonies scattered around the continent. Britain worried about interference from other European powers. To counter this threat and to boost development, it responded to Australian demands for self-rule. In 1901, Britain helped the colonies unite into the independent Commonwealth of Australia. The new country kept its ties to Britain by recognizing the British monarch as its head of state.

The Australian constitution drew on both British and American models. Unlike Britain and the United States, Australia quickly granted women the right to vote. In 1856, it also became the first nation to introduce the secret ballot.

✓ **Checkpoint** What effect did colonization have on Australia's indigenous population?

WITNESS HISTORY VIDEO

Watch *Australia: The Story of a Penal Colony* on the **Witness History Discovery School**™ video program to learn more about life in an Australian penal colony.

DISCOVERY SCHOOL

New Zealand's Story ⑬

Instruct

- **Introduce: Key Terms** Have students locate the key term ***Maori*** (in blue) in the text and explain its meaning. Have students make predictions about the impact of European colonization on the Maori.

- **Teach** Ask **How were the government and political institutions established in New Zealand similar to those established in Australia and Canada?** *(All created governments with elected parliaments and prime ministers and kept ties with Britain.)* Challenge students to explain the reasons they think Canada, Australia, and New Zealand won self-rule more quickly and easily than the colonies governed by Europeans in Asia and Africa.

- **Quick Activity** Display **Color Transparency 154: Maori Battles in New Zealand.** Use the lesson suggested in the transparency book to guide a discussion of why Maori efforts to resist colonization failed.
  ⬚ **Color Transparencies,** 154

Independent Practice

Have students access **Web Code nbp-2532** to take the **Geography Interactive Audio Guided Tour** and then answer the map skills questions in the text.

Monitor Progress

- To review this section, ask students to summarize the ways in which life was different for the Maori before and after European settlers moved to New Zealand.

- Check answers to map skills questions.

Answers

Map Skills
1. Review locations with students.
2. the deserts
3. Sample: mining of metals and sheepherding

✓ The Aborigines were killed or pushed out of areas desired by Europeans.

- Have students complete the Section Assessment.
- Administer the Section Quiz.

   **Teaching Resources, Unit 3**, p. 86
- To further assess student understanding, use

   Progress Monitoring Transparencies, 106

Reteach

If students need more instruction, have them read the section summary.

 Reading and Note Taking Study Guide, p. 145 (L3)

Adapted Reading and (L1) (L2) **Note Taking Study Guide**, p. 145

Spanish Reading and (L2) **Note Taking Study Guide**, p. 145

Extend (L4)

Ask students to conduct further research into the ways New Zealand, Australia, and Canada each developed its own national identity.

Answer

 Both were settled by the British and harmed indigenous populations. The Maori in New Zealand, who were farmers, were concentrated in a smaller area than the Aborigines in Australia, who were spread out and who hunted and gathered to support themselves.

New Zealand's Story

To the southeast of Australia lies New Zealand. In 1769, Captain Cook claimed its islands for Britain. Missionaries landed there in 1814 to convert the indigenous people, the **Maori** (MAH oh ree), to Christianity.

The Maori Struggle Unlike Australia, where the Aborigines were spread thinly across a large continent, the Maori were concentrated in a smaller area. They were descended from seafaring people who had reached New Zealand from Polynesia in the 1200s. The Maori were settled farmers. They were also determined to defend their land.

White settlers, who were attracted by New Zealand's mild climate and good soil, followed the missionaries. These settlers introduced sheep and cattle and were soon exporting wool, mutton, and beef. In 1840, Britain annexed New Zealand.

As colonists poured in, they took over more and more of the land, leading to fierce wars with the Maori. Many Maori died in the struggle. Still more perished from disease, alcoholism, and other misfortunes that followed European colonization. By the 1870s, resistance crumbled. The Maori population had fallen drastically, from about 200,000 to less than 45,000 in 1896. Only recently has the Maori population started to grow once more.

Settlers Win Self-Government Like settlers in Australia and Canada, white New Zealanders sought self-rule. In 1907, they won independence, with their own parliament, prime minister, and elected legislature. They, too, preserved close ties to the British empire.

✔ **Checkpoint** Compare and contrast the European settlement of Australia and New Zealand.

Maori Traditions
The portrait below shows a Maori leader in 1882. Many Maori men of high social standing commissioned tattoos on their faces. Maori war canoes, like the one below, often carried distinctive carving.

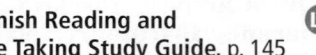

Progress Monitoring *Online*
For: Self-quiz with vocabulary practice
Web Code: nba-2531

SECTION 3 Assessment

Terms, People, and Places
1. For each term, person, or place listed at the beginning of the section, write a sentence explaining its significance.

Note Taking
2. **Reading Skill: Identify Causes and Effects** Use your completed chart to answer the Focus Question: How were the British colonies of Canada, Australia, and New Zealand settled, and how did they win self-rule?

Comprehension and Critical Thinking
3. **Sequence** What steps led to Canadian self-rule?
4. **Compare** Compare the European settlement of Australia with that of Canada.
5. **Identify Causes** Why did the Maori fight colonists in New Zealand?
6. **Synthesize Information** What ethnic tensions did Australia, Canada, and New Zealand face?

● **Writing About History**
Quick Write: Focus Your Time To stay focused as you respond to a short answer or extended-response question on a test, plan to spend a quarter of the allotted time on prewriting, half on drafting, and the remaining quarter on revising. Write a short answer response to the following prompt using a 20-minute time limit. Time yourself to practice staying within the appropriate time limit during each stage.
● Compare how Canada and Australia gained self-rule.

---

1. Sentences should reflect an understanding of each term, person, or place listed at the beginning of the section.
2. French and British colonists settled in Canada. Australia was first settled as a penal colony. Missionaries helped settle New Zealand. All forced out indigenous people as a result of settlement. All won self-rule from Britain fairly peacefully.
3. Upper Canada and Lower Canada were created; the Act of Union (1840) provided an elected legislature for domestic issues; the Dominion of Canada was created by the British North America Act.
4. Canada was first settled by French and British colonists; Australia by British prisoners.
5. to defend their land and settlements
6. Canada—between French and British settlers, with Native Americans and métis; Australia—between Aborigines and British settlers; New Zealand—between British settlers and Maori

● **Writing About History**
Responses should show an answer well-supported by specific details.

For additional assessment, have students access **Progress Monitoring** *Online* at **nba-2531.**

Sugar cane, a Latin American cash crop

Benito Juárez is the central figure of this detail from Mexican artist Diego Rivera's mural *Sunday Afternoon in Alameda Park*.

WITNESS HISTORY ◀)) AUDIO

La Reforma

The Mexican reformer Benito Juárez criticized the continuing inequality in Mexico:

66 The constitution of 1824 was a compromise between progress and reaction, and [that compromise was a] seedbed of the incessant convulsions [disorders] that the Republic has suffered, and that it will still suffer while society does not recover its balance by making effective the equality of rights and duties of all citizens and of all persons who inhabit the national territory, without privileges, without exemptions [exceptions], without monopolies, and without odious distinctions 99

Focus Question How did Latin American nations struggle for stability, and how did industrialized nations affect them?

Economic Imperialism in Latin America

Objectives
- Describe the political problems faced by Mexico and other new Latin American nations.
- List the ways industrialized nations effected Latin America.

Terms, People, and Places

regionalism	peonage
caudillo	Monroe Doctrine
Benito Juárez	Panama Canal
La Reforma	

Note Taking

Reading Skill: Recognize Multiple Causes As you read, record the causes of instability in Latin America in a chart similar to this one. Then give an example of how each cause affected Mexico.

Instability in Latin America	
Causes	**Mexican Example**

Despite bright hopes, democracy failed to take root in most of the newly independent nations of Latin America in the 1800s. Instead, wealth and power remained in the hands of the few. At the same time, new technology such as refrigerated ships helped to intertwine the economies of nations that were thousands of miles apart. Latin American economies became increasingly dependent upon those of more developed countries. Britain, and later the United States, invested heavily in Latin America.

Lingering Political Problems

Simón Bolívar had hoped to create strong ties among the nations of Latin America. But feuds among leaders, geographic barriers, and local nationalism shattered that dream of unity. In the end, 20 separate nations emerged.

These new nations wrote constitutions modeled on that of the United States. They set up republics with elected legislatures. However, true democracy failed to take hold. During the 1800s, many succumbed to revolts, civil war, and dictatorships.

The Colonial Legacy Many of the problems in the new nations had their origins in colonial rule. The existing social and political hierarchy barely changed. Creoles simply replaced *peninsulares* as the ruling class. The Roman Catholic Church kept its privileged position and still controlled huge amounts of land.

Objectives

As you teach this section, keep students focused on the following objectives to help them answer the Section Focus Question and master core content.

- Describe the political problems faced by Mexico and other new Latin American nations.

- List the ways industrialized nations affected Latin America.

Prepare to Read

Build Background Knowledge ⒧⒊

Remind students that Latin America experienced a long period of colonial rule. Ask students to predict how centuries of foreign domination might have affected attitudes toward imperialist powers.

Set a Purpose ⒧⒊

- **WITNESS HISTORY** Read the selection aloud or play the audio.

   AUDIO **Witness History Audio CD,** La Reforma

  Ask **What is Benito Juárez's main criticism of Mexican society?** (*that all citizens are not treated equally*) **What is the result of these inequalities?** (*They have led to disorder.*)

- **Focus** Point out the Section Focus Question and write it on the board. Tell students to refer to this question as they read. (*Answer appears with Section 4 Assessment answers.*)

- **Preview** Have students preview the Section Objectives and the list of Terms, People, and Places.

- **Note Taking** Have students read this section using the Guided Questioning strategy (TE, p. T20). As they read, have students fill in the chart listing the causes of instability in Latin America.

   Reading and Note Taking Study Guide, p. 146

Vocabulary Builder

Use the information below and the following resources to teach the high-use words from this section.
All in One Teaching Resources, Unit 3, p. 88; **Teaching Resources, Skills Handbook,** p. 3

High-Use Words	Definitions and Sample Sentences
enlightened, p. 440	*adj.* educated, informed It took an **enlightened** leader to reform the court system and reduce crime.
tangible, p. 441	*adj.* real or concrete The certificate was **tangible** proof that the student had completed the course.

Lingering Political Problems

Instruct

- **Introduce: Key Terms** Remind students that Simón Bolívar had hoped the wars for independence would lead to the creation of a "United States" of Latin America. Have students locate the key term *regionalism* (in blue) in the text and explain its meaning. Discuss how regionalism contributed to instability in Latin America.

- **Teach** Ask **What was the legacy of colonial rule for Latin American nations?** *(a rigid class system, social and political inequalities with special privileges for creoles and the Roman Catholic Church, limited voting rights, racial prejudice, limited land ownership)* **What were the consequences of regionalism and the rise of *caudillos*?** *(power struggles and frequent revolts, with privileged elites retaining power)*

Independent Practice

Have students write a paragraph explaining and giving evidence to support this statement from the text: "Many of the problems in the new nations had their origins in colonial rule."

Monitor Progress

- As students write their paragraphs, circulate to make sure that they have provided evidence to support their argument.

- As students fill in their charts, circulate to make sure they understand the key causes of instability in Latin America. For a completed version of the chart, see

  🏛 **Note Taking Transparencies**, 168A

Answer

✔ Inequalities remained, voting rights were limited, racial prejudices persisted, a small number of people owned most of the land, and regionalism hurt national unity.

For most people—mestizos, mulattoes, blacks, and Indians—life did not improve after independence. The new constitutions guaranteed equality before the law, but deep-rooted inequalities remained. Voting rights were limited. Many people felt the effects of racial prejudice. Small groups of people held most of the land. Owners of haciendas ruled their great estates, and the peasants who worked them, like medieval European lords.

The Search for Stability With few roads and no tradition of unity, **regionalism,** or loyalty to a local area, weakened the new nations. Local strongmen, called *caudillos* (kow THEE yohs), assembled private armies to resist the central government. At times, popular caudillos, occasionally former military leaders, gained national power. They looted the treasury and ruled as dictators. Power struggles led to frequent revolts that changed little except the name of the leader. In the long run, power remained in the hands of a privileged few who had no desire to share it.

As in Europe, the ruling elite in Latin America were divided between conservatives and liberals. Conservatives defended the traditional social order, favored press censorship, and strongly supported the Catholic Church. Liberals backed laissez-faire economics, religious toleration, greater access to education, and freedom of the press. Liberals saw themselves as <u>enlightened</u> supporters of progress but often showed little concern for the needs of the majority of the people.

Vocabulary Builder
<u>enlightened</u>—(en LYT und) *adj.* educated, informed

✔ **Checkpoint** What factors undermined democracy in post-independence Latin America?

Mexico's Struggle for Stability

During the 1800s, each Latin American nation followed its own course. Mexico provides an example of the challenges facing many Latin American nations. Large landowners, army leaders, and the Catholic Church dominated Mexican politics. However, bitter battles between conservatives and liberals led to revolts and the rise of dictators. Deep social divisions separated wealthy creoles from mestizos and Indians who lived in poverty.

Santa Anna and War With the United States Between 1833 and 1855, an ambitious and cunning *caudillo,* Antonio López de Santa Anna, gained and lost power many times. At first, he posed as a liberal reformer.

Life on a Hacienda
Peasant women process a crop grown on a hacienda in Mexico in the 1800s.

Soon, however, he reversed his stand and crushed efforts at reform.

In Mexico's northern territory of Texas, discontent grew. In 1835, settlers who had moved to Texas from the United States and other places revolted. After a brief struggle with Santa Anna's forces, the settlers gained independence from Mexico. They quickly set up an independent republic. Then in 1845 the United States annexed Texas. Mexicans saw this act as a declaration of war. In the fighting that followed, the United States invaded and defeated Mexico. In the Treaty of Guadalupe-Hidalgo, which ended the war, Mexico lost almost half its territory. The embarrassing defeat triggered new violence between conservatives and liberals.

La Reforma Changes Mexico In 1855, **Benito Juárez** (WAHR ez), a liberal reformer of Zapotec Indian heritage, and other liberals gained power and opened an era of reform known as **La Reforma.** Juárez offered hope to the oppressed people of Mexico. He and his fellow reformers revised the Mexican constitution to strip the military of power and end the special privileges of the Church. They ordered the Church to sell unused lands to peasants.

Conservatives resisted La Reforma and began a civil war. Still, Juárez was elected president in 1861 and expanded his reforms. His opponents turned to Europe for help. In 1863, Napoleon III sent troops to Mexico and set up Austrian archduke Maximilian as emperor.

For four years, Juárez's forces battled the combined conservative and French forces. When France withdrew its troops, Maximilian was captured and shot. In 1867, Juárez returned to power and tried to renew reform, but opponents resisted. Juárez died in office in 1872, never achieving all the reforms he envisioned. He did, however, help unite Mexico, bring mestizos into politics, and separate church and state.

Growth and Oppression Under Díaz After Juárez died, General Porfirio Díaz, a hero of the war against the French, staged a military coup and gained power. From 1876 to 1880 and 1884 to 1911, he ruled as a dictator. In the name of "Order and Progress," he strengthened the army, local police, and central government. He crushed opposition.

Under his harsh rule, Mexico made <u>tangible</u> economic advances. Railroads were built, foreign trade increased, some industry developed, and mining expanded. Growth, however, had a high cost. Capital for development came from foreign investors, to whom Díaz granted special rights. He also let wealthy landowners buy up Indian lands.

The rich prospered, but most Mexicans remained poor. Many Indians and mestizos fell into **peonage** to their employers. In the peonage system, hacienda owners would give workers advances on their wages and require them to stay on the hacienda until they had paid back what they owed. Wages remained low, and workers were rarely able to repay the hacienda owner. Many children died in infancy. Other children worked 12-hour days and never learned to read or write.

✓ **Checkpoint** What struggles did Mexico go through as it tried to find stability in the 1800s?

Remember the Alamo!
Mexican President Antonio López de Santa Anna (above) is well-known for his ruthless decision to give no quarter to the Texan defenders of the Alamo, a fort in San Antonio, Texas, during the Texas Revolution. The illustration above shows Texan defenders of the Alamo bravely fighting against overwhelming odds. *In what light does this illustration present the defenders of the Alamo?*

Vocabulary Builder
tangible—(TAN juh bul) *adj.* real or concrete

Mexico's Struggle for Stability

Instruct

- **Introduce: Vocabulary Builder**
  Have students read the Vocabulary Builder term and definition. Ask them to predict why the average Mexican would value seeing *tangible* proof of improving stability.

- **Teach** List the names of these political leaders on the board: Antonio López de Santa Anna, Benito Juárez, Porfirio Díaz. For each, have students list the leader's goals, his methods for achieving them, the effects of his actions, and his success at providing more stability and prosperity. Point out that though the government changed hands fairly frequently, these three leaders emerged and were able to hold power for most of this period.

- **Quick Activity** Have students write a letter to Juárez or Díaz identifying strengths and weaknesses of his leadership and explaining whether they think his policies and actions hurt or helped Mexico. Use the Think-Write-Pair-Share strategy (TE, p. T23) and have students compare their letters.

Independent Practice

Have students pick another nation in Latin America and write a short essay comparing its economic, social, and political challenges in the 1800s with those that were facing Mexico. Students might focus especially on social divisions, conflicts between liberals and conservatives, and regionalism.

Monitor Progress

To help students remember the key events of Mexico's struggle for stability, ask them to write one to three bullet points to summarize the text under each heading in the section.

History Background

Benito Juárez Throughout his life, Benito Juárez worked to overcome the legacies of colonial rule both for himself and for the Mexican people. Juárez was Mexico's first indigenous president. As a Zapotec, Juárez overcame strong barriers of prejudice against Native Americans. He began his formal education at age 12. After later earning a law degree, he entered public life. His first elected offices were as a member of the city council and then as governor of the state of Oaxaca. As governor, he earned a reputation for honesty, efficiency, and a modest lifestyle. He was respected for refusing to use public office to enrich himself or his family and friends. His goal was to turn his liberal ideas into political realities. Although he did not always succeed, his struggle brought hope to the poor and helped make him a national hero.

Answers

Caption They are determined heroically to defend themselves.

✓ It suffered defeat in war with the United States and lost land, faced social and economic inequalities, succumbed to civil war, and faced harsh rule by Díaz.

The Economics of Dependence L3

Instruct

- **Introduce** Discuss the word *dependence* in political and economic terms. Have students name factors that might lead to an unequal or dependent relationship between two countries. Then refer students to the map on this page. Have students use the map to make predictions about the trade relationship that would develop between Latin American countries and industrial nations like the United States.

- **Teach** Ask **How did Spanish and Portuguese policies prevent their Latin American colonies from developing their own economies?** *(Colonies had to sell raw materials to the parent country and buy manufactured goods from them, rather than manufacturing their own goods. Laws prevented trade with other countries and the creation of competitive local industries.)* **What happened to the cycle of dependence after political independence?** *(It continued, but with Britain and the United States replacing Spain and Portugal.)* **Why did many local industries fail to develop even after Latin America joined the world economy?** *(Only the elite benefited from foreign trade. The poor earned too little to buy consumer goods, so strong markets for local industries did not develop.)*

- **Quick Activity** Display **Color Transparency 155: Exports of Latin America and Selected Nations, About 1913.** Use the lesson suggested in the transparency book to guide a discussion about the cycle of dependence in Latin America.

  📖 **Color Transparencies,** 155

Answers

Map Skills
1. Review locations with students.
2. Sample: It is located right next to Latin America.
3. bananas and fish

442 New Global Patterns

Note Taking

Reading Skill: Identify Effects Use a chart like the one below to record how foreign influence, including that of the United States, affected Latin America.

Effects of Foreign Influence

The Economics of Dependence

Under colonial rule, mercantilist policies made Latin America economically dependent on Spain and Portugal. Colonies sent raw materials such as cash crops or precious metals to the parent country and had to buy manufactured goods from them. Strict laws kept colonists from trading with other countries and possibly obtaining goods at a lower price. In addition, laws prohibited the building of local industries that would have competed with the parent country. In short, the policies prevented the colonies from developing their own economies.

The Cycle of Economic Dependence After independence, this pattern changed very little. The new Latin American republics did adopt free trade, welcoming all comers. Britain and the United States rushed into the new markets, replacing Spain as Latin America's chief trading partners. But the region remained as economically dependent as before.

Foreign Influence Mounts In the 1800s, foreign goods flooded Latin America, creating large profits for foreigners and for a handful of local business people. Foreign investment, which could yield enormous profits, was often accompanied by local interference. Investors from Britain, the United States, and other nations pressured their own governments to take action if political events or reform movements in a Latin American country seemed to threaten their interests.

Some Economic Growth After 1850, some Latin American economies did grow. With foreign capital, they were able to develop mining and agriculture. Chile exported copper and nitrates, and Argentina expanded

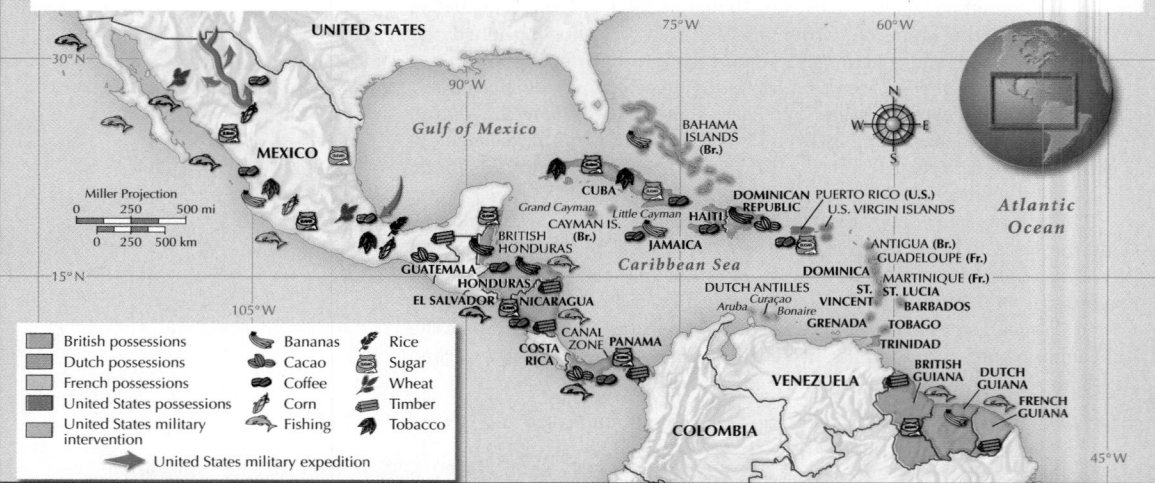

Geography *Interactive*
For: Audio guided tour
Web Code: nbp-2541

Imperialism in Latin America, 1898–1917

Map Skills In the early 1900s, European powers held possessions in Latin America. The United States often intervened to protect business interests there.

1. **Locate** (a) Cuba (b) Canal Zone (c) British Guiana (d) Honduras
2. **Location** Why did the United States have a particularly strong interest in Latin American affairs?
3. **Identify Point of View** What natural resources did the Dutch exploit in Dutch Guiana?

Differentiated Instruction

L4 Advanced Readers   L4 Gifted and Talented

Write the phrase "Create a new country" on the board. Ask students to identify the challenges that would face a group of leaders who are trying to create a country. Include issues such as providing for national defense, balance of power, and social welfare. Then have students do library or Internet research on one of the new Latin American countries. Students should provide a summary of how leaders handled these challenges in creating their new country.

its livestock and wheat production. Brazil exported the cash crops coffee and sugar, as well as rubber. By the early 1900s, both Venezuela and Mexico were developing important and lucrative oil industries.

Throughout the region, foreigners invested in modern ports and railroads to carry goods from the interior to coastal cities. European immigrants poured into Latin America. The newcomers helped to promote economic activity, and a small middle class emerged.

Thanks to trade, investment, technology, and migration, Latin American nations moved into the world economy. Yet internal development was limited. The tiny elite at the top benefited from the economic upturn, but very little trickled down to the masses of people at the bottom. The poor earned too little to buy consumer goods. Without a strong demand, many industries failed to develop.

✔ **Checkpoint** How did foreign influence and investment affect Latin America?

The Influence of the United States

As nations like Mexico tried to build stable governments, a neighboring republic, the United States, expanded across North America. Latin American nations began to feel threatened by the "Colossus of the North," the giant power that cast its shadow over the entire hemisphere.

The Monroe Doctrine In the 1820s, Spain plotted to recover its American colonies. Britain opposed any move that might close the door to trade with Latin America. British leaders asked American President James Monroe to join them in a statement opposing any new colonization of the Americas.

Monroe, however, wanted to avoid any "entangling alliance" with Britain. Acting alone, he issued the **Monroe Doctrine** in 1823. "The American continents," it declared, "are henceforth not to be considered as subjects for future colonization by any European powers." The United States lacked the military power to enforce the doctrine. But with the support of Britain's strong navy, the doctrine discouraged European interference. For more than a century, the Monroe Doctrine would be the key to United States policy in the Americas.

The United States Expands Into Latin America As a result of the war with Mexico, in 1848 the United States acquired the thinly populated regions of northern Mexico, gaining all or part of the present-day states of California, Arizona, New Mexico, Nevada, Utah, and Colorado. The victory fed dreams of future expansion. Before the century had ended, the United States controlled much of North America and was becoming involved in overseas conflicts.

For decades, Cuban patriots had battled to free their island from Spanish rule. As they began to make headway, the United States joined their cause, declaring war on Spain in 1898. The brief Spanish-American War ended in a crushing defeat for Spain. At the war's end, Cuba was granted independence. But in 1901, the United States forced Cubans to add the Platt Amendment to their constitution. The amendment gave the United States naval bases in Cuba and the right to intervene in Cuban affairs.

Analyzing Political Cartoons

Uncle Sam Takes Off This cartoon represents the entry of the United States into competition with European powers over new territory in the Eastern Hemisphere in the early 1900s.

 Uncle Sam represents the United States.

 The horse wears a saddle that reads "Monroe Doctrine."

C **European powers** watch in frustration.

1. What do the wheels on Uncle Sam's bicycle represent?
2. Why are the European powers shouting at Uncle Sam?

Independent Practice

- **Note Taking** Have students fill in the chart showing the effects of foreign influence on Latin America.
  ✎ **Reading and Note Taking Study Guide**, p. 146

- Have students access **Web Code nbp-2541** to take the **Geography Interactive Audio Guided Tour** and then answer the map skills questions in the text.

Monitor Progress

- As students fill in their charts, circulate to make sure they understand the ways in which foreign countries influenced Latin America. For a completed version of the chart, see
  ▥ **Note Taking Transparencies**, 168B
- Check answers to map skills questions.

History Background

Monroe Doctrine The Monroe Doctrine reflected the intention of the United States to make Latin America a U.S. sphere of influence. In 1823, when Monroe announced this policy, the United States was not yet a world power. If European nations had challenged the United States' assertion of control over Latin America, U.S. leaders would have had to turn to Britain for help. Over time, as the United States became a more powerful and prosperous nation, its assertion of unilateral authority in the region became more credible, though not more popular.

Answers

✔ Foreign investment helped Latin American economies develop to some extent, but their development mostly benefited the foreign investors and a small group of Latin American elites.

Analyzing Political Cartoons
1. Eastern and Western Hemispheres
2. They don't want the United States to interfere so much in the world.

The Influence of the United States

Instruct

- **Introduce** Remind students of the section title: Economic Imperialism in Latin America. Have students explain how economic imperialism is different from the imperialism of the colonial period. Have students make predictions about the consequences for Latin American nations of the involvement of the United States in their economies.

- **Teach** Create a four-column chart on the board, with columns labeled Country, U.S. Intervention, Purpose, and Outcome. Have the class work together to complete the chart. Then ask **What was the goal of the Monroe Doctrine?** (*to discourage European intervention in Latin America*) **Why did U.S. leaders add the Roosevelt Corollary to the Monroe Doctrine?** (*to protect U.S. investments in Latin America*)

- **Analyzing the Visuals** Have students study the Infographic on this page in groups. Have the groups list challenges faced by the canal builders. Taking these into account, ask students to consider why Panama didn't build the canal on its own.

Independent Practice

- **Primary Source** To help students understand how Latin Americans viewed intervention by the United States, have them read the excerpt from José Martí's *"Our America"* and complete the worksheet.

  All in One Teaching Resources, Unit 3, p. 94

- Have students fill in the Outline Map *Imperialism in Latin America* and label areas of U.S. influence.

  All in One Teaching Resources, Unit 3, p. 96

Monitor Progress

Circulate to make sure students are filling in their Outline Maps accurately. Administer the Geography Quiz.

All in One Teaching Resources, Unit 3, p. 97

Answers

Thinking Critically

1. to shorten the shipping distance between the East Coast and the West Coast
2. to protect the work force from the effects of disease

● INFOGRAPHIC

AN EPIC UNDERTAKING: PANAMA CANAL

The Panama Canal was a massive undertaking. The sheer scale of the project astounded engineers, politicians, and tourists. Building the canal cost the American government $352 million (about $7 billion in today's money). Workers excavated about 232 million cubic yards of dirt, rocks, and debris from the Canal Zone—enough debris to create a pyramid seven times the height of the Washington Monument, as one newspaper writer noted. Nearly six thousand workers died from industrial accidents or disease in the ten years it took to build the canal.

Despite many challenges, the builders would not give up. They completed the canal in 1914. The beginning of World War I in the summer of 1914, however, overshadowed what was to be its grand opening.

UNITED STATES • New York City
San Francisco
6,100 MILES
9,820 KILOMETERS
Atlantic Ocean
15,100 MILES
24,200 KILOMETERS
PANAMA CANAL
Pacific Ocean

▲ Playing cards featuring scenes from the canal's construction (above) helped to feed Americans' fascination with the canal.

◄ Two men (below) stand inside one of the canal lock's enormous gates. The gates allow water to flow in and out of the lock, raising or lowering ships to different levels.

▼ The tropical diseases malaria and yellow fever killed many workers. Quinine (below right) was used to treat some cases of malaria. The canal builders' massive efforts to kill disease-carrying mosquitoes, using methods, such as spraying swampy areas with oil (below left), were more effective.

Thinking Critically

1. **Draw Conclusions** Based on the map, why did Americans want to build a canal in Panama?
2. **Draw Inferences** Why was it important to control disease during the building of the canal?

Link to Science

Disease Fighter in Panama Building the Panama Canal required both scientific and engineering expertise. Early efforts by a French company to build the canal had failed in part because so many workers died of malaria and yellow fever. William Gorgas, an American disease and sanitation expert, solved the problem. Before coming to Panama, Gorgas had over-seen sanitation for the U.S. Army in Havana, Cuba. While there, he conducted many experiments to determine how mosquitoes transmit yellow fever. Gorgas realized that by draining swamps and other areas where mosquitoes breed, he could stop the spread of the deadly disease. His work led to the eradication of yellow fever from the Canal Zone.

The United States Interferes American investments in Latin America grew in the early 1900s. Citing the need to protect those investments, in 1904 the United States issued the Roosevelt Corollary to the Monroe Doctrine. Under this policy, the United States claimed "international police power" in the Western Hemisphere. When the Dominican Republic failed to pay its foreign debts, the United States sent in troops. Americans collected customs duties, paid off the debts, and remained for years.

Under the Roosevelt Corollary and then President William Howard Taft's policy of Dollar Diplomacy, American companies continued to invest in the countries of Latin America. To protect those investments, the United States sent troops to Cuba, Haiti, Mexico, Honduras, Nicaragua, and other countries in Central America and the Caribbean. As a result, like European powers in Africa and Asia, the United States became the target of increasing resentment and rebellion.

Building the Panama Canal From the late 1800s, the United States had wanted to build a canal across Central America. Panama was a proposed site. However, Panama belonged to Colombia, which refused to sell the United States land for the canal. In 1903, the United States backed a revolt by Panamanians against Colombia. The Panamanians quickly won independence and gave the United States control of the land to build the canal.

Construction began in 1904. Engineers solved many difficult problems in the course of building the canal. The **Panama Canal** opened in 1914. The canal cut the distance of a sea journey between such cities as New York and San Francisco by thousands of miles. It was an engineering marvel that boosted trade and shipping worldwide.

To people in Latin America, however, the canal was another example of "Yankee imperialism." Nationalist feeling in the hemisphere was often expressed as anti-Americanism. Panama did not gain complete control over the canal until 2000. It now forms a vital part of the Panamanian economy.

 Checkpoint How did the United States act as an imperialist power in Latin America?

Progress Monitoring *Online*
For: Self-quiz with vocabulary practice
Web Code: nba-2541

SECTION 4 Assessment

Terms, People, and Places

1. For each term, person, or place listed at the beginning of the section, write a sentence explaining its significance.

Note Taking

2. **Reading Skill: Recognize Multiple Causes** Use your completed charts to answer the Focus Question: How did Latin American nations struggle for stability, and how did industrialized nations affect them?

Critical Thinking and Comprehension

3. **Express Problems Clearly** What problems faced new nations in Latin America?
4. **Recognize Cause and Effect** How did the cycle of economic dependence continue after independence?
5. **Synthesize Information** Describe two ways the United States influenced Latin America.
6. **Draw Conclusions** Why might developing nations encourage foreign investment? Do you think foreign investors should have the right to intervene in another nations affairs to protect their investments? Explain.

● **Writing About History**

Quick Write: Support Your Ideas As you respond to a short-answer or extended-response question on a test, keep in mind that each sentence or paragraph should support your main idea. Omit information, no matter how interesting, that is not central to your argument. To practice, write an outline of an argument responding to the following extended-response prompt.

• Explain how American interference led to the building of the Panama Canal.

Section 4 Assessment

1. Sentences should reflect an understanding of each term, person, or place listed at the beginning of the section.
2. They struggled against unequal distribution of wealth and power, regionalism, and liberal-conservative conflicts. Industrialized nations increased trade and industrialization in Latin America, creating economic dependence. They often interfered in Latin American affairs.

3. little experience with self-government, uneven distribution of wealth and power, regionalism, frequent revolts
4. Latin American nations continued to export raw materials and import finished products.
5. It invested heavily in Latin American businesses and interfered politically and militarily in Latin American affairs.
6. Foreign capital helps local industries develop. Samples: Yes, their investment helps both parties. No, investors should

not interfere with local affairs just because they do business there.

● **Writing About History**

Outlines should be well organized and support main ideas with specific details.

For additional assessment, have students access **Progress Monitoring *Online*** at **Web Code nba-2541.**

- Have students use the Quick Study Guide to prepare for this chapter's test. Students may wish to refer to the following pages as they review:

Imperialism in Japan and Southeast Asia and the Pacific
Section 1, pp. 423–428; Section 2, pp. 429–433

Three British Colonies: Canada, Australia, and New Zealand
Section 3, pp. 434–438

The Cycle of Economic Dependence in Latin America
Section 4, pp. 442–443

Key Events in Worldwide Imperialism
Section 1, pp. 423–424, 428; Section 2, pp. 429, 430, 431; Section 3, pp. 435, 436, 438; Section 4, pp. 441, 445

- For additional review, remind students to refer to the **L3**

  Reading and Note Taking Study Guide
Note Taking Study Guide, pp. 140, 142, 144, 146
Section Summaries, pp. 141, 143, 145, 147

- Have students access **Web Code nbp-2562** for this chapter's **History Interactive** timeline, which includes expanded entries and additional events.

- If students need more instruction on analyzing timelines, have them read the **Skills Handbook,** p. SH30.

- When students have completed their study of the chapter, distribute Chapter Tests A and B.

  All in One Teaching Resources, Unit 3, pp. 98–103

For **Progress Monitoring Online,** refer students to the Self-test with vocabulary practice at **Web Code nba-2551.**

CHAPTER **13**

Quick Study Guide

Progress Monitoring Online
For: Self-test with vocabulary practice
Web Code: nba-2551

◼ Imperialism in Japan and Southeast Asia and the Pacific

Japan	Southeast Asia and the Pacific
• United States opens by show of force. • Meiji restoration begins modernization. • Japan becomes an imperialist power itself.	• European powers expand footholds. • Some countries resist, but succumb to European force. • Europeans gain resources and trade networks at expense of indigenous people.

◼ Three British Colonies: Canada, Australia, and New Zealand

British Colony	Settled by	Impact on Indigenous People	Gained Self-Rule From Britain
Canada	First France, then Britain	Native Americans forced to give up lands	1867
Australia	Britain, as penal colony	Aborigines suffered disastrously	1901
New Zealand	Britain, attracted by climate	Maori fought against settlers, population reduced drastically	1907

◼ The Cycle of Economic Dependence in Latin America

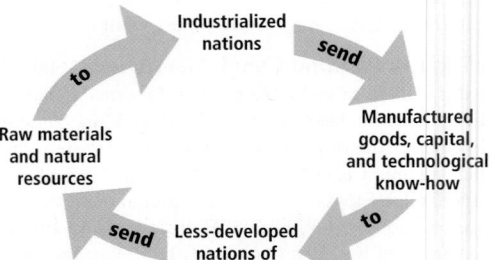

The relationship is unequal because the stronger, more developed nations control prices and terms of trade.

◼ Key Events in Worldwide Imperialism

Southeast Asia, the Pacific, and Japan
British Colonies and Latin America

1835

1840
Britain annexes New Zealand.

1850

1853
American ships commanded by Commodore Perry arrive in Japan.

1855
La Reforma begins in Mexico.

1858
France invades Vietnam.

1865

1867
Britain grants Canada self-rule.

1868
Meiji Restoration begins in Japan.

Differentiated Instruction   Solutions for All Learners

L1 Special Needs   L2 Less Proficient Readers

Use the following study guide resources to help students acquiring basic skills:

Adapted Reading and Note Taking Study Guide
Adapted Note Taking Study Guide, pp. 140, 142, 144, 146
Adapted Section Summaries, pp. 141, 143, 145, 147

L2 English Language Learners

Use the following study guide resources to help Spanish-speaking students:

Spanish Reading and Note Taking Study Guide
Spanish Note Taking Study Guide, pp. 140, 142, 144, 146
Spanish Section Summaries, pp. 141, 143, 145, 147

Concept Connector

Essential Question Review

To connect prior knowledge with what you have learned in this chapter, answer the questions below in your Concept Connector journal. Use the journal in the Reading and Note Taking Study Guide to record your answers (or go to www.phschool.com **Web Code: nbd-2507**).

1. **Cooperation** In response to Commodore Perry's demands, Japanese statesman Lord Ii suggested a strategy for dealing with the Americans:

   "Even though the Shogun's ancestors set up seclusion laws, they left the Dutch and the Chinese to act as a bridge…. Might this bridge not now be of advantage to us in handling foreign affairs, providing us with the means whereby we may for a time avert the outbreak of hostilities and then, after some time has elapsed, gain a complete victory?"

   Why did Lord Ii want to cooperate with the Americans? What steps did the Japanese take to "gain a complete victory?" Did this prove to be a good strategy for Japan? Why or why not?

2. **Geography's Impact** Location links the fate of Latin America with that of the United States. In the 1800s, ideas about independence springing from the American Revolution inspired independence leaders in Latin America, such as Simón Bolívar. However, in the late 1800s, the United States began to interfere more aggressively in the affairs of Latin American countries. Create a timeline tracking the relationship between the United States and Latin America from 1800 through 1914. Include a brief description of the significance of each event on the timeline.

3. **Migration** Native Americans made up the original population of Canada, Kooris inhabited Australia, and Maoris lived in New Zealand. Today, along with descendents of these early people, more of the inhabitants of these countries are of British ancestry. Explain the role migration played in changing the population of these lands.

■ Connections To Today

1. **Conflict: Unrest in Quebec** Although French-Canadian leaders agreed to confederation with the rest of Canada in 1867, the French-English question was never truly put to rest. Many French-Canadians continued to feel that the English-speaking majority in Canada threatened their unique French culture. In the late 1900s, a movement for an independent Quebec arose. Research the path of this movement and create a bulleted list of significant events that occurred within the last fifty years.

Languages Spoken in Canada Today

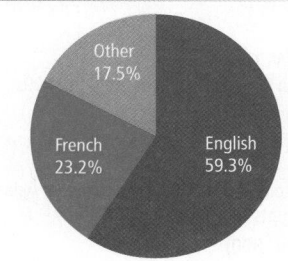

- Other 17.5%
- French 23.2%
- English 59.3%

SOURCE: The World Factbook Online

2. **Cooperation: Japan as a World Power** After its rapid modernization in the late 1800s, Japan took its place among the leading powers of the world. It asserted that power throughout the 1900s, with varying results. Today, Japan's economy is second in size only to that of the United States. Conduct research on Japan and write a paragraph describing its role in international affairs today.

1886 Britain annexes Burma.

1898 The Philippines declares independence from Spain.

1910 Japan annexes Korea.

History *Interactive*
For: Interactive timeline
Web Code: nbp-2562

| 1880 | 1895 | 1910 | 1925 |

1885 The Canadian Pacific Railway opens.

1904 The United States issues the Roosevelt Corollary.

1914 The Panama Canal opens.

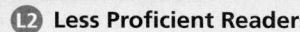

Differentiated Instruction — Solutions for All Learners

L1 Special Needs   L2 Less Proficient Readers

Use the following study guide resources to help students acquiring basic skills:

📑 **Adapted Reading and Note Taking Study Guide**

Adapted Concept Connector, pp. 242, 270, 281

L2 English Language Learners

Use the following study guide resources to help Spanish-speaking students:

📑 **Spanish Reading and Note Taking Study Guide**

Spanish Concept Connector, pp. 242, 270, 281

Concept Connector

Tell students that the main concepts for this chapter are Cooperation, Geography's Impact, and Cultural Diffusion, and then ask them to answer the Essential Question Review questions on this page. Discuss the Connections to Today topics and ask students to answer the questions that follow.

Essential Question Review

1. Japan could not defend itself against the U.S. Navy. Lord Ii wanted to cooperate until Japan built a strong military. The Meiji Restoration created a strong central government and bureaucracy and built a modern industrial economy. Japan modernized quickly and was soon strong enough to force Western powers to revise unequal treaties.

2. Timelines may include the following entries: Early 1800s—ideas from the American Revolution influence Latin American revolutionaries; 1823—Monroe Doctrine; 1867—U.S. pressures France to end its interference in Mexican civil war; 1899—U.S. fights for Cuban independence in Spanish-American War; 1904—Roosevelt Corollary; various military interventions.

3. Native cultures became less important as some colonized peoples came to believe in Western superiority. Cultural diffusion helped bring an end to colonialism as colonized people took on European ideas of nationalism and agitated for their own independence.

Connections to Today

1. Lists should include key events of the Quebec separatist movement.

2. Responses should reflect that Japan is a key player in international affairs, especially in East Asia.

For additional review of this chapter's core concepts, remind students to refer to the

 Reading and Note Taking Study Guide
Concept Connector, pp. 242, 270, 281

Chapter Assessment

Terms, People, and Places

1. Foreign pressure deepened resentment of the shogun's rule.

2. Japan's search for raw materials led to both conflicts.

3. reformed the government, modernized the army, adopted new technology, abolished slavery, gave women some choice in marriage

4. Canadian leaders unified Britain's North American colonies. Britain agreed with the British North America Act.

5. The treaty that ended the war gave the U.S. control of the Philippines. Cuba gained independence, but with U.S. intervention allowed.

6. Both regionalism and *caudillos* undermined governments. Some ruled as dictators, causing unrest.

Main Ideas

7. went from isolation and rigid feudal order to modern industrial economy and new political and social system, including central government and democratic constitution

8. They sought raw materials, Christian converts, and new markets for goods.

9. Siam tried to modernize to avoid colonization. Others tried to resist.

10. French and English colonists settled in Canada, where Native Americans also lived. The first Australian settlers were Aborigines; the first European settlers there were British convicts. The first settlers in New Zealand were the Maori; later British missionaries and settlers came.

11. British North America Act of 1867 made Canada self-governing; Australian colonies formed a commonwealth in 1901; New Zealand won independence in 1907.

12. the legacy of colonial rule, including social and political hierarchy with land and power held by elites; regionalism; rule by caudillos; political instability

13. Through the Monroe Doctrine, Roosevelt Corollary, and Dollar Diplomacy, the U.S. intervened in economic and political life.

Chapter Focus Question

14. caused the creation of both weak local economies closely tied to the industrial nations that ruled them and

---

Chapter Assessment

Terms, People, and Places

1. In what ways did **Matthew Perry's** opening of Japan lead to the **Meiji Restoration?**
2. How did the **Sino-Japanese** and **Russo-Japanese wars** spring out of Japan's new strength as a modernized nation?
3. What steps did **King Mongkut** take to help Siam avoid the fate of **French Indochina?**
4. How did Canada become a **dominion?**
5. Describe how the **Spanish-American War** affected both the Philippines and Cuba.
6. How did **regionalism** and *caudillos* weaken the stability of Latin American countries in the 1800s?

Main Ideas

Section 1 (pp. 784–790)
7. How did Japan change course in the late 1800s?

Section 2 (pp. 791–795)
8. Why were imperialist nations drawn to Southeast Asia and the Pacific?
9. How did the colonized peoples of Southeast Asia react to Western attempts to dominate the region?

Section 3 (pp. 796–800)
10. Describe settlement in Canada, Australia, and New Zealand.
11. How did these colonies gain independence?

Section 4 (pp. 801–807)
12. What factors caused instability in Latin America after independence?
13. How did the United States influence Latin America?

Chapter Focus question:
14. How did political and economic imperialism influence nations around the world?

Critical Thinking

15. **Compare** Compare Japan's response to Western imperialism to that of China. How were the two responses similar? How were they different?
16. **Identify Causes** In the image below, a Japanese woman wears Western clothing. What role did westernization play in helping both Japan and Siam avoid colonization by European nations?

17. **Connect to Geography** How did the creation of the Dominion of Canada encourage expansion?
18. **Synthesize Information** What principle did the United States express in the Monroe Doctrine? How did the Roosevelt Corollary alter the Monroe Doctrine?
19. **Draw Conclusions** List the benefits and disadvantages brought about by colonial rule. Do you think subject people were better or worse off as a result of the Age of Imperialism? Explain.

● Writing About History

In this chapter's four Section Assessments, you learned how to write for assessment.

Writing for Assessment Write an answer to one of the following extended response essay prompts. Spend only 40 minutes on the writing process. Consult page SH20 of the Writing Handbook for additional help.

- Analyze the effects of Japanese imperialism in Korea.
- Analyze the effects of American intervention in Latin America.

Prewriting
- Read both prompts and determine what you know about each. Choose the one whose topic you recall the most information about.

- Look for key words that will tell you what kind of answer to provide, such as "explain."

Drafting
- Focus your time by allowing 10 minutes for prewriting, 20 minutes for drafting, and 10 minutes for revising your response.
- Develop a thesis for your essay and make sure each piece of information supports it.

Revising
- Check that you open and close your response strongly, that each point supports your main idea, and that you've answered all aspects of the question.

---

economies based on producing raw materials and natural resources; introduced some technology and infrastructure; delayed self-government; slowed development of local political institutions

Critical Thinking

15. Both accepted unequal treaties. The Chinese resisted the British but were defeated. The Japanese modernized and became an industrial and military power.

16. Westernization often went hand in hand with Western-style modernization.

17. It provided a central government, which helped build a transcontinental railroad.

18. Americas were no longer open to colonization by European powers; U.S. had police power in the Western Hemisphere.

19. Benefits: provided technology and infrastructure. Disadvantages: economic dependence, deterred local growth. Encourage students to explain opinions.

Document-Based Assessment

The Imperialism Debate and the Philippines

After defeating Spain in Manila Bay in May 1898, American forces remained in the Philippines. In February 1899, the United States Senate voted to annex the Philippines. The Philippines were one aspect of the United States' efforts to compete with Europe in the scramble for new foreign markets, investment opportunities and raw materials. A great debate took place in the United States over the issue of imperialism, as the documents below show.

Document A

"I have been criticized a good deal about the Philippines, but don't deserve it. The truth is I didn't want the Philippines, and when they came to us, as a gift from the gods, I did not know what to do with them. . . . And one night late it came to me this way—I don't know how it was, but it came: (1) That we could not give them back to Spain—that would be cowardly and dishonorable; (2) that we could not turn them over to France and Germany—our commercial rivals in the Orient—that would be bad business and discreditable; (3) that we could not leave them to themselves—they were unfit for self-government—and they would soon have anarchy and misrule over there worse than Spain's was; and (4) that there was nothing left for us to do but to take them all, and to educate the Filipinos, and uplift and civilize and Christianize them . . ."

—From remarks to a visiting delegation of Methodist church leaders made by President William McKinley on November 21, 1899

Document B

"We hold that the policy known as imperialism is hostile to liberty and tends toward militarism, an evil from which it has been our glory to be free. . . . We maintain that governments derive their just powers from the consent of the governed. We insist that the subjugation of any people is "criminal aggression" and open disloyalty to the distinctive principles of our government.

We earnestly condemn the policy of the present National Administration in the Philippines. It seeks to extinguish the spirit of 1776 in those islands. . . . We denounce the slaughter of the Filipinos as a needless horror."

—From the Platform of the American Anti-Imperialist League, 1899

Document C

"Isn't Every American proud of the part that American soldiers bore in the relief of Pekin [i.e., Beijing, where some U.S. citizens were held hostage by the Boxers]? But that would have been impossible if our flag had not been in the Philippines.

Gen. Chaffee led two infantry regiments, the Ninth and the Fourteen, and one battery of the Fifth Artillery to Pekin. They did not come direct from the United States; there was no time. . . . But for these men and the marines from Manilla barracks, Minister Conger and his American comrades in the besieged legation would not have seen their country's flag, and would OWE THEIR RELIEF TO BRITISH, JAPANESE AND RUSSIANS.

When Mr. Bryan [Democratic candidate for president] tells you that the Philippines are worth nothing to America, you tell him to 'REMEMBER PEKIN!'"

—From a leaflet of the Republican Club of Massachusetts, 1900

Analyzing Documents

Use your knowledge of this chapter and Documents A, B, and C to answer questions 1–4.

1. In Document A, which of McKinley's four reasons for the takeover of the Philippines explained that important business interests were at stake?
   A 1
   B 2
   C 3
   D 4

2. In Document B, what is the meaning of "It seeks to extinguish the spirit of 1776 in those islands"?
   A The U.S. vowed never to give the Philippines its freedom.
   B The U.S. is undermining an independence movement that is like the American Revolution.
   C Self-government in the Philippines is inevitable.
   D The U.S. has the ability and the duty to educate Filipinos about self-government.

3. According to Document C, the Philippines are necessary to the United States as a(n)
   A source for raw materials.
   B outpost for Christian missionaries.
   C base for military actions.
   D market for U.S. goods.

4. William Jennings Bryan considered imperialism which he opposed, to be the top issue in the 1900 presidential campaign. Who would have received your vote, the Democratic candidate, Bryan, or the Republican, William McKinley? Give your reasons, using these documents and information from the chapter.

Document-Based Assessment

■ To help students understand the documents on this page, give them the following **TIP: As you review each document, use your knowledge of the subject as well as clues in the document to try to identify the writer's point of view.**

■ To provide students with further practice in answering Document-Based Assessment Questions, go to **Document-Based Assessment,** pp. 67–79

■ If students need more instruction on drawing inferences and conclusions, have them read the **Skills Handbook,** p. SH36.

● Writing About History

As students begin the assignment, refer them to page SH20 of the **Writing Handbook** for help in writing for assessment. Remind them of the steps they should take to complete their assignment, including prewriting, drafting, and revising. For help in revising, remind them to use the guidelines on page SH22 of the **Writing Handbook.**

Students' essays should have a clear thesis with supporting details and contain an introduction, a body, and a conclusion. They should show evidence of thoughtful consideration of the writing prompt selected and be free of grammatical and spelling errors. For scoring rubrics for writing assignments, see **Assessment Rubrics,** p. 8.

Answers

1. B
2. B
3. C
4. Students should express an opinion favoring either Bryan, who opposed imperialism, or McKinley, who supported it and should use specific evidence from the documents and the chapter to support their opinions.

World Wars and Revolutions
1910–1955

Unit Overview

Unit 4 presents the era from World War I through World War II and into the Cold War, including the Russian Revolution and nationalist struggles in Latin America, Africa, the Middle East, India, and China.

Chapter 14 examines World War I and also describes the Russian Revolution and the civil war that proceeded it.
Concepts: Conflict, Cooperation, Revolution

Chapter 15 explores nationalist conflicts in various parts of the world.
Concepts: Democracy, Impact of the Individual, Nationalism

Chapter 16 covers the years leading up to World War II, focusing on the dictatorships that arose in Italy, Germany, and the Soviet Union.
Concepts: Dictatorship, Human Rights, Science

Chapter 17 examines World War II and describes how the Cold War developed.
Concepts: Conflict, Cooperation, Democracy, Genocide, Technology

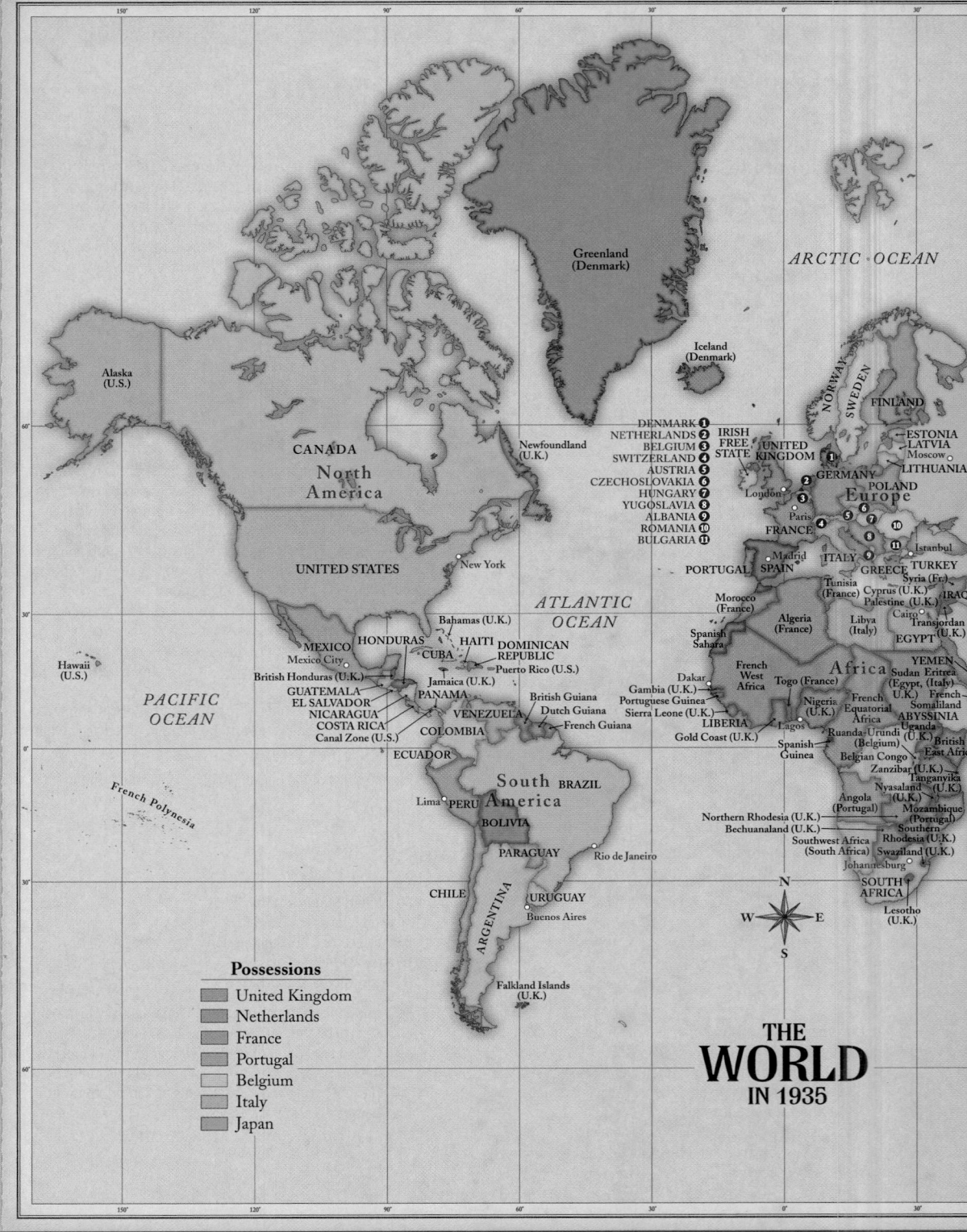

Possessions
- United Kingdom
- Netherlands
- France
- Portugal
- Belgium
- Italy
- Japan

THE WORLD IN 1935

About the Map

The Versailles treaty (1919), which ended World War I, punished Germany by taking away some of its territory and all of its overseas colonies. Other treaties dismantled Austria-Hungary and the Ottoman empire, both partners of Germany in the war. The victorious Allies, Britain and France, gained mandates to govern former German colonies in Africa and Ottoman lands in the Middle East. Japan gained control of Germany's Pacific possessions. Meanwhile, amid the turmoil of the Russian Revolution, Russia lost control of some lands. Several new Eastern European nations emerged from this reshuffling. Russia's new leaders formed the communist Soviet Union in 1922. After World War I, colonized peoples in Africa, Asia, and the Pacific had hoped that they would gain independence, yet the colonial powers maintained their grip. In 1931, Japan invaded northeastern China and established the colony of Manchukuo. The war between Japan and China that followed was one of the conflicts that led to World War II.

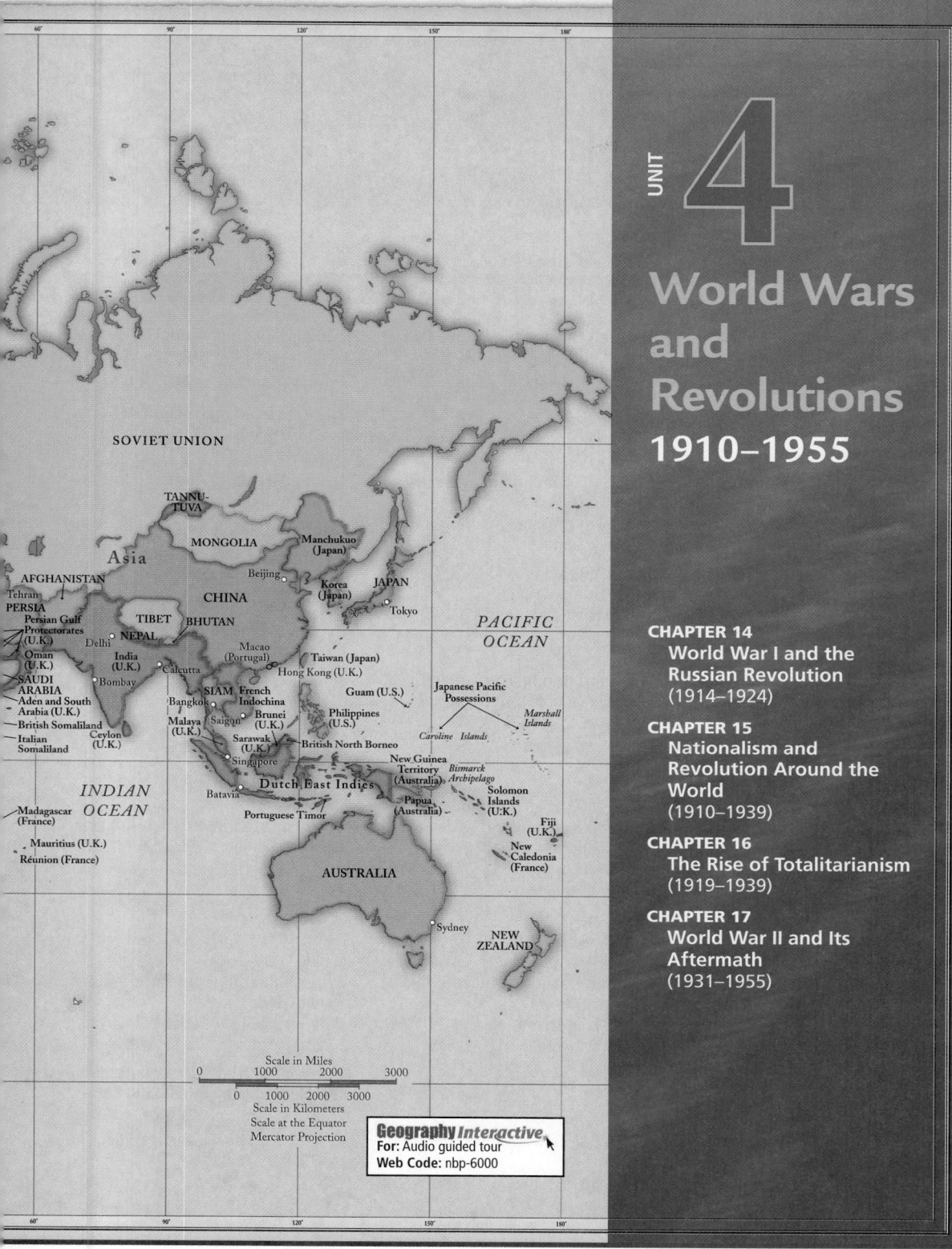

UNIT 4

World Wars and Revolutions
1910–1955

CHAPTER 14
World War I and the Russian Revolution
(1914–1924)

CHAPTER 15
Nationalism and Revolution Around the World
(1910–1939)

CHAPTER 16
The Rise of Totalitarianism
(1919–1939)

CHAPTER 17
World War II and Its Aftermath
(1931–1955)

Geographic Literacy

Tell students that the political map on these pages shows independent nations and colonies as they existed between World War I and World War II. Have them find Germany, Italy, the United Kingdom, and France on the map. Tell them that these European powers, along with the Soviet Union and the United States, played key roles in both world wars. Then ask **Which of these nations had colonial possessions in Africa in 1935?** *(United Kingdom, France, and Italy)* Have students find Japan on the map. Ask **What possessions did Japan control in East Asia and the Pacific?** *(Manchukuo, or Manchuria, as well as Korea, Taiwan, the Caroline Islands, and the Marshall Islands)* Then ask students to use the map to help them identify the main centers of political power in the world in 1935. *(Europe, especially France and the United Kingdom; Japan; the United States; and the Soviet Union)*

Looking Ahead

Ask students to read the chapter titles to the right of the map. Ask **Based on these titles and your study of the map, what do you predict you will learn about in this unit?** *(both world wars and the period between the wars, including various revolutions and nationalist struggles against imperialist powers)* Explain that students will also learn about the scientific, cultural, and social changes that took place after World War I, the misery caused by the Great Depression, and the origins of the Cold War.

A note on the projection:
Although the Mercator projection distorts the sizes of continents, it was widely used for maps after its invention in 1569.

> **Home Involvement**
> The *Letter Home* includes a summary of the World Wars and Revolutions content that students will be studying.
> **All in One** Teaching Resources, Unit 4, p. 1

World War I and the Russian Revolution

Section	Core Instruction L3	Differentiated Instruction L1 L2 L4	
Section 1 *The Great War Begins* ⏱ **2 periods, 1 block** **OBJECTIVES** ■ Describe how international rivalries and nationalism pushed Europe toward war. ■ Explain how the assassination in Sarajevo led to the start of World War I. ■ Analyze the causes and effects of the European alliance system. **Focus Question** *Why and how did World War I begin in 1914?*	**All in One Teaching Resources, Unit 4** Vocabulary Builder, p. 7 Reading Strategy, p. 8 Outline Map, p. 15 Section 1 Quiz, p. 2 **Reading and Note Taking Study Guide** Note Taking Study Guide, p. 148 Section 1 Summary, p. 149 **Note Taking Transparencies,** 169 **WITNESS HISTORY Audio CD** The Spark **Progress Monitoring Transparencies,** 108 **Color Transparencies,** 157 **Teaching Resources, Skills Handbook** Prereading the Chapter, pp. 1–2 Word Knowledge Rating Form, p. 3 K-W-L Chart, p. 4	**L1 Adapted Reading and Note Taking Study Guide** Note Taking Study Guide, p. 148 SN Section 1 Summary, p. 149 SN **L2 Adapted Reading and Note Taking Study Guide** Note Taking Study Guide, p. 148 LPR Section 1 Summary, p. 149 LPR **Spanish Reading and Note Taking Study Guide** Note Taking Study Guide, p. 148 ELL Section 1 Summary, p. 149 ELL **L4 Differentiated Instruction Activity,** Teacher's Edition, p. 456 AR, GT	*Guided Reading Audio (English/Spanish) SN *Student Edition Audio ELL **Differentiated Instruction Activity,** Teacher's Edition, p. 455 SN *Guided Reading Audio (Spanish) LPR, ELL *Student Edition Audio LPR **Differentiated Instruction Activity,** Teacher's Edition, p. 455 LPR, ELL **Extend Activity,** Teacher's Edition, p. 459 AR, GT
Section 2 *A New Kind of War* ⏱ **2 periods, 1 block** **OBJECTIVES** ■ Understand why a stalemate developed on the Western Front. ■ Describe how technology made World War I different from earlier wars. ■ Outline the course of the war on the Eastern Front, in other parts of Europe, in Turkey, and in the Middle East. ■ Summarize how colonies fought in the war. **Focus Question** *How and where was World War I fought?*	**All in One Teaching Resources, Unit 4** Section 2 Quiz, p. 2 Outline Map, p. 14 Geography Quiz, p. 16 **Reading and Note Taking Study Guide** Note Taking Study Guide, p. 150 Section 2 Summary, p. 151 **Note Taking Transparencies,** 170A–170B **WITNESS HISTORY Audio CD** A Soldier on the Western Front **Progress Monitoring Transparencies,** 109 **Color Transparencies,** 158, 159 **Witness History Discovery School™** video program, *World War I: A New Kind of War*	**L1 Adapted Reading and Note Taking Study Guide** Note Taking Study Guide, p. 150 SN Section 2 Summary, p. 151 SN **L2 Adapted Reading and Note Taking Study Guide** Note Taking Study Guide, p. 150 LPR Section 2 Summary, p. 151 LPR **L4 All in One Teaching Resources, Unit 4** Viewpoints: Soldier-Poets View World War I, p. 11 AR, GT Traveler's Tales: Isak Dinesan's Letters from Africa, p. 13	**Differentiated Instruction Activity,** Teacher's Edition, p. 463 SN **Spanish Reading and Note Taking Study Guide** Note Taking Study Guide, p. 150 ELL Section 2 Summary, p. 151 ELL **Differentiated Instruction Activity,** Teacher's Edition, p. 463 LPR, ELL **Extend Activity,** Teacher's Edition, p. 465 AR, GT

*Audio support is available for all sections.

Assessment Resources

- **Progress Monitoring Transparencies,** 108–112
- **SuccessTracker™,** Chapter 14
- **Document-Based Assessment,** pp. 80–94
- *ExamView*® **Test Bank CD-ROM,** Chapter 14
- **All in One Teaching Resources, Unit 4,** Chapter Tests A and B, pp. 17–22
- **Progress Monitoring** *Online* **Quizzes,** Chapter 14

Differentiated Instruction Key

L1 Special Needs	LPR Less Proficient Readers
L2 Basic to Average	AR Advanced Readers
L3 All Students	SN Special Needs Students
L4 Average to Advanced	GT Gifted and Talented
	ELL English Language Learners

Section	Core Instruction L3	Differentiated Instruction L1 L2 L4	
Section 3 *Winning the War* 🕐 **1.5 periods, .75 block** **OBJECTIVES** ■ Describe how World War I became a total war. ■ Explain the effect that years of warfare had on morale. ■ Analyze the causes and effects of American entry into the war. ■ Summarize events that led to the end of the war. **Focus Question** *How did the Allies win World War I?*	**All in One Teaching Resources, Unit 4** Section 3 Quiz, p. 4 **Reading and Note Taking Study Guide** Note Taking Study Guide, pp. 152–153 Section 3 Summary, p. 154 **Note Taking Transparencies,** 171 **WITNESS HISTORY Audio CD** An American War Song **Progress Monitoring Transparencies,** 110 **Color Transparencies,** 156, 160	**L1 Adapted Reading and Note Taking Study Guide** Note Taking Study Guide, pp. 152–153 SN Section 3 Summary, p. 154 SN **L2 Adapted Reading and Note Taking Study Guide** Note Taking Study Guide, pp. 152–153 LPR Section 3 Summary, p. 154 LPR **L4 All in One Teaching Resources, Unit 4** Primary Source: Kaethe Kollwitz's War Diary, p. 10 AR, GT	**Differentiated Instruction Activity,** Teacher's Edition, p. 468 SN **Spanish Reading and Note Taking Study Guide** Note Taking Study Guide, pp. 152–153 ELL Section 3 Summary, p. 154 ELL **Differentiated Instruction Activity,** Teacher's Edition, p. 468 LPR, ELL **Differentiated Instruction Activity,** Teacher's Edition, p. 470 AR, GT **Extend Activity,** Teacher's Edition, pp. 452c, 471 AR, GT
Section 4 *Making the Peace* 🕐 **1.5 periods, .75 block** **OBJECTIVES** ■ Analyze the costs of World War I. ■ Describe the issues faced by the delegates to the Paris Peace Conference. ■ Explain why many people were dissatisfied with the Treaty of Versailles and other peace settlements. **Focus Question** *What factors influenced the peace treaties that ended World War I, and how did people react to them?*	**All in One Teaching Resources, Unit 4** Section 4 Quiz, p. 5 **Reading and Note Taking Study Guide** Note Taking Study Guide, p. 155 Section 4 Summary, p. 156 **Note Taking Transparencies,** 172A–172B **WITNESS HISTORY Audio CD** Worth the Cost? **Progress Monitoring Transparencies,** 111	**L1 Adapted Reading and Note Taking Study Guide** Note Taking Study Guide, p. 155 SN Section 4 Summary, p. 156 SN **L2 Adapted Reading and Note Taking Study Guide** Note Taking Study Guide, p. 155 LPR Section 4 Summary, p. 156 LPR **L4 All in One Teaching Resources, Unit 4** Link to Literature: From "Pale Horse, Pale Rider," by Katharine Anne Porter, p. 12 AR, GT Biography: Woodrow Wilson, p. 9 AR, GT	**Differentiated Instruction Activity,** Teacher's Edition, p. 473 SN **Spanish Reading and Note Taking Study Guide** Note Taking Study Guide, p. 155 ELL Section 4 Summary, p. 156 ELL **Differentiated Instruction Activity,** Teacher's Edition, p. 473 LPR, ELL **Simulation: Paris Peace Conference,** pp. 86–89 AR, GT **Differentiated Instruction Activity,** Teacher's Edition, p. 475 AR, GT **Extend Activity,** Teacher's Edition, p. 476 AR, GT
Section 5 *Revolution and Civil War in Russia* 🕐 **1.5 periods, .75 block** **OBJECTIVES** ■ Explain the causes of the March Revolution. ■ Describe the goals of Lenin and the Bolsheviks in the November Revolution. ■ Outline how the Communists defeated their opponents in Russia's civil war. ■ Analyze how the Communist state developed under Lenin. **Focus Question** *How did two revolutions and a civil war bring about Communist control of Russia?*	**All in One Teaching Resources, Unit 4** Section 5 Quiz, p. 6 **Reading and Note Taking Study Guide** Note Taking Study Guide, p. 157 Section 5 Summary, p. 158 Concept Connector, pp. 237, 242, 291 **Note Taking Transparencies,** 173 **WITNESS HISTORY Audio CD** Voices From the Front **Progress Monitoring Transparencies,** 112 **Color Transparencies,** 161 **Witness History Discovery School™** video program, *The Fall of the Tsar*	**L1 Adapted Reading and Note Taking Study Guide** Note Taking Study Guide, p. 157 SN Section 5 Summary, p. 158 SN **L2 Adapted Reading and Note Taking Study Guide** Note Taking Study Guide, p. 157 LPR Section 5 Summary, p. 158 LPR Concept Connector, pp. 237, 242, 291 LPR **L4 Differentiated Instruction Activity,** Teacher's Edition, p. 478 AR, GT	**Concept Connector,** pp. 237, 242, 291 SN **Differentiated Instruction Activity,** Teacher's Edition, pp. 480, 482 SN **Spanish Reading and Note Taking Study Guide** Note Taking Study Guide, p. 157 ELL Section 5 Summary, p. 158 ELL Concept Connector, pp. 237, 242, 291 ELL **Differentiated Instruction Activity,** Teacher's Edition, pp. 480, 482 LPR, ELL **Extend Activity,** Teacher's Edition, p. 483 AR, GT

Author's Notes

Total War

The great fact about the war was that it involved national commitment to an extent seldom even approached before. To keep millions of men fed, clothed, armed, and supplied with munitions sufficient for four years of firing at each other over hundreds of miles of front lines required an unparalleled effort by the populations involved. World War I thus became the first total war in history.

Total war meant a total national commitment to, and involvement in, the great struggle. Governments took control of national economies as they had never dared do in peacetime. Government boards allocated raw materials, controlled transportation, regulated wages and prices, rationed food and other essentials. All able-bodied males were liable for conscription into the armed services.

Many women went into the war plants to produce the shells and guns their husbands and sons would use. Almost a million English women worked in munitions factories, and well over half a million French women. Others replaced men drafted for the war in other factories, on farms, as railway conductors, as milk deliverers, and in many other jobs.

New taxes, war loans, and a massive increase in the national debt of the warring countries were additional costs. A continual drain of food, fuel, clothing, and other essentials from the home front also resulted. Russians froze through icy northern winters, Germans went hungry, Austrians starved. Total war thus ravaged European economies even as it strengthened European governments.

This total mobilization of all the resources of great modern states was in its way as striking a feature of the Great War as the raking machine-gun fire and billowing clouds of mustard gas that turned European battlefields into no-man's-lands. And it would leave as long a legacy in battered European economies and in governments with newfound powers.

"World War I," one historian of the great debacle has written, "was really a vast global enterprise—Europe became an enormous cauldron into which men and resources from Asia, Africa, and America were poured."

—Anthony Esler, *The Human Venture*, (Upper Saddle River, New Jersey: Pearson Education 2004) pp. 605–606.

Extend Online

Propaganda Posters

Have students analyze propaganda posters from World War I. Ask them to compare posters from different nations and choose one poster to present to the class. Use the steps below to help students complete the activity.

Prepare for the Activity
Explain that each nation that fought in World War I used propaganda posters to influence public opinion. Governments aimed posters both at their own citizens to justify the war and at their enemy to instill fear. Some, like the one to the left, recruited men to enlist. Others promoted patriotism and self-sacrifice or raised resources.

Conduct the Activity For help in starting the activity, send students to **Web Code nbe-2601.** Students will view propaganda posters from France, Germany, Italy, Russia, Australia, Britain, and the United States. Have them note the similarities and differences in the images chosen by the various countries. After they view the posters, have them choose one and present it to the class. Be sure that students explain who the poster is aimed at, what the message is, and what techniques the poster uses to influence viewers.

Follow-Up Conduct a class discussion based on the following questions: What aspects of war are reflected in propaganda? What techniques do governments use to persuade people in wartime? What technique is most effective? Do you think you would be influenced by these posters?

Question-and-Answer Relationship L2

Understanding what a question is asking for will help students craft better answers. Explain the different types of questions below.

1. Right There— questions with answers that are found explicitly in one or two sentences in the book.

2. Think and Search— questions with answers that are found in several different paragraphs in the book.

3. Author and You— questions with answers that are not found directly in the book, but require you to think about what you've read.

4. On Your Own— questions with answers that are not found directly in the book and which you can answer out of your own knowledge.

Mapping Word Definitions L2

To help students learn unfamiliar words, introduce them to the strategy of mapping word definitions. Research shows this technique helps students develop the ability to investigate word meanings independently and provide elaborated definitions (as opposed to simple one- or two-word definitions).

Model mapping word definitions by using the following steps for the high-use word *withdrawal*, which can be found in context in Section 5.

■ Define the word in their own words—*the act of leaving*
■ Provide a synonym or example—*retreat, no longer taking part in something*
■ Use the word in a sentence—*Because half of the players were ill, the coach announced the team's withdrawal from the state championships.*
■ Provide a non-example—*return*

Modeling Reading and Writing Skills

Choosing an Organization Explain that in this chapter students will be writing a cause-and-effect essay. (See Writing About History, p. 486.) Point out that this type of essay requires a clear, consistent organization that makes it easy to follow the connections among events. Write these common ways of organizing on the board.

A Chronological Order
B Order of Importance

Explain that in chronological order, events are presented in sequence. In order of importance, events are presented in the order of their relative importance. Chronological order is effective when presenting a cause-and-effect chain, while order of importance is effective when presenting a series of causes of a single event. Help students match the types of organization with the following topics:

1. The events leading to World War I

2. The multiple effects of World War I

3. The multiple causes of the March Revolution

4. The events of Russia's Civil War
(Answers: A1, B2, B3, A4)

Cause and Effect Tell students that recognizing causes and effects helps them to clarify the relationships among events or situations. Point out that noting signal words can help them identify these relationships. Clue words such as *reason, because, produced,* and *purpose* indicate possible causes. Words such as *brought about, effect, led to, outcome, produced, reaction, result, so, then, therefore,* and *this* indicate possible effects.

Model how to identify cause-and-effect relationships by reading aloud the first sentence under *The Tsar Steps Down* in Section 5. Draw students' attention to the word *brought* and point out that this word signals an effect. The effect is the collapse of the monarchy. The cause of this collapse is the disasters on the battlefield and the shortages on the home front.

Teach With Technology
PresentationEXPRESS™
Premium DVD

- Teach this chapter's core content using **PresentationExpress™ Premium,** which includes dynamic lecture notes, interactive game shows, songs, videos, and the *ExamView® QuickTake* assessment tool.

- To introduce this chapter using **PresentationExpress™ Premium,** start by asking students **Which of the following statements do you most agree with: (A) War should be avoided at all costs. (B) War should be fought only to save innocent lives. (C) War is a noble pursuit. (D) War should be used to gain territory and increase power.** Take a class poll or record students' answers using the QuickTake feature and discuss their responses. Point out that in this chapter, they will read about the reasons why countries fought in World War I. Continue introducing the chapter using the chapter opener slide show and Witness History audio.

Technology Resources

- Student**EXPRESS** CD-ROM, Chapter 14
- Teacher**EXPRESS** CD-ROM, Chapter 14
- Presentation**EXPRESS™** **Premium DVD,** Chapter 14
- **WITNESS HISTORY** **Audio CD,** Chapter 14
- *ExamView* **Test Bank CD-ROM,** English and Spanish, Chapter 14
- **Guided Reading Audio,** Spanish, Chapter 14
- **Student Edition Audio,** Chapter 14
- **Witness History Discovery School**™ video program, *World War I: A New Kind of War* and *The Fall of the Tsar*
- **Experience It! Multimedia Pack**

14 World War I and the Russian Revolution
1914–1924

Bibliography

For the Teacher

Keegan, John. *The First World War.* Vintage Books, 2000.

MacMillan, Margaret. *Paris 1919.* Random House, 2003.

Tuchman, Barbara W. *The Guns of August.* Ballantine Books, 1994. First published 1962.

For the Student

L2 Cooper, Michael L. *Hell Fighters: African American Soldiers in World War I.* Lodestar Books, 1997.

L3 Wallas, Sarah and Svetlana Palmer, eds. *Intimate Voices from the First World War.* HarperCollins, 2004.

L4 Reed, John. *Ten Days That Shook the World.* Tantallon Press, 2002. First published 1919.

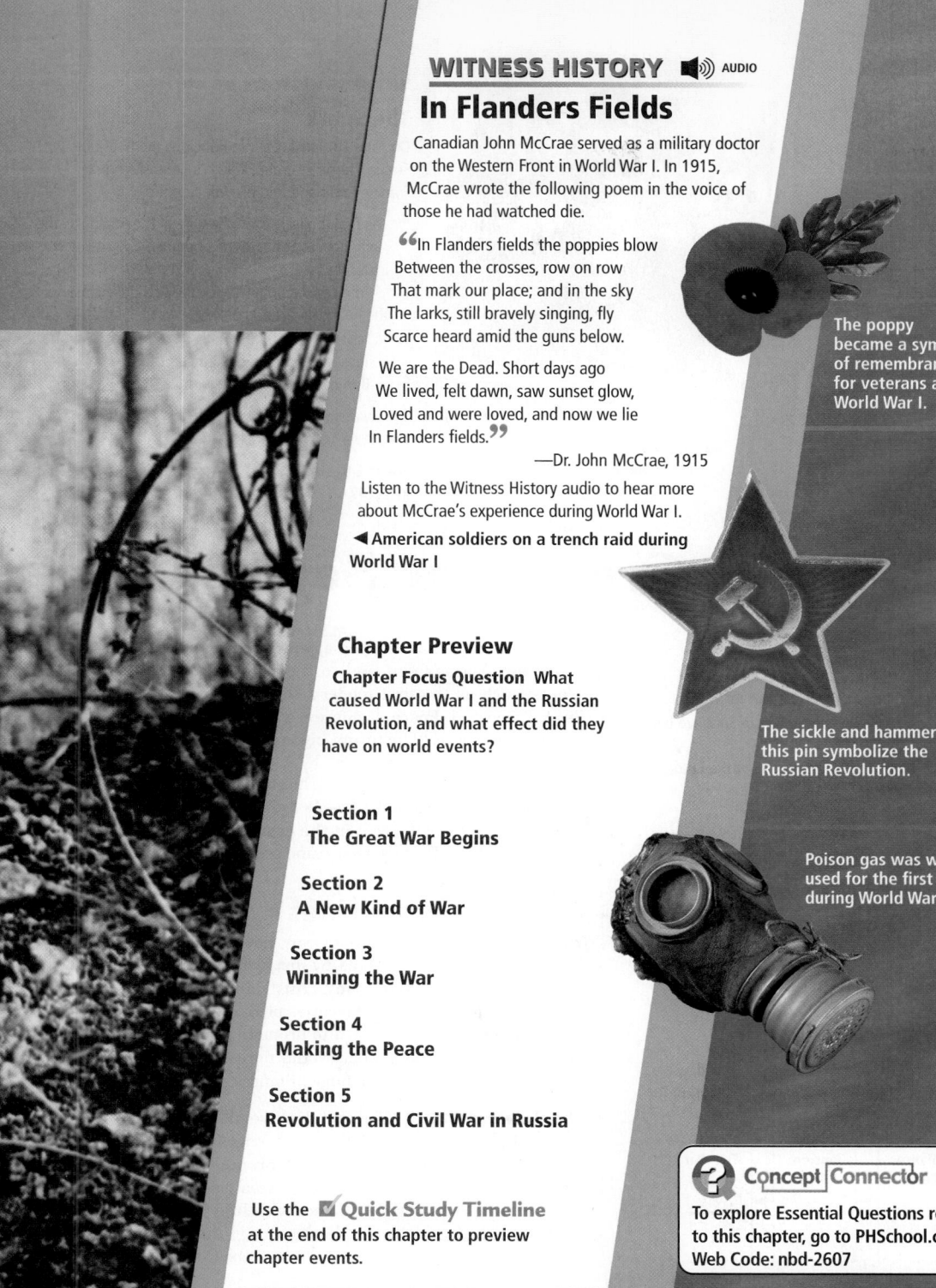

In Flanders Fields

Canadian John McCrae served as a military doctor on the Western Front in World War I. In 1915, McCrae wrote the following poem in the voice of those he had watched die.

❝In Flanders fields the poppies blow
Between the crosses, row on row
That mark our place; and in the sky
The larks, still bravely singing, fly
Scarce heard amid the guns below.

We are the Dead. Short days ago
We lived, felt dawn, saw sunset glow,
Loved and were loved, and now we lie
In Flanders fields.❞

—Dr. John McCrae, 1915

Listen to the Witness History audio to hear more about McCrae's experience during World War I.

◀ **American soldiers on a trench raid during World War I**

The poppy became a symbol of remembrance for veterans after World War I.

The sickle and hammer on this pin symbolize the Russian Revolution.

Poison gas was widely used for the first time during World War I.

Chapter Preview

Chapter Focus Question What caused World War I and the Russian Revolution, and what effect did they have on world events?

Section 1
The Great War Begins

Section 2
A New Kind of War

Section 3
Winning the War

Section 4
Making the Peace

Section 5
Revolution and Civil War in Russia

Use the ☑ **Quick Study Timeline** at the end of this chapter to preview chapter events.

? Concept Connector ONLINE

To explore Essential Questions related to this chapter, go to PHSchool.com
Web Code: nbd-2607

Chapter-Level Resources

All in One Vocabulary Builder; Reading Strategy; Enrichment; Outline Maps; Geography Quiz; Chapter Tests
- Document-Based Assessments
- AYP Monitoring Assessments
- *ExamView* Test Bank CD-ROM
- Guided Reading Audio (Spanish)
- Student Edition Audio

Previewing the Chapter

- **WITNESS HISTORY** Point out that Flanders is a region in northern Belgium where many devastating World War I battles were fought. John McCrae was a Canadian doctor who treated the wounded fresh from the battlefield. After burying a friend, he wrote the poem "In Flanders Fields." Read the Witness History selection aloud or play the accompanying audio. Ask students to list words that came to mind as they listened to the selection. Tell them that they will learn more about World War I and the people who fought and died in it in this chapter.

◀)) AUDIO **Witness History Audio CD,** In Flanders Field

- **Analyzing the Visuals** Ask students to study the photo of the American soldiers on a trench raid. Ask **What questions do the photo and the Witness History selection bring to mind?** *(Examples: What effects did the trenches and trench raids like these have on the war effort? Was World War I more deadly than previous wars?)* Write down their questions. Tell students you are keeping a copy of these questions so that they can go back and answer them after they have read the chapter.

- **Focus** Write the Chapter Focus Question on the board. Tell students to keep this question in mind as they read the chapter. *(Answer appears with Chapter Assessment answers.)* Have students preview the section titles for this chapter.

The following Teacher's Edition strategies are suitable for students of varying abilities.

L1 Special Needs Students, pp. 455, 463, 468, 473, 480, 482 **SN**

L2 English Language Learners, pp. 455, 463, 468, 473, 480, 482 **ELL**

L2 Less Proficient Readers, pp. 455, 463, 468, 473, 480, 482 **LPR**

L4 Gifted and Talented Students, pp. 456, 470, 475, 478 **GT**

L4 Advanced Readers, pp. 456, 470, 475, 478 **AR**

Note Taking Study Guide With Concept Connector Journal
For online access: Web code nbd-2607
For print alternative: Reading and Note Taking Study Guide booklet

Objectives

As you teach this section, keep students focused on the following objectives to help them answer the Section Focus Question and master core content.

■ Describe how international rivalries and nationalism pushed Europe toward war.

■ Explain how the assassination in Sarajevo led to the start of World War I.

■ Analyze the causes and effects of the European alliance system.

Prepare to Read

Build Background Knowledge Ⓛ3

Ask students to think about how European nationalism in the 1800s strengthened some countries, but weakened large empires. Have them predict how this situation might lead to problems in the early 1900s.

Set a Purpose Ⓛ3

■ **WITNESS HISTORY** Read the selection aloud or play the audio.
  🔊 AUDIO **Witness History Audio CD,** The Spark

  Ask **Who killed the Archduke and his wife?** *(Gavrilo Princip)* **Why might Princip have done this?** *(Sample: to make a statement about Serbian nationalism)* Tell students that they will learn more about the causes and consequences of the assassination as they read this section.

■ **Focus** Point out the Section Focus Question and write it on the board. Tell students to refer to this question as they read. *(Answer appears with Section 1 Assessment answers.)*

■ **Preview** Have students preview the Section Objectives and the list of Terms, People, and Places.

■ **Reading Skill** Have students use the *Reading Strategy: Summarize* worksheet.

All in One Teaching Resources, Unit 4, p. 8

▲ The assassin, Gavrilo Princip

◀ Austrian Archduke Francis Ferdinand and his wife Sophie

The Spark

On June 28, 1914, Gavrilo Princip, a member of a Serbian terrorist group, killed Austrian Archduke Francis Ferdinand and his wife Sophie.

❝ The first [bullet] struck the wife of the Archduke, the Archduchess Sofia, in the abdomen. . . . She died instantly.

    The second bullet struck the Archduke close to the heart. He uttered only one word, 'Sofia'—a call to his stricken wife. Then his head fell back and he collapsed. He died almost instantly. ❞
—Borijove Jevtic, co-conspirator

The assassinations triggered World War I, called "The Great War" by people at the time.

Focus Question Why and how did World War I begin in 1914?

The Great War Begins

Objectives
• Describe how international rivalries and nationalism pushed Europe toward war.
• Explain how the assassination in Sarajevo led to the start of World War I.
• Analyze the causes and effects of the European alliance system.

Terms, People, and Places

entente	ultimatum
militarism	mobilize
Alsace and Lorraine	neutrality

Note Taking

Reading Skill: Summarize As you read, use a chart to summarize the events that led up to the outbreak of World War I.

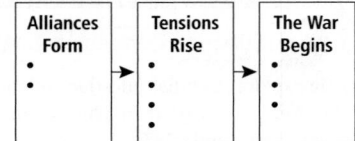

By 1914, Europe had enjoyed a century of relative peace. Idealists hoped for a permanent end to the scourge of war. International events, such as the first modern Olympic games in 1896 and the First Universal Peace Conference in 1899, were steps toward keeping the peace. "The future belongs to peace," said French economist Frédéric Passy (pa SEE).

Not everyone was so hopeful. "I shall not live to see the Great War," warned German Chancellor Otto von Bismarck, "but you will see it, and it will start in the east." It was Bismarck's prediction, rather than Passy's, that came true.

Alliances Draw Lines

While peace efforts were under way, powerful forces were pushing Europe towards war. Spurred by distrust of one another, the great powers of Europe—Germany, Austria-Hungary, Italy, Britain, France, and Russia—signed treaties pledging to defend one another. These alliances were intended to promote peace by creating powerful combinations that no one would dare attack. In the end, they had the opposite effect. Two huge alliances emerged.

The Triple Alliance The first of these alliances had its origins in Bismarck's day. He knew that France longed to avenge its defeat in the Franco-Prussian War. Sure that France would not attack Germany without help, Bismarck signed treaties with other powers. In 1882, he formed the Triple Alliance with Italy and Austria-Hungary. In 1914, when war did erupt, Germany and Austria-Hungary fought on the same side. They became known as the Central Powers.

Vocabulary Builder

Use the information below and the following resources to teach the high-use words from this section.
All in One Teaching Resources, Unit 4, p. 7; Teaching Resources, Skills Handbook, p. 3

High-Use Words	Definitions and Sample Sentences
status, p. 455	*n.* high standing or prestige The challenging team threatened our team's **status** as basketball champions.
overseas, p. 456	*adj.* across the sea, foreign Monica was hoping for **overseas** travel in her new job so she could learn about far-off cultures.

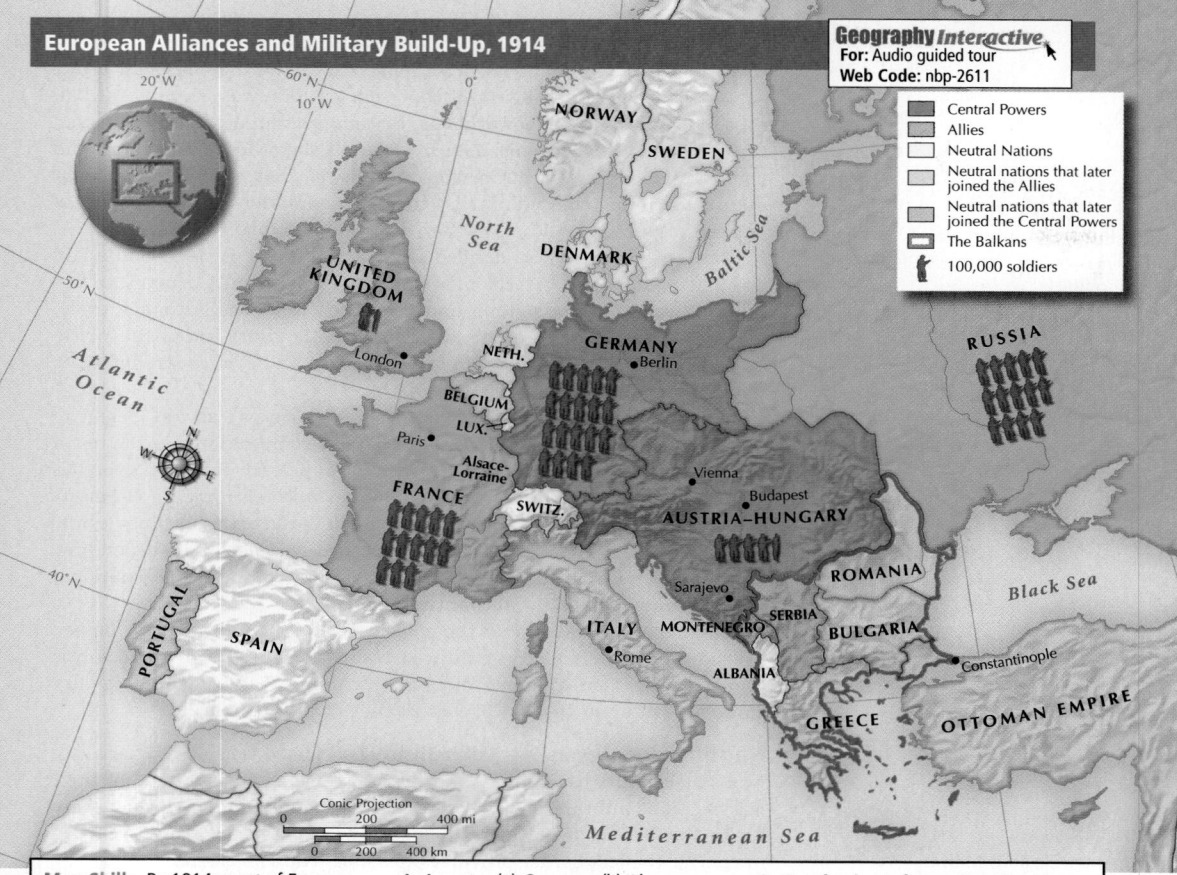

European Alliances and Military Build-Up, 1914

Geography *Interactive*
For: Audio guided tour
Web Code: nbp-2611

Legend:
- Central Powers
- Allies
- Neutral Nations
- Neutral nations that later joined the Allies
- Neutral nations that later joined the Central Powers
- The Balkans
- 100,000 soldiers

Map Skills By 1914, most of Europe was divided into two armed camps, the Allies and the Central Powers. Millions of troops stood ready for war.

1. **Locate** (a) Germany (b) Alsace-Lorraine (c) the Balkans (d) Serbia
2. **Regions** Why would Germans worry about the alliance between France and Russia?
3. **Synthesize Information** Based on the information on the map, which alliance do you think had the greater military advantage in 1914?

The Triple Entente A rival bloc took shape in 1893, when France and Russia formed an alliance. In 1904, France and Britain signed an **entente** (ahn TAHNT), a nonbinding agreement to follow common policies. Though not as formal as a treaty, the entente led to close military and diplomatic ties. Britain later signed a similar agreement with Russia. When war began, these powers became known as the Allies.

Other alliances also formed. Germany signed a treaty with the Ottoman empire. Britain drew close to Japan.

✔ **Checkpoint** What two large alliances took shape before the beginning of World War I?

Rivalries and Nationalism Increase Tension

The European powers jealously guarded their status. They competed for position in many areas. Two old empires, Austria-Hungary and Ottoman Turkey, struggled to survive in an age of nationalism.

Vocabulary Builder

status—(STAT us) *n.* high standing, rank, or prestige

Differentiated **Instruction** Solutions for All Learners

L1 Special Needs **L2 Less Proficient Readers**

To reinforce the concept of alliances, ask students to suppose they came across two groups of classmates involved in a fight. Each group asks them to join their side. Ask students the pros and cons of staying out of the fight. What are the the pros and cons of getting involved? How would they decide who to help? Then, have students compare and contrast their responses with the chart entitled "Reasons for Entering the War."

L2 English Language Learners

Use the following resources to help students acquire basic skills.

 **Adapted Reading and Note Taking Study Guide**

- Adapted Note Taking Study Guide, p. 148
- Adapted Section Summary, p. 149

■ **Note Taking** Have students read this section using the Structured Read Aloud strategy (TE, p. T20). As they read, have students fill in the chart summarizing the sequence of events leading to the start of World War I.

Reading and Note Taking Study Guide, p. 148

Teach

Alliances Draw Lines

L3

Instruct

- **Introduce: Key Terms** Draw students' attention to the key term *entente* (in blue) in the text. Explain that an entente is a type of alliance. Ask students to brainstorm why countries might form alliances.

- **Teach** Ask students to make a quick list of the countries in the Triple Alliance and the countries in the Triple Entente. Ask **Why did Germany form alliances with Italy and Austria-Hungary?** *(to protect itself against a potential attack by France and/or Russia)*

- **Quick Activity** Have students access **Web Code nbp-2611** to take the **Geography Interactive Audio Guided Tour** and then answer the map skills questions in the text.

Independent Practice

Have students fill in the Outline Map *Allies and Central Powers* and use a map key to identify the different alliances.

All in One **Teaching Resources, Unit 4, p. 15**

Monitor Progress

Circulate to make sure students are accurately filling in their Outline Maps.

Answers

Map Skills
1. Review locations with students.
2. France and Russia bordered Germany on two sides and could attack it from each direction.
3. The Allies appear to have a greater advantage. They have more troop strength and surrounded the major Central Powers.

✔ the Triple Alliance, made up of Germany, Italy, and Austria-Hungary; and the Triple Entente, made up of France, Britain, and Russia

Rivalries and Nationalism Increase Tension ⑬

Instruct

- **Introduce: Vocabulary Builder**
  Have students read the Vocabulary Builder terms and definitions. Then ask students to read the first three sentences under the heading Rivalries and Nationalism Increase Tension and the black headings underneath it. Ask students to predict why ***status*** might be important to Europe's great powers. How would ***overseas*** colonies affect their status?

- **Teach** Ask **How did Germany feel about the other great powers?** *(Germany felt that it was not respected enough by the other nations.)* **How did other great powers feel about Germany?** *(Britain feared Germany's economic potential and resented Germany' challenge to its navy; France was embittered towards Germany after it lost the Franco-Prussian War and the provinces of Alsace and Lorraine.)*

- **Quick Activity** Have students explain one effect of each of the following developments: (1) The French were defeated in the Franco-Prussian War and lost Alsace and Lorraine to Germany. (2) Russia felt kinship with other Slavic countries. (3) There was rising nationalism in Austria-Hungary and the Ottoman empire. (4) Germany gained territory as a result of the Moroccan crises. (5) Countries joined together in alliances.

Independent Practice

Break students into groups and assign them one of the following countries or empires: Britain, France, Germany, Russia, the Ottoman empire, Austria-Hungary, Serbia. Ask each group to write a few paragraphs describing the position of their country or countries on the eve of World War I. Then have each group present their position to the class.

Monitor Progress

As students fill in their charts, circulate to make sure they understand the events that led to World War I. For a completed version of the chart, see

📖 **Note Taking Transparencies,** 169

Answer

Caption by watching the parade, saluting the soldiers on horseback, and waving hats and handkerchiefs

Vocabulary Builder

overseas—(OH vur SEEZ) *adj.* across the sea; foreign

Germany's Glorious Military
Eager crowds watch a cavalry regiment, or group of troops serving on horseback, ride through Berlin in August 1914. Germany's army was known to be highly trained and well disciplined, making it a formidable fighting force. *How are the people pictured showing pride in their military?*

Competition Economic rivalries helped sour the international atmosphere. Germany, the newest of the great powers, was growing into an economic and military powerhouse. Britain felt threatened by its rapid economic growth. Germany, in turn, thought the other great powers did not give it enough respect. Germany also feared that when Russia caught up to other industrialized nations, its huge population and vast supply of natural resources would make it an unbeatable competitor.

Overseas rivalries also divided European nations. In 1905 and again in 1911, competition for colonies brought France and Germany to the brink of war in Morocco, then under France's influence. Although diplomats kept the peace, Germany did gain some territory in central Africa. As a result of the two Moroccan crises, Britain and France strengthened their ties against Germany.

With international tensions on the rise, the great powers began to build up their armies and navies. The fiercest competition was the naval rivalry between Britain and Germany. To protect its vast overseas empire, Britain had built the world's most respected navy. As Germany began acquiring overseas colonies, it began to build up its own navy. Suspicious of Germany's motives, Britain in turn increased naval spending. Sensational journalism dramatized the arms race and stirred national public opinion against rival countries.

The rise of **militarism,** or the glorification of the military, also helped to feed the arms race. The militarist tradition painted war in romantic colors. Young men dreamed of blaring trumpets and dashing cavalry charges—not at all the sort of conflict they would soon face.

Nationalism Aggressive nationalism also caused tension. Nationalism was strong in both Germany and France. Germans were proud of their new empire's military power and industrial leadership. The French were bitter about their 1871 defeat in the Franco-Prussian War and yearned to recover the lost border province of **Alsace and Lorraine.**

In Eastern Europe, Russia sponsored a powerful form of nationalism called Pan-Slavism. It held that all Slavic peoples shared a common nationality. As the largest Slavic country, Russia felt that it had a duty to lead and defend all Slavs. By 1914, it stood ready to support Serbia, a proud young nation that dreamed of creating a South Slav state.

Differentiated Instruction   Solutions for All Learners

L4 Advanced Readers   L4 Gifted and Talented Students

To help students recognize bias, read aloud the following headline from the New York *Sun,* written the day after the assassination: "Death of Francis Ferdinand Makes for Peace of Europe." The correspondent who wrote the headline believed that Europe would be more peaceful without the archduke, whose ideas on some issues had led to tension in the past. Assign students to write four additional headlines about the assassination of Archduke Francis Ferdinand and his wife, each from a separate country somehow involved in World War I. Remind students that before writing each headline, they should take into account the political viewpoints and biases that each newspaper might have had. Then have students display their headlines, and invite other students to identify and explain any biases that they see in each headline.

Two old multinational empires particularly feared rising nationalism. Austria-Hungary worried that nationalism might foster rebellion among the many minority populations within its empire. Ottoman Turkey felt threatened by nearby new nations, such as Serbia. If realized, Serbia's dream of a South Slav state could take territory away from both Austria-Hungary and Turkey.

In 1912, several Balkan states attacked Turkey and succeeded in taking a large area of land away from Turkish control. The next year, the Balkan states fought among themselves over the spoils of war. These brief but bloody Balkan wars raised tensions to a fever pitch. By 1914, the Balkans were called the "powder keg of Europe"—a barrel of gunpowder that a tiny spark might cause to explode.

✓ **Checkpoint** How did international competition and nationalism increase tensions in Europe?

The Powder Keg Ignites

As Bismarck had predicted, the Great War began in Eastern Europe. A regional conflict between tiny Serbia and the huge empire of Austria-Hungary grew rapidly into a general war.

Assassination in Sarajevo The crisis began when Archduke Francis Ferdinand of Austria-Hungary announced that he would visit Sarajevo (sa ruh YAY voh), the capital of Bosnia. Francis Ferdinand was the nephew and heir of the aging Austrian emperor, Francis Joseph. At the time of his visit, Bosnia was under the rule of Austria-Hungary. But it was also the home of many Serbs and other Slavs. News of the royal visit angered many Serbian nationalists. They viewed the Austrians as foreign oppressors. Some members of Unity or Death, a Serbian terrorist group commonly known as the Black Hand, vowed to take action.

The archduke ignored warnings of anti-Austrian unrest in Sarajevo. On June 28, 1914, he and his wife, Sophie, rode through Sarajevo in an open car. As the car passed by, a conspirator named Gavrilo Princip (GAV ree loh PREEN tseep) seized his chance and fired twice into the car. Moments later, the archduke and his wife were dead.

Austria Strikes Back The news of the assassination shocked Francis Joseph. Still, he was reluctant to go to war. The government in Vienna, however, saw the incident as an excuse to crush Serbia. In Berlin, Kaiser William II was horrified at the assassination of his ally's heir. He wrote to Francis Joseph, advising him to take a firm stand toward Serbia. Instead of urging restraint, Germany gave Austria a "blank check," or a promise of unconditional support no matter what the cost.

Austria sent Serbia a sweeping **ultimatum,** or final set of demands. To avoid war, said the ultimatum, Serbia must end all anti-Austrian agitation and punish any Serbian official involved in the murder plot. It must even let Austria join in the investigation. Serbia agreed to most, but not all, of the terms of Austria's ultimatum. This partial refusal gave Austria the opportunity it was seeking. On July 28, 1914, Austria declared war on Serbia.

✓ **Checkpoint** What happened because of the assassination of Francis Ferdinand and his wife?

History Background

What's in a Day? The date chosen for the Archduke Francis Ferdinand's visit to Sarajevo, June 28, was a special date in Serbian history. It was on that date in 1389 that Serbia had been conquered by the Ottoman empire. On the very same date in 1912, Serbia had at last freed itself from Turkish rule.

Serbian nationalists believed that Austria-Hungary's control of Bosnia oppressed the Slavs who lived there. The decision to visit Bosnia's capital on this day of all days inflamed the nationalists.

The date was also special to Francis Ferdinand and Sophie—it was their anniversary.

The Powder Keg Ignites

Instruct

■ **Introduce** Ask students to preview the black headings. Then have them predict why the emperor of Austria might have been hesitant to provoke a war with Serbia.

■ **Teach** Ask **Why did Austrian leaders send Serbia an ultimatum that they knew Serbian leaders would refuse to honor?** (They wanted to provoke a war in order to crush Serbia so it could not longer threaten the Austria-Hungarian empire.) **How did Germany encourage Austria's actions?** (Germany backed up Austria with a "blank check," giving the Austrian leaders more confidence in their course of action.)

■ **Quick Activity** Remind students that Austria-Hungary was the first party to declare war in what became World War I. Then tell students that many people later placed much of the blame for starting the war on Germany, not Austria-Hungary. As a class, brainstorm the arguments people might have used to blame Germany.

Independent Practice

Remind students of the Witness History in the beginning of the section. Have them write a brief paragraph explaining why Princip killed the Archduke and his wife. Ensure that they understand the long-term causes of the assassination.

Monitor Progress

To review this section, ask students to explain at what point they think war became inevitable. Ask them to list what actions either Austria or Serbia could have taken to avoid war.

Answers

BIOGRAPHY His desire for respect may have driven him to build up the German military, to win colonies, and to best the other European powers economically.

✓ Economic competition, imperial rivalries, and an arms race created antagonism between great powers. Nationalism contributed to the situation, and it threatened central authority in Austria-Hungary and the Ottoman empire.

✓ Austria blamed Serbia for the assassination and took the opportunity to attack Serbia. Germany backed Austria.

Alliances Kick In/Reaction to the War ⓛ③

Instruct

- **Introduce: Key Terms** Ask students to find the key term *mobilize* (in blue) in the text and explain its meaning. Remind students that Russia is the largest country in the alliance system. Have them speculate as to why Russia might mobilize its troops early. What is the drawback to this plan?

- **Teach** Austria's declaration of war on Serbia kicked off a chain reaction of events. Using the Idea Wave strategy (TE, p. T22), have students briefly note each event in the chain. Ask **How was France drawn into the war?** *(France supported its ally, Russia, and Germany demanded that France keep out of the conflict.)* **Why did Britain declare war?** *(Britain had an agreement guaranteeing Belgian neutrality. Britain declared war after Germany invaded Belgium on the way to France.)*

- **Quick Activity** Display **Color Transparency 157: The Schlieffen Plan.** Review the map with students. Use the lesson suggested in the transparency book to guide a discussion on the causes and consequences of the Schlieffen Plan.
  - 🏛 **Color Transparencies,** 157

Independent Practice

Have students study the political cartoon on this page. Tell them that leaders emphasized that their countries were fighting on the side of justice, and so could not be blamed for starting the war. Ask students to return to the groups with whom they wrote their position papers. Have them discuss how their assigned country or region might have spun events to avoid blame. Then have them amend their papers to include the start of the war.

Monitor Progress

- Make sure students understand the position of their country or region. If a group is having difficulty, direct them to the chart on this page.

- Check Reading and Note Taking Study Guide entries to ensure students understand the causes of World War I.

Answer

Chart Skills Russians might feel that Germany started the war because of their support of Austria-Hungary and eventual invasion of Belgium, which was a neutral country.

Reasons for Entering the War, July–August 1914

Country	Allied With	Reasons for Entering War
Austria-Hungary	Germany	Wanted to punish Serbia for encouraging terrorism
Germany	Austria-Hungary	Stood by its one dependable ally, Austria-Hungary
Serbia	Russia	Attacked by Austria-Hungary after assassination of Archduke
Russia	Serbia, France, Britain	Wanted to defend Slavic peoples in Serbia
France	Russia and Britain	Wanted to avoid facing Germany alone at a later date
Belgium	Neutral	Invaded by Germany
Britain	France and Russia	Outraged by invasion of Belgium

Chart Skills Who started the war? During the war, each side blamed the other. Afterward, the victorious Allies placed all blame on Germany, because it invaded Belgium. Today, historians still debate who should bear the blame for a catastrophe nobody wanted. **Using information from the chart, describe why Russians might feel that Germany started the war.**

Alliances Kick In

The war between Austria and Serbia might have been another "summer war," like most European wars of the previous century. However, the carefully planned alliances soon drew the great powers deeper into conflict.

Russia and France Back Serbia After Austria's declaration of war, Serbia turned to its ally, Russia, the champion of Slavic nations. From St. Petersburg, Nicholas II telegraphed William II. The tsar asked the kaiser to urge Austria to soften its demands. When this plea failed, Russia began to **mobilize,** or prepare its military forces for war. On August 1, Germany responded by declaring war on Russia.

Russia, in turn, appealed to its ally France. In Paris, nationalists saw a chance to avenge France's defeat in the Franco-Prussian War. Though French leaders had some doubts, they gave Russia the same kind of backing Germany offered to Austria. When Germany demanded that France keep out of the conflict, France refused. Germany then declared war on France.

Germany Invades Belgium By early August, the battle lines were hardening. Italy and Britain still remained uncommitted. Italy chose to stay neutral for the time being. **Neutrality** is a policy of supporting neither side in a war. Britain had to decide quickly whether or not to support its ally France. Then, Germany's war plans suddenly made the decision for Britain.

A cornerstone of Germany's military policy was a plan developed years earlier by General Alfred von Schlieffen (SHLEE fun). Germany's location presented the possibility of a two-front war—against France in the west and Russia to the east. The Schlieffen Plan was designed to avoid this problem. Schlieffen reasoned that Germany should move against France first because Russia's lumbering military would be slow to mobilize.

History Background

The War-Guilt Question Ever since the Treaty of Versailles forced Germany and its allies to accept responsibility for starting World War I, there has been continued debate as to who should bear this blame.

Scholarship moved away from blaming Germany in the 1920s and 1930s. Instead, it blamed the European leaders collectively. Some pointed to such long-term causes as nationalism and the alliance system. Others held that the war was a series of blunders.

In the 1960s, Fritz Fischer and other German historians suggested that German leaders' desire for world power may have been to blame. Fischer studied German war goals and concluded that the government intentionally incited the 1914 crisis. In the 2004 study *Cataclysm,* historian David Stevenson agreed but he also showed that each country could have gained from war and each took a calculated risk in engaging in it. The discussion continues.

However, Germany had to defeat France quickly so that its armies could then turn around and fight Russia.

To ensure a swift victory in the west, the Schlieffen Plan required German armies to march through neutral Belgium and then swing south behind French lines. The goal was to encircle and crush France's army. The Germans embarked on the plan by invading Belgium on August 3. However, Britain and other European powers had signed a treaty guaranteeing Belgian neutrality. Outraged by the invasion of Belgium, Britain declared war on Germany on August 4.

Once the machinery of war was set in motion, it seemed impossible to stop. Military leaders insisted that they must mobilize their forces immediately to accomplish their military goals. These military timetables made it impossible for political leaders to negotiate instead of fight.

✓ **Checkpoint** How did the alliance system deepen the original conflict between Austria-Hungary and Serbia into a general war?

Reaction to the War

Before the war, many countries were troubled by domestic problems. For example, Britain struggled with labor unrest and the issue of home rule in Ireland. Russia wrestled with problems stirred up by the Revolution of 1905. The outbreak of war brought a temporary relief from these internal divisions. A renewed sense of patriotism united countries. Governments on both sides emphasized that their countries were fighting for justice and a better world. Young men rushed to enlist, cheered on by women and their elders. Now that war had come at last, it seemed an exciting adventure.

British diplomat Edward Grey was less optimistic. As armies began to move, he predicted, "The lamps are going out all over Europe. We shall not see them lit again in our lifetime."

✓ **Checkpoint** Why were young men on both sides eager to fight when World War I started?

War Enthusiasm
People cheered as soldiers marched off to war. In this photograph, a woman is giving a soldier an apple to eat on his journey.

Assess and Reteach

Assess Progress
- Have students complete the Section Assessment.
- Administer the Section Quiz.
- [All in One] **Teaching Resources, Unit 4,** p. 2
- To further assess student understanding, use
  🏛 **Progress Monitoring Transparencies,** 108

Reteach
If students need more instruction, have them read the section summary.

 Reading and Note Taking Study Guide, p. 149

 Adapted Reading and Note Taking Study Guide, p. 149

 Spanish Reading and Note Taking Study Guide, p. 149

Extend
Have students debate the following question using evidence from the text: Are certain reasons for entering a war more justifiable than others?

Answers

✓ Alliances drew more and more countries into what began as a regional conflict. Russia stood by its ally, Serbia. France in turn stood by its ally, Russia. Undecided Britain was drawn in when Germany invaded neutral Belgium.

✓ Because of a renewed sense of patriotism, people rushed to fight for their homelands.

SECTION 1 Assessment

Progress Monitoring Online
For: Self-quiz with vocabulary practice
Web Code: nba-2611

Terms, People, and Places
1. For each term or place listed at the beginning of the section, write a sentence explaining its significance.

Note Taking
2. **Reading Skill: Summarize** Use your completed chart to answer the Focus Question: Why and how did World War I begin in 1914?

Comprehension and Critical Thinking
3. **Analyze Information** Why did European nations form alliances?
4. **Identify Central Issues** Why might the Balkans be called the "powder keg of Europe"?
5. **Recognize Causes** How did Austria's government react to the assassination of Archduke Francis Ferdinand?
6. **Determine Relevance** What role did geography play in the outbreak of World War I?

● **Writing About History**
Quick Write: Identify Causes and Effects Choose a specific event from the section and identify one cause and one effect of the event. Ask yourself the following questions:
- Why did this event happen? (cause)
- What happened as a result of this event? (effect)

Record your ideas in a chart that shows their cause-and-effect relationships.

Section 1 Assessment

1. Sentences should reflect an understanding of each term, person, or place listed at the beginning of the section.
2. After a long period of growing antagonism between allied blocs, Europe's great powers were drawn into a regional conflict by the alliances they had formed for protection.
3. to discourage rival countries from attacking them

4. Small nations in the Balkans had nationalistic goals, which threatened the Austria-Hungarian and Ottoman empires. A conflict in the Balkans would quickly spread because of the alliance system.
5. It issued an ultimatum to the Serbian government. When Serbia refused to meet all demands, Austria declared war.
6. Germany's location between France and Russia caused it to follow the Schlieffen

Plan and invade Belgium, which caused Britain to declare war on Germany.

● **Writing About History**
Charts should show an event from the section, such as Germany invading Belgium, with one valid cause and one valid effect.

For additional assessment, have students access **Progress Monitoring Online** at **Web Code nba-2611.**

Objectives

As you teach this section, keep students focused on the following objectives to help them answer the Section Focus Question and master core content.

- Understand why a stalemate developed on the Western Front.
- Describe how technology made World War I different from earlier wars.
- Outline the course of the war on the Eastern Front, in other parts of Europe, in Turkey, and in the Middle East.
- Summarize how colonies fought in the war.

Prepare to Read

Build Background Knowledge L3

Remind students that there had not been a large-scale European war since Napoleon's time. Have them predict how war might have changed since 1815.

Set a Purpose L3

- **WITNESS HISTORY** Read the selection aloud or play the audio.

  🔊 AUDIO **Witness History Audio CD,** A Soldier on the Western Front

  Ask **Why did the soldier find the singing of the birds so touching?** *(The peaceful, ordinary singing of the birds was such a contrast to the death and destruction surrounding him.)*

- **Focus** Point out the Section Focus Question and write it on the board. Tell students to refer to this question as they read. *(Answer appears with Section 2 Assessment answers.)*

- **Preview** Have students preview the Section Objectives and the list of Terms, People, and Places.

- **Note Taking** As they read, have students fill in the chart identifying details about the battlefronts.

  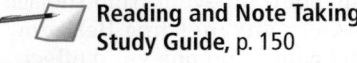 **Reading and Note Taking Study Guide,** p. 150

Answer

✓ Russia mobilized quickly in the east, causing Germany to divert troops there. The British and French stopped the weakened German advance at the Marne.

WITNESS HISTORY 🔊 AUDIO

▼ A wounded German soldier in 1915

A Soldier on the Western Front

❝ The blue French cloth mingled with the German grey upon the ground, and in some places the bodies were piled so high that one could take cover from shell-fire behind them. The noise was so terrific that orders had to be shouted by each man into the ear of the next. And whenever there was a momentary lull in the tumult of battle and the groans of the wounded, one heard, high up in the blue sky, the joyful song of birds! Birds singing just as they do at home in spring-time! It was enough to tear the heart out of one's body! ❞
—German soldier Richard Schmieder, writing from the trenches in France

Focus Question How and where was World War I fought?

World War I artillery shell ▶

A New Kind of War

Objectives
- Understand why a stalemate developed on the Western Front.
- Describe how technology made World War I different from earlier wars.
- Outline the course of the war on the Eastern Front, in other parts of Europe, in Turkey, and in the Middle East.
- Summarize how colonies fought in the war.

Terms, People, and Places
stalemate	convoy
zeppelin	Dardanelles
U-boat	T. E. Lawrence

Note Taking

Reading Skill: Identify Supporting Details Record important details about the various battlefronts of World War I in a flowchart.

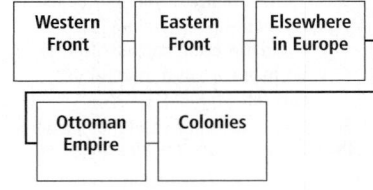

The Great War was the largest conflict in history up to that time. The French mobilized almost 8.5 million men, the British nearly 9 million, the Russians 12 million, and the Germans 11 million. "One out of every four men who went out to the World War did not come back again," recalled a survivor, "and of those who came back, many are maimed and blind and some are mad."

Stalemate on the Western Front

As the war began, German forces fought their way through Belgium toward Paris. The Belgians resisted more than German generals had expected, but the German forces prevailed. However, Germany's plans for a quick defeat of France soon faltered.

The Germans' Schlieffen Plan failed for several reasons. First, Russia mobilized more quickly than expected. After a few small Russian victories, German generals hastily shifted some troops to the east, weakening their forces in the west. Then, in September 1914, British and French troops pushed back the German drive along the Marne River. The first battle of the Marne ended Germany's hopes for a quick victory on the Western Front.

Both sides then began to dig deep trenches to protect their armies from fierce enemy fire. They did not know that the conflict would turn into a long, deadly **stalemate,** a deadlock in which neither side is able to defeat the other. Battle lines in France would remain almost unchanged for four years.

✓ **Checkpoint** How did the Allies stop the Germans from executing the Schlieffen Plan?

Vocabulary Builder

Use the information below and the following resources to teach the high-use words from this section.

All in One **Teaching Resources, Unit 4,** p. 7; **Teaching Resources, Skills Handbook,** p. 3

High-Use Words	Definitions and Sample Sentences
utilize, p. 463	*vt.* to put to practical use I **utilized** a new graphics program to make the sign.
confront, p. 463	*vt.* to face in opposition He **confronted** the student who had taken his book and asked her to return it.

The Western Front and the Eastern Front, 1914–1918

Geography *Interactive*
For: Interactive map and timeline
Web Code: nbp-2621

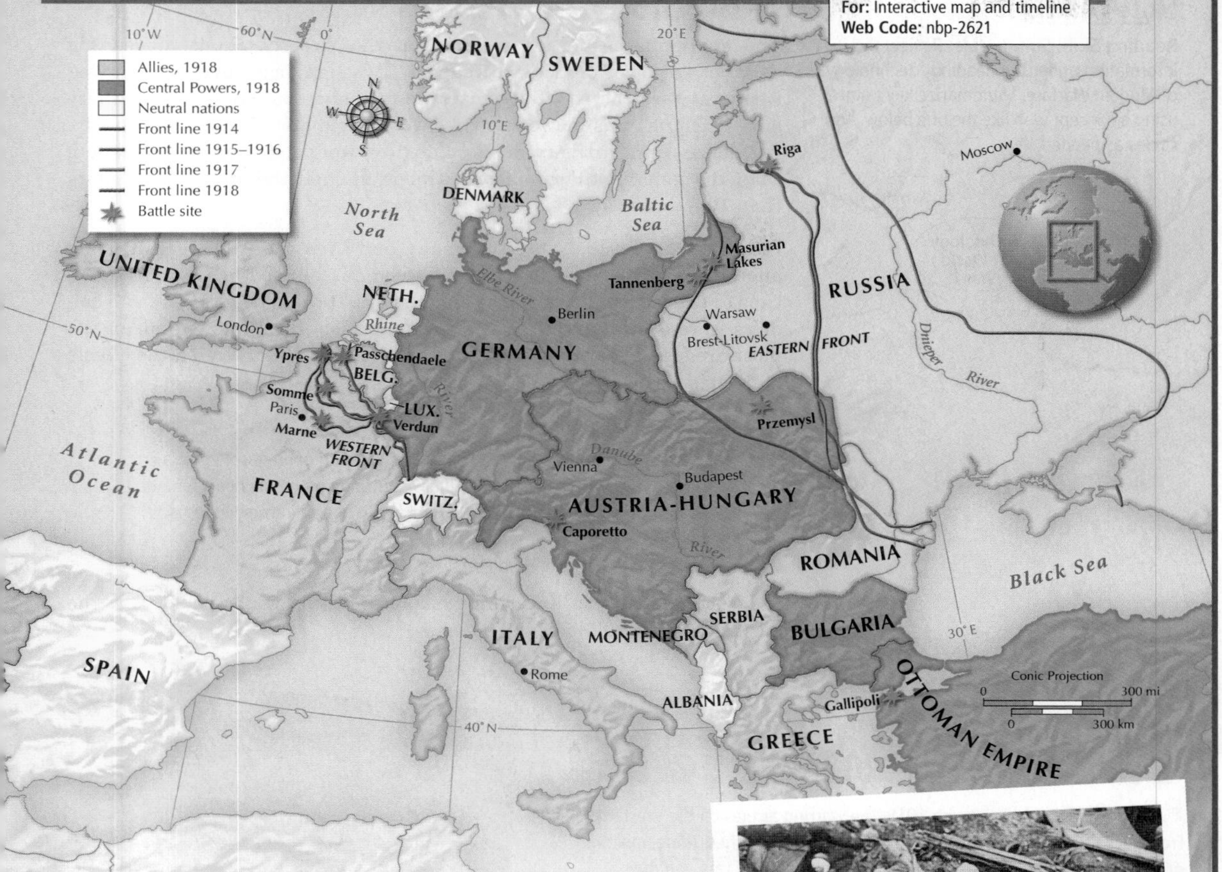

Legend:
- Allies, 1918
- Central Powers, 1918
- Neutral nations
- Front line 1914
- Front line 1915–1916
- Front line 1917
- Front line 1918
- ✶ Battle site

Map labels: NORWAY, SWEDEN, DENMARK, North Sea, Baltic Sea, UNITED KINGDOM, London, NETH., BELG., Ypres, Passchendaele, Somme, Paris, Marne, LUX., Verdun, WESTERN FRONT, FRANCE, SWITZ., Atlantic Ocean, SPAIN, Rhine, GERMANY, Berlin, Elbe River, Riga, Tannenberg, Masurian Lakes, Warsaw, Brest-Litovsk, EASTERN FRONT, RUSSIA, Moscow, Dnieper River, Przemysl, Danube, Vienna, Budapest, AUSTRIA-HUNGARY, Caporetto, ITALY, Rome, MONTENEGRO, SERBIA, ROMANIA, BULGARIA, Black Sea, ALBANIA, GREECE, Gallipoli, OTTOMAN EMPIRE

Conic Projection
0 — 300 mi
0 — 300 km

Map Skills World War I was fought on several fronts in Europe. Despite huge loss of life and property, the two sides came to a stalemate on the Western and Eastern fronts in 1915 and 1916.
1. **Locate** (a) Paris (b) Battle of the Marne (c) Verdun (d) Tannenberg
2. **Movement** Using the scale, describe how the battle lines moved on the Western Front from 1914 to 1918.
3. **Draw Inferences** Based on this map, why do you think many Russians were demoralized by the progress of the war?

The Human Cost To break the stalemate on the Western Front, both the Allies and the Central Powers launched massive offensives in 1916. German forces tried to overwhelm the French at Verdun (vur DUN). The French defenders held firm, sending up the battle cry "They shall not pass." The 11-month struggle cost more than a half a million casualties, or soldiers killed, wounded, or missing, on both sides.

An Allied offensive at the Somme River (sum) was even more costly. In a single grisly day, nearly 60,000 British soldiers were killed or wounded. In the five-month battle, more than one million soldiers were killed, without either side winning an advantage.

▲ Wounded soldiers on stretchers in Verdun in 1916

WITNESS HISTORY VIDEO

Watch *World War I: A New Kind of War* on the **Witness History Discovery School**™ video program to learn more about trench warfare.

Discovery SCHOOL

History Background

The Christmas Truce On December 24, 1914, on the front lines in Flanders, British troops reported an amazing sight: Christmas trees and lanterns along the German front line. They were even more amazed to see some Germans walking toward the British trenches shouting, "Hello! I want to talk to you!" So began the unofficial Christmas Truce. Ignoring orders from headquarters, small groups of enemy soldiers put down their arms. The enemies came together in no man's land and drank toasts and exchanged gifts such as chocolate or jam. They sang carols. One German recalled playing soccer against a Scottish regiment wearing kilts. After Christmas, the fighting began again.

Teach

Stalemate on the Western Front L3

Instruct

- **Introduce: Key Terms** Ask students to find the key term **stalemate** (in blue) in the text and explain its meaning. Tell them that the Allies and Central Powers fought to a stalemate in France. Ask them to predict why a stalemate will present problems.

- **Teach** Ask **How did the Schlieffen Plan fail?** (*Germany diverted troops from France to the Eastern Front, where Germany fought Russia. French troops, strengthened by British forces, stopped German forces at the first battle of the Marne.*) **What happened when the Schlieffen Plan failed?** (*stalemate, trench warfare*)

- **Quick Activity** Show students *World War I: A New Kind of War* from the **Witness History Discovery School**™ video program. Ask them to explain how new weapons affected the war. (*Answers should include the development of trench warfare and the increase in casualties of war.*)

Independent Practice

- **Web Code nbp-2621** will take students to an interactive map and timeline. Have students complete the interactivity and then answer the questions in the text.

- **Viewpoints** To help students better understand the shifts in attitude toward war, have them read *Soldier-Poets View World War I* and complete the worksheet.

  All in One Teaching Resources, Unit 4, p. 11

Monitor Progress

As students fill in their charts, circulate to make sure they understand how the different fronts impacted the war. For a completed version of the chart, see

▥ **Note Taking Transparencies,** 170A

Answers

Map Skills
1. Review locations with students.
2. They moved less than 150 miles, and not at all from 1915 to 1916.
3. Battle lines were pushed back far into Russian territory. The war was not going well for the Russians and it affected Russian civilians.

Technology of Modern Warfare

Instruct

- **Introduce: Vocabulary Builder**
Have students read the Vocabulary Builder term and definition. Then show **Color Transparency 158: Sopwith Camel.** Discuss with students how this aircraft was *utilized* in World War I.

  📖 **Color Transparencies,** 158

- **Teach** Using the Numbered Heads strategy (TE, p. T23), have students discuss how new or improved weapons affected the way war was fought. Ask **How did these weapons make trench warfare necessary?** *(Opposing sides dug trenches to protect themselves from the exploding shells and waves of bullets.)* **How did these weapons make warfare much deadlier than in Napoleon's day, when rifles were still hand-loaded?** *(The weapons were able to kill more people quicker.)* **Why would tanks have been useful on the Western Front?** *(Tanks would have been able to break through the barbed wire and ride over the uneven terrain of no man's land.)* **Why did tanks fail to break the stalemate?** *(The first tanks did not work properly.)*

- **Analyzing the Visuals** Direct students' attention to the Infographic on this page. Read the captions and discuss the visuals as a class. Ask students to use the visuals to describe what life was like in the trenches.

Independent Practice

<u>Note</u> Taking Have students fill in the concept web describing the technological innovations of World War I.

  ✏️ **Reading and Note Taking Study Guide,** p. 234

Monitor Progress

As students fill in their concept webs, circulate to make sure they understand the innovations developed during World War I. For a completed version of the concept web, see

  📖 **Note Taking Transparencies,** 170B

<u>N</u>ote **Taking**

Reading Skill: Summarize Review the information under the heading "Technology of Modern Warfare." Summarize key points using a concept web like the one below. Add circles as needed.

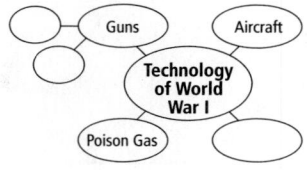

- Guns
- Aircraft
- **Technology of World War I**
- Poison Gas

Technology of Modern Warfare

The enormous casualties suffered on the Western Front proved the destructive power of modern weapons. Two significant new or improved weapons were the rapid-fire machine gun and the long-range artillery gun. Machine guns mowed down waves of soldiers. The shrapnel, or flying debris from artillery shells, killed or wounded even more soldiers than the guns. Artillery allowed troops to shell the enemy from more than 10 miles away.

Poison Gas In 1915, first Germany and then the Allies began using another new weapon—poison gas. Poison gas blinded or choked its victims or caused agonizing burns and blisters. It could be fatal. Though soldiers were eventually given gas masks, poison gas remained one of the most dreaded hazards of the war. One British soldier recalled the effects of being gassed:

> **Primary Source**
>
> ❝I suppose I resembled a kind of fish with my mouth open gasping for air. It seemed as if my lungs were gradually shutting up and my heart pounded away in my ears like the beat of a drum. . . . To get air into my lungs was real agony.❞
> —William Pressey, quoted in *People at War 1914–1918*

Poison gas was an uncertain weapon. Shifting winds could blow the gas back on the soldiers who launched it.

● INFOGRAPHIC

Trench Warfare

From the end of 1914 through 1918, the warring armies on the Western Front faced each other from a vast system of deep trenches. There, millions of soldiers lived out in the open, sharing their food with rats and their beds with lice. Between the opposing trench lines lay "no man's land." In this tract of land pocked with shell holes, every house and tree had long since been destroyed. Sooner or later, soldiers would go "over the top," charging into this manmade desert. With luck, the attackers might overrun a few enemy trenches. In time, the enemy would launch a counterattack, with similar results. The struggle continued, back and forth, over a few hundred yards of territory.

Soldiers peered over the edges of their trenches, watching for the next attack.

Soldiers ate, slept, and fought in trenches. ▶ Tea tins (above) supplied to British soldiers in World War I, contained 200 tablets of compressed tea.

Connect to Our World

Connections to Today Modern chemical warfare was first introduced in World War I when poison gas was used as a weapon. The use of the gas did not have a significant effect on the course of the war, mainly because protective measures such as gas masks were quickly developed. Still, poison gas inspired terror.

The Geneva Protocol of 1925 banned the use of chemical weapons, but not their production. As a result, these weapons continued to be used in warfare. The Nazis used Zyklon-B gas in World War II to kill millions in extermination camps. The United States used herbicides, such as Agent Orange, in Vietnam. In 1992, an international treaty called for the complete ban on production, stockpiling, and use of chemical weapons by 2007. The international community is still refining related treaties.

Tanks, Airplanes, and Submarines During World War I, advances in technology, such as the gasoline-powered engine, led the opposing forces to use tanks, airplanes, and submarines against each other. In 1916, Britain introduced the first armored tank. Mounted with machine guns, the tanks were designed to move across no man's land. Still, the first tanks broke down often. They failed to break the stalemate.

Both sides also used aircraft. At first, planes were <u>utilized</u> simply to observe enemy troop movements. In 1915, Germany used **zeppelins** (ZEP uh linz), large gas-filled balloons, to bomb the English coast. Later, both sides equipped airplanes with machine guns. Pilots known as "flying aces" <u>confronted</u> each other in the skies. These "dogfights" were spectacular, but had little effect on the course of the war on the ground.

Submarines proved much more important. German **U-boats**, nicknamed from the German word for submarine, *Unterseeboot*, did tremendous damage to the Allied side, sinking merchant ships carrying vital supplies to Britain. To defend against the submarines, the Allies organized **convoys**, or groups of merchant ships protected by warships.

✔ **Checkpoint** What made World War I much more deadly than previous wars?

Battle on Other European Fronts

On Europe's Eastern Front, battle lines shifted back and forth, sometimes over large areas. Even though the armies were not mired in trench warfare, casualties rose even higher than on the Western Front. The results were just as indecisive.

◀ **Trench Design**

Front line trenches were dug in a zigzag pattern to prevent the enemy from firing down the line.

Communications trenches, perpendicular to the front line trenches, served as routes for mail, food, supplies, reinforcements, and the transport of wounded soldiers.

Tanks, developed during the ▶ war, rolled on sturdy tracks, which allowed them to navigate through barbed wire and over the rough terrain of no man's land.

Messenger dogs, trained to leap over barbed wire, carried vital information to the front lines. ▼

Thinking Critically
1. **Determine Relevance** How did technological advances in machine guns and tanks affect soldiers in the trenches?
2. **Make Inferences** What effect do you think that trench warfare had on soldiers' morale?

War Around the World L3

Instruct

- **Introduce** Have students locate the Black Sea, the Mediterranean Sea, and Gallipoli on the map on this page. Ask them to predict why access to the Black Sea might be crucial to the Allies.

- **Teach** Ask **What happened at Gallipoli?** *(Allied troops fought Turkish troops to regain access to the Dardanelles. The Turkish troops pinned the Allies on the beaches. The Allies withdrew after 10 months of fighting and many deaths.)*

- **Quick Activity** Have students access **Web Code nbp-2622** to take the **Geography Interactive Audio Guided Tour** and then answer the map skills questions in the text.

Independent Practice

- Have students fill in the Outline Map *Major Battles of World War I*, labeling some of the key contests.

  All in One Teaching Resources, Unit 4, p. 14

- **Traveler's Tales** To help students better understand the effects of World War I in the African colonies, have them read the selection *Isak Dinesan's Letters from Africa* and answer the questions on the worksheet.

  All in One Teaching Resources, Unit 4, p. 13

Monitor Progress

- Circulate to make sure students are accurately filling in their Outline Maps, labeling the key battles of World War I. Administer the Geography Quiz.

  All in One Teaching Resources, Unit 4, p. 16

- Check Reading and Note Taking Study Guide entries to ensure that students understand that as fighting drew in non-European powers and soldiers from Europe's overseas colonies, World War I became a truly global conflict.

Answers

 The Eastern Front shifted over more area than the Western Front, with less trench warfare and even more casualties.

Map Skills It was bordered on two sides by Allied countries, Russia and British Egypt, and so faced fighting on several fronts.

Russian Losses on the Eastern Front In August 1914, Russian armies pushed into eastern Germany. Then, the Russians suffered a disastrous defeat at Tannenberg, causing them to retreat back into Russia. As the least industrialized of the great powers, Russia was poorly equipped to fight a modern war. Some troops even lacked rifles. Still, Russian commanders continued to send masses of soldiers into combat.

New Combatants in the Balkans and Southern Europe The Balkans were another battleground. In 1915, Bulgaria joined the Central Powers and helped defeat its old Balkan rival Serbia. Romania, hoping to gain some land in Hungary, joined the Allies in 1916, only to be crushed by the Central Powers.

Also in 1915, Italy declared war on Austria-Hungary and later on Germany. The Allies had agreed in a secret treaty to give Italy some Austrian-ruled lands inhabited by Italians. Over the next two years, the Italians and Austrians fought eleven battles along the Isonzo river, with few major breakthroughs. In October 1917, the Austrians and Germans launched a major offensive against the Italian position at Caporetto, also on the Isonzo. The Italians retreated in disarray. British and French forces later helped stop the Central Powers' advance into Italy. Still, Caporetto proved as disastrous for Italy as Tannenberg had been for Russia.

✓ **Checkpoint** In what way was the Eastern Front different from the Western Front?

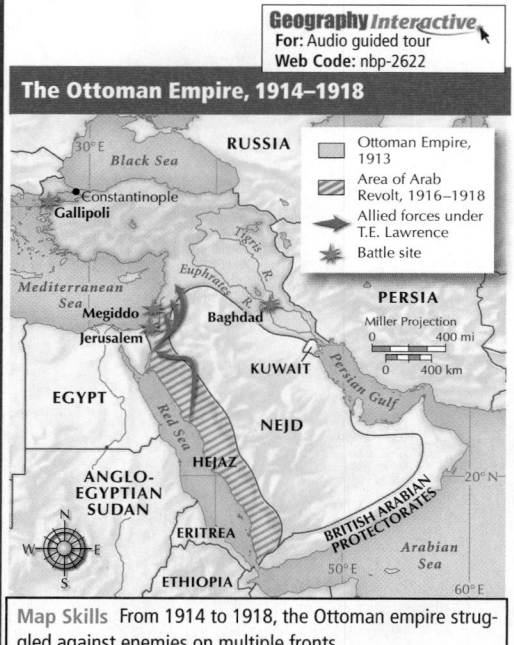

Geography *Interactive*
For: Audio guided tour
Web Code: nbp-2622

The Ottoman Empire, 1914–1918

Ottoman Empire, 1913

Area of Arab Revolt, 1916–1918

Allied forces under T.E. Lawrence

Battle site

RUSSIA

Black Sea

Constantinople
Gallipoli

Mediterranean Sea

Megiddo

Jerusalem

EGYPT

ANGLO-EGYPTIAN SUDAN

ERITREA

ETHIOPIA

Euphrates R.

Tigris R.

Baghdad

KUWAIT

PERSIA

Miller Projection
0   400 mi
0   400 km

Persian Gulf

NEJD

HEJAZ

Red Sea

BRITISH ARABIAN PROTECTORATES

Arabian Sea

30°E   50°E   60°E   20°N

Map Skills From 1914 to 1918, the Ottoman empire struggled against enemies on multiple fronts.

Location Given that Britain controlled Egypt at this time, describe how the Ottoman empire's location affected what happened to it during World War I.

War Around the World

Though most of the fighting took place in Europe, World War I was a global conflict. Japan, allied with Britain, used the war as an excuse to seize German outposts in China and islands in the Pacific.

The Ottoman Empire Joins the Central Powers Because of its strategic location, the Ottoman empire was a desirable ally. If the Ottoman Turks had joined the Allies, the Central Powers would have been almost completely encircled. However, the Turks joined the Central Powers in late October 1914. The Turks then cut off crucial Allied supply lines to Russia through the **Dardanelles,** a vital strait connecting the Black Sea and the Mediterranean.

In 1915, the Allies sent a massive force of British, Indian, Australian, and New Zealander troops to attempt to open up the strait. At the battle of Gallipoli (guh LIP uh lee), Turkish troops trapped the Allies on the beaches of the Gallipoli peninsula. In January 1916, after 10 months and more than 200,000 casualties, the Allies finally withdrew from the Dardanelles.

Meanwhile, Turkey was fighting Russia in the Caucasus mountains on Turkey's northern border. This region was home to ethnic Armenians, some of whom lived under Ottoman rule and some of whom lived under Russian rule. As Christians, the Armenians were a minority in the Ottoman empire and did not have the same rights as Muslims. As the Russians advanced in 1914, some

---

Link to Science

Communication During World War I
Although some trenches had a system of wires or cables to provide telephone service, both sides also used messenger dogs or carrier pigeons to communicate. Although well-trained, both dogs and pigeons could be injured while carrying messages or arrive too late to make a difference. However, in 1918, a pigeon saved the American 77th Division from almost certain destruction. The Americans were caught behind enemy lines and under heavy bombardment from their own artillery units. They released a pigeon with their location and this frantic message: "For heaven's sake, stop it." Although missing an eye and a leg, the pigeon reached the Allied lines. It delivered the message, and the shelling was stopped. The bird was later awarded a Distinguished Service Cross.

Turkish Armenians joined or helped the Russian army against the Turks. The Ottoman government used this cooperation as a reason to deport the entire Armenian population south to Syria and Mesopotamia. During the deportation, between 600,000 and 1.5 million Armenians died. Many were killed by planned massacres; others starved as they were forced to march with no food. Many Armenians fled to other countries, including the United States, leaving almost no Armenians in the historic Armenian homeland in Turkey.

On a third front, the Turks were hard hit in the Middle East. The Ottoman empire included vast areas of Arab land. In 1916, Arab nationalists led by Husayn ibn Ali (HOO sayn IB un AH lee) declared a revolt against Ottoman rule. The British government sent Colonel **T. E. Lawrence**—later known as Lawrence of Arabia—to support the Arab revolt. Lawrence led guerrilla raids against the Turks, dynamiting bridges and supply trains. Eventually, the Ottoman empire lost a great deal of territory to the Arabs, including the key city of Baghdad.

War and the Colonies European colonies were also drawn into the struggle. The Allies overran scattered German colonies in Africa and Asia. They also turned to their own colonies and dominions for troops, laborers, and supplies. Colonial recruits from British India and French West Africa fought on European battlefields. Canada, Australia, and New Zealand sent troops to Britain's aid.

People in the colonies had mixed feelings about serving. Some were reluctant to serve rulers who did not treat them fairly. Other colonial troops volunteered eagerly. They expected that their service would be a step toward citizenship or independence. As you will read, such hopes would be dashed after the war.

✔ **Checkpoint** How did World War I affect the Ottoman empire and European colonies and dominions?

Armenian Refugees
A group of Armenian refugees wait for their daily rations from Near East Relief, an American organization founded to help the surviving Turkish Armenians. Public opinion, especially in the United States, was sympathetic to the Armenians during and after World War I. However, the Allies' attempts to protect the Armenians through the treaty that ended the war with Turkey ultimately failed.

Section 2 Assessment

Progress Monitoring Online
For: Self-quiz with vocabulary practice
Web Code: nba-2621

Terms, People, and Places
1. For each term, person, or place listed at the beginning of the section, write a sentence explaining its significance.

Note Taking
2. **Reading Skill: Identify Supporting Details** Use your chart and concept web to answer the Focus Question: How and where was World War I fought?

Comprehension and Critical Thinking
3. **Draw Conclusions** Why did a stalemate develop on the Western Front?

4. **Synthesize Information** Describe three ways in which technology affected the war.
5. **Predict Consequences** Governments on both sides of World War I tried to keep full casualty figures and other bad news from reaching the public. What effect do you think news about disastrous defeats such as Tannenberg and Caporetto would have had on the attitudes of people back home?
6. **Recognize Causes** How did nationalism within the Ottoman Empire come into play during the war?

● **Writing About History**
Quick Write: Write a Thesis Statement Suppose that you are writing an essay on the effects of Ottoman Turkey's decision to join the Central Powers during World War I. Answer the questions below. Use your answers to create a thesis statement for the essay.
• Why were the Dardanelles important to the Allies?
• Who won the Battle of Gallipoli?
• What impact do you think Gallipoli had on the Russian war effort?

Erich Maria Remarque: *All Quiet on the Western Front*

Objective

■ Understand the point of view of a soldier on the Western Front.

Build Background Knowledge ⓛ

Ask students to remember what they have learned about trench warfare. Explain that, although the excerpt is quoted from a fictional novel, it is based on the real-life experiences of the author.

Instruct ⓛ

■ Ask students to work in pairs to identify the main idea and tone of the passage. *(Main idea: Paul sees the man he has killed as an individual rather than as an enemy, and regrets what he has done. Tone: sad, regretful, somewhat desperate.)*

■ Point out that Paul probably had to kill the Frenchman, or be killed by him. Ask **How did Paul's point of view change after the Frenchman died?** *(Once the Frenchman is dead, Paul can see him as a person rather than as a threat or an abstraction. He sees his face rather than his weapons, and realizes that the enemy is not very different from himself.)*

Monitor Progress

As a class, write a sentence summarizing Paul's experience. Discuss whether other soldiers on the Western Front might have felt the same way. How might soldiers today react to Paul's experience?

Thinking Critically

1. Sample: He can no longer stand the silence in the foxhole.
2. that enemy soldiers are fellow humans with lives and families

---

Erich Maria Remarque: *All Quiet on the Western Front*

Erich Maria Remarque (1898–1970) was wounded five times while serving in the German army during World War I. In 1929, he published *All Quiet on the Western Front,* which is often considered the greatest novel about World War I.

It follows the narrator, Paul Baumer, from eager recruit to disillusioned veteran. In this passage, Paul is trapped for hours in a foxhole with a French soldier he has just killed.

In the afternoon, about three, he is dead.

I breathe freely again. But only for a short time. Soon the silence is more unbearable than the groans. I wish the gurgling were there again, gasping hoarse, now whistling softly and again hoarse and loud.

It is mad, what I do. But I must do something. I prop the dead man up again so that he lies comfortably, although he feels nothing any more. I close his eyes. They are brown, his hair is black and a bit curly at the sides. . . .

The silence spreads. I talk and must talk. So I speak to him and say to him: "Comrade, I did not want to kill you. If you jumped in here again, I would not do it, if you would be sensible too. But you were only an idea to me before, an abstraction[1] that lived in my mind and called forth its appropriate response. It was that abstraction I stabbed. But now, for the first time, I see you are a man like me. I thought of your hand-grenades, of your bayonet[2], of your rifle; now I see your wife and your face and our fellowship. Forgive me, comrade. We always see it too late. Why do they never tell us that you are poor devils like us, that your mothers are just as anxious as ours, and that we have the same fear of death, and the same dying and the

▲ This painting is titled *Notre-Dame de Lorette—A Soldier Walks Through the Flooded Trenches.* It was painted by François Flameng, a French artist who was given access to the front lines by the French government.

same agony—Forgive me, comrade; how could you be my enemy? If we threw away these rifles and this uniform you could be my brother just like Kat and Albert. Take twenty years of my life, comrade, and stand up—take more, for I do not know what I can even attempt to do with it now."

It is quiet, the front is still except for the crackle of rifle fire. The bullets rain over, they are not fired haphazard, but shrewdly aimed from all sides. I cannot get out.

1. **abstraction** (ab STRAK shun) *n.* an idea or term that is developed from a concrete reality
2. **bayonet** (bay oh NET) *n.* a blade attached to an end of a rifle for stabbing in hand-to-hand combat

Thinking Critically
1. **Recognize Point of View** Why does Paul speak to the dead French soldier?
2. **Synthesize Information** What does Paul mean by "We always see it too late"?

History Background

Disillusionment With War *All Quiet on the Western Front,* a title that reflects the terse style of military communiqués, expresses the disillusionment with the war among participants who were shocked by the disparity between the rhetoric of patriotism and the reality of trench warfare. The book became an instant success, and in 1930 an American film was made based on it.

Nazis banned Remarque's books in 1933. Remarque, a German, left his homeland and became an American citizen. Then he settled in Switzerland after World War II, where he lived with his wife, the film star Paulette Goddard, until his death in 1970.

An American soldier bids goodbye to his sweetheart.

SECTION 3

WITNESS HISTORY ◀)) AUDIO

An American War Song

❝Over there, over there,
Send the word, send the word over there,
That the Yanks are coming,
The Yanks are coming…
We'll be over, we're coming over,
And we won't come back till it's over
Over there.❞
—George M. Cohan, from the song "Over There," written in 1917

Sheet music for the patriotic song "Over There"

On April 6, 1917, the United States declared war on Germany.

Focus Question How did the Allies win World War I?

Winning the War

Objectives
- Describe how World War I became a total war.
- Explain the effect that years of warfare had on morale.
- Analyze the causes and effects of American entry into the war.
- Summarize events that led to the end of the war.

Terms, People, and Places

total war	atrocity
conscription	Fourteen Points
contraband	self-determination
Lusitania	armistice
propaganda	

Note Taking

Reading Skill: Summarize As you read, use an outline to summarize the events in this section.

> I. Waging total war
>   A. Economies committed to war production
>   1. Conscription
>   2. Rationing
>   3. Price controls
>   B. Economic warfare

By 1917, European societies were cracking under the strain of war. Casualties on the fronts and shortages at home sapped morale. The stalemate dragged on, seemingly without end. Soon, however, the departure of one country from the war and the entry of another would tip the balance and end the stalemate.

Waging Total War

As the struggle wore on, nations realized that a modern, mechanized war required the channeling of a nation's entire resources into the war effort, or **total war.** To achieve total war, governments began to take a stronger role in directing the economic and cultural lives of their people.

Economies Committed to War Production Early on, both sides set up systems to recruit, arm, transport, and supply armies that numbered in the millions. All of the warring nations except Britain immediately imposed universal military **conscription,** or "the draft," which required all young men to be ready for military or other service. Britain, too, instituted conscription in 1916. Germany set up a system of forced civilian labor as well.

Governments raised taxes and borrowed huge amounts of money to pay the costs of war. They rationed food and other products, from boots to gasoline. In addition, they introduced other economic controls, such as setting prices and forbidding strikes.

Economic Warfare At the start of the war, Britain's navy formed a blockade in the North Sea to keep ships from carrying supplies in and out of Germany. International law allowed wartime blockades

Vocabulary Builder

Use the information below and the following resources to teach the high-use word from this section.
All in One Teaching Resources, Unit 4, p. 7; **Teaching Resources, Skills Handbook,** p. 3

High-Use Word	Definition and Sample Sentence
erode, p. 469	*vt.* to eat into or wear away The ocean tide **eroded** the rocks on the shore, turning them into smooth stones.

Objectives
As you teach this section, keep students focused on the following objectives to help them answer the Section Focus Question and master core content.

- Describe how World War I became a total war.
- Explain the effect that years of warfare had on morale.
- Analyze the causes and effects of American entry into the war.
- Summarize events that led to the end of the war.

Prepare to Read

Build Background Knowledge ⓛ3
Ask students to recall the devastation experienced by members of the military during the war. Have them predict how the war affected people on the home front.

Set a Purpose ⓛ3
- **WITNESS HISTORY** Read the selection aloud or play the audio.
   AUDIO **Witness History Audio CD,** An American War Song

  Ask **What is the tone of the song?** *(optimistic, excited, eager)* **What do you think was the purpose of this song?** *(to motivate troops)* **Do you think the song fulfills that purpose?** *(Answers will vary.)*

- **Focus** Point out the Section Focus Question and write it on the board. Tell students to refer to this question as they read. *(Answer appears with Section 3 Assessment answers.)*

- **Preview** Have students preview the Section Objectives and the list of Terms, People, and Places.

- **Note Taking** Have students read this section using the Paragraph Shrinking strategy (TE, p. T20). As they read, have students fill in the graphic organizer outlining events that led to the end of the war.

   Reading and Note Taking Study Guide, pp. 152–153

Teach

Waging Total War L3

Instruct

- **Introduce: Key Terms** Ask students to find the key term ***propaganda*** (in blue) in the text and explain its meaning. Point out that during World War I, governments used propaganda to raise morale and mobilize their citizens. Have students speculate on other ways that a government can try to control or influence public opinion.

- **Teach** Discuss the idea of a total war. Using the Numbered Heads strategy (TE, p. T23), ask **How did governments manipulate their economies to support the war?** *(raised taxes, borrowed money, rationed goods, set prices, and forbade strikes)* **How did Britain strike at Germany's economy?** *(Britain blockaded Germany, so that Germany could not import needed goods.)* **How did Germany strike at Britain's economy?** *(Germany tried to stop the flow of goods to Britain as well.)*

- **Analyzing the Visuals** Point out the propaganda art on this page. Discuss the effects this poster may have had on a viewer. Then display **Color Transparency 156:** *To the End,* **by Louis Raemaeker.** Use the lesson suggested in the transparency book to guide a discussion on how propaganda art was used in World War I.

  📖 **Color Transparencies,** 156

Independent Practice

Ask students to consider the role of conscription during war time. Have them write a paragraph explaining the benefits and drawbacks of conscription within a democracy.

Monitor Progress

As students write their responses, circulate to ensure they understand the role of conscription.

Answer

Caption It uses emotion by giving men something to fight for and appealing to their sense of family, safety, and moral obligation.

A German Submarine Sinks the *Lusitania*
The sinking of the British line *Lusitania* in 1915, illustrated below, was part of Germany's policy of unrestricted submarine warfare. The incident was featured in propaganda posters as evidence of German brutality. *How does the poster below use emotion to encourage men to enlist?*

to confiscate contraband, or military supplies and raw materials needed to make military supplies, but not items such as food and clothing. In spite of international law, the British blockade stopped both types of goods from reaching Germany. As the war progressed, it became harder and harder to feed the German and Austrian people. In Germany, the winter of 1916 and 1917 was remembered as "the turnip winter," because the potato crop failed and people ate turnips instead.

To retaliate, Germany used U-boats to create its own blockade. In 1915, Germany declared that it would sink all ships carrying goods to Britain. In May 1915, a German submarine torpedoed the British liner *Lusitania* off the coast of Ireland. Almost 1,200 passengers were killed, including 128 Americans. Germany justified the attack, arguing that the *Lusitania* was carrying weapons. When American President Woodrow Wilson threatened to cut off diplomatic relations with Germany, though, Germany agreed to restrict its submarine campaign. Before attacking any ship, U-boats would surface and give warning, allowing neutral passengers to escape to lifeboats. Unrestricted submarine warfare stopped—for the moment.

Propaganda War Total war also meant controlling public opinion. Even in democratic countries, special boards censored the press. Their aim was to keep complete casualty figures and other discouraging news from reaching the public. Government censors also restricted popular literature, historical writings, motion pictures, and the arts.

Both sides waged a propaganda war. Propaganda is the spreading of ideas to promote a cause or to damage an opposing cause. Governments used propaganda to motivate military mobilization, especially in Britain before conscription started in 1916. In France and Germany, propaganda urged civilians to loan money to the government. Later in the war, Allied propaganda played up the brutality of Germany's invasion of Belgium. The British and French press circulated tales of atrocities, horrible acts

Differentiated Instruction   Solutions for All Learners

L1 Special Needs   **L2 Less Proficient Readers**   **L2 English Language Learners**

Divide students into pairs. Have each pair construct a concept map of the strategies used to fight a total war. Students determine the main ideas surrounding this concept and determine supporting ideas for each main idea. Then have pairs use their concept maps to discuss why each strategy was important to winning the war.

Use the following study guide resources to help students acquiring basic skills:

📑 **Adapted Reading and Note Taking Study Guide**

- Adapted Note Taking Study Guide, pp. 152–153
- Adapted Section Summary, p. 154

committed against innocent people. Although some atrocities did occur, often the stories were distorted by exaggerations or completely made up.

Women Join the War Effort Women played a critical role in total war. As millions of men left to fight, women took over their jobs and kept national economies going. Many women worked in war industries, manufacturing weapons and supplies. Others joined women's branches of the armed forces. When food shortages threatened Britain, volunteers in the Women's Land Army went to the fields to grow their nation's food.

Nurses shared the dangers of the men whose wounds they tended. At aid stations close to the front lines, nurses often worked around the clock, especially after a big "push" brought a flood of casualties. In her diary, English nurse Vera Brittain describes sweating through 90-degree days in France, "stopping hemorrhages, replacing intestines, and draining and reinserting innumerable rubber tubes" with "gruesome human remnants heaped on the floor."

War work gave women a new sense of pride and confidence. After the war, most women had to give up their jobs to men returning home. Still, they had challenged the idea that women could not handle demanding and dangerous jobs. In many countries, including Britain, Germany, and the United States, women's support for the war effort helped them finally win the right to vote, after decades of struggle.

✔️ **Checkpoint** Why was it important for both sides to keep civilian morale high during the war?

Morale Collapses

Despite inspiring propaganda, by 1917 the morale of troops and civilians had plunged. Germany was sending 15-year-old recruits to the front. Britain was on the brink of bankruptcy.

War Fatigue Long casualty lists, food shortages, and the failure of generals to win promised victories led to calls for peace. Instead of praising the glorious deeds of heroes, war poets began denouncing the leaders whose errors wasted so many lives. British poet and soldier Siegfried Sassoon captured the bitter mood:

> **Primary Source**
>
> ❝You smug-faced crowds with kindling eye
> Who cheer when soldier lads march by,
> Sneak home and pray you'll never know
> The hell where youth and laughter go.❞
> —Siegfried Sassoon, "Suicide in the Trenches"

As morale collapsed, troops in some French units mutinied. In Italy, many soldiers deserted during the retreat at Caporetto. In Russia, soldiers left the front to join in a full-scale revolution back home.

Revolution in Russia Three years of war had hit Russia especially hard. Stories of incompetent generals and corruption <u>eroded</u> public confidence. In March 1917, bread riots in St. Petersburg erupted into a revolution that brought down the Russian monarchy. (You'll read more about the causes and effects of the Russian Revolution in Section 5.)

At first, the Allies welcomed the overthrow of the tsar. They hoped Russia would institute a democratic government and become a stronger

Vocabulary Builder
<u>eroded</u> (ee ROHD id)—*vt.* ate into or wore away

Morale Collapses ⓫

Instruct

- **Introduce: Vocabulary Builder**
  Have students read the Vocabulary Builder term and definition. Ask students to consider what might happen if support for the war *erodes*.

- **Teach** Ask **Why were people tired of war by 1917?** *(There were many casualties, food shortages, and few decisive victories.)* Remind students that the purpose of some propaganda was to raise morale. Ask **How could low morale hurt a country fighting a war?** *(Troops may refuse to continue fighting or not fight well; civilians may not work hard to contribute materials that support the war; both troops and civilians may rebel to end the war.)* **What happened in Russia, partly because of low morale?** *(The people rebelled and overthrew the government. Russia pulled out of the war.)*

Independent Practice

Primary Source To help students better understand the shift in morale, have them read the excerpt from *Kaethe Kollwitz's War Diary* and complete the worksheet.

⬛ **All in One** Teaching Resources, Unit 4, p. 10

Monitor Progress

- After students read *Kaethe Kollwitz's War Diary*, ask what the primary source has in common with the poem by Siegfried Sassoon (in the text). Ensure students understand that both pieces reflect a weariness and bitterness towards war.

- As students create their outlines, circulate to make sure they understand how the drop in morale affected the end of the war. For a completed version of the outline, see

  🏛 **Note Taking Transparencies,** 171

Answers

✔️ Total war demanded that civilians work tirelessly to produce and conserve goods needed to keep the war going. If civilians were unhappy, they might not work well or they might create domestic unrest that would upset war plans and demoralize soldiers.

BIOGRAPHY They could use the story as propaganda against the Germans, portraying them as brutal villains who executed a heroic and brave Englishwoman.

The United States Declares War/Victory at Last

Instruct

- **Introduce** Ask students to recall the state of the Allied cause in 1917. Have them predict how the entry of the United States on the side of the Allies will affect the morale of both sides.

- **Teach** Review the reasons the United States declared war against the Central Powers. Then point out that although the United States declared war in April 1917, troops did not arrive in Europe until 1918. Ask **How did the Central Powers try to take advantage of the delay?** *(They pushed to win the war before American troops arrived.)* **What was the outcome of this strategy?** *(The Germans pushed back troops on the Western Front, but were unable to win before American reinforcements arrived.)*

- **Quick Activity** Display **Transparency 160: The Fourteen Points.** Use the lesson suggested in the transparency book to guide a discussion about Wilson's terms for resolving the conflict.

  📖 Color Transparencies, 160

Independent Practice

Have students suppose that they are living in the United States during 1917. Ask them to write a letter to the editor explaining whether or not the United States should enter the war. Letters should refer to the Zimmerman Note and Germany's decision to resume unrestricted submarine warfare.

Monitor Progress

- As students work on their letters, circulate to ensure they understand how opinion on entering the war shifted during this time.

- Check Reading and Note Taking Study Guide entries for student understanding.

American Troops "Over There"
The arrival of fresh American troops in Europe throughout 1918 helped turn the tide of the war in favor of the Allies. Recruitment posters, like the one above, inspired soldiers to enlist. *How was the experience of American soldiers different from that of other Allied soldiers?*

ally. But later that year V. I. Lenin came to power with a promise to pull Russian troops out of the war. Early in 1918, Lenin signed the Treaty of Brest-Litovsk (brest lih TAWFSK) with Germany. The treaty ended Russian participation in World War I.

Russia's withdrawal had an immediate impact on the war. With Russia out of the struggle, Germany could concentrate its forces on the Western Front. In the spring of 1918, the Central Powers stood ready to achieve the great breakthrough they had sought for so long.

✓ **Checkpoint** How did Russia's loss of morale affect the strategic position of the Allies in World War I?

The United States Declares War

Soon after the Russian Revolution began, however, another event altered the balance of forces. The United States declared war on Germany. Many factors contributed to the decision of the United States to exchange neutrality for war in 1917.

Why Join the Allies? Many Americans supported the Allies because of cultural ties. The United States shared a cultural history and language with Britain and sympathized with France as another democracy. On the other hand, some German Americans favored the Central Powers. So did many Irish Americans, who resented British rule of Ireland, and Russian Jewish immigrants, who did not want to be allied with the tsar.

Germany had ceased submarine attacks in 1915 after pressure from President Wilson. However, in early 1917, Germany was desperate to break the stalemate. On February 1, the German government announced that it would resume unrestricted submarine warfare. Wilson angrily denounced Germany.

Also, in early 1917, the British intercepted a message from the German foreign minister, Arthur Zimmermann, to his ambassador in Mexico. In the note, Zimmermann authorized his ambassador to propose that Germany would help Mexico "to reconquer the lost territory in New Mexico, Texas, and Arizona" in return for Mexican support against the United States. Britain revealed the Zimmermann note to the American government. When the note became public, anti-German feeling intensified in the United States.

Declaring War In April 1917, Wilson asked Congress to declare war on Germany. "We have no selfish ends to serve," he stated. Instead, he painted the conflict idealistically as a war "to make the world safe for democracy" and later as a "war to end war."

The United States needed months to recruit, train, supply, and transport a modern army across the Atlantic. But by 1918, about two million American soldiers had joined the war-weary Allied troops fighting on the Western Front. Although relatively few American troops engaged in combat, their arrival gave Allied troops a much-needed morale boost. Just as important to the debt-ridden Allies was American financial aid.

Answers

✓ Poor morale, among other factors, led to revolution in Russia and Russia's eventual withdrawal from the war, which weakened the Allies.

Caption American soldiers came into the war supplied with resources and training, but hadn't experienced war on their home soil.

Differentiated Instruction Solutions for All Learners

L4 Advanced Readers

Divide the class into groups of three. Assign each group to create a talk show discussing whether America should join the war. Have one student in each group assume the role of the talk show host while the other two students act as guests on the show. The guests may choose one of these roles: a British government official waging total war, a British woman sup-

L4 Gifted and Talented Students

porting the war effort, an antiwar poet, a French soldier who has mutinied and deserted, and an American who believes that the United States should enter the war against Germany. Students should prepare for their roles by developing pertinent questions and answers. Then ask each group to present their show to the classroom audience.

The Fourteen Points Though he had failed to maintain American neutrality, Wilson still hoped to be a peacemaker. In January 1918, he issued the Fourteen Points, a list of his terms for resolving this and future wars. He called for freedom of the seas, free trade, large-scale reductions of arms, and an end to secret treaties. For Eastern Europe, Wilson favored self-determination, the right of people to choose their own form of government. Finally, Wilson urged the creation of a "general association of nations" to keep the peace in the future.

✔ **Checkpoint** What are three factors that led the United States to enter the war?

Victory at Last

A final showdown on the Western Front began in early 1918. The Germans badly wanted to achieve a major victory before eager American troops arrived in Europe. In March, the Germans launched a huge offensive that by July had pushed the Allies back 40 miles. These efforts exhausted the Germans, however, and by then American troops were arriving by the thousands. The Allies then launched a counterattack, slowly driving German forces back across France and Belgium. In September, German generals told the kaiser that the war could not be won.

Uprisings exploded among hungry city dwellers across Germany. German commanders advised the kaiser to step down. William II did so in early November, fleeing into exile in the Netherlands.

By autumn, Austria-Hungary was also reeling toward collapse. As the government in Vienna tottered, the subject nationalities revolted, splintering the empire of the Hapsburgs. Bulgaria and the Ottoman empire also asked for peace.

The new German government sought an armistice, or agreement to end fighting, with the Allies. At 11 A.M. on November 11, 1918, the Great War at last came to an end.

✔ **Checkpoint** Why did Germany ask the Allies for an armistice in November 1918?

Celebrating the Armistice
Around the globe, crowds celebrated the end of the war. Here, British and American soldiers and civilians wave the American and French flags in relief and jubilation.

SECTION 3 Assessment

Progress Monitoring Online
For: Self-quiz with vocabulary practice
Web Code: nba-2631

Terms, People, and Places
1. For each term, person, or place listed at the beginning of the section, write a sentence explaining its significance.

Note Taking
2. **Reading Skill: Summarize** Use your completed outline to answer the Focus Question: How did the Allies win World War I?

Comprehension and Critical Thinking
3. **Summarize** What measures did wartime governments take to control national economies and public opinion?
4. **Recognize Effects** What impact did wartime failures have on Russia?
5. **Draw Conclusions** Describe how the entry of United States into the war was a turning point.
6. **Analyze Information** Reread the poem by Siegfried Sassoon. What does it suggest about the effects of trench warfare?

● **Writing About History**
Quick Write: Gather Evidence to Support Thesis Statement Suppose you are writing an essay with the following thesis statement "Women played a critical role in World War I." Write three questions like the two below that would help you gather evidence to support this thesis.
● What types of things did women do during the war?
● Why was this work important?

Assess and Reteach

Assess Progress
■ Have students complete the Section Assessment.
■ Administer the Section Quiz.
▶ **All in One** Teaching Resources, Unit 4, p. 4
■ To further assess student understanding, use
  📖 **Progress Monitoring Transparencies**, 110

Reteach
If students need more instruction, have them read the section summary.

 **Reading and Note Taking** L3
Study Guide, p. 154

 Adapted Reading and L1 L2
Note Taking Study Guide, p. 154

 Spanish Reading and L2
Note Taking Study Guide, p. 154

Extend L4
See this Chapter's Professional Development pages for the Extend Online activity on propaganda in World War I.

Answers
✔ three of the following: unrestricted submarine warfare, cultural ties, the Zimmermann Note, Wilson's desire to "make the world safe for democracy"

✔ Its last drive failed because the Allies were renewed by American troops, and domestic unrest disrupted the government.

Section 3 Assessment

1. Sentences should reflect an understanding of each term, person, or place listed at the beginning of the section.
2. The Allies were weakened when Russia left the war, but were strengthened when the United States joined. The Germans attempted one last drive, but it failed and morale in Germany plummeted. The Allies were able to drive the Germans

back. The government in Germany toppled and the new one asked for peace.
3. raised taxes, borrowed money, rationed food and other supplies, introduced price controls, censored the press, and used propaganda to win support for the war
4. Food shortages and collapsing morale led to a revolution that overthrew the tsar.
5. U.S. financial aid helped the Allies, and U.S. troops helped drive back the German advance and boosted Allied morale.

6. that trench warfare was brutal and dehumanizing and amounted to suicide for soldiers

● **Writing About History**
Questions should relate to the main idea of the thesis and be useful for research.

For additional assessment, have students access **Progress Monitoring Online** at **Web Code nba-2631.**

Objectives

As you teach this section, keep students focused on the following objectives to help them answer the Section Focus Question and master core content.

- Analyze the costs of World War I.
- Describe the issues faced by the delegates to the Paris Peace Conference.
- Explain why many people were dissatisfied with the Treaty of Versailles and other peace settlements.

Prepare to Read

Build Background Knowledge ⒀

Ask students to recall World War I's effect on Britain and France. Based on their previous reading, have them predict these countries' goals for the peace negotiations.

Set a Purpose ⒀

- **WITNESS HISTORY** Read the selection aloud or play the audio.

  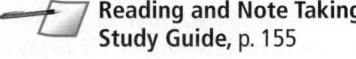 AUDIO **Witness History Audio CD,** Worth the Cost?

  Ask **What is Brittain's reaction to the peace negotiations?** *(She is unhappy with their outcome.)* **Why do you think Brittain had this reaction?** *(She may have hoped that the sacrifices her loved ones made would lead to a more positive resolution.)*

- **Focus** Point out the Section Focus Question and write it on the board. Tell students to refer to this question as they read. *(Answer appears with Section 4 Assessment answers.)*

- **Preview** Have students preview the Section Objectives and the list of Terms, People, and Places.

- **Note Taking** Have students read this section using the Guided Questioning strategy (TE, p. T20). As they read, have students fill in the concept web describing the costs of World War I.

  Reading and Note Taking Study Guide, p. 155

Lloyd George, Clemenceau, and Wilson (left to right) at the Paris Peace Conference. Above right, a medal sold to raise funds for wounded soldiers.

WITNESS HISTORY ◀🔊 AUDIO

Worth the Cost?

Vera Brittain, a British nurse, lost her brother Edward and her fiancé Roland on the battlefield.

❝ Although they would no doubt have welcomed the idea of a League of Nations, Roland and Edward certainly had not died in order that Clemenceau should outwit Lloyd George, and both of them bamboozle President Wilson, and all three combine to make the beaten, blockaded enemy pay the cost of the War. ❞
—Vera Brittain, *Testament of Youth*

Focus Question What factors influenced the peace treaties that ended World War I, and how did people react to the treaties?

Making the Peace

Objectives

- Analyze the costs of World War I.
- Describe the issues faced by the delegates to the Paris Peace Conference.
- Explain why many people were dissatisfied with the Treaty of Versailles and other peace settlements.

Terms, People, and Places

pandemic	radicals
reparations	collective security
	mandate

Note Taking

Reading Skill: Summarize As you read, summarize the main points of the text under the heading "The Costs of War" in a concept web like the one below.

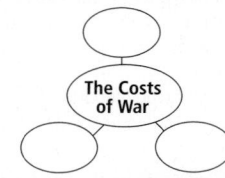

The Costs of War

Just weeks after the war ended, President Wilson boarded a steamship bound for France. He had decided to go in person to Paris, where Allied leaders would make the peace. Wilson was certain that he could solve the problems of old Europe. "Tell me what is right," Wilson urged his advisors, "and I'll fight for it." Sadly, it would not be that easy. Europe was a shattered continent. Its problems, and those of the world, would not be solved at the Paris Peace Conference, or for many years afterward.

The Costs of War

The human and material costs of the war were staggering. Millions of soldiers were dead, and even more wounded. The devastation was made even worse in 1918 by a deadly **pandemic** of influenza. A pandemic is the spread of a disease across a large area—in this case, the whole world. In just a few months, the flu killed more than 20 million people worldwide.

The Financial Toll In battle zones from France to Russia, homes, farms, factories, roads, and churches had been shelled into rubble. People had fled these areas as refugees. Now they had to return and start to rebuild. The costs of reconstruction and paying off huge war debts would burden an already battered world.

Shaken and disillusioned, people everywhere felt bitter about the war. The Allies blamed the conflict on their defeated foes and insisted that the losers make **reparations**, or payments for war damage. The stunned Central Powers, who had viewed the armistice as a cease-fire

Vocabulary Builder

Use the information below and the following resources to teach the high-use word from this section.
All in One **Teaching Resources, Unit 4,** p. 7; **Teaching Resources, Skills Handbook,** p. 3

High-Use Word	Definition and Sample Sentence
widespread, p. 475	*adj.* occurring in many places The decision to eat dinner now rather than later met with **widespread** approval among those who were hungry.

rather than a surrender, looked for scapegoats on whom they could blame their defeat.

Political Turmoil Under the stress of war, governments had collapsed in Russia, Germany, Austria-Hungary, and the Ottoman empire. Political radicals, or people who wanted to make extreme changes, dreamed of building a new social order from the chaos. Conservatives warned against the spread of bolshevism, or communism, as it was soon called.

Unrest also swept through Europe's colonial empires. African and Asian soldiers had discovered that the imperial powers were not as invincible as they seemed. Colonial troops returned home with a more cynical view of Europeans and renewed hopes for independence.

✓ **Checkpoint** What were some of the human, economic, and political costs of the war?

INFOGRAPHIC

The Costs of World War I

The war ended in 1918, but its effects would be felt for decades to come. More than 8.5 million men had died in battle. Twice that number had been wounded, many of them disabled for life. Historians estimate that from 6 to 13 million civilians also lost their lives as a result of the war. Many of the combatant nations had thrown all of their resources into the fight, leaving them little with which to rebuild. Below an American nurse tends to soldiers in France in 1918.

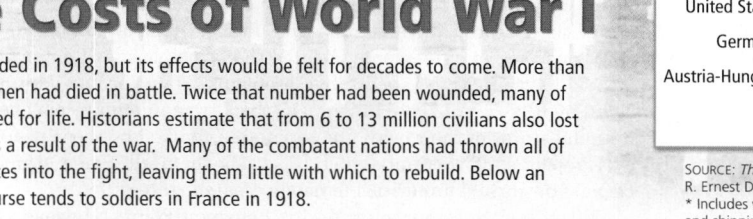

Financial Costs of the War*

British empire	$ $ $ $ $ $
France	$ $ $ $ $
Russia	$ $ $
United States	$ $ $
Germany	$ $ $ $ $ $
Austria-Hungary	$ $ $

$ Represents $10 billion

SOURCE: *The Harper Encyclopedia of Military History*, R. Ernest Dupuy and Trevor N. Dupuy
* Includes war expenditures, property losses, and shipping losses

Casualties of Mobilized Soldiers

■ Died   ■ Taken prisoner
■ Wounded and missing   ■ Unharmed

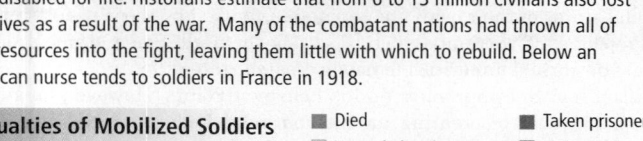

Central Powers

Germany: 16%, 36%, 10%, 38%

Austria-Hungary: 11%, 15%, 28%, 46%

Allies

British Empire: 10%, 23%, 65%, 2%

France: 16%, 27%, 6%, 51%

Russia: 24%, 14%, 21%, 41%

United States: 3%, 5%, 0.1%, 91.9%

SOURCE: *Encyclopædia Britannica*, 2004

Thinking Critically
1. **Draw Conclusions** Which two nations suffered the highest proportion of soldier deaths? Why were American casualties relatively low?
2. **Predict Consequences** What long-term impact might the number of casualties have on a country like France?

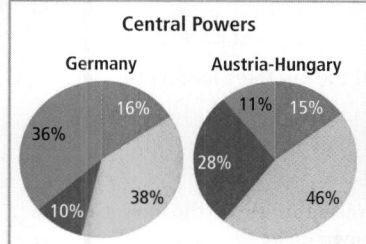

The Costs of War   L3

Instruct

■ **Introduce: Key Terms** Ask students to find the key term *reparations* (in blue) in the text and explain its definition. Ask them to predict the problems with making the defeated countries pay for war damage.

■ **Teach** Ask students to make a quick list of the costs of the war. Write their answers on the board. Using the Idea Wave strategy (TE, p. T35), ask students to compare Europe on the brink of war in 1914 to Europe in 1918. Discuss the sweeping changes brought about by the war, such as the collapse of the Austria-Hungarian and Ottoman empires.

■ **Analyzing the Visuals** Draw students' attention to the Infographic on this page. Ask them to summarize the information provided in the charts and graphs. Then have them use this information to predict how the costs of the war will affect how the various countries approach the peace negotiations.

Independent Practice

Link to Literature To help students better understand the effects of the influenza pandemic of 1918, have them read the selection *From "Pale Horse, Pale Rider" by Katharine Anne Porter* and complete the worksheet.

All in One Teaching Resources, Unit 4, p. 12

Monitor Progress

As students fill in their concept webs, circulate to make sure they understand the costs of war. For a completed version of the concept web, see

Note Taking Transparencies, 172A

Answers

✓ Due to the war, millions of soldiers and civilians lost their lives, property was destroyed, and several countries experienced political turmoil.

Thinking Critically
1. Germany and France; American casualties were lower because the United States entered the war several years after the other major nations.
2. As a smaller country, France would be hit harder with the loss of more soldiers, with widows and families who would be left without a means of financial support.

The Paris Peace Conference/The Treaty of Versailles ⓭

Instruct

- **Introduce** Tell students that Germany was forced to sign the Treaty of Versailles without any chance of negotiating its terms. Ask students to predict how this might lead to problems.

- **Teach** Using the Numbered Heads strategy (TE, p. T23), have students discuss the goals of each of the Big Three leaders. Then read aloud the background note French War Losses. Ask **Why might Clemenceau be more concerned with making Germany unable to fight another war than Wilson?** *(France borders Germany; the United States does not. France lost many more people than the United States, and more French property was destroyed).*

- **Quick Activity** Organize a debate on how self-determination both solved and created problems. Mention that self-determination allowed people to govern themselves, but that the division of ethnic groups was not always clean and neat.

Independent Practice

- **Biography** To help students better understand one of the leaders behind the treaty negotiations, have them read the biography *Woodrow Wilson* and complete the worksheet.

   **Teaching Resources, Unit 4,** p. 9

- **Note Taking** Have students fill in the table categorizing the treaty settlements and problems.

   Reading and Note Taking Study Guide, p. 155

Monitor Progress

- To review this section, ask students to explain how the Treaty of Versailles punished Germany.

- For a completed version of the table, see 🏛 **Note Taking Transparencies,** 172B

Answer

✔ Wilson wanted peace without revenge. Lloyd George wanted to please the British people by punishing Germany and getting money to fulfill his postwar goals. Clemenceau wanted to weaken Germany so that it could never threaten France again.

Note Taking

Reading Skill: Categorize One way to summarize information is to divide it into categories. In the table below, the left-hand column lists issues the world faced after World War I. As you read, categorize the information in the text in one of the second two columns.

Issue	Treaty Settlement	Problems
War Debt		
Fear of German Strength		
Nationalism		
Colonies and Other Non-European Territories		
League of Nations		

The Paris Peace Conference

The victorious Allies met at the Paris Peace Conference to discuss the fate of Europe, the former Ottoman empire, and various colonies around the world. The Central Powers and Russia were not allowed to take part in the negotiations.

Conflicting Goals Wilson was one of three strong leaders who dominated the Paris Peace Conference. He was a dedicated reformer and at times was so stubbornly convinced that he was right that he could be hard to work with. Wilson urged for "peace without victory" based on the Fourteen Points.

Two other Allied leaders at the peace conference had different aims. British prime minister David Lloyd George had promised to build a postwar Britain "fit for heroes"—a goal that would cost money. The chief goal of the French leader, Georges Clemenceau (KLEM un soh), was to weaken Germany so that it could never again threaten France. "Mr. Wilson bores me with his Fourteen Points," complained Clemenceau. "Why, God Almighty has only ten!"

Problems With the Peace Crowds of other representatives circled around the "Big Three" with their own demands and interests. The Italian prime minister, Vittorio Orlando (awr LAN doh), insisted that the Allies honor their secret agreement to give former Austro-Hungarian lands to Italy. Such secret agreements violated the principle of self-determination.

Self-determination posed other problems. Many people who had been ruled by Russia, Austria-Hungary, or the Ottoman empire now demanded national states of their own. The territories claimed by these peoples often overlapped, so it was impossible to satisfy them all. Some ethnic groups became unwanted minorities in newly created states.

Wilson had to compromise on his Fourteen Points. However, he stood firm on his goal of creating an international League of Nations. The League would be based on the idea of **collective security,** a system in which a group of nations acts as one to preserve the peace of all. Wilson felt sure that the League could correct any mistakes made in Paris.

 Checkpoint How did the goals of the Big Three leaders conflict at the Paris Peace Conference?

The Treaty of Versailles

In June 1919, the Allies ordered representatives of the new German Republic to sign the treaty they had drawn up at the palace of Versailles (vur SY) outside Paris. The German delegates were horrified. The treaty forced Germany to assume full blame for causing the war. It also imposed huge reparations that would burden an already damaged German economy. The reparations covered not only the destruction caused by the war, but also pensions for millions of Allied soldiers or their widows and families. The total cost of German reparations would later be calculated at $30 billion (the equivalent of about $2.7 trillion today).

Other parts of the treaty were aimed at weakening Germany. The treaty severely limited the size of the once-feared German military. It returned Alsace and Lorraine to France, removed hundreds of square miles of territory from western and eastern Germany, and stripped Germany of its overseas colonies. The treaty compelled many Germans to

---

History Background

French War Losses France did not suffer the greatest number of dead and wounded during the war. No other nation, however, suffered a greater *percentage* of its population dead or wounded. Of Frenchmen who were between 20 and 32 years old at the start of the war, more than half were killed. Property damage in northern France, where much of the fighting took place, included 300,000 houses destroyed and 20,000 factories or workshops ruined or badly damaged. Some 1,360,000 head of livestock were killed or confiscated. Bombing had ravaged thousands of acres of forest and farmland. This was the country that Georges Clemenceau represented at the Paris Peace Conference.

Europe, 1914

Europe, 1920

Geography *Interactive*
For: Audio guided tour
Web Code: nbp-2641

leave the homes they had made in Russia, Poland, Alsace-Lorraine, and the German colonies to return to Germany or Austria.

The Germans signed because they had no choice. However, German resentment of the Treaty of Versailles would poison the international climate for 20 years. It would help spark an even deadlier world war in the years to come.

✔ **Checkpoint** Why were the German delegates surprised when they read the treaty?

Outcome of the Peace Settlements

The Allies drew up separate treaties with the other Central Powers. Like the Treaty of Versailles, these treaties left <u>widespread</u> dissatisfaction. Discontented nations waited for a chance to revise the peace settlements in their favor.

Self-Determination in Eastern Europe Where the German, Austrian, and Russian empires had once ruled, a band of new nations emerged. Poland became an independent nation after more than 100 years of foreign rule. The Baltic states of Latvia, Lithuania, and Estonia fought for and achieved independence.

Three new republics—Czechoslovakia, Austria, and Hungary—rose in the old Hapsburg heartland. In the Balkans, the peacemakers created a new South Slav state, Yugoslavia, dominated by Serbia.

The Mandate System European colonies in Africa, Asia, and the Pacific had looked to the Paris Peace Conference with high hopes. Colonial leaders expected that the peace would bring new respect and an end to imperial rule. However, the leaders at Paris applied self-determination only to parts of Europe. Outside Europe, the victorious Allies added to

Map Skills The peace treaties that ended World War I redrew the map of Europe.

1. **Locate** (a) Lithuania (b) Czechoslovakia (c) Yugoslavia (c) Poland (d) Danzig
2. **Regions** Which countries lost territory in Eastern Europe?
3. **Draw Conclusions** Why might the distribution of territory after World War I leave behind widespread dissatisfaction?

Vocabulary Builder

widespread—(wyd SPRED) *adj.* occurring in many places

Outcome of the Peace Settlements   L3

Instruct

- **Introduce: Vocabulary Builder** Have students read the Vocabulary Builder term and definition. Ask them to consider how *widespread* dissatisfaction may unbalance the peace created by the treaties.

- **Teach** Ask **Was the principle of self-determination applied to areas outside Europe?** *(No.)* **What happened to these areas?** *(They became mandates.)* **Why might the mandate system cause widespread dissatisfaction?** *(Sample: Having fought alongside Europeans, people from other parts of the world may have felt they deserved the same treatment as Europeans.)*

- **Analyzing the Visuals** Ask students to study the two maps on this page. Tell them to trace the outlines of the former Austro-Hungarian and Russian empires on the map of Europe in 1920. Ask **What new countries were created from these former empires?** *(Austria, Hungary, Yugoslavia, Czechoslovakia, Poland, Lithuania, Latvia, Estonia, and Finland)*

Independent Practice

Have students access **Web Code nbp-2641** to take the **Geography Interactive Audio Guided Tour** and then answer the map skills questions in the text.

Monitor Progress

To review this section, ask students to list two ways the peace treaties succeeded and two ways they failed.

Answers

Map Skills
1. Review locations with students.
2. Germany, Russia, Austria-Hungary, Bulgaria
3. The defeated countries would have been unhappy to lose so much territory. Even Allied countries might have been disappointed that they did not gain more territory.

✔ They believed that the treaty would be based on the more lenient Fourteen Points.

Assess Progress

- Have students complete the Section Assessment.
- Administer the Section Quiz.
   **Teaching Resources, Unit 4**, p. 5
- To further assess student understanding, use
  📖 **Progress Monitoring Transparencies**, 111

Reteach

If students need more instruction, have them read the section summary.

✏️ **Reading and Note Taking Study Guide**, p. 156

✏️ **Adapted Reading and Note Taking Study Guide**, p. 156

✏️ **Spanish Reading and Note Taking Study Guide**, p. 156

Extend

Conduct the Unit 4 simulation, *Paris Peace Conference*, which examines the provisions of the peace treaties.

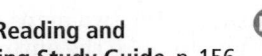 **Teaching Resources, Unit 4**, pp. 86–89

Answers

Analyzing Political Cartoons
1. the reparations that Germany had to make to the Allied countries
2. The cartoonist may have agreed with the ideas behind treaties but may have been more skeptical about their fairness and practicality.

 The United States did not join the League, and so did not have a leading role. The League was too weak to stop new wars from starting.

COME ALONG, GENTS, DINNER'S READY.

Analyzing Political Cartoons

This cartoon portrays one view of the peace treaties that ended World War I.

A The turkey symbolizes Germany.

B Britain holds a carving knife and fork, ready to carve the turkey.

C Other Allies await the feast.

1. What does carving up the turkey symbolize?
2. What attitude do you think that the cartoonist has towards the treaties?

---

their overseas empires. The treaties created a system of **mandates**, territories administered by Western powers. Britain and France gained mandates over German colonies in Africa. Japan and Australia were given mandates over some Pacific islands. The treaties handled lands that used to be part of the Ottoman empire as if they were colonies, too.

In theory, mandates were to be held until they were able to stand alone. In practice, they became European colonies. From Africa to the Middle East and across Asia, people felt betrayed by the peacemakers.

The League of Nations Offers Hope The Paris Peace Conference did offer one beacon of hope with the establishment of the League of Nations. More than 40 nations joined the League. They agreed to negotiate disputes rather than resort to war and to take common action against any aggressor state.

Wilson's dream had become a reality, or so he thought. On his return from Paris, Wilson faced resistance from his own Senate. Some Republican senators, led by Henry Cabot Lodge, wanted to restrict the treaty so that the United States would not be obligated to fight in future wars. Lodge's reservations echoed the feelings of many Americans. Wilson would not accept Lodge's compromises. In the end, the Senate refused to ratify the treaty, and the United States never joined the League.

The loss of the United States weakened the League's power. In addition, the League had no power outside of its member states. As time soon revealed, the League could not prevent war. Still, it was a first step toward something genuinely new—an international organization dedicated to maintaining peace and advancing the interests of all peoples.

✔️ **Checkpoint** Why did the League of Nations fail to accomplish Wilson's dreams?

SECTION 4 Assessment

Progress Monitoring Online
For: Self-quiz with vocabulary practice
Web Code: nba-2641

Terms, People, and Places
1. For each term, person, or place listed at the beginning of the section, write a sentence explaining its significance.

Note Taking
2. **Reading Skill: Summarize** Use your completed concept web and table to answer the Focus Question: What factors influenced the peace treaties that ended World War I, and how did people react to the treaties?

Comprehension and Critical Thinking
3. **Make Generalizations** Describe conditions in Europe after World War I.
4. **Draw Conclusions** How did the peace treaties both follow and violate the principle of self-determination?
5. **Draw Inferences** Wilson's closest advisor wrote of the Paris Peace Conference, "there is much to approve and much to regret." What do you think he might have approved? What might he have regretted?

● **Writing About History**
Quick Write: Choose an Organization Use an organizational strategy that suits the topic of your essay. For instance, if you are writing about one event with many causes, you might write one paragraph about each cause, followed by a paragraph that sums up the effects. If you are writing about a series of events, you might order your paragraphs chronologically.

Choose two topics from this section, one that suits the first type of organization and on that suits the second. Then write a brief outline for an essay about each.

Russia, Austria-Hungary, and the Ottoman empire.
4. In Eastern Europe, self-determination led to the creation of Czechoslovakia, Poland, the Baltic states, and Yugoslavia. However, by creating mandates outside Europe, the treaties ignored non-European peoples' right to self-determination.
5. Sample: Wilson's advisor probably approved the creation of the League of Nations and several new nations in

Eastern Europe and probably disapproved of the harsh treatment of Germany.

● **Writing About History**
Outlines should show a logical organization for each of the chosen topics.

For additional assessment, have students access **Progress Monitoring Online** at **Web Code nba-2641.**

A pin showing the Soviet hammer and sickle (left). A propaganda poster asks Russians to choose sides in the Russian Civil War (right).

WITNESS HISTORY AUDIO

Voices From the Front

" Mr. War Minister!
We, soldiers from various regiments,. . . ask you to end the war and its bloodshed at any cost…. If this is not done, then believe us when we say that we will take our weapons and head out for our own hearths to save our fathers, mothers, wives, and children from death by starvation (which is nigh). And if we cannot save them, then we'd rather die with them in our native lands than be killed, poisoned, or frozen to death somewhere and cast into the earth like a dog. "
—Letter from the front, 1917

The voices from the front joined voices at home, calling for change in Russia.

Focus Question How did two revolutions and a civil war bring about Communist control of Russia?

Revolution and Civil War in Russia

Objectives
- Explain the causes of the March Revolution.
- Describe the goals of Lenin and the Bolsheviks in the November Revolution.
- Outline how the Communists defeated their opponents in Russia's civil war.
- Analyze how the Communist state developed under Lenin.

Terms, People, and Places

proletariat	Cheka
soviet	commissar

Note Taking

Reading Skill: Summarize Copy the timeline below and fill it in as you read this section. When you finish, write two sentences that summarize the information in your timeline.

Russia enters
World War I.
|———|———|———|———|
1914   1916   1918   1920

The year 1913 marked the 300th anniversary of the Romanov dynasty. Everywhere, Russians honored the tsar and his family. Tsarina Alexandra felt confident that the people loved Nicholas too much to ever threaten him. "They are constantly frightening the emperor with threats of revolution," she told a friend, "and here,—you see it yourself—we need merely to show ourselves and at once their hearts are ours."

Appearances were deceiving. In March 1917, the first of two revolutions would topple the Romanov dynasty and pave the way for even more radical changes.

The March Revolution Ends Tsarism

In 1914, the huge Russian empire stretched from Eastern Europe east to the Pacific Ocean. Unlike Western Europe, Russia was slow to industrialize despite its huge potential. Landowning nobles, priests, and an autocratic tsar controlled the government and economy. Much of the majority peasant population endured stark poverty. As Russia began to industrialize, a small middle class and an urban working class emerged.

Unrest Deepens After the Revolution of 1905, Nicholas had failed to solve Russia's basic political, economic, and social problems. The elected Duma set up after the revolution had no real power. Moderates pressed for a constitution and social change. But Nicholas II, a weak and ineffective leader, blocked attempts to limit his authority. Like past tsars, he relied on his secret police

Vocabulary Builder

Use the information below and the following resources to teach the high-use words from this section.
All in One **Teaching Resources, Unit 4,** p. 7; **Teaching Resources, Skills Handbook,** p. 3

High-Use Words	Definitions and Sample Sentences
crucial, p. 478	*adj.* of vital importance I didn't hear the **crucial** information, so I couldn't answer the question.
withdrawal, p. 481	*n.* the act of leaving The **withdrawal** of the opposing candidate ensured that Mr. Ravek won the race.

SECTION 5 Step-by-Step Instruction

Objectives

As you teach this section, keep students focused on the following objectives to help them answer the Section Focus Question and master core content.

- Explain the causes of the March Revolution.
- Describe the goals of Lenin and the Bolsheviks in the November revolution.
- Outline how the Communists defeated their opponents in Russia's civil war.
- Analyze how the Communist state developed under Lenin.

Prepare to Read

Build Background Knowledge L3

Ask students to recall that Russia withdrew from World War I because of a revolution at home. Remind them that people had pressed for reform earlier, in 1905. Ask them to predict what caused the move toward revolution in 1917.

Set a Purpose L3

- **WITNESS HISTORY** Read the selection aloud or play the audio.
   AUDIO **Witness History Audio CD,** Voices From the Front

  Ask **How does the writer of the letter feel about the war?** *(He does not believe in it.)* **How have conditions at home affected his opinion?** *(His family's imminent starvation makes him want to help them instead of fighting.)*

- **Focus** Point out the Section Focus Question and write it on the board. Tell students to refer to this question as they read. *(Answer appears with Section 5 Assessment answers.)*

- **Preview** Have students preview the Section Objectives and the list of Terms, People, and Places.

- **Note Taking** Have students read this section using the Paragraph Shrinking strategy (TE, p. T20). As they read, have students fill in the timeline summarizing events in Russia.

  Reading and Note Taking Study Guide, p. 157

The March Revolution Ends Tsarism

Instruct

- **Introduce: Vocabulary Builder**
  Have students read the Vocabulary Builder term and definition. Ask them to predict how Russian soldiers felt about fighting without *crucial* equipment.

- **Teach** Draw a flowchart with three boxes on the board. Label the boxes Problems Before the War, Impact of the War, and The End of Tsarist Rule. Have students take turns coming to the board to note information from this subsection in the chart.

- **Quick Activity** Divide students into groups. Ask each group to create a list of problems that the provisional government faced after the tsar stepped down. Then, using the Think-Write-Pair-Share strategy (TE, p. T23), have students share their answers. Tell students to read further to see how the provisional government did or did not deal with these problems.

Independent Practice

Have students study the images on this page, and then reread the first paragraph under the section title again. Ask students to write a paragraph explaining why Tsarina Alexandra might have believed that the people would never revolt against the tsar.

Monitor Progress

As students write their paragraphs, check that they understand that although the tsar and his family were showered with celebrations, they had little contact with the Russian people themselves, and so did not understand their discontent.

Vocabulary Builder

crucial—(KROO shul) *adj.* of vital importance

The Tsar's Downfall

Tsarina Alexandra's reliance on the "mad monk" Gregory Rasputin (below left) to help her govern proved fatal for Rasputin, and ultimately for Alexandra. A lavish Fabergé egg (below right) details three centuries of Romanov tsars. *How do both images show the gulf between Russia's rulers and its people?*

and other enforcers to impose his will. A corrupt bureaucracy and an overburdened court system added to the government's problems.

Revolutionaries hatched radical plots. Some hoped to lead discontented peasants to overthrow the tsarist regime. Marxists tried to ignite revolution among the proletariat—the growing class of factory and railroad workers, miners, and urban wage earners. A revolution, they believed, would occur when the time was ripe.

Impact of World War I The outbreak of war in 1914 fueled national pride and united Russians. Armies dashed to battle with enthusiasm. But like the Crimean and Russo-Japanese wars, World War I quickly strained Russian resources. Factories could not turn out enough supplies. The transportation system broke down, delivering only a trickle of crucial materials to the front. By 1915, many soldiers had no rifles and no ammunition. Badly equipped and poorly led, they died in staggering numbers. In 1915 alone, Russian casualties reached two million.

In a patriotic gesture, Nicholas II went to the front to take personal charge. The decision proved a disastrous blunder. The tsar was no more competent than many of his generals. Worse, he left domestic affairs to the tsarina, Alexandra. In Nicholas' absence, Alexandra relied on the advice of Gregory Rasputin, an illiterate peasant and self-proclaimed "holy man." The tsarina came to believe that Rasputin had miraculous powers after he helped her son, who suffered from hemophilia, a disorder in which any injury can result in uncontrollable bleeding.

By 1916, Rasputin's influence over Alexandra had reached new heights and weakened confidence in the government. Fearing for the monarchy, a group of Russian nobles killed Rasputin on December 29, 1916.

The Tsar Steps Down By March 1917, disasters on the battlefield, combined with food and fuel shortages on the home front, brought the monarchy to collapse. In St. Petersburg (renamed Petrograd during the war), workers were going on strike. Marchers, mostly women, surged through the streets, shouting, "Bread! Bread!" Troops refused to fire on the demonstrators, leaving the government helpless. Finally, on the advice of military and political leaders, the tsar abdicated.

Duma politicians then set up a provisional, or temporary, government. Middle-class liberals in the government began preparing a constitution for a new Russian republic. At the same time, they continued the war against Germany.

Outside the provisional government, revolutionary socialists plotted their own course. In Petrograd and other cities, they set up soviets, or councils of workers and soldiers. At first, the soviets worked democratically within the government. Before long, though, the Bolsheviks, a radical socialist group, took charge. The leader of the Bolsheviks was a determined revolutionary, V. I. Lenin.

The revolutions of March and November 1917 are known to Russians as the February and October revolutions. In 1917, Russia still used an old calendar, which was 13 days behind the one used in Western Europe. Russia adopted the Western calendar in 1918.

✔ **Checkpoint** What provoked the March Revolution?

Answers

Caption The image of Rasputin shows that Tsarina Alexandra was out of touch with reality, while the Fabergé egg represents a detached royal family with no connection to their subjects.

✔ defeats on the front, shortages at home, and poor decisions by the tsar and government leaders

Differentiated

Instruction   Solutions for All Learners

L4 Advanced Readers   L4 Gifted and Talented Students

Remind students that World War I strained Russia's resources. The army suffered defeats, mass desertion, and violent rebellion. Ask students to assume the role of a newspaper report accompanying the Russian troops. Have them research and write an article describing how and why Russian troops turned against their officers and tsar to become the troops

of the Russian Revolution. Advise them to research and address such factors as socio-economic conditions, Bolshevik propaganda, conditions at the front, and the relations between the troops and their officers.

Lenin and the Bolsheviks

Vladimir Ilyich Ulyanov (ool YAHN uf) was born in 1870 to a middle-class family. He adopted the name Lenin when he became a revolutionary. When he was 17, his older brother was arrested and hanged for plotting to kill the tsar. The execution branded his family as a threat to the state and made the young Vladimir hate the tsarist government.

A Brilliant Revolutionary As a young man, Lenin read the works of Karl Marx and participated in student demonstrations. He spread Marxist ideas among factory workers along with other socialists, including Nadezhda Krupskaya (nah DYEZ duh kroop SKY uh), the daughter of a poor noble family. In 1895, Lenin and Krupskaya were arrested and sent to Siberia. During their imprisonment, they were married. After their release, they went into exile in Switzerland. There they worked tirelessly to spread revolutionary ideas.

Lenin's View of Marx Lenin adapted Marxist ideas to fit Russian conditions. Marx had predicted that the industrial working class would rise spontaneously to overthrow capitalism. But Russia did not have a large urban proletariat. Instead, Lenin called for an elite group to lead the revolution and set up a "dictatorship of the proletariat." Though this elite revolutionary party represented a small percentage of socialists, Lenin gave them the name Bolsheviks, meaning "majority."

In Western Europe, many leading socialists had come to think that socialism could be achieved through gradual and moderate reforms such as higher wages, increased suffrage, and social welfare programs. A group of socialists in Russia, the Mensheviks, favored this approach. The Bolsheviks rejected it. To Lenin, reforms of this nature were merely capitalist tricks to repress the masses. Only revolution, he said, could bring about needed changes.

In March 1917, Lenin was still in exile. As Russia stumbled into revolution, Germany saw a chance to weaken its enemy by helping Lenin return home. Lenin rushed across Germany to the Russian frontier in a special train. He greeted a crowd of fellow exiles and activists with this cry: "Long live the world-wide Socialist revolution!"

✓ **Checkpoint** Why did Germany want Lenin to return to Russia in 1917?

The November Revolution Brings the Bolsheviks to Power

Lenin threw himself into the work of furthering the revolution. Another dynamic Marxist revolutionary, Leon Trotsky, helped lead the fight. To the hungry, war-weary Russian people, Lenin and the Bolsheviks promised "Peace, Land, and Bread."

The Provisional Government's Mistakes Meanwhile, the provisional government, led by Alexander Kerensky, continued the war effort and failed to deal with land reform. Those decisions proved fatal. Most Russians were tired of war. Troops at the front were deserting in droves. Peasants wanted land, while city workers demanded an end to the desperate shortages.

● BIOGRAPHY

Vladimir Ilyich Lenin

Lenin (1870–1924) was the son of a teacher and his wife who lived in a little town on the Volga River. Vladimir lived with his parents and five siblings in a rented wing of a large house. By all accounts it was a happy home. Vladimir excelled at school and looked up to his older brother Alexander. But when Vladimir was 16, his father died. When he was 17, his beloved brother Alexander was hanged for plotting to kill the tsar.

Still reeling from the death of his brother, Vladimir enrolled at Kazan University. There he met other discontented young people. They united to protest the lack of student freedom in the university. Within three months, Vladimir was expelled for his part in the demonstrations. **How do you think Lenin's early life affected his later political ideas?**

Lenin and the Bolsheviks

Instruct

- **Introduce: Key Term** Review the definition of the key term *proletariat.* Remind students that Karl Marx's theories called for the proletariat to rise up and overthrow the bourgeoisie, creating a classless society where wealth and power would be shared equally among all people.

- **Teach** Ask students to briefly describe Lenin's life, after reading the text and the Biography on this page. Then ask **How did Lenin adapt Marx's theories to fit the Russian situation?** *(Although Russia lacked a large urban proletariat, Lenin started a movement that would form a "dictatorship of the proletariat" instead.)*

- **Quick Activity** Organize a debate on whether Lenin's adaptation of Marxism remained true to the spirit of Marxism.

Independent Practice

Have students suppose they are living in Russia in 1917. Ask them to write a diary entry either supporting or opposing Lenin's ideas. Entries should clearly explain how Lenin's ideas would help or harm Russia.

Monitor Progress

As students fill in their timelines, circulate to make sure they understand the sequence of events. For a completed version of the timeline, see

🏛 **Note Taking Transparencies,** 173

History Background

A Hard Man to Kill The death of Gregory Rasputin was perhaps even more bizarre than his strange life. Nobles feared his influence in the court. To get rid of him, in December 1916, a group of nobles lured Rasputin to the palace of Prince Felix Yusupov, where they served him poisoned cakes and wine. Rasputin was not affected. Next, Yusupov shot him through the chest with a revolver. Rasputin fell, but when the conspirators examined the body, Rasputin got to his feet and began to attack Yusupov.

Then Rasputin attempted to escape. He ran outside, but was shot again. The conspirators then clubbed him unconscious. After flinging Rasputin into the icy Neva River, they watched him sink. Later, the body of Rasputin—poisoned, shot, and badly beaten—was recovered from the river and autopsied. The cause of death? Drowning.

Answers

BIOGRAPHY Sample: The execution of his brother caused Lenin to question and reject the tsarist government.

✓ Germany hoped that Lenin would stir up trouble in Russia and disrupt Russia's war effort, which he did.

The November Revolution Brings the Bolsheviks to Power

Instruct

- **Introduce** Ask students to read the introductory sentences and the three black headings under The November Revolution Brings the Bolsheviks to Power. Have students predict what they will learn under each heading. Then have them read to find out whether their predictions were accurate.

- **Teach** Using the Idea Wave strategy (TE, p. T22), have students discuss the changes in government. Ask **What mistakes did the provisional government make?** *(It continued the war against public opinion and failed to resolve land disputes.)* **How did the Bolsheviks come to power?** *(The Russian people started to revolt. The Bolsheviks, promising peace, land, and bread, took over Petrograd and Moscow, ousting the provisional government almost bloodlessly.)* **What changes did the Bolsheviks make immediately?** *(They ended private ownership of land, gave land to peasants to use, and gave workers control of factories and mines.)*

- **Analyzing the Visuals** Draw students' attention to the Infographic on this page. Ask students to discuss how the events of World War I influenced events in Russia.

Independent Practice

Ask students to write a paragraph explaining why Lenin's promise of "Peace, Land, and Bread" was appealing to the Russian people.

Monitor Progress

Read aloud the black headings in this subsection and ask students to summarize the content under each.

Answer

✔ The soldiers, workers and peasants did not support the provisional government because the provisional government continued the war and did not address land reform.

In July 1917, the government launched the disastrous Kerensky offensive against Germany. By November, according to one official report, the army was "a huge crowd of tired, poorly clad, poorly fed, embittered men." Growing numbers of troops mutinied. Peasants seized land and drove off fearful landlords.

The Bolshevik Takeover Conditions were ripe for the Bolsheviks to make their move. In November 1917, squads of Red Guards—armed factory workers—joined mutinous sailors from the Russian fleet in attacking the provisional government. In just a matter of days, Lenin's forces overthrew the provisional government without a struggle.

The Bolsheviks quickly seized power in other cities. In Moscow, it took a week of fighting to blast the local government out of the walled Kremlin, the former tsarist center of government. Moscow became the Bolsheviks' capital, and the Kremlin their headquarters.

"We shall now occupy ourselves in Russia in building up a proletarian socialist state," declared Lenin. The Bolsheviks ended private ownership of land and distributed land to peasants. Workers were given control of the factories and mines. A new red flag with an entwined hammer and sickle symbolized union between workers and peasants. Throughout the land, millions thought they had at last gained control over their own lives. In fact, the Bolsheviks—renamed Communists—would soon become their new masters.

✔ **Checkpoint** How were the Bolsheviks able to seize power from the provisional government?

● **INFOGRAPHIC**

RUSSIA WAR AND REVOLUTION 1914 1920

1914
July
Russia enters World War I.

August
Germans defeat Russians at the Battle of Tannenberg.

1915
June–September
Russians retreat from German-Austrian offensive.

1917
March
The March Revolution forces Tsar Nicholas to abdicate. The Duma sets up a provisional government.

April
Lenin returns to Russia to instigate revolution. ▶

November
The provisional government fails to end the war and resolve internal problems. The November Revolution brings Bolsheviks to power.

Tsar Nicholas II (left), preoccupied by war, neglected unrest at home. Revolts erupted in March 1917 in response to poor leadership and equipment on the front and lack of food at home. ▶

Differentiated Instruction — Solutions for All Learners

L1 Special Needs   **L2 Less Proficient Readers**   **L1 English Language Learners**

Have students scan the headings and visuals in the section. Then create two columns on the board, for Tsarist rule and Communist rule. Have students volunteer information about the problems under each government, its motives, and its actions during this period. Then ask students to use this chart to compare life in Russia before and after the revolutions.

Use the following study guide resources to help students acquiring basic skills:

✎ **Adapted Reading and Note Taking Study Guide**

- Adapted Note Taking Study Guide, p. 157
- Adapted Section Summary, p. 158

Russia Plunges Into Civil War

After the Bolshevik Revolution, Lenin quickly sought peace with Germany. Russia signed the Treaty of Brest-Litovsk in March 1918, giving up a huge chunk of its territory and its population. The cost of peace was extremely high, but the Communist leaders knew that they needed all their energy to defeat a collection of enemies at home. Russia's withdrawal affected the hopes of both the Allies and the Central Powers, as you read in Section 3.

Opposing Forces For three years, civil war raged between the "Reds," as the Communists were known, and the counterrevolutionary "Whites." The "White" armies were made up of tsarist imperial officers, Mensheviks, democrats, and others, all of whom were united only by their desire to defeat the Bolsheviks. Nationalist groups from many of the former empire's non-Russian regions joined them in their fight. Poland, Estonia, Latvia, and Lithuania broke free, but nationalists in Ukraine, the Caucasus, and Central Asia were eventually subdued.

The Allies intervened in the civil war. They hoped that the Whites might overthrow the Communists and support the fight against Germany. Britain, France, and the United States sent forces to help the Whites. Japan seized land in East Asia that tsarist Russia had once claimed. The Allied presence, however, did little to help the Whites. The Reds appealed to nationalism and urged Russians to drive out the foreigners. In the long run, the Allied invasion fed Communist distrust of the West.

Vocabulary Builder

withdrawal—(with DRAW ul) *n.* the act of leaving

1918

March
Bolsheviks sign Treaty of Brest-Litovsk.

June–July
Civil war erupts between the Reds (Bolsheviks) and the Whites; the Reds execute the tsar and his family.

November
Allies sign armistice with Germany.

1920

November
Communist (Red) government wins civil war, after years of bloody fighting.

▲ The victorious Reds' symbol of worker and farmer unity—the hammer and sickle—comes to represent the new regime.

Thinking Critically

1. **Identify Central Issues** Describe Russia's performance in World War I.
2. **Draw Conclusions** How did involvement in World War I affect events within Russia?

Link to Geography

A Land of Many Nations Geography had long favored the growth of the Russian empire. The vast land stretching from Moscow had few natural obstacles to halt the advance of the Russian armies. For nearly four centuries, the empire grew steadily. This growth was a mixed blessing, however. In 1897, a census revealed that the Russians were a minority in their own empire. More than half the people under tsarist rule were not Russians. The population included Poles, Finns, Ukranians, Lithuanians, Latvians, Turkic peoples, and other groups.

Nationalism led to the rise of new political parties among the peoples. In addition to social and economic reform, the parties' leaders hoped for some degree of self-rule. Radicals dreamed of independent nations, which contributed to unrest in the Russian empire.

Russia Plunges Into Civil War

Instruct

■ **Introduce** Display **Color Transparency 161: Russia Before and After the Revolution 1914 and 1921.** Point out the borders of the Russian Empire before World War I and in 1921. Then point out the line of the Treaty of Brest-Litovsk. Ask **How did Russia's territory change from 1914 to 1921?** *(Russia lost control of the Baltic States, Finland, and Poland.)* Point out that Russia did not lose as much territory as it would have if the Treaty of Brest-Litovsk had stood. Ask students to consider how Russians may have felt about losing so much territory.

▥ **Color Transparencies,** 161

■ **Teach** Ask **Who were the Reds?** *(the Communists)* **the Whites?** *(a collection of groups who opposed the Reds)* **How did the Reds motivate the Russian people to support them?** *(by force and terror)*

■ **Quick Activity** Show students *The Fall of the Tsar* from the **Witness History Discovery School**™ video program. After watching the video, point out that the Bolsheviks murdered the tsar and his family in captivity. Ask them to explain why the Bolsheviks thought the tsar was dangerous. *(He served as a symbol of the old form of government; conservative Whites might have tried to bring him back to power.)*

Independent Practice

Have students review Lenin's promises of "Peace, Land, and Bread." Then have them write a paragraph explaining whether Lenin delivered on these promises by 1921.

Monitor Progress

As students work on their paragraphs, circulate to ensure their answers include examples from the text and show an understanding of Lenin's actions.

Answers

Thinking Critically

1. Russia performed poorly in the war; it was defeated by the Germans and continually retreated until it eventually withdrew in 1917.
2. Economic conditions got worse, and leaders were preoccupied with matters abroad. Revolutionaries were able to take advantage of the widespread unhappiness and bring about the overthrow of the provisional government.

Building the Communist Soviet Union

Instruct

- **Introduce** Ask students to recall that the Bolsheviks were an elite party representing just a small percentage of socialists. Based on their reading, ask students to predict how the new government set up by the Bolsheviks will operate after the end of the civil war.

- **Teach** Work with students to find evidence in the text to support the following generalizations: (1) In some ways, the Soviet Union remained similar to the old Russian empire. (2) Lenin retreated from pure communism. Write the evidence on the board.

- **Analyzing the Visuals** Have students look at the photograph on the next page. Ask them to describe the scene. Then ask **How did Lenin's New Economic Policy address some of the devastation caused by years of warfare?** *(It allowed for some people to develop economically and survive independent of government assistance.)*

Independent Practice

Have students work in groups to write one generalization of their own about the Soviet Union during this period.

Monitor Progress

Check the Reading and Note Taking Study Guide entries for student understanding. Check answers to map skills questions.

WITNESS HISTORY VIDEO

Watch *The Fall of the Tsar* on the **Witness History Discovery School™** video program to learn more about the end of the tsarist rule in Russia.

Brutality was common in the civil war. Counterrevolutionary forces slaughtered captured Communists and tried to assassinate Lenin. The Communists shot the former tsar and tsarina and their five children in July 1918 to keep them from becoming a rallying symbol for counterrevolutionary forces.

War Under Communism The Communists used terror not only against the Whites, but also to control their own people. They organized the **Cheka**, a secret police force much like the tsar's. The Cheka executed ordinary citizens, even if they were only suspected of taking action against the revolution. The Communists also set up a network of forced-labor camps in 1919—which grew under Stalin into the dreaded Gulag.

The Communists adopted a policy known as "war communism." They took over banks, mines, factories, and railroads. Peasants in the countryside were forced to deliver almost all of their crops to feed the army and hungry people in the cities. Peasant laborers were drafted into the military or forced to work in factories.

Meanwhile, Trotsky turned the Red Army into an effective fighting force. He used former tsarist officers under the close watch of **commissars**, Communist party officials assigned to the army to teach party principles and ensure party loyalty. Trotsky's passionate speeches roused soldiers to fight. So did the order to shoot every tenth man if a unit performed poorly.

The Reds' position in the center of Russia gave them a strategic advantage. The White armies were forced to attack separately from all sides. They were never able to cooperate effectively with one another. By 1921, the Communists had managed to defeat their scattered foes.

✔ **Checkpoint** How did the Red army defeat the White army to end the civil war?

Building the Communist Soviet Union

Russia was in chaos. Millions of people had died since the beginning of World War I. Millions more perished from famine and disease. Lenin faced the enormous problem of rebuilding a shattered state and economy.

New Government, Same Problems In 1922, Lenin's Communist government united much of the old Russian empire into the Union of Soviet Socialist Republics (USSR), or Soviet Union. The Communists produced a constitution that seemed both democratic and socialist. It set up an elected legislature, later called the Supreme Soviet, and gave all citizens over 18 the right to vote. All political power, resources, and means of production would belong to workers and peasants. The Soviet Union was a multinational state made up of European and Asian peoples. In theory, all the member republics shared certain equal rights.

Reality, however, differed greatly from theory. The Communist party, not the people, reigned supreme. Just as the Russian tsars had, the party used the army and secret police to enforce its will. Russia, which was the largest republic, dominated the other republics.

Lenin's New Economic Policy On the economic front, Lenin retreated from his policy of "war communism," which had brought the economy to near collapse. Under party control, factory and mine output had fallen. Peasants stopped producing grain, knowing the government would only seize it.

In 1921, Lenin adopted the New Economic Policy, or NEP. It allowed some capitalist ventures. Although the state kept control of banks, foreign trade, and large industries, small businesses were allowed to reopen for private profit. The government also stopped squeezing peasants for grain. Under the NEP, peasants held on to small plots of land and freely sold their surplus crops.

Lenin's compromise with capitalism helped the Soviet economy recover and ended armed resistance to the new government. By 1928, food and industrial production climbed back to prewar levels. The standard of living improved, too. But Lenin always saw the NEP as just a temporary retreat from communism. His successor would soon return the Soviet Union to "pure" communism.

Stalin Takes Over Lenin died in 1924 at the age of 54. His death set off a power struggle among Communist leaders. The chief contenders were Trotsky and Joseph Stalin. Trotsky was a brilliant Marxist thinker, a skillful speaker, and an architect of the Bolshevik Revolution. Stalin, by contrast, was neither a scholar nor an orator. He was, however, a shrewd political operator and behind-the-scenes organizer. Trotsky and Stalin differed on the future of communism. Trotsky urged support for a worldwide revolution against capitalism. Stalin, more cautious, wanted to concentrate on building socialism at home first.

Eventually, Stalin isolated Trotsky within the party and stripped him of party membership. Trotsky fled the country in 1929, but continued to criticize Stalin. In 1940, a Stalinist agent murdered Trotsky in Mexico.

In 1922, Lenin had expressed grave doubts about Stalin's ambitious nature: "Comrade Stalin . . . has concentrated an enormous power in his hands; and I am not sure that he always knows how to use that power with sufficient caution." Just as Lenin had warned, in the years that followed, Stalin used ruthless measures to win dictatorial power.

 Checkpoint How did the government and the economy under Lenin differ from "pure" communism?

Famine in Russia
Years of war took its toll on Russian people, like these starving families in the Volga region. An American journalist, accompanying an international relief team in Russia, described the horrible desolation. In village after village, he noted, "no one stirred from the little wooden house…where Russian families were hibernating and waiting for death."

Assess Progress

- Have students complete the Section Assessment.
- Administer the Section Quiz.
- **Teaching Resources, Unit 4,** p. 6
- To further assess student understanding, use
   Progress Monitoring Transparencies, 112

Reteach

If students need more instruction, have them read the section summary.

 Reading and Note Taking Study Guide, p. 158 **L3**

Adapted Reading and Note Taking Study Guide p. 158 **L1 L2**

 Spanish Reading and Note Taking Study Guide p. 158 **L2**

Extend **L4**

Assign half the class the American Revolution and the other half the Russian Revolution. Have each group research the ideology behind their revolution, the manner in which it was carried out, and its legacies. Then, have each group present its research.

Answer

 In the government Lenin set up, the Communist Party, not the people, controlled the government. The economy under the NEP allowed some capitalist ventures.

SECTION **5** Assessment

Terms, People, and Places
1. For each term, person, or place listed at the beginning of the section, write a sentence explaining its significance.

Note Taking
2. **Reading Skill: Summarize** Use your completed timeline to answer the Focus Question: How did two revolutions and a civil war bring about Communist control of Russia?

Comprehension and Critical Thinking
3. **Draw Conclusions** What were the causes of the March Revolution?
4. **Recognize Ideologies** How did Lenin adapt Marxism to conditions in Russia?
5. **Recognize Cause and Effect** What were the causes and effects of the civil war in Russia?
6. **Recognize Effects** Why did Lenin compromise between the ideas of capitalism and communism in creating the NEP?

Writing About History
Quick Write: Clarify Cause-and-Effect Transitions Writing clear transitions can help strengthen your points in a cause-and-effect essay. Connecting words like *since, as soon as, because* and *until* introduce causes. *Therefore, consequently, as a result,* and *then* introduce effects. Rewrite the sentence below to include a clear transition.
- Tsar Nicholas' government collapsed. He did not solve key problems.

Progress Monitoring Online
For: Self-quiz with vocabulary practice
Web Code: nba-2651

Section 5 Assessment

1. Sentences should reflect an understanding of each term, person, or place listed at the beginning of the section.
2. The first revolution toppled tsar rule and put a provisional government in place. The provisional government had little support, allowing it to be deposed by the Bolsheviks in the second revolution. After a civil war, the Bolsheviks finally drove their opponents out, and set up a Communist government and economy.
3. Russia's massive defeats in World War I, food and fuel shortages, and low confidence in the government
4. He called for an elite group to lead the revolution and set up a "dictatorship of the proletariat."
5. causes: resistance to Bolshevik rule, nationalist groups attempt to break away, Allies' desire to keep Russia in the war; effects: foreign intervention, loss of territory, country in chaos
6. to boost the economy, which war communism had brought to a near collapse

● Writing About History
Students should rewrite the sentences using appropriate cause-and-effect transitions.

For additional assessment, have students access **Progress Monitoring Online** at **Web Code nba-2651.**

- Have students use the Quick Study Guide to prepare for this chapter's tests. Students may wish to refer to the following pages as they review:

Causes and Effects of World War I
Section 1, pp. 454–459; Section 4, pp. 472–476; Section 5, p. 480

The Allies Fight the Central Powers
Section 1, pp. 455, 458–459; Section 2, pp. 461, 463–465; Section 3, pp. 470–471

Key Events in the Russian Revolution
Section 5, pp. 477–481

Key Events of World War I
Section 1, p. 457; Section 2, p. 461, Section 3, pp. 470–471; Section 4, pp. 474–475

- For additional review, remind students to refer to the

  Reading and Note Taking Study Guide
  Note Taking Study Guide, pp. 148, 150, 152–153, 155, 157
  Section Summaries, pp. 149, 151, 154, 156, 158

- Have students access **Web Code nbp-2662** for this chapter's *History Interactive* timeline, which includes expanded entries and additional events.

- If students need more instruction on analyzing timelines have them read the **Skills Handbook,** p. SH30.

- When students have completed their study of the chapter, distribute Chapter Tests A and B.

  All in One Teaching Resources, Unit 4, pp. 17–22

For **Progress Monitoring *Online*,** refer students to the Self-test with vocabulary practice at **Web Code nba-2661.**

Quick Study Guide

Progress Monitoring *Online*
For: Self-test with vocabulary practice
Web Code: nba-2661

■ Causes and Effects of World War I

Cause and Effect	
Long-Term Causes	**Immediate Causes**
• Rivalries among European powers • European alliance system • Militarism and arms race • Nationalist tensions in the Balkans	• Austria-Hungary's annexation of Bosnia and Herzegovina • Fighting in the Balkans • Assassination of Archduke Francis Ferdinand • Russian mobilization • German invasion of Belgium

↓

World War I	
Immediate Effects	**Long-Term Effects**
• Enormous cost in lives and property • Revolution in Russia • Creation of new nations in Eastern Europe • German reparations • German loss of overseas colonies • Balfour Declaration • League of Nations	• Economic impact of war debts on Europe • Stronger central governments • Emergence of United States and Japan as important powers • Growth of nationalism in colonies • Rise of fascism • Increased anti-Semitism in Germany • World War II

■ The Allies Fight the Central Powers

- ☐ Allies
- ☐ Colonial possessions of Allies
- ☐ Central Powers
- ☐ Colonial possessions of Central Powers

■ Key Events in the Russian Revolution

1914–1917 World War I pressures Russia.
March 1917 March Revolution causes tsar to abdicate; the provisional government takes power.
November 1917 Bolsheviks under Lenin topple provisional government (November Revolution).

■ Key Events of World War I

June 1914
Archduke Francis Ferdinand and his wife are assassinated in Sarajevo.

1916
More than two million soldiers are killed in the battle of Verdun and the battle of the Somme.

Chapter Events
Global Events

1914	1915	1916

August 1914
The Panama Canal opens.

January 1915
Japan tries to establish a protectorate over China with the

Differentiated Instruction   Solutions for All Learners

L1 Special Needs   L2 Less Proficient Readers
For students acquiring basic skills:

  Adapted Reading and Note Taking Study Guide
Adapted Note Taking, pp. 148, 150, 152–153, 155, 157
Adapted Summaries, pp. 149, 151, 154, 156, 158

L2 English Language Learners
For Spanish-speaking students:

  Spanish Reading and Note Taking Study Guide
Spanish Note Taking, pp. 148, 150, 152–153, 155, 157
Spanish Summaries, pp. 149, 151, 154, 156, 158

Concept Connector

Concept Connector

 Essential Question Review

To connect prior knowledge with what you have learned in this chapter, answer the questions below in your Concept Connector journal. Use the journal in the Reading and Note Taking Study Guide to record your answers (or go to www.phschool.com **Web Code:** nbd-2607).

1. **Conflict** By 1914, the Balkans were known as the "powder keg of Europe." That same year, a Serbian terrorist assassinated Austrian Archduke Francis Ferdinand and his wife. Write a paragraph explaining why, in addition to avenging the assassination, Austria-Hungary and Germany went to war against Serbia. Think about the following:
   • nationalism
   • international rivalries
   • militarism

2. **Revolution** Compare the Russian Revolution and the French Revolution. How were they similar and different? Create a chart comparing the two revolutions in the following categories:
   • causes
   • duration/phases
   • leaders
   • world reaction
   • results

3. **Cooperation** In his farewell address, President George Washington warned against "entangling alliances." Prewar treaties between European powers were intended to promote peace by creating alliances that no country would dare attack. Identify other reasons for the formation of these prewar European alliances. Do you think the true cause of World War I was entangling alliances? Why or why not?

■ Connections To Today

1. **Conflict: The Balkan Powder Keg** The formation of Yugoslavia after World War I fulfilled the dream of a South Slav state in the Balkans. Yet unrest continued, erupting as recently as 2008. Conduct research and create a timeline of major events in the Balkans from 1918 to the present.

2. **Genocide: Memory and the Armenian Genocide** The Republic of Turkey still maintains that the deportation of the Turkish Armenian population during World War I was a result of civil unrest, not a genocide. Armenian advocacy groups disagree and wage an ongoing campaign for recognition of the Armenians' experience as a planned genocide. Find out where the campaign stands now. Summarize your findings in an essay.

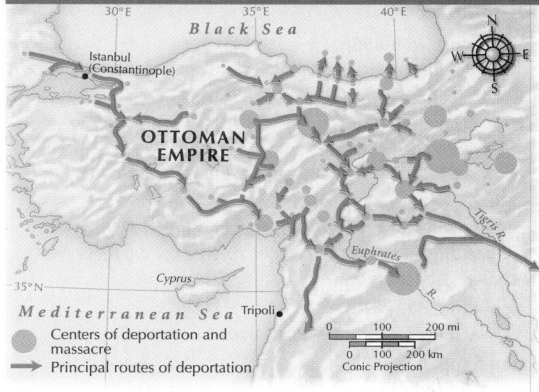

Armenian Genocide in the Ottoman Empire

● Centers of deportation and massacre
→ Principal routes of deportation

0   100   200 mi
0 100 200 km
Conic Projection

April 1917
The United States joins the Allies.

November 1918
Armistice with Germany ends the war.

April–May 1919
Delegates to the Paris Peace Conference draft the Treaty of Versailles.

1917   **1918**   **1919**

1918–1919
A deadly influenza pandemic sweeps across the world, killing more than 20 million people.

February 1919
The first Pan-African Congress meets in Paris.

History Interactive
For: Interactive timeline
Web Code: nbp-2662

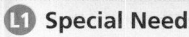

Differentiated Instruction **Solutions for All Learners**

 Special Needs **Less Proficient Readers**   **English Language Learners**

Use the following study guide resources to help students acquiring basic skills:

➧ **Adapted Reading and Note Taking Study Guide**
Adapted Concept Connector, pp. 237, 242, 291

Use the following study guide resources to help Spanish-speaking students:

➧ **Spanish Reading and Note Taking Study Guide**
Spanish Concept Connector, pp. 237, 242, 291

Concept Connector

Tell students that the main concepts for this chapter are Conflict, Revolution, and Cooperation, and then ask them to answer the Essential Question Review questions on this page. Discuss the Connections to Today topics and ask students to answer the questions that follow.

Essential Question Review

1. Nationalist pride drove the Germans to war and caused rebellion among minorities in Austria-Hungary. Germany, Britain, France, and Russia felt threatened by each other's power. Military conflict was glorified by the youth of Europe.

2. Charts should reflect a thorough understanding of the elements of both revolutions and include social unrest as a catalyst for both revolutions, and the phases of both revolutions, key leaders, world reaction, and the different outcomes of each conflict.

3. Answers will vary. Countries often form alliances to bolster trade or gain resources. Students might suggest that alliances were the true cause because they brought too many parties into conflict.

Connections to Today

1. Timelines should include accurate information about people and events in the Balkans through the present and include the creation of the separate states, the role of ethnic cleansing, Slobodan Milosevic, and the role of NATO.

2. Findings should include a current summary of the campaign for Armenian recognition as well as a summary of Turkey's position on the issue.

For additional review of this chapter's core concepts, remind students to refer to the

 Reading and Note Taking Study Guide
Concept Connector, pp. 237, 242, 291

Chapter Assessment

Terms, People, and Places

1. the Dardanelles
4. propaganda
2. stalemate
5. mandates
3. contraband
6. proletariat

Main Ideas

7. Many of the Great Powers were drawn into the war because of their alliances. Germany gave Austria-Hungary a "blank check" of support. Russia mobilized troops in order to support its ally, Serbia. France supported Russia because of its alliance. Britain declared war on Germany when Germany violated Belgian neutrality.

8. Troops dug miles of trench networks to protect themselves from fierce enemy fire. Occasionally, one side would attack the other. Many people were killed or wounded for very small gains.

9. Modern weapons were very deadly; submarines enabled the German navy to hurt British shipping; zeppelins, airplanes, and tanks were signs of warfare to come.

10. the United States; Russia; Russia's collapse allowed Germany to concentrate on the Western Front. The entry of the United States reinforced Allied positions on the Western Front.

11. It made Germany take blame for the war, ordered it to pay heavy reparations, limited the size of its military, stripped land from its borders, and took away its overseas colonies.

12. Millions of Russian soldiers died; the tsar, away at the front, neglected domestic affairs; popular discontent spread after battlefield defeats; and domestic shortages grew.

13. The Bolsheviks took power through an armed overthrow of the provisional government in November 1917.

Chapter Focus Question

14. World War I broke out because of rising international tensions and the European alliance system. It changed the nature of warfare and the map of Europe, and contributed to the downfall of tsarist Russia. Germany took on a burden of guilt and debt. The League of Nations was born. Radical Bolshevik changes turned Russia into the Soviet Union and transformed the international landscape.

Chapter Assessment

Terms, People, and Places

Choose the italicized term in parentheses that best completes each sentence.

1. The Allies tried to regain access to (*Alsace and Lorraine/the Dardanelles*) in the Battle of Gallipoli.
2. After the first battle of the Marne, the war on the Western Front turned into a/an (*entente/stalemate*) until 1918.
3. The British blockade kept both (*contraband/conscription*) and goods like food and clothing from reaching Germany.
4. Both sides used (*reparations/propaganda*) to influence public opinion as a part of total war.
5. After World War I, parts of the Middle East became (*soviets/mandates*) of Britain and France.
6. Lenin wanted to set up a "dictatorship of the (*Fourteen Points/proletariat*)" in Russia.

Main Ideas

Section 1 (pp. 454–459)
7. How did the alliance system that developed in the early 1900s help cause World War I?

Section 2 (pp. 460–465)
8. Describe trench warfare.
9. How did technology affect the way the war was fought?

Section 3 (pp. 467–471)
10. What nation joined the Allied war effort in 1917? What nation dropped out of the war in 1918? How did these two changes affect the war?

Section 4 (pp. 472–476)
11. How did the Treaty of Versailles punish Germany?

Section 5 (pp. 477–483)
12. How did World War I contribute to the collapse of the Russian monarchy?
13. How did the Bolsheviks take power in Russia?

Chapter Focus Question

14. What caused World War I and the Russian Revolution, and what effect did they have on world events?

Critical Thinking

15. **Geography and History** What role did geography play in Germany's war plans?
16. **Synthesize Information** Describe how World War I was a global war.

IN BELGIUM
HELP
THE NATIONAL COMMITTEE FOR RELIEF IN BELGIUM
TRAFALGAR BUILDINGS, TRAFALGAR SQUARE, LONDON

17. **Analyze Visuals** How did the poster above appeal to the emotions of its intended audience?
18. **Draw Inferences** What do you think Woodrow Wilson meant by "peace without victory"? Why do you think the European Allies were unwilling to accept this idea?
19. **Make Comparisons** In what ways did Soviet communism conform to the teachings of Marx? In what ways did it differ?

● **Writing About History**

In this chapter's five Section Assessments, you developed skills for writing a Cause-and-Effect essay.

Writing a Cause-and-Effect Essay World War I was a definitive event of the 1900s. Write an essay in which you analyze the causes and effects of an event that took place during the World War I era. Consider using one of the following topics: Archduke Francis Ferdinand's assassination or Russia's March Revolution.

Prewriting
• Choose the topic listed above that interests you most, or choose another topic that appeals to you.
• Consider multiple causes and immediate and long-term effects of the event you've chosen. Create a cause-and-effect chart to iden-

Drafting
• Develop a thesis and find information to support it.
• Choose an organizational structure for your essay.
• Write an introduction, several body paragraphs, and a conclusion. State the cause-and-effect relationship you are focusing on clearly in your introduction, and follow up your points in the conclusion.

Revising
• As you review your essay, make sure that each body paragraph supports or develops the cause-and-effect relationship you laid out in your thesis statement.
• Use the guidelines for revising your essay on page SH12 of the Writing Handbook.

Critical Thinking

15. Germany's location in between Russia and France led to a two-front war.

16. It involved people from countries all over the world. Colonial and dominion soldiers fought in Europe, and fighting went on in some colonies as well.

17. Viewers might pity the mother and child, fueling anger against the Germans who were blamed for causing such suffering.

18. Wilson did not want the losers punished or the winners to gain any greater power. Nations such as France and Britain had suffered heavily and wanted to be compensated for their losses and remove the threat of further German attacks.

19. The abolition of private property and businesses conformed with Marxist theory, but the rise of the Communist Party as an elite group violated it.

Document-Based Assessment

The United States Enters the War

The entry of the United States into the war in April 1917 was a turning point in World War I. The documents below describe different ways that the United States affected the war.

Document A

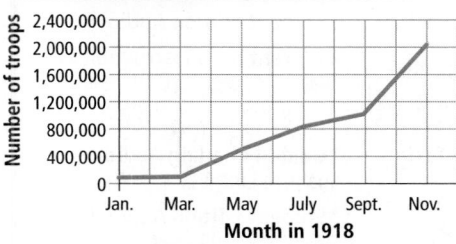

American Soldiers Arrive in Europe, 1918

SOURCE: *The First World War: An Eyewitness History*, Joe H. Kirchberger

Document B

"British shipping losses, especially since the declaration of unrestricted submarine warfare, had risen dangerously. . . . But the entry of the United States into the war made the German submarine warfare an evident failure, because thereafter the number of ships convoyed and the number of ships protecting the convoys was increased steadily. Convoys of ships transporting food, war materials, and troops arrived safely in Britain, and the rate of shipping construction soon exceeded the rate of loss."

—From ***The End of the European Era, 1890 to the Present,*** by Felix Gilbert and David Clay Large

Document C

Winston Churchill, who served in Britain's navy and army during World War I, wrote about the effect American troops had on their tired Allies.

"The impression made upon the hard-pressed French by this seemingly inexhaustible flood of gleaming youth in its first maturity of health and vigour was prodigious [amazing]. None were under twenty, and few were over thirty . . . the French Headquarters were thrilled with the impulse of new life. . . . Half trained, half organized, with only their courage, their numbers and their magnificent youth behind their weapons, they were to buy their experience at a bitter price. But this they were quite ready to do."

Document D

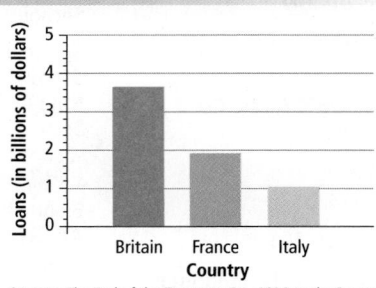

Loans From the United States to Allies

SOURCE: *The End of the European Era, 1890 to the Present,* Felix Gilbert and David Clay Large

Analyzing Documents

Use your knowledge of World War I and Documents A, B, C, and D to answer questions 1–4.

1. How would you describe the arrival of American troops in Europe in 1918?
   A slow at first, but rapid after March
   B steady throughout the year
   C rapid at first, but slow after March
   D No American troops arrived in Europe in 1918.

2. How did the United States navy help break Germany's submarine blockade of Britain?
   A by completely destroying the German submarine fleet
   B by finding new routes around the German submarine fleet
   C by strengthening the convoys
   D by sending supplies to France rather than Britain

3. Based on Document C, how did Churchill feel about American soldiers?
   A They were experienced, but had a poor attitude towards the war.
   B They were energetic and willing to fight, although not experienced.
   C They were well-trained and energetic.
   D They were neither energetic nor experienced.

4. **Writing Task** How did the United States help bring about the Allied victory in 1918? Use your knowledge of World War I and specific evidence from the documents to support your points.

● Writing About History

As students begin the assignment, refer them to page SH10 of the **Writing Handbook** for help in writing a cause-and-effect essay. Remind them of the steps they should take to complete their assignment, including prewriting, drafting, and revising. For help in revising, remind them to use the guidelines on page SH12 of the **Writing Handbook.**

Students' cause-and-effect essays should state the factors that caused the event they've written about and the effects that followed. They should be organized either in chronological order or order of relative importance, and should use supporting facts and details to illustrate causes and effects. For scoring rubrics for writing assignments see **Assessment Rubrics,** p. 8.

CHAPTER 15 Nationalism and Revolution Around the World

Section	Core Instruction L3	Differentiated Instruction L1 L2 L4	
Section 1 *Struggle in Latin America* ⏱ **1.5 periods, .75 block** **OBJECTIVES** ■ Identify the causes and effects of the Mexican Revolution. ■ Describe the Institutional Revolutionary Party (PRI) and the reforms it introduced in Mexico after the revolution. ■ Analyze the effects of nationalism in Latin America in the 1920s and 1930s. **Focus Question** *How did Latin Americans struggle for change in the early 1900s?*	**All in One Teaching Resources, Unit 4** Reading Strategy: Identify Causes and Effects, p. 29 Vocabulary Builder: Word Parts, p. 28 Section 1 Quiz, p. 23 **Reading and Note Taking Study Guide** Note Taking Study Guide, p. 159 Section 1 Summary, p. 160 **Note Taking Transparencies,** 174A–174B **WITNESS HISTORY Audio CD** Fighting for an Ideal **Progress Monitoring Transparencies,** 113 **Color Transparencies,** 162 **Teaching Resources, Skills Handbook** Prereading the Chapter, pp. 1–2 Word Knowledge Rating Form, p. 3 K-W-L, p. 4	**L1 Adapted Reading and Note Taking Study Guide** Note Taking Study Guide, p. 159 SN Section 1 Summary, p. 160 SN **L2 Adapted Reading and Note Taking Study Guide** Note Taking Study Guide, p. 159 LPR Section 1 Summary, p. 160 LPR **Spanish Reading and Note Taking Study Guide** Note Taking Study Guide, p. 159 ELL Section 1 Summary, p. 160 ELL **L4 All in One Teaching Resources, Unit 4** Biography: Emiliano Zapata p. 30 AR, GT	*Student Edition Audio SN **Differentiated Instruction Activity,** Teacher's Edition, p. 491 SN *Guided Reading Audio, Spanish LPR, ELL *Student Edition Audio LPR, ELL **Differentiated Instruction Activity,** Teacher's Edition, p. 491 LPR, ELL **Extend Activity,** Teacher's Edition, pp. 488c, 494 AR, GT
Section 2 *Nationalism in Africa and the Middle East* ⏱ **2 periods, 1 block** **OBJECTIVES** ■ Describe how Africans resisted colonial rule. ■ Analyze how nationalism grew in Africa. ■ Explain how Turkey and Persia modernized. ■ Summarize how European mandates contributed to the growth of Arab nationalism. ■ Understand the roots of conflict between Jews and Arabs in the Palestinian mandate. **Focus Question** *How did nationalism contribute to changes in Africa and the Middle East following World War I?*	**All in One Teaching Resources, Unit 4** Outline Map: Middle East After World War I, p. 35 Geography Quiz, p. 37 Section 2 Quiz, p. 24 **Reading and Note Taking Study Guide** Note Taking Study Guide, p. 161 Section 2 Summary, p. 162 **Note Taking Transparencies,** 175 **WITNESS HISTORY Audio CD** An African Protests Colonialism **Progress Monitoring Transparencies,** 114 **Color Transparencies,** 163 **Witness History Discovery School™** video program, *South Africa: The Rise of Apartheid*	**L1 Adapted Reading and Note Taking Study Guide** Note Taking Study Guide, p. 161 SN Section 2 Summary, p. 162 SN **L2 Adapted Reading and Note Taking Study Guide** Note Taking Study Guide, p. 161 LPR Section 2 Summary, p. 162 LPR **L4 All in One Teaching Resources, Unit 4** Link to Literature: "Prayer to the Masks," by Léopold Senghor, p. 31 AR, GT	**Differentiated Instruction Activity,** Teacher's Edition, p. 497 SN **Spanish Reading and Note Taking Study Guide** Note Taking Study Guide, p. 161 ELL Section 2 Summary, p. 162 ELL **Differentiated Instruction Activity,** Teacher's Edition, p. 497 LPR, ELL **Extend Activity,** Teacher's Edition, p. 502 AR, GT

Assessment Resources
- **Progress Monitoring Transparencies,** 113–117
- **SuccessTracker™,** Chapter 15
- **Document-Based Assessment,** pp. 80–94

- *ExamView®* **Test Bank CD-ROM,** Chapter 15
- **All in One Teaching Resources, Unit 4,** Chapter Tests A and B, pp. 38–43
- **Progress Monitoring** *Online* **Quizzes,** Chapter 15
- **Assessment Rubrics**

Differentiated Instruction Key
L1 Special Needs	**LPR** Less Proficient Readers
L2 Basic to Average	**AR** Advanced Readers
L3 All Students	**SN** Special Needs Students
L4 Average to Advanced	**GT** Gifted and Talented
	ELL English Language Learners

Section	Core Instruction L3	Differentiated Instruction L1 L2 L4

Section 3
India Seeks Self-Rule

 1 period, .5 block

OBJECTIVES
- Explain what motivated the Indian independence movement after World War I.
- Analyze how Mohandas Gandhi influenced the independence movement.
- Describe the impact of the Salt March on the independence movement.

Focus Question *How did Gandhi and the Congress party work for independence in India?*

Core Instruction

All in One Teaching Resources, Unit 4
Section 3 Quiz, p. 25

Reading and Note Taking Study Guide
Note Taking Study Guide, p. 163
Section 3 Summary, p. 164

Note Taking Transparencies, 163

WITNESS HISTORY Audio CD
Indian Frustration

Progress Monitoring Transparencies, 115

Differentiated Instruction

L1 Adapted Reading and Note Taking Study Guide
Note Taking Study Guide, p. 163 SN
Section 3 Summary, p. 164 SN

Differentiated Instruction Activity,
Teacher's Edition, p. 504 SN

L2 Adapted Reading and Note Taking Study Guide
Note Taking Study Guide, p. 163 LPR
Section 3 Summary, p. 164 LPR

Spanish Reading and Note Taking Study Guide
Note Taking Study Guide, p. 163 ELL
Section 3 Summary, p. 164 ELL

Differentiated Instruction Activity,
Teacher's Edition, p. 504 LPR

L4 All in One Teaching Resources, Unit 4
Viewpoints: The Impact of British Rule on India, p. 32 AR, GT

Extend Activity,
Teacher's Edition, p. 505 AR, GT

Section 4
Upheavals in China

 2 periods, 1 block

OBJECTIVES
- Explain the key challenges faced by the Chinese republic in the early 1900s.
- Analyze the struggle between two rival parties as they fought to control China.
- Describe how invasion by Japan affected China.

Focus Question *How did China cope with internal division and foreign invasion in the early 1900s?*

Core Instruction

All in One Teaching Resources, Unit 4
Section 4 Quiz, p. 26

Reading and Note Taking Study Guide
Note Taking Study Guide, p. 165
Section 4 Summary, p. 166

Note Taking Transparencies, 164A–164B

WITNESS HISTORY Audio CD
Change in China

Progress Monitoring Transparencies, 116

Color Transparencies, 164, 165

Differentiated Instruction

L1 Adapted Reading and Note Taking Study Guide
Note Taking Study Guide, p. 165 SN
Section 4 Summary, p. 166 SN

Differentiated Instruction Activity,
Teacher's Edition, p. 508 SN

L2 Adapted Reading and Note Taking Study Guide
Note Taking Study Guide, p. 165 LPR
Section 4 Summary, p. 166 LPR

Spanish Reading and Note Taking Study Guide
Note Taking Study Guide, p. 165 ELL
Section 4 Summary, p. 166 ELL

Differentiated Instruction Activity,
Teacher's Edition, p. 508 LPR, ELL

L4 All in One Teaching Resources, Unit 4
Biography: Jiang Jieshi, p. 33 AR, GT

Extend Activity,
Teacher's Edition, p. 511 AR, GT

Section 5
Conflicting Forces in Japan

 1.5 periods, .75 block

OBJECTIVES
- Explain the effects of liberal changes in Japan during the 1920s.
- Analyze how nationalists reacted to Japan's problems during the Great Depression.
- Describe how the militarists used their power in the 1930s.

Focus Question *How did Japan change in the 1920s and 1930s?*

Core Instruction

All in One Teaching Resources, Unit 4
Outline Map: Japanese Expansion, p. 36
Section 5 Quiz, p. 27

Reading and Note Taking Study Guide
Note Taking Study Guide, p. 167
Section 5 Summary, p. 166
Concept Connector, pp. 250, 278, 284

Note Taking Transparencies, 165

WITNESS HISTORY Audio CD
Japan in the Midst of Change

Progress Monitoring Transparencies, 117

Color Transparencies, 167

Differentiated Instruction

L1 Adapted Reading and Note Taking Study Guide
Note Taking Study Guide, p. 167 SN
Section 5 Summary, p. 168 SN
Concept Connector, pp. 250, 278, 284 SN

L2 Adapted Reading and Note Taking Study Guide
Note Taking Study Guide, p. 167 LPR
Section 5 Summary, p. 168 LPR
Concept Connector, pp. 250, 278, 284 LPR

Spanish Reading and Note Taking Study Guide
Note Taking Study Guide, p. 167 ELL
Section 5 Summary, p. 168 ELL
Concept Connector, pp. 250, 278, 284 ELL

Differentiated Instruction Activity,
Teacher's Edition, p. 513 LPR

L4 All in One Teaching Resources, Unit 4
Primary Source: An Account of the 1923 Tokyo Earthquake, p. 34 AR, GT

Differentiated Instruction Activity,
Teacher's Edition, p. 514 AR, GT

Extend Activity,
Teacher's Edition, p. 515 AR, GT

---

*Audio support is available for all sections.

Author's Notes

Scale of the Major Revolutions

Between 1911 and 1949, great ideological revolutions shook some of the largest nations in the world, including Russia, the largest in territory, and China, the largest in population. During this same period between the wars, less violent but nonetheless ideologically based independence movements gathered force on the Indian subcontinent—second only to China in population—and in many parts of Africa, the second largest continent. . . .

The Russian and Chinese revolutions in particular had much in common. They were based on Western ideologies and visions of social justice, and they anticipated a better social order. They became models for later generations of rebels in other parts of the world. But perhaps most important, they had *scale* in common.

They were fought over hundreds of thousands of square miles by millions of people. Their casualty totals dwarf those of the English, French, and American revolutions of earlier centuries. They changed the lives of hundreds of millions. And they dragged on, sometimes for decades, before a new social order was at last established, a new regime firmly in place. . . .

The many revolutions of the years between the wars are historic monuments of our century. They have given us crusaders such as Mahatma Gandhi, men of violence such as Pancho Villa, founders of new nations such as Lenin and Mao, transformers of whole societies by force, such as Stalin. They gave the world new powers—the Soviet Union and the People's Republic of China—which would play central parts in the history of most of the rest of the century.

Idealistic young rebels—and millions of other men and women—fell in hecatombs to bring these things to pass. Too often, once the guns were still, those who survived found their own lives little improved and their new governments at least as authoritarian as those they had overthrown.

In this also, they were typical of their times. For the most revolutionary of centuries was also the most politically authoritarian.

—Anthony Esler, *The Human Venture: From Prehistory to the Present,* (Upper Saddle River, New Jersey: Pearson Education, 2004), p. 625

Extend ● nline

Cultural Nationalism in Brazil

Have students research Brazilian artists from the early 1900s whose work reflects the cultural nationalism that swept through Brazil. Use the steps below to help students complete the activity.

Prepare for the Activity
Explain that in the early 1900s, Latin American artists, writers, and musicians began to reject European influences in favor of those from their own nations. In Mexico, cultural nationalism was reflected in the murals of Diego Rivera (shown at left) and other artists. In Brazil, artists such as Cândido Portinari and Emiliano Di Cavalcanti began to search for Brazilian themes and styles to use in their work. As the poet and critic Ronald de Carvalho wrote, "We are the sons of the hills and the forests. Stop thinking of Europe. Think of America."

Conduct the Activity For help in starting the activity, send students to **Web Code nbe-2701.** Students will view paintings by several artists and review their biographies. Ask them to write their own biography of one of the artists describe how that artist's work reflected the spirit of cultural nationalism in Brazil.

Follow-Up Conduct a class discussion based on the following questions: Why did art in Latin America have a strong European influence? Why might Latin Americans have wanted to avoid European trends in their art? How does cultural nationalism relate to economic and political nationalism?

Differentiated Instruction   Solutions for All Learners

Cornell Note Taking L1 L2

Learning to take notes efficiently will help students read the text and review key information. The Cornell Note Taking strategy provides students with a structured way to read and record core content.

1. Students draw a vertical line two and a half inches from the left-hand side of their notebook paper to create a Review Column.

2. Students take notes on the text material in the more spacious area to the right.

3. After taking notes on a section, students review their notes and in the Review Column write focused questions that elicit the specific content from the right-hand column. For example, if one section of the notes details African resistance to colonial rule, the student would write the review question "How did Africans resist colonial rule?" Formulating these review questions forces students to review the section content carefully and clarify the information.

4. To study their notes, students cover up the right side of the page, read the review questions, and quiz themselves by checking their understanding and recall of critical content, rather than passively rereading information.

5. Students can be encouraged or required to write a brief summary of each section in their own words at the end of their notes to strengthen their review and increase the likelihood that they will retain the information.

Modeling Reading and Writing Skills

State Your Thesis Explain that in this chapter students will be writing a persuasive essay. (See Writing About History, p. 518.) Remind students that a thesis statement should provoke valid arguments, and should then be supported and defended in the body of the essay. On the board, write the following thesis statements:

1. More authoritarian governments arose in Latin America in the 1930s.

2. Brazilian music is preferable to Argentine music.

3. Despite its problems, economic nationalism benefited Latin America.

Point out that the third one is the best thesis statement as it is the only one that can be argued based on facts. The first option is a straight fact, and the second option is a pure opinion.

Compare and Contrast Point out that comparing and contrasting helps students analyze information. Comparing examines similarities, while contrasting highlights differences. A Venn diagram provides an effective way to compare and contrast information. To make this graphic organizer, draw two overlapping circles. List differences in the outside portions and list similarities in the overlapping oval. Model this skill by going through the Infographic on African Resistance and comparing the ways different countries resisted imperialism.

Nationalism and Revolution Around the World
1910–1939

Teach With Technology

PresentationEXPRESS™
Premium DVD

- Teach this chapter's core content using **PresentationExpress™ Premium,** which includes dynamic lecture notes, interactive game shows, songs, videos, and the *ExamView® QuickTake* assessment tool.

- To introduce this chapter using **PresentationExpress™ Premium,** start by asking students **Which of the following statements do you most agree with? (A) People in colonies deserve to gain independence and should fight for it peacefully and forcefully. (B) People in colonies should prove that they deserve independence before the ruling country grants it. (C) There is no reason for people in colonies to be discontent with outside rule if the ruling country supports them economically. (D) There is no reason why people in colonies should be discontent with outside rule.** Take a class poll or record students' answers using the QuickTake feature and discuss their responses. Point out that, in this chapter, they will read about people in Africa and India beginning to fight for independence from their colonial rulers.

Technology Resources

- Student**EXPRESS** CD-ROM, Chapter 15

- Teacher**EXPRESS** CD-ROM, Chapter 15

- Presentation**EXPRESS**™ **Premium DVD,** Chapter 15

- **WITNESS HISTORY** Audio CD, Chapter 15

- *ExamView* **Test Bank CD-ROM,** English and Spanish, Chapter 15

- **Guided Reading Audio,** Spanish, Chapter 15

- **Student Edition Audio,** Chapter 15

- **Witness History Discovery School**™ video program, *South Africa: The Rise of Apartheid*

- **Experience It! Multimedia Pack**

Bibliography

For the Teacher

Chang, Iris. *The Rape of Nanking: The Forgotten Holocaust of World War II.* Basic Books, 1997.

Fenby, Jonathan. *Chiang Kai-shek: China's Generalissimo and the Nation He Lost.* Carroll & Graf, 2004.

McLynn, Frank. *Villa and Zapata: A History of the Mexican Revolution.* Carroll & Graf, 2001.

For the Student

L2 Hoobler, Dorothy and Thomas. *Showa: The Age of Hirohito.* Walker & Company, 1990.

L3 Harrison, Peter, ed. *African Nations and Leaders.* Series: History of Africa. Facts on File, 2003.

L4 Shields, Charles J. *Mohandas K. Gandhi.* Series: Overcoming Adversity. Chelsea, 2001.

Revolution in Mexico

This Mexican peasants' song from the early 1900s reflected many Mexican's desire for change under the rule of the dictator Porfirio Díaz:

“Our homes and humble dwellings
always full of sadness
living like animals
in the midst of riches.
On the other hand, the haciendados,
owners of lives and lands,
appear disinterested
and don't listen to our complaints.”

Listen to the Witness History audio to learn more about the Mexican Revolution.

◄ **General Carranza with some of his rebel forces during the Mexican Revolution**

Chapter Preview

Chapter Focus Question How did nationalism and the desire for change shape world events in the early 1900s?

Mexico's Coat of Arms

Beaded elephant mask from Africa

Section 1
Struggle in Latin America

Section 2
Nationalism in Africa and the Middle East

Section 3
India Seeks Self-Rule

Section 4
Upheavals in China

Section 5
Conflicting Forces in Japan

Japan's naval flag

Use the ✓ **Quick Study Timeline** at the end of this chapter to preview chapter events.

 Concept Connector ONLINE
To explore Essential Questions related to this chapter, go to PHSchool.com
Web Code: nbd-2707

Chapter-Level Resources

All-in-One Vocabulary Builder; Reading Strategy; Enrichments; Outline Maps; Geography Quiz; Chapter Tests
- Document-Based Assessments
- AYP Monitoring Assessments
- *ExamView*® Test Bank CD-ROM
- Guided Reading Audio (Spanish)
- Student Edition Audio

Previewing the Chapter

- **WITNESS HISTORY** Point out that by 1920, dictator Porfirio Díaz had been ruling Mexico for 35 years. Resentment was high. Read aloud the Witness History selection or play the accompanying audio. Ask students **What is the tone of this song?** *(mournful, sad)* **What inequalities does this song express?** *(inequalities of wealth, political power)* **Since the wealthy landowners, or haciendados, do not listen to the peasants' complaints, what do you predict the peasants will do?** *(revolt)*

  ◀》 AUDIO **Witness History Audio CD,** Revolution in Mexico

- **Analyzing the Visuals** Ask students to study the photograph of General Carranza and his rebel forces during the Mexican Revolution. Ask them to describe the rebel forces pictured. Tell students that in this chapter, they will learn how different regions struggled for change.

- **Focus** Write the Chapter Focus Question on the board. Tell students to keep this question in mind as they read the chapter. *(Answer appears with the Chapter Assessment answers.)* Have students preview the section titles for this chapter.

Differentiated Instruction Solutions for All Learners

The following Teacher's Edition strategies are suitable for students of varying abilities.

L1 Special Needs Students, pp. 853, 859, 866, 870 **SN**

L2 English Language Learners, pp. 853, 859, 870 **ELL**

L2 Less Proficient Readers, pp. 853, 859, 866, 870, 875 **LPR**

L4 Gifted and Talented Students, p. 876 **GT**

L4 Advanced Readers, p. 876 **AR**

Note Taking Study Guide With Concept Connector Journal
For online access: Web code nbd-2707
For print alternative: Reading and Note Taking Study Guide booklet

Step-by-Step Instruction

Objectives

As you teach this section, keep students focused on the following objectives to help them answer the Section Focus Question and master core content.

- Identify the causes and effects of the Mexican Revolution.
- Describe the Institutional Revolutionary Party (PRI) and the reforms it introduced in Mexico after the revolution.
- Analyze the effects of nationalism in Latin America in the 1920s and 1930s.

Prepare to Read

Build Background Knowledge **L3**

Remind students about the effects of nationalism on Europe in the 1800s. Then ask them to preview this section's headings and predict how nationalism might affect Latin America.

Set a Purpose **L3**

- **WITNESS HISTORY** Read the selection aloud or play the audio.
  - 🔊 AUDIO **Witness History Audio CD,** Fighting for an Ideal

  Ask **How does Ferreira describe his experience fighting in Mexico's Revolution?** *(He is glad that he fought with Zapata and others to realize an ideal.)* Ask students to predict what ideals the rebels were fighting for, and whether these ideals were realized.

- **Focus** Point out the Section Focus Question and write it on the board. Tell students to refer to this question as they read. *(Answer appears with Section 1 Assessment answers.)*

- **Preview** Have students preview the Section Objectives and the list of Terms, People, and Places.

- **Reading Skill** Have students use the *Reading Strategy: Identify Causes and Effects* worksheet.

  All in One Teaching Resources, Unit 4, p. 29

Mexican peasant revolutionaries

Coffee beans, one of Latin America's major export crops

WITNESS HISTORY 🔊 AUDIO

Fighting for an Ideal

Zeferino Diego Ferreira, a peasant soldier at the time of the Mexican Revolution, describes his feelings on fighting with the rebel leaders Pancho Villa and Emiliano Zapata:

❝ I am glad to have fought in the same cause with Zapata . . . and so many of my dear revolutionary friends who were left behind in the hills, their bones eaten by animals. I wasn't afraid. Just the opposite, I was *glad*. It's a *beautiful* thing to fight to realize an ideal. ❞

Mexico's revolution was a dramatic fight for reform, with mixed results.

Focus Question How did Latin Americans struggle for change in the early 1900s?

Struggle in Latin America

Objectives

- Identify the causes and effects of the Mexican Revolution.
- Describe the Institutional Revolutionary Party (PRI) and the reforms it introduced in Mexico after the revolution.
- Analyze the effects of nationalism in Latin America in the 1920s and 1930s.

Terms, People, and Places

haciendas	cultural nationalism
nationalization	Good Neighbor Policy
economic nationalism	

Note Taking

Reading Skill: Identify Causes and Effects As you read, note the causes and effects of the Mexican Revolution in a chart like the one below.

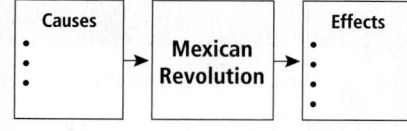

In the early 1900s, Latin America's economy was booming because of exports. Latin Americans sold their plentiful natural resources and cash crops to industrialized countries. In return, they bought products made in those countries. Meanwhile, foreign investors controlled many of Latin America's natural resources.

Stable governments helped to keep the region's economy on a good footing. Some Latin American nations, such as Argentina and Uruguay, had democratic constitutions. However, military dictators or small groups of wealthy landowners held the real power. The tiny ruling class kept the economic benefits of the booming economy for themselves. The growing middle class and the lower classes—workers and peasants—had no say in their own government. These inequalities troubled many Latin American countries, but in Mexico the situation led to an explosive revolution.

The Mexican Revolution

By 1910, the dictator Porfirio Díaz had ruled Mexico for almost 35 years, winning reelection as president again and again. On the surface, Mexico enjoyed peace and economic growth. Díaz welcomed foreign investors who developed mines, built railroads, and drilled for oil. However, underneath the surface, discontent rippled through Mexico. The country's prosperity benefited only a small group. Most Mexicans were mestizos or Indian peasants who lived in desperate poverty. Most of these peasants worked on **haciendas,** or

Vocabulary Builder

Use the information below and the following resources to teach the high-use words from this section.
All in One Teaching Resources, Unit 4, p. 28; **Teaching Resources, Skills Handbook,** p. 3

High-Use Words	Definitions and Sample Sentences
assets, p. 493	*n.* things of value The company's good location was one of its **assets.**
intervene, p. 494	*vi.* to come between two arguing factions My mother was always **intervening** to resolve my arguments with my sister.

large plantations, controlled by the landowning elite. Some peasants earned meager wages in factories and mines in Mexico's cities. Meanwhile, the growing urban middle class wanted democracy and the elite resented the power of foreign companies. All of these groups opposed the Diáz dictatorship.

The unrest boiled over in 1910 when Francisco Madero, a liberal reformer from an elite family, demanded free elections. Faced with rebellion in several parts of the country, Díaz resigned in 1911. Soon a bloody, complex struggle engulfed Mexico. (See below.)

✓ **Checkpoint** What political and economic factors helped to cause the Mexican Revolution?

● **INFOGRAPHIC**

THE MEXICAN REVOLUTION

Fighting raged across Mexico for over a decade. Peasants, small farmers, ranchers, and urban workers were drawn into the violent struggle. Women soldiers called *soldaderas* cooked, tended the wounded, and fought alongside the men. The struggle took a terrible toll. When it ended, the Mexican economy was in shambles and more than one million people were dead.

1 Faced with rebellion, Díaz resigned after holding power for almost 30 years.
◀ Porfirio Díaz

2 Madero, a liberal reformer, was democratically elected in 1911. But within two years he was assassinated by one of his generals, Victoriano Huerta.

Francisco Madero ▶

Emiliano Zapata ▼

Francisco "Pancho" Villa ▼

Victoriano Huerta

3 Huerta lost no time setting up his own dictatorship.

4 Villa, Zapata, and Carranza formed an uneasy coalition against Huerta. Villa and Zapata, peasants themselves, wanted to make broad changes to improve peasantsí lives. Carranza, a rich landowner, disagreed. After defeating Huerta, Carranza turned on Villa and Zapata and defeated them.

◀ Venustiano Carranza

Venustiano ▶ Carranza

5 Carranza became president of Mexico in 1917. A new constitution passed, but reforms were slow to materialize.

Thinking Critically
1. **Sequence** Describe the events of the Mexican Revolution.
2. **Draw Inferences** Why might Carranza feel that it was in his best interests to eliminate Zapata and Villa?

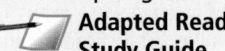
■ **Note Taking** Have students read this section using the Guided Questioning strategy (TE, p. T20) and fill in the chart showing the causes and effects of the Mexican Revolution.

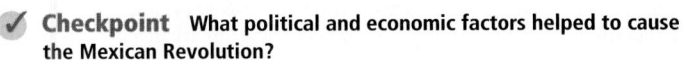 **Reading and Note Taking Study Guide,** p. 159

Teach

The Mexican Revolution ⓛ3

Instruct

■ **Introduce** After reading The Mexican Revolution, ask student to explain the inequality that existed in many Latin American countries. *(Wealth went to a small upper class and foreign investors.)*

■ **Teach** Ask students to list the groups unhappy with Díaz's rule and write their answers on the board. Then ask students to list each group's interest in the revolution, and write those responses on the board. *(rural peasants— land and better lives; urban workers— better wages; urban middle class— democratic government; elites—control over resources owned by foreign companies themselves)* Discuss ways the interests of these groups might conflict.

■ **Quick Activity** Refer students to the Infographic on this page. Read the text as a class. Have six students play the roles of the revolution's key players.

Independent Practice

Biography Have students read *Emiliano Zapata* and complete the worksheet.

All in One Teaching Resources, Unit 4, p. 30

Monitor Progress

Ask students to draw a brief timeline of the revolution.

Answers

✓ Elites resented the influence of foreign companies; poor rural peasants wanted land; poor urban workers wanted better wages; the urban middle class wanted a democratic government.

Thinking Critically
1. Díaz stepped down as a leader, and Madero was elected but assassinated by Huerta, who set up a dictatorship. Carranza, Villa, and Zapata defeated Huerta, then Carranza defeated Villa and Zapata and became president in 1917.
2. Answers should recognize that as a wealthy, conservative landowner, Carranza was threatened by the land reform policies of Zapata and Villa.

Revolution Leads to Change

Instruct

- **Introduce: Key Terms** Have students find the key term **nationalization** (in blue) in the text and define its meaning. Ask students to predict how nationalization will affect Mexico after the revolution.

- **Teach** Discuss the reforms instituted after the revolution. Ask **What were the main provisions of the Constitution of 1917?** *(land reform, labor protection, stronger government control over the economy, takeover of Church lands, and possible nationalization of resources)* **How did the PRI accommodate many groups in Mexican society, while keeping power for itself?** *(The PRI adopted some of each group's key goals.)* Point out the circle graph on land distribution on this page. Ask **Why do you think land distribution was such a key issue?** *(Sample: During Díaz's rule, those who held land held power. It was a way to get greater opportunity.)*

- **Quick Activity** Remind students that the PRI dominated Mexican politics from the 1930s to 2000. Organize students to debate whether PRI control was good or bad for Mexico. Have them consider the goals of the revolution, the importance of stability, and the location of power.

Independent Practice

Have students return to the chart of the various groups' interests. Ask them to note whether the aims of the various groups who fought in the revolution had been fulfilled by the 1930s.

Monitor Progress

As students complete their flowcharts, circulate to make sure they understand the major causes and effects of the Mexican Revolution. For a completed version of the flowchart, see

📖 **Note Taking Transparencies, 174A**

Answer

Caption Lázaro Cárdenas

A President of the People
Mexican President Lázaro Cárdenas greets people at a train station in the 1930s (below). Between 1915 and 1940, nearly 75 million acres of land was distributed to Mexico's people, fulfilling one of the goals of the Mexican Revolution. *Which president distributed the most land?*

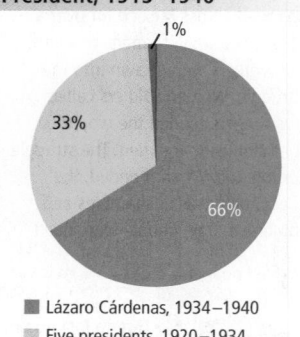

Land Distribution in Mexico by President, 1915–1940

- 1%
- 33%
- 66%

■ Lázaro Cárdenas, 1934–1940
■ Five presidents, 1920–1934
■ Venustiano Carranza, 1915–1920

SOURCE: Michael C. Meyer and William L. Sherman, *The Course of Mexican History*

Revolution Leads to Change

In 1917, voters elected Venustiano Carranza president of Mexico. That year, Carranza reluctantly approved a new constitution that included land and labor reform. With amendments, it is still in force today.

The Constitution of 1917 The Constitution of 1917 addressed three major issues: land, religion, and labor. The constitution strengthened government control over the economy. It permitted the breakup of large estates, placed restrictions on foreigners owning land, and allowed **nationalization**, or government takeover, of natural resources. Church land was made "the property of the nation." The constitution set a minimum wage and protected workers' right to strike.

Although the constitution gave suffrage only to men, it did give women some rights. Women doing the same job as men were entitled to the same pay. In response to women activists, Carranza also passed laws allowing married women to draw up contracts, take part in legal suits, and have equal authority with men in spending family funds.

The PRI Controls Mexico Fighting continued on a smaller scale throughout the 1920s, including Carranza's overthrow in 1920. In 1929, the government organized what later became the Institutional Revolutionary Party (PRI). The PRI managed to accommodate many groups in Mexican society, including business and military leaders, peasants, and workers. The PRI did this by adopting some of the goals of these groups, while keeping real power in its own hands. It suppressed opposition and dissent. Using all of these tactics, the PRI brought stability to Mexico and over time carried out many desired reforms. The PRI dominated Mexican politics from the 1930s until the free election of 2000.

Reforms Materialize At first, the Constitution of 1917 was just a set of goals to be achieved in the future. But in the 1920s and 1930s, as the government finally restored order, it began to carry out reforms.

In the 1920s, the government helped some Indian communities regain lands that had been taken from them. In the 1930s, under President Lázaro Cárdenas, millions of acres of land were redistributed to peasants

History Background

Mexico's Revolutionary Leaders Differences among Mexico's revolutionary leaders reflected sharp divisions in Mexican society. Zapata was an Indian from southern Mexico. Villa was a mestizo peasant from the north. Madero and Carranza were from upper-class, land-owning families. While Madero and Carranza supported democratic political reform, Villa and Zapata pushed for sweeping economic and social changes.

One thing the leaders did have in common, however, was a violent end. Huerta ordered Madero's death, only to die three years later after being released from an American jail. Zapata and Villa were both assassinated, Zapata by agents of Carranza. Carranza himself was murdered as he fled after being overthrown. Of the revolutionary-era leaders pictured on the previous page, only Porfirio Díaz died peacefully in exile.

under a communal land program. The government supported labor unions and launched a massive effort to combat illiteracy. Schools and libraries were set up. Dedicated teachers, often young women, worked for low pay. While they taught basic skills, they spread ideas of nationalism that began to bridge the gulf between the regions and the central government. As the revolutionary era ended, Mexico became the first Latin American nation to pursue real social and economic reforms for the majority of its people.

The government also took a strong role in directing the economy. In 1938, labor disputes broke out between Mexican workers and the management of some foreign-owned petroleum companies. In response, President Cárdenas decreed that the Mexican government would nationalize Mexico's oil resources. American and British oil companies resisted Cárdenas's decision, but eventually accepted compensation for their losses. Mexicans felt that they had at last gained economic independence from foreign influence.

 Checkpoint How did the Constitution of 1917 try to resolve some of the problems that started the revolution?

Nationalism at Work in Latin America

Mexico's move to reclaim its oil fields from foreign investors reflected a growing spirit of nationalism throughout Latin America. This spirit focused in part on ending economic dependence on the industrial powers, especially the United States, but it echoed throughout political and cultural life as well.

Economic Nationalism During the 1920s and 1930s, world events affected Latin American economies. After World War I, trade with Europe fell off. The Great Depression that struck the United States in 1929 spread around the world in the 1930s. Prices for Latin American exports plunged as demand dried up. At the same time, the cost of imported consumer goods rose. Latin America's economies, dependent on export trade, declined rapidly.

A tide of economic nationalism, or emphasis on home control of the economy, swept Latin American countries. They were determined to develop their own industries so they would not have to buy so many products from other countries. Local entrepreneurs set up factories to produce goods. Governments raised tariffs, or taxes on imports, to protect the new industries. Governments also invested directly in new businesses. Following Mexico's lead, some nations took over foreign-owned assets. The drive to create domestic industries was not wholly successful. Unequal distribution of wealth held back economic development.

Political Nationalism The Great Depression also triggered political changes in Latin America. The economic crisis caused people to lose faith in the ruling oligarchies and the ideas of liberal government. Liberalism, a belief in the individual and in limited government, was a European theory. People began to feel that it did not work in Latin America. However, ideas about what form a new type of government should take varied.

In the midst of economic crisis, stronger, authoritarian governments of different types rose in Latin American countries. People hoped that these governments could control, direct, and protect each country's economy more effectively.

Analyzing Political Cartoons

Nationalizing Oil In 1938, Mexican President Cárdenas nationalized foreign-owned oil companies. In response, some nations boycotted Mexican oil.
1. Why is Cárdenas shown standing on a pile of oil barrels?
2. Do you think the cartoonist is Mexican? Why or why not?

Vocabulary Builder
assets—(AS ets) *n.* things of value

Note Taking

Identify Effects As you read, identify the effects of nationalism in Latin America and record them a chart like the one below.

Effects of Latin American Nationalism		
Economic	Political	Cultural
•	•	•
•	•	•

- **Introduce: Vocabulary Builder** Have students read the Vocabulary Builder term and definition. Then refer students to the political cartoon on this page. Ask **What is the *asset* shown in this picture?** *(oil)* Use the Idea Wave strategy (TE, p. T22) and ask students to list the assets of their school or town.

- **Teach** Discuss the various aspects of nationalism. Ask **How did Latin Americans express nationalism economically?** *(by trying to grow domestic industry and by nationalizing existing foreign industry)* **How did political and cultural nationalism grow in Latin America?** *(Latin Americans began to reject European political ideas and European cultural influences, in favor of more indigenous Latin American ideas.)* **Did the Good Neighbor Policy support or undermine nationalism in Latin America?** *(It supported it.)*

- **Quick Activity** Display **Color Transparency 162: *Coffee Plantation*, by Candido Portinari.** Use the lesson suggested in the transparency book to guide a discussion on the ways cultural nationalism was expressed in Brazil.

  ⬛ **Color Transparencies,** 162

Independent Practice

- **Note Taking** Have students fill in the chart showing the effects of nationalism in Latin America.

  ✏️ **Reading and Note Taking Study Guide,** p. 159

Monitor Progress

- Circulate to make sure students understand the effects of nationalism in Latin America. For a completed version of the chart, see

  ⬛ **Note Taking Transparencies,** 174B

Answers

✓ It lessened the power of foreign investors and distributed land more equally.

Analyzing Political Cartoons
1. because he nationalized the oil industry in Mexico
2. Sample: Probably not, because the cartoon is in English and opposed the nationalization of oil, as did American and British oil companies.

Link to Literature

Mariano Azuela's *The Underdogs* One of the earliest works of Latin American cultural nationalism was Mariano Azuela's *Los de Abajo* (The Underdogs). The novel is based on Azuela's own experience fighting with Pancho Villa. It chronicles the Mexican Revolution from the point of view of a poor peasant who becomes a general in Villa's guerrilla army. Azuela's novel abandons European traditions to focus on colloquial, peasant speech; short action sentences with little description; and a series of brief episodes instead of a plot. The book describes a revolution sabotaged by corruption and greed, with disastrous results for the common people. At the end, the main character concludes, "The Revolution is a hurricane, and the man who goes into it is no longer a man, but just a miserable dry leaf driven by the wind."

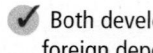

Mexico's Heritage
This stained glass image shows one variation of the Mexican coat of arms that appears on Mexico's flag today. An ancient prophecy dictated that the Aztec capital should be founded where scouts saw an eagle perched on a cactus growing out of a rock surrounded by water, holding a snake in its beak. Accordingly, the founders of Tenochtitlán were believed to have seen this sign in 1325 at the site of present-day Mexico City. The symbol is an emblem of Mexican nationalism. *Why do you think that an Aztec symbol is included on the Mexican flag?*

Vocabulary Builder
intervening—(in tur VEEN ing) *vi.* coming between two arguing factions

Cultural Nationalism By the 1920s, Latin American writers, artists, and thinkers began to reject European influences in culture as well. Instead, they took pride in their own culture, with its blend of Western and native traditions.

In Mexico, **cultural nationalism,** or pride in one's own culture, was reflected in the revival of mural painting, a major art form of the Aztecs and Maya. In the 1920s and 1930s, Diego Rivera, José Clemente Orozco (oh ROHS koh), David Alfaro Siqueiros (see KEH rohs), and other muralists created magnificent works. On the walls of public buildings, they portrayed the struggles of the Mexican people for liberty. The murals have been a great source of national pride ever since.

The Good Neighbor Policy During and after World War I, investments by the United States in the nations of Latin America soared. British influence declined. The United States continued to play the role of international policeman, <u>intervening</u> to restore order when it felt its interests were threatened.

During the Mexican Revolution, the United States stepped in to support the leaders who favored American interests. In 1914, the United States attacked the port of Veracruz to punish Mexico for imprisoning several American sailors. In 1916, the U.S. army invaded Mexico after Pancho Villa killed more than a dozen Americans in New Mexico. This interference stirred up anti-American feelings, which increased throughout Latin America during the 1920s. For example, in Nicaragua, Augusto César Sandino led a guerrilla movement against United States forces occupying his country.

In the 1930s, President Franklin Roosevelt took a new approach to Latin America and pledged to follow "the policy of the good neighbor." Under the **Good Neighbor Policy,** the United States pledged to lessen its interference in the affairs of Latin American nations. The United States withdrew troops stationed in Haiti and Nicaragua. It lifted the Platt Amendment, which had limited Cuban independence. Roosevelt also supported Mexico's nationalization of its oil companies. The Good Neighbor policy strengthened Latin American nationalism and improved relations between Latin America and the United States.

✔ **Checkpoint** Describe how economic and political nationalism in Latin America were related.

Progress Monitoring Online
For: Self-quiz with vocabulary practice
Web Code: nba-2711

 Assessment

Terms, People, and Places

1. What do each of the key terms listed at the beginning of the section, except "haciendas," have in common? Explain.

Note Taking

2. **Reading Skill: Identify Causes and Effects** Use your completed flow-charts to answer the Focus Question: How did Latin Americans struggle for change in the early 1900s?

Comprehension and Critical Thinking

3. **Recognize Causes** Describe three causes of the Mexican Revolution.

4. **Analyze Credibility** How did the PRI fulfill some goals of the revolution but not others?

5. **Identify Central Issues** How did nationalism affect Latin America?

6. **Summarize** How did Franklin Roosevelt change the policy of the United States toward Latin America?

● **Writing About History**

Quick Write: Write a Thesis Statement A persuasive essay seeks to convince its reader to accept the writer's position on a topic. To be effective, the thesis statement must state a position that provokes valid arguments. Write an effective thesis statement on the topic of economic nationalism in Latin America.

Mexican Murals

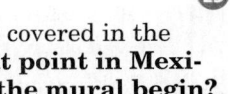

Diego Rivera ▶

During the 1920s and 1930s, the Mexican government commissioned artists to paint beautiful murals about revolutionary themes on the walls of public buildings. The murals were meant to help all Mexicans, even those who couldn't read, learn about the ideals of the Revolution.

The most famous Mexican muralist was Diego Rivera. The panel to the right is part of a huge work on Mexican history that Rivera painted on the stairway of the National Palace in Mexico City.

Zapata, Villa, and other revolutionaries appear at the top of the panel, holding a banner that reads "Tierra y Libertad" ("Land and Liberty")—Zapata's slogan.

The center of the composition shows an eagle sitting on a cactus. The eagle is part of a national symbol of Mexico. A variation of it appears on the current Mexican flag. However, here, the eagle holds the Aztec war symbol in its beak rather than the traditional serpent.

The bottom segment shows the conquest of Mexico by Hernán Cortés. Cortés's armies battle the native Aztecs.

Thinking Critically
1. **Make Inferences** Why do you think Diego Rivera has the Mexican eagle holding the Aztec war symbol rather than the serpent?
2. **Draw Conclusions** What do Rivera's murals reveal about how he viewed Mexican history?

Mexican Murals

Objectives
- Understand how artists present messages through their artwork.
- Describe how artwork relates to and shapes historical memory.

Build Background Knowledge ⬢
Remind students that Mexican murals were a form of cultural nationalism. Using the Idea Wave strategy (TE, p. T22), ask them to brainstorm ways that a mural would be an effective way of spreading nationalist ideas.

Instruct ⬢
- Discuss the periods covered in the mural. Ask **At what point in Mexican history does the mural begin?** *(with Cortés's conquest)* **At what point does it end?** *(with the Mexican Revolution)*
- Ask **What strikes you about the painting?** *(Answers will vary; students may note the bright colors or the complex composition.)* **Do you think the mural reflects a pride in Mexican history? Why or why not?** *(Answers will vary.)*

Monitor Progress
Divide the class into small groups. Ask students to pick a section of the mural not mentioned in the text, identify who is pictured, and describe that person's or group's role in Mexico's history. Ask them to consider why Rivera included the person in that section of the mural. Using the Numbered Heads strategy (TE, p. T23), have the groups share their findings with the class.

History Background

Diego Rivera In art school as a teen, Diego Rivera questioned why his teachers taught only European masters. After studying art in Europe, Rivera fought alongside Zapata. After five months, he fled back to Europe, but he remained a revolutionary. He met Picasso in Paris and studied Renaissance fresco techniques in Italy. He also learned more about the communist experiment in the Soviet Union. After the revolution, he returned to Mexico. The Mexican government commissioned him, with José Clemente Orozco and David Alfaro Siquieros, to create public murals honoring Mexico's national heritage. Rivera combined Mexican folk art with the fresco techniques he had learned in Italy to create unique murals, often with socialist themes.

Thinking Critically
1. Sample: Rivera may be emphasizing the role of war and conflict in Mexican history.
2. Sample: Rivera views Mexican history as a colorful pageant which combines Spanish and Indian strands to create a unique Mexican identity.

Objectives

As you teach this section, keep students focused on the following objectives to help them answer the Section Focus Question and master core content.

■ Describe how Africans resisted colonial rule.

■ Analyze how nationalism grew in Africa.

■ Explain how Turkey and Persia modernized.

■ Summarize how European mandates contributed to the growth of Arab nationalism.

■ Understand the roots of conflict between Jews and Arabs in the Palestinian mandate.

Prepare to Read

Build Background Knowledge L3

Remind students that many people in Africa and the Middle East helped the Allies during World War I. Ask them to predict how these people might expect to be treated after the war.

Set a Purpose

■ **WITNESS HISTORY** Read the selection aloud or play the audio.

🔊)) AUDIO **Witness History Audio CD,** An African Protests Colonialism

Ask students to paraphrase Jomo Kenyatta's words. Ask **What metaphor does Kenyatta use to dramatize the injustices of colonialism?** *(that of a house)*

■ **Focus** Point out the Section Focus Question and write it on the board. Tell students to refer to this question as they read. *(Answer appears with Section 2 Assessment answers.)*

■ **Preview** Have students preview the Section Objectives and the list of Terms, People, and Places.

■ **Note Taking** Have students read this section using the Paragraph Shrinking strategy (TE, p. T20). As they read, have students fill in the chart describing the rise of nationalism in Africa and the Middle East.

📝 **Reading and Note Taking Study Guide,** p. 161

A woman (right) carries a load of wood in the British colony of Kenya. A French poster (above) urges Europeans to visit Africa.

WITNESS HISTORY 🔊 AUDIO

An African Protests Colonialism

❝If you woke up one morning and found that somebody had come to your house, and had declared that house belonged to him, you would naturally be surprised, and you would like to know by what arrangement. Many Africans at that time found that, on land that had been in the possession of their ancestors from time immemorial, they were now working as squatters or as laborers.❞

—Jomo Kenyatta, Kenyan independence leader

Focus Question How did nationalism contribute to changes in Africa and the Middle East following World War I?

Nationalism in Africa and the Middle East

Objectives
• Describe how Africans resisted colonial rule.
• Analyze how nationalism grew in Africa.
• Explain how Turkey and Persia modernized.
• Summarize how European mandates contributed to the growth of Arab nationalism.
• Understand the roots of conflict between Jews and Arabs in the Palestinian mandate.

Terms, People, and Places

apartheid	Asia Minor
Pan-Africanism	Pan-Arabism
négritude movement	Balfour Declaration

Note Taking

Reading Skill: Identify Causes and Effects Record reasons for the rise of nationalism in Africa and the Middle East and its effects in a chart like the one below.

Rise of Nationalism		
Region	Reasons for Rise	Effects
Africa		
Turkey and Persia		
Middle East		

Jomo Kenyatta, quoted above, was a leader in Kenya's struggle for independence from British rule. During the 1920s and 1930s, a new generation of leaders, proud of their unique heritage, struggled to stop imperialism and restore Africa for Africans.

Africans Resist Colonial Rule

During the early 1900s, almost every part of Africa was a European colony. Agricultural improvements in some areas caused a boom in export crops. However, the colonizers exploited the boom solely for their own benefit.

Some Africans were forced to work on plantations or in mines run by Europeans. The money they earned went to pay taxes to the colonial government. In Kenya and Rhodesia, white settlers forced Africans off the best land. The few who kept their land were forbidden to grow the most profitable crops. Only Europeans could grow these. Also in Kenya, the British made all Africans carry identification cards, imposed a tax, and restricted where they could live or travel. In other parts of Africa, farmers kept their land but had to grow cash crops, like cotton, instead of food. This led to famines in some regions.

During World War I, more than one million Africans had fought on behalf of their colonial rulers. Many had hoped that their service would lead to more rights and opportunities. Instead, the situation remained mostly the same or even worsened.

Vocabulary Builder

Use the information below and the following resources to teach the high-use words from this section.
All in One **Teaching Resources, Unit 4,** p. 28; **Teaching Resources, Skills Handbook,** p. 3

High-Use Words	Definitions and Sample Sentences
assert, p. 499	*vt.* to maintain or defend She **asserted** that it was her turn to shower by taking over the bathroom.
advocate, p. 502	*vt.* to support or favor Because she was hungry, Maria **advocated** that the group eat first, and then work on the project.

Opposing Imperialism Many Western-educated Africans criticized the injustice of imperial rule. Although they had trained for professional careers, the best jobs went to Europeans. Inspired by President Woodrow Wilson's call for self-determination, Africans condemned the colonial system. In Africa, as in other regions around the world, socialism found a growing audience. Protests and opposition to imperialism multiplied.

Racial Segregation and Nationalism in South Africa Between 1910 and 1940, whites strengthened their grip on South Africa. They imposed a system of racial segregation. Their goal was to ensure white economic, political, and social supremacy. New laws, for example, restricted better-paying jobs in mines to whites only. Blacks were pushed into low-paid, less-skilled work. As in Kenya, South African blacks had to carry passes at all times. They were evicted from the best land, which was set aside for whites, and forced to live on crowded "reserves," which were located in dry, infertile areas.

Other laws chipped away at the rights of blacks. In one South African province, educated blacks who owned property had been allowed to vote in local elections. In 1936, the government abolished that right. The system of segregation set up at this time would become even stricter after 1948, when **apartheid** (uh PAHR tayt), a policy of rigid segregation, became law.

Yet South Africa was also home to a vital nationalist movement. African Christian churches and African-run newspapers demanded rights for black South Africans. They formed a political party, later known as the African National Congress (ANC), to protest unfair laws. Their efforts, however, had no effect on South Africa's white government. Still, the ANC did build a framework for political action in later years.

✔ **Checkpoint** In what ways did colonial powers try to control African life?

Nationalism and an "Africa for Africans"

In the 1920s, a movement known as **Pan-Africanism** began to nourish the nationalist spirit and strengthen resistance. Pan-Africanism emphasized the unity of Africans and people of African descent worldwide. Among its most inspiring leaders was Jamaica-born Marcus Garvey. He preached a forceful, appealing message of "Africa for Africans" and

WITNESS HISTORY VIDEO

Watch *South Africa: The Rise of Apartheid* on the **Witness History Discovery School**™ video program to explore the workings and origins of apartheid.

DISCOVERY SCHOOL

Segregation in South Africa
In the early 1900s, white people in South Africa began to force urban Africans to move to camps outside of the larger cities, such as this settlement outside of Cape Town. *Why do you think that the white people have forced the African people behind a barbed wire fence?*

Instruct

- **Introduce: Key Terms** Ask students to find the key term **Pan-Africanism** (in blue) in the text and explain its meaning. Ask students to predict how Marcus Garvey's idea of an "Africa for Africans" would strengthen the spirit of nationalism within Africa.

- **Teach** Review the ways the Pan-African movement promoted unity. Then ask **What did the Pan-African Congress accomplish?** *(It created a charter of rights for Africans, which the Western powers ignored, and established cooperation among African and African American leaders.)* **How did Léopold Senghor and other writers in the négritude movement foster pride in African culture?** *(They rejected negative views of Africa and protested colonial rule through their writing.)*

- **Analyzing the Visuals** Refer students to the Infographic on African Resistance. Ask volunteers to list the various forms of resistance. *(squatting on land, forming labor unions, developing political organizations)*

Independent Practice

Link to Literature To help students better understand how the négritude movement inspired pride in African accomplishments, have them read the selection *"Prayer to the Masks" by Léopold Senghor* and complete the worksheet.

All in One Teaching Resources, Unit 4, p. 31

Monitor Progress

Ask students to make a brief outline of this subsection to show their understanding of the Pan-African movement.

● INFOGRAPHIC

African Resistance

Opposition to imperialism grew among Africans in the 1920s and 1930s. Resistance took many forms. Those who had lost their lands to Europeans sometimes squatted, or settled illegally, on European-owned plantations. In cities, workers began to form labor unions, even though they were illegal under colonial law codes. Africans formed associations and political parties to express their opposition to the colonial system. Although large-scale revolts were rare, protests were common.

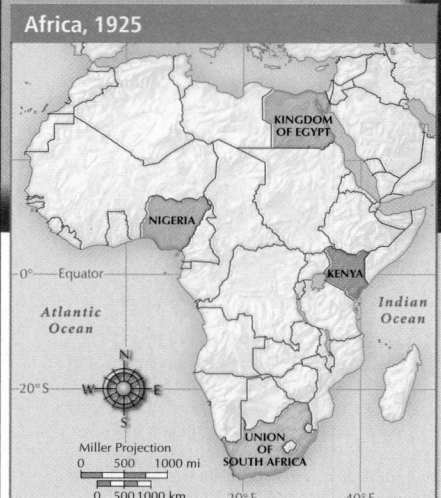

Africa, 1925

Nigeria
In 1929, Ibo market women in Nigeria denounced British policies. They demanded a voice in decisions that affected their markets (below). The "Women's War," as it was called, soon became a full-fledged revolt.

South Africa
In 1912, educated Africans organized a political party that later became the African National Congress (ANC). Its members worked through legal means, protesting laws that restricted the freedom of black Africans. One ANC member (left) gave a speaking tour in England to raise support for his cause.

demanded an end to colonial rule. Garvey's ideas influenced a new generation of African leaders.

Pan-African Congress Forges Ties African American scholar and activist W.E.B. DuBois (doo BOYS) organized the first Pan-African Congress in 1919. It met in Paris, where the Allies were holding their peace conference. Delegates from African colonies, the West Indies, and the United States called on the Paris peacemakers to approve a charter of rights for Africans. Although the Western powers ignored their demands, the Pan-African Congress established cooperation among African and African American leaders.

The Négritude Movement Shows Pride French-speaking writers in West Africa and the Caribbean further awakened self-confidence among Africans through the **négritude movement.** In the négritude movement, writers expressed pride in their African roots and protested colonial rule. Best known among them was the Senegalese poet Léopold Senghor, who celebrated Africa's rich cultural heritage. He fostered African pride by rejecting the negative views of Africa spread by colonial rulers. Later, Senghor would take an active role in Senegal's drive to independence, and he would serve as its first president.

Egypt Gains Independence African nationalism brought little political change, except to Egypt. Egyptians had suffered during World War I. After the war, protests, strikes, and riots forced Britain to grant Egypt independence in 1922. However, Britain still controlled Egypt's monarchy.

History Background

Léopold Senghor and the Négritude Movement The négritude movement developed during the 1930s to 1950s to protest mistreatment of Africa and its people by colonial powers. Léopold Senghor (1906–2001) of French West Africa (now the Republic of Senegal), the leading figure of négritude, also became a public figure greatly admired in his country and respected internationally. During the 1940s and 1950s, he worked to unify Africans politically.

After he successfully appealed to French president Charles de Gaulle, Senegal became a republic and soon after, in 1960, Senghor was elected its first president. Although their takes on négritude differed, Senghor inspired many other writers, such as Birago Diop and David Diop from Senegal; Jacques Rabemananjara of Madagascar; Mongo Beti and Ferdinand Oyone from Cameroon; and poet Tchicaya U Tam'si from the Congo.

Egypt

Simmering resistance to British rule in Egypt flared as World War I ended. Peasants, landowners, Christians, Muslims and Western-educated officials united behind the Wafd party, which launched strikes and protests (right). In 1922, the British finally agreed to declare Egypt independent. In fact, however, British troops stayed in Egypt to guard the Suez Canal, and Britain remained the real power behind Egypt's King Faud.

Kenya

Members of the Kikuyu ethnic group formed the Kikuyu Central Association in 1924. The Association protested the Kikuyu's loss of land, forced labor, heavy taxes, and the hated identification cards. The British jailed Harry Thuku (right) and other Kikuyu leaders, but protests continued.

Thinking Critically

1. **Make Comparisons** How did the methods of the ANC in South Africa differ from the Wafd party in Egypt?
2. **Determine Relevance** Why is it important to learn about early protest movements in Africa, despite the fact that most colonies did not gain independence until after World War II?

Displeased with this state of affairs, during the 1930s many young Egyptians joined an organization called the Muslim Brotherhood. This group fostered a broad Islamic nationalism that rejected Western culture and denounced corruption in the Egyptian government.

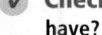 **Checkpoint** What significance does the phrase "Africa for Africans" have?

Turkey and Persia Modernize

Nationalist movements brought immense changes to the Middle East in the aftermath of World War I. The defeated Ottoman empire was near collapse in 1918. Its Arab lands, as you have read, were divided between Britain and France. However, in **Asia Minor,** the Turkish peninsula between the Black Sea and the Mediterranean Sea, Turks resisted Western control and fought to build a modern nation.

Atatürk Sets Goals In 1920, the Ottoman sultan reluctantly signed the Treaty of Sèvres, in which the empire lost its Arab and North African lands. The sultan also had to give up some land in Asia Minor to a number of Allied countries, including Greece. A Greek force landed in the city of Smyrna (now Izmir) to assert Greece's claims. Turkish nationalists, led by the determined and energetic Mustafa Kemal, overthrew the sultan, defeated the Greeks, and declared Turkey a republic. Kemal negotiated a new treaty. Among other provisions, the treaty called for about 1.3 million Greeks to leave Turkey, while some 400,000 Turks left Greece.

Vocabulary Builder

assert—(uh SURT) *vt.* maintain or defend

Turkey and Persia Modernize

Instruct

■ **Introduce: Vocabulary Builder** Have students read the Vocabulary Builder term and definition. Tell students that when Turkey's new leader, Atatürk, fought off the Greeks, he *asserted* Turkey's nationalist aims.

■ **Teach** Ask **What were Atatürk's goals for Turkey?** (*He wanted to strengthen Turkey as a nation by renegotiating the Treaty of Sèvres, then modernize and westernize Turkey. He also wanted to separate religion and government.*) Then direct students' attention to the Biography on the next page. **What reforms did Atatürk make to reach his goals?** (*replaced Islamic laws, calendar, days of rest, and schools with secular, westernized versions; changed the Turkish alphabet from an Arabic version to a Latin-based one, forced people to wear Western clothes, and removed some of the restrictions placed on women*) **How do you think people would react to these sweeping changes?** (*Sample: They might resist them.*)

Independent Practice

Ask students to write a letter from the perspective of an official in either Turkey or Persia that urges people to break with a long-standing tradition and adopt a new, Western custom, such as making Sunday a day of rest or adopting a Western style of dress. Tell them to consider the following questions: How would people resist this idea? What arguments should the letter use to be effective?

Monitor Progress

As students work on their writing, circulate to ensure that the letters are persuasive and that they recognize the tensions surrounding modernization and westernization.

Answers

Thinking Critically

1. The ANC protested legally and sought to reform specific laws while the Wafd Party protested violently with strikes and riots.
2. It shows that many countries had been working for independence for many years before they were finally granted it.

✓ It was used to encourage nationalism and an end to colonial rule, and it united Africans in their desire for independence.

Arab Nationalism in the Middle East ⓁⒶ

Instruct

■ **Introduce: Vocabulary Builder**
Have students read the Vocabulary Builder term and definition. Tell students that in the Middle East in the 1920s, British authorities *advocated* a plan to encourage Jewish settlement in Palestine. At the same time, Arab nationalists sought to create an Arab nation, which would include the Arabs who already lived in Palestine. Ask students to describe the conflict set up by these two plans.

■ **Teach** Discuss the goals of Pan-Arabism *(to unite Arabs in their own state)*. Then ask **How did the Paris Peace Conference affect Arabs?** *(Instead of Arabs gaining the independence they had been promised, some of their lands were made mandates of European powers.)* **How did the Balfour Declaration further undermine Pan-Arabism?** *(The Balfour Declaration encouraged Jewish settlement in Palestine, which was a part of the Arab homeland. The subsequent settlement further weakened Pan-Arab goals, and touched off a conflict that still rages today.)*

■ **Quick Activity** Ask students to come to the board and create a flowchart, detailing events in the Middle East from 1919 through the 1930s.

BIOGRAPHY

Atatürk (1881–1938)
"Atatürk" is the name that Mustafa Kemal gave himself when he ordered all Turkish people to take on surnames, or last names. It means "Father of the Turks." In 1920, he led Turkish nationalists in the fight against Greek forces trying to enforce the Treaty of Sèvres, establishing the borders of the modern Republic of Turkey. Once in power, he passed many reforms to modernize, Westernize, and secularize Turkey. Atatürk is still honored throughout Turkey today—his portrait appears on postage and all currency. **Why is Atatürk considered the "Father of the Turks"?**

Atatürk's Reforms in Turkey
- Replaced Islamic law with European model
- Replaced Muslim calendar with Western (Christian) calendar
- Moved day of rest from Friday to Sunday
- Closed religious schools and opened state schools
- Forced people to wear Western-style clothes
- Replaced Arabic alphabet with Latin alphabet
- Gave women the right to vote and to work outside the home.

Kemal later took the name Atatürk (ah tah TURK), meaning "father of the Turks." Between 1923 and his death in 1938, Atatürk forced through an ambitious program of radical reforms. His goals were to modernize Turkey along Western lines and to separate religion from government. To achieve these goals, Atatürk mandated that Islamic traditions in several fields be replaced with Western alternatives (see Biography).

Westernization Transforms Turkey Atatürk's government encouraged industrial expansion. The government built railroads, set up factories, and hired westerners to advise on how to make Turkey economically independent.

To achieve his reforms, Atatürk ruled with an iron hand. To many Turks, he was a hero who was transforming Turkey into a strong, modern power. Others questioned Atatürk's dictatorial powers and complete rejection of religion in laws and government. They believed that Islam could play a constructive role in a modern, civil state.

Nationalism and Reform at Work in Persia The success of Atatürk's reforms inspired nationalists in neighboring Persia (present-day Iran). Persian nationalists greatly resented the British and Russians, who had won spheres of influence over Persia in 1907. In 1925, an ambitious army officer, Reza Khan, overthrew the shah. He set up his own dynasty, with himself as shah.

Like Atatürk, Reza Khan rushed to modernize Persia and make it fully independent. He built factories, roads, and railroads and strengthened the army. He forced Persians to wear Western clothing and set up modern, secular schools. In addition, he moved to replace Islamic law with secular law and encouraged women to take part in public life. Muslim religious leaders fiercely condemned Reza Khan's efforts to introduce Western ways to the nation.

Reza Khan also persuaded the British company that controlled Persia's oil industry to give Persia a larger share of the profits and insisted that Persian workers be hired at all levels of the company. In the decades ahead, oil would become a major factor in Persia's economy and foreign policy.

 Checkpoint What did the reforms of Atatürk and Reza Khan have in common?

Arab Nationalism in the Middle East

Oil became a major factor throughout the Middle East during this period. The use of gasoline-powered engines in various vehicles during World War I showed that oil was the fuel of the future. Foreign companies began to move into the Middle East to exploit its large oil reserves.

Pan-Arabism Grows Partly in response to foreign influence, Arab nationalism grew after World War I and gave rise to **Pan-Arabism.** This nationalist movement was built on the shared heritage of Arabs who lived in lands from the Arabian Peninsula to North Africa. Today, this

---

Careers

Mediator Negotiations between warring factions, such as Arabs and Jews are often guided by professionals called *mediators*. Mediators also handle everyday conflicts between people who do not want to take their problem to a court of law. Couples, families, neighborhoods, and corporations all turn to mediators for help in resolving conflict. Mediators have good analytical abilities, listening skills, patience, and the ability to forge a creative compromise between two parties. Many mediators have college degrees. Some also have law degrees or a master's degree in mediation or dispute resolution. Others have degrees or experience in a field such as social work, counseling, or business. To become certified, mediators must receive training and complete an apprenticeship.

Answers

BIOGRAPHY because he led the fight to found and modernize the present Republic of Turkey

✓ Both were focused on modernizing industry and transportation, secularizing schools, and westernizing culture.

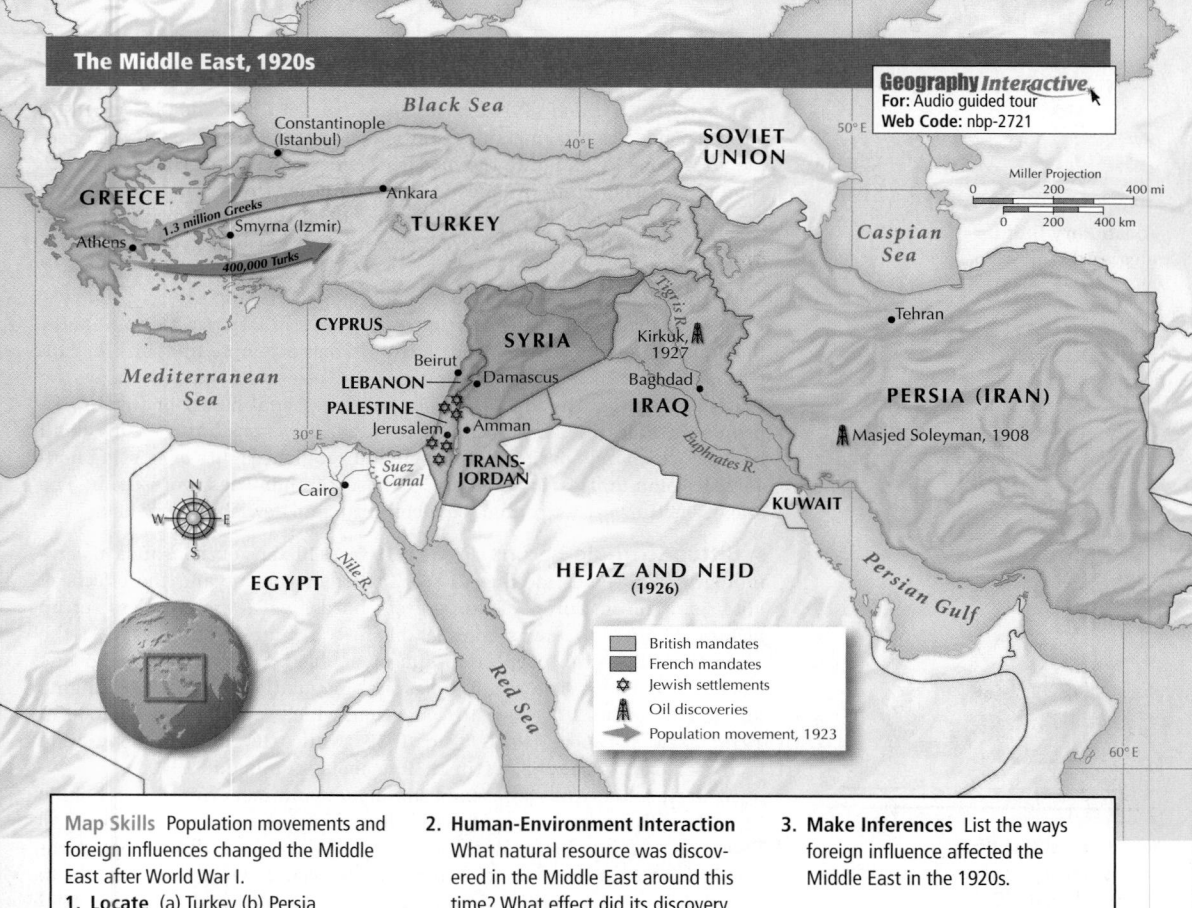

The Middle East, 1920s

Geography *Interactive*
For: Audio guided tour
Web Code: nbp-2721

Miller Projection

Black Sea

GREECE
1.3 million Greeks
Athens   Smyrna (Izmir)
400,000 Turks

Constantinople (Istanbul)

Ankara

TURKEY

SOVIET UNION

Caspian Sea

CYPRUS

Mediterranean Sea

SYRIA   Kirkuk, 1927
Beirut   Damascus
LEBANON
PALESTINE   Baghdad
Jerusalem   Amman   IRAQ
TRANS-JORDAN

Tehran

PERSIA (IRAN)

Masjed Soleyman, 1908

Cairo
Suez Canal

EGYPT

Nile R.

HEJAZ AND NEJD
(1926)

KUWAIT

Persian Gulf

Red Sea

British mandates
French mandates
Jewish settlements
Oil discoveries
Population movement, 1923

Map Skills Population movements and foreign influences changed the Middle East after World War I.
1. Locate (a) Turkey (b) Persia (c) Palestine (d) the Persian Gulf

2. Human-Environment Interaction What natural resource was discovered in the Middle East around this time? What effect did its discovery have on the region?

3. Make Inferences List the ways foreign influence affected the Middle East in the 1920s.

area includes Syria, Jordan, Iraq, Egypt, Algeria, and Morocco. Pan-Arabism emphasized the common history and language of Arabs and recalled the golden age of Arab civilization. The movement sought to free Arabs from foreign domination and unite them in their own state.

Betrayal at the Peace Conference Arabs were outraged by the European-controlled mandates set up at the Paris Peace Conference. During World War I, Arabs had helped the Allies against the Central Powers, especially the Ottoman empire. In return for their help, the Allies led the Arabs to believe that they would gain independence after the war. Instead, the Allies carved up the Ottoman lands, giving France mandates in Syria and Lebanon and Britain mandates in Palestine and Iraq. Later, Britain gave a large part of the Palestinian mandate, Trans-Jordan, to Abdullah for a kingdom.

Arabs felt betrayed by the West—a feeling that has endured to this day. During the 1920s and 1930s, their anger erupted in frequent protests and revolts against Western imperialism. A major center of turmoil was the British mandate of Palestine. There, Arab nationalists and Jewish nationalists, known as Zionists, increasingly clashed.

History Background

Kibbutzim During the early 1900s, many Jewish settlers in Palestine wanted to develop a new way of life. They organized collective farms, called *kibbutzim* (kee boot SEEM). Members shared belongings, labor, and proceeds. The settlements were communal, with cooking done in a central dining hall. Children were raised in a home, separate from their parents, so that women could join the kibbutz workforce.

Together, these settlers, called *kibbutzniks,* introduced new techniques of drainage and irrigation. They grew grain, fruit trees, and vegetables, and raised chickens and cows for meat. They planted cypress and palm trees to provide shade from the desert sun. Their efforts later helped the nation of Israel become a world leader in agricultural production.

Independent Practice

Have students fill in the Outline Map *Middle East After World War I* and label the location of the British and French mandates.

All in One Teaching Resources, Unit 4, p. 35

Monitor Progress

■ Have students access **Web Code nbp-2721** to take the **Geography Interactive Audio Guided Tour** and then answer the map skills questions in the text.

■ Check students' Outline Maps to make sure students are correctly labeling the location of the British and French mandates in the Middle East. Administer the Geography Quiz.

All in One Teaching Resources, Unit 4, p. 37

■ Check Reading and Note Taking Study Guide entries for student understanding.

Answers

Map Skills
1. Review locations with students.
2. oil; The discovery of oil caused foreign companies to begin moving to the Middle East to exploit the resource.
3. Britain controlled Palestine, Iraq, and Transjordan; France controlled Syria.

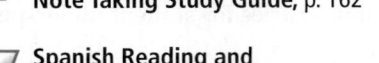

Vocabulary Builder

advocated—(AD vuh kayt id) *v.*
supported or favored

Two Views of One Place
Posters encouraged visitors and settlers to go to Palestine. At the same time, Palestinian Arabs tried to limit Jewish settlement in the area.

Promises in Palestine Since Roman times, Jews had dreamed of returning to the land of Judea, or Israel. In 1897, Theodor Herzl (HURT sul) responded to growing anti-Semitism, or prejudice against Jewish people, in Europe by founding the modern Zionist movement. His goal was to rebuild a Jewish state in Palestine. Among other things, violent pogroms against Jews in Russia prompted thousands of them to migrate to Palestine. They joined the small Jewish community that had lived there since biblical times.

During World War I, the Allies made two conflicting sets of promises. First, they promised Arabs their own kingdoms in former Ottoman lands, including Palestine. Then, in 1917, the British attempted to win the support of European Jews by issuing the **Balfour Declaration**. In it, the British advocated the idea of setting up "a national home for the Jewish people" in Palestine. The declaration noted, however, that "nothing shall be done which may prejudice the civil and religious rights of existing non-Jewish communities in Palestine." Those communities were Arab. The stage was thus set for conflict between Arab and Jewish nationalists.

A Bitter Struggle Begins From 1919 to 1940, tens of thousands of Jews immigrated to Palestine due to the Zionist movement and the effects of anti-Semitism in Europe. Despite great hardships, Jewish settlers set up factories, built new towns, and established farming communities. At the same time, the Arab population almost doubled. Some were immigrants from nearby lands. As a result, Palestine's population included a changing mix of newcomers. The Jewish population, which was less than 60,000 in 1919, grew to about 400,000 in 1936, while the Muslim population increased from about 568,000 in 1919 to about 1 million in 1940.

At first, some Arabs welcomed the money and modern technical skills that the newcomers brought with them. But as more Jews moved to Palestine, tensions between the two groups developed. Jewish organizations tried to purchase as much land as they could, while Arabs sought to slow down or stop Jewish immigration. Arabs attacked Jewish settlements, hoping to discourage settlers. The Jewish settlers established their own military defense force. For the rest of the century, Arabs and Jews fought over the land that Arabs called Palestine and Jews called Israel.

✓ **Checkpoint** Why did Palestine become a center of conflict after World War I?

SECTION 2 Assessment

Progress Monitoring *Online*
For: Self-quiz with vocabulary practice
Web Code: nba-2721

Terms, People, and Places

1. For each term, person, or place listed at the beginning of the section, write a sentence explaining its significance.

Note Taking

2. **Reading Skill: Identify Causes and Effects** Use your completed chart to answer the Focus Question: How did nationalism contribute to changes in Africa and the Middle East following World War I?

Comprehension and Critical Thinking

3. **Identify Central Issues** How did Africans resist colonial rule?

4. **Summarize** What are three examples of the rise of nationalism in Africa?

5. **Identify Central Issues** Why might Muslim religious leaders object to reforms in Turkey and Persia?

6. **Draw Conclusions** How did the Balfour Declaration affect the Middle East?

● Writing About History

Quick Write: Generate Arguments When you write a persuasive essay, you want to support your thesis statement with valid, convincing arguments. You'll need to read about your topic in order to formulate your list of arguments. Write down ideas for three arguments supporting the following thesis: The ANC was a valuable political party even though it did not affect the white-run government of South Africa for many years.

A Hindu servant serves tea to his mistress in colonial India.

WITNESS HISTORY 🔊 AUDIO

Indian Frustration

In the early 1900s, many Indians were dissatisfied with British rule. An early leader of the Indian National Congress party expressed his frustration with an unpopular policy to divide the province of Bengal into smaller sections:

❝ The scheme [to divide Bengal] . . . will always stand as a complete illustration of the worst features of the present system of bureaucratic rule—its utter contempt for public opinion, its arrogant pretensions to superior wisdom, its reckless disregard of the most cherished feelings of the people, the mockery of an appeal to its sense of justice, [and] its cool preference of [British civil service workers'] interests to those of the governed.❞
—Gopal Krishna Gokhale, 1905

Focus Question How did Gandhi and the Congress party work for independence in India?

India Seeks Self-Rule

Objectives

- Explain what motivated the Indian independence movement after World War I.
- Analyze how Mohandas Gandhi influenced the independence movement.
- Describe the impact of the Salt March on the course of the Indian independence movement.

Terms, People, and Places

Amritsar massacre	untouchables
ahimsa	boycott
civil disobedience	

Note Taking

Reading Skill: Identify Causes and Effects Recognizing causes and effects can help you understand the significance of certain events. In a chart like the one below, record the causes and effects of Gandhi's leadership of India's independence movement.

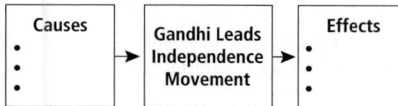

Tensions were running high in Amritsar, a city in northern India. Protests against British rule had sparked riots and attacks on British residents. On April 13, 1919, a large but peaceful crowd of Indians jammed into an enclosed field. The British commander, General Reginald Dyer, had banned public meetings, but the crowd either ignored or had not heard the order. As Indian leaders spoke, Dyer and 50 soldiers opened fire on the unarmed crowd, killing nearly 400 people and wounding more than 1,100. The **Amritsar massacre** was a turning point for many Indians. It convinced them that India needed to govern itself.

Calls for Independence

The tragedy at Amritsar was linked to broader Indian frustrations after World War I. During the war, more than a million Indians had served overseas. Under pressure from Indian nationalists, the British promised Indians greater self-government. But when the fighting ended, Britain proposed only a few minor reforms.

Since 1885, the Indian National Congress party, called the Congress party, had pressed for self-rule within the British empire. After Amritsar, it began to call for full independence. But party members were mostly middle-class, Western-educated elite who had little in common with the masses of Indian peasants. In the 1920s, a new leader named Mohandas Gandhi emerged and united Indians across class lines.

Gandhi came from a middle-class Hindu family. At age 19, he went to England to study law. Then, like many Indians, Gandhi

Vocabulary Builder

Use the information below and the following resources to teach the high-use word from this section.
All in One **Teaching Resources, Unit 4,** p. 28; **Teaching Resources, Skills Handbook,** p. 3

High-Use Word	Definition and Sample Sentence
discriminate, p. 504	*vi.* to treat differently because of a prejudice Jim Crow laws **discriminated** against African Americans.

SECTION 3 · Step-by-Step Instruction

Objectives

As you teach this section, keep students focused on the following objectives to help them answer the Section Focus Question and master core content.

- Explain what motivated the Indian independence movement after World War I.
- Analyze how Mohandas Gandhi influenced the independence movement.
- Define the impact of the Salt March on the course of the Indian independence movement.

Prepare to Read

Build Background Knowledge ⓛ3

Remind students that India provided Britain with natural resources and a market for goods. As in Africa, the colonial system benefited mainly Britain. Ask students to preview the section and write down one example of how Indians reacted against this system.

Set a Purpose ⓛ3

- **WITNESS HISTORY** Read the selection aloud or play the audio.
  🔊 AUDIO **Witness History Audio CD,** Indian Frustration

  Ask **What does Gokhale list as the "worst features" of British rule?** *(disregard for public opinion, belief in British superiority, insensitivity to Indian feelings)*

- **Focus** Point out the Section Focus Question and write it on the board. Tell students to refer to this question as they read. *(Answer appears with Section 3 Assessment answers.)*

- **Preview** Have students preview the Section Objectives and the list of Terms, People, and Places.

- **Note Taking** Have students read this section using the Structured Read Aloud strategy (TE, p. T20). As they read, have students fill in the chart on Gandhi's leadership.

   Reading and Note Taking Study Guide, p. 163

Teach

Calls for Independence/ The Power of Nonviolence/ Gandhi Takes a Stand L3

Instruct

- **Introduce: Vocabulary Builder** Have students read the Vocabulary Builder term and definition. Ask students to predict how fighting *discrimination* in South Africa influenced Gandhi when he returned to India.

- **Teach** Review India's desires for independence from Great Britain. **Name Gandhi's key ideas.** *(ahimsa, or nonviolence; satyagraha, or nonviolent resistance; civil disobedience, the refusal to obey unjust laws; democracy, or equal rights for all people)* **How did Gandhi put these ideas into practice?** *(He called for Indians to boycott British goods in favor of self-sufficiency; he encouraged nonviolent civil disobedience; he led symbolic protests, including one against the salt monopoly.)*

- **Quick Activity** Ask students to form groups and list reasons why Gandhi was effective. Have them share their responses with the class.

Independent Practice

Viewpoints Have students read *The Impact of British Rule on India* and complete the worksheet.

📘 **All in One Teaching Resources,** Unit 4, p. 32

Monitor Progress

- Make sure students understand the causes and effects of Gandhi's leadership. For a completed version of the chart, see 📺 **Note Taking Transparencies,** 176

Answers

Caption Sample: They might have been sympathetic to the nonviolent approach and shocked that the British resorted to violence.

✓ Indians felt that the British did not deliver the significant reforms promised during the war as an acknowledgment of their service. Incidents like the Amritsar massacre intensified dissatisfaction.

✓ They staged boycotts and other nonviolent protests. They increased their own industries so India would be more self-sufficient.

The Salt March
Gandhi's march to the sea to collect forbidden salt started out with Gandhi and 78 followers, but gathered strength as it progressed. As he picked up the first lump of salt, he declared, "With this, I am shaking the foundations of the British empire." *How do you think people in other countries would have reacted to British authorities using violence against this group?*

Vocabulary Builder
discriminated—(dih SKRIM ih nayt ed) *vi.* treated differently because of a prejudice

went to South Africa. For 20 years, Gandhi fought laws that discriminated against Indians in South Africa. In 1914, Gandhi returned to India. Soon, he became the leader of the Congress party.

✓ **Checkpoint** Why did Indians call for independence after World War I?

The Power of Nonviolence

Gandhi's ideas inspired Indians of all religious and ethnic backgrounds. His nonviolent protests caught the attention of the British government and the world.

Gandhi's Ideas Gandhi's theories embraced Hindu traditions. He preached the ancient doctrine of **ahimsa** (uh HIM sah), or nonviolence and reverence for all life. By using the power of love, he believed, people could convert even the worst wrongdoer to the right course of action. To fight against injustice, he advocated the use of nonviolent resistance.

Gandhi's philosophy reflected Western as well as Indian influences. He admired Christian teachings about love. He believed in the American philosopher Henry David Thoreau's ideas about **civil disobedience,** the refusal to obey unjust laws. Gandhi was also influenced by Western ideas of democracy and nationalism. He urged equal rights for all Indians, women as well as men. He fought hard to end the harsh treatment of **untouchables,** who were members of the lowest caste, or class.

Gandhi Sets an Example During the 1920s and 1930s, Gandhi launched a series of nonviolent actions against British rule. He called for Indians to **boycott,** or refuse to buy, British goods, especially cotton textiles. He worked to restore pride in India's traditional industries, making the spinning wheel a symbol of the nationalist movement. Gandhi's campaigns of civil disobedience attracted wide support.

✓ **Checkpoint** What methods did Indians under Gandhi use to resist British rule?

Gandhi Takes a Stand: The Salt March

To mobilize mass support, Gandhi decided to take a stand against the British salt monopoly, which he saw as a symbol of British oppression. Natural salt was available in the sea, but the British government required Indians to buy only salt sold by the monopoly.

Breaking the Law On March 12, 1930, Gandhi set out with 78 followers on a 240-mile march to the sea. As the tiny band passed through villages, crowds responded to Gandhi's message. By the time they reached the sea, the marchers numbered in the thousands. On April 6, Gandhi waded into the surf and picked up a lump of sea salt. He was soon arrested and jailed. Still, Indians followed his lead. Coastal villages started collecting salt. Indians sold salt on city streets. As Gandhi's campaign gained force, tens of thousands of Indians were imprisoned.

Steps Toward Freedom All around the world, newspapers criticized Britain's harsh reaction to the protests. Stories revealed how police brutally clubbed peaceful marchers who tried to occupy a government salt-works. Slowly, Gandhi's campaign forced Britain to hand over some power to Indians. Britain also agreed to meet other demands of the Congress party.

 **Checkpoint** What did the Salt March symbolize?

Looking Ahead

In 1939, a new world war exploded. Britain outraged Indian leaders by postponing independence and bringing Indians into the war without consulting them. Angry nationalists launched a campaign of noncooperation and were jailed. Millions of Indians, however, did help Britain during World War II.

When the war ended in 1945, India's independence could no longer be delayed. As it neared, Muslim fears of the Hindu majority increased. Conflict between Hindus and Muslims would trouble the new nation in the years to come.

 SECTION 3 Assessment

Progress Monitoring Online
For: Self-quiz with vocabulary practice
Web Code: nba-2731

Terms, People, and Places
1. Place each of the key terms listed at the beginning of the section into one of the following categories: politics, culture, or economy. Write a sentence for each term explaining your choice.

Note Taking
2. **Reading Skill: Identify Causes and Effects** Use your completed chart to answer the Focus Question: How did Gandhi and the Congress party work for independence in India?

Comprehension and Critical Thinking
3. **Identify Point of View** How did the Amritsar massacre affect the movement for Indian independence?
4. **Recognize Cause and Effect** Why do you think Gandhi was able to unite Indians when earlier attempts had not succeeded?
5. **Analyze Information** How did the Salt March force Britain to respond to Indian demands?

● Writing About History
Quick Write: Use Valid Logic In a persuasive essay, you must back up your conclusions with valid logic. One common pattern of weak logic is circular reasoning, where a writer simply restates ideas instead of defending them. Bring in an example of weak logic from recent editorials in your local paper. Include a paragraph explaining the problems with the author's logic.

Mohandas Gandhi: *Hind Swaraj*

Objective

■ Outline Gandhi's ideas behind the non-violent method of passive resistance.

Build Background Knowledge _{L3}

Remind students that Gandhi believed in using only peaceful means of protest. Tell them to write down the ideas underpinning this belief as they read.

Instruct _{L3}

Discuss Gandhi's underlying beliefs and how they led him to promote passive resistance. Ask **Why does soul-force involve sacrifice of self?** *(The person practicing soul-force must accept the consequences of breaking a law.)* **According to Gandhi, what would a person using body-force do to resist laws?** *(He or she would use violence.)* **What character traits would a person who practices passive resistance need?** *(courage, honesty, bravery, patience, thoughtfulness, self-discipline)*

Monitor Progress

Form students into groups and ask them to debate Gandhi's ideas. Which aspects of Gandhi's theories do they think work? Which do not work?

Thinking Critically

1. securing rights or bringing about change without using violence
2. Yes. Using soul-force, whether for a just or unjust cause, never involves violence toward others to accomplish a goal. The one who uses soul-force is the only one who gets hurt.

Mohandas Gandhi: *Hind Swaraj*

Mohandas Gandhi led a successful, peaceful revolution in India against British rule. In the following excerpt from his book *Hind Swaraj (Indian Home Rule)*, Gandhi explains the ideas behind his nonviolent method of passive resistance in the form of an imaginary conversation between an editor and a reader. *Hind Swaraj* was first published in 1909 in South Africa, but was banned in India.

Mohandas Gandhi ▶

Editor: Passive resistance is a method of securing rights by personal suffering; it is the reverse of resistance by arms. When I refuse to do a thing that is repugnant [offensive] to my conscience, I use soul-force. For instance, the government of the day has passed a law which is applicable to me. I do not like it. If by using violence, I force the government to repeal the law, I am employing what may be termed body-force. If I do not obey the law, and accept the penalty for its breach, I use soul-force. It involves sacrifice of self.

Everybody admits that sacrifice of self is infinitely superior to sacrifice of others. Moreover, if this kind of force is used in a cause that is unjust, only the person using it suffers. He does not make others suffer for his mistakes. Men have before now done many things which were subsequently found to have been wrong. No man can claim that he is absolutely in the right, or that a particular thing is wrong, because he thinks so, but it is wrong for him so long as that is his deliberate judgment. It is therefore meet [proper] that he should not do that which he knows to be wrong, and suffer the consequence whatever it may be. This is the key to the use of soul-force.

Reader: You would then disregard laws—this is rank disloyalty. We have always been considered a law-abiding nation. You seem to be going even beyond the extremists. They say that we must obey the laws that have been passed, but that, if the laws be bad, we must drive out the lawgivers even by force.

Editor: Whether I go beyond them or whether I do not is a matter of no consequence to either of us. We simply want to find out what is right, and to act accordingly. The real meaning of the statement that we are a law-abiding nation is that we are passive resisters. When we do not like certain laws, we do not break the heads of law-givers, but we suffer and do not submit to the laws.

Thinking Critically

1. **Identify Central Issues** What is the goal of passive resistance?
2. **Draw Conclusions** According to Gandhi, could soul-force ever be used to support an unjust cause? What does Gandhi mean when he says that a person using soul-force "does not make others suffer for his mistakes"?

History Background

Gandhi's Early Years Born on the coast near Bombay, Gandhi was married by his family at 13. His father was prime minister to three local rajas. His mother was deeply religious. Gandhi dreamed of studying medicine, but was forbidden because of his caste. Instead, he studied law in England. Unable to find work in Bombay, he accepted a position in South Africa. On a train there, Gandhi refused a white man's request that he leave the first-class carriage. As a result, he was thrown off the train at the next station. He spent the night meditating, and decided to dedicate himself to fighting racial injustice. While fighting injustice in South Africa, Gandhi began living a life of poverty and spiritual purity and developed his concept of *satyagraha*, or soul-force, "the quiet and irresistible pursuit of truth." Gandhi believed that the means used to achieve a goal would shape the outcome. Gandhi left South Africa in 1914, bringing his quest and his methods to India.

A family of refugees (right) flee a conflict between warlords in 1926.

Chinese currency showing Jiang Jieshi, the next leader of Sun Yixian's Guomindang party.

Objectives
- Explain the key challenges faced by the Chinese republic in the early 1900s.
- Analyze the struggle between two rival parties as they fought to control China.
- Describe how invasion by Japan affected China.

Terms, People, and Places

Twenty-One Demands   Guomindang
May Fourth Movement   Long March
vanguard

Note Taking

Reading Skill: Recognize Multiple Causes
Use a chart like the one below to record the causes of upheaval in the Chinese Republic.

Causes of Upheaval		

Change in China

Sun Yixian, "father" of modern China, painted a grim picture of China after the end of the Qing dynasty.

❝ But the Chinese people have only family and clan solidarity; they do not have national spirit. Therefore, even though we have four hundred million people gathered together in one China, in reality they are just a heap of loose sand. Today we are the poorest and weakest nation in the world and occupy the lowest position in international affairs. Other men are the carving knife and serving dish, we are the fish and the meat.❞

As Sun emphasized, China needed to change, but how and in what direction?

Focus Question How did China cope with internal division and foreign invasion in the early 1900s?

Upheavals in China

As the new Chinese republic took shape, nationalists like Sun Yixian (soon yee SHYAHN) set the goal of "catching up and surpassing the powers, east and west." But that goal would remain a distant dream as China suffered the turmoil of civil war and foreign invasion.

The Chinese Republic in Trouble

As you have read, China's Qing dynasty collapsed in 1911. The president of China's new republic, Sun Yixian (also called Sun Yat-sen) hoped to rebuild China on the Three Principles of the People—nationalism, democracy, and economic security for everyone. But he made little progress. China quickly fell into chaos in the face of the "twin evils" of warlord uprisings and foreign imperialism.

The Warlord Problem In 1912, Sun Yixian stepped down as president in favor of Yuan Shikai (yoo AHN shih KY), a powerful general. Sun hoped that Yuan would create a strong central government, but instead, the ambitious general tried to set up a new dynasty. The military, however, did not support Yuan, and opposition divided the nation. When Yuan died in 1916, China plunged into still greater disorder.

In the provinces, local warlords seized power. As rival armies battled for control, the economy collapsed and millions of peasants suffered terrible hardships. Famine and attacks by bandits added to their misery.

SECTION 4

Step-by-Step Instruction

Objectives

As you teach this section, keep students focused on the following objectives to help them answer the Section Focus Question and master core content.

- Explain the key challenges faced by the Chinese republic in the early 1900s.
- Analyze the struggle between two rival parties as they fought to control China.
- Describe how invasion by Japan affected China.

Prepare to Read

Build Background Knowledge L3

Remind students that China had struggled in the 1800s with foreign imperialism and domestic unrest. In 1911, the Republic of China was founded. Ask students to preview the section and predict what problems the new republic might face.

Set a Purpose L3

- **WITNESS HISTORY** Read the selection aloud or play the audio.

  🔊 AUDIO **Witness History Audio CD,** Change in China

  Ask **What metaphors does Sun use to describe China?** *(heap of loose sand; the fish and meat that other countries carve up)* **What is Sun's point?** *(He believes that China is weak.)*

- **Focus** Point out the Section Focus Question and write it on the board. Tell students to refer to this question as they read. *(Answer appears with Section 4 Assessment answers.)*

- **Preview** Have students preview the Section Objectives and the list of Terms, People, and Places.

- **Note Taking** Have students read this section using the Guided Questioning strategy (TE, p. T20). As they read, have students fill in the chart listing the causes of upheaval in China.

  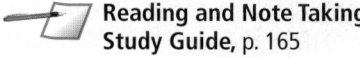 **Reading and Note Taking Study Guide,** p. 165

Teach

The Chinese Republic in Trouble ⑬

Instruct

■ **Introduce: Vocabulary Builder** Have students read the Vocabulary Builder term and definition. Ask students to brainstorm how an *intellectual* movement could lead to change.

■ **Teach** Ask **What were the "twin evils" that the fledgling Chinese republic faced?** *(Local warlords seized power over much of China; foreign powers also took advantage of China's weakness to expand their influence.)* **What were two reactions within China to the country's problems?** *(The May Fourth Movement sought to break with tradition and use Western thought to strengthen China against foreign domination; some people turned to the ideas of Marx and Lenin for solutions.)*

■ **Quick Activity** Display **Color Transparency 164: Demonstration of May 4th, 1919.** Use the lesson suggested in the transparency book to guide a discussion about the effect of the May Fourth Movement on Chinese culture.

 **Color Transparencies,** 164

Independent Practice

Have students outline the goals and methods of each of the following groups that competed for power in China in the early 1900s: warlords *(goal: local control; method: force),* the May Fourth Movement *(goal: strengthen China; method: change China's culture),* and the Japanese *(goal: expand Japanese influence in China; method: intimidation).*

Monitor Progress

As students fill in their charts, circulate to make sure they understand how warlord uprisings and foreign imperialism caused upheaval in China. For a completed version of the chart, see

 **Note Taking Transparencies,** 177A

Answer

✔ The warlord uprisings weakened China, allowing countries such as Japan to encroach upon China's possessions. Anger at China's inability to halt foreign imperialism led to the May Fourth Movement.

Note Taking

Reading Skill: Sequence Use a chart like the one below to sequence the fighting that went on among the Guomindang, the warlords, the Chinese Communists, and the Japanese from 1921 through 1937.

| 1926 Guomindang and Communists defeat warlords. | → | | → | |

Vocabulary Builder

intellectual—(in teh LEK choo ul) *adj.* involving the ability to reason or think clearly

Jiang Jieshi, Leader of the Guomindang Jiang Jieshi headed the Guomindang (Nationalist) government in China from the late 1920s until 1949.

Foreign Imperialism During this period of upheaval, foreign powers increased their influence over Chinese affairs. Foreign merchants, missionaries, and soldiers dominated the ports China had opened to trade.

During World War I, Japanese officials presented Yuan Shikai with the **Twenty-One Demands,** a list of demands that sought to make China a Japanese protectorate. With China too weak to resist, Yuan gave in to some of the demands. Then, in 1919, at the Paris Peace Conference, the Allies gave Japan control over some former German possessions in China. That news infuriated Chinese Nationalists.

May Fourth Movement In response, student protests erupted in Beijing on May 4, 1919, and later spread to cities across China. The protests set off a cultural and intellectual ferment known as the **May Fourth Movement.** Its goal was to strengthen China. Reformers sought to improve China's position by rejecting Confucian traditions and learning from the West. As in Meiji Japan, they hoped to use their new knowledge to end foreign domination.

Women played a key role in the May Fourth Movement. They joined marches and campaigned to end a number of traditional practices, including footbinding. Their work helped open doors for women in education and the economy.

The Appeal of Marxism Some Chinese turned to the revolutionary ideas of Marx and Lenin. The Soviet Union was more than willing to train Chinese students and military officers to become the **vanguard,** or elite leaders, of a communist revolution. By the 1920s, a small group of Chinese Communists had formed their own political party.

✔ **Checkpoint** How did warlord uprisings and foreign imperialism lead to the May Fourth movement?

Struggle for a New China

In 1921, Sun Yixian and his **Guomindang** (gwoh meen DAWNG) or Nationalist party, established a government in south China. Sun planned to raise an army, defeat the warlords, and spread his government's rule over all of China. When Western democracies refused to help, Sun accepted aid from the Soviet Union and joined forces with the small group of Chinese Communists. However, he still believed that China's future should be based on his Three Principles of the People.

Jiang Jieshi Leads the Nationalists After Sun's death in 1925, an energetic young army officer, Jiang Jieshi (jahng jeh shur), took over the Guomindang. Jiang Jieshi (also called Chiang Kai-Shek) was determined to smash the power of the warlords and reunite China, but he had little interest in either democracy or communism.

In 1926, Jiang Jieshi began the Northern Expedition in cooperation with the Chinese Communists. In the Northern Expedition, Jiang led the combined forces into northern China, crushing or winning over local warlords as he advanced and capturing Beijing. Jiang would go on to take control of a new government led by the Guomindang—but without the Communists.

Who Should Lead the New China?

The excerpts below present the views of China's two most influential leaders on who should direct the future of China. **Critical Thinking** *Who does each person think should lead China?*

One Strong Leader	Peasant Masses
The most important point of fascism is absolute trust in a sagely able leader. Aside from complete trust in one person, there is no other leader or ism. Therefore, with the organization, although there are cadre, council members, and executives, there is no conflict among them, there is only the trust in the one leader. The leader has final decision in all matters. —Jiang Jieshi, 1933	The broad peasant masses have risen to fulfill their historic mission . . . the democratic forces in the rural areas have risen to overthrow the rural feudal power. . . . To overthrow this feudal power is the real objective of the national revolution. What Dr. Sun Yat-sen [Yixian] wanted to do . . . but failed to accomplish, the peasants have accomplished in a few months. —Mao Zedong, 1927

In mid-campaign, Jiang seized the chance to strike at the Chinese Communist Party, which he saw as a threat to his power. The Communists were winning converts among the small proletariat in cities like Shanghai. Early in 1927, on orders from Jiang, Guomindang troops slaughtered Communist Party members and the workers who supported them. In Shanghai and elsewhere, thousands of people were killed. This massacre marked the beginning of a bitter civil war between the Communists and the Guomindang that lasted for 22 years.

Mao Zedong and the Communists Among the Communists who escaped Jiang's attack was a young revolutionary of peasant origins, Mao Zedong (mow dzuh doong) (also called Mao Tse-tung). Unlike earlier Chinese Communists, Mao believed that the Communists should seek support not among the small urban working class but among the large peasant masses.

Although the Communists were pursued at every turn by Guomindang forces, Mao was optimistic about eventual success. In southeastern China, Mao and the Communists redistributed land to peasants and promised other reforms.

The Long March Jiang Jieshi, however, was determined to destroy the "Red bandits," as he called the Communists. He led the Guomindang in a series of "extermination campaigns" against them. The Guomindang harassed Mao's retreating army throughout the **Long March** from 1934 to 1935. Mao's forces used guerrilla, or irregular hit-and-run, tactics to fight back. At the end of the Long March, the Communists set up a new base in a remote region of northern China. There, Mao rebuilt his forces and plotted new strategies for fighting the Guomindang.

During the march, the Communists enforced strict discipline. Soldiers were told to treat peasants politely, pay for goods they wanted, and avoid damaging crops. Such behavior made Mao's forces welcome among peasants, many of whom had suffered greatly at the hands of the Guomindang.

✓ **Checkpoint** How did the Communists manage to survive Jiang's "extermination campaigns"?

Mao Zedong, Leader of the Communists
Mao Zedong led the Chinese Communists through some of their darkest times, including the Long March.

Connect to Our World

Connections to Today Why use "Jiang Jieshi" when so many people may be more familiar with the name "Chiang Kai-Shek"? That spelling represented the sound of the Cantonese dialect version of the name in the Wade-Giles system, which was widely used until 1979. That year, *pinyin*—based on the Mandarin dialect spoken in Beijing—was decreed the official system by the Communist Chinese government. It had developed pinyin in 1958, in part to establish a single, dominant, national language in China. Because of its official status, and because it more accurately renders the sounds of the main dialect, pinyin today has generally replaced Wade-Giles. Hence "Jiang Jieshi." But for many widely known terms, the older form is often given in parentheses, e.g., Beijing (Peking).

Struggle for a New China ⓛ3

Instruct

- **Introduce** Jiang Jieshi once said "The Japanese are a disease of the skin. The Communists are a disease of the heart." Tell students that he used this belief to justify fighting the Chinese Communists rather than the invading Japanese in the 1930s. Ask students whether they agree with his reasoning.

- **Teach** Have students read the Viewpoints feature, then quickly describe each leader's key point. Ask **Which leader's theory was more "revolutionary," in the sense that it would bring broad changes?** *(If realized, Mao's; Jiang's theory would keep power in the hands of one person or very few, as it had been for centuries under various dynasties.)*

- **Quick Activity** Ask students to trace the route of the Long March on the map. Ask them to consider why the great hardships of the march actually strengthened the Chinese Communists. **Web Code nbp-2741** will take students to an interactive map and timeline. Have students complete the interactivity and then answer the questions in their text.

Independent Practice

- **Biography** Have students read the biography *Jiang Jieshi* and complete the worksheet.

  All in One Teaching Resources, Unit 4, p. 33

- **Note Taking** Have students fill in the chart sequencing events in the civil war in China.

  Reading and Note Taking Study Guide, p. 165

Monitor Progress

As students fill in their charts, circulate to make sure they understand the sequence of events in China's civil war. For a completed version of the chart, see

Note Taking Transparencies, 177B

Answers

COMPARING VIEWPOINTS Jiang: one strong leader (himself); Mao: the peasant masses

✓ On the Long March, the Communists retreated from Jiang's forces to a remote region in northern China and used guerrilla tactics to fight back as they marched.

Japanese Invasion

Instruct

- **Introduce: Vocabulary Builder**
  Have students read the Vocabulary Builder term and definition. Tell students that the leader of a *faction* of the Guomindang kidnapped Jiang and held him until he agreed to ally with the Communists against the Japanese. Ask students to speculate why this leader took such a drastic step.

- **Teach** Ask **What was the "rape of Nanjing"?** *(the destruction and cruelty perpetrated by the Japanese army after taking Nanjing in 1937)* **How did the Japanese invasion help to unify China?** *(The Guomindang stopped trying to stamp out the Communists, and the two parties worked together to fight the Japanese—for a time.)*

- **Quick Activity** Have the class suppose they live in China in 1931. Split the class into groups, and ask each group to create a persuasive pamphlet encouraging the warring Chinese factions to unite against a common enemy. Use the Numbered Heads strategy (TE, p. T23) and have groups present their pamphlets to the class.

Independent Practice

Ask students to create a concept web showing the different groups who helped the Chinese fight the Japanese and what each group contributed.

Monitor Progress

To ensure student understanding of the changes in China, have them review the section as a whole and note when and how Japan's actions affected events in China.

Answers

Map Skills
1. Review locations with students.
2. rivers, mountains
3. The Guomindang joined forces with the Communists when necessary to fight a common enemy (warlords, Japanese), but otherwise did their utmost to destroy them.

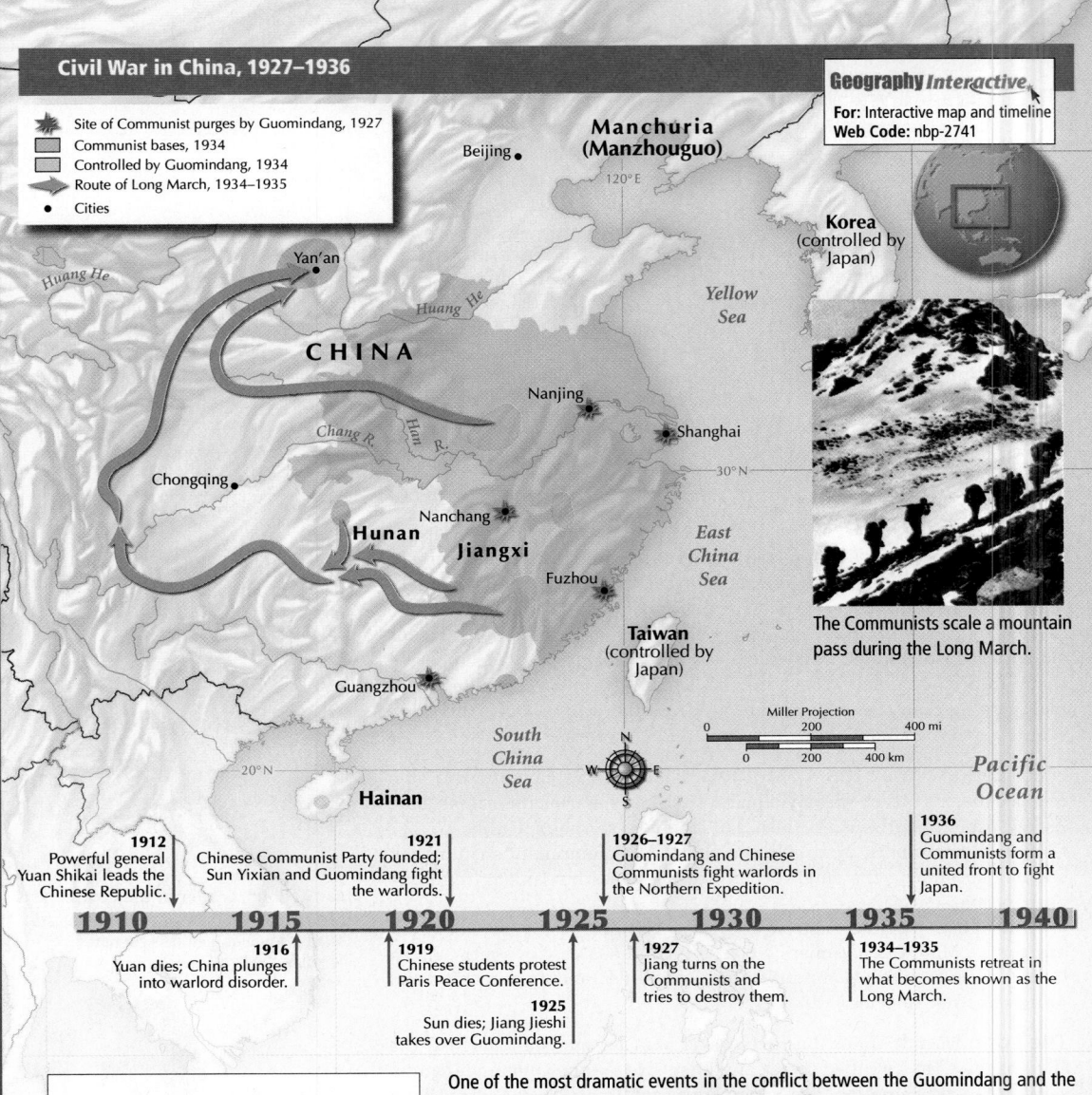

Civil War in China, 1927–1936

Legend:
- Site of Communist purges by Guomindang, 1927
- Communist bases, 1934
- Controlled by Guomindang, 1934
- Route of Long March, 1934–1935
- Cities

Geography *Interactive*
For: Interactive map and timeline
Web Code: nbp-2741

Manchuria (Manzhouguo)

Beijing

Korea (controlled by Japan)

Yellow Sea

CHINA

Huang He

Yan'an

Nanjing

Shanghai

Chongqing

Nanchang

Hunan   Jiangxi

Fuzhou

East China Sea

Taiwan (controlled by Japan)

Guangzhou

South China Sea

Hainan

Pacific Ocean

The Communists scale a mountain pass during the Long March.

Timeline:

- **1912** Powerful general Yuan Shikai leads the Chinese Republic.
- **1916** Yuan dies; China plunges into warlord disorder.
- **1919** Chinese students protest Paris Peace Conference.
- **1921** Chinese Communist Party founded; Sun Yixian and Guomindang fight the warlords.
- **1925** Sun dies; Jiang Jieshi takes over Guomindang.
- **1926–1927** Guomindang and Chinese Communists fight warlords in the Northern Expedition.
- **1927** Jiang turns on the Communists and tries to destroy them.
- **1934–1935** The Communists retreat in what becomes known as the Long March.
- **1936** Guomindang and Communists form a united front to fight Japan.

1910   1915   1920   1925   1930   1935   1940

Map Skills The Guomindang and the Communists waged a long and bitter war for control of China.
1. **Locate:** (a) Beijing (b) Shanghai (c) Jiangxi (d) Yan'an
2. **Movement** What natural features made the Long March difficult?
3. **Synthesize Information** Based on the map and timeline, describe the relationship between the Guomindang and the Communists.

One of the most dramatic events in the conflict between the Guomindang and the Communists was the epic retreat known as the Long March. During the Long March, Mao and about 100,000 of his followers fled the Guomindang. In the next year, they trekked more than 6,000 miles, facing daily attacks as they crossed rugged mountains and mighty rivers. Only about 8,000 marchers survived the ordeal. For decades, the Long March stood as a symbol of communist heroism and inspired new recruits to follow Mao. He claimed the great retreat as a victory. As he observed:

Primary Source

❝The Long March is also a seeding-machine. It has sown many seeds in eleven provinces, which will sprout, grow leaves, blossom into flowers, bear fruit, and yield a crop.❞
—Mao Zedong, "On the Tactics of Fighting Japanese Imperialism"

History Background

Mao Zedong Unlike Marx and Lenin, who came from wealthy families, Mao was born a peasant farmer. In a poem about his childhood, he wrote, "In delight I watched a thousand waves of growing rice." He loved learning and managed to pursue an education. At 18, he walked for days to join in Sun Yixian's revolution, but was disillusioned when warlords took over. In college, Mao and other student radicals watched and were influenced by Russia's 1918 revolution. However, Marxism was based on the rise of the proletariat, or industrial working class. China had only a small urban working class but an enormous peasant class. Mao believed that peasants could be the heart of China's revolution. Unlike Gandhi, Mao was willing to use ruthless measures to achieve his ideals of justice and equality. His struggle to gain control of China continued until 1949.

Japanese Invasion

While Jiang was pursuing the Communists across China, the country faced another danger. In 1931, Japan invaded Manchuria in northeastern China, adding it to the growing Japanese empire. As Japanese aggression increased, a <u>faction</u> within the Guomindang forced Jiang to form a united front with the Communists against Japan.

In 1937, the Japanese struck again, starting what became the Second Sino-Japanese War. Airplanes bombed Chinese cities, and Japanese troops overran eastern China, including Beijing and Guangzhou. Jiang Jieshi and his government retreated to the interior and set up a new capital at Chongqing (chawng CHING).

After a lengthy siege, Japanese troops marched into the city of Nanjing (nahn jing) on December 13. Nanjing was an important cultural center and had been the Guomindang capital before Chongqing. After the city's surrender, the Japanese killed hundreds of thousands of soldiers and civilians and brutalized still more. The cruelty and destruction became known around the world as the "rape of Nanjing."

The united Chinese fought back against the Japanese. The Soviet Union sent advisors and equipment to help. Great Britain, France, and the United States gave economic aid. The Guomindang and the Communists still clashed occasionally, but the united front stayed intact until the end of the war with Japan.

✔ **Checkpoint** How did the Japanese invasion help unify the Chinese temporarily?

Looking Ahead

The bombing of Pearl Harbor in 1941 brought the United States into the war against Japan and into an alliance with the Chinese. By the end of World War II, Jiang and the Guomindang controlled China's central government, but Mao's Communist Party controlled much of northern and central China. The Communists had organized hundreds of thousands of Chinese peasants at the village level, spreading their political ideas. Meanwhile, corruption grew in Jiang's government. Soon, the Communists would triumph, and Mao would impose revolutionary change on China.

Vocabulary Builder

faction—(FAK shun) *n.* a group within a larger group

SECTION 4 Assessment

Progress Monitoring Online
For: Self-quiz with vocabulary practice
Web Code: nba-2741

Terms, People, and Places

1. What do many of the key terms listed at the beginning of the section have in common? Explain.

Note Taking

2. **Reading Skill: Recognize Multiple Causes** Use your completed charts to answer the Focus Question: How did China cope with internal division and foreign invasion in the early 1900s?

Comprehension and Critical Thinking

3. **Identify Central Issues** Why did the new republic of China fall into chaos after 1912?
4. **Identify Point of View** Do you think that the retreating Communists' policy to pay for goods they wanted during the Long March was a good idea? Why or why not?
5. **Predict Consequences** How do you think the "rape of Nanjing" affected Japan's reputation around the world?

● **Writing About History**

Quick Write: Answer Opposing Arguments Every persuasive essay should present arguments that support the thesis *and* refute arguments that oppose the thesis. Your thesis for a persuasive essay is "The Long March ultimately helped the Chinese Communists' cause." Think of the strongest argument against this thesis, and then write a paragraph to refute that argument.

Objectives

As you teach this section, keep students focused on the following objectives to help them answer the Section Focus Question and master core content.

■ Explain the effects of liberal changes in Japan during the 1920s.

■ Analyze how nationalists reacted to Japan's problems during the Great Depression.

■ Describe how the militarists used their power in the 1930s.

Build Background Knowledge

Ask students to list what they know about Japan from the previous section and write each response on the board. Tell them that in this section, they will learn about these events from the Japanese perspective.

Set a Purpose L3

■ **WITNESS HISTORY** Read the selection aloud or play the audio.

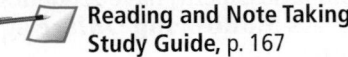 AUDIO **Witness History Audio CD,** Japan in the Midst of Change

Ask **According to the speaker, what are Japan's problems?** *(corrupt political parties and businesses that exploit the common people; weak diplomacy; corrupt education)* **What is the speaker's solution to these problems?** *(drastic change, revolution)*

■ **Focus** Point out the Section Focus Question and write it on the board. Tell students to refer to this question as they read. *(Answer appears with Section 5 Assessment answers.)*

■ **Preview** Have students preview the Section Objectives and the list of Terms, People, and Places.

■ **Note Taking** Have students read this section using the Guided Questioning strategy (TE, p. T20). As they read, have students fill in the table categorizing the events in Japan.

Reading and Note Taking Study Guide, p. 167

Japanese soldiers occupying a Chinese city in 1938

Japan in the Midst of Change

Groups with conflicting ideologies fought for control of Japan in the 1930s.

❝ Look straight at the present state of your fatherland, Japan! Where, we dare ask, can you find the genuine manifestation of the godliness of the Imperial Country of Japan? Political parties are blind in their pursuit of power and egoistic gains. Large enterprises are firmly in collusion with politicians as they suck the sweat and blood of the common people . . . Diplomacy is weak-kneed. Education is rotten to the core. Now is the time to carry out drastic, revolutionary change. Rise, and take action now!❞
—A Japanese ultranationalist criticizing the government, 1932

Focus Question How did Japan change in the 1920s and 1930s?

Conflicting Forces in Japan

Objectives
• Explain the effects of liberal changes in Japan during the 1920s.
• Analyze how nationalists reacted to Japan's problems during the Great Depression.
• Describe how the militarists used their power in the 1930s.

Terms, People, and Places

Hirohito
ultranationalist
Manchuria

Note Taking

Reading Skill: Understand Effects As you read this section, fill in the effects of two opposing outlooks in Japan in the 1920s and 1930s in a table like the one below.

Conflicting Forces in Japan	
Liberalism in the 1920s	Militarism in the 1930s
•	•
•	•
•	•

Solemn ceremonies marked the start of Emperor Hirohito's reign. In the Secret Purple Hall, the new emperor sat on the ancient throne of Japan. Beside him was his wife, the empress Nagako. Calling on the spirits of his ancestors, he pledged "to preserve world peace and benefit the welfare of the human race."

In fact, **Hirohito** reigned from 1926 to 1989—an astonishing 63 years. During those decades, Japan experienced remarkable successes and appalling tragedies. In this section, we will focus on the 1920s and 1930s, when the pressures of extreme nationalism and economic upheaval set Japan on a militaristic and expansionist path that would engulf all of Asia.

Japan on the Rise in the 1920s

In the 1920s, Japan moved toward greater prosperity and democracy. To strengthen its relationship with other countries, Japan drew back from some of its imperial goals in the 1920s. The country grew in international prestige. However, conflicts lurked beneath the surface. The economic crisis of the Great Depression in the 1930s would bring them to light.

Growth and Expansion After World War I During World War I, the Japanese economy enjoyed remarkable growth. Its exports to Allied nations soared. Heavy industrial production grew, making Japan a true industrial power.

Vocabulary Builder

Use the information below and the following resources to teach the high-use word from this section.
All in One **Teaching Resources, Unit 4,** p. 28; **Teaching Resources, Skills Handbook,** p. 3

High-Use Word	Definition and Sample Sentence
manipulate, p. 513	*vt.* to influence skillfully, often unfairly He **manipulated** his sister into agreeing to do his chores for the next week.

While Western powers battled in Europe, Japan expanded its influence throughout East Asia. Japan had already annexed Korea as a colony in 1910. During the war, Japan also sought further rights in China with the Twenty-One Demands. After the war, Japan took over former German possessions in East Asia, including the Shandong province in China.

Liberal Changes in the 1920s During the 1920s, Japan moved toward more widespread democracy. Political parties grew stronger. Elected members of the Diet—the Japanese parliament—exercised their power. In 1925, all adult men, regardless of class, won the right to vote. In addition, Western ideas about women's rights brought some changes. Overall, however, the status of Japanese women remained below that of men. They would not win suffrage, or the right to vote, until 1945.

Despite leaning toward greater democracy, political parties were <u>manipulated</u> by the zaibatsu (zy baht soo), Japan's powerful business leaders. The zaibatsu influenced the government through donations to political parties. They pushed for policies that favored international trade and their own interests.

Japan's aggressive expansion began to affect its economic relationship with the Western powers. To protect relations, moderate Japanese politicians decided to slow down foreign expansion. In 1922, Japan signed an agreement to limit the size of its navy with the United States, Britain, and France. It also agreed to leave Shandong. The government reduced military spending.

Problems Below the Surface Behind this well-being, Japan faced some grave problems. Rural peasants did not share in the nation's prosperity. They were still very poor. In the cities, factory workers earned low wages. Their poverty drew them to the socialist ideas of Marx and Lenin.

In the cities, members of the younger generation were also in revolt against tradition. They adopted Western fads and fashions. Also, they rejected family authority for the Western ideal of individual freedom, shocking their elders.

During the 1920s, tensions between the government and the military simmered not far below the surface. Conservatives, especially military officers, blasted government corruption, including payoffs by powerful zaibatsu. They also condemned Western influences for undermining basic Japanese values of obedience and respect for authority.

Although the economy grew throughout the 1920s, it experienced many highs and lows. One low point occurred when a devastating earthquake, one of the most destructive quakes in history, struck the Tokyo area in 1923. The earthquake and the widespread fires it caused resulted in the deaths of over 100,000 people and damaged more than 650,000 buildings. As many as 45 percent of surviving workers lost their jobs because so many businesses were destroyed. With help from the government, the Tokyo area gradually recovered—just as Japan faced a worldwide economic crisis.

✔ **Checkpoint** How did democratic participation in Japan both grow and stagnate in the 1920s?

Vocabulary Builder

<u>manipulated</u>—(muh NIP yoo layt id) *vt.* influenced skillfully, often unfairly

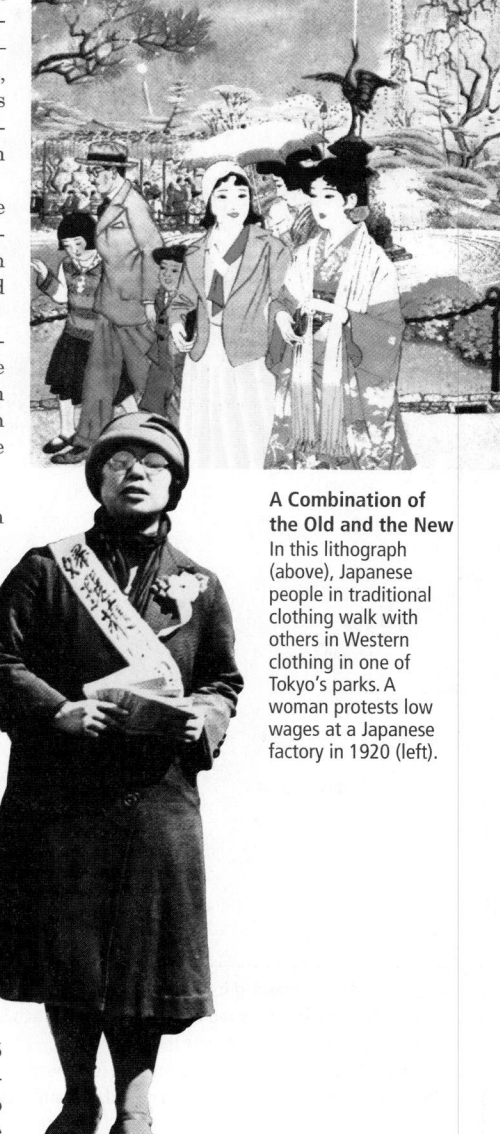

A Combination of the Old and the New In this lithograph (above), Japanese people in traditional clothing walk with others in Western clothing in one of Tokyo's parks. A woman protests low wages at a Japanese factory in 1920 (left).

Teach

Japan on the Rise in the 1920s   **L3**

Instruct

- **Introduce** Display **Color Transparency 166: Kobe, Japan in the 1880s.** Ask students to point out the evidence of Western influence in Japan. Ask students to predict how these new ideas will influence a country filled with old traditions.
  - 📽 **Color Transparencies,** 166

- **Teach** Ask students to add events to the list they created on the board in the Build Background Knowledge activity. Ask **How did Japanese foreign policy change during the 1920s?** *(Japan cut back on its expansionism in order to improve business relationships with the Western powers.)* **What were some sources of unrest in Japan in the 1920s?** *(Rural peasants and factory workers were very poor; young people revolted against tradition in favor of Western ideas; military leaders condemned political and business corruption and Western influence; the economy fluctuated quite a bit.)*

Independent Practice

Primary Source To help students learn more about the 1923 earthquake, have them read the selection *An Account of the 1923 Tokyo Earthquake* and complete the worksheet.

All in One **Teaching Resources, Unit 4,** p. 34

Monitor Progress

As students fill in their charts, circulate to make sure they understand the effects of the conflicting forces in Japan. For a completed version of the chart, see

📽 **Note Taking Transparencies,** 178

Differentiated Instruction   Solutions for All Learners

L2 Less Proficient Readers

To help visual learners, ask students to work in pairs and create a timeline of events in the 1920s. Have students categorize each event as positive or negative and make a mark above the timeline for a positive event, below the timeline for a negative event. Then have them connect these dots, and describe the pattern. Ensure students understand that Japan's behavior zigzagged between two opposite extremes during this time.

Use the following study guide resources to help students acquiring basic skills:

Adapted Reading and Note Taking Study Guide

- Adapted Note Taking Study Guide, p. 167
- Adapted Section Summary, p. 168

Answer

✔ All men were allowed to vote in 1925. However, rich *zaibatsu* had an undue influence on party politicians.

The Nationalist Reaction/ Militarists in Power L3

Instruct

- **Introduce** Refer students to the map on this page. Ask students to use the scale bar to compare the relative size of Japan to Manchuria. Then ask them to predict how Japan's small size fueled its desire to expand.

- **Teach** Ask students to list reasons for ultranationalists' discontent in the 1930s and write their responses on the board. Then ask **How did Japanese militarists rise to power in the 1930s?** *(Public opinion supported foreign conquest. Unrest, caused by assassinations and plots by extremist groups, caused the civilian government to bow to military control.)* Then display **Color Transparency 167: Japanese Military Build-Up, 1929–1941** and discuss the extent of Japan's military buildup and possible implications of that action.

  🏛 **Color Transparencies,** 167

- **Quick Activity** Have students access **Web Code nbp-2751** to take the **Geography Interactive Audio Guided Tour** and then answer the map skills questions in the text.

Independent Practice

Have students fill in the Outline Map *Japanese Expansion* and label the territory Japan added between 1918 and 1934.

All in One **Teaching Resources, Unit 4,** p. 36

Monitor Progress

- Circulate to make sure students are filling in their Outline Maps accurately.

- Check Reading and Note Taking Study Guide entries for student understanding.

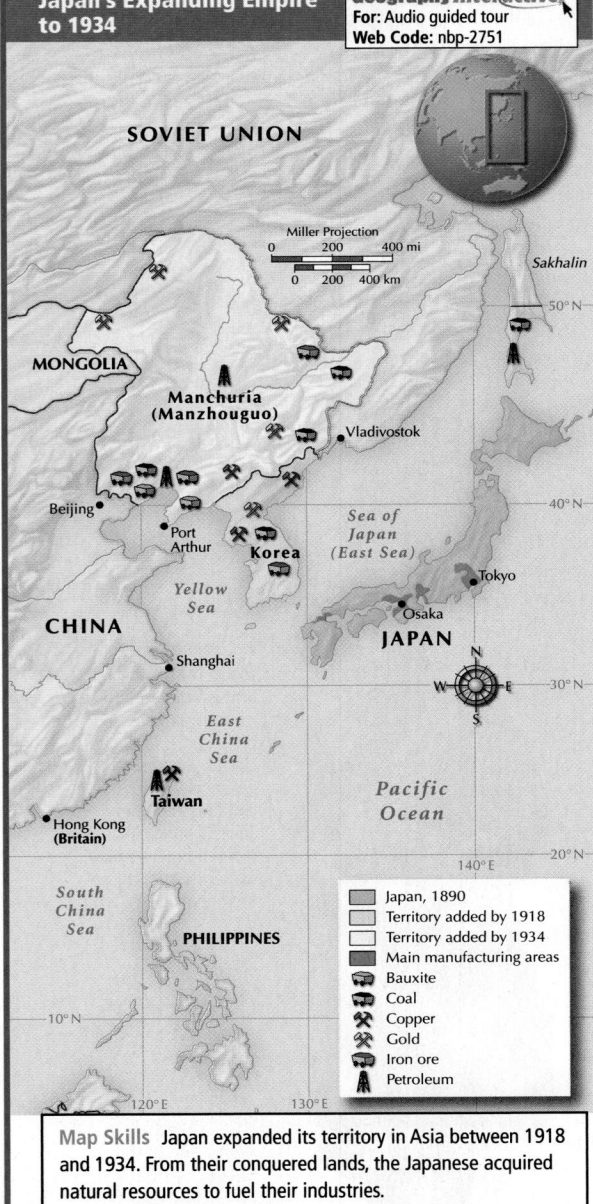

Japan's Expanding Empire to 1934

Geography *Interactive*
For: Audio guided tour
Web Code: nbp-2751

Miller Projection
0   200   400 mi
0   200   400 km

Legend:
- Japan, 1890
- Territory added by 1918
- Territory added by 1934
- Main manufacturing areas
- Bauxite
- Coal
- Copper
- Gold
- Iron ore
- Petroleum

Map Skills Japan expanded its territory in Asia between 1918 and 1934. From their conquered lands, the Japanese acquired natural resources to fuel their industries.

1. **Locate:** (a) Japan (b) Korea (c) Manchuria (d) Taiwan
2. **Region** Where were Japan's main manufacturing areas located?
3. **Draw Conclusions** What natural resource does Korea lack but Manchuria have?

The Nationalist Reaction

In 1929, the Great Depression rippled across the Pacific, striking Japan with devastating force. Trade suffered as foreign buyers could no longer afford to purchase Japanese silks and other exports. Unemployment in the cities soared, while rural peasants were only a mouthful from starvation.

Unrest Grows Economic disaster fed the discontent of the leading military officials and extreme nationalists, or **ultranationalists.** They condemned politicians for agreeing to Western demands to stop overseas expansion. Western industrial powers, they pointed out, had long ago grabbed huge empires. By comparison, Japan's empire was tiny.

Japanese nationalists were further outraged by racial policies in the United States, Canada, and Australia that shut out Japanese immigrants. The Japanese took great pride in their industrial achievements. They bitterly resented being treated as second-class citizens in other parts of the world.

As the economic crisis worsened, nationalists demanded renewed expansion. An empire in Asia, they argued, would provide much-needed raw materials as well as an outlet for Japan's rapidly growing population. They set their sights on the northern Chinese province of **Manchuria.** This region was rich in natural resources, and Japanese businesses had already invested heavily there.

The Manchurian Incident In 1931, a group of Japanese army officers provoked an incident that provided an excuse to seize Manchuria. They set explosives and blew up tracks on a Japanese-owned railroad line. Then, they claimed that the Chinese had committed the act. Claiming self-defense, the army attacked Chinese forces. Without consulting their own government, the Japanese military forces conquered all of Manchuria and set up a puppet state there that they called Manzhouguo (man choo KWOO). They brought in Puyi, the last Chinese emperor, to head the puppet state. When politicians in Tokyo objected to the army's highhanded actions, public opinion sided with the military.

When the League of Nations condemned Japanese aggression against China, Japan simply withdrew itself from the League. Soon, the Japanese government nullified the agreements limiting naval armament that it had signed with the Western democracies in the 1920s. The League's member states failed to take military action against Japanese aggression.

✓ **Checkpoint** How did the Great Depression lead to calls for renewed expansion?

Differentiated
Instruction   **Solutions for All Learners**

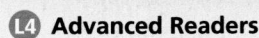 **Advanced Readers**   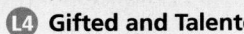 **Gifted and Talented**

Japan's invasion of Manchuria was the first real test of the League of Nations, created to avert a second world war. According to historian Thomas A. Bailey, "In a broad sense, collective security died and World War II was born in 1931 on the windswept plains of Manchuria. The League members had the economic and naval power to halt Japan, but lacked the courage

to act." Later, when Italy invaded Ethiopia in 1935, the League applied economic sanctions for the first time, but these were not effective.

Today the League has been replaced by the United Nations. Could the UN prevent a third world war? Assign students to debate the answer to this question.

Militarists in Power

In the early 1930s, ultranationalists were winning support from the people for foreign conquests and a tough stand against the Western powers. Members of extreme nationalist societies assassinated a number of politicians and business leaders who opposed expansion. Military leaders plotted to overthrow the government and, in 1936, briefly occupied the center of Tokyo.

Traditional Values Revived Civilian government survived, but the unrest forced the government to accept military domination in 1937. To please the ultranationalists, the government cracked down on socialists and suppressed most democratic freedoms. It revived ancient warrior values and built a cult around Emperor Hirohito, whom many believed was descended from the sun goddess. To spread its nationalist message, the government used schools to teach students absolute obedience to the emperor and service to the state.

More Expansion in China During the 1930s, Japan took advantage of China's civil war to increase its influence there. Japan expected to complete its conquest of China within a few years. But in 1939, while the two nations were locked in deadly combat, World War II broke out in Europe. That conflict swiftly spread to Asia.

In 1936, Japan allied with two aggressive European powers, Germany and Italy. These three powers signed the Tripartite Pact in September 1940, cementing the alliance known as the Axis Powers. That alliance, combined with renewed Japanese conquests, would turn World War II into a brutal, wide-ranging conflict waged not only across the continent of Europe but across Asia and the islands of the Pacific as well.

✔ **Checkpoint** What changes did militarists make when they came to power?

 BIOGRAPHY

Hirohito

Hirohito (1901–1989) became emperor of Japan in 1926. As emperor, according to Japanese tradition, he was the nation's supreme authority and a living god—no one could look at his face or even mention his name. In practice, however, he merely approved the policies that his ministers formulated.

Hirohito was a private man who preferred marine biology to power politics. As a result, his role in Japan's move toward aggression is unclear. Some historians believe that Hirohito did not encourage Japanese military leaders. Others assert that he was actively involved in expansionist policies. **Why was Hirohito given great respect?**

SECTION 5 Assessment

Progress Monitoring Online
For: Self-quiz with vocabulary practice
Web Code: nba-2751

Terms, People, and Places

1. For each term, person, or place listed at the beginning of the section, write a sentence explaining its significance.

Note Taking

2. **Reading Skill: Understand Effects** Use your completed chart to answer the Focus Question: How did Japan change in the 1920s and 1930s?

Comprehension and Critical Thinking

3. **Summarize** What changes occurred in Japan in the 1920s?
4. **Recognize Effects** How did nationalists respond to the Great Depression?
5. **Geography and History** What role did geography play in Japan's desire to expand its empire?
6. **Predict Consequences** Why might a nation turn to military leaders and extreme nationalists during a crisis?

● **Writing About History**
Quick Write: Decide on an Organizational Strategy Most persuasive essays follow this organization:
  I. Introduction, including thesis statement
  II. Second-strongest argument
  III. Answer to opposing arguments
  IV. Strongest argument
  V. Conclusion
Write a thesis statement based on the content of this section, and write an outline showing how you would organize your arguments.

Quick Study Guide

- Have students use the Quick Study Guide to prepare for this chapter's tests. Students may wish to refer to the following pages as they review:

Nationalism Around the World
Section 1, pp. 493–494; Section 2, pp. 496–502; Section 3, pp. 503–505; Section 4, pp. 507–511; Section 5, pp. 512–515

Key Leaders
Section 1, pp. 491–493; Section 2, pp. 499–500; Section 3, pp. 503–506; Section 4, pp. 508–511

Effects of World War I on World Events
Section 1, p. 493; Section 2, pp. 496–502; Section 5, pp. 514–515

Key Events in Latin America, Africa, and Asia
Section 1, pp. 490–493; Section 2, pp. 497–500; Section 3, p. 505; Section 4, pp. 508–509, 511

- For additional review, remind students to refer to the **L3**

  Reading and Note Taking Study Guide

Note Taking Study Guide, pp. 159, 161, 163, 165, 167
Section Summaries, pp. 160, 162, 164, 166, 168

- Have students access **Web Code nbp-2762** for this chapter's **History Interactive** timeline, which includes expanded entries and additional events.

- If students need more instruction on analyzing timelines, have them read the **Skills Handbook,** p. SH30.

- When students have completed their study of the chapter, distribute Chapter Tests A and B.

  All in One Teaching Resources, Unit 4, pp. 38–43

For **Progress Monitoring Online,** refer students to the Self-test with vocabulary practice at **Web Code nba-2761.**

Quick Study Guide

Progress Monitoring Online
For: Self-test with vocabulary practice
Web Code: nba-2761

■ Nationalism Around the World 1910–1939

Location	Goals	Expression
Mexico	To reject foreign influence	Nationalizing foreign companies; emphasizing Latin American culture
Africa	To fight for rights under colonial system	Organizing resistance, including protests, boycotts, strikes, squatting; founding of associations and political parties
Turkey and Persia	To strengthen countries by modernizing and westernizing	Secularizing daily life; adopting Western ways; building industry
The Middle East	To create a Pan-Arab state	Resisting mandate system; ongoing friction between Jewish settlers and Palestinians
India	To gain independence from British	Protesting British rule using nonviolent methods, under Gandhi's leadership
China	To lessen foreign domination of China	Resisting Japanese encroachment; attempting to strengthen China
Japan	To build an empire	Issuing the Twenty-One Demands; invading China multiple times

■ Key Leaders

Emiliano Zapata—Mexican land reformer
Venustiano Carranza—conservative Mexican president
Atatürk—father of modern Turkey
Reza Khan—modernizing Shah of Persia
Gandhi—Congress Party leader (led self-rule protest movement)
Jiang Jieshi—leader of Guomindang (Chinese Nationalists)
Mao Zedong—leader of Chinese Communist Party

■ Effects of World War I on World Events

Effects of World War I				
Trade fell off in Latin America after war.	Resistance to colonial rule grew when war service failed to improve treatment of African and Indian colonies.	Atatürk united Turkey and fought to renegotiate the Treaty of Sèvres.	The Allies broke promises in the Middle East, fostering bitterness.	Japan expanded its influence in China.

■ Key Events in Latin America, Africa, and Asia

Latin America and Africa

Asia

1910
Mexican Revolution begins.

1912
Black South Africans form a political party, which later becomes the African National Congress (ANC).

1917
A new Mexican constitution is passed, but fighting continues.

1910   1915   1920

1911
Sun Yixian and the Guomindang establish the Republic of China.

1923
Atatürk founds modern Turkey.

Differentiated Instruction   Solutions for All Learners

L1 Special Needs   **L2** Less Proficient Readers
For students acquiring basic skills:

Adapted Reading and Note Taking Study Guide
Adapted Note Taking, pp. 159, 161, 163, 165, 167
Adapted Section Summaries, pp. 160, 162, 164, 166, 168

L2 English Language Learners
For Spanish-speaking students:

Spanish Reading and Note Taking Study Guide
Spanish Note Taking, pp. 159, 161, 163, 165, 167
Spanish Section Summaries, pp. 160, 162, 164, 166, 168

Concept Connector

? Essential Question Review

To connect prior knowledge with what you have learned in this chapter, answer the questions below in your Concept Connector journal. Use the journal in the Reading and Note Taking Study Guide to record your answers (or go to www.phschool.com **Web Code: nbd-2707**).

1. **Democracy** Mohandas Gandhi used the power of nonviolence to protest British rule and achieve democratic reforms in India. Create a flowchart to describe how Gandhi's protests launched a democratic movement in India. Focus on the following:
   - the class system
   - civil disobedience
   - boycotts
   - the Salt March

2. **Impact of the Individual** In this chapter, you read about the influence of Jiang Jieshi and Mao Zedong in China. How were the goals of Jiang and Mao similar? How were their goals different? How did each of these leaders influence events in China?

3. **Nationalism** As you have read, During the 1920s and the 1930s, economic, political, and cultural nationalism in Latin American nations were triggered by world events. Do you think nationalism unified or divided the nations of Latin America? Write a paragraph that explains your point of view. Focus on the following:
   - the world economy
   - influence of the United States on Latin America
   - the types of governments that developed in Latin America

■ Connections to Today

1. **Conflict: The Zapatista Army of National Liberation** Although Emiliano Zapata was assassinated in 1919, the spirit of his movement has lived on. In the early 1990s, poverty-stricken Indian peasants in the southern state of Chiapas formed a revolutionary group named the Zapatista Army of National Liberation, after Zapata. Conduct research on the issues behind the Zapatista movement, and then create a chart comparing issues from the Mexican Revolution era to those of the Zapatistas today.

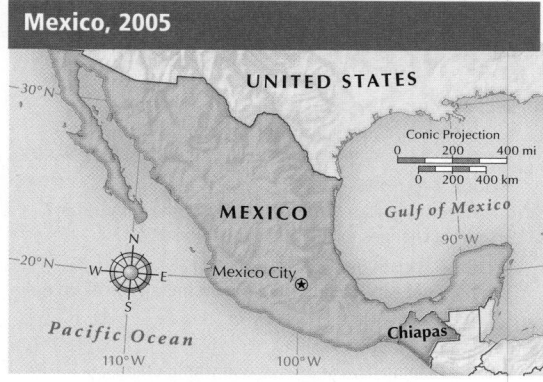

Mexico, 2005

2. **Conflict: Soweto, Then and Now** Soweto, a poor suburb of Johannesburg, South Africa, was a harsh symbol of apartheid. Soweto has changed since apartheid began to end in 1990, but poverty is still widespread. Conduct research and write two paragraphs about life in Soweto today.

History Interactive
For: Interactive timeline
Web Code: nbp-2762

1929	1938
Ibo women protest British policies in Nigeria.	Mexico nationalizes foreign-owned oil companies.

1925 — 1930 — 1935 — 1940

1925 Jiang Jieshi becomes the leader of the Guomindang in China.

1930 Thousands of Indians join Gandhi in the Salt March.

1937 The Japanese army captures Nanjing.

Concept Connector

Tell students that the main concepts for this chapter are Democracy, Impact of the Individual, and Nationalism, and then ask them to answer the Essential Question Review questions on this page. Discuss the Connections to Today topics and ask students to answer the questions that follow.

Essential Question Review

1. Flowcharts should show how Gandhi mobilized and inspired with his ideas of nonviolent protest.

2. Jiang Jieshi and Mao Zedong sought to unify China. But Jiang was only interested in national power and unity, while Mao wanted to empower the citizens. Jiang's legacy was a 22-year civil war. Mao's legacy was decades of communist rule in China.

3. Answers will vary. Nationalism both divided and unified, paving the way for later independence, but also helping to usher in failed policies. The Good Neighbor Policy of the U.S. strengthened Latin American nationalism.

Connections to Today

1. Charts should accurately compare the Zapatista movement with what was learned in this chapter about reform and economic and political nationalism in early twentieth-century Mexico. They should include the issues of land use, foreign influence, and resistance to one-party rule.

2. Answers should reflect valid research from reliable sources about life in modern-day Soweto. They should mention that Soweto residents today have more political power and better health care than in the apartheid years, but unemployment is still high.

For additional review of this chapter's core concepts, remind students to refer to the

 Reading and Note Taking Study Guide
Concept Connector, pp. 250, 278, 284

L3

Chapter Assessment

Terms, People, and Places

1. It is a desire for domestic control of the economy. In the early 1900s, Latin Americans nationalized many foreign-owned businesses and encouraged domestic industry.

2. It was the announcement of British support for Jewish settlement in Palestine. It went against Pan-Arabic aims to create a united Arab nation.

3. *Ahimsa* is a doctrine of nonviolence and reverence for all life. Civil disobedience is the refusal to obey unjust laws. Gandhi used the theory of nonviolence as a principle in his campaign, which included passive and active civil disobedience.

4. a list of demands given to Yuan Shikai, the leader of China, by Japanese leaders that would have made China a protectorate of Japan

5. Manchuria is a region of northern China that is rich in natural resources. Japanese ultranationalists, or extreme nationalists, created an excuse to invade and control Manchuria in 1931.

Main Ideas

6. unequal distribution of wealth and power, middle class agitation for democracy, upper class resentment of foreign control of business

7. It led to stronger central governments, less foreign influence, and more pride in Latin American cultures.

8. Pan-Africanism and the négritude movement bolstered pride in African culture.

9. Turkey and Persia modernized, while Palestine and other territories protested the mandate system.

10. by encouraging Indians to use non-violent protest and civil disobedience to force Britain to give India independence

11. First phase: Guomindang and Communists fought against warlords. Second phase: Guomindang and Communists fought each other for control of China.

12. Japan took over Manchuria in 1931 and invaded China again in 1937.

13. by expanding Japan's empire and getting access to more natural resources

---

Chapter Assessment

Terms, People, and Places

1. Define **economic nationalism**. How did this movement bring change to Latin America in the early 1900s?
2. What was the **Balfour Declaration**? Did it further or hinder the aims of **Pan-Arabism**? Explain.
3. Define **ahimsa** and **civil disobedience**. How did Gandhi use both in his campaign for self-rule in India?
4. What were the **Twenty-One Demands**? How were they an example of foreign imperialism in China?
5. Define **Manchuria** and **ultranationalist**. Describe how what happened in Manchuria was a result of ultranationalist aims in Japan.

Main Ideas

Section 1 (pp. 490–494)
6. What caused the Mexican Revolution?
7. How did nationalism affect Latin America in the early 1900s?

Section 2 (pp. 496–502)
8. How did African nationalism grow in the early 1900s?
9. What changes took place in the Middle East?

Section 3 (pp. 503–505)
10. How did Mohandas Gandhi help Indians work to gain self-rule?

Section 4 (pp. 507–511)
11. Describe the two phases of civil war in China.
12. How did Japan interfere in China in the 1930s?

Section 5 (pp. 512–515)
13. Describe how ultranationalists in Japan sought to solve Japan's economic problems during the Great Depression.

Chapter Focus Question
14. How did nationalism and the desire for change shape world events in the early 1900s?

● Writing About History

In this chapter's five Section Assessments, you developed skills for writing a persuasive essay.

Writing a Persuasive Essay In this chapter, you learned about how people in many different regions of the world struggled to change their lives in the early 1900s. Pick a major issue from one of these regions, choose a stance on it, and then write an essay that persuades the reader to believe in your point of view.

Prewriting
• Choose a topic that provokes a valid argument, not a topic on which most people would agree or disagree.
• Gather information about your topic to help you generate arguments.

Drafting
• Develop a thesis and arguments that support your position.
• Use an organizational structure to help build your argument.
• Write an introduction outlining your position and arguments on the topic, a body, and a conclusion.

Revising
• As you review your essay, look for and eliminate weak logic.
• Use the guidelines for revising your essay on page SH17 of the Writing Handbook.

Critical Thinking

15. **Draw Conclusions** How did the Good Neighbor Policy change the relationship between the United States and Latin America?
16. **Draw Inferences** How did Pan-Africanism affect people around the world?
17. **Recognize Cause and Effect** How did World War I affect relations between India and Britain?

18. **Analyzing Visuals** In the photo above, Mexican *soldaderas* stand with some male soldiers. How does this image embody some of the goals of the Mexican Revolution?
19. **Identify Central Issues** What three-sided struggle took place in China from 1937 to 1945?
20. **Predict Consequences** How were liberal changes in 1920s Japan reversed by ultranationalists in the 1930s?

Chapter Focus Question

14. Nationalism led many countries to resist foreign control or, in the case of Japan, to try to expand its own influence.

Critical Thinking

15. The United States lessened its interference in Latin American affairs.

16. It unified Africans and people of African descent.

17. Tensions increased when the British offered only small reforms after the war.

18. It shows that all Mexicans, including women, were united in overthrowing Díaz.

19. the struggle between the Communists, Guomindang, and Japanese

20. Ultranationalists restricted rights and renewed aggressive expansionist policies.

Document-Based Assessment

A Fistful of Salt

Mohandas Gandhi's campaign of nonviolent resistance was a potent weapon in the Indian struggle for independence from Britain. The documents below describe one hard-fought battle: the Salt March of 1930.

Document A

"Wherever possible, civil disobedience of the salt laws should be started. These laws can be violated in three ways. It is an offense to manufacture salt wherever there are facilities for doing so. The possession and sale of contraband salt, which includes natural salt or salt earth, [is] also an offense. The purchasers of such salt will be equally guilty. To carry away the natural salt deposits on the seashore is likewise violation of the law. So is the hawking of such salt. In short, you may choose any one or all of these devices to break the salt monopoly."

—Gandhi on the Salt March

Document B

"The Salt Satyagraha started with a dramatic long march by Gandhi and a group of picked companions from Sabarmati to the coast at Dandi, 240 miles away, where he proceeded to make salt illegally by boiling sea water. The march was a publicity enterprise of great power as the press followed the party's progress . . . As he journeyed . . ., deliberately challenging established authority, village headmen began to resign in large numbers . . . in April, [India's Viceroy, Lord] Irwin reported to London that in Gujarat 'the personal influence of Gandhi threatens to create a position of real embarrassment to the administration . . . as in some areas he has already achieved a considerable measure of success in undermining the authority of Government.'"

—From ***Modern India: The Origins of Asian Democracy***
by Judith M. Brown

Document C

"Suddenly, at a word of command, scores of native policemen rushed upon the advancing marchers and rained blows on their heads with their steel-shod *lathis*. Not one of the marchers even raised an arm to fend off the blows. They went down like ten-pins. . . . The survivors, without breaking ranks, silently and doggedly marched on until struck down."

—Webb Miller, a British journalist reporting on a march to the salt deposits at Dharsana

Document D

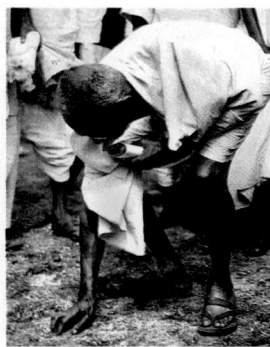

Gandhi picking up salt at the coastal village of Dandi in India, April 6, 1930

Analyzing Documents

Use your knowledge of India's struggle for self-rule and Documents A, B, C, and D to answer questions 1–4.

1. In Document A, Gandhi was mainly addressing
    A British authorities.
    B journalists around the world.
    C the British people.
    D the Indian people.

2. In Document B, the historian describes the effect of the Salt March on
    A the supply of salt.
    B the authority of the British government.
    C protesters in other countries.
    D Gandhi's health.

3. Which words from Document C reflect the attitude of the reporter toward the marchers?
    A suddenly, command
    B steel-shod *lathis*, ten-pins
    C fend, blows
    D silently, doggedly

4. **Writing Task** How was the Salt March a turning point in India's struggle for independence? Use what you have learned from these documents and the chapter in your response.

The Rise of Totalitarianism

Section	Core Instruction **L3**	Differentiated Instruction **L1** **L2** **L4**	
Section 1 *Postwar Social Changes* **2 periods, 1 block** **OBJECTIVES** ■ Analyze how Western society changed after World War I. ■ Describe the literary and artistic trends that emerged in the 1920s. ■ List several advances in modern scientific thought. **Focus Question** *What changes did Western society and culture experience after World War I?*	**All in One Teaching Resources, Unit 4** Vocabulary Builder: Word Origins, p. 49 Section 1 Quiz, p. 44 **Reading and Note Taking Study Guide** Note Taking Study Guide, p. 169 Section 1 Summary, p. 170 **Note Taking Transparencies**, 179 **WITNESS HISTORY Audio CD** The Jazz Age; Popular Culture in the Jazz Age **Progress Monitoring Transparencies**, 118 **Color Transparencies**, 168 **Teaching Resources, Skills Handbook** Prereading the Chapter, pp. 1–2 Word Knowledge Rating Form, p. 3 K-W-L Chart, p. 4	**L1** Adapted Reading and Note Taking Study Guide Note Taking Study Guide, p. 169 **SN** Section 1 Summary, p. 170 **SN** **L2** Adapted Reading and Note Taking Study Guide Note Taking Study Guide, p. 169 **LPR** Section 1 Summary, p. 170 **LPR** Spanish Reading and Note Taking Study Guide Note Taking Study Guide, p. 169 **ELL** Section 1 Summary, p. 170 **ELL** **L4** All in One Teaching Resources, Unit 4 Biography: Langston Hughes, p. 51 **AR, GT**	*Student Edition Audio **SN** Differentiated Instruction Activity, Teacher's Edition, pp. 523, 524 **SN** *Guided Reading Audio, Spanish **ELL** *Student Edition Audio **LPR** Differentiated Instruction Activity, Teacher's Edition, pp. 523, 524 **ELL** Extend Activity, Teacher's Edition, pp. 520c, 527 **AR, GT**
Section 2 *The Western Democracies Stumble* **1 period, .5 block** **OBJECTIVES** ■ Summarize the domestic and foreign policy issues Europe faced after World War I. ■ Compare the postwar economic situations in Britain, France, and the United States. ■ Describe how the Great Depression began and spread and how Britain, France, and the United States tried to address it. **Focus Question** *What political and economic challenges did the leading democracies face in the 1920s and 1930s?*	**All in One Teaching Resources, Unit 4** Reading Strategy: Identify Main Ideas, p. 50 Section 2 Quiz, p. 45 **Reading and Note Taking Study Guide** Note Taking Study Guide, p. 171 Section 2 Summary, p. 172 **Note Taking Transparencies**, 180A–180B **WITNESS HISTORY Audio CD** Brother, Can You Spare a Dime? **Progress Monitoring Transparencies**, 119 **Color Transparencies**, 169 **Witness History Discovery School™** video program, *The Great Depression and American Farmers*	**L1** Adapted Reading and Note Taking Study Guide Note Taking Study Guide, p. 171 **SN** Section 2 Summary, p. 172 **SN** **L2** Adapted Reading and Note Taking Study Guide Note Taking Study Guide, p. 171 **LPR** Section 2 Summary, p. 172 **LPR** **L4** All in One Teaching Resources, Unit 4 Viewpoints: The Red Scare, p. 52 **AR, GT**	Differentiated Instruction Activity, Teacher's Edition, p. 530 **SN** Spanish Reading and Note Taking Study Guide Note Taking Study Guide, p. 171 **ELL** Section 2 Summary, p. 172 **ELL** Differentiated Instruction Activity, Teacher's Edition, p. 530 **LPR, ELL** Differentiated Instruction Activity, Teacher's Edition, pp. 532, 534 **AR, GT** Extend Activity, Teacher's Edition, p. 535 **AR, GT**

Assessment Resources

- **AYP Monitoring Assessment**, Benchmark Test 3, pp. 44–46
- **Progress Monitoring Transparencies**, 118–122
- **SuccessTracker™**, Chapter 16
- **Document-Based Assessment**, pp. 80–94
- *ExamView*® Test Bank CD-ROM, Chapter 16
- **All in One Teaching Resources, Unit 4,** Chapter Tests A and B, pp. 59–64
- **Progress Monitoring *Online* Quizzes,** Chapter 16
- **Assessment Rubrics**

Differentiated Instruction Key

L1 Special Needs		**LPR**	Less Proficient Readers
L2 Basic to Average		**AR**	Advanced Readers
L3 All Students		**SN**	Special Needs Students
L4 Average to Advanced		**GT**	Gifted and Talented
		ELL	English Language Learners

Section	Core Instruction L3	Differentiated Instruction L1 L2 L4	

Section 3
Fascism in Italy

 2 periods, 1 block

OBJECTIVES
- Describe how conditions in Italy favored the rise of Mussolini.
- Summarize how Mussolini changed Italy.
- Understand the values and goals of fascist ideology.
- Compare and contrast fascism and communism.

Focus Question *How and why did fascism rise in Italy?*

All in One Teaching Resources, Unit 4
Section 3 Quiz, p. 46

Reading and Note Taking Study Guide
Note Taking Study Guide, p. 173
Section 3 Summary, p. 174

Note Taking Transparencies,
181A–181B

WITNESS HISTORY Audio CD
A New Leader: Mussolini

Progress Monitoring Transparencies, 120

Color Transparencies, 170

L1 Adapted Reading and Note Taking Study Guide
Note Taking Study Guide, p. 173 **SN**
Section 3 Summary, p. 174 **SN**

L2 Adapted Reading and Note Taking Study Guide
Note Taking Study Guide, p. 173 **LPR**
Section 3 Summary, p. 174 **LPR**

L4 All in One Teaching Resources, Unit 4
Link to Literature: From "The Sound of the Cicadas," by Arturo Vivante, p. 53 **AR, GT**

Differentiated Instruction Activity,
Teacher's Edition, p. 537 **SN**

Spanish Reading and Note Taking Study Guide
Note Taking Study Guide, p. 173 **ELL**
Section 3 Summary, p. 174 **ELL**

Differentiated Instruction Activity,
Teacher's Edition, p. 537 **LPR**

Extend Activity,
Teacher's Edition, p. 540 **AR, GT**

Section 4
The Soviet Union Under Stalin

 2.5 periods, 1.25 blocks

OBJECTIVES
- Describe the effects of Stalin's five-year plans.
- Explain how Stalin tried to control how people thought in the Soviet Union.
- List communist changes to Soviet society.
- Outline Soviet foreign policy under Stalin.

Focus Question *How did Stalin transform the Soviet Union into a totalitarian state?*

All in One Teaching Resources, Unit 4
Outline Map: The Soviet Union in the 1930s, p. 57
Geography Quiz, p. 58
Section 4 Quiz, p. 47

Reading and Note Taking Study Guide
Note Taking Study Guide, p. 175
Section 4 Summary, p. 176

Note Taking Transparencies, 182

WITNESS HISTORY Audio CD
The Heart of the Party; Anna Akmatova

Progress Monitoring Transparencies, 121

Color Transparencies, 171

L1 Adapted Reading and Note Taking Study Guide
Note Taking Study Guide, p. 175 **SN**
Section 4 Summary, p. 176 **SN**

L2 Adapted Reading and Note Taking Study Guide
Note Taking Study Guide, p. 175 **LPR**
Section 4 Summary, p. 176 **LPR**

L4 All in One Teaching Resources, Unit 4
Link to Literature: From *Darkness at Noon*, by Arthur Koestler, p. 54 **AR, GT**

Differentiated Instruction Activity,
Teacher's Edition, p. 545 **SN**

Spanish Reading and Note Taking Study Guide
Note Taking Study Guide, p. 175 **ELL**
Section 4 Summary, p. 176 **ELL**

Differentiated Instruction Activity,
Teacher's Edition, p. 545 **LPR, ELL**

Differentiated Instruction Activity,
Teacher's Edition, p. 544 **AR, GT**

Extend Activity,
Teacher's Edition, p. 549 **AR, GT**

Section 5
Hitler and the Rise of Nazi Germany

 2.5 periods, 1.25 blocks

OBJECTIVES
- Analyze the problems faced by the Weimar Republic.
- Describe the Nazi party's political, social, economic, and cultural policies.
- Summarize the rise of authoritarian rule in Eastern Europe in the 1920s and 1930s.

Focus Question *How did Hitler and the Nazi party establish and maintain a totalitarian government in Germany?*

All in One Teaching Resources, Unit 4
Outline Map: Fascist Governments in Europe, 1939, p. 56
Section 5 Quiz, p. 48

Reading and Note Taking Study Guide
Note Taking Study Guide, p. 177
Section 5 Summary, p. 178
Concept Connector, pp. 255, 275, 295

Note Taking Transparencies, 183

WITNESS HISTORY Audio CD
The Nazis in Control of Germany

Progress Monitoring Transparencies, 122

Color Transparencies, 173–174

L1 Adapted Reading and Note Taking Study Guide
Note Taking Study Guide, p. 177 **SN**
Section 5 Summary, p. 178 **SN**
Concept Connector, pp. 255, 275, 295 **SN**

L2 Adapted Reading and Note Taking Study Guide
Note Taking Study Guide, p. 177 **LPR**
Section 5 Summary, p. 178 **LPR**
Concept Connector, pp. 255, 275, 295 **LPR**

L4 All in One Teaching Resources, Unit 4
Viewpoints: Hitler's Propaganda Machine, p. 55 **AR, GT**

Differentiated Instruction Activity,
Teacher's Edition, p. 554 **SN**

Spanish Reading and Note Taking Study Guide
Note Taking Study Guide, p. 177 **ELL**
Section 5 Summary, p. 178 **ELL**
Concept Connector, pp. 255, 275, 295 **ELL**

Differentiated Instruction Activity,
Teacher's Edition, p. 554 **LPR, ELL**

Differentiated Instruction Activity,
Teacher's Edition, p. 551 **AR, GT**

Extend Activity,
Teacher's Edition, p. 555

Audio support is available for all sections.

CHAPTER PLANNER

Author's Notes

A Great Authoritarian Tide

Ideologically based dictatorships . . . rose in many lands in these dark years [after the War]. The most powerful of these governments are often described as totalitarian, vesting total power in a single highly ideological party and appealing to the total commitment of party members to the cause, the movement, and its leader.

Stalin brought Communist party power to a climax in Russia in the 1930s. The new regime built on the tsarist tradition of authoritarian rule but developed the bureaucracy, the army, and the secret police far beyond tsarist models. Communist repression cost the lives of millions of Russians—officially classified as enemies of the working class—in Stalinist work camps and prisons, or in the famines of the early 1930s.

Hitler's Nazi party rose to power in 1933, capitalizing on German resentment of the Versailles peace, disillusionment with democracy, and economic collapse. Once in power, Hitler suppressed rival parties, free elections, and free enterprise as he remilitarized his country. He bailed the nation out of the Depression with his public works and rearmament programs, and he unilaterally abrogated the Versailles Treaty. He also introduced Gestapo secret-police terror and SS death camps, massacring six million Jews and millions of others deemed biologically inferior to the "master race."

Mussolini's Fascists seized power in Italy in the early 1920s. In Japan, resentment of an unaggressive parliamentary regime and of *zaibatsu* big business allowed the militarists to dominate affairs in the 1930s. Through assassinations and the threat of a military coup, Japanese generals and admirals cowed civilian authorities into accepting increasingly nationalistic, imperialistic, and reactionary policies.

A great authoritarian wave seemed to be sweeping over the world. One-party rule, military dictatorship, and other forms of autocratic government rose to power in many East European, South American, and Middle Eastern nations. Under the pressure of great economic and political problems, people seemed to be turning their backs on democracy.

—Anthony Esler, *The Human Venture: From Prehistory to the Present*, (Upper Saddle River, New Jersey: Pearson Education, 2004), p. 650

Extend Online

The Harlem Renaissance

Have students analyze poems written during the Harlem Renaissance, such as the one below by Langston Hughes, and describe how it fits into the context of the period. Use the steps below to help students complete the activity.

> " They'll see how beautiful I am
> And be ashamed—
>
> I, too, am America. "
> —Langston Hughes,
> "I, Too, Sing America"

Prepare for the Activity Explain that a cultural awakening in African American literature took place in the early 1900s. Based in Harlem, a New York City neighborhood where many African Americans lived, the movement called critical attention to their lives. Writers such as Hughes, Countee Cullen, Claude McKay, and Zora Neale Hurston explored and celebrated their experiences through poems, essays, short stories, and novels.

Conduct the Activity For help in starting the activity, send students to **Web Code nbe-2801.** Students will read several poems written during this period and choose one to share with the class. Have them read the selected passage out loud, give their interpretation of its meaning, and explain how it reflects the social changes taking place after World War I.

Follow-Up Conduct a class discussion based on the following questions: Why might these poems have inspired pride in African American culture? How did these poems celebrate African American experiences? How was the Harlem Renaissance related to Pan-Africanism and the négritude movement discussed in the previous chapter?

Differentiated Instruction   Solutions for All Learners

Utilizing Images L1 L2

The importance of images in a world history classroom cannot be stressed enough. Photographs, political cartoons, paintings, and artifacts can help students comprehend concepts addressed in the text. For example, a political cartoon can visually represent two candidates' stances on an issue, and a painting can reveal the context of an era through its depiction of clothing.

Suggest that students use the visuals to compare and contrast concepts. For example, the flappers' style of the 1920s seems more "radical" when compared to its predecessor, Victorian dresses that covered the entire arm and leg. Overall, visuals can make an individual, event, or time period "come alive" by giving students concrete examples of what they are studying. As you come across each visual, ask students to describe what they are seeing and ask them to make connections to the text.

Layered Timelines L2

Too often, high school students have difficulty placing important events in their correct context. They may not understand simultaneous developments across a continent. A large timeline at the front of the classroom can help students make these connections.

To help students sequence events, create a layered timeline. At the front of the classroom, hang up a timeline that marks the years. Students will make timelines that show events in different countries, to help them see the general trend of dictators coming to power across Europe.

To begin, divide the class into groups and have each group create a timeline for one country discussed in this chapter: Germany, the Soviet Union, Italy, the United States, Great Britain, and France. Have them list the important events and sequence them correctly on the timeline. Then, have each group place its timeline on the wall either above or below the one marking years. Ask students to use this layered timeline to draw three to five conclusions about Europe in the 1930s.

Modeling Reading and Writing Skills

Choose a Topic Explain that in this chapter students will be writing a compare-and-contrast essay. (See Writing About History, p. 558.) Remind students that in this type of essay they will focus on similarities and differences. However, before they begin, they must ensure that their topic lends itself to a compare-and-contrast essay. On the board, write the following topics and ask students which topics would be suitable for a compare-and-contrast essay.

1. advances in science

2. development of cubism and surrealism after World War I

3. the rise of jazz and the rise of Stalin

4. the rise of dictators in Russia, Italy, and Germany

Point out that Topic 1 is too general for a compare-and-contrast essay. Topic 2 could be a good topic, as it compares two art styles during the same period. The same is true for Topic 4, as it compares similar items. However, in Topic 3, the items are too dissimilar to construct an effective thesis or essay.

Make Comparisons Explain to students that comparing two things can help them see how they are alike, despite their differences. This, in turn, can help students identify main ideas and make connections across time and space.

Model this skill by reading the information under the heading *The Democracies React to the Depression* in Section 2. Compare the ways in which Britain, France, and the United States responded to the Great Depression. Note that all three focused on labor issues and eased some of the economic hardship. Point out that you could then use this information to summarize how the democracies reacted to the Depression.

Teach With Technology

PresentationEXPRESS™
Premium DVD

- Teach this chapter's core content using **PresentationExpress™ Premium,** which includes dynamic lecture notes, interactive game shows, songs, videos, and the *ExamView® QuickTake* assessment tool.

- To introduce this chapter using **PresentationExpress™ Premium,** start by asking students **Which of the following statements do you most agree with? (A) A good leader should not be concerned about the rights of citizens. (B) A good leader should disregard the rights of citizens when they interfere with getting things done. (C) A good leader should disregard the rights of the citizens only in emergencies. (D) A good leader should never disregard the rights of citizens.** Take a class poll or record students' answers using the QuickTake feature and discuss their responses. Point out that in this chapter, they will read about how people turned to different types of leaders during tumultuous times in the 1920s and 1930s. Continue introducing the chapter using the chapter opener slide show and Witness History audio.

Technology Resources

- Student**EXPRESS** CD-ROM, Chapter 16

- Teacher**EXPRESS** CD-ROM, Chapter 16

- Presentation**EXPRESS**™ **Premium DVD,** Chapter 16

- **WITNESS HISTORY** Audio CD, Chapter 16

- *ExamView* **Test Bank CD-ROM,** English and Spanish, Chapter 16

- **Guided Reading Audio,** Spanish, Chapter 16

- **Student Edition Audio,** Chapter 16

- **Witness History Discovery School**™ video program, *The Great Depression and American Farmers*

- **Experience It! Multimedia Pack**

The Rise of Totalitarianism
1919–1939

Bibliography

For the Teacher
Clavin, Patricia. *The Great Depression in Europe, 1929–1939.* St. Martin's Press, 2000.

Fitzpatrick, Sheila. *Everyday Stalinism: Ordinary Life in Extraordinary Times: Soviet Russia in the 1930s.* Oxford University Press, 1999.

Pauley, Bruce F. *Hitler, Stalin and Mussolini: Totalitarianism in the Twentieth Century, 2nd ed.* Series: European History. Harlan Davidson, 2003.

For the Student
(L2) Brown, Gene. *Conflict in Europe (1914–1940).* Lerner Publishing Group, 1997.

(L3) Koestler, Arthur. *Darkness at Noon,* Harold Bloom, ed. and trans. Chelsea House Publishers, 2004. First published in 1940.

(L4) Zamyatin, Yevgeny. *We,* Translated by Clarence Brown. Penguin Books, 1993. First published in 1924.

WITNESS HISTORY AUDIO

Nazi Germany

Martin Niemöller, a Lutheran minister, preached against ruthless Nazi policies and was ultimately jailed. He later observed:

66 [The Nazis] came first for the Communists, and I didn't speak up because I wasn't a Communist. Then they came for the Jews, and I didn't speak up because I wasn't a Jew. Then they came for the Catholics, and I didn't speak up because I was a Protestant. Then they came for me, and by that time there was no one left to speak up. 99
—Martin Niemöller, quoted in *Time* magazine

Listen to the Witness History audio to learn more about totalitarian states in Europe.

◀ **Adolf Hitler surrounded by supporters at a Nazi party rally in 1934**

A toy replica of a Nazi storm trooper

A magazine cover showing a Jazz Age flapper

Chapter Preview

Chapter Focus Question What political and economic challenges did the Western world face in the 1920s and 1930s, and how did various countries react to these challenges?

Section 1
Postwar Social Changes

Section 2
The Western Democracies Stumble

Section 3
Fascism in Italy

Section 4
The Soviet Union Under Stalin

Section 5
Hitler and the Rise of Nazi Germany

A mug shot from a Soviet secret police file

Use the ☑ **Quick Study Timeline** at the end of this chapter to preview chapter events.

? Concept Connector ONLINE
To explore Essential Questions related to this chapter, go to PHSchool.com
Web Code: nbd-2807

Chapter-Level Resources

[All in One] Vocabulary Builder; Reading Strategy; Enrichments; Outline Maps; Geography Quiz; Chapter Tests
■ Document-Based Assessments
■ AYP Monitoring Assessments
■ *ExamView* Test Bank CD-ROM
■ Guided Reading Audio (Spanish)
■ Student Edition Audio

Previewing the Chapter

■ **WITNESS HISTORY** Explain that after Hitler came to power, he transformed Germany into a totalitarian state. Read aloud the Witness History selection or play the accompanying audio. Ask students **What point was Niemöller making in this observation?** *(The lack of opposition to Nazi persecutions allowed the Nazis to extend persecutions to additional groups.)* **Why do you think no one stood up to the persecutions?** *(Sample: People may have felt that if they stayed quiet, they could stay out of harm's way.)* Tell students that in this chapter, they will learn why so many people supported dictators such as Hitler.

◀)) AUDIO **Witness History Audio CD, Nazi Germany**

■ **Analyzing the Visuals** Ask students to study the photo of Hitler at a Nazi party rally in 1934. Ask **What questions do the photo and the Witness History selection bring to mind?** *(Samples: How did Hitler come to power? How did Hitler inspire such devotion within his troops? Why did no one stand up to him?)* Write down their questions. Tell students that you are keeping a copy of them to return to later.

■ **Focus** Write the Chapter Focus Question on the board. Tell students to keep this question in mind as they read the chapter. *(Answer appears with the Chapter Assessment answers.)* Have students preview the section titles for this chapter.

Note Taking Study Guide With Concept Connector Journal
For online access: Web code nbd-2807
For print alternative: Reading and Note Taking Study Guide booklet

---

Objectives

As you teach this section, keep students focused on the following objectives to help them answer the Section Focus Question and master core content.

- Analyze how Western society changed after World War I.
- Describe the literary and artistic trends that emerged in the 1920s.
- List several advances in modern scientific thought.

Prepare to Read

Build Background Knowledge ⬛

Remind students that in the early 1920s the Western world was still recovering from the effects of a disastrous war. Ask students to predict what problems might affect nations recovering from war.

Set a Purpose ⬛

- **WITNESS HISTORY** Read the selection aloud or play the audio. Ask **How does Zelda Fitzgerald describe a flapper?** *(rebellious, adventurous)*
  - 🔊 AUDIO **Witness History Audio CD,** The Jazz Age

- **Focus** Point out the Section Focus Question and write it on the board. Tell students to refer to this question as they read. *(Answer appears with Section 1 Assessment answers.)*

- **Preview** Have students preview the Section Objectives and the list of Terms, People, and Places.

- **Note Taking** Have students read this section using the Guided Questioning strategy (TE, p. T20). As they read, have them fill in the concept web with changes in society and culture.

  Reading and Note Taking Study Guide, p. 169

Jazz musician Louis Armstrong

WITNESS HISTORY 🔊 AUDIO

The Jazz Age

Many young people reacted to the trauma of World War I by rejecting the values of their parents. During the Jazz Age, this rebellion was exemplified by a new type of young woman—the flapper.

❝The Flapper awoke from her lethargy [tiredness] . . . bobbed her hair, put on her choicest pair of earrings and a great deal of audacity [boldness] and rouge, and went into the battle. She flirted because it was fun to flirt and . . . refused to be bored chiefly because she wasn't boring. . . . Mothers disapproved of their sons taking the Flapper to dances, to teas, to swim, and most of all to heart.❞
—Zelda Fitzgerald, flapper and wife of author F. Scott Fitzgerald

Focus Question What changes did Western society and culture experience after World War I?

Postwar Social Changes

Objectives

- Analyze how Western society changed after World War I.
- Describe the literary and artistic trends that emerged in the 1920s.
- List several advances in modern scientific thought.

Terms, People, and Places

flapper	psychoanalysis
Prohibition	abstract
speakeasies	dada
Harlem Renaissance	surrealism

Note Taking

Reading Skill: Identify Supporting Details Use a concept web like the one below to record details related to the main ideas of this section.

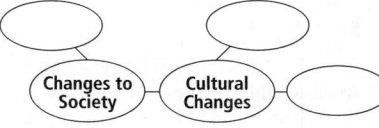

The catastrophe of World War I shattered the sense of optimism that had grown in the West since the Enlightenment. Despair gripped survivors on both sides as they added up the staggering costs of the war. It seemed as though a whole generation of young men had been lost on the battlefields. In reaction, the society and culture of Europe, the United States, and many other parts of the world experienced rapid changes.

Changes in Society After World War I

During the 1920s, new technologies helped create a mass culture shared by millions in the world's developed countries. Affordable cars, improved telephones, and new forms of media such as motion pictures and radio brought people around the world closer together than ever before.

The Roaring Twenties In the 1920s, many radios tuned into the new sounds of jazz. In fact, the 1920s are often called the Jazz Age. African American musicians combined Western harmonies with African rhythms to create jazz. Jazz musicians, like trumpeter Louis Armstrong and pianist Duke Ellington, took simple melodies and improvised endless subtle variations in rhythm and beat. They produced original music, and people loved it. Much of today's popular music has been influenced by jazz.

Vocabulary Builder

Use the information below and the following resources to teach the high-use words from this section.
All in One Teaching Resources, Unit 4, p. 49; **Teaching Resources, Skills Handbook,** p. 3

High-Use Words	Definitions and Sample Sentences
emancipation, p. 523	*n.* freeing from bondage or restraint Although I only visited my aunt for one week, I couldn't wait for my **emancipation** from all the rules of her house.
spontaneously, p. 525	*adv.* caused by inner forces, self-generated Although no one lit a match, the dried wood shavings **spontaneously** caught fire.

While Europe recovered from the war, the United States experienced a boom time. Europeans embraced American popular culture, with its greater freedom and willingness to experiment. The nightclub and the sounds of jazz were symbols of that freedom.

After the war, rebellious young people, disillusioned by the war, rejected the moral values and rules of the Victorian Age and chased after excitement. One symbol of rebellious Jazz Age youth was the liberated young woman called the **flapper**. The first flappers were American, but their European sisters soon adopted the fashion. Flappers rejected old ways in favor of new, exciting freedom.

Women's Lives Flappers were highly visible, but they were a small minority. Most women saw limited progress in the postwar period. During the war, women had held a wide range of jobs. Although most women left those jobs when the war ended, their war work helped them win the vote in many Western countries. A few women were elected to public office, such as Texas governor Miriam Ferguson or Lady Nancy Astor, the first woman to serve in the British Parliament.

By the 1920s, labor-saving devices had become common in middle-class homes. Washing machines, vacuum cleaners, and canned foods lightened the burden of household chores. Some women then sought work outside the home or did volunteer work to help the less fortunate.

In the new atmosphere of <u>emancipation</u>, women pursued careers in many areas—from sports to the arts. Women golfers, tennis players, swimmers, and pilots set new records. Women worked as newspaper reporters, published bestselling novels, and won recognition as artists. Most professions, though, were still dominated by men.

Reactions to the Jazz Age Not everyone approved of the freewheeling lifestyle of the Jazz Age. For example, many Americans supported **Prohibition**, a ban on the manufacture and sale of alcoholic beverages. For almost 90 years, social activists had waged an intense campaign against the abuse of alcohol. Finally, they gained enough support to get the Eighteenth, or Prohibition, Amendment ratified in 1919. Prohibition was meant to keep people from the negative effects of drinking. Instead, it caused an explosion of organized crime and **speakeasies,** or illegal bars. The Amendment was repealed in 1933.

In the United States in the early 1900s, a Christian fundamentalist movement swept rural areas. Fundamentalists support traditional Christian ideas about Jesus and believe that all of the events described in the Bible are literally true. Popular fundamentalist preachers traveled around the country holding inspirational revival meetings. Some used the new technology of radio to spread their message.

In 1925, a biology teacher in Tennessee named John T. Scopes was tried for teaching evolution in his classroom. His action broke a law that barred any teaching that went against the Bible's version of creation. The teacher was found guilty in the well-publicized Scopes trial, but many fundamentalists believed that the proceedings had hurt their cause.

✓ **Checkpoint** Describe the Jazz Age and some of the reactions to it.

Vocabulary Builder
<u>emancipation</u>—(ee man suh PAY shun) *n.* freedom from restrictions

Life Under Prohibition
A well-dressed couple waits to enter an illicit speakeasy (below right). Members of the United States Prohibition Service wore badges (below left) when they raided speakeasies and breweries and fought bootleggers such as Al Capone. *What does the clothing the couple is wearing tell you about who could afford to go to speakeasies?*

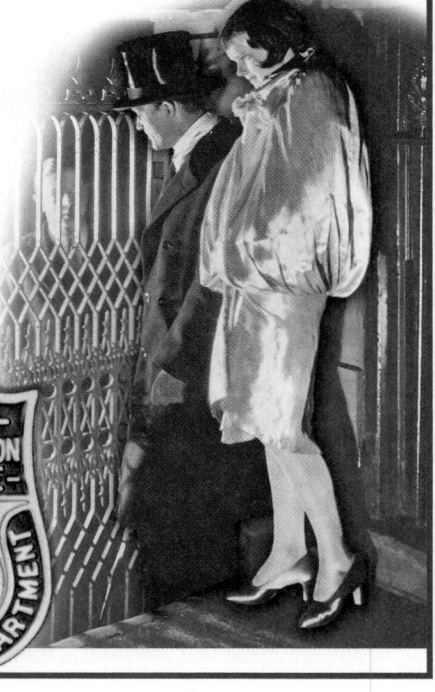

Teach

Changes in Society After World War I

Instruct

- **Introduce: Vocabulary Builder**
  Have students read the Vocabulary Builder term and definition. Then have them reread the Witness History passage. Ask **How did flappers illustrate women's *emancipation* in the Jazz Age?** *(They showed that many women felt free to do the things they wanted rather than what was traditionally expected of them.)*

- **Teach** Discuss the social changes that took place after World War I. Ask **How did new technologies in the 1920s contribute to postwar changes?** *(They helped form a mass culture. Labor-saving devices became common in middle-class homes, enabling more women to work outside the home.)* **What was the reaction to these new ideas and life styles?** *(Some people stressed the value of traditional beliefs, such as fundamentalism.)*

- **Quick Activity** Web Code nbp-2811 will take students to interactive audio and visuals. Have students complete the interactivity on Popular Culture in the Jazz Age and then answer the questions in the text.

Independent Practice

Remind students that the changing manners and culture of the 1920s created a "generation gap" between young people and their elders. Have them write a paragraph explaining whether manners and culture create a similar gap today.

Monitor Progress

As students fill in their concept webs, circulate to make sure they understand the postwar changes in society. For a completed version of the concept web, see

🏛 **Note Taking Transparencies,** 179

Differentiated Instruction   Solutions for All Learners

L1 Special Needs   L2 English Language Learners

To help students understand the generalization "Roaring Twenties," ask them to list things a member of an older generation might say about the music or clothing of teenagers today. Point out that the 1920s signified an abandonment of Victorian-era ideals. Then have students look through the visuals and think about how members of an older generation may have responded about the youth of the 1920s. For instance, point out the image on the next page of a flapper on the cover of *McClure's* magazine. Have students compare this with the image of the Victorian-era women on page 360. How would the flapper's dress, which exposes her arms and legs, be considered a dramatic departure from Victorian fashion?

Answers

Caption They were higher class people who could afford to buy expensive clothes.

✓ Some people embraced rebelliousness and experimentation, symbolized by the new sound of jazz. Meanwhile, others supported the Prohibition amendment, and fundamentalists supported traditional Christian ideas.

The New Literature

Instruct

- **Introduce** Read aloud the quotation from *The Sun Also Rises*, under A Loss of Faith: "I did not care what it was all about. All I wanted to know was how to live in it." Ask students to think about how the quote expresses the feelings of many young people in the 1920s. Ask **Based on this selection, how would you describe the literature of the 1920s?** *(bleak, pessimistic)*

- **Teach** Discuss the developments in literature. Ask **What did writers like James Joyce and Virginia Woolf explore with their use of stream of consciousness?** *(people's hidden thoughts)* **What did the writing of the Harlem Renaissance explore?** *(aspects of the African American experience)* Using the Numbered Heads strategy (TE, p. T23), discuss how these developments in literature reflected developments in society.

- **Quick Activity** Ask a volunteer to read aloud the passage from William Butler Yeats's poem on this page. Ask **How is this poem typical of the literature of the postwar period?** *(It reflects a sense of uncertainty, of a civilization falling apart.)*

Independent Practice

Biography To help students better understand the Harlem Renaissance, have them read the biography *Langston Hughes* and complete the worksheet.

All in One Teaching Resources, Unit 4, p. 51

Monitor Progress

To help students review the section so far, ask them to reread the black headings and summarize the information under each heading.

Popular Culture in the
JAZZ AGE

During the Jazz Age, new ideas and new technology transformed the daily lives of many Americans and Europeans. New, reasonably priced cars allowed the middle-class population to travel with greater ease. People used better telephones to communicate across great distances in an instant. Silent movie stars had fans on every continent. Radios brought news, music, and sports into homes throughout the Western world.

▲ An image of a flapper dancing to jazz music on the cover of *McClure's* magazine

Daily Life in the United States, 1920s		
	1922	**1929**
Households with radios	60,000	10.25 million
Daily local telephone calls	55,160	79,141
Motion picture attendance per week	40 million	80 million
Dwellings with electricity	40%	68%

SOURCE: *Historical Statistics of the United States, Colonial Times to 1970*

More and more ▶ families were able to afford cars.

▲ Jazz Age flappers shocked their elders by bobbing, or cutting short, their hair and wearing skirts far shorter than those of prewar fashions. They went out on dates unchaperoned, enjoyed wild new dance fads such as the Charleston, smoked cigarettes, and drank in nightclubs.

The New Literature

In the 1920s, war novels, poetry, plays, and memoirs flowed off the presses. *All Quiet on the Western Front* by German novelist Erich Remarque, and other works like it, exposed the grim horrors of modern warfare. These works reflected a powerful disgust with war.

A Loss of Faith To many postwar writers, the war symbolized the moral breakdown of Western civilization. In 1922, the English poet T. S. Eliot published *The Waste Land*. This long poem portrays the modern world as spiritually empty and barren. In *The Sun Also Rises*, the American novelist Ernest Hemingway shows the rootless wanderings of young people who lack deep convictions. "I did not care what it was all about," says the narrator. "All I wanted to know was how to live in it." Many of these authors, including Hemingway and F. Scott Fitzgerald, left the United States and moved to Paris. Gertrude Stein, an American writer living in Paris, called them the "lost generation." Her label caught on. It referred to Stein's literary friends, and their generation as a whole.

In 1921, the Irish poet William Butler Yeats summed up the mood of many in postwar Europe and the United States:

> **Primary Source**
>
> 66 Things fall apart; the centre cannot hold;
> Mere anarchy is loosed upon the world,
> The blood-dimmed tide is loosed, and everywhere
> The ceremony of innocence is drowned. 99
> —William Butler Yeats, "The Second Coming"

Literature of the Inner Mind Some writers experimented with stream of consciousness. In this technique, a writer appears to present a character's random thoughts and feelings without imposing any logic or order. In the novel *Mrs. Dalloway*, British novelist Virginia Woolf used stream of consciousness to explore the thoughts of people going through the

---

Differentiated
Instruction   Solutions for All Learners

L1 Special Needs   **L2** English Language Learners

To help students understand the concept of the Lost Generation, write on the board these definitions of the word *lost*: cannot be found, cannot find the way to some place, confused, or totally involved in something. Ask students to list other possible definitions. Have students determine which defintion is most appropriate for Gertrude Stein's literary friends.

Use the following resources to help students acquire basic skills.

 **Adapted Reading and Note Taking Study Guide**

- Adapted Note Taking Study Guide, p. 169
- Adapted Section Summary, p. 170

Listening to the ▶ radio was a family activity.
🔊 AUDIO

History *Interactive*
For: For Interactive Audio and Visuals
Web Code: nbp-2811

Thinking Critically
1. **Draw Inferences** Why do you think the flapper is considered the symbol of the Jazz Age?
2. **Draw Conclusions** How did technology affect daily life in the United States during the Jazz Age?

Silent movie ▲ star Charlie Chaplin

New Scientific Theories

Instruct

- **Introduce** Ask students to read this subsection's introductory sentences and preview the black headings. Then have them predict how new theories will challenge long-held ideas about the world.

- **Teach** Discuss the effects that the scientific theories of the early 1900s have had on society. Ask **Why did Curie's and Einstein's theories seem unsettling to the general public?** *(They seemed to reinforce the sense of old certainties falling apart and a universe that seemed beyond human understanding.)* **How did Fleming's discovery of penicillin affect people's lives?** *(It led to the development of antibiotics, which revolutionized the medical treatment of infections.)* **How did Freud's work have an impact beyond medicine?** *(It led artists to explore the subconscious mind.)*

Independent Practice

Ask students to work in small groups to explore the effects of one scientific discovery covered, such as Fleming's discovery of penicillin. How did the everyday lives of people change due to this discovery? Did the discovery have an immediate effect or did it affect later generations?

Monitor Progress

To check student understanding, point out the picture of Marie Curie on the next page. Ask students to draw connections between her pioneering work and the influence of flappers on society. How did both reject the traditional roles of women?

---

ordinary actions of their everyday lives. In *Finnegans Wake,* the Irish novelist James Joyce explored the inner mind of a hero who remains sound asleep throughout the novel.

The Harlem Renaissance Also during the 1920s, an African American cultural awakening called the **Harlem Renaissance** began in Harlem, a neighborhood in New York City that was home to many African Americans. African American writers and artists expressed their pride in their unique culture. James Weldon Johnson, Jean Toomer, and Zora Neale Hurston explored the African American experience in their novels and essays. The poets Claude McKay and Langston Hughes experimented with new styles, while Countee Cullen adapted traditional poetic forms to new content.

✔ **Checkpoint** How did postwar authors show disillusionment with prewar institutions?

New Scientific Theories

It was not only the war that fostered a sense of uncertainty. New scientific discoveries challenged long-held ideas about the nature of the world. Discoveries made in the late 1800s and early 1900s showed that the atom was more complex than anyone suspected.

Marie Curie and Radioactivity In the early 1900s, the Polish-born French scientist Marie Curie and others found that the atoms of certain elements, such as radium and uranium, spontaneously release charged particles. As scientists studied radioactivity further, they discovered that

Vocabulary Builder
spontaneously—(spahn TAY nee us lee) *adv.* caused by inner forces, self-generated

---

History Background

Notable Records In the 1920s, records and phonograph players were not new. Yet during this decade, record sales soared. Record companies adopted the small disc format for recordings, making record production easy and records themselves convenient for consumers. Double-sided records offered music fans a relatively inexpensive way to hear many of their favorite bands. In 1927 alone, Americans bought over 100 million jazz records. Recordings by acts such as Louis Armstrong's Hot Five brought jazz to remote areas that rarely saw live bands. These phonograph records made the rapid spread of jazz music possible, and for the first time turned music and music production into a major industry.

Answers

Thinking Critically
1. Sample: She embodies a rejection of traditional values and a new way of doing things.
2. More people had access to electricity, telephones, radios, and the movies. They were also able to travel more because of faster and more affordable cars.

✔ Sample: by writing about the horrors of modern warfare and moral emptiness, and by experimenting with new styles of writing

Modern Art and Architecture

Instruct

- **Introduce** Ask students to recall how writers and musicians rejected traditional values and styles after World War I. Point out the Kandinsky painting on the next page. Ask students how this, too, reflects that same rejection of traditional styles. Then have them predict how the public would react to this new art form.

- **Teach** Explore the new styles artists developed during and after the war, from cubism and dada to surrealism. Ask **Why did critics call the new artists** *fauves,* **or wild beasts?** *(because the colors and odd distortions seemed wild to them)* **What did surrealism have in common with the stream-of-consciousness technique and Freud's work?** *(They all attempted to explore the unconscious mind.)*

- **Quick Activity** Display **Color Transparency 168:** *The Persistence of Memory,* **by Salvador Dali.** Remind students that surrealists rejected rational thought, which they felt had led to the devastation of World War I. Discuss the meaning of the painting's title. Then use the lesson suggested in the transparency book to guide a discussion on Dali's painting.

  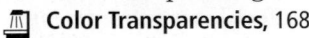 Color Transparencies, 168

Independent Practice

In groups, have students create a chart, listing the name of each new artistic movement, its style, its key artists, and what it stood for. Then ask them to create an image in one of those styles.

Monitor Progress

- To check student understanding of this section, ask students to summarize the ways in which dadaists and surrealists each reflected a new view of the world.

- Check Reading and Note Taking Study Guide entries for student understanding.

Answers

BIOGRAPHY

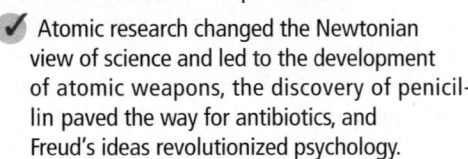

Marie Curie

Marie Curie (1867–1934) won two Nobel prizes, one in physics and one in chemistry. Still, like many other women, she struggled to balance her work with home duties. "I have a great deal of work," she said, "what with the housekeeping, the children, the teaching, and the laboratory, and I don't know how I shall manage it all."

Curie won worldwide fame for her groundbreaking research on radioactivity. But she paid a high price for knowledge. Although she shrugged off the health dangers, she died from radiation poisoning. **Why do you think Marie Curie's achievements were unique for her time?**

---

it can change atoms of one element into atoms of another. Such findings proved that atoms are not solid and indivisible.

Einstein's Theory of Relativity In 1905 and 1916, the German-born physicist Albert Einstein introduced his theories of relativity. Einstein argued that measurements of space and time are not absolute but are determined by the relative position of the observer. Einstein's ideas raised questions about Newtonian science, which compared the universe to a machine operating according to absolute laws.

In 1934, building on Curie's and Einstein's theories, Italian physicist Enrico Fermi and other scientists around the world discovered atomic fission, or the splitting of the nuclei of atoms in two. This splitting produces a huge burst of energy. In the 1940s, Fermi (now an American), along with fellow American physicists J. Robert Oppenheimer and Edward Teller, would use this discovery to create the devastating atomic bomb.

In the postwar years, many scientists came to accept the theories of relativity. To the general public, however, Einstein's ideas were difficult to understand. They seemed to further reinforce the unsettling sense of a universe whirling beyond the understanding of human reason.

Fleming Discovers Penicillin In 1928, the Scottish scientist Alexander Fleming made a different type of scientific discovery. He accidentally discovered a type of nontoxic mold that kills bacteria, which he called "penicillin." Later, other scientists used Fleming's work to develop antibiotics, which are now used all over the world to treat infections.

Freud Probes the Mind The Austrian physician Sigmund Freud (froyd) also challenged faith in reason. He suggested that the subconscious mind drives much of human behavior. Freud said that learned social values such as morality and reason help people to repress, or check, powerful urges. But an individual feels constant tension between repressed drives and social training. This tension, argued Freud, may cause psychological or physical illness. Freud pioneered psychoanalysis, a method of studying how the mind works and treating mental disorders. Although many of his theories have been discredited, Freud's ideas have had an extraordinary impact far beyond medicine.

 Checkpoint How did scientific discoveries in the 1920s change people's views of the world?

Modern Art and Architecture

In the early 1900s, many Western artists rejected traditional styles. Instead of trying to reproduce the real world, they explored other dimensions of color, line, and shape. Painters like Henri Matisse (ma TEES) utilized bold, wild strokes of color and odd distortions to produce works of strong emotion. He and fellow artists outraged the public and were dubbed *fauves* (fohv), or wild beasts, by critics.

New Directions in Painting While Matisse continued in the fauvist style, other artists explored styles based on new ideas. Before World War I, the Spanish artist Pablo Picasso and the French artist Georges Braque (brak) created a revolutionary new style called cubism. Cubists painted three-dimensional objects as complex patterns of angles and planes, as if they were composed of fragmented parts.

Later, the Russian Vasily Kandinsky and the Swiss Paul Klee moved even further away from representing reality. Their artwork was **abstract,** composed only of lines, colors, and shapes, sometimes with no recognizable subject matter at all.

During and after the war, the **dada** movement burst onto the art world. Dadaists rejected all traditional conventions and believed that there was no sense or truth in the world. Paintings and sculptures by Jean Arp and Max Ernst were intended to shock and disturb viewers. Other dadaist artists created collages, photomontages, or sculptures made of objects they found abandoned or thrown away.

Cubism and dada both helped to inspire **surrealism,** a movement that attempted to portray the workings of the unconscious mind. Surrealism rejected rational thought, which had produced the horrors of World War I, in favor of irrational or unconscious ideas. The Spanish surrealist Salvador Dali used images of melting clocks and burning giraffes to suggest the chaotic dream state described by Freud.

New Styles of Architecture Architects, too, rejected classical traditions and developed new styles to match a new world. The famous Bauhaus school in Germany influenced architecture by blending science and technology with design. Bauhaus buildings feature glass, steel, and concrete but have little ornamentation. The American architect Frank Lloyd Wright held that the function of a building should determine its form. He used materials and forms that fit a building's environment.

✓ **Checkpoint** What effect did World War I have on art movements in the 1920s?

Looking Ahead

Stunned by the trauma of World War I, many people sought to change the way they thought and acted during the turbulent 1920s. As nations recovered from the war, people began to feel hope rising out of their disillusionment. But soon, the "lost generation" would face a new crisis—this one economic—that would revive many old problems and spark new conflicts.

Abstract Art
Vasily Kandinsky painted *Swinging* (above) in 1925. He used geometrical shapes to convey the feeling of movement that the title suggests. **Analyzing Art** *How does* Swinging *show the abstract style of art that Kandinsky pioneered?*

Progress Monitoring Online
For: Self-quiz with vocabulary practice
Web Code: nba-2811

SECTION 1 Assessment

Terms, People, and Places

1. What do many of the key terms listed at the beginning of the section have in common? Explain.

Note Taking

2. **Reading Skill: Identify Supporting Details** Use your completed concept web to answer the Focus Question: What changes did Western society and culture experience after World War I?

Comprehension and Critical Thinking

3. **Determine Relevance** How did flappers symbolize changes in Western society during the 1920s?
4. **Identify Point of View** How did the ideas of Einstein and Freud contribute to a sense of uncertainty?
5. **Synthesize Information** Choose one postwar writer and one postwar artist. Explain how the work of each reflected a new view of the world.

● **Writing About History**

Quick Write: Choose a Topic The topic of a compare-and-contrast essay must involve two things that are neither nearly identical nor extremely different. Think of a topic from this section that would be a good candidate for a compare-and-contrast essay. Show why it would be a good topic by listing categories in which the two items could be compared and contrasted.

Answers

Analyzing Art   It uses lines, shapes, and colors to portray a feeling of movement.

✓ Artists rejected traditional representations and began to look for new and modern ways of expression.

Section 1 Assessment

1. Many of the terms relate to social or cultural history.
2. Disillusioned by World War I, the younger generation rebelled against Victorian values. Writers expressed a similar loss of faith and artists revolted against traditional styles and created new ways of viewing the world. Advances in science revolutionized scientific thought.
3. Flappers symbolized the rejection of the moral values and rules of the Victorian Age.
4. Einstein argued that measurements of space and time are not absolute, thus raising questions about Newtonian science and reinforcing the image of a universe beyond human understanding. Freud's ideas that the subconscious mind drives much human behavior seemed to challenge faith in reason.
5. Answers should indicate an understanding of how the writer or artist reflected a rejection of traditional views of reality.

● **Writing About History**

Responses should include a topic from this section and two items that could be compared and contrasted.

Pablo Picasso

Objectives

■ Gain a better understanding of Picasso's artwork.

■ Understand the significance of Picasso in the development of modern art.

Build Background Knowledge ⒧₃

Ask students if they have visited an art museum or art gallery. Ask them to list the different styles of art they may have seen there. Tell them they will learn about the different styles used by one artist, Picasso.

Instruct ⒧₃

■ For each image, ask students to read the caption and describe the image. Ask students what they notice about Picasso's use of color, lines, and shape. Ask **Why do you think Picasso used so many different styles to create his artwork?** *(Sample: Perhaps his tastes and goals changed over time; perhaps he enjoyed experimenting with new techniques.)*

■ Direct students to *Still Life With Violin*. Ask students if they can see the parts of the violin. Point out that cubism rejected the traditional ways of representing objects in a natural or realistic way by adapting such techniques as perspective. Ask **How are *Still Life With Violin* and *Hand With Flowers* similar?** *(They both show a two-dimensional image.)*

Monitor Progress ⒧₃

To review this section, ask students to reread the first sentence in the introductory paragraph. Ask students to explain why his work is considered to be so significant.

Thinking Critically

1. *Mother and Child* is a realistic representation of a scene, while *Still Life With Violin* is a cubist representation broken into abstract angles and shapes, rendering the objects almost unrecognizable.
2. Picasso's style ranged from realistic (*Mother and Child*), to abstract and cubist (*Still Life With Violin*), and back to representational (*Hand With Flowers*). He also ventured into different media like sculpture.

Pablo Picasso

The painter Pablo Picasso was one of the most important artists of the last century. Picasso and his friend Georges Braque together developed the art movement known as Cubism. The movement began around 1907 and continued through the First World War into the 1920s. Picasso's work continued to develop until his death in 1973 at the age of 91. Here are some of his best known artworks.

Picasso in his studio working on a sculpture

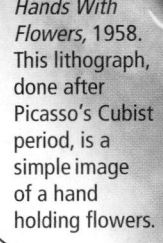

Still Life With Violin, 1912. In this Cubist still life, the objects, which include a violin, are fragmented into so many views that they are barely distinguishable.

Mother and Child, 1901. The years 1901 to 1904 are known as Picasso's Blue Period. Following the death of a close friend, Picasso used the color blue in many paintings to express his sadness.

Hands With Flowers, 1958. This lithograph, done after Picasso's Cubist period, is a simple image of a hand holding flowers.

Thinking Critically

1. **Compare** Describe the differences between *Mother and Child* and *Still Life With Violin*.
2. **Synthesize Information** Describe how Picasso's style changed over time, based on the artworks shown here.

History Background

The Artist's Life Born in Malaga, Spain, in 1881, Picasso's talent was recognized by his father, a professor of drawing, at an early age. The young artist had his first exhibition at age 13. Although he attended art school in Barcelona as a teenager, he disappointed his family by dropping out to develop his own style. He moved to Paris in 1904 and spent most of the rest of his life in France.

Still, he took a keen interest in Spain. During the Spanish Civil War, he supported the Republican (antifascist) side and painted his famous mural called *Guernica* for Spain to show at the 1937 World's Fair. *Guernica* is a powerful anti-war piece. The fascists won the civil war in 1939, and maintained power until the 1970s. Picasso never returned to Spain.

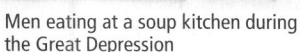

Tin cup

Men eating at a soup kitchen during the Great Depression

WITNESS HISTORY  AUDIO

Brother, Can You Spare a Dime?

In the early 1930s, a worldwide economic depression threw thousands out of work and into lives of poverty. The song below summed up the mood of the time:

❝ They used to tell me I was building a dream
With peace and glory ahead—
Why should I be standing in line,
Just waiting for bread?

Once I built a railroad, I made it run,
Made it race against time.
Once I built a railroad, now it's done—
Brother, can you spare a dime? ❞

— from the song "Brother, Can You Spare a Dime?," lyrics by E.Y. "Yip" Harburg & Jay Gorney. Published by Glocca Morra Music (ASCAP) & Gorney Music (ASCAP). Administered by Next Decade Entertainment, Inc. All rights reserved. Used by permission.

Focus Question What political and economic challenges did the leading democracies face in the 1920s and 1930s?

The Western Democracies Stumble

Objectives
- Summarize the domestic and foreign policy issues Europe faced after World War I.
- Compare the postwar economic situations in Britain, France, and the United States.
- Describe how the Great Depression began and spread and how Britain, France, and the United States tried to address it.

Terms, People, and Places

Maginot Line	finance
Kellogg-Briand Pact	Federal Reserve
disarmament	Great Depression
general strike	Franklin D. Roosevelt
overproduction	New Deal

Note Taking

Reading Skill: Identify Main Ideas Record main ideas from the first part of this section in a table like the one below.

Postwar Issues			
Country	Politics	Foreign Policy	Economics

In 1919, the three Western democracies—Britain, France, and the United States—appeared powerful. They had ruled the Paris Peace Conference and boosted hopes for democracy among the new nations of Eastern Europe. Beneath the surface, however, postwar Europe faced grave problems. To make matters worse, many members of the younger generation who might have become the next great leaders had been killed in the war.

Politics in the Postwar World

At first, the most pressing issues were finding jobs for returning veterans and rebuilding war-ravaged lands. Economic problems fed social unrest and made radical ideas more popular.

Party Struggles in Britain In Britain during the 1920s, the Labour party surpassed the Liberal party in strength. The Labour party gained support among workers by promoting a gradual move toward socialism. The Liberal party passed some social legislation, but it traditionally represented middle-class business interests. As the Liberal party faltered, the middle class began to back the Conservative party, joining the upper class, professionals, and farmers. With this support, the Conservative party held power during much of 1920s. After a massive strike of over three million workers in 1926, Conservatives passed legislation limiting the power of workers to strike.

Vocabulary Builder

Use the information below and the following resources to teach the high-use words from this section.
All in One Teaching Resources, Unit 4, p. 49; **Teaching Resources, Skills Handbook**, p. 3

High-Use Words	Definitions and Sample Sentences
suppress, p. 530	*vt.* to put down by force, subdue The police **suppressed** the protestors after violence erupted.
affluent, p. 532	*adj.* rich, wealthy It was an **affluent** neighborhood with several mansions, and our modest house looked out of place.

SECTION **2** Step-by-Step Instruction

Objectives

As you teach this section, keep students focused on the following objectives to help them answer the Section Focus Question and master core content.

- Summarize the domestic and foreign policy issues Europe faced after World War I.
- Compare the postwar economic situations in Britain, France and the United States.
- Describe how the Great Depression began and spread and how Britain, France, and the United States tried to address it.

Prepare to Read

Build Background Knowledge ⓛ
Remind students that after World War I, diplomats wanted to ensure peace. Have students predict the foreign policy issues that Europe might face in the 1920s.

Set a Purpose ⓛ

- **WITNESS HISTORY** Read the selection aloud or play the audio.

   AUDIO **Witness History Audio CD,** Brother, Can You Spare a Dime?

  Ask **How would you paraphrase the song?** (*The singer had been promised peace and glory and had helped build a railroad, but now he was poor and depended on charity for food.*)

- **Focus** Point out the Section Focus Question and write it on the board. Tell students to refer to this question as they read. (*Answer appears with Section 2 Assessment answers.*)

- **Preview** Have students preview the Section Objectives and the list of Terms, People, and Places.

- **Reading Skill** Have students use the *Reading Strategy: Identify Main Ideas* worksheet.

  All in One Teaching Resources, Unit 4, p. 50

- **Note Taking** Have students read this section using the Structured Read Aloud (TE, p. T20). As they read, have students fill in the table identifying postwar issues.

   Reading and Note Taking Study Guide, p. 171

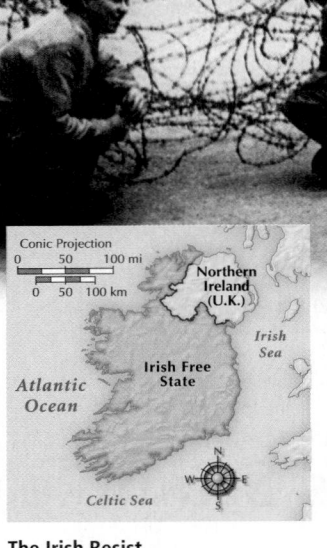

Politics in the Postwar World

L3

Instruct

- **Introduce: Vocabulary Builder**
  Have students read the Vocabulary Builder term and definition. Then have them look at the image on this page. Ask them to predict what group would be **suppressed** by the British. *(the Irish)*

- **Teach** Compare unrest in Britain, France, and the United States in the 1920s. Ask **What problems did France and Britain share?** *(disagreements between parties)* **What caused unrest in the United States?** *(Fear of radicals led to the Red Scare.)*

- **Quick Activity** Have students reread the first sentence after the heading France's Troubled Peace: "Like Britain, France emerged from World War I both a victor and a loser." Ask them to explain the meaning of this sentence.

Independent Practice

Viewpoints To help students better understand the ongoing debate between national security and civil liberties, have them read the selection *The Red Scare* and complete the worksheet.

All in One Teaching Resources, Unit 4, p. 52

Monitor Progress

As students fill in their tables, circulate to make sure they understand the issues that faced Britain, France, and the United States after the war. For a completed version of the table, see

Note Taking Transparencies, 180A

The Irish Resist

Members of the Irish Republican Army prepare to resist the British occupation of Dublin in 1921 by erecting a barbed wire barricade. The Irish Free State, established in 1922, was a compromise between the opposing sides, but peace was short-lived.

Vocabulary Builder

suppressed—(suh PRESD) *vt.* put down by force, subdued

Irish Independence at Last Britain still faced the "Irish question." In 1914, Parliament passed a home-rule bill that was shelved when the war began. On Easter 1916, a small group of militant Irish nationalists launched a revolt against British rule. Although the Easter Rising was quickly suppressed, it stirred wider support for the Irish cause. When Parliament again failed to grant home rule in 1919, members of the Irish Republican Army (IRA) began a guerrilla war against British forces and their supporters. In 1922, moderates in Ireland and Britain reached an agreement. Most of Ireland became the self-governing Irish Free State. The largely Protestant northern counties remained under British rule. However, the IRA and others fought for decades against the division.

France's Troubled Peace Like Britain, France emerged from World War I both a victor and a loser. Political divisions and financial scandals plagued the government of the Third Republic. Several parties—from conservatives to communists—competed for power. The parties differed on many issues, including how to get reparations payments from Germany. A series of quickly changing coalition governments ruled France.

"The Red Scare" and Isolationism in the United States In contrast, the United States emerged from World War I in good shape. A late entrant into the war, it had suffered relatively few casualties and little loss of property. However, the United States did experience some domestic unrest. Fear of radicals and the Bolshevik Revolution in Russia set off a "Red Scare" in 1919 and 1920. Police rounded up suspected foreign-born radicals, and a number were expelled from the United States.

The "Red Scare" fed growing demands to limit immigration. Millions of immigrants from southern and eastern Europe had poured into the United States between 1890 and 1914. Some native-born Americans sought to exclude these newcomers, whose cultures differed from those of earlier settlers from northern Europe. In response, Congress passed laws limiting immigration from Europe. Earlier laws had already excluded or limited Chinese and Japanese immigration.

✓ **Checkpoint** What political issues did each of the three democracies face after World War I?

Differentiated Instruction Solutions for All Learners

L1 Special Needs **L2 Less Proficient Readers**

To help students understand the contemporary definitions of socialism, liberalism, and conservatism, draw a line on the board to illustrate a spectrum. From left to right, place the words *Socialist, Liberal, Moderate* (in the middle), and *Conservative*. Explain that this spectrum measures each group's beliefs in the appropriate amount of government involvement in the

L2 English Language Learners

economy. To the right are Conservatives, those who want very little or no government involvement in economics. To the extreme left are Socialists, who oppose a free market economy and prefer the greatest amount of government involvement in economics. Explain how the labels *left* and *right* are used for these political positions.

Answer

✓ Great Britain faced political division and the demands of the Irish for self-government. France was plagued by political divisions and financial scandals. The United States had to deal with the fear of radicalism and growing demands for limits on immigration.

Postwar Foreign Policy

In addition to problems at home, the three democracies faced a difficult international situation. The peace settlements caused friction, especially in Germany and among some ethnic groups in Eastern Europe.

Arguing Allies France's chief concern after the war was securing its borders against Germany. The French remembered the German invasions of 1870 and 1914. To prevent a third invasion, France built massive fortifications called the **Maginot Line** (ma zhee NOH) along its border with Germany. However, the line would not be enough to stop another German invasion in 1940.

In its quest for security, France also strengthened its military and sought alliances with other countries, including the Soviet Union. It insisted on strict enforcement of the Versailles treaty and complete payment of reparations. France's goal was to keep the German economy weak.

Britain disagreed with this aim. Almost from the signing of the Treaty of Versailles, British leaders wanted to relax the treaty's harsh treatment of Germany. They feared that if Germany became too weak, the Soviet Union and France would become too powerful.

The Search for Peace Despite disagreements, many people worked for peace in the 1920s. Hopes soared in 1925 when representatives from seven European nations signed a series of treaties at Locarno, Switzerland. These treaties settled Germany's disputed borders with France, Belgium, Czechoslovakia, and Poland. The Locarno treaties became the symbol of a new era of peace.

The **Kellogg-Briand Pact,** which was sponsored by the United States in 1928, echoed the hopeful "spirit of Locarno." Almost every independent nation signed this agreement, promising to "renounce war as an instrument of national policy." In this optimistic spirit, the great powers pursued **disarmament,** the reduction of armed forces and weapons. The United States, Britain, France, Japan, and other nations signed treaties to reduce the size of their navies. However, they failed to agree on limiting the size of their armies.

From its headquarters in Geneva, Switzerland, the League of Nations encouraged cooperation and tried to get members to make a commitment to stop aggression. In 1926, after signing the Locarno agreements, Germany joined the League. Later, the Soviet Union was also admitted.

The League's Weakness The peace was fragile. Although the Kellogg-Briand Pact outlawed war, it provided no way of enforcing the ban. The League of Nations, too, was powerless to stop aggression. In 1931, the League vigorously condemned Japan's invasion of Manchuria, but did not take military action to stop it. Ambitious dictators in Europe noted the League's weakness and began to pursue aggressive foreign policies.

✓ **Checkpoint** How did the Treaty of Versailles affect the relationship between France and Britain?

Analyzing Political Cartoons

An End to War? The Kellogg-Briand Pact raised hopes for an end to war. But not everyone was so optimistic, as this 1929 American cartoon shows.

Ⓐ Kellogg-Briand Pact framed as a fire insurance policy

Ⓑ Adequate navy as a fire extinguisher

Ⓒ Uncle Sam looking at both

1. Do you think that the cartoonist feels that a fire insurance policy is enough to prevent a fire?
2. What point do you think the cartoonist is making about the Kellogg-Briand Pact?

HAVING AN INSURANCE POLICY DOESN'T MEAN YOU CAN DO WITHOUT FIRE PREVENTION

History Background

Maginot Line Most of the Maginot Line, a masterpiece of engineering, was built underground with connecting tunnels that stretched for miles. Main forts, placed strategically to protect river crossings and crossroads, were located about every three to five miles. These were self-contained underground structures more than 20 feet beneath the surface. Large enough to accommodate about 1,200 men, the forts contained barracks, kitchens, infirmaries, storage areas, telephone systems, electrical generation systems, and railways to move supplies. All that could be seen above ground were the barrels of the huge guns and gun placements. In the end, the line failed to prevent a German invasion. In 1940 German troops simply bypassed the Maginot Line and marched into France through the Ardennes forest.

Instruct

■ **Introduce: Vocabulary Builder** Have students read the Vocabulary Builder term and definition. Based on their previous reading, have them predict which postwar nation(s) would be the most *affluent* and which would face economic problems.

■ **Teach** On the board, draw a three-column chart with the title "Postwar Economics." Label the columns *Britain, France,* and *United States.* Ask students to supply the information about the economic condition of each nation after World War I, and write their answers on the board. *(Britain: lost overseas trade, was deep in debt, had outdated factories, and suffered severe unemployment, worker unrest and strikes. France: helped by German reparations and territories gained from Germany, but suffered economic swings. U.S.: became world's leading economic power, experienced boom years, produced many consumer goods, and contributed loans and investments to aid European recovery.)*

Independent Practice

Have students reread the paragraph under The United States Booms. In pairs, have them create a list of the pros and cons of economic interdependence. Using the Idea Wave strategy (TE, p. T22), ask groups to share their lists with the class.

Monitor Progress

To review the section so far, have students summarize the economic situation of each Western power.

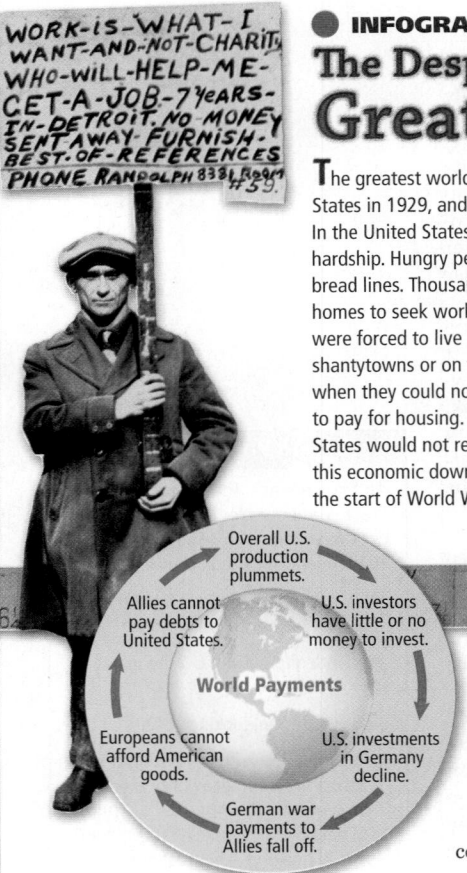

▲ A man tries to find work (above). The cycle of war payments helped spread the Great Depression to Europe.

Vocabulary Builder
affluent—(AF loo unt) *adj.* rich, wealthy

Unemployment led people to visit soup kitchens like the one below in Berlin. In New York and other cities, bread lines spanned multiple city blocks (below right), and many people became homeless (far right).

The greatest worldwide depression in history began in the United States in 1929, and soon spread to touch most parts of the world. In the United States alone, millions lost their jobs and endured great hardship. Hungry people visited soup kitchens or waited in long bread lines. Thousands of people left their homes to seek work in cities. Some were forced to live in makeshift shantytowns or on the streets when they could no longer afford to pay for housing. The United States would not recover from this economic downturn until the start of World War II.

World Payments cycle:
- Overall U.S. production plummets.
- U.S. investors have little or no money to invest.
- U.S. investments in Germany decline.
- German war payments to Allies fall off.
- Europeans cannot afford American goods.
- Allies cannot pay debts to United States.

Postwar Economics

The war affected economies all over the world, hurting some and helping others. Britain and France both owed huge war debts to the United States. Both relied on reparation payments from Germany to pay back their loans. Meanwhile, the crushing reparations and other conditions hurt Germany's economy.

Britain and France Recover Britain faced serious economic problems in the 1920s. It was deeply in debt, and its factories were out of date. Unemployment was severe. Wages remained low, leading to worker unrest and frequent strikes. In 1926, a **general strike**, or strike by workers in many different industries at the same time, lasted nine days and involved some three million workers.

In comparison, the French economy recovered fairly rapidly. Financial reparations and territories gained from Germany helped. Still, economic swings did occur, adding to an unstable political scene.

Despite these problems, Europe made a shaky recovery during the 1920s. Economies returned to peacetime manufacturing and trade. Veterans gradually found jobs, although unemployment never ceased to be a problem. Middle-class families enjoyed a rising standard of living.

The United States Booms In contrast, the United States emerged from the war as the world's leading economic power. In the affluent 1920s, middle-class Americans enjoyed the benefits of capitalism. American loans and investments backed the recovery in Europe. As long as the American economy prospered, the global economy remained stable.

✔ **Checkpoint** How did the war and its peace treaties affect the international economy?

Differentiated Instruction Solutions for All Learners

L4 Advanced Readers   L4 Gifted and Talented

Draw this "vicious cycle" graphic organizer on the board for students to analyze: People are not buying goods. → There is too much supply. → Companies lay off workers to save money. → Fewer people have extra money. → People are not buying goods. Ask students to work in groups and answer the following questions: (1) Where should a government intervene if it were to try to interrupt this cycle? For instance, should a government focus on buying up a company's excess supply? Should it give its citizens money to buy goods? (2) How did the United States, France, and Britain address this issue during the 1930s?

Answer

✔ The cycle of war debt and reparations made Europe's economic recovery shaky, while the United States boomed.

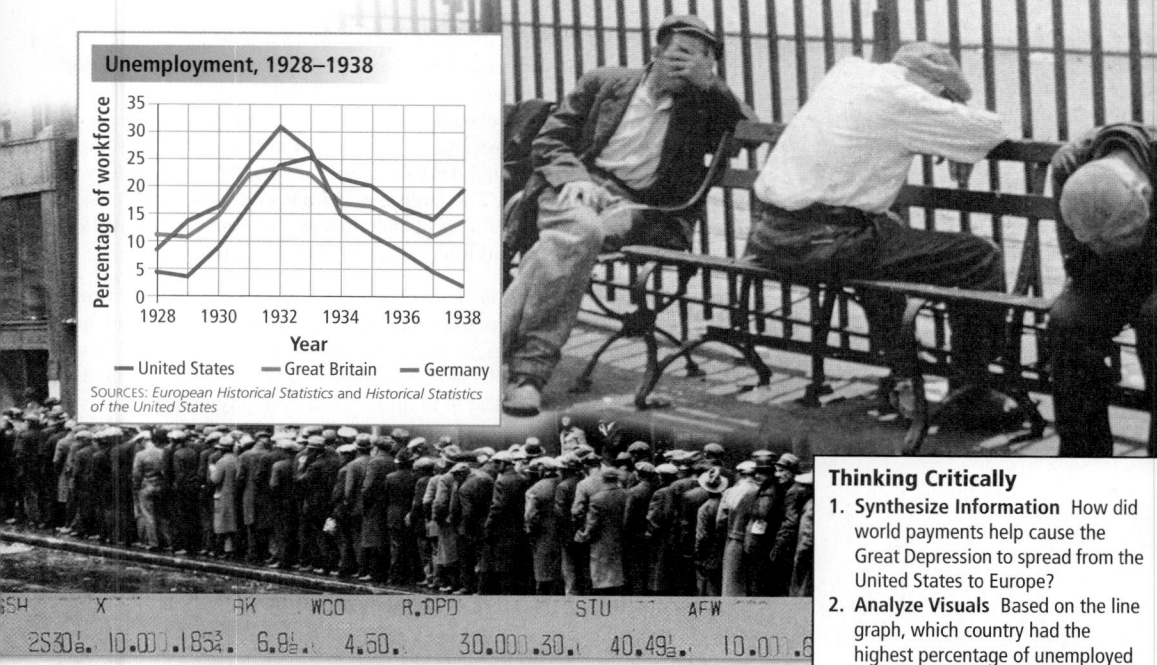

Unemployment, 1928–1938

Percentage of workforce

1928 1930 1932 1934 1936 1938

Year

— United States — Great Britain — Germany

SOURCES: *European Historical Statistics* and *Historical Statistics of the United States*

Thinking Critically

1. **Synthesize Information** How did world payments help cause the Great Depression to spread from the United States to Europe?
2. **Analyze Visuals** Based on the line graph, which country had the highest percentage of unemployed people in 1932? In 1938?

The Great Depression

This prosperity did not last. At the end of the 1920s, an economic crisis began in the United States and spread to the rest of the world, leaving almost no corner untouched.

Falling Demand and Overproduction The wealth created during the 1920s in the United States was not shared evenly. Farmers and unskilled workers were on the losing end. Though demand for raw materials and agricultural products had skyrocketed during the war, demand dwindled and prices fell after the war. Farmers, miners and other suppliers of raw materials suffered. Because they earned less, they bought less. At the same time, better technology allowed factories to make more products faster. This led to **overproduction,** a condition in which the production of goods exceeds the demand for them. As demand slowed, factories cut back on production and workers lost their jobs.

Crash and Collapse Meanwhile, a crisis in finance—the management of money matters, including the circulation of money, loans, investments, and banking—was brewing. Few saw the danger. Prices on the New York Stock Exchange were at an all-time high. Eager investors acquired stocks through risky methods. To slow the run on the stock market, the **Federal Reserve,** the central banking system of the United States, which regulates banks, raised interest rates in 1928 and again 1929. It didn't work. Instead, the higher interest rates made people nervous about borrowing money and investing, thereby hurting demand.

In the autumn of 1929, jitters about the economy caused many people to sell their stocks at once. Financial panic set in. Stock prices crashed, wiping out the fortunes of many investors. The **Great Depression,** a painful time of global economic collapse, had begun quietly in the

Note Taking

Reading Skill: Identify Main Ideas To help you to remember what you've read, use a chart like the one below to record the main ideas of the next two subsections.

The Great Depression		
Causes	Effects	Reactions
•	•	•
•	•	•
•	•	•

Link to Economics

An Interesting Theory During the Great Depression, one in four Americans was jobless. From 1928 to 1930, the unemployment rate in Great Britain doubled. Many people began to doubt that the economy could correct itself. During these uncertain times, British economist John Maynard Keynes put out a revolutionary economic theory. In his 1936 work, *The General Theory of Employment, Interest, and Money,* he showed how government actions might push the economy out of its depressed state. With this, he provided an economic basis for the creation of a government jobs program to reduce high unemployment. Many governments, looking to justify their decisions to increase spending, readily agreed with Keynes's conclusions. Keynes's work would influence economic policy for much of the twentieth century.

Instruct

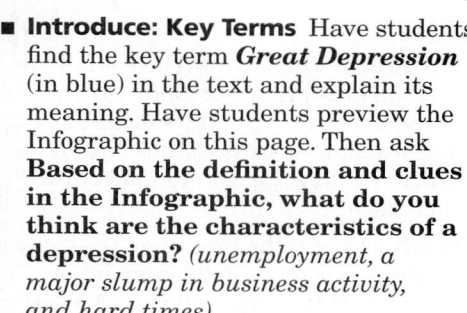

- **Introduce: Key Terms** Have students find the key term *Great Depression* (in blue) in the text and explain its meaning. Have students preview the Infographic on this page. Then ask **Based on the definition and clues in the Infographic, what do you think are the characteristics of a depression?** *(unemployment, a major slump in business activity, and hard times)*

- **Teach** Discuss how the economic crisis developed in the United States. Ask **What are three causes of the Great Depression?** *(less demand for raw materials, overproduction of manufactured goods, the crash of the stock market)* **How did the beginning of the depression in the United States affect world markets?** *(The U.S. economy was part of an international network of trade and finance; as its economy faltered, the economies that relied on it faltered, too.)*

- **Quick Activity** Show students *The Great Depression and American Farmers* from the **Witness History Discovery School™** video program. Ask them **Why were American farmers hit hard by the depression?** *(They had not shared equally in the wealth generated by the boom in the 1920s.)*

Independent Practice

Note Taking Have students begin to fill in the chart identifying the causes and effects of the Great Depression.

Reading and Note Taking Study Guide, p. 171

Monitor Progress

As students fill in their charts, circulate to make sure they understand the downward spiral set in motion by the American economic crisis in the 1920s. For a completed version of the chart, see

Note Taking Transparencies, 180B

Answers

Thinking Critically

1. Because European countries were dependent on American loans and investment, they were hit hard when the American economy failed.
2. Germany; the United States

The Democracies React to the Depression Ⓛ③

Instruct

- **Introduce: Key Terms** Have students find the key term ***New Deal*** (in blue) in the text and explain its meaning. Ask students to predict the ways in which the New Deal would affect the depression.

- **Teach** Discuss the programs the three Western powers each adopted in an effort to lift the Depression. Ask **Was the New Deal successful?** *(Partially; though it was not able to end the Great Depression, it did ease its effects on millions of Americans.)* Ask students to propose other ways nations might have dealt with the problem.

- **Quick Activity** Display **Color Transparency 169: WPA Mural.** Use the lesson suggested in the transparency book to guide a discussion on how the New Deal supported artists and provided work, as can be seen in this mural funded by the New Deal.

  🏛 **Color Transparencies,** 169

Independent Practice

Tell students that FDR's New Deal programs expanded the government's role in the daily lives of Americans. Many Americans disliked this trend. In groups, have students stage a debate on this question, with one side defending the New Deal and the other criticizing it.

Monitor Progress

- Check Reading and Note Taking Study Guide entries for student understanding.

- Point out the diagram on the next page. To review this section so far, ask students to explain how the New Deal illustrates John Maynard Keynes's ideas on economic recovery.

Answers

✓ The policies made people less likely to invest, which further hurt demand and eventually contributed to the closure of many banks and businesses.

Caption Drought and erosion allowed windstorms to pick up and carry topsoil away across the plains.

Watch *The Great Depression and American Farmers* on the **Witness History Discovery School**™ video program to learn more about the impact of the Great Depression on rural Americans.

Discovery SCHOOL

The Dust Bowl
In Dorothea Lange's famous 1936 photo *Migrant Mother, Nipomo, California,* a mother looks into the future with despair. She migrated to escape scenes like the one below, where huge dust storms buried farm equipment in Dallas, Texas. *How did geography help aggravate the depression in the United States?*

---

summer of 1929 with decreasing production. The October stock market crash aggravated the economic decline.

In 1931, the Federal Reserve again increased the interest rate, with an even more disastrous effect. As people bought and invested less, businesses closed and banks failed, throwing millions out of work. The cycle spiraled steadily downward. The jobless could not afford to buy goods, so more factories had to close, which in turn increased unemployment. People slept on park benches and lined up to eat in soup kitchens.

The Depression Spreads The economic problems quickly spread around the world. American banks stopped making loans abroad and demanded repayment of foreign loans. Without support from the United States, Germany suffered. It could not make its reparations payments. France and Britain were not able to make their loan payments.

Desperate governments tried to protect their economies from foreign competition. The United States imposed the highest tariffs in its history. The policy backfired when other nations retaliated by raising their tariffs. In 1932 and 1933, global world trade sank to its 1900 level. As you have read, the Great Depression spread misery from the industrial world to Latin America, Africa, and Asia.

✓ **Checkpoint** How did the Federal Reserve's policies affect the Great Depression?

The Democracies React to the Depression

The governments of Britain, France, and the United States, like others around the world, tried to find ways to lift the Depression. None of their methods provided a quick fix, but they did alleviate some of the suffering.

Britain and France Search for Solutions In response to the Depression, Britain set up a coalition government made up of leaders from all three of its major political parties. The government provided some unemployment benefits but failed to take decisive action to improve the economy. By 1931, one in every four workers was unemployed.

The Great Depression took longer to hurt France than some other countries. However, by the mid-1930s, France was feeling the pinch of decreased production and unemployment. In response, several leftist parties united behind the socialist leader Leon Blum. His Popular Front government tried to solve labor problems and passed some social legislation. But it could not satisfy more radical leftists. Strikes soon brought down Blum's government. Democracy survived, but the country lacked strong leadership able to respond to the clamor for change.

Differentiated Instruction Solutions for All Learners

Ⓛ④ **Gifted and Talented**

Historians still debate whether Roosevelt's New Deal helped the U.S. economy recover from the Great Depression, and whether the New Deal was worth the increase in government spending. To examine these questions, have student groups conduct a cost-benefit analysis of government spending during this period. Each group should determine whether U.S. government spending had benefits equal to or greater than the cost. First have groups gather data on government spending and gross domestic product from 1929 to 1940. Then ask them to consider: Did government spending raise gross domestic product during this period? What other factors might account for any increase in gross domestic product? Was the increase in government spending justified? For background and historical sources, go to **Web Code nbe-2802.**

Roosevelt Offers the United States a New Deal Meanwhile, in the United States, President Herbert Hoover firmly believed that the government should not intervene in private business matters. Even so, he did try a variety of limited measures to solve the crisis. Nothing seemed to work. In 1932, Americans elected a new President, **Franklin D. Roosevelt.** "FDR" argued that the government had to take an active role in combating the Great Depression. He introduced the **New Deal,** a massive package of economic and social programs.

Under the New Deal, the federal government became more directly involved in people's everyday lives than ever before. New laws regulated the stock market and protected bank deposits. Government programs created jobs and gave aid to farmers. A new Social Security system provided pensions for the elderly and other benefits.

As the New Deal programs were being put into effect, a natural disaster in 1934 hit several central states. After years of drought and over-farming, huge winds blew across the plains. The winds picked up and carried away the topsoil exposed by erosion, creating the Dust Bowl. The storms destroyed crops, land, and equipment. Thousands of farmers lost their land. Many migrated to the cities of the West Coast in search of work and a new life.

The New Deal failed to end the Great Depression, although it did ease the suffering for many. Still, some critics fiercely condemned FDR's expansion of the role of government. The debate about the size and role of the federal government continues to this day.

Loss of Faith in Democracy As the Depression wore on, many people lost faith in the ability of democratic governments to solve the problems of the modern world. Postwar disillusionment, soothed by the few good years of the 1920s, turned into despair in Europe. Misery and hopelessness created fertile ground for extremists who promised radical solutions.

✓ **Checkpoint** How did the government of the United States react to the Depression?

Economic Theories and the Great Depression

According to classical economists, free market economies naturally regulate their own highs and lows. The government should interfere as little as possible. The economist John Maynard Keynes argued that during a depression, the government should step in and spend more to bring the economy back up to its full productive capacity.

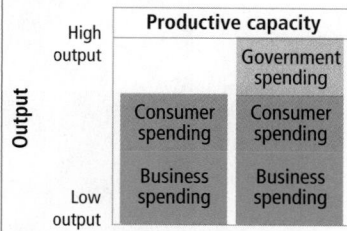

	Productive capacity	
High output		Government spending
	Consumer spending	Consumer spending
Low output	Business spending	Business spending

Output (vertical axis label)

Diagram Skills *What role did Keynes envision for government in the economy?*

Progress Monitoring Online
For: Self-quiz with vocabulary practice
Web Code nba-2821

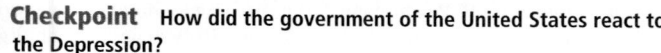

SECTION 2 Assessment

Terms, People, and Places

1. For each term, person, or place listed at the beginning of the section, write a sentence explaining its significance.

Note Taking

2. **Reading Skill: Identify Main Ideas** Use your completed table and chart to answer the Focus Question: What political and economic challenges did the leading democracies face in the 1920s and 1930s?

Comprehension and Critical Thinking

3. **Synthesize Information** How did Britain and France emerge from World War I as both victors and losers?

4. **Predict Consequences** What steps did the major powers take to protect the peace? Why did these moves have limited effects?

5. **Recognize Cause and Effect** Explain how each of the following contributed to the outbreak or spread of the Great Depression: (a) falling demand, (b) Federal Reserve Board, and (c) financial crisis.

6. **Identify Central Issues** How did the Great Depression affect political developments in the United States?

● **Writing About History**

Quick Write: Make a Venn Diagram A useful way to gather details for a compare-and-contrast essay is to use a Venn diagram. Place similarities between two ideas in the overlapping part of the circles; place differences in the parts that don't overlap. Create a Venn diagram for an essay on the following thesis statement: The United States was in better shape than Britain and France after World War I.

Assess Progress

- Have students complete the Section Assessment.
- Administer the Section Quiz.

All in One Teaching Resources, Unit 4, p. 45

- To further assess student understanding, use

   Progress Monitoring Transparencies, 119

Reteach

If students need more instruction, have them read the section summary.

 Reading and Note Taking Study Guide, p. 172

 Adapted Reading and Note Taking Study Guide, p. 172

Spanish Reading and Note Taking Study Guide, p. 172

Extend

Tell students that the Great Depression started in the United States and Europe, but its effects spread all over the world. Ask them to look into how the Depression affected one of the following regions: Southeast Asia, Latin America, Africa south of the Sahara.

Answers

Diagram Skills to provide additional spending during a depression

✓ At first, by providing only minimal assistance but under Roosevelt's New Deal, jobs were created, farmers received aid, Social Security was introduced, and the stock market regulated.

Section 2 Assessment

1. Sentences should reflect an understanding of each term, person, or place listed at the beginning of the section.
2. After the war, democracies struggled to rebuild war-ravaged land. In later years, they faced political and social unrest and the spread of an economic crisis.
3. Britain and France, with American help, defeated Germany. Both, however, faced serious political divisions and economic fragility.
4. They signed several treaties and relied on the League of Nations to halt aggression; the pacts and the League did not have the power to enforce their goals.
5. (a) Falling demand led to overproduction. (b) When the Federal Reserve Board raised interest rates, people bought less and invested less. (c) The financial crisis of 1929 aggravated the downward cycle.
6. Under the New Deal, the federal government became more directly involved in the lives of Americans than ever before.

● **Writing About History**

The Venn diagram should reflect facts from the section.

For additional assessment, have students access **Progress Monitoring Online** at **Web Code nba-2821.**

Objectives

As you teach this section, keep students focused on the following objectives to help them answer the Section Focus Question and master core content.

■ Describe how conditions in Italy favored the rise of Mussolini.

■ Summarize how Mussolini changed Italy.

■ Understand the values and goals of fascist ideology.

■ Compare and contrast fascism and communism.

Prepare to Read

Build Background Knowledge ⓛ3

Remind students about the problems that followed World War I. Have students speculate on how these problems could help pave the way for the rise of dictators, such as Mussolini and Hitler.

Set a Purpose ⓛ3

■ **WITNESS HISTORY** Read the selection aloud or play the audio.

🔊 AUDIO **Witness History Audio CD,** A New Leader: Mussolini

Ask **According to this description, how did people react to Mussolini?** *(joy, enthusiasm)* Ask students to predict the future of such a charismatic leader.

■ **Focus** Point out the Section Focus Question and write it on the board. Tell students to refer to this question as they read. *(Answer appears with Section 3 Assessment answers.)*

■ **Preview** Have students preview the Section Objectives and the list of Terms, People, and Places.

■ **Note Taking** Have students read this section using the Paragraph Shrinking strategy (TE, p. T20). As they read, have students fill in the flowchart identifying the main ideas of this section.

Reading and Note Taking Study Guide, p. 173

An image from a magazine of Benito Mussolini leading his nation to war ▶

◀ Italian national flag during Mussolini's rule

WITNESS HISTORY 🔊 AUDIO

A New Leader: Mussolini

In the early 1920s, a new leader named Benito Mussolini arose in Italy. The Italian people were inspired by Mussolini's promises to bring stability and glory to Italy.

❝ [Only joy at finding such a leader] can explain the enthusiasm [Mussolini] evoked at gathering after gathering, where his mere presence drew the people from all sides to greet him with frenzied acclamations. Even the men who at first came out of mere curiosity and with indifferent or even hostile feelings gradually felt themselves fired by his personal magnetic influence. . . . ❞
—Margherita G. Sarfatti, *The Life of Benito Mussolini* (tr. Frederic Whyte)

Focus Question How and why did fascism rise in Italy?

Fascism in Italy

Objectives
- Describe how conditions in Italy favored the rise of Mussolini.
- Summarize how Mussolini changed Italy.
- Understand the values and goals of fascist ideology.
- Compare and contrast fascism and communism.

Terms, People, and Places

Benito Mussolini	totalitarian state
Black Shirts	fascism
March on Rome	

Note Taking

Reading Skill: Identify Main Ideas Find the main points of the text under the first two headings and record them in a flowchart like the one below.

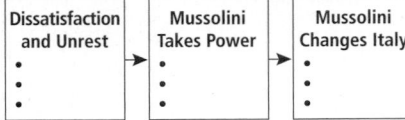

Dissatisfaction and Unrest	→	Mussolini Takes Power	→	Mussolini Changes Italy
•		•		•
•		•		•
•		•		•

"I hated politics and politicians," said Italo Balbo. Like many Italian veterans of World War I, he had come home to a land of economic chaos and political corruption. Italy's constitutional government, he felt, "had betrayed the hopes of soldiers, reducing Italy to a shameful peace." Disgusted and angry, Balbo rallied behind a fiercely nationalist leader, Benito Mussolini. Mussolini's rise to power in the 1920s served as a model for ambitious strongmen elsewhere in Europe.

Mussolini's Rise to Power

When Italy agreed to join the Allies in 1915, France and Britain secretly promised to give Italy certain Austro-Hungarian territories. When the Allies won, Italy received some of the promised territories, but others became part of the new Yugoslavia. The broken promises outraged Italian nationalists.

Disorders within Italy multiplied. Inspired in part by the revolution in Russia, peasants seized land, and workers went on strike or seized factories. Amid the chaos, returning veterans faced unemployment. Trade declined and taxes rose. The government, split into feuding factions, seemed powerless to end the crisis.

A Leader Emerges Into this turmoil stepped **Benito Mussolini.** The son of a socialist blacksmith and a teacher, Mussolini had been a socialist in his youth. During the war, however, he rejected socialism

---

Vocabulary Builder

Use the information below and the following resources to teach the high-use words from this section.
All in One Teaching Resources, Unit 4, p. 49; Teaching Resources, Skills Handbook, p. 3

High-Use Words	Definitions and Sample Sentences
proclaim, p. 538	*vt.* to announce officially After the election, the mayor **proclaimed** her victory to the awaiting constituents.
ideology, p. 539	*n.* a system of ideas that guides an individual, movement, or political program Anti-war protests were driven by a pacifist **ideology.**

for intense nationalism. In 1919, he organized veterans and other discontented Italians into the Fascist party. They took the name from the Latin *fasces,* a bundle of sticks wrapped around an ax. In ancient Rome, the fasces symbolized unity and authority.

Mussolini was a fiery and charismatic speaker. He promised to end corruption and replace turmoil with order. He also spoke of reviving Roman greatness, pledging to turn the Mediterranean into a "Roman lake" once again.

Mussolini Gains Control Mussolini organized his supporters into "combat squads." The squads wore black shirts to emulate an earlier nationalist revolt. These **Black Shirts,** or party militants, rejected the democratic process in favor of violent action. They broke up socialist rallies, smashed leftist presses, and attacked farmers' cooperatives. Fascist gangs used intimidation and terror to oust elected officials in northern Italy. Many Italians accepted these actions because they, too, had lost faith in constitutional government.

In 1922, the Fascists made a bid for power. At a rally in Naples, they announced their intention to go to Rome to demand that the government make changes. In the **March on Rome,** tens of thousands of Fascists swarmed towards the capital. Fearing civil war, King Victor Emmanuel III asked Mussolini to form a government as prime minister. Mussolini entered the city triumphantly on October 30, 1922. He thus obtained a nominally legal, constitutional appointment from the king to lead Italy.

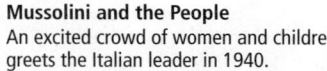 **Checkpoint** How did postwar disillusionment contribute to Mussolini's rise?

Mussolini's Rule

At first, Fascists held only a few cabinet posts in the new government. By 1925, though, Mussolini had assumed more power and taken the title Il Duce (eel DOO chay), "The Leader." He suppressed rival parties, muzzled the press, rigged elections, and replaced elected officials with Fascist supporters. In 1929, Mussolini received support from Pope Pius XI in return for recognizing Vatican City as an independent state, although the pope continued to disagree with some of Mussolini's goals. In theory, Italy remained a parliamentary monarchy. In fact, it was a dictatorship upheld by terror. Critics were thrown into prison, forced into exile, or murdered. Secret police and propaganda bolstered the regime.

State Control of the Economy To spur economic growth and end conflicts between owners and workers, Mussolini brought the economy under state control. However, he preserved capitalism. Under Mussolini's corporate state, representatives of business, labor, government, and the Fascist

Mussolini and the People
An excited crowd of women and children greets the Italian leader in 1940.

Mussolini's Rule ⑬

Instruct

- **Introduce** Ask students to preview the headings and visuals in this section. Then ask students to recall how Mussolini rose to power. Based on their previous reading and visuals in this section, have students predict what kind of leader Mussolini will be.

- **Teach** Discuss the ways in which Mussolini imposed a totalitarian regime in Italy. Then ask **Why is control of the media important in a totalitarian state?** *(It enables the state to censor information and spread propaganda.)* **What was Fascist policy regarding children?** *(Fascist youth groups taught strict discipline and children learned about the glories of ancient Rome.)*

- **Quick Activity** Display **Color Transparency 170: *The Triumph of Mussolini*, by W. Schulz.** Use the lesson suggested in the transparency book to guide a discussion on the political cartoon satirizing Mussolini.

  🏛 **Color Transparencies, 170**

Independent Practice

Link to Literature To help students understand how fascism was integrated into the school day, have them read the selection from *"The Sound of the Cicadas," by Arturo Vivante* and complete the worksheet.

All in One **Teaching Resources, Unit 4,** p. 53

Monitor Progress

To review this section, ask students to summarize how Mussolini ruled Italy.

Answer

✔ Fascist rule changed Italy's government to a dictatorship upheld by terror, brought the economy under state control, and altered domestic life.

Vocabulary Builder
proclaimed—(proh KLAYMD) *vt.*
announced officially

party controlled industry, agriculture, and trade. Mussolini's system favored the upper classes and industrial leaders. Although production increased, success came at the expense of workers. They were forbidden to strike, and their wages were kept low.

The Individual and the State In Mussolini's new system, loyalty to the state replaced conflicting individual goals. To Fascists, the glorious state was all-important, and the individual was unimportant except as a member of the state. Men, women, and children were bombarded with slogans glorifying the state and Mussolini. "Believe! Obey! Fight!" loudspeakers blared and posters <u>proclaimed</u>. Men were urged to be ruthless, selfless warriors fighting for the glory of Italy. Women were pushed out of paying jobs. Instead, Mussolini called on women to "win the battle of motherhood." Those who bore more than 14 children were given a medal by Il Duce himself.

Shaping the young was a major Fascist goal. Fascist youth groups toughened children and taught them to obey strict military discipline. Boys and girls learned about the glories of ancient Rome. Young Fascists marched in torchlight parades, singing patriotic hymns and chanting, "Mussolini is always right." By the 1930s, a generation of young soldiers stood ready to back Il Duce's drive to expand Italian power.

✔ **Checkpoint** How did the Fascist party transform Italy's government and economy?

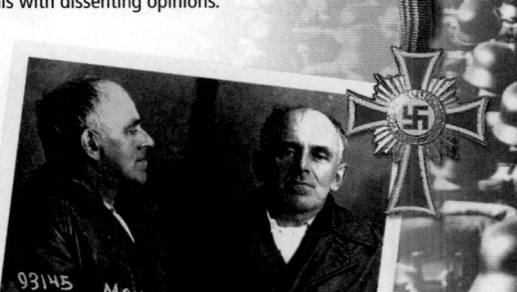

● **INFOGRAPHIC**

The Makings of a *Totalitarian* State

As part of a propaganda drive, German mothers received medals for bearing several children. ▶

In totalitarian Italy, Mussolini's government tried to dominate every part of the lives of Italians. Mussolini's totalitarian state became a model for others, although his rule in Italy was not as absolute as that of Stalin in the Soviet Union or Adolf Hitler in Germany. Still, all three governments shared the following basic features: (1) a single-party dictatorship with blind obedience to a single leader, (2) state control of the economy, (3) use of police spies and terror to enforce the will of the state, (4) government control of the media to indoctrinate and mobilize citizens through propaganda, (5) use of schools and youth organizations to spread ideology to children, and (6) strict censorship of artists and intellectuals with dissenting opinions.

◀ The dictators built cults of personality around themselves. At left, a statue of Stalin in a heroic pose, and (inset) Mussolini depicted working alongside Italian builders.

A photo from the Soviet secret police file on Osip Mandelstam, who was sent to the Gulag for writing poems unsympathetic to Stalin. ▶

History Background

All in the Family One of Mussolini's most prominent supporters and assistants was his son-in-law, Galeazzo Ciano. Ciano married Mussolini's favorite daughter, Edda, in 1930. He then served as a diplomat in China before leading a bomber squadron in the Ethiopian War. When Ciano returned to Italy, he climbed high in the Fascist hierarchy, eventually becoming foreign minister in 1936. Many thought that Ciano was Mussolini's natural successor. However, as Italy's position in World War II worsened, Ciano joined with others on the Fascist Grand Council to call on Mussolini to resign. Caught by Mussolini's government in northern Italy, he was tried for treason and executed by a shot in the back in January 1944—despite his close relationship with Mussolini. Ciano's secret diaries, published in 1946, provide a window into behind-the-scenes maneuvering in Fascist Italy.

The Nature of Fascism

Mussolini built the first **totalitarian state.** In this form of government, a one-party dictatorship attempts to regulate every aspect of the lives of its citizens. Other dictators, notably Stalin and Hitler, followed Mussolini's lead. Mussolini's rule was fascist in nature, as was Hitler's, but totalitarian governments rise under other kinds of ideology as well, such as communism in Stalin's Soviet Union.

What Is Fascism? Historians still debate the real nature of Mussolini's fascist <u>ideology</u>. Mussolini coined the term, but fascists had no unifying theory as Marxists did. Today, we generally use the term **fascism** to describe any centralized, authoritarian government that is not communist whose policies glorify the state over the individual and are destructive to basic human rights. In the 1920s and 1930s, though, fascism meant different things in different countries.

All forms of fascism, however, shared some basic features. They were rooted in extreme nationalism. Fascists glorified action, violence, discipline, and, above all, blind loyalty to the state. Fascists also pursued aggressive foreign expansion. Echoing the idea of "survival of the fittest," Fascist leaders glorified warfare as a noble struggle for survival.

Fascists were also antidemocratic. They rejected faith in reason and the concepts of equality and liberty. To them, democracy led to corruption and weakness and put individual or class interests above national goals. Instead, fascists emphasized emotion and the supremacy of the state.

Note Taking

Reading Skill: Identify Main Ideas Use a table like the one below to record information about fascism.

What Is Fascism?	
Values	
Characteristics	
Differences From Communism	
Similarities to Communism	

Vocabulary Builder

<u>ideology</u>—(ih dee AHL uh jee) *n.* a system of ideas that guides an individual, movement, or political program

▼ Huge numbers of people turned out for Nazi Party rallies.

▼ Mussolini spread his ideal of Italian military supremacy to Italian children through the Young Fascists.

Thinking Critically
1. **Draw Inferences** Why did totalitarian governments try to win the loyalty of their nations' young people?
2. **Recognize Ideologies** Why did leaders honor women for having many children?

The Nature of Fascism/ Looking Ahead **L3**

Instruct

- **Introduce: Vocabulary Builder** Have students read the Vocabulary Builder term and definition. Using the Idea Wave strategy (TE, p. T22), ask students to list examples of modern political ***ideologies.***

- **Teach** Ask students to identify the main characteristics of fascist governments, and write their responses on the board. Ask **How did fascist values differ from democratic principles and goals?** (*Unlike democracy, fascism rejected the concepts of equality and liberty, placed national goals above individual interests, and emphasized the role of emotion over reason.*)

- **Analyzing the Visuals** Refer students to the Infographic on this page. Ask students to describe how each image illustrates some of the features of totalitarian states. (*Sample: The photo from the the Soviet secret police file shows the use of terror to enforce the will of the state; the Young Fascists show the indoctrination of children.*)

Independent Practice

Note Taking Have students fill in the table recording information about fascism.

📄 **Reading and Note Taking Study Guide,** p. 173

Monitor Progress

As students fill in their tables, circulate to make sure they understand the values and characteristics of fascism. For a completed version of the table, see

📖 **Note Taking Transparencies,** 181B

Answers

Thinking Critically
1. to create a constant flow of people willing to serve the government
2. to reinforce traditional roles and to create as many new soldiers and loyal citizens as possible

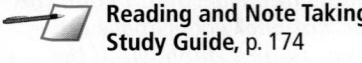

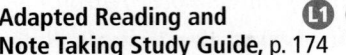
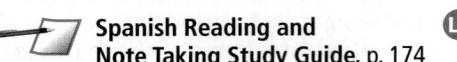

A Fascist Childhood
Children were required to use notebooks that featured fascist drawings and quotes from Mussolini.

The Appeal of Fascism Given its restrictions on individual freedom, why did fascism appeal to many Italians? First, it promised a strong, stable government and an end to the political feuding that had paralyzed democracy in Italy. Mussolini projected a sense of power and confidence at a time of disorder and despair. Mussolini's intense nationalism also revived national pride.

At first, newspapers in Britain, France, and North America applauded the discipline and order of Mussolini's government. "He got the trains running on time," admirers said. Only later, when Mussolini embarked on a course of foreign conquest, did Western democracies protest.

Fascism Compared to Communism Fascists were the sworn enemies of socialists and communists. While communists worked for international change, fascists pursued nationalist goals. Fascists supported a society with defined classes. They found allies among business leaders, wealthy landowners, and the lower middle class. Communists touted a classless society. They won support among both urban and agricultural workers.

Despite such differences, the products of these two ideologies had much in common. Both drew their power by inspiring a blind devotion to the state, or a charismatic leader as the embodiment of the state. Both used terror to guard their power. Both flourished during economic hard times by promoting extreme programs of social change. In both, a party elite claimed to rule in the name of the national interest.

✔ **Checkpoint** Describe the similarities between fascism and communism.

Looking Ahead

Three systems of government competed for influence in postwar Europe. Democracy endured in Britain and France but faced an uphill struggle in hard times. Communism emerged in Russia and won support elsewhere. In Italy, fascism offered a different option. As the Great Depression spread, other nations—most notably Germany—looked to fascist leaders.

SECTION 3 Assessment

Terms, People, and Places

1. For each term listed at the beginning of the section, write a sentence explaining its significance.

Note Taking

2. Reading Skill: Identify Main Ideas Use your completed flowchart and table to answer the section Focus Question: How and why did fascism rise in Italy?

Comprehension and Critical Thinking

3. Recognize Cause and Effect What problems did Italy face after World War I? How did these problems help Mussolini win power?

4. Summarize Describe one of Mussolini's economic or social goals, and explain the actions he took to achieve it.

5. Compare and Contrast List two similarities and two differences between fascism and communism.

6. Identify Point of View Mussolini said, "Machines and women are the two main causes of unemployment." (a) What do you think he meant? (b) How did Mussolini's policies reflect his attitude toward women?

● **Writing About History**
Quick Write: Write a Thesis Statement A compare-and-contrast thesis statement should introduce the items you are comparing and the point you intend to make. Which of the following thesis statements would work best for a compare-and-contrast essay?

- Fascism and communism are very different ideologies, but they both led to the imposition of totalitarian governments.
- Fascism led to a totalitarian government in Italy.

DICTATORSHIP

Why do people sometimes support dictators?

In This Chapter

Following World War I, European countries experienced economic and political turmoil. In Germany, money was worth so little that people used it as fuel for cooking (right). As society seemed to unravel, desperate people looked to strong leaders to create stability. In some countries, people were willing to give up individual freedoms to gain security and order.

Throughout History

48 B.C.– 44 B.C. Julius Caesar forces the Roman Senate to grant him absolute power and initiates reforms.

1547–1580 A.D. Ivan the Terrible, the Russian tsar, organizes agents of terror to enforce his will.

1920s Mussolini promises to restore order to Italy and revive its Roman greatness.

1930s Stalin uses terror and censorship to strengthen his power over the Soviet people.

1934 Hitler's extreme nationalism, racism, and economic goals appeal to many German people.

1950s–1970s Military leaders in Brazil, Argentina, and Chile use force to seize and maintain power.

Continuing Today

To maintain power, dictators like Kim Jong-Il of North Korea (below) create a cult of personality. They present themselves as heroic figures and people are encouraged to view them as an objects of worship.

21st Century Skills

TRANSFER Activities

1 **Analyze** Throughout history, how have dictators maintained control?

2. **Evaluate** What are the dangers of giving up rights in order to gain stability and order?

3. **Transfer** Complete a Web quest in which you speak out against a modern dictator; record your thoughts in the Concept Connector Journal; and learn to make a video. Web Code nbh-2808

History Background

Dictator . . . Then and Now In the ancient Roman republic, the term *dictator* held a very different meaning than it does today. The word comes from the Latin root *dicere* meaning "to speak." In ancient Rome, dictators were given power for the express purpose of helping the state through times of crisis. They usually resigned after the crisis was resolved, with a term limit of only six months. They were chosen by democratic means, after being recommended by the Senate and confirmed by an assembly of the people. Even then, after 300 B.C., their powers were limited—the people could appeal their decisions.

When Julius Caesar became dictator in 47 B.C., the powers he assumed went far beyond those outlined traditionally for the role. When he made himself dictator for life in 44 B.C., he changed the meaning of the word *dictator* forever.

Dictatorship

Objectives

■ Understand the conditions that lead people to support dictators.

■ Describe the methods that dictators use to maintain power.

■ Complete a Web Quest on dictatorship.

Build Background Knowledge (L3)

To check students' understanding of dictatorship, ask them to define the term ***totalitarian state***. *(a form of government in which a one-party dictatorship attempts to regulate every aspect of the lives of its citizens)*. Ask students to identify three ways life in the United States might be different if we lived in a dictatorship.

Instruct (L3)

■ Direct students' attention to the Essential Question: **Why do people sometimes support dictators?** Have students provide specific examples from the text that describe conditions that led people to support dictators. How might a person explain his or her support for a leader who later turned out to be a dictator?

■ Ask students to look at Continuing Today and the corresponding image. Have students describe ways that dictators can create a cult of personality. Then ask students to explain how the media influences our perceptions of people and events.

■ Assign the Web Quest activity.

Concept Connector

Concept Connector Have students fill in the Web Quest reflection question on dictatorship in their Concept Connector Journal.

 Reading and Note Taking Study Guide, p. 256

Monitor Progress (L3)

Circulate to make sure that students are filling in their Concept Connector Journal. Ensure they understand how dictators gain power.

Transfer Activities

1. Dictators have used military power, new laws, fear, censorship, propaganda, and security forces.

2. If a society gives up its rights to gain order, those rights could be lost forever.

3. Students' work should be evaluated against the rubric at Web Code nbh-2808.

Objectives

As you teach this section, keep students focused on the following objectives to help them answer the Section Focus Question and master core content.

■ Describe the effects of Stalin's five-year plans.

■ Explain how Stalin tried to control how people thought in the Soviet Union.

■ List communist changes to Soviet society.

■ Outline Soviet foreign policy under Stalin.

Prepare to Read

Build Background Knowledge ⓛ③

Remind students that Lenin founded the Soviet state, and after he died in 1924, Stalin took power. Ask them to recall what else they already know about Stalin.

Set a Purpose ⓛ③

■ **WITNESS HISTORY** Read the selection aloud or play the audio.

◀》 AUDIO **Witness History Audio CD,** The Heart of the Party

Ask **Based on clues in the image and selection from _Pravda_, what do you think the official view of Stalin was?** _(He was to be viewed as the ideal leader.)_ Ask students to speculate what Soviets may have secretly thought of him.

■ **Focus** Point out the Section Focus Question and write it on the board. Tell students to refer to this question as they read. _(Answer appears with Section 4 Assessment answers.)_

■ **Preview** Have students preview the Section Objectives and the list of Terms, People, and Places.

■ **Note Taking** Have students read this section using the Paragraph Shrinking strategy (TE, p. T20). As they read, have students fill in the chart with the main ideas about Stalin's rule in the Soviet Union.

/ **Reading and Note Taking Study Guide,** p. 175

In this propaganda image, children surround a gentle Stalin.

WITNESS HISTORY ◀》 AUDIO

The Heart of the Party

On the occasion of Stalin's sixtieth birthday, the Communist party newspaper, _Pravda_, or "Truth," printed this praise of Stalin:

❝ There is no similar name on the planet like the name of Stalin. It shines like a bright torch of freedom, it flies like a battle standard for millions of laborers around the world. . . . Stalin is today's Lenin! Stalin is the brain and heart of the party! Stalin is the banner of millions of people in their fight for a better life.❞

Far from helping people fight for a better life, Stalin's ruthless policies brought suffering and death to millions of Soviets.

Focus Question How did Stalin transform the Soviet Union into a totalitarian state?

The Soviet Union Under Stalin

Objectives

• Describe the effects of Stalin's five-year plans.
• Explain how Stalin tried to control how people thought in the Soviet Union.
• List communist changes to Soviet society.
• Outline Soviet foreign policy under Stalin.

Terms, People, and Places

command economy   russification
collectives   atheism
kulaks   Comintern
Gulag
socialist realism

Note Taking

Reading Strategy: Identify Main Ideas Summarize the main points of the section in a chart like the one below.

The Soviet Union Under Stalin		
Five-Year Plans	Methods of Control	Daily Life

In January 1924, tens of thousands of people lined up in Moscow's historic Red Square. They had come to view the body of Lenin, who had died a few days earlier. Lenin's widow, Nadezhda Krupskaya, wanted to bury him simply next to his mother. Communist party officials—including Joseph Stalin—wanted to preserve Lenin's body and put it on permanent display. In the end, Lenin's body was displayed in Red Square for more than 65 years. By preserving Lenin's body, Stalin wanted to show that he would carry on the goals of the revolution. However, in the years that followed, he used ruthless measures to control the Soviet Union and its people.

A Totalitarian State

Karl Marx had predicted that under communism the state would eventually wither away. Under Stalin, the opposite occurred. He turned the Soviet Union into a totalitarian state controlled by a powerful and complex bureaucracy.

Stalin's Five-Year Plans Once in power, Stalin imposed government control over the Soviet Union's economy. In the past, said Stalin, Russia had suffered because of its economic backwardness. In 1928, he proposed the first of several "five-year plans" aimed at building heavy industry, improving transportation, and increasing farm output. He brought all economic activity under government control. The government owned all businesses and distributed all

Vocabulary Builder

Use the information below and the following resources to teach the high-use words from this section.
All in One **Teaching Resources, Unit 4,** p. 49; **Teaching Resources, Skills Handbook,** p. 3

High-Use Words	Definitions and Sample Sentences
conform, p. 546	_vi._ to obey a set of standards Elena hated plaid skirts but had to **conform** to the school's mandatory dress code.
access, p. 548	_n._ the ability to get and use Because he worked in the principal's office, he had **access** to all the students' records.

resources. The Soviet Union developed a **command economy,** in which government officials made all basic economic decisions. By contrast, in a capitalist system, the free market determine most economic decisions. Privately owned businesses compete to win the consumer's choice. This competition regulates the price and quality of goods.

Mixed Results in Industry Stalin's five-year plans set high production goals, especially for heavy industry and transportation. The government pushed workers and managers to meet these goals by giving bonuses to those who succeeded—and by punishing those who did not. Between 1928 and 1939, large factories, hydroelectric power stations, and huge industrial complexes rose across the Soviet Union. Oil, coal, and steel production grew. Mining expanded, and new railroads were built.

Despite the impressive progress in some areas, Soviet workers had little to show for their efforts. Some former peasants did become skilled factory workers or managers. Overall, though, the standard of living remained low. Central planning was often inefficient, causing shortages in some areas and surpluses in others. Many managers, concerned only with meeting production quotas, turned out large quantities of low-quality goods. Consumer products such as clothing, cars, and refrigerators were scarce. Wages were low and workers were forbidden to strike. The party restricted workers' movements.

Forced Collectivization in Agriculture Stalin also brought agriculture under government control, but at a horrendous cost. The government wanted farmers to produce more grain to feed workers in the cities. It also hoped to sell grain abroad to earn money.

As you have read, under Lenin's New Economic Plan (NEP), peasants had held on to small plots of land. Many had prospered. Stalin saw that system as being inefficient and a threat to state power. Stalin wanted all peasants to farm on either state-owned farms or **collectives,** large farms owned and operated by peasants as a group. On collectives, the government would provide tractors, fertilizers, and better seed, and peasants would learn modern farm methods. Peasants would be permitted to keep their houses and personal belongings, but all farm animals and implements were to be turned over to the collective. The state set all prices and controlled access to farm supplies.

Some peasants did not want to give up their land and sell their crops at the state's low prices. They resisted collectivization by killing farm animals, destroying tools, and burning crops. Stalin was furious. He believed that **kulaks,** or wealthy farmers, were behind the resistance. He responded with brutal force. In 1929, Stalin declared his intention to "liquidate the kulaks as a class." To this end, the government confiscated kulaks' land and sent them to labor camps. Thousands were killed or died from overwork.

Even after the "de-kulakization," angry peasants resisted by growing just enough to feed themselves. In response, the government seized all of their grain to meet industrial goals, purposely leaving the peasants to starve. In 1932, this ruthless policy, combined with poor harvests, led to a terrible

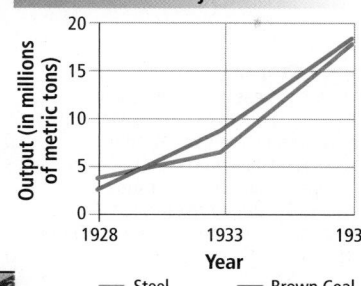

Effects of the Five-Year Plans on Soviet Industry

Output (in millions of metric tons) vs Year

— Steel   — Brown Coal

SOURCE: B.R. Mitchell, *European Historical Statistics, 1750–1970*

"Industrialism is the Path to Socialism" As this 1928 poster proclaims, Stalin's government saw rapid industrialization as the key to the success of the Soviet Union. *Using the line graph, describe the effect of the Five-Year Plans on steel and brown coal output.*

Instruct

- **Introduce: Key Terms** Have students find the key term *command economy* (in blue) in the text. Point out that Stalin's government took complete control over of the Soviet Union's economy; in other words, it was the government who "commanded" the economy. Then ask students to explain the difference between a command economy and a capitalist economy.

- **Teach** Ask students to list the goals of Stalin's five-year plans. Then ask **Why did some peasants resist the collectivization plan?** *(They did not want to give up their farms and sell crops at the low prices set by the state.)* **How did Stalin respond to this resistance?** *(He sent kulaks, or well-to-do farmers, to labor camps and seized all grain, leaving people to starve.)*

- **Quick Activity** Direct students to the graph on the next page, Soviet Agriculture Output, 1928 and 1932, and have them answer the caption question. Then ask **What were the effects of the collectivization plan on Soviet life?** *(Though it did not increase farm output, it increased Stalin's control of the peasantry. It also led to the Terror Famine.)*

Connect to Our World

Connections to Today For many years, Ukrainian interest groups have worked for international recognition of the Terror Famine. This was a deliberate Soviet policy meant to destroy the will of the Ukrainian people. Their quest is in some ways similar to that of Armenian groups who hope to gain recognition of the genocide of Armenians that took place in the Ottoman empire during World War I.

A big step for Ukrainians occured in 1984 when the U.S. Congress set up the Commission on the Ukraine Famine to compile the information available on the famine. The Committee concluded: "There is no doubt that large numbers of inhabitants of the Ukrainian SSR and the North Caucasus Territory starved to death in a man-made famine in 1932–1933, caused by the seizure of the 1932 crop by Soviet authorities."

Answer

Caption The output for each more than quadrupled.

Independent Practice

Have students write two statements, one that argues for collectivization and one that argues against it. Using the Think-Write-Pair-Share strategy (TE, p. T23), have students share and discuss their statements.

Monitor Progress

As students complete their charts, circulate to make sure they list collectivization as one of the main points of the five-year plans. For a completed version of the chart, see

📖 **Note Taking Transparencies,** 182

famine. Later called the Terror Famine, it caused between five and eight million people to die of starvation in the Ukraine alone.

Although collectivization increased Stalin's control of the peasantry, it did not improve farm output. During the 1930s, grain production inched upward, but meat, vegetables, and fruits remained in short supply. Feeding the population would remain a major problem in the Soviet Union.

✔ **Checkpoint** How did Stalin take control of the Soviet Union's economic life?

Stalin's Terror Tactics

In addition to tactics like the Terror Famine, Stalin's Communist party used secret police, torture, and violent purges to ensure obedience. Stalin tightened his grasp on every aspect of Soviet life, even stamping out any signs of dissent within the Communist elites.

Terror as a Weapon Stalin ruthlessly used terror as a weapon against his own people. He perpetrated crimes against humanity and systematically violated his people's individual rights. Police spies did not hesitate to open private letters or plant listening devices. Nothing appeared in print without official approval. There was no free press, and no safe method of voicing protest. Grumblers or critics were rounded up and sent to the **Gulag,** a system of brutal labor camps, where many died.

The Great Purge Even though Stalin's power was absolute, he still feared that rival party leaders were plotting against him. In 1934, he launched the Great Purge. During this reign of terror, Stalin and his secret police cracked down especially on Old Bolsheviks, or party activists from the early days of the revolution. His net soon widened to target army heroes, industrial managers, writers, and ordinary citizens. They were charged with a wide range of crimes, from counterrevolutionary plots to failure to meet production quotas.

Between 1936 and 1938, Stalin staged a series of spectacular public "show trials" in Moscow. Former Communist leaders confessed to all kinds of crimes after officials tortured them or threatened their families or friends. Many of the purged party members were never tried but were sent straight to the Gulag. Secret police files reveal that at least four million people were purged during the Stalin years. Some historians estimate the toll to be much greater.

Results of the Purge The purges increased Stalin's power. All Soviet citizens were now well aware of the consequences of disloyalty. However, Stalin's government also paid a price. Among the purged were experts in industry, economics, and engineering, and many of the Soviet Union's most talented

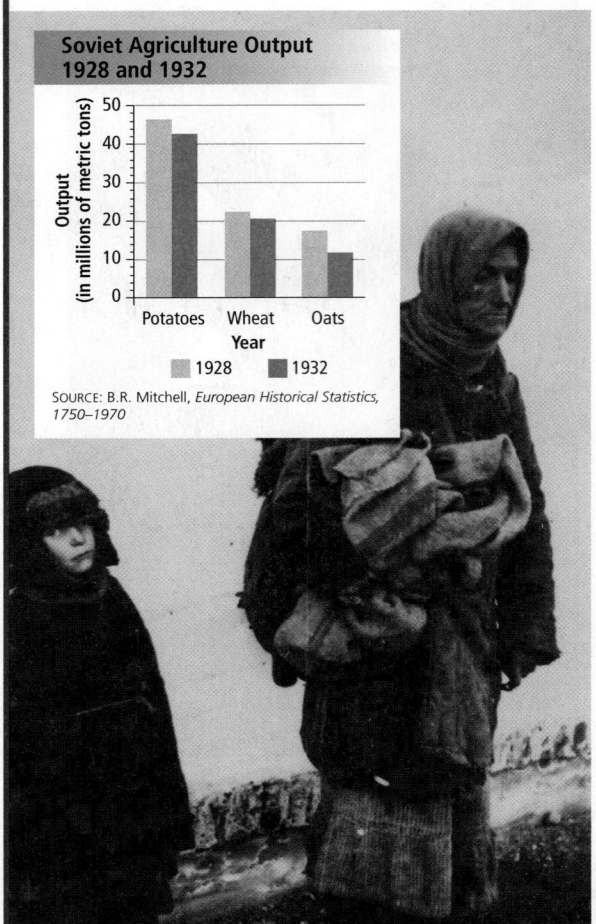

Food as a Weapon
In 1932, when peasants failed to meet unrealistic crop quotas, Stalin retaliated by seizing all of their grain to sell on the market, leaving millions to starve. Below, a woman and her son search for food during the famine. *Describe the effect of Stalin's ruthless policies on the production of oats, wheat, and potatoes.*

Soviet Agriculture Output 1928 and 1932

Output (in millions of metric tons)

■ 1928   ■ 1932

SOURCE: B.R. Mitchell, *European Historical Statistics, 1750–1970*

Differentiated Instruction   Solutions for All Learners

L4 Gifted and Talented   **L4 Advanced Readers**

Tell students that the Gulag looms large in the cultural life of the former Soviet Union. It is the subject of Nobel Prize winner Aleksandr Solzhenitsyn's first book, *One Day in the Life of Ivan Denisovitch*, in which Solzhenitsyn draws from his own Gulag experience to chronicle a typical day in a prison camp. Ask students to conduct further research to learn more about conditions in a

Gulag. Then ask them to write a fictional letter from a Gulag prisoner to a family member, describing what life is like as a prisoner. The letter should include details about daily life in the camp, the prisoner's views on the Communist government, and the prisoner's hopes for the future after getting out of prison.

Answers

✔ Stalin's government took control of all businesses, distributed all resources, and made all basic economic decisions.

Caption Output of potatoes, wheat, and oats all fell between 1928 and 1932.

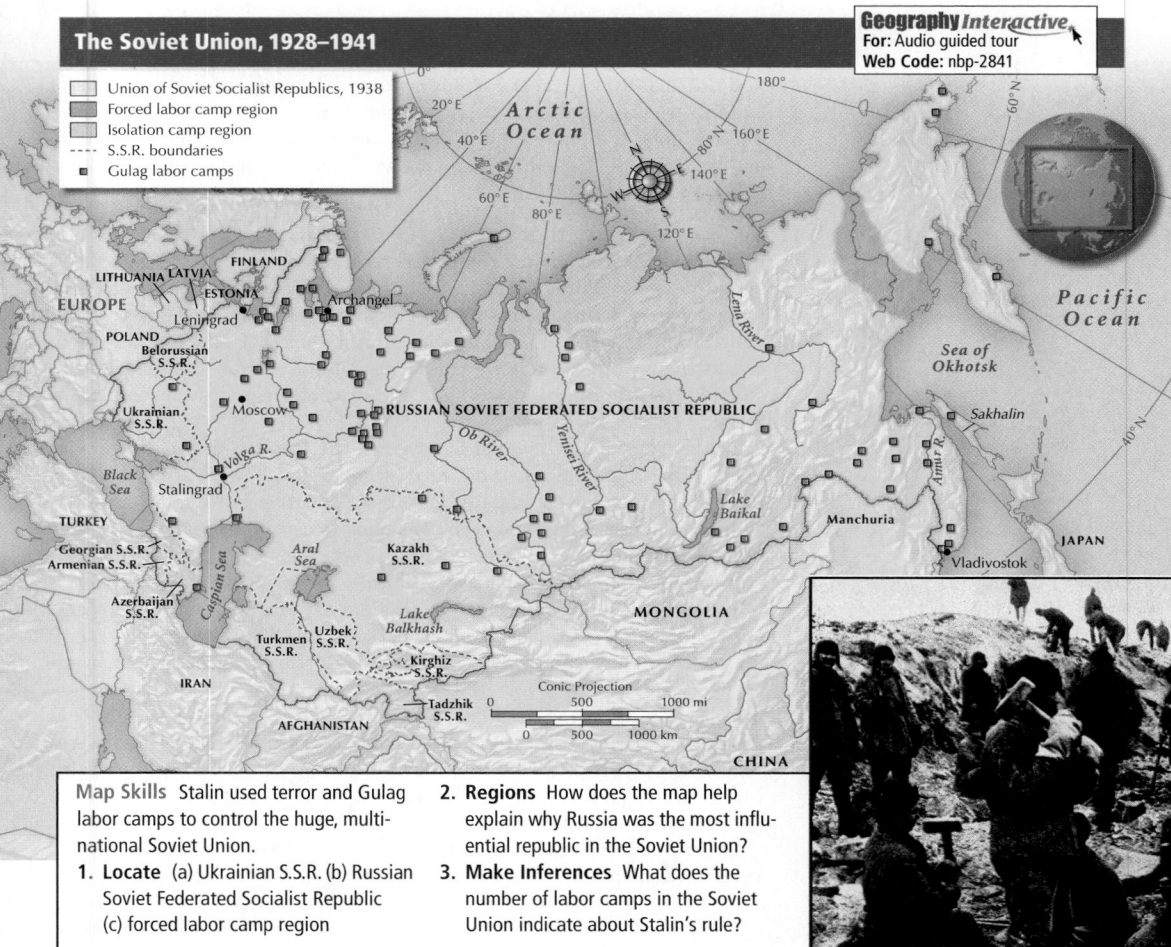

The Soviet Union, 1928–1941

Geography *Interactive*
For: Audio guided tour
Web Code: nbp-2841

Legend:
- Union of Soviet Socialist Republics, 1938
- Forced labor camp region
- Isolation camp region
- ---- S.S.R. boundaries
- ▪ Gulag labor camps

Map Skills Stalin used terror and Gulag labor camps to control the huge, multinational Soviet Union.

1. **Locate** (a) Ukrainian S.S.R. (b) Russian Soviet Federated Socialist Republic (c) forced labor camp region
2. **Regions** How does the map help explain why Russia was the most influential republic in the Soviet Union?
3. **Make Inferences** What does the number of labor camps in the Soviet Union indicate about Stalin's rule?

A Gulag labor camp in 1934

writers and thinkers. The victims included most of the nation's military leaders and about half of its military officers, a loss that would weigh heavily on Stalin in 1941, when Germany invaded the Soviet Union.

✔ Checkpoint In what ways did Stalin's terror tactics harm the Soviet Union?

Communist Attempts to Control Thought

At the same time that he was purging any elements of resistance in Soviet society, Stalin also sought to control the hearts and minds of Soviet citizens. He tried to do this by tirelessly distributing propaganda, censoring opposing ideas, imposing Russian culture on minorities, and replacing religion with communist ideology.

Propaganda Stalin tried to boost morale and faith in the communist system by making himself a godlike figure. He used propaganda as a tool to build up a "cult of personality" around himself. Using modern technology, the party bombarded the public with relentless propaganda. Radios

---

Differentiated Instruction Solutions for All Learners

L1 Special Needs **L2 Less Proficient Readers**

Ask students to refer to the Infographic on totalitarianism in the previous section. Have them create a table, listing the six basic features of a totalitarian state in one column, and how those basic features played out in Stalin's Soviet Union in a second column. For a review at the end of the chapter, consider asking students to add columns for Italy and Germany.

L2 English Language Learners

Use the following resources to help students acquire basic skills.

Adapted Reading and Note Taking Study Guide
- Adapted Note Taking Study Guide, p. 175
- Adapted Section Summary, p. 176

Stalin's Terror Tactics **L3**

Instruct

■ **Introduce** Display **Color Transparency 170: *Gulag Prisoners*, by Nikolai Getman** to show a painting from the Gulag. Tell students that Stalin used the threat of these labor camps to control life in the Soviet Union. Ask students to predict other methods that Stalin used.

🎨 **Color Transparencies,** 170

■ **Teach** Ask **What was the Great Purge?** *(the arrest and execution of hundreds of thousands of people whom Stalin suspected of disloyalty)* **How did the purges increase Stalin's power?** *(They made all Soviet citizens aware of the consequences of disagreement or disloyalty, and they replaced old revolutionaries with young party members loyal to Stalin.)* **How do you think this affected Soviets' feelings toward their government?** *(Sample: It probably made them feel either more loyal or become more secretive.)*

■ **Quick Activity** Have students access **Web Code nbp-2841** to take the **Geography Interactive Audio Guided Tour** and then answer the map skills questions in the text.

Independent Practice

Link to Literature To help students better understand Stalinist Russia, have them read the selection from Arthur Koestler's *Darkness at Noon* and complete the worksheet.

All in One **Teaching Resources, Unit 4,** p. 54

Monitor Progress

■ Check answers to map skills questions.

■ Refer students to the image of the Gulag on this page. To review this section, ask students to list Stalin's terror tactics.

Answers

Map Skills
1. Review locations with students.
2. Russia was the largest republic and the capital, Moscow, was located there.
3. that Stalin needed the threat of labor camps to guarantee his dominance

✔ The country lost many of its intellectual and military leaders.

Communist Attempts to Control Thought

Instruct

- **Introduce: Vocabulary Builder** Have students read the Vocabulary Builder term and definition. Ask them if they have ever felt pressure to **conform** to a set of rules or customs from their parents or peers. Ask what it would be like if they felt this pressure from the state. Explain that those were the daily conditions in Stalinist Russia.

- **Teach** Ask **How did Stalin control cultural life in the Soviet Union?** *(by distributing propaganda, censoring ideas, promoting Russification, and destroying religion)* **How do you think people reacted to the policy of Russification?** *(Sample: They probably resented it, because previously, they had been encouraged to celebrate their autonomy.)*

- **Quick Activity** Read the Primary Source selection aloud or play the accompanying audio. Ask **How long has Akhmatova's son been in prison?** *(almost a year and a half)* **What feelings does Akhmatova describe in this poem?** *(fear, desperation)* **Based on clues in this feature, how effective do you think censorship was in controlling writers?** *(Students may suggest that it was ineffective, as writers continued to work in secrecy, or they may suggest that it was effective, because writers could not publish or share their ideas with others within the Soviet Union.)*

🔊 AUDIO **Witness History Audio CD,** Anna Akhmatova

Independent Practice

To help students recognize propaganda, have them write two propaganda pieces for two different newspapers. One should be a statement in support of Stalin's policies and should be similar to the quote from *Pravda* at the beginning of the section. The other should be a statement that an illegal anti-Stalinist newspaper might have printed. Both should incorporate facts about Stalin's policies in some way.

Monitor Progress

As students write their statements, circulate to make sure they understand how the two newspapers would have different views of Stalin's policies.

Vocabulary Builder

conform—(kun FAWRM) *vi.* to obey a set of standards

Soviet Art
In this Socialist Realist sculpture, a factory worker and a collective farmer raise the hammer and sickle together.

Anna Akhmatova (ahk MAH tuh vuh), one of Russia's greatest poets, could not publish her works because she had violated state guidelines. Still, she wrote secretly. In this passage from "Requiem," she describes the ordeal of trying to visit her 20-year-old son, imprisoned during the Stalinist terrors:

Primary Source

66 For seventeen long months my pleas,
My cries have called you home.
I've begged the hangman on my knees,
My son, my dread, my own.
My mind's mixed up for good, and I'm
No longer even clear
Who's man, who's beast, nor how much time
Before the end draws near. 99
—Anna Akhmatova, "Requiem"
(tr. Robin Kemball) 🔊 AUDIO

---

and loudspeakers blared into factories and villages. In movies, theaters, and schools, citizens heard about communist successes and the evils of capitalism. Billboards and posters urged workers to meet or exceed production quotas. Headlines in the Communist party newspaper *Pravda,* or "Truth," linked enemies at home to foreign agents seeking to overthrow the Communist regime.

Censorship and the Arts At first, the Bolshevik Revolution had meant greater freedom for Soviet artists and writers. Under Stalin, however, the heavy hand of state control also gripped the arts. The government controlled what books were published, what music was heard, and which works of art were displayed. Stalin required artists and writers to create their works in a style called **socialist realism.** Its goal was to show Soviet life in a positive light and promote hope in the communist future.

In theory, socialist realism followed in the footstep of Russian greats Tolstoy and Chekhov; in practice it was rarely allowed to be realistic. Socialist realist novels usually featured a positive hero, often an engineer or scientist, battling against the odds to accomplish a goal. Popular themes for socialist-realist visual artists were peasants, workers, heroes of the revolution, and—of course—Stalin.

If they refused to <u>conform</u> to government expectations, writers, artists, and composers faced government persecution. The Jewish poet Osip Mandelstam, for example, was imprisoned, tortured, and exiled for composing a satirical verse that was critical of Stalin. Out of fear for his wife's safety, Mandelstam finally submitted to threats and wrote an "Ode to Stalin." Boris Pasternak, who would later win fame for his novel *Doctor Zhivago,* was afraid to publish anything at all during the Stalin years. Rather than write in the favored style of socialist realism, he translated foreign literary works instead.

Despite restrictions, some Soviet writers produced magnificent works. Yevgeny Zamyatin's classic anti-Utopian novel *We* became well known outside of the Soviet Union, but was not published in his home country until 1989. The novel depicts a nightmare future in which people go by numbers, not names, and the "One State" controls people's thoughts. *And Quiet Flows the Don,* by Mikhail Sholokhov, passed the censor. The novel tells the story of a man who spends years fighting in World War I, the Russian Revolution, and the civil war. Sholokhov later won the Nobel Prize for literature.

Russification Yet another way Stalin controlled the cultural life of the Soviet Union was by promoting a policy of **russification,** or making a nationality's culture more Russian. By 1936, the U.S.S.R. was made up of 11 Soviet Socialist Republics. The Russian Soviet Federated Socialist Republic consisted of the old Russian heartland and was the largest and dominant republic. The other

---

Link to Humanities

Sergei Eisenstein and Early Soviet Cinema
In the Soviet Union, filmmakers used motion pictures to express revolutionary ideals. "Of all the arts, for us the cinema is the most important," said Lenin, who valued film as a propaganda tool.

In 1925, director Sergei Eisenstein's *Battleship Potemkin* went far beyond propaganda to become true art. Eisenstein worked with a technique called *montage,* in which two or more images are juxtaposed in order to convey an emotional impact or a new idea. Eisenstein won international acclaim for his use of this technique in *Battleship Potemkin.* In fact, many critics consider the film to be the best ever made. It was also the last film over which Eisenstein had full control. Like other Soviet artists, Eisenstein was constrained by government regulations and expectations after Stalin's takeover.

SSRs, such as Uzbek and the Ukraine, were the homelands of other nationalities and had their own languages, historical traditions, and cultures. At first, Stalin encouraged the autonomy, or independence, of these cultures. However, in the late 1920s, Stalin turned this policy on its head and systematically tried to make the cultures of the non-Russian SSRs more Russian. He appointed Russians to high-ranking positions in non-Russian SSRs and required the Russian language to be used in schools and businesses.

War on Religion The Communist party also tried to strengthen its hold on the minds of the people by destroying their religious faith. In accordance with the ideas of Marx, **atheism,** or the belief that there is no god, became an official state policy. Early on, the Communists targeted the Russian Orthodox Church, which had strongly supported the tsars. Many priests and other religious leaders were among those killed in the purges or sent to die in prison camps. Other religions were persecuted as well. At one show trial, 15 Roman Catholic priests were charged with teaching religion to the young, a counterrevolutionary activity. The state seized Jewish synagogues and banned the use of Hebrew. Islam was also officially discouraged.

The Communists tried to replace religion with their own ideology. Like a religion, communist ideology had its own "sacred" texts—the writings of Marx and Lenin—and its own shrines, such as the tomb of Lenin. Portraits of Stalin replaced religious icons in Russian homes. However, millions of Soviets continued to worship, in private and sometimes in public, in defiance of the government's prohibitions.

 Checkpoint How did Stalin use censorship and propaganda to support his rule?

Soviet Society Under Stalin

The terror and cultural coercion of Stalin's rule made a mockery of the original theories and promises of communism. The lives of most Russians did change. But, while the changes had some benefits, they were often outweighed by continuous shortages and restricted freedoms.

The New Elite Takes Control The Communists destroyed the old social order of landowning nobles at the top and peasants at the bottom. But instead of creating a society of equals as they promised, they created a society where a few elite groups emerged as a new ruling class. At the head of society were members of the Communist party. Only a small fraction of Soviet citizens could join the party. Many who did so were motivated by a desire to get ahead, rather than a belief in communism.

The Soviet elite also included industrial managers, military leaders, scientists, and some artists and writers. The elite enjoyed benefits denied to most people. They lived in the best apartments in the cities and rested at the best vacation homes in the country. They could shop at special

The Party Versus the Church
To weaken the power of the Russian Orthodox Church, the party seized church property and converted churches into offices and museums. Here, Red Army soldiers carry off religious relics from a Russian church. *How might the policy of destroying churches in such a public way have backfired on the party?*

Soviet Society Under Stalin
Instruct
L3

- **Introduce: Vocabulary Builder** Ask students if they know what the word *elite* means. (*a small, privileged group or ruling class*) Ask them who they think probably comprised the elite in Soviet society. (*members of the Communist party*) Then have them read the Vocabulary Builder term and definition. Ask **What do you think the elites would gain *access* to that the rest of Russia probably would not?** (*better housing, better jobs, better food*)

- **Teach** Ask **How did life change under Soviet rule for those not in the elite party?** (*Though they had access to free schooling, free medical care, and inexpensive housing, key necessities remained scarce.*)

- **Quick Activity** Divide the class into small groups. Using the Idea Wave strategy (TE, p. T22), ask students to decide whether or not women's lives improved under Soviet rule.

Independent Practice
Have students fill in the Outline Map *The Soviet Union in the 1930s* and label the SSRs and the major industrial centers.

All in One Teaching Resources, Unit 4, p. 57

Monitor Progress
Circulate to make sure students are correctly labeling the SSRs on their Outline Maps. Administer the Geography Quiz.

All in One Teaching Resources, Unit 4, p. 57

History Background

The Russian Orthodox Church The Russian Orthodox Church survived more than half a century of Communist persecution. Under Stalin, clergy were often imprisoned and killed because of their beliefs. Church buildings were destroyed or converted for government uses. The government softened its policy towards the church in the late 1940s, but then cracked down again under Khrushchev and Brezhnev in the 1950s and 1960s.

After the fall of the Communist government in 1991, the Church experienced a revival in the Russian Federation. Its membership has swelled to perhaps as many as 80 million people. One Muscovite put it this way: "The Orthodox Church is perhaps the last, lone symbol of Russian national identity to have survived communism more or less intact. People . . . want and need such a symbol."

Answers

Caption For the religious, it would encourage secret worship and dislike of the Communist Party.

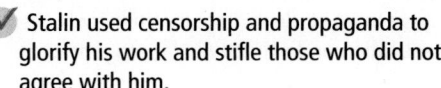 Stalin used censorship and propaganda to glorify his work and stifle those who did not agree with him.

Soviet Foreign Policy

Instruct

- **Introduce: Key Terms** Have students find the key term ***Comintern*** (in blue) in the text and explain its meaning. Ask **What was its purpose?** *(to encourage worldwide revolution)* Ask students to speculate on how Western nations might view this goal.

- **Teach** Ask **What foreign policy goals did both Lenin and Stalin pursue?** *(to bring about a worldwide revolution and to win the support of other countries)* Lead students in a discussion of how these goals were incompatible. Then ask **What progress did the Soviet Union make toward the goal of winning the support of other nations?** *(It slowly won recognition from Western powers, increased trade with them, and joined the League of Nations.)*

Independent Practice

Have students make a Venn diagram comparing the goals and practices of Stalin and Lenin. Have them refer back to Chapter 14 for more information on Lenin.

Monitor Progress

- To review this section, ask students to summarize the Soviet Union's foreign policy goals. *(to bring about worldwide revolution, to gain support of other nations)*

- Check Reading and Note Taking Study Guide entries for student understanding.

Vocabulary Builder

access—(AK ses) *n.* the ability to get and use

Crowded Lives

At the start of the first Five-Year Plan, millions of Soviets moved from the country to cities to take jobs in new industrial plants. This influx led to extremely crowded living conditions. These men gather in close quarters in a Soviet hostel in the early 1930s. *How does this photograph reflect the drawbacks of a centrally planned command economy?*

stores for scarce consumer goods. On the other hand, Stalin's purges often fell on the elite.

Benefits and Drawbacks Although excluded from party membership, most people did enjoy several new benefits. The party required all children to attend free Communist-built schools. The state supported technical schools and universities as well. Schools served many important goals. Educated workers were needed to build a modern industrial state. The Communist party also set up programs for students outside school. These programs included sports, cultural activities, and political classes to train teenagers for party membership. However, in addition to important basic skills, schools also taught communist values, such as atheism, the glory of collective farming, and love of Stalin.

The state also provided free medical care, day care for children, inexpensive housing, and public recreation. While these benefits were real, many people still lacked vital necessities. Although the state built massive apartment complexes, housing was scarce. Entire families might be packed into a single room. Bread was plentiful, but meat, fresh fruit, and other foods remained in short supply.

Women in the Soviet Union Long before 1917, women such as Nadezhda Krupskaya and Alexandra Kollontai worked for the revolution, spreading radical ideas among peasants and workers. Under the Communists, women won equality under the law. They gained access to education and a wide range of jobs. By the 1930s, many Soviet women were working in medicine, engineering, or the sciences. By their labor, women contributed to Soviet economic growth. They worked in factories, in construction, and on collectives. Within the family, their wages were needed because men and women earned the same low salaries.

✔ **Checkpoint** How did Communist schools benefit the state and the Communist party?

Answers

Caption The people in the photograph seem to be living in cramped and crowded conditions, indicating the failure of planning to meet people's needs.

✔ Schools taught communist values but also gave more students opportunities for higher education and extracurricular programs.

History Background

Educating the Youth The Soviet government used schools and youth groups to indoctrinate young people with communist ideals. One Soviet reader for elementary students began with this assertion: "The first country of socialism in the world became the first country of children's happiness in the world."

The Communist Party also set up three youth groups: the Little Octobrists, for young children, the Young Pioneers, for children ages 9 to 14, and the Komsomol, for young Soviets ages 14 to 28. Komsomol members were often given better scholarships and jobs than non-members. They were also favored for Communist Party membership, with all of its advantages.

Soviet Foreign Policy

Between 1917 and 1939, the Soviet Union pursued two very different goals in foreign policy. As Communists, both Lenin and Stalin wanted to bring about the worldwide revolution that Marx had predicted. But as Soviets, they wanted to guarantee their nation's security by winning the support of other countries. The result of pursuing these two different goals was a contradictory and generally unsuccessful foreign policy.

In 1919, Lenin formed the Communist International, or **Comintern.** The purpose of the Comintern was to encourage world-wide revolution. To this end, it aided revolutionary groups around the world and urged colonial peoples to rise up against imperialist powers.

The Comintern's support of revolutionary groups outside the Soviet Union and its propaganda against capitalism made Western powers highly suspicious of the Soviet Union. In the United States, fear of Bolshevik plots led to the "Red Scare" in the early 1920s. Britain broke off relations with the Soviet Union when evidence revealed Soviet schemes to turn a 1926 strike into a revolution. Even so, the Soviet Union slowly won recognition from Western powers and increased trade with capitalist countries. It also joined the League of Nations. However, mistrust still poisoned relations, especially after the Great Purge.

✔ **Checkpoint** How did the Soviet Union's foreign policy goals contradict one another?

Looking Ahead

By the time Stalin died in 1953, the Soviet Union had become a military superpower and a world leader in heavy industry. Yet Stalin's efforts exacted a brutal toll. The Soviet people were dominated by a totalitarian system based on terror. The reality of communism fell far short of Lenin's promises. Most people in the Soviet Union lived meager lives compared with people in the West.

SECTION **4** Assessment

Progress Monitoring Online
For: Self-quiz with vocabulary practice
Web Code: nba-2841

Terms, People, and Places

1. What do many of the key terms listed at the beginning of the section have in common? Explain.

Note Taking

2. **Reading Skill: Identify Main Ideas** Use your completed chart to answer the section Focus Question: How did Stalin transform the Soviet Union into a totalitarian state?

Comprehension and Critical Thinking

3. **Identify Effects** What were the goals and results of Stalin's five-year plans? How did the effects differ between industry and agriculture?

4. **Contrast** How did the command economy under Stalin differ from a capitalist economy?

5. **Synthesize Information** What methods did Stalin use to create a totalitarian state?

6. **Synthesize Information** One historian has said that socialist realism was "communism with a smiling face." What do you think he meant?

7. **Compare** Compare life under Stalin's rule with life under the Russian tsars.

● **Writing About History**

Quick Write: Choose an Organization Compare-and-contrast essays are often organized either point by point or by block. The first organization involves a discussion of one idea first, followed by the discussion of another, and emphasizes the two ideas. The second discusses all of the similarities, followed by all the differences, and emphasizes the comparison or contrast itself. Write an outline for each type for an essay comparing and contrasting the results of the Five-Year Plans in industry and agriculture.

Assess and Reteach

Assess Progress

- Have students complete the Section Assessment.
- Administer the Section Quiz.
- **All in One Teaching Resources, Unit 4,** p. 47
- To further assess student understanding, use
  📖 **Progress Monitoring Transparencies,** 121

Reteach

If students need more instruction, have them read the section summary.

 Reading and Note Taking Study Guide, p. 176 **L3**

 Adapted Reading and Note Taking Study Guide, p. 176 **L1 L2**

 Spanish Reading and Note Taking Study Guide, p. 176 **L2**

Extend

Tell students that in the 1990s, the breakup of the Soviet Union led to a revival of religion, particularly the Russian Orthodox Church. Ask students to form groups and discuss this question: **Why do you think the Soviets were unsuccessful in their attempt to destroy religion?**

Answer

✔ By aiding revolutionary groups in other countries and urging colonial peoples to rise up against imperialist powers, the Soviet Union also undermined potential trade relationships.

Section 4 Assessment

1. Most of the terms apply to changes that resulted from Communist rule.
2. Stalin brought all economic activity under government control, and he used terror tactics to control Soviet life.
3. The five-year plans were aimed at building up and improving industry and agriculture. The plans resulted in progress in industry but failed to increase agricultural output. Peasants resisted collectivization.
4. Command: government controls economy; Capitalist: free market controls most economic decisions.
5. tightened control and used force to punish opposition or protest
6. Soviet policy dictated that artists could only show Soviet life in a positive light.
7. Both repressed opposition, rejected democracy, tried to build up industry, and carried out programs of russification. However, the tsars supported religion whereas Stalin opposed it.

● **Writing About History**

Students' outlines should reflect understanding of the two types of organization.

For additional assessment, have students access **Progress Monitoring Online** at **Web Code nba-2841.**

Objectives

As you teach this section, keep students focused on the following objectives to help them answer the Section Focus Question and master core content.

- Analyze the problems faced by the Weimar Republic.
- Describe the Nazi party's political, social, economic, and cultural policies.
- Summarize the rise of authoritarian rule in Eastern Europe in the 1920s and 1930s.

Prepare to Read

Build Background Knowledge 🄲

Ask the students to recall the terms of the peace treaty forced on Germany after World War I. Ask students to speculate how the people of Germany probably felt about those terms.

Set a Purpose 🄲

- **WITNESS HISTORY** Read the selection aloud or play the audio.

  Ask **What did the narrator fear most that night?** *(She was afraid of being killed.)* **What does her experience suggest about the Nazis' methods?** *(Sample: ruthless)*

  🔊 AUDIO **Witness History Audio CD,** The Nazis in Control of Germany

- **Focus** Point out the Section Focus Question and write it on the board. Tell students to refer to this question as they read. *(Answer appears with Section 5 Assessment answers.)*

- **Preview** Have students preview the Section Objectives and the list of Terms, People, and Places.

- **Note Taking** Have students read this section using the Guided Questioning strategy (TE, p. T20). As they read, have students fill in the flowchart identifying main ideas about Germany after World War I.

  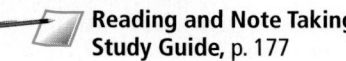
  Reading and Note Taking Study Guide, p. 177

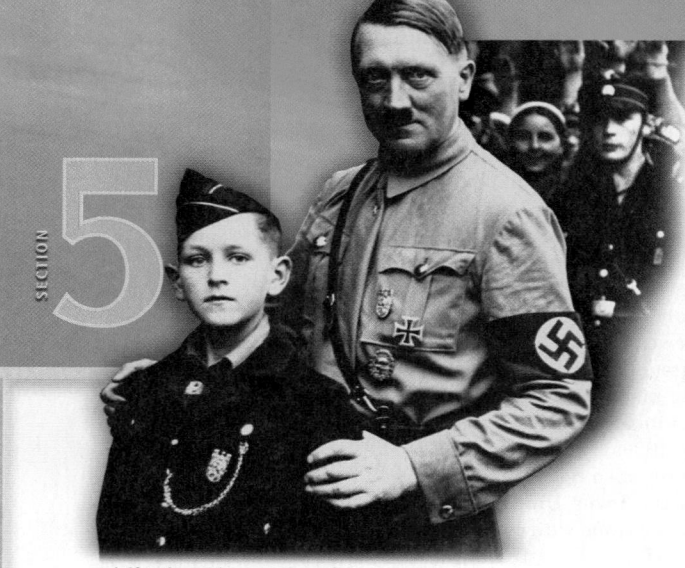

Adolf Hitler with a member of a Nazi youth organization

WITNESS HISTORY 🔊 AUDIO

The Nazis in Control of Germany

In the 1930s, Adolf Hitler and the Nazi party brought hope to Germans suffering from the Great Depression. On the dark side of Hitler's promises was a message of hate, aimed particularly at Jews. A German Jewish woman recalls an attack on her family during *Kristallnacht*, a night in early November 1938 when Nazi mobs attacked Jewish homes and businesses.

❝ They broke our windowpanes, and the house became very cold. . . . We were standing there, outside in the cold, still in our night clothes, with only a coat thrown over. . . . Then they made everyone lie face down on the ground . . . 'Now, they will shoot us,' we thought. We were very afraid. ❞

Focus Question How did Hitler and the Nazi party establish and maintain a totalitarian government in Germany?

Hitler and the Rise of Nazi Germany

Objectives

- Analyze the problems faced by the Weimar Republic.
- Describe the Nazi party's political, social, economic, and cultural policies.
- Summarize the rise of authoritarian rule in Eastern Europe in the 1920s and 1930s.

Terms, People, and Places

chancellor	Gestapo
Ruhr Valley	Nuremberg Laws
Third Reich	

Note Taking

Reading Skill: Identify Main Ideas As you read, summarize the section's main ideas in a flowchart like the one below.

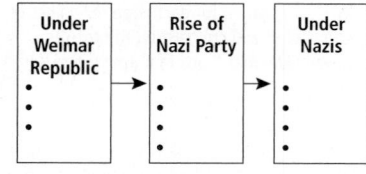

In November 1923, a German army veteran and leader of an extremist party, Adolf Hitler, tried to follow Mussolini's example by staging a small-scale coup in Munich. The coup failed, and Hitler was soon behind bars. But Hitler proved to be a force that could not be ignored. Within a decade, he made a new bid for power. This time, he succeeded by legal means.

Hitler's rise to power raises disturbing questions that we still debate today. Why did Germany, which had a democratic government in the 1920s, become a totalitarian state in the 1930s? How could a ruthless, hate-filled dictator gain the enthusiastic support of many Germans?

The Weimar Republic's Rise and Fall

As World War I drew to a close, Germany tottered on the brink of chaos. Under the threat of a socialist revolution, the kaiser abdicated. Moderate leaders signed the armistice and later, under protest, the Versailles treaty.

In 1919, German leaders drafted a constitution in the city of Weimar (VY mahr). It created a democratic government known as the Weimar Republic. The constitution set up a parliamentary system led by a **chancellor,** or prime minister. It gave women the vote and included a bill of rights.

Vocabulary Builder

Use the information below and the following resources to teach the high-use words from this section.
All-in-One Teaching Resources, Unit 4, p. 49; **Teaching Resources, Skills Handbook,** p. 3

High-Use Words	Definitions and Sample Sentences
passive, p. 551	*adj.* not active, nonviolent Dogs actively seek affection by barking, while cats prefer a **passive** approach.
regime, p. 554	*n.* a government in power There had been many attempts by neighboring nations to overthrow the current **regime,** which was known for brutality and abuse of the people.

Political Struggles The republic faced severe problems from the start. Politically, it was weak because Germany, like France, had many small parties. The chancellor had to form coalitions that easily fell apart.

The government, led by moderate democratic socialists, came under constant fire from both the left and right. Communists demanded radical changes like those Lenin had brought to Russia. Conservatives—including the old Junker nobility, military officers, and wealthy bourgeoisie—attacked the government as too liberal and weak. They longed for another strong leader like Bismarck. Germans of all classes blamed the Weimar Republic for the hated Versailles treaty. Bitter, they looked for scapegoats. Many blamed German Jews for economic and political problems.

Runaway Inflation Economic disaster fed unrest. In 1923, when Germany fell behind in reparations payments, France occupied the coal-rich Ruhr Valley (roor). Germans workers in the Ruhr protested using passive resistance and refused to work. To support the workers, the government continued to pay them, and printed huge quantities of paper money to do so. Inflation soon spiraled out of control, spreading misery and despair. The German mark became almost worthless. An item that cost 100 marks in July 1922 cost 944,000 marks by August 1923. Salaries rose by billions of marks, but they still could not keep up with skyrocketing prices. Many middle-class families saw their savings wiped out.

Recovery and Collapse With help from the Western powers, the government did bring inflation under control. In 1924, the United States gained British and French approval for a plan to reduce German reparations payments. Under the Dawes Plan, France withdrew its forces from the Ruhr, and American loans helped the German economy recover. Germany began to prosper. Then, the Great Depression hit, reviving memories of the miseries of 1923. Germans turned to an energetic leader, Adolf Hitler, who promised to solve the economic crisis and restore Germany's former greatness.

Weimar Culture Culture flourished in the Weimar Republic even as the government struggled through crisis after crisis. The tumultuous times helped to stimulate new cultural movements, such as dadaist art and Bauhaus architecture. Berlin attracted writers and artists from around the world, just as Paris did. The German playwright Bertolt Brecht sharply criticized middle-class values with *The Three-Penny Opera*. The artist George Grosz, through scathing drawings and paintings, blasted the failings of the Weimar Republic. However, many believed that this modern culture and the Weimar Republic itself were not in keeping with Germany's illustrious past.

✔ **Checkpoint** What political and economic problems did the Weimar Republic face?

The Nazi Party's Rise to Power

Adolf Hitler was born in Austria in 1889. When he was 18, he went to Vienna, then the capital of the multinational Hapsburg empire. German Austrians

Vocabulary Builder

passive—(PAS iv) *adj.* not active, nonviolent

Inflation Rocks Germany
A man uses German marks to paper his wall because it costs less than buying wallpaper. At the height of the inflation, it would have taken 84,000 fifty-million mark notes like the one below, to equal a single American dollar. *Why would inflation hit middle class people with modest savings hard?*

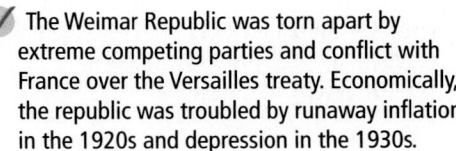

REICHSBANKNOTE ※ 084002
Fünfzig Millionen Mark
zahlt die Reichsbankhauptkasse in Berlin gegen diese
Banknote dem Einlieferer. Vom 1. Januar 1924 ab
kann diese Banknote aufgerufen und unter Umtausch
gegen andere gesetzliche Zahlungsmittel eingezogen
werden. Berlin, den 1. September 1923   MM–S
REICHSBANKDIREKTORIUM

Teach

The Weimar Republic's Rise and Fall   **L3**

Instruct

- **Introduce: Vocabulary Builder** Have students read the Vocabulary Builder term and definition. Ask **In what ways were the actions of the German workers *passive*?** *(They refused to work.)* Remind students that as they read in the previous chapter, Gandhi advocated *passive* resistance. Have students list other examples of *passive* resistance.

- **Teach** Ask students to list the problems that troubled the Weimar Republic. Write their responses on the board. *(weak government, demands for social change from the communists, attacks from conservatives who wanted a strong leader in charge, blame for the Versailles treaty, runaway inflation, reparations payments, and depression in the 1930s)* Ask **Why do you think culture flourished in the Weimar Republic despite the government's problems?** *(Sample: Artists may have felt inspired to speak out or depict the unrest and bitterness engendered by the republic's many problems.)*

Independent Practice

Ask students to work in small groups and decide what factor may have been the most significant in Hitler's coming to power and explain their choice. *(Samples: Germany had been eager for a strong leader; Hitler promised to restore Germany's former greatness.)* Then, using the Numbered Heads strategy (TE, p. T23), have students share their answers.

Monitor Progress

As students fill in their flowcharts, circulate to make sure they understand the main ideas of this section. For a completed version of the flowchart, see
▥ **Note Taking Transparencies**, 183

Differentiated Instruction   Solutions for All Learners

L4 Gifted and Talented   L4 Advanced Readers

Tell students that Weimar-era Germany experienced similar social and cultural movements to those in the United States and other parts of Europe in the 1920s. Ask students to choose which of the following areas is of greatest interest to them: painting, literature, music, architecture. Ask them to investigate developments in their area of interest in Weimar, Germany, in the 1920s and present their findings in a chart, piece of artwork, essay, or other type of product.

Answers

Caption They would go through their savings very fast.

✔ The Weimar Republic was torn apart by extreme competing parties and conflict with France over the Versailles treaty. Economically, the republic was troubled by runaway inflation in the 1920s and depression in the 1930s.

The Nazi Party's Rise to Power ⑬

Instruct

- **Introduce** Display **Color Transparency 172: Hitler at Nuremberg Stadium.** Based on clues in the photograph of Hitler giving a speech at Nuremberg Stadium, have students predict what kind of leader he would be.

  📖 **Color Transparencies,** 172

- **Teach** Ask students to briefly describe Hitler's life, after reading the text and the Biography on this page. Then ask **What actions and promises enabled Hitler to become dictator of Germany?** *(He made use of the frustrations brought on by the depression and fear of communists to gain the support of many Germans. After his appointment as chancellor, he suppressed all opposition.)* **What ideas did Hitler put forward in *Mein Kampf*?** *(his brand of extreme nationalism, racism, and anti-Semitism)*

Independent Practice

Have students make a timeline, charting the Nazi party's rise to power.

Monitor Progress

As students create their timelines, circulate to ensure they understand the conditions that paved the way to Hitler's rise to power.

Answers

BIOGRAPHY to understand how events from his upbringing would have affected his later actions

✔ The Nazi party's ideology was based on anti-Semitism, pride in Germany's past, and revenge for the Treaty of Versailles. Hitler planned to defy the Versailles treaty, create jobs, and bring Germany back to greatness.

BIOGRAPHY

Adolf Hitler
As a boy, Adolf Hitler (1889–1945) became obsessed with Germany's 1871 victory in the Franco–Prussian War. "The great historic struggle would become my greatest spiritual experience," he later wrote. "I became more and more enthusiastic about everything . . . connected with war."

In school, young Hitler was known as a ringleader. One of his teachers recalled, "He demanded of his fellow pupils their unqualified obedience." He failed to finish high school and was later crushed when he was rejected by art school.

After Hitler came to power, he used his elite guard of storm troopers to terrorize his opponents. But when he felt his power threatened, Hitler had leaders of the storm troopers murdered during the "Night of the Long Knives" on June 30, 1934. **Why do you think historians study Hitler's upbringing?**

---

made up just one of many ethnic groups in Vienna. Yet they felt superior to Jews, Serbs, Poles, and other groups. While living in Vienna, Hitler developed the fanatical anti-Semitism, or prejudice against Jewish people, that would later play a major role in his rise to power.

Hitler went to Germany and fought in the German army during World War I. In 1919, he joined a small group of right-wing extremists. Like many ex-soldiers, he despised the Weimar government, which he saw as weak. Within a year, he was the unquestioned leader of the National Socialist German Workers, or Nazi, party. Like Mussolini, Hitler organized his supporters into fighting squads. Nazi "storm troopers" fought in the streets against their political enemies.

Hitler's Manifesto In 1923, as you have read, Hitler made a failed attempt to seize power in Munich. He was arrested and found guilty of treason. While in prison, Hitler wrote *Mein Kampf ("My Struggle")*. It would later become the basic book of Nazi goals and ideology.

Mein Kampf reflected Hitler's obsessions—extreme nationalism, racism, and anti-Semitism. Germans, he said, belonged to a superior "master race" of Aryans, or light-skinned Europeans, whose greatest enemies were the Jews. Hitler's ideas were rooted in a long tradition of anti-Semitism. In the Middle Ages, Christians persecuted Jews because of their different beliefs. The rise of nationalism in the 1800s caused people to identify Jews as ethnic outsiders. Hitler viewed Jews not as members of a religion but as a separate race. (He defined a Jew as anyone with one Jewish grandparent.) Echoing a familiar right-wing theme, he blamed Germany's defeat in World War I on a conspiracy of Marxists, Jews, corrupt politicians, and business leaders.

In his recipe for revival, Hitler urged Germans everywhere to unite into one great nation. Germany must expand, he said, to gain *Lebensraum* (LAY buns rowm), or living space, for its people. Slavs and other inferior races must bow to Aryan needs. To achieve its greatness, Germany needed a strong leader, or Führer (FYOO rur). Hitler was determined to become that leader.

Hitler Comes to Power After less than a year, Hitler was released from prison. He soon renewed his table-thumping speeches. The Great Depression played into Hitler's hands. As unemployment rose, Nazi membership grew to almost a million. Hitler's program appealed to veterans, workers, the lower middle classes, small-town Germans, and business people alike. He promised to end reparations, create jobs, and defy the Versailles treaty by rearming Germany.

With the government paralyzed by divisions, both Nazis and Communists won more seats in the Reichstag, or lower house of the legislature. Fearing the growth of communist political power, conservative politicians turned to Hitler. Although they despised him, they believed they could control him. Thus, with conservative support, Hitler was appointed chancellor in 1933 through legal means under the Weimar constitution.

Within a year, Hitler was dictator of Germany. He and his supporters suspended civil rights, destroyed the socialists and Communists, and disbanded other political parties. Germany became a one-party state. Like Stalin in Russia, Hitler purged his own party, brutally executing Nazis he felt were disloyal. Nazis learned that Hitler demanded unquestioning obedience.

 Checkpoint Describe the Nazi party's ideology and Hitler's plans for ruling Germany.

History Background

The Fortunes of the Young Hitler As a young man, Hitler moved to Vienna from the Austrian countryside to try to become an artist. Although he had some talent, the Academy of Fine Arts denied him entry twice. He remained in Vienna, living in poverty. However, he soon found his niche—as a soldier in the German army during World War I. He served bravely and received an unusual number of awards. He was wounded in the Battle of the Somme in 1916, and again when he was gassed in 1918. After the war, Hitler finally gained financial security with the publication of his manifesto, *Mein Kampf,* in 1925. When he became chancellor of Germany in 1933, sales skyrocketed, making him a millionaire.

The Third Reich Controls Germany

Once in power, Hitler and the Nazis moved to build a new Germany. Like Mussolini, Hitler appealed to nationalism by recalling past glories. Germany's First Reich, or empire, was the medieval Holy Roman Empire. The Second Reich was the empire forged by Bismarck in 1871. Under Hitler's new **Third Reich,** he boasted, the German master race would dominate Europe for a thousand years.

To combat the Great Depression, Hitler launched large public works programs (as did Britain and the United States). Tens of thousands of people were put to work building highways and housing or replanting forests. Hitler also began a crash program to rearm Germany and schemed to unite Germany and Austria. Both measures were a strong repudiation, or rejection, of the hated Versailles treaty.

Germany Becomes a Totalitarian State To achieve his goals, Hitler organized an efficient but brutal system of totalitarian rule. Nazis controlled all areas of German life—from government to religion to education. Elite, black-uniformed troops, called the SS, enforced the Führer's will. His secret police, the Gestapo (guh STAH poh), rooted out opposition. The masses, relieved by belief in the Nazis' promises, cheered Hitler's accomplishments in ending unemployment and reviving German power. Those who worried about Hitler's terror apparatus quickly became its victims or were cowed into silence in fear for their own safety.

The Campaign Against the Jews Begins In his fanatical anti-Semitism, Hitler set out to drive Jews from Germany. In 1935, the Nazis passed the **Nuremberg Laws,** which deprived Jews of German citizenship and placed severe restrictions on them. They were prohibited from marrying non-Jews, attending or teaching at German schools or universities, holding government jobs, practicing law or medicine, or publishing

"Night of Broken Glass"
On the night of November 9, 1938, and into the next day, German mobs smashed the windows of Jewish homes and businesses, looted Jewish shops, and burned synagogues. Many Jewish people were dragged from their homes and beaten in the streets. Not only did the Nazi government authorize these attacks, it made the Jewish victims pay for the damage.

Link to Economics

Hitler's Popularity Hitler promised Germany an economic recovery—and he delivered it. As most of the world was gripped by the Great Depression, Hitler launched a massive public works program. Millions of Germans were employed constructing superhighways, office buildings, sports arenas, public housing, and military materials. As a result, unemployment dropped from six million in 1932 to one million in 1936. By 1938, there was a shortage of workers and women began taking jobs outside the home. Between 1932 and 1938, the standard of living for employed Germans rose by more than 20 percent. For the masses of ordinary Germans, those who were not Jews, Slavs, Gypsies, communists, or other persecuted minorities, Hitler had produced an economic miracle.

The Third Reich Controls Germany

Instruct

- **Introduce: Key Terms** Ask students to find the key terms *Gestapo* and *Nuremberg Laws* (in blue) in the text and explain their meanings. Ask students to write a sentence that relates these two terms to each other and describes their significance to Nazi Germany.

- **Teach** Ask **What did Hitler do in defiance of the Versailles treaty?** *(built up Germany's military and schemed to unite Austria and Germany)* **How did Hitler expand his control over the German people?** *(He brought business and labor under his control; he indoctrinated young people with Nazi ideology; he limited women's roles; he organized a system of terror and repression of opposition; he placed severe restrictions on Jews; he demanded that education and the arts reflect Nazi values; and he sought to replace religion with his racial creed.)*

- **Quick Activity** Ask students to look at the images on this page and the next page. Read the captions and discuss the visuals as a class. Ask students to use the visuals to describe what life was like in the Third Reich.

Independent Practice

Viewpoints To help students better understand the propaganda techniques used by Hitler, have them read the selection *Hitler's Propaganda Machine* and complete the worksheet.

All in One Teaching Resources, Unit 4, p. 55

Monitor Progress

Have students reread the black headings and summarize the content under each one. Ensure that students understand that Hitler's regime was based on totalitarian control of the German state and people.

Authoritarian Rule in Eastern Europe

Instruct

- **Introduce** Remind students that the entire world faced economic problems from 1919 to 1939. Ask them to recall how Britain, France, Italy, and Germany responded to this challenge and then have them predict how the nations in Eastern Europe would react to the same challenge.

- **Teach** Ask **What problems did the new nations in Eastern Europe face in the postwar years?** *(lack of capital to develop industry, social inequalities, little experience in democracy, ethnic and religious tensions)* **Where did dictators use these problems to gain power?** *(every Eastern European country except Czechoslovakia and Finland)* **How were these dictators similar to Hitler?** *(They promised order and won the support of the military and the wealthy, and they used Jews as scapegoats for many problems.)*

- **Quick Activity** Display **Color Transparency 173: Ethnic Groups of Eastern Europe, 1936.** Use the lesson suggested in the transparency book to guide a discussion on how these ethnic groups were a source of conflict after World War I.

  📺 **Color Transparencies, 173**

Independent Practice

Have students fill in the Outline Map *Fascist Governments in Europe, 1939* and label the areas taken over by fascist dictators.

All in One Teaching Resources, Unit 4, p. 56

Monitor Progress

- Circulate to make sure students are filling in their Outline Maps accurately. Ensure students have shaded Czechoslovakia and Finland as the two Eastern European countries not under fascist rule.

- Check Reading and Note Taking Study Guide entries for student understanding.

Answer

✔ The Nazi party maintained power by keeping some of Hitler's promises and brutally cracking down on dissent.

---

books. Nazis beat and robbed Jews and roused mobs to do the same. Many German Jews fled, seeking refuge in other countries.

Night of Broken Glass On November 7, 1938, a young Jew whose parents had been mistreated in Germany shot and wounded a German diplomat in Paris. Hitler used the incident as an excuse to stage an attack on all Jews. *Kristallnacht* (krih STAHL nahkt), or the "Night of Broken Glass," took place on November 9 and 10. Nazi-led mobs attacked Jewish communities all over Germany, Austria, and the annexed portions of Czechoslovakia. Before long, Hitler and his henchmen were making even more sinister plans for what they called the "Final Solution"—the extermination of all Jews.

Nazi Youth To build for the future, the Nazis indoctrinated young people with their ideology. In passionate speeches, the Führer spewed his message of racism. He urged young Germans to destroy their so-called enemies without mercy. On hikes and in camps, the "Hitler Youth" pledged absolute loyalty to Germany and undertook physical fitness programs to prepare for war. School courses and textbooks were rewritten to reflect Nazi racial views.

Like Fascists in Italy, Nazis sought to limit women's roles. Women were dismissed from upper-level jobs and turned away from universities. To raise the birthrate, Nazis offered "pure-blooded Aryan" women rewards for having more children. Still, Hitler's goal to keep women in the home and out of the workforce applied mainly to the privileged. As German industry expanded, women factory workers were needed.

Purging German Culture The Nazis also sought to purge, or purify, German culture. They denounced modern art, saying that it was corrupted by Jewish influences. They condemned jazz because of its African roots. Instead, the Nazis glorified old German myths such as those re-created in the operas of Richard Wagner (VAHG nur).

Hitler despised Christianity as "weak" and "flabby." He sought to replace religion with his racial creed. To control the churches, the Nazis combined all Protestant sects into a single state church. They closed Catholic schools and muzzled the Catholic clergy. Although many clergy either supported the new regime or remained silent, some courageously spoke out against Hitler.

✔ **Checkpoint** How did the Nazi party maintain its control of Germany?

Vocabulary Builder

regime—(ruh ZHEEM) *n.* a government in power

Nazi Book Burnings

Nazis burned books of which they disapproved, such as *All Quiet on the Western Front,* in huge, organized public bonfires. The Nazis viewed Remarque's novel as an insult to the German military.

Authoritarian Rule in Eastern Europe

Like Germany, most new nations in Eastern Europe slid from democratic to authoritarian rule in the postwar era. In 1919, a dozen countries were carved out of the old Russian, Austro-Hungarian, Ottoman and German empires. Although they differed from one another in important ways, they faced some common problems. They were small countries whose rural agricultural economies lacked capital to develop industry. Social and economic inequalities separated

---

Differentiated Instruction   Solutions for All Learners

L1 Special Needs   L2 Less Proficient Readers

Review the locations of the countries mentioned under the heading "Authoritarian Rule in Eastern Europe" by directing students to look at the map titled "Europe, 1920" on page 373. Then ask students to work as partners to create a concept web with "Causes of Unrest in Eastern Europe" in the central circle and the individual causes stemming out of that center.

L2 English Language Learners

Use the following resources to help students acquire basic skills.

✏️ **Adapted Reading and Note Taking Study Guide**

- Adapted Note Taking Study Guide, p. 177
- Adapted Section Summary, p. 178

poor peasants from wealthy landlords. None had much experience with the democratic process. Further complicating the situation, tensions leftover from World War I hindered economic cooperation between countries. Each country in the region tried to be independent of its neighbors, which hurt all of them. The region was hit hard by the Great Depression.

Ethnic Conflict Old rivalries between ethnic and religious groups created severe tensions. In Czechoslovakia, Czechs and Slovaks were unwilling partners. Serbs dominated the new state of Yugoslavia, but restless Slovenes and Croats living there pressed for independence. In Poland, Hungary, and Romania, conflict flared among various ethnic groups.

Democracy Retreats Economic problems and ethnic tensions contributed to instability, which in turn helped fascist rulers gain power. In Hungary, military strongman Nicholas Horthy (HAWR tay) overthrew a Communist-led government in 1919. By 1926, the military hero Joseph Pilsudski (peel SOOT skee) had taken control over Poland. Eventually, right-wing dictators emerged in every Eastern European country except Czechoslovakia and Finland. Like Hitler, these dictators promised order and won the backing of the military and wealthy. They also turned to anti-Semitism, using Jewish people as scapegoats for many national problems. Meanwhile, strong, aggressive neighbors eyed these small, weak states of Eastern Europe as tempting targets.

✓ **Checkpoint** Why did authoritarian states rise in Eastern Europe after World War I?

Notable Jewish Figures of Europe, Early 1900s

Person	Achievements
Marc Chagall	Forerunner of Surrealism
Gustav Mahler	Composed symphonies and conducted many major orchestras
Arnold Schoenberg	Pioneered new styles of music
Franz Kafka	Influential style of surrealist writing
Albert Einstein	Important scientist
Sigmund Freud	Founder of psychoanalysis
Edmund Husserl	Founder of phenomenology movement
Rudolph Lipschitz	Worked on number theory and potential theory

The table above lists a few of the notable Jewish people whose exceptional talents flew in the face of Hitler's claims of Aryan superiority. Some of these people fled Europe in the face of the Nazi regime. **Chart Skills** *Describe how losing some of its leading thinkers might have hurt Nazi Germany.*

Section 5 Assessment

Progress Monitoring Online
For: Self-quiz with vocabulary practice
Web Code: nba-2851

Terms, People, and Places
1. Place each of the terms listed at the beginning of the section into one of the following categories: politics, culture, or economy. Write a sentence explaining your choice.

Note Taking
2. **Reading Skill: Identify Main Ideas** Use your completed flowchart to answer the section Focus Question: How did Hitler and the Nazi Party establish and maintain a totalitarian government in Germany?

Comprehension and Critical Thinking
3. **Express Problems Clearly** List three problems faced by the Weimar Republic.

4. **Recognize Ideologies** What racial and nationalistic ideas did Nazis promote?
5. **Summarize** What were some of the restrictions that Hitler placed on German Jews?
6. **Demonstrate Reasoned Judgment** Do you think that there are any reasons why a government would be justified in banning books or censoring ideas? Explain.
7. **Identify Effects** Why did dictators gain power in much of Eastern Europe?
8. **Draw Conclusions** Both Stalin and Hitler instituted ruthless campaigns against supposed enemies of the state. Why do you think dictators need to find scapegoats for their nation's ills?

● **Writing About History**
Quick Write: Use Compare-and-Contrast Transitions Use strong transitions to help readers navigate your compare-and-contrast essays. Words such as *however, but, nevertheless, yet, likewise, similarly,* and *instead* signal comparison-and-contrast relationships. Add one of these words to the statements below to clarify their meanings.
• Hitler's rise was based on hate. He was a popular leader.
• Germany became a fascist state. Many of the countries of Eastern Europe became fascist states.

■ Have students use the Quick Study Guide to prepare for this chapter's test. Students may wish to refer to the following pages as they review:

Causes and Effects of the Great Depression
Section 2, pp. 532–535; Section 3, pp. 536–537; Section 4, pp. 542–543; Section 5, pp. 551–552

Three Totalitarian States: Italy, the Soviet Union, and Germany
Section 3, pp. 536–540; Section 4, pp. 536–538; Section 5, pp. 552–554

Some Cultural Figures of the Post World War I Era
Section 1, pp. 522–528

Key Events in Europe and the United States, 1919–1939
Section 2, pp. 529–534; Section 3, pp. 536–537; Section 4, pp. 542–544; Section 5, pp. 550–554

■ For additional review, remind **L3** students to refer to the

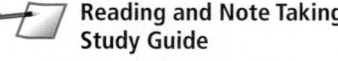 **Reading and Note Taking Study Guide**

Note Taking Study Guide, pp. 169, 171, 173, 175, 177
Section Summaries, pp. 170, 172, 174, 176, 178

■ Have students access **Web Code nbp-2862** for this chapter's **History** *Interactive* timeline, which includes expanded entries and additional events.

■ If students need more instruction on analyzing timelines, have them read the **Skills Handbook,** p. SH30.

■ When students have completed their study of the chapter, distribute Chapter Tests A and B.

All in One Teaching Resources, Unit 4, pp. 59–64

For **Progress Monitoring** *Online,* refer students to the Self-test with vocabulary practice at **Web Code nba-2861.**

Quick Study Guide

Progress Monitoring *Online*
For: Self-test with vocabulary practice
Web Code: nba-2861

■ Causes and Effects of the Great Depression

Cause and Effect	
Long-Term Causes	**Immediate Causes**
• Worldwide interrelationship of governments and economies • Gold standard • Overproduction of goods • Agricultural slump • Uneven distribution of wealth	• Falling demand • Financial crisis kicked off by New York stock market crash • Banks demand repayment of loans • American loans to other countries dry up • Without capital, businesses and factories fail

↓

Worldwide Economic Depression	
Immediate Effects	**Long-Term Effects**
• Vast unemployment and misery • Protective tariffs imposed • Countries abandon gold standard • Loss of faith in capitalism and democracy • Authoritarian leaders emerge	• Rise of fascism and Nazism • Governments experiment with social programs • People blame scapegoats • World War II begins

■ Three Totalitarian States: Italy, the Soviet Union, and Germany

Country	Dictator in Power	Ideology	Example of Terror Tactics
Italy	Benito Mussolini in power in 1922	Fascist; Fanatic nationalism	Black Shirts suppressed dissent.
Soviet Union	Joseph Stalin in power in 1924	Communist	Stalin sent millions to Gulag labor camps.
Germany	Adolf Hitler in power in 1933	Fascist; Racial policies of hatred, aimed particularly at Jews	Nazis began to restrict and terrorize German Jews.

■ Some Cultural Figures of the Post World War I Era

Literature
Ernest Hemingway
Virginia Woolf
Langston Hughes
Mikhail Sholokhov

Music and Theater
Louis Armstrong
Bertolt Brecht

Visual Arts
Pablo Picasso
Jean Arp
Salvador Dali
Frank Lloyd Wright
George Grosz
Vasily Kandinsky

■ Key Events in Europe and the United States, 1919–1939

Britain, France, and the United States
Germany, Italy, and the Soviet Union

1919–1920
Red Scare sweeps the United States.

1920

1919
The Weimar Republic is established in Germany.

1922
Benito Mussolini comes to power after the March on Rome.

1925
Seven European nations sign the Locarno treaties, raising hopes for world peace.

1926
More than three million workers in several different industries strike in Britain.

1925

Differentiated Instruction   **Solutions for All Learners**

L1 Special Needs   **L2** Less Proficient Readers

For students acquiring basic skills:

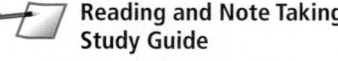 **Adapted Reading and Note Taking Study Guide**

Adapted Note Taking, pp. 169, 171, 173, 175, 177
Adapted Section Summaries, pp. 170, 172, 174, 176, 178

L2 English Language Learners

For Spanish-speaking students:

Spanish Reading and Note Taking Study Guide

Spanish Note Taking, pp. 169, 171, 173, 175, 177
Spanish Section Summaries, pp. 170, 172, 174, 176, 178

Concept Connector

Essential Question Review

To connect prior knowledge with what you have learned in this chapter, answer the questions below in your Concept Connector journal. Use the journal in the Reading and Note Taking Study Guide to record your answers (or go to www.phschool.com **Web Code:** nbd-2807). In addition, record information about the following concept:

• Dictatorship: Mussolini and Hitler

1. **Dictatorship** As the Western democracies stumbled after World War I, totalitarian governments gained power in Italy, Germany, and the Soviet Union. Summarize social, political, and economic conditions in postwar Europe. Then create a list of reasons that explain why an average citizen living in postwar Europe in the 1920s or early 1930s might support a dictator.

2. **Human Rights** Mussolini, Hitler, and Stalin were brutal dictators. In disregard for human rights, political opponents were murdered, imprisoned, or exiled. But terror was not the dictator's only weapon. Give examples of other methods they used to maintain power, strengthen their totalitarian states, and strip people of their human rights. Focus on the following:
   • culture
   • education
   • propaganda

3. **Science and Technology** In the 1940s, scientists built on Marie Curie's research on radioactivity and Albert Einstein's theories of relativity to develop atomic energy. How do these discoveries demonstrate the benefits and costs of technology?

■ Connections To Today

1. **Dictatorship: North Korea's Kim Jong Il** Dictatorship as a form of government still exists today. Kim Jong Il (below), head of a communist totalitarian regime in North Korea, is considered among the most dangerous of the present-day dictators. In fact, Kim has been described as "Stalinist." Kim took over as dictator from his father, Kim Il-Sung, in 1994. Since then, he has violated the civil liberties of his own people, and he has destabilized international relations in the region with claims that North Korea possesses nuclear weapons. Research Kim Jong Il's record in North Korea and write two paragraphs comparing his regime to Stalin's in Russia.

2. **Political Systems: The Former Soviet Union** The Soviet Union came to an end in 1991. Its collapse produced 14 new republics, besides the Russian Federation, as each of the former SSRs became independent. The transition was not easy. Choose one of the following countries and then research and write a brief report on its transition from SSR to independent republic: Armenia, Azerbaijan, Belarus, Estonia, Georgia, Kazakhstan, Kyrgyzstan, Latvia, Lithuania, Moldova, Tajikistan, Turkmenistan, Ukraine, Uzbekistan.

Concept Connector

Tell students that the main concepts for this chapter are Dictatorship, Human Rights, and Science, and then ask them to answer the Essential Question Review questions on this page. Discuss the Connections to Today topics and ask students to answer the questions that follow.

Essential Question Review

1. Summaries should reference the political and economic turmoil of postwar Britain, France, Ireland, Italy, the Soviet Union, and Germany. The list of reasons might include economic insecurity, hatred and intolerance, nationalist fervor, and the desire for a strong leader and stability.

2. To increase their power, dictators attempt to control media through censorship. They appeal to nationalist sentiments with propaganda. They bring the economy under government control. They take control of education and suppress intellectuals.

3. The work of Einstein and Curie has been instrumental in the creation of clean energy in nuclear power plants, but it has also lead to the creation of weapons of mass destruction.

Connections to Today

1. Paragraphs should include accurate information about North Korea as well as the Soviet Union's totalitarian regime and include both similarities and differences.

2. Reports should focus on a former SSR and include information on its transition to independence, such as the type of government, the ethnic background of its people, and the role of Communist influence.

For additional review of this **L3** chapter's core concepts, remind students to refer to the

Reading and Note Taking Study Guide
Concept Connector, pp. 255, 275, 295

1929	1930	1933
The Great Depression begins in the United States.	**Construction on the Maginot Line begins on the border of France and Germany.**	**Prohibition is repealed in the United States.**

History *Interactive*
For: Interactive timeline
Web Code: nbp-2862

1930   1935

1928	1932	1933	1935
Joseph Stalin launches the first of his Five-Year Plans in the Soviet Union.	**Stalin's ruthless policies, combined with failed crops, cause mass starvation in the Soviet Union.**	**Adolf Hitler becomes chancellor of Germany.**	**The Nazi Party in Germany passes the Nuremberg Laws, limiting the rights of Jews.**

Chapter Assessment

Terms, People, and Places

1. flapper
2. Benito Mussolini
3. disarmament
4. totalitarian state
5. Franklin Delano Roosevelt
6. Harlem Renaissance
7. Ruhr Valley

Main Ideas

8. World War I ended the sense of optimism that had grown in the West since the Enlightenment. Some disillusioned young people rejected traditional values and standards for newer attitudes. The work of many writers and artists reflected these changes.

9. The Locarno treaties settled Germany's disputed borders and became the symbol of a new era of peace. In the Kellogg-Briand Pact almost all nations agreed not to use war as a method of national policy. The League of Nations sought to get nations to commit to the end of war. With no way of enforcing a ban on war, all these efforts failed to halt aggression.

10. The Great Depression caused misery and hard times throughout the world and helped lead to the rise of Nazism in Germany.

11. Fascism is an ideology that glorifies the state over the individual and demands blind loyalty to a national leader. It rejects the concepts of democracy and human rights.

12. The Fascists brought the Italian economy under state rule, glorified the state, and indoctrinated the Italian youth with nationalist ideas.

13. The government imposed control over industry and agriculture and also over people's lives. Secret police used violent methods to enforce compliance. Many political prisoners were sent to forced labor camps.

14. After being elected chancellor in 1933, Hitler imposed a system of repression and glorification of the state.

Chapter Focus Question

15. Challenges: the aftermath of World War I and suffering brought on by the Great Depression; reaction: some countries worked within their democratic structure to solve problems, others turned to strong leaders and totalitarian governments.

Chapter Assessment

Terms, People, and Places

Match the following terms with the definitions below.

flapper	Benito Mussolini
Harlem Renaissance	command economy
Franklin Delano Roosevelt	Gulag
disarmament	Ruhr Valley
totalitarian state	Third Reich

1. rebellious young woman of the 1920s
2. leader of the first modern fascist state
3. reduction of armed forces and weapons
4. government in which a one-party dictatorship regulates every aspect of citizens' lives
5. president of the United States who established the New Deal to help Americans during the Great Depression
6. African American cultural movement in the 1920s and 1930s
7. coal-rich industrial region of Germany

Main Ideas

Section 1 (pp. 522–527)
8. How did Western culture and society change in reaction to World War I?

Section 2 (pp. 529–535)
9. Describe the search for peace in the 1920s and its results.
10. What were the effects of the Great Depression?

Section 3 (pp. 536–540)
11. What is fascism?
12. How did Mussolini's fascist regime rule Italy?

Section 4 (pp. 542–549)
13. Summarize conditions in the Soviet Union under Stalin.

Section 5 (pp. 550–555)
14. How did Hitler establish a totalitarian state in Germany?

Chapter Focus Question
15. What political and economic challenges did the Western world face in the 1920s and 1930s, and how did various countries react to these challenges?

Critical Thinking

16. **Synthesize Information** How did the literature and art of the 1920s reflect the influence of World War I?
17. **Identify Causes** What imbalances helped cause the Great Depression of the 1930s?
18. **Recognize Ideologies** Why did the ideology of fascism appeal to many Italians?
19. **Compare Points of View** Describe the similarities and differences between fascism and communism.
20. **Recognize Propaganda** Why was propaganda an important tool of totalitarian dictators?
21. **Make Comparisons** Both Germany under Hitler and the Nazis and the Soviet Union under Stalin and the Communists were totalitarian states. How was totalitarian rule similar in these two countries? How did Nazi totalitarianism differ from that of the Communist Soviet Union?

● Writing About History

In this chapter's five Section Assessments, you developed skills for writing a compare-and-contrast essay.

Writing a Compare-and-Contrast Essay The period between World War I and World War II was a time of rapid change with some serious crises of its own. Write a compare-and-contrast essay on one of the following pairs of ideas: society before and after World War I, solutions to alleviate the Great Depression in the United States and in Germany, fascism compared to democracy in the 1920s and 1930s, or a topic of your own choosing.

Prewriting
• Choose a valid topic for your essay by choosing two things that are neither too similar nor wildly different.

• Choose categories in which the two items could be compared and contrasted.
• Use a Venn diagram to gather and record details for your essay.

Drafting
• Develop a thesis that introduces the items you are comparing and the point you intend to make by the comparison.
• Outline how you will organize your arguments and the details that will support them.
• Write an introduction explaining what you are comparing and contrasting, a body, and a conclusion that restates your main points.

Revising
• Use the guidelines for revising your essay on page SH12 of the Writing Handbook.

Critical Thinking

16. Some writers' work reflected an aversion to war and the moral breakdown of Western civilization. Many artists turned away from trying to reproduce reality.

17. More goods were being produced than consumers could afford to buy. Also, wealth in the United States was unevenly distributed.

18. Fascism promised a strong, stable government and tried to revive national pride.

19. Under communism the state controls all economic activity, while fascism preserves capitalism, though under the control of a dictatorship. Both communism and fascism glorify the state over the individual and do not respect human rights.

20. It helped totalitarian leaders control and indoctrinate people with their ideology.

21. Responses should list similar totalitarian features and differences between communism and Nazi ideology.

Document-Based Assessment

Hitler's Rise to Power

In 1919, Hitler joined the National Socialist German Workers Party, later known as the Nazi party. It was a marginal party that only received one million votes in 1924. By 1932, however, the Nazi party, with Hitler at its helm, was Germany's largest party. Many factors contributed to Hitler's surprising rise to power, as the documents below illustrate.

Document A

This poster, displayed in Berlin in 1932, tells voters: "We want work and bread! Elect Hitler!"

Document B

"The National Socialist movement must strive to eliminate the disproportion between our population and our area—viewing this latter as a source of food as well as a basis for power politics. . . . We must hold unflinchingly to our aim . . . to secure for the German people the land and soil to which they are entitled. . . ."

—From ***Mein Kampf*** by Adolf Hitler

Document C

". . . [T]hough the Fuehrer's anti-Semitic programme furnished the National Socialist party in the first instance with a nucleus and a rallying-cry, it was swept into office by two things with which the "Jewish Problem" did not have the slightest connexion. On the one side was economic distress and the revulsion against Versailles; on the other, chicanery and intrigue. . . . Hitler and his party had promised the unhappy Germans a new heaven and a new earth, coupled with the persecution of the Jews. Unfortunately, a new heaven and earth cannot be manufactured to order. But a persecution of the Jews can. . . ."

—From ***The Jewish Problem*** by Louis Golding, 1939

Document D

"The Versailles settlement was seen as a means by which Germany's enemies aimed to keep the Reich prostrate forever and had to be overturned not merely to restore the status quo ante, but to allow Germany to expand and seize the "living space" that it allegedly needed in the east. And violence was viewed as the means by which to achieve a Third Reich and a German-dominated Europe—by smashing the democratic Weimar "system," destroying Marxism, solving the "Jewish question," breaking the "chains of Versailles," and building up the armed forces so that Germany again could go to war."

—From ***Nazism and War*** by historian Richard Bessel

Analyzing Documents

Use your knowledge of the rise of Nazism in Germany and Documents A, B, C, and D to answer questions 1–4.

1. Document A focuses on which factor that aided Hitler's rise to power?
   A anger over World War I
   B social considerations
   C the economy
   D racial and religious prejudice

2. According to Document C, the Nazis persecuted the Jews, because
   A most Germans hated them.
   B they wanted to keep attention from other problems.
   C they had already achieved their other goals.
   D their opponents were all Jews.

3. According to Document D, the Nazis' main goal was to
   A dominate Europe.
   B get revenge for the Treaty of Versailles.
   C stop communism.
   D end democracy.

4. Explain why Germany was fertile soil for the Nazis following World War I. Give your reasons, using these documents and information from the chapter.

● Writing About History

As students begin the assignment, refer them to p. SH10 of the **Writing Handbook** for help in writing a compare-and-contrast essay. Remind them of the steps they should take to complete their assignment, including prewriting, drafting, and revising. For help in revising, remind them to use the guidelines on p. SH12 of the **Writing Handbook.**

Students' compare-and-contrast essays should have a clear thesis that introduces the subjects to be compared and the main point to be made. They should include details that reveal the similarities and differences between the subjects and use transitions to make the relationships clear. The essays should also contain an introduction, a body, and a conclusion and be free of grammatical and spelling errors. For scoring rubrics for writing assignments, see **Assessment Rubrics,** p. 8.

World War II and Its Aftermath

Section	Core Instruction L3	Differentiated Instruction L1 L2 L4	

Section 1
From Appeasement to War

 2 periods, 1 block

OBJECTIVES
- Analyze the threat to world peace posed by dictators in the 1930s and how the Western democracies responded.
- Describe how the Spanish Civil War was a "dress rehearsal" for World War II.
- Summarize the ways in which continuing Nazi aggression led Europe to war.

Focus Question *What events unfolded between Chamberlain's declaration of "peace for our time" and the outbreak of a world war?*

All in One **Teaching Resources, Unit 4**
Reading Strategy: Recognize Sequence, p. 71
Vocabulary Builder: Word Maps, p. 70
Section 1 Quiz, p. 65

Reading and Note Taking Study Guide
Note Taking Study Guide, p. 179
Section 1 Summary, p. 180

Note Taking Transparencies, 184A–184B

WITNESS HISTORY **Audio CD**
A Desperate Peace

Progress Monitoring Transparencies, 123

Color Transparencies, 174

Teaching Resources, Skills Handbook
Prereading the Chapter, pp. 1–2
Word Knowledge Rating Form, p. 3
K-W-L Chart, p. 4

L1 **Adapted Reading and Note Taking Study Guide**
Note Taking Study Guide, p. 179 **SN**
Section 1 Summary, p. 180 **SN**

L2 **Adapted Reading and Note Taking Study Guide**
Note Taking Study Guide, p. 179 **LPR**
Section 1 Summary, p. 180 **LPR**

Spanish Reading and Note Taking Study Guide
Note Taking Study Guide, p. 179 **ELL**
Section 1 Summary, p. 180 **ELL**

L4 **All in One** **Teaching Resources, Unit 4**
Viewpoints: Can Hitler Be Trusted?, p. 72 **AR, GT**

*Student Edition Audio **SN**

Differentiated Instruction Activity, Teacher's Edition, p. 563 **SN**

*Guided Reading Audio, Spanish **ELL**

*Student Edition Audio **LPR**

Differentiated Instruction Activity, Teacher's Edition, p. 563 **LPR**

Extend Activity, Teacher's Edition, p. 567 **AR, GT**

Section 2
The Axis Advances

 2 periods, 1 block

OBJECTIVES
- Describe how the Axis powers came to control much of Europe, but failed to conquer Britain.
- Summarize Germany's invasion of the Soviet Union.
- Understand the horror of the genocide the Nazis committed.
- Describe the role of the United States before and after joining World War II.

Focus Question *Which regions were attacked and occupied by the Axis powers, and what was life like under their occupation?*

All in One **Teaching Resources, Unit 4**
Section 2 Quiz, p. 66

Reading and Note Taking Study Guide
Note Taking Study Guide, p. 181
Section 2 Summary, p. 182

Note Taking Transparencies, 185A–185B

WITNESS HISTORY **Audio CD**
Janina's War Story; Winston Churchill, June 4, 1940; Surviving the Blitz

Progress Monitoring Transparencies, 124

Color Transparencies, 175

L1 **Adapted Reading and Note Taking Study Guide**
Note Taking Study Guide, p. 181 **SN**
Section 2 Summary, p. 182 **SN**

L2 **Adapted Reading and Note Taking Study Guide**
Note Taking Study Guide, p. 181 **LPR**
Section 2 Summary, p. 182 **LPR**

L4 **All in One** **Teaching Resources, Unit 4**
Primary Source: From *The Diary of a Young Girl*, by Anne Frank, p. 73 **AR, GT**
Link to Literature: From *Night*, by Elie Wiesel, p. 74 **AR, GT**

Differentiated Instruction Activity, Teacher's Edition, pp. 571, 575 **SN**

Spanish Reading and Note Taking Study Guide
Note Taking Study Guide, p. 181 **ELL**
Section 2 Summary, p. 182 **ELL**

Differentiated Instruction Activity, Teacher's Edition, pp. 571, 575 **LPR, ELL**

Differentiated Instruction Activity, Teacher's Edition, p. 572 **AR, GT**

Extend Activity, Teacher's Edition, pp. 560c, 576 **AR, GT**

*Audio support is available for all sections.

Assessment Resources
- **Progress Monitoring Transparencies,** 123–127
- **Test Prep,** Unit Study Sheets, pp. 103–105; Unit Test, pp. 34–37
- **SuccessTracker™,** Chapter 17
- **Document-Based Assessment,** pp. 80–94
- *ExamView®* **Test Bank CD-ROM,** Chapter 17

- **All in One** **Teaching Resources, Unit 4,** Chapter Tests A and B, pp. 80–85
- **Progress Monitoring** *Online* **Quizzes,** Chapter 17
- **Assessment Rubrics**

Differentiated Instruction Key

L1 Special Needs		**LPR** Less Proficient Readers	
L2 Basic to Average		**AR** Advanced Readers	
L3 All Students		**SN** Special Needs Students	
L4 Average to Advanced		**GT** Gifted and Talented	
		ELL English Language Learner	

Section	Core Instruction L3	Differentiated Instruction L1 L2 L4	
Section 3 *The Allies Turn the Tide* ⏱ **2 periods, 1 block** **OBJECTIVES** ■ Understand how nations devoted all of their resources to fighting World War II. ■ Explain how Allied victories began to push back the Axis powers. ■ Describe D-Day and the Allied advance toward Germany. **Focus Question** *How did the Allies begin to push back the Axis powers?*	**All in One Teaching Resources, Unit 4** Outline Map: Europe and North Africa, p. 77 Geography Quiz, p. 79 Section 3 Quiz, p. 67 **Reading and Note Taking Study Guide** Note Taking Study Guide, p. 183 Section 3 Summary, p. 184 **Note Taking Transparencies**, 186 **WITNESS HISTORY Audio CD** Support the War! **Progress Monitoring Transparencies**, 125 **Color Transparencies**, 176, 177 **Witness History Discovery School™** video program, *Triumph at Normandy*	**L1 Adapted Reading and Note Taking Study Guide** Note Taking Study Guide, p. 183 SN Section 3 Summary, p. 184 SN **L2 Adapted Reading and Note Taking Study Guide** Note Taking Study Guide, p. 183 LPR Section 3 Summary, p. 184 LPR **L4 Differentiated Instruction Activity,** Teacher's Edition, p. 582 AR, GT	**Differentiated Instruction Activity,** Teacher's Edition, pp. 580, 584 SN **Spanish Reading and Note Taking Study Guide** Note Taking Study Guide, p. 183 ELL Section 3 Summary, p. 184 ELL **Differentiated Instruction Activity,** Teacher's Edition, pp. 580, 584 LPR, ELL **Extend Activity,** Teacher's Edition, p. 583 AR, GT
Section 4 *Victory in Europe, the Pacific* ⏱ **1 period, .5 block** **OBJECTIVES** ■ Describe the reasons for the final defeat of the Nazis. ■ Summarize how the Allies began to push back the Japanese in the Pacific. ■ Explain the American strategy for ending the war against Japan and the consequences of that strategy. **Focus Question** *How did the Allies finally defeat the Axis powers?*	**All in One Teaching Resources, Unit 4** Outline Map: The War in the Pacific, p. 78 Section 4 Quiz, p. 68 **Reading and Note Taking Study Guide** Note Taking Study Guide, p. 185 Section 4 Summary, p. 186 **Note Taking Transparencies**, 187 **WITNESS HISTORY Audio CD** A Soldier Remembers **Progress Monitoring Transparencies**, 126 **Color Transparencies**, 178	**L1 Adapted Reading and Note Taking Study Guide** Note Taking Study Guide, p. 185 SN Section 4 Summary, p. 186 SN **L2 Adapted Reading and Note Taking Study Guide** Note Taking Study Guide, p. 185 LPR Section 4 Summary, p. 186 LPR **L4 All in One Teaching Resources, Unit 4** Primary Source: From *Hiroshima*, by John Hersey, p. 75	**Differentiated Instruction Activity,** Teacher's Edition, p. 587 SN **Spanish Reading and Note Taking Study Guide** Note Taking Study Guide, p. 185 ELL Section 4 Summary, p. 186 ELL **Differentiated Instruction Activity,** Teacher's Edition, p. 587 LPR, ELL **Extend Activity,** Teacher's Edition, p. 589 AR, GT
Section 5 *The End of World War II* ⏱ **2 periods, 1 block** **OBJECTIVES** ■ Describe the issues faced by the Allies after World War II ended. ■ Summarize the organization of the United Nations. ■ Analyze how new conflicts developed among the former Allies after World War II. **Focus Question** *What issues arose in the aftermath of World War II and how did new tensions develop?*	**All in One Teaching Resources, Unit 4** Section 5 Quiz, p. 69 **Reading and Note Taking Study Guide** Note Taking Study Guide, pp. 187–188 Section 5 Summary, p. 189 Concept Connector, pp. 237, 242, 250, 267, 295 **Note Taking Transparencies**, 188 **WITNESS HISTORY Audio CD** The War is Over! **Progress Monitoring Transparencies**, 127 **Color Transparencies**, 179	**L1 Adapted Reading and Note Taking Study Guide** Note Taking Study Guide, pp. 187–188 Section 5 Summary, p. 189 Concept Connector, pp. 237, 242, 250, 267, 295 **L2 Adapted Reading and Note Taking Study Guide** Note Taking Study Guide, pp. 187–188 LPR Section 5 Summary, p. 189 LPR Concept Connector, pp. 237, 242, 250, 267, 295 LPR **L4 All in One Teaching Resources, Unit 4** Biography: Harry Truman, p. 76 AR, GT	**Differentiated Instruction Activity,** Teacher's Edition, p. 592 **Spanish Reading and Note Taking Study Guide** Note Taking Study Guide, pp. 187–188 ELL Section 5 Summary, p. 189 ELL Concept Connector, pp. 237, 242, 250, 267, 295 ELL **Differentiated Instruction Activity,** Teacher's Edition, p. 592 LPR **Differentiated Instruction Activity,** Teacher's Edition, p. 591 AR, GT **Extend Activity,** Teacher's Edition, p. 594 AR, GT

Author's Notes

Causes of World War II

Given what has been said about the nature of totalitarian governments, it is easy to see World War II as a splendid illustration of the "devil theory" of history—aggressive dictators on one side, democracies on the other. Certainly, Germany, Italy, and Japan were aggressive, militaristic, and expansionist in the 1930s. On the other hand, Stalin's Russia was as totalitarian as Hitler's Germany, and "Uncle Joe" at least finished the war on the Allied side. . . .

A related approach having much appeal because it seems to carry a message for our time is to see the cause of the war as Allied appeasement of Axis aggression. Again, there is much truth in this view, as will be apparent when we follow the grim sequence of crises down the thirties to the final confrontation over Poland in 1939. Yet this approach also is incomplete, for it does little to explain why the Axis powers were aggressive and expansionist in the first place.

Deeper, long-range causes for the Second World War include the World Depression, the Versailles peace after World War I, and perhaps, some deeply disturbing features of the global political order.

The Great Depression certainly accounted in significant part for Hitler's rise to power and for the decline of party government in Japan. Military expenditures were also a good way for Hitler and other totalitarian leaders to put people back to work in a hurry. Perhaps most important, however, the Depression left the Western democracies badly weakened in the 1930s. Preoccupied by domestic problems . . . democratic leaders found appeasement and the avoidance of the confrontation as natural as aggressive rhetoric was to the heads of militarized totalitarian states. . . .

Though they didn't know it then, revisionist dictators demanding justice and defenders of the international status quo pointing to the sanctity of treaties, militarists and appeasers, aggressive politicians, and peoples who were simply too busy with the Depression to care about the international situation all in their different ways contributed to the coming of the biggest war in history.

—Anthony Esler, *The Human Venture: From Prehistory to the Present*, (Upper Saddle River, New Jersey: Pearson Education, 2004), pp. 654–655

Extend Online

Kindertransport

Have students research first-person accounts of the Kindertransport, which allowed nearly 10,000 children to escape Nazi persecution. Ask them to read selections to the class. Use the steps below to help students complete the activity.

Prepare for the Activity Explain that as Hitler's persecution increased, Jewish parents were desperate to get their children to safety. In what became known as "The Kindertransport," children from Central Europe were sent to England to live in orphanages or with foster families. Many never saw their parents again.

Conduct the Activity For help in starting the activity, send students to **Web Code nbe-2901.** Students will read first-person accounts of the Kindertransport and present excerpts of their choosing to the class. Be sure that students explain who wrote the excerpt, the circumstances in which it was written, and why they chose it.

Follow-Up Conduct a class discussion based on the following questions: To what extraordinary lengths must people go in times of war? How did the war create heroes out of the ordinary people who took in the Kindertransport children? What other acts of moral courage take place during times of war?

Differentiated Instruction   Solutions for All Learners

Making Predictions ⓵ ⓶

One way to help struggling readers learn effective reading skills is to have students practice making predictions. To begin, offer these guidelines and model the process.

1. Preview the pictures in the section prior to reading the text.

2. Ask questions prompted by the graph, photograph, or painting.

3. Make predictions that will answer these questions.

4. Read the text and answer the questions they think were addressed.

Finding Patterns in History ⓸

Learning to find patterns in history helps students make connections among events and time periods and to see relevance to their own times. Comparing World War I and World War II requires higher-level thinking and presents an excellent opportunity for this exercise.

Suggest that students keep a "Patterns Diary" in which they make comparisons between the two world wars as they read this chapter. One column should be labeled World War I and the other World War II. Categories may include:

- causes
- countries and leaders
- life on the homefront
- military technology
- human costs of war
- effects

Students may also work together to brainstorm their own list of categories. When they have completed their reading, have students draw three to five conclusions from their Patterns Diaries.

Modeling Reading and Writing Skills

Organizing Topics Explain that in this chapter students will be writing a research report. (See Writing About History, p. 598.) Point out that research writing needs to be effectively organized in order to communicate clearly with an audience. Write these common ways of organizing on the board and label them A–C.

A Chronological Order
B Part-to-Whole Order
C Order of Importance

Explain that in chronological order, events are presented in sequence. In part-to-whole order, aspects or parts of a larger topic are described one by one to build a complete picture. In order of importance, details are presented from most to least important. Help students match the three types of organization with the following topics:

1. safety and driving, including the importance of following the rules of the road and ensuring one is wide awake when behind the wheel

2. the Jazz Age, including literature, music, and social change

3. the events that led to World War I
(Answers: A3; B2; C1)

Sequence Tell students that when you see events in sequence, you appreciate how one event follows the other in chronological order. Point out that noting the order in which events take place can help you understand and remember them.

Model how to recognize sequence by reading aloud the first paragraph under *Hitler Defies World War I Treaty* in Section 1. Draw students' attention to the first word of the second sentence *(first)* and point out that this word signals the beginning of a sequence of events. The first event is that Hitler built up the German military. The next sentence in the paragraph begins with the word *Then,* which indicates an event that takes place after the first one. The second event is that Hitler sent troops into the Rhineland.

Teach With Technology

PresentationEXPRESS™
Premium DVD

- Teach this chapter's core content using **PresentationExpress™ Premium,** which includes dynamic lecture notes, interactive game shows, songs, videos, and the *ExamView® QuickTake* assessment tool.

- To introduce this chapter using **PresentationExpress™ Premium,** start by asking students **Which of the following statements do you most agree with? (A) Civilians should expect to be attacked if their country goes to war. (B) Civilians should expect to be attacked away from the battlefront only if they are aiding in the war effort. (C) Civilians should expect to be attacked only if they are supporting troops at the battlefront. (D) Civilians should expect to be free from deliberate attack even at the battlefront.** Take a class poll or record students' answers using the QuickTake feature and discuss their responses. Point out that in this chapter, they will read about how civilians became embroiled in World War II. Continue introducing the chapter using the chapter opener slide show and Witness History audio.

Technology Resources

- Student**EXPRESS** CD-ROM, Chapter 17

- Teacher**EXPRESS** CD-ROM, Chapter 17

- Presentation**EXPRESS™ Premium DVD,** Chapter 17

- **WITNESS HISTORY Audio CD,** Chapter 17

- *ExamView* **Test Bank CD-ROM,** English and Spanish, Chapter 17

- **Guided Reading Audio,** Spanish, Chapter 17

- **Student Edition Audio,** Chapter 17

- **Witness History Discovery School™** video program, *Triumph at Normandy*

- **Experience It! Multimedia Pack**

World War II and Its Aftermath
1931–1955

Bibliography

For the Teacher

Commanger, Henry Steele, and Donald L. Miller. *The Story of World War II.* New York: Simon & Schuster, 2001. First published in 1945.

Kirk, Tim, and Anthony McElligott, eds. *Opposing Fascism: Community, Authority, and Resistance in Europe.* New York: Cambridge University Press, 1999.

Willmott, H. P., et al., eds. *World War II.* London: DK, 2004.

For the Student

L2 Gottfried, Ted. *Children of the Slaughter: Young People of the Holocaust.* Brookfield, Conn.: Twenty-First Century Books, 2001.

L3 Levine, Ellen. *Darkness Over Denmark: The Danish Resistance and the Rescue of the Jews.* New York: Holiday House, 2000.

L4 Hersey, John. *Hiroshima.* New York: Vintage, 1989.

WITNESS HISTORY 🔊 AUDIO

A City Lies in Ruins

March 6, 1944—The Allies' mission to bomb Berlin, Germany, includes 810 bombers plus 800 fighter escorts. The stream of aircraft stretches a mile wide and a half-mile deep and takes more than half an hour to pass over any given point. Approaching the city, the bombers press on through flak—anti-aircraft fire from the ground—"so thick you can walk on it." Then, bomb bay doors open, and their payloads rain down on the city.

Listen to the Witness History audio to hear more about the Allied bombing efforts.

◀ Cologne, Germany, in ruins, 1944

Chapter Preview

Chapter Focus Question How did aggressive world powers emerge, and what did it take to defeat them during World War II?

Section 1
From Appeasement to War

Section 2
The Axis Advances

Section 3
The Allies Turn the Tide

Section 4
Victory in Europe and the Pacific

Section 5
The End of World War II

Use the ☑ Quick Study Timeline at the end of this chapter to preview chapter events.

Japanese pilot's goggles recovered from Pearl Harbor

"Cricket" noisemakers used by Allied paratroopers to locate each other after landing

Thanks to PENICILLIN
...He Will Come Home!

FROM ORDINARY MOLD—
the Greatest Healing Agent of this War!

SCHENLEY LABORATORIES, INC.

An advertisement praising the benefits of penicillin

? Concept Connector ONLINE

To explore Essential Questions related to this chapter, go to PHSchool.com
Web Code: nbd-2907

Previewing the Chapter

■ **WITNESS HISTORY** Explain that late in the war, Allied bombers struck deep within Germany, resulting in massive destruction of German cities, but ultimately ensuring Allied victory. Read the Witness History selection aloud or play the accompanying audio. Then ask students to list words that came to mind as they listened to the Witness History selection. Be sure that they understand the danger and high stakes of the Allied bombing missions.

🔊 AUDIO **Witness History Audio CD,** A City Lies in Ruins

■ **Analyzing the Visuals** Ask students to study the photo of the young refugee resting her bags amidst the destruction of the German city of Cologne. Ask **What questions do the photo and the Witness History selection bring to mind?** *(Sample: Why did the Allies risk the lives of so many pilots to bomb cities like Cologne? What effects did bombing raids like this have on Germany's war effort and on the morale of German people? Was it right to bring the war to civilians in this way?)* As students offer questions, write them down. Tell students you will keep a copy of the questions so that they can go back and answer them after reading the chapter.

■ **Focus** Write the Chapter Focus Question on the board. Tell students to keep this question in mind as they read the chapter. *(Answer appears with Chapter Assessment answers.)* Have students preview the section titles for this chapter.

Objectives

As you teach this section, keep students focused on the following objectives to help them answer the Section Focus Question and master core content.

- Analyze the threat to world peace posed by dictators in the 1930s and how the Western democracies responded.
- Describe how the Spanish Civil War was a "dress rehearsal" for World War II.
- Summarize the ways in which continuing Nazi aggression led Europe to war.

Build Background Knowledge 🔳

Ask students to recall the rise of dictators during the early 1930s. Based on their previous reading, have them predict what they think the dictators will do next.

Set a Purpose 🔳

- **WITNESS HISTORY** Read the selection aloud or play the audio.

  🔊)) AUDIO **Witness History Audio CD,** A Desperate Peace

  Ask **What is the main idea of Chamberlain's speech?** (*He believes he has achieved an agreement that means lasting peace with Germany.*) Ask students to predict how long the peace will last.

- **Focus** Point out the Section Focus Question and write it on the board. Tell students to refer to this question as they read. (*Answer appears with Section 1 Assessment answers.*)

- **Preview** Have students preview the Section Objectives and the list of Terms, People, and Places.

- **Reading Skill** Have students use the *Reading Strategy: Recognize Sequence* worksheet.

  All in One Teaching Resources, Unit 4, p. 71

- **Note Taking** As students read, have them fill in the table sequencing the events that led to World War II.

  Reading and Note Taking Study Guide, p. 179

SECTION **1**

A Desperate Peace

British Prime Minister Neville Chamberlain spoke to a jubilant crowd upon returning to London from a conference with Adolf Hitler in Munich, Germany, in September 1938:

> 66 For the second time in our history, a British Prime Minister has returned from Germany bringing peace with honor. I believe it is peace for our time . . . Go home and get a nice quiet sleep. 99

Focus Question What events unfolded between Chamberlain's declaration of "peace for our time" and the outbreak of a world war?

Neville Chamberlain and headlines announcing the Munich Pact

From Appeasement to War

Objectives

- Analyze the threat to world peace posed by dictators in the 1930s and how the Western democracies responded.
- Describe how the Spanish Civil War was a "dress rehearsal" for World War II.
- Summarize the ways in which continuing Nazi aggression led Europe to war.

Terms, People, and Places

appeasement	Francisco Franco
pacifism	Anschluss
Neutrality Acts	Sudetenland
Axis powers	Nazi-Soviet Pact

Note Taking

Reading Skill: Recognize Sequence As you read, keep track of the sequence of events that led to the outbreak of World War II by completing a table like the one below.

Acts of Aggression	
Japan	
Italy	
Germany	
Spain	

After the horrors of World War I, Western democracies desperately tried to preserve peace during the 1930s while ignoring signs that the rulers of Germany, Italy, and Japan were preparing to build new empires. Despite the best efforts of Neville Chamberlain and other Western leaders, the world was headed to war again.

Aggression Goes Unchecked

Throughout the 1930s, challenges to peace followed a pattern. Dictators took aggressive action but met only verbal protests and pleas for peace from the democracies. Mussolini, Hitler, and the leaders of Japan viewed that desire for peace as weakness and responded with new acts of aggression. With hindsight, we can see the shortcomings of the democracies' policies. These policies, however, were the product of long and careful deliberation. At the time, some people believed they would work.

Japan Overruns Manchuria and Eastern China One of the earliest tests had been posed by Japan. Japanese military leaders and ultranationalists thought that Japan should have an empire equal to those of the Western powers. In pursuit of this goal, Japan seized Manchuria in 1931. When the League of Nations condemned the aggression, Japan simply withdrew from the organization. Japan's easy success strengthened the militarist faction in Japan. In 1937, Japanese armies overran much of eastern China, starting the Second Sino-Japanese War. Once again, Western protests did not stop Japan.

Vocabulary Builder

Use the information below and the following resources to teach the high-use words from this section.

All in One Teaching Resources, Unit 4, p. 70; **Teaching Resources, Skills Handbook,** p. 3

High-Use Words	Definitions and Sample Sentences
sanctions, p. 563	*n.* penalties Too many traffic tickets could result in **sanctions,** such as the loss of your license.
technology, p. 567	*n.* scientific advances applied to practical purposes New in space **technology** made it possible for astronauts to walk on the moon.

Hitler Remilitarizes Germany
Hitler rebuilt the German military during the 1930s in defiance of the Treaty of Versailles. The government's investment in armaments also helped pull Germany out of the Great Depression. Here, German police march in goose step as Hitler salutes in the background. *How did rearmament affect the rest of Germany?*

Italy Invades Ethiopia In Italy, Mussolini decided to act on his own imperialist ambitions. Italy's defeat by the Ethiopians at the battle of Adowa in 1896 still rankled. In 1935, Italy invaded Ethiopia, located in northeastern Africa. Although the Ethiopians resisted bravely, their outdated weapons were no match for Mussolini's tanks, machine guns, poison gas, and airplanes. The Ethiopian king Haile Selassie (HY luh suh lah SEE) appealed to the League of Nations for help. The League voted <u>sanctions</u> against Italy for violating international law. But the League had no power to enforce the sanctions, and by early 1936, Italy had conquered Ethiopia.

Hitler Goes Against the Treaty of Versailles By then, Hitler, too, had tested the will of the Western democracies and found it weak. First, he built up the German military in defiance of the treaty that had ended World War I. Then, in 1936, he sent troops into the "demilitarized" Rhineland bordering France—another treaty violation.

Germans hated the Versailles treaty, and Hitler's successful challenge made him more popular at home. The Western democracies denounced his moves but took no real action. Instead, they adopted a policy of **appeasement,** or giving in to the demands of an aggressor in order to keep the peace.

Keeping the Peace The Western policy of appeasement developed for a number of reasons. France was demoralized, suffering from political divisions at home. It could not take on Hitler without British support. The British, however, had no desire to confront the German dictator. Some even thought that Hitler's actions constituted a justifiable response to the terms of the Treaty of Versailles, which they believed had been too harsh on Germany.

In both Britain and France, many saw Hitler and fascism as a defense against a worse evil—the spread of Soviet communism. Additionally, the Great Depression sapped the energies of the Western democracies. Finally, widespread **pacifism,** or opposition to all war, and disgust with the destruction from the previous war pushed many governments to seek peace at any price.

Vocabulary Builder
<u>sanctions</u>—(SANGK shunz) *n.* penalties

Aggression Goes Unchecked

Instruct

■ **Introduce: Vocabulary Builder** Have students read the Vocabulary Builder term and definition. Use the Idea Wave strategy (TE, p. T22) and ask **What is an example of a** *sanction* **that a school might use to penalize disruptive students?** *(Sample: detention, suspension, removal from a sports team)*

■ **Teach** Trace Japanese, Italian, and German aggression during the 1930s. Ask **Why were these countries aggressors during this time?** *(They each wanted to fulfill imperialist ambitions.)* **Why didn't the Western democracies stop this aggression?** *(France was struggling with divisions at home; the British did not want to confront the dictators; some people thought Hitler's actions were justified in light of the Versailles Treaty; many saw fascism as preferable to communism; pacifism was widespread.)*

■ **Quick Activity** Point out that during the 1930s, many pacifists were working to avoid war at all costs. Have students, in small groups, discuss the following questions: What is pacifism and could it be a wise policy? Would students have supported pacifist goals if they had lived in the 1930s?

Independent Practice

Ask students to take the role of a French political leader during the 1930s and choose an act of aggression by one of the Axis powers. Have students write a brief speech outlining what they think the act of aggression shows about the country undertaking it, how they think their country should respond, and why that is the best response.

Monitor Progress

As students complete their tables, circulate to make sure they understand the growing aggression of the dictatorships. For a completed version of the table, see
📖 **Note Taking Transparencies, 184A**

Answer

Caption helped its economy, raised morale, increased Hitler's popularity

Spain Collapses Into Civil War

Instruct

- **Introduce** Have students read the red heading Spain Collapses Into Civil War. Ask students to predict the impact that this war will have on the rest of Europe. Then have them read to find out whether their predictions were accurate.

- **Teach** Discuss the effects of the Spanish Civil War. Ask **How was the Spanish Civil War another step in the march toward world war?** *(The Nazis were able to experiment with their new weapons; it produced open conflict between fascist and anti-fascist forces; it probably increased fears of spreading fascism.)*

Independent Practice

Break students into small groups and assign each group one of the following countries: Germany, Italy, the Soviet Union, Britain, France, or the United States. Have each group identify which side its country took in the Spanish Civil War (or whether it took no side at all) and find reasons for that choice. Then have the groups report their findings to the class.

Monitor Progress

Point out the Faces of Aggression photos. To help students review the section so far, ask them to briefly explain the significance of each of the leaders pictured.

Faces of Aggression

Three leaders in Europe and one in Japan launched ambitious plans to increase their power.

● Benito Mussolini—Italy

● Adolf Hitler—Germany

● Tojo Hideki—Japan

● Francisco Franco—Spain

As war clouds gathered in Europe in the mid-1930s, the United States Congress passed a series of Neutrality Acts. One law forbade the sale of arms to any nation at war. Others outlawed loans to warring nations and prohibited Americans from traveling on ships of warring powers. The fundamental goal of American policy, however, was to avoid involvement in a European war, not to prevent such a conflict.

Rome-Berlin-Tokyo Axis In the face of the apparent weakness of Britain, France, and the United States, Germany, Italy, and Japan formed what became known as the Rome-Berlin-Tokyo Axis. Known as the Axis powers, the three nations agreed to fight Soviet communism. They also agreed not to interfere with one another's plans for territorial expansion. The agreement cleared the way for these anti-democratic, aggressor powers to take even bolder steps.

✓ **Checkpoint** Describe the German, Italian, and Japanese drives for empire.

Spain Collapses Into Civil War

In 1936, a local struggle in Spain polarized public opinion throughout Europe. Trouble in Spain started in 1931, when popular unrest against the old order forced the king to leave Spain. A republic was set up with a new, more liberal constitution. The government passed a series of controversial reforms, taking land and privileges away from the Church and old ruling classes. Still, leftists demanded more radical reforms. Conservatives, backed by the military, rejected change.

In 1936, a conservative general named Francisco Franco led a revolt that touched off a bloody civil war. Fascists and supporters of right-wing policies, called Nationalists, rallied to back Franco. Supporters of the republic, known as Loyalists, included Communists, Socialists, and those who wanted democracy.

People from other nations soon jumped in to support both sides. Hitler and Mussolini sent arms and forces to help Franco. The Soviet Union sent soldiers to fight against fascism alongside the Spanish Loyalists. Although the governments of Britain, France, and the United States remained neutral, individuals from those countries, as well as other countries, also fought with the Loyalists. Anti-Nazi Germans and anti-Fascist Italians joined the Loyalist cause as well.

Both sides committed horrible atrocities. The ruinous struggle took more than 500,000 lives. One of the worst horrors was a German air raid on Guernica, a small Spanish market town, in April 1937. German planes dropped their load of bombs, and then swooped low to machine-gun anyone who had survived the bombs. Nearly 1,000 innocent civilians were killed. To Nazi leaders, the attack on Guernica was an experiment to identify what their new planes could do. To the rest of the world, it was a grim warning of the destructive power of modern warfare.

By 1939, Franco had triumphed. Once in power, he created a fascist dictatorship similar to the dictatorships of Hitler and Mussolini. He rolled back earlier reforms, killed or jailed enemies, and used terror to promote order.

✓ **Checkpoint** How did the Spanish Civil War involve combatants from other countries?

Answers

✓ Japan seized Manchuria in 1931 and invaded eastern China in 1937. Italy invaded Ethiopia in 1935 and conquered it the following year. Hitler built up the German military and sent troops into the Rhineland.

✓ Hitler and Mussolini sent arms and forces to help the fascist Franco; Stalin sent troops to fight against him; people from other countries who opposed fascism volunteered to fight on the side of the Loyalists.

Link to Humanities

Picasso's *Guernica* In 1937, the Spanish republican government commissioned Pablo Picasso to paint a memorial to the destruction of Guernica. His painting, titled simply *Guernica*, is filled with fragmented structures and broken human bodies. In a scene of overwhelming anguish and suffering, a wailing mother holds her dead child; a distraught woman rushes from a building; and other people appear with arms and heads extended in the pain of death.

Picasso also made extensive use of symbolism in this work. A horse may stand for Spain under attack; a bull, familiar from Spanish bullfighting and folk tales, could represent human irrationality. An electric light may symbolize the destructive power of modern technology, while an oil lamp might show humanity's resistance to war's atrocities. In *Guernica*, Picasso shows how war's destructive power and irrational nature can unleash terror and torment on humankind.

German Aggression Continues

In the meantime, Hitler pursued his goal of bringing all German-speaking people into the Third Reich. He also took steps to gain "living space" for Germans in Eastern Europe. Hitler, who believed in the superiority of the German people, thought that Germany had a right to conquer the Slavs to the east. Hitler claimed, "I have the right to remove millions of an inferior race that breeds like vermin."

Hitler's aggressive plans also served economic purposes. Production of military equipment would benefit German industry, which would also gain new raw materials and markets in the east.

Austria Annexed By March, 1938, Hitler was ready to engineer the Anschluss (AHN shloos), or union of Austria and Germany. When Austria's chancellor refused to agree to Hitler's demands, Hitler sent in the German army to "preserve order." To indicate his new role as ruler of Austria, Hitler made a speech from the Hofburg Palace, the former residence of the Hapsburg emperors.

The Anschluss violated the Versailles treaty and created a brief war scare. Some Austrians favored annexation. Hitler quickly silenced any Austrians who opposed it. And since the Western democracies took no action, Hitler easily had his way.

The Czech Crisis Germany turned next to Czechoslovakia. At first, Hitler insisted that the three million Germans in the Sudetenland (soo DAY tun land)—a region of western Czechoslovakia—be given autonomy. Czechoslovakia was one of only two remaining democracies in Eastern Europe. (Finland was the other.) Still, Britain and France were not willing to go to war to save it. As British and French leaders searched for a peaceful solution, Hitler increased his demands. The Sudetenland, he said, must be annexed to Germany.

Note Taking

Reading Skill: Recognize Sequence
Complete this timetable of German aggression as you read.

German Aggression	
March 1938	
September 1938	
March 1939	
September 1939	

Germany in Czechoslovakia
A Sudeten woman grieves while dutifully saluting Hitler's troops (below). German tanks roll through Wenceslas Square in Prague (left).

German Aggression Continues

L3

Instruct

- **Introduce: Key Terms** Direct students' attention to the key term *Anschluss* (in blue). Explain that it comes from the German language. Have them use the phonetic guide to practice the pronunciation. Then ask **Name a few other political unifications that have involved Germany.** *(Sample: the unification of different German states in 1871; the unification of East and West Germany after the Cold War)*

- **Teach** Review Hitler's invasion path. Discuss why Hitler thought he had a right to invade these regions. Read aloud the quotation at the end of the first paragraph on this page ("I have the right . . . breeds like vermin.") and discuss students' responses.

- **Quick Activity** Remind students of Chamberlain's assertion that he had achieved "peace for our time." Ask **What were the responses of other leaders to Chamberlain's claim?** *(Neither Daladier nor Churchill agreed.)* Have students engage in a brief debate between those who would have favored appeasement and those who would have opposed it.

Independent Practice

- **Note Taking** Have students fill in the timetable sequencing Germany's acts of aggression.

   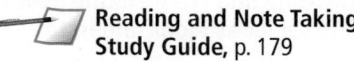 **Reading and Note Taking Study Guide**, p. 179

- **Viewpoints** To help students better understand the debates that took place in Europe in the 1930s, have them read the excerpts in *Can Hitler Be Trusted?* and complete the worksheet.

   All in One Teaching Resources, Unit 4, p. 72

Monitor Progress

As students fill in their timetables, circulate to make sure they list the demands Hitler made at the Munich Conference. For a completed version of the timetable, see

   Note Taking Transparencies, 184B

History Background

Aryan or Not? Nineteenth-century Europeans believed that around 1500 B.C., a group called Aryans had swept into South Asia, conquered the people already living there, and imposed their culture upon them. The Aryans were thought to have been behind civilization's most brilliant advances. One theory held the Aryans were descended from northern Europeans, and that Germanic or Nordic peoples were the purest and most advanced of all the Aryans, and therefore superior to people of other origins. In recent years, most scholars have rejected the ideas that the Aryans originated in Europe or invaded South Asia. Instead they believe that the group known as Aryans developed in South Asia and drew heavily on the existing culture of that region. Thus, the theories that Hitler based his government upon were not only morally wrong, but untrue as well.

Europe Plunges Toward War

Instruct

- **Introduce: Vocabulary Builder** Have students read the Vocabulary Builder term and definition. Ask students to speculate on why the use of *technology* in World War I would make Europe hesitant to start another war. *(Sample: World War I was so destructive because of advances in technology, and weapons had advanced even further since that time.)*

- **Teach** Explain that, as Churchill predicted, appeasement failed, and Europe was plunged into war. Ask **What event made the democracies willing to fight?** *(Hitler's invasion of the rest of Czechoslovakia)* **What event provoked the war?** *(his invasion of Poland)*

- **Analyzing the Visuals** Display **Color Transparency 174:** *Wonder How Long the Honeymoon Will Last?* Use the lesson suggested in the transparency book to guide a discussion on the political cartoon and its view on the Nazi-Soviet Pact.
  - 📖 **Color Transparencies,** 174

Independent Practice

Have students access **Web Code nbp-2911** to take the **Geography Interactive Audio Guided Tour** and then answer the map skills questions in the text.

Monitor Progress

- Check Reading and Note Taking Study Guide entries for student understanding.
- Check the answers to map skills questions.

Answers

✔ He wanted to bring all German-speaking people into the Third Reich.

Map Skills
1. Review locations with students.
2. It is a narrow strip of land separating East Prussia from the rest of Germany.
3. Sample: Denmark, the Netherlands, Belgium, France, Poland, Switzerland, Yugoslavia; because those were the countries that bordered Germany and Italy

---

At the Munich Conference in September 1938, British and French leaders again chose appeasement. They caved in to Hitler's demands and then persuaded the Czechs to surrender the Sudetenland without a fight. In exchange, Hitler assured Britain and France that he had no further plans to expand his territory.

"Peace for Our Time" Returning from Munich, British Prime Minister Neville Chamberlain told cheering crowds that he had achieved "peace for our time." He told Parliament that the Munich Pact had "saved Czechoslovakia from destruction and Europe from Armageddon." French leader Edouard Daladier (dah lahd yay) reacted differently to the joyous crowds that greeted him in Paris. "The fools, why are they cheering?" he asked. British politician Winston Churchill, who had long warned of the Nazi threat, judged the diplomats harshly: "They had to choose between war and dishonor. They chose dishonor; they will have war."

✔ **Checkpoint** Why did Hitler feel justified in taking over Austria and the Sudetenland?

Geography *Interactive*
For: Audio guided tour
Web Code: nbp-2911

Aggression in Europe and Africa to September, 1939

Map Skills Between 1936 and 1939, Germany and Italy repeatedly threatened peace in Europe.
1. **Locate** (a) Austria (b) Rhineland (c) Poland
2. **Regions** The strip of land between East Prussia and the rest of Germany is called the Polish Corridor. Why is that an appropriate name for the region?
3. **Predict Consequences** Which countries in 1939 were probably the most likely targets for future acts of German or Italian aggression? Explain.

Germany, 1935
Occupied by Germany, 1936
Occupied by Germany, 1938–1939
Italy and Italian territories, 1935
Occupied by Italy, 1935–1939

Connect to Our World

Connections to Today When the British and French leaders returned from the Munich Conference in 1938, the people of their nations cheered. The French leader Edouard Daladier, however, expressed concern about whether the agreement would prove wise. Daladier was correct, of course, in that the agreement did not satisfy Hitler's appetite for conquest.

In late 1990, another aggressive dictator, Saddam Hussein of Iraq, took over a small, neighboring country—the oil-rich nation of Kuwait. This time, world leaders chose to form a coalition, sanctioned by the United Nations and led by the United States, to force the dictator to retreat from Kuwait. After brief military operations, the coalition freed Kuwait. However, the coalition did not drive Saddam from power in Iraq—a step many predicted that the coalition members would regret.

Europe Plunges Toward War

Just as Churchill predicted, Europe plunged rapidly toward war. In March 1939, Hitler broke his promises and gobbled up the rest of Czechoslovakia. The democracies finally accepted the fact that appeasement had failed. At last thoroughly alarmed, they promised to protect Poland, most likely the next target of Hitler's expansion.

Nazi-Soviet Pact In August 1939, Hitler stunned the world by announcing a nonaggression pact with his great enemy—Joseph Stalin, the Soviet dictator. Publicly, the Nazi-Soviet Pact bound Hitler and Stalin to peaceful relations. Secretly, the two agreed not to fight if the other went to war and to divide up Poland and other parts of Eastern Europe between them.

The pact was based not on friendship or respect but on mutual need. Hitler feared communism as Stalin feared fascism. But Hitler wanted a free hand in Poland. Also, he did not want to fight a war with the Western democracies and the Soviet Union at the same time. For his part, Stalin had sought allies among the Western democracies against the Nazi menace. Mutual suspicions, however, kept them apart. By joining with Hitler, Stalin tried to protect the Soviet Union from the threat of war with Germany and grabbed a chance to gain land in Eastern Europe.

Invasion of Poland On September 1, 1939, a week after the Nazi-Soviet Pact, German forces invaded Poland. Two days later, Britain and France declared war on Germany. World War II had begun.

The devastation of World War I and the awareness of the destructive power of modern <u>technology</u> made the idea of more fighting unbearable. Unfortunately, the war proved to be even more horrendous than anyone had imagined.

✔ **Checkpoint** What convinced Britain and France to end their policy of appeasement? Why?

Why the West Appeased Hitler

- Fear of the destructive power of modern technology
- Widespread pacifism following World War I
- Hitler's actions seen as a justifiable response to the harsh Treaty of Versailles
- Widespread economic depression
- Hitler's fascism seen as a defense against Soviet communism
- Faith in diplomacy and compromise
- Misreading of Hitler's intentions

Chart Skills Agree or disagree with the following statement: "World War II was in large part a continuation of World War I." Provide evidence from the chart and your knowledge of history to support your view.

Vocabulary Builder

technology—(tek NAHL uh jee) *n.* scientific advances applied to practical purposes

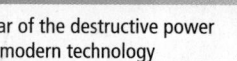

Assessment

Progress Monitoring Online
For: Self-quiz with vocabulary practice
Web Code: nba-2911

Terms, People, and Places

1. For each term, person, or place listed at the beginning of the section, write a sentence explaining its significance.

Note Taking

2. **Reading Skill: Recognize Sequence** Use your completed tables to answer the Focus Question: What events unfolded between Chamberlain's declaration of "peace for our time" and the outbreak of a world war?

Comprehension and Critical Thinking

3. **Identify Central Issues** How did the Western democracies respond to the aggression of the Axis powers during the 1930s?

4. **Synthesize Information** Why did Germany and Italy become involved in the Spanish Civil War?

5. **Recognize Cause and Effect** How was the Munich Conference a turning point in the road toward world war?

6. **Analyze Information** Why do you think some historians call the period between 1919 and 1939 the 20-year truce?

● **Writing About History**

Quick Write: Explore a Topic Choose one specific event from this section and write a series of questions that you could use to direct research on the topic. For example, on the formation of the Rome-Berlin-Tokyo Axis you could ask

- How did the Axis benefit each of the member countries?
- How did the Axis clear the way for the members to take even bolder aggressive actions?

Objectives

As you teach this section, keep students focused on the following objectives to help them answer the Section Focus Question and master core content.

- Describe how the Axis powers came to control much of Europe, but failed to conquer Britain.
- Summarize Germany's invasion of the Soviet Union.
- Understand the horror of the genocide the Nazis committed.
- Describe the role of the United States before and after joining World War II.

Prepare to Read

Build Background Knowledge L3

Remind students that the German attack on Poland signaled the outbreak of the war. Ask them to preview the section and predict what will happen next.

Set a Purpose L3

- **WITNESS HISTORY** Read the selection aloud or play the audio.

  AUDIO **Witness History Audio CD,** Janina's War Story

  Ask **How does Janina describe the German attack on Poland?** (Sample: loud, destructive, confusing, horrifying) **How do you predict airplanes might be used in World War II?** (Sample: for bombing, transportation, reconnaissance)

- **Focus** Point out the Section Focus Question and write it on the board. Tell students to refer to this question as they read. (Answer appears with Section 2 Assessment answers.)

- **Preview** Have students preview the Section Objectives and the list of Terms, People, and Places.

- **Note Taking** Have students read this section using the Structured Read Aloud strategy (TE, p. T20). As they read, have students fill in the flowchart sequencing events in World War II.

  Reading and Note Taking Study Guide, p. 181

▶ Janina Sulkowska in the early 1930s

▶ German fighter plane

🔊 AUDIO

Janina's War Story

❝ It was 10:30 in the morning and I was helping my mother and a servant girl with bags and baskets as they set out for the market. . . . Suddenly the high-pitch scream of diving planes caused everyone to freeze. . . . Countless explosions shook our house followed by the *rat-tat-tat* of strafing machine guns. We could only stare at each other in horror. Later reports would confirm that several German Stukas had screamed out of a blue sky and . . . dropped several bombs along the main street— and then returned to strafe the market. The carnage was terrible. ❞

—Janina Sulkowska, Krzemieniec, Poland, September 12, 1939

Focus Question Which regions were attacked and occupied by the Axis powers, and what was life like under their occupation?

The Axis Advances

Objectives

- Describe how the Axis powers came to control much of Europe, but failed to conquer Britain.
- Summarize Germany's invasion of the Soviet Union.
- Understand the horror of the genocide the Nazis committed.
- Describe the role of the United States before and after joining World War II.

Terms, People, and Places

blitzkrieg	General Erwin Rommel
Luftwaffe	concentration camps
Dunkirk	Holocaust
Vichy	Lend-Lease Act

Note Taking

Reading Skill: Recognize Sequence Sequence events as you read in a flowchart.

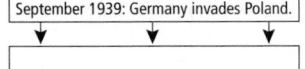

Diplomacy and compromise had not satisfied the Axis powers' hunger for empire. Western democracies had hoped that appeasement would help establish a peaceful world order. But Nazi Germany, Fascist Italy, and imperial Japan plunged ahead with their plans for conquest.

The Axis Attacks

On September 1, 1939, Nazi forces stormed into Poland, revealing the enormous power of Hitler's **blitzkrieg,** or "lightning war." The blitzkrieg utilized improved tank and airpower technology to strike a devastating blow against the enemy. First, the **Luftwaffe,** or German air force, bombed airfields, factories, towns, and cities, and screaming dive bombers fired on troops and civilians. Then, fast-moving tanks and troop transports pushed their way into the defending Polish army, encircling whole divisions of troops and forcing them to surrender.

While Germany attacked from the west, Stalin's forces invaded from the east, grabbing lands promised to them under the Nazi-Soviet Pact. Within a month, Poland ceased to exist. Because of Poland's location and the speed of the attacks, Britain and France could do nothing to help beyond declaring war on Germany.

Hitler passed the winter without much further action. Stalin's armies, however, forced the Baltic states of Estonia, Latvia, and

Vocabulary Builder

Use the information below and the following resources to teach the high-use words from this section.
All in One Teaching Resources, Unit 4, p. 70; **Teaching Resources, Skills Handbook,** p. 3

High-Use Words	Definitions and Sample Sentences
available, p. 569	*adj.* ready for use; at hand After Susan ran out of butter, she had to use whatever ingredients were **available**.
nullified, p. 571	*vt.* made invalid After the students were caught cheating, the instructor **nullified** their exam grades.

Lithuania to agree to host bases for the Soviet military. Soviet forces also seized part of Finland, which put up stiff but unsuccessful resistance.

The Miracle of Dunkirk During that first winter, the French hunkered down behind the Maginot Line. Britain sent troops to wait with them. Some reporters referred to this quiet time as the "phony war." Then, in April 1940, Hitler launched a blitzkrieg against Norway and Denmark, both of which soon fell. Next, his forces slammed into the Netherlands and Belgium.

In May, German forces surprised the French and British by attacking through the Ardennes Forest in Belgium, an area that was considered invasion proof. Bypassing the Maginot Line, German troops poured into France. Retreating British forces were soon trapped between the Nazi army and the English Channel. In a desperate gamble, the British sent all <u>available</u> naval vessels, merchant ships, and even fishing and pleasure boats across the channel to pluck stranded troops off the beach of **Dunkirk.** Despite German air attacks, the improvised armada ferried more than 300,000 troops to safety in Britain. This heroic rescue raised British morale.

France Falls Meanwhile, German forces headed south toward Paris. Italy declared war on France and attacked from the south. Overrun and demoralized, France surrendered. On June 22, 1940, Hitler forced the French to sign the surrender documents in the same railroad car in which Germany had signed the armistice ending World War I. Following the surrender, Germany occupied northern France. In the south, the Germans set up a "puppet state," with its capital at **Vichy** (VEE shee).

Some French officers escaped to England and set up a government-in-exile. Led by Charles de Gaulle, these "free French" worked to liberate their homeland. Within France, resistance fighters used guerrilla tactics against German forces.

Operation Sea Lion With the fall of France, Britain stood alone in Western Europe. Hitler was sure that the British would sue for peace. But Winston Churchill, who had replaced Neville Chamberlain as prime minister, had other plans. Faced with this defiance, Hitler made plans for Operation Sea Lion—the invasion of Britain. In preparation for the invasion, he launched massive air strikes against the island nation.

Beginning in August 1940, German bombers began a daily bombardment of England's southern coast. For a month, Britain's Royal Air Force valiantly battled the Luftwaffe. Then, the Germans changed their tactics. Instead of bombing military targets in the south, they began to bomb London and other cities.

Germany Launches the Blitz German bombers first appeared over London late on September 7, 1940. All through the night, relays of aircraft showered high explosives and firebombs on the sprawling capital. The bombing continued for 57 nights in a row and then sporadically until the next May. These bombing attacks are known as "the blitz." Much of London was destroyed, and thousands of people lost their lives.

Vocabulary Builder

available—(uh VAYL uh bul) *adj.* ready for use; at hand

YOUR COURAGE
YOUR CHEERFULNESS
YOUR RESOLUTION
WILL BRING
US VICTORY

Winston Churchill's defiance gave voice to the determination of the British. *How did Churchill give weight to his speech?*

Primary Source

❝We shall defend our island, whatever the cost may be, we shall fight on the beaches, we shall fight on the landing grounds, we shall fight in the fields and in the streets, we shall fight in the hills; we shall never surrender.❞
—*Winston Churchill, June 4, 1940* AUDIO

History Background

The Trick of the Hitler Two-Step After the surrender of France, the Western Allies saw news reels and photographs that seemingly showed a delighted Hitler doing a victory dance on the very spot where Germany had surrendered at the close of World War I. This humiliating image was continually shown in movie theaters and newspapers across Britain, the United States and Canada. It enraged viewers. However, the footage was really a clever editing trick by propagandist John Grierson, then the managing director of Canada's Wartime Information Board. When he received footage of Hitler stamping his foot once, he edited the frames and looped them to show Hitler doing a dance. The Allies then continuously aired the fake footage to rally the public to join the war effort.

Teach

The Axis Attacks ⓛ₃

Instruct

- **Introduce: Vocabulary Builder** Have students read the Vocabulary Builder term and definition. Ask **How did Germany use the technology *available* to it to strike at the Allies?** *(Germany used airplanes and high explosives in a "blitz" against its enemies.)* Explain to students that *blitz* is short for *blitzkrieg*, which means "lightning war" in German.

- **Teach** Trace the Axis advance at the beginning of the war. Ask **How did the Axis powers achieve victories in 1939 and 1940?** *(by striking fast, using the awesome power of modern technology, and never giving the enemy time to prepare or defend itself)* **Which side do you think was winning at the end of 1942?** *(the Axis because they controlled most of Europe and had won important victories in Africa)*

- **Quick Activity** Have students look at the Battle of Britain. To begin, read aloud or play the audio selection from the Primary Source. Then direct students to look at the Infographic on Surviving the Blitz, on the next page, and play that audio selection. Discuss the many ways in which the war hurt ordinary people. Then remind students that Britain had a strong navy. Ask **Why do you think the air strikes were important to Germany's plan to invade Britain?** *(Because Britain had a strong navy, Germany would need to ensure that it had control of the air in order to successfully invade the country.)*

🔊 AUDIO **Witness History Audio CD,** Winston Churchill, June 4, 1940

Answer

Caption by using repetition and showing determination

Independent Practice

Have students write a series of six to eight newspaper headlines that summarize the course of the war from the invasion of Poland to the German decision to break off the Battle of Britain. Encourage them to include not only battles but also important speeches by leaders involved in the war. Remind them that newspaper headlines should be short but informative.

Monitor Progress

- As students fill in their flowcharts, circulate to make sure they are sequencing the events in Europe and in Africa correctly. For a completed version of the flowchart, see

  📖 **Note Taking Transparencies,** 185A

- To review each country's status in 1941, ask students to create a three-column chart with the headings *Free of German Control, Axis Power,* and *Conquered by Axis.*

SURVIVING THE BLITZ

From 1940 to 1941, Germany tried to pummel Britain into submission during a months-long bombing campaign known as "the blitz." From September through May, German pilots targeted London with night after night of bombing, but other cities such as Liverpool, Glasgow, and Belfast became targets, too. These nighttime raids sent ordinary civilians scrambling for safety—in crowded public shelters, in homemade shelters, or even in the London Underground. During the blitz, German bombers killed more than 40,000 British civilians and damaged millions of homes. AUDIO 🔊

◄ Fearing poisonous gas attacks, the British government issued gas masks to its citizens. However, gas was never used against British civilians.

Small gestures of kindness helped Londoners deal with the effects of bombing raids. ▼

MOTHERS
Send them
out of
London

▲ Nearly three million people were evacuated from Britain's cities to the safer countryside.

London did not break under the blitz. Defiantly, Parliament continued to meet. Citizens carried on their daily lives, seeking protection in shelters and then emerging to resume their routines when the all-clear sounded. Even the British king and queen chose to support Londoners by joining them in bomb shelters rather than fleeing to the countryside.

Hitler Fails to Take Britain German planes continued to bomb London and other cities off and on until May 1941. But contrary to Hitler's hopes, the Luftwaffe could not gain air superiority over Britain, and British morale was not destroyed. In fact, the bombing only made the British more determined to turn back the enemy. Operation Sea Lion was a failure.

Africa and the Balkans Axis armies also pushed into North Africa and the Balkans. In September 1940, Mussolini ordered forces from Italy's North African colony of Libya into Egypt. When the British army repulsed these invaders, Hitler sent one of his most brilliant commanders, **General Erwin Rommel,** to North Africa. The "Desert Fox," as he was called, chalked up a string of successes in 1941 and 1942. He pushed the British back across the desert toward Cairo, Egypt.

In October 1940, Italian forces invaded Greece. They encountered stiff resistance, and in 1941 German troops once again provided reinforcements. Both Greece and Yugoslavia were added to the growing Axis empire. Even after the Axis triumph, however, Greek and Yugoslav

Link to Science

The Role of Radar Britain's Royal Air Force (RAF) was greatly outnumbered during the Battle of Britain, but it managed to fend off German attacks with remarkable success. One reason for this success was a new technology: radar (short for *r*adio *d*etecting *a*nd *r*anging), in which high frequency radio waves were emitted from stations. When those waves hit an object—like a German plane—they bounced off it and were sent back to the transmitter. A signal then appeared on a screen showing the object's distance, direction, and, over time, speed. Britain had 21 long-range radar stations that could detect an enemy plane at a distance of 140 miles (225 kilometers). Reports from radar stations were fed to an information clearing-house near London. There, experts tracked the movements of enemy planes and telephoned information to RAF headquarters, which could order planes into the air to meet each attack.

During air raids, some 60,000 Londoners sought shelter in the Underground, or subway, each night. Thousands of others slept in church crypts, basements, and other underground shelters.

Thinking Critically
1. **Draw Conclusions** What lessons might the British have learned from their experience of the blitz?
2. **Make Inferences** Why do you think that the blitz failed to break the morale of the British people?

guerrillas plagued the occupying forces. Meanwhile, both Bulgaria and Hungary had joined the Axis alliance. By 1941, the Axis powers or their allies controlled most of Europe.

✔ **Checkpoint** Which regions fell under Axis rule between 1939 and 1941?

Germany Invades the Soviet Union

After the failure in Britain, Hitler turned his military might to a new target—the Soviet Union. The decision to invade the Soviet Union helped relieve Britain. It also proved to be one of Hitler's costliest mistakes.

An Unstoppable German Army Stalls In June 1941, Hitler <u>nullified</u> the Nazi-Soviet Pact by invading the Soviet Union in Operation Barbarossa, a plan which took its name from the medieval Germanic leader, Frederick Barbarossa. Hitler made his motives clear. "If I had the Ural Mountains with their incalculable store of treasures in raw materials," he declared, "Siberia with its vast forests, and the Ukraine with its tremendous wheat fields, Germany under National Socialist leadership would swim in plenty." He also wanted to crush communism in Europe and defeat his powerful rival, Stalin.

Hitler unleashed a new blitzkrieg in the Soviet Union. About three million German soldiers invaded. The Germans caught Stalin unprepared.

Vocabulary Builder

<u>nullified</u>—(NUL uh fyd) *vt.* made invalid

Germany Invades the Soviet Union

Instruct

- **Introduce: Vocabulary Builder** Have students read the Vocabulary Builder term and definition. Ask **How did Hitler's invasion of the Soviet Union *nullify* the Nazi-Soviet Pact?** *(Hitler had promised that Germany would not fight the Soviet Union.)*

- **Teach** Ask **Why did Hitler want to conquer the Soviet Union?** *(He wanted its resources and he wanted to crush communism in Europe and break Stalin's power.)* **How far did German troops advance in the first few months?** *(They reached deep into the Soviet Union and were about to capture Moscow and Stalingrad.)* **What prevented the Germans from gaining victory?** *(stout defenses of those cities and Leningrad; the winter weather)* **How did Hitler's invasion of the Soviet Union work against him?** *(It led to cooperation between the Soviet Union and Britain and tied up troops and supplies with a fierce new enemy.)*

Answers

✔ Poland, Norway, Denmark, the Netherlands, Belgium, France, parts of the region of North Africa, Greece, and Yugoslavia. In addition, Bulgaria and Hungary joined the Axis.

Thinking Critically
1. Sample: to be resourceful, to be defiant
2. Sample: The bombings angered the British people and rallied their support for their country.

Independent Practice

Tell students to take the role of someone living in Leningrad in 1942, during the German siege. Have them write a journal entry describing what life was like within the city, including the shelling from German artillery, the physical destruction, and the difficulties of finding food and water. Encourage them to describe how they feel about the hardships they face. Invite volunteers to share their journal entries with the class.

Monitor Progress

To review this section, ask **What role did the climate of the Soviet Union play in its battle to halt the German invasion?** *(The extreme winter weather stalled the German advance.)*

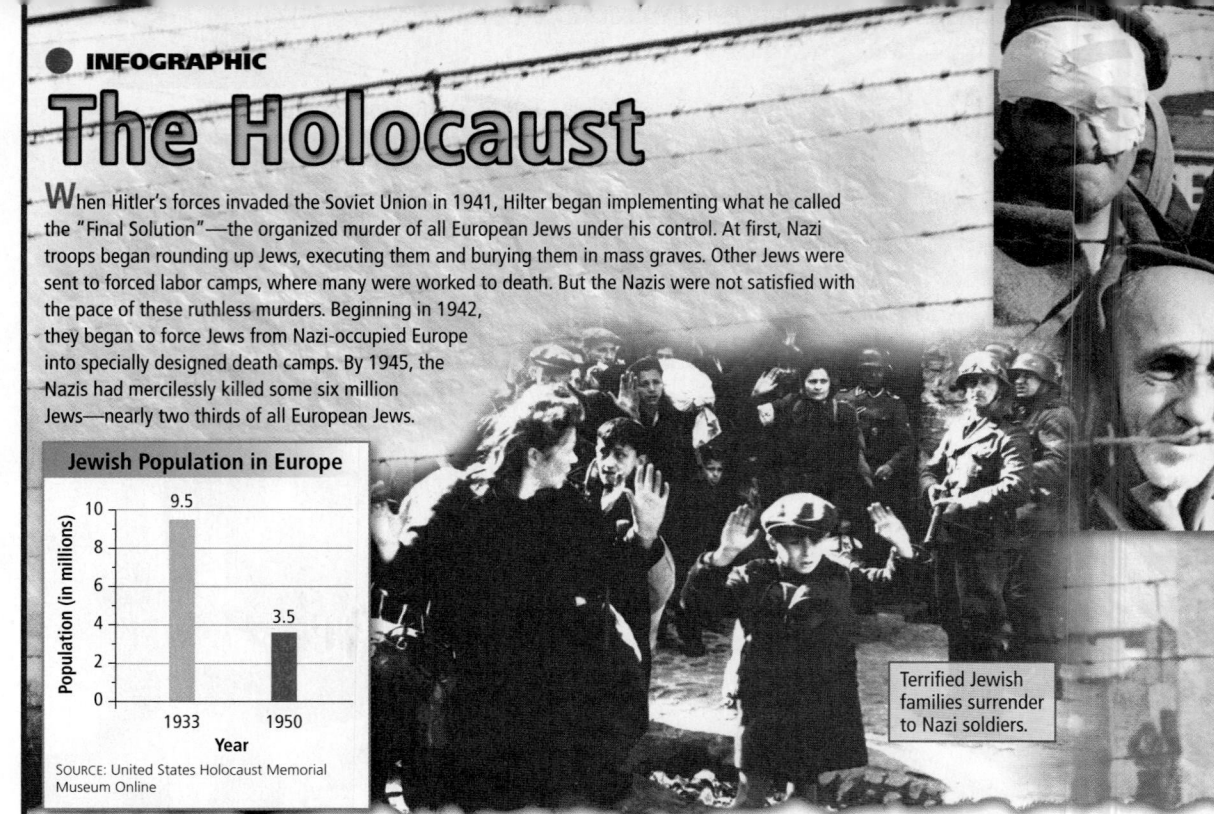

The Holocaust

When Hitler's forces invaded the Soviet Union in 1941, Hilter began implementing what he called the "Final Solution"—the organized murder of all European Jews under his control. At first, Nazi troops began rounding up Jews, executing them and burying them in mass graves. Other Jews were sent to forced labor camps, where many were worked to death. But the Nazis were not satisfied with the pace of these ruthless murders. Beginning in 1942, they began to force Jews from Nazi-occupied Europe into specially designed death camps. By 1945, the Nazis had mercilessly killed some six million Jews—nearly two thirds of all European Jews.

Jewish Population in Europe

Population (in millions)

- 1933: 9.5
- 1950: 3.5

Year

SOURCE: United States Holocaust Memorial Museum Online

Terrified Jewish families surrender to Nazi soldiers.

His army was still suffering from the purges that had wiped out many of its top officers.

The Soviets lost two and a half million soldiers trying to fend off the invaders. As they were forced back, Soviet troops destroyed factories and farm equipment and burned crops to keep them out of enemy hands. But they could not stop the German war machine. By autumn, the Nazis had smashed deep into the Soviet Union and were poised to take Moscow and Leningrad (present-day St. Petersburg).

There, however, the German advance stalled. Like Napoleon's Grand Army in 1812, Hitler's forces were not prepared for the fury of "General Winter." By early December, temperatures plunged to –40°F (–4°C). Thousands of German soldiers froze to death.

Germany's Siege of Leningrad The Soviets, meanwhile, suffered appalling hardships. In September 1941, the two-and-a-half-year siege of Leningrad began. Food was rationed to two pieces of bread a day. Desperate Leningraders ate almost anything. For example, they boiled wallpaper scraped off walls because its paste was said to contain potato flour.

Although more than a million Leningraders died during the siege, the city did not fall to the Germans. Hoping to gain some relief for his exhausted people, Stalin urged Britain to open a second front in Western Europe. Although Churchill could not offer much real help, the two powers did agree to work together.

✔ **Checkpoint** What caused Hitler's invasion of the Soviet Union to stall?

Answer

✔ It was stalled by Soviet resistance, the difficulty of the harsh winter and by Stalin's tactics of destroying equipment and burning crops to keep resources and food out of German hands.

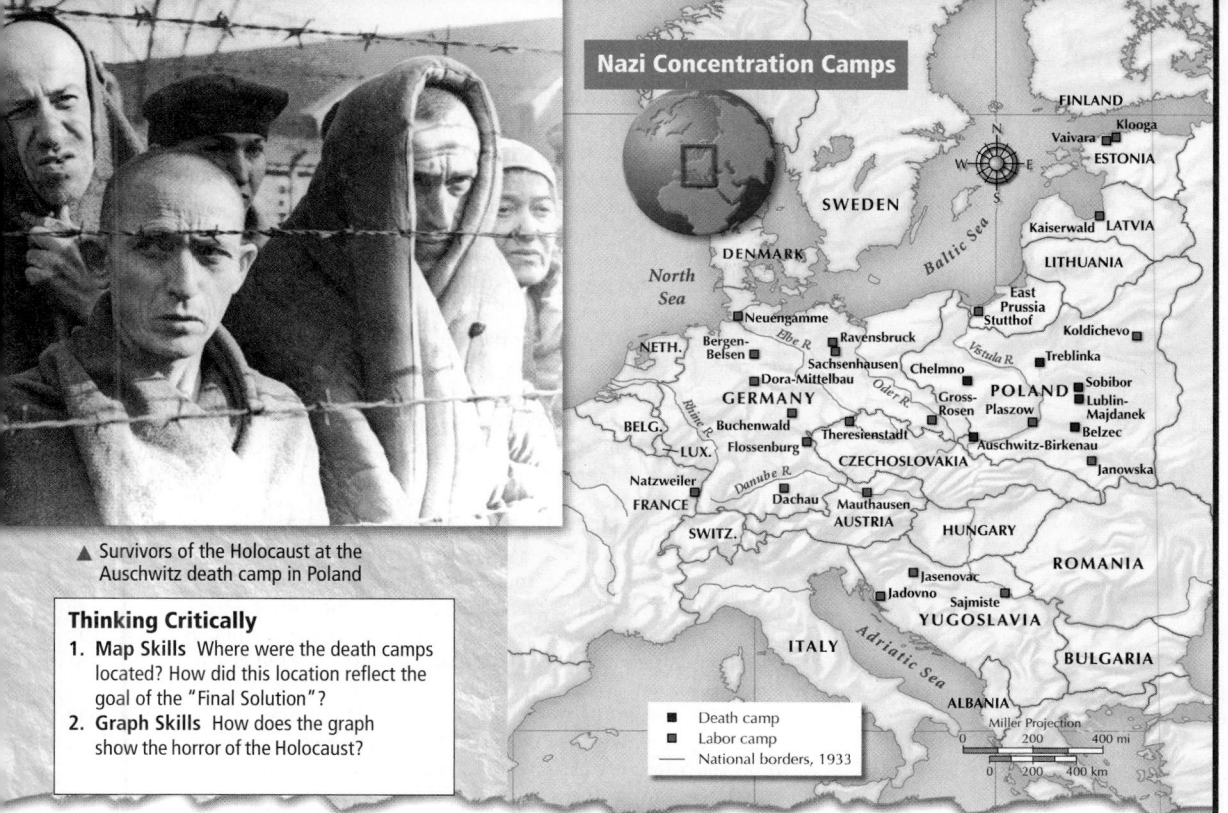

Nazi Concentration Camps

Survivors of the Holocaust at the Auschwitz death camp in Poland

■ Death camp
■ Labor camp
— National borders, 1933

Miller Projection
0   200   400 mi
0   200   400 km

Thinking Critically
1. **Map Skills** Where were the death camps located? How did this location reflect the goal of the "Final Solution"?
2. **Graph Skills** How does the graph show the horror of the Holocaust?

Life Under Nazi and Japanese Occupation

While Nazi forces rampaged across Europe, the Japanese military conquered an empire in Asia and the Pacific. Each set out to build a "new order" in the occupied lands.

Hitler's "New Order" Hitler's new order grew out of his racial obsessions. As his forces conquered most of Europe, Hitler set up puppet governments in Western European countries that were peopled by Aryans, or light-skinned Europeans, whom Hitler and his followers believed to be a "master race." The Slavs of Eastern Europe were considered to be an inferior "race." They were shoved aside to provide more "living space" for Germans, the strongest of the Aryans.

To the Nazis, occupied lands were an economic resource to be plundered and looted. The Nazis systematically stripped conquered nations of their works of art, factories, and other resources. To counter resistance movements that emerged in occupied countries, the Nazis took savage revenge, shooting hostages and torturing prisoners.

But the Nazis' most sinister plans centered on the people of the occupied countries. During the 1930s, the Nazis had sent thousands of Jewish people and political opponents to **concentration camps,** detention centers for civilians considered enemies of the state. Over the course of the war, the Nazis forced these people, along with millions of Polish and Soviet Slavs and people from other parts of Europe, to work as slave laborers. Prisoners were poorly fed and often worked to death.

N**ote Taking**

Reading Skill: Identify Supporting Details In a concept web like the one below, fill in details about how the Nazis and Japanese military treated people under their power during World War II. Add circles as necessary.

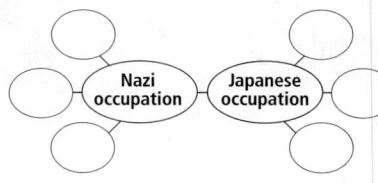

Nazi occupation   Japanese occupation

Life Under Nazi and Japanese Occupation

Instruct

- **Introduce** Direct students' attention to the photograph of Jewish families being led off by Nazi soldiers in the Infographic on the Holocaust. Discuss the emotions shown on the people's faces. Ask students to predict what this photograph reveals about how the Nazis treated the civilians they conquered.

- **Teach** Ask **What ideology was the basis for the Nazis' brutal treatment of conquered peoples?** (belief that so-called Aryans, especially Germans, were a superior race and that all others were inferior, especially Jews, Slavs, and the Roma) **How did the Nazis put these beliefs into practice?** (They forced conquered peoples from these groups into slave labor in work camps and in concentration camps; millions were systematically killed. They also targeted political opponents, the elderly, the disabled, and homosexuals.)

- **Quick Activity** Discuss the issue of who bears the greatest responsibility for the murders committed in the German "death camps"—Hitler and the few other top officials who developed the plan to create the camps and execute people, or the many people who carried out that effort by running the camps under orders.

Answers

Thinking Critically
1. in Poland near the work camps; it shows that all detainees might eventually be moved from work camps to death camps and reveals the Nazis' ruthless policies towards Slavs and Central European Jews
2. It depicts the dramatic drop in the Jewish population of Europe.

Independent Practice

- **Note Taking** Have students fill in the concept web with details on how the Nazis and the Japanese military treated people under their occupation.

  Reading and Note Taking Study Guide, p. 181

- **Primary Source** To further explore the life of Jewish people in occupied Europe, have students read the excerpt from *The Diary of A Young Girl* by Anne Frank and complete the worksheet.

  All in One Teaching Resources, Unit 4, p. 73

- **Link to Literature** To help students develop a deeper understanding of the gruesome reality of the Final Solution, have students read the excerpt from Elie Wiesel's *Night* and complete the worksheet.

  All in One Teaching Resources, Unit 4, p. 74

Monitor Progress

As students complete their concept webs, circulate to make sure they understand how the Nazi and Japanese forces treated people under their power during World War II. For a completed version of the concept web, see

Note Taking Transparencies, 185B

The Nazis Commit Genocide At the same time, Hitler pursued a vicious program to kill all people he judged "racially inferior," particularly Europe's Jews. The Nazis also targeted other groups who did not meet the Aryan racial ideal, including Slavs, Romas (Gypsies), homosexuals, and the disabled. Political and religious leaders who spoke out against Nazism also suffered abuse. Starting in 1939, the Nazis forced Jews in Poland and other countries to live in ghettos, or sections of cities where Jewish people were confined. Many died from starvation, disease, overwork, and the harsh elements. By 1941, however, German leaders had devised plans for the "Final Solution of the Jewish problem"—the genocide of all European Jews.

To accomplish this goal, Hitler had six special "death camps" built in Poland. The Nazis shipped "undesirables" from all over occupied Europe to the camps. There, Nazi engineers designed the most efficient means of killing millions of men, women, and children.

As the prisoners reached the camps, they were stripped of their clothes and valuables. Their heads were shaved. Guards separated men from women and children from their parents. The young, elderly, and sick were targeted for immediate killing. Within a few days, they were herded into "shower rooms" and gassed. The Nazis worked others to death or used them for perverse "medical" experiments. By 1945, the Nazis had massacred some six million Jews in what became known as the **Holocaust.** Nearly six million other people were killed as well.

Jewish people resisted the Nazis even though they knew their efforts could not succeed. In July 1942, the Nazis began sending Polish Jews from the Warsaw ghetto to the Treblinka death camp at a rate of about 5,000 per day. In the spring of 1943, knowing that their situation was hopeless, the Jews took over the ghetto and used a small collection of guns and homemade bombs to damage the Nazi forces as much as possible. On May 16, the Nazis regained control of the ghetto and eliminated the remaining Warsaw Jews. Still, their courage has inspired many over the years.

In some cases, friends, neighbors, or strangers protected Jews. Italian peasants hid Jews in their villages. Denmark and Bulgaria saved almost

The Japanese in China
Since 1937, the Japanese had been trying to expand into Asia by taking over China. Although the Japanese occupied much of Eastern China, the Chinese refused to surrender. The occupying Japanese treated the Chinese brutally. Below, Japanese soldiers load Chinese civilians onto trucks to take them to an execution ground during the sacking of Nanjing in 1937.

History Background

Resisting Nazi Rule Across Europe, ordinary citizens resisted Nazi rule by hiding Jewish people or helping them escape to find safety. In Denmark, where few German troops were stationed, the Danish people smuggled almost all of the country's Jews to the safety of Sweden. Another pocket of resistance was Le Chambon, in Vichy France, where villagers provided a safe haven for 5,000 Jews.

Even in the death camps themselves, some Jews fought back. In October 1944, for example, a group of Jews in the Auschwitz death camp destroyed one of the gas chambers. The rebels were all killed. One woman, Rosa Robota, was tortured for days before she was hanged. "Be strong and have courage," she called out to the camp inmates whom the Nazis forced to watch her execution.

all their Jewish populations. Many people, however, pretended not to notice what was happening. Some even became collaborators and cooperated with the Nazis. In France, the Vichy government helped ship thousands of Jewish people to their deaths. Strict immigration policies in many Western countries as well as conscious efforts to block Jewish immigration prevented many Jews from gaining refuge elsewhere.

The scale and savagery of the Holocaust are unequaled in history. The Nazis deliberately set out to destroy the Jews for no reason other than their religious and ethnic heritage. Today, the record of that slaughter is a vivid reminder of the monstrous results of racism and intolerance.

Japan's Brutal Conquest Japanese forces took control across Asia and the Pacific. Their self-proclaimed mission was to help Asians escape Western colonial rule. In fact, the real goal was a Japanese empire in Asia. The Japanese invaders treated the Chinese, Filipinos, Malaysians, and other conquered people with great brutality, killing and torturing civilians throughout East and Southeast Asia. The occupiers seized food crops, destroyed cities and towns, and made local people into slave laborers. Whatever welcome the Japanese had first met as "liberators" was soon turned to hatred. In the Philippines, Indochina, and elsewhere, nationalist groups waged guerrilla warfare against the Japanese invaders.

✔ **Checkpoint** How did Hitler's views about race lead to the murder of six million Jewish people and millions of Slavs, Gypsies, and others?

Japan Attacks the United States

When the war began in 1939, the United States declared its neutrality. Still, although isolationist feeling remained strong, many Americans sympathized with those who battled the Axis powers. As one of those sympathizers, President Franklin Delano Roosevelt (FDR) looked for ways around the Neutrality Acts to provide warships and other aid to Britain as it stood alone against Hitler.

American Involvement Grows In March 1941, FDR persuaded Congress to pass the **Lend-Lease Act.** It allowed him to sell or lend war materials to "any country whose defense the President deems vital to the defense of the United States." The United States, said Roosevelt, would not be drawn into the war, but it would become "the arsenal of democracy," supplying arms to those who were fighting for freedom.

To show further support, Roosevelt met secretly with Churchill on a warship in the Atlantic in August 1941. The two leaders issued the Atlantic Charter, which set goals for the war—"the final destruction of the Nazi tyranny"—and for the postwar world. They pledged to support "the right of all peoples to choose the form of government under which they will live" and called for a "permanent system of general security."

Japan and the United States Face Off When war broke out in Europe in 1939, the Japanese saw a chance to grab European possessions in Southeast Asia. The rich resources of the region, including oil, rubber, and tin, would be of immense value in fighting its war against the Chinese.

In 1940, Japan advanced into French Indochina and the Dutch East Indies. In response, the United States banned the sale of war materials, such as iron, steel, and oil, to Japan. Japanese leaders saw this move as a threat to Japan's economy and its Asian sphere of influence.

Meeting at Sea
President Roosevelt and Prime Minister Churchill issued the Atlantic Charter in August 1941.

Assess Progress L3

- Have students complete the Section Assessment.

- Administer the Section Quiz.

All in One Teaching Resources, Unit 4, p. 66

- To further assess student understanding, use

   Progress Monitoring Transparencies, 124

Reteach

If students need more instruction, have them read the section summary.

Reading and Note Taking Study Guide, p. 182 L3

Adapted Reading and Note Taking Study Guide, p. 182 L1 L2

Spanish Reading and Note Taking Study Guide, p. 182 L2

Extend L4

See this chapter's Professional Development pages for the Extend Online activity on the Kindertransport.

Answers

Caption The direct attack on the United States caused the United States to end its isolationist policies and enter the war.

✓ The United States banned the sale of war materials to Japan. This hampered Japanese expansion efforts in Southeast Asia and threatened the Japanese economy.

Damage at Pearl Harbor

U.S. ships sunk or damaged	19
U.S. aircraft destroyed	188
Americans killed	2,348
Americans injured	1,109

SOURCE: *Columbia Encyclopedia, Sixth Edition*

December 7, 1941
On the sleepy Sunday morning of December 7, 1941, the military complex at Pearl Harbor was suddenly jolted awake by a surprise attack. Planes screamed down from the sky, dropping bombs and torpedoes. Americans were shocked and horrified by the attacks. *How did Pearl Harbor change the isolationist policies of the United States?*

Japan and the United States held talks to ease the growing tension. But extreme militarists, such as General Tojo Hideki, hoped to expand Japan's empire, and the United States was interfering with their plans.

Attack on Pearl Harbor With talks at a standstill, General Tojo ordered a surprise attack. Early on December 7, 1941, Japanese airplanes bombed the American fleet at Pearl Harbor in Hawaii. The attack took the lives of about 2,400 people and destroyed battleships and aircraft. The next day, a grim-faced President Roosevelt told the nation that December 7 was "a date which will live in infamy." He asked Congress to declare war on Japan. On December 11, Germany and Italy, as Japan's allies, declared war on the United States.

Japanese Victories In the long run, the Japanese attack on Pearl Harbor would be as serious a mistake as Hitler's invasion of the Soviet Union. But in the months after Pearl Harbor, possessions in the Pacific fell to the Japanese one by one. The Japanese captured the Philippines and other islands held by the United States. They overran the British colonies of Hong Kong, Burma, and Malaya, and advanced deeper into the Dutch East Indies and French Indochina. By 1942, the Japanese empire stretched from Southeast Asia to the western Pacific Ocean.

✓ **Checkpoint** Why did Japanese leaders view the United States as an enemy?

SECTION **2 Assessment**

Progress Monitoring Online
For: Self-quiz with vocabulary practice
Web Code: nba-2921

Terms, People, and Places

1. For each term, person, or place listed at the beginning of the section, write a sentence explaining its significance.

Note Taking

2. **Reading Skill: Recognize Sequence** Use your completed flowchart and concept web to answer the Focus Question: Which regions were attacked and occupied by the Axis powers, and what was life like under their occupation?

Comprehension and Critical Thinking

3. **Summarize** Describe Hitler's blitzkrieg tactics.

4. **Recognize Effects** Referring to the Battle of Britain in 1940, Winston Churchill said "Never in the field of human conflict was so much owed by so many to so few." What did he mean?

5. **Recognize Ideologies** Hitler translated his hatred into a program of genocide. How do ethnic, racial, and religious hatreds weaken society?

● **Writing About History**

Quick Write: Gather Information Use the library and reliable Internet sources to find information about Pearl Harbor. Create a source card for each book or Web site you use. Then create note cards to record and organize at least three pieces of information.

Section 2 Assessment

1. Sentences should reflect an understanding of each term, person, or place listed at the beginning of the section.
2. Germany and Italy controlled most of Europe and some of North Africa, Japan attacked China and Southeast Asia and many islands in the Pacific. Both Germany and Japan treated the civilians they encountered with brutality.

3. Blitzkrieg tactics used advanced technology to overwhelm enemy forces. First, airplanes bombed a region, then fast-moving ground troops moved in to surround the enemy forces.
4. The RAF, although relatively small, was able to protect Britain.
5. Sample: By perpetuating prejudice and cruelty, such hatreds cause conflict and may eventually lead to the loss of valuable members of society.

● **Writing About History**

Source cards should contain basic publication information for the source. The three note cards should each contain information and should cite the source card.

For additional assessment, have students access **Progress Monitoring Online** at **Web Code nba-2921.**

British poster encouraging women to work in factories to increase production

American medal awarded for supporting the war

WITNESS HISTORY 🔊 AUDIO

Support the War!

For the Allies to succeed against the relentless Axis war machine, everyone—on the home front as well as on the battlefield—had to work tirelessly. Ships needed to be built in a matter of days, not months. Airplanes, tanks, and ammunition had to be mass-produced. As factories converted to war production, the production of consumer goods such as automobiles ceased. All efforts were focused on the massive production of the materials of war.

Focus Question How did the Allies begin to push back the Axis powers?

The Allies Turn the Tide

Objectives
- Understand how nations devoted all of their resources to fighting World War II.
- Explain how Allied victories began to push back the Axis powers.
- Describe D-Day and the Allied advance toward Germany.

Terms, People, and Places

Rosie the Riveter	Stalingrad
aircraft carrier	D-Day
Dwight Eisenhower	Yalta Conference

Note Taking

Recognize Sequence In a flowchart like the one below, sequence the events that turned the tide of the war towards the Allies.

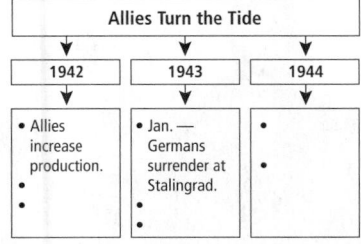

Allies Turn the Tide		
▼	▼	▼
1942	1943	1944
▼	▼	▼
• Allies increase production. • •	• Jan. — Germans surrender at Stalingrad. • •	• •

As 1942 began, the Allies were in trouble. German bombers flew unrelenting raids over Britain, and the German army advanced deep into the Soviet Union. In the Pacific, the Japanese onslaught seemed unstoppable. But helped by extraordinary efforts on the home front and a series of military victories, the tide was about to turn.

All-Out War

To defeat the Axis war machine, the Allies had to commit themselves to total war. Total war means nations devote all of their resources to the war effort.

Governments Increase Power To achieve maximum war production, democratic governments in the United States and Great Britain increased their political power. They directed economic resources into the war effort, ordering factories to stop making cars or refrigerators and to turn out airplanes or tanks instead. Governments implemented programs to ration or control the amount of food and other vital goods consumers could buy. They raised money by holding war bond drives, in which citizens lent their government certain sums of money that would be returned with interest later. Prices and wages were also regulated. While the war brought some shortages and hardships, the increase in production ended the unemployment of the depression era.

Under the pressures of war, even democratic governments limited the rights of citizens, censored the press, and used propaganda to win public support for the war. In the United States and Canada, many citizens of Japanese descent lost their jobs, property, and civil rights. Many Japanese Americans and Japanese Canadians were even interned in camps after their governments

Vocabulary Builder

Use the information below and the following resources to teach the high-use words from this section.
All in One Teaching Resources, Unit 4, p. 70; Teaching Resources, Skills Handbook, p. 3

High-Use Words	Definitions and Sample Sentences
incessant, p. 582	*adj.* uninterrupted; ceaseless Because of the **incessant** rain yesterday, we never made it to the beach.
inevitable, p. 583	*adj.* unavoidable; inescapable The soccer squads' victory in the state finals seemed **inevitable**, because the team had outplayed its competitor during the entire game.

SECTION 3

Step-by-Step Instruction

Objectives
As you teach this section, keep students focused on the following objectives to help them answer the Section Focus Question and master core content.

- Understand how nations devoted all of their resources to fighting World War II.
- Explain how Allied victories began to push back the Axis powers.
- Describe D-Day and the Allied advance toward Germany.

Prepare to Read

Build Background Knowledge L3
Using a map of the world, point to an area of fighting at this stage of the war and ask volunteers to summarize the Axis and Allied positions there. Guide students to see that the Axis had the upper hand almost everywhere.

Set a Purpose L3
- **WITNESS HISTORY** Read the selection aloud or play the audio.
  🔊 AUDIO **Witness History Audio CD,** Support the War!

  Ask **What will the Allies need to carry out this great effort?** *(raw materials and workers)* **With so many men going to fight in the war, who will fill the need for workers?** *(women)*

- **Focus** Point out the Section Focus Question and write it on the board. Tell students to refer to this question as they read. *(Answer appears with Section 3 Assessment answers.)*

- **Preview** Have students preview the Section Objectives and the list of Terms, People, and Places.

- **Note Taking** Have students read this section using the Paragraph Shrinking strategy (TE, p. T20). As they read, have students fill in the flowchart describing the sequence of events that turned the tide of the war.

 Reading and Note Taking Study Guide, p. 183

All-Out War

Instruct

- **Introduce** Display **Color Transparency 176: World War II Poster.** Have students also look at the British poster on the previous page. Discuss how posters, advertisements, and movies helped to instill patriotism and a desire to cooperate in the war effort.
  🏛 **Color Transparencies,** 176

- **Teach** Ask **Why would Britain and the United States need to ration, or limit, the amount of consumer goods available?** *(to preserve supplies for the war effort)* **What impact did increased production have on the economy?** *(It finally ended the depression.)*

- **Quick Activity** Ask **Why did Allied governments intern people with Japanese and German ancestry in camps?** *(from fear that they were security risks)* Using the Numbered Heads strategy (TE, p. T23), ask students to discuss the following: In times of war, does a government have the right to take away civil liberties?

Independent Practice

Have students take the role of an American woman who has entered the workforce for the first time and write a letter to a male relative in the army. Have them explain why they wanted to work.

Monitor Progress

As students complete their flowcharts, circulate to make sure they correctly identify and sequence the key events. For a completed version of the flowchart, see

🏛 **Note Taking Transparencies,** 186

Answers

✔ converted factories from making consumer goods to making airplanes, tanks, and ships; rationed goods; regulated wages and prices; worked to recruit all members of society to the war effort

Caption Sample: Naval warfare became less predictable; enemy ships no longer had to be very close to each other to engage in battle.

---

decided that they were a security risk. The British took similar action against German refugees. Some 40 years later, both the United States and Canada provided former internees with reparations, or payment for damages, but for many the compensation came too late.

Women Help Win the War As men joined the military, millions of women around the world replaced them in essential war industry jobs. Women, symbolized by the character **"Rosie the Riveter"** in the United States, built ships and planes and produced munitions.

British and American women served in the armed forces in many auxiliary roles—driving ambulances, delivering airplanes, and decoding messages. In occupied Europe, women fought in the resistance. Marie Fourcade, a French woman, helped downed Allied pilots escape to safety. Soviet women served in combat roles. Soviet pilot Lily Litvak, for example, shot down 12 German planes before she herself was killed.

✔ **Checkpoint** How did the Allies mobilize all of their resources for the war effort?

The Allies Forge Ahead

The years 1942–1943 marked the turning point of the war. The Allies won victories on four fronts—the Pacific, North Africa and Italy, the Soviet Union, and France—to push back the Axis tide.

Japanese Navy Battered In the Pacific, the Japanese suffered their first serious setback at the Battle of the Coral Sea. The battle lasted for five days in May 1942. For the first time in naval history, the enemy ships never even saw each other. Attacks were carried out by planes launched from **aircraft carriers,** or ships that transport aircraft and accommodate the take-off and landing of airplanes. The Japanese were prevented from seizing several important islands. More importantly, the Americans sank one Japanese aircraft carrier and several cruisers and destroyers.

This Allied victory was followed by an even more impressive win at the Battle of Midway in June 1942, which was also fought entirely from the air. The Americans destroyed four Japanese carriers and more than 250 planes. The battle was a devastating blow to the Japanese. After Midway, Japan was unable to launch any more offensive operations.

The Big Three Plot Their Strategy After the United States entered the war, the Allied leaders met periodically to hammer out their strategy.

Air War in the Pacific
Allied forces won decisive victories in the Coral Sea and at Midway Island. The Japanese pilots below may have taken part in these battles, which were fought from planes launched from aircraft carriers. *How do you think aircraft carriers changed naval warfare?*

History Background

Social Impact of War To meet the needs of total war, Americans of all backgrounds joined the armed forces. Filipino and Korean Americans were especially eager to fight, not only to aid the Allied effort, but also to liberate their homelands from Japanese conquest. African Americans were initially limited to support roles, but soon were given the opportunity to fight in combat. African American soldiers went on to win nearly 800 medals.

The war also provided new opportunities at home. At first, defense industries did not want to hire African Americans. In 1942, President Roosevelt issued Executive Order 8802, which banned discrimination in job training programs and in defense industries. He also set up the Fair Employment Practices Committee, to review charges of job discrimination. By the end of the war, nearly two million African Americans worked in defense factories.

INFOGRAPHIC
Technology That Helped Win the War

Deadlier bombs, machines that broke secret codes, dive-bombers—all of these technologies gave those who used them a military advantage. Scientists and engineers on both sides of World War II created and improved technologies at a fast and furious pace in a desperate effort to win the war.

Nylon replaced ▶ silk as a lightweight material used to make parachutes.

◀ Radar uses the behavior of electromagnetic waves to detect objects. It helped defenders to "see" and destroy planes before they could reach their targets.

▼ Improved sonar technology allowed submarines to use sound waves underwater to "see" enemy submarines.

Thinking Critically
1. **Draw Conclusions** Radar helped the British win the Battle of Britain. Explain why it made such a difference.
2. **Determine Relevance** How did Hitler use technology in his blitzkrieg tactics?

In 1942, the "Big Three"—Roosevelt, Churchill, and Stalin—agreed to focus on finishing the war in Europe before trying to end the war in Asia.

From the outset, the Allies distrusted one another. Churchill and Roosevelt feared that Stalin wanted to dominate Europe. Stalin believed the West wanted to destroy communism. None of the new Allies wanted to risk a breakdown in their alliance, however. At a conference in Tehran, Iran, in late 1943, Churchill and Roosevelt yielded to Stalin by agreeing to let the borders outlined in the Nazi-Soviet Pact stand, against the wishes of Poland's government-in-exile. However, Stalin also wanted Roosevelt and Churchill to open a second front against Germany in Western Europe to relieve the pressure on the Soviet Union. Roosevelt and Churchill replied that they did not yet have the resources. Stalin saw the delay as a deliberate policy to weaken the Soviet Union.

Allied Victory in North Africa In North Africa, the British led by General Bernard Montgomery fought Rommel. After the fierce Battle of El Alamein in November 1942, the Allies finally halted the Desert Fox's advance. Allied tanks drove the Axis back across Libya into Tunisia.

Later in 1942, American General **Dwight Eisenhower** took command of a joint British and American force in Morocco and Algeria. Advancing on Tunisia from the west, the Allies trapped Rommel's army, which surrendered in May 1943.

Link to Math

The Enigma Code Intelligence work helped produce the American victory at Midway—and that work owed its success in part to a Polish mathematician. In the 1930s, the Germans developed a machine called Enigma that allowed them to put military communications in code. Polish mathematician Marian Rejewski led a team that cracked the code. The Polish team gave their information to the British, who developed a new device that decoded messages created by a revised version of Enigma. The Germans had given an Enigma machine to the Japanese, and the Americans created their own machine to decode it. As a result, American naval intelligence officers intercepted Japanese plans to attack Midway. That allowed the navy to have a fleet lying in wait to beat back the Japanese attack.

The Allies Forge Ahead ⓭
Instruct

- **Introduce: Key Terms** Have students find the key term *aircraft carrier* (in blue) in the text. Point out that Japan was more than 3,000 miles from some of its conquests in Southeast Asia. Ask **Why do you think *aircraft carriers* were such a vital part of the war effort?** *(Sample: Large fleets were needed to move airplanes, troops, and supplies around the vast area of the Pacific.)*

- **Teach** Have students refer to the map of the Pacific theater in Section 4 and locate the Battles of Coral Sea and Midway. Then have them refer to the map of the European theater on the next spread to see the location of El Alamein, the points where Italy was invaded, and the site of Stalingrad. Ask **How did these battles turn the tide for the Allies?** *(Midway and the Coral Sea badly damaged Japanese power, preventing Japan from launching any further offensive operations. El Alamein and Stalingrad stopped the Axis powers at their farthest advance. The invasion of Italy was the first assault on the Axis' homelands.)*

- **Analyzing the Visuals** To help students visualize the battle of Stalingrad, display **Color Transparency 177: Battle of Stalingrad.** Ask a volunteer to read the description of the battle from the text. As the student reads each sentence, point to the map to show where the action took place. Then use the lesson suggested in the transparency book to guide a discussion.

  ▥ **Color Transparencies,** 177

Answers

Thinking Critically
1. because it allowed the British to know when German planes were coming and where they were going
2. Improved aircraft and tank technology helped Hitler to overwhelm his opponents.

Independent Practice

- Have students fill in the Outline Map *Europe and North Africa*.

  All in One Teaching Resources, Unit 4, p. 77

- Have students access **Web Code nbp-2931** to take the **Geography Interactive Audio Guided Tour** and then answer the map skills questions in the text.

Monitor Progress

- Have students write a brief paragraph explaining why Churchill, Roosevelt, and Stalin cooperated during the war, what agreements they reached in their 1942 conference, and what factors caused problems among them.

- Circulate to make sure students have correctly labeled their Outline Maps. Administer the Geography Quiz.

  All in One Teaching Resources, Unit 4, p. 79

The Pain of Defeat
German prisoners are marched through the snowy streets of Stalingrad after their defeat by the Soviet army.

Allies Advance Through Italy

With North Africa under their control, the Allies were able to cross the Mediterranean into Italy. In July 1943, a combined British and American army landed first in Sicily and then in southern Italy. They defeated the Italian forces there in about a month.

After the defeats, the Italians overthrew Mussolini and signed an armistice, but fighting did not end. Hitler sent German troops to rescue Mussolini and stiffen the will of Italians fighting in the north. For the next 18 months, the Allies pushed slowly up the Italian peninsula, suffering heavy losses against strong German resistance. Still, the Italian invasion was a decisive event for the Allies because it weakened Hitler by forcing him to fight on another front.

Germans Defeated at Stalingrad

A major turning point occurred in the Soviet Union. After their lightning advance in 1941, the Germans were stalled outside Moscow and Leningrad. In 1942, Hitler launched a new offensive. This time, he aimed for the rich oil fields of the south. His troops, however, got only as far as **Stalingrad**.

The Battle of Stalingrad was one of the costliest of the war. Hitler was determined to capture Stalin's namesake city, and Stalin was equally determined to defend it. The battle began when the Germans surrounded the city. As winter closed in, a bitter street-by-street, house-by-house struggle raged. A German officer wrote that soldiers fought for two weeks for a single building. Corpses "are strewn in the cellars, on the landings and the staircases," he said. In November, the Soviets encircled their attackers. Trapped, without food or ammunition and with no hope of rescue, the German commander finally surrendered in January 1943.

After the Battle of Stalingrad, the Red Army took the offensive and drove the invaders out of the Soviet Union entirely. Hitler's forces suffered irreplaceable losses of both troops and equipment. By early 1944, Soviet troops were advancing into Eastern Europe.

 Checkpoint How did the Allies push back the Axis powers on four fronts?

The Allies Push Toward Germany

By 1944, the Western Allies were at last ready to open a second front in Europe by invading France. Allied leaders under Eisenhower faced the enormous task of planning the operation and assembling troops and supplies. To prepare the way for the invasion, Allied bombers flew constant missions over Germany. They targeted factories and destroyed aircraft that might be used against the invasion force. They also bombed railroads and bridges in France.

The D-Day Assault

The Allies chose June 6, 1944—known as **D-Day**—for the invasion of France. Just before midnight on June 5, Allied planes dropped paratroopers behind enemy lines. Then, at dawn, thousands of ships ferried 156,000 Allied troops across the English Channel. The troops

Answer

✓ Midway blocked the Japanese advance in the Pacific. El Alamein was the beginning of the end of German control of North Africa. The invasion of Italy attacked one of the Axis home lands. Stalingrad destroyed a large German army in the east.

Differentiated Instruction   Solutions for All Learners

L2 Less Proficient Readers

Tell students that many historians consider the Battle of Stalingrad to be the key turning point in World War II. Work with students to help them to find reliable internet sources and grade-level reference sources about the battle. Then challenge them to describe or illustrate one of the aspect battle—for example, the military movements or daily life in the city.

Use the following resources to help students acquire basic skills.

📑 **Adapted Reading and Note Taking Study Guide**

- Adapted Note Taking Study Guide, p. 183
- Adapted Section Summary, p. 184

Geography *Interactive*
For: Interactive map and timeline
Web Code: nbp-2931

Map Skills Axis power reached its height in Europe in 1942. Then the tide began to turn.

1. **Locate** (a) Vichy France (b) Soviet Union (c) El Alamein (d) Normandy (e) Berlin

2. **Place** Describe the extent of Axis control in 1942.

3. **Make Inferences** How did geography both help and hinder Allied advances?

Legend:
- Europe Axis powers, 1942
- Maximum Axis control, 1942
- Neutral nations, 1942
- Allied territory, 1942
- Allied advances
- Major battles

Conic Projection
0   200   400 mi
0   200   400 km

Timeline:

1942 — **1943** — **1944** — **1945** — **1946**

- **Jan 1943** Germans surrender at Stalingrad
- **Jul 1943** Allied forces land in Sicily
- **Jan 1945** Soviets enter Warsaw
- **May 7, 1945** Germany surrenders
- **Nov 1942** British defeat Germans at El Alamein
- **Sep 1943** Italians surrender to Allies
- **Jun 6, 1944** D-Day invasion at Normandy
- **Mar 1945** British and American forces cross Rhine

The Allies Push Toward Germany

L3

Instruct

- **Introduce: Vocabulary Builder**
  Have students read the Vocabulary Builder terms and definitions. Give them the following sentence and ask which term would best fill in the blank to complete the sentence: **The _____ attacks on German cities were repeated against Japan.** *(incessant)*

- **Teach** Ask **Why did the Americans and British wait until 1944 to invade France?** *(They said they were not ready until then.)* **How long did it take the Allied forces to liberate Paris and all of France?** *(about two and half months to regain Paris and another month to free the rest of France)* **What kinds of targets did the Allies bomb in Germany in 1944?** *(military bases, factories, railroads, oil depots, and cities)* **Why was it important for the Allied leaders to meet early in 1945?** *(They were closing in on Germany from both sides by that time, and the war in Europe was nearing an end; they had to agree on the strategy to end the war and on post-war arrangements.)*

- **Quick Activity** Show students *Triumph at Normandy* from the **Witness History Discovery School**™ video program. Ask volunteers to describe some of the planning and resources needed to carry out the D-Day invasion of Normandy.

Answers

Map Skills

1. Review locations with students.

2. The Axis controlled all of Eastern and Western Europe except the neutral nations (Sweden, Ireland, Portugal, Spain, and Switzerland) and the United Kingdom, which was fighting them. They also controlled the western part of the Soviet Union and almost all of North Africa.

3. helped: They could attack Germany from all sides; hindered: The Americans and British had to move resources through the Atlantic to North Africa and southern Europe.

Careers

Cartographer Mapmakers, or cartographers, make maps that show geographic data—latitude and longitude, the distance between objects, and the height or depth of physical features—or other data, such as political boundaries, the location of economic resources, and living patterns. They usually learn their skills by taking a college degree. They also need strong computer skills. Mapping technicians help cartographers carry out their work. They turn information taken from observations of the land into data that can be incorporated onto maps. These workers need less training than cartographers, and the demand for them is expected to grow more rapidly than for cartographers in the future. However, they earn less than people in cartography, which is considered a more advanced career.

Independent Practice

- Have each student select one of the three leaders, Churchill, Stalin, or Roosevelt. Have them learn more about this leader and then write an obituary, which summarizes his role and achievements during World War II.

- Have students take the role of a soldier who fought at D-Day and write a letter to family members back home describing the experience.

Monitor Progress

- Have students create an outline of the subsection The Allies Push Toward Germany that organizes and highlights the key points.

- Check Reading and Note Taking Study Guide entries for student understanding.

BIOGRAPHY

Churchill
Winston Churchill (1874–1965) was a staunch antisocialist and defender of the British Empire. As a member of Parliament, he loudly warned the British of the threat posed by Nazi Germany. After Neville Chamberlain's government failed to defend Norway from Hitler, Churchill replaced him as prime minister on May 10, 1940. Within seven weeks, France had surrendered, and Nazi forces threatened Britain. Churchill's courage and defiance steeled British resolve in the darkest days of the war when Britain stood alone against the Nazis. **How did Churchill inspire the British people?**

Roosevelt
In 1933, Franklin Delano Roosevelt (1882–1945) started his first term as president, promising to bring the United States out of the Great Depression. During his second term, FDR lent, and then gave, millions of dollars in war supplies to the struggling British. Japan's attack on Pearl Harbor quickly brought the United States into the war. From the start of American involvement, Roosevelt took the lead in establishing alliances among all countries fighting the Axis powers—including the Soviet Union. **How did Roosevelt influence World War II before Pearl Harbor?**

Stalin
Joseph Stalin (1879–1953) was born Joseph Dzhugashvili (joo gush VYEE lyee). He changed his name to Stalin, meaning "man of steel," after he joined the Bolshevik underground in the early 1900s. Stalin emerged as the sole ruler of the Soviet Union in the 1920s, and he maintained an iron grasp on the nation until his death in 1953. When Hitler's army invaded the Soviet Union and threatened Moscow in 1941, Stalin refused to leave the capital city. He eventually forced the Germans into retreat. **Why would Churchill and Roosevelt have distrusted Stalin?**

WITNESS HISTORY VIDEO

Watch *Triumph at Normandy* on the **Witness History Discovery School**™ video program to experience the planning and execution of the D-Day invasion.

DISCOVERY SCHOOL

fought their way to shore amid underwater mines and raking machine-gun fire. As one soldier who landed in the first wave of D-Day assault recalled,

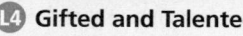
Primary Source

66 It all seemed unreal, a sort of dreaming while awake, men were screaming and dying all around me. . . I honestly could have walked the full length of the beach without touching the ground, they were that thickly strewn about. 99
—Melvin B. Farrell, *War Memories*

Still, the Allied troops clawed their way inland through the tangled hedges of Normandy. In early August, a massive armored division under American General George S. Patton helped the joint British and American forces break through German defenses and advance toward Paris. Meanwhile, other Allied forces sailed from Italy to land in southern France. In Paris, French resistance forces rose up against the occupying Germans. Under pressure from all sides, the Germans retreated. On August 25, the Allies entered Paris. Within a month, all of France was free.

Vocabulary Builder
incessant—(in SES unt) *adj.* uninterrupted, ceaseless

Allies Continue to Advance By this time, Germany was reeling under incessant, round-the-clock bombing. For two years, Allied bombers had hammered military bases, factories, railroads, oil depots, and cities.

Answer

BIOGRAPHY Churchill: with his courage and defiant attitude; Roosevelt: He gave supplies and guidance to help the British fight the Nazis; Stalin: because he showed ruthlessness in killing or exiling all his rivals before gaining power and because he had earlier allied himself with Hitler

Differentiated Instruction Solutions for All Learners

L4 Advanced Readers   L4 Gifted and Talented

Point out that the war saw heavy use of air attacks on cities. Explain that cities often held key military targets, such as factories, railroad depots, bridges, and oil facilities. They also held millions of people, however, and targeting during World War II was not precise. Have students investigate the issue of the bombing carried out during the war and write an essay exploring whether the targeting of cities was justified, not justified, or justified in some cases but not others. Remind students to offer facts as well as well-reasoned arguments to support their opinions.

The goal of this kind of bombing was to cripple Germany's industries and destroy the morale of its civilians. In one 10-day period, bombing almost erased the huge industrial city of Hamburg, killing 40,000 civilians and forcing one million to flee their homes. In February 1945, Allied raids on Dresden, not an industrial target, but considered one of the most beautiful cities in Europe, killed as many as 135,000 people.

After freeing France, Allied forces battled toward Germany. As their armies advanced into Belgium in December, Germany launched a massive counterattack. At the bloody Battle of the Bulge, which lasted more than a month, both sides took terrible losses. The Germans were unable to break through. The battle delayed the Allied advance from the west, but only for six weeks. Meanwhile, the Soviet army battled through Germany and advanced on Berlin from the east. Hitler's support within Germany was declining, and he had already survived one assassination attempt by senior officers in the German military. By early 1945, the defeat of Germany seemed <u>inevitable</u>.

Uneasy Agreement at Yalta In February 1945, Roosevelt, Churchill, and Stalin met again at Yalta, in the southern Soviet Union. Once again, the Big Three planned strategy in an atmosphere of distrust. Stalin insisted that the Soviet Union needed to maintain control of Eastern Europe to be able to protect itself from future aggression. Churchill and Roosevelt favored self-determination for Eastern Europe, which would give people the right to choose their own form of government. However, Churchill and Roosevelt needed Stalin's help to win the war.

At the **Yalta Conference,** the three leaders agreed that the Soviet Union would enter the war against Japan within three months of Germany's surrender. In return, Churchill and Roosevelt promised Stalin that the Soviets would take possession of southern Sakhalin Island, the Kuril Islands, and an occupation zone in Korea. They also agreed that Germany would be temporarily divided into four zones, to be governed by American, French, British, and Soviet forces. Stalin agreed to hold free elections in Eastern Europe. However, as you will read later, growing mistrust would later cause a split between the Allies.

 Checkpoint What agreements did Churchill, Roosevelt, and Stalin come to at Yalta?

Vocabulary Builder
<u>inevitable</u>—(in EV ih tuh bul) *adj.* unavoidable, inescapable

---

SECTION **3** Assessment

Progress Monitoring *Online*
For: Self-quiz with vocabulary practice
Web Code: nba-2931

Terms, People, and Places
1. For each term, person, or place listed at the beginning of the section, write a sentence explaining its significance.

Note Taking
2. **Reading Skill: Recognize Sequence** Use your completed timeline to answer the Focus Question: How did the Allies begin to push back the Axis powers?

Comprehension and Critical Thinking
3. **Analyze Information** How did democratic governments mobilize their economies for war?
4. **Determine Relevance** Explain why the battles of Midway, El Alamein, and Stalingrad were important turning points in the war.
5. **Predict Consequences** Why didn't the Yalta Conference lead to lasting unity among the Big Three leaders?

● **Writing About History**
Quick Write: Develop a Thesis A thesis statement summarizes the main idea of your research paper. The thesis statement should express an idea that can be defended or refuted. It should also be narrow enough to be addressed clearly in your writing.

Based on what you have read, write a thesis statement for an essay explaining the importance of the Battle of Stalingrad.

D-Day

Objectives

■ Identify the obstacles that Allied forces encountered in reaching and gaining control of the beaches of Normandy.

■ Evaluate the resources the Allies brought to the landing and how those resources contributed to its success.

Build Background Knowledge L3

Ask students to name major turning points in the war. *(Battles of Coral Sea and Midway, El Alamein, the invasion of Italy, Battle of Stalingrad)* Then explain that D-Day belongs on this list as well since it launched a new front in the west—forcing the Germans to commit resources and troops to yet another area—and proved that German troops could not keep the Allies out of France.

Instruct L3

■ Direct students' attention to the map at the top of the left-hand page. Ask **What is the purpose of this map?** *(to show where Allied troops left Britain and where they landed in France)* **In what part of France did they land?** *(Normandy)* **What were the code names of the beaches on which they landed, and which Allied troops had responsibility for which beach?** *(Americans—Utah and Omaha; British—Gold and Sword; Canadians—Juno)*

■ Ask volunteers to read aloud the captions that describe the obstacles the Allies faced on D-Day. Ask **Which facts are the most impressive or startling?** *(Answers will vary but should show an appreciation for the vast number of ships, planes, troops, and equipment the Allies amassed as well as the serious dangers they encountered before and on the beaches.)*

D-DAY

In the earliest hours of June 6, 1944, the Allies launched a surprise invasion of Normandy in France—the largest amphibious, or land and water, invasion in history. More than 156,000 Allied troops crossed the English Channel. Thousands of these troops landed on the beaches, fighting and clawing their way up the steep cliffs under heavy German fire. Paratroopers dropped from the sky. By the end of the day, about 2,500 men had given their lives. But by August, the Allies had made their way to Paris and freed it from German control.

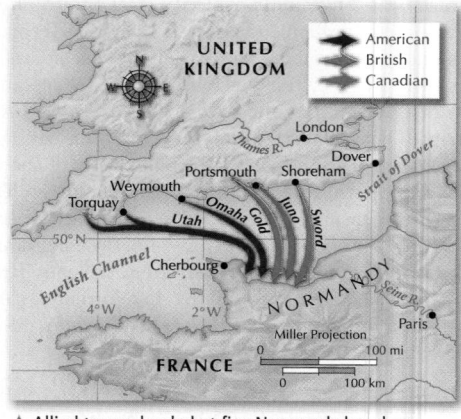

▲ Allied troops landed at five Normandy beaches, code-named Utah, Omaha, Gold, Juno, and Sword.

Overcoming Hitler's Defenses at Normandy

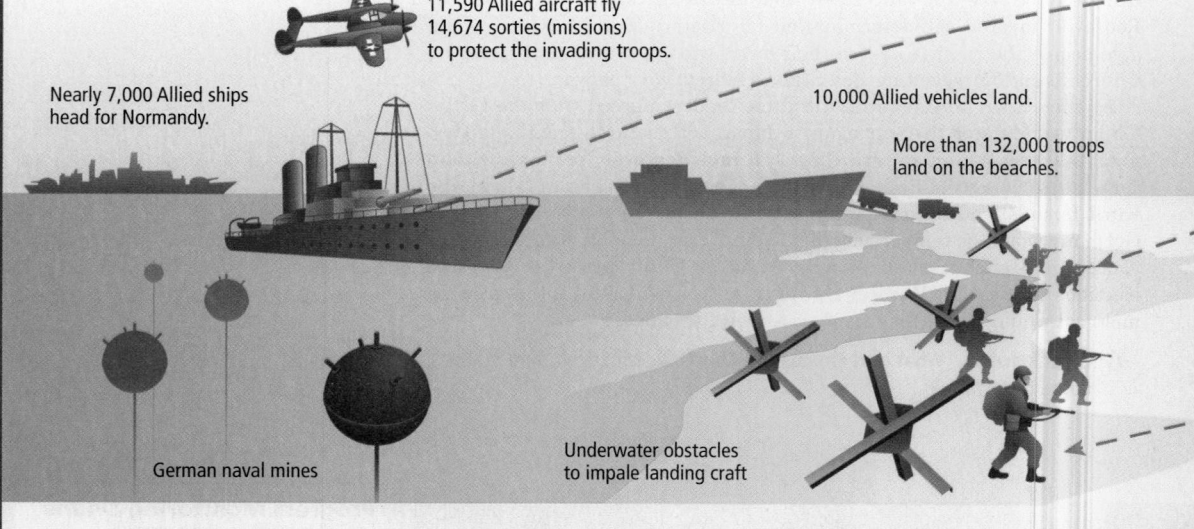

11,590 Allied aircraft fly 14,674 sorties (missions) to protect the invading troops.

Nearly 7,000 Allied ships head for Normandy.

10,000 Allied vehicles land.

More than 132,000 troops land on the beaches.

German naval mines

Underwater obstacles to impale landing craft

Allied troops faced daunting obstacles on D-Day. Naval mines threatened ships trying to land. Steel obstacles on the beaches could rip the bottoms out of landing craft at high tide. The Germans waited atop the steep cliffs.

▼ British special forces storm the beach.

L1 Special Needs   **L2 Less Proficient Readers**   **L2 English Language Learners**

For visual learners and students who need help with basic skills, direct their attention to the diagram titled Overcoming Hitler's Defenses at Normandy. Remind students that the diagram shows the many obstacles that Allied troops faced on D-Day as they worked to overcome Hitler's Defenses at Normandy. Tell students

that the diagram moves from left to right and can be divided roughly into quarters. Ask four volunteers to explain what the Allies are doing and what obstacles they have to overcome in each quarter. *(For example, on the far left, the Allies are approaching Normandy on ships but must avoid German naval mines.)*

Allied Troop Strengths and Casualties on D-Day		
Country	Troops	Estimated Casualties*
United States	73,000	6,603
Britain	61,715	2,700
Canada	21,400	946
Allied Total	**156,115**	**10,249**

*includes those killed, wounded, missing, and captured
SOURCE: The D-Day Museum Online

▲ Wounded Allied soldiers after the battle

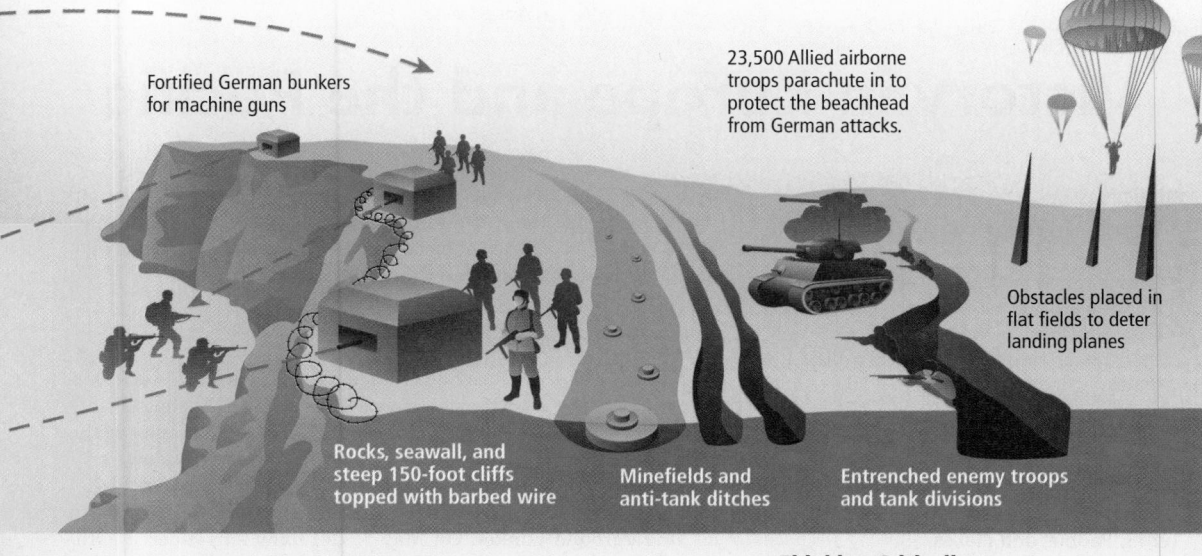

Fortified German bunkers for machine guns

23,500 Allied airborne troops parachute in to protect the beachhead from German attacks.

Obstacles placed in flat fields to deter landing planes

Rocks, seawall, and steep 150-foot cliffs topped with barbed wire

Minefields and anti-tank ditches

Entrenched enemy troops and tank divisions

▼ Omaha Beach at the end of D-Day

Thinking Critically

1. **Chart Skills** Which of the Allies suffered the greatest losses on D-Day?
2. **Draw Conclusions** Why do you think the D-Day landings were made on beaches instead of at established harbors?
3. **Diagram Skills** What do you think was the greatest obstacle the Allies had to overcome on D-Day? Explain.

History *Interactive*
For: interactive map, audio, and more
Visit: PHSchool.com
Web Code: nbp-2932

Step-by-Step Instruction

Objectives

As you teach this section, keep students focused on the following objectives to help them answer the Section Focus Question and master core content.

- Describe the reasons for the final defeat of the Nazis.
- Summarize how the Allies began to push back the Japanese in the Pacific.
- Explain the American strategy for ending the war against Japan and the consequences of that strategy.

Prepare to Read

Build Background Knowledge L3

Have the class recap the situation in Europe and the Pacific as presented so far in the chapter. Explain that in this section, they will learn how the war ended.

Set a Purpose L3

- **WITNESS HISTORY** Read the selection aloud or play the audio.

  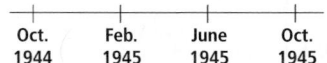 AUDIO **Witness History Audio CD,** A Soldier Remembers

  Have students look at the photograph that accompanies the Witness History extract. Ask **What attitude or mood does the soldier show?** *(Sample: relaxation, confidence)* **How does that relate to the words of the passage?** *(Lt. Ramsey speaks of his renewed hope when he heard that MacArthur had returned.)*

- **Focus** Point out the Section Focus Question and write it on the board. Tell students to refer to this question as they read. *(Answer appears with Section 4 Assessment answers.)*

- **Preview** Have students preview the Section Objectives and the list of Terms, People, and Places.

- **Note Taking** Have students read this section using the Structured Read Aloud strategy (TE, p. T20). As they read, have them fill in the timeline with events that led to the end of the war.

  Reading and Note Taking Study Guide, p. 185

1st Marine Division patch from Guadalcanal

Allied soldier in the Pacific

WITNESS HISTORY ◀)) AUDIO

A Soldier Remembers

A defeated General Douglas MacArthur left the Philippines in 1942. As he departed, he pledged his determination to free the islands with the words "I shall return." In October 1944, that pledge became a reality when MacArthur landed on the Philippine island of Leyte. As one soldier recalled,

❝When I heard that he had returned, I finally had the feeling that I might have a chance of living through the war. . . . [O]nce they landed in Leyte, I knew it was only a question of hanging on for a few more months and I would be able to live through it.❞
—Edwin Ramsey

Focus Question How did the Allies finally defeat the Axis powers?

Victory in Europe and the Pacific

Objectives
- Describe the reasons for the final defeat of the Nazis.
- Summarize how the Allies began to push back the Japanese in the Pacific.
- Explain the American strategy for ending the war against Japan and the consequences of that strategy.

Terms, People, and Places

V-E Day	kamikaze
Bataan Death March	Manhattan Project
Douglas MacArthur	Hiroshima
island-hopping	Nagasaki

Note Taking

Reading Skill: Recognize Sequence Use a timeline like the one below to sequence the events that led to the defeat of the Axis powers.

Oct. 1944	Feb. 1945	June 1945	Oct. 1945

By early spring 1945, the war in Europe was nearing its end, and the Allies turned their attention to winning the war in the Pacific. There remained a series of bloody battles ahead, as well as an agonizing decision for American President Harry Truman.

Nazis Defeated

By March 1945, the Allies had crossed the Rhine into western Germany. From the east, Soviet troops closed in on Berlin. In late April, American and Russian soldiers met and shook hands at the Elbe River. All over Europe, Axis armies began to surrender.

In Italy, guerrillas captured and executed Mussolini. As Soviet troops fought their way into Berlin, Hitler committed suicide in his underground bunker. On May 7, Germany surrendered. Officially, the war in Europe ended the next day, May 8, 1945, which was proclaimed **V-E Day** (Victory in Europe). After just 12 years, Hitler's "thousand-year Reich" was bomb-ravaged and in ruins.

The Allies were able to defeat the Axis powers in Europe for a number of reasons. Because of the location of Germany and its allies, they had to fight on several fronts simultaneously. Hitler, who took almost complete control over military decisions, made some poor ones. He underestimated the ability of the Soviet Union to fight his armies.

The enormous productive capacity of the United States was another factor. By 1944, the United States was producing twice as much as all of the Axis powers combined. Meanwhile, Allied bombing hindered German production. Oil became so scarce because of

Vocabulary Builder

Use the information below and the following resources to teach the high-use word from this section.
All in One Teaching Resources, Unit 4, p. 70; Teaching Resources, Skills Handbook, p. 3

High-Use Word	Definition and Sample Sentence
objective, p. 588	*n.* something worked toward; a goal Karl decided that his **objective** for this summer would be to improve his ability to play chess.

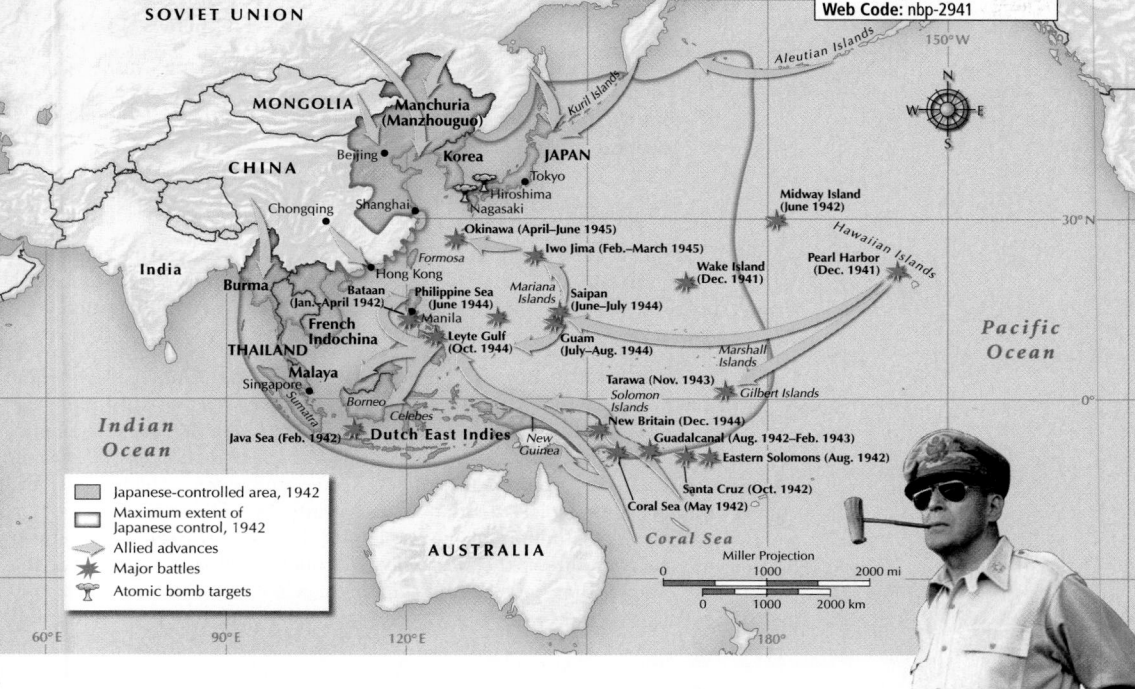

World War II in the Pacific, 1941–1945

Map Skills After the Battle of Midway, the Allies took the offensive in the Pacific. They gradually worked their way north towards Japan itself.

1. **Locate** (a) Japan (b) Pearl Harbor (c) Iwo Jima (d) Okinawa (e) Hiroshima (f) Manila
2. **Regions** Describe the extent of Japanese control in 1942.
3. **Draw Conclusions** How did geography make it difficult for Japan to maintain control of its empire?

Geography *Interactive*
For: Audio guided tour
Web Code: nbp-2941

Japanese-controlled area, 1942
Maximum extent of Japanese control, 1942
Allied advances
Major battles
Atomic bomb targets

General Douglas MacArthur

bombing that the Luftwaffe was almost grounded by the time of the D-Day invasion. With victory in Europe achieved, the Allies now had to triumph over Japan in the Pacific.

✓ **Checkpoint** How did the Allied forces finally defeat the Germans?

Struggle for the Pacific

Until mid-1942, the Japanese had won an uninterrupted series of victories. They controlled much of Southeast Asia and many Pacific islands. By May 1942, the Japanese had gained control of the Philippines, killing several hundred American soldiers and as many as 10,000 Filipino soldiers during the 65-mile **Bataan Death March.** One survivor described the ordeal as "a macabre litany of heat, dust, starvation, thirst, flies, filth, stench, murder, torture, corpses, and wholesale brutality that numbs the memory." Many Filipino civilians risked—and sometimes lost—their lives to give food and water to captives on the march.

After the battles of Midway and the Coral Sea, however, the United States took the offensive. That summer, United States Marines landed at Guadalcanal in the Solomon Islands. Victory at Guadalcanal marked the

Differentiated Instruction — Solutions for All Learners

L1 Special Needs   L2 Less Proficient Readers

To help students track Allied advances, have them turn the information on the map into a chart. Tell them to create a four-column chart with the headings *China and Korea, Southeast Asia, Pacific Islands,* and *Japan.* Then have them use the information from the map and text to fill in the dates of Allied advances on each area and the regions taken in those attacks.

L2 English Language Learners

Use the following resources to help students acquire basic skills.

Adapted Reading and Note Taking Study Guide

■ Adapted Note Taking Study Guide, p. 185
■ Adapted Section Summary, p. 186

Nazis Defeated/Struggle for the Pacific L3

Instruct

- **Introduce: Vocabulary Builder** Have students read the Vocabulary Builder term and definition. Ask **What was the Allies' *objective* in the island-hopping campaign?** *(to provide stepping stones toward an attack on Japan itself)*

- **Teach** Ask **How did its location play into Germany's defeat?** *(It was surrounded by enemies.)* **How did the Allies combine ground, naval, and air power to chip away at Japanese defenses?** *(Ground troops captured different islands as part of the island-hopping campaign; the navy blockaded Japan; and air power bombed Japanese cities and industries.)*

- **Quick Activiy** Have students access **Web Code nbp-2941** to take the **Geography Interactive Audio Guided Tour** and then answer the map skill questions in the text.

Independent Practice

Have students fill in the Outline Map *War in the Pacific.*

All in One Teaching Resources, Unit 4, p. 78

Monitor Progress

- For a completed version of the flowchart, see
  Note Taking Transparencies, 187
- Circulate to make sure students are filling in their Outline Maps accurately. Ensure students have created keys for their maps.

Answers

✓ The following factors helped the Allies defeat the Germans: Germany's location; poor decisions by Hitler; superior U.S. productive capacity

Map Skills
1. Review locations with students.
2. By 1942, Japan controlled a large portion of the Pacific; Southeast Asia; and large parts of northern and eastern China.
3. Japan's empire was far-flung, and many of its outposts were on isolated islands, making it difficult to supply and defend its empire.

Defeat for Japan

Instruct

■ **Introduce** Direct students' attention to the photograph of the mushroom cloud at the bottom of the left page. Then direct them to the photograph of Hiroshima on the top of the right page. Finally, display **Color Transparency 178:** *Hiroshima,* **by Toshimitsu Imai.** Discuss this image's more human view of the devastation caused by the bomb.

  📽 **Color Transparencies,** 178

■ **Teach** Ask **What behavior did Japanese fighters show in the battles of Iwo Jima and Okinawa and in the air?** *(willingness to fight to the death rather than surrender)* **How do you think this behavior affected the decision to use the atomic bomb?** *(Sample: It probably worried American decision makers when they thought about invading Japan.)* **Why did the Americans drop the second atomic bomb?** *(Japan continued to refuse to surrender even after the dropping of the first bomb and the Soviet invasion of Manchuria.)*

■ **Quick Activity** The decision to drop the atomic bombs is one of the most controversial presidential decisions in history. Have students debate Truman's decision. They might consult Web sites that carry first-person accounts of survivors to learn more about the effects of the bomb. They should also consider the American military estimates of the casualties—Japanese as well as American—that would result from an invasion of Japan.

Independent Practice

Primary Source To help students better understand the impact of atomic weapons, have them read the selection from John Hersey's *Hiroshima* and complete the worksheet.

  All in One **Teaching Resources, Unit 4,** p. 75

Monitor Progress

Check Reading and Note Taking Study Guide entries for student understanding.

Answers

✔ island-hopping

Caption Sample: because they were worried about the harm and destruction it could cause

---

Vocabulary Builder
objective—(ub JEK tiv) *n.* something worked toward; a goal

beginning of an **"island-hopping"** campaign. The goal of the campaign was to recapture some Japanese-held islands while bypassing others. The captured islands served as steppingstones to the next <u>objective</u>. In this way, American forces, led by General **Douglas MacArthur,** gradually moved north towards Japan. By 1944, the United States Navy, commanded by Admiral Chester Nimitz, was blockading Japan, and American bombers pounded Japanese cities and industries. In October 1944, MacArthur began the fight to retake the Philippines. The British, meanwhile, were pushing Japanese forces back into the jungles of Burma and Malaya.

✔ **Checkpoint** What strategy did General MacArthur use to fight the Japanese in the Pacific?

Defeat for Japan

With war won in Europe, the Allies poured their resources into defeating Japan. By mid-1945, most of the Japanese navy and air force had been destroyed. Yet the Japanese still had an army of two million men. The road to victory, it appeared, would be long and costly.

Invasion or the Bomb? In bloody battles on the islands of Iwo Jima from February to March 1945 and Okinawa from April to July 1945, the Japanese had shown that they would fight to the death rather than surrender. Beginning in 1944, some young Japanese men chose to become **kamikaze** (kah muh KAH zee) pilots who undertook suicide missions, crashing their explosive-laden airplanes into American warships.

While Allied military leaders planned for invasion, scientists offered another way to end the war. Scientists understood that by splitting the atom, they could create an explosion far more powerful than any yet known. Allied scientists, some of them German and Italian refugees, conducted research, code-named the **Manhattan Project,** racing to harness the atom. In July 1945, they successfully tested the first atomic bomb at Alamogordo, New Mexico.

News of this test was brought to the new American president, Harry Truman. Truman had taken office after Franklin Roosevelt died unexpectedly on April 12. He realized that the atomic bomb was a terrible new force for destruction. Still, after consulting with his advisors, and

Nuclear Blast
The world's first nuclear explosion instantly vaporized the tower from which it was launched. Seconds later an enormous blast sent searing heat across the desert and knocked observers to the ground. Shown here is an atomic bomb's characteristic mushroom cloud. *Why might the scientists who created the bomb have counseled leaders not to use it?*

History Background

The Brain Drain Both before and during World War II, thousands of people emigrated from Europe to escape the brutal police of the fascist states. This massive migration included gifted artists, scholars, and scientists, many of whom were Jewish. Among the scientists were specialists who played vital roles in the Manhattan Project, in which the United States developed the first atomic bombs. Hitler showed little concern for the negative impact that the departure of these brilliant minds would have on German science. He once said, "If the dismissal of Jewish scientists means the annihilation of contemporary German science, we shall do without science for a few years."

determining that it would save American lives, he decided to use the new weapon against Japan.

At the time, Truman was meeting with other Allied leaders in the city of Potsdam, Germany. They issued a warning to Japan to surrender or face "complete destruction" and "utter devastation." When the Japanese ignored the warning, the United States took action.

Utter Devastation On August 6, 1945, an American plane dropped an atomic bomb over the city of **Hiroshima.** The bomb flattened four square miles and instantly killed more than 70,000 people. In the months that followed, many more would die from radiation sickness, a deadly after-effect of exposure to radioactive materials.

On August 8, the Soviet Union declared war on Japan and invaded Manchuria. Again, Japanese leaders did not respond. The next day, the United States dropped a second atomic bomb, this time on the city of **Nagasaki.** More than 40,000 people were killed in this second explosion.

Finally, on August 10, Emperor Hirohito intervened, an action unheard of for a Japanese emperor, and forced the government to surrender. On September 2, 1945, the formal peace treaty was signed on board the American battleship *Missouri,* anchored in Tokyo Bay.

Hiroshima in Ruins
The atomic bomb reduced the center of Hiroshima to smoldering ruins (top left), but the full effect of the bomb would take years to materialize. A woman (above) pays respects to the victims of the atomic bomb at the Memorial Cenotaph in Peace Memorial Park in Hiroshima. A cenotaph is a monument that honors people who are buried elsewhere.

✔ **Checkpoint** What strategies did the Allies use to end the war with Japan?

Assess and Reteach

Assess Progress L3

- Have students complete the Section Assessment.

- Administer the Section Quiz.

All in One Teaching Resources, Unit 4, p. 68

- To further assess student understanding, use

  📖 **Progress Monitoring Transparencies,** 126

Reteach

If students need more instruction, have them read the section summary.

 Reading and Note Taking Study Guide, p. 186 L3

 Adapted Reading and Note Taking Study Guide, p. 186 L1 L2

 Spanish Reading and Note Taking Study Guide, p. 186 L2

Extend L4

Have students write an essay explaining whether they think President Truman was right or wrong in approving the use of atomic bombs on Hiroshima and Nagasaki. Remind them that if they disagree with Truman's decision, they need to explain how they think the war would have ended otherwise and what casualties, Japanese as well as American, would have been suffered.

Answer

✔ The Americans dropped two atomic bombs on Japan, and the Soviets invaded Manchuria.

SECTION 4 Assessment

Progress Monitoring *Online*
For: Self-quiz with vocabulary practice
Web Code: nba-2941

Terms, People, and Places
1. For each term, person, or place listed at the beginning of the section, write a sentence explaining its significance.

Note Taking

2. **Reading Skill: Recognize Sequence** Use your completed flowchart to answer the Focus Question: How did the Allies finally defeat the Axis powers?

Comprehension and Critical Thinking
3. **Determine Relevance** How did the location of the Axis powers in Europe contribute to their defeat?
4. **Draw Inferences** What factors besides ending the war in the Pacific might have contributed to President Harry Truman's decision to drop the atomic bomb?

● **Writing About History**

Quick Write: Make an Outline Once you have a thesis and have gathered research on your topics, you must choose an organization. Some choices are compare and contrast, order of importance, chronological, and cause and effect. Using one of these organizations, create an outline for the following thesis statement: The atomic bomb was a decisive weapon in World War II.

Section 4 Assessment

1. Sentences should reflect an understanding of each term, person, or place listed at the beginning of the section.
2. Germany lost because its position made it vulnerable to attack on two sides; Hitler underestimated the ability of the Soviet Union to fight; U.S. productive capacity was large enough to supply the Allies with vital equipment; and Allied bombing seri-ously damaged German production. Japan lost because its far-flung empire was hard to defend; the island-hopping campaign worked; and the U.S. developed and used atomic bombs.
3. Germany was forced to defend itself on two fronts, a difficult task. Japan had difficulty defending its far-flung empire.
4. Sample: wanting to show the Soviets that the U.S. had a powerful weapon

● **Writing About History**
Students' outlines should include sections detailing the war situation before the atomic bombs were dropped and the results of their use.

For additional assessment, have students access **Progress Monitoring *Online*** at **Web Code nba-2941.**

Step-by-Step Instruction

Objectives

As you teach this section, keep students focused on the following objectives to help them answer the Section Focus Question and master core content.

■ Describe the issues faced by the Allies after World War II ended.

■ Summarize the organization of the United Nations.

■ Analyze how new conflicts developed among the former Allies in the years after World War II.

Prepare to Read

Build Background Knowledge L3

Discuss with students how the phrase "The enemy of my enemy is my friend." applies to the United States and the Soviet Union during World War II. Then have them predict what will happen once their common enemy is defeated.

Set a Purpose L3

■ **WITNESS HISTORY** Read the selection aloud or play the audio.

🔊 AUDIO **Witness History Audio CD,** The War Is Over!

Ask **What is Truman's tone?** *(serious; grateful to the people who served in the armed forces)* **How does that contrast with the tone of the photograph and the newspaper headline?** *(The couple kissing and the headline both show joy and excitement.)*

■ **Focus** Point out the Section Focus Question and write it on the board. Tell students to refer to this question as they read. *(Answer appears with Section 5 Assessment answers.)*

■ **Preview** Have students preview the Section Objectives and the list of Terms, People, and Places.

■ **Note Taking** Have students read this section using the Paragraph Shrinking strategy (TE, p. T20). As they read, have students fill in an outline of the section.

📖 **Reading and Note Taking Study Guide,** pp. 187–188

▲ Newspaper headline on the day Japan surrendered

▶ A sailor embraces a nurse when the end of the war is announced.

The War Is Over!

American President Harry Truman made these remarks on the day the Japanese surrendered:

❝ Our first thoughts, of course—thoughts of gratefulness and deep obligation—go out to those of our loved ones who have been killed or maimed in this terrible war. On land and sea and in the air, American men and women have given their lives so that this day of ultimate victory might come and assure the survival of a civilized world . . . ❞

Focus Question What issues arose in the aftermath of World War II and how did new tensions develop?

The End of World War II

Objectives

• Describe the issues faced by the Allies after World War II ended.

• Summarize the organization of the United Nations.

• Analyze how new conflicts developed among the former Allies after World War II.

Terms, People, and Places

Nuremberg	Marshall Plan
United Nations (UN)	North Atlantic Treaty
Cold War	Organization (NATO)
Truman Doctrine	Warsaw Pact

Note Taking

Reading Skill: Recognize Sequence Sequence the events following World War II by creating an outline of this section. Use the outline below as a starting point.

```
I. The War's Aftermath
   A. Devastation
      1. As many as 50 million dead
      2.
```

Even as the Allies celebrated victory, the appalling costs of the war began to emerge. The war had killed as many as 50 million people around the world. In Europe alone, over 30 million people had lost their lives, more than half of them civilians. The Soviet Union suffered the worst casualties, with over 20 million dead. As they had after World War I, the Allies faced difficult decisions about the future.

The War's Aftermath

"Give me ten years and you will not be able to recognize Germany," said Hitler in 1933. Indeed, Germany in 1945 was an unrecognizable ruin. Parts of Poland, the Soviet Union, Japan, China, and other countries also lay in ruins. Total war had gutted cities, factories, harbors, bridges, railroads, farms, and homes. Over twenty million refugees wandered Europe. Amid the devastation, hunger, disease, and mental illness took their toll for years after the fighting ended. As they had after World War I, the Allies faced difficult decisions about the future.

Horrors of the Holocaust Numbers alone did not tell the story of the Nazi nightmare in Europe or the Japanese brutality in Asia. During the war, the Allies were aware of the existence of Nazi concentration camps and death camps. But only at war's end did they learn the full extent of the inhumanity of the Holocaust. American General Dwight Eisenhower, who visited the camps, was stunned to come "face to face with indisputable evidence of Nazi brutality and ruthless disregard of every sense of decency."

Vocabulary Builder

Use the information below and the following resources to teach the high-use words from this section.

🔲 **Teaching Resources, Unit 4,** p. 70; **Teaching Resources, Skills Handbook,** p. 3

High-Use Words	Definitions and Sample Sentences
convene, p. 591	*vi.* to meet; assemble The student council **convened** every month in the cafeteria to plan events.
invoke, p. 594	*vt.* to resort to; to call upon In order to finish preparing the food before the guests arrived, I **invoked** the help of my brothers.

War Crimes Trials At wartime meetings, the Allies had agreed that Axis leaders should be tried for "crimes against humanity." In Germany, the Allies held war crimes trials in **Nuremberg,** where Hitler had staged mass rallies in the 1930s. Nearly 200 Germans and Austrians were tried, and most were found guilty. A handful of top Nazis received death sentences. Others were imprisoned. Similar war crimes trials were held in Japan. Many of those accused of war crimes were never captured or brought to trial. However, the trials showed that political and military leaders could be held accountable for actions in wartime.

Occupying Allies The war crimes trials further discredited the totalitarian ideologies that had led to the war. Yet disturbing questions remained. Why had ordinary people in Germany, Poland, France, and elsewhere accepted—and even collaborated in—Hitler's "Final Solution"?

The United States felt that strengthening democracy would ensure tolerance and peace. The Western Allies built new governments in occupied Germany and Japan with democratic constitutions to protect the rights of all citizens. In Japan, the occupying forces under General MacArthur helped Japanese politicians to create a new constitution that gave power to the Japanese people, rather than the emperor.

✓ **Checkpoint** Why did the Allies hold war crimes trials for Axis leaders?

Establishing the United Nations

In April 1945, delegates from 50 nations <u>convened</u> in San Francisco to draft a charter for the **United Nations (UN).** The UN would play a greater role in world affairs than did its predecessor, the League of Nations.

Under the UN Charter, each of the member nations has one vote in the General Assembly. A much smaller body called the Security Council has greater power. Each of its five permanent members—the United States, the Soviet Union (today Russia), Britain, France, and China—has the right to veto any council decision. The goal was to give these great powers the authority to ensure the peace. The Security Council has the power to apply economic sanctions or send a peace-keeping military force to try to resolve disputes. Differences among the nations on the Security Council, most notably the United States and the Soviet Union, have often kept the UN from taking action. Since the fall of the Soviet Union in 1991, more peacekeeping delegations have been approved.

The UN's work would go far beyond peacekeeping. The organization would take on many world problems—from preventing the outbreak of disease and improving education to protecting refugees and helping nations to develop economically. UN agencies like the World Health Organization and the Food and Agricultural Organization have provided aid for millions of people around the world.

✓ **Checkpoint** Compare and contrast the United Nations and the League of Nations.

Casualties of World War II

	Military Dead*	Military Wounded*	Civilian Dead*
Allies			
Britain	264,000	277,000	93,000
France	213,000	400,000	350,000
China	1,310,000	1,753,000	1,000,000
Soviet Union	7,500,000	14,012,000	15,000,000
United States	292,000	672,000	6,000
Axis Powers			
Germany	3,500,000	5,000,000	780,000
Italy	242,000	66,000	153,000
Japan	1,300,000	4,000,000	672,000

World War II resulted in enormous casualties and disruption. Afterwards, millions of displaced Europeans, like the Germans above, searched for relatives they had been separated from during the war. **Chart Skills** *Which nation suffered the greatest number of both civilian and military casualties?*

* All figures are estimates.
SOURCE: *Encyclopædia Britannica; The Harper Encyclopedia of Military History,* R. Ernest Dupuy and Trevor N. Dupuy

Vocabulary Builder
<u>convened</u>—(kun VEEND) *vi.* met; assembled

Instruct

■ **Introduce: Vocabulary Builder**
Have students read the Vocabulary Builder term and definition. Ask **What was the purpose of the courts *convened* in Nuremburg after the end of the war?** *(to try German and Austrian officials for war crimes)*

■ **Teach** Ask **How did the war crimes trials help in creating new governments in Germany and Japan?** *(They helped discredit the old leaders who had led the countries into war and committed such terrible crimes.)* **How was the United Nations meant to maintain peace?** *(by giving the Security Council the power to apply economic sanctions or send troops to enforce its decisions)* **What issues besides peacekeeping has the United Nations become involved in over the years?** *(preventing the outbreak of disease, improving education, protecting refugees, economic development)*

Independent Practice

Have students consider the status of the United Nations Security Council in today's world. Tell them to write an essay that addresses how relevant the present permanent members are in the world today.

Monitor Progress

As students complete their outline, circulate to make sure they understand which detail to include. For a completed version of the outline, see
⌂ **Note Taking Transparencies,** 188

Answers

✓ to hold them accountable for "crimes against humanity"

Chart Skills the Soviet Union

✓ Sample: The Security Council gave the United Nations the authority to enforce its decisions, which the League of Nations never had; the United States belonged to the United Nations but not to the League of Nations.

The Alliance Breaks Apart

Instruct

- **Introduce: Key Terms** Direct students' attention to the key term *Cold War* (in blue). Ask **Why was the conflict between the United States and the Soviet Union called a "cold" war?** Guide students to see that while these nations were bitter rivals, and although both were involved in shooting wars at times during the long Cold War, they never fought each other directly.

- **Teach** Ask **What were Stalin's goals in Eastern Europe?** *(communist leadership in those countries; to create a set of nations that could act as a buffer between the Soviet Union and Germany)* **What were Roosevelt and Churchill's goals?** *(free elections so people could choose whatever leaders they wanted)* **What was the outcome?** *(Stalin made sure that communists took control in those countries.)*

Independent Practice

Divide the class into halves to debate the following statement: "The Cold War was inevitable." Remind those who take the opposing view that they must specify what steps could have been taken—by both sides—to avoid it.

Monitor Progress

Remind students that the Cold War arose in part from different goals or beliefs held by American and Soviet leaders and from actions taken by both countries. Have them create a two-column chart with the headings *Goals/Beliefs* and *Actions*. Then have them list appropriate details from the text under each heading.

Answer

 reparations in Germany and the nature of the governments of Eastern Europe

The Alliance Breaks Apart

Amid the rubble of war, a new power structure emerged. In Europe, Germany was defeated. France and Britain were exhausted. Two other powers, the United States and the Soviet Union, emerged as the new world leaders. The United States abandoned its traditional policy of isolationism to counter what President Truman saw as the communist threat.

Differences Grow Between the Allies During the war, the Soviet Union and the nations of the West had cooperated to defeat Nazi Germany. After the war's end, the Allies set up councils made up of foreign ministers from Britain, France, China, the United States, and the Soviet Union to iron out the peace agreements discussed at various conferences during the war. The councils concluded peace agreements with several Axis nations in 1947. However, reparations in Germany and the nature of the governments of Eastern Europe caused divisions to deepen between the former Allies. Conflicting ideologies and mutual distrust soon led to the conflict known as the Cold War. The Cold War was a state of tension and hostility between nations aligned with the United States on one side and the Soviet Union on the other, without armed conflict between the major rivals.

The Cold War Begins Stalin had two goals in Eastern Europe. First, he wanted to spread communism in the area. Second, he wanted to create a buffer zone of friendly governments as a defense against Germany, which had invaded Russia during World War I and again in 1941.

As the Red Army had pushed German forces out of Eastern Europe, it had left behind occupying forces. At wartime conferences, Stalin tried to persuade the West to accept Soviet influence in Eastern Europe. The Soviet dictator pointed out that the United States was not consulting the Soviet Union about peace terms for Italy or Japan, both of which were defeated and occupied by American and British troops. In the same way, the Soviet Union would determine the fate of the Eastern European lands that it occupied.

Roosevelt and Churchill rejected Stalin's view, making him promise "free elections" in Eastern Europe. Stalin ignored that pledge. Most Eastern European countries had existing Communist parties, many of which had actively resisted the Nazis during the war. Backed by the Red Army, these local Communists in Poland, Czechoslovakia, and elsewhere destroyed rival political parties and even assassinated democratic leaders. By 1948, pro-Soviet communist governments were in place throughout Eastern Europe.

✔ **Checkpoint** What post-war issues caused the Western Allies and the Soviet Union to disagree?

New Conflicts Develop

Stalin soon showed his aggressive intentions outside of Eastern Europe. In Greece, Stalin backed communist rebels who were fighting to overturn a right-wing monarchy supported by Britain. By 1947, however, Britain could no longer afford to defend Greece. Stalin was also menacing Turkey in the Dardanelles.

A Widening Gulf
Although Stalin and Truman were friendly at the Potsdam Conference (above), this Soviet propaganda poster from 1949 shows that relations between the two nations were becoming strained. The poster urges support "For a stable peace! Against those who would ignite a new war." The small caricatures of Churchill and Uncle Sam in the lower corner indicate who "those" people are.

Differentiated Instruction Solutions for All Learners

L1 Special Needs **L2 Less Proficient Readers**

Pair less proficient readers with advanced readers. Have the latter students write each key event in the section on a separate slip of paper, without including the dates. Have the less proficient readers put the events in the correct order and fill in the dates. Have their partners confirm the answers and help them review any events they placed or dated incorrectly.

Use the following resources to help students acquire basic skills.

Adapted Reading and Note Taking Study Guide

- Adapted Note Taking Study Guide, pp. 187–188
- Adapted Section Summary, p. 189

The Truman Doctrine Truman took action. On March 12, 1947, Truman outlined a new policy to Congress: "I believe that it must be the policy of the United States to support free peoples who are resisting attempted subjugation by armed minorities or by outside pressures." This policy, known as the **Truman Doctrine**, was rooted in the idea of containment, limiting communism to the areas already under Soviet control.

The Truman Doctrine would guide the United States for decades. It made clear that Americans would resist Soviet expansion in Europe or elsewhere in the world. Truman soon sent military and economic aid and advisors to Greece and Turkey so that they could withstand the communist threat.

The Marshall Plan Postwar hunger and poverty made Western European lands fertile ground for communist ideas. To strengthen democratic governments, the United States offered a massive aid package, called the **Marshall Plan.** Under it, the United States funneled food and economic assistance to Europe to help countries rebuild. Billions of dollars in American aid helped war-shattered Europe recover rapidly.

President Truman also offered aid to the Soviet Union and its satellites, or dependent states, in Eastern Europe. However, Stalin declined and forbade Eastern European countries to accept American aid. Instead, he promised help from the Soviet Union in its place.

Germany Stays Divided Defeated Germany became another focus of the Cold War. The Soviet Union took reparations for its massive war losses by dismantling and moving factories and other resources in its occupation zone to help rebuild the Soviet Union. France, Britain, and the United States also took some reparations out of their portions of Germany. However, Western leaders wanted the German economy to recover in order to restore political stability to the region. The Western Allies decided to unite their zones of occupation. Then, they extended the Marshall Plan to western Germany. The Soviets were furious at Western moves to rebuild the German economy and deny them further reparations. They strengthened their hold on eastern Germany.

The Berlin Airlift
After World War II, Germany, and Berlin within it, was divided into communist and noncommunist zones. In the photo below, children in West Berlin greet a plane delivering supplies during the Berlin Airlift.

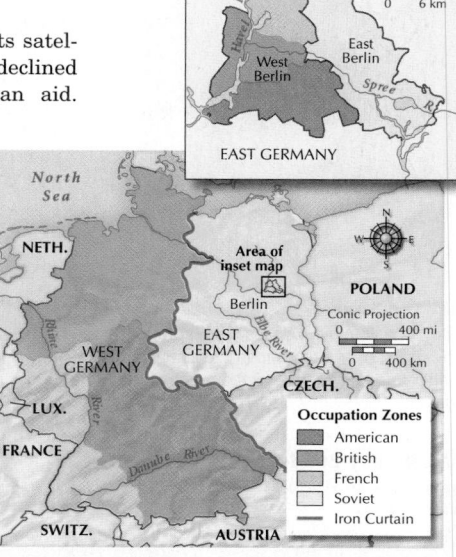

Occupation Zones
- American
- British
- French
- Soviet
- Iron Curtain

Instruct

■ **Introduce: Vocabulary Builder**
Have students read the Vocabulary Builder term and definition. Ask **What policy was *invoked* by presidents after Truman to explain steps they took to block the spread of communism?** *(the Truman Doctrine; containment)*

■ **Teach** Ask **Why did Truman announce the Truman Doctrine?** *(as a result of growing Soviet power in general and to block communist gains in Greece and Turkey in particular)* **How was the Marshall Plan related to that doctrine?** *(The United States provided aid to European countries to help them rebuild in the belief that doing so would strengthen democratic governments and prevent communists from taking control.)* **Why did Stalin block Marshall Plan aid in Eastern Europe?** *(He feared that American aid would influence countries there in favor of the United States.)* **What was the effect of the forming Cold War on Germany?** *(It remained divided and developed into two separate nations.)*

■ **Quick Activity** Display **Color Transparency 179: NATO and Warsaw Pact Member Nations.** Ask volunteers to read the names of the countries in each alliance aloud while other volunteers show their locations on a wall map of Europe. When the exercise is complete, discuss why the two alliances were sometimes referred to as "the West" (NATO) and "the East" (the Warsaw Pact).

▥ Color Transparencies, 179

Independent Practice

Biography To help students better understand the president who led the country as World War II ended and the Cold War began, have them read the biography *Harry Truman* and complete the worksheet.

All in One Teaching Resources, Unit 4, p. 76

Monitor Progress

Check Reading and Note Taking Study Guide entries for student understanding.

History Background

The Berlin Airlift The planes of the Berlin Airlift, or "Operation Vittles," carried more than 2.3 million tons of food, coal, and supplies into Berlin. Planes landed all day, every day. A new plane touched down every 3 minutes, was unloaded in 17, and then took off to receive another load. The operation was so successful that Berlin's two airfields could not handle all the traffic. American soldiers and German civilians—about 17,000 of them—had to build a third airfield to handle the traffic. Lieutenant Gail Halvorsen came up with the idea for a part of the airlift called "Operation Little Vittles." Soldiers formed tiny parachutes out of handkerchiefs, which were used to drop fruit, candy, and gum to Berlin's children.

Assess Progress

- Have students complete the Section Assessment.

- Administer the Section Quiz.

 **Teaching Resources, Unit 4,** p. 69

- To further assess student understanding, use

 Progress Monitoring Transparencies, 127

Reteach

If students need more instruction, have them read the section summary.

Reading and Note Taking Study Guide, p. 189 **L3**

Adapted Reading and Note Taking Study Guide, p. 189 **L1 L2**

Spanish Reading and Note Taking Study Guide, p. 189 **L2**

Extend **L4**

Point out that some people criticize the United Nations, saying that it does not use resources efficiently and that the United States should not put its foreign policy goals or actions at the mercy of UN approval. Have students write an essay expressing their opinion on the proper role of the United States within the United Nations.

Answer

✓ containment, the policy of trying to prevent the expansion of communism

---

The Red Menace
Films like *The Red Menace* (1949) dramatized the threat of communism in the United States and formed a vital part of the propaganda war.

Vocabulary Builder
invoked—(in VOKED) *vt.* resorted to; called upon

Germany thus became a divided nation. In West Germany, the democratic nations allowed the people to write their own constitution and regain self-government. In East Germany, the Soviet Union installed a socialist dictatorship under Stalin's control.

The Berlin Airlift Stalin's resentment at Western moves to rebuild Germany triggered a crisis over Berlin. Even though it lay deep within the Soviet zone, the former German capital was occupied by all four victorious Allies. In June 1948, Stalin tried to force the Western Allies out of Berlin by sealing off every railroad and highway into the Western sectors of the city. The Western powers responded to the blockade by mounting a round-the-clock airlift. For more than a year, cargo planes supplied West Berliners with food and fuel. Their success forced the Soviets to end the blockade. Although the West had won, the crisis deepened.

Opposing Alliances Tensions continued to grow. In 1949, the United States, Canada, and ten other countries formed a new military alliance called the **North Atlantic Treaty Organization (NATO).** Members pledged to help one another if any one of them were attacked.

In 1955, the Soviet Union responded by forming its own military alliance, the **Warsaw Pact.** It included the Soviet Union and seven satellites in Eastern Europe. Unlike NATO, however, the Warsaw Pact was often invoked by the Soviets to keep its satellites in order. The Warsaw Pact cemented the division of Europe into "eastern" and "western" blocs. In the East were the Soviet-dominated countries of Eastern Europe. These countries were communist in name but dictatorships in practice, like the Soviet Union itself. In the West were the Western democracies, led by the United States.

The Propaganda War Both sides participated in a propaganda war. The United States spoke of defending capitalism and democracy against communism and totalitarianism. The Soviet Union claimed the moral high ground in the struggle against Western imperialism. Yet linked to those stands, both sides sought world power.

 Checkpoint What foreign policy pattern did the United States establish with the Truman Doctrine?

SECTION **5** Assessment

Progress Monitoring *Online*
For: Self-quiz with vocabulary practice
Web Code: nba-2951

Terms, People, and Places
1. What do many of the key terms listed at the beginning of the section have in common? Explain.

Note Taking
2. **Reading Skill: Recognize Sequence** Use your completed outline to answer the Focus Question: What issues arose in the aftermath of World War II and how did new tensions develop?

Comprehension and Critical Thinking
3. **Compare and Contrast** How did the peace made after World War II differ from that made after World War I?
4. **Identify Central Issues** What was the main purpose of the UN when it was founded?
5. **Recognize Causes** List two causes of the Cold War.
6. **Draw Conclusions** Why is it important to remember the inhumanity of the Holocaust?

● **Writing About History**
Quick Write: Credit Sources When you use quotes or ideas from your sources in your paper, you must give proper credit. One way to do this is to list the author and page number of the material you have used in parentheses following the statement. Then, include a bibliography at the end of your paper. Research a topic from this section and write a paragraph using two sources. Credit the sources where appropriate and list them at the end.

Section 5 Assessment

1. Sample: The Truman Doctrine and the Marshall Plan were U.S. steps taken early in the Cold War, which was based on rivalry between the U.S.-led alliance of NATO and the Soviet-led alliance of the Warsaw Pact.
2. Issues: the status of Germany and free elections in Eastern Europe. Tensions: the Americans and the Soviets were threatened by each other's actions.

3. Sample: After World War II, the Allies made stronger efforts to reform the political systems of the defeated nations and tried to create a stronger international organization.
4. to ensure peace
5. conflict over reparations in Germany and communism in Eastern Europe, conflicting ideologies, and mutual distrust.
6. Sample: to have a better chance of preventing something similar from happening in the future

● **Writing About History**
Students' paragraphs should cite information from at least two sources, and those sources should be identified appropriately.

For additional assessment, have students access **Progress Monitoring *Online*** at **Web Code nba-2951.**

GENOCIDE

Why do people sometimes commit the crime of genocide?

Concept Connector

Genocide

Objectives

- Understand the ultimate goal of those who commit genocide.
- Describe factors that have led people to commit genocide.
- Complete the Web Quest on genocide.

In This Chapter

Hitler's Final Solution involved rounding up all the Jews in German-held territory (right). Millions were then brutally killed in death camps. British Prime Minister Winston Churchill called this well-organized plan of mass murder "a crime that has no name." After the war, the United Nations gave the crime a name: genocide. Genocide is any act committed with the intention of destroying an entire national, ethnic, racial or religious group.

Throughout History

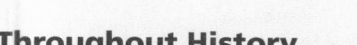

- **1500s** European guns and disease kill millions of Native Americans in the Americas.

- **1915–1916** Muslim Turks slaughter members of the Armenian Christian minority in the Ottoman Empire.

- **1938** Nazis urge mobs to attack and rob German Jews during Krisstallnacht.

- **1994** Ethnic conflict in Rwanda leads to the murder of 800,000 Tutsis and moderate Hutus.

- **2004** Arab militias in Sudan unleash violence against non-Arab Muslim villagers in Darfur.

Continuing Today

In recent times, countries on the Balkan peninsula and in Africa have witnessed widespread violence against ethnic or religious minorities. The struggle in Darfur has driven thousands of refugees into refugee camps (below), where they depend on international relief agencies for food and medical help.

Build Background Knowledge L3

Ask students to explain how the Nuremberg Laws affected Jews in Nazi Germany. *(Jews could not hold government jobs, practice law or medicine, teach or attend German schools or universities, or marry non-Jews)* Ask: **How did the Nuremberg laws set the stage for greater discrimination against the Jewish people?**

Instruct L3

- Direct students' attention to the Essential Question: **Why do people sometimes commit the crime of genocide?** Have students read In This Chapter. Ask: **How do you think other Jewish people responded to a scene like this?**

- Have students review the Throughout History time line. Ask: **What conditions lead to genocide?** Have students consider what responsibilities other nations have when they know a nation is engaged in genocide.

- Assign the Web Quest activity.

Independent Practice

Concept Connector Have students fill in the Web Quest reflection question on genocide in their Concept Connector Journal.

 Reading and Note Taking Study Guide, p. 268

Monitor Progress

Circulate to make sure that students are filling in their Concept Connector Journal. Ensure they understand the factors that cause people to commit genocide.

21st Century Skills

TRANSFER Activities

1. **Analyze** Throughout history, what motives have led people to commit genocide?

2. **Infer** Under what conditions is genocide more likely to occur?

3. **Transfer** Complete a Web quest in which you document the motives for genocide; record your thoughts in the Concept Connector Journal; and learn to make a video. Web Code nbh-2908

Connect to Our World

Connections to Today The Nuremberg Trials marked the first time in history that individuals were put on trial for genocide. After the trials, the new United Nations approved a convention that defined genocide as actions taken to kill, injure, or harm a particular group of people or to prevent them from having or rearing children. Such actions are considered an international crime whether they take place in a period of war or peace, and are punishable even if they are directed by a country's government against its own citizens. In recent years, international courts have tried people, including leaders, from Serbia and Rwanda for their role in organizing and carrying out genocide. No agreement has yet been reached on trying those who carried out the Cambodian genocide, however.

Transfer Activities

1. Motives for genocide include extreme nationalism, fear of others, religious persecution.
2. Genocide is more likely to occur under repressive, authoritarian, or totalitarian governments.
3. Students' work should be evaluated against the rubric at Web Code nbh-2908.

- Have students use the Quick Study Guide to prepare for this chapter's tests. Students may wish to refer to the following pages as they review:

Key Causes of World War II
Section 1, pp. 562–567

Key Political Leaders
Section 1, pp. 562–567; Section 2, pp. 569–572, 575–576; Section 3, pp. 578–580, 582–583; Section 4, pp. 588–589; Section 5, pp. 592–594

The Allies vs. the Axis
Section 3, pp. 577–583

Reasons for Allied Victory
Section 4, pp. 586–589

Key Events of World War II
Section 1, pp. 564–567; Section 2, pp. 569–574, 575–576; Section 3, pp. 578–585; Section 4, pp. 587–589

- For additional review, remind **L3** students to refer to the

  Reading and Note Taking Study Guide
  Note Taking Study Guide, pp. 179, 181, 183, 185, 187–188
  Section Summaries, pp. 180, 182, 184, 186, 189

- Have students access **Web Code nbp-2962** for this chapter's *History Interactive* timeline, which includes expanded entries and additional events.

- If students need more instruction on analyzing timelines, have them read the **Skills Handbook,** p. SH30.

- When students have completed their study of the chapter, distribute Chapter Tests A and B.

  All in One Teaching Resources, Unit 4, pp. 80–85

For **Progress Monitoring *Online*,** refer students to the Self-test with vocabulary practice at **Web Code nba-2961.**

Progress Monitoring *Online*
For: Self-test with vocabulary practice
Web Code: nba-2961

Key Causes of World War II

- Failure of World War I peace settlement, Treaty of Versailles
- Global economic depression
- Fascism, militarism, and imperialism in Germany, Italy, and Japan
- Weakness of the League of Nations
- British and French appeasement

The Allies vs. the Axis

As the map below shows, most of the world was divided into areas controlled by the Allies or the Axis powers during the war.

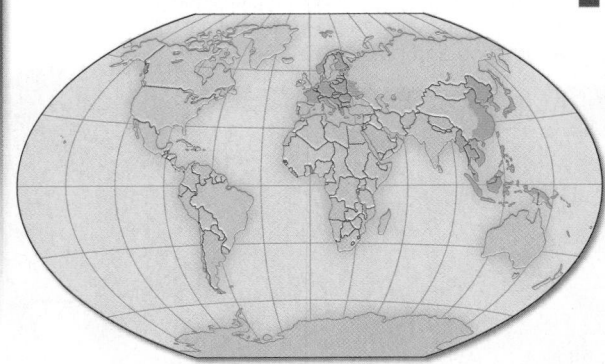

Allies or under Allied control, July 1943
Axis or under Axis control, July 1943
Neutral, July 1943

Key Political Leaders

Allies
Franklin Delano Roosevelt, *U.S. president*
Harry S Truman, *U.S. president*
Neville Chamberlain, *British prime minister*
Winston Churchill, *British prime minister*
Joseph Stalin, *Soviet dictator*
Charles de Gaulle, *leader of Free French*

Axis Powers
Adolf Hitler, *German dictator*
Benito Mussolini, *Italian dictator*
Hirohito, *Japanese emperor*
Tojo Hideki, *Japanese prime minister*

Reasons for Allied Victory

Location of Germany—surrounded by enemies
Location of Japan—dependent on imported goods
Poor military decisions by Axis leaders
Huge productive capability of the United States
Better technology developed and used by Allies

Key Events of World War II

Sept. 1939
Germany invades Poland. France and Britain declare war on Germany.

June–July 1940
France falls to Germany. Germany begins Battle of Britain.

June 1941
Germany invades the Soviet Union.

Europe and Africa
The Pacific

1939   1940   1941

Sept. 1940
Japan signs Tripartite Pact with Germany and Italy.

Dec. 1941
Japan attacks Pearl Harbor.

Differentiated Instruction   Solutions for All Learners

L1 Special Needs   **L2 Less Proficient Readers**
Use the following study guide resources to help students acquiring basic skills:

    Adapted Reading and Note Taking Study Guide
Adapted Note Taking Study Guide, pp. 179, 181, 183, 185, 187–188
Adapted Summaries, pp. 180, 182, 184, 186, 189

L2 English Language Learners
Use the following study guide resources to help Spanish-speaking students:

    Spanish Reading and Note Taking Study Guide
Spanish Note Taking Study Guide, pp. 179, 181, 183, 185, 187–188
Spanish Summaries, pp. 180, 182, 184, 186, 189

Concept Connector

 Essential Question Review

To connect prior knowledge with what you have learned in this chapter, answer the questions below in your Concept Connector journal. Use the journal in the Reading and Note Taking Study Guide to record your answers (or go to www.phschool.com Web Code: nbd-2907). In addition, record information about the following concepts:

- Cooperation: United Nations
- Conflict: World War II
- Technology: Nuclear Power

1. **Democracy** During World War II, the United States government interned Japanese Americans in camps, citing security concerns. This was a curtailment of American citizens' individual rights. Do you think such actions are ever justified by a democratic government? Why or why not?

2. **Genocide** In *Mein Kampf*, Hitler said that Germans were a "master race" whose greatest enemies were the Jews. In 1935, the Nazis passed the Nuremberg Laws, which deprived Jews of German citizenship. The Nazis massacred six million Jews in the Holocaust. Read the Witness History at the beginning of Chapter 16. Then suggest reasons why ordinary Germans and other Europeans accepted, or even collaborated in, Hitler's "Final Solution." Focus on the following:
   - conditions in Depression-era Europe
   - anti-Semitism
   - propaganda
   - Nazi occupation

■ Connections to Today

1. **Conflict: The Arab-Israeli Conflict** Partly in response to the horrors of the Holocaust, the United Nations created a plan to divide the Palestine Mandate into two states—one Arab and one Jewish. Jews accepted the plan, but Arabs rejected it. When the Jewish state of Israel was born in 1948, the surrounding Arab countries invaded Israel. Between 1956 and 1973, three more wars erupted between Israel and Arab states. Conflict between Arabs and Israelis continued into the early 2000s despite many attempts at peace. What historical reasons did the United Nations have for creating a Jewish state in the Palestine Mandate?

Jewish Migration to Israel

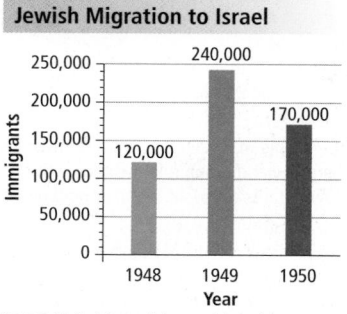

SOURCE: United States Holocaust Memorial Museum Online

2. **Cooperation: The United Nations Is Established** Fifty nations met in April 1945 to draft a charter for the United Nations. Today, the UN's work goes far beyond peacekeeping to include economic development, disease prevention, and refugee protection. Conduct research and write two paragraphs about a program sponsored by the UN in the last five years.

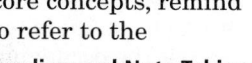
History Interactive
For: Interactive timeline
Web Code: nbp-2962

Nov. 1942 The Allies push Rommel back in North Africa.	**Jan. 1943** Germans surrender at Stalingrad.	**June 1944** D-Day invasion of Normandy	**May 1945** Germany surrenders.

1942　**1943**　**1944**　**1945**

June 1942 Japan defeated at Battle of Midway.	**Feb. 1943** Japan defeated at Guadalcanal.	**Oct. 1944** Japan defeated at Battle of Leyte Gulf.	**Aug–Sept. 1945** U.S. drops atomic bombs on Hiroshima and Nagasaki, Japan. Japan surrenders.

Concept Connector

Tell students that the main concepts for this chapter are Cooperation, Conflict, Democracy, Genocide, and Technology and then ask them to answer the Essential Question Review questions on this page. Discuss the Connections to Today topics and ask students to answer the questions that follow.

Essential Question Review

1. Students should give reasons for their position on the question of whether democratic governments are justified in curtailing the rights of citizens. For example, they might argue that the curtailment of certain rights is a way to better protect the majority of citizens.

2. Responses will vary. Reasons include post-war economic desperation, hatred of Jews and others that are different, powerful nationalist propaganda, and the desire to be on the winning or more powerful side of the conflict.

Connections to Today

1. Responses should recognize the desire of the world community to provide a homeland for Jews after the horrors of the Holocaust.

2. Paragraphs should summarize the activities of one of the UN's programs in the last five years. Some examples might include UN involvement in Bosnia or Rwanda.

For additional review of this (L3) chapter's core concepts, remind students to refer to the

Reading and Note Taking Study Guide
Concept Connector, pp. 237, 242, 250, 267, 295

Chapter Assessment

Terms, People, and Places

1. *Anschluss*—the union of Germany and Austria; *appeasement*—giving in to the demands of an aggressor to keep the peace; The British and French did nothing when Hitler took Austria.

2. "lightning war"; Speed and firepower allow the attacker to overrun defenders.

3. Normandy, in northern France; D-Day signaled the beginning of the liberation of France.

4. Leaders agreed that the Soviet Union would join the war against Japan within three months of Germany's surrender and that Germany would be temporarily divided. It signaled trouble to come because the three leaders did not trust each other.

5. the world's first atomic bombs; They dropped two on Japanese cities, which led the Japanese to surrender.

6. By giving aid to European countries, it helped them rebuild and thus strengthened their democracies.

Main Ideas

7. Japan overran Manchuria and Eastern China; Italy conquered Ethiopia; Germany rearmed and seized Austria and Czechoslovakia; Germany, Italy, and Japan signed an agreement of cooperation; and Germany and the Soviet Union signed a pact.

8. Sample: through the fighting of the RAF and because the British people remained determined to resist

9. They treated them brutally; these tactics were meant to suppress all opposition, although conquered peoples fought against the occupying powers.

10. by allowing the fighting countries to greatly increase their ability to produce needed weapons and supplies

11. advanced in the Soviet Union, North Africa then Italy, and France, carried out extensive bombing

12. island hopping, supplemented by bombing of the Japanese islands

13. Sample: disagreements over the status of Germany and Eastern Europe

Chapter Focus Question

14. They arose in several countries due to the effects of World War I and the Great Depression. It took an all-out

---

Chapter Assessment

Terms, People, and Places

1. Define **appeasement** and **Anschluss.** How was Hitler's Anschluss an example of British and French appeasement?
2. Define **blitzkrieg.** What were the advantages of this war tactic?
3. Where did the **D-Day** invasion take place? What was its significance?
4. What happened at the **Yalta Conference**? How did it foreshadow later events?
5. What technological advantage did the **Manhattan Project** give the Allies? How was it used?
6. Describe how the **Marshall Plan** was part of the **Truman Doctrine.**

Main Ideas

Section 1 (pp. 560–565)
7. Summarize the steps that Axis powers took to achieve world power prior to World War II.

Section 2 (pp. 566–574)
8. How did the people of Britain fend off a German invasion?
9. How did Germany and Japan rule the people they conquered? How did this contribute to their hold on power?

Section 3 (pp. 575–583)
10. How did government control of economic production help defeat Germany and Japan?
11. Summarize how the Allies defeated Germany.

Section 4 (pp. 584–587)
12. What strategy did the Allies use to defeat Japan?

Section 5 (pp. 588–593)
13. What conflicts emerged between the former Allies after the end of World War II?

Chapter Focus Question
14. How did aggressive world powers emerge, and what did it take to defeat them during World War II?

Critical Thinking

15. **Recognize Cause and Effect** How did the World War I peace settlement help cause World War II?
16. **Analyze Information** What lessons does the Holocaust have for people today?

17. **Analyzing Cartoons** How does this cartoon reflect the cause of Hitler's defeat?
18. **Predict Consequences** The Atlantic Charter called for the establishment of a "permanent system of general security." What form did this "system" take when it was established following the war?
19. **Synthesize Information** Was participation by the United States crucial to winning the war? Explain.
20. **Draw Conclusions** Which battle was most important in the war in Europe? In the war in the Pacific? Explain.

● Writing About History

In this chapter's five Section Assessments, you developed skills for writing a research report.

Writing a Research Report The history of World War II includes many stories of great courage and personal sacrifice. Write a research report on one of the following topics in which you describe the actions of the person or group: the Kindertransport, Oskar Schindler, Miep Gies, Raoul Wallenberg, Dietrich Bonhoeffer. Consult pages SH13–SH15 of the Writing Handbook for additional help.

Prewriting
- Do some preliminary research on each of the topics listed above.

- Choose the topic that interests you most and take notes about the people involved and the personal risks they took.
- Create a set of questions about the topic and gather additional resources.

Drafting
- Develop a working thesis and choose information to support the thesis.
- Make an outline organizing the report.
- Write an introduction in which you explain why the topic is interesting, a body, and a conclusion.

Revising
- Use the guidelines for revising your report on page SH15 of the Writing Handbook.

---

war, with dedicated national resources and the loss of millions of lives, to defeat them.

Critical Thinking

15. Sample: Germans hated the Versailles Treaty, so Hitler's defiance of it helped him gain popularity.

16. Sample: A powerful leader can exert enormous influence. Ordinary people are capable of unspeakable atrocities.

17. It shows that he was surrounded and choked from all sides by the Soviet Union, Britain, and the United States.

18. the United Nations, which had the power to enforce peace through economic sanctions or military force

19. Sample: Yes, its military and productive capabilities were crucial factors.

20. Accept any well-reasoned answer.

Document-Based Assessment

The Decision to Use the Atomic Bomb

Perhaps no decision in American history has been more hotly debated than Harry S. Truman's decision to drop atomic bombs on Hiroshima and Nagasaki, Japan, in August 1945. Documents A and B are two historians' views on Truman's decision.

Document A

"It was believed with deep apprehension that many thousands, probably tens of thousands, of lives of Allied combatants would have been spent in the continuation of our air and sea bombardment and blockade. . . . But the people who would have suffered most, had the war gone on much longer and their country invaded, were the Japanese. One American incendiary air raid on the Tokyo area in March 1945 did more damage and killed and injured more Japanese than the bomb on Hiroshima."

—From *The Atomic Bomb and the End of World War II* by Herbert Feis

Document B

"Even without the use of the atomic bombs, the war would probably have ended before an American invasion of Kyushu [one of the four main islands of Japan] became necessary. Conditions in Japan were steadily deteriorating . . . The destruction of cities from B-29 raids, diminishing food supplies, [and] decreased public morale fostered enough discontent to worry the emperor and his advisors. . . . Even without the atomic attacks, it seems likely that the emperor at some point would have acted in the same way that he did in the aftermath of Hiroshima to end the war."

—From *Prompt and Utter Destruction: Truman and the Use of Atomic Bombs Against Japan* by J. Samuel Walker

Document C

In the spring of 1945, the Allies' island-hopping campaign in the Pacific brought them closer to the heart of Japan. When American troops invaded first the island of Iwo Jima, then the island of Okinawa, the Japanese fought fiercely, but unsuccessfully, to keep them from gaining control. They knew that the Allies planned to use the islands as a base for an invasion of Japan itself.

Troops Killed at Iwo Jima and Okinawa, 1945		
Battle	Japanese troops killed	American troops killed
Iwo Jima	21,000	6,800
Okinawa	100,000	12,000

SOURCE: Encyclopaedia Brittannica

Document D

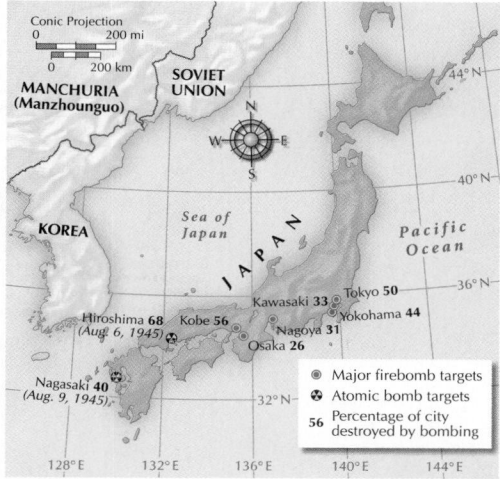

Analyzing Documents

Use your knowledge of World War II and Documents A, B, C, and D to answer questions 1–4.

1. Which of the following cities experienced the most damage from the American bombing raids?
   A Tokyo
   B Yokohama
   C Hiroshima
   D Osaka

2. Which of the following statements BEST summarizes Herbert Feis's explanation for Truman's use of the atomic bomb?
   A Use of the atomic bombs would cause more destruction.
   B Use of the atomic bombs would save lives.
   C Use of the atomic bombs would ensure surrender.
   D Use of the atomic bombs would make it more difficult for Japan to rebuild its military.

3. J. Samuel Walker's main argument against the use of atomic bombs is that
   A atomic bombs were more destructive than conventional bombs.
   B an American invasion would not have been as destructive as the bombs.
   C the war would have ended anyway.
   D the Japanese emperor opposed the use of atomic bombs.

4. **Writing Task** Which of the historians quoted in Documents A and B do you agree with most strongly? Why? Use your knowledge of World War II and specific evidence from the documents to support your opinion.

Document-Based Assessment

- To help students understand the documents on this page, give them the following **TIP: Analyze each of the points made in the documents arguing for and against the use of the bomb by writing down the main fact or reason each author presents and judging how important and persuasive you think it is.**

- To provide students with further practice in answering Document-Based Assessment Questions, go to **Document-Based Assessment,** pp. 80–94

- If students need more instruction on comparing viewpoints, have them read the **Skills Handbook,** p. SH30.

Writing About History

As students begin the assignment, refer them to p. SH13 of the **Writing Handbook** for help in writing a research paper. Remind them of the steps they should take to complete their assignment, including prewriting, drafting, and revising. For help in revising, remind them to use the guidelines on p. SH15 of the **Writing Handbook.**

Students' research papers should tell the story of one of the people or groups specified and explain how that person or group demonstrated courage or personal sacrifice. They should contain an introduction, a body, and a conclusion. They should show evidence of reflection and be free of grammatical and spelling errors. For scoring rubrics for writing assignments, see **Assessment Rubrics,** p. 8.

Answers

1. C
2. B
3. C
4. Responses should indicate which historian they agree with and effectively explain why using specific evidence from the documents and the chapter to support their conclusions.

The World Since 1945
1945–Present

Unit Overview

Unit 5 surveys significant events and developments throughout the world since the end of World War II.

Chapter 18 focuses on the Cold War, describing the rivalry between democratic and communist countries, how it manifested itself in various conflicts and confrontations, and how it finally ended with the collapse of the Soviet Union.
Concepts: Cooperation, Dictatorship, Empire, Human Rights

Chapter 19 explains how new nations emerged in South Asia, Southeast Asia, Africa, and the Middle East.
Concepts: Dictatorship, Geography's Impact, Nationalism, Revolution

Chapter 20 describes conflicts that have plagued regions of Africa, the Middle East, and elsewhere.
Concepts: Dictatorship, Genocide, Human Rights, Impact of the Individual

Chapter 21 examines the challenges facing developing nations and details the progress they have made.
Concepts: Dictatorship, Economic Systems, Revolution

Chapter 22 depicts the world today, focusing on major issues facing humankind.
Concepts: Cooperation, Democracy, Economic Systems, Technology, Trade

THE **WORLD** TODAY

About the Map

Today the world has more than 190 independent states. Very few traditional colonies remain. After 1945, many new nations in Africa, Latin America, Asia, and the Pacific gained their independence. Some achieved independence through patient negotiation, while others pursued armed struggle. Others simply received their independence from their former colonizer. Colonial boundaries usually served as boundaries of the newly independent states. This meant that diverse ethnic groups were thrown together to build a new nation. Their differences often led to conflict and political instability. During the decades after World War II, the United States and the Soviet Union both led groups of nations around the world in a global rivalry called the Cold War. The breakup of the Soviet Union in 1991 and the fall of communist governments in Eastern Europe led to independence for several new nations in Central Asia and Eastern Europe. The largest of these is Russia.

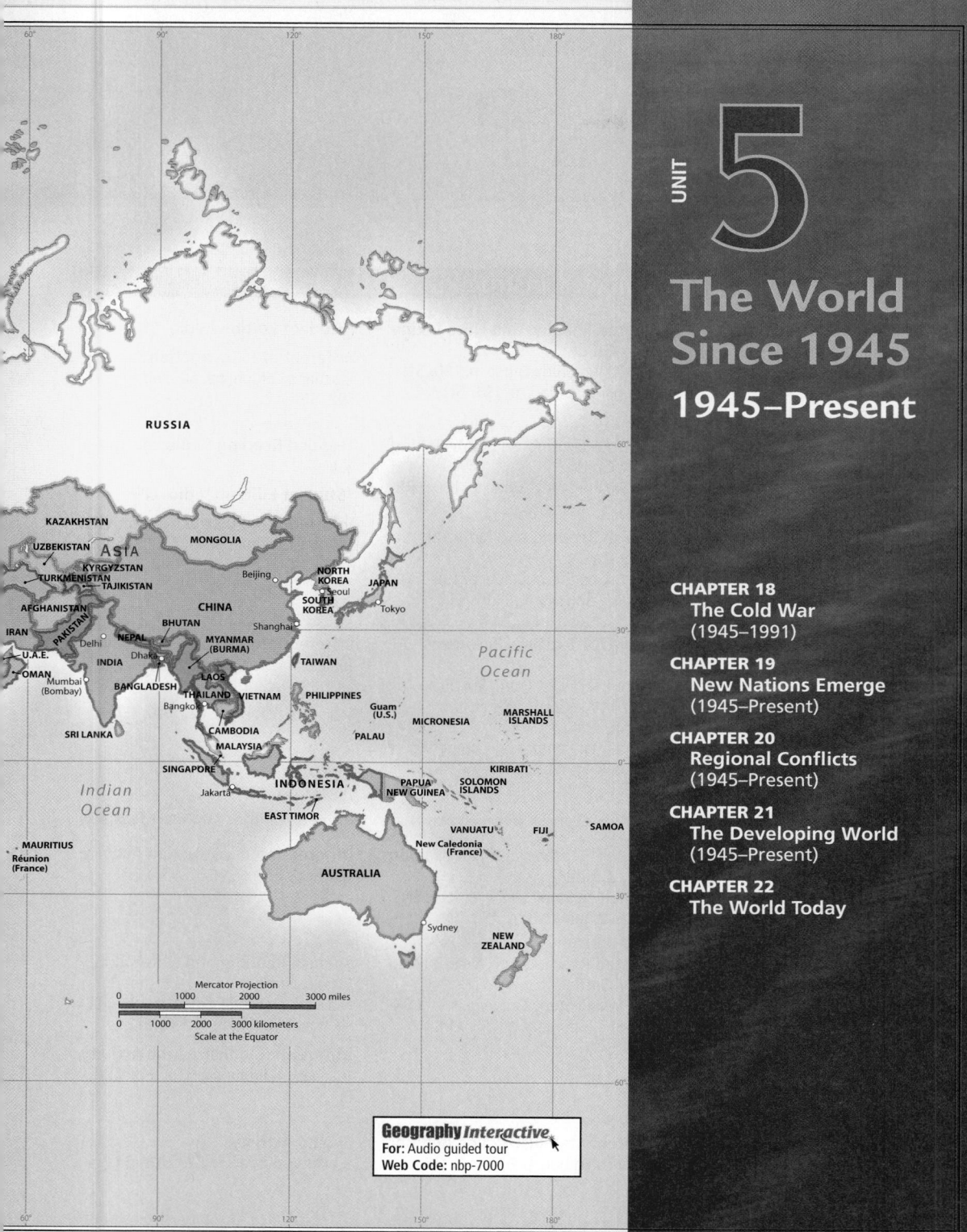

5

The World Since 1945

1945–Present

CHAPTER 18
The Cold War
(1945–1991)

CHAPTER 19
New Nations Emerge
(1945–Present)

CHAPTER 20
Regional Conflicts
(1945–Present)

CHAPTER 21
The Developing World
(1945–Present)

CHAPTER 22
The World Today

Geography *Interactive*
For: Audio guided tour
Web Code: nbp-7000

Geographic Literacy

Point out that the map on these pages shows all the countries in the world today. Explain that the former colonial powers remain among the world's richest nations, while many former colonies, known as developing nations, remain poor. Ask **If many of the world's richest nations are former colonial powers, which countries do you think are rich today?** *(The United States, European nations, and Japan)* Tell them that Canada and Australia are also among the world's rich nations and that the rich nations are also known as developed nations. Then ask **Which regions contain former colonies, many of which are poor, or developing nations?** *(Latin America, Africa, and much of Asia)* Have students use this information to explain why so many migrants seek entry into developing nations *(to find work),* and have them suggest some likely paths that these migrations might take. *(from Latin America north to the United States and Canada; from Africa north to Europe; from Asia west to Europe; from Asia east to Japan; from Asia southeast to Australia)*

Looking Ahead

Ask students to read the chapter titles to the right of the map. Ask **Based on these titles and your study of the map, what do you predict you will learn about in this unit?** *(the political conflicts and economic issues that have challenged the world since 1945)* Explain that students will also learn about the expansion of democracy throughout the world, environmental challenges, terrorism, and advances in science and technology.

A note on the projection:
Although the Mercator projection distorts the sizes of continents, it was widely used for maps after its invention in 1569.

Home Involvement
The *Letter Home* includes a summary of the World Since 1945 content that students will be studying.
All in One Teaching Resources, Unit 5, p. 1

All in One Unit 5 Directory

Section	Core Instruction **L3**	Differentiated Instruction **L1 L2 L4**	

Section 1
The Cold War Unfolds

 3 periods, 1.5 blocks

OBJECTIVES
- Understand how two sides faced off in Europe during the Cold War.
- Learn how nuclear weapons threatened the world.
- Understand how the Cold War spread globally.
- Compare and contrast the Soviet Union and the United States in the Cold War.

Focus Question *What were the military and political consequences of the Cold War in the Soviet Union, Europe, and the United States?*

Core Instruction:

All in One Teaching Resources, Unit 5
Reading Strategy: Summarize, p. 8
Vocabulary Builder: Make Connections, p. 7
Outline Map: Cold War World, p. 14
Geography Quiz, p. 16
Section 1 Quiz, p. 2

Reading and Note Taking Study Guide
Note Taking Study Guide, p. 190
Section 1 Summary, p. 191

Note Taking Transparencies, 189

WITNESS HISTORY Audio CD
An Iron Curtain, The Cuban Missile Crisis

Progress Monitoring Transparencies, 128

Color Transparencies, 181, 182

Witness History Discovery School™
video programs, *The Rise and Fall of the Berlin Wall* and *Showdown: The Cuban Missile Crisis*

L1 Adapted Reading and Note Taking Study Guide
Note Taking Study Guide, p. 190 **SN**
Section 1 Summary, p. 191 **SN**

L2 Adapted Reading and Note Taking Study Guide
Note Taking Study Guide, p. 190 **LPR**
Section 1 Summary, p. 191 **LPR**

Spanish Reading and Note Taking Study Guide
Note Taking Study Guide, p. 190 **ELL**
Section 1 Summary, p. 191 **ELL**

L4 All in One Teaching Resources, Unit 5
Link to Literature: From *The Gulag Archipelago* by Aleksandr Solzhenitsyn, p. 9 **AR, GT**
Viewpoints: Comparing Competing Economic Systems, p. 10 **AR, GT**

*Student Edition Audio SN

Differentiated Instruction Activity,
Teacher's Edition, pp. 605, 607, 608 **SN**

*Guided Reading Audio, Spanish **ELL**

*Student Edition Audio LPR

Differentiated Instruction Activity,
Teacher's Edition, pp. 605, 607, 608, 610 **LPR, ELL**

Differentiated Instruction Activity,
Teacher's Edition, p. 609 **GT**

Extend Activity,
Teacher's Edition, p. 612 **AR, GT**

Section 2
The Industrialized Democracies

 2 periods, 1 block

OBJECTIVES
- Understand how the United States prospered and expanded opportunities.
- Explain how Western Europe rebuilt its economy after World War II.
- Describe how Japan was transformed.

Focus Question *How did the United States, Western Europe, and Japan achieve economic prosperity and strengthen democracy during the Cold War years?*

Core Instruction:

All in One Teaching Resources, Unit 5
Section 2 Quiz, p. 3

Reading and Note Taking Study Guide
Note Taking Study Guide, p. 192
Section 2 Summary, p. 193

Note Taking Transparencies, 190

WITNESS HISTORY Audio CD
The Marshall Plan

Progress Monitoring Transparencies, 129

Color Transparencies, 180, 183

L1 Adapted Reading and Note Taking Study Guide
Note Taking Study Guide, p. 192 **SN**
Section 2 Summary, p. 193 **SN**

L2 Adapted Reading and Note Taking Study Guide
Note Taking Study Guide, p. 192 **LPR**
Section 2 Summary, p. 193 **LPR**

L4 Differentiated Instruction Activity,
Teacher's Edition, p. 617 **AR, GT**

Differentiated Instruction Activity,
Teacher's Edition, p. 619 **SN**

Spanish Reading and Note Taking Study Guide
Note Taking Study Guide, p. 192 **ELL**
Section 2 Summary, p. 193 **ELL**

Differentiated Instruction Activity,
Teacher's Edition, pp. 615, 619 **LPR, ELL**

Extend Activity,
Teacher's Edition, p. 622 **AR, GT**

---

*Audio support is available for all sections.

Assessment Resources
- **Progress Monitoring Transparencies,** 128–132
- **SuccessTracker™,** Chapter 18
- **Document-Based Assessment,** pp. 95–109
- ***ExamView® Test Bank CD-ROM,** Chapter 18
- **All in One Teaching Resources, Unit 5,** Chapter Tests, pp. 17–22
- **Progress Monitoring *Online* Quizzes,** Chapter 18
- **Assessment Rubrics**

Differentiated Instruction Key
- **L1** Special Needs
- **L2** Basic to Average
- **L3** All Students
- **L4** Average to Advanced
- **LPR** Less Proficient Readers
- **AR** Advanced Readers
- **SN** Special Needs Students
- **GT** Gifted and Talented
- **ELL** English Language Learner

Section	Core Instruction (L3)	Differentiated Instruction (L1) (L2) (L4)	
Section 3 *Communism Spreads in East Asia* **2 periods, 1 block** **OBJECTIVES** ■ Analyze China's communist revolution. ■ Describe China's role as a "wild card" in the Cold War. ■ Explain how war came to Korea and how the two Koreas followed different paths. **Focus Question** *What did the Communist victory mean for China and the rest of East Asia?*	**All in One Teaching Resources, Unit 5** Section 3 Quiz, p. 4 **Reading and Note Taking Study Guide** Note Taking Study Guide, p. 194 Section 3 Summary, p. 195 **Note Taking Transparencies,** 191 **WITNESS HISTORY Audio CD** Communist Victory in China **Progress Monitoring Transparencies,** 130 **Color Transparencies,** 184	(L1) **Adapted Reading and Note Taking Study Guide** Note Taking Study Guide, p. 194 **SN** Section 3 Summary, p. 195 **SN** (L2) **Adapted Reading and Note Taking Study Guide** Note Taking Study Guide, p. 194 **LPR** Section 3 Summary, p. 195 **LPR** (L4) **Differentiated Instruction Activity,** Teacher's Edition, p. 628 **GT**	**Spanish Reading and Note Taking Study Guide** Note Taking Study Guide, p. 194 **ELL** Section 3 Summary, p. 195 **ELL** **Differentiated Instruction Activity,** Teacher's Edition, pp. 624, 628 **LPR** **Extend Activity,** Teacher's Edition, p. 629 **AR, GT**
Section 4 *War in Southeast Asia* **2 periods, 1 block** **OBJECTIVES** ■ Describe events in Indochina after World War II. ■ Learn how America entered the Vietnam War. ■ Understand how the Vietnam War ended. ■ Analyze Southeast Asia after the war. **Focus Question** *What were the causes and effects of war in Southeast Asia, and what was the American role in this region?*	**All in One Teaching Resources, Unit 5** Section 4 Quiz, p. 5 **Reading and Note Taking Study Guide** Note Taking Study Guide, p. 196 Section 4 Summary, p. 197 **Note Taking Transparencies,** 192 **WITNESS HISTORY Audio CD** America's Role in Vietnam; The Vietnam War **Progress Monitoring Transparencies,** 131	(L1) **Adapted Reading and Note Taking Study Guide** Note Taking Study Guide, p. 196 **SN** Section 4 Summary, p. 197 **SN** (L2) **Adapted Reading and Note Taking Study Guide** Note Taking Study Guide, p. 196 **LPR** Section 4 Summary, p. 197 **LPR** (L4) **Differentiated Instruction Activity,** Teacher's Edition, p. 637 **AR, GT**	**Differentiated Instruction Activity,** Teacher's Edition, pp. 631, 632 **SN** **Spanish Reading and Note Taking Study Guide** Note Taking Study Guide, p. 196 **ELL** Section 4 Summary, p. 197 **ELL** **Differentiated Instruction Activity,** Teacher's Edition, pp. 631, 632 **LPR, ELL** **Extend Activity,** Teacher's Edition, p. 635 **AR, GT**
Section 5 *The End of the Cold War* **3 periods, 1.5 blocks** **OBJECTIVES** ■ Understand how the Soviet Union declined. ■ Analyze the changes that transformed Eastern Europe. ■ Explain how communism declined worldwide and the United States became the sole superpower. **Focus Question** *What were the causes and effects of the end of the Cold War?*	**All in One Teaching Resources, Unit 5** Outline Map: The Soviet Union After the Breakup, p. 15 Geography Quiz, p. 16 Section 5 Quiz, p. 6 **Reading and Note Taking Study Guide** Note Taking Study Guide, p. 198 Section 5 Summary, p. 199 Concept Connector, pp. 242, 255, 262, 275 **Note Taking Transparencies,** 193 **WITNESS HISTORY Audio CD** A Democratic Transformation **Progress Monitoring Transparencies,** 132 **Color Transparencies,** 185	(L1) **Adapted Reading and Note Taking Study Guide** Note Taking Study Guide, p. 198 **SN** Section 5 Summary, p. 199 **SN** Concept Connector, pp. 242, 255, 262, 275 **SN** (L2) **Adapted Reading and Note Taking Study Guide** Note Taking Study Guide, p. 198 **LPR** Section 5 Summary, p. 199 **LPR** Concept Connector, pp. 242, 255, 262, 275 **LPR** (L4) **All in One Teaching Resources, Unit 5** Biography: Fidel Castro, p. 11 **AR, GT** Biography: Mikhail Gorbachev, p. 12 **AR, GT** Viewpoints: Two Views on the Reunification of Germany, p. 13 **AR, GT**	**Differentiated Instruction Activity,** Teacher's Edition, p. 639 **SN** **Spanish Reading and Note Taking Study Guide** Note Taking Study Guide, p. 198 **ELL** Section 5 Summary, p. 199 **ELL** Concept Connector, pp. 242, 255, 262, 275 **ELL** **Differentiated Instruction Activity,** Teacher's Edition, pp. 639, 642 **LPR, ELL** **Differentiated Instruction Activity,** Teacher's Edition, p. 643 **AR, GT** **Extend Activity,** Teacher's Edition, p. 644 **AR, GT**

Author's Notes

Coexistence and Détente

Over four decades, the Cold War brought the world rebellions, revolutions, wars, and confrontation between the superpowers. The Cold War also, however, turned out to be much more subtle and complicated than a survey of these open clashes might suggest. And in the end, the conflict terminated—dramatically enough, but without the final showdown many had feared.

There was, however, a wide range of nonmilitary contention between the United States and the Soviet Union. There were propaganda broadsides aimed at their own people and at "world opinion." There was espionage of all sorts, from the most sophisticated electronic gear to old-fashioned spying. There was intense technological and economic competition, ranging from the battle to see who could produce the most tungsten or toothbrushes to the race to the moon. And there was, of course, the unending arms race.

Accompanying these varied forms of competition, however, were repeated attempts to improve relations between America and the Soviet Union. Under such rubrics as "coexistence" or *détente,* these efforts provided a counterpoint of hope that the world could avoid a third global war in the twentieth century.

A number of summit meetings occurred between the two states and a great many consultations between the foreign ministers, ambassadors, and other lesser officials of the two governments. Direct electronic communications between the White House and the Kremlin were set up for easy and quick discussions when problems arose. Trade relations, while fluctuating with other aspects of the relationship, repeatedly provided a splendid opportunity for America to market its habitual agricultural overproduction and for the Soviet Union to import lifesaving quantities of grain. . . .

And in fact a number of agreements were negotiated limiting arms development in the two superstates—though this proved in the long run perhaps the most difficult problem of all for the two armed camps.

—Anthony Esler, *The Human Venture: From Prehistory to the Present,* (Upper Saddle River, New Jersey: Pearson Education, 2004), p. 690

Extend Online

Cold War Crises

Have students research the major crises of the Cold War. Ask them to present their findings to the class, using visuals such as maps, charts, and copies of photos to enhance their presentations. Use the steps below to help students complete the activity.

Prepare for the Activity Explain that the Cold War gave rise to a series of crises in which tensions between the two superpowers increased. The most important of these were the Korean War, the 1956 Polish and Hungarian crises, the Cuban missile crisis, the Vietnam War, the crisis posed by the Solidarity movement in Poland, the Soviet invasion of Afghanistan, and the fall of the Soviet Union.

Conduct the Activity For help in starting the activity, send students to **Web Code nbe-3002.** Students will select one of the Cold War crises listed above and research it. Students may work in groups, with each group researching different events. Have students find out how the crisis developed, its significance in the history of the Cold War, the human impact, and the resolution.

Follow-Up Have each student or group of students present the results of their research to the class. Have students explain how their crisis illustrates an important event in the Cold War.

Differentiated Instruction Solutions for All Learners

Oral History L1 L2

To help students become engaged in more recent historical events, have them conduct an oral history. First, have students select a focus for the oral history. It could be either a topic, such as the Cold War, or a question, such as how successful desegregation was during the 1960s and 1970s. As a class, draft specific questions for an interview. The class can use these questions with a guest speaker or with their own interviewee. Offer students a choice as to how they will report their findings: multimedia presentation, essay, poster, or skit. You may recommend that they record the interview with a camcorder, tape recorder, or MP3 player and then incorporate clips or sound bites into their presentation.

To conclude the activity, have students compare and contrast their findings with a partner and with the information presented in their text. Remind students to analyze their sources when they compare findings. For example, an interviewee who experienced desegregation while serving in the army may view its results differently from someone who was a teacher in an inner-city public school.

Identifying Viewpoints L4

As you present events in the text, ask students to analyze the accompanying visuals. To begin, have students look at the visuals in the text and answer the following questions:

1. Who produced or sponsored the image?

2. Who is the target audience? How is the message tailored specifically to them?

3. What is implied in this image?

4. What tools are used to create the message?

5. What perspective is absent from the image? What is left out of the image that might be important to know?

Modeling Reading and Writing Skills

Gather Information Tell students that in this chapter, they will be writing a problem-solution essay. (See Writing About History, p. 648.) When explaining a problem or proposing a solution, students must persuade the audience that they are describing a real problem and that their proposed solution is likely to work.

On the board, write the following types of evidence that can be used to present convincing detail:

A statistics
B expert opinion
C comparable situations

Explain that statistics provide relevant numerical data that can back up a claim. Expert opinion includes the advice of those who have experience related to the problem, while comparable situations describe how real-life scenarios were resolved. Ask students to brainstorm places where they might look to find each type of support-

ing detail for a problem-solution essay on ways to encourage European unity.

Interpret Nonliteral Meanings Explain to students that literal language means exactly what it says. Nonliteral language, on the other hand, uses images or comparisons to communicate an idea more vividly. When students come across these phrases, they should ask themselves what the phrase means and how it makes the author's point.

Model this skill by reading aloud the first three sentences in the second paragraph of the Primary Source excerpted from Václav Havel's New Year's Address. Point out the phrase *fell morally ill*. Explain that one's morals cannot literally become sick or frail. This image suggests a corruption of the country's ideals and beliefs.

The Cold War
1945–1991

Teach With Technology

PresentationEXPRESS™
Premium DVD

■ Teach this chapter's core content using **PresentationExpress™ Premium,** which includes dynamic lecture notes, interactive game shows, songs, videos, and the *ExamView® QuickTake* assessment tool.

■ To introduce this chapter using **PresentationExpress™ Premium,** start by asking students **Which of the following statements do you most agree with? (A) Nations should develop nuclear weapons to strengthen their defenses. (B) Nations should develop nuclear weapons only if their enemies have them. (C) Nations should agree with their enemies to ban nuclear weapons, as their potential for destruction outweighs their benefits for defense. (D) Nations should not develop nuclear weapons, even if their enemies have them.** Take a class poll or record students' answers using the QuickTake feature and discuss their responses. Point out that in this chapter, they will read about the arms race that developed during the Cold War.

Technology Resources

■ Student**EXPRESS** CD-ROM, Chapter 18

■ Teacher**EXPRESS** CD-ROM, Chapter 18

■ Presentation**EXPRESS™** Premium DVD, Chapter 18

■ **WITNESS HISTORY** Audio CD, Chapter 18

■ *ExamView* Test Bank CD-ROM, English and Spanish, Chapter 18

■ **Guided Reading Audio,** Spanish, Chapter 18

■ **Student Edition Audio,** Chapter 18

■ **Witness History Discovery School™** video program, *The Rise and Fall of the Berlin Wall* and *Showdown: The Cuban Missile Crisis*

■ **Experience It! Multimedia Pack**

Bibliography

For the Teacher

Chang, Jung. *Wild Swans: Three Daughters of China.* New York: Simon & Schuster, 1991.

Frankel, Max. *High Noon in the Cold War: Kennedy, Khruschev, and the Cuban Missile Crisis.* New York: Ballantine Books, 2004.

Rosenberg, Tina. *The Haunted Land: Facing Europe's Ghosts After Communism.* New York: Vintage Books, 1996.

For the Student

L2 Chen, Da. *China's Son: Growing Up in the Cultural Revolution.* New York: Delacorte Press, 2001.

L3 *First They Killed My Father: A Daughter of Cambodia Remembers.* New York: HarperCollins, 2000.

WITNESS HISTORY AUDIO

Berlin Is Walled In

On August 13, 1961, the first morning after the Berlin Wall was built, thousands of East Berliners arrived at the main border crossing hoping to travel to West Berlin. Transportation Police, or Trapos, blocked the way. Robert Lochner recalls, "A timid old woman . . . asked one of the Trapos when the next train would go to West Berlin. Sneeringly he answered: 'None of that anymore, grandma. You are all now caught in a mousetrap.'" Listen to the Witness History audio to hear more about the Berlin Wall.

◀ **East German guards watch the newly built Berlin Wall.**

Chapter Preview

Chapter Focus Question How did the Cold War develop, how did it shape political and economic life in individual nations, and how did it end?

Section 1
The Cold War Unfolds

Section 2
The Industrialized Democracies

Section 3
Communism Spreads in East Asia

Section 4
War in Southeast Asia

Section 5
The End of the Cold War

Use the ☑ **Quick Study Timeline** at the end of this chapter to preview chapter events.

U.S. President Ronald Reagan

Pin promoting the Soviet reforms that helped to end the Cold War

U.S. military helicopter over Vietnam

 Concept Connector ONLINE
To explore Essential Questions related to this chapter, go to PHSchool.com
Web Code: nbd-3007

Chapter-Level Resources

All-in-One Vocabulary Builder; Reading Strategy; Enrichments; Outline Maps; Geography Quiz; Chapter Tests
- Document-Based Assessments
- AYP Monitoring Assessments
- *ExamView* Test Bank CD-ROM
- Guided Reading Audio Spanish
- Student Edition Audio

Previewing the Chapter

- **WITNESS HISTORY** Read the Witness History selection aloud or play the accompanying audio. Ask students to explain the events described in this selection in their own words. Ask **What does the Transportation Police mean by the term "mousetrap"?** *(They are caught within the walls and cannot escape.)* Tell them that before the wall went up, 2,000 residents of East Berlin were crossing into West Berlin each day. Ask **Why do you think East Berliners want to cross into West Berlin?** *(Sample: to escape the constrictions of communism)*

  ◀))) AUDIO **Witness History Audio CD,** Berlin Is Walled In

- **Analyzing the Visuals** Ask students to study the photo of the Berlin Wall. Ask **What do you think life is like for the people who live nearby?** *(Sample: that people nearby felt trapped and that life near a wall is restricting)* Tell students to read this chapter to understand the events that led to this photo.

- **Focus** Write the Chapter Focus Question on the board. Tell students to keep this question in mind as they read the chapter. *(Answer appears with the Chapter Assessment answers.)* Have students preview the section titles for this chapter.

Note Taking Study Guide With Concept Connector Journal
For online access: Web code nad-3007
For print alternative: Reading and Note Taking Study Guide booklet

SECTION 1

Step-by-Step Instruction

Objectives

As you teach this section, keep students focused on the following objectives to help them answer the Section Focus Question and master core content.

- Understand how two sides faced off in Europe during the Cold War.
- Learn how nuclear weapons threatened the world.
- Understand how the Cold War spread globally.
- Compare and contrast the Soviet Union and the United States in the Cold War.

Prepare to Read

Build Background Knowledge L3

Ask students to recall some of the conflicts that remained at the end of World War II. Ask them to predict ways that the Soviet Union and United States might clash in the postwar years.

Set a Purpose L3

- **WITNESS HISTORY** Read the selection aloud or play the audio.

   AUDIO **Witness History Audio CD,** An Iron Curtain

  Ask **According to Churchill, who controls the states of Central and Eastern Europe?** *(the Soviet Union, whose capital is Moscow)*

- **Focus** Point out the Section Focus Question and write it on the board. Tell students to refer to this question as they read. *(Answer appears with Section 1 Assessment answers.)*

- **Preview** Have students preview the Section Objectives and the list of Terms, People, and Places.

- **Reading Skill** Have students use the *Reading Strategy: Summarize* worksheet.

  All in One Teaching Resources, Unit 5, p. 8

- **Note Taking** Have students read this section using the Guided Questioning strategy (TE, p.T20). As they read, have students fill in the chart showing the consequences of the Cold War.

  Reading and Note Taking Study Guide, p. 190

Winston Churchill

WITNESS HISTORY ◀)) AUDIO

An Iron Curtain

In 1946, Winston Churchill, former prime minister of Britain, spoke of an "iron curtain" sealing off the countries in Eastern Europe that the Soviet Union had occupied at the end of World War II:

“ [A]n iron curtain has descended [fallen] across the Continent. Behind that line lie all the capitals of the ancient states of Central and Eastern Europe. . . . [A]ll these famous cities . . . lie in what I must call the Soviet sphere, and are all subject . . . to a very high . . . measure of control from Moscow.”

Focus Question What were the military and political consequences of the Cold War in the Soviet Union, Europe, and the United States?

The Cold War Unfolds

Objectives
- Understand how two sides faced off in Europe during the Cold War.
- Learn how nuclear weapons threatened the world.
- Understand how the Cold War spread globally.
- Compare and contrast the Soviet Union and the United States in the Cold War.

Terms, People, and Places

superpowers	John F. Kennedy
anti-ballistic missiles (ABMs)	ideology
Ronald Reagan	Nikita Khrushchev
détente	Leonid Brezhnev
Fidel Castro	containment

Note Taking

Reading Skill: Summarize Sum up the consequences of the Cold War in the United States, Europe, and the Soviet Union in a chart like the one below.

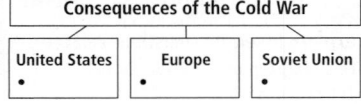

Consequences of the Cold War

United States	Europe	Soviet Union
•	•	•

After World War II devastated Europe and Japan, two great powers remained: the United States and the Soviet Union. These two nations were known as **superpowers,** or nations stronger than other powerful nations. The Cold War between these superpowers cast a shadow over the world for more than 40 years.

Two Sides Face Off in Europe

Cold War confrontation began in Europe, where the two superpowers' armies confronted each other after World War II. Each superpower formed a European military alliance made up of the nations that it occupied or protected. The United States led the North Atlantic Treaty Organization, or NATO, in Western Europe. The Soviet Union led the Warsaw Pact in Eastern Europe. The two alliances in Europe faced each other along the Iron Curtain, the tense line between the democratic West and the communist East.

A Wall Divides Berlin Berlin was a key focus of Cold War tensions. The city was split into democratic West Berlin and communist East Berlin. In the 1950s, West Berlin became a showcase for West German prosperity. A massive exodus of low-paid East Germans, unhappy with communism, fled into West Berlin. To stop the flight, East Germany built a wall in 1961 that sealed off West Berlin. When completed, the Berlin Wall was a massive concrete barrier, topped with barbed wire and patrolled by guards. The wall showed that workers, far from enjoying a communist paradise, had to be forcibly kept from fleeing.

Vocabulary Builder

Use the information below and the following resources to teach the high-use word from this section.
All in One Teaching Resources, Unit 5, p. 7; **Teaching Resources, Skills Handbook,** p. 3

High-Use Word	Definition and Sample Sentence
comprise, p. 608	*vt.* to be made up of The school **comprises** students from three different towns.

Eastern Europe Resists Other explosions of Cold War tension included revolts against Soviet domination in East Germany, Poland, Hungary, and Czechoslovakia. One of the earliest revolts occurred in East Berlin. In 1953, some 50,000 workers confronted the Soviet army in the streets of the German capital. The uprising spread to other East German cities, but the demonstrators could not stand up to Russian tanks.

In 1956, Eastern Europeans challenged Soviet authority in the name of economic reform in both Poland and Hungary. Poles were responding in part to Soviet-backed mass arrests of noncommunist leaders and government seizures of private lands and industry. Hungarian leader Imre Nagy (nahj) went furthest, ending one-party rule and seeking to pull his country out of the Warsaw Pact. In response, Soviet troops launched a massive assault that overwhelmed resistance. Nagy was later executed.

In early 1968, Czechoslovak leader Alexander Dubček introduced greater freedom of expression and limited democracy. This blossoming of freedom came to be known as the "Prague Spring." Soviet leaders feared that democracy would threaten communist power and Soviet domination. Warsaw Pact troops launched a massive invasion of Czechoslovakia in August of that year to put an end to these freedoms.

✓ **Checkpoint** How was Europe divided, and what were three consequences of its division?

Nuclear Weapons Threaten the World

One of the most terrifying aspects of the Cold War was the arms race that began right after World War II. At first, the United States was the only nuclear power. By 1949, however, the Soviet Union had also developed nuclear weapons. By 1953, both sides had developed hydrogen bombs, which are much more destructive than atomic bombs.

Critics argued that a nuclear war would destroy both sides. Yet each superpower wanted to be able to deter the other from launching its nuclear weapons. Both sides engaged in a race to match each other's new weapons. The result was a "balance of terror." Mutually assured destruction—in which each side knew that the other side would itself be

WITNESS HISTORY VIDEO

Watch *The Rise and Fall of the Berlin Wall* on the **Witness History Discovery School**™ video program to experience the dramatic history of the wall that divided a nation.

Discovery SCHOOL

Soviet Nuclear Missiles
Every year on May 1, the Soviet Union demonstrated its military and nuclear strength in a parade through Moscow's Red Square. *Why might the Soviet Union have wanted to show off its nuclear might?*

Nuclear Weapons Threaten the World ⓭

Instruct

- **Introduce** Ask students to describe nuclear weapons and share what they know about the role of these weapons in ending World War II. Point out that people vividly remembered the atomic destruction at Hiroshima and Nagasaki. Do students think that nuclear power was an asset or a liability for nations of the world? Would students have supported nuclear proliferation or disarmament during the Cold War period?

- **Teach** Have students look at the chart on this page. Identify the major agreements: SALT, ABM Treaty, START. As students read, have them list in their notes the main features of each treaty. Ask **Why were these treaties necessary?** (*The United States and Soviet Union were building up nuclear weapons arsenals to threaten each other. People feared that nuclear destruction would result from this arms race.*) **What did each treaty seek to do?** (*control and limit the spread and use of nuclear weapons*)

Independent Practice

Ask students to list the steps the two sides took to reduce the threat of Cold War. Then ask them to choose which step was most significant and write a one-paragraph essay explaining why. Use the Think-Write-Pair-Share strategy (TE, p. T23) and have students share their work.

Monitor Progress

- To check student understanding, ask them to reread the black headings and summarize the information under each one.

- As students work on their paragraphs, circulate to ensure their paragraphs include sound reasoning.

Answers

Chart Skills The Nuclear Test Ban Treaty banned just atmospheric testing; SALT II went on to limit numbers of weapons; START required actual weapons reductions.

✓ Neither side wanted to start a destructive war that would devastate both sides. Both sides eventually signed treaties to limit nuclear weapons.

Arms Control Agreements		
Date	Agreement	Effect
1963	Nuclear Test Ban Treaty	Banned testing of nuclear weapons in the atmosphere
1972	SALT I Interim Agreement	Froze existing number of weapons held by each side
1972	SALT I Anti-Ballistic Missile Treaty	Set strict limits on missiles that could shoot down missiles from the other side
1979	SALT II Treaty	Set absolute limit on number of weapons each side could hold
1991	START Treaty	Required both sides to reduce the number of weapons each held

Chart Skills Compare the Nuclear Test Ban Treaty, the SALT II Treaty, and the START Treaty. *How did each of the later treaties advance beyond the treaty that came before it?*

SOURCE: *Encyclopaedia Britannica*

---

destroyed if it launched its weapons—discouraged nuclear war. Still, the world's people lived in constant fear of nuclear doom.

Limiting Nuclear Weapons To reduce the threat of nuclear war, the two sides met at disarmament talks. Although mutual distrust slowed progress, the rival powers did reach some agreements. In 1969, the United States and the Soviet Union began Strategic Arms Limitation Talks (SALT) to limit the number of nuclear weapons held by each side. In 1972 and 1979, both sides signed agreements setting these limits.

One of these agreements limited **anti-ballistic missiles (ABMs),** or missiles that could shoot down other missiles from hostile countries. ABMs were seen as a particular threat to the balance of terror because, by giving one side some protection against the other, they might encourage the protected side to attack. They were also seen as a technology that could provoke a renewed arms race. During the 1980s, U.S. President **Ronald Reagan** launched a program to build a "Star Wars" missile defense against nuclear attack. Critics objected that this program would violate the ABM treaty. Nonetheless, the two sides signed the Strategic Arms Reduction Treaty (START) in 1991.

Building Détente American and Soviet arms control agreements led to an era of **détente** (day TAHNT), or relaxation of tensions, during the 1970s. The American strategy under détente was to restrain the Soviet Union through diplomatic agreements rather than by military means. The era of détente ended in 1979, when the Soviet Union invaded Afghanistan.

Stopping the Spread of Nuclear Weapons By the late 1960s, Britain, France, and China had developed their own nuclear weapons. However, many world leaders worked to keep the arms race from spreading any further. In 1968, many nations signed the Nuclear Non-Proliferation Treaty (NPT). These nations agreed not to develop nuclear weapons or to stop the proliferation, or spread, of nuclear weapons.

✓ **Checkpoint** What factors discouraged the use of nuclear weapons during the Cold War?

The Cold War Goes Global

Although the Cold War began in Central Europe, it quickly spread around the world. When World War II ended, the Soviets were assisting communist forces in China and Korea. American leaders saw that the United States faced a conflict as global as the two world wars that had preceded it. They therefore developed policies to respond to challenges anywhere in the world.

Building Alliances and Bases As part of its strategy to contain Soviet power, the United States reached out to the rest of the world both diplomatically and militarily. The NATO alliance with Europe's democracies was only one of several regional alliances.

Link to Technology

The Hydrogen Bomb After the Soviets exploded an atomic bomb in 1949, U.S. politicians and scientists began to debate whether to develop a hydrogen bomb, which would be one thousand times more destructive than the atomic bomb. Many scientists, including J. Robert Oppenheimer, who led the project to develop the atomic bomb, were opposed on both moral and practical grounds. Yet the threat of the Soviet Union developing it first grew too great for many politicians. Soon after it was discovered that the Soviet Union had been given U.S. preliminary data on the hydrogen bomb, Truman approved the project. First he asked his advisors, "Can the Russians do it?" "Yes," they said. Truman replied, "We have no choice. We'll go ahead."

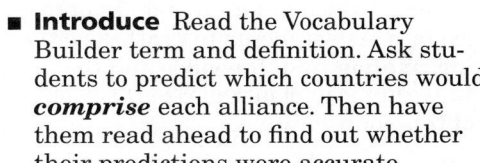

UNITED STATES

SOVIET UNION

TURKEY

Area of inset map

AFGHANISTAN

LEBANON

IRAN

ISRAEL

IRAQ

CUBA

Atlantic Ocean

KOREA

VIETNAM

CAMBODIA

Pacific Ocean

EL SALVADOR

NICARAGUA

MALAYSIA

Pacific Ocean

CONGO

ANGOLA

Indian Ocean

CHILE

30°N

0°

30°S

150°W   120°W   90°W   30°W   0°   30°E   60°E   90°E   120°E   150°E

Robinson Projection

2000   4000 mi

0   2000   4000 km

■ Soviet Union and allies
□ Other communist countries
■ United States and allies
□ Other noncommunist countries
★ Cold War conflicts

ICELAND

30°W   20°W   10°W   0°   10°E   20°E   40°E   50°E

60°N

Atlantic Ocean

NORWAY   FINLAND

SWEDEN

50°N

IRELAND   UNITED KINGDOM   *North Sea*   DENMARK   *Baltic Sea*

SOVIET UNION

NETH.   EAST GER.   POLAND

BELGIUM

LUX.   WEST GERMANY   CZECH.

40°N

FRANCE   SWITZ.   AUST.   HUNG.

ITALY   ROMANIA

PORTUGAL   SPAIN   YUGOSLAVIA   *Black Sea*

BULGARIA

ALB.   TURKEY

GREECE

Mediterranean Sea

Conic Projection

0   300   600 mi

0   300   600 km

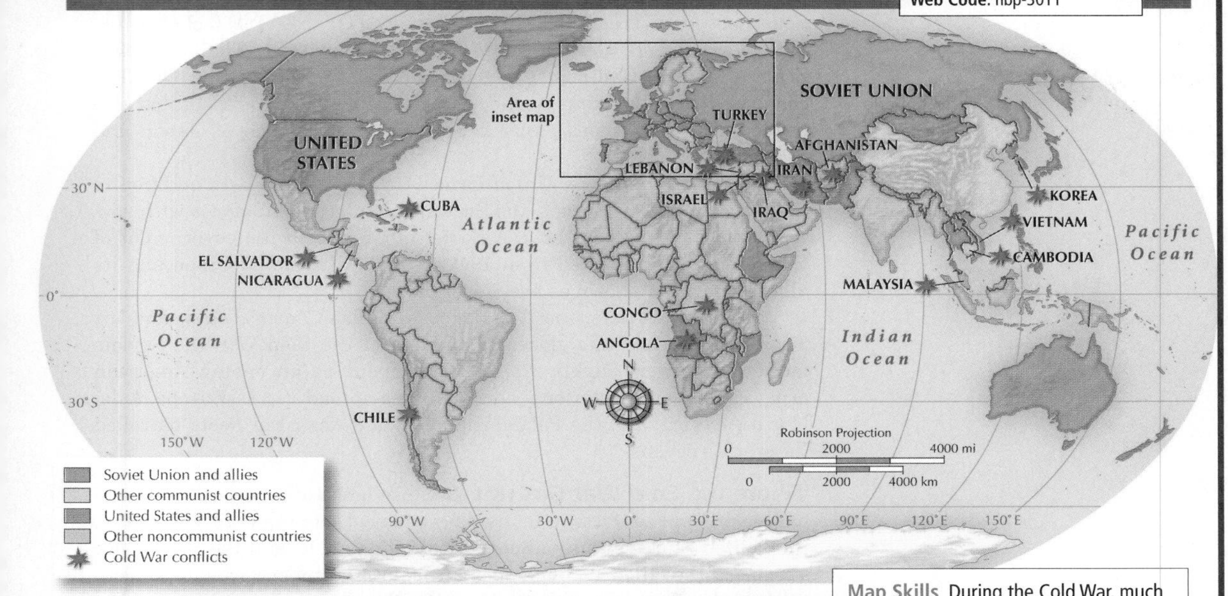

Map Skills During the Cold War, much of the world was divided into two powerful alliances, led by the United States and the communist Soviet Union. Communism reached its maximum extent around 1977, the date of this map. The inset shows details in Europe.
1. **Locate** (a) the Soviet Union (b) the United States (c) Poland
2. **Location** Where were most Cold War conflicts located in relation to the two alliances shown on the map?
3. **Draw Inferences** Why might Cold War conflicts be concentrated as they are?

◀ Soviet troops in Afghanistan

The Cold War Goes Global

Instruct L3

- **Introduce** Read the Vocabulary Builder term and definition. Ask students to predict which countries would **comprise** each alliance. Then have them read ahead to find out whether their predictions were accurate.

- **Teach** Review the ways that the Cold War spread across the globe and the key moments in which it flared into shooting battles and crises. Display **Color Transparency 181: Europe During the Cold War.** Ask **How did the Cold War become a global conflict?** (*Nations around the world allied themselves with either the United States or the Soviet Union.*) **Why did the Cold War sometimes get "hot"?** (*The United States and Soviet Union competed for influence in areas such as Southeast Asia by supporting local forces with weapons and military advice.*)

  📖 **Color Transparencies,** 181

- **Quick Activity** Web Code nbp-3011 will take students to an interactive map on the Cold War world. Have students complete the interactivity and then answer the questions in the text.

L1 Special Needs   **L2 Less Proficient Readers**

Use the map on this page to reinforce why Cuba's fall to communism was such a significant threat to the United States. Have students locate the United States and the Soviet Union on the map. Then have them locate Cuba and note how close it is to Florida. Ask students to explain the threat to a partner.

Use the following resources to help students acquire basic skills.

✏️ **Adapted Reading and Note Taking Study Guide**

■ Adapted Note Taking Study Guide, p. 190
■ Adapted Section Summary, p. 191

Answers

Map Skills
1. Review locations with students.
2. in countries near the Soviet Union or its allies
3. Sample: because of the U.S. policy of containment of Soviet power

■ **Quick Activity** Show students *Show-down: The Cuban Missile Crisis* from the **Witness History Discovery School**™ video program. Ask them to explain. Ask students to synthesize the information from the video and the Infographic and summarize the events of this confrontation.

Vocabulary Builder

comprised—(kum PRYZD) *vt.* was made up of

In 1955, the United States and its allies formed another alliance, the Southeast-Asia Treaty Organization (SEATO). SEATO included the United States, Britain, France, Australia, Pakistan, Thailand, New Zealand, and the Philippines. The Central Treaty Organization (CENTO) comprised Britain, Turkey, Iran, and Pakistan. The United States also formed military alliances with individual nations, such as Japan and South Korea.

Meanwhile, the Soviet Union formed its own alliances. In addition to the Warsaw Pact in Europe, the Soviet Union formed alliances with governments in Africa and Asia. A Soviet alliance with the government of Communist China lasted from 1949 to 1960. The Soviet Union and its allies were often known as the Soviet bloc.

Unlike the Soviets, the Americans established army, navy, and air force bases around the globe. By the end of the Cold War, the Soviets faced the military nightmare of encirclement by an enemy. American army camps, naval stations, and air bases spread across Europe, Asia, North America, and the Pacific islands, while American fleets patrolled the world's oceans.

Where the Cold War Got Hot Because both superpowers had a global reach, local conflicts in many places played into the Cold War. Often, the United States and its allies supported one side, and the Soviet bloc supported the other. Through such struggles, the superpowers could confront each other indirectly rather than head to head. Political shifts around the world added to Cold War tensions. When communist forces won control of mainland China in 1949, the United States feared that a tide of communism would sweep around the world. During this period, European colonies in Africa and Asia demanded independence. As colonies battled for independence, liberation leaders and guerrillas frequently sought help from one or the other Cold War power.

On occasion, the Cold War erupted into "shooting wars," especially in Asia. Both Korea and Vietnam were torn by brutal conflicts in which the United States, the Soviet Union, and China played crucial roles. More commonly, however, the superpowers provided weapons, training, or other aid to opposing forces in Asia, Africa, or Latin America.

Cuba Goes Communist The most serious Cold War conflict in the Western Hemisphere involved the Latin American island nation of Cuba, just 90 miles off the coast of Florida. In the 1950s, **Fidel Castro** organized an armed rebellion against the corrupt dictator who then ruled Cuba. By 1959, Castro had led his guerrilla army to victory and set about transforming the country. This transformation is known as the Cuban Revolution. Castro sought the support of the Soviet Union. He nationalized businesses and put most land under government control. In addition, Castro severely restricted Cubans' political freedom. Critics of the new regime were jailed or silenced, and hundreds of thousands fled to Florida.

The United States attempted to bring down the communist regime next door. In 1961, President **John F. Kennedy** supported an invasion attempt by U.S.-trained Cuban exiles. The Bay of Pigs Invasion, known for the bay where the invaders came ashore in Cuba, quickly ended in failure when Castro's forces captured the invaders. The United States imposed a trade embargo on Cuba that remains in effect today.

Differentiated
Instruction   **Solutions for All Learners**

L1 Special Needs   **L2 Less Proficient Readers**   **L2 English Language Learners**

To help students master vocabulary, have them make a list of this section's Vocabulary Builder terms and Key Terms and People. Encourage students to include in the list additional terms that may be new to them, such as *exodus, prosperity,* and *domination.* Then have them create flashcards with the term on one side

and its definition (or, in the case of Key People, an identifying statement) on the other. For English Language Learners, you may wish to have students add explanations in their first language to go with the flashcards. Pair students and have them quiz each other, using the flashcards.

Cuban Missiles Spark a Crisis In 1962, the Soviet Union sent nuclear missiles to Cuba. President Kennedy responded by imposing a naval blockade that prevented further Soviet shipments. Kennedy demanded that the Soviet Union remove its nuclear missiles from Cuba, and for a few tense days, the world faced a risk of nuclear war over the issue. Finally, however, Soviet Premier Nikita Khrushchev agreed to remove the Soviet missiles, and war was averted.

✓ **Checkpoint** How did the U.S. and the Soviet Union confront each other around the world during the Cold War?

WITNESS HISTORY VIDEO

Watch *Showdown: The Cuban Missile Crisis* on the **Witness History Discovery School**™ video program to experience the dramatic showdown between the Soviet Union and the United States.

Discovery
SCHOOL

● **INFOGRAPHIC**

THE CUBAN MISSILE *CRISIS*

In the summer of 1962, the United States learned that the Soviet Union was shipping nuclear missiles to Cuba, less than 100 miles off the coast of Florida. President John F. Kennedy demanded that the Soviet Union remove the missiles from Cuba. In October 1962, the United States imposed a naval blockade on Cuba. For one week, a tense confrontation brought the world to the brink of nuclear war. Finally, on October 28, Khrushchev agreed to remove the Soviet missiles.

▲ Soviet Premier Nikita Khrushchev

◀ U.S. President John F. Kennedy

During the U.S. naval blockade, the U.S. Navy surrounded Cuba with ships. (See the map below). In this photo, the USS *Barry* inspects the cargo of a Soviet freighter returning from Cuba.

KIDIZER TRAILERS
2 MISSILE TRANSPORTERS
OXIDIZER TRAILER
6 MISSILE TRANSPORTERS
PROB IRBM PROPELLANT TRAILERS
ERECTOR
3 MISSILE TRANSPORTERS

This aerial photo shows Soviet missiles being unloaded at a Cuban port.

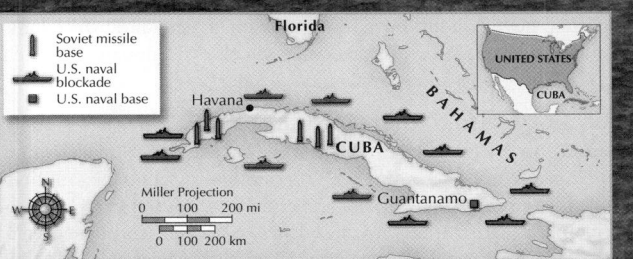
Soviet missile base
U.S. naval blockade
U.S. naval base
Florida
UNITED STATES
CUBA
Havana
B A H A M A S
CUBA
Miller Projection
0   100   200 mi
0   100 200 km
Guantanamo

Thinking Critically
1. **Map Skills** Considering Cuba's location on the map, why did Soviet nuclear missiles on the island pose a threat to the United States?
2. **Draw Conclusions** Why might Khrushchev have agreed to withdraw the missiles from Cuba?

Independent Practice

■ Direct students to the Infographic on the Cuban Missile Crisis and ask them to study the photos and captions. Then play the accompanying audio. Have students work in pairs to summarize the issues and events of the crisis in their own words and to answer the Thinking Critically questions.

🔊 AUDIO **Witness History Audio CD,** The Cuban Missile Crisis

■ Have students fill in the Outline Map *Cold War World* and label the allies of the Soviet Union and the United States.

All in One Teaching Resources, Unit 5, p. 14

Monitor Progress

■ Circulate to make sure that students are filling in their Outline Maps by accurately identifying communist and democratic nations. Administer the Geography Quiz.

All in One Teaching Resources, Unit 5, p. 16

■ Check answers to map skills questions.

Differentiated
Instruction   Solutions for All Learners

L4 Gifted and Talented

Tell students that during the Cuban Missile Crisis, President Kennedy publicly demanded that the Soviet missiles be removed, or "face American military action." Yet privately, he promised not to invade Cuba. A little while later, the U.S. quietly withdrew American missiles from Turkey. After this confrontation, the two sides set up a "hot line," or direct line of communication. Ask students to discuss the value of having public, private, and back channel negotiations. Ask **Why would the heads of state want to have a direct line of communication?** *(Sample: to avoid any misinterpretations, which may happen when multiple people pass on a message)*

Answers

✓ The two nations confronted each other militarily, by supporting opposing sides in local conflicts, and politically, by assembling opposing alliances.

Thinking Critically
1. because of its close proximity to U.S. soil
2. Sample: He didn't want to start a nuclear war.

The Soviet Union in the Cold War

L3

Instruct

- **Introduce: Key Terms** Ask students to find the key term *ideology* (in blue) in the text and define its meaning. Point out that during the Cold War, the Soviet Union sought to advance its ideology within its nation and within other nations. Is it possible to persuade all the people of a nation to follow a single ideology? What might be some advantages and disadvantages of this approach to governing?

- **Teach** Trace the ways that Soviet leaders supported Soviet ideology. Ask **What was Stalin's approach to leadership?** *(He brutally controlled all aspects of Soviet life and attempted to purge the society of influences he disliked.)* **How was Soviet leader Khrushchev similar to and different from Stalin?** *(Khrushchev denounced Stalin's methods and eased central control, but maintained Soviet goals and political control.)*

- **Quick Activity** Display **Color Transparency 182:** *No Time To Take A Bow,* by Clifford Baldowski. Have students discuss ways that the cartoon reflects the image of Soviet leadership portrayed within the Soviet Union during the Cold War.

  🖳 **Color Transparencies,** 182

Independent Practice

In groups, have students chart or illustrate the succession of leaders in the Soviet Union and the dissidents who resisted them. Challenge them to identify the forces in conflict—control and freedom. Use the Numbered Heads strategy (TE, p. T23) to have groups share their work with the class.

Monitor Progress

To review Soviet policies, ask students to explain why a leader such as Khrushchev might have called for peaceful coexistence with the West.

Answer

Chart Skills Sample: In communist countries, government-controlled economies limited consumer choices; in capitalist countries, consumers have more choices because they make economic decisions.

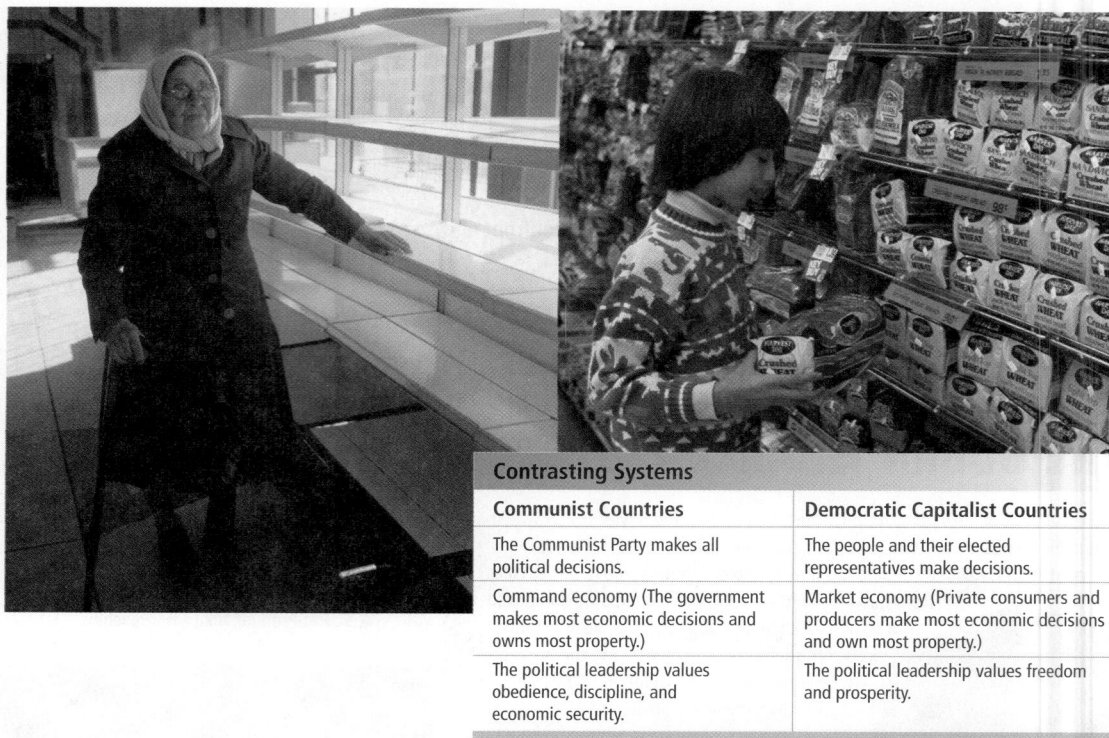

Contrasting Systems	
Communist Countries	**Democratic Capitalist Countries**
The Communist Party makes all political decisions.	The people and their elected representatives make decisions.
Command economy (The government makes most economic decisions and owns most property.)	Market economy (Private consumers and producers make most economic decisions and own most property.)
The political leadership values obedience, discipline, and economic security.	The political leadership values freedom and prosperity.

Chart Skills The communist system often offered few choices for consumers, such as for the Russian woman above. By contrast, capitalist societies provided a wealth of choices for consumers, such as for the American girl at the right. *What facts in the chart above help to explain the different experiences of consumers under these contrasting systems?*

The Soviet Union in the Cold War

Victory in World War II brought few rewards to the Soviet people. Stalin continued his ruthless policies. He filled labor camps with "enemies of the state" and seemed ready to launch new purges when he died in 1953.

Soviet Communism In the Soviet Union, the government controlled most aspects of public life. Communists valued obedience, discipline, and economic security. They sought to spread their communist **ideology,** or value system and beliefs, around the globe. The Soviet Union also aimed to spread its communist command economy to other countries. In command economies, government bureaus make most economic decisions. They often make decisions for political reasons that do not make much economic sense. The government owns most property.

Stalin's Successors Hold the Line After Stalin's death in 1953, **Nikita Khrushchev** (KROOSH chawf) emerged as the new Soviet leader. In 1956, he shocked top Communist Party members when he publicly denounced Stalin's abuse of power. Khrushchev maintained the Communist Party's political control, but he closed prison camps and eased censorship. He called for a "peaceful coexistence" with the West.

Differentiated Instruction   Solutions for All Learners

L2 Less Proficient Readers

To help students better understand the Cold War rivalry, have them make a chart comparing the Soviet Union and the United States. Ensure they include not only the economic and political value systems, but also leaders, policies, and conditions under each government. Have students share their work with a partner. If they are having difficulty, have them refer to the chart in the Quick Study Guide, p. 646. Then have them use their completed charts to write one to two sentences comparing the two superpowers.

Khrushchev's successor, Leonid Brezhnev (BREZH nef) held power from the mid-1960s until he died in 1982. Under Brezhnev, critics faced arrest and imprisonment.

Some Soviets Bravely Resist Despite the risk of punishment, some courageous people dared to criticize the government. Andrey Sakharov (SAH kuh rawf), a distinguished Soviet scientist, spoke out for civil liberties. Brezhnev's government silenced him. As a Soviet soldier during World War II, Aleksandr Solzhenitsyn (sohl zhuh NEET sin) wrote a letter to a friend criticizing Stalin. He was sent to a prison camp. Under Khrushchev, he was released and wrote fiction that drew on his experience as a prisoner. His writing was banned in the Soviet Union, and in 1974 he was exiled. Despite the government's actions, Sakharov and Solzhenitsyn inspired others to resist communist policies.

 Checkpoint How did the Soviet government handle critics of its policies?

The United States in the Cold War

The Cold War was not just a military rivalry. It was also a competition between two contrasting economic and political value systems. Unlike the communist countries, the democratic, capitalist countries, led by the United States, gave citizens the freedom to make economic and political choices. These nations valued freedom and prosperity.

Free Markets While communist countries had command economies, capitalist countries had market economies. In market economies, producers and consumers make economic decisions. Prices are based on supply and demand in a free market. Property is privately owned. Producers compete to offer the best products for the lowest prices. By deciding what to buy, consumers ultimately decide which products are produced. Producers who win consumers' business make profits and grow.

The United States economy is basically a market economy. However, the United States and Western Europe have what can be called mixed economies, because their governments have an economic role.

Containing the Soviet Union America's basic policy toward communist countries was known as containment. This was a strategy of containing communism, or keeping it within its existing boundaries and preventing further expansion. This strategy meant supporting any government facing invasion or internal rebellion by communists.

Living With Nuclear Dangers The nuclear threat led many people in the United States and other countries to build fallout shelters. Fallout shelters

Preparing for a Nuclear Attack
"Duck and cover" air-raid drills were common during the Cold War, even though it is doubtful that ducking and covering would offer much protection in an actual nuclear attack. *What does this photo suggest about Americans' fears during the Cold War?*

Instruct

- **Introduce: Key Terms** Ask students to find the key term *containment* (in blue) in the text and explain its meaning. Tell them that the desire to contain Soviet influence became a key factor in U.S. foreign and even domestic policy during the Cold War era. Have students speculate on the kinds of decisions this policy might have led to for the U.S. government. How could this focus lead to a fear of communism in the United States?

- **Teach** Review the ways that containment affected U.S. foreign and domestic policy. Ask **What were the ways that the United States and Soviet Union competed during the Cold War?** *(militarily, politically, and economically)* **What was the goal of containment?** *(to limit communist power and influence)* **How did the United States pursue this goal politically and militarily?** *(It supported governments facing a communist threat or invasion with military aid and political support.)*

- **Analyzing the Visuals** Have students compare the images on the previous page. Then have them use the Contrasting Systems chart to summarize the differences between market and command economies. Ask students how these economic systems were supported by the United States and Soviet governments.

Independent Practice

Viewpoints To help students better understand the differences between command and market economies, have them read the selection *Comparing Competing Economic Systems* and complete the worksheet.

 Teaching Resources, Unit 5, p. 10

Monitor Progress

Check Reading and Note Taking Study Guide entries for student understanding.

Answers

☑ The Soviet government arrested and imprisoned critics of its policies.

Caption Fears were widespread and part of everyday life.

Assess Progress

- Have students complete the Section Assessment.
- Administer the Section Quiz.

 **Teaching Resources, Unit 5,** p. 2

- To further assess student understanding, use

   Progress Monitoring Transparencies, 128

Reteach

If students need more instruction, have them read the section summary.

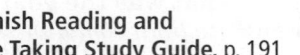 **Reading and Note Taking Study Guide,** p. 191

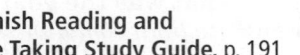 **Adapted Reading and Note Taking Study Guide,** p. 191

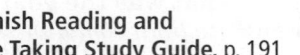 **Spanish Reading and Note Taking Study Guide,** p. 191

Extend

See this chapter's Professional Development pages for the Extend Online activity on the Cold War crisis.

Answer

✓ The United States sought to remove communist influences at home and sought to contain Soviet power overseas.

Red Scare Culture
Pop culture during the "red scare" of the 1940s and 1950s reflected the fears of the times. "I Was a Communist for the FBI" thrilled movie-goers in 1951.

were structures, often underground, designed to protect people from fallout, or radioactive particles from a nuclear explosion. In 1961, the U.S. government launched a community fallout shelter program to create fallout shelters in public and commercial buildings, stocked with a two-week supply of food for the surrounding population. The fear of nuclear attack reached a peak in the United States during the Cuban missile crisis of 1962. Thousands of Americans built private fallout shelters underneath their backyards.

From the 1950s into the 1970s, American schools conducted air-raid drills in anticipation of a nuclear attack. These drills were nearly as common as fire drills. Children were trained to duck underneath desks and crouch with their hands over their heads. Although this would not have protected them from an actual nuclear explosion, the drills reflected the widespread fear of nuclear war.

Seeking Enemies Within Cold War fears led to a "red scare" within the United States. During the late 1940s and early 1950s, many Americans feared that communists inside the United States might try to undermine the U.S. government. Around 1950, Senator Joseph McCarthy led a hunt for suspected American communists. McCarthy became notorious for unproven charges. Accusing innocent people of communism, and the fear that this created, became known as McCarthyism. McCarthy's influence, however, faded after he attacked the patriotism of the United States Army.

During the same period, the House Un-American Activities Committee (HUAC) led a similar campaign to identify supposed communist sympathizers. HUAC was made up of members of the U.S. House of Representatives. In 1947, the Committee sought to expose communist sympathizers in Hollywood's movie industry. People who had flirted with communist ideas in their youth and later rejected them were labeled as communists. Many who were labeled in this way were no longer able to get decent jobs.

✓ **Checkpoint** How did America respond to the threat of communism at home and overseas?

SECTION **1** **Assessment**

Progress Monitoring Online
For: Self-quiz with vocabulary practice
Web Code: nba-3011

Terms, People, and Places

1. For each term, person, or place listed at the beginning of the section, write a sentence explaining its significance.

Note Taking

2. **Reading Skill: Summarize** Use your completed chart to answer the Focus Question: What were the military and political consequences of the Cold War in the Soviet Union, Europe, and the United States?

Comprehension and Critical Thinking

3. **Make Generalizations** What kinds of conflicts resulted from the global confrontation between the two superpowers?

4. **Draw Inferences** How did the buildup of nuclear weapons discourage their use?

5. **Make Comparisons** Identify similarities and differences between the Soviet Union and the United States during the Cold War.

● **Writing About History**

Quick Write: Understand the Purpose To write a problem-solution essay, you first need to understand the purpose of this type of essay. In this section, you learned that the superpowers' possession of nuclear weapons posed a risk of nuclear war. Write sentences answering each of the following questions: What makes this issue a problem? What benefit comes from solving this problem?

---

1. Sentences should reflect an understanding of each term, person, or place listed at the beginning of the section.

2. The U.S. and Soviet Union built up huge nuclear arsenals, but then worked to limit them through treaties. The U.S. led Western Europe, while the Soviet Union dominated Eastern Europe. Germany was divided between East and West. Eastern Europe resisted Soviet influence. The U.S.

and Soviet Union supported opposing sides in global conflicts between communism and democracy.

3. Tense struggles for influence developed in many parts of the world; a few of these flared into actual military conflicts.

4. It made each side in the Cold War resist using weapons for fear of unleashing devastating nuclear attack.

5. Both nations feared each other and both tried to influence other nations to share their views. The U.S. experienced free-

dom, economic prosperity, and anxiety over communism.

● **Writing About History**

Sentences should reflect that the risk is possible total destruction and that the benefits are relief from anxiety, greater safety for all, and decreased focus on military buildup.

For additional assessment, have students access **Progress Monitoring Online** at **Web Code nba-3011.**

Concept Connector

COOPERATION

With whom should we cooperate and why?

In This Chapter

Cooperation between the United States and the Soviet Union broke down as soon as Germany was defeated. Each superpower developed its own network of allies, NATO and the Warsaw Pact, and built large nuclear arsenals. Faced with the possibility of devastating war, American and Soviet leaders (right) negotiated treaties that gradually reduced the number of nuclear weapons.

Throughout History

400s B.C. Greek city-states unite to defeat the Persians.

1200s A.D. Hanseatic League promotes trade in northern Europe.

Late 1500s Five Iroquois groups form the Iroquois League to keep peace among themselves.

Late 1800s European and American workers form unions to improve pay and working conditions.

2000s The Kyoto Protocol to reduce greenhouse gas emissions is signed by 140 countries.

"LET'S GET A LOCK FOR THIS THING"

NUCLEAR WAR

FALLOUT SHELTER
CAPACITY 1730

Continuing Today

Despite political differences, many nations come together every four years to take part in the Olympic Games. Athletes compete in individual and team events.

21st Century Skills

TRANSFER Activities

1. **Analyze** What goals have motivated people to cooperate throughout history?

2. **Evaluate** Why is it sometimes necessary to cooperate with an enemy?

3. **Transfer** Complete a Web quest in which you, as Secretary of State, consider whether or not to cooperate with a new regime in the Middle East; record your thoughts in the Concept Connector Journal; and learn to make a video. Web Code nbh-3008

History Background

Smallpox Countries also cooperate to rid the world from infectious diseases such as polio and smallpox. For example, in 1958, Soviet epidemiologist Viktor Zhdanov called for the global eradication of smallpox; this disease is thought to have killed more people than any other infectious disease. In a political move designed to help American-Soviet relations, President Lyndon Johnson endorsed this idea in 1965. Then the

World Health Organization put together an international team of doctors and health workers, who worked with local governments to contain outbreaks of smallpox and inoculate the population against it. In 1966, the year the program began, two million people per year were dying from smallpox. By 1977, the last known natural case occurred in Somalia.

Objectives

As you teach this section, keep students focused on the following objectives to help them answer the Section Focus Question and master core content.

- Understand how the United States prospered and expanded opportunities.
- Explain how Europe rebuilt its economy after World War II.
- Describe how Japan was transformed.

Prepare to Read

Build Background Knowledge L3

Ask students to recall the devastation caused by World War II. Based on their previous reading, ask them to predict challenges facing Europe and Japan after the war.

Set a Purpose L3

- **WITNESS HISTORY** Read the selection aloud or play the audio.

  AUDIO **Witness History Audio CD,** The Marshall Plan

  Ask **What were the goals of the Marshall Plan?** *(to rebuild the economies of war-torn Europe and Japan in the postwar years)* **How could achieving these goals help the United States?** *(The United States wanted to form alliances with vital, independent, and democratic nations.)*

- **Focus** Point out the Section Focus Question and write it on the board. Tell students to refer to this question as they read. *(Answer appears with Section 2 Assessment answers.)*

- **Preview** Have students preview the Section Objectives and the list of Terms, People, and Places.

- **Note Taking** Have students read this section using the Paragraph Shrinking strategy (TE, p. T20). As they read, have them fill in the chart with changes in the industrialized democracies.

  Reading and Note Taking Study Guide, p. 192

Marshall Plan poster

Marshall Plan food aid being distributed in France

WITNESS HISTORY AUDIO

The Marshall Plan

In a speech at Harvard University in June 1947, U.S. Secretary of State George Marshall made the case for the Marshall Plan, a United States assistance program for Western Europe.

❝ Our policy is directed not against any country or doctrine but against hunger, poverty, desperation, and chaos. Its purpose should be the revival of a working economy in the world so as to permit the emergence of . . . conditions in which free institutions can exist. ❞

Focus Question How did the United States, Western Europe, and Japan achieve economic prosperity and strengthen democracy during the Cold War years?

The Industrialized Democracies

Objectives

- Understand how the United States prospered and expanded opportunities.
- Explain how Western Europe rebuilt its economy after World War II.
- Describe how Japan was transformed.

Terms, People, and Places

recession	Konrad Adenauer
suburbanization	welfare state
segregation	European Community
discrimination	gross domestic product
Dr. Martin Luther King, Jr.	(GDP)

Note Taking

Reading Skill: Categorize Keep track of changes in the industrialized democracies with a chart like the one below.

Economic and Political Changes in the Industrialized Democracies

United States	Western Europe	Japan
•	•	•
•	•	•
•	•	•

The industrialized democracies of North America, Western Europe, and Japan grew in prosperity and went through social change during the Cold War. Throughout this period, the United States was the world's wealthiest and most powerful country. By the end of the Cold War, however, Western Europe and Japan rivaled the United States economically.

America Prospers and Changes

In the postwar decades, American businesses expanded into markets around the globe. The dollar was the world's strongest currency. Foreigners flocked to invest in American industry and to buy U.S. government bonds. America's wealth was a model for other democracies and a challenge to the stagnant economies of the communist world.

America Plays a Central Role During the Cold War, the United States was a global political leader. The headquarters of the League of Nations had been symbolically located in neutral Switzerland. The headquarters of the newly formed United Nations was built in New York City.

The United States also played a leading economic role. America had emerged untouched from the horrendous destruction of the Second World War. Other nations needed American goods and services, and foreign trade helped the United States achieve a long postwar boom. The long postwar peace among democratic nations

Vocabulary Builder

Use the information below and the following resources to teach the high-use word from this section.

Teaching Resources, Unit 5, p. 7; **Teaching Resources, Skills Handbook,** p. 3

High-Use Word	Definition and Sample Sentence
prosper, p. 616	*vi.* to succeed, thrive, do well Gina **prospered** in college; she got excellent grades and made many friends.

helped to spread this boom worldwide. The World Bank, an international agency that finances world economic development, was headquartered in Washington, D.C. The International Monetary Fund (IMF), which oversees the finances of the world's nations, was based there as well.

The Postwar American Boom America's economic strength transformed life in the United States itself. During the 1950s and 1960s, boom times prevailed. Recessions, or periods when the economy shrinks, were brief and mild. Although segments of the population were left behind, many Americans prospered in the world's wealthiest economy. As Americans grew more affluent, many moved from the cities to the suburbs. The movement to communities outside an urban core is known as suburbanization. Suburbanites typically lived in single-family houses with lawns and access to good schools. Suburban highways allowed residents to commute to work by car.

During the postwar decades, many Americans also moved to the Sunbelt, or the states in the South and Southwest of the United States. Jobs in these states were becoming more plentiful than in the industrialized North, and the warmer climate was an added bonus. The growing availability of air conditioning and water for irrigation in states such as Arizona helped make the movement to the Sunbelt possible.

The wide popularity of American culture abroad vividly illustrated the global influence of the United States. The world embraced twentieth-century art forms such as American movies, television, and rock-and-roll music. American originals such as Elvis Presley, musical comedies, Hollywood romances, and action movies had a worldwide following.

The federal government contributed to the economic boom. Under President Truman, Congress created programs that helped veterans, the elderly, and the poor. Truman's successor, Dwight Eisenhower, approved government funding to build a vast interstate highway system. Government programs also made it easier for people to buy homes.

Moving to the Suburbs
This cartoon from the 1950s shows a family moving from the city to the suburbs. The photo below shows a suburb in New York in 1954. *Why might suburbs such as this attract families from cities?*

Teach

America Prospers and Changes

Instruct

■ **Introduce** Point out the images on this page. Ask students to describe what these images reveal about American life and culture during the 1950s. Have them predict how America will prosper and change in the postwar years. Then have students read to find out whether their predictions were accurate.

■ **Teach** Review ways that America's economy was tied to global events. Ask **What factors helped America's economy thrive in the postwar years?** *(America's economy was undamaged in World War II and prospered after the war, so it could produce goods much needed by recovering nations. Foreign trade helped fund huge economic expansion.)* **How did America's economic prosperity affect the lives of people in the United States and abroad?** *(Many Americans were able to buy consumer goods and move to the suburbs; people abroad invested in American industry and looked to the United States as an economic model.)*

■ **Quick Activity** Discuss the effects of American culture on the global community. Ask students how this may have contributed to today's conflicts between Western and Muslim cultures.

Independent Practice

Have students create a chart showing causes and effects discussed in this section. Model the first entry on the board as *Cause: lack of WW II damage; Effect: U.S. economy prospers during postwar years.*

Monitor Progress

As students fill in their charts, circulate to make sure they have correctly categorized social, political, and economic changes. For a completed version of the chart, see

📖 **Note Taking Transparencies,** 190

Answer

Caption because of the additional living space and the opportunity to own some land

Democracy Expands Opportunities

Instruct

- **Introduce: Vocabulary Builder** Have students read the Vocabulary Builder term and definition. Ask students to predict what segments of the American population will *prosper* after World War II. Have them predict which segments will struggle to gain additional rights. Then have them read ahead to see if their predictions were accurate.

- **Teach** Write each black heading on the board. Ask students to volunteer phrases or sentences to put under each one. Then ask **What problems faced America's democracy during the 1950s and 1960s?** *(African Americans, other minorities, and women were denied equal rights in education, housing, and other areas. Economic opportunities were limited for many Americans.)* **How did Americans respond to these problems?** *(Many protested for equal rights, both within and outside the government. The government moved to support needy Americans.)*

- **Quick Activity** On the board, post King's "I have a dream" quotation from the text *("I have a dream that one day this nation will rise up. . . . all men are created equal.")* Then refer them to the biography of King on this page. Ask students to connect King's words with his actions and biography. Then have them summarize his goals and hopes for equal rights in America, particularly for African Americans.

The Oil Shock of the 1970s
In 1973 and 1974, a reduction in the supply of oil led to shortages and higher prices for gasoline. In the photos above, motorists wait on line to fill up with scarce gasoline.

An Oil Shock Brings Recession However, America's growing dependence on the world economy brought problems. In the early 1970s, a political crisis in the Middle East led to decreased oil exports. Oil prices soared worldwide. Waiting in long lines for scarce and expensive gasoline, Americans became aware of their dependence on imported oil and on global economic forces.

In America and in the other industrialized democracies, which were even more dependent on imported oil, higher prices for oil left businesses and consumers with less to spend on other products. The decades of postwar prosperity ended with a serious recession in 1974. During the 1970s and 1980s, the world's economies suffered a series of recessions alternating with years of renewed prosperity.

 Checkpoint How was the U.S. economy linked to the broader global economy during the Cold War?

Vocabulary Builder
prospered—(PRAHS purd) *vi.* succeeded, thrived, did well

Democracy Expands Opportunities

Although America prospered after World War II, the American promise of equality and opportunity had not yet been fulfilled for ethnic minorities and women. In the postwar decades, these groups demanded equality. In American politics, liberals and conservatives offered contrasting programs to increase opportunities for the American people.

Segregation and Discrimination The prosperity of the postwar years failed to benefit all Americans equally. Although slavery had been abolished a century before, many states denied equality to African Americans and other minority groups. These groups faced legal **segregation,** or forced separation, in education and housing. Minorities also suffered **discrimination**—unequal treatment or barriers—in jobs and voting. After World War II, President Harry Truman desegregated the armed forces. Then, in 1954, the U.S. Supreme Court made a landmark ruling, *Brown* v. *Board of Education of Topeka,* declaring that segregated schools were unconstitutional.

History Background

Gandhi and the Civil Rights Movement The U.S. Civil Rights Movement was heavily influenced by the ideas of Mahatma Gandhi. The Indian leader's nonviolent protests, which helped free India from British rule in the 1940s, set a standard for peaceful civil disobedience that many civil rights activists, including Martin Luther King, Jr., openly emulated. One such act sparked the Civil Rights Movement in 1955, when Rosa Parks refused to give up her seat to a white man on a public bus.

Caesar Chavez, who fought for farm workers' rights through the United Farm Workers' union, also found inspiration in Gandhi's sacrifices. Like Gandhi, Chavez enacted boycotts and hunger strikes to gain attention to his cause. One of his strikes in 1988 lasted for 36 days.

Answer

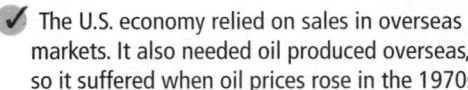 The U.S. economy relied on sales in overseas markets. It also needed oil produced overseas, so it suffered when oil prices rose in the 1970s.

Americans Demand Civil Rights By 1956, a gifted preacher, Dr. Martin Luther King, Jr., had emerged as a leader of the civil rights movement. This movement aimed to extend equal rights to all Americans, and particularly African Americans. King organized boycotts and led peaceful marches to end segregation in the United States. In 1963, King made a stirring speech. "I have a dream," he proclaimed, "that one day this nation will rise up and live out the true meaning of its creed: 'We hold these truths to be self-evident, that all men are created equal.'"

Americans of all races joined the civil rights movement. Their courage in the face of sometimes brutal attacks stirred the nation's conscience. Asians, Latinos, Native Americans, and other groups joined African Americans in demanding equality. The U.S. Congress outlawed public segregation, protected voting rights, and required equal access to housing and jobs. Poverty, unemployment, and discrimination still plagued many African Americans. However, some were elected to political office or gained top jobs in business and the military.

Women Demand Equality Women too faced discrimination in employment and other areas. Inspired by the civil rights movement, women fought gender-based discrimination during the 1960s and 1970s. The women's rights movement won laws banning discrimination against women. More women also gained higher salaries and positions in politics and business.

The Government's Role Grows During the 1960s, the government further expanded social programs to help the poor and disadvantaged. Under Presidents John F. Kennedy and Lyndon Johnson, both Democrats,

BIOGRAPHY

MARTIN LUTHER KING, Jr.
Dr. Martin Luther King, Jr. (1929–1968) was born in Atlanta, Georgia, and grew up in the segregated American South. He earned a doctorate in divinity in 1955 and became a minister at a church in Montgomery, Alabama. Beginning that year, King helped lead the Montgomery Bus Boycott to protest segregation on the city's buses. In the years that followed, King emerged as the most respected leader of the American civil rights movement. He was repeatedly attacked and jailed for his beliefs. He helped organize the massive March on Washington, D.C., for civil rights in 1963. He gave his famous "I Have a Dream" speech at this event. King lived to see the passage of the Civil Rights Act of 1965 that outlawed segregation. However, he was killed in 1968 by an assassin.
How did King's actions show courage?

Independent Practice
Have students create a timeline showing how the government expanded between the 1950s and 1970s, and then contracted in the 1980s. Ensure that students' timelines include both social and economic policy.

Monitor Progress
As students complete their timelines, circulate to confirm that the information is accurate, that the events are in sequence, and that they recognize the ebb and flow of government's control from the 1950s to the 1980s.

Differentiated
Instruction   Solutions for All Learners

L4 Gifted and Talented   L4 Advanced Readers

Tell students that by the 1970s, most of America's minority groups were represented by at least one prominent civil rights group and that each group's goals and tactics varied. La Raza defended the rights of Mexican Americans. The American Indian Movement protested the treatment of Native Americans, demanding the return of tribal lands seized by the U.S. government. Some groups such as the Black Panther Party and the Nation of Islam, led by Malcolm X, did not always espouse or adhere to the principle of non-violence. Yet the majority of activists were content using politics and persuasion to reach their goals. Have students choose two groups, research their methods, and create a chart comparing and contrasting their methods and their effectiveness.

Answer

BIOGRAPHY He continually put his life and freedom at risk for his beliefs.

Western Europe Rebuilds

Instruct

■ **Introduce** Read aloud the Primary Source selection. Ask students to summarize what it says about postwar Berlin. Remind students of the terrible physical and economic havoc wrought by World War II.

■ **Teach** Create two columns on the board, labeled *Problems* and *Solutions*. Have students list the problems that Western Europe faced in the postwar years and the steps nations took to solve those problems. Write their answers on the board. Discuss the role of the Marshall Plan, colonial independence, and the welfare state in both problems and solutions. Then display **Color Transparency 180: European Nations Grant Aid Under the Marshall Plan** to illustrate the European recipients of Marshall Plan aid.

🏛 Color Transparencies, 180

■ **Analyzing the Visuals** Direct students to the photo on this page. Ask them to describe the factors that contributed to conditions in Germany before and after World War II. Challenge them to explain how West Germany was able to recover so quickly, and why other nations, such as Britain, faced slower recoveries.

Congress funded Medicare, providing health care for the elderly. Other programs offered housing for the poor.

Republicans Respond In the 1980s, President Reagan and the Republican Party called for cutbacks in taxes and government spending. They argued that cutting taxes was the best way to improve opportunities for Americans. Congress ended some social programs, reduced government regulation of the economy, and cut taxes. At the same time, however, military spending increased.

The combination of increased spending and tax cuts greatly increased the national budget deficit, or the shortfall between what the government spends and what it receives in taxes and other income. To deal with the deficit, Republicans pushed for deeper cuts in social and economic programs, including education, welfare, and environmental protection.

✔ **Checkpoint** Over time, how did the U.S. government expand opportunities for Americans?

Western Europe Rebuilds

Americans arriving in Europe as liberators or occupiers in 1945 were astonished at the damage that the war had inflicted. Germany in particular lay in ruins. Many Europeans had suffered grievously. However, Western Europe recovered economically more rapidly than anyone had expected—and then moved on to even higher standards of living.

Germany Divided and Reunited At the end of World War II, the United States, Britain, and France—all democracies—occupied the western portion of Germany. The Soviet Union occupied eastern Germany. The goal had been to hold elections throughout Germany for a single German government, but disputes between the Soviet Union and the Western powers led to Germany's division into two separate countries by 1949. West Germany became a member of NATO, while East Germany became a member of the Warsaw Pact. For 40 years, differences between the two Germanys widened.

Primary Source

❝There are no homes, no shops, no transportation, no government buildings. Only a few walls. . . . Berlin can now be regarded only as a geographical location heaped with mountainous mounds of debris.❞
—*New York Herald Tribune,* May 3, 1945

Wartime Destruction in Germany
Many German cities suffered serious wartime damage. In this photo, civilians walk through the rubble left by wartime bombing in Nuremberg, Germany, in 1945. *What challenges would residents of a city face after such heavy destruction?*

Answers

✔ The U.S. government stepped in to end segregation and discrimination; to improve life for veterans, the elderly, and the poor; and to expand transportation and housing opportunities.

Caption loss of electricity, possible homelessness, uncertainty about cleaning up and rebuilding

History Background

The Vision of Lyndon B. Johnson The tall Texan dreamed of ridding the United States of poverty and inequality. When Lyndon B. Johnson became president, he oversaw sweeping social reforms. First, he helped get Kennedy's pending legislation passed. The Civil Rights Act of 1964 outlawed discrimination. The Voting Rights Act of 1965 and the Twenty-Fourth constitutional amendment expanded the right to vote.

Johnson added his own vision, the Great Society, and declared a war on poverty. The first piece of legislation, The Economic Opportunity Act of 1964, introduced Medicare and Medicaid. Yet these programs did not do enough to mend the fractured society. The culture would continue to break apart over politics, the war in Vietnam, racism, and other issues.

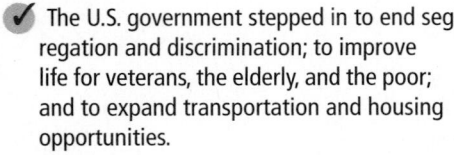

Independent Practice
Have students write a short paragraph
supporting or opposing the European
welfare state. Each position should
clearly explain how the welfare state
would help or harm its citizens. Tell
students to adopt the voice of a group
in European society that held one of
these views.

Monitor Progress
As students complete their paragraphs,
circulate to review aspects of the welfare
state. Confirm that students have accurately described its features, chosen an
appropriate group, and successfully
developed an argument for or against the
welfare state.

While West Germany had a democratic government, East Germany
was a communist state. While West Germany enjoyed an economic boom,
East Germany's command economy stagnated. Before the Berlin Wall
was built, millions of East Germans fled to the freedom and prosperity of
West Germany. After the wall was built, some East Germans still managed to escape, but others were shot as they tried to cross the border.

In 1989, as Soviet communism declined, Germany moved toward
reunification. Without Soviet backing, East German communist leaders
were unable to maintain control. They were forced to reopen their western borders. Quickly, East Germans demanded reunification with the
West. In 1990, German voters approved reunification.

West Germany's "Economic Miracle" Early in the Cold War, the
United States rushed aid to its former enemy through the Marshall Plan
and other programs. It wanted to strengthen West Germany against
communist Eastern Europe. From 1949 to 1963, **Konrad Adenauer**
(AHD uh now ur) was West Germany's chancellor, or prime minister. He
guided the rebuilding of cities, factories, and trade. Because many of its
old factories had been destroyed, Germany built a modern and highly
productive industrial base. Despite high taxes to pay for the recovery,
West Germans created a booming industrial economy.

Britain's Narrowed Horizons Britain's economy was slow to recover
after the war. Despite U.S. assistance through the Marshall Plan, Britain
could no longer afford a large military presence overseas. Therefore, Britain abandoned its colonial empire in the face of demands for independence. After several years of economic hardship, however, Britain's
economy recovered during the 1950s and 1960s. Although Britain did not
enjoy a boom like Germany's, its living standard did improve.

Other European Nations Prosper Most European nations emerged
from World War II greatly weakened. Like Britain, European colonial
powers such as Belgium and the Netherlands gave in to demands for
independence from former colonies. France was forced to abandon its

The Iron Curtain Divides Germany
While the Berlin Wall divided the city of
Berlin, a much longer series of concrete
walls, barbed wire, and watchtowers ran
along the border between East and West
Germany, forming part of the Iron
Curtain. *Why might East Germany have
built a fortified border such as this?*

Answer

Caption to keep people living in East Germany
from crossing the border at any point as well as
to create an atmosphere of intimidation

Japan Is Transformed 🔳

Instruct

- **Introduce: Key Terms** Ask students to locate the key term **gross domestic product** (in blue) in the text and to explain its meaning. Explain that Japan's gross domestic product (GDP) soared in the postwar years. Given the total destruction Japan experienced during World War II, ask students to consider how the nation might have achieved such an economic transformation.

- **Teach** Trace the changes in Japan's political and economic structure after World War II. Ask **How did Japan change in the postwar years?** *(It became a democracy and successfully rebuilt its industrialized economy.)* **What role did other nations play in Japan's changing economy?** *(The United States provided military protection and economic assistance, distributed land to landless farmers, and, with other nations, bought great quantities of Japan's export products.)*

- **Quick Activity** Display **Color Transparency 183: Japan's Economic Recovery After World War II.** Use the lesson suggestion in the transparency book to guide a discussion on Japan's transformation.

  📖 **Color Transparencies,** 183

Building Britain's Welfare State
Britain's Labour Party won support after World War II by expanding social programs and the government's role in the economy.

empire after bloody colonial wars in Vietnam and Algeria drained and demoralized the country.

Most Western European countries had suffered serious wartime damage. Like West Germany, they received U.S. assistance through the Marshall Plan. As in West Germany, this helped them to build more modern and productive facilities. During the 1950s and 1960s, most of Europe enjoyed an economic boom. Living standards improved greatly for most Dutch, Belgians, French, and Italians. Poorer European countries, such as Spain and Ireland, were able to attract outside investment that led to economic growth.

Building the Welfare State In the postwar decades, Europeans worked to secure their economic prosperity. From the 1950s through the 1970s, European nations expanded social benefits to their citizens. During this time, many European nations also moved toward greater economic cooperation.

Many European political parties, and particularly those representing workers, wanted to extend the welfare state. A welfare state is a country with a market economy but with increased government responsibility for the social and economic needs of its people. The welfare state had its roots in the late 1800s. During that period, Germany, Britain, and other nations had set up basic old-age pensions and unemployment insurance.

After 1945, European governments expanded these social programs. Both the middle class and the poor enjoyed increased benefits from national healthcare, unemployment insurance, and old-age pensions. Other programs gave aid to the poor and created an economic cushion to help people get through difficult times.

However, the welfare state brought high taxes and greater government regulation of private enterprise. In Britain, France, and elsewhere, governments took over basic industries such as railroads, airlines, and steel. Conservatives, or people who favor free markets and a limited role for government, condemned this drift from the free enterprise system toward socialism.

Limiting the Welfare State In 1979, British voters turned to the Conservative Party, which denounced the welfare state as costly and inefficient. The Conservatives were led by Margaret Thatcher. Thatcher's government reduced social welfare programs and returned government-owned industries to private control. Faced with soaring costs, other European nations also moved to limit social welfare benefits and to privatize state-owned businesses during the 1980s and 1990s.

Toward European Unity Greater economic cooperation helped fuel Europe's economic boom during the 1950s and 1960s. In 1952, six nations—West Germany, the Netherlands, Belgium, Luxembourg, France, and Italy—set up the European Coal and Steel Community. This agency established free trade in coal and steel among member states by eliminating tariffs, or fees, and other barriers that limited trade. This small start spurred economic growth across Western Europe and led to further regional cooperation.

In 1957, the same six European nations signed a treaty to form the European Economic Community, later known simply as the **European Community.** This was an organization dedicated to establishing free trade among member nations for all products. The European Community

Connect to Our World

Connections to Today Japan's economic recovery after World War II was evident in the two cities destroyed by atomic bombs: Hiroshima and Nagasaki. Before they were attacked, Hiroshima was mainly a military center and Nagasaki was a major shipbuilding center. After the war, Japan's new capitalist economy spurred large rebuilding projects. Modern architec-

tural marvels were built, large parks and monuments were constructed in memory of the victims, and new industries developed. Today, Hiroshima is the largest industrial city in its region, home to numerous rubber, chemical, and automobile factories. Nagasaki is once again a major shipbuilding center, and now also supports a large tourism industry.

gradually ended tariffs and allowed workers and capital to move freely across national borders. In later years, the European Community expanded to include Britain and other European countries.

✓ **Checkpoint** What were some advantages and disadvantages of the welfare state in Europe?

Japan Is Transformed

In 1945, Japan, like Germany, lay in ruins. It had suffered perhaps the most devastating damage of any nation involved in World War II. Tens of thousands of Japanese were homeless and hungry.

American Occupiers Bring Changes Under General Douglas MacArthur, the Japanese emperor lost all political power. Japan's new constitution established a parliamentary democracy. Occupation forces also introduced social reforms. They opened the education system to all people, with legal equality for women. A land-reform program bought out large landowners and gave land to landless farmers. The United States also provided funds to rebuild Japan's cities and economy.

In 1952, the United States ended the occupation and signed a peace treaty with Japan. Still, the two nations kept close ties. American military forces maintained bases in Japan, which in turn was protected by American nuclear weapons. The two countries were also trading partners, eventually competing with each other in the global economy.

Japan Develops a Democracy Over the years, democracy took root in Japan. The Liberal Democratic Party (LDP) dominated the government from the 1950s to the 1990s. The LDP, however, differs from political parties in the United States. The LDP is a coalition, or alliance, of factions that compete for government positions.

Peace Comes to Japan
A 1945 poster printed by a Japanese bank encourages people to "make a bright future for Japan."

明るい日本 みんなの力で
住友銀行

Land Reform Benefits Japanese Farmers
Japan's postwar land reform redistributed land from wealthy landlords to small farmers such as the ones in this photo. *How would ownership of land benefit farmers?*

Link to Humanities

Akira Kurosawa One of the twentieth century's finest film directors, Akira Kurosawa was the first Japanese director to win an audience and acclaim outside Japan's borders, thus opening the Japanese cinema to the West. Born in Tokyo in 1920, Kurosawa was a talented painter who took a job as an assistant director at a film studio. His movies, with their rich visuals and rich ideas, have influenced numerous filmmakers in Hollywood and Hollywood has, in turn, influenced his own moviemaking. For example, he directed the epic *The Seven Samurai* because he wanted to make a Japanese western. This film, which follows seven unemployed samurai who are hired by peasant farmers to defend their village, was later remade as an American western, *The Magnificent Seven*.

Independent Practice

Have students write a paragraph comparing and contrasting Japan's postwar transformation with that of Germany's. Encourage students to find the common and disparate factors in the experiences of these two nations. If students are having trouble, recommend they draw a Venn diagram to help them organize the information.

Monitor Progress

■ As students work on their paragraphs, circulate to ensure they are using examples from both Japan's and Germany's recovery efforts to show the similarities and differences between the two nations.

■ Check Reading and Note Taking Study Guide entries for student understanding.

Answers

✓ Advantages included expanded social benefits such as old-age pensions and unemployment insurance. Disadvantages included higher taxes and greater government regulation, or control of industry.

Caption by giving them a source of capital, or wealth

Japan's Economic Miracle
By the 1970s and 1980s, Japan prospered by manufacturing products to be sold overseas, such as the televisions being assembled in this photo.

An Economic Miracle Relies on Exports Like Western Europe, Japan achieved an economic miracle between 1950 and 1970. Its **gross domestic product (GDP)** soared year after year. GDP is the total value of all goods and services produced in a nation within a particular year.

Japan's success was built on producing goods for export. At first, Japan sold textiles. Later, it shifted to selling steel and machinery. By the 1970s, Japanese cars, cameras, and televisions found eager buyers on the world market. Soon, a wide range of Japanese electronic goods were competing with Western, and especially American, products.

How did Japan enjoy such success? After World War II, Japan, like Germany, had to rebuild from scratch. Also like Germany, it had successfully industrialized in the past, so it quickly built efficient, modern factories that outproduced older industries in the West. With American military protection, Japan spent little money on its own military and could invest more in its economy. In addition, Japan benefited from an educated and skilled workforce. Finally, the government protected home industries by imposing tariffs and regulations that limited imports.

These policies, along with the high quality of Japanese exports, resulted in a trade surplus for Japan. That is, Japan sold more goods overseas than it bought from other countries. By the 1980s, United States manufacturers were angered by what they saw as unfair competition, and the United States pushed Japan to open its economy to more imports. However, Japan's trade surplus persisted.

✔ **Checkpoint** What factors explain Japan's economic success in the decades after World War II?

SECTION **2** Assessment

Progress Monitoring *Online*
For: Self-quiz with vocabulary practice
Web Code: nba-3021

Terms, People, and Places

1. Place each of the key terms at the beginning of the section into one of the following categories: politics, culture, or the economy. Write a sentence for each term explaining your choice.

Note Taking

2. **Reading Skill: Categorize** Use your completed chart to answer the Focus Question: How did the United States, Western Europe, and Japan achieve economic prosperity and strengthen democracy during the Cold War years?

Comprehension and Critical Thinking

3. **Compare Points of View** How did Democrats and Republicans differ on the best ways to improve opportunity for Americans?

4. **Make Comparisons** How was the economic development of Western Europe during the Cold War years similar to or different from that of Japan?

5. **Make Generalizations** How was trade important to the economic development of Western Europe, the United States, and Japan during the postwar decades?

● **Writing About History**

Quick Write: Brainstorm Possible Solutions To write a problem-solution essay, you first need to brainstorm possible solutions to a problem you have defined. In this section, you learned that European welfare states offered social benefits but that these benefits were very costly. List possible solutions to this problem, and explain the advantages and disadvantages of each.

Chinese communist soldier marching into Beijing, 1949

The "little red book" of quotations from Mao Zedong

WITNESS HISTORY 🔊 AUDIO

Communist Victory in China

On September 21, 1949, at a rally in the Chinese capital, Beijing, the victorious communist leader Mao Zedong said:

❝ We have closed our ranks and defeated both domestic and foreign oppressors through the People's War of Liberation and the great people's revolution, and now we are proclaiming the founding of the People's Republic of China. ❞

Focus Question What did the communist victory mean for China and the rest of East Asia?

Communism Spreads in East Asia

Objectives
- Analyze China's Communist Revolution.
- Describe China's role as a "wild card" in the Cold War.
- Explain how war came to Korea and how the two Koreas followed different paths.

Terms, People, and Places

collectivization	Kim Il Sung
Great Leap Forward	Syngman Rhee
Cultural Revolution	Pusan Perimeter
38th parallel	demilitarized zone

Note Taking

Reading Skill: Summarize Complete this chart to summarize the effects of the Communist Revolution on China and the impact of the Cold War on China and Korea.

```
        Impact of Communism and
        the Cold War in East Asia
    ┌───────────┬───────────┬───────────┐
    │  Chinese  │ China in  │ Korea in  │
    │ Communist │  the      │  the      │
    │ Revolution│ Cold War  │ Cold War  │
    ├───────────┼───────────┼───────────┤
    │  •        │  •        │  •        │
    │  •        │  •        │  •        │
    │  •        │  •        │  •        │
    │           │  •        │           │
    └───────────┴───────────┴───────────┘
```

In the late 1940s, communism made advances in East Asia. With their victory in China in 1949, the Communists gained control of one fifth of the world's people.

China's Communist Revolution

By the end of World War II, the Chinese Communists had gained control of much of northern China. After Japan's defeat, Communist forces led by Mao Zedong (Mao Tse-tung) fought a civil war against Nationalists headed by Jiang Jieshi (jahng jeh shur). Battles raged until Mao's forces swept to victory and set up the People's Republic of China. The defeated Nationalists fled to the island of Taiwan, off the Chinese coast. After decades of struggle, China was finally under Communist control.

How the Communists Won Mao's Communists triumphed for several reasons. Mao had won the support of China's huge peasant population. Peasants had long suffered from brutal landlords and crushing taxes. The Communists redistributed land to poor peasants and ended oppression by landlords.

While support for the Communists grew, the Nationalists lost popularity. Nationalist policies had led to widespread economic hardship. Many Chinese people also resented corruption in Jiang's government and the government's reliance on support from Western "imperialist" powers. They hoped that the Communists would build a new China and end foreign domination.

Widespread support for the Communists in the countryside helped them to capture rail lines and surround Nationalist-held cities. One after another, these cities fell, and Mao's People's Liberation Army

 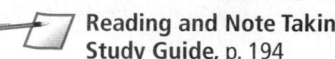

China's Communist Revolution L3

Instruct

- **Introduce** Have students read the introductory paragraph and the black headings under China's Communist Revolution. Have students predict what challenges China will face during its Communist Revolution. Then have students read to find out whether their predictions were accurate.

- **Teach** Review the key events of China's Communist Revolution. Discuss the revolution's goals and its methods. Then ask **How did China change as a result of its Communist Revolution?** (*It became a communist nation with a centralized government and economy. Its people endured great suffering because of the government's brutal policies and poor decisions.*)

- **Quick Activity** Have students read the biography of Mao Zedong on this page and review the visuals in this section. Discuss what qualities or characteristics enabled Mao to capture a nation's support and allowed him to carry out extreme policies.

Independent Practice

Remind students of Chinese efforts to identify and eliminate "counterrevolutionaries," particularly during the Cultural Revolution. Using the Think-Write-Pair-Share strategy (TE, p. T23), have students write a paragraph on whether this policy was in the nation's long-term interest.

Monitor Progress

Ask students to reread the black headings and summarize the content under each one.

BIOGRAPHY

Mao Zedong
During the mid-1950s, divisions arose within the Communist Party in China. In response, Mao Zedong (1893–1976) launched a campaign under the slogan "Let a hundred flowers bloom, let a hundred thoughts contend." Mao hoped that by offering people the opportunity to openly express their views he would gain more support. When people began to criticize the Communist Party, however, Mao ended the campaign. Of the nearly 550,000 Chinese who had spoken out, thousands were executed and hundreds of thousands were exiled to the countryside to "rectify their thinking through labor." **What methods did Mao use to keep power for himself?**

Vocabulary Builder
communes—(KAHM yoonz) *n.* commonly owned and operated farms or communities

---

emerged victorious. After their victory against the Nationalists, the Communists conquered Tibet in 1950. In 1959, Tibet's most revered religious leader, the Dalai Lama, was forced to flee the country.

Changing Chinese Society Mao Zedong built a Communist one-party totalitarian state in the People's Republic of China. Communist ideology guided the government's efforts to reshape the economy and society that China had inherited from the dynastic period. The Communist government discouraged the practice of Buddhism, Confucianism, and other traditional Chinese beliefs. Meanwhile, the government seized the property of rural landlords and urban business owners throughout China.

Opponents of the Communists were put down as "counterrevolutionaries." Many thousands of people who had belonged to the propertied middle class, or "bourgeoisie," were accused of counterrevolutionary beliefs. They were then beaten, sent to labor camps, or killed.

With Soviet help, the Chinese built dams and factories. To boost agriculture, Mao at first distributed land to peasants. Soon, however, he called for **collectivization,** or the forced pooling of peasant land and labor, in an attempt to increase productivity.

The Great Leap Forward Fails From 1958 to 1960, Mao led a program known as the **Great Leap Forward.** He urged people to make a superhuman effort to increase farm and industrial output. In an attempt to make agriculture more efficient, he created communes. A typical commune brought together several villages, thousands of acres of land, and up to 25,000 people. Rural communes set up small-scale "backyard" industries to produce steel and other products.

The Great Leap Forward, however, proved to be a dismal failure. Backyard industries turned out low-quality, useless goods. The commune system cut food output partly by removing incentives for individual farmers and families, leading to neglect of farmland and food shortages. Bad weather added to the problems and led to a terrible famine. Between 1959 and 1961, as many as 55 million Chinese are thought to have starved to death.

The Cultural Revolution Disrupts Life China slowly recovered from the Great Leap Forward by reducing the size of communes and taking a more practical approach to the economy. However, in 1966, Mao launched the Great Proletarian **Cultural Revolution.** Its goal was to purge China of "bourgeois" tendencies. He urged young Chinese to experience revolution firsthand, as his generation had.

Answer

BIOGRAPHY He executed anyone who threatened his power and sent critics to the countryside for forced labor.

Differentiated
Instruction   Solutions for All Learners

L2 Less Proficient Readers

Have students identify each change in China mentioned in the text and give examples of how those changes led to upheaval in that country. Then ask students to draw a flowchart of the events of the Chinese Communist Revolution.

Use the following resources to help students acquire basic skills.

Adapted Reading and Note Taking Study Guide
- Adapted Note Taking Study Guide, p. 194
- Adapted Section Summary, p. 195

In response, teenagers formed bands of Red Guards. Waving copies of the "little red book," *Quotations From Chairman Mao Tse-tung* [Zedong], Red Guards attacked those they considered bourgeois. The accused were publicly humiliated or beaten, and sometimes even killed. Skilled workers and managers were forced to leave their jobs and do manual labor on rural farms or in forced labor camps. Schools and factories closed. The economy slowed, and civil war threatened. Finally, Mao had the army restore order.

✓ **Checkpoint** What were the main successes and failures of the Chinese Communist Revolution?

China, the Cold War's "Wild Card"

In 1949, the triumph of the Communists in China had seemed like a gain for the Soviet Union and a loss for the United States and its democratic allies. The number of people under communist rule had more than tripled. China's role in the Cold War, however, proved to be more complex than a simple expansion of communist power.

Split With the Soviet Union The People's Republic of China and the Soviet Union were uneasy allies in the 1950s. Stalin sent economic aid and technical experts to help China modernize, but distrust between the two countries created tensions. Some of these tensions dated back to territorial disputes between tsarist Russia and dynastic China. By 1960, border clashes and disputes over ideology led the Soviets to withdraw all aid and advisors from China. Western fears of a strong alliance between the Soviet Union and China had proved unfounded.

Promoting the Cultural Revolution
The Cultural Revolution poster above shows soldiers holding "little red books" and urges them to "destroy all enemies." The photo to the left shows Chinese soldiers waving their "little red books" during this same period. *What do these images suggest about freedom of speech and freedom of thought during the Cultural Revolution in China?*

Independent Practice

Tell students to suppose they are a team of specialists assigned to prepare a briefing for the U.S. President, so he can stay abreast of events. Have them prepare a brief but thorough report on relations with China and Taiwan during the Cold War, including the pros and cons of the current situation. Ensure students understand the inherent compromises in the U.S. position.

Monitor Progress

As students fill in their charts, circulate to make sure they understand how China's Communist Revolution affected the nation. For a completed version of the chart, see

📖 **Note Taking Transparencies,** 191

Washington Plays the China Card Relations between China and the United States were even more complex. After Jiang Jieshi (Chiang Kai-shek) fled to Taiwan, the United States supported his Nationalist government as the rightful representative of China. Washington refused diplomatic recognition of the mainland People's Republic of China, which American leaders saw as a communist threat to all of Asia.

As the Cold War dragged on, however, the United States took a second look at the People's Republic. From the American point of view, there were strategic advantages to improving relations with Communist China after its split with the Soviet Union. By "playing the China card," as this strategy was sometimes called, the United States might isolate the Soviets between NATO in the west and a hostile China in the east.

The United States allowed the People's Republic to replace Taiwan in the United Nations in 1971. A year later, U.S. President Richard Nixon visited Mao in Beijing. Finally, in 1979, the United States set up formal diplomatic relations with China.

Taiwan and the Nationalists Jiang Jieshi's government continued to rule Taiwan under martial law as a one-party dictatorship. Not until the late 1980s did Taiwan's government end martial law and allow opposition

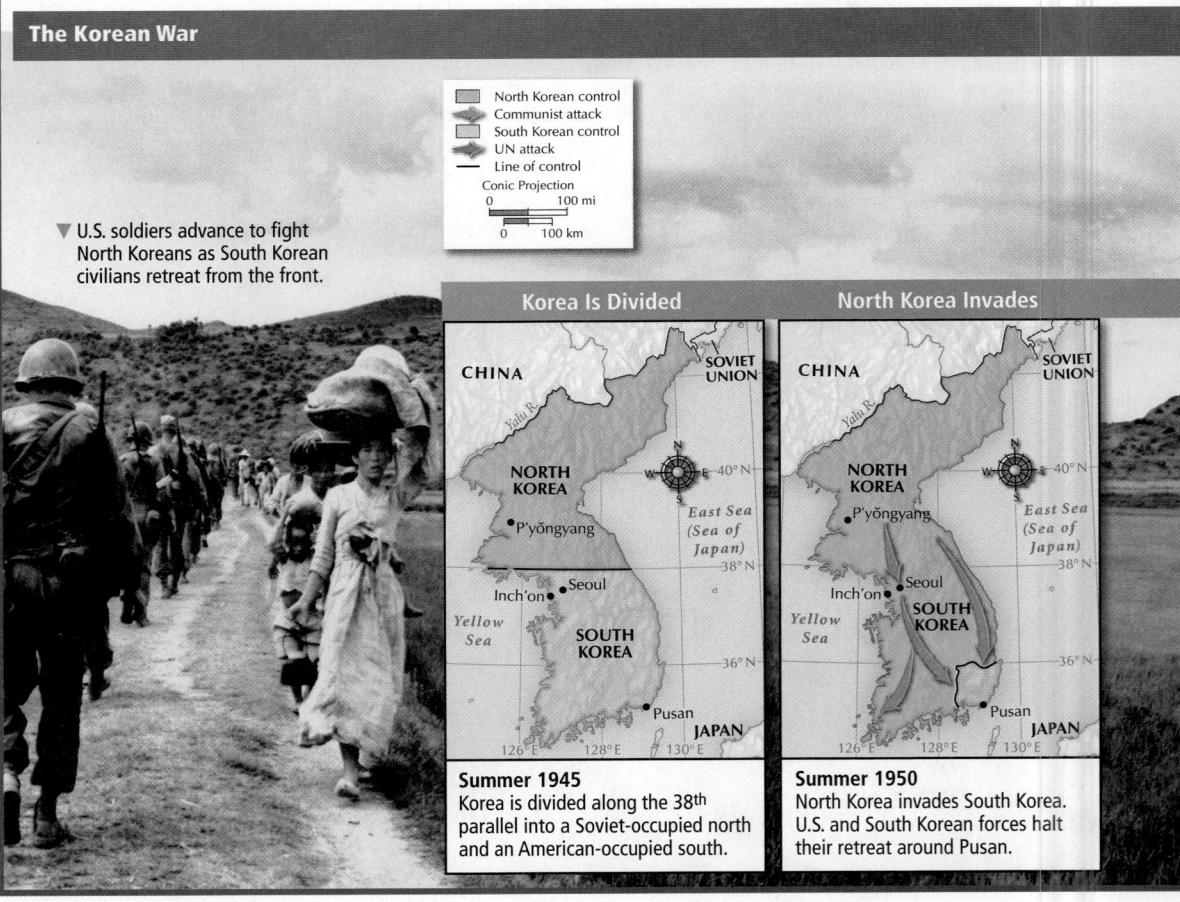

The Korean War

- North Korean control
- Communist attack
- South Korean control
- UN attack
- Line of control
- Conic Projection
  - 0 — 100 mi
  - 0 — 100 km

▼ U.S. soldiers advance to fight North Koreans as South Korean civilians retreat from the front.

Korea Is Divided

CHINA · SOVIET UNION · NORTH KOREA · P'yŏngyang · East Sea (Sea of Japan) · 40°N · 38°N · Inch'on · Seoul · Yellow Sea · SOUTH KOREA · 36°N · Pusan · JAPAN · 126°E · 128°E · 130°E

Summer 1945
Korea is divided along the 38th parallel into a Soviet-occupied north and an American-occupied south.

North Korea Invades

CHINA · SOVIET UNION · NORTH KOREA · P'yŏngyang · East Sea (Sea of Japan) · 40°N · 38°N · Inch'on · Seoul · Yellow Sea · SOUTH KOREA · 36°N · Pusan · JAPAN · 126°E · 128°E · 130°E

Summer 1950
North Korea invades South Korea. U.S. and South Korean forces halt their retreat around Pusan.

Connect to Our World

Connections to Today Since 1949, the People's Republic of China has considered Taiwan a "rebel province" that must be reunited with the parent country. In 1995, the Chinese drove home that point by conducting two months of missile tests and live-fire exercises in the island's waters.

In 1999, Taiwanese President Lee Teng-hui created a new uproar when he insisted that China deal with Taiwan as a separate state. The Chinese responded angrily, renewing their threats of force against Taiwan. In Beijing, the *People's Daily* compared Taiwan's efforts to influence China to "an ant trying to topple a tree."

parties. Mainland China saw Taiwan as a breakaway province and threatened military action when Taiwanese politicians proposed declaring the island's formal independence. In the long term, the mainland government insisted that Taiwan be rejoined with China. Taiwan's government resisted such pressure.

✔ **Checkpoint** How did China's relationships with the Soviet Union and the United States change during the Cold War?

War Comes to Korea

The nation of Korea occupies a peninsula on China's northeastern border. Like East and West Germany, Korea was split in two by rival forces after World War II. And like other divided lands, the two Koreas found themselves on opposite sides in the Cold War.

A Divided Nation Korea was an independent kingdom until Japan conquered it in the early twentieth century. After Japan's defeat in World War II, Soviet and American forces agreed to divide Korea temporarily along the 38th **parallel** of latitude. However, North Korea, ruled by the

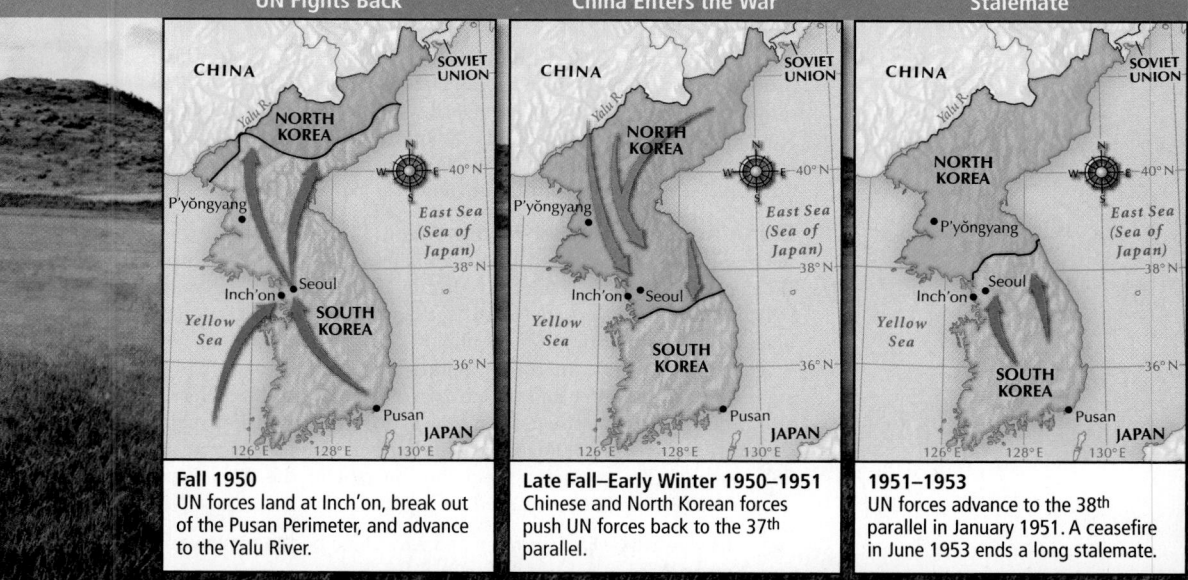

Map Skills In June 1950, North Korea invaded South Korea. U.S. troops made up the bulk of the UN force that aided South Korea. When UN troops neared the Chinese border, communist China sent troops to aid North Korea.

1. **Locate** (a) the 38th parallel (b) Pusan (c) Inch'on (d) Yalu River
2. **Movement** Which nation gained new territory by the end of the war?
3. **Draw Conclusions** How might UN forces have avoided war with China?

Geography *Interactive*
For: Audio guided tour
Web Code: nbp-3031

UN Fights Back

Fall 1950
UN forces land at Inch'on, break out of the Pusan Perimeter, and advance to the Yalu River.

China Enters the War

Late Fall–Early Winter 1950–1951
Chinese and North Korean forces push UN forces back to the 37th parallel.

Stalemate

1951–1953
UN forces advance to the 38th parallel in January 1951. A ceasefire in June 1953 ends a long stalemate.

Link to Geography

Frostbite in Korea U.S. troops in Korea were not only fighting Communism; they also fought frostbite. The troops first landed in Korea during the summer, when the temperature was high, the air humid. The military was not prepared for the Korean winters, when Siberian air masses flowed south over the country; the temperature typically dipped below zero. Sol- diers camped outside during the harsh conditions. During one battle at the Chosin Reservoir, the temperature reached 40 degrees below zero, yet the troops still wore summer uniforms. In the first year of battle alone, an estimated 5,300 troops suffered some form of frostbite. By war's end, the number would be in the tens of thousands.

War Comes to Korea ⑬

Instruct

- **Introduce** Explain that in the postwar years, Koreans fought a civil war over political and ideological control of their nation. Ask students what, given the Cold War climate of the period, they think the central issues might be in that war.

- **Teach** Write the headings *North Korea* and *South Korea* on the board. Ask students to supply details describing the two nations. Write their answers on the board. Then ask **What role did the United Nations and China each play in the conflict between the two Koreas?** (*The United Nations sent mostly American military aid to support South Korea, and China sent military aid to support North Korea.*)

- **Quick Activity** Ask a volunteer to define the word *stalemate* and explain how this word applies to the Korean War. Then ask student groups to discuss and explain why each side in the Korean War fought so hard and how living in this divided land might have affected the Korean people.

Independent Practice

Have students access **Web Code nbp-3031** to take the **Geography Interactive Audio Guided Tour** and then answer the map questions in the text.

Monitor Progress

Check answers to map skills questions.

Answers

✔ China's relationship with the Soviet Union deteriorated during the Cold War because of rivalries over ideology and borders. China's relationship with the United States improved as the Cold War progressed, because the United States saw China as a useful partner in its conflict with the Soviet Union.

Map Skills

1. Review locations with students.
2. Both the North and South gained and lost territory during the war, but ultimately the border was restored to a position close to the 38th parallel.
3. by avoiding the Chinese border

Two Koreas

L3

Instruct

- **Introduce** Tell students that the text compares a divided Korea to a divided Germany. Ask them to predict how these nations would be similar, politically and ideologically. What roles were these areas likely to play in the Cold War conflict?

- **Teach** Draw a Venn diagram on the board, labeled *Korea, Germany,* and *Both.* Have students supply facts to compare and contrast the two divided nations. Ask **In what ways were divided Korea and divided Germany similar?** *(Both were divided into communist command economies and capitalist market economies. In both cases, capitalists thrived and communists struggled.)* **How did they differ?** *(South Korea was not democratic, while West Germany was. North Korea had one dictator, while East Germany had many leaders. Korea remained divided after the Cold War while Germany was unified.)*

- **Quick Activity** Invite students to suggest reasons why command economies seem to stagnate, while market economies seem to thrive.

Independent Practice

Have students use the Venn diagram on the board to write a paragraph comparing and contrasting the economies and the postwar developments of North Korea and South Korea.

Monitor Progress

As students work on their paragraphs, circulate to ensure they understand the differences between a market economy and a command economy.

Winter Battle Scene in Korea
U.S. soldiers rest after winning a battle for a snowy hill in Korea, February 1951. *Based on the photograph, what advantage did these soldiers gain by winning control of this hill?*

dictator **Kim Il Sung,** became a communist ally of the Soviet Union. In South Korea, the United States backed the dictatorial—but noncommunist—leader, **Syngman Rhee.**

North Korean Attack Brings a United Nations Response Both leaders wanted to rule the entire country. In early 1950, Kim Il Sung called for a "heroic struggle" to reunite Korea. North Korean troops attacked in June of that year and soon overran most of the south. The United Nations Security Council condemned the invasion. The United States then organized a United Nations force to help South Korea.

United Nations forces were made up mostly of Americans and South Koreans. Although U.S. troops arrived in early July, North Korean troops continued to advance until United Nations forces stopped them in August along a line known as the **Pusan Perimeter.** This perimeter was centered on the port city of Pusan, in the southeastern corner of the Korean peninsula.

In September 1950, United Nations troops landed on the beaches around the port of Inch'on, behind enemy lines. These U.S.-led troops quickly captured Korea's north-south rail lines and cut off North Korean troops from their supply of food and ammunition. North Korean forces in the south soon surrendered. By November, United Nations forces had advanced north to the Yalu River, along the border of China.

China Reverses United Nations Gains The success of the U.S.-led forces alarmed China. In late November, Mao Zedong sent hundreds of thousands of Chinese troops to help the North Koreans. In tough winter fighting, the Chinese and North Koreans forced United Nations troops back to the south of the 38th parallel.

The Korean War turned into a stalemate. Finally, in 1953, both sides signed an armistice, or end to fighting. Nearly two million North Korean and South Korean troops remained dug in on either side of the **demilitarized zone** (DMZ), an area with no military forces, near the 38th parallel. The armistice held for the rest of the Cold War, but no peace treaty was ever negotiated.

✓ **Checkpoint** Explain when and why China became involved in the Korean War.

L2 Less Proficient Readers

In small groups, have students create a Venn diagram to record the comparisons made in the section between the Two Koreas and the Two Germanys during the Cold War. This will help them organize the information and make connections across regions. Then discuss with students what might account for the differences between these divided nations *(Sample: geography, culture, history, economics).*

L4 Gifted and Talented

Have students research the current state of affairs of North and South Korea. Ask them to answer the following questions: How does each country's current situation compare to that of the 1950s? What is the United States' current relationship with each country? How have events from the Cold War influenced these relations?

Answers

Caption relative safety and a better vantage point

✓ China got involved in the Korean War when it felt threatened by UN forces on its borders. China wanted to help the Communist North Koreans.

Two Koreas

Like the two Germanys, North and South Korea developed separately after the armistice—North Korea as a communist command economy, South Korea as a capitalist market economy. As in Germany, the capitalist portion of the country had an economic boom and rising standards of living, while the communist zone went through economic stagnation and decline. Also as in Germany, the United States gave economic and military aid to capitalist South Korea, while the Soviets helped the communist north.

Unlike democratic West Germany, however, South Korea was governed by a series of dictators and military rulers during much of the Cold War. Unlike East Germany, where a series of officials led the communist government, a single dictator controlled North Korea throughout the Cold War. Whereas Germany was reunited at the end of the Cold War, Korea remained divided.

South Korea Recovers After the war, South Korea slowly rebuilt its economy. By the mid-1960s, South Korea's economy had leapt ahead. After decades of dictatorship and military rule, a prosperous middle class and fierce student protests pushed the government to hold direct elections in 1987. These elections began a successful transition to democracy. Despite the bloody Korean War, most South Koreans during the Cold War years wanted to see their ancient nation reunited, as did many North Koreans. All Koreans shared the same history, language, and traditions. For many, this meant more than Cold War differences.

North Korea Digs In Under Kim Il Sung, the command economy increased output for a time in North Korea. However, in the late 1960s, economic growth slowed. Kim's emphasis on self-reliance kept North Korea isolated and poor. The government built a personality cult around Kim, who was constantly glorified as the "Great Leader" in propaganda. Even after its Soviet and Chinese allies undertook economic reforms in the 1980s, North Korea clung to hard-line communism.

✔ **Checkpoint** How did North Korea's economic performance compare to South Korea's?

SECTION 3 Assessment

Progress Monitoring Online
For: Self-quiz with vocabulary practice
Web Code: nba-3031

Terms, People, and Places

1. For each term, person, or place listed at the beginning of the section, write a sentence explaining its significance.

Note Taking

2. **Reading Skill: Summarize** Use your completed chart to answer the Focus Question: What did the communist victory mean for China and the rest of East Asia?

Comprehension and Critical Thinking

3. **Recognize Ideologies** What ideologies did Mao's programs to transform China reflect?
4. **Draw Inferences** How did the United States use the changing relationship between China and the Soviet Union to its own advantage?
5. **Predict Consequences** How might the history of Korea have been different if United Nations forces had not stepped in to oppose the North Korean invasion in 1950?

● Writing About History

Quick Write: Write a Thesis Statement To write a problem-solution essay, you need to choose the best solution to a problem. In this section, you learned that both North and South Koreans wanted to reunify their country, but that Cold War differences got in the way. List possible solutions to Korea's Cold War division and write a thesis statement arguing for the best solution.

Answer

✔ North Korea's economic performance was dismal compared with the prosperity experienced in South Korea.

Section 3 Assessment

1. Sentences should reflect an understanding of each term, person, or place listed at the beginning of the section.
2. Communist victory meant communist rule in China and in North Korea, as well as the introduction of a wild card in the conflict between the United States and the Soviet Union.
3. They reflected an opposition to "bourgeois" property owners and a belief in totalitarian state control.
4. The United States improved ties with China in order to isolate the Soviet Union.
5. Without the United Nations' involvement, communist aggression might have succeeded in Korea entirely and the nation would not now be divided.

● Writing About History

Answers should include a thesis statement arguing for a solution. One possible solution includes a coalition government that represents both democratic and communist views.

For additional assessment, have students access **Progress Monitoring Online** at Web Code nba-3031.

Objectives

As you teach this section, keep students focused on the following objectives to help them answer the Section Focus Question and master core content.

■ Describe events in Indochina after World War II.

■ Learn how America entered the Vietnam War.

■ Understand how the Vietnam War ended.

■ Analyze Southeast Asia after the war.

Prepare to Read

Build Background Knowledge ⒃

Inform students that from 1954 to 1975 Vietnam was divided into two separate states. Ask students to recall other nations that were divided during this same period *(Germany, Korea)* and the reasons for those divisions.

Set a Purpose

■ **WITNESS HISTORY** Read the selection aloud or play the audio.
  ■)) AUDIO **Witness History Audio CD,** America's Role in Vietnam

  Ask **What is the main idea of President Kennedy's comment?** *(He believed that civil wars could only be won by the people within a nation, not with outside forces.)*

■ **Focus** Point out the Section Focus Question and write it on the board. Tell students to refer to this question as they read. *(Answer appears with Section 4 Assessment answers.)*

■ **Preview** Have students preview the Section Objectives and the list of Terms, People, and Places.

■ **Note Taking** Have students read this section using the Guided Questioning strategy (TE, p. T20). As they read, have students fill in the chart summarizing events connected to the wars in Southeast Asia.
  ◢ **Reading and Note Taking Study Guide,** p. 196

U.S. military helicopter in Vietnam

America's Role in Vietnam

In a television interview on September 2, 1963, U.S. President John F. Kennedy referred to U.S. support for the noncommunist government of South Vietnam. He did not foresee that five years later, more than 500,000 Americans would be fighting a bloody and divisive war there.

❝ I don't think that unless a greater effort is made by the Government to win popular support that the war can be won out there. . . . We can help them, we can give them equipment, we can send our men out there as advisors, but they have to win it, the people of Viet-nam, against the Communists. ❞

Focus Question What were the causes and effects of war in Southeast Asia, and what was the American role in this region?

A family watches President Kennedy speak on television.

War in Southeast Asia

Objectives
• Describe events in Indochina after World War II.
• Learn how America entered the Vietnam War.
• Understand how the Vietnam War ended.
• Analyze Southeast Asia after the war.

Terms, People, and Places

guerrillas	Viet Cong
Ho Chi Minh	Tet Offensive
Dienbienphu	Khmer Rouge
domino theory	Pol Pot

Note Taking

Reading Skill: Summarize Complete a chart like the one below to summarize the events connected to the wars in Southeast Asia.

War in Southeast Asia		
Indochina After World War II	Vietnam War	Aftereffects of War
•	•	•

Southeast Asia's wars were, for many local participants, nationalist struggles against foreign domination. Like Korea, however, Southeast Asia eventually played a part in the global Cold War.

Indochina After World War II

In mainland Southeast Asia after World War II, an agonizing liberation struggle tore apart the region once known as French Indochina. The nearly 30-year conflict had two major phases. First was the war against the French, dating from 1946 to 1954. Second was the Cold War conflict that involved the United States and raged from 1955 to 1975.

Indochina Under Foreign Rule The eastern part of mainland Southeast Asia, or Indochina, was conquered by the French during the 1800s. The Japanese overran Indochina during World War II, but faced fierce resistance, especially in Vietnam, from local **guerrillas** (guh RIL uz), or small groups of loosely organized soldiers making surprise raids. The guerrillas, determined to be free of all foreign rule, turned their guns on the European colonialists who returned after the war. The guerrillas were strongly influenced by communist opposition to European colonial powers.

Ho Chi Minh Fights the French After the Japanese were defeated, the French set out in 1946 to re-establish their authority in Indochina. In Vietnam, they faced guerrilla forces led by

---

Vocabulary Builder

Use the information below and the following resources to teach the high-use word from this section.
All in One Teaching Resources, Unit 5, p. 7; **Teaching Resources, Skills Handbook,** p. 3

High-Use Word	Definition and Sample Sentence
terminate, p. 634	*vt.* to finish, bring to an end
	His job was **terminated** when his manager realized that he'd been stealing.

Ho Chi Minh (hoh chee min). Ho was a nationalist and communist who had fought the Japanese. He then fought the French in what is known as the First Indochina War. An unexpected Vietnamese victory at the bloody battle of Dienbienphu (dyen byen foo) in 1954 convinced the French to leave Vietnam. Cambodia and Laos had meanwhile gained their independence separately.

Vietnam Is Divided After 1954, however, the struggle for Vietnam became part of the Cold War. At an international conference that year, Western and communist powers agreed to a temporary division of Vietnam. Ho's communists controlled North Vietnam. A noncommunist government led by Ngo Dinh Diem (ngoh din dee EM), supported by the United States, ruled South Vietnam. The agreement called for elections to reunite the two Vietnams. These elections were never held, largely because the Americans and Ngo Dinh Diem feared that the Communists would win.

Some South Vietnamese preferred Ho Chi Minh, a national hero, to the South Vietnamese government backed by the United States, a foreign power. But Ho's communist rule in the North alienated some Vietnamese. Many Catholic and pro-French Vietnamese fled to the south.

The United States supported Ngo Dinh Diem's regime against what American leaders saw as the communist threat from North Vietnam. Meanwhile, Ngo Dinh Diem's dictatorial regime alienated many Vietnamese with its corruption and brutal tactics against political opponents.

By the early 1960s, communist guerrilla fighters had appeared in the jungles of South Vietnam. Many of them were South Vietnamese, but they received strong support from the north. Many saw their fight as a nationalist struggle to liberate Vietnam from foreign domination.

✓ **Checkpoint** Why did Vietnamese guerrillas fight the French in Indochina?

America Enters the Vietnam War

American foreign policy planners saw the situation in Vietnam as part of the global Cold War. They developed the **domino theory**—the view that a communist victory in South Vietnam would cause noncommunist governments across Southeast Asia to fall to communism, like a row of dominoes. America's leaders wanted to prevent this from happening.

The War Intensifies Ho Chi Minh remained determined to unite Vietnam under communist rule. He continued to aid the National Liberation Front, or **Viet Cong**, the communist rebels trying to overthrow South Vietnam's government. At first, the United States sent only supplies and military advisors to South Vietnam. Later, it sent thousands of troops, turning a local struggle into a major Cold War conflict.

BIOGRAPHY

Ho Chi Minh

Ho Chi Minh (1890–1969) was born in central Vietnam at a time when Vietnam was under French colonial control. Ho discovered communism while working abroad and quickly adapted it to his struggle against French rule back in Vietnam. While Soviet communism gave a leading role to urban workers, Ho saw rural peasants as the driving force behind a successful revolution. Ho was more interested in national liberation than following a Soviet communist model. As president of North Vietnam, he led his people first against French control and later against the U.S-backed South Vietnamese government. **How did Ho Chi Minh's approach to communism differ from the Soviet model?**

Teach

Indochina After World War II **L3**

Instruct

■ **Introduce** Write the term *nationalist* on the board and review its meaning, as discussed in Section 3. Explain that nationalism fueled the desire of Southeast Asia's people to fight foreign powers for control. In the context of the Cold War, what problems do students think might result from this desire?

■ **Teach** Write the date *1954* on the board. Trace events of conflict in Southeast Asia before and after this date. Ask **Why was Ho Chi Minh fighting the French in Vietnam?** *(He wanted them to leave and allow Vietnam independence. He wanted to make Vietnam a communist country.)* **Why and how was Vietnam divided after 1954?** *(Vietnam was divided by world nations after the French left in 1954. Communists in the North struggled for control with anti-communists in the South. The Soviet Union and United States each supported the groups that shared their own ideologies.)*

■ **Quick Activity** Have students read the biography of Ho Chi Minh in the text. Then in groups, have them discuss the following question: *Why do you think that revolutions are so often led by passionate nationalists?*

Independent Practice

To help students better understand the unfolding conflict in Vietnam, have them create a timeline of events covered in this section. For additional guidance, refer them to the information on the board.

Monitor Progress

As students fill in their charts, circulate to make sure they understand the events connected to the wars in Southeast Asia. For a completed version of the chart, see

📖 **Note Taking Transparencies,** 192

Answers

BIOGRAPHY He shifted the focus from urban workers to rural peasants and focused on national liberation.

✓ Vietnamese guerillas fought the French in an effort to win independence.

America Enters the Vietnam War L3

Instruct

■ **Introduce: Key Terms** Have students locate the key term ***domino theory*** (in blue) in the text. If possible, demonstrate its meaning for students with actual dominoes. Point out that due to this theory, the United States invested enormous resources in Vietnam.

■ **Teach** Discuss the turning points and the key issues in the early part of the Vietnam War. Ask **What happened at the Gulf of Tonkin in 1964?** *(The North Vietnamese attacked a U.S. Navy destroyer that they thought had assisted South Vietnamese raids nearby. The North Vietnamese may have attacked again three days later, but this is uncertain. President Johnson told Congress that the destroyer had been attacked twice, without mentioning the South Vietnamese raids.)* **What advantage did the Vietcong have over American troops?** *(They knew the countryside and often had the support of the local population.)*

■ **Quick Activity** Discuss the Infographic with students. Have them review the images and read the captions. Play the accompanying audio. Ask students to describe what it might be like to fight a war in the jungle. Then ask students to use the map to explain the domino theory. *(The domino theory asserted that if South Vietnam fell to communism, Cambodia, Thailand, and Laos would, one by one, follow suit.)*

🔊 AUDIO **Witness History Audio CD,** The Vietnam War

Independent Practice

Direct students to the text on the next page that describes the American military draft during the Vietnam War. Review the opposing viewpoints about it. Have students write a short persuasive paragraph arguing for or against a draft in the United States.

Monitor Progress

As students write their paragraphs, check that their answers include a clearly stated opinion and evidence to support that opinion.

INFOGRAPHIC

THE VIETNAM WAR

The Vietnam War thrust American soldiers into an alien and dangerous environment of jungles and swamps. The Viet Cong guerrillas were often local villagers, so it was hard for American soldiers to tell friend from foe. Local guerrillas' knowledge of the land allowed them to hide behind vegetation or behind the earthen banks of canals before a surprise ambush. The map at the right shows how North Vietnam delivered supplies to the Viet Cong in South Vietnam along the Ho Chi Minh Trail. These supply lines and the Viet Cong's knowledge of the land made the Viet Cong a deadly foe, even against the better-equipped American forces.

🔊 AUDIO

Viet Cong guerrillas train in a ditch for combat against American soldiers.

An American soldier sits on the bank of a canal during a skirmish with Viet Cong snipers. Vietnamese children are clinging to their mothers nearby, trying to stay low to avoid gunfire.

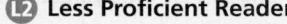
▲ This 1966 calendar may have belonged to one of the 58,000 American soldiers killed in the Vietnam War. It was left at the Vietnam Veterans Memorial in Washington, D.C., by a visitor.

On August 1, 1964, South Vietnamese commandos conducted raids on North Vietnamese islands in the Gulf of Tonkin. The following day, the North Vietnamese attacked a nearby U.S. Navy destroyer, the *Maddox,* which they mistakenly believed had assisted the South Vietnamese raids. Three days later, sailors on the *Maddox* thought that they had been attacked a second time, although it seems likely that their sonar and radar equipment were malfunctioning due to heavy seas.

U.S. President Johnson reported the attacks to Congress without mentioning the South Vietnamese raids or the doubts about the second attack. Believing that the attacks had been unprovoked, Congress passed the Gulf of Tonkin Resolution on August 7, 1964. The resolution authorized the President to take all necessary measures to prevent further aggression in Southeast Asia.

After the resolution passed, the United States began bombing targets in North Vietnam. Eventually, more than 500,000 American troops were committed to the war. At the same time, both the Soviet Union and China sent aid—but no troops—to help North Vietnam.

Differentiated
Instruction   Solutions for All Learners

L1 Special Needs   **L2 Less Proficient Readers**

Have visual learners use the images on these pages to learn more about the conditions in the Vietnam War. Ask volunteers to describe what is occurring in each visual and to read aloud the caption. Then ask students to list the advantages the Viet Cong had *(Sample: They knew the terrain and were friendly with the local villagers.)*

The Vietnam War, 1968–1975

CHINA

NORTH VIETNAM
• Dien Bien Phu
Haiphong
• Hanoi

LAOS

Gulf of Tonkin

Hainan

• Vientiane

Mekong R.

Hué •
• Danang

➤ Tet Offensive, 1968
- North Vietnam's final offensive, 1975
--- Ho Chi Minh Trail
■ American bases

THAILAND

CAMBODIA

Gulf of Thailand

Phnom Penh •

SOUTH VIETNAM
Saigon •

Mekong Delta

South China Sea

Miller Projection
0   100   200 mi
0   100   200 km

▲ This American soldier is patrolling a swamp in the Mekong Delta in the summer of 1969.

During the Vietnam era, young American men were required to register for the military draft. Men were then selected for the draft in a random lottery. Many saw fighting for their country as their patriotic duty. However, to avoid being drafted, some military-age American men left the country and sought refuge in other nations not involved in the war.

Guerrilla War Like the French in Vietnam, America faced a guerrilla war. The rebels in South Vietnam tended to be local peasants. They thus knew the countryside much better than their American enemies. They also knew the local people. Villagers frequently offered them safe haven against foreign troops. The close connections between guerrilla fighters and the villagers turned the Vietnamese villages themselves into military targets. Supplies for the guerrillas came from the north, following trails that wound through the jungles of neighboring Cambodia and Laos. In response, American aircraft and ground troops crossed the borders of these nations, drawing them into the war.

The Tet Offensive Despite massive American support, South Vietnam failed to defeat the communist guerrillas and their North Vietnamese allies. In 1968, guerrilla forces came out of the jungles and attacked American and South Vietnamese forces in cities all across the south. The assault was unexpected because it took place during Tet, the Vietnamese New Year. The communists lost many of their best troops and did not

History Background

A Turning Point Despite huge casualties, the Tet Offensive turned the tide for North Vietnam. Communist forces attacked some 100 cities and military bases, including the embassy in Saigon. The battle convinced the American public that the war could not continue at current levels. Soon after, President Johnson announced he would not run for re-election.

When General William Westmoreland requested 206,000 additional troops, Johnson refused and declared that bombing north of the 20th parallel would cease. This opened the way for negotiations with Hanoi. By October, peace talks were under way, although a cease fire would be still be five years away.

The Vietnam War Ends

Instruct

■ **Introduce** Write the following quotation on the board: *"I want to get out, but I don't want to give up."* Tell students that as the nation's involvement in Vietnam expanded, Americans became fiercely divided about the war. Have students recall what they have learned about America's many wars. Ask **Why would Americans find it hard to give up in a war?** *(They had seldom lost one.)*

■ **Teach** Review the problems the U.S. military had in Vietnam and trace the growing division of views at home. Ask **Why did many Americans come to oppose United States involvement in the Vietnam War?** *(Many Americans had been killed, taken prisoner, or were missing, yet the United States military seemed to be making little progress.)* **Why and how did United States involvement end?** *(It ended because of increasing opposition at home and limited success on the battlefield. The United States agreed to withdraw and left the Vietnamese to resolve their differences.)*

Independent Practice

Ask students to write a paragraph summarizing the events at the end of the Vietnam War.

Monitor Progress

To help students review the section so far, ask them to explain why the Vietnam War was so painful for many Americans.

Answers

Thinking Critically

1. to halt further advances of troops and supplies from North Vietnam along the Ho Chi Minh Trail and to be able to attack Vietnam from the west
2. It was difficult to distinguish Viet Cong guerrillas from local villagers; swamps and dense vegetation made it easy for guerrillas, who were more familiar with the land, to hide and lie in ambush.

Southeast Asia After the War

Instruct

- **Introduce** Remind students that after American withdrawal, Vietnam fell under communist rule. Over time, this communist rule extended to neighboring Cambodia. Ask students what they think it would be like to live under communist rule.

- **Teach** Review the brutal reign of Pol Pot with students. Ask **Why do you think Pol Pot was willing to kill his own people?** *(He was a dictator. He believed in removing all opposition to his views. He believed in removing Western influences.)* **How did communist rule affect Cambodia? How did it affect Vietnam?** *(In Cambodia, it led to brutal terror by Pol Pot and to the murder of more than a million Cambodians. In Vietnam, it led to a flood of refugees and persistent poverty.)*

- **Quick Activity** Have students return to the domino theory. In groups, ask them to explain its outcome in Southeast Asia.

Independent Practice

Assign small groups the following countries: China, Korea, Vietnam, and Cambodia. Then ask each group to create a list of how their country became involved in the Cold War. Rearrange the small groups so there is an "expert" on each country in each group. Have students take turns teaching about their area of expertise. Then as a class, make a master list.

Monitor Progress

Check Reading and Note Taking Study Guide entries for student understanding.

Peace Necklace
The peace sign on this necklace was a popular symbol of protest against the Vietnam War.

hold any cities against American counterattacks. Nevertheless, the bloody **Tet Offensive** marked a turning point in public opinion in the United States.

✔ **Checkpoint** How did the domino theory lead the United States to send troops to Vietnam?

The Vietnam War Ends

As the fighting continued, civilian deaths caused by the bombing of North Vietnam and growing American casualties inflamed antiwar opinion in the United States. Growing numbers of American troops were prisoners of war (POWs) or missing in action (MIAs). Some Americans began to think that the Vietnam War was a quagmire, or swamp, in which the United States was becoming more and more bogged down.

More Americans Oppose the War As the war continued, the nation became deeply and bitterly divided over the ongoing struggle. Many Americans of all ages continued to support the war effort in Vietnam. Others wanted to end the loss of lives. More and more young people turned out for massive street demonstrations, all part of a growing antiwar movement. It was clear that an increasing number of Americans wanted no more "body bags" coming back or television footage of burned Vietnamese villages. At the same time, many agreed with a housewife who said, "I want to get out, but I don't want to give up."

America Withdraws In the end, American leaders decided that they had to get out of Vietnam. Faced with conflict at home and abroad, President Lyndon Johnson, who had presided over the massive expansion of the war in the 1960s, decided not to run for a second term. Johnson also opened peace talks with North Vietnam in Paris.

Although American troops had seldom lost a battle in the long struggle, they had not destroyed the Vietnamese Communists' determination to keep fighting. Johnson's successor, President Nixon, came under increasing pressure to <u>terminate</u> American involvement. Nixon finally negotiated the Paris Peace Accord in January 1973. This agreement established a cease-fire, or a halt in fighting. The United States agreed to withdraw its troops, and North Vietnam agreed not to send any more troops into the South. The accord left South Vietnam to determine its own future and set a goal of peaceful reunification with the North.

North Vietnam Wins the War Two years after American troops had withdrawn from the country, the North Vietnamese conquered South Vietnam. The South Vietnamese capital, Saigon, was renamed Ho Chi Minh City in 1976 in honor of the late leader. The North Vietnamese capital, Hanoi, became the capital of the reunited nation.

✔ **Checkpoint** Why did the United States withdraw its troops from Vietnam?

Southeast Asia After the War

After the American withdrawal from Vietnam, some dominos did fall. Both Cambodia and Laos ended up with governments dominated by Communist Vietnam. However, the falling dominos stopped at the

Link to Government

Limits on the Office of the President In the 1970s, the legacy of Vietnam was fresh in the minds of many U.S. citizens. Most of the blame for the war fell on the presidents who perpetuated it. Then the Watergate scandal occurred. Many Americans, including legislators, decided that the presidency had to change. Starting in 1973, Congress approved legislation that would weaken and check the president's power. The War Powers Act of 1973 limited a president's ability to use military forces overseas. The Arms Export Control Act took away a president's previous ability to supply arms to other countries. Congress also took a greater role in overseeing such agencies as the FBI and CIA.

former borders of French Indochina. Other parts of Southeast Asia remained thoroughly capitalist, if less than democratic.

Tragedy in Cambodia During the Vietnam War, fighting had spilled over into neighboring Cambodia. In 1970, the United States bombed North Vietnamese supply routes in Cambodia and then briefly invaded the country. Afterwards, the **Khmer Rouge** (kuh MEHR roozh), a force of Cambodian communist guerrillas, gained ground in Cambodia. Finally, in 1975, the Khmer Rouge overthrew the Cambodian government.

Led by the brutal dictator **Pol Pot,** the Khmer Rouge unleashed a reign of terror. To destroy all Western influences, they drove people from the cities and forced them to work in the fields. They slaughtered, starved, or worked to death more than a million Cambodians, about a third of the population.

In the end, it took a Vietnamese invasion to drive Pol Pot and his Khmer Rouge back into the jungle. Vietnam imposed an authoritarian government on Cambodia, but they at least ended the genocide.

Vietnam Under the Communists In the newly reunited Vietnam, the communist victors imposed a harsh rule of their own on the south. Hundreds of thousands of Vietnamese fled their country, most in small boats. Many of these "boat people" drowned. Survivors landed in refugee camps in neighboring countries. Eventually, some settled in the United States. Meanwhile, Vietnam had to rebuild a land destroyed by war. Recovery was slow due to a lack of resources and an American-led embargo, or blockage of trade. For years, the country remained mired in poverty.

✓ **Checkpoint** How did communist Vietnam dominate parts of Southeast Asia after the Vietnam War?

Fleeing Communist Control
These South Vietnamese refugees are fleeing their country after communist forces took control in April 1975. Refugees who fled in small boats like this one were known as "boat people." *Why might people choose to flee across the open ocean in a small boat like this one?*

Section 4 Assessment

Terms, People, and Places

1. For each term, person, or place listed at the beginning of the section, write a sentence explaining its significance.

Note Taking

2. Reading Skill: Summarize Use your completed chart to answer the Focus Question: What were the causes and effects of war in Southeast Asia, and what was the American role in this region?

Comprehension and Critical Thinking

3. Draw Conclusions Why did the French withdraw from Indochina in the 1950s?

4. Summarize How did a local struggle in Vietnam become a major Cold War conflict?

5. Compare Points of View What different opinions did Americans have about U.S. involvement in the Vietnam War?

6. Synthesize Information When the text states that "dominos fell" after the Vietnam War, what does this mean?

● **Writing About History**

Quick Write: Write a Supporting Paragraph To write a problem-solution essay, you need to provide arguments to support a proposed solution to a problem. In this section, an American was quoted as wanting to "get out" of South Vietnam without giving up on it. Write a thesis statement proposing a way to do this. Based on the text or your own ideas, write a paragraph with arguments supporting your thesis statement.

Progress Monitoring *Online*
For: Self-quiz with vocabulary practice
Web Code: nba-3041

Section 4 Assessment

1. Sentences should reflect an understanding of each term, person, or place listed at the beginning of the section.

2. Causes: A desire for independence led to war with the French; struggle between Communist and noncommunist groups led to a civil war that became part of a larger Cold War. Effects: widespread death and destruction and the spread of communist rule; America entered the war to prevent the spread of communism.

3. They were losing the battle against guerrilla forces led by Ho Chi Minh.

4. The United States entered the war on South Vietnam's side to stop the spread of communism, while the Soviet Union and China supported communist North Vietnam.

5. Many Americans felt it was a quagmire and that America should withdraw. Others felt America needed to stay in Southeast Asia to avoid the spread of communism.

6. Some nations in Southeast Asia fell under communist rule.

● **Writing About History**
Responses should reflect a specific thesis statement.

For additional assessment, have students access **Progress Monitoring** *Online* at **Web Code nba-3041.**

The Fall of the Soviet Union

Objectives

- Understand the key events and people that contributed to the fall of the Soviet Union.
- Trace the impact of the fall of the Soviet Union on other nations.

Build Background Knowledge **L3**

Ask students to recall what they learned about the economic progress of the Soviet Union after World War II. Ask **How might Soviet citizens and leaders feel after many years of economic stagnation?** *(They would probably feel frustrated and perhaps ready for a change.)* Based on their previous reading, ask students to predict likely factors that led to the fall of the Soviet Union.

Instruct **L3**

- Walk students through the photos and captions. Ask **Who were some of the key players in the collapse of the Soviet Union?** *(Mikhail Gorbachev and Boris Yeltsin)* Ask students to create a timeline of the events leading to the fall of the Soviet Union and to use the 1991 and 1992 maps to explain the changes that occurred after the breakup. Then ask **What might it have been like to live in the Soviet Union during this time of transition?** *(It was probably exciting, but also scary and unsettling.)*

THE FALL OF THE SOVIET UNION

Soviet president Mikhail Gorbachev was due to sign a treaty that would reduce the power of the Soviet government. On August 18, 1991, two days before the signing, a committee of Communist hardliners detained Gorbachev at his summer home. The next day, the committee announced to the nation that Gorbachev had resigned and that they were taking control of the government. The committee sent columns of tanks and troops to take control of the capital, Moscow. (See photo at the right.) However, Boris Yeltsin, the president of Russia, the largest Soviet republic, defied the hardliners. Yeltsin called on thousands of Russians to resist the unlawful takeover. Finally, on August 21, the hardliners gave up their takeover and ordered Soviet troops to retreat from Moscow. Yeltsin's defeat of the hardliners led a few months later to the breakup of the Soviet Union.

◄ Soviet president
Mikhail Gorbachev

Soviet Union, 1991

Arctic Ocean

EUROPE

Baltic Sea

Black Sea

Caspian Sea

SOVIET UNION

ASIA

Pacific Ocean

Conic Projection
0   500   1000 mi

0   500   1000 km

History Background

Fall of the Soviet Union The only domino effect communism truly saw was during its decline in Europe in 1989, when nation after nation rejected their ruling regimes and forged freer governments. During that summer, Poland held elections and voted out the communist party. Hungary quickly followed. Then East Germans began clamoring for the right to go to West Germany. Soon the Berlin Wall fell and spurred the peaceful communist overthrow in Czechoslovakia and the violent one in Romania, not to mention the dissolution of communism in Albania and Bulgaria. All told, eight countries abandoned communism within six months.

History *Interactive*

For: Interactive timeline, audio, and more
Visit: www.PHSchool.com
Web Code: nbp-3041

Independent Practice

History *Interactive* To enrich and extend the lesson, have students access this unit's History Interactive map, audio, and slide show at **Web Code nbp-3041.**

Monitor Progress

To confirm students' understanding, have them focus on the visuals. Ask them to explain the significance of each image.

▲ Russian president Boris Yeltsin, holding a sheet of paper at left, stands atop a Soviet tank on August 19, 1991, and calls on Russians to resist the attempted takeover of the Soviet Union by hardliners. Behind him, a supporter holds a Russian flag. Yeltsin's success in defying the takeover broke the power of the central Soviet government and led to the independence of Russia and the other Soviet republics.

◄ Stanislav Shushkevich (left), president of Belarus; Boris Yeltsin (center), president of Russia; and Leonid Kravchuk (right), president of Ukraine, agreed on December 8, 1991, to dissolve the Soviet Union, effective at the end of 1991.

Thinking Critically
1. **Analyze Images** Why is it significant that Russian President Yeltsin is standing on top of a Soviet tank in the photo at the top of the page?
2. **Synthesize Information** How did the events of August 1991 cause the Soviet government to lose power to Russia?
3. **Map Skills** Based on the maps, why would Russia's wish for independence lead to the Soviet Union's breakup?

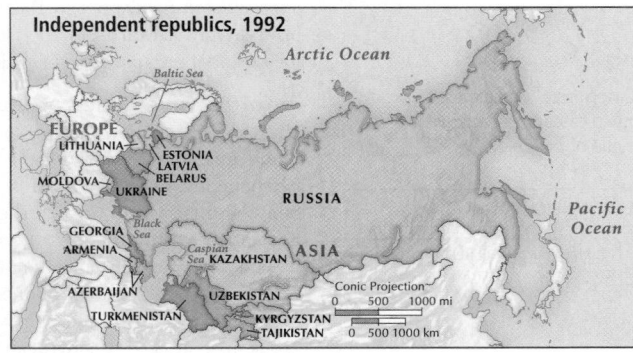

Independent republics, 1992

L4 Gifted and Talented   L4 Advanced Readers

In 1984, Jaroslav Seifert, a Czech poet, won the Nobel Peace Prize for Literature. He wrote the following about Eastern Europe: "For us, there is no Eastern Europe. It is a collection of countries. . . . You should not see us as a single country." Write this statement on the board and discuss the meaning of it with students. Ask students how the events in 1989 reflect this attitude.

Thinking Critically
1. It shows that the Soviet Union, as represented by its army, had lost power to Soviet republics such as Russia, as represented by its president, Yeltsin.
2. Popular support for Yeltsin showed that Soviet central power had lost support among Russians and other Soviet citizens.
3. Russia is by far the largest and most influential of the former Soviet republics. Other republics would follow Russia's lead.

Objectives

As you teach this section, keep students focused on the following objectives to help them answer the Section Focus Question and master core content.

- Understand how the Soviet Union declined.

- Analyze the changes that transformed Eastern Europe.

- Explain how communism declined worldwide and the United States became the sole superpower.

Prepare to Read

Build Background Knowledge L3

Ask students to recall the economic struggles experienced in the postwar years by the Soviet Union, East Germany, and other communist-led nations. Based on their previous reading, ask them to predict how these nations will seek to change their economic and political systems.

Set a Purpose L3

- **WITNESS HISTORY** Read the selection aloud or play the audio.

  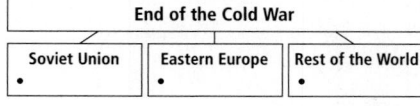 AUDIO **Witness History Audio CD,** A Democratic Transformation

  Ask **What mood does Stefan Heym describe?** *(a mood of jubilation and excitement)* **How could you link opening a window to taking down a wall?** *(Both allow for greater movement and communication.)*

- **Focus** Point out the Section Focus Question and write it on the board. Tell students to refer to this question as they read. *(Answer appears with Section 5 Assessment answers.)*

- **Preview** Have students preview the Section Objectives and the list of Terms, People, and Places.

- **Note Taking** Have students read this section using the Paragraph Shrinking strategy (TE, p. T20). As they read, have students fill in the flowchart categorizing Cold War events by region.

  Reading and Note Taking Study Guide, p. 198

Bessere Politik – nur mit neuer Regierung

Demonstrators in East Berlin, November 4, 1989

Soviet pin promoting "openness, democracy, and restructuring"

WITNESS HISTORY 🔊 AUDIO

A Democratic Transformation

On November 4, 1989, hundreds of thousands of people demonstrated for democracy in the streets of East Berlin. Never before had so many dared to speak out. Speaking to the crowd, author Stefan Heym captured the mood:

❝ Dear friends, fellow citizens, it is as if someone had thrown open the window after all the years of stagnation. . . . What a transformation! ❞

Ultimately, the transformation in Eastern Europe led to the end of the Cold War.

Focus Question What were the causes and effects of the end of the Cold War?

The End of the Cold War

Objectives

- Understand how the Soviet Union declined.
- Analyze the changes that transformed Eastern Europe.
- Explain how communism declined worldwide and the United States became the sole superpower.

Terms, People, and Places

mujahedin	Lech Walesa
Mikhail Gorbachev	Solidarity
glasnost	Václav Havel
perestroika	Nicolae Ceausescu

Note Taking

Reading Skill: Categorize Complete a flowchart like the one below to categorize each event connected to the end of the Cold War.

End of the Cold War		
Soviet Union	**Eastern Europe**	**Rest of the World**
•	•	•

The global Cold War between two armed camps led by the United States and the Soviet Union lasted almost half a century. In the years around 1990, however, the struggle finally ended. The much-feared nuclear confrontation between the two superpowers never came about, but the end was as clear as any military victory.

The Soviet Union Declines

Western fears of growing Soviet power did not come true. In fact, Soviet communism was doomed. Signs of the weakness of the Soviet system had in fact been visible from the beginning.

A Hollow Victory Stalin's Soviet Union emerged from World War II as a superpower with an Eastern European sphere of influence stretching from the Baltic to the Balkans. Victory, however, brought few rewards to the Soviet people. Stalin continued to fill forced labor camps with "enemies of the state."

Reforms Give Way to Repression Under Stalin's successor, Nikita Khrushchev, Soviets enjoyed greater freedom of speech. Some government critics were freed from prisons and labor camps. Khrushchev oversaw a shift in economic priorities away from heavy industry and toward the production of consumer goods. But Khrushchev remained firmly committed to a command economy.

The thaw in Moscow inspired some East Europeans to move toward greater independence. However, Khrushchev himself remained a determined cold warrior. When Hungarians tried to break free of Soviet control in 1956, Khrushchev sent tanks in to

Vocabulary Builder

Use the information below and the following resources to teach the high-use word from this section.
All in One Teaching Resources, Unit 5, p. 7; **Teaching Resources, Skills Handbook,** p. 3

High-Use Word	Definition and Sample Sentence
incentive, p. 639	*n.* something that encourages a person to take action or work harder. The beautiful weather acted as an **incentive** for me to quickly finish my work so I could go outside and enjoy it.

enforce obedience, and his successor, Leonid Brezhnev, did the same thing when Czechs challenged the Soviets in the "Prague spring" of 1968.

The Command Economy Stagnates The Soviet Union rebuilt its shattered industries after World War II, using equipment stripped from Germany. The government poured resources into science and technology, launching *Sputnik I,* the first artificial satellite, in 1957.

Yet the Soviet economy faced severe problems. Collectivized agriculture remained so unproductive that Russia, a grain exporter in tsarist times, had to import grain to feed its people. The Soviet command economy could not match Western market economies in producing consumer goods. Soviet shoes and television sets were far inferior, while such luxuries as clothes washers or automobiles remained rare.

Central economic planning led to inefficiency and waste. A huge bureaucracy decided what and how much to produce. Government planners in Moscow, however, knew little about local needs. They chose to produce many unneeded goods. Consumers' needs often were not met. Although workers were paid low wages, lifetime job security gave them little <u>incentive</u> to produce better-quality goods.

Unlike the economies of Western Europe and the United States, which experienced booms during the Cold War, the economies of Eastern Europe and the Soviet Union stagnated. People saw little improvement in their standards of living and envied the prosperity of the West. Soviet economic inferiority made it impossible for the Soviet Union to keep up with the United States in the arms race and in military preparedness.

Cracking Under the Burden of Military Commitments As you have read, Soviet-American relations swung between confrontation and détente during the Cold War. Meanwhile, both sides maintained large military budgets and built expensive nuclear weapons.

Vocabulary Builder

<u>incentive</u>—(in SEN tiv) *n.* something that encourages a person to take action or work harder

Soviet Tanks Bring Repression

A boy watches Soviet tanks in the Hungarian capital, Budapest, in 1956. The Soviet Union sent tanks to stop Hungary's attempt to take an independent course. *What does this suggest about the independence of Eastern European countries such as Hungary during the Cold War?*

Teach

The Soviet Union Declines

Instruct L3

- **Introduce: Vocabulary Builder**
  Have students read the Vocabulary Builder term and definition. Use the Idea Wave strategy (TE, p. T22) and ask students to list the ***incentives*** for them to do well in school. *(Sample: get into college, get a good job)*

- **Teach** Review the problems that the Soviet Union had in the postwar era. Write the names *Stalin, Khrushchev,* and *Gorbachev* on the board. Have students supply information about the problems each leader faced and the policies or reforms each took in response. Discuss the pressures that ultimately caused the Soviet Union and its command economy to collapse.

- **Analyzing the Visuals** Refer students to the political cartoon on the next page. Have students discuss its meaning with a partner. Then discuss this as a class.

Differentiated Instruction Solutions for All Learners

L1 Special Needs L2 Less Proficient Readers

Direct students to choose three key events discussed in this section and create illustrations for a newspaper reporting on these events *(Sample: Gorbachev tries reform).* Then display the red headings from the text on a bulletin board. Ask students to display their drawings underneath the appropriate heading. To review this content, discuss the events illustrated under each heading.

Use the following resources to help students acquire basic skills.

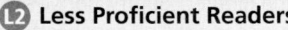 **Adapted Reading and Note Taking Study Guide**

■ Adapted Note Taking Study Guide, p. 198
■ Adapted Section Summary, p. 199

Answer

Caption that they had little real independence

Independent Practice

Have students fill in the Outline Map *The Soviet Union After the Breakup.*

All in One Teaching Resources, Unit 5, p. 15

Monitor Progress

- As students fill in their flowcharts, circulate to make sure they understand the importance of the failing Soviet economy in the end of the Cold War. For a completed version of the flowchart, see

  📖 **Note Taking Transparencies,** 193

- Circulate to make sure that students have completed the Outline Map correctly and have accurately labeled the former Soviet republics.

The arms race put a particular strain on the inefficient Soviet command economy. And when U.S. President Ronald Reagan launched a new round of missile development, it was clear that the Soviet economy could not afford to match it.

Soviets Have Their Own "Vietnam" in Afghanistan In 1979, the Soviet Union became involved in a long war in Afghanistan, an Islamic country just south of the Soviet Union. A Soviet-supported Afghan government had tried to modernize the nation. Its policies included social reforms and land redistribution that would reduce the power of regional landlords. Afghan landlords—who commanded armed men as warlords—and Muslim conservatives charged that both policies threatened Islamic tradition. When these warlords took up arms against the government, Soviet troops moved in.

Battling **mujahedin** (moo jah heh DEEN), or Muslim religious warriors, in the mountains of Afghanistan, however, proved as difficult as fighting guerrillas in the jungles of Vietnam had been for Americans. By the mid-1980s, the American government began to smuggle modern weaponry to the mujahedin. The Soviets had years of heavy casualties, high costs, and few successes. Like America's Vietnam War, the struggle in Afghanistan provoked a crisis in morale for the Soviets at home.

Gorbachev Tries Reform In 1985, an energetic new leader, **Mikhail Gorbachev** (GAWR buh chawf), came to power in the Soviet Union. With the economy in bad shape and the war dragging on in Afghanistan, Gorbachev was eager to bring about reforms. The changes he urged, however, soon spiraled out of control.

Gorbachev sought to avoid Cold-War confrontations. He signed arms control treaties with the United States and pulled Soviet troops out of Afghanistan.

At home, he called for **glasnost,** or openness. He ended censorship and encouraged people to discuss the country's problems openly. He also urged **perestroika** (pehr uh STROY kuh), or restructuring, of the government and economy. To improve efficiency, he reduced the size of the bureaucracy and backed limited private enterprise. His reforms made factory managers rather than central planners responsible for decisions. They also allowed farmers to sell produce on the free market.

Analyzing Political Cartoons

The Crumbling Soviet Union This cartoon shows Soviet leader Mikhail Gorbachev with an egg-shaped head sitting on a wall marked with the national symbol of the Soviet Union. The cartoon draws on the nursery rhyme *Humpty Dumpty.*

1. What does the cartoon suggest about the state of the Soviet Union under Gorbachev?
2. What does it imply about Gorbachev's future?
3. How does this cartoon communicate ideas without using any words?

Link to Literature

Russian Writers Due to strict censorship laws, books by many of Russia's greatest writers were not available during the Cold War. When Gorbachev introduced glasnost, censorship faded. Russians were introduced to the works of writers that were admired and respected around the world but little known in the mother country. Boris Pasternak's *Dr. Zhivago,* which is cited as possibly the greatest Russian novel of the twentieth century, was new to Russians, as was Vladimir Nabokov's *Lolita,* the story of a grown man who falls in love with a young girl.

Answers

Analyzing Political Cartoons

1. that it was unstable politically
2. It was uncertain how much longer he would be able to maintain leadership.
3. by drawing on recognizable symbolism from a common nursery rhyme and connecting it to larger political themes

An Empire Crumbles Gorbachev's reforms, however, brought economic turmoil. Shortages grew worse and prices soared. Factories that could not survive without government help closed, leading to high unemployment. Those whose jobs were threatened denounced the reforms. Other critics demanded even more radical changes.

Gorbachev's policies also fed unrest across the Soviet empire. Eastern European countries from Poland to Bulgaria broke out of the Soviet orbit beginning in 1989. The Baltic States—Estonia, Latvia, and Lithuania—which the Soviet Union had seized in 1940, regained full independence in 1991. Russia's postwar empire seemed to many to be collapsing. Soviet hard-liners tried to overthrow Gorbachev that year and restore the old order. Their attempted coup failed, but it further weakened Gorbachev, who soon resigned as president.

At the end of 1991, the remaining Soviet republics separated to form 12 independent nations, in addition to the three Baltic States. The largest of these was Russia, which had most of the population and territory of the former Soviet Union. The next largest were Kazakhstan and Ukraine. Maps of Europe and Asia had to be redrawn to reflect the new political boundaries. After 69 years, the Soviet Union had ceased to exist.

✔ **Checkpoint** How did Gorbachev's policies lead to a new map of Europe and Asia?

Changes Transform Eastern Europe

The Soviet Union had maintained control over its Eastern European satellites by force. When Gorbachev introduced glasnost and perestroika in the Soviet Union, Eastern Europeans began to seek greater freedom in their own countries. As the Soviet Union crumbled, Eastern Europeans demanded an end to Soviet domination. This time they got it.

Demands for Freedom Increase As you have read, unrest had long simmered across the Soviet bloc. Many Eastern Europeans opposed communist rule. Nationalists resented Russian domination. Revolts had erupted in Poland, Hungary, Czechoslovakia, and elsewhere in the 1950s and 1960s. In the 1980s, demands for change mounted once again.

Hungary Quietly Reforms In 1968, when Czechoslovakia's defiance of Soviet control led to a Soviet invasion, Hungary quietly introduced modest economic reforms. Because Hungary remained loyal to the Warsaw Pact and maintained communist political control, it was allowed to go ahead with these reforms, which included elements of a market economy. During the 1970s, Hungary expanded its market economy. During the late 1980s, under the spirit of glasnost, Hungarians began to criticize the communist government more openly. Economic troubles led to greater discontent. Finally, in 1988 and 1989, under public pressure, the communist government allowed greater freedoms. New political parties were allowed to form, and the western border with Austria was opened.

Poland Embraces Solidarity Poland led the way in the new surge of resistance that shattered the Soviet satellite empire. In 1980, economic hardships ignited strikes by shipyard workers. Led by **Lech Walesa** (lek vah WEN suh), they organized **Solidarity,** an independent labor union. It won millions of members and demanded political as well as economic change.

Defending Lithuania's Independence
This woman, holding a Lithuanian flag, is guarding Lithuania's parliament building and TV tower from Soviet troops that tried and failed to regain control after Lithuania declared independence in January 1991.

Instruct

- **Introduce: Key Terms** Recall with students the terms *glasnost* and *perestroika.* Discuss how these ideas of openness and restructuring led to dramatic change within the Soviet Union. Ask students to predict how nations under Soviet influence might use these ideas to reshape their relationship with the Soviet Union.

- **Teach** Trace the changes that occurred in the nations of Eastern Europe. Ask **What changes occurred in these nations?** *(They shifted from communism to democracy and from command economies to market economies.)* **Why were they seeking change at this time?** *(Communism and command economies had brought economic stagnation, social unrest, and anger. It was a time ripe for change, as glasnost, perestroika, and the collapse of the Soviet Union loosened the grip of Soviet control.)*

- **Quick Activity** Display **Color Transparency 185: The Cold War: Freeze to Thaw.** Use the lesson suggested in the transparency guide to discuss the link between the collapse of the Soviet Union and the reunification of Germany.

  🏛 **Color Transparencies,** 185

Independent Practice

- **Viewpoints** Have students read the selection *Two Views on the Reunification of Germany* and answer the questions that follow.

   **Teaching Resources, Unit 5,** p. 13

- Have students write a paragraph describing the changes that transformed Eastern Europe during the 1980s.

Monitor Progress

As students work on their paragraphs, circulate to ensure students understand the changes transforming this region.

Answer

✔ Gorbachev's policies led to the weakening of centralized communist power in the Soviet Union. As a result, countries under the Soviet domination broke free, and the republics of the USSR separated into 15 independent nations.

Communism Declines Around the World

L3

Instruct

- **Introduce** Ask students to read the introductory paragraph and the black headings under Communism Declines Around the World. Have students predict what they will learn under each heading. Then have them read to find out if their predictions were accurate.

- **Teach** Discuss each of the nations described in the text: China, Korea, Vietnam, and Cuba. Ask **How did these nations change economically and politically?** *(China and Vietnam moved toward market economies, but remained under Communist Party political control. North Korea and Cuba changed little politically or economically.)* **How did such changes affect people in China and North Korea?** *(Though the Chinese made no major political reforms, they did experience economic prosperity. North Korea grew increasingly rigid, unable to provide for its people.)*

- **Analyzing the Visuals** Have students describe the photo on the next page. Ask **How does this photo symbolize the changes occurring in China?** *(Under a market economy, the Chinese had access to a wide selection of modern consumer goods.)* **How might increased economic access lead people to want increased political freedom?** *(It makes people aware of having choices and aware of the freedoms others have elsewhere in the world.)*

Independent Practice

Biography To expand students' understanding of Cuba's decline, have them read the biography *Fidel Castro* and answer the questions on the worksheet.

All in One Teaching Resources, Unit 5, p. 11

Monitor Progress

Return to the introductory text: *(Although political dictatorships still prevailed, rigid, government-run economies sometimes gave way to freer, more productive economic systems.)* Have students use examples from the text to explain and support this statement.

Answer

Caption They would not want workers to have too much control.

Lech Walesa and Solidarity
Lech Walesa, at the left, speaks at a shipyard workers' strike in August 1980. The following month, he helped found the Polish national union known as Solidarity (Solidarnosc in Polish). At the right, Poles defy the government by holding a banner for the outlawed Solidarity union in 1983. *Why would a communist government ban a labor union?*

Under pressure from the Soviet Union, the Polish government outlawed the union and arrested its leaders, including Walesa. Still, unrest continued. Walesa became a national hero, and the Polish government eventually released him from prison. Pope John Paul II visited Poland, met with Solidarity leaders, and criticized communist policies. The pope was the former Karol Wojtyla, archbishop of the Polish city of Cracow.

East Germans Demand Change Unlike Poland or Hungary, East Germany resisted Gorbachev's calls for change. In 1988, the rigidly communist East German government banned Soviet publications, because it considered glasnost subversive. East Germany's communists blocked moves toward a market economy or greater political freedom. However, East Germans could watch television broadcasts from West Germany. They were thus intensely aware how much more prosperity and political freedom existed on the other side of the Berlin Wall. When Hungary opened its border with Austria in 1989, thousands of East Germans fled through Hungary and Austria to West Germany. Thousands more held demonstrations across East Germany demanding change.

Communist Governments Fall In the late 1980s, Gorbachev declared that he would not interfere with Eastern European reforms. Poland legalized Solidarity and, in 1989, held the first free elections in 50 years. A year later, Lech Walesa was elected president of Poland. The new government began a difficult, but peaceful, transition from a command economy to a market economy.

A flowering of opposition and reform movements spread across the Eastern European countries. By late 1989, a powerful democracy movement was sweeping throughout the region. Everywhere, people took to the streets, demanding reform. One by one, communist governments fell. In Czechoslovakia, **Václav Havel** (VAHTS lahv HAH vul), a dissident writer and human rights activist, was elected president. In East Germany, the gates of the Berlin Wall were opened, and the country started down the road to reunification with West Germany. Most changes came

Differentiated Instruction   Solutions for All Learners

L2 Less Proficient Readers   L2 English Language Learners

To help students distill significant facts about Eastern European countries, ask them to create a historical map of Eastern Europe. To begin, have them take out their Outline Maps of The Soviet Union. Explain that maps sometimes include labels, or call-outs, that give historical information about an area on the map. Have them use the information in this section to create call-outs for the following countries: Yugoslavia, Hungary, Czechoslovakia, Poland, East Germany, and Romania. Call-outs should include the year the event took place and be enclosed in a box on the map near the appropriate country with a line from the box to the country. Call-outs should be short, such as "1956: Imre Nagy gains power in Hungary."

peacefully, but when Nicolae Ceausescu (chow SHES koo), Romania's longtime dictator, refused to step down, he was overthrown and executed.

For the first time since 1939, Eastern European countries were free. They dissolved the Warsaw Pact in 1991 and requested that Russian troops leave. By then, the Soviet Union itself had crumbled.

Czechoslovakia Splits Czechoslovakia was a relatively new nation, formed in 1918 at the breakup of the Austro-Hungarian Empire. Before 1918, the country's Czech and Slovak ethnic groups—each with its own language and traditions—had lived separately. After Czechoslovakia's founding, Czechs dominated the country's government. During World War II, Czechoslovakia was conquered and partitioned, or divided, by Nazi Germany. Czechoslovakia was reunified under communist control after the war. When the communists lost power in 1989, some Slovaks began to call for independence. In 1992, the Slovaks and Czechs peacefully agreed to divide Czechoslovakia into the new nations of Slovakia and the Czech Republic.

✓ **Checkpoint** How did glasnost in the Soviet Union lead to the end of communism in Eastern Europe?

Communism Declines Around the World

The collapse of communism in the Soviet bloc affected communist countries from China to Castro's Cuba. Many were already suffering economic decline by the 1980s as their command economies stagnated. Although political dictatorships still prevailed, rigid, government-run economies sometimes gave way to freer, more productive economic systems.

China Builds on Deng's Reforms Gorbachev had urged the leaders of other communist states to consider both political and economic changes. China's leaders, building on Deng Xiaoping's 1980s economic reforms, generated an amazing economic boom in the 1990s. China became a major producer of consumer goods and achieved double-digit growth rates.

China's government undertook no major political reforms. However, as the global economic crisis that began in 2008 led to factory closings, protests by unemployed workers increased. China's government responded with a $600 billion stimulus package to retrain workers and improve productivity.

Vietnam and North Korea Differ Communist Vietnam established diplomatic relations with the United States in the 1990s. Vietnam also began to change economically, encouraging tourism and becoming a leading exporter of coffee.

North Korea, on the other hand, hunkered down in grim isolation, rejecting all reforms. Its rigidly totalitarian regime often proved unable to feed its own

Capitalism Comes to China
Chinese consumers shop for mobile phones in this recent photo. *Do the activities in this photo reflect a command economy or a market economy? Explain why.*

The United States as Sole Superpower

Instruct

■ **Introduce** Recall with students the Cold War military standoff between the Soviet Union and the United States, and how this led to equal global power for each nation. Ask students to predict how the collapse of the Soviet Union might affect the global status of the United States.

■ **Teach** Discuss with students the new role in which America found itself after the collapse of the Soviet Union. Ask **What did the end of the Soviet Union mean for the United States?** *(It left the United States with the responsibility of being the world's only superpower.)* **How did Americans react to this new role?** *(Some Americans embraced this role, while others felt it added too much risk and expense to foreign policy.)*

■ **Quick Activity** Review with students the ways that nations around the world reacted to U.S. global supremacy. Ask **How did different nations view America's unrivaled power?** *(Many found it offensive, while others still saw America as a champion of freedom.)* Organize students to briefly debate what America's role should be within the global community.

Independent Practice

Challenge students to think of one current world situation in which the United States has acted as the sole superpower. If necessary, suggest events in Iraq during 2004. Have students write a few sentences describing how the world reacted to America's actions in Iraq.

Monitor Progress

Check Reading and Note Taking Study Guide entries for student understanding.

Differentiated Instruction   Solutions for All Learners

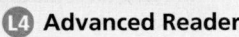 **Gifted and Talented**   **Advanced Readers**

Remind students that the fall of communism affected many countries around the globe. Have students find out more about one of these nations. Ask students to choose one country that was communist during the Cold War and conduct research in the library or online and write a three paragraph report on the country today. Have them answer the following questions: How have daily conditions changed for most people? How did the decline of the Soviet Union affect this country?

Answers

✓ Glasnost in the Soviet Union led to a loosening of Soviet control over Eastern Europe and to greater ability for Eastern European nations to openly resist and criticize Soviet rule.

Caption a market economy because there are a large number of goods for sale, reflecting a healthy, competitive economy

people, leading to hundreds of thousands of deaths. A 2007 agreement to dismantle its nuclear weapons program in exchange for U.S. aid seemed to founder as the decade drew to a close.

Cuba Declines Cuba's economy, deprived of Soviet support and still crippled by American sanctions, deteriorated. Many felt that communism in Cuba would not outlive its leader, Fidel Castro. In 2006, the ailing Castro surrendered control of the government to his younger brother Raúl, who allowed some market reforms.

✓ **Checkpoint** How did communist countries react differently to the collapse of the Soviet bloc?

The United States as Sole Superpower

With the collapse of its great rival, the United States was widely recognized as the only remaining superpower. After years of thin budgets, Russia's armed forces seemed weak and ineffective. Only the United States could project its power around the world.

The United States thus emerged as the world's leading military power. From time to time, the United States exercised this power. Beginning in the 1990s, the United States staged several military missions around the world. You will learn more about these in upcoming chapters.

Americans seemed unsure of their proper role in the world. Some objected to the risk and expense of being "the world's policeman." Others, however, believed that the United States should play an even more aggressive part in world affairs.

America's unrivaled power produced mixed reactions around the world. When the Soviet threat had loomed, American power had been seen as a valuable counterweight. Some continued to see the United States as a protector of freedom. With no rival threat in sight, however, people in many parts of the world were less pleased to see any single nation as powerful as the United States had become.

✓ **Checkpoint** Why did America's position as the sole superpower produce mixed reactions?

SECTION 5 **Assessment**

Terms, People, and Places

1. For each term, person, or place listed at the beginning of the section, write a sentence explaining its significance.

Note Taking

2. **Reading Skill: Categorize** Use your completed chart to answer the Focus Question: What were the causes and effects of the end of the Cold War?

Comprehension and Critical Thinking

3. **Draw Conclusions** Why was the Soviet Union unable to keep up with the market economies of the West?
4. **Summarize** How did Gorbachev's reforms lead to the breakup of the Soviet empire?
5. **Recognize Cause and Effect** Why were Eastern Europeans able to break free of communist governments and Soviet domination in the late 1980s?
6. **Draw Inferences** How did the collapse of the Soviet Union affect the power of other countries around the world?

● Writing About History

Quick Write: Gather Evidence To write a problem-solution essay, you need to gather evidence to support a proposed solution to a problem. In this section, you learned that rigidly communist countries faced isolation and economic decline after the fall of the Soviet Union. Identify a solution to this problem and gather evidence to support your solution. Then write a paragraph with a thesis statement proposing a solution. Include the evidence you have gathered in support of your thesis statement.

Václav Havel: *New Year's Address*

Václav Havel was a leading dissident and human rights activist in communist Czechoslovakia. When the "democracy movement" swept through Eastern Europe in 1989, Havel was elected president. In the following speech delivered on January 1, 1990, Havel asks the citizens of Czechoslovakia to accept responsibility for their past and to move forward in building a democracy. Havel calls on Czechs and Slovaks to be active participants in their new democracy.

Václav Havel

O ur country is not flourishing. The enormous creative and spiritual potential of our nations is not being used sensibly. Entire branches of industry are producing goods that are of no interest to anyone.... [W]e have today the most contaminated environment in Europe....

But all this is still not the main problem. The worst thing is that we live in a contaminated moral environment. We fell morally ill because we became used to saying something different from what we thought. We learned not to believe in anything, to ignore each other, to care only about ourselves. Concepts such as love, friendship, compassion, humility, or forgiveness lost their depth and dimensions.... Only a few of us were able to cry out loud that the powers that be should not be all-powerful....

We had all become used to the totalitarian system and accepted it as an unchangeable fact and thus helped to perpetuate it. In other words, we are all ... responsible for the operation of the totalitarian machinery....

Why do I say this? It would be very unreasonable to understand the sad legacy of the last forty years as something alien, which some distant relative bequeathed to us. On the contrary, we have to accept this legacy as a sin we committed against ourselves. If we accept it as such, we will understand that it is up to us all, and up to us only, to do something about it. We cannot blame the previous rulers for everything, not only because it would be untrue but also because it could blunt the duty that each of us faces today, namely, the obligation to act independently, freely, reasonably, and quickly. Let us not be mistaken: the best government in the world, the best parliament and the best president, cannot achieve much on their own. And it would also be wrong to expect a general remedy from them only. Freedom and democracy include participation and therefore responsibility from us all.

Czechoslovak democracy demonstrators

Thinking Critically
1. **Identify Point of View** Who does Havel hold responsible for Czechoslovakia's totalitarian past?
2. **Draw Conclusions** What does Havel see as the solution to his country's problems?

Václav Havel: *New Year's Address*

Objective
■ Understand Havel's argument that democracy involves responsibility on the part of citizens.

Build Background Knowledge ⓛ₃
Ask students to recall the changes that took place in Czechoslovakia in 1989. Have them identify ways that communism and democracy involved citizen participation in the governments. (*Communism gave citizens few choices and left almost total control with the government. Democracy involved citizens in making regular choices about the nation's policies.*)

Instruct ⓛ₃
■ Direct students' attention to the introduction at the top of the page. Then ask **What does Havel believe citizens must do?** (*He believes they must take responsibility and participate in building a democracy.*)
■ Discuss with students the problems Havel sees ahead for his people. Ask **How had life under a totalitarian system made people less prepared to participate in democracy?** (*It made them used to accepting total control instead of sharing responsibility.*)

Monitor Progress
To confirm students' understanding, ask them to briefly summarize Havel's views.

History Background

The Writer's Life While campaigning for democracy in Czechoslovakia, Václav Havel was arrested many times. His offenses included organizing dissidents and writing plays and essays that implied that the Czech government was absurd, demoralizing, and corrupt. (In his best known play, *The Memorandum*, office workers are forced to speak a nonsensical language under the assumption that it will make them communicate with each other more effectively.) Once in power, Havel was criticized for being too soft and too thoughtful an administrator, and he often admitted he felt personally unsuited to be president. However, his policies brought civil liberties and rights to his country.

Thinking Critically
1. all the citizens of Czechoslovakia
2. shared responsibility and participation from everyone

Quick Study Guide

- Have students use the Quick Study Guide to prepare for this chapter's test. Students may wish to refer to the following pages as they review:

Cold War Contrasts
Section 1, pp. 605–612; Section 2, pp. 614–617, 621–622

Cold War Hot Spots
Section 3, pp. 627–629; Section 4, pp. 630–634

Steps in the Collapse of the Soviet Empire
Section 5, pp. 636–643

Key Events of the Cold War
Section 1, pp. 604, 608–609; Section 2, p. 618; Section 3, pp. 623–624, 627–629; Section 4, pp. 631–634, pp. 636–637; Section 5, pp. 641–643

- For additional review, remind **L3** students to refer to the

 **Reading and Note Taking Study Guide**

Note Taking Study Guide, pp. 190, 192, 194, 196, 198
Section Summaries, pp. 191, 193, 195, 197, 199

- Have students access **Web Code nbp-3061** for this chapter's **History Interactive** timeline, which includes expanded entries and additional events.

- If students need additional instruction on analyzing timelines, have them read the **Skills Handbook,** p. SH30.

- When students have completed their study of the chapter, distribute Chapter Tests A and B.

All in One Teaching Resources, Unit 5, pp. 17–22

For **Progress Monitoring Online,** refer students to the Self-test with vocabulary practice at **Web Code nba-3061.**

Quick Study Guide

Progress Monitoring *Online*
For: Self-test with vocabulary practice
Web Code: nba-3061

■ Cold War Contrasts

Communist Countries	Industrialized Democracies
Compete in arms race to maintain "balance of terror."	Compete in arms race to maintain "balance of terror."
Form Warsaw Pact. China follows separate path.	Form NATO and SEATO.
Seek to spread communism.	Seek to contain communism.
Command economies	Market economies
Economic stagnation, low standards of living	Economic "miracles," prosperity with scattered recessions
Repression of dissent, labor camps	Free expression, but fears lead to an episode of McCarthyism
Power is closely held by communist parties.	Democracy is established in Japan, civil rights movement extends democracy in the United States.
Lost arms race.	Won arms race.

■ Cold War Hot Spots

Korea	Vietnam
Divided into communist north and noncommunist, U.S.-supported south.	Divided into communist north and noncommunist, U.S.-supported south.
China provided troops to support North Korea.	China and the Soviet Union provided economic and military aid, but not troops, to North Vietnam.
The United States led United Nations troops supporting South Korea.	The United States and some allies provided troops to support South Vietnam.
Warfare mainly involved regular troops.	Viet Cong fighting in the south were mainly guerrillas.
United States troops remained in South Korea after war.	United States troops withdrew before the war ended.
Korean War ended in a stalemate between the two sides and a ceasefire.	Vietnam War ended when North Vietnam defeated South Vietnam and reunited the country.

■ Steps in the Collapse of the Soviet Empire

- The command economy could not create wealth or raise living standards as quickly as market economies.
- The Soviet Union could not afford the expense of maintaining a "balance of terror" in the arms race.
- East Europeans resisted communism and Soviet control.
- Soviet military failure in Afghanistan led to calls for change.
- Reforms in Russia included glasnost, or freedom of expression, and perestroika, or market reforms.

- East Germans forced their government to open the Berlin Wall.
- Eastern European nations rejected Soviet control and adopted market economies and democracy.
- Glasnost led to drive for independence by Soviet ethnic minorities and the breakup of the Soviet Union.
- Soviet Union was divided into 15 independent nations.
- The Warsaw Pact was dissolved.

■ Key Events of the Cold War

| 1945 World War II ends in Europe. | 1949 Germany is divided. | 1959 Fidel Castro leads communist revolution in Cuba. |

Americas, Europe, and Soviet Union

1945 **1955**

East and Southeast Asia

1945 — World War II ends in Asia.
1949 — Mao Zedong leads communists to victory in China.
1950–1953 — Korean War

L1 Special Needs   **L2 Less Proficient Readers**

For students acquiring basic skills:

 **Adapted Reading and Note Taking Study Guide**
Section Note Taking Study Guide, pp. 190, 192, 194, 196, 198
Section Summaries, pp. 191, 193, 195, 197, 199

L2 English Language Learners

For Spanish-speaking students:

 **Spanish Reading and Note Taking Study Guide**
Section Note Taking Study Guide, pp. 190, 192, 194, 196, 198
Section Summaries, pp. 191, 193, 195, 197, 199

Concept Connector

 ## Essential Question Review

To connect prior knowledge with what you have learned in this chapter, answer the questions below in your Concept Connector journal. Use the journal in the Reading and Note Taking Study Guide to record your answers (or go to www.phschool.com Web Code: nbd-3007). In addition, record information about the following concepts:

• Cooperation: European Community

1. **Empire** During the 1950s and 1960s, Soviet military forces crushed democratic reforms in East Germany, Poland, Hungary, and Czechoslovakia. By the mid-1980s, the weakness of the Soviet system was becoming apparent. Compare the decline of the Soviet empire to the decline of the Ottoman empire (Chapter 10). Identify any similarities. Then identify the single most important reason for the fall of communist governments in Eastern Europe.

2. **Dictatorship** Mao Zedong built a one-party totalitarian state in China. Critics and opponents were labeled "counter-revolutionaries" and beaten, exiled, or killed. How do you think adult Chinese might have viewed the Cultural Revolution? Did the Cultural Revolution strengthen Mao's hold on China? Focus on:
   • Red Guards
   • propaganda
   • forced labor camps
   • civil war

3. **Human Rights** After World War II, the American promise of equality and opportunity had not yet been fulfilled for minorities and women. African Americans and other minority groups faced segregation and discrimination. What tactics did these groups use to gain their civil rights? What were the results? Think about:
   • protests
   • spending power
   • legislation

■ Connections to Today

1. **Conflict: India and Pakistan** The Cold War was a tense standoff between the United States and the Soviet Union, with only brief outbreaks of actual fighting. Since India and Pakistan gained independence in 1947, the two countries have engaged in a similar conflict. This conflict involves occasional fighting, often involving guerrillas in the disputed Kashmir region. Since 1998, both India and Pakistan have had nuclear weapons. Using recent news articles and the Internet, research the current state of this conflict. How is it similar to the Cold War? How is it different?

Kashmir Sweater

2. **Democracy: The Global Spread of Democracy** This chapter describes the spread of democracy to West Germany and Japan and later to Eastern Europe. Using an encyclopedia, research the move to democracy in an Eastern European country. Then research a move to democracy in a country in Latin America, East Asia, or Africa. How was the transition to democracy similar or different in these two countries?

1961
Berlin Wall is built.

1989
Eastern Europeans overthrow communist rulers.

1991
The Soviet Union breaks up and the Cold War ends.

1965   **1975**   **1985**   **1995**

1964
U.S. enters the Vietnam War.

1975
Vietnam War ends with North Vietnamese victory.

1976
Mao Zedong dies.

 History *Interactive*
For: Interactive timeline
Web Code: nbp-3061

 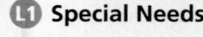 

 Special Needs   **Less Proficient Readers**

Use the following study guide resources to help students acquiring basic skills:

Adapted Reading and Note Taking Study Guide
Adapted Concept Connector, pp. 242, 255, 262, 275

 **English Language Learners**

Use the following study guide resources to help Spanish-speaking students:

Spanish Reading and Note Taking Study Guide
Spanish Concept Connector, pp. 242, 255, 262, 275

 # Concept Connector

Tell students that the main concepts for this chapter are Cooperation, Dictatorship, Empire, and Human Rights, and then ask them to answer the Essential Question Review questions on this page. Discuss the Connections to Today topics and ask students to answer the questions that follow.

Essential Question Review

1. Responses should indicate that both the Ottoman Empire and Soviet Union declined because of antiquated policies, corruption, and the rebellion of provinces. The introduction of reforms in the Soviet Union led Eastern European governments to seek greater freedoms and caused the collapse of communism.

2. Responses will vary. Students might suggest that Chinese adults viewed the cultural revolution with fear. But other adults might have been swept up by Mao's propaganda. While in the short term, the Cultural Revolution demonstrated Mao's power, in the long run, it contributed to his decline.

3. Answers should mention that these groups used boycotts, peaceful marches, and lobbying for legislation to increase their rights. The results were changes in laws to help create greater equality.

Connections to Today

1. Sample: Both conflicts included a military standoff with nuclear weapons. India and Pakistan, however, had a direct conflict between two nations. The United States and the Soviet Union never confronted each other directly. Instead each fought through allies or against the other's allies.

2. Responses should reflect accurate information and good organization.

For additional review of this chapter's core concepts, remind students to refer to the **L3**

Reading and Note Taking Study Guide
Concept Connector, pp. 242, 255, 262, 275

647

Chapter Assessment

Terms, People, and Places

1. containment
2. Ho Chi Minh
3. European Community
4. 38th parallel
5. recession
6. détente

Main Ideas

7. The Soviet Union pursued communist ideas while the United States and Western Europe followed democratic principles. The Cold War developed as each built up its military to protect and advance its own ideology.

8. a balance of terror based on mutually assured destruction coupled with a series of disarmament talks

9. The civil rights and women's movements expanded democracy, while the country enjoyed economic prosperity.

10. As trade increased, the economies of these nations prospered.

11. The U.S. strongly opposed Communist China for its support of North Korea in the Korean War, and saw it as a threat to Asia. After China's split with the Soviet Union, however, the U.S. saw China as a useful partner in opposing Soviet power.

12. It believed that communism in Vietnam would spread through the region.

13. They loosened the government's hold on the economy and fueled unrest.

14. The Soviet republics gained independence, and Eastern European nations moved toward democracy; in Germany the Berlin Wall was removed and the nation reunited.

Chapter Focus Question

15. The Cold War developed as a result of a power struggle between the U.S. and the Soviet Union. It led to fear in the U.S. and economic stagnation and political repression in communist countries. It ended when these factors became unbearable for citizens and leaders in communist countries.

Critical Thinking

16. Sample: frustrated because they were now unable to travel freely or sad because they were unable to visit family on the opposite side

17. Postwar demand for exports, the ability to rebuild infrastructure and

---

Chapter Assessment

Terms, People, and Places

Choose the italicized term in parentheses that best completes each sentence.

1. The United States aimed to prevent the spread of communism through a policy of (*containment/glasnost*).
2. (*Ngo Dinh Diem/Ho Chi Minh*) was the leader of North Vietnam.
3. European nations eliminated barriers to trade by establishing the (*welfare state/European Community*).
4. At the end of the Korean War, a cease-fire line was established near the (*38th parallel/Pusan Perimeter*).
5. A period of economic decline is a (*budget deficit/recession*).
6. During the 1970s, the United States and the Soviet Union had a period of reduced Cold War tensions known as (*collectivization/détente*).

Main Ideas

Section 1 (pp. 604–612)
7. How did the Cold War develop in the Soviet Union, Europe, and the United States?
8. What were the main features of the nuclear arms race?

Section 2 (pp. 614–622)
9. How did political and economic life change during the Cold War years in the United States?
10. What was the relationship between economic growth and trade in Western Europe and Japan?

Section 3 (pp. 623–629)
11. How did the Korean War influence U.S. relations with Communist China? How did those relations change as a result of hostility between China and the Soviet Union?

Section 4 (pp. 630–635)
12. Why did the United States enter the Vietnam War?

Section 5 (pp. 638–644)
13. How did Gorbachev's reforms lead to the breakup of the Soviet Union?
14. What events marked the end of the Cold War?

Chapter Focus Question
15. How did the Cold War develop, how did it shape political and economic life in individual nations, and how did it end?

Critical Thinking

16. **Analyze Visuals** Turn to the photo of the Berlin Wall on the first page of this chapter. How do you think that the Berliners in this photo felt about the wall that had been built through their city?

17. **Make Comparisons** What factors contributed to economic booms after World War II in Western Europe, the United States and Japan? Why was the economic performance of Eastern Europe and the Soviet Union different?

18. **Draw Inferences** You have read that the leaders of the Soviet Union retained power in Poland and elsewhere in Eastern Europe for over forty years. How were they able to do so despite lacking the consent of the governed?

19. **Predict Consequences** During the Cold War, many nations formed alliances with one superpower for protection against the other. After the Cold War, the United States emerged as the sole superpower. How might this change the nature of alliances?

20. **Recognize Cause and Effect** Which factors allowed North Vietnam to achieve victory over South Vietnam? What were some consequences of North Vietnam's victory in Vietnam and other parts of Southeast Asia?

● **Writing About History**

In this chapter's five Section Assessments, you developed skills to write a problem-solving essay.

Writing a Problem-Solution Essay Write a problem-solution essay on one of the Cold War problems listed below. Problems to address include the military standoff on the Iron Curtain, the arms race, and the division of Germany, Korea, or Vietnam. Consult page SH10 of the Writing Handbook for additional help.

Prewriting
• Go online or do library research to find evidence on each of the problems listed above.
• Choose the problem that interests you most and take notes about the evidence you find.

• Decide on the best solution to this problem and gather the evidence that supports your solution.

Drafting
• Write a first paragraph stating the problem and explaining why it is important.
• Write a thesis statement arguing for your solution to the problem.
• Write a second paragraph beginning with your thesis statement, followed by sentences providing evidence to support your thesis.

Revising
• Use the guidelines for revising your report on page SH12 of the Writing Handbook.

---

industry after wartime destruction, and skilled workers fueled economic booms. Eastern Europe and the Soviet Union had command economies that were slower to recover.

18. by suppressing free speech, imprisoning or exiling people, and making an example out of those who disagreed

19. Countries formerly allied with the Soviet Union had to forge new alliances with the United States or survive without such alliances and support.

20. North Vietnam's communist allies in South Vietnam knew the land and had the support of local populations, which led to North Vietnam's victory in the South. The victorious Vietnamese communists used their strength to back communist governments in neighboring Cambodia and Laos.

Document-Based Assessment

Cold War Chills

The United States and the Soviet Union confronted each other in the Cold War—a global conflict that included a nuclear arms race. In Document A, Nikita Khrushchev discusses the border fortifications that prevented East Germans from entering West Germany. In Document B, U.S. Vice President Richard Nixon warns Khrushchev about restricting western access to Berlin.

Document A

"Seeing that their government had reasserted control over its own frontiers, the East Germans were heartened by the solidification and fortification of their state. . . . I know there are people who claim that the East Germans are imprisoned in paradise and that the gates of the Socialist paradise are guarded by armed troops. I'm aware that a defect exists, but I believe it's a necessary and only temporary defect."

—From ***Khrushchev Remembers*** by Nikita Khrushchev

Document B

". . . I hope the Prime Minister has understood all the implications of what I said," Nixon went on, with an oblique [indirect] reference to Berlin. "What I mean is that the moment we place either one of these powerful nations, through an ultimatum, in a position where it has no choice but to accept dictation or fight, then you are playing with the most destructive force in the world."

Khrushchev: (flushed, wagging a finger near Nixon's face): We too are giants. If you want to threaten, we will answer threat with threat.

Nixon: We never engage in threats.

Khrushchev: You wanted indirectly to threaten me. But we have means at our disposal that can have very bad consequences.

Nixon: We have too.

—From ***Time***, August 3, 1959

Document C

Divided Germany and Berlin, 1949–1990

Document D

Fortifications that kept East Germans from crossing into West Germany

Analyzing Documents

Use your knowledge of the Cold War and Documents A, B, C, and D to answer questions 1–4.

1. The author's purpose in Document A was to
   A explain East German discipline.
   B offer a balanced perspective on the Cold War.
   C argue for a fortified barrier between East and West Germany.
   D explain the role of the Soviet Union in East Germany.

2. The tone of the exchange in Document B is
   A friendly and joking.
   B tense and hostile.
   C cautious.
   D businesslike.

3. Document C shows that
   A West Berlin was located inside West Germany.
   B the border between East and West Germany passed through Berlin.
   C East Germany surrounded West Germany.
   D two East German borders separated West Berlin from West Germany.

4. **Writing Task** How was the Cold War fought? Use what you have read in the chapter, along with these documents, to write a response.

Document-Based Assessment

- To help students understand the documents on the page, give them the following **TIP: Read the documents several times to make sure you understand them.**

- To provide students with further practice in answering Document-Based Assessment Questions, go to

  Document-Based Assessment, pp. 95–109

- If students need more instruction on synthesizing information, have them read the **Skills Handbook,** p. SH33.

● Writing About History

As students begin the assignment, refer them to p. SH10 of the **Writing Handbook** for help in writing an expository essay. Remind them of the steps they should take to complete their assignment, including prewriting, drafting, and revising. For help in revising, remind them to use the guidelines on p. SH12 of the **Writing Handbook.**

Students' problem-and-solution essays should identify a problem, propose a solution, and reflect thorough research. They should contain an introduction, a body, and a conclusion. They should show evidence of reflection and be free of grammatical and spelling errors. For scoring rubrics for writing assignments, see **Assessment Rubrics,** p. 8.

Answers

1. C
2. B
3. D
4. Responses should show a clear understanding of the issues and should use specific evidence from the documents and the chapter to support students' conclusions.

CHAPTER 19
New Nations Emerge

Section	Core Instruction L3	Differentiated Instruction L1 L2 L4

Section 1
Independent Nations of South Asia

🕐 **1.5 periods, .75 block**

OBJECTIVES
- Understand why independence brought partition to South Asia.
- Describe how Indian leaders built a new nation.
- Summarize how Pakistan and Bangladesh grew apart.
- Explain how India and Pakistan pursued independence from the superpowers in their foreign relations.

Focus Question *How did nationalist demands for independence affect South Asia and the world?*

All in One Teaching Resources, Unit 5
Reading Strategy: Identify Causes and Effects, p. 28
Vocabulary Builder, p. 27
Section 1 Quiz, p. 23

Reading and Note Taking Study Guide
Note Taking Study Guide, p. 200
Section 1 Summary, p. 201

Note Taking Transparencies, 194

WITNESS HISTORY Audio CD
Fleeing Amid Religious Violence

Progress Monitoring Transparencies, 133

Color Transparencies, 187, 188

Teaching Resources, Skills Handbook
Prereading the Chapter, pp. 1–2
Word Knowledge Rating Form, p. 3
K-W-L Chart p. 4

Witness History Discovery School™
video program, *Pakistan: Improving Education*

L1 Adapted Reading and Note Taking Study Guide
Note Taking Study Guide, p. 200 SN
Section 1 Summary, p. 201 SN

L2 Adapted Reading and Note Taking Study Guide
Note Taking Study Guide, p. 200 LPR
Section 1 Summary, p. 201 LPR

Spanish Reading and Note Taking Study Guide
Note Taking Study Guide, p. 200 ELL
Section 1 Summary, p. 201 ELL

L4 All in One Teaching Resources, Unit 5
Viewpoints: The Creation of Pakistan, p. 29 AR, GT
Biography: Indira Gandhi, p. 30 AR, GT
Literature: From "Under the Banyan Tree," by R.K. Narayan, p. 32 AR, GT

***Student Edition Audio SN**

Differentiated Instruction Activity, Teacher's Edition, p. 655 SN

***Guided Reading Audio, Spanish ELL**

***Student Edition Audio LPR**

Differentiated Instruction Activity, Teacher's Edition, p. 655 LPR, ELL

Differentiated Instruction Activity, Teacher's Edition, p. 656 AR, GT

Extend Activity, Teacher's Edition, p. 657 AR, GT

Section 2
New Nations of Southeast Asia

🕐 **1.5 periods, .75 block**

OBJECTIVES
- Explain the political and economic contrasts in mainland Southeast Asia.
- Understand how Indonesia's size posed challenges.
- Summarize how the Philippines sought democracy.

Focus Question *What challenges did Southeast Asian nations face after winning independence?*

All in One Teaching Resources, Unit 5
Section 2 Quiz, p. 24

Reading and Note Taking Study Guide
Note Taking Study Guide, p. 202
Section 2 Summary, p. 203

Note Taking Transparencies, 195

WITNESS HISTORY Audio CD
All for All

Progress Monitoring Transparencies, 134

Color Transparencies, 186, 192

L1 Adapted Reading and Note Taking Study Guide
Note Taking Study Guide, p. 202 SN
Section 2 Summary, p. 203 SN

L2 Adapted Reading and Note Taking Study Guide
Note Taking Study Guide, p. 202 LPR
Section 2 Summary, p. 203 LPR

L4 Extend Activity,
Teacher's Edition, pp. 650c, 661 AR, GT

Differentiated Instruction Activity, Teacher's Edition, p. 660 SN

Spanish Reading and Note Taking Study Guide
Note Taking Study Guide, p. 202 ELL
Section 2 Summary, p. 203 ELL

Differentiated Instruction Activity, Teacher's Edition, p. 660 LPR, ELL

*Audio support is available for all sections.

Assessment Resources
- **Progress Monitoring Transparencies,** 133–136
- **SuccessTracker™,** Chapter 19
- **Document-Based Assessment,** pp. 95–109
- **ExamView® Test Bank CD-ROM,** Chapter 19

- **All in One Teaching Resources, Unit 5,** Chapter Tests, pp. 37–42
- **Progress Monitoring Online Quizzes,** Chapter 19
- **Assessment Rubrics**

Differentiated Instruction Key
L1 Special Needs	LPR Less Proficient Readers
L2 Basic to Average	AR Advanced Readers
L3 All Students	SN Special Needs Students
L4 Average to Advanced	GT Gifted and Talented
	ELL English Language Learner

Section	Core Instruction **L3**	Differentiated Instruction **L1 L2 L4**	
Section 3 *African Nations Gain Independence* **1.5 periods, .75 block** **OBJECTIVES** ■ Describe how Africa's colonies gained independence. ■ Explain how Africans built new nations. ■ Analyze the recent histories of five African nations. **Focus Question** *What challenges did new African nations face?*	**All in One Teaching Resources, Unit 5** Section 3 Quiz, p. 25 Outline Map: Independence in Africa, p. 34 Geography Quiz, p. 36 **Reading and Note Taking Study Guide** Note Taking Study Guide, p. 204 Section 3 Summary, p. 205 **Note Taking Transparencies,** 196 **WITNESS HISTORY Audio CD** Kenya Achieves Independence **Progress Monitoring Transparencies,** 135 **Color Transparencies,** 189, 190, 191	**L1 Adapted Reading and Note Taking Study Guide** Note Taking Study Guide, p. 204 SN Section 3 Summary, p. 205 SN **L2 Adapted Reading and Note Taking Study Guide** Note Taking Study Guide, p. 204 LPR Section 3 Summary, p. 205 LPR **L4 Differentiated Instruction Activity,** Teacher's Edition, p. 664 AR, GT	**Differentiated Instruction Activity,** Teacher's Edition, p. 665 SN **Spanish Reading and Note Taking Study Guide** Note Taking Study Guide, p. 204 ELL Section 3 Summary, p. 205 ELL **Differentiated Instruction Activity,** Teacher's Edition, p. 665 LPR, ELL **Extend Activity,** Teacher's Edition, p. 668 AR, GT
Section 4 *The Modern Middle East* **2.5 periods, 1.25 blocks** **OBJECTIVES** ■ Analyze the diversity of the Middle East and the political challenges it has faced. ■ Explain the region's conflicts over resources and religion. ■ Outline the history of nation-building in three Middle Eastern nations. **Focus Question** *What were some similarities and differences in the nations of the Middle East?*	**All in One Teaching Resources, Unit 5** Outline Map: Nations of the Middle East, p. 35 Section 4 Quiz, p. 26 **Reading and Note Taking Study Guide** Note Taking Study Guide, p. 206 Section 4 Summary, p. 207 Concept Connector, pp. 255, 270, 284, 291 **Note Taking Transparencies,** 197 **WITNESS HISTORY Audio CD** Remembering Nasser **Progress Monitoring Transparencies,** 136	**L1 Adapted Reading and Note Taking Study Guide** Note Taking Study Guide, p. 206 SN Section 4 Summary, p. 207 SN Concept Connector, pp. 255, 270, 284, 291 SN **L2 Adapted Reading and Note Taking Study Guide** Note Taking Study Guide, p. 206 LPR Section 4 Summary, p. 207 LPR Concept Connector, pp. 255, 270, 284, 291 LPR **L4 All in One Teaching Resources, Unit 5** Biography: Gamal Abdel Nasser, p. 31 AR, GT Primary Source: From *Egypt's Liberation: The Philosophy of the Revolution*, by Gamal Abdel Nasser, p. 33 AR, GT	**Differentiated Instruction Activity,** Teacher's Edition, p. 671 SN **Spanish Reading and Note Taking Study Guide** Note Taking Study Guide, p. 206 ELL Section 4 Summary, p. 207 ELL Concept Connector, pp. 255, 270, 284, 291 ELL **Differentiated Instruction Activity,** Teacher's Edition, p. 671 LPR, ELL **Differentiated Instruction Activity,** Teacher's Edition, p. 674 AR, GT **Extend Activity,** Teacher's Edition, p. 675 AR, GT

CHAPTER PLANNER

Author's Notes

The Liberation Struggle

The great liberation [of Africa from European colonialism] dramatically transformed the global political picture. A total of ninety new countries emerged between the mid-1940s and the 1990s. Well over a billion people—a third of the earth's population—gained their independence of foreign rule. . . .

The liberation struggles were a complex, confusing business, but some general patterns can be detected.

The leaders of the various movements for colonial emancipation tended to be both Westernized and charismatic. As Western-educated people, they could deal effectively with their European rulers. The internationally known poet Léopold Senghor of French West Africa and Kwame Nkrumah of the British Gold Coast colony (today's Ghana), educated in France and in Britain and the United States, had no trouble dealing effectively with Westerners. As charismatic figures, flamboyant personalities such as Sukarno of the Dutch East Indies (Indonesia) and saintly ones such as Mahatma Gandhi in India could move their own people to action.

The strength of many colonial revolts also resided in powerful independence parties put together by the new colonial leadership. These intensely nationalistic organizations were strongly centralized on the person of the leader. They helped to overcome regional, religious, tribal, or other differences within the colony, to articulate common demands, and to mobilize mass support for challenges to colonial authority. After independence was achieved, however, these parties tended to become a stronger focus for loyalty than the new nation itself. In some places, they became the core of one-party governments.

In some of the emerging nations, as we shall see, bitter and sometimes long-drawn-out revolutions were fought before independence was achieved. In general, however, a relatively low level of violence—by comparison, say, with the long revolutions of the first half of the century—accompanied the great liberation.

—Anthony Esler, *The Human Venture: From Prehistory to the Present*, (Upper Saddle River, New Jersey: Pearson Education, 2004), pp. 695–696

Extend Online

History in the Making

Using the steps below, have students research recent events in a country in one of the regions covered in this chapter (South Asia, Southeast Asia, Africa, or the Middle East). Have students discuss their findings in class.

Prepare for the Activity Explain that each country in the regions discussed in this chapter has its own history and has had unique challenges and successes. These countries have dealt with many of the themes of the chapter, such as ethnic and religious diversity, the search for peace and political stability, and the struggle for democracy.

Conduct the Activity For help in starting the activity, send students to **Web Code nbe-3101.** Each student will research a country from one of the regions covered. Have students find out how their country has dealt with any ethnic or religious diversity, political unrest, whether the country has a democratic government, and what challenges the country currently faces. Have students write a one-paragraph summary of their findings and be prepared to discuss them in class.

Follow-Up Conduct a class discussion based on the following questions: How have nations in Africa and Asia dealt with ethnic and religious diversity? What progress have countries in these regions made in moving toward democracy?

Differentiated Instruction   Solutions for All Learners

Give One, Get One

Use the following steps to help foster independent reflection and peer interaction before a class discussion.

1. Pose a thought-provoking question to the class.

2. Allow students time to consider what they may already know about the topic and jot down potential responses.

3. Ask students to place a check mark next to the two or three ideas that they perceive as their strongest and then draw a line after their final idea to separate their ideas from those that they will gather from classmates.

4. Give students a set amount of time (about eight to ten minutes) to get up from their seats and share ideas with a classmate. After finding a partner, the two students should exchange papers and quietly read each other's ideas. Then they should discuss the ideas briefly, select one idea from their partner's list, and add it to their own, making sure to accurately copy the idea and their partner's name. Then have students exchange partners.

5. At the end of the exchange period, facilitate a unified class discussion. Call on a volunteer to share one new idea acquired from a conversation partner. The student whose idea has just been reported will then share the next idea, pulled from a different conversation partner.

Modeling Reading and Writing Skills

Gathering Information Tell students that in this chapter, they will be writing a problem-solution essay (See Writing About History, p. 678). When proposing a solution to a problem, students must persuade their audience that their proposed solution is likely to work.

On the board, write the following types of evidence that can be used to present convincing detail:

A Statistics
B Expert opinion
C Comparable situations

Explain that statistics provide relevant numerical data that can be used to back up a claim. Expert opinion includes the advice of those who have experience related to the problem, while comparable situations describe how similar real-life scenarios were resolved. Ask students to brainstorm places where they might look to find each type of supporting detail for a problem-solution essay on ways to encourage European unity.

Analyze Text Structure Remind students that authors organize their text to suit a specific purpose. For example, an advertisement and a newspaper article will probably be set up differently, since the advertisement's goal is to persuade, while the article's goal is to inform. Write these guidelines for evaluating text structure on the board:

1. Head structure: What is the largest head on the page? What information do these heads provide?

2. Images: What images are included? Where? How do the images support information in the text? What is their purpose?

3. Organization: What information appears on the first page? Why? What information appears inside? Why?

To model this skill, show students the text structure of Section 2 and the Infographic on Religious Diversity in Southeast Asia within that section. Note that the main text is structured so it effectively compares and contrasts points about the new nations in this region. The Infographic, however relies more heavily on visuals and uses a map and graph to depict the region's religious diversity.

<CHAPTER>

19 New Nations Emerge
1945–Present

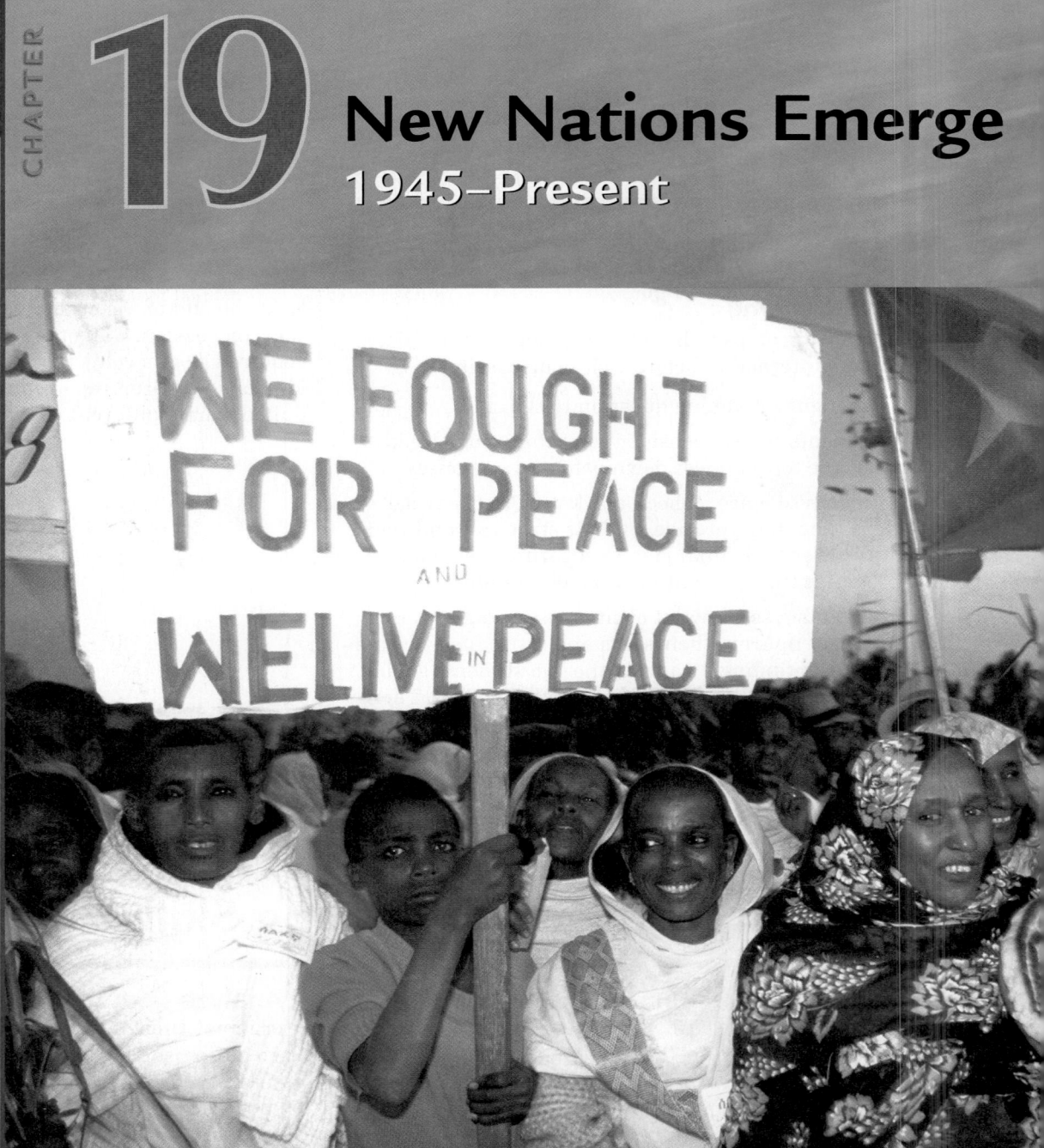

Bibliography

For the Teacher
Bose, Sumantra. *Kashmir: Roots of Conflict, Paths to Peace.* Harvard University Press, 2003.
Cooper, Frederick. *Africa Since 1940: The Past of the Present.* Series: New Approaches to African History. Cambridge University Press, 2002.
Nafisi, Azar. *Reading Lolita in Tehran: A Memoir in Books.* New York: Random House, 2003.

For the Student
- L4 Hakakian, Roya. *Journey from the Land of No: A Girlhood Caught in Revolutionary Iran.* New York: Crown Publishers, 2004.
- L3 Shilington, Kevin. *Independence in Africa.* Raintree Steck-Vaughn, 1998.
- L2 Long, Cathryn J. *The Middle East in Search of Peace.* Millbrook, 1996.

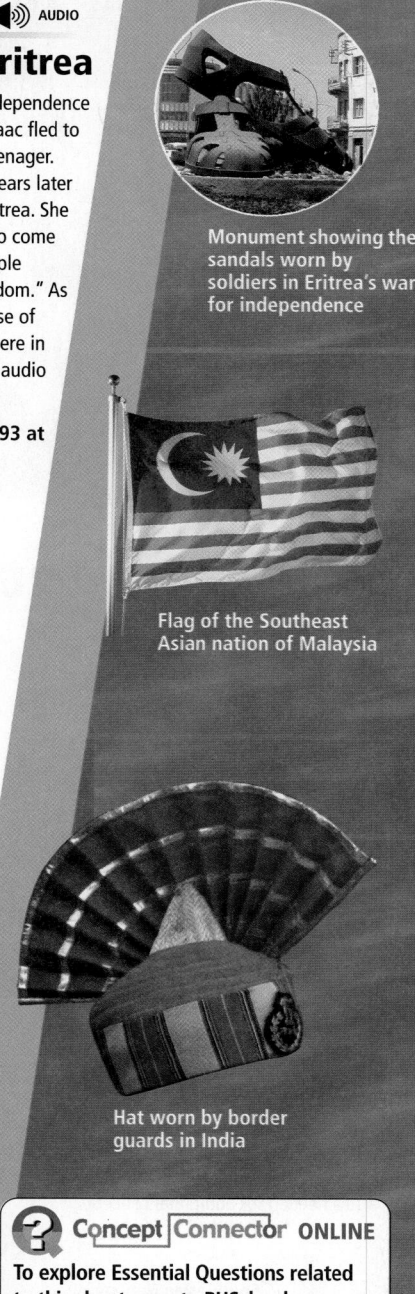

WITNESS HISTORY AUDIO

Independence in Eritrea

To escape the dangers of the war for independence in the African nation of Eritrea, Almaz Isaac fled to America as a refugee when she was a teenager. When Eritrea won its independence ten years later and peace returned, Almaz returned to Eritrea. She said, "This is the first time I've been able to come back, to see my family. We waited, our people fought, and now this is it. We have our freedom." As in Eritrea, independence brought a new sense of hope to many countries in Africa and elsewhere in recent decades. Listen to the Witness History audio to hear more about independence in Africa.

◄ **Eritreans celebrate independence in 1993 at the end of their long war for freedom.**

Chapter Preview

Chapter Focus Question How did former European colonies gain independence, and what challenges did they face after independence?

Use the ☑ **Quick Study Timeline** at the end of this chapter to preview chapter events.

Monument showing the sandals worn by soldiers in Eritrea's war for independence

Flag of the Southeast Asian nation of Malaysia

Hat worn by border guards in India

Concept Connector ONLINE
To explore Essential Questions related to this chapter, go to PHSchool.com
Web Code: nbd-3107

Chapter-Level Resources

All in One Vocabulary Builder; Reading Strategy; Enrichments; Outline Maps; Geography Quiz; Chapter Tests
- Document-Based Assessments
- AYP Monitoring Assessments
- *ExamView* Test Bank CD-ROM
- Guided Reading Audio (Spanish)
- Student Edition Audio

Previewing the Chapter

- **WITNESS HISTORY** Have students locate Eritrea on a map. Explain that most African countries gained independence directly from European colonial powers. Eritrea had been an Italian colony, but it was taken over by Ethiopia after World War II. It finally gained independence from Ethiopia in 1993. Read the Witness History selection aloud or play the accompanying audio. Ask students to predict challenges that a newly independent country might face. Tell them that they will learn more about the many countries that gained their independence after World War II in this chapter.

  ◄)) AUDIO **Witness History Audio CD,** Independence in Eritrea

- **Analyzing the Visuals** Ask students to study the photo of Eritreans celebrating their country's independence. Ask **What challenges does the sign held by the woman suggest that Eritrea faced after independence?** *(preventing conflicts within the country; finding peacetime work for former fighters)* Have students discuss ways in which independence might make it easier or more difficult to meet those challenges.

- **Focus** Write the Chapter Focus Question on the board. Tell students to keep this question in mind as they read the chapter. *(Answer appears with the Chapter Assessment answers.)* Have students preview the section titles for this chapter.

Differentiated Instruction   Solutions for All Learners

The following Teacher's Edition strategies are suitable for students of varying abilities.

L1 Special Needs Students, pp. 655, 660, 665, 671 **SN**

L2 English Language Learners, pp. 655, 660, 665, 671 **ELL**

L2 Less Proficient Readers, pp. 655, 660, 665, 671 **LPR**

L4 Gifted and Talented Students, pp. 656, 664, 674 **GT**

L4 Advanced Readers, pp. 656, 664, 674 **AR**

Note Taking Study Guide With Concept Connector Journal
For online access: Web code nbd-3107
For print alternative: Reading and Note Taking Study Guide booklet

Objectives

As you teach this section, keep students focused on the following objectives to help them answer the Section Focus Question and master core content.

- Understand why independence brought partition to South Asia.
- Describe how Indian leaders built a new nation.
- Summarize how Pakistan and Bangladesh grew apart.
- Explain how India and Pakistan pursued independence from the superpowers in their foreign relations.

Prepare to Read

Build Background Knowledge L3

Ask students to recall conflicts within India's nationalist movement before World War II. Have them predict challenges that the newly-independent region might face.

Set a Purpose L3

- **WITNESS HISTORY** Read the selection aloud or play the audio.

   AUDIO **Witness History Audio CD,** Fleeing Amid Religious Violence

  Ask **What does Damyanti Sahgal's account suggest about the conflict between Hindus and Muslims?** (*It was intense and full of hatred.*)

- **Focus** Point out the Section Focus Question and write it on the board. Tell students to refer to this question as they read. (*Answer appears with Section 1 Assessment answers.*)

- **Preview** Have students preview the Section Objectives and the list of Terms, People, and Places.

- **Reading Skill** Have students use the *Reading Strategy: Identify Causes and Effects* worksheet.

  All in One Teaching Resources, Unit 5, p. 28

- **Note Taking** Have students use the Structured Read Aloud strategy (TE, p. T20). As they read, have them fill in the concept web with causes and effects.

  Reading and Note Taking Study Guide, p. 200

A family of refugees flees the religious violence that broke out during the partition of India.

Hat worn by Indian border guards along the border with Pakistan

WITNESS HISTORY))) AUDIO

Fleeing Religious Violence

At independence, India was partitioned, or divided, into India and Pakistan, a new, largely Muslim country. Damyanti Sahgal, a Hindu, describes fleeing from Hindu-Muslim violence during the partition.

66 When we came close to Amritsar, we found that they had started stopping trains, killing people in them, but we were lucky. Everyone said put your windows up, they are cutting down people. 99

While people in India and Pakistan welcomed independence, they had to live with the violence of partition and its legacy of distrust.

Focus Question How did nationalist demands for independence affect South Asia and the world?

Independent Nations of South Asia

Objectives

- Understand why independence brought partition to South Asia.
- Describe how Indian leaders built a new nation.
- Summarize how Pakistan and Bangladesh grew apart.
- Explain how India and Pakistan pursued independence from the superpowers in their foreign relations.

Terms, People, and Places

partition	Indira Gandhi
Sikhs	Punjab
Kashmir	Golden Temple
Jawaharlal Nehru	Bangladesh
dalits	nonalignment

Note Taking

Reading Skill: Identify Causes and Effects Fill in a concept web like this one to keep track of causes and effects of events in South Asia. Add ovals as needed for additional concepts.

At the same time that the Cold War was unfolding, a global independence movement was reshaping the world. Among the first new nations to win independence were the former British colonies of South Asia.

Independence Brings Partition

Nationalists in British-ruled India had demanded self-rule since the late 1800s. As independence neared, however, a long-simmering issue surfaced. What would happen to the Muslim minority in a Hindu-dominated India?

Two New Nations Emerge Like Mohandas Gandhi, most of the leaders and members of the Congress Party were Hindus. However, the party wanted a unified India that would include both Muslims and Hindus. The Muslim League, led by Muhammad Ali Jinnah, had a different view of liberation. The Muslim League feared discrimination against the Muslim minority in a unified India. Therefore, the Muslim League demanded the creation of a separate nation, called Pakistan, that would include the parts of British India where Muslims formed a majority. In the 1940s, tensions between Muslims and the Hindu majority in British India led to increasing violence.

After World War II, the British government decided that it could no longer afford to resist Indian demands for independence.

Vocabulary Builder

Use the information below and the following resources to teach the high-use word from this section.
All in One Teaching Resources, Unit 5, p. 27; **Teaching Resources, Skills Handbook,** p. 3

High-Use Word	Definition and Sample Sentence
compel, p. 655	*v.* to make to or force One teacher **compelled** his students come to school for a study session on Saturday.

As independence approached, violence between Hindus and Muslims accelerated. In response, Britain decided to accept the idea of **partition,** or dividing the subcontinent into two nations. Hindu-dominated India, and Pakistan, which had a Muslim majority, both won independence on August 13, 1947.

Refugees Flee Amid Violence However, Hindus and Muslims still lived side by side in many cities and rural areas. As soon as the new borders became known, millions of Hindus on the Pakistani side of the borders packed up their belongings and fled to the new India. At the same time, millions of Muslims fled into newly created Pakistan. An estimated 10 million people fled their homes, most of them on foot.

Muslims fleeing along the crowded roads into Pakistan were slaughtered by Hindus and **Sikhs** (seeks), members of an Indian religious minority. Muslims massacred Hindu and Sikh neighbors. Around one million people died in these massacres. Others died of starvation and exposure on the road.

Struggles Over Kashmir Since independence, India and Pakistan have fought a series of wars over **Kashmir,** a state in the Himalayas. In 1947, Kashmir's Hindu ruler tried to join India. However, Kashmir's Muslim majority wanted to be part of Pakistan. For decades, Kashmiri separatists, often supported by Pakistani militants, have fought Indian troops. Indian and Pakistani forces have also battled along Kashmir's mountainous border. Today, Kashmir remains a flashpoint in the tense relations between India and Pakistan.

South Asian Nations

Geography *Interactive*
For: Audio guided tour
Web Code: nbp-3111

Under Chinese control

CHINA

AFGHANISTAN

Pakistani Kashmir

Indian Kashmir

Miller Projection
0   250   500 mi
0   250   500 km

PAKISTAN

BHUTAN

NEPAL

Ganges River

Tropic of Cancer

Arabian Sea

INDIA

BANGLADESH

MYANMAR

Bay of Bengal

15°N

Disputed area
Map shows boundaries of 2005

N
W   E
S

60°E   MALDIVES   75°E   SRI LANKA   90°E

Map Skills The former British colony of India had become the independent nations of Pakistan, India, and Bangladesh by 1971. The region's other nations had also achieved independence by that date. The status of Kashmir, however, remained in dispute.

1. **Locate** (a) Bangladesh (b) Pakistani Kashmir (c) Indian Kashmir
2. **Regions** Which other nation also has a stake in the Kashmir conflict?
3. **Make Inferences** Bangladesh was once part of Pakistan. How might its location have contributed to its people's desire for independence?

Teach

Independence Brings Partition

Instruct

- **Introduce: Key Terms** Direct students to the key term *partition* in the section title and (in blue) in the text, and ask them to explain its meaning. Have students predict the problems that might arise when an entire nation is partitioned. How might this affect individuals and their communities?

- **Teach** Display **Color Transparency 188: The Partition of India.** Trace the path from British-ruled India to the independent nations of India and Pakistan. Ask **Has partition led to peace? Explain.** (*No, India and Pakistan continue to fight over control of Kashmir and to engage in a nuclear arms race.*)

  📖 **Color Transparencies, 188**

- **Quick Activity** Have students access **Web Code nbp-3111** to take the **Geography Interactive Audio Guided Tour** and then answer the map skills questions in the text.

Independent Practice

- **Viewpoints** To help students better understand the debate over the partitioning of India, have them read the selection *The Creation of Pakistan* and complete the worksheet.

  All in One Teaching Resources, Unit 5, p. 29

- Display **Color Transparency 187: South Asia.** Have students locate Kashmir. Then ask them to write a paragraph explaining how the region's geography contributes to the conflict over its control.

  📖 **Color Transparencies, 187**

Monitor Progress

Check answers to map skills questions.

Answers

Map Skills
1. Review locations with students.
2. China
3. Sample: Because it is far from the rest of Pakistan, its people might want a separate state.

Building a Modern Nation

 L3

Instruct

- **Introduce** Recall with students the issues of religion at the heart of the conflict between India and Pakistan. Explain that while many Muslims left India, many stayed. Ask students why they think religion divided people so sharply. Use the Idea Wave strategy (TE, p. T22) and ask students to suggest things that would help Indian Hindus and Muslims to live together in peace.

- **Teach** Create two columns on the board, labeled *Social Challenges* and *Religious Challenges*. Have students fill in the problems India faced in each area. Have students use the chart on the next page to identify the main religious groups in India. Then discuss how religion has played a role in creating conflicts and influencing people's attitudes since independence.

- **Quick Activity** Ask student groups to choose one of India's social or religious challenges and propose solutions to that issue. For example, students might discuss ways to reduce tensions between Muslims and Hindus, or between the government and separatist Sikhs in Punjab.

Independent Practice

Biography To help students better understand the first female leader of India and her role in leading the new nation through challenging times, have them read the biography *Indira Gandhi* and complete the worksheet.

All in One Teaching Resources, Unit 5, p. 30

Monitor Progress

- To help students review the section so far, have them write one sentence for each black heading, stating the main idea of that subsection.

- As students fill in their concept webs, circulate to make sure they understand the causes and effects of partition. For a completed version of the concept web, see

  📖 Note Taking Transparencies, 194

Answer

✔ Each country wants to control this region, which is home to both Muslims and Hindus.

 654 New Nations Emerge

A Nuclear Arms Race In the 1970s, first India and then Pakistan developed nuclear weapons programs. By 1998, both nations had successfully tested nuclear weapons. The emergence of these two nuclear powers alarmed neighbors in South Asia and the world, in part because of the ongoing hostility between India and Pakistan. Another concern was the danger that extremists might get access to nuclear technology or even nuclear weapons.

Conflict Divides Sri Lanka The island of Ceylon won freedom from Britain in 1948. Later, it took the name Sri (sree) Lanka. Most Sri Lankans are Buddhists who speak Sinhalese. However, a large Tamil-speaking Hindu minority lives in the north and east. The Sri Lankan government favored the Sinhalese majority, which angered many Tamils. In the late 1970s, Tamil rebels battled to set up their own separate nation. For three decades, terrorism and brutality fed a deadly conflict between government forces and Tamil rebels. By 2009, the government had regained control of Tamil-held towns, but peace was by no means assured.

✔ **Checkpoint** Why was Kashmir a source of conflict between India and Pakistan?

Building a Modern Nation

At independence, India established a parliamentary democracy. Although India remains the world's largest democracy, it has faced many challenges. Ethnic and religious tensions threatened its unity. Its people speak over 100 languages and many dialects. Hundreds of millions of Indians lived in desperate poverty. Despite unrest and diversity, India has emerged as a major world power.

Strong Leaders During its early decades, India benefited from strong leadership. The Congress Party, which had spearheaded the independence movement, worked to turn India into a modern nation. From 1947 to 1964, **Jawaharlal Nehru,** leader of the Congress Party, was India's prime minister. He promoted economic growth and social change. Under Nehru, food output rose, but so did India's population. The government encouraged family planning to reduce the birthrate, but with limited success.

Although India's 1947 constitution banned discrimination against **dalits,** or people in the lowest castes, discrimination based on caste continued. Nehru's government set aside jobs and places in universities for dalits and other lower-caste Indians. Still, higher-caste Hindus generally got better schooling and jobs.

Later, Nehru's daughter, **Indira Gandhi,** served as prime minister for most of the years between 1966 and 1984. She led India with a firm hand and challenged traditional discrimination against women.

Religious Conflicts India was a land of many religions. A majority of Indians were Hindu, but millions were Muslim, Sikh, Christian, or Buddhist. At times, religious divisions led to violence.

Some Sikhs wanted independence for **Punjab,** a prosperous, largely Sikh state in northern India. In 1984, armed Sikh separatists

Indira Gandhi
Prime Minister Indira Gandhi led India from 1966 to 1977 and again from 1980 to 1984.

Connect to Our World

Connections to Today Some estimate that since 1987, the fight over Kashmir has claimed more than 60,000 lives. India believes that Kashmir rightly belongs to India and that it must protect Kashmir's Hindu minority; Pakistan supports Kashmir's Muslim majority and its right to self-rule. Now that both countries have tested nuclear weapons, this struggle has potentially disastrous repercussions. When fighting broke out between the two nuclear powers in 1999,

the world held its breath. After eleven weeks, both sides backed down.

Indian and Pakistani leaders are making efforts toward peace. In 2001, when an earthquake ravaged northwestern India, Pakistan's General Pervez Musharraf sent aid. In 2003, the two countries declared a ceasefire and began talks. U.S. and British envoys have pressured both sides for peace.

took dramatic action. They occupied the **Golden Temple,** the holiest Sikh shrine. When Indira Gandhi sent troops to oust them, bloody fighting erupted. Soon after, Gandhi was assassinated by her Sikh bodyguards, igniting terrible violence.

In the late 1980s, the Hindu nationalist party, Bharatiya Janata Party (BJP) challenged the secular, or nonreligious, Congress Party. The BJP wanted a government based on Hindu traditions and sometimes encouraged violence against Muslims.

✔ **Checkpoint** How did the Indian government try to improve conditions for lower castes?

Pakistan and Bangladesh Separate

Pakistan gained independence in 1947, at the same time as India. Geographically, it was a divided country, with West Pakistan and East Pakistan located on either side of India. A thousand miles of Indian territory separated the two regions, and India made trade and travel between the two Pakistans difficult.

Bangladesh Breaks Away From the start, West Pakistan dominated the government even though East Pakistan had a larger population. The government concentrated most economic development programs in West Pakistan, while East Pakistan remained deep in poverty. Most people in East Pakistan were Bengalis, while West Pakistan was home to other ethnic groups. Many Bengalis resented governmental neglect of East Pakistan.

In 1971, Bengalis in East Pakistan declared independence. They named their country **Bangladesh,** or "Bengali nation." When the Pakistani army tried to crush the rebellion, India sent forces to help Bangladesh. Pakistan was then <u>compelled</u> to recognize the new country.

Pakistan's Shaky Government After independence, Pakistan struggled to build a stable government. Power shifted back and forth between elected civilian leaders and military rulers. Tensions among the country's diverse ethnic groups posed problems. The fiercely independent people in the northwestern "tribal areas" were left largely on their own and resisted government control. The activities of Islamic fundamentalists created tension. The fundamentalists wanted a government that followed strict Islamic principles, while other Pakistanis wanted greater separation between religion and state.

Ongoing Challenges In 2008, after nine years in power, General Pervez Musharraf allowed elections. Before the election, Islamic extremists assassinated one of the candidates, Benazir Bhutto, a popular former prime minister. Pakistan's new civilian government faced tough challenges, including the global economic recession.

Meanwhile, support for Islamic fundamentalist groups based in Pakistan grew, especially in the northwest. In November 2008, Islamic militants from Pakistan launched terror attacks on hotels and tourists in Mumbai, India, fueling tensions between the hostile neighbors.

Religions of India

Religion	Population (millions)	Percentage	Regional Concentration
Hinduism	828	80.5	Throughout India
Islam	138	13.4	Kashmir, Northern India, Southwest Coast
Christianity	24	2.3	Northeastern India, Southwest Coast
Sikhism	19	1.9	Northwestern India
Buddhism	8	0.8	Northeastern India, West Coast
Others	11	1.0	Throughout India

Chart Skills What is India's largest minority religion? Where do most of its followers live?

SOURCE: Census of India 2001

WITNESS HISTORY VIDEO

Watch *Pakistan: Improving Education* on the **Witness History Discovery School**™ video program to see how teachers are being trained in Pakistan's countryside.

Vocabulary Builder

<u>compelled</u>—(kum PELD) *v.* made to or forced

Finding an Independent Path L3

Instruct

- **Introduce: Key Terms** Ask students to find the key term *nonalignment* (in blue) in the text and explain its meaning. Ask them to recall that during the Cold War, the Soviet Union and the United States sought to advance their influence over other nations. Ask students to speculate on how people in newly independent nations might react to those attempts. How might less powerful nations work together to resist the influence of the Soviet Union and the United States?

- **Teach** Describe how India and Pakistan worked to organize newly independent states. Ask **What was nonalignment?** *(a policy of remaining politically and diplomatically independent from both the United States and Soviet Union)* **How did nonalignment unite newly independent nations?** *(Many wanted to remain neutral—or nonaligned—in the Cold War struggle between the United States and Soviet Union.)* **Why might newly independent nations be particularly interested in nonalignment?** *(They had recently emerged from external colonial control and wished to avoid control by the United States or Soviet Union.)*

Independent Practice

Tell students to suppose that they are representatives at the 1961 meeting of nonaligned states. Have them write an argument in favor of the movement's goals. Have each student state how the movement will benefit the student's newly independent state.

Monitor Progress

- As students work on their arguments, check that they understand why newly independent states would be particularly interested in avoiding outside influences.

- Check Reading and Note Taking Study Guide entries for student understanding.

Answer

Caption Sample: Frequent floods disrupt the economy and cause damage to houses and businesses.

Islamic traditions were strong in the rugged border area between Pakistan and Afghanistan. When the Soviet Union invaded Afghanistan in 1979, one million Afghan refugees fled into Pakistan. There, many joined Islamic fundamentalist groups to battle the invaders.

After Russia withdrew from Afghanistan, the Taliban, an extreme Islamist group, seized power with the support of Pakistan. The Taliban backed Al Qaeda, which launched terrorist attacks on the United States in 2001. When U.S. forces invaded Afghanistan and overthrew the Taliban, its supporters fled into Pakistan. They set up strongholds in northwestern Pakistan, where their influence spread. Pakistan's government had limited success fighting the terrorists. However, it was angered by American missile attacks on suspected terrorists within its borders.

Bangladesh Struggles Bangladesh ranks among the world's poorest, most crowded countries. Its population, more than half as large as that of the United States, lives in an area the size of Alabama. The flat Ganges Delta, just a few feet above sea level, covers much of the country. Bangladesh has suffered repeatedly from devastating tropical storms and floods.

Floods Ravage Bangladesh
Summer rains often flood much of low-lying Bangladesh. Here, aid workers bring supplies to a family trapped on the roof of their home. *How might frequent floods hurt efforts to improve conditions in Bangladesh?*

Differentiated
Instruction   Solutions for All Learners

L4 Advanced Readers   **L4 Gifted and Talented**

South Asian nations were among the first in the world to elect women as leaders. The first was Sri Lanka, which elected Sirimavo Bandaranaike prime minister in 1960. Her daughter, Chandrika Kumaratunga, later became prime minister and then president. Indira Gandhi became India's prime minister in 1966. In 1988, Pakistan elected Benazir Bhutto prime minister.

Bangladesh has elected two women as prime ministers: Khaleda Zia and Sheikh Hasina. Have each student research one of these women and design a poster about her with text and pictures. Then hold a discussion about their similarities (for example, all were daughters or wives of popular politicians who were assassinated) and the challenges they faced.

Geographic conditions made it hard for the government to ease the desperate poverty that most people endure. One hopeful program, however, came from the Grameen Bank, founded by Bangladeshi economist Muhammad Yunus. It gave tiny loans, or "microcredit" to poor people so they could open small businesses. Although microcredit helped only a few, it offered a model to poor nations around the world. In 2006, Yunus was awarded the Nobel Peace Prize for his efforts.

✓ **Checkpoint** How did geography pose challenges for Bangladesh?

Finding an Independent Path

India and Pakistan were among the first of more than 90 new nations to emerge after World War II. By the 1930s, nationalist movements had taken root in European colonies across Africa, Asia, and the Middle East. After World War II, nationalist leaders such as Gandhi and Nehru insisted on independence. After India and Pakistan gained independence, nationalist leaders in Africa and other regions demanded the same for their countries.

India, Pakistan, and other new nations condemned colonialism and rejected Cold War expansion and the divisions between the West and the Soviet Union. In response, they sought **nonalignment,** or political and diplomatic independence from the Cold War superpowers. In 1955, India and Pakistan helped organize a conference of newly independent nations in Bandung, Indonesia, which marked the birth of the nonaligned movement.

The Nonaligned Movement had its first formal meeting in 1961 in Yugoslavia. India was a leader of the nonaligned movement, which came to include more than 100 nations, mainly in Asia, Africa, and Latin America. Because they rejected both the Western allies, or the First World, and the Soviet alliance, or the Second World, the Nonaligned Movement was seen as the voice of a "Third World" of countries.

✓ **Checkpoint** What global role did India and Pakistan play after independence?

SECTION 1
Assessment

Progress Monitoring *Online*
For: Self-quiz with vocabulary practice
Web Code: nba-3111

Terms, People, and Places
1. For each term, person, or place in the beginning of the section, write a sentence explaining its significance.

Note Taking
2. **Reading Skill: Identify Causes and Effects** Use your completed concept web to answer the Focus Question: What were the consequences of independence in South Asia for the region and for the world?

Comprehension and Critical Thinking
3. **Recognize Cause and Effect** Why did the partition of British India cause refugees to flee?
4. **Express Problems Clearly** What problems did India's religious diversity pose?
5. **Summarize** Why did Bangladesh separate from Pakistan?
6. **Draw Conclusions** How did a policy of nonalignment influence the relations of India and Pakistan with the Cold War superpowers?

● Writing About History
Quick Write: Outline Your Topic To write a compare-and-contrast essay, you need to consider two subjects and find similarities and differences between them. In this section, you learned that India and Pakistan share a common history but were separated at independence. Write features of each country's history in three lists: a list of features specific to India, a list of features specific to Pakistan, and a list of features shared by both countries.

Assess and Reteach

Assess Progress (L3)
- Have students complete the Section Assessment.
- Administer the Section Quiz.

  All in One Teaching Resources, Unit 5, p. 23
- To further assess student understanding, use

  🏛 **Progress Monitoring Transparencies,** 133

Reteach
If students need more instruction, have them read the section summary.

 Reading and Note Taking Study Guide, p. 201 (L3)

 Adapted Reading and Note Taking Study Guide, p. 201 (L1)(L2)

 Spanish Reading and Note Taking Study Guide, p. 201 (L2)

Extend (L4)
Link to Literature Have students read from *Under the Banyan Tree* by R.K. Narayan and complete the worksheet.

All in One Teaching Resources, Unit 5, p. 32

Answers

✓ Bangladesh lies just a few feet above sea level at the mouth of the Ganges River. As a result, it experiences frequent floods and tropical storms. In addition, it is densely populated.

✓ They helped organize the international Nonaligned Movement.

Section 1 Assessment

1. Sentences should reflect an understanding of each term, person, or place listed at the beginning of the section.
2. Nationalist demands led to independence in South Asia. After independence, India and Pakistan led the nonalignment movement, which included over 100 nations.
3. Religious violence between Muslims and Hindus drove people to flee areas where their religion was in the minority.
4. India faced religious unrest between majority Hindus and minority Sikhs and Muslims.
5. The people of East Pakistan broke away to form Bangladesh because they felt that West Pakistanis dominated the government of Pakistan.
6. Both Pakistan and India sought to avoid control by either superpower, in accordance with nonalignment.

● Writing About History
India: religious diversity with a Hindu majority; Pakistan: Muslim domination, division into Pakistan and Bangladesh amid ethnic conflict; Both: colonized by Britain, gained independence after WWII, nuclear weapons, poverty, nonalignment policy

For additional assessment, have students access **Progress Monitoring *Online*** at Web Code nba-3111.

Objectives

As you teach this section, keep students focused on the following objectives to help them answer the Section Focus Question and master core content.

- Explain the political and economic contrasts in mainland Southeast Asia.
- Understand how Indonesia's size posed challenges.
- Summarize how the Philippines sought democracy.

Prepare to Read

Build Background Knowledge ⏹

Ask students to recall the conflicts that emerged in India, Pakistan, and Sri Lanka after independence. Based on their previous reading, ask students to predict the challenges the nations of neighboring Southeast Asia will face as *they* gain independence.

Set a Purpose ⏹

- **WITNESS HISTORY** Read the selection aloud or play the audio.

  🔊 AUDIO **Witness History Audio CD,** All for All

  Ask **What was Sukarno advocating?** *(He felt that Indonesians must overcome religious or other differences and work together to build a successful new state in Indonesia.)*

- **Focus** Point out the Section Focus Question and write it on the board. Tell students to refer to this question as they read. *(Answer appears with Section 2 Assessment answers.)*

- **Preview** Have students preview the Section Objectives and the list of Terms, People, and Places.

- **Note Taking** Have students read this section using the Guided Questioning strategy (TE, p. T20). As they read, have students fill in the concept web recording effects of recent developments on Southeast Asia.

  📋 **Reading and Note Taking Study Guide,** p. 202

Indonesia's flag

WITNESS HISTORY 🔊 AUDIO

All for All

Most Southeast Asian nations are home to diverse people speaking many languages and practicing different religions. Indonesia's independence leader, Sukarno, stressed the importance of unity for his nation:

66 [W]e are establishing an Indonesian state which all of us must support. All for all. Not the Christians for Indonesia, not the Islamic group for Indonesia . . . but the Indonesians for Indonesia—all for all! 99

Achieving unity was one of many challenges that Indonesia faced after independence.

Focus Question What challenges did Southeast Asian nations face after winning independence?

Sukarno, Indonesia's first president

New Nations of Southeast Asia

Objectives

- Explain the political and economic contrasts in mainland Southeast Asia.
- Understand how Indonesia's size posed challenges.
- Summarize how the Philippines sought democracy.

Terms, People, and Places

autocratic	East Timor
Aung San Suu Kyi	Ferdinand Marcos
Sukarno	Benigno Aquino
Suharto	Corazon Aquino

Note Taking

Reading Skills: Understand Effects Fill in a concept web like the one below to keep track of the effects of recent historical processes in Southeast Asia. Add to it as needed for additional concepts in the section.

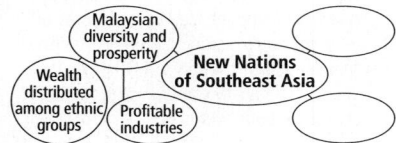

Southeast Asia includes part of the Asian mainland and thousands of islands that stretch from the Indian Ocean to the South China Sea. In 1939, most of the region was under colonial rule by European nations or the United States. During World War II, Japan seized the region. After the war, nationalist groups demanded independence and resisted reoccupation by European nations.

Mainland Contrasts

Mainland Southeast Asia is a region of contrasts. Thailand and Malaysia have mostly prospered as market economies, although they have been affected by global financial crises. However, nearby Myanmar has suffered under a brutal **autocratic,** or repressive, government with unlimited power.

Malaysia Prospers British colonies on the Malay Peninsula and the island of Borneo gained independence in the 1950s and joined to form the nation of Malaysia. The oil-rich monarchy of Brunei, on Borneo, and the prosperous city-state of Singapore gained independence as separate nations.

Malaysia has a very diverse population. People of Chinese and Indian descent have long dominated business. They have made the nation a Southeast Asian leader in profitable industries such as rubber and electronics. The government, however, has tried to include the Malay majority in the country's prosperity. The result has been a more equal distribution of wealth in Malaysia than in most countries in the region.

Vocabulary Builder

Use the information below and the following resources to teach the high-use word from this section.

All in One Teaching Resources, Unit 5, p. 27; **Teaching Resources, Skills Handbook,** p. 3

High-Use Word	Definition and Sample Sentence
predominant, p. 661	*adj.* most common or numerous Although buses are the **predominant** way of getting to school, I ride my bicycle.

Myanmar Suffers Burma won independence from Britain in 1948 and took the name Myanmar in 1989. Ethnic tensions and a repressive government have plagued the country. The Burmese majority dominated other ethnic groups. The harsh military government limited foreign trade, and living standards remained low.

Under mounting pressure, the military held elections in 1990. When an opposition party won the election, the military rejected the results. It put the opposition leader, Aung San Suu Kyi, (awn sahn soo chee) under house arrest, and jailed, killed, or exiled many opponents. In 1991, Suu Kyi won the Nobel Peace Prize for her "nonviolent struggle for democracy and human rights." For twenty years, the military has silenced demands for new elections and crushed peaceful demonstrations by Buddhist monks. It even prevented humanitarian aid from reaching areas of Myanmar that were devastated by a cyclone in 2008.

✔ **Checkpoint** How did Malaysia's approach to ethnic diversity differ from Myanmar's?

Indonesia's Size Poses Challenges

After World War II, the Netherlands attempted to regain power in Indonesia, formerly the Dutch East Indies. The Dutch, however, were forced to give up their possessions when the Indonesian government declared independence in 1949 after the Japanese defeat.

Geography and diversity posed an obstacle to unity in Indonesia. Indonesia includes more than 13,000 islands, many very small but some as large as European nations. Javanese make up almost half of the population, but there are hundreds of other ethnic groups. About 90 percent of Indonesians are Muslims, but the population includes substantial Christian, Buddhist, and Hindu minorities.

Seeking Stability At independence, Indonesia formed a parliamentary government under its first president, Sukarno. But Sukarno shifted from democracy to authoritarian rule. In 1967, an army general, Suharto, seized power. Suharto claimed that communists were responsible for an earlier attempt by military officers to overthrow the government and ordered the slaughter of hundreds of thousands of communists and suspected communists. For decades, Suharto imposed his will on Indonesia. A financial crisis finally forced Suharto to resign from power in 1998.

Since then, elected governments have worked to build democracy, strengthen the economy, and fight corruption. Indonesia is home to the world's largest Muslim population. But Islamic extremists have challenged Indonesia's long tradition of religious tolerance. Islamic terrorist groups in Indonesia have targeted foreigners and non-Muslims and threatened the stability of the government.

East Timor Fights for Freedom Indonesia seized East Timor in 1975, just after it had been granted independence by Portugal. However, most East Timorese wanted independence. For years, the government battled the mostly Catholic East Timorese. East Timor finally won independence from Indonesia in 2002. This very poor new nation struggled to meet its people's need for jobs and decent living standards.

Brunei's Oil Wealth
A few Southeast Asian nations such as Indonesia have oil and gas reserves. This oil well produces revenues for Brunei (broo NY), a tiny kingdom located on the island of Borneo.

History Background

A History of Diversity Indonesia is a diverse nation made up of thousands of islands and hundreds of different ethnic groups. Before independence, Indonesia was a Dutch colony. Before Dutch rule, however, Indonesia was made up of hundreds of independent sultanates and chiefdoms. Some parts of Indonesia, such as the provinces of Aceh and Papua, resisted Dutch rule right into the 1900s and have continued to resist Indonesian rule to this day. While a majority of Indonesians live on the crowded island of Java, even Java has three main ethnic groups, not including its sizable ethnic Chinese minority. A majority of Indonesians are Muslims, but most ethnic Chinese are Buddhists, and substantial Christian minorities exist on several islands. The island of Bali is noted for its ancient Hindu culture, brought by travelers from India more than a thousand years ago.

Indonesia's Size Poses Challenges/The Philippines Seeks Democracy L3

Instruct

- **Introduce** Ask students to recall some of the problems large nations such as the Soviet Union or Pakistan have faced due to their size or the isolation of their parts. Explain that both Indonesia and the Philippines are large groups of islands. Ask students to speculate how size and isolation might challenge these new nations.

- **Teach** Review the challenges that Indonesia faced in the years after independence. Discuss how the nation fell victim to dictatorship and how the nation faced ethnic and religious conflicts and natural disaster. Ask **How did Indonesia's geography influence its recent history?** (*The nation's size and ethnic diversity has led to regional movements for independence, and its location has left it vulnerable to tsunamis.*) Then discuss the challenges that the Philippines faced after its independence.

- **Quick Activity** Display **Color Transparency 186: Religions of Southeast Asia.** Then have students study the Infographic on Religious Diversity in Southeast Asia on this page. Have student groups discuss how diversity can both help and challenge a nation such as Indonesia or the Philippines.

  🏛 **Color Transparencies,** 186

Independent Practice

Have students create a timeline showing key events in the Philippines between 1945 and the present. Then ask students to write a sentence highlighting at least one cause-and-effect relationship reflected in the timeline.

Monitor Progress

As students complete their timelines, circulate to confirm that their information is accurate, that events are in sequence, and that they recognize the cause-and-effect relationships present.

Answers

Thinking Critically
1. the majority
2. Those groups are not a majority in any specific region of Malaysia. Instead, they are spread throughout the country.

✔ Diversity of religious, ethnic, and political groups has led to conflict and violence.

● INFOGRAPHIC

RELIGIOUS DIVERSITY IN SOUTHEAST ASIA

Southeast Asia is one of the world's most religiously diverse regions. This diversity is a result of its history as a crossroads between South and East Asia. In some countries, such as Indonesia and the Philippines, religious differences have played a part in civil conflicts. In others, such as Malaysia and Singapore, people of different religions live together in peace.

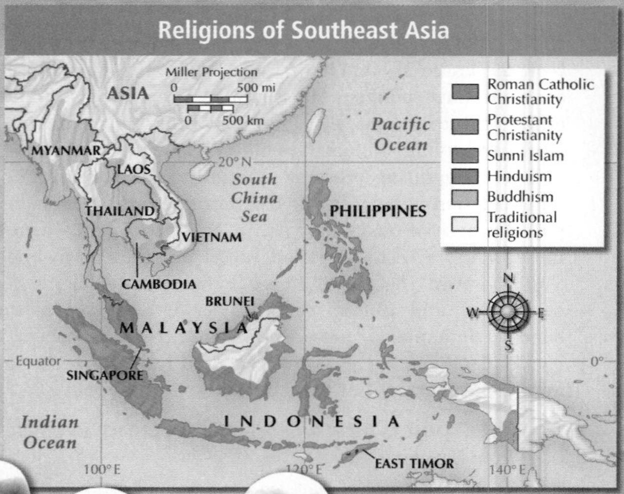

Islam links many Southeast Asians to other parts of the Muslim world. The Indonesian Muslim woman to the left is attending a prayer service for peace in the Middle East.

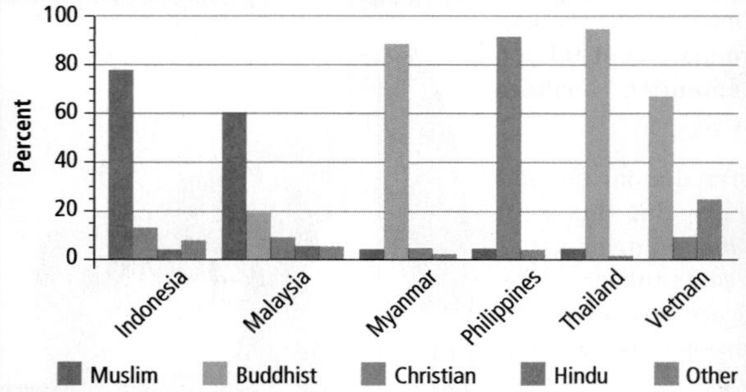

Religions of Southeast Asia

Legend:
- Roman Catholic Christianity
- Protestant Christianity
- Sunni Islam
- Hinduism
- Buddhism
- Traditional religions

Religious Composition of Major Southeast Asian Nations

(Bar graph: Percent, 0 to 100, for Indonesia, Malaysia, Myanmar, Philippines, Thailand, Vietnam)

Legend: ■ Muslim ■ Buddhist ■ Christian ■ Hindu ■ Other

SOURCE: *Encyclopaedia Britannica*

Buddhism plays an important role in the lives of many mainland Southeast Asians. In Thailand, all young Buddhist men are expected to live for at least a short time as monks, such as the ones in this photo.

Thinking Critically
1. **Graph Skills** Based on the graph, are the people in the two photos members of their country's majority or minority religion?
2. **Map Skills** Notice that some religious groups shown on the graph for Malaysia do not have distinct areas on the map. What might explain this?

Ethnic Conflicts and Natural Disasters Religious and ethnic conflicts fueled violence in parts of Indonesia. In the Moluccas, a group of eastern islands, fighting between Muslims and Christians killed thousands. Discrimination against Chinese people led to vicious attacks. Rebels in Papua, on the island of New Guinea, sought independence, as did Muslim separatists in Aceh (AH chay) in the northwest.

Natural disasters have added to Indonesia's troubles. In 2004, a tsunami (tsoo NAH mee), or giant wave, devastated the coast of Aceh and killed more than 100,000 people. The tsunami also ravaged Thailand, Sri Lanka, and other lands around the Indian Ocean. Following the disaster, rebels in Aceh and the Indonesian government signed a peace accord. Helped by international aid donors, they worked together to rebuild Aceh.

✔ **Checkpoint** How has diversity posed challenges to Indonesia?

Differentiated Instruction · Solutions for All Learners

L1 Special Needs **L2 Less Proficient Readers**

Have students create a three-column chart. In the first column, they should list Malaysia, Myanmar, Indonesia, East Timor, and the Philippines. In the next column, they should fill in each country's majority religion. Have them use the Infographic on this page to find that information. Finally, have them list key information about each country in the third column.

L2 English Language Learners

Use the following resources to help students acquire basic skills:

✏ **Adapted Reading and Note Taking Study Guide**
- Adapted Note Taking Study Guide, p. 202
- Adapted Section Summary, p. 203

The Philippines Seeks Democracy

Like Indonesia, the Philippines include thousands of islands with diverse ethnic and religious groups. Catholics are <u>predominant</u>, but many Muslims live in the south. In 1946, the Philippines gained independence after almost 50 years of American rule. American influence remained strong through military and economic aid.

Marcos Becomes a Dictator Although the Filipino constitution set up a democratic government, a wealthy elite controlled politics and the economy. The peasant majority was poor. For years, the government battled Huks (hooks), local communists with strong peasant support. **Ferdinand Marcos,** elected president in 1965, abandoned democracy. He became a dictator and cracked down on basic freedoms. He even had **Benigno Aquino** (beh NEE nyoh ah KEE noh), a popular rival, murdered.

Filipinos Demand Democracy When Marcos finally held elections in 1986, voters chose **Corazon Aquino** (kawr ah SOHN), the widow of the slain Benigno. Marcos tried to deny the results, but massive protests forced him to resign during the "people power" revolution. Under Aquino and her successors, this fragile democracy survived, despite many political scandals. Economic growth was limited, and poverty remained widespread. With the highest birth rate in Asia, the population continues to rise rapidly, straining already limited resources.

Clashes With Rebels Continue For decades, various rebel groups have waged guerrilla wars across the Philippines. Some rebels were communists. Others were Muslim separatists. Some Muslim rebels have links to international terrorist groups such as Al Qaeda. In the early 2000s, the Filipino government accepted aid from its ally, the United States, to fight rebels and pursue President George W. Bush's "war on terror."

✓ **Checkpoint** Why has the Philippines had trouble preserving its democracy?

Vocabulary Builder

<u>predominant</u>—(pree DAHM uh nunt) *adj.* most common or numerous

---

SECTION 2 Assessment

Progress Monitoring *Online*
For: Self-quiz with vocabulary practice
Web Code: nba-3121

Terms, People, and Places
1. For each term, person, or place listed at the beginning of the section, write a sentence explaining its significance.

Note Taking
2. **Reading Skill: Understand Effects** Use your completed concept web to answer the Focus Question: What challenges did Southeast Asian nations face after winning independence?

Comprehension and Critical Thinking
3. **Make Comparisons** Why did policies toward ethnic diversity lead to prosperity in Malaysia but to conflict in other parts of Southeast Asia?
4. **Synthesize Information** How have religious and ethnic diversity affected the recent history of Indonesia?
5. **Draw Inferences** What conclusions might separatist movements in Indonesia draw from East Timor's successful independence struggle?
6. **Recognize Cause and Effect** What causes explain the overthrow of Ferdinand Marcos?

● **Writing About History**
Quick Write: Evaluate Your Topic To write a compare-and-contrast essay, you can organize your ideas in a point-by-point comparison. In this section, you learned that Malaysia and Indonesia are both ethnically diverse. Draft two sentences for an essay. In each sentence, compare or contrast an aspect of ethnic diversity in one of these countries with a related aspect of ethnic diversity in the other.

Section 2 Assessment

1. Sentences should reflect an understanding of each term, person, or place listed at the beginning of the section.
2. Southeast Asian nations faced challenges of religious and ethnic conflict, poverty, natural disasters, and popular struggles to replace dictatorships with democracies.
3. Malaysia's policies to aid disadvantaged ethnic groups brought internal peace and economic prosperity. In other countries, such as Indonesia and Myanmar, ethnic discrimination led to violence.
4. It has brought deadly violence and discrimination and has led to independence struggles in Papua New Guinea and Aceh.
5. Independence is hard to achieve, and it brings a challenging responsibility for economic development.
6. the murder of his rival and the protests in Manila

Assess and Reteach

Assess Progress ⓛ3

- Have students complete the Section Assessment.
- Administer the Section Quiz.

All in One Teaching Resources, Unit 5, p. 24

- To further assess student understanding, use
   📖 **Progress Monitoring Transparencies,** 134

Reteach

If students need more instruction, have them read the section summary.

 Reading and Note Taking Study Guide, p. 203 ⓛ3

 Adapted Reading and Note Taking Study Guide, p. 203 ⓛ1 ⓛ2

Spanish Reading and Note Taking Study Guide, p. 203 ⓛ2

Extend ⓛ4

See this chapter's Professional Development pages for the Extend Online activity on history in the making.

Answer

✓ Guerilla rebels, poverty, a high birth rate, and a lack of economic growth have held the Philippines back.

● **Writing About History**
Sentences should include information about ethnic diversity in both nations, and each one should focus on a specific feature.

For additional assessment, have students access **Progress Monitoring *Online*** at **Web Code nba-3121.**

Objectives

As you teach this section, keep students focused on the following objectives to help them answer the Section Focus Question and master core content.

- Describe how Africa's colonies gained independence.
- Explain how Africans built new nations.
- Analyze the recent histories of five African nations.

The Union Jack, the flag of the United Kingdom, flew over many African countries before independence.

WITNESS HISTORY ◀)) AUDIO

Kenya Achieves Independence

A scene from a novel by Ngugi wa Thiong'o describes the moment of independence in Nairobi, Kenya's capital:

❝A minute before midnight, lights were put out. . . . In the dark, the Union Jack [British flag] was quickly lowered. When next the lights came on the new Kenya flag was . . . waving in the air.❞
—Ngugi wa Thiong'o, *A Grain of Wheat*

Kenya was one of more than 40 African nations that gained independence from European colonial powers in the decades after World War II.

Focus Question What challenges did new African nations face?

Britain's Prince Philip and Queen Elizabeth II congratulate Jomo Kenyatta as his nation, Kenya, gains independence in 1963.

African Nations Gain Independence

Objectives
- Describe how Africa's colonies gained independence.
- Explain how Africans built new nations.
- Analyze the recent histories of five African nations.

Terms, People, and Places

savannas	Mobutu Sese Seko
Kwame Nkrumah	Islamist
Jomo Kenyatta	Katanga
coup d'état	Biafra

Note Taking

Reading Skill: Identify Causes and Effects Fill in a concept web like this one to keep track of the causes and effects of independence in Africa.

Colonists demand rights → Independent African Nations

In new nations all across Africa, crowds celebrated their freedom, while bands played each country's new national anthem. However, even as independence celebrations took place, the new nations of Africa faced tough challenges.

New Nations Emerge in Africa

After World War II, European colonial powers could no longer afford to hold onto their colonies. As nationalist demands forced Britain to withdraw from India, African leaders, too, pressed for independence.

A Geographically Diverse Continent Africa is the world's second-largest continent, more than three times the size of the United States. Tropical rain forests cover central Africa's Congo Basin and coastal West Africa. Vast **savannas,** or grasslands with scattered trees, make up interior West Africa, East Africa, and much of central and southern Africa. Africa has the world's largest desert—the Sahara—in the north and the smaller Kalahari Desert in the south, as well as fertile coastal strips in North and South Africa.

Africa's people are concentrated in the most fertile areas, such as the savanna and forest regions of Nigeria and the moist highlands of East Africa. These regions produce enough food to support large populations. Like people in other parts of the world, however, millions of Africans were migrating, or moving, from rural areas to cities.

Africa has rich deposits of minerals such as gold ore, copper ore, and diamonds. Some African nations produce valuable cash crops, including coffee and cacao—used to make chocolate. Some regions also have large oil reserves. European powers had established colonies in Africa to tap into these natural resources.

Nationalist Leaders Demand Freedom By the 1950s, nationalist movements in Africa had grown stronger. Skilled organizers such as Kwame Nkrumah (KWAH may un KROO muh) in Gold Coast (later Ghana), Jomo Kenyatta in Kenya, and Léopold Senghor (sahn GAWR) in Senegal led independence movements in their own countries.

Most African nations won independence through largely peaceful means. Drained by World War II, European powers had few resources to resist the pressure to give up their colonial empires. The struggle for freedom turned violent, however, in a few colonies where large numbers of Europeans had settled, such as Kenya and Algeria.

✓ **Checkpoint** Why did some African countries have to fight for independence?

New Nations Build Governments

Some new nations enjoyed peace and had democratic governments. Others were plunged into crisis by civil war, military rule, or corrupt dictators. In recent decades, a number of African nations have taken steps toward democracy.

Challenges to Unity The new nations of Africa faced many difficulties, including the need to unify their people. European colonial powers had drawn boundaries around their colonies without regard to the many rival ethnic groups living in a particular region. At independence, most African nations included a patchwork of peoples with different languages, religions, and traditions. Within these new nations, people often felt their first loyalty was to their own ethnic group, not to a distant national government. As a result, conflict between different ethnic groups plagued many new nations.

Dictators Gain Power Many leaders of the new nations were heroes of the liberation struggle. Some chose to build one-party states. These leaders claimed that multiparty systems encouraged disunity. In time, these one-party governments became repressive, and some liberation leaders became dictators. Dictators often used their positions to enrich themselves and their supporters at the expense of the nation.

When bad or corrupt governments led to civil unrest, the military seized power in many countries. More than half of all African nations suffered military coups (kooz). A coup, or coup d'état (koo day TAH) is the forcible overthrow of a government. Some military rulers were brutal tyrants. Others tried to end corruption and improve conditions. Military leaders usually promised to restore civilian rule. But in many cases, they only surrendered power when they were toppled by another coup.

Moves Toward Democracy By the 1990s, some African nations were moving away from strongman rule. Western

Mineral Resources
A miner in the West African nation of Sierra Leone sifts gravel to find rough diamonds. Minerals are important to the economy of many African nations.

New Nations Build Governments **L3**

Instruct

- **Introduce: Key Terms** Ask students to locate the key term *coup d'état* (in blue) in the text and explain its meaning. Point out that more than half of Africa's new nations suffered military coups. Ask students to predict why there were so many changes of power and struggles for control in the emerging nations of Africa. Have students read to confirm or adjust their ideas.

- **Teach** Discuss how colonial rule contributed to the post-independence power struggles in many African nations. Highlight the different factions that competed for influence, including former colonial powers, and trace the trend toward democracy. Use the Numbered Heads strategy (TE, p. T23) and ask **Why did many Africans lack loyalty to their new national governments?** *(National boundaries had been drawn by European colonial powers without regard to ethnic composition. Africans had greater loyalty to their ethnic group than to their nation.)* **What role did former colonial powers play in African power struggles?** *(Many former colonial powers retained strong business interests and economic influence.)* **How have African nations moved toward democracy?** *(Many have legalized opposition parties and lifted censorship. Some nations have held multiparty elections for the first time.)*

- **Quick Activity** Web Code nbp-3131 will take students to an interactive map. Have students complete the interactivity and then answer the questions in the text.

Answers

✔️ More and more Africans have demanded democracy. In addition, Western governments and the World Bank have used economic pressure to require democratic reforms.

Caption Sample: They could provide financial support and influence those who visit their markets.

---

governments and lenders, such as the World Bank, demanded political reforms before granting loans. In response, some governments allowed opposition parties to emerge and expanded freedom of expression. In nations such as Nigeria, Tanzania, and Benin, multiparty elections were held, removing long-ruling leaders from office.

The Superpowers Compete for Influence Even after African nations won independence, colonial powers and foreign companies often retained control of businesses and resources in these former colonies. Many new nations remained dependent on their former colonial rulers for aid, trade, and investment.

The new nations were also buffeted by the Cold War. Both the United States and the Soviet Union competed for military and strategic advantage through alliances with several African countries. The United States, for example, backed **Mobutu Seso Seko,** the dictator of Zaire (now called the Democratic Republic of Congo). It wanted to counter Soviet influence in nearby Angola. During the 1970s, the United States backed Somalia, while the Soviet Union supported neighboring Ethiopia. Both African countries were important because they controlled access to the Red Sea, a vital world-shipping route.

✔️ **Checkpoint** Why have some African nations taken steps toward democracy in recent years?

The Stories of Five African Nations

While the new nations of Africa faced many of the same challenges, each nation had a unique history. To gain a better understanding of the process of nation-building in Africa, we will examine the recent histories of five important nations.

Ghana In 1957, Ghana was the first African nation south of the Sahara to win independence. Britain had called this colony Gold Coast, for its rich mineral resources. Under independence leader Kwame Nkrumah, it took the name Ghana, after the ancient West African kingdom.

As president, Nkrumah supported socialism and government ownership of major industries. He backed the building of a huge dam to provide electric power, but the project left Ghana with massive debts. Nkrumah's government became increasingly corrupt and dictatorial. In 1966, Nkrumah was toppled by the first of several military coups.

This pattern repeated itself in many new African nations. Large costly projects, often poorly planned, left many countries in debt to foreign lenders. Coups and dictators became common.

Market Women in Ghana
In West African countries such as Ghana, women have traditionally sold goods in the markets. These women wait for customers with a display of food and other goods. *Why might political candidates in Ghana and elsewhere seek support from local market women?*

Independence in Africa

Map Skills From the late 1800s until the 1950s and 1960s, most African countries were colonies of European powers, which drew their borders. Most African nations gained independence during the 1950s and 1960s.

Geography *Interactive*
For: Interactive map
Web Code: nbp-3131

1. **Locate** (a) Kenya (b) Democratic Republic of the Congo (c) Angola (d) Ghana

2. **Regions** Which was the last of the Democratic Republic of the Congo's neighbors to gain independence?

3. **Draw Conclusions** When must the Cold War conflict involving independent Angola have taken place?

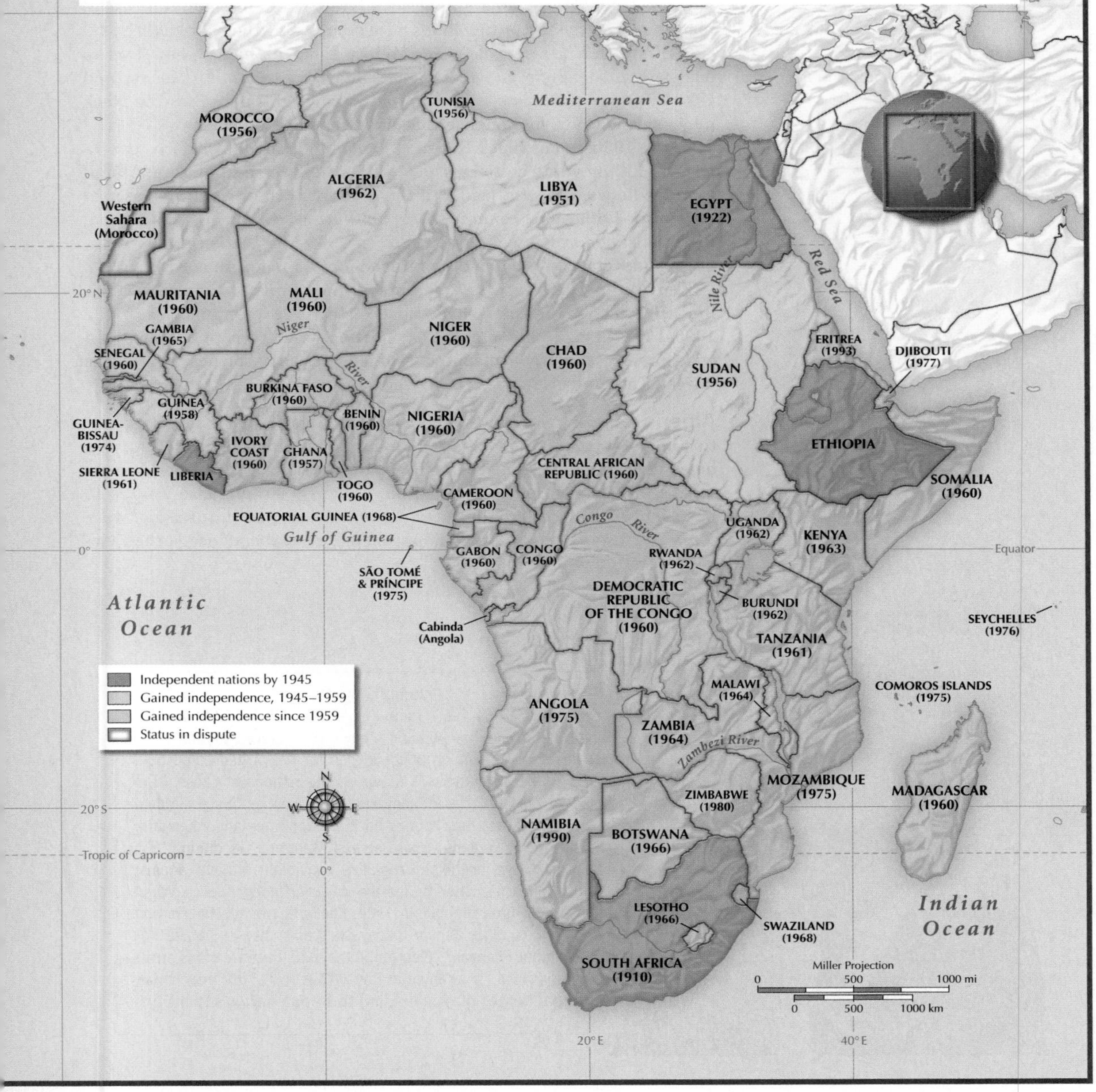

TUNISIA (1956)

Mediterranean Sea

MOROCCO (1956)

ALGERIA (1962)

LIBYA (1951)

EGYPT (1922)

Western Sahara (Morocco)

20°N

MAURITANIA (1960)

MALI (1960)

Niger

NIGER (1960)

CHAD (1960)

SUDAN (1956)

ERITREA (1993)

Red Sea

Nile River

DJIBOUTI (1977)

GAMBIA (1965)

SENEGAL (1960)

River

BURKINA FASO (1960)

GUINEA (1958)

GUINEA-BISSAU (1974)

BENIN (1960)

NIGERIA (1960)

IVORY COAST (1960)

GHANA (1957)

SIERRA LEONE (1961)

LIBERIA

TOGO (1960)

EQUATORIAL GUINEA (1968)

CAMEROON (1960)

CENTRAL AFRICAN REPUBLIC (1960)

ETHIOPIA

SOMALIA (1960)

Gulf of Guinea

SÃO TOMÉ & PRÍNCIPE (1975)

0°

GABON (1960)

CONGO (1960)

Congo River

UGANDA (1962)

KENYA (1963)

Equator

Cabinda (Angola)

DEMOCRATIC REPUBLIC OF THE CONGO (1960)

RWANDA (1962)

BURUNDI (1962)

TANZANIA (1961)

SEYCHELLES (1976)

Atlantic Ocean

ANGOLA (1975)

MALAWI (1964)

ZAMBIA (1964)

Zambezi River

COMOROS ISLANDS (1975)

Independent nations by 1945
Gained independence, 1945–1959
Gained independence since 1959
Status in dispute

MOZAMBIQUE (1975)

ZIMBABWE (1980)

MADAGASCAR (1960)

20°S

NAMIBIA (1990)

BOTSWANA (1966)

Indian Ocean

Tropic of Capricorn

0°

LESOTHO (1966)

SWAZILAND (1968)

SOUTH AFRICA (1910)

Miller Projection
0   500   1000 mi
0   500   1000 km

N   W   E   S

20°E   40°E

Differentiated Instruction   Solutions for All Learners

L1 Special Needs   **L2 Less Proficient Readers**

Ask pairs of students to locate each of the five nations discussed in this section, describe where in Africa each is located, and name the date each gained independence. Then have pairs create a chart that lists how each of the five nations gained independence and what kind of government it has now.

L2 English Language Learners

Use the following resources to help students acquire basic skills:

 **Adapted Reading and Note Taking Study Guide**

■ Adapted Note Taking Study Guide, p. 204
■ Adapted Section Summary, p. 205

Independent Practice

Have students fill in the Outline Map *Independence in Africa*.

All in One Teaching Resources, Unit 5, p. 34

Monitor Progress

■ Circulate to make sure students are accurately labeling the nations in Africa on their Outline Maps. Administer the Geography Quiz.

All in One Teaching Resources, Unit 5, p. 36

■ Check answers to map skills questions.

Answers

Map Skills
1. Review locations with students.
2. Angola
3. after 1975

Instruct

- **Introduce** Have a volunteer read this subtitle and the paragraph beneath it. Discuss why each nation's experience in facing the challenges of independence might vary. Invite students to suggest reasons, such as geography, ethnic makeup, or external influences, and then have them read to confirm or revise their ideas.

- **Teach** Write the names of the five nations on the board: Ghana, Kenya, Algeria, Democratic Republic of Congo, and Nigeria. Have students list features of each nation's history, including its former colonial ruler, key leaders, types of government, and current form of government. Write their answers on the board.

- **Quick Activity** Direct students' attention to the Biography of Jomo Kenyatta and other information about Kenyatta on this page. Discuss the Biography question, inviting students' thoughts on the importance of dynamic political leaders in inspiring change.

Vocabulary Builder

ensure—(en SHOOR) *v.* make sure or certain, guarantee

In the 1980s, Jerry Rawlings, a military officer, took power in a coup. He strengthened the economy and moved Ghana toward democracy. In 1992, Rawlings allowed multiparty elections and was chosen president. Other elections followed. Although the economy suffered from falling prices for cocoa and gold, its main exports, Ghana made progress toward improving life for its people. The recent discovery of offshore oil raised hopes for more economic growth.

Kenya While Ghana made a peaceful transition to freedom, Kenya faced an armed struggle. A large number of white settlers had built successful plantations on the fertile highlands once occupied by the Kikuyu (kee KOO yoo), Kenya's largest ethnic group. White Kenyans had passed laws to <u>ensure</u> their domination over the black majority. Nationalist leader and Kikuyu spokesman Jomo Kenyatta had long sought justice for the black majority and called for nonviolent means to end oppressive laws.

In the 1950s, some black Kenyans turned to guerrilla warfare, attacking and killing white settlers. The British called them Mau Mau. Claiming that he was a secret leader of the Mau Mau, the British imprisoned Kenyatta. Both sides committed terrible atrocities during this period, and thousands of Kikuyu were killed. In 1963, the British finally withdrew, and Kenyatta became the first leader of an independent Kenya.

Kenyatta and his successor dominated the country for decades. They limited freedom of expression and resisted free elections. Since the 1990s, Kenya has held multiparty elections, but corruption remained widespread. In 2007, a disputed election sparked violence and ethnic unrest. The conflict hurt tourism—one of Kenya's largest industries.

Algeria Like Kenya, the French colony of Algeria had a large population of European settlers. Over one million French people called Algeria home and were determined to remain part of France. The French government, which had recently lost its Asian colony, Vietnam, also wanted to hold onto Algeria, especially after deposits of oil and natural gas were discovered there. As a result, the struggle for independence turned violent in the 1950s.

BIOGRAPHY

Jomo Kenyatta

On December 12, 1963, Jomo Kenyatta (c. 1894–1978) watched the flag of an independent Kenya rise above Nairobi. After 50 years, his dream of independence for Kenya had come true. Early in life, Kenyatta was drawn to the nationalist cause. "The land is ours," declared Kenyatta, who was a Kikuyu. "When Europeans came, they kept us back and took our land." Kenyatta spent time in England, where he met Mahatma Gandhi in 1932. Back in Kenya, he helped organize nonviolent protests against British injustices. Later, he led the drive for independence. When Kenya became a republic in 1964, Kenyatta was elected its first president. To black Kenyans, Kenyatta was known as "Mzee," or "Wise Elder." Kenyans celebrate October 20, the date of his arrest by the British, as Kenyatta Day. **What role do you think national heroes play in helping to form a nation's identity?**

Answer

BIOGRAPHY Sample: They inspire people to support their nation and make the ideals of the nation appealing to people of different backgrounds.

History Background

A History of Repression Colonialism in Algeria left a bitter legacy. Under French rule, Muslims faced discrimination. French settlers owned and operated large farms, businesses, and industries while Algerian Muslims labored on tiny farms or in menial jobs. Muslims were prevented from taking an active role in government. In the 1950s, resentment erupted into guerrilla war. The French moved two million Algerians to internment camps in the desert, where thousands perished. Algerians responded with terrorist attacks. Nearly a million Algerians and 10,000 French soldiers died overall. Since independence, Algeria has experienced cycles of repression and violence. In the 1990s, attacks by government and opposition forces killed up to 150,000 civilians.

An Election Celebration
Citizens of Mauritania, in West Africa, celebrate the reelection of the country's president in 2003. *Why did many nations have difficulty building democratic governments?*

Algerian nationalists set up the National Liberation Front, which turned to guerrilla warfare to win freedom. From 1954 to 1962, more than one million Algerians were killed in this bloody conflict. When public opinion in France finally turned against the war, Algeria won independence.

Algerian nationalists set up the National Liberation Front, which turned to guerrilla warfare to win freedom. From 1954 to 1962, more than one million Algerians were killed in this bloody conflict. When public opinion in France finally turned against the war, Algeria won independence.

Algeria's oil and gas resources have helped it economically. Politically, it has suffered through periods of military rule and internal conflict. During the 1970s, the government nationalized, or took over, foreign-owned companies and created a command economy. Since the 1980s, Algeria has been moving toward a market economy.

By the 1990s, a growing struggle had erupted between the military and **Islamists,** people who want a government based on Islamic law and beliefs. In 1992, the Algerian government allowed free elections. When an Islamist party won, the military rejected the results. For seven years, civil war raged between Islamist militants and the military, leaving as many as 150,000 dead. The violence slowed after 1999, but tensions remained.

Democratic Republic of Congo The Democratic Republic of Congo (or Congo) covers a vast region of central Africa. It includes a million square miles of rain forest and savanna centered on the Congo River basin. Congo was a Belgian colony, and the Belgians were eager to keep control of Congo's rich resources, such as copper and diamonds.

When Congo gained independence in 1960, it was not prepared for self-government. The new nation included 14 million people from more than 200 separate groups. Competing economic interests and rival political leaders soon plunged Congo into civil war when the copper-rich **Katanga** province broke away. Belgian mining companies supported Katanga, hoping to control its mineral resources. The Cold War superpowers backed rival leaders, further complicating the fighting. The United Nations ended the Katanga rebellion in 1963.

Link to Literature

Wole Soyinka In 1986 Nigerian writer Wole Soyinka became the first black African to receive the Nobel Prize for Literature. Soyinka has written plays, poetry, and novels that combine Western influences with his native Yoruba folklore, song, and dance. Soyinka writes in English, and his works criticize both excessive nostalgia for the African past and unthinking embrace of the West. He attacks the corruption and tyranny of colonialism and of Africa's modern governments. "I have one abiding religion—human liberty," Soyinka says. In the 1960s, Soyinka was arrested by Nigeria's repressive government and kept mainly in solitary confinement for more than two years. His notes, written on toilet paper and paper scraps using self-made ink, were later published as a prison diary. Forced into exile in 1994, Soyinka returned to Nigeria in 1998.

Assess Progress

- Have students complete the Section Assessment.
- Administer the Section Quiz.

 **Teaching Resources, Unit 5**, p. 25

- To further assess student understanding, use

   Progress Monitoring Transparencies, 135

Reteach

If students need more instruction, have them read the section summary.

 Reading and Note Taking Study Guide, p. 205

Adapted Reading and Note Taking Study Guide, p. 205

Spanish Reading and Note Taking Study Guide, p. 205

Extend

Display **Color Transparency 189: *The Lullaby* by Tapfuma Gutsa.** Have students respond to the sculpture, discussing how it reflects the struggles and experiences of Africans in the post-colonial era.

 Color Transparencies, 189

Answer

✔ They are both regions within a larger African nation that possess valuable natural resources. Both rebelled and sought independence but suffered defeat at the hands of the more powerful national military force.

In 1965, Colonel Joseph Mobutu, later known as Mobutu Sese Seko, seized power. For 32 years, Mobutu's harsh, corrupt rule brought poverty and unrest to Congo. Rebels finally forced Mobutu from power in 1997. But civil war again raged as rival military leaders battled to control Congo's mineral riches.

The country's first free elections in 41 years brought Joseph Kabila to power in 2006. As on and off violence continued in the eastern region, Kabila had to reduce corruption, calm ethnic tensions, protect Congo's mineral resources, and heal the scars caused by decades of war.

Nigeria Nigeria, on the coast of West Africa, includes diverse people and climates. Nigeria's huge population is the largest in Africa. Its people belong to more than 250 ethnic groups, speak many languages, and practice different religions. The dominant groups are the mainly Christian Ibo (EE boh) and Yoruba (YOH roo buh) in the south, and the Muslim Hausa (HOW suh) in the north.

Nigeria won independence peacefully from Britain in 1960. The next year, oil was discovered, raising hopes for the country's economic future. Instead, the country faced military coups, corruption, and economic crises. In 1966, the Ibo people in the oil-rich south rebelled and set up the independent Republic of **Biafra.** A brutal civil war led to famine, the death of an estimated half million people, and the end of Biafra's independence.

Between 1996 and 1999, the military was in and out of power in Nigeria. Military leaders ruled with an iron hand but failed to improve Nigeria's government or its economy. In 1999, Nigeria again held elections. A new civilian government introduced reforms to strengthen the economy and restore political freedom.

Because Nigeria relied heavily on oil exports, it was affected by the rise and fall of oil prices. Nigeria also faced ethnic and religious violence. In the north, Islamists wanted strict Sharia law. In the oil-producing Niger Delta region, local people were bitter about the environmental damage caused by oil drilling, and the huge profits going to foreign companies. Armed groups attacked pipelines and held foreign oil workers for ransom.

Nigeria's Oil Industry
This oil worker is drilling for oil in southeastern Nigeria. Nigeria's vital oil industry is threatened by conflict in this oil-producing region.

✔ **Checkpoint** How did Katanga and Biafra reflect the challenges that new African nations faced after independence?

SECTION 3 Assessment

Progress Monitoring Online
For: Self-quiz with vocabulary practice
Web Code: nba-3131

Terms, People, and Places

1. Place each of the key terms at the beginning of the section into one of the following categories: politics, economy, or geography. Write a sentence for each term explaining your choice.

Note Taking

2. **Reading Skill: Identify Causes and Effects** Use your completed concept web to answer the Focus Question: What challenges did new African nations face?

Comprehension and Critical Thinking

3. **Make Comparisons** Why did some countries gain independence peacefully, while others faced violent struggles?
4. **Identify Central Issues** Why did the Cold War superpowers seek alliances with African nations?
5. **Express Problems Clearly** Based on what you have read about Algeria, what problems caused the civil war in Algeria?
6. **Draw Conclusions** How have religious and ethnic divisions affected Nigeria's history?

● **Writing About History**

Quick Write: Provide Elaboration To write a compare-and-contrast essay, you need to provide examples that support the main point of the essay. Suppose that the point of your essay is to compare and contrast challenges faced by Algeria and Nigeria since independence. Draft two sentences for an essay. In each sentence, give examples that compare or contrast a challenge faced by these countries.

---

1. Sentences should reflect an understanding of each term, person, or place listed at the beginning of the section.
2. creating national unity amid ethnic diversity; promoting democracy; combating dictatorship; achieving economic independence from colonial powers; and ending government corruption
3. Some colonial powers were more willing than others to allow independence. Places where European settlers had lived for a long time saw more European resistance and thus more violence.
4. They both wanted military and strategic advantage in Africa, so they could advance their global dominance.
5. violence, repression, and a lack of democracy
6. Divisions have led to conflict, which has undermined democracy by allowing the military to seize power several times.

● **Writing About History**

Sentences should compare or contrast a challenge faced by the two countries. For example, they could focus on the common features of military coups or religious conflicts.

For additional assessment, have students access **Progress Monitoring *Online*** at **Web Code nba-3131.**

Kwame Nkrumah: *Autobiography*

Kwame Nkrumah led the people of Gold Coast in their quest for independence from Britain. After succeeding in 1957, Nkrumah became the first prime minister and renamed the country Ghana. In this excerpt from his *Autobiography*, Nkrumah speaks of the need to establish economic independence as a means of maintaining political independence. Nkrumah describes the difficult work of building an independent economy.

▲ Prime Minister Kwame Nkrumah of Ghana

I ndependence for the Gold Coast was my aim. It was a colony, and I have always regarded colonialism as the policy by which a foreign power binds territories to herself by political ties with the primary object of promoting her own economic advantage. No one need be surprised if this system has led to disturbances and political tension in many territories. There are few people who would not rid themselves of such domination if they could. . . .

I saw that the whole solution to [our] problem lay in political freedom for our people, for it is only when a people are politically free that other races can give them the respect that is due to them. It is impossible to talk of equality of races in any other terms. No people without a government of their own can expect to be treated on the same level as peoples of independent sovereign[1] states. It is far better to be free to govern or misgovern yourself than to be governed by anybody else. . . .

Once this freedom is gained, a greater task comes into view. All dependent[2] territories are backward in education, in science, in agriculture, and in industry. The economic independence that should follow and maintain political independence demands every effort from the people, a total mobilization of brain and manpower resources. What other countries have taken three hundred years or more to achieve, a once dependent territory must try to accomplish in a generation if it is to survive. . . .

▲ Ghana's leaders—including Kwame Nkrumah, at center—celebrate Ghana's independence in 1957.

1. **sovereign** (SAHV run) *adj.* not subject to any other power
2. **dependent** (dee PEN dunt) *adj.* subject to the power of another

Thinking Critically
1. **Identify Point of View** What does Nkrumah think the people of a dependent territory must do before they can achieve economic independence?
2. **Draw Inferences** Based on Nkrumah's remarks, what makes economic independence difficult for newly independent nations to achieve?

History Background

Kwame Nkrumah When Kwame Nkrumah helped design Ghana's new national flag, he chose the Pan-African colors and a black star symbolizing his hope that Ghana would be a beacon of independence for all of Africa. Nkrumah built modern roads, schools, and universities, the Volta Dam for hydroelectric power, and an aluminum industry. He also spent lavishly on his goal of liberating and uniting all of Africa.

However, as other countries gained freedom, they resisted unification. Meanwhile, the once-thriving Ghana became mired in foreign debt, and Nkrumah resorted to more and more repressive tactics to maintain control. In 1966 the army overthrew Nkrumah. The rejoicing populace destroyed his statues and renamed the roads and buildings that had been named for him.

Kwame Nkrumah: *Autobiography*

Objective
■ Understand Kwame Nkrumah's impact on the development of independent Ghana.

Build Background Knowledge L3
Ask students to recall the changes that took place as South Asian and Southeast Asian nations pushed for independence. Ask **Why do you think people everywhere want to control their own destiny?** (*Sample: The desire for self-rule is inherent in the human urge for freedom.*)

Instruct L3
■ Direct students' attention to the introduction at the top of the text page. Ask **What does Nkrumah believe new nations must do?** (*He believes that new nations must achieve economic independence in order to maintain political independence.*)

■ Discuss with students the goals Nkrumah has for his country, and the problems he foresees if those goals are not met. Ask **How does Nkrumah equate economic and political independence?** (*He believes that economic dependence is a facet of colonialism and that economic independence is needed to maintain political independence.*) **What problems does Nkrumah think his people will face in achieving economic and political independence?** (*They will have to mobilize all of their resources to achieve in a generation what other nations have taken centuries to achieve.*)

Monitor Progress
To confirm students' understanding, ask them to briefly summarize Nkrumah's views.

Thinking Critically
1. They must put all their resources and efforts into modernizing the country.
2. They must make up for being centuries behind more established nations in their economic development.

Objectives

As you teach this section, keep students focused on the following objectives to help them answer the Section Focus Question and master core content.

- Analyze the diversity of the Middle East and the political challenges it has faced.
- Explain the region's conflicts over resources and religion.
- Outline the history of nation-building in three Middle Eastern nations.

Prepare to Read

Build Background Knowledge ⓛ₃

Ask students to recall the differences between those seeking modern democracies and those who favored tradition and religion in Pakistan and elsewhere. Then ask them to predict how the tension between religion and modernity might affect the mainly Muslim Middle East.

Set a Purpose ⓛ₃

- **WITNESS HISTORY** Read the selection aloud or play the audio.

  🔊 AUDIO **Witness History Audio CD,** Remembering Nasser

  Ask **How does Nasser Rabbat describe the crowd?** *(excited, proud of Gamal Abdel Nasser, because he was to unite the Arabs)* Discuss why Arab nationalism would be an important force in the Middle East after World War II.

- **Focus** Point out the Section Focus Question and write it on the board. Tell students to refer to this question as they read. *(Answer appears with Section 4 Assessment answers.)*

- **Preview** Have students preview the Section Objectives and the list of Terms, People, and Places.

- **Note Taking** As students read, have them fill in the concept web with causes and effects in the Middle East.

  📝 **Reading and Note Taking Study Guide,** p. 206

Egypt's leader, Gamal Abdel Nasser, greets children in 1956.

Islamic ornamental writing from a mosque in Iran

WITNESS HISTORY 🔊 AUDIO

Remembering Nasser

As a young boy in Syria, Nasser Rabbat recalls seeing the Arab leader, Gamal Abdel Nasser.

❝One of my earliest memories dates back to the winter of 1960 when I was almost four years old. I remember . . . screaming with the crowd around us 'Nasser, Nasser.' . . . I had been taught . . . to be proud of . . . Nasser, 'the unifier of the Arabs' and 'the leader of our new renaissance.'❞

—Nasser Rabbat, "On being named Nasser"

In the decades after World War II, nationalism was a major force shaping Middle Eastern nations from Egypt and Israel to Turkey and Iran.

Focus Question What were some similarities and differences in the nations of the Middle East?

The Modern Middle East

Objectives

- Analyze the diversity of the Middle East and the political challenges it has faced.
- Explain the region's conflicts over resources and religion.
- Outline the history of nation-building in three Middle Eastern nations.

Terms, People, and Places

kibbutz	Anwar Sadat
secular	Mohammad Mosaddeq
hejab	Ruhollah Khomeini
Suez Canal	theocracy
Gamal Abdel Nasser	

Note Taking

Reading Skill: Identify Causes and Effects Fill in a concept web like this one to keep track of events in the Middle East since 1945.

In the 1950s, leaders like Egypt's Gamal Abdel Nasser set out to build strong nations across the Middle East. Most Middle Eastern countries were poor—only a few had rich oil reserves. Autocratic governments and internal divisions hindered progress throughout the region.

Diversity Brings Challenges

The Middle East, as we use the term in this chapter, is the region stretching from Egypt in the west to Iran in the east and from Turkey in the north to the Arabian Peninsula in the south. Though most people in the region today are Muslims, there are also Christian communities and the predominantly Jewish nation of Israel. Most countries have large ethnic or religious minorities.

Mandates Gain Independence After World War I, Britain and France were given mandates over parts of the Middle East. During the 1930s and 1940s, nationalists demanded an end to European control, and the mandates became the independent states of Iraq, Syria, Lebanon, Jordan, and Israel.

Kurds Seek Rights In the Middle East, as elsewhere, new nations faced challenges from ethnic minorities that demanded self rule, or even independence. The Kurds are an ethnic group with their own language and culture, and are an important minority in Turkey, Iran, and Iraq.

Vocabulary Builder

Use the information below and the following resources to teach the high-use word from this section.

All in One Teaching Resources, Unit 5, p. 27; **Teaching Resources, Skills Handbook,** p. 3

High-Use Word	Definition and Sample Sentence
doctrine, p. 673	*n.* teachings, principles, or beliefs People around the world have adopted Gandhi's **doctrine** of nonviolence.

Kurds faced discrimination and harsh treatment, especially in Iraq and Turkey. In Turkey, Kurdish rebels resisted government efforts to suppress their culture. Thousands died fighting the government. In Iraq, a Kurdish rebellion after the 1991 Gulf War was brutally suppressed. As you will read, Kurds form one of the three main groups sharing power in Iraq. However, some Kurds still want their own state.

Israel Is Founded As you have learned, Britain supported a Jewish national homeland in part of its Palestine Mandate. The horrific experience of Jews in the Holocaust added to worldwide support for a Jewish homeland. Jews, including many Holocaust survivors, sought to migrate there after World War II. In 1947, the UN drew up a plan to divide the Palestine Mandate into an Arab and a Jewish state. Jews accepted the plan, but Arabs rejected it. They felt that all of Palestine should belong to them.

After Britain withdrew from Palestine in 1948, Jews proclaimed the independent State of Israel. Arab states launched the first of several wars against Israel but were defeated. Israel developed rapidly. A skilled workforce built businesses. Kibbutzim produced crops for export. A **kibbutz** (kih BOOTS) is a collective farm. Israel attracted Jews from around the world, including Jews expelled from other Middle Eastern lands.

The conflicts of 1948 created enormous refugee problems. As a result of the war, hundreds of thousands of Palestinian Arabs fled their homes

The Middle East Today

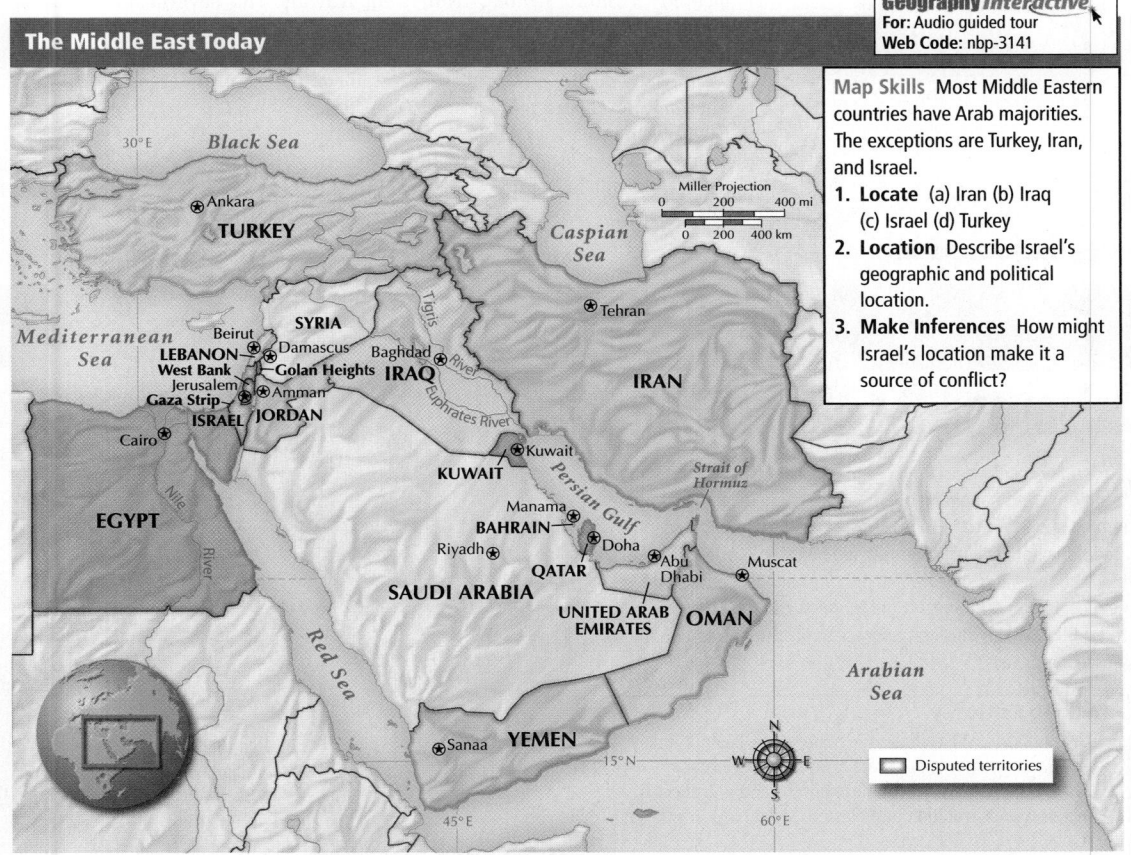

Geography *Interactive*
For: Audio guided tour
Web Code: nbp-3141

Map Skills Most Middle Eastern countries have Arab majorities. The exceptions are Turkey, Iran, and Israel.
1. **Locate** (a) Iran (b) Iraq (c) Israel (d) Turkey
2. **Location** Describe Israel's geographic and political location.
3. **Make Inferences** How might Israel's location make it a source of conflict?

Diversity Brings Challenges (L3)

Instruct

- **Introduce** Show students the map on this page. Recall that most of these borders were drawn by European powers after World War I without regard for ethnic or religious divisions. Recall the difficulties African nations faced because national borders did not match ethnic divisions. Ask students to predict how such borders might lead to difficulties in the Middle East.

- **Teach** Discuss the challenges facing Kurds in the region. Ask **Where do the Kurds live, and how does this location affect their independence?** *(The Kurds live in an area straddling Turkey, Iran, and Iraq. As a result, they have no integral or unified nation.)* Then trace the development of Israel. Ask **When was Israel founded and why?** *(Israel was founded after World War II to reestablish a Jewish state in the ancient homeland and to provide a safe homeland for Jews who survived the Holocaust.)*

- **Quick Activity** Have students access **Web Code nbp-3141** to take the **Geography Interactive Audio Guided Tour** and then answer the map skills questions in the text.

Independent Practice

Have students fill in the Outline Map *Nations of the Middle East.*

All in One Teaching Resources, Unit 5, p. 35

Monitor Progress

- Circulate to make sure students are filling in their Outline Maps accurately.
- Check answers to map skills questions.

Answers

Map Skills
1. Review locations with students.
2. It is located in a narrow strip of land along the Mediterranean Sea. It borders disputed territories as well as several countries with Arab majorities.
3. Its small size and location next to disputed territories might make it a focus of conflicts with surrounding nations.

Sources of Conflict

Instruct

- **Introduce: Key Terms** Have students find the key terms *secular* and *hejab* (in blue) in the text and explain their meanings. Point out that in many Middle Eastern nations, those advocating secular government and law struggle for control with those advocating traditions such as the *hejab*. Ask how each of these approaches might appeal to citizens of the Middle East.

- **Teach** Discuss the central conflicts in the Middle East over resources and religion. Have students identify views on both sides of each issue. Ask **What resource plays a large role in Middle Eastern economies?** *(oil)* **Why is this resource so important to the balance of power in the region?** *(There is a huge global demand for oil. As a result, nations with control over oil reserves can wield power regionally and globally.)*

- **Analyzing the Visuals** Discuss the Infographic with students. Have them review the images and read the captions. Ask students what it might be like to live as a woman in an Islamic society. Have them read the chart and describe what it shows about access to education and jobs in the Middle East.

Independent Practice

Stage a debate about paths to development in the Middle East. Have one team present arguments in favor of westernization and modernization. Have the other team present the opposing viewpoint in favor of traditionalism.

Monitor Progress

As students fill in their concept webs, circulate to make sure they understand the causes and effects of change in the Middle East. For a completed version of the concept web, see

 Note Taking Transparencies, 197

Answers

✔ People supported a Jewish homeland because centuries of persecution and genocide had threatened Jewish survival.

Thinking Critically
1. women's literacy
2. They combine elements of both traditions, as shown by the women wearing athletic pants, sneakers, and headscarves, and the artist using Western influences in his art.

---

in Israeli territory. The UN set up camps in neighboring areas to house them. Hundreds of thousands of Jews from Arab lands were also driven from their homes. Both sides feel embittered by the displacements.

Political Systems Limit Freedom Most Middle Eastern nations have had autocratic governments. In some countries, nationalist military leaders seized power. In other countries, such as Jordan and Saudi Arabia, hereditary monarchs remained in power. Only Israel and Turkey had stable multiparty democratic systems by 2005.

✔ **Checkpoint** Why did many people around the world support a Jewish homeland in Palestine?

Sources of Conflict

Some Middle Eastern nations sit atop vast oil and gas reserves. These oil-rich nations have prospered. Although these countries have helped their less fortunate neighbors, many Middle Eastern nations struggled economically. Meanwhile, Muslims have disagreed over the role of Islam in a modern society.

Supplying the World With Oil The huge oil resources of the Middle East gave it strategic, global importance. The largest oil resources were located in Saudi Arabia, Iran, Iraq, Kuwait, and several small states along the Persian Gulf. In 1960, these nations, along with Venezuela, set up the Organization of Petroleum Exporting Countries (OPEC). OPEC wanted to end the power of Western oil companies and determine oil production quotas and prices. In 1973, Middle Eastern members of OPEC used oil as a weapon. They stopped oil shipments to countries that had supported Israel in the

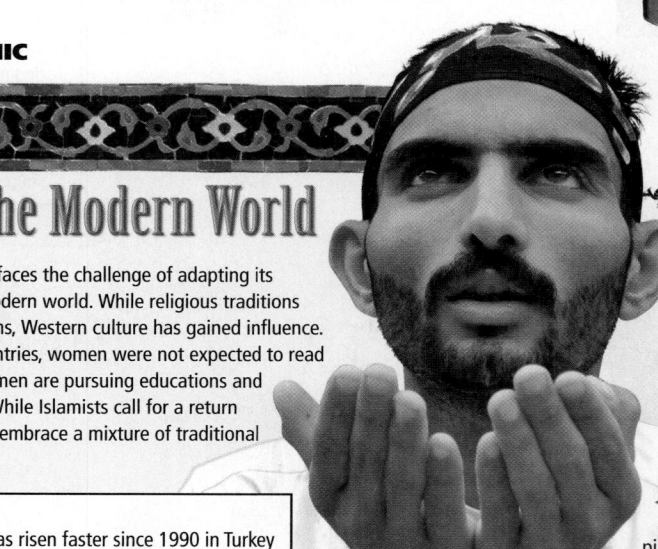

● **INFOGRAPHIC**

Islam and the Modern World

Like other religions, Islam faces the challenge of adapting its traditions to a changing modern world. While religious traditions remain important to Muslims, Western culture has gained influence. Traditionally, in Islamic countries, women were not expected to read or write. Today, Muslim women are pursuing educations and new career opportunities. While Islamists call for a return to tradition, many Muslims embrace a mixture of traditional and modern ways.

The Iraqi artist ▲ Hassan Massoudy combines the Islamic tradition of calligraphy, or ornamental writing, with abstract Western styles.

◀ The basic principles of Islam, such as pilgrimage and prayer, remain important to modern Muslims, such as the Iraqi pilgrim to the left.

Thinking Critically
1. **Graph Skills** Which has risen faster since 1990 in Turkey and Saudi Arabia, men's literacy or women's literacy?
2. **Analyze Visuals** How do these photos and art reflect a mix of Islamic tradition and Western styles?

Connect to Our World

Connections to Today Many Westerners find it difficult to understand *hejab*, or Islamic guidelines for women's dress. In recent decades, some educated Muslim women have returned to wearing hejab as an expression of their religious beliefs or as a refusal to imitate Western culture. Westerners often see hejab as representing the oppression of women, but some Muslim women see it as a way of deemphasizing gender. As one Egyptian student put it, "I think of Muslim dress as a kind of uniform. I can sit in class with men and there is no question of attraction and so on—we are all involved in the same business of learning." Because Muslim women wear hejab as a way to avoid calling attention to themselves, many find it very disturbing when people in the United States stare at them and their garments.

Yom Kippur War. This oil embargo triggered a worldwide recession. Since then, OPEC has focused on setting production quotas.

Islam in the Modern World After independence, some Middle Eastern countries adopted Western-style **secular,** or nonreligious, governments. At the same time, Western cultural influences grew. In cities, people bought imported goods from the West, wore Western fashions, and watched American television shows and movies.

Some Muslims claimed that secular Western culture was undermining Islamic society. They called for a return to Sharia, or Islamic law based on the Quran. These conservative reformers, known as Islamists, blamed social and economic ills on the West. Only a renewed commitment to Islamic <u>doctrine</u>, they declared, could improve conditions in the Muslim world. Many Muslims welcomed the Islamist movement as a way to cope with rapid social and economic changes. Although some people advocated violence to achieve their goals, most Muslims opposed Islamic extremists.

Changes Affect Women's Lives Conditions for women vary greatly across the Middle East. In most countries, women won equality before the law. Educated women entered professions such as law and medicine. In Turkey, Egypt, and Syria, many urban women gave up the **hejab,** or traditional Muslim headscarf, or wearing loose, ankle-length garments meant to conceal. Some women, however, embraced these traditions as a symbol of their Islamic faith.

In religiously conservative countries like Saudi Arabia and Iran, women must follow Islamic traditions, such as wearing the hejab. In many Middle Eastern countries, girls are less likely to attend school than boys, because of a traditional belief that girls do not need a formal education for their expected roles as wives and mothers. Women's rights movements, however, have challenged these traditions.

✔ **Checkpoint** Why did Islamists oppose secular government and culture in the Muslim world?

Vocabulary Builder

<u>doctrine</u>—(DAHK trin) *n.* teachings, principles, or beliefs

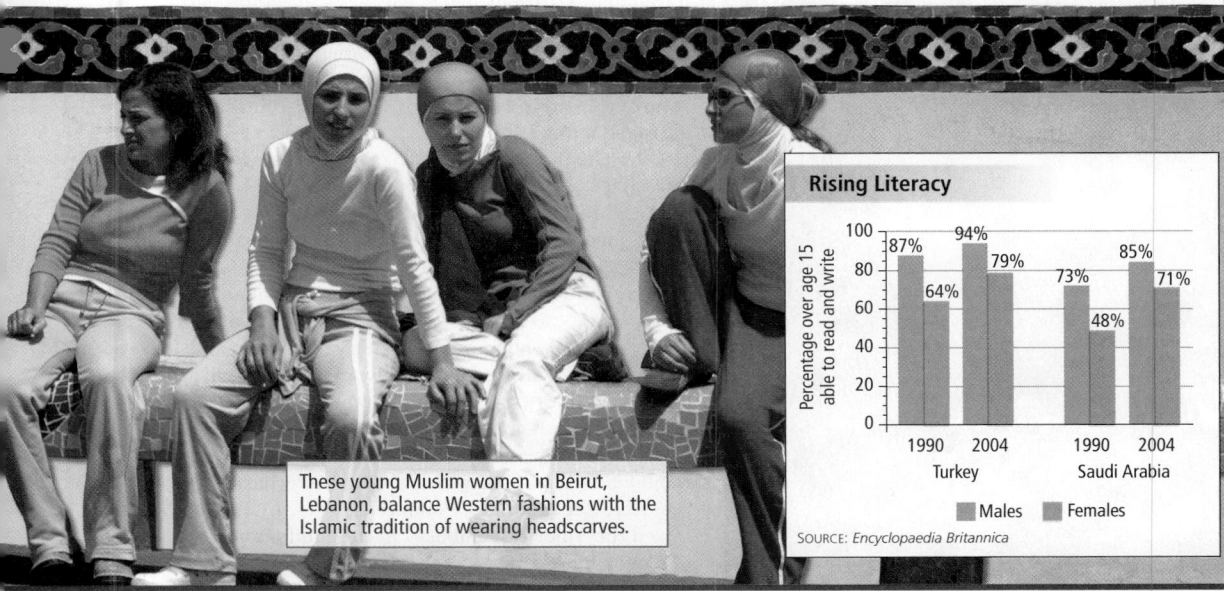

These young Muslim women in Beirut, Lebanon, balance Western fashions with the Islamic tradition of wearing headscarves.

Rising Literacy

Percentage over age 15 able to read and write

	Turkey		Saudi Arabia	
	1990	2004	1990	2004
Males	87%	94%	73%	85%
Females	64%	79%	48%	71%

■ Males   ■ Females

SOURCE: *Encyclopaedia Britannica*

History Background

Shirin Ebadi In 2003, Shirin Ebadi became the first Iranian and the first Muslim woman to win the Nobel Peace Prize. Born in 1947, Ebadi studied law, as her father had done. In 1969, she became Iran's first female judge. In 1975, she became president of the Tehran city court. After the 1979 Islamic revolution, she was dismissed as a judge. Unable even to practice law, Ebadi wrote books on civil rights and children's rights. In 1995, she obtained a law license and began taking controversial civil rights and child abuse cases. In 1997, Ebadi circulated evidence of the slaying of dissidents by right-wing factions. She was jailed for 23 days in solitary confinement and barred from practicing law for five years. Ebadi believes "there is no contradiction between an Islamic republic, Islam, and human rights."

Building Nations in the Middle East   L3

Instruct

■ **Introduce** Write the word *oil* on the board and ask students to describe its importance in modern American society. Remind students that several nations in the Middle East have large oil reserves. Ask **How might interest in Middle East oil influence United States actions and policies in the region?** *(It might encourage the United States to ensure its access to the region's large oil reserves.)*

■ **Teach** Ask students to identify the various forces that are shaping the Middle East today. List these on the board, adding to students' ideas if necessary. *(nationalism, Western influence, religious differences, vital resources, Islamic reforms, and women's roles)* Define and discuss each term as it applies to individual nations in the Middle East. Then, ask students to rank these forces in the order of their importance to the Middle East. Use the Think-Write-Pair-Share strategy (TE, p. T23) and have students share their rankings with one another.

■ **Quick Activity** Have students, in groups, create a chart comparing the leadership of Gamal Abdel Nasser, Ayatollah Khomeini, and the Saudi royal family. What views did each leader have about modernization and about relations with the United States?

Answer

✔ Islamists feel that secular government has led to social and economic ills. They believe that returning to Islamic principles will solve these problems.

Independent Practice

■ **Biography** To help students better understand Egypt's role as a leader in the Arab world, have them read *Gamal Abdel Nasser* and complete the worksheet.

All in One **Teaching Resources, Unit 5**, p. 31

■ Return to the Witness History quotation at the beginning of this section. Ask students if the Middle East has achieved the unity and renaissance that Nasser Rabat mentioned.

Monitor Progress

Check Reading and Note Taking Study Guide entries to confirm that students have accurately identified causes and effects of historical processes in the Middle East.

An Islamist Government
Iran's political leaders, who are Muslim clergymen, gather in 2003 to commemorate the death of Ayatollah Khomeini, a religious leader and the founder of Iran's Islamist government. The leaders are seated beneath a giant portrait of Khomeini. *How does promoting the memory of Khomeini help to justify rule by religious leaders?*

Building Nations in the Middle East

Across the Middle East, leaders sought to build strong and prosperous nations. However, in the years since World War II, each nation has faced different challenges.

Egypt, a Leader in the Arab World Egypt has the largest population of the Arab nations. While most of Egypt is desert, its large population is crammed into the narrow Nile River valley. Egypt's location is strategically important, because it shares a long border with Israel and controls the **Suez Canal,** which links Europe with Asia and East Africa.

In 1952, **Gamal Abdel Nasser** seized power in Egypt. Determined to modernize Egypt and stop Western domination, Nasser nationalized the Suez Canal in 1956, ending British and French control. Although Britain and France responded militarily, the United States and the Soviet Union forced them to withdraw. Nasser's Arab nationalism made him popular throughout the Arab world. Nasser led two unsuccessful wars against Israel. To counter U.S. support for Israel, Egypt relied on Soviet aid. Egypt's foreign relations thus took on Cold War significance.

In 1979, Nasser's successor, **Anwar Sadat,** became the first Arab leader to make peace with Israel. Sadat also weakened ties with the Soviet Union and sought U.S. aid. However, Islamists denounced the undemocratic government's failure to end corruption and poverty. In 1981, Muslim fundamentalists assassinated Sadat. Under Sadat's appointed successor, Hosni Mubarak, extremists turned to terrorist attacks, and harsh government crackdowns tended to increase support for Islamists.

Iran's Islamic Revolution Because of its vast oil fields, Iran was a focus of Cold War interest. Iran's ruler, Shah Mohammad Reza Pahlavi, favored the West but faced nationalist critics at home, led by **Mohammad Mosaddeq** (MAW sah dek). When Mosaddeq was elected prime minister in 1951, he nationalized the foreign-owned oil industry. With American help, the shah ousted Mosaddeq and returned Iran's oil industry to Western control. This move outraged many Iranians.

Over the next decades, the shah used oil wealth to build industries and redistribute land to peasants. He also gave new rights to women. Opposition to the shah grew, especially among the Islamic clergy. In response, the shah's secret police terrorized critics.

The shah's foes rallied behind Ayatollah **Ruhollah Khomeini** (ROO hoh lah koh MAY nee). The ayatollah, a religious leader, condemned Western influences and accused the shah of violating Islamic law. In 1979, massive protests drove the shah from power. Khomeini and his supporters proclaimed an Islamic republic.

The new government was a **theocracy,** or government by religious leaders. They ran the country based on Islamic law. Like the shah, they silenced critics. In 1979, Islamists seized the American embassy in the capital and held 52 hostages for more than a year. The new Islamic republic soon

Differentiated Instruction   Solutions for All Learners

L4 Advanced Readers   L4 Gifted and Talented

This section focuses on the tensions between Islamic religious traditions and Western ideas and practices in the Muslim Middle East. Using this section as a starting point, have students conduct research either online or in the library on the dimensions of this tension in Iran and Saudi Arabia. Encourage students to find recent accounts of both nations in periodicals. Based on their research, have them compare these two oil-rich Muslim nations. Have students answer the following questions: What are the similarities and the differences between these two nations? What are the relationships between their governments and fundamentalist religious leaders? What tensions have arisen from their governments' relations with Western powers?

Answer

Caption It enforces the idea that he was a successful leader and validates the religious-based government.

faced a long, bloody war with its neighbor, Iraq, and tense relations with the West. The United States imposed economic sanctions and accused Iran of backing terrorists. After the 2003 U.S. occupation of Iraq, American officials accused Iran of providing weapons to Iraqi fighters for use against U.S. forces. Iran was also accused of using nuclear research as a cover for developing nuclear weapons.

Oil, Religion, and Threats to Stability Saudi Arabia, a vast desert land, has the world's largest oil reserves. It also includes Islam's holy land. Since the 1920s, kings from the Sa'ud (sah OOD) family have ruled Saudi Arabia. They justify their rule by their commitment to the strict Wahhabi sect of Sunni Islam.

However, Saudi Arabia's economic development after World War II depended on massive oil exports to the Western world. In return, Saudi leaders relied on the military support of the United States. Although Saudi Arabia joined the OPEC oil embargo in 1973, the nation's rulers quickly returned to their cooperative relationship with the West.

To build support within the country, the royal family backed fundamentalist religious leaders. However, some of these leaders and their followers criticized the kingdom's close ties to the West. They also charged that Western influence in the kingdom violated Islamic principles.

Increasingly, opponents of the kingdom's Western ties adopted violent or terrorist tactics. Attacks on western targets included an attack on a U.S. military compound in 1996 and another on a U.S. consulate in 2004. These attacks threatened to disrupt the Saudi oil industry, which depends on Western expertise. Some feared that growing unrest could threaten the country's ability to supply oil vital to the world's economy.

Other oil-rich monarchies along the Persian Gulf, such as Kuwait, Bahrain, Qatar, and the United Arab Emirates, face similar threats. In Kuwait, Qatar, and the U.A.E., foreign citizens are a majority of the population. In Bahrain, there has been growing opposition among the majority of the people, who follow Shiite Islam, toward Bahrain's royal family, who follow the Sunni branch of Islam.

✔ **Checkpoint** What were Ayatollah Khomeini's reasons for opposing the shah?

SECTION 4 Assessment

Progress Monitoring *Online*
For: Self-quiz with vocabulary practice
Web Code: nba-3141

Terms, People, and Places
1. For each term, person, or place listed in the beginning of the section, write a sentence explaining its significance.

Note Taking
2. **Reading Skill: Identify Causes and Effects** Use your completed concept web to answer the Focus Question: What were some main similarities and differences in the nations of the Middle East?

Comprehension and Critical Thinking
3. **Summarize** How was the Holocaust connected to the birth of Israel?
4. **Identify Central Issues** What changes in government policies did the Islamists seek?
5. **Draw Conclusions** Why did Egypt attract the interest of the superpowers during the Cold War?
6. **Synthesize Information** How has the Saudi royal family's support for fundamentalism made their kingdom more unstable in recent years?

● **Writing About History**
Quick Write: Revise Your Writing When you write a compare-and-contrast essay, combining short sentences can improve your writing. Write a short sentence that states a fact about a Middle Eastern country. Write a second sentence stating a similar or different fact about another Middle Eastern country. Revise your sentences by joining them into a single sentence that compares or contrasts these facts, using conjunctions such as *while, whereas, yet, both, and,* or *also.*

- Have students use the Quick Study Guide to prepare for this chapter's test. Students may wish to refer to the following pages as they review:

Common Themes in New Nations
Section 1, pp. 652–657; Section 2, pp. 659–661; Section 3, pp. 663–668; Section 4, pp. 670–675

Leaders of New Nations
Section 1, pp. 654–655; Section 2, pp. 659, 661; Section 3, pp. 663–666, 669; Section 4, pp. 670, 674–675

New Nations Emerge
Section 1, pp. 653–656; Section 2, pp. 658–659, 661; Section 3, pp. 664, 666–668; Section 4, p. 671

Key Events in the Emergence of New Nations
Section 1, pp. 653, 655–656; Section 2, pp. 659, 661; Section 3, pp. 662–668; Section 4, pp. 671–674

- For additional review, remind students to refer to the **L3**

  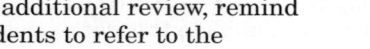 **Reading and Note Taking Study Guide**

Section Note Taking Study Guide, pp. 200, 202, 204, 206
Section Summaries, pp. 201, 203, 205, 207

- Have students access **Web Code nbp-3151** for this chapter's *History Interactive* timeline, which includes expanded entries and additional events.

- If students need more instruction on analyzing timelines, have them read the **Skills Handbook,** p. SH30.

- When students have completed their study of the chapter, distribute Chapter Tests A and B.

  All in One Teaching Resources, Unit 5, pp. 37–42

For **Progress Monitoring Online,** refer students to the Self-test with vocabulary practice at **Web Code nba-3151.**

CHAPTER **19**

Quick Study Guide

Progress Monitoring *Online*
For: Self-test with vocabulary practice
Web Code: nba-3151

■ Common Themes in New Nations

- Borders drawn by European colonial powers left nations with diverse religions and ethnic groups.
- Ethnic and religious diversity has brought conflicts.
- Military coups, one-party systems, and dictatorships kept some countries from achieving democracy.
- Citizens and foreign lenders have forced former dictatorships to hold elections and transition to democracy.
- Natural resources such as oil have been a source of wealth for some nations but have fueled conflicts in others.
- During the Cold War, the United States and Soviet Union competed for influence, particularly in regions with natural resources such as oil, or locations near strategic waterways.

■ Leaders of New Nations

- Jawaharlal Nehru, *first prime minister of India*
- Indira Gandhi, *first female prime minister of India*
- Aung San Suu Kyi, *leader of Myanmar democracy movement*
- Sukarno, *founder and first president of Indonesia*
- Suharto, *military dictator of Indonesia*
- Corazon Aquino, *democratic president of the Philippines*
- Kwame Nkrumah, *founder and first president of Ghana*
- Jomo Kenyatta, *founder and first president of Kenya*
- David Ben-Gurion, *first prime minister of Israel*
- Gamal Abdel Nasser, *an Arab nationalist and first president of Egypt*
- Mohammad Reza Pahlavi, *shah of Iran*
- Ruhollah Khomeini, *leader of the religious government of Iran*

■ New Nations Emerge

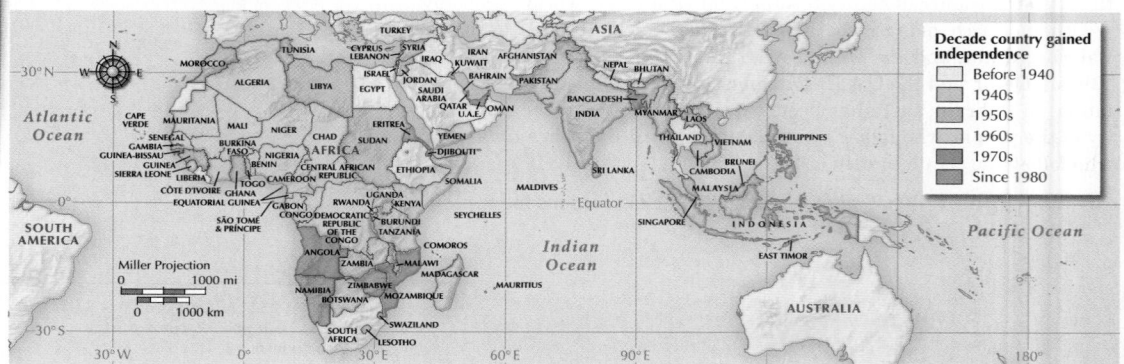

Decade country gained independence
- Before 1940
- 1940s
- 1950s
- 1960s
- 1970s
- Since 1980

■ Key Events in the Emergence of New Nations

Africa and the Middle East

South and Southeast Asia

1946 Syria and Jordan gain independence.

1947 India and Pakistan win independence after partition.

1948 Israel is founded.

1956–1966 More than 30 African nations win independence.

1966 Suharto establishes military dictatorship in Indonesia.

| 1940 | 1950 | 1960 | 1970 |

Differentiated Instruction   Solutions for All Learners

L1 Special Needs   L2 Less Proficient Readers
For students acquiring basic skills:

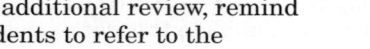 **Adapted Reading and Note Taking Study Guide**
Adapted Section Note Taking Study Guide, pp. 200, 202, 204, 206
Adapted Section Summaries, pp. 201, 203, 205, 207

L2 English Language Learners
For Spanish-speaking students:

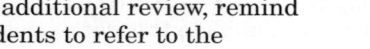 **Spanish Reading and Note Taking Study Guide**
Spanish Section Note Taking Study Guide, pp. 200, 202, 204, 206
Spanish Section Summaries, pp. 201, 203, 205, 207

Concept Connector

⍰ Essential Question Review

To connect prior knowledge with what you have learned in this chapter, answer the questions below in your Concept Connector journal. Use the journal in the Reading and Note Taking Study Guide to record your answers (or go to www.phschool.com **Web Code:** nad-3107).

1. **Revolution** Between 1946 and 1970, European colonies around the world won independence. Choose one of these colonies and compare its struggle for independence with the American Revolution, which brought independence to the United States in the late 1700s. Consider the following:
   - the presence or the absence of military conflict
   - the challenge of forming stable governments after independence

2. **Nationalism** Although India has large religious minorities, the Bharatiya Janata Party (BJP) promoted Hindu nationalism, or the idea that India should favor the Hindu majority and the Hindu religion. How do you think the BJP's stand affected peace and stability in India?

3. **Dictatorship** In many African nations that gained independence after World War II, dictators seized power and established one-party political systems. These leaders claimed that multiparty systems encouraged disunity. Do you think the dictators' concerns were genuine? What appeal might the disunity argument have for citizens of a newly independent nation?

4. **Geography's Impact** The world's largest reserves of oil are located in the Middle East. What impact has the location of this valuable resource had on global politics and the economy?

■ Connections to Today

1. **Conflict: Struggles for Independence** Former European colonies such as Algeria had to fight deadly wars to win their independence. Today, in different parts of the world, people continue to fight for independence. Examples include Darfur, where rebels have fought against Sudan, and Papua, where rebels seek independence from Indonesia. Research one of these regions. Explain why this region is fighting for independence.

2. **Belief Systems: World Religions** In this chapter, you have seen that religions remain an important force in today's world. Turn to the Concept Connector Handbook on Culture at the back of your textbook. There you will find a list of world religions and their key beliefs. List the beliefs, traditions, customs, and sacred writings of Judaism, Christianity, Islam, Buddhism, and Hinduism. Then, using reliable sources from the Internet or a library, research and list the present-day geographic distribution of each of these religions.

1973 OPEC oil embargo

1979 Iranian revolution

1990–2002 African nations move toward democracy.

Mid-2000s Tensions grow between Iran and the West.

1980   1990   2000   2010

1971 Bangladesh wins independence.

1986 "People power" revolution in the Philippines

1998 Indonesia returns to democracy.

History _Interactive_
For: Interactive timeline
Web Code: nbp-3151

Concept | Connector ⍰

Tell students that the main concepts for this chapter are Revolution, Nationalism, Dictatorship, and Geography's Impact and then ask them to answer the Essential Question Review questions on this page. Discuss the Connections to Today topics and ask students to answer the questions that follow.

Essential Question Review

1. Some nations gained independence without military conflict. For others, independence came only after a military conflict like the American Revolution. Many new nations in Africa and Asia had greater difficulty forming stable governments than did early America.

2. Sample: Favoring the Hindu majority likely increased religious tensions, so it did not contribute to peace or stability.

3. Responses will vary. Students might suggest that the rulers honestly believed in what they were doing, or that they might have only done it for power. The disunity argument might be appealing to some citizens because of their fear of chaos and disorder in a new nation.

4. Oil has influenced how the United States and other powers interact with Middle Eastern nations. While it is a significant source of wealth for a number of nations, oil (along with religious and ethnic conflict) continues to cause division in the Middle East.

Connections to Today

1. Explanations should state the main reasons why the chosen region is seeking independence. For example, in Sudan, rebels in Darfur seek freedom from Arab domination.

2. Responses should provide accurate information about each of these five religions, including beliefs, traditions, customs, sacred writings, and geographic distribution.

For additional review of this   **L3**
chapter's core concepts, remind students to refer to the

📝 **Reading and Note Taking Study Guide**
Concept Connector, pp. 255, 270, 284, 291

Chapter Assessment

Terms, People, and Places

1. theocracy
2. Corazon Aquino
3. Indira Gandhi
4. kibbutz
5. nonalignment
6. coup d'état

Main Ideas

7. to provide separate nations for Muslims and Hindus, who had been fighting

8. Divisions along ethnic or religious lines sometimes brought violent conflicts.

9. Myanmar struggles under a brutal dictatorship. Indonesia and the Philippines have fragile democracies. Malaysia has a more stable democracy.

10. Most African nations won their independence during the 1950s and 1960s, either through political pressure or armed battle.

11. resistance from European colonial settlers, ethnic strife resulting from European-drawn national boundaries that ignored ethnic divisions, and single-party political systems and dictatorships

12. Islamists have condemned Western influences in the Middle East and called for governments based on fundamentalist Islamic principles.

Chapter Focus Question

13. Former colonies gained independence either through political pressure or armed resistance. They faced challenges of forming democratic governments, resolving ethnic and religious conflicts, and deciding how much to modernize.

Critical Thinking

14. In both Indonesia and the Philippines, popular protest has forced non-democratic leaders from office and demanded democratic reforms.

15. In Iran, religious conservatism led to the overthrow of the Shah and the establishment of a theocracy. In Israel, the desire for a Jewish homeland led to the founding of an entirely new nation. In Saudi Arabia, women's liberties are restricted based on a conservative interpretation of Islamic law.

16. Refugees are desperate to flee from their homes despite uncomfortable and crowded conditions.

Chapter Assessment

Terms, People, and Places

Match the following definitions with the terms listed below.

Indira Gandhi	coup d'état
nonalignment	theocracy
Corazon Aquino	kibbutz

1. rule by religious leaders
2. a political leader in the Philippines
3. the first female prime minister of India
4. a collective farm
5. political and diplomatic independence
6. the forcible overthrow of a government

Main Ideas

Section 1 (pp. 650–655)
7. Why was British India divided into India and Pakistan?
8. How did religious and ethnic diversity pose challenges for South Asian nations after independence?

Section 2 (pp. 656–659)
9. Compare the nations of Southeast Asia in the progress that they have made toward democracy.

Section 3 (pp. 660–667)
10. How did African nations win their independence? How did this differ among nations?
11. What obstacles slowed progress toward democracy for some African nations?

Section 4 (pp. 668–673)
12. How has the Islamist movement affected politics in the Middle East?

Chapter Focus Question
13. How did former European colonies gain independence, and what challenges did they face after independence?

Critical Thinking

14. **Draw Conclusions** How did the Philippines and Indonesia achieve democracy?
15. **Synthesize Information** How has religion influenced the recent history of the Middle East?
16. **Analyzing Visuals** The photograph below shows refugees from the partition of India and Pakistan. What does it suggest about conditions for these refugees?

17. **Make Comparisons** Compare the impact of ethnic and religious diversity on the histories of India and Pakistan.
18. **Analyze Information** How have the natural resources of the Middle East affected its recent history?
19. **Draw Conclusions** How were African nations affected by military rule and dictatorships? Support your conclusions with examples.
20. **Recognize Cause and Effect** What have been some lasting effects of colonial rule on African nations?

● Writing About History

In this chapter's four Section Assessments, you learned how to write a compare-contrast essay.

Writing a Compare-Contrast Essay Write a compare-contrast essay on the post-independence histories of two countries covered in different sections of this chapter. Discuss similarities and differences in the histories of the two countries. Consult page SH10 of the Writing Handbook for additional help.

Prewriting
• Go online or do library research to find information about the post-independence histories of countries covered in this chapter.

• Choose two countries that interest you and take notes about the challenges these countries faced.
• Gather evidence that supports comparisons and contrasts between these countries.

Drafting
• Write a first paragraph with a thesis statement and details about similarities between the two countries.
• Write a second paragraph with a topic sentence and details about differences between the two countries.

Revising
• Use the guidelines for revising your report on page SH12 of the Writing Handbook.

17. In India, religious diversity has been the main source of conflict and has led to violence between the majority Hindus and minority Muslims and Sikhs. In Pakistan, ethnic conflict has been important. Ethnic conflict led Bangladesh to declare independence from Pakistan.

18. Oil has brought great wealth to parts of the Middle East. It has also made the region strategically important to the United States and other oil importers.

19. Military rule and dictatorships led to widespread conflict, corruption, and economic disruption in nations such as the Congo, Algeria, and Nigeria.

20. Economic influence from former colonial powers continues in some nations. The arbitrary national divisions created by European colonizers have led to many ethnic and religious conflicts.

Document-Based Assessment

The Kashmir Question

In 1947, British India was partitioned into Hindu-majority India and Muslim-majority Pakistan. Kashmir is claimed by both India and Pakistan and has been a battleground between the two countries. The documents below help to show why the "Kashmir problem" remains worrisome today.

Document A

Hum kya chahtey? Azaadi! (What do we want? Freedom!)

—Slogan in Kashmir Valley

Document B

"Mr. Jinnah and his colleagues in the Muslim League, the creators of Pakistan, had always considered that the Vale of Kashmir at least would form part of the new Islamic State . . . When in 1933 Choudhri Rahmat Ali coined the word Pakistan as a suitable name for the State, he intended the letter K in 'Pak' to stand for Kashmir. The geographical and historical links between the Panjab and the Vale of Kashmir were so close that it was inevitable that the two regions should find themselves combined in the thoughts of the protagonists of a separate Islamic State."

—From ***Crisis in Kashmir, 1947–1966*** by Alastair Lamb

Document C

Document D

Religions of Kashmir, 1941

Other 3%
Hinduism 20%
Islam 77%

SOURCE: *Census of India, 1941*

Document E

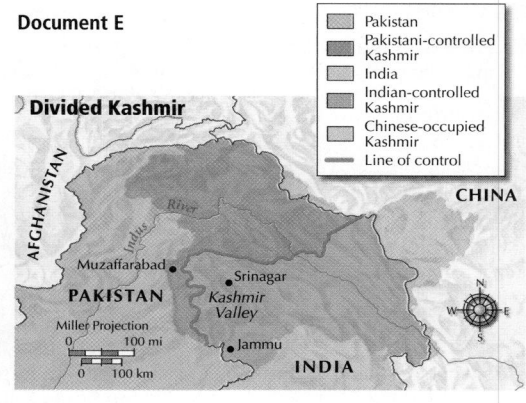

Divided Kashmir

- Pakistan
- Pakistani-controlled Kashmir
- India
- Indian-controlled Kashmir
- Chinese-occupied Kashmir
- Line of control

Analyzing Documents

Use your knowledge of World War II and Documents A, B, C, D, and E to answer questions 1–4.

1. According to Document B, Kashmir and Pakistan share
   A the same heroes and poets.
   B a similar history and geography.
   C the same language and literature.
   D similar architecture and art.

2. What argument does the billboard in Document C support?
   A India is a diverse country, and the region of Kashmir is an important part of it.
   B India will never let go of Kashmir.
   C Kashmir is more beautiful than other parts of India.
   D Indians are tired of dealing with Kashmir and its thorny problems.

3. According to Document D, Kashmir's population
   A is evenly balanced among its different religions.
   B is about one-half Hindu and "Other."
   C only has two religious affiliations.
   D is more than three-quarters Muslim.

4. **Writing Task** Why has Kashmir continued to be a volatile spot for so long? What are the main causes of the conflict there? Use information from these documents along with information from the chapter to write your response.

● Writing About History

As students begin the assignment, refer them to p. SH10 of the **Writing Handbook** for help in writing a comparison-contrast essay. Remind them of the steps they should take to complete their assignment, including prewriting, drafting, and revising. For help in revising, remind them to use the guidelines on p. SH12 of the **Writing Handbook.**

Students' essays should focus on two countries from different sections of this chapter and show similarities and differences in at least two features. They should be well organized and contain an introduction, a body, and a conclusion. They should be free of grammatical and spelling errors. For scoring rubrics for writing assignments, see **Assessment Rubrics,** p. 8.

Answers

1. B
2. A
3. D
4. Responses should show an understanding of the causes of conflict in Kashmir and should use specific evidence from the documents and the chapter to support their conclusions.

CHAPTER 20

Regional Conflicts

Section	Core Instruction ⑬	Differentiated Instruction ① ② ④

Section 1
Conflicts Divide Nations

🕐 **.5 period, .25 block**

OBJECTIVES
- Explain the complex causes of ethnic and religious conflicts.
- Describe how war ravaged Chechnya.
- Understand how Yugoslavia broke apart.

Focus Question *Why have ethnic and religious conflicts divided some nations?*

Core Instruction

All in One Teaching Resources, Unit 5
Reading Strategy: Recognize Sequence, p. 47
Vocabulary Builder, p. 46
Outline Map: Former Yugoslavia, p. 53
Section 1 Quiz, p. 43

Reading and Note Taking Study Guide
Note Taking Study Guide, p. 208
Section 1 Summary, p. 209

Note Taking Transparencies, 198

WITNESS HISTORY Audio CD
A Young Girl in Wartime

Progress Monitoring Transparencies, 137

Color Transparencies, 193, 194

Teaching Resources, Skills Handbook
Prereading the Chapter, pp. 1–2
Word Knowledge Rating Form, p. 3
K-W-L Chart, p. 4

Differentiated Instruction

① **Adapted Reading and Note Taking Study Guide**
Note Taking Study Guide, p. 208 **SN**
Section 1 Summary, p. 209 **SN**

② **Adapted Reading and Note Taking Study Guide**
Note Taking Study Guide, p. 208 **LPR**
Section 1 Summary, p. 209 **LPR**

Spanish Reading and Note Taking Study Guide
Note Taking Study Guide, p. 208 **ELL**
Section 1 Summary, p. 209 **ELL**

④ **All in One Teaching Resources, Unit 5**
Primary Source: A Family in Sarajevo, p. 48 **AR, GT**

*Student Edition Audio **SN**
Differentiated Instruction Activity, Teacher's Edition, p. 684 **SN**

*Guided Reading Audio, Spanish **ELL**
*Student Edition Audio **LPR**
Differentiated Instruction Activity, Teacher's Edition, p. 684 **LPR, ELL**

Differentiated Instruction Activity, Teacher's Edition, p. 683 **AR, GT**
Extend Activity, Teacher's Edition, p. 685 **AR, GT**

Section 2
Struggles in Africa

🕐 **2 periods, 1 block**

OBJECTIVES
- Understand South Africa's struggle for freedom.
- Describe how struggles for independence and Cold War rivalries brought decades of conflict to South Africa's neighbors.
- Analyze how ethnic conflicts killed millions in Rwanda and Sudan.

Focus Question *Why have conflicts plagued some African countries?*

Core Instruction

All in One Teaching Resources, Unit 5
Section 2 Quiz, p. 44

Reading and Note Taking Study Guide
Note Taking Study Guide, p. 210
Section 2 Summary, p. 211

Note Taking Transparencies, 199A–199B

WITNESS HISTORY Audio CD
Recovering from Genocide

Progress Monitoring Transparencies, 138

Color Transparencies, 195, 196

Witness History Discovery School™
video program, *Nelson Mandela and the End of Apartheid*

Differentiated Instruction

① **Adapted Reading and Note Taking Study Guide**
Note Taking Study Guide, p. 210 **SN**
Section 2 Summary, p. 211 **SN**

② **Adapted Reading and Note Taking Study Guide**
Note Taking Study Guide, p. 210 **LPR**
Section 2 Summary, p. 211 **LPR**

④ **All in One Teaching Resources, Unit 5**
Viewpoints: Abolishing Apartheid, p. 51 **AR, GT**
Biography: Nelson Mandela, p. 52 **AR, GT**
Unit 5 Simulation: Beyond Apartheid, pp. 103–106 **AR, GT**

Differentiated Instruction Activity, Teacher's Edition, p. 688 **SN**

Spanish Reading and Note Taking Study Guide
Note Taking Study Guide, p. 210 **ELL**
Section 2 Summary, p. 211 **ELL**

Differentiated Instruction Activity, Teacher's Edition, p. 688 **LPR, ELL**

Extend Activity, Teacher's Edition, p. 690 **AR, GT**

---

*Audio support is available for all sections.

Section	**Core Instruction** L2	**Differentiated** Instruction L1 L2 L4

Section 3
Conflicts in the Middle East

 2 periods, 1 block

OBJECTIVES
■ Understand why Arabs and Israelis have fought over land.
■ Explain why civil war ravaged Lebanon.
■ Outline Iraq's long history of conflict.

Focus Question *What are the causes of conflict in the Middle East?*

Core Instruction

 All in One **Teaching Resources, Unit 5**
Outline Map: Israel and the Occupied Territories, p. 54
Geography Quiz, p. 55
Section 3 Quiz, p. 45

Reading and Note Taking Study Guide
Note Taking Study Guide, p. 212
Section 3 Summary, p. 213
Concept Connector, pp. 255, 267, 275, 278

Note Taking Transparencies, 200

WITNESS HISTORY Audio CD
Two Peoples Claim the Same Land

Progress Monitoring Transparencies, 139

Color Transparencies, 197, 198

Differentiated Instruction

L1 **Adapted Reading and Note Taking Study Guide**
Note Taking Study Guide, p. 212 SN
Section 3 Summary, p. 213 SN
Concept Connector, pp. 255, 267, 275, 278 SN

L2 **Adapted Reading and Note Taking Study Guide**
Note Taking Study Guide, p. 212 LPR
Section 3 Summary, p. 213 LPR
Concept Connector, pp. 255, 267, 275, 278 LPR

L4 **All in One** **Teaching Resources, Unit 5**
Viewpoints: The Creation of the State of Israel, p. 50 AR, GT
Primary Source: Sowing "Seeds of Peace," by Sara Rimer, p. 49 AR, GT

Differentiated Instruction Activity,
Teacher's Edition, pp. 693, 696 SN

Spanish Reading and Note Taking Study Guide
Note Taking Study Guide, p. 212 ELL
Section 3 Summary, p. 213 ELL
Concept Connector, pp. 255, 267, 275, 278 ELL

Differentiated Instruction Activity,
Teacher's Edition, pp. 693, 696 LPR, ELL

Differentiated Instruction Activity,
Teacher's Edition, p. 694 AR, GT

Extend Activity,
Teacher's Edition, pp. 680c, 697 AR, GT

Assessment Resources

- **Progress Monitoring Transparencies,** 137–139
- **SuccessTracker™,** Chapter 20
- **Document-Based Assessment,** pp. 95–109
- *ExamView*® **Test Bank CD-ROM,** Chapter 20
- **All in One** **Teaching Resources, Unit 5,** Chapter Tests, pp. 56–61
- **Progress Monitoring** *Online* **Quizzes,** Chapter 20
- **Assessment Rubrics**

Differentiated Instruction **Key**

L1 Special Needs	**LPR** Less Proficient Readers
L2 Basic to Average	**AR** Advanced Readers
L3 All Students	**SN** Special Needs Students
L4 Average to Advanced	**GT** Gifted and Talented
	ELL English Language Learner

Author's Notes

Struggle in South Africa

No amount of international pressure, guerrilla assault, or domestic resistance seemed to shake the grip of European settlers in the Republic of South Africa [during the time that other African nations were emerging from European rule]. There the winds were blowing all the other way during the postwar decades, for this was the period that saw the imposition of the system of *apartheid* on South Africa.

The colonial and precolonial history of South Africa is a complex story of peoples, rights, and freedoms in conflict. Though British colonists . . . dominated the state economically in the twentieth century, the Dutch-descended Afrikaners held political power. The condition of the indigenous Africans in South Africa had always

been drastically inferior to that of the Europeans. But at the end of World War II the ruling Afrikaner Nationalist party set out to codify that inferiority in a system of discriminatory racial legislation reminiscent of the old Jim Crow laws in the American South.

Apartheid means "apartness" and the physical separation of the ethnic communities was clearly one purpose of the apartheid laws passed in the years around 1950. Europeans, black Africans, Asians, and others were to live in separate areas, be educated in separate schools, work at different jobs, find recreation in separate places. Marriages between Europeans and others were made illegal. Black Africans had to carry passes in white areas.

But it was, of course, more than a matter of separation. Black Africans were confined to the least productive

lands, the least pleasant living places; the best jobs were closed to them; they could not be elected to parliament. Apartheid meant separate and *un*equal, and all Africa knew it.

For decades after the imposition of apartheid, then, South Africa was caught up in a tragic, brutal confrontation, a struggle of guerrillas and counterinsurgency, of border raids and military incursions. South Africa was pitted against a handful of states on its borders—from Tanzania in the east to Angola in the west. Liberal foreign governments increasingly excluded South Africa from trade, capital markets, and even athletic competitions to punish it for its racist policies.

—Anthony Esler, *The Human Venture: From Prehistory to the Present*, (Upper Saddle River, New Jersey: Pearson Education 2004), pp. 700–701

Extend Online

The Israeli-Palestinian Conflict

Using the following steps, have students research recent developments in the Israeli-Palestinian conflict. Have students write a paragraph about their findings and prepare for a classroom discussion about the conflict.

Prepare for the Activity Tell students that there are many different perspectives on the Israeli-Palestinian conflict among Israelis, Palestinians, and people living outside the region. Explain that understanding the different perspectives on the conflict can help in understanding the conflict itself.

Conduct the Activity For help in starting the activity, send students to Web Code nbe-3201. Each student will research recent developments in the Palestinian-Israeli conflict. You may assign students to focus in groups on different aspects of the conflict or have students work individually. Have students write a one-paragraph summary of their findings and be prepared to discuss their findings in class.

Follow-Up Conduct a class discussion based on the following questions: What are the main concerns of Palestinians today? What are the main concerns of Israelis? How might the conflict be resolved peacefully?

Differentiated Instruction   Solutions for All Learners

Descriptive Phrases L2

To further English language learners' acquisition of vocabulary, ask them to create descriptive phrases for key terms, people, and places. Assign students to work either individually or with a partner and find examples of the terms, people and places listed at the beginning of each section in the chapter in their text. Instruct students to create a bulleted list of descriptive phrases and adjectives that describe their given topic. Provide students with a thesaurus to assist them with the assignment. Then ask students to read their list of descriptive phrases to the class. Allow members of the class to guess what is being described. Write the list of possible terms, people, and places on the board to assist students in guessing correctly.

Historical Precedents L4

Modern events do not happen in a vacuum; they are usually shaped by many preceding causes and situations. Students should place the regional conflicts studied in this chapter within the greater context of world history. Ask them to draw upon previously learned information to understand the motives and perspectives of those involved in the conflicts.

To help students develop an understanding of the continuum of history, ask them to formulate a list of causes of events being studied, such as the fighting in Kosovo or the conflict in the Middle East. Then have them determine which cause was the most significant in ultimately shaping the outcome of the event. As a class, vote on which cause was the most significant. Ask students, if this cause were removed, might the event have been altered or prevented?

Modeling Reading and Writing Skills

Choosing a Topic
Explain that in this chapter students will be writing a research paper. (See Writing About History, p. 700). Remind students that when they choose a topic for a research paper, they should pick one that interests them, has enough information available to present a full discussion of the topic, and yet is narrow enough to cover fully in a short report. Ask students to think of some things that they would like to learn more about. Have students share their topics with the group.

Take one of their suggested topics and write it on the board. Then have students think of similar and more narrowly focused ideas. Explain that this kind of process helps to focus on a topic that is both interesting and manageable. Have students follow the same procedure in beginning their own topic search for their research paper. Suggest that they list, diagram, or make a chart of their ideas.

Distinguish Fact and Opinion
Explain that when reading primary and secondary sources, students should distinguish between facts and opinions. Remind students that facts can be proven true, while opinions are beliefs. Though they may be valid, they cannot be proved.

To model this skill, read aloud the Witness History Primary Source that opens Section 1. Point out that the facts are that a shell fell in the park, the park is in front of Zlata's house, many people were hurt, and Nina died. These can all be proved true. The opinion is that Nina was "such a sweet, nice" girl, because this statement cannot be proved.

Teach With Technology

PresentationEXPRESS™
Premium DVD

- Teach this chapter's core content using **PresentationExpress™ Premium,** which includes dynamic lecture notes, interactive game shows, songs, videos, and the ***ExamView®*** *QuickTake* assessment tool.

- To introduce this chapter using **PresentationExpress™ Premium,** start by asking students **Which of the following statements do you most agree with? (A) Ethnic and religious differences inevitably cause conflicts. (B) Ethnic and religious conflicts can be avoided only by separating different ethnic and religious groups. (C) While different ethnic and religious groups can coexist peacefully, there will be tensions because one group will always be privileged. (D) Different ethnic and religious groups can live together without tensions when no group enjoys an advantage over another.** Take a class poll or record students' answers using the QuickTake feature and discuss their responses. Point out that in this chapter, they will read about regional conflicts around the world.

Technology Resources

- Student**EXPRESS** CD-ROM, Chapter 20

- Teacher**EXPRESS** CD-ROM, Chapter 20

- Presentation**EXPRESS™ Premium DVD,** Chapter 20

- **WITNESS HISTORY** Audio CD, Chapter 20

- *ExamView* **Test Bank CD-ROM,** English and Spanish, Chapter 20

- **Guided Reading Audio,** Spanish, Chapter 20

- **Student Edition Audio,** Chapter 20

- **Witness History Discovery School™** video program, *Nelson Mandela and the End of Apartheid*

- **Experience It! Multimedia Pack**

Regional Conflicts
1945–Present

Bibliography

For the Teacher

Malcolm, Noel. *Kosovo: A Short History.* New York: New York University Press, 1998.

Ross, Dennis. *The Missing Peace: The Inside Story of the Fight for Middle East Peace.* New York: Farrar, Straus and Giroux, 2004.

For the Student

L2 Ellis, Deborah. *Three Wishes: Palestinian and Israeli Children Speak.* Toronto: Groundwood Books, 2004.

L3 Armstrong, Jennifer, ed. *Shattered: Stories of Children and War.* New York: Knopf Books for Young Readers, 2002.

WITNESS HISTORY AUDIO

Life in a War Zone

For more than a year, hostile troops surrounded the city of Sarajevo in Bosnia and fired down on it from the hills above. Zlatko Dizdarevic, a journalist in Sarajevo, wrote this journal entry during the conflict:

❝It's been a relentless morning. Shells are falling close by us, perhaps closer than ever before. The official alert remains in force; so does our private and personal alert. We evaluate our chances, run risks, and keep hoping.**❞**

Listen to the Witness History audio to hear more about the war in Bosnia.

◀ **A boy dodging sniper fire to get water, Sarajevo, Bosnia, 1993**

Zlata's Diary, a teenage girl's account of the conflict in Bosnia

Chapter Preview

Chapter Focus Question Why have deadly conflicts plagued some regions of the world?

Nelson Mandela, who led a struggle against racial discrimination and became president of South Africa

Section 1
Conflicts Divide Nations

Section 2
Struggles in Africa

Section 3
Conflicts in the Middle East

A fallen statue of Saddam Hussein, the dictator of Iraq, who was overthrown by American troops

Use the ☑ **Quick Study Timeline** at the end of this chapter to preview chapter events.

 Concept Connector ONLINE

To explore Essential Questions related to this chapter, go to PHSchool.com
Web Code: nbd-3207

Chapter-Level Resources

■ **All in One** Vocabulary Builder; Reading Strategy; Enrichments; Outline Maps; Geography Quiz; Chapter Test
■ Document-Based Assessments
■ AYP Monitoring Assessments
■ *ExamView* Test Bank CD-ROM
■ Guided Reading Audio, Spanish
■ Student Edition Audio CD

Previewing the Chapter

■ **WITNESS HISTORY** Point out that Sarajevo is the capital of Bosnia, which faced a deadly regional conflict during the 1990s. Much of the city lies in a valley and faced daily bombing and sniper fire from the surrounding hills. Zlatko Dizdarevic recorded his experiences in the embattled city in a diary. Read the Witness History selection aloud or play the accompanying audio. Ask students to predict how this kind of conflict would affect people's lives. Tell them that they will learn more in this chapter about regional conflicts, including their causes and effects.

■))) AUDIO **Witness History Audio CD,** Life in a War Zone

■ **Analyzing the Visuals** Ask students to study the photo of the Bosnian boy risking sniper fire to get water. Ask **Why would someone risk being shot to get water?** *(because water supplies must have been disrupted in safe areas, and a lack of water is also deadly)* Have students discuss how this kind of warfare would affect people's ability to make a living, raise children, or vote in democratic elections.

■ **Focus** Write the Chapter Focus Question on the board. Tell students to keep this question in mind as they read the chapter. *(Answer appears with Chapter Assessment answers.)* Have students preview the section titles for this chapter.

Differentiated Instruction   Solutions for All Learners

The following Teacher's Edition strategies are suitable for students of varying abilities.

L1 Special Needs Students, pp. 684, 688, 693, 696 **SN**

L2 English Language Learners, pp. 684, 688, 693, 696 **ELL**

L2 Less Proficient Readers, pp. 684, 688, 693, 696 **LPR**

L4 Gifted and Talented Students, pp. 683, 694 **GT**

L4 Advanced Readers, pp. 683, 694 **AR**

Note Taking Study Guide With Concept Connector Journal
For online access: Web code: nbd-3207
For print alternative: Reading and Note Taking Study Guide booklet

Objectives

As you teach this section, keep students focused on the following objectives to help them answer the Section Focus Question and master core content.

- Explain the complex causes of ethnic and religious conflicts.
- Describe how war ravaged Chechnya.
- Understand how Yugoslavia broke apart.

Build Background Knowledge **L3**

Ask students to recall that, after World War I, Serbians dominated the multiethnic state of Yugoslavia, Soviet Russia included many ethnic minorities, and Ireland was divided along religious lines. Ask students to predict the challenges in these regions.

Set a Purpose **L3**

- **WITNESS HISTORY** Read the selection aloud or play the audio.

  AUDIO **Witness History Audio CD,** A Young Girl in Wartime

  Ask **What does Zlata describe in her journal entry?** *(the death of a friend when a bomb falls on the park where Zlata used to play)* **What is Zlata's tone? Is she surprised?** *(She sounds resigned, as if this has happened before.)* **What does Zlata's experience suggest about everyday life in Sarajevo in 1992?** *(It was full of violence.)*

- **Focus** Point out the Section Focus Question and write it on the board. Tell students to refer to this question as they read. *(Answer appears with Section 1 Assessment answers.)*

- **Preview** Have students preview the Section Objectives and the list of Terms, People, and Places.

- **Reading Skill** Have students use the *Reading Strategy: Recognize Sequence* worksheet.

All in One Teaching Resources, Unit 5, p. 47

Zlata Filipovic in 1994

A Young Girl in Wartime

Zlata Filipovic (fee LEEP uh vich) was 11 years old in 1992 when she began a diary about her life in war-torn Sarajevo, the capital of Bosnia. Here is an excerpt:

❝ Today a shell fell on the park in front of my house, the park where I used to play and sit with my girl-friends. A lot of people were hurt . . . AND NINA IS DEAD . . . She was such a sweet, nice little girl.❞
—Zlata Filipovic, *Zlata's Diary*

Bosnia is just one of the nations that have faced ethnic, religious, or national conflicts in recent decades.

Focus Question Why have ethnic and religious conflicts divided some nations?

Conflicts Divide Nations

Objectives
- Explain the complex causes of ethnic and religious conflicts.
- Describe how war ravaged Chechnya.
- Understand how Yugoslavia broke apart.

Terms, People, and Places

Northern Ireland	Slobodan Milosevic
Good Friday Agreement	ethnic cleansing
Chechnya	Kosovo
multiethnic	

Note Taking

Reading Skill: Recognize Sequence Fill in a flowchart like the one below to keep track of the sequence of events in the conflicts in Northern Ireland, Chechnya, and Yugoslavia.

Sequence of Conflicts		
Northern Ireland	**Chechnya**	**Yugoslavia**
• 1922: Six Irish counties vote to remain in the United Kingdom.	•	•
•	•	•

In recent decades, wars have raged in many parts of the world. These conflicts had complex causes. But rivalries between different ethnic, religious, and nationalist groups have often led to civil wars and regional conflicts.

Sources of Conflict

Nationalism led to the creation of many new nations after World War II. Many of these nations were former colonies or mandates. Their borders had been drawn by European powers with little concern for ethnic, religious, or regional differences. As a result, these new nations had culturally diverse populations. In some cases, minorities controlled the government and imposed their will on the majority. Often, the majority ethnic or religious group dominated the government and the economy and oppressed other groups.

War in Sri Lanka Discrimination, or unfair treatment, based on language, ethnicity, and culture has frequently set one group against another. In the island nation of Sri Lanka, discrimination and violence by majority Sinhalese Buddhists against Tamil-speaking Hindus led to rebellion. Since 1983, Tamil rebels, known as the Tamil Tigers, have fought to establish a separate Tamil homeland. The Tamil Tigers used terrorist tactics and guerrilla warfare. Peace talks held in 2002 led to a truce that slowed, but did not end the violence. However, by early 2009, government troops had toppled several Tamil rebel strongholds in a final push to end the 25-year-old civil war.

Vocabulary Builder

Use the information below and the following resources to teach the high-use word from this section.
All in One Teaching Resources, Unit 5, p. 46; Teaching Resources, Skills Handbook, p. 3

High-Use Word	Definition and Sample Sentence
dominate, p. 684	*v.* to control or have power over The high school squad **dominated** the game against the middle school team.

Divisions in Canada Some countries, such as Canada, have found peaceful ways to resolve internal conflicts. Although Canada is mostly English-speaking, the province of Quebec is mainly French-speaking. At times, many people in Quebec wanted to separate from Canada. While a few separatists turned to violence, most worked within Canada's democratic system to protect their language and culture.

Troubles in Northern Ireland Religious and economic discrimination fueled a long struggle in Northern Ireland. When Ireland won independence in 1922, Britain kept control of **Northern Ireland,** the six northern counties that had a Protestant majority. Faced with discrimination, minority Catholics demanded civil rights and unification with the rest of Ireland. Protestants wanted Northern Ireland to remain part of Britain.

In the 1960s, extremists on both sides turned to violence and terrorism. The mostly Catholic Irish Republican Army (IRA) attacked Protestants, while armed Protestant groups targeted Catholics. The violence, known as "the Troubles," raged for three decades. Finally, in 1998, both sides signed a peace accord, known as the **Good Friday Agreement.** Protestants and Catholics set up a power-sharing government in 2007. Although there have been isolated acts of violence, most people hoped that peace would last after years of conflict.

✓ **Checkpoint** Why did conflict break out in Northern Ireland?

Russia and Its Neighbors

Ethnic and religious tensions in Russia and in several former Soviet republics fueled conflicts within Russia. In 1994, separatists in **Chechnya** tried to break away from Russian rule. Chechnya was home to diverse ethnic and religious groups, including Muslim Chechens.

Russia crushed the Chechen revolt, killing many civilians. During two wars and nearly ten years of fighting, both sides committed atrocities. In the early 2000s, Chechen rebels launched terrorist attacks on Moscow, and killed school children in the city of Beslan. By 2009, a Russian-backed leader was rebuilding Chechnya, despite occasional violence.

In the oil-rich former Soviet republic of Azerbaijan, Azeris are the majority. In the region of Nagorno-Karabakh, however, ethnic Armenians outnumbered Azeris. When Armenians declared independence, fierce fighting raged. The Armenians gained control of the region, creating one million Azeri refugees.

In Georgia, another former Soviet republic, two provinces, South Ossetia and Abkhazia, wanted to break away. Russia backed the separatists. In 2008, after Georgia attacked separatists in South Ossetia, fighting erupted between Russian and Georgian troops. International pressure soon ended the conflict, but tensions remained high.

✓ **Checkpoint** What were the causes of the conflicts that erupted in the former Soviet Union?

Grozny in Ruins
Russian forces destroyed Grozny, the capital of Chechnya, during the fighting in 2000. The city was later rebuilt.

Contrasting Ethnic Relations

Nation	Political System	Ethnic Conflict
Sri Lanka	Limits rights of minority groups	Has led to violence
Canada	Protects minority groups	Resolved democratically

Chart Skills Based on the chart and the information in this section, explain why the response of the ethnic minority to discrimination in Sri Lanka differed from that in Canada.

■ **Note Taking** Have students read this section using the Guided Questioning strategy (TE, p. T20). As they read, have students fill in the flowchart.

✎ **Reading and Note Taking Study Guide,** p. 208

Teach

Sources of Conflict/ Russia and Its Neighbors L3

Instruct

■ **Introduce** Point out that in some societies, such as ours, people of different ethnic and religious backgrounds generally live together without violent conflict. Ask students to predict why ethnic and religious differences might fuel violence in some societies.

■ **Teach** Create a three-column chart on the board, labeled *Country, Conflict,* and *Status of Conflict.* Ask students about Sri Lanka, Canada, Northern Ireland, and Chechnya. Ensure that students understand why ethnic and religious differences did or did not lead to violence in each country.

Independent Practice

Have students view the photograph on this page and read the caption. Use the Think-Write-Pair-Share strategy (TE, p. T23) and have them write an alternative caption that includes reasons for destruction. Then have students suppose the image shows destruction in Northern Ireland and write a different caption for the image.

Monitor Progress

As students fill in their flowcharts, circulate to make sure they understand the sequences of events in Northern Ireland, Chechnya, and Yugoslavia. For a completed version of the flowchart, see

▥ **Note Taking Transparencies,** 198

Answers

Chart Skills Canada's political system allows minority groups to take political action, while in Sri Lanka, the political system limits minority rights and has driven some minority members to take violent action.

✓ Minority Catholics faced discrimination, while majority Protestants opposed Catholics' goal of Irish unification.

✓ Ethnic and religious divisions and nationalism led to conflict.

Yugoslavia Breaks Apart

Instruct

- **Introduce: Vocabulary Builder**
  Have students read the Vocabulary Builder term and definition. Then tell students that Yugoslavia was made up of different geographic republics, and that people in each republic were divided along ethnic lines. Ask students what might be the consequences if one ethnic group in Yugoslavia sought to **dominate** the others?

- **Teach** Display **Color Transparency 194: Conflict in Yugoslavia.** Discuss the issues that led to conflict in Croatia, Bosnia, and Kosovo. Then ask **Which group played a role in all three conflicts?** (Serbs)
  ▥ Color Transparencies, 194

- **Quick Activity** Have students access **Web Code nbp-3211** to take the **Geography Interactive Audio guided tour** and then answer the map skills questions in the text.

Independent Practice

- **Primary Source** To help students better understand the conflict in Yugoslavia, have them read the selection *A Family in Sarajevo* and complete the worksheet.
  All in One Teaching Resources, Unit 5, p. 48

- Have students fill in the Outline Map *Former Yugoslavia* and label the new republics.
  All in One Teaching Resources, Unit 5, p. 53

Monitor Progress

- Circulate to make sure students are filling in their Outline Maps accurately. Check answers to map skills questions.

- Check Reading and Note Taking Study Guide entries for student understanding.

Answers

Map Skills

1. Review locations with students.
2. Slovenia
3. Bosnia is located between Serbia, where Serbs dominate, and Croatia, where Croatians dominate.

Yugoslavia Breaks Apart

Ethnic, nationalist, and religious tensions tore Yugoslavia apart during the 1990s. Before 1991, Yugoslavia was **multiethnic,** or made up of several ethnic groups. These groups included Serbs, Montenegrins, and Macedonians, who were Orthodox Christians; Croats and Slovenes, who were Roman Catholics; and the mostly Muslim Bosniaks and Albanians. A majority of Yugoslavians—including the Serbs, Montenegrins, Croats, and Bosniaks—all spoke the same language, Serbo-Croatian, but these groups had different religions. Albanians, Slovenes, and Macedonians spoke minority languages.

Yugoslavia was made up of six republics, similar to states in the United States. These were Slovenia, Croatia, Serbia, Bosnia and Herzegovina (often known as Bosnia for short), Montenegro, and Macedonia. Each republic had a dominant ethnic group but also was home to ethnic minorities. Serbs formed the majority in Serbia but were an important ethnic minority in several of the other republics. Serbs <u>dominated</u> Yugoslavia, which was held together and controlled by its Communist Party.

Republics Break Away The fall of communism fed nationalist unrest throughout Yugoslavia. The Serbian-dominated government tried to preserve the country. In 1991, however, Slovenia and Croatia declared independence. This move triggered fighting between Croats and the Serbian minority within Croatia. Macedonia and Bosnia soon broke away from Yugoslavia as well, leaving only Serbia and Montenegro. In 2006, Montenegro also went its own way, separate from Serbia.

Civil War Devastates Bosnia When Bosnia declared independence in 1992, civil war erupted among Bosniaks, Serbs, and Croats. Bosnian Serbs wanted to set up their own government. They received money and arms from Serbian president **Slobodan Milosevic** (mih LOH shuh vich), an extreme Serb nationalist. The largest group in Bosnia, the Muslim Bosniaks, lived scattered across Bosnia. They did not want the country divided into ethnic regions.

During the war, all sides committed atrocities. Bosnian Serbs conducted a vicious campaign of **ethnic cleansing.** This meant killing people from other ethnic groups or forcibly removing them from their homes to create ethnically "pure" areas, in this case for Serbs. Tens of thousands of Bosniaks and Croats were brutalized or killed, sometimes in mass executions. Croat and Bosniak fighters took revenge. Croats launched an ethnic cleansing campaign to drive ethnic Serbs from parts of Croatia.

Finally, NATO air strikes against the Bosnian Serb military forced the warring parties to the peace table. Guided by the United States, the rival groups signed the Dayton Accords, ending the war in 1995. An international force helped maintain a fragile peace in Bosnia.

Vocabulary Builder

<u>dominate</u>—(DAHM uh nayt) *v.* to control or have power over

---

Former Yugoslavia in 2008

Geography *Interactive*
For: Audio guided tour
Web Code: nbp-3211

AUSTRIA
Ljubljana
SLOVENIA • Zagreb
CROATIA
HUNGARY
Drava R.
Tisa R.
Danube R.
Sava R.
Belgrade
BOSNIA AND HERZEGOVINA
SERBIA
Sarajevo
ROMANIA
Morava R.
Danube R.
Adriatic Sea
MONTE-NEGRO
KOSOVO
Podgorica
Pristina
BULGARIA
ITALY
Skopje
MACEDONIA
ALBANIA
GREECE

Yugoslavia, 1990
National border

Conic Projection
0   50   100 mi
0   50   100 km

Map Skills The former nation of Yugoslavia had broken apart into six new nations by 2006. In 2008, Kosovo declared its independence from Serbia.
1. **Locate** (a) Sarajevo (b) Serbia (c) Kosovo
2. **Location** Which new nation does not share a border with Serbia on any side?
3. **Make Inferences** How did the location of Bosnia and Herzegovina put it at risk of becoming involved in conflicts between Serbians and Croatians?

Differentiated Instruction — Solutions for All Learners

L1 Special Needs   L2 Less Proficient Readers

To help students understand Yugoslavia's breakup, have them look at the map on this page. Note that Serbs once dominated all of Yugoslavia, although they are the majority only in Serbia. Have students list the countries that once made up Yugoslavia and discuss why they declared independence. Discuss the challenges posed by ethnic diversity in Bosnia.

L2 English Language Learners

Use the following resources to help students acquire basic skills.

Adapted Reading and Note Taking Study Guide
- Adapted Note Taking Study Guide, p. 208
- Adapted Section Summary, p. 209

The Fight for Kosovo As Bosnia reached a tense peace, a crisis broke out in the Serbian province of Kosovo. Over the centuries, many Albanians, mostly Muslim, had settled in Kosovo. By the 1990s, they made up about 90 percent of Kosovo's population. The rest of the population was mostly Serb.

In 1989, Serbian leader Slobodan Milosevic began oppressing Kosovo Albanians. By the mid-1990s, a small guerrilla force of Kosovo Albanians had emerged. It attacked Serbian targets. Milosevic rejected international peace efforts and stepped up a campaign of ethnic cleansing against Kosovo Albanians. In response, NATO launched air attacks against Serbia in 1999.

The air strikes forced Milosevic to withdraw Serbian forces from Kosovo. UN and NATO forces then supervised a tense peace. After years of negotiation, Kosovo declared independence in 2008. While Kosovo Albanians celebrated, Serbs angrily protested. For them, Kosovo was a historic part of Serbia. A small NATO force remained in Kosovo to keep the peace between the majority Albanians and the minority Serbs.

Fighters in Kosovo
Kosovo Albanians claim an area after Serbian forces withdrew in 1999. *What does this photograph suggest about relations between Albanians and Serbs in Kosovo?*

✓ **Checkpoint** How did the breakup of Yugoslavia lead to ethnic cleansing in Bosnia and Herzegovina?

SECTION 1 Assessment

Progress Monitoring *Online*
For: Self-quiz with vocabulary practice
Web Code: nba-3211

Terms, People, and Places
1. What do many of the terms, people, and places listed at the beginning of the section have in common? Explain.

Note Taking
2. **Reading Skill: Recognize Sequence** Use your completed flowchart to answer the Focus Question: Why have ethnic and religious conflicts divided some nations?

Comprehension and Critical Thinking
3. **Synthesize Information** How might Malaysia and Singapore serve as examples of to how to resolve ethnic conflict in the nations that make up the former Yugoslavia?
4. **Predict Consequences** Do you think Kosovo will be able to maintain its independence and resolve the conflict between Albanians and Serbs?
5. **Draw Conclusions** Why do you think Russia intervened in Georgia's conflict with its provinces?

● **Writing About History**
Quick Write: Explore a Topic To write a research report, you first need to frame questions that will help you to explore your topic. Choose one of the conflicts in this section and write a series of questions that you could try to answer through research. For example, if you choose the Northern Ireland conflict, you might ask why the IRA has been reluctant to turn over weapons, or who has been responsible for recent attacks in Northern Ireland.

Objectives

As you teach this section, keep students focused on the following objectives to help them answer the Section Focus Question and master core content.

- Understand South Africa's struggle for freedom.
- Describe how struggles for independence and Cold War rivalries brought decades of conflict to South Africa's neighbors.
- Analyze how ethnic conflicts killed millions in Rwanda and Sudan.

Prepare to Read

Build Background Knowledge ⓛ

Ask students to recall that Africa's borders were drawn by colonial powers without regard for ethnic divisions. Based on their previous reading, have students predict how this colonial history might lead to conflict in African nations.

Set a Purpose ⓛ

- **WITNESS HISTORY** Read the selection aloud or play the audio.

  🔊 AUDIO **Witness History Audio CD,** Recovering From Genocide

  Ask **What is the main idea of Kofi Annan's speech?** *(Rwanda's example shows that nations can overcome their divisive pasts and unite to move forward.)*

- **Focus** Point out the Section Focus Question and write it on the board. Tell students to refer to this question as they read. *(Answer appears with Section 2 Assessment answers.)*

- **Preview** Have students preview the Section Objectives and the list of Terms, People, and Places.

- **Note Taking** Have students read this section using the Paragraph Shrinking strategy (TE, p. T20). As they read, have students fill in the flowchart sequencing events in South Africa and its neighbors.

  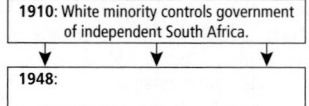 **Reading and Note Taking Study Guide,** p. 210

Since 1994, peace has returned to Rwanda. This recent photo shows Rwandan boys running home after school.

Struggles in Africa

Objectives

- Understand South Africa's struggle for freedom.
- Describe how struggles for independence and Cold War rivalries brought decades of conflict to South Africa's neighbors.
- Analyze how ethnic conflicts killed millions in Rwanda and Sudan.

Terms, People, and Places

apartheid	Desmond Tutu
African National Congress (ANC)	F.W. de Klerk
	Hutus
Sharpeville	Tutsis
Nelson Mandela	Darfur

Note Taking

Reading Skill: Recognize Sequence Keep track of the sequence of events in the conflicts in South Africa and its neighbors. Add boxes as needed.

```
┌─────────────────────────────────────┐
│ 1910: White minority controls       │
│ government of independent South      │
│ Africa.                              │
└─────────────────────────────────────┘
      ↓          ↓          ↓
┌─────────────────────────────────────┐
│ 1948:                                │
└─────────────────────────────────────┘
```

In the 1950s and 1960s, many new nations won independence in Africa. National unity, however, was hard to achieve. Most African nations were home to diverse ethnic groups. Often, people did not even share a common language. They spoke dozens of local languages. Religious differences and longstanding rivalries further divided people within a nation.

After independence, a single ethnic group often dominated a nation's government and economy at the expense of other groups. The Cold War further complicated matters, as you have read. As a result, several African nations suffered internal conflicts and civil war.

South Africa Struggles for Freedom

In South Africa, the struggle for freedom was different from that elsewhere in Africa. In 1910, South Africa achieved self-rule from Britain. Freedom, however, was limited to white settlers. The black majority was denied the right to vote. Whites made up less than 20 percent of the population but controlled the government and the economy. The white-minority government passed racial laws that severely restricted the black majority.

Apartheid Divides South Africa After 1948, the government expanded the existing system of racial segregation, creating what was known as **apartheid,** or the separation of the races. Under apartheid, all South Africans were registered by race: Black,

White, Colored (people of mixed ancestry), Asian. Supporters of apartheid claimed it would allow each race to protect its culture. In fact, the policy was designed to keep white control over South Africa.

Under apartheid, nonwhites faced many restrictions. Blacks were treated like foreigners in their own land. Under the pass laws, they had to get permission to travel. Other laws banned marriages between the races and <u>stipulated</u> segregated restaurants, beaches, and schools. Black workers were paid less than whites for the same job. Blacks could not own land in most areas. Low wages and inferior schooling condemned most blacks to poverty.

The Struggle for Majority Black Rule Black South Africans resisted apartheid. The **African National Congress (ANC)** emerged as the main party opposed to apartheid and led the struggle for majority rule. In the 1950s, the government imposed strict new rules to separate the races. The ANC organized marches, boycotts, and strikes. In 1960, police gunned down 69 men, women, and children during a peaceful protest in **Sharpeville,** a black township. The government then outlawed the ANC and cracked down on other groups that opposed apartheid.

The Sharpeville massacre led some ANC activists to shift from nonviolent protest to armed struggle. Some leaders, like **Nelson Mandela,** went underground. As an ANC leader, Mandela had first mobilized young South Africans to peacefully resist apartheid laws. As government oppression grew, Mandela joined ANC militants who called for armed struggle against the white-minority government. In the early 1960s, Mandela was arrested, tried, and condemned to life in prison for treason. Even in prison, he remained a powerful symbol of the struggle for freedom.

In the 1980s, demands for an end to apartheid and for Mandela's release increased. Many countries, including the United States, imposed economic sanctions on South Africa. In 1984, black South African bishop **Desmond Tutu** won the Nobel Peace Prize for his nonviolent opposition to apartheid.

Ending Apartheid Outside pressure and protests at home finally convinced South African president **F. W. de Klerk** to end apartheid. In 1990, he lifted the ban on the ANC and freed Mandela. In 1994, South Africans of every race were allowed to vote for the first time.

Vocabulary Builder

<u>stipulated</u>—(STIP yuh layt ed)
v. required, specified

WITNESS HISTORY VIDEO

Watch *Nelson Mandela and the End of Apartheid* on the **Witness History Discovery School**™ video program to learn about the struggle against apartheid.

The Sharpeville Massacre
When South African police opened fire on peaceful demonstrators at Sharpeville in 1960, many demonstrators ran for their lives. *How might this police action lead anti-apartheid activists to give up on peaceful methods?*

Link to Literature

Literature of Protest Alan Paton's novel *Cry, the Beloved Country* was a stinging rebuke of South Africa's apartheid policy. Paton's novel helped focus world attention on the injustices of South African society. The author later became a founding member and leader of an anti-apartheid party. His words and actions led South Africa's all-white government to punish him by taking away his passport for ten years, preventing Paton from traveling abroad. Other South African writers also penned works that criticized the apartheid system. They include playwright Athol Fugard and novelists Nadine Gordimer and J.M. Coetzee. Both Gordimer (1991) and Coetzee (2003) won Nobel Prizes for Literature.

Teach

Struggles for Freedom/ Struggles in Southern Africa L3

Instruct

- **Introduce: Key Terms** Have students find the key term **apartheid** (in blue) in the text and explain its meaning. Then refer them to the feature on the next page and describe apartheid's impact on South Africa.

- **Teach** To show a map of South Africa under apartheid, display **Color Transparency 195: South Africa.** Then trace the roots of apartheid and its effects in South Africa and its neighbors. Ask **Who claimed control of South Africa after independence in 1910, and why?** *(The white minority claimed control of the government in order to maintain its position of power and status.)* **How did apartheid help the white minority achieve its goals?** *(By limiting the rights of the non-white majority, the white minority could maintain power.)* **How did South Africa affect its neighbors?** *(Its government supported white minority government in some surrounding countries, and it viewed new nations with black majority rule as a threat, so it aided rebel fighters.)* Then discuss the events that led to the end of apartheid in South Africa.

  🏛 **Color Transparencies,** 195

- **Quick Activity** Show students *Nelson Mandela and the End of Apartheid* from the **Witness History Discovery School**™ video program. Ask them to explain why so many South Africans participated in the ANC-led civil disobedience. *(Answers should recognize that the majority of South Africans were damaged by apartheid. They had little to lose and, without votes, no way to change the system other than civil disobedience.)*

Answer

Caption Activists might conclude that peaceful protests were ineffective and turn to military means instead.

Independent Practice

- **Biography** To help students understand a key figure in South Africa's history, have them read the biography *Nelson Mandela* and complete the worksheet.

  All in One **Teaching Resources, Unit 5**, p. 52

- **Viewpoints** To extend students' understanding of apartheid, have them read the selection *Abolishing Apartheid* and complete the worksheet.

  All in One **Teaching Resources, Unit 5**, p. 51

Monitor Progress

As students fill in their flowcharts, circulate to make sure that they understand the sequence of events in South Africa. For a completed version of the flowchart, see

Note Taking Transparencies, 199A

Answers

Caption nearly 80 percent

Graph Skills Black

✔ President de Klerk ended apartheid in response to international pressures such as economic sanctions and internal pressures such as ongoing protests.

For more than 40 years, apartheid shaped the lives of the black majority and of whites and other minorities in South Africa. Whites made up less than one fifth of South Africa's population, as you can see in the graph at the right. However, apartheid gave whites not only political power, but also control of South Africa's best lands and economic resources. This hurt blacks, Asians, and people of mixed backgrounds economically and socially. *Based on the information in the graph and elsewhere in this section, about what percentage of South Africa's population suffered from apartheid?*

South Africa's Population by Race

Colored (mixed race) 8.6%
Asian (Indian) 2.6%
White 13.6%
Black 75.2%

SOURCE: *CIA World Factbook*, 2005

Graph Skills This graph shows South Africa's population by race. The percentages have changed little since the years of apartheid. Which racial group is the majority in South Africa?

▲ Apartheid gave many white South Africans a life of privilege.

Apartheid required all non-whites to get legal permits to travel within their own country and to carry these in a passbook like the one shown here. ▼

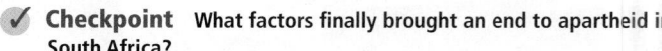

Deprived of opportunities, many black South Africans lived in poverty.

Voters chose Nelson Mandela as president in South Africa's first multiracial election. Mandela worked to heal the country's wounds. "Let us build together," he declared. He welcomed old foes into his government, including whites who had supported apartheid.

Since 1994, South Africa has faced huge challenges. With majority rule, black South Africans expected a better life. Although South Africa was a rich, industrial country, it had limited resources to spend on housing, education, and other programs. The income and education gap between blacks and whites remained large. Poverty and unemployment were high among blacks. The AIDS epidemic hit South Africa severely. As South Africa's government struggled with these problems, the global economic slowdown created new challenges.

✔ **Checkpoint** **What factors finally brought an end to apartheid in South Africa?**

Struggles in Southern Africa

Most African nations achieved independence through peaceful means during the 1950s and 1960s. In southern Africa, however, the road to freedom was marked by some long, violent struggles. For many years, the apartheid government of South Africa supported white minority rule in neighboring nations.

Differentiated Instruction **Solutions for All Learners**

L1 Special Needs **L2 Less Proficient Readers**

As students read this section, have them look for evidence that U.S. Cold War concerns or South Africa's fear of the ANC affected conflicts in South Africa's neighbors. Have students, working in pairs, make a list of these details. Then have each pair use their lists to write a sentence summarizing how South Africa and the United States affected these conflicts.

L2 English Language Learners

Use the following resources to help students acquire basic skills.

Adapted Reading and Note Taking Study Guide

- Adapted Note Taking Study Guide, p. 210
- Adapted Section Summary, p. 211

Zimbabwe As African nations won independence, whites in Southern Rhodesia refused to share power with the black majority. Conservative whites, led by Ian Smith, declared independence in 1965. For years, black guerrilla groups fought for majority rule. In 1980, after a ceasefire and elections, the country gained independence and was renamed Zimbabwe.

Robert Mugabe, a liberation leader, was elected president. Although popular at first, Mugabe grew increasingly dictatorial. He cracked down on opponents and was accused of electoral fraud. Despite international pressure and an economic crisis, the aging Mugabe held onto power.

Angola and Mozambique While Britain and France gave up their African possessions, Portugal clung fiercely to its colonies of Angola and Mozambique. In response, nationalist groups waged a long guerrilla war. In 1975, after Portugal finally agreed to withdraw, Angola and Mozambique celebrated independence.

Both countries then faced brutal civil wars fueled by Cold War rivalries. Because some liberation leaders had ties to the Soviet Union or the ANC, the United States and South Africa aided a rebel group in Angola. South Africa also supported a rebel group in Mozambique. The fighting continued until 1992 in Mozambique, and 2002 in Angola. Decades of war had ravaged both countries, which slowly began to rebuild.

 Checkpoint Why did fighting continue after Angola and Mozambique achieved independence?

Ethnic Conflicts Fuel Power Struggles

After independence, ethnic conflicts plagued several African nations. The causes were complex. Historic resentments divided ethnically diverse nations. Unjust governments and regional rivalries fed ethnic violence.

Rwanda and Burundi Power struggles between ethnic groups led to a deadly genocide in Rwanda, a small central African nation. The country was home to two main ethnic groups. **Hutus** were the majority group, but **Tutsis** had long dominated Rwanda. Both groups spoke the same language, but they had different traditions. After independence, Hutu violence against Tutsis increased.

Tensions worsened in early 1994, after the presidents of Rwanda and neighboring Burundi were killed in a suspicious plane crash. Extremist Hutu officials urged civilians to turn on their Tutsi neighbors. At least 800,000 Tutsis and moderate Hutus were slaughtered. Millions of Rwandans lost their homes to destructive mobs. Even as the death toll rose, the world community was slow to act to stop the genocide.

In July 1994, a Tutsi exile army conquered Rwanda and set up a unity government. Those accused of genocide faced trials in an international court.

Nearby Burundi faced similar ethnic tensions between Hutus and Tutsis. In 1993, Tutsi military officers killed Burundi's Hutu president in a failed coup attempt. Violence erupted, but did not lead to genocide as in Rwanda. In 2005, voters approved a new constitution that guaranteed both Hutu and Tutsi participation in the government and military.

Strife in Sudan Genocide also took place in oil-rich Sudan. Since independence, Sudan's Arab Muslim north has dominated the non-Muslim, non-Arab south. Sudan's Muslim government even tried to impose Islamic law in non-Muslim areas. For decades, rebel groups in the south

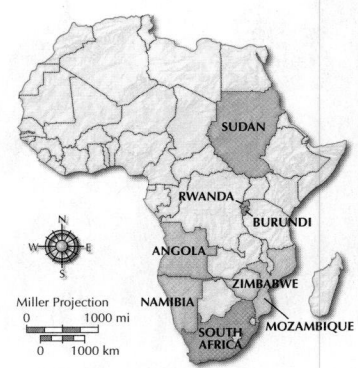

Note Taking

Reading Skill: Identify Causes and Effects Fill in a concept web like the one below to keep track of the causes and effects of the conflicts in Rwanda and Sudan.

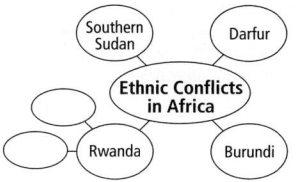

Ethnic Conflicts Fuel Power Struggles

Instruct

■ **Introduce: Key Terms** Have students locate the key terms *Hutus* and *Tutsis* (in blue) in the text and explain their meanings. Recall with students the causes of other ethnic conflicts, such as those in Bosnia. Ask students what causes might lead to an outcome of violent conflict between Hutus and Tutsis.

■ **Teach** Trace the path of civil war and ethnic conflict in Rwanda, Burundi, and Sudan. Discuss the human costs of these conflicts, both in terms of immediate death and injury as well as the longer-term costs of community destruction and residual tensions.

■ **Quick Activity** Using the Think-Write-Pair-Share strategy (TE, p. T23), have students discuss the following questions: Why do you think international communities hesitated to intervene? What qualities will it take for communities so torn apart by strife to heal their wounds and live again as neighbors?

Independent Practice

Note Taking Have students fill in the concept web listing causes and effects of conflicts in Rwanda and Sudan.

Reading and Note Taking Study Guide, p. 210

Monitor Progress

As students fill in their concept webs, circulate to make sure they understand the events that led to civil war in Rwanda and ethnic conflict in Sudan. For a completed version of the concept web, see

Note Taking Transparencies, 199B

Connect to Our World

Civic Responsibility South Africans who opposed apartheid found many peaceful ways to work against the system. Some wrote articles, books, and speeches describing its injustice and inhumanity. Others demonstrated against the government or worked for opposition parties. All those actions were risky, because the government of South Africa often cracked down on critics. Ameri-cans, whose rights of free speech, petition, and assembly are guaranteed by the Constitution, have many avenues open to them for voicing their opinions and working to promote changes in their laws. They can write to newspapers or magazines, organize petition-signing drives or e-mail campaigns, or write to elected officials. Which methods do students think are most effective?

Answer

 Civil wars continued as groups struggled for control of newly independent nations. These wars were fueled by U.S. and South African concerns over new nations' links to the Soviet Union or the ANC.

Assess Progress

- Have students complete the Section Assessment.

- Administer the Section Quiz.

All in One Teaching Resources, Unit 5, p. 44

- To further assess student understanding, use

   Progress Monitoring Transparencies, 138

Reteach

If students need more instruction, have them read the section summary.

 Reading and Note Taking Study Guide, p. 211

Adapted Reading and Note Taking Study Guide, p. 211

 Spanish Reading and Note Taking Study Guide, p. 211

Extend

Conduct the unit simulation, *Looking Beyond Apartheid,* which helps students understand why so many South Africans found difficulty in moving beyond this issue.

All in One Teaching Resources, Unit 5, pp. 103–106

Answers

Caption Villagers would be unable to resist an attack, and many could lose their lives.

✓ In both Rwanda and Darfur, the killings of members of different ethnic groups and the destruction of villages had some government support. In both countries, those accused of genocide faced charges brought by the International Criminal Court.

Terror in Darfur
Arab militias, known as *janjaweed* or "bandits," spread terror across Darfur. Mounted gangs burned homes and murdered non-Arab villagers in a campaign of ethnic cleansing. *How might an attack by the janjaweed affect unarmed villagers?*

battled northern political domination. The fighting also spilled into neighboring Chad. Sudan's north-south conflict killed millions and displaced many more.

In 2005, the Sudanese government and rebels in the south agreed to a peace accord. However, in 2004, fighting worsened in the western region of **Darfur.** With government backing, Arab militias conducted widespread killings of civilians. They burned homes and drove farmers off the land.

The United States and other countries sent humanitarian aid to the refugees. Sudan allowed UN peacekeepers into the region, but they were unable to end the violence. In 2009, the International Criminal Court charged Sudan's president with crimes against humanity.

✓ **Checkpoint** How was the conflict in Rwanda similar to the conflict in Darfur?

SECTION 2 Assessment

Progress Monitoring *Online*
For: Self-quiz with vocabulary practice
Web Code: nba-3221

Terms, People, and Places
1. For each term, person, or place listed at the beginning of the section, write a sentence explaining its significance.

Note Taking
2. **Reading Skill: Recognize Sequence** Use your completed flowchart to answer the Focus Question: Why have conflicts plagued some African countries?

Comprehension and Critical Thinking
3. **Analyze Information** Was apartheid a product of a democratic system of government? Explain.

4. **Summarize** What was South Africa's role in the conflicts that plagued its neighbors from the 1960s to the 1990s?
5. **Make Comparisons** How was the ethnic conflict in Burundi similar to or different from the conflict in Rwanda?
6. **Synthesize Information** A newspaper headline read, "Looking at Darfur, Seeing Rwanda." Explain what that headline meant. How did the world community respond to genocide after the events in Rwanda?

● **Writing About History**
Quick Write: Gather Information To write a research report, you need to gather information about your topic. Choose one of the conflicts in this section and gather facts about the topic from the library or reliable sources online. Make a list of facts about your topic.

Section 2 Assessment

1. Sentences should reflect an understanding of each term, person, or place listed at the beginning of the section.
2. because people of differing racial, religious, and ethnic groups have sought power at one another's expense
3. No, it was instituted by the white minority, which had denied democratic rights to the nonwhite majority.

4. South Africa supported white minority rule and groups that opposed governments with ties to the ANC.
5. Both were between Hutus and Tutsis, but there was no genocide in Burundi.
6. It raises concerns that, as in Rwanda, the international community will hesitate to act to stop genocide.

● **Writing About History**
Facts should reflect careful and organized research. Lists should include key details and source information.

For additional assessment, have students access **Progress Monitoring *Online*** at Web Code nba-3221.

Nelson Mandela: *Glory and Hope*

Nelson Mandela delivered this speech after having been elected president in South Africa's first multiracial election in 1994. Knowing that the injustices of apartheid would be hard to overcome, Mandela asked the people to work together for peace and justice.

Students in South Africa after the end of apartheid

Today, all of us do, by our presence here, and by our celebrations ... confer glory and hope to newborn liberty.

Out of the experience of an extraordinary human disaster that lasted too long must be born a society of which all humanity will be proud.

Our daily deeds as ordinary South Africans must produce an actual South African reality that will reinforce humanity's belief in justice, strengthen its confidence in the nobility of the human soul and sustain all our hopes for a glorious life for all. . . .

The time for the healing of the wounds has come. . . .

The time to build is upon us.

We have, at last, achieved our political emancipation.[1] We pledge ourselves to liberate all our people from the continuing bondage of poverty, deprivation, suffering, gender and other discrimination. . . .

We have triumphed in the effort to implant hope in the breasts of the millions of our people. We enter into a covenant[2] that we shall build the society in which all South Africans, both black and white, will be able to walk tall, without any fear in their hearts, assured of their inalienable right to human dignity—a rainbow nation at peace with itself and the world. . . .

We understand it still that there is no easy road to freedom.

We know it well that none of us acting alone can achieve success.

We must therefore act together as a united people, for national reconciliation,[3] for nation building, for the birth of a new world.

Let there be justice for all. Let there be peace for all. Let there be work, bread, water, and salt for all. . . . The sun shall never set on so glorious a human achievement!

1. **emancipation** (ee man suh PAY shun) *n.* the gaining of freedom from bondage or control by others
2. **covenant** (KUV uh nunt) *n.* a binding and solemn pledge to do something
3. **reconciliation** (rek un sil ee AY shun) *n.* a settling of differences that results in harmony

Thinking Critically

1. **Identify Alternatives** When apartheid ended, there was a danger of a backlash by blacks against whites who supported apartheid. How does Mandela's speech respond to that danger?
2. **Draw Inferences** In addition to political freedom, what further freedoms does Mandela call for in his speech?

Nelson Mandela with supporters in 1994

PRIMARY SOURCE

Nelson Mandela: *Glory and Hope*

Objective

- Understand the importance of Nelson Mandela to the development of post-apartheid South Africa.

Build Background Knowledge L3

Ask students to recall the struggle of black South Africans to gain citizenship rights and an end to apartheid. Ask students what role Nelson Mandela played in that struggle. (*He was an important leader in the ANC, spent many years in prison, and emerged to become South Africa's first post-apartheid president.*)

Instruct L3

- Direct students' attention to the introduction at the top of the text page. Ask **What does Mandela want people to do?** (*work together to overcome the injustices and wounds of apartheid*)

- Discuss with students the hopes that Mandela has for South Africa and the challenges he thinks must be overcome. Ask **What tone does Mandela set for moving forward as one nation?** (*He sets a tone of forgiveness.*) **What do you think Mandela views as the greatest challenge to South Africa's future?** (*unity*)

Monitor Progress

To confirm students' understanding, ask them to briefly summarize Mandela's speech and the views it represents.

History Background

Mandela and de Klerk Both Nelson Mandela and F.W. de Klerk showed extraordinary statesmanship in working together to bring about the peaceful end of apartheid in South Africa. Before acting formally to dismantle the system, de Klerk carried on private talks with leaders from the country's four officially recognized groups: White, Black, Colored, and Asian. He released many political prisoners besides Mandela and pushed the country's Parliament to repeal apartheid laws despite conservative opposition. His actions were validated in 1992 when nearly 70 percent of the nation's voters—only whites at the time—voted approval of the end of apartheid. Mandela, in turn, worked to avoid ethnic divisions among the nation's blacks and brought de Klerk into the first majority-rule government he formed in 1994. Both men were rewarded for their work by jointly winning the Nobel Peace Prize in 1993.

Thinking Critically

1. He says that all South Africans should be able to walk tall without fear, in peace.
2. He calls for freedom from poverty, deprivation, suffering, and discrimination.

Objectives

As you teach this section, keep students focused on the following objectives to help them answer the Section Focus Question and master core content.

- Understand why Arabs and Israelis fought over land.
- Explain why civil war ravaged Lebanon.
- Outline Iraq's long history of conflict.

Prepare to Read

Build Background Knowledge L3

Review the key historical issues that affected the modern Middle East. *(independence from colonial powers, the formation of Israel, the growing world demand for oil, and conflicts between Islamists and secularists)* Ask students to predict likely conflicts in the modern Middle East.

Set a Purpose L3

- **WITNESS HISTORY** Read the selection aloud or play the audio.

  🔊 AUDIO **Witness History Audio CD,** Two Peoples Claim the Same Land

  Ask **What is the main idea of the quotations?** *(Both groups descend from Abraham.)*

- **Focus** Point out the Section Focus Question and write it on the board. Tell students to refer to this question as they read. *(Answer appears with Section 3 Assessment answers.)*

- **Preview** Have students preview the Section Objectives and the list of Terms, People, and Places.

- **Note Taking** Have students read this section using the Structured Read Aloud strategy (TE, p. T20). As they read, have students fill in the flowchart sequencing events in Middle East conflicts.

  Reading and Note Taking Study Guide, p. 212

SECTION 3

An Israeli soldier and a Palestinian Arab pass each other in the street.

WITNESS HISTORY 🔊 AUDIO

Two Peoples Claim the Same Land

Many Jewish Israelis believe that the quotation from the Bible, below, promises Israel to the Jewish people as descendants of Abraham (Abram). Many Muslims also believe that they are the spiritual heirs to Abraham, as stated in the Quran. They too feel entitled to the land as part of Abraham's legacy. Representatives of both peoples have lived in the land for centuries.

66 On that day the LORD made a covenant with Abram, saying, 'To your descendants I give this land. . . .' 99
—Genesis 15:18

66 He [Allah] has chosen you and has placed no hardship on you in practicing your religion—the religion of your father Abraham. 99
—Quran 22:78

Focus Question What are the causes of conflict in the Middle East?

Conflicts in the Middle East

Objectives
- Understand why Arabs and Israelis fought over land.
- Explain why civil war ravaged Lebanon.
- Outline Iraq's long history of conflict.

Terms, People, and Places

occupied territories	Saddam Hussein
Yasir Arafat	no-fly zone
intifada	weapons of mass
Yitzhak Rabin	destruction (WMDs)
Jerusalem	insurgent
militia	

Note Taking

Reading Skill: Recognize Sequence Keep track of the sequence of events in the conflicts in the Middle East with a flowchart like the one below.

```
         Middle Eastern Conflicts
   ┌──────────────┬──────────────┬──────────────┐
   │ Arab-Israeli │   Lebanon    │     Iraq     │
   │   Conflict   │              │              │
   ├──────────────┼──────────────┼──────────────┤
   │ • 1948: Israel│ •           │ •           │
   │   is founded │              │              │
   │ •            │ •           │ •           │
   └──────────────┴──────────────┴──────────────┘
```

For decades, the Middle East has been the focus of conflicts that have had a global impact. The Middle East commands vast oil resources and key waterways such as the Persian Gulf. During the Cold War, both the United States and the Soviet Union wanted access to the oil and the waterways. Since the end of the Cold War, Western nations have acted to prevent regional powers from interfering with the region's oil supply. Meanwhile, the persistent dispute between Israelis and Palestinian Arabs has added to tensions.

Arabs and Israelis Fight Over Land

Modern Israel was established in 1948 in accordance with the United Nations Partition Plan. The Palestinian Arabs regarded the UN action as illegitimate and rejected the state offered to them. Conflicting claims to this land led to repeated violence. After the 1948 war that followed Israel's founding, Israel and its Arab neighbors fought three more wars, in 1956, 1967, and 1973. In these wars, Israel defeated Arab forces and gained more land. Between the wars, Israel faced guerrilla and terrorist attacks. Repeatedly, the United States tried to bring about peace.

Israel Controls the Occupied Territories In the 1967 war, in response to hostility by its neighbors, Israeli forces took control of territories occupied by Jordan and Egypt since 1948, including the West Bank, East Jerusalem, and the Gaza Strip. They also took control of the Sinai Peninsula from Egypt and the Golan Heights from Syria. In 1973, these nations attacked Israel on Yom Kippur, one of the holiest days of the Jewish year.

Vocabulary Builder

Use the information below and the following resources to teach the high-use word from this section.
All in One Teaching Resources, Unit 5, p. 46; **Teaching Resources, Skills Handbook,** p. 3

High-Use Word	Definition and Sample Sentence
diverse, p. 695	*adj.* multiple, varied, different
	Because Molly keeps such a **diverse** mix of pets, friends tease that she runs a farm.

In the 1973 war, Arabs failed to regain the regions they had lost to Israel, called by Palestinians the **occupied territories.** Israel's government later helped Jewish settlers build homes in settlements in these territories, causing more bitterness among the Palestinians.

Palestinian Attacks Bring Israeli Response For decades, the Palestinian Liberation Organization (PLO) led the struggle against Israel. Headed by **Yasir Arafat,** the PLO had deep support among Palestinians. The PLO called for the destruction of Israel. It attacked Israelis at home and abroad. The PLO gained world attention with airplane hijackings and the killing of Israeli athletes at the 1972 Olympic games.

In 1987, Palestinians in the occupied territories started to resist Israel with **intifadas,** or uprisings. Demanding an end to Israeli occupation, young Palestinians stoned and fired on Israeli troops. Suicide bombers blew up buses, stores, and clubs in Israel, killing many civilians. Israel responded by sealing off and raiding Palestinian towns and targeting terrorist leaders. Many Palestinian civilians lost their lives in these raids.

Seeking Peace Despite the violence, the United States, the UN, and other nations pushed for peace. Golda Meir, Israel's first woman prime minister, was planning peace talks when Arab nations attacked in 1973. As you have read, Israel and Egypt signed a peace accord in 1979. Israel then returned the Sinai Peninsula to Egypt. In 1994, Jordan's King Hussein made peace with Israel. However, talks between Syria and Israel failed over various issues, including control of the Golan Heights.

In 1993, Yasir Arafat and Israeli Prime Minister **Yitzhak Rabin** (rah BEEN) signed the Oslo Accords. This plan gave Palestinians in Gaza and the West Bank limited self-rule under a Palestinian Authority. The PLO recognized Israel's right to exist and pledged to stop terrorist attacks on Israel. Arafat led the Palestinian Authority until his death in 2004.

A City Sacred to Many
Jerusalem is dotted with many places that are sacred to the Jewish people, Christians, and Muslims. This photograph shows the Western Wall, a Jewish holy place. In the background is the Dome of the Rock, an important Islamic shrine. *How might Jerusalem's sacred status make it harder to resolve competing Israeli and Palestinian Arab claims to the city?*

Teach

Arabs and Israelis Fight Over Land **L3**

Instruct

- **Introduce** Point out that the photograph on this page shows a place holy to Jews in the foreground and one holy to Muslims in the middle ground. Remind students that Jerusalem is a city holy to Jews, Christians, and Muslims. Strong feelings of religious entitlement have added to the conflict. Ask students to predict how these feelings would affect the conflict over land.

- **Teach** Display **Color Transparency 198: Israel and the Occupied Territories.** Trace the factors influencing ongoing conflict between Israelis and Palestinians. Ask **Why are Israelis and Palestinians at odds?** *(Both claim land in what is now Israel and the occupied territories.)* **What circumstances might bring an end to the cycle of violence?** *(Answers will vary but could include an end to suicide attacks, increased security so that people feel safe, and elimination of poverty in the region.)*

  Color Transparencies, 198

- **Quick Activity** Web Code nbp-3231 will take students to an interactive map based on the map in the Infographic on the next page. Have students complete the interactivity and then answer the questions in the text.

L1 Special Needs   **L2 Less Proficient Readers**
Have students create a timeline from 1947 to the present. As they read the text, have them label the appropriate year or span of years on the timeline with the major events in the Arab-Israeli conflict, including steps toward peace. Then have them write two or three sentences that sum up the current situation.

L2 English Language Learners
Use the following resources to help students acquire basic skills.

  Adapted Reading and Note Taking Study Guide
  ■ Adapted Note Taking Study Guide, p. 212
  ■ Adapted Section Summary, p. 213

Answer

Caption Sample: Because people care deeply about their religion, they may be less likely to compromise on issues of claims to religious sites.

Independent Practice

■ Have students fill in the Outline Map *Israel and the Occupied Territories*.

All in One Teaching Resources, Unit 5, p. 54

■ **Viewpoints** To help students better understand the different views on the creation of the state of Israel in 1948, have them read the selection *The Creation of the State of Israel* and complete the worksheet.

All in One Teaching Resources, Unit 5, p. 50

■ **Primary Source** To provide students with one solution to the Israeli-Palestinian conflict, have them read the selection *Sowing "Seeds of Peace" by Sara Rimer* and complete the worksheet.

All in One Teaching Resources, Unit 5, p. 49

Monitor Progress

■ As students fill in their flowcharts, circulate to make sure they can trace the sequence of events in Middle East conflicts. For a completed version of the flowchart, see

📖 Note Taking Transparencies, 200

■ Circulate to make sure students are filling in their Outline Maps accurately. Administer the Geography Quiz.

All in One Teaching Resources, Unit 5, p. 55

● **INFOGRAPHIC**

The Israeli-Palestinian Conflict

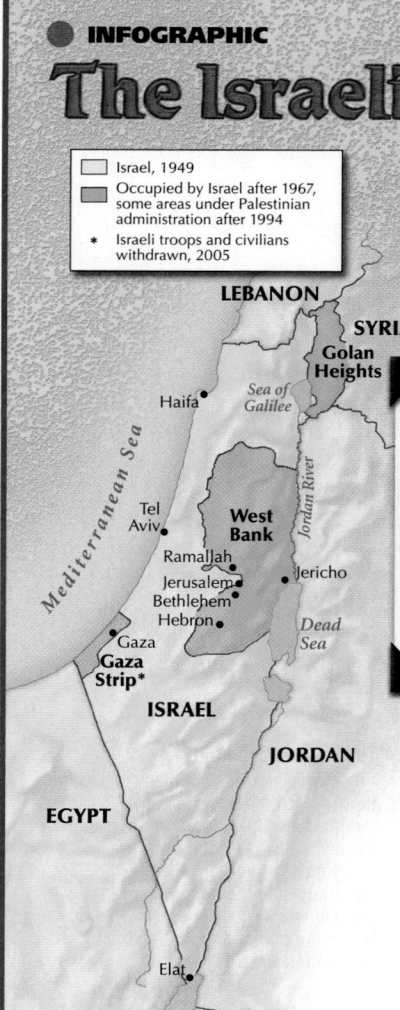

Map legend:
- Israel, 1949
- Occupied by Israel after 1967, some areas under Palestinian administration after 1994
- * Israeli troops and civilians withdrawn, 2005

Labels: LEBANON, SYRIA, Golan Heights, Haifa, Sea of Galilee, Mediterranean Sea, Tel Aviv, West Bank, Jordan River, Ramallah, Jerusalem, Jericho, Bethlehem, Hebron, Dead Sea, Gaza, Gaza Strip*, ISRAEL, JORDAN, EGYPT, Elat

Conflict has dragged on for years in the region. Palestinian Arabs resent the Israeli occupation. Some have responded with suicide bombings targeting Israeli civilians. Israeli forces have responded with attacks on Palestinian militants that have also killed some civilians. Hopes for peace in the region center on ending this cycle of violence and retaliation.

◀ Palestinian suicide bombers have set off deadly explosions in public places that have killed Israeli civilians. The bus in this photo was torn apart by a bomb carried by a Palestinian terrorist.

Ongoing Violence Although Arafat's successor, Mahmoud Abbas (ah BAHS), pledged to stop Palestinian attacks on Israel, violence continued. Fierce divisions split the Palestinian Authority between Fatah, the party of Arafat and his successors, and Hamas, a radical Islamist group. Hamas was funded by Iran and rejected Israel's right to exist. After its impressive victory in the 2006 Palestinian parliamentary election, Hamas seized control of Gaza in 2007, ousting Fatah supporters.

In response, Israel imposed an economic blockade on Gaza, allowing only humanitarian aid to enter. Hamas used Gaza as a launching ground for rocket attacks on Israel. In early 2009, Israeli forces invaded the densely populated Gaza Strip to stop the attacks. A short destructive war resulted in high civilian casualties and ended in a shaky ceasefire.

Obstacles to Peace Decades of conflict and mistrust make peace hard to achieve. Many issues pose obstacles. One issue is land claims. Palestinians who were forced off their lands in earlier wars want the "right of return," or the right to resettle on their lands in Israel. Israelis oppose this right, which could overwhelm the Jewish state with large numbers of Palestinians.

A second obstacle to peace is the issue of Jewish settlements in the West Bank, an area claimed by Palestinians. In the early 2000s, the Israeli government forced Jewish settlers to leave Gaza. Palestinians also insist that Jewish settlers must leave the West Bank.

A third stumbling block is **Jerusalem,** a city sacred to Jews, Christians, and Muslims. Israel occupied Arab East Jerusalem in 1967. Later, it added East Jerusalem to Israel and made the city the capital of Israel. The government allowed Muslims and Christians to control their holy sites within the city. Palestinians, however, insist that East Jerusalem must be the capital of any Palestinian state.

Differentiated
Instruction   Solutions for All Learners

L4 Advanced Readers   **L4 Gifted and Talented**

To challenge students to solve historical problems, have them conduct library or Internet research on Palestinian claims to land within Israel and Israeli claims to land within the disputed areas. Have them create a list of arguments both for and against Palestinian claims to a right of return. Then have them write a letter to the editor on this issue. Their letters should propose a solution and use arguments based on their research. For scoring rubrics for letters to the editor, see **Assessment Rubrics**, p. 9.

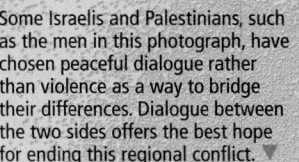

Israeli counterattacks in the occupied territories have killed Palestinians, including some civilians. Some 20,000 people attended this funeral for Palestinians killed in an Israeli attack.

Some Israelis and Palestinians, such as the men in this photograph, have chosen peaceful dialogue rather than violence as a way to bridge their differences. Dialogue between the two sides offers the best hope for ending this regional conflict. ▼

History *Interactive*
For: Interactive map
Web Code: nap-3231

Economic Output per Person

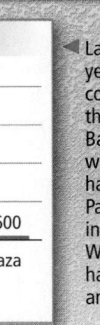

Economic output per person (U.S. dollars)

- Israel: $19,800
- West Bank: $800
- Gaza: $600

SOURCE: *CIA World Factbook*, 2005

◀ Lack of development, years of conflict, and corruption have crippled the economy of the West Bank and Gaza. Meanwhile, Palestinian attacks have forced Israel to limit Palestinians' access to jobs in Israel. Poverty in the West Bank and Gaza Strip has led to desperation among Palestinians.

Over time, the Israeli-Palestinian conflict has fueled the anger of radical Islamist groups around the world. The growing popularity of Hamas and Hezbollah, a radical Islamist group based in Lebanon, created more conflict. These groups reject Israel's right to exist and condemn its ally, the United States, as well as moderate Arab governments involved in the peace process.

By the early 2000s, the United States, the European Union, Russia, and the UN supported a plan known as the "road map" to peace in the Middle East. It supports a two-state solution, with peaceful coexistence between Israel and a stable, democratic Palestinian state. To achieve this, it called for an end to violence and terrorism. Some Israeli and Palestinian leaders accepted the plan, while Iran and radical Islamist groups rejected it.

 Checkpoint What obstacles have prevented peace between Israel and the Palestinians?

Civil War Ravages Lebanon

Historically, Lebanon was a thriving center of commerce. Its population included <u>diverse</u> ethnic and religious groups. After Lebanon won independence, the government depended on a delicate balance among Arab Christian sects, Sunni and Shiite Muslims, and Druze, people with a religion related to Islam. Arab Christians held the most power, but local strongmen controlled their own districts with private armies.

Growing Tensions By the 1970s, the Arab-Israeli conflict was contributing to problems in nearby Lebanon. As Palestinian refugees fled into Lebanon after each new conflict with Israel, Lebanon's Muslim population grew to outnumber Christians. Tensions rose as PLO guerrillas disguised as refugees then crossed the border to attack Israel.

Thinking Critically

1. **Graph Skills** How does economic output in the West Bank and Gaza Strip compare with that in Israel?
2. **Draw Conclusions** How might violence by both sides tend to prolong the Palestinian-Israeli conflict?

Vocabulary Builder

<u>diverse</u>—(dih VURS) *adj.* multiple, varied, different

History Background

Shiites and Sunnis The split between Sunni and Shiite Muslims dates back to the middle 600s A.D., just a few decades after Islam first appeared. Muhammad's son-in-law, named Ali, was the fourth caliph, or spiritual and temporal ruler, of Islam after Muhammad. He died in a struggle between his followers and others. The Shiites believe that only Ali and his descendants are the legitimate leaders of the Islamic world. Shiites number between 60 and 80 million people, which is about one in every ten Muslims. They are a majority in Iran and Iraq, though there are sizable Shiite communities in other nations. Shiites have rarely had political power outside of modern Iran. Shiite religious leaders have guided Iran's government since the Islamic revolution of 1979.

Instruct

- **Introduce: Vocabulary Builder** Have students read the Vocabulary Builder term and definition. Ask them to recall the overflow of conflicts in the former Yugoslavia. Ask students to speculate why one conflict in a region with *diverse* groups living in close contact can fuel other conflicts so easily.

- **Teach** Discuss the delicate political balance among ethnic and religious groups in independent Lebanon. Use the Numbered Heads Strategy (TE, p.T23) and ask **How did the Israeli-Palestinian conflict affect the delicate balance of power in Lebanon?** *(It added Palestinian Muslims to Lebanon, such that they outnumbered Christians. Attacks on Israel from Lebanon brought Israeli counterattacks.)* **How did Israel and Syria intervene in the civil war in Lebanon?** *(Israel invaded to destroy bases that threatened Israel. Syria attacked in response.)* **How is the Lebanese civil war similar to others you have read about?** *(People of different ethnicities and religions fought over access to power.)*

- **Quick Activity** Organize students to debate the following statement: Israel had the right to attack PLO bases in Lebanon as a way of protecting itself.

Independent Practice

Ask students to find news articles describing the current situation in Lebanon. Have students write a paragraph comparing recent developments to the situation described in the text. How has it changed? How has Lebanon's situation remained the same?

Monitor Progress

Read aloud the red heading and the black headings that follow. Ask students to briefly summarize each subsection.

Answers

 Obstacles included land claims by Palestinians within Israel, Israeli settlements in the West Bank, and conflicting claims to Jerusalem.

Thinking Critically

1. Economic output is much lower in the West Bank and Gaza Strip.
2. Violence by each side would tend to increase distrust and calls for vengeance toward the other side.

Iraq's History of Conflict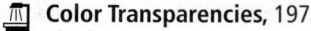

Instruct

- **Introduce** Display a current newspaper describing the situation in Iraq. Then ask students what they know about Iraqi history, including the time prior to Saddam Hussein and the Iran-Iraq War of the 1980s. Remind students of Iraq's oil wealth. Ask them to predict how this might play a role in conflicts in Iraq.

- **Teach** Review Saddam Hussein's rise to power. Discuss why Saddam Hussein seized land from Iran, invaded Kuwait, and defied UN restrictions. Invite students' thoughts on the U.S.-led invasion of 2002, and on the events that have followed in Iraq. Ask students what they think will happen next in Iraq.

- **Quick Activity** Display **Color Transparency 197: Ethnoreligious Groups in Iraq.** Use the lesson suggested in the transparency book to guide a discussion on the reasons that ethnoreligious distribution has contributed to Iraq's history of conflict.

  Color Transparencies, 197

Independent Practice

Direct students' attention to the photos on this page and the next. Have them write a caption that could fit with the two pictures if they were displayed together. Captions should explain how Iraq's situation changed from one picture to the other.

Monitor Progress

Check Reading and Note Taking Study Guide entries for student understanding.

Civil War and Conflict With Israel In 1975, Lebanon was plunged into civil war. Christian and Muslim **militias,** or armed groups of citizen soldiers, battled each other. In 1982, Israel invaded southern Lebanon to stop cross-border attacks. Syria occupied eastern Lebanon. UN peacekeepers tried to end the fighting but withdrew after hundreds were killed by suicide bombers. After 16 years, Lebanese leaders finally restored order. Beirut, the ruined capital, was slowly rebuilt.

Deep divisions remained in Lebanon. Rival militias controlled different regions. In 2006, Hezbollah attacked Israel from southern Lebanon, sparking a war that lasted just over a month. The war killed civilians in both Israel and Lebanon and caused widespread damage across Lebanon. Despite the costs, Hezbollah, backed by Syria and Iran, remained popular among Lebanon's Shiite Muslims. In 2008, a new power-sharing agreement was reached in Lebanon. The agreement increased Hezbollah's power, but contained a pledge that no faction would use its weapons within Lebanon.

✔ **Checkpoint** How did an influx of Palestinians contribute to conflict in Lebanon?

Iraq's History of Conflict

Since the 1950s, ethnic and religious divisions, oil resources, and border disputes have led to conflict in Iraq. During the Cold War, the United States and the Soviet Union competed for influence in Iraq, which had vast oil reserves and was strategically located on the Persian Gulf.

Iraq was carved out of the Ottoman Empire after World War I. Its population included Sunni and Shiite Arabs as well as Kurds. Although Shiites formed a majority in Iraq, Sunni Arabs controlled the government. Kurds, who lived in the north, distrusted the government and wanted self-rule. Divisions among these groups fed tensions in Iraq.

The Iran-Iraq War In 1980, Iraqi dictator, **Saddam Hussein,** took advantage of turmoil in neighboring Iran following its Islamic revolution by seizing a disputed border region. His action sparked a long, costly war.

Iraq used superior weapons and poison gas to stop waves of Iranian soldiers. After both sides attacked foreign oil tankers and oil fields in the Persian Gulf, the United States sent naval forces to protect shipping lanes. The war ended in a stalemate in 1988. For both Iran and Iraq, the human and economic toll was enormous.

During the war, Saddam Hussein brutally repressed a Kurdish revolt in the north. He also used chemical weapons on Kurdish civilians. His actions sparked outrage and charges of genocide.

The 1991 Gulf War In 1990, Iraq invaded its oil-rich neighbor, Kuwait. Saddam Hussein claimed that Kuwait was historically part of Iraq. In fact, he wanted control of Kuwait's vast oil fields and greater access to the Persian Gulf.

The United States saw Saddam's move not only as illegal, but also as a threat to its ally, Saudi Arabia, and to the oil resources of the region. It formed an international coalition to drive Iraq out of Kuwait. In the 1991 Gulf War, the U.S.-led coalition operated under the UN banner. It quickly crushed Iraqi forces and freed Kuwait.

Saddam Hussein's Dictatorship
Saddam Hussein, shown here in a propaganda poster in 1982, turned Iraq into a brutal police state, in which critics were tortured and killed.

Despite defeat, Saddam Hussein remained in power. He brutally crushed revolts by Shiite Muslims and the minority Kurds. He used torture and terror to impose his will.

Saddam Defies the UN To protect the Shiites and Kurds, the UN set up **no-fly zones,** or areas where Iraqi aircraft were banned. The UN also tried to discover if Saddam Hussein was building **weapons of mass destruction (WMDs),** or nuclear, biological, and chemical weapons. It imposed economic sanctions on Iraq to limit its oil sales and its use of oil profits. For years, Saddam Hussein defied the UN.

U.S. Forces Invade After the 2001 terrorist attacks, the United States claimed that Saddam Hussein had weapons of mass destruction and was supporting terrorists. It formed a coalition that invaded Iraq in 2003. Coalition forces toppled Saddam, who was later tried and executed for war crimes by a new Iraqi government.

Backed by U.S. and coalition forces, Shiite, Kurdish, and Sunni leaders wrote a constitution and held national elections in 2005. Efforts to rebuild Iraq were hampered by guerrilla attacks and suicide bombings. **Insurgents,** or rebels, from rival Shiite and Sunni groups targeted civilians and government workers.

Civil War Threatens Iraq By 2005, ethnic and religious divisions had pushed the country to the brink of civil war. The United States and Britain worked to train the Iraqi military and police. In 2007, the United States increased troop levels in a "surge" to end the fighting. The violence and death tolls declined.

Iraq's Shiite-led government faced many obstacles. It needed to promote reconciliation among bitterly divided factions. Sunnis claimed that the new government failed to represent their interests. Kurds in the north still sought autonomy. Much of the country's oil industry had been destroyed. An estimated 2 million Iraqi refugees remained outside the country.

Despite the troubles, Iraqi leaders grew more confident. They expanded their security forces and agreed to a withdrawal of all U.S. troops by 2011.

✔ **Checkpoint** Why has conflict persisted in Iraq since the defeat of Saddam Hussein?

Urban Warfare in Iraq
Iraqi foot soldiers accompany a U.S. military vehicle. They are patrolling a war-torn neighborhood of Baghdad, Iraq's capital, in 2007. U.S. and Iraqi forces worked together to try to stop violence between Sunni and Shiite forces.

SECTION 3 Assessment

Progress Monitoring Online
For: Self-quiz with vocabulary practice
Web Code: naa-3231

Terms, People, and Places
1. What do each of the terms, people, and places listed at the beginning of the section have in common? Explain.

Note Taking
2. Reading Skill: Recognize Sequence Use your finished flowchart to answer the Focus Question: What are the causes of conflict in the Middle East?

Comprehension and Critical Thinking
3. Draw Conclusions Why has the Arab-Israeli conflict been so difficult to resolve?
4. Identify Central Issues What were the causes of Lebanon's civil war?
5. Synthesize Information Why did the UN impose economic sanctions in Iraq after the 1991 Gulf War?

● **Writing About History**
Quick Write: Make an Outline To write a research report, you need to make an outline that organizes information that you have gathered. Suppose that you are writing a research report on the Arab-Israeli conflict. Make an outline that organizes the information in this section about that conflict.

Quick Study Guide

- Have students use the Quick Study Guide to prepare for this chapter's test. Students may wish to refer to the following pages as they review:

Conflicts in Iraq
Section 3, pp. 696–697

Conflicts in Former Yugoslavia
Section 1, pp. 684–685

Locations of Regional Conflicts
Section 1, pp. 682–684; Section 2, pp. 686–690; Section 3, pp. 692–697

Key Events of Regional Conflicts
Section 1, pp. 683–685; Section 2, pp. 686–687, 689; Section 3, pp. 692–693, 695–697

- For additional review, remind students to refer to the **L3**

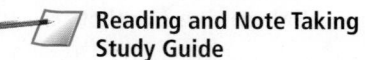

Reading and Note Taking Study Guide
Note Taking Study Guide, pp. 208, 210, 212
Section Summaries, pp. 209, 211, 213

- Have students access **Web Code nbp-3241** for this chapter's **History Interactive** timeline, which includes expanded entries and additional events.

- If students need more instruction on analyzing timelines, have them read the **Skills Handbook, p. SH30.**

- When students have completed their study of the chapter, distribute Chapter Tests A and B.

All in One Teaching Resources, Unit 5, p. 56–61

For **Progress Monitoring Online**, refer students to the Self-test with vocabulary practice at **Web Code nba-3241.**

Quick Study Guide

Progress Monitoring Online
For: Self-test with vocabulary practice
Web Code: nba-3241

■ Conflicts in Iraq

Conflict	Duration	Main Events
Iran-Iraq War	1980–1988	Saddam Hussein tried to seize an Iranian border region. Saddam used chemical weapons against Kurds.
Gulf War	1990–1991	Saddam Hussein invaded Kuwait. Coalition led by United States defeated Saddam's army and freed Kuwait.
Iraq War	2003–	Coalition led by the United States defeated Saddam Hussein's forces and occupied Iraq. Fighting with insurgents continued after Saddam's defeat in 2003.

■ Conflicts in Former Yugoslavia

Area of Conflict	Duration	Main Events
Croatia	1991–1995	Croatian forces fought with ethnic Serbs and the Yugoslav army over ethnic Serb areas. Serbs faced ethnic cleansing.
Bosnia	1992–1995	Ethnic Serbs, Croats, and Muslim Bosniaks fought each other. Muslims faced ethnic cleansing by Serbs.
Kosovo	1996–1999	Ethnic Albanians clashed with the Yugoslav army. Yugoslav forces attempted ethnic cleansing of Albanians.

■ Locations of Regional Conflicts

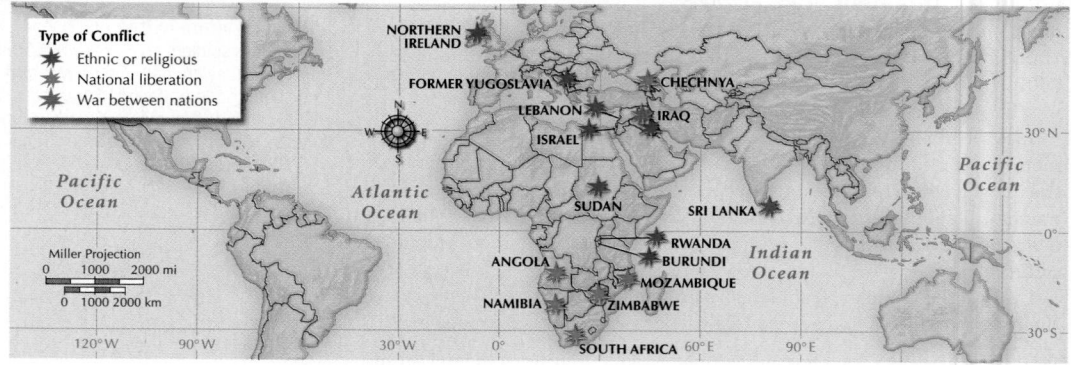

Type of Conflict
- ✷ Ethnic or religious
- ✷ National liberation
- ✷ War between nations

■ Key Events of Regional Conflicts

1948 South Africa expands apartheid system.

1960 Sharpeville massacre marks violent turn in anti-apartheid struggle.

Late 1960s Conflict in Northern Ireland turns violent.

Africa and Europe
Middle East

| 1940 | 1950 | 1960 | 1970 |

1948 Israel's founding brings attack by Arab neighbors.

1967 Israel gains territory in the 1967 war, and Palestinians increase attacks on Israel.

Differentiated Instruction Solutions for All Learners

L1 Special Needs L2 Less Proficient Readers
For students acquiring basic skills:

Adapted Reading and Note Taking Study Guide
Adapted Note Taking, pp. 208, 210, 212
Adapted Section Summaries, pp. 209, 211, 213

L2 English Language Learners
For Spanish-speaking students:

Spanish Reading and Note Taking Study Guide
Spanish Note Taking, pp. 208, 210, 212
Spanish Section Summaries, pp. 209, 211, 213

Concept Connector

Essential Question Review

To connect prior knowledge with what you have learned in this chapter, answer the questions below in your Concept Connector journal. Use the journal in the Reading and Note Taking Study Guide to record your answers (or go to www.phschool.com Web Code: nbd-3207). In addition, record information about the following concepts:

• Impact of the Individual: Nelson Mandela

1. **Dictatorship** Iraq was carved out of the old Ottoman empire after World War I, without regard for the ethnic and religious divisions of the population. Differences between Sunni Arabs, Shiite Arabs, and Kurds often led to conflicts. Given these differences, why might Iraqis support a dictator like Saddam Hussein? Identify at least one other reason for Iraqi support of Saddam Hussein.

2. **Genocide** During Bosnia's civil war, Bosnian Serbs conducted a campaign of ethnic cleansing—killing people from other ethnic groups or forcibly removing them from their homes to create ethnically "pure" areas. Croat and Bosnian fighters responded by launching ethnic cleansing campaigns against Serbs in Croatia. Suggest other possible motives for ethnic cleansing.

3. **Human Rights** After 1948, South Africa's government created apartheid, or the separation of the races. Because apartheid was designed to protect white control over South Africa, blacks were treated like foreigners in their own land. What restrictions did black South Africans face under apartheid? How did the ANC respond to apartheid? What factors caused South African president F.W. de Klerk to end apartheid?

■ Connections to Today

1. **Democracy** In this chapter, you read that Canada's democracy has allowed ethnic differences to be resolved peacefully, rather than through violent conflict. Through democratic means, the French-speaking majority in Quebec has secured rights for their language in Canada, even though French speakers are a minority in Canada (see the graphs below). Use the library and online research to identify another country where a democratic system has recently helped bring a peaceful resolution to ethnic differences. Compare your country's ethnic politics to those in Canada.

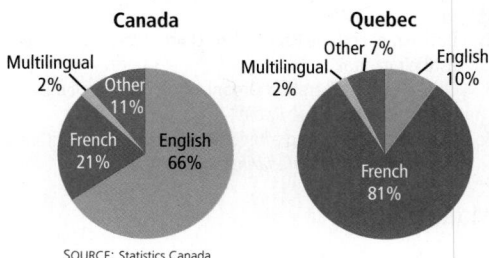

Canada
Multilingual 2%
Other 11%
French 21%
English 66%

Quebec
Other 7%
Multilingual 2%
English 10%
French 81%

SOURCE: Statistics Canada

2. **Cooperation** In this chapter, you learned that members of the NATO military alliance cooperated to end ethnic cleansing and warfare in Kosovo in 1999. Use the library and online research to identify a more recent case in which cooperation among concerned nations has helped to bring peace to a country involved in a violent conflict. How does this recent case compare to what you learned about Kosovo?

History *Interactive*
For: Interactive timeline
Web Code: nbp-3241

1992 Ethnic conflict erupts in Bosnia.	**1994** Open elections bring end of apartheid in South Africa.	**1999** Brutal ethnic conflict in Kosovo brings NATO intervention.

1980   1990   2000   2010

1975 Lebanon plunges into civil war.

1991 U.S.-led coalition defeats Iraq in Gulf War.

2003– U.S.-led coalition occupies Iraq and faces ongoing resistance.

Concept Connector

Tell students that the main concepts for this chapter are Dictatorship, Genocide, Human Rights, and Impact of the Individual, and then ask them to answer the Essential Question Review questions on this page. Discuss the Connections to Today topics and ask students to answer the questions that follow.

Essential Question Review

1. Iraqis may have supported Hussein because he could control conflicting ethnic groups and bring order to the country. Some Iraqis may have supported Hussein out of fear: Opposition could have resulted in imprisonment or death.

2. Possible motives for ethnic cleansing include greed and fear. People may have been forced from their homes so ethnic cleansers could take their property; people who opposed ethnic cleansing could become targets.

3. Under apartheid, blacks needed permission to travel, could not own land in most areas, were segregated, and paid less than whites for the same job. The ANC organized marches, boycotts, and strikes to oppose apartheid. When that failed, the ANC turned to armed struggle. After countries imposed economic sanctions on South Africa and Desmond Tutu won the Nobel Peace Prize for opposing apartheid, F.W. de Klerk ended apartheid.

Connections to Today

1. Comparisons should recognize the main features of Canada's ethnic politics, such as a democratic process, and should identify similar or contrasting features in another country.

2. Comparisons should consider a country like Kosovo, where warfare ended only because of international intervention, and should identify similarities and differences with Kosovo.

For additional review of this chapter's core concepts, remind students to refer to the **L3**

 **Reading and Note Taking Study Guide**
Concept Connector, pp. 255, 267, 275, 278

Chapter Assessment

Terms, People, and Places

1. Chechnya
2. the Good Friday Agreement
3. Nelson Mandela
4. Hutus
5. Jerusalem
6. Yasir Arafat
7. insurgent

Main Ideas

8. In places where different ethnic groups share in the economic rewards and the political process, these groups can work out their differences peacefully.

9. Serbs had dominated Yugoslavia. When Yugoslavia broke up, Serbs fought to retain dominance in regions where they were a minority. This led to widespread ethnic conflict.

10. International pressure and internal resistance to apartheid led white and black leaders to work out a peaceful transition to majority rule.

11. historic resentments between ethnic groups, unjust governments, and regional rivalries

12. Both Israeli Jews and Palestinian Arabs claim the same land as their own. They have fought over the right to control that land, particularly the city of Jerusalem, which is sacred to both.

13. Ethnic and religious divisions and insurgent attacks led to conflict.

Chapter Focus Question

14. Sample: Conflicts have plagued some regions of the world when one ethnic or religious group has denied the rights of others or tried to dominate them, or when a nation has appeared to pose a threat to neighboring nations.

Critical Thinking

15. Sample: International powers could set up a constitutional structure to ensure that political power and economic resources are fairly distributed among the ethnic groups in Bosnia or Kosovo. However, the dominant group might reject its loss of power.

16. The majority of South Africans were black South Africans, who had been excluded from political power and economic participation for generations. It was important that this majority be allowed to rule and gain opportunities after years of white and colonial domination.

Chapter Assessment

Terms, People, and Places

Choose the italicized term in parentheses that best completes each sentence.

1. Muslim nationalists in (*Kosovo/Chechnya*) have fought to free their homeland from Russian control.
2. There were hopes that (*the Good Friday Agreement/ethnic cleansing*) would provide for a peaceful resolution of the conflict in Northern Ireland.
3. (*Desmond Tutu/Nelson Mandela*) led the struggle against apartheid even when he was imprisoned for his role in the African National Congress.
4. In Rwanda, extremist (*Hutus/Tutsis*), the country's ethnic majority, slaughtered members of the country's ethnic minority in 1994.
5. Both Israel and the Palestinians claim (*Mecca /Jerusalem*) as their capital.
6. The Palestine Liberation Organization was headed by (*Yasir Arafat/Yitzhak Rabin*).
7. Efforts to rebuild Iraq after Saddam Hussein's overthrow were slowed by (*intifada/insurgent*) attacks.

Main Ideas

Section 1 (pp. 682–685)
8. Why does ethnic diversity lead to violent conflicts in some places but not in others?
9. How did Yugoslavia's breakup lead to ethnic conflicts?

Section 2 (pp. 686–690)
10. How did South Africa overcome apartheid?
11. What factors contributed to Africa's deadly ethnic conflicts?

Section 3 (pp. 692–697)
12. Explain the basic causes of the Israeli-Palestinian conflict.
13. Why did the removal of Saddam Hussein's regime fail to bring peace to Iraq?

Chapter Focus Question
14. Why have deadly conflicts plagued some regions of the world?

Critical Thinking

15. **Predict Consequences** Identify possible solutions to the ethnic conflicts in Bosnia and Kosovo and predict the consequences of these solutions.
16. **Draw Conclusions** Why was the idea of majority rule important to people in South Africa and in neighboring African countries?
17. **Express Problems Clearly** What are the main problems that have stood in the way of a peace settlement between Palestinians and Israelis?
18. **Recognize Cause and Effect** How did Saddam Hussein's policies cause suffering for Iraqis?
19. **Analyzing Visuals** What is the main message of the cartoon below? How might violence have been prevented in these countries?

● Writing About History

In this chapter's three Section Assessments, you developed skills for writing a research report.

Writing a Research Report This chapter discusses several ethnic and regional conflicts. Choose one of the conflicts covered or find another conflict that interests you. Write a research report on the causes of the conflict, how the conflict unfolded, and how it was resolved or might be resolved. Consult page SH13 of the Writing Handbook for additional help.

Prewriting
• Do online or library research to read background materials about your conflict.
• Take notes on relevant details, events, and the people involved in the conflict.

• Create a set of questions about your conflict and gather additional resources.

Drafting
• Develop a working thesis about the cause of this conflict—for example, is the main issue control of land, government policies, or some other issue?
• Make an outline to organize a report that supports your thesis. Find information from your research that supports each part of your outline.
• Write an introduction explaining your thesis, a body, and a conclusion.

Revising
• Use the guidelines for revising your report on page SH15 of the Writing Handbook.

---

17. Palestinians claim a right to return to lands they once owned within Israel. Israelis were determined to remain in settlements established within the mainly Palestinian West Bank, and both sides wanted Jerusalem to be their capital. Both sides have used violence against the other, and this has increased fear and undermined trust.

18. He treated his opponents, ethnic Kurds, and Shiites brutally, and his attacks on neighboring countries led to deadly wars and international sanctions that caused great suffering for Iraqis.

19. The cartoon questions the commitment of powerful nations to intervene to prevent genocide. Such intervention might have prevented deadly violence in Rwanda and Sudan.

Document-Based Assessment

The Palestinian Question

In 1947, the United Nations drew up a plan dividing the Palestine Mandate into two states, Jewish and Arab, which the Arabs rejected. The next year, Israel was established as an independent nation according to the United Nations guidelines. As a result of the 1967 war, Israel gained control of the West Bank and Gaza. Israeli troops and civilians withdrew from Gaza in 2005. Palestinians still do not have an independent state of their own. Despite ongoing conflict between Israelis and Palestinians, many on both sides still hope for peace.

Document A

UN Partition Plan, 1947

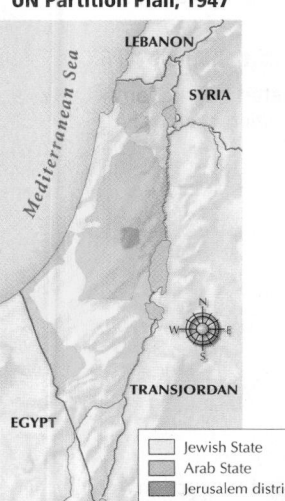

Jewish State
Arab State
Jerusalem district

Document B

Israel and Occupied Territories, 2005

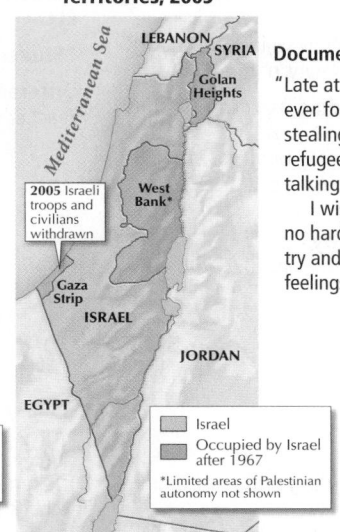

2005 Israeli troops and civilians withdrawn

West Bank*

Gaza Strip

Israel
Occupied by Israel after 1967
*Limited areas of Palestinian autonomy not shown

Document C

"As I have said, we came to Palestine to do away with the help-lessness of the Jewish people through our own endeavors. Therefore, you will realize what it meant for us to watch from here millions of Jews being slaughtered during these years of war. . . . We Jews only want that which is given naturally to all peoples of the world to be masters of our own fate . . . . We are certain that given an opportunity of bringing in large masses of Jews into this country, of opening the doors of Palestine to all Jews who wish to come here, we can . . . create a free Jewish society built on the basis of cooperation, equality, and mutual aid."

—From **"The Zionist Case"** by Golda Meir (speech given March 25, 1946)

Document D

"Late at night when everything is quiet I think about how I will ever forgive the Israelis for what they did to me. I don't mean stealing my homeland, killing my people, turning me into a refugee, or depriving me from having a Palestinian state. I'm talking about myself—what they did to my personality.

I wish I had a normal life: no tension, no rage, no hatred, no hard feelings toward anybody. Even if they leave my country and give me back my rights, how will I overcome these feelings inside me?"

—From **"Children of a Tenth-Class God?"** by Nihaya Qawasmi (1998)

Analyzing Documents

Use your knowledge of the Palestinian-Israeli conflict and Documents A, B, C, and D to answer questions 1–4.

1. According to Documents A and B, what is the present status of the area outlined in the UN Partition Plan?
   A It is divided between Israel and neighboring countries.
   B Palestine is now an independent nation.
   C Part of it is the State of Israel, part is occupied by Israel, and part is ruled by the Palestinians.
   D It is divided among three independent nations.

2. In Document C, "helplessness" refers to
   A Israel's inability to help the Palestinians.
   B the inability of Jews in Palestine to help Jews in Nazi territory.
   C the inability of Palestinians to change their attitude toward Israel.
   D the inability of the Allies to do anything about Nazi atrocities.

3. Which words best describe the feelings of the author of Document D toward Israel?
   A acceptance and understanding
   B discouragement and fear
   C anger and resentment
   D trust and hope

4. **Writing Task** What are the prospects for a peaceful settlement of the Palestinian question? Use the documents on this page along with information from the chapter to write a short essay on this topic.

● Writing About History

As students begin the assignment, refer them to p. SH13 of the **Writing Handbook** for help in writing a research paper. Remind them of the steps they should take to complete their assignment, including prewriting, drafting, and revising. For help in revising, remind them to use the guidelines on p. SH15 of the **Writing Handbook**.

Students' research papers should accurately identify the conflict and its participants, analyze the key causes of the conflict and their historical origins, and advance an idea about how the conflict might be resolved. They should be free of grammatical and spelling errors. For scoring rubrics for writing assignments, see **Assessment Rubrics,** p. 8.

Document-Based Assessment

- To help students understand the documents on the page, give them the following **TIP: As you review each document, use your knowledge of the subject as well as clues in the document to identify the point of view of the writer.**

- To provide students with further practice in answering Document-Based Assessment Questions, go to **Document-Based Assessments,** pp. 95–109

- If students need more instruction on comparing viewpoints, have them read the **Skills Handbook,** p. SH32.

Answers

1. C
2. B
3. C
4. Responses should show a clear understanding of the issues at the root of the Israeli-Palestinian conflict, including conflicting claims to the land, and should analyze the prospect for peace. Students should use specific evidence from the documents and the chapter to support their conclusions.

The Developing World

Section	Core Instruction (L3)	Differentiated Instruction (L1) (L2) (L4)
Section 1 *The Challenges of Development* 🕐 **2 periods, 1 block** **OBJECTIVES** ■ Understand the paths that nations in Asia, Africa, and Latin America have taken in developing strong economies. ■ Describe some obstacles to development in the global South. ■ Explain how development is changing patterns of life in the developing world. **Focus Question** *How have the nations of the developing world tried to build better lives for their people?*	**All in One Teaching Resources, Unit 5** Reading Strategy, p. 67 Vocabulary Builder, p. 66 Outline Map: Developed and Developing Nations, p. 73 Section 1 Quiz, p. 62 **Reading and Note Taking Study Guide** Note Taking Study Guide, p. 214 Section 1 Summary, p. 215 **Note Taking Transparencies**, 201 **WITNESS HISTORY Audio CD** Building a Better Life **Progress Monitoring Transparencies**, 140 **Color Transparencies**, 200, 203 **Teaching Resources, Skills Handbook** Prereading the Chapter, pp. 1–2 Word Knowledge Rating Form, p. 3 K-W-L Chart, p. 4	**(L1) Adapted Reading and Note Taking Study Guide** Note Taking Study Guide, p. 214 SN Section 1 Summary, p. 215 SN **(L2) Adapted Reading and Note Taking Study Guide** Note Taking Study Guide, p. 214 LPR Section 1 Summary, p. 215 LPR **Spanish Reading and Note Taking Study Guide** Note Taking Study Guide, p. 214 ELL Section 1 Summary, p. 215 ELL **(L4) Extend Activity,** Teacher's Edition, pp. 702c, 708 AR, GT	*Student Edition Audio SN **Differentiated Instruction Activity,** Teacher's Edition, p. 705 SN *Guided Reading Audio, Spanish ELL *Student Edition Audio LPR **Differentiated Instruction Activity,** Teacher's Edition, p. 705 LPR
Section 2 *Africa Seeks a Better Future* 🕐 **2 periods, 1 block** **OBJECTIVES** ■ Describe the choices African nations had to make as they began to develop their economies. ■ Understand obstacles that African nations faced in their search for well-being. ■ Analyze the challenges faced by a developing nation by taking a closer look at Tanzania. **Focus Question** *What challenges have African nations faced in their effort to develop their economies?*	**All in One Teaching Resources, Unit 5** Section 2 Quiz, p. 63 **Reading and Note Taking Study Guide** Note Taking Study Guide, p. 216 Section 2 Summary, p. 217 **Note Taking Transparencies**, 202 **WITNESS HISTORY Audio CD** Plundering Forests at Gunpoint **Progress Monitoring Transparencies**, 141 **Color Transparencies**, 199, 201	**(L1) Adapted Reading and Note Taking Study Guide** Note Taking Study Guide, p. 216 SN Section 2 Summary, p. 217 SN **(L2) Adapted Reading and Note Taking Study Guide** Note Taking Study Guide, p. 216 LPR Section 2 Summary, p. 217 LPR **(L4) All in One Teaching Resources, Unit 5** Viewpoints: Saving Africa's Environment?, p. 68 AR, GT	**Differentiated Instruction Activity,** Teacher's Edition, p. 711 SN **Spanish Reading and Note Taking Study Guide** Note Taking Study Guide, p. 216 ELL Section 2 Summary, p. 217 ELL **Differentiated Instruction Activity,** Teacher's Edition, p. 711 LPR **Extend Activity,** Teacher's Edition, p. 713 AR, GT **Color Transparency 199**

*Audio support is available for all sections.

Section	Core Instruction L3	Differentiated Instruction L1 L2 L4	

Section 3
China and India: Two Giants of Asia

 2 periods, 1 block

OBJECTIVES
■ Analyze how China has reformed its economy but limited freedom.
■ Describe the continuing challenges that China faces.
■ Understand how India has faced poverty but built a stronger economy.
■ Explain important Indian social reforms.

Focus Question *How do China and India compare in building strong economies and democratic governments?*

All in One Teaching Resources, Unit 5
Section 3 Quiz, p. 64

Reading and Note Taking Study Guide
Note Taking Study Guide, p. 218
Section 3 Summary, p. 219

Note Taking Transparencies, 203

WITNESS HISTORY Audio CD
A Violent Crackdown

Progress Monitoring Transparencies, 142

Color Transparencies, 202

L1 **Adapted Reading and Note Taking Study Guide**
Note Taking Study Guide, p. 218 **SN**
Section 3 Summary, p. 219 **SN**

L2 **Adapted Reading and Note Taking Study Guide**
Note Taking Study Guide, p. 218 **LPR**
Section 3 Summary, p. 219 **LPR**

L4 **All in One Teaching Resources, Unit 5**
Primary Source: "The Outlook for China, Human Rights," by Harry Wu, p. 70 **AR, GT**
Biography: Mother Teresa, p. 69 **AR, GT**

Differentiated Instruction Activity, Teacher's Edition, p. 717 **SN**

Spanish Reading and Note Taking Study Guide
Note Taking Study Guide, p. 218 **ELL**
Section 3 Summary, p. 219 **ELL**

Differentiated Instruction Activity, Teacher's Edition, p. 717 **LPR, ELL**

Differentiated Instruction Activity, Teacher's Edition, p. 715 **AR, GT**

Extend Activity, Teacher's Edition, p. 718 **AR, GT**

Section 4
Latin America Builds Democracy

 2 periods, 1 block

OBJECTIVES
■ Analyze how Latin America grappled with poverty.
■ Describe Latin America's difficult road to democracy.
■ Understand the struggle for democracy in Argentina.

Focus Question *What challenges have Latin American nations faced in recent decades in their struggle for democracy and prosperity?*

All in One Teaching Resources, Unit 5
Outline Map: Nations of Latin America, p. 74
Geography Quiz, p. 75
Section 4 Quiz, p. 65

Reading and Note Taking Study Guide
Note Taking Study Guide, pp. 220–221
Section 4 Summary, p. 222
Concept Connector, pp. 237, 262, 295, 300

Note Taking Transparencies, 204

WITNESS HISTORY Audio CD
A Daily Struggle

Progress Monitoring Transparencies, 143

Color Transparencies, 204

Witness History Discovery School™
video program, *Making a Living in Peru*

L1 **Adapted Reading and Note Taking Study Guide**
Note Taking Study Guide, pp. 220–221 **SN**
Section 4 Summary, p. 222 **SN**

L2 **Adapted Reading and Note Taking Study Guide**
Note Taking Study Guide, pp. 220–221 **LPR**
Section 4 Summary, p. 222 **LPR**
Concept Connector, pp. 237, 262, 295, 300 **LPR**

L4 **All in One Teaching Resources, Unit 5**
Viewpoints: Democracy in Latin America, p. 71 **AR, GT**
Biography: Pablo Neruda, p. 72 **AR, GT**

Concept Connector, pp. 237, 262, 295, 300 **SN**

Differentiated Instruction Activity, Teacher's Edition, p. 721 **SN**

Spanish Reading and Note Taking Study Guide
Note Taking Study Guide, pp. 220–221 **ELL**
Section 4 Summary, p. 222 **ELL**
Concept Connector, pp. 237, 262, 295, 300 **ELL**

Differentiated Instruction Activity, Teacher's Edition, p. 721 **ELL**

Differentiated Instruction Activity, Teacher's Edition, p. 722 **AR, GT**

Extend Activity, Teacher's Edition, p. 726 **AR, GT**

Assessment Resources
• **Progress Monitoring Transparencies,** 140–143
• **SuccessTracker™,** Chapter 21
• **Document-Based Assessment,** pp. 95–109
• *ExamView*® **Test Bank CD-ROM,** Chapter 21

• **All in One Teaching Resources, Unit 5,** Chapter Test, pp. 76–81
• **Progress Monitoring *Online* Quizzes,** Chapter 21
• **Assessment Rubrics**

Differentiated Instruction Key
L1 Special Needs		**LPR**	Less Proficient Readers
L2 Basic to Average		**AR**	Advanced Readers
L3 All Students		**SN**	Special Needs Students
L4 Average to Advanced		**GT**	Gifted and Talented
		ELL	English Language Learner

CHAPTER PLANNER

Author's Notes

Poverty, Dependency, Debt

The traditional way of acquiring money to pay for development was through the export of what Third World countries had to sell: raw materials or agricultural products. The new nations thus joined Latin America as commodity exporters, shipping overseas vast quantities of coffee, tea, sugar, bananas, copra, palm oil, wheat, beef, rubber, oil, copper, iron, uranium, bauxite.

When the prices of these products of the southern earth were high, as in the 1960s, the South did passably well—and invested commensurately in new projects. When the prices went down in the world markets, as they did in the 1970s and 1980s, the new countries suffered. Commodity prices, furthermore, were frequently deter-mined not by Third World producers, but by speculators in First World countries or by what Second World governments were willing to pay. Desperate for foreign exchange, the countries of the global South often cut back even on subsistence agriculture in order to put more land into export crops—and hence had to import food. The result was a very serious set of export-related problems.

Another major category of difficulty was the sort of dependency syndrome that had afflicted Latin America for so long. Third World countries in general depended on other nations for both manufactured goods and energy—meaning mostly oil. Again, a crucial factor in the economic development of the global South was beyond their control, in the hands of oil sheiks and European or American or Japanese manufacturers.

Another fundamental problem for developing nations followed directly from those of commodity exports and dependency. This was the huge debt that many countries in the South incurred, particularly over the 1970s and 1980s, because the other way to capitalize development projects was to borrow money. . . . When these loans began to come due, the countries of the south found commodity prices still low, the cost of dependency for oil and essential manufactured goods still high. Many of them could not repay the loans or even make interest payments on them—unless they borrowed more money.

—Anthony Esler, *The Human Venture: From Prehistory to the Present,* (Upper Saddle River, New Jersey: Pearson Education, 2004), pp. 736–737

Extend Online

Measuring Development

Have students compare data on developing countries. Use the steps below to help students complete the activity.

Prepare for the Activity Explain that there are many ways to measure a country's level of development. One common measure is gross domestic product (GDP, or economic output) per capita (per person). However, some social scientists feel that other statistics, such as life expectancy or literacy, are more important. Together, these numbers make it possible to judge a country's strengths and weaknesses in the area of development.

Conduct the Activity For help in starting the activity, send students to **Web Code nbe-3301,** where they can access data tables for every country. Assign students to groups and have students compare two developing countries in the same developing region (Latin America, Africa, or Asia excluding Japan). Members of the group should prepare graphs comparing the two countries on three or four statistics measuring development. Have them present their research to the class. Each group should discuss the strengths and weaknesses of each country.

Follow-Up Conduct a class discussion based on the following questions: How might each country build on its strengths and overcome its weaknesses in the area of development?

Differentiated Instruction   Solutions for All Learners

Mapping Concepts ⓛⓛ

Concept terms such as *development* and *urbanization* are not only complex, but they are also pervasive in social studies. They warrant more extensive instruction than terms such as *caucus* or *suffrage*, which are less conceptually demanding. Model this using the following steps.

1. On the board, create a concept organizer to be filled in together as you teach the concept.

2. Pronounce the term—*compromise*.

3. Provide students with a contextually rich sentence—*A successful marriage involves plenty of give and take; one must make many compromises.*

4. Guide students in coming up with synonyms for the term—*give and take, working it out, agreement.*

5. Guide students to analyze the contextual sentence and synonyms and clarify the essential attributes of the concept as they list them on their concept organizer form—*Compromises always involve each party getting less than they want, give and take, discussion and mutual respect.*

6. Record examples of the new concept on the organizer—taking care to link directly to the attributes noted in the previous step—*agreeing on a curfew with your parents, two nations reaching a peace treaty, Republicans and Democrats agreeing on a bill.*

7. Elicit from students additional examples of the concept. Be sure to insist students justify their examples using the attributes—*two friends compromising on which movie to see.*

8. Provide non-examples that do NOT have all of the attributes—*being told to do all of your homework, no matter what.*

9. Provide additional examples and non-examples and coach students through the process of evaluating them until they are fairly proficient with the new concept.

10. Coach students in writing a "show you know" sentence using the new concept on their organizer—*Friendship involves making many compromises.*

11. When completed, the concept organizer provides students with information that can be used in a form to explain additional examples they may encounter.

Modeling Reading and Writing Skills

Evaluating Online Sources Explain that in this chapter students will be writing a research paper. (See Writing About History, p. 730). Remind students that when conducting research, they should use credible, accurate sources. To improve accuracy of the information gathered, provide students with these guidelines:

1. Identify the sponsor of the Web site. Examine the sponsor's credentials and expertise. Determine if the sponsor has any bias.

2. Check the time of the last update of the Web site to ensure the information is current.

3. Use several sources to confirm information.

To model this skill, write the following possible sources on the board. For each one, have students decide whether or not it would be a good source to use for a research paper.

• Personal home page updated daily (*No, because the individual has no incentive to make sure the information is accurate.*)

• Web site sponsored by a publisher of reference materials (*Yes, because the group has an incentive to make sure the information is accurate.*)

• Government Web site last updated three years ago (*No, because the site will not have up-to-date information.*)

• Web site sponsored by a political group or business (*Possibly. Students should look at the information carefully, because the site might present biased information favorable to the sponsors' interests.*)

Draw Inferences Tell students that when reading, they may need to recognize an implied message. By differentiating between what is stated explicitly and what is implied, they can draw inferences.

To model this skill, read aloud the Witness History Primary Source selection that opens Section 1. Point out the explicitly stated facts: Begum slept in a cow shed and spent her days begging, until she received a loan from Grameen Bank. What can be inferred is that organizations are providing new economic opportunities to the poor.

Teach With Technology

PresentationEXPRESS™
Premium DVD

- Teach this chapter's core content using **PresentationExpress™ Premium,** which includes dynamic lecture notes, interactive game shows, songs, videos, and the *ExamView® QuickTake* assessment tool.

- To introduce this chapter using **PresentationExpress™ Premium,** start by asking students the following question: **Which of the following statements do you most agree with? (A) Poor, or developing, countries should avoid any damage to the environment in their effort to improve standards of living. (B) Poor countries should limit the damage to the environment as they raise living standards. (C) Raising living standards is more important than protecting the environment for poor countries. (D) Poor countries have to expect environmental damage if they want to raise living standards.** Take a class poll using the QuickTake feature, and discuss their responses. Point out that in this chapter, they will read about environmental issues faced by poor, or developing, countries. Continue introducing the chapter using the Witness History audio.

Technology Resources

- Student**EXPRESS** CD-ROM, Chapter 21

- Teacher**EXPRESS** CD-ROM, Chapter 21

- Presentation**EXPRESS**™ **Premium DVD,** Chapter 21

- **WITNESS HISTORY** Audio CD, Chapter 21

- *ExamView* Test Bank CD-ROM, English and Spanish, Chapter 21

- **Guided Reading Audio,** Spanish, Chapter 21

- **Student Edition Audio,** Chapter 21

- **Witness History Discovery School**™ video program, *Making a Living in Peru*

- **Experience It! Multimedia Pack**

The Developing World
1945–Present

Bibliography

For the Teacher

French, Howard W. *A Continent for the Taking: The Tragedy and Hope of Africa.* Knopf, 2004.

Jha, Prem Shankar *Perilous Road to Market: The Political Economy of Reform in Russia, India, and China.* London: Pluto Press, 2002.

Winn, Peter. *Americas: The Changing Face of Latin America and the Caribbean.* Berkeley: University of California Press, 1999.

For the Student

L1 Keeler, Stephen *The Changing Face of China.* London: Hodder and Stoughton, 2002.

L2 Hadden, Gerry. *Teenage Refugees from Guatemala Speak Out.* New York: Rosen, 1997.

L3 Lekuton, Joseph Lemasolai. *Facing the Lion: Growing Up Maasai on the African Savanna.* Washington, D.C.: National Geographic, 2003.

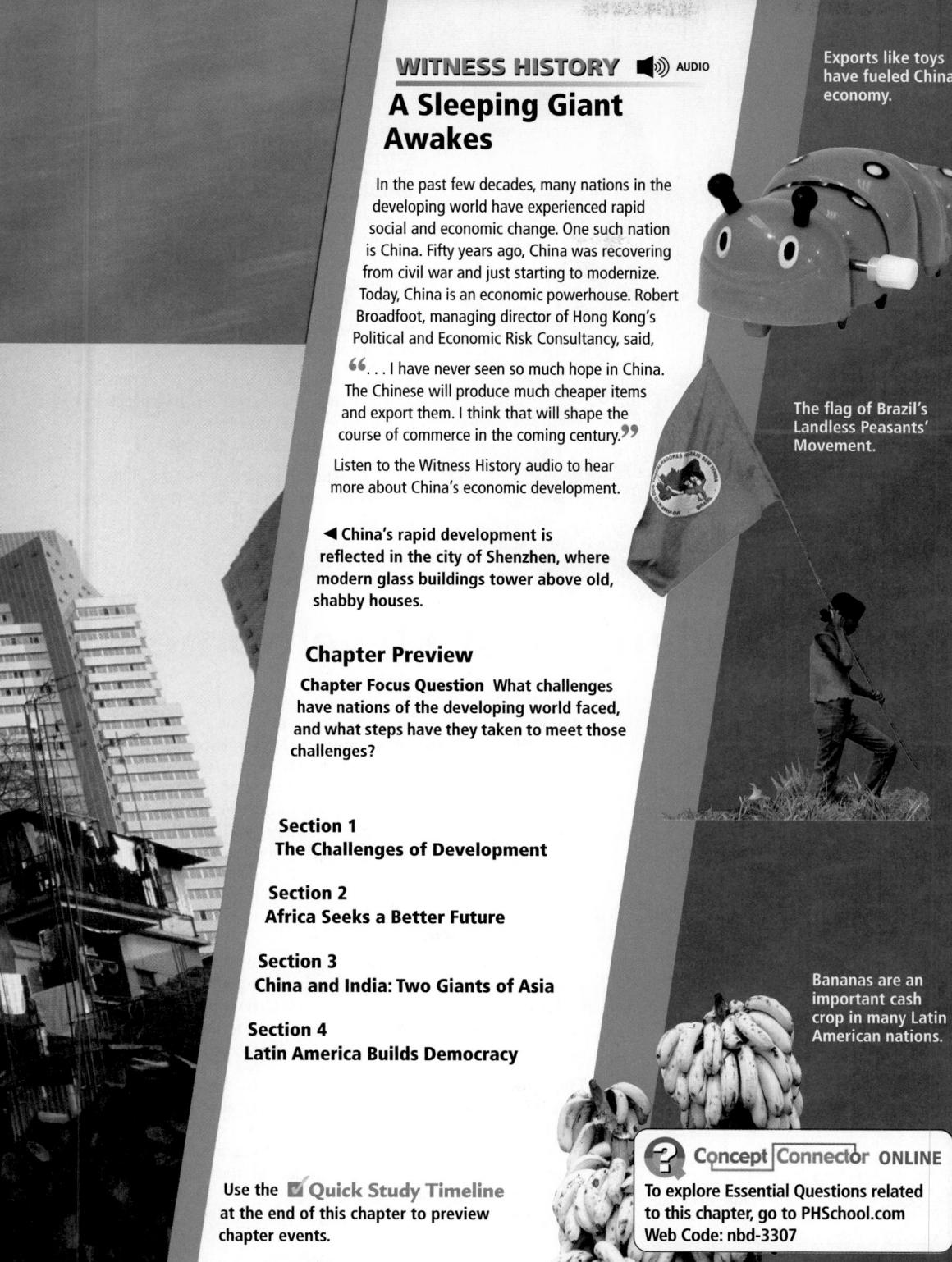

A Sleeping Giant Awakes

In the past few decades, many nations in the developing world have experienced rapid social and economic change. One such nation is China. Fifty years ago, China was recovering from civil war and just starting to modernize. Today, China is an economic powerhouse. Robert Broadfoot, managing director of Hong Kong's Political and Economic Risk Consultancy, said,

66 . . . I have never seen so much hope in China. The Chinese will produce much cheaper items and export them. I think that will shape the course of commerce in the coming century. 99

Listen to the Witness History audio to hear more about China's economic development.

◀ China's rapid development is reflected in the city of Shenzhen, where modern glass buildings tower above old, shabby houses.

Exports like toys have fueled China's economy.

The flag of Brazil's Landless Peasants' Movement.

Bananas are an important cash crop in many Latin American nations.

Chapter Preview

Chapter Focus Question What challenges have nations of the developing world faced, and what steps have they taken to meet those challenges?

Section 1
The Challenges of Development

Section 2
Africa Seeks a Better Future

Section 3
China and India: Two Giants of Asia

Section 4
Latin America Builds Democracy

Use the ✓ **Quick Study Timeline** at the end of this chapter to preview chapter events.

? Concept Connector ONLINE
To explore Essential Questions related to this chapter, go to PHSchool.com
Web Code: nbd-3307

Chapter-Level Resources

All in One Vocabulary Builder; Reading Strategy; Enrichment; Outline Maps; Geography Quiz; Chapter Tests
- Document-Based Assessments
- AYP Monitoring Assessments
- *ExamView* Test Bank CD-ROM
- Guided Reading Audio (Spanish)
- Student Edition Audio

Previewing the Chapter

- **WITNESS HISTORY** Point out that the old and the new coexist today in much of Africa, Asia, and Latin America, a region known as the developing world. Explain that nations in this region are working to build stronger economies and create higher standards of living. China is one such nation. Read the Witness History selection aloud or play the accompanying audio. Ask **What is the speaker's view of China's future?** *(He is very optimistic and sees China as a major economic power.)* Tell students that they will find out whether Bradford's prediction is correct as they read the chapter ahead.

🔊 AUDIO **Witness History Audio CD,** A Sleeping Giant Awakes

- **Analyzing the Visuals** Ask students to study the photo of Shenzhen, China. Ask **What questions do the photo and the Witness History selection bring to mind?** *(Examples: Why are there both old and new buildings? What opportunities will the schoolgirl have?)* Write down students' questions and tell students that you are keeping a copy of these questions so that they can go back and answer them after they have read the chapter.

- **Focus** Write the Chapter Focus Question on the board. Tell students to keep this question in mind as they read the chapter. *(Answer appears with Chapter Assessment answers.)* Have students preview the section titles for this chapter.

Note Taking Study Guide With Concept Connector Journal
For online access: Web code: nad-3307
For print alternative: Reading and Note Taking Study Guide booklet

Objectives

As you teach this section, keep students focused on the following objectives to help them answer the Section Focus Question and master core content.

- Understand the paths that nations in Asia, Africa, and Latin America have taken in developing strong economies.
- Describe some obstacles to development in the global South.
- Explain how development is changing patterns of life in the developing world.

A loan recipient poses with the cows she bought to help generate income.

Bangladesh's currency, the taka

WITNESS HISTORY 🔊 AUDIO

Building a Better Life

Bangladeshi Laily Begum used to sleep in a cow shed and spend her days begging. Then she got a loan for $119 from Grameen Bank, a Bangladesh-based organization that lends money to the poor. She bought a cow and began to build her own business selling milk. Today she and her husband own several shops and a restaurant.

❝ People now come to me for help . . . I can feed myself and my family, and now other people look at me and they treat me with respect. ❞
—Laily Begum, February 12, 1998

Focus Question How have the nations of the developing world tried to build better lives for their people?

The Challenges of Development

Objectives

- Understand the paths that nations in Asia, Africa, and Latin America have taken in developing strong economies.
- Describe some obstacles to development in the global South.
- Explain how development is changing patterns of life in the developing world.

Terms, People, and Places

development	Green Revolution
developing world	fundamentalists
literacy	shantytowns
traditional economies	

Note Taking

Reading Skill: Identify Supporting Details Expand this chart to record details about development as you read.

```
                    Development
    ┌──────────────┬──────────────┬──────────────┐
    │  Economic    │  Obstacles   │  Changes in  │
    │  Change      │              │  Patterns    │
    │              │              │  of Life     │
    │  •           │  •           │  •           │
    │  •           │  •           │  •           │
    │              │  •           │              │
```

Many new nations emerged in Africa and Asia in the decades after World War II. These new nations, along with countries in Latin America, focused on development. **Development** means building stable governments, improving agriculture and industry, and raising standards of living. The nations working toward development in Africa, Asia, and Latin America are known collectively as the **developing world.** From the beginning, nations in the developing world faced many challenges.

Goals of Development

At independence, new nations wrote constitutions that set up representative governments and protected the rights of citizens. Their leaders also pushed to build strong modern economies. Since a modern economy needs well-trained workers, developing nations built schools to increase **literacy,** or the ability to read and write.

The Global South The developing world is sometimes called the global South because it is located mostly south of the Tropic of Cancer. The global South holds 75 percent of the world's people and much of its natural resources. It was poor, however, compared to the global North, the rich industrial nations located mostly north of the Tropic of Cancer.

Transforming Economies Leaders of new nations in the developing world set ambitious economic goals. They wanted to increase food output, develop industry, construct roads, airports, and railroads and build power plants.

Despite these goals, much of the developing world still lived and worked in traditional economies. Traditional economies are undeveloped economic systems that rely on custom and tradition, using simple tools and methods of production passed down from earlier generations. In traditional economies, most people are farmers or craftspeople who make or grow enough to meet their own needs. They trade any surplus, or extra, for goods they cannot make themselves.

Economic Policies Developing nations needed vast amounts of capital to finance projects to modernize their economies. After independence, some political leaders tried to speed development by replacing traditional and market economies with government-led command economies. This meant that governments owned most businesses and controlled farming.

To pay for development, many countries <u>procured</u> large loans from banks and governments in the global North. When poor economic conditions made it difficult for these countries to repay their loans, lenders insisted that developing countries sell government businesses, hold free elections, and establish market economies. Lenders required these changes so developing countries could pay off debts and be eligible for new loans.

Vocabulary Builder

<u>procure</u>—(proh KYOOR) *v.* obtain, make an effort to get

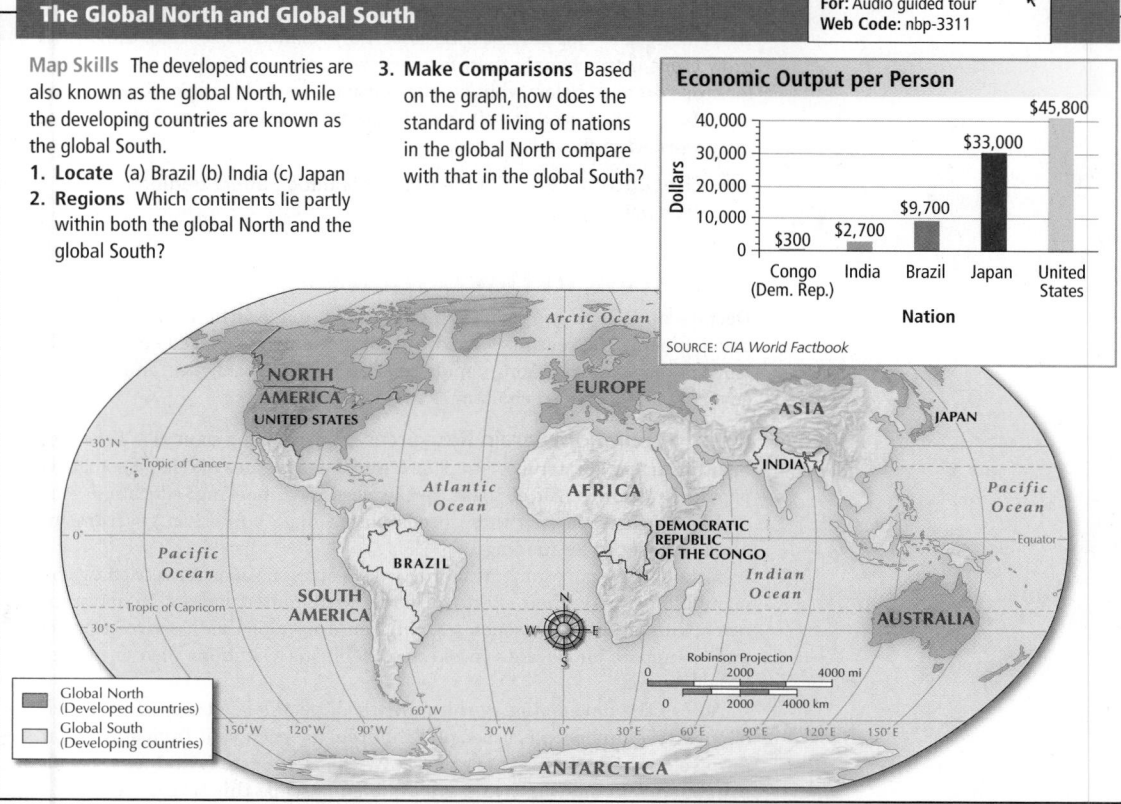

The Global North and Global South

Geography *Interactive*
For: Audio guided tour
Web Code: nbp-3311

Map Skills The developed countries are also known as the global North, while the developing countries are known as the global South.
1. **Locate** (a) Brazil (b) India (c) Japan
2. **Regions** Which continents lie partly within both the global North and the global South?

3. **Make Comparisons** Based on the graph, how does the standard of living of nations in the global North compare with that in the global South?

Economic Output per Person

$45,800
$33,000
$9,700
$300 $2,700

Congo (Dem. Rep.) | India | Brazil | Japan | United States
Nation

SOURCE: *CIA World Factbook*

Global North (Developed countries)
Global South (Developing countries)

Goals of Development L3

Instruct

- **Introduce: Key Terms** Ask students to find the key term ***development*** (in blue) in the text and provide its meaning. Explain that here the word is used to describe the process of making a society wealthier, or more ***developed.*** Use the Idea Wave strategy (TE, p. T22) and ask students predict the challenges that might occur in trying to develop an entire nation.

- **Teach** Trace the path developing nations have taken from traditional to market economies. Ask **What are the main features of a traditional economy?** *(property owned by families or ethnic groups; economic activity and consumer choice limited by custom; production limited to fulfilling needs of the group)* **How did colonization change traditional economies?** *(Many were replaced by market economies.)*

- **Quick Activity** Display **Color Transparency 200: Global Economic Trends**. Use the lesson suggested in the transparency book to summarize and contrast trends in the global North with those in the global South.
  📖 **Color Transparencies,** 200

Independent Practice

Have students access **Web Code nbp-3311** to take the **Geography Interactive Audio Guided Tour** and then answer the map skills questions in the text.

Monitor Progress

- As students fill in their charts, circulate to make sure they understand the obstacles to and effects of development in the global South. For a completed version of the chart, see
  📖 **Note Taking Transparencies,** 201

- Check answers to map skills questions.

Differentiated Instruction   Solutions for All Learners

L1 Special Needs   **L2 Less Proficient Readers**

Ask students to create a concept web for the concept of development. Have them list synonyms, definitions, essential features, and examples. See this chapter's Professional Development pages for more on creating a concept web. Then ask students to list things a country would need to build a stronger economy. *(skilled workers, electricity, transportation)*

Use the following resources to help students acquire basic skills.

 **Adapted Reading and Note Taking Study Guide**

- Adapted Note Taking Study Guide, p. 214
- Adapted Section Summary, p. 215

Answers

Map Skills
1. Review locations with students.
2. Asia and North America
3. It is much higher in the global North.

Obstacles to Development L3

Instruct

- **Introduce** Ask students to read the introductory paragraph and three black headings under the red heading Obstacles to Development. Have them predict the effects of each obstacle. Then have them read to find out whether their predictions were accurate.

- **Teach** Create a cause-and-effect chart on the board. Have students fill in the problems faced by poor people of the developing world. Help students see the difficulty of breaking the cycle of poverty.

- **Quick Activity** Display **Color Transparency 203: Challenges Facing Developing Countries.** Have students identify challenges to development and explain how each one hinders the development process.

  📽 **Color Transparencies,** 203

Independent Practice

Have students work in groups to choose one economic obstacle facing developing nations and brainstorm possible solutions. Use the Numbered Heads strategy (TE, p. T23) and have groups share their work with the class.

Monitor Progress

To check students' understanding, have them write one cause-and-effect statement for each black heading. Discuss how, if at all, each cause could be modified to improve the outcome or effect.

Answer

✓ Farmers with smaller plots could not afford the new technology. Since big landowners could use the technology to produce crops more cheaply, crop prices fell below what smaller farmers needed to earn a living. Many were forced out of business.

After developing countries shifted to market economies, companies and individuals from the global North invested in industries in these countries. Investors put money into businesses that produced income for them, but were not always best for the developing nations's economy.

The Green Revolution During the 1950s and 1960s, new high-yield seeds, fertilizers, and pesticides, along with mechanical equipment such as tractors, were introduced in many parts of the developing world. These new products, along with new methods of farming, are known as the Green Revolution. The Green Revolution raised farm output in developing countries. But it had unforeseen consequences. Only big landowners could afford these new tools and methods. Because they farmed more land, they could grow crops more cheaply than farmers with small plots. As a result, prices for crops dropped below what smaller farmers needed to make to earn a living. Many were forced to sell their farms to big landowners. They became farm workers or moved to cities.

 Checkpoint How did the Green Revolution affect traditional economies?

Obstacles to Development

Despite ambitious goals, many new nations made little progress toward development. The reasons varied, but many countries shared similar problems. Poverty, rapidly rising populations, economic dependence, and unstable governments all posed challenges to development.

Rising Populations Strain Resources In developing countries, improved healthcare and greater food supplies lowered death rates and led to explosive population growth. All of these people need food, housing, education, jobs, and healthcare. Meeting these needs puts a huge burden on governments already strapped for funding.

Although the governments of many developing nations have tried to slow population growth, their efforts have met with limited success. In many cultures with traditional economies, children are valued as a source of labor and a support for parents in old age. Religious traditions also encourage large families.

Across the developing world, millions of people are trapped in a cycle of poverty. Many people, especially children, die each year from starvation, disease, and other effects of poverty. Without education and jobs, people cannot earn living wages and are unable to escape this tragic cycle.

History Background

The People Behind the Green Revolution
American scientist Norman Borlaug helped start the Green Revolution. He created a new kind of wheat that helped Mexico triple its grain production. This news reached Chidambaram Subramaniam, who was in charge of India's agriculture. Worried about his country's chronic food shortages, Subramaniam flew thousands of tons of Borlaug's seeds to India and brought Borlaug to teach farmers how to grow them. Wheat production in India soared by 60 percent. For his work, Borlaug won the 1970 Nobel Peace Prize.

Critics say that the use of fertilizer and pesticide along with his grain hurts the environment. Borlaug points out that by producing higher yields, his approach prevents deforestation that would result from the need to clear more land for farming.

Different Kinds of Labor
A mechanical harvester cuts rice in South America, while women in West Africa prepare fields for planting. *How do traditional economies affect economic development?*

Economic Dependence Despite their efforts to build industry, many developing nations remain economically dependent on their former colonial rulers. Western nations had used their colonies as sources of raw materials. They used the raw materials to produce manufactured goods that they sold to their colonies.

This pattern continued after colonies won their independence. Industrialized countries purchase agricultural goods and raw materials from the developing world. In turn, the industrial nations provide technology, investment, and manufactured goods to developing countries. However, in recent years, lower labor costs have led Western companies to relocate their manufacturing operations to the global South.

Some developing nations produce only a single export crop or commodity, such as sugar or cocoa. Their economies depend on global demand for the commodity. If demand weakens and prices drop, their economies suffer.

Unstable Governments Civil wars and other conflicts hinder development in some countries. Poor leadership and corrupt governments also prevent growth. Dictators spend resources on weapons instead of on education or healthcare. Corrupt leaders loot their nations' treasuries and allow a culture of bribery to thrive.

✓ **Checkpoint** How did population growth affect developing nations?

Patterns of Life Change

Economic development has unleashed great changes across the developing world. Just as the Industrial Revolution disrupted traditional ways of life in Europe and North America, economic development is now transforming life in the global South.

Women's Lives Change In the developing world, the move away from traditional ways of life has brought new opportunities for women. New constitutions granted equality to women, at least on paper. In some countries, such as India, Argentina, and Liberia, women have served as heads of state. Although women still have less access to education than men, the gap has narrowed. Women are joining the work force in growing numbers and contributing their skills to their nations' wealth.

Child Labor In traditional economies, children worked alongside parents, farming or herding to meet the family's needs. When development forces people off their farms, they often move to cities and take low-paying

manufacturing jobs. Because these jobs do not pay enough to cover basic needs, parents depend on the low wages that children earn in factory jobs to survive. In India, around 44 million children work for pay. In Pakistan, children make up 10 percent of the workforce.

Religious Revivals In recent decades, religious revivals have swept many developing nations. Some religious leaders are called **fundamentalists,** because they call for a return to what they see as the fundamental, or basic values of their faiths. Many seek political power to oppose changes that undermine their valued religious traditions.

Rapid Growth of Cities Across the developing world, people have flooded into cities to escape rural poverty and find jobs. Besides economic opportunities, cities offer attractions such as entertainment and sports. With no money and few jobs, most newcomers settle in **shantytowns,** crowded, dangerous slums on the edges of cities. These crime-ridden slums lack basic services such as running water, electricity, or sewer systems.

✔ **Checkpoint** How did development change life for women?

Mumbai: A Divided City
In Mumbai, India, the poverty of slums stands in stark contrast to the comfortable high-rise apartments of wealthier city dwellers. *How did rapid population growth create problems for cities?*

SECTION 1 Assessment

Progress Monitoring *Online*
For: Self-quiz with vocabulary practice
Web Code: nba-3311

Terms, People, and Places

1. For each term, person, or place listed at the beginning of the section, write a sentence explaining its significance.

Note Taking

2. **Reading Skill: Identify Supporting Details** Use your completed chart to answer the Focus Question: How have the nations of the developing world tried to build better lives for their people?

Comprehension and Critical Thinking

3. **Summarize** In general, what are the economic goals of developing nations?
4. **Categorize** What are the differences between the global North and the global South?
5. **Identify Central Issues** Why do developing countries remain dependent on former colonial powers or other industrialized countries?
6. **Predict Consequences** How might modern products and technologies weaken traditional cultures?

● Writing About History

Quick Write: Explore a Topic Choose one challenge facing developing nations and write a series of questions you could use to direct research on the topic. For example, on the topic of industrialization in developing nations you could ask:
- Which five developing nations have the highest level of industrialization today?
- What industries do these nations engage in?

 **Concept** **Connector**

THE ESSENTIAL **?**

DEMOCRACY

Under what conditions is democracy most likely to succeed?

In This Chapter

Developing countries have had to overcome many obstacles in order to establish democratic governments. Poverty, illiteracy, political corruption, and inequality among ethnic groups are among the factors that have stood in their way. The education of children like these (right) will be critical to the future of democratic government everywhere.

Throughout History

400s B.C. The Athenian leader, Pericles, believes all citizens should take part in government.

400s B.C. Plebeians in ancient Rome demand and get the right to elect their own officials.

1215 A.D. English nobles force King John to sign the Magna Carta, limiting the power of the king.

1776 The American colonies wage a war to gain independence and the right to rule themselves.

1930s Germany, facing economic and social problems, turns away from democracy.

Continuing Today

Zimbabwe went from being a model of development to one of the poorest nations in the world under the leadership of Robert Mugabe. Mugabe has ruthlessly held on to power, threatening anyone who has challenged him.

21st Century Skills

? TRANSFER Activities

1. **Analyze** Throughout history, how have people gained the right to a say in government?

2. **Explain** How can democratic government be undermined?

3. **Transfer** Complete a Web quest in which you compare a democratic and a non-democratic country; record your thoughts in the Concept Connector Journal; and learn to make a video. Web Code nbh-3308

History Background

Views of Democracy Discuss these comments about democracy made over the years:
- Jonathan Swift: "All government without the consent of the governed is the very definition of slavery."
- Thomas Jefferson: "Information is the currency of democracy."
- Abraham Lincoln: "No man is good enough to govern another man without that other's consent."

- Winston Churchill: "No one pretends that democracy is perfect or all-wise. Indeed, it has been said that democracy is the worst form of government except for all those others that have been tried from time to time."
- Reinhold Niebuhr: "Man's capacity for justice makes democracy possible; but man's inclination to injustice makes democracy necessary."

Concept **Connector**

Democracy

Objectives
- Understand the characteristics of a democracy.
- Understand the conditions that could undermine a democracy.
- Complete a Web Quest on democracy.

Build Background Knowledge L3
Check students' understanding of the term *democracy*. Have students describe two characteristics of a democratic society and of an undemocratic society. Review students' Concept Connector Journal entries for this theme.

Instruct
- Direct students' attention to the essential question: **Under what conditions is democracy most likely to succeed?**
- Have students read In This Chapter and look at the corresponding picture. Ask: **Why is education critical to a successful democracy?**
- Review the South African cartoon on Zimbabwe. Have volunteers explain what is happening in each panel. Provide help with unfamiliar terms. Ask: **Why would a democracy have no chance of survival in such an environment?**
- Assign the Web Quest on Democracy.

Independent Practice
Concept **Connector** Have students fill in the reflection question on the Web Quest on democracy in their Concept Connector Journal.

📝 **Reading and Note Taking Study Guide**, p. 253

Monitor Progress
Circulate to make sure that students are filling in their Concept Connector Journal. Ensure they understand how democracy occurs.

Transfer Activities
1. People have gotten together and forced their governments to give them more say.
2. Democracy can be limited by poverty, illiteracy, corruption, censorship, police intimidation and other dictatorial tactics.
3. Students' work should be evaluated against the rubric at Web Code nbh-3308.

709

Objectives

As you teach this section, keep students focused on the following objectives to help them answer the Section Focus Question and master core content.

- Describe the goals of developing nations in Africa.
- Understand the obstacles that African nations faced as they pursued development.
- Analyze the challenges faced by a developing nation by taking a closer look at Tanzania.

Prepare to Read

Build Background Knowledge ⓛ

Point out that for a country to develop, it needs to build up industry, transportation systems, public education, and health care. Have students predict why achieving these goals might be difficult in Africa.

Set a Purpose ⓛ

- **WITNESS HISTORY** Read the selection aloud or play the audio.
  - ◀)) AUDIO **Witness History Audio CD,** Plundering Forests at Gunpoint

  Ask **What problem does Yao describe?** (*Gangs are cutting and selling teak trees.*) **How does this affect Yao's people?** (*They are much poorer because of the loss of the valuable resources.*)

- **Focus** Point out the Section Focus Question and write it on the board. Tell students to refer to this question as they read. (*Answer appears with Section 2 Assessment answers.*)

- **Preview** Have students preview the Section Objectives and the list of Terms, People, and Places.

- **Note Taking** Have students read this section using the Structured Read Aloud strategy (TE, p. T20). As they read, have students fill in the concept web recording main ideas about economic, social, and environmental challenges to development in Africa.

  Reading and Note Taking Study Guide, p. 216

A Nigerian child stands in front of the massive trunk of a felled ironwood tree.

WITNESS HISTORY ◀)) AUDIO
Plundering Forests

Civil wars, economic development, and the demand for valuable woods have led to the destruction of ancient African forests. In Ivory Coast, also known as Côte d'Ivoire (koht dee VWAHR), rebels cut trees to sell for money to buy weapons. Illegal logging is devastating local economies. A village chief, Kouadio Yao (KWAH dyoh yow) , told a UN worker of watching helplessly as valuable teak trees were chopped down:

❝ If someone came with a gun, would you be able to stop them and demand that they pay for the trees? What I do know is that because of the conflict, we have lost everything.**❞**
—Integrated Regional Information Networks (IRIN), December 23, 2004

Focus Question What challenges have African nations faced in their effort to develop their economies?

Africa Seeks a Better Future

Objectives
- Describe the goals of developing nations in Africa.
- Understand the obstacles that African nations faced as they pursued development.
- Analyze the challenges faced by a developing nation by taking a closer look at Tanzania.

Terms, People, and Places

socialism	endangered species
desertification	Wangari Maathai
urbanization	sustainable development

Note Taking

Reading Skill: Identify Main Ideas As you read, use a concept web to record the main ideas in this section and to note details that support those main ideas.

More than fifty new nations emerged in Africa in the decades after World War II. African nations are a large part of the developing world. As they set out to build stable governments and modern economies, they faced serious challenges.

Making Economic Choices

In Africa, as elsewhere, development meant building productive economies and raising standards of living. To achieve these goals, African nations had to establish industries, build transportation systems, increase literacy, and reduce poverty. Many countries had little capital to invest in such projects. Each nation had to make difficult choices about how to achieve their goals.

Socialism or Capitalism Many newly independent nations were attracted to socialism, a system in which the people as a whole own all property and operate all businesses. Through socialism, the new nations hoped to reduce dependence on their former colonial rulers and end the inequalities between rich and poor. To regulate the economy, socialism relied on large, generally inefficient bureaucracies.

Some nations chose capitalism, or market economies with private ownership of property, as a path to development. To get the huge sums needed for development, they turned to foreign lenders to invest capital in new industries. These countries often had more efficient economies, but foreign owners took more profits out of the country.

Vocabulary Builder

Use the information below and the following resources to teach the high-use word from this section.
Teaching Resources, Unit 5, p. 66; **Teaching Resources, Skills Handbook,** p. 3

High-Use Word	Definition and Sample Sentence
subsidize, p. 711	*v.* to support with government spending
	Local governments **subsidized** the rebuilding of houses that had been destroyed by a hurricane.

Cash Crops or Food Governments tried to raise development funds by producing cash crops for export, such as coffee or cotton. Some nations also relied on exports of a single commodity, such as copper or oil. However, dependence on a single crop or commodity is risky, because it puts economies at the mercy of sudden price changes in the market.

Because land used for cash crops could not be used to produce food, some countries had to buy costly imported food. To prevent unrest among the urban poor, many governments kept food prices artificially low. However, low prices discouraged local farmers from growing food crops. Governments then had to <u>subsidize</u> part of the cost of importing food.

✔ **Checkpoint** Why did governments promote cash crops?

Obstacles to Progress

Developing African nations faced numerous problems. The challenges included deadly civil wars, rapid population growth, epidemics, and damage to the environment and wildlife.

Drought Brings Starvation From time to time, droughts struck parts of Africa, killing livestock and crops. The Sahel, a semi-desert region just south of the Sahara, was especially hard hit in the late 1960s. The drought, which lasted for decades, led to famine. Overgrazing and farming in this fragile area removed topsoil and led to **desertification,** or a change of semi-dry land into desert. International relief efforts eased the famine, but wars that raged in several countries in the Sahel added to the suffering.

The AIDS Epidemic Since the 1980s, the deadly disease AIDS (Acquired Immune Deficiency Syndrome) has spread across Africa. AIDS is caused by HIV, a virus that damages the body's ability to fight infections. In South Africa and Botswana, up to one third of adults were infected with HIV. More than 11 million children in Africa have been orphaned by the AIDS epidemic.

The loss of so many skilled and productive workers hurt the economies of African countries. A global effort to combat AIDS led to the development of drugs to treat people infected with HIV. African nations set up treatment programs and worked hard to stop the spread of AIDS.

People Move to Cities African nations experienced rapid **urbanization,** or the movement of people from rural areas to cities. The newcomers hoped to find a better life. Instead, millions faced unemployment, terrible living conditions, and crime. However, in much of West Africa, the growth of cities has provided increased opportunities for women, who have historically dominated urban markets as traders.

Urbanization also brought people from different ethnic groups together and helped replace ethnic loyalties with a larger national identity. But modern urban lifestyles weakened traditional cultures and undermined ethnic and kinship ties. Despite rapid urbanization, most people in Africa still lived in villages.

Vocabulary Builder

subsidize—(SUB suh dyz) *v.* support with government spending

Displaced by Drought
A Sudanese mother and children escape famine caused by years of drought. *How can geography affect migration patterns?*

Differentiated
Instruction Solutions for All Learners

L1 Special Needs **L2 Less Proficient Readers**

Students may use the visuals in this section to learn about challenges in Africa. Have them read the headings under Facing Obstacles to Well-Being. Then ask **What obstacles does the photo on this page show?** *(drought, famine)* Then have students look at the Infographic on endangered species on the next page. Ask **What two threats to the environment are shown here?** *(poaching, urbanization)*

Use the following resources to help students acquire basic skills.

 Adapted Reading and Note Taking Study Guide

■ Adapted Reading Strategies, p. 216
■ Adapted Section Summary, p. 217

Teach

Making Economic Choices   **L3**

Instruct

■ **Introduce: Vocabulary Builder** Have students read the Vocabulary Builder term and definition. Have them explain why a government might have to **subsidize** food imports.

■ **Teach** Create a two-column chart on the board, labeling one column "Socialism" and the other "Capitalism." Have students fill in the chart with the pros and cons of each economic system. Then have students fill in pros and cons in another two-column chart, with columns labeled "Cash Crops" and "Food."

■ **Quick Activity** Display **Color Transparency 201: Major World Industrial Regions and Mineral Resources.** Have students identify major industrial regions and places that practice subsistence farming and commercial farming. Point out that commercial farming requires capital investments in equipment. Then discuss how this would pose a challenge in developing nations.

🖳 **Color Transparencies,** 201

Independent Practice

Divide the class into two groups. One group should briefly debate the issue of socialism versus capitalism in developing countries, and the other group should briefly debate the issue of cash crops versus food. Students from the group that is not debating should determine which side of the debate has the stronger argument.

Monitor Progress

As students fill in their concept webs, circulate to make sure they understand the obstacles that face developing nations in Africa. For a completed version of the concept web, see

🖳 **Note Taking Transparencies,** 202

Answers

✔ to increase national income and fund development

Caption People can be forced to migrate because of drought and other natural disasters.

Obstacles to Progress/
Tanzania: A Closer Look ⬤ L3

Instruct

■ **Introduce: Key Terms** Ask students to find the key term *desertification* (in blue) in the text and explain its meaning. Tell students that desertification is just one of several social and environmental challenges in Africa today. Invite them to predict others.

■ **Teach** Have students create a chart on the board listing the challenges Africans face and how each issue makes development difficult for African nations. Then discuss the challenges facing Tanzania and the decisions Tanzania has made regarding capitalism versus socialism and cash crops versus food.

■ **Quick Activity** Refer students to the Infographic on endangered species on this page. Have them discuss in groups the factors that contribute to species endangerment and why some African nations might have a hard time protecting endangered wildlife. Use the Numbered Heads strategy (TE, p. T23) to have each group summarize its findings for the class.

Independent Practice

Viewpoints To help students better understand different viewpoints, have them read the selection *Saving Africa's Environment?* and complete the worksheet.

All in One Teaching Resources, Unit 5, p. 68

Monitor Progress

Check Reading and Note Taking Study Guide entries for student understanding.

Answers

Thinking Critically

1. As their habitats have been disrupted and shrunk, many forest species have become endangered.
2. Sample: by making the wildlife a source of jobs, and therefore worth more to local people alive than dead

✔ Advantages: increased opportunities for women in urban markets, greater diversity, development of national identity; Disadvantages: weakening of traditional culture, environmental threats

● **INFOGRAPHIC**

ENDANGERED SPECIES

The threats to Africa's endangered species include a loss of habitats and poaching, or illegal hunting. The map below shows that most of Africa's forests have been disturbed or cut down. However, Africans have taken steps to save their rich wildlife. Earnings from tourism have given local people a stake in saving these animals' lives.

▶ Elephants have been killed for their valuable tusks.

▲ Foreign demand for leopard skins has encouraged illegal killing of leopards.

▲ Africa's wildlife draw foreign tourists, who provide a steady income to local guides and tour operators. This gives Africans a stake in preventing poaching.

◀ African nations have set aside preserves to protect endangered species such as these mountain gorillas in Rwanda.

Undisturbed forest
Disturbed forest
Formerly forested land

Miller Projection
0   1000 mi
0   1000 km

Thinking Critically
1. **Draw Conclusions** Based on the map at the right, how have changes in Africa's forest cover affected its forest species?
2. **Synthesize Information** How might wildlife tourism discourage poaching in Africa?

Development Hurts the Environment In Africa, as elsewhere, urbanization, population growth, farming, and logging led to the destruction of Africa's animal habitats. As habitats were destroyed, some animals became **endangered species,** or species threatened with extinction. Foreign demand for elephant tusks to make ivory, or for rare pelts or furs, has encouraged impoverished Africans to kill endangered animals, even when it is illegal.

In Kenya, **Wangari Maathai** (mah THY) an environmental activist, started the Green Belt Movement. She was inspired to plant trees with women to help them meet basic needs, such as energy, clean drinking water, and nutritious food. Maathai wanted to heal the land, empower women, and promote **sustainable development,** or development that meets the needs of the present without compromising the ability of future generations to meet their own needs.

✔ **Checkpoint** What are some advantages and disadvantages of urbanization in Africa?

Tanzania: A Closer Look

Tanganyika, a large country in East Africa, gained independence in the early 1960s and later merged with the island state of Zanzibar to form the republic of Tanzania. Julius Nyerere, the country's first president, wanted to raise the standard of living for Tanzania's impoverished, population.

African Socialism Tanzania had little capital or technology. Most people were farmers. The country's main exports were coffee, cotton, tea, and tobacco. To improve life for Tanzanians, Nyerere's government embraced what he called "African socialism." This was based on village traditions of cooperation and shared responsibility.

The government took over banks, businesses, and factories. In a program of rural development called *ujaama* (pulling together), farmers were encouraged to move to large villages and work on collective farms. The goal was to increase output and produce surplus crops for export.

Nyerere's experiment failed, partly because farmers did not want to leave their own land for collective farms. Agricultural output did not rise. However, Tanzania did make important advances in education and healthcare during this period.

Debt Leads to Reforms The experiment created a huge and inefficient government bureaucracy. The expense of this huge bureaucracy, along with high oil prices, plunged Tanzania into debt. In 1985, President Nyerere resigned. Tanzania's new leaders introduced economic reforms, cutting the size of government and promoting a market economy. By 2003, Tanzania's debt was being reduced through participation in an IMF/World Bank program.

Outlook Today, Tanzania still has an overwhelming agricultural economy. Although Tanzania remains poor, its economy received a boost in the early 2000s from the opening of a huge new gold mine. The government planned to use gold mine profits along with foreign aid to reduce poverty and improve basic services.

✔ **Checkpoint** What was the result of Tanzania's experiment with socialism?

Wangari Maathai

While working with a women's rights group, Kenyan activist Wangari Maathai (born in 1940) came up with the idea of getting ordinary women involved in tree-planting projects. In 1977, she launched the Green Belt Movement (GBM). This grassroots organization promotes reforestation and controlled wood cutting to ensure a sustainable supply of wood fuel. The group also sought jobs for women in Kenya, Tanzania, and other East African countries. In 2004, Maathai became the first African woman to be awarded the Nobel Peace Prize. Today, Maathai continues to work with the GBM. She is also a member of Kenya's government. **In what ways might planting trees help improve women's lives?**

Progress Monitoring *Online*
For: Self-quiz with vocabulary practice
Web Code: nba-3321

SECTION 2 Assessment

Terms, People, and Places
1. For each term or person listed at the beginning of the section, write a sentence explaining its significance.

Note Taking
2. **Reading Skill: Identify Main Ideas** Use your completed concept web to answer the Focus Question: What challenges have African nations faced in their effort to develop their economies?

Comprehension and Critical Thinking
3. **Summarize** What obstacles kept many African nations from developing strong economies?
4. **Synthesize Information** Why have African nations had trouble feeding their people?
5. **Draw Inferences** Urbanization is a problem for many developing nations. Why do you think this is?
6. **Summarize** Why did socialism in Tanzania fail?

● **Writing About History**
Quick Write: Gather Information Review the material in this section on social issues in Africa. For each problem, list the causes, the effects, and any actions that have been taken to solve that problem.

Section 2 Assessment

1. Sentences should reflect an understanding of each term, person, or place listed at the beginning of the section.
2. debt, lack of capital, civil war, disease, urbanization, population growth, and environmental problems
3. They needed capital to invest in development and had to borrow it from foreign investors.
4. overpopulation, drought, civil war, dependence on cash crops, and failed socialist economies
5. Urbanization puts pressure on public services. Poor countries lack money to extend these services to so many new people.
6. Farmers would not leave their land for collective farms, and farm output did not rise. In addition, the government became inefficient, and the cost of government contributed to Tanzania's increasing debt.

● **Writing About History**
Example: major cause of urban poverty is migration; effect is overcrowding, joblessness; possible action is developing higher-yielding crops so that people can make a living by farming.

For additional assessment, have students access **Progress Monitoring** *Online* at **Web Code nba-3321.**

Objectives

As you teach this section, keep students focused on the following objectives to help them answer the Section Focus Question and master core content.

- Analyze how China has reformed its economy but limited freedom.
- Describe the continuing challenges that China faces.
- Understand how India has faced poverty but built a stronger economy.
- Explain important Indian social reforms.

Prepare to Read

Build Background Knowledge L3

Point out that China and India are among the world's largest and most populous nations. Ask students to speculate on how this might make development more challenging.

Set a Purpose L3

- **WITNESS HISTORY** Read the selection aloud or play the audio.

  ◀))) AUDIO **Witness History Audio CD,** A Violent Crackdown

  Ask **What is the young man in front of the tanks trying to do?** *(stop the tanks)* **What does the military action in Tiananmen Square suggest about China's government?** *(It was unwilling to tolerate a range of political views.)*

- **Focus** Point out the Section Focus Question and write it on the board. Tell students to refer to this question as they read. *(Answer appears with Section 3 Assessment answers.)*

- **Preview** Have students preview the Section Objectives and the list of Terms, People, and Places.

- **Note Taking** Have students read this section using the Paragraph Shrinking strategy (TE, p. T20). As they read, have students fill in the table listing the main ideas about reform and change in China and India.

  ◢ **Reading and Note Taking Study Guide,** p. 218

A man tries to stop a line of tanks heading into the crowd of protesters in Tiananmen Square (top). Protesters erect a statue of the goddess of democracy in front of a poster of Mao (right).

WITNESS HISTORY ◀))) AUDIO

A Violent Crackdown

When students and other Chinese citizens protested to demand more political freedom in the 1980s, the government cracked down. Cheng Zhen, a student, describes what she saw in Beijing's Tiananmen (TYEN ahn mun) Square on the night of June 4, 1989.

❝ [A]t about 2 A.M. we . . . could see that the troops were already in the square, and we quickly ran to the other side. . . . While I was running, I noticed a young man ahead of me. He picked up a bottle on the ground, and was about to throw it at the troops, angry because they were holding up their guns and firing. Suddenly, he fell to the ground. . . . He was shot. . . . ❞
—BBC News Online, June 2, 2004

Focus Question What are the similarities and differences between the economies and governments of China and India?

China and India: Two Giants of Asia

Objectives
- Analyze how China has reformed its economy but limited freedom.
- Describe the continuing challenges that China faces.
- Understand how India has faced poverty but built a stronger economy.
- Explain important Indian social reforms.

Terms, People, and Places

Deng Xiaoping	Mumbai
Tiananmen Square	Mother Teresa
one-child policy	dalits
Kolkata	

Note Taking

Reading Skill: Identify Main Ideas As you read, make a table like this one to record the main ideas.

Reform and Change in China and India		
Type	**China**	**India**
Economic	• Free market •	
Political		

China and India dominate much of Asia. Together, they are home to about two-fifths of the world's population. China is a major industrial nation. Although India's economy is smaller, like China, it is a leading Asian and global power. Over the last 60 years, China and India have taken different paths toward development.

China Mixes Reform and Repression

Mao Zedong, China's communist revolutionary leader, died in 1976. After Mao's death, more moderate leaders took control of China. By 1981, **Deng Xiaoping** (dung show ping), had taken a new approach to China's economy. Deng was a practical reformer, more interested in improving economic output than in political purity. "I don't care if a cat is black or white," he declared, "as long as it catches mice."

Modernizing the Economy Deng's program, the Four Modernizations, emphasized agriculture, industry, science, and defense. The plan allowed some features of a free market, such as some private ownership of property. Communes, or collectively owned farms, were dismantled, and peasant families were allotted plots of farmland in what was called the "responsibility system." Farmers still did not own the land, and the government took a share of their

---

Vocabulary Builder

Use the information below and the following resources to teach the high-use word from this section.

All in One Teaching Resources, Unit 5, p. 66; **Teaching Resources, Skills Handbook,** p. 3

High-Use Word	Definition and Sample Sentence
disperse, p. 715	*v.* to break up and scatter The police ordered the crowd to **disperse** and leave the area.

crops. However, farmers could sell any surplus produce and keep their profits. Chinese entrepreneurs were allowed to set up businesses. Managers of state-run factories were given more freedom, but they had to make their plants more efficient. Deng also welcomed foreign capital and technology. Investors from Japan, Hong Kong, Taiwan, and Western nations invested heavily in Chinese firms.

Economic reforms brought a surge of growth. In coastal cities, foreign investment created an economic boom. Some Chinese enjoyed an improved standard of living. They bought refrigerators, televisions, and cars. On the other hand, crime and corruption increased and a growing economic and regional gap developed between poor rural farmers and wealthy city dwellers.

The Government Crushes Protests Economic reforms and increased contact with the West led some Chinese to demand greater political freedom. In the late 1980s, students, workers, and others created a democracy movement similar to those sweeping across Eastern Europe. However, Deng and other Chinese leaders refused to allow democratic reforms.

In 1989, thousands of protesters, many of them students, occupied Tiananmen (TYEN ahn mun) Square, a huge public plaza in Beijing. They raised banners calling for democracy. The government ordered the protesters to <u>disperse.</u> When they refused, the government sent in troops and tanks. Thousands of demonstrators were killed or wounded in the Tiananmen Square Massacre. Many others were imprisoned and tortured. The crackdown showed that the communist government was determined to keep control.

China Limits Population Growth China's population, at more than 1.3 billion, is the largest in the world. In the 1980s, the government imposed a **one-child policy,** which limited urban families to a single child, and rural families to two children. The goal was to keep population growth from hurting economic development. The government enforced the policy with fines and other penalties. Although the one-child policy was harshly condemned, it did slow population growth.

☑ **Checkpoint** How did economic reforms benefit China?

China Faces Ongoing Challenges

Economic reforms had more than quadrupled China's economic output by the early 2000s. China's industrial power made it a growing rival of the United States. China's achievements—symbolized by the newly built Beijing National Stadium—were displayed to the world when it hosted the 2008 summer Olympic games. But the country still faced serious internal challenges.

Growth Brings Problems Boom times led to rapid urbanization as millions of rural workers flooded into China's cities. Urban newcomers worked for low wages in manufacturing jobs. Although

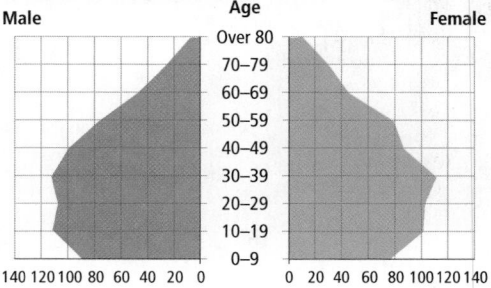

China, Estimated Population by Age and Gender, 2008

Male | Age | Female
Population (in millions)
140 120 100 80 60 40 20 0 | 0 20 40 60 80 100 120 140

Graph Skills China's population growth has slowed in recent years due to government efforts like the one-child policy, encouraged in the billboard below. *According to the graph, in what age groups is most of China's population concentrated? What might this mean for China's future?*

SOURCE: U.S. Census Bureau, International Data Base

一对夫妇只生一个孩子

China Faces Ongoing Challenges L3

Instruct

■ **Introduce** Ask students to define "human rights" in their own words. Then have volunteers come to the board and list an important human right. Point out that while China's economy has surged ahead, its record on human rights has remained poor.

■ **Teach** Ask **Why did China's government want to limit population growth?** *(They felt population growth could damage economic development.)* **What health problems has economic growth caused?** *(air and water pollution, the spread of AIDS and other diseases)* **How have human rights suffered?** *(Critics have been jailed, free speech has been curtailed, Tibetans have been repressed.)*

■ **Quick Activity** Have students study the graphs and photos on this page on the economic rise of China and India. Ask **What details in the photo of Shanghai suggest economic growth?** *(the construction, the woman's cell phone and shopping bag)* **How does the photo of the man voting suggest the difference in the political structure of the two countries?** *(India is a democracy, while China has a communist government.)* Discuss the questions posed in the introduction.

Independent Practice

Primary Source To help students better understand human rights issues in China, have them read the selection *The Outlook for China, Human Rights* by *Harry Wu* and complete the worksheet.

All in One Teaching Resources, Unit 5, p. 70

Monitor Progress

Read aloud the two red headings on China and the black headings that follow. Ask students to briefly summarize each subsection.

Answers

Caption China; it shifted to a free-market economy and welcomed foreign investment.

✔ Factories closed and unemployment rose. Workers returned to rural family homes. The government passed a stimulus package to improve productivity and retrain workers.

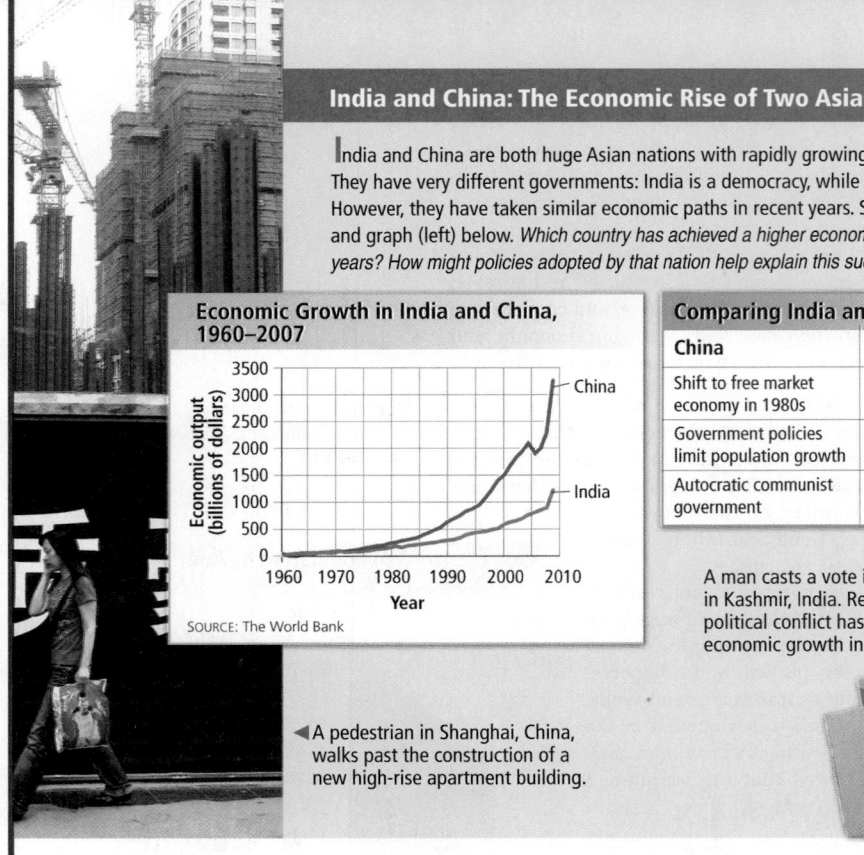

India and China: The Economic Rise of Two Asian Giants

India and China are both huge Asian nations with rapidly growing populations. They have very different governments: India is a democracy, while China is communist. However, they have taken similar economic paths in recent years. Study the chart (right) and graph (left) below. *Which country has achieved a higher economic output in recent years? How might policies adopted by that nation help explain this success?*

Economic Growth in India and China, 1960–2007

SOURCE: The World Bank

Comparing India and China

China	India
Shift to free market economy in 1980s	Shift to free market economy in 1980s
Government policies limit population growth	Population growth remains a serious issue
Autocratic communist government	Democratic government

A man casts a vote in an election in Kashmir, India. Religious and political conflict has limited economic growth in that region.

◀ A pedestrian in Shanghai, China, walks past the construction of a new high-rise apartment building.

these workers lived in poverty, their needs strained local resources. Rapid development brought other problems. Industrial production led to dangerously polluted air and water. In 2007, China's Ministry of Health said that pollution caused hundreds of thousands of premature deaths each year. Increased travel and trade helped spread AIDS and other diseases across China.

The global economic recession that began in 2008 took its toll. Chinese factories closed as overseas orders fell. As the economy slowed and unemployment rose, many workers returned to family homes in rural areas. Protests by unemployed urban workers increased. To prevent social unrest, the government announced an economic stimulus package to improve productivity and retrain workers

Human Rights Abuses Despite the global outcry after the Tiananmen Square massacre, China continued to jail critics and limit freedom. Human rights activists inside and outside China protested abuses such as the use of prison labor to produce cheap goods for export and the suppression of Tibetan culture and rights. China's trading partners called for an end to human rights abuses. Party leaders said that outsiders had no right to try to impose "Western-style" ideas of human rights on China. However, China's cabinet issued the country's first human rights action plan in 2009. It included the right to question government policies.

✔ **Checkpoint** How did the global economic recession affect China?

Link to Geography

Three Gorges Dam In the mid-1990s, China began construction on the world's largest dam. Located on the Chang (Yangtze) River, Three Gorges Dam is 607 feet high and 1.4 miles long and will hold a reservoir 370 miles long. The dam—expected to have cost as much as $75 billion to build—has sparked controversy. Officials say it will protect millions from floods, generate electric power for one of the country's most underdeveloped regions, and improve navigation along the river. Critics point out that the new lake is flooding 13 cities and 140 towns, forcing some 1.5 million people to relocate. They charge that the lake is destroying important archaeological sites and that the dam will lead to greater pollution as industrial areas are flooded.

India Builds a Modern Economy

Like China, India is a big country with a large, diverse population and widespread poverty. After gaining independence in 1947, India set up a democratic government and planned to develop a modern economy.

Agriculture and Industry Expand Like other developing nations, India was determined to use modern technology to expand agriculture and industry. The government followed a socialist model, using five-year plans to set economic goals and manage resources. Development, however, was uneven. India built some industries, but it lacked oil and natural gas, key resources for economic growth. Instead, it had to rely on costly imported oil.

India benefited from the Green Revolution. High-yield crops, chemical fertilizers, and better irrigation systems increased output. Still, most farmers used traditional methods and relied on seasonal rains for water. They produced enough to survive, but little surplus.

By the 1980s, an economic slowdown and outside pressure pushed India toward a market economy. Some industries were privatized and limits on foreign investment were eased. During the 1990s, Indian textiles, technology, and other industries saw rapid expansion. By 2000, India was a leader in information technology, providing computer software services to the world. Although India's booming economy slowed after 2008 as a result of the global recession, it stood ready to move ahead when economic conditions improved.

Population Growth and Poverty In India, as in China, rapid population growth hurt efforts to improve living conditions. As food output rose, so did demand. More than one-third of Indians lived in poverty, unable to meet basic needs for food, clothing, and shelter. The growing population put added pressure on India's healthcare system, which faced additional challenges after 1990 from the spread of AIDS.

The population boom and the labor-saving methods of the Green Revolution led millions of rural families to migrate to cities. But overcrowded cities like Kolkata (or Calcutta) and Mumbai (or Bombay) could not provide jobs

Bangalore: A Customer Support Center Workers in Bangalore, India, serve as customer service operators for American and European companies. To make callers feel more comfortable, the operators are trained in English and American slang. *How do you expect the customer service industry to change as more countries develop?*

India Builds a Modern Economy/Reforming Indian Society

Instruct

■ **Introduce** Have students read the first paragraph on this page. Ask them to consider reasons why India's efforts toward economic development and reform might be different from or similar to China's.

■ **Teach** Ask **How did India seek economic development?** *(First, it used command economy elements such as five-year plans and promotion of the Green Revolution. Later, it shifted to a free-market system.)* **How successful were these policies?** *(The first two policies did not work very well, the first due to lack of resources and the second due to the large number of rural farmers without the means to use technology. Under the free-market system, some industries developed rapidly.)* **How did economic development lead to social change?** *(It led to increased education and mobility, which in turn affected traditional ways of life.)*

■ **Quick Activity** Display **Color Transparency 202: World Per Capita GDP.** Have students review the map and identify India's GDP per capita. Use the lesson suggested in the transparency book to guide a discussion on developing economies.

🏛 **Color Transparencies,** 202

Independent Practice

Biography To help students better understand the terrible poverty in India's cities, have them read the biography *Mother Teresa* and complete the worksheet.

All in One **Teaching Resources, Unit 5,** p. 69

Monitor Progress

Check Reading and Note Taking Study Guide entries for student understanding.

Differentiated Instruction   Solutions for All Learners

L1 Special Needs   **L2 Less Proficient Readers**   **L2 English-Language Learners**

Have students look at the photographs on this page and the next. Then have them write a brief explanation of how either one or both of the pictures relate to each of the following topics:
- modernizing the economy
- growing urbanization
- changing women's roles
- democracy

Use the following resources to help students acquire basic skills.

 **Adapted Reading and Note Taking Study Guide**
■ Adapted Note Taking Study Guide, p. 218
■ Adapted Section Summary, p. 219

Answer

Caption Sample: Customer service operators may have to learn to deal with people from more than one country.

Assess Progress

■ Have students complete the Section Assessment.

■ Administer the Section Quiz.

All in One Teaching Resources, Unit 5, p. 64

■ To further assess student understanding, use

🏛 **Progress Monitoring Transparencies,** 142

Reteach

If students need more instruction, have them read the section summary.

 Reading and Note Taking Study Guide, p. 219

 Adapted Reading and Note Taking Study Guide, p. 219

 Spanish Reading and Note Taking Study Guide, p. 219

Extend

Ask students to suppose they are diplomats for either China or India. Have them write a speech introducing their nation's economic challenges and social reforms at a meeting of diplomats from the global South. They should define issues common to all developing nations and specific efforts in their nation.

Answers

✓ India's textile and technology industries grew rapidly, and by 2000, India was providing computer software services to the world.

✓ by setting aside jobs and university spots for dalits

Combating Poverty
Mother Teresa, shown with children in Calcutta, inspired others to help people living in poverty.

for everyone or even basic services, such as water or sewage systems. To help the urban poor, **Mother Teresa,** a Roman Catholic nun, founded the Missionaries of Charity in Calcutta. This group provided food and medical care to thousands. Still, millions more remained in desperate need.

The Indian government supported family planning but did not adopt the harsh policies that were used in China. Efforts to slow population growth had limited success. Poor families, especially in rural areas, saw children as an economic resource to work the land and care for parents in old age.

✓ **Checkpoint** How did market reforms affect India's economy during the 1990s?

Reforming Indian Society

In India, as elsewhere, urbanization, education, and the growth of a modern economy undermined traditional ways of life. These changes benefited India's lowest social castes and women. In the cities, many people adopted western-style clothing and bought modern consumer goods. Yet most Indians still lived in villages and followed traditional ways.

Caste Discrimination Persists India's constitution banned discrimination against **dalits,** or people of the lowest caste. To improve conditions, the government set aside jobs and places in universities for members of these groups. However, discrimination based on caste continued.

Women Make Progress India's constitution granted equal rights to women. In the cities, girls from well-to-do families were educated. Women entered many professions. Some, like Indira Gandhi, won political office. Girls from poor families, however, received little or no education. Although women in rural areas worked the land or contributed to household industries, few received wages. Across India, women organized self-help groups to start small businesses and improve their lives.

✓ **Checkpoint** How did the Indian government try to improve the status of dalits?

SECTION 3 **Assessment**

Terms, People, and Places

1. For each term, person, or place listed at the beginning of the section, write a sentence explaining its significance.

Note Taking

2. **Reading Skill: Identify Main Ideas** Use your completed table to answer the Focus Question: What are the similarities and differences between the economies and governments of China and India?

Comprehension and Critical Thinking

3. **Identify Central Issues** What obstacles to economic development does China still face?

4. **Draw Inferences** How did the Green Revolution contribute to urbanization in India?

5. **Summarize** What economic goals has the Indian government pursued and how has it met these goals?

6. **Predict Consequences** Do you think that China can continue to develop economically without making political reforms? Explain.

● Writing About History

Quick Write: Write a Conclusion Choose one subheading from this section—for example "Reforming Indian Society." After rereading the text under that subheading, write a conclusion that summarizes the information.

1. Sentences should reflect an understanding of each term, person, or place listed at the beginning of the section.
2. China has seen stronger economic growth than India, but its government has rejected democracy. India is a stable democracy that has seen modest economic growth.
3. economic inequality, poverty, rapid urbanization, and disease
4. It drove many small farmers, who could not afford the capital investment required, to flee their farms for the cities.
5. It has aimed to strengthen and expand its agriculture and industry. It has had some success by reforming agriculture, privatizing some industries, and easing restrictions on foreign investment.
6. Samples: No, a lack of democratic rights will lead to political unrest that will hurt economic development. Yes, as long as economic development continues, the government will be able to avoid political reforms.

● Writing About History
Conclusions should be at least a paragraph long and reflect the key ideas of the subheading.

For additional assessment, have students access **Progress Monitoring *Online*** at **Web Code nba-3331.**

Brotherhood by Octavio Paz

Mexican poet, essayist, and critic Octavio Paz (1914–1998) was one of Latin America's great modern writers. Besides enjoying enormous success as an author, he was also a diplomat. Paz held diplomatic positions in France and India, where he was exposed to different schools of literature. In France, he explored surrealism. This literary movement encouraged the expression of the irrational and freed Paz to write beyond the limits of literal meaning. In India, Paz studied Buddhism, which also influenced his work. However, even as he contributed to the global culture, Paz maintained his national identity. He thought and wrote much about Mexico, its past, and its place in the modern world. In 1990, Paz became the first Mexican writer to receive the Nobel Prize for Literature. The poem below is dedicated to the Greek scientist and geographer Ptolemy (TAHL uh mee), who wrote one of the most influential astronomy texts of the ancient world.

▲ Octavio Paz

Brotherhood	Hermandad
Homage to Claudius Ptolemy	*Homenaje a Claudio Ptolomeo*
I am a man: little do I last	Soy hombre: duro poco
and the night is enormous.	y es enorme la noche.
But I look up:	Pero miro hacia arriba:
the stars write.	las estrellas escriben.
Unknowing I understand:	Sin entender comprendo:
I too am written,	también soy escritura
and at this very moment	y en este mismo instante
someone spells me out.	alguien me deletrea.

Thinking Critically

1. **Analyze Literature** What do you think is the meaning of the lines "I am a man: little do I last / and the night is enormous"?
2. **Draw Conclusions** Why do you think Paz chose the title "Brotherhood" for this poem?

History Background

Ptolemy The astronomer and mathematician Ptolemy lived in Egypt in the second century A.D. In his most influential work, known as the *Almagest,* he recorded years of observations about stars and planets. It was on the basis of those observations that he developed his theory—based on carefully worked-out mathematics—that the sun, stars, and planets revolved around the earth. He was primarily responsible for the theory of an Earth-centered universe that prevailed in medieval Europe.

Octavio Paz: *Brotherhood*

Objectives

- Understand the importance of the Mexican writer Octavio Paz.
- Appreciate an example of Paz's poetry.

Build Background Knowledge ⓛ

Discuss how people everywhere want to maintain their individual and national identities even as they reach for greater global interaction. Point out that the poem *Brotherhood* reflects this desire. Then ask volunteers to read the poem aloud in English, as well as in the original Spanish if possible.

Instruct ⓛ

Discuss the ideas expressed in Paz's poem. Ask **Why do you think Paz dedicated a poem to Ptolemy?** *(He is interested in how ideas from the past can help him understand his own experience.)* **What do you think the last four lines of the poem mean?** *(Sample: Each person leaves a story for those who come after.)*

Monitor Progress

To confirm students' understanding, ask them to summarize the poem in a single sentence.

Thinking Critically

1. Human life is brief, but the stars and sky last forever.
2. He wanted to convey that he feels a sense of brotherhood with Claudius Ptolemy as well as with the rest of mankind.

Objectives

As you teach this section, keep students focused on the following objectives to help them answer the Section Focus Question and master core content.

■ Analyze how Latin America grappled with poverty.

■ Describe Latin America's difficult road to democracy.

■ Understand the struggle for democracy in Argentina.

Prepare to Read

Build Background Knowledge **L3**

Ask students to recall how economic growth has challenged rural people. Based on their previous reading, have students predict how this issue might affect Latin America.

Set a Purpose **L3**

■ **WITNESS HISTORY** Read the selection aloud or play the audio.

🔊 AUDIO **Witness History Audio CD,** A Daily Struggle

Ask **What does this selection suggest about life for the rural poor who move to cities?** (*It's hard to succeed financially.*)

■ **Focus** Point out the Section Focus Question and write it on the board. Tell students to refer to this question as they read. (*Answer appears with Section 4 Assessment answers.*)

■ **Preview** Have students preview the Section Objectives and the list of Terms, People, and Places.

■ **Note Taking** Have students read this section using the Guided Questioning strategy (TE, p. T20). As they read, have students fill in the graphic organizer outlining main ideas and supporting details about development in Latin America.

 Reading and Note Taking Study Guide, pp. 220–221

A woman at a municipal dump in Mexico collects garbage to sell.

WITNESS HISTORY 🔊 AUDIO

A Daily Struggle

Carolina Maria de Jesus (day zhay ZOOS) faced a life of hardship in the slums of São Paulo (sow POW loh), Brazil. Like millions of other poor, rural people, she came to the city hoping to improve her life. Instead, to buy food, she spent her days combing through garbage for paper, cans, and other scraps to sell. In her diary, de Jesus described her daily struggle against poverty:

66 July 16 . . . I went to Senhor Manuel, carrying some cans to sell. . . . He gave me 13 [coins]. I kept thinking that I had to buy bread, soap, and milk. . . . The 13 [coins] wouldn't make it. I returned . . . to my shack, nervous and exhausted. I thought of the worrisome life that I led. Carrying paper, washing clothes for children, staying in the street all day long.99
—Carolina Maria de Jesus, *Child of the Dark*

Focus Question What challenges have Latin American nations faced in recent decades in their struggle for democracy and prosperity?

Latin America Builds Democracy

Objectives
• Analyze how Latin America grappled with poverty.
• Describe Latin America's difficult road to democracy.
• Understand the struggle for democracy in Argentina.

Terms, People, and Places

import substitution	Sandinista
agribusiness	contra
liberation theology	indigenous
Organization of	Juan Perón
American States	Mothers of the
(OAS)	Plaza de Mayo

Note Taking

Reading Skill: Identify Main Ideas and Supporting Details As you read this section, make an outline like the one below.

> I. Economic and Social Forces
>   A. Society
>   1.
>   2.

Latin America comprises Mexico, Central America, the Caribbean, and South America. It includes 33 independent nations, ranging from small islands, such as Grenada, to giant Brazil.

For decades, Latin American nations have faced political, economic, and social challenges similar to those of other developing nations—rapid population growth, poverty, illiteracy, political instability, and authoritarian governments.

Latin America Grapples With Poverty

From the 1950s to the 1980s, economic development failed to change deep-rooted inequalities in many Latin American countries. Due to inequality and growing populations, most countries saw little improvement in living standards.

Promoting Industry and Agriculture In Latin America, as in other developing regions, nations often relied heavily on a single cash crop or commodity to earn money for needed imports. If harvests failed or if world demand fell, their economies were hard hit.

To reduce their dependence on imported goods, many Latin American governments adopted a policy of **import substitution,** or manufacturing goods locally to replace imports. This policy, pursued mainly in the 1950s and 1960s, was a mixed success. Many of the new industries needed government help or foreign capital to survive.

Vocabulary Builder

Use the information below and the following resources to teach the high-use word from this section.
All in One **Teaching Resources, Unit 5,** p. 66; **Teaching Resources, Skills Handbook,** p. 3

High-Use Word	Definition and Sample Sentence
allege, p. 725	*v.* to assert, charge, claim After the robbery, the police **alleged** that the neighbor had stolen the diamonds.

Latin America: Economic Activity

Geography *Interactive*
For: Interactive map
Web Code: nbp-3341

Map Skills Latin American nations have been diversifying their economies in recent decades.

1. **Locate** (a) Venezuela (b) Nicaragua (c) Brazil (d) Haiti

2. **Region** Which region is the least diversified? What factors might explain this?

3. **Synthesize Information** Locate the areas on the map with manufacturing and trade. Are those areas likely to be near cities or countryside? Explain.

▲ Mexican men harvest tangerines, carrying baskets weighing up to 200 pounds.

▲ A man works at an off-shore oil rig in Venezuela. Like many oil companies in Venezuela, the company he works for is foreign-owned.

Key
- Forestry
- Livestock raising
- Mainly commercial farming
- Mainly subsistence farming
- Manufacturing and trade
- Little or no activity
- Petroleum (oil)

Equal Area Projection
0   500   1000 mi
0   500   1000 km

UNITED STATES
Atlantic Ocean
Gulf of Mexico
MEXICO
BAHAMAS
CUBA
DOMINICAN REPUBLIC
HAITI
JAMAICA
U.S. Virgin Islands (U.S.)
British Virgin Islands (U.K.)
ST. KITTS AND NEVIS
ANTIGUA AND BARBUDA
Puerto Rico (U.S.)
Guadeloupe (Fr.)
Martinique (Fr.)
DOMINICA
BARBADOS
ST. LUCIA
ST. VINCENT & THE GRENADINES
GRENADA
TRINIDAD AND TOBAGO
BELIZE
GUATEMALA
HONDURAS
EL SALVADOR
NICARAGUA
Caribbean Sea
COSTA RICA
PANAMA
VENEZUELA
GUYANA
SURINAME
French Guiana (Fr.)
COLOMBIA
ECUADOR
Equator
PERU
BRAZIL
BOLIVIA
Pacific Ocean
PARAGUAY
CHILE
URUGUAY
ARGENTINA
Atlantic Ocean
Falkland Islands (U.K.)
Tropic of Cancer
Tropic of Capricorn
20° N
0°
20° S
40° S
120° W 100° W 80° W 60° W 40° W 20° W

Teach

Latin America Grapples With Poverty

Instruct

■ **Introduce: Key Terms** Draw students' attention to the key term *agribusinesses* (in blue) in the text. Point out that much of the best farmland in Latin America belongs to these giant commercial farms. Discuss how this might affect individual farmers.

■ **Teach** Using the Idea Wave strategy (TE, p. T22), have students list the challenges facing governments in Latin America. Ask **Why has the gap between rich and poor grown in Latin America?** *(Most benefits of economic growth went to the wealthy elite, who in turn discouraged reforms that might spread these benefits to all.)* **How did population growth reinforce poverty?** *(It gave farmers more mouths to feed, and cities more citizens to house and absorb.)* Discuss the ways religions have reached out to the poor.

Differentiated Instruction   Solutions for All Learners

L1 Special Needs   L2 English Language Learners

Have students study the map and the key. Then, for each type of activity in the key, have them list at least two countries that show that activity. Encourage them to find one country in South America and one country outside of South America if possible. Then ask students to use this information to write a one sentence summary of economic activity in Latin America.

Use the following resources to help students acquire basic skills.

Adapted Reading and Note Taking Study Guide

■ Adapted Note Taking Study Guide, pp. 220–221
■ Adapted Section Summary, p. 222

Answers

Map Skills
1. Review locations with students.
2. Central America and most of the West Indies show only subsistence and commercial farming. They tend to lack landscape suitable for much livestock raising, and they tend to lack the resources and capital for forestry and manufacturing.
3. Sample: near cities because of large labor pools and infrastructure

- **Analyzing the Visuals** Have students analyze the Infographic on Brazil's efforts to combat poverty. Discuss the causes of poverty in Brazil and ask volunteers to explain the efforts to combat it.

- **Quick Activity** Show students *Making a Living in Peru* from the **Witness History Discovery School**™ video program and discuss how some people in Peru have been able to combat poverty.

Independent Practice

Web Code nbp-3341 will take students to an interactive map. Have students complete the interactivity and then answer the questions in the text.

Monitor Progress

- As students fill in their outlines, circulate to make sure they understand the main challenges facing Latin American development. For a completed version of the outline, see

  📖 **Note Taking Transparencies,** 204

- Check answers to map skills questions.

WITNESS HISTORY VIDEO

Watch *Making a Living in Peru* on the **Witness History Discovery School**™ video program to learn how economic challenges affect ordinary Latin Americans.

DISCOVERY
SCHOOL

● INFOGRAPHIC
FIGHTING POVERTY IN BRAZIL

More than a quarter of Brazil's population lives on less than two dollars a day. A minority controls most of the country's wealth and income. In recent years, though, better jobs and education have provided more opportunities for many Brazilians. The country's steady economic growth, shown in the graph at right, has helped make these improvements possible.

◄ In Brazil's countryside, most land is owned by a wealthy few. In this photo, members of the Landless Peasants' Movement occupy a large privately owned ranch.

To escape rural poverty, many ▶ Brazilians seek better-paying urban employment, such as the factory job shown here.

In time, Latin American governments moved away from import substitution because of its high cost. Instead, they have tried to generate income by promoting exports. Specifically, they have focused on developing a variety of cash crops and encouraging industries that they hope will produce goods for export.

Governments also backed efforts to open more land to farming through irrigation and the clearing of forests. Much of the best farmland belongs to **agribusinesses,** or giant commercial farms owned by multinational corporations. In Central America and Brazil, developers continue to clear tropical rain forests for use as farmland. This practice has had environmental costs, as you will read in the next chapter.

A Growing Gap One major obstacle to progress in Latin America is the uneven distribution of wealth. In many countries, a tiny elite controls the land, businesses, and factories. These powerful groups oppose changes that might undermine their position. As a result, the gap between the rich and the poor has widened, fueling discontent.

Poverty Latin American nations, like the rest of the developing world, experienced a population explosion that contributed to poverty. Although population growth rates slowed somewhat in the 1990s, economies were hard-pressed to keep pace with growing populations. Overall, the population of Latin America was 570 million in 2008.

In rural areas, population pressures made life more difficult for peasant farmers. Even though a family might own a small plot to grow their own food, most farmers worked on the estates of large landowners for low wages. Their wages pay for needed essentials like clothing, tools, and the food they cannot grow themselves.

Harsh conditions and limited land drove millions of peasants to the cities. Today, more than half of all people in Latin America live in cities. Some newcomers found jobs in factories, offices, and stores. Many more, like Carolina de Jesus, survive by working odd jobs. They fill the shantytowns on the edges of Latin American cities such as Mexico City and São Paulo. The shantytowns in these cities are among the largest in the world.

The World Today

Section	Core Instruction **L3**	Differentiated Instruction **L1** **L2** **L4**	

Section 1
Industrialized Nations After the Cold War

 1 period, .5 block

OBJECTIVES
- Examine social, political, and economic trends in Europe after the Cold War.
- Analyze how the United States' and Russia's shifting roles have affected the balance of global power.
- Understand how important economic changes have affected Asia since the end of the Cold War.

Focus Question *How did the end of the Cold War affect industrialized nations and regions around the world?*

All in One Teaching Resources, Unit 5
Reading Strategy: Compare and Contrast, p. 88
Vocabulary Builder, p. 87
Outline Map: Europe Today, p. 94
Outline Map: The Pacific Rim, p. 95
Geography Quiz, p. 96
Section 1 Quiz, p. 82

Reading and Note Taking Study Guide
Note Taking Study Guide, p. 223
Section 1 Summary, p. 224

Note Taking Transparencies, 205

WITNESS HISTORY Audio CD
The Nations of Europe Unite

Progress Monitoring Transparencies, 144

Color Transparencies, 206

Teaching Resources, Skills Handbook
Prereading the Chapter, pp. 1–2
Word Knowledge Rating Form, p. 3
K-W-L Chart, p. 4

L1 Adapted Reading and Note Taking Study Guide
Note Taking Study Guide, p. 223 **SN**
Section 1 Summary, p. 224 **SN**

L2 Adapted Reading and Note Taking Study Guide
Note Taking Study Guide, p. 223 **LPR**
Section 1 Summary, p. 224 **LPR**

Spanish Reading and Note Taking Study Guide
Note Taking Study Guide, p. 223 **ELL**
Section 1 Summary, p. 224 **ELL**

L4 Extend Activity,
Teacher's Edition, p. 737 **AR, GT**

*Student Edition Audio **SN**

Differentiated Instruction Activity, Teacher's Edition, p. 735 **SN**

*Guided Reading Audio, Spanish **LPR, ELL**

*Student Edition Audio **LPR, ELL**

Differentiated Instruction Activity, Teacher's Edition, p. 735 **LPR, ELL**

Section 2
Globalization

 2 periods, 1 block

OBJECTIVES
- Describe the ways in which countries around the world are interdependent.
- Understand how international treaties and organizations make global trade possible.
- Analyze the costs and benefits of global trade.

Focus Question *How is globalization affecting economies and societies around the world?*

All in One Teaching Resources, Unit 5
Section 2 Quiz, p. 83

Reading and Note Taking Study Guide
Note Taking Study Guide, p. 225
Section 2 Summary, p. 226

Note Taking Transparencies, 206

WITNESS HISTORY Audio CD
A Connected World

Progress Monitoring Transparencies, 145

Color Transparencies, 207, 208

L1 Adapted Reading and Note Taking Study Guide
Note Taking Study Guide, p. 225 **SN**
Section 2 Summary, p. 226 **SN**

L2 Adapted Reading and Note Taking Study Guide
Note Taking Study Guide, p. 225 **LPR**
Section 2 Summary, p. 226 **LPR**

L4 Extend Activity,
Teacher's Edition, p. 742 **AR, GT**

Differentiated Instruction Activity, Teacher's Edition, p. 739 **SN**

Spanish Reading and Note Taking Study Guide
Note Taking Study Guide, p. 225 **ELL**
Section 2 Summary, p. 226 **ELL**

Differentiated Instruction Activity, Teacher's Edition, p. 739 **LPR, ELL**

*Audio support is available for all sections.

Assessment Resources
- **AYP Monitoring Assessments,** Benchmark Test 4, pp. 47–49; Final Outcome Test, pp. 50–52
- **Progress Monitoring Transparencies,** 144–148
- **Test Prep,** Unit Study Sheets, pp. 106–109; Unit Test, pp. 38–44; Second Semester Exam, pp. 57–68; Whole Course Exam, pp. 69–86
- **SuccessTracker™,** Chapter 22
- **Document-Based Assessment,** pp. 95–109
- **ExamView® Test Bank CD-ROM,** Chapter 22
- **All in One Teaching Resources, Unit 5,** Chapter Tests, pp. 97–102
- **Progress Monitoring Online Quizzes,** Chapter 22
- **Assessment Rubrics**

Differentiated Instruction Key
- **L1** Special Needs
- **L2** Basic to Average
- **L3** All Students
- **L4** Average to Advanced
- **LPR** Less Proficient Readers
- **AR** Advanced Readers
- **SN** Special Needs Students
- **GT** Gifted and Talented
- **ELL** English Language Learner

Brazilians have also escaped from poverty through education, such as this adult literacy class. ▼

Economic Growth in Brazil, 1970–2007

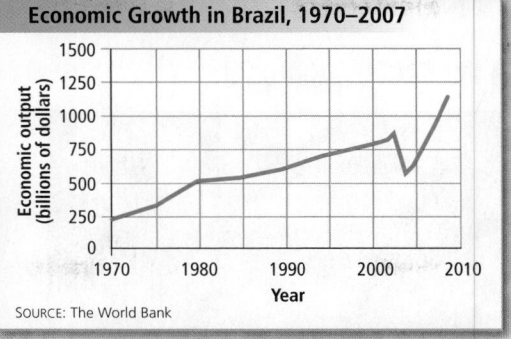

SOURCE: The World Bank

Thinking Critically
1. **Make Generalizations** How did Brazil's economic output change from 1970 to 2002?
2. **Synthesize Information** How did this change help Brazilians to move out of poverty?

Churches Help the Poor The Catholic Church remained a powerful force across Latin America. Although it was often tied to the ruling class, some church leaders spoke up for the poor. During the 1960s and 1970s, many priests, nuns, and church workers crusaded for social justice and an end to poverty. This movement, known as liberation theology, urged the church to become a force for reform. Meanwhile, evangelical Protestant groups won converts among the poor in many countries.

✔ **Checkpoint** How did the gulf between the rich and the poor cause problems in Latin America?

Dictatorships and Democracy

Democracy was difficult to achieve in Latin American nations plagued by poverty and inequality. From the 1950s on, many groups pressed for reforms. They included liberals, socialists, urban workers, peasants, and Catholic priests and nuns. Although they differed over how to achieve their goals, all wanted to improve conditions for the poor. Conservatives, however, resisted reforms. Conflict between conservatives and reformers contributed to political unrest in many nations.

Military Leaders Seize Power Between the 1950s and 1970s, as social unrest grew, military leaders in Argentina, Brazil, Chile, and other nations seized power. Claiming the need for order, they imposed harsh, autocratic regimes. These military rulers outlawed political parties, censored the press, and closed universities. They also imprisoned and executed thousands. "Death squads" linked to the government murdered many more. Latin American writers, such as Pablo Neruda of Chile and Gabriel García Márquez of Colombia, went into exile after speaking out against repressive governments or social inequality.

Threats of Revolution Beginning in the 1950s, leftist guerrillas battled repressive governments across much of Latin America. They believed that only socialism could end inequalities. Others were nationalists who opposed economic and cultural domination by the United States.

Dictatorships and Democracy

Instruct

■ **Introduce** Create a chart on the board that lists characteristics of military control and of democracy. Point out that in many Latin American nations, groups that advocate democracy have struggled against military control.

■ **Teach** Discuss the power struggle that has raged in much of Latin America. Have students identify the different participants and explain their views. Then ask **How did Latin America's political struggles evolve in the 1990s and early 2000s?** *(Several nations, such as El Salvador, have moved toward greater democracy.)* **Why does the U.S. have such strong views about events in Latin America?** *(These nations are just to the south of the United States, so events there can affect citizens here.)*

Answers

Thinking Critically
1. It steadily increased.
2. It created more jobs and educational opportunities.

✔ Political unrest grew as attempts at reform were defeated by the wealthy elite that controls the means of production.

Independent Practice

■ **Biography** To help students better understand the role writers played in Latin American politics, have them read the biography *Pablo Neruda* and complete the worksheet.

All in One Teaching Resources, Unit 5, p. 72

■ Have students fill in the Outline Map *Nations of Latin America* and highlight nations that might be of particular interest to the United States due to their geography.

All in One Teaching Resources, Unit 5, p. 74

Monitor Progress

Circulate to make sure students are filling in their Outline Maps accurately. Administer the Geography Quiz.

All in One Teaching Resources, Unit 5, p. 75

BIOGRAPHY

Lula da Silva

As a child, Luíz Inácio Lula da Silva sold peanuts and shined shoes on the streets of São Paulo, Brazil. The son of poor peasants with eight children, the boy did not learn to read and write until he was 10 years old. From this humble background, Lula, as he is called, rose to become president of Brazil. Lula left school at age 14 to become a metal worker in a factory. Ambitious and bright, he worked his way up and took courses to improve his skills. Lula also became active in workers rights issues. A fierce union leader, he helped start the Workers' Party, which became a major political force in Brazil. Even though he vigorously supported workers' rights, Lula gradually moved the party platform from revolutionary idealism to practical goals. Lula ran three times for president before finally winning the office in 2002 on his fourth try. As president, he expanded social programs and tried to narrow the huge gap between rich and poor in Brazil. When he won a second term in 2006, Lula declared, "The foundation is in place and now we have to get to work." **How does Lula's life illustrate both the problems and successes of development in Brazil?**

Cold War fears about the spread of Marxism complicated moderate reform efforts. Many Latin American conservatives saw any call for reform as a communist threat. These groups were often supported by the United States.

Civil Wars Shake Central America Several Central American nations were torn by civil wars as revolutionaries battled authoritarian governments. In 1954, the United States helped the Guatemalan military overthrow an elected, leftist government. Leftists and others fought the military regime, which responded savagely. The military targeted Guatemala's **indigenous,** or native people, slaughtering tens of thousands. The fighting ended in the 1990s, after the government finally held elections and signed a peace accord with leftist guerillas.

In the 1970s and 1980s, reformers and revolutionaries challenged El Salvador's landowning and military elite. One reformer, Archbishop Oscar Romero, preached liberation theology until he was assassinated while celebrating mass in 1980. A brutal civil war shook El Salvador until the rebels and the military agreed to a UN-backed peace plan in 1991.

In 1979, the **Sandinistas,** socialist rebels in Nicaragua, toppled the ruling Somoza family. The Sandinistas introduced land reform and tried to redistribute wealth to the country's poor. Claiming that Nicaragua could become "another Cuba," United States President Ronald Reagan financed the **contras,** guerrillas who fought the Sandinistas. Fighting raged until a 1990 compromise brought peace and multiparty elections.

Progress Toward Democracy By the 1990s, pressure from democracy activists and foreign lenders led military rulers to restore civilian rule. Argentina, Brazil, Chile, and other countries held elections. In some countries, such as Brazil, Venezuela, and Bolivia, leftist leaders won office. These new leaders challenged U.S. economic and political dominance over the region.

In Mexico, which had escaped military rule, demands for reform grew. There, a single party—the Institutional Revolutionary Party (PRI)—had controlled the government for 70 years. It claimed to represent all groups in Mexican society. But in reality, PRI bosses moved forcefully against any serious opposition.

Under pressure, the PRI made some reforms in the1990s. In 2000, Vicente Fox became the first candidate from an opposition party to be elected president. Fox and his successor, conservative Felipe Calderón, faced tough challenges, ranging from desperate rural poverty, to crime, corruption, and violent drug gangs.

 Checkpoint What conditions led to civil wars in many Latin American countries?

Latin America and the United States

Politically, a fact of life for Latin Americans has been the looming presence of the United States. An economic and military giant, the United

---

Careers

Interpreter and Translator Interpreters and translators help people who use different languages to communicate with one another. Interpreters take part in conversations, translating the words of one person into a language understood by the other. Translators work on pieces of writing, such as articles or books. Both kinds of workers must thoroughly understand each of the languages. They must be able to translate not just words, but also ideas and feelings.

Many interpreters and translators have college degrees and learn about the culture where the language is spoken. Others enroll in special language schools. Facility with languages, good interpersonal skills, and travel or study abroad are all helpful. As more people from Latin America settle in the United States, many institutions have a growing need for people who can interpret and translate between Spanish and English.

Answer

BIOGRAPHY Sample: As a child, Lula lived in poverty and had to quit school to help his family. However, as the economy developed, he was able to get an education, improve his life, and join and eventually lead the government.

States has dominated the **Organization of American States (OAS)**, a group formed in 1948 to promote democracy, economic cooperation, and peace in the Americas. Today, Latin America and the United States are still closely linked. The United States is the region's most important investor and trading partner.

Despite these links, the United States and Latin American nations view each other very differently. The United States sees itself as the defender of democracy and capitalism in the region. It also provides much-needed aid. While many Latin Americans admire the wealth of the United States, they resent what they see as its political, economic, and cultural domination. However, in 2000, when the United States honored its 1977 treaty and turned control of the Panama Canal over to Panama, many Latin American nations welcomed it as a sign of respect for Panama's independence.

The United States Intervenes During the Cold War, the United States backed anti-communist dictators in Latin America. On several occasions, it intervened militarily to stop the spread of communism. As you have read, in 1954, the United States helped overthrow Guatemala's leftist government. In 1961, President John F. Kennedy supported the Bay of Pigs invasion of Castro's Cuba. Since that failed invasion, the United States has imposed economic sanctions on Cuba. In 1973, the United States secretly backed the military coup that toppled Chile's democratically elected socialist president, Salvador Allende (ah YEN day), putting military dictator, Augusto Pinochet (pee noh SHAY), in power.

In 1994, a UN force led by the United States stepped into Haiti to restore its elected leader three years after a military coup. In 2004, the U.S. withdrew, leaving UN peacekeepers the job of restoring democracy to poverty-stricken, hurricane-ravaged Haiti.

The War on Drugs In the 1980s, illegal drug use grew in the United States, leading the U.S. government to declare a "war on drugs." The United States tried to stop illegal drugs from being smuggled into the country from Colombia, Peru, Bolivia, and elsewhere. It pressed Latin American governments to destroy drug crops and crush the drug cartels, or criminal gangs that ran the drug trade.

Governments cooperated, but critics in Latin America <u>alleged</u> that the main problem was growing demand for illegal drugs in the United States. Efforts to stop the drug trade led drug gangs to bribe government officials and hire assassins to kill judges, journalists, and others who worked against them. In 1989, U.S. forces invaded Panama and arrested its president, Manuel Noriega (noh ree AY guh), for drug trafficking. He was later tried and convicted.

Migration Poverty and unrest led many people to flee their homes in Latin America for the United States. Many entered the country legally. A large number were illegal immigrants. Their remittances, or the earnings they sent home, helped raise the standard of living for their families in Latin America. As the economic slowdown worsened after 2008, many newcomers lost their jobs and returned to their homelands.

✓ **Checkpoint** Why do people in Latin America have mixed reactions to the United States?

Vocabulary Builder

allege—(uh LEJ) *v.* assert, charge, claim

Democracy in Mexico

Mexican president Felipe Calderón waves after being sworn in on December 1, 2006. Although his opponent claimed that he was elected unfairly, international observers and Mexico's courts rejected these claims. *What does the free election of two presidents in a row suggest about the stability of Mexico's democracy?*

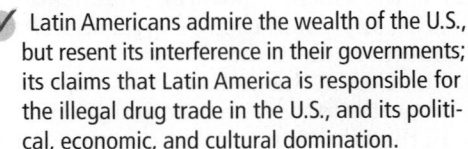

Instruct

- **Introduce** Write the words *military control* and *oppression* on the board. Ask **How are these issues connected?** *(Military control often includes oppression.)* **How might they have limited Argentina's economic development?** *(The violence and unrest that often accompany oppression make it hard to do business.)*

- **Teach** Help students create a timeline on the board to trace the path of economic development and political change in Argentina.

- **Analyzing the Visuals** Direct students' attention to the photos on the next page of the Mothers of the Disappeared. Discuss how the loss of many young people, as well as the rage and fear among families left behind, might fuel further instability.

Independent Practice

Display **Color Transparency 204: Chavez and Allende.** Have students work in groups to discuss the significance of the image, in which the president of Venezuela is holding a poster of assassinated Chilean president Allende.

 **Color Transparencies,** 204

Monitor Progress

Check Reading and Note Taking Study Guide entries to confirm that students have accurately identified main ideas about development and democracy in Latin America.

Answers

Caption It suggests that Mexico's democracy is becoming stronger and more stable.

✓ Latin Americans admire the wealth of the U.S., but resent its interference in their governments; its claims that Latin America is responsible for the illegal drug trade in the U.S., and its political, economic, and cultural domination.

Assess and Reteach

Assess Progress

- Have students complete the Section Assessment.
- Administer the Section Quiz.

All in One Teaching Resources, Unit 5, p. 65

- To further assess student understanding, use

 Progress Monitoring Transparencies, 143

Reteach

If students need more instruction, have them read the section summary.

 Reading and Note Taking Study Guide, p. 222

 Adapted Reading and Note Taking Study Guide, p. 222

 Spanish Reading and Note Taking Study Guide, p. 222

Extend

Viewpoints To help students better understand different viewpoints on democracy, have them read the selection *Democracy in Latin America* and complete the worksheet.

All in One Teaching Resources, Unit 5, p. 71

Answer

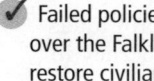 Failed policies and its loss to Britain in the war over the Falkland Islands forced the military to restore civilian rule.

Argentina Survives Upheavals

Once the most prosperous country in Latin America, Argentina enjoyed a robust economy based on exports of beef and grain. It attracted millions of immigrants. But since the Great Depression of the 1930s, Argentina has experienced more than 60 years of political and economic upheavals.

Military Rule From 1946 to 1955, nationalist president **Juan Perón** enjoyed great support from workers. He increased the government's economic role, boosted wages, and backed labor unions. He also suppressed opposition.

When Perón's policies led to an economic crisis, he was ousted in a 1955 military coup. Although Perón was reelected in 1973, the military was in and out of power for two decades. In 1976, as a wave of political unrest swept Argentina, the military again seized control. As the military battled leftist guerrillas, it waged a "dirty war" of torture and murder against its own citizens. As many as 20,000 people were kidnapped by the government and disappeared. Every week, women, known as the **Mothers of the Plaza de Mayo,** marched in Buenos Aires, the capital of Argentina. They demanded to know what had happened to their missing sons and daughters.

Remembering the Disappeared
The Mothers of the Plaza de Mayo demanded to know the fate of family members who had disappeared under military rule.

Democracy Is Restored By 1983, failed policies and a lost war with Britain over the Falkland Islands forced the military to restore civilian rule and allow elections. A financial crisis in 2001 devastated Argentina's economy and brought widespread poverty. Argentina's democracy survived the economic crisis and its economy recovered after 2003. However, like other Latin American nations, Argentina's economic progress was undermined by the 2008 global recession.

✔ **Checkpoint** Why did the military restore civilian rule in Argentina?

SECTION 4 Assessment

Progress Monitoring Online
For: Self-quiz with vocabulary practice
Web Code: nba-3341

Terms, People, and Places
1. For each term or person listed at the beginning of the section, write a sentence explaining its significance.

Note Taking
2. **Reading Skill: Identify Main Ideas and Supporting Details** Use your completed outline to answer the Focus Question: What challenges have Latin American nations faced in recent decades in their struggle for democracy and prosperity?

Comprehension and Critical Thinking
3. **Draw Conclusions** How has U.S. involvement in Latin America affected the region?
4. **Analyze Information** Explain the impact of social inequality on politics in Argentina.
5. **Make Inferences** What do you think was the appeal of liberation theology to people in Latin American nations?

● Writing About History
Quick Write: Develop a Working Thesis and Choose Supporting Information Reread the information in this section or review your outline. Then develop a thesis statement that expresses what you think is the main idea of this section. Locate details within the text that support your thesis statement. Evaluate your thesis to be sure that the details support it, and if not, revise it accordingly.

Section 4 Assessment

1. Sentences should reflect an understanding of each term, person, or place listed at the beginning of the section.
2. Answers include poverty, urbanization, debt, and population growth, as well as military rule and civil war.
3. The United States has given aid, been an important trade partner, and participated in the OAS. But to avert communist takeovers during the Cold War, the United States sometimes supported dictatorships.
4. Social inequality has often meant that wealthy elite groups retain control of political power in order to protect the status quo.
5. Sample: Liberation theology spoke to the poor and powerless and brought attention to their plight.

● Writing About History
Thesis statements should be no more than one to two sentences, and should clearly state a main idea. Students should list at least three details from the section that support this main idea.

For additional assessment, have students access **Progress Monitoring Online** at **Web Code nba-3341.**

Mario Vargas Llosa:
Latin America—The Democratic Option

In this speech delivered in 1987, Peruvian novelist, playwright, and journalist Mario Vargas Llosa (BAHR gahs YOH sah) (born 1936) discussed the state of democracy in Latin America. He also described the changes that he believed were needed to maintain and extend that democracy.

The democratization of Latin America, even though it has today an unprecedented[1] popular base, is very fragile. To maintain and extend this popular base, governments will have to prove to their citizens that democracy means not only the end of political brutality but progress—concrete benefits in areas such as labor, health, and education, where so much remains to be done. But, given Latin America's current economic crisis, when the prices of its exports are hitting record lows and the weight of its foreign debt is crushing, those governments have virtually no alternative but to demand that their citizens—especially the poor—make even greater sacrifices than they've already made. . . .

A realistic and ethically sound approach that our creditors could take would be to demand that each debtor nation pay what it can without placing its stability in jeopardy. . . .

If we want democracy to take hold in our countries, our most urgent task is to broaden it, give it substance and truth. Democracy is fragile in so many countries because it is superficial[2], a mere framework within which institutions and political parties go about their business in their traditionally arbitrary, bullying way. . . .

Perhaps the hardest struggle we Latin Americans will have will be against ourselves. Centuries of intolerance, of absolute truths, of despotic governments, weigh us down—and it won't be easy to shake that burden off. The tradition of absolute power that began with our pre-Columbian empires, and the tradition that might makes right that the Spanish and Portuguese explorers practiced, were perpetuated in the nineteenth century, after our independence, by our *caudillos*[3] and our oligarchies[4], often with the blessing or direct intervention of foreign powers.

▲ Mario Vargas Llosa in 1997

1. **unprecedented** (un PRES uh den tid) *adj.* new; never having happened before
2. **superficial** (soo pur FISH ul) *adj.* shallow; on the surface
3. **caudillos** (kow THEE yohs) *n. pl.* military dictators
4. **oligarchies** (AHL ih gahr keez) *n. pl.* governments run by a few powerful individuals or families

Thinking Critically
1. **Synthesize Information** According to Vargas Llosa, what currently threatens democracy in Latin America?
2. **Recognize Cause and Effect** How has Latin America's past led to the region's difficulty in maintaining democracy?

PRIMARY SOURCE

Mario Vargas Llosa:
Latin America—The Democratic Option

Objective
■ Understand the views of Mario Vargas Llosa on changes needed to support democracy in Latin America.

Build Background Knowledge ⓛ3
Based on their knowledge of other regions in the developing world, ask students to predict the challenges faced by Latin American nations as they sought economic development and political stability. *(Answers include extreme poverty and a history of totalitarian governments.)*

Instruct ⓛ3
■ Direct students' attention to the introduction at the top of the page and ask **Who is Mario Vargas Llosa, and what concerns does he discuss in this speech?** *(He is a Peruvian writer interested in understanding and supporting Latin American democracy.)*

■ Discuss the goals Vargas Llosa has for Latin America and the obstacles he sees to reaching those goals. Ask **How does Vargas Llosa view Latin American democracy?** *(He believes it is fragile, because people in the region do not have a long experience or history with it.)* **What must Latin Americans do to strengthen their democracies?** *(They must overcome historical forces, such as intolerance and the tradition of absolute power. They must make democracy more than just a superficial framework for undemocratic practices.)*

Monitor Progress
To confirm students' understanding, ask them to briefly summarize Vargas Llosa's views.

History Background

Vargas Llosa Explains His Interest in Politics
In 1990, Mario Vargas Llosa ran for president in Peru. Although he lost the election, he remained involved in Peruvian politics. Vargas Llosa explained his interest as a writer in politics in a speech he gave in 2000:

"In 1953 when I entered the University of San Marcos my country was a military dictatorship, as were many Latin American countries. . . . So it was very difficult if you were young and living in those circumstances not to become aware of the importance of politics in life. Even if you wanted to be a writer and only a writer, politics was there presenting you with all kinds of difficulties and obstacles. . . . So I was pushed to participate first of all in the political debate and then in political action."

Thinking Critically
1. a lack of economic progress
2. Sample: Latin America's long history of authoritarian rulers has left it with traditions that are at odds with democracy.

- Have students use the Quick Study Guide to prepare for this chapter's test. Students may wish to refer to the following pages as they review:

Key Problems Facing Developing Nations
Section 1, pp. 705–708; Section 2, pp. 711–712; Section 3, pp. 714–718; Section 4, pp. 720, 722–726

Economic Output for Selected Developing Nations
Section 1, pp. 704–706; Section 2, pp. 710, 713; Section 3, pp. 714–715, 717; Section 4, pp. 721–724

Global North and Global South
Section 1, pp. 704–705

Key Events in the Developing World
Section 1, p. 706; Section 2, p. 711; Section 3, pp. 714–715, 717; Section 4, pp. 720, 725–726

- For additional review, remind students to refer to the **L3**

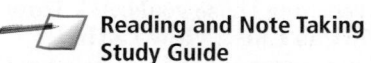
Reading and Note Taking Study Guide
Note Taking Study Guide, pp. 214, 216, 218, 220–221
Section Summaries, pp. 215, 217, 219, 222

- Have students access **Web Code nbp-3351** for this chapter's **History Interactive** timeline, which includes expanded entries and additional events.

- If students need more instruction on analyzing timelines, have them read the **Skills Handbook,** p. SH30.

For **Progress Monitoring Online,** refer students to the Self-test with vocabulary practice at **Web Code nba-3351.**

CHAPTER
21
Quick Study Guide

Progress Monitoring *Online*
For: Self-test with vocabulary practice
Web Code: nba-3351

■ Key Problems Facing Developing Nations

- rapid population growth
- urbanization
- widespread poverty
- food shortages
- economic dependence on foreign lenders and on exports
- repressive, authoritarian governments
- diseases
- environmental damage
- poor education

■ Economic Output for Selected Developing Nations

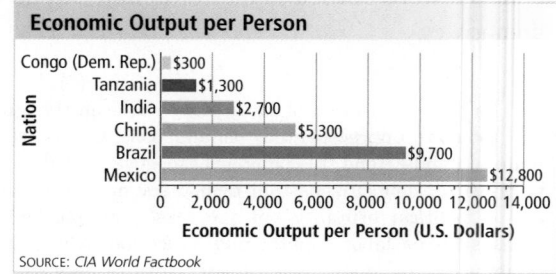

Economic Output per Person

Nation	Economic Output per Person (U.S. Dollars)
Congo (Dem. Rep.)	$300
Tanzania	$1,300
India	$2,700
China	$5,300
Brazil	$9,700
Mexico	$12,800

SOURCE: *CIA World Factbook*

■ Global North and Global South

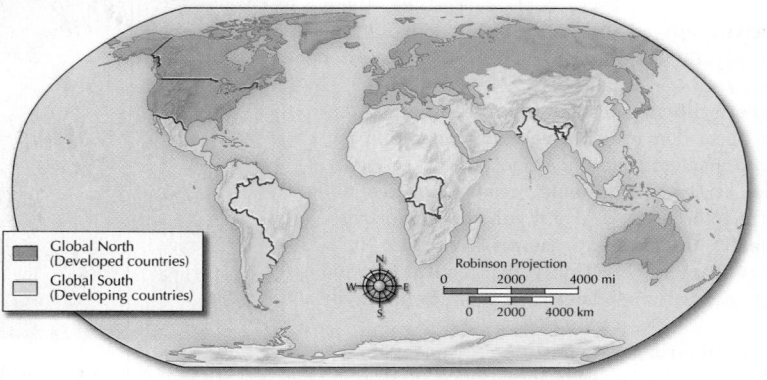

Global North (Developed countries)
Global South (Developing countries)

Robinson Projection
0   2000   4000 mi
0   2000   4000 km

■ Key Events in the Developing World

1950s–1960s
Green Revolution transforms agriculture.

Africa and Asia
Latin America

1940   1950   1960   1970

1946
Juan Perón is elected president of Argentina.

1950s–1960s
Latin American countries pursue policy of import substitution.

Differentiated
Instruction   Solutions for All Learners

L1 Special Needs   **L2 Less Proficient Readers**   **L2 English Language Learners**
For students acquiring basic skills:

Adapted Reading and Note Taking Study Guide
Adapted Note Taking, pp. 214, 216, 218, 220–221
Adapted Section Summaries, pp. 215, 217, 219, 222

For Spanish-speaking students:

Spanish Reading and Note Taking Study Guide
Spanish Note Taking, pp. 214, 216, 218, 220–221
Spanish Section Summaries, pp. 215, 217, 219, 222

Concept Connector

 Essential Question Review

To connect prior knowledge with what you have learned in this chapter, answer the questions below in your Concept Connector journal. Use the journal in the Reading and Note Taking Study Guide to record your answers (or go to www.phschool.com **Web Code:** nbd-3307).

1. **Economic Systems** Developing countries face economic challenges as they industrialize and urbanize. Choose one of the nations described in this chapter. Discuss how that nation's economic development created challenges for its people. Consider some of the following in your response:
   - poverty and the gap between the rich and poor
   - lack of resources for healthcare, education, and food
   - human rights

2. **Dictatorship** The United States sees itself as the defender of democracy and free markets in Latin America. However, from the 1950s to the 1980s, the United States helped overthrow democratically elected governments and install dictators in some Latin American countries. Provide a list of reasons that explain why the United States government would support dictators or repressive governments in Latin America. Think about the following:
   - Cold War
   - policy of containment
   - economy

3. **Revolution** During the French Revolution, the poor and the middle classes rebelled against privileged monarchs and aristocrats. During the Russian Revolution, the Communists mobilized working people to overthrow the privileged rulers of Russia. How do recent rebellions in Latin America, for example in Guatemala or Nicaragua, compare with earlier revolutions? Consider social and economic inequalities and ideologies or belief systems.

■ Connections to Today

1. **Cooperation** In this chapter, you read about cooperation between the United States and the nations of Latin America. In recent years, cooperation among Latin American nations and between the United States and Latin America has spread to include economic development. Mercosur is a trade alliance among South American nations. Meanwhile, the United States has proposed trade alliances with Chile and Central American nations. Refer to online news services or other sources to learn about Latin American trade alliances today. Investigate whether cooperation in the area of trade has spread in recent years within Latin America and between Latin America and the United States.

2. **Nationalism** In this chapter, you learned that during the 1950s and 1960s many developing nations tried to decrease their economic dependence on foreign investors by developing their own industries. Then, in the 1980s and 1990s, many of these nations put more emphasis on foreign trade and investment, often under pressure from foreign lenders. However, the pendulum has begun to swing back toward economic independence. After 2000, China, Argentina, and other nations put the economic concerns of their own people ahead of those of foreign investors. Why might a nation choose a course of economic independence? Consult news sources to find out how countries that resisted foreign economic pressure have fared in recent years.

Timeline:

1976	1981	1989	1994	2005
Military coup in Argentina	Deng Xiaoping reforms China's economy.	Tiananmen Square massacre	Open elections bring end of apartheid in South Africa.	China has one of the world's largest economies.

1980   1990   2000   2010

1980s Civil wars wrack Central American nations.

1990s Latin American nations move toward democracy.

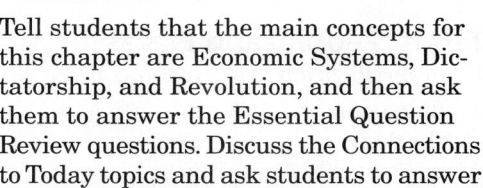

History *Interactive,*
For: Interactive timeline
Web Code: nbp-3351

Differentiated Instruction   Solutions for All Learners

L1 Special Needs L2 Less Proficient Readers

Use the following resources to help students acquiring basic skills:

✎ **Adapted Reading and Note Taking Study Guide**
Adapted Concept Connector, pp. 237, 262, 295, 300

L2 English Language Learners

Use the following resources to help Spanish-speaking students:

✎ **Spanish Reading and Note Taking Study Guide**
Spanish Concept Connector, pp. 237, 262, 295, 300

Concept Connector

Essential Question Review

1. Responses should note that free-market economies generally result in greater economic progress. As urban manufacturing centers grow, a wealth gap develops between the rich and the rural poor. Countries with rapidly growing populations have few resources for healthcare or education. Raising cash crops leaves less land to produce food. Repressive governments place economic development over the rights of citizens.

2. Responses should note that during the Cold War, the U.S. backed dictators to stop the spread of communism. Because even moderate reforms were seen as a threat to democracy and capitalism, the U.S. also prevented socialist governments from gaining power. Protecting its many business interests was a significant reason for U.S. support of Latin American dictators.

3. Responses should note that poverty, the uneven distribution of land and wealth, and repressive governments spurred Latin American revolutions. Many revolutionaries believed socialism could solve these inequalities. But unlike earlier revolutions, repressive Latin American governments had the military support of the United States.

Connections to Today

1. Answers should accurately refer to current information about trade relations within Latin America and between Latin America and the United States, for example, through discussion of NAFTA.

2. Responses should discuss countries such as Argentina or China that pursued economic independence and assess their economic success.

L3

For additional review of this chapter's core concepts, remind students to refer to the

✎ **Reading and Note Taking Study Guide**
Concept Connector, pp. 237, 262, 295, 300

Chapter Assessment

Terms, People, and Places

1. desertification
2. liberation theology
3. developing world
4. urbanization
5. Tiananmen Square
6. Green Revolution

Main Ideas

7. Answers include overpopulation, urbanization, poverty, famine, low literacy, lack of industry, a weak economy, and civil unrest.

8. global North: wealthy industrialized nations; global South: poor, developing nations

9. Most were unable to meet the needs of citizens or to strengthen their economies.

10. She is an activist and Nobel-prize winner who started a tree-planting organization in East Africa called the Green Belt Movement.

11. They allowed private property, some features of free markets, and other economic reforms but would not extend political freedoms or democratic rights.

12. It faced poverty and a rising population, lacked oil and gas, and started with a socialist government that did not allow much foreign investment.

13. When there was political unrest or an economic crisis, the military often took over the government and established authoritarian rule.

14. Vicente Fox's election victory ended one-party rule.

Chapter Focus Question

15. Challenges: poverty, population growth, famine, disease, urbanization, crushing debt, lack of industry, weak economies, civil unrest, repression, and environmental damage; Steps to meet challenges: establishing free markets and inviting foreign investment; improving education and healthcare; using technology to improve farming; and democratic reforms

Critical Thinking

16. It has put pressure on local and national governments to try to provide public services and has led to poverty and high unemployment.

Chapter Assessment

Terms, People, and Places

Complete each sentence by choosing the correct answer from the list of terms below. You will not use all the terms.

desertification
developing world
Green Revolution
liberation theology
sustainable development
Tiananmen Square
urbanization
Mumbai

1. In parts of Africa, drought and over-farming have brought about the _____ of land that was previously farmable.
2. Many Catholic clergy were part of a movement known as _____ that called for social justice and an end to poverty.
3. New nations attempting to improve their economies and achieve higher living standards are known as the _____.
4. Many poorer nations have seen rapid _____, or the movement of rural people to the cities.
5. In 1989, troops had a deadly encounter with protesters in _____.
6. The use of new technologies in the mid-1900s for improving crop production was known as the _____.

Main Ideas

Section 1 (pp. 704–708)
7. Summarize the challenges faced by most developing nations.
8. Compare and contrast the global North with the global South.

Section 2 (pp. 710–713)
9. How successful were new African nations that tried to develop by creating command economies?
10. Who is Wangari Maathai and what was her role in sustainable development efforts in Africa?

Section 3 (pp. 714–718)
11. After Mao's death, what reforms did China's government make and what reforms did they block?
12. What were the main challenges to economic growth in India?

Section 4 (pp. 720–726)
13. What role did the military play in the governments of Latin America?
14. Describe the democratic progress that was made in Mexico in 2000.

Chapter Focus Question
15. What challenges have nations of the developing world faced and what steps have they taken to meet those challenges?

Critical Thinking

16. **Synthesize Information** How has rapid population growth affected developing nations?
17. **Draw Conclusions** Which problem facing developing nations do you think is the most important one to solve? Explain your answer.
18. **Analyze Images** How does the photo of Mumbai at the end of Section 1 reflect some of the challenges facing developing nations? Explain your answer.
19. **Make Inferences** Many developing nations are ruled by dictators or by one party, as in China. Does autocratic rule help or hurt economic progress? Explain.
20. **Cause and Effect** How did the Cold War affect the United States' relations with Latin American nations?

● Writing About History

In this chapter's four Section Assessments, you developed skills to write a research report.

Writing a Research Report As governments in the developing world struggle to grow their economies and improve the well being of their citizens, they may set policies that cause damage to the environment and threaten local plant and animal species. Write a research report in which you discuss how one developing nation you read about in this chapter is balancing economic development with environmental concerns. Consult page SH13 of the Writing Handbook for additional help.

Prewriting
• Do online or library research to read background materials about developing nations.

• Choose a developing nation and take notes on relevant details, events, and the people.
• Create a set of questions about your developing nation and gather additional resources.

Drafting
• Develop a thesis about this nation's economic status—for example, is it succeeding or failing?
• Make an outline to organize the report. Then choose information from your research that supports each part of your outline.
• Write an introduction explaining your thesis, a body, and a conclusion.

Revising
• Use the guidelines for revising your report on page SH15 of the Writing Handbook.

---

17. Responses may refer to any of the major problems discussed, such as poverty, population growth, debt, environmental damage, or repressive governments, and must be well-reasoned and supported with facts.

18. It shows poverty, overcrowding, and joblessness caused by migration from rural areas to cities.

19. Samples: Unresponsive governments can generate popular unrest and restrictions that may hurt economic growth. Autocratic governments can promote economic development by limiting population and implementing reforms.

20. In order to prevent the Soviet Union from gaining allies in Latin America, the United States intervened when it believed that revolutions might bring socialist governments into power or when it wanted to help topple socialist leaders.

Document-Based Assessment

China's Economy

China has one of the fastest-growing economies in the world. Many who once thought of China as backward now see the country as a lively economic giant. Though China's economic gains are impressive, China's critics see a dark underside, as Documents C and D illustrate.

Document A

"China's annual GDP [gross domestic product, or economic output] growth has averaged more than 8 percent in the past 25 years, and in 2003, its GDP grew by a record-breaking 9.1 percent. . . . Noting these economic achievements as well as the complete success of China's first manned space flight in 2003, Premier Wen Jiabao in his annual address to the NPC [National People's Congress] in March 2004 pointed to a national strength that has reached new heights. . . ."

—From **China Internet Information Center**, May 4, 2005

Document B

Chinese workers assemble electronic parts.

Document C

". . . China has not changed in non-economic matters . . . [T]he leadership remains deaf to democracy and human rights. Religion is on a tight leash. . . . Basic legal safeguards are non-existent in the judicial system, and prison conditions are harsh. Privacy rights are routinely violated, and the government maintains tight restrictions on freedom of speech and the press. Increased control and monitoring of the Internet has led to arrest of dissidents, and most "Netizens" practice self-censorship, or face the long arm of the law. Freedom of association and assembly are virtually non-existent. . . ."

—From **"Only China's Economy Has Changed"** in *Taipei Times*, April 29, 2005, by Robert Bedeski

Document D

"China's grim 19th century style mines—many of them little more than holes in the ground—claimed yet more lives this week. A gas explosion ripped through the Sunjiawan coal mine in the northeastern province of Liaoning on Monday, killing at least 210. . . . They were just the latest casualties in a familiar story of mining accidents, which routinely claim the lives of dozens of young miners every month. . . . Many of those who die belong to China's growing underclass. They are desperately impoverished boys and men from rural villages."

—From **The Wall Street Journal**, February 18, 2005, by Sara Davis and Mickey Spiegel

Analyzing Documents

Use your knowledge of China's economic reforms and Documents A, B, C, and D to answer questions 1–4.

1. The author of Document A is best described as a
   A harsh critic of China's economic inequality.
   B strong supporter of China's economic policies.
   C shrewd observer of China's social system.
   D half-hearted supporter of the socialist market economy.

2. What is the main point of Document C?
   A China's social progress is equal to the country's economic gains.
   B China's human rights record is poor, despite economic progress.
   C China's economic progress outweighs any human rights problems.
   D China's economic success has led a commitment to human rights.

3. Some critics of China say that China's new wealth has not been evenly shared. According to Document D, one of the groups that has been left out is
   A people from the large cities.
   B young people.
   C women.
   D males from rural villages.

4. Do the current leaders of China deserve praise or criticism? Give your opinions based on the documents on this page and information from the chapter.

● Writing About History

As students begin the assignment, refer them to p. SH13 of the **Writing Handbook** for help in writing a research paper. Remind them of the steps they should take to complete their assignment, including prewriting, drafting, and revising. For help in revising, remind them to use the guidelines on p. SH15 of the **Writing Handbook.**

Students' research papers should have a clear thesis with supporting details and contain an introduction, a body, and a conclusion. Their papers should show evidence of thoughtful and thorough research and use correct bibliographical form. Papers should focus on one nation from the chapter and provide information on its current state of economic development, its environmental challenges, and its environmental policies. For scoring rubrics for writing assignments, see **Assessment Rubrics,** p. 8.

Section	Core Instruction ㉹	Differentiated Instruction ㉵ ㉶ ㉷	

Section 3
Social and Environmental Challenges

🕐 **1 period, .5 block**

OBJECTIVES
- Explain the causes and effects of global poverty, disasters, and disease.
- Analyze whether the basic human rights of people around the world are being upheld.
- Discuss the environmental challenges that have resulted from industrial development.

Focus Question *How do poverty, disease, and environmental challenges affect people around the world today?*

All in One Teaching Resources, Unit 5
Section 3 Quiz, p. 84

Reading and Note Taking Study Guide
Note Taking Study Guide, p. 227
Section 3 Summary, p. 228

Note Taking Transparencies, 207

WITNESS HISTORY Audio CD
Giant Waves Arrive

Progress Monitoring Transparencies, 146

Color Transparencies, 210, 211

㉵ Adapted Reading and Note Taking Study Guide
Note Taking Study Guide, p. 227 SN
Section 3 Summary, p. 228 SN

㉶ Adapted Reading and Note Taking Study Guide
Note Taking Study Guide, p. 227 LPR
Section 3 Summary, p. 228 LPR

㉷ All in One Teaching Resources, Unit 5
Primary Source: "Put Your Love in Action" by Mother Teresa, p. 91 AR, GT
Viewpoints: Approaches to the Environment, p. 89 AR, GT
Link to Literature: From *A Song Flung Up to Heaven*, by Maya Angelou, p. 90 AR, GT

Differentiated Instruction Activity,
Teacher's Edition, p. 745 SN

Spanish Reading and Note Taking Study Guide
Note Taking Study Guide, p. 227 ELL
Section 3 Summary, p. 228 ELL

Differentiated Instruction Activity,
Teacher's Edition, pp. 745, 749 LPR, ELL

Differentiated Instruction Activity,
Teacher's Edition, p. 747 AR, GT

Extend Activity,
Teacher's Edition, pp. 732c, 751 AR, GT

Section 4
Security in a Dangerous World

🕐 **2 periods, 1 block**

OBJECTIVES
- Explain why nuclear, biological, and chemical weapons threaten global security.
- Analyze the various terrorist groups and why they are becoming more and more dangerous.
- Describe the various ways in which the United States and other nations have responded to terrorism.

Focus Question *What kinds of threats to national and global security do nations face today?*

All in One Teaching Resources, Unit 5
Section 4 Quiz, p. 85

Reading and Note Taking Study Guide
Note Taking Study Guide, p. 229
Section 4 Summary, p. 230

Note Taking Transparencies, 208

WITNESS HISTORY Audio CD
Taking a Stand

Progress Monitoring Transparencies, 147

Witness History Discovery School™
video program, *The Taliban in Afghanistan*

㉵ Adapted Reading and Note Taking Study Guide
Note Taking Study Guide, p. 229 SN
Section 4 Summary, p. 230 SN

㉶ Adapted Reading and Note Taking Study Guide
Note Taking Study Guide, p. 229 LPR
Section 4 Summary, p. 230 LPR

㉷ All in One Teaching Resources, Unit 5
Biography: Albert Einstein, p. 92 AR, GT

Differentiated Instruction Activity,
Teacher's Edition, p. 755 AR, GT

Differentiated Instruction Activity,
Teacher's Edition, p. 754 SN

Spanish Reading and Note Taking Study Guide
Note Taking Study Guide, p. 229 ELL
Section 4 Summary, p. 230 ELL

Differentiated Instruction Activity,
Teacher's Edition, p. 754 LPR

Extend Activity,
Teacher's Edition, p. 757 AR, GT

Section 5
Advances in Science and Technology

🕐 **1 period, .5 block**

OBJECTIVES
- Describe the exploration of space and the practical applications that resulted from it.
- Analyze the development and impact of the computer revolution.
- Explain how advances in medicine and biotechnology have shaped life today.

Focus Question *How have advances in science and technology shaped the modern world?*

All in One Teaching Resources, Unit 5
Section 5 Quiz, p. 86

Reading and Note Taking Study Guide
Note Taking Study Guide, p. 231
Section 5 Summary, p. 232
Concept Connector, pp. 242, 250, 259, 295, 300

Note Taking Transparencies, 209

WITNESS HISTORY Audio CD
A Giant Leap for Mankind; Twentieth Century Scientific Milestones

Progress Monitoring Transparencies, 148

Color Transparencies, 205, 209

Witness History Discovery School™
video program, *The Space Race*

㉵ Adapted Reading and Note Taking Study Guide
Note Taking Study Guide, p. 231 SN
Section 5 Summary, p. 232 SN
Concept Connector, pp. 242, 250, 259, 295, 300 SN

㉶ Adapted Reading and Note Taking Study Guide
Note Taking Study Guide, p. 231 LPR
Section 5 Summary, p. 232 LPR
Concept Connector, pp. 242, 250, 259, 295, 300 LPR

㉷ All in One Teaching Resources, Unit 5
Traveler's Tale: The First Earthrise, p. 93 AR, GT

Extend Activity,
Teacher's Edition, p. 763 AR, GT

Differentiated Instruction Activity,
Teacher's Edition, p. 759 SN

Spanish Reading and Note Taking Study Guide
Note Taking Study Guide, p. 231 ELL
Section 5 Summary, p. 232 ELL
Concept Connector, pp. 242, 250, 259, 295, 300 ELL

Differentiated Instruction Activity,
Teacher's Edition, p. 759 LPR, ELL

Author's Notes

The Ties That Globalize

A striking embodiment of the evolving international order around 2000 was a growing number of what we might call *global people,* true citizens of the world whose lives and labors were helping to weld the world's many communities into one. These new global citizens included business people, diplomats, military personnel, representatives of international agencies and charitable organizations, American Peace Corps volunteers, overseas Chinese merchants in Asia, and Indian computer experts who swarmed to California's Silicon Valley. Global people were immigrants and expatriates and compulsive travelers. . . .

A major globalizing structure was the web of *technological links* which brought the peoples of the planet closer together. In the nineteenth century, the age of steam and telegraphy had strapped the continents across with rail lines, bound one continent to another with shipping lanes, and provided instantaneous telegraphic communication around the world. In the twentieth century, the automobile and the airplane, the super-tanker and the high-speed train had further revolutionized transport, while the telephone, radio, television, computer, and world wide web had transformed communications. Never had the world's peoples been physically so close as they were as the millennium dawned.

Closely related to these technological links were the growing *economic ties* that bound the nations of the world more closely with every passing decade. When the European empires crumbled after World War II, the economic relationships between the western nations and their former colonies forged in earlier centuries survived. Raw materials and industrial products, investment capital and labor in search of employment flowed with increasing freedom around the globe. Critics stressed the exploitative dimension of these ties, dubbing them "economic imperialism." But the growing global economy bound both parties. A third-world country that negotiated a development loan incurred an immense debt which it would find desperately hard to repay. But default on a loan large enough to help a whole nation could put the biggest western bank in jeopardy.

—Anthony Esler, *The Human Venture: From Prehistory to the Present,* (Upper Saddle River, New Jersey: Pearson Education, 2004), pp. 770–771

Extend Online

Picturing the Environment

Have students review photographs that depict environmental issues. Use the steps below to help students complete the activity.

Prepare for the Activity Explain that photographs of the environment can offer insights that are difficult to convey in words. To help students learn as much as possible from the photographs in this activity, ask students to consider the following questions: What information does this photograph present? Why did the photographer choose the scene shown in this photograph? What conclusions can I draw from this photograph?

Conduct the Activity For help in starting the activity, send students to **Web Code nbe-3401,** where they can access environmental photographs. Have students view these photos and write a paragraph summarizing their observations.

Follow-Up Conduct a class discussion based on the following questions: How did these photographs expand your knowledge of environmental issues? What did you learn about the environment in other parts of the world? How are the environmental issues in other parts of the world similar to or different from environmental issues in your hometown?

Making Connections to Today ⓛ2

Students are more engaged when they understand why the information matters to them. To provide relevancy, ask students to find examples of this chapter's themes in newspapers or magazines. Ask students to bring in their examples and share their findings with the class. This activity will not only encourage students to read more outside of class, it will also reinforce why studying world history matters today. Some possible themes include the following:

- global disease
- global poverty
- global warming
- human rights
- natural disasters
- hunger and famine
- mass migration
- nuclear weapons
- pollution
- terrorism

Making Connections to Today ⓛ4

Strong readers have a keen interest in current world events that should be utilized. Have students look through newspapers and magazines for examples of the same themes listed in the left column. Then ask students to rewrite a section of text, adding in the additional examples. Follow the steps below:

1. Ask students to choose a section of text from this chapter. Be sure that this selection discusses a problem in the world today.

2. Ask students to research further examples of the problem and develop a thorough understanding of its effect on the global community.

3. Have students rewrite or revise the chosen selection of text to reflect the new information. Students should adjust the conclusions as needed.

Modeling Reading and Writing Skills

Revising Tell students that in this chapter they will be writing a persuasive essay. (See Writing About History, p. 767.) Point out that in a persuasive essay, students need to support their conclusions with valid logic. After writing the first draft, they should go back and revise their essay to eliminate faulty logic, such as circular reasoning and either/or statements. Explain that circular reasoning is when the author merely restates an idea, rather than defending or advancing the argument. Either/or statements ignore other possibilities.

To model this, begin by writing on the board the following statement: "Winter is the best season because there are so many things to do. Because summer, spring, and fall have few activities, winter is the best season." Tell students that this is an example of circular reasoning. Point out that the second sentence merely repeats the idea of the first sentence; it does not give proof that there are more winter activities, nor does it persuade the reader

that having a large number of activities makes one season better than another.

Identify Evidence Remind students that before they accept an author's conclusion, they should identify the author's evidence. Then they should evaluate that evidence to ensure that it supports the conclusion.

To model this skill, read aloud the text under the black heading Russia is Remade. Point out the conclusion: Russia struggled to change to a market economy. Next, identify the evidence: Yeltsin privatized businesses, unemployment and prices rose, criminals flourished, and gangs preyed on new businesses. Together, all those statements are credible evidence that supports the conclusion: Russia struggled with the change.

The World Today

Teach With Technology

PresentationEXPRESS™
Premium DVD

■ Teach this chapter's core content using **PresentationExpress™ Premium,** which includes dynamic lecture notes, interactive game shows, songs, videos, and the ***ExamView*** *QuickTake* assessment tool.

■ To introduce this chapter using **PresentationExpress™ Premium,** start by asking students **Which of the following statements do you most agree with? (A) The best way to deal with global challenges is for each nation to look out for itself. (B) Nations should cooperate only with other nations that share their points of view. (C) Cooperation among all nations is necessary to address global challenges. (D) National interests have lost importance in the face of global challenges, which should be addressed by international bodies such as the United Nations.** Take a class poll using the QuickTake feature and discuss their responses. Point out that in this chapter, they will read about issues that have shaped our world in recent years. Continue introducing the chapter using the chapter opener slide show and Witness History audio.

Technology Resources

■ Student**EXPRESS** CD-ROM, Chapter 22

■ Teacher**EXPRESS** CD-ROM, Chapter 22

■ Presentation**EXPRESS™ Premium DVD,** Chapter 22

■ **WITNESS HISTORY** Audio CD, Chapter 22

■ ***ExamView*** **Test Bank CD-ROM,** English and Spanish, Chapter 22

■ **Guided Reading,** Spanish, Chapter 22

■ **Student Edition Audio,** Chapter 22

■ **Witness History Discovery School™** video program, *The Taliban in Afghanistan* and *The Space Race*

■ **Experience It! Multimedia Pack**

Bibliography

For the Teacher

Ehrlich, Paul R. and Anne H. *One With Nineveh: Politics, Consumption, and the Human Future.* Washington: Island Press, 2004.

Farmer, Paul. *Infections and Inequalities: The Modern Plagues.* University of California Press, 2001.

Friedman, Thomas L. *The World Is Flat: A Brief History of the Twenty-first Century.* New York: Farrar, Straus & Giroux, 2005.

For the Student

L4 Egendorf, Laura, ed. *Terrorism.* San Diego: Greenhaven Press, 2004.

L3 Cuomo, Kerry Kennedy. *Speak Truth to Power: Human Rights Defenders Who Are Changing Our World.* New York: Crown, 2000.

L2 January, Brendan. *Globalize it!* Brookfield, Conn.: Twenty-First Century Books, 2003.

A Changing World

In 2001, Mongolia's prime minister declared that "in order to survive we have to stop being nomads." His words—and his plans to settle 90% of Mongolia's people in cities by the year 2030—came as a shock to a people who have been nomadic herders for centuries. At the same time, his idea seemed inevitable. Listen to the Witness History audio to hear more about how Mongolians are struggling to modernize without losing their traditions.

◀ A Mongolian nomadic family uses a satellite dish on their tent to feed their solar-powered television.

Chapter Preview

Chapter Focus Question What are the major issues facing the world today?

Section 1
Industrialized Nations After the Cold War

Section 2
Globalization

Section 3
Social and Environmental Challenges

Section 4
Security in a Dangerous World

Section 5
Advances in Science and Technology

Use the ☑ Quick Study Timeline at the end of this chapter to preview chapter events.

Logo for the international aid organization CARE

Euro coin

NASA seal

❓ Concept | Connector ONLINE

To explore Essential Questions related to this chapter, go to PHSchool.com
Web Code: nbd-3407

Chapter-Level Resources

All-in-One Vocabulary Builder; Reading Strategy; Enrichments; Outline Maps; Geography Quiz; Chapter Tests
- Document-Based Assessments
- AYP Monitoring Assessments
- *ExamView* Test Bank CD-ROM
- Guided Reading Audio CD (Spanish)
- Student Edition on Audio CD

Previewing the Chapter

- **WITNESS HISTORY** Have students locate Mongolia on a map and explain that traditionally Mongolians have been nomadic herders. Read the Witness History selection aloud or play the accompanying audio. Then ask students to name other cultures like those in Mongolia that are struggling to modernize. Tell them that they will read more about the challenges of modernization in the chapter ahead.

  ◀)) AUDIO **Witness History Audio CD,** A Changing World

- **Analyzing the Visuals** Ask students to study the photo of rural Mongolia. Point out that traditionally people there live in a round tent called a *yurt*, which can be packed up and moved as they travel with their herds. Ask **What evidence of modernization can be seen in the photo?** *(the satellite dish and the woman's clothing)* **How might this image be different if a photographer returns to this location in 20 years?** *(A permanent town may have been built or the people may have moved to cities.)* Ask students what will have been gained or lost by the changes they mention.

- **Focus** Write the Chapter Focus Question on the board. Tell students to keep this question in mind as they read the chapter. *(Answer appears with Chapter Assessment answers.)* Have students preview the section titles for this chapter.

Note Taking Study Guide With Concept Connector Journal
For online access: Web code: nad-3407
For print alternative: Reading and Note Taking Study Guide booklet

Objectives

As you teach this section, keep students focused on the following objectives to help them answer the Section Focus Question and master core content.

■ Examine social, political, and economic trends in Europe after the Cold War.

■ Analyze how the United States' and Russia's shifting roles have affected the balance of global power.

■ Understand how important economic changes have affected Asia since the end of the Cold War.

Build Background Knowledge L3

Based on their previous reading about the end of the Cold War, have students predict events in the Soviet Union and the West in subsequent years.

Set a Purpose L3

■ **WITNESS HISTORY** Read the selection aloud or play the audio.

🔊)) AUDIO **Witness History Audio CD,** The Nations of Europe Unite

Ask **How does the photo illustrate the main idea of the treaty excerpt?** (*It supports uniting all of Europe despite differences in culture.*)

■ **Focus** Point out the Section Focus Question and write it on the board. Tell students to refer to this question as they read. (*Answer appears with Section 1 Assessment answers.*)

■ **Preview** Have students preview the Section Objectives and the list of Terms, People, and Places.

■ **Reading Skill** Have students use the *Reading Strategy: Compare and Contrast* worksheet.

All in One Teaching Resources, Unit 5, p. 88

■ **Note Taking** Have students read this section using the Structured Read Aloud strategy (TE, p. T20). As they read, have students fill in the chart showing post–Cold War developments.

Reading and Note Taking Study Guide, p. 223

A euro coin

Turks celebrate their country's efforts to join the European Union (EU).

WITNESS HISTORY 🔊)) AUDIO

The Nations of Europe Unite

❝ Resolved to mark a new stage in the process of European integration . . . Recalling the historic importance of the ending of the division of the European continent and the need to create firm bases for the construction of the future Europe . . . Desiring to deepen the solidarity between their peoples while respecting their history, their culture, and their traditions . . . [We] have decided to establish a European Union . . . ❞
—The Maastricht Treaty on the European Union, 1992

Focus Question How did the end of the Cold War affect industrialized nations and regions around the world?

Industrialized Nations After the Cold War

Objectives
• Examine social, political, and economic trends in Europe after the Cold War.
• Analyze how the United States' and Russia's shifting roles have affected the balance of global power.
• Understand how important economic changes have affected Asia since the end of the Cold War.

Terms, People, and Places

European Union	Vladimir Putin
euro	surplus
default	deficit
Barack Obama	Pacific Rim

Note Taking

Reading Skill: Compare and Contrast Create a chart to compare and contrast developments in industrialized nations after the Cold War.

Europe	Russia/United States	Asia
• 1991 Germany reunified	•	•
•	•	•

The end of the Cold War created favorable conditions for the spread of democracy. It also marked the beginning of a new global economy. Growing economic ties and increased international trade would become a driving force shaping the world in the new millennium.

The New Face of Europe

The collapse of communism ended decades of division between communist Eastern Europe and democratic Western Europe. Trade, business, travel, and communications across the continent became easier. European nations faced common problems such as large-scale immigration from the developing world, growing discrimination against foreigners, and rising unemployment.

Germany Reunifies After more than 45 years of division, East and West Germany were reunited in 1990. Germans welcomed reunification, but they paid a high price. East Germany's economy and infrastructure were weak and had to be modernized. Unemployment rose in the former East Germany when inefficient communist-era factories were closed. West Germans paid higher taxes to finance the rebuilding of the eastern part of the country.

Reunification brought social problems. Racist groups, such as neo-Nazis, a hate group modeled on the Nazi party, blamed immigrants for the country's problems and viciously attacked foreign workers. The vast majority of Germans condemned such actions. Twenty years after reunification, Germany remained an economic giant and a strong European leader.

Vocabulary Builder

Use the information below and the following resources to teach the high-use word from this section.
All in One Teaching Resources, Unit 5, p. 87; **Teaching Resources, Skills Handbook**, p. 3

High-Use Word	Definition and Sample Sentence
inflation, p. 736	*n.* a rise in prices linked to an increase in the amount of money available. During the French Revolution, **inflation** forced peasants to pay extremely high prices for bread.

NATO Evolves The collapse of the Soviet Union ended the Warsaw Pact. Many of the nations of Eastern Europe wanted to join NATO. Poland, Hungary, and the Czech Republic joined in 1999, soon followed by other countries. Russia disliked NATO's eastward expansion, but agreed to a NATO-Russia Council to consult on issues of common interest.

Europe was changing and NATO had to reassess its purpose. Many NATO officials believed that NATO's primary goal should be that of peacekeeper and protector of human rights. Following terrorist attacks in the United States, Europe, and elsewhere, the fight against terrorism has become a priority for the alliance.

The European Union Expands Like NATO, the European Economic Community expanded over the years to add nations from Eastern Europe. In 1993, the European Economic Community became the **European Union (EU),** a group of European nations that work together to promote a freer flow of capital, labor, services, and goods. Members also cooperate on security matters.

In 2002, the **euro** became the common currency for most of Western Europe. By then, EU passports had replaced national passports. Today, the expanded EU has the world's largest economy and competes with economic superpowers like the United States and Japan.

Some European leaders supported even greater economic and political unity for the region. However, many ordinary citizens felt loyalty to their own nations, not to the EU. They opposed more change. Also, the economies of Eastern Europe were weaker than those in the West, causing worries about the EU's overall economic outlook.

Turkey, long a member of NATO, wants full membership in the EU. But Turkey's application faced opposition because of its poor record on human rights and other issues. Also, some Europeans are concerned about admitting countries with large Muslim populations into the EU. They worry that if the EU changes too quickly, it will be less stable.

✓ **Checkpoint** What challenges did Germany face after reunification?

The European Union

Geography *Interactive*
For: Audio guided tour
Web Code: nbp-3411

Map Skills By 2007, 27 countries had joined the EU.
1. **Locate** (a) The Netherlands (b) Turkey (c) Germany (d) Croatia
2. **Identify** Which nations are applicant nations?
3. **Draw Inferences** How does geography help explain why these nations applied for EU membership later than many other nations?

Member of EU
Applicant nation
Non-EU nations

Teach

The New Face of Europe

Instruct

■ **Introduce** Ask students to read the red heading: *The New Face of Europe.* What do they think this means? How might Europe have changed? Ask them to recall events in Europe during the Cold War. Then have them read to find out how these earlier events led to new changes in Europe in recent years.

■ **Teach** Have students list key events from the subsection on the board: Germany reunified; European Union established; NATO reassessed. Work with students to describe each event.

■ **Quick Activity** Display **Color Transparency 206: Taipei 101.** Discuss how the image encapsulates the sense of hope and the potential of technology of the post–Cold War era.
🏛 **Color Transparencies,** 206

Independent Practice

■ Have students fill in the Outline Map *Europe Today* and indicate whether each country is a member of the EU.
All in One **Teaching Resources, Unit 5,** p. 94

■ Have students access **Web Code nbp-3411** to take the **Geography Interactive Audio Guided Tour** and then answer the map skills questions in the text.

Monitor Progress

■ Circulate to make sure students are filling in their Outline Maps correctly. Administer the Geography Quiz.
All in One **Teaching Resources, Unit 5,** p. 96

■ Check answers to map skills questions.

■ As students fill in their charts, circulate to make sure they list post–Cold War developments in Europe. For a completed version of the chart, see
🏛 **Note Taking Transparencies,** 205

Answers

Map Skills
1. Review locations with students.
2. Croatia, Macedonia, and Turkey
3. They are far from the original EU nations of Western Europe.

Global Power Shifts/ Changes in Asia

Instruct

- **Introduce: Vocabulary Builder**
  Have students read the Vocabulary Builder term and definition. Ask students to predict why *inflation* would contribute to Russia's struggle to create a market economy. *(People could afford fewer products, leading to idle factories and unemployment.)*

- **Teach** Create two columns on the board, labeled *Then* and *Now*. Have students add information to describe the global power balance before and after the Soviet Union's collapse and the Asian economy before and after the 1990s. Discuss factors that influenced each change and invite students' ideas about the future of each nation discussed in the subsections.

- **Quick Activity** Have students work in groups to develop ideas for political cartoons on changes or issues in Russia, the United States, or countries in the Pacific Rim. If time allows, have them sketch their cartoons and share them with the class. Use the Numbered Heads strategy (TE, p. T23) and have groups share their work with the class.

Independent Practice

Have students fill in the Outline Map *The Pacific Rim.*

All in One **Teaching Resources, Unit 5,** p. 95

Monitor Progress

- Circulate to make sure that students are filling in their Outline Maps correctly with nations of the Pacific Rim.

- Check Reading and Note Taking Study Guide entries to confirm that students have accurately listed developments in Europe, Russia, the United States, and Asia.

Answers

✔ Germany has faced economic challenges such as integrating East Germany's weak economy and social challenges such as racist groups within the nation.

Caption When demand falls in one country, it creates an economic chain reaction, as suppliers in other counties cut back on production.

✔ Russia defaulted on its foreign debt. High inflation and the collapse of the ruble forced banks and businesses to close. Unemployment rose and corruption plagued the government.

Vocabulary Builder

inflation—(in FLAY shun) *n.* a rise in prices linked to an increase in the amount of money available

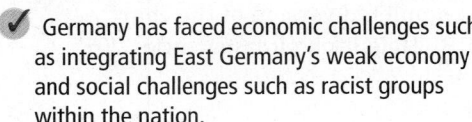
Meeting Economic Challenges
World leaders, including U.S. President Barack Obama, met at the G20 Summit in 2009 to discuss solutions to global economic problems. *Why might economic problems in one country affect the economy of other nations?*

Global Power Shifts

After the Soviet Union collapsed and the Cold War ended, the balance of global power shifted. The United States became the world's sole superpower. Recently, though, Russia has reemerged as a powerful force.

Russia Rebuilds Russia faced hard times after the breakup of the Soviet Union. In an effort to shift to a market economy, Russia's president, Boris Yeltsin, privatized many state-run industries and collective farms. This change brought great hardships to many Russians as unemployment and prices soared.

In 1998, Russia barely avoided financial collapse. It **defaulted,** or failed to make payments, on much of its foreign debt. High inflation and the collapse of the ruble, Russia's currency, forced many banks and businesses to close. People lost their savings and jobs, although some Russians did prosper in the new economy.

In 2000, **Vladimir Putin** was elected president in Russia's second free election. Putin, who served two terms, projected toughness and competence and helped rebuild Russia's economy. However, his government was plagued by corruption and Putin came under fire for increasing the power of the central government at the expense of peoples' civil liberties. Putin's handpicked successor, Dmitri Medvedev, was sworn in as president in May 2008. The next day, Putin was appointed prime minister by Russia's Parliament. While Russia benefited from rising prices for its oil and gas exports, the 2008 global economic slowdown posed challenges for Russia, as it did for other nations.

As Russia rebounded, it defended its interests, which sometimes caused tensions with the West. Despite UN sanctions against Iran, Russia assisted Iran with its nuclear energy program. In 2008, Russia sent troops into neighboring Georgia to help two breakaway regions gain independence.

The United States Faces New Challenges As the world's only superpower, the United States had a great deal of military and political influence. After the terrorist attacks on the United States in September 2001, President George W. Bush declared a "war on terror." In 2002, the United States sent forces to Afghanistan, where the terrorist plot had been hatched. The next year, U.S. forces invaded Iraq and toppled its dictator Saddam Hussein. When **Barack Obama,** the nation's first African American President, took office in January 2009, U.S. forces still occupied Afghanistan and Iraq. Obama had to decide the future course of U.S. policy toward both countries.

The United States weathered economic ups and downs. An economic boom in the 1990s produced a budget **surplus,** or money left over after expenditures. During George W. Bush's presidency, slower growth, massive military spending, and tax cuts for the wealthiest Americans led to a huge budget **deficit,** or gap between what the government spends and what it takes in through taxes and other measures.

In 2008, a financial crisis shook the American economy, sparking a global recession. Millions of Americans lost their jobs as businesses cut back or closed. President Obama responded with a multibillion dollar economic stimulus package that called for increased federal spending and tax cuts to revive the economy and create millions of new jobs.

✔ **Checkpoint** What troubles did Russia face after the collapse of the Soviet Union?

Changes in Asia

As the Cold War ended, Asia experienced the successes and downturns of being part of the global economy.

The Pacific Rim A major force in the global economy is the Pacific Rim, the many Asian nations that border the Pacific Ocean. The Pacific Ocean first became a highway for world trade in the 1500s. By the mid-1900s, links across the Pacific had grown dramatically. By the 1990s, the volume of trade across the Pacific was greater than that across the Atlantic. Some analysts predict that the 2000s will be the "Pacific century" because of this region's potential for further growth.

Japan and China For decades, Japan dominated the Asian Pacific Rim. But in the 1990s, as Japan suffered a long economic downturn, China's economy boomed. However, the global recession that began in 2008 hurt China's export-based economy.

The Asian Tigers Among the powerhouses of the Pacific Rim were Taiwan, Hong Kong, Singapore, and South Korea. Although they differed in important ways, all had quickly modernized and industrialized by the 1980s. All four were influenced to some degree by China, and Confucian traditions of loyalty, hard work, and consensus. Each stressed education as a way to increase worker productivity.

Because of their economic success, these countries were nicknamed the "Asian tigers" or "four tigers." The Asian tigers first focused on light industries, such as textiles. As their economies grew, they shifted to higher-priced exports, such as electronics. Their stunning growth was due in part to low wages, long hours, and other worker sacrifices. Like other export-driven economies, the Asian tigers were hurt by the 2008 global economic slowdown.

✓ **Checkpoint** Why did the Asian Tigers enjoy strong economic growth?

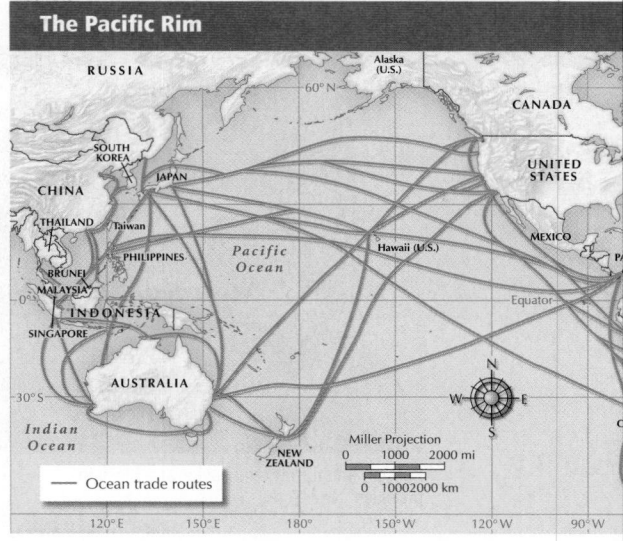

The Pacific Rim

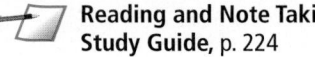

Pacific Powerhouse
The countries of the Pacific Rim have geographic, cultural, and economic ties. The region is a major center of ocean trade routes, shown on the map above.

SECTION 1 Assessment

Progress Monitoring Online
For: Self-quiz with vocabulary practice
Web Code: nba-3411

Terms, People, and Places
1. For each term, person, or place listed at the beginning of the section, write a sentence explaining its significance.

Note Taking
2. **Reading Skill: Compare and Contrast** Use your completed chart to answer the Focus Question: How did the end of the Cold War affect industrialized nations and regions around the world?

Comprehension and Critical Thinking
3. **Determine Relevance** How did the collapse of the Soviet Union affect organizations such as NATO and the EU?
4. **Draw Conclusions** Do you think an American investor would choose to invest large sums of money in Russia? Why or why not?
5. **Analyze Information** Why is the Pacific Rim seen as an important link in the global economy?

● **Writing About History**
Quick Write: Write a Thesis Statement To persuade someone in an essay, you must have a strong opinion on a subject and express it clearly in a thesis statement. Write a single sentence that expresses the main point you want to make about developments in the industrialized world after the Cold War.

Section 1 Assessment

1. Sentences should reflect an understanding of each term, person, or place listed at the beginning of the section.
2. Germany: faced challenges of reunification; Europe: faced challenges of regional unification; Russia: lost superpower status and struggled to establish market economy; U.S.: became only superpower; Asia: gained global economic importance.
3. The EU faced the challenge of absorbing Eastern European nations, whose economies are much weaker. NATO had to focus on a new mission.
4. Samples: Yes, because the economy is so huge and contains many potential customers; No, because the economy is unstable.
5. It has enormous potential for growth, traditions that stress productivity, and a location conducive to trade.

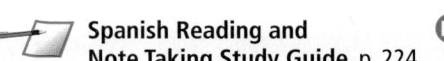
● **Writing About History**
Thesis statements should reflect knowledge of the chapter content, for example: The end of the Cold War created great challenges and great opportunities for industrialized nations.

For additional assessment, have students access **Progress Monitoring Online** at **Web Code nba-3411.**

Objectives

As you teach this section, keep students focused on the following objectives to help them answer the Section Focus Question and master core content.

■ Describe the ways in which countries around the world are interdependent.

■ Understand how international treaties and organizations make global trade possible.

■ Analyze the costs and benefits of global trade.

Prepare to Read

Build Background Knowledge ⓛ

Ask students to recall the goals of the European Union. Discuss the growth of the Asian Tigers and how this has affected the global economy. Then ask students to predict ways that nations of the world might draw closer together economically and politically.

Set a Purpose ⓛ

■ **WITNESS HISTORY** Read the selection aloud or play the audio.

🔊 AUDIO **Witness History Audio CD,** A Connected World

Ask **How does Mike Moore expect people to react to globalization? Why?** *(with varied emotions, because it is a complex and powerful issue that changes people's lives dramatically)*

■ **Focus** Point out the Section Focus Question and write it on the board. Tell students to refer to this question as they read. *(Answer appears with Section 2 Assessment answers.)*

■ **Preview** Have students preview the Section Objectives and the list of Terms, People, and Places.

■ **Note Taking** Have students read this section using the Paragraph Shrinking strategy (TE, p. T20). As they read, have students fill in the Venn Diagram listing how globalization has affected both developing and developed nations.

📏 **Reading and Note Taking Study Guide,** p. 225

WITNESS HISTORY 🔊 AUDIO

A Connected World

❝ Few topics are as controversial as globalization. That is hardly surprising. It is the defining feature of our time. Bringing distant markets and people across the world together is a huge change that affects everyone, whether they are peasants in India, students in London, or bankers in New York.❞

—Mike Moore, director-general of the WTO, 2000

Focus Question How is globalization affecting economies and societies around the world?

Russian immigrants sell caviar at a kiosk in Brooklyn, New York.

Globalization

Objectives

• Describe the ways in which countries around the world are interdependent.

• Understand how international treaties and organizations make global trade possible.

• Analyze the costs and benefits of global trade.

Terms, People, and Places

globalization	World Trade Organization
interdependence	(WTO)
outsourcing	protectionism
multinational	bloc
corporation	sustainability

Note Taking

Reading Skill: Compare and Contrast As you read, use the Venn diagram to track how globalization has affected developed and developing nations.

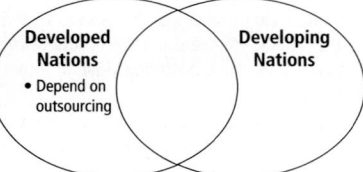

Globalization defines the world of the post-Cold War. **Globalization** refers to the process by which national economies, politics, cultures, and societies become integrated with those of other nations around the world. Globalization began on a small scale 500 years ago, with the European Age of Exploration. By the 2000s, globalization was occurring at a dramatic, unprecedented pace.

An Interdependent World

One major effect of globalization is economic interdependence. **Interdependence** is the dependence of countries on each other for goods, resources, knowledge, and labor from other parts of the world. Improvements in transportation and communication, the spread of democratic systems, and the rise of free trade—the buying and selling of goods by private individuals and corporations in a free market—have made the world increasingly interdependent. The spread of goods and ideas has even led to the development of a global culture. All of these links, from economic to cultural, have created both challenges and opportunities.

Doing the World's Work The world's rich and poor nations are linked. The nations of the developed world control much of the world's capital, trade, and technology. Yet they increasingly depend on largely low-paid workers in developing countries to produce manufactured goods cheaply. Companies in industrial nations also choose to outsource jobs. **Outsourcing** is the practice of sending work to the developing world in order to save money or increase efficiency. Many technological jobs have been outsourced to India, Russia, China, and the Philippines.

Vocabulary Builder

Use the information below and the following resources to teach the high-use word from this section.

🔲 **Teaching Resources, Unit 5,** p. 87; **Teaching Resources, Skills Handbook,** p. 3

High-Use Word	Definition and Sample Sentence
asset, p. 739	*n.* any property that has exchange value
	My aunt plans to buy a store, so she sold her house as an **asset** to pay for it.

Multinational Corporations Grow Globalization has led to the growth of huge, powerful, multinational corporations. **Multinational corporations** have <u>assets</u> in many countries and sell their goods and services worldwide. These corporations have invested heavily in the developing world. They brought new technology to industries, built factories, improved transportation networks and provided jobs. Critics, however, have blasted multinational corporations for taking large profits out of developing countries, causing environmental damage, and paying workers low wages.

Global Economic Crises Globalization led to financial interdependence in the world's markets. As a result, an economic crisis in one country or region can have a global impact. In 1997, a financial crisis struck Thailand and quickly spread across Asia. A 2008 banking crisis in the United States and Europe set off global shockwaves as world stock markets plunged. Wealthy nations shored up their economies with economic stimulus packages and costly bailout plans for banks and other troubled industries. Developing countries felt the impact as prices for their goods fell and international aid decreased.

Oil Prices Rise and Fall Energy resources play a huge role in the global economy. All nations, for example, need oil for transportation and to manufacture products ranging from plastics to fertilizers. Any change in the global oil supply can have a huge impact worldwide.

In 1973, OPEC limited oil exports and raised prices, creating shortages and hurting economies throughout the world. Since then, whenever oil prices have risen sharply, people have faced economic uncertainties. In 2008, oil prices shot up, partly because the growing economy in China, India, and elsewhere led to increased demand. When the global economic crisis slowed demand, prices fell. This sudden, rapid change in oil prices has led to renewed calls to develop alternative energy sources. Still, the world has remained largely dependent on oil.

Geography *Interactive*
For: Audio guided tour
Web Code: nbp-3421

Vocabulary Builder

<u>asset</u>—(AS et) *n.* any property that has exchange value

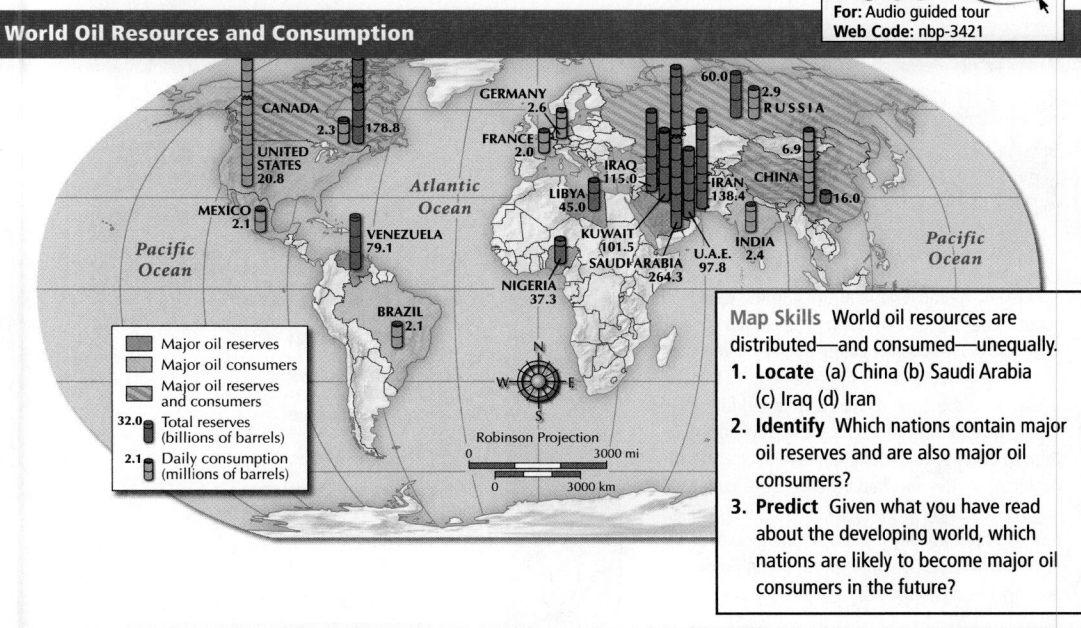

World Oil Resources and Consumption

CANADA 2.3 178.8
UNITED STATES 20.8
MEXICO 2.1
Atlantic Ocean
Pacific Ocean
VENEZUELA 79.1
BRAZIL 12.1
GERMANY 2.6
FRANCE 2.0
LIBYA 45.0
NIGERIA 37.3
IRAQ 115.0
KUWAIT 101.5
SAUDI ARABIA 264.3
U.A.E. 97.8
IRAN 138.4
60.0
2.9 RUSSIA
6.9
CHINA 16.0
INDIA 2.4
Pacific Ocean

Robinson Projection
0   3000 mi
0   3000 km

Major oil reserves
Major oil consumers
Major oil reserves and consumers
32.0 Total reserves (billions of barrels)
2.1 Daily consumption (millions of barrels)

Map Skills World oil resources are distributed—and consumed—unequally.
1. **Locate** (a) China (b) Saudi Arabia (c) Iraq (d) Iran
2. **Identify** Which nations contain major oil reserves and are also major oil consumers?
3. **Predict** Given what you have read about the developing world, which nations are likely to become major oil consumers in the future?

Differentiated
Instruction Solutions for All Learners

L1 Special Needs **L2 Less Proficient Readers**

Have students work in pairs to explain how *interdependence* (defined on the previous page) is illustrated by the map titled "World Oil Resources and Consumption." Ask them how nations that are oil consumers and nations with oil reserves are interdependent. Have them discuss the advantages and disadvantages of interdependence as it relates to oil.

L2 English Language Learners

Use the following resources to help students acquire basic skills.

 **Adapted Reading and Note Taking Study Guide**

■ Adapted Note Taking Study Guide, p. 225
■ Adapted Section Summary, p. 226

Teach

An Interdependent World **L3**

Instruct

- **Introduce: Key Term** Ask students to find the key term *interdependence* (in blue) in the text and explain its meaning. Use the Idea Wave strategy (TE, p. T22) and ask them to identify ways that nations can be interdependent. Write their answers on the board.

- **Teach** Link students' lists to the section content, focusing on economic links such as the use of low-cost labor to produce goods for wealthy nations; the global reach of multinational corporations; financial ties among nations; and the role of energy resources. For each category, have students suggest one way that global interdependence has been positive and one way it has been negative, either for developing or developed nations.

- **Quick Activity** Display **Color Transparency 207: Global Interdependence.** Have students use the information on the chart to explain ways the nations of the world are interdependent.
  Color Transparencies, 207

Independent Practice

Have students access **Web Code nbp-3421** to take the **Geography Interactive Audio Guided Tour** and then answer the map skills questions in the text.

Monitor Progress

- As students fill in their Venn Diagrams, circulate to make sure they list effects of globalization on developing and developed nations. For a completed version of the Venn Diagram, see
  Note Taking Transparencies, 206

- Check answers to Map Skills questions.

Answers

Map Skills
1. Review locations with students.
2. Russia and China
3. Answers may include any nations in Africa, South America, or Asia that are moving ahead in development.

Global Trade Organizations and Treaties ⑬

Instruct

- **Introduce** Ask students to recall how the EU strives to foster and build on interdependence among member nations. Have students predict ways that other regional and international organizations might respond to global interdependence. What goals might they have? What problems might they face?

- **Teach** Using the Numbered Heads strategy (TE, p. T23), have students list each global organization or treaty on the board. For each, have students describe the organization or treaty and explain its impact on globalization. Discuss the goals of each, as well as any problems that have resulted. Ask students how their reading confirmed or revised their predictions about goals and problems.

- **Quick Activity** Display **Color Transparency 208:** *Man/Life/Problem Solving,* **by Joel Nakamura.** Ask students what the painting's main idea is and how it relates to the controversial issue of globalization.

  🏛 **Color Transparencies,** 208

Independent Practice

Have students examine the Infographic *Coffee: From Shrub to Cup.* Ask them to create a simple flowchart showing how coffee is produced. For each step on the chart, have them fill in whether the step mainly affects the developing world or the developed world.

Monitor Progress

Circulate to confirm that students are creating accurate flowcharts. Then discuss how coffee production illustrates both the advantages and disadvantages of globalization. *(For example, consumers in the wealthy, developed world are able to enjoy coffee that is grown far away. However, farmers in the developing world receive a very small share of the price paid by the consumer.)*

Answer

✔ A reduction in oil production can lead to higher energy prices around the world, resulting in higher manufacturing and transportation costs worldwide.

Debt Hurts the Developing World Developing nations borrowed heavily in order to modernize. In the 1980s, bank interest rates rose as the world economy slowed. As demand for their goods fell, poor nations could not repay their debts or even interest on their loans. Their economies stalled as they spent much of their export incomes on payments to foreign creditors.

The debt crisis hurt rich nations, too. Banks were stuck with billions of dollars of bad debts. To ease the crisis, lenders made agreements with debtor nations to lower interest rates or allow more time to repay their loans. Some debts were canceled. In return, debtor nations had to accept market reforms to help improve their economies. Debt has remained a major issue throughout the developing world.

✔ **Checkpoint** How do changes in the supply of oil affect economies around the world?

Global Trade Organizations and Treaties

Many international organizations and treaties connect people and nations around the world. These organizations have various goals, such as supporting development, settling economic issues, and promoting free trade.

International Organizations Expand The United Nations is an international organization whose membership has grown from 50 nations in 1945 to 192 in 2009. As a result, its global role has expanded. The UN has sent peacekeepers to many trouble spots, including Cambodia, Congo, and the Balkans. In addition, the UN deals with economic and social development, human rights, humanitarian aid, and international law.

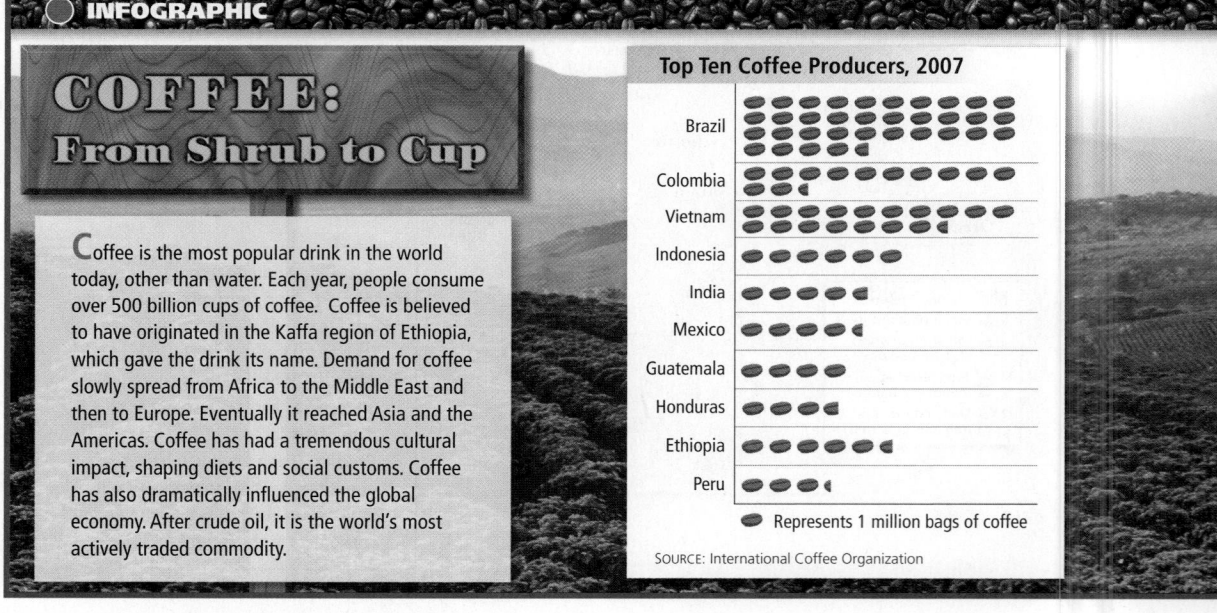

INFOGRAPHIC

COFFEE: From Shrub to Cup

Coffee is the most popular drink in the world today, other than water. Each year, people consume over 500 billion cups of coffee. Coffee is believed to have originated in the Kaffa region of Ethiopia, which gave the drink its name. Demand for coffee slowly spread from Africa to the Middle East and then to Europe. Eventually it reached Asia and the Americas. Coffee has had a tremendous cultural impact, shaping diets and social customs. Coffee has also dramatically influenced the global economy. After crude oil, it is the world's most actively traded commodity.

Top Ten Coffee Producers, 2007

Brazil
Colombia
Vietnam
Indonesia
India
Mexico
Guatemala
Honduras
Ethiopia
Peru

Represents 1 million bags of coffee

SOURCE: International Coffee Organization

Link to Economics

Outsourcing Improved communications technologies and the removal of barriers to trade have made it easier for companies in the developed world to move jobs to developing countries, where the pay is lower. This process, known as outsourcing or offshoring, allows companies to cut labor costs. During the 1980s and 1990s, outsourcing mainly affected manufacturing jobs, but, since 2000, more service jobs have moved to developing countries. Critics of outsourcing say that these moves threaten the strength of the United States economy, which depends on such jobs. Advocates respond that outsourcing helps the American economy, by allowing companies to sell products and services to consumers at lower prices and by improving companies' profits.

Other organizations deal with economic issues. The World Bank, for example, offers loans and technical advice to developing nations. The International Monetary Fund (IMF) encourages global economic growth, promotes international monetary cooperation, and helps developing nations solve economic problems. It also lends to countries in crisis.

Organizations not affiliated with governments also provide aid. These nongovernmental organizations (NGOs) perform a variety of functions, such as monitoring human rights, supplying disaster relief, and providing medical care. The International Red Cross is an example of an NGO.

Treaties Promote Global Trade A variety of international treaties help regulate world trade. The General Agreement on Tariffs and Trade (GATT) was signed in 1947 to expand world trade and reduce tariffs, or taxes on imported goods. In 1995, more than 100 nations joined to form the World Trade Organization (WTO) to strengthen GATT. Its goal was to set global rules to ensure that trade flows as smoothly and as freely as possible. The WTO opposes protectionism, or the use of tariffs and other restrictions that protect a country's home industries against international competition. The Group of Eight (G-8) is an organization of industrialized nations that meets annually to discuss a wide range of economic and other issues. The G-8 consists of Canada, France, Germany, Great Britain, Italy, Japan, Russia, and the United States.

Regional Trade Many nations have formed regional blocs, or groups, to boost trade and meet common needs. Among the largest is the EU (European Union.) In 1994, NAFTA (North American Free Trade Association) set out to ease restrictions and promote trade among the United States, Canada, and Mexico. APEC (Asia-Pacific Economic Cooperation) was formed to further trade among Pacific Rim nations. OPEC, representing oil-producing countries, regulates the production of oil to stabilize the market. Regional trade groups like these work to lower trade

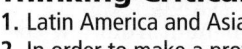

The Fair Trade Movement ▶
The fair trade movement seeks to ensure that coffee growers receive fair prices for their crops and have decent living and working conditions. Coffee that has met these conditions is stamped with the fair trade logo.

Growing Coffee
A worker in Thailand picks raw coffee beans from a shrub. Less than 10 percent of the money made from coffee actually goes to the grower.

Drinking Coffee
By the time coffee beans are turned into cups of coffee in the developed world, they have passed through the hands of many middlemen and have been re-sold a number of times. The coffee crop that a small farmer earned $8,000 for growing is worth nearly a million dollars to the people who sell it.

Thinking Critically
1. **Chart Skills** What regions are the top 5 coffee producers located in?
2. **Draw Inferences** Why does a crop of coffee become more expensive each time it is sold by middlemen?

Anti-Globalization in Action
In 1999, an anti-globalization demonstration led to rioting when thousands of protesters disrupted WTO meetings in Seattle, Washington.

barriers and encourage the free exchange of goods and services. Often, regional organizations like the African Union (AU), deal with both economic and political issues.

✓ **Checkpoint** How does the IMF help developing nations?

Costs and Benefits of Global Trade

With advanced communications and increased economic ties, globalization is expected to increase in the years ahead. Yet the debate about the impact of globalization on people and nations around the world continues.

Benefits Global trade provides consumers with a greater variety of goods and services. And because many people compete to provide these goods and services, prices are generally lower. People in the industrial world, especially, benefited from these changes.

Millions of people worldwide moved from rural areas to cities. There, they often had better access to education and health care. Globalization introduced people to new ideas, technologies, and communications. The money that developing nations earn from trade can be used to improve infrastructure, raise standards of living, and provide better services. Nations that practice free trade often become more democratic.

The Anti-Globalization Movement Critics point to the costs of free trade and globalization. Generally, anti-globalizers focus on poverty. They claim that rich nations exploit, or take advantage of, poor countries by raising their debt and lowering their standard of living. Some anti-globalizers target the World Bank and the IMF. Although these organizations provide aid to ease economic problems, they also require developing nations to make tough reforms and cut costly social programs. Anti-globalizers also oppose the United States, which is seen as the force behind policies they oppose.

Environmentalists claim that industries eager for profits encourage too-rapid development, endangering **sustainability,** or development that balances people's needs today while preserving the environment for future generations.

✓ **Checkpoint** How has globalization improved the lives of people around the world?

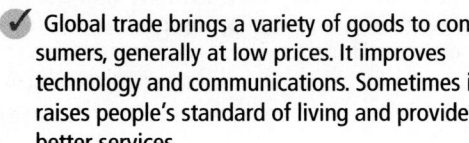 **Assessment**

Terms, People, and Places

1. What do each of the key terms listed at the beginning of the section have in common? Explain.

Note Taking

2. **Reading Skill: Compare and Contrast** Use your completed Venn diagram to answer the Focus Question: How is globalization affecting economies and societies around the world?

Comprehension and Critical Thinking

3. **Make Comparisons** Which countries benefit more from economic interdependence—developed or developing countries? Explain.

4. **Draw Inferences** Given what you have read in this section, do you think developing nations would support or oppose globalization?

5. **Demonstrate Reasoned Judgment** Do you think that increased globalization is inevitable? Explain.

● Writing About History

Quick Write: Generate Arguments One of the most effective ways to persuade is to address both sides of the topic you are covering. Create a chart to record facts about globalization. In one column, record the facts that support your position on globalization. In the second column, note arguments that could be used to attack your position.

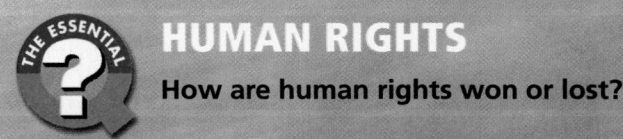

HUMAN RIGHTS

How are human rights won or lost?

Human Rights

Objectives
- Define human rights.
- Understand how basic rights have changed.
- Complete a web quest on human rights.

In This Chapter

What rights are basic to all human beings? The Declaration of Independence lists "life, liberty, and the pursuit of happiness." In 1948, the United Nations Declaration of Human Rights added more, including the rights to own property and to enjoy a basic standard of living. The Grameen Bank has granted loans to many poor women (right) to help them start businesses and provide for their families.

Throughout History

100s B.C. Romans enslave captives taken in war.

1100s A.D. Under King Henry II, England develops an early jury system.

1300s Smaller medieval African societies reach decisions by general agreement.

1800s Women actively seek social and political equality in Britain and the United States.

1980s Trade embargos are used to pressure South Africa to end apartheid.

Continuing Today

Limitation of human rights continues to be an issue in China. Members of the Chinese community in Australia protest severe abuses of freedom of belief and freedom of speech in their homeland.

21st Century Skills

TRANSFER Activities

1. Analyze Throughout history, how have people's rights been limited?

2. Evaluate What role does economic power play in gaining or maintaining human rights?

3. Transfer Complete a Web quest in which you act as a human rights "watch dog"; record your thoughts in the Concept Connector Journal; and learn to make a video. Web Code nbh-3408.

Build Background Knowledge

Have students brainstorm for a list of rights they believe everyone should have. Write these on the board. Then have students rank them in order of importance. Narrow the list to highlight the top ten rights according to your students.

Instruct

- Direct students' attention to the Essential Question: **How are human rights won or lost?** Have students read In This Chapter. Ask: **Which rights are in the Declaration of Independence? What other rights were considered basic by the United Nations in 1948?**

- Have students look at Continuing Today and the corresponding image. Ask: **What do the protestors want? Why do you think these rights have been limited?**

- Have students recall times in history when rights were restricted and discuss what caused the loss of rights.

- Assign the Web Quest on human rights.

Independent Practice

Concept Connector Have students fill in the Web Quest reflection question on human rights in their Concept Connector Journal.

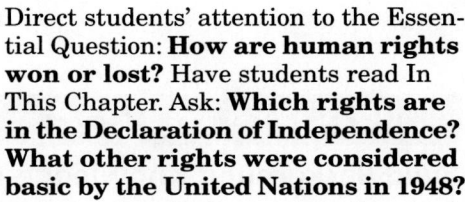

Reading and Note Taking Study Guide, p. 277

Monitor Progress

Circulate to make sure that students are filling in their Concept Connector Journal. Ensure they understand how human rights are won or lost.

Transfer Activities

1. People did not have guaranteed rights. For example, there was no protection for captives in war, people could not disagree with rulers, and there was no security for personal privacy or property.

2. Possible answer: Trade embargos and sanctions have been used to pressure nations to provide equitable rights to their citizens. People have boycotted or gone on strike to gain their rights.

3. Students' work should be evaluated against the rubric at Web Code nbh-3408.

Objectives

As you teach this section, keep students focused on the following objectives to help them answer the Section Focus Question and master core content.

■ Explain the causes and effects of global poverty, disasters, and disease.

■ Analyze whether the basic human rights of people around the world are being upheld.

■ Discuss the environmental challenges that have resulted from industrial development.

Prepare to Read

Build Background Knowledge L3

Ask students to recall their study of developing nations in the previous chapter. As a class, draw up a list of challenges that these nations might face today.

Set a Purpose L3

■ **WITNESS HISTORY** Read the selection aloud or play the audio.

🔊 AUDIO **Witness History Audio CD,** Giant Waves Arrive

Ask **How might a tidal wave, or tsunami, affect a region?** *(It could cause suffering, death, and destruction. Problems might include homelessness, lack of drinkable water, disease, and loss of crops, jobs, and businesses.)*

■ **Focus** Point out the Section Focus Question and write it on the board. Tell students to refer to this question as they read. *(Answer appears with Section 3 Assessment answers.)*

■ **Preview** Have students preview the Section Objectives and the list of Terms, People, and Places.

■ **Note Taking** Have students read this section using the Guided Questioning strategy (TE, p. T20). As they read, have students fill in the chart comparing aspects of globalization.

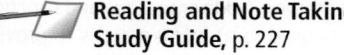 **Reading and Note Taking Study Guide,** p. 227

WITNESS HISTORY 🔊 AUDIO

Giant Waves Arrive

On December 26, 2004, an Indonesian man named Harmi went to the beach with hundreds of other people. An earthquake had hit his village, and people gathered to watch the sea recede from the beach.

❝ Suddenly . . . oh my God . . . there was a thundering sound from the sea. I saw the rolls of the waves ten meters (33 feet) high . . . the waves came three times. The worst was the second one, which swallowed thousands of houses in our village.❞

Harmi's village was completely destroyed.

Focus Question How do poverty, disease, and environmental challenges affect people around the world today?

A family in Indonesia tries to make their way to shelter after tsunamis destroyed their village in 2004. Aid organizations like CARE (logo above) worked to bring relief to the devastated region.

Social and Environmental Challenges

Objectives

• Explain the causes and effects of global poverty, disasters, and disease.

• Analyze whether the basic human rights of people around the world are being upheld.

• Discuss the environmental challenges that have resulted from industrial development.

Terms, People, and Places

tsunami	acid rain
epidemic	deforestation
famine	erosion
refugee	global warming

Note Taking

Reading Skill: Compare Use a chart like this one to compare aspects of globalization.

Apects of Globalization		
Poverty/Disease	**Human Rights**	**Environmental Issues**
• Natural disasters	•	•
	•	•

Globalization involves much more than economic links and the spread of technology. It has brought all kinds of social and environmental issues to the world's attention. Poverty, disease, environmental threats, and human rights may originate in countries or regions. But they have global dimensions that often require global solutions.

Global Poverty, Disasters, and Disease

Half of the world's population, or almost 3 billion people, live on less than $2 a day. Almost 1 billion people cannot read or write. About 790 million people in the developing world suffer from hunger—many from extreme hunger. Millions suffer from life-threatening diseases. Although these are problems mainly of the developing world, they affect the nations of the developed world as well.

Causes of Poverty Experts cannot agree on the exact number of people living in poverty worldwide, in part because there are many ways to measure poverty. Experts do agree about some trends, however. First, the gap between rich and poor nations is huge and growing. Second, some progress has been made toward reducing poverty, but it has been uneven. India and China, for example, have enjoyed economic growth, which has meant fewer people overall living in poverty there, but extreme poverty still persists.

Vocabulary Builder

Use the information below and the following resources to teach the high-use words from this section.

All in One Teaching Resources, Unit 5, p. 87; **Teaching Resources, Skills Handbook,** p. 3

High-Use Words	Definitions and Sample Sentences
inhibit, p. 745	*v.* to hold back or keep from some action Nick's severe stage fright often **inhibits** him from performing at all.
fluctuation, p. 751	*n.* swing; rising and falling of something The **fluctuations** of Uncle Steve's heart rate concerned his doctors.

Poverty is a complex issue with many causes. Many poor nations owe billions in debt and have no extra money to spend to improve living conditions. Political upheavals, civil war, corruption, and poor planning also inhibit efforts to reduce poverty worldwide. Rapid population growth—especially in India, China, and the nations of Africa and Latin America—has made it harder for countries to provide basic services.

Organizations like the World Bank believe that erasing poverty is essential to global security and peace. In this spirit, they call on poor nations to limit population growth. They also encourage rich nations to forgive the debt of poor nations, making more funds available for education, healthcare, and other services.

Natural Disasters Affect Millions In 2004, a huge underwater earthquake in the Indian Ocean triggered a massive tidal wave, or **tsunami** (tsoo NAH mee). It swept over islands and the coasts of 11 countries ringing the Indian Ocean. More than 160,000 people were killed, mainly in Indonesia, Thailand, Sri Lanka, and India. Millions were left homeless or lost their livelihood.

Natural disasters range from earthquakes, floods, and avalanches to droughts, fires, hurricanes, and volcanic eruptions. They strike all over the world all the time. They cause death, destruction, and unsanitary

Vocabulary Builder

inhibit—(in HIB it) v. to hold back or keep from some action

MALARIA: WHEN A MOSQUITO STRIKES

Malaria is a disease that kills more than a million people a year worldwide, mostly children. Malaria is a parasite that is usually found in unsanitary conditions, especially stagnant water, in warm climates. Mosquitoes who breed on water pick up the parasite and then pass it to humans when they bite them. Forty percent of the world's population is at risk for contracting malaria, especially in developing countries. *Why do you think malaria is a risk mainly in developing countries?*

Global Malaria Risk	
	Significant
	Low
	None

An African child receives a malaria vaccination.

Workers plan a new sewage project in Pakistan.

Teach

Global Poverty, Disasters, and Disease　**L3**

Instruct

■ **Introduce** Display **Color Transparency 211: Historical Map Set: World Population.** Review the population growth from 1600 to the present. Then display **Color Transparency 210: World Population Density.** Ask students to identify areas of greatest population density. Ask **Are the economies of these areas developing or developed?** Then ask students to speculate on the social and environmental problems densely populated areas might have. Have students list their ideas and read to confirm or revise them.
　　🏛 **Color Transparencies, 210, 211**

■ **Teach** Review causes of global poverty and disease, and discuss how regional conflicts and natural disasters can contribute to these problems. Use the Numbered Heads strategy (TE, p. T23) and ask **What are the main causes of famine?** *(drought and war)* **Why do refugees leave their homelands?** *(poverty, war, famine, natural disasters, persecution)* **How do the problems of disease and poverty in developing nations affect developed nations?** *(Developed nations receive large numbers of immigrants, many of them unskilled and poor; travelers carry diseases from developing nations to developed nations; developed nations must help with relief efforts against disease and poverty.)*

■ **Quick Activity** Direct students to the feature on malaria on this page and explain that malaria is one of the most common threats to health in the developing world. Ask **Why is malaria such a threat in these regions?** *(warm climates, poor sanitation due to poverty, lack of medical care)* **Why is it so hard to control?** *(Developing nations have little money to spend on even basic health needs and public welfare.)*

Answer

Caption Many developing countries have warm climates, and they lack the resources to correct unsanitary conditions.

Independent Practice

- Ask students to study the chart Top Five Destination Countries for International Migrants and answer the Chart Skills question.

- **Primary Source** To help illustrate a positive example and give a human voice to combating poverty, have students read the selection from Mother Teresa's *"Put Your Love in Action"* and complete the worksheet.

  All in One Teaching Resources, Unit 5, p. 91

Monitor Progress

- As students fill in their charts, circulate to make sure they correctly list the effects of social and environmental challenges on regions around the world. For a completed version of the chart, see

  📖 Note Taking Transparencies, 207

- Check students' responses to the Chart Skills question.

Answer

Chart Skills Sample: employment and educational opportunities; freedom from war and persecution

---

conditions that often lead to disease. Even a local disaster can disrupt the economy of an entire country and have a ripple effect on the global economy. For example, a recent typhoon destroyed Myanmar's rice-producing region, leading to the threat of famine in that country. One benefit of globalization is that news of natural disasters spreads instantly and triggers a quick aid response.

Global Diseases With millions of people on the move daily, diseases can spread rapidly. Still, health experts, working together, can often identify and limit outbreaks of many diseases. In the early 2000s, air travelers spread SARS (severe acute respiratory syndrome), a respiratory disease, from China to more than two dozen countries. Health officials took quick action to stop the SARS outbreak. Other diseases, including the avian flu (bird flu), mad cow disease, West Nile virus, swine flu (H1N1), and influenza have raised concerns about the global spread of disease. Diseases often spread before health officials know they exist. Globalization has meant that health experts around the world cooperate to quickly identify and contain outbreaks of disease.

Some diseases have proved hard to contain. When a disease spreads rapidly, it is called an **epidemic.** HIV/AIDS is an epidemic that began in the 1980s. HIV/AIDS has taken a staggering human and economic toll worldwide, especially in southern Africa and Southeast Asia. An estimated 25 million people have died from HIV/AIDS and as many as 40 million are infected with HIV. By 2010, the treatment and prevention of AIDS had been a global priority for a decade. In some nations, education about how to prevent the transmission of AIDS had lowered infection rates. Despite progress, HIV/AIDS continues to spread, especially in Asia and Eastern Europe.

Ending Hunger and Famine For tens of millions of people, hunger poses a daily threat. A major problem is that food does not get distributed to the people who need it most—especially in countries racked by poverty and civil strife. Hunger escalates into **famine** when large numbers of people in a region or country face death by starvation.

Natural disasters can cause famine. Human activity can also cause famine. War disrupts food distribution. During the 1970s and 1980s, civil wars raging in Ethiopia and Sudan intensified the effects of drought, leading to famine. Each side in the conflict tried to keep relief supplies from reaching the other. In many instances, only the efforts of international aid groups have saved millions of people from starvation.

Global Migration Globalization has led to a vast movement of people around the world. Although some people choose to migrate to find jobs or reunite with their families, millions more are **refugees,** people who are forced to move because of poverty, war, persecution, natural disasters, or other crises.

Many migrants find jobs and homes and create better lives in their new countries. But others face hostility and discrimination. Many people in developed countries resent immigrants, who they claim take away jobs and services from natural-born citizens. Millions of migrants, both legal and illegal, head to Europe, Asia, and North

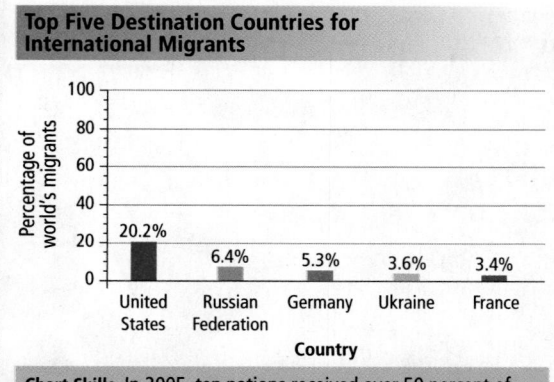

Top Five Destination Countries for International Migrants

United States 20.2%
Russian Federation 6.4%
Germany 5.3%
Ukraine 3.6%
France 3.4%

Chart Skills In 2005, ten nations received over 50 percent of the world's total migrants. *What characteristics of the top five destination nations might attract migrants?*

SOURCE: *United Nations, Trends in Total Migrant Stock, 2005*

History Background

Changing U.S. Immigration Policies Until the early 20th century, the United States placed few restrictions on immigration from Europe, though immigrants from Asia faced obstacles. Beginning in the 1920s, the United States sharply limited immigration. In the 1960s, the United States again opened the way for expanded immigration. However, regulations still limited the number of legal immigrants. To get around those limits, many immigrants crossed the border between Mexico and the United States illegally. Latin American immigrants became an important part of the work force in some states. When President Bush took office in 2001, he had hoped to make it easier for Latin Americans to work in the United States legally. However, terrorist attacks in 2001 created great concern about the safety of the U.S. borders. New security measures have made it more difficult to cross along the Mexican border.

America. Each year, the United States alone receives about one million legal immigrants and 300,000 or more illegal immigrants. Since World War II, Germany has welcomed large numbers of Turkish, Italian, and Russian immigrants to make up for the part of the labor force that was lost in two world wars.

As migration has grown, so has the smuggling of human beings across borders. Many illegal immigrants pay smugglers large sums to help them reach their destinations. In 2006, the United Nations estimated that human smuggling was a $10 billion-a-year global industry.

✔ **Checkpoint** What are some of the causes of famine and migration?

Human Rights

In 1948, UN members approved the Universal Declaration of Human Rights. It stated that all people are entitled to basic rights "... without distinction of any kind, such as race, colour, sex, language, religion, political or other opinion, national or social origin, property, birth or other status." In 1975, nations signing the Helsinki Accords guaranteed such basic rights as freedom of speech, religion, and the press as well as the rights to a fair trial, to earn a living, and to live in safety. Despite such agreements, human rights abuses—ranging from arbitrary arrest to torture and slavery—occur daily around the world.

The Role of the World Community Human rights abuses are not new, but globalization has brought them to the attention of the world in a new way. And the spread of democracy has forced people to question how human rights abuses can still happen in a modern world. In response, the world community has pressed countries to end abuses. In the 1980s, for example, economic pressure was used against South Africa to end apartheid, its system of legalized segregation.

Sometimes there is no stable government to pressure, or direct pressure does not work. Still, the UN, the United States, and human rights groups monitor and report on human rights violations, from Afghanistan, to Bosnia, to Congo. They even monitor human rights in nations that are part of the developed world, such as Russia.

Women Work for Rights For decades, a global women's movement has focused attention on the needs of women worldwide. The UN Charter supported "equal rights for men and women." By 1950, women had won the right to vote in most European nations, as well as in Japan, China, Brazil, and other countries. In most African nations, both women and men won the vote when their countries gained independence. Women have headed governments in Britain, Israel, India, Pakistan, the Philippines, and elsewhere.

Still, a report to the UN noted that while women represent half of the world's people, "they perform nearly two thirds of all working hours, receive only one tenth of the world's income, and own less than one percent of world property." The UN and other groups thus carefully monitor the human rights of women. They also condemn violence and discrimination against women. More than 165 countries have ratified a new women's human rights treaty.

An Illegal Crossing
Each year tens of thousands of illegal immigrants, like this family, risk their lives to cross the border between Mexico and the United States. *What factors lead people to risk their lives in illegal border crossings?*

Human Rights ⓛ₃

Instruct

- **Introduce** Ask students to define the term *human rights*. If necessary, explain its meaning. What human rights do students think should be protected around the world? Why might these human rights be especially fragile in developing nations?

- **Teach** Use the Idea Wave strategy (TE, p. T22) and ask students to list the human rights problems that affect women, children, and indigenous groups around the world. Ask students to summarize features of each group's problems, and then to find similarities. To help them draw conclusions, ask **How does lack of economic power make people vulnerable to human rights abuses?** *(Those without economic power, because of age or physical dependence, cannot escape abuse as easily as those with more options.)*

- **Analyzing the Visuals** Direct students to the photo on the next page of the young woman learning to read. Ask students to explain why education is so important to ending human rights abuses against women and others. *(People with more education have greater economic power and thus are less vulnerable to human rights abuses.)*

Answers

✔ Famine can be caused by natural disasters and political instability; migration is often caused by the desire for greater opportunity or the need to escape difficult conditions.

Caption poverty, rapid population growth, hunger, famine, natural disaster, a search for a better life and more opportunity

Independent Practice

■ **Link to Literature** To help students better understand human rights issues, have them read the selection from Maya Angelou's *A Song Flung Up to Heaven* and complete the worksheet.

All in One **Teaching Resources, Unit 5**, p. 90

■ Have students write a letter to the editor calling for action to protect children against human rights abuses. If time permits, students might first research the topic of protecting the rights of children online or in the library. In their letters, students should refer to specific types of abuse either mentioned in the text or uncovered through their research. They should also propose specific ways to protect the rights of children.

Monitor Progress

As students work on their letters, circulate to ensure that they are mentioning specific instances of abuse of children and proposing specific solutions for those instances of abuse.

Answers

Caption People might seek out and buy these products so that they can support organizations that work to end child labor.

✔ Children are forced to work for low wages in horrible conditions and to serve as soldiers or even slaves.

748 The World Today

Ending Child Labor
RUGMARK, an organization that works to end child labor, sponsors the education of South Asian students like this girl. The RUGMARK label on her sleeve also appears on carpets and rugs that were made without child labor. *What effect might labels like this one have on people's buying habits?*

Women in the Developed and Developing Worlds In the developed world, more and more women now work outside their homes. They have gained high-profile jobs as business owners and executives, scientists, and technicians. Yet women often receive less pay for the same job that men do, and many must balance demanding jobs with child-rearing and housework. Still, many women do not have the option of not working, because many families need two incomes just to maintain a decent standard of living. Poor families need two incomes just to survive.

The education gap has been narrowing in developing nations, and women from the middle and elite classes have entered the workforce in growing numbers. Still, women often shoulder a heavy burden of work. In rural areas, especially in Africa where many men have migrated to cities to work, women do much of the farm work in addition to household tasks. In other regions, such as Southeast Asia, young women often leave home in search of work to support the family or to pay for their brothers' education. In many places, cultural traditions still confine women to the home or segregate men and women in the workplace.

Protecting Children Worldwide, children suffer terrible abuses. A 2005 UN report showed that half of the world's children suffer the effects of extreme poverty, armed conflict, and AIDS. Children are also the targets of human rights violations. In some nations, children are forced to serve as soldiers or even slaves. The resulting abuses not only damage children but also hurt a country's hope for the future. In 1989, the UN General Assembly approved the Convention on the Rights of the Child. This human rights treaty sets standards for basic rights for children, including the right to life, liberty, education, and healthcare. But ensuring these rights has proved difficult or even impossible.

In developing countries, tens of millions of children between the ages of 5 and 14 do not attend school. Instead, they work full time. Often, these child laborers work long hours in dangerous, unhealthy conditions for little pay. Many are physically abused by their employers and live in conditions of near slavery. Still, their families need the income the children earn. In some cases, children must work to pay off a family's debt. Human rights groups, the UN, and developed nations have focused a spotlight on child labor in order to end such practices.

Indigenous Peoples Face Challenges Indigenous peoples—including Native Americans, Aborigines in Australia, and Maoris in New Zealand—face discrimination and other abuses. Often, their lands have been forcibly taken. In South America, for example, developers have pushed into once-isolated areas, threatening the ways of life of indigenous peoples. Many Indians have died of diseases carried by the newcomers. During Guatemala's long civil war, the government targeted Mayan villagers, killing tens of thousands. The UN has worked to set standards to protect the rights of indigenous peoples.

✔ **Checkpoint** How are the human rights of children around the world violated?

Development and the Environment

Since earliest times, people have taken what they wanted from the environment. In the past, damage was limited because the world's population was small and technology was simple. Industrialization and the world

History Background

The Legacy of Colonialism In many parts of the world, threats to the rights of indigenous people date back to the arrival of European colonists. In Guatemala, persecution of the Maya Indians dates back to 1523, when Pedro de Alvarado, a Spaniard, conquered the local Maya. Under Spanish rule, the conquered Maya were forced to work as agricultural laborers for Spanish landlords. Native Americans in other Spanish colonies, such as Mexico and Peru, faced a similar plight. Even in colonies with few European settlers, indigenous people have suffered. For example, the Dutch conquered the western half of New Guinea in the nineteenth century. After the Dutch East Indies gained independence as Indonesia, the people of Java dominated the country politically. The indigenous New Guineans, or Papuans, have faced land seizures and brutal repression by the Javanese-dominated Indonesian military.

Health of the World Today

In the year 2000, the world population stood at just over 6 billion people. In 2050, it is projected to reach over 9 billion. The world's population in 2000 was sharply divided in terms of health and access to resources. Despite improvements in agriculture, medicine, and technology, huge numbers of people around the world lacked adequate food and access to safe water. Disease threatened some regions more than others. And in certain areas, poverty-stricken people made up the majority of the population.

Access to Safe Water

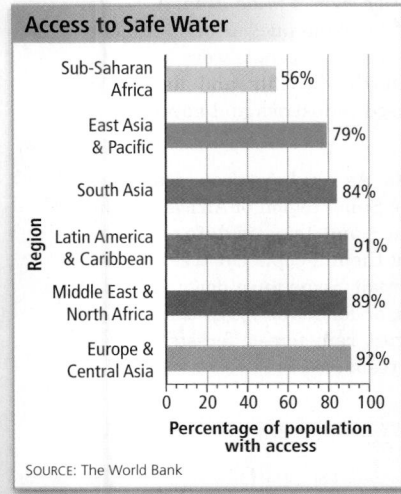

SOURCE: The World Bank

Many people around the world have no access to safe water. Drinking and using unsafe water spreads unsanitary conditions and disease.

Global HIV/AIDS Mortality

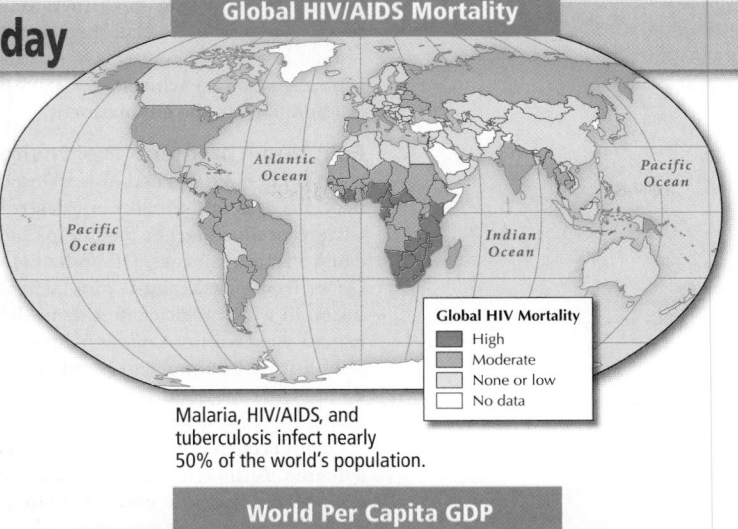

Global HIV Mortality
- High
- Moderate
- None or low
- No data

Malaria, HIV/AIDS, and tuberculosis infect nearly 50% of the world's population.

World Per Capita GDP

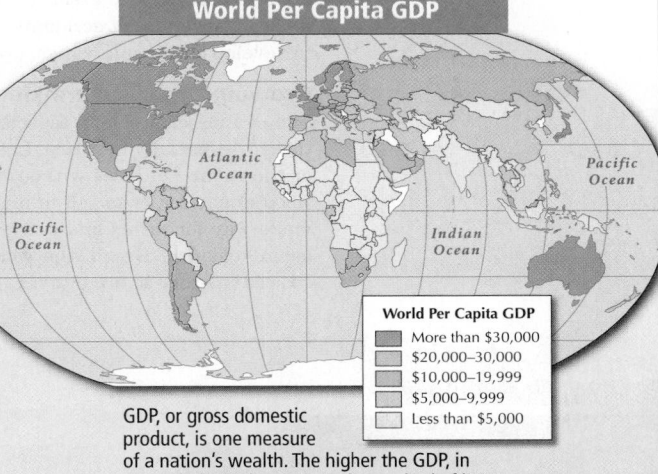

World Per Capita GDP
- More than $30,000
- $20,000–30,000
- $10,000–19,999
- $5,000–9,999
- Less than $5,000

GDP, or gross domestic product, is one measure of a nation's wealth. The higher the GDP, in general, the higher a nation's standard of living.

African farmers work with a member of a Japanese agricultural exchange program. These kinds of programs can help countries increase their GDP. ▶

History Interactive
For: Interactive world health statistics
Web Code: nbp-3431

Thinking Critically

1. **Map Skills** Which regions have high rates of disease and low percentages of their population with access to safe water?
2. **Compare** Compare the HIV/AIDS map and the chart with the map of global GDP. What can a nation's GDP suggest about the health of its people?

Development and the Environment ⓛ

Instruct

- **Introduce** Explain that the conflict between people's needs and the environment's fragility is longstanding. However, given the changes in technology and the growth of population in the last 100 years, how do students think that conflict may have deepened? What special challenges might this create for people in developing nations?

- **Teach** Draw a seesaw on the board and label the ends *Development* and *The Environment*. Discuss with students how emphasizing one end of the balance might affect the issue on the other end. Ask **What pollution problems have resulted from development?** *(erosion of topsoil, polluted soil and water, acid rain, nuclear leakages)* Then ask students to explain the links between development and desertification and deforestation.

- **Quick Activity** Have students discuss and debate which is more important: development or protecting the environment. Urge them to link the discussion to a current issue, such as oil exploration in the Arctic National Wildlife Refuge.

Answers

Thinking Critically
1. Sub-Saharan Africa, East Asia, and South Asia
2. The lower a nation's GDP, the less healthy its people are.

- **Web Code nbp-3431** will take students to interactive maps and charts related to the Infographic on the previous page. Have students complete the interactivity and then answer the questions in the text.

- **Viewpoints** To provide students with the perspective of environmentalists on global issues, have them read the selection *Approaches to the Environment* and complete the worksheet.

All in One Teaching Resources, Unit 5, p. 89

Monitor Progress

- Have students write a summary sentence about each black subheading under Development and the Environment.

- Check Reading and Note Taking Study Guide entries for student understanding.

population explosion have increased the damage done to the environment. As you have read, development improves lives and strengthens economies—but at a price. One of the great challenges of the twenty-first century is how to achieve necessary development without causing permanent damage to the environment.

Pollution Threatens the Environment Since the 1970s, environmentalists have warned about threats to the environment. Strip mining provides ores for industry but destroys land. Chemical pesticides and fertilizers produce larger food crops but harm the soil and water and may cause certain cancers. Oil spills pollute waterways and kill marine life. Gases from power plants and factories produce **acid rain**, a form of pollution in which toxic chemicals in the air fall back to Earth as rain, snow, or hail. Acid rain has damaged forests, lakes, and farmland.

Pollution from nuclear plants is another concern. In 1986, an accident at the Chernobyl nuclear power plant in the Soviet Union exposed people, crops, and animals to deadly radiation over a wide area. A similar accident occurred in 1978 at the Three Mile Island nuclear plant in Pennsylvania. Although the fallout was limited and no people were killed, the accident sparked a great debate about the benefits and hazards of nuclear power. Such accidents have caused industries and governments to develop better safety measures.

Growing Deserts, Shrinking Forests As you have read, desertification is a major problem, especially in the Sahel region of Africa. Another threat—especially in Africa, Latin America, and Asia—is **deforestation**, or the cutting of trees without replacing them. People cut trees for firewood or shelter, or to sell in markets abroad. Some burn down forests to make way for farms and cattle ranches, or for industry. In the Amazon basin region of Brazil, the world's largest rain forest, forests are also cleared in order to tap into rich mineral resources.

BIOGRAPHY

Edward O. Wilson

As a child in Alabama, Edward O. Wilson (1929–) developed a love for nature. His poor eyesight and limited physical strength encouraged him to focus on ants—small creatures that he could hold and look at closely. Wilson never grew out of his "bug period," becoming a renowned professor of biology at Harvard. In recent years, Wilson has increasingly focused his attention on environmental issues. In his 2002 book *The Future of Life*, he writes about how Earth's growing human population is affecting the planet and its resources. Calling the 2000s the "Century of the Environment," he appeals to "science and technology, combined with foresight and moral courage," to meet modern environmental challenges. *Why does Wilson believe that "foresight and moral courage" are needed to preserve the environment?*

Link to Science

Biodiversity Edward O. Wilson was famous for promoting awareness of biodiversity, or biological diversity. Healthy ecosystems contain a rich variety of species, each of which plays a role in the biological processes of the ecosystem. For example nitrogen-fixing plants make the soil more fertile, flowering plants provide food for herbivores, or plant-eating animals, and fungi, bacteria, and other microorganisms decompose dead plants and animals. Biodiversity gives an ecosystem resilience. If one species faces disease or other threats, another may be able to fill its niche in the ecosystem. Tropical ecosystems, particularly rain forests, tend to be especially rich in species. Their biodiversity is threatened today by economic and population pressures, including the cutting of forests for timber and to clear land for agriculture.

Answer

BIOGRAPHY People need foresight in order to make decisions that protect the future well-being of the environment, rather than pursue short-term gain; they need courage to convince people to plan for the future.

Once forests are cleared, rains wash nutrients from the soil, destroying its fertility. Deforestation also causes **erosion,** or the wearing away of land, which encourages flooding. The deforestation of rain forests is particularly worrisome. Rain forests like the Amazon play a key role in absorbing poisonous carbon dioxide from the air and releasing essential oxygen. They are also home to millions of animal and plant species, many of which have become extinct because of deforestation.

Global Warming Another environmental challenge—one that is hotly debated—is **global warming.** Global warming refers to the rise of Earth's surface temperature over time. A rise in Earth's temperature could bring about changes such as the following: a rise in sea level, changes in weather patterns, increased desertification in some areas, and an increase in precipitation in others. Because climates in some areas could become colder, many scientists prefer to call the trend "climate change."

Scientists agree that Earth's temperature has risen slightly over the past century. Many scientists think that this warming comes from gases released into the atmosphere by human activity such as the burning of fossil fuels. These "greenhouse" gases trap warmth in Earth's atmosphere. Some scientists, however, and many policymakers, argue that global warming is due to natural <u>fluctuations</u> in Earth's climate.

The debate over a treaty called the Kyoto Protocol points to a central challenge facing world leaders: Does economic development have to conflict with protecting the environment? The treaty, signed by 140 countries, with the major exceptions of the United States and Australia, went into effect in 2005. Its purpose is to lower the emissions of carbon dioxide and other "greenhouse" gases that contribute to global warming. Many developing nations refuse to sign because they say they must exploit their resources in order to develop fully. The United States has not signed the Kyoto Protocol because it believes the treaty could strain economic growth. Nations that have signed the treaty, however, argue that developed nations must lead the way in slowing emissions.

✓ **Checkpoint** What kinds of environmental issues do people face today?

Vocabulary Builder
<u>fluctuation</u>—(fluk choo AY shun) *n.* swing; rising and falling of something

---

SECTION 3 Assessment

Progress Monitoring *Online*
For: Self-quiz with vocabulary practice
Web Code: nba-3431

Terms, People, and Places
1. Place each of the key terms at the beginning of the section into one of the following categories: politics, culture, government, economy, or environment. Write a sentence for each term explaining your choice.

Note Taking
2. **Reading Skill: Compare** Use your completed chart to answer the Focus Question: How do poverty, disease, and environmental challenges affect people around the world today?

Comprehension and Critical Thinking
3. **Synthesize Information** How are global poverty, disease, disasters, and migration linked to each other? How might they be linked to globalization?
4. **Identify Central Issues** Why is protecting human rights not a central issue for many developing countries?
5. **Identify Assumptions** What assumptions can you make about the lack of participation on the part of some nations in the Kyoto Protocol?

● **Writing About History**
Quick Write: Decide on an Organizational Strategy Make a draft of a persuasive essay about social and environmental challenges. Your draft should include a thesis statement, begin with your second-strongest argument, and conclude with your strongest argument. To organize most efficiently, rank your remaining arguments from weakest to strongest.

Section 3 Assessment

1. Sentences should reflect an understanding of each term, person, or place listed at the beginning of the section, as well as the proper categorization.
2. Poverty, disease, and environmental challenges limit development, create economic difficulties, and contribute to human rights abuses.
3. Poverty, disease, and disasters often cause people to migrate. Globalization may be contributing to these problems by improving travel and communications and introducing new employment patterns that disrupt traditional cultures and local economies.
4. In many developing nations, the need to survive dominates all other needs.
5. These nations feel that the limitations of the Kyoto Treaty will impede their economic development.

Assess and Reteach

Assess Progress L3
- Have students complete the Section Assessment.
- Administer the Section Quiz.

All in One **Teaching Resources, Unit 5,** p. 84
- To further assess student understanding use
  📺 **Progress Monitoring Transparencies,** 146

Reteach
If students need more instruction, have them read the section summary.

 **Reading and Note Taking Study Guide,** p. 228 L3

 Adapted Reading and Note Taking Study Guide, p. 228 L1 L2

 Spanish Reading and Note Taking Study Guide, p. 228 L2

Extend L4
See this chapter's Professional Development pages for the Extend Online activity on the environment.

Answer

✓ chemical pollution of our land, air, and water, as well as global warming, soil erosion, deforestation, and desertification

---

● **Writing About History**
Drafts should reflect a clearly stated thesis, supported by at least three arguments. The strongest argument should appear last and should lead into a strong conclusion.

For additional assessment, have students access **Progress Monitoring *Online*** at **Web Code nba-3431.**

Aung San Suu Kyi: *Freedom From Fear*

Objective

- Understand the importance of courage for Aung San, Suu Kyi, Myanmar's leading human rights and democracy advocate.

Build Background Knowledge **L3**

Describe the struggle for democracy in Myanmar after that nation, formerly known as Burma, achieved independence from Great Britain. *(A military government ruled, limiting foreign trade. Living standards were low. The government rejected the 1990 elections, which had elected Aung San Suu Kyi and her party, and viciously suppressed the opposition.)*

Instruct **L3**

- Direct students' attention to the introduction at the top of the page. Then ask **Why has Aung San Suu Kyi been jailed and restricted by the Myanmar government?** *(She opposes its dictatorship and speaks out for democracy.)*

- Discuss with students the issue of courage under oppression. Ask **According to Suu Kyi, why does oppression create fear?** *(People are afraid all the time for their physical safety, their livelihood, and their future.)* **How does Suu Kyi believe that courage plays a role in resisting oppression?** *(It gives people a way to keep hoping, to believe that in the end ideas such as truth and justice will endure and dominate over fear and oppression.)*

Monitor Progress

To confirm students' understanding, ask them to briefly summarize Suu Kyi's views about courage.

Thinking Critically

1. because fear is not the natural condition of people in a civilized society
2. Examples should be supported with details that illustrate the person's lack of fear.

Aung San Suu Kyi: *Freedom From Fear*

Aung San Suu Kyi, leader of Myanmar's National League for Democracy and winner of the Nobel Peace Prize, has worked courageously for human rights and democracy in her country. Because of her opposition to Myanmar's ruling military junta, she was held under house arrest from 1989 to 1995 and severely restricted thereafter. In this essay, Aung San Suu Kyi describes the need for courage when living under an oppressive government.

▲ Aung San Suu Kyi

Fearlessness may be a gift but perhaps more precious is the courage acquired through endeavor, courage that comes from cultivating the habit of refusing to let fear dictate one's actions, courage that could be described as 'grace under pressure'—grace which is renewed repeatedly in the face of harsh, unremitting[1] pressure.

Within a system which denies the existence of basic human rights, fear tends to be the order of the day. Fear of imprisonment, fear of torture, fear of death, fear of losing friends, family, property or means of livelihood, fear of poverty, fear of isolation, fear of failure. A most insidious[2] form of fear is that which masquerades as common sense or even wisdom, condemning as foolish, reckless, insignificant or futile the small, daily acts of courage which help to preserve man's self-respect and inherent[3] human dignity. It is not easy for a people conditioned by fear under the iron rule of the principle that might is right to free themselves from the enervating[4] miasma[5] of fear. Yet even under the most crushing state machinery courage rises up again and again, for fear is not the natural state of civilized man.

The wellspring[6] of courage and endurance in the face of unbridled power is generally a firm belief in the sanctity of ethical principles combined with a historical sense that despite all setbacks the condition of man is set on an ultimate course for both spiritual and material advancement. ... It is man's vision of a world fit for rational, civilized humanity which leads him to dare and to suffer to build societies free from want and fear. Concepts such as truth, justice and compassion cannot be dismissed as trite[7] when these are often the only bulwarks[8] which stand against ruthless power.

▲ Burmese children living in Bangladesh protested for the release of Aung San Suu Kyi on the occasion of the Burmese foreign minister's visit to Bangladesh.

1. **unremitting** (un rih MIT ing) *adj.* not letting up
2. **insidious** (in SID ee us) *adj.* meant to harm
3. **inherent** (in HIHR unt) *adj.* part of one's basic nature
4. **enervating** (EN ur vayt ing) *adj.* weakening or destroying
5. **miasma** (my AZ muh) *n.* harmful atmosphere or influence
6. **wellspring** (WEL spring) *n.* source
7. **trite** (tryt) *adj.* overused; uninteresting
8. **bulwark** (BOOL wurk) *n.* serving as a defense

Thinking Critically

1. **Identify Main Ideas** Why does the author believe that even in harsh, cruel societies courage will rise up again and again?
2. **Apply Information** Give one example of a person refusing to let fear dictate his or her actions.

History Background

Sharing Her People's Suffering After independence Myanmar (then known as Burma) had a democratic form of government, until the military seized power in 1962. It has ruled brutally ever since. When the military first took power, Suu Kyi was a high school student in India, where her mother was serving as Burma's ambassador. She lived overseas until 1988, when she decided to return to Burma. She became a leader of the democracy movement. In 1989, the military placed her under house arrest. Nonetheless, her party won a national election in 1990. The country's military rulers rejected the election results. Suu Kyi was not released until 1995. However, the government continued to harass her and her followers. She was again detained in 2000 but she was released in 2002. The next year, the military once again placed Suu Kyi under house arrest and sharply limited her contact with others.

SECTION 4

WITNESS HISTORY AUDIO

Taking a Stand

In the fall of 2002, United States President George W. Bush delivered a speech on international security before the United Nations in New York:

❝ We must choose between a world of fear and a world of progress. We cannot stand by and do nothing while dangers gather. We must stand up for our security and for the permanent rights and for the hopes of mankind.❞

—George W. Bush, Remarks at the United Nations General Assembly, September 12, 2002

Focus Question What kinds of threats to national and global security do nations face today?

President Bush emphasizes the importance of national security in a speech to U.S. Coast Guard members in 2003.

Security in a Dangerous World

Objectives
- Explain why nuclear, biological, and chemical weapons threaten global security.
- Analyze the various terrorist groups and why they are becoming more and more dangerous.
- Describe the various ways in which the United States and other nations have responded to terrorism.

Terms, People, and Places

proliferate   Afghanistan
terrorism   Taliban
al Qaeda

N̲o̲te Taking

Reading Skill: Compare and Contrast Use the chart to compare threats to global security.

Threats to Security	
Nuclear Weapons	Nuclear weapons unsecured in former Soviet Union

The end of the Cold War seemed to promise an end to global conflict and the threat of nuclear war. However, since the fall of the Iron Curtain, new and unpredictable threats continue to haunt the world.

The Threat of Modern Weapons

During the Cold War, the United States and the Soviet Union built huge arsenals of nuclear weapons. When the Cold War ended, those weapons still existed. Since then, keeping nuclear, chemical, and biological weapons out of the hands of dangerous groups has become an important issue.

The Nuclear Nonproliferation Treaty In 1968, during a thaw in the Cold War, the United States, the Soviet Union, and 60 other nations signed the Nuclear Nonproliferation Treaty (NPT). The purpose of the treaty was to ensure that nuclear weapons did not proliferate, or rapidly spread to nations that had no nuclear weapons. Since then, the treaty has been renewed, with 189 nations agreeing not to develop or possess nuclear weapons.

The International Atomic Energy Agency (IAEA) monitors nations regularly to check that they comply with the treaty. Three nations have not signed the NPT: India, Israel, and Pakistan. All three have nuclear weapons. India and Pakistan's testing of nuclear weapons in 1998 raised fears of a nuclear arms race in Asia. A few signers of the NPT, such as Iran, have tried to sidestep the treaty by acquiring nuclear technology that they claim is being used to develop nuclear power as an energy source.

Objectives

As you teach this section, keep students focused on the following objectives to help them answer the Section Focus Question and master core content.

- Explain why nuclear, biological, and chemical weapons threaten global security.

- Analyze the various terrorist groups and why they are becoming more and more dangerous.

- Describe the various ways in which the United States and other nations have responded to terrorism.

Prepare to Read

Build Background Knowledge **L3**

Ask students to recall the dangers of the Cold War. Explain that today the world faces attacks by terrorists, or violent extremists. Ask students to list some recent examples of terrorism.

Set a Purpose **L3**

- **WITNESS HISTORY** Read the selection aloud or play the audio.

   AUDIO **Witness History Audio CD,** Taking a Stand

  Ask **What is the main idea of President Bush's comment?** *(He believes that the United States must take actions to limit terrorism rather than live with the fear of it.)*

- **Focus** Point out the Section Focus Question and write it on the board. Tell students to refer to this question as they read. *(Answer appears with Section 4 Assessment answers.)*

- **Preview** Have students preview the Section Objectives and the list of Terms, People, and Places.

- **N̲o̲te Taking** Have students read this section using the Structured Read Aloud strategy (TE, p. T20). As they read, have students fill in the chart comparing threats to global security.

  Reading and Note Taking Study Guide, p. 229

Vocabulary Builder

Use the information below and the following resources to teach the high-use word from this section.
All in One **Teaching Resources, Unit 5,** p. 87; **Teaching Resources, Skills Handbook,** p. 3

High-Use Word	Definition and Sample Sentence
priority, p. 757	*n.* something deemed of greater importance than other things Brad's biggest **priority** was playing guitar, although his mother insisted that he finish high school first.

The Threat of Modern Weapons ⓛ₃

Instruct

- **Introduce: Key Terms** Ask students find the key term ***proliferate*** (in blue) in the text and explain its meaning. Point out that a main worry in the twenty-first century is that weapons of mass destruction will proliferate around the world. Ask students to brainstorm problems that might result from this. What steps might nations take to control the spread of weapons?

- **Teach** Point out the term ***weapons of mass destruction*** in the text. Trace events that have led to the existence of these weapons. Discuss issues that threaten the security of existing weapons arsenals. Ask **Why are WMDs more of a threat today than in the past?** *(Nations and groups that do not respect international law have them.)*

- **Quick Activity** Have students work in small groups to discuss the following issue: Some nations say that, like the U.S., they want nuclear weapons for defense. Do individual nations have the right to decide to acquire nuclear weapons? Why or why not? Use the Numbered Heads strategy (TE, p. T23) to have students share their responses with the class.

Independent Practice

- Have students write a journal entry describing their concerns about WMDs. Clarify that you will not read the entry.

- **Biography** To have students learn more about the development of nuclear weapons, have them read the biography *Albert Einstein* and complete the worksheet. Then have them consider the positive and negative effects of Einstein's work.

 **Teaching Resources, Unit 5,** p. 92

Monitor Progress

As students fill in their charts, circulate to make sure they can identify and differentiate types of global threats. For a completed version of the chart, see

🏛 **Note Taking Transparencies,** 208

Answer

✔ to limit the proliferation, or spread, of nuclear weapons and technology

---

Russia's Nuclear Weapons During the 1990s, the United States and Russia agreed to reduce their nuclear arsenals. However, after the collapse of the Soviet Union, Russia's nuclear weapons were scattered across a vast territory. With aid from the United States and Europe, Russia dismantled, or took apart, some nuclear weapons. Despite the agreements however, both the United States and Russia held on to their nuclear stockpiles.

A Risky Situation
Vials of the bacteria that cause plague were left improperly secured in Kazakhstan by Soviet scientists.

Weapons of Mass Destruction As you have read, weapons of mass destruction (WMDs) include nuclear, biological, and chemical weapons. Nuclear weapons include the atomic bomb. Biological weapons refer mainly to germs that can be released into the air or into water supplies. Chemical weapons are toxins, such as nerve gas and mustard gas.

Recently, however, the danger from WMDs has grown, as terrorist groups and "rogue states"— nations that ignore international law and threaten other nations—try to acquire them. One concern is that terrorists will seize nuclear weapons during transport. Another fear is that terrorists, or those who sympathize with their causes, will gain access to nuclear weapons programs in countries with unstable governments, such as Pakistan.

✔ **Checkpoint** What was the purpose of the NPT?

Terrorism Threatens Global Security

Since the 1990s, the world has witnessed a growing threat from terrorism. **Terrorism** is the use of violence by groups of extremists to achieve political goals. Terrorists' goals range from getting political prisoners released to gaining territory or autonomy for a particular ethnic group. Terrorists have bombed buildings, slaughtered civilians, police, and soldiers, and assassinated political leaders. Although terrorists have seldom achieved their larger goals, they have inflicted terrible damage and generated widespread fear.

Terrorists use headline-grabbing tactics to draw attention to their demands. They might attack hotels and tourists in Mumbai, bomb commuter trains in Madrid, or blow themselves up as "suicide bombers" to kill Israeli or Iraqi civilians. Terrorism has led to greater international cooperation between governments in an effort to prevent further attacks.

Regional Terrorist Groups Regional terrorist groups have operated in the developed world for decades. For 30 years, the Irish Republican Army (IRA) used terrorist tactics to force Britain out of Northern Ireland. Protestant paramilitary groups loyal to Great Britain responded with the same tactics. During the Cold War, the communist Red Brigade in Italy used violence in an attempt to gain power. The ETA, a Basque terrorist group, wants the Spanish government to grant independence to the Basque region in northern Spain.

In South America, leftist groups like the Shining Path in Peru and FARC in Colombia use kidnappings, murder, and bombings to overthrow national governments. They finance their operations with the sale of illegal drugs. In Asia, terrorist activities were linked to the long conflict between India and Pakistan over Kashmir.

Differentiated Instruction Solutions for All Learners

ⓛ₁ Special Needs   **ⓛ₂ Less Proficient Readers**

To help students connect their studies to current events, have them look through recent news. Ask them to use the Internet, newspapers, or magazines to find images and stories related to the content of the section. Have students present their findings to the class and explain how they relate to the text.

Use the following resources to help students acquire basic skills.

 Adapted Reading and Note Taking Study Guide

- Adapted Note Taking Study Guide, p. 229
- Adapted Section Summary, p. 230

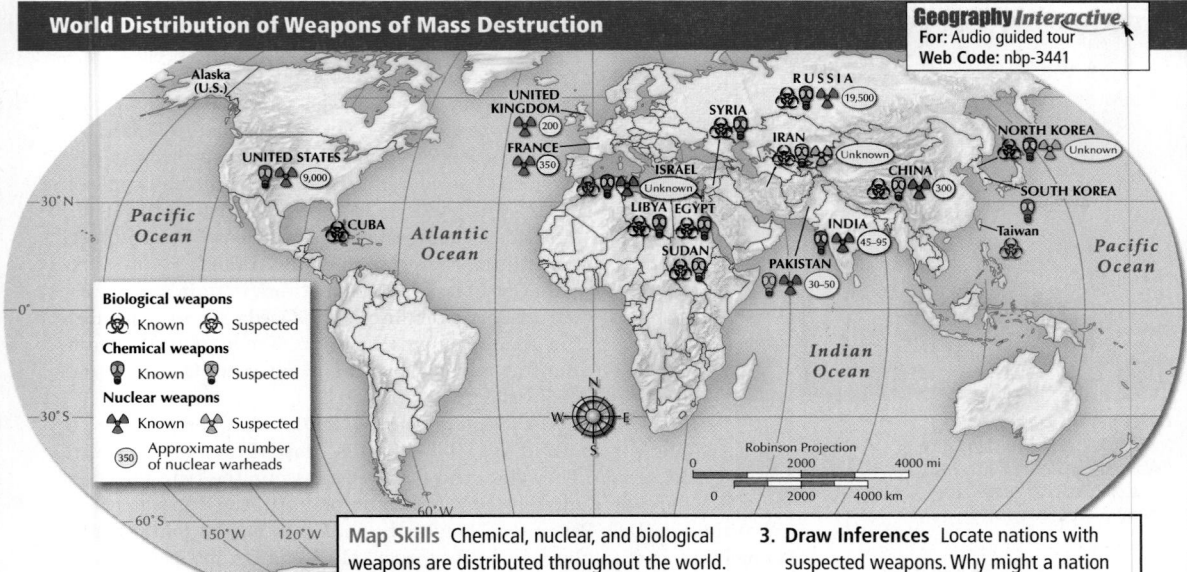

World Distribution of Weapons of Mass Destruction

Geography *Interactive*
For: Audio guided tour
Web Code: nbp-3441

RUSSIA (19,500)

Alaska (U.S.)

UNITED KINGDOM (200)

SYRIA

IRAN (Unknown)

NORTH KOREA (Unknown)

FRANCE (350)

ISRAEL (Unknown)

CHINA (300)

SOUTH KOREA

UNITED STATES (9,000)

LIBYA EGYPT

INDIA (45–95)

Taiwan

CUBA

SUDAN

PAKISTAN (30–50)

Pacific Ocean

Atlantic Ocean

Indian Ocean

Pacific Ocean

30°N / 0° / 30°S / 60°S

150°W / 120°W / 60°W

Biological weapons
Known / Suspected
Chemical weapons
Known / Suspected
Nuclear weapons
Known / Suspected
(350) Approximate number of nuclear warheads

Robinson Projection
0 2000 4000 mi
0 2000 4000 km

Map Skills Chemical, nuclear, and biological weapons are distributed throughout the world.
1. **Locate** (a) Sudan (b) North Korea (c) Israel (d) India.
2. **Describe** Which nations have stockpiles of biological, chemical, and nuclear weapons?
3. **Draw Inferences** Locate nations with suspected weapons. Why might a nation choose to be secretive about its stores of dangerous weapons?

Conflicts in the Middle East Decades of conflict between Israel and its neighbors helped fuel the spread of terrorism. In 1964, a group of Arabs founded the Palestine Liberation Organization (PLO), with the goal of creating an independent Palestinian state. In its early years, the PLO used terrorist methods.

The PLO renounced terrorism in 1988. Meanwhile, other terrorist groups have emerged and continue their calls for the establishment of a Palestinian state and the destruction of Israel. The Al-Aqsa Martyrs Brigade, Hamas, Hezbollah, and Islamic Jihad are among the groups that practice terror to achieve their goals. They found support in poverty-stricken Palestinian refugee camps in Gaza and trained suicide bombers to attack Israeli targets.

Islamic Fundamentalism By the 1980s, Islamic fundamentalism was on the rise. This conservative reform movement wanted to revive Islamic values and install governments that strictly followed Islamic law, or Sharia. The Islamist movement was partly a response to the rise of secular governments in many Muslim nations and the impact of Western culture. It was also a backlash against foreign support for Israel and the presence of foreign powers in the Middle East. Islamic fundamentalists made Israel or Western nations scapegoats for their problems.

The 1979 Iranian revolution brought an Islamist government to power. Later, an Islamist group called the Taliban gained power in Afghanistan. Fundamentalist movements have also emerged in countries from Algeria to Indonesia. Iran and Saudi Arabia have both provided financial support for terrorist organizations.

Al Qaeda Attacks Some Islamic fundamentalists turned to terrorism. The most widely known Islamic terrorist organization is **al Qaeda**

Terrorism Threatens Global Security **L3**

Instruct

- **Introduce: Key Terms** Ask students find the key term *terrorism* (in blue) in the title. Work as a class to agree on a definition, then have a student read the definition in the text. Have students recall what they just read about WMDs. Ask students how the spread of WMDs would change the threat of terrorism.

- **Teach** Discuss the terrorist threat. Ask **What tactics do terrorists use?** *(headline-grabbing tactics like bombings of public places and poison gas attacks)* **What are their goals?** *(to make political demands, such as control of territory or freedom for prisoners, through the use of violence and to try to frighten nations into meeting those demands)* **Why is terrorism so difficult to control?** *(Terrorists can hide in the general population; they will use extreme measures to achieve their ends.)*

- **Quick Activity** Read the following sentence from the text to students: "Terrorists generally have failed to achieve their greater goals." Ask students to consider why they think terrorists continue their actions. How do they justify these actions?

Independent Practice

Have students access **Web Code nbp-3441** to take the **Geography Interactive Audio Guided Tour** and then answer the map skills questions in the text.

Monitor Progress

- Check answers to map skills questions.
- Ask students to write a one-sentence summary of each black heading under Terrorism Threatens Global Security.

L4 Advanced Readers   **L4 Gifted and Talented**

The complicated and ever-changing nature of national security in the age of terrorism presents an opportunity for more in-depth analysis of the issues presented in this section. Consider having these students read all or parts of Thomas Friedman's book *Longitudes and Attitudes: Exploring the World After September 11th*. This collection of Friedman's newspaper columns delves into the roots of modern global terrorism and the battle to stop it. Students can write a review of the book following their reading. Alternatively, have students consult a variety of print and online sources on issues surrounding the War on Terrorism and then present a critical review of their findings to the class.

Answers

Map Skills
1. Review locations with students.
2. the United States, United Kingdom, France, Israel, Libya, Egypt, Sudan, Syria, Pakistan, India, China, Russia, North Korea, South Korea
3. Sample: It might not want world opinion to turn against it or it might want to retain an advantage over its enemies.

Response to Terrorism

❸

Instruct

■ **Introduce** Tell students that after September 11, 2001, America looked for ways to defend itself. As the nation explored different ways to do this, debates arose about which methods were effective or in the nation's best interests. Ask students to share their knowledge about the methods and debates.

■ **Teach** Write *Afghanistan* and *Iraq* on the board. Have students summarize U.S. military actions in these locations and identify the reasons for those actions. Ask **How did Americans feel about U.S. military action in Afghanistan and Iraq?** *(Many supported them; some opposed the actions.)* Have students identify steps the United States has taken to improve security.

■ **Quick Activity** Show students *The Taliban in Afghanistan* from the **Witness History Discovery School**™ video program. Then discuss how the Taliban enforced a harsh interpretation of Islam in Afghanistan and how it was finally removed from power by a U.S.-led military coalition after it was linked to the terrorist attacks of September 11, 2001.

Independent Practice

Have students write a paragraph for or against the following statement: America should have gone to war against Iraq. Clarify that you will not read the entry.

Monitor Progress

Check Reading and Note Taking Study Guide entries to confirm that students have accurately identified and compared threats to global security.

A Dangerous Leader
New York City police stand near a "Wanted" poster in 2001. *How does bin Laden threaten the United States' security?*

WITNESS HISTORY VIDEO

Watch *The Taliban in Afghanistan* on the **Witness History Discovery School**™ video program to learn about Islamic fundamentalism in Afghanistan.

Discovery
SCHOOL

Vocabulary Builder
priority—(pry AWR uh tee) *n.* something deemed of greater importance than other things

(ahl KY duh), which means "the Base" in Arabic. The founder and leader of al Qaeda is Osama bin Laden, a wealthy Saudi businessman.

In the 1980s, bin Laden joined Muslim fighters battling Soviet forces in Afghanistan. Later, he broadened his goals to include the overthrow of governments considered "un-Islamic" and the expulsion of non-Muslims from Muslim countries. In the 1990s, bin Laden mobilized al Qaeda to expel U.S. interests and military power from Saudi Arabia.

Al Qaeda built a global network to train and finance terrorist activities. In 1998, al Qaeda terrorists bombed the American embassies in Kenya and Tanzania. But the major blow came when al Qaeda struck inside the United States.

On September 11, 2001, al Qaeda terrorists hijacked four airplanes in the United States. Most of the hijackers were from Saudi Arabia. They slammed two airplanes into the twin towers of the World Trade Center in New York and one into the Pentagon near Washington, D.C. Passengers fought the hijackers on the fourth flight, which crashed on the way to its target. More than 2,500 people were killed in the attacks.

✔ **Checkpoint** What are the goals of Islamic fundamentalists?

Response to Terrorism

Al Qaeda's attack on the United States triggered a startling global shake-up. Governments around the world questioned their ability to keep their citizens safe. In the United States, President George W. Bush declared a "war on terror" in general, and against al Qaeda in particular.

New Security Measures After the 2001 attacks, the United States made national security a top priority. To this end, the government strengthened and reorganized its intelligence services and passed new counterterrorism laws. In the United States and elsewhere, there were more rigorous security measures at airports and public buildings. A long-term effort was launched to find out how terrorist groups were funded, with the goal of cutting off terrorists' money supply and limiting their activities. The United States worked with other countries to coordinate intelligence about terrorist groups.

These measures were costly. In addition, some believed the federal government was using the threat of terrorism to increase its power and violate the constitutional rights and freedoms of its citizens. But many felt that the threat was serious enough to justify extreme measures.

War in Afghanistan As part of its "war on terror," the United States made it a priority to find and punish the organizers of the 2001 attacks. Osama bin Laden was based in Afghanistan. The government of Afghanistan, an extreme Islamic fundamentalist group called the Taliban, refused U.S. demands to surrender the terrorists. The United States then formed a coalition of nations to invade Afghanistan. In 2002, with the help of Afghan warlords, American and allied forces overthrew the Taliban and drove al Qaeda into hiding or flight. Bin Laden and many Taliban leaders escaped capture.

Answers

Caption Bin Laden leads al Qaeda, which carried out the September 11, 2001, attacks on the United States and has threatened further attacks.

✔ They want to install governments that strictly follow Islamic law and reduce the presence of Western powers in the Middle East.

History Background

Civil Liberties and the War on Terrorism
Two months after the September 11 attacks in 2001, Congress passed the Patriot Act. Congress's action reflected an urgent desire to protect the nation, even at the cost of certain freedoms. Among the act's most hotly debated provisions were new laws allowing the federal government easier access to private records, including personal financial, library, travel, phone, and medical records that had previously been off-limits to the government without a court-issued warrant. It also became easier for the government to conduct phone taps and other surveillance. Civil liberties advocates argued that fighting terrorism did not justify eroding the rights of American citizens. Proponents of the law countered that the government needed expanded powers to protect the nation.

Coalition forces helped Afghanistan hold elections for a new government. The new government lifted many harsh Taliban laws, such as those that forbid girls and women from getting an education. From hideouts along the Pakistan border, Taliban fighters resisted the new government and its Western allies. The war soon spilled into neighboring Pakistan, where Taliban and al Qaeda fighters took refuge.

War in Iraq In 2003, President Bush urged Congress to agree to an invasion of Iraq, citing intelligence reports that said Iraq was secretly producing WMDs. The Bush administration also suggested that Iraq was involved in the 2001 terrorist attacks against the United States. The war was bitterly debated among Americans and around the world, because no WMDs were found after the U.S. invasion.

A 2008 report by the Senate Intelligence Committee said that prior to the invasion, the Bush administration had repeatedly exaggerated the threat posed by Iraq. The report also revealed that there had been no credible intelligence to support the Bush administration's claims that Iraq was developing nuclear weapons, or that Iraq had longstanding ties to terrorist groups.

Threats From Iran and North Korea When Iran announced a plan to develop nuclear power plants in the early 2000s, the United States and other nations feared that Iran truly intended to develop nuclear weapons. Although Iran insisted its nuclear energy program was for peaceful purposes, the UN Security Council imposed some sanctions on Iran.

For years, North Korea violated its agreement under the Nuclear Nonproliferation Treaty and worked on developing nuclear weapons. Tensions grew as the United States tried to pressure North Korea's regime to stop its nuclear weapons program. In 2003, North Korea withdrew from the NPT. In 2006, it tested a small nuclear bomb.

Many people feared that if Iran or North Korea developed nuclear weapons, that nuclear technology could be passed on to terrorist groups. A nuclear-armed Iran or North Korea also posed threats to their regions and to world peace.

✔ **Checkpoint** Why did the United States invade Iraq?

Iran's Nuclear Plans
Iranians form a chain around a nuclear research facility to show their support for their country's nuclear program. *Why do Western nations object to the program?*

SECTION **4** Assessment

Progress Monitoring *Online*
For: Self-quiz with vocabulary practice
Web Code: nba-3441

Terms, People, and Places
1. For each term, person, or place listed at the beginning of the section, write a sentence explaining its significance.

Note Taking
2. **Reading Skill: Compare and Contrast** Use your completed chart to answer the Focus Question: What kinds of threats to national and global security do nations face today?

Comprehension and Critical Thinking
3. **Draw Inferences** Why might the United States and Russia be reluctant to fully commit to nuclear disarmament?
4. **Predict Consequences** How might nations around the world react should Middle Eastern nations democratically elect Islamic fundamentalist governments?
5. **Demonstrate Reasoned Judgment** Do you think that "preemptive" wars, or wars waged to prevent other wars or attacks, are sometimes necessary? Explain your answer.

● **Writing About History**
Quick Write: Draft the Opening Paragraph The paragraph that opens your essay is the place to grab the reader's interest. Remember that if the reader loses interest after reading the first paragraph, he or she is unlikely to continue reading. Draft an opening paragraph about threats to global security, using specific details to grab the reader's interest. An opening such as "There are many threats to global security" is much less compelling than a description of a specific threat.

Assess Progress Ⓛ③
- Have students complete the Section Assessment.
- Administer the Section Quiz.
- All in One **Teaching Resources, Unit 5**, p. 85
- To further assess student understanding use
  📖 **Progress Monitoring Transparencies,** 147

Reteach
If students need more instruction, have them read the section summary.

 **Reading and Note Taking** Ⓛ③
Study Guide, p. 230

 **Adapted Reading and** Ⓛ① Ⓛ②
Note Taking Study Guide, p. 230

Spanish Reading and Ⓛ②
Note Taking Study Guide, p. 230

Extend Ⓛ④
Organize students in discussion groups. Ask them to consider how the military actions taken by the United States aimed to improve U.S. security and how successful those actions have been. How else might the United States respond to terrorist threats?

Answers

Caption They believe that Iran may be developing nuclear weapons, which it might use to threaten neighbors or pass on to terrorists.

✔ President Bush claimed that Iraq was producing WMDs.

Section 4 Assessment

1. Sentences should reflect an understanding of each term, person, or place listed at the beginning of the section.
2. Nations face threats from weapons of mass destruction, such as nuclear, chemical, and biological weapons, and from terrorist groups.
3. Both nations might feel that they might need nuclear weapons for defense against others who have these weapons.

4. Sample: Most will be disappointed; some would accept the nations' decisions while others might try to make changes.
5. Students should support their answers with specific examples from various periods of history. They may also create hypothetical examples to help explain their answers.

● **Writing About History**
A well-constructed opening paragraph should contain a thesis statement, but it should also begin with a hook, or opening, that engages readers with specific details.

For additional assessment, have students access **Progress Monitoring** *Online* at **Web Code nba-3441.**

Objectives

As you teach this section, keep students focused on the following objectives to help them answer the Section Focus Question and master core content.

- Describe the exploration of space and the practical applications that resulted from it.
- Analyze the development and impact of the computer revolution.
- Explain how advances in medicine and biotechnology have shaped life today.

Prepare to Read

Build Background Knowledge L3

Ask students to recall the discussion of globalization in Section 2 of this chapter and the many ways in which nations are interdependent. Based on their previous reading, ask students to suggest the role that technology plays in globalization.

Set a Purpose L3

- **WITNESS HISTORY** Read the selection aloud or play the audio.

  ◀)) AUDIO **Witness History Audio CD,** A Giant Leap for Mankind

  Ask **What did Neil Armstrong mean by his statement?** *(that his physical step symbolized the greater step that human beings were making by beginning an entirely new era of exploration)*

- **Focus** Point out the Section Focus Question and write it on the board. Tell students to refer to this question as they read. *(Answer appears with Section 5 Assessment answers.)*

- **Preview** Have students preview the Section Objectives and the list of Terms, People, and Places.

- **Note Taking** Have students read this section using the Paragraph Shrinking strategy (TE, p. T20). As they read, have students fill in the chart comparing the impacts of modern science and technology.

  ✎ **Reading and Note Taking Study Guide,** p. 231

A logo of the National Aeronautic and Space Administration (NASA)

Buzz Aldrin walks on the moon in 1969. The space capsule that he traveled in is reflected on his visor.

WITNESS HISTORY ◀)) AUDIO

A Giant Leap for Mankind

On July 20, 1969, American astronauts Neil Armstrong and Edwin Aldrin landed on the moon after a four-day trip in the spacecraft *Apollo 11*. Stepping out onto the powdery surface, Armstrong—the first person ever to have walked on the moon—said, "That's one small step for man, one giant leap for mankind." Those words electrified a nation and defined a new era of world history.

Focus Question How have advances in science and technology shaped the modern world?

Advances in Science and Technology

Objectives
- Describe the exploration of space and the practical applications that resulted from it.
- Analyze the development and impact of the computer revolution.
- Explain how advances in medicine and biotechnology have shaped life today.

Terms, People, and Places

artificial satellite	biotechnology
International Space Station (ISS)	laser
	genetics
personal computer (PC)	genetic engineering
Internet	

Note Taking

Reading Skill: Compare Use the chart to compare the impacts of modern science and technology.

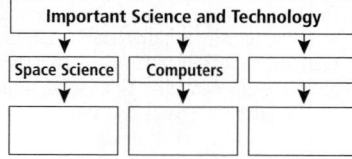

People in the past half century have used various terms to describe the age they live in, including "the atomic age," the "electronic age," and the "automobile age." All of these labels have one thing in common: their connection to modern science and technology. Since 1945, scientific research and technological development have had a transforming effect on human history. Startling new inventions, the computer revolution, and advances in the life sciences have redefined the world we live in and the lives we lead.

Exploring and Making Use of Space

By the second half of the twentieth century, there were few places on Earth that people had not begun to explore. Space was seen as the "final frontier"—an unknown world filled with opportunity. Within a few short decades, people had traveled to this frontier and had used its resources to help develop practical applications that transformed their lives.

The Space Race Begins Rockets are projectiles or vehicles propelled by the ejection of burning gasses from the rear of the rocket. In the early twentieth century, pioneers in rocketry like the American physicist Robert Goddard probed the potential of liquid-fueled rockets. From the beginning, Goddard believed that a rocket could carry people to the moon. At first people met his ideas with disbelief. Increasingly, German scientists took interest in Goddard's work, prompting him to work with great secrecy.

Vocabulary Builder

Use the information below and the following resources to teach the high-use word from this section.
All in One **Teaching Resources, Unit 5,** p. 87; **Teaching Resources, Skills Handbook,** p. 3

High-Use Word	Definition and Sample Sentence
manipulation, p. 763	*n.* the skillful handling of something with the purpose of achieving a specific result
	Jana's skillful **manipulation** of the puppets made them seem almost real.

Nevertheless, during World War II German scientists, led by Wernher von Braun, developed Germany's "secret weapon," the V-2 rockets that flew across the English Channel to rain down on London.

During the Cold War, the United States and the Soviet Union competed with each other to build both rocket-propelled weapons and rocketry for the purpose of space exploration. Von Braun, who moved to the United States after World War II, became a leader in the American missiles and space program. In 1957, the space age began when the Soviet Union launched into orbit *Sputnik*, the first **artificial satellite,** or man-made object that orbits a larger body. In 1969, the United States Apollo program landed the first man on the moon. Both superpowers also explored the military uses of space and sent spy satellites to orbit Earth. Since the end of the Cold War, the United States and Russia have cooperated in joint space ventures.

Space Science Develops In the decades since *Sputnik* and *Apollo*, rockets have been launched to other planets and beyond. Robotic space vehicles have penetrated the mists of Venus and the rings of Saturn, landed on Mars, and circled the moons of Jupiter. Rocket missions have various goals. They can take scientific measurements, release permanent satellites or telescopes, and if they are manned, conduct medical or biological experiments. They can also provide information about the composition and formation of the universe itself.

Increasingly, nations have worked together to explore space. For example, Russia, the United States, Canada, Japan, and several countries in Europe are developing the **International Space Station (ISS).**

WITNESS HISTORY VIDEO

Watch *The Space Race* on the **Witness History Discovery School**™ video program to experience the superpowers struggle to win the space race.

Traveler's Tales

EYEWITNESS ACCOUNT

An Astronaut Views Earth From Space

Alan Bean is an American astronaut who participated in the United States' Apollo 12 moon-landing project. In 1969, Bean became the fourth person to walk on the moon. Deeply moved by his experience, he began taking art lessons upon his return to Earth to express visually what he had seen. He resigned from NASA in 1981 to devote himself to painting. The excerpt below, taken from a book about the Apollo mission that he wrote and illustrated, describes the view from the moon.

66It was incredible to stand on the moon… and take a moment to reflect on all the dedicated people it took to get us there for America. We were the lucky ones. The stars were not visible because the sunlight reflecting from the bright lunar surface caused the irises of our eyes to contract, just as they do on earth at night when standing on a brightly lit patio. As we looked up, the sky was a deep, shiny black. I guessed that deep, shiny black was the color one sees looking into infinity . . . . I thought: Can all the people we know, all the people we love, who we've seen on TV, or read about in the newspapers, all be up there on that tiny blue-and-white marble? Earth—small but so lovely—was easily the most beautiful object we could see from the moon. It was a wondrous moment.99

—*Alan Bean,*
from *Apollo*, 1998

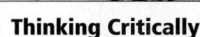

Thinking Critically
1. **Draw Inferences** Why does Bean call the astronauts the "lucky ones"?
2. **Analyze Information** How does Bean contrast his view of Earth with that of the lunar sky? What point does he make by contrasting these two views?

Teach

Exploring and Making Use of Space   L3

Instruct

■ **Introduce** Show students *The Space Race* from the **Witness History Discovery School**™ video program. Discuss the Cold War space race between the world's two superpowers.

■ **Teach** Review the different ways nations have explored and used space. Write the term *space race* on the board and ask students to define and describe it. Then discuss how interaction between nations about the use of space has changed since the end of the Cold War.

■ **Quick Activity** Have students read the Traveler's Tales feature on this page and paraphrase Astronaut Alan Bean's statement to a partner and answer the questions. Then extend their understanding of the feature by asking them to read the selection *The First Earthrise* and complete the worksheet.

All in One Teaching Resources, Unit 5, p. 93

Independent Practice

Have students read the red heading *Exploring and Making Use of Space*. Ask them to create a bulleted list of the ways that people have explored and used space. Urge them to read for new ways that they can add to their list. Use the Think-Write-Pair-Share strategy (TE, p. T23) and have students compare their lists.

Monitor Progress

As students fill in their charts, circulate to make sure students have accurately listed impacts of modern science and technology. For a completed version of the chart, see

Note Taking Transparencies, 209

Answers

Thinking Critically
1. They were able to see Earth from a unique perspective that few people have experienced.
2. The stars were not visible because of the brightness of the lunar surface, which Bean likens to standing on a brightly lit patio; looking into the blackness was like looking into infinity.

The Computer Revolution 🔞

Instruct

- **Introduce** Recall with students the *revolutions* about which they have read, including the Scientific Revolution and the Industrial Revolution. Discuss the characteristics of a revolution. Ask students what the term *computer revolution* could mean. What does the term suggest about the impact of computers on modern life?

- **Teach** Trace the changes that have occurred since computers were invented. Ask **How have computers evolved?** *(They have become faster, smaller, and widely available for individuals and businesses.)* **How does the Internet play a role in modern life?** *(It allows people to communicate instantly; it allows information to be shared around the world.)*

- **Quick Activity** Display **Color Transparency 209: Communications Technology, Selected Countries.** Use the lesson suggested in the transparency book to guide a discussion on how advances in communications technology are shaping the global community.

🖵 **Color Transparencies,** p. 209

Answer

✔ It is a multinational project to build a space station for international research.

Construction on the ISS began in 1998. When it is completed in 2010, it will serve as a space laboratory, allowing scientists from many different countries to observe space, conduct research, and develop new space-related technologies.

The Impact of Artificial Satellites The thousands of artificial satellites that orbit Earth have a number of very specific applications. These applications can be divided into three groups—communications, observation, and navigation. Communications satellites relay information that is used in advanced communications, including television, telephone, and high-speed data transmission. Observation satellites observe Earth, providing data to scientists, weather forecasters, and military planners. Navigation satellites beam precise locations to ship captains and others who need to navigate Earth's surface.

By 2000, artificial satellites had revolutionized global communications. Maintaining stationary orbits over specific points on Earth's surface, artificial satellites can transmit phone messages or television pictures anywhere on Earth. Linked to cell phones or computers, they allow people separated by thousands of miles to communicate instantly.

✔ **Checkpoint** What is the International Space Station and what is its significance?

The Computer Revolution

The invention of the computer in the twentieth century caused an unprecedented information revolution. Very few aspects of modern life remain untouched by computers. Computers run businesses and power plants, help scientists conduct advanced research, and when connected to satellites, make global communications possible. The development of computer technology has given rise to the term "Information Age."

INFOGRAPHIC

Twentieth Century Scientific Milestones

Developing Nuclear Energy

During World War II, the United States was determined to create an atomic bomb that could be used against the Axis Powers. Scientists including Albert Einstein, J. Robert Oppenheimer, Enrico Fermi, and Edward Teller participated in the Manhattan Project, as it was called. The project achieved success in 1945 with the explosion of a test bomb in New Mexico.

◄ Einstein and Oppenheimer in 1947

Link to Geography

Technology and Modern Life Advances in technology have changed both where and how people today live. The growth of car ownership and major highways has provided better access to rural areas. Air conditioning has made life in hot climates more bearable. Improved water infrastructures have made farming much easier in dry climates, and dams have produced valuable hydroelectric power to surrounding regions. For example, the Hoover Dam, located along the Colorado River on the Arizona-Nevada border and the Aswan Dam on the Nile, provide not only flood control, but also irrigation for surrounding areas and over thousands of megawatts of hydroelectric power. Technological advances have allowed people to flourish and industry to boom even in lands facing challenging climates.

Early Computers A computer is a device for making mathematical calculations and for storing, processing, and rapidly manipulating data. Computers have made it possible to preserve vast amounts of data. And when linked up in a vast network, they have brought written communication over enormous distances instantaneously.

The first electronic computers, built in the 1940s, were huge, slow machines. Later, thanks to inventions like the silicon chip, the computer was reduced in size. **Personal computers,** or **PCs,** became widely available in the 1970s for individual users, both at work and at home. By inserting basic programs into the machine, the user could perform complex and difficult tasks quickly and easily.

Over the next few decades, PCs replaced typewriters and account books in homes and businesses worldwide. At the same time, computer technology spread into many different fields. Computerized robots operate in factories. Computers remotely control satellites and probes in space and students use them in school classrooms. And computers increasingly aid scientists and architects in developing models to predict disasters, understand environmental changes, and plan urban development.

The Internet In the 1970s, various branches of the U.S. government along with groups in several American universities led efforts to link computer systems together via cables and satellites. By the 1990s, the "Internet" or "World Wide Web" was well established, again revolutionizing information technology. Using the **Internet,** a person can instantly communicate with other users around the world. The same person can also instantly access vast storehouses of information of all sorts.

By 2000, the Internet had grown to a gigantic network, linking individuals, governments, and businesses around the world. E-commerce, or buying and selling on the Internet, contributed to economic growth. The Internet also began to shape life in developing nations.

Breakthroughs in Medicine

Twentieth-century discoveries in medicine had a major impact on people around the world. For example, in 1952 researcher Jonas Salk (left) developed a vaccine for polio. Polio is a virus that spreads rapidly among people, especially children, causing paralysis. Before Salk's discovery, around 20,000 people in the United States contracted polio each year. Because of Salk's vaccine, the disease is extremely rare in the world today.

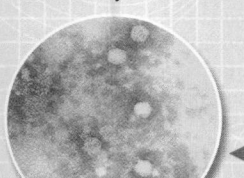

◀ the polio virus

DNA ▶ sequencer

Expanding the Science of Genetics

The study of genes was not new to the twentieth century. The work of James Watson and Francis Crick, (right) however, dramatically transformed the science of genetics. In 1953, the two men discovered the basic structure of DNA—the material in the chromosomes of all cells that determines how every organism functions. This discovery revolutionized the study of heredity and paved the way for genetic engineering.

Thinking Critically
1. **Draw Inferences** Why did Albert Einstein later regret his work on the Manhattan Project?
2. **Cause and Effect** How did the discovery of DNA affect the field of genetics? ◀)) AUDIO

Link to Technology

The Internet Brings Change When the Internet was first invented, pundits announced that it would change the way we live. In the United States, the Internet has changed people's ways of getting information and news, ways of shopping, and even ways of meeting socially. In many foreign countries, computers and the Internet have also brought significant change. For instance, in Peru, farmers have been able to increase their profits by selling their products online—some farmers report earning five times their former profit. In Africa, the Internet has helped farmers prepare for droughts and fend off potential famine. In China, Internet outrage after a prisoner died in police custody led the government to change laws on how it detains prisoners.

Independent Practice

■ Have students read the Infographic Twentieth Century Scientific Milestones. Ask students to explain which of the inventions mentioned affect their lives and how. Then have students, working in small groups, rank which inventions they think are the most important and why. Ask them to identify ethical or political issues that may relate to these technologies, such as genetic engineering and the safe storage of nuclear wastes. Then take a class vote on the most important invention and discuss the result.

■ Play the Witness History audio selection on Albert Einstein, and have student pairs discuss this selection. Have them answer the following questions: **What does he say is responsible for our progress?** *(intelligence)* **What is Einstein concerned about?** *(Sample: that fear and suspicion will triumph over reason, that nuclear weapons will be used)* **According to Einstein, what must people do to protect society?** *(build institutions based on law and justice to govern the atomic bomb and other weapons)*

◀)) AUDIO **Witness History Audio CD,** Twentieth Century Scientific Milestones

Monitor Progress

Have students write a brief paragraph explaining why the development and spread of computers is seen as a *revolution*.

Answers

Thinking Critically
1. because it lead to the development of nuclear weapons that threatened the world with enormous damage
2. It paved the way for genetic engineering, or the rearrangement of genetic material.

Advances in Medicine and Biotechnology ⑬

Instruct

- **Introduce: Key Terms** Ask students to notice the key term **biotechnology** in the red heading. What do they think biotechnology is? Clarify that *bio* means "life." Discuss other types of technology that students have read about. Ask students to suggest ways that technology could affect life. Have them read to find out whether their ideas on biotechnology are accurate.

- **Teach** Write the categories *medicine* and *biotechnology* on the board. Discuss the different breakthroughs described in the text, and ask students to define and describe each. List the breakthroughs under the appropriate category.

- **Quick Activity** Have students read the feature *A Global Food Evolves* on this page. Discuss the various stages in the development of modern corn and the importance of corn as a food and energy source today. Then help students develop a statement that frames a debate about genetic engineering, such as *Genetic engineering is the solution to world hunger.* If time allows, allow students to conduct full-scale debates based on their statement.

Independent Practice

Have students choose one of the breakthroughs they listed during the Teach activity and explain its significance to a classmate.

Monitor Progress

Check Reading and Note Taking Study Guide entries to make sure students have accurately listed different impacts of science and technology.

Answer

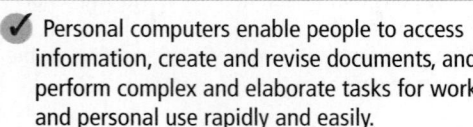

✔ Personal computers enable people to access information, create and revise documents, and perform complex and elaborate tasks for work and personal use rapidly and easily.

A GLOBAL FOOD EVOLVES

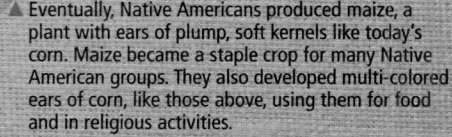

What we now know as corn originally grew as a wild grass in the Americas. Thousands of years ago, ancient peoples began experimenting with this grass, carefully selecting good seeds and nurturing plants. About 7,000 years ago, Native Americans near present-day Mexico City developed small ears of corn, calling them *maize*. Indians throughout the Americas, and then European settlers, constantly experimented with corn to produce bigger and better ears. The experimentation still continues today.

▲ Eventually, Native Americans produced maize, a plant with ears of plump, soft kernels like today's corn. Maize became a staple crop for many Native American groups. They also developed multi-colored ears of corn, like those above, using them for food and in religious activities.

◄ Ancient wild corn was called *teosinte* (tee oh SIN tee). Teosinte kernels, hard and nut-like, grew on thick grassy stalks. Over thousands of years Native Americans domesticated teosinte, carefully preserving the seeds of the plants that produced the best ears.

▲ A biotechnology worker cuts into an ear of corn to extract a section of DNA, or genetic material, that will be used to improve the next corn crop. By selecting only specific DNA, scientists can transfer only the genes that will result in desirable crop traits, such as hardiness or resistance to insects.

At the beginning of the twenty-first century, about 6 percent of the world's population could access the Internet. By 2010, it is estimated that about one third of the world's population will have access to the Internet—connecting them to a new world of ideas and information.

✔ **Checkpoint** What impact have personal computers had on people's lives?

Advances in Medicine and Biotechnology

Science and technology have revolutionized our understanding and our control of both human life and other forms of life on this planet. Developments in medicine and **biotechnology**, the application of biological research to industry, engineering, and technology, have resulted in new ways to combat and prevent disease.

Breakthroughs Transform Medicine In the postwar era, pioneers in the life sciences such as Dr. Jonas Salk became household names. Before the Salk vaccine, the paralyzing disease polio had crippled thousands of children and adults—including President Franklin D. Roosevelt. Other medical researchers developed vaccines to help prevent the spread of smallpox and other diseases.

Breakthroughs in surgery also transformed the field of medicine. In the 1970s, surgeons learned to transplant organs, including the human heart, to save lives. **Lasers** made many types of surgery safer and more precise. Lasers are high-energy light beams that surgeons use to cut or repair tissues and organs. Scientists have also had success in treating some cancers, a disease that affects the global population. In recent decades, computers and other technologies have become partners with doctors in diagnosing and treating disease. They have also made it easier for people to share information, thus making diseases easier to treat.

History Background

The Growth of the Sun Belt The development of advanced electronic and communications technologies since 1950 has been closely tied to suburbanization and the growth of the Sunbelt in the United States. Many technological industries built research and manufacturing facilities in suburbs or in the growing metropolitan areas of the Sunbelt. This has particularly affected states such as North Carolina, Texas, Arizona, and California. States in the Sun Belt—roughly the region in the United States south of the 37th degree of latitude—also offer people a more moderate climate than northern regions. The Sun Belt states have also benefited from the construction of the interstate highway system and an abundance of land for development. As a consequence, their population has grown faster than most other U.S. states.

Biotechnology and Genetic Engineering In the past couple of decades, the field of biotechnology has exploded. Biotechnology companies make products including vaccinations, medicines, and industrial bacteria that can be used to treat waste or clean up toxic spills.

Biotechnology is closely related to the fields of genetics and genetic engineering, which have also made dramatic advances in recent years. **Genetics** is the study of genes and heredity, while **genetic engineering** is the <u>manipulation</u> of genetic material to produce specific results. Beginning in the 1950s, genetic researchers, spearheaded by Rosalind Franklin, J. D. Watson, and F.H.C. Crick, examined the chemical code carried by all living things. Their research established the central role of DNA—deoxyribonucleic acid—in the chromosomes that determine human heredity. Their work revealed the "double helix," spiral-shaped DNA that carries hereditary traits from parents to children.

Ongoing genetic research has produced new drug therapies to fight human diseases. Research has also created new strains of fruits and vegetables that are intended to resist disease or thrive in conditions that usually inhibit growth. Genetic cloning, or the process of creating identical organisms from the cell of a host organism, has many practical applications in raising livestock and in biological research.

Biotechnology and genetic engineering have brought benefits, but also debate. Some people believe that genetically modified foods are unnatural and potentially dangerous. The possibility of cloning genetically identical mammals—including human beings—has also raised ethical questions about the role of science in creating and changing life.

Standards of Living Rise As you have read, science and technology have often had a direct and powerful impact on human life. Advances in diagnosing and treating disease and increased agricultural output have raised life expectancies worldwide, as well as standards of living. Yet great challenges still remain, from overpopulation to disasters to corrupt governments. In the decades ahead, people will continue to look for ways to solve global problems, using whatever tools they have.

✓ **Checkpoint** How have scientific advances affected people's standard of living?

Vocabulary Builder

<u>manipulation</u>—(muh nip yoo LAY shun) *n.* the skillful handling of something with the purpose of achieving a specific result

---

SECTION 5 Assessment

Progress Monitoring *Online*
For: Self-quiz with vocabulary practice
Web Code: nba-3451

Terms, People, and Places
1. What do each of the key terms listed at the beginning of the section have in common? Explain.

Note Taking
2. **Reading Skill: Compare** Use your completed chart to answer the Focus Question: How have advances in science and technology shaped the modern world?

Comprehension and Critical Thinking
3. **Synthesize Information** Considering the history of the Cold War, explain why the United States and Russia competed against each other to achieve dominance in the space race.
4. **Recognize Cause and Effect** What impact has the computer revolution had on globalization?
5. **Express Problems Clearly** Biotechnology has provided many benefits, but many people worry about its long-term effects. Explain why this is so.

● **Writing About History**
Quick Write: Write a Conclusion Write a conclusion that restates your thesis, sums up the supporting details, and leaves readers with a final impression. This final impression can be a memorable statement or even a call to action. As you write a conclusion about science and technology in the modern world, consider what basic impression you want the reader to remember about the topic, even if he or she takes nothing else away from the essay.

 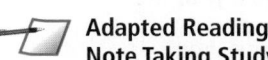

Section 5 Assessment

1. Sentences should reflect an understanding of each term, person, or place listed at the beginning of the section.
2. Science and technology have increased life expectancies, improved standards of living, enhanced communications and navigation, and facilitated space exploration.
3. Each nation felt that winning the space race would show the superiority of its political system. In addition, domination in space could play a role in the arms race.
4. It has brought nations into closer contact and allowed individuals access to global information and the ability to communicate and trade globally.
5. Some people fear that biotechnology will change food in unsafe ways; some also fear that it could give people dangerous power to create or change life.

● **Writing About History**
Conclusions should refer back to a specific thesis statement and summarize data that supports that statement. In addition, responses should end by asking readers to consider an idea or take an action.

For additional assessment, have students access **Progress Monitoring** *Online* at Web Code nba-3451.

Quick Study Guide

- Have students use the Quick Study Guide to prepare for this chapter's test. Students may wish to refer to the following pages as they review:

Key Components of Globalization
Section 2, pp. 738–742

Major Challenges to Society Today
Section 3, pp. 744–751; Section 4, pp. 753–757

Influential Technology of the Twentieth Century
Section 5, pp. 758–763

Important Industrialized Regions
Section 1, pp. 734–737

Recent World Events
Section 1, pp. 734–735; Section 2, pp. 739–741; Section 3, pp. 745, 750; Section 4, pp. 756–757

- For additional review, remind students to refer to the **L3**

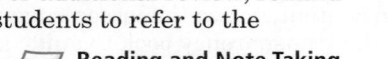 **Reading and Note Taking Study Guide**

Note Taking Study Guide, pp. 223, 225, 227, 229, 231
Section Summaries, pp. 224, 226, 228, 230, 232

- Have students access **Web Code nbp-3461** for this chapter's **History Interactive** timeline, which includes expanded entries and additional events.

- If students need more instruction on analyzing timelines, have them read the **Skills Handbook,** p. SH30.

- When students have completed their study of the chapter, distribute Chapter Tests A and B.

  All in One **Teaching Resources, Unit 5,** pp. 97–102.

> For **Progress Monitoring Online,** refer students to the Self-test with vocabulary practice at **Web Code nba-3461.**

CHAPTER 22

Quick Study Guide

> **Progress Monitoring Online**
> **For:** Self-test with vocabulary practice
> **Web Code:** nba-3461

■ Key Components of Globalization

- Interdependence: dependence of countries on goods, resources, knowledge, and labor from other parts of the world
- Advances in communications and transportation
- Rise of huge multinational corporations
- Far-reaching effects of financial crisis, shortages of natural resources, and debt
- Rise of global economy with many global organizations and treaties

■ Influential Technology of the Twentieth Century

Technology	Description	Uses
Artificial satellite	Man-made object that orbits a larger body	Space exploration; spying and other military purposes; scientific research; navigation; communications
Computer	Device for storing, processing, and rapidly manipulating data	Creating and preserving data; making businesses and homes run more efficiently; controlling satellites and factories
Internet	Network of world computer systems linked by cables and satellites	Instant communication with users around world; instant data retrieval; means of commerce
Biotechnology	Application of biological research to industry	Vaccinations and medicines; industrial bacteria; genetic engineering

■ Major Challenges to Society Today

- Global poverty, disasters, and disease
- Ensuring human rights for all, including women, children, and indigenous peoples
- Environmental problems including pollution, deforestation, desertification, and climate change
- Threat of misuse of nuclear technology and weapons of mass destruction
- Terrorism

■ Important Industrialized Regions

Region	Description	Role in Global Economy
The United States	Worldís only superpower	Important world leader; largest trading country in world
The European Union	Union of 25 European nations with distinct governments but common economic, political, and cultural institutions	Currently includes over half of European nations and is growing; world's largest trading region
The Pacific Rim	Geographical region that includes the countries that border the Pacific Ocean	With many countries and huge populations, potential to be major player in global economy

■ Recent World Events

1986	1990	1995
Nuclear accident occurs in Chernobyl.	**Germany is reunited.**	**The WTO forms.**

1985 **1990** **1995**

1988	1994
Osama bin Laden forms al Qaeda.	**NAFTA is created.**

Differentiated Instruction **Solutions for All Learners**

L1 Special Needs **L2 Less Proficient Readers**

Use the following study guide resources to help students acquiring basic skills:

 Adapted Reading and Note Taking Study Guide

Note Taking Study Guide, pp. 223, 225, 227, 229, 231
Section Summaries, pp. 224, 226, 228, 230, 232

L2 English Language Learners

Use the following study guide resources to help Spanish-speaking students:

Spanish Reading and Note Taking Study Guide

Note Taking Study Guide, pp. 223, 225, 227, 229, 231
Section Summaries, pp. 224, 226, 228, 230, 232

Concept Connector

 Essential Question Review

To connect prior knowledge with what you have learned in this chapter, answer the questions below in your Concept Connector journal. Use the journal in the Reading and Note Taking Study Guide to record your answers (or go to www.phschool.com **Web Code:** nbd-3407). In addition, record information about the following concepts:

- Trade: United States trade in the twentieth century
- Economic systems: Globalization

1. **Technology** Since their introduction, personal computers have become more common around the world. If everyone in the world could have access to a computer and the Internet, how might society, culture, and the economy change?

2. **Trade** The formation of the European Union improved the economy of many nations in Europe and created a sense of unity. But not all people and all member nations were equally happy with the many changes. What were some of the unintended consequences of the formation of the EU?

3. **Cooperation** Is the work of NGOs essential in the 21st century? Think about the work that organizations like the International Red Cross do. Are there situations in which an NGO would be better suited to provide relief than a government or an organization like the United Nations? Why might groups of people in some situations be more likely to welcome aid from an NGO than from a government?

4. **Democracy** Look at the image at the start of this chapter. Artificial satellites can transmit phone messages or television pictures anywhere on Earth. Do you think better communication will lead to the spread of democracy? Explain.

■ Connections to Today

1. **Advances in Science: Medical Procedures** In 1954, American doctor Joseph Murray performed the first organ transplant, successfully transplanting a kidney from a man into his twin brother. In 2004, nearly 30,000 organ transplants were performed. Think about the issues that people grappled with decades ago as they considered the ethics of organ transplantation. Then choose a medical procedure that is being debated today. (Possibilities might include stem cell research, genetic cloning, or the use of surrogate mothers.) Research your topic and then write two paragraphs: one that supports the procedure and one that opposes it.

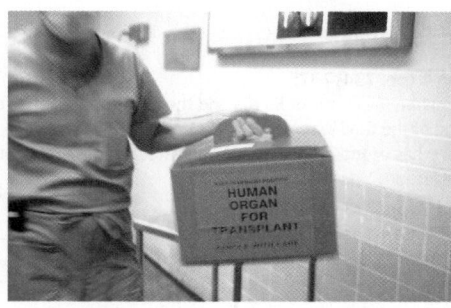

2. **Cultural Diffusion: Spread of Popular Culture** During the 20th century, American popular culture—especially American movies, music, and clothing—influenced people around the world. Consider the factors necessary for cultural diffusion. Why is popular culture from the United States widely influential? Predict which countries' popular culture will become widely influential in the early 21st century.

| 1997 **The Asian financial crisis hits.** | | Sept. 11, 2001 **Al Qaeda attacks the United States.** | | **History** *Interactive* **For:** Interactive timeline **Web Code:** nbp-3461 | | |

| **2000** | | **2005** | | **2010** | |

| | 2000 **Vladimir Putin is elected president of Russia.** | October 2001 **The United States begins war on the Taliban in Afghanistan.** | Dec. 26, 2004 **Tsunami devastates Southeast Asia.** | 2007 **The United States commits more troops to Iraq and Afghanistan.** |

Concept Connector

Tell students that the main concepts for this chapter are Trade, Technology, Cooperation, Democracy, and Human Rights, and then ask them to answer the Essential Question Review questions on this page. Discuss the Connections to Today topics and ask students to answer the questions that follow.

Essential Question Review

1. Responses should suggest that a computer and Internet access would bring users new ideas and information.

2. Responses should note that member countries did not foresee efforts by Eastern European countries to join the EU. Members fear that countries with weaker economies, along with rapid change, will destabilize the EU. Others worry about cultural differences between members.

3. NGOs are essential in their ability to enter situations of high political or ethnic tension. Because they do not represent any particular government or nation, they are neutral and thus more easily accepted.

4. Students may agree that communication devices could result in democratic reforms. Images of violence by governments against its citizens; violations of laws; and abuses of authority can be easily photographed and transmitted to large audiences, creating demands for democracy.

Connections to Today

1. Paragraphs should accurately explain the procedure and the supporting and opposing positions about it.

2. Cultural diffusion is aided by rapid communication, as disseminated by American film, television, and print media around the world. In addition, people from the United States travel frequently. Countries likely to influence culture in the twenty-first century could be from Asia, as these economies are growing rapidly.

For additional review of this **L3** chapter's core concepts, remind students to refer to the

Reading and Note Taking Study Guide
Concept Connector, pp. 242, 250, 259, 295, 300

Chapter Assessment

Terms, People, and Places

1. deficit
2. protectionism
3. Famine
4. Islamic fundamentalism
5. Artificial satellites

Main Ideas

6. Since Russia no longer controlled Eastern Europe or the other former Soviet republics, the U.S. became the world's sole superpower.

7. Japan's economy has slowed down, while China, Taiwan, Hong Kong, Singapore, and South Korea have had strong economic growth.

8. Economic interdependence is the dependence of countries on one another for resources, knowledge, and labor. It has increased with improvements in transportation and communications and the rise of free trade.

9. Globalization has exposed people to new ideas and technologies. However, it may allow rich nations to exploit poorer nations, and it could lead to increased economic imbalances.

10. national debts, lack of money to improve living standards, political unrest, poor government planning, and rapid population growth

11. pollution, nuclear accidents, growing deserts, shrinking forests, and global warming

12. Russia has lacked the money or the ability to dismantle or secure nuclear materials properly.

13. Al Qaeda is an Islamic fundamentalist group that has initiated repeated terrorist attacks against the U.S. and its interests abroad. They were responsible for the September 11, 2001, attacks on the World Trade Center.

14. Space exploration has led to new knowledge and advances in communications technology. Computers link people to each other and to information, speeding up many business processes.

Chapter Focus Question

15. Major issues include the changing balance of economic and political power; globalization; global poverty, disease, and natural disasters; human rights; environmental issues; the world's stockpile of WMDs; terrorism; and the wise use of technology.

Chapter Assessment

Chapter Assessment

Terms, People, and Places

Choose the italicized term in parentheses that best completes each sentence.

1. A *(deficit/default)* is the gap between what a government spends and what it takes in through taxes and other resources.
2. One of the WTO's basic policies is its opposition to *(outsourcing/protectionism)*.
3. *(Famine/Acid rain)* is a particular concern in areas where there has been a natural disaster.
4. The belief that society should be governed by Islamic law is known as *(Islamic fundamentalism/terrorism)*.
5. *(Genetics/Artificial satellites)* have revolutionized communications.

Main Ideas

Section 1 (pp. 734–737)
6. Describe the status of Russia and the United States after the end of the Cold War.
7. How has economic power in Asia shifted over the past couple of decades?

Section 2 (pp. 738–742)
8. What are the main characteristics of economic interdependence?
9. Summarize the benefits and costs of globalization.

Section 3 (pp. 744–751)
10. What are the main causes of poverty?
11. Describe some of the environmental challenges of the 21st century.

Section 4 (pp. 753–757)
12. Why are nuclear weapons a particular problem in Russia?
13. What is al Qaeda, and why is it such a threat?

Section 5 (pp. 758–763)
14. Summarize the impact of science and technology on modern life.

Chapter Focus Question
15. What are the major issues facing the world today?

● Writing About History

In this chapter's five Section Assessments, you developed skills to write a persuasive essay.

Write a Persuasive Essay Choose a topic that interests you—and that you have a strong opinion about—and then write a persuasive essay. You may choose your own topic or select from the following: free trade, global warming, the war on terrorism, WMDs, or HIV/AIDS. Consult page SH16 of the Writing Handbook for additional help.

Prewriting
• Do library or Internet research to read about each of the topics listed above.
• List questions about the topic and gather sources.

Critical Thinking

16. **Analyze Information** Which region do you think will be the most important economically during the next half-century: the EU, the Pacific Rim, or the United States? Explain your answer.
17. **Predict Consequences** What might be the global impact if terrorists cut off supplies of natural gas or another important resource to a large American city?
18. **Geography and History** Consider the space race of the late 1900s. Why have nations throughout history found it important to explore frontiers?
19. **Recognize Cause and Effect** In this chapter you have read about how economic and technological changes have had an impact on people around the world. How might these changes also affect people's values and beliefs?

"Nothing's labeled. How are we supposed to know which fruit has been genetically engineered?"

20. **Analyze Visuals** What point is the cartoonist making about genetically modified foods in the cartoon above?
21. **Recognize Cause and Effect** How does outsourcing jobs affect both the home country and the country where the jobs are outsourced?
22. **Draw Inferences** How can globalization bring about a stronger commitment to human rights? How can it encourage human rights abuses, such as child labor?

Drafting
• Develop your thesis and select persuasive arguments that support it.
• Organize and write the essay, using your second best argument in the introduction and your best argument in the conclusion.
• Include an example that many people can relate to.

Revising
• Use the guidelines for revising your report on page SH17 of the Writing Handbook.

Critical Thinking

16. Sample: The Pacific Rim will be the most important due to strong economic growth.

17. That city's economy would grind to a halt, and the United States might take military action to restore the supply.

18. Frontiers offer nations access to new resources and new areas of influence.

19. Awareness of other beliefs and values could bring both greater tolerance and a loss of traditional values.

20. that genetically modified food is different from other food

21. Outsourcing creates jobs in the country where the jobs are outsourced and eliminates some jobs in the home country.

22. Globalization can increase commitment to human rights by making people everywhere aware of suffering around the world. But it can encourage abuses by creating markets for products created by child labor or unsafe labor practices.

Document-Based Assessment

The Use of Alternative Energy

For many scientists, politicians, and citizens, energy consumption is a troubling issue. Most people agree that the world is too dependent on fossil fuels, which are not renewable. However, intense debate surrounds the questions of which alternate energy sources we should focus on and how quickly we need to have them developed.

Document A

U. S. Energy Consumption by Energy Source, 2007

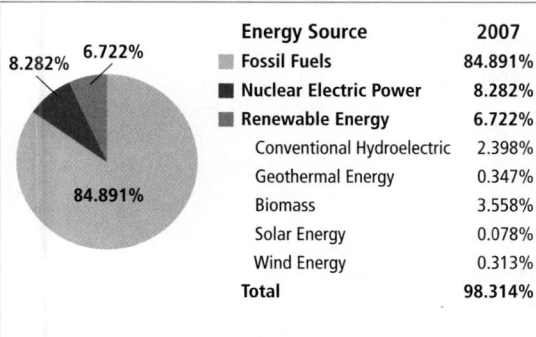

Energy Source	2007
Fossil Fuels	84.891%
Nuclear Electric Power	8.282%
Renewable Energy	6.722%
Conventional Hydroelectric	2.398%
Geothermal Energy	0.347%
Biomass	3.558%
Solar Energy	0.078%
Wind Energy	0.313%
Total	**98.314%**

SOURCE: *Energy Information Administration, 2003–2007*
Note: Percentages may not equal 100 due to rounding.

Document B

"As we approach the end of the twentieth century there is no single thing we can do that will have as large an impact on the people of the world during the new century than the development of solar power satellites. They will bring prosperity, an opportunity for the poor nations of the earth to achieve true freedom from want, healing of our environment, and open the vast new frontier of space to all of us.

. . . With the development of solar power satellites we will tap directly into the power of the sun and save the world from impending chaos. There will be hope for the future as we enter the twenty-first century."

—From ***Sun Power*** by Ralph Nansen

Document C

"Renewables are not without their drawbacks. Solar and wind farms cannot generate much electricity on cloudy or still days. As intermittent energy sources, they require vast systems to store the energy they produce, or must rely on the rest of the electrical system for backup. And despite federal subsidies to spur technological innovation, renewable sources have not become economical enough to seriously challenge fossil fuels in an open market."

—From ***CQ Researcher,*** November 7, 1997

Analyzing Documents

Use your knowledge of global issues and Documents A, B, and C to answer questions 1–4.

1. Which document is supported by the actual U.S. energy consumption data shown in Document A?
   A Document B
   B Document C
   C both Documents B and C
   D neither Document B nor C

2. Which statement best describes the viewpoint of the author of Document B?
   A Biomass generators are a better alternative to fossil fuel than solar powered satellites.
   B Solar powered satellites are the most promising alternative to fossil fuel.
   C Solar powered satellites are not realistic or cost effective as an alternative to fossil fuel.
   D More research must be carried out to determine whether solar powered satellites are a realistic alternative to fossil fuel.

3. According to Document C, all are drawbacks of renewables except which of the following?
   A They are intermittent energy sources.
   B They are not cost-efficient.
   C They rely on traditional electricity sources.
   D They are worse for the environment.

4. **Writing Task** What does our energy future hold? Make some predictions for 50 years in the future. Use information from these documents along with information from the chapter to support your predictions.

Document-Based Assessment

■ To help students understand the documents on the page, give them the following **TIP: As you study each document, write down at least one main idea from it. Use statements in the text, captions on photographs, and titles on maps, charts, and graphs to help you.**

■ To provide students with further practice in answering Document-Based Assessment Questions, go to 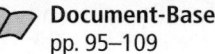 **Document-Based Assessment,** pp. 95–109

■ If students need more instruction on analyzing graphic data, have them read the **Skills Handbook,** p. SH28.

● Writing About History

As students begin the assignment, refer them to page SH16 of the **Writing Handbook** for help in writing a persuasive essay. Remind them of the steps they should take to complete their assignment, including prewriting, drafting, and revising. For help in revising, remind them to use the guidelines on page SH17 of the **Writing Handbook**.

Students' essays should define the issue under discussion, advance a clearly stated position, and support that position with specific reasons and evidence. They should contain an introduction, a body, and a conclusion. They should show evidence of reflection and be free of grammatical and spelling errors. For scoring rubrics for writing assignments, see **Assessment Rubrics,** p. 8.

Answers

1. B
2. B
3. D
4. Sample: Rising energy demands will force us to reduce our reliance on fossil fuels and increase the output of renewable energy technologies.

Contents

Overview

The Concept Connector Handbooks are a source of useful information for students as well as a versatile instruction tool for teachers. They provide students with a collection of basic definitions, explanations, and facts and figures that will support their study of world history. The handbooks can be presented at the beginning of the course to teach core concepts, or they can be presented at the end of the course to help prepare students for tests. You can also use them as a reference throughout the year.

Each handbook—Atlas and Geography, History, Economics, Science and Technology, Government and Civics, and Culture—is supported by a set of key concepts that help students see patterns across time and space. These concepts appear throughout the program in Concept Connector features, review materials, and worksheets. The concepts are distributed among the subject areas as follows:

- **Atlas and Geography:** Geography's Impact, Migration
- **History:** Conflict, Cooperation, Empire, Genocide, Nationalism, Revolution
- **Economics:** Economic Systems, Trade
- **Science and Technology:** Science and Technology
- **Government and Civics:** Democracy, Dictatorship, Political Systems
- **Culture:** Belief Systems, Cultural Diffusion, Human Rights, Impact of the Individual

Spanish doubloons

Lithuanian woman, 1991

The Concept Connector Handbooks provide you with reference information that will make it easier for you to compare key concepts and events across time and place.

Ancient Egypt

Great Wall of China

Detail of the Bayeux Tapestry

Concept Connector

Contents

Background

The Concept Connector Handbooks enable students to realize that history is not merely a sequence of events. The six handbook categories represent broad subject areas that students will explore throughout the textbook. Together, these areas cover all the major learning strands related to world history.

The handbooks explain basic concepts, often in the form of a glossary or table. They also connect events across time and place through timelines, maps, and other graphics. Students' awareness of these connections is essential to their critical understanding of world history. Some handbooks also contain additional information that can help students gain new perspectives.

Overview

Students need geography skills to understand the movement of people, the expansion of empires, the value of trade, the role of natural resources, and many other aspects of world history. The Atlas and Geography Handbook opens with a map of landforms and bodies of water. The map is paired with a glossary of the same geographic terms that are illustrated on the map. The following several pages present an atlas that depicts the physical and political world.

Test Preparation

■ **Glossary** Have groups of students create flashcards for the Glossary of Geographic Terms on the next two pages. Ask them to use the flashcards to help them learn the descriptions of each natural feature. Then have students create a story about the migration of a family across the landscape shown in the map titled Landforms and Bodies of Water. Stories should include most, if not all, of the geographic terms. Each group should then present their story to the class, using the map as a visual aid.

■ **Atlas** Have students examine the series of political and physical maps. Ask them to point out similarities and differences between the political and physical maps of the different continents. Invite pairs of students to quiz each other about the content of particular maps or pairs of maps. They might, for example, ask what the capital of a particular country is or what the elevation of a particular city is. The maps can also be used to review information presented in the text and maps. For example, after reading about World War II, students might be asked to show, on one of the maps of Europe, how Allied armies retook the continent from the Axis powers.

What Is Geography?

Geography is the study of Earth's features, including its people, their surroundings, and the resources available to them. By describing the human environment in different times and places, geographers have added to our knowledge of world history. Often those geographers must draw conclusions from limited evidence. For example, studies might turn up common artistic styles or religious rituals in two widely separated groups of people. A geographer might conclude that the groups traded with each other and, in the process, developed shared cultural traits. Geographers use their favorite tool, the map, to show the results of their observations.

Landforms and Water Bodies

volcano · flood plain · mesa · plateau · butte · canyon · bay · strait · island · isthmus · peninsula

Glossary of Geographic Terms

basin
an area that is lower than surrounding land areas; some basins are filled with water

bay
a part of a larger body of water that extends into the land

butte
a small, high, flat-topped landform with cliff-like sides

canyon
a deep, narrow valley with steep sides; often has a stream flowing through it

cataract
a large waterfall or steep rapids

delta
a plain at the mouth of a river, often triangular in shape, formed when sediment is deposited by flowing water

flood plain
a broad plain on either side of a river, formed when sediment settles during floods

glacier
a huge, slow-moving mass of snow and ice

hill
an area that rises above surrounding land and has a rounded top; lower and usually less steep than a mountain

island
an area of land completely surrounded by water

isthmus
a narrow strip of land that connects two larger areas of land

mesa
a high, flat-topped landform with cliff-like sides; larger than a butte

Bibliography

For the Teacher

Boehm, Richard and Sarah Bednarz. *Geography for Life: National Geography Standards.* National Council for Geographic Education, 1994.

Natoli, Salvatore J. *Strengthening Geography in the Social Studies,* Bulletin No. 81. National Council for the Social Studies, 1988.

For the Student

Black, Jeremy, ed. *World History Atlas.* Dorling Kindersley, 2005.

Ross, Val. *The Road to There: Mapmakers and Their Stories.* Tundra, 2003.

Waldman, Carl, et al. *Encyclopedia of Exploration.* Facts on File, 2004.

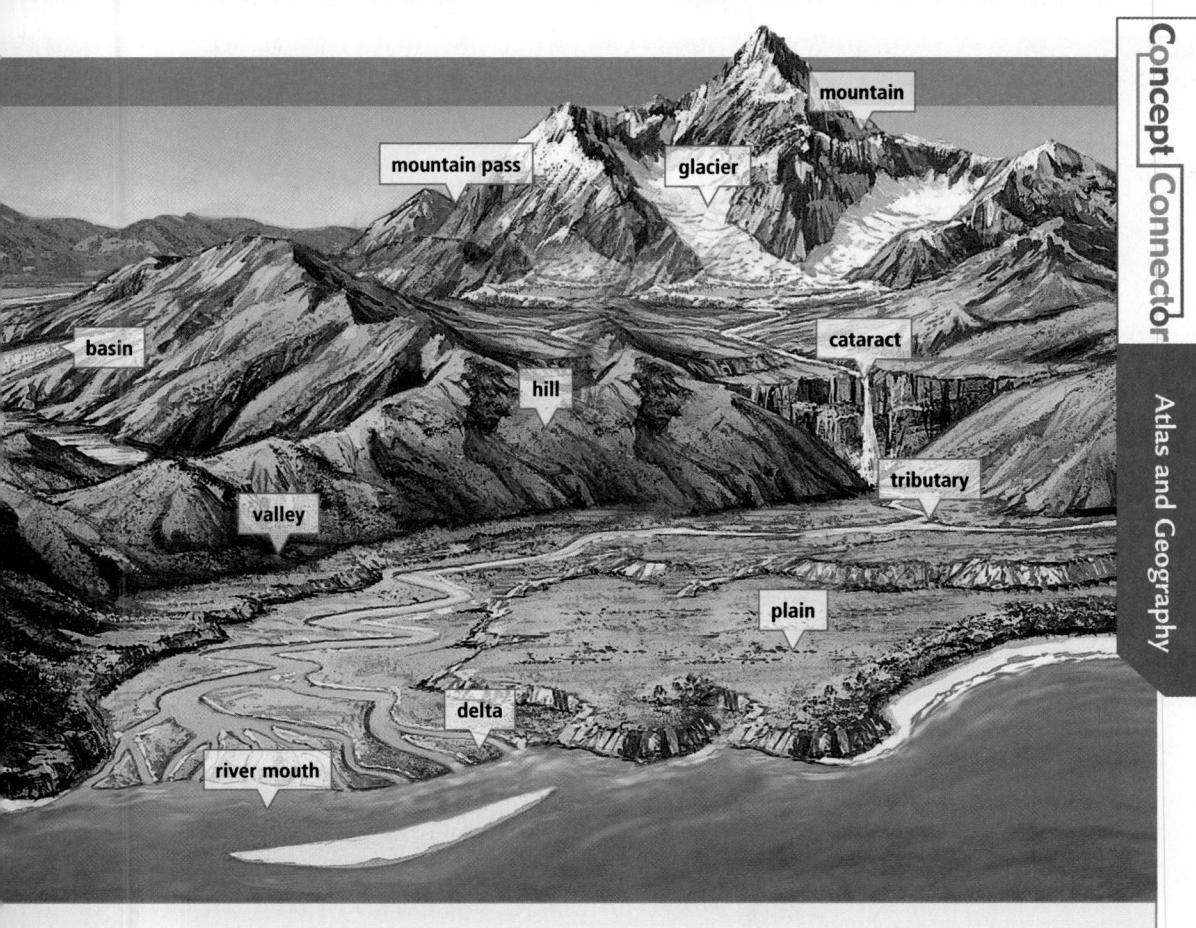

mountain
a landform that rises steeply at least 2,000 feet (610 m) above surrounding land; usually wide at the bottom and rising to a narrow peak or ridge

mountain pass
a gap between mountains

peninsula
an area of land almost completely surrounded by water and connected to the mainland by an isthmus

plain
a large area of flat or gently rolling land

plateau
a large, flat area that rises above the surrounding land; at least one side has a steep slope

river mouth
the point where a river enters a lake or sea

strait
a narrow stretch of water that connects two larger bodies of water

tributary
a river or stream that flows into a larger river

valley
a low stretch of land between mountains or hills; land that is drained by a river

volcano
an opening in the Earth's surface through which molten rock, ashes, and gases from the Earth's interior escape

Differentiated Instruction — Solutions for All Learners

L1 Special Needs   L2 Less Proficient Readers   L2 English Language Learners

Students can use the map to help them to understand the geographic terms in the glossary, and they can use the terms in the glossary to help them to clarify differences among the landforms and water bodies shown

on the map. Have students work back and forth between these two sources of geographic information until they have a clear understanding of all the natural features.

Atlas and Geography

The World: Political

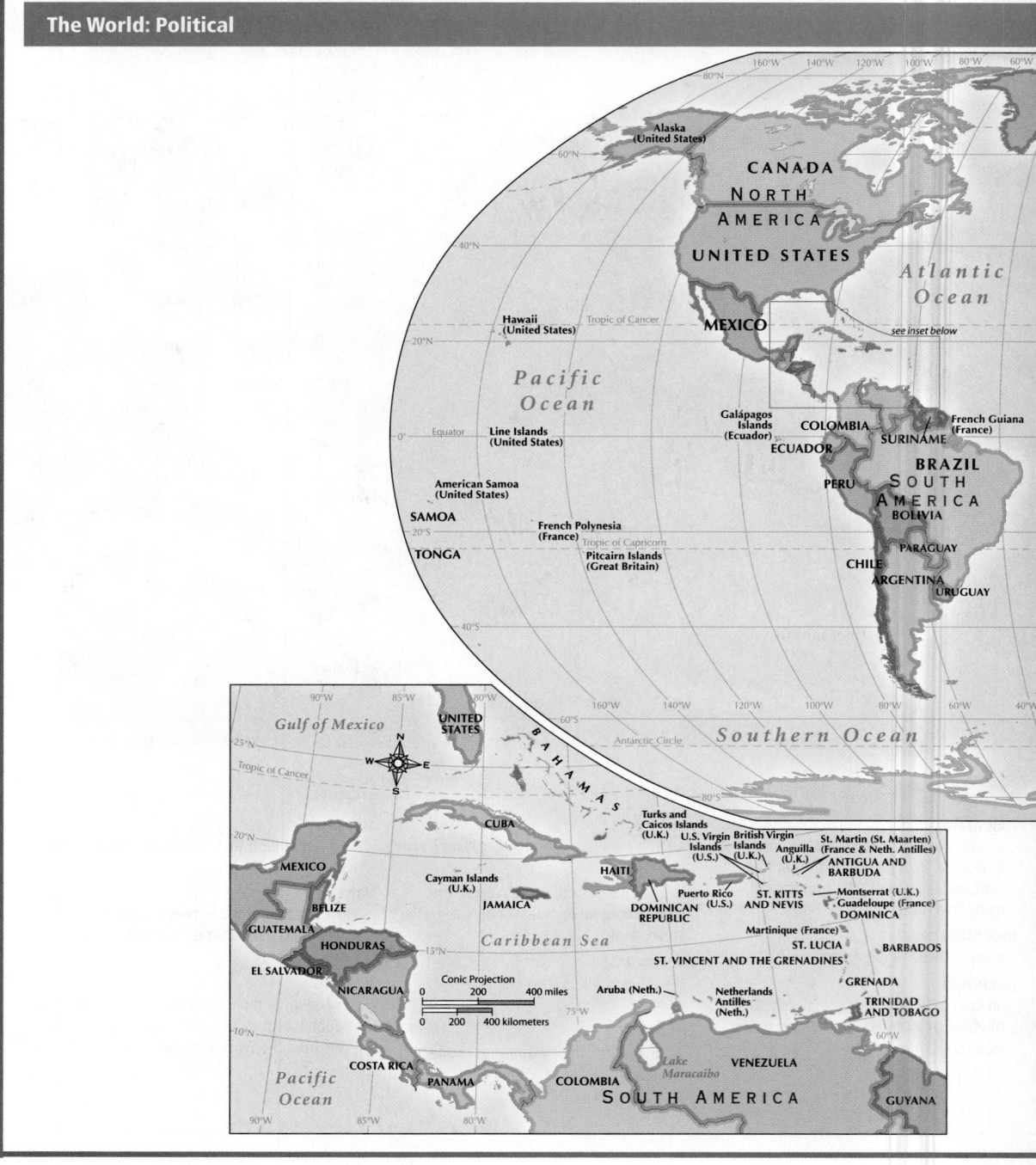

History Background

Historical Regions Geographers divide the world into continents and other geographical regions based on such attributes as physical features and climate. Historians, or more precisely, history itself, has also carved out regions that often vary from those of geographers. These regions have evolved based on their political or cultural characteristics. Examples include Western Europe, the West, Eastern Europe, the Balkans, East Asia, South Asia (or the Indian subcontinent), the Middle East, Southeast Asia, the West Indies, the East Indies, the Spice Islands, North Africa, West Africa, Sub-Saharan Africa, Palestine (Holy Land), and Mesoamerica. Students should be able to locate these historical regions and explain their relevance in world history.

Concept Connector

Atlas and Geography

Differentiated
Instruction   Solutions for All Learners

L4 Advanced Readers   L4 Gifted and Talented

To extend students' understanding of inset maps, ask them to study the inset maps within this political map of the world. Have them identify how the inset maps differ from the main map. *(Land areas are larger; additional features are labeled; more lines of latitude and* *longitude appear; the scale differs; the projection differs.)* Ask students to draw a conclusion about the value of inset maps. Then ask them to list other places in this atlas where an inset map might be useful and what that inset map could illustrate.

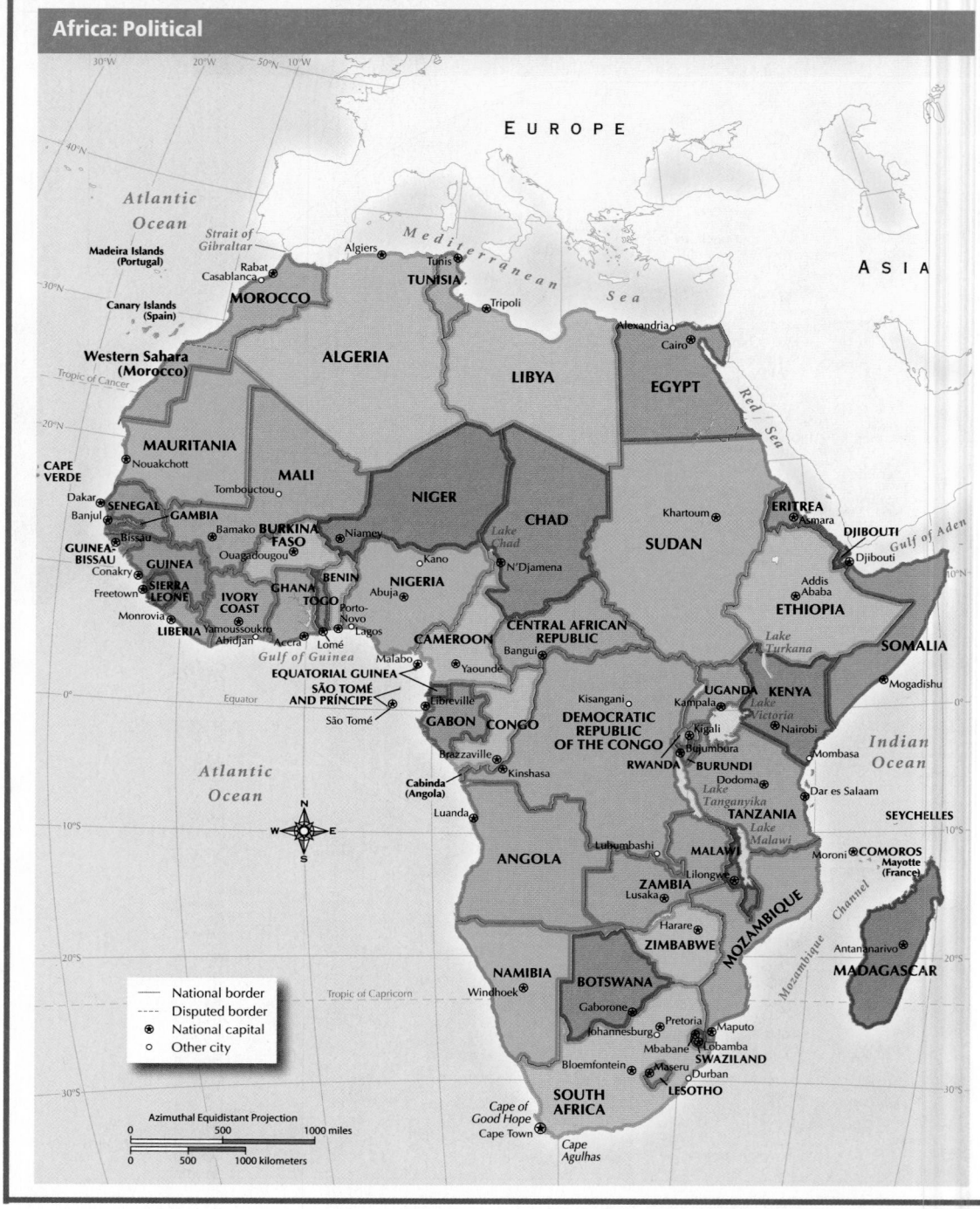

Africa: Political

EUROPE

ASIA

Atlantic Ocean

Strait of Gibraltar

Algiers

Tunis

Mediterranean Sea

Madeira Islands (Portugal)

Rabat

Casablanca

MOROCCO

TUNISIA

Tripoli

Alexandria

Cairo

Canary Islands (Spain)

Western Sahara (Morocco)

Tropic of Cancer

ALGERIA

LIBYA

EGYPT

Red Sea

MAURITANIA

Nouakchott

MALI

Tombouctou

NIGER

CHAD

Khartoum

ERITREA

Asmara

DJIBOUTI

Gulf of Aden

CAPE VERDE

Dakar

SENEGAL

Banjul

GAMBIA

Bamako

BURKINA FASO

Niamey

Lake Chad

SUDAN

Djibouti

Bissau

GUINEA-BISSAU

GUINEA

Conakry

Ouagadougou

Kano

N'Djamena

Addis Ababa

SIERRA LEONE

Freetown

IVORY COAST

GHANA

BENIN

TOGO

NIGERIA

Abuja

ETHIOPIA

Monrovia

LIBERIA

Yamoussoukro

Abidjan

Accra

Porto-Novo

Lomé

Lagos

CAMEROON

CENTRAL AFRICAN REPUBLIC

Lake Turkana

SOMALIA

Malabo

Gulf of Guinea

Yaoundé

Bangui

UGANDA

KENYA

Mogadishu

EQUATORIAL GUINEA

SÃO TOMÉ AND PRÍNCIPE

Libreville

Kisangani

Kampala

Lake Victoria

Equator

São Tomé

GABON

CONGO

DEMOCRATIC REPUBLIC OF THE CONGO

Kigali

Nairobi

Brazzaville

RWANDA

Bujumbura

BURUNDI

Mombasa

Indian Ocean

Cabinda (Angola)

Kinshasa

Dodoma

Dar es Salaam

Atlantic Ocean

Luanda

Lake Tanganyika

TANZANIA

SEYCHELLES

Lubumbashi

MALAWI

Lake Malawi

Moroni

COMOROS

Mayotte (France)

ANGOLA

ZAMBIA

Lilongwe

Lusaka

Harare

MOZAMBIQUE

Mozambique Channel

Antananarivo

NAMIBIA

ZIMBABWE

BOTSWANA

MADAGASCAR

Tropic of Capricorn

Windhoek

Gaborone

Pretoria

Maputo

Johannesburg

Mbabane

Lobamba

SWAZILAND

Bloemfontein

Maseru

Durban

LESOTHO

Cape of Good Hope

SOUTH AFRICA

Cape Town

Cape Agulhas

— National border
--- Disputed border
⊗ National capital
○ Other city

Azimuthal Equidistant Projection

0   500   1000 miles

0   500   1000 kilometers

Africa: Physical

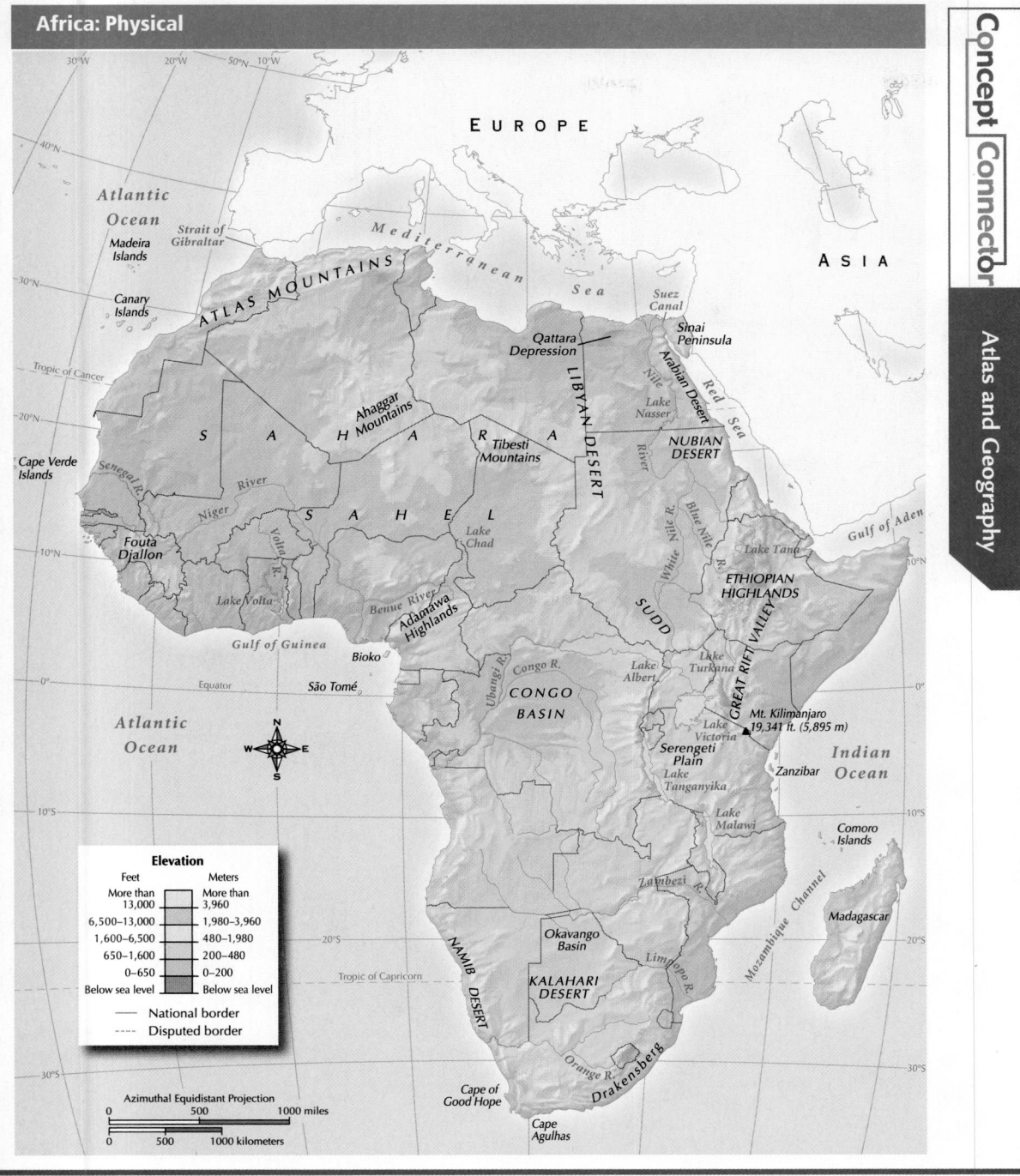

EUROPE

ASIA

Atlantic
Ocean

Madeira
Islands

Strait of
Gibraltar

Mediterranean   Sea

Canary
Islands

Tropic of Cancer

ATLAS MOUNTAINS

Suez
Canal

Sinai
Peninsula

Qattara
Depression

LIBYAN DESERT

Arabian Desert

Red Sea

Nile

Lake
Nasser

Ahaggar
Mountains

S   A   H   A   R   A

Tibesti
Mountains

NUBIAN
DESERT

Cape Verde
Islands

Senegal R.

River

Niger

S   A   H   E   L

Lake
Chad

River

White Nile R.

Blue Nile R.

Lake Tana

Gulf of Aden

Fouta
Djallon

Volta R.

Lake Volta

Benue River

Adamawa
Highlands

ETHIOPIAN
HIGHLANDS

Gulf of Guinea

Bioko

SUDD

Ubangi R.

Congo R.

Lake
Albert

Lake
Turkana

GREAT RIFT VALLEY

Equator

São Tomé

CONGO
BASIN

Lake
Victoria

Mt. Kilimanjaro
19,341 ft. (5,895 m)

Atlantic
Ocean

N
W   E
S

Serengeti
Plain

Lake
Tanganyika

Zanzibar

Indian
Ocean

Lake
Malawi

Comoro
Islands

Elevation

Feet	Meters
More than 13,000	More than 3,960
6,500–13,000	1,980–3,960
1,600–6,500	480–1,980
650–1,600	200–480
0–650	0–200
Below sea level	Below sea level

—— National border
---- Disputed border

Zambezi R.

Mozambique Channel

Madagascar

Okavango
Basin

Limpopo R.

NAMIB DESERT

KALAHARI
DESERT

Tropic of Capricorn

Azimuthal Equidistant Projection

0   500   1000 miles

0   500   1000 kilometers

Orange R.

Drakensberg

Cape of
Good Hope

Cape
Agulhas

30°W   20°W   50°N   10°W

40°N

30°N

20°N

10°N

0°

10°S

20°S

30°S

Atlas and Geography

Asia: Political

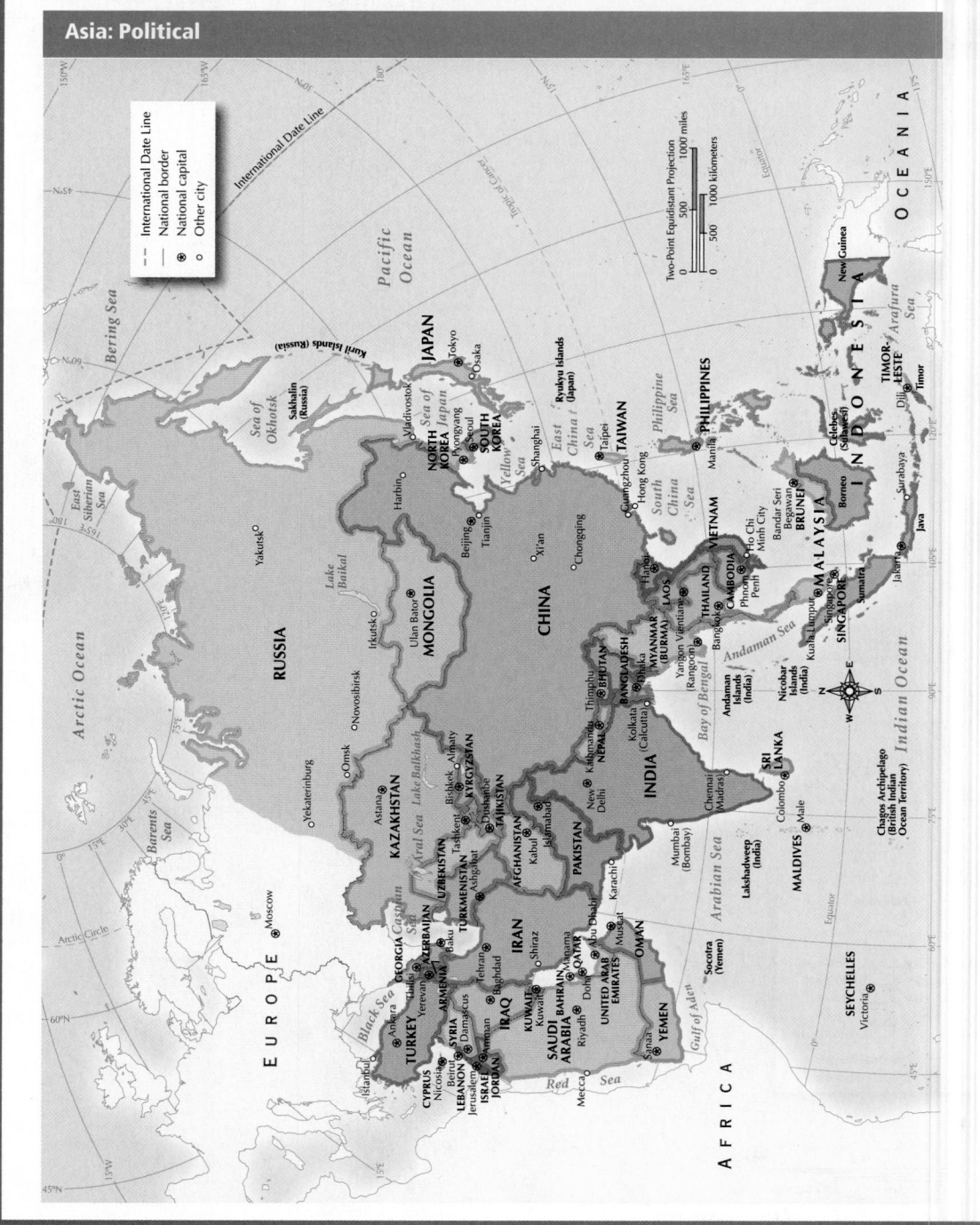

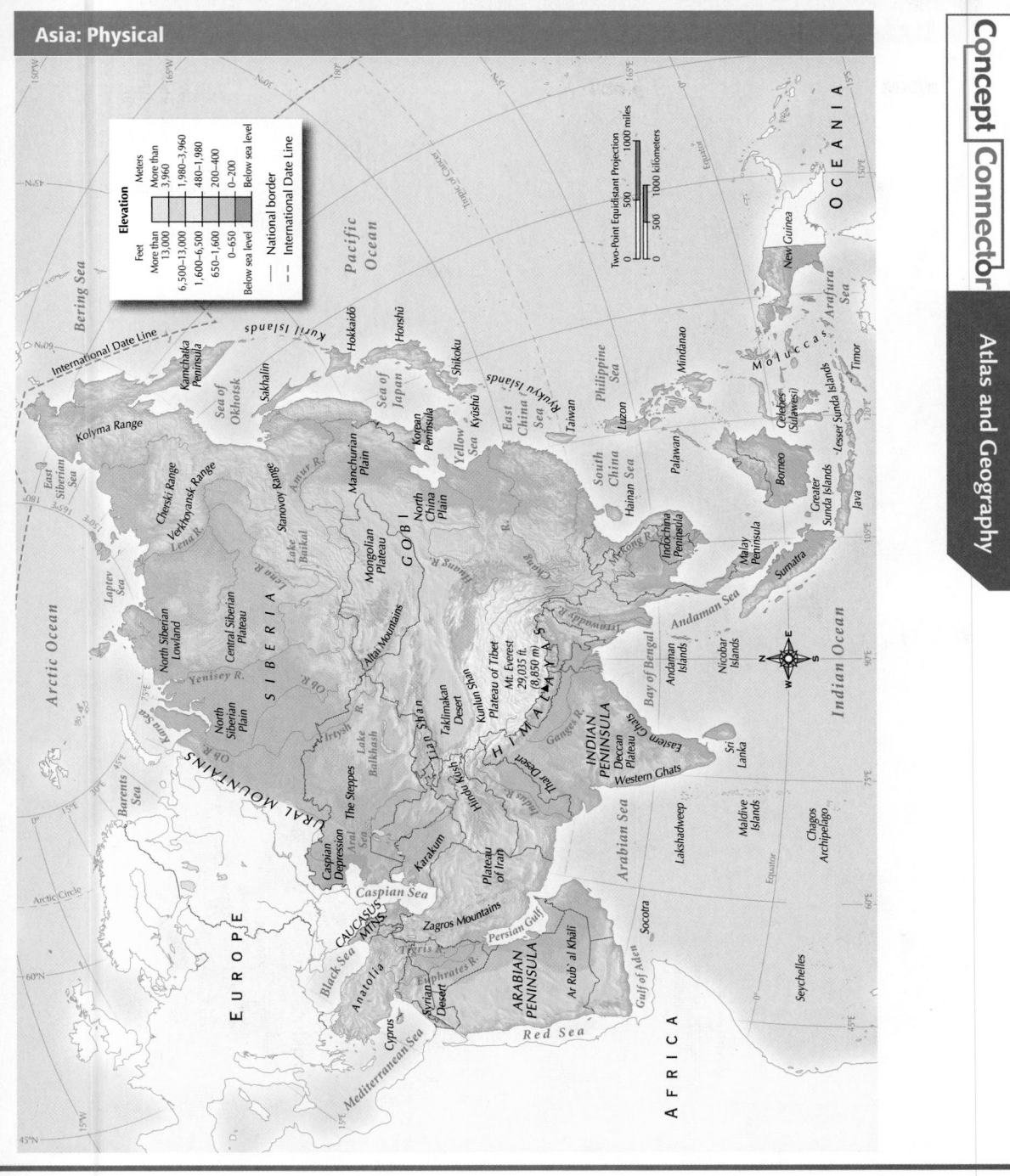

Asia: Physical

Elevation

Feet	Meters
More than 13,000	More than 3,960
6,500–13,000	1,980–3,960
1,600–6,500	480–1,980
650–1,600	200–400
0–650	0–200
Below sea level	Below sea level

— National border
-- International Date Line

Two-Point Equidistant Projection

Atlas and Geography

Europe: Political

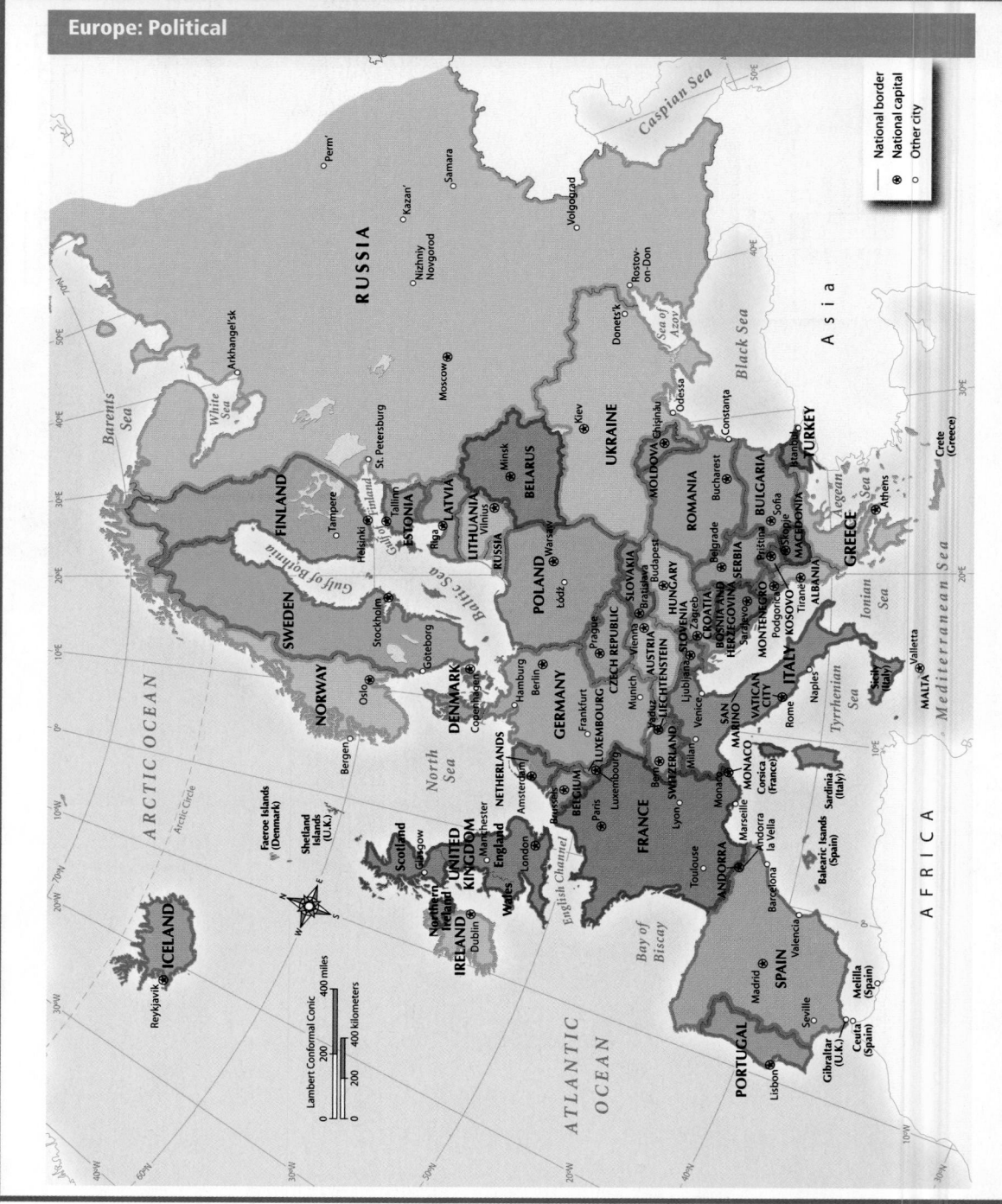

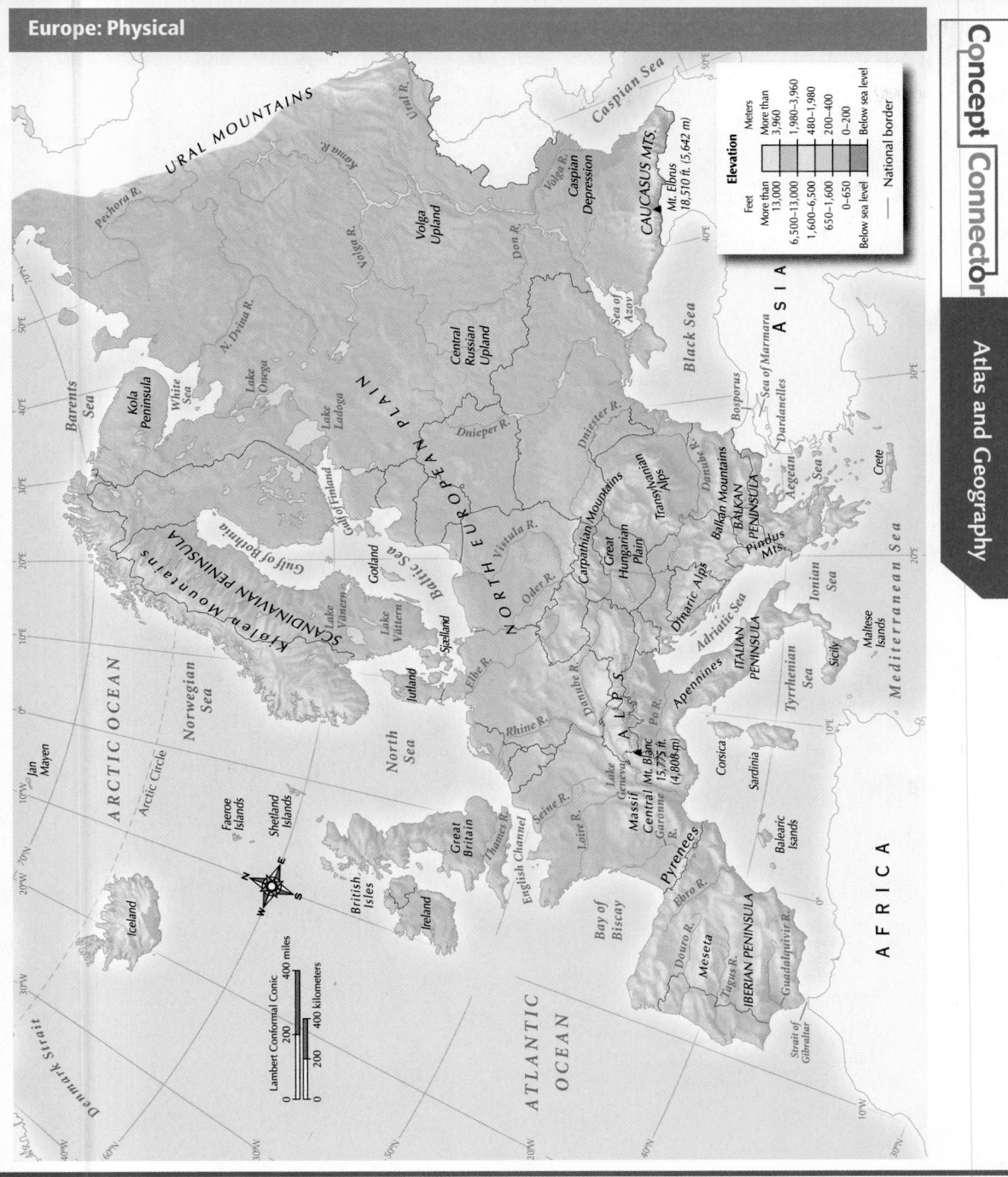

Elevation

Feet	Meters
More than 13,000	More than 3,960
6,500–13,000	1,980–3,960
1,600–6,500	480–1,980
650–1,600	200–400
0–650	0–200
Below sea level	Below sea level

— National border

Concept Connector

Atlas and Geography

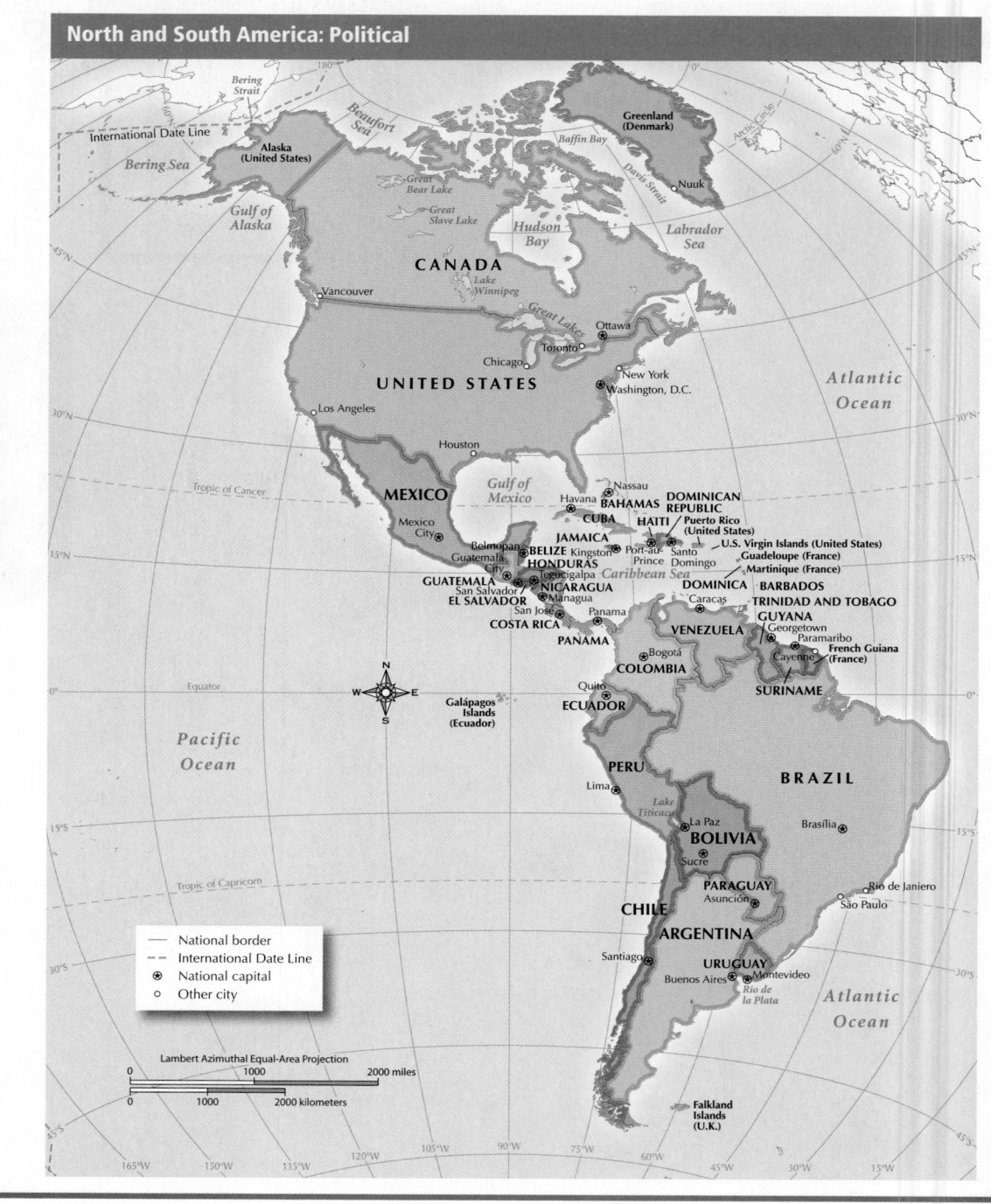

Atlas and Geography

North and South America: Political

- — National border
- – – International Date Line
- ⊛ National capital
- ○ Other city

Lambert Azimuthal Equal-Area Projection

0 1000 2000 miles

0 1000 2000 kilometers

North and South America: Physical

Mt. McKinley (Denali) 20,320 ft. (6,194 m)

Aconcagua 22,834 ft. (6,960 m)

Elevation

Feet		Meters
More than 13,000		More than 3,960
6,500–13,000		1,980–3,960
1,600–6,500		480–1,980
650–1,600		200–400
0–650		0–200
Below sea level		Below sea level

—— National border

- - - International Date Line

Lambert Azimuthal Equal-Area Projection

0   1000   2000 miles

0   1000   2000 kilometers

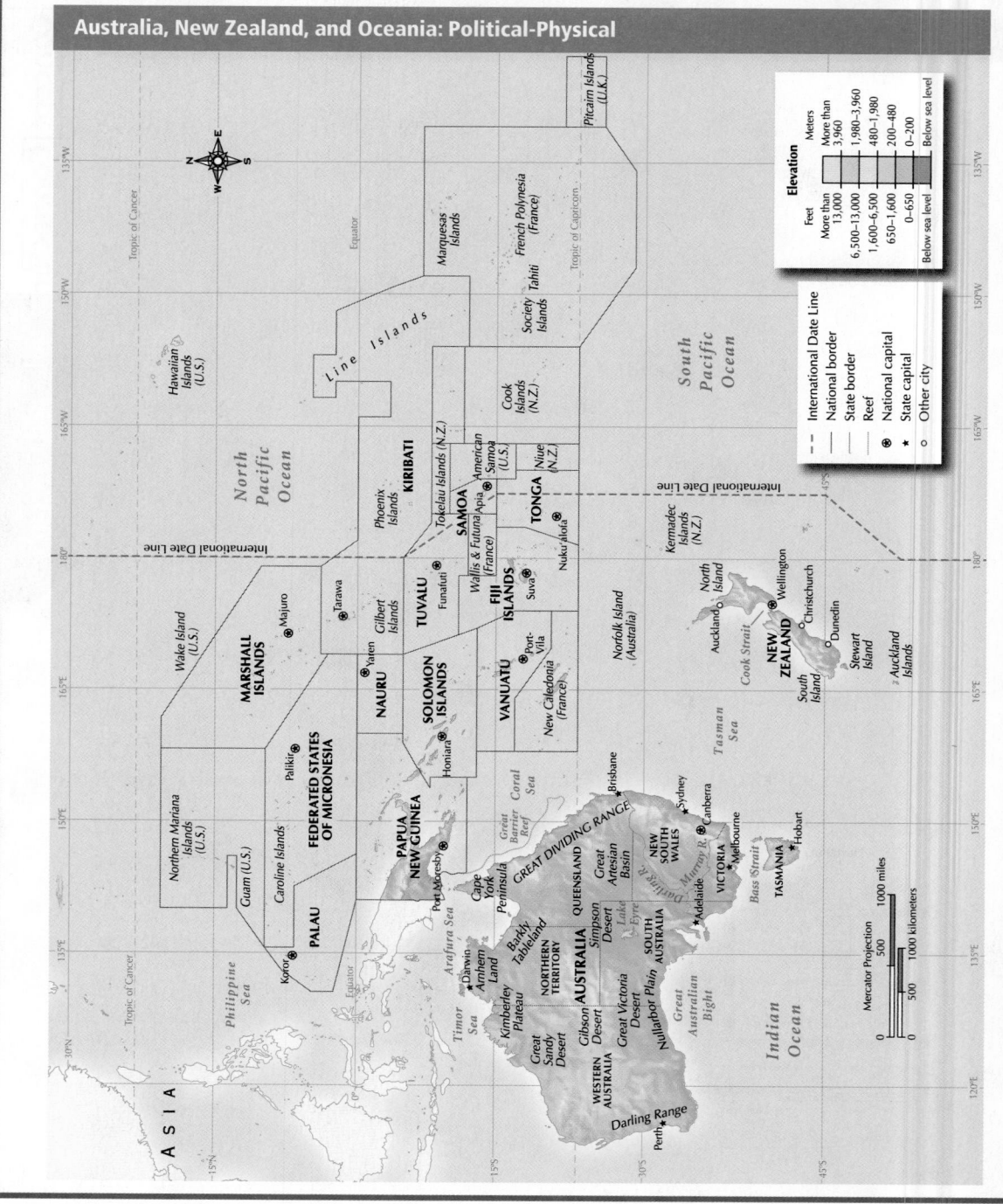

Australia, New Zealand, and Oceania: Political-Physical

Elevation

Feet	Meters
More than 13,000	More than 3,960
6,500–13,000	1,980–3,960
1,600–6,500	480–1,980
650–1,600	200–480
0–650	0–200
Below sea level	Below sea level

- – – International Date Line
- —— National border
- —— State border
- Reef
- ⊛ National capital
- ★ State capital
- ○ Other city

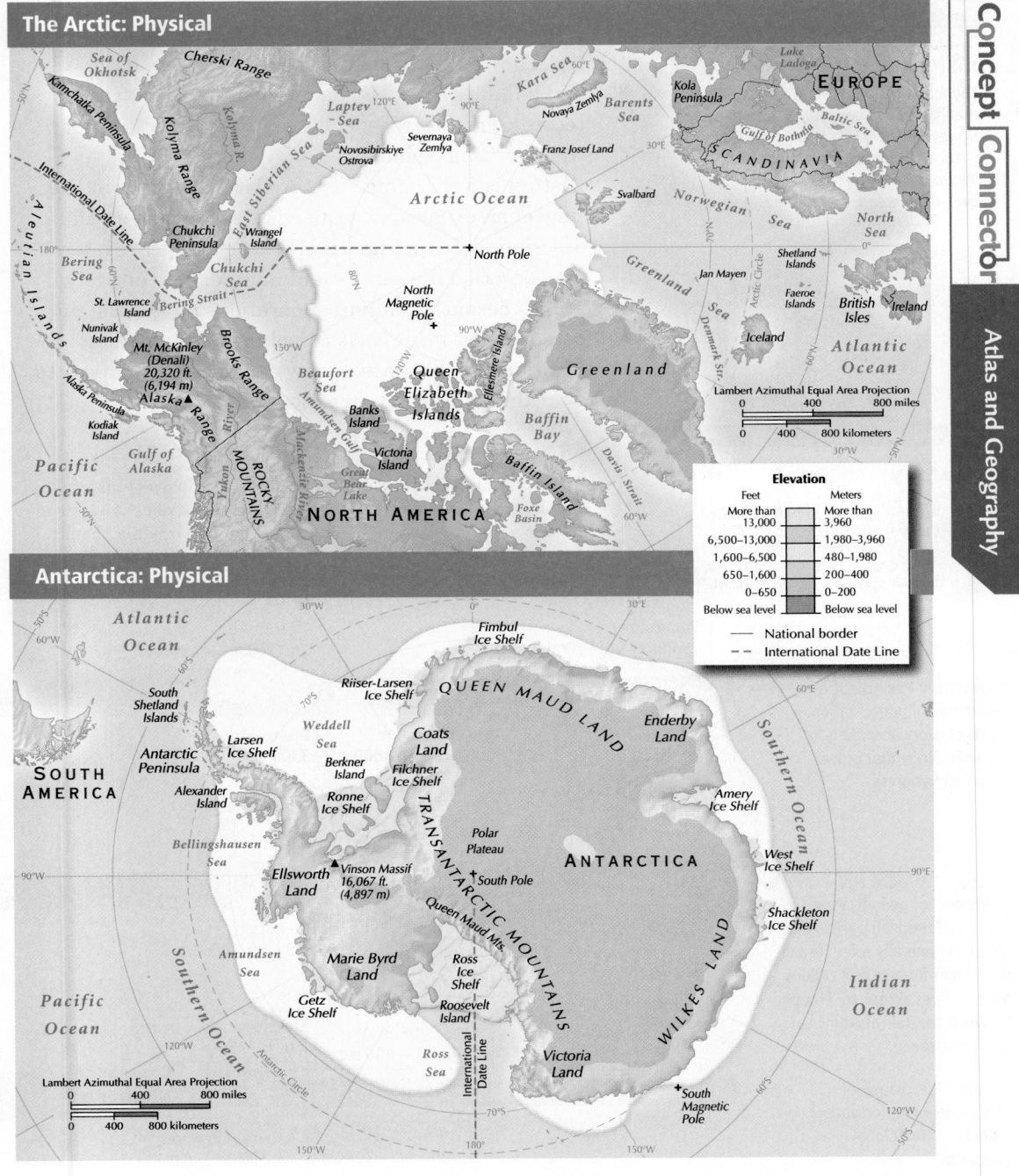

The Arctic: Physical

Sea of Okhotsk
Kamchatka Peninsula
Cherski Range
Kolyma Range
Kolyma R.
Laptev Sea
120°E
Novosibirskiye Ostrova
Severnaya Zemlya
East Siberian Sea
Kara Sea
60°E
Novaya Zemlya
Barents Sea
Franz Josef Land
30°E
Kola Peninsula
Gulf of Bothnia
Baltic Sea
Lake Ladoga
EUROPE
SCANDINAVIA

International Date Line
Aleutian Islands
180°
Bering Sea
Chukchi Peninsula
Wrangel Island
Chukchi Sea
Arctic Ocean
North Pole
Svalbard
Norwegian Sea
Greenland Sea
Jan Mayen
Arctic Circle
Shetland Islands
North Sea
0°
60°N
St. Lawrence Island
Bering Strait
Nunivak Island
80°N
North Magnetic Pole
90°W
Faeroe Islands
Iceland
British Isles
Ireland
Denmark Str.
Atlantic Ocean

Mt. McKinley (Denali) 20,320 ft. (6,194 m)
Alaska ▲
Brooks Range
150°W
120°W
Beaufort Sea
Queen Elizabeth Islands
Ellesmere Island
Greenland
60°N

Kodiak Island
Alaska Peninsula
Yukon River
Alaska Range
ROCKY MOUNTAINS
Mackenzie River
Amundsen Gulf
Banks Island
Victoria Island
Great Bear Lake
Baffin Bay
Baffin Island
Davis Strait

Pacific Ocean
Gulf of Alaska
NORTH AMERICA
Foxe Basin
60°W

Lambert Azimuthal Equal Area Projection
0 — 400 — 800 miles
0 — 400 — 800 kilometers
30°W

Elevation

Feet	Meters
More than 13,000	More than 3,960
6,500–13,000	1,980–3,960
1,600–6,500	480–1,980
650–1,600	200–400
0–650	0–200
Below sea level	Below sea level

— National border
-- International Date Line

Antarctica: Physical

Atlantic Ocean
30°W
0°
30°E
Fimbul Ice Shelf
60°S
60°E
Riiser-Larsen Ice Shelf
QUEEN MAUD LAND
Enderby Land
Southern Ocean
South Shetland Islands
70°S
Weddell Sea
Larsen Ice Shelf
Coats Land
Antarctic Peninsula
Berkner Island
Filchner Ice Shelf
Amery Ice Shelf
SOUTH AMERICA
Alexander Island
Ronne Ice Shelf
TRANSANTARCTIC MOUNTAINS
Polar Plateau
ANTARCTICA
West Ice Shelf
90°W
Bellingshausen Sea
Vinson Massif 16,067 ft. (4,897 m) ▲
South Pole
90°E
Ellsworth Land
Queen Maud Mts.
Shackleton Ice Shelf
Amundsen Sea
Marie Byrd Land
Ross Ice Shelf
WILKES LAND
Indian Ocean
Pacific Ocean
120°W
Getz Ice Shelf
Roosevelt Island
Victoria Land
Southern Ocean
Antarctic Circle
Ross Sea
International Date Line
South Magnetic Pole
120°E
150°W
180°
150°E
70°S
60°S

Lambert Azimuthal Equal Area Projection
0 — 400 — 800 miles
0 — 400 — 800 kilometers

Overview

This handbook begins by giving students a historian's perspective on the history of the world, along with some basic dating methods and periodization timelines. It also offers a continent-by-continent chronology of major events, again in timeline form. The remaining pages explore conquest, conflict, and cooperation through tables, lists, and a map.

Test Preparation

- **Timeline Quiz** Ask students to prepare a list of five multiple-choice questions that test the skill of reading timelines. They should base their questions on the timelines in this handbook. Have pairs of students take each other's test.

- **Essay** Point out the definitions of imperialism, colonialism, nationalism, and revolution in the student text. Have students consider how imperialism or colonialism might lead to nationalism and revolution. Ask them to write an essay exploring the cause-and-effect relationships among these concepts. Encourage students to use the tables titled Selected Empires in World History and Selected Conflicts in World History for examples that fit the points they are making in their essays.

Concept Connector Handbooks

History

Historians study how people lived in the past. They might examine their tools, weapons, jewelry, and building sites, but they rely mainly on written records. For this reason, we say that history began when writing began.

History is a changing story. A historian living at the time of an event may write what seems like a valid description, but a historian writing 100 years later may describe the same event another way entirely. This is because different generations have different perspectives on, or ways of looking at, history. In addition, as time passes, new evidence may appear to alter the interpretation of an event.

History and Prehistory

You might think of history as everything that has ever happened. For historians, however, history began around 5,000 years ago with the appearance of writing in two civilizations—Sumer and Egypt. Everything before that is prehistory.

Prehistory   **3000 B.C.**   **History**

Writing systems appear in Sumer (above) and in Egypt *c.* 3000 B.C.*

* The *c.* before the date is Latin for *circa*, meaning iaround " or "approximately."

Major Eras in World History

Historians attempt to make sense of vast stretches of history by dividing them into periods. This periodization makes it easier to discuss a group of events by relating them to a broader theme.

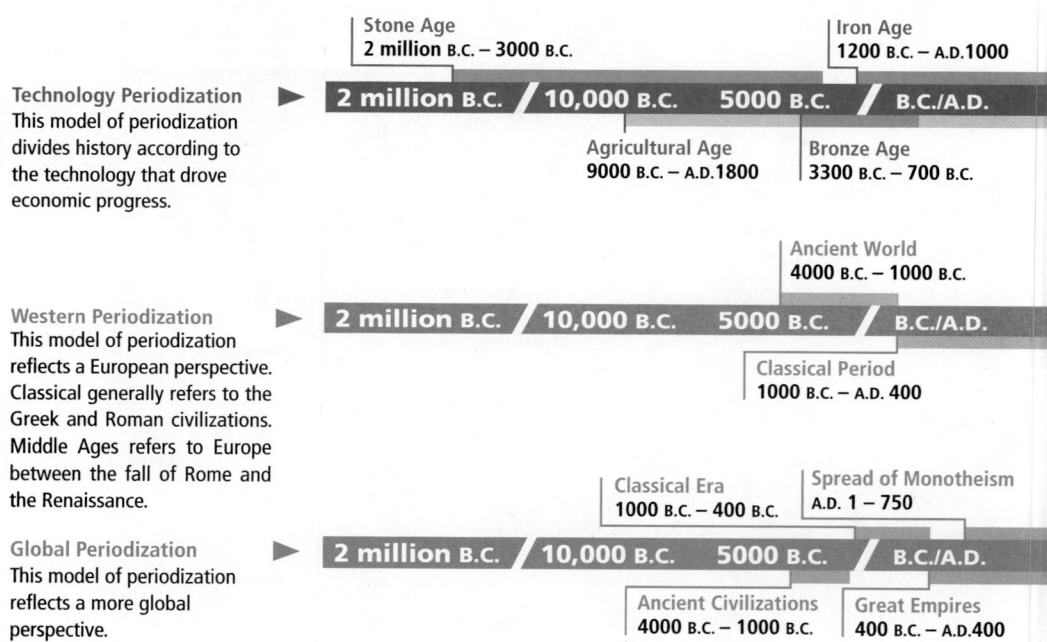

Technology Periodization
This model of periodization divides history according to the technology that drove economic progress.

| Stone Age | Iron Age |
| 2 million B.C. – 3000 B.C. | 1200 B.C. – A.D.1000 |

2 million B.C. / 10,000 B.C. 5000 B.C. / B.C./A.D.

| Agricultural Age | Bronze Age |
| 9000 B.C. – A.D.1800 | 3300 B.C. – 700 B.C. |

Western Periodization
This model of periodization reflects a European perspective. Classical generally refers to the Greek and Roman civilizations. Middle Ages refers to Europe between the fall of Rome and the Renaissance.

Ancient World
4000 B.C. – 1000 B.C.

2 million B.C. / 10,000 B.C. 5000 B.C. / B.C./A.D.

Classical Period
1000 B.C. – A.D. 400

Global Periodization
This model of periodization reflects a more global perspective.

Classical Era
1000 B.C. – 400 B.C.

Spread of Monotheism
A.D. 1 – 750

2 million B.C. / 10,000 B.C. 5000 B.C. / B.C./A.D.

Ancient Civilizations
4000 B.C. – 1000 B.C.

Great Empires
400 B.C. – A.D.400

Bibliography

For the Teacher

Diamond, Jared. *Guns, Germs, and Steel: The Fates of Human Societies.* Norton, 1999.

Kohn, George Childs. *Dictionary of Historic Documents,* rev. ed. Facts On File, 2003.

Roberts, J. M. *Ancient History: From the First Civilizations to the Renaissance.* Duncan Baird, 2004.

For the Student

Brewer, Paul. *Warfare in the Ancient World.* Raintree Steck-Vaughan, 1999.

Corrick, James A. *The Industrial Revolution.* Lucent, 1998.

Williams, Brian. *The Modern World: From the French Revolution to the Computer Age.* Bedrick, 1994.

Your textbook is divided this way, into units. Each unit deals with a period, or era, in world history. There are endless ways to categorize the past, depending on one's point of view. The timelines below show three different examples of periodization.

Decades, Centuries, and Millenniums

Most nations today use a standard calendar that dates events from the believed birth of Jesus. For dates preceding his birth, this calendar uses the abbreviation b.c. ("before Christ"). For dates after his birth, it uses A.D. (anno Domini, Latin for "in the year of our Lord"). An alternative version of this calendar uses the abbreviations B.C.E. and C.E. meaning "Before the Common Era" and "Common Era."

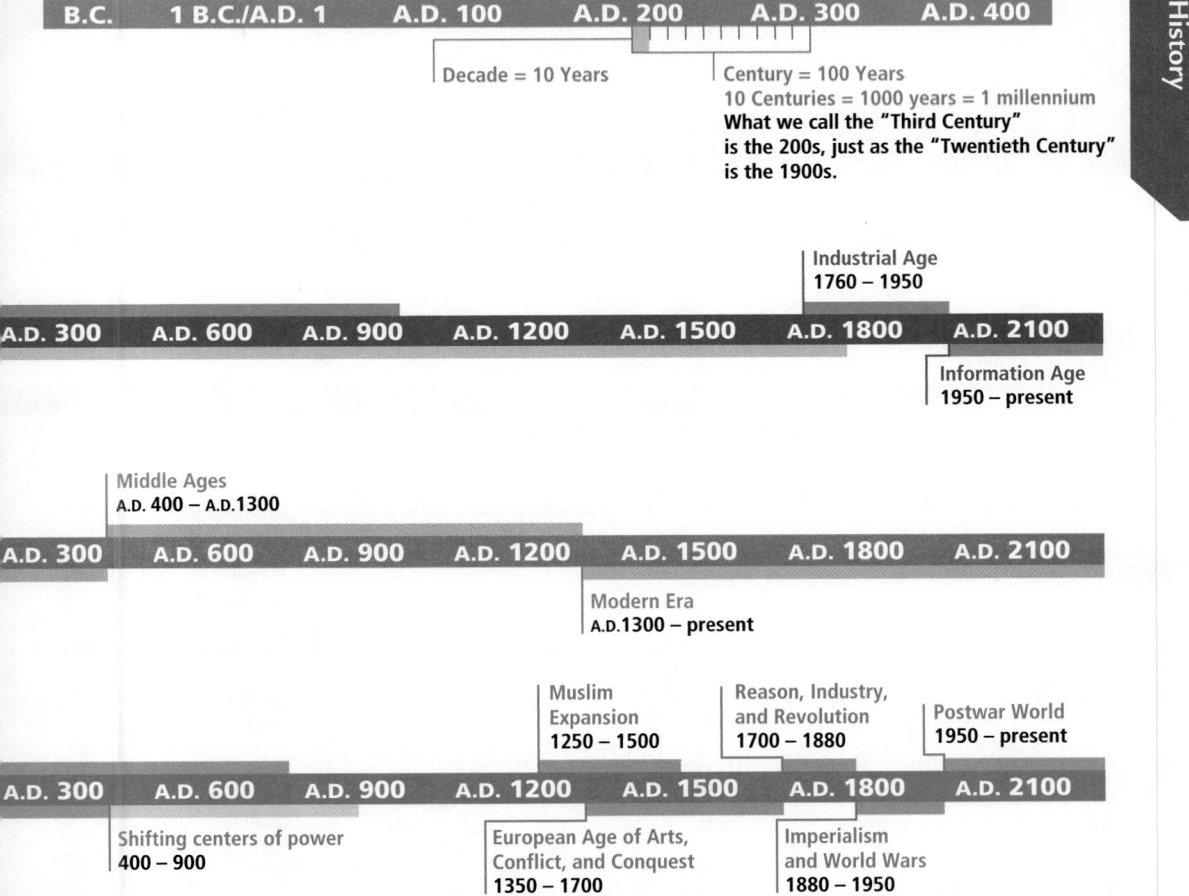

B.C. | 1 B.C./A.D. 1 | A.D. 100 | A.D. 200 | A.D. 300 | A.D. 400

Decade = 10 Years

Century = 100 Years
10 Centuries = 1000 years = 1 millennium
What we call the "Third Century" is the 200s, just as the "Twentieth Century" is the 1900s.

Industrial Age
1760 – 1950

A.D. 300 | A.D. 600 | A.D. 900 | A.D. 1200 | A.D. 1500 | A.D. 1800 | A.D. 2100

Information Age
1950 – present

Middle Ages
A.D. 400 – A.D. 1300

A.D. 300 | A.D. 600 | A.D. 900 | A.D. 1200 | A.D. 1500 | A.D. 1800 | A.D. 2100

Modern Era
A.D. 1300 – present

Muslim Expansion
1250 – 1500

Reason, Industry, and Revolution
1700 – 1880

Postwar World
1950 – present

A.D. 300 | A.D. 600 | A.D. 900 | A.D. 1200 | A.D. 1500 | A.D. 1800 | A.D. 2100

Shifting centers of power
400 – 900

European Age of Arts, Conflict, and Conquest
1350 – 1700

Imperialism and World Wars
1880 – 1950

Analyzing the Visuals

■ Have students look at the visual that shows the split between history and prehistory. Ask **Are events that occurred in 5000 B.C. considered prehistory or history?** *(prehistory)* **Why?** *(because the appearance of writing determines the point at which history begins, and 5000 B.C. is 2,000 years before the first appearance of writing)*

■ Then point out the timeline on this page that illustrates decades and centuries and the shift from B.C. to A.D. Ask **What is one year that occurred during the seventeenth century?** *(any of the 1600s—technically, 1601–1700)* Point out that there is no year zero, because the shift from B.C. to A.D. is set at the estimated point of Jesus' birth, not the entire year of his birth. The year preceding that point is 1 B.C. The year following that point is A.D. 1.

■ Finally, discuss the timelines that represent three models of periodization. Ask **What era are we living in today, according to the technology model of periodization?** *(the Information Age)* **Why do you think the Industrial Revolution is referenced in both the technological and global models of periodization?** *(because it had both technological and global consequences)*

Analyzing the Visuals

■ Point out the timelines on these two pages. Be sure students know the meaning of the turning point symbol. Ask **What events shown on these timelines took place within 50 years of the date Columbus reached the Caribbean?** *(Height of Aztec empire, Ottoman Turks conquer Constantinople, Gutenberg Bible printed, Sonni Ali founds Songhai, Atlantic slave trade grows)* **Which, if any, of these events can you connect to Columbus's voyage?** *(Columbus, who sailed for Spain, can be connected to the Aztecs, who reached their height around the same time that the Spanish conquered them. He can also be connected to the slave trade, which the Spanish initiated.)*

■ Now have students look at the line graph on this page. Ask **What is the approximate population of the world today?** *(between 6 and 7 billion)* **What is the trend you see in the graph up to the year A.D. 1000?** *(very slow but steady growth of population)* **What is the trend since around A.D. 1700?** *(sharply faster growth of the population)* **What would need to happen to sharply change the modern trend?** *(much lower birth rates or higher death rates)*

History

World Regional Timelines

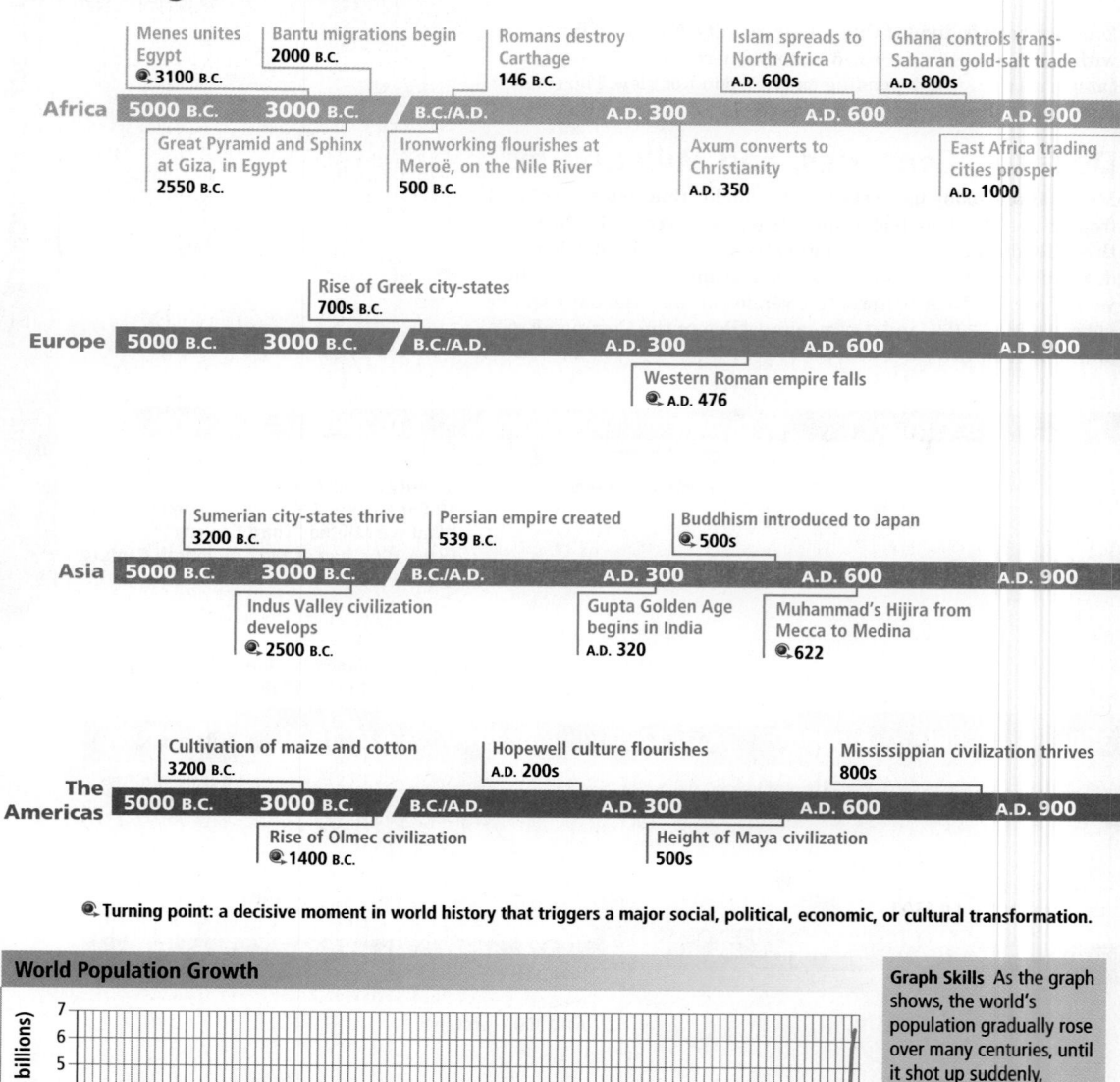

🔎 Turning point: a decisive moment in world history that triggers a major social, political, economic, or cultural transformation.

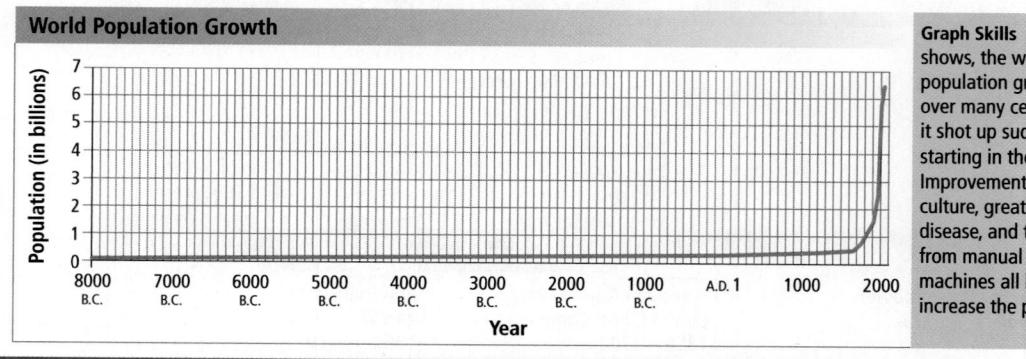

Graph Skills As the graph shows, the world's population gradually rose over many centuries, until it shot up suddenly, starting in the 1700s. Improvements in agriculture, greater control of disease, and the shift from manual labor to machines all helped to increase the population.

History Background

Population Growth The population of the world did not reach 1 billion through all of human history until A.D. 1800. The population rose to 2 billion just 130 years later, in 1930. Thirty years after that, it reached 3 billion (1960); fourteen years after that 4 billion (1974); thirteen years later 5 billion (1987); and twelve years later 6 billion (1999). Today, the two most populous countries are China, with 1.3 billion people, and India, with 1.1 billion people. The population of the United States is a distant third, at 302 million.

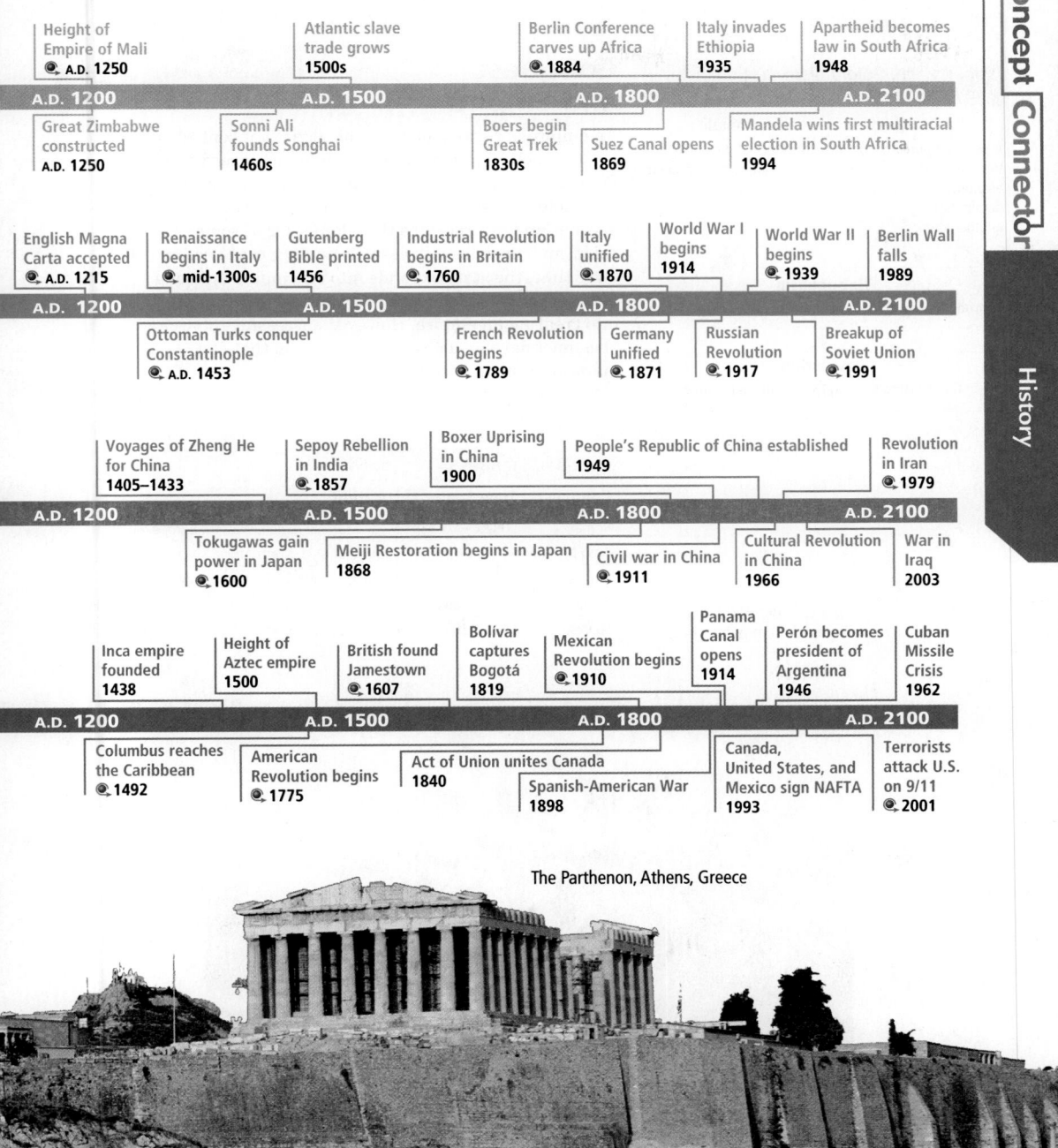

Africa timeline

Height of Empire of Mali
A.D. 1250

Atlantic slave trade grows
1500s

Berlin Conference carves up Africa
1884

Italy invades Ethiopia
1935

Apartheid becomes law in South Africa
1948

A.D. 1200 — A.D. 1500 — A.D. 1800 — A.D. 2100

Great Zimbabwe constructed
A.D. 1250

Sonni Ali founds Songhai
1460s

Boers begin Great Trek
1830s

Suez Canal opens
1869

Mandela wins first multiracial election in South Africa
1994

Europe timeline

English Magna Carta accepted
A.D. 1215

Renaissance begins in Italy
mid-1300s

Gutenberg Bible printed
1456

Industrial Revolution begins in Britain
1760

Italy unified
1870

World War I begins
1914

World War II begins
1939

Berlin Wall falls
1989

A.D. 1200 — A.D. 1500 — A.D. 1800 — A.D. 2100

Ottoman Turks conquer Constantinople
A.D. 1453

French Revolution begins
1789

Germany unified
1871

Russian Revolution
1917

Breakup of Soviet Union
1991

Asia timeline

Voyages of Zheng He for China
1405–1433

Sepoy Rebellion in India
1857

Boxer Uprising in China
1900

People's Republic of China established
1949

Revolution in Iran
1979

A.D. 1200 — A.D. 1500 — A.D. 1800 — A.D. 2100

Tokugawas gain power in Japan
1600

Meiji Restoration begins in Japan
1868

Civil war in China
1911

Cultural Revolution in China
1966

War in Iraq
2003

Americas timeline

Inca empire founded
1438

Height of Aztec empire
1500

British found Jamestown
1607

Bolívar captures Bogotá
1819

Mexican Revolution begins
1910

Panama Canal opens
1914

Perón becomes president of Argentina
1946

Cuban Missile Crisis
1962

A.D. 1200 — A.D. 1500 — A.D. 1800 — A.D. 2100

Columbus reaches the Caribbean
1492

American Revolution begins
1775

Act of Union unites Canada
1840

Spanish-American War
1898

Canada, United States, and Mexico sign NAFTA
1993

Terrorists attack U.S. on 9/11
2001

The Parthenon, Athens, Greece

History Background

The Parthenon The Athenian leader Pericles ordered the building of the Parthenon, dedicated to the goddess Athena Parthenos, in the mid-400s B.C. Colorful sculptures adorned the white marble building, which is 101 feet wide and 228 feet long. The Parthenon stood largely as built for some 800 years until, in the mid-400s A.D., it was turned into a Christian church. In 1460, after the Ottoman Turks took control of Athens, the Parthenon became a mosque, with a minaret built into one corner. During a battle between the Turks and an army from Venice, munitions stored in the Parthenon exploded, damaging the central part of the structure. After 1800, many sculptures, including the famed Elgin marbles, were removed to museums and other locations in Britain, France, Denmark, and elsewhere.

Analyzing the Visuals

■ Point out the picture of Columbus landing in the Americas. Ask students to draw on their existing knowledge and ask **What are the occupations of the men pictured here?** *(military men and one religious figure)* **How can you tell this?** *(The soldiers carry swords and a rifle; the priest is dressed in religious clothing, carries a cross, and has a cross on his belt.)* **What does the combination of military and religious figures suggest about these men?** *(They are prepared to defend themselves or take military action, and they have strong religious convictions.)* **What does it suggest about what their conquest will be like?** *(They will use force to subdue the inhabitants of the Americas; they will try to convert the inhabitants to Christianity.)* Tell students that this painting depicts the start of an empire. Have them look at the table above the picture to determine which empire started with Columbus. *(the Spanish empire)*

■ Point out the definition of nationalism given in the chart at the top left of this page. Then direct students' attention to the flag at the top right. Tell students that this is the flag of Giovine Italia, or Young Italy, a group founded by the Italian nationalist Giuseppe Mazzini with the goal of freeing their homeland from the Italian princes and Austrians who controlled Italy. Encourage students to try to translate the Italian slogan on the flag, based on similar English words. *("Union, Power, and Liberty!!")*

History

Flag of Giovine Italia, 1833

UNIONE. FORZA E LIBERTA !!

Imperialism, Colonialism, Nationalism, and Revolution

Imperialism	**Colonialism**
A policy of pursuing, often through conquest, the economic and political domination of another state.	A policy of politically dominating a dependent territory or people.

↓ ↓

Nationalism
A strong feeling of pride in, or devotion to, one's nation.

↓

Revolution
The overthrow of a government from within.

Conquest and Empire

An empire is a group of states or territories controlled by one ruler. Empires often form in a haphazard way. For example, a small state with a strong army successfully defends itself against one neighboring state after another and incorporates their lands. Or at some point, an able ruler aggressively seeks more territory. Over time, the state expands into an empire. A strong military and able leadership are two factors that go into creating an empire. However, successful empires also must develop a government system that can maintain control of conquered peoples.

Selected Empires in World History

Conquests	Time Span	Location
Roman	509 B.C.–A.D. 180	Mediterranean region, Western Europe, Britain
Arab Muslim	A.D. 624–750	Southwest Asia, North Africa, Spain
Mongol	1206–1294	China, Central Asia, Eastern Europe
Ottoman	1299–1566	Southwest Asia, North Africa, Balkans, Eastern Europe
Spanish	1492–1560	Mexico, Central America, South America, Cuba, Florida

First Landing of Columbus by Frederick Kemmelmeyer

Major Conflicts in World History

This table shows selected major wars and conquests. Hundreds of other conflicts, large and small, have occurred throughout history. The cause of a conflict may be as simple as "I want what you have." For example, the basic need for food—and the land to grow it on—has been a prime cause of war. But most of the time, the reasons for wars are more complex. They can involve intertwining economic, political, religious, and cultural forces.

A sans-culotte figure from the French Revolutionary period

Selected Conflicts in World History

Conflict	Time Span	Location	Combatants
Persian Wars	499–448 B.C.	Greece	Greeks vs. Persians
Peloponnesian War	431–404 B.C.	Greece	Athens vs. Sparta
Punic Wars	264–146 B.C.	Mediterranean region	Rome vs. Carthage
Crusades	A.D. 1096–1291	Southwest Asia	Christians vs. Muslims
Hundred Years' War	1337–1443	France	England vs. France
Wars of King Philip II	1571–1588	Europe	Spain vs. Dutch Netherlands; Spain vs. England
Thirty Years' War	1618–1648	Central Europe (German states)	Holy Roman Empire, Spain, Poland, and others vs. Netherlands, Sweden, France, and others
English Civil War	1642–1649	England	Parliament (Roundheads) vs. Charles I and supporters (Cavaliers)
Seven Years' War (includes French and Indian War)	1756–1763	Europe; North America; India	Austria, Russia, and France vs. Prussia and Britain; Britain and its American colonies vs. France and its Native American allies; Britain vs. France
American Revolution	1775–1783	North America	Britain vs. its American colonies
French Revolution	1789–1799	France	Reformers (mainly middle class and peasants) vs. Louis XVI and supporters (mainly nobles and clergy)
Napoleonic Wars (end of the French Revolution)	1799–1815	Europe	France vs. combined European powers
Latin American Wars of Independence	1802–1824	Latin America	Colonies in Latin America vs. France and Spain
American Civil War	1860–1865	United States	North (Unionists) vs. South (Secessionists)
World War I	1914–1918	Europe (mainly France and Russia)	Allied powers vs. Central powers
World War II	1939–1945	North Africa, Europe, East Asia, Pacific Islands	Allies vs. Axis powers
Korean War	1950–1953	Korea	North Korea and China vs. South Korea and United States
Vietnam War	1959–1975	Vietnam	North Vietnam vs. South Vietnam and the United States

Analyzing the Visuals

Point out the French revolutionary on this page. Have students use the table on this same page to find information about the French Revolution. Ask **Did the French Revolution occur before or after the American Revolution?** *(after)* **Would you say that France or French fighters have participated in a significant way or in a minor way in the major conflicts of world history?** *(Students should consider that besides the conflicts located in France or in which France is a named combatant, the French also participated in the Crusades and in World War II, as well as in the precursor to the Vietnam War, known as the First Indochina War.)*

History Background

Warfare Warfare is probably as old as humankind. The earliest wars involved hand-to-hand combat—grisly, painful, and horrifying for the combatants. Weapons included clubs, axes, spears, and, later, swords. The bow and arrow changed the tactics of warfare somewhat by giving armies the ability to fight from a distance. Gunpowder, too, allowed troops to fire at each other across an open space. Still, most battles ended with pairs of soldiers fighting each other face to face. In today's world of high-flying bombers, helicopter gunships, and assault rifles, enemy forces rarely engage in close combat. Nevertheless, warfare remains grisly, painful, and horrifying—not only for the combatants but also for the innocent civilians who so often get caught in the crossfire.

Analyzing the Visuals

■ Direct students' attention to the map on these pages. Ask **Which of these regional organizations encompass nearly an entire continent?** *(the North American Free Trade Agreement, the African Union, Southern Common Market, and the European Union)* Point out the asterisks and the footnote. Then ask **What is the main purpose of most of these organizations?** *(economic development through free trade)* **Which of these organizations are you most familiar with, and why?** *(Students should be familiar with NAFTA, because it includes the United States. Students should also recognize the European Union, a fairly new organization that is growing and is the subject of ongoing news reports. They might also be familiar with the Commonwealth of Independent States, because it emerged from the fall of the Soviet Union—an event of great significance in modern history.)*

■ Make clear to students that many other international organizations exist, including those listed in the box on the next page. Ask students what they know about the United Nations, beyond the information provided here. Briefly discuss the importance of using cooperation to achieve world peace.

Regional Organizations

Through treaties, nations with common regional interests often work together to improve themselves politically, economically, and socially.

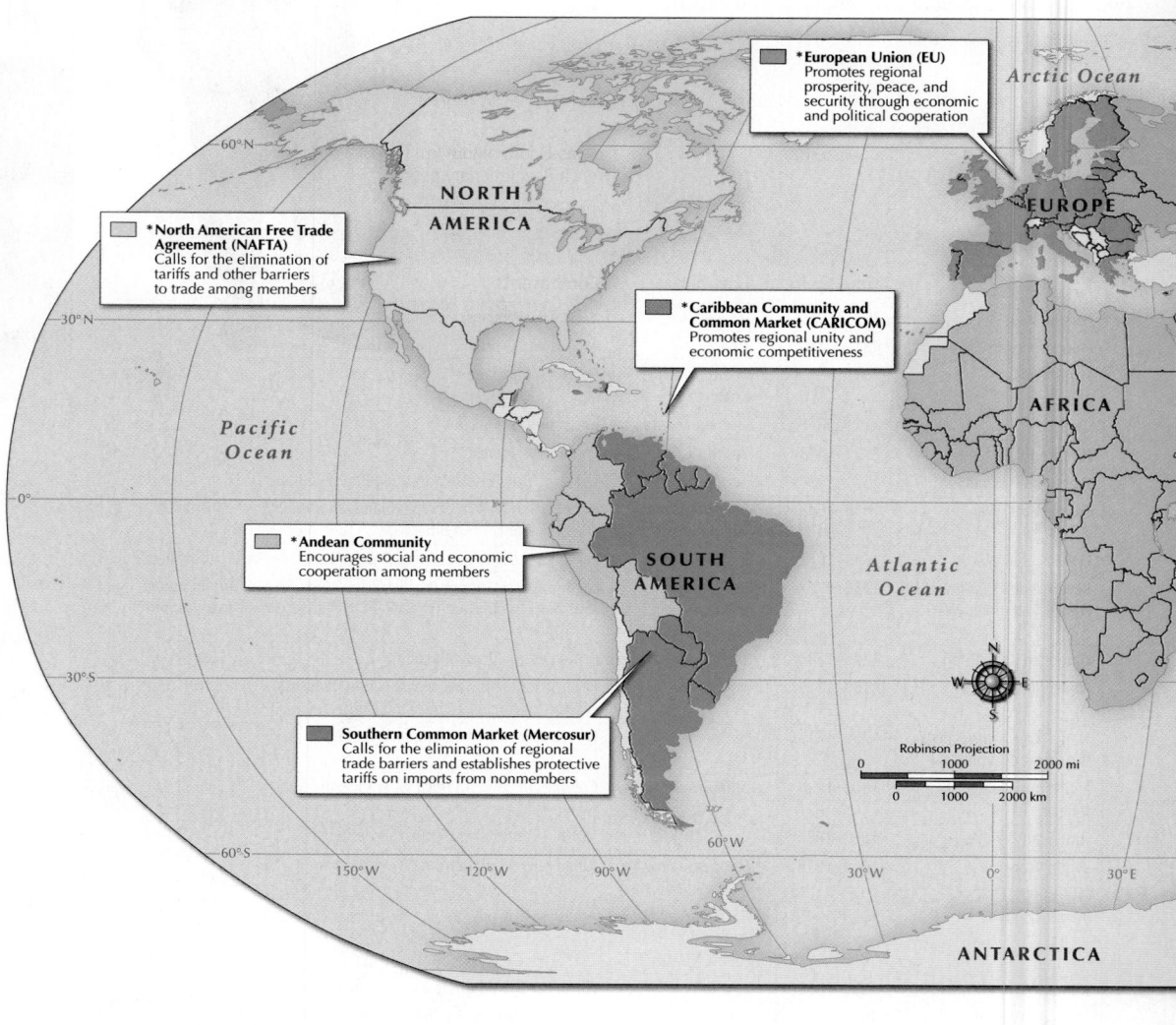

*European Union (EU)
Promotes regional prosperity, peace, and security through economic and political cooperation

*North American Free Trade Agreement (NAFTA)
Calls for the elimination of tariffs and other barriers to trade among members

*Caribbean Community and Common Market (CARICOM)
Promotes regional unity and economic competitiveness

*Andean Community
Encourages social and economic cooperation among members

Southern Common Market (Mercosur)
Calls for the elimination of regional trade barriers and establishes protective tariffs on imports from nonmembers

Robinson Projection
0   1000   2000 mi
0   1000   2000 km

History Background

European Union The European Union (EU) is but the latest form taken by an organization that was launched by six nations in 1952 as the European Coal and Steel Community (ECSC). The six nations—France, West Germany, Belgium, the Netherlands, Luxembourg, and Italy—aimed to eliminate tariffs and quotas on coal and steel within the ECSC. In 1957, these nations formed the European Economic Community (EEC) to establish a free trade zone among its member states. In 1967, the ECSC, the EEC, and Euratom combined to form the European Communities (EC), which several other European nations joined. Further European integration came about in 1991, when a treaty created the EU, with 12 member states, a number that had swelled to 27 by 2007.

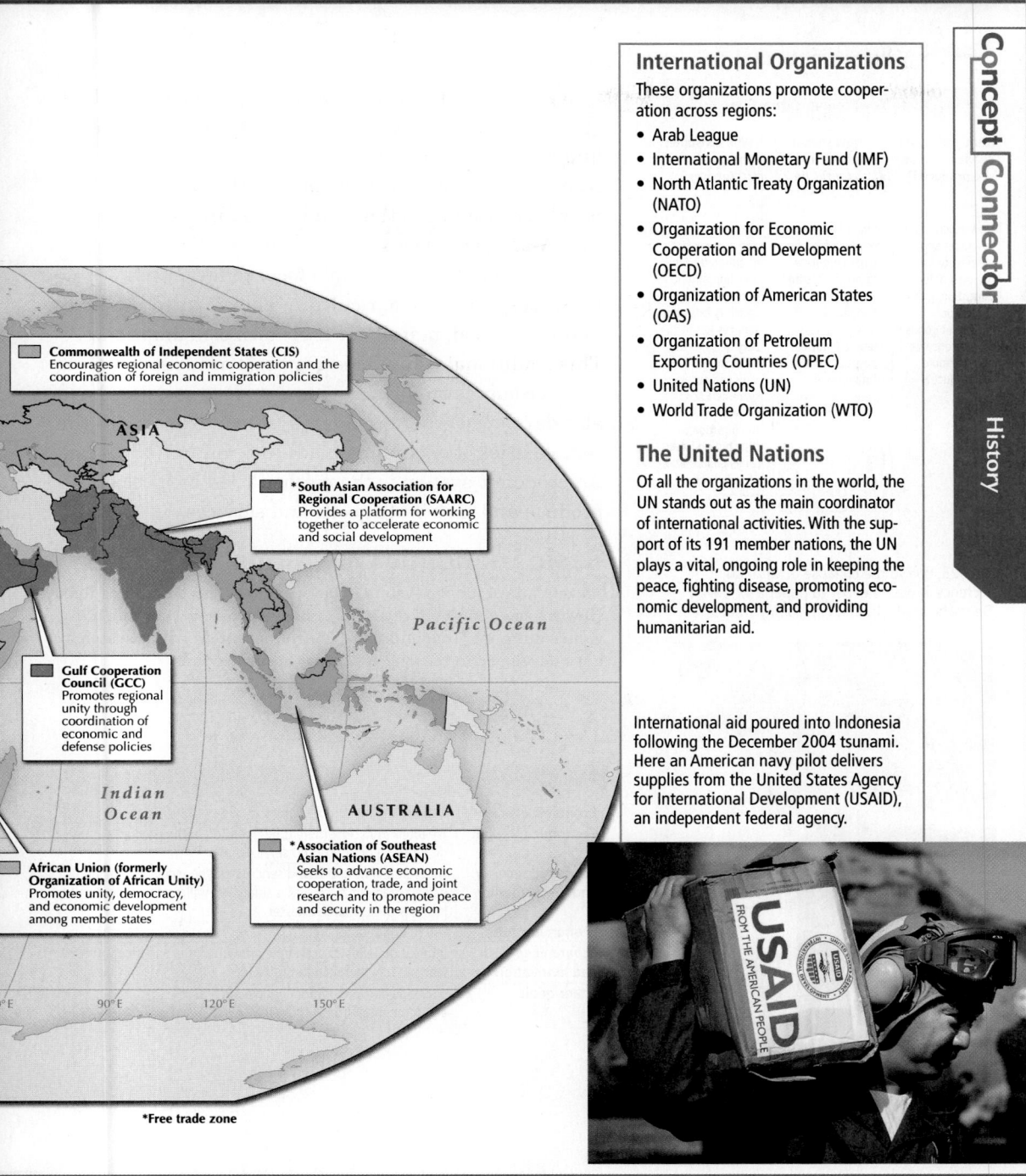

Commonwealth of Independent States (CIS)
Encourages regional economic cooperation and the coordination of foreign and immigration policies

ASIA

*South Asian Association for Regional Cooperation (SAARC)
Provides a platform for working together to accelerate economic and social development

Pacific Ocean

Gulf Cooperation Council (GCC)
Promotes regional unity through coordination of economic and defense policies

Indian Ocean

AUSTRALIA

African Union (formerly Organization of African Unity)
Promotes unity, democracy, and economic development among member states

*Association of Southeast Asian Nations (ASEAN)
Seeks to advance economic cooperation, trade, and joint research and to promote peace and security in the region

*Free trade zone

0° E   90° E   120° E   150° E

International Organizations

These organizations promote cooperation across regions:

- Arab League
- International Monetary Fund (IMF)
- North Atlantic Treaty Organization (NATO)
- Organization for Economic Cooperation and Development (OECD)
- Organization of American States (OAS)
- Organization of Petroleum Exporting Countries (OPEC)
- United Nations (UN)
- World Trade Organization (WTO)

The United Nations

Of all the organizations in the world, the UN stands out as the main coordinator of international activities. With the support of its 191 member nations, the UN plays a vital, ongoing role in keeping the peace, fighting disease, promoting economic development, and providing humanitarian aid.

International aid poured into Indonesia following the December 2004 tsunami. Here an American navy pilot delivers supplies from the United States Agency for International Development (USAID), an independent federal agency.

History Background

United Nations The United Nations celebrated its sixtieth anniversary on October 24, 2005. Since its founding at the close of World War II, the UN has expanded greatly but has maintained one goal above all others: to promote peace in the world. The predecessor to the UN was the League of Nations, formed after World War I with the intention of preventing another major war. The League's fatal flaw was its unwillingness in the 1930s to stand up against German, Italian, and Japanese aggression, which led to World War II. Countries lost faith in the value of the League, but not in its principles. Franklin Roosevelt and Winston Churchill reaffirmed those principles in the Atlantic Charter. In 1941, this document paved the way for a new organization, known as the UN, that would promote peace and cooperation.

Overview

This handbook links economics with history by presenting the three key economic questions that all societies must answer. The answers reveal how those societies have chosen to organize their economies in order to reach their economic goals. The handbook goes on to identify and describe four modern economic systems and the interdependence of economies throughout the modern world.

Test Preparation

- **Student Quiz** Ask students to write an example of an economic activity that would take place in a modern economic system. For example, for a mixed economy, a student might write "The government works with a shoe company to construct a new factory." Have students read their examples to the class, and have other students determine the economic system.

- **Flashcards** Students might also make flashcards for terms in the glossary on the following pages. Have them quiz one another, by holding up either the term or its definition.

Analyzing the Visuals

- Ask students to read the three key economic questions. Ask **How are a society's economic goals linked to the three key questions?** (*Depending on how it values different economic goals, a society might answer the questions differently.*)

- Ask **What is the man in the photograph using to cover the wall?** (*German paper money*) Tell them that after World War I, Germany's currency lost most of its value. This economic crisis helped extremists like Adolf Hitler gain power. Ask **Why would an economic crisis lead people to seek radical changes in leadership?** (*When people cannot find jobs or feed their families, they tend to blame government policies and support politicians who promise to fix the economy.*)

Economics

Three Key Economic Questions		
What goods and services should be produced?	**How should goods and services be produced?**	**Who consumes the goods and services?**
How much of our resources should we devote to national defense, education, public health, or consumer goods? Which consumer goods should we produce?	Should we produce food on large corporate farms or on small family farms? Should we produce electricity with oil, nuclear power, coal, or solar power?	How do goods and services get distributed? The question of who gets to consume which goods and services lies at the very heart of the differences between economic systems. Each society answers the question of distribution based on its combination of social values and goals.

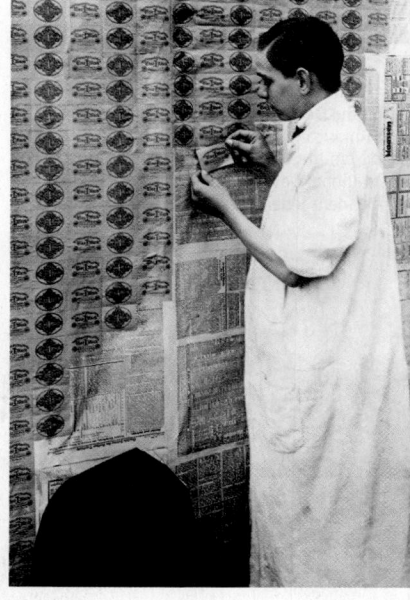

In 1923, due to the collapse of German currency, it was cheaper to paper a wall with Deutsche marks than it was to buy wallpaper.

I n every society throughout history, people have had access to resources, such as water, fertile land, and human labor. Yet everywhere in the world, people's resources are limited. Economics is the study of how people choose to use their limited resources to meet their wants and needs.

Until modern times, people focused largely on resources related to agriculture. They farmed the land to produce food, mainly for their own consumption. This traditional way of meeting basic needs still defines some economies today. However, modern societies have also developed other economic systems to deal with the complexities of expanding trade and industrialization. An economic system is the method used by a society to produce and distribute goods and services.

Basic Economic Questions

Through its economic system, society answers three key questions. How a society answers these questions depends on how much it values different economic goals. Four different economic systems have developed in response to these three questions.

Economic Goals	
Economic efficiency	Making the most of resources
Economic freedom	Freedom from government intervention in the production and distribution of goods and services
Economic security and predictability	Assurance that goods and services will be available, payments will be made on time, and a safety net will protect individuals in times of economic disaster
Economic equity	Fair distribution of wealth
Economic growth and innovation	Innovation leads to economic growth, and economic growth leads to a higher standard of living.
Other goals	Societies pursue additional goals, such as environmental protection.

Bibliography

For the Teacher
Bentley, Jerry H. *Old World Encounters: Cross-Cultural Contacts and Exchanges in Pre-Modern Times.* Oxford University Press, 1993.

Cameron, Rondo, et al. *A Concise Economic History of the World: From Paleolithic Times to the Present,* 4th ed. Oxford University Press, 2002.

Buchholz, Todd G., et al. *New Ideas from Dead Economists: An Introduction to Modern Economic Thought,* Plume Books, 1999.

For the Student
Cozic, Charles P., ed. *Global Resources.* Greenhaven Press, 1998.

Downing, David. *Capitalism.* Heinemann, 2002.

January, Brendan. *Globalize It! The Stories of the IMF, The World Bank, the WTO—and Those Who Protest.* Lerner, 2003.

Sold! The Origins of Money and Trade. Runestone, 1994.

Modern Economic Systems

A society's economic system reflects how that society answers the three key economic questions. Different systems produce different results in terms of productivity, the welfare of workers, and consumer choice. This table provides information about the main economic systems in the world today.

A Grameen Bank officer meets with loan recipients in India.

Modern Economic Systems

	Description	Origin	Location Today
Traditional	People make economic decisions based on custom or habit. They produce what they have always produced and just as much as they need, using long-established methods.	Accompanied the rise of agriculture and home crafts	Mainly in rural areas within developing nations
Market (Capitalist, Free-Enterprise)	Economic decisions are made in the marketplace through interactions between buyers and sellers according to the laws of supply and demand. Individual capitalists own the means of production. Government regulates some economic activities and provides such ¡publi c goods" as education.	Capitalism has existed since the earliest buying and selling of goods in a market. The market economic system developed in response to Adam Smith's ideas and the shift from agriculture to industry in the 1800s.	Canada, Germany, Japan, United States, and a handful of other nations
Centrally Planned (Command, Socialist, Communist)	Central government planners make most economic decisions for the people. In theory, the workers own the means of production. In practice, the government does. Some private enterprise, but government dominates.	In the 1800s, criticism of capitalism by Karl Marx and others led to calls for distributing wealth according to need. After the 1917 Russian Revolution, the Soviet Union developed the first command economy.	Communist countries, including China, Cuba, North Korea, and Vietnam
Mixed (Social Democratic, Liberal Socialist)	A mix of socialism and free enterprise in which the government plays a significant role in making economic decisions.	The Great Depression of the 1930s ended laissez-faire capitalism in most countries. People insisted that government take a stronger role in fixing economic problems. The fall of communism in Eastern Europe in the 1990s ended central planning in most countries. People insisted on freer markets.	Most nations, including Brazil, France, India, Italy, Poland, Russia, Sweden, and the United Kingdom

Analyzing the Visuals

- Ask **Which economic system is the oldest?** *(traditional)* **Which economic system came about as a response to an existing system?** *(centrally planned)* **What was the existing system?** *(market)* **How do these two systems differ?** *(In a market system, economic decisions are made in the marketplace, with little government interference. In a centrally planned system, central government planners make most economic decisions.)*

- Explain that the Grameen Bank offers small loans to poor, mostly rural women who use the money to start up small businesses. Ask **Which economic system is best represented in this picture?** *(market)* **What character traits should an entrepreneur have?** *(Sample: perseverance, courage, imagination, thrift)*

 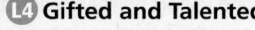

Differentiated Instruction Solutions for All Learners

L4 Advanced Readers **L4 Gifted and Talented**

To extend students' understanding of economic systems, ask them to create a fictional modern economy. First, briefly review how a society answers the three economic questions based on its economic goals, and how its economic system reflects those answers. Then, have students pick one or more economic goals (making sure they don't conflict), write detailed answers to the three economic questions, and then choose the economic system that best suits their goals and answers. Students should be prepared to explain their results. Tell them that they can modify their goals and answers if needed for their choices to work together.

Analyzing the Visuals

- Direct students' attention to the two-page map of trade organizations. Ask **Which trade organization includes countries from southern and eastern South America?** *(Mercosur)* **Which organizations are in Asia?** *(OPEC and ASEAN)* Tell students that trade organizations move to eliminate tariffs and trade barriers among member countries. Ask **What is the advantage of joining a regional trade organization?** *(Lower trade barriers and the absence of taxes on imported goods encourage trade within the organization by giving member countries access to more markets, which should strengthen their economies.)*

- Point out the illustration of NAFTA on this page. Ask **What three countries make up NAFTA?** *(the United States, Canada, and Mexico)* **Why is this puzzle an effective way of representing NAFTA?** *(Sample: The puzzle pieces fit together to make a whole, just as NAFTA brings together the economies of North America. Each country has goods and services needed by the other countries.)*

Economics

Major Trade Organizations

This map shows the major regional trade associations in the world today. In addition, 147 countries belong to the World Trade Organization (WTO). The WTO works to encourage trade by reducing tariffs, promoting international agreements, and mediating trade disputes among member nations.

This illustration represents the cooperation among nations involved in NAFTA.

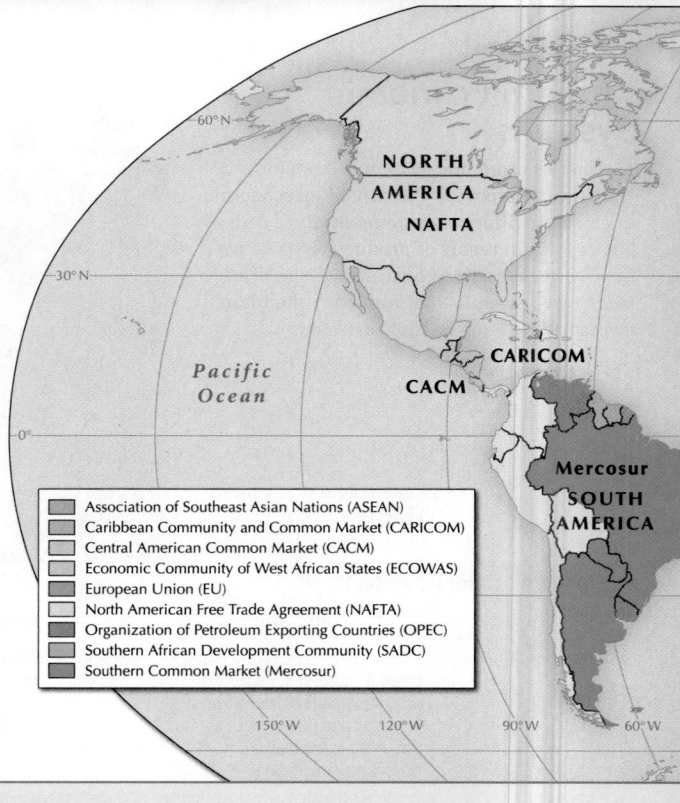

- Association of Southeast Asian Nations (ASEAN)
- Caribbean Community and Common Market (CARICOM)
- Central American Common Market (CACM)
- Economic Community of West African States (ECOWAS)
- European Union (EU)
- North American Free Trade Agreement (NAFTA)
- Organization of Petroleum Exporting Countries (OPEC)
- Southern African Development Community (SADC)
- Southern Common Market (Mercosur)

Glossary of Economic Terms

barter
the direct exchange of one set of goods or services for another

budget
a plan for income and spending

capital
any human-made resource that is used to create other goods or services

communism
a political system characterized by a centrally planned economy with all economic and political power resting in the hands of the central government

currency
coins and paper bills used as money

depression
a recession that is especially long and severe

developed nation
industrialized country with a higher average level of material well-being

developing nation
country with limited industrialization and a lower average level of material well-being

economic system
the method used by a society to produce and distribute goods and services

entrepreneur
ambitious leader who combines land, labor, and capital to create and market new goods or services

export
a good that is sent to another country for sale

free enterprise
an economic system that permits the conduct of business with minimal government intervention

goods
physical objects such as clothes or shoes

import
a good that is brought in from another country for sale

industrialization
the extensive organization of an economy for the purpose of manufacturing

History Background

Developed and Developing Economies
Developed economies, also known as advanced economies, have thoroughly industrialized. Their citizens enjoy the highest income levels in the world. The remaining countries have developing economies, which means that they are in the process of industrializing. The developing economies with the lowest per capita incomes are also known as the least developed countries. They chiefly export primary goods—such as crops or raw minerals—and import finished products. Many people there live in poverty. A third category encompasses the countries of Eastern Europe and the former Soviet Union. These have been called countries in transition, and their people's income levels lie somewhere between those in developed and developing countries.

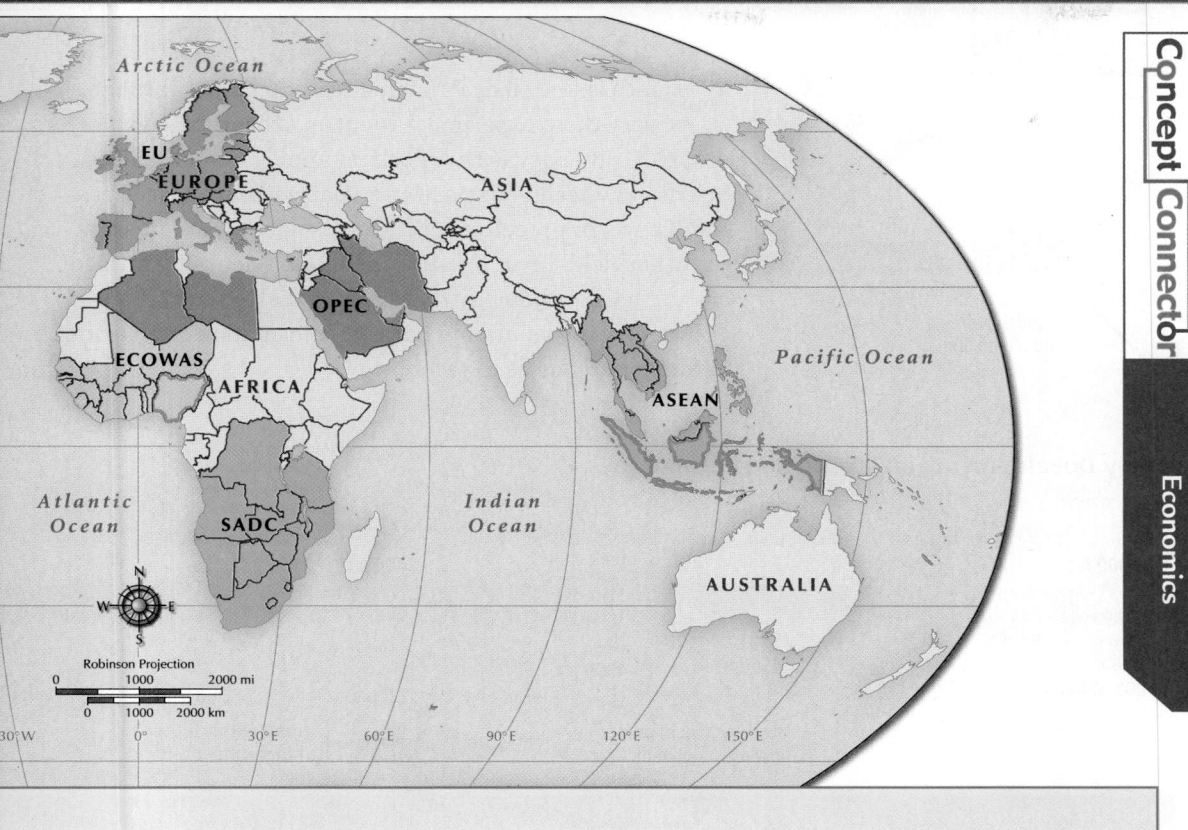

inflation
a general increase in prices

law of demand
economic law that states that consumers buy more of a good when its price decreases and less when its price increases

law of supply
tendency of suppliers to offer more of a good at a higher price

market
an arrangement that allows buyers and sellers to exchange things

market economy
economic system in which decisions on production and consumption of goods and services are based on voluntary exchange in markets

mixed economy
economic system that combines tradition and the free market with limited government involvement

opportunity cost
the most desirable alternative given up as the result of a decision

recession
a prolonged economic contraction

scarcity
limited quantities of resources to meet unlimited wants

socialism
a social and political philosophy based on the belief that democratic means should be used to evenly distribute wealth throughout a society.

tariff
a tax on imported goods

tax
a required payment to a government

traditional economy
economic system that relies on habit, custom, or ritual to decide questions of production and consumption of goods and services

welfare
government aid to the poor

Differentiated Instruction   Solutions for All Learners

L1 Special Needs   **L2 Less Proficient Readers**   **L2 English Language Learners**

Have students read each term and definition in the glossary and then offer an example of each. They might act out the example (such as *barter*), draw an example (such as *budget*), point to an example in the classroom (such as *goods* or *currency*), or give an example from experience or from their textbook.

Overview

This handbook presents key developments in science and technology. It consists mainly of four timelines. Be sure students see that each of the timelines runs across all four pages of the handbook. The timelines cover developments in science and technology, medicine, communication, and transportation. Together they reveal a story of progress in understanding the natural world and applying that knowledge in practical ways.

Test Preparation

Divide the class into groups and assign each group a period of years from the timelines. Have each group choose three different developments in science and technology from their period and do more research on them. They should determine the following: the inventor, if any, the society in which the development occurred, what life was like in that society at the time, what major historical events were taking place there and elsewhere around that time, and what effect the development had on the world. Have each group, in chronological order, present its findings to the class.

Analyzing the Visuals

Have students study one particular period across all four timelines to get an idea of the level of advancement of human beings at that time. Write the date *3000 B.C.* on the board. Ask **How did some civilizations communicate at this time?** *(through pictogram writing)* **How did they travel over water?** *(by dugout canoe or square-sailed ship)* **If one civilization had access to all the developments in science and technology available in 3000 B.C., what might their day-to-day lives have been like?** *(Students should describe how people acquired food, made tools, communicated, and traveled.)*

Concept Connector Handbooks

Science and Technology

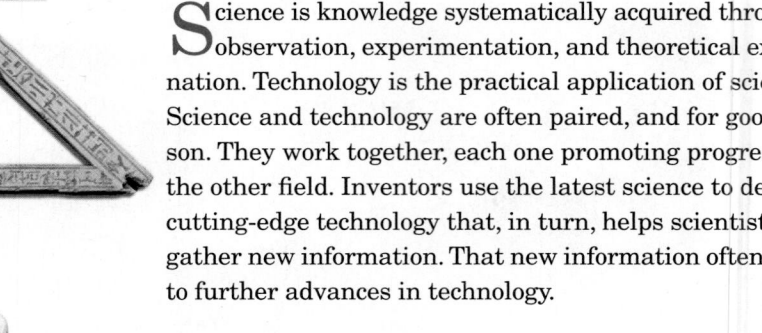

▲ Egyptian A-frame and plumb line

Science is knowledge systematically acquired through observation, experimentation, and theoretical explanation. Technology is the practical application of science. Science and technology are often paired, and for good reason. They work together, each one promoting progress in the other field. Inventors use the latest science to develop cutting-edge technology that, in turn, helps scientists gather new information. That new information often leads to further advances in technology.

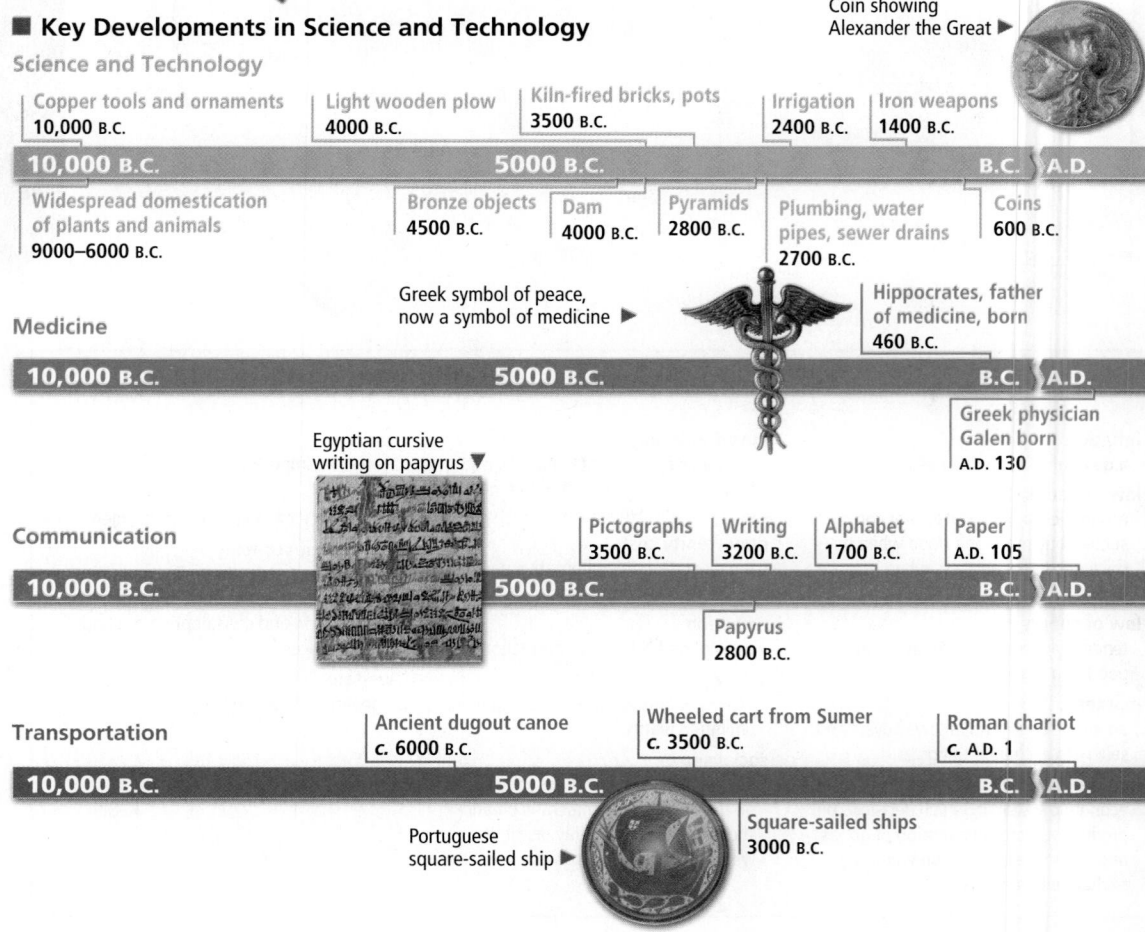

■ **Key Developments in Science and Technology**

Coin showing Alexander the Great ▶

Science and Technology

| Copper tools and ornaments 10,000 B.C. | Light wooden plow 4000 B.C. | Kiln-fired bricks, pots 3500 B.C. | | Irrigation 2400 B.C. | Iron weapons 1400 B.C. |

10,000 B.C.   5000 B.C.   B.C. / A.D.

| Widespread domestication of plants and animals 9000–6000 B.C. | Bronze objects 4500 B.C. | Dam 4000 B.C. | Pyramids 2800 B.C. | Plumbing, water pipes, sewer drains 2700 B.C. | Coins 600 B.C. |

Greek symbol of peace, now a symbol of medicine ▶

Hippocrates, father of medicine, born 460 B.C.

Medicine

10,000 B.C.   5000 B.C.   B.C. / A.D.

Greek physician Galen born A.D. 130

Egyptian cursive writing on papyrus ▼

Communication

| | | | Pictographs 3500 B.C. | Writing 3200 B.C. | Alphabet 1700 B.C. | Paper A.D. 105 |

10,000 B.C.   5000 B.C.   B.C. / A.D.

Papyrus 2800 B.C.

Transportation

| | Ancient dugout canoe c. 6000 B.C. | Wheeled cart from Sumer c. 3500 B.C. | Roman chariot c. A.D. 1 |

10,000 B.C.   5000 B.C.   B.C. / A.D.

Portuguese square-sailed ship ▶

Square-sailed ships 3000 B.C.

Bibliography

For the Teacher

Boorstin, Daniel. *The Discoverers.* Random House, 1983.

McClellan, James E., et al. *Science and Technology in World History: An Introduction.* Johns Hopkins University Press, 1998.

Trefil, James S., ed. *The Encyclopedia of Science and Technology.* Routledge, 2001.

For the Student

Bridgman, Roger. *1000 Inventions and Discoveries.* Dorling Kindersley, 2003.

McGowen, Tom. *The Beginnings of Science.* Twenty-First Century, 1998.

Reid, Struan. *Inventions and Trade.* Silver Burdett, 1994.

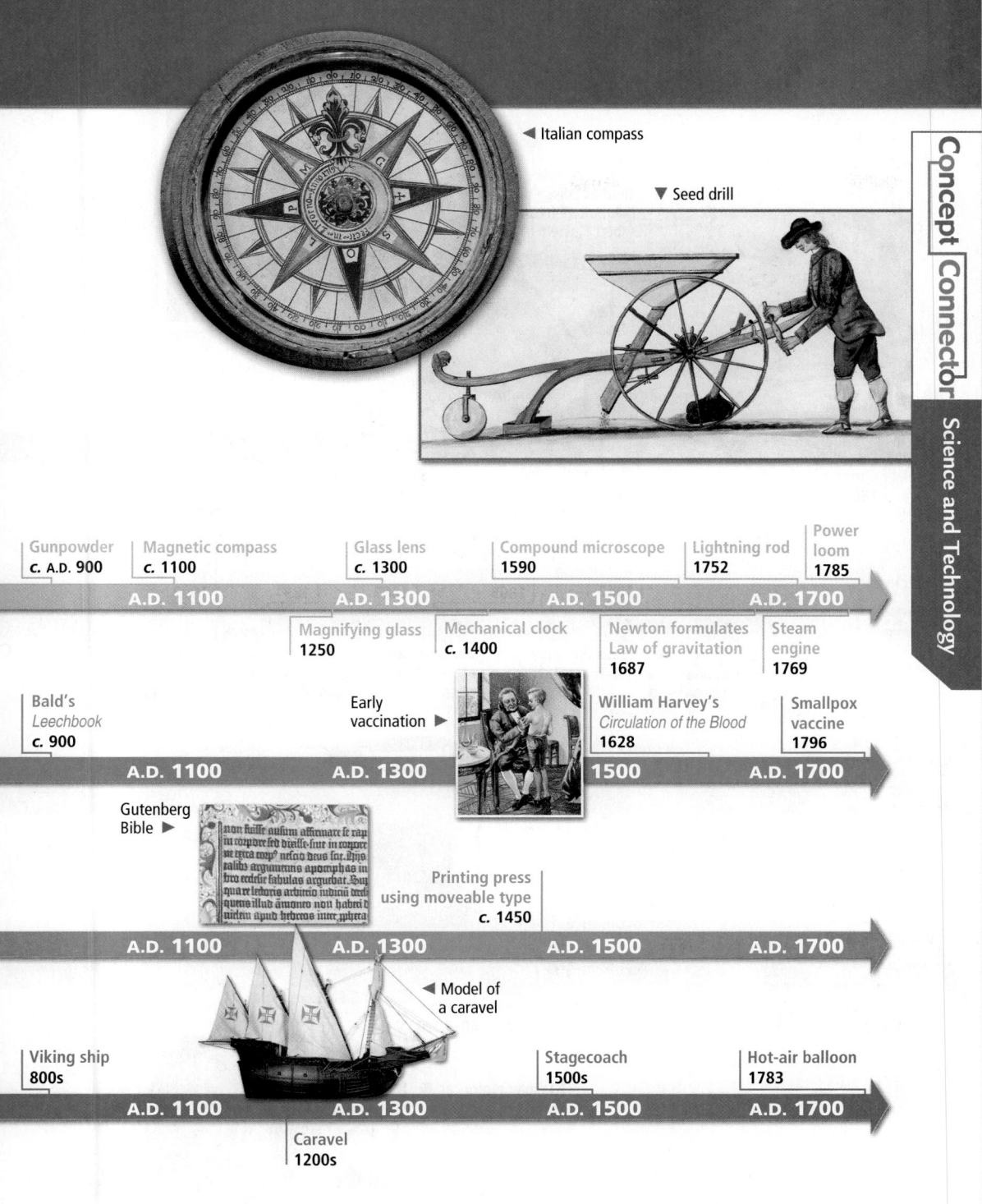

◄ Italian compass

▼ Seed drill

Analyzing the Visuals

Point out the compass and the ship on this page. Ask **When was the magnetic compass invented?** *(around A.D. 1100)* **When did Christopher Columbus sail to the Americas?** *(1492)* **What effect do you think the invention of the magnetic compass had on European exploration of the Americas?** *(The compass greatly helped mariners stay on course as they traveled across the open ocean.)*

Gunpowder c. A.D. 900	Magnetic compass c. 1100	Glass lens c. 1300	Compound microscope 1590	Lightning rod 1752	Power loom 1785

A.D. 1100   A.D. 1300   A.D. 1500   A.D. 1700

Magnifying glass 1250   Mechanical clock c. 1400   Newton formulates Law of gravitation 1687   Steam engine 1769

Bald's *Leechbook* c. 900   Early vaccination ►   William Harvey's *Circulation of the Blood* 1628   Smallpox vaccine 1796

A.D. 1100   A.D. 1300   1500   A.D. 1700

Gutenberg Bible ►

Printing press using moveable type c. 1450

A.D. 1100   A.D. 1300   A.D. 1500   A.D. 1700

◄ Model of a caravel

Viking ship 800s   Stagecoach 1500s   Hot-air balloon 1783

A.D. 1100   A.D. 1300   A.D. 1500   A.D. 1700

Caravel 1200s

Analyzing the Visuals

Point out the picture of Albert Einstein, whose theory of relativity revolutionized the science of physics. Ask **When did Einstein present his theory of relativity?** *(1905)* **Did Einstein's theory come before or after the theory of evolution?** *(46 years after)* **What development shown on these two pages do you think has had the greatest impact on the modern world?** Use student responses to initiate a discussion of the importance of science and technology.

Science and Technology

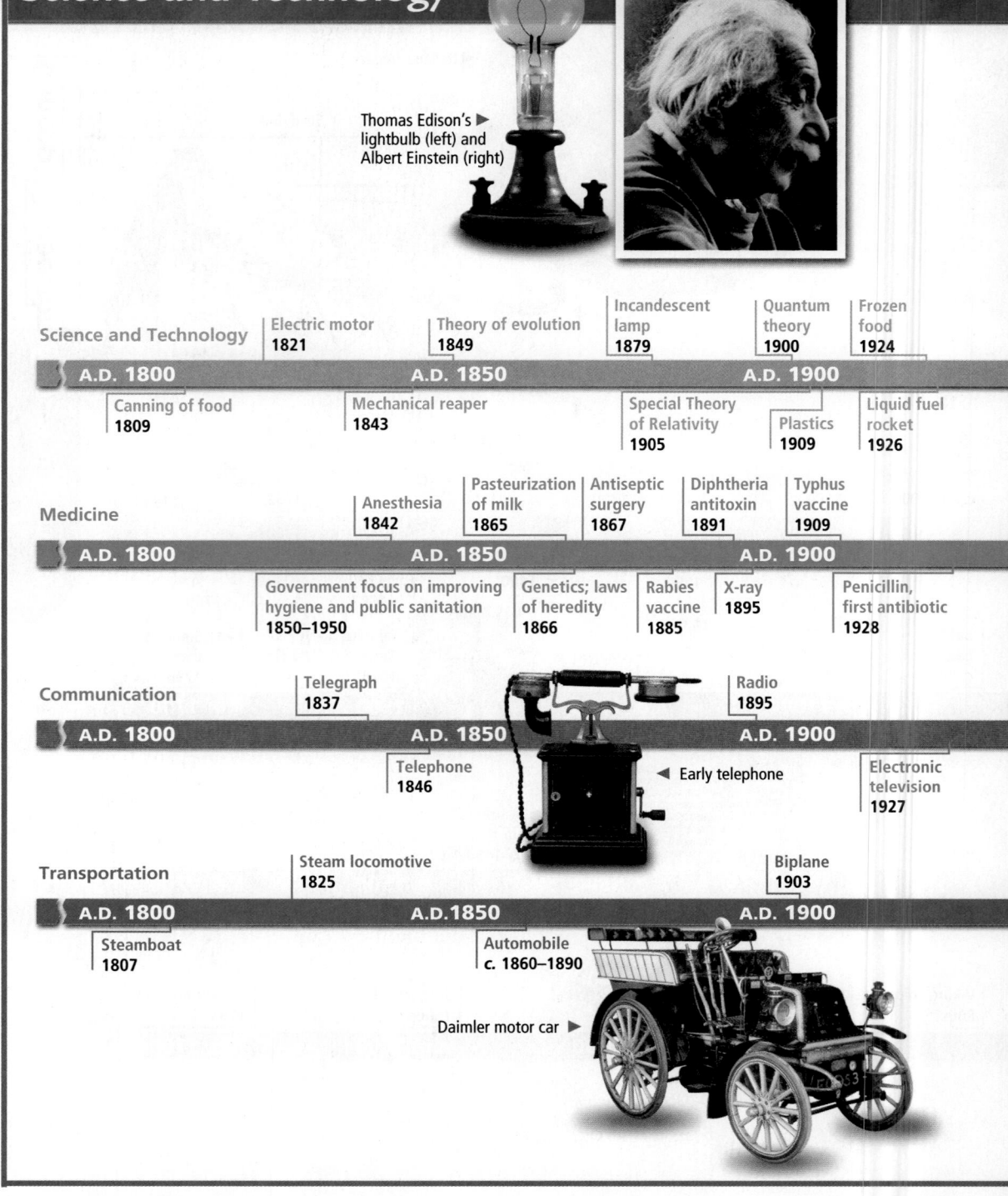

Thomas Edison's ▶
lightbulb (left) and
Albert Einstein (right)

Science and Technology

			Incandescent lamp 1879	Quantum theory 1900	Frozen food 1924
	Electric motor 1821	Theory of evolution 1849			

A.D. 1800 — A.D. 1850 — A.D. 1900

Canning of food 1809 • Mechanical reaper 1843 • Special Theory of Relativity 1905 • Plastics 1909 • Liquid fuel rocket 1926

Medicine

Anesthesia 1842 • Pasteurization of milk 1865 • Antiseptic surgery 1867 • Diphtheria antitoxin 1891 • Typhus vaccine 1909

A.D. 1800 — A.D. 1850 — A.D. 1900

Government focus on improving hygiene and public sanitation 1850–1950 • Genetics; laws of heredity 1866 • Rabies vaccine 1885 • X-ray 1895 • Penicillin, first antibiotic 1928

Communication

Telegraph 1837 • Radio 1895

A.D. 1800 — A.D. 1850 — A.D. 1900

Telephone 1846 • ◀ Early telephone • Electronic television 1927

Transportation

Steam locomotive 1825 • Biplane 1903

A.D. 1800 — A.D. 1850 — A.D. 1900

Steamboat 1807 • Automobile c. 1860–1890

Daimler motor car ▶

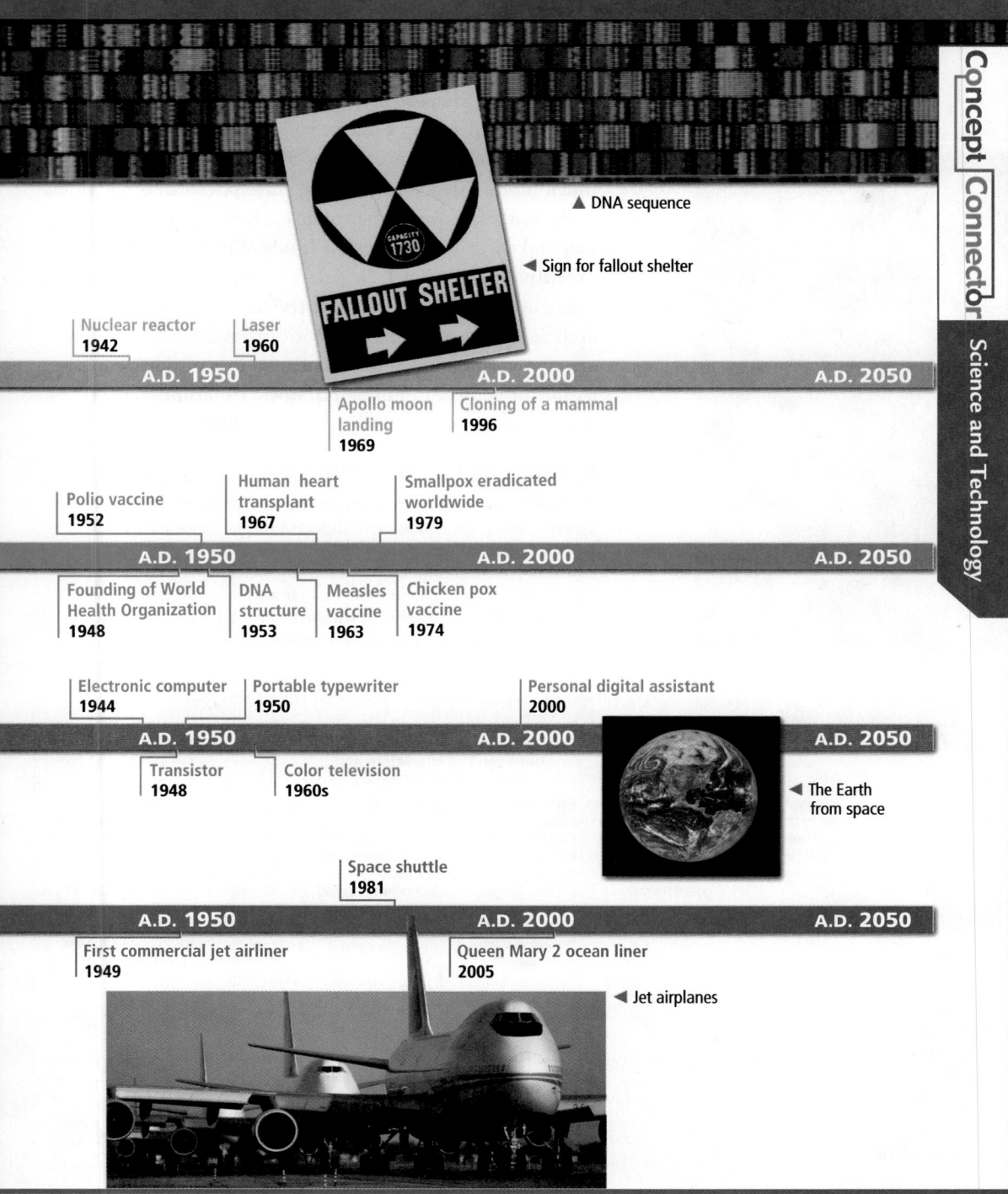

▲ DNA sequence

◄ Sign for fallout shelter

| Nuclear reactor | Laser |
| 1942 | 1960 |

A.D. 1950　　　**A.D. 2000**　　　**A.D. 2050**

| Apollo moon landing | Cloning of a mammal |
| 1969 | 1996 |

| Polio vaccine | Human heart transplant | Smallpox eradicated worldwide |
| 1952 | 1967 | 1979 |

A.D. 1950　　　**A.D. 2000**　　　**A.D. 2050**

| Founding of World Health Organization | DNA structure | Measles vaccine | Chicken pox vaccine |
| 1948 | 1953 | 1963 | 1974 |

| Electronic computer | Portable typewriter | Personal digital assistant |
| 1944 | 1950 | 2000 |

A.D. 1950　　　**A.D. 2000**　　　**A.D. 2050**

| Transistor | Color television |
| 1948 | 1960s |

◄ The Earth from space

| Space shuttle |
| 1981 |

A.D. 1950　　　**A.D. 2000**　　　**A.D. 2050**

| First commercial jet airliner | Queen Mary 2 ocean liner |
| 1949 | 2005 |

◄ Jet airplanes

History Background

Telescope Improvements in a single tool can help in the advancement of science over centuries. In the early 1600s, Galileo used a homemade refracting telescope to map landforms on Earth's moon, discover four of Jupiter's moons, and study nearby stars. Steady improvements since then have resulted in sophisticated modern telescopes that are helping scientists look back at the early universe to see how stars, galaxies, and planetary systems evolved.

However, these telescopes have a problem: Earth's atmosphere distorts the images they receive. In 1990, space-shuttle technology allowed NASA to place the Hubble Space Telescope into orbit above the distorting atmosphere. Since then, its amazingly sharp images have helped scientists measure the rate of expansion of the universe, prove the existence of black holes, and observe in greater detail the birth and death of stars.

Overview

This handbook presents information about the various forms that government has taken throughout history. It discusses the main differences between federal and unitary government, presidential and parliamentary government, and democracy and dictatorship. During most of world history, governments have been ruled through some type of dictatorship. The handbook describes several of these types.

The study of government is a key element of civics. Knowing about various forms of government gives students a perspective for understanding their own political system and their rights and responsibilities as citizens of a democracy.

Test Preparation

■ **Review Chart** Have students draw a table to show the similarities and differences between federal and unitary, presidential and parliamentary, and democratic and dictatorial governments.

■ **Glossary** Ask students to make flashcards for the Glossary of Political Terms. Then encourage students to quiz each other.

Analyzing the Visuals

■ Direct students to the photo of the Ukrainians on this page. Explain that supporters of the opposition candidate for president took part in what was called the Orange Revolution, a series of protests aiming to end government corruption and voting fraud in Ukraine. Ukraine's Supreme Court agreed with the protesters, leading to this celebration. Ask **Are public protests acceptable in a democracy?** *(yes)* **Are they acceptable in a dictatorship?** *(no)* Remind students that the United States was founded by people who protested that their rights were being violated.

■ Point out the chart on this page. Ask **Which two countries in the chart are dictatorships?** *(Cuba and Syria)* **Do you think that dictatorships tend to be unitary or federal?** *(unitary)* **Why?** *(Dictatorships concentrate power in the hands of the few; they are not inclined to divide or share power.)*

Concept Connector Handbooks

Government and Civics

Presidential elections in Ukraine, 2004

The main purpose of government is to create and enforce a society's public policies. Public policies cover such matters as defense, crime, taxation, and much more. Governments must have power in order to make and carry out public policies. Every government has and exercises three basic kinds of power: legislative, executive, and judicial. Legislative refers to the power to make laws. Executive refers to the power to enforce laws. Judicial refers to the power to interpret laws. These powers of government are often outlined in a nation's constitution, or body of fundamental laws. Different forms of government exercise their powers in different ways.

Forms of Government

Political scientists classify governments in order to help them describe, compare, and analyze different forms. Three particularly helpful classifications involve determining (1) the geographic distribution of governmental power within the state, (2) the relationship between the legislative and executive branches of the government, and (3) who can participate in the government. As the chart shows, modern forms of government vary widely.

Forms of Government

Country	Where is the power?		What is the relationship between the legislative and executive branches?		Who can participate?	
	Unitary: All powers held by the government belong to a single, central agency.	**Federal**: The powers of government are divided between a central government and several regional governments.	**Parliamentary**: The executive branch is made up of the prime minister, or premier, and that officials' cabinet. The prime minister and cabinet are members of the legislative branch, or parliament.	**Presidential**: The executive and legislative branches of government are separate, independent of each other, and coequal.	**Democracy**: Supreme political authority rests with the people, who choose a small group of individuals to act as their representatives to carry out the day-to-day conduct of government.	**Dictatorship**: The government is not accountable to the people for its policies or for how they are carried out. Those who rule do not represent or consider the will of the people.
Botswana	✓		✓		✓	
Brazil		✓		✓	✓	
Costa Rica	✓		✓		✓	
Cuba	✓		✓			✓
France	✓			✓	✓	
India		✓	✓		✓	
Syria	✓			✓		✓
United States		✓		✓	✓	

Bibliography

For the Teacher

Finer, Samuel E. *The History of Government from the Earliest Times.* Oxford University Press, 1999.

National Standards for Civics and Government. Center for Civic Education, 1994.

Woodruff, Paul. *First Democracy: The Challenge of an Ancient Idea.* Oxford University Press, 2004.

For the Student

Luthringer, Chelsea. *So What Is Citizenship Anyway?* Rosen, 1999.

Nardo, Don. *Democracy.* Lucent, 1994.

Tocqueville, Alexis de. *Democracy in America.* Everyman's Library, 1994.

Federal vs. Unitary Government

Today, about two dozen nations, including the United States, have a federal system of government. In this kind of system, two levels of government—central and state—divide power between them. In the unitary system, which is more common by far, all powers belong to the central government. One disadvantage of a federal system is its inefficiency. People must obey two sets of laws, which may overlap or even conflict. In a unitary system, one government governs all the people directly, even though it may yield certain powers to the states. On the other hand, a federal system allows for checks on the power of the central government and for some diversity of laws in regions with a distinctive culture, history, or language.

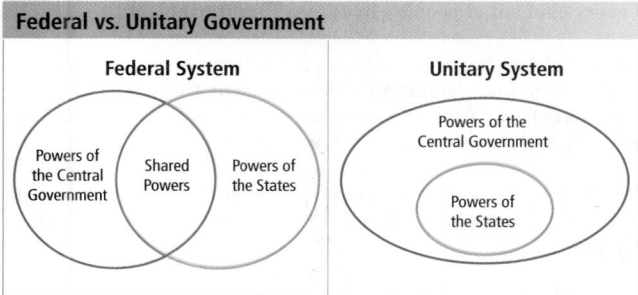

Federal vs. Unitary Government

Federal System

Powers of the Central Government — Shared Powers — Powers of the States

Unitary System

Powers of the Central Government — Powers of the States

Presidential and Parliamentary Governments

The Presidential Relationship Voters elect the legislature and the chief executive, who is part of the executive branch. The legislative and executive branches are independent and coequal.

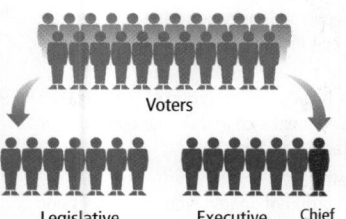

Voters

Legislative Branch

Executive Branch — Chief Executive

The Parliamentary Relationship Voters elect the legislature. The chief executive is drawn from the legislature.

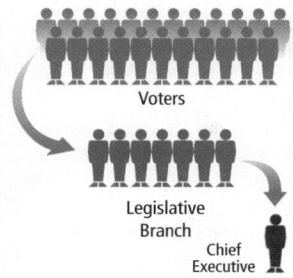

Voters

Legislative Branch

Chief Executive

Concept Connector

Government and Civics

Basic Concepts of Democracy

1. A recognition of the fundamental worth and dignity of every person. At various times, the welfare of one or a few individuals is subordinate to the interests of the many in a democracy. For example, a democratic society may force people to pay a tax or obey traffic signals.

2. A respect for the equality of all persons. The democratic concept of equality insists that all people are entitled to equality of opportunity and equality before the law—not necessarily equal distribution of wealth.

3. A faith in the majority rule and an insistence upon minority rights. In a democracy, the will of the people and not the dictate of the ruling few determine public policy. Unchecked, however, a majority could destroy its opposition and, in the process, destroy democracy. Thus, democracy insists upon majority rule restrained by minority rights.

4. An acceptance of the necessity of compromise. In a democracy, public decision making must be largely a matter of give-and-take among the various competing interests. People must compromise to find the position most acceptable to the largest number. Compromise is the process of blending and adjusting competing views and interests.

5. An insistence upon the widest possible degree of individual freedom. In a democracy, each individual must be as free to do as he or she pleases as far as the freedom of all will allow. Oliver Wendell Holmes once had this to say about the relative nature of each individual's rights: "The right to swing my fist ends where the other man's nose begins."

Analyzing the Visuals

- Have students look at the diagram titled Federal vs. Unitary Government. Ask **In which system is the central government stronger?** *(the unitary system)* **How do the two governmental systems differ in the way they distribute power?** *(In a federal system the powers of the central government and of the states are fairly equal and some powers are shared. In a unitary system, the central government holds all the power; any power wielded by the states comes from the central government.)* **Which system probably experiences more squabbling between the central and state governments, and why?** *(the federal system, because the central and state governments might have trouble sharing some powers or avoiding the occasional usurping of the other's powers)*

- Now point out the Presidential and Parliamentary Governments diagrams. Ask **Who elects the chief executive in a presidential government?** *(the voters)* **Who chooses the chief executive in a parliamentary government?** *(the legislative branch)* **In which system might the chief executive be more responsive to the citizens, and why?** *(presidential, because the chief executive is directly elected by the voters)*

Differentiated
Instruction Solutions for All Learners

L1 Special Needs **L2 Less Proficient Readers** **L2 English Language Learners**

Review the Basic Concepts of Democracy, as listed in the box on this page. Start by writing the following words and phrases on the board: *fundamental worth, dignity, equality, majority rule, minority rights, compromise, individual freedom.* Ask students to read

these words and phrases and suggest the meaning of each. Have them use a dictionary as needed to clarify meanings. Then proceed to discuss each of the concepts and why it is important.

Analyzing the Visuals

Tell students that each of the leaders shown on these pages was a dictator. Nevertheless, each had the support of a large part, if not most, of the population. Ask **Which leaders appear to reflect the typical militaristic character of an authoritarian government? How can you tell?** *(Adolf Hitler, Saddam Hussein, Mao Zedong; they are all wearing military uniforms.)* **Which leaders appear to be sensitive to the finer aspects of life? How can you tell?** *(Mehmed II, who is sniffing a flower; Louis XIV, who is riding a fine horse; Catharine the Great; all three are wearing fashionable clothing.)* Discuss the various forms of dictatorship described in the text. Challenge students to give examples of each.

Catherine the Great of Russia

Louis XIV of France

Mehmed II of the Ottoman Empire

Forms of Dictatorship

Typically militaristic in character, an authoritarian or dictatorial regime usually acquires political power by force and may turn to foreign aggression to enhance its military strength and prestige. Authoritarianism has taken several related forms throughout history.

Absolutism   A system in which the ruler holds complete authority over the government and the lives of the people. Some absolute monarchs ruled according to the principle of divine right. Modern forms of absolutism include military dictatorships that try to control every element of people's lives (see Totalitarianism).

Despotism   Absolute rule with no constitutional restraints. The term *despot* was an honorable title in ancient times. Later, absolute monarchs who favored reforms became known as enlightened despots. Today, despot refers to a brutal and oppressive ruler.

Autocracy   The concentration of power in one individual or group that uses force to maintain absolute control and smother any political opposition.

Glossary of Political Terms

bureaucracy
a large, complex administrative structure that handles the everyday business of government

citizen
a member of a state or nation who is entitled to full civil rights

civil service
those civilian employees who perform the administrative work of government

compromise
an adjustment of opposing principles or systems by modifying some aspect of each

constitution
the body of fundamental laws setting out the principles, structures, and processes of a government

foreign policy
everything a nation's government says and does in world affairs

immigrant
a person legally admitted as a permanent resident of a country

jury
a legally chosen group of persons who hear evidence and decide questions of fact in a court case

nation
a group of people who share the same way of life and live in the same area and under the same central government

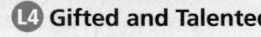

Differentiated
Instruction   **Solutions for All Learners**

L4 Advanced Readers   L4 Gifted and Talented

Point out that the regimes of the leaders depicted here varied greatly. Ask students to research one or more of these dictators to determine which form of dictatorship best applies to their government. Have students present their conclusions, along with supporting details, to the class.

Totalitarianism A form of absolutism in which the government sweeps away existing political institutions and exerts complete control over nearly every aspect of the society. In this system, a supreme leader often becomes the sole source of society's rules.

Communism An ideology that, in theory, calls for ownership of all land and other productive property by the workers. In practice, a system of repressive, single-party government that completely controls its citizens' lives and stifles all opposition.

Fascism A form of government that seeks to renew society by demanding citizens' complete devotion to the state. Often led by a dictator who strictly controls industry and labor, denies freedom and individual rights, and uses police and the military to silence opposition.

Adolf Hitler of Germany

Mural of Saddam Hussein

Mao Zedong's Little Red Book

politics
the activities of those who run or seek to run a government

rule of law
idea that all citizens, including government officials, are subject to the law

sovereign
having supreme power within its own territory

state
a group of people living in a defined territory who have a government with the power to make and enforce law without the consent of any higher authority

suffrage
the right to vote

tax
a charge levied by government on persons or property to meet public needs

treaty
a formal agreement between two or more sovereign states

History Background

Mao's Little Red Book By the 1960s, Chinese Communist leader Mao Zedong had become a revered, godlike figure, especially to members of the People's Liberation Army (PLA). Lin Biao, the head of the PLA, gathered many of Mao's sayings and writings into a book called the *Quotations of Chairman Mao Tse-Tung*. He ordered all PLA soldiers to memorize the material, which presented Mao's ideas about a variety of political and social issues. During the Cultural Revolution of the 1970s, the book was required reading for students at all grade levels, and workers studied it as well. Mao's quotations came to be seen as infallible. Unofficially, all Chinese citizens were expected to carry a copy of the book with them at all times, and they could be punished for failing to do so. The pocket-sized Western version of this book, with its bright red cover, became known as *The Little Red Book.*

Overview

Culture can be a difficult concept for students to grasp. Encourage them to read and discuss the introductory paragraphs of this handbook until they have a clear sense of the concept. This handbook focuses on three major aspects of culture—language, religion, and the arts. Language clearly serves to differentiate cultures. If you cannot speak a people's language, you cannot participate fully in their culture. Historically, religion provided a similar barrier, although today, religions such as Christianity and Islam have spread their influence far beyond their places of origin. Art can still reflect a particular society, but in an age of instantaneous communication, artists are influenced by works from all over the world and from many historical eras.

The Culture Handbook includes a large chart showing Major World Religions/Belief Systems. Be sure students have enough time to read and digest the information presented there. Students should also take time to study the list of Major Art Movements, which are presented in chronological order.

Test Preparation

Ask groups of students to create multiple-choice questions drawn from the charts in this handbook. Have them follow each question with four possible answers. Invite each group to test the rest of the class with their questions.

Analyzing the Visuals

Direct students' attention to the chart titled Principal Languages of the World. Ask **Which language is spoken by the most people?** *(Mandarin Chinese)* **How many people speak English as their first language?** *(309 million)* Explain that Portugal has a population of 10.6 million. Ask **Given this information how do you explain that 177 million people speak Portuguese as their first language?** *(Portugal, like other European countries, established colonies throughout the world, and many people in those colonies continue to speak Portuguese.)*

Concept Connector Handbooks

Culture

Culture is a way of life, or a set of values and behaviors, that people in a society learn, share, and pass on from generation to generation. Culture mainly involves what people think, what they do, and what they create. It consists of such elements as language, religion, art, social organization, and technology. Cultures can change over time. Some elements are forgotten, and others are improved or replaced. Still others are picked up from outside cultures. This spread of ideas, customs, and technologies from one culture to another is known as cultural diffusion. Historically, cultures have spread mainly through trade, migration, and conquest.

World Languages

Language is a part of culture. Yet it is also the main tool by which people transmit their culture. Many thousands of languages have arisen since humans first began to communicate. Some 6,800 of those languages still survive. Related languages can be grouped into language families.

Principal Languages of the World

Language	Speakers* (in millions)
Mandarin (Chinese)	873
Spanish	322
English	309
Hindi	180
Portuguese	177
Bengali	171
Russian	145
Japanese	122
German	95
Wu (Chinese)	77

* estimated number for whom this is their first language

Sign in a Native American language and English (above); fragment of a Dead Sea scroll, written in ancient Hebrew (below)

Major Belief Systems

Most of the world's major belief systems have existed for more than 2,000 years. Today, if the world included only 1,000 people, 330 of them would be Christian, 215 would be Muslim, 149 would be Hindu, 140 would follow no religion, 59 would be Buddhist, 37 would follow Chinese traditional religions, and 41 would hold primal-indigenous beliefs.

Bibliography

For the Teacher

Deutscher, Guy. *The Unfolding of Language: An Evolutionary Tour of Mankind's Greatest Invention.* Metropolitan Books, 2005.

Farrington, Karen. *Historical Atlas of Religions.* Checkmark Books, 2002.

Onians, John, ed. *Atlas of World Art.* Oxford University Press, 2004.

For the Student

Breuilly, Elizabeth, et al. *Religions of the World: The Illustrated Guide to Origins, Beliefs, Traditions and Festivals.* Facts on File, 1997.

Davidson, Rosemary. *Take a Look: An Introduction to the Experience of Art.* Viking, 1994.

Levinson, David. *Human Environments: A Cross-Cultural Encyclopedia.* ABC-CLIO, 1995.

Major World Religions/Belief Systems

	Leading Figures; Dates	Key Beliefs	Writings	Number of Followers
Buddhism	Siddhartha Gautama (the Buddha); late sixth to fourth century B.C.	No gods, but buddhas, or "enlightened ones" exist; reincarnation (cycle of birth, death, and rebirth); the Four Noble Truths: (1) suffering is a part of life; (2) selfish desire leads to suffering; (3) desire can be overcome; (4) the Eightfold Path leads away from desire, toward release from the cycle of birth, death, and rebirth	*Tripitaka (The Three Baskets)*; the sutras; the tantras	373 million
Chinese Traditional Religions (blend of Buddhism, Confucianism, and Daoism)	Blending began in the A.D. 900s	Reincarnation (from Buddhism); virtuous way of life (from Confucianism); acting in harmony with nature and avoiding aggressive action (from Daoism)	*Dao de Jing (The Way of Power)*; *Zhuangzi* (named after the greatest interpreter of Daoism); (see also Buddhism and Confucianism)	398 million
Christianity	Jesus of Nazareth; early first century A.D.	One God; to save humans, God sent Jesus, who suffered, died, and rose from the dead; the Trinity: three figures (God the Father, God the Son, and God the Holy Spirit) united as one; love God above all else	The Bible: the Old Testament (Hebrew Bible) and the New Testament; various creeds and statements of faith	2.07 billion
Confucianism	Confucius; around 500 B.C.	No gods; not an organized religion, but a system of moral conduct based on the teachings of Confucius; kindness, love, and respect lead to a virtuous way of life	The *Lun yü (Analects)*; the *Wu-ching (Five Classics)*; the *Ssu Shu (Four Books)*	6.43 million (mainly in Korea)
Hinduism	No founder or central institution; around 1500 B.C.	Brahman, the ultimate God, is the source of all existence; many lesser gods, the main ones being Vishnu and Siva; reincarnation; law of karma (actions in one life affect next life); ahimsa (principle of noninjury or nonviolence)	The Vedas, sutras, epics, and puranas	837 million
Islam	Muhammad; early A.D. 600s	One God, Allah; Five Pillars, or duties: (1) profession of faith; (2) prayer; (3) charity; (4) fasting; (5) pilgrimage to Mecca in Saudi Arabia	Quran	1.25 billion
Judaism	Abraham; around 2000 B.C.	One God; God made a covenant, with Abraham and the Jewish people that if they obey God's commands, God will make Israel a great nation; moral actions are more important than beliefs	Hebrew Bible: The Torah (the "Law"), the Nevi'im (the "Prophets"), and the Ketuvim (the "Writings"); oral tradition, written as the Talmud	14.6 million
primal-indigenous (includes tribal religions, animism, shamanism, and paganism)	Such religions have existed since prehistoric times	May be a high god; nature spirits (powerful life forces inhabiting the elements of nature); communication with spirits through prayers and offerings ensures the support of the spirits	none	238 million
Shinto	No founder; well established by the A.D. 500s	Many gods; Kami (superior, mystical, or divine powers) are the sources of human life; main deity is sun goddess Amaterasu O-mikami; each person is worthy of respect; truthfulness and purification (physical and spiritual) bring the blessings of the kami	No central sacred scripture; chief books: *Kojiki (Records of Ancient Matters)* and *Nihon shoki (Chronicles of Japan)*	2.68 million
Sikhism (combines elements of Hinduism and Islam)	Nanak; around A.D. 1500	One God; reincarnation; meditation can release one from the cycle of reincarnation; law of karma; all humans are equal	*Adi Granth (First Book)*	24.3 million

Analyzing the Visuals

Point out the table on this page. Give students time to familiarize themselves with the headings. Then ask **Which of these belief systems is the oldest?** *(primal-indigenous)* Write the answer on the board, and then have students put all the belief systems in chronological order according to their founding. Then ask **How are Judaism, Christianity, and Islam similar?** *(All three are monotheistic—followers believe in one God.)* **How do the beliefs of Hindus differ from those of Jews, Christians, and Muslims?** *(Hindus have an ultimate God but also many lesser gods; their belief in reincarnation and karma are not found in the other religions.)* **How does Confucianism differ from all the other religions and belief systems?** *(It is not an organized religion but a system of moral conduct.)* **How does religion serve to create differences between cultures? For example, how are the lives of Muslims different from the lives of Sikhs?** *(Organized religions have rules that affect one's way of life. Muslims' duties include setting time aside for fasting and prayer; Sikhs are expected to meditate.)*

Differentiated Instruction   Solutions for All Learners

L1 Special Needs   L2 Less Proficient Readers

To help students better understand the chart on this page, start by asking them to read the title and the names of all the religions and belief systems in the first column. Then have them read the four column headings. Ask **What information will this table provide?** *(For each religion or belief system, the table provides information about its founding, beliefs, sacred writings, and followers.)* Model an examination of the first row, asking and answering questions such as **Who founded Buddhism?** and **What do Buddhists believe?** Then use a similar technique to elicit information from students about other religions.

Have students look at all the works of art on these two pages and read the captions. Point out that the central box only covers major art movements in Western culture. Suggest to students that they read the descriptions in the box to help them understand and date each work. Ask **How are the terms organized in this box?** *(by chronology)* **Which work of art appeals to you most? Why? Which one is least appealing? Why?** *(Encourage students to back up their opinions even if they can say only that the work gives them a good or bad feeling or impression.)*

Culture

The Arts

The arts tell much about a culture. Ancient civilizations produced artists only after they were capable of generating an agricultural surplus. Some people could then be spared from the fields to devote themselves to other pursuits, including the arts. Works of art, from paintings and sculptures to music, dance, and writing, reflect the culture in which the artist lived. Notice the variations among the arts presented in these pictures. Think about what each picture says about the culture that produced it.

▲ Neoclassical bust of Napoleon by Antonio Canova, c. 1802

Romantic poet, writer, and artist William Blake's *Songs of Innocence*, 1789 ▼

Major Art Movements

classicism
Greek and Roman art; emphasis on harmony, proportion, balance, and simplicity

byzantine
500s–1400s, Europe, Russia

Romanesque
late eleventh century, Europe

Gothic
1100s–1400s, Europe; cathedral architecture and religious art

Renaissance
c. 1400–1600, Europe; Leonardo, Michelangelo, Raphael

mannerism
c. 1520–1600, Europe; Parmigianino

baroque
seventeenth and early eighteenth centuries, Europe; Bernini, Caravaggio, Rubens

rococo
eighteenth century, Europe; Fragonard

neoclassicism
late eighteenth and early nineteenth centuries, Europe; revival of ancient Greek and Roman art; David, Canova

romanticism
late eighteenth to mid-nineteenth century, Europe, United States; Delacroix, Géricault, Turner, Blake, Hudson River school

Barbizon School
c. 1840–1870, France; landscapes; Rousseau, Corot, Millet

realism
nineteenth century, Europe and United States; Daumier, Courbet, Eakins

impressionism
late nineteenth century, France and United States; Monet, Renoir, Cassatt

pointillism
1880s, France; Seurat, Signac

Costume from Georg Friedrich Handel's baroque opera *Agrippina*, 1709 (right) ▶

Pointillist painting by Georges Seurat, *Porte-en-Bessin*, 1888 (far right) ▶

Differentiated Instruction   Solutions for All Learners

🄻🄸 **Advanced Readers**   🄻🄸 **Gifted and Talented**

To help students gain a better understanding of the differences between ancient and modern art, assign pairs of students to research the visual arts of a region or country that they choose, such as East Asia, South Asia, Latin America, West Africa, Sub-Saharan Africa, or Europe. Have them prepare a presentation to compare and contrast examples of the region's ancient and modern visual arts. Remind students that the visual arts include painting, sculpture, architecture, printmaking, and decorative arts.

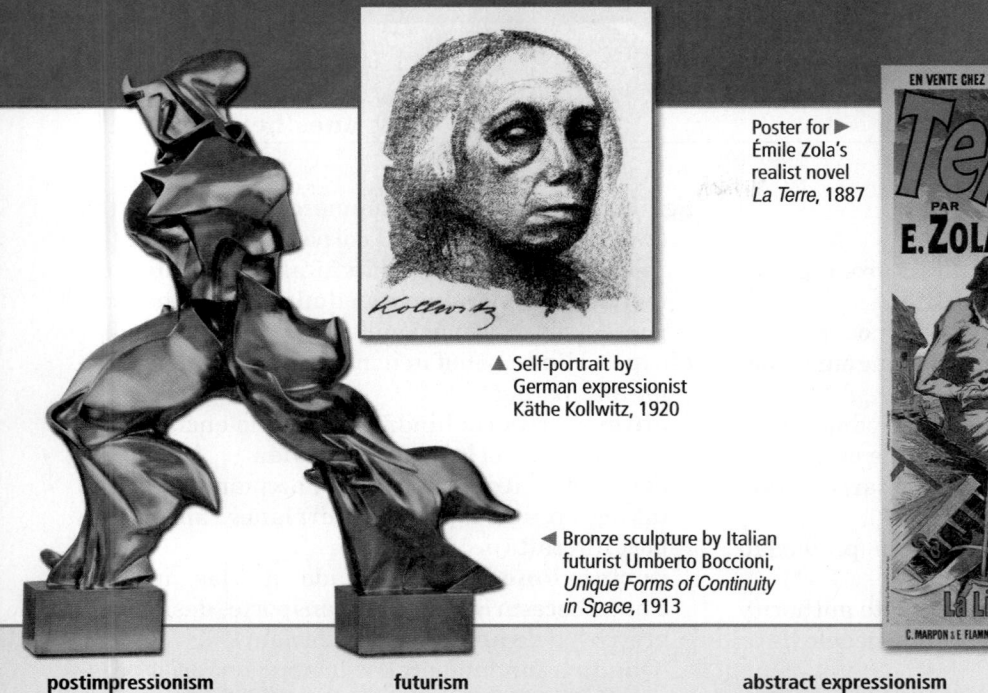

Poster for ▶
Émile Zola's
realist novel
La Terre, 1887

▲ Self-portrait by
German expressionist
Käthe Kollwitz, 1920

◀ Bronze sculpture by Italian
futurist Umberto Boccioni,
*Unique Forms of Continuity
in Space*, 1913

postimpressionism
late nineteenth century, France;
Cézanne, Van Gogh, Gauguin

art nouveau
late nineteenth century, Europe;
decorative arts

cubism
early twentieth century, Europe;
Picasso, Braque

fauvism
c. 1905–1908, France; pure, bold
colors applied in a spontaneous
manner; Matisse

expressionism
c. 1905–1925, northern Europe;
Rouault, Kokoschka, Schiele

futurism
c. 1909–1919, Italy; Boccioni

constructivism
c. 1915, Russia; abstract style using
non-traditional materials;
Rodchenko, Tatlin, Gabo, Pevsner

dadaism
c. 1915–1923, France; rejected
accepted aesthetic standards;
Duchamp

surrealism
1920s–1930s, Europe; Magritte, Dalí,
Miró, Ernst, de Chirico

art deco
1920s–1930s; decorative arts characterized by sleek lines and slender
forms

abstract expressionism
1940s, New York City; Pollock,
de Kooning, Motherwell, Kline

minimalism
late 1950s, United States; Judd,
Martin, Kelly

color field painting
1950s, United States; Newman,
Rothko, Frankenthaler

pop art
1950s, United States; Warhol,
Lichtenstein, Oldenburg

conceptual art
1960s and 1970s, interna-
tional; questioned the definition of "art"

Sculpture for a park in Minneapolis
by pop artist Claes Oldenburg,
Spoonbridge and Cherry, 1988 ▼

History Background

Patrons of the Arts The ancient Greek statesman Pericles, the Persian shah Abbas, the Japanese shogun Minamoto Yoritomo, and the American computer whiz Bill Gates all have something in common. They all have been great patrons of the arts. Throughout history, peo-ple of wealth and power have supported all manner of artistic endeavor, from painting and sculpture to music and dance. In the Western world, Pope Julius II stands

out for the support he gave to the famous Renaissance artists Bramante, Raphael, and Michelangelo. Julius also worked together with Michelangelo on ideas for the Sistine Chapel ceiling. In return for their support, painters would often create portraits of their patrons, and musicians would compose music in their honor. Both Raphael and Michelangelo drew celebrated por-traits of Pope Julius.

A

abdicate to give up or step down from power (p. 236)

abdicar renunciar de un puesto de poder

abolition movement the campaign against slavery and the slave trade (p. 365)

movimiento por la abolición campaña contra la esclavitud y contra el tráfico de esclavos

absentee landlord one who owns a large estate but does not live there (p. 367)

dueño ausente dueño de una gran propiedad que no vive en ella

absolute monarch ruler with complete authority over the government and lives of the people he or she governs (p. 144)

monarca absoluto gobernante que tiene autoridad absoluta sobre la administración y la vida de los que están bajo su mando

abstract style of art composed of lines, colors, and shapes, sometimes with no recognizable subject matter at all (p. 527)

abstracto estilo de arte compuesto de líneas, colores y formas, y que a veces no tiene un tema reconocible

acid rain a form of pollution in which toxic chemicals in the air come back to Earth in the form of rain, snow, or hail (p. 750)

lluvia ácida forma de polución en la que los productos químicos tóxicos que se encuentran en el aire vuelven a la tierra en la lluvia, nieve o granizo

acropolis highest and most fortified point within a Greek city-state (p. 16)

acrópolis el punto más alto y fortificado de una ciudad-estado griega

Afghanistan an Islamic country in Central Asia; invaded by the Soviet Union in 1979; later home to the radical Islamist Taliban and the terrorist al Qaeda (pp. 170, 757)

Afganistán país islámico en Asia Central; invadido por la Unión Soviética en 1979; más tarde hogar de los radicales islamistas Talibán y de los terroristas de al Qaeda

African National Congress (ANC) the main organization that opposed apartheid and pushed for majority rule in South Africa; later a political party (p. 687)

Congreso Nacional Africano (ANC, por sus siglas en inglés) principal organización que se opuso al apartheid y que abogó por el gobierno de la mayoría de Sudáfrica; posteriormente, partido político

agribusinesses giant commercial farms, often owned by multinational corporations (p. 722)

industria agropecuaria inmensas granjas comerciales, generalmente administradas por corporaciones multinacionales

ahimsa Hindu belief in nonviolence and reverence for all life (p. 504)

ahimsa creencia hindú en la no violencia y en el respeto a todas las formas de vida

aircraft carriers ships that accommodate the taking off and landing of airplanes, and transport aircraft (p. 578)

portaaviones buque dotado de las instalaciones necesarias para el transporte, despegue y aterrizaje de aparatos de aviación

al Qaeda a fundamentalist Islamic terrorist organization led by Saudi Arabian Osama bin Laden (p. 756)

al Qaeda organización fundamentalista islámica terrorista liderada por el saudí Osama bin Laden

alliance formal agreement between two or more nations or powers to cooperate and come to one another's defense (p. 111)

alianza acuerdo formal de cooperación y defensa mutua entre dos o más naciones o potencias

Alsace and Lorraine provinces on the border of Germany and France, lost by France to Germany in 1871; regained by France after World War I (p. 456)

Alsacia y Lorena provincias en la frontera entre Alemania y Francia, que Alemania arrebató a Francia en 1871, y que Francia recuperó después de la Primera Guerra Mundial

Amritsar massacre an incident in 1919 in which British troops fired on an unarmed crowd of Indians (p. 503)

masacre de Amritsar incidente en 1919 en el que las tropas británicas dispararon contra un grupo de indios indefensos

anarchist someone who wants to abolish all government (p. 342)

anarquista persona que quiere abolir toda forma de gobierno

ancien régime old order; system of government in pre-revolution France (p. 210)

ancien regime antiguo orden; sistema de gobierno en la Francia prerevolucionaria

anesthetic drug that prevents pain during surgery (p. 247)

anestesia fármaco que suprime el dolor durante la cirugía

annex add a territory to an existing state or country (pp. 232, 332)

anexar agregar un territorio a un estado o país existente

Anschluss union of Austria and Germany (p. 565)

Anschluss unión de Austria y Alemania

anti-ballistic missiles (ABMs) missiles that can shoot down other missiles (p. 606)

misiles anti-balísticos (ABM, por sus siglas) misiles que pueden derribar otros misiles

apartheid a policy of rigid segregation of non-white people in the Republic of South Africa (pp. 497, 686)

apartheid política de estricta separación racial en Sudáfrica que fue abolida en 1989

appeasement policy of giving in to an aggressor's demands in order to keep the peace (p. 563)

contemporización política de aceptación de las exigencias de un agresor para mantener la paz

aristocracy government headed by a privileged minority or upper class (p. 16)

aristocracia gobierno encabezado por una minoría privilegiada o de clase alta

armada fleet of ships (p. 145)

armada flota de barcos

armistice agreement to end fighting in a war (p. 471)

armisticio acuerdo para dejar de luchar en una guerra

artificial satellite man-made object that orbits a larger body in space (p. 759)

satélite artificial objeto artificial que gira en el espacio alrededor de un cuerpo más grande

artisan a skilled craftsperson (p. 5)

artesano trabajador cualificado que hace objetos a mano

Asante kingdom kingdom that emerged in the 1700s in present-day Ghana and was active in the slave trade (p. 92)

reino Asante reino que surgió en el siglo XVIII en el actual Ghana y que tenía comercio de esclavos

Asia Minor the Turkish peninsula between the Black Sea and the Mediterranean Sea (p. 499)

Asia Menor la península turca entre el Mar Negro y el Mar Mediterráneo

assembly line production method that breaks down a complex job into a series of smaller tasks (p. 301)

cadena de montaje método de producción que divide un trabajo complejo en una serie de tareas menores

atheism belief that there is no god (p. 547)

ateísmo creencia de que no existen dioses

atrocity horrible act committed against innocent people (p. 468)

atrocidad acto brutal cometido en contra de inocentes

autocratic having unlimited power (pp. 169, 658)

autocrático que tiene poder ilimitado

autonomy self-rule (p. 274)

autonomía autogobierno

Axis powers group of countries led by Germany, Italy, and Japan that fought the Allies in World War II (p. 564)

Potencias del Eje grupo de países liderado por Alemania, Italia y Japón que luchó contra los Aliados durante la Segunda Guerra Mundial

B

balance of power distribution of military and economic power that prevents any one nation from becoming too strong (p. 152)

equilibrio de poder distribución del poder military y económico que evita que una nación se vuelva demasiado fuerte

balance of trade difference between how much a country imports and how much it exports (p. 411)

balance commercial diferencia entre lo que importa y exporta un país

Balfour Declaration statement issued by the British government in 1917 supporting the establishment of a homeland for Jews in Palestine (p. 502)

Declaración Balfour declaración hecha por el gobierno británico en 1917 en la que apoyaba la constitución de un estado judío en Palestina

Bangladesh literally "Bengali nation," nation east of India that was formerly part of Pakistan (p. 655)

Bangladesh literalmente significa "nación bengalí"; país al este de India que antiguamente formaba parte de Pakistán

baroque ornate style of art and architecture popular in the 1600s and 1700s (p. 189)

barroco estilo artístico y arquitectónico elaborado que se dio en los siglos XVII y XVIII

Bastille fortress in Paris used as a prison; French Revolution began when Parisians stormed it in 1789 (p. 215)

Bastilla fortificación en París usada como prisión; la Revolución Francesa empezó cuando los parisinos la asaltaron en 1789

Bataan Death March during World War II, the forced march of Filipino and American prisoners of war under brutal conditions by the Japanese military (p. 587)

Jornada de la Muerte desde Bataan episodio acaecido durante la Segunda Guerra Mundial, en el que prisioneros de guerra filipinos y estadounidenses fueron obligado a marchar bajo condiciones brutales por parte de militares japoneses

Biafra region of southeastern Nigeria that launched a failed bid for independence from Nigeria in 1966, launching a bloody war (p. 668)

Biafra región del sudeste de Nigeria que lanzó un fallido intento de independizarse de Nigeria en 1966, y por el que se desató una cruenta guerra

biotechnology the application of biological research to industry, engineering and technology (p. 762)

biotecnología la aplicación de investigaciones biológicas en la industria, la ingeniería y la tecnología

Black Shirt any member of the militant combat squads of Italian Fascists set up under Mussolini (p. 537)

Camisa Negra cualquier miembro de las escuadras militantes de combate de los fascistas italianos que estableció Mussolini

blitzkrieg lightning war (p. 568)

blitzkrieg guerra relámpago o guerra intensa y muy breve

bloc a group of nations acting together in support of one another (p. 741)

bloque grupo de naciones que actúan conjuntamente en apoyo mutuo

Boer War (1899–1902) a war in which Great Britain defeated the Boers of South Africa (p. 396)

Guerra Boer (1899–1902) guerra en la que Gran Bretaña venció a los Boer de Sudáfrica

Boers Dutch people who settled in Cape Town, Africa, and eventually migrated inland (p. 93)

Boers holandeses establecidos en Ciudad del Cabo, África, que con el tiempo emigraron hacia el interior

bourgeoisie the middle class (p. 211)

burguesía clase media

Boxer Uprising anti-foreign movement in China from 1898–1900 (p. 414)

Rebelión Bóxer movimiento en contra de los extranjeros ocurrido en China de 1898 a 1900

boyar landowning noble in Russia under the tsars (p. 169)

boyar noble ruso que poseía tierras en la época de los zares (p. 169)

boycott refuse to buy (p. 504)

boicot negarse a comprar

brahman in the belief system established in Aryan India, the single spiritual power that resides in all things (p. 8)

brahman en el sistema de creencias establecido en la India aria, el único poder espiritual que reside en todas las cosas

C

cabinet parliamentary advisors to the king who originally met in a small room, or "cabinet" (p. 160)

gabinete miembros del parlamento consejeros del rey que originalmente se reunían en un pequeño cuarto o "gabinete"

cahier notebook used during the French Revolution to record grievances (p. 214)

memorándum cuaderno usado durante la Revolución Francesa para anotar los agravios

calculus a branch of mathematics in which calculations are made using special symbolic notations; developed by Isaac Newton (p. 76)

cálculo rama de las matemáticas en la que los cálculos se hacen con notaciones simbólicas especiales; fue desarrollado por Isaac Newton

caliph successor to Muhammad as political and religious leader of the Muslims (p. 32)

califa sucesor de Mahoma como líder religioso político de los musulmanes

canonize recognize a person as a saint (p. 67)

canonizar reconocer a una persona como santo

Cape Town seaport city and legislative capital of South Africa; was the first Dutch colony in Africa (p. 93)

Ciudad del Cabo ciudad portuaria y capital legislativa de Sudáfrica; fue la primera colonia holandesa en África

capital money or wealth used to invest in business or enterprise (p. 251)

capital dinero o bienes que se usan para invertir en negocios o empresas

capital offense crime punishable by death (p. 365)

ofensa capital crimen que puede castigarse con la muerte

capitalism economic system in which the means of production are privately owned and operated for profit (p. 131)

capitalismo sistema económico por el que los medios de producción son propiedad privada y se administran para obtener beneficios

cartel a group of companies that join together to control the production and price of a product (p. 304)

cartel asociación de grandes corporaciones formada para controlar la producción y el precio de un producto

cartographer mapmaker (p. 85)

cartógrafo persona que hace mapas

caste in traditional Indian society, an unchangeable social group into which a person is born (p. 8)

casta grupo social en la sociedad tradicional de India, en el que una persona nace y del que no se puede cambiar

caudillo military dictator in Latin America (p. 440)

caudillo dictador militar en América Latina

censorship restriction on access to ideas and information (p. 189)

censura restricción en el acceso a ideas o información

chancellor the highest official of a monarch, prime minister (pp. 331, 550)

canciller oficial con más rango dentro de una monarquía, primer ministro

Chechnya a republic within Russia where rebels have fought for independence from Russia (p. 683)

Chechenia república dentro del territorio ruso en la que grupos rebeldes luchan por su independencia de Rusia

Cheka early Soviet secret police force (p. 482)

Cheka una de las primeras fuerzas policiales secretas soviética

chivalry a code of conduct for knights during the Middle Ages (p. 26)

caballería código de conducta para los caballeros durante la Edad Media

circumnavigate to travel completely around the world (p. 89)

circunnavegar viajar alrededor del mundo

city-state a political unit that includes a city and its surrounding lands and villages (p. 6)

ciudad estado unidad política compuesta por una ciudad y las tierras y aldeas que la rodean

civil disobedience the refusal to obey unjust laws (p. 504)

desobediencia civil negarse a obedecer leyes injustas

civil war war fought between two groups of people in the same nation (p. 113)

guerra civil guerra en la que luchan dos grupos de personas de una misma nación

coalition temporary alliance of various political parties (p. 374)

coalición alianza temporal de varios partidos políticos

Cold War state of tension and hostility between nations aligned with the United States on one side and the Soviet Union on the other that rarely led to direct armed conflict (p. 592)

Guerra Fría estado de tensión y hostilidad entre las naciones alineadas con Estados Unidos, por una parte, y con la Unión Soviética, por la otra, que salvo raras excepciones desembocó en un conflicto armado

collective large farm owned and operated by peasants as a group (p. 543)

granja colectiva granja grande que pertenece a campesinos que la administran en grupo

collective security system in which a group of nations acts as one to preserve the peace of all (p. 474)

seguridad colectiva sistema por el que un grupo de naciones actúa como una para preservar la paz común

collectivization the forced joining together of workers and property into collectives, such as rural collectives that absorb peasants and their land (p. 624)

colectivización unión forzada de trabajadores y propiedad en colectivos, como colectivos rurales que absorben a campesinos y sus tierras

colossus giant (p. 348)

coloso gigante

Columbian Exchange the global exchange of goods, ideas, plants and animals, and disease that began with Columbus' exploration of the Americas (p. 129)

Intercambio colombino intercambio global de bienes, ideas, plantas, animales y enfermedades que comenzaron con la exploración de las Américas por parte de Colón

Comintern Communist International, international association of communist parties led by the Soviet Union for the purpose of encouraging worldwide communist revolution (p. 549)

Comintern Internacional Comunista, asociación internacional de partidos comunistas liderada por la Unión Soviética con el propósito de extender por el mundo una revolución comunista

command economy system in which government officials make all basic economic decisions (p. 543)

economía controlada sistema en el que los funcionarios del gobierno toman todas las decisiones económicas básicas

commissar Communist party officials assigned to the army to teach party principles and ensure party loyalty during the Russian Revolution (p. 482)

comisario funcionario del partido comunista asignado al ejército para enseñar los principios del partido y para asegurar la lealtad al mismo durante la revolución rusa

communism form of socialism advocated by Karl Marx; according to Marx, class struggle was inevitable and would lead to the creation of a classless society in which all wealth and property would be owned by the community as a whole (p. 263)

comunismo forma de socialismo defendido por Karl Marx; según Marx, la lucha de clases era inevitable y llevaría a la creación de una sociedad sin clases en la que toda la riqueza y la propiedad pertenecería a la comunidad como un todo

compact an agreement among people (p. 122)

pacto acuerdo

compromise an agreement in which each side makes concessions; an acceptable middle ground (p. 68)

compromiso acuerdo en el que cada parte hace concesiones; un término medio aceptable

concentration camp detention center for civilians considered enemies of the state (p. 573)

campo de concentración centro de detención de los civiles que se considera enemigos del estado

Concert of Europe a system in which Austria, Russia, Prussia, and Great Britain met periodically to discuss any problems affecting the peace in Europe; resulted from the post-Napoleon era Quadruple Alliance (p. 600)

Concierto de Europa sistema por el cual Austria, Rusia, Prusia y Gran Bretaña se reunían periódicamente para discutir cualquier problema que afectara a la paz en Europa; resultado de la Cuádruple Alianza de la era postnapoleónica

concession special economic rights given to a foreign power (p. 404)

concesión derechos económicos especiales que se dan a un poder extranjero

confederation unification (p. 435)

confederación unificación

Congress of Vienna assembly of European leaders that met after the Napoleonic era to piece Europe back together; met from September 1814 to June 1815 (p. 237)

Congreso de Viena asamblea de líderes europeos que se reunió después de la era napoleónica para reconstruir Europa; se reunieron desde septiembre de 1814 a junio de 1815

conquistador Spanish explorers who claimed lands in the Americas for Spain in the 1500s and 1600s (p. 110)

conquistador los exploradores españoles que apropiaron tierras en América para España en los siglos XVI y XVII

conscription "the draft," which required all young men to be ready for military or other service (p. 467)

conscripción llamado a filas que exigía que todos los hombres jóvenes estuvieran listos para el servicio militar u otro servicio

constitutional government government whose power is defined and limited by law (p. 160)

gobierno constitucional gobierno cuyo poder está definido y limitado por las leyes

containment the U.S. strategy of keeping communism within its existing boundaries and preventing its further expansion (p. 611)

contención estrategia de Estados Unidos de mantener el comunismo dentro de sus fronteras existentes y de prevenir su expansión

Continental System blockade designed by Napoleon to hurt Britain economically by closing European ports to British goods; ultimately unsuccessful (p. 232)

sistema continental bloqueo diseñado por Napoleón para dañar a Gran Bretaña económicamente que consistía en cerrar los puertos europeos a los productos británicos; con el tiempo no tuvo éxito

contraband during wartime, military supplies and raw materials needed to make military supplies that may legally be confiscated by any belligerent (p. 468)

contrabando durante el tiempo de guerra, provisiones militares y materias primas necesarios para fabricar artículos militares, y que pueden ser confiscados legalmente por cualquiera de las partes beligerantes

contras guerrillas who fought the Sandinistas in Nicaragua (p. 724)

contras grupo guerrillero que luchó contra los sandinistas en Nicaragua

convoy group of merchant ships protected by warships (p. 463)

convoy grupo de barcos mercantes protegidos por barcos de guerra

corporation business owned by many investors who buy shares of stock and risk only the amount of their investment (p. 303)

corporación empresa propiedad de muchos inversores que compran acciones y que sólo arriesgan el monto de su inversión

Council of Trent a group of Catholic leaders that met between 1545 and 1563 to respond to Protestant challenges and direct the future of the Catholic Church (p. 69)

Concilio de Trento grupo de líderes católicos que se reunieron entre 1545 y 1563 para tratar los retos protestantes y liderar el futuro de la Iglesia Católica

coup d'état the forcible overthrow of a government (p. 663)

golpe de estado derrocamiento por la fuerza de un gobierno

creole person in Spain's colonies in the Americas who was an American-born descendent of Spanish settlers (pp. 118, 283)

criollo descendiente de colonos españolas nacido en las colonias españolas de América

Crimean War war fought mainly on the Crimean Peninsula between the Russians and the British, French, and Turks from 1853–1856 (p. 349)

Guerra de Crimea guerra librada principalmente en la península de Crimea entre los rusos y los británicos, franceses y turcos entre 1853 y 1856

Crusades a series of wars from the 1000s through the 1200s in which European Christians tried to win control of the Holy Land from Muslims (p. 29)

Cruzadas serie de guerras entre el siglo XI y el siglo XIII en las que los cristianos europeos intentaron ganar el control sobre los musulmanes de la Tierra Santa

cult of domesticity idealization of women and the home (p. 313)

culto a lo doméstico idealización de las mujeres y del hogar

cultural diffusion the spread of ideas, customs, and technologies from one people to another (p. 6)

difusión cultural divulgación de ideas, costumbres y tecnología de un pueblo a otro

cultural nationalism pride in one's country's culture (p. 494)

nacionalismo cultural orgullo de la cultura del país propio

Cultural Revolution a Chinese Communist program in the late 1960s to purge China of non-revolutionary tendencies that caused economic and social damage (p. 624)

Revolución Cultural programa de la China comunista a finales de la década de 1960 que pretendía eliminar de China todas las tendencias no revolucionarias y que causó daños económicos y sociales

cuneiform in the ancient Middle East, a system of writing that used wedge-shaped marks (p. 7)

cuneiforme en el antiguo Oriente Medio, sistema de escritura cuyos caracteres tenían forma de cuña

D

dada artistic movement in which artists rejected tradition and produced works that often shocked their viewers (p. 527)

dadaísmo movimiento artístico en el que los artistas rechazaban la tradición y producían obras que a menudo sorprendían a su público

daimyo warrior lord directly below the shogun in feudal Japan (p. 36)

daimio señor de la Guerra que en el Japón feudal estaba directamente abajo del shogun

dalits outcastes or members of India's lowest caste (pp. 654, 718)

dalits (o intocables) los marginados o miembros de las castas más bajas de India

Dardanelles vital strait connecting the Black Sea and the Mediterranean Sea in present-day Turkey (p. 464)

Dardanelos estrecho de vital importancia que conecta el Mar Negro y el Mar Mediterráneo en la actual Turquía

Darfur a region in western Sudan where ethnic conflict threatened to lead to genocide (p. 690)

Darfur región occidental de Sudán donde un conflicto étnico amenaza con provocar un genocidio

D-Day code name for the day that Allied forces invaded France during World War II, June 6, 1944 (p. 582)

Día D nombre en clave del día en que las fuerzas aliadas invadieron Francia durante la Segunda Guerra Mundial (6 de junio de 1944)

default fail to make payments (p. 736)

cese de pagos imposibilidad de realizar pagos

deficit gap between what a government spends and what it takes in through taxes and other sources (p. 736)

déficit diferencia entre los gastos de un gobierno y las recaudaciones por impuestos y otras fuentes de ingresos

deficit spending situation in which a government spends more money than it takes in (p. 213)

gasto deficitario situación en la que un gobierno gasta más de lo que recauda

deforestation the destruction of forest land (pp. 408, 750)

deforestación destrucción de tierras forestales

demilitarized zone a thin band of territory across the Korean peninsula separating North Korean forces from South Korean forces; established by the armistice of 1953 (p. 628)

zona desmilitarizada estrecha franja de tierra que cruza la península de Corea y que separa las fuerzas de Corea del Norte y las fuerzas de Corea del Sur; establecida por el armisticio de 1953

democracy government in which the people hold ruling power (p. 17)

democracia forma de gobierno en el que la soberanía reside en el pueblo

depopulation reduction in the number of people in an area (p. 165)

despoblación reducción del número de la población en una zona

desertification process by which fertile or semi-desert land becomes desert (p. 711)

desertización proceso por el que la tierra fértil o semifértil se convierte en desierto

détente the relaxation of Cold War tensions during the 1970s (p. 606)

distensión relajamiento de las tensiones de la Guerra Fría en los años 70

developing world nations working toward development in Africa, Asia, and Latin America (p. 704)

mundo en desarrollo países en vías de desarrollo de á frica, Asia y Latinoamérica

development the process of building stable governments, improving agriculture and industry, and raising the standard of living (p. 704)

desarrollo proceso de establecer gobiernos estables, mejorar la agricultura, la industria y las condiciones de vida

Diaspora the spreading of the Jews beyond their historic homeland (p. 7)

Diáspora diseminación de los judíos más allá de su patria histórica

Dienbienphu small town and former French army base in northern Vietnam; site of the battle that ended in a Vietnamese victory, the French withdrawal from Vietnam, and the securing of North Vietnam's independence (p. 631)

Dienbienphu pequeño pueblo y antigua base del ejército francés en el norte de Vietnam; lugar de la batalla que terminó con la victoria vietnamita, la expulsión de los franceses de Vietnam y la obtención de la independencia de Vietnam del Norte

diet assembly or legislature (pp. 63, 425)

dieta asamblea o cuerpo legislativo

direct democracy system of government in which citizens participate directly in the day-to-day affairs of government rather than through elected representatives (p. 17)

democracia directa sistema de gobierno en el que los ciudadanos participan directamente en lugar de hacerlo a través de representantes electos en los asuntos diarios del gobierno

disarmament reduction of armed forces and weapons (p. 531)

desarme reducción del ejército y del armamento

discrimination unequal treatment or barriers (p. 616)

discriminación tratamiento desigual o barreras

dissenter Protestant whose views and opinions differed from those of the Church of England (p. 155)

disidente protestante cuyos puntos de vista y opiniones diferían de los de la Iglesia de Inglaterra

divine right belief that a ruler's authority comes directly from God (p. 144)

derecho divino creencia de que la autoridad de un gobernante proviene directamente de Dios

dominion self-governing nation (p. 435)

dominio nación que se gobierna a sí misma

domino theory the belief that a communist victory in South Vietnam would cause noncommunist governments across Southeast Asia to fall to communism, like a row of dominoes (p. 631)

teoría del dominó creencia de que una victoria comunista en Vietnam del Sur podría causar que los gobiernos no comunistas del sudeste de Asia cayeran bajo dominio del comunismo, como una fila de fichas de dominó

Dreyfus affair a political scandal that caused deep divisions in France between Royalists and liberals and republicans; centered on the 1894 wrongful conviction of Alfred Dreyfus, a Jewish officer in the French army (p. 375)

Caso Dreyfus escándalo político que causó divisiones profundas en Francia entre los realistas, liberales y republicanos; basado en la in justa condena en 1894 de Alfred Dreyfus, un oficial judío del ejérci to francés

Dual Monarchy the monarchy of Austria-Hungary (p. 344)

    monarquía dual monarquía de Austria-Hungría

Duma elected national legislature in Russia (p. 353)

    Duma en Rusia, asamblea legislative nacional electa

Dunkirk port in France from which 300,000 Allied troops were evacuated when their retreat by land was cut off by the German advance in 1940 (p. 569)

    Dunkirk puerto de Francia desde donde fueron evacuadas 300,000 tropas aliadas en 1940 al ser bloqueada su retirada terrestre por el avance del ejército alemán

Dutch East India Company a trading company established by the Netherlands in 1602 to protect and expand its trade in Asia (p. 96)

    Compañía Holandesa de las Indias Orientales compañía de comercio establecida por Holanda en 1602 para proteger y aumentar su comercio con Asia

dynamo a machine used to generate electricity (p. 301)

    dínamo máquina que se usa para generar electricidad

dynastic cycle rise and fall of Chinese dynasties according to the Mandate of Heaven (p. 9)

    ciclo dinástico florecimiento y caída de las dinastías chinas de acuerdo con el Mandato del Cielo

dynasty ruling family (p. 9)

    dinastía familia gobernante

E

East Timor a former Portuguese colony, seized by Indonesia, that gained independence in 2002 (p. 659)

    Timor Oriental antigua colonia portuguesa, ocupada por Indonesia, que obtuvo su independencia en 2002

economic nationalism an emphasis on domestic control and protection of the economy (p. 493)

    nacionalismo económico énfasis en el control nacional y en la protección de la economía

Edict of Nantes law issued by French king Henry IV in 1598 giving more religious freedom to French Protestants (p. 148)

    Edicto de Nantes ley promulgada por el rey francés Enrique IV en 1598 por la que se concedía mayor libertad religiosa a los protestantes frances (p. 148)

elector one of seven German princes who would choose the Holy Roman emperor (p. 163)

elector uno de los siete príncipes germanos que elegían al emperador del Sacro Romano

electorate body of people allowed to vote (p. 361)

    electorado conjunto de personas a quienes se permite votar

elite upper class (p. 398)

    élite clase alta

emancipation granting of freedom to serfs or slaves (p. 349)

    emancipación concesión de libertad a esclavos o siervos

emigration movement away from one's homeland (p. 342)

    emigración trasladarse de su propio país a otro

émigré person who flees his or her country for political reasons (p. 220)

    exiliado persona que deja su país por razones políticas

empire a group of states or territories controlled by one ruler (p. 5)

    imperio grupo de estados o territorios controlados por un gobernante

enclosure the process of taking over and consolidating land formerly shared by peasant farmers (p. 248)

    cercamiento proceso de consolidar y apropiarse de una tierra que anteriormente compartían campesinos

encomienda right the Spanish government granted to its American colonists to demand labor or tribute from Native Americans (p. 116)

    encomienda derecho a exigir tributo o trabajo a los natives americanos, que el gobierno español otorgó a sus colonos en América

endangered species species threatened with extinction (p. 712)

    especies en vías de extinción especies amenazadas de extinción, es decir, de desaparición

English Bill of Rights series of acts passed by the English Parliament in 1689 that limited the rights of the monarchy and ensured the superiority of Parliament (p. 159)

    Declaración de derechos de los ingleses serie de leyes aprobadas por el parlamento inglés en 1689 que limitaba los derechos de la monarquía y establecía la primacía del parlamento

engraving art form in which an artist etches a design on a metal plate with acid and then uses the plate to make multiple prints (p. 57)

    grabado forma de arte en la que un artista graba un diseño con ácido en una placa de metal y después la usa para producir múltiples impresiones

enlightened despot absolute ruler who used his or her power to bring about political and social change (p. 191)

déspota ilustrado gobernante absoluto que usa su poder para precipitar cambios políticos y sociales

entente nonbinding agreement to follow common policies (p. 455)

entendimiento acuerdo no vinculante de seguir normas comunes

enterprise a business organization in such areas as shipping, mining, railroads, or factories (p. 251)

empresa entidad empresarial en áreas como transportes, minería, ferrocariles o fábricas

entrepreneur person who assumes financial risk in the hope of making a profit (pp. 131, 251)

empresario persona que asume riesgos financieros con la esperanza de obtener beneficios

epidemic outbreak of a rapidly spreading disease (p. 746)

epidemia brote de una enfermedad que se extiende rápidamente

erosion the wearing away of land (p. 751)

erosión el desgaste paulatino de la tierra

estate social class (p. 210)

estado clase social

Estates-General legislative body made up of representatives of the three estates in pre-revolutionary France

Estados Generales cuerpo legislativo formado por representantes de los tres estados en la Francia prerevolucionaria

ethnic cleansing the killing or forcible removal of people of different ethnicities from an area by aggressors so that only the ethnic group of the aggressors remains (p. 684)

limpieza étnica la matanza o expulsión forzosa de personas de diferentes grupos étnicos de una zona, llevadas a cabo por agresores para que su grupo étnico tenga permanencia exclusiva

ethnic group large group of people who share the same language and cultural heritage (p. 31)

étnico grupo grande de personas que comparten el idioma y la herencia cultural

euro common currency used by member nations of the European Union (p. 735)

euro moneda común usada por las naciones que pertenecen a la Unión Europea

European Community an international organization dedicated to establishing free trade among its European member nations (p. 620)

Comunidad Europea organización internacional dedicada a establecer un comercio libre entre sus naciones europeas miembros de todos los productos

European Union an international organization made up of over two dozen European nations, with a common currency and common policies and laws (p. 735)

Unión Europea organización internacional compuesta por más de dos docenas de países, con una misma moneda, y políticas y leyes en común

excommunication exclusion from the Roman Catholic Church as a penalty for refusing to obey Church law (p. 28)

excomunión exclusión de la Iglesia Católica Romana como castigo por rehusar obedecer la ley de la Iglesia

expansionism policy of increasing the amount of territory a government holds (p. 377)

expansionismo política de aumentar el territorio que posee un gobierno

extraterritoriality right of foreigners to be protected by the laws of their own nation (p. 412)

extraterritorialidad derecho de los extranjeros a recibir protección de las leyes de su propio país

F

faction dissenting group of people (p. 217)

facción grupo de disidentes

famine a severe shortage of food in which large numbers of people starve (p. 746)

hambruna escasez severa de alimentos por la que perece gran número de personas

fascism any centralized, authoritarian government system that is not communist whose policies glorify the state over the individual and are destructive to basic human rights (p. 539)

fascismo cualquier sistema de gobierno autoritario centralizado no comunista cuya política glorifica al estado o encima del individuo y que destruye los derecho humanos fundamentales

federal republic government in which power is divided between the national, or federal, government and the states (p. 201)

república federal gobierno en el que el poder se divide entre el gobierno nacional o federal y los estados

Federal Reserve central banking system of the United States, which regulates banks (p. 533)

Reserva Federal sistema central de banca de Estados Unidos que regula los bancos

feudalism loosely organized system of government in which local lords governed their own lands but owed military service and other support to a greater lord (p. 26)

feudalismo sistema de gobierno poco organizado en el que los señores gobierna han sus propias tierras, pero debían servicio militar y otras formas de apoyo a un superior

fief in medieval Europe, an estate granted by a lord to a vassal in exchange for service and loyalty (p. 26)

estado feudal durante la Edad Media, terreno que un señor cedía a un vasallo a cambio de servicio y lealtad

filial piety respect for parents (p. 15)

piedad filial respeto hacia los padres

finance the management of money matters including the circulation of money, loans, investments, and banking (p. 533)

finanzas o gestión de los asuntos monetarios incluyendo la circulación de dinero, préstamos, inversiones y banca

First Sino-Japanese War conflict between China and Japan in 1894–1895 over control of Korea (p. 427)

Primera guerra sino-japonesa conflicto entre China y Japón de 1894 a 1895 por el control de Corea

Flanders a region that included parts of present-day northern France, Belgium, and the Netherlands; was an important industrial and financial center of northern Europe during the Middle Ages and Renaissance (p. 57)

Flandes región que incluye partes de los actuales norte de Francia, Bélgica y Holanda; fue un importante centro industrial y financiero del norte de Europa durante la Edad Media y el Renacimiento

flapper in the United States and Europe in the 1920s, a rebellious young woman (p. 523)

flapper mujer joven y rebelde en los años 20 en Estados Unidos y Europa

Florence a city in the Tuscany region of northern Italy that was the center of the Italian Renaissance (p. 50)

Florencia ciudad de la región de Toscana en el norte de Italia que fue el centro del Renacimiento italiano

Fourteen Points list of terms for resolving World War I and future wars outlined by American President Woodrow Wilson in January 1918 (p. 471)

Catorce puntos lista de condiciones para resolver la Primera Guerra Mundial y futuras guerras, esbozada por el presidente estadounidense Woodrow Wilson en enero de 1918

free trade trade between countries without quotas, tariffs, or other restrictions (p. 364)

libre comercio comercio entre países, sin cuotas, tasas u otras restricciones

French and Indian War war between Britain and France in the Americas that happened from 1754 to 1763; it was part of a global war called the Seven Years' War (p. 124)

Guerra franco-india guerra entre Gran Bretaña y Francia en América, que duró desde 1754 a 1763; fue parte de una guerra global que se conoció como la Guerra de los Siete Años

French Indochina Western name for the colonial holdings of France on mainland Southeast Asia—present-day Vietnam, Laos, and Cambodia (p. 430)

Indochina francesa nombre occidental para las colonias de Francia en el sudeste asiático continental

fundamentalists religious leaders who call for a return to what they see as the fundamental, or basic, values of their faiths (p. 708)

fundamentalistas líderes religiosos que abogan por el retorno de lo que consideran ser los valores fundamentales, o básicos, de sus creencias

G

general strike strike by workers in many different industries at the same time (p. 532)

huelga general huelga de trabajadores de muchas industrias diferentes al mismo tiempo

genetic engineering manipulation of living organisms' chemical code in order to produce specific results (p. 763)

ingeniería genética alteración del código genético que portan todas las formas de vida con el fin de producir resultados específicos

genetics a branch of biology dealing with heredity and variations among plants and animals (p. 763)

genética rama de la biología que trata sobre la herencia y las variaciones entre sí de los animales y las plantas

Geneva Swiss city-state which became a Calvinist theocracy in the 1500s; today a major city in Switzerland (p. 65)

Ginebra ciudad estado suiza que se convirtió en una teocracia calvinista en el siglo XVI; en la actualidad es una de las principales ciudades de Suiza

genocide deliberate attempt to destroy an entire religious or ethnic group (p. 402)

genocidio intento deliberado de destruir la totalidad de un grupo religioso o étnico

germ theory the theory that infectious diseases are caused by certain microbes (p. 305)

teoría de los gérmenes teoría de que las enfermedades infecciosas son causadas por ciertos microbios

Gestapo secret police in Nazi Germany (p. 553)

Gestapo policía secreta de la Alemania nazi

ghetto separate section of a city where members of a minority group are forced to live (p. 71)

gueto área separada de una ciudad donde se fuerza a vivir a los miembros de una minoría

glasnost "openness" in Russian; a Soviet policy of greater freedom of expression introduced by Mikhail Gorbachev in the late 1980s (p. 640)

glasnost "apertura" en ruso; política soviética de mayor libertad de expresión introducida por Mikhail Gorbachev a finales de la década de 1980

global warming the rise of Earth's surface temperature over time (p. 751)

calentamiento global el aumento de la temperatura de la superficie terrestre a través del tiempo

globalization the process by which national economies, politics, cultures, and societies become integrated with those of other nations around the world (p. 738)

globalización proceso mediante el cual las economías nacionales, la política, la cultura y la sociedades se integran con las de otros países del mundo

Goa a state in western India; formerly a coastal city that was made the base of Portugal's Indian trade (p. 95)

Goa estado en el oeste de India; antiguamente una ciudad costera que se convirtió en la base del comercio en la India de Portugal

Golden Temple the Sikh religion's holiest shrine (p. 655)

Templo Dorado santuario de mayor peso sagrado de la religión sikh

Good Friday Agreement an agreement to end the conflict in Northern Ireland signed in 1998 by Protestants and Catholics (p. 683)

Acuerdo del Viernes Santo acuerdo firmado por protestantes y católicos en 1998 para poner fin al conflicto en Irlanda del Norte

Good Neighbor Policy policy in which American President Franklin Roosevelt promised that the United States would interfere less in Latin American affairs (p. 494)

Política del Buen Vecino politica con la que el presidente estadounidense Franklin Roosevelt prometio que Estados Unidos interferiria menos en los asuntos de America Latina

gravity force that pulls objects in Earth's sphere to the center of Earth (p. 76)

gravedad fuerza que atrae los objetos dentro de la esfera terrestre al centro de la Tierra

Great Depression a painful time of global economic collapse, starting in 1929 and lasting until about 1939 (p. 533)

Gran Depresión período nefasto de colapso de la economía mundial que empezó en 1929 y duró hasta 1939

Great Leap Forward a Chinese Communist program from 1958 to 1960 to boost farm and industrial output that failed miserably (p. 624)

Gran Salto hacia Adelante programa de la China comunista de 1958 a 1960 para aumentar la producción agrícola e industrial que fracasó miserablemente

Green Revolution the improved seeds, pesticides, mechanical equipment, and farming methods introduced in the developing world beginning in the 1950s (p. 706)

revolución verde la introducción, en los países en vías de desarrollo durante la década de 1950, de semillas, pesticidas, equipo mecánico y métodos de agricultura perfeccionados

griot professional storyteller in early West Africa (p. 35)

griot antiguo narrador de historias profesional en África occidental

gross domestic product (GDP) the total value of all goods and services produced in a nation within a particular year (p. 622)

producto interior bruto (PIB) valor total de todos los productos y servicios producidos en una nación en un determinado año

Guangzhou a coastal city in southeastern China, also known as Canton (p. 100)

Guangzhou ciudad costera del sudeste de China, también conocida como Cantón

guerrilla a soldier in a loosely organized force making surprise raids (p. 631)

guerrilla pequeños grupos de soldados pertenecientes a una fuerza poco organizada que despliega ataques por sorpresa

guerrilla warfare fighting carried on through hit-and-run raids (p. 235)

guerra de guerrillas lucha que se caracteriza por rápidos ataques y retiradas

guild in the Middle Ages, an association of merchants or artisans who cooperated to uphold standards of their trade and to protect their economic interests (p. 27)

gremio en la Edad Media, asociación de mercaderes o artesanos que cooperaban para mantener los valores de sus oficios y para proteger sus intereses económicos

guillotine device used during the Reign of Terror to execute thousands by beheading (p. 226)

guillotina aparato usado durante el Reinado del Terror para decapitar a miles de personas

Gulag in the Soviet Union, a system of forced labor camps in which millions of criminals and political prisoners were held under Stalin (p. 544)

Gulag en la Unión Soviética, un sistema de campos de trabajo forzado donde millones de criminales y prisioneros políticos fueron detenidos durante el gobierno de Stalin

Guomindang Nationalist party; active in China 1912 to 1949 (p. 508)

Guomindang partido nacionalista, activo en China entre 1912 y 1949

H

hacienda a large plantation (p. 490)
hacienda plantación grande

hajj one of the Five Pillars of Islam, the pilgrimage to Mecca that all Muslims are expected to make at least once in their lifetime (p. 32)

hayyi uno de los Cinco Pilares del Islam, la peregrinación a la Meca que se espera hagan todos los musulmanes por lo menos una vez en la vida

Hapsburg empire Central European empire that lasted from the 1400s to the 1900s and at its height included the lands of the Holy Roman Empire and the Netherlands (p. 142)

Imperio Habsburgo imperio centroeuropeo que duró desde el siglo XV hasta el siglo XX, y que en su plenitud abarcó los territorios del Sacro Imperio Romano y Holanda

Harlem Renaissance an African American cultural movement in the 1920s and 1930s, centered in Harlem (p. 525)

Renacimiento de Harlem movimiento cultural afroamericano durante las décadas de 1920 y 1930, que estaba centrado en Harlem

hejab headscarves and loose-fitting, ankle-length garments meant to conceal the body (p. 673)

hejab velos, pañuelos y prendas de vestir amplias y hasta los tobillos cuya finalidad es ocultar el cuerpo

heliocentric based on the belief that the sun is the center of the universe (p. 72)

heliocéntrico sistema basado en la creencia de que el Sol es el centro del universo

hierarchy system of ranking groups (p. 6)
jerarquía sistema que clasifica a las personas de una sociedad

Hiroshima mid-sized city in Japan where the first atomic bomb was dropped in August, 1945 (p. 589)

Hiroshima ciudad de tamaño medio de Japón donde fue lanzada la primera bomba atómica en agosto de 1945

Holocaust the systematic genocide of about six million European Jews by the Nazis during World War II (p. 574)

Holocausto el genocidio sistemático por parte de los nazis de alrededor de seis millones de judíos europeos durante la Segunda Guerra Mundial

home rule local self-government (p. 369)
autogobierno autogobierno local

homogeneous society society that has a common culture and language (p. 426)

sociedad homogénea sociedad que tiene un lenguaje y una cultura común

Huguenots French Protestants of the 1500s and 1600s (p. 148)

Hugonotes protestantes franceses de los siglos XVI y XVII

humanism an intellectual movement at the heart of the Renaissance that focused on education and the classics (p. 49)

humanismo movimiento intelectual durante el auge del Renacimiento que se centraba en la educación y los clásicos

humanities study of subjects such as grammar, rhetoric, poetry, and history, that were taught in ancient Greece and Rome (p. 49)

humanidades estudio de asignaturas como la gramática, la retórica, poesía e historia que se enseñaban en las antiguas Grecia y Roma

Hutus the group that forms the majority in Rwanda and Burundi (p. 689)

Hutus grupo mayoritario de Ruanda y Burundi

hypothesis an unproved theory accepted for the purposes of explaining certain facts or to provide a basis for further investigation (p. 74)

hipótesis teoría sin probar aceptada con el propósito de explicar determinados hechos o de proveer una base para una investigación posterior más profunda

I

ideology system of thought and belief (pp. 272, 610)

ideología sistema de pensamiento y creencias

immunity natural protection, resistance (p. 111)

immunidad protección natural, resistencia

imperialism domination by one country of the political, economic, or cultural life of another country or region (p. 388)

imperialismo dominio por parte de un país de la vida política, económica o cultural de otro país o región

import substitution manufacturing goods locally to replace imports (p. 720)

sustitución de importaciones la producción local de bienes para reemplazar su importación

impressionism school of painting of the late 1800s and early 1900s that tried to capture fleeting visual impressions (p. 322)

impresionismo escuela de pintura de finales del siglo XIX y principios del siglo XX que trataba de captar impresiones visuales fugaces

indemnity payment for losses in war (p. 412)

indemnización compensación como pago por pérdidas de guerra

indigenous original or native to a country or region (pp. 436, 725)

indígena originario o nativo de un país o región

indulgence in the Roman Catholic Church, pardon for sins committed during a person's lifetime (p. 62)

indulgencia perdón por los pecados cometidos en vida concedido por la Iglesia Católica Romana

inflation economic cycle that involves a rapid rise in prices linked to a sharp increase in the amount of money available (p. 130)

inflación ciclo económico caracterizado por un rápida subida de los precios ligada a un aumento rápido del dinero disponible

insurgents rebel forces (p. 697)

insurgentes fuerzas rebeldes

intendant official appointed by French king Louis XIV to govern the provinces, collect taxes, and recruit soldiers (p. 150)

intendente oficial publico nombrado por el rey francés Luis XIV para gobernar las provincias, recaudar impuestos y reclutar soldados

interchangeable parts identical components that can be used in place of one another in manufacturing (p. 301)

repuestos intercambiables componentes idénticos que pueden usarse unos en lugar de otros en el proceso de producción

interdependence mutual dependence of countries on goods, resources, labor, and knowledge from other parts of the world (p. 738)

interdependencia dependencia mutua de los países con los de otras partes del mundo en cuanto a productos, recursos, mano de obra y conocimientos

International Space Station (ISS) an artificial structure built and maintained by a coalition of nations with the purpose of research (p. 759)

Estación Espacial Internacional (ISS, por sus siglas en inglés) estructura artificial construida y mantenida por una coalición de naciones con el fin de llevar a cabo investigaciones

Internet a huge international computer network linking millions of users around the world (p. 761)

Internet inmensa red internacional de computadoras que une a millones de ususarios en todo el mundo

intifada Palestinian Arab uprisings against the Israeli occupation (p. 693)

intifadas levantamientos de árabes palestinos en contra de la ocupación israelí

Islamist a person who wants government policies to be based on the teachings of Islam (p. 667)

islamista persona que desea que las políticas del gobierno tengan su fundamento en las enseñanzas del Islam

island-hopping during World War II, Allied strategy of recapturing some Japanese-held islands while bypassing others (p. 588)

salto entre islas estrategia aliada durante la Segunda Guerra Mundial de retomar algunas de las islas ocupadas por los japoneses e ignorar y pasar de largo de otras

J

Jacobin member of a radical political club during the French Revolution (p. 221)

jacobino miembro de un club político radical durante la Revolución Francesa

Jerusalem capital of the Jewish state of Judea in ancient times and capital of the modern State of Israel; city sacred to Jews, Muslims, and Christians (p. 694)

Jerusalén capital del estado judío de Judea en la antigüedad, y capital del actual estado de Israel; ciudad sagrada para los judíos, musulmanes y cristianos

jury group of people sworn to make a decision in a legal case (p. 28)

> **jurado** grupo de personas que han prestado juramento par tomar una decisión en un caso legal

K

kaiser emperor of Germany (p. 333)

> **kaiser** emperador de Alemania

kamikaze Japanese pilot who undertook a suicide mission (p. 588)

> **kamikaze** piloto japonés que emprendía una misión suicida

Kashmir a former princely state in the Himalayas, claimed by both India and Pakistan, which have fought wars over its control (p. 653)

> **Cachemira** antiguo estado principesco de los Himalayas, reclamado tanto por India como Pakistán, y por cuyo control han librado varias guerras

Katanga a province of the Democratic Republic of the Congo with rich copper and diamond deposits that tried to gain independence from Congo in 1960 (p. 667)

> **Katanga** provincia de la República Democrática del Congo con ricos depósitos de cobre y diamantes, que intentó independizarse del Congo en 1960

Kellogg-Briand Pact an international agreement, signed by almost every nation in 1928, to stop using war as a method of national policy (p. 531)

> **Pacto de Kellogg-Briand** acuerdo internacional firmado por casi todas las naciones en 1928 para erradicar el uso de la guerra como un metodo de politica nacional

Khmer Rouge a political movement and a force of Cambodian communist guerrillas that gained power in Cambodia in 1975 (p. 635)

> **Khmer Rouge** movimiento político y fuerza guerrillera comunista de Camboya que llegó al poder en ese país en 1975

kibbutz a collective farm in Israel (p. 671)

> **kibbutz** en Israel, granja comunitaria

kiva large underground chamber that the Anasazi used for religious ceremonies and political meetings (p. 21)

> **kiva** gran sala subterránea que usaban los anazasi para ceremonias religiosas y reuniones políticas

knight a European noble who served as a mounted warrior (p. 26)

> **caballero** noble europeo que servía como guerrero montado

Knossos an ancient Minoan city on the island of Crete

> **Cnosos** antigua ciudad minoica en la isla de Creta

Kolkata a large city in India, also known as Calcutta (p. 718)

> **Kolkata** ciudad grande de India, conocida también como Calcuta

Kosovo a province of Serbia with an Albanian ethnic majority that was the site of an ethnic conflict during the 1990s (p. 685)

> **Kosovo** provincia de Serbia de mayoría étnica albanesa que sufrió un conflicto étnico durante la década de 1990

kulak wealthy peasant in the Soviet Union in the 1930s (p. 543)

> **campesino** adinerado de la Unión Soviética en la década de 1930

Kulturkampf Bismarck's "battle for civilization," in which his goal was to make Catholics put loyalty to the state above their allegiance to the Church (p. 336)

> **Kulturkampf** "batalla por civilización" de Bismarck, cuyo objetivo era que los católicos pusieran la lealtod al estado por encima de la lealtad a la Iglesia

L

La Reforma an era of liberal reform in Mexico from 1855 to 1876 (p. 441)

> **La Reforma** era de reforma liberal en México desde 1855 a 1876

labor union workers' organization (p. 256)

> **sindicato** organización de trabajadores

laissez faire policy allowing business to operate with little or no government interference (p. 186)

> **laissez faire** política que permite a los negocios y empresas operar con poca o ninguna interferencia del gobierno

laser a high-energy light beam that can be used for many purposes including surgery, engineering, and scientific research (p. 762)

> **láser** haz luminoso de alta energía que puede ser usado para muchos fines, entre ellos la cirugía, la ingeniería y la investigación científica

legitimacy principle by which monarchies that had been unseated by the French Revolution or Napoleon were restored (p. 238)

legitimidad principio por el que las monarquías que habían sido derrocadas por la Revolución Francesa o por Napoleón fueron restituidas

Lend-Lease Act act passed by the United States Congress in 1941 that allowed the president (FDR) to sell or lend war supplies to any country whose defense was considered vital to the United States (p. 575)

Ley de Préstamo y Arriendo decreto aprobado por el Congreso de Estados Unidos en 1941 que permitió al presidente (FDR) vender o arrendar materiales de guerra a cualquier país cuya defensa fuese considerada de vital importancia para Estados Unidos

levée morning ritual during which nobles would wait upon French king Louis XIV (p. 150)

recepción matutina ritual de la mañana en el que los nobles atendían al rey Luis XIV

libel knowing publication of false and damaging statements (p. 375)

libelo publicación intencional de declaraciones falsas que perjudican a alguien

liberation theology movement within the Catholic Church that urged the church to become a force for reform, social justice, and put an end to poverty (p. 723)

teología de la liberación movimiento dentro de la Iglesia Católica que urgía a la iglesia a liderar un llamamiento por la reforma, la justicia social el fin de la pobreza

limited monarchy government in which a constitution or legislative body limits the monarch's powers (p. 160)

monarquía limitada gobierno en el que la constitución o el cuerpo legislativo limitan los poderes de la monarquía

Line of Demarcation line set by the Treaty of Tordesillas dividing the non-European world into two zones, one controlled by Spain and the other by Portugal (p. 88)

Línea de demarcación línea establecida por el Tratado de Tordesillas que dividía el mundo fuera de Europa en dos zonas: una controlada por España y otra por Portugal

literacy the ability to read and write (p. 704)

alfabetismo capacidad de leer y escribir

Liverpool city and one of the largest ports in England; first major rail line linked Liverpool to Manchester in 1830 (p. 253)

Liverpool ciudad y uno de los puertos más grandes de Inglaterra; línea importante de ferrocarril unió Liverpool con Manchester en 1830

Long March epic march in which a group of Chinese Communists retreated from Guomindang forces by marching over 6,000 miles (p. 509)

Gran Marcha marcha épica en la que un grupo de comunistas chinos marcharon en retirada de las fuerzas del Guomindang por más de 6,000 millas

Louisiana Purchase territory purchased by Thomas Jefferson from France in 1803 (p. 377)

Compra de Luisiana territorio que Thomas Jefferson compró a Francia en 1803

Luftwaffe German air force (p. 568)

Luftwaffe fuerza aérea alemana

Lusitania British liner torpedoed by a German submarine in May 1915 (p. 468)

Lusitania crucero británico torpedeado por un submarino alemán en mayo de 1915

M

Macao region of southeastern China made up of a peninsula and two islands, a Portuguese territory from the mid-1800s to 1999 (p. 100)

Macao región al sudeste de China formada por una península y dos islas; fue territorio portugués desde mediados del siglo XIX a 1999

Maginot Line massive fortifications built by the French along the French border with Germany in the 1930s to protect against future invasions (p. 531)

Línea Maginot fortificaciones masivas construídas por los franceses a lo largo de la frontera france sa con Alemania en la década de 1930 para protegerse contra invasiones futuras

Mahdi a Muslim savior of the faith (p. 400)

Mahdi salvador musulmán de la fe

Malacca a state and coastal city in southwestern Malaysia, was an early center of the spice trade (p. 95)

Malacca estado y ciudad costera en el sudoeste de Malasia; fue uno de los primeros centros del comercio de especias

Malindi a coastal town in southeastern Kenya (p. 90)

Malindi pueblo costero al sudeste de Kenia

Manchester city in England; one of the leading industrial areas; example of an Industrial Revolution city; first major rail line linked Manchester to Liverpool in 1830 (p. 253)

Manchester ciudad de Inglaterra; una de las principales áreas industriales; ejemplo de ciudad de la Revolución Industrial; la primera línea importante de ferrocarril unió Manchester con Liverpool en 1830

Manchuria historic province in northeastern China; rich in natural resources (p. 514)

Manchuria provincia histórica en el noreste de China; rica en recursos naturales

Manchus people originally from Manchuria, north of China, who conquered the Ming dynasty and ruled China as the Qing dynasty from the mid-1600s to the early 1900s (p. 101)

manchus personas originalmente de Manchuria, al norte de China, que derrotaron a la dinastía Ming y gobernaron como la dinastía Chin desde mediados del siglo XVII a principios del siglo XX

mandate after World War I, a territory administered by a Western power (p. 476)

mandato territorio administrado por un poder occidental después de la Primera Guerra Mundial

Manhattan Project code name for the project to build the first atomic bomb during World War II (p. 588)

Proyecto Manhattan nombre en clave del proyecto para la fabricación de la primera bomba atómica durante la Segunda Guerra Mundial

Manifest Destiny American idea that the United States should stretch across the entire North American continent (p. 377)

Destino Manifiesto idea estadounidense de que Estados Unidos debería extenderse hasta ocupar todo el continente norteamericano

manor during the Middle Ages in Europe, a lord's estate which included one or more villages and the surrounding lands (p. 26)

señorío durante la Edad Media en Europa, propiedad de un señor que incluía uno o más pueblos y sus terrenos adyacentes

Maori indigenous people of New Zealand (p. 438)

maoríe pueblo indígena de Nueva Zelanda

March on Rome planned march of thousands of Fascist supporters to take control of Rome; in response Mussolini was given the legal right to control Italy (p. 537)

Marcha sobre Roma marcha planeada de miles de simpatizantes fascistas sobre Roma para tomar su control; en respuesta a ella a Mussolini se le concedió el derecho legal del control de Italia

Marseilles French port city; troops marched to a patriotic song as they marched from this city, the song eventually became the French national anthem (p. 228)

Marsella ciudad portuaria francesa; las tropas que marcharon al ritmo de una canción patrió-tica desde esta ciudad inspiraron el himno nacional francés

Marshall Plan massive aid package offered by the United States to Europe to help countries rebuild after World War II (p. 593)

Plan Marshall paquete de ayuda a gran escala ofrecido por Estados Unidos a Europa para apoyar la reconstrucción de los países después de la Segunda Guerra Mundial

May Fourth Movement cultural movement in China that sought to reform China and make it stronger (p. 508)

Movimiento del Cuatro de Mayo movimiento cultural de China que se centró en reformar China y hacerla más fuerte

means of production farms, factories, railways, and other large businesses that produce and distribute goods (p. 263)

medios de producción granjas, fábricas, ferrocarriles y otros grandes negocios que producen y distribuyen mercancías

Meiji Restoration in Japan, the reign of emperor Meiji from 1868 to 1912 which was marked by rapid modernization and industrialization (p. 424)

restauración de Meiji en Japón, reino del emperador Meiji desde 1868 a 1912 que fue marcado por la rápida modernización e industrialización

mercantilism policy by which a nation sought to export more than it imported in order to build its supply of gold and silver (p. 132)

mercantilismo política por la que una nación trataba de exportar más de lo que importaba para aumentar sus reservas de o ro y plata

mercenary soldier serving in a foreign army for pay (p. 165)

mercenario soldado que sirve en un ejército extranjero a cambio de dinero

messiah savior sent by God (p. 19)

mésias salvador enviado por Dios

mestizo person in Spain's colonies in the Americas who was of Native American and European descent (pp. 118, 283)

mestizo persona de las colonias españolas de América descendiente de nativos y europeos

métis people of mixed Native American and French Canadian descent (p. 436)

métis pueblo de descendientes con mezcla de indígenas americanos y franceses canadienses

Middle Passage the leg of the triangular trade route on which slaves were transported from Africa to the Americas (p. 125)

Travesía Intermedia parte de la ruta del comercio triangular en la que los esclavos eran transportados desde África a las Américas

militarism glorification of the military (p. 456)

militarismo glorificación de las fuerzas armadas

militias armed groups of citizen soldiers (p. 696)

milicias grupos armados de soldados-ciudadanos

missionary someone sent to do religious work in a territory or foreign country (p. 91)

misioneros personas enviadas para hacer trabajos religiosos en un territorio u otro país

mobilize prepare military forces for war (p. 458)

mobilizar preparar las fuerzas militares para la guerra

Moluccas a group of islands in eastern Indonesia; was the center of the spice trade in the 1500s and 1600s (p. 84)

Molucas grupo de islas en el este de Indonesia; fue el centro del comercio de especias en los siglos XVI y XVII

Mombasa a city in southeastern Kenya, located on a small coastal island (p. 90)

Mombasa ciudad al sudeste de Kenia, localizada en una pequeña isla costera

monarchy government in which a king or queen exercises central power (p. 16)

monarquía gobierno en el que el poder reside en el rey o la reina

monopoly complete control of a product or business by one person or group (p. 92)

monopolio control total de un producto o negocio por una persona o grupo

monotheistic believing that there was only one god (p. 7)

monoteísta creencia en un solo dios

Monroe Doctrine American policy of discouraging European intervention in the Western Hemisphere (p. 443)

Doctrina Monroe política estadounidense de rechazo a la intervención europea en el hemisferio occidental

mosque Muslim house of worship (p. 33)

mezquita templo musulmán

Mothers of the Plaza de Mayo a movement of women who protested weekly in a central plaza in the capital of Argentina against the disappearance or killing of relatives (p. 726)

Madres de la Plaza de Mayo asociación de mujeres que se reunían semanalmente en una céntrica plaza de la capital de Argentina para protest por la desaparición o asesinato de sus familiares

Mughal empire Muslim empire that ruled most of northern India from the mid-1500s to the mid-1700s; also known as the Mogul or Mongol empire (p. 95)

imperio Mughal imperio musulmán que gobernó la mayor parte del norte de India desde mediados del siglo XVI a mediados del siglo XVIII; también se conoce como imperio Mogul o Mongol

mujahedin Muslim religious warriors (p. 640)

mujaedin guerreros religiosos musulmanes

mulatto in Spain's colonies in the Americas, person who was of African and European descent (pp. 118, 283)

mulato en las colonias españolas de América descendiente de africanos y europeos

multiethnic made up of several ethnic groups (p. 684)

multiétnico compuesto de varios grupos étnicos

multinational corporation company with branches in many countries (p. 739)

corporación multinacional empresa con sucursales en muchos países

Mumbai a large city in India, also known as Bombay (p. 718)

Mumbai ciudad grande de India, conocida también como Bombay

mutiny revolt, especially of soldiers or sailors against their officers (p. 128)

motín revuelta, especialmente de soldados y marineros contra sus oficiales

mutual-aid societies self-help groups to aid sick or injured workers (p. 308)

sociedades de ayuda mutua grupos de apoyo establecidos para ayudar a los trabajadores enfermos o heridos en accidentes laborales

mystic person who devotes his or her life to seeking direct communion with divine forces (p. 8)

místico persona que dedica su vida a buscar la comunión directa con las fuerzas divinas

Nagasaki a coastal city in southern Japan on the island of Kyushu; city in Japan where the second atomic bomb was dropped in August, 1945 (pp. 103, 589)

Nagasaki ciudad costera en el sur de Japón en la isla de Kyushu; ciudad de Japón donde fue lanzada la segunda bomba atómica en agosto de 1945

Napoleonic Code body of French civil laws introduced in 1804; served as model for many nations' civil codes (p. 231)

Código Napoleónico cuerpo de las leyes civiles francesas presentadas en 1804, que sirvieron como modelo para los códigos civiles de muchos países

nationalism a strong feeling of pride in and devotion to one's country (p. 228)

nacionalismo fuerte sentimiento de orgullo y devoción hacia el país propio

nationalization takeover of property or resources by the government (p. 492)

nacionalización apropiación de propiedades o recursos por parte del gobierno

natural law rules of conduct discoverable by reason (p. 182)

leyes naturales normas de conducta que se pueden descubrir mediante la razón

natural right right that belongs to all humans from birth, such as life, liberty, and property (p. 183)

derecho natural derecho que pertenece a todos los humanos desde el nacimiento: vida, libertad y propiedad

Nazi-Soviet Pact agreement between Germany and the Soviet Union in 1939 in which the two nations promised not to fight each other and to divide up land in Eastern Europe (p. 567)

Pacto nazi-soviético acuerdo en 1939 entre Alemania y la Unión Soviética mediante el cual las dos naciones prometen no atacarse mutuamente y dividirse entre sí territorio de Europa del Este

négritude movement movement in which writers and artists of African descent expressed pride in their African heritage (p. 498)

movimiento de la negritud movimiento en el que los escritores y artistas descendientes de africanos expresabansu orgullo por la herencia africana

neutrality policy of supporting neither side in a war (p. 458)

neutralidad política de mantenerse al margen en una guerra

Neutrality Acts a series of acts passed by the United States Congress from 1935 to 1939 that aimed to keep the United States from becoming involved in World War II (p. 564)

Leyes de Neutralidad serie de decretos aprobados por el Congreso de Estados Unidos de 1935 a 1939 con el fin de evitar la implicación del país en la Segunda Guerra Mundial

New Deal a massive package of economic and social programs established by FDR to help Americans during the Great Depression (p. 535)

Nuevo Tratado paquete masivo de programas económicos y sociales establecidos por FDR para ayudar a los estadounidenses durante la Gran Depresión

New France French possessions in present-day Canada from the 1500s to 1763 (p. 120)

Nueva Francia posesiones francesas en el actual Canadá desde el siglo XVI a 1763

nirvana in Buddhist belief, union with the universe and release from the cycle of rebirth (p. 14)

nirvana en el budismo, unión con el universo y liberación del ciclo de la reencarnación

no-fly zones in Iraq, areas where the United States and its allies banned flights by Iraqi aircraft after the 1991 Gulf War (p. 697)

zonas de exclusión del espacio aéreo zonas de Iraq en las que Estados Unidos y sus aliados prohibieron el vuelo a la aviación iraquí después de la Guerra del Golfo en 1991

nomad a person who moves from place to place in search of food (p. 4)

nómada persona que se traslada de un lugar a otro en busca de alimentos

nonalignment political and diplomatic independence from both Cold War powers (p. 656)

no alineación independencia política y diplomática de ambas potencias de la guerra fría

North Atlantic Treaty Organization (NATO) a military alliance between several North Atlantic states to safeguard them from the presumed threat of the Soviet Union's communist bloc; countries from other regions later joined the alliance (p. 594)

Organización del Tratado del Atlántico Norte (OTAN) alianza militar entre varios estados del Atlántico norte para salvaguardarlos de la supuesta amenaza del bloque comunista liderado por la Unión Soviética; más tarde se incorporarían a la alianza países de otras regiones

Northern Ireland the northern portion of the island of Ireland, a part of the United Kingdom that has had a long religious conflict (p. 683)

Irlanda del Norte parte norte de la isla de Irlanda y territorio del Reino Unido, que ha sufrido un conflicto religioso durante mucho tiempo

nuclear family family unit consisting of parents and children (p. 35)

familia nuclear unidad familiar que consta de los padres y sus hijos

Nuremberg a city in southern Germany where Hitler staged Nazi rallies in the 1930s, and where Nazi war crimes trials were held after World War II (p. 591)

Nuremberg ciudad del sur de Alemania donde Hitler escenificó manifestaciones nazis durante la década de 1930, y donde se celebraron los juicios por crímenes de guerra nazis después de la Segunda Guerra Mundial

Nuremberg Laws laws approved by the Nazi Party in 1935, depriving Jews of German citizenship and taking some rights away from them (p. 553)

Leyes de Nuremberg leyes aprobadas por el partido nazi en 1935, que eliminaba algunos de los derechos de los judíos en Alemania

O

occupied territories areas controlled by a nation that are part of another entity; Palestinians use this term for certain lands Israel gained after the 1967 war. (p. 693)

territorios ocupados zonas controladas por una nación que forman parte de otra entidad. Los palestinos usan esta palabra para referirse a los territorios ocupados por Israel después de la guerra de 1967

oligarchy government in which ruling power belongs to a few people (pp. 16, 161)

oligarquía gobierno en el que el poder está en manos de unas pocas personas

one-child policy a Chinese government policy limiting urban families to a single child (p. 715)

política de un sólo hijo medida del gobierno chino que limita a las familias urbanas a tener únicamente un hijo

Open Door Policy American approach to China around 1900, favoring open trade relations between China and other nations (p. 414)

Política de puertas abiertas política estadounidense con respecto a China a principios del siglo XX, que abogaba por las libres relaciones comerciales entre China y otras naciones

Opium War war fought between Great Britain and China over restrictions to foreign trade (p. 412)

Guerra del opio guerra librada entre Gran Bretaña y China por las restricciones sobre el comercio exterior

Organization of American States (OAS) a group formed in 1948 to promote democracy, economic cooperation, and human rights in the Americas (p. 724)

Organización de los Estados Americanos grupo formado en 1948 con el fin de promover la democracia, la cooperación económica y los derechos humanos en las Américas

outpost a distant military station or a remote settlement (p. 96)

fuerte fronterizo estación militar distante o asentamiento lejano

outsourcing the practice of sending work to companies in the developing world in order to save money or increase efficiency (p. 738)

subcontratación práctica empresarial de enviar trabajo a compañías de países en vías de desarrollo con el fin de ahorrar dinero o aumentar el rendimiento

overproduction condition in which production of goods exceeds the demand for them (p. 533)

superproducción condición en la que la producción de mercancías excede la demanda

Oyo empire Yoruba empire that arose in the 1600s in present-day Nigeria and dominated its neighbors for a hundred years (p. 92)

imperio Oyo el imperio Yoruba que surgió en el siglo XVII en la actual Nigeria y dominó a sus vecinos durante cien años

P

Pacific Rim vast region of nations, including countries in Southeast Asia, East Asia, and the Americas, that border the Pacific Ocean (p. 737)

Cuenca del Pacífico vasta región de naciones, que incluye los países del sureste y este asiático y de las Américas, que limitan con el océano Pacífico

pacifism opposition to all war (p. 563)

pacifismo oposición a las guerras

Pan-Africanism movement which began in the 1920s that emphasized the unity and strength of Africans and people of African descent around the world (p. 497)

Panafricanismo movimiento que empezó en la década de 1920 que se centraba en la unidad y fuerza de los africanos y personas con ascendencia africana en todo el mundo

Panama Canal man-made waterway connecting the Atlantic and Pacific oceans (p. 445)

Canal de Panamá canal artificial que conecta los océanos Atlántico y Pacífico

Pan-Arabism movement in which Arabs sought to unite all Arabs into one state (p. 500)

Panarabismo movimiento en el que los árabes pretendían unir a todos los árabes en un sólo estado

pandemic spread of a disease across a large area, country, continent, or the entire world (p. 472)

pandemia propagación de una enfermedad a una gran área, país, continente o al mundo entero

parliamentary democracy a form of government in which the executive leaders (usually a prime minister and cabinet) are chosen by and responsible to the legislature (parliament), are also members of it (p. 362)

democracia parlamentaria forma de gobierno en la que la dirección ejecutiva (normalmente un primer ministro y un gabinete) es elegida por la asamblea legislativa (parlamento) y controlada por la misma, además de formar parte de ella

partition a division into pieces (pp. 173, 189, 653)

partición división en partes

pasha provincial ruler in the Ottoman empire (p. 401)

bajá gobernante provincial del imperio otomano

paternalistic the system of governing a country as a father would a child (p. 394)

paternalista sistema de gobernar un país como un padre lo hace con su hijo

patrician in ancient Rome, member of the landholding upper class (p. 18)

patricio miembro de la clase alta terrateniente en la antigua Roma

patron a person who provides financial support for the arts (p. 50)

mecenas persona que proporciona apoyo financiero a la cultura y las artes

Peace of Westphalia series of treaties that ended the Thirty Years' War (p. 165)

Paz de Westfalia serie de tratados por los que se puso fin a la Guerra de los Treinta Años

penal colony place where people convicted of crimes are sent (pp. 365, 437)

colonia penal lugar al que se manda a los condenados por crímenes

peninsulare member of the highest class in Spain's colonies in the Americas (pp. 118, 283)

peninsular miembro de la clase más alta en las colonias españolas de América

peon worker forced to labor for a landlord in order to pay off a debt (p. 116)

peón trabajador forzado a trabajar para un terrateniente para pagar una deuda

peonage system by which workers owe labor to pay their debts (p. 442)

peonaje sistema en el que los trabajadores deben trabajo como pago por sus deudas

perestroika "restructuring" in Russian; a Soviet policy of democratic and free-market reforms introduced by Mikhail Gorbachev in the late 1980s (p. 640)

perestroika "reestructuración" en ruso; política soviética de reformas democráticas y de libre mercado que introdujo Mikhail Gorbachev a finales de la década de 1980

personal computer (PC) a small computer meant to be used by individuals or small businesses (p. 761)

computadora personal (PC, por sus siglas en inglés) pequeña computadora diseñada para uso individual o por parte de pequeñas empresas

perspective artistic technique used to give paintings and drawings a three-dimensional effect (p. 50)

perspectiva técnica artística usada para lograr el efecto de tercera dimensión en dibujos y pinturas

pharaoh title of the rulers of ancient Egypt (p. 6)

faraón título de los gobernantes del antiguo Egipto

Philippines a country in southeastern Asia made up of several thousand islands (p. 97)

Filipinas país al sudeste de Asia formado por varios miles de islas

philosophe French for "philosopher"; French thinker who desired reform in society during the Enlightenment (p. 184)

philosophe palabra francesa que significa "filósofo"; pensador francés que abogaba por reformas en la sociedad durante la Ilustración

pictograph a simple drawing that looks like the object it represents (p. 5)

pictografía dibujo sencillo que se parece al objeto que representa

Pilgrims English Protestants who rejected the Church of England (p. 122)

peregrinos protestantes ingleses que rechazaron la Iglesia de Inglaterra

plantation large estate run by an owner or overseer and worked by laborers who live there (p. 91)

plantación gran propiedad administrada por un dueño o capataz y cultivada por trabajadores que viven en ella

plebian in ancient Rome, member of the lower class, including farmers, merchants, artisans, and traders (p. 18)

plebeyo en la antigua Roma, miembro de clase baja, que incluía granjeros, mercaderes, artesanos y comerciantes

plebiscite ballot in which voters have a direct say on an issue (p. 231)

plebiscito votación en la que los votantes expresan su opinión sobre un tema en particular

pogrom violent attack on a Jewish community (p. 351)

pogrom ataque violento de una multitud hacia una comunidad judía

polis city-state in ancient Greece (p. 16)

polis ciudad-estado de la antigua Grecia

polytheistic believing in many gods (p. 9)

politeísta creencia en muchos dioses

popular sovereignty basic principle of the American system of government which asserts that the people are the source of any and all governmental power, and government can exist only with the consent of the governed (p. 198)

soberanía popular principio básico del sistema de gobierno estadounidense en el que se determina que el pueblo es la fuente de todo poder gubernamental, y que el gobierno sólo puede existir con el consentimiento de los gobernados

predestination Calvinist belief that God long ago determined who would gain salvation (p. 65)

predestinación creencia calvinista de que Dios decidió hace mucho tiempo quién conseguiría la salvación

premier prime minister (p. 374)

premier primer ministro

price revolution period in European history when inflation rose rapidly (p. 130)

revolución del precio período en la historia de Europa en que la inflación aumentó rápidamente

privateer privately owned ship commissioned by a government to attack and capture enemy ships, especially merchant's ships (p. 119)

corsario barco privado comisionado por un gobierno para atacar y capturar barcos enemigos, especialmentelos barcos mercantes

Prohibition a ban on the manufacture and sale of alcoholic beverages in the United States from 1920 to 1933 (p. 523)

Prohibición restricción de la fabricación y venta de bebidas alcohólicas en Estados Unidos desde 1920 a 1933

proletariat working class (pp. 263, 478)

proletariado clase trabajadora (p. 263)

proliferate to multiply rapidly (p. 753)

proliferar multiplicarse rápidamente

propaganda spreading of ideas to promote a cause or to damage an opposing cause (p. 468)

propaganda divulgación de ideas para promover cierta causa o para perjudicar una causa opuesta

prophet spiritual leader who interprets God's will (p. 7)

profeta líder espiritual a quien se le atribuye la interpretación de la voluntad de Dios

protectionism the use of tariffs and other restrictions to protect a country's home industries against competition (p. 741)

proteccionismo el uso de aranceles y otras medidas restrictivas para proteger a las empresas de un país de la competencia

protectorate country with its own government but under the control of an outside power (p. 391)

protectorado país con su propio gobierno pero que está bajo el control de una potencia exterior

provisional temporary (p. 373)

provisional temporal

Prussia a strong military state in central Europe that emerged in the late 1600s (p. 166)

Prusia estado centroeuropeo militarmente poderoso que emergió a finales del siglo XVII

psychoanalysis a method of studying how the mind works and treating mental disorders (p. 526)

psicoanálisis método que estudia el funcionamiento de la mente y trata los trastornos mentales

Punjab state in northwestern India with a largely Sikh population (p. 654)

Punjab estado del noroeste de India de población mayoritariamente sikh

purdah isolation of women in separate quarters (p. 408)

purdah aislamiento de las mujeres en recintos separadas

Pusan Perimeter a defensive line around the city of Pusan, in the southeast corner of Korea, held by South Korean and United Nations forces in 1950 during the Korean War; marks the farthest advance of North Korean forces (p. 628)

Perímetro de Pusan línea defensiva alrededor de la ciudad de Pusan, en el sudeste de Corea, custodiada por Corea del Sur y las fuerzas de las Naciones Unidas en 1950 durante la Guerra de Corea; marca el mayor avance de las fuerzas de Corea del Norte

putting-out system a system developed in the eighteenth century in which tasks were distributed to individuals who completed the work in their own homes; also known as cottage industry (p. 252)

sistema de trabajo a domicilio sistema desarrolla do en el siglo XVIII en el que las tareas se distribúan a individuos quienes completaban el trabajo en sus hogares; tambien se conoce como industria familiar

Q

Qing dynasty dynasty established by the Manchus in the mid 1600s and lasted until the early 1900s; China's last dynasty (p. 101)

dinastía Chin dinastía establecida por los manchus a mediados del siglo XVII que duró hasta principios del siglo XX; fue la última dinastía china

R

racism belief that one racial group is superior to another (p. 318)

racismo creencia de que un grupo racial es superior a otro

radicals those who favor extreme changes (pp. 276, 473)

radicales persona que quiere hacer cambios extremos

realism nineteenth-century artistic movement whose aim was to represent the world as it is (p. 320)

realismo movimiento artístico del siglo XIX cuyo objetivo era representar el mundo tal como es

Realpolitik realistic politics based on the needs of the state (p. 332)

Realpolitik política realista basada en las necesidades del estado

recession period of reduced economic activity (pp. 278, 615)

recesión periodo de reducción de la actividad económica

refugee a person who flees from home or country to seek refuge elsewhere, often because of political upheaval or famine (pp. 351, 746)

refugiado persona que abandona su hogar o país en busca de refugio en otro lugar, a menudo como consecuencia de inestabilidad política o hambruna

regionalism loyalty to a local area (p. 440)

regionalismo lealtad a un área local

Reich German empire (p. 333)

Reich imperio alemán

Reign of Terror time period during the French Revolution from September 1793 to July 1794 when people in France were arrested for not sup-porting the revolution and many were executed (p. 225)

Reinado del terror período durante la Revolución Francesa desde septiembre de 1793 a julio de 1794, en el que la gente en Francia era arresta da por no apoyar la revolución; mucha gente fue ejecutada

reincarnation in Hindu belief, the rebirth of the soul in another bodily form (p. 14)

reencarnación según la creencia hindú, renacimiento del alma en otra forma corporal

reparation payment for war damage, or damage caused by imprisonment (p. 472)

indemnización pago por daños causados por guerra o encarcelamiento

repeal cancel (p. 365)

revocar cancelar

republic system of government in which officials are chosen by the people (pp. 18, 221)

república sistema de gobierno en el que los gobernantes son elegidos por el pueblo

revenue money taken in through taxes (p. 121)

rentas públicas dinero que se recauda por impuestos

rococo personal, elegant style of art and architecture made popular during the mid-1700s that featured designs with the shapes of leaves, shells, and flowers (p. 189)

rococó estilo de arte y arquitectura elegante y personal que se hizo popular a mediados del siglo XVIII y que incluía diseños con formas de hojas, conchas y flores

romanticism nineteenth-century artistic movement that appealed to emotion rather than reason (p. 319)

romanticismo movimiento artístico del siglo XIX que apelaba a la emoción más que a la razón

Rosie the Riveter popular name for women who worked in war industries during World War II (p. 578)

Rosita la Remachadora nombre popularmente dado a las mujeres que trabajaban en las fábricas de armamento durante la Segunda Guerra Mundial

rotten borough rural town in England that sent members to Parliament despite having few or no voters (p. 360)

"distrito podrido" en Inglaterra, ciudad rural que enviaba miembros al parlamento a pesar de no tener o tener pocos votantes

Ruhr Valley coal-rich industrial region of Germany (p. 551)

Valle del Ruhr región industrial alemana rica en carbón

russification making a nationality's culture more ethnically Russian (p. 546)

rusificación hacer la cultura nacionalista más étnicamente rusa

Russo-Japanese War conflict between Russia and Japan in 1904–1905 over control of Korea and Manchuria (p. 428)

Guerra ruso-japonesa conflicto entre Rusia y Japón de 1904 a 1905 por el control de Corea y Manchuria

S

sacraments sacred ritual of the Roman Catholic Church (p. 29)

sacramento ritual sagrado de la Iglesia Católica Romana

salon informal social gathering at which writers, artists, *philosophes,* and others exchanged ideas (p. 189)

salón reuniones sociales informales en las que escritores, artistas, filósofos y otros intercambiaban ideas

samurai member of the warrior class in Japanese feudal society (p. 36)

samurai miembro de la clase guerrera en la sociedad japonesa feudal

Sandinistas a socialist political movement and party that held power in Nicaragua during the 1980s (p. 724)

sandinistas partido y movimiento político socialista que gobernó Nicaragua durante la década de 1980

sans-culotte working-class man or woman who made the French Revolution more radical; called such because he or she wore long trousers instead of the fancy knee breeches that the upper class wore (p. 221)

sans-culotte hombre o mujer de la clase obrera que hicieron la Revolución Francesa más radical; llamados así porque llevaban pantalones largos a la rodilla como los que llevaba en vez de los pantalones ajustados la clase altas a la rodilla como los que llevaba la clase alta

sati Hindu custom that called for a widow to join her husband in death by throwing herself on his funeral pyre (p. 406)

sati costumbre hindú que requería que la esposa se uniera a su marido en la muerte arrojándose a su pira funeraria

savanna grassy plain with irregular patterns of rainfall (p. 662)

sabana planicie con pastizales cuyo régimen de lluvias es irregular

schism permanent division in a church (p. 30)

cisma división permanente de una iglesia

scientific method careful, step-by-step process used to confirm findings and to prove or disprove a hypothesis (p. 74)

método científico proceso cuidadoso y de varios pasos que se usa para confirmar descubrimientos y para aprobar o desaprobar una hipótesis

scorched-earth policy military tactic in which soldiers destroy everything in their path to hurt the enemy (p. 235)

política de tierra quemada táctica militar en la que los soldados destruyen todo lo que tienen a su paso para perjudicar al enemigo

scribe in ancient civilizations, a person specially trained to read, write, and keep records (p. 7)

escriba en las civilizaciones antiguas, persona especialmente educada para leer, escribir y mantener registros

secede withdraw (p. 379)

separar retirarse

secret ballot votes cast without announcing them publicly (p. 361)

voto secreto votos que se dan sin hacerlos públicos

sect a subgroup of a major religious group (p. 19)

secta subgrupo de un grupo religioso importante

secular having to do with worldly, rather than religious, matters; nonreligious (pp. 27, 673)

secular que tiene que ver más con asuntos mundanos que religiosos; no religioso

segregation forced separation by race, sex, religion, or ethnicity (pp. 379, 616)

segregación separación forzada por razón de raza, sexo, religión o etnia

self-determination right of people to choose their own form of government (p. 471)

autodeterminación derecho de los pueblos a elegir su propia forma de gobierno

sepoy Indian soldier who served in an army set up by the French or English trading companies (pp. 98, 406)

sepoy soldado indio que sirvió en un ejército establecido por las compañías de comercio francesas o inglesas

serf in medieval Europe, a peasant bound to the lord's land (p. 26)

siervo en la Europa medieval, campesino vinculado a las tierras del señor

shantytowns slums of flimsy shacks (p. 708)
   barrio de chabolas barrios muy pobres de casuchas endebles

Sharpeville a black township in South Africa where the government killed anti-apartheid demonstrators in 1960 (p. 687)
   Sharpeville municipio sudafricano habitado por personas de raza negra donde el gobierno mató a decenas de manifestantes antiapartheid en 1960

shogun in Japanese feudal society, supreme military commander, who held more power than the emperor (p. 37)
   shogún en la sociedad feudal japonesa, jefe militar supremo con más poder que el emperador

Sino-Japanese War war between China and Japan in which Japan gained Taiwan (p. 414)
   Guerra Sinojaponesa guerra entre China y Japón por la que Japón obtuvo el control de Taiwán

smelt melt in order to get the pure metal away from its waste matter (p. 249)
   refinar fundir mineral para separar el mineral puro de las impurezas

social contract an agreement by which people gave up their freedom to a powerful government in order to avoid chaos (p. 183)
   contrato social acuerdo mediante el cual el pueblo cede sus libertades a un gobierno poderoso para evitar el caos

social democracy political ideology in which there is a gradual transition from capitalism to socialism instead of a sudden violent overthrow of the system (p. 264)
   democracia social ideología política en la que hay una transición gradual del capitalismo al socialismo en vez de un derrocamiento violento del sistema

social gospel movement of the 1800s that urged Christians to do social service (p. 318)
   evangelio social movimiento del siglo XIX que urgía a los cristianos a que hicieran servicios sociales

social welfare programs to help certain groups of people (p. 337)
   bienestar social programas para ayudar a ciertos grupos de personas

socialism system in which the people as a whole rather than private individuals own all property and operate all businesses (pp. 263, 710)

socialismo sistema en el que el pueblo como un todo, en vez de los individuos, son dueños de todas la propiedades y manejan todos los negocios

socialist realism artistic style whose goal was to promote socialism by showing Soviet life in a positive light (p. 546)
   realismo socialista estilo artistico cuyo objetivo era promover el socialismo mostrando la vida en la Union Sovietica desde un perspectiva postiva

Solidarity a Polish labor union and democracy movement (p. 641)
   Solidaridad sindicato laboral y movimiento democrático polaco

sovereign having full, independent power (p. 96)
   soberano tener poder pleno e independiente

soviet council of workers and soldiers set up by Russian revolutionaries in 1917 (p. 478)
   soviet consejo de trabajadores y soldados establecido por los revolucionarios rusos en 1917

Spanish-American War conflict between the United States and Spain in 1898 over Cuban independence (p. 431)
   Guerra entre Estados Unidos y España (Guerra hispano-estadounidense) conflicto entre Estados Unidos y España en 1898 por la independencia de Cuba

speakeasies illegal bars (p. 523)
   speakeasies bares ilegales

sphere of influence area in which an outside power claims exclusive investment or trading privileges (p. 391)
   esfera de influencia área sobre la que un poder exterior se reserva privilegios comerciales o la exclusividad de realizar inversiones

St. Petersburg capital city and major port that Peter the Great established in 1703 (p. 170)
   San Petersburgo ciudad y capital con un puerto importante, establecida en 1703 por Pedro el Grande

stalemate deadlock in which neither side is able to defeat the other (p. 460)
   estancamiento punto muerto en una confrontación, en el que ninguna de las partes puede vencer a la otra

Stalingrad now Volgograd, a city in southwestern Russia that was the site of a fierce battle during World War II (p. 580)
   Stalingrado actual Volgogrado; ciudad del sudoeste de Rusia donde se libró una encarnizada batalla durante la Segunda Guerra Mundial

Stamp Act law passed in 1765 by the British Parliament that imposed taxes on items such as newspapers and pamphlets in the American colonies; repealed in 1766 (p. 197)

Ley del Timbre ley promulgada en 1765 por el Parlamento Británico que imponía gravámenes a artículos como diarios y panfletos en las colonias americanas; revocada en 1766

standard of living measures the quality and availability of necessities and comforts in a society (p. 309)

estándar de vida medida de la calidad y disponibilidad de las necesidades básicas y de los lujos en una sociedad

stock shares in a company (p. 303)

acciones títulos o valores de una compañía

suburbanization the movement to built-up areas outside of central cities (p. 615)

suburbanización proceso de construcción en áreas fuera del centro de la ciudad

Sudetenland a region of western Czechoslovakia (p. 565)

Sudetenland región occidental de la antigua Checoslovaquia

Suez Canal a canal linking the Red Sea and Indian Ocean to the Mediterranean Sea, which also links Europe to Asia and East Africa (pp. 372, 674)

Canal de Suez canal que une el Mar Rojo y el Océano índico con el Mar Mediterráneo, que a la vez une Europa con Asia y África Oriental

suffrage right to vote (p. 224)

sufragio derecho al voto

sultan Muslim ruler (pp. 33, 402)

sultán gobernante musulmán

superpower a nation stronger than other powerful nations (p. 604)

superpotencia nación suficientemente poderosa para influir en los actos y políticas de otras naciones poderosas

surplus an amount that is more than needed, excess (p. 736)

excedente cantidad de algo superior a lo que se necesita; exceso

surrealism artistic movement that attempts to portray the workings of the unconscious mind (p. 527)

surrealismo movimiento artístico que trata de mostrar el funcionamiento del inconsciente

sustainability the ability to meet the needs of the present without compromising the needs of future generations (p. 742)

sostenibilidad capacidad de satisfacer las necesidades actuales sin poner en peligro las necesidades de generaciones futuras

sustainable development development that meets the needs of the present without compromising the ability of future generations to meet their own needs (p. 712)

desarrollo sostenible desarrollo que cubre las necesidades del presente sin perjudicar la capacidad de las generaciones futuras de cubrir sus necesidades

T

Taiping Rebellion peasant revolt in China (p. 413)

Rebelión Taiping revuelta campesina en China

Taliban Islamic fundamentalist faction that ruled Afghanistan for nearly ten years until ousted by the United States in 2002 (p. 757)

Talibán facción islámica fundamentalista que gobernó Afganistán durante casi diez años hasta que fue expulsada por Estados Unidos en 2002

tariff tax on imported goods (p. 133)

tasa impuesto a mercancías importadas

temperance movement campaign to limit or ban the use of alcoholic beverages (p. 314)

campaña de moderación campaña para limitar o prohibir el uso de bebidas alcohólicas

tenement multistory building divided into crowded apartments (p. 256)

apartamento de vecindad edificio de varios pisos dividido en apartamentos donde vive mucha gente

Tennis Court Oath famous oath made on a tennis court by members of the Third Estate in France (p. 214)

Juramento del juego de pelota famoso juramento hecho en una cancha de frontón por los miembros del Tercer Estado en Francia

Tenochtitlán capital city of the Aztec empire, on which modern-day Mexico City was built (p. 111)

Tenochtitlán capital del imperio azteca, sobre la cual se construyó la actual Ciudad de México

terrorism deliberate use of random violence, especially against civilians, to achieve political goals (p. 754)

terrorismo uso deliberado de la violencia indiscriminada, especialmente en contra de civiles, para lograr fines políticos

Tet Offensive a massive and bloody offensive by communist guerrillas against South Vietnamese and American forces on Tet, the Vietnamese New Year, 1968; helped turn American public opinion against military involvement in Vietnam (p. 634)

Ofensiva Tet ofensiva masiva y sangrienta de las guerrillas comunistas contra los sudvietnamitas y las fuerzas estadounidenses durante el Tet, el Nuevo Año vietnamita, en 1968; ayudó a que la opinión pública estadouniden se se volviera en contra de la ocupación militar en Vietnam

theocracy government run by religious leaders

teocracia gobierno administrado por líderes religiosos (pp. 65, 675)

Third Reich official name of the Nazi party for its regime in Germany, held power from 1933 to 1945 (p. 553)

Tercer Reich nombre oficial del partido nazi durante su mandato en Alemania; mantuvo el poder desde 1933 a 1945

38th parallel an imaginary line marking 38 degrees of latitude, particularly the line at 38 degrees of latitude north across the Korean Peninsula, dividing Soviet forces to the north and American forces to the South after World War II (p. 627)

paralelo 38 línea imaginaria que marca los 38 grados de latitud, en particular la línea a 38 grados de latitud norte que cruza la península coreana, que dividía las fuerzas soviéticas al norte y las fuerzas estadounindenses al sur después de la Segunda Guerra Mundial

Tiananmen Square a huge public plaza at the center of China's capital, Beijing (p. 715)

Plaza de Tiananmen inmensa plaza pública en el centro de Beijing, la capital de China

Tokyo capital of Japan, on the eastern coast of Japan (p. 424)

Tokio capital de Japón, ubicada en la costa este de Japón

total war channeling of a nation's entire resources into a war effort (p. 467)

estado de guerra canalización de todos los recursos de una nación hacia la guerra

totalitarian state government in which a one-party dictatorship regulates every aspect of citizens' lives (p. 539)

estado totalitario gobierno en el que una dictadura de partido único regula todos los aspectos de la vida de los ciudadanos

trade deficit situation in which a country imports more than it exports (p. 411)

déficit comercial situación en la que un país importa más de lo que exporta

trade surplus situation in which a country exports more than it imports (p. 411)

excedente commercial situación en la que un país exporta más de lo que importa

traditional economies undeveloped economic systems that rely on custom and tradition (p. 704)

economía de subsistencia sistemas económicos sin desarrollar que dependen de costumbres y tradiciones

Treaty of Paris treaty of 1763 that ended the Seven Years' War and resulted in British dominance of the Americas (p. 124)

Tratado de París en 1763, tratado que terminó con la Guerra de los Siete Años y resultó en el dominio británico de las Américas

Treaty of Paris peace treaty made final in 1783 that ended the American Revolution (p. 200)

Tratado de París tratado de paz de 1783 que dio final a la Revolución Americana

Treaty of Tordesillas treaty signed between Spain and Portugal in 1494 which divided the non-European world between them (p. 88)

Tratado de Tordesillas tratado firmado por España y Portugal en 1494 por el que se dividían entre ellos el mundo fuera de Europa

triangular trade colonial trade routes among Europe and its colonies, the West Indies, and Africa in which goods were exchanged for slaves (p. 125)

comercio triangular ruta colonial de comercio entre Europa y sus colonias en las Indias Occidentales y África, en donde las mercancías se cambiaban por esclavos

tributary state independent state that has to acknowledge the supremacy of another state and pay tribute to its ruler (p. 36)

estado tributario estado independiente que debe reconocer la supremacía de otro estado y pagar tributo a su gobernante

tribute payment that conquered peoples may be forced to pay their conquerors (p. 20)

tributo pago que los conquistadores podían obligar a pagar a los pueblos conquistados

Truman Doctrine United States policy, established in 1947, of trying to contain the spread of communism (p. 593)

Doctrina Truman estrategia política establecida en 1947 con el propósito de contener la expansión del comunismo

tsar title of the rule of the Russian empire (p. 31)

zar título del regente del imperio ruso

tsunami very large, damaging wave caused by an earthquake or very strong wind (p. 745)

tsunami ola enorme y destructiva causada por un terremoto o vientos muy fuertes

turnpike private road built by entrepreneurs who charged a toll, or fee, to travelers who used it (p. 252)

autopista de peaje carretera construida con capital privado; el dueño de la carretera cobra una tarifa a los viajeros por usarla

Tutsis the main minority group in Rwanda and Burundi (p. 689)

Tutsis principal minoría de Ruanda y Burundi

Twenty-One Demands list of demands given to China by Japan in 1915 that, if agreed to, would have made China a protectorate of Japan (p. 508)

Veintiuna Exigencias lista de exigencias dadas por Japón a China en 1915 por las que, si hubiera estado de acuerdo, China se habría convertido en un protectorado de Japón

U

U-boat German submarine (p. 463)

U-Boat submarino alemán

ultimatum final set of demands (p. 457)

ultimátum serie final de exigencias

ultranationalist extreme nationalist (p. 514)

ultranacionalista nacionalista radical

United Nations (UN) international organization established after World War II with the goal of maintaining peace and cooperation in the international community (p. 591)

Naciones Unidas (ONU) organización internacional establecida después de la Segunda Guerra Mundial con el propósito de preservar la paz y la cooperación en la comunidad internacional

universal manhood suffrage right of all adult men to vote (p. 273)

sufragio universal masculino derecho de todos los hombres adultos a votar

untouchable in India, a member of the lowest caste (p. 504)

intocable en India, miembro de la casta más baja

urban renewal the process of fixing up the poor areas of a city (p. 306)

renovación urbana reconstrucción de las áreas pobres de una ciudad

urbanization movement of people from rural areas to cities (pp. 254, 711)

urbanización movimiento de personas de las áreas rurales a las ciudades

utilitarianism idea that the goal of society should be to bring about the greatest happiness for the greatest number of people (p. 261)

utilitarismo idea de que el objetivo de la sociedad debería ser lograr la mayor felicidad para el mayor número de personas

utopian idealistic or visionary, usually used to describe a perfect society (p. 58)

utópico idealista o visionario, normalmente se usa para describir una sociedad perfecta

V

V-E Day Victory in Europe Day, May 8, 1945, the day the Allies won World War II in Europe (p. 586)

Día de la Victoria en Europa (Día del Armisticio) (8 de mayo de 1945) día en que los aliados vencieron en Europa durante la Segunda Guerra Mundial

vanguard group of elite leaders (p. 508)

vanguardia grupo de líderes de la élite

vassal in medieval Europe, a lord who was granted land in exchange for service and loyalty to a greater lord, (p. 26)

vasallo durante la Edad Media, señor a quien se le cedía un terreno a cambio de servicio y lealtad al señor más importante

vernacular everyday language of ordinary people (p. 29)

vernáculo lenguaje diario de la gente corriente

Versailles royal French residence and seat of government established by King Louis XIV (p. 150)

Versalles residencia de la realeza francesa y sede de gobierno establecidos por el rey Luis XIV

viceroy representative who ruled one of Spain's provinces in the Americas in the king's name; one who governed in India in the name of the British monarch (pp. 115, 407)

virrey representante que regía una de las provincias de España en las Américas en nombre del rey; quien gobernaba en India en nombre del monarca británico

Vichy city in central France where a puppet state governed unoccupied France and the French colonies (p. 569)

Vichy ciudad en el centro de Francia desde donde un gobierno títere dirigió la Francia no ocupada y las colonias francesas

Viet Cong communist rebels in South Vietnam who sought to overthrow South Vietnam's government; received assistance from North Vietnam (p. 631)

Vietcong rebeldes comunistas en Vietnam del Sur que buscaban derrotar el gobierno de Vietnam del Sur; recibieron ayuda de Vietnam del Norte

W

War of the Austrian Succession series of wars in which various European nations competed for power in Central Europe after the death of Hapsburg emperor Charles VI (p. 166)

Guerra de Sucesión Austriaca serie de guerras en las que diversos países europeos lucharon por la hegemonía en centroeuropa después de la muerte de Carlos IV, emperador Habsburgo

warm-water port port that is free of ice year-round (p. 170)

puerto de aguas templadas puerto en el que sus aguas nunca se congelan a lo largo del año

Warsaw Pact mutual-defense alliance between the Soviet Union and seven satellites in Eastern Europe set up in 1955 (p. 594)

Pacto de Varsovia alianza de defensa mutua establecida en 1955 entre la Unión Soviética y siete países de Europa del Este pertenecientes a su esfera de influencia

weapons of mass destruction (WMDs) biological, nuclear, or chemical weapons (p. 697)

armas de destrucción masiva (ADM) armas biológicas, nucleares o químicas

welfare state a country with a market economy but with increased government responsibility for the social and economic needs of its people (p. 620)

estado de bienestar país con una economía de Mercado, pero con un gobierno con mayor responsabilidad sobre las nece sidades económicas de su pueblo

westernization adoption of western ideas, technology, and culture (p. 169)

occidentalización adopción de ideas, tecnología y cultura occidentales

Wittenberg a city in northern Germany, where Luther drew up his 95 theses (p. 63)

Wittenberg ciudad al norte de Alemania donde Lutero redactó sus 95 tesis

women's suffrage right of women to vote (p. 314)

sufragio femenino derecho de las mujeres a votar

World Trade Organization (WTO) international organization set up to facilitate global trade (p. 741)

Organización Mundial del Comercio (OMC) organización internacional constituida para facilitar el comercio en el ámbito mundial

Y

Yalta Conference meeting between Churchill, Roosevelt, and Stalin in February 1945 where the three leaders made agreements regarding the end of World War II (p. 583)

Conferencia de Yalta reunión mantenida en febrero de 1945 entre Churchill, Roosevelt y Stalin en la que los tres mandatarios alcanzaron un acuerdo con respecto a la finalización de la Segunda Guerra Mundial

Yorktown, Virginia location where the British army surrendered in the American Revolution (p. 200)

Yorktown, Virginia lugar donde el ejército británico se rindió en la Revolución Americana

Z

zaibatsu since the late 1800s, powerful banking and industrial families in Japan (p. 426)

zaibatsu familias japonesas de banqueros e industriales poderosos desde finales del siglo XIX

zemstvos local elected assembly set up in Russia under Alexander II (p. 349)

zemstvos asambla local electa que se estableció en Rusia en la época de Alejandro II

zeppelin large gas-filled balloon (p. 463)

zepelín dirigible, globo grande lleno de gas

ziggurat in ancient Mesopotamia, a large, stepped platform thought to have been topped by a temple dedicated to a city's chief god or goddess (p. 6)

zigurat templo piramidal de la antigua Mesopotamia dedicado al dios o diosa principal de una ciudad

Zionism a movement devoted to rebuilding a Jewish state in Palestine (p. 375)

zionismo movimiento dedicado a la reconstrucción del estado judío en Palestina

INDEX

Italicized letters after page numbers refer to the following:
c = chart; *g* = graph; *m* = map; *p* = picture; *q* = primary source
Items in blue refer to Teacher's Edition pages.

Abbas, Mahmoud   **Alberta**

INDEX

INDEX

INDEX

Staff Credits

The people who make up the **World History © 07** team—representing design services, editorial, editorial services, educational technology, marketing, market research, photo research and art development, production services, publishing processes, and rights & permissions—are listed below. Bold type denotes core team members.

Marla Abramson, Leann Davis Alspaugh, Scott Andrews, Helene Avraham, Renee Beach, Eytan Bernstein, Suzanne Biron, Stephanie Bradley, **Peter Brooks,** Kerry Lyn Buckley, Lynn Burke, Kerry Cashman, Geoffrey Cassar, Todd Christy, Lori-Anne Cohen, Alan Dalgleish, Laura Edgerton-Riser, Anne Falzone, Tom Ferreira, Lara Fox, Elizabeth Good, Ellen Welch Granter, **Diane Grossman,** Julie Gurdin, **Mary Ann Gundersen,** Mary Hanisco, Salena Hastings, Lance Hatch, Brian Heyward, Margaret Higgins, Katharine Ingram, Tim Jones, Judie Jozokos, Lynne Kalkanajian, Courtney Lane, Ruth Lopriore, **Grace Massey, Constance J. McCarty,** Michael McLaughlin, Claudi Mimo, Xavier Niz, Carrie O'Connor, Mark O'Malley, Linda Punskovsky, **Deborah Nicholls,** Jen Paley, Jonathan Penyack, **Gabriela Perez-Fiato,** Judi Pinkham, Jennifer Ribnicky, Marcy Rose, Rashid Ross, Robyn Salbo, **Colleen Searson,** Greg Slook, Laurel Smith, **Lisa Smith-Ruvalcaba,** Kara Stokes, Ana Sofia Villaveces, Rachel Winter, **Sarah Yezzi**

Additional Credits

Paul Astwood, Gaylord Brynolfson, Sandra M. Graff, Lynette Haggard, John Judge, Kevin Keane, Beth Kun, Susan Nimmo, Kim Schmidt, Jan Shapiro, Ted Smykal, Erin Sunderland, Paula Wehde

Vendor

Pronk & Associates Inc.

Maps

XNR Productions, Inc.: SH25, SH27, SH28, SH29, 5, 7, 9, 15, 17, 31, 33, 35, 37, 39, 41, 44–45, 51, 70, 81, 85, 92, 100–101, 113, 123, 127, 134–135, 136, 143, 164, 170, 173, 178–179, 192, 196, 203, 233, 237, 239, 251, 278, 285, 287, 294–295, 299, 316–317, 331, 339, 341, 345, 354, 373, 380, 395, 403, 407, 412, 416, 431, 435, 437, 442, 444, 450–451, 459, 465, 468, 479, 490, 491, 498, 501, 510, 514, 517, 530, 545, 566, 572, 578, 581, 584, 587, 593, 595, 596, 599, 600–601, 607, 609, 613, 626, 627, 633, 636, 637, 649, 653, 660, 665, 671, 676, 679, 684, 689, 694, 698, 701, 705, 712, 721, 735, 737, 739, 745, 749, 755, 769, 772–773, 774, 775, 776, 777, 778, 779, 780, 781, 782, 783, 790–791, 794–795

Illustrations

Kenneth Batelman **567, 584–585;** Kerry Cashman **SH13, SH26, SH39,** 2–3, 12–13, 24–25, 52–53, 58–59, 68–69, 74, 75, 78–79, 86–87, 100–101, 104–105, 112–113, 118, 126–127, 134–135, 136–137, 144, 147, 151, 156–157, 172, 174–175, 190, 196, 200, 202–203, 204–205, 212, 219, 226–227, 240–241, 252, 262, 266–267, 278–279, 287, 290–291, 304, 312–313, 315, 321, 324–325, 341, 350–351, 354–355, 362–363, 368, 372–373, 378, 382–383, 403, 406–407, 412–413, 416–417, 424–425, 432, 444, 446–447, 466–467, 477, 484–485, 490–491, 491, 498–499, 516–517, 524–525, 532–533, 538–539, 556–557, 570–571, 572–573, 579, 584–585, 596–597, 607, 609, 626–627, 632–633, 646–647, 676–677, 688, 692–693, 698–699, 716, 728–729, 740–741, 745, 749, 759, 760–761, 762, 764–765, 770–771, 784, 784–785, 785, 786–787, 796–797, 798–799, 801, 806–807; Ellen Welch Granter **SH2, SH3, SH4, SH9, SH10, SH12, SH13, SH15, SH16, SH17, SH21, SH28, SH39;** Kevin Jones Associates 220, 252, 273, 302, 350; Jen Paley **SH5, SH20, SH23, SH35,** 48, 56, 61, 64, 66, 72, 78, 84, 90, 95, 99, 104, 110, 115, 118, 120, 125, 129, 131, 134, 135, 136, 142, 144, 148, 154, 160, 163, 168, 172, 182, 188, 192, 193, 195, 201, 204, 210, 216, 223, 230, 240, 246, 247, 250, 254, 255, 260, 266, 272, 275, 276, 280, 283, 290, 298, 300, 305, 308, 312, 313, 319, 324, 327, 330, 334, 338, 343, 348, 354, 360, 364, 368, 371, 377, 382, 382, 388, 392, 400, 405, 410, 411, 416, 417, 422, 426, 429, 434, 439, 442, 444, 446, 447, 462, 464, 466, 471, 476, 477, 478, 481, 490, 491, 492, 493, 496, 503, 507, 508, 512, 516, 522, 524, 529, 533, 535, 536, 539, 542, 543, 544, 550, 555, 556, 562, 565, 567, 568, 572, 573, 576, 577, 585, 586, 590, 591, 596, 597, 599, 606, 610, 614, 623, 630, 638, 646, 652, 655, 658, 660, 662, 670, 673, 679, 682, 683, 686, 688, 689, 692, 695, 698, 699, 704, 705, 710, 714, 715, 716, 720, 723, 728, 734, 738, 740, 744, 746, 749, 753, 758, 764, 767, 786, 788, 789, 792, 793, 800, 801, 804, 805; Ted Smykal **SH4, SH6, SH7, SH8, SH9, SH10, SH11, SH14, SH15, SH16, SH17, SH18, SH19, SH21, 131, 192, 316, 636, 660, 672, 727**

Cover and Title Page

Ann Ronan Picture Library/HIP/The ImageWorks

Table of Contents

xii, T, Photograph by Frank Khoury National Museum of African Art Smithsonian Institution; B, © Erich Lessing/Art Resource; **xiii,** Michael Holford; **xiv,** T, Joe Sohm/Chromosohm/VOA; B, Science Museum/SSPL; **xv,** © Christie's Images/CORBIS; **xvi,** Inset, The Granger Collection, New York; **xvi-xvii,** © Bettmann/CORBIS; **xviii,** photolibrary; **xix,** Ron Giling/Das Fotoarchiv; **xxiii,** Robertstock; **xxiv,** Bildarchiv Preussischer Kulturbesitz/Art Resource, NY; **xvi,** L, Frank Nowikowski; **xx,** L, © Wanda Beaver; R, © Photos by Eric L. Johnson/Courtesy of the Museum of World War II, Natick MA; Background, Time Life Pictures/Getty Images

Skills Handbook

SH1, © Jose Luis Pelaez, Inc./CORBIS; **SH2,** © IT Stock Free/AGE Fotostock; **SH3,** © Ed Bock/CORBIS; **SH6,** © Bananastock/PictureQuest; **SH13,** Public Record Office/HIP/The Image Works; **SH22,** Arthur Tilley/Getty Images; **SH24,** © Roger Wood/CORBIS; **SH29,** Keystone/Getty Images; **SH30,** North Wind Picture Archives; **SH31,** © Arcadio/Cartoonists & Writers Syndicate; **SH33,** The Science Museum/Science & Society Picture Library; **SH36,** Bettman/CORBIS; The Granger Collection, New York; **SH38,** © Charles Gupton/CORBIS

Review Unit

c, Reunion des Musees Nationaux/Art Resource; **0,** TL, Archivo Iconografico, S;A/Corbis; BL, © Archivo Iconografico, S.A./CORBIS; **0–1,** B, © ArtWolfe/Getty Images; **1,** TR, Réunion des Musées Nationaux/Art Resource, NY; BR, © Dirk Bakker; **2,** TR, Werner Forman/Art Resource, NY; TL, © Archivo Iconografico, S.A./CORBIS; BL, © Robert Frerck/Odyssey Productions, Inc.; **3,** T, The Art Archive/Museum of Mankind; B, Copyright of Christie's Images Inc., 2004; **4,** Erich Lessing/Art Resource, NY; **6,** © Archivo Iconografico, S.A./CORBIS; **8,** The Metropolitan Museum of Art, Gift of R. H. Ellsworth Ltd., in honor of Susan Dilon, 1987 (1987.80.1); Photograph by Bruch White; Photograph © 1994 The Metropolitan Museum of Art; **9,** CM Dixon/HIP/The Image Works; **11,** Yang Liu/CORBIS; **12,** T, Ronald Sheridan/Ancient Art & Architecture Collection Ltd; B, © Danny Lehman/CORBIS; **13,** MR, The Metropolitan Museum of Art, Purchase, Elaine Rosenberg Gift and funds from various donors, 1998. (1998.37); Photograph © 2001 The Metropolitan Museum of Art; T, John Bigelow Taylor/Art Resource, NY; M, By permission of the British Library; Or.8212/480–484 paper fragments from Loulan; M, The Trustees of The British Museum; B, © Richard A; Cooke/CORBIS; **14,** Photri Microstock; **16,** Réunion des Musées Nationaux/Art Resource, NY; **18,** Réunion des Musées Nationaux/Art Resource, NY; **19,** Erich Lessing/Art Resource, NY; **20,** akg-images/Francois Guénet; **21,** George H. Huey/CORBIS; **23,** © Francesco Venturi/CORBIS; Richard Bergmann/Photo Researchers, Inc.; © Michael Reynolds/epa/CORBIS; **24,** TL, Los Angeles County Museum of Art, The Nasli M.; TR, Werner Forman/Art Resource, NY; M, ArkReligion.com; B, © Gianni Dagli Orti/CORBIS; **25,** T, The Granger Collection, New York; M, The Art Archive/Archaeological Museum Lima/Mireille Vautie; BL, Time Life Pictures/Getty Images; R, Prisma/ANCIENT ART & ARCHITECTURE COLLECTION LTD; **26,** Bridgeman Art Library; **27,** T, Kunsthistorisches Museum, Vienna, Austria/Bridgeman Art Library; B, Archivo Iconografico, S.A./CORBIS; **28,** L, akg-images; R, Giraudon/Art Resource, NY; **29,** The Art Archive/San Francesco Assisi/Dagli Orti; **30,** San Vitale, Ravenna, Italy/Bridgeman Art Library; **32,** Topkapi Palace Museum, Istanbul, Turkey/Bridgeman Art Library; **34,** © Dirk Bakker; **36,** The Art Archive/British Library; **36–37,** Panorama Stock; **41,** Getty Images; page, The Art Archive/Biblioteca Nacional Madrid/Laurie Platt Winfrey; Getty Images; **42,** ASSOCIATED PRESS/Shizuo Kambayashi; **43,** Visuals Unlimited/CORBIS; Edifice/CORBIS; Peter Yates/Photo Researchers, Inc.

Chapter One

46c, The Granger Collection; **46–47,** © Vittoriano Rastelli/CORBIS; **47,** T, Arte & Immagini srl/Corbis; M, The Pierpont Morgan Library/Art Resource, NY; B, HIP/Art Resource, NY; **48,** L, Scala/Art Resource, NY; R, Ashley Simmons/Alamy Images; **49,** The Bridgeman Art Library/Getty Images; **50,**

Bibliotheque Nationale, Paris; **52,** M, Dorling Kindersley; R, Private Collection/Bridgeman Art Library; L, Scala/Art Resource, NY; **52–53,** The Image Bank/Getty Images; **53,** R, Mary Evans Picture Library; L, Dorling Kindersley; **54,** Mary Evans Picture Library; **55,** Archivo Iconografico, S;A/Corbis; **56,** L, Mary Evans Picture Library; R, The Pierpont Morgan Library/Art Resource, NY; **57,** Archivo Iconografico, S.A./Corbis; **58,** Scala/Art Resource, NY; **59,** TR, Dorling Kindersley; M, Erich Lessing/Art Resource, NY; L, Erich Lessing/Art Resource, NY; BR, Susannah Price/Dorling Kindersley; **60,** T, Mary Evans Picture Library; B, Andrea Pistolesi/Getty Images, Inc.; M, Dorling Kindersley; **61,** L, AAAC/Topham/The Image Works; R, London College of Printing/Dorling Kindersley; **62,** Bildarchiv Preussischer Kulturbesitz/Art Resource, NY; **63,** © The Corcoran Gallery of Art/CORBIS; **65,** Erich Lessing/Art Resource, NY; **66,** L, National Trust Photographic Library/Derrick E; Witty/The Image Works; R, HIP/Art Resource, NY; **67,** Fine Art Photographic Library/Corbis; **68,** Inset, The Granger Collection; **68–69,** Background, © Michael Busselle/CORBIS; **69,** L, Mary Evans Picture Library; R, The Granger Collection; **71,** Erich Lessing/Art Resource, NY; **72,** L, The Granger Collection, New York; R, Gustavo Tomsich/Corbis; **73,** L, The Granger Collection; R, © Reuters/CORBIS; **74,** R, Maximilian Stock Ltd;/Photo Researchers, Inc.; TL, Kevin Fleming/Corbis; BL, Royalty-Free/Corbis; **75,** R, AAAC/Topham/The Image Works; L, Glasgow University Library, Scotland/Bridgeman Art Library; **77,** GILDAS RAFFENEL/epa/CORBIS; Bridgeman Art Library/Robert-Fleury, Joseph-Nicolas (1797-1890); **78,** Scala/Art Resource, NY; **79,** T, FRANK & EARNEST, © Thaves/Dist. by Newspaper Enterprise Association, Inc.; The Pierpont Morgan Library/Art Resource, NY; The Granger Collection; **80,** T, Scala/Art Resource, NY; B, © Vittoriano Rastelli/CORBIS

Chapter Two

82c, Masterfile; **82–83,** Instituto Portugues de Museus; **83,** T, V & A Museum/Art Resource; B, © Christie's Images/CORBIS; **84,** R, Bridgeman Art Library; L, Ann Ronan Picture Library/The Image Works; **86,** L, The Granger Collection; R, National Maritime Museum; **86–87,** Museu de Marinha, The Granger Collection; **87,** TL, Antiquarian Images; TR, Michael Holford; M, HIP/Scala/Art Resource; **88,** Preus-

sischer Kulturbesitz/Art Resource, NY; **90,** L, Topham/The Image Works; R, Museum of African Art/Smithsonian Institution; **91,** Michael Holford; **93,** Werner Forman/Art Resource; **94,** B, The Art Archive/Museo de Arte Antiga; T, Metropolitan Museum of Art, Gift of Ernest Anspach, 1999 (199;295;4) Photograph (c) 2002 Metropolitan Museum of Art; **95,** R, Rainer Daehnhardt/Portuguese Academy of Antique Arms; L, British Library; **96,** R, Maritime Museum of Rotterdam; L, Royal Collection (c) 2005, Her Majesty Queen Elizabeth II; **97,** Rijksmuseum Amsterdam; **98,** British Library; **99,** L, The Ricci Institute, University of San Francisco; R, Vatican Library; **100,** The British Museum/The Image Works; **101,** M, © Christie's Images/CORBIS; L, The Granger Collection; R, British Museum/HIP/The Image Works; **102,** Cleveland Musuem of Art; **103,** Michael Holford; **104,** L, The British Museum/The Image Works; R, HIP/Scala/Art Resource, NY; **105,** Cleveland Musuem of Art; **106,** T, The Granger Collection; B, Instituto Portugues de Museus; **107,** T, Giraudon/Art Resource; B, Granger Collection

Chapter Three

108c, Ira Block; **108–109,** Schalkwijk/Art Resource, NY; **109,** T, Erich Lessing/Art Resource, NY; Musee Departemental des Antiquites, Rouen, France/Bridgeman Art Library; B, © Canadian Museum of Civilization, catalogue no. D-1511, image no. S90–1861; **110,** Biblioteca Medicea-Laurenziana/Florence Bridgeman Art Library; **111,** T, The Granger Collection; B, Biblioteque Nationale de France; **112,** Inset, akg-images; **112–113,** Background, Corbis; **113,** Frank Nowikowski; **114,** Ira Block; **115,** Hispanic Society of New York; **116,** Divisao de Documentacao Fotografica-Instituto Portugues De Museus; **117,** Dan Lehmann/Corbis; **118,** Joseph Martin/AKG Images; **119,** Musee Departemental des Antiquites, Rouen, France/Bridgeman Art Library; **120,** R, © Lee Snider/Photo Images/CORBIS; L, (c) Canadian Museum of Civilization, catalogue # 989.56.1, photo Merle Toole, #S90–640; **121,** Corbis; **122,** Michael Schwarz/Image Works; **123,** TR, National Museum of Natural History/Smithsonian Institution; BL, The Newark Musseum/Art Resource, NY; TL, Victoria & Albert Museum, London/Art Resource, NY; BR, New York Historical Society; **124,** Gunter Marx; **125,** L, Royal Albert Museum/Bridgeman Art Library; R, Chicago Historical

Society; **126,** B, Ariadne Van Zandbergen/Lonely Planet Images; T, Corbis; **126–127,** Background, Corbis; T, © Royalty-Free/Corbis; **127,** T, British Library; B, British Library; **128,** Bettmann/Corbis; **129,** R, The Art Archive; L, (c) Canadian Museum of Civilization, catalogue no. D-1511, image no. S90–1861; **130,** R, Francis C. Mayer/Corbis; L, Bancroft Library/UC-Berkeley; **131,** Background, © Darrell Gulin/CORBIS; R, RF/Corbis; M, Corbis; **132,** R, Robert Harding Image Library; L, Journal-Courier/Steve Warmowski/The Image Works; **133,** Erich Lessing/Art Resource, NY; **134,** M, Julie Habel/Corbis; BL, © Ed Quinn/CORBIS; R, © PoodlesRock/CORBIS; TL, © Carlos Goldin/CORBIS; **135,** BL, Kim Blaxland/Getty Images; MR, Ira Block; TL, Corbis; BR, Ron Giling/Peter Arnold Inc.; TR, © Liba Taylor/CORBIS; **136,** © Steve Vidler/eStock Photo; **137,** TR, Levine/Roberts; BR, Lisa Knouse Braiman/Business Week; L, Stock Montage; **138,** R, National Gallery of Art; L, Schalkwijk/Art Resource, NY; **139,** Mary Evans Picture Library

Chapter Four

140c, Fine Art Photographic Library/Corbis; **140–141,** Erich Lessing/Art Resource, NY; **141,** B, Museums On Line; M, Dorling Kindersley; T, Erich Lessing/Art Resource; **142,** L, Bettmann/Corbis; Background, L, Bettmann/Corbis; R, Archivo Iconographica, S.A./Corbis; **144,** L, Bridgeman Art Library; MR, British Library/Bridgeman Art Library; Background, The National Maritime Museum; TR, Archivo Iconographica, S.A./Corbis; TL, Archivo Iconographica, S.A./Corbis; **145,** Bridgeman Art Library; **146,** Bridgeman Art Library; **147,** T, Art Resource, NY; B, Mary Evans Picture Library; **148,** L, Versailles, châteaux de Versailles et de Trianon/RMN/Art Resource; R, Bata Shoe Museum; **149,** © National Gallery Collection; By kind permission of the Trustees of the National Gallery, London/CORBIS; **151,** Background, T, Superstock; Background, B, Reunion des Musees Nationaux/Art Resource; TL, Scala/Art Resource, NY; BR, Topham/The Image Works; MR, Victoria & Albert Museum/Art Resource, NY; **153,** © The Gallery Collection/CORBIS; © STEPHEN MORRISON/epa/CORBIS; **154,** Art Resource, NY; **155,** Archivo Iconographico S.A./Corbis; **156,** TR, The Granger Collection; BR, British Museum/HIP/The Image Works; L, Fine Art Photographic Library/Corbis; **157,**

TR, Bridgeman Art Library; L, Mary Evans Picture Library; B, The Granger Collection; **158,** Background, HIP/The Image Works; Inset, Dorling Kindersley; **159,** B, The Granger Collection; T, Atwater Kent Museum/Bridgeman Art Library; **162,** B, The Parliamentary Archives; T, Corbis; **163,** L, Erich Lessing/Art Resource, NY; R, Royal Armouries; **166,** Archivo Iconographica, S.A./Corbis; **167,** Mary Evans Picture Library; **168,** R, Corbis; L, Corbis; **169,** The Granger Collection; **171,** Corbis; **172,** BL, The Granger Collection; Inset, C, Museums On Line; Background, B, Sovfoto; TR, akg-images; **174,** R, Mary Evans Picture Library; L, Royal Armouries; **175,** T, The Granger Collection; B, Bata Shoe Museum; **176,** Archivo Iconographica, S.A./Corbis; **177,** Bridgeman Art Library

Chapter Five

180c, SuperStock, Inc; **180–181,** Réunion des Musées Nationaux/Art Resource, NY; **181,** T, Réunion des Musées Nationaux/Art Resource, NY; M, Bridgeman Art Library; B, The Granger Collection; **182,** Background, © Archivo Iconografico, S.A./Corbis; Inset, Musée Marmottan/Dorling Kindersley; **183,** The Granger Collection; **184,** R, Chateau de Versailles, France, Lauros/Giraudon/Bridgeman Art Library; L, Réunion des Musées Nationaux/Art Resource, NY; **185,** L, The Granger Collection; R, Royalty-Free/Corbis; **186,** © Archivo Iconografico, S.A./Corbis; **187,** T, The Granger Collection; B, © Archivo Iconografico, S.A./Corbis; **188,** Inset, Bettmann/Corbis; Background, Bildarchiv der Osterreichische Nationalbibliothek; **189,** The Granger Collection; **190,** L, Victoria & Albert Museum/Art Resource; **190–191,** Bridgeman Art Library; Background, T, Russ Lappa; Background, B, Russ Lappa; **191,** Inset, L, John Heseltine/Corbis; Inset, M, Francis G. Mayer/Corbis; R, Dorling Kindersley; **192,** L, Kurpfalzisches Museum, Heidelberg, Germany/The Bridgeman Art Library; R, Museum of Tropinin and His Contemporaries, Moscow, Russia/Bridgeman Art Library; M, © Archivo Iconografico, S.A./Corbis; **194,** Background, © Archivo Iconografico, S.A./Corbis; TL, Zuma/Corbis; BL, Reuters/Corbis; **195,** L, The Granger Collection; R, The Granger Collection; **196,** Joe Sohm/Chromosohm/VOA; **197,** SuperStock, Inc.; **198,** L, National Portrait Gallery, Smithsonian Institution/Art Resource, NY; M, Reunion des Musees Nationaux/Art Resource; R, © The Corcoran

Gallery of Art/CORBIS; **199,** Bridgeman Art Library; **200,** Background, The Granger Collection; **202,** Inset, Bettmann/Corbis; **202–203,** Bettmann/Corbis; **203,** Inset, L, Bettmann/Corbis; Inset, R, Hulton/Getty Images, Inc.; Background, T, Library of Congress; **204,** The Granger Collection; **205,** T, Steve Artley; B, British Library, London, UK/Bridgeman Art Library; **206,** R, Christie's Images/Corbis; L, The Granger Collection; **207,** Corbis

Chapter Six
208c, British Library, London, UK/Bridgeman Art Library; **208–209,** Giraudon/Art Resource, NY; **209,** T, Musee de L'Histoire Vivante, Montreuil, France, Archives Charmet/Bridgeman Art Library; M, Erich Lessing/Art Resource, NY; B, Scala/Art Resource, NY; **210,** T, Erich Lessing/Art Resource, NY; B, The Granger Collection, NY; **211,** Snark/Art Resource, NY; **212,** TR, Giraudon/Art Resource, NY; B, Musee de la Ville de Paris, Musee Carnavalet, Paris, France, Archives Charmet/Bridgeman Art Library; TL, Musee du Ranquet, Clermont-Ferrand, France/Giraudon/Bridgeman Art Library; **213,** Musee Carnavalet, Paris, France, Lauros/Giraudon/Bridgeman Art Library; **214,** Background, Chateau de Versailles, France/Bridgeman Art Library; Inset, Giraudon/Art Resource, NY; **215,** RÈunion des MusÈes Nationaux/Art Resource; **216,** Réunion des Musées Nationaux/Art Resource, NY; **217,** (c) Judith Miller/Dorling Kindersley/Bill & Myrtle Aquilino; **218,** Background, Chateau de Versailles, France, Giraudon/Bridgeman Art Library; Inset, AKG Images; **221,** Giraudon/Art Resource, NY; **222,** Musee de la Ville de Paris, Musee Carnavalet, Paris, France, Giraudon/Bridgeman Art Library; **223,** The Art Archive/Bibliothèque des Arts Décoratifs Paris/Dagli Orti; **224,** Leonard de Selva/CORBIS; **225,** Giraudon/Art Resource, NY; **226,** L, Musee de la Ville de Paris, Musee Carnavalet, Paris, France, Giraudon/Bridgeman Art Library; R, The Art Archive/Musée Carnavalet Paris/Dagli Orti; M, Hulton Archive/Getty Images; **227,** TL, Hulton-Deutsch Collection/Corbis; BL, Musee de la Revolution Francaise, Vizille, France/Bridgeman Art Library; R, Max Alexander/Dorling Kindersley Media Library; **228,** T, British Library, London, UK/Bridgeman Art Library; B, Erich Lessing/Art Resource, NY; **229,** T, Réunion des Musées Nationaux/Art Resource, NY; B, Erich Lessing/Art Resource, NY; **230,** T, Scala/Art Resource, NY; B, Private Collection/Bridgeman Art Library; **231,** Giraudon/Art Resource, NY; **233,** Scala/Art Resource, NY; **234,** Musee des Beaux-Arts, Rouen, France Lauros/Giraudon/Bridgeman Art Library; **235,** Giraudon/Art Resource, NY; **236,** Bibliotheque Nationale, Paris, France, Archives Charmet/Bridgeman Art Library; **238,** Giraudon/Art Resource, NY; **239,** Randy Faris/CORBIS; **240,** Cleveland Museum of Art; **241,** B, Private Collection/Bridgeman Art Library; T, © Riyadh Biji/Reuters/Corbis; **242,** R, The Fotomas Index; L, Giraudon/Art Resource, NY; **243,** Giraudon/Art Resource, NY

Chapter Seven
244c, National Railway Museum/Science and Society Picture Library; **244–245,** © NRM/Pictorial Collection/SSPL/The Image Works; **245,** T, National Railway Museum/Science and Society Picture Library; M, Bettman/CORBIS; B, Austrian Archives/CORBIS; **246,** NRM/SSPL/The Image Works; **247,** Time Life Pictures/Getty Images; **248,** Inset, Bettmann/CORBIS; B, The Granger Collection, New York; **249,** photolibrary; **250,** L, Fine Art Photographic Library, London/Art Resource, NY; R, National Railway Museum/Science and Society Picture Library; **251,** Science Museum/SSPL; **254,** Mary Evans Picture Library; **255,** Hulton Archive/Getty Images; **257,** T, Mary Evans Picture Library; B, Manchester Archives and Local Studies; **258,** Museum of London; **259,** Hulton-Deutsch Collection/CORBIS; **260,** Hulton-Deutsch Collection/CORBIS; **261,** B, The Granger Collection, New York; T, Fine Art Photographic Library/Art Resource, NY; **262,** L, Topham/The Image Works; R, The Stapleton Collection/Bridgeman Art Library; **264,** B, Austrian Archives/CORBIS; T, The Granger Collection, New York; **265,** © Daniel Leclair/Reuters/CORBIS; Image Works/Mary Evans Picture Library Ltd.; **266,** L, akg-images; R, Mary Evans Picture Library; **267,** T, Peter Titmuss/Alamy; B, The Art Archive/Museo Historico Nacional Buenos Aires/Dagli Orti; **268,** NRM/Pictorial Collection/SSPL/The Image Works; **269,** Image Select/Art Resource, NY

Chapter Eight
270c, North Wind Picture Archives; **270–271,** The Art Archive/Simon Bolivar Amphitheatre Mexico/Dagli Orti; **271,** T, Coleccion Museo Nacional de Columbia, Bogota; M, Musee des Tissus de Lyon/Pierre Verrier/Museum-Images 2003; BR, The Granger Collection, New York; **272,** Hadtorteneti Muzeum, Budapest, Hungary/Archives Charmet/Bridgeman Art Library International; **274,** R, Igor Ursic/Chancery of HRH Crown Prince Alexander/The Royal Palace in Belgrade; L, Igor Ursic/Chancery of HRH Crown Prince Alexander/The Royal Palace in Belgrade; **276,** R, Musée des Tissus de Lyon/Pierre Verrier/Museum-Images 2003; L, North Wind Picture Archive; **277,** Musee de la Ville de Paris, Musee Carnavalet, Paris, France, Lauros/Giraudon/Bridgeman Art Library; **278,** ullstein bild/The Granger Collection, New York; **279,** L, Private Collection, Archives Charmet/Bridgeman Art Library; M, ullstein bild/The Granger Collection, New York; R, Louvre, Paris, France/Bridgeman Art Library International; Background, ullstein bild/The Granger Collection, New York; **280,** Scala/Art Resource, NY; **281,** The Granger Collection, New York; **282,** GLEB GARANICH/Reuters/CORBIS; The Granger Collection, New York; **283,** L, The Art Archive/Museo Nacional Bogota/Dagli Orti; R, Coleccion Museo Nacional de Columbia, Bogota; **284,** Chateau de Versailles, France/Bridgeman Art Library International; **285,** Bettmann/CORBIS; **287,** TM, Bettmann/CORBIS; TL, The Granger Collection, New York; B, The Granger Collection, New York; TR, The Art Archive/Archaeological and Ethnological Museum Quito Ecuador/Dagli Orti; **288,** The Art Archive/Miramare Museum Trieste/Dagli Orti (A); **289,** North Wind Picture Archives; **290,** North Wind Picture Archives; **291,** T, Reuters/Corbis; M, The Art Archive/Bibliothéque des Art Décoratifs Paris/Marc Charmet; B, Popular Book Co. Ltd.; **292,** T, age fotostock/SuperStock; B, The Art Archive/Simon Bolivar; **293,** akg-images

Chapter Nine
296c, Réunion des Musées Nationaux/Art Resource, NY; **296–297,** Photo by Lewis W. Hine/George Eastman House/Getty Images; **297,** MR, Mary Evans/The Women's Library; BR, © SSPL/The Image Works; TR, © Jacqui Hurst/CORBIS; **299,** Mary Evans Picture Library; Lewis B Hine/AKG Images; **300,** SSPL/The Image Works; **301,** B, Mary Evans Picture Library; T, SSPL/The Image Works; **302,** L, © SSPL/The Image Works; MR, The Art Archive/Dagli Orti; TR, © Michael Holford; BR, © ScienceMuseum,London/HIP/The Image Works; **303,** Hulton-Deutsch Collection/Corbis; **304,**

Library of Congress; **305,** Background, Topham/The Image Works; Inset, Bettmann/Corbis; **306,** Bettmann/Corbis; **307,** Hulton-Deutsch Collection/Corbis; **309,** The Art Archive/Musée de l'Affiche Paris/Dagli Orti; **310,** Inset, The Advertising Archives; R, Leland J. Prater/Corbis; **310–311,** © SSPL/The Image Works; **311,** TL, © Scala/Art Resource, NY; B, Siri Schwartzman/Prentice Hall; TR, © Michael Nicholson/CORBIS; M, Science Museum/Science & Society Picture Library; **312,** L, Underwood & Underwood/Corbis; R, Mary Evans/The Women's Library; **313,** B, Corbis; T, Museum of London/Topham-HIP/The Image Works; Background, Philip de Bay/Corbis; Inset, Museum of London, UK/Bridgeman Art Library; **314,** Hulton Archive Photos/Getty Images Inc.; **315,** Topham/The Image Works; **316,** TL, Tui De Roy/Minden Pictures; BL, Renee Lynn/Photo Researchers, Inc.; TR, Kevin Schafer/Corbis; BR, Oriol Alamany/Corbis; **317,** BR, The Granger Collection, New York; TR, Michael Nicholson/Corbis; TL, Mary Evans Picture Library; Inset, ML, © Kevin Schafer/CORBIS; Inset, BL, © Tony Arruza/CORBIS; Inset, TL, © Tom Brakefield/Superstock; **318,** Underwood & Underwood/Corbis; **319,** Albert Bierstadt (American, 1830–1902)Hetch Hetchy Canyon Oil on canvas, 1875 Gift of Mrs. E. H. Sawyer and Mrs. A. L. Williston; Mount Holyoke College Art Museum, South Hadley, Massachusetts; **320,** Archivo Iconografico, S.A./Corbis; **321,** TR, Erich Lessing/Art Resource, NY; BR, Bettmann/Corbis; BL, Private Collection, Archives Charmet/Bridgeman Art Library; TL, Thomas Jefferson University; **322,** Erich Lessing/Art Resource, NY; **323,** BL, Art Resource; T, Art Resource; BR, © Superstock Inc./Superstock; **324,** Dave King (c) Dorling Kindersley, Courtesy of The Science Museum, London; **325,** Private Collection/The Bridgeman Art Library; **326,** R, © Christie's Images/SuperStock; L, © Jacqui Hurst/CORBIS; **327,** Copyright © North Wind Picture Archives/North Wind Picture Archives—All rights reserved

Chapter Ten
328c, Snark/Art Resource, NY; **328–329,** AKG Images; **329,** T, Judith Miller Archive/Dorling Kindersley; M, Istituto Mazziniano/Museo Risorgimento, Genova; B, Andy Crawford/Dorling Kindersley; **330,** L, Index Stock Imagery, Inc.; R, Judith Miller Archive/Dorling Kindersley; **331,** Deutsches Historiches Museum; **332,**

ACKNOWLEDGMENTS

Background, AKG Images; Inset, Deutsches Historiches Museum; **334,** L, PPP/Popperfoto/Retrofile; R, Alison Harris/Dorling Kindersley; **335,** The Granger Collection, New York; **336,** Mary Evans Picture Library/WEIMAR ARCHIVE; **337,** AKG Images; **338,** L, Alinari/Art Resource, NY; R, Istituto Mazziniano/Museo Risorgimento, Genova; **339,** L, © Istituto per la Storia del Risorgimento Italiano; R, © Istituto per la Storia del Risorgimento Italiano; **340,** TM, Private Collection, Ken Welsh/Bridgeman Art Library; TR, Alinari/Art Resource, NY; TL, Private Collection, Alinari/Bridgeman Art Library; B, The Granger Collection, NY; **341,** Alinari/Art Resource, NY; **342,** L, Private Collection, Archives Charmet/Bridgeman Art Library; **343,** R, Karl Shone/Dorling Kindersley; **346,** Mary Evans Picture Library; **347,** © The Art Archive/CORBIS/; © Brooks Kraft/Sygma/CORBIS; **348,** (c) 1999 North Wind Picture; **349,** B, Private Collection/Bridgeman Art Library; T, Andy Crawford/Dorling Kindersley; **350,** HIP/Art Resource, NY; **351,** The Granger Collection, New York; **352,** B, Snark/Art Resource, NY; T, Mary Evans Picture Library; **354,** Bettmann/Corbis; **355,** B, Granger Collection, NY; T, Musée Carnavalet Paris/Dagli Orti/The Art Archive; **356,** T, Giraudon/Art Resource, NY; B, AKG Images; **357,** Greater London Council, UK/Bridgeman Art Library

Chapter Eleven

358c, © Royalty-Free/Corbis; **358–359,** Blackburn Museum and Art Gallery, Lancashire, UK/Bridgeman Art Library; **359,** T, AKG Images; M, By permission of People's History Museum; B, © Bettmann/CORBIS; **360,** L, Hulton Archive/Getty Images; R, Victoria & Albert Museum, London/Art Resource, NY; **361,** (C) THE BRIDGEMAN ART LIBRARY; **362,** R, AKG Images; MR, Palace of Westminster, London, UK,/Bridgeman Art Library; L, Corbis; ML, AKG Images; **363,** L, Private Collection/Bridgeman Art Library; M, Mary Evans Picture Library; R, PA/EMPICS; **364,** Bettmann/Corbis; **365,** Anti-Slavery International; **366,** Mary Evans Picture Library; **367,** T, By permission of People's History Museum; B, TUC Library Collections, London Metropolitan University; **368,** MR, The Illustrated London News Picture Library, London, UK/Bridgeman Art Library; TR, Holt Studios Int./Photo Researchers, Inc.; Background, L, Miki Duisterhof/Getty Images, Inc.; BR, Trustees of the Watts

Gallery, Compton, Surrey, UK/Bridgeman Art Library; L, Sean Sexton Collection/Corbis; **370,** Bradford Art Galleries and Museums, West Yorkshire, UK/Bridgeman Art Library; National Geographic/Getty Images; **371,** R, Erich Lessing/Art Resource, NY; L, Hulton Archive/Getty Images; **372,** Inset, Hulton Archive/Getty Images; **372–373,** Background, Hulton Archive/Getty Images; **373,** BR, Musee de la Poste, Paris, France, Archives Charmet/BridgemanArt Library; TR, The Granger Collection, NY; **374,** Dave G. Houser/Corbis; **375,** AKG Images; **376,** Musee National de l'Education, Rouen, France, Archives Charmet/Bridgeman Art Library; **377,** Stockbyte/Getty Images, Inc.; **378,** BR, Smithsonian Institution/Office of Imaging, Printing, and Photographic Services; BL, American Philosophical Society; Background, American Philosophical Society; T, Kevin R. Morris/Bohemian Nomad Picturemakers/Corbis; **379,** New-York Historical Society/Bridgeman Art Library; **380,** L, Pajaro Valley Historical Association; M, Oakland Museum of California; R, Benjamin Franklin Reinhart, An Evening Halt - Emigrants Moving to the West in 1840, 1867, Oil on canvas, 40 x 70 in., Corcoran Gallery of Art, Washington, D.C., Gift of Mr. and Mrs. Lansdell K. Christie, 59.21.; **382,** Mary Evans Picture Library; **383,** Mary Evans Picture Library/The Women's Library; **384,** T, The Granger Collection, NY; B, AKG Images; **385,** Musee de la Ville de Paris, Musee Carnavalet, Paris, France, Archives Charmet/Bridgeman Art Library

Chapter Twelve

386c, Private Collection/Bridgeman Art Library; **386–387,** © Hulton-Deutsch Collection/CORBIS; **387,** M, Private Collection/Bridgeman Art Library; B, Ashmolean Museum, University of Oxford,Bridgeman Art Library; T, British Library; **388,** L, Mary Evans Picture Library; R, AKG-Images; **389,** National Archives UK; **390,** Roger Viollet/Topham/The Image Works; **391,** Hulton Archive/Getty Images, Inc.; **392,** © AKG Images; **393,** The Royal Collection (c) 2005, Her Majesty Queen Elizabeth II; **394,** T, Mary Evans Picture Library; B, AKG Images; **396,** ML, The Granger Collection; **397,** Mary Evans Picture Library; **398,** Popperfoto/Robertstock; **399,** © Mansell/Time & Life Pictures/Getty Images; **400,** L, © Corbis; All Rights Reserved; R, Ashmolean Museum, University of Oxford,Bridgeman Art

Library; **401,** AKG Images; **403,** Background, Public Record Office/HIP/The Image Works; Inset, The Granger Collection; **404,** Hulton/Getty Images; **405,** R, British Library; L, Hulton Archive/Getty Images, Inc.; **406,** Inset, R, British Library/HIP/The Image Works; L, Mary Evans Picture Library; Inset,L, Royal Armories; **406–407,** Inset T, Royal Armouries; Background T, The Art Archive/Company of Girdlers/Eileen Tweedy; **407,** R, Mary Evans Picture Library; **408,** Inset,T, AFP/Getty Images, Inc.; Inset, B, Paul A. Souders/Corbis; Background, Colin Garatt/Corbis; **410,** Edward VII receiving Maharajahs and Dignitaries Prior to his Coronation by Albert E. Harris (fl.1917) Roy Miles Fine Paintings/The Bridgeman Art Library; Newscom; **411,** R, Bridgeman Art Library; L Garry Black/Masterfile; **412,** L, British Museum/HIP/The Image Works; **413,** R, Harvard-Yenching Library, Harvard University; L, Panorama Stock; **414,** Corbis; **415,** Time-Life Pictures/Getty Images, Inc.; **416,** L, Bridgeman Art Library; R, British Library/HIP/The Image Works; **417,** Topham/The Image Works; **418,** T, The Granger Collection, New York; B, Time-Life Pictures/Getty Images, Inc

Chapter Thirteen

420c, Andy Crawford © Dorling Kindersley; **420–421,** Peter Harholdt/CORBIS; **421,** T, The Granger Collection, New York; M, photolibrary;co/Index Stock Imagery; B, SSPL/The Image Works; **422,** L, Topham/The Image Works; R, Andy Crawford (c) Dorling Kindersley; **423,** B, The Art Archive/British Museum; **424–425,** Réunion des Musées Nationaux/Art Resource, NY; **425,** R, From the website of the National Diet Library (http,//www.ndl.go.jp/); L, trove;net/Index Stock Imagery; **426,** T, Old Japan Picture Library; **427,** B, Rykoff Collection/CORBIS; **428,** Mary Evans Picture Library; **429,** B, Crown Agents; T, Mary Evans Picture Library; **430,** R, Courtesy National Archives, photo no; 350-P-AD-3–3; L, Bettman/CORBIS; **432,** TR, Getty Images; TM, Roy Miles Fine Paintings/Bridgeman Art Library International; TL, © Horace Bristol/CORBIS; BR, Ray Moller/Dorling Kindersley © Royal Pavilion Museum and Art Galleries, Brighton; Background, Crown Agents; BL, Prentice Hall; **434,** TL, Art Gallery of Ontario, Toronto, Canada/Bridgeman Art Library; TR, © Royalty-Free/Corbis; **436,** T, photolibrary.co/Index Stock Imagery; B, Mary Evans Picture Library; **438,** Inset, Auckland

Art Gallery Toi o Tamaki, Gift of Mr H E Partridge, 1915; Background, Historical Picture Archive/CORBIS; **439,** L, Robert Frerck/Odyssey/Chicago © Banco de Mexico Diego Rivera Museum Trust; R, © Royalty-Free/Corbis; **440,** The Art Archive/National History Museum Mexico City/Dagli Orti; **441,** R, Private Collection/Bridgeman Art Library International; L, The Art Archive/National History Museum Mexico City/Dagli Orti; **443,** Bettman/CORBIS; **444,** BL, Image courtesy Smithsonian Institution; T, Image courtesy Smithsonian Institution; BR, SSPL/The Image Works; Background, Corbis; **446,** T, Dorling Kindersley; B, © Werner Forman/CORBIS; **447,** © Royalty-Free/Corbis; **448,** B, The Art Archive/National History Museum Mexico City/Dagli Orti; T, © Asian Art & Archaeology, Inc./CORBIS

Chapter Fourteen

452c, The Granger Collection, NY; **452–453,** The Art Archive/Imperial War Museum; **453,** T, © C Squared Studios/Getty Images; M, Andy Crawford/Dorling Kindersley; B, SSPL/The Image Works; **454,** L, © Bettmann/CORBIS; R, ULLSTEIN - Ullstein Bild; **456–457,** © CORBIS; **457,** The Granger Collection, New York; **458,** John McCutchson/The Chicago Tribune, 1914 Photo, Ken Karp; **459,** Jacques Moreau/Archives Larousse, Paris, France/Bridgman Art Library; **460,** L, © Hulton-Deutsch Collection/CORBIS; R, Imperial War Museum, London/Dorling Kindersley; **461,** Snark/Art Resource, NY; **462,** R, © ULLSTEIN-Zennig; L, © SSPL/The Image Works; **462–463,** Foto Marburg/Art Resource, NY; **463,** TR, ENA/Popperfoto/Robertstock/Retrofile; BR, © The Tank Museum; **465,** © Bettmann/CORBIS; **466,** Mary Evans Picture Library; **467,** L, © CORBIS; R, The Granger Collection, New York; **468,** B, Snark/Art Resource, NY; T, © David Pollack/CORBIS; **469,** © Hulton-Deutsch Collection/CORBIS; **470,** B, The Granger Collection, New York; T, © A. R. Coster/Hulton Archive/Getty Images; **471,** © CORBIS; **472,** R, SSPL/The Image Works; L, © Bettmann/CORBIS; **473,** B, © CORBIS; T, © Bettmann/CORBIS; **476,** SSPL/The Image Works; **477,** L, Andy Crawford/Dorling Kindersley; R, akg-images; **478,** L, C.Walker/Topham/The Image Works; R, AP Photo/Wonders Exhibit; **479,** © Hulton Archive/Getty Images; **480,** Inset, Christie's Images, London, UK/The Bridgeman Art Library; Background, akg-images; **481,** L, Novosti/The

Bridgeman Art Library; R, Topham/The Image Works; **483,** © Topical Press Agency/Hulton Archive/Getty Images; **484,** L, © Bettmann/CORBIS; M, Snark/Art Resource, NY; R, Imperial War Museum, London/Dorling Kindersley; **485,** L, The Granger Collection, New York; R, © Bettmann/CORBIS; **486,** T, The Imperial War Museum, London; B, C.Walker/Topham/The Image Works

Chapter Fifteen
488c, (detail) photograph ©The Detroit Institute of Arts, 1995. Palacio Nacional stairway, Mexico City © Dirk Bakker, photographer; **488–489,** Corbis; **489,** T, Frank Nowikowski; M, Bridgeman Art Library; B, Martin Plomer (c) Dorling Kindersley; **490,** R, Courtesy Susan Frost; L, Fernando Bueno/Getty Images; **491,** TL, Bettmann/Corbis; Center L, Bettmann/Corbis; Center, R, Bettmann/Corbis; BR, Bettmann/Corbis; BL Grouping, Center, Bettmann/Corbis; BL Groupling, L, Bettmann/Corbis; TR, Bettmann/Corbis; BL Grouping, R, Bettmann/Corbis; **492,** Bettmann/Corbis; **493,** Library of Congress; **494,** Frank Nowikowski; **495,** B, (detail) photograph © The Detroit Institute of Arts, 1995; Palacio Nacional stairway, Mexico City © Dirk Bakker, photographer; T, Time Life Pictures/Getty Images Inc.; **496,** R, Jackson Davis Collection/Universit of Virginia Library; L, Image courtesy of The Advertising Archives; **497,** National Library of South Africa; **498,** T, Bartko-Reher-GbR; B, Dept of Historical Papers/William Cullen Library; **498–499,** WorldSat International Inc.; **499,** CORBIS; **500,** The Granger Collection; **502,** Library of Congress; **503,** Corbis; **506,** Bettmann/Corbis; **507,** T, Corbis; B, Panorama Stock; **508,** The Granger Collection; **509,** Bettmann/CORBIS; **510,** Sovfoto; **512,** Time Life Pictures/Getty Images; **513,** B, Mansell Collection/Getty Images, Inc.; T, Random House Publishing Group; **514,** DAP/The Image Works; **515,** Hulton/Getty Images, Inc.; **516,** L, Bettmann/Corbis; R, The Granger Collection; **517,** B, The Granger Collection; T, Library of Congress; **518,** T, Center for American History/University of Texas; B, Bettmann/Corbis; **519,** DPA/The Image Works

Chapter Sixteen
520–521, Time-Life Getty Images, Inc. **521,** T, Prentice Hall; M, Library of Congress; B, David King Collection; **522,** © Bettmann/Corbis; **523,** R, Culver Pictures, Inc.; L, Drug Enforce-ment Administration; **524,** L, Under-wood & Underwood/Corbis; Inset, Library of Congress; **524–525,** Corbis; **525,** Inset, Topham/The Image Works; R, Corbis; **526,** Robertstock; **527,** Tate Gallery/Art Resource; **528,** BM, Fogg Art Museum/Harvard University/Bridgeman Art Library; BL, Scala/Art Resource, NY; BR, Art Resource, NY; Background, Roger Viollet/Topham/The Image Works; **529,** L, Corbis; R, Dorling Kindersley; **530,** Bettmann/Corbis; **531,** The Granger Collection; **532,** L, Detroit News; R, AkG Images; **532–533,** M, Collection of the Museum of American Finance; **533,** L, © Bettmann/CORBIS; R, Mary Evans Picture Library; **534,** Inset, The Granger Collection; Background, Roger-Viollet/Topham/The Image Works; **536,** T, Mary Evans Picture Library; B, Dorling Kindersley; **537,** Time-Life/Getty Images, Inc.; **538,** L, Museum of the Revolution, Moscow/Dorling Kindersley; R, Imperial War Museum, London/Dorling Kindersley; Inset R, David King Collection; Inset L, Stefano Bianchetti/Corbis; **538–539,** Bettmann/Corbis; **539,** Bettmann/Corbis; **540,** From the Fry Collection of Italian History and Culture; By courtesy of the Department of Special Collections, General Library System, University of Wisconsin-Madison; **541,** Korea News Service/Reuters/CORBIS; Bettmann/CORBIS; **542,** David King Collection; **543,** David King Collection; **544,** London Express/Getty Images; **545,** David King Colllection; **546,** Andy Crawford/Dorling Kindersley; **547,** David King Collection; **548,** David King Collection; **550,** © Corbis; **551,** Inset, Corbis; Background, Corbis; **552,** Mary Evans Picture Library; **553,** D.O.W./US Holocaust Memorial Museum; The views or opinions expressed in this book, and the context in which the images are used, do not necessarily reflect the views or policy of, nor imply approval or endorsement by, the United States Holocaust Memorial Museum; **554,** Feltz/Topham/The Image Works; **556,** L, Andy Crawford/Dorling Kindersley; R, Dorling Kindersley; **557,** T, A/P Wide World Photos; B, Drug Enforcement Administration; **558,** Corbis

Chapter Seventeen
560–561, Time Life Pictures/Getty Images; **561,** T, © Photos by Eric L. Johnson/Courtesy of the Museum of World War II, Natick MA; M, © Photos by Eric L. Johnson/Courtesy of the Museum of World War II, Natick MA; B, The Advertising Archive; **562,** R, Getty Images; L, Photo by London Express/Getty Images; **563,** R, © Photos by Eric L. Johnson/Courtesy of the Museum of World War II, Natick MA; L, Getty Images; **564,** T, © Bettmann/CORBIS; TM, © Corbis; BM, © Corbis; B, © Corbis; **565,** R, Time Life Pictures/Getty Images; L, Getty Images; **568,** L, © Wanda Beaver; R, © Museum of Flight/CORBIS; **569,** © Photos by Eric L. Johnson/Courtesy of the Museum of World War II, Natick MA; **570,** TR, © Photos by Eric L. Johnson/Courtesy of the Museum of World War II, Natick MA; L, © Photos by Eric L. Johnson/Courtesy of the Museum of World War II, Natick MA; R, © CORBIS; **571,** © Bettmann/CORBIS; **572,** B, © Copyright 2000 Corbis; **572–573,** Inset, © Topham/The Image Works; Background, USHMM, courtesy of Mark Chrzanowski; **574,** Panorama Stock; **575,** AP/Wide World; **576,** AP/Wide World Photos; **577,** TL, The Granger Collection, New York; TR, © Ellen Granter; **578,** R, © Corbis; All Rights Reserved; L, © Bettmann/CORBIS; **579,** L, Hulton|Archive by Getty Images; R, Hulton Archive/Getty Images; B, Geoff Dann (c) Dorling Kindersley, Courtesy of the Imperial War Museum, London; Background, © Corbis; **580,** © Corbis; All Rights Reserved; **582,** © Bettmann/CORBIS; **584,** © Topham/The Image Works; **585,** T, © CORBIS; B, © Corbis; All Rights Reserved; **586,** R, Photo courtesy of the Military & Historical Image Bank; L, AP/Wide World Photos; **587,** AP/Wide World Photos; **588,** AP/Wide World Photos; **589,** T, Time Life Pictures/Getty Images; B, Richard Klune/Corbis; **590,** R, Alfred Eisenstaedt/Time-Life Pictures/Getty Images; L, Dorling Kindersley; **591,** T, (c) Dorling Kindersley, Courtesy of Andrew L Chernack; B, Hulton Deutsch/Corbis; **592,** T, Corbis; B, Library of Congress; **593,** © Bettmann/CORBIS; **594,** The Michael Barson Collection; **595,** Lynsey Addario/CORBIS; Bildarchiv Preussischer Kulturbesitz/Art Resource, NY; **596,** L, © Corbis; R, © Photos by Eric L. Johnson/Courtesy of the Museum of World War II, Natick MA; M, © Photos by Eric L. Johnson/Courtesy of the Museum of World War II, Natick MA; **597,** R, Hiroshima Peace Memorial Museum; L, © Photos by Eric L. Johnson/Courtesy of the Museum of World War II, Natick MA; **598,** T, © Photos by Eric L. Johnson/Courtesy of the Museum of World War II, Natick MA; B, Time Life Pictures/Getty Images

Chapter Eighteen
602c, Getty Images; **602–603,** © Photos**12**;com/Polaris Images; **603,** T, © Jacques M. Chenet/CORBIS; M, Russ Lappa; B, © Bettmann/CORBIS; **604,** L, © Photos**12**;com/Polaris; R, Getty Images; **605,** Alamy Images; **606,** © Bettmann/CORBIS; **607,** © PATRICK ROBERT/CORBIS SYGMA; **609,** TL, © KEYSTONE/GAMMA; TR, © Bettmann/CORBIS; Background, © Bettmann/CORBIS; BR, © AP/Wide World Photos; **610,** L, © Peter Turnley/CORBIS; R, © Bob Rowan; Progressive Image/CORBIS; **611,** © AP/Wide World Photos; **612,** Copyright © Courtesy Everett Collection/Everett Collection; **613,** Newscom; The Herblock Foundation; Getty Images; **614,** B, © David Seymour/Magnum Photos; T, Library of Congress; **615,** T, Reprinted from Electrical Merchandising, July 1957; Courtesy The State Museum of Pennsylvania; B, © Bettmann/CORBIS; **616,** L, © Corbis; R, © AP/Wide World Photos; **617,** © Bob Adelman/Magnum Photos; **618,** © Photos**12**;com/Polaris; **619,** © Brian Rose; **620,** © Topham/The Image Works; **621,** B, © Horace Bristol/CORBIS; TR, Imatake Shichiro/Prentice Hall; **622,** © Charles Gupton/Getty Images; **623,** L, © Baldwin H. Ward & Kathryn C. Ward/CORBIS; R, © Dave Bartruff/CORBIS; **624,** © Bettmann/CORBIS; **625,** R, Collection of the International Institute of Social History, Amsterdam; L, © GAMMA; **626–627,** BR, © Bettmann/CORBIS; **628,** © CORBIS; **630,** L, © Hulton/Getty; R, © Bettmann/CORBIS; **631,** © Time Life Pictures/Getty Images; **632,** BR, © AP/Wide World Photos; TR, © AP/Wide World Photos; BL, © Nathan Benn/CORBIS; TL, © Prentice Hall School Division; **632–633,** Background, © Bettmann/CORBIS; **634,** Russ Lappa/Prentice Hall; **635,** © Dirck Halstead/Getty Images; **636,** L, © ANTICOLI LIVIO/GAMMA; R, © AP/Wide World Photo; **637,** T, AP Photo; B, © HIRES CHIP/GAMMA; **638,** L, © AP/Wide World Photo; R, Russ Lappa; **639,** © Bettmann/CORBIS; **640,** Punch; **641,** © Pascal Le Segretain/CORBIS SYGMA; **642,** R, Time Life Pictures/Getty Images; L, © POLOGNE GDANSK **0880**/GAMMA; **643,** Ricky Wong/Bloomberg News;/Landov; **645,** T, © Liba Taylor/CORBIS; B, © Jacques Langevin/CORBIS SYGMA; **646,** © Dave Bartruff/CORBIS; **647,** TR, TOLES © 2002 The Buffalo News; Reprinted with permission of UNIVERSAL PRESS SYNDICATE; All rights reserved; BR, © ANTICOLI LIVIO/GAMMA; L, © Bettmann/CORBIS; **648,** © Photos12;com/Polaris Images; **649,** © Martyn Goddard/CORBIS

ACKNOWLEDGMENTS

Chapter Nineteen

650c, PhotoDisc/Getty Images; **650–651,** Alexis Orand/Gamma; **651, M,** PhotoDisc/Getty Images; **T,** Andrew England/AP/Wide World Photo; **B,** AP/Wide World Photos; **652, L,** Henri Cartier-Bresson/Magnum Photos; **R,** AP/Wide World Photos; **654,** Bettmann/Corbis; **655,** Phoenix Art Museum, Arizona, Gift of George P; Bickford/Bridgeman Art Library; **656,** Mike Goldwater/Network Photographers; **658, L,** Howard Sochurek//Time Life Pictures/Getty Images; **R,** Bernard Napthine/Lonely Planet Images; **659,** Christopher Furlong/Getty Images; **660, L,** EPA/Empics; **R,** AP Photo/Sakchai Lalit; **662, R,** Corbis; **L, M & E** Bernheim/Woodfin Camp & Associates; **663,** Fredrik Naumann/Panos Pictures; **664,** Christian Sappa/Network Photographers; **666,** Keystone/Getty Images; **667,** Ben Curtis/AP/Wide World Photos; **668,** Eric Miller/Panos Pictures; **669, T,** © Bettmann/CORBIS; **B,** Mark Kauffman/Time Life Pictures/Getty Images; **670, L,** Bettmann/Corbis; **R,** Patrick Ben Luke Syder/Lonely Planet Images; **672,** LANGE JACQUES/PARIS MATCH/GAMMA; **B,** Marco Di Lauro/Getty Images; **T,** Hassan Massoudy/ARS/Banque d'Images, ADAGP/Art Resource, NY; **674,** AP/Wide World Photos; **676, R,** Bettmann/Corbis; **BL,** Corbis; **TL,** Corbis; **677, T,** Mindaugas Kulbis/AP/Wide World Photos; **BL,** Christopher Furlong/Getty Images; **BR,** AP/Wide World Photos; **678, T,** Henri Cartier-Bresson/Magnum Photos; **B,** EPA/Empics; **679,** EPA/Empics

Chapter Twenty

680c, AP/Wide World Photos; **680–681,** © SAZY LAURENT/GAMMA; **681, T,** Prentice Hall; **M,** © Graeme Williams/South Photographs; **B,** Corbis; **682,** Les Stone/Corbis Sygma; **683,** TURESSON/PRESSENS BILD/GAMMA; **685,** OTHoNIEL/GAMMA; **686,** Dieter Telemans/Panos Pictures; **687,** Ian Berry/Magnum Photos; **688, TL,** David Turnley/Corbis; **BL,** Frankenfeld/SOUTH LIGHT/GAMMA; **R,** UN Photo Library; **690,** Espen Rasmussen/AFP/Getty Images; **691, B,** David Turnley/Corbis; **T,** Owen Franken/Corbis; **692,** Nasser Shiyoukhi/Ap/Wide World Photos; **693,** Ziv Koren/Polaris Images; **694,** Ap/Wide World Photos; **695, R,** AP Photo/Jacqueline Arzt; **L,** QUIDU NOEL/GAMMA; **696,** Peter Jordan/Network; **697,** © WISSAM AL-OKAILI/AFP/Getty Images; **698,** Ian Berry/Magnum Photos; **699,**

MICHAEL EVSTAFIEV/AFP/Getty Images; **700, R,** Carlson © 2004 Milwaukee Journal Sentinel/UPI; **L,** © SAZY LAURENT/GAMMA

Chapter Twenty-One

702c, © Prentice Hall; **702–703,** Tischler Fotografen/Peter Arnold, Inc.; **703, B,** © Corbis; **T,** Prentice Hall; **M,** EVARISTO SA/AFP/Getty Images; **704, L,** Zed Nelson/Panos Pictures; **R,** © Prentice Hall; **706,** Ron Giling/Peter Arnold, Inc.; **707,** Clive Shirley/Panos Pictures; **708,** Mark Henley/Panos Pictures; **709,** Zapiro; IPNStock; **710,** Mark Edwards/Peter Arnold, Inc.; **711,** Liba Taylor/Panos Pictures; **712, L,** Fiona Teede-UNEP/Peter Arnold, Inc.; **M,** ABPL/Nigel Dennis/Animals Animals-Earth Scenes; Background, Cyril Ruoso/Minden Pictures; **R,** Betty Press/Panos Pictures; **713,** William Campbell/Corbis; **714, B,** Peter Turnley/Corbis; **T,** Jeff Widener/AP/Wide World Photos; **715,** Barry Lewis/Network; **716, L,** Eugene Hoshiko/AP/Wide World Photos; **R,** © Findlay Kember/Polaris; **717,** Christopher Brown/Polaris; **718,** Kapoor Baldev/Sygma/Corbis; **719,** Barriopedro, EFE/AP/Wide World Photos; **720,** Janet Jarman/Corbis; **721, R,** Russell Gordon/Das Fotoarchiv/Peter Arnold, Inc.; **L,** David Rochkind/Polaris; **722, L,** Paulo Santos-Interfoto/AP/Wide World Photos; **R,** Paulo Santos/AP Wide World Photos; **723,** Anders Gunnartz/Peter Arnold, Inc.; **724,** Dado Galdieri/AP/Wide World Photos; **725,** © AP Photo/Dario Lopez-Mills; **726, T,** Rafael Wollmann/Gamma; **B,** ALI BURAFI/AFP/Getty Images; **727,** Inset, Steve Northup/Timepix/Time Life Pictures/Getty Images; Background, Corbis; **728, R,** Image Port/Index Stock Imagery, Inc.; **L,** © Bettmann/CORBIS; **729,** © Dennis Galante/Corbis; **730,** Jorgen Schytte/Peter Arnold, Inc.; **731,** China Photos/Reuters/Corbis

Chapter Twenty-Two

732–733, Gordon Wiltsie; **733, M,** © Matthias Kulka/CORBIS; **B,** NASA; **T,** CARE; **734, L,** AFP/Gettty Images; **R,** © Matthias Kulka/CORBIS; **736,** AFP/Getty Images, Inc.**738,** David Grossman/The Image Works; **740, B,** Russell Gordon/Das Fotoarchiv/Peter Arnold; **T,** Corel Corporation; **741, BL,** Mike Yamashita, Inc.; **BR,** Bananastock/Picturequest; **T,** Transfair USA; **742,** Paul A. Souders/Corbis; **743,** AFP/Getty Images; Newscom; ©Rafiqur Rahman/Reuters/CORBIS; **744, L,** Getty Images, Inc.; **R,** CARE; **745,** Inset B,

Noah Poritz/Photo Researchers, Inc.; Inset T, Photo Researchers, Inc.; Background, Caroline Penn/Corbis; **747, T,** Phil Huber/Black Star; **B,** Michael Newman/PhotoEdit; **748,** RUGMARK; **749,** Ron Giling/Das Fotoarchiv; **750,** AP/Wide World Photos; **752, T,** Alison Wright/The Image Works; **B,** Shawkat Khan/AFP/Getty Images, Inc.; **753,** Larry Downing/Reuters/Corbis; **754,** Lynn Johnson/Aurora; **756, T,** Russell Boyce/Reuters/Corbis; **757,** © RAHEB HOMAVANDI/Reuters/Landov; **758, L,** Photo Researchers; **R,** NASA; **759, T,** ESA/Corbis; **B,** Corbis; **760,** Background, Los Alamos National Laboratory/Photo Researchers, Inc.; **L,** Alfred Eisenstaedt/Time & Life Pictures/Getty Images; **R,** Bettmann/Corbis; **761, R,** Photo Researchers, Inc.; **M,** Photo Researchers, Inc.; **L,** Phototake; **762, M,** John Doebly/University of Wisconsin; **R,** Grant Heilman Photography; **L,** Jim Richardson/Corbis; **764,** Russell Boyce/Reuters/Corbis; **765, T,** Custom Medical Stock Photo, Inc.; **B,** © AP Photo/Rafiq Maqbool; **766, T,** Cartoon Stock; **B,** AFP/Getty Images, Inc.

Concept Connector Handbooks

768, T, Archivo Iconographica, S.A./Corbis; **BL,** © Pascal Le Segretain/CORBIS SYGMA; **768–769,** Musee de la Tapisserie, Bayeux, France/www.bridgeman.co.uk; **769,** Free Agents Limited/CORBIS; **784,** © Robert Frerck/Odyssey Productions, Inc.; **787,** Anders Blomqvist/Lonely Planet Images; **788, B,** National Gallery of Art; **789,** Giraudon/Art Resource, NY; **791,** AP/Wide World Photos; **792,** Corbis; **793,** Rafiqur Rahman/Reuters America LLC; **794,** Lisa Knouse Braiman/Business Week; **796, TL,** The Granger Collection, New York; **TR,** A. Eaton/Ancient Art & Architecture Collection; **MR,** Comstock/SuperStock; **ML,** © Michael Holford; **B,** V & A Museum/Art Resource; **797, TL,** National Maritime Museum; **TR,** Time Life Pictures/Getty Images; **MR,** Mary Evans Picture Library/Photo Researchers, Inc.; **ML,** The Pierpont Morgan Library/Art Resource, NY; **B,** Museu de Marinha; **798, TL,** © Michael Holford; **TR,** Alfred Eisenstaedt/Time & Life Pictures/Getty Images; **M,** The Art Archive/Dagli Orti; **B,** © ScienceMuseum,London/HIP/The Image Works; **799, T,** Photo Researchers, Inc.; **M,** Getty Images; **BR,** ESA/Corbis; **BL,** Chris Sorensen Photography; **800,** © James Hill; **802, TL,** Versailles, château de Versailles et de Trianon/RMN/Art Resource; **BL,** Giraudon/Art Resource, NY; **R,** Museum of Tropinin

and His Contemporaries, Moscow, Russia/Bridgeman Art Library; **803, TR,** © Corbis; **BR,** Peter Jordan/Network; **L,** © Dave Bartruff/CORBIS; **804, T,** Gunter Marx; **B,** The Granger Collection, New York; **806, TL,** Scala/Art Resource, NY; **TR,** © Fitzwilliam Museum, University of Cambridge, UK; **BL,** © Archivo Iconografico, S.A./CORBIS; **BR,** Erich Lessing/Art Resource, NY; **807, TL,** Art Resource/The Museum of Modern Art; **TM,** Copyright ARS, NY;/Art Resource, NY; **TR,** © Historical Picture Archive/CORBIS; **B,** © Jeff Greenberg/eStockPhoto

Text
Grateful acknowledgment is made to the following for copyrighted material:

ACT, Inc.
Excerpt from "Writing Test Scores" from *www.act.org.* Copyright © 2005 by Act, Inc. All rights reserved. Reproduced by permission.

Ardis Publishing
From "Requiem" from *Selected Poems* by Anna Ahkmatova, translation copyright © 1974 by Robin Kemball. Reprinted with the permission of The Overlook Press (Ardis Publishers).

Cambridge University Press
From *Hind Swaraj* by Mohandas K. Gandhi (Anthony J. Parel, editor.), copyright © 1997 by Anthony J. Parel, editor. Reprinted with the permission of Cambridge University Press.

The College Board
Excerpt from "The SAT Scoring Guide" from *www.collegeboard.com.* Reproduced by permission. Copyright © 2005 collegeboard.com. All rights reserved.

Harcourt Education Ltd.
From *On Trial for my Country* by Stanlake Samkange. Reprinted by permission of Harcourt Education Limited.

Houghton Mifflin Company
From *Stolen Continents* by Ronald Wright. Copyright © 1992 by Ronald Wright. Reprinted by permission of Houghton Mifflin Company. All rights reserved.

Indiana University Press
Song: "Our homes and humble dwellings . . ." from *The Mexican Corrido as a Source for Interpretive Study of Modern Mexico (1870–1950)* by Merle E. Simmons. Copyright © 1957 by Merle E. Simmons.

New Directions Publishing Corporation
"Brotherhood" by Octavio Paz, translated by Eliot Weingberger, from *Collected Poems 1957–1987,* copyright © 1986 by Octavio Paz and Eliot Weinberger. Reprinted by permission of New Directions Publishing Corp. "Hermandad" by Octavio Paz, from *Collected Poems 1957–1987,* copyright © 1986 by Octavio Paz. Reprinted by permission of New Directions Publishing Corp.

Next Decade Entertainment, Inc.
"Brother Can You Spare a Dime?" by E.Y. "Yip" Harburg and Jay Gorney. Published by Glocca Morra Music (ASCAP) and Gorney Music (ASCAP). Administered by Next Decade Entertainment, Inc. All rights reserved. Used by permission.

W. W. Norton & Company, Inc.
from *The Prince: A Norton Critical Edition, Second Edition* by Niccolo Machiavelli, translated by Robert M. Adams. Copyright © 1992, 1977 by W. W. Norton & Company, Inc. Used by permission of W. W. Norton & Company, Inc.

Pearson Education
Esler, Anthony, *The Human Venture: From Prehistory to the Present,* 10/E, © 2004. Reprinted by permission of Pearson Education, Inc., Upper Saddle River, New Jersey.

The Estate of Paulette Goddard Remarque c/o Richard Kay/Pryor, Cashamn, Sherman & Flynn
Excerpt from *All Quiet on the Western Front* by Erich Maria Remarque. "Im Western Nichts Neues," copyright 1928 by Ullstein A.G.; Copyright renewed © 1956 by Erich Maria Remarque. "All Quiet On The Western Front," copyright 1929, 1930 by Little, Brown and Company; copyright renewed 1957, 1958 by Erich Maria Remarque. Reprinted by permission. All rights reserved.

The Polish Institute of Arts and Sciences of America
"The Bronze Horseman" by Alexander Pushkin. Copyright © The Estate of Waclaw Lednicki. Used by permission of The Estate of Waclaw Lednicki, on behalf of The Polish Institute of Arts and Sciences of America.

University of California Press, Inc.
Excerpt from "The Bronze Horseman" by Alexander Pushkin, translated by Waclaw Lednicki from *Waclaw Lednicki, Pushkin's Bronze Horseman* (Berkeley, CA: University of California Press, 1955). Used by permission.

University of Oklahoma Press
From "Two: Invasion" by Ralph L. Roys, ed. From *The Book of Chilam Balam of Chumayel.* Copyright © 1992 by Ronald Wright. Used with permission of the University of Oklahoma Press.

Vintage Books
From *Open Letters: Selected Writings 1965–1990* by Vaclav Havel, translated by Paul Wilson, copyright © 1991 by A.G. Brain. Preface/translation copyright © 1985, 1988, 1991 by Paul Wilson. Used by permission of Alfred A. Knopf, a division of Random House, Inc.

Note: Every effort has been made to locate the copyright owner of material reprinted in this book. Omissions brought to our attention will be corrected in subsequent editions.

Professional Development Bibliography

Baumann, J.F. and Kameenui, E.J. (2004), *Vocabulary Instruction: From Research to Practice.* New York: Guilford Press.

Coxhead, Averil. "A New Academic Word List." *TESOL Quarterly* (Summer 2000): 213–238.

Hamot, Gregory, et al, *Media Literacy in Social Studies Teacher Education: Relating Meaning to Practice,* 1997.

Schleppegrell, M. "Linguistic Features of the Language of Schooling." *Linguistics and Education,* 12, no. 4 (2002): 431–459.

Snow, C., et al. 2002. Reading for Understanding: Toward an R&D Program in *Reading Comprehension.* Santa Monica: The Rand Corporation, 2002.

Xue, G., and Nation, I.S. P. "A University Word List." *Language Learning and Communication* (1984): 215–229.